18e

INTERMEDIATE FINANCIAL ACCOUNTING

Earl K. Stice, PhD
Brigham Young University

James D. Stice, PhD
Brigham Young University

SOUTH-WESTERN
CENGAGE Learning™

Australia • Brazil • Canada • Mexico • Singapore • Spain • United Kingdom • United States

SOUTH-WESTERN
CENGAGE Learning™

Intermediate Financial Accounting, 18e
Earl K. Stice, James D. Stice

Vice President of Editorial, Business: Jack W. Calhoun
Editor-in-Chief: Rob Dewey
Senior Acquisitions Editor: Matthew Filimonov
Developmental Editor: Lauren Athmer and Leslie Kauffman/LEAP Publishing Services, Inc.
Editorial Assistant: Ann Mazzaro
Marketing Manager: Natalie Livingston
Marketing Coordinator: Nicki Parsons
Marketing Communications Manager: Elizabeth Shipp
Production Manager: Patricia Matthews Boies
Content Project Manager: Corey Geissler
Media Editor: Jessica Robbe
Frontlist Buyer, Manufacturing: Doug Wilke
Production Service: LEAP Publishing Services, Inc.
Compositor: Knowledgeworks Global Limited
Senior Art Director: Stacy Jenkins Shirley
Internal Designers: c miller design/Beckmeyer Design
Cover Designer: Patti Hudepohl
Cover Images: © Getty/Digital Vision
Permissions Account Manager, Text: John Hill
Permissions Account Manager, Images/Media: Deanna Ettinger
Photo Credits:
B/W Image: Getty Images/rubberball
Cover Image: Shutterstock Images/Sergej Khakimullin

Library of Congress Control Number: 2010942870

International Edition:

ISBN-13: 978-0-538-47972-1
ISBN-10: 0-538-47972-8

Cengage Learning International Offices

Asia
www.cengageasia.com
tel: (65) 6410 1200

Australia/New Zealand
www.cengage.com.au
tel: (61) 3 9685 4111

Brazil
www.cengage.com.br
tel: (55) 11 3665 9900

India
www.cengage.co.in
tel: (91) 11 4364 1111

Latin America
www.cengage.com.mx
tel: (52) 55 1500 6000

UK/Europe/Middle East/Africa
www.cengage.co.uk
tel: (44) 0 1264 332 424

Represented in Canada by Nelson Education, Ltd.
tel: (416) 752 9100 / (800) 668 0671
www.nelson.com

Cengage Learning is a leading provider of customized learning solutions with office locations around the globe, including Singapore, the United Kingdom, Australia, Mexico, Brazil, and Japan. Locate your local office at: **www.cengage.com/global**

For product information: **www.cengage.com/international**
Visit your local office: **www.cengage.com/global**
Visit our corporate website: **www.cengage.com**

Printed in China by China Translation & Printing Services Limited.
1 2 3 4 5 15 14 13 12 11

PREFACE

Currency + Context = Motivation

Motivation

From the smallest mom-and-pop retailer to the largest multinational corporation, businesses of all sizes are recognizing that accounting professionals are no longer simply "number crunchers" but rather essential partners in achieving the fundamental goals of their organization. When people understand accounting's critical role in managing a business and making business decisions, they are **motivated** to learn accounting. That is why *Intermediate Financial Accounting, 18e* provides a powerful connection between accounting and business today with:

- **Business strategy cases** at the start of each chapter that describe how a real-world firm such as MicroStrategy struggled with revenue recognition and the pressures on management to interpret revenue as positively as possible;
- **Coverage of high-interest and current topics** such as **earnings management, fair value,** and **International Financial Reporting Standards (IFRS)** as well as other issues that are driving accounting in today's business environment;
- **FASB codification activities** that link FASB research with real business situations and help readers understand both how to research and use authoritative guidance as well as why that guidance is important;
- **Real-world end-of-chapter case activities** that use the financial results of companies such as The Walt Disney Company, The Boston Celtics, Hewlett-Packard, and Dell to help readers connect accounting to business.

CURRENCY—Current and Relevant Coverage

One look at the business pages of any newspaper shows how illusory long-term success can be. Yesterday's runaway successes can quickly find themselves derailed by the new realities of today's business world. This is the first text to provide a real-world perspective that links accounting functions to the activities of business.

International Financial Reporting Standards topics, indicated by this symbol throughout the text, help students understand how accounting practices differ from country to country and reflect the increasingly global nature of business.

The international environment of business is dramatically changing the landscape of accounting. The Financial Accounting Standards Board (FASB) and the International Accounting Standards Board (IASB) are working together to develop one set of accounting standards to be used by companies in countries around the world. No longer is the United States making the rules for the rest of the world to follow. Instead, the FASB and the IASB are working hand-in-hand as financial accounting standards converge at a pace that was not dreamed of even five years ago.

The international environment has greatly affected this textbook. Every chapter discusses relevant accounting standards and developments from both a U.S. and a global perspective. Each chapter begins with a discussion of the accounting standards and procedures used by companies complying with U.S. GAAP. Then those areas where U.S. GAAP and international accounting standards are significantly different are discussed so that the reader can understand how accounting standards around the world are similar and how they are different. A chapter on **Accounting in a Global Market** further emphasizes the role of International Financial Reporting Standards.

The objective of this approach is to develop in students the ability to see beyond the borders of the United States and understand that the global business environment is leading to global accounting standards. Users of this text will understand that they are not just learning U.S. GAAP. Instead, they are being prepared to be active participants in a global accounting environment with the ability to understand and apply international accounting standards as well as U.S. accounting standards.

Fair Value Accounting is another major topic affecting the accounting environment. The credit crisis of 2008 is blamed by some on the inappropriate use of fair value accounting. A module details the "why," "when," "where," and "how" for using fair values in financial statements. Because this concept of fair value accounting is so important and affects so many of the principles and topics discussed later in the text, it has been placed near the front of the text following the discussion of the financial statements.

A Chapter on Earnings Management in Part 1 establishes a framework for the remainder of the course. Students come to understand the importance and ramifications of earnings management through current, real-world examples, extracts from SEC enforcement actions, business press analysis, and the extensive use of academic research findings.

A new FASB Codification feature presents a relevant issue and related question in order to assist students in understanding how to use the FASB's new codification in research. This feature is found in each chapter and includes a description of the issue at hand, a specific question pertaining to that given issue, and suggestions for "Searching the Codification" in order to guide students in the right direction for research. Each feature includes an answer section at the end of the chapter, so that students can check their research and adjust their technique as needed. References throughout the textbook have been updated to reflect the FASB ASC (Accounting Standards Codification).

FASB CODIFICATION

The Issue: You are the accountant for a company in the carpet cleaning business. Because of your company's innovative cleaning system (no harsh detergents, no damaging brushes, and extremely small carbon footprint), you have been very successful and have begun to drive your competitors out of business. In fact, just today your company's CEO has decided to start buying a number of your competitors. As you walked out the door at the end of the day, she said: "You had better learn how to account for a bargain purchase."

The Question: What is a bargain purchase, and why is a bargain purchase likely to arise in this situation?

Searching the Codification: Bargain purchases are covered in this chapter, but you would like to show your boss that you can find accounting standards for yourself in the authoritative literature. The best place to start is in Topic 805 (Business Combinations), which is in the "Broad Transactions" collection of topics.

The Answer: The authoritative accounting standards relative to bargain purchases are described on page 10-43.

Up-to-Date *Intermediate Financial Accounting, 18e* has been **completely updated** to reflect the latest changes in accounting standards, practices, and techniques. The real company information has been revised to account for recent changes in financial statements and other company reports.

EX 9-6 SCHEDULE OF COST OF GOODS MANUFACTURED

Bartlett Corporation
Schedule of Cost of Goods Manufactured
For the Year Ended December 31, 2013

Direct materials:		
Raw materials inventory, January 1, 2013	$ 21,350	
Purchases	107,500	
Cost of raw materials available for use	$128,850	
Less: Raw materials inventory, December 31, 2013	22,350	
Raw materials used in production		$106,500
Direct labor		96,850
Manufacturing overhead:		
Indirect labor	$ 40,000	
Factory supervision	29,000	
Depreciation—factory buildings and equipment	20,000	
Light, heat, and power	18,000	
Factory supplies	15,000	
Miscellaneous manufacturing overhead	12,055	134,055
Total manufacturing costs		$337,405
Add: Work in process inventory, January 1, 2013		29,400
		$366,805
Less: Work in process inventory, December 31, 2013		26,500
Cost of goods manufactured		$340,305

CONTEXT—Business Activities Emphasized in Organization

No other text works harder to demonstrate accounting's integral importance to an organization's decision-making capabilities. This book is organized as much as possible around the essential interrelationship between accounting procedures and the activities of business to provide students with the context behind the accounting that is discussed. The innovative structure is unsurpassed in preparing students to serve as trusted advisors on the front lines of business.

In an effort to streamline the sequence of chapters in the text, the table of contents accounts for a more traditional balance sheet order of topics while still maintaining the structure of covering topics as they relate to business activities. The investing chapters fall before the financing chapters, which results in a more familiar order of presentation for instructors and students.

Part 1—Foundations of Financial Accounting provides students with the fundamentals of financial accounting, including a full chapter on Earnings Management, and concludes with a module that covers the Time Value of Money as well as a module on Fair Value.

Part 2—Routine Activities of a Business gets down to business, integrating accounting into management by exploring operating and investing activities.

Part 3—Additional Activities of a Business examines financing activities, leases, income taxes, and employee compensation.

Part 4—Other Dimensions of Financial Reporting rounds out the comprehensive coverage with earnings per share; derivatives, contingencies, business segments, and interim reports; accounting changes; and financial statement analysis; as well as extended coverage of IFRS, which is found in the separate chapter, Accounting in a Global Market.

Why and How Framework follows each learning objective, as the authors provide additional reinforcement of the critical concepts by highlighting both the procedural aspects (the "how") as well as the context (or "why") for which they are applied. As they move through the chapter, students gain a greater understanding of both elements and can rationalize why businesses account for things the way they do. By exposing students to the "why" behind each concept, students are being trained to realize the business implications of various decisions made by companies and can take their careers head-on.

Supporting this framework are a number of critical-thinking elements that allow students to stretch their minds into the analysis of the relevant topics, a skill that will also be crucial as they move on in their studies and careers.

Overview of the Accounting Process

1 **Identify and explain the basic steps in the accounting process (accounting cycle).**

WHY It is important to understand how accounting information flows through an organization and how that information is captured by the accounting information system.

HOW The accounting process, often referred to as the accounting cycle, generally includes the following steps: analyze business documents, journalize transactions, post to ledger accounts, prepare a trial balance, prepare adjusting entries, prepare financial statements, close the nominal accounts, and prepare a post-closing trial balance.

Statement of Cash Flows "Revisited" in Chapter 21 provides coverage of the statement of cash flows in the second semester of the course. The book continues to provide a full chapter early in the text (Chapter 5) addressing the statement of cash flows and integrates this financial statement throughout the text, which results in the most comprehensive treatment of this important subject available.

Opening Scenario Questions are critical-thinking questions that follow the updated real company chapter openers. Solutions are provided at the end of each chapter so students can check their answers as they think about how they would approach accounting-related issues that businesses face.

QUESTIONS

1. Why do you think the price-to-sales ratio (as opposed to the price-earnings ratio) is often used in valuing the stocks of start-up technology companies, especially those related to the Internet?
2. On Monday, March 20, 2000, MicroStrategy issued a press release stating that revenues for the year 1999 were about $155 million, not $205 million as previously announced. This represented a drop of 24% in reported revenue. Why did a drop of just 24% in reported revenue result in a stock price drop of 62%? In other words, why wasn't the drop in stock price also 24%?
3. In early March 2000, MicroStrategy's board of directors received word that the company's auditor was requesting a revenue restatement. The board was reluctant to go forward with the restatement because of fears (justified, as it turns out) that the restatement would hurt the company's stock price. List and explain two or three arguments that you, as a member of the board, could have made in support of the restatement.

Answers to these questions can be found on page 8-41.

STOP&THINK

It would seem that the physical capital maintenance concept would provide the best theoretical measure of "well-offness." However, use of the physical capital maintenance concept of measuring income involves many practical difficulties. Identify ONE of those practical difficulties from the list below.

a) Difficulty in estimating depreciation lives
b) Difficulty in implementing internal control procedures
c) Difficulty in providing cash flow information
d) Difficulty in obtaining fair market values of assets and liabilities

Stop & Think multiple-choice questions have been written by the authors to accompany the Stop & Think boxed features. These critical-thinking boxes, found in every chapter, allow students to test their knowledge and then consult the answers found at the end of the chapter.

FYI

Before 2002, all gains and losses resulting from the early extinguishment of debt were reported as extraordinary. This classification was ended with the release of pre-Codification *SFAS No. 145* (now in FASB ASC paragraph 470-50-45-1); these gains and losses are now considered ordinary, subject to the normal criteria for extraordinary items.

FYI margin boxes often provide additional context to an important topic by emphasizing additional points of interest.

! CAUTION

The most common error when computing bad debt expense is to confuse the two methods—percentage of sales and percentage of receivables. Remember that when you are using the percentage-of-sales method, bad debt expense is computed and the balance in the allowance account is then determined. When you are using the percentage-of-receivables method, the balance in the allowance account is computed, and then the amount of bad debt expense for the period is determined.

Caution provide students with important points to consider when thinking about more complex concepts and topics.

REVERSE SOLVABLE

New "Reverse Solvable" Problems at the end of chapters, identified by an icon, ask students to demonstrate mastery of relationships and accounting concepts by working with incomplete information and completing the missing information before completing the assignment.

Chapter Updates and Enhancements

Chapter 1

- New chapter-opening vignette focusing on the global financial crisis
- New extended discussion of FASB Accounting Standards Codification
- Update on the standard-setting process
- Introduction of the revised GAAP hierarchy and revised discussion of GAAP overall
- Further explanation of the convergence of U.S. GAAP and IASB standards
- New extended coverage of U.S. GAAP and IFRS similarities and differences

Chapter 2

- New discussion of *IFRS for SMEs* as alternative option to full-blown provisions of U.S. GAAP or IFRS
- New feature "Using the FASB's Codification"

Chapter 3

- Updated and revised opening case on Coca-Cola
- New feature "Using the FASB's Codification"
- New analysis of the proposed new balance sheet format
- Revised coverage on minority interest as related to the consolidated balance sheet

Chapter 4

- Updated exhibits
- New feature "Using the FASB's Codification"
- New, continued analysis (from Chapter 3) of the proposed new balance sheet format

Chapter 5

- Revised chapter-opening vignette regarding Circle K
- New feature "Using the FASB's Codification"
- Revised FASB-IFRS-Codification Summary

Chapter 6

- Updated exhibits
- Revised to reflect economic and housing crises

Time Value of Money Module

- Revised end-of-chapter material to reflect recent updates

Fair Value Module

- Revised to acknowledge pre-Codification provisions
- New FASB ASC references

Chapter 7

- Updated chapter-opening vignette to reflect global economic crisis
- New FASB ASC references
- New feature "Using the FASB's Codification"
- Updated exhibits

Chapter 8

- Revised Learning Objectives
- Expanded discussion of internal controls
- Updated and expanded discussion of Subtopic 605-25
- New review of some of the topics addressed in SAB 101
- Updated and expanded discussion of the asset-and-liability approach to revenue recognition that is currently being developed as a joint effort of the FASB and the IASB
- New feature "Using the FASB's Codification"
- Updated data and exhibits

Chapter 9

- New feature "Using the FASB's Codification"
- Updated data and exhibits

Chapter 10

- Updated references to FASB ASC throughout
- Discussion of pre-Codification material as well
- New feature "Using the FASB's Codification"
- Updated data and exhibits

Chapter 11

- Updated references to FASB ASC throughout
- New feature "Using the FASB's Codification"
- Updated data and exhibits

Chapter 12

- Updated references to FASB ASC throughout
- New feature "Using the FASB's Codification"
- Updated data and exhibits
- Updated discussion on the use of the fair value option for the reporting of financial assets and liabilities

Chapter 13

- Updated discussion of "perpetual approach" and both the FASB's and the IASB's opinions on it
- Updated references to FASB ASC throughout
- New feature "Using the FASB's Codification"
- Updated data and exhibits

Chapter 14

- Updated references to FASB ASC throughout
- New feature "Using the FASB's Codification"
- Updated data and exhibits
- Updated discussion on the classification of investment securities according to IFRS
- Updated discussion on equity method accounting according to IFRS

Chapter 15

- Updated chapter-opening vignette data
- Updated references to FASB ASC throughout
- New feature "Using the FASB's Codification"
- Updated data and exhibits
- Revised discussion of the profit deferral rule

Chapter 16

- New discussion regarding the FASB's attempts to use accounting theory to define what "income tax expense" means
- Updated references to FASB ASC throughout
- New feature "Using the FASB's Codification"
- Expanded discussion of accounting for uncertain tax provisions

Chapter 17

- Updated chapter-opening vignette to address the global economic crisis and health care reform
- Updated references to FASB ASC throughout
- New feature "Using the FASB's Codification"
- New coverage of the IASB Exposure Draft, April 2010
- Updated information regarding GM and the effects of the economic crisis

Chapter 18

- New chapter-opening vignette focusing on China's position in the global economic world
- Updated references to FASB ASC throughout
- New feature "Using the FASB's Codification"
- Revised discussion on participating securities and the two-class method

Chapter 19

- Updated references to FASB ASC throughout
- New feature "Using the FASB's Codification"
- Added discussion of how IFRS affects derivatives, contingencies, business segments, and interim reports
- Analysis of pre-Codification provisions and the effects of FASB ASC in regards to these provisions
- Additional coverage of the accounting for contingent liabilities and contingent assets

Chapter 20

- Updated references to FASB ASC throughout
- New coverage of the proper reporting of accounting changes according to FASB ASC
- New feature "Using the FASB's Codification"
- Updated exhibits and data

Chapter 21

- Revised comprehensive example of the statement of cash flows using Tesco, one of the largest supermarket chains in the United Kingdom
- New discussion of the FASB–IASB project on financial statement presentation
- Updated exhibits and data
- Updated references to FASB ASC throughout

Chapter 22

- Updated information regarding the economic crisis
- Revised information on the IASB
- Expanded discussion on the transfer of provision sources (U.S. GAAP vs. IFRS)
- Updated key differences between U.S. GAAP and IFRS
- Updated references to FASB ASC throughout
- New feature "Using the FASB's Codification"

Chapter 23

- Updated chapter-opening vignette information and data
- Updated references to FASB ASC throughout
- New feature "Using the FASB's Codification"

Reinforce Student Understanding

Unmatched End-of-Chapter Material

Widely regarded as providing the most varied and expansive set of problem assignments available, *Intermediate Financial Accounting, 18e* continues to raise the bar to new heights. Only *Intermediate Financial Accounting* features such a diverse set of traditional exercises, problems, and cases:

- 15–25 Questions per chapter to help assimilate chapter content
- More than 400 Practice Exercises written by the authors
- Discussion Cases for homework or class discussion
- Exercises to reinforce key concepts or applications

- Problems that integrate several concepts or techniques
- Sample CPA Exam Questions written to provide students with similar problems commonly found on the CPA exam
- Selected Exercises or Problems that have accompanying spreadsheet templates, marked with an icon

SPREADSHEET

REVERSE SOLVABLE

"Reverse Solvable" Problems at the end of chapters, identified by an icon, ask students to demonstrate mastery of relationships and accounting concepts by working with incomplete information to determine the data that is missing from the exercise, before completing the assignment.

Case Materials have been designed to help accelerate the development of essential skills in critical thinking, communication, research, and teamwork. Retention and application of key concepts build as future accountants and business professionals take advantage of a wide range of tools found in this innovative section. These cases satisfy the skills-based curriculum endorsed by the AICPA's Core Competency Framework and the recommendations of the Accounting Education Change Commission (AECC).

Deciphering Actual Financial Statements Cases enable students to analyze financial data from recent annual reports from companies such as The Walt Disney Company, Coca-Cola, and the Boston Celtics.

Researching Accounting Standards Cases ask students to visit the FASB's Web site to access designated pronouncements as they are applied to each chapter's topics.

Ethical Dilemma Assignments help develop the critical-thinking skills students will need as they wrestle with the business world's many "gray" issues.

Case 7-73 **Ethical Dilemma**

You recently graduated from college with your accounting degree. Your father's best friend is the director of the accounting department of a small manufacturing firm in the area, and you accepted a position on his staff. After a month on the job, you have noticed several deficiencies in the cash controls for the company. For example, the individual making the daily deposits at the bank is also in charge of updating accounts receivable. You also notice that the petty cash fund is under general control of everyone in the office (that means that no one person has ultimate responsibility) and that vouchers are seldom completed when cash is removed from the fund. You bring your concerns to the attention of your boss, your father's friend, and he comments:

> "I appreciate your concerns. I knew when we hired you that you were sharp, but you need to understand that not everything is done by the book here. We trust our employees. If we were to enforce rigid controls on cash, it would create a nontrusting work environment. We don't want that. Sure, a little money may turn up missing now and then, but it is a small price to pay. Now, don't you worry about it anymore."

What do you do now? Would you be comfortable working in an environment where there is a lack of control on cash? If a significant sum of money were to turn up missing and the control system was unable to determine who was responsible, what would that do to the trusting work environment? And remember, big sums of money never turned up missing until you came to work at the company.

The Cumulative Spreadsheet Analysis Case builds upon the lessons of each chapter to give students the opportunity to demonstrate and reinforce their understanding. Found at the end of Chapters 2–5, 7–20, and 23, each exercise requires students to create a spreadsheet that allows for numerous variables to be modified and their effects to be monitored. By the end of the course, students have constructed a spreadsheet that enables them to forecast operating cash flows for five years in the future, adjust forecasts for the most reasonable operating parameters, and analyze the impact of a variety of accounting assumptions based on the reported numbers.

Case 2-52 **Cumulative Spreadsheet Analysis**

Beginning with Chapter 2, each chapter in this text will include a spreadsheet assignment based on the financial information of a fictitious company named Skywalker Enterprises. The assignments start out simple—in this chapter you are not asked to do much more than set up financial statement formats and input some numbers. In succeeding chapters, the spreadsheets will get more complex so that by the end of the course you will have constructed a spreadsheet that allows you to forecast operating cash flows for five years in the future, adjust your forecast depending on the operating parameters that you think are most reasonable, and analyze the impact of a variety of accounting assumptions on the reported numbers.

So, let's get started with the first spreadsheet assignment.

Bonus Content

Web-Based Chapter Enhancements

In response to instructor requests, subject-enhancing material from previous editions of the text is available on the companion Web site. The result is a streamlined, easier-to-use text that provides ample supplement material for important topics.

CHAPTER	WEB MATERIAL
2	Illustration of Special Journals and Subsidiary Ledgers
5	Statement of Cash Flows—Indirect Method
7	Petty Cash Fund
8	Deposit Method: Franchising Industry
10	Complexities in Accounting for Capitalized Interest
13	Quasi-Reorganizations Complexities in Accounting for Stock-Based Compensation
14	Changes in Classification Involving the Equity Method
15	Real Estate Leases
16	Intraperiod Tax Allocation
17	Details of Accounting for Postretirement Benefits Other Than Pensions Detailed Pension Present Value Calculations
22	Foreign Currency
23	Impact of Changing Prices on Financial Statements

Give your students instant feedback and an online learning tool that will propel them forward in this course!

Introducing CengageNOW™ for Stice/Stice: *Intermediate Financial Accounting, 18e*

CengageNOW is an online homework solution in accounting that delivers better student outcomes—NOW! CengageNOW encourages practice with the textbook homework that is central to success in accounting with author-written homework from the textbook, automatic grading and tracking student progress, and course management tools, including gradebook.

CengageNOW includes:

- End-of-chapter homework from the textbook written by the authors
- Integrated eBook
- Personalized Study Plan with pre-test, study plan based on students' individual weak areas, and post-test
- Ability to run reports to gauge individual class/student dynamics, report at institutional level or to accrediting bodies based on outcomes
- Flexible course management tools

CengageNOW offers:

- Easy-to-use course management options that offer flexibility and continuity from one semester to another. Includes all end-of-chapter questions, Test Bank, eBook, study resources, and personalized learning plan. CengageNOW includes everything you and your students need to be successful.
- Different levels of feedback and engaging student resources to guide students through material and solidify learning.
- "**Smart Entry**" helps eliminate common typos and errors to help students do their best work and understand the concept behind each answer.
- The ability to analyze student work from the gradebook and generate reports on learning outcomes for accreditation and other purposes.
- Robust assignment options allow you to control your course and make the system work best for you and your students:
    - Set prerequisites for assignments or extra credit
    - Control the amount of feedback you give students
    - Control the rigor of assignments by selecting different question types or grading methods
    - Easily change point values of questions or individual student grades

What Is a Personalized Study Plan? It is offered in CengageNOW as a diagnostic tool with a Pre-Test, Customized Study Plan, and Post-Test for each chapter. It offers valuable study assets to empower students to master concepts. The resources available with the personalized study plan for *Intermediate Financial Accounting, 18e* are:

- Crossword Puzzles
- Key Terms
- Flashcards
- Student PowerPoint Slides
- QuizBowl game
- eBook by learning objective

To order CengageNOW with Stice/Stice: *Intermediate Financial Accounting, 18e*, contact your sales representative to decide which purchasing option best suits your classroom and students' needs.

For Instructors

Comprehensive Instructor Supplement Package

An unsurpassed package of supplementary resources allows you to make the most of your time while providing valuable assignments and assessment for your students.

To access the online instructor's resources for this text, please visit www.cengage.com/international and search for Stice/Stice: *Intermediate Financial Accounting, 18e* by author, title, or ISBN in the search bar.

Solutions Manual, prepared by James D. Stice and Earl K. Stice, Brigham Young University.

This manual contains independently verified answers to all end-of-chapter questions, cases, exercises, and problems, written by the authors. These are available on the companion Web site, www.cengage.com/international.

Instructor's Resource Manual, prepared by Ira W. Bates, Florida A&M University.

This manual enhances class preparation with objectives, chapter outlines, teaching suggestions and strategies, and topical overviews of end-of-chapter materials. It also features assignment classifications with level of difficulty and estimated completion time, suggested readings on chapter topics, and transparency masters. A new transition guide has been added to make the move from 17e to 18e easier. The result is a comprehensive resource integration guide to supplement the course. Available on the companion Web site, www.cengage.com/international.

Test Bank and ExamView®, prepared by Fernando Rodriguez.

The revised and expanded test bank is available in both Word files and computerized ExamView versions. Test items include multiple-choice questions and short examination problems for each chapter, along with solutions. Analysis problems are included to coincide with the emphasis on decision making in the text. Available electronically on the companion website, www.cengage.com/international.

Instructor's PowerPoint® Slides, prepared by Doug Cloud, Professor Emeritus, Pepperdine University.

Hundreds of slides in PowerPoint format can be used in on-screen lecture presentations or printed out and used as traditional overheads. Additionally, they can be printed and distributed to students, allowing students to concentrate on the professor instead of hurrying to copy down information. Available on the companion Web site, www.cengage.com/international.

Create a Custom Solution that Fits Your Exact Needs! This service develops personalized solutions to meet your business education needs. Match your learning materials to your syllabus and create the perfect learning solution. Consider the following when looking at your customization options for Stice/Stice: *Intermediate Financial Accounting, 18e*:

- Remove chapters you do not cover or rearrange their order, creating a streamlined and efficient text.
- Add your own material to cover new topics or information or to easily provide students with content you are currently printing and handing out to them, saving you time in planning and providing students a fully integrated course resource.
- Add additional material such as cases or chapters from other textbooks.

For Students

SPREADSHEET

Excel Enhanced Spreadsheet Templates, prepared by Beth Woods, *Accuracy Counts*. Excel templates with validations are provided on the Web site for solving selected end-of-chapter exercises and problems that are identified in the text with a spreadsheet icon.

Robust Product Support Web Site

A robust Web site provides a wealth of resources for you and your students in *Intermediate Financial Accounting* at no additional cost! With a multitude of chapter-enhancing features and study aids, these resources will allow students to excel in class and save you time in planning!

Book Resources Available

- Expanded Material Topics
- Instructor's PowerPoint Slides
- Instructor's Resource Manual
- Solutions Manual
- Transparency Masters

Available for Every Chapter

- Check Figures
- Crossword Puzzles
- Enhanced Spreadsheet Templates

- Interactive Quizzes
- Key Terms Flashcards
- Learning Objectives
- Problem Solving Strategy Guide
- Student PowerPoint Slides

To access additional course materials, please visit www.cengagebrain.com. At the CengageBrain.com home page, search for the ISBN of your title (from the back cover of your book) using the search box at the top of the page. This will take you to the product page where these resources can be found.

Acknowledgments and Thanks

Relevant pronouncements of the Financial Accounting Standards Board and other authoritative publications are paraphrased, quoted, discussed, and referenced throughout the text. We are indebted to the American Accounting Association, the American Institute of Certified Public Accountants, the Financial Accounting Standards Board, and the Securities and Exchange Commission for material from their publications.

We'd like to thank the following reviewers for their comments and suggestions that helped shape this latest edition:

Florence Atiase, *University of Texas at Austin*
Al Case, *Southern Oregon University*
Kimberly D. Charland, *Kansas State University*
Douglas deVidal, *University of Texas at Austin*
Kenneth R. Henry, *Florida International University*
Donald Hoppa, *Roosevelt University*
Florence R. Kirk, *State University of New York at Oswego*
Lisa Koonce, *University of Texas at Austin*
Danny S. Litt, *University of California–Los Angeles*
Mostafa Maksy, *Northeastern Illinois University*
Dawn W. Massey, *Fairfield University*
Tommy Moores, *University of Nevada–Las Vegas*
Robert Tezevant, *University of Southern California*

In addition, we would like to thank those who provided comments on recent editions of Intermediate Financial Accounting:

Charlene Abendroth, *California State University, Hayward*
Thomas Badley, *Baker College of Port Huron*
Ira W. Bates, Ph.D., *Florida A&M University*
Daisy Beck, *Louisiana State University*
Martin J. Birr, *Kelley School of Business, Indiana University*
Tiffany Bortz, *University of Texas—Dallas*
Bruce Branson, *North Carolina State University*
Russell F. Briner, *University of Texas—San Antonio*
Helen Brubeck, CA, CPA, *San Jose State University*
Bob Brush, *Cecil Community College*
Suzanne Busch, *California State University, Hayward*
Jane E. Campbell, *Kennesaw College*
Al Case, CPA, *Southern Oregon University*
Gyan Chandra, *Miami University—Oxford*
Kimberly D. Charland, *Kansas State University*
Janice Cobb, *Texas Christian University*
Elizabeth C. Conner, *University of Colorado—Denver*
Teresa L. Conover, *University of North Texas*
David A. Cook, *Calvin College*
Patricia Davis, *Keystone College*
Dan S. Deines, *Kansas State University*
Laura DeLaune, *Louisiana State University*
Susan W. Eldridge, *University of Nebraska—Omaha*
Alan H. Falcon, *Loyola Marymont University*
Michael Farina, *Cerritos College*
Richard Fern, *Eastern Kentucky University*
Mary A. Flanigan, *Longwood College*
Jennifer J. Gaver, *University of Georgia*

Lucille S. Genduso, Ed. S CPA, *Nova Southeastern University*
Joseph Godwin, *Grand Valley State University*
C. Terry Grant, *Mississippi College*
Albert J. Hannan, *The College of Notre Dame of Maryland*
Dr. Chuck Harter, *North Dakota State University*
Clayton H. Hock, *Miami University—Oxford*
Inam Hussain, *Purdue University*
Laura L. Ilcisin, *University of Nebraska—Omaha*
Afshad J. Irani, *University of New Hampshire*
Sharon S. Jackson, *Samford University*
Keith L. Jones, *George Mason University*
Burch T. Kealey, *University of Nebraska—Omaha*
Florence R. Kirk, *SUNY—Oswego*
Gordon Klein, *UCLA*
Mark Kohlbeck, *University of Wisconsin—Madison*
Ellen L. Landgraf, CPA, Ph.D., *Loyola University—Chicago*
Dr. Janice E. Lawrence, *University of Nebraska—Lincoln*
Patsy Lee, *University of Texas—Arlington*
Anne C. Lewis, *Edgecombe Community College*
Sharon M. Lightner, *San Diego State University*
Tim M. Lindquist, *University of Northern Iowa*
Walter J. Luchini, *Champlain College*
Barbara Marotta, *Northern Virginia Community College*
Bernard McNeal, *Bowie State*
David Middleton, *Indiana Institute of Technology*
Jacquelyn Sue Moffitt, Ph.D., *Louisiana State University*
Paula Morris, *Kennesaw State University*
Brian Nagle, *Duquesne University*
Bruce L. Oliver, *Rochester Institute of Technology*
Gyung Paik, *Brigham Young University*
Mary Phillips, *North Carolina Central University*
Richard M. Piazza, *University of North Carolina at Charlotte*
Chuck Pier, *Appalachian State University*
J. Marion Posey, *Pace University*
K. K. Raman, *University of North Texas*
Randall Rentfro, *Florida Atlantic University*
Mary Ann Reynolds, *Western Washington University*
John Rossi, *Moravian College*
Joe Sanders, *Indiana State University*
Donald T. Scala, BBA, MS, *Adelphia University*
Bunney Schmidt, *Utah Valley State College*
Victoria Shoaf, *St. John's University*
Alice Sineath, *Forsyth Technical Community College*
William P. Sloboda, *Gallaudet University*
Sheldon R. Smith, *Utah Valley State College*
Brian B. Stanko, Ph.D., CPA, *Loyola University—Chicago*
Vic Stanton, *University of California, Berkeley*
Undine Stinnette, *Roosevelt University*
John J. Surdick, *Xavier University*
Gary Taylor, *The University of Alabama*
Robert Trezevant, *University of Southern California*
Rebecca Toppe Shortridge, *Ball State University*
Carmelita Troy, *University of Maryland, College Park*
Richard A. Turpin, *The University of Tennessee at Chattanooga*
Robin Wagner, *San Francisco State University*
Scott H. Wang, *Davenport University*
George P. Wentworth, *Brenau University*
Kent Williams, *Indiana Wesleyan University*

Finally, we would like to give special recognition to the following contributors to the Intermediate Financial Accounting *text project:*

Ira W. Bates, *Florida A&M University* ■ Instructor's Manual
Gary Bower, *Community College of Rhode Island* ■ Text and Solutions Verification
Doug Cloud, Professor Emeritus, *Pepperdine University* ■ PowerPoint Slides
Fernando Rodriguez ■ Test Bank
Beth Woods, *Accuracy Counts* ■ Spreadsheets

E. Kay Stice James D. Stice

ABOUT THE AUTHORS

AA

An author team for over 50 years.

Earl K. Stice

Earl K. Stice is the PricewaterhouseCoopers Professor of Accounting in the School of Accountancy and Information Systems at Brigham Young University where he has been on the faculty since 1998. He holds bachelor's and master's degrees from Brigham Young University and a Ph.D. from Cornell University. Dr. Stice has taught at Rice University, the University of Arizona, Cornell University, and the Hong Kong University of Science and Technology (HKUST). He won the Phi Beta Kappa teaching award at Rice University and was twice selected at HKUST as one of the ten best lecturers on campus. Dr. Stice has also taught in a variety of executive education and corporate training programs in the United States, Hong Kong, China, and South Africa, and he is currently on the executive MBA faculty of the China Europe International Business School in Shanghai. He has published papers in the *Journal of Financial and Quantitative Analysis, The Accounting Review, Review of Accounting Studies,* and *Issues in Accounting Education*, and his research on stock splits has been cited in *Business Week*, *Money*, and *Forbes*. Dr. Stice has presented his research results at seminars in the United States, Finland, Taiwan, Australia, and Hong Kong. He is co-author of *Accounting: Concepts and Applications*, 9th edition, and *Financial Accounting: Reporting and Analysis*, 7th edition. Dr. Stice and his wife, Ramona, are the parents of seven children: Derrald, Han, Ryan Marie, Lorien, Lily, Taraz, and Kamila. They also have four grandchildren.

James D. Stice

James D. Stice is the W. Steve Albrecht Professor of Accounting in the Marriott School of Management at Brigham Young University. He also serves as an Associate Dean in the Marriott School. He holds bachelor's and master's degrees from BYU and a Ph.D. from the University of Washington, all in accounting. Professor Stice has been on the faculty at BYU since 1988. During that time, he has been selected by graduating accounting students as "Teacher of the Year" on numerous occasions. He was selected by his peers in the Marriott School at BYU to receive the "Outstanding Teaching Award" in 1995, and in 1999 he was selected by the University to receive its highest teaching award, the Maeser Excellence in Teaching Award. Professor Stice is also a visiting professor for INSEAD's MBA Program in France. Professor Stice has published articles in *The Journal of Accounting Research, The Accounting Review, Decision Sciences*, *Issues in Accounting Education*, *The CPA Journal*, and other academic and professional journals. In addition to this text, he has published two other textbooks: *Financial Accounting: Reporting and Analysis*, 7th edition, and *Accounting: Concepts and Applications*, 9th edition. In addition to his teaching and research, Dr. Stice has been involved in executive education for such companies as IBM, Bank of America, and Ernst & Young and currently serves on the board of directors of Nutraceutical Corporation. Dr. Stice and his wife, Kaye, are the parents of seven children: Crystal, JD, Ashley, Whitney, Kara, Skyler, and Cierra. They also have ten grandchildren.

ABOUT THE AUTHORS

An author team for over 50 years.

Earl K. Stice

Earl K. Stice is the PricewaterhouseCoopers Professor of Accounting in the School of Accountancy and Information Systems at Brigham Young University where he has been on the faculty since 1998. He holds bachelor's and master's degrees from Brigham Young University and a Ph.D. from Cornell University. Dr. Stice has taught at Rice University, the University of Arizona, Cornell University, and the Hong Kong University of Science and Technology (HKUST). He won the Phi Beta Kappa teaching award at Rice University and was twice selected at HKUST as one of the ten best lecturers on campus. Dr. Stice has also taught in a variety of executive education and corporate training programs in the United States, Hong Kong, China, and South Africa, and he is currently on the executive MBA faculty of the China Europe International Business School in Shanghai. He has published papers in the *Journal of Financial and Quantitative Analysis*, *The Accounting Review*, *Review of Accounting Studies*, and *Issues in Accounting Education*, and his research on stock splits has been cited in *Business Week*, *Money*, and *Forbes*. Dr. Stice has presented his research results at seminars in the United States, Finland, Taiwan, Australia, and Hong Kong. He is co-author of *Accounting: Concepts and Applications*, 9th edition, and *Financial Accounting: Reporting and Analysis*, 7th edition. Dr. Stice and his wife, Ramona, are the parents of seven children: Derrald, Han, Ryan Marie, Lorien, Lily, Taraz, and Kamila. They also have four grandchildren.

James D. Stice

James D. Stice is the W. Steve Albrecht Professor of Accounting in the Marriott School of Management at Brigham Young University. He also serves as an Associate Dean in the Marriott School. He holds bachelor's and master's degrees from BYU and a Ph.D. from the University of Washington, all in accounting. Professor Stice has been on the faculty at BYU since 1988. During that time, he has been selected by graduating accounting students as "Teacher of the Year" on numerous occasions. He was selected by his peers in the Marriott School at BYU to receive the "Outstanding Teaching Award" in 1995, and in 1999 he was selected by the University to receive its highest teaching award, the Maeser Excellence in Teaching Award. Professor Stice is also a visiting professor for INSEAD's MBA Program in France. Professor Stice has published articles in *The Journal of Accounting Research*, *The Accounting Review*, *Decision Sciences*, *Issues in Accounting Education*, *The CPA Journal*, and other academic and professional journals. In addition to this text, he has published two other textbooks: *Financial Accounting: Reporting and Analysis*, 7th edition, and *Accounting: Concepts and Applications*, 9th edition. In addition to his teaching and research, Dr. Stice has been involved in executive education for such companies as IBM, Bank of America, and Ernst & Young and currently serves on the board of directors of Nutraceutical Corporation. Dr. Stice and his wife, Kaye, are the parents of seven children: Crystal, J.D., Ashley, Whitney, Kara, Skyler, and Cierra. They also have ten grandchildren.

BRIEF CONTENTS

BC

P1 PART ONE: FOUNDATIONS OF FINANCIAL ACCOUNTING

P2 PART TWO: ROUTINE ACTIVITIES OF A BUSINESS

P3 PART THREE: ADDITIONAL ACTIVITIES OF A BUSINESS

P4 PART FOUR: OTHER DIMENSIONS OF FINANCIAL REPORTING

CONTENTS

PART ONE: FOUNDATIONS OF FINANCIAL ACCOUNTING

P2 PART TWO: ROUTINE ACTIVITIES OF A BUSINESS

EM EXPANDED MATERIAL

CHAPTER 1 Financial Reporting

LEARNING OBJECTIVES

1. Describe the purpose of financial reporting and identify the primary financial statements.
2. Explain the function of accounting standards and describe the role of the FASB in setting those standards in the United States.
3. Recognize the importance of the SEC, AICPA, AAA, and IRS to financial reporting.
4. Realize the growing importance and relevance of international accounting issues to the practice of accounting in the United States and understand the role of the IASB in international accounting standard setting.
5. Understand the significance of the FASB's conceptual framework in outlining the qualities of good accounting information, defining terms such as asset and revenue, and providing guidance about appropriate recognition, measurement, and reporting.
6. Identify career opportunities related to accounting and financial reporting and understand the importance of personal ethics in the practice of accounting.

It all started with a French accountant named René Ricol. In mid- 2008, Mr. Ricol was commissioned by French President Nicolas Sarkozy to write a report on the impact of the worldwide financial crisis of 2007 and 2008.[1] This 148-page report covers a variety of topics including the origins of the crisis, the ongoing response by governments and business, and 30 detailed recommendations for additional actions. But on page 53, Mr. Ricol wrote something that was to have explosive consequences. He wrote: "At present, it is important to ensure that . . . a level playing field between European and U.S. [accounting] rules is achieved." By implication, according to Mr. Ricol, one reason that European banks were having such severe difficulties in the third quarter of 2008 was that U.S. accounting rules were giving an advantage to U.S. banks.

[1] René Ricol, "Report to the President of the French Republic on the Financial Crisis," September 2008.

Hannelore Foerster/Bloomberg/Getty Images

Mr. Sarkozy passed Mr. Ricol's report along to the assembled EU Finance Ministers, who happened to be meeting in Paris. These ministers were shocked—shocked to learn that U.S. accounting rules were creating an "unlevel playing field" to the advantage of U.S. banks. The Finance Ministers issued a communiqué on October 7, 2008, calling for: "[T]he necessity of avoiding any distortion of treatment between U.S. and European banks due to differences in accounting rules . . . We also consider that the issue of asset reclassification must be resolved quickly . . . We expect this issue to be solved by the end of the month, with the objective to implement as of the third quarter."[2]

So, to whom was the call to arms addressed? To the International Accounting Standards Board (IASB), based in London and designated by the European Union as the approved source of accounting standards for all EU nations. IASB standards, collectively known as International Financial Reporting Standards (IFRS), are also recognized as the source of generally accepted accounting principles in every sizeable economy in the world . . . every sizeable economy except one, the United States.

Attention turned to Sir David Tweedie, chairman of the IASB. Sir David was told that the IASB had three days to revise IFRS. Three *days*? The due process requirements of both the IASB and its U.S. counterpart, the FASB, typically result in proposed accounting standards being circulated and discussed for *years*, not days. However, Sir David was told that without an immediate rule change, the EU would go around the IASB and unilaterally change the accounting rules for companies in its constituent countries. It is reported that Sir David considered resigning.[3] However, in order to live to fight another day, he succumbed to the EU pressure and rushed through the accounting change.

So, what was this accounting rule that was viewed as threatening the very survival of European banks? The accountants call it "fair value accounting," and in the business press it is often called "mark-to-market accounting." For companies, such as banks, that actively trade stocks and bonds, the mark-to-market rule says that the investments must be reported on the company's books at current market value, with any paper gains or losses (called "unrealized" gains or losses by the accountants) being reported in the company's income statement. Well, during the third quarter of 2008 (from July 2008 through September 2008), there had been HUGE paper losses for banks and other investors all over the world. These losses reduced the recorded capital of banks and threatened to put many banks in violation of their regulatory capital requirements. So, you can see why banks in particular were upset at "mark-to-market accounting." Note: No one seemed to complain much about mark-to-market accounting in the years when the market was up.

Back to Mr. Ricol. He claimed to have found a provision in the U.S. accounting rules that allowed U.S. banks to reclassify their investment securities into a category that accountants call "held to maturity." The important thing about held-to-maturity securities is that they are reported in the balance sheet at their original cost, not their current market value, with any changes in value being ignored. Thus, this appears to be a loophole that U.S. banks could use to sidestep the harsh impact of mark-to-market accounting. At least that is the way this U.S. rule was explained to the EU Finance Ministers. What the Finance Ministers were not told is that this reclassification is so rare that no one can think of an example of a U.S. company ever actually doing it. In addition, the U.S. rule requires the reclassification to "held-to-maturity" to be done at the prevailing market value on the date of the reclassification, so any paper gains or losses must be recorded in full on that day. This doesn't seem like much of a loophole. But remember, the EU Finance Ministers probably weren't given a full briefing on all the aspects of the U.S. rule; they were only told that this U.S. loophole allowed U.S. banks to avoid mark-to-market accounting, thus appearing to create an unlevel international playing field with European banks being the losers.

Now the story gets really interesting. In drafting the hasty revision to its rules, someone in the IASB (no one is saying who) made the IASB version of this reclassification rule applicable retroactively to July 1, 2008. Very clever. The IASB rule was approved on October 13, 2008, two weeks AFTER the end of the fiscal third quarter of the year.[4] By

[2] Ecofin Council of 7 October 2008, "Immediate responses to financial turmoil."

[3] David Jetuah, "Tweedie nearly quit after fair value change," *Accountancy Age*, November 12, 2008.

[4] "Reclassification of Financial Assets—Amendments to *IAS 39 Financial Instruments: Recognition and Measurement and IFRS 7 Financial Instruments: Disclosures*," International Accounting Standards Board, London, October 2008.

that time, European banks were able to see which of their investments had gone up and which had gone down during the third quarter. This new IASB rule allowed the European banks to roll back the clock to July 1, 2008, and, with the benefit of hindsight, designate some investments to be accounted for using mark-to-market accounting (probably the ones that they now knew went up during the third quarter) and some investments to be reclassified as "held to maturity" at the value existing as of July 1 (probably the ones that they knew, with hindsight, went down during the third quarter).

So, this IASB rule revision, intended to "level" the international playing field, substantially tilted the playing field in favor of those European banks that chose to use it. Some European banks quickly backed away from this blatant manipulation of the accounting rules for their benefit. For example, in its third quarter 2008 financial report, **BNP Paribas** specifically stated that: "BNP Paribas did not use, in the third quarter 2008, the amendment to the *IAS 39* accounting standard authorising the transfer of certain assets . . . from the trading book to other portfolios."[5] On the other hand, **Deutsche Bank** gratefully used the retroactive provision to turn a loss into a profit. Without the retroactive reclassifications, Deutsche Bank would have reported a pre-tax loss of €732 million for the third quarter. With the reclassifications, Deutsche Bank was able report a pre-tax profit of €93 million, which it proudly hailed in its third quarter report.[6]

There are certainly historical examples of U.S. politicians putting pressure on the FASB to revise its rules for some perceived benefit or another. But in the United States the FASB is somewhat shielded from these pressures by the Securities and Exchange Commission (SEC). Internationally, there is no global SEC, so the IASB was left on its own to experience the full force of the European Union's political pressure. Predictably, when faced with an EU ultimatum, the IASB buckled.

Across the Atlantic, U.S. regulators and the U.S. business community could only stand back and watch this political power play with a mixture of amazement and disgust. As of October 2008, the SEC had an announced policy, a "time line," for shifting all U.S. accounting rulemaking responsibility to the IASB by 2014. This policy stemmed from two incontrovertible facts: (1) global capital markets demand a uniform set of accounting rules, and (2) the world will never accept "Yankee" control of this one-world standard. So, the SEC had the choice of either watching the international harmonization parade go by or getting in line behind the IASB banner. However, the October 2008 IASB debacle caused both the SEC and the U.S. business community to reevaluate the benefits of ceding standard-setting power to the IASB, an organization that had now revealed itself as being subject to powers more interested in the well being of European banks than in any abstract notion of global accounting harmony. It was time to rethink the "time line."

SEC Chairman Mary Shapiro was never as enthusiastic about international accounting convergence as was her predecessor, Christopher Cox. She was fearful of "convergence" really being a "race to the bottom" in terms of a degradation in the quality of the U.S. financial reporting environment. During 2009, Chairman Shapiro said cautiously that the "time line" was on hold until the SEC determined exactly how it wanted to proceed.

The SEC's new international accounting convergence "work plan" was announced on February 24, 2010.[7] The SEC is still convinced that "a single set of high-quality globally accepted accounting standards would benefit U.S. investors." However, the SEC has expressed concern about both the quality of the international standards and the process by which those standards are set. Specifically, before ceding standard-making authority to the IASB (or any other international body, for that matter), the SEC wants to ensure that "accounting standards are set by an independent standard-setter and for the benefit of investors." The implication is that the SEC wants to be convinced that the IASB won't again cave in to EU pressure to twist an accounting rule to the benefit of European banks or some other powerful EU constituency. The SEC's "work plan" also states that the SEC will not switch over to IFRS until 2015, at the earliest.

So, what has been the result of that report written by René Ricol? The primary result has been to bring home, dramatically, the remaining barriers to

[5] BNP Paribas Press Release, "Results as at 30 September 2008," November 5, 2008, Paris.

[6] Deutsche Bank, "Interim Report as of September 30, 2008," October 2008, Frankfurt am Main, pages 2 and 53.

[7] SEC Press Release 2010-27, "SEC Approves Statement on Global Accounting Standards," U.S. Securities and Exchange Commission, February 24, 2010, Washington, D.C.

international convergence in financial reporting. The U.S. business community was forced to face the reality that it really doesn't want its reporting rules set by a London-based group that is essentially controlled by the European Union. In addition, all interested parties, both in the United States and overseas, have seen that the IASB differs from the FASB in one extremely important way—the pronouncements of the FASB have the force of law because the regulatory power of the SEC is behind them. But who will enforce the pronouncements of the IASB? Who will ensure that the provisions are applied in a consistent way in each country around the world? Will it ever really be possible to have one truly global set of accounting standards, uniformly interpreted, implemented, and audited? For now, it looks like the answer may be: No.

? QUESTIONS

1. What is "mark-to-market accounting"?
2. When the IASB adopted its amended rule in October 2008, what was significant about the fact that the rule was written so that companies could apply the rule retroactively to July 1, 2008?
3. What impact did the October 2008 IASB debacle have in the United States?

Answers to these questions can be found on page 1-37.

In this text you will learn about many of the key accounting issues integral to an understanding of the October 2008 IASB case described above: the accounting for investment securities in Chapter 14, fair value accounting in the Fair Value Module, and the ongoing effort by the IASB and the FASB to achieve convergence on a globally accepted set of high-quality accounting standards. In fact, this IASB-FASB convergence is such an important issue that it is discussed in every chapter in this book, starting with this one.

As the October 2008 IASB case illustrates, the intricacies of accounting often result in differences of opinion as to what accounting methods are appropriate and the level of disclosure that should be required of companies. Arguments over appropriate accounting are facts of life because accounting involves judgment. Even in cases that don't involve financial statement scandal or political intrigue, the management of a company is likely to have some accounting disagreements with the independent auditor before the company's financial statements are released. If a company falters, outside analysts are sure to find accounting judgments with which, in retrospect, they disagree. If the FASB or IASB propose a new accounting rule, it is certain that some business executives will proclaim the rule to be utterly absurd. This is not because managers are sleazy, conniving, and self-serving (although such managers certainly exist); it is because the business world is a complex place filled with complex transactions, and reasonable people can disagree about how to account for those transactions. As the chapters in this book will explain in detail, accounting for the complex transactions that are commonplace today is much more than the simple "bean-counting" image portrayed of accounting in the popular press.

Your introductory accounting course gave you an overview of the primary financial statements and touched briefly on such topics as revenue recognition, depreciation, leases, pensions, deferred taxes, LIFO, and financial instruments. In intermediate financial accounting, all these topics are back, bigger and better than ever. Now, instead of getting an overview, you will actually get the nuts and bolts. Yes, some of these topics are complex—they are complex because the business world is a complex place. However, when you complete your course in intermediate financial accounting, you will be quite comfortable with a set of financial statements. In fact, you will probably find yourself skipping the statements themselves and turning directly to the really interesting reading—the notes.

Now is an exciting time to be studying accounting. Students have been learning double-entry bookkeeping for more than 500 years. Now it will be your privilege to witness the transformation of financial reporting via the twin forces of internationalization and information technology. Over the next five years, the increased integration of the worldwide market for capital will finally force diverse national accounting practices to converge to one global standard, with the United States being one of the last countries to accept that global standard. This text will help you understand the "how and why" of this process. In the longer term, the power of computers to create and analyze huge databases will change the very nature of accounting. Users will not learn about companies through a few pages of financial statements and notes but, ultimately, through online access to the raw financial data. It isn't clear what "accounting" will entail in the technological future, but it is certain that those professionals trained in the underlying concepts of accounting and in the importance of accounting judgment and accounting estimates will be best able to make the transition. This book is intended to prepare you for the future.

Accounting and Financial Reporting

1 **Describe the purpose of financial reporting and identify the primary financial statements.**

WHY **The purpose of financial reporting is to aid interested parties in evaluating a company's past performance and in forecasting its future performance. The information about past events is intended to improve future operations and forecasts of future cash flows.**

HOW **Internal users have the ability to receive custom-designed accounting reports. External users must rely on the general-purpose financial statements. The five major components of the financial statements are:**

- Balance sheet
- Income statement
- Statement of cash flows
- Explanatory notes
- Auditor's opinion

The overall objective of accounting is to provide information that can be used in making economic decisions.

> Accounting is a service activity. Its function is to provide quantitative information, primarily financial in nature, about economic entities that is intended to be useful in making economic decisions—in making reasoned choices among alternative courses of action.[8]

Several key features of this definition should be noted.

- Accounting provides a vital service in today's business environment. The study of accounting should not be viewed as a theoretical exercise—accounting is meant to be a practical tool.
- Accounting is concerned primarily with quantitative financial information that is used in conjunction with qualitative evaluations in making judgments.

[8] *Statement of the Accounting Principles Board No. 4*, "Basic Concepts and Accounting Principles Underlying Financial Statements of Business Enterprises" (New York: American Institute of Certified Public Accountants, 1970), par. 40.

- Accounting information is used in making decisions about how to allocate scarce resources. Economists and environmentalists remind us constantly that we live in a world with limited resources. The better the accounting system that measures and reports the costs of using these resources, the better decisions can be made for allocating them.
- Although accountants place much emphasis on reporting what has already occurred, this past information is intended to be useful in making economic decisions about the future.

> **! CAUTION**
>
> Remember that accounting information is only one type of information used in decision making. In many cases, qualitative data are more useful than quantitative data.

Users of Accounting Information

Who uses accounting information and what information do they require to meet their decision-making needs? In general, all parties interested in the financial health of a company are called stakeholders. Stakeholder users of accounting information are normally divided into two major classifications:

- Internal users, who make decisions directly affecting the internal operations of the enterprise
- External users, who make decisions concerning their relationship to the enterprise

Major internal and external stakeholder groups are listed in Exhibit 1-1.

EX 1-1 MAJOR INTERNAL AND EXTERNAL STAKEHOLDER GROUPS

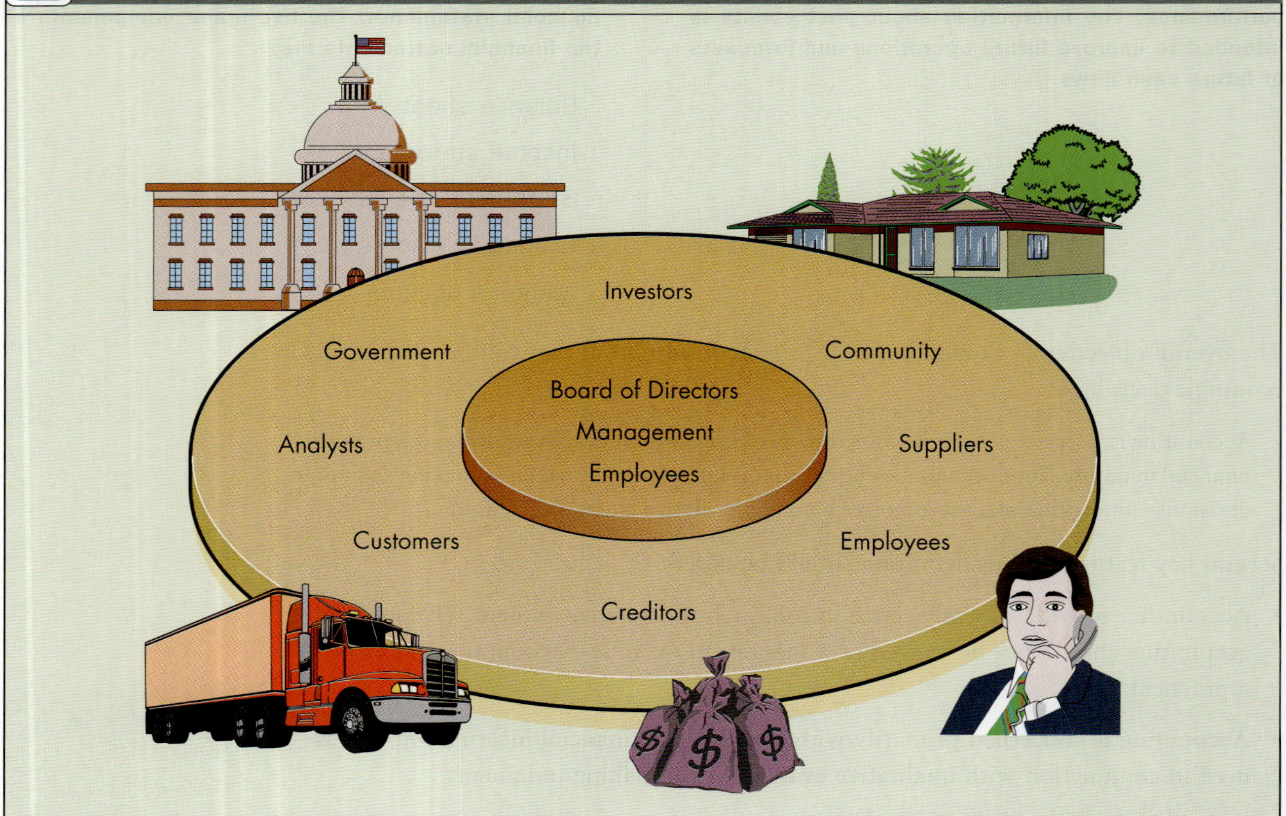

Internal users need information to assist in planning and controlling company operations and managing company resources. The accounting system must provide timely information needed to control day-to-day operations and to make major planning decisions such as:

- Do we make this product or another one?
- Do we build a new production plant or expand existing facilities?

Management accounting (sometimes referred to as *managerial* or *cost accounting*) is concerned primarily with financial reporting for internal users. Internal users, especially management, have control over the accounting system and can specify precisely what information is needed and how the information is to be reported.

Financial accounting focuses on the development and communication of financial information for external users. As a company grows and expands, it often finds its need for cash to be greater than that provided from profitable operations. In this situation, it will turn to people or organizations external to the company for funding. These external users need assurances that they will receive a return on their investment. Thus, they require information about the company's past performance because this information will allow them to forecast how the company can be expected to perform in the future.

Companies compete for external funding because external users have a variety of investment alternatives. The accounting information provided to external users aids in determining (1) whether a company's operations are profitable enough to justify additional funding and (2) how risky a company's operations are in order to determine what rate of return is necessary to compensate capital providers for the investment risk.

The types of decisions made by external users vary widely; therefore, their information needs are highly diverse. As a result, two groups of external users, creditors and investors, have been identified as the principal external users of financial information. Creditors need information about the profitability and stability of the company to decide whether to lend money to the company and, if so, what interest rate to charge. Investors (both existing stockholders and potential investors) need information concerning the safety and profitability of their investment.

Incentives

As mentioned, companies often need external funding if they are to compete in the marketplace. Thus, the managers of these companies have an incentive to provide information that will attract external funding. They want to present information to external users that will make it appear as though their companies will be profitable in the future.

In their pursuit of external funding, management may not be as objective in evaluating and presenting accounting information as external users would like. As a result, care must be taken to ensure that accounting information is neutral. Standards have been established and safeguards have been implemented in an attempt to ensure that accounting information is neutral and objective.

Financial Reporting

Most accounting systems are designed to generate information for both internal and external reporting. The external information is much more highly summarized than the information reported internally. Understandably, a company does not want to disclose every detail of its internal financial dealings to outsiders. For this reason, external financial reporting is governed by an established body of standards or principles that are designed to carefully define what information a firm must disclose to outsiders. Financial accounting standards also establish a uniform method of presenting information so that financial reports for different companies can be more easily compared. The development of these standards is discussed in some detail later in this chapter.

This textbook focuses on financial accounting and external reporting. The general-purpose financial statements are the centerpiece of financial accounting. These financial statements include the balance sheet, income statement, and statement of cash flows.

The three major financial statements, along with the explanatory notes and the auditor's opinion, are briefly described here.

- The balance sheet reports, as of a certain point in time, the resources of a company (the assets), the company's obligations (the liabilities), and the net difference between its assets and liabilities, which represents the equity of the owners. The balance sheet addresses these fundamental questions: What does a company own? What does it owe?
- The income statement reports, for a certain interval, the net assets generated through business operations (revenues), the net assets consumed (expenses), and the difference, which is called *net income*. The income statement is the accountant's best effort at measuring the economic performance of a company for the given period.
- The statement of cash flows reports, for a certain interval, the amount of cash generated and consumed by a company through the following three types of activities: operating, investing, and financing. The statement of cash flows is the most objective of the financial statements because it is somewhat insulated from the accounting estimates and judgments needed to prepare a balance sheet and an income statement.

FYI

The cash flow statement is the most recent of the primary financial statements. It has been required only since 1988.

- Accounting estimates and judgments are outlined in the notes to the financial statements. In addition, the notes contain supplemental information as well as information about items not included in the financial statements. Using financial statements without reading the notes is like preparing for an intermediate financial accounting exam by just reading the table of contents of the textbook—you get the general picture, but you miss all of the important details. Each financial statement routinely carries the following warning printed at the bottom of the statement: "The notes to the financial statements are an integral part of this statement."
- Auditors, working independently of a company's management and internal accountants, examine the financial statements and issue an auditor's opinion about the fairness of the statements and their adherence to proper accounting principles. The opinion is based on evidence gathered by the auditor from

STOP&THINK

In addition to the financial statements, the management of a company has a variety of other methods of communicating financial information to external users. Which ONE of the following is NOT one of those methods?

a) Press releases
b) Postings on the Internet
c) Interviews with financial reporters
d) Paid advertisements in the financial press
e) Preparation and dissemination of detailed operating budgets
f) Public meetings with analysts, institutional investors, and other interested parties

EX 1-2 RELATIVE FREQUENCY OF AUDIT OPINIONS

Types of Audit Opinions Relative Frequency For the Year 2006	Companies
UNQUALIFIED: Financial statements are in accordance with generally accepted accounting principles. They are consistent, and all material information has been disclosed.	2,369
UNQUALIFIED, WITH EXPLANATORY LANGUAGE: The opinion is unqualified, but the auditor has felt it necessary to emphasize some item with further language.	3,624
QUALIFIED: Either the audit firm was somehow constrained from performing all the desired tests, or some item is accounted for in a way with which the auditor disagrees.	5
NO OPINION: The auditor refuses to express an opinion, usually because there is great uncertainty about whether the audited firm will be able to remain in business.	0
ADVERSE: The financial statements are not in accordance with generally accepted accounting principles.	1
Total	5,999

Source: Standard and Poor's COMPUSTAT. The database includes firms traded on the New York, American, and NASDAQ exchanges.

the detailed records and documents maintained by the company and from a review of the controls over the accounting system. Obviously, there is a motivation on the part of management to present the financial information in the most favorable manner possible. It is the responsibility of the auditors to review management's reports and to independently decide whether the reports are indeed representative of the actual conditions existing within the enterprise. The auditor's opinion adds credibility to the financial statements. The types of opinions issued by auditors, along with their relative frequencies, are outlined in Exhibit 1-2. As you can see, the audit opinion is almost always "unqualified."

The financial statements and accompanying notes (certified by the auditor's opinion) have historically been the primary mode of communicating financial information to external users.

Development of Accounting Standards

2 **Explain the function of accounting standards and describe the role of the FASB in setting those standards in the United States.**

WHY **By defining which accounting methods to use and how much information to disclose, accounting standards save time and money for accountants. Users also benefit because they can learn one set of accounting rules to apply to all companies.**

HOW **The Financial Accounting Standards Board (FASB) sets accounting standards in the United States. The FASB is a private-sector body and has no legal authority. Accordingly, the FASB must carefully balance theory and practice in order to maintain credibility in the business community. The issuance of a new accounting standard is preceded by a lengthy public discussion. The Emerging Issues Task Force (EITF) works under the direction of the FASB and formulates a timely expert consensus on how to handle new issues not yet covered in FASB pronouncements.**

Consider this situation. A company decides to pay its managers partly in cash and partly in the form of options to buy the company's stock. The options would be very valuable if the company's stock price were to increase but would be worthless if the company's stock price were to decline. Because the company gives these potentially valuable options to employees, cash salaries don't need to be as high.

Should the value of the options be reported as salary expense or not? (You'll learn the answer to this surprisingly explosive question in Chapter 13.) One alternative is to let each company decide for itself. Users then must be careful about comparing the financial statements of two companies that have accounted for the same thing differently. Another alternative is to have one standard accounting treatment. Who sets the standard?

Accounting principles and procedures have evolved over hundreds of years in response to changes in business practices. The formal standard-setting process that exists today in the United States, however, has developed in just the past 75 years. The triggering event was the Stock Market Crash of 1929. In the aftermath of the crash, many market observers claimed that stock prices had been artificially inflated through questionable accounting practices. The Securities and Exchange Commission (SEC) was created to protect the interests of investors by ensuring full and fair disclosure. The SEC was also given specific legal authority to establish accounting standards for companies desiring to publicly issue shares in the United States. The emergence of the SEC forced the U.S. accounting profession to unite and to become more diligent in developing accounting principles. This led over time to the formation of a series of different private-sector organizations, each having the responsibility of issuing accounting standards. These organizations, their publications, and the time they were in existence are identified in Exhibit 1-3. The SEC has generally allowed these private-sector organizations to make the accounting standards in the United States. These standards are commonly referred to as generally accepted accounting principles (GAAP). Remember, however, that the SEC retains the legal authority to establish U.S. accounting standards if it so chooses.

Financial Accounting Standards Board

The Financial Accounting Standards Board (FASB) is currently recognized as the private-sector body responsible for the establishment of U.S. accounting standards. The FASB was organized in 1973, replacing the Accounting Principles Board (APB). The APB was replaced because it had lost credibility in the business community and was seen as being too heavily influenced by accountants. As a result, the five full-time members of the FASB are drawn from a variety of backgrounds—auditing, corporate accounting, financial services, and academia.[9] The members are required to sever all connections with their firms or institutions prior to assuming membership on the Board. Members are appointed for 5-year terms and are eligible for reappointment to one additional term. Headquartered in Norwalk, Connecticut, the Board has its own research staff and a 2009 operating budget of $29.1 million, much of which comes from fees levied under the Sarbanes-Oxley Act on companies publicly traded in the United States.

Appointment of new Board members is done by the Financial Accounting Foundation (FAF). The FAF is an independent, self-perpetuating body that, like the FASB, is made up of representatives from the accounting profession, the business world, government, and academia. However, the FAF has no standard-setting power, and its members are not full time. The FAF serves somewhat like a board of directors, overseeing the operations of the FASB.

[9] When it was initially established, the FASB was structured to have seven Board members. This number was reduced to five on July 1, 2008. In August 2010, it was announced that the FASB would return to seven board members in 2011.

EX 1-3 U.S. ACCOUNTING STANDARD-SETTING BODIES

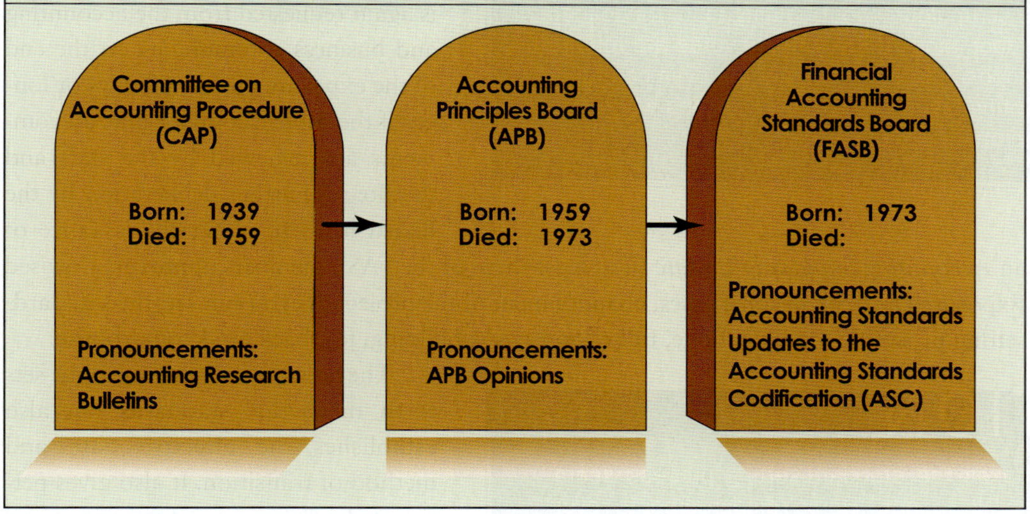

In addition to overseeing the FASB, the FAF is also responsible for selecting and supporting members of the Governmental Accounting Standards Board (GASB). The GASB was established in 1984 and sets financial accounting standards for state and local government entities.

The Standard-Setting Process

The major functions of the FASB are to study accounting issues and to establish accounting standards. These standards are published as Accounting Standards Updates. The FASB has also issued Statements of Financial Accounting Concepts that provide a framework within which specific accounting standards can be developed. The conceptual framework of the FASB is detailed later in the chapter.

The hallmark of the FASB's standard-setting process is openness. Because so many companies and individuals are impacted by the FASB's standards, the Board is meticulous about holding open meetings and inviting public comment. At any given time, the Board has a number of major projects under way. For example, as of May 10, 2010, the FASB was engaged in 23 agenda projects, 17 of which are joint projects with the International Accounting Standards Board (IASB), which is described later in this chapter. These FASB projects address fundamental issues such as revenue recognition and the distinction between liabilities and equity as well as technical issues relating to very complex business transactions such as insurance contracts.

Each major project undertaken by the Board involves a lengthy process. The FASB staff assembles background information and the Board holds public meetings before a decision is made to even add a project to the FASB's formal agenda. After more study and further hearings, the Board often issues a report summarizing its *Preliminary Views*, which identifies the principal issues involved with the topic. This document includes a discussion of the various points of view as to the resolution of the issues, as well as an extensive bibliography, but it does not include specific conclusions. Interested parties are invited to comment either in writing or orally at a public hearing.

After comments from interested parties have been evaluated, the Board meets as many times as necessary to resolve the issues. These meetings are open to the public, and the agenda is published in advance. From these meetings, the Board develops an Exposure Draft of a statement that includes specific recommendations for financial accounting and reporting.

FYI

The FASB is quite scrupulous about holding all of its deliberations in public. In fact, since three (of five) votes are required to pass a FASB proposal, Board members are even careful not to discuss accounting issues at social occasions when three or more Board members are present.

After the Exposure Draft has been issued, reaction to the new document is again requested from the accounting and business communities. At the end of the exposure period, 60 days or longer if the topic is a major one, all comments are reviewed by the staff and the Board. Further deliberation by the Board leads to either the issuance of an *Accounting Standards Update* (if at least three of the FASB members approve), a revised Exposure Draft, or, in some cases, abandonment of the project. As you can see, the standard-setting process is a political one, full of consensus building, feedback, and compromise.

CAUTION

This description makes the standard-setting process seem orderly and serene. It is not. Fierce disagreements over accounting standards are common, and some people hate the FASB.

The final statement not only sets forth the actual standards but also establishes the effective date and method of transition. It also gives pertinent background information and the basis for the Board's conclusions, including reasons for rejecting significant alternative solutions. If any members dissent from the majority view, they may include the reasons for their dissent as part of the document. These dissents are interesting reading. For example, the dissent to the standard on the statement of cash flows (released in 1987) reveals that the Board members disagreed about a fundamental issue—whether payment of interest is an operating activity or a financing activity.[10]

Emerging Issues Task Force The methodical, sometimes slow, nature of the standard-setting process has been one of the principal points of criticism of the FASB. There seems to be no alternative to the lengthy process, however, given the philosophy that arriving at a consensus among members of the accounting profession and other interested parties is important to the Board's credibility.

In an effort to overcome this criticism and provide more timely guidance on issues, in 1984 the FASB established the Emerging Issues Task Force (EITF). The EITF assists the FASB in the early identification of emerging issues that affect financial reporting. Members of the EITF include the senior technical partners of the major national CPA firms plus representatives from major associations of preparers of financial statements. In addition, observers from the SEC, the AICPA, and the IASB (three organizations discussed later in this chapter) are invited to participate in the EITF discussions. The EITF meets periodically, typically at least once every quarter.

As an emerging issue is discussed, an attempt is made to arrive at a consensus treatment for the issue. If a consensus is reached by the EITF, that consensus must then be

[10] Three of the seven members of the FASB dissented to the issuance of the standard on the statement of cash flows. Prior to 1991, a majority of the seven-member board (four members) was the minimum requirement for approval of an Exposure Draft or a final statement of standards. This requirement was changed to a minimum approval of five members, or to what has been referred to as a "super-majority." A number of close, 4–3, votes that resulted in standards not favored by many businesspeople led to strong pressure on the Financial Accounting Foundation to change the voting requirements. Although not favored by members of the FASB, the change was made in 1990. In April 2002, the voting requirement was changed back to 4–3 as an attempt to increase the efficiency and speed of the Board's deliberations. When the number of Board members was reduced from seven to five on July 1, 2008, the simple majority rule (three out of five) was retained.

approved by a majority of the FASB members. That consensus opinion then defines the generally accepted accounting treatment unless and until the FASB decides to reconsider the issue. The EITF not only helps the FASB and its staff to better understand emerging issues but also in many cases determines that no immediate FASB action is necessary.

The consensus opinions of the EITF are published as Accounting Standards Updates. These updates are identified by a two-part number; the first part represents the year the issue was discussed, and the second part identifies the update number for that year. For example, among the consensuses reached in 2010 was Update No. 2010-17, "Milestone Method of Revenue Recognition," which deals with the timing of the reporting of revenue in long-term projects involving significant performance milestones such as the completion of certain regulatory requirements in a pharmaceutical study. [Note: We will talk about revenue recognition at length in Chapter 8.] Although many of the issues are very specialized by topic and industry, the importance of the EITF to the standard-setting process cannot be overemphasized. Because discussions rarely last more than a day or two and a consensus is reached on a majority of the issues discussed, timely guidance is provided to the accounting profession without the lengthy due process of the FASB.

FASB Accounting Standards Codification™ As you saw in the discussion above, both the FASB standards and the EITF consensus opinions are published as Accounting Standards Updates. These Updates serve as formal notification that the official body of generally accepted accounting standards (GAAP) has been updated. This official source of U.S. GAAP is called the FASB Accounting Standards Codification (ASC) and is found on the FASB's Web site at **asc.fasb.org.**

Prior to the launching of the FASB ASC in July 2009, the FASB standards and the EITF consensus opinions were made available as numbered lists of items. So, if you wanted to know about the accounting for research and development costs, for example, you had to know that the accounting for normal R&D costs was contained in FASB Statement of Financial Accounting Standards No. 2 (released in 1974), unless the R&D cost was for software development, in which case the accounting was described in Statement No. 86 (released in 1985). In other words, for everyone except the experienced practitioners and the old accounting professors who had been around for a thousand years, finding a specific accounting rule on a specific topic involved a primitive hunt-and-peck strategy.

The FASB ASC employs a topical menu structure. Accounting topics are grouped under nine broad categories. Each category contains a collection of topics. For example, under the Presentation group of topics, you can find Topic 210 on the balance sheet, Topic 230 on the statement of cash flows, Topic 260 on earnings per share, and more. Under the Broad Transactions group of topics, you can find Topic 805 on business combinations, Topic 840 on leases, and more. A list of topic groupings and individual topics is given in Exhibit 1-4.[11]

Within each Topic, the accounting standard content is organized in additional menus leading eventually down to the paragraph level. A paragraph in the FASB ASC is identified with a four-part address: Topic-Subtopic-Section-Paragraph. For example, the paragraph that explains that cash paid for interest is to be classified in the statement of cash flows as an operating activity is FASB ASC 230-10-45-17.

[11] For those who have a subscription to the "Professional View" of the FASB ASC, key word searches are also possible. The "Basic View" is free, and instructions for registering for the "Basic View" are given in this chapter. The "Professional View" costs about $800 per year. However, your college or university accounting department may have registered for free student access to the "Professional View." Ask your instructor.

- The first number, 230, designates the topic Statement of Cash Flows (which is in the Presentation group of topics).
- The second number, 10, indicates that this is an Overall issue, or subtopic. Other types of subtopics provide standards for particular types of transactions or industries. For example, under Topic 230, there are subtopics explaining statement of cash flow issues related to foreign currency exchange rates, cash flows in the film industry, and others.
- The third number, 45, indicates that this section addresses "Other Presentation Matters." The set of sections under each subtopic is standardized. For most subtopics

EX 1-4 TOPICS IN THE FASB ACCOUNTING STANDARDS CODIFICATION AS OF MAY 2010

General Principles	
105	Generally Accepted Accounting Principles

Presentation	
205	Presentation of Financial Statements
210	Balance Sheet
215	Statement of Shareholder Equity
220	Comprehensive Income
225	Income Statement
230	Statement of Cash Flows
235	Notes to Financial Statements
250	Accounting Changes and Error Corrections
255	Changing Prices
260	Earnings Per Share
270	Interim Reporting
272	Limited Liability Entities
274	Personal Financial Statements
275	Risks and Uncertainties
280	Segment Reporting

Assets	
305	Cash and Cash Equivalents
310	Receivables
320	Investments—Debt and Equity Securities
323	Investments—Equity Method and Joint Ventures
325	Investments—Other
330	Inventory
340	Other Assets and Deferred Costs
350	Intangibles—Goodwill and Other
360	Property, Plant, and Equipment

Liabilities	
405	Liabilities
410	Asset Retirement and Environmental Obligations
420	Exit or Disposal Cost Obligations
430	Deferred Revenue
440	Commitments
450	Contingencies
460	Guarantees
470	Debt
480	Distinguishing Liabilities from Equity

Equity	
505	Equity

Revenue	
605	Revenue Recognition

Expenses	
705	Cost of Sales and Services
710	Compensation—General
712	Compensation—Nonretirement Postemployment Benefits
715	Compensation—Retirement Benefits
718	Compensation—Stock Compensation
720	Other Expenses
730	Research and Development
740	Income Taxes

Broad Transactions	
805	Business Combinations
808	Collaborative Arrangements
810	Consolidation
815	Derivatives and Hedging
820	Fair Value Measurements and Disclosures
825	Financial Instruments
830	Foreign Currency Matters
835	Interest
840	Leases
845	Nonmonetary Transactions
850	Related Party Disclosures
852	Reorganizations
855	Subsequent Events
860	Transfers and Servicing

Note: The specific Industry topics are omitted from this list of topics. Go to **asc.fasb.org** to see the entire list.

you will see a section (10) on Objectives, another section (30) on how accounting items are to be initially measured, and so forth.

- Finally, the fourth number (17) indicates the exact paragraph where the text of the accounting standard is found. In this case, FASB ASC paragraph 230-10-45-17 reads as follows (in part): "All of the following are cash outflows for operating activities . . . (d) Cash payments to lenders and other creditors for interest."

In this textbook you will see many, many references to the FASB ASC. Any person who plans to work in a field where financial statements are prepared or used needs to become comfortable with the Codification. Each chapter in this book includes a short research exercise to give you practice finding things in the ASC. And the end of each chapter includes a matrix that summarizes the FASB ASC material relating to the items covered in that chapter. This matrix also includes references to the old pre-Codification standard numbers, just in case you run across a long-time accountant who has refused to learn the new Codification references. Finally, these end-of-chapter matrices contain the corresponding references to the international accounting standards, which are discussed later in this chapter.

FASB Summary Remember this: The FASB has no enforcement power. Legal authority to set U.S. accounting standards rests with the SEC. FASB standards are "generally accepted," meaning that, overall, the FASB standards are viewed by the business community as being good accounting. However, the credibility of the FASB has fluctuated through the years as different issues have been resolved. For example, within the past 10 years the business community has been outraged by proposed standards for accounting for stock-based compensation and for goodwill. In both of those cases (which are discussed in Chapters 13 and 10, respectively), the FASB was forced to significantly revise its initial proposal. The FASB's job has been described as a "balancing act" between theoretical correctness and practical acceptability.

In addition to the FASB, several other bodies impact accounting standards and are important in other ways to the practice of accounting. Some of these bodies are discussed here.

Other Organizations Important to Financial Reporting

3 **Recognize the importance of the SEC, AICPA, AAA, and IRS to financial reporting.**

WHY **Financial accounting rules are not created by the FASB in a vacuum, and numerous groups provide input into the development of accounting standards.**

HOW ***Securities and Exchange Commission (SEC).*** **To speed the improvement of disclosure, the SEC sometimes implements broad disclosure requirements in areas still being deliberated by the FASB.**

American Institute of Certified Public Accountants (AICPA). **The AICPA establishes some accounting guidance, particularly in areas related to specific industries.**

American Accounting Association (AAA). **The AAA helps disseminate research results and facilitates improvements in accounting education.**

Internal Revenue Service (IRS). **Financial accounting is not the same as tax accounting. However, many specifics learned in intermediate financial accounting are similar to the corresponding tax rules.**

Securities and Exchange Commission

The SEC was created by an act of Congress in 1934. Its primary role is to regulate the issuance and trading of securities by corporations to the general public. Prior to offering securities for sale to the public, a company must file a registration statement with the Commission that contains financial and organizational disclosures. In addition, all publicly held companies are required to furnish annual financial statements (called a *10-K filing*), quarterly financial statements (*10-Q filing*), and other periodic information about significant events (*8-K filing*). The SEC also requires companies to have their external financial statements audited by independent accountants.

FYI

The first chairman of the SEC was Joseph P. Kennedy, father of the late President John F. Kennedy.

The Commission's intent is not to prevent the trading of speculative securities but to insist that investors have adequate information. As a result, the SEC is vitally interested in financial reporting and the development of accounting standards. The Commission carefully monitors the standard-setting process. The Commission also brings to the Board's attention emerging problems that need to be addressed and sends observers to meet with the EITF.

When the Commission was formed, Congress gave it power to establish accounting principles as follows:

> The Commission may prescribe, in regard to reports made pursuant to this title, the form or forms in which the required information shall be set forth, the items or details to be shown in the balance sheet and the earning statement, and the methods to be followed in the preparation of reports in the appraisal or valuation of assets and liabilities. . . .[12]

The Commission has generally refrained from fully using these powers, preferring to work through the private sector in the development of standards. Throughout its existence, however, the Commission has issued statements pertaining to accounting and auditing issues. These SEC statements are authoritative for companies that are publicly traded in the United States. This fact is made clear in FASB ASC paragraph 105-10-05-1, as follows.

> Rules and interpretive releases of the Securities and Exchange Commission (SEC) under authority of federal securities laws are also sources of authoritative GAAP for SEC registrants. In addition to the SEC's rules and interpretive releases, the SEC staff issues Staff Accounting Bulletins that represent practices followed by the staff in administering SEC disclosure requirements, and it utilizes SEC Staff Announcements and Observer comments made at Emerging Issues Task Force meetings to publicly announce its views on certain accounting issues for SEC registrants.

The formal SEC rules are found in the Code of Federal Regulations (CFR). For example, on March 4, 2008, Chapter II of Title 17 of the CFR was amended by the SEC to allow non-U.S. companies to use International Accounting Standards, instead of U.S. GAAP, in their financial statement filings with the SEC. This is an extremely interesting development that will be discussed in more detail later in this chapter.

Although the SEC is generally supportive of the FASB, there have been disagreements between the two bodies. One of the most public of these disagreements occurred in the late 1970s and concerned the accounting for oil and gas exploratory costs. The FASB issued a

[12] Securities Exchange Act of 1934, Section 13(b).

standard in 1977, and the SEC publicly opposed the standard; the FASB finally succumbed to the pressure and reversed its position in 1979. In recent years, the SEC and FASB have increased their efforts at behind-the-scenes coordination and consultation. Still, the two bodies are not in complete harmony. For example, the SEC has been impatient with the FASB's slow progress on improving financial reporting. Often, the SEC establishes broad disclosure requirements in an area while the FASB deliberates about the specific accounting rules. In recent years, this was the pattern with stock-based compensation, environmental disclosures, and derivatives.

As mentioned above, the SEC requires all publicly traded companies in the United States to have their financial statements audited. The auditors of those financial statements must be registered and periodically inspected by the Public Company Accounting Oversight Board (PCAOB), which is a private-sector organization created by the Sarbanes-Oxley Act of 2002. The SEC has congressional authority to oversee the PCAOB's activities.

American Institute of Certified Public Accountants

The American Institute of Certified Public Accountants (AICPA) is the professional organization of practicing certified public accountants (CPAs) in the United States. The organization was founded in 1887, and it publishes a monthly journal, the *Journal of Accountancy*. (*Note*: Anyone interested in current developments in accounting should regularly read the *Journal of Accountancy*.) The AICPA has several important responsibilities, including certification and continuing education for CPAs, quality control, and standard setting.

The AICPA is responsible for preparing and grading the Uniform CPA Examination. This computer-based examination is offered year round in authorized testing centers around the United States. In addition to passing the examination, an individual must meet the state education and experience requirements in order to obtain state certification as a CPA. Most states now require CPAs to meet continuing education requirements in order to retain their licenses to practice. The AICPA assists its members in meeting these requirements through an extensive Continuing Professional Education (CPE) program.

The AICPA is also concerned with maintaining the integrity of the profession through its Code of Professional Conduct and through a quality control program, which includes a process of peer review of CPA firms conducted by other CPAs. For CPA firms that audit publicly traded clients, these AICPA peer reviews are now somewhat overshadowed by the registration and inspection program of the PCAOB mentioned previously.

Prior to the formation of the FASB, accounting principles were established under the direction of the AICPA. Both the CAP and the APB were AICPA committees. Although the FASB replaced the APB as the official standard-setting body for the profession, the AICPA continues to influence the establishment of accounting standards. The AICPA helps the FASB identify emerging issues and communicates the concerns of CPAs on accounting issues to the FASB. In addition, the AICPA frequently establishes the specialized standards that relate to particular industries. For example, in *Statement of Position (SOP) 04-2*, the AICPA issued a set of rules for the accounting for a variety of real estate time-sharing transactions.

American Accounting Association

The American Accounting Association (AAA) is an organization for accounting professors, with 6,052 academic members as of August 2009. The AAA sponsors national and regional meetings where accounting professors discuss technical research and share innovative teaching techniques and materials. The AAA also organizes working committees of professors to study and comment on accounting standards issues. In addition, the AAA publishes a number of academic journals, including *The Accounting Review*, a quarterly research journal, and *Accounting Horizons*, which contains articles addressing many real-world accounting problems. In fact, *Accounting Horizons* is an excellent journal to read for more depth on intermediate financial accounting issues.

One of the most significant actions of the AAA is to motivate and facilitate curriculum revision. As the accounting profession changes, it is critical that accounting educators continually revise their curricula to keep pace with these changes. The AAA provides forums for educators to share ideas about changes in curriculum and rewards innovative curriculum revision efforts. For example, in 1993 our university (Brigham Young University) was given the *Innovation in Accounting Education Award* for the integrative revision of our intermediate financial accounting, managerial accounting, tax, audit, and information systems courses. By the way, our university received this accounting education innovation award again in 2007 (the only university to receive it twice), but we probably shouldn't tell you any more because you might think we are bragging.

FYI

Ask your instructor if he or she is a member of the AAA.

Internal Revenue Service

Tax accounting and financial accounting are different, but the popular perception is that they are one and the same. Tax accounting and financial accounting were designed with different purposes in mind. In the **Thor Power Tool** case (1979), the Supreme Court stated:

> The primary goal of financial accounting is to provide useful information to management, shareholders, creditors, and others properly interested; the major responsibility of the accountant is to protect these parties from being misled. The primary goal of the income tax system, in contrast, is the equitable collection of revenue. . . .

Although this text on intermediate financial accounting is not a study of income tax accounting, the U.S. tax rules as administered by the Internal Revenue Service (IRS) will still be discussed from time to time. In most areas, financial accounting and tax accounting are closely related. For example, your study of leases, depreciation, and inventory valuation in this text will aid your understanding of the corresponding tax rules.

What Is GAAP?

With all of these different bodies (FASB, EITF, AICPA, and SEC) being involved with accounting rules and accounting guidance, what is GAAP? Historically, the Auditing Standards Board of the AICPA has defined GAAP in the context of the phrase included in the standard auditor's opinion: "present fairly . . . in conformity with generally accepted accounting principles."[13] Both the SEC and the AICPA have recognized the FASB as the body entrusted with establishing GAAP in the United States. So, it is the FASB that determines what GAAP is. With the activation of the FASB Accounting Standards Codification in July 2009, the FASB clarified exactly which accounting rules and statements are "authoritative" GAAP and which are merely nonauthoritative suggestions. In FASB ASC paragraph 105-10-05-1, the FASB clearly states that the standards contained in the Codification itself are "the source of authoritative generally accepted accounting principles (GAAP) recognized by the FASB." In paragraph 3 of the same section, the FASB

[13] *Statement of Auditing Standards No. 69*, "The Meaning of Present Fairly in Conformity with Generally Accepted Accounting Principles in the Independent Auditor's Report" (New York: AICPA, December 1991).

states: "Accounting and financial reporting practices not included in the Codification are nonauthoritative. . . . The appropriateness of other sources of accounting guidance depends on its relevance to particular circumstances, the specificity of the guidance, the general recognition of the issuer or author as an authority, and the extent of its use in practice." These sources of nonauthoritative guidance include widely recognized industry practices, the standards of the IASB (discussed later in this chapter), FASB Concepts Statements (also discussed later in this chapter), and even lowly accounting textbooks such as the one you are reading right now. The chapters in this textbook will, of course, focus on the authoritative standards in the FASB ASC.

For firms required to file financial statements with the SEC, the SEC rules and interpretive releases have the same authority as the FASB's Codification. These authoritative pronouncements are of particular importance to auditors because Rule 203 of the AICPA Code of Professional Conduct specifies that an auditor must not express an unqualified opinion when there is a material departure from these authoritative pronouncements.

In the description of the authoritative pronouncements, note that the Statements of Financial Accounting Concepts are relegated to a low-priority position, equal in authority with accounting textbooks(!). The FASB plans to address this issue in a broader project to improve the conceptual framework. As discussed later in this chapter, the conceptual framework embodied in the Statements of Financial Accounting Concepts forms an increasingly important foundation for all financial accounting standards.

FASB CODIFICATION

The Issue: You were at a party last night and, inevitably, the conversation turned to accounting and the FASB. You were embarrassed to learn that ALL of your friends have registered for access to the FASB Accounting Standards Codification (ASC). They were swapping amusing stories about various standards they had been looking at that day in the FASB ASC. You could feel your friends giving you the collective cold shoulder when it became obvious that you had never even seen the FASB ASC.

The Question: What are the steps I need to go through to register for access to the FASB ASC?

Searching the Codification: You start by going to **asc.fasb.org**. Follow the steps to register as a "New User." If you get stuck, take a look at the solution for this Codification item.

The Answer: The correct process is described on page 1-38.

International Accounting Issues

4 **Realize the growing importance and relevance of international accounting issues to the practice of accounting in the United States and understand the role of the IASB in international accounting standard setting.**

WHY **Because business is increasingly conducted across national borders, companies must be able to use their financial statements to communicate with external users all over the world. As a result, divergent national accounting practices are converging to an overall global standard.**

HOW **The International Accounting Standards Board (IASB) is an international body that releases financial reporting standards. IASB standards have become the accepted worldwide standard.**

Divergent national accounting practices around the world can have an extremely significant impact on reported financial statements. With the increasing integration of the worldwide economy, these accounting differences have become impossible to ignore. For example, to raise debt or equity capital, many non-U.S. firms, such as **Sony**, **British Petroleum**, and **Nokia**, list their securities on U.S. exchanges and borrow from U.S. financial institutions. The number of non-U.S. companies listed on the New York Stock Exchange (NYSE) has increased substantially in recent years. As of May 2010, over 450 foreign share issues (from more than 45 countries) were trading on the NYSE. In addition, many U.S. companies have listed their shares on foreign exchanges; for example, **Boeing**'s shares trade on the Amsterdam, Brussels, London, Swiss, and Tokyo stock exchanges. U.S. companies also do substantial amounts of business in foreign currencies; **Disney** has significant amounts of business denominated in Japanese yen, European euros, British pounds, and Canadian dollars.

The international nature of business requires companies to be able to make their financial statements understandable to users all over the world. The significant differences in accounting standards that exist throughout the world complicate both the preparation of financial statements and the understanding of these financial statements by users.

International Differences in GAAP

As will be noted throughout this text, there are some differences between U.S. GAAP and GAAP of other countries. The good news is that the fundamental concepts underlying accounting practice are the same around the world. As a result, a solid understanding of U.S. GAAP will allow you to quickly grasp the variations that exist in different countries. Throughout this book, we will include specific coverage of the areas in which significant differences exist in accounting practices around the world. One other piece of good news is that the demands of international financial statement users are forcing accountants around the world to harmonize differing accounting standards. Accordingly, the differences that currently exist will gradually diminish over time.

International Accounting Standards Board

Just as the FASB establishes accounting standards for U.S. entities, other countries have their own standard-setting bodies. In an attempt to harmonize conflicting standards, the International Accounting Standards Board (IASB) was formed in 1973 to develop worldwide accounting standards. Like the FASB, the IASB develops proposals, circulates these among interested organizations, receives feedback, and then issues a final pronouncement. The 15 Board members of the IASB come from many countries and represent a variety of professional backgrounds.[14]

As of May 2010, the 15 Board members included individuals from the United States, the United Kingdom, France, Sweden, China, Australia, South Africa, Brazil, and Japan. Most of the Board members are CPAs with audit experience, but in May 2010 the IASB also included a financial analyst and several people with national regulatory experience.

The early standards of the IASB were primarily catalogs of the diverse accounting practices then used worldwide. Recent IASB projects have been more focused and innovative. For example, the substance of IASB decisions on improving earnings-per-share reporting was embraced by the FASB. In fact, the FASB and the IASB worked closely to develop compatible standards. In 2002, the IASB and the FASB entered into a joint agreement, called

[14] The IASB will be expanded to 16 members by 2012.

the Norwalk Agreement, in which they pledged to work together to develop a set of "fully compatible" accounting standards as soon as possible, and to continue to work together to make sure that those standards stay compatible. This joint effort is proceeding along two fronts. First, the IASB and the FASB have identified several accounting standard issues on which they could achieve full compatibility without too much difficulty. These issues include the accounting for some inventory costs, accounting for the exchange of nonmonetary assets, and the reporting of accounting changes, all of which have been completed, and the computation of earnings per share, which is still in progress. Second, the IASB and FASB are working together on larger projects involving fundamental issues such as revenue recognition, the accounting for business combinations, and a joint conceptual framework.

The accounting standards produced by the IASB are referred to as *International Financial Reporting Standards (IFRS)* and *International Accounting Standards (IAS)*. The difference between these two sets of standards is merely one of timing; the IASB standards issued before 2001 are called *IAS* and those issued since 2001 are called *IFRS*. In practice, the entire body of IASB standards is referred to simply as *IFRS*. The international counterpart of the FASB's Emerging Issues Task Force (EITF) is called the International Financial Reporting Interpretations Committee (IFRIC), which was called the Standing Interpretations Committee (SIC) before 2002.

IFRSs are envisioned to be a set of standards that can be used by all companies regardless of where they are based. In fact, IFRS will supplement or even replace standards set by national standard setters such as the FASB. IASB standards have gained widespread acceptance throughout the world. And as mentioned earlier, in 2008 the SEC began allowing non-U.S. companies with shares trading on U.S. stock exchanges to issue their financial reports using IASB standards. Before this change, all non-U.S. companies wishing to have their shares traded in the United States were required to provide financial statements in accordance with U.S. GAAP. Historically, financial disclosure requirements in the United States have been the strictest in the world, and foreign companies have been reluctant to provide the U.S. GAAP disclosures. With the new SEC rule, the number of non-U.S. companies listed on U.S. stock exchanges may increase dramatically.

As mentioned in the opening scenario for this chapter, the SEC is considering whether to allow U.S. companies to use IASB standards, rather than FASB standards, in the financial reports that they provide to their U.S. shareholders. If this happens, the FASB may cease to exist. So pay attention because the next few years will be momentous ones in terms of the history of accounting standard setting. However, lest you despair over losing your good friend (the FASB) about whom you have just been reading, remember from the opening scenario of this chapter that the current SEC "work plan" does not envision a U.S. switch to

FYI

In 2001, the IASB restructured itself as an independent body with closer links to national standard-setting bodies. At that time, the IASB adopted its current name and dropped its original name of the International Accounting Standards Committee (IASC).

STOP&THINK

Consider these four organizations: FASB, AICPA, SEC, and IASB. Which ONE do you think will be making U.S. GAAP ten years from now?

a) FASB
b) AICPA
c) SEC
d) IASB

IFRS until 2015 at the earliest. Remember, there are lots of issues of enforcement and independence to work out before the SEC turns the reins over to the IASB. In this textbook, you will learn both U.S. GAAP and, where there are substantive differences, IFRS.

In order to prepare you for a professional world in which both FASB and IASB standards will be used, both sets of standards will be covered in this textbook. The focus will be on FASB standards, but you will also receive comprehensive exposure to the IASB standards in each major topic area throughout the chapters of the text. In addition, Chapter 22 contains capstone coverage of International Accounting Standards.

A Conceptual Framework of Accounting

5 **Understand the significance of the FASB's conceptual framework in outlining the qualities of good accounting information, defining terms such as *asset* and *revenue*, and providing guidance about appropriate recognition, measurement, and reporting.**

WHY **The conceptual framework allows for the systematic adaptation of accounting standards to a changing business environment. The FASB uses the conceptual framework to aid in an organized and consistent development of new accounting standards. In addition, learning the FASB's conceptual framework allows one to understand and, perhaps, anticipate future standards.**

HOW **The conceptual framework outlines the objectives of financial reporting and the qualities of good accounting information, precisely defines commonly used terms such as *asset* and *revenue*, and provides guidance about appropriate recognition, measurement, and reporting. Recording an item in the accounting records through a journal entry is called *recognition*. To be recognized, an item must meet the definition of an element and be measurable, relevant, and reliable.**

A strong theoretical foundation is essential if accounting practice is to keep pace with a changing business environment. Accountants are continually faced with new situations, technological advances, and business innovations that present new accounting and reporting problems. These problems must be dealt with in an organized and consistent manner. The conceptual framework plays a vital role in the development of new standards and in the revision of previously issued standards. Recognizing the importance of this role, the FASB stated that fundamental concepts "guide the Board in developing accounting and reporting standards by providing . . . a common foundation and basic reasoning on which to consider merits of alternatives."[15] In a very real sense, then, the FASB itself is a primary beneficiary of a conceptual framework.

In addition, when accountants are confronted with new developments that are not covered by GAAP, a conceptual framework provides a reference for analyzing and resolving emerging issues. Thus, a conceptual framework not only helps in understanding existing practice but also provides a guide for future practice.

Nature and Components of the FASB's Conceptual Framework

Serious attempts to develop a theoretical foundation of accounting can be traced to the 1930s. Among the leaders in such attempts were accounting educators, both individually and collectively, as a part of the American Accounting Association (AAA). In 1936,

[15] *Statement of Financial Accounting Concepts No. 6*, "Elements of Financial Statements" (Stamford, CT: Financial Accounting Standards Board, December 1985), p. i.

the Executive Committee of the AAA began issuing a series of publications devoted to accounting theory, the last of which was published in 1965 and entitled "A Statement of Basic Accounting Theory." During the period from 1936 to 1973, the AAA and the AICPA issued several additional publications in their attempt to develop a conceptual foundation for the practice of accounting.[16]

Although these publications made significant contributions to the development of accounting thought, no unified structure of accounting theory emerged from these efforts. When the FASB was established in 1973, it responded to the need for a general theoretical framework by undertaking a comprehensive project to develop a "conceptual framework for financial accounting and reporting." This project has been described as an attempt to establish a so-called constitution for accounting.

The conceptual framework project was one of the original FASB agenda items. Because of its significant potential impact on many aspects of financial reporting and, therefore, its controversial nature, progress was deliberately slow. The project had high priority and received a large share of FASB resources. In February 2000, after almost 30 years, the FASB issued the last of seven Statements of Financial Accounting Concepts (usually referred to as *Concepts Statements*), which provide the basis for the conceptual framework.[17]

! CAUTION

Don't think that the conceptual framework is a useless exercise in accounting theory. Since its completion, the framework has significantly affected the nature of many accounting standards.

The seven Concepts Statements address four major areas.

1. *Objectives:* What are the purposes of financial reporting?
2. *Qualitative characteristics:* What are the qualities of useful financial information?
3. *Elements:* What is an asset? a liability? a revenue? an expense?
4. *Recognition, measurement, and reporting:* How should the objectives, qualities, and elements definitions be implemented?

[16] Among the most prominent of these publications were the following:

- Maurice Moonitz, *Accounting Research Study No. 1*, "The Basic Postulates of Accounting" (New York: American Institute of Certified Public Accountants, 1961).
- William A. Paton and A. C. Littleton, "An Introduction to Corporate Accounting Standards, Monograph 3" (Evanston, IL: American Accounting Association, 1940).
- Thomas H. Sanders, Henry R. Hatfield, and W. Moore, "A Statement of Accounting Principles" (New York: American Institute of Accountants, Inc., 1938).
- Robert T. Sprouse and Maurice Moonitz, *Accounting Research Study No. 3*, "A Tentative Set of Broad Accounting Principles for Business Enterprises" (New York: American Institute of Certified Public Accountants, 1962).
- *Statement of the Accounting Principles Board No. 4*, "Basic Concepts and Accounting Principles Underlying Financial Statements of Business Enterprises" (New York: American Institute of Certified Public Accountants, October 1970).
- *Report of the Study Group on the Objectives of Financial Statements*, "Objectives of Financial Statements" (New York: American Institute of Certified Public Accountants, October 1973).

[17] The seven Concepts Statements issued by the FASB are

(1) Objectives of Financial Reporting by Business Enterprises
(2) Qualitative Characteristics of Accounting Information
(3) Elements of Financial Statements of Business Enterprises
(4) Objectives of Financial Reporting by Nonbusiness Organizations
(5) Recognition and Measurement in Financial Statements of Business Enterprises
(6) Elements of Financial Statements (a replacement of No. 3, broadened to include not-for-profit as well as business enterprises)
(7) Using Cash Flow Information and Present Value in Accounting Measurements

Objectives of Financial Reporting

Without identifying the goals for financial reporting (e.g., who needs what kind of information and for what reasons), accountants cannot determine the recognition criteria needed, which measurements are useful, or how best to report accounting information. The key financial reporting objectives outlined in the conceptual framework are as follows:

- Usefulness
- Understandability
- Target audience: investors and creditors
- Assessing future cash flows
- Evaluating economic resources
- Primary focus on earnings

Usefulness The overall objective of financial reporting is to provide information that is useful for decision making. The FASB states

> Financial reporting should provide information that is useful to present and potential investors and creditors and other users in making rational investment, credit, and similar decisions.[18]

Understandability Financial reports cannot and should not be so simple as to be understood by everyone. Instead, the objective of understandability recognizes a fairly sophisticated user of financial reports, that is, one who has a reasonable understanding of accounting and business and who is willing to study and analyze the information presented.[19] In other words, the information should be comprehensible to someone like you.

Target Audience: Investors and Creditors Although there are many potential users of financial reports, the objectives are directed primarily toward investors and creditors. Other external users, such as the IRS or the SEC, can require selected information from individuals and companies. Investors and creditors, however, must rely to a significant extent on the information contained in the periodic financial reports supplied by management. In addition, information useful to investors and creditors in most cases will be useful to other external users (i.e., customers and employees).

Assessing Future Cash Flows Investors and creditors are interested primarily in a company's future cash flows. Creditors expect interest and loan principals to be paid in cash. Investors desire cash dividends and sufficient cash flow to allow the business to grow. Thus, financial reporting should provide information that is useful in assessing amounts, timing, and uncertainty (risk) of prospective cash flows.

Evaluating Economic Resources Financial reporting should also provide information about a company's assets, liabilities, and owners' equity to help investors, creditors, and others evaluate the financial strengths and weaknesses of the enterprise and its liquidity and solvency. Such information will help users determine the financial condition of a company, which, in turn, should provide insight into the prospects of future cash flows.

[18] *Statement of Financial Accounting Concepts No. 1*, par. 34.
[19] Ibid.

Primary Focus on Earnings Information about company earnings, measured by accrual accounting, generally provides a better basis for forecasting future performance than does information about current cash receipts and disbursements. Thus, the FASB states that "the primary focus of financial reporting is information about a company's performance provided by measures of earnings and its components."[20]

Qualitative Characteristics of Accounting Information

The overriding objective of financial reporting is to provide useful information. This is a very complex objective because of the many reporting alternatives. To assist in choosing among financial accounting and reporting alternatives, the conceptual framework identifies the qualitative characteristics of useful accounting information. The key characteristics discussed here are as follows:

- Benefits greater than cost
- Relevance
- Reliability
- Comparability
- Materiality

The relationships among these characteristics and their components are illustrated in Exhibit 1-5.

Benefits Greater Than Cost Information is like other commodities in that it must be worth more than the cost of producing it. The difficulty in assessing cost effectiveness of financial reporting is that the costs and benefits, especially the benefits, are not always evident or easily measured. In addition, the costs are borne by an identifiable and vocal constituency, the companies required to prepare financial statements. The benefits are spread over the entire economy. Thus, the FASB more frequently hears complaints about the expected cost of a new standard than it hears praise about the expected benefits. In the majority of its recent standards, the FASB has included a section attempting to describe the expected costs and benefits of the standard.

Relevance The FASB describes relevance as "making a difference." Qualities of relevant information are as follows:

- Feedback value
- Predictive value
- Timeliness

Relevant information normally provides both feedback value and predictive value at the same time. Feedback on past events helps confirm or correct earlier expectations. Such information can then be used to help

AP Photo/Dave Martin

The estimated cost of environmental cleanup represents a trade-off of relevance and reliability.

[20] *Statement of Financial Accounting Concepts No. 1*, par. 43.

EX 1-5 QUALITATIVE CHARACTERISTICS OF ACCOUNTING INFORMATION

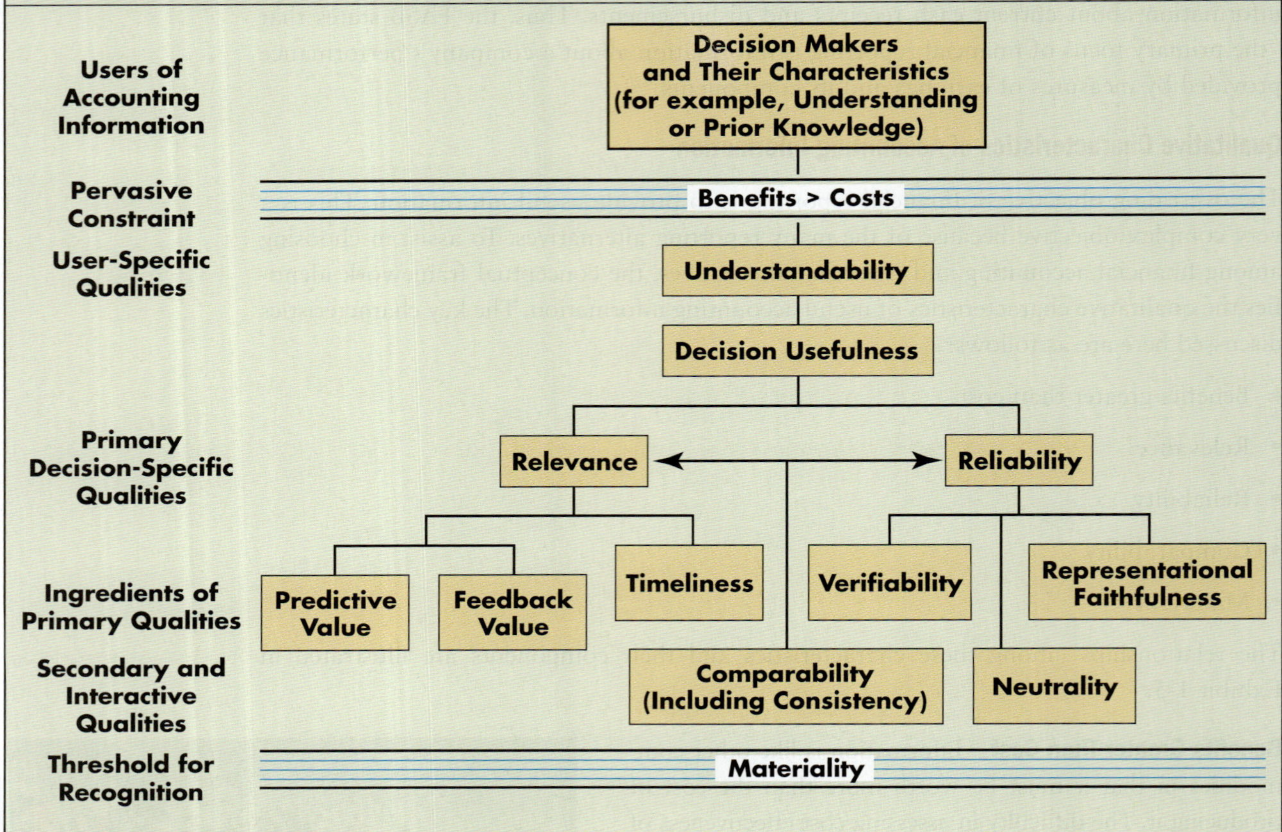

Source: *Statement of Financial Accounting Concepts No. 2.*

predict future outcomes. For example, when a company presents comparative income statements, an investor has information to compare last year's operating results with this year's. This provides a general basis for evaluating prior expectations and for estimating what next year's results might be.

Timeliness is essential for information to "make a difference" because if the information becomes available after the decision is made, it isn't of much use. Financial reporting is increasingly criticized on the timeliness dimension because in the age of information technology, users are becoming accustomed to getting answers overnight, not at the end of a year or a quarter.

Reliability Information is reliable if it is relatively free from error and represents what it claims to represent. Reliability does not mean absolute accuracy. Information that is based on judgments and that includes estimates and approximations cannot be totally accurate, but it should be reliable. The objective, then, is to present the type of information in which users can have confidence. Such information must have the following:

- Verifiability
- Representational faithfulness
- Neutrality

Verifiability implies consensus. Accountants seek to base the financial statements on measures that can be verified by other trained accountants using the same measurement methods. Representational faithfulness means that there is agreement between a measurement and the economic activity or item that is being measured.

Neutrality is similar to the all-encompassing concept of "fairness." If financial statements are to satisfy a wide variety of users, the information presented should not be biased in favor of one group of users to the detriment of others. Neutrality also suggests that accounting standard setters should not be influenced by potential effects a new rule will have on a particular company or industry. In practice, neutrality is very difficult to achieve because firms that expect to be harmed by a new accounting rule often lobby vigorously against the proposed standard.

Many of the difficult decisions in choosing appropriate accounting practices boil down to a choice between relevance and reliability. Emphasizing reliability results in long preparation times as information is double-checked, and there is an avoidance of estimates and forecasts that cloud the data with uncertainty. On the other hand, relevance often requires the use of instant information full of uncertainty. A good illustration is information regarding expected environmental cleanup costs. Toxic waste cleanup takes years, and any forecast of the total expected cleanup cost is full of assumptions. These forecasts are not very reliable, but they are extremely relevant—ask any company that has ever purchased property without considering the potential environmental liabilities. As the world has filled with competing sources of instant information, the accounting standards have slowly moved toward more relevance and less reliability.

Comparability The essence of comparability is that information becomes much more useful when it can be related to a benchmark or standard. The comparison may be with data for other firms or it may be with similar information for the same firm but for other periods of time. Comparability of accounting data for the same company over time is often called consistency. Comparability requires that similar events be accounted for in the same manner on the financial statements of different companies and for a particular company for different periods. It should be recognized, however, that uniformity is not always the answer to comparability. Different circumstances may require different accounting treatments.

Materiality Materiality deals with this specific question: Is the item large enough to influence the decision of a user of the information? Quantitative guidance concerning materiality is lacking, so managers and accountants must exercise judgment in determining whether an item is material. All would agree that an item causing net income to change by 10% is material. How about 1%? Most accountants would say an item changing net income by 1% is immaterial unless the item results from questionable income manipulation or something else indicative of broader concern. Remember that there is no definitive numerical materiality threshold—the accountant must use his or her judgment. In recognition of the importance of the concept of materiality, the SEC released *Staff Accounting Bulletin (SAB) No. 99* in August 1999 to offer additional guidance on this concept. The SEC confirmed that materiality can never be boiled down to a simple numerical benchmark. However, the SEC said that, in terms of an auditor considering whether an item is material, extra scrutiny should be given to items that change a loss to a profit, that allow a company to meet analyst earnings expectations, or that allow management to meet a bonus threshold that otherwise would have been missed.

What About Conservatism? No discussion of the qualities of accounting information is complete without a discussion of conservatism, which historically has been the guiding principle behind many accounting practices. The concept of conservatism can be summarized as follows: When in doubt, recognize all losses but don't recognize any gains. In formulating the conceptual framework, the FASB did not include conservatism in the list of qualitative characteristics (see Exhibit 1-5). Nevertheless, conservatism is an important concept. Financial statements that are deliberately biased to understate assets and profits lose the characteristics of relevance and reliability.

Since the conceptual framework was formulated, the accounting standards have moved away from conservatism. For example, recognition of unrealized gains on financial instruments is now required in contrast to the conservative lower-of-cost-or-market rule in existence when the conceptual framework was written. However, as pointed out by the FASB in *Concepts Statement No. 2*, there is still a place for practical conservatism. When two estimates are equally likely, the prudent decision is to use the more conservative number. This approach provides a counterbalance to the natural optimism and exaggeration of managers and entrepreneurs.

! CAUTION

Although the conceptual framework excludes conservatism from its list of qualitative characteristics, most practicing accountants are still conservative in making their estimates and judgments.

Elements of Financial Statements

The FASB definitions of the 10 basic financial statement elements are listed in Exhibit 1-6. These elements compose the building blocks upon which financial statements are constructed. These definitions and the issues surrounding them are discussed in detail as the elements are introduced in later chapters.

Recognition, Measurement, and Reporting

To recognize or not to recognize . . . THAT is the question. One way to report financial information is to boil down all the estimates and judgments into one number and then use that one number to make a journal entry. This is called recognition. The key assumptions and estimates are then described in a note to the financial statements. Another approach is to skip the journal entry and just rely on the note to convey the information to users. This is called disclosure.

The recognition versus disclosure question has been at the heart of many accounting standard controversies and compromises in recent years. Two examples follow.

- The business community absolutely refused to accept the FASB's decision to require recognition of the value of employee stock options as compensation expense. The FASB initially compromised by requiring only disclosure of the information but finally insisted that, starting in 2006, businesses must recognize the expense rather than just disclose it.
- The FASB has used disclosure requirements to give firms some years of practice in reporting the fair value of financial instruments. Some standards now require recognition of those fair values, and the FASB provides extensive guidance on the use of and required disclosures regarding fair value measurements in the financial statements.

The conceptual framework provides guidance in determining what information should be formally incorporated into financial statements and when. These concepts are discussed here under the following three headings:

- Recognition criteria
- Measurement
- Reporting

EX 1-6 ELEMENTS OF FINANCIAL STATEMENTS

Assets are probable future economic benefits obtained or controlled by a particular entity as a result of past transactions or events.

Liabilities are probable future sacrifices of economic benefits arising from present obligations of a particular entity to transfer assets or provide services to other entities in the future as a result of past transactions or events.

Equity, or Net Assets, is the residual interest in the assets of an entity that remains after deducting its liabilities.

Investments by Owners are increases in equity of a particular business enterprise resulting from transfers to it from other entities of something valuable to obtain or increase ownership interests (or equity) in it. Assets are most commonly received as investments by owners, but that which is received may also include services or satisfaction or conversion of liabilities of the enterprise.

Distributions to Owners are decreases in equity of a particular business enterprise resulting from transferring assets, rendering services, or incurring liabilities by the enterprise to owners. Distributions to owners decrease ownership interests (or equity) in an enterprise.

Comprehensive Income is the change in equity of a business enterprise during a period from transactions and other events and circumstances from nonowner sources. It includes all changes in equity during a period except those resulting from investments by owners and distributions to owners.

Revenues are inflows or other enhancements of assets of an entity or settlement of its liabilities (or a combination of both) from delivering or producing goods, rendering services, or other activities that constitute the entity's ongoing major or central operations.

Expenses are outflows or other using up of assets or incurrences of liabilities (or a combination of both) from delivering or producing goods, rendering services, or carrying out other activities that constitute the entity's ongoing major or central operations.

Gains are increases in equity (net assets) from peripheral or incidental transactions of an entity and from all other transactions and other events and circumstances affecting the entity except those that result from revenues or investments by owners.

Losses are decreases in equity (net assets) from peripheral or incidental transactions of an entity and from all other transactions and other events and circumstances affecting the entity except those that result from expenses or distributions to owners.

Source: *Statement of Financial Accounting Concepts No. 6, pp. ix–x.*

Recognition Criteria For an item to be formally recognized, it must meet one of the definitions of the elements of financial statements.[21] For example, a receivable must meet the definition of an asset to be recorded and reported as such on a balance sheet. The same is true of liabilities, owners' equity, revenues, expenses, and other elements. An item must also be reliably measurable in monetary terms to be recognized. For example, as mentioned earlier, many firms have obligations to clean up environmental damage. These obligations fit the definition of a liability, and information about them is relevant to users, yet they should not be recognized until they can be reliably quantified. Disclosure is preferable to recognition in situations in which relevant information cannot be reliably measured.

Measurement Closely related to recognition is measurement. Five different measurement attributes are currently used in practice.

[21] *Statement of Financial Accounting Concepts No. 5*, "Recognition and Measurement in Financial Statements of Business Enterprises" (Stamford, CT: Financial Accounting Standards Board, December 1984), par. 63.

Most inventories are valued at historical cost—the cash equivalent price exchanged for the goods at the date of acquisition.

1. Historical cost is the cash equivalent price exchanged for goods or services at the date of acquisition. (Examples of items measured at historical cost: land, buildings, equipment, and most inventories.)
2. Current replacement cost is the cash equivalent price that would be exchanged currently to purchase or replace equivalent goods or services. (Example: some inventories that have declined in value since acquisition.)
3. Fair value is the cash equivalent price that could be obtained by selling an asset in an orderly transaction. (Example: many financial instruments.)
4. Net realizable value is the amount of cash expected to be received from the conversion of assets in the normal course of business. (Example: accounts receivable.)
5. Present (or discounted) value is the amount of net future cash inflows or outflows discounted to their present value at an appropriate rate of interest. (Examples: long-term receivables, long-term payables, and long-term operating assets determined to have suffered an impairment in value.)

! CAUTION

You will be doing lots of present value calculations during your course in intermediate financial accounting. Check the batteries in your calculator.

On the date an asset is acquired, all five of these measurement attributes have approximately the same value. The differences arise as the asset ages, business conditions change, and the original acquisition price becomes a less relevant measure of future economic benefit.

Current accounting practice in the United States is said to be based on historical costs, although, as illustrated, each of the five measurement attributes is used. Still, historical cost is the dominant measure and is used because of its high reliability. Many users believe that current replacement costs or fair values, though less reliable, are more relevant than historical costs for future-oriented decisions. Here we see the classic trade-off between relevance and reliability. In recent years we have seen an increasing emphasis on relevance and thus a movement away from historical cost. Most financial instruments are now reported at fair value, and the present value of forecasted cash flows is becoming a more common measurement attribute. The importance of forecasted cash flow information is evidenced by the fact that the most recent addition to the conceptual framework (*Concepts Statement No. 7* adopted in February 2000) outlines the appropriate approach to computing the present value of cash flows. In spite of this trend, the United States still lags behind other countries in the use of market values in financial statements. For example, many British companies report their land and buildings at estimated market values.

Reporting The conceptual framework indicates that a "full set of financial statements" is necessary to meet the objectives of financial reporting. Included in the recommended set of general-purpose financial statements are reports that show the following:

- Financial position at the end of the period
- Earnings (net income) for the period
- Cash flows during the period
- Investments by and distributions to owners during the period
- Comprehensive income (total non-owner changes in equity) for the period

The first three items have obvious reference to the three primary financial statements: balance sheet, income statement, and statement of cash flows. By the way, at the time the conceptual framework was formulated, there was no requirement to prepare a statement of cash flows. One of the early consequences of the completed conceptual framework was an increased emphasis on cash flow and the addition of the cash flow statement to the set of primary financial statements. The fourth reporting recommendation is typically satisfied with a statement of changes in owners' equity. Finally, a statement of comprehensive income is intended to summarize all increases and decreases in equity except for those arising from owner investments and withdrawals. Comprehensive income differs from earnings in that it includes unrealized gains and losses not recognized in the income statement. Examples of these unrealized gains and losses include those arising from foreign currency translations, changes in the value of available-for-sale securities, and changes in the value of certain derivative contracts. Although the concept of comprehensive income has been discussed by the FASB for 20 years, it was finally operationalized in 1998. Beginning in that year, companies were required to provide, in at least one place, information relating to these unrealized gains and losses.

For financial reporting to be most effective, all relevant information should be presented in an unbiased, understandable, and timely manner. This is sometimes referred to as the full disclosure principle. Because of the cost-benefit constraint discussed earlier, however, it would be impossible to report all relevant information. Further, too much information could adversely affect understandability and, therefore, decision usefulness. Those who provide financial information must use judgment in determining what information best satisfies the full disclosure principle within reasonable cost limitations.

Two final points to remember are that the financial statements represent just one part of financial reporting and that financial reporting is just one vehicle used by companies to communicate with external parties. Exhibit 1-7 illustrates the total information spectrum. In one way, this chart is somewhat misleading. Financial reporting is represented as four-fifths of the information spectrum, with other information comprising the other fifth. In reality, the proportions are probably reversed. In a world where online information is available 24 hours a day, the accounting profession faces the challenge of maintaining the relevance of financial reporting in the information spectrum.

Traditional Assumptions of the Accounting Model

The FASB conceptual framework is influenced by several underlying assumptions, although these assumptions are not addressed explicitly in the framework. These five basic assumptions are

- Economic entity
- Going concern

EX 1-7 TOTAL INFORMATION SPECTRUM

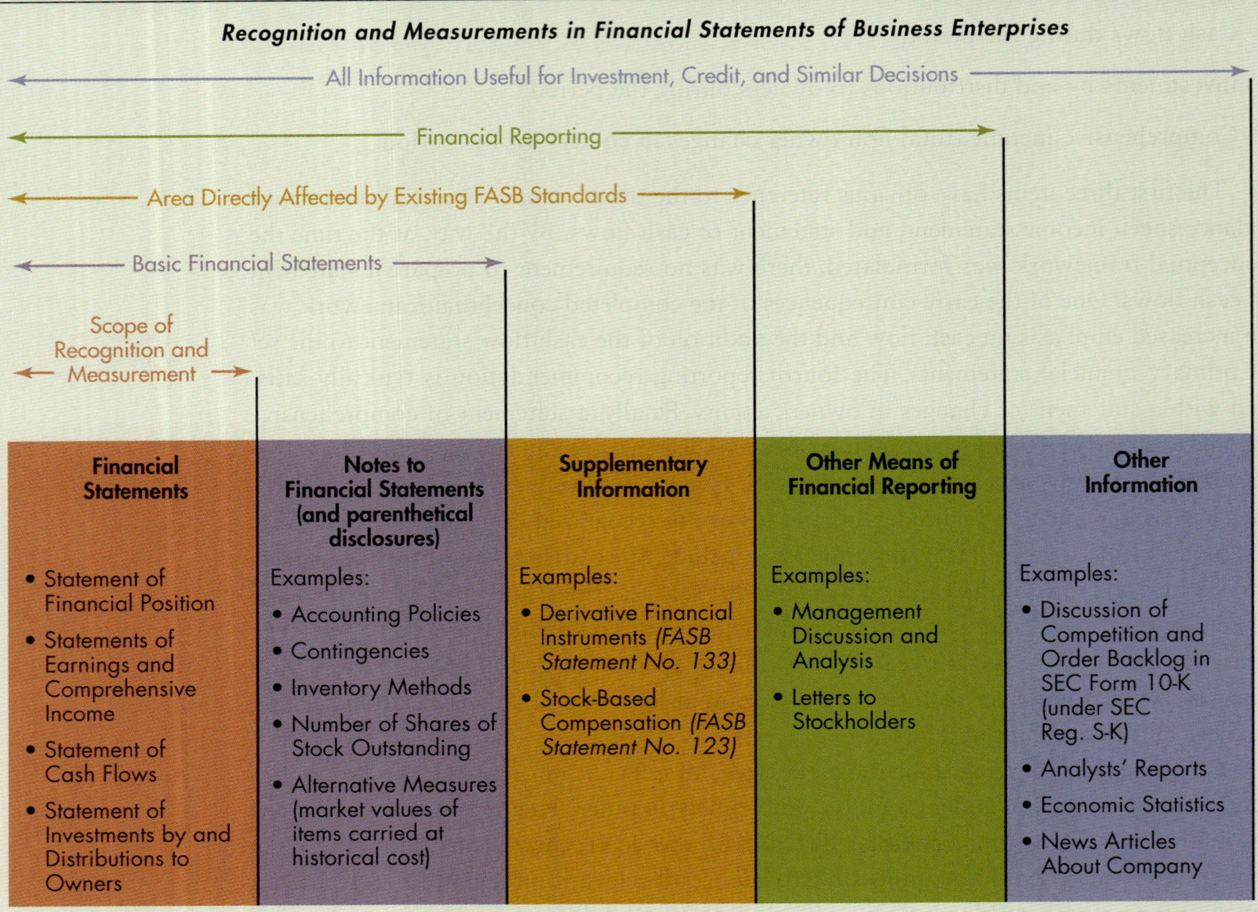

Source: Adapted from *Statement of Financial Accounting Concepts No. 5.*

- Arm's-length transactions
- Stable monetary unit
- Accounting period

The business enterprise is viewed as a specific economic entity separate and distinct from its owners and any other business unit. Identifying the exact extent of the economic entity is difficult with large corporations that have networks of subsidiaries and subsidiaries of subsidiaries with complex business ties among the members of the group. The *keiretsu* in Japan (groups of large firms with ownership in one another and interlocking boards of directors) are an extreme example. At the other end of the spectrum, it is often very difficult to disentangle the owner's personal transactions from the transactions of a small business.

In the absence of evidence to the contrary, the entity is viewed as a going concern. This continuity assumption provides support for the preparation of a balance sheet that reports costs assignable to future activities rather than market values of properties that would be realized in the event of voluntary liquidation or forced sale. This same assumption calls for the preparation of an income statement reporting only such portions of revenues and costs as are allocable to current activities.

Transactions are assumed to be arm's-length transactions. That is, they occur between independent parties, each of which is capable of protecting its own interests. The problem of related-party transactions was at the heart of the **Enron** scandal. Concern about Enron's accounting and business practices escalated dramatically when it was discovered that Enron's CFO was also managing partnerships that were buying assets from Enron.

Transactions are assumed to be measured in stable monetary units. Because of this assumption, changes in the dollar's purchasing power resulting from inflation have traditionally been ignored. To many accountants, this is a serious limitation of the accounting model. In the late 1970s, when inflation was in double digits in the United States, the FASB adopted a standard requiring supplemental disclosure of inflation-adjusted numbers. However, because inflation has remained fairly low for the past twenty years, interest in inflation-adjusted financial statements died in the United States, and the standard was repealed. Of course, many foreign countries with historically high inflation routinely require inflation-adjusted financial statements.

Because accounting information is needed on a timely basis, the life of a business entity is divided into specific accounting periods. By convention, the year has been established as the normal period for reporting, supplemented by interim quarterly reports. Even this innocent traditional assumption has come under fire. Many users want "flash" reports and complain that a quarterly reporting period is too slow. On the other hand, U.S. business leaders often claim that the quarterly reporting cycle is too fast and forces managers to focus on short-term profits instead of on long-term growth. Many other countries require financial statements only semiannually.

Impact of the Conceptual Framework

The conceptual framework provides a basis for consistent judgments by standard setters, preparers, users, auditors, and others involved in financial reporting. A conceptual framework will not solve all accounting problems but if used on a consistent basis over time, it should help improve financial reporting.

The impact of the conceptual framework has been seen in many ways. For example, in *Concepts Statement No. 5,* the FASB outlines the need for a Statement of Comprehensive Income that would contain all of the changes in the value of a company during a period whether those value changes were created by operations, by changes in market values, by changes in exchange rates, or by any other source. This Statement of Comprehensive Income is now a required statement (see FASB ASC Section 220). In addition, the existence of this statement as a place to report changes in market values of assets has facilitated the adoption of standards that result in more relevant values in the balance sheet. Examples are the market values of investment securities and the market values of derivatives. Without the conceptual framework to guide the creation of these standards, their provisions would have been even more controversial than they were.

Related to the conceptual framework is the push toward more "principles-based" accounting standards. In theory, principles-based standards would not include any exceptions to general principles and would not include detailed implementation and interpretation guidance. Instead, a principles-based standard would have a strong conceptual foundation and be applicable to a variety of circumstances by a practicing accountant using his or her professional judgment. A number of accounting standards in the United States, including those dealing with the accounting for leases and derivatives, are full of exceptions, special cases, and tricky implementation rules requiring hundreds of pages of detailed interpretation. The cry for an emphasis on principles-based standards is a reaction to the huge costs of trying to understand and use these voluminous, detailed standards. The ideal of basing accounting standards on a strong conceptual foundation is what motivated the FASB's conceptual framework project in the first place and which continues to motivate the FASB and the IASB to work on a joint conceptual framework (with some parts expected to be completed as soon as 2010).

The framework discussed in this chapter will be a reference source throughout the text. In studying the remaining chapters, you will see many applications and a few exceptions to the theoretical framework established here. An understanding of the overall theoretical framework of accounting should make it easier for you to understand specific issues and problems encountered in practice.

Rules vs. Principles

The most prominent difference between U.S. GAAP and IFRS is that U.S. GAAP contains many more detailed rules. In fact, a shorthand description is that U.S. GAAP is "rules oriented" and IFRS are "principles oriented." This is best summarized in a startling statistic—the entire body of U.S. accounting rules is estimated to occupy 25,000 pages. In contrast, the entire body of IFRS is estimated to occupy 2,500 pages. The theory with IFRS is that the application details in individual circumstances will be determined by the professional judgment of the accountant herself or himself.

For years the FASB has been prodded to transition from a rules approach to a principles approach.[22] In July 2003, the SEC submitted a report to Congress recommending that the FASB move toward "objectives-oriented standards" which would have the following characteristics.

- Be based on an improved and consistently applied framework
- Clearly state the accounting objective of the standard
- Provide sufficient detail and structure so that the standard can be operationalized and applied on a consistent basis
- Minimize exceptions from the standard
- Avoid use of percentage tests ("bright-lines") that allow financial engineers to achieve technical compliance with the standard while evading the intent of the standard

As you can see, an improved conceptual framework is a key element of this transition from rules to principles. Since receipt of this SEC report, the FASB, in conjunction with the IASB, has been moving toward more principles-based standards. The question that continues to be asked in the U.S. business community is whether principles-based accounting standards will work in the U.S. legal environment. Accountants and auditors are concerned that they can never be sure their application of the accounting "principle," without the detailed guidance of rules, will bear up under the after-the-fact scrutiny of trial lawyers, juries, and judges. We'll just have to see what happens.

[22] *Study Pursuant to Section 108(d) of the Sarbanes-Oxley Act of 2002 on the Adoption by the United States Financial Reporting System of a Principles-Based Accounting System*, Securities and Exchange Commission, July 2003.

Careers in Financial Accounting and the Importance of Personal Ethics

6 **Identify career opportunities related to accounting and financial reporting and understand the importance of personal ethics in the practice of accounting.**

WHY **Accounting-related jobs are much more challenging and varied than that of the stereotypical bookkeeper with green eyeshades. Financial statement numbers impact the decisions of the public so accountants bear an ethical responsibility to provide unbiased information.**

HOW **Public accounting firms provide other customer services in addition to auditing. Because all companies have some financial reporting responsibilities, many financial accounting career opportunities are available in industry. In addition, a background in accounting, the language of business, is useful for any career in business. Without a commitment to strong personal ethical behavior, an accountant exercising judgment in preparing financial statements can bias the statements for personal or company gain.**

If you are like most students who take intermediate financial accounting, you aren't taking this class as a general social science elective. You intend to pursue a career in an accounting-related field. This introductory chapter closes with a brief discussion of some of the careers in accounting. One piece of advice: The best career move you can make right now (in addition to taking this class, of course) is to become familiar with your school's job placement office. Ask the people there where the jobs are and what kinds of candidates employers are hiring. Have them help you get started crafting a "killer" résumé. Find out about summer internships. The sooner you start gathering information and establishing a network of contacts, the better.

The three major career areas in financial accounting are:

1. Public accounting
2. Corporate accounting
3. User (analyst, banker, consultant)

Public Accounting

Public accountants do not work for a single business enterprise. Rather, they provide a variety of services for many different individual and business clients. In essence, a public accountant is a freelance accountant, an accountant for hire. Public accountants practice either individually or in firms.

A CPA is a certified public accountant. As mentioned earlier in connection with the discussion of the AICPA, in order to become a CPA, an individual must pass the CPA exam and satisfy education and work experience requirements that differ somewhat from state to state. One of the most significant (and controversial) developments in CPA licensing is the requirement adopted in many states that one must have 150 college credit hours (five years of full-time education) in order to become a CPA.

Traditionally, the most prominent role of CPAs has been as independent auditors of financial statements. Almost all large publicly held corporations are audited by a few large CPA firms. Listed in alphabetical order, the four largest firms are **Deloitte & Touche**, **Ernst & Young**, **KPMG**, and **PricewaterhouseCoopers**. Each of these firms is an international organization with many offices in the United States and abroad. Many small businesses are serviced by regional and local CPA firms, including a large number of sole practitioners. In these smaller firms, the role of auditing is often less important than the areas of tax reporting and planning and systems consulting. A CPA in a smaller firm is expected to be something of an accounting generalist as opposed to the more specialized positions of CPAs in large regional and national firms.

Corporate Accounting

Public accountants move from client to client as accountants for hire. Of course, businesses also employ their own staffs of in-house accountants. A large business enterprise employs financial accountants who are primarily concerned with external financial reporting; management accountants who are primarily concerned with internal financial reporting; tax accountants who prepare the necessary federal, state, and local tax returns and advise management in matters relating to taxation; and internal auditors who review the work performed by accountants and others within the enterprise and report their findings to management. In smaller organizations, there is less specialization and more combining of responsibility for the various accounting functions.

> **FYI**
> You might also consider a career as an accounting instructor. Ask your instructor what he or she thinks.

Not all CPAs are public accountants. Individuals who start their careers in public accounting and become CPAs often leave public accounting after a few years and join the in-house accounting staff of a business. Typically, the company they join is one of the clients they audited or consulted for as a public accountant. In fact, this is the most common career path for college graduates who start out working for one of the large accounting firms.

User (Analyst, Banker, Consultant)

Believe it or not, not everyone in the world wants to become an accountant. Many students take intermediate financial accounting in preparation for becoming a user of financial statements. Credit analysts in large banks are required to have a strong working knowledge of accounting to be able to evaluate the financial statements of firms seeking loans. Investment bankers and brokerage firms employ staffs of analysts to evaluate potential clients and to provide financial statement analysis services to customers. Consulting firms advise clients on how to improve operations. These days, most accounting-related consulting jobs require strong skills in information technology.

The Importance of Personal Ethics

Personal ethics is not a topic one typically expects to study in an intermediate financial accounting course. However, accounting-related scandals such as the one involving Enron have demonstrated that personal ethics and financial reporting are inextricably connected. The flexibility inherent in the assumptions underlying the preparation of financial statements means that an accountant can intentionally deceive financial statement users and yet still technically be in compliance with GAAP. Thus, our financial reporting system is of limited value if the accountants who operate the system do not have strong personal ethics.

Most of us believe that intentionally trying to deceive others is wrong. You will be reminded throughout this text that accounting choices often impact real economic decisions such as whether to grant a loan, make an investment, or fire an employee. Real economic decisions impact peoples' lives, and it is sobering to think that accountants have this power in their hands. Your personal ethical standards are of paramount importance.

Overview of Intermediate Financial Accounting

This chapter has briefly described financial reporting and the accounting standard-setting process, introduced the organizations (and their acronyms) that all accountants should know, outlined the FASB conceptual framework (the "constitution" of accounting), discussed the major accounting-related careers, and reminded you of the importance of personal ethics. In the next four chapters, we will review everything you learned in introductory financial accounting, starting with the accountant's basic tools of analysis, the journal entry and the T-account. The text then covers the accounting standards for the different aspects of a business: operating, investing, and financing. The text concludes with individual chapters on a number of important topics such as deferred taxes, derivative financial instruments, and earnings per share.

As mentioned at the start of this chapter, now is an exciting time to be studying accounting because things are changing so fast. For example, one of the topics most discussed currently is the accounting for financial instruments. Thirty years ago when we took intermediate financial accounting, the accounting for financial instruments was a minor topic. The important point is that we really can't know what the important accounting issues will be thirty years from now. The best preparation for this unknown future is to learn the existing accounting rules, to understand how these rules arose, and to recognize the underlying concepts. That is the aim of this textbook.

? SOLUTIONS TO OPENING SCENARIO QUESTIONS

1. Mark-to-market accounting is the practice of reporting investment securities in the balance sheet at their current market value. For securities that are in an active trading portfolio, the unrealized gains and losses (the "paper" gains and losses) are reported as part of net income.
2. The fact that the rule was retroactive allowed the European banks to roll back the clock to July 1, 2008, and, with the benefit of knowing which securities had increased and which had decreased in value, designate some investments to be accounted for using mark-to-market accounting (probably the ones that they now knew went up during the third quarter) and some investments to be reclassified as "held to maturity" at the value existing as of July 1 (probably the ones that they knew, with hindsight, went down during the third quarter).
3. The primary result of the October 2008 IASB debacle has been to highlight the remaining barriers to international convergence in financial reporting. The U.S. business community was forced to face the reality that it really doesn't want its reporting rules set by a London-based group that is essentially controlled by the European Union. In addition, all interested parties, both in the United States and overseas, have seen that the IASB differs from the FASB in one extremely important way—the pronouncements of the FASB have the force of law because the regulatory power of the SEC is behind them. Who will enforce the pronouncements of the IASB?

SOLUTIONS TO STOP & THINK

1. (Page 1-8) The correct answer is E. Detailed operating budgets are an example of managerial accounting information. This budget information would typically not be revealed to external users.
2. (Page 1-21) The correct answer is a matter of personal opinion. As the business world becomes more global, the need for accounting rules that apply across borders increases. In ten years, it is most likely that an international standard-setting body will be issuing accounting rules that apply to the global economy.

SOLUTION TO USING THE FASB'S CODIFICATION

1. Go to **asc.fasb.org**.
2. On the right side of the screen, click on the word "Order" in the "New User" box. You can also see the "Academic User" box. Your school's accounting department may have registered for academic access. If so, your instructor will have the information you need in order to log in.
3. The "Professional View," at the top of the page, costs over $800. Because this is your first experience with the FASB ASC, it is probably better to choose the "Basic View," at the bottom of the page, which is free. Click "Select."
4. Type in your email address. Don't worry about security—they aren't going to ask for any personal data beyond your name and address. In addition, this is the FASB we are talking about. You can trust them. Click "Submit."
5. Enter your personal data. Then click to submit the data.
6. Accept the terms of the agreement.
7. Gleefully check out with your total bill being $0.00.
8. You are in. You should get an email confirmation of your registration. However, even before you get the email, you can go right to **asc.fasb.org** and log in as a Registered User by clicking in the bottom box on the right side of the ASC home page.
9. Enjoy! Each chapter in this textbook will contain an exercise that will require you to search the FASB ASC. Hint: Don't forget your FASB password. And it wouldn't hurt to tell your mom that you are officially registered with the FASB, with a password and everything. Nothing could make a mother prouder.

REVIEW CHAPTER 1

LEARNING OBJECTIVES

1 Describe the purpose of financial reporting and identify the primary financial statements.

The purpose of financial reporting is to aid interested parties in evaluating the company's past performance and in forecasting its future performance. The information about past events is intended to improve future operations and forecasts of future cash flows.

Internal users have the ability to receive custom-designed accounting reports. External users must rely on the general-purpose financial statements. The five major components of the financial statements follow:

- Balance sheet
- Income statement
- Statement of cash flows
- Explanatory notes
- Auditor's opinion

2 **Explain the function of accounting standards and describe the role of the FASB in setting those standards in the United States.**

Accounting standards help accountants meet the information demands of users by providing guidelines and limits for financial reporting. Accounting standards also improve the comparability of financial reports among different companies. There are many different ways to account for the same underlying economic events, and users are never satisfied with the amount of financial information they receive—they always want to know more. By defining which methods to use and how much information to disclose, accounting standards save time and money for accountants. Users also benefit because they can learn one set of accounting rules to apply to all companies.

The Financial Accounting Standards Board (FASB) sets accounting standards in the United States. The FASB is a private-sector body and has no legal authority. Accordingly, the FASB must carefully balance theory and practice in order to maintain credibility in the business community. The issuance of a new accounting standard is preceded by a lengthy public discussion. The Emerging Issues Task Force (EITF) works under the direction of the FASB. The EITF formulates a timely expert consensus on how to handle new issues not yet covered in FASB pronouncements. The authoritative accounting standards are contained in the FASB Accounting Standards Codification.

3 **Recognize the importance of the SEC, AICPA, AAA, and IRS to financial reporting.**

- *Securities and Exchange Commission (SEC).* The SEC has legal authority to establish U.S. accounting rules but generally allows the FASB to set the standards. To speed the improvement of disclosure, the SEC sometimes implements broad disclosure requirements in areas still being deliberated by the FASB.
- *American Institute of Certified Public Accountants (AICPA).* The AICPA is a key professional organization of practicing accountants. The AICPA administers the CPA exam, polices the practices of its members, and establishes some accounting guidance, particularly related to specific industries.
- *American Accounting Association (AAA).* The AAA is the professional organization of accounting professors. The AAA helps disseminate research results and facilitates improvements in accounting education.
- *Internal Revenue Service (IRS).* Financial accounting is not the same as tax accounting. However, many specifics learned in intermediate financial accounting are similar to the corresponding tax rules.

4 **Realize the growing importance and relevance of international accounting issues to the practice of accounting in the United States and understand the role of the IASB in international accounting standard setting.**

Because business is increasingly conducted across national borders, companies must be able to use their financial statements to communicate with external users all over the world. As a result, divergent national accounting practices are converging to an overall global standard.

The International Accounting Standards Board (IASB) is an international body whose goal is to prepare a comprehensive set of financial accounting standards than can be used anywhere in the world. IASB standards have gained almost universal acceptance worldwide.

5 **Understand the significance of the FASB's conceptual framework in outlining the qualities of good accounting information, defining terms such as *asset* and *revenue*, and providing guidance about appropriate recognition, measurement, and reporting.**

The conceptual framework allows for the systematic adaptation of accounting standards to a changing business environment. The FASB uses the conceptual framework to aid in an organized and consistent development of new accounting standards. In addition, learning the FASB's conceptual framework allows one to understand and, perhaps, anticipate future standards.

The conceptual framework outlines the objectives of financial reporting and the qualities of good accounting information, precisely defines commonly used terms such as *asset* and *revenue*, and provides guidance about appropriate recognition, measurement, and reporting.

The key financial reporting objectives are as follows:

- Usefulness
- Understandability
- Target audience of investors and creditors
- Assessment of future cash flows and existing economic resources
- Primary focus on earnings

Qualities of useful accounting information are the following:

- Benefits greater than cost
- Relevance—feedback value, predictive value, and timeliness
- Reliability—verifiability, representational faithfulness, and neutrality
- Comparability
- Materiality

Recording an item in the accounting records through a journal entry is called *recognition*. To be recognized, an item must meet the definition of an element and be measurable, relevant, and reliable.

The following are the five measurement attributes used in practice:

- Historical cost
- Current replacement cost
- Fair value
- Net realizable value
- Present (or discounted) value

A full set of financial statements includes a balance sheet, income statement, statement of cash flows, statement of changes in owners' equity, and statement of comprehensive income.

6 Identify career opportunities related to accounting and financial reporting and understand the importance of personal ethics in the practice of accounting.

Public accountants are freelance accountants who provide auditing, tax, and a variety of other customer services. In addition, since all companies have some financial reporting responsibilities, there are many financial accounting career opportunities in industry. Because accounting is the language of business, any business career requires a familiarity with financial accounting. Finally, our financial reporting system is of limited value if the accountants who operate the system do not have strong personal ethics.

FASB-IASB CODIFICATION SUMMARY

Topic	U.S. GAAP	IASB
Accounting standard setter	Financial Accounting Standards Board (FASB)	International Accounting Standards Board (IASB)
Financial accounting standards	FASB Accounting Standards Codification (ASC)	• International Financial Reporting Standards (IFRS) • International Accounting Standards (IAS)
Group to address issues of interpretation or for which no formal standard currently exists	Emerging Issues Task Force (EITF)	• International Financial Reporting Interpretations Committee (IFRIC) • Standing Interpretations Committee (SIC) before 2002

KEY TERMS

Accounting 1-5
Accounting periods 1-33
Accounting Principles Board (APB) 1-10
Accounting Standards Updates 1-11
American Accounting Association (AAA) 1-17
American Institute of Certified Public Accountants (AICPA) 1-17
Arm's-length transactions 1-33
Certified public accountants (CPAs) 1-17
Comparability 1-27
Comprehensive income 1-31
Conceptual framework 1-22
Conservatism 1-27
Consistency 1-27
Creditors 1-7
Current replacement cost 1-30
Disclosure 1-28
Economic entity 1-32
Emerging Issues Task Force (EITF) 1-12
Exposure Draft 1-11
Fair value 1-30
Feedback value 1-25
Financial accounting 1-7
Financial Accounting Foundation (FAF) 1-10
Financial Accounting Standards Board (FASB) 1-10
Full disclosure principle 1-31
Generally accepted accounting principles (GAAP) 1-10
General-purpose financial statements 1-8
Going concern 1-32
Governmental Accounting Standards Board (GASB) 1-11
Historical cost 1-30
Internal Revenue Service (IRS) 1-18
International Accounting Standards Board (IASB) 1-20
Investors 1-7
Management accounting 1-7
Materiality 1-27
Net realizable value 1-30
Neutrality 1-27
Predictive value 1-25
Present (or discounted) value 1-30
Recognition 1-28
Relevance 1-25
Reliability 1-26
Representational faithfulness 1-27
Securities and Exchange Commission (SEC) 1-10
Stable monetary units 1-33
Stakeholders 1-6
Statement of changes in owners' equity 1-31
Statements of Financial Accounting Concepts 1-11
Timeliness 1-26
Verifiability 1-26

QUESTIONS

1. *Accounting* has been defined as a service activity. Who is served by accounting and how do they benefit?
2. How does the fact that there are limited resources in the world relate to accounting information?
3. Accounting is sometimes characterized as dealing only with the past. Give examples of how accounting information can be of value in dealing with the future.
4. Distinguish between management accounting and financial accounting.
5. What five items make up the general-purpose financial statements?
6. Contrast the roles of an accountant and an auditor.
7. Why are independent audits necessary?
8. What conditions led to the establishment of accounting standard-setting bodies in the United States?
9. Describe the structure of the FASB. Where does the FASB get its operating funds?
10. What are the differences in purpose and scope of the FASB Accounting Standards Codification and the FASB Statements of Financial Accounting Concepts?
11. What characteristics of the standard-setting process are designed to increase the acceptability of standards established by the FASB?
12. (a) What role does the EITF play in establishing accounting standards? (b) Why can it meet this role more efficiently than the FASB?
13. How does the SEC influence the setting of accounting standards?
14. What is the AICPA? The AAA?
15. Explain the relationship between financial accounting rules and tax accounting rules.
16. Why is standard setting such a difficult and complex task?
17. What constitutes authoritative GAAP in the United States?
18. Why are differing national accounting standards converging to a common global standard?
19. What is the IASB? What is the SEC position regarding IASB standards?
20. List and explain the main reasons why a conceptual framework of accounting is important.
21. Identify the major objectives of financial reporting as specified by the FASB.
22. One objective of financial reporting is understandability. Understandable to whom?
23. Why is it so difficult to measure the cost effectiveness of accounting information?
24. Distinguish between the qualities of relevance and reliability.
25. Does reliability imply absolute accuracy? Explain.
26. Define *comparability*.
27. Of what value is consistency in financial reporting?

28. What is the current numerical materiality standard in accounting?
29. What is conservatism in accounting? What is an example of conservatism in accounting practice?
30. Identify the criteria that an item must meet to qualify for recognition.
31. Identify and describe five different measurement attributes.
32. Briefly describe the five traditional assumptions that influence the conceptual framework.
33. What is the most common career path for a college graduate who starts out in public accounting?
34. What user careers require a knowledge of intermediate financial accounting issues?

EXERCISES

Exercise 1-1
LO5

Elements of Financial Reporting

For each of the following items, identify the financial statement element being discussed.

1. Changes in equity during a period except those resulting from investments by owners and distributions to owners.
2. The net assets of an entity.
3. The result of a transaction requiring the future transfer of assets to other entities.
4. An increase in assets from the delivery of goods that constitutes the entity's ongoing central operations.
5. An increase in an entity's net assets from incidental transactions.
6. An increase in net assets through the issuance of stock.
7. Decreases in net assets from peripheral transactions of an enterprise.
8. The payment of a dividend.
9. Outflows of assets from the delivery of goods or services.
10. Items offering future value to an entity.

Exercise 1-2
LO5

Objectives of Financial Reporting

For each of the following independent situations, identify the relevant objective(s) of financial reporting that the company could be overlooking. Discuss each of these objectives.

1. The president of Daughters, Inc. believes that the financial statements should be prepared for use by management only, because they are the primary decision makers.
2. Sparkling Tile Co. believes that financial statements should reflect only the present financial standing and cash position of the firm and should not provide any future-oriented data.
3. The vice president of Greed Enterprises, Inc. believes that the financial statements are to present only current-year revenues and expenses, not to disclose assets, liabilities, and owners' equity.
4. Lohan Co. has a policy of providing disclosures of only its assets, liabilities, and owners' equity.
5. Bob Building, Inc. always discloses the assets, liabilities, and owners' equity of the firm along with the revenues and expenses. Bob's management believes that these items provide all of the information relevant to investing decisions.

Exercise 1-3
LO5

Assumptions of Financial Reporting

In each of the following independent situations, an example is given involving one of the five traditional assumptions of the accounting model. For each situation, identify the assumption involved (briefly explain your answer).

1. A subsidiary of Parent Inc. was exhibiting poor earnings performance for the year. In an effort to increase the subsidiary's reported earnings, Parent Inc. purchased products from the subsidiary at twice the normal markup.

2. When preparing the financial statements for MacNeil & Sons, the accountant included certain personal assets of MacNeil and his sons.
3. The operations of Uintah Savings & Loan are being evaluated by the federal government. During their investigations, government officials have determined that numerous loans made by top management were unwise and have seriously endangered the future existence of the savings and loan.
4. Pine Valley Ski Resort has experienced a drastic reduction in revenues because of light snowfall for the year. Rather than produce financial statements at the end of the fiscal year, as is traditionally done, management has elected to wait until next year and present results for a two-year period.
5. Colobri Inc. has equipment that was purchased in 2001 at a cost of $150,000. Because of inflation, that same equipment, if purchased today, would cost $225,000. Management would like to report the asset on the balance sheet at its current value.

Exercise 1-4

LO5

Conceptual Framework Terminology

Match the numbered statements below with the lettered terms. An answer (letter) may be used more than once, and some terms require more than one answer (letter).

1. Key ingredients in quality of relevance.
2. Traditional assumptions that influence the FASB's conceptual framework.
3. The idea that information should represent what it purports to represent.
4. An important constraint relating to costs and benefits.
5. An example of conservatism.
6. The availability of information when it is needed.
7. Recording an item in the accounting records.
8. Determines the threshold for recognition.
9. Implies consensus.
10. Transactions between independent parties.

(a) Cost effectiveness	(h) Timeliness
(b) Representational faithfulness	(i) Materiality
(c) Recognition	(j) Predictive value
(d) Verifiability	(k) Economic entity
(e) Time periods	(l) Lower-of-cost-or-market rule
(f) Unrealized	(m) Phrenology
(g) Completeness	(n) Arm's-length transactions

Exercise 1-5

LO5

Aspects of the FASB's Conceptual Framework

Determine whether the following statements are true or false. If a statement is false, explain why.

1. Comprehensive income includes changes in equity resulting from distributions to owners.
2. Timeliness and predictive value are both characteristics of relevant information.
3. The tendency to recognize favorable events early is an example of conservatism.
4. The conceptual framework focuses primarily on the needs of internal users of financial information.
5. The seven Statements of Financial Accounting Concepts are considered part of generally accepted accounting principles.
6. The overriding objective of financial reporting is to provide information for making economic decisions.
7. The term *recognition* is synonymous with the term *disclosure*.
8. Once an accounting method is adopted, it should never be changed.

Exercise 1-6

LO5

Trade-Off Between Qualitative Characteristics

In each of the following independent situations, an example is given requiring a trade-off between the qualitative characteristics discussed in the text. For each situation, identify the relevant characteristics and briefly discuss how satisfying one characteristic may involve not satisfying another.

1. The book value of an office building is approaching its originally estimated salvage value of $100,000. However, its fair value has been estimated at $10 million. The company's management would like to disclose to financial statement users the current value of the building on the balance sheet.
2. JCB Industries has used the FIFO inventory method for the past 20 years. However, all other major competitors use the LIFO method of accounting for inventories. JCB is contemplating a switch from FIFO to LIFO.
3. Hobson Inc. is negotiating with a major bank for a significant loan. The bank has asked that a set of financial statements be provided as quickly after the year-end as possible. Because invoices from many of the company's suppliers are mailed several weeks after inventory is received, Hobson Inc. is considering estimating the amounts associated with those liabilities to be able to prepare its financial statements more quickly.
4. Starship Inc. produces and sells satellites to government and private industries. The company provides a warranty guaranteeing the performance of the satellites. A recent space launch placed one of its satellites in orbit, and several malfunctions have occurred. At year-end, Starship Inc.'s auditors would like the company to disclose the potential liability in the notes to the financial statements. Officers of Starship Inc. believe that the satellite can be repaired in orbit and that disclosure of a contingency such as this would unnecessarily bias the financial statements.

Exercise 1-7
LO5

Applications of Accounting Characteristics and Concepts

For each situation listed, indicate by letter the appropriate qualitative characteristic(s) or accounting concept(s) applied. A letter may be used more than once, and more than one characteristic or concept may apply to a particular situation.

1. Goodwill is recorded in the accounts only when it arises from the purchase of another entity at a price higher than the fair value of the purchased entity's identifiable assets.
2. Land is valued at cost.
3. All payments out of petty cash are debited to Miscellaneous Expense.
4. Plant assets are classified separately as land or buildings, with an accumulated depreciation account for buildings.
5. Periodic payments of $2,300 per month for services of R. Robertson, who is the sole proprietor of the company, are reported as withdrawals.
6. Small tools used by a large manufacturing firm are recorded as expenses when purchased.
7. Investments in equity securities are initially recorded at cost.
8. A retail store estimates inventory rather than taking a complete physical count for purposes of preparing monthly financial statements.
9. A note describing the company's possible liability in a lawsuit is included with the financial statements even though no formal liability exists at the balance sheet date.
10. Depreciation on plant assets is consistently computed each year by the straight-line method.

(a) Understandability
(b) Verifiability
(c) Timeliness
(d) Representational faithfulness
(e) Neutrality
(f) Relevance
(g) Going concern
(h) Economic entity
(i) Historical cost
(j) Measurability
(k) Materiality
(l) Comparability

Exercise 1-8
LO5

Sample CPA Exam Questions

1. One of the elements on a financial statement is comprehensive income. Comprehensive income excludes changes in equity resulting from which of the following?
   (a) Loss from discontinued operations
   (b) Unrealized loss from foreign currency translation
   (c) Dividends paid to stockholders
   (d) Unrealized loss on investments in noncurrent marketable equity securities
2. According to the FASB conceptual framework, the objectives of financial reporting for business enterprises are based on
   (a) generally accepted accounting principles.
   (b) reporting on management's stewardship.
   (c) the need for conservatism.
   (d) the needs of users of the information.
3. Statements of Financial Accounting Concepts are intended to establish
   (a) generally accepted accounting principles in financial reporting by business enterprises.
   (b) the meaning of "Present fairly in accordance with generally accepted accounting principles."
   (c) the objectives and concepts for use in developing standards of financial accounting and reporting.
   (d) the hierarchy of sources of generally accepted accounting principles.
4. According to Statements of Financial Accounting Concepts, neutrality is an ingredient of reliability? Of relevance?
   (a) Yes Yes
   (b) Yes No
   (c) No Yes
   (d) No No
5. According to the FASB conceptual framework, which of the following statements conforms to the realization concept?
   (a) Equipment depreciation was assigned to a production department and then to product unit costs.
   (b) Depreciated equipment was sold in exchange for a note receivable.
   (c) Cash was collected on accounts receivable.
   (d) Product unit costs were assigned to cost of goods sold when the units were sold.

Exercise 1-9
LO5

Measurement Attributes and Going Concern Problems

One of the underlying assumptions of the accounting model is the going concern assumption. When this assumption is questionable, valuation methods used for assets and liabilities may differ from those used when the assumption is viable. For each of the following situations, identify the measurement attribute that would most likely be used if the company is not likely to remain a going concern.

1. Plant and equipment are carried at an amortized cost on a straight-line basis of $2,100,000.
2. Bonds with a maturity price of $1,500,000 and interest in arrears of $400,000 are reported as a noncurrent liability.
3. Accounts receivable are carried at $600,000, the gross amount charged for sales. No allowance for doubtful accounts is reported.
4. The reported LIFO cost of inventory is $250,000.
5. Investments in a subsidiary company are recorded at initial cost plus undistributed profits.

CASES

Discussion Case 1-10

How Should I Invest?

Assume that you just inherited $1 million. You are aware that numerous studies have shown that investments in equity securities (stocks) give the highest rate of return over the long run. However, you are not sure in which companies you should invest. You send for and receive the annual reports of several companies in three growth industries.

In making your investment decision, what useful information would you expect to find in the following?

1. The balance sheet
2. The income statement
3. The statement of cash flows

Discussion Case 1-11

The Advantage of Internal Users

Emilio Valdez worked for several years as a loan analyst for a large bank. He recently left the bank and took a management position with Positron, a high-tech manufacturing firm. Emilio prepared for his first management meeting by extensively analyzing Positron's external financial statements. However, in the meeting, the other managers referred to lots of information that Emilio hadn't found in the financial statements. In addition to using the financial statements, the other managers were using computer printouts and reports unlike anything Emilio had seen in his years at the bank. After the meeting, Monique Vo, one of Emilio's associates, offered the following advice: "Emilio, you have to remember that you are an internal user now, not an external user." What does Monique mean?

Discussion Case 1-12

We Aren't Getting What We Expect

Quality Enterprises Inc. issued its 2012 financial statements on February 22, 2013. The auditors expressed a "clean" opinion in the audit report. On July 14, 2013, the company filed for bankruptcy as a result of the inability to meet currently maturing long-term debt obligations. Reasons cited for the action include (1) large losses on inventory due to overproduction of product lines that did not sell, (2) failure to collect on a large account receivable due to the customer's bankruptcy, and (3) a deteriorating economic environment caused by a severe recession in the spring of 2013. Joan Stevens, a large stockholder with a large number of Quality shares, is concerned about the fact that a company with a clean audit opinion could have financial difficulty leading to bankruptcy just four months after the audit report was issued. "Where were the auditors?" she inquired. In reply, the auditors contend that on December 31, 2012, the date of the financial statements, the statements were presented in accordance with GAAP. What is an auditor's responsibility for protecting users from losses? Are auditors and investors in agreement on what an audit should provide?

Discussion Case 1-13

Does Lobbying Improve the Quality of Accounting Standards?

The "due process" system of the FASB encourages public input into the standard-setting process. It invites written comments, holds public hearings, and often changes proposed standards in response to this input. However, some observers have suggested that this process makes the setting of accounting standards less a technical exercise and more a political one. Parties are known to lobby for or against proposed standards according to their economic interests.

1. How would accounting standard setting be improved by eliminating lobbying?
2. How would accounting standard setting be harmed by eliminating lobbying?

Discussion Case 1-14

How Important Are Economic Consequences?

FASB ASC Subtopic 715-60 requires companies to recognize a liability for their obligation to pay for retirees' health care. Prior to this rule, most companies recognized no liability for their health care promises to employees, although an economic liability certainly existed. Many companies used the adoption of the FASB rule as an excuse to cut retiree health benefits, claiming that the FASB had suddenly created this liability. Thus, it seems that an FASB accounting rule had an economic impact on retirees. Recognizing that accounting rules can have economic consequences, sometimes unintended and undesirable, should the impact on society be an important consideration for the FASB in setting accounting standards?

Discussion Case 1-15

ifrs

Who Needs International Accounting?

Tom Obstinate is disgusted by all of the emphasis being put on international accounting issues. Tom plans to practice accounting in the United States, with U.S. companies, using U.S. GAAP. Accordingly, Tom sees no reason to know anything about the International Accounting Standards Board or cross-national differences in accounting practices. Is there any merit in Tom's view? What might you say to Tom to get him to reconsider his position?

Discussion Case 1-16

You Need More Education!

For more than three decades, accounting professionals, accounting educators, and accounting bodies have debated requiring more education for those entering the public accounting profession. In 1988, the AICPA passed a resolution mandating 150 college credit hours as a minimum educational requirement for all new members of its organization after 1999. This requirement placed added pressure on state legislators to pass new accounting legislation, and during the 1990s, an increasing number of states passed the "150-hour rule." Some groups, however, oppose this move and argue that it is restrictive to entry of minority groups and that it will unnecessarily reduce the number of accounting graduates and put accounting educators "out of work" as students opt for less expensive educational alternatives.

Why does the accounting profession recommend more education for new accounting professionals? Why would some groups resist this move? As an accounting student, were you deterred in your decision to major in accounting because of the "150-hour rule"? Why or why not?

Discussion Case 1-17

Let's Play by the IRS Rules

Little attempt is made to reconcile the accounting standard differences between the IRS and the FASB. These differences are recognized as arising from differences in the objectives of the two bodies. However, the existence of differences requires companies to keep two different sets of records in some areas: records that follow the FASB pronouncements and those that follow the IRS rules and regulations.

Historically, the financial accounting standards in some countries have closely followed the tax rules established by the respective government. What applies for taxes often applies for the balance sheet and the income statement as well.

What are the advantages of merging accounting standards for taxes and financial reporting? What are the disadvantages? What would it take to change a system so deeply ingrained in the business fabric of either the United States or other countries?

Discussion Case 1-18

Cash Flow vs. Earnings

The FASB concluded in *Concepts Statement No. 1* that investors and creditors are interested in an enterprise's future cash flows. However, the Board further stated that the primary focus of financial reporting is information about earnings. If an investor or creditor is interested in future cash flows, why isn't the focus on an examination of a firm's past cash flows? What are the limitations associated with using cash flows to measure the performance of an enterprise? Conversely, what are the risks to an investor or creditor of focusing solely on accrual-based earnings figures?

Discussion Case 1-19

What Is an Asset?

Conserv Corporation, a computer software company, is trying to determine the appropriate accounting procedure to apply to its software development costs. Management is considering capitalizing the development costs and amortizing them over several years. Alternatively, they are considering charging the costs to expense as soon as they are incurred. You, as an accountant, have been asked to help settle this issue. Which definitions of financial statement elements would apply to these costs? Based on this information, what accounting procedure would you recommend and why?

Discussion Case 1-20

Which Measurement Attribute Is Right for Bonds Payable?

Companies regularly obtain money through the issuance of bonds. The market value of bonds changes daily and on any given day is a function of many factors including economic variables, interest rates, industry developments, and firm specific information. Should bonds be reported on the books of the issuer at their market value on the balance sheet date? at their historical selling price? at their discounted present value? or at their eventual maturity value? For each of these measurement attributes, identify and discuss the issues associated with each attribute.

Discussion Case 1-21

But We Need Only One Accounting Standard—Fairness

In the 1970s, a leader in the accounting profession proposed that there really needed to be only one underlying standard to govern the establishment of generally accepted accounting principles. That standard was identified as *fairness*. Financial statements should be prepared so that they are fair to all users: management, labor, investors, creditors. As changes occur in society, financial reporting should change to fairly reflect each user's needs. Because the financial statements are the responsibility of management, such a standard would require management to determine what reporting methods would be fair. What advantages do you see to this proposal? What would be management's most serious problem in applying a fairness standard?

Discussion Case 1-22

And Then There Were Four

The existence of just four large CPA firms that service virtually all of the major industrial and financial companies and thus dominate the accounting profession has led to criticism through the years.

1. What dangers do you see from the dominance of a few large CPA firms? What advantages?
2. During the 1980s and 1990s, mergers among the large public accounting firms reduced the Big 8 to the Big 5. The death of **Arthur Andersen** (because of the **Enron** scandal) reduced the number to four. One reason offered for the mergers was that they improved the ability of the merging firms to provide the broad array of consulting services that provided an increasing share of the revenues of the large accounting firms. What problems do you think intensified as public accounting firms earned an ever-larger share of their income from consulting?

Case 1-23

Deciphering Financial Statements (The Walt Disney Company)

Locate the 2009 financial statements for **The Walt Disney Company** on the Internet and consider the following questions:

1. How well did Disney do financially during the year ended October 3, 2009? (*Hint*: Look at the income statement.)
2. Comment on the level of detail in Disney's balance sheet. Should there be more balance sheet categories or fewer?
3. In 2009, was Disney's net cash from operations sufficient to pay for its investments in parks, resorts, and other property and in the acquisition of other businesses?
4. Look at the notes to the financial statements. You will find 18 of them. Which ones seem to give you the most new information?
5. Find the auditor's opinion. Who is Disney's auditor? Was the 2009 audit opinion unqualified?

Case 1-24

Deciphering Financial Statements (McDonald's Corporation)

The following information comes from the 2009 financial statements of **McDonald's Corporation.**

Conventional franchise arrangements generally include a lease and a license and provide for payment of initial fees, as well as continuing rent and royalties to the Company based upon a percent of sales with minimum rent payments that parallel the Company's underlying leases and escalations (on properties that are leased). Under this arrangement, franchisees are granted the right to operate a restaurant using the McDonald's System and, in most cases, the use of a restaurant facility, generally for a period of 20 years. These franchisees pay related occupancy costs including property taxes, insurance and maintenance. Affiliates and developmental licensees operating under license agreements pay a royalty to the Company based upon a percent of sales, and may pay initial fees.

The results of operations of restaurant businesses purchased and sold in transactions with franchisees were not material to the consolidated financial statements for periods prior to purchase and sale.

Revenues from franchised restaurants consisted of:

In millions	2009	2008	2007
Rents	$4,841.0	$4,612.8	$4,177.2
Royalties	2,379.8	2,275.7	1,941.1
Initial fees	65.4	73.0	57.3
Revenues from franchised restaurants	$7,286.2	$6,961.5	$6,175.6

Future minimum rent payments due to the Company under existing franchise arrangements are:

In millions	Owned sites	Leased sites	Total
2010	$ 1,218.1	$ 1,076.0	$ 2,294.1
2011	1,177.3	1,042.9	2,220.2
2012	1,144.5	1,011.5	2,156.0
2013	1,105.1	972.4	2,077.5
2014	1,062.1	924.8	1,986.9
Thereafter	8,495.8	6,782.5	15,278.3
Total minimum payments	$14,202.9	$11,810.1	$26,013.0

This $26.0 billion amount represents the future minimum payments that McDonald's expected to receive from its franchisees as of December 31, 2009.

1. Using the element definition from the conceptual framework, should this $26.0 billion be recorded as an asset in McDonald's 2009 balance sheet? Why or why not?
2. If your answer in part (1) is yes, what measurement attribute should be used in reporting the asset?

Case 1-25

Writing Assignment (Should the SEC replace the FASB?)

Imagine that you have been selected to compete with students from other universities in presenting a case considering whether the FASB should be abolished and its standard-setting role taken over by the SEC.

Prepare a one-page summary outlining the major arguments for and against the SEC replacing the FASB.

Case 1-26 **Ethical Dilemma (Should you manipulate your reported income?)**

Accounting standards place limits on the set of allowable alternative accounting treatments, but the accountant must still exercise judgment to choose among the remaining alternatives. In making those choices, which of the following should the accountant seek to do?

1. Maximize reported income.
2. Minimize reported income.
3. Ignore the impact of the accounting choice on income and just focus on the most conceptually correct option.

Would your answer change if this were a tax accounting class? Why or why not?

CHAPTER 2 A REVIEW OF THE ACCOUNTING CYCLE

LEARNING OBJECTIVES

1. Identify and explain the basic steps in the accounting process (accounting cycle).
2. Analyze transactions and make and post journal entries.
3. Make adjusting entries, produce financial statements, and close nominal accounts.
4. Distinguish between accrual and cash-basis accounting.
5. Discuss the importance and expanding role of computers to the accounting process.

Tom Clancy typed the first draft of his first novel, *The Hunt for Red October*, on an **IBM** Selectric typewriter while still holding down his full-time job as an insurance agent. The book was published in October 1984, and sales took off when it became known that the book was President Ronald Reagan's favorite. To date, Clancy has published a total of nine novels featuring the reluctant hero, Jack Ryan, and two featuring Ryan's son. The stories have been so popular that Clancy has commanded a $25 million advance per book.

In *The Hunt for Red October*, Jack Ryan, who was trained as a historian, is a part-time analyst for the CIA. By the sixth novel in the series, *Debt of Honor*, a well-earned reputation for being a "good man in a storm" has landed Ryan, against his wishes, in the position of serving as the president's national security advisor. Jack Ryan's abilities are tested as an international crisis is touched off when a group of Japanese businessmen gain control of their government and determine that the only way to save the Japanese economy is through neutralization of U.S. power in the Pacific.

The first act of war against the United States is not an attack on a military target but on the bookkeeping system used by U.S. stock exchanges. A computer virus injected into the program used to record trades on all the major U.S. stock exchanges is activated at noon on Friday. The records of all trades made after that time are eliminated so that

Jin Lee/Bloomberg/Getty Images

No trading house, institution, or private investor could know what it had bought or sold, to or from whom, or for how much, and none could therefore know how much money was available for other trades, or for that matter, to purchase groceries over the weekend. (Tom Clancy, *Debt of Honor*, page 312)

The uncertainty created by the destruction of the stock exchanges' bookkeeping records threatens to throw the U.S. economy into a tailspin and distract U.S. policy makers from other moves being made by Japan in the Pacific. Jack Ryan saves the world as we know it and restores the U.S. economy to sound footing by . . . well, it wouldn't be fair to say—you'll have to read the book. Suffice it to say that a key part of the restoration plan is the repair of the stock exchanges' bookkeeping system.

This fictitious attack was an eerie precursor to the actual attack on the World Trade Center in New York City on September 11, 2001. In addition to the tragic loss of life, this attack also closed the New York Stock Exchange (NYSE) for four business days; it reopened the following Monday. The market fell by 7.1% when trading resumed. The impact on the U.S. economy could have been even greater if Wall Street firms had not had disaster recovery and data backup plans in place. In fact, within two months (November 9, 2001), the Dow Jones Industrial Average had recovered to its pre-attack level.

QUESTIONS

1. What would be the consequences to a customer if her bank could not tell her if her paycheck (which is direct deposited) had in fact been deposited? What would be the consequences to the bank?
2. Suppose the Internal Revenue Service and employers had no system established to track the amount of income tax withheld from employee salaries. How would taxpayers demonstrate to the U.S. government that they had paid taxes? How would the government verify tax payments?

Answers to these questions can be found on page 2-25.

These two examples, one fictitious and one tragically real, make a very good point: The business world in which we live and work would not be able to operate, for even one day, without a reliable method for recording the effects of transactions. A systematic method of recording transactions is necessary if companies such as IBM and **General Electric** (and even local music stores and Internet vendors) are to generate information with which to make sound business decisions.

This information is summarized in a variety of reports prepared from accounting records to assist users in making better economic decisions. Examples include the following:

1. General-purpose financial statements prepared for external user groups, primarily current or potential investors and creditors, who are involved financially with an enterprise but who are not a part of its management team.
2. Reports received by user groups within organizations, especially those in managerial positions, to assist them in planning and controlling the day-to-day operations of their organizations.
3. Tax returns and similar reports prepared to comply with Internal Revenue Service (IRS) requirements.
4. Special reports required by various regulatory agencies such as the Securities and Exchange Commission (SEC).

Each of these reports is based on data that are the result of an accounting system and a set of procedures collectively referred to as the accounting process or the accounting cycle. While this process follows a fairly standard set of procedures that has existed for centuries, the exact nature of the accounting system used to collect and report the data depends on the type of business, its size, the volume of transactions processed, the degree of automation employed, and other related factors. Every accounting system, however, should be designed to provide accurate information on a timely and efficient basis. At the same time, the system must provide controls that are effective in preventing mistakes and guarding against dishonesty.

Historically, accounting systems were maintained by hand and referred to as *manual systems*. Such systems continue to be used effectively in some situations. In today's business environment, however, most companies use computers to collect, process, and analyze financial information. Has the computer changed the accounting process? It allows businesses to collect and analyze much more information and do it quickly, but the computer has not changed the underlying accounting concepts involved—debits still equal credits; assets still equal liabilities plus owners' equity.

The purpose of this chapter is to review the basic steps of the accounting process including a brief review of debits and credits and the mechanics of bookkeeping. Get ready for a discussion of double-entry accounting, a system described by the German poet Goethe as "an absolutely perfect one."[1]

Overview of the Accounting Process

1 **Identify and explain the basic steps in the accounting process (accounting cycle).**

WHY **It is important to understand how accounting information flows through an organization and how that information is captured by the accounting information system.**

HOW **The accounting process, often referred to as the accounting cycle, generally includes the following steps: analyze business documents, journalize transactions, post to ledger accounts, prepare a trial balance, prepare adjusting entries, prepare financial statements, close the nominal accounts, and prepare a post-closing trial balance.**

As you will recall from your introductory accounting class, the accounting process (or accounting cycle) consists of two interrelated parts, (1) the recording phase and (2) the reporting phase. The recording phase is concerned with collecting information about economic transactions and events and distilling that information into a form useful to the accounting process. For most businesses, the recording function is based on double-entry accounting procedures. In the reporting phase, the recorded information is organized and summarized using various formats for a variety of decision-making purposes. The two phases overlap because the recording of transactions is an ongoing activity that does not stop at the end of an accounting period but continues uninterrupted while events of the preceding period are being summarized and reported. The recording and reporting phases of the accounting process are reviewed and illustrated in this chapter. The form and content of the basic financial statements are discussed in depth and illustrated in Chapters 3, 4, and 5.

[1] Johann Wolfgang von Goethe, *Wilhelm Meister's Apprenticeship and Travels*. Translated by Thomas Carlyle. Chapman and Hall, 1824.

The accounting process, illustrated in Exhibit 2-1, generally includes the following steps in a well-defined sequence:

Recording Phase

1. **Business documents are analyzed.** Analysis of the documentation of business activities provides the basis for making an initial record of each transaction.
2. **Transactions are recorded.** Based on the supporting documents from step 1, transactions are recorded using journal entries.
3. **Transactions are posted.** Transactions, as classified and recorded, are posted to the appropriate accounts.

Reporting Phase

4. **A trial balance of the accounts in the general ledger is prepared.** The trial balance simply lists every account in the ledger along with its current debit or credit balance. This step in the reporting phase provides a general check on the accuracy of recording and posting.
5. **Adjusting entries are recorded.** Before financial statements can be prepared, all relevant information that has not been recorded must be determined and appropriate adjustments made. Adjusting entries must be recorded and posted so the accounts are current prior to the preparation of financial statements.
6. **Financial statements are prepared.** Statements summarizing operations and showing the financial position and cash flows are prepared from the information obtained from the adjusted accounts.
7. **Nominal accounts are closed.** Balances in the nominal (temporary) accounts are closed into the retained earnings account. This closing process results in beginning each

EX 2-1 THE ACCOUNTING PROCESS

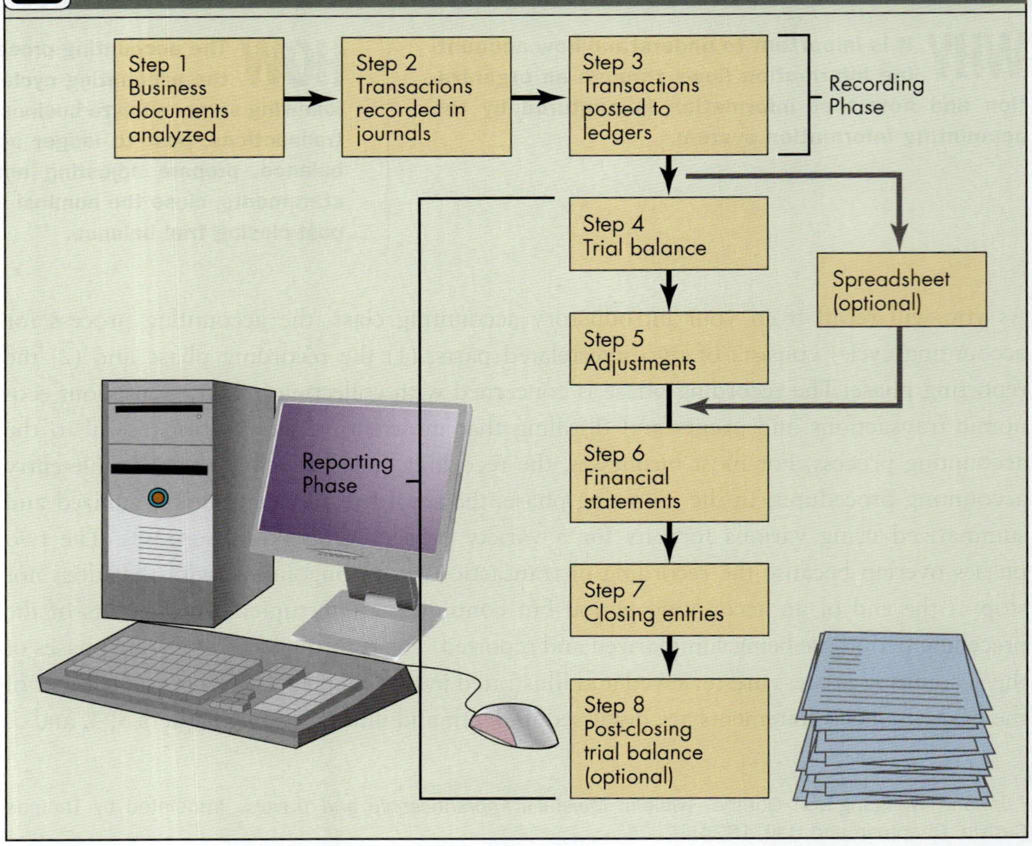

accounting period with zero balances in all nominal accounts.

8. **A post-closing trial balance may be prepared** to determine the equality of the debits and credits after posting the adjusting and closing entries.

FYI

As noted in Exhibit 2-1, an optional spreadsheet can be used for the reporting process. This spreadsheet has columns for the trial balance, adjustments, an adjusted trial balance, and the financial statements. All accounts with their balances are listed on the spreadsheet in the appropriate columns. Computer spreadsheets are often used to facilitate this process.

Before we are immersed in the details associated with the accounting process, it is important to remember that functions such as journalizing, posting, and closing are bookkeeping functions. You must be familiar with the mundane details of bookkeeping and know how to analyze transactions in terms of debits and credits, but you should not expect to spend your entire accounting career doing bookkeeping. As an accountant, you will spend a great deal of your time in designing information systems, analyzing complex transactions, and interpreting accounting results. A knowledge of the fundamentals of bookkeeping provides a foundation upon which these activities are based. These activities are vital to the management of an organization.

STOP&THINK

Which of the following would NOT be the role of a bookkeeper?

a) Analyzing and recording routine transactions
b) Posting journal entries
c) Interpreting accounting results
d) Preparing a post-closing trial balance

Recording Phase

2 **Analyze transactions and make and post journal entries.**

WHY **Transactions are events that transfer or exchange goods or services between or among two or more entities. These transactions provide the foundation for information captured by the accounting system.**

HOW **Business documents, such as invoices, provide evidence that transactions have occurred as well as the data required to record the transactions in the accounting records. The data are recorded with journal entries using a system of double-entry accounting. The journal entries are subsequently posted to ledger accounts.**

Accurate financial statements can be prepared only if the results of business events and activities have been properly recorded. Certain events, termed transactions, involve the transfer or exchange of goods or services between two or more entities. Examples of business transactions include the purchase of merchandise or other assets from suppliers and the sale of goods or services to customers. In addition to transactions, other events and circumstances can affect the assets, liabilities, and owners' equity of the business. Some of those events and circumstances also must be recorded. Examples include the recognition of depreciation on plant assets or a decline in the market value of inventories and investments.

As indicated, the recording phase involves analyzing business documents, journalizing transactions, and posting to the ledger accounts. Before discussing these steps, the system of double-entry accounting will be reviewed because virtually all businesses use this procedure in recording their transactions.

Double-Entry Accounting

As explained in Chapter 1, financial accounting rests on a foundation of basic assumptions, concepts, and principles that govern the recording, classifying, summarizing, and reporting of accounting data. Double-entry accounting is an old and universally accepted system for recording accounting data. With double-entry accounting, each transaction is recorded in a way that maintains the equality of the basic accounting equation:

Assets = Liabilities + Owners' equity

To review how double-entry accounting works, recall that a debit is an entry on the left side of an account and a credit is an entry on the right side. The debit/credit relationships of accounts were explained in detail in your introductory accounting course. Exhibit 2-2 summarizes these relationships for a corporation. You will note that assets, expenses, and dividends are increased by debits and decreased by credits. Liabilities, capital stock, retained earnings, and revenues are increased by credits and decreased by debits. Note that while dividends reduce retained earnings, they are not classified as an expense and are not reported on the income statement.

> **! CAUTION**
>
> Remember that *debit* does not mean good (or bad) and *credit* does not mean bad (or good). *Debit* means left, and *credit* means right.

Journal entries provide a systematic method for summarizing a business event's effect on the accounting equation. Every journal entry involves a 3-step process:

1. Identify the accounts involved with an event or transaction.
2. Determine whether each account increased or decreased (this information, coupled with the answer to step 1, will tell you if the account was debited or credited).
3. Determine the amount by which each account was affected.

EX 2-2 DEBIT AND CREDIT RELATIONSHIPS OF ACCOUNTS

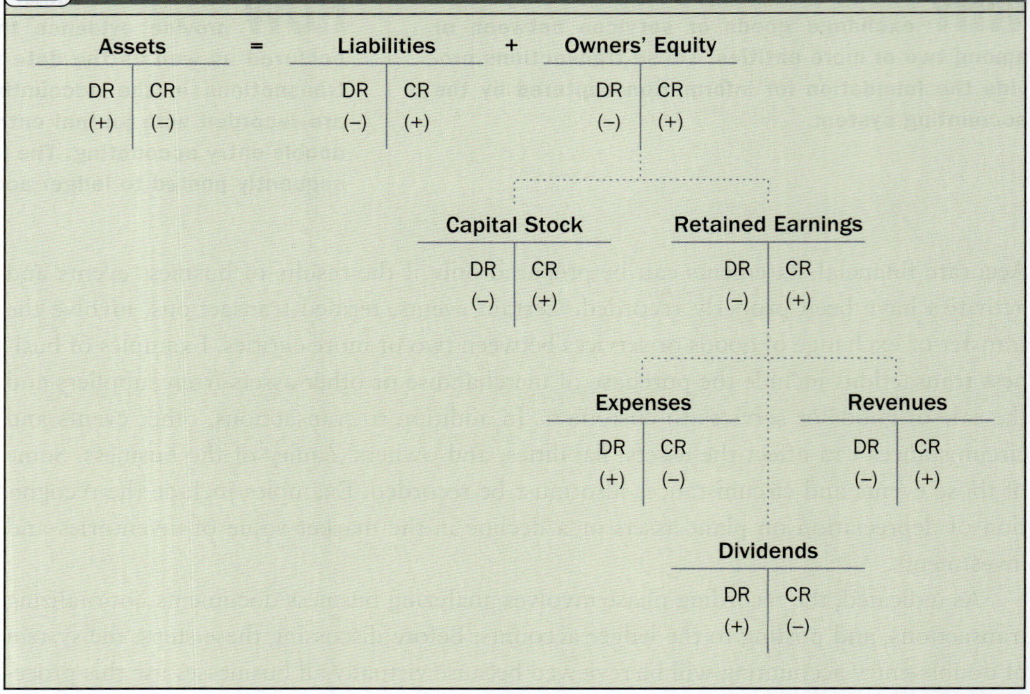

This 3-step process, properly applied, will always result in a correct journal entry. Note that this process is used whether the accounting is being done manually or with a computer.

To illustrate double-entry accounting, consider the transactions and journal entries shown in Exhibit 2-3 and their impact on the accounting equation. In studying this illustration, you should note that for each transaction, total debits equal total credits. Therefore, the equality of the accounting equation is maintained.

To summarize, you should remember the following important features of double-entry accounting:

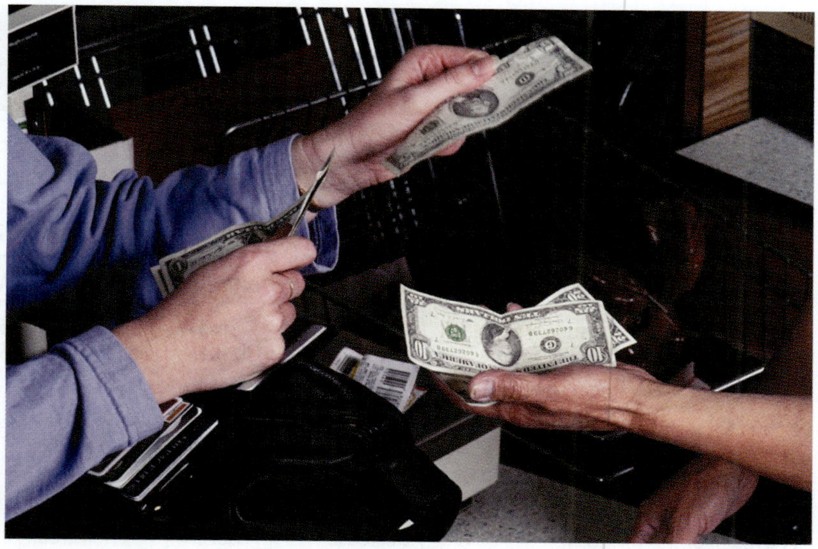

Rim Light/PhotoLink/Photodisc/Getty Images

Purchasing groceries at your local supermarket is a common example of a business transaction. Can you identify the accounts involved with this transaction?

CAUTION

Note in Exhibit 2-2 that dividends reduce retained earnings, but they are not classified as an expense and are not reported on the income statement.

1. Assets are increased by debits and decreased by credits.
2. Liability and owners' equity accounts are increased by credits and decreased by debits.
3. Owners' equity for a corporation includes capital stock accounts and the retained earnings account.
4. Revenues, expenses, and dividends relate to owners' equity through the retained earnings account.
5. Expenses and dividends are increased by debits and decreased by credits because they reduce owners' equity.
6. Revenues are increased by credits and decreased by debits.
7. The difference between total revenues and total expenses for a period is net income (loss), which increases (decreases) owners' equity through the retained earnings account.

With this brief overview of the accounting equation and journal entries, we are now ready to proceed through the steps in the accounting process.

Analyzing Business Documents

The recording phase begins with an analysis of the documentation showing what business activities have occurred. Normally, a business document, or source document, is the first record of each transaction. Such a document offers detailed information concerning the transaction. The business documents provide support for the data to be recorded in the journals. Copies of sales invoices, for example, are the evidence in support of sales transactions; canceled checks provide data concerning cash disbursements; and the corporation minutes book supports entries authorized by action of the board of directors. Documents underlying each recorded transaction provide a means of verifying the accounting records and thus form a vital part of the information and control systems.

EX 2-3 DOUBLE-ENTRY ACCOUNTING: ILLUSTRATIVE TRANSACTIONS AND JOURNAL ENTRIES

	Three-Step Process				
Transaction	**(1) Identify Accounts.**	**(2) Increase or Decrease?**	**(1) and (2) together indicate whether an account is debited or credited.**	**(3) By How Much?**	**Journal Entry**
Investment by shareholder in a corporation, $10,000	Cash Capital Stock	Increase Increase	Asset ↑ = debit Owners' equity ↑ = credit	$10,000 $10,000	Cash 10,000 Capital Stock 10,000
Purchase of supplies on account, $5,000	Supplies Accounts Payable	Increase Increase	Asset ↑ = debit Liability ↑ = credit	$5,000 $5,000	Supplies 5,000 Accounts Payable 5,000
Payment of wages expense, $2,500	Cash Wages Expense	Decrease Increase	Asset ↓ = credit Expenses ↑ = debit	$2,500 $2,500	Wages Expense 2,500 Cash 2,500
Collection of accounts receivable, $1,000	Cash Accounts Receivable	Increase Decrease	Asset ↑ = debit Asset ↓ = credit	$1,000 $1,000	Cash 1,000 Accounts Receivable 1,000
Payment of account payable, $500	Cash Accounts Payable	Decrease Decrease	Asset ↓ = credit Liability ↓ = debit	$500 $500	Accounts Payable 500 Cash 500
Sale of merchandise on account, $20,000	Accounts Receivable Sales	Increase Increase	Asset ↑ = debit Revenues ↑ = credit	$20,000 $20,000	Accounts Receivable 20,000 Sales 20,000
Purchase of equipment: $15,000 down payment plus $40,000 long-term note	Cash Equipment Notes Payable	Decrease Increase Increase	Asset ↓ = credit Asset ↑ = debit Liability ↑ = credit	$15,000 $55,000 $40,000	Equipment 55,000 Cash 15,000 Notes Payable 40,000
Payment of cash dividend, $4,000	Cash Dividends	Decrease Increase	Asset ↓ = credit Dividends ↑ = debit	$4,000 $4,000	Dividends 4,000 Cash 4,000

Journalizing Transactions

Once the information provided on business documents has been analyzed, transactions are recorded in chronological order in the appropriate journals. In some small businesses, all transactions are recorded in a single journal. Most business enterprises, however, maintain various special journals designed to meet their specific needs as well as a general journal. A special journal is used to record a particular type of frequently recurring transaction. Special journals are commonly used, for example, to record each of the following types of transactions: sales, purchases, cash disbursements, and cash receipts. A general journal is used to record all transactions for which a special journal is not maintained. As illustrated below, a general journal shows the transaction date and the accounts affected and allows for a brief description of each transaction. Special journals are illustrated and explained in the Web Material associated with this chapter (see **www.cengage.com/international**).

GENERAL JOURNAL Page 24

Date		Description	Post. Ref.	Debit	Credit
2013					
July	1	Dividends	330	25,000	
		Dividends Payable	260		25,000
		Declared semiannual cash dividend on common stock.			
	10	Equipment	180	7,500	
		Notes Payable	220		7,500
		Issued note for new equipment.			
	31	Payroll Tax Expense	418	2,650	
		Payroll Taxes Payable	240		2,650
		Recorded payroll taxes for month.			

Posting to the Ledger Accounts

An account is used to summarize the effects of transactions on each element of the expanded accounting equation. For example, the cash account is used to provide detail for all transactions involving the inflow (debit) and outflow (credit) of cash. A ledger is a collection of accounts maintained by a business. The specific accounts required by a business unit vary depending on the nature of the business, its properties and activities, the information to be provided on the financial statements, and the controls to be employed in carrying out the accounting functions.

Information recorded in the journals is transferred to appropriate accounts in the ledger. This transfer is referred to as posting. Note that posting is a copying process; it involves no new analysis. Ledger accounts for Equipment and Notes Payable are presented by illustrating the posting of the July 10 transaction from the preceding general journal. The posting reference (J24) indicates that the transaction was transferred from page 24 of the general journal. Note that the account numbers for Equipment (180) and Notes Payable (220) are entered in the Posting Reference column of the journal.

GENERAL LEDGER

Account EQUIPMENT **Account No.** 180

Date		Item	Post. Ref.	Debit	Credit	Balance
2013						
July	1	Balance				10,550
	10	Purchase Equipment	J24	7,500		18,050

Account NOTES PAYABLE **Account No.** 220

Date		Item	Post. Ref.	Debit	Credit	Balance
2013						
July	1	Balance				5,750
	10	Purchase Equipment	J24		7,500	13,250

It is often desirable to establish separate ledgers for detailed information in support of balance sheet or income statement items. The general ledger includes all accounts appearing on the financial statements, and separate subsidiary ledgers afford additional detail in support of certain general ledger accounts. For example, a single accounts receivable account is usually carried in the general ledger, and individual customer accounts are recorded in a subsidiary accounts receivable ledger. The general ledger account that summarizes the detailed information in a subsidiary ledger is known as a control account. Thus, Accounts

> **STOP&THINK**
>
> The computer is very valuable in the posting process because it reduces the types of errors that can be made. Which of the following posting errors could a person make that a computer would not?
>
> a) Posting to the wrong account
> b) Posting the wrong amount
> c) Posting a debit to a specific account instead of a credit
> d) A well-functioning computer would not make any of these mistakes

Receivable is considered a control account. Subsidiary ledger accounts are illustrated in the Web Material associated with this chapter (see **www.cengage.com/international**).

Depending primarily on the number of transactions involved, amounts may be posted to ledger accounts on a daily, weekly, or monthly basis. If a computer system is being used, the posting process may be done automatically as transactions are recorded.

At the end of an accounting period, when the posting process has been completed, the balances in the ledger accounts are used for preparing the trial balance.

Reporting Phase

3 **Make adjusting entries, produce financial statements, and close nominal accounts.**

WHY **Adjusting entries are required at the end of an accounting period to update accounts so that the data are current and accurate. Closing entries are required so that each new accounting period can be accounted for independent of other periods.**

HOW **Adjusting entries are made at the end of an accounting period prior to preparing the financial statements for that period. Generally, the required adjustments are the result of analysis rather than based on new transactions. At the end of each accounting cycle, the nominal or temporary accounts must be transferred through the closing process to real or permanent accounts. The nominal accounts are left with a zero balance and are ready to receive transaction data for the new accounting period. The real accounts remain open and carry their balances forward to the new period.**

As noted earlier, the objective of the accounting process is to produce financial statements and other reports that will assist various users in making economic decisions. Once the recording phase is completed, the data must be summarized and organized into a useful format. The remaining steps of the accounting process are designed to accomplish this purpose. These steps will be illustrated using data from Rosi, Inc., a hypothetical merchandising company, for the year ended December 31, 2013.

Preparing a Trial Balance

After all transactions for the period have been posted to the ledger accounts, the balance for each account is determined. Every account will have either a debit, credit, or zero balance. A trial balance is a list of all accounts and their balances. The trial balance, therefore, indicates whether total debits equal total credits and thus provides a general check on the accuracy of recording and posting. When debits equal credits in a trial balance, however, it is no guarantee that the accounts are correct. For example, a journal entry involving a debit to Accounts Receivable could have been incorrectly posted as a debit to the notes receivable account. The trial balance would indeed balance, but the accounts would be in error. Thus, a balanced trial balance provides no guarantee of accuracy. However, a trial balance that does not balance indicates that we needn't go further into the reporting phase of the accounting process. An error exists somewhere and must be detected and corrected before proceeding. If we elect to proceed without correcting the error, we have one guarantee—the financial statements will contain errors. The trial balance for Rosi, Inc., is presented below.

FYI

A fundamental difference between the trial balance and the financial statements is that no external users ever see the trial balance. Most managers have never seen a trial balance. It serves as the basis for the preparation of the financial statements but is not an information source to either management or external users.

Rosi, Inc.
Trial Balance
December 31, 2013

	Debit	Credit
Cash	$ 83,110	
Accounts Receivable	106,500	
Allowance for Bad Debts		$ 1,610
Inventory	45,000	
Prepaid Insurance	8,000	
Interest Receivable	0	
Land	114,000	
Buildings	156,000	
Accumulated Depreciation—Buildings		39,000
Furniture & Equipment	19,000	
Accumulated Depreciation—Furniture & Equipment		3,800
Accounts Payable		37,910
Unearned Rent Revenue		0
Salaries and Wages Payable		0
Interest Payable		0
Income Taxes Payable		0
Dividends Payable		3,400
Bonds Payable		140,000
Common Stock, $0.10 par		150,000
Retained Earnings		103,900
Dividends	13,600	
Sales		479,500
Cost of Goods Sold	159,310	
Salaries and Wages Expense	172,450	
Heat, Light, and Power Expense	32,480	
Payroll Tax Expense	18,300	
Advertising Expense	18,600	
Bad Debt Expense	0	
Depreciation Expense—Buildings	0	
Depreciation Expense—Furniture & Equipment	0	
Insurance Expense	0	
Interest Revenue		1,100
Rent Revenue		2,550
Interest Expense	16,420	
Income Tax Expense	0	
Totals	$962,770	$962,770

Preparing Adjusting Entries

As discussed in the previous section, transactions generally are recorded in a journal in chronological order and then posted to the ledger accounts. The entries are based on the best information available at the time. Although the majority of accounts are up to date at the end of an accounting period and their balances can be included in the financial statements, some accounts require adjustment to reflect current circumstances. In general, these accounts are not updated throughout the period because it is impractical or inconvenient to make such entries on a daily or weekly basis. At the end of each accounting period, in order to report all asset, liability, and owners' equity amounts properly and to recognize all revenues and expenses for the period on an accrual basis, accountants are required to make any necessary adjustments prior to preparing the financial statements. The entries that reflect these adjustments are called adjusting entries.

> **FYI**
>
> **Disney**'s 1998 balance sheet included in its annual report did not balance. The preparers of that balance sheet transposed two numbers, and the result was a $9 (million) error. The balance sheet in the 1998 10-K that was filed with the SEC did not contain the transposition error.

One difficulty with adjusting entries is that the need for an adjustment is not signaled by a specific event such as the receipt of a bill or the receipt of cash from a customer. Rather, adjusting entries are recorded on the basis of an analysis of the circumstances at the close of each accounting period. This analysis involves just two steps:

1. Determine whether the amounts recorded for all assets and liabilities are correct. If not, debit or credit the appropriate asset or liability account. In short, fix the balance sheet.
2. Determine what revenue or expense adjustments are required as a result of the changes in recorded amounts of assets and liabilities indicated in step 1. Debit or credit the appropriate revenue or expense account. In short, fix the income statement.

It should be noted that these two steps are interrelated and may be reversed. That is, revenue and expense adjustments may be considered first to fix the income statement, indicating which asset and liability accounts need adjustment to fix the balance sheet. As you will see, each adjusting entry involves at least one income statement account and one balance sheet account. T-accounts are helpful in analyzing adjusting entries and will be used in the illustrations that follow.

The areas most commonly requiring analysis to see whether adjusting entries are needed include the following:

Transactions where cash will be exchanged in a future period

1. Unrecorded assets
2. Unrecorded liabilities

Transactions where cash has been exchanged in a prior period

3. Prepaid expenses
4. Unearned revenues

Transactions involving estimates

For most transactions, the revenue or expense recognition and the flow of cash occur in the same accounting period. For those transactions, no adjustments are necessary as the entire transaction is accounted for in one accounting period. In some instances, the recognition of revenues and expenses and the flow of cash may occur in different accounting periods. In those instances, an adjusting entry is required to ensure that the proper amount of revenue and/or expense is recorded in each accounting period.

As we illustrate and discuss adjusting entries, remember that the basic purpose of adjustments is to make account balances current in order to report all asset, liability, and owners' equity amounts properly and to recognize all revenues and expenses for the period on an accrual basis. This is done so that the income statement and the balance sheet will reflect the proper operating results and financial position, respectively, at the end of the accounting period.

The adjusting entry part of the accounting process is illustrated using the adjusting data for Rosi, Inc., presented as follows.

Adjusting Data for Rosi, Inc.
December 31, 2013

Unrecorded Assets:

(a) Interest on notes receivable, $250.

Unrecorded Liabilities:

(b) Salaries and wages, $2,150.

(c) Interest on bonds payable, $5,000.

(d) Federal and state income taxes, $8,000.

Prepaid Expenses:

(e) Prepaid insurance remaining at year-end, $3,800.

Unearned Revenues:

(f) Unearned rent revenue remaining at year-end, $475.

Estimates:

(g) Depreciation Expense for buildings, 5% per year.

(h) Depreciation Expenses for furniture and equipment, 10% per year.

(i) The Allowance for Bad Debts is to be increased by $1,100.

Transactions Where Cash Will Be Exchanged in a Future Period

In cases where work is performed in the current period but cash does not flow until a future period, an adjusting entry must be made to ensure that revenue is recognized (if you are the one who did the work) in the current period or that an expense is recognized (if the work was done on your behalf) in the current period. These adjusting entries are referred to as accrual entries, and there are generally two types: unrecorded (or accrued) receivables and unrecorded (or accrued) liabilities.

Unrecorded Assets In accordance with the revenue recognition principle of accrual accounting, revenues should be recorded when earned, regardless of when the cash is received. If revenue is earned but not yet collected in cash, a receivable exists. To ensure that all receivables are properly reported on the balance sheet in the correct amounts, an analysis should be made at the end of each accounting period to see whether there are any revenues that have been earned but have not yet been collected or recorded. These unrecorded receivables are earned and represent amounts that are receivable in the future; therefore, they should be recognized as assets.

In recording unrecorded assets, an asset account is debited and a revenue account is credited. The illustrative entry recognizing the unrecorded receivable (and the accrued revenue) for Rosi, Inc., is as follows:

(a) Interest Receivable	250	
Interest Revenue		250
To record accrued interest on notes receivable.		

After this adjusting entry has been journalized and posted, the receivable will appear as an asset on the balance sheet, and the interest revenue will be reported on the income statement. Through the adjusting entry, the asset (receivable) accounts are properly stated and revenues are appropriately reported.

Unrecorded Liabilities Just as assets are created from revenues being earned before they are collected or recorded, liabilities can be created by expenses being incurred prior to being paid or recorded. These expenses, along with their corresponding liabilities, should be recorded when incurred, no matter when they are paid. Thus, adjusting entries are required at the end of an accounting period to recognize any unrecorded liabilities in the proper period and to record the corresponding expenses. As the expense is recorded (increased by a debit), the corresponding liability is also recorded (increased by a credit), showing the entity's obligation to pay for the expense. If such adjustments are not made, the net income measurement for the period will not reflect all appropriate expenses and the corresponding liabilities will be understated on the balance sheet.

The adjusting entries to record unrecorded liabilities (and accrued expenses) for Rosi, Inc., are as follows:

(b) Salaries and Wages Expense	2,150	
Salaries and Wages Payable		2,150
To record accrued salaries and wages.		
(c) Interest Expense	5,000	
Interest Payable		5,000
To record accrued interest on bonds.		
(d) Income Tax Expense	8,000	
Income Taxes Payable		8,000
To record income taxes.		

Transactions Where Cash Has Been Exchanged in a Prior Period

For some transactions, cash has changed hands before the revenue is earned or the expense is incurred. If the revenue is not earned or the expense is not incurred prior to the end of the period, then an adjusting entry to reflect that fact is required.

Prepaid Expenses Payments that a company makes in advance for items normally charged to expense are known as prepaid expenses. An example would be the payment of an insurance premium for three years. Theoretically, every resource acquisition is an asset, at least temporarily. Thus, the entry to record an advance payment should be a debit to an asset account (Prepaid Expenses) and a credit to Cash, showing the exchange of cash for another asset.

An expense is the using up of an asset. For example, when supplies are purchased, they are recorded as assets; when they are used, their cost is transferred to an expense account. The purpose of making adjusting entries for prepaid expenses is to show the complete or partial consumption of an asset. If the original entry is to an asset account, the adjusting entry reduces the asset to an amount that reflects its remaining future benefit and at the same time recognizes the actual expense incurred for the period.

> **! CAUTION**
>
> Prepaid Expenses is a tricky name for an asset. Assets are reported in the balance sheet. Don't make the mistake of including Prepaid Expenses with the expenses on the income statement.

For the unrecorded assets and liabilities discussed earlier, there was no original entry; the adjusting entry was the first time these items were recorded in the accounting records. For prepaid expenses, this is not the case. Because cash has already been paid (in the case of prepaid expenses), an original entry has been made to record the cash transaction. Therefore, the amount of the adjusting entry is the difference between what the updated balance should be and the amount of the original entry already recorded.

The method of adjusting for prepaid expenses depends on how the expenditures were originally entered in the accounts. They could have been recorded originally as debits to (1) an asset account or (2) an expense account. Both methods, if consistently applied, result in the same end result. Thus, both methods are equally correct. An individual company would choose one method or the other and apply it each period.

Original debit to an asset account. If an asset account was originally debited (Prepaid Insurance in this example), the adjusting entry requires that an expense account be debited for the amount applicable to the current period and the asset account be credited. The asset account remains with a debit balance that shows the amount applicable to future periods. An adjusting entry for Prepaid Insurance for Rosi, Inc., illustrates this situation as follows:

	Debit	Credit
(e) Insurance Expense	4,200	
Prepaid Insurance		4,200
To record expired insurance ($8,000 – $3,800 = $4,200).		

Because the asset account Prepaid Insurance was originally debited, as shown in the trial balance, the amount of the prepayment ($8,000) must be reduced to reflect only the $3,800 that remains unexpired. The following T-accounts illustrate how this adjusting entry, when posted, would affect the accounts.

Prepaid Insurance

Debit		Credit	
Beg. Bal.	8,000		
		Adj. (e)	4,200
End. Bal.	3,800		

Insurance Expense

Debit		Credit
Beg. Bal.	0	
Adj. (e)	4,200	
End. Bal.	4,200	

Original debit to an expense account. If an expense account was originally debited (Insurance Expense in this example), the adjusting entry requires that an asset account be debited for the amount applicable to future periods and the expense account be credited. The expense account then remains with a debit balance representing the amount applicable to the current period. For example, if Rosi, Inc., had originally debited Insurance Expense for $8,000, the adjusting entry would be as follows:

Prepaid Insurance	3,800	
Insurance Expense		3,800
To record prepaid insurance ($8,000 – $4,200 = $3,800).		

The following T-accounts illustrate the effect that this adjusting entry would have on the relevant accounts.

Prepaid Insurance

	Debit	Credit
Beg. Bal.	0	
Adj.	3,800	
End. Bal.	3,800	

Insurance Expense

	Debit		Credit
Beg. Bal.	8,000	Adj.	3,800
End. Bal.	4,200		

Note that regardless of which method is used, the ending balance in each account is the same. In this example, using either method results in an ending balance in Prepaid Insurance and Insurance Expense of $3,800 and $4,200, respectively.

CAUTION

The original debit to an asset account makes more sense conceptually. Remember, however, that the account balances reported in the financial statements are what matter; the working balances that exist in the accounting records on a day-to-day basis are not as important.

Unearned Revenues Amounts received before the actual earning of revenues are known as unearned revenues. They arise when customers pay in advance of the receipt of goods or services. Because the company has received cash but has not yet given the customer the purchased goods or services, the unearned revenues are in fact liabilities. That is, the company must provide something in return for the amounts received. For example, a building contractor may require a deposit before proceeding on construction of a house. Upon receipt of the deposit, the contractor has unearned revenue, a liability. The contractor must construct the house to earn the revenue. If the house is not built, the contractor will be obligated to repay the deposit.

The method of adjusting for unearned revenues depends on whether the receipts for undelivered goods or services were recorded originally as credits to (1) a revenue account or (2) a liability account.

Original credit to a revenue account. If a revenue account was originally credited (Rent Revenue in this example), this account is debited and a liability account is credited for the revenue applicable to a future period. The revenue account remains with a credit balance representing the earnings applicable to the current period. As indicated in the trial balance for Rosi, Inc., rent receipts are recorded originally in the rent revenue account. Unearned revenue at the end of 2013 is $475, and it is recorded as follows:

(f) Rent Revenue	475	
Unearned Rent Revenue		475
To record unearned rent revenue.		

The following T-accounts illustrate the effect that this adjusting entry would have on the related accounts.

Unearned Rent Revenue

		Beg. Bal.	0
		Adj. (f)	475
		End. Bal.	475

Rent Revenue

		Beg. Bal.	2,550
Adj. (f)	475		
		End. Bal.	2,075

Original credit to a liability account. If a liability account was originally credited (Unearned Rent Revenue), this account is debited and a revenue account is credited for the amount applicable to the current period. The liability account remains with a credit balance that shows the amount applicable to future periods. For example, if Rosi, Inc., had originally credited Unearned Rent Revenue for $2,550, the adjusting entry (along with affected T-accounts) would be as follows:

Unearned Rent Revenue	2,075	
Rent Revenue		2,075
To record rent revenue ($2,550 – $475).		

Unearned Rent Revenue

		Beg. Bal.	2,550
Adj.	2,075		
		End. Bal.	475

Rent Revenue

		Beg. Bal.	0
		Adj.	2,075
		End. Bal.	2,075

Again, note that using either method results in exactly the same balances for the income statement and balance sheet accounts.

Transactions Involving Estimates

In addition to timing differences associated with cash flows and the recognition of revenues and/or expenses, a third type of adjusting entry involves estimates. Accountants must constantly use judgment when applying the accrual accounting model. Questions such as "for how many periods will a machine generate revenues" or "how many of our credit customers will not pay" must be answered and reflected in the financial statements. The answers to these questions involve estimates. Two common types of these adjusting entries involve depreciation and bad debts.

Asset Depreciation Charges to operations for the use of buildings, furniture, and equipment must be recorded at the end of the period. In recording asset depreciation, operations are charged with a portion of the asset's cost, and the carrying value of the asset is reduced by that amount. A reduction in an asset for depreciation is usually recorded by a credit to a contra account, Accumulated Depreciation. A contra account (or offset account) is set up to record subtractions from a related account.

Adjustments at the end of the year for depreciation for Rosi, Inc., are as follows:

(g) Depreciation Expense—Buildings	7,800	
Accumulated Depreciation—Buildings		7,800
To record depreciation on buildings at 5% per year.		
(h) Depreciation Expense—Furniture & Equipment	1,900	
Accumulated Depreciation—Furniture & Equipment		1,900
To record depreciation on furniture and equipment at 10% per year.		

Bad Debts Invariably, when a business allows customers to purchase goods and services on credit, some of the accounts receivable will not be collected, resulting in a charge to income for bad debt expense. Under the accrual concept, an adjustment should be made for the estimated expense in the current period rather than when specific accounts actually become uncollectible in later periods. This practice produces a better matching of revenues and expenses and therefore a better income measurement. Using this procedure, operations are charged with the estimated expense, and receivables are reduced by means of a contra account, Allowance for Bad Debts. To illustrate, the adjustment for Rosi, Inc., at the end of the year, assuming the allowance account is to be increased by $1,100, would be as follows:

(i) Bad Debt Expense	1,100	
Allowance for Bad Debts		1,100
To adjust for estimated bad debt expense.		

We should emphasize two characteristics of adjusting entries. First, adjusting entries made at the end of an accounting period *do not involve cash*. Cash has either changed hands prior to the end of the period (as is the case with prepaid expenses or unearned revenues), or cash will change hands in a future period (as is the case with many unrecorded receivables and unrecorded liabilities). It is precisely because cash is not changing hands on the last day of the accounting period that most adjusting entries must be made.

Second, each adjusting entry involves a balance sheet account and an income statement account. In each case requiring adjustment, we are either generating an asset, using up an asset, recording an incurred but unrecorded expense, or recording revenue that has yet to be earned. Knowing that each adjusting entry has at least one balance sheet and one income statement account makes the adjustment process a little easier. Once you have determined that an adjusting entry involves a certain balance sheet account, you can then focus on identifying the corresponding income statement account that requires adjustment.

Preparing Financial Statements

Once all accounts have been brought up to date through the adjustment process, financial statements are prepared. Financial statements can be prepared directly from the data in the adjusted ledger accounts. The data must only be organized into appropriate sections and categories so as to present them as simply and clearly as possible. The following process describes how the financial statements are prepared from the information taken from the trial balance:

1. Identify all revenues and expenses—these account balances are used to prepare the income statement.
2. Compute net income—subtract expenses from revenues.
3. Compute the ending retained earnings balance—Retained Earnings from the previous period is the starting point. Net income (computed in step 2) is added to the beginning retained earnings balance and dividends for the period are subtracted.
4. Prepare a balance sheet using the balance sheet accounts from the trial balance and the modified retained earnings balance computed from step 3.

Once the financial statements are prepared, explanatory notes are written. These notes clarify the methods and assumptions used in preparing the statements. In addition, the auditor must review the financial statements to make sure they are accurate, reasonable, and in accordance with generally accepted accounting principles. Finally, the financial statements are distributed to external users who analyze them in order to learn more about the financial condition of the company.

How long does it take for large corporations to complete the accounting process to the point at which financial statements are available? For December 31 year-end firms, financial statement preparation is usually completed in February. The date of Disney's audit opinion (a rough measure of when financial statement preparation is essentially complete) for the fiscal year ended October 3, 2009, is December 2, 2009. For firms with publicly traded shares, the SEC requires the annual financial statements to be released within 60 days of fiscal year-end. The data used to prepare financial statements can be taken directly from the adjusted account balances in the ledger, or a spreadsheet may be used. Financial statements are prepared by determining which accounts go on which financial statement, appropriately listing those accounts, and summing to obtain totals.

Using a Spreadsheet

An optional step in the accounting process is to use a spreadsheet (also called a work sheet) to facilitate the preparation of adjusting entries and financial statements. The availability of computer spreadsheets, such as Microsoft® Excel, makes the preparation of a spreadsheet quite easy. Remember, however, that preparing a spreadsheet is not a required step. As indicated, financial statements can be prepared directly from data in adjusted ledger account balances.

When a spreadsheet is constructed, trial balance data are listed in the first pair of columns. The adjusting entries are listed in the second pair of columns. Sometimes a third pair of columns is included to show the trial balance after adjustment. Account balances, as adjusted, are carried forward to the appropriate financial statement columns. A spreadsheet for a merchandising enterprise includes a pair of columns for the income statement accounts and a pair for the balance sheet accounts. There are no columns for the statement of cash flows because this statement requires additional analysis of changes in account balances for the period. A spreadsheet for Rosi, Inc., is shown on page 2-20. All adjustments illustrated previously are included.

Closing the Nominal Accounts

Once adjusting entries have been formally recorded in the general journal and posted to the ledger accounts, the books are ready to be closed in preparation for a new accounting period. During this closing process, the nominal (temporary) account balances are transferred to a real (permanent) account, leaving the nominal accounts with a zero balance. Nominal accounts include all income statement accounts plus the dividends account for a corporation. The real account that receives the closing amounts from the nominal accounts is Retained Earnings. Because it is a real account, this and all other balance sheet accounts remain open and carry their balances forward to the new period.

The mechanics of closing the nominal accounts are straightforward. All revenue accounts with credit balances are closed by being debited; all expense accounts with debit balances are closed by being credited. This process reduces these temporary accounts to a zero balance. The difference between the closing debit amounts for revenues and the credit amounts for expenses is net income (or net loss) and is an increase (or decrease) to Retained Earnings. Dividends are also closed at the end of each period. The closing of Dividends serves to reduce Retained Earnings. Thus, the closing entries for revenues, expenses, and Dividends can be made directly to Retained Earnings, as shown at the top of page 2-21.

FYI

No account on the trial balance shows up on both the income statement and the balance sheet.

CAUTION

Students often make the mistake of using the beginning retained earnings balance on the end-of-year balance sheet. As we shall see in the next section, the ending retained earnings balance is arrived at when the books are closed for the year.

Rosi, Inc.
Trial Balance
December 31, 2013

	Trial Balance		Adjustments		Income Statement		Balance Sheet	
	Debit	**Credit**	**Debit**	**Credit**	**Debit**	**Credit**	**Debit**	**Credit**
Cash	83,110						83,110	
Accounts Receivable	106,500						106,500	
Allowance for Bad Debts		1,610		(i) 1,100				2,710
Inventory	45,000						45,000	
Prepaid Insurance	8,000			(e) 4,200			3,800	
Interest Receivable	0		(a) 250				250	
Land	114,000						114,000	
Buildings	156,000						156,000	
Accumulated Depreciation—Buildings		39,000		(g) 7,800				46,800
Furniture & Equipment	19,000						19,000	
Accumulated Depreciation—Furniture & Equipment		3,800		(h) 1,900				5,700
Accounts Payable		37,910						37,910
Unearned Rent Revenue		0		(f) 475				475
Salaries and Wages Payable		0		(b) 2,150				2,150
Interest Payable		0		(c) 5,000				5,000
Income Taxes Payable		0		(d) 8,000				8,000
Dividends Payable		3,400						3,400
Bonds Payable		140,000						140,000
Common Stock, $0.10 par		150,000						150,000
Retained Earnings		103,900						103,900
Dividends	13,600						13,600	
Sales		479,500				479,500		
Cost of Goods Sold	159,310				159,310			
Salaries and Wages Expense	172,450		(b) 2,150		174,600			
Heat, Light, and Power Expense	32,480				32,480			
Payroll Tax Expense	18,300				18,300			
Advertising Expense	18,600				18,600			
Bad Debt Expense	0		(i) 1,100		1,100			
Depreciation Expense—Buildings	0		(g) 7,800		7,800			
Depreciation Expense—Furniture & Equipment	0		(h) 1,900		1,900			
Insurance Expense	0		(e) 4,200		4,200			
Interest Revenue		1,100		(a) 250		1,350		
Rent Revenue		2,550	(f) 475			2,075		
Interest Expense	16,420		(c) 5,000		21,420			
Income Tax Expense	0		(d) 8,000		8,000			
Totals	962,770	962,770	30,875	30,875	447,710	482,925	541,260	506,045
Net Income					35,215			35,215
					482,925	482,925	541,260	541,260

Revenues	xx	
Retained Earnings		xx
To close revenues to Retained Earnings.		
Retained Earnings	xx	
Expenses		xx
To close expenses to Retained Earnings.		
Retained Earnings	xx	
Dividends		xx
To close Dividends to Retained Earnings.		

The closing entries for Rosi, Inc., follow.

Closing Entries

2013			
Dec. 31	Sales	479,500	
	Interest Revenue	1,350	
	Rent Revenue	2,075	
	Retained Earnings		482,925
	To close revenue accounts to Retained Earnings.		
31	Retained Earnings	447,710	
	Cost of Goods Sold		159,310
	Salaries and Wages Expense		174,600
	Heat, Light, and Power		32,480
	Payroll Tax Expense		18,300
	Advertising Expense		18,600
	Bad Debt Expense		1,100
	Depreciation Expense—Buildings		7,800
	Depreciation Expense—Furniture & Equipment		1,900
	Insurance Expense		4,200
	Interest Expense		21,420
	Income Tax Expense		8,000
	To close expense accounts to Retained Earnings.		
31	Retained Earnings	13,600	
	Dividends		13,600
	To close Dividends to Retained Earnings.		

The following T-accounts (revenues and expenses have each been combined into one account for illustrative purposes) illustrate the effect the closing process has on the nominal accounts and Retained Earnings.

Expenses (All)

Bal.	447,710	Closing	447,710
End. Bal.	0		

Dividends

Bal.	13,600	Closing	13,600
End. Bal.	0		

Revenues (All)

Closing	482,925	Bal.	482,925
		End. Bal.	0

Retained Earnings

		Beg. Bal.	103,900
Closing	447,710		
Closing	13,600		
		Closing	482,925
		End. Bal.	125,515

Preparing a Post-Closing Trial Balance

After the closing entries are posted, a post-closing trial balance can be prepared to verify the equality of the debits and credits for all real accounts. Recall that real accounts are only those accounts shown on the balance sheet. The post-closing trial balance represents the end of the accounting cycle. The post-closing trial balance for Rosi, Inc., follows:

Rosi, Inc.
Post-Closing Trial Balance
December 31, 2013

	Debit	Credit
Cash	$ 83,110	
Accounts Receivable	106,500	
Allowance for Bad Debts		$ 2,710
Inventory	45,000	
Prepaid Insurance	3,800	
Interest Receivable	250	
Land	114,000	
Buildings	156,000	
Accumulated Depreciation—Buildings		46,800
Furniture & Equipment	19,000	
Accumulated Depreciation—Furniture & Equipment		5,700
Accounts Payable		37,910
Unearned Rent Revenue		475
Salaries and Wages Payable		2,150
Interest Payable		5,000
Income Taxes Payable		8,000
Dividends Payable		3,400
Bonds Payable		140,000
Common Stock, $0.10 par		150,000
Retained Earnings		125,515
Totals	$527,660	$527,660

Accrual Versus Cash-Basis Accounting

4 Distinguish between accrual and cash-basis accounting.

WHY The FASB has indicated that accrual accounting generally provides a better basis for financial reports, especially in reporting earnings, than does information showing only cash receipts and disbursements.

HOW Accrual accounting recognizes revenues when they are earned, not necessarily when cash is received. Similarly, expenses are recognized and recorded under accrual accounting when they are incurred, not necessarily when cash is paid. Some organizations (and most individuals) use cash-basis accounting, which recognizes revenues when cash is received and expenses when cash is paid. However, both the FASB and SEC require a statement of cash flows to be presented along with an accrual-based income statement and a balance sheet as the primary financial statements of an enterprise.

The procedures described in the previous sections are those required in a double-entry system based on accrual accounting. Accrual accounting recognizes revenues as they are earned, not necessarily when cash is received. Expenses are recognized and recorded when they are incurred, not necessarily when cash is paid. Accrual accounting provides for a better matching of revenues and expenses during an accounting period and generally results in financial statements that more accurately reflect a company's financial position and results of operations.[2]

Some accounting systems are based on cash receipts and cash disbursements instead of accrual accounting. Cash-basis accounting procedures frequently are found in organizations not requiring a complete set of double-entry records. Such organizations might include small, unincorporated businesses and some nonprofit organizations. Professionals engaged in service businesses, such as CPAs, dentists, and engineers, also have traditionally used cash accounting systems. Even many of these organizations, however, periodically use professional accountants to prepare financial statements and other required reports on an accrual basis.

Discussion continues as to the appropriateness of using cash accounting systems, especially as a basis for determining tax liabilities. The FASB, in *Concepts Statement No. 1*, indicates that accrual accounting provides a better basis for financial reports than does information showing only cash receipts and disbursements.

The AICPA's position, however, is that the cash basis is appropriate for some small companies and especially for companies in the service industry. Accordingly, accountants will continue to be asked on occasion to convert cash-based records to generally accepted accrual-based financial statements. The procedures involved are illustrated in the Web Material associated with this chapter (see **www.cengage.com/international**).

The AICPA calls cash-basis accounting an example of an "other comprehensive basis of accounting," or OCBOA. The most common alternatives to the accrual basis of accounting are the cash basis and the income tax basis.[3]

In July 2009, the IASB released a document detailing yet another accounting alternative to full GAAP. This alternative is called *IFRS for SMEs*, where "SME" stands for "small and medium-sized entities." The IASB intends this set of condensed standards to be appropriate for private companies around the world that have no need for all of the full-blown provisions of IFRS or U.S. GAAP. Because these standards fill just 230 pages, compared to 2,500 pages for IFRS and 25,000 pages for U.S. GAAP, implementation of *IFRS for SMEs* is certainly an attractive low-cost alternative for a small or medium-sized private company. The IASB has made this set of standards available for free to anyone who wants to use them. Go ahead and take a look at **www.iasb.org**.

[2] In *Concepts Statement No. 6*, the FASB discusses the concept of accrual accounting and relates it to the objectives of financial reporting. *Statement of Financial Accounting Concepts No. 6*, "Elements of Financial Statements" (Stamford, CT: Financial Accounting Standards Board, December 1985).

[3] See Thomas A. Ratcliffe, "OCBOA: Financial statements," *Journal of Accountancy*, October 2003, Vol. 196, Issue No. 4, p. 71. This article describes the AICPA's standards for auditing financial statements prepared under another comprehensive basis of accounting. These auditing standards are contained in the AICPA's Statement on Auditing Standards (SAS) No. 62, *Special Reports*.

FASB CODIFICATION

The Issue: Because you are excited about your accounting class, you have spent a couple of days preparing a personal balance sheet. Of course, you have carefully used the principles of accrual accounting. Your brother, an extremely dense and unpleasant person, is now making fun of you. He claims that the FASB itself has stated that personal financial statements are to be prepared using the cash basis. You would love to put your brother in his place and show him that you are right and he is wrong ... again.

The Question: What is the proper basis for preparing a personal balance sheet?

Searching the Codification: The best place to start is with the FASB ASC topic group labeled "Presentation." In that menu you will find Topic 274, Personal Financial Statements. Look to see what basis should be used to recognize items that are reported in a personal balance sheet.

The Answer: The correct treatment is described on page 2-26.

Computers and the Accounting Process

5 **Discuss the importance and expanding role of computers to the accounting process.**

WHY **Computers play an increasing role in today's business environment as well as society in general.**

HOW **In the past, many companies used manual systems to record, classify, summarize, and report accounting data. Today, most companies use computers and electronic technology as an integral part of their accounting systems. In the future, technological advances will continue to significantly impact the accounting process of recording and reporting data for decision-making purposes.**

As an organization grows in size and complexity, its recording and summarizing processes become more involved, and it seeks to improve efficiency and reduce costs. Some enterprises could find that a system involving primarily manual operations is adequate in meeting their needs. Most find that information-processing needs can be handled effectively only through the use of computers.

The computer revolution has rapidly changed society and the way business is conducted and, therefore, the way accounting functions are performed. The 1990s are referred to as the *Decade of Networking*, indicating that the PCs on people's desks in the 1980s were increasingly being interconnected. The new millennium has seen increased use of the Internet, with business-to-business (B2B) and business-to-consumer (B2C) applications proliferating. The opportunities for information exchange have expanded exponentially. However, despite their tremendous capabilities, computers cannot replace skilled accountants. A computer, for example, does not know the difference between inventory and supplies until someone (the accountant) specifies the accounts involved in the transaction. Instead of reducing the responsibilities of accountants, the existence of computers places increased demands on them in directing the operations of the computer systems to ensure the use of appropriate procedures. For example, a poorly designed computer system may leave no document trail with which to verify accounting records. Although all arithmetical operations can be assumed to be done accurately by computers, the validity of the output data depends on the adequacy of the instructions given the computer. Unlike a human accountant, a computer cannot think for itself but must be given explicit instructions for performing each operation. Computers have certain advantages in that the accountant can be sure every direction will be carried out precisely. On the other hand, computers place a great responsibility on the information systems designer to anticipate any unusual situations that will require special consideration or judgment by an accountant.

A recent development in the use of computers in financial reporting is the spread of XBRL. XBRL, which stands for eXtensible Business Reporting Language, is a method of embedding computer-readable tags in financial report documents. With these XBRL tabs, a company's financial statements can be downloaded directly into a spreadsheet where they can be compared to the financial statements of other companies that have also been downloaded. The use of XBRL greatly simplifies the process of analyzing financial statement data. The SEC initially required the use of XBRL for all financial statements filed by large public companies, and in June 2011 the requirement is extended to all companies publicly traded on U.S. stock exchanges. In the FASB's *Accounting Standards Codification*, XBRL elements are listed in many of the topic areas.

The question to be asked is this: If computers now take care of all of the routine accounting functions, why does an accounting student need to know anything about debits, credits, journals, posting, T-accounts, and trial balances? Good question. First, even though computers now do most of the routine work, the essence of double-entry accounting is unchanged from the days of quill pens and handwritten ledgers. Thus, the understanding of the process explained in this chapter is still relevant to a computer-based accounting system. Second, with or without computers, the use of debits, credits, and T-accounts still provides an efficient and widespread shorthand method of analyzing transactions. At a minimum, all businesspeople should be familiar enough with the language of accounting to understand, for example, why a credit balance in the cash account or a debit balance in Retained Earnings is something unusual enough to merit investigation. Finally, an understanding of the accounting cycle—analyzing, recording, summarizing, and preparing—gives one insight into how information flows within an organization. Great advantages accrue to those who understand information flow.

? SOLUTIONS TO OPENING SCENARIO QUESTIONS

1. If a customer could not tell if a deposit was made to her account, she would be unable to tell if the checks she had written would clear her account. If a bank cannot confirm for a customer that a deposit had been made, then the customer would search for a bank that could provide that basic service.

2. The burden of proof for tax payments would shift to the taxpayers. They would have to provide evidence that tax payments had been made. Currently, employers typically provide that evidence. The government would then need to have a system to match payments received from taxpayers with specific taxpayers. Fortunately for us, this system is already in place.

SOLUTIONS TO STOP & THINK QUESTIONS

1. (Page 2-5) The correct answer is C. Accountants and analysts interpret the accounting results for an accounting period.
2. (Page 2-10) The correct answer is D. If a computer is programmed properly, it will not post incorrect amounts, it will not post to incorrect accounts, and it will not mix its debits and credits.

SOLUTION TO USING THE FASB'S CODIFICATION

In Topic 274, you should find Section 274-10-25. There, in a very concise statement (in paragraph 1) that should silence your brother forever (at least on this issue), the FASB states: "Assets and liabilities shall be recognized on the accrual basis of accounting."

So, once again your brother is wrong.

REVIEW **CHAPTER 2**

LEARNING OBJECTIVES

1 Identify and explain the basic steps in the accounting process (accounting cycle).

The accounting process, often referred to as the *accounting cycle*, generally includes the following steps in a well-defined sequence: analyze business documents, journalize transactions, post to ledger accounts, prepare a trial balance, prepare adjusting entries, prepare financial statements (using a spreadsheet or working from the adjusted individual accounts), close the nominal accounts, and prepare a post-closing trial balance. This process of recording, classifying, summarizing, and reporting of accounting data is based on an old and universally accepted system called *double-entry accounting*.

2 Analyze transactions and make and post journal entries.

Transactions are events that transfer or exchange goods or services between or among two or more entities. Business documents, such as invoices, provide evidence that transactions have occurred as well as the data required to record the transaction in the accounting records. The data are recorded with journal entries using a system of double-entry accounting. The journal entries are subsequently posted to ledger accounts.

3 Make adjusting entries, produce financial statements, and close nominal accounts.

Adjusting entries are made at the end of an accounting period prior to preparing the financial statements for that period. Adjusting entries are often required to update accounts so that the data are current and accurate. Generally, the required adjustments are the result of analysis rather than based on new transactions. Once adjusting entries are journalized and posted, the balance sheet, income statement, and statement of cash flows can be prepared and reported.

At the end of each accounting cycle, the balances in the nominal or temporary accounts must be transferred through the closing process to real or permanent accounts. The nominal accounts (all income statement accounts plus dividends) are left with a zero balance and are ready to receive transaction data for the new accounting period. The real (balance sheet) accounts remain open and carry their balances forward to the new period.

4 Distinguish between accrual and cash-basis accounting.

Accrual accounting recognizes revenues when they are earned, not necessarily when cash is received. Similarly, expenses are recognized and recorded under accrual accounting when they are incurred, not necessarily when cash is paid. Some organizations (and most individuals) use cash-basis accounting, which recognizes revenues when cash is received and expenses when cash is paid. The FASB has indicated that accrual accounting generally provides a better basis for financial reports, especially in reporting earnings, than does information showing only cash receipts and disbursements. However, both the FASB and SEC require a statement of cash flows to be presented along with an accrual-based income statement and a balance sheet as the primary financial statements of an enterprise.

5 Discuss the importance and expanding role of computers to the accounting process.

Computers play an increasing role in today's business environment as well as society in general. In the past, many companies used manual systems to record, classify, summarize, and report accounting data. Today, most companies use computers and electronic technology as an integral part of their accounting systems. In the future, technological advances will continue to significantly impact the accounting process of recording and reporting data for decision-making purposes.

KEY TERMS

Account 2-9
Accounting cycle 2-3
Accounting process 2-3
Accounting system 2-3
Accrual accounting 2-23
Adjusting entries 2-12
Business document 2-7
Cash-basis accounting 2-23
Closing entries 2-21
Contra account 2-17
Control account 2-10
Credit 2-6
Debit 2-6
Double-entry accounting 2-6
General ledger 2-9
General journal 2-8
Journal entry 2-6
Journals 2-8
Ledger 2-9
Nominal (temporary) account 2-19
Post-closing trial balance 2-22
Posting 2-9
Prepaid expenses 2-14
Real (permanent) account 2-19
Source document 2-7
Special journal 2-8
Subsidiary ledgers 2-9
Transactions 2-5
Trial balance 2-10
Unearned revenues 2-16
Unrecorded liabilities 2-14
Unrecorded receivables 2-13

QUESTIONS

1. What types of reports are generated from the accounting system?
2. What are the main similarities and differences between a manual and an automated accounting system?
3. Distinguish between the recording and reporting phases of the accounting process.
4. List and describe the steps in the accounting process. Why are these steps necessary? Are any steps optional?
5. Under double-entry accounting, what are the debit/credit relationships of accounts?
6. Distinguish between (a) real and nominal accounts, (b) general journal and special journals, and (c) general ledger and subsidiary ledgers.
7. Explain the nature and the purpose of (a) adjusting entries and (b) closing entries.
8. As Beechnut Mining Company's independent certified public accountant, you find that the company accountant posts adjusting and closing entries directly to the ledger without formal entries in the general journal. How would you evaluate this procedure in your report to management?

9. Give three common examples of contra accounts. Explain why contra accounts are used.
10. Payment of insurance in advance may be recorded in either (a) an expense account or (b) an asset account. Which method would you recommend? What periodic entries are required under each method?
11. Describe the nature and purpose of a work sheet.
12. What effect, if any, does the use of a work sheet have on the sequence of the reporting phase of the accounting process?
13. From the following list of accounts, determine which ones should be closed and whether each would normally be closed by a debit or by a credit entry.

Cash	Land	Depreciation Expense	Advertising Expense
Rent Expense	Interest Revenue	Sales	Notes Payable
		Retained Earnings	Dividends
		Capital Stock	Accounts Payable
		Accounts Receivable	

14. Distinguish between accrual and cash-basis accounting.
15. Is greater accuracy achieved in financial statements prepared from double-entry accrual data as compared with cash data? Explain.
16. What are the major advantages of computers as compared with manual processing of accounting data?
17. One of your clients overheard a computer manufacturer sales representative saying that the computer will make the accountant obsolete. How would you respond to this comment?

PRACTICE EXERCISES

Practice 2-1
LO2

Journalizing

Make the journal entry (or entries) necessary to record the following transaction: Sold merchandise costing $14,000 for $22,000. Of the $22,000, $4,000 was received in cash and the remainder was on account. Assume a perpetual inventory system, meaning that the inventory reduction is recorded at the time of the sale.

Practice 2-2
LO2

Journalizing

Make the journal entry (or entries) necessary to record the following transaction: Purchased equipment with a fair market value of $100,000. Paid $10,000 cash as a down payment and signed two notes for the remaining cost—a 6% note for $20,000 that must be repaid (with interest) in six months and an 8% note for $70,000 that must be repaid (with interest) in two years.

Practice 2-3
LO2

Journalizing

Make the journal entry (or entries) necessary to record the following transaction: Sold land that had an original cost of $50,000. Received $40,000 cash. Also received a piece of equipment with a fair value of $90,000.

Practice 2-4
LO2

Journalizing

Make the journal entry (or entries) necessary to record the following transaction: Declared and paid a $12,000 cash dividend to shareholders.

Practice 2-5
LO2

Journalizing

Make the journal entry (or entries) necessary to record the following transaction: Gave land to an employee. The land originally cost $52,000, and it had that same value on the date it was given to the employee. This land was given in exchange for services rendered by the employee.

Practice 2-6
LO2

Posting

The beginning balance in the cash account was $10,000. During the month, the following four journal entries (involving cash) were recorded:

		Debit	Credit
a.	Cash	2,775	
	Sales		2,775
b.	Accounts Payable	1,500	
	Cash		1,500
c.	Utilities Expense	6,200	
	Cash		6,200
d.	Cash	4,100	
	Gain		2,150
	Land		1,950

Create a Cash T-account and post the entries to this account. Compute an ending balance.

Practice 2-7

LO2

Posting

The beginning balance in the accounts payable account was $8,000. During the month, the following four journal entries (involving accounts payable) were recorded:

		Debit	Credit
a.	Inventory	2,700	
	Accounts Payable		2,700
b.	Accounts Payable	6,500	
	Cash		6,500
c.	Accounts Payable	200	
	Inventory		200
d.	Inventory	3,000	
	Cash		450
	Accounts Payable		2,550

Create an Accounts Payable T-account and post the entries to this account. Compute an ending balance.

Practice 2-8

LO3

Trial Balance

Use the following account balance information to construct a trial balance:

Cost of Goods Sold	$ 9,000
Accounts Payable	1,450
Paid-In Capital	2,000
Cash	750
Sales	10,000
Dividends	700
Retained Earnings (beginning)	1,000
Inventory	4,000

Practice 2-9

LO3

Trial Balance

Use the following account balance information to construct a trial balance:

Salary Expense	$24,000
Unearned Service Revenue	1,600
Paid-In Capital	3,000
Cash	3,500
Service Revenue	32,000
Rent Expense	5,300
Retained Earnings (beginning)	1,200
Prepaid Rent Expense	5,000

Practice 2-10
LO3

Income Statement

Prepare two income statements, one using the information in Practice 2–8 and the other using the information in Practice 2–9.

Practice 2-11
LO3

Balance Sheet

Prepare two balance sheets, one using the information in Practice 2–8 and the other using the information in Practice 2–9.

Practice 2-12
LO3

Adjusting Entries

Make the adjusting journal entry necessary at the end of the period in the following situation: Equipment depreciation for the year was computed to be $5,500.

Practice 2-13
LO3

Adjusting Entries

Make the adjusting journal entry necessary at the end of the period in the following situation: Bad debts created by selling on credit during the year are estimated to be $1,200. So far, none of these accounts have been specifically identified and written off as uncollectible.

Practice 2-14
LO3

Adjusting Entries

Make the adjusting journal entry necessary at the end of the period in the following situation: On August 1, the company borrowed $10,000 under a 1-year loan agreement. The annual interest rate is 8%. As of the end of the year, no entry has yet been made to record the accrued interest on the loan.

Practice 2-15
LO3

Adjusting Entries

Make the adjusting journal entry necessary at the end of the period in the following situation: On August 1, the company paid $3,600 in advance for 12 months of rent, with the rental period beginning on August 1. This $3,600 was recorded as Prepaid Rent. As of the end of the year, no entry has yet been made to adjust the amount initially recorded.

Practice 2-16
LO3

Adjusting Entries

Make the adjusting journal entry necessary at the end of the period in the following situation: On June 1, the company received $9,600 in advance for 12 months of service to be provided, with the service period beginning on June 1. This $9,600 was recorded as Unearned Service Revenue. The service is provided evenly throughout the year. As of the end of the year, no entry has yet been made to adjust the amount initially recorded.

Practice 2-17
LO3

Closing Entries

Make the closing entry (or entries) necessary to close the following accounts:

Cost of Goods Sold	$ 7,000
Accounts Payable	900
Paid-In Capital	1,500
Cash	3,200
Sales	11,000
Dividends	900
Retained Earnings (beginning)	1,200
Inventory	3,500

Practice 2-18
LO3

Closing Entries

Make the closing entry (or entries) necessary to close the following accounts:

Salary Expense	$18,000
Unearned Service Revenue	4,700
Paid-In Capital	2,000
Cash	800
Service Revenue	20,000
Rent Expense	6,400
Retained Earnings (beginning)	1,500
Prepaid Rent Expense	3,000

EXERCISES

Exercise 2-19

LO3

REVERSE SOLVABLE

Determining Income from Equity Account Analysis

An analysis of Goulding, Inc., disclosed changes in account balances for 2013 and the following supplementary data. From these data, calculate the net income or loss for 2013. (*Hint*: Net income can be thought of as the increase in net assets resulting from operations.)

Cash	$21,300	increase
Accounts Receivable	5,000	decrease
Inventory	14,000	increase
Equipment	58,000	increase
Accounts Payable	2,000	increase

Goulding sold 4,000 shares of its $5 par stock for $8 per share and received cash in full. Dividends of $20,000 were paid in cash during the year. Goulding borrowed $40,000 from the bank and made interest payments of $5,000. Goulding had no other loans payable. Interest of $2,000 was payable at December 31, 2013. There was no interest payable at December 31, 2012. Equipment of $15,000 was donated by stockholders during the year.

Exercise 2-20

LO2, LO3

Recording Transactions in T-Accounts

Georgia Supply Corporation, a merchandising firm, prepared the following trial balance as of October 1:

	Debit	Credit
Cash	$150,000	
Accounts Receivable	21,540	
Inventory	32,680	
Land	15,400	
Building	14,000	
Accounts Payable		$ 9,190
Mortgage Payable		23,700
Common Stock		140,000
Retained Earnings		60,730
Totals	$233,620	$233,620

Georgia Supply engaged in the following transactions during October 2013. The company records inventory using the perpetual system.

Oct. 1 Sold merchandise on account to the Tracker Corporation for $12,000; terms 2/10, n/30, FOB shipping point. Tracker paid $350 freight on the goods. The merchandise cost $6,850.

5 Purchased inventory costing $10,250 on account; terms n/30.

7 Received payment from Tracker for goods shipped October 1.

Oct. 15 The payroll paid for the first half of October was $22,000. (Ignore payroll taxes.)

18 Purchased a machine for $8,600 cash.

22 Declared a dividend of $0.45 per share on 45,000 shares of common stock outstanding.

27 Purchased building and land for $62,500 in cash and a $112,500 mortgage payable, due in 30 years. The land was appraised at $75,000 and the building at $150,000.

1. Prepare T-accounts for all items in the October 1 trial balance and enter the initial balances.

2. Record the October transactions directly to the T-accounts.
3. Prepare a new trial balance as of the end of October.

Exercise 2-21
LO2

REVERSE SOLVABLE

Analysis of Journal Entries

For each of the following journal entries, write a description of the underlying event.

	Account	Debit	Credit
1.	Cash	300	
	Accounts Receivable		300
2.	Accounts Payable	400	
	Inventory		400
3.	Cash	5,000	
	Loan Payable		5,000
4.	Cash	200	
	Accounts Receivable	700	
	Sales		900
	Cost of Goods Sold	550	
	Inventory		550
5.	Prepaid Insurance	200	
	Cash		200
6.	Dividends	250	
	Dividends Payable		250
7.	Retained Earnings	1,000	
	Dividends		1,000
8.	Insurance Expense	50	
	Prepaid Insurance		50
9.	Inventory	600	
	Cash		150
	Accounts Payable		450
10.	Allowance for Bad Debts	46	
	Accounts Receivable		46
11.	Interest Expense	125	
	Interest Payable		125
12.	Wages Payable	130	
	Wages Expense	75	
	Cash		205
13.	Accounts Payable	500	
	Cash		490
	Purchase Discounts		10

Exercise 2-22
LO3

Accrual Errors

Spilker Aviation, Inc., failed to make year-end adjustments to record accrued salaries and recognize interest receivable on investments over the last three years as follows:

	2011	2012	2013
Accrued salaries	$21,000	$17,500	$26,000
Interest receivable	8,500	11,400	12,100

What impact would the correction of these errors have on the net income for these three years? Ignore income taxes.

Exercise 2-23

LO3

Adjusting and Correcting Entries

Upon inspecting the books and records for Wernli Company for the year ended December 31, 2013, you find the following data:

(a) A receivable of $640 from Hatch Realty is determined to be uncollectible. The company maintains an allowance for bad debts for such losses.
(b) A creditor, E. F. Bowcutt Co., has just been awarded damages of $3,500 as a result of breach of contract by Wernli Company during the current year. Nothing appears on the books in connection with this matter.
(c) A fire destroyed part of a branch office. Furniture and fixtures that cost $12,300 and had a book value of $8,200 at the time of the fire were completely destroyed. The insurance company has agreed to pay $7,000 under the provisions of the fire insurance policy.
(d) Advances of $950 to salespersons have been previously recorded as sales salaries expense.
(e) Machinery at the end of the year shows a balance of $19,960. It is discovered that additions to this account during the year totaled $4,460, but of this amount, $760 should have been recorded as repairs. Depreciation is to be recorded at 10% on machinery owned throughout the year but at one-half this rate on machinery purchased or sold during the year.

Record the entries required to adjust and correct the accounts. (Ignore income tax consequences.)

Exercise 2-24

LO3

REVERSE SOLVABLE

Analyzing Adjusting Entries

Guidecom Consulting Company initially records prepaid items as assets and unearned items as liabilities. Selected account balances at the end of the current and prior year follow. Accrued expenses and revenues are adjusted only at year-end.

	Adjusted Balances, December 31, 2012	Adjusted Balances, December 31, 2013
Prepaid Rent	$ 5,100	$3,400
Salaries and Wages Payable	2,100	4,700
Unearned Consulting Fees	18,200	7,800
Interest Receivable	800	2,100

During 2013, Guidecom Consulting paid $14,000 for rent and $40,000 for wages. It received $112,000 for consulting fees and $3,200 as interest.

1. Provide the entries that were made at December 31, 2013, to adjust the accounts to the year-end balances shown above.
2. Determine the proper amount of Rent Expense, Salaries and Wages Expense, Consulting Fees Revenue, and Interest Revenue to be reported on the current-year income statement.

Exercise 2-25

LO3

Adjusting Entries

The following accounts were taken from the trial balance of Cole Company as of December 31, 2013:

Sales	$70,000
Interest Revenue	3,000
Equipment	52,000
Accumulated Depreciation—Equipment	8,000
Inventory	23,000
Advertising Expense	1,500
Selling Expense	7,500
Interest Expense	2,000

Given the information below, make the necessary adjusting entries.

(a) The equipment has an estimated useful life of ten years and a salvage value of $4,000. Depreciation is calculated using the straight-line method.
(b) Of selling expense, $1,500 has been paid in advance.
(c) Interest of $800 has accrued on notes receivable.
(d) Of advertising expense, $440 was incorrectly debited to Selling Expense.

Exercise 2-26
LO3

Adjusting Entries

In analyzing the accounts of Sydney Corporation, the adjusting data listed below are determined on December 31, the end of an annual fiscal period.

(a) The prepaid insurance account shows a debit of $6,000, representing the cost of a 2-year earthquake insurance policy dated July 1.
(b) On August 1, Rent Revenue was credited for $9,450, representing revenue from subrental for a 7-month period beginning on that date.
(c) Purchase of advertising materials for $3,550 during the year was recorded in the advertising expense account. On December 31, advertising materials costing $500 are on hand.
(d) On November 1, $4,200 was paid for rent for a 6-month period beginning on that date. The rent expense account was debited.
(e) Miscellaneous Office Expense was debited for office supplies of $950 purchased during the year. On December 31, office supplies of $125 are on hand.
(f) Interest of $534 has accrued on notes payable.

1. Give the adjusting entry for each item.
2. What sources would provide the information for each adjustment?

Exercise 2-27
LO3

SPREADSHEET

Adjusting Entries

The following data were obtained from an analysis of the accounts of Noble Distributor Company as of March 31, 2013, in preparation of the annual report. Noble records current transactions in nominal accounts. What are the appropriate adjusting entries?

(a) Prepaid Insurance has a balance of $14,100. Noble has the following policies in force:

Policy	Date	Term	Cost	Coverage
A	1/1/2013	2 years	$ 5,400	Shop equipment
B	12/1/2012	6 months	2,700	Delivery equipment
C	7/1/2012	3 years	18,000	Buildings

(b) Unearned Subscription Revenue has a balance of $56,250. The following subscriptions were collected in the current year. There are no other unexpired subscriptions.

Effective Date	Amount	Term
July 1, 2012	$27,000	1 year
October 1, 2012	22,200	1 year
January 1, 2013	28,800	1 year
April 1, 2013	20,700	1 year

(c) Interest Payable has a balance of $825. Noble owes a 10%, 90-day note for $45,000 dated March 1, 2013.
(d) Supplies has a balance of $2,190. An inventory of supplies revealed a total of $1,410.
(e) Salaries Payable has a balance of $9,750. The payroll for the 5-day workweek ended April 3 totaled $11,250.

Exercise 2-28

LO3

REVERSE SOLVABLE

Reconstructing Adjusting Entries

For each situation, reconstruct the adjusting entry that was made to arrive at the ending balance. Assume statements and adjusting entries are prepared only once each year.

1. Prepaid Insurance:

Balance beginning of year	$3,600
Balance end of year	4,300

   During the year, an additional business insurance policy was purchased. A 1-year premium of $1,200 was paid and charged to Prepaid Insurance.

2. Accumulated Depreciation:

Balance beginning of year	$103,400
Balance end of year	106,100

   During the year, a depreciable asset that cost $10,700 and had a carrying value of $5,300 was sold for $6,000.The disposal of the asset was recorded correctly.

3. Unearned Rent:

Balance beginning of year	$12,000
Balance end of year	8,000

   Warehouse quarterly rent received in advance is $14,000. During the year, equipment was rented to another company at an annual rent of $6,000. The quarterly rent payments were credited to Rent Revenue; the annual equipment rental was credited to Unearned Rent.

4. Salaries Payable:

Balance beginning of year	$29,480
Balance end of year	36,540

   Salaries are paid biweekly. All salary payments during the year were debited to Salaries Expense.

Exercise 2-29

LO3

Adjusting and Closing Entries and Post-Closing Trial Balance

Below is the trial balance for Boudreaux Company as of December 31.

	Debit	Credit
Cash	$ 72,000	
Accounts Receivable	365,000	
Inventory	52,000	
Prepaid Expenses	36,000	
Land	70,000	
Plant and Equipment	1,254,000	
Other Assets	1,275,000	
Accounts Payable		$ 154,000
Wages, Interest, and Taxes Payable		218,000
Unearned Revenue		42,000
Long-Term Debt		1,190,000
Other Liabilities		297,000
Common Stock		195,000
Retained Earnings		915,000
Dividends	211,000	
Sales		2,762,000
Interest Revenue		29,000
Costs of Goods Sold	1,565,000	

(Continued)

	Debit	Credit
Selling, General, and Administrative Expenses	615,000	
Interest Expense	82,000	
Income Tax Expense	205,000	
Totals	$5,802,000	$5,802,000

Consider the following additional information:

(a) Boudreaux uses a perpetual inventory system.
(b) The prepaid expenses were paid on September 1 and relate to a 3-year insurance policy that went into effect on September 1.
(c) The unearned revenue relates to rental of an unused portion of the corporate offices. The $42,000 was received on April 1 and represents payment in advance for one year's rental.
(d) Plant and Equipment includes $15,000 for routine equipment repairs that were erroneously recorded as equipment purchases. The repairs were made on December 30.
(e) Other Assets includes $7,000 for miscellaneous office supplies, which were purchased in mid-October. An end-of-year count reveals that only $4,200 of the office supplies remain.
(f) Selling, General, and Administrative Expenses incorrectly includes $13,000 for office furniture purchases (Other Assets). The purchases were made on December 30.
(g) Inventory erroneously includes $7,500 of inventory that Boudreaux had purchased on account but that was returned to the supplier on December 28 because of unsatisfactory quality.

1. Record the entries necessary to adjust the books.
2. Record the entries necessary to close the books. Assume the adjustments in (1) do not affect Income Tax Expense.
3. Prepare a post-closing trial balance.

Exercise 2-30

LO3

Adjusting and Closing Entries and Post-Closing Trial Balance

Accounts of Pioneer Heating Corporation at the end of the first year of operations showed the following balances. In addition, prepaid operating expenses are $4,000, and accrued sales commissions payable are $5,900. Investment revenue receivable is $1,000. Depreciation for the year on buildings is $4,500 and on machinery, $5,000. Federal and state income taxes for the year are estimated at $18,100.

	Debit	Credit
Cash	$ 39,000	
Inventory	50,000	
Investment	50,000	
Land	70,000	
Buildings	180,000	
Machinery	100,000	
Accounts Payable		$ 65,000
Common Stock		320,000
Additional Paid-In Capital		40,000
Sales		590,000
Cost of Goods Sold	230,000	
Sales Commissions	200,000	
General Operating Expenses	101,000	
Investment Revenue		5,000
Totals	$1,020,000	$1,020,000

1. Prepare the necessary entries to adjust and close the books.
2. Prepare a post-closing trial balance.

Exercise 2-31
LO3

Closing Entries

Dylan's Taxidermy Corporation reports revenues and expenses of $142,300 and $91,500, respectively, for the period. Give the remaining entries to close the books assuming the ledger reports Additional Paid-In Capital of $400,000 and Retained Earnings of $125,000. Dividends during the year amounting to $29,200 were recorded in a dividends account.

Exercise 2-32
LO3

Closing Entries

An accountant for Jolley, Inc., a merchandising enterprise, has just finished posting all year-end adjusting entries to the ledger accounts and now wishes to close the appropriate account balances in preparation for the new period.

1. For each of the accounts listed, indicate whether the year-end balance should be (a) carried forward to the new period, (b) closed by debiting the account, or (c) closed by crediting the account.

(a)	Cash	$ 25,000
(b)	Sales	75,000
(c)	Dividends	3,500
(d)	Inventory	7,500
(e)	Selling Expenses	7,900
(f)	Capital Stock	100,000
(g)	Wages Expense	14,400
(h)	Dividends Payable	4,000
(i)	Cost of Goods Sold	26,500
(j)	Accounts Payable	12,000
(k)	Accounts Receivable	140,000
(l)	Prepaid Insurance	16,000
(m)	Interest Receivable	1,500
(n)	Sales Discounts	4,200
(o)	Interest Revenue	6,500
(p)	Supplies	8,000
(q)	Retained Earnings	6,500
(r)	Accumulated Depreciation	2,000
(s)	Depreciation Expense	1,800

2. Give the necessary closing entries.
3. What was Jolley's net income (loss) for the period?

PROBLEMS

Problem 2-33
LO2

Journal Entries

Selfish Gene Company is a merchandising firm. The following events occurred during the month of May. (*Note*: Selfish Gene maintains a perpetual inventory system.)

May 1 Received $40,000 cash as new stockholder investment.
3 Purchased inventory costing $8,000 on account from Dawkins Company; terms 2/10, n/30.
4 Purchased office supplies for $500 cash.
4 Held an office party for the retiring accountant. Balloons, hats, and refreshments cost $150 and were paid for with office staff contributions.
5 Sold merchandise costing $7,500 on account for $14,000 to Richard Company; terms 3/15, n/30.

8 Paid employee wages of $2,000. Gross wages were $2,450; taxes totaling $450 were withheld.
9 Hired a new accountant; agreed to a first-year salary of $28,000.
9 Paid $1,500 for newspaper advertising.
10 Received payment from Richard Company.
12 Purchased a machine for $6,400 cash.
15 Declared a cash dividend totaling $25,000.
18 Sold merchandise costing $13,000 for $3,000 cash and $21,000 on account to Feynman Company; terms n/30.
19 Paid Dawkins Company account in full.
22 Company executives appeared on the cover of a national newsmagazine. Related article extolled Selfish Gene's labor practices, environmental concerns, and customer service.
23 Market value of Selfish Gene's common stock rose by $150,000.
25 Purchased a building for $15,000 cash and a $135,000 mortgage payable.
29 Paid dividends declared on May 15.

Instructions:

1. Record the preceding events in general journal form.
2. Which event do you think had the most significant economic impact on Selfish Gene Company? Are all economically relevant events recorded in the financial records?

Problem 2-34

LO2, LO3

SPREADSHEET

Account Classification and Debit/Credit Relationship

Instructions: Using the format provided, identify for each account, including an asterisk for contra accounts:

1. Whether the account will appear on a balance sheet (B/S), income statement (I/S), or neither (N)
2. Whether the account is an asset (A), liability (L), owners' equity (OE), revenue (R), expense (E), or other (O)
3. Whether the account is real or nominal
4. Whether the account will be "closed" or left "open" at year-end
5. Whether the account normally has a debit (Dr.) or a credit (Cr.) balance

Account Title	(1) B/S, I/S, N	(2) A, L, OE, R, E, O	(3) Real or Nominal	(4) Closed or Open	(5) Debit (Dr.) or Credit (Cr.)
Example: Cash	B/S	A	Real	Open	Dr.

(a) Unearned Rent Revenue
(b) Accounts Receivable
(c) Inventory
(d) Accounts Payable
(e) Prepaid Rent
(f) Mortgage Payable
(g) Sales
(h) Cost of Goods Sold
(i) Dividends
(j) Dividends Payable
(k) Interest Receivable
(l) Wages Expense
(m) Interest Revenue
(n) Supplies
(o) Accumulated Depreciation
(p) Retained Earnings

(q) Discount on Bonds Payable
(r) Goodwill
(s) Additional Paid-In Capital

Problem 2-35
LO3
SPREADSHEET

Adjusting Entries

On December 31, Trinkets Supply Company noted the following transactions that occurred during 2013, some or all of which might require adjustment to the books.

(a) Payment of $4,300 to suppliers was made for purchases on account during the year and was not recorded.
(b) Building and land were purchased on January 2 for $190,000. The building's fair value was $141,000 at the time of purchase. The building is being depreciated over a 30-year life using the straight-line method, assuming no salvage value.
(c) Of the $52,000 in Accounts Receivable, 7% is estimated to be uncollectible. Currently, Allowance for Bad Debts shows a debit balance of $1,100.
(d) On September 1, $80,000 was loaned to a customer on a 12-month note with interest at an annual rate of 11%.
(e) During 2013, Trinkets Supply received $15,200 in advance for services, 80% of which will be performed in 2014. The $15,200 was credited to Sales Revenue.
(f) The interest expense account was debited for all interest charges incurred during the year and shows a balance of $2,300. However, of this amount, $300 represents a discount on a 60-day note payable, due January 30, 2014.

Instructions:
1. Give the necessary adjusting entries to bring the books up to date.
2. Indicate the net change in income as a result of the foregoing adjustments.

Problem 2-36
LO3
REVERSE SOLVABLE

Analysis of Adjusting Entries

The accountant for Save More Company made the following adjusting entries on December 31, 2013.

(a) Prepaid Rent	1,800	
Rent Expense		1,800
(b) Advertising Materials	1,700	
Advertising Expense		1,700
(c) Rent Revenue	900	
Unearned Revenue		900
(d) Office Supplies	1,000	
Office Supplies Expense		1,000
(e) Prepaid Insurance	1,050	
Insurance Expense		1,050

Further information is provided as follows:

(a) Annual rent is paid in advance every October 1.
(b) Advertising materials are purchased at one time (June 1) and are used evenly throughout the year.
(c) Annual rent is received in advance every March 1.
(d) Office supplies are purchased every July 1 and used evenly throughout the year.
(e) Yearly insurance premium is payable each August 1.

Instructions: For each adjusting entry, indicate the original transaction entry that was recorded.

Problem 2-37

LO3

SPREADSHEET

Adjusting Entries

The bookkeeper for Joe's Hardware Co. records all revenue and expense items in nominal accounts during the period. The following balances, among others, are listed on the trial balance at the end of the fiscal period, December 31, 2013, before accounts have been adjusted:

	Dr. (Cr.)
Accounts Receivable	$123,000
Allowance for Bad Debts	(2,700)
Interest Receivable	3,200
Discount on Notes Payable	300
Prepaid Real Estate and Personal Property Tax	1,600
Salaries and Wages Payable	(7,600)
Discount on Notes Receivable	(1,800)
Unearned Rent Revenue	(5,200)

Inspection of the company's records reveals the following as of December 31, 2013:

(a) Uncollectible accounts are estimated at 4% of the accounts receivable balance.

(b) The accrued interest on investments totals $3,900.

(c) The company borrows cash by discounting its own notes at the bank. Discounts on notes payable at the end of 2013 are $1,200.

(d) Prepaid real estate and personal property taxes are $1,600, the same as at the end of 2012.

(e) Accrued salaries and wages are $8,300.

(f) The company accepts notes from customers, giving its customers credit for the face of the note less a charge for interest. At the end of each period, any interest applicable to the succeeding period is reported as a discount. Discounts on notes receivable at the end of 2013 are $1,300.

(g) Part of the company's properties had been sublet on September 15, 2012, at a rental of $2,100 per month. The arrangement was terminated at the end of one year.

Instructions: Give the adjusting entries required to bring the books up to date.

Problem 2-38

LO3, LO4

Cash to Accrual Adjusting Entries and Income Statement

Gee Enterprises records all transactions on the cash basis. Greg Gee, company accountant, prepared the following income statement at the end of the company's first year of operations:

Gee Enterprises
Income Statement
For the Year Ended December 31, 2013

Sales		$261,400
Selling and administrative expenses:		
Salaries expense	$78,000	
Rent expense	45,000	
Commission expense	37,800	
Equipment	30,000	
Utilities expense	29,000	
Insurance expense	6,000	
Interest expense	3,000	228,800
Net income		$ 32,600

You have been asked to prepare an income statement on the accrual basis. The following information is given to you to assist in the preparation:

(a) Amounts due from customers at year-end were $28,000. Of this amount, $3,000 will probably not be collected.
(b) Salaries of $11,000 for December 2013 were paid on January 5, 2014. Ignore payroll taxes.
(c) Gee rents its building for $3,000 a month, payable quarterly in advance. The contract was signed on January 1, 2013.
(d) The bill for December's utility costs of $2,700 was paid January 10, 2014.
(e) Equipment of $30,000 was purchased on January 1, 2013. The expected life is five years, no salvage value. Assume straight-line depreciation.
(f) Commissions of 15% of sales are paid on the same day cash is received from customers.
(g) A 1-year insurance policy was issued on company assets on July 1, 2013. Premiums are paid annually in advance.
(h) Gee borrowed $50,000 for one year on May 1, 2013. Interest payments based on an annual rate of 12% are made quarterly, beginning with the first payment on August 1, 2013.
(i) The income tax rate is 40%. No prepayments of income taxes were made during 2013.

Instructions:

1. Prepare adjusting entries to convert the books from a cash to an accrual basis.
2. Prepare the income statement for the year ended December 31, 2013, based on the entries in (1).

Problem 2-39
LO3

Adjusting and Closing Entries

Account balances taken from the ledger of Builders' Supply Corporation on December 31, 2013, before adjustment, follow information relating to adjustments on December 31, 2013:

(a) Allowance for Bad Debts is to be increased to a balance of $3,000.
(b) Buildings are depreciated at the rate of 5% per year.
(c) Accrued selling expenses are $3,840.
(d) There are supplies of $780 on hand.
(e) Prepaid insurance relating to 2014 totals $720.
(f) Accrued interest on long-term investments is $240.
(g) Accrued real estate and payroll taxes are $900.
(h) Accrued interest on the mortgage is $480.
(i) Income taxes are estimated to be 30% of the income before income taxes.

Cash	$ 24,000
Accounts Receivable	72,000
Allowance for Bad Debts	1,380
Inventory	87,570
Long-Term Investments	15,400
Land	69,600
Buildings	72,000
Accumulated Depreciation—Buildings	19,800
Accounts Payable	35,000
Mortgage Payable	68,800
Capital Stock, $10 par	180,000
Retained Earnings, December 31, 2012	14,840
Dividends	13,400

Sales	$246,000
Sales Returns	4,360
Sales Discounts	5,400
Cost of Goods Sold	114,370
Selling Expenses	49,440
Office Expenses	21,680
Insurance Expense	1,440
Supplies Expense	5,200
Taxes—Real Estate and Payroll	7,980
Interest Revenue	660
Interest Expense	2,640

Instructions:

1. Prepare a trial balance.
2. Journalize the adjustments.
3. Journalize the closing entries.
4. Prepare a post-closing trial balance.

(*Note:* Although not required, the use of a spreadsheet is recommended for the solution of this problem.)

Problem 2-40

LO3

Adjusting and Closing Entries and Post-Closing Trial Balance

Data for adjustments at December 31, 2013, are as follows:

(a) Taipei International uses a perpetual inventory system.
(b) An analysis of Accounts Receivable reveals that the appropriate year-end balance in Allowance for Bad Debts is $750.
(c) Equipment depreciation for the year totaled $32,000.
(d) A recheck of the inventory count revealed that goods costing $5,600 were wrongly excluded from ending inventory. The goods in question were not shipped until January 3, 2014. A related receivable for $8,200 was also mistakenly recorded.
(e) Interest on the note payable has not been accrued. The note was issued on March 1, 2013, and the interest rate is 12%.
(f) The balance in Insurance Expense represents $3,000 that was paid for a 1-year policy on October 1. The policy went into effect on October 1.
(g) Dividends totaling $7,800 were declared on December 25. The dividends will not be paid until January 15, 2014. No entry was made.

Taipei International Corporation
Unadjusted Trial Balance
December 31, 2013

	Debit	Credit
Cash	$ 31,500	
Accounts Receivable	25,000	
Allowance for Bad Debts		$ 250
Inventory	41,700	
Equipment	190,000	
Accumulated Depreciation—Equipment		51,000
Accounts Payable		31,000
Notes Payable		70,000
Wages Payable		8,000

Income Taxes Payable		6,500
Common Stock		40,000
Retained Earnings		34,100
Sales Revenue		310,000
Interest Revenue		12,000
Cost of Goods Sold	205,250	
Wages Expense	45,000	
Interest Expense	3,200	
Utilities Expense	6,000	
Insurance Expense	3,000	
Advertising Expense	5,000	
Income Tax Expense	7,200	
Totals	$562,850	$562,850

Instructions:

1. Journalize the necessary adjusting entries. (Ignore income tax effects.)
2. Journalize the necessary closing entries.
3. Prepare a post-closing trial balance.
4. Can a company pay dividends in a year in which it has a net loss? Can a company owe income taxes in a year in which it has a net loss?

Problem 2-41

LO3

Preparation of Work Sheet

Account balances taken from the ledger of High Flying Logistics Co. on December 31, 2013, follow:

Cash	$ 42,000
Accounts Receivable	86,000
Allowance for Bad Debts	2,400
Inventory	97,000
Long-Term Investments	31,500
Land	62,300
Buildings	142,500
Accumulated Depreciation—Buildings	32,560
Accounts Payable	51,800
Mortgage Payable	122,500
Capital Stock, $5 par	200,000
Retained Earnings, December 31, 2012	26,950
Dividends	40,540
Sales	431,000
Sales Returns	9,560
Sales Discounts	8,440
Cost of Goods Sold	203,420
Selling Expenses	58,300
Office Expenses	44,200
Insurance Expense	12,000
Supplies Expense	5,100
Taxes—Real Estate and Payroll	15,800
Interest Revenue	750
Interest Expense	9,300

Information relating to adjustments on December 31, 2013, follows:

(a) Allowance for Bad Debts is to be increased by $2,200.
(b) Buildings have a salvage value of $7,500. They are being depreciated at the rate of 10% per year.
(c) Accrued selling expenses are $9,300.
(d) There are supplies of $850 on hand.
(e) Prepaid insurance relating to 2014 totals $3,800.
(f) Total interest revenue earned in 2013 is $1,900.
(g) Accrued real estate and payroll taxes are $3,550.
(h) Accrued interest on the mortgage is $1,980.
(i) Income tax is estimated to be 40% of income.

Instructions: Prepare a work sheet showing the net income and balance sheet totals for the year ending December 31, 2013.

Problem 2-42

LO3

SPREADSHEET

Preparation of Work Sheet and Adjusting and Closing Entries

The following account balances are taken from the general ledger of Whitni Corporation on December 31, 2013, the end of its fiscal year. The corporation was organized January, 2005.

Cash	$ 40,250
Notes Receivable	16,500
Accounts Receivable	63,000
Allowance for Bad Debts (credit balance)	650
Inventory, December 31, 2013	94,700
Land	80,000
Buildings	247,600
Accumulated Depreciation—Buildings	18,000
Furniture and Fixtures	15,000
Accumulated Depreciation—Furniture and Fixtures	9,000
Notes Payable	18,000
Accounts Payable	72,700
Common Stock, $100 par	240,000
Retained Earnings	129,125
Sales	760,000
Sales Returns and Allowances	17,000
Cost of Goods Sold	465,800
Utilities Expense	16,700
Property Tax Expense	10,200
Salaries and Wages Expense	89,000
Sales Commissions Expense	73,925
Insurance Expense	18,000
Interest Revenue	2,600
Interest Expense	2,400

Data for adjustments at December 31, 2013, are as follows:

(a) Depreciation (to nearest month for additions): furniture and fixtures, 10%; buildings, 4%.
(b) Additions to the buildings costing $150,000 were completed June 30, 2013.
(c) Allowance for Bad Debts is to be increased to a balance of $2,500.
(d) Accrued expenses: sales commissions, $700; interest on notes payable, $45; property taxes, $6,000.

(e) Prepaid expenses: insurance, $3,200.
(f) Accrued revenue: interest on notes receivable, $750.
(g) The following information is also to be recorded:
   (1) On December 30, the board of directors declared a quarterly dividend of $1.50 per share on common stock, payable January 25, 2014, to stockholders of record January 15, 2014.
   (2) Income taxes for 2013 are estimated at $15,000.
   (3) The only charges to Retained Earnings during the year resulted from the declaration of the regular quarterly dividends.

Instructions:

1. Prepare an 8-column spreadsheet. There should be a pair of columns each for trial balance, adjustments, income statement, and balance sheet.
2. Prepare all the journal entries necessary to record the effects of the foregoing information and to adjust and close the books of the corporation.

CASES

Discussion Case 2-43

Where Is Your Cash Box?

Consider the following account of a veterinarian attempting to hire his first bookkeeper:

Miss Harbottle, the prospective bookkeeper, paused at the desk, heaped high with incoming and outgoing bills and circulars from drug firms with here and there stray boxes of pills and tubes of udder ointment.

Stirring distastefully among the mess, she extracted the dog-eared old ledger and held it up between finger and thumb. "What's this?"

Siegfried trotted forward. "Oh, that's our ledger. We enter the visits into it from our day book, which is here somewhere." He scrabbled about on the desk. "Ah, here it is. This is where we write the calls as they come in."

She studied the two books for a few minutes with an expression of amazement that gave way to grim humor. She straightened up slowly and spoke patiently. "And where, may I ask, is your cash box?"

"Well, we just stuff it in there, you know." Siegfried pointed to the pint pot on the corner of the mantelpiece. "Haven't got what you'd call a proper cash box, but this does the job all right."

Miss Harbottle looked at the pot with horror. Crumpled cheques and notes peeped over the brim at her; many of their companions had burst out on the hearth below. "And you mean to say that you go out and leave that money there day after day?"

"Never seems to come to any harm." Siegfried replied.

"And how about your petty cash?"

Siegfried gave an uneasy giggle. "All in there, you know. All cash—petty and otherwise."

(Excerpted from James Herriot, *All Creatures Great and Small*, New York: St. Martin's Press, 1972.)

Situations similar to the one described here are not unusual for small businesses. How does a business survive with such bad bookkeeping?

Discussion Case 2-44

To Record or Not to Record

Explain why each of the following hypothetical events would not be recorded in a journal entry.

1. A famous and much-beloved movie star is secretly filmed by an investigative news team using your company's product when she in fact has an endorsement contract with your company's major competitor.
2. Two of your firm's top vice presidents have a bitter argument and will probably never speak to each other again.
3. Your company's chief research chemist is killed in a plane crash.

4. Because of unfavorable economic news, consumer confidence is shaken, and the stock market falls by 10%.
5. You, a small business owner, buy a sofa for your home. You pay with a check drawn on your personal, not your business, checking account.
6. **Disney** decides to build the next Walt Disney World near a large piece of property you own.

Discussion Case 2-45

Is It Time to Revolutionize the Recording of Business Events?

Jim Price and Elaine Bijard are taking an accounting systems course at their local university. They are intrigued with the rapid advances in technology and communication that are occurring in the computer world. Today's lecture was especially thought provoking. Professor Hansen stated that it is no longer necessary or even desirable to record business events in sequential order as has been traditionally done in accounting journals. The better approach is to capture all data related to a business event in a computer database, including accounting, marketing, and production data, and to prepare reports for many different users from a single source. The database would be a management information database, not just one for accounting reports.

Jim argues that such an approach would make it more difficult for accountants to keep control of input and ensure the integrity of their financial reports, but Elaine feels that the sooner the accountants recognize the potential, the better they can serve management's varied needs. What advantages and disadvantages do you see coming from a database approach to recording? How can Jim's objections be met?

Discussion Case 2-46

When Cash Basis Is Different from Accrual Basis

Alice Guth operates a low-impact aerobics studio. Alice has been in business for three years and has always had her financial statements prepared on a cash basis. This year, Alice's accountant has suggested that accrual-based financial statements would give a more accurate picture of the performance of the business. Alice's friend Frank Geller tells her that, in his experience, accrual-based financial statements tell pretty much the same story as cash-basis statements.

Under what circumstances would the cash basis and the accrual basis of accounting yield quite different pictures of a firm's operating performance? Under what circumstances would the cash basis and the accrual basis show approximately the same picture?

Discussion Case 2-47

The Impact of Computers on Financial Reporting

Computers have drastically altered the way accounting records are maintained. Almost all businesses now keep the bulk of their accounting records on computers. However, the financial statements are still prepared methodically on only a quarterly and annual basis (for public companies). What types of changes in companies' financial statements are likely to occur over the next 10 to 15 years as a result of the increasing ability to disseminate information online?

Discussion Case 2-48

But I Need More Timely Information!

Julie is successful in her position as a consultant for Worldwide Enterprises. She has selectively invested her money in stocks of several companies. She receives the annual reports and faithfully analyzes them as she was taught in her university accounting class. She is concerned, however, with the impact that events have on the financial reports between years. Julie understands that quarterly reports are available from the companies upon request but that they are not audited and thus may not be reliable. She wonders whether they can be trusted. Even quarterly reports might not be frequent enough. Wouldn't it be useful if she could use her computer to interrogate the company's computer and obtain information anytime she wanted it?

She decides to write for advice from the chief accountants of the companies in which she holds stock. As chief accountant, how would you address Julie's concerns?

Case 2-49 **Deciphering Financial Statements (Lockheed Martin Corporation)**

Locate the 2009 financial statements for **Lockheed Martin Corporation** on the Internet.

Reconstruct the company's adjusted trial balance as of December 31, 2009.

Case 2-50 **Writing Assignment (I am going to be an accountant—not a bookkeeper!)**

Some accounting students feel that the mechanics of accounting (journal entries and T-accounts) are for bookkeepers. Because these students are training to be accountants, they see no need to spend a great deal of time studying these mechanics.

In one page, explain why accountants must have a thorough understanding of journal entries and T-accounts, even though these tools are mostly the domain of bookkeepers.

Case 2-51 **Ethical Dilemma (The art of making adjusting entries)**

Refer back to the section of the chapter entitled "Preparing Adjusting Entries." Who determines how long buildings and furniture and equipment are to last? Who determines the dollar amount of accounts receivable that are doubtful?

Suppose we were to change our asset depreciation on the buildings and the furniture and equipment from 5% and 10% to 4% and 8%, respectively. What would be the effect on net income? Would it increase or decrease? Likewise, suppose our estimate of the balance in Allowance for Bad Debts was reduced to $1,000. What would be the effect on net income?

Is the adjusting entry process an exact science where accountants can determine exactly how well a company has done for a period? Or is accounting an art that requires significant judgment on the part of the accountant?

What are the dangers for the accountant when making an estimate in an area (like Bad Debts) where significant judgment is required?

Case 2-52 **Cumulative Spreadsheet Analysis**

Beginning with Chapter 2, each chapter in this text will include a spreadsheet assignment based on the financial information of a fictitious company named Skywalker Enterprises. The assignments start out simple—in this chapter you are not asked to do much more than set up financial statement formats and input some numbers. In succeeding chapters, the spreadsheets will get more complex so that by the end of the course you will have constructed a spreadsheet that allows you to forecast operating cash flows for five years in the future, adjust your forecast depending on the operating parameters that you think are most reasonable, and analyze the impact of a variety of accounting assumptions on the reported numbers.

So, let's get started with the first spreadsheet assignment.

1. The following numbers are for Skywalker Enterprises for 2013.

Short-Term Loans Payable	$ 30
Unearned Revenue	35
Interest Expense	27
Paid-In Capital	150
Cash	30
Other Long-Term Liabilities	253
Dividends	0
Accumulated Depreciation	27
Other Long-Term Assets	40
Inventory	459
Cost of Goods Sold	1,557
Long-Term Debt	621
Investment Securities (current)	70
Income Tax Expense	12

Retained Earnings (as of January 1, 2013)	$ 93
Receivables	81
Long-Term Investments	250
Sales	2,100
Accounts Payable	222
Other Equity	72
Property, Plant, and Equipment	597
Other Operating Expenses	480

Your assignment is to create a spreadsheet containing a balance sheet and an income statement for Skywalker Enterprises.

2. Skywalker is wondering what its balance sheet and income statement would have looked like if the following numbers were changed as indicated.

	Change	
	From	**To**
Sales	$2,100	$2,190
Cost of Goods Sold	1,557	1,650
Other Operating Expenses	480	495

Create a second spreadsheet with the numbers changed as indicated. (*Note:* After making these changes, your balance sheet may no longer balance.) Eliminate any discrepancy by increasing or decreasing Short-Term Loans Payable as much as necessary.

P1 FOUNDATIONS OF FINANCIAL ACCOUNTING

Chris Rank/Bloomberg News/Landov

CHAPTER 3 The Balance Sheet and Notes to the Financial Statements

LEARNING OBJECTIVES

1. Describe the specific elements of the balance sheet (assets, liabilities, and owners' equity), and prepare a balance sheet with assets and liabilities properly classified into current and noncurrent categories.
2. Identify the different formats used to present balance sheet data.
3. Analyze a company's performance and financial position through the computation of financial ratios.
4. Recognize the importance of the notes to the financial statements, and outline the types of disclosures made in the notes.
5. Understand the major limitations of the balance sheet.

"Every man in uniform gets a bottle of Coca-Cola for 5 cents, wherever he is and whatever it costs." So said Robert Woodruff, **Coca-Cola** chairman, as U.S. soldiers entered the fighting in World War II. By 1941, Coca-Cola was such a part of U.S. life that Coke also became part of the war machine. In 1943, General Dwight Eisenhower requested the necessary equipment and bottles to refill 10 million Coca-Colas for soldiers in the European theater. Allied Headquarters in North Africa operated 64 bottling plants during the war.

From its beginnings in Atlanta, Georgia, in which 1886 sales averaged 9 drinks per day, to its current worldwide presence in which 2009 sales averaged 1.6 billion servings per day, Coca-Cola has grown to the point that it is now the most recognizable trademark on the planet—with sales in over 200 countries around the world.

Pharmacist Dr. John S. Pemberton mixed the first kettle of Coca-Cola in his backyard in 1886. Frank Robinson, Pemberton's bookkeeper and partner, named the drink and came up with the unique script that is Coke's signature. Bottled Coke (in contrast to Coca-Cola served at a soda fountain) was first offered in 1894, and five years later, Joseph Whitehead and Benjamin Thomas purchased the exclusive rights to bottle Coca-Cola for $1. Within 20 years, 1,000 bottlers around the world were bottling Coke. In 1915, the contoured bottle that symbolizes Coca-Cola was developed, and its shape was finally granted a patent in 1977.

With Coca-Cola's remarkable success, one must wonder what company executives were thinking in 1985 when they made a historic blunder. In April of

EX 3-1 COCA-COLA'S BALANCE SHEET

The Coca-Cola Company and Subsidiaries
Consolidated Balance Sheets
December 31, 2009 and 2008
(In millions except par value)

ASSETS	**2009**	**2008**
CURRENT ASSETS		
Cash and cash equivalents	$ 7,021	$ 4,701
Short-term investments	2,130	—
TOTAL CASH, CASH EQUIVALENTS, AND SHORT-TERM INVESTMENTS	9,151	4,701
INVESTMENTS		
Marketable securities	62	278
Trade accounts receivable, less allowances of $55 and $51, respectively	3,758	3,090
Inventories	2,354	2,187
Prepaid expenses and other assets	2,226	1,920
TOTAL CURRENT ASSETS	17,551	12,176
EQUITY METHOD INVESTMENTS	6,217	5,316
OTHER INVESTMENTS, PRINCIPALLY BOTTLING COMPANIES	538	463
OTHER ASSETS	1,976	1,733
PROPERTY, PLANT AND EQUIPMENT—net	9,561	8,326
TRADEMARKS WITH INDEFINITE LIVES	6,183	6,059
GOODWILL	4,224	4,029
OTHER INTANGIBLE ASSETS	2,421	2,417
TOTAL ASSETS	**$48,671**	**$40,519**
LIABILITIES AND EQUITY		
CURRENT LIABILITIES		
Accounts payable and accrued expenses	$ 6,657	$ 6,205
Loans and notes payable	6,749	6,066
Current maturities of long-term debt	51	465
Accrued income taxes	264	252
TOTAL CURRENT LIABILITIES	13,721	12,988
LONG-TERM DEBT	5,059	2,781
OTHER LIABILITIES	2,965	3,011
DEFERRED INCOME TAXES	1,580	877
THE COCA-COLA COMPANY SHAREOWNERS' EQUITY		
Common stock, $0.25 par value; Authorized—5,600 shares; Issued—3,520 and 3,519 shares, respectively	880	880
Capital surplus	8,537	7,966
Reinvested earnings	41,537	38,513
Accumulated other comprehensive income (loss)	(757)	(2,674)
Treasury stock, at cost—1,217 and 1,207 shares, respectively	(25,398)	(24,213)
EQUITY ATTRIBUTABLE TO SHAREOWNERS OF THE COCA-COLA COMPANY	24,799	20,472
EQUITY ATTRIBUTABLE TO NONCONTROLLING INTERESTS	547	390
TOTAL EQUITY	25,346	20,862
TOTAL LIABILITIES AND EQUITY	**$48,671**	**$40,519**

that year, the company changed its secret formula, terminated the original Coke, and introduced "new" Coke. The public reaction was overwhelmingly negative, with consumers organizing and calling for the return of the original. After four months, the company reintroduced the original formula as Coca-Cola Classic.

Today, over 17,000 soft drink servings from The Coca-Cola Company are consumed around the world every second of every day.

Owning the most valuable brand name in the world (**Interbrand**, an international brand valuation company, estimated the value of the Coca-Cola brand name in 2009 at $68.734 billion), one might expect Coca-Cola's balance sheet to contain a significant amount assigned to this asset. One look at the company's balance sheet (see Exhibit 3-1), however, reveals that very little is recorded on Coke's balance sheet related to its intangible assets.

As illustrated with the brand name example, Coke's balance sheet is interesting as much for what it excludes as for what it includes. As an additional example, Coke owns approximately 34% of **Coca-Cola Enterprises**, a bottling company. Coca-Cola Enterprises has $15.5 billion in liabilities; however, because The Coca-Cola Company does not own a controlling interest (more than 50%) of this bottler, none of these liabilities are reported in Coke's balance sheet. Coke also owns significant percentages (but less than 50%) of other bottlers, which together report approximately $19.5 billion in liabilities. Again, Coke reported none of these liabilities in its balance sheet.

Coke's balance sheet appears relatively simple—deceptively simple. Although we are each comfortable with accounts such as Cash, Inventory, Accounts Payable, and Reinvested (or Retained) Earnings, a firm's balance sheet becomes much more complex as its business gets more complex. It is important that we understand what the balance sheet tells us, what it does not tell us, and the role that the financial statement notes play in assisting us in interpreting the financial statements.

? QUESTIONS

1. As stated above, the Coca-Cola trademark has been estimated to be worth $68.734 billion. The value of this trademark is NOT reported in the Coca-Cola balance sheet in Exhibit 3-1, but trademarks valued at $6.183 billion are reported in 2009. What do you think is the difference between these trademarks and the original Coca-Cola trademark?
2. The liabilities of the Coca-Cola bottlers of which The Coca-Cola Company owns a significant percentage total $35 billion. As stated above, NONE of these liabilities is included in the balance sheet of The Coca-Cola Company. Look at Exhibit 3-1—what amount of total liabilities does The Coca-Cola Company report as of December 31, 2009?
3. Look at Exhibit 3-1. As of December 31, 2009, which amount is greater—total current assets or total current liabilities? If you were a banker making a short-term loan to a company, would you prefer that company to have more current assets or more current liabilities?

Answers to these questions can be found on page 3-37.

Coca-Cola's balance sheet, like the balance sheet of any company, lists the organization's accounting assets and liabilities. However, this does not mean that the balance sheet includes complete, up-to-date information about all of the organization's economic resources and obligations. As described in Chapter 1, the choice of how to include information in the financial statements is often a trade-off between relevance and reliability. The balance sheet has been criticized for being *too* reliable, with too many assets being recorded at historical cost instead of market value, and with many important economic assets (such as **Microsoft**'s installed base of customers or **Intel**'s market dominance) not being recorded at all. A characteristic of recent FASB statements is an effort to improve the relevance of the balance sheet.

Even with its limitations, the balance sheet is still *the* fundamental financial statement. In fact, the income statement and statement of cash flows can be thought of as simply providing supplemental information about certain balance sheet accounts: The income statement gives a detailed description of some of the yearly changes in retained earnings, and the statement of cash flows details the reasons for the change in the cash balance.

This chapter focuses on the strengths and limitations of the balance sheet and describes how companies report their assets, liabilities, and owners' equity. The chapter also introduces some financial ratios used to analyze the balance sheet and outlines the type of information contained in the notes to the financial statements.

Elements of the Balance Sheet

1 **Describe the specific elements of the balance sheet (assets, liabilities, and owners' equity), and prepare a balance sheet with assets and liabilities properly classified into current and noncurrent categories**

WHY **Identification and measurement of assets and liabilities is fundamental to the practice of accounting. Assets and liabilities are usually separated into current and noncurrent categories so that a financial statement user can assess the firm's ability to meet its obligations as they come due.**

HOW **Conceptual definitions, traditional accounting practice, and, in some cases, specific accounting standards determine when economic items should be reported as accounting assets or liabilities. Current items are those expected to be used or paid within one year. When classifying assets and liabilities, the key considerations are how management intends to use an asset and when it expects to pay a liability.**

Twenty years after his victory at the Battle of Hastings in 1066, William the Conqueror commissioned a royal survey of all the property in England. The survey was described as follows by one of the defeated Anglo-Saxons:

> He sent his men all over England into every shire and had them find out how many hundred hides there were in the shire, or what land and cattle the king himself had in the country, or what dues he ought to have in twelve months from the shire. Also, he had a record made of how much land his archbishops had, and his bishops and his abbots and his earls, and what or how much everybody had who was occupying land in England, in land or cattle, and how much money it was worth.

EX 3-2 DEFINITIONS OF ASSET, LIABILITY, AND EQUITY

Balance Sheet

Asset:	**Liability:**
Probable future economic benefit obtained or controlled by a particular entity as a result of past transactions or events.	Probable future sacrifice of economic benefit arising from a present obligation of a particular entity to transfer assets or provide services to other entities in the future as a result of past transactions or events.
	Equity:
	Residual interest in the assets of an entity that remains after deducting its liabilities. In a business enterprise, the equity is the ownership interest.

Source: *Statement of Financial Accounting Concepts No. 6*, "Elements of Financial Statements." pars. 25, 35, and 49.

The survey thoroughly frightened the people of England, and it was called "Domesday [or Doomsday] Book" because it caused them to think of the final reckoning at the Last Judgment.[1]

Had the original Doomsday Book also included a listing of all the obligations, or liabilities, of the people of England, it would have comprised a balance sheet for England as of the year 1086. A balance sheet is a listing of an organization's assets and liabilities as of a certain point in time. The difference between assets and liabilities is called equity. Equity can be thought of as the amount of the assets that the owners of the organization can really call their own, the amount that would be left if all the liabilities were paid. The balance sheet is an expression of the basic accounting equation[2]:

$$\text{Assets} = \text{Liabilities} + \text{Owners' equity}$$

The three elements found on the balance sheet were precisely defined in Chapter 1. These definitions are repeated in Exhibit 3-2.

These definitions contain several key words and phrases that are briefly discussed here.

- *Probable*. Contrary to popular belief, accounting is not an exact science. Business is full of uncertainty, and this is acknowledged by the inclusion of the word *probable* in the definitions of assets and liabilities.
- *Future economic benefit*. Although the balance sheet summarizes the results of past transactions and events, its primary purpose is to help forecast the future. Hence, the only items included as assets and liabilities are those with implications for the future.
- *Obtained or controlled*. Accountants have a phrase, "substance over form," meaning that financial statements should reflect the underlying economic substance, not the superficial

[1] Elizabeth M. Hallam, *Domesday Book Through Nine Centuries* (Thomas and Hudson, 1986), pp. 16, 17.
[2] In abbreviated form, the basic accounting equation can be expressed as $A = L + E$. This can be rearranged algebraically to yield $E = A - L$. Notice the similarity with Einstein's famous equation: $E = mc^2$. Researchers thus far have had no luck in finding an underlying connection that would unify the fields of physics and accounting.

legal form. If a company economically controls the future economic benefits associated with an item, that item qualifies as an asset whether it is legally owned or not.

- *Obligation.* This term includes legal commitments as well as moral, social, and implied obligations. Again, the phrase "substance over form" applies.
- *Transfer assets or provide services.* Most liabilities involve an obligation to transfer assets in the future. However, an obligation to provide a service is also a liability. For example, having received your tuition check, your college or university now has a liability to you to provide top-notch education.
- *Past transactions or events.* Assets and liabilities arise from transactions or events that have already happened. Consider a company that promises in April to pay a student $4,000 for a summer internship starting in June. If the company declares bankruptcy in May, does the student get to collect the $4,000? No, because the transaction, the actual summer internship work, has not yet occurred.[3]

STOP&THINK

Alternatively, *asset* could be defined as everything legally owned by a company, and *liability* defined as all legal obligations. Which ONE of the following would NOT be a problem of these legalistic definitions?

a) Companies would be tempted to hire teams of lawyers to carefully craft contracts in order to obtain favorable accounting classification of assets and liabilities.
b) Companies could use legal technicalities in order to hide their economic liabilities in legally separate companies.
c) These law-based definitions of assets and liabilities would put too much power into the hands of the FASB.
d) The identification of accounting assets and liabilities would be greatly influenced by changing governmental standards of ownership.

Assets include financial items such as cash, receivables, and investments in financial instruments. Assets also include costs that are expected to provide future economic benefits. For example, expenditures made for inventories, equipment, and patents are expected to help generate revenues in future periods. Most assets are measured in terms of historical cost. As mentioned in Chapter 1 and as outlined later in this chapter, however, some assets are measured in terms of replacement cost, market value, net realizable value, or discounted present value.

Liabilities include obligations with amounts denominated in precise monetary terms, such as accounts payable and long-term debt. The amounts of other liabilities must be estimated based on expectations about future events. These types of liabilities include warranties, pension obligations, and environmental liabilities.

The total liability amount measures the amounts of the assets of the company that are claimed by various creditors. Owners' equity measures the amounts of the total assets of the company that remain and are thus claimed by the ownership group. Owners' equity equals the net assets of a company, or the difference between total assets and total liabilities. Owners' equity arises from investment by owners and is increased by net income and decreased by net losses and distributions to owners. Other items that can impact owners' equity are outlined later in the chapter.

[3] Whether the transaction has already occurred is sometimes difficult to determine. For example, if the student signs a summer internship contract guaranteeing payment of $4,000 whether or not any work is done, the contract signing itself might be viewed as creating an asset for the student and a liability for the company. This exact issue is important in determining the proper accounting treatment for long-term leases.

Classified Balance Sheets

Although there are no standard categories that must be used, the general framework for a balance sheet shown in Exhibit 3-3 is representative and will be used in this chapter. Balance sheet items are generally classified as current (or short-term) items and noncurrent (or long-term) items. How long is *current*? For most companies, *current* means one year or less. Accordingly, assets expected to be used and liabilities expected to be paid or otherwise satisfied within a year are current items. When assets and liabilities are so classified, the difference between current assets and current liabilities may be determined. This difference is referred to as the company's working capital—the liquid buffer available in meeting financial demands and contingencies of the near future.

EX 3-3 CATEGORIES OF A CLASSIFIED BALANCE SHEET

ASSETS

Current assets:
- Cash
- Investment securities
- Accounts and notes receivable
- Inventories
- Other current assets, such as prepaid expenses

Noncurrent assets:
- Investments
- Property, plant, and equipment
- Intangible assets
- Other noncurrent assets, such as deferred income tax assets

LIABILITIES

Current liabilities:
- Accounts and notes payable
- Accrued expenses
- Current portion of long-term obligations
- Other current liabilities, such as unearned revenues

Noncurrent liabilities:
- Long-term debt, such as notes, bonds, and mortgages payable
- Long-term lease obligations
- Deferred income tax liabilities
- Other noncurrent liabilities, such as pension obligations

OWNERS' EQUITY

Contributed capital:
- Capital stock
- Additional paid-in capital

Retained earnings

Other equity, such as treasury stock (a subtraction)

Accumulated other comprehensive income

The division of assets and liabilities into just two categories—current and noncurrent—is in some sense an arbitrary partition. Users of financial statements could desire a different partition. For example, some users exclude inventory when evaluating a company's working capital position. Users are certainly free to recast the balance sheet in whatever manner they wish. However, although there is some arbitrariness in the current/noncurrent classifications, its popularity among users as an indication of liquidity suggests that the classification does meet the test of decision usefulness.

Current Assets

The most common current assets are cash, receivables, and inventories. As depicted in Exhibit 3-4, the normal operating cycle involves the use of cash to purchase inventories, the sale of inventories resulting in receivables, and ultimately the cash collection of those receivables. In some industries, such as lumber and shipbuilding, this normal operating cycle is longer than one year. When the operating cycle is longer than a year, the length of the operating cycle should be used in defining current assets and liabilities. In practice, almost all companies use the 1-year period.[4]

In addition to cash, receivables, and inventories, current assets typically include prepaid expenses and investments in certain securities. Prepaid items are a bit different from other current assets in that they are not expected to be converted into cash within a year. Instead, their expiration makes it possible to conserve cash that otherwise would have been required. Prepayments for periods extending beyond a year should be reported as noncurrent assets.

Debt and equity securities (often called bonds and stocks) that are purchased mainly with the intent of reselling the securities in the short term are called trading securities. Trading securities are classified as current assets. Other investments in debt and equity

EX 3-4 OPERATING CYCLE

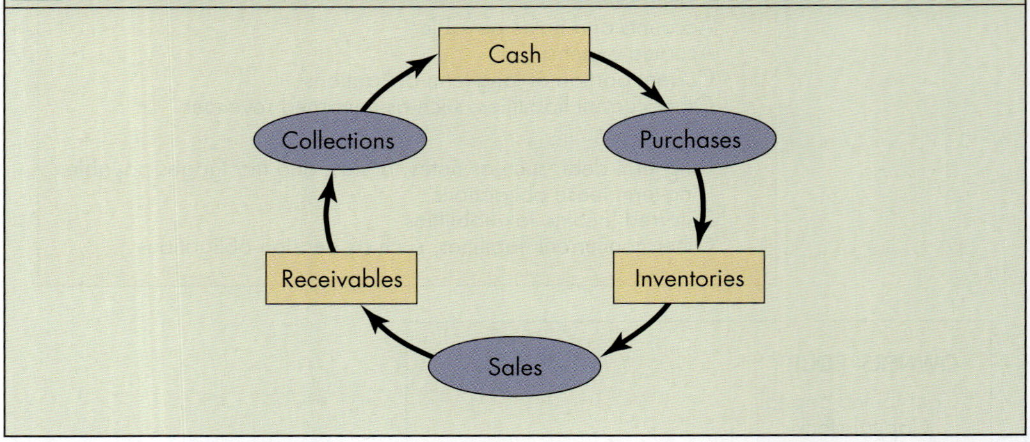

[4] In classifying items not related to the operating cycle, a 1-year period is always used as the basis for current classification. For example, a note receivable due in 15 months that arose from the sale of land held as an investment would be classified as noncurrent even if the normal operating cycle exceeds 15 months.

securities are classified as current or noncurrent depending on whether management intends to convert them into cash within one year or one operating cycle, whichever is longer.[5]

The reported amounts for current assets are measured in a variety of ways. Cash and receivables are reported at their net realizable values. Thus, current receivable balances are reduced by allowances for estimated uncollectible accounts. Investments in debt and equity securities are reported, in most cases, at current market value. Inventories are reported at cost (FIFO, LIFO, etc.) or on the lower-of-cost-or-market basis. Prepaid expenses are reported at their historical costs.

Current assets are normally listed on the balance sheet before the noncurrent assets and in the order of their liquidity, with the most liquid terms (those closest to cash) first. This ordering is a tradition, not a requirement. Most utilities and insurance companies reverse the order and report their longer-lived assets first. In addition, as illustrated later, non-U.S. companies frequently start their balance sheets with their long-term assets.

Some exceptions to the normal classification of assets should be noted. If management intends to use an asset for a noncurrent purpose, that asset should be classified as noncurrent in spite of the usual classification. For example, cash that is restricted to a noncurrent use (e.g., for the acquisition of noncurrent assets or for the liquidation of noncurrent debts) should not be included in current assets. Similarly, land that is held for resale within the coming year should be classified as current. The overriding criterion is management intent.

> **! CAUTION**
>
> As illustrated with current assets, a balance sheet is not restricted to reporting historical cost.

Noncurrent Assets

Assets not qualifying for presentation under the current heading are classified under a number of noncurrent headings. Noncurrent assets may be listed under separate headings, such as Investments; Property, Plant, and Equipment; Intangible Assets; and Other Noncurrent Assets.

Investments Investments held for such long-term purposes as regular income, appreciation, or ownership control are reported under the heading Investments. Debt and equity securities purchased as investments that management does not intend to sell in the coming year are classified as long-term investments. Acquisitions of the stock of other companies made in order to exert influence or control over the actions of those companies are accounted for using the equity method, which is explained in Chapter 14.These investments are classified as long-term investments. The Investments heading also includes other miscellaneous investments not used directly in the operations of the business, such as land held for investment purposes. Many long-term investments are reported at cost. However, more and more long-term assets are being reported at current market values. These deviations from cost will be discussed in later chapters.

Property, Plant, and Equipment Properties of a tangible and relatively permanent character that are used in the normal business operations are reported under Property, Plant, and Equipment or other appropriate headings such as Land, Buildings, and Equipment. Land, buildings, machinery, tools, furniture, fixtures, and vehicles are included in this section

[5] FASB ASC paragraphs 210-10-45-1(f) and 320-10-45-2.

FYI

When an investment in another company represents majority ownership of that company, no single investment amount is reported in the balance sheet. Instead, all of the individual assets and liabilities of the other company are included, or consolidated, in the balance sheet.

of the balance sheet. If an asset, such as land, is being held for speculation, it should be classified as an investment rather than under the heading Property, Plant, and Equipment. Tangible properties, except land, are normally reported at cost less accumulated depreciation. If the current value of a tangible property is less than its depreciated cost, the asset is said to be impaired. Guidelines for when and how to recognize asset impairments are given in Chapter 11.

Intangible Assets The long-term rights and privileges of a nonphysical nature acquired for use in business operations are often reported under the heading Intangible Assets. Included in this class are items such as goodwill, patents, trademarks, franchises, copyrights, formulas, leaseholds, and customer lists. Intangible assets are an increasingly important part of most companies' economic value; accordingly, the FASB has placed more emphasis on the accounting for intangibles. Some intangible assets are depreciated, or amortized, in the same way as tangible assets. However, many intangible assets, including goodwill, are not amortized on a systematic basis. Instead, these intangible assets are regularly tested to determine whether their value has been impaired. The details of accounting for intangibles are in Chapters 10 and 11.

Other Noncurrent Assets Those noncurrent assets not suitably reported under any of the previous classifications may be listed under the general heading "Other Noncurrent Assets" or may be listed separately under special descriptive headings. Such assets include, for example, long-term advances to officers, long-term receivables, deposits made with taxing authorities and utility companies, and deferred income tax assets. Deferred income tax assets arise when taxable income exceeds reported income for the period and the difference is expected to "reverse" in future periods. One common source of deferred income tax assets is large restructuring charges (including write-downs in asset values and recognition of relocation obligations) that are not yet deductible for income tax purposes; the deferred income tax asset reflects the expected future tax benefits that will arise when the elements of the restructuring charge become tax deductible in the future. The computation and reporting of deferred income tax assets is somewhat complex as well as interesting (as will be explained in Chapter 16).

Photodisc/Getty Images

Properties used in normal business operations, such as the printing press shown here, are classified as "property, plant, and equipment" on the balance sheet.

Current Liabilities

Current liabilities are those obligations that are reasonably expected to be paid using current assets or by creating other current liabilities. Generally, if a liability is reasonably expected to be paid within 12 months, it is classified as current. As with receivables, payables arising from the normal operating activities may be classified as current even if they are not to be paid within 12 months as long as they are to be paid within the operating cycle, which may exceed 12 months.

In addition to accounts payable and short-term borrowing, current liabilities also include amounts for accrued expenses. Common accruals include salaries and wages, interest, and taxes. The Current Liabilities section also includes amounts representing the portion of the long-term obligations due to be satisfied within one year.

The current liability classification generally does not include the following items that normally would be considered current.

- *Debts to be liquidated from a noncurrent sinking fund.* A sinking fund consists of cash and investment securities that have been accumulated for the stated purpose of repaying a specific loan. If the sinking fund is classified as a noncurrent asset, the associated loan is also classified as noncurrent.
- *Short-term obligations to be refinanced.* If a short-term loan is expected to be refinanced (either with a new long-term loan or with the issuance of equity) or paid back with the proceeds of a replacement loan, the existing short-term loan will not require the use of current assets even though it is scheduled to mature within a year. To reflect the economic substance of this situation, the existing loan is not classified as current as long as (1) the intent of the company is to refinance the loan on a long-term basis and (2) the company's intent is evidenced by an actual refinancing after the balance sheet date but before the financial statements are finalized or by the existence of an explicit refinancing agreement.[6]

> **FYI**
>
> The international standard for classification of short-term obligations to be refinanced is slightly different. According to *IAS 1*, for the obligation to be classified as long term the refinancing must take place by the balance sheet date, not the later date when the financial statements are finalized. The FASB is considering adopting this more stringent condition.

Callable Obligations Classification problems can arise when an obligation is callable by a creditor because it is difficult to determine exactly when the obligation will be paid. A callable obligation is one that is payable on demand and thus has no specified due date. If the terms of an agreement specify that an obligation is due on demand or will become due on demand within one year from the balance sheet date, the obligation should be classified as current.[7]

A loan can become callable because the debtor violates the provisions of the debt agreement. Loan agreement clauses that identify specific deficiencies (e.g., missing two consecutive interest payments) that can cause a loan to be immediately callable are referred to as objective acceleration clauses. If these specific deficiencies exist as of the balance sheet date, the associated liability should be classified as current unless the lender has agreed to waive the right to receive immediate payment or the deficiency has been fixed (e.g., an interest payment made) by the time the financial statements are issued.

In some cases, the debt agreement does not specifically identify the circumstances under which a loan will become callable, but it does indicate some general conditions that permit

[6] FASB ASC paragraph 470-10-45-14.
[7] FASB ASC paragraph 470-10-45-10.

the lender to accelerate the due date. This type of provision is known as a subjective acceleration clause because the violation of the conditions cannot be objectively determined. Examples of the wording in such clauses are "if the debtor fails to maintain satisfactory operations . . ." or "if a material adverse change occurs. . . ." If invoking of the clause is deemed probable, the liability should be classified as a current liability. If invoking of the clause is considered to be reasonably possible but not probable, only a note disclosure is necessary, and the liability continues to be classified as noncurrent.[8]

FYI

Large banks have entire "compliance" departments that verify whether borrowers are following the terms of their loan agreements.

Noncurrent Liabilities

Obligations not reasonably expected to be paid or otherwise satisfied within 12 months (or within the operating cycle if it exceeds 12 months) are classified as *noncurrent liabilities*. Noncurrent liabilities are generally listed under separate headings, such as Long-Term Debt, Long-Term Lease Obligations, Deferred Income Tax Liability, and Other Noncurrent Liabilities.

Long-Term Debt Long-term notes, bonds, mortgages, and similar obligations not requiring the use of current funds for their retirement are generally reported on the balance sheet under the heading Long-Term Debt.

Long-term debt is reported at its discounted present value, which is initially measured by the proceeds from the debt issuance. When the amount borrowed is not the same as the amount ultimately required to be repaid, called the *maturity value*, a discount or premium is included as an adjustment to the maturity value to ensure that the debt is reported at its discounted present value. A discount should be subtracted from the amount reported for the debt, and a premium should be added to the amount reported for the debt.

When a note, a bond issue, or a mortgage formerly classified as a long-term obligation becomes payable within a year, it should be reclassified and presented as a current liability except when the obligation is to be refinanced, as discussed earlier, or is to be paid out of a fund classified as noncurrent.

Long-Term Lease Obligations Some leases of property, plant, and equipment are financially structured so that they are essentially debt-financed purchases. The FASB has established criteria to determine which leases are to be accounted for as purchases, or capital leases, rather than as ordinary operating leases. In accounting for capital leases, the present value of the future minimum lease payments is recorded as a long-term liability. That portion of the present value due within the next year is classified as a current liability. The long-term lease obligation reported by some firms is often more interesting for what it doesn't include than for what it does include. For example, as of May 31, 2009, the present value of future minimum lease payments for capital leases for **FedEx** was $280 million. At the same time, the present value of future minimum lease payments for operating leases (an amount *not* reported in the balance sheet) was approximately $7.6 billion. Be patient; in Chapter 15, you will learn more about leases than you ever wanted to know.

Deferred Income Tax Liability Almost all large companies include a deferred income tax liability in their balance sheets. This liability can be thought of as the income tax expected

[8] FASB ASC paragraph 470-10-45-2.

to be paid in future years on income that has already been reported in the income statement but which, because of the tax law, has not yet been taxed. The liability is valued using the enacted income tax rates expected to prevail in the future when the income is taxed. However, because the liability is not reported at its present (discounted) value, some analysts disregard it when evaluating a company's debt position. The accounting for deferred income taxes is very complex and controversial and has been the subject of considerable debate.

Other Noncurrent Liabilities Those noncurrent liabilities not suitably reported under the separate headings outlined earlier may be listed under this general heading or may be listed separately under special descriptive headings. Examples of such long-term liabilities are pension plans and obligations resulting from advance collections on long-term contracts.

Contingent Liabilities Past activities or circumstances may give rise to possible future liabilities although obligations do not exist on the date of the balance sheet. These possible claims are known as contingent liabilities. They are potential obligations involving uncertainty as to possible losses. As future events occur or fail to occur, this uncertainty will be resolved. A good example of a contingent liability is the cosigner's obligation on a co-signed loan. The cosigner has no existing obligation but may have one in the future, depending on whether the borrower defaults on the loan.

Contingent liabilities are accounted for according to the judgment of management about the probability of the contingent obligation's becoming an actual obligation. If a future payment is considered probable, the liability should be recorded by a debit to a loss account and a credit to a liability account. If future payment is possible, the contingent nature of the loss is disclosed in a note to the financial statements. If future payment is remote, no accounting action is necessary.[9]

A contingent liability is distinguishable from an estimated liability. An estimated liability is a definite obligation with only the amount of the obligation in question and subject to estimation at the balance sheet date. Examples of estimated liabilities are pensions, warranties, and deferred taxes. Some liabilities combine the characteristics of contingent and estimated liabilities. A good example is a company's obligation for environmental cleanup

CAUTION

This description makes it sound as if accounting for contingencies is cookbook simple, but the words "probable" and "possible" represent very complex concepts. For example, when exactly does a future event (such as a thunderstorm tomorrow) stop being possible and start being probable?

STOP&THINK

The current/noncurrent classification scheme is only one way to split assets and liabilities into two groups. Below are three alternate 2-way classification schemes. Which one would be most useful for: (1) A financial analyst trying to compare the company's core business with the core businesses of similar companies? (2) A U.S. congressperson concerned about the relocation of operations overseas? (3) An analyst trying to estimate the current market value of a company?

a) Located in the United States and located in a non-U.S. country
b) Used in the primary line of business and used in secondary lines of business
c) Measured at current fair value and measured on some other basis

[9] FASB ASC paragraphs 450-20-25-2, 450-20-50-3, 460-10-50-2.

costs. In many cases, a company is not certain it is liable for environmental damage until the obligation is confirmed in the courts. However, even after the cleanup obligation is verified, estimating its amount is quite difficult; the cleanup typically extends over several years, the amount of the cost to be shared by other polluting companies is uncertain, and governmental environmental regulations can change at any time. If no reasonable estimate of an obligation can be made, it is not recognized as a liability in the balance sheet, but the nature of the obligation is disclosed in the financial statement notes. Chapter 19 contains more details on the accounting for contingent and estimated liabilities.

Owners' Equity

The method of reporting the owners' equity varies with the form of the business unit. Business units are typically divided into three categories: proprietorships, partnerships, and corporations.[10] In the case of a proprietorship, the owner's equity in assets is reported by means of a single capital account. The balance in this account is the cumulative result of the owner's investments and withdrawals as well as past earnings and losses. In a partnership, capital accounts are established for each partner. Capital account balances summarize the investments and withdrawals and shares of past earnings and losses of each partner and thus measure the partners' individual equities in the partnership assets.

In a corporation, the difference between assets and liabilities is referred to as stockholders' (shareholders') equity or *owners' equity*. In presenting the owners' equity on the balance sheet, a distinction is made between the equity originating from the stockholders' investments, referred to as contributed capital or paid-in capital, and the equity originating from earnings, referred to as retained earnings.

Most financial statement analysis calculations use total stockholders' equity and do not distinguish between contributed capital and retained earnings. However, for some purposes the distinction can be very important. Historically, companies could legally pay cash dividends only in an amount not exceeding the retained earnings balance. This legal restriction has been relaxed in most states, but the retained earnings amount is still viewed as an informal limit to cash dividend payments.

Contributed Capital Contributed (or paid-in) capital is generally reported in two parts: (1) capital stock and (2) additional paid-in capital. The amount reported on the balance sheet as capital stock usually reflects the number of shares issued multiplied by the par value or stated value per share. Historically, par value was the market value of the shares at the time of their issue. In cases where shareholders invested less than the par value of the stock, courts sometimes held that the shareholders were contingently liable for the difference if corporate resources were insufficient to satisfy creditors. Today, most stocks are issued with low or no par values; par value no longer has much significance.

The two types of capital stock are preferred stock and common stock. In general, preferred stockholders are paid a fixed annual cash dividend and have a higher likelihood of

[10] In addition to these three general categories, there are many hybrids. Some of these are limited partnerships, S corporations, and limited liability companies (LLCs). In general, these organizations are taxed as partnerships but have some of the limited liability advantages of a corporation. All of the large accounting firms are organized as limited liability partnerships (LLP) to insulate uninvolved partners from client lawsuits directed at individual partners. According to IRS records, about 70% of U.S. businesses are organized as sole proprietorships.

recovering their investment if the company goes bankrupt.[11] Common stockholders are the real owners of the corporation; they vote for the board of directors and have legal ownership of the corporate assets after the claims of all creditors and preferred stockholders have been satisfied. For accounting purposes, when a corporation has issued more than one class of stock, the stock of each class is reported separately.

Additional paid-in capital represents investments by stockholders in excess of the par or stated value of the capital stock. Additional paid-in capital is also affected by a whole host of diverse transactions such as stock repurchases, stock dividends, share retirements, and stock conversions. In a sense, additional paid-in capital is the "dumping ground" of the Equity section.

Retained Earnings The amount of undistributed earnings of past periods is reported as retained earnings. An excess of dividends and losses over earnings results in a negative retained earnings balance called a deficit. As detailed in Chapter 13, retained earnings can also be reduced as a result of stock retirements and the issuance of stock dividends. A sample of large positive and negative retained earnings balances for U.S. companies is given in Exhibit 3-5.

EX 3-5 LARGE POSITIVE AND NEGATIVE RETAINED EARNINGS BALANCES FOR THE YEAR 2009 (IN MILLIONS)

Company Name	Retained Earnings
Exxon	$276,937
General Electric	126,363
Citigroup	77,440
Qwest	(42,953)
JDS Uniphase	(68,538)
Time Warner	(97,148)

Source: Standard and Poor's *COMPUSTAT.*

Portions of retained earnings are sometimes reported as restricted and unavailable as a basis for cash dividends. This ensures that a company does not distribute cash dividends to shareholders to the extent that the ability to repay creditors or make other planned expenditures comes into question. Retained earnings restrictions can be part of a loan agreement or can be voluntarily adopted by a company (called an *appropriation*). These restrictions are usually disclosed in a financial statement note.

Other Equity In addition to the two major categories of contributed capital and retained earnings, the Equity section can include a couple of other items: treasury stock and accumulated other comprehensive income. These are described in detail in later chapters, but they are briefly discussed here.

[11] In essence, preferred stock is an investment that has some of the characteristics of a loan: fixed periodic payment, no vote for the board of directors, and higher priority than common stock in case of bankruptcy liquidation. Increasingly, finance wizards are creating securities that combine characteristics of both debt and equity. The accounting question is where to put these creations. Distinguishing between debt and equity is addressed more fully in Chapter 13.

Treasury stock. When a company buys back its own shares, accountants call the repurchased shares treasury stock. Treasury shares can be retired, or they can be retained and reissued later. When the shares are retained, the amount paid to repurchase the treasury stock is usually shown as a subtraction from total stockholders' equity. In essence, a treasury stock purchase returns funds to shareholders.

Accumulated other comprehensive income. Beginning in 1998, the FASB required companies to summarize changes in owners' equity exclusive of net income and contributions by and distributions to owners. This summary, termed other comprehensive income, is typically provided by companies as part of their statement of stockholders' equity. The corresponding balance sheet item reflecting the cumulative total of these items over the years is titled Accumulated Other Comprehensive Income. The three most common components are certain unrealized gains and losses on investments, foreign currency adjustments, and certain unrealized gains and losses on derivative contracts.

FYI

For those interested in stock tips, buy the stocks of companies that announce treasury stock purchases. Those companies tend to outperform the market in the three to four years following the announcement.

Unrealized gains and losses on available-for-sale securities. Available-for-sale securities are those that were not purchased with the immediate intention to resell but also are not meant to be held permanently. These securities are reported in the balance sheet at their current market values. The unrealized gains and losses from market value fluctuations are not included in the income statement but are instead shown as a separate equity item.[12]

Foreign currency translation adjustments. Almost every U.S. multinational corporation has a foreign currency translation adjustment in its Equity section. This adjustment arises from the change in the equity of foreign subsidiaries (as measured in terms of U.S. dollars) that occurs during the year as a result of changes in foreign currency exchange rates. These adjustments are discussed in Chapter 22.

Unrealized gains and losses on derivatives. A derivative is a financial instrument, such as an option or a future, that derives its value from the movement of a price, an exchange rate, or an interest rate associated with some other item. For example, an option to purchase a stock becomes more valuable as the price of the stock increases, and the right to purchase foreign currency at a fixed exchange rate becomes more valuable as that foreign currency becomes more expensive. As will be discussed in Chapter 19, companies often use derivatives in order to manage their exposure to risk stemming from changes in prices and rates. Some of the unrealized gains and losses from the fluctuations in the value of derivatives are reported as part of accumulated other comprehensive income.

Minority interest. When one company owns controlling interest (more than 50%) of the common stock of one or more other companies, the financial results of this group of companies are combined into a set of consolidated financial statements. The objective of consolidated financial statements is to reflect in one set of financial statements the results of all companies owned or controlled by the parent corporation. In the consolidated balance

[12] One never knows where controversy and compromise will rear their ugly heads. Accounting purists hoped to include these unrealized gains and losses in the income statement. Companies (particularly banks) fearful of the volatility that this would add to the income statement opposed the treatment. This equity item is the FASB's compromise.

sheet, minority (or noncontrolling) interest is the amount of equity investment made by outside shareholders to consolidated subsidiaries that are not 100% owned by the parent. For example, if the parent owns 80% of the subsidiary, then the minority interest is the amount of financing provided by the outside shareholders who own the other 20% of the subsidiary. This minority interest is reported as part of owners' equity, but it is clearly listed separately from the parent's owners' equity.[13]

International reserves. The first thing one notices about the Equity portion of the balance sheets of many foreign companies, particularly those from countries influenced by the British accounting tradition, is the extended description of the company's "reserves." In familiar terms, reserves are merely different equity categories similar in nature, depending on the reserve, to additional paid-in capital or to restricted retained earnings. Reserve accounting is very important because in many foreign countries the legal ability to pay cash dividends is strictly tied to the balances in various reserve accounts. Common reserve category titles are revaluation reserve and capital redemption reserve. Reserves are discussed in more detail in Chapter 13, which is devoted to the Equity section.

Offsets on the Balance Sheet

As illustrated in the preceding discussion, a number of balance sheet items are reported at gross amounts not reflecting their actual values, thus requiring the recognition of offset balances in arriving at proper valuations. In the case of assets, for example, an allowance for bad debts is subtracted from the sum of the customer accounts in reporting the net amount estimated as collectible; accumulated depreciation is subtracted from the related buildings and equipment balances in reporting the costs of the assets still assignable to future revenues.

FASB CODIFICATION

The Issue: You have just started working as a business manager for a local medical practice. As one of your first tasks, you have been asked to get the financial statements in shape to take to the bank to request a $500,000 loan for the practice. You have been examining the most recent balance sheet and noticed that there are no reported long-term liabilities. You are surprised to see this because you know that the practice has an existing 5-year loan for $350,000. You asked one of the doctors about this and were told that the $350,000 loan was omitted because the doctors know that they have sufficient cash, in their personal savings, to pay the loan if needed. Thus, instead of going to the trouble of putting their personal cash in the business balance sheet, along with the $350,000 loan amount, they have just offset the two. Voilà.

The Question: Is there any accounting rule that specifically states that assets and liabilities shouldn't be offset in the way the doctors are doing? Are there any exceptions to the no-offset rule?

Searching the Codification: This issue relates to balance sheet presentation, so we should start with the Presentation group of topics in the FASB's Codification. One of the topics in that group is Topic 210—Balance Sheet. If we are lucky, "Offsetting" is one of the subtopics in the Balance Sheet topic.

The Answer: The correct treatment is described on page 3-38.

[13] FASB ASC paragraph 810-10-45-16.

In the case of liabilities, a loan discount is subtracted from the maturity value of the loan in reporting the loan at its discounted present value. In the Stockholders' Equity section of the balance sheet, treasury stock is deducted in reporting total stockholders' equity.

The types of offsets described here, utilizing contra accounts, are required for proper reporting of particular balance sheet items. In addition, accounting rules require some assets and liabilities to be offset against one another, resulting in just one net amount being reported in the balance sheet. For example, a company's pension obligation is offset against the assets in the pension fund, and only the net number goes into the balance sheet. Deferred tax assets and liabilities are also offset against each other.

The cases just described are the exceptions. The general rule is that assets, liabilities, and equities should not be offset when compiling the balance sheet. Offsetting, or netting, can significantly reduce the information value of the balance sheet. If offsetting were taken to its extreme, the balance sheet would be just one line, total equity, embodying total liabilities offset against total assets.

Format of the Balance Sheet

2 Identify the different formats used to present balance sheet data.

WHY **The arrangement of items within the balance sheet is meant to emphasize certain items and to highlight important relationships.**

HOW **In most industries, assets and liabilities are listed in order of their liquidity with cash first, followed by the other current items. For some industries, particularly those with large investments in long-term assets, property, plant, and equipment items are listed first.**

When preparing a balance sheet, the order of asset and liability classifications may vary, but most businesses emphasize working capital position and liquidity, with assets and liabilities presented in the order of their liquidity. An exception to this order is generally found in the Property, Plant, and Equipment section where the more permanent assets with longer useful lives are listed first. The balance sheet of The Coca-Cola Company, reproduced in Exhibit 3-1, is an example of current assets and of current liabilities being listed first.

As mentioned earlier, in some industries, such as the utility industry, the investment in plant assets is so significant that these assets are placed first on the balance sheet. Also, because long-term financing is so important in these industries, the equity capital and long-term debt obtained to finance plant assets are listed before current liabilities. To illustrate this type of presentation, the 2008 balance sheet for **Consolidated Edison** is given in Exhibit 3-6. Consolidated Edison, established in 1884, provides electric service to almost all of New York City.[14]

As seen in the Consolidated Edison illustration in Exhibit 3-6, balance sheets are generally presented in comparative form. With comparative reports for two or more dates, information is made available concerning the nature and trend of financial changes taking place within the periods between balance sheet dates. Currently, a minimum of two years of balance sheets and three years of income statements and cash flow statements are required by the SEC to be included in the annual report to shareholders.

[14] In 2009, Consolidated Edison reordered its balance sheet and began using the more common sequencing with current assets first, then long-term assets, and so forth.

EX 3-6 CONSOLIDATED EDISON, INC.

Consolidated Edison, Inc.
Consolidated Balance Sheet
December 31, 2008 and 2007

(Millions of Dollars)	At December 31, 2008	2007
Assets		
Utility Plant, at Original Cost (Note A)		
Electric	$17,483	$15,979
Gas	3,696	3,403
Steam	1,849	1,755
General	1,795	1,732
Total	24,823	22,869
Less: Accumulated depreciation	5,079	4,784
Net	19,744	18,085
Construction work in progress	1,109	1,028
Net Utility Plant	**20,853**	**19,113**
Non-Utility Plant (Note A)		
Non-utility property, less accumulated depreciation of $40 and $36 in 2008 and 2007, respectively	20	18
Non-utility property held for sale (Note V)	—	778
Construction work in progress	1	5
Net Plant	**20,874**	**19,914**
Current Assets		
Cash and temporary cash investments (Note A)	74	210
Accounts receivable—customers, less allowance for uncollectible accounts of $58 and $47 in 2008 and 2007, respectively	952	970
Accrued unbilled revenue (Note A)	131	149
Other receivables, less allowance for uncollectible accounts of $6 in 2008 and 2007	339	288
Fuel oil, at average cost	37	44
Gas in storage, at average cost	325	215
Materials and supplies, at average cost	154	146
Prepayments	697	119
Fair value of derivative assets	162	98
Recoverable energy costs (Notes A and B)	172	213
Deferred derivative losses	260	45
Current assets held for sale (Note V)	—	40
Other current assets	16	13
Total Current Assets	**3,319**	**2,550**
Investments (Note A)	**356**	**378**
Deferred Charges, Regulatory Assets and Noncurrent Assets		
Goodwill (Note K)	411	408
Intangible assets, less accumulated amortization of $2 and $1 in 2008 and 2007, respectively	5	2
Regulatory assets (Note B)	8,105	4,511
Noncurrent assets held for sale (Note V)	—	88
Other deferred charges and noncurrent assets	428	411
Total Deferred Charges, Regulatory Assets and Noncurrent Assets	**8,949**	**5,420**
Total Assets	**$33,498**	**$28,262**

The accompanying notes are an integral part of these financial statements.

	2008	2007
Capitalization and Liabilities		
Capitalization		
Common shareholders' equity (See Statement of Common Shareholders' Equity)	$ 9,698	$ 9,076
Preferred stock of subsidiary (See Statement of Capitalization)	213	213
Long-term debt (See Statement of Capitalization)	9,232	7,611
Total Capitalization	**19,143**	**16,900**
Minority Interests	—	43

EX 3-6 CONSOLIDATED EDISON, INC. (Continued)

Consolidated Edison, Inc.
Consolidated Balance Sheet

(Millions of Dollars)	At December 31, 2008	2007
Noncurrent Liabilities		
Obligations under capital leases (Note J)	17	22
Provision for injuries and damages (Note G)	169	161
Pensions and retiree benefits	4,511	938
Superfund and other environmental costs (Note G)	250	327
Uncertain income taxes	118	155
Asset retirement obligations (Note R)	115	110
Fair value of derivative liabilities	120	15
Noncurrent liabilities held for sale (Note V)	—	61
Other noncurrent liabilities	79	95
Total Noncurrent Liabilities	**5,379**	**1,884**
Current Liabilities		
Long-term debt due within one year	482	809
Notes payable	363	840
Accounts payable	1,161	1,187
Customer deposits	265	249
Accrued taxes	57	26
Accrued interest	139	149
Accrued wages	88	82
Fair value of derivative liabilities	192	76
Deferred derivative gains (Note B)	23	10
Deferred income taxes—recoverable energy costs (Note L)	70	86
Current liabilities held for sale (Note V)	—	28
Other current liabilities	365	309
Total Current Liabilities	**3,205**	**3,851**
Deferred Credits and Regulatory Liabilities		
Deferred income taxes and investment tax credits (Notes A and L)	4,999	4,465
Regulatory liabilities (Note B)	737	1,097
Other deferred credits	35	22
Total Deferred Credits and Regulatory Liabilities	**5,771**	**5,584**
Total Capitalization and Liabilities	**$33,498**	**$28,262**

Format of Foreign Balance Sheets

Foreign balance sheets are frequently presented with property, plant, and equipment and intangibles listed first. In addition, foreign balance sheets frequently list the current assets and the current liabilities together and label the difference between the two as net current assets or working capital. This manner of reporting the current items reflects the business reality that a person starting a company needs to get long-term financing (long-term debt and equity) to finance the acquisition of long-term assets as well as to finance the portion of current assets that can't be acquired by incurring current liabilities. For example, if a company can acquire all of its inventory through credit purchases (accounts payable) and if the supplier

STOP&THINK

From the information in Exhibit 3-7, compute total assets for British Telecommunications as of March 31, 2009.

a) £18,559 million
b) £29,274 million
c) £24,540 million
d) £21,052 million
e) £32,630 million

will wait for payment until the inventory is sold and the cash collected, no long-term financing is needed to purchase the initial stock of inventory.

An example of a typical foreign balance sheet is provided in Exhibit 3-7, which contains the March 31, 2009, balance sheet of **British Telecommunications**. In addition to the format

EX 3-7 2009 BALANCE SHEET OF BRITISH TELECOMMUNICATIONS

British Telecommunications
Balance Sheet
At 31 March 2009

	2009 (In millions of British pounds)
Non current assets	
Intangible assets	£ 3,788
Property, plant and equipment	15,405
Derivative financial instruments	2,456
Investments	55
Retirement benefit asset	—
Associates and joint ventures	132
Trade and other receivables	322
Deferred tax assets	1,103
	23,261
Current assets	
Inventories	121
Trade and other receivables	4,185
Derivative financial instruments	244
Investments	163
Cash and cash equivalents	1,300
	6,013
Current liabilities	
Loans and other borrowings	1,542
Derivative financial instruments	340
Trade and other payables	7,215
Current tax liabilities	1
Provisions	254
	9,352
Total assets less current liabilities	**£19,922**
Non current liabilities	
Loans and other borrowings	£12,365
Derivative financial instruments	427
Retirement benefit obligations	3,973
Other payables	794
Deferred tax liabilities	1,728
Provisions	466
	19,753
Equity	
Ordinary shares	408
Share premium	62
Capital redemption reserve	27
Other reserves	1,301
Retained (loss) earnings	(1,656)
Total parent shareholders' equity	**142**
Minority interests	27
Total equity	**169**
	£19,922

difference already mentioned, this balance sheet also reflects several other differences between a U.S. balance sheet and the balance sheet of a foreign company. The most obvious of these differences is in terminology. However, with some thought and a little accounting intuition, one can deduce that the item "ordinary shares" is what we would call "common stock," "share premium" is "additional paid-in capital," and so forth. Of course, there is more to accounting than formatting and terminology. Because British Telecommunications reports using International Financial Reporting Standards (IFRS), there are some slight differences in the company's reported numbers compared to what would be reported if British Telecommunications was a U.S. company reporting according to U.S. GAAP. Those U.S. GAAP-IFRS differences will be addressed throughout this textbook.

Balance Sheet Analysis

3 **Analyze a company's performance and financial position through the computation of financial ratios.**

WHY **A financial statement number, in isolation, tells you very little. To really understand the financial statements, you must look at relationships among the numbers.**

HOW **Computing a financial ratio is simply a matter of dividing one financial statement number by another. Ratios of balance sheet numbers reveal information about financing choices and liquidity. Ratios of a balance sheet and an income statement number tell you about how efficiently an asset is being managed.**

The purpose of classifying and ordering balance sheet items is to make the balance sheet easier to use. Look at Exhibit 3-8 and compare the two balance sheets for the fictitious Techtronics Corporation. The balance sheet on the left is just a list of assets, liabilities, and equities in alphabetical order, like a simple account listing. The balance sheet on the right uses the classification and ordering format described in the previous section. You decide which is easier to interpret.

The Techtronics numbers will be used to illustrate standard balance sheet analysis techniques. The simple techniques described in this overview will probably not help you to pick "winning" stocks and become a millionaire, but they are a start. It is said that Warren Buffett (worth about $40 billion at last count) picks his investments only after "a careful balance sheet analysis."[15]

Balance sheet information is analyzed in two major ways:

1. Relationships between balance sheet amounts
2. Relationships between balance sheet and income statement amounts

In general, relationships between financial statement amounts are called financial ratios.

Relationships Between Balance Sheet Amounts

Financial ratios comparing one balance sheet amount to another yield information about the operating and financial structure of a business. Three examples, which are discussed here, are liquidity, overall leverage, and asset mix.

[15] Robert Lenzner and David S. Fondiller, "The Not-So-Silent Partner," *Forbes*, January 22, 1996, p. 78.

EX 3-8 TECHTRONICS' BALANCE SHEET, WITH AND WITHOUT CLASSIFICATION

Techtronics Corporation
Balance Sheet
December 31, 2013

WITHOUT CLASSIFICATION

Assets	
Buildings and equipment (net of accumulated depreciation of $228,600)	$ 732,900
Cash	52,650
Intangible assets	165,000
Inventories	296,000
Investments	128,000
Investment securities	67,350
Land	76,300
Other noncurrent assets	37,800
Prepaid expenses	32,900
Receivables (less allowance for bad debts)	363,700
Total assets	$1,952,600
Liabilities	
Accounts payable	$ 312,700
Accrued expenses	46,200
Bonds payable	165,000
Current portion of long-term debt	62,000
Deferred tax liability	126,700
Long-term lease obligations	135,000
Notes payable—current	50,000
Notes payable—noncurrent	100,000
Other current liabilities	28,600
Other noncurrent liabilities	72,500
Total liabilities	$1,098,700
Stockholders' Equity	
Additional paid-in capital	$ 375,000
Common stock	170,000
Retained earnings	308,900
Total stockholders' equity	$ 853,900
Total liabilities and stockholders' equity	$1,952,600

WITH CLASSIFICATION

Assets	
Current assets:	
Cash	$ 52,650
Investment securities	67,350
Receivables (less allowance for bad debts)	363,700
Inventories	296,000
Prepaid expenses	32,900
Total current assets	$ 812,600
Noncurrent assets:	
Investments	$ 128,000
Land	76,300
Buildings and equipment (net of accumulated depreciation of $228,600)	732,900
Intangible assets	165,000
Other noncurrent assets	37,800
Total noncurrent assets	$1,140,000
Total assets	$1,952,600
Liabilities	
Current liabilities:	
Notes payable	$ 50,000
Accounts payable	312,700
Accrued expenses	46,200
Current portion of long-term debt	62,000
Other current liabilities	28,600
Total current liabilities	$ 499,500
Noncurrent liabilities:	
Notes payable	$ 100,000
Bonds payable	165,000
Long-term lease obligations	135,000
Deferred tax liability	126,700
Other noncurrent liabilities	72,500
Total noncurrent liabilities	$ 599,200
Total liabilities	$1,098,700
Stockholders' Equity	
Contributed capital:	
Common stock	$ 170,000
Additional paid-in capital	375,000
	$ 545,000
Retained earnings	308,900
Total stockholders' equity	$ 853,900
Total liabilities and stockholders' equity	$1,952,600

Liquidity The relationship between current assets and current liabilities can be used to evaluate the liquidity of a company. Liquidity is the ability of a firm to satisfy its short-term obligations. Many companies with fantastic long-run potential have been killed by short-run liquidity problems.

A common indicator of the overall liquidity of a company is the current ratio. The current ratio is computed by dividing total current assets by total current liabilities. For Techtronics, the current ratio is computed as follows:

$$\text{Current ratio: } \frac{\text{Current assets}}{\text{Current liabilities}} = \frac{\$812,600}{\$499,500} = 1.63$$

Historically, the rule of thumb has been that a current ratio below 2.0 suggests the possibility of liquidity problems. However, advances in information technology have enabled companies to be much more effective in minimizing the need to hold cash, inventories, and other current assets. As a result, current ratios for successful companies these days are frequently less than 1.0. Note that this is just a rule of thumb; proper evaluation of a company's liquidity involves comparing the current year's current ratio to current ratios in prior years and comparing the company's current ratio to those for other companies in the same industry.

Minimum current ratio requirements are frequently included in loan agreements. A typical agreement might state that if the current ratio falls below a certain level, the lender can declare the loan in default and require immediate repayment. This type of minimum current ratio restriction forces the borrower to maintain its liquidity and gives the lender an increased assurance that the loan will be repaid. When loan covenant restrictions are violated, the lender usually waives the right to immediate repayment, sometimes in exchange for a renegotiation of the loan at a higher interest rate. Exhibit 3-9 contains the 2009 current ratios for selected companies. Note that **eBay** and Microsoft have higher current ratios relative to the other companies. This is an indication of the need for liquidity in technology industries. As technology changes, companies in that industry need to be able to quickly adapt, and that ability requires liquidity. Note also the low current ratio of **Disney**, for example. At first glance you might think that 1.33 is dangerously low. Before jumping to that conclusion, think about what Disney's current assets are. Disney has cash and accounts receivable but very little inventory. They make movies and they run theme parks and these ventures require very little inventory. Therefore, the "secret" for Disney's low current ratio is its ability to collect its receivables quickly and reinvest the money into long-term productive assets.

Another ratio used to measure a firm's liquidity is the quick ratio, also known as the acid-test ratio. This ratio is computed as total *quick assets* divided by total current liabilities, where quick assets are defined as cash, investment securities, and net receivables. For Techtronics, the quick ratio is computed as follows:

$$\text{Quick ratio: } \frac{\text{Cash} + \text{Securities} + \text{Receivables}}{\text{Current liabilities}} = \frac{\$483,700}{\$499,500} = 0.97$$

The quick ratio indicates how well a firm can satisfy existing short-term obligations with assets that can be converted into cash without difficulty. For a bank considering a three-month loan or for a supplier considering selling to a company on short-term credit, the quick ratio yields information about the likelihood it will be repaid. Techtronics' quick ratio indicates it has $0.97 in quick assets for every $1.00 in current liabilities.

A lender wants to lend on a short-term basis to a company with high current and quick ratios, thus ensuring repayment. However, maintaining an excessively high current ratio is an inefficient use of company resources. Having excess investment securities will increase a company's current and quick ratios, giving comfort to lenders, but the resources used to buy those excess securities might be better utilized by buying trucks or buildings, paying off debts, or if nothing else, returning the cash to the owners for their personal use.

EX 3-9 SELECTED 2009 RATIOS

	Coca-Cola	Disney	McDonald's	Microsoft	eBay
Current ratio	1.28	1.33	1.14	1.82	2.32
Debt ratio	47.92%	43.87%	53.57%	49.21%	25.10%
Asset mix—PP&E*	19.64%	36.00%	71.24%	9.67%	7.14%
Asset turnover	0.64	0.57	0.75	0.75	0.47
Return on assets	14.02%	5.24%	15.06%	18.71%	12.98%
Return on equity	27.52%	9.80%	32.43%	36.83%	17.33%

* PP&E = property, plant, and equipment

A common characteristic of almost all financial ratios is that a ratio that deviates too much from the norm, either above or below, indicates a possible problem.[16]

> **! CAUTION**
>
> A current ratio that is too high can also indicate trouble. Excess current assets, resulting in a high current ratio, can represent an inefficient use of resources. Cash management and just-in-time inventory systems are designed to keep current asset levels low.

Overall Leverage Comparing the amount of liabilities to the amount of assets held by a business indicates the extent to which borrowed funds have been used to leverage the owners' investments and increase the size of the firm. One frequently used measure of leverage is the debt ratio, computed as total liabilities divided by total assets. The debt ratio is frequently used as an indicator of the overall ability of a company to repay its debts. An intuitive interpretation of the debt ratio is that it represents the proportion of borrowed funds used to acquire the company's assets. For Techtronics, the debt ratio is computed as follows:

$$\text{Debt ratio: } \frac{\text{Total liabilities}}{\text{Total assets}} = \frac{\$1{,}098{,}700}{\$1{,}952{,}600} = 0.56$$

In other words, Techtronics borrowed 56% of the money it needed to buy its assets. The higher the debt ratio, the higher the likelihood that some of the debt might not be repaid. The general rule of thumb is that debt ratios should be below 50%. Again, this varies widely from one industry to the next. A bank, for example, could easily have a debt ratio in excess of 95%.

See Exhibit 3-9; eBay has the lowest debt ratio, with each of the other companies having a debt ratio around 50%. As a general rule, companies in mature industries have a higher amount of debt than in newer industries because the proven track records of the companies make lenders willing to provide more debt financing.

Asset Mix A large fraction of a bank's assets is in financial investments, either loans receivable or securities. Property, plant, and equipment (PP&E) compose only a small fraction of

[16] Working capital management involves making sure a company does not have excess resources tied up in the form of cash, receivables, and inventory. An example is a just-in-time inventory system. An excess $1 million in working capital implicitly increases finance charges by $100,000 per year if the interest rate on borrowing is 10%.

a bank's assets. By comparison, the bulk of the assets of an electric utility is property, plant, and equipment. A company's asset mix, the proportion of total assets in each asset category, is determined to a large degree by the industry in which the company operates.

Asset mix is calculated by dividing each asset amount by the sum of total assets. For example, to determine what fraction of Techtronics' assets is buildings and equipment, perform the following calculation:

$$\frac{\text{Buildings and equipment}}{\text{Total assets}} = \frac{\$732{,}900}{\$1{,}952{,}600} = 0.38$$

Techtronics holds 38% of its assets in the form of buildings and equipment. To determine whether this proportion is appropriate requires looking at the comparable number for other firms in Techtronics' industry. We can tell, for example, that Techtronics is probably not an electric utility, since property, plant, and equipment are 62% ($20,874,000,000/$33,498,000,000) of the total assets of Consolidated Edison in 2008 (see Exhibit 3-6). Similar computations and comparisons can be done with any of the asset categories.

Not surprisingly, **McDonald's** has a large amount of its assets invested in property, plant, and equipment as shown in Exhibit 3-9. It is also not surprising that Microsoft and eBay have very little invested in these long-term assets. What is somewhat surprising is Coca-Cola's low level of investment in PP&E. As mentioned at the beginning of the chapter, however, many of Coca-Cola's bottling facilities are owned by subsidiaries and are not reported on Coca-Cola's balance sheet.

Relationships Between Balance Sheet and Income Statement Amounts

Financial ratios comparing balance sheet and income statement amounts reveal information about a firm's overall profitability and about how efficiently the assets are being used. For this discussion, the following income statement data will be assumed for Techtronics: sales, $4,000,000; net income, $150,000.

Efficiency Techtronics' balance sheet reveals that it has $1,952,600 in assets. Are those assets being used efficiently? A financial ratio that gives an overall measure of company efficiency is called asset turnover and is computed as follows:

$$\text{Asset turnover: } \frac{\text{Sales}}{\text{Total assets}} = \frac{\$4{,}000{,}000}{\$1{,}952{,}600} = 2.05$$

Techtronics' asset turnover ratio of 2.05 means that for each dollar of assets, Techtronics is able to generate $2.05 in sales. The higher the asset turnover ratio, the more efficient the company is at using its assets to generate sales.

As indicated in Exhibit 3-9, Microsoft and McDonald's are the most efficient of the five companies in using assets to generate sales. Every dollar of Microsoft or McDonald's assets generates $0.75 in annual revenue.

Similar computations can be made for specific assets. The general principle is that in measuring whether a company has too much or too little of an asset, the amount of that asset is compared to an income statement item indicating the amount of business activity related to that asset. For example, evaluating the level of inventory involves comparing the inventory level to cost of goods sold for the year. Specific efficiency ratios for accounts receivable, inventory, and fixed assets will be described in the appropriate chapters later in the text.

Overall Profitability Techtronics' net income was $150,000. Is that a lot? It depends. If Techtronics is a small backyard computer-repair business, net income of $150,000 is a lot. If Techtronics is a multinational consumer electronics firm, net income of only $150,000 is terrible. To appropriately measure profitability, net income must be compared to some measure of the size of the investment. Two financial ratios used to assess a firm's overall profitability are return on assets and return on equity. Companies purchase assets with the intent of using them to generate profits. Return on assets is computed as follows:

$$\text{Return on assets: } \frac{\text{Net income}}{\text{Total assets}} = \frac{\$150{,}000}{\$1{,}952{,}600} = 7.7\%$$

Techtronics' return on assets of 7.7% means that one dollar of assets generated 7.7 cents in net income. As with all ratios, this number must be evaluated in light of Techtronics' return on assets in previous years and the ratios for other firms in the same industry.

Note from Exhibit 3-9 that Microsoft stands out in terms of profitability, with Disney bringing up the rear. The 18.7% return on assets earned by Microsoft is unusually high.

One important factor not included when using return on assets to evaluate profitability is the effect of leverage. The stockholders of Techtronics did not have to invest the entire $1,952,600 needed to purchase the assets; they leveraged their investment through borrowing. Return on equity (ROE) measures the percentage return on the actual investment made by stockholders and is computed as follows:

$$\text{Return on equity: } \frac{\text{Net income}}{\text{Stockholder's equity}} = \frac{\$150{,}000}{\$853{,}900} = 17.6\%$$

Techtronics stockholders earned 17.6 cents for each dollar of equity investment. Computing return on equity is like taking a child's temperature: This one number is a summary indicator of the health of the entity. As a rule of thumb, companies with return on equity significantly below 15% are doing poorly. Companies with return on equity consistently above 15% are doing well.

! CAUTION

A low ROE tells you only that a company is sick. Other financial ratios are the diagnostic tools used to pinpoint the exact nature of the illness.

Coca-Cola demonstrates how the effective use of debt can be of benefit to shareholders. Coca-Cola's shareholders earned a 27.5% return on their investment in 2009 (Exhibit 3-9). Contrast that with eBay's return of 17.3%. Also note that because eBay has a small debt ratio, there is a relatively small difference between the company's return on assets and its return on equity.

Proposed New Balance Sheet Format

The FASB and the IASB are currently engaged in a long-term project to restructure the way information is presented in the financial statements.[17] The focus of this effort is to

[17] "Preliminary Views on Financial Statement Presentation," Norwalk, CT: Financial Accounting Standards Board, October 16, 2008.

EX 3-10

Techtronics Corporation
Balance Sheet (restructured according to FASB-IASB proposal)
December 31, 2013

BUSINESS			
Operating			
Current assets:			
Receivables (less allowance for bad debts)	$ 363,700		
Inventories	296,000		
Prepaid expenses	32,900		
Total short-term assets		$ 692,600	
Land	$ 76,300		
Buildings and equipment (net of accumulated depreciation of $228,600)	732,900		
Intangible assets	165,000		
Other long-term assets	37,800		
Total long-term assets		1,012,000	
Accounts payable	$ (312,700)		
Accrued expenses	(46,200)		
Other current liabilities	(28,600)		
Total short-term liabilities		(387,500)	
Other long-term liabilities		(72,500)	
Net operating assets		1,244,600	
Investing			
Investment securities (short-term)	$ 67,350		
Investments (long-term)	128,000		
Total investing assets		195,350	
NET BUSINESS ASSETS			**$1,439,950**
FINANCING			
Financing assets			
Cash		52,650	
Financing liabilities			
Notes payable	$ (50,000)		
Current portion of long-term debt	(62,000)		
Total short-term financing liabilities		(112,000)	
Notes payable	$ (100,000)		
Bonds payable	(165,000)		
Long-term lease obligations	(135,000)		
Total long-term financing liabilities		(400,000)	
Total financing liabilities		(512,000)	
NET FINANCING LIABILITIES			**(459,350)**
INCOME TAXES			
Deferred tax liability			(126,700)
NET ASSETS			**$ 853,900**
EQUITY			
Common stock	$ (170,000)		
Additional paid-in capital	(375,000)		
Retained earnings	(308,900)		
TOTAL EQUITY			**$ (853,900)**

clearly separate financial statement items that are related to a company's business activities from items that are related to other activities such as income taxes or financing. To give you an idea of what a restructured balance sheet might look like under this new proposal, the Techtronics balance sheet in Exhibit 3-8 has been reformatted and now appears in Exhibit 3-10.

Take a look at Exhibit 3-10 and note the following.

- The balance sheet contains four major sections: business, financing, income taxes, and equity. For a company that has decided to cease some of its operations, a fifth section would include the assets and liabilities related to "discontinued operations."
- Items related to activities associated with a company's financial operations (making investments and borrowing money) are reported separately from items related to the actual day-to-day function of the business. Responsibility for these items belongs to the treasury and financial people in the company, not to the people conducting the actual business operations.
- Items related to income taxes are also highlighted and reported separately. One way to think of this is that the people who run the business on a daily basis don't have anything to do with filing the income tax returns, planning income tax strategy, and so forth.
- This format makes it a little difficult to add up the traditional measures of total assets and total liabilities. The proposed restructuring would also require supplemental disclosure of these traditional numbers.

Under the current plan (as of May 2010), this proposed restructuring of the financial statements, which will also impact the income statement and the statement of cash flows, is expected to be jointly announced by the FASB and the IASB in 2011 and will be phased in over the succeeding years. Of course, lots could happen between now and then. But there is a strong sentiment for restructuring the financial statements to highlight a company's core business. So, take a good look at Exhibit 3-10: It could be your first look at the future.

Notes to the Financial Statements

4 **Recognize the importance of the notes to the financial statements, and outline the types of disclosures made in the notes.**

WHY **The notes to the financial statements contain information relating to assumptions made, accounting methods applied, and other information relevant to those using the financial statements. Users must understand this information in order to properly interpret the numbers contained in the financial statements.**

HOW **The following important information is included in the financial statement notes: A description of the accounting policies, details of summary totals, disclosure of significant items that fail to meet the recognition criteria, and supplemental information required by FASB and SEC standards.**

The basic financial statements do not provide all of the information desired by users. Among other things, creditors and investors need to know what methods of accounting were used by the company to arrive at the balances in the accounts. Sometimes the additional information desired is descriptive and is reported in narrative form. In other cases, additional numerical data are reported. To interpret the numbers contained in the financial statements and make useful comparisons with other companies, one must be able to read the notes and understand the assumptions applied.

The following types of notes are typically included by management as support to the basic financial statements.

- Summary of significant accounting policies.
- Additional information (both numerical and descriptive) to support summary totals found on the financial statements, usually the balance sheet. This is the most common type of note used.
- Information about items that are not reported on the basic statements because the items fail to meet the recognition criteria but are still considered to be significant to users in their decision making.
- Supplementary information required by the FASB or the SEC to fulfill the full disclosure principle.

These notes are considered to be an integral part of the financial statements and, unless specifically excluded, are covered by the auditor's opinion.

Summary of Significant Accounting Policies

GAAP requires that information about the accounting principles and policies followed in arriving at the amounts in the financial statements be disclosed to the users. The FASB Accounting Standards Codification contains the following statement:

> Information about the accounting policies adopted by an entity is essential for financial statement users. When financial statements that are issued ... purport to present fairly financial position, cash flows, and results of operations in accordance with generally accepted accounting principles (GAAP), a description of all significant accounting policies of the entity shall be included as an integral part of the financial statements.[18]

Examples of the required disclosures of accounting policies include those relating to subsidiaries that have been included in the consolidated statements, depreciation methods (is straight-line used?), inventory valuation method (FIFO, LIFO, or something else?), implementation of any accounting changes, and special revenue recognition practices. This information is usually included as the initial note or as a separate summary preceding the notes to the financial statements. The summary of significant accounting policies for The Walt Disney Company is presented in Notes 2 and 3 to the company's 2009 financial statements. Much of the discussion is devoted to new accounting standards released by the FASB during the preceding year. Companies are required to outline the new standards that they are adopting for the first time. For example, in 2009 Disney reported that it was "assessing the potential effect" of a new FASB rule regarding the timing of the reporting of revenue from contracts that contain multiple elements. Companies are required to outline what impact, if any, the future adoption of new accounting standards will have on their financial statements.

Additional Information to Support Summary Totals

In order to prepare a balance sheet that is brief enough to be understandable but complete enough to meet the needs of users, notes are added that provide either quantitative or narrative information to support the postretirement amounts. For example, only

[18] FASB ASC paragraph 235-10-50-1.

summary totals for property, plant, and equipment and long-term debt are given in the balance sheet itself; the breakdown of these two items by category is usually given in the notes. Most large firms also have extended notes relating to leases, income taxes, and postemployment benefits. If a firm has entered into long-term leases, the length of the leases and the required future payments are outlined in a note. The income tax note identifies the major areas of difference between a company's financial accounting and tax accounting records. The tax note is also the place one has to look to find out what a company's actual income tax bill is. The postretirement benefit note describes a company's pension plan and plan for coverage of retiree medical benefits. Examination of this note reveals the large amount of information that underlies the single summary numbers recognized in the balance sheet. Examples of these are Note 10 (income taxes) and Note 11 (pensions) to Disney's 2009 financial statements. Disney also includes notes detailing the summary totals for other assets (Note 14) and borrowings (Note 9).

FYI

Financial statements in the United Kingdom are usually much more condensed than U.S. financial statements. For example, all current assets and current liabilities are often summed and reported as one net number. The details are given in the notes.

Information About Items Not Included in Financial Statements

As discussed in Chapter 1, items included in the financial statements must meet certain recognition criteria. Even though an item might not meet the criteria for recognition in the statements, information concerning the item might be relevant to users. Loss contingencies are good examples of this type of item. As discussed earlier, if the probability of paying a contingent liability is estimated as "possible" or if the contingent liability is "probable but not reasonably estimable," the contingency should not be recognized but should be disclosed in the notes to the financial statements. The information provided should include as much data as possible to assist the user in evaluating the risk of the loss contingency. Along these lines, most large companies have an interesting note describing the lawsuits outstanding against them.

Conceptually, disclosure should not be an alternative to recognition. In other words, if an item meets the recognition criteria given in Chapter 1, it should be included in the financial statements themselves, not just disclosed in a note. However, recall that the FASB's standard-setting process has been described as a "balancing act" between conceptual purity and business practicality. One of the tools in this balancing act is disclosure. Two examples are the accounting for stock-based compensation and for derivative financial instruments.

- In 1993, the FASB tentatively decided to require firms to recognize as compensation expense the value of stock options given to employees. This decision caused an angry uproar in the business community. After deliberation, the FASB decided to use note disclosure as a compromise; recognition of the stock option values was not required; the values needed only be disclosed in a note. After this experience with disclosure, in 2004 the FASB again decided to require firms to recognize a stock option expense (starting in 2006).[19]

[19] FASB ASC Topic 218—Compensation-Stock Compensation, originally found in pre-Codification *Statement of Financial Accounting Standards No. 123* and *No. 123(R)*.

- With derivative financial instruments (e.g., options, futures, swaps, and other exotic financial contracts), the FASB responded to a public demand (backed by requests from the SEC) for more information about derivatives by requiring extensive disclosure.[20] This disclosure standard was a stopgap measure while the FASB studied the issue further with the view of establishing a recognition standard (which was accomplished in 1998).

STOP&THINK

In analyzing a company, do users care whether they get the information from the financial statements themselves or from the notes? The answer to this question is "yes, in some circumstances." To understand this better, identify in which ONE of the following circumstances the financial analyst would be MOST LIKELY to prefer recognition over disclosure.

a) The analyst is performing a detailed financial statement analysis on a single company.

b) The analyst is performing a detailed financial statement comparison of two companies.

c) The analyst is performing a summary analysis of 50 different companies in 12 different industries.

One of the accounting controversies involved in the **Enron** scandal that exploded in 2001 and 2002 was the inadequacy of the disclosure in the notes to Enron's financial statements. For example, the existence of the controversial LJM2 investment partnerships, which were used to "hedge" (some would say "hide") $1 billion in Enron investment losses, was not disclosed anywhere in Enron's financial statements notes and was outlined in just three brief paragraphs in the company's proxy statement (which is sent to all shareholders in advance of the annual shareholder meeting).

Supplementary Information

The FASB and SEC require that supplementary information must be reported in separate schedules. For example, the FASB requires the disclosure of quarterly information for certain companies. While the information in these notes is important to the users, it may not be covered by the auditors' opinion. A note that is not covered by the opinion is marked "unaudited."

Another category of supplementary information is business segment information. For companies with geographically dispersed operations, this segment information outlines the results for the different geographic segments. For example, Coca-Cola reports that only 26.4% (2009) of its net operating revenues come from North America. For firms with diverse product lines (such as **PepsiCo**, with substantial operations in soft drinks and snack foods), segment information for the different product lines is presented.[21]

In addition to FASB requirements, the SEC also requires the disclosure of supplemental information about financial statement information for those publicly traded firms falling under the SEC's jurisdiction. For example, if the level of property, plant, and equipment is significant, the SEC requires a firm to provide details about changes in gross property, plant, and equipment and about changes in accumulated depreciation. The SEC also requires disclosure of the details of the changes in short-term borrowing and the average interest rate on short-term loans during the period.

[20] FASB ASC Section 815-10-50, originally found in pre-Codification *Statement of Financial Accounting Standards No. 119*.

[21] FASB ASC Topic 280—Segment Reporting.

EX 3-11 SUBSEQUENT EVENT INTERVAL

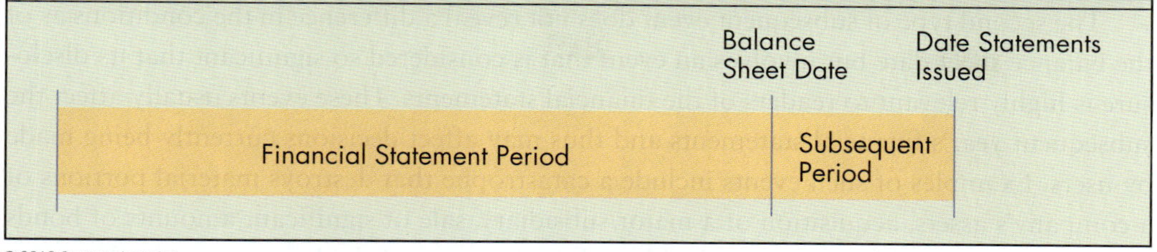

Subsequent Events

Although a balance sheet is prepared as of a given date, it is usually between one and three months before the financial statements are issued and made available to external users. For example, the SEC requires large publicly traded companies to file their financial statements within 60 days of the fiscal year-end. During this time, the accounts are analyzed, adjusting entries are prepared, and for most companies, an independent audit is completed. During this "subsequent period," business doesn't shut down while the accountants huddle over the books. Business continues, and events could take place that have an impact upon the balance sheet and the other basic financial statements for the preceding year. Some of these events could even affect the amounts reported in the statements. These events are referred to in the accounting literature as subsequent events or post-balance sheet events. This subsequent period is illustrated in Exhibit 3-11.

Two different types of subsequent events require consideration by management and evaluation by the independent auditor.[22]

- Those that require retroactive recognition and thus affect the amounts to be reported in the financial statements for the preceding accounting period.
- Those that do not require recognition but should be disclosed in the notes to the financial statements.

The first type of subsequent event usually provides additional information that affects the amounts included in the financial statements. The reported amounts in several accounts, such as Allowance for Bad Debts, Warranty Liability, and Income Taxes Payable, reflect estimates of the expected value. These estimates are based on information available as of a given date. If a subsequent event provides new information that shows that the conditions existing as of the balance sheet date were different from those assumed when making the estimate, a change in the amount to be reported in the financial statements is required.

To illustrate this type of event, assume that a month after the balance sheet date, the company learns that a major customer has filed for bankruptcy. This information was not known as of the balance sheet date, and only ordinary provisions were made in determining the Allowance for Bad Debts. In all likelihood, the customer was already in financial difficulty at the balance sheet date, but it was not general knowledge. The filing of bankruptcy reveals that the conditions at the balance sheet date were different than those

[22] FASB ASC Topic 855–Subsequent Events.

assumed in preparing the statements, and a further adjustment to both the balance sheet and income statement is indicated.

The second type of subsequent event does not reveal a difference in the conditions as of the balance sheet date but involves an event that is considered so significant that its disclosure is highly relevant to readers of the financial statements. These events usually affect the subsequent year's financial statements and thus may affect decisions currently being made by users. Examples of such events include a catastrophe that destroys material portions of a company's assets, acquisition of a major subsidiary, sale of significant amounts of bonds or capital stock, and losses on receivables when the cause of the loss occurred subsequent to the balance sheet date. Information about this type of event is included in the notes to the financial statements and serves to notify the reader that the subsequent event could affect the predictive value of the statements.

The most common types of subsequent events reported by companies include events associated with debt refinancing, debt reduction, or incurring significant amounts of new debt; post-balance sheet developments associated with litigation; and changes in the status of a proposed merger or acquisition. Of course, many business events that occur during this subsequent period are related only to the subsequent year and therefore have no impact on the preceding year's financial statements.

As an example of the types of disclosure associated with subsequent events, the following items were discussed in Note 35 to the financial statements of **General Motors** dated December 31, 2009:

- A discussion of the financial statement impact of currency revaluations conducted by the Venezuelan government in early 2010
- The February 2010 sale of 1% of a joint venture (reducing GM's ownership to 49%) to a Hong Kong subsidiary of Shanghai Automotive Industry Corp (SAIC)—in essence, GM gave up joint control in exchange for some cash
- The February 2010 failure to complete a deal to sell HUMMER to a Chinese company
- The successful February 2010 sale of Saab to a Dutch company
- The progress of talks with the German government about the future of Opel
- The March 2010 partial repayment of loans received from the U.S. and Canadian governments

As you can see from these subsequent events notes, the period from the balance sheet date of December 31, 2009, to the financial statement issuance date on April 7, 2010, was a busy one for General Motors. (*Note:* Because of the company's ongoing restructuring, it was allowed to delay its financial statement issuance beyond the usual requirement of 60 days for companies publicly traded in the United States.)

International Accounting for Subsequent Events The International Accounting Standards Board (IASB) has released a standard, IAS 10, dealing specifically with the accounting for subsequent events. This standard, which was originally issued in September 1974 and was revised in December 2003, is essentially the same as the accounting employed in the United States. Specifically, IAS 10 requires that companies adjust the reported amounts of assets and liabilities if events occurring after the balance sheet date provide additional information about conditions that existed at the balance sheet date. In addition, IAS 10 requires that disclosure be made of significant subsequent events even if those events do not impact the valuations reported in the balance sheet.

Limitations of the Balance Sheet

5 **Understand the major limitations of the balance sheet.**

WHY **Before users can appropriately use the information contained in the balance sheet, they must understand what the information implies and, just as importantly, what it does not imply.**

HOW **The balance sheet often does not provide an accurate reflection of the value of a business. Reasons for this include the use of historical cost instead of current values, omission of some economic assets from the balance sheet, and failure to make adjustments for inflation. The difference between balance sheet value and market value is captured in the book-to-market ratio (book value of equity divided by market value of equity), which is usually less than 1.0.**

Notwithstanding its usefulness, the balance sheet has some serious limitations. External users often need to know a company's worth. The balance sheet, however, does not generally reflect the current value of a business. A favorite ratio among followers of the stock market is the book-to-market ratio, computed as total book value of common equity divided by total market value of common equity. The book-to-market ratio reflects the difference between the balance sheet value of a company and the company's actual market value.[23] A company's book-to-market ratio is almost always less than 1.0 because many assets are reported at historical cost, which is usually less than market value, and other assets are not included in the balance sheet at all. In addition, many intangible economic assets, such as a reputation for superior products or customer service, are not recognized in the balance sheet. Accordingly, the balance sheet numbers often very poorly reflect what a company is worth.

The graph in Exhibit 3-12 shows the average book-to-market ratio, from 1924 through 2008, of the 30 companies making up the Dow Jones Industrial Average. Note the fairly steady decrease from an average book-to-market ratio of about 1.0 in 1980 to about 0.3 in 2008. This means that, in 2008, the accounting book value of the equity of the average company included in the Dow Jones Industrial Average was just 30% as large as the market value of the equity of that company. This low book-to-market ratio reflects the increasing importance of unreported, intangible assets as service and technology companies have become a more significant part of the U.S. economy.

A related problem with the balance sheet is the instability of the dollar, the standard accounting measuring unit in the United States. Because of general price changes in the economy, the dollar does not maintain a constant purchasing power, yet the historical costs of resources and equities shown on the balance sheet are not adjusted for changes in the purchasing power of the measuring unit. The result is a balance sheet that reflects assets, liabilities, and equities in terms of unequal purchasing power units. Some elements, for example, may be stated in terms of 1980 dollars and some in terms of current-year dollars. The variations in purchasing power of the amounts reported in the balance sheet make comparisons among companies, and even within a single company, less meaningful.

[23] Research into the behavior of stock prices has found that firms with high book-to-market ratios tend to outperform the market in future years. See Eugene F. Fama and Kenneth R. French, "The Cross-Section of Expected Stock Returns," *The Journal of Finance*, June 1992, p. 427. No one is sure why high book-to-market-ratio firms outperform the market. One suggestion is that the accounting numbers partially reflect fundamental underlying value, and a high book-to-market ratio indicates that the market is currently undervaluing a company.

EX 3-12 AVERAGE BOOK-TO-MARKET RATIO OF COMPANIES LISTED IN THE DOW JONES INDUSTRIAL AVERAGE: 1924–2008

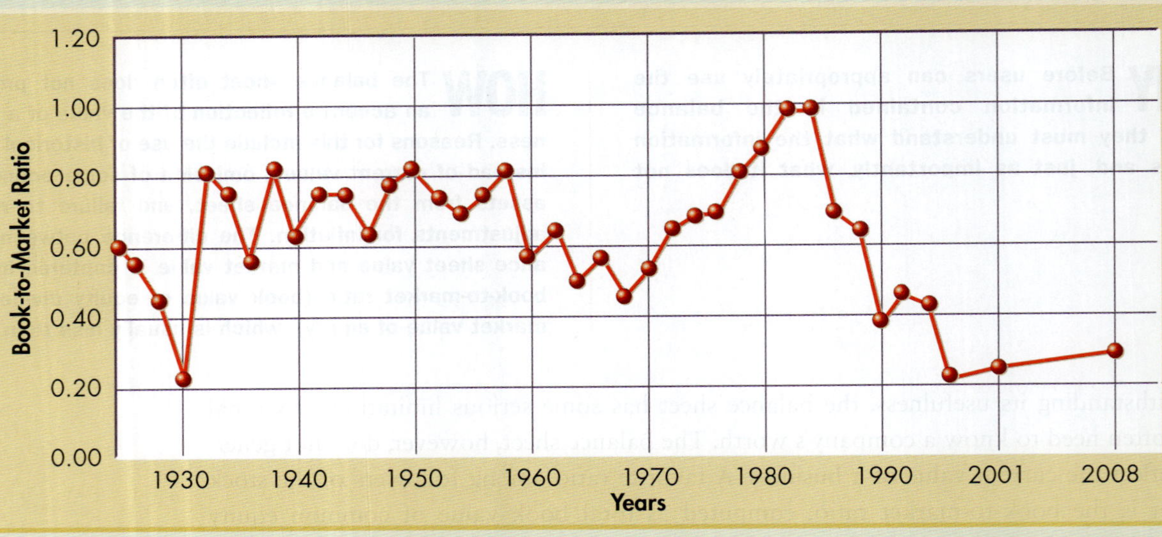

Source: *The Wall Street Journal*, March 30, 1999, p. C14. The original source has been augmented with data from www.djindexes.com.

An additional limitation of the balance sheet, also related to the need for comparability, is that all companies do not classify and report all like items similarly. For example, titles and account classifications vary; some companies provide considerably more detail than others; and some companies with apparently similar transactions report them differently. Such differences make comparisons difficult and diminish the potential value of balance sheet analysis.

As mentioned, some entity resources and obligations are not reported on the balance sheet. For example, as mentioned at the beginning of the chapter in connection with Coca-Cola, the company's reputation and worldwide market presence are among its most valuable resources, yet those economic assets are not shown on the balance sheet because measuring them in monetary terms is quite difficult. The assumptions of the traditional accounting model identified in Chapter 1, specifically the requirements of arm's-length transactions or events measurable in monetary terms, add to the objectivity of balance sheet disclosures but at the same time cause some information to be omitted that is likely to be relevant to certain users' decisions.

One other limitation of the balance sheet is the increasing use of off-balance-sheet financing. In fact, a key aspect of the famous Enron accounting scandal was Enron's creative use of financing arrangements (with exotic names such as Rhythms and Raptor) to avoid reporting large amounts of debt in the company's balance sheet. In an off-balance-sheet financing arrangement, a company borrows money to purchase an asset or to fund an activity (such as research), but is able to take advantage of the accounting rules to avoid reporting a balance sheet obligation for the borrowed funds. For example, a section in Chapter 12 describes how companies use joint ventures to achieve off-balance-sheet financing. In addition, Chapter 15 demonstrates how companies can use leases to finance asset purchases through borrowing but avoid showing the associated debt on the balance sheet.

SOLUTIONS TO OPENING SCENARIO QUESTIONS

1. The original Coca-Cola trademark is a "homegrown" intangible asset. Traditional accounting in the United States does not report an estimated value for homegrown intangibles in the balance sheet. The trademark values that are reported in the balance sheet of The Coca-Cola Company are values for trademarks that the company has purchased over the years, such as Minute Maid.
2. Total liabilities as of December 31, 2009, are \$23.325 billion (\$13.721 billion for current liabilities + \$5.059 billion for long-term debt + \$2.965 billion for other liabilities + \$1.580 billion for deferred income taxes). Note that this amount of reported liabilities is much smaller than the amount of unreported liabilities of the Coca-Cola bottlers of which The Coca-Cola Company owns a substantial percentage.
3. As of December 31, 2009, current assets total \$17.551 billion, and current liabilities total \$13.721 billion. All other things being equal, a banker making a short-term loan to a company would prefer current assets of that company to be much more than current liabilities. This historical rule of thumb has been that the desired level of current assets is twice as much as current liabilities. If this were the case, the banker would have a greater likelihood of having the short-term loan repaid because the borrowing company already has enough current assets to be able to repay all of its existing current liabilities. In the case of Coca-Cola, with a long history of generating cash from operations, a banker would take some comfort from its track record.

SOLUTIONS TO STOP & THINK

1. (Page 3-6) The correct answer is C. Actually, defining assets and liabilities in terms of legal statutes would severely limit the FASB's influence. One of the key roles of the FASB is to apply the definitions in the conceptual framework to determine when assets and liabilities should be recognized. Legalistic definitions would take this exercise out of the FASB's hands and transfer it to the lawmakers responsible for contract law.
2. (Page 3-13)
   (a) A financial analyst trying to compare the company's core business with the core businesses of similar companies—Classification (b). This classification allows the analyst to compare the assets and liabilities associated with the primary lines of business of various companies.
   (b) A U.S. congressperson concerned about the relocation of operations overseas—Classification (a). This classification allows the congressperson to see how much of a company's assets and liabilities are located outside the United States. The congressperson would also be able to see the trend over time.
   (c) An analyst trying to estimate the current market value of a company—Classification (c). This classification allows the analyst to see what fraction of a company's assets is not reported at current fair value. This gives the analyst an idea of how much the company's market value might vary from its reported balance sheet value.
3. (Page 3-20) The correct answer is B. Total assets is the sum of current assets and long-term (fixed) assets. For British Telecommunications as of March 31, 2009, the amount of total assets is £29,274 million (£23,261 million + £6,013 million). Note that this is not the same total amount shown in the balance sheet—the balance sheet amount is total assets minus current liabilities.
4. (Page 3-32) The correct answer is C. When the analyst is doing a detailed analysis of one or two companies, then he or she can make any desired financial statement adjustments using note disclosure. Such adjustments might be necessary to make a company comparable to some benchmark or to make the financial statements of two different companies comparable. However, these detailed adjustments using note disclosure become expensive and time consuming when many companies are involved. In such a case, the analyst prefers to have all of the relevant data summarized and recognized in the financial statements themselves.

SOLUTION TO USING THE FASB'S CODIFICATION

In FASB ASC 210-20-05-1 we read the following: "This Subtopic provides criteria for offsetting amounts related to certain contracts and provides guidance on presentation. It is a general principle of accounting that the offsetting of assets and liabilities in the balance sheet is improper except if a right of setoff exists."

The "right of setoff" is defined as follows: "A right of setoff is a debtor's legal right, by contract or otherwise, to discharge all or a portion of the debt owed to another party by applying against the debt an amount that the other party owes to the debtor."

This "right of setoff" doesn't describe the situation with the doctors and their $350,000 bank loan. The "right of setoff" would exist if I owe you $1,000, and you owe me $1,000, and my contract with you allowed me to cancel my debt to you by "setting off" the amount you owe to me. I could then offset those amounts and eliminate both from my balance sheet.

To make a proper balance sheet for the medical practice, you need to include the existing $350,000 loan ... unless the doctors want to pull some of that cash out of their personal accounts and repay the loan.

REVIEW **CHAPTER 3**

LEARNING OBJECTIVES

1 **Describe the specific elements of the balance sheet (assets, liabilities, and owners' equity), and prepare a balance sheet with assets and liabilities properly classified into current and noncurrent categories.**

A balance sheet is a listing of a company's assets, liabilities, and equities as of a certain point in time.

- Assets are probable future economic benefits obtained or controlled as a result of past transactions or events.
- Liabilities are probable future sacrifices of economic benefits arising from present obligations to transfer assets or provide services in the future as a result of past transactions or events.
- Equity is the net assets of an entity, that is, the amount that remains after total liabilities have been deducted from total assets.

For balance sheet reporting, assets and liabilities are often separated into current and noncurrent categories. Current items are those expected to be used or paid within one year or within the normal operating cycle, whichever is longer.

When classifying assets and liabilities, the key considerations are how management intends to use an asset and when it expects to pay a liability.

Equity arises from owner investment, is increased by net income, and is decreased by losses and by distributions to owners. Equity is also impacted by stock repurchases, unrealized security gains and losses, and foreign exchange rate fluctuations.

2 **Identify the different formats used to present balance sheet data.**

In most industries in the United States, assets and liabilities are listed in order of their liquidity with current items first. For some industries, particularly those with large investments in long-term assets, current items are not listed first. In addition, in other countries, the format of the balance sheet can vary widely.

3 **Analyze a company's performance and financial position through the computation of financial ratios.**

Balance sheet information is most often analyzed by looking at relationships between different balance sheet amounts and relationships between balance sheet and income statement amounts. Relationships between financial statement amounts are called *financial ratios*.

4 **Recognize the importance of the notes to the financial statements, and outline the types of disclosures made in the notes.**

The information in the financial statements is supported by explanatory notes. The notes include a description of the accounting policies, details of summary totals, disclosure of significant items that fail to meet the recognition criteria, and supplemental information required by FASB and SEC standards.

Note disclosure also sometimes relates to subsequent events. *Subsequent events* are significant events occurring between the balance sheet date and the date the financial statements are issued. Subsequent events come in two varieties: those requiring immediate retroactive recognition in the financial statements and those requiring only note disclosure.

5 **Understand the major limitations of the balance sheet.**

The balance sheet often does not provide an accurate reflection of the value of a business. Reasons for this include the use of historical cost instead of current values, omission of some assets from the balance sheet, and failure to make adjustments for inflation. The balance sheet does not measure the market value of a company. The difference between balance sheet value and market value is captured in the book-to-market ratio (book value of equity divided by market value of equity), which is usually less than 1.0.

FASB-IASB CODIFICATION SUMMARY

ifrs

Topic	FASB Accounting Standards Codification	Original FASB Standard	Corresponding IASB Standard	Differences between U.S. GAAP and IFRS
Classified balance sheet	*Section 210-10-05 par. 4* *Section 210-10-45 par. 1 through 12*	*ARB 43 Ch, 3A par. 4-8*	*IAS 1 par. 60-61*	No substantial differences in the descriptions and definitions of current assets and current liabilities
Classification of short-term obligations to be refinanced	*Section 470-10-45 par. 14*	*SFAS No. 6 par. 10-11*	*IAS 1 par. 72*	Under IFRS, for a short-term obligation to be classified as long term, the refinancing must take place by the balance sheet date.
Subsequent events	*Topic 855*	*SFAS No. 165*	*IAS 10*	No substantial differences

KEY TERMS

Acid-test ratio 3-24
Additional paid-in capital 3-14
Asset mix 3-26
Assets 3-5
Asset turnover 3-26
Balance sheet 3-5
Book-to-market ratio 3-35
Callable obligation 3-11
Capital stock 3-14
Common stock 3-14
Contingent liabilities 3-13
Contributed capital 3-14
Corporations 3-14
Current assets 3-8
Current liabilities 3-10
Current ratio 3-24
Debt ratio 3-25
Deferred income tax assets 3-10
Deferred income tax liability 3-12
Deficit 3-15
Derivative 3-16
Equity 3-5
Estimated liability 3-13
Financial ratios 3-22

QUESTIONS

1. What three elements are contained in a balance sheet?
2. What is the importance of the term *probable* in the definition of an asset?
3. "Liabilities are obligations denominated in precise monetary terms." Do you agree or disagree? Explain.
4. What does the difference between current assets and current liabilities measure?
5. What criteria are generally used (a) in classifying assets as current? (b) in classifying liabilities as current?
6. Indicate under what circumstances each of the following can be considered noncurrent: (a) cash and (b) receivables.
7. How can expected refinancing impact the classification of a liability?
8. (a) What is a subjective acceleration clause?
   (b) What is an objective acceleration clause?
   (c) How do these clauses in debt instruments affect the classification of a liability?
9. Distinguish between contingent liabilities and estimated liabilities.
10. How do the Equity sections of proprietorships, partnerships, and corporations differ from one another?
11. What are the three major categories in a corporation's Equity section?
12. Under what circumstances may offset balances be properly recognized on the balance sheet?
13. In what order are assets usually listed in the balance sheet?
14. What are financial ratios?
15. Explain how the asset turnover ratio provides a measure of a company's overall efficiency.
16. What one financial ratio summarizes everything about the performance of a company? How is it computed?
17. What are the major types of notes attached to the financial statements?
18. How has the FASB used note disclosure as a tool of compromise?
19. What are some examples of supplementary information included in the notes to financial statements?
20. Under what circumstances does a subsequent event lead to a journal entry for the previous reporting period?
21. "The balance sheet does not reflect the value of a business." Do you agree or disagree? Explain.

PRACTICE EXERCISES

Practice 3-1
LO1

Working Capital

Using the following information, compute **working capital**:

Cost of Goods Sold	$ 9,000
Accounts Payable	2,400
Paid-In Capital	1,950
Cash	700
Sales	10,000
Accrued Wages Payable	225
Dividends	500
Retained Earnings (beginning)	1,000
Inventory	2,500

Practice 3-2
LO1

Current Assets
Using the following information, compute total **current assets**:

Goodwill	$ 9,000
Prepaid Expenses	1,100
Paid-In Capital	1,750
Cash	400
Property, Plant, and Equipment	10,000
Investment Securities (trading)	250
Accounts Receivable	700
Retained Earnings	1,000
Inventory	4,000

Practice 3-3
LO1

Current Liabilities
Using the following information, compute total **current liabilities**:

Accrued Income Taxes Payable	$ 9,000
Notes Payable (due in 14 months)	1,100
Paid-In Capital	1,750
Treasury Stock	400
Current Portion of Long-Term Debt	10,000
Unearned Revenue	315
Accounts Payable	700
Retained Earnings	1,000
Additional Paid-In Capital	4,000

Practice 3-4
LO1

Classification of Short-Term Loans to Be Refinanced
The company has the following three loans payable scheduled to be repaid in June of next year. As of December 31 of this year, identify which of the three should be classified as current and which should be classified as noncurrent.

(a) The company intends to repay Loan A when it comes due in June. In September, the company intends to get a new loan of equal amount from the same bank.
(b) The company intends to refinance Loan B when it comes due. The refinancing contract will be signed in May *after* the financial statements for this year have been released.
(c) The company intends to refinance Loan C when it comes due. The refinancing contract will be signed in January *before* the financial statements for this year have been released.

Practice 3-5
LO1

Callable Obligations
The company has the following three loans. As of December 31 of this year, identify which of the three should be classified as current and which should be classified as noncurrent.

(a) On July 15 of next year, Loan A will become payable on demand.
(b) Loan B is scheduled to be repaid in three years. In addition, the loan agreement specifies that if the company's current ratio falls below 1.5, the loan becomes payable on demand. On December 31, the current ratio is 1.8.
(c) Loan C is scheduled to be repaid in three years. In addition, the loan agreement specifies that if the company's "general financial condition deteriorates significantly," the loan becomes payable on demand. As of December 31, it is reasonably possible that this clause will be invoked.

Practice 3-6

LO1

Contingent Liabilities

The company has the following three potential obligations. Describe how each will be reported in the financial statements.

(a) The company has promised to make fixed pension payments to employees after they retire. The company is not certain how long the employees will work or how long they will live after they retire.

(b) The company has been sued by a group of shareholders who claim that they were deceived by the company's financial reporting practices. It is possible that the company will lose this lawsuit.

(c) The company is involved in litigation over who must clean up a toxic waste site near one of the company's factories. It is probable, but not certain, that the company will be required to pay for the cleanup.

Practice 3-7

LO1

Stockholders' Equity

Using the following information, compute: (a) total contributed capital, (b) ending retained earnings, and (c) total stockholders' equity:

Additional Paid-In Capital, Common	$8,200
Accounts Payable	1,300
Total Expenses	5,650
Preferred Stock, at par	3,450
Common Stock, at par	170
Sales	9,700
Treasury Stock	375
Dividends	950
Retained Earnings (beginning)	6,500
Additional Paid-In Capital, Preferred	150

Practice 3-8

LO1

Stockholders' Equity

Using the following information, compute (a) total contributed capital, (b) total accumulated other comprehensive income, and (c) total stockholders' equity:

Additional Paid-In Capital, Common	$9,000
Common Stock, at par	400
Cumulative Translation Adjustment (equity reduction), ending	2,000
Treasury Stock	700
Retained Earnings (post closing, or ending)	1,500
Cumulative Unrealized Gain on Available-for-Sale Securities, ending	1,100

Practice 3-9

LO2

Format of Foreign Balance Sheet

Following is a balance sheet presented in standard U.S. format. Rearrange this balance sheet to be in standard British format. Don't worry about differences in terminology; use the U.S. labels, but present the information in the British format.

Current Assets:	
Cash	$ 500
Inventory	2,000
Total current assets	$ 2,500
Noncurrent Assets:	
Property, plant, and equipment	$ 8,000
Long-term investments	1,700
Total noncurrent assets	$ 9,700
Total assets	$12,200

Current Liabilities:	
Accounts payable	$ 300
Short-term loans payable	1,100
Total current liabilities	$ 1,400
Noncurrent Liabilities:	
Long-term debt	$ 3,000
Stockholders' Equity:	
Common stock, at par	$ 50
Additional paid-in capital	2,000
Retained earnings	5,750
Total stockholders' equity	$ 7,800
Total liabilities and stockholders' equity	$12,200

Practice 3-10
LO3

Current Ratio

Use the following information to compute the current ratio:

Accounts Payable	$3,700
Paid-In Capital	3,650
Cash	750
Sales	9,500
Accrued Wages Payable	615
Inventory	6,300

Practice 3-11
LO3

Quick Ratio

Use the following information to compute the quick ratio:

Long-Term Loan Payable	$ 1,100
Accounts Receivable	1,750
Cash	400
Cost of Goods Sold	10,000
Accrued Wages Payable	315
Inventory	4,000

Practice 3-12
LO3

Debt Ratio

Use the information in Practice 3-3 to compute the debt ratio. Assume that the list includes all liability and equity items.

Practice 3-13
LO3

Debt Ratio

Use the information in Practice 3-7 to compute the debt ratio. Assume that the list includes all liability and equity items.

Practice 3-14
LO3

Asset Mix

Use the information in Practice 3-9 to compute the proportion of total assets in each of the following asset categories.

(a) Inventory
(b) Property, Plant, and Equipment

Practice 3-15
LO3

Asset Mix

Use the information in Practice 3-2 to compute the proportion of total assets in each of the following asset categories. Assume that the list contains all the asset items.

(a) Inventory
(b) Property, Plant, and Equipment

Practice 3-16
LO3

Measure of Efficiency

Refer to Practice 3-9. Sales for the year totaled $50,000. Compute asset turnover.

Practice 3-17
LO3

Return on Assets

Refer to Practice 3-9. Net income for the year totaled $3,600. Compute return on assets.

Practice 3-18
LO3

Return on Equity

Refer to Practice 3-9. Net income for the year totaled $2,000. Compute return on equity.

Practice 3-19
LO4

Accounting for Subsequent Events

On December 31, the warranty liability was estimated to be $150,000. On January 16 of the following year, results of a study done before December 31 were received. These study results indicate that products would require a much larger amount of warranty repairs than expected; total warranty repairs will be $215,000 instead of the estimated $150,000. The financial statements were issued on February 20. What amount should be reported as warranty liability in the December 31 balance sheet?

Practice 3-20
LO4

Accounting for Subsequent Events

On December 31, the warranty liability was estimated to be $100,000. On January 16 of the following year, it was learned that one week before, on January 9, poor-quality materials were introduced into the production process. This mistake is expected to create an additional $87,000 in warranty repairs. The financial statements were issued on February 20. What amount should be reported as warranty liability in the December 31 balance sheet?

Practice 3-21
LO5

Book-to-Market Ratio

Refer to Practice 3-9. As of the end of the year, the total market value of shares outstanding was $10,000. Compute the book-to-market ratio.

EXERCISES

Exercise 3-22
LO1

Asset Definition

Using the definition of an asset from FASB *Concepts Statement No. 6*, indicate whether each of the following should be listed as an asset by Ingalls Company.

(a) Ingalls has legal title to a coal mine in a remote location. Historically, the mine has yielded more than $25 million in coal. Engineering estimates suggest that no additional coal is economically extractable from the mine.
(b) Ingalls employs a team of five geologists who are widely recognized as worldwide leaders in their field.
(c) Several years ago, Ingalls purchased a large meteor crater on the advice of a geologist who had developed a theory claiming that vast deposits of iron ore lay underneath the crater. The crater has no other economic use. No ore has been found, and the geologist's theory is not generally accepted.
(d) Ingalls claims ownership of a large piece of real estate in a foreign country. The real estate has a current market value of over $225 million. The country

expropriated the land 35 years ago, and no representative of Ingalls has been allowed on the property since.

(e) Ingalls is currently negotiating the purchase of an oil field with proven oil reserves totaling 5 billion barrels.

Exercise 3-23
LO1

Liability Definition

Using the definition of a liability from FASB *Concepts Statement No. 6*, indicate whether each of the following should be listed as a liability by Pauli Company.

(a) Pauli was involved in a highly publicized lawsuit last year. Pauli lost and was ordered to pay damages of $125 million. The payment has been made.
(b) In exchange for television advertising services that Pauli received last month, Pauli is obligated to provide the television station with building maintenance service for the next four months.
(c) Pauli contractually guarantees to replace any of its stain-resistant carpets if they are stained and can't be cleaned.
(d) Pauli estimates that its total payroll for the coming year will exceed $35 million.
(e) In the past, Pauli has suffered frequent vandalism at its storage warehouses. Pauli estimates that losses due to vandalism during the coming year will total $3 million.

Exercise 3-24
LO5

Book-to-Market Ratio

The following information relates to two companies, designated Company A and Company B. One of the companies is a traditional steel manufacturer. The other is a successful Internet retailer. Using the following information, identify which is which, and explain your answer.

	Reported Stockholders' Equity	Total Market Value of Equity
Company A.	$15,000	$82,000
Company B.	15,000	11,000

Exercise 3-25
LO1

Balance Sheet Preparation

From the following list of accounts, prepare a balance sheet showing all balance sheet items properly classified. (No monetary amounts are to be recognized.)

Accounts Payable
Accounts Receivable
Accumulated Depreciation—Buildings
Accumulated Depreciation—Equipment
Advertising Expense
Allowance for Bad Debts
Bad Debt Expense
Bonds Payable
Buildings
Cash
Common Stock
Cost of Goods Sold
Deferred Income Tax Liability
Depreciation Expense—Buildings
Dividends
Equipment
Estimated Warranty Expense Payable (current)

Gain on Sale of Investment Securities
Gain on Sale of Land
Goodwill
Income Tax Expense
Income Taxes Payable
Interest Receivable
Interest Revenue
Inventory
Investment in Subsidiary
Investment Securities (Trading)
Land
Loss on Purchase Commitments
Miscellaneous General Expense
Net Pension Asset
Notes Payable (current)
Paid-In Capital from Sale of Treasury Stock
Paid-In Capital in Excess of Stated Value
Patents
Premium on Bonds Payable
Prepaid Insurance
Property Tax Expense
Purchase Discounts
Purchases
Retained Earnings
Salaries Payable
Sales
Sales Salaries
Travel Expense

Exercise 3-26
LO1, LO2

Preparation of Corrected Balance Sheet

The following balance sheet was prepared for Jared Corporation as of December 31, 2013.

Jared Corporation
Balance Sheet
December 31, 2013

Assets		**Liabilities and Owners' Equity**	
Current assets:		Current liabilities:	
Cash	$ 12,500	Accounts payable	$ 3,400
Investment securities	8,000	Other current liabilities	2,000
Accounts receivable, net	21,350	Total current liabilities	$ 5,400
Inventory	31,000	Long-term liabilities	32,750
Other current assets	14,200	Total liabilities	$ 38,150
Total current assets	$ 87,050		
Noncurrent assets:		Owners' equity:	
Property, plant, and equipment, net	$ 64,800	Common stock	$ 50,000
Treasury stock	4,500	Retained earnings	81,800
Other noncurrent assets	13,600	Total owners' equity	$131,800
Total noncurrent assets	$ 82,900		
Total assets	$169,950	Total liabilities and owners' equity	$169,950

The following additional information relates to the December 31, 2013, balance sheet.

(a) Cash includes $4,000 that has been restricted to the purchase of manufacturing equipment (a noncurrent asset).
(b) Investment securities include $2,750 of stock that was purchased in order to give the company significant ownership and a seat on the board of directors of a major supplier.
(c) Other current assets include a $4,000 advance to the president of the company. No due date has been set.
(d) Long-term liabilities include bonds payable of $10,000. Of this amount, $2,500 represents bonds scheduled to be redeemed in 2014.
(e) Long-term liabilities also include a $7,000 bank loan. On May 15, the loan will become due on demand.
(f) On December 21, dividends in the amount of $15,000 were declared to be paid to shareholders of record on January 25. These dividends have not been reflected in the financial statements.
(g) Cash in the amount of $19,000 has been placed in a restricted fund for the redemption of preferred stock in 2014. Both the cash and the stock have been removed from the balance sheet.
(h) Property, plant, and equipment includes land costing $8,000 that is being held for investment purposes and that is scheduled to be sold in 2014.

Based on the information provided, prepare a corrected balance sheet.

Exercise 3-27

LO1

Balance Sheet Classification

State how each of the following accounts should be classified on the balance sheet.

(a) Treasury Stock
(b) Retained Earnings
(c) Vacation Pay Payable
(d) Foreign Currency Translation Adjustment
(e) Allowance for Bad Debts
(f) Liability for Pension Payments
(g) Investment Securities (Trading)
(h) Paid-In Capital in Excess of Stated Value
(i) Leasehold Improvements
(j) Goodwill
(k) Receivables—U.S. Government Contracts
(l) Advances to Salespersons
(m) Premium on Bonds Payable
(n) Inventory
(o) Patents
(p) Unclaimed Payroll Checks
(q) Income Taxes Payable
(r) Subscription Revenue Received in Advance
(s) Interest Payable
(t) Deferred Income Tax Asset
(u) Tools
(v) Deferred Income Tax Liability

Exercise 3-28

LO1

Balance Sheet Classification

A balance sheet contains the following classifications:

(a) Current assets
(b) Investments
(c) Property, plant, and equipment
(d) Intangible assets
(e) Other noncurrent assets
(f) Current liabilities
(g) Long-term debt
(h) Other noncurrent liabilities
(i) Capital stock
(j) Additional paid-in capital
(k) Retained earnings

Indicate by letter how each of the following accounts would be classified. Place a minus sign (–) for all accounts representing offset or contra balances.

1. Discount on Bonds Payable
2. Stock of Subsidiary Corporation
3. 12% Bonds Payable (due in 6 months)
4. U.S. Treasury Bills
5. Income Taxes Payable
6. Sales Taxes Payable
7. Estimated Claims under Warranties for Service and Replacements
8. Par Value of Stock Issued and Outstanding
9. Unearned Rent Revenue (6 months in advance)
10. Long-Term Advances to Officers
11. Interest Receivable
12. Preferred Stock Retirement Fund
13. Trademarks
14. Allowance for Bad Debts
15. Dividends Payable
16. Accumulated Depreciation
17. Trading Securities
18. Prepaid Rent
19. Prepaid Insurance
20. Deferred Income Tax Asset

Exercise 3-29
LO1

SPREADSHEET

REVERSE SOLVABLE

Balance Sheet Relationships

On the Clark and Company Inc. balance sheet, indicate the amount that should appear for each of the items (a) through (n) on the balance sheet.

Clark and Company Inc.
Consolidated Balance Sheet
December 31, 2013

Assets

Current assets:			
Cash		$ 24,250	
Investment securities		(a)	
Accounts and notes receivable	$ (b)		
Allowance for doubtful accounts and notes receivable	7,851	121,664	
Inventories		197,682	
Other current assets		14,227	
Total current assets			$ (c)
Noncurrent assets:			
Property, plant, and equipment	$694,604		
Accumulated depreciation	(d)	$398,832	
Other noncurrent assets		13,217	
Total noncurrent assets			412,049
Total assets			$792,514

Liabilities and Owners' Equity

Current liabilities:			
Accounts payable		$ (e)	
Payable to banks		34,236	
Income taxes payable		9,211	
Current installments of long-term debt		6,341	
Accrued expenses		7,100	
Total current liabilities			$ (f)

Noncurrent liabilities:			
Long-term debt		$ (g)	
Deferred income tax liability		41,218	
Minority interest in subsidiaries		4,201	
Total noncurrent liabilities			205,410
Total liabilities			$350,782
Contributed capital:			
Preferred stock, no par value (authorized 1,618 shares; issued 1,115 shares)		$ 12,392	
Common stock, $1 par value per share (authorized 60,000 shares; issued 21,842 shares)	$ (h)		
Additional paid-in capital	(i)	(j)	
Total contributed capital		$ (k)	
Retained earnings		390,625	
Total contributed capital and retained earnings		$ (l)	
Less: Treasury stock, at cost (1,229 shares)		27,038	
Total owners' equity			$ (m)
Total liabilities and owners' equity			$ (n)

Exercise 3-30

LO1, LO3

SPREADSHEET

Balance Sheet Schedules

In its annual report to stockholders, Hakobe Inc. presents a condensed balance sheet with detailed data provided in supplementary schedules.

1. From the adjusted trial balance of Hakobe, prepare the following sections of the balance sheet, properly classifying all accounts as to balance sheet categories:

   (a) Current assets
   (b) Property, plant, and equipment
   (c) Intangible assets
   (d) Total assets
   (e) Current liabilities
   (f) Noncurrent liabilities
   (g) Owners' equity
   (h) Total liabilities and owners' equity

2. Compute the current ratio and debt ratio for Hakobe.

Hakobe Inc.
Adjusted Trial Balance
December 31, 2013

	Debit	Credit
Cash	$ 43,700	
Investment securities (trading)	15,000	
Notes receivable—trade debtors	22,000	
Accrued interest on notes receivable	2,100	
Accounts receivable	79,500	
Allowance for doubtful accounts		$ 4,600
Inventory	59,300	
Prepaid expenses	8,200	
Accounts payable		57,600
Notes payable—trade creditors		11,000
Accrued interest on notes payable		950
Land	103,000	
Buildings	192,000	

(Continued)

	Debit	Credit
Accumulated depreciation—buildings		$ 21,000
Equipment	$ 37,000	
Accumulated depreciation—equipment		5,900
Patents	85,000	
Franchises	82,110	
Bonds payable, 8%—issue 1 (mature 12/31/15)		65,000
Bonds payable, 12%—issue 2 (mature 12/31/17)		125,000
Accrued interest on bonds payable		7,500
Premium on bonds payable—issue 1		2,500
Discount on bonds payable—issue 2	12,500	
Mortgage payable		72,000
Accrued interest on mortgage payable		4,320
Capital stock, par value $1; 10,000 shares authorized; 5,000 shares issued		5,000
Additional paid-in capital		123,700
Retained earnings		251,340
Treasury stock—at cost (500 shares)	16,000	
	$757,410	$757,410

Exercise 3-31

LO4

Preparation of Notes to Financial Statements

The following information was used to prepare the financial statements for Delta Chemical Company. Prepare the necessary notes to accompany the statements.

Delta uses the LIFO inventory method on its financial statements. If the FIFO method were used, the ending inventory balance would be reduced by $50,000 and net income for the year would be reduced by $35,000 after taxes. Delta depreciates its equipment using the straight-line method. Revenue is generally recognized when inventory is shipped unless it is sold on a consignment basis. The current value of the equipment is $525,000, as contrasted to its depreciated cost of $375,000.

Delta has borrowed $350,000 on a 10-year note at 14% interest. The note is due on July 1, 2020. Delta's equipment has been pledged as collateral for the loan. The terms of the note prohibit additional long-term borrowing without the express permission of the holder of the note. Delta is planning to request such permission during the next fiscal year.

The board of directors of Delta is currently discussing a merger with another chemical company. No public announcement has yet been made, but it is anticipated that additional shares of stock will be issued as part of the merger. Delta's balance sheet will report receivables of $126,000. Included in this figure is a $25,000 advance to the president of Delta, $30,000 of notes receivable from customers, $10,000 in advances to sales representatives, and $70,000 of accounts receivable from customers. The reported balance reflects a deduction for anticipated collection losses.

Exercise 3-32

LO4

Reporting Financial Information

For each of the following items, indicate whether the item should be reflected in the 2013 financial statements for Tindall Company. If the item should be reflected, indicate whether it should be reported in the financial statements themselves or by note disclosure.

(a) As of December 31, 2013, the company holds $12.1 million of its own stock that it purchased in the open market and is holding for possible reissuance.

(b) As of December 31, 2013, the company was in violation of certain loan covenants. The violation does not cause the loans to be callable immediately but does increase the interest charge by 2.0%.

(c) The company's reported Provision for Income Taxes includes $4.2 million in current taxes and $7.8 million in deferred taxes.

(d) As of December 31, 2013, accounts receivable in the amount of $7.1 million are estimated to be uncollectible.
(e) The Environmental Protection Agency is investigating the company's procedures for disposing of toxic waste. Outside consultants have estimated that the company may be liable for fines of up to $10 million.
(f) During 2013, the company had a gain on the sale of manufacturing assets.
(g) During 2013, a long-term insurance agreement was signed. The company paid five years of insurance premiums in advance.
(h) The company uses straight-line depreciation for all tangible, long-term assets.
(i) During 2013, the company hired three prominent research chemists away from its chief competitor.
(j) Reported long-term debt is composed of senior subordinated bonds payable, convertible bonds payable, junior subordinated bonds payable, and capital lease obligations.
(k) Early in 2014, a significant drop in raw material prices caused the company's stock price to rise in anticipation of sharply increased profits for the year.

Exercise 3-33
LO3

Computation of Financial Ratios

Schlofman Company has the following assets.

Cash	$ 20,000
Accounts receivable	60,000
Inventory	105,000
Property, plant, and equipment	220,000
Total assets	$405,000

Companies in Schlofman's industry typically have the following asset mix: cash, 7%; accounts receivable, 15%; inventory, 18%; property, plant, and equipment, 60%.

Compared to other companies in its industry, Schlofman has too much of one asset. Which one? Show your computations.

Exercise 3-34
LO3

Computation of Financial Ratios

The following data are from the financial statements of Riverton Company.

Current assets	$ 55,000
Total assets	150,000
Current liabilities	25,000
Total liabilities	95,000
Net income	18,000
Sales	275,000

Compute Riverton's current ratio, debt ratio, asset turnover, return on assets, and return on equity.

Exercise 3-35
LO1

Computation of Working Capital

From the following data, compute the working capital for Hales Shipping Co. at December 31, 2013.

Cash in general checking account	$ 34,000
Cash in fund to be used to retire bonds in 2017	59,000
Cash held to pay sales taxes	18,000
Notes receivable—due February 2015	113,000
Accounts receivable	113,000
Inventory	111,000
Prepaid insurance—for 2014	15,000

Vacant land held as investment	$350,000
Used equipment to be sold	9,000
Deferred tax asset—to be recovered in 2015	12,000
Accounts payable	79,000
Note payable—due July 2014	27,000
Note payable—due January 2015	18,000
Bonds payable—maturity date 2017	249,000
Salaries payable	11,000
Sales taxes payable	23,000
Goodwill	54,000

Exercise 3-36
LO4

Classification of Subsequent Events

The following events occurred after the end of the company's fiscal year but before the annual audit was completed. Classify each event as to its impact on the financial statements, that is, (1) reported by changing the amounts in the financial statements, (2) reported in notes to the financial statements, or (3) does not require reporting. Include support for your classification.

(a) Major customer went bankrupt due to a deteriorating financial condition.
(b) Company sustained extensive hurricane damage to one of its plants.
(c) Company lost a major lawsuit that had been pending for two years.
(d) Increasing U.S. trade deficit may have impact on company's overseas sales.
(e) Company sold a large block of preferred stock.
(f) Preparation of current year's income tax return disclosed that an additional $25,000 is due on last year's return.
(g) Company's controller resigned and was replaced by an audit manager from the company's audit firm.

PROBLEMS

Problem 3-37
LO1, LO3

Computing Balance Sheet Components

Denton Equipment Inc. furnishes you with the following list of accounts.

Accounts Payable	$ 66,000
Accounts Receivable	40,000
Accumulated Depreciation	44,000
Advances to Salespersons	10,000
Advertising Expense	72,000
Allowance for Bad Debts	10,000
Bonds Payable	100,000
Cash	22,000
Certificates of Deposit	16,000
Common Stock (par)	100,000
Deferred Income Tax Liability	46,000
Equipment	215,500
Inventory	75,000
Investment in Rowe Oil Co. Stock (40% of outstanding stock owned for control purposes)	76,500
Investment in Siebert Co. Stock (trading securities)	21,000
Paid-In Capital in Excess of Par	42,500
Premium on Bonds Payable	6,000
Prepaid Insurance	6,000

Rent Revenue	$37,000
Rent Revenue Received in Advance (4 months)	12,000
Retained Earnings	97,500
Taxes Payable	10,000
Tools	52,000

Instructions:

1. From the preceding list of accounts, determine working capital, total assets, total liabilities, and owners' equity per share of stock (75,000 shares outstanding).
2. Assume net income of $20,000. Compute current ratio, debt ratio, and return on equity.

Problem 3-38

LO1, LO3

SPREADSHEET

Classified Balance Sheet

Following is a list of account titles and balances for Pennington Investment Corporation as of January 31, 2013.

Accounts Payable	$ 92,400
Accounts Receivable	158,200
Accumulated Depreciation—Buildings	139,500
Accumulated Depreciation—Machinery and Equipment	116,300
Additional Paid-In Capital—Common Stock	605,000
Allowance for Doubtful Notes and Accounts Receivable	24,700
Buildings	320,000
Cash Fund for Stock Redemption	17,500
Cash in Banks	8,320
Cash on Hand	96,250
Claim for Income Tax Refund	4,000
Common Stock, $1 par	55,000
Employees' Income Taxes Payable	4,360
Income Taxes Payable	18,000
Interest Payable	5,790
Interest Receivable	2,700
Inventory	201,500
Investment Securities (trading)	83,750
Investments in Undeveloped Properties	193,500
Land	213,000
Machinery and Equipment	165,500
Miscellaneous Supplies Inventory	4,200
Notes Payable (current)	68,320
Notes Payable (due in 2016)	63,800
Notes Receivable (current)	32,960
Preferred Stock, $5 par	285,000
Prepaid Insurance	3,900
Retained Earnings	11,410
Salaries and Wages Payable	15,700

Instructions:

1. Prepare a properly classified balance sheet.
2. Assume net income of $300,000 and sales of $7,000,000. Compute the current ratio, debt ratio, and asset turnover.

Problem 3-39
LO1, LO4

Classified Balance Sheet—Including Notes

Adjusted account balances and supplemental information for Brockbank Research Corp. as of December 31, 2013, are as follows:

Accounts Payable	$ 32,160
Accounts Receivable—Trade	57,731
Accumulated Depreciation—Leasehold Improvements and Equipment	579,472
Additional Paid-In Capital	265,000
Allowance for Bad Debts	1,731
Automotive Equipment	132,800
Cash	25,600
Cash Fund for Bond Retirement	3,600
Common Stock	35,000
Deferred Income Tax Liability	45,000
Dividends Payable	37,500
Franchises	12,150
Furniture, Fixtures, and Store Equipment	769,000
Insurance Claims Receivable	120,000
Inventories	201,620
Investment in Unconsolidated Subsidiary	80,000
Land	6,000
Leasehold Improvements	65,800
7½%–12% Mortgage Notes Payable	200,000
Notes Payable—Banks (due in 2014)	12,000
Notes Payable—Trade	63,540
Patent Licenses	57,402
Prepaid Insurance	5,500
Profit Sharing, Payroll, and Vacation Payable	40,000
Retained Earnings	225,800

Supplemental information is as follows:

(a) Depreciation is provided by the straight-line method over the estimated useful lives of the assets.
(b) Common stock is $1 par, and 35,000 of the 100,000 authorized shares were issued and are outstanding.
(c) The cost of an exclusive franchise to import a foreign company's ball bearings and a related patent license are being amortized on the straight-line method over their remaining lives: franchise, 10 years; patents, 15 years.
(d) Inventories are stated at the lower of cost or market; cost was determined by the specific identification method.
(e) Insurance claims based on the opinion of an independent insurance adjustor are for property damages at the central warehouse. These claims are estimated to be two-thirds collectible in the following year and one-third collectible thereafter.
(f) The company leases all of its buildings from various lessors. Estimated fixed-lease obligations are $50,000 per year for the next 10 years. The leases do not meet the criteria for capitalization.
(g) The company is currently in litigation over a claimed overpayment of income tax of $13,000. In the opinion of counsel, the claim is valid. The company is contingently liable on guaranteed notes worth $12,000.

Instructions: Prepare a properly classified balance sheet. Include all notes and parenthetical notations necessary to properly disclose the essential financial data.

Problem 3-40
LO1, LO4

Classification of Liabilities

The accountant for Sierra Corp. prepared the following schedule of liabilities as of December 31, 2013.

Accounts payable	$ 85,000
Notes payable—trade	19,000
Notes payable—bank	80,000
Wages and salaries payable	1,500
Interest payable	14,300
Mortgage note payable—10%	60,000
Mortgage note payable—12%	150,000
Bonds payable	200,000
Total	$609,800

The following additional information pertains to these liabilities.

(a) All trade notes payable are due within six months of the balance sheet date.
(b) Bank notes payable include two separate notes payable to First Interstate Bank.
  1. A $30,000, 8% note issued March 1, 2011, payable on demand. Interest is payable every six months.
  2. A 1-year, $50,000, 11½% note issued January 2, 2013. On December 30, 2013, Sierra negotiated a written agreement with First Interstate Bank to replace the note with a 2-year, $50,000, 10% note to be issued January 2, 2014.

(c) The 10% mortgage note was issued October 1, 2010, with a term of 10 years. Terms of the note give the holder the right to demand immediate payment if the company fails to make a monthly interest payment within 10 days of the date the payment is due. As of December 31, 2013, Sierra is three months behind in paying its required interest payment.
(d) The 12% mortgage note was issued May 1, 2007, with a term of 20 years. The current principal amount due is $150,000. Principal and interest are payable annually on April 30. A payment of $22,000 is due April 30, 2014. The payment includes interest of $18,000.
(e) The bonds payable are 10-year, 8% bonds, issued June 30, 2004.

Instructions: Prepare the Liabilities section of the December 31, 2013, classified balance sheet for Sierra Corp. Include notes as appropriate. Assume the interest payable accrual has been computed correctly.

Problem 3-41
LO1, LO2

Corrected Balance Sheet

The following balance sheet was prepared by the accountant for Midway Company.

Midway Company
Balance Sheet
June 30, 2013

Assets

Cash	$ 44,500
Investment securities—Trading (includes long-term investment of $275,000 in stock of Bahen Builders)	328,700
Inventories (net of amount still due suppliers of $50,000)	585,100
Prepaid expenses (includes a deposit of $25,000 made on inventories to be delivered in 18 months)	66,000
Property, plant, and equipment (excluding $60,000 of equipment still in use, but fully depreciated)	270,000
Goodwill (based on estimate by the president of Midway Company)	85,000
Total assets	$1,379,300

Liabilities and Owners' Equity

Notes payable ($95,000 due in 2015)	$ 150,000
Accounts payable (not including amount due to suppliers of inventory—see above)	190,000
Long-term liability under pension plan	49,000
Retained earnings restricted for building expansion	112,000
Accumulated depreciation	90,000
Taxes payable	37,000
Bonds payable (net of discount of $25,000)	300,000
Deferred income tax liability	71,000
Common stock (15,000 shares, $1 par)	15,000
Additional paid-in capital	227,200
Unrestricted retained earnings	138,100
Total liabilities and owners' equity	$1,379,300

Instructions: Prepare a corrected classified balance sheet using appropriate account titles.

Problem 3-42

LO1

Classified Balance Sheet

The financial position of St. Charles Ranch is summarized in the following letter to the corporation's accountant.

Dear Dallas:

The following information should be of value to you in preparing the balance sheet for St. Charles Ranch as of December 31, 2013. The balance of cash as of December 31 as reported on the bank statement was $43,825. There were still outstanding checks of $9,320 that had not cleared the bank, and cash on hand of $10,640 was not deposited until January 4, 2014.

Customers owed the company $40,500 at December 31. We estimated 6% of this amount will never be collected. We owe suppliers $37,000 for poultry feed purchased in November and December. About 75% of this feed was used before December 31.

Because we think the price of grain will rise in 2014, we are holding 10,000 bushels of wheat and 5,000 bushels of oats until spring. The market value at December 31 was $3.50 per bushel of wheat and $1.50 per bushel of oats. We estimate that both prices will increase 15% by selling time. We are not able to estimate the cost of raising this product.

St. Charles Ranch owns 1,850 acres of land. Two separate purchases of land were made as follows: 1,250 acres at $200 per acre in 1991 and 600 acres at $400 per acre in 1996. Similar land is currently selling for $800 per acre. The balance of the mortgage on the two parcels of land is $250,000 at December 31; 10% of this mortgage must be paid in 2014.

Our farm buildings and equipment cost us $176,400 and on the average are 40% depreciated. If we were to replace these buildings and equipment at today's prices, we believe we would be conservative in estimating a cost of $300,000.

We have not paid property taxes of $5,500 for 2014 billed to us in late November. Our estimated income tax for 2013 is $18,500. A refund claim for $2,800 has been filed relative to the 2011 income tax return. The claim arose because of an error made on the 2011 return.

The operator of the ranch will receive a bonus of $9,000 for 2013 operations. It will be paid when the entire grain crop has been sold.

As you may recall, we issued 14,000 shares of $1 par stock upon incorporation. The ranch received $290,000 as net proceeds from the stock issue. Dividends of $30,000 were declared last month and will be paid on February 1, 2014.

The new year appears to hold great promise. Thanks for your help in preparing this statement.

Sincerely,

Frank K. Santiago
President, St. Charles Ranch

Instructions: Based on this information, prepare a properly classified balance sheet as of December 31, 2013.

Problem 3-43

LO1

SPREADSHEET

Corrected Balance Sheet

The bookkeeper for Chordwise Music, Inc., reports the following balance sheet amounts as of June 30, 2013.

Current assets	$286,800
Other assets	630,600
Current liabilities	158,920
Other liabilities	200,000
Owners' equity	558,480

A review of account balances reveals the following data.

(a) An analysis of current assets discloses the following:

Cash	$ 51,000
Investment securities—trading	40,000
Accounts receivable	68,300
Inventories, including advertising supplies of $3,500	127,500
	$286,800

(b) Other assets include the following:

Property, plant, and equipment:	
Depreciated book value (cost, $775,000)	$554,500
Deposit with a supplier for merchandise ordered for August delivery	10,700
Goodwill recorded on the books to cancel losses incurred by the company in prior years	65,400
	$630,600

(c) Current liabilities include the following:

Payroll payable		$ 4,050
Taxes payable		8,870
Rent payable		7,700
Accounts payable		
Total owed to suppliers on account	$111,300	
Less: 6-month note received from a supplier who purchased some used equipment on June 29, 2013	5,000	106,300
Notes payable		32,000
		$158,920

(d) Other liabilities include the following:

10% mortgage on property, plant, and equipment, payable in semiannual installments of $20,000 through June 30, 2018	$200,000

(e) Owners' equity includes the following:

Preferred stock: 15,000 shares outstanding ($20 par value)	$300,000
Common stock: 175,000 shares at $1 stated value	175,000
Additional paid-in capital	83,480
	$558,480

(f) Common shares were originally issued for $495,000, but the losses of the company for the past years were charged against additional paid-in capital.

Instructions: Using the account balances and related data, prepare a corrected balance sheet showing individual asset, liability, and owners' equity balances properly classified.

Problem 3-44
LO1

Corrected Balance Sheet

The following balance sheet is submitted to you for inspection and review.

Appalachian Freight Company
Balance Sheet
December 31, 2013

Assets	
Cash	$ 45,050
Accounts receivable	112,500
Inventories	204,000
Prepaid insurance	8,800
Property, plant, and equipment	376,800
Total assets	$747,150
Liabilities and Owners' Equity	
Miscellaneous liabilities	$ 3,600
Loan payable	76,200
Accounts payable	75,250
Capital stock	134,000
Paid-in capital	458,100
Total liabilities and owners' equity	$747,150

In the course of the review, you find the following data:

(a) The possibility of uncollectible accounts on accounts receivable has not been considered. It is estimated that uncollectible accounts will total $4,800.

(b) The amount of $45,000 representing the cost of a large-scale newspaper advertising campaign completed in 2013 has been added to the inventories because it is believed that this campaign will benefit sales of 2014. It is also found that inventories include merchandise of $16,250 received on December 31 that has not yet been recorded as a purchase.

(c) The books show that property, plant, and equipment have a cost of $556,800 with depreciation of $180,000 recognized in prior years. However, these balances include fully depreciated equipment of $85,000 that has been scrapped and is no longer on hand.

(d) Miscellaneous liabilities of $3,600 represent salaries payable of $9,500, less noncurrent advances of $5,900 made to company officials.

(e) Loan payable represents a loan from the bank that is payable in regular quarterly installments of $6,250.

(f) Tax liabilities not shown are estimated at $18,250.

(g) Deferred income tax liability arising from temporary differences totals $44,550. This liability was not included in the balance sheet.
(h) Capital stock consists of 6,250 shares of preferred 6% stock, par $20, and 9,000 shares of common stock, stated value $1.
(i) Capital stock had been issued for a total consideration of $283,600; the amount received in excess of the par and stated values of the stock has been reported as paid-in capital. Net income and dividends were recorded in Paid-In Capital.

Instructions: Prepare a corrected balance sheet with accounts properly classified.

Problem 3-45
LO1

Corrected Balance Sheet

The accountant for Delicious Bakery prepares the following condensed balance sheet.

Delicious Bakery
Condensed Balance Sheet
December 31, 2013

Current assets	$53,415
Less: Current liabilities	29,000
Working capital	$24,415
Add: Other assets	75,120
	$99,535
Less: Other liabilities	3,600
Investment in business	$95,935

A review of the account balances disclosed the following data.

(a) An analysis of the current asset grouping revealed the following:

Cash	$10,600
Accounts receivable (fully collectible)	12,500
Notes receivable (notes of customer who has been declared bankrupt and is unable to pay anything on the obligations)	1,000
Investment securities—trading, at cost (market value $2,575)	4,250
Inventory	20,965
Cash surrender value of insurance on officers' lives	4,100
Total current assets	$53,415

The inventory account was found to include supplies costing $425, a delivery truck acquired at the end of 2013 at a cost of $2,100, and fixtures at a depreciated value of $10,400. The fixtures had been acquired in 2005 at a cost of $12,500.

(b) The total for other assets was determined as follows.

Land and buildings at cost of acquisition, July 1, 2011	$92,000
Less balance due on mortgage, $16,000, and accrued interest on mortgage, $880 (mortgage is payable in annual installments of $4,000 on July 1 of each year together with interest for the year at that time at 11%)	16,880
Total other assets	$75,120

It was estimated that the land at the time of the purchase was worth $30,000. Buildings as of December 31, 2013, were estimated to have a remaining life of 17½ years.

(c) Current liabilities represented balances that were payable to trade creditors.
(d) Other liabilities consisted of withholding, payroll, real estate, and other taxes payable to the federal, state, and local governments. However, no recognition was given the accrued salaries, utilities, and other miscellaneous items totaling $350.

(e) The company was originally organized in 2006 when 5,000 shares of no-par stock with a stated value of $5 per share were issued in exchange for business assets that were recognized on the books at their fair market value of $55,000.

Instructions: Prepare a corrected balance sheet with the items properly classified.

Problem 3-46

LO1

Classified Balance Sheet

Blake Matthews incorporated his paper manufacturing operations on January 1, 2013, by issuing 5,000 shares of $1 par common stock to himself. The following balance sheet for the new corporation was prepared.

Looseleaf Corporation
Balance Sheet
January 1, 2013

Cash	$ 15,000
Accounts receivable	55,000
Inventory	105,000
Equipment	110,000
Total	$285,000
Accounts payable—suppliers	$ 85,000
Capital stock, $1 par	5,000
Additional paid-in capital	195,000
Total	$285,000

During 2013, Looseleaf Corporation engaged in the following transactions.

(a) Looseleaf Corporation produced paper costing $395,000. Paper costs consisted of the following: $307,000, raw materials purchased; $48,000, labor; and $40,000, overhead. Looseleaf Corporation paid the $85,000 owed to suppliers as of January 1 and $210,000 of the $307,000 of raw materials purchased during the year. All labor, except for $6,000, and recorded overhead were paid in cash during the year. Other operating expenses of $8,500 were incurred and paid in 2013.

(b) Paper costing $320,000 was sold during 2013 for $390,000. All sales were made on credit, and collections on receivables were $350,000.

(c) Looseleaf Corporation purchased machinery (fair market value = $245,000) by trading in old equipment costing $140,000 and paying $105,000 in cash. There is no accumulated depreciation on the old equipment as it was revalued when the new corporation was formed.

(d) Looseleaf Corporation issued an additional 15,000 shares of common stock for $10 per share and declared a dividend of $1.75 per share to all stockholders of record as of December 31, 2013, payable on January 15, 2014.

(e) Depreciation expense for 2013 was $45,000. The allowance for bad debts after year-end adjustments is $4,000.

Instructions: Prepare a properly classified balance sheet for Looseleaf Corporation as of December 31, 2013.

Problem 3-47

LO4

Sample CPA Exam Questions

1. Which of the following is the true purpose of information presented in notes to the financial statements?

   (a) To provide disclosures required by generally accepted accounting principles.
   (b) To correct improper presentation in the financial statements.
   (c) To provide recognition of amounts not included in the totals of the financial statements.
   (d) To present management's responses to auditor comments.

2. Which of the following information should be included in Melay, Inc.'s 2013 summary of significant accounting policies?

   (a) Property, plant, and equipment is recorded at cost with depreciation computed principally by the straight-line method.
   (b) During 2013, the Delay Segment was sold.
   (c) Business segment 2013 sales are Alay, $1M; Belay, $2M; and Celay, $3M.
   (d) Future common share dividends are expected to approximate 60% of earnings.

CASES

Discussion Case 3-48

The Ten Largest Companies in the United States

Forbes annually provides a list of the most valuable companies in the world. The top 10 most valuable companies in the United States, from the 2010 Forbes 2000, follow.

(In billions of U.S. dollars)	Net Income ($bil)	Assets ($bil)	Market Value ($bil)
ExxonMobil	19.28	233.32	308.77
Microsoft	16.26	82.10	254.52
Wal-Mart Stores	14.34	170.71	205.37
Berkshire Hathaway	8.06	297.12	190.86
Apple	9.36	53.93	189.51
Procter & Gamble	13.05	135.29	184.47
Johnson & Johnson	12.27	94.68	174.90
General Electric	11.03	781.82	169.65
Google	6.52	40.50	169.38
Bank of America	6.28	2,223.30	167.63

As an analyst for a securities broker, you are asked the following questions concerning some of the figures.

1. **Microsoft** has total assets of $82 billion but a stock market value of $255 billion. How can a company be worth more than its total assets?
2. Compute for each company the ratio of total assets to total market value. What factors must the market be considering in valuing these companies that are not captured on the companies' balance sheets?
3. The price-earnings ratio, often called the *P/E ratio*, is defined as market price per share divided by earnings per share. Alternatively, the P/E ratio can be computed as total market value divided by net income. Compute the P/E ratios for the preceding companies. What factors do you think influence P/E ratios?

Discussion Case 3-49

Which Company Is Which?

Following are summaries of the balance sheets of five companies. The amounts are all stated as a percentage of total assets. The five companies are

- **BankAmerica**, a large bank
- **Kelly Services**, a firm that provides temporary employees
- **Yahoo!**, an Internet company
- **McDonald's**, a fast-food company
- **Consolidated Edison**, a utility serving New York City

	A	B	C	D	E
Receivables	59.1	4.0	4.0	62.9	3.1
Inventories	0.0	1.9	0.0	0.0	0.4
Other current assets	20.6	1.8	71.1	23.8	3.2
Land, buildings, and equipment	11.7	79.3	2.4	1.5	81.1
Other long-term assets	8.6	13.1	22.4	11.8	12.3
Short-term payables	42.1	6.6	12.9	26.8	8.5
Other current liabilities	0.0	1.3	0.0	57.8	4.1
Long-term liabilities	0.0	48.4	0.9	8.0	39.5
Equity	57.9	43.6	86.2	7.4	47.8

Match each balance sheet summary (A–E) with the appropriate company. Justify your choices.

Discussion Case 3-50

We've Got You Now!

The Piedmont Computer Company has brought legal action against ATC Corporation for alleged monopolistic practices in the development of software. The claim has been pending for two years, with both sides accumulating evidence to support their positions. The case is now ready for trial. ATC Corporation has offered to settle out of court for $500,000, but Piedmont is asking for $5,000,000.

If financial statements must be issued prior to the court action, how should ATC reflect this contingent claim?

Discussion Case 3-51

How Can We Live with Debt Covenant Requirements?

Bohr Company has a credit agreement with a syndicate of banks. In order to impose some limitations on Bohr's financial riskiness, the credit agreement requires Bohr to maintain a current ratio of at least 1.4 and a debt ratio of 0.55 or less.

The following summary data reflect a projection of Bohr's balance sheet for the coming year-end.

Current assets	$1,200,000
Long-term assets	1,800,000
Current liabilities	900,000
Long-term liabilities	800,000
Equity	1,300,000

The following information has also been prepared.

(a) If Bohr were to use FIFO instead of LIFO for inventory valuation, ending inventory would increase by $50,000.

(b) The amounts listed for long-term assets and liabilities include the anticipated purchase (and associated mortgage payable) of a building costing $100,000, or Bohr can lease the building instead. The lease would qualify for treatment as an operating lease.

(c) Projected amounts include a planned declaration of cash dividends totaling $40,000 to be paid next year. Bohr has consistently paid dividends of equivalent amounts.

As a consultant to Bohr, you are asked to respond to the following two questions.

1. What steps can Bohr take to avoid violating the current ratio constraint?
2. What steps can Bohr take to avoid violating the debt ratio constraint? Of the steps that you propose, which ones do you think the banks had in mind when they imposed the loan covenants? If you had assisted the banks in drawing up the loan covenants, how would you have written them differently to avoid unintended consequences?

Discussion Case 3-52

Are Current Values Necessary for Valuing Investment Assets?

First Federal Finance Co. has a large investment securities portfolio. In the "old days," First Federal was allowed to value these securities at the lower of cost or market. U.S. GAAP now requires current market valuation on the balance sheet for most securities. As a banker, you do not consider current value reporting to be necessary. Indeed, you feel it unfairly harms your reported performance.

As a banker, why would current value accounting be threatening to you? How would you respond to these concerns if you were a member of the FASB?

Discussion Case 3-53

What Should We Tell the Stockholders?

Technology Unlimited, Inc., uses a fiscal year ending June 30. The auditors completed their review of the 2013 financial statements on September 8, 2013. They discovered the following subsequent events between June 30 and September 8.

(a) Technology split its common stock 2 for 1 on August 15. Prior to the split, Technology had outstanding 100,000 shares of $1 par common stock.

(b) A major customer, Diatride Company, declared bankruptcy on August 1. The customer owed Technology $75,000 on June 30. No payment had been received as of September 8. It is estimated that creditors will receive only 15% of outstanding claims.

(c) Technology completed negotiations to purchase Liston Development Labs on July 18. The purchase price was $525,000 cash and a 4-year, $250,000, 10% note.

(d) A $750,000 lawsuit against Technology was filed on August 15. It is too early to measure the loss potential.

(e) A general decline in stock market values for technology stocks occurred during the first week of September. Technology Unlimited's market value per share dropped from $42.50 to $28.00 in this week.

The auditors have requested that you prepare the subsequent event note that should accompany the financial statements for the year ending June 30, 2013. Only those events that require disclosure should be included in your note. Justify the exclusion of any events from your note.

Discussion Case 3-54

What Does this British Balance Sheet Mean?

Jonathan Atwood, a student from England, shows you the following balance sheet from his father's British company. Jonathan knows that you are studying accounting and asks you to look at the statement. You immediately recognize some differences between this statement and the ones you have been studying in your textbook.

		Group 31 December		Company 31 December	
		2013	2012	2013	2012
	NOTES	£m	£m	£m	£m
Fixed Assets					
Intangibles	13	304.0	307.4	—	—
Tangible assets	14	978.8	822.5	16.8	16.2
Investments	15	16.7	25.2	938.9	679.3
		1,299.5	1,155.1	955.7	695.5
Current Assets					
Stock	16	328.2	334.8	—	—
Debtors	17	554.1	548.2	113.4	210.8
Investments—short-term loans and deposits		118.0	33.3	5.1	23.5
Cash at bank and in hand		62.6	57.4	—	—
		1,062.9	973.7	118.5	234.3

		Group		Company	
		31 December		31 December	
		2013	2012	2013	2012
	NOTES	£m	£m	£m	£m
Creditors: amounts falling due within one year					
Borrowings	18	(136.3)	(133.7)	(175.0)	(74.6)
Other	19	(825.9)	(809.2)	(98.4)	(234.7)
Net current assets (liabilities)		100.7	30.8	(154.9)	(75.0)
Total assets less current liabilities		1,400.2	1,185.9	800.8	620.5
Other Liabilities					
Creditors: amounts falling due after more than one year					
Borrowings	18	(407.9)	(381.4)	(54.2)	(80.4)
Other	19	(12.0)	(8.5)	(26.4)	(42.1)
Provisions for liabilities and charges	20	(96.4)	(115.5)	0.5	1.2
		(516.3)	(505.4)	(80.1)	(121.3)
		883.9	680.5	720.7	499.2
Capital and Reserves					
Called-up share capital	21	174.7	173.6	174.7	173.6
Share premium account	22	381.6	217.4	381.6	217.4
Revaluation reserve	22	95.8	36.7	2.4	1.1
Profit and loss account	22	115.8	167.6	162.0	107.1
		767.9	595.3	720.7	499.2
Minority interests		116.0	85.2	—	—
		883.9	680.5	720.7	499.2

1. Identify the differences that exist between this British statement and those prepared using the standards and conventions of the United States.
2. Evaluate the differences, identifying strengths and weaknesses of each nation's approach.

Discussion Case 3-55

Why Is Our Book-to-Market Ratio So High?

Aiga Company is a leading manufacturer of household plumbing materials. Aiga does not make the high-profile faucets and fixtures; instead, it makes the pipes and other connections that are usually out of sight under kitchen and bathroom sinks. You are Aiga Company's chief financial officer. You are scheduled to meet with an irate group of stockholders. These stockholders read a recent business press article that explained that the average book-to-market ratio for the 10 most valuable companies in the United States is below 0.10. The article then claimed that companies with book-to-market ratios above 0.50 are probably run by mediocre managers who are unable to inspire market confidence in their companies. Aiga has a book-to-market ratio of 0.65. What will you say to the irate stockholders?

Case 3-56

Deciphering Financial Statements (The Walt Disney Company)

Locate the 2009 financial statements for **The Walt Disney Company** on the Internet.

1. Compute a current ratio for Disney as of October 3, 2009. How does this current ratio compare with the prior year's current ratio?
2. Compute Disney's asset turnover for 2009. Was the company more or less efficient in 2009 compared to 2008?
3. What method of inventory valuation does Disney use?
4. What method of depreciation does Disney use?

5. What material commitments and contingencies does Disney report in the notes to its 2009 financial statements?
6. What percentage of Disney's 2009 operating income was generated in the "United States and Canada" geographic segment?

Case 3-57 **Deciphering Financial Statements (Boston Celtics)**

The **Boston Celtics** are the most successful team in professional basketball history. Teams led by Bill Russell, Larry Bird, and Kevin Garnett have won a total of 17 NBA championships. The Celtics are also an unusual professional sports team because ownership shares in the Celtics were at one time publicly traded (on the New York Stock Exchange as "Boston Celtics Limited Partnership"). As such, the Celtics were required to file financial statements with the SEC each quarter. The June 30, 2001, balance sheet of "Celtics Basketball Holdings" follows.

Boston Celtics Limited Partnership
and Subsidiaries
Consolidated Balance Sheets

	June 30, 2001	June 30, 2000
ASSETS		
CURRENT ASSETS		
Cash and cash equivalents	$12,572,324	$14,941,632
Accounts receivable	3,250,212	5,799,898
Prepaid expenses and other current assets	601,184	636,551
TOTAL CURRENT ASSETS	16,423,720	21,378,081
PROPERTY AND EQUIPMENT, net	1,200,556	1,144,785
NATIONAL BASKETBALL ASSOCIATION FRANCHISE, net of amortization of $2,776,318 in 2001 and $2,622,078 in 2000	3,393,263	3,547,503
INVESTMENT IN NBA MEDIA VENTURES, LLC	5,018,420	4,263,420
OTHER ASSETS	125,060	776,815
	$26,161,019	$31,110,604
LIABILITIES AND PARTNERS' CAPITAL (DEFICIT)		
CURRENT LIABILITIES		
Accounts payable and accrued expenses	$23,506,664	$24,478,303
Deferred game revenues	6,498,726	9,204,607
Deferred compensation—current portion	1,226,316	1,278,410
TOTAL CURRENT LIABILITIES	31,231,706	34,961,320
NOTES PAYABLE TO BANK	50,000,000	50,000,000
DEFERRED COMPENSATION—noncurrent portion	5,182,821	6,369,646
OTHER NONCURRENT LIABILITIES		708,000
PARTNERS' CAPITAL (DEFICIT)		
Celtics Basketball Holdings, LP—General Partner	1,015	1,008
Celtics Pride GP—Limited Partner	(29,111,174)	(29,437,209)
Castle Creek Partners, LP—Limited Partner	(31,144,430)	(31,493,235)
	(60,254,589)	(60,929,436)
Celtics Basketball, LP—General Partner	1,081	1,074
TOTAL PARTNERS' CAPITAL (DEFICIT)	(60,253,508)	(60,928,362)
	$26,161,019	$31,110,604

1. From June 2000 to June 2001, the Celtics' total assets decreased by approximately $5 million. What assets accounted for most of the decrease? Of course, total liabilities and equity also decreased by $5 million; what liability or equity items accounted for most of the decrease?
2. As of June 30, 2001, the Celtics have their NBA franchise recorded, net of amortization, at approximately $3.393 million. What original value was recorded for the NBA franchise? Over how many years is the NBA franchise being amortized? In what year was the NBA franchise originally recorded?
3. Partners' capital as of June 30, 2001, is about negative $60.3 million. How can partners' capital become negative?
4. The Celtics reported a liability for deferred compensation totaling $6,409,137 ($1,226,316 + $5,182,821). However, the notes to the financial statements revealed the following: "Celtics Basketball has employment agreements with officers, coaches, and players of the Boston Celtics basketball team. Certain of the contracts provide for guaranteed payments which must be paid even if the employee is injured or terminated." The Celtics then disclose that the total amount of these guaranteed payments is $254.585 million. Explain the vast difference between the $6.4 million deferred compensation liability reported in the balance sheet and the $254.585 million compensation obligation disclosed in the notes.

Case 3-58 **Deciphering Financial Statements (Safeway, Kroger, and Supervalu)**

Safeway operates 1,775 supermarkets in the United States and Canada. In the United States, Safeway is located principally in the Western, Southwestern, Rocky Mountain, Midwestern, and Mid-Atlantic regions. **Kroger** operates 2,468 stores in Northeastern, Western, Midwestern, and Southern states. **Supervalu** operates 2,349 stores throughout the United States. Selected financial statement information for 2009 for these three companies follows (in millions of U.S. dollars).

	Kroger	Safeway	Supervalu
Total Current Assets	$ 7,450.00	$ 3,825.30	$ 3,711.00
Total Assets	$23,093.00	$14,963.60	$16,436.00
Inventory	$ 4,902.00	$ 2,508.90	$ 2,342.00
Total Current Liabilities	$ 7,714.00	$ 4,237.80	$ 4,167.00
Total Liabilities	$18,187.00	$10,017.20	$13,549.00
Property, Plant, and equipment	$13,929.00	$10,282.70	$ 7,026.00
Cost of goods sold	$58,958.00	$27,986.00	$31,444.00
Net income	$ 70.00	$ (1,097.50)	$ 393.00
Sales	$76,733.00	$40,850.70	$40,597.00

1. For each of the three companies, compute the following ratios:
   (a) Current ratio
   (b) Debt ratio
   (c) Asset turnover
   (d) Return on equity
2. Which company uses its inventory most efficiently? Which company uses its property, plant, and equipment most efficiently?
3. What dangers might there be in making ratio comparisons without viewing the financial statement notes for the individual companies?

Case 3-59 **Deciphering Financial Statements (Diageo)**

Diageo is a United Kingdom (UK) consumer products firm, best known in the United States for the following brand names: Smirnoff, Johnnie Walker, J&B, Gordon's, Seagram's, and Guinness. Diageo's 2009 consolidated balance sheet follows.

Diageo
Consolidated Balance Sheet
30 June 2009
(In millions of pounds)

Non-current assets		
Intangible assets	6,215	
Property, plant and equipment	2,268	
Biological assets	37	
Investments in associates	2,045	
Other investments	231	
Other receivables	18	
Other financial assets	364	
Deferred tax assets	672	
Post employment benefit assets	41	
		11,891
Current assets		
Inventories	3,162	
Trade and other receivables	2,031	
Other financial assets	98	
Cash and cash equivalents	914	
		6,205
Total assets		18,096
Current liabilities		
Borrowings and bank overdrafts	(890)	
Other financial liabilities	(220)	
Trade and other payables	(2,173)	
Corporate tax payable	(532)	
Provisions	(172)	
		(3,987)
Non-current liabilities		
Borrowings	(7,685)	
Other financial liabilities	(99)	
Other payables	(30)	
Provisions	(314)	
Deferred tax liabilities	(621)	
Post employment benefit liabilities	(1,424)	
		(10,173)
Total liabilities		(14,160)
Net assets		3,936
Equity		
Called up share capital	797	
Share premium	1,342	
Other reserves	3,282	
Retained deficit	(2,200)	
Equity attributable to equity shareholders of the parent company		3,221
Minority interests		715
Total equity		3,936

Re-create Diageo's June 30, 2009, balance sheet using U.S. terminology and a standard U.S. format. (*Note*: The other reserves item has no counterpart in the United States. For purposes of this exercise, add the other reserves to "called up share capital.")

Case 3-60 **Deciphering Financial Statements (Consolidated Edison)**

Refer to the 2009 balance sheet for **Consolidated Edison**, reproduced in Exhibit 3-6 on pages 3-19–3-20.

1. Compute the following financial ratios for Consolidated Edison for 2008:
   (a) Debt ratio (total liabilities/total assets)
   (b) Current ratio (current assets/current liabilities)
   (c) Long-term debt as a percentage of total capitalization
   (d) Long-term debt as a percentage of "net plant"
2. For Consolidated Edison, which of the four ratios computed in part (1) is the most informative? The least informative? Explain.

Case 3-61 **Writing Assignment (Unrecorded assets should stay unrecorded)**

You are a member of the most popular student club on campus, the Accounting Antidefamation Organization. Recently, the field of accounting was savagely attacked in an article written by a militant economics student group and published in the student newspaper. The article charged that the balance sheet is stupid, outdated, and useless and cited as an example the accounting practice of not recognizing many intangible assets. As a specific illustration, the article claimed that the name recognition, reputation, and goodwill of the **Coca-Cola** trademark are worth over $67 billion, but these assets are not recorded in Coca-Cola's balance sheet.

You have been asked by the editor of the student newspaper to respond in writing to this vicious assault by the economics students. Don't cave in to the pressure—argue persuasively why these unrecorded assets should stay unrecorded.

Case 3-62 **Ethical Dilemma (Dodging a loan covenant violation)**

You are on the accounting staff of Chisos Manufacturing Company. Chisos has a $100 million loan with Rio Grande National Bank. One of the covenants associated with the loan is that Chisos must maintain a current ratio greater than 1.5.

As of January 20, 2013, preliminary financial statement numbers for the year ended December 31, 2012, have been compiled. It looks like Chisos will violate the current ratio loan covenant. Violation could be very costly in two ways. First, Rio Grande National Bank has historically raised the interest rate one-half of a point on loans with covenant violations. Second, a violation will increase the perceived riskiness of Chisos and make future borrowing more costly.

The 2012 financial statement numbers are just preliminary, and the senior accounting staff of Chisos has discussed the following two options to avoid violation:

1. Reclassify "long-term investment property" as "short-term property held for sale." Doing this would require a statement from management that the intention is to sell the property within one year. Actually, Chisos intends to hold the property for several more years, and the property classification would be changed back to long-term next year when the threat of covenant violation has hopefully disappeared.
2. Reclassify certain short-term loans as long-term on the basis that Chisos will refinance the loans. Technically, this is true. However, Chisos has no formal refinancing commitment and will not have one until some time in June.

You have been chosen to present the findings of the accounting staff to the board of directors. What points will you emphasize in your presentation?

Case 3-63 **Cumulative Spreadsheet Analysis**

This spreadsheet assignment is a continuation of the spreadsheet assignment given in Chapter 2. If you completed that assignment, you have a head start on this one.

1. Refer back to the financial statement numbers for Skywalker Enterprises for 2013 (given in part 1 of the Cumulative Spreadsheet Analysis assignment in Chapter 2). Revise those financial statements by making the following changes:

   - Change the paid-in capital amount from $150 to $200.
   - In the Equity section of the balance sheet, insert a treasury stock amount of negative $60.

   The remaining amount of the "other equity" mentioned in Chapter 2 is accumulated other comprehensive income.

   - Increase amount of long-term debt from $621 to $671.
   - In the Asset section of the balance sheet, insert an intangible asset amount of $100.

   Using the revised balance sheet and income statement, create spreadsheet cell formulas to compute and display values for the following ratios.

   - Current ratio
   - Debt ratio
   - Asset turnover
   - Return on assets
   - Return on equity

2. Determine the impact of each of the following transactions on the ratio values computed in Question 1. Treat each transaction independently; that is, before determining the impact of each new transaction you should reset the financial statement values to their original amounts. The transactions that follow are assumed to occur on December 31, 2013.

   (a) Collected $60 cash from customer receivables.
   (b) Purchased $90 in inventory on account.
   (c) Purchased $300 in property, plant, and equipment. The entire amount of the purchase was financed with a mortgage. Principal repayment for the mortgage is due in 10 years.
   (d) Purchased $300 in property, plant, and equipment. The entire amount of the purchase was financed with new stockholder investments.
   (e) Borrowed $60 with a short-term loan payable. The $60 was paid out as a dividend to stockholders.
   (f) Received $60 as an investment from stockholders. The $60 was paid out as a dividend to stockholders.
   (g) The long-term debt amount of $671 includes $90 in short-term loans payable that Skywalker hopes to refinance. Skywalker has no explicit agreement with the bank to refinance the loan and does not expect to finalize the refinancing until the last quarter of 2014.
   (h) During the first week in January 2014, Skywalker learned that, of the $459 reported as inventory as of December 31, 2013, $45 is completely obsolete and worthless. The inventory had become obsolete during the last quarter of 2013, but the facts had not been verified until early 2014.

CHAPTER 4 The Income Statement

LEARNING OBJECTIVES

1. Define the concept of income.
2. Explain why an income measure is important.
3. Explain how income is measured, including the revenue recognition and expense-matching concepts.
4. Understand the format of an income statement.
5. Describe the specific components of an income statement.
6. Compute comprehensive income and prepare a statement of stockholders' equity.
7. Construct simple forecasts of income for future periods.

Eliza Grace Symonds was an accomplished pianist, a feat additionally notable because she was deaf. Eliza met and married Melville Bell, who was the son of a famous elocutionist, Alexander Graham Bell. Melville's career followed that of his father. Eliza and Melville had three sons; the second son was named Alexander Graham Bell after his paternal grandfather. Young Alexander Graham Bell demonstrated an early interest in speech. In 1871, at the age of 24, Bell began teaching deaf children to speak at the Boston School for Deaf Mutes. Bell's approach was somewhat unorthodox because, at the time, it was common practice to teach deaf mutes only to sign or to simply institutionalize them. Mabel Hubbard, who would become Bell's wife, was one of his students.

Bell's interest in speech caused him to try to develop what he called the "harmonic telegraph." Samuel Morse completed his first telegraph line in 1843, allowing communication using Morse code between two points, and Bell was interested in transmitting speech in a similar way.

> **FYI**
> Long after inventing the telephone, Bell continued his work with the deaf. In gratitude for his work, Helen Keller dedicated her autobiography to him.

At an electrical machine shop, Bell met

Comstock Images/Jupiter Images

Thomas Watson. At the time, Watson was a repair mechanic and model maker who was regularly assigned to work with inventors. As Watson learned more of Bell's "harmonic telegraph," the two formed a partnership. In 1876, Bell, while working on their invention, spilled some battery acid and uttered those now-famous words, "Mr. Watson, come here. I want you!" On March 7, 1876, Bell was issued patent number 174,465, covering "the method of, and apparatus for, transmitting vocal or other sounds telegraphically . . . by causing electrical undulations, similar in form to the vibrations of the air accompanying the said vocal or other sounds."

The **Bell Telephone Company** immediately presented immense competition to the **Western Union Telegraph Company**, which was developing its own telephone technology. Western Union hired Thomas Edison to develop a competing system, forcing the Bell Telephone Company to sue Western Union for patent infringement—and win. The Bell Telephone Company would be forced in subsequent years to defend its patent in more than 600 cases.

Alexander Graham Bell had little interest in the day-to-day operations of his company. Instead, he preferred studying science and nature. In 1888 he founded the National Geographic Society. Upon his death on August 2, 1922, in a tribute to their inventor, all the phones in the nation were silent for one minute.

The Bell Telephone Company was to become the **American Telephone and Telegraph Company (AT&T)** in 1899. AT&T first transmitted the human voice across the Atlantic Ocean in 1915, and in 1927, AT&T introduced commercial transatlantic phone service at a cost of $75 for five minutes. Numerous AT&T inventions followed, including the transistor (1947), the first microwave relay system (1950), the laser (1958), and the first communications satellite (1962).

AT&T functioned as a regulated monopoly until January 1, 1984, when after an 8-year legal battle with the U.S. federal government, AT&T agreed to get out of the local telephone service business by divesting itself of its regional Bell operating companies. On that day, AT&T shrunk from 1,009,000 employees to 373,000. In an interesting twist, one of the original seven regional Bell companies, **Southwestern Bell**, changed its name to **SBC Communications** and eventually bought three of the other regional companies and finally bought the original parent, AT&T, as well. The combination of these companies now uses the "AT&T" name. Exhibit 4-1 outlines the fate of the other regional Bells.

In recent years, all of this merger activity at AT&T has resulted in steady profits. For example, AT&T's 2009 financial statements reported the following income numbers (in millions):

	2009	2008	2007
Revenue	123,018	124,028	118,928
Operating income.	21,492	23,063	20,404
Income from continuing operations	12,843	13,128	12,147
Net income	12,843	13,128	12,147
Comprehensive income	15,184	(3,810)	16,885

In your parents' young adult years, they knew only one phone company—AT&T, or "Ma Bell" as it was sometimes called back then. These days, you have a confusing array of phone services, including AT&T, to choose from. And by the time your children enter college, AT&T might be just a historical curiosity.

EX 4-1 FATE OF THE PIECES FROM THE 1984 AT&T BREAKUP

1984 Breakup	Where Are They in 2010?
	Companies comprising "AT&T" in 2010:
original AT&T	Purchased by SBC Communications in 2005
Ameritech	Purchased by SBC Communications in 1999
Bell South	Purchased by new AT&T in 2006
Pacific Telesis	Purchased by SBC Communications in 1997
Southwestern Bell	Renamed SBC Communications
	Companies included in Verizon in 2010:
Nynex	Purchased by Bell Atlantic in 1997
Bell Atlantic	Merged with GTE to form Verizon in 2000
	Company included in Qwest in 2010:
U S West	Purchased by Qwest in 2000

QUESTIONS

1. By what percentage did AT&T's revenue increase from 2007 to 2009?
2. By what percentage did AT&T's net income increase from 2007 to 2009?
3. AT&T's comprehensive income was down substantially in 2008. What factors can cause a decrease in comprehensive income?

Answers to these questions can be found on page 4-41.

In this chapter, we focus on one of the primary financial statements, the income statement. By analyzing the various components of the income statement, you will understand how the performance of a business is reported to financial statement users and how reported performance can change over time as a company changes the nature of its operations. In addition, we will discuss the format of the income statement, its more common components, and ways in which income statements from around the world differ as to the information they contain and the presentation of that information.

Income: What It Is and What It Isn't

1 Define the concept of income.

WHY **Income provides the best accounting measure of a firm's economic performance.**

HOW **Income measures the amount that an entity could return to its investors and still leave the entity as well-off at the end of the period as at the beginning. The FASB has chosen to measure income using the financial capital maintenance concept.**

Individuals often confuse income with cash flows. Is income equal to the amount of cash generated from the successful operations of a business? No. For a variety of reasons, most of them related to accrual accounting, income and cash flows from operations are seldom the same number. Because both income and cash flows provide measures of a firm's performance, which provides the best measure? The FASB, in its conceptual framework, stated that "information about earnings and its components measured by accrual accounting generally provides a better indication of enterprise performance than information about current cash receipts and payments."[1] Information regarding cash flows is important. In fact, Chapter 5 focuses entirely on the statement of cash flows. Research supports the FASB's assertion, however, that the best indicator of a firm's performance is income.[2] So, an understanding of income, what it measures, and its components is essential in understanding and interpreting a firm's financial situation.

[1] *Statement of Financial Accounting Concepts No. 1*, "Objectives of Financial Reporting by Business Enterprises" (Stamford, CT: Financial Accounting Standards Board, 1984), par. 44.
[2] For example, see Gary C. Biddle, Robert M. Bowen, and James S. Wallace, "Does EVA® Beat Earnings? Evidence on Associations with Stock Returns and Firm Values," *Journal of Accounting and Economics*, December 1997, p. 301.

So, what is income? All of the varying ways to measure income share a common basic concept: Income is a return over and above the investment. One of the more widely accepted definitions of income states that it is the amount that an entity could return to its investors and still leave the entity as well-off at the end of the period as it was at the beginning.[3] What does it mean, however, to be "as well-off," and how can this be measured? Most measurements are based on some concept of capital or ownership maintenance. The FASB considered two concepts of capital maintenance in its conceptual framework: financial capital maintenance and physical capital maintenance.

Financial Capital Maintenance Concept of Income Determination

The financial capital maintenance concept assumes that a company has income "only if the dollar amount of an enterprise's net assets (assets – liabilities or, in other words, owners' equity) at the end of a period exceeds the dollar amount of net assets at the beginning of the period after excluding the effects of transactions with owners."[4] To illustrate, assume that Kreidler, Inc., had the following assets and liabilities at the beginning and at the end of a period.

	Beginning of Period	End of Period
Total assets	$510,000	$560,000
Total liabilities	430,000	390,000
Net assets (owners' equity)	$ 80,000	$170,000

If there were no investments by owners or distributions to owners during the period, income would be $90,000, the amount of the increase in net assets. Assume, however, that owners invested $40,000 in the business and received distributions (dividends) of $15,000. Income for the period would be $65,000, computed as follows:

Net assets, end of period	$170,000
Net assets, beginning of period	80,000
Change (increase) in net assets	$ 90,000
Deduct investment by owners	(40,000)
Add distributions (dividends) to owners	15,000
Income	$ 65,000

Physical Capital Maintenance Concept of Income Determination

Another way of defining capital maintenance is in terms of physical capital maintenance. Under this concept, income occurs "only if the physical productive capacity of the enterprise at the end of a period . . . exceeds the physical productive capacity at the beginning of the same period, also after excluding the effects of transactions with owners."[5] This concept requires that productive assets (inventories, buildings, and equipment) be valued at fair market values. Productive capital is maintained only if the current costs of these capital assets are maintained. Consider the beginning net asset value of $80,000 in the previous example. Now assume that, because of rising prices of buildings, inventory,

[3] Although many economists and accountants have adopted this view, a basic reference is J. R. Hicks' widely accepted book, *Value and Capital*, 2nd ed. (Oxford University Press, 1946).

[4] *Statement of Financial Accounting Concepts No. 5*, "Recognition and Measurement in Financial Statements of Business Enterprises" (Stamford, CT: Financial Accounting Standards Board, 1984), par. 47.

[5] Ibid.

equipment, and so forth, in order to maintain the same productive capacity the company would have had to have $100,000 in net asset value by the end of the year. If the ending net asset value were $170,000, as before, and new investments and dividends were as shown, income would be $45,000 rather than $65,000. The $20,000 difference would be the amount necessary to "maintain physical productive capacity" and would not be part of income.

The FASB considered carefully these two ways of viewing income, and it adopted the financial capital maintenance concept as part of its conceptual framework. The acceptance of the financial capital maintenance concept rescued accountants from the difficult task of trying to measure productive capacity. Measuring income using the concept of financial capital maintenance, however, still leaves the question of how to value the net asset balance. Many suggest that net assets should be measured at their unexpired historical cost values as is often done. Others believe that replacement values or disposal values should be used. Some would include as assets intangible resources, such as human resources, goodwill, and geographic location, that have been attained over time without specifically identified payments. Others believe that only resources that have been acquired in arm's-length exchange activities should be included.

STOP&THINK

It would seem that the physical capital maintenance concept would provide the best theoretical measure of "well-offness." However, use of the physical capital maintenance concept of measuring income involves many practical difficulties. Identify ONE of those practical difficulties from the list below.

a) Difficulty in estimating depreciation lives
b) Difficulty in implementing internal control procedures
c) Difficulty in providing cash flow information
d) Difficulty in obtaining fair market values of assets and liabilities

Likewise, controversy has developed over the recognition and measurement of liabilities. Should future claims against the entity for items such as pensions, warranties, and deferred income taxes be valued at their discounted values, at their future cash flow values, or eliminated completely from the financial statements until events clearly define the existence of a specific liability? The reported income under the financial maintenance concept varies widely depending on when and how the assets, liabilities, and changes in the valuation of assets and liabilities are measured. As it stands currently, a combination of historical costs, fair values, present values, and other valuation measures are used to measure a firm's "well-offness."

Why Is a Measure of Income Important?

2 **Explain why an income measure is important.**

WHY **Income measurement is important to business and economic decisions that result in the allocation of resources, which in turn contributes to the standard of living in society.**

HOW **Accrual accounting rules in general, and the financial accounting standards established by the FASB in particular, establish the rules of accounting income measurement in the United States. As such, these rules and standards have the power to impact the allocation of societal resources.**

The recognition, measurement, and reporting (display) of business income and its components are considered by many to be the most important tasks of accountants. The users of financial statements who must make decisions regarding their relationship with the company are almost always concerned with a measure of its success in using the resources committed to its operation. Has the activity been profitable? What is the trend of profitability? Is it increasingly profitable, or is there a downward trend? What is the most probable result for future years? Will the company be profitable enough to pay interest on its debt and dividends to its stockholders and still grow at a desired rate? These and other questions all relate to the basic question: What is income?

Information about the components of income is important and can be used to help predict future income and cash flows. Not only can this information be helpful to a specific user, but it is also of value to the economy. As discussed in Chapter 1, many groups utilize accounting information, and accountants play a key role in providing information that will assist in allocating scarce resources to the most efficient and effective organizations or groups.

In the United States, the FASB has specified that financial accounting information is designed with investors and creditors in mind, while at the same time recognizing that many other groups will find the resulting information useful as well. Of course, accrual-based financial accounting information is not suited for every possible use. For example, governments, both federal and state, rely heavily on income taxes as a source of their revenues. The income figure used for assessing taxes is based on laws passed by Congress and regulations applied by the IRS and various courts. The income determined for financial reporting, however, is determined by adherence to accounting standards (GAAP) developed by the accounting profession. Thus, the amount of income reported to creditors and investors may not be the same as the income reported for tax purposes. Many items are the same for both types of reporting, but there are some significant differences. Most of these differences relate to the specific purposes Congress has for taxing income. Governments use an income figure as a base to assess taxes, but they must use one that relates closely with the ability of the taxpayer to pay the computed tax. For example, accrual accounting requires companies to defer recognition of revenues that are received before they are earned. Income tax regulations, however, often require these unearned revenues to be reported as income as soon as they are received in cash.

As mentioned in previous chapters, the increasing globalization of business is providing the impetus for a movement toward a unified body of International Accounting Standards. However, because financial accounting information plays different roles in different countries, it is probably not reasonable to assume that one set of standards can fit the business, legal, and cultural settings of every country in the world. For example, countries can be separated, broadly speaking, into two groups: code law countries and common law countries.[6] In code law countries, such as Germany and Japan, accounting standards have historically been set by legal processes. In such an environment, financial accounting numbers serve a variety of functions, including the determination of the amount of income tax and cash dividends to be paid. In common law countries, such as the United States and the United Kingdom, accounting standards are set in response to market forces. In a common law setting, financial accounting numbers are used more for informational purposes, not for deciding how the economic pie gets split among taxes, dividends, wages, and so forth. Given the significantly different roles played by financial accounting numbers in code law and common law countries, it may be unreasonable to expect one set of standards to work worldwide.

[6] Ray Ball, S. P. Kothari, and Ashok Robin, "The Effect of International Institutional Factors on Properties of Accounting Earnings," *Journal of Accounting and Economics*, February 2000, p. 1.

Accounting standards also play a different role in developing economies as compared to developed economies. In China, for example, the rudimentary state of the auditing and legal infrastructure makes the application of judgment-based accounting standards extremely problematic.[7] In a developing economy, it may be more important for financial reporting to satisfactorily fulfill its essential bookkeeping function rather than attempt to provide sophisticated investment information relevant for only a small set of companies trying to attract foreign investment. The fundamental question is this: How are accounting standards designed for use by international financial analysts going to help a domestic Chinese company with no plans to seek foreign investment and with a desire only to improve the monitoring of managers and the allocation of resources?

This text focuses on principles of accounting that are the supporting foundation for financial accounting and reporting as practiced in the United States. Income for tax purposes will be discussed, but only as it is used to determine the income tax expense and other tax-related amounts reported in the financial statements. Differences between U.S. and foreign accounting practices will be discussed where appropriate throughout the text.

How Is Income Measured?

3 **Explain how income is measured, including the revenue recognition and expense-matching concepts.**

WHY **The recognition of revenue begins the process of computing income. Expenses are then matched with revenues when those revenues are recognized.**

HOW **Income is measured as the difference between resource inflows (revenues and gains) and outflows (expenses and losses) over a period of time. Revenues are recognized when (1) they are realized or realizable and (2) they have been earned through substantial completion of the activities involved in the earning process. Expenses are matched against revenues directly, in a systematic or rational manner, or are immediately recognized as a period expense.**

Comparing the net assets at two points in time, as was done previously in introducing the concept of financial capital maintenance, yields a single net income figure. However, this procedure discloses no detail concerning the components of income. To provide this detail, accountants have adopted a transaction approach to measuring income that stresses the direct computation of revenues and expenses. As long as the same measurement method is used, income will be the same under the transaction approach as with a single income computation.

The transaction approach, sometimes referred to as the *matching method*, focuses on business events that affect certain elements of financial statements, namely, revenues, expenses, gains, and losses. Income is measured as the difference between resource inflows (revenues and gains) and outflows (expenses and losses) over a period of time. Definitions for the four income elements are presented in Exhibit 4-2 as an aid to the following discussion.

As studying these definitions will indicate, by defining gains and losses in terms of changes in equity after providing for revenues, expenses, investments, and distributions to the owners, income determined by the transaction approach will be the same income as

[7] Bing Xiang, "Institutional Factors Influencing China's Accounting Reforms and Standards," *Accounting Horizons*, June 1998, p. 105.

EX 4-2 COMPONENT ELEMENTS OF INCOME

- **Revenues** are inflows or other enhancements of assets of an entity or settlements of its liabilities (or a combination of both) from delivering or producing goods, rendering services, or carrying out other activities that constitute the entity's ongoing major or central operations.
- **Expenses** are outflows or other "using up" of assets of an entity or incurrences of liabilities (or a combination of both) from delivering or producing goods, rendering services, or carrying out other activities that constitute the entity's ongoing major or central operations.
- **Gains** are increases in equity (net assets) from peripheral or incidental transactions of an entity and from all other transactions and other events and circumstances affecting the entity except those that result from revenues or investments by owners.
- **Losses** are decreases in equity (net assets) from peripheral or incidental transactions of an entity and from all other transactions and other events and circumstances affecting the entity except those that result from expenses or distributions to owners.

Source: *Statement of Financial Accounting Concepts No. 6*, "Elements of Financial Statements" (Stamford, CT: Financial Accounting Standards Board, December 1985), p. x.

that determined under financial capital maintenance. However, by identifying intermediate income components, the transaction approach provides detail to assist in predicting future cash flows.

The key problem in recognizing and measuring income using the transaction approach is deciding when an "inflow or other enhancements of assets" has occurred and how to measure the "outflows or other 'using up' of assets." The first issue is identified as the revenue recognition problem, and the second issue is identified as the expense recognition, or expense-matching, problem.

STOP&THINK

Take a close look at Exhibit 4-2. Why is it important to disclose separately revenues and gains?

a) To distinguish between the profits generated by a company's core business and the profits generated by secondary, or peripheral, activities.
b) To distinguish between profits generated through selling goods and profits generated through selling services.
c) To distinguish between profits generated through business activities and profits generated through investments by owners.
d) To distinguish between profits generated through the enhancement of assets and profits generated through the settlement of liabilities.

Revenue and Gain Recognition

The transaction approach requires a clear definition of when income elements should be recognized, or recorded, in the financial statements. Under the GAAP of accrual accounting, revenue recognition does not necessarily occur when cash is received. The FASB's conceptual framework identifies two factors that should be considered in deciding when revenues and gains should be recognized: realization and the earnings process. Revenues and gains are generally recognized when

1. they are realized or realizable, and
2. they have been earned through substantial completion of the activities involved in the earnings process.[8]

Put in simple terms, revenues are recognized when the company generating the revenue has provided the bulk of the goods or services it promised (substantial completion) for the

[8] *Statement of Financial Accounting Concepts No. 5*, par. 83.

customer and when the customer has provided payment or at least a valid promise of payment (realizable) to the company. That is, the company has lived up to its end of an agreement, and the customer has the intention of paying.

Emma Lee/Life File/Photodisc/Getty Images

Construction contracts are an example of revenue that is recognized as services are performed.

In order for revenues and gains to be realized, inventory or other assets must be exchanged for cash or claims to cash, such as accounts receivable. Revenues are realizable when assets held or assets received in an exchange are readily convertible to known amounts of cash or claims to cash. The earnings process criterion relates primarily to revenue recognition. Most gains result from transactions and events, such as the sale of land or a patent, that involve no earnings process. Thus, being realized, or realizable, is of more importance in recognizing gains.

Application of these two criteria to certain industries and companies within these industries has resulted in recognition of revenue at different points in the revenue-producing cycle. This cycle can be a lengthy one. For a manufacturing company, it begins with the development of proposals for a certain product by an individual or by the research and development department and extends through planning, production, sale, collection, and finally expiration of the warranty period. Consider, for example, the revenue-producing cycle for **Ford Motor Company**. Engineers develop plans and create models and prototypes. Actual production of vehicles then occurs, followed by delivery to dealers for sale to customers. All new vehicles are warranted against defect, in some cases for several years. All of these steps, which can take more than 10 years, are involved in generating sales revenue. If a failure occurs at any step, revenue may be seriously curtailed or even completely eliminated, yet there is only one aggregate revenue amount for the entire cycle, the selling price of the product.

> **FYI**
>
> Most firms specify their revenue recognition policies in the notes to the financial statements. For example, the notes to **Disney's** financial statements disclose the corporation's revenue recognition policies for movie tickets, video sales, movie licensing, TV advertising, Internet advertising, merchandise licensing, and theme park sales.

For a service company, the revenue-producing cycle begins with an agreement to provide a service and extends through the planning and performance of the service to the collection of the cash and final proof through the passage of time that the service has been adequately performed. As an example, consider the revenue-producing cycle of **PricewaterhouseCoopers (PwC)**, one of the large accounting firms. For a typical audit, much of the planning and preparation occurs before the actual on-site visit. The on-site visit is then followed by an accumulation of data and the preparation of an audit report. And with increasing legal actions being taken against professionals, such as doctors and accountants, one could argue that the revenue-producing cycle does not end until the possibility of legal claims for services performed is remote, a period that extends until years after the actual service is provided.

Although some accountants have argued for recognizing revenue on a partial basis over these extended production or service periods, the prevailing practice has been to select one point in the cycle that best meets the revenue recognition criteria. Both of these criteria are generally met at the point of sale, which is generally when goods are delivered or services are rendered to customers and payment or a promise of payment is received. Thus, revenue for automobiles sold to dealers by Ford Motor Company will be recognized when the cars are shipped to the dealers. Similarly, PwC will record its revenue from audit and tax work when the services have been performed and billed. In both examples, the earnings process is deemed to be substantially complete, and the cash or receivable from the customer meets the realization criterion. Although the "point-of-sale" practice is the most common revenue recognition point, there are notable variations to this general rule.[9] The following discussion is merely an introduction to the subtleties associated with revenue recognition. A more complete treatment is given in Chapter 8.

Earlier Recognition

1. If a market exists for a product so that its sale at an established price is practically ensured without significant selling effort, revenues may be recognized at the point of completed production. Examples of this situation may occur with certain precious metals and agricultural products that are sold in liquid and reliable markets at easily-determinable prices.[10] In these situations, revenue is recognized when the mining or production of the goods is complete because the earnings process is considered to be substantially complete and the existence of a virtually guaranteed purchaser provides evidence of realizability. An example of this method of revenue recognition is provided by a Canadian mining company, **Kinross Gold Corporation**; the appropriate note from Kinross' financial statements is reproduced in Exhibit 4-3. According to the note, Kinross recognizes revenue prior to the point of sale with the expected sales price to be received being recorded in a current asset account, Bullion Settlements. Note that Kinross accounts for Kubaka bullion differently from its other ores; revenue recognition for Kubaka bullion occurs when it is sold. The Kubaka gold is produced in eastern Russia. For international purposes under *IAS 41*, gains and losses from increases and decreases in the fair value of biological assets (such as cows) and agricultural produce (such as harvested wheat) are recognized when they occur, without waiting until the items are subsequently sold. Similar treatment

STOP&THINK

Why do you think Kinross waits to recognize revenue from the sale of Kubaka gold until the gold is actually sold?

a) Revenue from the sale of a product can never be recognized until after the product is actually sold.
b) Uncertainty surrounds the ultimate shipment and sale of gold produced in the remote regions of eastern Russia.
c) Revenue from the sale of a product can never be recognized until after the cash from the sale is actually collected.
d) GAAP forbids the recognition of any revenue at the time of production.

ifrs

[9] Accounting Principles Board, *Statement No. 4*, "Basic Concepts in Accounting Principles Underlying Financial Statements of Business Enterprises" par. 152, October 1970. In 1999, the SEC released *SAB No. 101*, which gives specific guidance about when to recognize revenue. *SAB 101* is discussed in Chapter 8. In 2002, the FASB began a "Revenue Recognition" project in which the earnings and realization criteria would be replaced with an emphasis on the creation and extinguishment of performance obligations. As of June 2010, a final revised revenue recognition standard was expected to be released in 2011.

[10] Companies in these industries may recognize revenue prior to the point of sale, but a survey of revenue recognition policies for companies in these industries reveals that the vast majority recognize revenue at the point of sale. For example, Kinross Gold, which is used as an illustration, changed its accounting policy for revenue recognition effective January 1, 2001, so that revenue is now recognized upon shipment and passage of title to the customer. SEC rules adopted in 1999 frown on the recognition of revenue before delivery to a customer has taken place. See Chapter 8 for more details.

EX 4-3 KINROSS GOLD CORPORATION REVENUE RECOGNITION NOTE DISCLOSURE

Gold and silver poured, in transit and at refineries, are recorded at net realizable value and included in bullion settlements and other accounts receivable, with the exception of Kubaka bullion. The estimated net realizable value of Kubaka bullion is included in inventory until it is sold.

is allowed, but not required, under U.S. GAAP (see FASB ASC Section 905-330-35 Agriculture—Inventory—Subsequent Measurement).

2. If a product or service is contracted for in advance, revenue may be recognized as production takes place or as services are performed, especially if the production or performance period extends over more than one fiscal year. The percentage-of-completion and proportional performance methods of accounting have been developed to recognize revenue at several points in the production or service cycle rather than waiting until the final delivery or performance takes place. This exception to the general point-of-sale rule is necessary if the qualitative characteristics of relevance and representational faithfulness are to be met. Construction contracts for buildings, roads, and dams, and contracts for scientific research are examples of situations in which these methods of revenue recognition occur. In all cases when this revenue recognition variation is employed, a firm, enforceable contract must exist to meet the realizability criterion, and an objective measure of progress toward completion must be attainable to measure the degree of completeness. As an example of this type of revenue recognition, **The Boeing Company** indicates in its notes (see Exhibit 4-4) that a portion of its revenues are recognized prior to the point of sale.

Later Recognition

3. If collectibility of assets received for products or services is considered doubtful, revenues and gains may be recognized as the cash is received. The installment sales and cost recovery methods of accounting have been developed to recognize revenue under these conditions. Sales of real estate, especially speculative recreational property, are often recorded using this variation of the general rule. In these cases, although the earnings process has been substantially completed, the questionable receivable fails to meet the realization criterion. For example, **Rent-A-Center** operates rent-to-own stores where consumers can obtain furniture, televisions, and other consumer goods on a rent-to-own basis. A big concern for Rent-A-Center is collecting the full amount of cash due under a rental contract.

EX 4-4 THE BOEING COMPANY NOTE ON REVENUE RECOGNITION

Sales related to fixed-price contracts are recognized as deliveries are made except for certain fixed-price contracts that require substantial performance over an extended period before deliveries begin, for which sales are recorded based on attainment of performance milestones.

Losses from natural disasters, such as earthquakes, are recognized immediately.

In fact, Rent-A-Center states that only 25% of its customers complete the full term of their agreement. With such a high likelihood of customers stopping payments on their rental agreements, Rent-A-Center recognizes revenue from a specific contract only gradually as the cash is actually collected. The general point-of-sale rule will be assumed for examples in this text unless specifically stated otherwise. Variations on this rule are discussed fully in Chapter 8.

Expense and Loss Recognition

In order to determine income, not only must criteria for revenue recognition be established, but also the principles for recognizing expenses and losses must be clearly defined. Some expenses are directly associated with revenues and can thus be recognized in the same period as the related revenues. Other expenditures are not recognized currently as expenses because they relate to future revenues and therefore are reported as assets. Still other expenses are not associated with specific revenues and are recognized in the time period when paid or incurred. Expense recognition, then, is divided into three categories: (1) direct matching, (2) systematic and rational allocation, and (3) immediate recognition.

Direct Matching Relating expenses to specific revenues is often referred to as the matching process. For example, the cost of goods sold is clearly a direct expense that can be "matched" with the revenues produced by the sale of goods and reported in the same time period as the revenues are recognized. Similarly, shipping costs and sales commissions usually relate directly to revenues.[11]

Direct expenses include not only those that have already been incurred but also include anticipated expenses related to revenues of the current period. After delivery of goods to customers, there are still costs of collection, bad debt losses from uncollectible receivables, and possible warranty costs for product deficiencies. These expenses are directly related to revenues and should be estimated and matched against recognized revenues for the period.

Systematic and Rational Allocation The second general expense recognition category involves assets that benefit more than one accounting period. The cost of assets such as buildings, equipment, patents, and prepaid insurance are spread across the periods of expected benefit in some systematic and rational way. Generally, it is difficult, if not impossible, to relate these expenses directly to specific revenues or to specific periods, but it is clear that they are necessary if the revenue is to be earned. Examples of expenses that are included in this category are depreciation and amortization.

[11] *Statement of Financial Accounting Concepts No. 6*, "Elements of Financial Statements" (Stamford, CT: Financial Accounting Standards Board, December 1985), par. 144.

Immediate Recognition Many expenses are not related to specific revenues but are incurred to obtain goods and services that indirectly help to generate revenues. Because these goods and services are used almost immediately, their costs are recognized as expenses in the period of acquisition. Examples include most administrative costs, such as office salaries, utilities, and general advertising and selling expenses.

Immediate recognition is also appropriate when future benefits are highly uncertain. For example, expenditures for research and development may provide significant future benefits, but these benefits are usually so uncertain that the costs are written off in the period in which they are incurred.

Most losses also fit in the immediate recognition category. Because they arise from peripheral or incidental transactions, they do not relate directly to revenues. Examples include losses from disposition of used equipment, losses from natural catastrophes such as earthquakes or tornadoes, and losses from disposition of investments.

Gains and Losses from Changes in Market Values

An exception to the transaction approach in the recognition of gains and losses arises when gains or losses are recognized in the wake of changes in market values. For example, some investment securities, called trading securities (as explained fully in Chapter 14), are purchased by a company with the express intent of making money on short-term price fluctuations. Accordingly, even in the absence of a transaction to sell the trading securities, a gain (if the price of the securities has increased) or a loss (if the price of the securities has decreased) is recognized. Similarly, when a long-term asset such as a building has decreased substantially in value, a loss is recognized even though the building has not been sold and no transaction has occurred. (These impairment losses are explained in Chapter 11.)

The transaction approach is deeply ingrained in accounting practice. A primary attraction of the transaction approach is its reliability—increases and decreases in asset values can be verified by observing the transaction prices. However, as with the case of the trading securities mentioned in the preceding paragraph, many important economic factors influence a company even in the absence of explicit transactions. Because of the information relevance of these changes in market values, more and more of these market value gains and losses are being recognized as part of income. As described more fully in Chapter 8, the FASB is currently working on a "revenue recognition" project that may go even further in stepping away from the transaction approach to instead embrace a focus on changes in values of assets and liabilities.

Form of the Income Statement

4 **Understand the format of an income statement.**

WHY Companies can use various formats when presenting income. The resulting income figure will be the same, regardless of the format used. However, the level of detail and the ability to compare will be influenced by the format chosen.

HOW The general format of an income statement is to subtract cost of goods sold and operating expenses from operating revenues to derive operating income. Gains and losses are then included to arrive at income from continuing operations. Irregular and extraordinary items are reported separately to determine net income.

All income statements prepared in accordance with GAAP report the same basic type of information and have certain common display features. Some sections of the income statement, especially irregular and extraordinary items, are specified by FASB pronouncements. Others have become standardized by wide usage.

Traditionally, the income from continuing operations category has been presented in multiple-step form. With the multiple-step form, the income statement is divided into separate sections (referred to as "intermediate components" in FASB *Concepts Statement No. 5*), and various subtotals are reported that reflect different levels of profitability. The income statement of **IBM**, shown in Exhibit 4-5, illustrates a multiple-step income statement. With the multiple-step form, the costs are partitioned so that intermediate components of income are presented. For example, IBM discloses gross profit, income before taxes, and net income in its income statements.

EX 4-5 INTERNATIONAL BUSINESS MACHINES INCOME STATEMENT

Consolidated Statement of Earnings (USD $) In Millions, except Share data	12 Months Ended Dec. 31, 2009	Dec. 31, 2008	Dec. 31, 2007
Revenue:			
Services	$55,128	$ 58,892	$54,057
Sales	38,300	42,156	42,202
Financing	2,331	2,582	2,526
Total revenue	95,758	103,630	98,786
Cost:			
Services	37,146	40,937	39,160
Sales	13,606	15,776	16,552
Financing	1,220	1,256	1,345
Total cost	51,973	57,969	57,057
Gross profit	43,785	45,661	41,729
Expense and other income:			
Selling, general and administrative	20,952	23,386	22,060
Research, development and engineering (Note Q)	5,820	6,337	6,153
Intellectual property and custom development income	(1,177)	(1,153)	(958)
Other (income) and expense	(351)	(298)	(626)
Interest expense (Notes K & L)	402	673	611
Total expense and other income	25,647	28,945	27,240
Income from continuing operations before income taxes	18,138	16,715	14,489
Provision for income taxes (Note P)	4,713	4,381	4,071
Income from continuing operations	13,425	12,334	10,418
Discontinued operations:			
Income/(loss) from discontinued operations, net of tax			0
Net income	$13,425	$ 12,334	$10,418
Earnings/(loss) per share of common stock, assuming dilution:			
Continuing operations (Note R)	$ 10.01	$ 8.89	$ 7.15
Discontinued operations (Note R)			$0
Total (Note R)	$ 10.01	$ 8.89	$ 7.15
Earnings/(loss) per share of common stock, basic:			
Continuing operations (Note R)	$ 10.12	$ 9.02	$ 7.27
Discontinued operations (Note R)			$0
Total (Note R)	$ 10.12	$ 9.02	$ 7.27
Weighted-average number of common shares outstanding:			
Assuming dilution	1,341,352,754	1,387,797,198	1,456,880,751
Basic	1,327,157,410	1,369,367,069	1,433,935,221

For discussion purposes, we will use the multiple-step income statement for Techtronics Corporation shown in Exhibit 4-6. This hypothetical income statement contains more categories and more detail than is usually found in actual published financial statements. It has become common practice to issue highly condensed statements, with details and supporting schedules provided in notes to the statements. The potential problem with this practice is that the condensed statements may not provide as much predictive and feedback value as statements that provide more detail about the components of income directly on the statement.

EX 4-6 TECHTRONICS CORPORATION INCOME STATEMENT

Techtronics Corporation
Income Statement
For the Year Ended December 31, 2013

Revenue:			
Sales		$800,000	
Less: Sales returns and allowances	$ 12,000		
Sales discounts	8,000	20,000	$780,000
Cost of goods sold:			
Beginning inventory		$125,000	
Net purchases	$630,000		
Freight-in	32,000	662,000	
Cost of goods available for sale		$787,000	
Less ending inventory		296,000	491,000
Gross profit			$289,000
Operating expenses:			
Selling expenses:			
Sales salaries	$ 46,000		
Advertising expense	27,000		
Miscellaneous selling expenses	12,000	$ 85,000	
General and administrative expenses:			
Officers' and office salaries	$ 44,000		
Taxes and insurance	26,500		
Depreciation and amortization expense	30,000		
Bad debt expense	8,600		
Miscellaneous general expense	9,200	118,300	203,300
Operating income			$ 85,700
Other revenues and gains:			
Interest revenue		$ 12,750	
Gain on sale of investment		37,000	49,750
Other expenses and losses:			
Interest expense		$ (18,250)	
Loss on sale of equipment		(5,250)	(23,500)
Income from continuing operations before income taxes			$111,950
Income taxes on continuing operations			33,585
Income from continuing operations			$ 78,365
Discontinued operations:			
Loss from operations of discontinued business component (including loss on disposal of $16,000)		$ (51,000)	
Income tax benefit		15,300	(35,700)
Extraordinary gain (net of income taxes of $5,370)			12,530
Net income			$ 55,195
Change in translation adjustment		$ (2,450)	
Increase in unrealized gains on available-for-sale securities		1,180	(1,270)
Comprehensive income			$ 53,925
Earnings per common share:			
Income from continuing operations			$ 1.57
Discontinued operations			(0.71)
Extraordinary gain			0.25
Net income			$ 1.11

The Techtronics income statement differs from most published statements in other ways. For example, to simplify the illustration of the various income components, only one year is presented for Techtronics. To comply with SEC requirements, income statements of public companies are presented in comparative form for three years (see Exhibit 4-5). Comparative financial statements enable users to analyze performance over multiple periods and identify significant trends that might impact future performance. Also note that the Techtronics income statement is for a single business entity, but public companies often present consolidated financial statements that combine the financial results of a "parent company," such as IBM, with other companies that it owns, called *subsidiaries*.

All actual company statements illustrated in this chapter are consolidated statements.[12]

Components of the Income Statement

5 Describe the specific components of an income statement.

WHY **Through careful grouping and sequencing of the income statement items, important business relationships are highlighted, and the results of the continuing core operations of the company are emphasized.**

HOW **Most companies will include some or all of the following specific components in the income statement: Revenue, Cost of goods sold, Gross profit, Operating expenses, Operating income, Other revenues and gains, Other expenses and losses, Income from continuing operations before income taxes, Income taxes on continuing operations, Income from continuing operations, Discontinued operations, and Extraordinary items.**

In the following sections, the content of the income statement will be discussed and illustrated using the statement for Techtronics Corporation. Variations in current reporting practices will be examined and illustrated with income statements of actual companies. Finally, the requirement to supplement reported net income with a measure of comprehensive income will be discussed.

Income from Continuing Operations

The Techtronics Corporation income statement has two major categories of income: (1) income from continuing operations and (2) irregular or extraordinary items. Income from continuing operations includes all revenues and expenses and gains and losses arising from the ongoing operations of the firm. In the Techtronics example, income from continuing operations includes six separate sections as follows.

1. Revenue
2. Cost of goods sold
3. Operating expenses
4. Other revenues and gains
5. Other expenses and losses
6. Income taxes on continuing operations

[12] Throughout this text, we will use many actual companies to illustrate financial reporting concepts and practices. You will observe many variations in statement titles, terminology, level of detail, and other aspects of reporting. As a result, you will develop an appreciation of the diversity in financial reporting and the ability to understand financial information presented in a wide variety of terms and formats.

Also, a review of the Techtronics income statement discloses several subtotals in the income from continuing operations category. These subtotals are identified as follows.

1. Gross profit (Revenue – Cost of goods sold)
2. Operating income (Gross profit – Operating expenses)
3. Income from continuing operations before income taxes (Operating income + Other revenues and gains – Other expenses and losses)
4. Income from continuing operations (Income from continuing operations before income taxes – Income taxes on continuing operations)

Each of these major sections and related subtotals is discussed separately as a way to help you better understand current practices in reporting income from continuing operations. Then, we will examine the irregular and extraordinary components of income.

Revenue Revenue reports the total sales to customers for the period less any sales returns and allowances or discounts. This total should not include additions to billings for sales taxes and excise taxes that the business is required to collect on behalf of the government. These billing increases are properly recognized as current liabilities instead of as revenues because the sales tax and excise tax amounts must be forwarded to the appropriate government agency. Sales returns and allowances and sales discounts should be subtracted from gross sales in arriving at net sales revenue. When the sales price is increased to cover the cost of freight to the customer and the customer is billed accordingly, freight charges paid by the company should also be subtracted from sales in arriving at net sales. Freight charges not passed on to the buyer are recognized as selling expenses.

Cost of Goods Sold In any merchandising or manufacturing enterprise, the cost of goods relating to sales for the period must be determined. As illustrated in the Techtronics Corporation income statement, cost of goods available for sale is first determined. This is the sum of the beginning inventory, net purchases, and all other buying, freight, and storage costs relating to the acquisition of goods. (The net purchases balance is developed by subtracting purchase returns and allowances and purchase discounts from gross purchases, not shown.) Cost of goods sold is then calculated by subtracting the ending inventory from the cost of goods available for sale.

When the goods are manufactured by the seller, additional elements enter into the cost of goods sold. Besides material costs, a company incurs labor and overhead costs to convert the material from its raw material state to a finished good. A manufacturing company has three inventories rather than one: raw materials, goods in process, and finished goods. Techtronics Corporation is a merchandising company. The cost of goods sold for a manufacturing company is illustrated in Chapter 9.

Gross Profit For most merchandising and manufacturing companies, cost of goods sold is the most significant expense on the income statement. Because of its size, firms pay particular attention to changes in cost of goods sold relative to changes in sales. Gross profit is the difference between revenue from net sales and cost of goods sold; gross profit percentage, computed by dividing gross profit by revenue from net sales, provides a measure of profitability that allows comparisons for a firm from year to year. For **General Motors**, gross profit is the difference between the cost to manufacture a car and the price GM charges to dealers who buy cars. In a supermarket, gross profit is the difference between retail selling price and wholesale cost.

Gross profit is an important number. If a company is not generating enough from the sale of a product or service to cover the costs directly associated with that product or service, that company will not be able to stay in that line of business for long. For example, if IBM sells a mainframe computer for $126,000 and the materials, labor, and overhead costs associated with producing that computer are $139,000, the gross profit of negative $13,000 suggests that IBM is in serious difficulty. After all, with a negative gross profit, IBM would not be able to pay for advertising, executive salaries, interest expense, and so forth.

For example, using information from IBM's income statement in Exhibit 4-5, we can compute a gross profit percentage for each type of revenue.

IBM Corporation
Gross Profit Percentage

	2009	2008	2007
Services	32.6%	30.5%	27.6%
Sales	64.5%	62.6%	60.8%
Financing	47.7%	51.4%	46.8%
Total	45.7%	44.1%	42.2%

This analysis reveals that IBM's overall gross profit percentage has increased over the 3-year period from 2007 to 2009. This increase can be attributed to increases in the gross profit percentage in each of the three reported categories.

Operating Expenses Operating expenses may be reported in two parts: (1) selling expenses and (2) general and administrative expenses. Selling expenses include items such as sales salaries and commissions and related payroll taxes, advertising and store displays, store supplies used, depreciation of store furniture and equipment, and delivery expenses. General and administrative expenses include officers' and office salaries and related payroll taxes, office supplies used, depreciation of office furniture and fixtures, telephone, postage, business licenses and fees, legal and accounting services, contributions, and similar items. For manufacturers, charges related jointly to production and administrative functions should be allocated in an equitable manner between manufacturing overhead and operating expenses.

Operating Income Operating income measures the performance of the fundamental business operations conducted by a company and is computed as gross profit minus operating expenses. A general rule of thumb is that all expenses are operating expenses except interest expense and income tax expense. Accordingly, another name for operating income is *earnings before interest and taxes (EBIT)*.

Operating income tells users how well a business is performing in the activities unique to that business, separate from the financing and income tax management policies that are handled at the corporate headquarters level. For example, operating income allows you to evaluate **Wal-Mart**'s overall ability to choose store locations, establish pricing strategies, train and retain workers, and manage relations with its suppliers. Operating income does not tell you anything about the interest cost of Wal-Mart's loans or how successful Wal-Mart's tax planners have been at structuring and locating operations to minimize income taxes.

FASB CODIFICATION

The Issue: You have recently started working for an engineering company. The company is in the process of developing optical switches that will make computer memory storage and data transmission 200 times faster than current technology allows. The optical switches are still in the development stage, and the company has not yet shipped any products or recognized any revenue.

The CEO of the company is preparing to make a presentation to a group of venture capitalists. As part of the presentation, the CEO wants to provide the venture capitalists with a complete set of audited financial statements (balance sheet, income statement, and statement of cash flows). The CEO has heard that for a development stage company, the accounting rules are different. For example, items that would be recorded as expenses for a normal operating company can instead be viewed as investments in the future and recorded as assets by a development stage company. With this approach, the income statement of the engineering company won't look too bad even though the company has not yet had any revenue.

The CEO has asked you to confirm her general understanding of the accounting rules for development stage companies.

The Question: For development stage companies, can some expenses be reported not as expenses but instead as assets?

Searching the Codification: There are two different ways to get started on this one. First, you can go to the "Industry" set of topics and find Topic 915 (Development Stage Entities). Alternatively, you can go to the "Presentation" set of topics and find Topic 205 (Presentation of Financial Statements). Either way you start, you will end up at Subtopic 915-205 (Development Stage Entities—Presentation of Financial Statements). In the Glossary for this Subtopic, you can see that a "Development Stage Entity" is one for which either no operations have commenced or, if operations have commenced, no significant revenue has been generated. This certainly describes the optical switch company for which you work. Now it is time to find the answer to the question: *Hint:* You will find the most useful information in Section 45 (Other Presentation Matters).

The Answer: The accounting for expenses in development stage companies is discussed on page 4-41.

Other Revenues and Gains This section usually includes items identified with the peripheral activities of the company. Examples include revenue from financial activities, such as rents, interest, and dividends, and gains from the sale of assets such as equipment or investments. A gain reported on the income statement represents a net amount, that is, the difference between selling price and cost. This differs from revenues, which are reported in total separately from related expenses.

Other Expenses and Losses This section is parallel to the previous one but results in deductions from, rather than increases to, operating income. Examples include interest expense and losses from the sale of assets. Losses, like gains, are reported at their net amounts.

A particularly controversial type of loss arises when companies propose a restructuring of their operations. A restructuring typically causes some assets to lose value because they no longer fit in a company's strategic plans. A restructuring also creates additional costs associated with the termination or relocation of employees. For example, in the notes to its financial statements, AT&T disclosed that its operating expenses for 2000 included a restructuring charge of $7.029 billion resulting from a combination of asset impairment charges (write-downs) and other one-time restructuring and exit costs to make the company more cost efficient in the future. The controversy over restructuring charges stems from the fact that companies exercise considerable discretion in determining the amount of a restructuring charge. The fear is that companies can use this discretion as a tool for manipulating the amount of reported net income. For example, companies that are already faced with the prospect of poor reported performance for a year may intentionally overstate the cost of a restructuring. The motivation for this so-called big-bath approach is that if a company is going to report poor results anyway, it makes sense to gather up all the bad news in the company and report it at the same time, thus diluting the effect of any single bad news item. Historically, if this approach was followed, reported performance in the years following the big-bath year would appear much improved, in large part because the restructuring charge resulted in many expenses of future years being estimated and reported as one lump sum in the big-bath year. In 2002, the FASB issued a clarifying standard to reduce the flexibility companies have to strategically estimate and recognize big-bath restructuring charges.[13]

The largest restructuring charge (to date) was recognized by **Time Warner** (then called AOL Time Warner) in 2002. The company recognized a total of $99.737 billion in restructuring charges, almost all of which related to write-downs of goodwill associated with the AOL and Time Warner merger in early 2001. This astronomical restructuring charge also contributed to Time Warner having the distinction of reporting the largest single-year net loss in history, $98.696 billion (on revenues of $40.961 billion!).

Income from Continuing Operations Before Income Taxes Subtracting other revenues and gains and other expenses and losses from operating income results in income from continuing operations before taxes.

Income Taxes on Continuing Operations Income tax expense is the sum of all the income tax consequences of all transactions undertaken by a company during a year. Some of those tax consequences may occur in the current year, and some may occur in future years. When transitory, irregular, or extraordinary items are reported, total taxes for the period must be allocated among the various components of income. One income tax amount is reported for all items included in the income from continuing operations category; it is presented as the last section in the category. In contrast, each item in the transitory, irregular, or extraordinary items category is reported net of its income tax effect, referred to as "net of income tax." This separation of income taxes into different sections of the income statement is referred to as intraperiod income tax allocation. The Web Material (**www.cengage.com/international**) associated with Chapter 16 includes extensive coverage of intraperiod income tax allocation.

For example, in 2009 IBM generated enough taxable income to require it to pay $1.567 billion in income taxes in cash for the year. However, in 2009 IBM also entered into transactions creating tax liabilities that the company will pay in future years. Even though

> **! CAUTION**
>
> Keep in mind that while a transaction may result in a gain or loss for one company, that same transaction may be treated differently for another. For example, if an office supplies store sells its delivery truck to a used car dealer, a gain or loss occurs for the office supplies store. However, when the used car dealer sells the delivery truck, the proceeds will be considered revenue. Why the different treatment? In the first instance, the sale of the truck is a peripheral activity. In the second case, the sale of the truck results from the dealer's ongoing operations.

[13] FASB ASC Topic 420 (Exit or Disposal Cost Obligations).

those taxes will not be paid until future years, they are recognized as an expense in the period in which they are incurred. So, as seen in Exhibit 4-5, IBM reports income tax expense of $4.713 billion for 2009, which represents the net tax effects, both now and in the future, of all transactions entered into during the year.

In the Techtronics illustration, an income tax rate of 30% was assumed. Thus, the amount of income tax related to continuing operations is $33,585 ($111,950 × 0.30). The same tax rate is applied to all income components in the Techtronics example. In practice, however, intraperiod income tax allocation may involve different rates for different components of income. This results from graduated tax rates and special, or alternative, rates for certain types of gains and losses.

Income from Continuing Operations A key purpose of financial accounting is to provide interested parties with information that can be used to predict how a company will perform in the future. Therefore, financial statement users desire an income amount that reflects the aspects of a company's performance that are expected to continue into the future. This is labeled Income from Continuing Operations. Income from continuing operations is computed by subtracting interest expense, income tax expense, and other gains and losses from operating income.

Transitory, Irregular, and Extraordinary Items

Components of income that are reported separately after income from continuing operations are sometimes called below-the-line items. These items arise from transactions and events that are not expected to continue to impact reported results in future years. Reporting these items and their related tax effects separately from continuing operations provides more informative disclosure to users of financial statements, helping them assess the income and cash flows the reporting company can be expected to generate in future years. Two types of transactions and events are reported in this manner: (1) discontinued operations and (2) extraordinary items. In addition to these two items, the effects of changes in accounting principles, changes in estimates, and changing prices also influence the income statement and related disclosures. Each of these items is discussed in turn.

Discontinued Operations A common irregular item involves the disposition of a separately identifiable component of a business either through sale or abandonment. The component of the company disposed of may be a major line of business, a major class of customer, a subsidiary company, or even just a single store with separately identifiable operations and cash flows. The size of the discontinued activity is not the factor that determines whether it is reported as a discontinued operation. Instead, to qualify as discontinued operations for reporting purposes, the operations and cash flows of the component must be clearly distinguishable from other operations and cash flows of the company, both physically and operationally, as well as for financial reporting purposes. For example, closing down one of five product lines in a plant in which the operations and cash flows from all of the product lines are intertwined would not be an example of a discontinued operation. Similarly, shifting production or marketing functions from one location to another would not be classified as a discontinued operation.

Management may decide to dispose of a component of a business for many reasons, such as the following:

- The component may be unprofitable.
- The component may not fit into the long-range plans for the company.

- Management may need funds to reduce long-term debt or to expand into other areas.
- Management may be fearful of a corporate takeover by new investors desiring to gain control of the company.

As companies constantly seek to fine-tune their strategic focus, they sometimes seek to sell peripheral operational components, especially unprofitable ones, and to consolidate the company around its principal business operations.

Regardless of the reason that a company sells a business component, the discontinuance of a substantial portion of company operations is a significant event. Therefore, information about discontinued operations should be presented explicitly to readers of financial statements.

Reporting requirements for discontinued operations. When a company discontinues operating a component of its business, future comparability requires that all elements that relate to the discontinued operation be identified and separated from continuing operations. Thus, in the Techtronics Corporation income statement illustrated in Exhibit 4-6, the first category after income from continuing operations is discontinued operations. The category is separated into two subdivisions: (1) the current-year income or loss from operating the discontinued component, in this case a $35,000 loss, plus any gain or loss on the disposal of the component, in this case a $16,000 loss, and (2) disclosure of the overall income tax impact of the income or loss associated with the component, in this case a tax benefit of $15,300. As previously indicated, all below-the-line items are reported net of their respective tax effects. If the item is a gain, it is reduced by the tax on the gain. If the item is a loss, it is deductible against other income and thus its existence saves income taxes. The overall company loss can thus be reduced by the tax savings arising from being able to deduct the loss from otherwise taxable income.

Frequently, the disposal of a business component is initiated during the year but not completed by the end of the fiscal year. To be classified as a discontinued operation for reporting purposes, the ultimate disposal must be expected within one year of the period for which results are being reported. Accordingly, if a company made a decision in 2013 to dispose of a business component in April 2014, in the 2013 income statement the results of the operations of that business component should be reported as discontinued operations.

To illustrate the reporting for discontinued operations, consider the following example. Thom Beard Company has two divisions, A and B. The operations and cash flows of these two divisions are clearly distinguishable, so they both qualify as business components. On June 20, 2013, Thom Beard decides to dispose of the assets and liabilities of Division B; it is probable that the disposal will be completed early next year. The revenues and expenses of Thom Beard for 2013 and for the preceding two years are as follows:

	2013	2012	2011
Sales—A	$10,000	$9,200	$8,500
Total nontax expenses—A	8,800	8,100	7,500
Sales—B	7,000	8,100	9,000
Total nontax expenses—B	7,900	7,500	7,700

During the later part of 2013, Thom Beard disposed of a portion of Division B and recognized a pretax loss of $4,000 on the disposal. The income tax rate for Thom Beard Company is 40%. The 2013 comparative income statement would appear as follows:

	2013	2012	2011
Sales	$10,000	$9,200	$8,500
Expenses	8,800	8,100	7,500
Income before income taxes	$ 1,200	$1,100	$1,000
Income tax expense (40%)	480	440	400
Income from continuing operations	$ 720	$ 660	$ 600
Discontinued operations:			
Income (loss) from operations (including loss on disposal in 2013 of $4,000)	(4,900)	600	1,300
Income tax expense (benefit)—40%	(1,960)	240	520
Income (loss) on discontinued operations	(2,940)	360	780
Net income	$(2,220)	$1,020	$1,380

Notice that this method of reporting allows users to distinguish between the part of Thom Beard's business that will continue to generate income in the future and the part that will not. This reporting format makes it much easier for financial statement users to attempt to forecast how Thom Beard will perform in subsequent years.

The reporting requirements for discontinued operations are contained in FASB ASC Subtopic 205-20.[14] On the balance sheet, assets and liabilities associated with discontinued components that have not yet been completely disposed of as of the balance sheet date are to be listed separately in the asset and liability sections of the balance sheet. Also, in addition to the summary income or loss number reported in the income statement, the total revenue associated with the discontinued operation should be disclosed in the financial statement notes. The objective of these disclosures is to report information that will assist external users in assessing future cash flows by clearly distinguishing normal recurring earnings patterns from those activities that are not expected to continue in the future yet are significant in assessing the total results of company operations for the current and prior years.

According to *International Financial Reporting Standard (IFRS) 5*, companies with discontinued operations must disclose the following: the amounts of revenue, expenses, and pretax profit or loss attributable to the discontinued operations and related income tax expense. In addition, separate disclosure of the assets, liabilities, and cash flows of the discontinued operations should be made. IFRS 5 differs from U.S. GAAP in that IFRS 5 requires separate disclosure of the cash flows of the discontinued operations; this requirement does not exist in U.S. GAAP. In addition, IFRS 5 requires that a discontinued operation be "a separate major line of business or geographical area of operations" (IFRS 5 par. 32); under U.S. GAAP, the discontinued operation need not be a major line of business but must only have operations and cash flows that can be separately identified.

The reporting practices with respect to discontinued operations in the United Kingdom represent an interesting alternative to the U.S. approach. For example, in complying with *Financial Reporting Standard (FRS) 3* of the Accounting Standards Board in the United Kingdom, **British Telecommunications (BT)** provided the following information in its 2002 profit and loss account (income statement).

[14] FASB ASC Subtopic 205-20 (Presentation of Financial Statements—Discontinued Operations).

(In millions of £)	2002
Total turnover (sales)	
Ongoing activities	£21,815
Discontinued activities	2,827
Total operating profit	
Ongoing activities	(1,489)
Discontinued activities	(371)

This approach provides more information to financial statement users than does the U.S. approach because it allows for a comparison of the relative size and operating profitability of the continuing and discontinued operations.

Extraordinary Items According to FASB ASC Subtopic 225-20, extraordinary items are events and transactions that are both unusual in nature and infrequent in occurrence. Thus, to qualify as extraordinary, an item must "possess a high degree of abnormality and be of a type clearly unrelated to, or only incidentally related to, the ordinary and typical activities of the entity . . . [and] be of a type that would not reasonably be expected to recur in the foreseeable future. . . ."[15]

The intent of this standard is to restrict the items that can be classified as extraordinary. The presumption of the FASB is that an item should be considered ordinary and part of the company's continuing operations unless evidence clearly supports its classification as an extraordinary item. Examples of gains and losses that should *not* be reported as extraordinary items are as follows.

- The write-down or write-off of receivables, inventories, equipment leased to others, or intangible assets.
- The gains or losses from exchanges or remeasurement of foreign currencies, including those relating to major devaluations and revaluations.
- The gains or losses on disposal of a segment of a business.
- Other gains or losses from sale or abandonment of property, plant, or equipment used in the business.
- The effects of a strike.
- The adjustment of accruals on long-term contracts.

For example, companies have reported as extraordinary items litigation settlements and write-offs of assets in foreign countries where expropriation risks were high.

Some items may not meet both criteria for extraordinary items but may meet one of them. Although these items do not qualify as extraordinary, they should be disclosed separately as part of income from continuing operations, either before or after operating income. Examples of these items include strike-related costs, obsolete inventory write-downs, and gains and losses from liquidation of investments. Most of us would consider the costs created by the September 11, 2001, World Trade Center attack to be the ultimate extraordinary item. However, these costs were *not* reported as extraordinary in 2001 income statements. The Emerging Issues Task Force determined that the economic effects of the World Trade Center attack were so pervasive as to make it impossible to separate the direct costs stemming from the attack from the economic costs (including lost revenue) created by the transformation of the economic landscape created by the attack.

[15] FASB ASC paragraph 225-20-45-2.

In 2000 and 2001, **Verizon**'s financial statements exhibited examples of restructuring charges, extraordinary items, and catastrophic items that seemed extraordinary but were accounted for as part of ordinary operations. In 2001, Verizon reported a restructuring charge of $1.596 billion related to employee severance costs in the wake of the **Bell Atlantic–GTE** merger that created Verizon. In 2000, Verizon reported a $1.027 billion extraordinary loss (net of tax) stemming from the FCC-mandated sale of overlapping wireless services. See Exhibit 4-7 for Verizon's disclosure regarding costs created by the World Trade Center attack.

> **FYI**
>
> Before 2002, all gains and losses resulting from the early extinguishment of debt were reported as extraordinary. This classification was ended with the release of pre-Codification *SFAS No. 145* (now in FASB ASC paragraph 470-50-45-1); these gains and losses are now considered ordinary, subject to the normal criteria for extraordinary items.

In an interesting departure from U.S. GAAP, the IASB does not allow for any income or expense items to be classified as "extraordinary," neither in the income statement itself nor in the notes to the financial statements. In the "Basis for Conclusions" for *IAS 1*, the IASB states that the normal risks of business involve unexpected and heretofore unexperienced events. In other words, the items classified as "extraordinary events" under U.S. GAAP are considered to be just another part of business by the IASB.

Changes in Accounting Principles Although consistency in application of accounting principles increases the usefulness and comparability of the financial statements, the conditions of some occasions justify a change from one accounting principle to another. Occasionally a company will change an accounting principle (such as from LIFO to FIFO) because a change in economic conditions suggests that an accounting change will provide better information. More frequently, a change in accounting principle occurs because the FASB issues a new pronouncement requiring a change in principle; if GAAP is to be followed, the company has no choice but to change to conform with the new standard.

When there is a change in accounting principle or method, a company is required to determine how the income statement would have been different in past years if the new accounting method had been used all along. To improve comparability, income statements

EX 4-7 VERIZON DISCLOSURE REGARDING SEPTEMBER 11, 2001, WORLD TRADE CENTER ATTACK

Note 2: Accounting for the Impact of the September 11, 2001, Terrorist Attacks

The terrorist attacks on September 11th resulted in considerable loss of life and property, as well as to exacerbate weakening economic conditions. Verizon was not spared any of these effects, given our significant operations in New York and Washington, D.C.

The primary financial statement impact of the September 11th terrorist attacks pertains to Verizon's plant, equipment and administrative office space located either in, or adjacent to the World Trade Center complex, and the associated service restoration efforts. During the period following September 11th, we focused primarily on service restoration in the World Trade Center area and incurred costs, net of estimated insurance recoveries, totaling $285 million pretax ($172 million after-tax, or $.06 per diluted share) as a result of the terrorist attacks.

Verizon's insurance policies are limited to losses of $1 billion for each occurrence and include a deductible of $1 million. As a result, we accrued an estimated insurance recovery of approximately $400 million in 2001, of which approximately $130 million has been received. The costs and estimated insurance recovery were recorded in accordance with Emerging Issues Task Force *Issue No. 01-10*, "Accounting for the Impact of the Terrorist Attacks of September 11, 2001."

for all years presented (for example, for all three years if three years of comparative data are provided) must be restated using the new accounting method. The beginning balance of Retained Earnings for the oldest year presented reflects an adjustment for the cumulative income effect of the accounting change on the net incomes of all preceding years for which a detailed income statement is not presented.

As an illustration of the accounting for a change in accounting principle, consider the following example. Brandoni Company started business in 2011. In 2013, the company decided to change its method of computing cost of goods sold from FIFO to LIFO. To keep things simple, assume that Brandoni has only two expenses: cost of goods sold and income tax expense. The income tax rate for all items is 40%. The following sales and cost of goods sold information are for 2011–2013:

	2013	2012	2011
Sales	$8,000	$8,000	$8,000
Cost of goods sold—old method (FIFO)	5,600	6,100	7,500
Cost of goods sold—new method (LIFO)	4,500	4,500	4,500

The first impact of the change in inventory valuation method is to reduce cost of goods sold in 2013. The $4,500 cost of goods sold under the new method would be reported in the normal fashion in the income statement, and the $1,100 ($5,600 – $4,500) current-year impact of the accounting principle change would be disclosed in the notes to the financial statements. The 2013 comparative income statement would appear as follows:

	2013	2012	2011
Sales	$8,000	$8,000	$8,000
Cost of goods sold	4,500	4,500	4,500
Income before income taxes	$3,500	$3,500	$3,500
Income tax expense (40%)	1,400	1,400	1,400
Net income	$2,100	$2,100	$2,100

One drawback of this retroactive restatement approach is that the comparative income statements for 2011 and 2012 that are presented in the 2013 financial statements do NOT report the same 2011 and 2012 cost of goods sold and net income that were reported in the original 2011 and 2012 income statements. However, this drawback is more than compensated by the interyear comparability that is provided through retroactive restatement.

The approach described above for reporting the impact of a change in accounting principle is derived from FASB ASC Topic 250 (Accounting Changes and Error Corrections). This standard is modeled on *International Accounting Standard (IAS) 8*. Formerly, the FASB required companies to report the cumulative income effect (for all past years) of an accounting change as a single item in the current year's income statement. To increase international comparability of financial statements, the FASB decided in 2005 to change U.S. GAAP to conform with the international standard. The accounting for changes in accounting principles is discussed more fully in Chapter 20.

Changes in Estimates In reporting periodic revenues and in attempting to properly match those expenses incurred to generate current-period revenues, accountants must continually make judgments. The numbers reported in the financial statements reflect these judgments and are based on estimates of such factors as the number of years of useful life for depreciable assets, the amount of uncollectible accounts expected, and the amount of warranty liability to be recorded on the books. These and other estimates are made using the best available information at the statement date. However, conditions may subsequently change, and the estimates may need to be revised. Naturally, changing either revenue or expense amounts affects the income statement. The question is whether the previously reported income measures should be revised or whether the changes should impact only current and future periods.

Changes in estimates should be reflected in the current period (the period in which the estimate is revised) and in future periods, if any, that are affected. No retroactive adjustments are to be made for a change in estimate. These changes are considered a normal part of the accounting process, not errors made in past periods.

To illustrate the computations for a change in estimate, assume that Springville Manufacturing Co., Inc., purchased a milling machine at a cost of $100,000. At the time of purchase, it was estimated that the machine would have a useful life of 10 years. Assuming no salvage value and that the straight-line method is used, the depreciation expense is $10,000 per year ($100,000/10). At the beginning of the fifth year, however, conditions indicated that the machine would be used for only three more years. Depreciation expense in the fifth, sixth, and seventh years should reflect the revised estimate, but depreciation expense recorded in the first four years would not be affected. Because the book value at the end of four years is $60,000 ($100,000 – $40,000 accumulated depreciation), annual depreciation charges for the remaining three years of estimated life would be $20,000 ($60,000/3). The following schedule summarizes the depreciation charges over the life of the asset:

Year	Depreciation
1	$ 10,000
2	10,000
3	10,000
4	10,000
5	20,000
6	20,000
7	20,000
Total (accumulated) depreciation	$100,000

Effects of Changing Prices The preceding presentation of revenue and expense recognition has not addressed the question of how, if at all, changing prices are to be recognized under the transaction approach. As indicated in Chapter 1, accountants have traditionally ignored this phenomenon, especially when gains would result from recognition. When an economy experiences high rates of inflation, users of financial statements become concerned that the statements do not reflect the impact of these changing prices. When the inflation rates are lower, this user concern decreases. When the price change rates are increasing, added pressure to adjust the financial statements is exerted by users of the income statement. Many foreign countries with high inflation rates require adjustments to remove the inflation effects. **McDonald**'s addresses the effects of inflation in its 10-K filed with the SEC. This note disclosure (included in Exhibit 4-8) indicates that McDonald's is able to deal with inflation through a quick turnover of inventory and by increasing prices in those locations where costs change rapidly. Disclosure related to the impact of changing prices is encouraged, but not required, in FASB ASC Topic 255 (Changing Prices).

EX 4-8 MCDONALD'S—NOTE DISCLOSURE

The Company has demonstrated an ability to manage inflationary cost increases effectively. This is because of rapid inventory turnover, the ability to adjust menu prices, cost controls and substantial property holdings—many of which are at fixed costs and partly financed by debt made less expensive by inflation.

Net Income or Loss

Income or loss from continuing operations combined with the results of discontinued operations and extraordinary items provides users a summary measure of the firm's performance for a period: net income or net loss. This figure is the accountant's attempt to summarize in one number a company's overall economic performance for a given period. In the absence of any irregular items, net income is the same as income from continuing operations.

From the preceding discussion, you can see that when someone refers to a company's "income" or "profit," the person could be referring to any one of a host of numbers: gross profit, operating income, income from continuing operations, or net income. It is important to learn to be very specific when discussing a company's income. After all, comparing one company's net income to another company's operating income would be like comparing apples to oranges.

In order to compare this period's results with prior periods or with the performance of other firms, net income is divided by net sales to determine the return on sales. This measurement represents the net income percentage per dollar of sales. For example, **The Walt Disney Company** reported the following returns on sales.

	2009	2008	2007
Return on sales	9.15%	11.70%	13.20%

Compare these results with a sample of returns on sales from various companies in different industries, shown in Exhibit 4-9.

When computing the return on sales, keep in mind that net income may include extraordinary or irregular items that can distort the results and hamper comparability. Adjustments may be needed in the analysis to account for such items.

Earnings per Share An individual shareholder is interested in how much of a company's net income is associated with his or her ownership interest. As a result, the income

EX 4-9 RETURN ON SALES

	2009	2008	2007
AT&T	10.4%	10.6%	10.2%
Microsoft	24.9%	29.3%	27.5%
IBM	14.0%	11.9%	10.5%
McDonald's	20.0%	18.3%	10.5%

statement reports earnings per share (EPS), which is the amount of net income associated with each common share of stock. For example, in Exhibit 4-5 basic EPS for IBM in 2009 was $10.12. This means that an owner of 100 shares of IBM stock has claim on $1,012 ($10.12 EPS × 100 shares) of the $13.425 billion in IBM net income available to common shareholders for 2009.

To illustrate the importance of earnings per share, consider the following example. For the years 2011–2013, James Caird Company had net income, average shares outstanding, and earnings per share as follows:

	2013	2012	2011
Net income	$10,000	$6,000	$2,500
Average shares outstanding	10,000	5,000	1,000
Earnings per share (EPS)	$1.00	$1.20	$2.50

Note that if one looks only at the growth in net income, it appears that the shareholders of James Caird are doing very well, with net income growth rates of 140% in 2012 and 67% in 2013. However, a look at the data on shares outstanding reveals that this growth in net income has been driven by a substantial increase in the size of the company as evidenced by the large increases in shares outstanding. When viewed on a per-share basis, performance was actually steadily declining from 2011 to 2013; one of the original shareholders who earned $2.50 for each share owned in 2011 earned only $1.00 for each of those same shares in 2013.

Companies often disclose two earnings-per-share numbers. Basic EPS reports earnings based solely on shares actually outstanding during the year. Basic earnings per share is computed by dividing income available to common shareholders (net income less dividends paid to or promised to preferred shareholders) by the average number of common shares outstanding during the period.

Diluted earnings per share reflects the existence of stock options or other rights that can be converted into shares in the future. For example, in addition to having shares outstanding, a company could also have granted stock options that allow the option holders to buy shares of stock at some predetermined price. At present, the option holders don't own shares of stock, but they can acquire them from the company at any time. In other cases, a company might borrow money but also give the right to the lender to exchange the loan for shares of stock at some predetermined price. Diluted EPS is computed to give financial statement users an idea about the potential impact on EPS of the exercise of existing stock options or other rights to acquire shares.

IBM reports basic earnings per share and diluted earnings per share in 2009 of $10.12 and $10.01, respectively (see Exhibit 4-5). If all options and other convertible items that are likely to be converted were in fact converted into shares of IBM stock, the effect on IBM's earnings per share would be to reduce it by $0.10. A small difference of $0.10 (about 1% of basic EPS) indicates that IBM does not have many options and convertible securities outstanding.

Historically, the accounting rules in the United States governing the computation of EPS have been unnecessarily complex. In the mid-1990s, the FASB initiated a project, in conjunction with the IASB, to both improve U.S. accounting practice with respect to EPS and to increase international agreement on this important accounting issue. In 1997, the FASB and IASB issued almost identical standards prescribing the methods of computing the basic and diluted EPS numbers outlined earlier. This represented not only a big

ifrs

improvement in U.S. accounting practice but also was a milestone in that it was the first time that the FASB and the IASB worked jointly to issue an accounting standard.

When presenting EPS figures, separate earnings-per-share amounts are computed by dividing income from continuing operations and each irregular or extraordinary item by the weighted average number of shares of common stock outstanding for the reporting period.[16]

For example, the Techtronics Corporation income statement (Exhibit 4-6) shows earnings per common share of $1.57 for income from continuing operations, a $0.71 loss from discontinued operations, and $0.25 for extraordinary gain, for a total of $1.11 for net income. These figures were derived by dividing each identified component of net income by 50,000 shares of common stock outstanding during the period. When a company has only common stock outstanding, computing EPS is very straightforward. The computations become more complex, however, when a company has certain types of securities outstanding, such as convertible stock and stock options. These and other types of securities are discussed in Chapter 13, and more detail on the computation of earnings per share is given in Chapter 18.

Earnings per share is often used to calculate a firm's price-earnings (P/E) ratio. This ratio expresses the market value of common stock as a multiple of earnings and allows investors to evaluate the attractiveness of a firm's common stock. The price-earnings ratio is computed by dividing the market price per share of common stock by the annual basic EPS. Instead of using the average market value of shares for the period covered by earnings, the latest market value is normally used. *The Wall Street Journal* reports P/E ratios for most listed companies on a daily basis. Assuming that Techtronics Corporation's stock closed with a market value of $14.25 per share on December 31, 2013, its P/E ratio would be computed as follows:

$$\text{P/E ratio} = \frac{\text{Market value of per share}}{\text{Earnings per share}} = \frac{\$14.25}{\$1.11} = 12.8$$

To get an idea of how price-earnings ratios vary across time, consider the information contained in Exhibit 4-10. This exhibit summarizes data for thousands of companies over a 20-year period. The companies included in the analysis are the largest publicly traded companies in the United States, determined each year by ranking all publicly traded companies by market value and then computing the P/E ratios for the half with the largest market values. Note that over this 20-year period, P/E ratios tended to increase.

In general, the following types of firms have *higher* than average P/E ratios.

- Firms with strong future growth possibilities
- Firms with earnings for the year lower than average because of a nonrecurring event (e.g., a large write-off, a natural disaster)
- Firms with substantial unrecorded assets (e.g., appreciated land, unrecorded goodwill)
- In general, the following types of firms have *lower* than average P/E ratios.
- Firms with earnings for the year higher than average because of a nonrecurring event (e.g., a one-time gain)
- Firms perceived as being very risky

[16] FASB ASC Topic 260 (Earnings per Share).

EX 4-10 P/E RATIOS OVER TIME FOR LARGE, PUBLICLY TRADED U.S. COMPANIES

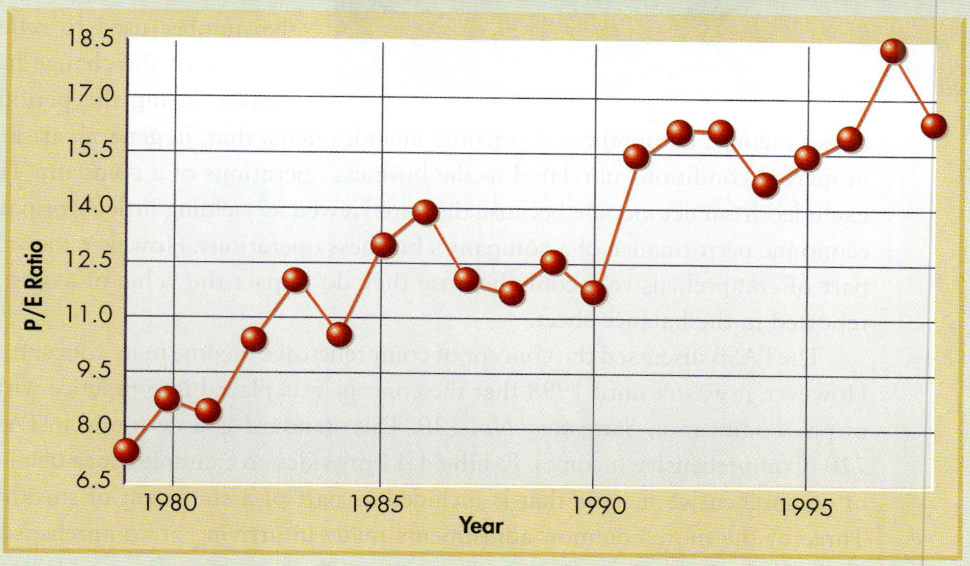

Comprehensive Income and the Statement of Stockholders' Equity

6 Compute comprehensive income and prepare a statement of stockholders' equity.

WHY In its conceptual framework, the FASB suggests reporting comprehensive income reflecting all changes in equity during a period except those resulting from investments by owners and distributions to owners. Comprehensive income is the number used to reflect an overall measure of the change in a company's wealth during the period.

HOW In addition to net income, comprehensive income includes items that, in general, arise from changes in market conditions unrelated to the business operations of a company. Most companies include a report of comprehensive income as part of the statement of stockholders' equity. The statement of stockholders' equity also includes changes in equity other than those related to income.

The FASB requires companies to provide an additional measure of income: comprehensive income. This measure of a company's performance includes items in addition to those included in net income. Companies can either provide this additional information in a separate financial statement or include it as a part of the statement of stockholders' equity. In this section, we discuss both comprehensive income and the statement of stockholders' equity.

Comprehensive Income

Recall from the beginning of this chapter that a general definition of income is the increase in a company's wealth during a period. The wealth of a company is impacted in a variety of ways that have nothing to do with the business operations of the company. For

FYI

The FASB allows, even encourages, a separate statement of comprehensive income. However, almost all companies report comprehensive income in the statement of changes of stockholders' equity.

example, changes in exchange rates can cause the U.S. dollar value of a company's foreign subsidiaries to increase or decrease. Comprehensive income is the number used to reflect an overall measure of the change in a company's wealth during the period. In addition to net income, comprehensive income includes items that, in general, arise from changes in market conditions unrelated to the business operations of a company. These items are excluded from net income because they are viewed as yielding little information about the economic performance of a company's business operations. However, they are reported as part of comprehensive income because they do impact the value of assets and liabilities reported in the balance sheet.

The FASB discussed the concept of comprehensive income in its conceptual framework. However, it wasn't until 1998 that the concept was placed into practice with the issuance of pre-Codification *Statement No. 130*. This standard is now found in FASB ASC Topic 220 (Comprehensive Income). Exhibit 4-11 provides an example (**Coca-Cola**) of a statement of comprehensive income that is included as part of a statement of stockholders' equity. Three of the more common adjustments made in arriving at comprehensive income are (1) foreign currency translation adjustments, (2) unrealized gains and losses on available-for-sale securities, and (3) deferred gains and losses on derivative financial instruments.

Foreign Currency Translation Adjustment During 2009, there was an increase in the value of the currencies (relative to the U.S. dollar) in the countries where Coca-Cola has foreign subsidiaries. Thus, the U.S. dollar value of the net assets of those subsidiaries increased

EX 4-11 COCA-COLA'S STATEMENT OF STOCKHOLDERS' EQUITY FOR 2009

	2009	2008	2007
(In millions except per share data)			
EQUITY ATTRIBUTABLE TO SHAREOWNERS OF THE COCA-COLA COMPANY			
NUMBER OF COMMON SHARES OUTSTANDING			
Balance at beginning of year	**2,312**	2,318	2,318
Stock issued to employees exercising stock options	**—**	—	8
Purchases of treasury stock	**(26)**	(18)	(35)
Treasury stock issued to employees exercising stock options	**17**	12	23
Treasury stock issued to former shareholders of glacéau	**—**	—	4
Balance at end of year	**2,303**	2,312	2,318
COMMON STOCK			
Balance at beginning of year	**$ 880**	$ 880	$ 878
Stock issued to employees related to stock compensation plans	**—**	—	2
Balance at end of year	880	880	880
CAPITAL SURPLUS			
Balance at beginning of year	**7,966**	7,378	5,983
Stock issued to employees related to stock compensation plans	**339**	324	1,001
Tax (charge) benefit from employees' stock option and restricted stock plans	**(6)**	(1)	(28)
Stock-based compensation	**238**	265	309
Stock purchased by former shareholders of glacéau	**—**	—	113
Balance at end of year	8,537	7,966	7,378

EX 4-11 (Continued)

	2009	2008	2007
REINVESTED EARNINGS			
Balance at beginning of year	**38,513**	36,235	33,468
Cumulative effect of the adoption of new accounting guidance for pension and other postretirement plans	**—**	(8)	—
Cumulative effect of the adoption of new accounting guidance for uncertain tax positions	**—**	—	(65)
Net income attributable to shareowners of The Coca-Cola Company	**6,824**	5,807	5,981
Dividends (per share — $1.64, $1.52 and $1.36 in 2009, 2008 and 2007, respectively)	**(3,800)**	(3,521)	(3,149)
Balance at end of year	41,537	38,513	36,235
ACCUMULATED OTHER COMPREHENSIVE INCOME (LOSS)			
Balance at beginning of year	**(2,674)**	626	(1,291)
Net foreign currency translation adjustment	**1,824**	(2,285)	1,575
Net gain (loss) on derivatives	**34**	1	(64)
Net change in unrealized gain on available-for-sale securities	**(52)**	(44)	14
Net change in pension liability	**111**	(972)	392
Net other comprehensive income (loss)	**1,917**	(3,300)	1,917
Balance at end of year	**(757)**	(2,674)	626
TREASURY STOCK			
Balance at beginning of year	**(24,213)**	(23,375)	(22,118)
Stock issued to employees related to stock compensation plans	**333**	243	428
Stock purchased by former shareholders of glacéau	**—**	—	66
Purchases of treasury stock	**(1,518)**	(1,081)	(1,751)
Balance at end of year	**(25,398)**	(24,213)	(23,375)
TOTAL EQUITY ATTRIBUTABLE TO SHAREOWNERS OF THE COCA-COLA COMPANY	**$ 24,799**	$ 20,472	$ 21,744
EQUITY ATTRIBUTABLE TO NONCONTROLLING INTERESTS			
Balance at beginning of year	**$ 390**	$ 342	$ 333
Net income attributable to noncontrolling interests	**82**	67	46
Net foreign currency translation adjustment	**49**	(25)	1
Dividends paid to noncontrolling interests	**(14)**	(20)	(23)
Contributions by noncontrolling interests	**40**	31	41
Disposal of subsidiaries	**—**	(5)	(56)
TOTAL EQUITY ATTRIBUTABLE TO NONCONTROLLING INTERESTS	**$ 547**	$ 390	$ 342
COMPREHENSIVE INCOME			
Consolidated net income	**$ 6,906**	$ 5,874	$ 6,027
Consolidated net other comprehensive income (loss)	**1,966**	(3,325)	1,918
CONSOLIDATED COMPREHENSIVE INCOME	**$ 8,872**	$ 2,549	$ 7,945

$1.824 billion during the year. This increase was not the result of good business performance by Coca-Cola; it was simply a function of the ebb and flow of the worldwide economy. This "gain" is not reported as part of net income but is included in the computation of comprehensive income. **PepsiCo**, Coca-Cola's major competitor, was exposed to similar market conditions during the year and reported an increase in comprehensive income for foreign currency changes of $66 million.

Unrealized Gains and Losses on Available-for-Sale Securities To maintain a liquid reserve of assets that can be converted into cash if needed, most companies purchase an investment portfolio of stocks and bonds. For example, as of December 31, 2009, Coca-Cola owned $398 million in securities that had been classified as "available for sale," meaning Coca-Cola does not intend to actively trade the securities in this portfolio but has them available to be sold if the need for cash arises. These securities are reported in the balance sheet at their current market value. As the market value of these securities fluctuates, Coca-Cola experiences "unrealized" gains and losses. An unrealized gain or loss is the same as what is sometimes called a paper gain or loss, meaning that because the security has not yet been sold, the gain or loss is only on paper.

Because available-for-sale securities are not part of a company's operations, the associated unrealized gains and losses are excluded from the computation of net income and are instead reported as part of comprehensive income. During 2009, Coca-Cola recorded a $52 million loss on its available-for-sale portfolio; this amount was reported as a decrease in comprehensive income.

Deferred Gains and Losses on Derivative Financial Instruments Companies frequently use derivative financial instruments to hedge their exposure to risk stemming from changes in prices and rates. As prices and rates change, the value of a derivative based on that price or rate also changes. As with available-for-sale securities, these value changes give rise to unrealized gains and losses. In some cases, these unrealized gains and losses on derivatives are included in net income and offset gains or losses on the items that were being hedged. In other cases, the reporting of the unrealized gains and losses on derivatives in net income is delayed until a subsequent year; in the meantime, the unrealized gains and losses are reported as part of comprehensive income. In 2009, Coca-Cola reported unrealized derivative gains of $34 million as part of comprehensive income. Additional discussion of derivatives is given in Chapter 19.

A few other comprehensive income items exist in addition to the three just described. For example, in 2009 Coca-Cola reported an increase of $111 million in comprehensive income stemming from a reduction of Coca-Cola's reported pension liability. The key point to remember is that these items represent changes in assets and liabilities reported in the balance sheet that are not deemed to reflect a company's own economic performance and are therefore excluded from the computation of net income. The net effect of each of these adjustments is to report a total comprehensive income of $8.872 billion in 2009, a net increase of $1.966 billion from the reported amount of net income.

The Statement of Stockholders' Equity

Most companies include a report of comprehensive income as part of the statement of stockholders' equity. This is not the required method of disclosure, but it appears to be the disclosure chosen by most companies.

The statement of stockholders' equity also includes changes in equity other than those related to income. As the Coca-Cola example in Exhibit 4-11 illustrates, new share issues, treasury stock repurchases, dividends declared, and miscellaneous other transactions related to the equity of a company are disclosed in this statement. A more detailed discussion of the different types of equity transactions is included in Chapter 13.

Also included in this statement (or as a separate statement of retained earnings) are adjustments to Retained Earnings. The two general types of retained earnings adjustments are (1) prior-period adjustments and, as indicated earlier, (2) adjustments arising from some changes in accounting principles. Prior-period adjustments arise primarily when an error occurs in one period but is not discovered until a subsequent period. Prior-period adjustments are discussed in Chapter 20.

Proposed New Income Statement Format As mentioned in Chapter 3, the FASB and the IASB are currently engaged in a long-term project to restructure the way information is presented in the financial statements.[17] The focus of this effort is to clearly separate financial statement items that are related to a company's business activities from items that are related to other activities such as income taxes or financing. To give you an idea of what a restructured income statement might look like under this new proposal, the Techtronics income statement in Exhibit 4-6 (with some of the detail, including earnings per share data, omitted) has been reformatted and now appears in Exhibit 4-12.

Take a look at Exhibit 4-12 and note the following.

- When compared to the proposed change in the format of the balance sheet (see Chapter 3), this proposed new format for the income statement is really not that different from what we have been using for years.

EX 4-12

Techtronics Corporation
Statement of Comprehensive Income (restructured according to FASB-IASB proposal)
For the Year Ended December 31, 2013

BUSINESS	
Operating	
Sales	$ 780,000
Cost of goods sold	(491,000)
Gross profit	$ 289,000
Selling expenses	(85,000)
General and administrative expenses:	(118,300)
Loss on sale of equipment	(5,250)
Gain (called "extraordinary" in Exhibit 4-6)	17,900
Operating income	$ 98,350
Investing	
Interest revenue	$ 12,750
Gain on sale of investment	37,000
Total investing income	$ 49,750
TOTAL BUSINESS INCOME	$ 148,100
FINANCING	
Interest expense	(18,250)
Income from continuing operations before income taxes	$ 129,850
INCOME TAX	
Total income tax expense ($33,585 + $5,370)	(38,955)
Income from continuing operations	$ 90,895
DISCONTINUED OPERATIONS	
Loss from operations of discontinued business component (including loss on disposal of $16,000)	$ (51,000)
Income tax benefit	15,300
NET LOSS ON DISCONTINUED OPERATIONS	(35,700)
NET INCOME	$ 55,195
OTHER COMPREHENSIVE INCOME (net of tax)	
Foreign currency translation adjustment	$ (2,450)
Unrealized gains on available-for-sale securities	1,180
TOTAL OTHER COMPREHENSIVE INCOME	$ (1,270)
TOTAL COMPREHENSIVE INCOME	$ 53,925

[17] "Preliminary Views on Financial Statement Presentation," Norwalk, CT: Financial Accounting Standards Board, October 16, 2008.

- The income statement contains five major sections: business, financing, income taxes, discontinued operations, and other comprehensive income.
- This income statement does NOT include a separate line for extraordinary items. As mentioned earlier in this chapter, IFRS does NOT allow for the separate reporting of extraordinary items with the rationale that anything that happens to a business is part of the normal risk of running a business. The proposed new income statement format incorporates this provision of IFRS.
- Comprehensive income is an integral part of the proposed new statement, as evidenced by the statement title: "Statement of Comprehensive Income." The Techtronics illustration in Exhibit 4-6 does include comprehensive income on the face of the income statement, but in practice this presentation is rare. Current practice in the United States, as illustrated for Coca-Cola in Exhibit 4-11, is that comprehensive income is reported in an obscure place in the statement of changes in stockholders' equity. The new income statement structure would put increased emphasis on comprehensive income.

As stated in Chapter 3, this proposed restructuring of the financial statements is expected to be jointly announced by the FASB and the IASB in 2011 and will be phased in over the succeeding years.

Forecasting Future Performance

7 **Construct simple forecasts of income for future periods.**

WHY **An important use of an income statement is to forecast income in future periods.**

HOW **Good forecasting requires an understanding of what underlying factors determine the level of a revenue or an expense. Most financial statement forecasting exercises start with a forecast of sales, which establishes the expected scale of operations in future periods. Some balance sheet and income statement items increase naturally as the level of sales increases. Other balance sheet and income statement items change in response to a company's long-term strategic plans. Examples include property, plant, and equipment and depreciation expense.**

Financial statements report past results, but financial statement users are often interested in what will happen in the future. Therefore, an important skill for financial statement users to develop is using past financial statements to predict the future. This section presents a simple demonstration of how to use historical financial statement information to forecast a future income statement and balance sheet.

The key to a good financial statement forecast is identifying which underlying factors determine the level of a certain revenue or expense. For example, the level of cost of goods sold is closely tied to the level of sales, whereas the level of interest expense is only weakly tied to sales and is instead a direct function of the level of interest-bearing debt.

Most forecasting exercises start with a forecast of sales. The sales forecast indicates how fast the company is expected to grow and represents the general volume of activity expected in the company. This expected volume of activity influences the amount of assets that are needed to do business, which in turn determines the level of financing required. In

EX 4-13 HISTORICAL FINANCIAL DATA FOR DERRALD COMPANY

Balance Sheet	2013
Cash	$ 10
Other current assets	250
Property, plant, and equipment, net	300
Total assets	$ 560
Accounts payable	$ 100
Bank loans payable	300
Total stockholders' equity	160
Total liabilities and stockholders' equity	$ 560
Income Statement	
Sales	$1,000
Cost of goods sold	700
Gross profit	$ 300
Depreciation expense	30
Other operating expenses	170
Operating profit	$ 100
Interest expense	30
Income before taxes	$ 70
Income taxes	30
Net income	$ 40

short, for the resulting forecasted financial statements to be reliable, an accurate projection of sales is critical. The starting point for a sales forecast is last year's sales, with an addition for expected year-to-year growth based on the average sales growth experienced in previous years. This crude sales forecast should then be refined using as much company-specific information as is available. For example, in forecasting McDonald's sales, one should try to determine how many new outlets McDonald's expects to open during the coming year. The resulting sales forecast is the basis on which to forecast the remainder of the balance sheet, income statement, and statement of cash flows information.

Exhibit 4-13 contains financial statement information for the hypothetical Derrald Company. This information will be used as the basis for a simple forecasting exercise. The 2013 information for Derrald Company is historical information.

Forecast of Balance Sheet Accounts

Not all balance sheet accounts change according to the same process. Some items increase naturally as sales volume increases. Others increase only in response to specific long-term expansion plans, and other balance sheet items change only in response to specific financing choices made by management. How these different processes impact the forecast of a balance sheet is outlined next.

Natural Increase If Derrald Company plans to increase its sales volume by 40% in 2014, it seems logical to assume that Derrald will need about 40% more cash with which to handle this increased volume of business. In other words, the increased level of activity itself will create the need for more cash. The same is true of other current assets, such as accounts receivable and inventory, and of current operating liabilities, such as accounts payable and wages payable. In short, a planned 40% increase in the volume of Derrald's business means that, in the absence of plans to significantly change its methods of operation, Derrald will also experience a 40% increase in the levels of its current operating assets and liabilities. These forecasted natural increases are reflected in the forecasted balance sheet contained in Exhibit 4-14.

Long-Term Planning Long-term assets, such as property, plant, and equipment, do not increase naturally as sales volume increases. Instead, the addition of a new factory building, for example, occurs only as the result of a long-term planning process. Thus, a business anticipating an increase of sales in the coming year of only 10% may expand its productive capacity by 50% as part of its long-term strategic plan. Similarly, a business forecasting 25% sales growth may plan to use existing excess capacity to handle the entire sales increase without any increase in long-term assets. In short, forecasting future levels of long-term assets requires some knowledge of a company's strategic expansion plan. It is assumed that we know that Derrald Company plans to increase its property, plant, and equipment from \$300 in 2013 to \$500 in 2014. This forecasted increase is reflected in Exhibit 4-14.

Financing Choices The levels of long-term debt and of stockholders' equity are determined by management's decisions on how to best obtain financing. In fact, management often uses forecasted financial statements, prepared under a variety of different financing scenarios, to help determine financing choices. Because detailed treatment of the field of corporate finance is beyond the scope of this discussion, we will merely assume that Derrald is planning to finance its operations in 2014 by increasing its bank loans payable

EX 4-14 FORECASTED BALANCE SHEET AND INCOME STATEMENT FOR DERRALD COMPANY

Balance Sheet	2013	2014 Forecasted	Basis for Forecast
Cash	\$ 10	\$ 14	40% natural increase
Other current assets	250	350	40% natural increase
Property, plant, and equipment, net	300	500	management decision
Total assets	\$560	\$864	
Accounts payable	\$100	\$140	40% natural increase
Bank loans payable	300	524	management decision
Total stockholders' equity	160	200	management decision
Total liabilities and stockholders' equity	\$560	\$864	

Income Statement	2013	2014 Forecasted	Basis for Forecast
Sales	\$1,000	\$1,400	40% increase
Cost of goods sold	700	980	70% of sales, same as last year
Gross profit	\$ 300	\$ 420	
Depreciation expense	30	50	10% of PPE, same as last year
Other operating expenses	170	238	17% of sales, same as last year
Operating profit	\$ 100	\$ 132	
Interest expense	30	52	10% of bank loans, same as last year
Income before taxes	\$ 70	\$ 80	
Income taxes	30	34	43% of pretax, same as last year
Net income	\$ 40	\$ 46	

from $300 to $524 and by increasing stockholders' equity from $160 to $200. These forecasted increases are shown in Exhibit 4-14. Notice that the forecasted balance sheet for 2014 has total assets of $864 and total liabilities and stockholders' equity of $864. The numerical discipline imposed by the structure of the balance sheet ensures that the forecasted asset increases are consistent with Derrald Company's plans for additional financing.

Forecast of Income Statement Accounts

The amount of some expenses is directly tied to the amount of sales for the year. Derrald Company's sales are forecasted to increase by 40% in 2014, so it is reasonable to predict that cost of goods sold will increase by the same 40%. Another way to perform this calculation is to assume that the ratio of cost of goods sold to sales remains constant from year to year. Thus, because cost of goods sold was 70% of sales in 2013 ($700/$1,000 = 70%), cost of goods sold should increase to $980 ($1,400 × 0.70) in 2014, as shown in Exhibit 4-14. Similarly, other operating expenses, such as wages and shipping costs, are also likely to maintain a constant relationship with the level of sales.

The amount of a company's depreciation expense is determined by how much property, plant, and equipment the company has. In 2013, Derrald Company had $30 of depreciation expense on $300 of property, plant, and equipment, that is, depreciation was 10% ($30/$300). If the same relationship holds in 2014, Derrald can expect to report depreciation expense of $50 ($500 × 0.10).

Interest expense depends on how much interest-bearing debt a company has. In 2013, Derrald Company reported interest expense of $30 with bank loans payable of $300. These numbers imply that the interest rate on Derrald's loans is 10% ($30/$300). Because the bank loans payable are expected to increase to $524 in 2014, Derrald can expect interest expense for the year of $52 ($524 × 0.10 = $52).

As shown in Exhibit 4-14, the assumptions made so far imply that Derrald's income before taxes in 2014 will total $80. Income tax expense is determined by how much pretax income a company has. The most reasonable assumption to make is that a company's tax rate, equal to income tax expense divided by pretax income, will stay constant from year to year. Derrald's tax rate in 2013 was 43% ($30/$70), which when applied to the forecasted pretax income of $80 for 2014, implies that income tax expense in 2014 will total $34 ($80 × 0.43).

The complete forecasted income statement for 2014 indicates that Derrald Company's income for the year will be $46. The quality of this forecast is only as good as the assumptions that underlie it. To determine how much impact the assumptions can have, it is often useful to conduct a sensitivity analysis. This involves repeating the forecasting exercise using a set of pessimistic and a set of optimistic assumptions. Thus, one can construct worst-case, standard-case, and best-case scenarios to use in making decisions with the forecasted numbers.

Financial statement forecasting is used to construct an estimate of how well a company will perform in the future. This forecasting exercise is useful for bankers worried about whether they can recover their money if they make a loan to a company and for investors who want to determine how much to invest in a company. Forecasted financial statements are also useful to company management for evaluating alternate strategies and determining whether the planned operating, investing, and financing activities appropriately mesh together. The Derrald Company example used in this chapter will also be used in Chapter 5 to illustrate how to forecast a company's statement of cash flows.

EX 4-15 SUMMARY OF PROCEDURES FOR REPORTING IRREGULAR, NONRECURRING, OR UNUSUAL ITEMS*

Where Reported	Category	Description	Examples
Part of income from continuing operations.	Changes in estimates.	Normal recurring changes in estimating future amounts. Included in normal accounts.	Changes in building and equipment lives, changes in estimated loss from uncollectible accounts receivable, changes in estimate of warranty liability.
	Unusual gains and losses, not considered extraordinary.	Unusual or infrequent, but not both. Related to normal operations. Material in amount. Shown in other revenues and gains or other expenses and losses.	Gains or losses from sale of assets, investments, or other operating assets. Write-off of inventories as obsolete.
On income statement, but after income from continuing operations.	Discontinued operations.	Disposal of completely separate business component. Include gain or loss from sale or abandonment.	Sale by conglomerate company of separate line of business, such as milling company selling restaurant segment.
	Extraordinary items.	Both unusual and infrequent. Not related to normal business operations. Material in amount.	Material gains and losses from some casualties or legal claims if meet criteria.
As adjustments to retained earnings on the balance sheet.	Prior-period adjustments and changes in accounting principles.	Material correction of errors; earliest retained earnings balance reported when a retroactive adjustment is made.	Failure to depreciate fixed assets; mathematical error in computing inventory balance; retroactive adjustment for new FASB standard.

* This chart describes the usual case. Exceptions to the descriptions occasionally do occur.

Concluding Comments

This chapter highlights the need for users of the income statement to use care with terminology. For example, income can mean gross profit, operating income, income from continuing operations, net income, or comprehensive income. One must be very careful with accounting terminology.

The income statement summarizes a firm's performance in its primary business activities (operating income) as well as peripheral activities (income from continuing operations). The income statement also includes two "below-the-line" items that are treated somewhat differently than other items included on the income statement. These are summarized in Exhibit 4-15.

The statement of stockholders' equity includes other changes in a company's equity and often includes comprehensive income. Comprehensive income is a relatively new operational measure, and it will be interesting to see how the financial community uses this information in making investment decisions.

? SOLUTIONS TO OPENING SCENARIO QUESTIONS

1. 3.4% = ($123,018 – $118,928)/$118,928.
2. 5.7% = ($12,843 – $12,147)/$12,147.
3. As explained in this chapter, the factors that impact comprehensive income are (1) net income and (2) unrealized gains and losses from market movements in investment values or foreign currency exchange rates. The large negative comprehensive income for AT&T in 2008 was primarily the result of a drop in the value of the investments held by AT&T's employee pension fund. Pension accounting is discussed in Chapter 17.

SOLUTIONS TO STOP & THINK

1. (Page 4-5) The correct answer is D. Measuring physical well-offness would require firms to obtain fair market value measures of each of their assets and liabilities each period. The difficulties of obtaining these measures along with the associated costs would, in most cases, cause the costs of the information to exceed its benefits.
2. (Page 4-8) The correct answer is A. Revenues and expenses are associated with what a business does. That is, they relate to a company's central activities. An investor or creditor would want to evaluate a business's performance in its central activities. Additional information relating to gains and losses associated with the peripheral activities of a business would be useful but should not be combined with revenues and expenses for reporting purposes.
3. (Page 4-10) The correct answer is B. Recall that revenue recognition at the time of production is acceptable when sale at an established price is practically assured. For the gold produced by Kinross in eastern Russia, enough uncertainty surrounds the shipment and sale of the gold that revenue is not recognized until the actual sale occurs.

SOLUTION TO USING THE FASB'S CODIFICATION

FASB ASC paragraph 915-205-45-1 says the following: "Financial statements issued by a development stage entity shall present financial position, results of operations, and cash flows in conformity with the generally accepted accounting principles (GAAP) that apply to established operating entities." In short, a development stage company must use the same accounting standards used by regular companies. So, the answer to your CEO's question is "No. A development stage company must report expenses using the same standards used by regular companies."

FASB ASC Subtopic 915-205 comes from pre-Codification *SFAS No. 7,* which was adopted by the FASB in 1975. Before SFAS No. 7, special accounting practices used in development stage companies included: "(a) deferral of all types of costs without regard to their recoverability, (b) nonassignment of dollar amounts to shares of stock issued for consideration other than cash, and (c) offset of revenue against deferred costs." (*SFAS No. 7,* par. 2)

REVIEW **CHAPTER 4**

LEARNING OBJECTIVES

1 Define the concept of income.

Income is a return over and above the investment of the owners. It measures the amount that an entity could return to its investors and still leave the entity as well off at the end of the period as at the beginning. Two concepts can be used to measure "well-offness": financial capital maintenance (the dollar amount of net assets) and physical capital maintenance (physical productive capacity). The FASB has chosen to use the financial capital maintenance concept in measuring income.

2 Explain why an income measure is important.

Many consider the recognition, measurement, and reporting of income to be among the most important tasks performed by accountants. Many individuals use this measure for business and economic decisions that result in the allocation of resources, which in turn contributes to the standard of living in society.

3 Explain how income is measured, including the revenue recognition and expense-matching concepts.

Income is measured as the difference between resource inflows (revenues and gains) and outflows (expenses and losses) over a period of time. Revenues are recognized when (1) they are realized or realizable and (2) they have been earned through substantial completion of the activities involved in the earning process. Usually, this is at the point of sale of goods or services. Expenses are matched against revenues directly, in a systematic and rational manner, or are immediately recognized as a period expense.

4 **Understand the format of an income statement.**

The general format of a multiple-step income statement is to subtract cost of goods sold and operating expenses from operating revenues to derive operating income. Gains and losses are then included to arrive at income from continuing operations. Regardless of the format, irregular and extraordinary items are disclosed separately to determine net income.

5 **Describe the specific components of an income statement.**

Most companies will report on some or all of the following specific components of an income statement:

- Revenue
- Cost of goods sold
- Gross profit
- Operating expenses
- Operating income
- Other revenues and gains
- Other expenses and losses
- Income from continuing operations before income taxes
- Income taxes on continuing operations
- Income from continuing operations
- Discontinued operations
- Extraordinary items

6 **Compute comprehensive income and prepare a statement of stockholders' equity.**

In its conceptual framework, the FASB suggests reporting comprehensive income reflecting all changes in equity during a period except those resulting from investments by owners and distributions to owners. Comprehensive income is the number used to reflect an overall measure of the change in a company's wealth during the period. In addition to net income, comprehensive income includes items that, in general, arise from changes in market conditions unrelated to the business operations of a company. Most companies include a report of comprehensive income as part of the statement of stockholders' equity. The statement of stockholders' equity also includes changes in equity other than those related to income.

7 **Construct simple forecasts of income for future periods.**

An important use of an income statement is to forecast income in future periods. Good forecasting requires an understanding of what underlying factors determine the level of a revenue or an expense. Most financial statement forecasting exercises start with a forecast of sales, which establishes the expected scale of operations in future periods. Some balance sheet items increase naturally as the level of sales increases; examples of such accounts are cash, accounts receivable, inventory, and accounts payable. Other balance sheet items, such as property, plant, and equipment, change in response to a company's long-term strategic plans. Finally, the amounts of the balance sheet items associated with financing, such as long-term debt and paid-in capital, are determined by the financing decisions made by a company's management.

Some income statement items, such as cost of goods sold, maintain a constant relationship with sales. Depreciation expense is more likely to be related to the amount of a company's property, plant, and equipment. Interest expense is tied to the balance in interest-bearing debt. Finally, income tax expense is typically a relatively constant percentage of income before taxes.

FASB-IASB CODIFICATION SUMMARY

ifrs

Topic	FASB Accounting Standards Codification	Original FASB Standard	Corresponding IASB Standard	Differences between U.S. GAAP and IFRS
Discontinued operations	*Subtopic 205-20*	*SFAS No. 144*	*IFRS 5*	Under IFRS, a discontinued operation must be a major line of business or geographic segment. Also, under IFRS, separate disclosure must be made of the cash flows of the discontinued operations.
Extraordinary items	*Subtopic 225-20*	*APB Opinion No. 30*	*IAS 1 par. 87*	Under IFRS, no income or expense items are allowed to be classified as "extraordinary."
Change in accounting principle	*Section 250-10-45 par. 1-16* *Section 250-10-50 par. 1- 3*	*SFAS No. 154 par. 4-18* *APB No. 28 par. 28*	*IAS 8 par. 14-31*	No substantial differences

KEY TERMS

Comparative financial statements 4-16
Comprehensive income 4-32
Consolidated financial statements 4-16
Discontinued operations 4-21
Earnings per share (EPS) 4-29
Expense recognition 4-12
Expenses 4-8
Extraordinary items 4-24
Financial capital maintenance 4-4
Gains 4-8
Gross profit 4-17
Gross profit percentage 4-17
Income 4-4
Income from continuing operations 4-16
Intraperiod income tax allocation 4-20
Losses 4-8
Matching 4-12
Multiple-step form 4-14
Operating income 4-18
Physical capital maintenance 4-4
Price-earnings ratio (P/E ratio) 4-30
Prior-period adjustments 4-34
Restructuring charge 4-19
Return on sales 4-28
Revenue recognition 4-8
Revenues 4-8
Transaction approach 4-7

QUESTIONS

1. FASB *Concepts Statement No. 1* states, "The primary focus of financial reporting is information about an enterprise's performance provided by measures of earnings and its components." Why is it unwise for users of financial statements to focus too much attention on the income statement?

2. After the necessary definitions and assumptions that support the determination of income have been made, what are the two methods of income measurement that may be used to determine income? How do they differ?

3. What different measurement methods may be applied to net assets in arriving at income under the capital maintenance approach?
4. Income as determined by income tax regulations is not necessarily the same as income reported to external users. Why might there be differences?
5. What is the difference between a code law country and a common law country?
6. How are revenues and expenses different from gains and losses?
7. What two factors must be considered in deciding the point at which revenues and gains should be recognized? At what point in the revenue cycle are these conditions usually met?
8. Name three exceptions to the general rule that assumes revenue is recognized at the point of sale. What is the justification for these exceptions?
9. What guidelines are used to match costs with revenues in determining income?
10. What are some possible disadvantages of a multiple-step income statement?
11. Identify the major sections (components of income) that are included in a multiple-step income statement.
12. What are restructuring charges, and why do they generate controversy?
13. What is the meaning of "intraperiod" income tax allocation?
14. Pop-Up Company has decided to sell its lid manufacturing division even though the division is expected to show a small profit this year. The division's assets will be sold to another company at a loss of $10,000. What information (if any) should Pop-Up disclose in its financial reports with respect to this division?
15. Which of the following would not normally qualify as an extraordinary item?
    (a) The write-down or write-off of receivables.
    (b) Major devaluation of foreign currency.
    (c) Loss on sale of plant and equipment.
    (d) Gain from early extinguishment of debt.
    (e) Loss due to extensive flood damage to an asphalt company in Las Vegas, Nevada.
    (f) Loss due to extensive earthquake damage to a furniture company in Los Angeles, California.
    (g) Farming loss due to heavy spring rains in the Northwest.
16. Explain briefly the difference in accounting treatment of (a) a change in accounting principle and (b) a change in accounting estimate.
17. Under IASB standards, how is a change in accounting principle reported?
18. What is the general practice in reporting earnings per share?
19. Define *comprehensive income*. How does it differ from net income?
20. What is the starting point for the preparation of forecasted financial statements?
21. Describe the process one should use in forecasting depreciation expense.

PRACTICE EXERCISES

Practice 4-1
LO1

Financial Capital Maintenance

The company had the following total asset and total liability balances at the beginning and the end of the year:

	Beginning	Ending
Total assets	$365,000	$625,000
Total liabilities	230,000	280,000

During the year, the company received $100,000 in new investment funds contributed by the owners. Using the financial capital maintenance concept, determine the company's income for the year.

Practice 4-2
LO1

Physical Capital Maintenance

Refer to Practice 4-1. Assets with the same productive capacity as the assets comprising the $365,000 beginning asset balance had a current cost of $437,000 at the end of the year. Using the physical capital maintenance concept, determine the company's income for the year.

Practice 4-3
LO3

Computation of Income Using Matching

The company sells custom-designed engineering equipment. During the most recent year, the company received the following customer orders:

For Machine A, selling price = \$125,000, production cost = \$67,000
For Machine B, selling price = \$235,000, production cost = \$140,000
For Machine C, selling price = \$72,000, production cost = \$41,000
For Machine D, selling price = \$370,000, production cost = \$150,000

Machines A and C were completed and shipped during the year; the total revenue from the sale of these machines will be reported in the income statement for the year. Machines B and D have not yet been completed; the total production cost incurred so far for these two machines is \$240,000. The revenue from the sale of these two machines will *not* be reported in the income statement for the year. Using the transaction approach (the matching method), compute the company's income for the year.

Practice 4-4

LO3

Revenue Recognition

The following information describes the company's sales for the year:

(a) A sale for \$100,000 was made on March 23. As of the end of the year, all work associated with the sale has been completed. Unfortunately, the customer is a significant credit risk and the collection of the cash for the sale is very uncertain. No cash has been collected as of the end of the year.
(b) A sale for \$130,000 was made on July 12. The \$130,000 cash for the sale was collected in full on July 12. The work associated with the sale has not yet begun but is expected to be completed early next year.
(c) A sale for \$170,000 was made on November 17. No cash has been collected as of the end of the year, but all of the cash is expected to be collected early next year. As of the end of the year, all of the work associated with the sale has been completed.

How much revenue should be recognized for the year?

Practice 4-5

LO3

Expense Recognition

The following information describes the company's costs incurred during the year:

	Amount of Cost	Expense Recognition Method	Length of Allocation Period	Matched Revenue Recognized?
(a)	\$30,000	Direct matching	Not applicable	Yes
(b)	70,000	Immediate recognition	Not applicable	Not applicable
(c)	27,000	Rational allocation	3 years	Not applicable
(d)	27,000	Immediate recognition	Not applicable	Not applicable
(e)	45,000	Rational allocation	5 years	Not applicable
(f)	50,000	Direct matching	Not applicable	No

How much expense should be recognized for the year?

Practice 4-6

LO4

Multiple-Step Income Statement

Using the following information, prepare a multiple-step income statement.

Cost of goods sold	\$ 6,000
Interest expense	1,100
Selling and administrative expense	750
Cash	400
Sales	10,000
Extraordinary gain (net of income taxes)	250
Dividends	700
Retained earnings (beginning)	1,000
Income tax expense (on continuing operations)	1,200

Practice 4-7
LO4

Multiple-Step Income Statement

Using the following information, prepare a multiple-step income statement.

Cost of goods sold	$ 8,000
Interest expense	900
Selling and administrative expense	1,000
Cash	600
Sales	13,000
Accrued wages payable	320
Dividends	500
Retained earnings (beginning)	700
Income tax expense	1,000

Practice 4-8
LO5

Computation of Gross Profit Percentage

Refer to the **IBM** information in Exhibit 4-5. Compute the overall gross profit percentage for 2007, 2008, and 2009.

Practice 4-9
LO5

Income from Continuing Operations

Refer to the **IBM** information in Exhibit 4-5. Compute income from continuing operations as a percentage of total revenue for 2007, 2008, and 2009.

Practice 4-10
LO5

Computation of Income from Continuing Operations

Use the following information to compute *income from continuing operations*. Assume that the income tax rate on all items is 40%.

Cost of goods sold	$ 5,000
Interest expense	900
Income (loss) from discontinued operations	(1,500)
Selling and administrative expense	1,450
Extraordinary loss	(350)
Sales	12,000
Dividends	750
Loss on sale of discontinued operations	(300)

Practice 4-11
LO5

Computation of Income from Discontinued Operations

Fleming Company has two divisions, E and N. Both qualify as business components. In 2013, the firm decides to dispose of the assets and liabilities of Division N; it is probable that the disposal will be completed early next year. The revenues and expenses of Fleming for 2012 and 2013 are as follows:

	2013	2012
Sales—E	$5,000	$4,600
Total nontax expenses—E	4,400	4,100
Sales—N	3,500	5,100
Total nontax expenses—N	3,900	4,500

During the later part of 2013, Fleming disposed of a portion of Division N and recognized a pretax loss of $2,000 on the disposal. The income tax rate for Fleming Company is 30%. Prepare the 2013 comparative income statement.

Practice 4-12
LO5

Computation of Income from Discontinued Operations

Refer to the data in Practice 4-11. Repeat the exercise, assuming that Division E is being discontinued. Also assume that instead of a $2,000 pretax loss on the disposal, there was a $1,500 pretax gain.

Practice 4-13
LO5

Gains and Losses on Extraordinary Items

Use the following information to compute *income from continuing operations* and *net income*. Assume that the income tax rate on all items is 35%.

Cost of goods sold	$14,000
Interest expense	2,400
Loss from an unusual but frequent event	(3,000)
Selling and administrative expense	2,250
Loss from an unusual and infrequent event	(800)
Sales	25,000
Gain from a normal but infrequent event	1,350
Dividends	1,000

Practice 4-14
LO5

Cumulative Effect of a Change in Accounting Principle

The company started business in 2011. In 2013, the company decided to change its method of computing oil and gas exploration expense. The company has only two expenses: oil and gas exploration expense and income tax expense. The following sales and oil and gas exploration expense information are for 2011–2013:

	2013	2012	2011
Sales	$5,000	$3,000	$2,000
Oil and gas exploration expense—old method	1,000	600	400
Oil and gas exploration expense—new method	700	1,200	1,500

Prepare the 2013 comparative income statement. The income tax rate for all items is 30%.

Practice 4-15
LO5

Accounting for Changes in Estimates

A building was purchased for $100,000 on January 1, 2008. It was estimated to have no salvage value and to have an estimated useful life of 20 years. On January 1, 2013, the estimated useful life was changed from 20 years to 30 years. Compute depreciation expense for 2013. Use straight-line depreciation.

Practice 4-16
LO5

Return on Sales

Use the following information to compute return on sales.

Earnings per share	$1.67
Cost of goods sold	$10,000
Cash	$550
Sales	$15,000
Market price per share	$20
Net income	$320
Total stockholders' equity	$6,700

Practice 4-17
LO5

Earnings per Share

For the years 2011–2013, Robbins Soccer Company had net income and average shares outstanding as follows:

	2013	2012	2011
Net income	$12,250	$9,000	$5,500
Average shares outstanding	3,500	3,000	2,000

What was the percentage of change in earnings per share (EPS) in 2012? In 2013?

Practice 4-18
LO5

Price-Earnings (P/E) Ratio
Refer to Practice 4-16. Use that information to compute the price-earnings ratio.

Practice 4-19
LO6

Comprehensive Income
Use the following information to compute *net income* and *comprehensive income*. For simplicity, ignore income taxes.

Income from continuing operations	$ 9,000
Unrealized loss on available-for-sale securities	(1,700)
Dividends	850
Extraordinary loss	(1,200)
Foreign currency translation adjustment (equity increase)	1,500

Practice 4-20
LO7

Forecasted Balance Sheet
The following balance sheet asset information is for 2013:

Cash	$ 100
Accounts receivable	500
Inventory	1,000
Land	2,500
Plant and equipment (net)	5,000

Sales are expected to increase by 25% in 2014. No new land will be needed to support this increased level of sales. This sales increase will require significantly expanded production capacity; net plant and equipment will increase by 40%. Prepare a forecast of the Assets section of the 2014 balance sheet.

Practice 4-21
LO7

Forecasted Income Statement
The following balance sheet information represents actual data for 2013 and forecasted data for 2014:

	Actual 2013	Forecasted 2014
Current assets	$2,000	$2,600
Property, plant, and equipment (net)	5,000	6,000
Accounts payable	500	650
Long-term debt	4,000	5,000
Total stockholders' equity	2,500	2,950

The actual income statement for 2013 is as follows:

Sales	$10,000
Cost of goods sold	6,000
Depreciation expense	1,000
Interest expense	400
Income before income taxes	$ 2,600
Income tax expense	910
Net income	$ 1,690

Sales are expected to increase by 30% in 2014. Prepare a forecasted income statement for 2014.

EXERCISES

Exercise 4-22
LO3

Expense Recognition

For each of the following items, indicate whether the expense should be recognized using (1) direct matching, (2) systematic and rational allocation, or (3) immediate recognition. Provide support for your answer.

(a) Johnson & Smith, Inc., conducts cancer research. The company's hope is to develop a cure for the deadly disease. To date, its efforts have proven unsuccessful. It is testing a new drug, Ebzinene, which has cost $400,000 to develop.
(b) **Sears** offers warranties on many of the products it sells. Although the warranty periods range from days to years, Sears can reasonably estimate warranty costs.
(c) Stocks Co. recently signed a 2-year lease agreement on a warehouse. The entire cost of $15,000 was paid in advance.
(d) John Clark assembles chairs for the Stone Furniture Company. The company pays Clark on an hourly basis.
(e) Hardy Co. recently purchased a fleet of new delivery trucks. The trucks are each expected to last for 100,000 miles.
(f) Taylor Manufacturing Inc. regularly advertises in national trade journals. The objective is to acquire name recognition, not to promote a specific product.

Exercise 4-23
LO3

Revenue Recognition

Indicate which of the following transactions or events gives rise to the recognition of revenue in 2013 under the accrual basis of accounting. If revenue is not recognized, what account, if any, is credited?

(a) On December 15, 2013, Howe Company received $20,000 as rent revenue for the 6-month period beginning January 1, 2014.
(b) Monroe Tractor Co., on July 1, 2013, sold one of its tractors and received $10,000 in cash and a note for $50,000 at 12% interest, payable in one year. The fair market value of the tractor is $60,000.
(c) Oswald, Inc., issued additional shares of common stock on December 10, 2013, for $30,000 above par value.
(d) Balance Company received a purchase order in 2013 from an established customer for $10,200 of merchandise. The merchandise was shipped on December 20, 2013. The company's credit policy allows the customer to return the merchandise within 30 days and a 3% discount if paid within 20 days from shipment.
(e) Gloria, Inc., sold merchandise costing $2,000 for $2,500 in August 2013. The terms of the sale are 15% down on a 12-month conditional sales contract, with title to the goods being retained by the seller until the contract price is paid in full.
(f) On November 1, 2013, Jones & Whitlock entered into an agreement to audit the 2013 financial statements of Lehi Mills for a fee of $35,000. The audit work began on December 15, 2013, and will be completed around February 15, 2014.

Exercise 4-24
LO3

Revenue Recognition

For each of the following transactions, events, or circumstances, indicate whether the recognition criteria for revenues and gains are met and provide support for your answer.

(a) An order of $25,000 for merchandise is received from a customer.
(b) The value of timberlands increases by $40,000 for the year due to normal growth.
(c) Accounting services are rendered to a client on account.
(d) A 1991 investment was made in land at a cost of $80,000. The land currently has a fair market value of $107,000.
(e) Cash of $5,600 is collected from the sale of a gift certificate that is redeemable in the next accounting period.

(f) Cash of $7,500 is collected from subscribers for subscription fees to a monthly magazine. The subscription period is 2 years.

(g) You owe a creditor $1,500, payable in 30 days. The creditor has cash flow difficulties and has agreed to allow you to retire the debt in full with an immediate payment of $1,200.

Exercise 4-25
LO7

Forecasted Income Statement

Romney and Associates wishes to forecast its net income for the year 2014. Romney has assembled balance sheet and income statement data for 2013 and has also done a forecast of the balance sheet for 2014. In addition, Romney has estimated that its sales in 2014 will rise to $3,600. This information is summarized in the following table.

Balance Sheet	2013	2014 Forecasted
Cash	$ 40	$ 48
Other current assets	450	540
Property, plant, and equipment (net)	500	700
Total assets	$ 990	$1,288
Accounts payable	$ 190	$ 228
Bank loans payable	500	400
Total stockholders' equity	300	660
Total liabilities and stockholders' equity	$ 990	$1,288

Income Statement	2013	2014 Forecasted
Sales	$3,000	$3,600
Cost of goods sold	1,200	
Gross profit	$1,800	
Depreciation expense	100	
Other operating expenses	1,440	
Operating profit	$ 260	
Interest expense	50	
Income before taxes	$ 210	
Income taxes	84	
Net income	$ 126	

Instructions:

Prepare a forecasted income statement for 2014. Clearly state what assumptions you make.

Exercise 4-26
LO7

Forecasted Balance Sheet and Income Statement

Ryan Company wishes to prepare a forecasted income statement and a forecasted balance sheet for 2014. Ryan's balance sheet and income statement for 2013 follow.

Balance Sheet	2013
Cash	$ 10
Other current assets	250
Property, plant, and equipment, net	800
Total assets	$1,060
Accounts payable	$ 100
Bank loans payable	700
Total stockholders' equity	260
Total liabilities and stockholders' equity	$1,060

Income Statement	2013
Sales	$1,000
Cost of goods sold	750
Gross profit	$ 250
Depreciation expense	40
Other operating expenses	80
Operating profit	$ 130
Interest expense	70
Income before taxes	$ 60
Income taxes	20
Net income	$ 40

In addition, Ryan has assembled the following forecasted information regarding 2014:

(a) Sales are expected to increase to $1,500.
(b) Ryan expects to become more efficient at utilizing its property, plant, and equipment in 2014. Therefore, Ryan expects that the sales increase will not require any increase in property, plant, and equipment. Accordingly, the year 2014 property, plant, and equipment balance is expected to be $800.
(c) Ryan's bank has approved a new long-term loan of $200. This loan will be in addition to the existing loan payable.

Instructions:
Prepare a forecasted balance sheet and a forecasted income statement for 2014. Clearly state what assumptions you make.

Exercise 4-27
LO6

Statement of Comprehensive Income
Svedin Incorporated provides the following information relating to 2013:

Net income	$14,200
Unrealized losses on available-for-sale securities	1,285
Foreign currency translation adjustment	287
Deferred loss on derivatives	315

The foreign currency adjustment resulted from a weakening in the currencies of Svedin's foreign subsidiaries relative to the U.S. dollar. The deferred loss on derivatives required the recognition of a liability with a resulting decrease in equity. (*Note*: These items represent the results of events occurring during 2013, not the cumulative result of events in prior years.)

1. Determine the effect that each of these items would have when computing comprehensive income for 2013. Explain your rationale.
2. Prepare a statement of comprehensive income for Svedin Incorporated for 2013.

Exercise 4-28
LO5

SPREADSHEET

Analysis and Preparation of Income Statement
The selling expenses of Caribou Inc. for 2013 are 13% of sales. General expenses, excluding doubtful accounts, are 25% of cost of goods sold but only 15% of sales. Doubtful accounts are 2% of sales. The beginning inventory was $136,000, and it decreased 30% during the year. Income from operations for the year before income taxes of 30% is $160,000. Extraordinary gain, net of tax of 30%, is $21,000. Prepare an income statement, including earnings-per-share data, giving supporting computations. Caribou Inc. has 130,000 shares of common stock outstanding.

Exercise 4-29
LO4, LO5

Classification of Income Statement Items
Where in a multiple-step income statement would each of the following items be reported?

(a) Purchase discounts
(b) Gain on early retirement of debt

(c) Interest revenue
(d) Loss on sale of equipment
(e) Casualty loss from hurricane
(f) Sales commissions
(g) Loss on disposal of business component
(h) Income tax expense
(i) Gain on sale of land
(j) Sales discounts
(k) Loss from long-term investments written off as worthless
(l) Direct labor cost
(m) Vacation pay of office employees
(n) Ending inventory

Exercise 4-30

LO4, LO5

Multiple-Step Income Statement

From the following list of accounts, prepare a multiple-step income statement in good form showing all appropriate items properly classified, including disclosure of earnings-per-share data. (No monetary amounts are to be reported.)

Accounts Payable
Accumulated Depreciation—Office Building
Accumulated Depreciation—Office Furniture and Fixtures
Advertising Expense
Allowance for Bad Debts
Bad Debt Expense
Cash
Common Stock, $1 par (10,000 shares outstanding)
Depreciation Expense—Office Building
Depreciation Expense—Office Furniture and Fixtures
Dividend Revenue
Dividends Payable
Dividends Receivable
Extraordinary Gain (net of income taxes)
Federal Unemployment Tax Payable
Freight-In
Goodwill
Income Tax Expense
Income Taxes Payable
Insurance Expense
Interest Expense—Bonds
Interest Expense—Other
Interest Payable
Interest Receivable
Interest Revenue
Inventory—beginning
Inventory—ending
Loss from Discontinued Operations (net of income taxes)
Miscellaneous General Expense
Miscellaneous Selling Expense
Office Salaries Expense
Office Supplies
Office Supplies Expense
Officers' Salaries Expense
Property Taxes Expense
Purchase Discounts
Purchase Returns and Allowances
Purchases
Retained Earnings

Royalties Received in Advance
Royalty Revenue
Salaries and Wages Payable
Sales
Sales Discounts
Sales Returns and Allowances
Sales Salaries and Commissions
Sales Taxes Payable

Exercise 4-31
LO4, LO6

Multiple-Step Income Statement and Statement of Retained Earnings
Jacksonville Window Co. reports the following for 2013:

Retained earnings, January 1	$335,200
Selling expenses	$290,200
Sales revenue	$1,420,000
Interest expense	$14,100
General and administrative expenses	$224,800
Cost of goods sold	$790,000
Dividends declared this year	$40,000
Tax rate for all items	40%
Average shares of common stock outstanding during the year	30,000

Prepare a multiple-step income statement (including earnings-per-share data) and a statement of retained earnings for Jacksonville.

Exercise 4-32
LO6

REVERSE SOLVABLE

Correction of Retained Earnings Statement
J. Mair has been employed as a bookkeeper at Problems Inc. for a number of years. With the assistance of a clerk, Mair handles all accounting duties, including the preparation of financial statements. The following is a statement of earned surplus prepared by Mair for 2013:

Problems Inc.
Statement of Earned Surplus for 2013

Balance at beginning of year		$ 76,843
Additions:		
Change in estimate of 2013 amortization expense	$ 3,100	
Gain on sale of land	17,420	
Interest revenue	3,900	
Profit and loss for 2013	12,760	
Total additions		37,180
Total		$114,023
Deductions:		
Increased depreciation due to change in estimated life	$ 6,400	
Dividends declared and paid	12,000	
Loss on sale of equipment	2,490	
Loss from major casualty (extraordinary)	25,310	
Total deductions		46,200
Balance at end of year		$ 67,823

Instructions:

1. Prepare a schedule showing the correct net income for 2013. (Ignore income taxes.)

2. Prepare a retained earnings statement for 2013.
3. Explain why you have changed the retained earnings statement.

Exercise 4-33
LO5

Change in Estimate

Borgquist Corporation purchased a patent on January 2, 2010, for $600,000. Its original life was estimated to be 10 years. However, in December of 2013, Borgquist's controller received information proving conclusively that the product protected by the Borgquist patent would be obsolete within three years. Accordingly, the company decided to write off the unamortized portion of the patent cost over four years beginning in 2013. How would the change in estimate be reflected in the accounts for 2013 and subsequent years?

Exercise 4-34
LO5

Reporting Items on Financial Statements

Under what classification would you report each of the following items on the financial statements?

(a) Revenue from sale of obsolete inventory.
(b) Loss on sale of the fertilizer production division of a lawn supplies manufacturer.
(c) Loss stemming from expropriation of assets by a foreign government.
(d) Gain resulting from changing asset balances to adjust for the effect of excessive depreciation charged in error in prior years.
(e) Loss resulting from excessive accrual in prior years of estimated revenues from long-term contracts.
(f) Costs incurred to purchase a valuable patent.
(g) Net income from the discontinued dune buggy operations of a custom car designer.
(h) Costs of rearranging plant machinery into a more efficient order.
(i) Error made in capitalizing advertising expense during the prior year.
(j) Gain on sale of land to the government.
(k) Loss from destruction of crops by a hailstorm.
(l) Additional depreciation resulting from a change in the estimated useful life of an asset.
(m) Gain on sale of long-term investments.
(n) Loss from spring flooding.
(o) Sale of obsolete inventory at less than book value.
(p) Additional federal income tax assessment for prior years.
(q) Loss resulting from the sale of a portion of a business component.
(r) Costs associated with moving a U.S. business to Japan.
(s) Loss resulting from a patent that was recently determined to be worthless.

Exercise 4-35
LO5

Change in Accounting Principle

In 2013, Compliance Industries changed its method of inventory valuation. The summary effect of those changes is as follows:

	Old Method	New Method
Cost of goods sold—2013	$25,000	$19,000
Cost of goods sold—2012	29,000	21,000
Cost of goods sold—2011	31,000	24,000
Cost of goods sold—2010 and before	51,000	38,000

Net income was $128,000, $119,000, and $98,000 for 2013, 2012, and 2011, respectively. The income tax rate is 30%.

1. Compute the reported net income for each year if three years of financial statements are issued at the end of 2013.

2. Compute the amount of adjustment that would be made to Retained Earnings as of January 1, 2011.

Exercise 4-36
LO5

Intraperiod Income Tax Allocation

Nephi Corporation reported the following income items before tax for the year 2013:

Income from continuing operations before income taxes	$260,000
Loss from operations of a discontinued business component	70,000
Gain from disposal of a business component	40,000
Extraordinary gain	110,000

The income tax rate is 35% on all items. Prepare the portion of the income statement beginning with Income from continuing operations before income taxes for the year ended December 31, 2013, after applying proper intraperiod income tax allocation procedures.

Exercise 4-37
LO3

Calculation of Net Income

Changes in the balance sheet account balances for the Bubble Bobble Co. during 2013 follow. Dividends declared during 2013 were $18,000. Calculate the net income for the year assuming that no transactions other than the dividends affected retained earnings.

	Increase (Decrease)
Cash	$ 38,500
Accounts Receivable	57,000
Inventory	(32,500)
Buildings and Equipment (net)	160,000
Patents	(4,000)
Accounts Payable	(45,000)
Bonds Payable	135,000
Capital Stock	25,000
Additional Paid-In Capital	35,000

Exercise 4-38
LO5

Discontinued Operations

Jason Bond Company operates two restaurants, one in Valencia and one in Saugus. The operations and cash flows of each of the two restaurants are clearly distinguishable. During 2013, Jason Bond decided to close the restaurant in Saugus and sell the property; it is probable that the disposal will be completed early next year. The revenues and expenses of Jason Bond for 2013 and for the preceding two years are as follows:

	2013	2012	2011
Sales—Valencia	$60,000	$48,000	$40,000
Cost of goods sold—Valencia	26,000	22,000	18,000
Other expenses—Valencia	14,000	13,000	12,000
Sales—Saugus	23,000	30,000	52,000
Cost of goods sold—Saugus	14,000	19,000	20,000
Other expenses—Saugus	17,000	16,000	15,000

The other expenses do not include income tax expense. During the later part of 2013, Jason Bond sold much of the kitchen equipment of the Saugus restaurant and recognized a pretax gain of $15,000 on the disposal. The income tax rate for Jason Bond is 35%.

Prepare the 3-year comparative income statement for 2011–2013.

Exercise 4-39
LO5

Discontinued Operations

On May 31, 2013, top management of Stafford Manufacturing Co. decided to dispose of an unprofitable business component. An operating loss of $210,000 associated with the component was incurred during the year. The plant facilities associated with the business segment were sold on November 30, and a $23,000 gain was realized on the sale of the plant assets.

(a) Assuming a 40% tax rate, prepare the discontinued operations section of Stafford Manufacturing Co.'s income statement for the year ending December 31, 2013.

(b) What additional information about the discontinued segment would be provided by Stafford Manufacturing if it were reporting using the accounting standards of the United Kingdom?

PROBLEMS

Problem 4-40
LO4, LO6

Single-Step Income Statement

McGrath Co. on June 30, 2013, reported a retained earnings balance of $1,475,000 before closing the books. The books of the company showed the following account balances on June 30, 2013:

Sales	$2,870,000
Inventory: July 1, 2012	150,000
June 30, 2013	175,000
Sales Returns and Allowances	120,000
Purchases	1,520,000
Purchase Discounts	32,000
Dividends Declared	300,000
Selling and General Expenses	283,000
Interest Revenue	72,000
Income Taxes	270,900

Instructions:

Prepare a multiple-step income statement and a retained earnings statement. McGrath Co. has 275,000 shares of common stock outstanding.

Problem 4-41
LO3, LO5

Revenue Recognition and Preparation of Income Statement

Manchester Company manufactures and sells robot-type toys for children. Under one type of agreement with the dealers, Manchester is to receive payment upon shipment to the dealers. Under another type of agreement, Manchester receives payments only after the dealer makes the sale. Under this latter agreement, toys may be returned by the dealer. Manchester's president desires to know how the income statement would differ under these two methods over a 2-year period.

The following information is made available for making the computations:

Sales price per unit:	
If paid after shipment	$7
If paid after sale, with right of return	$8
Cost to produce per unit (assume fixed quantity of toys is produced)	$4
Expected bad debt percentage of sales if revenue recognized at time of shipment	4%
Expected bad debt percentage of sales if revenue recognized at time of sale	1%
Selling expenses—2013	$30,000
Selling expenses—2014	$21,000
General and administrative expenses—2013 and 2014	$16,000

Quantity Shipped and Sold	2014	2013
Units shipped to dealers	38,000	32,000
Units sold by dealers	28,000	18,000

Instructions:

1. Prepare comparative income statements for 2013 and 2014 for each of the two types of dealer agreements assuming the company began operations in 2013.
2. Discuss the implications of the revenue recognition method used for each of the dealer agreements.

Problem 4-42

LO3, LO4

Revenue and Expense Recognition

On December 31, 2013, Hadley Company provides the following pre-audit income statement for your review:

Sales	$185,000
Cost of goods sold	(94,000)
Gross profit	$ 91,000
Rent expense	(18,000)
Advertising expense	(6,000)
Warranty expense	(8,000)
Other expenses	(15,000)
Net income	$ 44,000

The following information is also available:

(a) Many of Hadley's customers pay for their orders in advance. At year-end, $18,000 of orders paid for in advance of shipment have been included in the sales figure.

(b) Hadley introduced and sold several products during the year with a 30-day, money-back guarantee. During the year, customers seldom returned the products. Hadley has not included in revenue or in cost of goods sold those items sold within the last 30 days that included the guarantee. The revenue is $16,000, and the cost associated with the products is $7,500.

(c) On January 1, 2013, Hadley prepaid its building rent for 18 months. The entire amount paid, $18,000, was charged to Rent Expense.

(d) On July 1, 2013, Hadley paid $24,000 for general advertising to be completed prior to the end of 2013. Hadley's management estimates that the advertising will benefit a 2-year period and, therefore, has elected to charge the costs to the income statement at the rate of $1,000 a month.

(e) Hadley has collected current cost information relating to its inventory. The cost of goods sold, if valued using current costing techniques, is $106,000.

(f) In past years, Hadley has estimated warranty expense using a percentage of sales. Hadley estimates future warranty costs relating to 2013 sales will amount to 5% of sales. However, during 2013, Hadley elected to charge costs to warranty expense as costs were incurred. Hadley spent $8,000 during 2013 to repair and replace defective inventory sold in current and prior periods.

Instructions:

1. For each item of additional information, identify the revenue or expense recognition issue.
2. Prepare a revised income statement using the information provided.

Problem 4-43
LO5

Intraperiod Income Tax Allocation

The following information relates to Spiker Manufacturing Inc. for the fiscal year ended July 31, 2013. Assume that there are no tax rate changes, a 30% tax rate applies to all items reported in the income statement, and there are no differences between financial and taxable income.

Taxable income, year ending July 31, 2013	$1,015,000
Nonoperating items included in taxable income:	
Extraordinary gain	121,000
Loss from disposal of a business component	(130,000)
Prior-year error resulting in income overstatement for fiscal year 2012;	
tax refund to be requested	90,000
Retained earnings, August 1, 2012	2,520,000

Instructions:

Prepare the income statement for Spiker Manufacturing Inc. beginning with Income from continuing operations before income taxes and the retained earnings statement for the fiscal year ended July 31, 2013. Apply intraperiod income tax allocation procedures to both statements.

Problem 4-44
LO5, LO6
SPREADSHEET

Reporting Special Income Items

Plush Textiles Inc. shows a retained earnings balance on January 1, 2013, of $580,000. For 2013, the income from continuing operations was $240,000 before income tax. Following is a list of special items:

Income from operations of a discontinued textiles division	$22,000
Loss on the sale of the textiles division	60,000
Extraordinary gain	31,000
Correction of sales understatement in 2012 (net of income taxes of $17,500	
to be paid when amended 2012 return is filed)	32,500
Omission of depreciation charges of prior years (a claim has been filed for	
an income tax refund of $6,400)	16,000

Income taxes paid during 2013 were $87,200, which consisted of the tax on continuing operations, plus $8,800 resulting from operations of the discontinued textiles division and $12,400 from the extraordinary gain, less a $24,000 tax reduction for the loss on the sale of the textiles division. Dividends of $45,000 were declared by the company during the year (30,000 shares of common stock are outstanding).

Instructions:

Prepare the income statement for Plush Textiles Inc. beginning with Income from continuing operations before income taxes. Include an accompanying retained earnings statement.

Problem 4-45
LO5

Discontinued Operations in Process

In 2013, Laetner Industries decided to discontinue its Laminating Division, a separately identifiable component of Laetner's business. At December 31, Laetner's year-end, the division has not been completely sold. However, negotiations for the final and complete sale are progressing in a positive manner, and it is probable that the disposal will be completed within a year. Analysis of the records for the year disclosed the following relative to the Laminating Division.

Operating loss for the year	$89,900
Loss on disposal of some Laminating Division assets during 2013	5,000
Expected operating loss in 2014 preceding final disposal	45,000
Expected gain in 2014 on disposal of division	20,000

Instructions:
Assuming a 35% tax rate, prepare the Discontinued Operations section of Laetner Industries' income statement for the year ending December 31, 2013.

Problem 4-46
LO5

Financial Statement Analysis—Ratios
The following financial statement information for Tronics Inc. is available:

(In thousands)	2013	2012	2011
Sales	$6,041	$5,872	$5,324
Cost of goods sold	3,202	2,877	2,396
Operating expenses	1,991	1,779	1,578
Income taxes	165	222	280

The following information relates to the firm's common stock for the same period:

	2013	2012	2011
Shares outstanding	1,000	1,000	1,000
Market value per share at year-end	$8.13	$12.25	$15.32

Instructions:
1. For each year compute
   (a) Gross profit percentage.
   (b) Return on sales.
   (c) Price-earnings ratio.
2. Do you notice any significant trends as a result of this analysis?

Problem 4-47
LO4, LO5, LO6
SPREADSHEET

Income and Retained Earnings Statements
Selected account balances of Connell Company for 2013 along with additional information as of December 31 are as follows:

Bad Debt Expense	$ 32,000
Delivery Expense	425,000
Depreciation Expense—Delivery Trucks	29,000
Depreciation Expense—Office Building	25,000
Depreciation Expense—Office Equipment	10,000
Depreciation Expense—Store Equipment	25,000
Dividend Revenue	35,000
Dividends	165,000
Employee Pension Expense	190,000
Freight-In	145,000
Gain on Sale of Office Equipment	8,000
Income Taxes, 2013	427,425
Interest Revenue	10,000
Inventory, January 1, 2013	775,000
Loss on Sale of Investment Securities	20,000
Loss on Write-Down of Obsolete Inventory	75,000
Miscellaneous General Expenses	45,000
Miscellaneous Selling Expenses	50,000

Officers' and Office Salaries	$ 550,000
Property Taxes Expense	100,000
Purchase Discounts	47,700
Purchases	4,633,200
Retained Earnings, January 1, 2013	550,000
Sales	8,125,000
Sales Discounts	55,000
Sales Returns and Allowances	95,000
Sales Salaries	521,000

(a) Inventory was valued at year-end as follows:

Cost	$825,000
Write-down of obsolete inventory	75,000
	$750,000

(b) Number of Connell shares of stock outstanding: 60,000

Instructions:
Prepare a multiple-step income statement and statement of retained earnings for the year ended December 31, 2013.

Problem 4-48
LO4, LO5

Corrected Income Statement
A newly hired staff accountant prepared the pre-audit income statement of Be Fit Recreation Incorporated for the year ending December 31, 2013.

Net revenues		$645,000
Cost of goods sold		305,200
Gross profit		$339,800
Expenses:		
Sales salaries and commissions	$116,400	
Officers' and office salaries	121,000	
Depreciation	64,000	
Advertising expense	18,700	
Other general and administrative expenses	16,300	
		336,400
Income from continuing operations		$ 3,400
Discontinued operations:		
Gain on disposal of business segment		32,000
Income before income taxes		$ 35,400
Income taxes (30%)		10,620
Net income		$ 24,780
Earnings per common share (10,000 shares outstanding)		$ 2.48

The following information was obtained by Be Fit's independent auditor.

(a) Net revenues in the income statement included the following items.

Sales returns and allowances	$ 8,700
Interest revenue	5,300
Interest expense	9,400
Loss on sale of short-term investment	2,800
Extraordinary gain	13,300

(b) Of the total depreciation expense reported in the income statement, 40% relates to stores and store equipment, 60% to office building and equipment.
(c) At the beginning of 2013, management decided to close one of Be Fit's retail stores. Be Fit is a large company and does not attempt to prepare complete financial reports for each individual store. The inventory and equipment were moved to another Be Fit store, and the land and building were sold on July 1, 2013, at a pretax gain of $32,000. This amount has been reported under discontinued operations.
(d) The income tax rate is 30%.

Instructions:
Prepare a corrected multiple-step income statement for the year ended December 31, 2013.

Problem 4-49
LO4, LO5
SPREADSHEET

Analysis of Income Items—Multiple-Step Income Statement Preparation
On December 31, 2013, analysis of Sayer Sporting Goods' operations for 2013 revealed the following.

(a) Total cash collections from customers, $105,260.
(b) December 31, 2012, inventory balance, $12,180.
(c) Total cash payments, $92,450.
(d) Accounts receivable, December 31, 2012, $22,150.
(e) Accounts payable, December 31, 2012, $10,830.
(f) Accounts receivable, December 31, 2013, $18,920.
(g) Accounts payable, December 31, 2013, $7,120.
(h) General and administrative expenses total 25% of sales. This amount includes the depreciation on store and equipment.
(i) Selling expenses of $12,352 total 20% of gross profit.
(j) No general and administrative or selling expense liabilities existed at December 31, 2013.
(k) Wages and salaries payable at December 31, 2012, $4,450.
(l) Depreciation expense on store and equipment total 12% of general and administrative expenses.
(m) Shares of stock issued and outstanding, 5,000.
(n) The income tax rate is 40%.

Instructions:
Prepare a multiple-step income statement for the year ended December 31, 2013.

Problem 4-50
LO4, LO5, LO6

Corrected Income and Retained Earnings Statements
Selected pre-adjustment account balances and adjusting information of Sunset Cosmetics Inc. for the year ended December 31, 2013, are as follows:

Retained Earnings, January 1, 2013	$440,670
Sales Salaries and Commissions	35,000
Advertising Expense	16,090
Legal Services	2,225
Insurance and Licenses	8,500
Travel Expense—Sales Representatives	4,560
Depreciation Expense—Sales/Delivery Equipment	6,100
Depreciation Expense—Office Equipment	4,800
Interest Revenue	700
Utilities Expense	6,400
Telephone and Postage Expense	1,475
Supplies Inventory	2,180
Miscellaneous Selling Expenses	2,200

Dividends	$ 29,000
Dividend Revenue	7,150
Interest Expense	4,520
Allowance for Bad Debts (Cr. balance)	370
Officers' Salaries Expense	36,600
Sales	495,200
Sales Returns and Allowances	11,200
Sales Discounts	880
Gain on Sale of Assets	18,500
Inventory, January 1, 2013	89,700
Inventory, December 31, 2013	20,550
Purchases	173,000
Freight-In	5,525
Accounts Receivable, December 31, 2013	261,000
Gain from Discontinued Operations (before income taxes)	40,000
Extraordinary Loss (before income taxes)	72,600
Shares of common stock outstanding	39,000

Adjusting information:

(a)	Cost of inventory in the possession of consignees as of December 31, 2013, was not included in the ending inventory balance	$33,600
(b)	After preparing an analysis of aged accounts receivable, a decision was made to increase the allowance for bad debts to a percentage of the ending accounts receivable balance	3%
(c)	Purchase returns and allowances were unrecorded. They are computed as a percentage of purchases (not including freight-in)	6%
(d)	Sales commissions for the last day of the year had not been accrued.	
	Total sales for the day	$3,600
	Average sales commissions as a percent of sales	3%
(e)	No accrual had been made for a freight bill received on January 3, 2014, for goods received on December 29, 2013	$800
(f)	An advertising campaign was initiated November 1, 2013. This amount was recorded as prepaid advertising and should be amortized over a 6-month period. No amortization was recorded	$1,818
(g)	Freight charges paid on sold merchandise and not passed on to the buyer were netted against sales. Freight charge on sales during 2013	$4,200
(h)	Interest earned but not accrued	$690
(i)	Depreciation expense on a new forklift purchased March 1, 2013, had not been recognized. (Assume that all equipment will have no salvage value and the straight-line method is used. Depreciation is calculated to the nearest month.)	
	Purchase price	$7,800
	Estimated life in years	10
(j)	A "real" account is debited upon the receipt of supplies.	
	Supplies on hand at year-end	$1,600
(k)	Income tax rate (on all items)	35%

Instructions:

Prepare a corrected multiple-step income statement and a retained earnings statement for the year ended December 31, 2013. Assume all amounts are material.

Problem 4-51

LO6

Comprehensive Income Statement

The following information for the year ending December 31, 2013, has been provided for Calle Company.

Sales	$530,000
Cost of goods sold	305,600
Foreign translation adjustment (net of income taxes)	51,000
Selling expenses	76,200
Extraordinary gain (net of income taxes)	36,800
Correction of inventory error (net of income taxes)	33,460
General and administrative expenses	57,300
Income tax expense	20,100
Gain on sale of investment	10,800
Proceeds from sale of land at cost	81,000
Dividends	11,200

Instructions:

Prepare a statement of comprehensive income for Calle Company. (*Note*: Both the foreign translation adjustment and the correction of the inventory error involve a reduction in equity.)

Problem 4-52

LO7

Forecasted Balance Sheet and Income Statement

Lorien Company wishes to prepare a forecasted income statement and a forecasted balance sheet for 2014. Lorien's balance sheet and income statement for 2013 follow.

Balance Sheet	**2013**
Cash	$ 40
Other current assets	350
Property, plant, and equipment, net	1,000
Total assets	$1,390
Accounts payable	$ 100
Bank loans payable	1,000
Paid-in capital	100
Retained earnings	190
Total liabilities and stockholders' equity	$1,390

Income Statement	**2013**
Sales	$1,000
Cost of goods sold	350
Gross profit	$ 650
Depreciation expense	200
Other operating expenses	250
Operating profit	$ 200
Interest expense	120
Income before taxes	$ 80
Income taxes	20
Net income	$ 60

In addition, Lorien has assembled the following forecasted information regarding 2014:

(a) Sales are expected to increase to $1,200.

(b) Lorien does not expect to buy any new property, plant, and equipment during 2014. (*Hint:* Think about how depreciation expense in 2014 will affect the net reported amount of property, plant, and equipment.)

(c) Because of adverse banking conditions, Lorien does not expect to receive any new bank loans in 2014.
(d) Lorien plans to pay cash dividends of $15 in 2014.

Instructions:

1. Prepare a forecasted balance sheet and a forecasted income statement for 2014. Clearly state what assumptions you make.
2. If you construct your forecasted balance sheet in (1) correctly, total forecasted paid-in capital for 2014 should be negative. Is this possible? Explain.

Problem 4-53
LO5

Sample CPA Exam Question

During January 2013, Doe Corp. agreed to sell the assets and product line of its Hart division. The sale was completed on January 15, 2014; on that date, Doe recognized a gain on disposal of $900,000. Hart's operating losses were $600,000 for 2013 and $50,000 for the period January 1 through January 15, 2014. The income tax rate is 40%. What amount of net gain (loss) from discontinued operations should be reported in Doe's comparative 2014 and 2013 income statements?

	2014	2013
a.	$ 0	$ 150,000
b.	150,000	0
c.	510,000	(360,000)
d.	540,000	(390,000)

CASES

Discussion Case 4-54

How Can My Company Have Income but No Cash?

Max Stevenson owns a local drug store. During the past few years, the economy has experienced a period of high inflation. Stevenson has had the policy of withdrawing cash from his business equal to 80% of the company's reported net income. As the business has grown, he has had a CPA prepare the company's financial statements and tax returns. The following is a summary of the company's income statement for the current year:

Revenue	$565,000
Cost of goods sold (drugs, etc.)	395,000
Gross profit on items sold	$170,000
Operating expenses (including taxes)	110,000
Net income	$ 60,000

Even though the business has reported net income each year, it has experienced severe cash flow shortages. The company has had to pay higher prices for its inventory as the company has tried to maintain the same quantity and quality of its goods. For example, last year's cost of goods sold had a historical cost of $250,000 and a replacement cost of $295,000. The current year's cost of goods sold has a replacement cost of $440,000. Stevenson's personal cash outflows have also grown faster than his withdrawals from the company due to increasing personal demands.

Stevenson asks you as a financial advisor how the company can have income of $60,000 yet he and the company still have a shortage of cash.

Discussion Case 4-55

When Should Revenue Be Recognized?

Stan Crowfoot is a renowned sculptor who specializes in Native American sculptures. Typically, a cast is prepared for each work to permit the multiple reproduction of the pieces. A limited number of copies are made for each sculpture, and the mold is destroyed after the number is reached. Limiting the number of pieces enhances the price, and most of the pieces have initially sold for $2,000 to $4,000. To encourage sales, Stan has a liberal return policy that permits customers to return any unwanted piece for a period of up to one year from the date of sale and receive a full refund.

Do you think Stan should recognize revenue (1) when the piece is produced and cast in bronze, (2) when the goods are delivered to the customer, or (3) when the period of return has passed? Justify your answer in terms of the FASB conceptual framework.

Discussion Case 4-56

We Just Changed Our Minds

Management for Marlowe Manufacturing Company decided in 2012 to discontinue one of its unsuccessful product lines. (The product line does not meet the definition of a business component.) The planned discontinuance involved obsolete inventory, assembly lines, and packaging and advertising supplies. It was estimated that a loss of $250,000 would result from the decision, and this estimate was recorded as a restructuring charge in the 2012 income statement. In 2013, new management was appointed, and it was decided that the unsuccessful product line could be turned around with a more aggressive marketing policy. The change was made, and indeed the product began to make money. The new management wants to reverse the adjustment made the previous year and remove the liability for the estimated loss.

How should the 2012 estimated loss be reported in the 2013 income statement? How should the 2013 reversal of the 2012 action be reported in the 2013 financial statements?

Discussion Case 4-57

The Sure-Fire Computer Software

Flexisoft Company has had excellent success in developing business software for computers. Management has followed the accounting practice of deferring the research costs for the software until sufficient sales have developed to cover the software cost. Because of past successes, management believes it is improper to charge software research costs directly to expense as current GAAP requires.

What are the pros and cons of immediately deferring or expensing these costs?

Discussion Case 4-58

Accrual Accounting

Near the end of the fiscal year, preliminary financial results revealed that Stancomb Wills Company was in danger of not meeting corporate performance goals. According to an article in the business press, top executives at Stancomb Wills responded by deferring many expenses "beyond accepted accounting norms, and revenue was inappropriately booked far in advance." These practices had the effect of "making the current quarter look more profitable." The top executives of Stancomb Wills were hoping that an upturn in the economy would spur sales that would provide additional profits to cover the deceptive accounting practices.

1. How are expenses deferred and revenues booked (recorded) in advance? What would the journal entries be?
2. Why would top executives encourage these misleading accounting practices?
3. None of the top executives who ordered the misstatements actually made the journal entries. If you were Stancomb Wills' accountant, what would you have done?
4. Is the independent auditor responsible for detecting these types of misstatements?

Discussion Case 4-59

Financial Statement Analysis—Ratios

Shawn O'Neil owns two businesses, a drug store and a retail department store.

	Drug Store	Department Store
Net sales	$1,050,000	$670,000
Cost of goods sold	950,000	560,000
Other expenses	39,500	66,500

Which business earns more income? Which business has the higher gross profit percentage? Return on sales? Which business would you consider more profitable?

Case 4-60 **Deciphering Financial Statements (The Walt Disney Company)**

Locate the 2009 financial statements for **The Walt Disney Company** on the Internet.

1. Did Disney have any below-the-line items in 2009? Explain.
2. Disney's net income decreased from $4,427 million in 2008 to $3,307 million in 2009. Identify the major reasons for the decrease.
3. Imagine that you are a financial analyst asked to generate a forecast of Disney's net income for 2010. You know that generally the best place to start in forecasting next year's net income is this year's net income. Given this starting point, look at the items in Disney's 2009 income statement and make a forecast of 2010 net income.
4. What was Disney's comprehensive income for 2009?
5. Of Disney's four major segments—media networks, parks and resorts, studio entertainment, and consumer products—which generated the most revenue in 2009? The most operating income? Which had the highest operating profit margin (operating income/revenue)?
6. What percent of total revenue does Disney generate within the United States and Canada?
7. How does Disney recognize revenue from broadcast advertising? From advance theme park ticket sales?
8. Does Disney expense its film and television costs using direct matching, systematic and rational allocation, or immediate recognition?
9. How does Disney expense its parks, resorts, and other properties?

Case 4-61 **Deciphering Financial Statements (Coca-Cola)**

The computation of comprehensive income for 2009 for **Coca-Cola** is presented in Exhibit 4-11 on pages 4-32–4-33.

1. Which is greater in 2009—Coca-Cola's net income or comprehensive income?
2. With respect to the currencies in the countries where Coca-Cola has foreign subsidiaries—did those currencies get stronger or weaker, relative to the U.S. dollar, in 2009? Explain.
3. Did Coca-Cola's available-for-sale securities portfolio increase or decrease in value during 2009? Explain.

Case 4-62 **Deciphering Financial Statements (Wells Fargo & Company)**

Wells Fargo & Company is the fourth largest bank in the U.S. (based on consolidated asset data gathered by the Federal Reserve as of March 31, 2010). Its consolidated statement of income follows.

Consolidated Statement of Income (USD $) In Millions, except Per Share data	12 Months Ended Dec. 31, 2009	Dec. 31, 2008	Dec. 31, 2007
Interest income			
Trading assets	$ 918	$ 177	$ 173
Securities available for sale	11,319	5,287	3,451
Mortgages held for sale	1,930	1,573	2,150
Loans held for sale	183	48	70
Loans	41,589	27,632	29,040
Other interest income	335	181	293
Total interest income	56,274	34,898	35,177
Interest expense			
Deposits	3,774	4,521	8,152
Short-term borrowings	222	1,478	1,245

Consolidated Statement of Income (USD $) In Millions, except Per Share data	12 Months Ended Dec. 31, 2009	Dec. 31, 2008	Dec. 31, 2007
Long-term debt	5,782	3,756	4,806
Other interest expense	172	0	0
Total interest expense	9,950	9,755	14,203
Net interest income	46,324	25,143	20,974
Provision for credit losses	21,668	15,979	4,939
Net interest income after provision for credit losses	24,656	9,164	16,035
Noninterest income			
Service charges on deposit accounts	5,741	3,190	3,050
Trust and investment fees	9,735	2,924	3,149
Card fees	3,683	2,336	2,136
Other fees	3,804	2,097	2,292
Mortgage banking	12,028	2,525	3,133
Insurance	2,126	1,830	1,530
Net gains from trading activities	2,674	275	544
Net gains (losses) on debt securities available for sale (includes impairment losses of $1,012, consisting of $2,352 of total other-than-temporary impairment losses, net of $1,340 recognized in other comprehensive income, for the year ended December 31, 2009)	(127)	1,037	209
Net gains (losses) from equity investments (includes impairment losses of $655 for the year ended December 31, 2009)	185	(757)	864
Operating leases	685	427	703
Other	1,828	850	936
Total noninterest income	42,362	16,734	18,546
Noninterest expense			
Salaries	13,757	8,260	7,762
Commission and incentive compensation	8,021	2,676	3,284
Employee benefits	4,689	2,004	2,322
Equipment	2,506	1,357	1,294
Net occupancy	3,127	1,619	1,545
Core deposit and other intangibles	2,577	186	158
FDIC and other deposit assessments	1,849	120	34
Other	12,494	6,376	6,347
Total noninterest expense	49,020	22,598	22,746
Income before income tax expense	17,998	3,300	11,835
Income tax expense	5,331	602	3,570
Net income before noncontrolling interests	12,667	2,698	8,265
Less: Net income from noncontrolling interests	392	43	208
Wells Fargo net income	12,275	2,655	8,057
Wells Fargo net income applicable to common stock	$ 7,990	$ 2,369	$ 8,057
Per share information			
Earnings per common share	$1.76	$0.70	$2.41
Diluted earnings per common share	$1.75	$0.70	$2.38
Dividends declared per common share	$0.49	$1.30	$1.18
Average common shares outstanding	4,545.20	3,378.10	3,348.50
Diluted average common shares outstanding	4,562.70	3,391.30	3,382.80

1. How is this income statement different from all the other income statements illustrated in this chapter?
2. For a merchandising firm, gross profit represents sales less cost of goods sold. For Wells Fargo, what component of the income statement would be similar to gross profit?
3. Compute the following ratios for each of the years 2007–2009: (a) Total interest expense/Total interest income, (b) Incentive compensation/Salaries, and (c) Employee benefits/Salaries.
4. Comment on the ratios you computed in part (3), particularly any trends.
5. The average loans receivable balance for Wells Fargo during 2009 was $801,036 million. The average amount of deposits during 2009 was $802,710 million. Using the income statement data, comment on the average interest rate Wells Fargo pays to its depositors, the average interest rate Wells Fargo earns on its loans receivable, and the spread between these two rates.
6. The market value of Wells Fargo's stock at the end of each year was $26.99, $29.48, and $30.19 for the years 2009, 2008, and 2007, respectively. Compute the firm's price-earnings ratio for each year. Use diluted earnings per share. Is it increasing or decreasing over time?

Case 4-63

Deciphering Financial Statements (Apple Inc.)

Apple Inc. is one of the country's most successful computer technology companies. The company designs, manufactures, and sells computers, digital music devices, communication devices, and various software products. The company's net income has increased each year since 2002, and in 2009, Apple sold 10.396 million computers, 54.132 million iPods, and 20.731 million iPhones. Information relating to the company's business segments can be found in the company's annual report, an excerpt of which follows.

Net Sales by Operating Segment:	**2009**	**2008**	**2007**
Americas net sales	$18,887	$16,447	$11,907
Europe net sales	11,810	9,233	5,469
Japan net sales	2,279	1,728	1,084
Retail net sales	6,656	7,292	4,362
Other Segments net sales (a)	3,273	2,791	1,756
Total net sales	$42,905	$37,491	$24,578
Operating Income			
Americas	$ 6,637	$ 4,874	$ 2,998
Europe	4,296	3,022	1,350
Japan	961	549	233
Retail	1,677	1,661	876
Other Segments (c)	1,121	775	389
Other corporate expenses, net (a)	(2,242)	(2,038)	(1,197)
Stock-based compensation expense	(710)	(516)	(242)
Total operating income	$11,740	$ 8,327	$ 4,407
Assets			
Americas	$ 1,882	$ 1,678	$ 1,250
Europe	1,352	1,069	586
Japan	483	272	158
Retail	1,344	1,139	908
Other Segments (c)	543	405	249
Corporate Assets	41,897	31,608	21,727
Total Assets	$47,501	$36,171	$24,878

1. Where does Apple generate most of its revenues? Its profits?
2. The profitability of each dollar of revenue is measured by the ratio (Operating income/Net sales). Compute this ratio for each of Apple's five operating segments in 2009. Which segment has the highest profitability per dollar of revenue?
3. The extent to which a segment uses its assets to efficiently generate revenues is measured by the ratio (Net sales/Assets). Compute this asset turnover ratio for each of Apple's five operating segments in 2009. Which segment has the highest number of dollars of revenue generated for each dollar of assets?
4. The return on assets ratio (Operating income/Assets) measures how well a segment combines profitability and efficiency to generate profits with the existing assets. Compute return on assets for each of Apple's five operating segments in 2009. Which segment has the highest operating profit generated for each dollar of assets?
5. Based on your answers to parts (1) and (2), how critical is Apple's Retail segment to the company's overall success? Before you answer this question, think about how the company is able to sell and promote its computers and other products.

Case 4-64

Deciphering Financial Statements (Ford Motor Company)

The consolidated statement of income for **Ford Motor Company** appears below.

	2009	2008	2007
AUTOMOTIVE			
Sales	105,893	129,165	154,379
Costs and expenses			
Cost of sales	100,016	127,102	142,587
Selling, administrative and other expenses	8,583	11,356	13,660
Goodwill impairment	—	—	2,400
Total costs and expenses	108,599	138,458	158,647
Operating income/(loss)	(2,706)	(9,293)	(4,268)
Interest expense	1,515	2,061	2,363
Interest income and other non-operating income/(expense), net (Note 20)	5,433	(563)	1,550
Income/(Loss) before income taxes — Automotive	1,212	(11,917)	(5,081)
FINANCIAL SERVICES			
Revenues	12,415	15,949	16,193
Costs and expenses			
Interest expense	5,313	7,744	8,675
Depreciation	3,937	9,109	6,289
Operating and other expenses	738	965	1,220
Provision for credit and insurance losses	1,030	1,874	668
Total costs and expenses	11,018	19,692	16,852
Other income/(loss), net (Note 20)	552	1,149	1,869
Equity in net income/(loss) of affiliated companies	(135)	13	14
Income/(Loss) before income taxes — Financial Services	1,814	(2,581)	1,224
TOTAL COMPANY			
Income/(Loss) before income taxes	3,026	(14,498)	(3,857)
Provision for/(Benefit from) income taxes (Note 23)	69	63	(1,333)
Income/(Loss) from continuing operations	2,957	(14,561)	(2,524)
Income/(Loss) from discontinued operations (Note 24)	5	9	41
Net income/(loss)	2,962	(14,552)	(2,483)
Less: Income/(Loss) attributable to noncontrolling interests	245	214	312
Net income/(loss) attributable to Ford Motor Company	2,717	(14,766)	(2,795)

1. What do you notice about the way revenues and expenses are partitioned?
2. For the Automotive division, compute the ratio (Cost of sales/Sales) for each of the three years presented. Interpret the results.
3. Look at the operating results for the Automotive division. Is there any good news for Ford in these results?
4. Depreciation expense is reported by the Financial Services division but not by the Automotive division. Explain why this is so.
5. Which of the company's two divisions seems to be performing better over time?
6. Is Ford a car company that finances autos or a finance company that makes cars?

Case 4-65

Writing Assignment (What are the benefits of a restructuring charge?)

Write a one-page paper identifying the benefits, both from an economic and a financial reporting perspective, that a company might reap through recognizing a big-bath restructuring charge.

Case 4-66

Ethical Dilemma

Far from being an exact science, accounting involves estimation and judgment. Consider the case of Dwight Nelson, chief financial officer of Pilot Enterprises. Pilot is a relatively young, privately held company with thoughts of going public in the near future. The owners of the business would like to include in the prospectus (a document containing information about the company and its past performance) financial statements that support their assertion that Pilot is a successful company with a bright future.

The problem is the income statement for the past year shows a slight decrease in income from the prior period. When Dwight presented this information to the board of directors, he was told to revise the income statement. He was specifically counseled to review his estimates associated with bad debt expense, warranty expense, and estimated useful life of depreciable assets. He was invited to present his "revised" income statement to the board when it showed a 5% increase over last period's net income—anything less would not do.

After reviewing the assumptions made regarding uncollectibles, warranties, and depreciation, Dwight found that he could revise his estimates and obtain the 5% target increase in income. But he did not feel that the revised income statement properly reflected the performance of Pilot for the period.

1. What are the risks to Dwight of revising the income statement to meet the target?
2. What are the risks to Dwight of not revising the income statement?

Case 4-67

Cumulative Spreadsheet Analysis

This spreadsheet assignment is a continuation of the spreadsheet assignment given in Chapter 3. If you completed that assignment, you have a head start on this one. Refer back to part (1) of the Cumulative Spreadsheet Analysis assignment in Chapter 3. Clearly state any additional assumptions that you make.

Skywalker wishes to prepare a *forecasted* balance sheet and a *forecasted* income statement for 2014. Use the financial statement numbers for 2013 [given in part (1) of the Cumulative Spreadsheet Analysis assignment in Chapter 3] as the basis for the forecast, along with the following additional information. (*Note*: Use "Paid-in-Capital" to solve.)

(a) Sales in 2014 are expected to increase by 40% over 2013 sales of $2,100.
(b) In 2014, Skywalker plans to acquire new property, plant, and equipment for $240.
(c) The $480 in operating expenses reported in 2013 breaks down as follows: $15 depreciation expense and $465 other operating expenses.
(d) No new long-term debt will be acquired in 2014.
(e) No cash dividends will be paid in 2014.
(f) New short-term loans payable will be acquired in an amount sufficient to make Skywalker's current ratio in 2014 exactly equal to 2.0.

(g) Skywalker does not plan to repurchase any additional shares of stock in 2014.

(h) Because changes in future prices and exchange rates are impossible to predict, Skywalker's best estimate is that the balance in accumulated other comprehensive income will remain unchanged in 2014.

(i) Assume that investment securities, long-term investments, other long-term assets, and intangible assets will increase at the same rate as sales (40%) in 2014.

(j) In the absence of more detailed information, assume that other long-term liabilities will increase at the same rate as sales (40%) in 2014.

Note: Because the amounts of all other items are specified by the information and assumptions listed above, use the Paid-in Capital amount to make the balance sheet balance.

Sandy Huffaker/Bloomberg/Getty Images

P1 FOUNDATIONS OF FINANCIAL ACCOUNTING

CHAPTER 5 Statement of Cash Flows and Articulation

LEARNING OBJECTIVES

1. Describe the circumstances in which the cash flow statement is a particularly important companion of the income statement.
2. Outline the structure of and information reported in the three main categories of the cash flow statement: operating, investing, and financing.
3. Compute cash flow from operations using either the direct or the indirect method.
4. Prepare a complete statement of cash flows and provide the required supplemental disclosures.
5. Assess a firm's financial strength by analyzing the relationships among cash flows from operating, investing, and financing activities and by computing financial ratios based on cash flow data.
6. Demonstrate how the three primary financial statements tie together, or articulate, in a unified framework.
7. Use knowledge of how the three primary financial statements tie together to prepare a forecasted statement of cash flows.

Karl Eller started out in the billboard business. After his company was acquired by **Gannett**, he sat on the firm's board and was one of a group of directors who opposed Gannett's risky plan to start up the first U.S. national daily newspaper, *USA Today*. He left Gannett and went to **Columbia Pictures**, where he was one of the driving forces behind the purchase of Columbia by **Coca-Cola**. (Columbia Pictures was subsequently purchased again, this time by **Sony** in one of the most overpriced Hollywood deals of all time—but that is another story.) In 1983, Mr. Eller went into the convenience store business and took on the challenge of transforming **Circle K** from a regional 1,200-store convenience store chain centered in Arizona into the second-largest chain in the United States (behind **7-Eleven**). At its peak, Circle K operated 4,685 stores in 32 states.

Circle K's rapid expansion was financed through long-term borrowing. Its long-term debt increased from $41 million in 1983, when Mr. Eller took over, to $1.2 billion in 1990. The interest on this large debt, along with increased price competition from convenience stores operated by oil companies, combined to squeeze Circle K's profits.[1] Net income dropped from a record high of $60 million in 1988 to $15 million in 1989. For the year ended April 30, 1990, Circle K reported a loss of $773 million. In May 1990, Circle K filed for Chapter 11 bankruptcy protection.

As illustrated in Exhibit 5-1, at the same time it was reporting the disastrous $773 million loss, Circle K was reporting a record high positive cash flow from operations of more than $100 million. How could Circle K report positive cash flow at the same time it was reporting a record-breaking net loss? There are many causes for a difference between accrual net income and cash flow; these causes are discussed in this chapter. In Circle K's case, there were three primary contributing factors:

- *Much of the reported loss was due to a $639 million restructuring charge. For example, goodwill previously recorded as a $300 million asset was written off. This drastically reduced net income but did not affect cash flow.*
- *Circle K added $75 million to its estimated liability for environmental cleanup charges resulting from leaky underground gasoline storage tanks. Again, this charge reduced income but did not involve an immediate cash outflow.*
- *Financial distress forced Circle K to make its operations more efficient. One result was that Circle K reduced its inventory by $65 million in 1990. This action increased cash flow because $65 million in cash was liberated that otherwise would have been tied up in the form of gasoline, beer, and Twinkies®.*

In 1991, Circle K again showed positive cash flow from operations while reporting a large net loss. In an interesting twist, this positive cash flow was partially a result of the bankruptcy filing. When a company files for Chapter 11 bankruptcy, the courts allow the company to cease making interest payments on its old debts. During the fiscal year ended April 30, 1990, the year before the bankruptcy filing, Circle K paid more than $100 million in interest. In 1991, after the filing, Circle K paid only $6 million in interest. In addition, the bankruptcy filing strengthened the willingness of suppliers to sell to Circle K on credit because bankruptcy laws place postbankruptcy lenders near the top of the creditor priority list. As a result, Circle K's accounts payable increased $80 million in 1991. This accounts payable increase freed up cash that otherwise would have been used to pay current bills.

Because of this positive cash flow from operations, Circle K was able to stay in business while its management devised a reorganization plan. As part of its bankruptcy restructuring, Circle K replaced Karl Eller as chief executive officer (CEO) in 1990. Following a lengthy debate among the creditors, Circle K's bankruptcy reorganization plan was formally approved by a federal bankruptcy court judge, and in 1993 Circle K was purchased for $400 million by a diverse group of private investors from Barcelona, Kuwait, and Pittsburgh. Subsequently, Circle K was taken over by **Tosco**, the largest independent refiner and marketer of petroleum products in the United States.[2] In September 2001, Tosco itself was acquired by **Phillips Petroleum**, temporarily combining the Circle K brand under the same umbrella as 76 and Phillips 66. In 2003, Circle K was acquired by a Canadian company, **Alimentation Couche-Tard**.

And what about Mr. Eller, who started this whole thing? Well, you can't keep a good entrepreneur down. Karl Eller returned to his roots and became CEO of **Eller Media**, the largest billboard company in the United States.[3] On April 10, 1997, Eller Media was acquired by **Clear Channel Communications**, which has billboards across the United States and in the United Kingdom and operates radio and TV stations in the United States, Mexico, Australia, and New Zealand. Mr. Eller served on the board of directors of Clear Channel until his retirement in 2001 at age 73. As of May 2010, Mr. Eller, a longtime sports fan, was serving on the NCAA Leadership Advisory Board of Directors along with other luminaries such as Peyton Manning and Fred Smith, chairman of FedEx Corporation. How is that for landing on your feet?

[1] Roy J. Harris Jr., "Karl Eller of Circle K, Always Pushing Luck, Now Lives to Regret It," *The Wall Street Journal*, March 28, 1990, p. A1.
[2] Jonathan Auerbach and Louise Lee, "Circle K Pact Gives Tosco Fuel Injection," *The Wall Street Journal,* February 20, 1996, p. A4. (Interestingly, Tosco's corporate headquarters were in Stamford, Connecticut, the same city where the FASB was formerly located—small world.)
[3] William P. Barrett, "The Phoenix of Phoenix," *Forbes,* January 1, 1996, p. 44.

EX 5-1 CIRCLE K INCOME VS. CASH FLOW

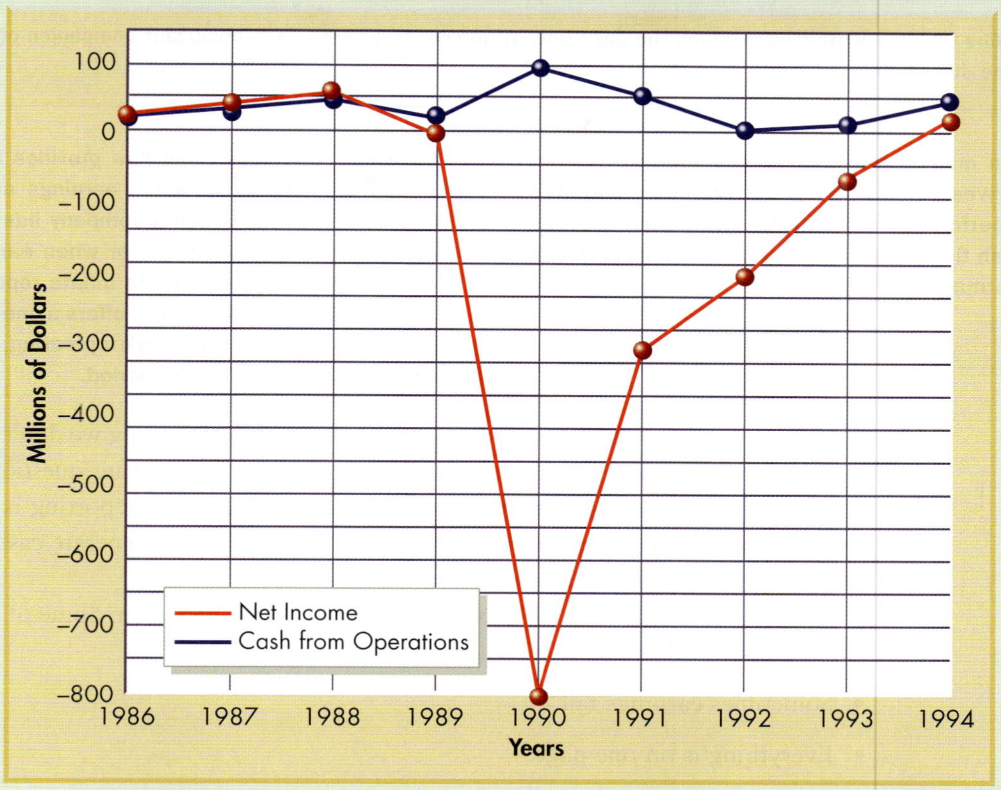

? QUESTIONS

1. How was Circle K able to report a record amount of positive operating cash flow at the same time it was reporting an income statement loss of $773 million?
2. How did filing for Chapter 11 bankruptcy help Circle K's cash flow situation?
3. In what kind of business did Karl Eller both start and end his business career?

Answers to these questions can be found on page 5-34.

The Circle K case illustrates that cash flow data sometimes reveal aspects of operations not captured by earnings. In addition, recall that assessing the amounts, timing, and uncertainty of future cash flows is one of the primary objectives of financial reporting.[4] The statement that provides information needed to meet this objective is a statement of cash flows. This chapter provides an overview of reporting cash flows and outlines the techniques for preparing and analyzing a cash flow statement.

[4] *Statement of Financial Accounting Concepts No. 1*, "Objectives of Financial Reporting by Business Enterprises" (Stamford, CT: Financial Accounting Standards Board, 1978), par. 37.

What Good Is a Cash Flow Statement?

1 **Describe the circumstances in which the cash flow statement is a particularly important companion of the income statement.**

WHY **In many situations, the income statement gives an incomplete picture of a company's economic performance. In those situations, a statement of cash flows provides another assessment of a firm's performance.**

HOW **Operating cash flow provides a reality check in cases in which earnings are of questionable value such as when a company has reported large one-time noncash expenses or when earnings management may have been used to inflate reported earnings. The cash flow statement also offers a one-page summary of the results of a company's operating, investing, and financing activities for the period.**

The key question is whether a cash flow statement tells us anything we don't already know from the balance sheet and income statement. This is a legitimate question because the conceptual framework says that the primary focus of financial reporting is earnings, and earnings information is a better indicator of a firm's ability to generate cash in the future than is current cash flow information.

To answer the question: Yes, we need the cash flow statement. Some of the important reasons discussed in this chapter follow.

- Sometimes earnings fail.
- Everything is on one page.
- It is used as a forecasting tool.

Sometimes Earnings Fail

In some situations, net income does not give us an accurate picture of the economic performance of a company for a certain period. Three such scenarios are illustrated here by reference to actual company examples: (1) the Circle K scenario, (2) the Home Depot scenario, and (3) the KnowledgeWare scenario.

The Big Loss Scenario When a company reports large noncash expenses, such as write-offs, depreciation, and provisions for future obligations, earnings may give a gloomier picture of current operations than is warranted. As discussed in the opening scenario of the chapter, Circle K reported record losses in the same years it was reporting record positive cash flow from operations. In such cases, cash flow from operations is a better indicator of whether the company can continue to honor its commitments to creditors, customers, employees, and investors in the near term. Don't misunderstand this to mean that a reported loss is nothing to worry about as long as cash flow is positive; the positive cash flow indicates that business can continue for the time being, but the reported loss may hint at looming problems in the future.

> **! CAUTION**
>
> Note that the heading to this section says that "sometimes" earnings fail. In most cases, net income is the single best measure of a firm's economic performance.

The Rapid Growth Scenario Rapidly growing firms use large amounts of cash to expand inventory. In addition, cash collections on the growing accounts receivable often lag behind the need to pay creditors. In these cases, reported earnings may be positive, but operations are actually consuming rather than generating cash. This can make it difficult to service debt and satisfy investors' demands for cash dividends. For example, in the mid-1980s, **The Home Depot** was faced with a crisis as exponential sales growth necessitated operating cash infusions every year in spite of the fact that earnings were positive.[5] The lesson is this: For high-growth companies, positive income is no guarantee that sufficient cash flow is there to service current needs.

The Reality Check Scenario Accounting assumptions are the heart of accrual accounting. For companies entering phases in which it is critical that reported earnings look good, those assumptions can be stretched—sometimes to the breaking point. Such phases include just before making a large loan application, just before the initial public offering of stock (when founding entrepreneurs cash in all those years of struggle and sweat), and just before being bought out by another company. In these cases, cash flow from operations, which is not impacted by accrual assumptions, provides an excellent reality check for reported earnings. For example, in 1994, **KnowledgeWare**, an Atlanta-based software company, was acquired by **Sterling Software**. Negotiations over the purchase price were thrown into chaos when it was disclosed that KnowledgeWare had been overly optimistic with its revenue recognition assumptions. At the time, one accounting professor commented: "Cash from operations is the critical number investors should be looking at when evaluating one of these companies."[6]

Everything Is on One Page

As discussed in more detail later, the cash flow statement includes information on operating, investing, and financing activities. In essence, everything you ever wanted to know about a company's performance for the year is summarized in this one statement. How successful were operations for the year? Look at the Operating Activities section. What new investments were made in property, plant, and equipment? Look in the Investing Activities section. Where did the money come from this year to finance all this stuff? See the Financing Activities section. If you were stuck on a desert island and could receive only a single financial statement each year (by bottle floated in on the waves), you would probably choose the cash flow statement.

It Is Used as a Forecasting Tool

When forecasting the future, a cash flow statement is an excellent tool to analyze whether the operating, investing, and financing plans are consistent and workable. To do this, one constructs a pro forma, or projected, cash flow statement. A pro forma cash flow statement is a prediction of what the actual cash flow statement will look like in future years if the operating, investing, and financing plans are implemented. For example, most lenders would be reluctant to loan money to a company to finance new investing activities when the pro forma cash flow statement indicates that there will be no positive operating cash flow to repay the loan. Construction of a pro forma cash flow statement is illustrated later in this chapter.

[5] The cash flow problems of Home Depot in 1985 are the subject of a very popular Harvard Business School case written by Professor Krishna Palepu.

[6] Timothy L. O'Brien, "KnowledgeWare Accounting Practices Are Questioned," *The Wall Street Journal*, September 7, 1994, p. B2.

FASB CODIFICATION

The Issue: You have interrupted a successful acting career and are now following your dream of studying accounting. However, you still have a fondness for the film industry. You recently overheard an extremely disturbing conversation between two accounting professors. One of the professors said to the other: "Yes, exploitation is one of the primary operating cash outflows in the film business."

You are shocked to hear such an unfair characterization of the business where you got your start. You are planning to confront this professor and denounce him for voicing such an odious stereotype. However, before you visit the offending professor in his office, you want to do some research in the accounting standards to find out a bit more about accounting in the film industry, particularly as it relates to operating cash outflows.

The Question: What has "exploitation" got to do with operating cash outflows in the film business?

Searching the Codification: This is a great opportunity to use the Industry topics in the FASB Codification. Under the Industry topics, you should see the collection of Entertainment topics in the group 92X. One of those entertainment industries is Topic 926—Films. A look at the menu under this topic should allow you to find some information on the statement of cash flows in the film industry.

The Answer: The correct treatment is described on page 5-34.

Structure of the Cash Flow Statement

2 **Outline the structure of and information reported in the three main categories of the cash flow statement: operating, investing, and financing.**

WHY **The statement of cash flows is divided into three sections to allow users to determine how the company is both generating and using cash in each general activity of the business.**

HOW **A financial statement user can gain much insight into the current state of a company by comparing the magnitudes of cash flows from operating, investing, and financing activities. For young companies, operating cash flow is sometimes negative. For mature, successful "cash cows," operating cash flow is more than enough to pay for investing activities.**

A statement of cash flows explains the change during the period in cash and cash equivalents. A cash equivalent is a short-term, highly liquid investment that can be converted easily into cash. To qualify as a cash equivalent, an item must be[7]:

1. Readily convertible to cash
2. So near to its maturity that there is insignificant risk of changes in value due to changes in interest rates

Generally, only investments with original maturities of three months or less qualify as cash equivalents. Original maturity in this case is determined from the date an investment is acquired by the reporting entity, which often does not coincide with the date

[7] FASB ASC Section 230-10-20 (Glossary)—Cash equivalents.

the security is issued. For example, both a 3-month U.S. Treasury bill and a 3-year Treasury note purchased three months prior to maturity qualify as cash equivalents. However, if the Treasury note were purchased three years ago, it would not qualify as a cash equivalent during the last three months prior to its maturity.[8] In addition to U.S. Treasury obligations, cash equivalents can include items such as money market funds and commercial paper. Investments in marketable equity securities (common and preferred stock) normally would not be classified as cash equivalents because such securities have no maturity date.

Not all investments qualifying as cash equivalents need be reported as such. Management establishes a policy concerning which short-term, highly liquid investments are to be treated as cash equivalents. Once a policy is established, management should disclose which items are being treated as cash equivalents in presenting its cash flow statement. Any change in the established policy should be disclosed.

Three Categories of Cash Flows

In the statement of cash flows, cash receipts and payments are classified according to three main categories:

- Operating activities
- Investing activities
- Financing activities

Exhibit 5-2 summarizes the major types of cash receipts and cash payments included in each category and includes the income statement and balance sheet accounts that are typically related to each category in the statement of cash flows.

Operating Activities Operating activities include those transactions and events associated with the revenues and expenses that enter into the determination of net income. Cash receipts from selling goods or from providing services are the major cash inflows for most businesses. Other cash receipts come from interest, dividends, and similar items. Major cash outflows include payments to purchase inventory and to pay wages, taxes, interest, utilities, rent, and similar expenses. The net amount of cash provided or used by operating activities is the key figure in a statement of cash flows. In the same way that net income is used to summarize everything in an income statement, net cash from operations is the "bottom line" of the cash flow statement.

> **! CAUTION**
>
> Whether an activity is an operating activity depends upon the nature of the business. The purchase of machinery is an investing activity for a manufacturing business, but it is an operating activity for a machinery sales business.

Although cash inflows from interest or dividends logically might be classified as investing or financing activities, the FASB decided to classify them as operating activities. The guiding principle is that the Operating Activities section contains the cash flow effects of revenues and expenses included in the income statement.

Investing Activities The primary investing activities are the purchase and sale of land, buildings, equipment, and other assets not generally held for resale. In addition, investing activities

[8] Ibid.

EX 5-2 MAJOR CASH RECEIPTS AND PAYMENTS BY CATEGORY

Operating Activities

Cash receipts from:	Cash payments for:
Sale of goods or services	Inventory purchases
Sale of trading securities*	Wages and salaries
Interest revenue	Taxes
Dividend revenue	Interest expense
	Other expenses (e.g., utilities, rent)
	Purchase of trading securities*

Related items: income statement; current operating assets; current operating liabilities; some long-term operating assets and liabilities

*Cash flows associated with trading securities are usually, but not always, classified as operating activities.

Investing Activities

Cash receipts from:	Cash payments for:
Sale of plant assets	Purchase of plant assets
Sale of a business segment	Purchase of nontrading securities
Sale of nontrading securities	Making loans to other entities
Collection of principal on loans	

Related items: property, plant, and equipment; long-term investments; other long-term assets

Financing Activities

Cash receipts from:	Cash payments for:
Issuance of stock	Cash dividends
Borrowing (e.g., bonds, notes, mortgages)	Repayment of loans
	Repurchase of stock (treasury stock)

Related items: short-term and long-term debt; common stock; treasury stock; dividends

STOP&THINK

There is conceptual difficulty in categorizing some cash flow items into just one of the three cash flow activities specified by the FASB. Two items that the FASB insists be classified as operating activities can be classified in other ways, or even in their own categories, according to the IASB. Look at the list below and identify these two problematic items.

a) Payment of wages and payment for inventory purchases
b) Payment of rent and payment of insurance
c) Payment of interest and payment of income taxes
d) Payment of utilities and payment for repairs

include the purchase and sale of financial instruments not intended for trading purposes, as well as the making and collecting of loans. These activities occur regularly and result in cash receipts and payments, but they are not classified as operating activities because they relate only indirectly to the central, ongoing operation of a business.

Financing Activities Financing activities include transactions and events whereby cash is obtained from or repaid to owners (equity financing) and creditors (debt financing). For example, the cash proceeds from issuing stock or bonds would be classified under financing activities. Similarly, payments to reacquire stock (treasury stock) or to retire bonds and the payment of dividends are considered financing activities.

The nature of financing activities is the same no matter what industry a company is in, but operating and investing activities differ considerably across industries. For example, the operating and investing activities of a supermarket chain are quite different from those of a sand and gravel company. However, for both companies, the process of borrowing money, selling stock, paying cash dividends, and repaying loans is almost the same.

Cash Flow Pattern The normal pattern of positive inflows or negative outflows of cash reported in the cash flow statement is as follows:

- Cash from operating activities, +
- Cash from investing activities, −
- Cash from financing activities, + or −

Most companies (73% in the United States in 2006) generate positive cash flow from operations. In fact, several periods of negative cash from operations is a sure indicator of financial trouble. In normal times, most companies use cash to expand or enhance long-term assets, so cash from investing activities is usually negative (83% of the time in the United States in 2006). A company with positive cash flows from investing activities is selling off its long-term assets faster than it is replacing them.

No general statements can be made about cash flows from financing activities; in healthy companies the number can be either positive or negative. As an example, positive cash flows from financing activities can be a sign of a young company that is expanding so fast that operations cannot provide enough cash to finance the expansion. Hence, additional cash must come from financing. Negative cash flows from financing activities might be exhibited by a mature company that has reached a stable state and has surplus cash from operations that can be used to repay loans or to pay higher cash dividends. Accordingly, a company's cash flow pattern is a general reflection of where the company is in its life cycle. As shown in Exhibit 5-3, a young or rapidly growing company requires cash inflows from financing activities in order to pay for its capital expansion (investing activities) and to subsidize negative operating cash flow resulting from a buildup in inventories and receivables. In a company that has stopped growing and is focused on maintaining its position, cash from operations is sufficient to finance the replenishment of long-term assets and to pay dividends to the investors. Finally, a mature, successful company (sometimes called a *cash cow*) generates so much cash from operations that it can pay for capital expansion and have cash left over to repay loans, pay cash dividends, and even repurchase shares of stock.

> **FYI**
>
> A contender for the world record "cash cow" year is **ExxonMobil** in 2008. In that year, ExxonMobil's operating cash flow of $59.7 billion was enough to pay for its investing activities ($15.5 billion), repay debt ($0.5 billion), pay cash dividends ($8.1 billion), and repurchase stock ($35.7 billion).

Further discussion of the interpretation of the cash flow pattern is in a later section of this chapter.

Noncash Investing and Financing Activities

Some investing and financing activities affect an entity's financial position but not the entity's cash flow during the period. For example, equipment may be purchased with a note payable, or land may be acquired by issuing stock. Such noncash investing and financing activities should be disclosed separately, either in the notes to the financial statements or in an accompanying schedule, but not in the cash flow statement itself.[9] For example, when

[9] FASB ASC paragraph 230-10-50-3.

EX 5-3 CASH FLOW PATTERNS OVER THE LIFE OF A COMPANY

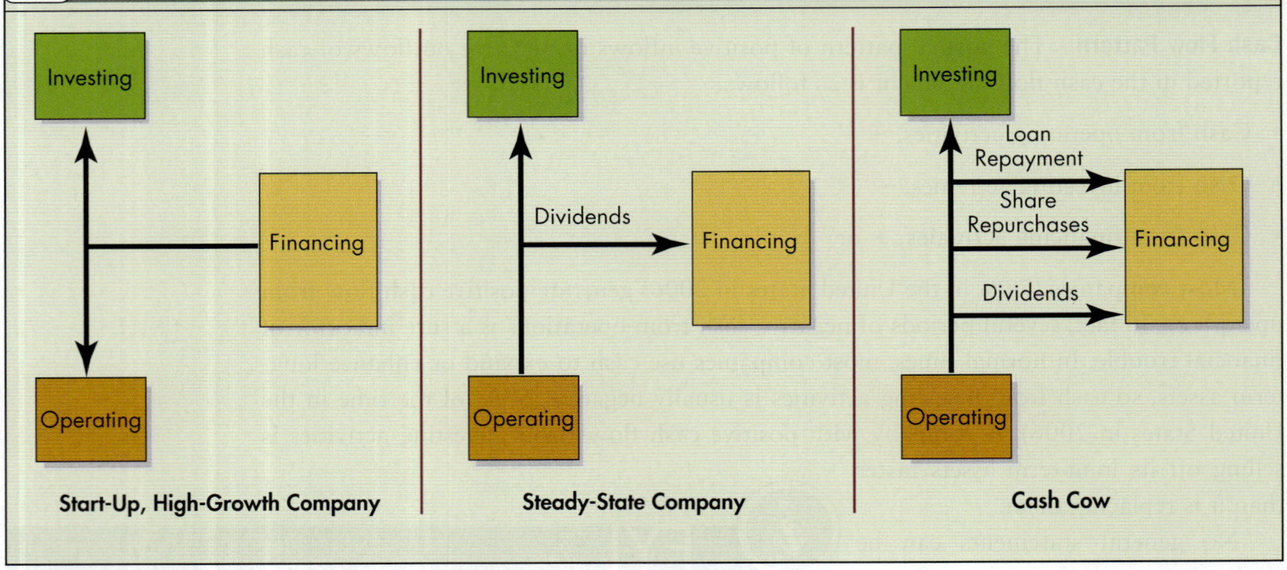

Chevron Corporation acquired a 50% interest in a joint venture with Kazakhstan to develop the Tengiz oil field, the $709 million deferred portion of the acquisition price was disclosed in the notes to Chevron's financial statements as a noncash transaction.

ifrs

Cash Flow Categories under *IAS 7*

A cash flow statement has been required under IFRS since 1992. The provisions of *IAS 7*, *Statement of Cash Flows*, are more flexible than the U.S. rules contained FASB *ASC Section 230* (originally *SFAS No. 95*). Total cash flow, operating plus investing plus financing, is the same under both sets of rules, but a few common types of cash flows can be classified in different categories depending on whether U.S. GAAP or IFRS is used to make the categorization. A summary of those differences is given below.

Type of Cash Flow	U.S. GAAP—*ASC Section 230*	IFRS—*IAS 7*
Cash paid for interest (associated with interest expense)	Operating activity	Operating or financing activity
Cash paid for income taxes (associated with income tax expense)	Operating activity	Usually operating activity, but can be split among operating, investing, and financing depending on the nature of the transaction giving rise to the tax payment
Cash received from interest (associated with interest revenue)	Operating activity	Operating or investing activity
Cash received from dividends (associated with dividend revenue)	Operating activity	Operating or investing activity
Cash paid for dividends (not an income statement item)	Financing activity	Financing or operating activity

The key number in a cash flow statement is total operating cash flow. As you can see from the table above, total operating cash flow for a company using IFRS could be greater than, less than, or the same as what the same company would report under U.S. GAAP, depending on the classification choices made under IFRS.

The particulars for computing operating cash flow, as illustrated in the next section, are slightly different under IFRS if some of the items above are classified differently from what is required under U.S. GAAP. Those slight differences are demonstrated in Chapter 21 when we revisit the statement of cash flows.

Reporting Cash Flow from Operations

3 Compute cash flow from operations using either the direct or the indirect method.

WHY **The accounting standards allow for two different ways of reporting cash from operations—the indirect and the direct method. Both methods result in the same amount.**

HOW **The direct method is a recap of the income statement with the objective of reporting how much cash was received or disbursed in association with each income statement item. The indirect method starts with net income and then reports adjustments for operating items not involving cash flow.**

EX 5-4 GENERAL FORMAT FOR A STATEMENT OF CASH FLOWS—INTEL CORPORATION 2009 (AMOUNTS IN MILLIONS)

Cash provided by (or used for):	
Operating activities	$11,170
Investing activities	(7,965)
Financing activities	(2,568)
Net increase (decrease) in cash and cash equivalents	$ 637
Cash and cash equivalents at beginning of year	3,350
Cash and cash equivalents at end of year	$ 3,987

Exhibit 5-4 illustrates the general format, with details omitted, for a statement of cash flows using data from **Intel**'s statement of cash flows. The statement should report the net cash provided by or used in operating, investing, and financing activities and the net effect of total cash flow on cash and cash equivalents during the period. The information is to be presented in a manner that reconciles beginning and ending cash and cash equivalent amounts.[10]

The preparation of the Investing and Financing Activities sections of the statement of cash flows is straightforward. The Operating Activities section, however, is more complex. Operating cash flow is actually a simple concept: It is merely the difference between cash

[10] Additional disclosures are required in reconciling the change in cash and cash equivalents for a company that has subsidiaries located in foreign countries. Because of changes in exchange rates, the U.S. dollar equivalent of foreign cash balances can change during the year even if the foreign subsidiary enters into no transactions. If the amount is material, the effect of this change is shown as a separate line in the cash flow statement of U.S. multinationals.

EX 5-5 RELATIONSHIP BETWEEN NET INCOME AND OPERATING CASH FLOW

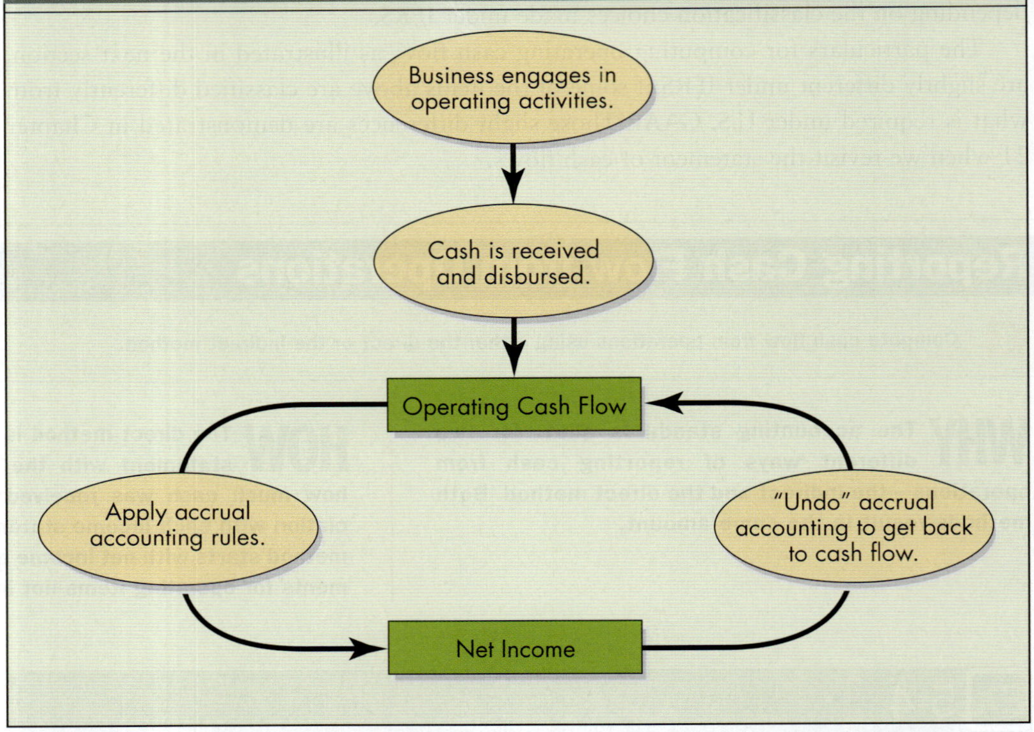

received and cash disbursed for operating activities. The computation of operating cash flow is difficult because accounting systems are designed to adjust cash flow numbers to arrive at accrual net income. Computing operating cash flow requires undoing all the accrual accounting adjustments. This is illustrated in Exhibit 5-5.

Two methods may be used in calculating and reporting the amount of net cash flow from operating activities: the indirect method and the direct method. The most popular method used in reported financial statements is the indirect method; it is used by approximately 95% of large U.S. corporations.

> **! CAUTION**
> The choice of the direct or indirect method is not a way to manipulate the amount of reported cash flow from operations. Both methods yield the same number.

The direct method is essentially a reexamination of each income statement item with the objective of reporting how much cash was received or disbursed in association with the item. For example, for the item Sales in the income statement, there is a corresponding item in the cash flow statement called *cash collected from customers*. For cost of goods sold, the corresponding item is *cash paid for inventory*. To prepare the Operating Activities section using the direct method, one must adjust each income statement item for the effects of accruals.

The indirect method begins with net income as reported on the income statement and adjusts this accrual amount for any items that do not affect cash flow. The adjustments are of three basic types.

- Revenues and expenses that do not involve cash inflow or outflow.
- Gains and losses associated with investing or financing activities.

- Adjustments for changes in current operating assets and liabilities that indicate non-cash sources of revenues and expenses.

Both methods produce identical results—that is, the same amount of net cash flow provided by (or used in) operations. The indirect method is favored and used by most companies because it is relatively easy to apply and it reconciles the difference between net income and the net cash flow provided by operations. Many users of financial statements favor the direct method because it reports directly the sources of cash inflow and outflow without the potentially confusing adjustments to net income. The FASB considered the arguments for both methods, and although the Board favored the clarity of the direct method, it finally permitted either method to be used.[11]

The choice of the indirect or direct method affects only the Operating Activities section. The Investing and Financing Activities sections are exactly the same regardless of which method is used to report cash flow from operations.

Operating Activities: Simple Illustration

The following data for Orchard Blossom Company are used to illustrate both the direct and the indirect methods:

Orchard Blossom Company
Selected Balance Sheet and Income Statement Data

	End of Year	Beginning of Year
Balance sheet:		
Cash	$ 25	$ 15
Accounts receivable	60	40
Inventory	75	100
Wages payable	10	7
Income statement:		
Sales	$150	
Cost of goods sold	(80)	
Wages expense	(25)	
Depreciation expense	(30)	
Net income	$ 15	

Direct Method The best way to do the direct method is to systematically go down the list of income statement items and calculate how much cash is associated with each item.

Sales and cash collected from customers. The beginning accounts receivable balance, along with sales for the year, constitutes potential collections from customers. The ending accounts receivable balance represents accounts not collected. Thus, cash collected from customers is computed as follows:

	Beginning accounts receivable	$ 40
+	Sales	150
=	Cash available for collection	$190
−	Ending accounts receivable	60
=	Cash collected from customers	$130

[11] FASB ASC paragraphs 230-10-45-25 and 28.

Note that a faster way to do this is to adjust the $150 sales amount by the $20 change in accounts receivable. The question is whether to add or subtract the $20. An increase in accounts receivable means less cash, so subtract the $20 increase ($150 – $20 = $130).

Cost of goods sold and cash paid for inventory. The ending inventory balance, along with cost of goods sold for the year, represents the total amount of inventory the company must have purchased some time in the past. The beginning inventory balance represents inventory purchased in prior years. Thus, inventory purchased this year is computed as follows:

	Ending inventory	$ 75
+	Cost of goods sold	80
=	Required inventory	$155
–	Beginning inventory	100
=	Inventory purchased this year	$ 55

Alternatively, adjust the $80 cost of goods sold amount by the $25 change in inventory. Should you add or subtract the $25? First, remember that in the absence of any inventory changes, the $80 in cost of goods sold would have represented an $80 OUTFLOW to replenish the inventory that was sold. A decrease in inventory during the year means that you purchased less than you sold, so less cash was paid to replenish the inventory. Accordingly, add the decrease in inventory (–$80 + $25 = –$55) to arrive at the net $55 outflow for inventory purchased during the year.

> **! CAUTION**
>
> Students who try to prepare cash flow statements solely by memorization of rules (e.g., add all decreases) usually end up getting only 50% of their computations correct. The best approach is to stop and use your business intuition.

Note that in this simple illustration, all inventory is paid for in cash. A subsequent illustration in this chapter will show how to make adjustments for accounts payable.

Wages expense and cash paid for wages. The beginning wages payable balance, along with wages expense for the year, constitutes the total obligation to employees. The ending wages payable balance represents the amount of that obligation not yet paid. Thus, cash paid to employees for wages is computed as follows:

	Beginning wages payable	$ 7
+	Wages expense	25
=	Total obligation to employees	$32
–	Ending wages payable	10
=	Cash paid for wages	$22

This can also be computed by adding the $3 increase in wages payable to the $25 cash outflow represented by wages expense (–$25 + $3 = –$22). You ADD the $3 increase because the increase represents wages that were not paid in cash during the year.

Depreciation expense. Here's a trick question: How much cash is paid for depreciation? None, because depreciation is a noncash expense.

The Operating Activities section of Orchard Blossom's cash flow statement, using the direct method, appears as follows:

Orchard Blossom Company
Statement of Cash Flows
Operating Activities: Direct Method

Cash collected from customers	$130
Cash paid for inventory	(55)
Cash paid for wages	(22)
Cash paid for depreciation	0
Net cash from operating activities	$ 53

Of course, in a proper cash flow statement, there would be no line for cash paid for depreciation. It is included here only to remind you that no cash is paid for depreciation.

Indirect Method With the indirect method, we start with net income, which incorporates the net effect of all the income statement items, and then report the adjustments necessary to convert all income statement items into cash flow numbers. Only the adjustments themselves are reported. As with the direct method, the best way to perform the indirect method is to go right down the income statement, item by item.

Sales. What adjustment is necessary to convert this item to a cash flow number? The $20 increase in accounts receivable means that cash collected is $20 less than the $150 sales number indicates. So, the necessary adjustment to convert net income into cash flow is to subtract the $20 increase in accounts receivable.

Cost of goods sold. The $25 decrease in inventory means that although cost of goods sold of $80 is included in the income statement, less cash was used to purchase inventory than is suggested by the cost of goods sold number. Therefore, add the $25 inventory decrease to convert net income into cash flow.

Wages expense. The income statement includes a $25 subtraction for wages expense. However, the $3 increase in wages payable indicates that not all of that $25 wages expense was paid in cash. Accordingly, the $3 increase in wages payable is added to net income.

Depreciation expense. The $30 depreciation expense is a noncash expense. Because it was subtracted in computing net income, it must be added back to net income in computing cash flow. Add the $30 depreciation expense to net income.

The Operating Activities section of Orchard Blossom's cash flow statement, using the indirect method, follows.

Orchard Blossom Company
Statement of Cash Flows
Operating Activities: Indirect Method

Net income	$15
Plus: Depreciation	30
Less: Increase in accounts receivable	(20)
Plus: Decrease in inventory	25
Plus: Increase in wages payable	3
Net cash from operating activities	$53

Note that net cash from operating activities, commonly referred to as *cash flow from operations*, is the same, $53, whether the direct or the indirect method is used. Also note that depreciation is the first item listed after net income. This is the traditional presentation. This ordering is unfortunate because it reinforces two wrong ideas.

- Depreciation is a source of cash. *Wrong.*
- Cash flow is equal to net income plus depreciation. *Wrong.*

Depreciation is not a source of cash.[12] Depreciation is added back to net income to offset the effect of subtracting depreciation expense in the original computation of net income. The net effect is to eliminate depreciation in the computation of cash flow.

The definition "cash flow equals net income plus depreciation" is widely used. A quick look at Orchard Blossom's indirect method Operating Activities section shows, however, that the "net income plus depreciation" definition ignores all of the changes in current assets and current liabilities. Sometimes the changes in current items cancel (as they almost do in Orchard Blossom's case), so "net income plus depreciation" can be a good estimate of true cash from operations. However, many times, particularly with rapidly expanding firms, the current item changes do not cancel out. In those situations, true cash from operations is much lower than the "net income plus depreciation" definition would indicate. The "net income plus depreciation" definition is used widely in finance, and many finance professors believe it with all their hearts. Don't let them deceive you.

FYI

One advantage of the indirect method is that it highlights how cash flow can be improved in the short run by adjusting operating procedures. In the Orchard Blossom example, both cutting back on inventory levels and slowing payments of wages increased the amount of cash generated by operations.

Comparison of Direct and Indirect Methods The computations of Orchard Blossom's net income and operating cash flow are compared as follows:

Income Statement		Adjustments		Cash Flows from Operations	
Sales	$150	− 20	(increase in accounts receivable)	$130	Cash collected from customers
Cost of goods sold	(80)	+ 25	(decrease in inventory)	(55)	Cash paid for inventory
Wages expense	(25)	+ 3	(increase in wages payable)	(22)	Cash paid for wages
Depreciation expense	(30)	+ 30	(not a cash flow item)	0	
Net income	$ 15	+ 38	net adjustment	$ 53	Cash flows from operations

With the direct method of reporting cash from operations, each of the individual cash flow items is reported. The Operating Activities section of a statement of cash flows prepared using the direct method is, in effect, a cash-basis income statement and involves reporting the shaded information from the following work sheet.

[12] Depreciation is not a source of cash in a financial accounting context. However, when income taxes are considered, the depreciation tax deduction lowers the income tax liability. Thus, when analyzing the cash flow of a business or a project, the depreciation tax deduction is a source of cash to the extent that it lowers the amount of income taxes paid. This issue is covered in most textbook discussions of capital budgeting.

Income Statement		Adjustments		Cash Flows from Operations	
Sales	$150	− 20	(increase in accounts receivable)	$130	Cash collected from customers
Cost of goods sold	(80)	+ 25	(decrease in inventory)	(55)	Cash paid for inventory
Wages expense	(25)	+ 3	(increase in wages payable)	(22)	Cash paid for wages
Depreciation expense	(30)	+ 30	(not a cash flow item)	0	
Net income	$ 15	+ 38	net adjustment	$ 53	Cash flows from operations

With the indirect method, only net income and the adjustments are reported. Therefore, the Operating Activities section of the statement of cash flows for Orchard Blossom includes the shaded information in the following table.

Income Statement		Adjustments		Cash Flows from Operations	
Sales	$150	− 20	(increase in accounts receivable)	$130	Cash collected from customers
Cost of goods sold	(80)	+ 25	(decrease in inventory)	(55)	Cash paid for inventory
Wages expense	(25)	+ 3	(increase in wages payable)	(22)	Cash paid for wages
Depreciation expense	(30)	+ 30	(not a cash flow item)	0	
Net income	$ 15	+ 38	net adjustment	$ 53	Cash flows from operations

Both methods of reporting operating cash flow have advantages. The primary advantage of the direct method is that it is very straightforward and intuitive. The primary advantage of the indirect method is that it highlights the factors that cause net income and cash from operations to differ. As mentioned earlier, almost all large U.S. companies use the indirect method. Some actual examples of the large differences that can exist between income and cash from operations are given in Exhibit 5-6.

EX 5-6 LARGE DIFFERENCES BETWEEN INCOME AND CASH FROM OPERATIONS FOR THE YEAR 2009 (IN MILLIONS OF U.S. DOLLARS)

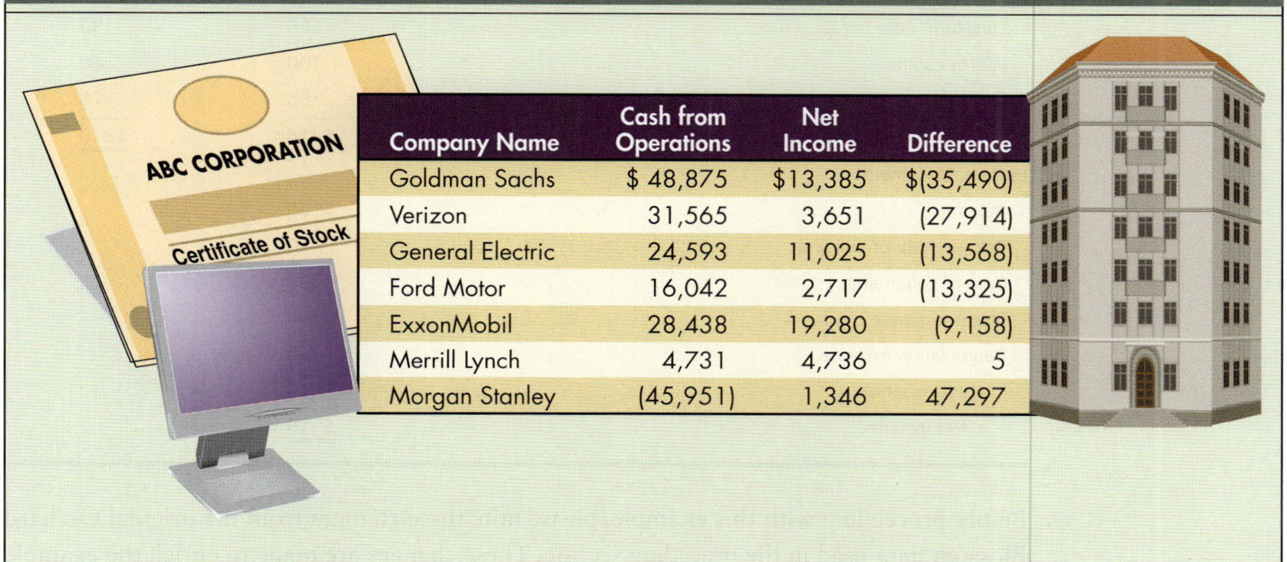

Company Name	Cash from Operations	Net Income	Difference
Goldman Sachs	$ 48,875	$13,385	$(35,490)
Verizon	31,565	3,651	(27,914)
General Electric	24,593	11,025	(13,568)
Ford Motor	16,042	2,717	(13,325)
ExxonMobil	28,438	19,280	(9,158)
Merrill Lynch	4,731	4,736	5
Morgan Stanley	(45,951)	1,346	47,297

Preparing a Complete Statement of Cash Flows

4 **Prepare a complete statement of cash flows and provide the required supplemental disclosures.**

WHY **A complete statement of cash flows summarizes all of the important activities—operating, investing, and financing—undertaken by a company during a given period.**

HOW **Basic information to prepare the three sections of the cash flow statement comes from the balance sheet and income statement, as follows:**

- **Operating—income statement adjusted for changes in current operating assets and liabilities.**
- **Investing—changes in long-term assets.**
- **Financing—changes in long-term liabilities and in owners' equity.**

In this section, we will expand the Orchard Blossom Company example into a comprehensive problem in order to illustrate the preparation of a complete statement of cash flows. For this example, we will need complete balance sheet data as of the beginning and end of the year, as well as income statement data for the year. These data are as follows:

Orchard Blossom Company
Complete Balance Sheet and Income Statement Data

	End of Year	Beginning of Year
Balance Sheet:		
Cash	$ 25	$ 15
Accounts receivable	60	40
Inventory	75	100
Land	120	105
Buildings	200	160
Accumulated depreciation	(66)	(50)
Total assets	$414	$370
Accounts payable	$ 50	$ 37
Wages payable	10	7
Long-term debt	169	190
Paid-in capital	100	60
Retained earnings	85	76
Total liabilities and equity	$414	$370
Income Statement:		
Sales	$150	
Gain on sale of building	10	
Cost of goods sold	(80)	
Wages expense	(25)	
Depreciation expense	(30)	
Interest expense	(10)	
Net income	$ 15	

Before proceeding with this example, please note three changes from the original Orchard Blossom data used in the preceding section. These changes are made to enrich the example so that it will illustrate all of the major items you need to learn at this point with respect to preparing a complete statement of cash flows.

- Accounts payable have been added to the balance sheet. This will change the operating cash flow calculation done previously. We will assume that all of these accounts payable relate to inventory purchases.
- Interest expense has been added to the income statement. This will change the operating cash flow calculation done previously.
- A gain on sale of building has been added to the income statement. From supplemental information (not found in the balance sheet or income statement), we learn that buildings with an original cost of $36 and a book value of $22 were sold for a total of $32, resulting in the reported gain of $10 ($32 sales price – $22 book value). The sale of a building is an investing activity, yet the gain is shown as part of net income, which we use as our basis for computing operating cash flow. We will have to be careful how we handle this gain.

The following 6-step process outlines a systematic method that can be used in analyzing the income statement and comparative balance sheets in preparing a statement of cash flows:

1. Compute how much the cash balance changed during the year. The statement of cash flows is not complete until the sum of cash from operating, investing, and financing activities exactly matches the total change in the cash balance during the year.
2. Convert the income statement from an accrual-basis to a cash-basis summary of operations. This is done in three steps.
   (a) Eliminate expenses that do not involve the outflow of cash, such as depreciation expense.
   (b) Eliminate gains and losses associated with investing or financing activities to avoid counting these items twice.
   (c) Adjust for changes in the balances of current operating assets and operating liabilities because these changes indicate cases in which the operating cash flow associated with an item does not match the revenue or expense reported for that item.

The final result of these adjustments is that net income is converted into cash flow from operating activities.

3. Analyze the long-term assets to identify the cash flow effects of investing activities. Changes in property, plant, and equipment may indicate that cash has either been spent or received.
4. Analyze the long-term debt and stockholders' equity accounts to determine the cash flow effects of any financing transactions. These transactions include borrowing or repaying debt, issuing or buying back stock, and paying dividends. Also, examine changes in short-term loan accounts; borrowing and repaying under short-term arrangements are also classified as financing activities.
5. Make sure that the total net cash flow from operating, investing, and financing activities is equal to the net increase or decrease in cash as computed in step 1. Then, prepare a formal statement of cash flows by classifying all cash inflows and outflows according to operating, investing, and financing activities. The net cash flows from each of the three main activities should be highlighted.
6. Prepare supplemental disclosure, including the disclosure of any significant investing or financing transactions that did not involve cash. This disclosure is done outside the

cash flow statement itself. The types of transactions disclosed in this way include the purchase of land by issuing stock and the retirement of bonds by issuing stock. In addition, supplemental disclosure of cash paid for interest expense and taxes is required.

We will illustrate this 6-step process using the expanded information from the Orchard Blossom example. Because we will prepare the statement of cash flows without reference to the detailed cash flow transaction data, we are going to have to make some informed inferences about cash flows by examining the balance sheet and income statement accounts.

Step 1. Compute How Much the Cash Balance Changed During the Year. Orchard Blossom began the year with a cash balance of \$15 and ended with a cash balance of \$25. Thus, our target in preparing the statement of cash flows is to explain why the cash account increased by \$10 during the year.

Step 2. Convert the Income Statement from an Accrual-Basis to a Cash-Basis Summary of Operations. Recall that converting accrual net income into cash from operations involves eliminating noncash expenses, removing the effects of gains and losses, and adjusting for the impact of changes in current operating asset and liability balances. These adjustments are shown in the work sheet, Exhibit 5-7, and are explained below. Many of the adjustment are the same as those illustrated in the simple Orchard Blossom example in the previous section.

Depreciation expense (adjustment A1). The first adjustment involves adding the amount of depreciation expense. As explained previously, because depreciation expense does not involve an outflow of cash, and because depreciation was initially subtracted to arrive at net income, this adjustment effectively eliminates depreciation from the computation of cash from operations. It can be seen in the far right column of the work sheet in Exhibit 5-7 that adjustment A1 results in a \$0 (–\$30 + \$30 = \$0) cash flow effect from depreciation.

Gain on sale of building (adjustment B1). Adjustment must also be made for any gains or losses included in the computation of net income. Orchard Blossom sold buildings during the year and recorded a gain of \$10 on the sale. The \$32 cash flow effect of the building sale (mentioned above) will be shown in the Investing Activities section of the cash flow statement. To avoid counting any part of the \$32 sales amount twice, the gain should be

EX 5-7 ADJUSTMENTS TO CONVERT ORCHARD BLOSSOM'S ACCRUAL NET INCOME TO CASH FROM OPERATIONS

	Income Statement		Adjustments		Cash Flows from Operations
Sales	\$150	C1	\$(20)	Increase in accounts receivable	\$130
Gain on sale of building	10	B1	(10)	Investing activity item	0
Cost of goods sold	(80)	C2	25	Decrease in inventory	(42)
		C3	13	Increase in accounts payable	
Wages expense	(25)	C4	3	Increase in wages payable	(22)
Depreciation expense	(30)	A1	30	Not a cash flow item	0
Interest expense	(10)			No interest payable balance	(10)
Net income	\$ 15		\$ 41		\$ 56

excluded from the Operating Activities section. However, the gain has already been added in the computation of net income. In order to exclude the gain from the Operating Activities section, it must be subtracted from net income. If there had been a loss on the building sale, that loss would be added back to net income in the Operating Activities section so that it would not impact cash flows from operations. The full $32 cash flow impact of the sale of this building (to be analyzed later) is reported in the Investing Activities section.

Ryan McVay/Getty Images

A company's statement of cash flows must reflect the amount of cash paid for inventory during the year. For example, in the computation of cash from operations, Reebok must reduce the cost of goods sold number to reflect that part of the inventory sold in the current period was actually purchased in the prior period.

Changes in current assets and liabilities. The remaining adjustments (C1–C4 in Exhibit 5-7) are needed because the computation of accrual net income involves reporting revenues and expenses when economic events occur, not necessarily when cash is received or paid. The timing differences between the receipt or payment of cash and the earning of revenue or the incurring of an expense are reflected in the shifting balances in the current operating assets and liabilities. This is illustrated through a discussion of each of Orchard Blossom's current operating asset and liability accounts.

Accounts receivable (adjustment C1). Recall from our analysis earlier in the chapter that the amount of cash Orchard Blossom collected from customers during the year differed from sales for the period. The $20 increase in accounts receivable is subtracted, as shown in Exhibit 5-7.

Inventory (adjustment C2). The statement of cash flows should reflect the amount of cash paid for inventory during the year, which is not necessarily the same as the cost of inventory sold. Orchard Blossom's inventory decreased by $25 during the year, indicating that the amount of inventory purchased during the year was less than the amount of inventory sold. Accordingly, in the computation of cash from operations we must reduce the cost of goods sold number to reflect the fact that part of the inventory sold this period was actually purchased last period. To reduce cost of goods sold (which is subtracted in the computation of net income), the adjustment involves adding $25, as shown in Exhibit 5-7. This addition of $25 represents an increase in cash flow because less cash was used to replenish inventory during the year.

Accounts payable (adjustment C3). The balance in Orchard Blossom's accounts payable account increased by $13 during the year. This increase occurred because Orchard Blossom paid for less than it bought from its suppliers during the year. The adjustment necessary to reflect this reduction in cash outflow is to add $13 in computing cash from operations, shown as adjustment C3 in Exhibit 5-7. As seen in the exhibit, total cash paid to purchase inventory during the year was $42.

Wages expenses (adjustment C4). The balance in Orchard Blossom's wages payable account increased by $3 during the year. This increase occurred because Orchard Blossom did not pay all wages due to its employees during the year. The adjustment necessary to reflect this reduction in cash outflow for wages is to add $3 in computing cash from operations, shown as adjustment C4 in Exhibit 5-7. Again, when the wages payable account increases, the company has more cash because cash was conserved and not used to pay its operating obligations.

Interest expense. Because an interest payable account does not exist, we can safely assume that all interest expense was paid for in cash. Therefore, there is no need for an adjustment. If there were an interest payable account, the reasoning used when analyzing the accounts payable and wages payable accounts would apply.

Note that the total cash inflow from operating activities is $56, which is $3 more than the $53 we computed in the earlier example. The $3 difference arises because in this expanded example we included $10 in interest expense (which reduces operating cash flow by $10) and also included a $13 increase in the accounts payable balance (which increases operating cash flow by $13). The net effect is to increase operating cash flow by $3 relative to the previous simple example.

Step 3. Analyze the Long-Term Assets to Identify the Cash Flow Effects of Investing Activities. Orchard Blossom reports two long-term asset accounts.

- Land
- Buildings

We will analyze each of these in turn to determine how much cash flow was associated with each during the year.

Land. The land account increased by $15 ($120 – $105) during the year. This could be a combination of purchases and sales of land. Because there is no indication of land sales during the year, we conclude that the $15 represents the price of new land purchased during the year.

Buildings. The balance in Orchard Blossom's buildings account increased by $40 ($200 – $160) during the year. In the absence of any other information, this increase would suggest that Orchard Blossom purchased buildings with a cost of $40. However, in this case, additional information mentioned above is available indicating that buildings were sold for $32 during the year. This $32 cash proceeds from the sale is a cash inflow from investing activities. This building sale complicates our calculations so that we aren't yet sure how much was paid to purchase new buildings during the year.

A useful way to summarize all of the purchase and sale information for buildings is to reconstruct the T-accounts for both the buildings account and the associated accumulated depreciation account. Those T-accounts appear as follows:

Buildings			
Beg. Bal.	160		
Purchases	[76]	36	Historical cost of items sold
End. Bal.	200		

Accumulated Depreciation			
		50	Beg. Bal.
Accum. dep. on items sold	[14]	30	Dep. exp.
		66	End. Bal.

The amounts in boxes (amount of purchases and amount of accumulated depreciation associated with the items sold) can be inferred given the other information. With this information, we can compute whether the sale of buildings resulted in a gain or in a loss as follows:

Cash proceeds (given earlier)	$32
Book value of items sold ($36 – $14)	22
Gain on sale of buildings	$10

The existence of a $10 gain is confirmed in the Orchard Blossom income statement. Note that with the income statement information and the amounts inferred using the T-accounts above, we could have traced backward and computed the cash proceeds from the sale of the buildings and equipment. The T-accounts are very useful devices for structuring the information that we have so that we can infer the missing values needed to complete the statement of cash flows.

Step 4. Analyze the Long-Term Debt and Stockholders' Equity Accounts to Determine the Cash Flow Effects of Any Financing Transactions. Long-term debt accounts increase when a company borrows more money—an inflow of cash—and decrease when the company pays back the debt—an outflow of cash. In the case of Orchard Blossom, we observe that the company's balance in Long-Term Debt decreased by $21 ($190 – $169) during the year. Accordingly, we can infer that Orchard Blossom repaid $21 in loans during the year. This $21 loan repayment represents cash used by financing activities. The same analysis would apply to short-term debt. The $40 ($200 – $160) increase in Orchard Blossom's paid-in capital account during the year represents a cash inflow from the issuance of new shares of stock. This cash inflow is reported as part of cash from financing activities.

The retained earnings account increases from the recognition of net income (an operating activity), decreases as a result of net losses (also an operating activity), and decreases through the payment of dividends (a financing activity). In the absence of detailed information, it is possible to infer the amount of dividends declared by identifying the unexplained change in the retained earnings account balance. An efficient way to do this is to recreate the retained earnings T-account as follows:

Retained Earnings

		76	Beg. Bal.
Dividends	6	15	Net income
		85	End. Bal.

So, the amount of dividends paid during the year was $6. Of course, it is usually the case that the amount of dividends paid is disclosed somewhere in the financial statements. However, you never know the level of detailed information to which you will have access. And, after all, it is a relatively simple (and fun!) analytical exercise.

Step 5. Prepare a Formal Statement of Cash Flows. Based on our analyses of the income statement and balance sheet accounts, we have identified all inflows and outflows of cash for Orchard Blossom for the year, and we have categorized those cash flows based on the type of activity. The resulting statement of cash flows (prepared using the indirect method, which is by far the more common method of presentation) is shown in Exhibit 5-8. Note that the statement indicates that the total change in cash for the year is an increase of $10, which matches the $10 increase (from $15 to $25) shown on the balance sheet.

Step 6. Prepare Supplemental Disclosure. Two categories of supplemental disclosure are associated with the statement of cash flows. These are as follows:

- Cash paid for interest and income taxes
- Noncash investing and financing activities

EX 5-8 COMPLETE STATEMENT OF CASH FLOWS FOR ORCHARD BLOSSOM COMPANY

Orchard Blossom Company
Statement of Cash Flows
For the Year Ended December 31

Cash flows from operating activities:		
Net income		$ 15
Adjustments:		
Add: Depreciation expense	$ 30	
Subtract: Gain on sale of building	(10)	
Subtract: Increase in accounts receivable	(20)	
Add: Decrease in inventory	25	
Add: Increase in accounts payable	13	
Add: Increase in wages payable	3	41
Net cash provided by operating activities		$ 56
Cash flows from investing activities:		
Sold buildings	$ 32	
Purchased land	(15)	
Purchased buildings	(76)	
Net cash used by investing activities		(59)
Cash flows from financing activities:		
Issued stock to shareholders	$ 40	
Repaid long-term debt	(21)	
Paid dividends	(6)	
Net cash provided by financing activities		13
Net increase in cash		$ 10
Beginning cash balance		15
Ending cash balance		$ 25

Cash paid for interest and income taxes. FASB *ASC Topic 230* requires separate disclosure of the cash paid for interest and for income taxes during the year. When the direct method is used, the amounts of cash paid for interest and for income taxes are part of the Operating Activities section, so no additional disclosure is needed. When the indirect method is used, these amounts must be shown separately, either at the bottom of the cash flow statement, or in an accompanying note. In the case of Orchard Blossom (which has no income taxes), the supplemental information might be presented as follows:

Supplemental Disclosure:	
Cash paid for interest	$10

Noncash investing and financing activities. When a company has significant noncash transactions, such as purchasing property, plant, and equipment by issuing debt or in exchange for shares of stock, these transactions must be disclosed in the notes to the financial statements. Orchard Blossom did not have any of these noncash transactions, so no additional disclosure is necessary in this case.

This Orchard Blossom example includes all the common items that are encountered in preparing a statement of cash flows. In Chapter 21, we will revisit the statement of cash flows and learn how to handle some more complex items.

Using Cash Flow Data to Assess Financial Strength

5 **Assess a firm's financial strength by analyzing the relationships among cash flows from operating, investing, and financing activities and by computing financial ratios based on cash flow data.**

WHY **Patterns of positive and negative cash flow in the three categories of operating, investing, and financing yield insights into the health and current strategy of a business.**

HOW **Data from the cash flow statement can be used in conjunction with balance sheet and income statement data to compute financial ratios.**

Various analytical techniques are used to assess a company's financial strength. Key variables are profitability, efficiency, leverage, and liquidity. By tradition, analysts have concentrated on the relationships captured in the income statement and the balance sheet. More and more emphasis is now placed, however, on cash flows and the relationships of data reported on the cash flow statement in conjunction with the income statement and the balance sheet.

Cash Flow Patterns

It is possible to gain useful insights about a company by analyzing the relationships among the three cash flow categories. Exhibit 5-9 shows the eight different possible patterns. Patterns 1 and 8 are unusual. Pattern 1 might exist when a firm is experiencing positive cash flows from all three activities and is seeking to significantly increase its cash position for some strategic reason. Pattern 8 shows negative cash flows from all activities and could exist, even in the short-term, only if a company had existing cash reserves to draw upon. Patterns 2 through 4 show positive operating cash flows that are sufficient by themselves (pattern 2) or are supplemented by investing (pattern 3) or financing (pattern 4) activities to settle debt, pay owners, or expand the business. Patterns 5 through 7 are not healthy over the long term, because operating cash shortfalls have to be covered by selling long-term assets and/or by securing external financing.

These cash flow patterns stress the importance of operating cash flows. A positive operating cash flow allows a company to pay its bills, its creditors, and its shareholders and to grow and expand. A negative operating cash flow means a company has to look at other sources of cash, which eventually dry up if operations are not successful.

Cash Flow Ratios

The data from a cash flow statement also can be used to compute selected ratios that help determine a company's financial strength. If such ratios are compared for the same company over a period of time or with other companies in the same industry, they can be helpful in evaluating relative performance. To illustrate the computation of selected cash flow ratios, selected data from Circle K's 1989 and 1988 financial statements (before Circle K's disastrous year in 1990) will be used (Exhibit 5-10).

> **FYI**
>
> Most courses in financial statement analysis still make only passing mention of cash flow ratios. Familiarity with the ratios discussed in this section is a quick and easy way to set oneself apart from the crowd.

EX 5-9 ANALYSIS OF CASH FLOW STATEMENT: PATTERNS

	CF from Operating	CF from Investing	CF from Financing	General Explanation
#1	+	+	+	Company is using cash generated from operations and from sale of assets and from financing to build up pile of cash—very liquid company—possibly looking for acquisition.
#2	+	−	−	Company is using cash flow generated from operations to buy fixed assets and to pay down debt or pay owners.
#3	+	+	−	Company is using cash from operations and from sale of fixed assets to pay down debt or pay owners.
#4	+	−	+	Company is using cash from operations and from borrowing (or from owner investment) to expand.
#5	−	+	+	Company's operating cash flow problems are covered by sale of fixed assets and by borrowing or by shareholder contributions.
#6	−	−	+	Company is growing rapidly but has shortfalls in cash flow from operations and from purchase of fixed assets financed by long-term debt or new investment.
#7	−	+	−	Company is financing operating cash flow shortages and payments to creditors and/or stockholders via sale of fixed assets.
#8	−	−	−	Company is using cash reserves to finance operation shortfall and pay long-term creditors and/or investors.

Source: Michael T. Dugan, Benton E. Gup, and William D. Samson, "Teaching the Statement of Cash Flows," *Journal of Accounting Education*, Vol. 9, 1991, p. 36.

Cash Flow to Net Income Perhaps the most important cash flow relationship is the relationship between cash from operations and reported net income. The cash-flow-to-net-income ratio reflects the extent to which accrual accounting assumptions and adjustments have been included in computing net income. The formula is cash from operations divided by net income. For Circle K, computation of the cash-flow-to-net-income ratios is as follows:

	1989	1988
Cash from operations	$57,767	$84,333
Net income	÷15,414	÷60,411
Cash-flow-to-net-income ratio	3.75	1.40

In general, the cash-flow-to-net-income ratio has a value more than 1.0 because of the existence of significant noncash expenses (such as depreciation) that reduce reported net income but have no impact on cash flow. For a given company, the cash-flow-to-net-income

EX 5-10 SELECTED CASH FLOW DATA FOR CIRCLE K FOR 1988 AND 1989

(In thousands of dollars)	1989	1988
Net income	$ 15,414	$ 60,411
Cash from operations	57,767	84,333
Cash paid for capital expenditures	193,338	233,087
Cash paid for acquisitions	68,139	147,500
Cash paid for interest	89,928	49,267
Cash paid for income taxes	11,233	28,439

ratio should remain fairly stable from year to year. A significant increase in the ratio, such as that reported by Circle K in 1989, indicates that accounting assumptions were instrumental in reducing reported net income. This ratio reveals that, from the standpoint of management concerned about being able to pay the bills and creditors concerned about timely repayment of loans, Circle K's performance in 1989 was actually somewhat better than indicated by just looking at net income. From the numbers reported earlier in the chapter, it is apparent that the same was true in 1990 when the reported net loss was $773 million but the cash generated by operations was $108 million.

Cash Flow Adequacy As defined earlier, a *cash cow* is a business that is generating enough cash from operations to completely pay for all new plant and equipment purchases with cash left over to repay loans or to distribute to investors. The cash flow adequacy ratio, computed as cash from operations divided by expenditures for fixed asset additions and acquisitions of new businesses, indicates whether a business is a cash cow. Computation of the cash flow adequacy ratio for Circle K is as follows:

	1989	1988
Cash from operations	$ 57,767	$ 84,333
Cash paid for capital expenditures	$193,338	$233,087
Cash paid for acquisitions	68,139	147,500
Cash required for investing activities	$261,477	$380,587
Cash flow adequacy ratio	0.22	0.22

The calculations indicate that in both 1988 and 1989, Circle K's cash from operations fell well short of being able to pay for its expansion. This means that Circle K was forced to seek substantial amounts of external financing, either new debt or additional funds from investors, during both years.

FYI

Cash paid for dividends is sometimes added to the denominator of the cash flow adequacy ratio. With this formulation, the ratio indicates whether operating cash flow is sufficient to pay for both capital additions and regular dividends to stockholders.

Cash Times Interest Earned Because interest payments must be made with cash, an informative indicator of a company's interest-paying ability compares cash generated by operations to cash paid for interest. This cash times interest earned ratio is computed for Circle K as follows:

	1989	1988
Cash from operations	$ 57,767	$ 84,333
Cash paid for interest	89,928	49,267
Cash paid for income taxes	11,233	28,439
Cash before interest and taxes	$158,928	$162,039
Cash paid for interest	÷ 89,928	÷ 49,267
Cash times interest earned ratio	1.77	3.29

Pretax cash flow is used because interest is paid before any taxes are deducted. From this calculation, we can see that Circle K's creditors experienced a significant drop in security in 1989 because Circle K's operations generated only 1.77 times the amount of cash that was needed in order to make its required interest payments. Ultimately, the inability to continue making its interest payments forced Circle K into bankruptcy.[13]

Articulation: How the Financial Statements Tie Together

6 Demonstrate how the three primary financial statements tie together, or articulate, in a unified framework.

WHY Complete understanding and intelligent use of financial statements requires familiarity with how the three primary financial statements are quantitatively linked.

HOW The essence of financial statement articulation is summarized in these three relationships.

a. Balance sheet and income statement—The income statement for the year details the change in the retained earnings balance (less dividends) for the year.

b. Balance sheet and statement of cash flows—The statement of cash flows details the change in the cash balance for the year.

c. Income statement and statement of cash flows—The important accrual adjustments made during the year explain the difference between the income statement and the Operating section of the statement of cash flows.

In an accounting context, articulation means that the three primary financial statements are not isolated lists of numbers but are an integrated set of reports on a company's financial health. The statement of cash flows contains the detailed explanation for why the balance sheet cash amount changed from beginning of year to end of year. The income statement, combined with the amount of dividends declared during the year, explains the change in retained earnings shown in the balance sheet. Cash from operations in the statement of cash flows is transformed into net income through the accounting adjustments applied to the raw cash flow data. These relationships are illustrated in Exhibit 5-11 using the financial statement numbers from the Orchard Blossom Company example in the preceding section.

[13] For additional cash flow ratios, see Don E. Giacomino and David E. Mielke, "Cash Flows: Another Approach to Ratio Analysis," *Journal of Accountancy*, March 1993, p. 57.

The balance sheet can be viewed as the mother of all financial statements, with the statement of cash flows merely giving some details about changes in the cash balance in the balance sheet and the income statement merely giving some details about changes in the retained earnings balance. Of course, before we get too carried away in our admiration of the balance sheet, we should remind ourselves that these "mere changes" in the cash balance and the retained earnings balance capture much of what business is all about.

Now let's take a detailed look at Exhibit 5-11. Note that the $10 increase in cash during the year, from a beginning balance of $15 to an ending balance of $25, is explained by the sum of the cash flows from operating, investing, and financing activities reported in the statement of cash flows. The $9 increase in the retained earnings balance during the year, from a beginning balance of $76 to an ending balance of $85, is explained by the $15 net income, reported in the income statement, less the $6 paid in dividends. The link between the statement of cash flows (or, more precisely, the Operating section of the statement of cash flows) and the income statement is the accrual adjustments made during the year. One of the beauties of the indirect method of reporting cash flow from operating activities is that these accrual adjustments are summarized in one place. Look back at Exhibit 5-8 and see that the body of the Operating Activities section is a listing of the net effects of the operating accrual adjustments made during the year.

The articulation diagram in Exhibit 5-11 gives just a glimpse of the interrelationships among the financial statements. As you saw when we prepared the Investing Activities section of the Orchard Blossom Company statement of cash flows, the beginning and ending balances in the buildings and accumulated depreciation accounts, along with reported

EX 5-11 ARTICULATION OF THE FINANCIAL STATEMENTS

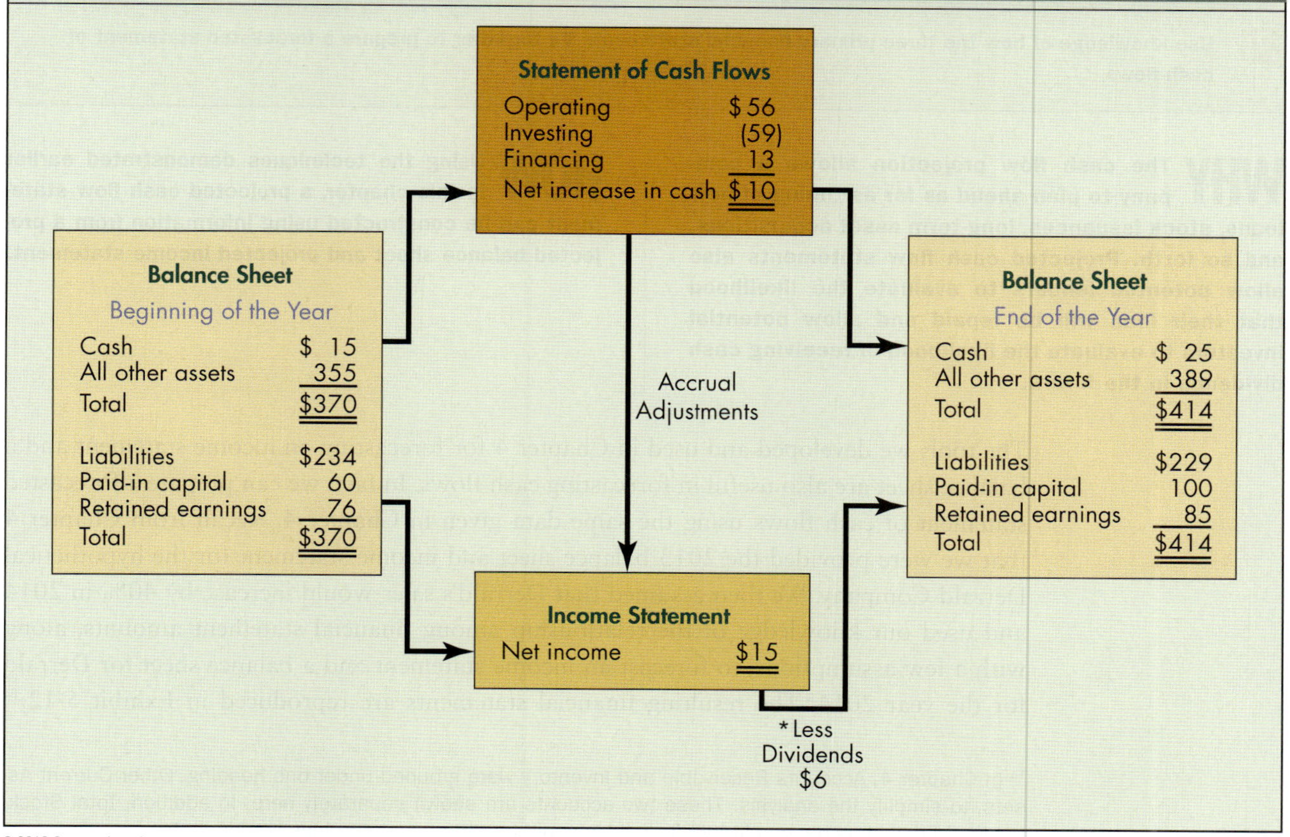

Depreciation Expense from the income statement, combine to indicate the amount of cash flow from investing activities as reported in the statement of cash flows. Similarly, the changes in long-term debt and paid-in capital are explained in the Financing Activities section of the statement of cash flows. Look again at Exhibit 5-11 and imagine a complex web connecting the beginning and ending balance sheets with the income statement and the statement of cash flows; this web represents the complete articulation of the financial statements.

The articulation of the three primary financial statements is perhaps the most beautiful, and useful, aspect of the financial accounting model. The constraints of this articulation framework require that all of the recorded transactions and the accrual assumptions for a company for a year must fit together and add up. In Chapter 6, we will discuss some of the practices of earnings management that are attempted by desperate managers seeking to make their company look better on paper. Earnings management can deceive financial statement users for a limited time, but the inexorable requirements of financial statement articulation mean that ultimately any deception practiced in the income statement will show up as increasingly unlikely amounts in the balance sheet and increasingly disturbing differences between net income and operating cash flow.

Similarly, the articulation of the financial statements is an important disciplinary tool in making financial forecasts. In the concluding section of this chapter, you will learn how to prepare a forecasted statement of cash flows. Because the financial statements must articulate, you will be able to clearly see that assumptions about building purchases and dividend payments ripple through all three financial statements, and no financial plan is complete until all of these ripple effects have been analyzed, recorded, and articulated.

Forecasted Statement of Cash Flows

7 **Use knowledge of how the three primary financial statements tie together to prepare a forecasted statement of cash flows.**

WHY **The cash flow projection allows a company to plan ahead as far as timing of new loans, stock issuances, long-term asset acquisitions, and so forth. Projected cash flow statements also allow potential lenders to evaluate the likelihood that their loan will be repaid and allow potential investors to evaluate the likelihood of receiving cash dividends in the future.**

HOW **Using the techniques demonstrated earlier in this chapter, a projected cash flow statement can be constructed using information from a projected balance sheet and projected income statement.**

The tools we developed and used in Chapter 4 for forecasting an income statement and a balance sheet are also useful in forecasting cash flows. In fact, we can prepare a forecasted statement of cash flows using the same data given in Chapter 4. Recall from Chapter 4 that we were provided the 2013 balance sheet and income statement for the hypothetical Derrald Company. We then assumed that Derrald's sales would increase by 40% in 2014 and used our knowledge of the relationship among financial statement amounts, along with a few assumptions, to forecast an income statement and a balance sheet for Derrald for the year 2014. The resulting financial statements are reproduced in Exhibit 5-12.[14]

[14] In Chapter 4, Accounts Receivable and Inventory were grouped under one heading, Other Current Assets, to simplify the analysis. These two accounts are shown separately here. In addition, Total Stockholders' Equity has been split into its paid-in capital and retained earnings components.

EX 5-12 FORECASTED BALANCE SHEET AND INCOME STATEMENT FOR DERRALD COMPANY

Balance Sheet	2013	2014 Forecasted	Basis for Forecast
Cash	$ 10	$ 14	40% natural increase
Accounts receivable	100	140	40% natural increase
Inventory	150	210	40% natural increase
Property, plant, and equipment, net	300	500	management decision
Total assets	$560	$864	
Accounts payable	$100	$140	40% natural increase
Bank loans payable	300	524	management decision
Paid-in capital	50	50	management decision
Retained earnings	110	150	plus net income less dividends
Total liabilities and stockholders' equity	$560	$864	

Income Statement	2013	2014 Forecasted	Basis for Forecast
Sales	$1,000	$1,400	40% increase
Cost of goods sold	700	980	70% of sales, same as last year
Gross profit	$ 300	$ 420	
Depreciation expense	30	50	10% of PP&E, same as last year
Other operating expenses	170	238	17% of sales, same as last year
Operating profit	$ 100	$ 132	
Interest expense	30	52	10% of bank loan, same as last year
Income before taxes	$ 70	$ 80	
Income taxes	30	34	43% of pretax, same as last year
Net income	$ 40	$ 46	

Using the same 6-step process for preparing a statement of cash flows that was described earlier in the chapter, we can use the data in Exhibit 5-12 to construct a forecasted statement of cash flows for Derrald Company for 2014.

Step 1. Compute the Change in Cash. Cash is forecasted to increase by $4 ($14 − $10) from 2013 to 2014. Hence, we know that the sum of cash from operating, investing, and financing activities in the forecasted statement of cash flows must be $4.

Step 2. Convert the Income Statement from an Accrual Basis to a Cash Basis. Beginning with the forecasted income statement, the following adjustments are necessary:

	Income Statement	Adjustments	Cash Flows from Operations
Sales	$1,400	A. −40	$ 1,360
Cost of goods sold	(980)	B. −60	(1,000)
		C. +40	
Depreciation expense	(50)	D. +50	0
Other operating expenses	(238)	E. 0	(238)
Interest expense	(52)	F. 0	(52)
Income taxes	(34)	G. 0	(34)
Net income	$ 46		$ 36

Adjustment A. Accounts Receivable is forecasted to increase by $40 ($140 – $100) during 2014, indicating that more sales will be made during the year than will be collected in cash. To compute cash collected from customers, sales must be reduced by the amount of the $40 forecasted increase in Accounts Receivable.

Adjustment B. Inventory is forecasted to increase by $60 ($210 – $150), indicating that more inventory will be purchased than will be sold. This $60 Inventory increase represents an additional cash outflow.

Adjustment C. Accounts Payable is forecasted to increase by $40 ($140 – $100), signifying that not all inventory that will be purchased on account during 2014 will be paid for during 2014. Thus, the Accounts Payable increase represents a cash savings.

Adjustment D. Forecasted depreciation expense of $50 does not involve cash and must be added back in computing cash from operating activities.

Adjustments E through G. For this example, we are assuming that the accounts payable account relates strictly to the purchase of inventory and that all other expenses involving the outflow of cash are paid for immediately. As a result, there are no payable accounts relating to other operating expenses, interest, or taxes. If payable accounts relating to these expenses were to exist, the analysis would be similar to that conducted for Accounts Payable: Increases would be added (indicating a cash savings by allowing the payable to increase) and decreases would be subtracted (indicating an additional outflow of cash to reduce the payable balance).

The resulting Operating section of the forecasted statement of cash flows indicates that Derrald Company will generate $36 from operations in 2014.

Step 3. Analyze the Long-Term Asset Accounts. The only long-term asset account is Property, Plant, and Equipment (PP&E). PP&E is forecasted to increase from $300 to $500 in 2014. Note that the PP&E amount is reported "net," meaning that accumulated depreciation is subtracted from the reported PP&E amount rather than being shown as a separate amount. As a result, the "net" PP&E amount can be affected by any of three events: purchase of new PP&E (an addition), sale of old PP&E (a subtraction), and depreciation of existing PP&E (a subtraction). Using the forecasted information, and assuming that no old PP&E will be sold during 2014, we can conclude the following.

	Beginning PP&E	$300
	PP&E to be sold during the year	0
–	PP&E depreciation	(50)
=	Ending PP&E without purchase of new PP&E	$250

The fact that the projected ending PP&E balance is $500 implies that Derrald Company expects to purchase $250 ($500 – $250) in new PP&E during 2014. This $250 forecasted purchase represents cash to be used for investing activities.

Step 4. Analyze the Long-Term Debt and Stockholders' Equity Accounts. The bank loans payable account is projected to increase from $300 to $524. This difference of $224 represents a cash inflow from financing. Because Paid-In Capital is projected to remain at $50, Derrald Company is not expecting to raise any new cash by issuing shares of stock during 2014.

The $40 ($150 – $110) projected increase in Retained Earnings must be analyzed in light of expected net income for 2014. Because Derrald Company is expected to have net income of $46 in 2014, it must also be expecting to pay dividends of $6 to result in the net increase in Retained Earnings of $40. The $6 forecasted dividend payment is reported as a cash outflow from financing activities.

Step 5. Prepare the Statement of Cash Flows. All information necessary to prepare the forecasted statement of cash flows is now assembled. The forecasted statement is shown in Exhibit 5-13, with forecasted operating cash flows being reported using the indirect method. Note that the sum of the forecasted operating, investing, and financing cash flows ($36 – $250 + $218) is equal to the total forecasted change in cash of $4.

Step 6. Disclose Any Significant Noncash Activities. Derrald Company does not anticipate any significant noncash activities during 2014, so the forecasted cash flow statement completely summarizes the important events that are expected to occur.

From the forecasted cash flow statement, we can see that Derrald's expected operating cash flow will not be nearly enough to pay for the additional PP&E it expects to acquire during 2014. As a result, Derrald plans to make up the shortfall with a significant $224 increase in its bank loan payable account. When used internally, the projected statement of cash flows allows Derrald Company to plan ahead; Derrald can start investigating the likelihood of obtaining such a large new loan. Alternatively, Derrald could consider scaling back the expansion plans if obtaining the required financing doesn't appear feasible. An external user, such as a bank, can use the forecasted cash flow statement to see whether it seems likely that Derrald can continue to meet its existing obligations. An investor can use the projected cash flow statement to evaluate the likelihood that Derrald will be able to continue making dividend payments. In summary, construction of a full set of projected financial statements—a balance sheet, an income statement, and a statement of cash flows—allows the financial statement user to see whether a company's strategic plans concerning operating, investing, and financing activities are consistent with one another.

EX 5-13 FORECASTED STATEMENT OF CASH FLOWS FOR DERRALD COMPANY FOR 2014

Derrald Company
Forecasted Statement of Cash Flows
For the Year Ended December 31, 2014

Cash flows from operating activities:		
Net income		$ 46
Adjustments:		
Add depreciation	$ 50	
Subtract increase in accounts receivable	(40)	
Subtract increase in inventory	(60)	
Add increase in accounts payable	40	
		(10)
Net cash provided by operating activities		$ 36
Cash flows from investing activities:		
Purchase of property, plant, and equipment	$(250)	
Net cash used in investing activities		(250)
Cash flows from financing activities:		
Borrowing (bank loan payable)	$ 224	
Payment of dividends	(6)	
Net cash provided by financing activities		218
Net increase in cash		$ 4
Beginning cash balance		10
Ending cash balance		$ 14

Conclusion

This chapter has been an overview of the statement of cash flows. Along with the balance sheet and the income statement, the statement of cash flows is one of the three primary financial statements. However, because it is relatively new (required only since 1988), it sometimes does not receive the emphasis that it deserves. Cash flow variables and ratios are only now starting to make it into the mainstream of financial statement analysis. You are now a cash flow statement expert; be patient with those who have not yet caught the vision.

All basic aspects of cash flow reporting and disclosure have been covered in this chapter. Additional complexities are introduced in later chapters as appropriate. An expanded discussion, incorporating these complexities, is provided in Chapter 21. You might start thinking now about how that will be affected by revenue recognition assumptions, FIFO and LIFO, capitalize or expense decisions, operating leases, bonds issued at a discount, stock splits, and dividends. Chapter 21 also includes material on international differences in the statement of cash flows.

SOLUTIONS TO OPENING SCENARIO QUESTIONS

1. Some of the expenses included in Circle K's $773 million loss were noncash expenses. Two examples are the $300 million write-off of goodwill and the $75 million expense recorded for estimated future environmental cleanup costs. In addition, Circle K reduced its inventory level by $65 million, which doesn't affect the computation of net income but does free up $65 million in cash.
2. Under Chapter 11 bankruptcy protection, Circle K was able to reduce the cash it paid for interest in 1991 by $100 million. In addition, collection protection given to new creditors allowed Circle K to increase its accounts payable by $80 million, freeing up a substantial amount of cash.
3. Karl Eller started and ended his business career in the billboard business.

SOLUTION TO STOP & THINK

1. (Page 5-8) The correct answer is C. Conceptually, payment of interest can be thought of as a financing activity. And because income taxes relate to all activities (for example, income tax must be paid on a gain from the sale of land, which is an investing activity), one could argue that categorization of the payment of income taxes depends on the underlying activity that gave rise to these income taxes. The IASB provides flexibility in the classification of the payment of interest and income taxes. In addition, as explained in this chapter, although the FASB requires these items to be classified as operating activities, it also requires that these two specific items be separately disclosed so that financial statement users can reclassify them, if desired, to meet their own needs.

SOLUTION TO USING THE FASB'S CODIFICATION

The glossary in FASB ASC Subtopic 926-230-20 includes the following definition of "exploitation costs" in the film industry: "All direct costs (including marketing, advertising, publicity, promotion, and other distribution expenses) incurred in connection with the distribution of a film."

So, exploitation is indeed a primary operating cash outflow in the film industry. However, the word "exploitation" as used in the accounting standards does not have the same meaning as it does in everyday speech. By the way, it does seem extremely insensitive of the accountants to use the term "exploitation" when talking about marketing, advertising, publicity, and promotion.

REVIEW CHAPTER 5

LEARNING OBJECTIVES

1 Describe the circumstances in which the cash flow statement is a particularly important companion of the income statement.

A cash flow statement is an important companion to the income statement. When noncash expenses are high, earnings gives an overly pessimistic view of a company's performance; cash flow from operations could give a better picture. In addition, the operations of rapidly growing companies can consume cash even when reported net income is positive. Finally, the cash flow statement provides a reality check in situations in which companies have an incentive to bias the accrual accounting assumptions.

The cash flow statement offers a one-page summary of the results of a company's operating, investing, and financing activities for the period. A pro forma, or projected, cash flow statement is an excellent tool to analyze whether a company's operating, investing, and financing plans are consistent and workable.

2 Outline the structure of and information reported in the three main categories of the cash flow statement: operating, investing, and financing.

The three sections of a cash flow statement are operating, investing, and financing. Significant noncash investing and financing transactions must also be disclosed.

- *Operating*. For purposes of preparing a cash flow statement, operating activities are those activities that enter into the calculation of net income. Net cash provided by operating activities is the "bottom line" of the cash flow statement.
- *Investing*. The primary investing activities are the purchase and sale of land, buildings, equipment, and nontrading financial instruments.
- *Financing*. Financing activities involve the receipt of cash from and the repayment of cash to owners and creditors. An exception is that the payment of interest is considered an operating activity.
- *Noncash investing and financing transactions*. These include the purchase of long-term assets in exchange for the issuance of debt or stock.

3 Compute cash flow from operations using either the direct or the indirect method.

There are two ways to present cash flow from operations: the direct method and the indirect method. The direct method is more intuitive; the indirect method emphasizes a reconciliation between net income and cash flow. Almost all companies use the indirect method.

The direct method is a recap of the income statement with the objective of reporting how much cash was received or disbursed in association with each income statement item.

The indirect method starts with net income and then reports adjustments for operating items not involving cash flow. The three types of adjustments are

- Revenues and expenses that do not involve cash inflows or outflows
- Gains and losses associated with investing or financing activities
- Adjustments for changes in current operating assets and liabilities that indicate noncash sources of revenues and expenses

Net cash from operations is the same whether it is computed using the direct method or the indirect method.

4 Prepare a complete statement of cash flows and provide the required supplemental disclosures.

Basic information to prepare the three sections of the cash flow statement comes from the following portions of the balance sheet and the income statement:

- Operating—income statement and current assets and liabilities
- Investing—long-term assets
- Financing—long-term liabilities and owners' equity

A complete cash flow statement is not prepared until each income statement item has been considered, all changes in balance sheet items have been explained, and the net change in cash has been exactly reconciled.

Six steps to preparing a cash flow statement are as follows:

1. Determine the change in cash (including cash equivalents). This is the target number.
2. Operating activities—analyze each income statement item and the changes in all current operating assets and operating liabilities.
3. Investing activities—analyze the changes in all noncurrent assets, such as land, buildings, and so forth.
4. Financing activities—analyze the changes in all noncurrent liabilities, all owners' equity accounts, and all nonoperating current liabilities.
5. Prepare a formal statement of cash flows, reconciling the beginning and ending cash balances. If the sum of operating, investing, and financing activities does not equal the total balance sheet change in cash, something in the cash flow statement is wrong. Fix it.
6. Prepare supplemental disclosure, including the disclosure of any significant investing or financing transactions that did not involve cash.

5 Assess a firm's financial strength by analyzing the relationships among cash flows from operating, investing, and financing activities and by computing financial ratios based on cash flow data.

Patterns of positive and negative cash flow in the three categories of operating, investing, and financing yield insights into the health and current strategy of a business. Most companies have positive cash from operations and negative cash from investing activities.

Data from the cash flow statement can be used in conjunction with balance sheet and income statement data to compute financial ratios.

6 Demonstrate how the three primary financial statements tie together, or articulate, in a unified framework.

Complete understanding of financial statements requires familiarity with how the three primary financial statements are linked together. This linkage is called financial statement articulation. The essence of financial statement articulation is summarized in these three relationships.

(a) Balance sheet and income statement—The income statement for the year details the change in the retained earnings balance (less dividends) for the year.

(b) Balance sheet and statement of cash flows—The statement of cash flows details the change in the cash balance for the year.

(c) Income statement and statement of cash flows—The important accrual adjustments made during the year explain the difference between the income statement and the Operating section of the statement of cash flows.

7 Use knowledge of how the three primary financial statements tie together to prepare a forecasted statement of cash flows.

A projected cash flow statement can be constructed using information from a projected balance sheet and income statement. The cash flow projection allows a company to plan ahead as far as timing of new loans, stock issuances, long-term asset acquisitions, and so forth. Projected cash flow statements also allow potential lenders to evaluate the likelihood that the loan will be repaid and allow potential investors to evaluate the likelihood of receiving cash dividends in the future.

FASB-IASB CODIFICATION SUMMARY

ifrs

Topic	FASB Accounting Standards Codification	Original FASB Standard	Corresponding IASB Standard	Differences between U.S. GAAP and IFRS
Definition of cash equivalents	*Section 230-10-20 (Glossary)—Cash equivalents*	*SFAS No. 95 par. 8*	*IAS 7 par. 7*	No substantial differences
Noncash investing and financing activities	*Section 230-10-50 par. 3*	*SFAS No. 95 par. 32*	*IAS 7 par. 43*	No substantial differences
Direct and indirect methods	*Section 230-10-45 par. 25,28*	*SFAS No. 95 par. 27-28*	*IAS 7 par. 18-19*	No substantial differences
Classification of interest paid	*Section 230-10-45 par. 17(d)*	*SFAS No. 95 par. 23(d)*	*IAS 7 par. 33*	U.S. GAAP—operating IFRS—operating or financing
Classification of income taxes paid	*Section 230-10-45 par. 17(c)*	*SFAS No. 95 par. 23(c)*	*IAS 7 par. 35*	U.S. GAAP—operating IFRS—operating, investing, or financing
Classification of interest received	*Section 230-10-45 par. 16(b)*	*SFAS No. 95 par. 22(b)*	*IAS 7 par. 33*	U.S. GAAP—operating IFRS—operating or investing
Classification of dividends received	*Section 230-10-45 par. 16(b)*	*SFAS No. 95 par. 22(b)*	*IAS 7 par. 33*	U.S. GAAP—operating IFRS—operating or investing
Classification of dividends paid	*Section 230-10-45 par. 15(a)*	*SFAS No. 95 par. 20(a)*	*IAS 7 par. 34*	U.S. GAAP—financing IFRS—operating or financing

KEY TERMS

Articulation 5-28
Cash equivalent 5-6
Cash flow adequacy ratio 5-27
Cash-flow-to-net-income ratio 5-26
Cash times interest earned ratio 5-28
Direct method 5-12
Financing activities 5-8
Indirect method 5-12
Investing activities 5-7
Noncash investing and financing activities 5-9
Operating activities 5-7
Pro forma cash flow statement 5-5
Statement of cash flows 5-6

QUESTIONS

1. Under what circumstances does cash flow from operations offer a clearer picture of a company's performance than does net income?
2. What criteria must be met for an item to be considered a cash equivalent in preparing a statement of cash flows?
3. What are the three categories in a statement of cash flows? What types of items are included in each?
4. What is the normal pattern of cash flow (positive or negative) for operating, investing, and financing activities?

5. Either the direct method or the indirect method may be used to report cash flows from operating activities. What is the difference in approach for the two methods?
6. Why do many users prefer the direct method? Why do the majority of preparers prefer the indirect method?
7. How is depreciation expense handled when the direct method is used? The indirect method?
8. What is wrong with the statement, "Cash flow is equal to net income plus depreciation"?
9. Why does the FASB treat interest payments as an operating activity rather than as a financing activity?
10. When preparing a cash flow statement, what is the "target number"?
11. When using the direct method, what items must be considered in the calculation of cash paid for inventory purchases?
12. How is a loss on the sale of a long-term asset treated when using the direct method? The indirect method?
13. Is the purchase of securities an operating activity or an investing activity? Explain.
14. What supplemental disclosures are required by the FASB if a company elects to use the direct method in preparing its statement of cash flows? What disclosures are required if the indirect method is used?
15. How are significant noncash investing and financing transactions reported in connection with a statement of cash flows?
16. How is interest paid classified in a statement of cash flows under the provisions of FASB ASC Topic 230?
17. On average, which number is larger, net income or cash from operations? Explain.
18. What does it mean when the value of a company's cash flow adequacy ratio is less than 1.0?
19. The income statement provides detail as to transactions that occurred during the period relating to what balance sheet account? The statement of cash flows provides detail as to the transactions that occurred during the period relating to what balance sheet account?
20. A forecasted statement of cash flows allows management to plan ahead. What information is contained in the statement that can be used for planning purposes?
21. How can external users use a forecasted statement of cash flows?

PRACTICE EXERCISES

Practice 5-1
LO2

Cash and Cash Equivalents

A company reports the following information as of the end of the year. Using the information, determine the total amount of cash and cash equivalents.

(a) Investment securities of $10,000. These securities are common stock investments in 30 companies that compose the Dow Jones Industrial average. As a result, the stocks are very actively traded in the market.
(b) Investment securities of $7,250. These securities are U.S. government bonds. The bonds are 30-year bonds; they were purchased on December 31 at which time they had two months to go until they mature.
(c) Cash of $3,400 in the form of coin, currency, savings accounts, and checking accounts.
(d) Investment securities of $6,600. These securities are commercial paper (short-term IOUs from other companies). The term of the paper is nine months; they were purchased on December 31 at which time they had four months to go until they mature.

Practice 5-2
LO2

Three Categories of Cash Flows

Using the following information, compute cash flow from operating activities, cash flow from investing activities, and cash flow from financing activities.

		Cash Inflow (Outflow)
(a)	Cash received from sale of a building	$ 4,200
(b)	Cash paid for interest	(600)
(c)	Cash paid to repurchase shares of stock (treasury stock)	(1,100)
(d)	Cash collected from customers	13,400
(e)	Cash paid for dividends	(930)
(f)	Cash paid for income taxes	(1,850)

Practice 5-3

LO2

Cash Flow Patterns

Identify which of the following cash flow patterns most likely belongs to (1) a start-up, high-growth company; (2) a steady-state company; and (3) a cash cow.

	Operating Cash Flow	Investing Cash Flow	Financing Cash Flow
Company A	$30,000	$(27,000)	$ (1,500)
Company B	(10,000)	(27,000)	40,000
Company C	40,000	(27,000)	(10,000)

Practice 5-4

LO2

Noncash Investing and Financing Activities

Combining the following information, compute the total amount of (1) cash flow from investing activities and (2) cash flow from financing activities.

(a) Purchased a building for $120,000. Paid $40,000 and signed a mortgage with the seller for the remaining $80,000.

(b) Executed a debt-equity swap: replaced a $67,000 loan by giving the lender shares of common stock worth $67,000 on the date the swap was executed.

(c) Purchased land for $100,000. Signed a note for $35,000 and gave shares of common stock worth $65,000.

(d) Borrowed $56,000 under a long-term loan agreement. Used the cash from the loan proceeds as follows: $15,000 for purchase of additional inventory, $30,000 to pay cash dividends, and $11,000 to increase the cash balance.

Practice 5-5

LO3

General Format for a Statement of Cash Flows

Organize the following summary information into the proper format for a statement of cash flows.

Cash balance, beginning of year	$ 2,800
Cash flow from financing activities	5,000
Total stockholders' equity, end of year	24,300
Cash flow from operating activities	6,200
Cash balance, end of year	4,600
Cash flow from investing activities	(9,400)
Total stockholders' equity, beginning of year	21,500

Practice 5-6

LO3

Cash Collected from Customers

Using the following information, compute cash collected from customers.

Sales	$10,000
Cost of goods sold	5,300
Operating expenses	3,800

	End of Year	Beginning of Year
Prepaid operating expenses	$ 700	$1,000
Accounts payable	1,200	1,350
Inventory	2,100	2,500
Accounts receivable	1,375	1,400

Practice 5-7
LO3

Cash Paid for Inventory Purchases
Refer to the information in Practice 5-6. Compute cash paid for inventory purchases. (*Note*: All Accounts Payable relate to inventory purchases.)

Practice 5-8
LO3

Cash Paid for Operating Expenses
Refer to the information in Practice 5-6. Compute cash paid for operating expenses.

Practice 5-9
LO3

Direct Method
Using the following income statement and cash flow adjustment information, prepare the Operating Cash Flow section of the statement of cash flows using the *direct* method.

Sales	$7,800
Cost of goods sold	3,100
Interest expense	450
Depreciation expense	600
Net income	$3,650

Adjustments:
(a) Interest payable *increased* by $80.
(b) Accounts receivable *decreased* by $320.
(c) Inventory *decreased* by $180.
(d) Accounts payable *decreased* by $210. (*Note*: All accounts payable relate to inventory purchases.)

Practice 5-10
LO3

Indirect Method
Refer to Practice 5-9. Prepare the Operating Cash Flow section of the statement of cash flows using the *indirect* method.

Practice 5-11
LO4

Complete Statement of Cash Flows from Detailed Data
Using the following information, prepare a complete statement of cash flows.

(a)	Cash balance, beginning	$ 1,500
(b)	Cash paid to purchase inventory	7,800
(c)	Cash received from sale of a building	4,750
(d)	Cash paid for interest	450
(e)	Cash paid to repay a loan	1,000
(f)	Cash collected from customers	11,200
(g)	Cash balance, ending	?
(h)	Cash received from issuance of new shares of common stock	1,200
(i)	Cash paid for dividends	780
(j)	Cash paid for income taxes	1,320
(k)	Cash paid to purchase machinery	1,950

Practice 5-12
LO3

Operating Cash Flow: Gains and Losses
Using the following information, compute cash flow from operating activities. (*Note*: With the limited information given, only the indirect method can be used.)

Increase in accounts receivable	$ 300
Decrease in income taxes payable	170
Depreciation	1,000
Net income	250
Gain on sale of equipment	440
Loss on sale of building	210

Practice 5-13
LO3

Operating Cash Flow: Restructuring Charges

Using the following information, compute cash flow from operating activities. (*Note*: With the limited information given, only the indirect method can be used.)

Decrease in inventory	$ 300
Increase in wages payable	170
Restructuring charge	2,300
Depreciation	1,000
Net income	500

The restructuring charge consists of two elements: (1) $1,500 for the write-down in value of certain assets and (2) $800 for recognition of an obligation to relocate employees; none of the relocation has yet taken place.

Practice 5-14
LO3

Operating Cash Flow: Deferred Income Taxes

Using the following information, compute cash paid for income taxes.

Reported income tax expense	$35,500

	End of Year	Beginning of Year
Income taxes payable	$ 2,950	$ 2,560
Deferred income tax liability	32,100	28,600

Practice 5-15
LO3

Operating Cash Flow: Deferred, or Unearned, Sales Revenue

Using the following information, compute cash collected from customers.

Sales	$10,000

	End of Year	Beginning of Year
Accounts receivable	$1,250	$1,430
Deferred sales revenue	1,000	750

Practice 5-16
LO3

Operating Cash Flow: Prepaid Operating Expenses

Using the following information, compute cash paid for operating expenses.

Operating expenses:	
Depreciation	$10,000
Insurance	7,500
Wages	14,600
Total operating expenses	$32,100

	End of Year	Beginning of Year
Prepaid insurance	$1,500	$1,430
Wages payable	600	750

Practice 5-17
LO4

Computing Cash Paid to Purchase Property, Plant, and Equipment

Using the following information, compute cash paid to purchase property, plant, and equipment.

Depreciation expense	$9,700

	End of Year	Beginning of Year
Property, plant, and equipment	$134,000	$124,000
Accumulated depreciation	32,000	41,000

During the year, property, plant, and equipment with an original cost of $28,000 was sold for a gain of $6,500.

Practice 5-18
LO4

Computing Cash Received from the Sale of Property, Plant, and Equipment
Refer to Practice 5-17. Compute the amount of cash received from the sale of the property, plant, and equipment.

Practice 5-19
LO4

Computing Cash Paid for Dividends
Using the following information, compute cash paid for dividends.

Net income	$10,000

	End of Year	Beginning of Year
Retained earnings	$112,000	$106,000
Paid-in capital	50,000	44,000
Cash	1,300	1,000
Dividends payable	200	450

Practice 5-20
LO5

Computing Cash Flow Ratios
Using the following information, compute the following ratios: (1) cash-flow-to-net-income, (2) cash flow adequacy, and (3) cash times interest earned.

Net income	$18,000
Cash flow from operating activities	21,000
Cash paid for capital expenditures	23,500
Cash paid for acquisitions	11,000
Cash paid for interest	3,800
Cash paid for income taxes	6,700

Practice 5-21
LO6

Articulation
Use the following information to answer the questions below:

Dividends declared and paid	$ 8,000
Cash from investing activities	(25,000)
Cash from financing activities	(8,000)

	End of Year	Beginning of Year
Cash	$ 22,500	$ 12,000
Other assets	210,000	227,000
Liabilities	106,500	117,000
Common stock	21,000	21,000
Retained earnings	105,000	?

Compute the (a) cash from operating activities and (b) net income.

Practice 5-22
LO7

Preparing a Forecasted Statement of Cash Flows
The following balance sheet and income statement information includes actual data for 2013 and forecasted data for 2014:

	Actual 2013	Forecasted 2014
Cash	$ 100	$ 130
Accounts receivable	600	780
Inventory	1,300	1,690
Property, plant, and equipment (net)	5,000	6,300
Accounts payable	500	650
Long-term debt	4,000	5,000
Paid-in capital	1,000	1,400
Retained earnings	1,500	1,850
Sales	$10,000	$13,000
Cost of goods sold	6,000	7,800
Depreciation expense	1,000	1,200
Interest expense	400	500
Income before income taxes	$ 2,600	$ 3,500
Income tax expense	910	1,225
Net income	$ 1,690	$ 2,275

Prepare a forecasted statement of cash flows for 2014. Use the indirect method of reporting cash flow from operating activities.

EXERCISES

Exercise 5-23
LO2
SPREADSHEET

Classification of Cash Flows

Indicate whether each of the following items would be classified as (1) an operating activity, an investing activity, or a financing activity or (2) as a noncash transaction or noncash item.

(a) Cash collected from customers.
(b) Cash paid to suppliers for inventory.
(c) Cash received for interest on a nontrade note receivable.
(d) Cash received from issuance of stock.
(e) Cash paid for dividends.
(f) Cash received from bank on a loan.
(g) Cash paid for interest on a loan.
(h) Cash paid to retire bonds.
(i) Cash paid to purchase stock of another company as a long-term investment.
(j) Cash received from the sale of a business segment.
(k) Cash paid for property taxes.
(l) Cash received for dividend revenue.
(m) Cash paid for wages.
(n) Cash paid for insurance.
(o) Preferred stock retired by issuing common stock.
(p) Depreciation expense for the year.
(q) Cash paid to purchase machinery.
(r) Cash received from the sale of land.

Exercise 5-24
LO5

Cash Flow Ratios

Following are data from the financial statements for Houma Company.

Houma Company
Selected Financial Statement Data
For the Years Ended December 31, 2013 and 2012

	2013	2012
Net income	$35,500	$ 65,200
Cash from operating activities	28,900	158,130
Cash paid for purchase of fixed assets	42,000	156,000
Cash paid for interest	26,000	24,000
Cash paid for income taxes	15,000	25,670

Compute the following for both 2012 and 2013:

1. Cash-flow-to-net-income ratio
2. Cash flow adequacy ratio
3. Cash times interest earned ratio

Exercise 5-25
LO2

Cash Flow Analysis

State how each of the following items would be reflected on a statement of cash flows.

(a) Securities classified as available for sale were purchased for $4,200.
(b) Buildings were acquired for $210,000, the company paying $60,000 cash and signing an 11% mortgage note, payable in five years, for the balance.
(c) Cash of $54,200 was paid to purchase a business whose assets consisted of inventory, $16,700; furniture and fixtures, $8,400; land and buildings, $20,100; and goodwill, $9,000.
(d) A cash dividend of $2,600 was declared in the current period, payable at the beginning of the next period.
(e) Accounts Payable shows a decrease for the period of $1,250.

Exercise 5-26
LO2

Cash Receipts and Cash Payments

The accountant for Alpine Hobby Stores prepared the following selected information for the year ended December 31, 2013:

	Dec. 31, 2013	Dec. 31, 2012
(a) Equipment	$56,500	$62,000
(b) Accumulated Depreciation	13,900	12,800
(c) Long-Term Debt	20,000	25,000
(d) Common Stock	16,000	12,000

Equipment with a book value of $18,000 was sold for $16,000 cash. The original cost of the equipment was $21,000.

Determine the cash inflows and outflows during 2013 associated with each of the accounts listed. Indicate how the cash flows for each item would be presented on the statement of cash flows.

Exercise 5-27
LO3

SPREADSHEET

Preparing the Operating Activities Section of a Statement of Cash Flows

Norrington Trading Co. provides the following income statement for 2013:

Sales	$675,400
Cost of goods sold	243,500
Gross margin	$431,900
Depreciation expense	51,000

Salaries expense	$124,600
Interest expense	11,300
Other expenses	98,700
Income taxes expense	44,000
Net income	$102,300

In addition, the following balance sheet information is available:

	Dec. 31, 2013	Dec. 31, 2012
Accounts receivable	$52,000	$47,000
Inventory	78,100	72,300
Prepaid other expenses	5,600	6,700
Accounts payable	53,600	52,300
Interest payable	800	1,200
Income taxes payable	5,200	3,400

Using the format presented in the chapter, prepare the Operating Activities section of the statement of cash flows and present that information using (a) the direct method and (b) the indirect method.

Exercise 5-28

LO3

Preparing the Operating Activities Section of the Statement of Cash Flows

Anakin, Inc., provides the following account balances for 2013 and 2012:

	Dec. 31, 2013	Dec. 31, 2012
Accounts Receivable	$ 19,100	$15,500
Inventory	25,440	27,200
Accounts Payable	21,650	22,400
Salaries Payable	1,500	1,350
Sales	278,700	
Cost of Goods Sold	197,000	
Depreciation Expense	16,700	
Salaries Expense	35,200	
Other Expenses	24,300	

Using the format presented in the chapter, prepare the Operating Activities section of the statement of cash flows and present that information using (a) the direct method and (b) the indirect method.

Exercise 5-29

LO6

REVERSE SOLVABLE

Articulation

The following information is available for Santiago Inc.:

	Dec. 31, 2013	Dec. 31, 2012
Cash	$ 141,000	$ 97,000
Retained earnings	665,000	543,000
Cash from operating activities	?	
Cash from investing activities	(483,000)	
Cash from financing activities	(287,000)	
Dividends declared and paid	47,000	
Net income	?	

Compute the following for 2013:

1. Net income
2. Cash from operating activities

Exercise 5-30
LO6

Articulation

The following information is available for Kelsey Inc. (*Note*: All inventory is purchased on account, and Accounts Payable relates only to the purchase of inventory.)

	Dec. 31, 2013	Dec. 31, 2012
Accounts receivable	$?	$75,000
Inventory	72,000	83,000
Accounts payable	56,000	44,000
Sales	540,000	
Cost of goods sold	?	
Cash collected from customers	551,000	
Cash paid for inventory	?	
Inventory purchased on account	279,000	

Compute the following for 2013:

1. The ending balance in accounts receivable
2. The amount of cash paid for inventory
3. The amount of cost of goods sold

Exercise 5-31
LO7

Forecasted Balance Sheet, Income Statement, and Statement of Cash Flows

(*Note*: This exercise uses the same information used in Exercise 4-26.) Ryan Company wishes to prepare a forecasted income statement, balance sheet, and statement of cash flows for 2014. Ryan's balance sheet and income statement for 2013 follow:

Balance Sheet	2013
Cash	$ 10
Other current assets	250
Property, plant, and equipment, net	800
Total assets	$1,060
Accounts payable	$ 100
Bank loans payable	700
Total stockholders' equity	260
Total liabilities and stockholders' equity	$1,060

Income Statement	2013
Sales	$1,000
Cost of goods sold	750
Gross profit	$ 250
Depreciation expense	40
Other operating expenses	80
Operating profit	$ 130
Interest expense	70
Income before taxes	$ 60
Income taxes	20
Net income	$ 40

In addition, Ryan has assembled the following forecasted information regarding 2014.

(a) Sales are expected to increase to $1,500.
(b) Ryan expects to become more efficient at utilizing its property, plant, and equipment in 2014. Therefore, Ryan expects that the sales increase will not require any overall increase in property, plant, and equipment. Accordingly, the year 2014 property, plant, and equipment balance is expected to be $800.
(c) Ryan's bank has approved a new long-term loan of $200. This loan will be in addition to the existing loan payable.
(d) Ryan Company does not anticipate paying any dividends in the coming year.

Instructions:

1. Prepare a forecasted balance sheet for 2014. Clearly state what assumptions you make.
2. Prepare a forecasted income statement for 2014. Clearly state what assumptions you make.
3. Prepare a forecasted statement of cash flows for 2014. Use the indirect method of reporting cash from operating activities. (*Hint*: In computing cash paid to purchase new property, plant, and equipment, don't forget to consider the effect of depreciation expense in 2014.)

Exercise 5-32

LO7

Forecasted Income Statement and Statement of Cash Flows

(*Note*: This exercise uses the same information used in Exercise 4-25.) Romney and Associates wishes to forecast its net income for the year 2014. In addition, for planning purposes Romney intends to construct a forecasted statement of cash flows for 2014. Romney has assembled balance sheet and income statement data for 2013 and has forecast a balance sheet for 2014. In addition, Romney has estimated that its sales in 2014 will rise to $3,600 and does not anticipate paying any dividends in the coming year. This information is summarized here.

Balance Sheet	2013	2014 Forecasted
Cash	$ 40	$ 48
Other current assets	450	540
Property, plant, and equipment (net)	500	700
Total assets	$990	$1,288
Accounts payable	$190	$ 228
Bank loans payable	500	400
Total stockholders' equity	300	660
Total liabilities and stockholders' equity	$990	$1,288

Income Statement	2013	2014 Forecasted
Sales	$3,000	$3,600
Cost of goods sold	1,200	
Gross profit	$1,800	
Depreciation expense	100	
Other operating expenses	1,440	
Operating profit	$ 260	
Interest expense	50	
Income before taxes	$ 210	
Income taxes	84	
Net income	$ 126	

Instructions:

1. Prepare a forecasted income statement for 2014. Clearly state what assumptions you make.
2. Prepare a forecasted statement of cash flows for 2014. Use the indirect method of reporting cash from operating activities. (*Hint*: In computing cash paid to purchase new property, plant, and equipment, don't forget to consider the effect of depreciation expense in 2014.)

Exercise 5-33

LO3, LO4

SPREADSHEET

Cash Computations

A comparative balance sheet, income statement, and additional information for Shillig Doors Inc. follow.

Shillig Doors Inc.
Condensed Comparative Income Statement
For the Years Ended December 31, 2013 and 2012

	2013	2012
Net sales	$3,946,000	$3,112,000
Cost of goods sold	2,385,000	2,364,000
Gross profit	$1,561,000	$ 748,000
Expenses	792,000	506,000
Net income	$ 769,000	$ 242,000

Shillig Doors Inc.
Comparative Balance Sheet
December 31, 2013 and 2012

	2013	2012
Assets		
Current assets:		
Cash	$ 131,000	$ 102,000
Available-for-sale securities	400,000	—
Accounts receivable	409,000	372,000
Inventory	289,000	304,000
Prepaid expenses	36,000	24,000
Total current assets	$1,265,000	$ 802,000
Property, plant, and equipment	$ 656,000	$ 541,000
Accumulated depreciation	(81,000)	(42,000)
	$ 575,000	$ 499,000
Total assets	$1,840,000	$1,301,000
Liabilities and Stockholders' Equity		
Current liabilities:		
Accounts payable	$ 191,000	$ 174,000
Accrued expenses	124,000	110,000
Dividends payable	165,000	100,000
Total current liabilities	$ 480,000	$ 384,000
Notes payable—due 2015	210,000	106,000
Total liabilities	$ 690,000	$ 490,000

(*Continued*)

	2013	2012
Stockholders' equity:		
Common stock	$ 625,000	$ 600,000
Retained earnings	525,000	211,000
Total stockholders' equity	$1,150,000	$ 811,000
Total liabilities and stockholders' equity	$1,840,000	$1,301,000

Additional information for Shillig:

(a) All accounts receivable and accounts payable relate to trade merchandise.
(b) The proceeds from the notes payable were used to finance plant expansion.
(c) Capital stock was sold to provide additional working capital.

Compute the following for 2013:

Cash collected from accounts receivable, assuming all sales are on account.
Cash payments made on accounts payable to suppliers, assuming that all purchases of inventory are on account.
Cash payments for dividends.
Cash receipts that were not provided by operations.
Cash payments for assets that were not reflected in operations.

Exercise 5-34

LO3, LO4

SPREADSHEET

Statement of Cash Flows—Indirect Method

Following is information for Goulding Manufacturing Company:

(a) Long-term debt of $500,000 was retired at face value.
(b) New machinery was purchased for $62,000.
(c) Common stock with a par value of $100,000 was issued for $160,000.
(d) Dividends of $22,000 declared in 2012 were paid in January 2013, and dividends of $30,000 were declared in December 2013, to be paid in 2014.
(e) Net income was $450,700. Included in the computation were depreciation expense of $70,000 and intangible assets amortization of $10,000.

	Dec. 31, 2013	Dec. 31, 2012
Current assets:		
Cash and cash equivalents	$191,700	$130,000
Accounts receivable	175,000	156,000
Inventory	178,000	160,000
Current liabilities:		
Accounts payable	64,000	87,400
Dividends payable	30,000	22,000
Interest payable	12,900	7,000
Wages payable	26,500	17,000

Prepare a statement of cash flows for the year ended December 31, 2013, using the indirect method.

Exercise 5-35

LO3, LO4

Format of Statement of Cash Flows with Indirect Method

From the following information for Carter Corporation, prepare a statement of cash flows for the year ended December 31, 2013, using the indirect method.

Amortization of patent	$ 4,000
Depreciation expense	7,000
Issuance of common stock	25,000
Issuance of new bonds payable	30,000

(Continued)

Net income	$55,000
Payment of dividends	22,500
Purchase of equipment	33,200
Retirement of long-term debt	40,000
Sale of land (includes $6,000 gain)	35,000
Decrease in accounts receivable	2,100
Increase in inventory	1,200
Increase in accounts payable	1,500
Increase in cash	56,700
Cash balance, January 1, 2013	82,800

Exercise 5-36
LO3

Cash Flow from Operations—Indirect Method

The following information was taken from the comparative financial statements of Tulip Corporation:

Net income for year	$ 75,000
Sales revenue	450,000
Cost of goods sold (except depreciation)	275,000
Depreciation expense for year	50,000
Amortization of intangible assets for year	20,000
Interest expense on short-term debt for year	5,200
Dividends declared and paid during year	35,000

Selected account balances:

	Beginning of Year	End of Year
Accounts Receivable	$22,000	$15,000
Inventory	35,000	40,000
Accounts Payable	47,500	52,000
Interest Payable	1,200	400

Using the indirect method, compute the net amount of cash provided by (used in) operating activities for the year.

Exercise 5-37
LO3

Cash Flow from Operations—Indirect Method

The following information was taken from the books of Tapwater Company. Compute the amount of net cash provided by (used in) operating activities during 2013 using the indirect method.

	Dec. 31, 2013	Dec. 31, 2012
Accounts receivable	$18,900	$16,750
Accounts payable	11,500	14,000
Accumulated depreciation (no plant assets retired during year)	29,000	22,000
Inventories	24,500	20,000
Other current liabilities	5,000	3,000
Prepaid insurance	950	2,000
Net income	35,500	—

Exercise 5-38
LO3

Cash Flow from Operations—Direct Method

Based on the information given in Exercise 5-36 and using the direct method, compute the net amount of cash provided by (used in) operating activities for the year.

Exercise 5-39
LO3

Cash Flow from Operations—Direct Method

A summary of revenues and expenses for Norwalk Company for 2013 follows:

Sales	$7,200,000
Cost of goods manufactured and sold	3,500,000
Gross profit	$3,700,000
Selling, general, and administrative expenses	2,300,000
Income before income taxes	$1,400,000
Income taxes	500,000
Net income	$ 900,000

Net changes in working capital accounts for 2013 were as follows:

	Debit	Credit
Cash	$104,000	
Trade Accounts Receivable	420,000	
Inventories		$110,000
Prepaid Expenses (selling and general)	15,000	
Accrued Expenses (75% of increase related to manufacturing activities and 25% to general operating activities)		48,000
Income Taxes Payable		54,000
Trade Accounts Payable		170,000

Depreciation on plant and equipment for the year totaled $700,000; 60% was related to manufacturing activities and 40% to general and administrative activities.

Prepare a schedule of net cash provided by (used in) operating activities for the year using the direct method.

PROBLEMS

Problem 5-40
LO3

Preparing the Operating Activities Section of the Statement of Cash Flows

Podracer Productions provides the following income statement for the year ended December 31, 2013:

Sales	$1,530,600
Cost of goods sold	895,400
Gross margin	$ 635,200
General expenses	255,400
Depreciation expense	23,500
Salaries expense	114,300
Operating income	$ 242,000
Interest revenue	17,250
Interest expense	(12,500)
Loss on sale of equipment	(9,500)
Income before income taxes	$ 237,250
Income tax expense	85,500
Net income	$ 151,750

In addition, Podracer provides the following balance sheet information:

	Dec. 31, 2013	Dec. 31, 2012
Accounts receivable	$250,400	$225,400
Interest receivable	2,100	2,250
Inventory	74,300	59,550
Prepaid general expenses	17,600	14,000
Accounts payable	39,500	46,300
Accrued general expenses	19,500	21,750
Interest payable	900	1,100
Income taxes payable	11,500	9,750
Salaries payable	8,700	5,400

Instructions: Using the simultaneous analysis matrix illustrated in the text, prepare the Operating Activities section of the statement of cash flows using (1) the direct method and (2) the indirect method.

Problem 5-41
LO3, LO4

Statement of Cash Flows—Indirect Method

Comparative balance sheet data for Tanzanite Imporium follow. In addition, new equipment was purchased for $60,000, payment consisting of $40,000 cash and a long-term note for $20,000. The short-term note payable was arranged with a supplier to finance inventory purchases on credit. Cash dividends of $15,000 were paid in 2013; all other changes to retained earnings were caused by the net income for 2013, which amounted to $92,200.

	Dec. 31, 2013	Dec. 31, 2012
Cash and cash equivalents	$ 42,000	$ 33,000
Accounts receivable	84,000	77,000
Inventory	95,700	131,000
Property, plant, and equipment	560,000	500,000
Accumulated depreciation—property, plant, and equipment	(231,500)	(210,000)
Total assets	$ 550,200	$ 531,000
Short-term notes payable	$ —	$ 30,000
Accounts payable	81,000	69,000
Long-term notes payable	110,000	90,000
Bonds payable	60,000	120,000
Common stock, $1 par	35,000	35,000
Additional paid-in capital	165,000	165,000
Retained earnings	99,200	22,000
Total liabilities and stockholders' equity	$ 550,200	$ 531,000

Instructions: Prepare a statement of cash flows for the year ended December 31, 2013, using the indirect method.

Problem 5-42
LO3, LO4

Statement of Cash Flows—Indirect Method

The following information was taken from the records of Glassett Produce Company for the year ended June 30, 2013.

Borrowed on long-term notes	$15,000
Issued capital stock	45,000
Purchased equipment	18,000
Net income	33,500
Purchased treasury stock	5,000
Paid dividends	29,000
Depreciation expense	21,000
Retired bonds payable	65,000
Patent amortization	3,000
Sold long-term investment (at cost)	7,200
Increase in cash	14,800
Decrease in inventories	6,300
Increase in accounts receivable	9,200
Increase in accounts payable	10,000
Cash balance, July 1, 2012	22,000

Instructions:

1. From the information given, prepare a statement of cash flows using the indirect method.
2. Briefly explain what an interested party would learn from studying the cash flow statement for Glassett Produce Company.

Problem 5-43

LO3, LO4

Statement of Cash Flows—Indirect Method

The following information was obtained from analysis of selected accounts of Orlando Company for the year ended December 31, 2013.

Increase in long-term debt	$ 57,000
Purchase of treasury stock	52,000
Depreciation and amortization	197,000
Gain on sale of equipment (included in net income)	6,000
Proceeds from issuance of common stock	184,000
Purchase of equipment	434,000
Proceeds from sale of equipment	20,000
Payment of dividends	49,000
Net income	375,000
Increase (decrease) in working capital accounts:	
Cash	45,000
Accounts receivable	229,000
Inventories	275,000
Trade notes payable	167,000
Accounts payable	124,000
Income taxes payable	(34,000)
Cash balance, January 1, 2013	120,000

Instructions: From the information given, prepare a statement of cash flows using the indirect method.

Problem 5-44

LO3, LO4

Statement of Cash Flows—Direct Method

Based on an analysis of the cash and other accounts, the following information was provided by the controller of Black Iron, Inc., a manufacturer of wood-burning stoves, for the year 2013.

(a) Cash sales for the year were $210,000; sales on account totaled $240,000.
(b) Cost of goods sold was 50% of total sales.
(c) All inventory is purchased on account.

(d) Depreciation on equipment was $86,000 for the year.
(e) Amortization of patent was $9,000.
(f) Collection of accounts receivable was $98,000.
(g) Payments on accounts payable for inventory equaled $123,000.
(h) Rent expense paid in cash was $40,700.
(i) Cash of $580,000 was obtained by issuing 40,000 shares of $10 par stock.
(j) Land worth $425,000 was acquired in exchange for a $400,000 bond.
(k) Equipment was purchased for cash at a cost of $287,000.
(l) Dividends of $115,000 were declared.
(m) Dividends of $52,000 that had been declared the previous year were paid.
(n) A machine used on the assembly line was sold for $26,000. The machine had a book value of $19,000.
(o) Another machine with a book value of $2,300 was scrapped and was reported as an ordinary loss. No cash was received on this transaction.
(p) The cash account had a balance of $79,000 on January 1, 2013.

Instructions: Use the direct method to prepare a statement of cash flows for Black Iron, Inc., for the year ended December 31, 2013.

Problem 5-45
LO3, LO4

Statement of Cash Flows—Indirect Method
Comparative balance sheet data for the partnership of Bond and Wallin follow.

	Dec. 31, 2013	Dec. 31, 2012
Cash	$ 15,000	$ 12,500
Accounts receivable	24,200	27,000
Inventory	105,400	91,000
Prepaid expenses	4,100	5,350
Furniture and fixtures	65,500	41,000
Accumulated depreciation	(40,250)	(25,250)
Total assets	$173,950	$151,600
Accrued expenses	$ 9,000	$ 6,700
Accounts payable	22,425	32,875
Long-term note	21,300	—
Ryan Bond, capital	69,350	56,150
Trent Wallin, capital	51,875	55,875
Total liabilities and stockholders' equity	$173,950	$151,600

Net income for the year was $22,000, and this was transferred in equal amounts to the partners' capital accounts. Additional changes in the capital accounts arose from additional investments and withdrawals by the partners. The change in the furniture and fixtures account arose from a purchase of additional furniture; part of the purchase price was paid in cash, and a long-term note was issued for the balance.

Instructions: Using the indirect method, prepare a statement of cash flows for 2013.

Problem 5-46
LO3, LO4

Statement of Cash Flows—Indirect Method
Sparkling Cleaner Company reported net income of $7,450 for 2013 but has been showing an overdraft in its bank account in recent months. The manager has contacted you as the auditor for an explanation. The comparative balance sheet was given to you for examination, along with the following information.

(a) Equipment was sold for $1,700, its cost was $3,000, and its book value was $800. The gain was reported as Other Revenue.
(b) Cash dividends of $4,870 were paid.

Sparkling Cleaner Company
Comparative Balance Sheet

	Dec. 31, 2013		Dec. 31, 2012	
Assets				
Current assets:				
Cash		$ (1,100)		$ 3,950
Accounts receivable		4,100		2,300
Inventory		3,250		1,150
Prepaid insurance		90		210
Total current assets		$ 6,340		$ 7,610
Land, buildings, and equipment:				
Land		$15,200		$15,200
Buildings	$ 35,000		$ 35,000	
Less: Accumulated depreciation	(16,500)	18,500	(15,000)	20,000
Equipment	$ 28,350		$ 24,150	
Less: Accumulated depreciation	(20,900)	7,450	(17,900)	6,250
Total land, buildings, and equipment		$41,150		$41,450
Total assets		$47,490		$49,060
Liabilities and Stockholders' Equity				
Current liabilities:				
Accounts payable		$ 3,600		$ 2,800
Income taxes payable		950		1,850
Wages payable		1,100		2,150
Notes payable—current portion		3,000		4,500
Total current liabilities		$ 8,650		$11,300
Long-term liabilities:				
Notes payable		11,250		14,250
Stockholders' equity:				
Capital stock	$ 19,500		$ 18,000	
Retained earnings	8,090		5,510	
Total stockholders' equity		27,590		23,510
Total liabilities and stockholders' equity		$47,490		$49,060

Instructions: Prepare a statement of cash flows using the indirect method.

Problem 5-47
LO3, LO4

Statement of Cash Flows—Direct Method

The table below shows the account balances of Novations, Inc., at the beginning and end of the company's accounting period.

Debits	Dec. 31, 2013	Jan. 1, 2013
Cash and Cash Equivalents	$176,400	$ 58,000
Accounts Receivable	32,000	26,600
Inventory	21,000	25,400
Prepaid Insurance	5,600	4,000
Long-Term Investments (at cost)	6,000	16,800
Equipment	80,000	66,000
Treasury Stock (at cost)	10,000	20,000
Cost of Goods Sold	368,000	
Operating Expenses	185,000	
Income Tax Expense	37,600	
Loss on Sale of Equipment	1,000	
Total debits	$922,600	$216,800

Credits	Dec. 31, 2013	Jan. 1, 2013
Accumulated Depreciation—Equipment	$ 19,000	$ 18,000
Accounts Payable	7,000	11,200
Interest Payable	1,000	2,000
Income Taxes Payable	12,000	8,000
Notes Payable—Long-Term	16,000	24,000
Common Stock	110,000	100,000
Paid-In Capital in Excess of Par	32,000	30,000
Retained Earnings	19,600*	23,600
Sales	704,000	
Gain on Sale of Long-Term Investments	2,000	
Total credits	$922,600	$216,800

* Preclosing balance.

The following additional information is available:

(a) All purchases and sales were on account.
(b) Equipment costing $10,000 was sold for $3,000; a loss of $1,000 was recognized on the sale.
(c) Among other items, the operating expenses included depreciation expense of $7,000; interest expense of $2,800; and insurance expense of $2,400.
(d) Equipment was purchased during the year by issuing common stock and by paying the balance ($12,000) in cash.
(e) Treasury stock was sold for $4,000 less than it cost; the decrease in owners' equity was recorded by reducing Retained Earnings. No dividends were paid during the year.

Instructions:

1. Prepare a statement of cash flows for the year ended December 31, 2013, using the direct method of reporting cash flows from operating activities.
2. Comment on the lack of dividend payment. Does a "no-dividend" policy seem appropriate under the current circumstances for Novations, Inc.?

Problem 5-48
LO3, LO4, LO6

Income Statement and Statement of Cash Flows—Indirect Method
Refer to the data for Novations, Inc., in Problem 5-47.

Instructions:

1. Prepare an income statement for Novations, Inc., for the year ended December 31, 2013.
2. Prepare a statement of cash flows for the year ended December 31, 2013, using the indirect method.

Problem 5-49
LO6
REVERSE SOLVABLE

Articulation
The following data are for Ernst Company. (*Note*: All inventory is purchased on account, and Accounts Payable relates only to the purchase of inventory.)

	Dec. 31, 2013	Dec. 31, 2012
BALANCE SHEET DATA (partial)		
Accounts receivable	$ 72,000	$65,000
Inventory	54,000	41,000
Prepaid rent	?	8,000
Accounts payable	44,000	52,000
Wages payable	23,000	?

INCOME STATEMENT DATA	
Sales	$485,000
Cost of goods sold	?
Wages expense	?
Rent expense	22,000
Other expenses	121,000
Net income	?
CASH FLOW DATA	
Net income	?
+/– Change in accounts receivable	(7,000)
+/– Change in inventory	(13,000)
+/– Change in accounts payable	(8,000)
+/– Change in prepaid rent	?
+/– Change in wages payable	6,000
Cash from operating activities	?
OTHER DATA	
Cash collected from customers	?
Cash paid for inventory	?
Inventory purchased on account	230,000
Cash paid for rent	27,000
Cash paid for wages	81,000
Cash paid for other expenses	121,000

Instructions: Compute the following:

1. The ending balance in the prepaid rent account.
2. The beginning balance in the wages payable account.
3. The amount of Cost of Goods Sold for 2013.
4. The amount of Wages Expense for 2013.
5. The amount of reported Net Income for 2013.
6. The amount of cash collected from customers during 2013.
7. The amount of cash paid for inventory during 2013.

Problem 5-50

LO5

Analysis of Cash Flow Data

The following summary data are for Gwynn Company:

	2013	2012	2011
Cash	$ 85,000	$ 75,000	$ 70,000
Other current assets	480,000	420,000	390,000
Current liabilities	325,000	270,000	290,000
Depreciation expense	57,000	51,000	44,000
Net income	59,000	50,000	45,000

All current assets and current liabilities relate to operations.

Instructions:

1. Compute net cash provided by (used in) operating activities for 2012 and 2013.
2. How would the numbers you computed in (1) change if Gwynn had decided to delay payment of $40,000 in accounts payable from late 2012 to early 2013? This will increase both Cash and Accounts Payable as of December 31, 2012; the December 31, 2013, amounts will be unaffected.

3. Ignore the change described in (2). How would the numbers you computed in (1) change if Gwynn had decided to delay purchase of $40,000 of inventory for cash from late 2012 to early 2013? This will increase cash but decrease inventory as of December 31, 2012; the December 31, 2013, amounts will be unaffected.
4. Can net cash from operations be manipulated? Explain your answer.

Problem 5-51
LO3

Definitions of Cash Flow
The following summary information is for Numbers Company:

	2013	2012	2011	2010
Net income	$ 90	$ 90	$ 90	$ 90
Depreciation expense	40	40	40	40
Change in accounts receivable	+15	−30	0	+20
Change in inventory	+10	−25	+15	−5
Change in accounts payable	+30	0	−20	+15

Instructions:

1. Compute net cash provided by (used in) operating activities for Numbers Company for the years 2010 through 2013.
2. One definition of *cash flow* often used in financial analysis is "net income + depreciation." Use this definition to compute cash flow for Numbers Company for the years 2010 through 2013.
3. Under what circumstances is the "net income + depreciation" measure of cash flow a good estimate of actual cash flow from operations? Under what circumstances is it a particularly misleading measure?

Problem 5-52
LO5

Cash Flow Analysis
Following are data from the financial statements for Drury Lane Company:

Drury Lane Company
Selected Financial Statement Data
For the Years Ended December 31, 2013 and 2012
(In millions of dollars)

	2013	2012
Sales	$ 90,000	$85,000
Total assets	105,000	98,000
Stockholders' equity	34,000	32,000
Net income	9,200	8,500
Cash from operations	12,300	20,100
Cash paid for capital expenditures	13,100	12,900
Cash paid for acquisitions	2,800	900
Cash paid for interest	1,800	1,500
Cash paid for income taxes	3,300	3,000

Instructions:

1. Compute the following for 2012 and 2013.
   (a) Return on sales
   (b) Return on assets
   (c) Return on equity
   (d) Cash-flow-to-net-income ratio

(e) Cash flow adequacy ratio
(f) Cash times interest earned ratio

2. In which year did Drury Lane Company perform better, 2012 or 2013? Explain your answer.
3. Drury Lane Company intends to sell a large block of newly issued stock to the public in the first half of 2014. Given your computations in (1), what questions would you like to ask of Drury Lane's management before investing in the newly issued stock?

Problem 5-53
LO7

Forecasted Balance Sheet, Income Statement, and Statement of Cash Flows
(*Note*: This problem uses the same information used in Problem 4-52.) Lorien Company wishes to prepare a forecasted income statement, a forecasted balance sheet, and a forecasted statement of cash flows for 2014. Lorien's balance sheet and income statement for 2013 follow:

Balance Sheet	**2013**
Cash	$ 40
Other current assets	350
Property, plant, and equipment, net	1,000
Total assets	$1,390
Accounts payable	$ 100
Bank loans payable	1,000
Paid-in capital	100
Retained earnings	190
Total liabilities and stockholders' equity	$1,390

Income Statement	**2013**
Sales	$1,000
Cost of goods sold	350
Gross profit	$ 650
Depreciation expense	200
Other operating expenses	250
Operating profit	$ 200
Interest expense	120
Income before taxes	$ 80
Income taxes	20
Net income	$ 60

In addition, Lorien has assembled the following forecasted information for 2014.

(a) Sales are expected to increase to $1,200.
(b) Lorien does not expect to buy any new property, plant, and equipment during 2014. (*Hint*: Think about how depreciation expense in 2014 will affect the reported amount of property, plant, and equipment.)
(c) Because of adverse banking conditions, Lorien does not expect to receive any new bank loans in 2014.
(d) Lorien plans to pay cash dividends of $15 in 2014.

Instructions:

1. Prepare a forecasted balance sheet, a forecasted income statement, and a forecasted statement of cash flows for 2014. Clearly state what assumptions you make. Use the indirect method for reporting cash from operating activities.

2. If you have constructed your forecasted cash flow statement correctly, you will see that Lorien plans to distribute cash to shareholders through two different means in 2014. Which of these methods involves distributing an equal amount of cash for each share owned? Which of these methods channels the cash to shareholders who are the least optimistic about the prospects of the company?

Problem 5-54
LO3

Sample CPA Exam Questions

1. Accounts Receivable has a beginning balance of $425,000 and an ending balance of $437,000. Cash collected from customers during the period was $1,263,000. Sales for the period were:
   (a) $1,251,000.
   (b) $1,263,000.
   (c) $1,275,000.
   (d) $1,287,000.

2. Ruse Inc. reported net income for 2013 of $174,000. Ruse also reported the following related to its current assets and liabilities:

	Dec. 31, 2013	Dec. 31, 2012
Accounts receivable	$ 84,000	$ 86,000
Inventory	117,000	101,000
Accounts payable	150,000	140,000

What amount should be reported by Ruse Inc. as cash provided by operating activities in the statement of cash flows?
   (a) $150,000
   (b) $170,000
   (c) $178,000
   (d) $198,000

3. In the statement of cash flows (using the indirect method), an increase in interest payable should be presented as a(n):
   (a) subtraction from net income in the Operating Activities section.
   (b) addition to net income in the Operating Activities section.
   (c) subtraction in the Financing Activities section.
   (d) addition in the Financing Activities section.

CASES

Discussion Case 5-55

Is Depreciation a Source of Cash?

Brad Berrett and Jim Wong are roommates in college. Berrett is an accounting major, and Wong is a finance major. Both recently studied the statement of cash flows in their classes. Wong's finance professor stated that depreciation is a major source of cash for some companies. Berrett's accounting professor indicated in class that depreciation cannot be a source of cash because cash is not affected by the recording of depreciation.

Berrett and Wong wonder which professor is correct. Explain the positions taken by both professors and indicate which viewpoint you support and why.

Discussion Case 5-56

Where Does All the Money Go?

Price Auto Parts has hired you as a consultant to analyze the company's financial position. One of the owners, DeeAnn Price, is in charge of the company's financial affairs. She makes all deposits and pays the bills but has an accountant prepare a balance sheet and an income statement once a year. The business has been quite profitable over the years. In fact, two years ago Price opened a second store and is now considering a third outlet. The economy has slowed, however, and the company's cash position has become very tight. The company is having an increasingly difficult time paying its bills. DeeAnn has not been able to explain satisfactorily to her partners what is happening. What factors should you consider, and what recommendations might you make to Price?

Discussion Case 5-57

Why Do We Have More Cash?

Hot Lunch Delivery Service has always had a policy to pay stockholders annual dividends in an amount exactly equal to net income for the year. Joe Alberg, the company's president, is confused because the Cash balance has been consistently increasing ever since Hot Lunch began operations five years ago in spite of its faithful adherence to the dividend policy. Assuming no errors have been made in the bookkeeping process, explain why this situation might occur.

Discussion Case 5-58

Which Method Should We Use: The Direct or the Indirect Method?

As the assistant controller of Do-It-Right Company, you have been given the assignment to study FASB *ASC Topic 230* and make recommendations on how the company should prepare its statement of cash flows. Specifically, you are to indicate which method—the direct or the indirect—should be used in reporting cash flows from operating activities. Which method do you recommend and why?

Discussion Case 5-59

Some Accountant You Are!

Early in the year 2014, John Roberts, a recent graduate of Southeast State College, delivers the financial statements shown below to Laura Dennis of Dennis, Inc. After a quick review, Dennis exclaims, "What do you mean I had net income of $20,000? I borrowed $40,000 from the bank and my cash balance decreased by $2,000. I must have had a loss! Some accountant you are!" How should Mr. Roberts answer Ms. Dennis?

Dennis, Inc.
Comparative Balance Sheet
December 31, 2013 and 2012

	2013	2012
Assets		
Cash	$ 3,000	$ 5,000
Accounts receivable	18,000	8,000
Inventory	20,000	15,000
Equipment (at cost)	52,000	20,000
Accumulated depreciation	(10,000)	(5,000)
Total assets	$ 83,000	$43,000
Liabilities and Stockholders' Equity		
Accounts payable	$ 4,000	$ 9,000
Notes payable—long-term	40,000	—
Common stock, $1 par	2,000	2,000
Additional paid-in capital	18,000	18,000
Retained earnings	19,000	14,000
Total liabilities and stockholders' equity	$ 83,000	$ 43,000

Dennis, Inc.
Combined Statement of Income and Retained Earnings
For the Year Ended December 31, 2013

Sales		$240,000
Cost of goods sold	$150,000	
Operating expenses (including depreciation of $5,000)	70,000	220,000
Net income		$ 20,000
Add: Retained earnings, January 1, 2013		14,000
Deduct: Dividends paid		(15,000)
Retained earnings, December 31, 2013		$ 19,000

Discussion Case 5-60

The Secret of Cash Flow Patterns

Kara Nemrow, a security analyst for Primer Mead & Co., asserts that she can tell more about a company's financial condition by looking at the trends of the negative or positive cash flows in the three categories than from other information found in the financial statements. She illustrates her theory with the following pattern of cash flows for Atlas Security over the past three years.

	2013	2012	2011
Net income	–	+	+
Cash flows from:			
Operating activities	–	–	+
Financing activities	+	+	+
Investing activities	+	+	+

How do you think Kara would analyze this pattern? Do you agree that analyzing cash flow patterns provides superior analytical information?

Discussion Case 5-61

W. T. Grant: What Is "Cash Flow"?

The case of **W. T. Grant** is a classic in cash flow analysis. During the 1960s and 1970s, Grant was one of the largest retailers in the United States, with more than 1,200 stores nationwide. Grant was a stable New York Stock Exchange firm that had paid cash dividends every year since 1907. However, the inability of Grant's operations to generate positive cash flow indicated the existence of serious problems. From 1966 through 1973, while Grant's net income was steady at about $35 million per year, cash flow from operations was negative in every year except 1968 and 1969, and even in those years the positive cash flow generated was insignificant in amount. The results for the fiscal year ended January 31, 1973, are the most striking. Net income for the year was $38 million. A frequently used measure of "cash flow" (net income and depreciation) suggested that W. T. Grant's operations generated $48 million in cash. However, actual cash flow generated by operations for the year was a negative $120 million. In October 1975, Grant filed for bankruptcy, and by early 1976, the company was liquidated and ceased to exist.

What might have caused the "net income + depreciation" measure of cash flow to be positive when in fact actual cash flow from operations was negative? Under what circumstances is the "net income + depreciation" measure of cash flow a good estimate of actual cash flow from operations? When is it a bad measure?

SOURCES: James A. Largay III and Clyde P. Stickney, "Cash Flows, Ratio Analysis and the W. T. Grant Company Bankruptcy," *Financial Analysts Journal*, July/August 1980, pp. 51–54; and *Moody's Handbook of Common Stocks*, 2nd quarterly ed. (1973).

Case 5-62

Deciphering Financial Statements (The Walt Disney Company)

Locate the 2009 financial statements for **The Walt Disney Company** on the Internet and consider the following questions:

1. Does Disney use the direct method or the indirect method? Explain.
2. Analyze Disney's overall cash flow picture for 2007, 2008, and 2009 in light of the positive or negative cash flow patterns for the three categories of cash flows.
3. In the notes to Disney's financial statements, *cash and cash equivalents* is defined. What is that definition?
4. What is the largest dollar item in the Operating Activities section of Disney's 2009 statement of cash flows? Explain exactly what is represented by this item.
5. What would Disney's operating cash flow have been in 2009 if interest and taxes paid were not considered to be operating items?
6. Companies often compute earnings before interest, taxes, depreciation, and amortization (EBITDA). This number is used as an approximation of operating cash flow before interest and taxes. Using the information in Disney's income statement and statement of cash flows, compute EBITDA for 2009. Compare EBITDA to your answer in (5), and explain why there is a difference.

Case 5-63

Deciphering Financial Statements (Lockheed Martin Corporation)

Lockheed Martin Corporation is a well-known producer of advanced aircraft, missiles, and space hardware. Lockheed Martin is most famous for its super-secret research and development division, nicknamed the "Skunk Works." Among the high-tech aircraft developed at the Skunk Works are the SR-71 Blackbird spy plane and the F-117A Stealth fighter.

The consolidated statement of cash flows from Lockheed Martin's 2009 annual report is reproduced below.

When investors and analysts use the term *cash flow*, they can mean a variety of things. Some common definitions of cash flow are as follows:

(a) Net income + Depreciation
(b) Cash flow from operating activities
(c) Cash flow from operating activities + Cash paid for interest + Cash paid for income taxes
(d) Cash flow from operating activities − Capital expenditures − Dividends

Lockheed Martin Corporation
CONSOLIDATED STATEMENT OF CASH FLOWS

	Year ended December 31,		
(in millions)	**2009**	**2008**	**2007**
Operating Activities			
Net earnings	$ 3,024	$3,217	$3,033
Adjustments to reconcile net earnings to net cash provided by operating activities:			
Depreciation and amortization	750	727	666
Amortization of purchased intangibles	104	118	153
Stock-based compensation	154	155	149
Excess tax benefits on stock-based compensation	(21)	(92)	(124)
Deferred income taxes	542	72	110
Contributions related to our qualified defined benefit plans	(1,482)	(109)	(335)
Changes in operating assets and liabilities:			
Receivables	(719)	(333)	(324)
Inventories	(233)	(183)	(57)
Accounts payable	(21)	(141)	(66)
Customer advances and amounts in excess of costs incurred	482	313	394

(in millions)	Year ended December 31, 2009	2008	2007
Other	$ 593	$ 677	$ 639
Net cash provided by operating activities	3,173	4,421	4,238
Investing Activities			
Expenditures for property, plant, and equipment	(852)	(926)	(940)
Acquisition of businesses/investments in affiliates	(435)	(233)	(337)
Net proceeds from (payments for) short-term investments	(279)	272	48
Other	48	(20)	24
Net cash used for investing activities	(1,518)	(907)	(1,205)
Financing Activities			
Issuances of common stock and related amounts	40	250	350
Repurchases of common stock	(1,851)	(2,931)	(2,127)
Excess tax benefits on stock-based compensation	21	92	124
Common stock dividends	(908)	(737)	(615)
Issuance of long-term debt, net of related costs	1,464	491	—
Repayments of long-term debt	(242)	(1,103)	(32)
Net cash used for financing activities	(1,476)	(3,938)	(2,300)
Effect of exchange rate changes on cash and cash equivalents	44	(56)	3
Net (decrease) increase in cash and cash equivalents	223	(480)	736
Cash and cash equivalents at beginning of year	2,168	2,648	1,912
Cash and cash equivalents at end of year	$ 2,391	$ 2,168	$ 2,648
Supplemental Disclosure Information Cash paid during the year for:			
Interest	$ 286	$ 320	$ 327
Taxes	986	1,234	1,131

Instructions:

1. Using the data from Lockheed's statement of cash flows, compute values for the four measures of *cash flow* defined above for 2007, 2008, and 2009. Use net earnings as *net income*. For *capital expenditures*, use expenditures for property, plant, and equipment.
2. One of the definitions (a) through (d) is sometimes given the title *free cash flow* because it indicates the amount of discretionary cash generated by a business. Free cash flow is thought of as the amount of cash that an owner can remove from a business without harming its long-term potential. Which of these four definitions do you think applies to free cash flow? Explain.
3. A leveraged buyout (LBO) is the purchase of a company using borrowed money. The idea behind an LBO is to borrow the money, buy the company, and then repay the loan using the cash flow generated by the purchased company. Which of the four definitions of cash flow do you think would be particularly useful to someone considering an LBO? Explain.

Case 5-64 **Deciphering Financial Statements (The Coca-Cola Company)**

The following data were obtained from the cash flow statements (prepared using the indirect method) of **The Coca-Cola Company** from 2006 through 2009. All amounts are in millions of U.S. dollars.

	2009	2008	2007	2006
Net income	$ 6,906	$ 5,874	$ 6,027	$ 5,080
Cash from operating activities	8,186	7,571	7,150	5,957
Cash from investing activities	(4,149)	(2,363)	(6,719)	(1,700)

Cash from financing activities				
Issuances of debt	$14,689	$4,337	$9,979	$ 617
Payments of debt	(12,326)	(4,308)	(5,638)	(2,021)
Issuances of stock	662	586	1,619	148
Purchases of stock for treasury	(1,518)	(1,079)	(1,838)	(2,416)
Dividends	(3,800)	(3,521)	(3,149)	(2,911)
At January 1, 2006, the following items had the indicated balances:				
Cash				$ 4,701
Paid-In Capital from Common Stock (includes par value and additional paid-in capital)				6,369
Retained Earnings				31,299
Treasury Stock				19,644

Instructions:

1. Using the information given, estimate the December 31, 2009, balances in the following accounts.
   (a) Cash
   (b) Paid-In Capital from Common Stock
   (c) Retained Earnings
   (d) Treasury Stock
2. Comment on the size of the December 31, 2009, balance in the paid-in capital from common stock account in relation to the balance in the treasury stock account.

Case 5-65

Writing Assignment (Where is your statement of cash flows?)

You are a senior credit analyst for Far West Bank. The president of Moran Auto Sales has asked you for a loan of $2,000,000. Moran's accountant has compiled and submitted a current balance sheet and income statement. Moran has had moderate income over the past three years but has found itself short of cash and therefore in need of the loan.

After receiving the statements, you call Moran's accountant and indicate that the financial statements are not complete; you need to see a statement of cash flows. The accountant argues, "Everything on a statement of cash flows comes from the other two statements. Why make me do the additional work? Just analyze what we sent."

Your task now is to write a memo to the president of Moran Auto Sales convincing her that a statement of cash flows is essential for you to properly evaluate Moran's loan application.

Case 5-66

Ethical Dilemma (Is the price right?)

You are a finance and accounting analyst for Bunscar Company and have been with the firm for five years. Bunscar is a closely held corporation—all of the shares are owned by the founder, Ryan Brown, and by other longtime employees. Bunscar is preparing to issue stock for the first time in an initial public offering (IPO). Of great interest is the initial selling price of the stock because that will determine how much Brown and the others will reap from the sale of their shares.

The board of directors has put together an analysis proposing that the initial selling price be set at $15 per share. Because Brown and the other insiders intend to sell 10 million shares, this price will bring them $150 million. The analysis relies heavily on the trend in Bunscar's earnings, which have grown sharply, particularly in the past year.

You have the reputation of possessing the best presentation skills in the company. The board of directors has asked you to present the $15-per-share proposal to the investment banking firm that will handle Bunscar's IPO. This is your big chance.

As you review the board's analysis in preparing your presentation, you notice that no mention is made of Bunscar's cash flow from operations (CFO). CFO has been fairly steady for the past few years; at the same time, earnings have more than doubled. In the past year, when earnings increased 65%, CFO actually declined slightly. After some investigation, you find that Bunscar has become very loose in its assumptions about when revenue should be recognized. In fact, putting the revenue and cash flow numbers together, you conclude that most of Bunscar's earnings increase has come from questionable revenue that probably will never be collected in cash. It seems clear to you that Bunscar's accounting assumptions have been manipulated to make reported income look as good as possible to increase the IPO selling price.

Your presentation is scheduled for the day after tomorrow. What should you do?

Case 5-67

Cumulative Spreadsheet Analysis

This spreadsheet assignment is a continuation of the spreadsheet assignments given in earlier chapters. If you completed those assignments, you have a head start on this one.

Refer back to the instructions for preparing the revised financial statements for 2013 as given in part (1) of the Cumulative Spreadsheet Analysis assignment in Chapter 3.

1. Skywalker wishes to prepare a *forecasted* balance sheet, a *forecasted* income statement, and a *forecasted* statement of cash flows for 2014. Use the financial statement numbers for 2013 as the basis for the forecast, along with the following additional information.

   (a) Sales in 2014 are expected to increase by 40% over 2013 sales of $2,100.
   (b) In 2014, Skywalker expects to acquire new property, plant, and equipment costing $240.
   (c) The $480 in operating expenses reported in 2013 breaks down as follows: $15 depreciation expense and $465 other operating expenses.
   (d) No new long-term debt will be acquired in 2014.
   (e) No cash dividends will be paid in 2014.
   (f) New short-term loans payable will be acquired in an amount sufficient to make Skywalker's current ratio in 2014 exactly equal to 2.0.
   (g) Skywalker does not anticipate repurchasing any additional shares of stock during 2014.
   (h) Because changes in future prices and exchange rates are impossible to predict, Skywalker's best estimate is that the balance in accumulated other comprehensive income will remain unchanged in 2014.
   (i) In the absence of more detailed information, assume that investment securities, long-term investments, other long-term assets, and intangible assets will all increase at the same rate as sales (40%) in 2014.
   (j) In the absence of more detailed information, assume that other long-term liabilities will increase at the same rate as sales (40%) in 2014.

   (*Note*: The forecasted balance sheet and income statement were constructed as part of the spreadsheet assignment in Chapter 4; you can use that spreadsheet as a starting point if you have completed that assignment.) In addition, assume the following:

   (k) The investment securities are classified as available for sale. Accordingly, cash from the purchase and sale of these securities is classified as an investing activity.
   (l) Transactions impacting other long-term assets and other long-term liabilities accounts are operating activities.

   [*Hint*: Construction of the forecasted statement of cash flows for 2014 involves analyzing the forecasted income statement for 2014 along with the balance sheets for 2013 (actual) and 2014 (forecasted).]

2. Repeat (1) with the following change in assumptions:

   (a) Sales growth in 2014 is expected to be 25%.
   (b) Sales growth in 2014 is expected to be 50%.

3. Comment on the forecasted values of cash from operating activities in 2014, assuming that sales will grow at 25%, 40%, and 50%, respectively.

AP Photo/Douglas Healey

CHAPTER 6 Earnings Management

LEARNING OBJECTIVES

1. Identify the factors that motivate earnings management.
2. List the common techniques used to manage earnings.
3. Critically discuss whether a company should manage its earnings.
4. Describe the common elements of an earnings management meltdown.
5. Explain how good accounting standards and ethical behavior by accountants lower the cost of obtaining capital.

Chester Carlson was a patent attorney. He was frustrated at the time and expense involved in producing copies of patent documents. Copies of text documents could be produced by retyping them with carbon paper inserted between multiple sheets of blank typing paper. Drawings were reproduced by sending them out to be professionally photographed. Carlson pondered how he might make single copies of any sort of document right in the office with just the push of a button. Carlson had a technical background, having graduated from Cal Tech and worked at **Bell Labs** for a time. Accordingly, he was aware of the fairly recent discovery of the photoconductivity of some materials. These materials, when exposed to light, were transformed from electrical insulators to electrical conductors. Carlson combined the phenomena of photoconductivity and static electricity to devise a process for making copies; he applied for his first patent in 1937.

Patent application notwithstanding, Chester Carlson didn't have the necessary engineering skills to bring his copying process to life. Accordingly, he hired a young engineer, and the two of them worked on the process in a back room behind a beauty parlor in Astoria, Long Island. They made their first successful copy on October 22, 1938; the text of the copy was "10-22-38 Astoria." Carlson called the process "electrophotography." This was later changed to *xerography*, from the Greek words for dry (xeros) and writing (graphein). The five steps in xerography are outlined in Exhibit 6-1; as you can tell from the description and from your experience with copy machines today, the general xerography process is the same today as it was back in 1938.

Chester Carlson approached 20 companies with his new process, but none were interested. For several years, **IBM** considered buying the patent from Carlson but ultimately decided against it. Finally, in 1944 Carlson was able to convince **Batelle Memorial Institute** of Columbus, Ohio, to commercially develop his xerography process. Batelle was to get 60% of the proceeds, leaving Carlson with 40%. The progress of Batelle scientists was slow initially because of their continuing work on war-related research. By 1946, after the conclusion of World War II, the Batelle researchers had refined xerography to the point at which it was commercially viable. On January 2, 1947, Batelle licensed the process to **Haloid Company**, a producer of photographic paper based in Rochester, New York, for $50,000 plus royalties on sales. When this deal was signed, Chester Carlson quit his job as a patent attorney and prepared to sit back and let the sales royalties roll in. He soon realized that there was still much work to be done before Haloid could mass-produce xerography machines; Carlson was back at his job within a month. Ultimately, Chester Carlson wound up with $2 million and 150,000 shares of Haloid stock.

Haloid produced its first xerography machine, the Xerox Model A, in 1949. This initial model required the user to perform 14 steps and took 45 seconds to make a single copy. Between 1949 and 1961, Haloid invested more than $90 million in improving its xerography machines. In 1959, Haloid released the Xerox 914. Following the practice of renting, rather than selling, its machines made popular by IBM, Haloid was able to place 20,000 Xerox 914 machines by 1962. Each machine produced yearly rental revenue averaging $4,000, and it had cost Haloid just $2,500 to manufacture each machine. Haloid became the original high-tech, high-flying glamour stock; the company had a price-earnings ratio of over 100 in 1961. In that same year, Haloid changed its name to **Xerox**.

FYI

Xerox has been so successful in the copy machine business that the company has had difficulty preserving the trademark status of the word *xerox*. Like the words *aspirin, escalator,* and *zipper,* which were once the trade names of specific products, the word *xerox* runs the risk of passing into generic usage and losing its legal protection. For example, on its Web site, Xerox advises that the word "xerox" never be used as a verb.

Through the 1960s and 1970s, Xerox continued to be a very profitable company known for its innovative products. In 1970, the company opened its Palo Alto Research Center (PARC) near Stanford University. During the 1970s, many of the products developed at PARC were truly 20 years ahead of their time. For example, by 1974 PARC researchers had developed a personal computer, the Alto, that employed a Windowslike screen, allowed the user to execute commands by pointing and clicking with a mouse, and was networked with other machines through Ethernet. In 1977, PARC researchers were able to add the computer industry's first laser printer to this networked configuration. Unfortunately for Xerox, the traditional East Coast executives of the company didn't share the enthusiasm for personal computers expressed by the West Coast PARC researchers. The Alto (and its successor, the Star) were never fully embraced

EX 6-1 THE FIVE KEY STEPS IN XEROGRAPHY

1. A plate (or drum) made of a photoconductive material is charged with positive static electricity. The original material used by Chester Carlson was sulfur; commonly used photoconductive materials now are selenium, germanium, and silicon.
2. The plate is exposed to light reflected from the page to be copied. Where the light falls on the photoconductive material, the material becomes an electrical conductor and the positive charge is dissipated. In the shadows (corresponding to the image to be copied), the positive static charge remains.
3. The plate is dusted with a negatively charged powder, the toner. The toner particles stick to the positively charged areas of the plate, duplicating the image to be copied.
4. A piece of paper that has been supercharged with positive static electricity is placed over the plate. The negatively charged toner is attracted away from the plate by the supercharged paper.
5. The paper is heated, melting the toner and fusing the image onto the paper.

by either customers (because of their relatively high price) or the Xerox sales force. Xerox stopped producing personal computers in the early 1980s.

FYI

On March 17, 1988, **Apple Computer** brought suit against **Microsoft**, claiming that Windows 2.03 illegally copied the "look and feel" of the Apple Macintosh graphical user interface. Reportedly, Bill Gates' response was that both he and Apple cofounder Steve Jobs had taken the idea from PARC.

In the 1980s, Xerox faced stiff competition from Japanese copy machine makers such as **Canon** and **Ricoh**. Xerox was able to maintain its profitability through aggressive cost cutting and improvement in quality. Then in the 1990s, Xerox faced another threat as companies focused more on "digital documents," calling into question the need for large-scale paper copy machines. Xerox fought back again with its digital and color copiers and its slogan, "The Document Company." Through mid-1999, the Xerox business strategy seemed to be working. In July 1999, the company's shares were trading for $50 each, and financial analysts were expecting the next year (fiscal 2000) to be a record-breaking one, with earnings forecasted to top $3.00 per share (compared to the $2.67 per share expected to be reported in fiscal 1999).

Unknown to analysts and investors in July 1999, the favorable revenue and earnings numbers reported by Xerox from 1997 through 1999 were more the result of accounting manipulations than effective business practices. As revealed through a subsequent SEC investigation, Xerox had accelerated the recognition of revenue and boosted reported earnings through the use of both non-GAAP (generally accepted accounting principles) accounting practices and changes in GAAP accounting practices that were not disclosed to financial statement users. Descriptions of some of these practices follow:

Lease discount rates in Brazil. Xerox sometimes accounts for the lease of a copy machine as a sale, with financing provided by Xerox. This is entirely acceptable and is discussed in Chapter 15 in the section on sales-type leases. A sales-type lease involves both initial sales revenue and interest revenue over the life of the lease. An accounting assumption about the appropriate interest rate associated with the financing aspect of the lease determines the mix between initial sales revenue and subsequent interest revenue. For example, assume that a copy machine is leased for 10 years with annual lease payments of $1,000. Over the life of the lease, total revenue of $10,000 (10 years × $1,000) will be recognized. If it is assumed that the appropriate interest rate is 6%, immediate sales revenue is $7,360 (the present value of $1,000 per year for 10 years at a 6% discount rate), and interest revenue over the life of the lease is $2,640 ($10,000 – $7,360). In contrast, if the appropriate interest rate is assumed to be 25%, immediate sales revenue is $3,571, and subsequent interest revenue is $6,429. The key difference between sales revenue and interest revenue is that the sales revenue is reported immediately whereas the interest revenue is spread over the life of the lease. To increase reported revenue in its Brazilian subsidiary, Xerox's accounting staff assumed interest rates as low as 6% when accounting for its leases. This assumption was made even though Xerox's own borrowing rate in Brazil was in excess of 25%. Xerox did not disclose details about this key accounting assumption to financial statement users.

Income tax refund receivable in the United Kingdom. In 1995, Xerox won a tax dispute in the United Kingdom. As a result, the company was entitled to a refund of $237 million in overpaid taxes. Xerox recorded this victory by debiting tax refund receivable. However, instead of crediting income for the entire $237 million immediately, as required by GAAP, Xerox deferred much of the income to be recognized in future periods. As explained later in the chapter, this is known as creating a "cookie jar reserve." Basically, through this accounting procedure Xerox was free to recognize the $237 million in income in whatever quarter it needed in order to meet performance targets or analyst expectations.

Bad debts and sales returns at Xerox Mexico. In the mid-1990s, the managers of Xerox Mexico relaxed credit standards for customers in order to increase sales to meet revenue targets set by corporate headquarters. This practice did increase immediate sales, but it also increased the estimated amount of bad debts by $127 million. To avoid recognizing this $127 million in bad debts, the managers of Xerox Mexico renegotiated the credit terms, lengthening payment periods for delinquent accounts to maintain the appearance that the accounts were actually collectible. In addition, Xerox Mexico received $27 million in sales returns from 1996 through 2000. To avoid recording this return of merchandise (and associated reduction in net sales), secret warehouses were rented to store the returned merchandise. Again, these activities were done in order to allow the managers of Xerox Mexico to meet the aggressive targets imposed by Xerox company headquarters.

In total, Xerox accelerated the reporting of more than $6 billion in revenue in the period 1997–2000 and increased reported earnings by $1.4 billion during the same period. At the peak of the earnings manipulation in 1998, more than 30% of Xerox's reported earnings stemmed from undisclosed changes in accounting practices. An SEC investigation uncovering Xerox's accounting abuses resulted in a $10 million fine for the company; at the time, this was the largest fine ever imposed for misleading financial reporting.

FYI

The corporate headquarters of Xerox is located in Norwalk, Connecticut. This is also the home of the FASB!

Until 2001, Xerox's auditor was **KPMG**. KPMG required Xerox to make many adjustments to its financial statements over the 1997–2000 period. For example, when Xerox proposed the creation of an off-balance-sheet entity dubbed "Project Mozart," KPMG stood firm against the plan because it appeared to be a blatant attempt to transfer reported losses from the Xerox income statement to the Project Mozart income statement. In addition, in early 2000, KPMG refused to sign off on the 1999 audit until Xerox had completed an internal investigation of its accounting practices and had made a number of restatements. As a result of this firm stance by KPMG, the Xerox financial statements for the year ended December 31, 1999, were not released until June 7, 2000. However, many businesspeople and regulators argue that KPMG was not tough enough. In response to the KPMG claim that the vast majority of the $6 billion overstatement in revenue by Xerox stemmed from honest differences in accounting judgment and estimates, Lynn E. Turner, at the time an accounting professor at Colorado State University and former chief accountant of the SEC, said, "As I tell my students, they will flunk if they can't get the answers on their homework any closer than to the nearest billion dollars." In April 2005, KPMG agreed to pay $22 million to settle a civil suit filed by the SEC stemming from the Xerox audit.

SOURCES: James Bandler and Mark Maremont, "KPMG's Auditing with Xerox Tests Toughness of SEC," *The Wall Street Journal*, May 6, 2002, p. A1.

Richard Hamner, "There Isn't Any Profit Squeeze at Xerox," *Fortune*, July 1962, pp. 151–155 and 208–216.

Jeremy Kahn, "The Paper Jam from Hell," *Fortune*, November 13, 2000.

"Publishing: Revolution Ahead?" *Time*, November 1, 1948, pp. 82–83.

"Printing With Powders," *Fortune*, June 1949, pp. 113–122.

Securities and Exchange Commission, Plaintiff, v. Xerox Corporation, Defendant, Civil Action No. 02-272789 (DLC), April 11, 2002.

Lynn E. Turner, "Just a Few Rotten Apples? Better Audit Those Books," *The Washington Post*, July 14, 2002, p. B1.

QUESTIONS

1. What business events of the 1980s and 1990s put pressure on Xerox's reported profits?
2. What was done by the managers of Xerox Mexico to avoid reducing reported net sales for $27 million in returned merchandise?
3. What happened to KPMG as a result of its work auditing the financial statements of Xerox?

Answers to these questions can be found on page 6-31.

The final outcomes of this exercise in earnings and revenue management at Xerox were all negative. By August 2002, after all of the public revelations and accounting restatements had been assimilated by the market, Xerox's total market value had fallen to $5 billion. Xerox also bore a tarnished reputation that will take years to restore; by April 2010, the company's market value had only risen back to $15 billion, a far cry from its $46 billion peak in 1999. The CEO and CFO who presided over Xerox during the accounting manipulations were let go, and a group of six former Xerox executives agreed to personally pay more than $20 million to settle SEC charges. KPMG lost the Xerox audit engagement, with the $60 million in fees earned by the successor auditor in 2001 alone. The biggest loser, however, was the U.S. economy. The crisis in investor confidence sparked by the relentless barrage of accounting scandals in 2001 and 2002 helped lower stock values in the United States by more than 20%, eliminating in excess of $2 trillion in wealth for U.S. investors.

This chapter explores the topic of earnings management. Because accounting numbers are so important in so many decisions, there is a predictable tendency of managers to try to manipulate the reported numbers to be as favorable as possible. And because financial accounting involves so many judgments and estimates, such manipulation is possible. In this chapter we will discuss the common techniques used to manage earnings, as well as the difficult issue of whether it is in the best interest of a company to try to manage its reported earnings. We will also walk through the typical sequence of events associated with an earnings management catastrophe. The Xerox case that started the chapter is an accurate model of the mess that can result from managers trying to manipulate reported accounting numbers to try to compensate for lackluster operating performance. The chapter ends with a discussion of the great value that can be added to an economy by good accounting standards and ethical accountants.

Motivation for Earnings Management

1 Identify the factors that motivate earnings management.

WHY Understanding the economic motivations behind earnings management allows the financial statement preparer, the auditor, and the financial statement user to identify circumstances in which reported earnings are more likely to have been managed.

HOW Four factors typically motivate managers to manage reported earnings: attempts to meet internal targets, to meet external expectations, to smooth reported income, and to window dress the financial statements in advance of an IPO or a loan application.

Numbers are very important in framing peoples' opinions. Rarely do we question how the numbers are computed. For example, the too-close-to-call U.S. presidential election of 2000 resulted in very close scrutiny of the voting process in Florida. This close scrutiny made all of us aware that rather than just take vote totals as a given, we should instead exercise more care and healthy skepticism about vote tabulation in future elections. As another example, U.S. federal government budget decisions are not made based on some theoretical "real economic" budget surplus or deficit but are based on the reported surplus or deficit. Pressure to raise or lower taxes, to increase or cut spending, to elect different representatives, and so forth, are based on that one reported number, and hardly anyone delves into how the number is computed. In the government budgetary arena, the following statement, though perhaps a bit overstated, still contains a grain of truth:

> Perception dictates policy,
> accounting determines perception,
> therefore, accounting rules the world.

Reported numbers have a similar power to frame opinions in the corporate arena. Because reported net income is the number that receives the most attention, it is also the number that corporate managers might be most tempted to manipulate. This section describes four reasons for managing reported earnings. These aren't necessarily good reasons, as illustrated in the Xerox opening scenario and as discussed more fully later in the chapter. However, they do reflect the forces that are often spoken of as pushing managers to manipulate reported earnings. These four reasons are as follows:

1. Meet internal targets.
2. Meet external expectations.
3. Provide income smoothing.
4. Provide window dressing for an IPO or a loan.

Each of these earnings management motivations will be discussed in turn in this section.

Meet Internal Targets

As discussed in the Xerox scenario at the beginning of the chapter, managers in Xerox Mexico felt pressured by corporate earnings and revenue targets and resorted to relaxing credit standards, biasing estimates of bad debts, and finally fraudulently concealing sales returns. One of the most notorious examples of accounting manipulation to meet internal goals is the **MiniScribe** case from 1989. To meet the nearly impossible earnings targets set by the flamboyant and volatile CEO, employees of MiniScribe, a seller of disk drives, reportedly resorted to shipping disk drive boxes filled with bricks to meet sales targets at the end of a quarter.

Internal earnings targets represent an important tool in motivating managers to increase sales efforts, control costs, and use resources more efficiently. As with any performance measurement tool, however, it is a fact of life that the person being evaluated will have a tendency to forget the economic factors underlying the measurement and instead focus on the measured number itself. If you doubt this tendency, consider whether during this intermediate financial accounting course you have maintained your focus solely on learning financial accounting or whether you have occasionally concentrated primarily on scoring points to get a good grade.

Academic research has also confirmed that the existence of earnings-based internal bonuses contributes to the incidence of earnings management. For example, research has demonstrated that managers subject to an earnings-based bonus plan are more likely to manage earnings upward if they are close to the bonus threshold and are also more likely to manage earnings downward if reported earnings are substantially in excess of the maximum bonus level.[1] This latter tendency basically means that managers have a tendency to defer some earnings "for a rainy day," which could occur the next period when operating results are not as favorable. This tendency has been found using company-level information as well as using earnings reported by managers of divisions of

[1] P. Healy, "The Effect of Bonus Schemes on Accounting Decisions," *Journal of Accounting and Economics*, 1985, p. 85.

companies.[2] Because the existence of an earnings-based bonus plan increases the incentive of managers to manipulate the reported numbers, auditors consider such plans a risk factor as they plan the nature and extent of their audit work.

Meet External Expectations

A wide variety of external stakeholders has an interest in a company's financial performance. For example, employees and customers want a company to do well so that it can survive for the long run and make good on its long-term pension and warranty obligations. Suppliers want assurance that they will receive payment and, more important, that the purchasing company will be a reliable purchaser for many years into the future. For these stakeholders, signs of financial weakness, such as reporting negative earnings, are very bad news indeed. Accordingly, we shouldn't be surprised that in some companies when the initial computations reveal that a company will report a net loss, the company's accountants are asked to go back to the accrual judgments and estimates to see whether just a few more dollars of earnings can be squeezed to obtain positive earnings. If this scenario is true, we should expect that there should be a lower-than-expected number of companies with earnings just a little bit negative and a higher-than-expected number of companies with earnings just a little bit positive. This result should occur because any company that has a small negative earnings number has a strong incentive to try to use accounting assumptions to nudge the earnings into positive territory. This intuition is verified by the earnings distribution information reproduced in Exhibit 6-2. As seen in the diagram, annual net income for an average company is equal to about 7% of the company's market value. And except around zero, the numerical distribution of companies that have net income above and below that average amount follows the familiar bell-shaped curve. However, just below zero you can see a trough in the distribution, indicating that the number of companies with earnings just below zero is significantly lower than expected. In addition, there is a lump on the distribution just above zero, indicating that the number of companies with earnings just above zero is significantly greater than expected. This simple picture provides strong evidence that companies manage earnings to avoid reporting losses and disappointing external stakeholders.

> **FYI**
>
> As China prepared to apply for World Trade Organization (WTO) membership, the official Chinese government target was 8% economic growth in 1998. Government officials biased the reported numbers upward, concealing the fact that actual growth was just 4%. See Nicholas R. Lardy, "Integrating China into the Global Economy," Brookings Institution Press, 2002.

> **FYI**
>
> According to *CFO.com*, chief financial officer (CFO) turnover among the Fortune 500 increased by 21% from 2003 to 2004. Failing to meet analysts' earnings expectations and the pressure to comply with Sarbanes-Oxley were cited as the most frequent causes for the turnover of CFOs. See Lisa Yoon, "CFO Resignations Soared in 2004," *CFO.com*, April 5, 2005.

Financial analysts are a very important set of external financial statement users. In addition to making buy and sell recommendations about shares of a company's stock, financial analysts also generate forecasts of company earnings. Extensive research has shown that announcing net income less than the income forecast by analysts results in a

[2] F. Guidry, A. Leone, and S. Rock, "Earnings-Based Bonus Plans and Earnings Management by Business-Unit Managers," *Journal of Accounting and Economics*, 1999, p. 113.

EX 6-2 STANDARDIZED DISTRIBUTION OF ANNUAL NET INCOME

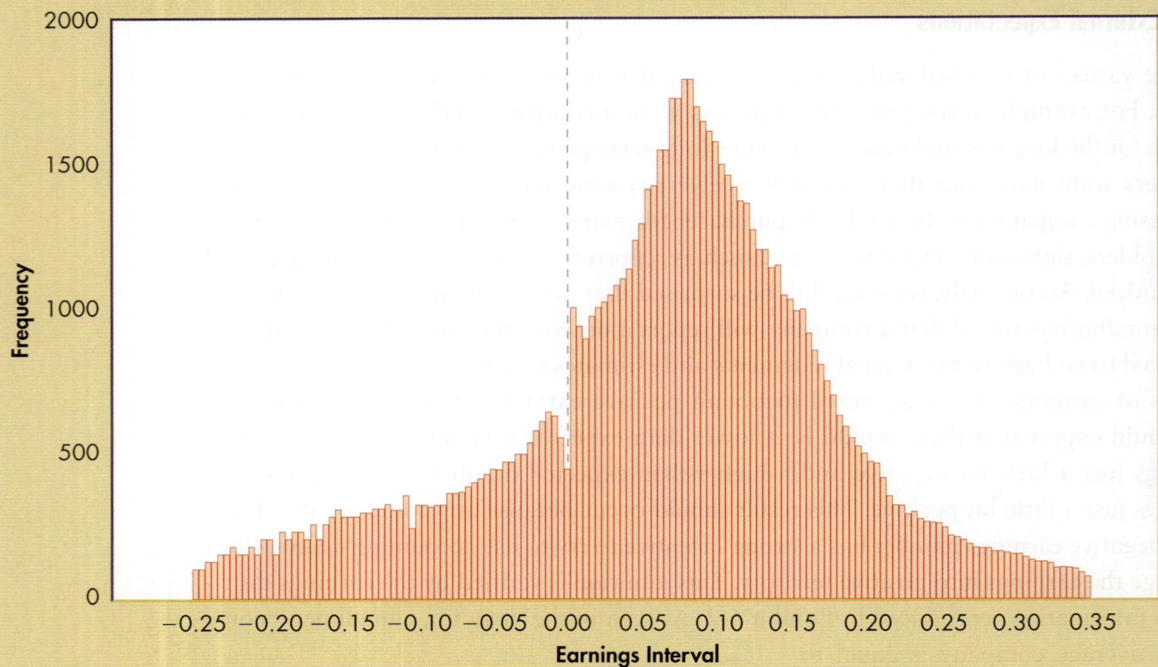

Observations are computed as net income divided by beginning-of-year market value. For example, 0.05 represents net income that is 5% of market value. "Frequency" is the number of observations in a given earnings interval.

Source: D. Burgstahler and I. Dichev, "Earnings Management to Avoid Earnings Decreases and Losses," *Journal of Accounting and Economics*, 1997, p. 99. The diagram is from Figure 3 on page 109.

drop in stock price. As a result, companies have an incentive to manage earnings to make sure that the announced number is at least equal to the earnings expected by analysts.

The uncanny ability of many companies to consistently meet analysts' earnings expectations would not be possible unless those companies were practicing at least some earnings management. For example, until the unexpected earnings decline associated with the September 11, 2001, World Trade Center attack, **General Electric** had met or exceeded analysts' earnings expectations for 29 consecutive quarters. Microsoft met or exceeded analysts' expectations for 52 quarters in a row, a streak that ended in the first quarter of 2000. Streaks like this defy the laws of probability. If analysts make an unbiased forecast of earnings and if companies don't make any efforts to manage earnings to reach the forecasted level, reported earnings should exceed the forecast half the time and fall short of the forecast half the time. In this setting, a string of 52 quarters in a row of meeting or beating analysts' forecast has a 1-in-4.5 quadrillion chance of occurring randomly. Research has demonstrated that managers not only manage earnings to make sure they meet analysts' forecasts but also provide overly pessimistic "guidance" to analysts to ensure that the forecasts made are not too high to reach.[3]

[3] D. Matsumoto, "Management's Incentives to Avoid Negative Earnings Surprises," *The Accounting Review*, July 2002, p. 483.

Provide Income Smoothing

Examine the time series of earnings for Company A and Company B shown in Exhibit 6-3. For Company A, the amount of earnings increases steadily for each year from Year 1 through Year 10. For Company B, the earnings series is like a roller coaster ride. Companies A and B have the same earnings in Year 1, the same earnings in Year 10, and the same total earnings over the 10-year period included in the graph. At the end of Year 10, if you were asked which company you would prefer to loan money to or to invest in, you would almost certainly choose Company A. The earnings stream of Company A gives you a sense of stability, reliability, and reduced risk.

Now imagine yourself as the chief executive officer of Company B. You know that through aggressive accounting assumptions, you can strategically defer or accelerate the recognition of some revenues and expenses and smooth your reported earnings stream to be exactly like that shown for Company A. Would you be tempted to do so? Of course you would. The practice of carefully timing the recognition of revenues and expenses to even out the amount of reported earnings from one year to the next is called income smoothing. By making a company appear to be less volatile, income smoothing can make it easier for a company to obtain a loan on favorable terms and easier to attract investors.[4]

The champion of all income-smoothing companies is General Electric. In fact, GE's ability to report steadily increasing earnings is legendary. As of the end of 2001, General

EX 6-3 INCOME SMOOTHING

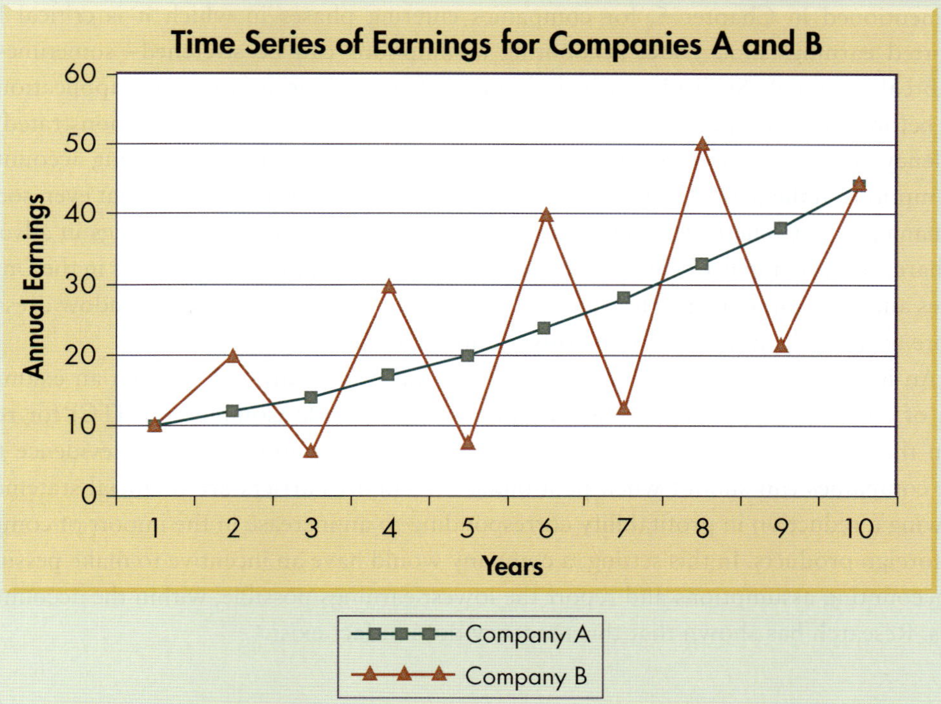

[4] See R. Dye, "Earnings Management in an Overlapping Generations Model," *Journal of Accounting Research*, 1988, p. 195; and B. Trueman and S. Titman, "An Explanation for Accounting Income Smoothing," *Journal of Accounting Research* (supplement), 1988, p. 127. For a more general discussion of earnings management, see K. Schipper, "Commentary on Earnings Management," *Accounting Horizons*, December 1989, p. 91.

Electric had reported 105 consecutive quarters of earnings growth (a streak that ended in 2002). GE's business structure is particularly well suited to earnings management because of the company's large number of diverse operating units (financial services, heavy manufacturing, home appliances, and so forth). A large one-time loss reported by one business unit can frequently be matched with an offsetting gain reported by another unit. By carefully timing the recognition of these gains and losses, GE can avoid reporting earnings that bounce up and down from quarter to quarter. For example, in its press release announcing results for the fourth quarter of 2001, GE reported that its **GE Capital Services** subsidiary reported a $642 million after-tax gain from the restructuring of its investment in a global satellite partnership. During the same quarter, GE Capital Services reported a $656 million after-tax loss associated with its exit from certain unprofitable insurance and financing product lines. The timing of one of these transactions could have been delayed so that it would have occurred in the first quarter of 2002, but by making sure that they were both recognized in the same quarter, General Electric was able to show a more smooth earnings stream. In 1994, an article in *The Wall Street Journal* accused General Electric of income smoothing.[5] Shortly after the article came out, one of GE's financial executives was speaking to a group of accounting professors, one of whom was brazen enough to ask if it were true that GE practiced income smoothing. The GE executive quietly smiled and responded, "Well, the timing of the recognition of some of our gains and losses has been rather fortuitous"—the implication of the response being that, of course, GE did all that it could, within the accounting rules, to smooth reported earnings.

Provide Window Dressing for an IPO or a Loan

As mentioned in Chapter 5, for companies entering phases in which it is critical that reported earnings look good, accounting assumptions can be stretched—sometimes to the breaking point. Such phases include just before making a large loan application or just before the initial public offering (IPO) of stock. Many studies have demonstrated the tendency of managers in U.S. companies to boost their reported earnings using accounting assumptions in the period before an IPO.[6] A study of IPOs in China found that even socialist managers in Chinese state-owned enterprises manipulate reported earnings in advance of shares of the company being sold to the public.[7] If both capitalist managers in the United States and socialist managers in China are engaged in the same pattern of window dressing before an IPO, the phenomenon is truly a universal one.

An interesting case of reverse window dressing was discovered through an examination of companies applying to the U.S. International Trade Commission (ITC) for relief from the importation of competing foreign products. Important pieces of evidence that U.S. companies can submit when petitioning for import barriers are financial statements showing a reduction in profitability corresponding to an increase in the import of competing foreign products. In this setting, a company would have an incentive to make pessimistic accounting assumptions and report the lowest earnings possible, within the accounting rules. Research has shown that this tendency does in fact exist.[8]

[5] Randall Smith, Steven Lipin, and Amal Kumar Naj, "Managing Profits: How General Electric Damps Fluctuations in its Annual Earnings," *The Wall Street Journal*, November 3, 1994, p. A1.

[6] As one example, see S. Teoh, T. Wong, and G. Rao, "Are Accruals during Initial Public Offerings Opportunistic?" *Review of Accounting Studies*, May 1998, p. 175.

[7] J. Aharony, J. Lee, and T. Wong, "Financial Packaging of IPO Firms in China," *Journal of Accounting Research*, 2000, p. 103.

[8] J. Jones, "Earnings Management during Import Relief Investigations," *Journal of Accounting Research*, 1991, p. 193.

This section has outlined a number of settings in which managers have strong economic incentives to manipulate reported earnings. Whether a manager should attempt to manage earnings is the topic of a later section in this chapter.

Earnings Management Techniques

2 List the common techniques used to manage earnings.

WHY **Maintaining the credibility of the financial reporting model involves constant adaptation by regulators, standard setters, auditors, and financial statement preparers because managers under pressure (aided by accountants) are constantly inventing and perfecting new earnings management techniques.**

HOW **Earnings management generally involves a series of increasingly aggressive steps. Those steps include strategic matching of one-time gains and losses, change in methods or estimates with full disclosure, change in methods or estimates with little or no disclosure, non-GAAP accounting, and fictitious transactions.**

With all of the incentives to manage earnings mentioned in the previous section, it isn't surprising that managers occasionally do use the flexibility inherent in accrual accounting to actually manage earnings. The more accounting training one has, the easier it is to see ways in which accounting judgments and estimates can be used to "enhance" the reported numbers. In fact, there have been nationwide seminars on exactly how to effectively manage earnings. One popular seminar sponsored by the National Center for Continuing Education in 2001 was "How to Manage Earnings in Conformance with GAAP." The target audience for the 2-day seminar was described as CFOs, CPAs, controllers, auditors, bankers, analysts, and securities attorneys.

Using the concepts of accrual accounting and the accounting standards that have been promulgated, accountants add information value by using estimates and assumptions to convert the raw cash flow data into accrual data. However, the same flexibility that allows accountants to use professional judgment to produce financial statements that accurately portray a company's financial condition also allows desperate managers to manipulate the reported numbers. The following sections describe the common techniques used in managing earnings.

FYI

In the wake of the accounting scandals that occurred in 2001 and 2002, the National Center for Continuing Education decided to change the title of the earnings management seminar to "How to Detect Manipulative Accounting Practices." However, the course outline was exactly the same as the original "How to Manage Earnings" seminar.

Earnings Management Continuum

Not all earnings management schemes are created equal. The continuum in Exhibit 6-4 illustrates that earnings management can range from savvy timing of transactions to outright fraud. This section provides examples of each activity on the earnings management continuum. Keep in mind that in most companies, earnings management, if it is practiced at all, does not extend beyond the savvy transaction timing found at the left end of the continuum in Exhibit 6-4. However, because of the importance and economic significance of the catastrophic reporting failures that are sometimes associated with companies that engage in more elaborate earnings management, the entire continuum is discussed here.

EX 6-4 THE EARNINGS MANAGEMENT CONTINUUM

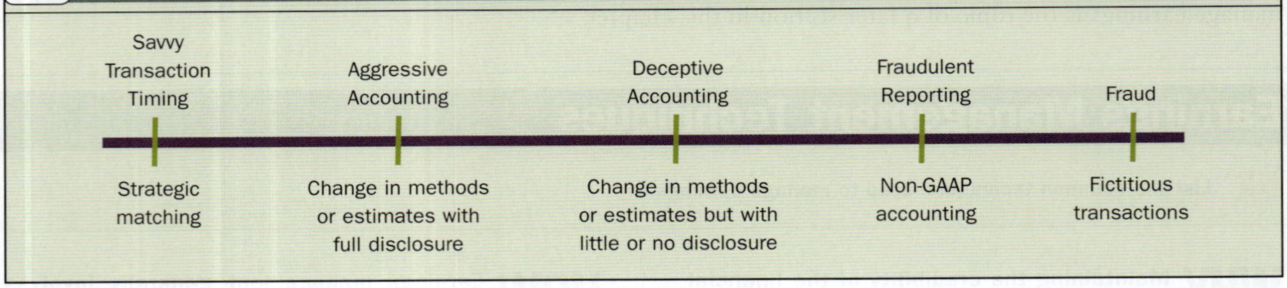

Strategic Matching As mentioned in the earlier discussion of income smoothing, General Electric is the acknowledged master at timing its transactions so that large one-time gains and losses occur in the same quarter, resulting in a smooth upward trend in reported earnings. Through awareness of the benefits of consistently meeting earnings targets or of reporting a stable income stream, a company can make extra efforts to ensure that certain key transactions are completed quickly or delayed so that they are recognized in the most advantageous quarter.

Change in Methods or Estimates with Full Disclosure Companies frequently change accounting estimates respecting bad debts, return on pension funds, depreciation lives, and so forth. For example, in 1998 **Delta Air Lines** increased the depreciation life for some of its aircraft from 20 to 25 years, reducing depreciation expense and increasing pretax income by $92 million. Although such changes are a routine part of adjusting accounting estimates to reflect the most current information available, they can be used to manage the amount of reported earnings. Because the impact of such changes is fully disclosed, any earnings management motivation could be detected by financial statement users willing to do a little detective work.

Change in Methods or Estimates with Little or No Disclosure In contrast to the accounting changes referred to in the preceding paragraph, other accounting changes are sometimes made without full disclosure. For example, the Xerox opening scenario reported that the company changed the estimated interest rate used in recording sales-type leases without describing the change in the notes to the financial statements. One might debate whether the new estimated interest rate was more appropriate, but what is certain is that failing to disclose the impact of the change misled financial statement users. These users evaluated the reported earnings of Xerox under the incorrect assumption that the results were compiled using a consistent set of accounting methods and estimates and could therefore be meaningfully compared to prior-year results. As indicated by the label in Exhibit 6-4, this constitutes deceptive accounting.

Non-GAAP Accounting Toward the right end of the earnings management continuum lies the earnings management tool that can be politely called "non-GAAP accounting." A more descriptive label in many cases is "fraudulent reporting," although non-GAAP accounting can also be the result of inadvertent errors. For example, part of the accounting deception practiced by **Enron** was the inappropriate use of special-purpose entities (SPEs). SPEs are small companies affiliated with, and often indirectly controlled by, a larger company. It is clear that some (although certainly not all) of Enron's SPEs were established for the express purpose of hiding information from financial statement users. In so doing, Enron violated the spirit of the accounting standards. In some cases, Enron also violated the letter of the standards by using SPE accounting when it was not allowed under GAAP. As another example, it was revealed in 2002 that **WorldCom** had capitalized (i.e., recognized as an asset) $3.8 billion in expenditures for local phone access charges that should have been reported as operating expenses. By the way, when the smoke finally cleared on the WorldCom scandal, the estimate of the total amount of accounting fraud climbed to $11 billion.

Fictitious Transactions The opening scenario for this chapter mentioned that managers at Xerox Mexico rented secret warehouses in which to store returned merchandise to avoid recording the returns. This is an example of outright fraud, which is the deceptive concealment of transactions (like the sales returns) or the creation of fictitious transactions. A classic example of the latter is the famous **ZZZZ Best** case. The founder of ZZZZ Best, a carpet cleaning and fire damage restoration business, started inventing sales contracts to meet increasing operating performance expectations by banks and investors. For example, ZZZZ Best claimed to have a contract for a $2.3 million restoration job on an eight-story building in Arroyo Grande, California, a town that had no buildings over three stories.

The five items displayed in Exhibit 6-4 also mirror the progression in earnings management strategies followed by individual companies. These activities start small and legitimately and really reflect nothing more than the strategic timing of transactions to smooth reported results. In the face of operating results that fall short of targets, a company might make some cosmetic changes in accounting estimates to meet earnings expectations but would fully disclose these changes to avoid deceiving serious financial statement users. If operating results are far short of expectations, an increasingly desperate management might cross the line into deceptive accounting by making accounting changes that are not disclosed or by violating GAAP completely. Finally, when the gap between expected results and actual results is so great that it cannot be closed by any accounting assumption, a manager who is still fixated on making the target number must resort to out-and-out fraud by inventing transactions and customers. The key things to remember are that the forces encouraging managers and accountants to manage earnings are real and that if one is not aware of those forces, it is easy to gradually slip from the left side of the earnings management continuum to the right side.

Chairman Levitt's Top Five Accounting Hocus-Pocus Items

On September 28, 1998, then-SEC Chairman Arthur Levitt gave a speech at the New York University Center for Law and Business.[9] The title of Chairman Levitt's remarks was "The Numbers Game." He chose this occasion to proclaim the SEC's dismay over the increasing practice of earnings management. Mr. Levitt's comments at the banquet were so blunt and hit so close to home that it was reported that "first, people put down their forks, . . . then they pulled out notepads."[10] Mr. Levitt described five techniques of "accounting hocus-pocus" that summarized the most blatant abuses of the flexibility inherent in accrual accounting. A description of these five techniques follows. The discussion includes both a description of the abuses that prompted Chairman Levitt's comments as well as a description of how accounting standards and practices have been changed to address these abuses.

[9] A text of this entire landmark speech can be found at **http://www.sec.gov/news/speech/speecharchive/1998/spch220.txt**.

[10] Carol Loomis, "Lies, Damned Lies, and Managed Earnings," *Fortune*, August 2, 1999, p. 74.

FYI

Traditionally, companies have sometimes timed a big bath to coincide with a change in management. In this way, the "bath" year can be blamed on past management.

Big-Bath Charges Examine the time series of earnings for Company C and Company D shown in Exhibit 6-5. For Company C, the amount of earnings increases steadily until Year 5 when the trend turns around and earnings decrease steadily thereafter. For Company D, earnings drop dramatically in Year 5 but then are steady at $15 each year thereafter. Companies C and D have the same total earnings over the 10-year period included in the graph. At the end of Year 10, if you were asked which company you would prefer to loan money to or to invest in, you would almost certainly choose Company D. Any problems that Company D may have had appear to have been put behind it in Year 5, and the recent earnings picture exudes stability. In contrast, Company C's problems seem to be continuing without end. The big drop in earnings in Year 5 for Company D is an example of a "big bath." The concept behind a big bath is that if a company expects to have a series of hits to earnings in future years, it is better to try to recognize all of the bad news in one year, leaving future years unencumbered by continuing losses. One way to execute a big bath is through a large restructuring charge, as discussed in Chapter 4. As part of a restructuring charge, assets are written off and the expenses associated with future restructuring obligations are recognized immediately. Since Mr. Levitt's speech in 1998, the FASB has substantially limited the flexibility a company has to recognize a big-bath restructuring charge by adopting stricter rules on the accounting for impairment losses (FASB ASC Section 360-10-35) and on the timing of the recognition of restructuring obligations (FASB ASC Topic 420).

EX 6-5 A BIG BATH

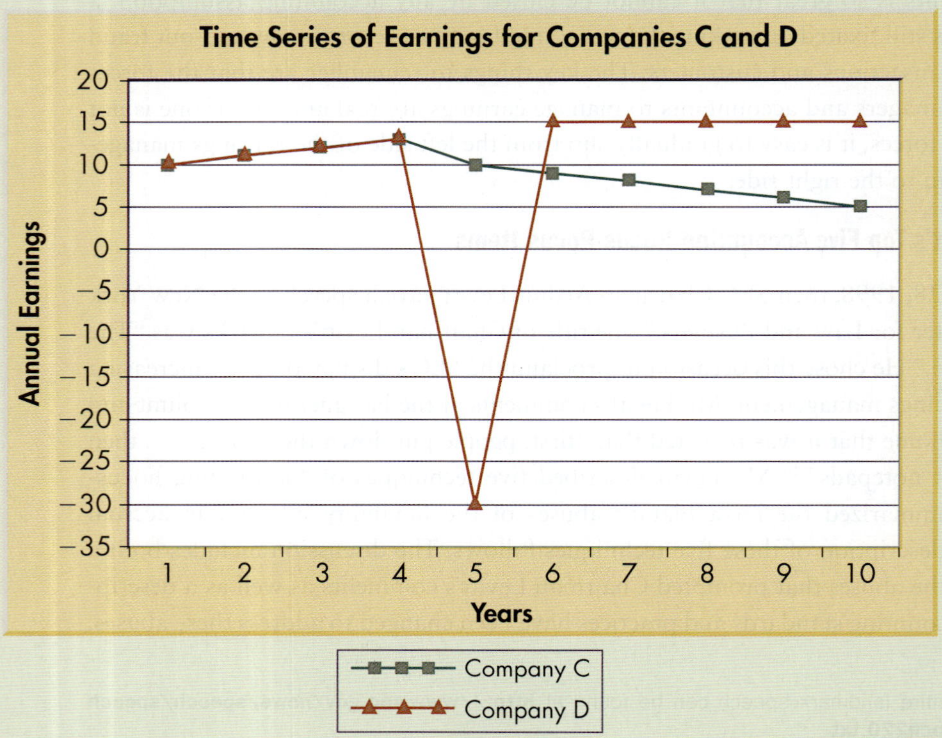

Creative Acquisition Accounting A key accounting task after one company has acquired another is the allocation of the total purchase price to the individual assets of the acquired company. This process is described in Chapter 10. A practice common at the time Mr. Levitt gave his speech was that of allocating a large amount of a purchase price to the value of ongoing research and development projects. As described in Chapter 10, at the time of Mr. Levitt's speech, the cost assigned to "purchased in-process R&D" was expensed immediately in accordance with the mandated U.S. GAAP treatment of all R&D expenditures. The net result of this treatment is similar to a big bath in that a large R&D expense is recorded in the acquisition year, and expenses in subsequent years are lower than they would have been if the purchase price had been allocated to a depreciable asset. Since 1998, new acquisition accounting rules have been adopted (FASB ASC Topic 805, Business Combinations); these standards give more extensive guidelines on how the purchase price in a business acquisition should be allocated. In the immediate aftermath of Mr. Levitt's speech, the SEC staff informed companies that they would be very skeptical in their review of the accounting for any business acquisition in which a large portion of the purchase price was allocated to in-process R&D.

Cookie Jar Reserves We are all familiar with the advice that in good times we should save for a rainy day. Companies sometimes follow this advice with respect to earnings. For example, by recognizing very high bad debt expense this year, when earnings are high even with the extra expense, a company has the flexibility of recognizing lower bad debt expense in future years when the earnings picture might not be so bright. Similarly, by recognizing some cash received as unearned revenue instead of revenue, a company is basically saving revenue for a rainy day or a future year or quarter in which there might be a threat that earnings would fall short of market expectations. Microsoft has been accused of doing exactly this. An SEC investigation into Microsoft's accounting for deferred revenue resulted in a 2002 order to "cease and desist" any further improper accounting practices. Since 1998, the SEC has released *Staff Accounting Bulletins (SAB) 101* and *104* (now in FASB ASC Section 605-10-S99), identifying more carefully the circumstances in which it is appropriate for a company to defer revenue.

Materiality As discussed in Chapter 1, auditors have traditionally used arbitrary quantitative benchmarks to define how big an amount must be to be considered material. Examples of such benchmarks are 1% of sales, 5% of operating income, or 10% of stockholders' equity. However, in this era of increasingly refined analyst expectations, falling short of the market's expectation of earnings by just one penny per share can cause a company to lose literally billions of dollars in market value. Thus, Chairman Levitt urged auditors to rethink their ideas about what is material and what is not. In particular, consider a company that uses a questionable accounting technique that changes reported earnings by a small amount, just 1%. Historically, the auditor would not withhold a favorable audit opinion based on this questionable accounting practice because the amount was deemed to be immaterial. However, assume that the use of the questionable accounting practice allows the company to meet analysts' earnings expectations. According to Chairman Levitt, the impact of that technique should be considered material. Thus, the auditor should not sign off on the audit opinion until the company had changed the practice or convinced the auditor that it was in accordance with GAAP. In 1999, the SEC released *SAB 99* (now in FASB ASC Section 250-10-S99) that outlines this more comprehensive definition of materiality.

Revenue Recognition More common than Microsoft's efforts to defer revenue are the efforts of companies to accelerate the reporting of revenue. In particular, start-up companies, eager to show operating results to lenders and potential investors, would like to report revenue when contracts are signed or partially completed rather than waiting until the promised product or service has been fully delivered. For example, the opening scenario for Chapter 8 describes the rise and fall of **MicroStrategy**, a software firm. When the operating performance of the company fell short of analysts' expectations in the third quarter of 1999, the company recognized \$17.5 million in revenue from a \$27.5 million multiyear licensing agreement that was signed very near the end of the quarter. Given that the company had not really provided any of the promised service in the short time that had elapsed since the signing of the contract, it would have been more appropriate not to report any revenue at all. However, to do so would have resulted in MicroStrategy's reporting a loss for the quarter on revenues that were 20% lower than revenues reported the quarter before. As mentioned earlier, in response to the abuses mentioned by Mr. Levitt the SEC released *SAB 101*, which reduces the flexibility companies have in the timing of revenue recognition. The revenue recognition guidance contained in *SAB 101* is described in detail in Chapter 8. As also described in Chapter 8, the FASB and IASB are in the midst of a joint project involving a comprehensive revisiting of the rules regarding when revenue should be reported.

As mentioned earlier, action has been taken to reduce the incidence of each of these five hocus-pocus items. However, this list is still a useful starting point to see how companies attempt to manage earnings. As new accounting standards and SEC regulations reduce or eliminate one particular type of earnings management, rest assured that resourceful managers and accountants will invent new ones, but these new techniques will be variations on the general theme shared by all of Chairman Levitt's hocus-pocus items. The exercise of judgment inherent in the accrual process gives desperate managers the ability to accelerate or defer the reporting of profit to best suit their purposes.

Pro Forma Earnings

An interesting twist in the practice of earnings management is the reporting of pro forma earnings. A pro forma earnings number is the regular GAAP earnings number with some revenues, expenses, gains, or losses excluded. The exclusions are made because, companies claim, the GAAP results do not fairly reflect the company's performance.

The concern with pro forma earnings is that companies can abuse the practice and report pro forma earnings merely in an effort to make their results seem better than they actually were. In fact, pro forma earnings have been labeled as "EBS," or "everything but the bad stuff."[11] There are many examples of questionable pro forma earnings reporting. For example, on August 8, 2001, **Waste Management** announced its earnings for the second quarter of 2001. Reported GAAP earnings were \$191 million, somewhat short of analysts' expectations. However, pro forma earnings were \$212 million for the quarter, beating analysts' expectations. The difference between GAAP earnings and pro forma earnings resulted because, on a pro forma basis, Waste Management decided to exclude \$1 million in truck-painting costs and \$30 million in consulting costs from the operating expenses. Waste Management's claim was that the trucks were painted early, making the paint job economically equivalent to a capital expenditure (an asset) rather than an expense. The consulting costs were part of a strategic improvement initiative; again, Waste Management

[11] Lynn Turner, SEC Chief Accountant, Remarks to the 39th Annual Corporate Counsel Institute, Northwestern University School of Law, Evanston, Illinois, October 12, 2000.

claimed that these costs were more appropriately reported as an asset rather than as an expense as required under GAAP.[12]

The key question with respect to pro forma earnings is whether the number helps financial statement users better understand a company or whether it is a blatant attempt to cover up poor performance. Research on this issue has revealed that both answers are correct. For many companies, the pro forma earnings number is in fact a better reflection of the underlying economic performance than is GAAP net income. Thus, a manager can use the flexibility of pro forma earnings reports to reveal additional, useful information. On the other hand, there is also evidence that some managers use a pro forma earnings release in an attempt to hide poor operating performance. A study of 1,149 pro forma earnings announcements made from January 1998 through December 2000 found that while only 38.7% of the announcing companies had GAAP earnings that met or exceeded analysts' expectations, the pro forma earnings numbers reported by these same companies met or exceeded analysts' expectations 80.1% of the time.[13]

One way to view the flexible reporting options a manager has in choosing what to report as "pro forma earnings" is that these options are just an exaggerated version of the options the same manager has in reporting GAAP earnings. If the manager is trustworthy, the GAAP earnings are reliable, and the manager can reveal even better information about the underlying economics of the business through appropriate adjustments in computing pro forma earnings. This advantage of pro forma earnings is offset (some would say swamped) by the opportunity that reporting pro forma earnings gives a desperate manager seeking to gloss over operating problems by reporting deceptively positive pro forma results. This potential for misleading reporting of pro forma earnings prompted the Financial Executives International (FEI) and the National Investor Relations Institute in April 2001 to recommend that firms give a reconciliation to GAAP net income whenever reporting pro forma numbers. This reconciliation highlights the adjustments made by management in reporting pro forma earnings. In 2003, the SEC formalized this requirement of providing a reconciliation between GAAP and pro forma earnings in its Regulation G. An example of one such reconciliation is reproduced in Exhibit 6-6. This illustration is for **Intuit Inc.**, maker of the popular software products QuickBooks, Quicken, and TurboTax. Note that the largest adjustment (for share-based compensation expense, which will be explained in Chapter 13) is a noncash item that Intuit believes does not relate to the company's core operating performance.

> **FYI**
>
> The first SEC cease and desist order with respect to pro forma earnings was issued to **Trump Hotels & Casino Resorts**. For the third quarter of 1999, Trump had a GAAP loss of $67 million. However, by excluding a one-time charge of $81 million, Trump was able to report pro forma earnings of $14 million, exceeding the prevailing analyst forecast of $12 million. What Trump deceptively failed to mention is that the $14 million in pro forma earnings included a $17 million one-time gain. See Securities and Exchange Commission, *Accounting and Auditing Enforcement Release No. 1499*, Administrative Proceeding File No. 3-10680, January 16, 2002.

This section has discussed the earnings management continuum, which illustrates how a company can imperceptibly slide from intelligent transaction timing to unquestionably fraudulent deception in its attempts to report the most attractive earnings possible. The five accounting hocus-pocus techniques are examples of the accounting tactics companies

[12] Aaron Elstein, "Unusual Expenses Raise Concerns," *The Wall Street Journal*, August 23, 2001, p. C1.
[13] N. Bhattacharya, E. Black, T. Christensen, and C. Larson, "Assessing the Relative Informativeness and Permanence of Pro Forma Earnings and GAAP Operating Earnings," *Journal of Accounting and Economics*, 2002.

EX 6-6 RECONCILIATION OF PRO FORMA EARNINGS TO GAAP EARNINGS

Intuit Inc.
GAAP to Pro Forma Operating Income Reconciliation

	Three Months Ended	
(in millions)	**January 31, 2010**	**January 31, 2009**
GAAP operating income	$139	$111
Amortization of purchased intangible assets	16	14
Acquisition-related charges	11	13
Professional fees for business combinations	3	—
Share-based compensation expense	37	34
Non-GAAP operating income	$206	$172

Share-based compensation expenses. These consist of non-cash expenses for stock options, restricted stock units and purchases of common stock under our Employee Stock Purchase Plan. When considering the impact of equity awards, we place greater emphasis on overall shareholder dilution rather than the accounting charges associated with those awards.

Amortization of purchased intangible assets and acquisition-related charges. When we acquire an entity, we are required by GAAP to record the fair values of the intangible assets of the entity and amortize them over their useful lives. Amortization of purchased intangible assets in cost of revenue includes amortization of software and other technology assets of acquired entities. Acquisition-related charges in operating expenses include amortization of other purchased intangible assets such as customer lists, covenants not to compete and trade names.

Professional fees for business combinations. We exclude from our non-GAAP financial measures the professional fees we incur to complete business combinations. These include investment banking, legal and accounting fees.

Gains and losses on marketable equity securities and other investments. We exclude from our non-GAAP financial measures gains and losses that we record when we sell or impair marketable equity securities and other investments.

use to manage earnings. Finally, pro forma earnings announcements can be either an effort by management to add information value to the reported GAAP numbers or a last-ditch attempt to meet earnings targets that were not attainable using generally accepted accounting principles. Keep in mind that accounting standards and SEC enforcement activities will undoubtedly change in the future to eliminate some earnings management techniques that are common now. However, desperate managers will continue to work with creative accountants to develop new ways for companies to manage their reported results.

Pros and Cons of Managing Earnings

3 **Critically discuss whether a company should manage its earnings.**

WHY **Financial reporting is a normal part of a company's overall public relations effort. As such, a responsible manager should consider what impact the financial statements will have on the company's ability to satisfy the needs of its stakeholders.**

HOW **We know that a company CAN manage its earnings; the question is whether a company SHOULD manage its earnings. An important guiding principle is that it is wrong to intentionally try to deceive others.**

The preceding two sections have discussed why and how a company manages earnings. This section explores the difficult issue of whether a company *should* manage earnings. The perfect-world response that a company should never manage earnings under any circumstances is both naïve in today's financial reporting environment and is also not necessarily correct. On the other hand, there can be great risk in starting down the slippery slope of managing reported results.

Financial Reporting as a Part of Public Relations

In the Web sites of most publicly traded companies, the financial statements can be found under the heading "Investor Relations." In essence, financial reporting is just a subcategory of public relations. A financial statement is one of a large number of vehicles that managers of a company use to communicate information about the company to the public. And as with other forms of corporate communications, a company must balance its desire to frame information in the best light possible with the need to maintain credibility with company stakeholders.

In the context of financial statements being one way for a company to communicate with the public, consider your answers to the following questions:

QUESTION Does a manager have an ethical and fiduciary responsibility to carefully manage the resources of a publicly traded company in order to maximize the value to the shareholders?

Answer. *Yes. In fact, this is the very definition of the responsibility of a corporate manager.*

> **FYI**
>
> Of course, a manager who spends too much time managing earnings, at the expense of pushing forward the strategic efforts of the company, is wasting corporate resources. One CEO estimated that 35% of his/her time was spent considering preliminary financial reports and providing earnings guidance to analysts and company stakeholders.

QUESTION Does the public perception of a company impact the company's success in terms of finding customers, securing relationships with suppliers, attracting employees, and obtaining cooperation from elected officials and regulators?

Answer. *Certainly. It is impossible to rally people to put their time and money behind a company unless they are convinced that the company can be successful.*

QUESTION Does the amount of reported earnings impact the public's perception of a company?

Answer. *Absolutely. Accounting net income is not the only piece of information relevant to assessing a company's viability, but it certainly is one influential data point.*

QUESTION Does a manager have a responsibility to manage reported earnings, within the constraints of generally accepted accounting principles?

Answer. *It is difficult to answer no to this question. In light of the answers to the preceding questions, it would be an irresponsible manager indeed who did not do all possible, within the constraints of GAAP, to burnish the company's public image.*

Is Earnings Management Ethical?

Refer back to Exhibit 6-4. Everyone agrees that the creation of fictitious transactions, at the far right side of the earnings management continuum, is unethical. But there the universal agreement ends with respect to what is and is not ethical. For example, managers and their auditors frequently disagree about what constitutes fraudulent, non-GAAP reporting. In the WorldCom example mentioned earlier, the company's CFO vigorously defended the capitalization rather than the expensing of the disputed $3.8 billion in local phone access charges. The CFO reiterated this defense, based on his understanding of the appropriate accounting standards, in a multi-day series of meetings with the external auditor and the audit committee.[14] In the view of the CFO, this "fraudulent reporting" was both ethical and in conformity with GAAP. As one moves even further to the left on the earnings management continuum, disagreement about whether a certain act is or is not ethical increases. For example, when a company makes an accounting change, how can a bright line be drawn between sufficient and deceptive disclosure? Who is to judge whether the strategic timing of gains and losses by General Electric is unethical or just prudent business practice?

Exhibit 6-7 contains a figure titled "The GAAP Oval." This oval represents the flexibility a manager has, within GAAP, to report one earnings number from among many possibilities based on different methods and assumptions. Clearly, reporting a number corresponding with points D or E, which are both outside the GAAP oval, is unethical. The difficult ethical question is whether the manager has a responsibility to try to report an earnings number exactly in the middle of the possible range, point B in Exhibit 6-7. Or does the manager have a responsibility to report the most conservative, worst-case number, point A in the exhibit? Is it wrong for the manager to try to use accounting flexibility to report an earnings number corresponding with point C, which is the highest possible earnings number that is still in conformity with GAAP? What cost is there, in terms of credibility, for a manager who makes a conservative set of accounting assumptions one year, perhaps when overall operating performance is good, and an aggressive set of assumptions the next year, perhaps to try to hide lackluster operating performance? Finally, note that the boundary of the oval is fuzzy, so it sometimes is not clear whether a certain set of computations is or is not in conformity with GAAP.

EX 6-7 THE GAAP OVAL

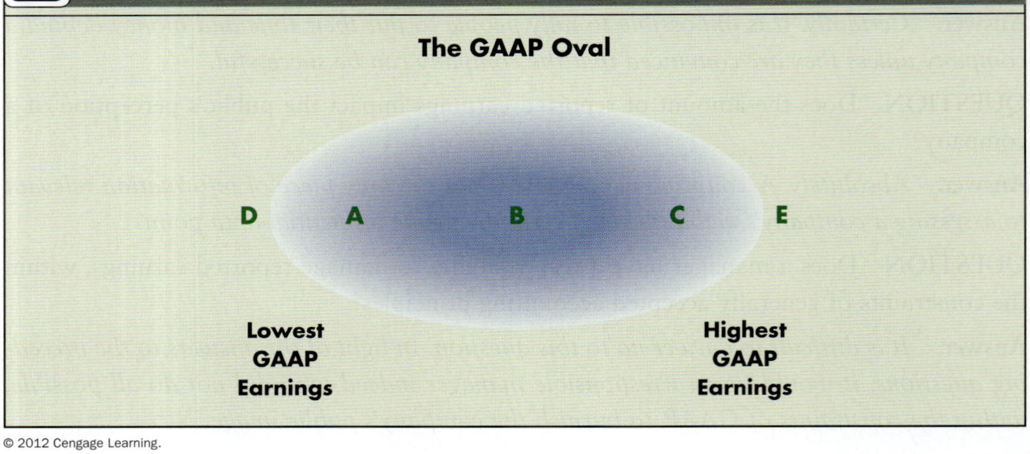

[14] Jared Sandberg, Deborah Solomon, and Rebecca Blumenstein, "Inside WorldCom's Unearthing of a Vast Accounting Scandal," *The Wall Street Journal*, June 27, 2002, p. A1. WorldCom's CFO, Scott Sullivan, later pleaded guilty to charges of conspiracy, securities fraud, and filing false statements. Mr. Sullivan was released from prison in 2009 after serving four years.

ARTHUR ANDERSEN: A TALE OF TWO CHOICES

As with any company that has a long history, **Arthur Andersen** has a number of internal legends that helped define its character over the years. One of these legends, included in the official history covering the firm's first 50 years, is as follows:

> About 1915, Mr. [Arthur] Andersen [the founder of the firm] was confronted with a difficult situation with respect to the financial statements of a midwestern interurban railway company. The company had distorted its earnings by deferring relatively large charges that properly should have been absorbed in current operating expenses. Mr. Andersen was insistent that the financial statements to which he attached his report should disclose the facts. The president of the company . . . came to Chicago and demanded that Mr. Andersen issue a report approving the company's procedure in deferring these operating charges. Mr. Andersen informed the president that there was not enough money in the city of Chicago to induce him to change his report. We lost the client, of course, at a time when the small firm was not having easy sailing, and the loss of a client was almost a life and death matter. The soundness of Mr. Andersen's judgment in this case was clearly indicated when, a few months later, the company was forced to file a petition in bankruptcy.

Contrast this account with the behavior of Arthur Andersen personnel associated with the Enron scandal. In connection with the Enron engagement, Andersen helped Enron structure special-purpose entities that were used to improve the reported accounting numbers of the Enron parent company. Andersen partners also failed to warn Enron's board of directors of their concerns about Enron's accounting. And finally, Andersen professionals shredded documents in a desperate attempt to cover up the firm's involvement in Enron's accounting deception. These questionable actions, taken without careful consideration of their long-term consequences, ultimately brought down the firm started by Mr. Andersen back in 1913.

Question:

1. In what specific ways can a reputation for unbending integrity help an audit firm? A manufacturing firm? A service firm?

Source: Arthur Andersen & Co., "The First Fifty Years: 1913–1963," Chicago, 1963, pp. 19–20.

Of course, whether a manager actually does manage earnings and whether he or she crosses the line and violates GAAP to do so is partially a function of the fear (and costs) of getting caught and of the general ethical culture of the company. It is also a function of the manager's personal ethics and ability to recognize that fraudulent and deceptive financial reporting is part of a continuum that starts with innocent window dressing but can end with full-scale fraud. There is no neon sign giving a final warning saying, "Beware: Don't cross this line!" Thus, each individual must be constantly aware of where he or she is with respect to the earnings management continuum in Exhibit 6-4 and the GAAP oval in Exhibit 6-7. Boards of directors and financial statement preparers should also be aware that, as a group, managers are notoriously overoptimistic about the future business prospects of their companies. A company policy of having a consistently conservative approach to accounting is a good counterbalance to managers who might try to justify optimistic accounting assumptions on the basis of a business turnaround that is "just around the corner."

FYI

Nonaccountants are under the impression that there is no GAAP oval. Instead, they believe that there is only a GAAP point, a single quantity that represents the one, true earnings number. Managers must be aware that this attitude can cause the public to be very unforgiving of companies that are found to have "innocently" managed earnings.

Personal Ethics

Personal ethics is not a topic one typically expects to study in an intermediate financial accounting course. However, the large number of accounting scandals in 2001 and 2002 demonstrated that personal ethics and financial reporting are inextricably connected. The GAAP oval shown in Exhibit 6-7 illustrates that companies can report a range of earnings numbers for a year and still be in strict conformity with GAAP. In other words, earnings management can and does occur without any violation of the accounting rules. If one takes a strictly legalistic view of the world, then it is clear that managers should manage earnings, when they have concluded that the potential costs in terms of lost credibility are outweighed by the financial reporting benefits, because earnings can be managed without violating any rules.

> **FYI**
>
> In an effort to increase the personal cost to company executives of allowing a company to report earnings that violate GAAP, the SEC in 2002 began requiring CEOs and CFOs to submit sworn statements asserting that they had personally confirmed that their company's financial statements contained no materially misleading items.

A contrasting view is that the practice of financial accounting is not a matter of simply applying a list of rules to a set of objective facts. Management intent often enters into the decision of how to report a particular item. For example, land is reported as a long-term asset in the balance sheet unless management intends to sell the land within one year of the balance sheet date. In the context of earnings management, an important consideration is whether savvy transaction timing or changes in accounting methods or estimates are done to better communicate the economic performance of the business to financial statement users or whether the earnings management techniques are used with the intent to deceive. And if earnings management is done to deceive, whom is management trying to deceive? If management is trying to deceive potential investors, lenders, regulatory authorities, employees, or other company stakeholders, then managing earnings poses a real risk of lost credibility in the future. One final important item should be considered—most people believe that intentionally trying to deceive others is wrong, regardless of the economic consequences.

Elements of Earnings Management Meltdowns

4 Describe the common elements of an earnings management meltdown.

WHY An earnings management meltdown does not occur in one step. A company goes through a lengthy process where a series of poor decisions eventually results in a bad outcome for the company, its investors, and the economy.

HOW An earnings management meltdown involves seven steps: downturn in business, pressure to meet expectations, attempted accounting solution, auditor's calculated risk, insufficient user skepticism, regulatory investigation, and massive loss of reputation.

Since the start of the new millennium, astounding numbers of catastrophic accounting failures have occurred. The list includes, but is not limited to, Xerox, Enron, **WorldCom**, **Lehman Brothers**, **Freddie Mac**, and undoubtedly many more by the time you read this chapter. Of course, the details of each failure are different, but they all stem from unsuccessful attempts to manage earnings, and they all have common elements. These common elements are outlined in the timeline in Exhibit 6-8 and are discussed in this section.

EX 6-8 SEVEN ELEMENTS OF AN EARNINGS MANAGEMENT MELTDOWN

1	2	3	4	5	6	7
Downturn in business	Pressure to meet expectations	Attempted accounting solution	Auditor's calculated risk	Insufficient user skepticism	Regulatory investigation	Massive loss of reputation

Downturn in Business

Excessive earnings management almost always begins with a downturn in business. When operating results are consistently good, the need for earnings management is not as great. For example, the first step along the path to accounting scandal for Xerox was a slowdown in sales associated with the increased use of digital documents in the United States and general business woes in the company's Mexican and Brazilian subsidiaries. WorldCom was caught in the massive collapse of the telecommunications companies. From 1997 through 2002, telecom companies spent $4 trillion (with a t!) laying fiber optic cable in the expectation of doubling or tripling of data traffic every quarter. When this volume of traffic didn't materialize, the aggregate market values of telecom companies dropped by $2.5 trillion.[15] In this industry setting, WorldCom was bound to feel some earnings pressure. For Enron, the company's rapid revenue growth partially masked a substantial decline in operating profitability. Exhibit 6-9 displays the return on assets (operating income/assets) of Enron's largest segment from 1996 through 2000. Note that the Enron accounting scandal did not break until late in 2001. You should note that return on assets was not only declining but it was also at a very low absolute level of less than 2%. This dwindling profitability increased the pressure on Enron's management to manage earnings.

EX 6-9 ENRON'S DECLINING OPERATING PROFITABILITY

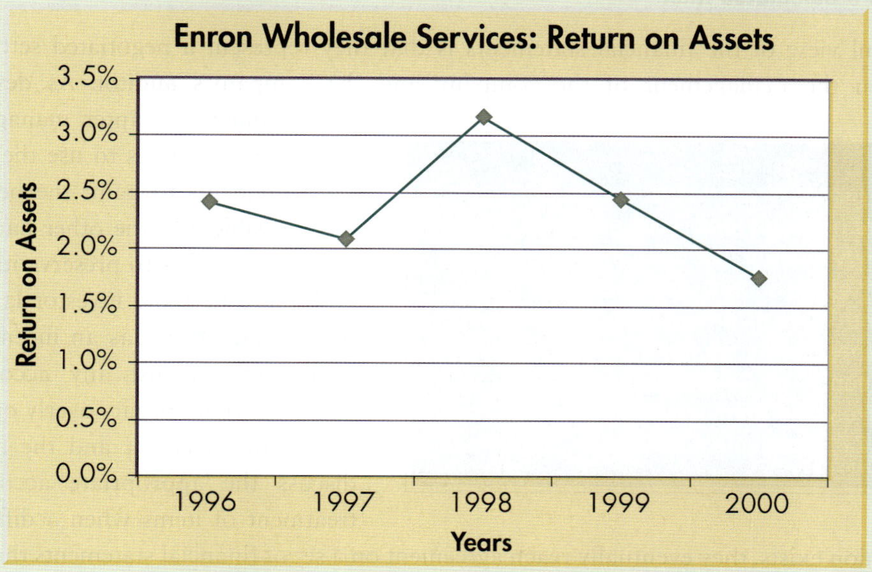

[15] Geoffrey Colvin, "When Scandal Isn't Sexy," *Fortune*, June 10, 2002.

Pressure to Meet Expectations

As mentioned earlier, a powerful factor motivating managers to manage earnings is the desire to continue to meet expectations, both internal and external. According to the SEC, without the accounting manipulations outlined at the beginning of the chapter, Xerox would have failed to meet analysts' earnings expectations in 11 of the 12 quarters in 1997, 1998, and 1999. As it was, Xerox met or exceeded expectations in each of the 12 quarters. As described in Chapter 8, when MicroStrategy fell short of market expectations in March 2000, the company's stock price started into a tailspin that reduced the value of the company by 99.9% within 16 months.

> **FYI**
>
> In 1993, the CFO for **Daimler-Benz** was concerned that the company was using loopholes in the German accounting standards to manage earnings and hide the company's poor operating performance, allowing management to delay making the tough decisions needed to fix the company. See Case 22-8 (and the associated solution) to find out what happened.

Attempted Accounting Solution

One response to a downturn in business and a looming failure to meet market expectations is to go back to the drawing board and try to improve the business. For example, as described in the opening scenario for Chapter 23, **Home Depot** was in exactly this situation at the beginning of 1986. The company's earnings had dropped and a disappointed market had reduced the value of Home Depot's stock by 23%. Home Depot's response in 1986 was to more efficiently manage inventory, cut overhead, and aggressively collect its outstanding accounts receivable. This approach propelled Home Depot to years of double-digit sales and earnings growth. Alternatively, when the accountants, instead of the operations or marketing people, are asked to return a company to profitability through earnings management, the solution is a temporary one at best. At worst, the counterproductive mentality associated with papering over a company's problems through earnings management can ultimately lead to even larger business problems.

Auditor's Calculated Risk

A useful view of the financial statements is that they represent a negotiated settlement between the management of the company and the company's auditor. As described throughout this chapter, management has many incentives to use the financial statements to paint the best picture possible. On the other hand, the audit firm wishes to preserve its reputation and to avoid investor lawsuits, so the audit firm has an incentive to push back against any accounting treatment that appears overly optimistic. As management and the auditor discuss the appropriate accounting treatment of items when a difference of opinion exists, they eventually reach agreement on a set of financial statements that both management and the auditor can sign and release to the public.

> **FYI**
>
> Companies that pay more nonaudit fees (such as for tax work) to auditors more frequently meet or just beat analysts' expectations through the use of accounting accruals. This is evidence that companies with more extensive economic ties with their auditor tend to manage earnings more. See R. Frankel, M. Johnson, and K. Nelson, "The Relation between Auditors' Fees for Nonaudit Services and Earnings Management," *The Accounting Review,* Vol. 77, Supplement 2002.

As you can imagine, an auditor is frequently required to decide whether to accept a debatable accounting treatment, engage in further discussions to try to convince management to abandon the treatment, or, as a final resort, withdraw from the audit. In making this decision, the auditor must balance the multiyear future revenues from continuing as a company's auditor with the potential costs of being swept up in an accounting scandal, losing valuable reputation, and perhaps losing a large lawsuit. Thus, the decision to sign the audit opinion is always a calculated risk.

One lesson we can learn from the Enron case is that all auditors, not just Arthur Andersen, had been underweighting the potential cost of signing an audit opinion on financial statements that contain questionable accounting. In the case of Enron and Arthur Andersen, this calculated risk by Andersen's Enron audit team resulted in the rapid demise of a venerable firm with the loss of the jobs of tens of thousands of Andersen employees along with billions of dollars in partners' equity. Probably more than any new regulation from the SEC or new law from Congress, this huge economic loss resulting from Andersen's calculated risk with respect to the Enron audit has caused other audit firms to be more careful and less willing to compromise on accounting treatments as the negotiated settlement over the financial statements is reached.

Insufficient User Skepticism

With the benefit of hindsight, it is often very easy to look back and see advance warning signs of an impending accounting scandal. For example, as we look now at Enron's declining return on asset numbers in Exhibit 6-9, we wonder why more people weren't skeptical about the company's fundamental operating performance before accounting scandal engulfed the company. In fact, in October 2001, just before the Enron earnings restatement that led to the company's bankruptcy less than two months later, 11 of the 13 financial analysts following Enron recommended the company's stock as a "buy" or "strong buy." Again, with the benefit of hindsight, it seems that even though Enron's published financial statements were misleadingly positive, there were still indications in those financial statements that should have led a skeptical analyst and investment community to question the company's fundamental business model.

FYI

An analysis of 26,000 analysts' recommendations as of April 2, 2001, revealed that only 0.3% of the recommendations were a "strong sale." By comparison, 67.7% of the recommendations were "buy" or "strong buy." See Lynn E. Turner, "The State of Financial Reporting Today: An Unfinished Chapter III," SEC Chief Accountant, Remarks at Glasser LegalWorks Third Annual SEC Disclosure & Accounting Conference, San Francisco, California, June 21, 2001.

The question of why financial statement users have historically not exhibited enough healthy skepticism is an interesting one without a definitive answer. One contributing factor is similar to the calculated risk idea mentioned earlier with respect to auditors. Financial statement users have usually accepted companies' financial statements at face value with the realization that there was some risk of deceptive reporting but without being sufficiently aware of the massive losses that might stem from that deception. Just as auditors are now weighing their risks in a new light after the large losses stemming from the Enron, WorldCom, and other accounting scandals, financial statement users are now exercising a greater degree of skepticism about reported financial results.

Another reason that analysts and the investment community have not exhibited enough financial statement skepticism is that these parties often stand to benefit economically as companies obtain loans, issue stock, set up complicated financing vehicles, and engage in merger and acquisition activity. Wall Street investment firms such as GE Capital,

J.P. Morgan Capital, **Merrill Lynch**, and **Morgan Stanley** all benefited as investors in the special-purpose entities that Enron used to keep some information off its balance sheet.

An extreme example of financial analysts intentionally overlooking poor performance comes in the case of the $100 million fine levied by the state of New York against Merrill Lynch. Investigation revealed that at the same time that the Merrill Lynch analysts were publicly recommending stocks as a "buy," they were internally circulating highly negative comments about those same stocks. For example, one stock, **InfoSpace**, was listed on Merrill Lynch's "Favored 15" buy list for four months in 2000 even though the firm's analysts were internally saying that InfoSpace was a "powder keg" and a "piece of junk" and that the analysts had received many "bad smell comments" about the company.[16] The motivation behind this public recommendation of stocks that the analysts privately were very skeptical about was as follows: "The research analysts were acting as quasi-investment bankers for the companies at issue, often initiating, continuing, and/or manipulating research coverage for the purpose of attracting and keeping investment banking clients."

Regulatory Investigation

Just as New York investigated the Merrill Lynch analyst team as described above, investigations are often conducted when companies are suspected of passing outside the boundary of the GAAP oval in Exhibit 6-7 into the area of fraudulent financial reporting. As described at the beginning of the chapter, the SEC launched an investigation of Xerox and uncovered evidence of systematic financial misrepresentation, resulting in a $10 million fine and a $22 million civil judgment being levied against Xerox. The SEC frequently investigates questionable accounting and requires the offending company to sign an order agreeing to "cease and desist" its misleading accounting practices.

In addition to regulatory investigations, fraudulent financial reporting can also lead to criminal charges. In the Enron case, for example, Arthur Andersen was convicted of obstruction of justice for its destruction of audit work papers.[17] Some Enron executives pleaded guilty to criminal charges, and one of the former CEOs of the company is currently sitting in a federal prison. As mentioned earlier, the CFO of WorldCom pleaded guilty to charges of fraud, and the CEO of WorldCom was found guilty of fraud in a highly publicized trial.

Massive Loss of Reputation

The final step in an earnings management meltdown is the huge loss of credibility experienced by the company that has been found to have manipulated its reported earnings. This loss of credibility harms all of the company's relationships and drastically impairs its economic value. As mentioned earlier, the SEC imposed $32 million in penalties on Xerox for its improper reporting practices. However, the amount of these penalties pales in comparison to the $764 million in market value that Xerox shareholders lost on April 3, 2001, the day after the company announced that it was delaying the release of its 2000 financial statements pending an additional review by the company's auditor. Overall, from the peak

[16] Affidavit in Support of an Inquiry by Eliot Spitzer, Attorney General of the State of New York, Pursuant to Article 23-A of the General Business Law of the State of New York with regard to the acts and practices of Merrill Lynch & Co., Inc., and others, April 2002.

[17] In a strange twist to the Enron and Arthur Andersen story, the U.S. Supreme Court later overturned the Arthur Andersen conviction because of erroneous instructions given by the judge to the jury. Unfortunately for Arthur Andersen, the firm's operations had long since ceased because of the loss of its reputation stemming from the conviction.

EX 6-10 SEVEN ELEMENTS OF AN EARNINGS MANAGEMENT MELTDOWN

1	2	3	4	5	6	7
Downturn in business	Pressure to meet expectations	Attempted accounting solution	Auditor's calculated risk	Insufficient user skepticism	Regulatory investigation	Massive loss of reputation

Through stage 5, the public is unaware of an earnings management meltdown.

of the earnings manipulation in 1999 to the final resolution of the accounting scandal in June 2002, Xerox shareholders lost approximately $40 billion in market value.

From 1997 through 2010, five major periods of decline in worldwide stock prices occurred. The first, in 1997, was touched off by a concern about the reliability of banking and financial information in a number of Asian countries. The second, in 2000, was primarily a return to reality after initial euphoria about the business possibilities associated with the Internet. The third decline occurred in 2001 in the wake of the political and economic uncertainty created by the September 11, 2001, attack on the World Trade Center. The fourth broad-based decline in stock values occurred in 2002 and was largely fueled by widespread uncertainty about the credibility of the financial reports of U.S. corporations. The fifth large decline occurred in 2008. Of course, this decline was a natural result of the real estate greed that had inflated U.S. real estate prices. However, the decline was made worse because of investor uncertainty about what was really inside the mortgage-backed securities that had flooded the market. This credibility crisis has graphically illustrated the real economic value of high-quality and transparent (i.e., easy to understand) financial reporting.

We close this section with one final thought about earnings management meltdowns. Refer to Exhibit 6-10, which repeats the seven elements of an earnings management meltdown. If we had been discussing this topic in 1999, the Xerox meltdown would have been at stage 5, meaning that the earnings management manipulations were in full swing, the auditor had made a calculated risk and signed off on past financial statements, and the investment community was bullish on Xerox's stock and pleasantly unaware of the catastrophe that was waiting to happen. Similarly, as you are reading this chapter, it is certain that some major corporations are at stage 5 of an earnings management meltdown about which the public is as yet completely oblivious. Accordingly, an attitude of healthy skepticism about financial reports is always appropriate, whether you are an accountant, an auditor, a financial analyst, a regulator, a private investor, or just a conscientious citizen.

Transparent Financial Reporting: The Best Practice

5 Explain how good accounting standards and ethical behavior by accountants lower the cost of obtaining capital.

WHY **High-quality accounting standards and vigorous regulatory enforcement activity reduce information risk, thereby lowering a company's cost of capital.**

HOW **The more reliable the information provided by a company, the more confidence potential investors can place in that information. High-quality information allows for better decision making. The ability to make better decisions reduces the risk to potential investors and creditors and thus reduces the cost of capital to a company.**

An important fact often forgotten by financial statement preparers and users is that the entire purpose of accounting, both financial and managerial, is to lower the cost of doing business. A good managerial accounting system allows managers more efficient access to the information needed to make good business decisions. Good financial accounting reduces the information uncertainty surrounding a company so that external parties, such as lenders and investors, do not bear as much risk when they provide financing to the company. This section explains how transparent financial reporting, even in a setting in which there are great incentives for managers to manipulate earnings in the short run, represents the best business practice for the long run.

What Is the Cost of Capital?

The cost of capital is the cost a company bears to obtain external financing. The cost of debt financing is simply the after-tax interest cost associated with borrowing the money. The cost of equity financing is the expected return (both as dividends and an increase in the market value of the investment) necessary to induce investors to provide equity capital. A company often computes its weighted-average cost of capital, which is the average of the cost of debt and equity financing weighted by the proportion of each type of financing.

A company's cost of capital is critical because it determines which long-term projects are profitable to undertake. In a capital budgeting setting, the cost of capital can be thought of as the *discount rate* or *hurdle rate* used in evaluating long-term projects. The higher the cost to obtain funds, the fewer long-term projects are profitable for the company to undertake. A project that makes economic sense to a company with a low cost of capital could very well be unprofitable to a company with a higher cost of capital.

FYI

Financial statements that have no credibility can actually be worse than no financial statements at all. When managers are willing to try to deceive lenders and investors through misleading financial reporting, those same lenders and investors naturally wonder what other types of deception the managers are attempting. This is called the "cockroach theory": If you discover one deceptive practice, there are likely to be more.

A key factor in determining a company's cost of capital is the risk associated with the company. For a very risky company, lenders and investors are going to require a higher return to induce them to provide capital to the company. Thus, the more risk associated with a company, the higher its cost of capital. One risk factor is the information risk associated with uncertainty about the company's future prospects. A company produces financial statements to better inform lenders and investors about its past performance; they can then use this information to make better forecasts of the company's future performance. Consequently, good financial statements reduce the uncertainty of lenders and investors so that they will provide financing at a lower cost. However, when the financial statements lose their credibility, they do nothing to reduce the information risk surrounding a company, and the company's cost of capital is higher.

The Role of Accounting Standards

Chapter 1 introduced you to the organizations important in setting accounting standards: the FASB, the AICPA, the SEC, and the IASB. In the context of our discussion here, it is useful to view each of these organizations as helping to lower the cost of capital. The FASB and the AICPA help lower the U.S. cost of capital by promulgating uniform recognition and disclosure standards for use by companies in the United States. In spite of the accounting scandals that have been discussed in this chapter, the financial reporting system in the

United States is still viewed as being the best in the world. Put another way, the extensive and high-quality accounting standards used in the United States result in financial statements that reduce information risk more than do the statements prepared under the standards used anywhere else in the world.

According to the SEC, its "primary mission . . . is to protect investors and maintain the integrity of the securities markets." In terms of financial reporting, this protection of investors means that the SEC monitors the accounting standard-setting process of the FASB, requires publicly traded companies to make quarterly financial statements available to investors on a timely basis, and, as in the case of Xerox, investigates (and punishes) cases of deceptive financial reporting. All of these actions increase the reliance that capital providers can place on the financial statements of companies trading on U.S. securities markets. Thus, the SEC's actions contribute toward reducing information risk and lowering the cost of capital.

The IASB is playing an increasingly important role in enhancing the credibility of international financial reporting. In the international arena, transparent and reliable financial reports are extremely important to providers of capital because the company requiring the investment capital may be in a different business environment and a different culture than those providing the capital. Therefore, the important efforts of the IASB also serve to lower the cost of capital by lowering information risk.

However, not everyone agrees that the mandated adoption of IFRS by U.S. companies will lower the cost of capital for those companies. U.S. GAAP is famous for containing detailed accounting rules. In contrast, IFRS is known for being based on general principles, with the detailed application being left up to the professional judgment of the accountant. By some counts, U.S. GAAP contains about 25,000 pages and IFRS contains just 2,500 pages; those extra 22,500 pages allow for a lot of detailed U.S. GAAP accounting guidance that doesn't exist under IFRS. The question being considered in the U.S. business community is whether principles-based accounting standards will work in the U.S. legal environment. Accountants and auditors are concerned that they can never be sure their application of the accounting "principle," without the detailed guidance of rules, will bear up under the after-the-fact scrutiny of trial lawyers, juries, and judges. And financial statement users are concerned that this increased reliance on accounting judgment will make the reported numbers under IFRS more vulnerable to management manipulation, increasing information risk and thus increasing the cost of capital. These are issues that will be played out over the next few years as the SEC guides the U.S. transition to IFRS.

The Necessity of Ethical Behavior

A nagging question concerns why accounting scandals continue to occur in the United States even when we have high-quality accounting standards supplemented by an active regulatory system. The answer to this question has been mentioned over and over in this chapter: Managers have strong economic incentives to report favorable financial results, and these incentives can lead to deceptive or fraudulent reporting. But managers also have strong incentives to maintain a reputation for credibility for both their company and for themselves personally. This existence of conflicting forces is not unique to the area of financial reporting. We are all faced with situations in which we have incentives to deceive or commit fraud. For example, the income tax collection system in the United States works reasonably well only because the vast majority of taxpayers honestly report their taxable income, even though they could benefit economically by understating their income. Without this voluntary compliance, the Internal Revenue Service would find it prohibitively costly to audit and investigate every Form 1040 to enforce tax compliance.

As all college students know, good grades make it easier to secure a spot on the interview schedules of campus recruiters. Thus, there are some incentives to cheat when writing papers or taking exams. As a result, the internal control systems surrounding the security of exams on some campuses are truly impressive. Other universities have found that an honor code, or a code of conduct, is a less costly way to reduce the incidence of cheating. For example, at Rice University in Houston, Texas, incoming students commit to abide by the university's Honor System. Under this system, class instructors are specifically prohibited from monitoring students during an examination. In place of this external monitoring, each student is required to write the following statement on his or her exam: "On my honor, I have neither given nor received any aid on this examination."

Accountants have their own honor system; it is called the *AICPA Code of Professional Conduct*. An important concept from this code of conduct is contained in the following paragraph:

> In discharging their professional responsibilities, members may encounter conflicting pressures. . . . In resolving those conflicts, members should act with integrity, guided by the precept that when members fulfill their responsibility to the public, clients' and employers' interests are best served.[18]

In essence, this paragraph says that ethical behavior is also the best long-run business practice. To illustrate that this is so, consider again the Xerox scenario that started this chapter. The deceptive accounting practices undertaken at Xerox to hide poor operating performance merely delayed the inevitable. When these problems were eventually revealed, the economic loss suffered by all Xerox stakeholders—investors, lenders, customers, employees—was greatly magnified because of the accounting deception. The company lost economic value not just because of reduced opinions about its operating performance but also because the company had lost its credibility. Xerox researchers and marketers may soon design and promote products that will reverse the company's operating woes, but the impairment of the company's credibility will not be reversed for many, many years.

In a perfectly rational world, efforts to manipulate public perception through earnings management would be fruitless because appropriately skeptical users of the financial data would be aware of the potential for earnings management and would perfectly adjust the reported numbers using alternative sources of information to remove any bias. However, the world is not perfectly rational. Rarely do financial statement users have the time or resources to unravel the potential manipulations in every set of numbers that they see. Instead, financial statement users rely on the soundness of the accounting standards, the integrity of the managers who prepared the numbers, and the skills and thoroughness of the auditors. One of the disappointing lessons stemming from the accounting scandals of 2001 and 2002 is that financial statement users probably placed too much unquestioning reliance on the reported financial statement numbers of some companies. Because of the large amounts of money lost by investors and creditors, they will be more skeptical in the future. Hopefully, one of the positive lessons drawn from these same scandals will be that society at large will see the massive impact that credible (or questionable) financial reporting can have on the economy. Hopefully, both users and preparers of financial statements will insist on transparency in reporting in order to reduce information risk and lower the cost of capital. And hopefully individual managers, accountants, and financial statement users will be reminded again that ethical behavior really is the best long-run business practice.

[18] *AICPA Code of Professional Conduct, Section 53–Article II: The Public Interest*, par. 02 (New York: AICPA, 19).

SOLUTIONS TO OPENING SCENARIO QUESTIONS

1. In the 1980s, Xerox faced stiff competition from Japanese copy machine makers. In the 1990s, Xerox faced another threat as companies focused more on "digital documents," calling into question the need for large-scale paper copy machines.
2. To avoid recording $27 million in sales returns, the Xerox Mexico managers rented secret warehouses to store the returned merchandise.
3. In April 2005, KPMG agreed to pay $22 million to settle a civil suit filed by the SEC stemming from the Xerox audit. In addition, KPMG lost the Xerox audit account, resulting in lost audit fees of tens of millions of dollars per year.

REVIEW CHAPTER 6

LEARNING OBJECTIVES

1 Identify the factors that motivate earnings management.

Four factors that motivate managers to manage reported earnings follow:

- Meet internal targets.
- Meet external expectations.
- Provide income smoothing.
- Provide window dressing for an IPO or a loan.

2 List the common techniques used to manage earnings.

The earnings management continuum contains the following five items:

- Strategic matching of one-time gains and losses
- Change in methods or estimates with full disclosure
- Change in methods or estimates with little or no disclosure
- Non-GAAP accounting
- Fictitious transactions

The five techniques of accounting hocus-pocus identified by then-Chairman Arthur Levitt of the SEC in 1998 are as follows:

- Big-bath charges
- Creative acquisition accounting
- Cookie jar reserves
- Materiality
- Revenue recognition

A pro forma earnings number is the regular GAAP earnings number with some revenues, expenses, gains, or losses excluded. Managers can use the flexibility of pro forma disclosures to reveal better information about a company's underlying economic performance. However, pro forma disclosures can also be used in an attempt to hide poor performance.

3 Critically discuss whether a company should manage its earnings.

Financial reporting is a normal part of a company's overall public relations effort. As such, a responsible manager should consider what impact the financial statements will have on the company's ability to satisfy the needs of its stakeholders. There is no "true" earnings number, and a manager is not necessarily expected to report earnings that are somewhere in the middle of the possible range of numbers. Computing earnings using non-GAAP methods is clearly unethical, but the boundary between GAAP and non-GAAP treatment is not always a bright line. If the intent in using earnings management techniques is to deceive, then most people would consider the earnings management wrong, independent of whether it was in strict conformity with GAAP.

4 Describe the common elements of an earnings management meltdown.

The seven stages in an earnings management meltdown are as follows:

- Downturn in business
- Pressure to meet expectations
- Attempted accounting solution
- Auditor's calculated risk
- Insufficient user skepticism
- Regulatory investigation
- Massive loss of reputation

At any given time, at least a few large corporations are somewhere in the middle of an earnings management meltdown that has not yet been publicly revealed.

5 Explain how good accounting standards and ethical behavior by accountants lower the cost of obtaining capital.

By reducing information risk, good financial reporting can lower a company's cost of capital. High-quality accounting standards and vigorous regulatory enforcement activity alone cannot ensure the credibility of financial reports. Without ethical behavior by individual managers and accountants, the regulatory cost to ensure credible financial statements would be prohibitively high. Because of the high value of a company's reputation, ethical financial reporting is also a good long-run business practice.

FASB-IASB CODIFICATION SUMMARY

ifrs

Topic	U.S. GAAP	IASB Standard
General characterization of the standards	Rules oriented. U.S. GAAP contains about 25,000 pages with lots of detailed guidance.	Principles oriented. IFRS contains just 2,500 pages with many detailed accounting decisions left up to the professional judgment of the accountant.

KEY TERMS

Big bath 6-14
Cost of capital 6-28
Cost of debt financing 6-28
Cost of equity financing 6-28
Earnings management continuum 6-11
GAAP oval 6-20
Income smoothing 6-9
Internal earnings target 6-6
Pro forma earnings number 6-16
Weighted-average cost of capital 6-28
Window dressing 6-10

QUESTIONS

1. What are the four factors that might motivate a manager to attempt to manage earnings?
2. (a) What is the purpose of internal earnings targets?
   (b) What is the risk associated with internal earnings targets?
3. What has academic research shown with respect to earnings-based bonus thresholds?
4. How do auditors react to the existence of an earnings-based bonus plan in the company being audited?
5. Explain the significance of the figure in Exhibit 6-2.
6. Explain the significance of a company meeting or beating analysts' earnings forecasts for many quarters in a row.

7. What does the term *income smoothing* mean?
8. **General Electric** has long been known as a company that smoothes its reported earnings. What is it about General Electric that makes it possible for the company to smooth earnings?
9. Research has discovered a phenomenon common to both capitalist managers in the West and socialist managers in China. What is this phenomenon?
10. Describe one setting in which a manager might have an incentive to manipulate the accrual assumptions so that lower earnings are reported.
11. The flexibility that is a key part of the estimates and judgments inherent in accrual accounting allows desperate managers to manipulate the reported numbers. Why not do away with this flexibility and just require companies to report raw cash flow data without any assumptions about bad debt percentage, depreciation life, estimated future warranty repairs, and so forth?
12. What are the five labels in the earnings management continuum (see Exhibit 6-4), and what general types of actions are associated with each label?
13. Is there anything wrong with using a different accounting estimate this year compared to last year so long as both estimates fall within a generally accepted range for your industry?
14. What are two potential causes of non-GAAP accounting?
15. Company A has created fictitious transactions to report more favorable earnings. Is it likely that this is the only action Company A has taken to manage earnings? Explain.
16. In 1998, then-SEC Chairman Arthur Levitt gave a speech in which he identified five techniques of accounting hocus-pocus. List those five techniques.
17. What is the benefit of "taking a big bath"?
18. What accounting actions have been taken since Chairman Levitt's speech in 1998 to limit the use of big-bath charges to manage earnings?
19. What type of company would be most likely to establish a cookie jar reserve?
20. In what way is the concept of materiality contained in *SAB 99* different from the traditional concept of materiality?
21. What major accounting action has been taken since Chairman Levitt's speech in 1998 to limit the abuse of revenue recognition to manage earnings?
22. What is a pro forma earnings number?
23. What is a benefit of a company's reporting a pro forma earnings number? What is a danger with pro forma earnings numbers?
24. With respect to pro forma earnings numbers, what recommendation made by the Financial Executives International (FEI) and the National Investor Relations Institute did the SEC endorse?
25. In what sense is financial reporting part of a company's general public relations effort?
26. Refer to the GAAP oval in Exhibit 6-7.
    (a) In what important way is point E different from point C?
    (b) In what important way is point A different from point C?
27. What factors influence whether a manager actually violates GAAP in an effort to manage earnings?
28. What is one way to distinguish between earnings management that is ethically right and earnings management that is ethically wrong?
29. What are the seven elements of an earnings management meltdown?
30. A manager being pressured to meet expectations in the face of a downturn in operating performance can be tempted to turn to an accounting solution and use accrual estimates and judgments to manage reported earnings. How else might the manager respond to this pressure?
31. What costs and risks is an auditor balancing when signing an audit opinion?
32. What economic incentives do financial analysts sometimes have for overlooking a company's glaring deficiencies and continuing to recommend it to investors as a "buy"?
33. When the SEC launches an investigation against a company and finds evidence of misleading financial reporting, historically what type of punishments has the SEC used?
34. The text of the chapter includes discussion of seven stages in an earnings management meltdown. At what stage does the earnings management meltdown become public knowledge?
35. What does the *cost of capital* mean?
36. How does financial reporting impact a company's cost of capital?
37. How do accounting standards impact the cost of capital?
38. According to the AICPA Code of Professional Conduct, what precept should guide members of the AICPA as they encounter conflicting pressures among their clients, investors, the business community, the government, and so forth?
39. What is the best long-run business practice?

CASES

Discussion Case 6-1

Should We Implement an Earnings-Based Bonus Plan?

Benjamin Vincent is the chief financial officer (CFO) of Annie Company. The company's chief executive officer (CEO) has asked Benjamin to design an incentive scheme that will motivate employees to focus more on the company's bottom-line results. Benjamin is considering a plan that will give each employee a bonus based on the company's reported net income for the year. Each employee will receive an amount equal to the company's earnings per share multiplied by either 10,000 times, 50,000 times, or 200,000 times, depending on the employee's level in the company. Last year, Annie Company's earnings per share was $1.32. Benjamin Vincent has asked you for your advice. In particular, he wants you to explain the *disadvantages* of having an earnings-based bonus system.

Discussion Case 6-2

We Only Need Another $100,000!

Chris Titera is the chief financial officer (CFO) for Dallas Company. It is January 10, and Chris has just finished compiling the preliminary financial results for the most recent fiscal year, which ended on December 31. The preliminary results indicate that Dallas lost $100,000 during the year. Dallas is a large company (with assets in excess of $1 billion), so the $100,000 loss is essentially the same as zero. However, the board of directors thinks that it conveys a very negative image for Dallas Company to report a loss for the year, even if the loss amount is very small. As a result, it has instructed Chris to look at the numbers again and see if he can turn this loss into a profit. What things can Chris do, as the CFO, to turn this loss into a profit? What concerns should Chris have?

Discussion Case 6-3

Are Financial Analysts Rational?

Stella Valerio is a financial analyst who follows Olsen Company and other companies in the same industry. You have just done a historical analysis of Stella's earnings forecasts for Olsen Company and noticed that its earnings have exceeded Stella's forecasted amount for 27 quarters in a row. You are wondering whether this is just a coincidence, whether Stella is an exceptionally bad forecaster, or whether other factors may be at work here.

Discussion Case 6-4

Income Smoothing and an IPO

You are an analyst for an investment fund that invests in initial public offerings (IPOs). You are looking at the financial statements of two companies, Clark Company and Durfee Company, that plan to go public soon. Net income for the past three years for the two companies has been as follows (in thousands):

Year	Clark Net Income	Durfee Net Income
2010	$10,000	$17,000
2011	14,000	1,000
2012	20,000	26,000

If both companies issue the same number of shares and if the initial share prices are the same, which of the two companies appears to be a more attractive investment? Explain your reasoning. What alternate sources of data would you look at to find out whether the reported earnings amounts accurately portray the business performance of these two companies over the past three years?

Discussion Case 6-5

Who Benefits When a State-Owned Enterprise Goes Public?

Dalian Company is a Chinese state-owned enterprise. This means that ownership of the company rests in one of the ministries of the Chinese central government. Ministry officials have decided to sell a portion (40%) of the government's ownership interest in Dalian to outside investors, including foreign investors. The proceeds from this initial public offering (IPO) will flow into the operating budget for the ministry.

Zhang Tianfu is Dalian Company's senior manager. He is preparing for the IPO. Among other things, he is working with the company's accountants to get the financial statements for the past three years ready for use by external investors. With respect to these financial statements, what conflicting incentives face Mr. Zhang as he prepares for the IPO?

Discussion Case 6-6

If It Isn't Fraud, Then It's Ethical

Cruella DeVil is the chief financial officer (CFO) of a local publicly traded company. She was recently invited to speak to accounting students at the local university. One of the students asked Cruella whether she thought earnings management was ethical. Cruella laughed and responded that her view was that anything that was not explicitly prohibited by the accounting standards or by government regulations was ethical. What do you think of Cruella's opinion?

Discussion Case 6-7

Managing Earnings in the Jubilee Year

Heidelberg Company has been in business for 100 years. The past three years have been trying ones for the company, which has reported operating losses in each of those three years. The board of directors is planning a huge, year-long celebration of the company's centennial year. The board has informed the company's controller that the company *must* report a profit in each quarter of the centennial year. The board has not told the controller how this is to be done, but the implication is that if the operating results are not enough to generate a profit, the controller must use accounting assumptions to push the company over the top. The controller has identified three areas in which Heidelberg Company has some flexibility in its accounting assumptions: depreciation, bad debts, and pension accounting. Describe specifically how the controller can use accounting assumptions in these three areas to improve Heidelberg's reported earnings. Also describe which set of financial statement users is most likely to be influenced by this earnings management in the centennial year financial statements.

Discussion Case 6-8

I Didn't Do It on Purpose!

You are a senior staff member in the office of the Chief Accountant of the Securities and Exchange Commission (SEC). You have been supervising a case brought against an audit firm. The audit client used non-GAAP accounting practices that allowed it to report annual earnings of $47.3 million instead of a loss of $15.0 million. Earnings in the preceding three years averaged $10 million per year. The auditor explains that this non-GAAP accounting practice was not detected during the audit because of innocent mistakes made by staff auditors. Your thorough investigation has not turned up any evidence that the audit firm intentionally allowed the client to use this non-GAAP practice. You must decide whether to formally sanction the audit firm or whether to drop the case because of lack of evidence of wrongful intent. What should you do?

Discussion Case 6-9

Earnings Management, Inc.

John Sleaze and Mary Scum run Earnings Management, Inc., a consulting business. They have the following items in their product line:

1. A database that lists types of depreciable assets and the minimum and maximum depreciation lives that have been accepted by auditors for each type of asset. The listing can be sorted by audit firm, so a client can know the minimums and maximums accepted by each individual audit firm.
2. A detailed analysis of the accounting rules on revenue recognition. The analysis reveals loopholes in the rules that companies can use to strategically time the recognition of revenue.
3. A comprehensive list of all accounting issues for which there is no generally accepted standard. This list can be viewed as an identification of all of the fuzzy

areas of accounting that a company might exploit if it desired to conduct earnings management.

4. A list of the local offices for each major audit firm that appear to have been the most "flexible" in signing off on aggressive accounting treatments by clients. In some cases, the list includes specific audit partners who have a reputation for being accommodating when a client firm wishes to use aggressive earnings management techniques.

You are an FBI agent investigating Earnings Management, Inc., for possible indictment on securities fraud and racketeering charges. Comment on whether you think John and Mary have committed any indictable offenses.

Discussion Case 6-10

I'm New Here; I Think I'll Take a Bath

Frank Elsholz is the new chief executive officer (CEO) of Kearl Street Company. You are the controller for Kearl Street; you have been with the company for 15 years. In connection with the preparation of this year's financial statements (the first prepared since the departure of the old management team), Frank has asked you to bring him a list of all long-term assets, both tangible and intangible, that have any chance of becoming impaired within the next three years. Some of Kearl Street's long-term assets have appreciated substantially since they were acquired, so there is little chance that they will be impaired in the foreseeable future. However, other assets could become impaired in the next three years, depending on what happens to local business conditions. If a long-term asset becomes impaired, its carrying value is written down and a loss is recognized, as explained in Chapter 11. You are curious about why the new CEO wants you to compile this list. Speculate on what you think Frank has in mind.

Discussion Case 6-11

Loading Up the Cookie Jar!

Lily Company has historically reported a bad debt expense amount of between 1% and 4% of sales. The percentage for any given year is a function of both the business conditions for the year and whether recent experience suggests that the estimates in past years have been too high or too low. For example, if estimates in past years have been too high, a lower amount of bad debt expense is recognized in the current year. Lily Company's board of directors has met to review the preliminary financial statements for the just-completed fiscal year. Assume that the board will decide on a bad debt estimate of either 1% or 4% of sales. Consider the following two scenarios:

Scenario 1. The preliminary earnings number for the year is very high, far higher than expected. However, Lily's board is concerned about future years; there is some indication of unsettled business conditions ahead.

Scenario 2. The preliminary earnings number for the year is quite low, lower than expected. The board has reason to be optimistic that Lily's operating performance will turn around next year.

What estimate (1% or 4%) do you think Lily's board will choose in each of the two scenarios? Explain your choices. What risks are there to Lily Company if the bad debt estimate is chosen using only the type of information given here?

Discussion Case 6-12

I Need to Recognize the Revenue Now!

The H.K. Clark Health Club sells lifetime memberships for $5,000 each. These memberships entitle a person to unlimited access to the club's weight room, exercise equipment, swimming pool, and sauna. Once a lifetime membership fee is paid, it is not refundable for any reason. According to the accounting rules, revenue from the sale of a lifetime membership must be deferred and recognized over the average expected time that a member will continue to use the club facilities. However, if the terms of the membership agreement are interpreted very favorably, a substantial portion of the $5,000 initial fee might be able to be recognized as revenue immediately. Kristen Qi and her partners own the health club. To overcome a cash shortage, they intend to seek a new loan from their bank. Kristen and her partners are meeting with their accountant to provide information for preparation of financial statements. What incentives would Kristen and her partners have for recognizing the entire amount of the lifetime membership fee as revenue at the time it is collected? Since the entire amount will ultimately be recognized anyway, what difference does the timing make? Do Kristen and her partners have any *economic* incentive to go ahead and defer the membership revenue in accordance with the accounting rules?

Discussion Case 6-13

How Should I Interpret the Pro Forma Number?

Worthington Company and Millward Company both reported pro forma earnings numbers in conjunction with their release of results for the most recent quarter. Both announcements included a reconciliation to GAAP earnings. These reconciliations are reproduced here.

Worthington Company
Pro Forma Earnings

(in thousands)	
GAAP earnings	$ 50,000
Add back amount expensed for an R&D project that resulted in a valuable new product	35,000
Subtract a one-time gain from the sale of a building	(17,000)
Pro forma earnings	$ 68,000

Millward Company
Pro Forma Earnings

(in thousands)	
GAAP earnings	$ 50,000
Add back expenses associated with a strategic realignment initiative	10,000
Add back employee training expenses	8,000
Pro forma earnings	$ 68,000

Which of the two pro forma earnings disclosures do you find to be the more informative? Explain.

Discussion Case 6-14

I'm an Accountant, Not a Public Relations Person!

Jacob Marley is the controller for Dickens Company. Marley has been with Dickens for more than 30 years. Marley is a dedicated employee and prides himself on the efficiency of his accounting department staff. Over the years, Marley has received many inquiries and suggestions from the board of directors of Dickens Company about appropriate accounting treatments, the magnitude of certain accounting estimates, and so forth, but he has never paid the slightest attention to any of the suggestions. Marley's view is that the process of generating the financial statement numbers is simply a matter of rigidly applying certain predetermined mathematical rules, and he does not welcome the input of the board of directors or anyone else. Marley also refuses to communicate with analysts, pension fund managers, and business press reporters who call to make inquiries about Dickens. Marley believes that the financial statements speak for themselves and need no clarification or amplification. Comment on the benefits and costs of Jacob Marley's approach to financial reporting to Dickens Company.

Discussion Case 6-15

GAAP Is a Point, Not an Oval!

You are the chief financial officer (CFO) of Clarke Company, which is publicly traded. At the annual shareholders' meeting you discussed the company's recent reported results. As part of your presentation, you illustrated the minimum and maximum values for net income that Lorien could have reported using a range of accounting assumptions other companies in your industry use. Your statement prompted a cry of outrage from one of the shareholders present at the meeting, who accused you of being an unprincipled liar. This shareholder stated that any suggestion that there is a range of possible net income values for a given company in a given year indicates an overly liberal approach to financial reporting. This shareholder has moved that your employment contract be immediately terminated because of an apparent lack of moral character. The shareholder's arguments have been persuasive to a large number of people at the meeting. What can you say to defend yourself?

Discussion Case 6-16

Is It Easier to Fix My Business if I'm a Private Company?

Tooele Company is publicly traded. However, its chief executive officer (CEO), Kara Brown, is considering taking the company private in a leveraged buyout (LBO). One of the primary motivations for the LBO is dissatisfaction with the amount of time Kara must spend each quarter giving guidance to analysts about what reported earnings will be, meeting with the accounting staff to see whether the company will meet its earnings targets, and then explaining the reported quarterly results to the business press. Comment on Kara's motivation for taking Tooele Company private.

Discussion Case 6-17

Do All Analysts Have the Same Incentives?

There are two general types of financial analysts:

- *Buy-side analyst.* An analyst employed by an entity, such as a mutual fund, which invests on its own accounts. Unlike that of the sell-side analysts employed by brokerage firms, research produced by buy-side analysts is usually unavailable outside the firm that hired the analyst.
- *Sell-side analyst.* An analyst employed by a brokerage firm or another firm that manages client accounts. Unlike that of the buy-side analysts employed by mutual funds, research produced by sell-side analysts is usually available to the public.

Some financial analysts have been criticized for making optimistic forecasts of the earnings of potential clients in order to curry favor with those potential clients. Do you think that this criticism is directed at buy-side analysts or sell-side analysts? Explain.

Discussion Case 6-18

Who Would Report if Reporting Were Voluntary?

Tarazania is a country with a small but active stock market. However, the country has no accounting standards; in fact, the issuance of financial statements is illegal. This odd law stems from the fact that the founding king of Tarazania once took an intermediate financial accounting course and was so overwhelmed by the chapter on the statement of cash flows that he vowed he would never view another financial statement again. As a result, none of the 100 companies with publicly traded stocks in Tarazania have ever made financial statements available to the public. Of course, each of these companies has prepared financial statements and other reports for use internally for years. Last week Tarazania's founding king died. His eldest daughter has now ascended to the throne. Her Majesty has been a secret aficionado of financial statements for years. One of her first official acts was to make the public release of financial statements legal but not mandatory. Of the 100 publicly traded companies in Tarazania, which will be the first to release its financial statements to the public? Will all 100 companies do so?

Discussion Case 6-19

Does It Pay to Lie?

Joseph Han has $10 million that he wishes to invest. He has identified two candidate companies: Company A and Company B. Both companies are privately held and have never yet released external financial statements. Joseph Han has some familiarity with the use of financial statements, but his knowledge is not perfect and he can be fooled. However, he has the ability to recognize blatant financial statement manipulation. As Companies A and B prepare their financial statements, they must consider the following three scenarios:

- *Scenario 1.* Both prepare transparent financial statements that faithfully reflect their underlying business performance. Joseph Han is impressed with both companies and invests $5 million in each.

- *Scenario 2*. One of the companies prepares deceptive financial statements. These financial statements look so good compared to the transparent financial statements prepared by the other company that Joseph Han instantly decides to invest $8 million in the deceptive company and nothing in the truthful company. To avoid putting all of his eggs in one basket, Joseph Han holds back $2 million and puts it in a bank savings account.
- *Scenario 3*. Both companies prepare deceptive financial statements. In carefully comparing these two glowing sets of financial statements, Joseph Han realizes that both sets of financial statements have been manipulated. He decides to invest $1 million in each company, as a speculation, and to put the remaining $8 million in a bank savings account.

Given these three scenarios, what is the best strategy for Companies A and B—to lie or to tell the truth? Will your answer change if Joseph Han announces his intention to make this same $10 million investment decision with respect to these two companies each year for the next 30 years?

Case 6-20

Deciphering Financial Statements (The Walt Disney Company)

In the press release announcing **Disney's** results for the first fiscal quarter of 2008 ending December 29, 2007, the company stated the following:

> The Walt Disney Company today reported earnings for its first fiscal quarter ended December 29, 2007. Diluted earnings per share (EPS) for the quarter were $0.63 . . . EPS in the prior-year quarter . . . were $0.79.

The prior-year quarter's EPS of $0.79 included $1.1 billion gains on the sales of Disney's interests in E! Entertainment and Us Weekly and a $48 million equity-based compensation plan modification charge. In aggregate, these items increased the prior-year quarter's EPS by $0.29.

1. By what percentage did Disney's EPS decrease from the end of its first fiscal quarter in 2007 to the end of its first fiscal quarter in 2008?
2. Suppose none of the non-operating transactions disclosed in the second paragraph had occurred in the first fiscal quarter of 2007. Compute the percentage change in EPS.

Case 6-21

Deciphering Financial Statements (Xerox)

As indicated in the case at the beginning of this chapter, **Xerox** was manipulating income between the years 1997 through 1999. Below are revenue, gross profit, net income, and operating cash flow data for Xerox for the years 1997 through 2000.

(in millions)	2000	1999	1998	1997
Revenues	$18,701	$19,228	$19,447	$18,144
Gross profit	7,601	9,003	9,580	9,036
Net income (loss)	(257)	1,424	395	1,452
Operating cash flow	(663)	1,224	(1,165)	472
Proceeds from securitization of finance receivables	0	1,495	0	0

The securitization of the finance receivables represents the sale of receivables to a third party. The cash inflow from the sale was shown in the Operating Activities section of the statement of cash flows.

Using these data, identify evidence that proves Xerox was managing its operating cash flow during this period.

Case 6-22 **Writing Assignment (Why did we manage earnings?)**

You are the controller for Cam-Ry Industries. Your company has recently received a large amount of unfavorable publicity because an SEC investigation uncovered a systematic 2-year effort by Cam-Ry's management to manipulate reported earnings. The primary motivation for this earnings management scheme was to consistently meet analysts' earnings expectations in order to keep the opinion of your company high in advance of an additional share offering that was to take place next year. The SEC has now formally sanctioned your company and fined it $350,000, and the investor backlash has lowered the company's share price and resulted in the cancellation of the planned share offering next year.

As controller, you were aware of the earnings management scheme. You failed to actively oppose the effort. However, the driving force behind the scheme was the former chief executive officer (CEO) who has now been replaced. Your former auditor has also been fired. The new CEO is attempting to mend all of the stakeholder relationships that have been strained because of the SEC revelation of the earnings management activity. The new CEO has assigned you to repair relations with Yosef Bank. The bank has provided a line of credit to Cam-Ry for over 15 years. You have personally represented Cam-Ry in its dealings with the bank. For the past five years, you have met frequently with DeeAnn Martinez, who is a senior vice president with the bank and the person assigned to the Cam-Ry account. Through mutual friends, you have heard that Martinez feels personally betrayed by you and no longer trusts you.

You are scheduled to meet with DeeAnn Martinez next week to discuss Cam-Ry's line of credit. In advance of that meeting, you have decided to write a one-page memo to Martinez in an attempt to mend your relationship. Write a draft of that memo.

Case 6-23 **Ethical Dilemma (What should you do with unpleasant and unwelcome audit evidence?)**

You are a manager with Doman & Detmer, a mid-sized local accounting firm. You have been with the firm for six years. Currently, you are working on the McMahon Company audit engagement. You are supervising a team of seven staff and senior accountants. Your direct supervisor, Giff Nielsen, is the partner in charge of the engagement. You were involved with the economic analysis of McMahon Company that was undertaken during the audit planning stage. A number of indicators suggest that McMahon has suffered a substantial downturn in its business this year. Accordingly, you are being very careful to see whether this downturn is properly reflected in the reported financial statement numbers.

In scrutinizing McMahon's sales near the end of the fiscal year, your audit team has detected a number of suspicious transactions. It appears that McMahon has shipped goods without receiving customer purchase orders. In addition, in several cases in which McMahon has received purchase orders, the goods shipped were two or three times the quantity ordered. Your audit team thinks that McMahon has been engaging in "channel stuffing," which is the shipment of excess goods to customers in order to boost reported sales in the current period.

You have taken the findings of your audit team to Giff Nielsen, the partner in charge of the audit, and have suggested that substantial additional audit tests be conducted to find out whether McMahon has in fact engaged in channel stuffing. Nielsen instructed you to ignore the channel stuffing evidence and proceed with the rest of the audit program. Nielsen is concerned about keeping the staff hours under budget on this engagement. In addition, Nielsen doesn't want to upset the senior management team of McMahon. McMahon's controller has already expressed some concern over the level of detailed testing that the Doman & Detmer audit team has conducted this year. McMahon's controller has hinted that McMahon is shopping around for a new auditor for next year. Because McMahon is one of the largest clients of Doman & Detmer, Giff Nielsen is afraid that his future with Doman & Detmer will be bleak if he loses McMahon as a client.

What should you do with the channel stuffing evidence assembled by your audit team?

M MODULE

Time Value of Money Review

The concept of the time value of money is very important in today's business world. No doubt you have studied this concept previously in basic accounting, finance, and business math classes. This module is intended as a review of the subject and includes illustrations of common applications.

The Time-Value-of-Money Concept

Decision makers, whether sports figures, entertainers, business executives, or parents saving for their children's college education, must try to adjust for the impact of interest and changing economic prices. Consider the following illustrative situations:

- You are in the market for a used car. A newspaper advertisement offers the vehicle you want with two payment options. You can choose between an immediate cash price of $22,500 or a 6% financing option with payments over five years of $395 at the end of each month. Which alternative purchase plan should you choose?
- You intend to provide income for your retirement. If you are 20 years old, how much must you invest now in order to establish a fund large enough to pay for your retirement in 45 years?
- Every month, millions of individuals make mortgage payments on their homes. Because part of each payment is interest, and therefore tax-deductible, a method is needed for calculating the interest portion of each payment. What are the procedures for determining the interest and principal portions of each payment over the life of the mortgage?

In each of the preceding situations, decisions must be made regarding inflows and outflows of money over an extended period of time. Making correct financial decisions requires that the time value of money be taken into account. This means that dollars to be received or paid in the future must be "discounted" or adjusted to their present value. Alternatively, current dollars may be "accumulated" or adjusted to their future value so that comparisons of dollar amounts at different time periods can be meaningful.

In the first example, you must decide whether to pay $22,500 cash now or make 60 monthly payments of $395. Assuming you have sufficient cash, wouldn't it be better to pay $22,500 for the car now instead of $23,700 (60 payments of $395) under the monthly payment plan? The answer to that question is, "Not necessarily." This decision requires that the alternatives be made comparable in terms of the time value of money, that is, the two alternatives must be stated at their respective present values.

The present value of the first alternative, the cash purchase, is simply the amount of cash to be paid currently, or $22,500. The present value of the second alternative is equal to the present value of each of the 60 payments, illustrated as follows.

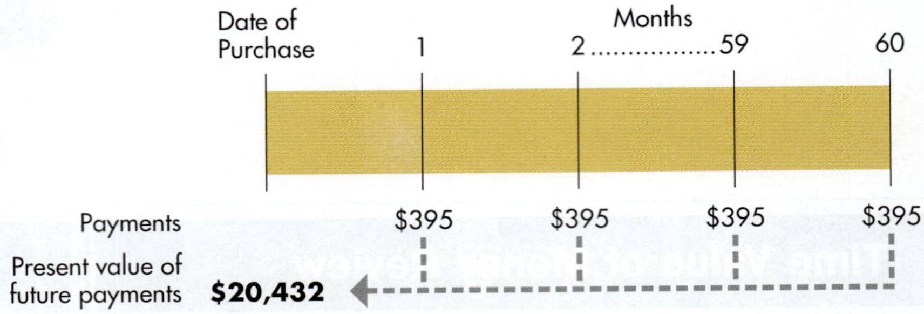

The total present value of the 60 payments of $395 each discounted to the date of purchase at 6% interest is approximately $20,432.[1] This amount is less than the $22,500 cash price the dealer is willing to accept. Therefore, assuming no other factors are relevant to your decision, you should purchase the car on the monthly payment plan. This conclusion and the other examples in the chapter ignore any tax implications, which may modify the decision in actual practice.

There are many business situations where present or future value techniques must be used in making financial decisions. Common applications in accounting include the following categories:

1. Valuing long-term notes receivable and payable where there is no stated rate of interest or where the stated rate does not reflect existing economic conditions.
2. Determining bond prices and using the effective-interest method for amortizing bond premiums or discounts.
3. Determining appropriate values for long-term capital leases and measuring the amount of interest expense and principal applicable to the periodic lease payments.
4. Accounting for pension funds, including interest accruals and amortization entries.
5. Analyzing investment alternatives.
6. Establishing amortization schedules for mortgages and measuring periodic payments on long-term purchase contracts.
7. Determining appropriate asset, liability, and equity values in mergers and business combinations.
8. Computing the amount that should be recorded for an impairment loss.
9. Estimating the fair value of intangible assets.

Because future and present value techniques are commonly used in business and have become increasingly important for accountants, this module explains these techniques and provides several illustrations of their use. The emphasis in the module is on present value techniques, because most applications in accounting require future amounts to be discounted to the present. Before future and present value techniques can be explained, however, the concept of interest must first be reviewed.

Computing the Amount of Interest

Money, like other commodities, is a scarce resource, and a payment for its use is generally required. This payment (cost) for the use of money is interest. For example, if $100

[1] As will be explained later, the $20,432 is determined by discounting an annuity of $395 for 60 months at an interest rate of 6% compounded monthly.

is borrowed, whether from an individual, a business, or a bank, and $110 is paid back, $10 in interest has been paid for the use of the $100. Thus, interest represents the excess cash paid or received over the amount of cash borrowed or loaned, illustrated as follows.

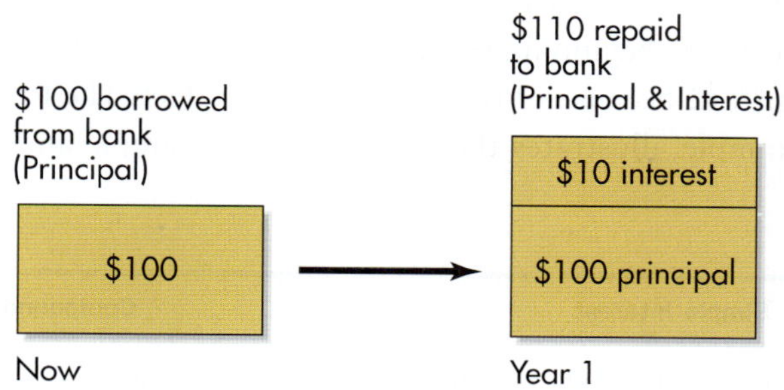

Simple Interest

Generally, interest is specified in terms of a percentage rate for a period of time, usually a year. For example, interest at 8% means the annual cost of borrowing an amount of money, called the principal, is equal to 8% of that amount. If $100 is borrowed for a period of one year at 8% annual interest, the total to be repaid is $108—the amount of the principal, $100, and the interest for a year, $8 ($100 × 0.08 × 1). Interest on a $1,000 note for six months at an annual rate of 8% is $40 ($1,000 × 0.08 × 6/12). In this case, the annual rate of 8% is multiplied by 6/12 (or 1/2 year) because interest is being computed for less than one year. Thus, the formula for computing simple interest is:

$$i = p \times r \times t,$$

where:

i = Amount of simple interest
p = Principal amount
r = Interest rate (per period)
t = Time (number of periods)

The Difference Between Simple and Compound Interest

The preceding formula applies to the computation of simple interest. Most transactions, however, involve compound interest. This means that the amount of interest earned for a certain period is added to the principal for the next period. Interest for the subsequent period is computed on the new amount, which includes both principal and accumulated interest.

The difference between simple and compound interest can be quite significant, particularly over a long period of time. Consider, for example, the case of Christopher Columbus. On October 12, 1492, Columbus landed in the Americas, and (although this is not well known) his first action was to deposit $100 in the First Bank of the Americas. The annual interest rate was 5%. On October 12, 2013, Columbus' heirs went to the bank to check the status of their ancestor's account. The bank manager informed them that certain records had been lost, and it was unknown whether Mr. Columbus had selected a simple or compound interest account. The heirs were given the option of making that choice now. After a few calculations, the heirs elected compound interest. Why? Using simple interest, the balance in Columbus' account had increased by $5 per year ($100 × 0.05) for 521 years to a current total of $2,705 ($100 principal + $2,605 interest). Using compound interest, the money in Columbus' account (which had been earning interest on the interest) totaled approximately $11.0 trillion.

Computing Compound Interest To illustrate the computation of compound interest, assume that $100 is deposited in a bank and left for two years at 6% annual interest. At the end of the first year, the $100 has earned $6 interest ($100 × 0.06 × 1). At the end of the second year, $6 has been earned for the first year, plus another $6.36 interest (6% on the $106 balance at the beginning of the second year). Thus, the total interest earned is $12.36 rather than $12 because of the compounding effect. The following table, based on the foregoing example, illustrates the computation of simple and compound interest for four years.

	Simple Interest			Compound Interest		
Year	**Computation**	**Interest**	**Total**	**Computation**	**Interest**	**Total**
1	($100 × 0.06)	$6	$106	($100.00 × 0.06)	$6.00	$106.00
2	($100 × 0.06)	6	112	($106.00 × 0.06)	6.36	112.36
3	($100 × 0.06)	6	118	($112.36 × 0.06)	6.74	119.10
4	($100 × 0.06)	6	124	($119.10 × 0.06)	7.15	126.25

The Effect of Compounding Periods The interest rate used in compound interest problems is the effective rate of interest and is generally stated as an annual rate, sometimes called "per annum." However, if the compounding of interest is for periods other than a year, the stated rate of interest must be adjusted. A comparable adjustment must be made to the number of periods. The interest rate per period equals the stated interest rate divided by the number of compoundings per period. And the number of periods equals the number of years times the number of compoundings per year. Thus, the adjustments required to the interest rate (i) and to the number of periods (n) for semiannual, quarterly, and monthly compounding of interest are as follows:

Example	Annual Compounding	Semiannual Compounding	Quarterly Compounding	Monthly Compounding
1.	i = 6%, n = 10	i = 3%, n = 20	i = 1.5%, n = 40	i = 0.5%, n = 120
2.	i = 12%, n = 5	i = 6%, n = 10	i = 3%, n = 20	i = 1%, n = 60
3.	i = 24%, n = 3	i = 12%, n = 6	i = 6%, n = 12	i = 2%, n = 36

As shown in the table, the semiannual compounding of interest requires the annual interest rate to be reduced by half and the number of periods to be doubled. Quarterly compounding of interest requires use of one-fourth the annual rate and four times the number of periods, and so forth. Because of this compounding effect, more interest is earned by an investor with semiannual interest than with annual interest, and more is earned with quarterly compounding than with semiannual compounding. Monthly compounding of interest is even better than quarterly compounding, from an investor's perspective.

Future and Present Value Techniques

Because money earns interest over time, $100 received today is more valuable than $100 received one year from today. Future and present value analysis is a method of comparing the value of money received or expected to be received at different time periods.

Analyses requiring comparisons of present dollars and future dollars may be viewed from one of two perspectives, the future or the present. If a future time frame is chosen, all cash flows must be accumulated to that future point. In this instance, the effect of interest is to increase the amounts or values over time so that the future amount is greater than the present amount. For example, \$500 invested today will accumulate to a future value of \$1,079 (rounded) in 10 years if 8% annually compounded interest is paid on the investment.

If, on the other hand, the present is chosen as the point in time at which to evaluate alternatives, all cash flows must be discounted from the future to the present. In this instance, the discounting effect reduces the amounts or values. To illustrate, if an investor is earning 10% annual interest on a note receivable that will pay \$10,000 in three years, what might the investor accept today in full payment, i.e., what is the present value of that note? The amount the investor should be willing to accept, assuming a 10% interest rate is satisfactory and that other considerations are held constant, is \$7,513, which is the discounted present value of the note. The rationale for the investor is that if the \$7,513 could be invested at 10%, compounded annually, it would accumulate to \$10,000 in three years.

As just illustrated, the future and present value situations involving single payments are essentially reciprocal relationships, and both future and present values are based on the concept of interest. Thus, if interest can be earned at 8% per year, the future value of \$100 one year from now is \$108. Conversely, assuming the same rate of interest, the present value of a \$108 payment due in one year is \$100 [\$108 ÷ (1 + 0.08)]. Similarly, \$100 to be received in one year, at an 8% annual interest rate, is worth \$92.59 today (\$100 ÷ 1.08), because \$92.59 invested at 8% will grow to \$100 in one year.

Use of Formulas

There are four common future and present value situations, each with a corresponding formula. Two of the situations deal with one-time, single payments or receipts (either future or present values), and the other two involve annuities (either future or present values).[2] An annuity consists of a series of equal payments over a specified number of equal time periods. For example, a contract calling for three annual payments of \$3,000 each would be an annuity. However, a similar contract requiring three annual payments of \$2,000, \$3,000, and \$4,000, respectively, would not be an annuity because the payments are not equal.

Without going into the derivations, the formulas for the four common situations are as follows:

1. Future Value of a Single Payment: $FV = P(1 + i)^n$ where:

   FV = Future value
   P = Principal amount to be accumulated
   i = Interest rate per period
   n = Number of periods

   Example. To calculate the future value of \$1,500 to be accumulated at 10% annual interest for five years.

   $FV = \$1,500\ (1 + 0.10)^5$
   $FV = \$2,416$ (rounded)

2. Present Value of a Single Payment: $PV = A\left[\frac{1}{(1+i)^n}\right]$ where:

   PV = Present value
   A = Accumulated amount to be discounted
   i = Interest rate per period
   n = Number of periods

[2] Hereafter in this module, the terms *payments* and *receipt* will be used interchangeably. A payment by one party in a transaction becomes a receipt to the other party and vice versa.

Example. To calculate the present value of \$2,416 to be discounted at 10% annual interest for five years.

$$PV = \$2{,}416\left[\frac{1}{(1 + 0.10)^5}\right]$$

$$PV = \underline{\underline{\$1{,}500}} \text{ (rounded)}$$

3. Future Value of an Annuity: $FV_n = R\left[\frac{(1 + i)^n - 1}{i}\right]$ where:

FV_n = Future value of an annuity
R = Annuity payment to be accumulated
i = Interest rate per period
n = Number of periods

Example. To calculate the future value of an annuity of \$2,000 for 10 years to be accumulated at 12% annual interest.

$$FV_n = \$2{,}000\left[\frac{(1 + 0.12)^{10} - 1}{0.12}\right]$$

$$FV_n = \underline{\underline{\$35{,}097}} \text{ (rounded)}$$

4. Present Value of an Annuity: $PV_n = R\left[\frac{1 - \frac{1}{(1 + i)^n}}{1}\right]$ where:

PV_n = Present value of an annuity
R = Annuity payment to be discounted
i = Interest rate per period
n = Number of periods

Example. To calculate the present value of an annuity of \$5,000 for three years to be discounted at 11% annual interest.

$$PV_n = \$5{,}000\left[\frac{1 - \frac{1}{(1 + 0.11)^3}}{0.11}\right]$$

$$PV_n = \underline{\underline{\$12{,}219}} \text{ (rounded)}$$

Use of Tables

In the previous examples, formulas were used to make the computations. As illustrated later, this is easily accomplished with a business calculator or with Excel. Alternatively, future and present value tables have been developed for each of the four situations. These tables, such as those provided on pages TVM–23 to TVM–28, are based on computing the value of \$1 for various interest rates and periods of time. Consequently, future and present value computations can be made by multiplying the appropriate table value factor for \$1 by the applicable single payment or annuity amount involved in the particular situation. Thus, the formulas for the four situations may be rewritten as follows:

1. Future Value of a Single Payment:

$FV = P(1 + i)^n$ or $FV = P(FVF_{\overline{n}|i})$ or simply

$FV = P(\text{Table I factor})$

where:

$FVF_{\overline{n}|i}$ = Future value factor for a particular interest rate (i) and for a certain number of periods (n) from Table I.

Example. (from example 1, previously illustrated):

FV = \$1,500 (1.6105 = Factor from Table I; n = 5; i = 10%)

FV = \$2,416 (rounded)

2. Present Value of a Single Payment:

$$PV = A\left[\frac{1}{(1+i)^n}\right] \text{ or } PV = A(PVF_{\overline{n}|i}) \text{ or simply}$$

PV = A(Table II factor)

where:

$PVF_{\overline{n}|i}$ = Present value factor for a particular interest rate (i) and for a certain number of periods (n) from Table II.

Example. (from example 2, previously illustrated):

PV = \$2,416 (0.6209 = Factor from Table II; n = 5; i = 10%)

PV = \$1,500 (rounded)

3. Future Value of an Annuity:

$$FV_n = R\left[\frac{(1+i)^n - 1}{i}\right] \text{ or } FV_n = R(FVAF_{\overline{n}|i}) \text{ or simply}$$

FV_n = R(Table III factor)

where:

$FVAF_{\overline{n}|i}$ = Future value annuity factor for a particular interest rate (i) and for a certain number of periods (n) from Table III.

Example. (from example 3, previously illustrated):

FV_n = \$2,000 (17.5487 = Factor from Table III; n = 10; i = 12%)

FV_n = \$35,097 (rounded)

4. Present Value of an Annuity:

$$PV_n = R\left[\frac{1 - \frac{1}{(1+i)^n}}{i}\right] \text{ or } PV_n = R(FVAF_{\overline{n}|i}) \text{ or simply}$$

PV_n = R(Table IV factor)

where:

$PVAF_{\overline{n}|i}$ = Present value annuity factor for a particular interest rate (i) and for a certain number of periods (n) from Table IV.

Example. (from example 4, illustrated previously):

PV_n = \$5,000 (2.4437 = Factor from Table IV; n = 3; i = 11%)

PV_n = \$12,219 (rounded)

Note that the answers obtained in the examples by using the tables are the same as those obtained using the formulas.

Business Calculator Keystrokes

The same future and present values computed in the previous examples can be obtained using a business calculator. The necessary keystrokes are illustrated below. (*Note:* The exact sequences of keystrokes illustrated are for a **Hewlett-Packard** business calculator; the keystrokes for other business calculators are similar if not exactly the same.)

1. Business Calculator Keystrokes for Future Value of a Single Payment:
   1500—Press [PV] (this is the initial, or present, amount)
   5—Press [N] (number of periods)
   10—Press [I] (interest rate per period; do *not* use decimals)
   Press [FV] for the answer = $2,415.7650 = $2,416 (rounded)

2. Business Calculator Keystrokes for Present Value of a Single Payment:
   2416—Press [FV] (this is the future amount)
   5—Press [N]
   10—Press [I]
   Press [PV] for the answer = $1,500.1459 = $1,500 (rounded)

3. Business Calculator Keystrokes for Future Value of an Annuity:
   2000—Press [PMT] (this the equal periodic payment)
   10—Press [N]
   12—Press [I]
   Press [FV] for the answer = $35,097.4701 = $35,097 (rounded)

4. Business Calculator Keystrokes for Present Value of an Annuity:
   5000—Press [PMT]
   3—Press [N]
   11—Press [I]
   Press [PV] for the answer
   = $12,218.5736
   = $12,219 (rounded)

! CAUTION

A common source of errors with business calculators is to forget to "Clear" the previous inputs before attempting a new present or future value computation.

Excel Spreadsheet Functions

Future and present values can also be computed using Microsoft Excel®. The relevant functions and inputs are illustrated below.

1. Excel Inputs for Future Value of a Single Payment:
   Press the "Insert Function," or f_x button, in Excel, and you can scan the menu of "Financial" functions and find the FV function. The function arguments for the FV function are as follows:

Excel Label	Your Input
Rate	Interest rate—enter 10% as "0.10"
Nper	Number of periods
Pmt	The amount of each annuity payment
Pv	The single initial amount
Type	Indication of whether the cash flows occur at the beginning or the end of the periods. If the future cash flows occur at the end of the periods, leave this field blank or insert a zero. If the future cash flows occur at the beginning of the periods, this is indicated by entering a 1 in this field.

To illustrate with the example used above, input the following into the FV function.

Excel Label	**Your Input**
Rate	0.10
Nper	5
Pmt	0—there is no annuity amount in this case, only an initial lump sum
Pv	1500
Type	0

Press "Enter" to see the answer of $2,416. Actually, the answer displayed is negative $2,416. Excel always returns negative numbers in its time value of money calculations. If this bothers you, a minus sign in front of the FV function converts these numbers to positive. Usually, you don't have to worry about the signs of the inputs and outputs of the Excel functions. The few cases where you do have to pay attention are illustrated later.

2. Excel Inputs for Present Value of a Single Payment:
   Press the "Insert Function," or f_x button, in Excel, and you can scan the menu of "Financial" functions and find the PV function. The function arguments for the PV function are as follows:

Excel Label	**Your Input**
Rate	Interest rate—enter 10% as "0.10"
Nper	Number of periods
Pmt	The amount of each annuity payment
Fv	The single future cash flow
Type	Indication of whether the cash flows occur at the beginning or the end of the periods. If the future cash flows occur at the end of the periods, leave this field blank or insert a zero. If the future cash flows occur at the beginning of the periods, this is indicated by entering a 1 in this field.

To illustrate with the example used above, input the following into the PV function.

Excel Label	**Your Input**
Rate	0.10
Nper	5
Pmt	0—there is no annuity amount in this case, only an initial lump sum
Fv	2416
Type	0

Press "Enter" to see the answer of $1,500.

3. Excel Inputs for Future Value of an Annuity:
   Using the FV function:

Excel Label	**Your Input**
Rate	0.12
Nper	10
Pmt	2000
Pv	0—there is no initial amount in this case, only an annuity
Type	0

Press "Enter" to see the answer of $35,097.

4. Excel Inputs for Present Value of an Annuity:
   Using the PV function:

Excel Label	**Your Input**
Rate	0.11
Nper	3
Pmt	5000
Fv	0—there is no final lump sum amount in this case, only an annuity
Type	0

Press "Enter" to see the answer of $12,219.

Business Applications

The following examples demonstrate the application of future and present value computations in solving business problems. Additional applications are provided in later sections as well as in the exercises at the end of the module.

Example 1—Future Value of a Single Payment Marywhether Company loans its president, Celia Phillips, \$45,000 to purchase a car. Marywhether accepts a note due in four years with interest at 10% compounded semiannually. How much cash does Marywhether expect to receive from Phillips when the note is paid at maturity?

Solution. This problem involves a single payment to be accumulated four years into the future. In many present and future value problems, a time line is helpful in visualizing the problem. (*Note:* Because of rounding, the sum of the interest amounts in the time line don't add precisely to the accumulating balance in each case.)

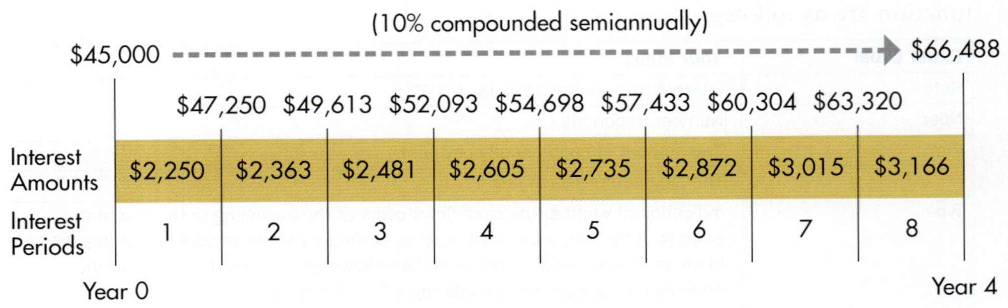

The \$45,000 must be accumulated for four years at 10% compounded semiannually. Table I may be used, and the applicable formula is:

FV = $P(FVF_{\overline{n}|i})$

where:

FV = The future value of a single payment
P = \$45,000
n = 8 periods (4 years × 2)
i = 5% effective interest rate per period (10% ÷ 2)
FV = \$45,000 (Table $I_{\overline{8}|5\%}$)
FV = \$45,000 (1.4775)
FV = \$66,488 (rounded)

In four years, Marywhether will expect to receive \$66,488, consisting of \$45,000 principal repayment and \$21,488 interest.

Business Calculator Keystrokes:

45,000—Press PV
8—Press N
5—Press I
Press FV for the answer = \$66,485.49497 = \$66,485 (rounded)

Excel Spreadsheet Function:
Using the FV function:

Excel Label	Your Input
Rate	0.05
Nper	8
Pmt	0
Pv	45000
Type	0

Press "Enter" to see the answer of $66,485.

Example 2—Present Value of a Single Payment Edgemont Enterprises holds a note receivable from a regular customer. The note is for $22,000, which includes principal and interest, and is due to be paid in exactly two years. The customer wants to pay the note now, and both parties agree that 10% is a reasonable annual interest rate to use in discounting the note. How much will the customer pay Edgemont Enterprises today to settle the obligation?

Solution. The single future payment must be discounted to the present value at the agreed upon annual rate of interest of 10%. Since this involves a present value computation of a single payment, Table II is used, and the applicable formula is:

$$PV = A(PVF_{\overline{n}|i})$$

where:

PV = The present value of a single payment
A = $22,000
n = 2 periods
i = 10% effective interest rate per period
PV = $22,000 (Table $II_{\overline{2}|10\%}$)
PV = $22,000 (0.8264)
PV = $18,181 (rounded)

The customer will pay approximately $18,181 today to settle the obligation.

Business Calculator Keystrokes:
22000—Press [FV]
2—Press [N]
10—Press [I]
Press [PV] for the answer = $18,181.8182 = $18,182 (rounded)

Excel Spreadsheet Function:
Using the PV function:

Excel Label	Your Input
Rate	0.10
Nper	2
Pmt	0
Fv	22000
Type	0

Press "Enter" to see the answer of $18,182.

Example 3—Present Value of Series of Unequal Payments Casper Sporting Goods Co. is considering a $1 million capital investment that will provide the following expected net receipts at the end of each of the next six years.

Year	Expected Net Receipts
1	$195,000
2	457,000
3	593,000
4	421,000
5	95,000
6	5,000

Casper will make the investment only if the rate of return is greater than 12%. Will Casper make the investment?

Solution. A series of unequal future receipts must be compared with a present single-payment investment. For such a comparison to be made, all future cash flows must be discounted to the present.

If the rate of return on the investment is greater than 12%, then the total of all yearly net receipts discounted to the present at 12% will be greater than the amount invested. Since the future receipts are not equal, this situation does not involve an annuity. Each receipt must be discounted individually. Table II is used, and the applicable formula is: $PV = A(PVF_{\overline{n}|i})$ where:

(1) Year = n	(2) A (Net Receipts)	(3) Table II $_{\overline{n}|12\%}$	(2) × (3) = (4) PV (Discounted Amount)
1	$195,000	0.8929	$ 174,116
2	457,000	0.7972	364,320
3	593,000	0.7118	422,097
4	421,000	0.6355	267,546
5	95,000	0.5674	53,903
6	5,000	0.5066	2,533
		Total	$1,284,515 (rounded)

The total discounted receipts are greater than the $1 million investment; thus, the rate of return is more than 12%. Therefore, other things being equal, Casper will invest. (*Note:* The problem is approached in the same way if a business calculator or an Excel spreadsheet is used. Computations similar to those in Example 2 are performed.)

Example 4—Future Value of an Annuity Boswell Co. owes an installment debt of $1,000 per quarter for five years. The creditor has indicated a willingness to accept an equivalent single payment at the end of the 5-year period instead of the series of equal payments made at the end of each quarter. If the money is worth 16% compounded quarterly, what is the equivalent single payment at the end of the contract period?

Solution. The equivalent single payment can be found by accumulating the quarterly $1,000 payments to the end of the contract period. Since the payments are equal, this is an annuity. Table III is used, and the applicable formula is:

$$FV_n = R(FVAF_{\overline{n}|i})$$

where:

FV_n	=	The unknown equivalent lump-sum payment
R	=	\$1,000 quarterly installment to be accumulated
n	=	20 periods (5 years × 4 quarters)
i	=	4% effective interest rate per period (16% ÷ 4)
FV_n	=	\$1,000 (Table III $_{\overline{12}|2\%}$)
FV_n	=	\$1,000 (29.7781)
FV_n	=	\$29,778 (rounded)

The \$29,778 paid at the end of five years is approximately equivalent to the 20 quarterly payments of \$1,000 each plus interest.

Business Calculator Keystrokes:

1000—Press [PMT]
20—Press [N]
4—Press [I]
Press [FV] for the answer = \$29,778.0786 = \$29,778 (rounded)

Excel Spreadsheet Function:
Using the FV function:

Excel Label	Your Input
Rate	0.04
Nper	20
Pmt	1000
Pv	0
Type	0

Press "Enter" to see the answer of \$29,778.

Example 5—Present Value of an Annuity Mary Sabin, proprietor of Sabin Appliance, received two offers for her last deluxe-model refrigerator. Jerry Sloan will pay \$6,500 in cash. Elise Jensen will pay \$7,000 consisting of a down payment of \$1,000 and 12 monthly payments of \$500. If the installment interest rate is 24% compounded monthly, which offer should Sabin accept?

Solution. In order to compare the two alternative methods of payment, all cash flows must be accumulated or discounted to one point in time. As illustrated by the following time line, the present is selected as the point of comparison.

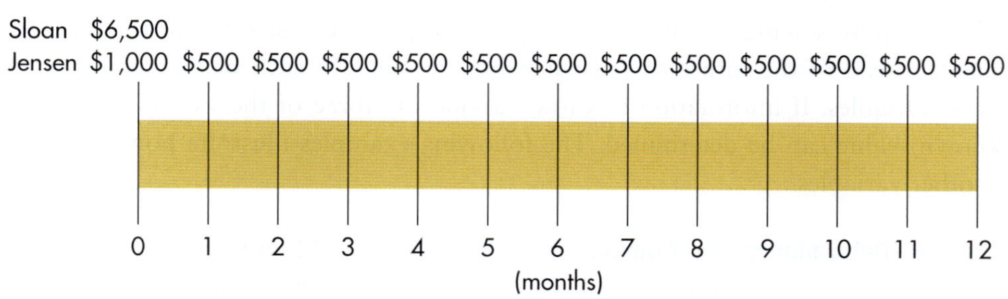

Sloan's offer is \$6,500 today. The present value of \$6,500 today is \$6,500. Jensen's offer consists of an annuity of 12 payments, plus \$1,000 paid today, which is not part of the annuity. The annuity may be discounted to the present by using Table IV and the applicable formula:

$PV_n \quad = \quad R(PVAF_{\overline{n|}i})$

where:

PV_n = Unknown present value of 12 payments
R = \$500 monthly payment to be discounted
n = 12 periods (1 year × 12 months)
i = 2% effective interest rate per period (24% ÷ 12)
PV_n = \$500 (Table $IV_{\overline{12|}2\%}$)
PV_n = \$500 (10.5753)
PV_n = \$5,288

Present value of Jensen's payments	\$5,288
Present value of Jensen's \$1,000 down payment	1,000
Total present value of Jensen's offer	\$6,288

Therefore, Sloan's offer of \$6,500 cash is more desirable than Jensen's offer.

Business Calculator Keystrokes:

500—Press [PMT]
12—Press [N]
2—Press [I]
Press [PV] for the answer = \$5,287.6706 = \$5,288 (rounded)

Excel Spreadsheet Function:
Using the PV function:

Excel Label	Your Input
Rate	0.02
Nper	12
Pmt	500
Fv	0
Type	0

Press "Enter" to see the answer of \$5,288.

Determining the Number of Periods, the Interest Rate, or the Amount of Payment

So far, the examples and illustrations have required solutions for the future or present values, with the other three variables in the formulas being given. Sometimes business problems require solving for the number of periods, the interest rate,[3] or the amount of payment instead of the future or present value amounts. In each of the formulas, there are four variables. If information is known about any three of the variables, the fourth (unknown) value can be determined. The following examples illustrate how to solve for these other variables.

Example 6—Determining the Number of Periods Rocky Mountain Survey Company wants to purchase new equipment at a cost of \$100,000. The company has \$88,850 available in cash but does not want to borrow the other \$11,150 for the purchase. If the company can invest the \$88,850 today at an interest rate of 12% compounded quarterly,

[3] When the interest is not known, it is properly called the *implicit rate of interest*, that is, the rate of interest implied by the terms of a contract or situation. (See Examples 7 and 10 in this module.)

how many years will it be before Rocky Mountain will have the $100,000 it needs to buy the equipment?

Solution. As illustrated below, Rocky Mountain Survey Company can invest $88,850 now at 12% interest compounded quarterly and needs to know how long it will take for this amount to accumulate to $100,000.

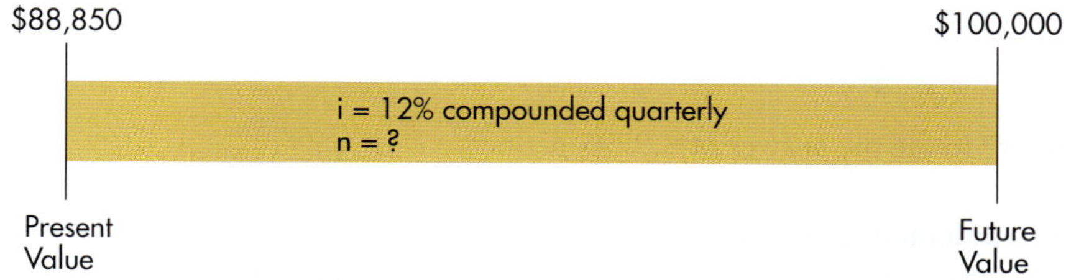

In this situation, involving both present values and future values, either Table I or Table II may be used. If Table I is used, the applicable formula is:

$$FV = P(FVF_{\overline{n}|i})$$
$$FV = P(\text{Table I factor})$$

The problem may be solved as follows:

$$\frac{FV}{P} = \text{Table I factor}$$

$$\frac{\$100{,}000}{\$88{,}850} = 1.1255$$

Reading down the 3% column (12% ÷ 4) in Table I, the factor value of 1.1255 is shown for n = 4. Therefore, it would take four periods (quarters) or one year for Rocky Mountain to earn enough interest to have $88,850 accumulate to a future value of $100,000.

If Table II is used, the applicable formula is:

$$PV = A(PVF_{\overline{n}|i})$$
$$PV = A(\text{Table II factor})$$

Solving,

$$\frac{PV}{A} = \text{Table II factor}$$

$$\frac{\$88{,}850}{\$100{,}000} = 0.8885$$

Reading down the 3% column in Table II, the factor of 0.8885 corresponds with n = 4 (quarters) or one year. This illustrates again the reciprocal nature of future and present values for single payments.

Business Calculator Keystrokes:

−88850—Press [PV] (enter as a negative number, signifying an initial cash outflow)
100000—Press [FV]
3—Press [I]
Press [N] for the answer = 3.9995 periods = 4 periods (rounded)

Excel Spreadsheet Function:

Solving for the number of periods requires the use of a new Excel function called NPER. Press the "Insert Function," or f_x button, in Excel, and you can scan the menu of "Financial" functions and find the NPER function. The function arguments for the NPER function are quite similar to those we have been using. Using the NPER function, make the following inputs:

Excel Label	Your Input
Rate	0.03
Pmt	0
Pv	−88850 (input as a negative number to signify an initial cash outflow)
Fv	100000
Type	0

Press "Enter" to see the answer of 3.9995 periods.

Example 7—Determining the Interest Rate The Hughes family wishes to purchase a used grand piano. The cost of the piano one year from now will be $5,800. If the family can invest $5,000 now, what annual interest rate must they earn on their investment to have $5,800 at the end of one year?

Solution. The Hughes family can invest $5,000 now and needs it to accumulate to $5,800 in one year. The rate of annual interest they need to earn can be computed as shown below.

If Table I is used, the applicable formula is:

$$FV = P(FVF_{\overline{n}|i})$$
$$FV = P(\text{Table I factor})$$
$$\frac{FV}{P} = \text{Table I factor}$$
$$\frac{\$5{,}800}{\$5{,}000} = 1.1600$$

Reading across the n = 1 row, the factor value 1.1600 corresponds to an annual effective interest rate of 16%. Therefore, the Hughes family would have to earn 16% annual interest to accomplish their goal. The same result is obtained if Table II is used to solve this problem.

Business Calculator Keystrokes:

–5000—Press PV (enter as a negative number, signifying an initial cash outflow)
5800—Press FV
1—Press N
Press I for the answer = 16.0000% = 16% (rounded)

Excel Spreadsheet Function:

Solving for the interest rate requires the use of a new Excel function called RATE. Press the "Insert Function," or f_x button, in Excel, and you can scan the menu of "Financial" functions and find the RATE function. The function arguments for the RATE function are quite similar to those we have been using. Using the RATE function, make the following inputs:

Excel Label	Your Input
Nper	1
Pmt	0
Pv	−5000 (input as a negative number to signify an initial cash outflow)
Fv	5800
Type	0

Press "Enter" to see the answer of 16.0%.

Example 8—Determining the Amount of Payment Provo 1st National Bank is willing to lend a customer $75,000 to buy a warehouse. The note will be secured by a 5-year mortgage and carry an annual interest rate of 12%. Equal payments are to be made at the end of each year over the 5-year period. How much will the yearly payment be?

Solution. This is an example of an unknown annuity payment. Since the present value ($75,000) is known, as well as the interest rate (12%) and the number of periods (5), the annuity payment can be determined using Table IV. The applicable formula is:

$$PV_n = R(PVAF_{\overline{n}|i})$$
$$PV_n = R(\text{Table IV factor})$$
$$\$75,000 = R(3.6048) \text{ (for } n = 5 \text{ and } i = 12\%)$$
$$\frac{\$75,000}{3.6048} = R$$
$$\underline{\underline{\$20,806}} \text{ (rounded)} = R$$

The payment on this 5-year mortgage would be approximately $20,806 each year.

Business Calculator Keystrokes:

75000—Press PV

5—Press N

12—Press I

Press PMT for the answer = $20,805.7299 = $\underline{\underline{\$20,806}}$ (rounded)

Excel Spreadsheet Function:

Solving for the payment amount requires the use of a new Excel function called PMT. Press the "Insert Function," or f_x button, in Excel, and you can scan the menu of "Financial" functions and find the PMT function. The function arguments for the PMT function are quite similar to those we have been using. Using the PMT function, make the following inputs:

Excel Label	Your Input
Rate	0.12
Nper	5
Pv	75000
Fv	0—this amount would represent a final balloon payment to be made at the end of the loan period, in addition to the regular payments
Type	0

Press "Enter" to see the answer of $20,806. Again, don't be distracted by the fact that the answer is a negative number.

Ordinary Annuity vs. Annuity Due

The illustrations up to this point have been fairly straightforward. In practice, however, complexities can arise that make it somewhat more difficult to perform future and present value calculations. One of these complexities involves the difference between an ordinary annuity and an annuity due.

Annuities are of two types: ordinary annuities (annuities in arrears) and annuities due (annuities in advance). The periodic receipts or payments for an ordinary annuity are made at the end of each period, and the last payment coincides with the end of the annuity term. The periodic receipts or payments for an annuity due are made at the beginning of the period, and one period of the annuity term remains after the last payment. These differences are illustrated below.

Ordinary Annuity of $1 for Three Years (10% annual interest)

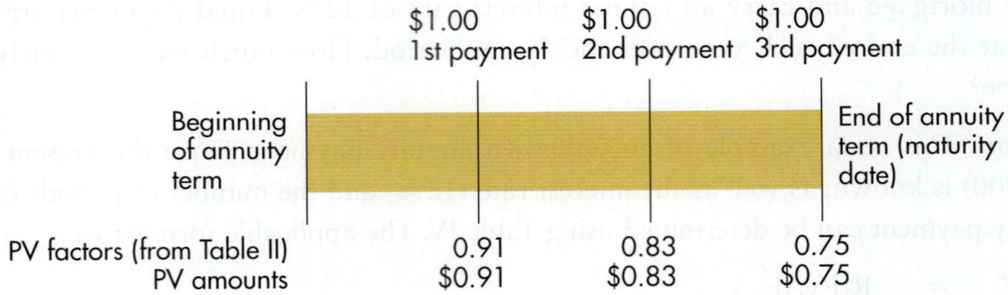

Therefore, assuming a 10% annual interest rate, the present value of an annuity of $1 per year to be received at the end of each of the next three years is $2.49 ($0.91 + $0.83 + $0.75). Notice that the last $1 is received on the maturity date, or the end of the annuity term.

Again assuming a 10% annual interest rate, the present value of an annuity of $1 per year to be received at the beginning of each of the next three years is $2.74 ($1.00 + $0.91 + $0.83). Notice here that the last payment is received one year prior to the maturity date.

Annuity Due of $1 for Three Years (10% annual interest)

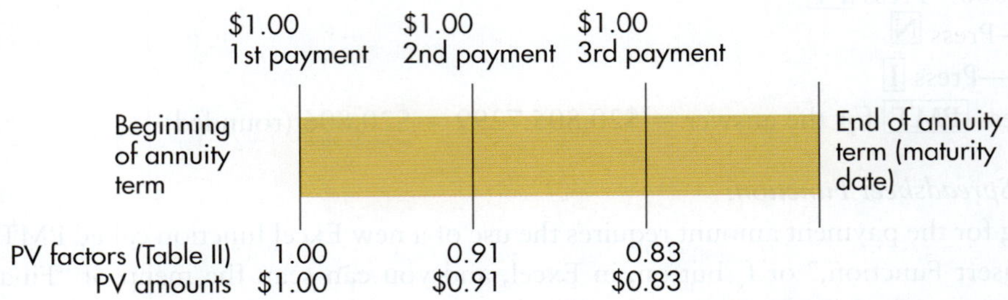

The difference in the two annuities is in the timing of the payments, and, therefore, how many interest periods are involved. As shown below, both annuities require three payments. However, the ordinary annuity payments are at the end of each period, so there are only two periods of interest accumulation; the annuity-due payments are in advance or at the beginning of the period, so there are three periods of interest accumulation.

Accumulation of Ordinary Annuity for Three Years

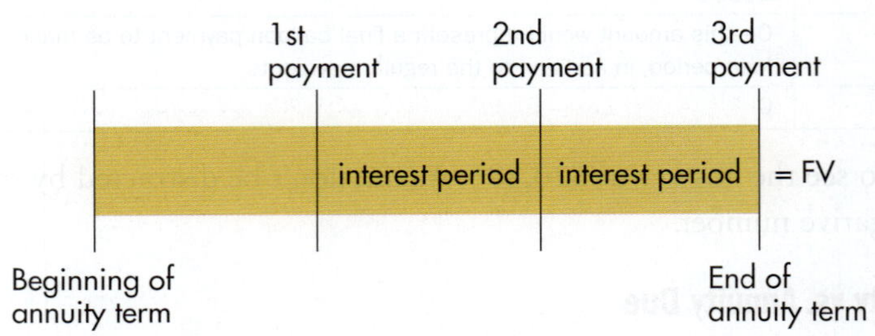

Accumulation of Annuity Due for Three Years

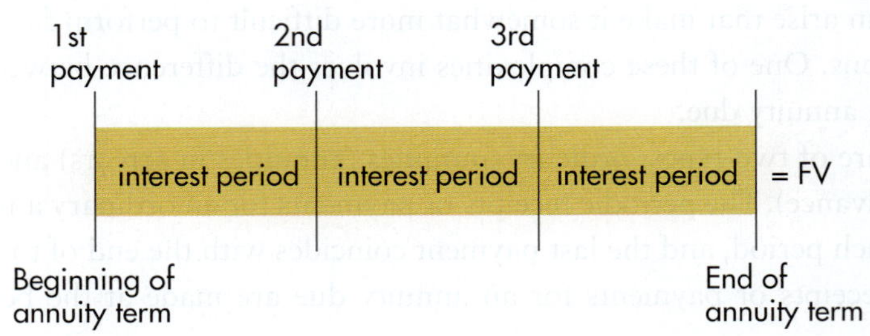

The preceding situation is exactly reversed when viewed from a present value standpoint. The ordinary annuity has three interest or discount periods, while the annuity due has only two periods, as shown below.

Present Value of Ordinary Annuity for Three Years

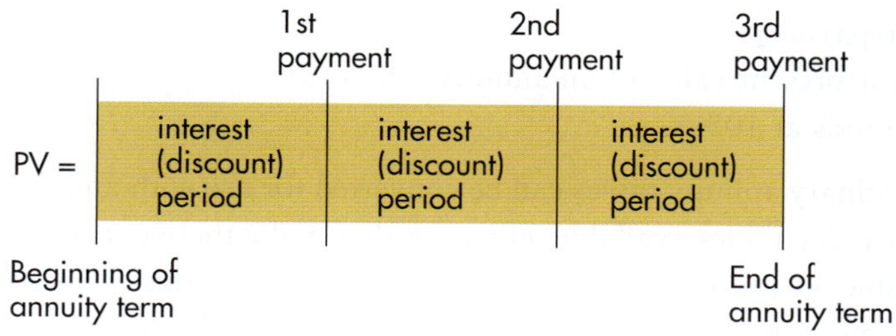

Present Value of Annuity Due for Three Years

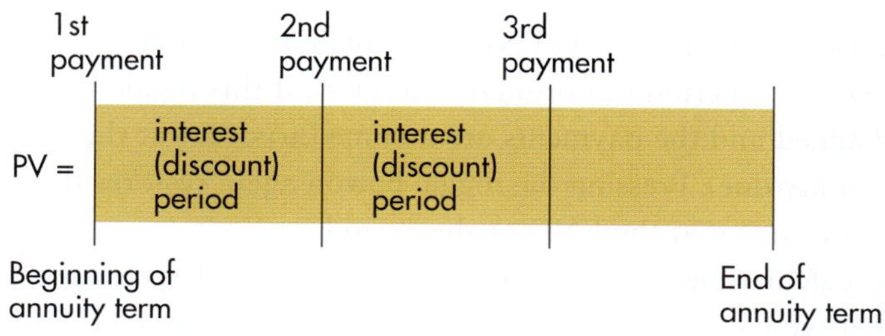

Even though most future and present value annuity tables are computed for ordinary annuities (payments at the end of the periods), these tables can be used for solving annuity-due problems where the payments are in advance. However, the following adjustments will be required:

1. To find the future value of an annuity due using ordinary annuity table values (Table III), select the appropriate table value for an ordinary annuity for one additional period (n + 1) and subtract the extra payment (which is 1.0000 in terms of the table value for $1.00). The formula is:

   $$FV_n = R(FVAF_{\overline{n+1}|i} - 1)$$

2. To find the present value of an annuity due using ordinary annuity table values (Table IV), select the appropriate table value for an ordinary annuity for one less period (n – 1) and add the extra payment (1.0000). The formula is:

   $$PV_n = R(PVAF_{\overline{n-1}|i} + 1)$$

By making the above adjustments, when payments are in advance, ordinary annuity tables may be used for all annuity situations. For example, the table value (Table III) for the future amount of an annuity due for three periods at 10% is:

(1) Factor for future value of an ordinary annuity of $1 for 4 periods (n + 1) at 10%	4.6410
(2) Less one payment.	1.0000
(3) Factor for future value of an annuity due of $1 for 3 periods at 10%	3.6410

The table value (Table IV) for the present value of an annuity due for three periods at 10% is:

(1) Factor for present value of an ordinary annuity of \$1 for 2 periods (n – 1) at 10%	1.7355
(2) Plus one payment	1.0000
(3) Factor for present value of an annuity due of \$1 for 3 periods at 10%	2.7355

As noted, ordinary annuity tables can be converted for use with annuity-due situations. There are annuity-due tables available, however, that make these conversions unnecessary. Table V and Table VI are provided for annuity-due factor values. Note that these table values are the same as those for Tables III and IV if annuity-due adjustments are made, as previously described.

Annuity-due calculations are very easy with a business calculator. The calculator has a toggle button, usually labeled "BEG/END." The default assumption is that the payments occur at the END of the period (an ordinary annuity). If this toggle button is pressed, the assumption is changed and the payments are assumed to occur at the beginning (BEG) of the period (an annuity due). Pressing the toggle button again restores the original assumption of payments occurring at the END of the period.

Annuity-due calculations are also very easy using Excel spreadsheet functions. For each function that we have used, all you have to do is to input a "1" instead of a "0" in the "Type" field.

The following examples illustrate the application of annuity-due calculations.

Example 9—Calculating Annuity-Due Values for Future Amounts Porter Corporation desires to accumulate funds to retire a \$200,000 bond issue at the end of 15 years. Funds set aside for this purpose can be invested to yield 8%. What annual payment, starting immediately, would provide the needed funds?

Solution. Annuity payments of an unknown amount, to be paid in advance, are to be accumulated toward a specific dollar amount at a known interest rate. Because the first payment is to be made immediately, all payments will fall due at the beginning of each period and an annuity due is used. Therefore, Table V is used. The appropriate formula is the same as that presented previously for an ordinary annuity, the only difference being the table in which the annuity factor is found.

$FV_n = R(FVAF_{\overline{n|}i})$

where:

FV_n = \$200,000

R = Unknown annual payment

n = 15 periods

i = 8% annual interest

$\$200,000 = R(\text{Table V}_{\overline{15|}8\%})$

$\$200,000 = R(29.3243)$

$\frac{\$200,000}{29.3243} = R$

$\underline{\underline{\$6,820}} = R$

Porter Corporation must deposit \$6,820 annually, starting immediately, to accumulate \$200,000 in 15 years at 8% annual interest.

Business Calculator Keystrokes:

Toggle so that the payments are assumed to occur at the beginning (BEG) of the period.

200000—Press [FV]

15—Press [N]

8—Press [I]

Press [PMT] for the answer = \$6,820.2861 = \$6,820 (rounded)

Excel Spreadsheet Function:

Using the PMT function:

Excel Label	Your Input
Rate	0.08
Nper	15
Pv	0—this amount would represent a separate, initial payment in addition to the initial regular payment
Fv	200000
Type	1—the "1" in this field represents the assumption that the first payment will occur immediately

Press "Enter" to see the answer of \$6,820.

Example 10—Calculating Annuity-Due Values for Present Values Utah Corporation has completed negotiations to lease equipment with a fair market value of \$45,897. The lease contract specifies semiannual payments of \$3,775 for 10 years beginning immediately. At the end of the lease, Utah Corporation may purchase the equipment for a nominal amount. What is the implicit annual rate of interest on the lease purchase?

Solution. This is a common application of an annuity-due situation in accounting since most lease contracts require payments in advance, i.e., at the beginning of the period rather than at the end of the period. The implicit interest rate must be computed for the present value of an annuity due. The present value is the fair market value of the equipment, and the payment is the lease payment. Table VI is used, and the applicable formula is:

$$PV_n = R(PVAF_{\overline{n|}i})$$

where:

$$PV_n = \$45,897$$
$$R = \$3,775$$
$$n = 20 \text{ periods } (10 \text{ years} \times 2 \text{ payments per year})$$
$$i = \text{The unknown semiannual interest rate}$$
$$\$45,897 = \$3,775 (\text{Table VI}_{\overline{20|}i})$$
$$\frac{\$45,897}{\$3,775} = 12.1581 = \text{Table VI}_{\overline{20|}i}$$
$$i = \underline{\underline{6\%}}$$

Examination of Table VI for 20 periods and a factor of 12.1581 shows i = 6%. The implicit annual interest rate is twice the semiannual rate, or 2 × 6% = 12%.

Business Calculator Keystrokes:

Toggle so that the payments are assumed to occur at the beginning (BEG) of the period.

−45897—Press [PV] (enter as a negative number)

3775—Press [PMT]

20—Press [N]

Press [I] for the answer = 5.9999665% = 6% (rounded)

Excel Spreadsheet Function:
Using the RATE function, make the following inputs:

Excel Label	Your Input
Nper	20
Pmt	3775
Pv	−45897 (input as a negative number to signify an initial cash outflow)
Fv	0—this amount would represent a final balloon payment to be made at the end of the lease period, in addition to the regular payments
Type	1

Press "Enter" to see the answer of 6.0%.

Concluding Comment

As noted in Chapter 1, the FASB's conceptual framework allows for various measurement attributes, one of which is discounted present values. This measurement attribute has received additional attention from the FASB. In February 2000, the FASB released *Statement of Financial Accounting Concepts No. 7,* "Using Cash Flow Information and Present Value in Accounting Measurement."

The work of the FASB on this topic is in response to the need for a comprehensive study of present-value-based measurements. The FASB has addressed the following issues: (1) under what circumstances an amount should be recognized in financial statements based on the present value of estimated future cash flows, (2) when is it appropriate to use the effective interest method in accounting allocations over the life of an asset or liability, (3) when the interest element involved with present-value-based measurements should be recognized as interest revenue or expense, and (4) how to reflect uncertainty in the calculation of present values.

This module has illustrated a few of the many business applications of present and future value measurement techniques. The application of these techniques in the computation of fair values for accounting purposes is illustrated in the Fair Value Module in this textbook.

Table I Future Value of a Single Payment

	1%	2%	3%	4%	5%	6%	7%	8%	9%	10%	11%	12%	14%	16%	20%
1	1.0100	1.0200	1.0300	1.0400	1.0500	1.0600	1.0700	1.0800	1.0900	1.1000	1.1100	1.1200	1.1400	1.1600	1.2000
2	1.0201	1.0404	1.0609	1.0816	1.1025	1.1236	1.1449	1.1664	1.1881	1.2100	1.2321	1.2544	1.2996	1.3456	1.4400
3	1.0303	1.0612	1.0927	1.1249	1.1576	1.1910	1.2250	1.2597	1.2950	1.3310	1.3676	1.4049	1.4815	1.5609	1.7280
4	1.0406	1.0824	1.1255	1.1699	1.2155	1.2625	1.3108	1.3605	1.4116	1.4641	1.5181	1.5735	1.6890	1.8106	2.0736
5	1.0510	1.1041	1.1593	1.2167	1.2763	1.3382	1.4026	1.4693	1.5386	1.6105	1.6851	1.7623	1.9254	2.1003	2.4883
6	1.0615	1.1262	1.1941	1.2653	1.3401	1.4185	1.5007	1.5869	1.6771	1.7716	1.8704	1.9738	2.1950	2.4364	2.9860
7	1.0721	1.1487	1.2299	1.3159	1.4071	1.5036	1.6058	1.7138	1.8280	1.9487	2.0762	2.2107	2.5023	2.8262	3.5832
8	1.0829	1.1717	1.2668	1.3686	1.4775	1.5938	1.7182	1.8509	1.9926	2.1436	2.3045	2.4760	2.8526	3.2784	4.2998
9	1.0937	1.1951	1.3048	1.4233	1.5513	1.6895	1.8385	1.9990	2.1719	2.3579	2.5580	2.7731	3.2519	3.8030	5.1598
10	1.1046	1.2190	1.3439	1.4802	1.6289	1.7908	1.9672	2.1589	2.3674	2.5937	2.8394	3.1058	3.7072	4.4114	6.1917
11	1.1157	1.2434	1.3842	1.5395	1.7103	1.8983	2.1049	2.3316	2.5804	2.8531	3.1518	3.4785	4.2262	5.1173	7.4301
12	1.1268	1.2682	1.4258	1.6010	1.7959	2.0122	2.2522	2.5182	2.8127	3.1384	3.4985	3.8960	4.8179	5.9360	8.9161
13	1.1381	1.2936	1.4685	1.6651	1.8856	2.1329	2.4098	2.7196	3.0658	3.4523	3.8833	4.3635	5.4924	6.8858	10.6993
14	1.1495	1.3195	1.5126	1.7317	1.9799	2.2609	2.5785	2.9372	3.3417	3.7975	4.3104	4.8871	6.2613	7.9875	12.8392
15	1.1610	1.3459	1.5580	1.8009	2.0789	2.3966	2.7590	3.1722	3.6425	4.1772	4.7846	5.4736	7.1379	9.2655	15.4070
16	1.1726	1.3728	1.6047	1.8730	2.1829	2.5404	2.9522	3.4259	3.9703	4.5950	5.3109	6.1304	8.1372	10.7480	18.4884
17	1.1843	1.4002	1.6528	1.9479	2.2920	2.6928	3.1588	3.7000	4.3276	5.0545	5.8951	6.8660	9.2765	12.4677	22.1861
18	1.1961	1.4282	1.7024	2.0258	2.4066	2.8543	3.3799	3.9960	4.7171	5.5599	6.5436	7.6900	10.5752	14.4625	26.6233
19	1.2081	1.4568	1.7535	2.1068	2.5270	3.0256	3.6165	4.3157	5.1417	6.1159	7.2633	8.6128	12.0557	16.7765	31.9480
20	1.2202	1.4859	1.8061	2.1911	2.6533	3.2071	3.8697	4.6610	5.6044	6.7275	8.0623	9.6463	13.7435	19.4608	38.3376
21	1.2324	1.5157	1.8603	2.2788	2.7860	3.3996	4.1406	5.0338	6.1088	7.4002	8.9492	10.8038	15.6676	22.5745	46.0051
22	1.2447	1.5460	1.9161	2.3699	2.9253	3.6035	4.4304	5.4365	6.6586	8.1403	9.9336	12.1003	17.8610	26.1864	55.2061
23	1.2572	1.5769	1.9736	2.4647	3.0715	3.8197	4.7405	5.8715	7.2579	8.9543	11.0263	13.5523	20.3616	30.3762	66.2474
24	1.2697	1.6084	2.0328	2.5633	3.2251	4.0489	5.0724	6.3412	7.9111	9.8497	12.2392	15.1786	23.2122	35.2364	79.4968
25	1.2824	1.6406	2.0938	2.6658	3.3864	4.2919	5.4274	6.8485	8.6231	10.8347	13.5855	17.0001	26.4619	40.8742	95.3962
26	1.2953	1.6734	2.1566	2.7725	3.5557	4.5494	5.8074	7.3964	9.3992	11.9182	15.0799	19.0401	30.1666	47.4141	114.4755
27	1.3082	1.7069	2.2213	2.8834	3.7335	4.8223	6.2139	7.9881	10.2451	13.1100	16.7386	21.3249	34.3899	55.0004	137.3706
28	1.3213	1.7410	2.2879	2.9987	3.9201	5.1117	6.6488	8.6271	11.1671	14.4210	18.5799	23.8839	39.2045	63.8004	164.8447
29	1.3345	1.7758	2.3566	3.1187	4.1161	5.4184	7.1143	9.3173	12.1722	15.8631	20.6237	26.7499	44.6931	74.0085	197.8136
30	1.3478	1.8114	2.4273	3.2434	4.3219	5.7435	7.6123	10.0627	13.2677	17.4494	22.8923	29.9599	50.9502	85.8499	237.3763
35	1.4166	1.9999	2.8139	3.9461	5.5160	7.6861	10.6766	14.7853	20.4140	28.1024	38.5749	52.7996	98.1002	180.3141	590.6682
40	1.4889	2.2080	3.2620	4.8010	7.0400	10.2857	14.9745	21.7245	31.4094	45.2593	65.0009	93.0510	188.8835	378.7212	1469.7716

Table II Present Value of a Single Payment

	1%	2%	3%	4%	5%	6%	7%	8%	9%	10%	11%	12%	14%	16%	20%
1	0.9901	0.9804	0.9709	0.9615	0.9524	0.9434	0.9346	0.9259	0.9174	0.9091	0.9009	0.8929	0.8772	0.8621	0.8333
2	0.9803	0.9612	0.9426	0.9246	0.9070	0.8900	0.8734	0.8573	0.8417	0.8264	0.8116	0.7972	0.7695	0.7432	0.6944
3	0.9706	0.9423	0.9151	0.8890	0.8638	0.8396	0.8163	0.7938	0.7722	0.7513	0.7312	0.7118	0.6750	0.6407	0.5787
4	0.9610	0.9238	0.8885	0.8548	0.8227	0.7921	0.7629	0.7350	0.7084	0.6830	0.6587	0.6355	0.5921	0.5523	0.4823
5	0.9515	0.9057	0.8626	0.8219	0.7835	0.7473	0.7130	0.6806	0.6499	0.6209	0.5935	0.5674	0.5194	0.4761	0.4019
6	0.9420	0.8880	0.8375	0.7903	0.7462	0.7050	0.6663	0.6302	0.5963	0.5645	0.5346	0.5066	0.4556	0.4104	0.3349
7	0.9327	0.8706	0.8131	0.7599	0.7107	0.6651	0.6227	0.5835	0.5470	0.5132	0.4817	0.4523	0.3996	0.3538	0.2791
8	0.9235	0.8535	0.7894	0.7307	0.6768	0.6274	0.5820	0.5403	0.5019	0.4665	0.4339	0.4039	0.3506	0.3050	0.2326
9	0.9143	0.8368	0.7664	0.7026	0.6446	0.5919	0.5439	0.5002	0.4604	0.4241	0.3909	0.3606	0.3075	0.2630	0.1938
10	0.9053	0.8203	0.7441	0.6756	0.6139	0.5584	0.5083	0.4632	0.4224	0.3855	0.3522	0.3220	0.2697	0.2267	0.1615
11	0.8963	0.8043	0.7224	0.6496	0.5847	0.5268	0.4751	0.4289	0.3875	0.3505	0.3173	0.2875	0.2366	0.1954	0.1346
12	0.8874	0.7885	0.7014	0.6246	0.5568	0.4970	0.4440	0.3971	0.3555	0.3186	0.2858	0.2567	0.2076	0.1685	0.1122
13	0.8787	0.7730	0.6810	0.6006	0.5303	0.4688	0.4150	0.3677	0.3262	0.2897	0.2575	0.2292	0.1821	0.1452	0.0935
14	0.8700	0.7579	0.6611	0.5775	0.5051	0.4423	0.3878	0.3405	0.2992	0.2633	0.2320	0.2046	0.1597	0.1252	0.0779
15	0.8613	0.7430	0.6419	0.5553	0.4810	0.4173	0.3624	0.3152	0.2745	0.2394	0.2090	0.1827	0.1401	0.1079	0.0649
16	0.8528	0.7284	0.6232	0.5339	0.4581	0.3936	0.3387	0.2919	0.2519	0.2176	0.1883	0.1631	0.1229	0.0930	0.0541
17	0.8444	0.7142	0.6050	0.5134	0.4363	0.3714	0.3166	0.2703	0.2311	0.1978	0.1696	0.1456	0.1078	0.0802	0.0451
18	0.8360	0.7002	0.5874	0.4936	0.4155	0.3503	0.2959	0.2502	0.2120	0.1799	0.1528	0.1300	0.0946	0.0691	0.0376
19	0.8277	0.6864	0.5703	0.4746	0.3957	0.3305	0.2765	0.2317	0.1945	0.1635	0.1377	0.1161	0.0829	0.0596	0.0313
20	0.8195	0.6730	0.5537	0.4564	0.3769	0.3118	0.2584	0.2145	0.1784	0.1486	0.1240	0.1037	0.0728	0.0514	0.0261
21	0.8114	0.6598	0.5375	0.4388	0.3589	0.2942	0.2415	0.1987	0.1637	0.1351	0.1117	0.0926	0.0638	0.0443	0.0217
22	0.8034	0.6468	0.5219	0.4220	0.3418	0.2775	0.2257	0.1839	0.1502	0.1228	0.1007	0.0826	0.0560	0.0382	0.0181
23	0.7954	0.6342	0.5067	0.4057	0.3256	0.2618	0.2109	0.1703	0.1378	0.1117	0.0907	0.0738	0.0491	0.0329	0.0151
24	0.7876	0.6217	0.4919	0.3901	0.3101	0.2470	0.1971	0.1577	0.1264	0.1015	0.0817	0.0659	0.0431	0.0284	0.0126
25	0.7798	0.6095	0.4776	0.3751	0.2953	0.2330	0.1842	0.1460	0.1160	0.0923	0.0736	0.0588	0.0378	0.0245	0.0105
26	0.7720	0.5976	0.4637	0.3607	0.2812	0.2198	0.1722	0.1352	0.1064	0.0839	0.0663	0.0525	0.0331	0.0211	0.0087
27	0.7644	0.5859	0.4502	0.3468	0.2678	0.2074	0.1609	0.1252	0.0976	0.0763	0.0597	0.0469	0.0291	0.0182	0.0073
28	0.7568	0.5744	0.4371	0.3335	0.2551	0.1956	0.1504	0.1159	0.0895	0.0693	0.0538	0.0419	0.0255	0.0157	0.0061
29	0.7493	0.5631	0.4243	0.3207	0.2429	0.1846	0.1406	0.1073	0.0822	0.0630	0.0485	0.0374	0.0224	0.0135	0.0051
30	0.7419	0.5521	0.4120	0.3083	0.2314	0.1741	0.1314	0.0994	0.0754	0.0573	0.0437	0.0334	0.0196	0.0116	0.0042
35	0.7059	0.5000	0.3554	0.2534	0.1813	0.1301	0.0937	0.0676	0.0490	0.0356	0.0259	0.0189	0.0102	0.0055	0.0017
40	0.6717	0.4529	0.3066	0.2083	0.1420	0.0972	0.0668	0.0460	0.0318	0.0221	0.0154	0.0107	0.0053	0.0026	0.0007

Table III Future Value of an Ordinary Annuity

	1%	2%	3%	4%	5%	6%	7%	8%	9%	10%	11%	12%	14%	16%	20%
1	1.0000	1.0000	1.0000	1.0000	1.0000	1.0000	1.0000	1.0000	1.0000	1.0000	1.0000	1.0000	1.0000	1.0000	1.0000
2	2.0100	2.0200	2.0300	2.0400	2.0500	2.0600	2.0700	2.0800	2.0900	2.1000	2.1100	2.1200	2.1400	2.1600	2.2000
3	3.0301	3.0604	3.0909	3.1216	3.1525	3.1836	3.2149	3.2464	3.2781	3.3100	3.3421	3.3744	3.4396	3.5056	3.6400
4	4.0604	4.1216	4.1836	4.2465	4.3101	4.3746	4.4399	4.5061	4.5731	4.6410	4.7097	4.7793	4.9211	5.0665	5.3680
5	5.1010	5.2040	5.3091	5.4163	5.5256	5.6371	5.7507	5.8666	5.9847	6.1051	6.2278	6.3528	6.6101	6.8771	7.4416
6	6.1520	6.3081	6.4684	6.6330	6.8019	6.9753	7.1533	7.3359	7.5233	7.7156	7.9129	8.1152	8.5355	8.9775	9.9299
7	7.2135	7.4343	7.6625	7.8983	8.1420	8.3938	8.6540	8.9228	9.2004	9.4872	9.7833	10.0890	10.7305	11.4139	12.9159
8	8.2857	8.5830	8.8923	9.2142	9.5491	9.8975	10.2598	10.6366	11.0285	11.4359	11.8594	12.2997	13.2328	14.2401	16.4991
9	9.3685	9.7546	10.1591	10.5828	11.0266	11.4913	11.9780	12.4876	13.0210	13.5795	14.1640	14.7757	16.0853	17.5185	20.7989
10	10.4622	10.9497	11.4639	12.0061	12.5779	13.1808	13.8164	14.4866	15.1929	15.9374	16.7220	17.5487	19.3373	21.3215	25.9587
11	11.5668	12.1687	12.8078	13.4864	14.2068	14.9716	15.7836	16.6455	17.5603	18.5312	19.5614	20.6546	23.0445	25.7329	32.1504
12	12.6825	13.4121	14.1920	15.0258	15.9171	16.8699	17.8885	18.9771	20.1407	21.3843	22.7132	24.1331	27.2707	30.8502	39.5805
13	13.8093	14.6803	15.6178	16.6268	17.7130	18.8821	20.1406	21.4953	22.9534	24.5227	26.2116	28.0291	32.0887	36.7862	48.4966
14	14.9474	15.9739	17.0863	18.2919	19.5986	21.0151	22.5505	24.2149	26.0192	27.9750	30.0949	32.3926	37.5811	43.6720	59.1959
15	16.0969	17.2934	18.5989	20.0236	21.5786	23.2760	25.1290	27.1521	29.3609	31.7725	34.4054	37.2797	43.8424	51.6595	72.0351
16	17.2579	18.6393	20.1569	21.8245	23.6575	25.6725	27.8881	30.3243	33.0034	35.9497	39.1899	42.7533	50.9804	60.9250	87.4421
17	18.4304	20.0121	21.7616	23.6975	25.8404	28.2129	30.8402	33.7502	36.9737	40.5447	44.5008	48.8837	59.1176	71.6730	105.9306
18	19.6147	21.4123	23.4144	25.6454	28.1324	30.9057	33.9990	37.4502	41.3013	45.5992	50.3959	55.7497	68.3941	84.1407	128.1167
19	20.8109	22.8406	25.1169	27.6712	30.5390	33.7600	37.3790	41.4463	46.0185	51.1591	56.9395	63.4397	78.9692	98.6032	154.7400
20	22.0190	24.2974	26.8704	29.7781	33.0660	36.7856	40.9955	45.7620	51.1601	57.2750	64.2028	72.0524	91.0249	115.3797	186.6880
21	23.2392	25.7833	28.6765	31.9692	35.7193	39.9927	44.8652	50.4229	56.7645	64.0025	72.2651	81.6987	104.7684	134.8405	225.0256
22	24.4716	27.2990	30.5368	34.2480	38.5052	43.3923	49.0057	55.4568	62.8733	71.4027	81.2143	92.5026	120.4360	157.4150	271.0307
23	25.7163	28.8450	32.4529	36.6179	41.4305	46.9958	53.4361	60.8933	69.5319	79.5430	91.1479	104.6029	138.2970	183.6014	326.2369
24	26.9735	30.4219	34.4265	39.0826	44.5020	50.8156	58.1767	66.7648	76.7898	88.4973	102.1742	118.1552	158.6586	213.9776	392.4842
25	28.2432	32.0303	36.4593	41.6459	47.7271	54.8645	63.2490	73.1059	84.7009	98.3471	114.4133	133.3339	181.8708	249.2140	471.9811
26	29.5256	33.6709	38.5530	44.3117	51.1135	59.1564	68.6765	79.9544	93.3240	109.1818	127.9988	150.3339	208.3327	290.0883	567.3773
27	30.8209	35.3443	40.7096	47.0842	54.6691	63.7058	74.4838	87.3508	102.7231	121.0999	143.0786	169.3740	238.4993	337.5024	681.8528
28	32.1291	37.0512	42.9309	49.9676	58.4026	68.5281	80.6977	95.3388	112.9682	134.2099	159.8173	190.6989	272.8892	392.5028	819.2233
29	33.4504	38.7922	45.2189	52.9663	62.3227	73.6398	87.3465	103.9659	124.1354	148.6309	178.3972	214.5828	312.0937	456.3032	984.0680
30	34.7849	40.5681	47.5754	56.0849	66.4388	79.0582	94.4608	113.2832	136.3075	164.4940	199.0209	241.3327	356.7868	530.3117	1181.8816
35	41.6603	49.9945	60.4621	73.6522	90.3203	111.4348	138.2369	172.3168	215.7108	271.0244	341.5896	431.6635	693.5727	1120.7130	2948.3411
40	48.8864	60.4020	75.4013	95.0255	120.7998	154.7620	199.6351	259.0565	337.8824	442.5926	581.8261	767.0914	1342.0251	2360.7572	7343.8578

Table IV Present Value of an Ordinary Annuity

	1%	2%	3%	4%	5%	6%	7%	8%	9%	10%	11%	12%	14%	16%	20%
1	0.9901	0.9804	0.9709	0.9615	0.9524	0.9434	0.9346	0.9259	0.9174	0.9091	0.9009	0.8929	0.8772	0.8621	0.8333
2	1.9704	1.9416	1.9135	1.8861	1.8594	1.8334	1.8080	1.7833	1.7591	1.7355	1.7125	1.6901	1.6467	1.6052	1.5278
3	2.9410	2.8839	2.8286	2.7751	2.7232	2.6730	2.6243	2.5771	2.5313	2.4869	2.4437	2.4018	2.3216	2.2459	2.1065
4	3.9020	3.8077	3.7171	3.6299	3.5460	3.4651	3.3872	3.3121	3.2397	3.1699	3.1024	3.0373	2.9137	2.7982	2.5887
5	4.8534	4.7135	4.5797	4.4518	4.3295	4.2124	4.1002	3.9927	3.8897	3.7908	3.6959	3.6048	3.4331	3.2743	2.9906
6	5.7955	5.6014	5.4172	5.2421	5.0757	4.9173	4.7665	4.6229	4.4859	4.3553	4.2305	4.1114	3.8887	3.6847	3.3255
7	6.7282	6.4720	6.2303	6.0021	5.7864	5.5824	5.3893	5.2064	5.0330	4.8684	4.7122	4.5638	4.2883	4.0386	3.6046
8	7.6517	7.3255	7.0197	6.7327	6.4632	6.2098	5.9713	5.7466	5.5348	5.3349	5.1461	4.9676	4.6389	4.3436	3.8372
9	8.5660	8.1622	7.7861	7.4353	7.1078	6.8017	6.5152	6.2469	5.9952	5.7590	5.5370	5.3282	4.9464	4.6065	4.0310
10	9.4713	8.9826	8.5302	8.1109	7.7217	7.3601	7.0236	6.7101	6.4177	6.1446	5.8892	5.6502	5.2161	4.8332	4.1925
11	10.3676	9.7868	9.2526	8.7605	8.3064	7.8869	7.4987	7.1390	6.8052	6.4951	6.2065	5.9377	5.4527	5.0286	4.3271
12	11.2551	10.5753	9.9540	9.3851	8.8633	8.3838	7.9427	7.5361	7.1607	6.8137	6.4924	6.1944	5.6603	5.1971	4.4392
13	12.1337	11.3484	10.6350	9.9856	9.3936	8.8527	8.3577	7.9038	7.4869	7.1034	6.7499	6.4235	5.8424	5.3423	4.5327
14	13.0037	12.1062	11.2961	10.5631	9.8986	9.2950	8.7455	8.2442	7.7862	7.3667	6.9819	6.6282	6.0021	5.4675	4.6106
15	13.8651	12.8493	11.9379	11.1184	10.3797	9.7122	9.1079	8.5595	8.0607	7.6061	7.1909	6.8109	6.1422	5.5755	4.6755
16	14.7179	13.5777	12.5611	11.6523	10.8378	10.1059	9.4466	8.8514	8.3126	7.8237	7.3792	6.9740	6.2651	5.6685	4.7296
17	15.5623	14.2919	13.1661	12.1657	11.2741	10.4773	9.7632	9.1216	8.5436	8.0216	7.5488	7.1196	6.3729	5.7487	4.7746
18	16.3983	14.9920	13.7535	12.6593	11.6896	10.8276	10.0591	9.3719	8.7556	8.2014	7.7016	7.2497	6.4674	5.8178	4.8122
19	17.2260	15.6785	14.3238	13.1339	12.0853	11.1581	10.3356	9.6036	8.9501	8.3649	7.8393	7.3658	6.5504	5.8775	4.8435
20	18.0456	16.3514	14.8775	13.5903	12.4622	11.4699	10.5940	9.8181	9.1285	8.5136	7.9633	7.4694	6.6231	5.9288	4.8696
21	18.8570	17.0112	15.4150	14.0292	12.8212	11.7641	10.8355	10.0168	9.2922	8.6487	8.0751	7.5620	6.6870	5.9731	4.8913
22	19.6604	17.6580	15.9369	14.4511	13.1630	12.0416	11.0612	10.2007	9.4424	8.7715	8.1757	7.6446	6.7429	6.0113	4.9094
23	20.4558	18.2922	16.4436	14.8568	13.4886	12.3034	11.2722	10.3711	9.5802	8.8832	8.2664	7.7184	6.7921	6.0442	4.9245
24	21.2434	18.9139	16.9355	15.2470	13.7986	12.5504	11.4693	10.5288	9.7066	8.9847	8.3481	7.7843	6.8351	6.0726	4.9371
25	22.0232	19.5235	17.4131	15.6221	14.0939	12.7834	11.6536	10.6748	9.8226	9.0770	8.4217	7.8431	6.8729	6.0971	4.9476
26	22.7952	20.1210	17.8768	15.9828	14.3752	13.0032	11.8258	10.8100	9.9290	9.1609	8.4881	7.8957	6.9061	6.1182	4.9563
27	23.5596	20.7069	18.3270	16.3296	14.6430	13.2105	11.9867	10.9352	10.0266	9.2372	8.5478	7.9426	6.9352	6.1364	4.9636
28	24.3164	21.2813	18.7641	16.6631	14.8981	13.4062	12.1371	11.0511	10.1161	9.3066	8.6016	7.9844	6.9607	6.1520	4.9697
29	25.0658	21.8444	19.1885	16.9837	15.1411	13.5907	12.2777	11.1584	10.1983	9.3696	8.6501	8.0218	6.9830	6.1656	4.9747
30	25.8077	22.3965	19.6004	17.2920	15.3725	13.7648	12.4090	11.2578	10.2737	9.4269	8.6938	8.0552	7.0027	6.1772	4.9789
35	29.4086	24.9986	21.4872	18.6646	16.3742	14.4982	12.9477	11.6546	10.5668	9.6442	8.8552	8.1755	7.0700	6.2153	4.9915
40	32.8347	27.3555	23.1148	19.7928	17.1591	15.0463	13.3317	11.9246	10.7574	9.7791	8.9511	8.2438	7.1050	6.2335	4.9966

Table V Future Value of an Annuity Due

	1%	2%	3%	4%	5%	6%	7%	8%	9%	10%	11%	12%	14%	16%	20%
1	1.0100	1.0200	1.0300	1.0400	1.0500	1.0600	1.0700	1.0800	1.0900	1.1000	1.1100	1.1200	1.1400	1.1600	1.2000
2	2.0301	2.0604	2.0909	2.1216	2.1525	2.1836	2.2149	2.2464	2.2781	2.3100	2.3421	2.3744	2.4396	2.5056	2.6400
3	3.0604	3.1216	3.1836	3.2465	3.3101	3.3746	3.4399	3.5061	3.5731	3.6410	3.7097	3.7793	3.9211	4.0665	4.3680
4	4.1010	4.2040	4.3091	4.4163	4.5256	4.6371	4.7507	4.8666	4.9847	5.1051	5.2278	5.3528	5.6101	5.8771	6.4416
5	5.1520	5.3081	5.4684	5.6330	5.8019	5.9753	6.1533	6.3359	6.5233	6.7156	6.9129	7.1152	7.5355	7.9775	8.9299
6	6.2135	6.4343	6.6625	6.8983	7.1420	7.3938	7.6540	7.9228	8.2004	8.4872	8.7833	9.0890	9.7305	10.4139	11.9159
7	7.2857	7.5830	7.8923	8.2142	8.5491	8.8975	9.2598	9.6366	10.0285	10.4359	10.8594	11.2997	12.2328	13.2401	15.4991
8	8.3685	8.7546	9.1591	9.5828	10.0266	10.4913	10.9780	11.4876	12.0210	12.5795	13.1640	13.7757	15.0853	16.5185	19.7989
9	9.4622	9.9497	10.4639	11.0061	11.5779	12.1808	12.8164	13.4866	14.1929	14.9374	15.7220	16.5487	18.3373	20.3215	24.9587
10	10.5668	11.1687	11.8078	12.4864	13.2068	13.9716	14.7836	15.6455	16.5603	17.5312	18.5614	19.6546	22.0445	24.7329	31.1504
11	11.6825	12.4121	13.1920	14.0258	14.9171	15.8699	16.8885	17.9771	19.1407	20.3843	21.7132	23.1331	26.2707	29.8502	38.5805
12	12.8093	13.6803	14.6178	15.6268	16.7130	17.8821	19.1406	20.4953	21.9534	23.5227	25.2116	27.0291	31.0887	35.7862	47.4966
13	13.9474	14.9739	16.0863	17.2919	18.5986	20.0151	21.5505	23.2149	25.0192	26.9750	29.0949	31.3926	36.5811	42.6720	58.1959
14	15.0969	16.2934	17.5989	19.0236	20.5786	22.2760	24.1290	26.1521	28.3609	30.7725	33.4054	36.2797	42.8424	50.6595	71.0351
15	16.2579	17.6393	19.1569	20.8245	22.6575	24.6725	26.8881	29.3243	32.0034	34.9497	38.1899	41.7533	49.9804	59.9250	86.4421
16	17.4304	19.0121	20.7616	22.6975	24.8404	27.2129	29.8402	32.7502	35.9737	39.5447	43.5008	47.8837	58.1176	70.6730	104.9306
17	18.6147	20.4123	22.4144	24.6454	27.1324	29.9057	32.9990	36.4502	40.3013	44.5992	49.3959	54.7497	67.3941	83.1407	127.1167
18	19.8109	21.8406	24.1169	26.6712	29.5390	32.7600	36.3790	40.4463	45.0185	50.1591	55.9395	62.4397	77.9692	97.6032	153.7400
19	21.0190	23.2974	25.8704	28.7781	32.0660	35.7856	39.9955	44.7620	50.1601	56.2750	63.2028	71.0524	90.0249	114.3797	185.6880
20	22.2392	24.7833	27.6765	30.9692	34.7193	38.9927	43.8652	49.4229	55.7645	63.0025	71.2651	80.6987	103.7684	133.8405	224.0256
21	23.4716	26.2990	29.5368	33.2480	37.5052	42.3923	48.0057	54.4568	61.8733	70.4027	80.2143	91.5026	119.4360	156.4150	270.0307
22	24.7163	27.8450	31.4529	35.6179	40.4305	45.9958	52.4361	59.8933	68.5319	78.5430	90.1479	103.6029	137.2970	182.6014	325.2369
23	25.9735	29.4219	33.4265	38.0826	43.5020	49.8156	57.1767	65.7648	75.7898	87.4973	101.1742	117.1552	157.6586	212.9776	391.4842
24	27.2432	31.0303	35.4593	40.6459	46.7271	53.8645	62.2490	72.1059	83.7009	97.3471	113.4133	132.3339	180.8708	248.2140	470.9811
25	28.5256	32.6709	37.5530	43.3117	50.1135	58.1564	67.6765	78.9544	92.3240	108.1818	126.9988	149.3339	207.3327	289.0883	566.3773
26	29.8209	34.3443	39.7096	46.0842	53.6691	62.7058	73.4838	86.3508	101.7231	120.0999	142.0786	168.3740	237.4993	336.5024	680.8528
27	31.1291	36.0512	41.9309	48.9676	57.4026	67.5281	79.6977	94.3388	111.9682	133.2099	158.8173	189.6989	271.8892	391.5028	818.2233
28	32.4504	37.7922	44.2189	51.9663	61.3227	72.6398	86.3465	102.9659	123.1354	147.6309	177.3972	213.5828	311.0937	455.3032	983.0680
29	33.7849	39.5681	46.5754	55.0849	65.4388	78.0582	93.4608	112.2832	135.3075	163.4940	198.0209	240.3327	355.7868	529.3117	1180.8816
30	35.1327	41.3794	49.0027	58.3283	69.7608	83.8017	101.0730	122.3459	148.5752	180.9434	220.9132	270.2926	406.7370	615.1616	1418.2579
35	42.0769	50.9944	62.2759	76.5983	94.8363	118.1209	147.9135	186.1021	235.1247	298.1268	379.1644	483.4631	790.6729	1300.0270	3538.0094
40	49.3752	61.6100	77.6633	98.8265	126.8398	164.0477	213.6096	279.7810	368.2919	486.8518	645.8269	859.1424	1529.9086	2738.4784	8812.6294

Table VI Present Value of an Annuity Due

	1%	2%	3%	4%	5%	6%	7%	8%	9%	10%	11%	12%	14%	16%	20%
1	1.0000	1.0000	1.0000	1.0000	1.0000	1.0000	1.0000	1.0000	1.0000	1.0000	1.0000	1.0000	1.0000	1.0000	1.0000
2	1.9901	1.9804	1.9709	1.9615	1.9524	1.9434	1.9346	1.9259	1.9174	1.9091	1.9009	1.8929	1.8772	1.8621	1.8333
3	2.9704	2.9416	2.9135	2.8861	2.8594	2.8334	2.8080	2.7833	2.7591	2.7355	2.7125	2.6901	2.6467	2.6052	2.5278
4	3.9410	3.8839	3.8286	3.7751	3.7232	3.6730	3.6243	3.5771	3.5313	3.4869	3.4437	3.4018	3.3216	3.2459	3.1065
5	4.9020	4.8077	4.7171	4.6299	4.5460	4.4651	4.3872	4.3121	4.2397	4.1699	4.1024	4.0373	3.9137	3.7982	3.5887
6	5.8534	5.7135	5.5797	5.4518	5.3295	5.2124	5.1002	4.9927	4.8897	4.7908	4.6959	4.6048	4.4331	4.2743	3.9906
7	6.7955	6.6014	6.4172	6.2421	6.0757	5.9173	5.7665	5.6229	5.4859	5.3553	5.2305	5.1114	4.8887	4.6847	4.3255
8	7.7282	7.4720	7.2303	7.0021	6.7864	6.5824	6.3893	6.2064	6.0330	5.8684	5.7122	5.5638	5.2883	5.0386	4.6046
9	8.6517	8.3255	8.0197	7.7327	7.4632	7.2098	6.9713	6.7466	6.5348	6.3349	6.1461	5.9676	5.6389	5.3436	4.8372
10	9.5660	9.1622	8.7861	8.4353	8.1078	7.8017	7.5152	7.2469	6.9952	6.7590	6.5370	6.3282	5.9464	5.6065	5.0310
11	10.4713	9.9826	9.5302	9.1109	8.7217	8.3601	8.0236	7.7101	7.4177	7.1446	6.8892	6.6502	6.2161	5.8332	5.1925
12	11.3676	10.7868	10.2526	9.7605	9.3064	8.8869	8.4987	8.1390	7.8052	7.4951	7.2065	6.9377	6.4527	6.0286	5.3271
13	12.2551	11.5753	10.9540	10.3851	9.8633	9.3838	8.9427	8.5361	8.1607	7.8137	7.4924	7.1944	6.6603	6.1971	5.4392
14	13.1337	12.3484	11.6350	10.9856	10.3936	9.8527	9.3577	8.9038	8.4869	8.1034	7.7499	7.4235	6.8424	6.3423	5.5327
15	14.0037	13.1062	12.2961	11.5631	10.8986	10.2950	9.7455	9.2442	8.7862	8.3667	7.9819	7.6282	7.0021	6.4675	5.6106
16	14.8651	13.8493	12.9379	12.1184	11.3797	10.7122	10.1079	9.5595	9.0607	8.6061	8.1909	7.8109	7.1422	6.5755	5.6755
17	15.7179	14.5777	13.5611	12.6523	11.8378	11.1059	10.4466	9.8514	9.3126	8.8237	8.3792	7.9740	7.2651	6.6685	5.7296
18	16.5623	15.2919	14.1661	13.1657	12.2741	11.4773	10.7632	10.1216	9.5436	9.0216	8.5488	8.1196	7.3729	6.7487	5.7746
19	17.3983	15.9920	14.7535	13.6593	12.6896	11.8276	11.0591	10.3719	9.7556	9.2014	8.7016	8.2497	7.4674	6.8178	5.8122
20	18.2260	16.6785	15.3238	14.1339	13.0853	12.1581	11.3356	10.6036	9.9501	9.3649	8.8393	8.3658	7.5504	6.8775	5.8435
21	19.0456	17.3514	15.8775	14.5903	13.4622	12.4699	11.5940	10.8181	10.1285	9.5136	8.9633	8.4694	7.6231	6.9288	5.8696
22	19.8570	18.0112	16.4150	15.0292	13.8212	12.7641	11.8355	11.0168	10.2922	9.6487	9.0751	8.5620	7.6870	6.9731	5.8913
23	20.6604	18.6580	16.9369	15.4511	14.1630	13.0416	12.0612	11.2007	10.4424	9.7715	9.1757	8.6446	7.7429	7.0113	5.9094
24	21.4558	19.2922	17.4436	15.8568	14.4886	13.3034	12.2722	11.3711	10.5802	9.8832	9.2664	8.7184	7.7921	7.0442	5.9245
25	22.2434	19.9139	17.9355	16.2470	14.7986	13.5504	12.4693	11.5288	10.7066	9.9847	9.3481	8.7843	7.8351	7.0726	5.9371
26	23.0232	20.5235	18.4131	16.6221	15.0939	13.7834	12.6536	11.6748	10.8226	10.0770	9.4217	8.8431	7.8729	7.0971	5.9476
27	23.7952	21.1210	18.8768	16.9828	15.3752	14.0032	12.8258	11.8100	10.9290	10.1609	9.4881	8.8957	7.9061	7.1182	5.9563
28	24.5596	21.7069	19.3270	17.3296	15.6430	14.2105	12.9867	11.9352	11.0266	10.2372	9.5478	8.9426	7.9352	7.1364	5.9636
29	25.3164	22.2813	19.7641	17.6631	15.8981	14.4062	13.1371	12.0511	11.1161	10.3066	9.6016	8.9844	7.9607	7.1520	5.9697
30	26.0658	22.8444	20.1885	17.9837	16.1411	14.5907	13.2777	12.1584	11.1983	10.3696	9.6501	9.0218	7.9830	7.1656	5.9747
35	29.7027	25.4986	22.1318	19.4112	17.1929	15.3681	13.8540	12.5869	11.5178	10.6086	9.8293	9.1566	8.0599	7.2098	5.9898
40	33.1630	27.9026	23.8082	20.5845	18.0170	15.9491	14.2649	12.8786	11.7255	10.7570	9.9357	9.2330	8.0997	7.2309	5.9959

KEY TERMS

Annuity TVM-5
Annuity due TVM-17
Compound interest TVM-3
Effective rate of interest TVM-4
Future value TVM-1
Future value of an annuity due TVM-19
Interest TVM-2
Ordinary annuity TVM-17
Present value TVM-1
Present value of an annuity due TVM-19
Principal TVM-3
Simple interest TVM-3

EXERCISES

Exercise M-1

Choosing between Purchase Alternatives

Foot Loose, Inc., needs to purchase a new shoelace-making machine. Machines Ready has agreed to sell Foot Loose the machine for $22,000 down and four payments of $5,700 to be paid in semiannual installments for the next two years. Do-It-Yourself Machines has offered to sell Foot Loose a comparable machine for $10,000 down and four semiannual payments of $9,000. If the current interest rate is 16%, compounded semiannually, which machine should Foot Loose purchase?

Exercise M-2

Choosing among Alternative Payment Plans

The following payment plans are offered on the purchase of a new freezer:

Plan A $375 cash.
Plan B 8 monthly payments of $55.
Plan C $100 cash down and six monthly payments of $50.

Which payment plan would you choose if interest is 24% annually, compounded monthly, if you are the purchaser? If you are the seller? (Assume ordinary annuities where applicable.)

Exercise M-3

Choosing between Alternative Investments

Heather Company has $10,000 to invest. One alternative will yield 10% per year, compounded annually for four years. A second alternative is to deposit the $10,000 in a bank that will pay 8% per year, compounded quarterly for four years. Which alternative should Heather select?

Exercise M-4

Choosing between Rent Payment Alternatives

Park City Construction is building a new office building, and management is trying to decide how rent payments for the office space should be structured. The alternatives are as follows:

Plan A Annual payment of $15,000 at the end of each year.
Plan B Monthly payments of $1,200 at the end of each month.

Assuming an interest rate of 12% compounded monthly, which payment schedule should Park City use?

Exercise M-5

Determining Purchase Price

Big Company purchased a machine on February 1, 2013, and will make seven semiannual payments of $28,000 beginning five years from the date of purchase. The interest rate will be 12%, compounded semiannually. Determine the purchase price of the machine.

Exercise M-6

Determining the Implicit Interest Rate

Valley Technical College needs to purchase some computers. Because the college is short of cash, Computer Sales Company has agreed to let Valley have the computers now and pay $2,500 per computer six months from now. If the current cash price is $2,404, what is the rate of interest Valley would be paying?

Exercise M-7

Determining Ordinary Annuity Payments

Determine the amount of the periodic payments needed to pay off the following purchases. Payments are made at the end of the period.

1. Purchase of a flat-screen TV for $2,410. Monthly payments are to be made for one year with interest at 24% per annum, compounded monthly.
2. Purchase of a waterskiing boat for $26,565. Quarterly payments are to be made for four years with interest at 8% per annum, compounded quarterly.
3. Purchase of a condominium for $65,500. Semiannual payments are to be made for 10 years with interest at 10% per annum, compounded semiannually.

Exercise M-8

Determining Unknown Quantities

Determine the unknown quantity for each of the following independent situations using the appropriate interest tables:

1. Megan wants to have $20,000 saved when she begins college. If Megan enters college in four years and interest is 8% compounded annually, how much will Megan need to save each year assuming equal deposits at the end of each year?
2. XYZ Company has obtained a bank loan to finance the purchase of an automobile for one of its executives. The terms of the loan require monthly payments at the end of each month of $585. If the interest rate is 18% compounded monthly and the car costs $15,850, for how many months will XYZ have to make payments?
3. Diaz Company is offering the following investment plan. If deposits of $250 are made semiannually for the next nine years, $7,726 will accrue. If interest is compounded semiannually, what is the approximate annual rate of interest on the investment?
4. Jack wants to buy a rental unit. For how many periods will he have to make annual deposits of $5,000 in order to accumulate $50,445, the price of the rental unit, if interest is 12% compounded annually? Assume deposits are made at the end of each year.

Exercise M-9

Determining Unknown Quantities

Determine the unknown quantity for each of the following independent situations using the appropriate interest tables:

1. Nancy and Jeff want to start a trust fund for their newborn son, Mark. They have decided to invest $3,000 today. If interest is 8% compounded semiannually, how much will be in the fund when Mark turns 20?
2. Nixon Corporation wants to establish a retirement fund. Management wants to have $1,000,000 in the fund at the end of 40 years. If fund assets will earn 12%, compounded annually, how much will need to be invested now?
3. How many payments would Star, Inc., need to make if it purchases a new building for $100,000 with annual payments made at the end of each year of $16,401.24 and interest of 16%, compounded annually?
4. An investment broker indicates that an investment of $10,000 in a CD for 10 years at the current interest rate will accumulate to $21,589. What is the current annual rate of interest if interest is compounded annually?

Exercise M-10

Unknown Interest Rates

Determine the annual interest rate that is needed for the following investments to accumulate to $50,000.

1. $10,414 for 20 years, interest compounded semiannually.
2. $7,102 for 10 years, interest compounded quarterly.
3. $33,778 for 10 years, interest compounded annually.

Exercise M-11

Unknown Annuity Amount

Lily Henry wants to buy her son a car for his 21st birthday. If Lily's son is turning 16 today, and interest is 8% per annum, compounded semiannually, what would Lily's semiannual investment need to be if the car will cost $30,000 and the first payment is made six months from today?

Exercise M-12

Unknown Interest Rates—Annuities

Determine the annual interest rate that is needed for the following annuities to accumulate to $25,000. Assume payments are made at the end of each period.

1. Annual payments of $4,095 for five years, interest compounded annually.
2. Semiannual payments of $5,715 for two years, interest compounded semiannually.
3. Quarterly payments of $1,864 for three years, interest compounded quarterly.

Exercise M-13

Unknown Investment Periods

Determine the number of periods for which the following amounts would have to be invested, under the terms specified, to accumulate to $10,000. Convert the number of periods to years.

1. $5,051 at 10% per annum, compounded semiannually.
2. $5,002 at 8% per annum, compounded annually.
3. $5,134 at 16% per annum, compounded quarterly.

Exercise M-14

Unknown Investment Periods—Annuities

Determine the number of periods for which the following annuity payments would have to be invested to accumulate to $20,000. Assume payments are made at the end of each period. Convert the number of periods to years.

1. Annual payments of $5,927 at 12% per annum, compounded annually.
2. Semiannual payments of $3,409 at 16% per annum, compounded semiannually.
3. Quarterly payments of $4,640 at 20% per annum, compounded quarterly.

Exercise M-15

Reciprocal Relationships: Future and Present Values

Determine the amount that must be deposited now at compound interest to provide the desired sum for each of the following:

1. Amount to be invested for 10 years at 6% per annum, compounded semiannually, to equal $17,000.
2. Amount to be invested for 2½ years at 8% per annum, compounded quarterly, to equal $5,000.
3. Amount to be invested for 15 years at 12% per annum, compounded semiannually, then reinvested at 16% per annum, compounded quarterly, for five more years to equal $25,000.
4. Amount to be invested at 8% per annum, compounded semiannually for three years, then $5,000 more added and the entire amount reinvested at the same rate for another three years, compounded semiannually, to equal $12,500.

Exercise M-16

Reciprocal Relationships: Future and Present Values

Determine the amount that would accumulate for the following investments:

1. $10,050 at 10% per annum, compounded annually for six years.
2. $650 at 12% per annum, compounded quarterly for 10 years.
3. $5,000 at 16% per annum, compounded annually for four years, and then reinvested at 16% per annum, compounded semiannually for four more years.
4. $1,000 at 8% per annum, compounded semiannually for five years, an additional $1,000 added and then the entire amount reinvested at 12% per annum, compounded quarterly for three more years.

Exercise M-17

Simple and Compound Interest

Dietrick Corporation borrowed $60,000 from its major shareholder, the president of the company, at an annual interest rate of 12%.

1. Assuming simple interest,
   (a) How much will Dietrick have to pay to settle its obligation if the loan is to be repaid in 12 months?
   (b) How much of the payment is interest?
   (c) How much will Dietrick have to pay if the loan is due in 18 months?
2. If the loan is paid off in 18 months and interest is compounded annually, how much will the company have to pay?
3. Compare the answers for (1c) and (2) and explain why they differ.

Exercise M-18

Computing Mortgage Payments with the Use of Formulas

George and Barbara Shrub would like to purchase a large white house and are evaluating their financing options. Bank A offers a 10-year mortgage at 12% annual interest, compounded monthly, with payments made at the end of each month. Bank B is offering a 10-year mortgage at 13% annual interest, compounded annually, with payments made at the end of each year. The purchase price of the white house is $300,000.

1. Use formulas to compute the following amounts:
   (a) The monthly payment for the Bank A mortgage.
   (b) The annual payment for the Bank B mortgage.
2. Which financing alternative would you advise the Shrubs to select?

MODULE

Fair Value

LEARNING OBJECTIVES

1. Understand the need for fair values in financial reporting.
2. Identify where fair values are used in the financial statements.
3. Define "fair value" and describe the valuation concepts used in determining fair value.
4. Use a variety of valuation models.
5. Prepare the Level 1, Level 2, and Level 3 fair value disclosures required under FASB ASC Topic 820, Fair Value Measurements and Disclosures.

The Need for Fair Values

1 **Understand the need for fair values in financial reporting.**

WHY The use of fair values in financial reporting is increasing. Accountants and users of financial statements can no longer pretend that financial reports are based completely on historical cost and ignore the practice of and principles behind valuation.

HOW Fair values are more common in financial reports because fair values have increased in business importance in recent years. Increasingly elaborate financial instruments and risk management practices have created financial statement elements for which historical cost is almost irrelevant, and fair value, and fluctuations in fair value, are extremely relevant.

Most observers of accounting, and even most accountants, have the mistaken view that financial reporting has always been firmly based on the foundation of historical cost. This is not true. For example, for a period of 10 years, the FASB, under the provisions of pre-Codification *SFAS No. 33*, required large companies to report the current value of noncurrent operating assets in a note to the financial statements. This requirement was rescinded in 1986 by pre-Codification *SFAS No. 89*. As an earlier example, before the formation of the SEC in 1934, it was common for U.S. companies to report the upward revaluation of property and equipment so that these long-term assets would be reported at their estimated fair values. However, by 1940 the SEC had effectively eliminated this practice, not by explicitly banning it, but through informal administrative pressure. Much of the suspicion about asset revaluations stemmed from a Federal Trade Commission investigation, completed in 1935, that uncovered a number of cases in the public utility industry in which a utility had improperly revalued assets upward to boost its rate base. This same issue remains a concern that many hold regarding fair value reporting today—can scheming managers manipulate reported fair value numbers to mislead banks, boards of directors, suppliers, customers, employees, and current and potential investors?

On the other hand, many financial statement users have complained for years about the *lack* of fair values in the financial statements. For example, in the late 1980s, the absence of advance warning of the $500 billion collapse of the savings and loan (S&L) industry was blamed in part on the failure of S&Ls to report the fair values of their loan portfolios. Reexamination of the accounting for financial institutions led to *SFAS No. 115* (now FASB ASC Topic 320, Investments—Debt and Equity Securities), which requires most investment securities to be reported at their fair values. The requirement in *SFAS No. 133* (now FASB ASC Topic 815, Derivatives and Hedging) that derivatives be reported at their fair values caused increased awareness and scrutiny of these financial instruments, which had historically been poorly understood and often overlooked.

So, the debate about reporting historical cost or fair value is not new. But it has heated up in recent years. Consider the two polar opposite views expressed below.

> "I recommend that FASB, with help from the SEC and from federal and state banking and insurance regulators, proceed to require fair-value measurements in all balance sheets for all assets and liabilities as soon as possible. When that happens, FASB will be able to dissolve, for we no longer will need accounting rules, much less a mountain of complex accounting rules such as we have today, and there will be no need for FASB."[1]—Walter P. Schuetze. Mr. Schuetze is the former chief accountant of the SEC and a charter member of the FASB.

> "[I]n the real world we are dealing with human beings who can (and will) be pressured and often tempted to manipulate accounting data. Thus what continues to be needed is an objective, transaction-based model with . . . historical cost as a control point. Accountants should not attempt to provide financial statements to meet the presumed needs of the short-term speculator, but instead should seek to meet the needs of the long-term shareholder and investor with reliable reports based on transactions, not guesses about values."[2]—Eugene H. Flegm. Mr. Flegm spent 28 years as an accountant at **General Motors**, 10 of those years as assistant comptroller.

There are at least two reasons for the increased interest regarding fair values in financial statements. First, the nature of global business has changed substantially in the past 20 years. Investing, financing, and risk management activities are much more elaborate and sophisticated. Computer-monitored risk management systems are constantly making automated trades and entering into derivative contracts in order to manage the complex jumble of risks to which modern corporations are exposed. As explained in Chapter 19, some of those risks are price risk (uncertainty about the future price of an asset), credit risk (uncertainty over whether other people or companies will do what they have agreed to do), interest rate risk (uncertainty about future interest rates), and exchange risk (uncertainty about future foreign exchange rates). Other risks include liquidity risk, theft risk, competitive risk, and business cycle risk. As quantitative techniques have improved and have allowed for the creation of complex financial instruments that aid in mitigating these risks, financial statement preparers and users have become aware that only the reporting of fair values accurately reflects the economic effects of these risk mitigation activities. For example, the historical cost focus of traditional accounting is misplaced with derivatives because derivatives often have little or no up-front historical cost. With derivatives, the

[1] Walter P. Schuetze, "In Defense of Fair Value," *The CPA Journal*, February 2006.

[2] Eugene H. Flegm, response to Walter P. Schuetze (*The CPA Journal*, February 2006), and *Accounting: How to Meet the Challenges of Relevance and Regulation* (Elsevier Ltd., 2004, Foreword).

subsequent changes in prices or rates are critical to determining the fair value of the derivative, yet these changes have frequently been ignored in traditional accounting.

Another reason for the increased interest regarding fair values in the financial statements is that intangible assets have increased dramatically in importance, so the computation of fair values upon a business acquisition is more difficult. As stated by former Federal Reserve Chairman Alan Greenspan: "Virtually unimaginable a half-century ago was the extent to which concepts and ideas would substitute for physical resources and human brawn in the production of goods and services."[3] As shown in Exhibit 3-12 in this textbook, the relation between the book value of a company and that company's market value has changed dramatically since 1980. Exhibit 3-12 illustrates that before 1980, between 60% and 80% of a company's market value was reflected in the reported asset and liability amounts in the balance sheet. Since 1995, balance sheets have reflected only about 20% of a company's market value. The difference stems, in large part, from the increased economic importance of intangible assets. The push for fair values in financial reporting is, in some sense, an early step in the effort to prevent financial statements from becoming an irrelevant historical curiosity.

In response to the forces described above as well as the demands of financial statement users, the FASB and IASB have determined that fair value is the most relevant measurement attribute for many assets and liabilities. Fair value is defined as "the price that would be received to sell an asset or paid to transfer a liability in an orderly transaction between market participants."[4] Because accounting has long been founded on a backbone of historical cost, the FASB and IASB are transitioning cautiously, item by item, to fair value.

A key step in this transition is FASB ASC Topic 820, which standardizes the definition of fair value and substantially expands the quality and quantity of fair value disclosures. These disclosures are explained and illustrated in this module. The FASB has also taken an additional bold step toward increased use of fair value by allowing companies a "fair value option" for the reporting of financial assets and liabilities.[5] As explained in Chapter 12, under the fair value option, a company has the option to report, at each balance sheet date, any or all of its financial assets and liabilities at their fair values on the balance sheet date. The number of financial reporting standards that require or permit the recognition of fair values will only increase in the future.

Where Are Fair Values Used in Financial Statements?

2 **Identify where fair values are used in the financial statements.**

WHY **Creating a list of the financial statement items for which fair value reporting is required or allowed brings home the pervasiveness of fair values in financial reporting.**

HOW **The FASB has standardized the use of fair values in existing accounting standards. Those standards impact many of the financial reporting areas addressed in this textbook. Those areas, and the location of the relevant coverage in this text, are summarized in this section.**

[3] Alan Greenspan, quoted in *Cracking the Value Code: How Successful Businesses Are Creating Wealth in the New Economy* [Richard E. S. Bolton, Barry D. Libert, and Steve M. Samek (HarperCollins, 2000)].

[4] FASB ASC Section 820-10-20, Glossary—Fair Value.

[5] FASB ASC Topic 825, Financial Instrument—Fair Value Option Subsections.

The purpose of this section of this fair value module is simple—to illustrate how widespread the use of fair value already is in financial statements. Below is a list of the financial statement uses of fair values. The list includes the item, a brief description of how fair value is used with that item, a U.S. GAAP reference (where appropriate), and the location of relevant coverage in this textbook.[6]

Financial Statement Item	Description of Use of Fair Value	U.S. GAAP Reference	Chapter Reference for this Textbook
Investment securities	Investment securities classified as trading or available for sale are reported in the balance sheet at their fair value on the balance sheet date.	Topic 320, Investments—Debt and Equity Securities	Chapter 14
Financial assets accounted for using the fair value option	Companies have the option of reporting almost any financial asset at its fair value in the balance sheet. Associated unrealized gains and losses are reported in the income statement.	Topic 825, Financial Instrument—Fair Value Option Subsections	Chapters 12 and 14
Long-term receivables	Long-term receivables are initially recorded at the discounted value of the future contractual cash receipts under the terms of the receivable. With the correct specification of the discount rate, this approximates the fair value, or the amount for which the receivable could be sold.	Subtopic 835-30, Imputation of Interest	Chapter 7
Pension plan assets	Pension plan assets are reported at their fair value on the balance sheet date. This fair value, along with the projected benefit obligation, are netted against each other, and a single amount is reported in the balance sheet.	Topic 715, Compensation—Retirement Benefits	Chapter 17
Assets acquired in a business combination	Assets acquired in a business combination are recorded in the books of the acquiring company at their fair value on the acquisition date.	Topic 805, Business Combinations	Chapter 10
Long-lived tangible assets that are impaired	If a long-lived tangible asset is determined to be impaired, is it written down to its fair value.	Section 360-10-35, Impairment or Disposal of Long-Lived Assets	Chapter 11
Intangible assets and goodwill that are impaired	If a long-lived intangible asset, including goodwill, is determined to be impaired, is it written down to its fair value.	Topic 350, Intangibles—Goodwill and Other	Chapter 11
Derivative instruments (asset or liability)	The fair value of all derivatives is recognized and reported in the balance sheet.	Topic 815, Derivatives and Hedging	Chapter 19
Financial liabilities accounted for using the fair value option	Companies have the option of reporting almost any financial liability at its fair value in the balance sheet. Associated unrealized gains and losses are reported in the income statement.	Topic 825, Financial Instrument—Fair Value Option Subsections	Chapter 12
Long-term payables	Long-term payables are initially recorded at the discounted value of the future contractual cash payments under the terms of the payable. With the correct specification of the discount rate, this approximates the fair value, or the amount which could be paid to transfer the payable obligation to a third party.	Subtopic 835-30, Imputation of Interest	Chapter 12
Liabilities assumed in a business combination	Liabilities assumed in a business combination are recorded in the books of the acquiring company at their fair value on the acquisition date.	Topic 805, Business Combinations	Chapter 10
Asset retirement obligation	An asset retirement obligation is recognized at its fair value at the time the obligation is incurred, and that same fair value is added to the cost of the long-term operating asset being acquired.	Topic 410, Asset Retirement and Environmental Obligations	Chapters 10 and 11
Valuation of nonmonetary items received such as assets or services	Nonmonetary assets or services are recorded at the fair value of the asset or service received or the asset or service given up, whichever is more clearly determinable.	Topic 845, Nonmonetary Transactions	Chapter 10

[6] Many of the items in this list are derived from Appendix E in the pre-codification standard *SFAS No. 157*.

As you can see from this list, fair values are already widely used in financial statements. FASB ASC Topic 820 does not require additional use of fair value beyond what is required in other statements. Instead, Topic 820 standardizes the definition of fair value, as explained in the next section.

What Is "Fair Value"?

3 **Define "fair value" and describe the valuation concepts used in determining fair value.**

WHY **A number of related, but different, definitions of "fair value" in the accounting standards have been created over the years. FASB ASC Topic 820 creates a standard "fair value" definition to be used in financial accounting.**

HOW **There are many possible ways to define "fair value" for financial reporting purposes. The FASB chose to define fair value as the price that would be received to sell an asset or paid to transfer a liability in an orderly transaction between market participants at the measurement date.**

Consider the following hypothetical example. In addition to her regular job as an accountant and financial analyst at a mid-sized local company, Lorien Franklin also buys and sells real estate. Specifically, she closely monitors land sales in the area, buys a plot of land when the price is right, holds on to the land while she carefully waits for the right buyer to come along (usually between six months and a year), and then sells the land. She has been doing this for 15 years and has many contacts and information sources in the local real estate market.

Lorien has decided to prepare a personal balance sheet and is considering the amount at which she should report the one piece of land that she currently owns. She has assembled the following facts about the land:

(a) One year ago when she purchased the land, she paid $220,000.
(b) Real estate prices have increased dramatically in the past year. Analysis of current land prices in the area indicates that Lorien would have to pay $260,000 to buy an equivalent piece of land now. Remember, however, that Lorien is an exceptionally skilled buyer; other market participants would probably have to pay more to buy that same piece of land.
(c) Lorien has assembled land sales data for the past three months for comparable pieces of land in the area. The sales prices have averaged $21.55 per square foot, with the low being $20.06 per square foot and the high being $24.78 per square foot. For general market transactions (not involving Lorien and her special skills), the price of $21.55 per square foot is a good indication of what a piece of land would sell for. Lorien's land contains 13,000 square feet.
(d) Based on her historical track record for selling land, Lorien will be able to sell this land for $310,000. It will cost her about $20,000 in various fees to finalize the sale.
(e) Lorien has determined that this land can be rented for $20,000 per year. Lorien has also determined that this rent revenue stream can be expected each year for the next 20 years. At the end of 20 years, Lorien estimates that the land can be sold for $400,000. The appropriate interest rate to use in valuing these future cash flows is 8%.

Lorien can use only a single number to report the value of the land in her balance sheet; at what value should Lorien report the land?

In *Statement of Financial Accounting Concepts No. 5*, the FASB describes five measurement attributes.[7] The amounts at which Lorien's land would be reported under each of these five measurement attributes are given below.

- *Historical cost*: Amount paid to acquire an asset (adjusted for depreciation). According to existing U.S. accounting rules, Lorien would report her land at its historical cost of $220,000. This number has the advantage of being verifiable and objective. However, it also has the disadvantage of being the least relevant of the five numbers.
- *Replacement cost*: Amount that would have to be paid to acquire the same or an equivalent asset. If Lorien were to report the land at $260,000, its replacement cost, she would be reflecting the general rise in land prices in the area. The $260,000 number is similar to the $220,000 number in that it is an entry price, meaning that it reflects the cost to Lorien to purchase the land. This $260,000 replacement cost can be viewed as merely an updated purchase price. The disadvantage of the replacement cost number is that it is hypothetical. The more active the real estate market, the more reliable is this hypothetical replacement cost.
- *Fair value*: The price that would be received to sell an asset in an orderly transaction between market participants.[8] The fair value of $280,150 ($21.55 average selling price per square foot × 13,000 square feet) reflects the amount that the land would be expected to sell for between two unrelated market participants. This hypothetical selling price is a general market price and does not factor in Lorien's above-average ability to negotiate in this market.
- *Net realizable value*: Amount of cash into which an asset is expected to be converted in due course of business less direct costs, if any, necessary to make that conversion. The net realizable value is $290,000 ($310,000 selling price less $20,000 in expected selling costs). This net realizable value of $290,000 is higher than the $280,150 fair value because it reflects Lorien's individual market skill in making land sales happen.
- *Present value of future cash flows*: Present or discounted value of future cash inflows into which an asset is expected to be converted. The present value of the future cash inflows is $282,182 (N = 20, I = 8%, PMT = $20,000, FV = $400,000 → PV = $282,182). One can argue that, conceptually, the present value of future cash flow *is* the fair value of an asset or a liability, and that market participants implicitly do present value calculations when settling on transaction prices in markets. The FASB confirms that present value techniques are one way of estimating fair value (see FASB ASC paragraph 820-10-55-4).

Which one number should Lorien include in her personal balance sheet? Well, if she wants to follow U.S. GAAP, she should report the land at its historical cost of $220,000. The $280,150 fair value (using the square footage estimation) reflects what the land would sell for between two random but informed market participants in an orderly transaction conducted today. At a minimum, this fair value number is extremely relevant. In fact, as companies and even whole national economies respond ever more rapidly to new information, the current data reflected in fair values will become increasingly relevant.

[7] *Statement of Financial Accounting Concepts No. 5*, "Recognition and Measurement in Financial Statements of Business Enterprises" (December 1984), par. 67. In *SFAC No. 5*, the concept of "fair value" is called "current market value."
[8] FASB ASC Section 820-10-20, Glossary—Fair Value.

In the glossary for Section 820-10-20, the FASB defines "fair value" as follows:

> Fair value is the price that would be received to sell an asset or paid to transfer a liability in an orderly transaction between market participants at the measurement date.

Note that this fair value definition covers both assets and liabilities. The introductory discussion in this module will focus on the fair value of assets.

In Topic 820, the FASB explains the key concepts associated with valuation. These concepts have been used for years by professional appraisers, and it certainly is not the intent of the FASB that all accountants become appraisers. However, with the increasing use of fair values in financial reporting, all accountants, auditors, and financial statement users should understand the key concepts used in defining and estimating fair values. These key concepts are as follows:

- The hypothetical transaction
- The principal (or most advantageous) market
- Market participants
- Highest and best use
- Valuation techniques
- Inputs to valuation techniques

The Hypothetical Transaction

Fair value is based on the price that would be received to sell an asset (or paid to transfer a liability) in a hypothetical transaction on the date of the measurement.[9] This hypothetical transaction is assumed to be an orderly one meaning that it is not a forced or hasty sale. In addition, this hypothetical transaction is assumed to occur between two unrelated, informed market participants. Thus, as a company seeks to determine the fair value of an asset it holds, it does not focus on the price it could receive in selling the asset; that amount is essentially equivalent to the net realizable value in the Lorien example given earlier. Instead, the company must determine what price would be acceptable to a seller without that particular company's special skills or unique handicaps.

The Principal (or Most Advantageous) Market

As explained in the previous paragraph, the hypothetical transaction is an orderly market transaction. Well, a natural question is: Which market? For some assets, there is a principal market in which that asset is typically traded. This principal market would be associated with the largest trading volume for the asset in question. For example, if the asset in question is a share of **Microsoft** stock, then the principal market is the NASDAQ market, and the relevant price in determining the fair value of the share of stock is the price at which a shareholder could sell the share in the NASDAQ market on the measurement date. Similarly, the principal market for trading pork belly futures is the Chicago Mercantile Exchange. If there is no one principal market in which a company could sell the asset, then the fair value should be determined using the price that could be obtained in the most advantageous market of those available.[10]

[9] FASB ASC paragraph 820-10-35-3.
[10] FASB ASC paragraphs 820-10-35-5 through 8.

Market Participants

As mentioned earlier, the price of the hypothetical transaction used to determine the fair value of an asset is the price that would occur between two unrelated, informed market participants. Specifically, the hypothetical market participants are knowledgeable about the asset in question, have the financial resources to buy and sell the asset, and are interested in buying or selling the asset.[11] For example, neither you nor the authors of this text have much knowledge of pork belly futures, so any price that we might agree to would not be appropriate to use in determining the fair value of a pork belly future because we are not knowledgeable, we probably don't have the necessary financial resources, and we are also probably not interested in buying or selling pork belly futures.

Highest and Best Use

A key assumption in appraising an asset is that in an unconstrained market with ample time given for market participants to consider whether they want to buy an asset, the asset will be sold to the market participant who will use that asset in the most valuable way and who will pay the highest price for the asset. In shorthand terms, it is assumed that the asset in question will be put to its "highest and best use."[12] For most financial assets, such as a share of stock, the "highest and best use" is on a stand-alone basis. For example, a share of Microsoft stock is not worth more or less if you also own a piece of undeveloped real estate and a license to operate a steel mill. In this case, it is said that the highest and best use of the share of Microsoft stock is "in exchange," meaning that the way to get the most value out of the share of stock is to exchange it, or sell it. In contrast, for many nonfinancial assets, such as a steel furnace used in producing raw steel, the highest and best use is "in use," meaning that the asset is most valuable when used in concert with other, related assets. Accordingly, a steel furnace is probably not of much worth to you or to the authors of this text, but it would be of great worth to a company that also owns a piece of undeveloped real estate and a license to operate a steel mill. When the highest and best use of an asset is "in use," in determining the fair value of the asset it is assumed that the hypothetical market participant who would purchase the asset also owns the related assets that would allow it to maximize the "in use" value of the purchased asset.

Valuation Techniques

In the field of asset appraisal, there are three primary asset valuation techniques: the market approach, the income approach, and the cost approach.[13] Each of these approaches is explained briefly here using the example of the determination of the fair value of a piece of commercial real estate.

Market Approach The market approach uses data from market prices for identical or similar assets. For example, in determining the fair value of a piece of commercial real estate, it is natural to look to the recent selling prices of similar pieces of real estate.

Income Approach The income approach is the general heading given to valuation techniques based directly or indirectly on discounted cash flow analysis. To use an income approach in estimating the fair value of a piece of commercial real estate, you would estimate the annual net cash flows to be generated by the property plus the amount for which

[11] FASB ASC paragraph 820-10-35-9.

[12] FASB ASC paragraphs 820-10-35-10 through 15.

[13] FASB ASC paragraphs 820-10-35-24 through 35.

the real estate could be sold at some terminal period. All of these cash flows would then be discounted to the present using an appropriate interest rate. Examples of discounted cash flow analysis are given later in this module.

Cost Approach The cost approach is based on the replacement cost of the asset. Often, the replacement cost is estimated based on what it would cost to replace the asset new, and then an adjustment is made for wear and tear to reflect the fact that the asset is used. The cost approach involves a subtle shift from the underlying concept of fair value because the cost approach is based on an entry price (the cost to buy) instead of an exit price (the price at which the asset can be sold). The cost approach might be used with commercial real estate if there are no other similar properties that have recently changed hands. For example, assume that the real estate involves the land, a building, and a surrounding parking lot. The cost approach would involve estimating how much it would cost to buy similar land and then the cost of constructing the building and the parking lot.

Illustrations of different applications of each of these approaches will be given later in this module.

Inputs to Valuation Techniques

All of the valuation techniques outlined above require data inputs in estimating a fair value. Some data inputs are independently verifiable such as market prices for shares of stock or selling prices for comparable pieces of commercial real estate. These are called *observable inputs*. In the absence of observable inputs based on market data, a company must use its own assumptions to generate reasonable estimates of the cash flow forecasts, discount rate assumptions, or other valuation inputs that would be used by market participants. These are called *unobservable inputs*. The FASB states that companies should maximize the use of observable inputs when estimating fair values.[14]

Examples of various valuation models, along with inputs to these models, are given in the next section.

Examples of Valuation Models

4 **Use a variety of valuation models.**

WHY **Preparers and users of financial statements do not necessarily need to be experts in valuation. However, anyone associated with financial reports containing fair values should understand the valuation process and the connection between the inputs to and outputs from common valuation models.**

HOW **Valuation models employ the use of both observable and unobservable inputs. Models that employ observable inputs focus on the adjustments necessary to convert the observed market data into a fair value for the asset in question. Models that employ unobservable inputs, such as models using the income approach, exhibit much greater sensitivity to the possible model inputs.**

The following simple valuation models are illustrated in this section:

- Market multiples
- Matrix pricing
- Discounted cash flows, finite period

[14] FASB ASC paragraph 820-10-35-36.

- Discounted cash flows, infinite period
- Adjusted replacement cost

Keep in mind that the objective of this module is not to train you to be a professional appraiser. Instead, you need a general understanding of common valuation models so that you can be an intelligent user of the fair value information you receive from expert appraisers for use in preparing financial reports, auditing financial reports, or interpreting financial reports.

Market Multiples

As part of a business acquisition, Taraz Company purchased two buildings. The buildings are to be reported in Taraz's books at their fair values on the purchase date. Each of the buildings is unique, so Taraz cannot look to other building sales to directly determine how much each building would bring in a sales transaction. However, Taraz has assembled the following market data, based on commercial real estate sales in the area in the past six months, which can be used to indirectly estimate the selling price of each of the buildings Taraz purchased.

Selling Price

	Square Feet				
Capitalization Rate	**10,000**	**20,000**	**30,000**	**40,000**	**50,000**
7%	$700,000	$1,425,000	$2,000,000	$2,500,000	$3,000,000
8%	625,000	1,250,000	1,750,000	2,250,000	2,625,000
9%	550,000	1,100,000	1,550,000	2,000,000	2,300,000
10%	500,000	1,000,000	1,400,000	1,800,000	2,100,000

Taraz has learned that the selling price of a building is related to both its size (shown in the table above in square feet) and by the expected stability in the rental income that the building could generate if it were rented. This expected stability is represented by the "capitalization rate," which is the amount of rental income that the building can generate divided by the building's price. A higher capitalization rate indicates that market participants view the future income stream as being more risky. This riskiness is related to location, nature of surrounding properties, and so forth.

For the two buildings it purchased, Taraz has measured the size and estimated a capitalization rate based on location and surrounding properties. These estimates for the two buildings are as follows:

	Square Feet	Capitalization Rate
Building 1	15,000	9%
Building 2	22,000	10%

The fair value of the two buildings can be estimated as follows:

Building 1

- Look at the 9% capitalization rate row.
- Based on square footage, Building 1 is exactly halfway between $550,000 and $1,100,000.
- Estimated fair value of Building 1 = $825,000 = $550,000 + 0.5($1,100,000 − $550,000)

Building 2

- Look at the 10% capitalization rate row.
- Based on square footage, Building 2 is 20% of the way from $1,000,000 to $1,400,000.
- Estimated fair value of Building 2 = $1,080,000 = $1,000,000 + 0.2($1,400,000 – $1,000,000)

Matrix Pricing

Han Company has purchased two corporate bonds as temporary investments. The bond investments are to be reported in Han's books at their fair values on the balance sheet date. Each of the bonds has unique terms, and the bonds are not traded in active markets, so Han cannot look to quoted market prices to directly determine how much each bond would bring in a sales transaction. However, Han has assembled the following matrix of bond price data for actively traded bonds which can be used to indirectly estimate the selling price of each of Han's bonds.

Bond Prices (% of par)

			Bond Ratings		
Term (in years)	**AAA**	**AA**	**A**	**BBB**	**BB**
2	103.85	103.56	102.71	102.37	100.29
5	103.66	102.53	101.45	100.17	98.50
10	101.64	100.29	99.56	98.54	91.98
20	95.66	91.49	90.00	89.31	82.06

Han has learned that the selling price of a bond is related to both its term (the number of years until the bond matures) and to the underlying riskiness of the company that issued the bond. (*Note*: Another important valuation variable is the coupon interest rate on the bond. In this example, that rate is assumed to be the same for all bonds and so is ignored in this analysis.) This underlying riskiness is represented by the "bond rating" which is a label attached to a bond by a bond rating agency such as **Standard & Poor's**. The rating agency assigns the rating after an analysis of the bond issuing company's finances and the strength of its industry. A lower bond rate (AAA is the highest in the table and BB is the lowest) indicates that rating agency views the bond issuing company as being more risky. The higher this risk, the lower the bond price if everything else is held constant. Also, somewhat independent of the underlying riskiness of the bond issuing company, the longer time until a bond matures the more risk is associated with the bond. Thus, holding all else constant, bonds with longer times to maturity have lower prices.

For the two bonds it purchased, Han has determined the time to maturity and has also looked up the bond rating from Standard & Poor's. These data for the two bonds are as follows:

	Term	**Bond Rating**
Bond 1	15	AA
Bond 2	6	BBB

The fair value of each of the two bonds can be estimated as follows. (*Note*: The par value of each of the bonds is $1,000, and the numbers given in the matrix of bond prices are expressed in terms of a percentage of par value.)

Bond 1

- Look at the AA bond rating column.
- Based on the term of the bond, Bond 1 is exactly halfway between 100.29 and 91.49.
- Estimated bond price as a percent of par = 95.89 = 100.29 − 0.5(100.29 − 91.49)
- Estimated price of Bond 1 = 0.9589 × $1,000 = $958.90

Bond 2

- Look at the BBB bond rating column.
- Based on the term of the bond, Bond 2 is 20% of the way from 100.17 to 98.54.
- Estimated bond price as a percent of par = 99.844 = 100.17 − 0.2(100.17 − 98.54)
- Estimated price of Bond 2 = 0.99844 × $1,000 = $998.44

Discounted Cash Flows, Finite Period

As described in FASB *Concepts Statement* No. 7, the present value of future cash flows can be used to estimate fair value in one of two ways. In the traditional approach, which is often used in situations in which the amount and timing of the future cash flows are determined by contract, the present value is computed using a risk-adjusted interest rate that incorporates expectations about the uncertainty of receipt of the future contractual cash flows. In the expected cash flow approach, a range of possible outcomes is identified, the present value of the cash flows in each possible outcome is computed (using the risk-free interest rate), and a weighted-average present value is computed by summing the present value of the cash flows in each outcome, multiplied by the estimated probability of that outcome. To illustrate the traditional and the expected cash flow approaches, consider the following two examples.[15]

Traditional Approach Intangible Asset A is the right to receive royalty payments in the future. The future royalty cash flows are $1,000 at the end of each year for the next five years. The risk-free interest rate is 5%; the receipt of these royalty cash flows is not certain, so a risk-adjusted interest rate of 12% is used in computing their present value. The fair value of Intangible Asset A is estimated as follows:

Business calculator keystrokes:

N = 5 years

I = 12%

PMT = $1,000

FV = $0 (there is no additional payment at the end of five years)

PV = $3,605

This $3,605 amount is the estimated fair value of the intangible asset.

[15] These examples are also found in the text of Chapter 10.

Expected Cash Flow Approach Intangible Asset B is a secret formula to produce a fast-food cheeseburger that contains 25 essential vitamins and minerals, reduces cholesterol levels, and replenishes the ozone layer. Future cash flows from the secret formula are uncertain; the following estimates have been generated, with the associated probabilities.

Outcome 1 10% probability of cash flows of $5,000 at the end of each year for 10 years

Outcome 2 30% probability of cash flows of $1,000 at the end of each year for 4 years

Outcome 3 60% probability of cash flows of $100 at the end of each year for 3 years

In the expected cash flow approach, the uncertainty of the future cash flows is not reflected in a risk-adjusted interest rate but is incorporated through the assessment of the various possible outcomes and the probabilities of each. Thus, the risk-free interest rate (5% in this case) is used in computing the present value of the cash flows in each outcome.

	Present Value	Probability	Probability Weighted Present Value
Outcome 1	$38,609	0.10	$3,861
Outcome 2	3,546	0.30	1,064
Outcome 3	272	0.60	163
Total estimated fair value			$5,088

This $5,088 amount is the estimated fair value of the intangible asset.[16]

Discounted Cash Flows, Infinite Period

Rockmimi Company has purchased a taxi cab company in Winnemucca, Nevada, at the beginning of Year 1. One of the assets of the acquired company is an operating license issued by the city of Winnemucca. These licenses are quite valuable, but they trade infrequently, and the last separate sale of a similar license was 15 years ago. Accordingly, Rockmimi has determined that an income approach is necessary to determine the fair value of the acquired operating license. Because similar licenses are sometimes sublicensed, or rented, in exchange for a royalty fee based on total taxi revenue, Rockmimi can use a "relief from royalty" method to estimate the fair value of the license. Rockmimi has determined that the prevailing market royalty rate for such an arrangement is 6.0%. Using this approach, the fair value of the license is the present value of the after-tax royalties that Rockmimi is avoiding by owning the license instead of being forced to rent it from someone else.

Rockmimi has generated the following inputs for use with the "relief from royalty" method:

- Royalty rate: 6.0% of total taxi cab revenue (before subtracting any expenses)
- Discount rate: 11.0%
- Expected taxi cab revenue in Year 1: $1,000

[16] In applying the expected cash flow approach, we really should take the analysis one step further and convert the expected cash flows into "certainty equivalents." The basic idea is that there is a lower amount of cash that you would accept for sure in exchange for a higher, uncertain amount. We will leave this more complete "certainty equivalent" analysis to a more detailed course in valuation.

- Expected growth rate in taxi cab revenue each year for Years 2 through 5: 20.0%. Rockmimi expects rapid revenue growth for the next five years, but then the growth will slow to a sustainable long-term level.
- Expected long-term growth rate in cab revenue each year after five years (Year 6 and beyond): 4.0%
- Income tax rate: 40%

As you can see, most of the inputs into this valuation model are unobservable with the important exception of the royalty rate of 6.0%, which is an observable input determined by reference to other similar royalty arrangements. Using these data, the fair value of the license is estimated to be $842, computed as follows:

						Growth 4.0%
	Year 1	**Year 2**	**Year 3**	**Year 4**	**Year 5**	**Years 5+**
Total annual revenue	$1,000	$1,200	$1,440	$1,728	$2,074	
Pretax royalty (6%)	$ 60	$ 72	$ 86	$ 104	$ 124	
Income taxes (40%)	24	29	34	42	50	
After-tax royalty	$ 36	$ 43	$ 52	$ 62	$ 74	$1,099
Discounted cash flow	$ 32	$ 35	$ 38	$ 41	$ 44	
Sum of discounted cash flow	$ 190					
Present value of "perpetuity"	652					
Total present value of cash flows	$ 842					

One number, $652, in this computation deserves extra explanation. The cash flows in Year 6 and after constitute an infinite series. This infinite series is not exactly a perpetuity because the payments are not equal but are instead growing at 4.0% per year. The $1,099 value is computed using the Gordon growth model that is illustrated in Chapter 23.

$$\text{Present Value} = \frac{\text{First "Perpetuity" Cash Flow}}{r - g}$$

where g is the expected growth rate and r is the discount rate. In this case, the calculation is as follows:

$$\text{First "Perpetuity" Cash Flow} = \$76.96 = \$74 \times 1.04$$

$$\text{Present Value of Year 5+ Cash Flows} = \$76.96 \div (0.110 - 0.040) = \$1{,}099$$

This $1,099 is the present value of the infinite series of cash flows as of one year before the first cash flow occurs. The first cash flow in this series occurs at the end of Year 6, so the $1,099 value is as of the end of Year 5. This amount must be discounted back five more years to the beginning of Year 1; this yields the $652 amount identified as the present value of the "perpetuity."

To a person unfamiliar with valuation models, the reporting of the $842 estimated fair value of the license gives the illusion that the fair value is a precise number. One reason it is useful to learn about the basics of valuation is to learn how sensitive some fair value estimates can be to changes in the inputs, especially unobservable inputs. For example, in this case, changes in the values of the discount rate (in the range from 7% to 15%) and the post-Year 5 growth rate (in the range from 2% to 6%) yield estimated fair values as low at $450 and as high as $5,800.

You can see that to assess the reliability of reported fair value numbers it is important for an accountant, an auditor, or a financial statement user to understand the basics of valuation.

Adjusted Replacement Cost

Kamaraz Company has purchased the site of a ski resort for $10 million. Kamaraz must now estimate the fair values of the assets acquired in the purchase in order to properly record the acquisition. One of the assets is a ski lift system that is still fully functional. Because ski lift systems are of necessity tied to specific resorts and the contours of the resort's ski runs, there is no practical way to directly determine a selling price for this particular system. However, Kamaraz can estimate how much it would cost to duplicate the system with new construction. That cost is $1,200,000. The existing system has been in use for five years, and such systems are typically assumed to have useful lives of 20 years with a 10% salvage value. In a process exactly analogous to the computation of depreciated book value, we can estimate a "depreciated" replacement cost of $930,000. The computations are as follows:

- ($1,200,000 − $120,000) ÷ 20 years = $54,000 "depreciation" per year
- 5 years × $54,000 "depreciation" per year = $270,000 total "depreciation"
- $1,200,000 replacement cost new − $270,000 "depreciation" = $930,000 adjusted replacement cost

This $930,000 adjusted replacement cost is a cost-based estimate of the fair value of the ski lift system.

It bears repeating again that the objective of this module is not to train you to be a professional appraiser. Instead, you must be familiar with the common valuation models so that you can better understand the valuations provided by professional appraisers and be better prepared to ask questions about the critical and influential inputs into the models.

Fair Value Disclosures

5 **Prepare the Level 1, Level 2, and Level 3 fair value disclosures required under FASB ASC Topic 820, Fair Value Measurements and Disclosures.**

WHY **The reliability of inputs into valuation models is not the same in all circumstances and for all models. As a result, the output from the models can vary substantially in reliability. In Topic 820, the FASB requires disclosures that help financial statement users assess the reliability of the fair values used in preparing the financial statements.**

HOW **Level 1 inputs are the most reliable and are quoted prices in active markets for identical assets or liabilities. Level 2 inputs are of intermediate reliability and are prices for similar (but not identical) assets or liabilities or observable market inputs used in a valuation model. Level 3 inputs are unobservable inputs such as internal cash flows forecasts, discount rate estimations, and so forth.**

Fair value measurements are generated with a combination of observable and unobservable inputs. Consider the example of Company A estimating the fair value of its investment in the common stock of Company B. Examples of observable inputs are the quoted price of Company B stock and market multiples (such as price-to-sales ratio, price-earnings ratio, and price-to-book ratio) for Company B and other companies in its industry. Examples of unobservable inputs are Company A's own estimate of the future cash flows to be generated by its investment in Company B and its estimate of the appropriate rate of return to use in valuing those cash flows. In using valuation techniques to generate fair values, the FASB requires companies to maximize the use of observable inputs and minimize the use of unobservable inputs.

The FASB has refined this observable/unobservable dichotomy into a 3-way "fair value hierarchy," as follows:

- Level 1 inputs—quoted prices in active markets for identical assets (or liabilities)
- Level 2 inputs—observable inputs other than quoted prices in active markets for identical assets (or liabilities)
- Level 3 inputs—unobservable inputs

In generating fair values, Level 1 inputs are preferable to Level 2 inputs, which in turn are preferable to Level 3 inputs. Back to the Company A valuation of its investment in Company B mentioned above, Company A should use the quoted price of Company B stock if such a price exists. In the absence of such a price, Company A should maximize its use of market multiples and other market data for similar companies. Finally, if no market-corroborated data exist relative to the fair value of Company B, then Company A should use its own internally generated cash flow and required rate of return estimates.

Clearly, a fair value generated with Level 1 inputs is more reliable and involves less uncertainty than a fair value generated with Level 3 inputs. Accordingly, under the provisions of Topic 820, a company is required to provide quantitative disclosure about the source of the inputs into its fair value computations.

These fair value disclosures fall into two categories. The first category is for assets (and liabilities) that are measured at fair value on a recurring basis. Examples are trading securities, available-for-sale securities, and derivatives. These items are reported at their fair values on every reporting date. For items measured at fair value on a recurring basis, the first required valuation input disclosure is a simple table with the assets as the rows and the three input levels as the columns. The example below is copied from FASB ASC paragraph 820-10-55-61.

($ in 000s)		**Fair Value Measurements at Reporting Date Using**		
Description	**12/31/XX**	**Quoted Prices in Active Markets for Identical Assets (Level 1)**	**Significant Other Observable Inputs (Level 2)**	**Significant Unobservable Inputs (Level 3)**
Trading securities	$115	$105	$10	
Available-for-sale securities	75	75		
Derivatives	60	25	15	$20
Venture capital investments	10			10
Total	$260	$205	$25	$30

To illustrate what additional information this disclosure provides beyond the summary fair value measurements, consider the values reported for the available-for-sale securities ($75) and the venture capital investments ($10). The data in this table tell the financial statement user that there is a large difference in the reliability of these two numbers even though both are reported as "fair value" numbers in the balance sheet. The $75 number is extremely reliable because, as noted in the table heading, it comes from "quoted prices in active markets for identical assets." In contrast, the $10 number is not as reliable because it stems from internal judgments and estimates that have not been corroborated by independent market observations.

The preceding paragraph highlights that the greatest concern regarding fair value numbers is with the numbers generated using Level 3 inputs. As a result, further disclosure is required for these fair values. An example is given in the table below.

($ in 000s)	**Fair Value Measurements Using Significant Unobservable Inputs (Level 3)**		
	Derivatives	**Venture Capital Investments**	**Total**
Beginning balance	$14	$11	$25
Total gains or losses (realized/unrealized)			
Included in earnings (or changes in net assets)	11	(3)	8
Included in other comprehensive income	4		4
Purchases, issuances, and settlements	(7)	2	(5)
Transfers in and/or out of Level 3	(2)	0	(2)
Ending balance	$20	$10	$30

This table presents a beginning and ending balance reconciliation, or rollforward, for the fair values generated using Level 3 inputs. In summary, for items measured at fair value on a recurring basis, an overall table is presented showing the relative magnitudes of fair values computed using Level 1, Level 2, and Level 3 inputs. In addition, a more detailed table is provided for the values generated using Level 3 inputs showing an explanation of the change in the fair value amounts from the beginning of the period to the end of the period.

Most balance sheet items are NOT reported at fair value on a recurring basis but are occasionally reported at fair value. A common example is impaired assets. The required disclosure for assets reported at fair value on a nonrecurring basis is given below. This table is copied from FASB ASC paragraph 820-10-55-64.

($ in millions)		**Fair Value Measurements Using**			
Description	**Year Ended 12/31/XX**	**Quoted Prices in Active Markets for Identical Assets (Level 1)**	**Significant Other Observable Inputs (Level 2)**	**Significant Unobservable Inputs (Level 3)**	**Total Gains (Losses)**
Long-lived assets held and used	$75		$75		$(25)
Goodwill	30			$30	(35)
Long-lived assets held for sale	26		26		(15)
					$(75)

You should first notice that with items reported at fair value on a nonrecurring basis, it is unlikely that Level 1 inputs will be available. Also, note that the final column, containing the gains and the losses, is a very condensed version of the second table, the rollforward table, required for the items that are reported at fair value on a recurring basis.

The Level 1, Level 2, and Level 3 disclosures required under Topic 820 help accountants, auditors, and financial statements users assess the reliability of the fair value numbers used in preparing the financial statements. Remember that the strong point of fair values is that they are very relevant, but the downside is that they sometimes lack reliability. The Topic 820 disclosures enable the assessment of that reliability.

FASB-IASB CODIFICATION SUMMARY

ifrs

Topic	FASB Accounting Standards Codification	Original FASB Standard	Corresponding IASB Standard	Differences between U.S. GAAP and IFRS
Fair values in financial reporting	*Topic 820*	*SFAS No. 157*	*Exposure Draft: Fair Value Measurement, May 2009*	No substantial differences. Both the FASB and the IASB plan to have revised fair value standards finalized by the end of 2010; the revised standards will be mutually consistent.

EXERCISES

Exercise FV-1
LO4

Adjusted Replacement Cost

Burton Dee Company has purchased the site of a gravel pit for $10 million. Burton Dee must now estimate the fair values of the assets acquired in the purchase in order to properly record the acquisition. One of the assets is a rock crushing system. This system includes a crusher, a conveyer belt, and a control room. Because rock crushing systems such as this are tailor made for the pit in which they are located, there is no practical way to directly determine a selling price for this particular system. However, Burton Dee can estimate how much it would cost to duplicate the system with new construction. That cost is $800,000. The existing system has been in use for seven years, and such systems are typically assumed to have a useful life of 16 years with a 5% salvage value.

Using these data, estimate the fair value of the rock crushing system.

Exercise FV-2
LO5

Disclosures for Items Reported at Fair Value on a Nonrecurring Basis

During the year, Nelson Company conducted an impairment analysis for three assets: a building, an operating license, and goodwill. The carrying values of the assets as of the beginning of the year were as follows: building, $20,000; operating license, $38,000; goodwill, $120,000. It was found that each one of the assets was impaired. Impairment losses were recognized as follows: building, $4,000; operating license, $23,000; goodwill, $94,000. The year-end fair values of all three of these assets were determined using internally generated data.

Prepare the Level 1, Level 2, and Level 3 disclosures required under Topic 820.

Exercise FV-3
LO5

Disclosures for Items Reported at Fair Value on a Recurring Basis

Didericksen Company has an investment portfolio containing three securities. Details about each of the securities are given below.

- *Security 1*: 1,000 shares purchased last year for $20 per share. At the beginning of this year, the shares were trading at $25 per share. At the end of this year, the shares were trading at $27 per share. The shares of Security 1 trade actively on the New York Stock Exchange. Didericksen holds these securities with the intent to make money through short-term fluctuations in price; they are classified as trading securities.

- *Security 2*: 30 bonds ($1,000 face value) purchased last year at 98.5. At the beginning of this year, the bonds were trading at 101.4. The bonds are thinly traded, so no quoted price is available near the end of this year. However, use of matrix pricing based on the trading prices of similar bonds indicates that the estimated price of the bonds is 97.8 at the end of this year. Didericksen classifies these securities as available for sale.
- *Security 3*: 500 shares in a real estate investment trust. Didericksen purchased 300 shares last year for $15 per share. At the beginning of this year, the estimated fair value of these shares was $18. During the year, Didericksen purchased another 200 shares at $16 per share. Didericksen classifies this as an available-for-sale investment. The shares in this real estate investment trust are privately held, and transactions are infrequent. As of the end of the year, Didericksen has used its own analysis to estimate the price per share to be $12.

Prepare the Level 1, Level 2, and Level 3 disclosures required under Topic 820.

Exercise FV-4
LO4

Use of Market Multiples

Pockey Company has assembled the following market data, based on commercial real estate sales in the area in the past six months, which can be used to indirectly estimate the selling price of a building the company purchased.

Selling Price

	Square Feet				
Capitalization Rate	**10,000**	**20,000**	**30,000**	**40,000**	**50,000**
7%	$700,000	$1,425,000	$2,000,000	$2,500,000	$3,000,000
8%	625,000	1,250,000	1,750,000	2,250,000	2,625,000
9%	550,000	1,100,000	1,550,000	2,000,000	2,300,000
10%	500,000	1,000,000	1,400,000	1,800,000	2,100,000

The building purchased by Pockey Company, which is called "Building Z," has 32,000 square feet and a capitalization rate of 9.3%.

What is the fair value of Building Z?

Exercise FV-5
LO4

Use of Market Multiples

Polly Company purchased three buildings. Polly has assembled the following market data, based on commercial real estate sales in the area in the past six months, which can be used to indirectly estimate the selling price of each of the buildings Polly purchased.

Selling Price

	Square Feet				
Capitalization Rate	**10,000**	**20,000**	**30,000**	**40,000**	**50,000**
7%	$700,000	$1,425,000	$2,000,000	$2,500,000	$3,000,000
8%	625,000	1,250,000	1,750,000	2,250,000	2,625,000
9%	550,000	1,100,000	1,550,000	2,000,000	2,300,000
10%	500,000	1,000,000	1,400,000	1,800,000	2,100,000

For the three buildings it purchased, Polly has measured the size and estimated a capitalization rate based on location and surrounding properties. These estimates for the three buildings are on page FV-20.

	Square Feet	Capitalization Rate
Building 3	38,000	7%
Building 4	41,000	8%
Building 5	46,000	10%

Estimate the fair value of each of the three buildings.

Exercise FV-6
LO4

Use of Matrix Pricing for Bonds

Bodie Company has purchased three corporate bonds as temporary investments. Bodie has assembled the following matrix of bond price data for actively traded bonds which can be used to indirectly estimate the selling price of each of Bodie's bonds.

Bond Prices (% of par)

	Bond Ratings				
Term (in years)	**AAA**	**AA**	**A**	**BBB**	**BB**
2	103.85	103.56	102.71	102.37	100.29
5	103.66	102.53	101.45	100.17	98.50
10	101.64	100.29	99.56	98.54	91.98
20	95.66	91.49	90.00	89.31	82.06

For the three bonds it purchased, Bodie has determined the time to maturity and has also looked up the bond rating from **Standard & Poor's**. These data for the three bonds are as follows:

	Term	Bond Rating
Bond 3	3	AAA
Bond 4	18	BB
Bond 5	9	A

Estimate the fair value of each of the three bonds. (*Note*: The par value of each of the bonds is $1,000, and the numbers given in the matrix of bond prices are expressed in terms of a percentage of par value.)

Exercise FV-7
LO4

Use of Matrix Pricing for Bonds

Below is a bond pricing matrix.

Bond Prices (% of par)

	Bond Ratings			
Term (in years)	**AAA**	**AA**	**A**	**BBB**
2	104	103	102	101
5	103	102	101	100
10	101	100	99	98
20	96	91	90	89

Company H owns a bond with a 13-year term and an AA rating. What is the fair value of this $1,000 bond? (*Note*: The par value of each of the bonds is $1,000, and the numbers given in the matrix of bond prices are expressed in terms of a percentage of par value.)

Exercise FV-8

LO4

Discounted Cash Flows, Infinite Period

Sophie Zincmann Company has purchased an auto repair business in Tucson, Arizona, at the beginning of Year 1. One of the assets of the acquired company is a business license issued by the city of Tucson. These licenses are valuable, but they trade infrequently, and the last separate sale of a similar license was 10 years ago. Accordingly, Sophie Zincmann has determined that an income approach is necessary to determine the fair value of the acquired business license. Because similar licenses are sometimes sublicensed, or rented, in exchange for a royalty fee based on total repair shop revenue, Sophie Zincmann can use a "relief-from-royalty" method to estimate the fair value of the license. Sophie Zincmann has determined that the prevailing market royalty rate for such an arrangement is 2.0%. Using this approach, the fair value of the license is the present value of the after-tax royalties that Sophie Zincmann is avoiding by owning the license. Sophie Zincmann has generated the following inputs for use with the "relief-from-royalty" method:

- Royalty rate: 2.0% of total repair shop revenue (before subtracting any expenses)
- Discount rate: 15.0%
- Expected repair shop revenue in Year 1: $300,000
- Expected growth rate in repair shop revenue each year for Years 2 through 5: 10.0%. Sophie Zincmann expects rapid revenue growth for the next five years, but then the growth will slow to a sustainable long-term level.
- Expected growth rate in repair shop revenue each year after five years (Year 6 and beyond): 3.0%
- Income tax rate: 30%

Using these data, estimate the fair value of the business license.

Exercise FV-9

LO4

Expected Cash Flow Approach

As part of a business combination, Mother Ryan Company acquired a customer list and a franchise agreement. Mother Ryan uses the expected cash flow approach for estimating the fair value of these two intangibles. The appropriate interest rate is 8%. The potential future cash flows from the two intangibles, and their associated probabilities, are as follows:

Customer List

Outcome 1 20% probability of cash flows of $40,000 at the end of each year for five years

Outcome 2 30% probability of cash flows of $18,000 at the end of each year for four years

Outcome 3 50% probability of cash flows of $9,000 at the end of each year for three years

Franchise Agreement

Outcome 1 10% probability of cash flows of $450,000 at the end of each year for 10 years

Outcome 2 20% probability of cash flows of $12,000 at the end of each year for four years

Outcome 3 70% probability of cash flows of $500 at the end of each year for three years

Using the expected cash flow approach, estimate the fair value of the customer list and of the franchise agreement.

CASES

This module concludes with two cases.

- Sprint Nextel 2007
- China Telecommunications Industry 2008

These cases allow you to explore various issues associated with asset valuation and fair value disclosures. These cases focus on the estimation of fair values of nonfinancial assets. Both cases are for companies in the telecommunications industry. The fact that companies in this industry have many intangible assets leads to interesting valuation questions.

Case FV-10

Fair Value and Impairment

Both **Sprint** and **Nextel** started business on the competitive fringes of the telecommunications industry. Until 1984, the phone business was dominated by the **AT&T** monopoly that stretched back to the time of Alexander Graham Bell. When founded in 1987, Nextel was originally called "Fleetcall" because it utilized wireless frequencies that had historically been used by taxi dispatchers. Sprint was formed from the combination of several companies including a local telephone company, founded in 1899, that had competed against AT&T in its monopoly days as well as a company that made wireless transmissions using the track right-of-way communication system of the **Southern Pacific Railroad**. Sprint and Nextel were formally united on August 12, 2005.

From a technology standpoint, the Sprint–Nextel merger presented a serious challenge. There are three common digital wireless technologies used around the world: GSM, CDMA, and iDEN. These different technologies vary based on, among other things, how they deal with the technical challenge of transmitting several calls at once. GSM (which was developed in Europe; the "GSM" stands for Groupe Spécial Mobile) is by far the most common mobile phone technology used worldwide. In the United States, GSM is used by AT&T and **T-Mobile**. CDMA (which stands for code division multiple access) is used in the United States by **Verizon** and, historically, by Sprint. iDEN (integrated digital enhanced network) was developed by **Motorola** and has been used for years by Nextel. These three technologies are mutually incompatible, so a cellular phone built to use CDMA doesn't work with a network designed around iDEN. Thus, when Sprint and Nextel merged, a huge issue was how to get the CDMA and iDEN systems of the two companies to work together. As of early 2008, Sprint Nextel was still using both technologies, which the company described in its 2007 10-K filing as a continuing risk, as follows: "Our wireless networks provide services utilizing CDMA and iDEN technologies. Wireless subscribers served by these two technologies represent a smaller portion of global wireless subscribers than the subscribers served by wireless networks that utilize GSM technology. As a result, our costs with respect to both CDMA and iDEN network equipment and handsets may continue to be higher than the comparable costs incurred by our competitors who use GSM technology, which places us at a competitive disadvantage."

The Sprint–Nextel merger also presented organizational behavior challenges. Sprint's management approach was described as "bureaucratic" in contrast to the "aggressive, entrepreneurial" approach of Nextel.[1] Many joint meetings "ended with Nextel employees storming out, leaving the Sprint side baffled. Sprint people thought Nextel made reckless decisions and spent money impulsively. Nextel people felt stifled by Sprint's process-oriented pace."

During 2007, it became apparent that the honeymoon was over at Sprint Nextel. Signs of distress included the following:

- Operating income in each quarter in 2007 was down compared to the same quarter in 2006. For the first three quarters, the total decrease was 63%.
- Average revenue per user (ARPU) declined during each quarter in 2007 compared to the same quarter in 2006. Sprint Nextel explained the decline as follows: "The

[1] Kim Hart, "No Cultural Merger at Sprint Nextel," *Washington Post*, November 24, 2007, p. D01.

decline in our average monthly voice revenue is primarily due to the loss of subscribers with higher priced service plans, while new subscribers and the subscribers acquired from the PCS Affiliates have lower priced service plans."

- The market value of the company, which had held steady at about $55 billion during the first three quarters of 2007, began on a long slide in the fourth quarter, dropping to $44 billion by the end of November and $37 billion by the end of the year.

This financial distress triggered a careful impairment analysis. This analysis included consideration of the recoverability of the cost of long-lived assets, both tangible and intangible, as well as an assessment of potential impairment of goodwill. The data underlying those analyses are detailed below.

(*Note*: These data are adapted from the 2007 10-K filing of Sprint Nextel; they represent an approximation of the actual data used in the internal impairment analysis conducted by Sprint Nextel.)

Impairment Analysis of Property, Plant, and Equipment
As described above, the impairment concerns center on the Wireless segment. Data on the property, plant, and equipment for the Wireless segment as of December 31, 2007, are as follows. (All numbers are in millions.)

Land	$ 277
Network equipment	30,764
Buildings and improvements	4,054
Non-network software, office equipment	2,844
Less: Accumulated depreciation	(18,545)
	19,394
Construction in progress	3,488
Property, plant, and equipment, net	$ 22,882

For purposes of an impairment test, Sprint Nextel groups property, plant, and equipment at the lowest organizational level for which the cash flows of the group "are largely independent of the cash flows of other groups of assets and liabilities." Sprint Nextel has determined that the segment level is the appropriate level at which to conduct this analysis.

Sprint Nextel is involved in an active market for the leasing of "cell and switch sites, real estate, information technology and network equipment and office space." Data from this active leasing market can be used to generate cash flow estimates for the property, plant, and equipment of the Wireless segment. Estimated annual lease payments for the property, plant, and equipment currently being used by the Wireless segment are as follows:

	Estimated Annual Lease Payment
Land	$ 30
Network equipment	2,840
Buildings and improvements	299
Non-network software, office equipment	437
Construction in progress*	1,073

*This estimated annual lease payment is for a completed asset. Construction in progress is 60% complete.

According to FASB ASC paragraph 360-10-35-31, "the remaining life of an asset group shall be based on the remaining useful life of the primary asset of the group." The primary asset is the depreciable asset "that is the most significant component asset from which the asset group derives its cash-flow-generating capacity." For the property, plant, and equipment of the Wireless segment, this asset is the network equipment which has, on average, a remaining useful life of eight years.

Impairment Analysis of Goodwill

Before any impairment charges, the net book value of the Wireless segment as of December 31, 2007, is $52,808, computed as follows:

Current assets	$ 7,414
Property, plant, and equipment, net	22,882
Intangible assets:	
Goodwill	30,664
FCC licenses	21,123
Customer relationships, net	4,203
Other definite-lived intangibles	1,835
Other assets	733
Total Wireless assets	$88,854
Current liabilities	$ 7,793
Long-term debt	17,521
Deferred tax liabilities	7,438
Other liabilities	3,294
Total Wireless liabilities	$36,046
Net book value of Wireless segment	$52,808

The total market value of Sprint Nextel at the end of each quarter during 2007 was as follows:

	Market Capitalization (in billions)
January 1, 2007	$54.2
March 31, 2007	53.8
June 30, 2007	58.8
September 30, 2007	54.1
December 31, 2007	37.4

All of Sprint Nextel's reported goodwill relates to the Wireless segment. The process used by Sprint Nextel to estimate the fair value of the Wireless segment is described as follows: "We [reduce] our stock price by the estimated value per share of our Wireline reporting unit and then [add] a control premium, as permitted by FASB guidance, to determine an estimate of the equity value of the wireless reporting unit."

One way to estimate the fair value of the Wireline segment is using a market-based approach based on price-to-sales and price-to-EBITDA ratios for publicly traded companies with similar operations. Data for this analysis are included below.

	Market Capitalization	Operating Revenues	EBITDA*
Qwest	$8.29	$13.73	$4.61
Level 3	4.96	4.31	0.76
Embarq	6.79	6.35	2.67
Windstream	6.00	3.26	1.67
Centurytel	3.80	2.70	1.37
Sprint Nextel Wireline segment	?	6.46	1.07

All numbers are for 2007 and are in billions.

*EBITDA = Earnings before interest, taxes, depreciation, and amortization

The "control premium" mentioned by Sprint Nextel is the additional value, above the value based on reported sales or cash flows, that accrues to an entity that controls a business operation. In this case, the control premium is that additional value from owning, or controlling, the Wireless segment and thus being able to make strategic decisions with respect to the use of the resources of the segment. Estimates in the academic literature place the magnitude of this premium at 5% to 10%.

Sprint Nextel also estimates the fair value of the Wireless segment through an income approach which involves the computation of the present value of an estimate of the cash flows to be generated by the segment. Data used in that analysis are as follows:

For computing weighted-average cost of capital	
Risk-free rate (12/31/2007)	4.0%
Equity premium	7.0%
Industry-average Beta	1.55
Interest rate on debt	7.0%
5-year growth forecast	
Annual growth in OIBDA*	13.0%
Annual growth in capital expenditures	10.0%
*OIBDA = Operating income before depreciation and amortization; this is equivalent to after-tax segment earnings.	
Terminal growth rate (after 5 years)	6.0%
Income tax rate for all years	38.0%
Reported amounts for 2007	
Segment earnings	$9,914
Capital expenditures	5,067

(*Note*: Total liabilities for Sprint Nextel as of December 31, 2007, were $42.1 billion.)

Estimation of Fair Value of Non-Goodwill Intangible Assets

As part of its Wireless segment goodwill impairment analysis, Sprint Nextel estimated the fair value of its intangible assets that are also associated with the Wireless segment. Data for Sprint Nextel's FCC licenses and customer relationships are given below. (*Note*: For this analysis, assume that book value approximates fair value for the "other definite-lived intangibles" and "other assets" reported for the Wireless segment.)

FCC Licenses

Sprint Nextel owns a number of FCC licenses. These licenses are essential to Sprint Nextel. The company wrote the following in its 2007 annual report: "We hold several kinds of FCC licenses to deploy our wireless services: 1.9 GHz personal communications services, or PCS, licenses utilized in our CDMA network, 800 MHz and 900 MHz licenses utilized in our iDEN network and 2.5 GHz licenses that we use for first generation wireless Internet access services. We also hold 2.5 GHz, 1.9 GHz and other FCC licenses that we currently do not utilize in our networks or operations. As long as we act within the requirements and constraints of the regulatory authorities, the renewal and extension of our licenses is reasonably certain at minimal cost. FCC licenses authorize wireless carriers to use radio frequency spectrum. That spectrum is a renewable, reusable resource that does not deplete or exhaust over time. We are not aware of any technology being developed that would render spectrum obsolete. Currently, there are no changes in the competitive or legislative environments that would put in question the future need for spectrum licenses."

One way to estimate the fair value of Sprint Nextel's FCC licenses is the "relief-from-royalty" approach. This method uses market royalty rates charged for the use of licenses similar to those owned by Sprint Nextel. Using this approach, the fair value of the licenses is the present value of the after-tax royalties that Sprint Nextel is avoiding by owning the licenses.

Of course, a key variable in this analysis is the royalty rate. A search in a proprietary royalty rate database revealed rates ranging from 2% to 8% with an average of 4.2%. The royalty is based on revenue, before the subtraction of any expenses.

Another key variable in the analysis is the average revenue per user, or ARPU. Sprint Nextel reports in its 2007 10-K filing that its ARPU for the fourth quarter of 2007 was $58 per month, down from $63 per month in the fourth quarter of 2005. Because of brisk competition among wireless service providers, Sprint Nextel expects ARPU to continue to decrease.

A summary of the data used in the relief-from-royalty valuation analysis is as follows:

Royalty rate	4.2%
Beginning monthly ARPU	$58
ARPU annual growth rate	–1.0%
Number of customers, 12/31/2007 (in thousands)	40,751
Income tax rate	38%
For the next five years:	
Annual growth rate in number of customers	13.0%
Terminal growth rate (after five years)	6.0%

Customer Relationships

As of December 31, 2007, Sprint Nextel had almost 41 million wireless customers. These customers represent an existing base of users that will continue to generate cash flows in the future. Assuming no new customers and normal attrition among these existing customers, the discounted present value of these after-tax cash flows, after removing a reasonable return on other assets employed, represents an estimate of the fair value of the customer relationships as of December 31, 2007.

A key variable in the value of the existing customer relationships is Sprint Nextel's normal monthly "churn rate," which is the percentage of customers who leave the company in a normal month. In its 2007 10-K filing, Sprint Nextel disclosed that its churn rate in the fourth quarter of 2007 was 2.3%. This rate has been fairly stable for the past three years, ranging from a high of 2.5% in the first quarter of 2005 to a low of 2.0% in the second quarter of 2007.

Another important factor in valuing Sprint Nextel's wireless customer relationships is the contribution margin associated with wireless revenue. Defining variable cost as the "cost of services and products" reported in Sprint Nextel's income statement, the overall company contribution margin percentage was 56.4% in 2005, 59.1% in 2006, and 57.2% in 2007. For the valuation analysis, a weighted average of the 2006 and 2007 percentages is used, with the 2007 percentage being given double weight. This weighted average contribution margin percentage is 57.8%.

To isolate the value associated with the customer relationships, it is necessary to subtract an estimate of the income generated by identifiable other assets. These assets include both the reported assets (less goodwill) of the Wireless segment of $58,190 ($88,854 – $30,664) plus the fair value in excess of book value of any of the recorded assets. The rate of return is the company's weighted average cost of capital.

A summary of the data used in the customer relationship valuation analysis is as follows:

Monthly churn rate	2.3%
Beginning monthly ARPU	$58
ARPU annual growth rate	–1.0%
Variable cost as a percent of revenue	42.2%
Income tax rate	38%

(*Note*: In this customer relationship valuation analysis, the economic life of the relationship is assumed to extend as far into the future as the excess cash flows are positive. With a monthly churn rate of 2.3%, this will probably be three or four years.)

Questions

1. Before any impairment write-down, the net recorded amount of Sprint Nextel's Wireless segment property, plant, and equipment as of December 31, 2007, is $22,882. Is the Wireless segment's property, plant, and equipment impaired? If so, what is the amount of any necessary impairment write-down?
2. Before any impairment write-down, the net recorded amount of Sprint Nextel's goodwill as of December 31, 2007, is $30,664. Is Sprint Nextel's goodwill impaired? If so, what is the amount of any necessary impairment write-down?
3. With respect to the Wireless segment's long-lived assets (tangible and intangible) described in the data given above, what Topic 820 fair value disclosures are necessary for the year ended December 31, 2007?
4. Refer to Question 1. How will your answer change if the discount rate you use is *increased* by 0.5% (50 basis points)? *Decreased* by 0.5%? Comment.
5. Refer to Question 2. How will your answer change if the discount rate you use is *increased* by 0.5% (50 basis points)? *Decreased* by 0.5%? Comment.
6. In conducting the goodwill impairment analysis, you used several different valuation techniques.

   - Wireless segment valuation using price-to-sales and price-to-EBITDA data for the Wireline segment
   - Wireless segment valuation using discounted cash flow analysis
   - FCC license valuation using a "relief-from-royalty" approach
   - Customer relationship valuation using discounted cash flow analysis

   Which one of these valuation techniques seems most reliable to you? Explain.

Case FV-11

Asset Values[2]

"Industry Shakeup Creates 3 Telecom Giants," ***China Daily*****, 25 May 2008**

In a brave industry shake-up, Beijing has ordered its six telecom companies to merge assets and create three hi-tech conglomerates that will compete with each other to offer fixed, mobile, broadband, and future telecom services. The overhaul is expected to have a long-lasting effect on a massive and rapidly growing market. China, with 1.3 billion people, is already the world leader in mobile phone and Internet users. The central government will issue three third-generation wireless licenses to the three mega companies after the overhaul is completed, sources told **chinadaily.com.cn**.

Under the plan revealed by Beijing over the weekend, the parent of **China Telecom Corporation** will buy a mobile phone network from **China Unicom Ltd**'s parent, which in turn will merge with the company that controls **China Netcom Corporation**. Industry analysts said that the reform will help China Telecom and China Netcom expand their operations to compete against **China Mobile Ltd**. The $105 billion industry has room to expand because six out of 10 people still don't own mobile phones and 82% of the population lacks Web connections. The reform is designed to foster "healthy market competition and prevent a monopoly by any," according to a joint statement, issued by the Ministry of Information Industry, Ministry of Finance, and the National Development and Reform Commission.

China Mobile Communications Corp., the state-owned parent of China Mobile Ltd., which is listed in Hong Kong, will take control of fixed-line operator **China Tietong Telecommunications Corporation**. China Telecom, China's biggest fixed-line company, will acquire Unicom's smaller mobile phone network, which provides services to 43 million customers based on the code-division multiple access technology used in Japan and South Korea. China Telecom will also get **China Satellite Communications Corporation**'s phone assets.

[2] Prepared by Professor Earl K. Stice with the cooperation of the School of Accountancy at The Chinese University of Hong Kong.

China Network Communications Corporation will merge with Unicom's parent to offer fixed-line and mobile-phone services based on the global system for mobile communications technology that is used in most of the world. Unicom had 125.4 million GSM customers as of the end of April, according to the company. Netcom, the nation's second-largest fixed-line company, had 108 million phone users.

China Mobile, which accounts for more than two-thirds of the nation's mobile phone users as customers, will take control of unlisted Tietong. Tietong, which means "railway telecom" in Chinese, had assets of 55.3 billion yuan as of the end of 2006. China Mobile, with 399.6 million customers as of April 30, posted a profit of 87.1 billion yuan last year. The company's dominance of China's wireless market helped its stock triple in the past two years, overtaking **General Electric** and **Microsoft** to become the world's fourth-largest company by market value.

Chinese regulators aim to boost competitiveness at fixed-line operators before the nation rolls out 3G high-speed wireless services, which will require billions of dollars in investments for network equipment. The government has said it plans to offer 3G during the Olympic Games in August. China had 583.5 million mobile phone users at the end of April, exceeding the combined populations of the United States and Japan.

Brief History of the Telecommunications Industry in China

When the People's Republic of China was proclaimed on October 1, 1949, the condition of the telecommunications system in China was primitive. Much of the pre-existing infrastructure had been destroyed during World War II and its aftermath. The first priority was to establish telephone lines linking Beijing with the large cities in China and then with the provincial capitals.[3] For many years, telecommunications services in China were provided through a government monopoly, China Telecom. In 1994, the Ministry of Information Industry (then called the Ministry of Electronic Industry) established China Unicom to provide paging and mobile phone services, with China Telecom maintaining its monopoly over fixed-line service. In 1999, China Telecom was split into three pieces: China Telecom which would continue with the monopoly fixed-line system, China Mobile to compete with China Unicom in the mobile phone sector, and China Satcom to offer satellite communications service. Then in 2002, the Chinese government split the monopoly fixed-line operations of China Telecom, creating China Netcom out of the fixed-line operations of China's 10 northern provinces (30% of the fixed-line network). China Telecom continued to operate fixed-line service in China's 21 southern provinces (70% of the fixed-line network). In the middle of all of this, in 2000, China Tietong was created out of the far-flung railway communications system in China.[4]

Mobile Phone Technology

There are three common digital wireless technologies used around the world: GSM, CDMA, and iDEN. These different technologies vary based on, among other things, how they deal with the technical challenge of transmitting several calls at once. GSM (which was developed in Europe; the "GSM" stands for Groupe Spécial Mobile) is by far the most common mobile phone technology used worldwide. In the United States, GSM is used by **AT&T** and **T-Mobile**; GSM is also the technology used by China Mobile. CDMA (which stands for code division multiple access) is used in the United States by **Verizon** and by **Sprint**. In China, China Unicom uses both GSM (74% of its subscribers) and CDMA (26% of its subscribers). iDEN (integrated digital enhanced network) was developed by **Motorola** and

[3] See the Wikipedia entry for "Communications in the People's Republic of China" at **http://en.wikipedia.org/wiki/Communications_in_the_People%27s_Republic_of_China**.

[4] In the United States, Sprint was formed from the combination of several companies including a company that made wireless transmissions using the track right-of-way communication system of the **Southern Pacific Railroad**.

has been used for years by **Nextel**. These three technologies are mutually incompatible, so a cellular phone built to use CDMA doesn't work with a network designed around GSM.

Summary Data for 2007

Summary performance data for the four publicly traded China telecommunications companies are given below. China Satcom and China Tietong are not publicly traded, so financial accounting data are not available.

	December 31, 2007	Fiscal 2007	Fiscal 2007	Fiscal 2007	Fiscal 2007	December 2007	December 2007
(billions of RMB)	Market Capitalization	Sales	Operating Profit	EBITDA	Net Income	Lines/ Subscribers (millions)	State Ownership
China Mobile	2,523.4	357.0	124.1	194.0	87.1	369.3	74.3%
China Telecom	466.6	178.7	37.0	89.3	23.7	256.0	70.9%
China Unicom	220.2	99.5	10.3	32.4	9.3	162.5	48.3%
China Netcom	141.9	84.0	18.6	41.2	12.1	130.6	74.1%

Terms of the Restructuring

On June 2, 2008, the following terms were released regarding the China telecommunications restructuring announced on May 25:

- China Unicom would acquire China Netcom for 165 billion yuan. This acquisition would be accomplished through a swap of 1.508 China Unicom shares for each China Netcom share.
- China Telecom would buy China Unicom's CDMA network and operations for 110 billion yuan. China Unicom had 42 million CDMA subscribers as of December 31, 2007. During 2007, China Unicom's CDMA business generated net income (after tax) of 0.8 billion yuan on total sales of 27.7 billion yuan.

Recording the Unicom/Netcom Business Combination

A crucial accounting issue regarding the acquisition of China Netcom by China Unicom is determining the amounts at which the acquired assets and liabilities of China Netcom will be initially recorded in the books of China Unicom. According to *IFRS 3* as well as FASB ASC Topic 805 (Business Combinations), acquired assets and liabilities are to be recognized in the books of the acquiring company at their fair values.

As of December 31, 2007, the recorded assets and liabilities of China Netcom are as follows (in millions of yuan):

Cash	5,395
Accounts receivable	8,458
Inventories	287
Prepayments	1,021
Due from holding companies	347
Fixed assets	156,948
Construction in progress	3,990
Lease prepayments	2,494
Intangible assets	1,552
Deferred tax assets	2,693
Other noncurrent assets	3,243
Total assets	186,428
Total liabilities	104,376

For simplicity, assume that the fair value of all recorded assets and liabilities of China Netcom is equal to their December 31, 2007, balance sheet value EXCEPT for the following:

- Accounts receivable
- Fixed assets
- Intangible assets

Detailed data for use in determining the fair values of these three asset categories are given below.

> Disclaimer: The detailed data presented below are generally consistent with telecommunication company valuation practices. However, they are hypothetical and almost certainly bear only a general resemblance to the actual data that China Unicom may use in estimating the fair values of the assets, both tangible and intangible, it acquires in the combination with China Netcom.

Valuation Analysis of Accounts Receivable
There is some evidence that the net carrying amount for accounts receivable as reported in the December 31, 2007, balance sheet may overstate the fair value of the receivables. A detailed aging analysis of the accounts receivable is as follows:

	Amount	Uncollectible Estimate
0–30 days	3,546	1.0%
31–60 days	1,639	3.0%
61–90 days	1,363	15.0%
91–150 days	1,763	40.0%
Over 150 days	1,545	80.0%
Total	9,856	

Valuation Analysis of Fixed Assets
China Netcom purchases, rather than leases, the large majority of its fixed assets. However, there exists an active worldwide market for the leasing of telecommunications network equipment. In addition, there are markets in China for the leasing of both buildings and office furniture and equipment. Estimated annual lease payments for the fixed assets currently being used by China Netcom are as follows:

(in millions of RMB)	Estimated Annual Lease Payment
Buildings	2,670
Telecom networks and equipment	25,780
Furniture and other equipment	2,130

In the notes to its financial statements, China Netcom discloses the following with respect to the estimated useful lives of its fixed assets:

Buildings	8 to 30 years
Telecommunications networks and equipment	5 to 10 years
Furniture, fixture, motor vehicles and other equipment	5 to 10 years

Valuation Analysis of Intangible Assets
China Netcom has recorded intangible assets with a book value of 1.552 billion yuan. Assume that this recorded amount is equal to the fair value of these recorded intangibles. China Netcom also has important unrecorded intangibles, as explained below.

Licenses
In its 2007 20-F filing with the Securities and Exchange Commission (SEC) in the United States, China Netcom explained the regulatory restrictions under which it operates. "The Group's operations are subject to the supervision of and regulation by the PRC Government. The Ministry of Information Industry (MII), pursuant to the authority delegated by the PRC's State Council, is responsible for formulating the policies and regulations for the telecommunications industry in China, including granting licenses, allocating frequency spectrum, formulating interconnection and settlement arrangements between telecommunications operators, enforcing industry regulations and reviewing tariffs for domestic services." The licenses granted by the MII are essential to China Netcom. The company wrote the following in its 20-F filing: "If these approvals or licenses were revoked or suspended, our business and operations would be materially and adversely affected." In summary, among the most valuable economic assets of China Netcom are the operating licenses it holds to offer fixed-line telephone services. However, because these licenses were acquired at zero or only nominal cost, their value is not reflected in China Netcom's 2007 balance sheet.

One way to estimate the fair value of China Netcom's operating licenses is the "relief-from-royalty" approach. This method uses market royalty rates charged for the use of licenses similar to those held by China Netcom. Using this approach, the fair value of the licenses is the present value of the after-tax royalties that China Netcom is avoiding by holding the licenses.

Of course, a key variable in this analysis is the royalty rate. A search in a proprietary royalty rate database revealed rates ranging from 2% to 8%, with an average of 4.2%. The royalty is based on revenue, before the subtraction of any expenses.

Another key variable in the analysis is the average revenue per user, or ARPU, which is a common measure in the telecommunications industry. China Netcom had a *monthly* ARPU of ¥53.6, down from ¥54.6 in 2006. This decrease represents the offsetting effects of an increase from a shift from fixed-line to broadband customers and a decrease from an overall, worldwide decline in telecommunications prices to consumers. China Netcom expects these trends to continue into the foreseeable future (i.e., the next five years). However, total users (fixed-line plus broadband) increased slightly from 128.4 million at the end of 2006 to 130.6 million at the end of 2007; this slightly increasing trend is also expected to continue as customers continue to switch away from fixed-line phones to mobile phones but as the number of broadband customers increases.

A summary of the data to be used in the relief-from-royalty valuation analysis is as follows:

Discount rate	10.0%
Royalty rate	4.2%
Beginning monthly ARPU	¥53.6
ARPU annual growth rate	–1.8%
Dec. 31, 2007 lines/subscribers (millions)	130.6
Income tax rate	25%
For the next five years:	
Annual growth rate in number of customers	1.7%
Terminal growth rate (after five years)	0.0%

Customer Relationships
As of December 31, 2007, China Netcom had 110.8 million fixed-line customers (this established customer relationship analysis ignores the 19.8 million relatively new

broadband customers). These fixed-line customers represent an existing base of users that will continue to generate cash flows in the future. Assuming no new customers and normal attrition among these existing customers as these customers continue to migrate from fixed-line to mobile phones, the discounted present value of these after-tax cash flows, after removing a reasonable return on other assets employed, represents an estimate of the fair value of the customer relationships as of December 31, 2007.

A key variable in the value of the existing customer relationships is China Netcom's normal "churn rate," which is the percentage of fixed-line customers who leave the company. It is estimated that China Netcom's annual churn rate is 15.0%. This rate is expected to continue for the foreseeable future.

Another important factor in valuing China Netcom's fixed-line customer relationships is the contribution margin associated with fixed-line revenue. Fixed-line revenue totaled 59.2 billion yuan in 2007. Variable cost was 46% of revenue.

To isolate the value associated with customer relationships, it is necessary to subtract an estimate of the income generated by identifiable other assets. These assets include both the reported assets of China Netcom of 186.4 billion yuan plus the fair value in excess of book value of any of the recorded assets plus the fair value of any unrecorded intangibles such as licenses. For simplicity, the rate of the return is assumed to be 10%.

A summary of the data used in the customer relationship valuation analysis is as follows:

Discount rate	10.0%
Annual churn rate	–15.0%
Beginning monthly ARPU	¥53.6
ARPU annual growth rate	–1.8%
Variable cost as a percent of revenue	46.0%
Income tax rate	25%

(*Note*: In this customer relationship valuation analysis, because of the volatile nature of the telecommunications industry, the economic life of the existing fixed-line relationships is assumed to be three years.)

Questions

1. Briefly outline the effect of the China telecommunications industry restructuring announced in May 2008. In particular, explain how this restructuring will condense six companies into three, and list the business segments that will end up in each of the remaining three.
2. How will this restructuring into three mega-companies foster "healthy market competition and prevent a monopoly by any"?
3. For each of the four Chinese telecommunications companies with publicly available data, compute price-to-sales, price-to-EBITDA, and price-to-earnings ratios as of December 31, 2007. Also compute the market capitalization per subscriber. Comment.
4. Discuss why fixed-line subscribers and profits have different valuation multiples than do mobile phone subscribers and profits.
5. Evaluate the 165 billion yuan price tag for the acquisition of China Netcom by China Unicom. Do you think the price is too high or too low? Defend your answer.
6. Evaluate the 110 billion yuan price tag for the purchase of China Unicom's CDMA network and operations by China Telecom. Do you think China Telecom is paying too much or too little? Defend your answer.
7. What evidence would a company use to generate the type of uncollectible accounts percentages given in the case? Given those percentages, what is the fair value of China Netcom's accounts receivable? Ignore the time value of money.

8. Using the lease payment data in the case material, estimate the fair value of each of China Netcom's three fixed asset categories. For simplicity, assume that the appropriate discount rate to use in computing the fair value of the fixed assets is 10% for each of the asset categories.
9. Estimate the fair value of China Netcom's operating licenses.
10. Estimate the fair value of China Netcom's fixed-line customer relationships.
11. Compute the amount of goodwill that China Unicom should recognize when it records the acquisition of China Netcom.

P2 ROUTINE ACTIVITIES OF A BUSINESS

CHAPTER 7 THE REVENUE/RECEIVABLES/ CASH CYCLE

LEARNING OBJECTIVES

1. Explain the normal operating cycle of a business.
2. Prepare journal entries to record sales revenue, including the accounting for bad debts and warranties for service or replacement.
3. Analyze accounts receivable to measure how efficiently a firm is using this operating asset.
4. Discuss the composition, management, and control of cash, including the use of a bank reconciliation.
5. Recognize appropriate disclosures for presenting sales and receivables in the financial statements.

EM EXPANDED MATERIAL

6. Explain how receivables may be used as a source of cash through secured borrowing or sale.
7. Describe proper accounting and valuation of notes receivable.
8. Understand the impact of uncollectible accounts on the statement of cash flows.

A. P. Giannini was born in 1870 in San Jose, California. When Giannini was seven, his father was killed. His mother remarried, and the family moved to San Francisco where Giannini's stepfather started a fruit wholesaling business. Giannini worked full-time in the business and by age 19 was made a junior partner in what was by then the most successful fruit wholesaling firm on the West Coast. He invested his profits in San Francisco real estate and by age 31 was financially secure enough to retire.

Giannini's retirement was an active one. He continued to manage his real estate portfolio, and he was a member of the board of directors of **Columbus Savings & Loan Association**, which was San Francisco's first Italian-owned bank. In spite of its immigrant roots, Columbus Savings followed the practice of the other area banks, lending only a portion of the deposits it took in to a few large local businesses and sending the rest to the money center banks in New York and Chicago. Giannini was disturbed to see that the farmers, merchants, and workers he was accustomed

AP Photo/Chuck Burton

to dealing with were not able to get loans. When he was unable to get Columbus to change the policy, he quit the board and vowed to start his own bank. On October 17, 1904, A. P. Giannini, a man with no prior experience as a banker, embarked on a second career by opening the Bank of Italy in a converted saloon in San Francisco.

By April 1906, Giannini's bank was still an obscure little bank in the Italian section of town. On the morning of April 18, 1906, San Francisco was rocked by the worst earthquake in its history. About one-third of the town was destroyed, and 500 people were killed. In the quake's aftermath, many local business and civic leaders advocated a slow rebuilding, with a moratorium on all building loans for six months. Giannini disagreed strongly: "Gentlemen, you are making a vital mistake. The time for doing business is right now. Tomorrow morning I am putting a desk on Washington Street wharf with a Bank of Italy sign over it. Any man who wants to rebuild San Francisco can come there and get as much cash as he needs to do it."

Giannini's little bank would eventually grow to become one of the largest banks in the world—**Bank of America**. As of December 31, 2009, Bank of America reported total assets exceeding $2.2 trillion, making it the largest commercial bank in the United States in terms of assets (although only the fifth largest worldwide). Bank of America's largest asset is its loan portfolio, which totals $863 billion; Bank of America's loan portfolio alone is almost four times as large as **ExxonMobil**'s entire asset base (at $233 billion). As you can imagine, with a loan portfolio of this size, Bank of America is continually dealing with customers who don't pay. In 2009, Bank of America recognized an expense of $48.6 billion for loans that it does not expect its customers to repay.

QUESTIONS

1. What do you think is a bank's largest revenue category? Its largest expense category?
2. Loans made by banks can be lumped into two general categories: consumer loans and commercial, or business, loans. Bank of America had total loans outstanding of $863 billion as of the end of 2009. Do you think most of these loans were to individuals (consumer loans) or to businesses (commercial loans)?
3. Bank of America reports a "net charge-off ratio" for each major loan category. This ratio is computed as the amount of loans in a category that were written off during the year, divided by the average daily loan balance in that category during the year. The four largest categories of consumer loans for Bank of America in 2009 were residential mortgages, home equity loans, direct/indirect consumer loans, and domestic credit cards. Which one of these four loan categories do you think had the lowest net charge-off ratio? The highest net charge-off ratio?

Answers to these questions can be found on page 7-41.

Our discussion of the income statement in Chapter 4 focused our attention on the importance of net income in the decisions made by investors and creditors. In this and the subsequent chapter, we focus on the event that begins the income-producing process—the sale. Because the financial statements are interrelated, a study of the sale contained in the income statement is also a study of the resulting accounts receivable and/or cash contained in the balance sheet.

Exhibit 7-1 illustrates the time line associated with the revenue/receivables/cash cycle. The chapter will begin with a discussion of the events relating to this time line. We will first discuss the journal entries that result from the sale of goods or services. With this

EX 7-1 REVENUE/RECEIVABLES/CASH TIME LINE

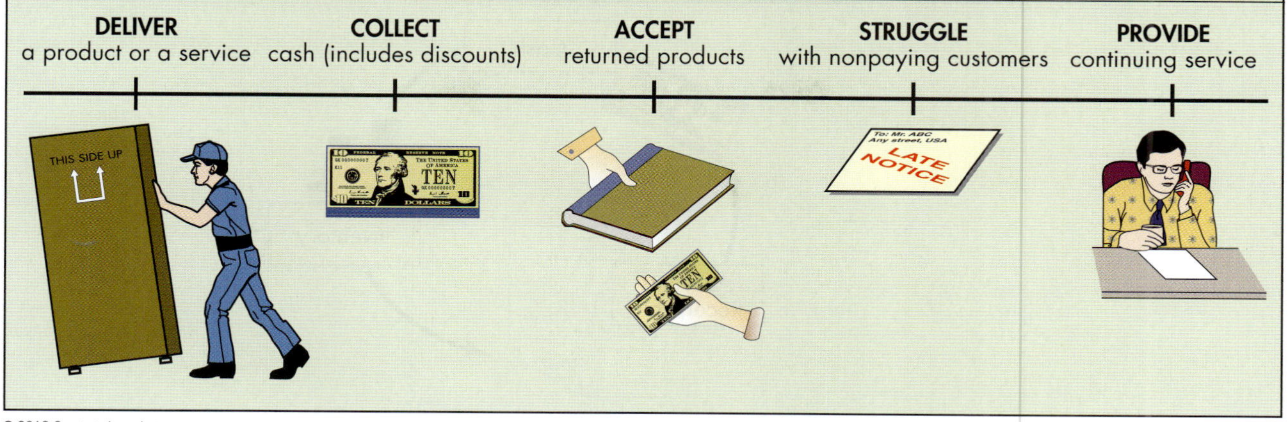

background, we then introduce additional complexities associated with sales—sales discounts, sales returns and allowances, bad debts, and warranties—and their effect on the financial statements. As illustrated by the large amount of bad debt expense recognized by Bank of America in 2009, proper recognition of revenues and the valuation of receivables can have a very significant impact on the financial statements.

Once we discuss the events relating to the revenue/receivables/cash cycle, we also present and discuss methods for monitoring accounts receivable, cash management and control, and the presentation of sales, receivables, and cash on the financial statements. In the Expanded Material section of this chapter, we discuss how receivables can be used as a source of cash. The chapter concludes with a discussion of the impact of bad debt expense on computing cash flows from operations. Chapter 8 contains a further discussion of the important issues surrounding revenue recognition.

The Operating Cycle of a Business

1 Explain the normal operating cycle of a business.

WHY **Because the operating cycle is the lifeblood of every business, understanding a company's operating cycle is the first step in appropriately accounting for the company's operations.**

HOW **The sale of goods or services results in the receipt of cash and/or the recording of an account receivable. The account receivable is then collected, the resulting cash is reinvested in the business, and the operating cycle begins again.**

The normal operating cycle of a business involves purchasing inventory (using either cash or credit), which is then sold, often on account. Once the receivable is collected, the cycle begins again. This cycle, illustrated in Exhibit 7-2, continually repeats itself and is the lifeblood of any business enterprise. An understanding of this operating cycle (which involves the recognition of revenue, the recording of a receivable, and the subsequent collection of cash) is critical if you

FYI

When a company accepts another company's credit card (such as Visa, MasterCard, and American Express) as payment, the credit card company charges a service fee. This fee is recognized as an expense by the seller.

EX 7-2 THE OPERATING CYCLE

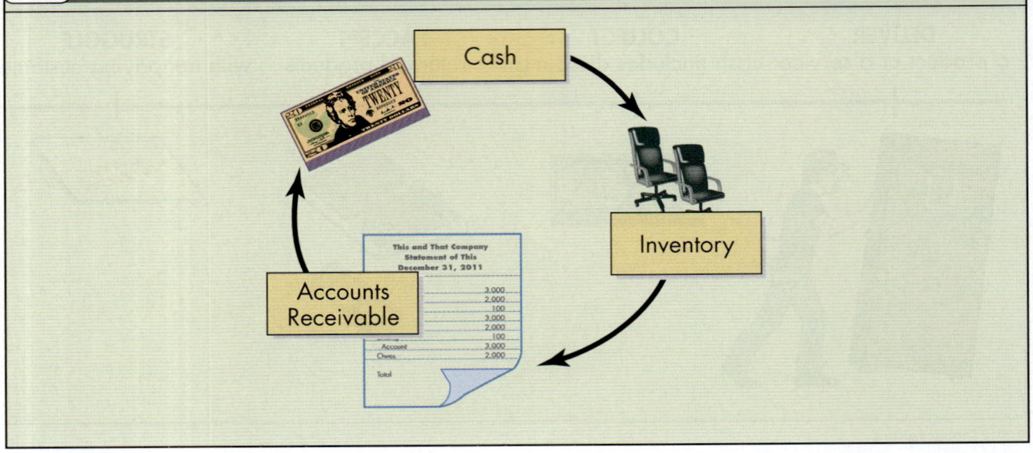

are to understand how businesses operate and the role of accounting information in that business. Thus, we begin our detailed discussion of accounting with a look at the revenue/receivables/cash cycle.

The recognition of revenue is generally related to the recognition of accounts receivable. Because revenues are generally recorded when the earning process is complete and a valid promise of payment (or payment itself) is received, it follows that a receivable arising from the sale of goods is generally recognized when title to the goods passes to a bona fide buyer. The point at which title passes may vary with the terms of the sale; therefore, it is normal practice to recognize the receivable when goods are shipped to the customer. It is at this point in time that the revenue recognition criteria are normally satisfied. Revenue should not be recognized for goods shipped on approval when the shipper retains title until there is a formal acceptance, or for goods shipped on consignment when the shipper retains title until the goods are sold by the consignee. Receivables for services to customers are properly recognized when the services are performed. It is worth again mentioning that the complexities of revenue recognition (and there are many) are discussed in Chapter 8.

The entry for recognizing revenue and a receivable from the sale of goods or services is as follows:

Accounts Receivable	xx	
Sales		xx

When the amount is collected, Accounts Receivable is credited, and Cash is debited as follows:

Cash	xx	
Accounts Receivable		xx

For department stores and major oil and gas companies that have their own credit cards, a significant portion of revenues arises from sales using these credit cards. For example, **Target** has both a Target credit card and a Target Visa card (although as of April 2010, all new cards issued are Target cards). By maintaining its own credit card, Target makes money both from its store operations as well as financial income from its credit card receivables portfolio.

Before we move on and introduce some additional aspects of sales, let's take a moment and discuss the different types of receivables that are typical. In its broadest sense, the term *receivables* is applicable to all claims against others for money, goods, or services. For accounting purposes, however, the term is generally employed in a narrower sense to designate claims expected to be settled by the receipt of cash.

STOP&THINK

Consider the question of why a company would sell on account in the first place. In other words, why not just have a policy of "all sales are for cash"? Which ONE of the following is the most reasonable explanation for why companies sell on account?

a) Allowing customers to buy on credit attracts more customers.
b) The creation of accounts receivable allows a company to more precisely manage its asset mix.
c) An excess of cash sales can overwhelm a company's cash management system.
d) State incorporation laws require businesses with more than $100,000 in total assets to allow customers to buy on credit.

In classifying receivables, an important distinction is made between trade and nontrade receivables. Trade receivables, generally the most significant category of receivables, result from the normal operating activities of a business, that is, credit sales of goods or services to customers. Trade receivables may be evidenced by a formal written promise to pay and classified as notes receivable. In most cases, however, trade receivables are unsecured "open accounts," often referred to simply as *accounts receivable*.

Accounts receivable represent an extension of short-term credit to customers. Payments are generally due within 30 to 90 days. The credit arrangements are typically informal agreements between seller and buyer supported by such business documents as invoices, sales orders, and delivery contracts. Normally, trade receivables do not involve interest, although an interest or service charge may be added if payments are not made within a specified period. Trade receivables are the most common type of receivable and are generally the most significant in total dollar amount.

Nontrade receivables include all other types of receivables. They arise from a variety of transactions, such as (1) the sale of securities or property other than inventory, (2) deposits to guarantee contract performance or expense payment, (3) claims for rebates and tax refunds, and (4) dividends and interest receivable. Nontrade receivables should be summarized in appropriately titled accounts and reported separately in the financial statements. Another way of classifying receivables relates to the current or short-term versus noncurrent or long-term nature of receivables. As indicated in Chapter 3, the *current assets* classification, as broadly conceived, includes all receivables identified as collectible within one year or the normal operating cycle, whichever is longer. Thus, for classification purposes, all trade receivables are considered current receivables; each nontrade item requires separate analysis to determine whether it is reasonable to assume that it will be collected within one year. Noncurrent receivables are reported under the

Russell Illig/Photodisc/Getty Images

Companies must pay a fee for accepting another company's credit card. What do you think this fee is for?

Investments or Other Noncurrent Assets caption or as a separate item with an appropriate description.

In summary, receivables are classified in various ways, for example, as accounts or notes receivable, as trade or nontrade receivables, and as current or noncurrent receivables. These categories are not mutually exclusive. For example, accounts receivable are trade receivables and are current; notes receivable may be trade receivables and therefore current in some circumstances, but they may be nontrade receivables, either current or noncurrent, in other situations. The classifications used most often in practice and throughout this book will be simply *accounts receivable*, *notes receivable*, and *other receivables*.

Accounting for Sales Revenue

2 Prepare journal entries to record sales revenue, including the accounting for bad debts and warranties for service or replacement.

WHY Once a sale is recorded, the matching principle requires that expenses associated with the sale, such as estimated bad debt and warranty expenses, be recorded in the period of the sale.

HOW Bad debts are estimated using one of two methods: percentage of sales or percentage of receivables. Each of these methods involves estimating the likelihood that some receivables will not be collected. The warranty obligation is quantified by estimating, based on past experience, the probable amount of future warranty costs; this amount is recognized as an expense in the period of the associated sale.

The amount of sales or revenues is always the largest item on the income statement (if it's not, the company has bigger problems to worry about than how to account for transactions), and accounts receivable is typically one of the largest current assets on a company's balance sheet. The large magnitude of these two account balances should not, however, cause us to overlook some additional aspects of sales transactions. Although these items are significantly smaller when compared to sales and receivables, knowledge of them is critical in properly accounting for the transactions of a company. The items we will examine in this section include the following:

- *Discounts*—Discounts are offered at the time of the sale or at the time of payment.
- *Sales Returns and Allowances*—Returns and allowances occur subsequent to the sale and can occur before or after payment has been made.
- *Accounting for Bad Debts*—Once a credit sale is made, the issue of collection remains. Bad debts must be estimated in any period in which credit sales are made or accounts receivable are outstanding.
- *Warranties for Service or Replacement*—Long after a sale occurs and collection is made, a warranty period associated with that sale may still be in place.

Discounts

Many companies bill their customers at a gross sales price less an amount designated as a trade discount. The discount may vary by customer, depending on the volume of business or size of order from the customer. In effect, the trade discount reduces the *list* sales price to the *net* sales price actually charged the customer. This net price is the amount at which the receivable and corresponding revenue should be recorded; the list price is merely the starting point in the price negotiation between buyer and seller.

Another type of discount is a cash (sales) discount offered to customers by some companies to encourage prompt payment of bills. Cash discounts may be taken by the customer only if payment is made within a specified period of time, generally 30 days or less. Receivables are generally recorded at their gross amounts, without regard to any cash discount offered. If payment is received within the discount period, Sales Discounts (a contra account to Sales) is debited for the difference between the recorded amount of the receivable and the total cash collected. This method (called the *gross method*), which is simple and widely used, is illustrated as follows with credit terms of 2/10, n/30 (2% discount if paid within 10 days, net amount due in 30 days).

Cash (Sales) Discounts—Gross Method

Sales of $1,000; terms 2/10, n/30:		
Accounts Receivable	1,000	
Sales		1,000
Partial payment of $300, received within discount period:		
Cash	294	
Sales Discounts	6	
Accounts Receivable		300
Payment of the remaining $700, received after discount period:		
Cash	700	
Accounts Receivable		700

The net method of accounting for sales discounts records the sale and the receivable net of the discount. Using the preceding example, the receivable and the sale would be recorded at $980 ($1,000 × 0.98). If payment is not made within the discount period, the additional amount paid by the customer through failure to take the sales discount would be recorded in a revenue account. Illustrations of the journal entries using the net method follow.

Cash (Sales) Discounts—Net Method

Sales of $1,000; terms 2/10, n/30:		
Accounts Receivable	980	
Sales		980
Partial payment of $294, received within discount period:		
Cash	294	
Accounts Receivable		294
Payment of the remaining $700, received after discount period:		
Cash	700	
Sales Discounts Not Taken		14
Accounts Receivable ($700 × 0.98)		686

Sales Returns and Allowances

In the normal course of business, some goods will be returned by customers and some allowance will have to be made for factors such as goods damaged during shipment,

FYI

Contra accounts are used because they often yield valuable information. For example, suppose Firm A and Firm B both have net sales of $10,000. Firm A has gross sales of $1,000,000 and sales returns of $990,000. Firm B has gross sales of $10,000 and no sales returns. Might this information affect decisions made about these two firms?

spoiled or otherwise defective goods, or shipment of an incorrect quantity or type of goods. When an allowance is necessary, net sales and accounts receivable are reduced. To illustrate, assume that red sweaters costing $600 are sold to a customer for $1,000. The customer calls and states that green sweaters were ordered and should have been shipped. Rather than return the sweaters, the customer agrees to keep the sweaters in return for a reduction in the price—an allowance—of $200. The entry to record this sales allowance is as follows:

Sales Returns and Allowances	200	
Accounts Receivable		200

Although the debit could be made directly to Sales, reducing the Sales amount, the use of a separate contra account preserves the information about the original amount of Sales. Knowledge of the amount of Sales Returns and Allowances relative to total Sales may be useful to management.

Suppose that instead of an allowance, the customer elects to return the sweaters. The return is recorded as follows:

Sales Returns and Allowances	1,000	
Accounts Receivable		1,000
Inventory	600	
Cost of Goods Sold		600

As will be discussed in Chapter 9, management must ensure that inventory is not recorded in the books at more than its current value. This lower-of-cost-or-market test is especially important for damaged inventory, as is often the case with returned inventory.

The Valuation of Accounts Receivable–Accounting for Bad Debts

Theoretically, all receivables should be valued at an amount representing the present value of the expected future cash receipts. Because accounts receivable are short term, usually being collected within 30 to 90 days, the amount of interest is small relative to the amount of the receivable. Consequently, the accounting profession has chosen to ignore the interest element for these trade receivables.[1]

Instead of valuing accounts receivable at a discounted present value, they are reported at their net realizable value, that is, their expected cash value. This means that accounts receivable should be recorded net of estimated uncollectible items. The objective is to report the receivables at the amount actually expected to be collected in cash.

Uncollectible Accounts Receivable Invariably, some receivables will prove uncollectible. The simplest method for recognizing the loss from these uncollectible accounts is to debit an expense account, such as Doubtful Accounts Expense, Bad Debt Expense, or Uncollectible Accounts Expense, and credit Accounts Receivable at the time it is determined

[1] FASB ASC paragraph 835-30-15-3(a).

that an account cannot be collected. This approach is called the direct write-off method and is often used by small businesses because of its simplicity. Although the recognition of uncollectibles in the period of their discovery is simple and convenient, this method does not provide for the matching of expenses with current revenues and does not report receivables at their net realizable value. Therefore, use of the direct write-off method is not allowed under generally accepted accounting principles. The following sections describe the procedures used in estimating uncollectibles with the allowance method, which is required by GAAP.[2]

FYI

The direct write-off method of accounting for bad debts is the method required by the IRS in most cases when computing taxable income.

Establishing an allowance for bad debts. When using the allowance method, the amount of receivables estimated to be uncollectible is recorded by a debit to Bad Debt Expense and a credit to Allowance for Bad Debts. The terminology for these account titles may vary somewhat. For example, other possibilities for Allowance for Bad Debts include Allowance for Uncollectible Accounts and Allowance for Doubtful Accounts. The expense account title usually is consistent with that of the allowance account.

The allowance for bad debts account is a contra asset account that is offset against Accounts Receivable, resulting in the Accounts Receivable balance being reported at its net realizable value. The credit side of the allowance account represents estimated future uncollectible accounts. The debit side of the account reflects verified uncollectible accounts. If a large credit balance builds up in the account over time, this indicates that estimated bad debts are running higher than actual bad debts and that the estimation technique being used may need to be revised.

A typical entry to recognize bad debt expense, normally made as an end-of-the-period adjustment, is as follows:

Bad Debt Expense	xx	
Allowance for Bad Debts		xx
To record estimated uncollectible accounts receivable for the period.		

The expense would be reported as a selling or general and administrative expense, and the allowance account would be shown as a deduction from Accounts Receivable, thereby reporting the net realizable amount of the receivables.

Writing off an uncollectible account under the allowance method. When positive evidence is available concerning the partial or complete worthlessness of an account, the account is written off by a debit to the allowance account, which was previously established, and a credit to Accounts Receivable. Positive evidence of a reduction in value is found in the bankruptcy, death, or disappearance of a debtor, failure to enforce collection legally, or barring of collection by the statute of limitations. Write-offs should be supported by evidence of the uncollectibility of the accounts from appropriate parties, such as courts, lawyers, or credit agencies. The entry to write off an uncollectible receivable is as follows:

Allowance for Bad Debts	xx	
Accounts Receivable		xx
To record the write-off of an uncollectible account.		

[2] FASB ASC paragraphs 310-10-35-7 through 9.

Note that no entry is made to Bad Debt Expense at this time. That entry was made when the allowance was established. The expense was thus estimated and recorded in the period when the sale was made, not necessarily in the period when a particular account was verified as being uncollectible.

Occasionally, an account that has been written off as uncollectible is unexpectedly collected. Entries are required to reverse the write-off entry and to record the collection. Assuming an account of $1,500 was written off as uncollectible but was subsequently collected, the following entries would be made at the time of collection.

Accounts Receivable	1,500	
Allowance for Bad Debts		1,500
To reverse the entry made to write off the account.		
Cash	1,500	
Accounts Receivable		1,500
To record collection of the account.		

For many companies, the issue of collection of accounts previously written off is not significant. For companies in some industries, however, it is a multimillion-dollar issue. For example, in 2009, Bank of America recovered $1.8 billion of loans that had been previously written, or charged, off. Exhibit 7-3 provides the note from Bank of America's 2009 10-K filing, which illustrates that over the preceding three years, Bank of America recovered over $4.5 billion in accounts previously charged off.

To summarize using a T-account, the allowance account typically increases (with a credit) as estimates of bad debts are made and recognized as an expense, and decreases (with a debit) as actual bad debts are identified and written off. In addition, the allowance account will increase if accounts that had previously been written off are subsequently recovered; the reason for this increase is that, if the original bad debt estimate was correct, the recovery of one would-be bad debt means that there must still be another bad debt out there somewhere.

Allowance for Bad Debts	
Actual bad debts written off	Estimated bad debt expense
	Recovery of previously written off bad debts

EX 7-3 BANK OF AMERICA'S NOTE DISCLOSURE RELATING TO RECOVERIES

(Dollars in millions)	2009	2008	2007
Allowance for loan and lease losses, January 1	$23,071	$11,588	$ 9,016
Loans and leases charged off	(35,483)	(17,666)	(7,730)
Recoveries of loans and leases previously charged off	1,795	1,435	1,250
Net charge-offs	(33,688)	(16,231)	(6,480)
Provision for loan and lease losses	48,366	26,922	8,357
Write-downs on consumer purchased impaired loans	(179)	n/a	n/a
Other	(370)	792	695
Allowance for loan and lease losses, December 31	$37,200	$23,071	$11,588

FYI

For a firm in a steady state, that is, one that has been in business for a number of years and has a stable level of accounts receivable, bad debt expense estimated on current year's credit sales will be approximately the same as actual write-offs.

Estimating uncollectibles based on percentage of sales. The estimate for uncollectible accounts may be based on sales for the period or the amount of receivables outstanding at the end of the period. When a sales basis is used, the amount of uncollectible accounts in past years relative to total sales provides a percentage of estimated uncollectibles. This percentage may be modified by expectations based on current experience. Because doubtful accounts occur only with credit sales, it is logical to develop a percentage of doubtful accounts based on credit sales of past periods. This percentage is then applied to credit sales of the current period. However, because extra work may be required in maintaining separate records of cash and credit sales or in analyzing sales data, the percentage is frequently developed in terms of total sales. Unless there is considerable periodic fluctuation in the proportion of cash and credit sales, the percentage-of-total-sales method will normally give satisfactory results.

To illustrate, if 2% of sales is considered doubtful in terms of collection and sales for the period are $100,000, the charge for Bad Debt Expense would be 2% of the current period's sales, or $2,000. Note that any existing balance in the allowance account resulting from past period charges to Bad Debt Expense is ignored. The entry for this period is simply as follows:

Bad Debt Expense.	2,000	
Allowance for Bad Debts		2,000
To record estimated bad debt expense for the period ($100,000 × 0.02 = $2,000).		

The percentage-of-sales method for estimating bad debts is widely used in practice because it is simple to apply. Companies often use this method to estimate bad debts periodically during the year and then adjust the allowance account at year-end in relationship to the Accounts Receivable balance, as explained in the next section.

Estimating uncollectibles based on Accounts Receivable balance. Instead of using a percentage of sales to estimate bad debts, companies may base their estimates on a percentage of total accounts receivable outstanding. This method emphasizes the relationship between the Accounts Receivable and the Allowance for Bad Debts balances. For example, if total Accounts Receivable are $50,000 and it is estimated that 3% of those accounts will be uncollectible, the allowance account should have a balance of $1,500 ($50,000 × 0.03). If the allowance account already has a $600 credit balance from prior periods, the current-period adjusting entry is as follows:

Bad Debt Expense.	900	
Allowance for Bad Debts		900
To record estimated bad debt expense for the period ($1,500 required balance − $600 current balance = $900 adjustment).		

After posting this entry, the balance in the allowance account would be $1,500, or 3% of total Accounts Receivable. Note that this method adjusts the existing balance to the desired balance based on a percentage of total receivables outstanding. If, in the example, the allowance account had a $200 debit balance caused by writing off more bad debts than had been estimated previously, the adjusting entry would be for $1,700 in order to bring the allowance account to the desired credit balance of $1,500, or 3% of total receivables.

The most commonly used method for establishing an allowance based on outstanding receivables involves aging receivables. Individual accounts are analyzed to determine those not yet due and those past due. Past-due accounts are classified in terms of the length of the period past due. An analysis sheet used in aging accounts receivable is shown below.

Overdue balances can be evaluated individually to estimate the collectibility of each item as a basis for developing an overall estimate. An alternative procedure is to develop a series of estimated loss percentages and apply these to the different receivables classifications. ICO Products' calculation of the allowance on the latter basis is illustrated below.

ICO Products, Inc.
Analysis of Receivables
December 31, 2013

Customer	Amount	Not Yet	Not More Than 30 Days Past Due	31–60 Days Past Due	61–90 Days Past Due	91–180 Days Past Due	181–365 Days Past Due	More Than One Year Past Due
A. B. Andrews	$ 450			$ 450				
B. T. Brooks	300				$100	$200		
B. Bryant	200		$ 200					
L. B. Devine	2,100	$ 2,100						
K. Martinez	200						$200	
M. A. Young	1,400	1,000		100	300			
Total	$47,550	$40,000	$3,000	$1,200	$650	$500	$800	$1,400

ICO Products, Inc.
Estimated Amount of Uncollectible Accounts
December 31, 2013

Classification	Balances	Uncollectible Accounts Experience Percentage	Accounts Estimated Amount of Uncollectible
Not yet due	$40,000	2%	$ 800
Not more than 30 days past due	3,000	5	150
31–60 days past due	1,200	10	120
61–90 days past due	650	20	130
91–180 days past due	500	30	150
181–365 days past due	800	50	400
More than one year past due	1,400	80	1,120
	$47,550		$2,870

Just as with the previous method based on a percentage of total receivables outstanding, Bad Debt Expense is debited and Allowance for Bad Debts is credited for an amount bringing the allowance account to the required balance. Assuming uncollectibles estimated at $2,870 as shown in the ICO Products calculation and a credit balance of $620 in the allowance account before adjustment, the following entry is made:

Bad Debt Expense	2,250	
Allowance for Bad Debts		2,250
To record bad debt expense for the period ($2,870 required balance − $620 current balance = $2,250 adjustment).		

The aging method provides the most satisfactory approach to the valuation of receivables at their net realizable amounts. Furthermore, data developed through aging receivables may be quite useful to management for purposes of credit analysis and control.

> **CAUTION**
>
> The most common error when computing bad debt expense is to confuse the two methods—percentage of sales and percentage of receivables. Remember that when you are using the percentage-of-sales method, bad debt expense is computed and the balance in the allowance account is then determined. When you are using the percentage-of-receivables method, the balance in the allowance account is computed, and then the amount of bad debt expense for the period is determined.

Corrections to allowance for bad debts. As previously indicated, the Allowance for Bad Debts balance is established and maintained by means of adjusting entries at the close of each accounting period. If the allowance provisions are too large, the allowance account balance will be unnecessarily inflated and earnings and accounts receivable will be understated; if the allowance provisions are too small, the allowance account balance will be inadequate, and both accounts receivable and earnings will be overstated.

Care must be taken to see that the allowance balance follows the credit experience of the particular business. The process of aging receivables at different intervals may be employed as a means of checking the allowance balance to be certain that it is being maintained satisfactorily. Such periodic reviews may indicate a need for a correction in the allowance as well as a change in the rate or in the method employed.

When the uncollectible accounts experience approximates the estimated losses, the allowance procedure may be considered satisfactory, and no adjustment is required. When it appears that there has been a failure to estimate uncollectible accounts accurately, resulting in an allowance balance that is clearly inadequate or excessive, an adjustment is in order. The effect of this change in accounting estimate would be reported in the current and future periods as an ordinary item on the income statement, usually as an addition to or subtraction from Bad Debt Expense.

The actual write-off of receivables as uncollectible by debits to the allowance account and credits to the receivables account may temporarily result in a debit balance in the allowance account. A debit balance arising in this manner does not mean necessarily that the allowance is inadequate; debits to the allowance account simply predate the end-of-period adjustment for uncollectible accounts. Once an adjustment is made, the allowance account will have a credit balance. Think about what it would mean if, after adjustment, the allowance account still had a debit balance—when combined with the balance in Accounts Receivable, it would mean that you expect to receive more than you are owed, which is a very low probability event.

Warranties for Service or Replacement

As you have just read, bad debts must be estimated so that proper expenses can be matched with revenues in the period in which the revenues were earned. The same is true in the case of warranties. Many companies agree to provide free service on units failing to perform

FYI

Many companies that sell items such as electronics or appliances make large amounts of profits by selling *maintenance agreements*. Because of the high profit margins associated with these agreements, salespersons are often given big incentives to sell them. Some consumer magazines have warned readers that these maintenance agreements are not cost effective and should not be purchased.

satisfactorily or to replace defective goods. When these agreements, or warranties, involve only minor costs, such costs may be recognized in the periods incurred. When these agreements involve significant future costs and when experience indicates that a definite future obligation exists, estimates of such costs should be made and matched against current revenues.[3]

Such estimates are usually recorded by a debit to an expense account and a credit to a liability account. Subsequent costs of fulfilling warranties are debited to the liability account and credited to an appropriate account, for example, Cash or Inventory. As was the case with the allowance for bad debts account, the debit side of the estimated liability under warranties account tracks actual warranty costs while the credit side of the account represents estimated costs.

To illustrate accounting for warranties, consider the following example. MJW Video & Sound sells compact stereo systems with a 2-year warranty. Past experience indicates that 10% of all systems sold will need repairs in the first year and 20% will need repairs in the second year. The average repair cost is $50 per system. The number of systems sold in 2012 and 2013 was 5,000 and 6,000, respectively. Actual repair costs were $12,500 in 2012 and $55,000 in 2013; it is assumed that all repair costs involved cash expenditures.

2012	Warranty Expense	75,000	
	Estimated Liability under Warranties		75,000
	To record estimated warranty expense based on systems sold (5,000 × 0.30 × $50 = $75,000).		
	Estimated Liability under Warranties	12,500	
	Cash		12,500
	To record cost of actual repairs in 2012.		
2013	Warranty Expense	90,000	
	Estimated Liability under Warranties		90,000
	To record estimated warranty expense based on systems sold (6,000 × 0.30 × $50 = $90,000).		
	Estimated Liability under Warranties	55,000	
	Cash		55,000
	To record cost of actual repairs in 2013.		

Periodically, the warranty liability account should be analyzed to see whether the actual repairs approximate the estimate. Adjustment to the percentages used in estimating future warranty obligations will be required if experience differs materially from the

[3] FASB ASC paragraphs 460-10-25-5 through 7. This guidance relates to warranties that are not separately sold but instead are included in the overall price of the product. For separately priced warranties, the revenue for the sale should be divided between the product and the warranty service. Revenue associated with providing the warranty service is recognized in a straight-line fashion over the term on the separately price warranty. See FASB ASC paragraphs 605-20-25-1 through 6.

estimates. These adjustments are changes in estimates and are reported prospectively, that is, in current and future periods. If sales and repairs in the preceding example are assumed to occur evenly through two years, analysis of the liability account at the end of 2013 shows that the ending balance of $97,500 ($75,000 + $90,000 − $12,500 − $55,000) is reasonably close to the predicted amount of $100,000 based upon the 10% and 20% estimates. (*Note:* Assuming that sales occur evenly throughout the year is mathematically the same as assuming that all of the sales occur halfway through the year.)

Computation:	
2012 sales still under warranty for 6 months:	
$50 × [5,000 units × (6/12 × 0.20)]	$ 25,000
2013 sales still under warranty for 18 months:	
$50 × [6,000 units × (6/12 × 0.10) + 6,000 units × (12/12 × 0.20)]	75,000
Total	$100,000

On occasion, an estimate may differ significantly from actual experience. Misleading financial statements may result if an adjustment is not made. In those instances, an adjustment is made to the liability account in the current period. Continuing the previous example, assume that warranty costs incurred in 2013 were only $35,000. Then the ending balance of $117,500 would be much higher than the $100,000 estimate. If the $17,500 difference was considered to be material, an adjustment to warranty expense would be made in 2013 as follows:

Estimated Liability under Warranties	17,500	
Warranty Expense		17,500
To record adjustment of estimate for warranty repairs.		

FASB CODIFICATION

The Issue: Your company sells lawn care equipment—lawn mowers, aerators, trimmers, and so forth. Your salespersons are trained to aggressively sell extended warranty agreements to all customers. These extended warranty agreements are a HUGE profit center for your business. To give the salespersons an incentive to sell these agreements, your company pays the salespersons a 30% commission on every extended warranty they sell.

The Question: What is the proper accounting treatment for these commissions—should they be recognized as an expense in the period they are paid, or should they be deferred and amortized as an expense over the warranty agreement period?

Searching the Codification: On this one, we are going to cheat just a little bit. We note in the chapter that regular warranties are discussed in FASB ASC paragraphs 460-10-25-5 through 7. Let's go there and see if we can pick up any clues about the accounting for commissions on separately priced warranties.

The Answer: The correct treatment is described on page 7-42.

Monitoring Accounts Receivable

3 **Analyze accounts receivable to measure how efficiently a firm is using this operating asset.**

WHY **The effective management of accounts receivable is critical to the operation of any business that sells on credit.**

HOW **The most commonly used tool to monitor receivables is the average collection period, which reflects the average number of days that lapse between the time a sale is made and the time cash is collected.**

Managers as well as external users of financial information need to measure how efficiently a firm is utilizing its operating assets, particularly significant working capital elements such as receivables, inventories, and accounts payable. The most common relationship used to monitor receivables is the average collection period.

Average Collection Period

Average receivables are sometimes expressed in terms of the average collection period, which reflects the average number of days that elapse between the time that a sale is made and the time that cash is collected. Average receivables outstanding divided by average daily sales gives the average collection period. This measure is computed for the WS Corporation as illustrated here.

	2013	2012
Average receivables	$397,500	$354,250
Net sales	$1,425,000	$1,650,000
Average daily sales (net sales/365)	$3,904	$4,521
Average collection period (average receivables/average daily sales)	102 days	78 days

This same measurement can be obtained by dividing the number of days in the year by the receivables turnover. Accounts receivable turnover is determined by dividing net sales by the average trade accounts receivable outstanding during the year. In developing an average receivables amount, the average of the beginning-of-year and end-of-year balances is normally used; however, a better measure of the average balance can be obtained using quarterly or monthly balances.

Accounts receivable turnover rates for WS Corporation for 2013 and 2012 are computed as follows:

	2013	2012
Net sales	$1,425,000	$1,650,000
Net receivables:		
Beginning of year	$375,000	$333,500
End of year	$420,000	$375,000
Average receivables [(beginning balance + ending balance)/2]	$397,500	$354,250
Receivables turnover for year	3.6 times	4.7 times

The value computed for receivables turnover represents the average number of revenue/receivables/cash cycles completed by the firm during the year.

In some cases, instead of computing the average collection period for the entire year, it may be more useful to report the average collection period for the receivables existing at the end of the period. This information would be significant in evaluating current position and, particularly, the receivable position as of a given date. This information for WS Corporation is computed as follows:

	2013	2012
Receivables at end of year	$420,000	$375,000
Average daily sales	$3,904	$4,521
Average collection period (end of year)	108 days	83 days

What constitutes a reasonable average collection period varies with individual businesses. For example, if merchandise is sold on terms of net 45 days, a 40-day average collection period would be reasonable, but if terms are net 30 days, a receivable balance equal to 40 days' sales would indicate slow collections. The average collection period for a number of companies is given in Exhibit 7-4. Notice the difference between the 93-day average collection period of **Caterpillar**, a company that makes its money selling and financing heavy equipment, and the 5-day average collection period of **Home Depot**, which emphasizes the sales of inventory and devotes relatively little effort to credit issues. Also, note the relatively short 6-day average collection period for **Sears**. Before Sears sold its in-house credit card business to **Citicorp** in 2003, Sears routinely had an average collection period in excess of 200 days, driven by the long time period that Sears credit card customers took to pay for their credit purchases.

Sales activity just before the close of a period should be considered when interpreting accounts receivable measurements. If sales are unusually light or heavy just before the end of the fiscal period, this affects total receivables as well as the related measurements. When such unevenness prevails, it may be better to analyze accounts receivable according to their due dates, as was illustrated earlier in the chapter.

The problem of minimizing accounts receivable without losing desirable business is important. Receivables often do not earn interest revenue, and the cost of carrying them

EX 7-4 AVERAGE COLLECTION PERIOD (IN DAYS) FOR 2009

Company	Average Collection Period
Caterpillar	92.7
ExxonMobil	31.7
Home Depot	5.3
McDonald's (franchise fees)	49.9
Microsoft	77.4
Sears	6.2

must be covered by the profit margin. The longer the accounts are carried without interest being earned, the smaller will be the percentage return realized on invested capital.

To attract business, credit frequently is granted for relatively long periods. The cost of granting long-term credit should be considered. Assume that a business has average daily sales of $5,000 and average accounts receivable of $250,000, which represents 50 days' sales. If collections and the credit period can be improved so that accounts receivable represent only 30 days' sales, accounts receivable will be reduced to $150,000. Assuming a total cost of 10% to carry and service the accounts, the $100,000 decrease would yield annual savings of $10,000.

Cash Management and Control

4 Discuss the composition, management, and control of cash, including the use of a bank reconciliation.

WHY **Because cash is the most liquid of assets, safeguards must be in place to ensure the proper handling of and accounting for it.**

HOW **A common cash control is the use of a bank reconciliation. A bank reconciliation requires accountants to reconcile the bank statement's cash balance with the balance recorded on the company's books. Any differences are identified, and appropriate adjusting entries and corrections are made.**

To this point, our focus has been primarily on revenues and receivables. However, revenues and receivables have value because they will eventually be converted to cash. Cash is important because it provides the basis for measurement and accounting for all other items. Another reason that cash is so important is that individuals, businesses, and even governments must maintain an adequate liquidity position; that is, they must have a sufficient amount of cash on hand to pay obligations as they come due if they are to remain viable operating entities. In the early stages of its conceptual framework project, the FASB identified the need to report information on cash and liquidity as one of the key objectives of financial reporting. This emphasis eventually led to the requirement of providing a statement of cash flows as one of the primary financial statements.

In striking contrast to the importance of cash as a key element in the liquidity position of an entity is its unproductive nature. Because cash is the measure of value, it cannot expand or grow unless it is converted into other properties. Cash kept under a mattress, for example, will not grow or appreciate, whereas land may increase in value if held. Excessive balances of cash on hand are often referred to as *idle cash*. Efficient cash management requires available cash to be continuously working in one of several ways as part of the operating cycle or as a short-term or long-term investment. The management of cash is therefore a critical business function.

Because cash is the most liquid of all assets, it is also the one that needs to be safeguarded the most. Thus, we will spend some time discussing cash and its equivalents as well the most common safeguard—a bank reconciliation—often employed to ensure the proper accounting for cash.

Composition of Cash

Cash is the most liquid of current assets. To be reported as "cash," an item must be readily available and not restricted for use in the payment of current obligations. A general guideline is whether an item is acceptable for deposit at face value by a bank or other financial institution.

Items that are classified as cash include coin and currency on hand and unrestricted funds available on deposit in a bank, which are often called demand deposits, because they can be withdrawn upon demand. Demand deposits include amounts in checking, savings, and money market deposit accounts. Petty cash funds or change funds and negotiable instruments, such as personal checks and cashiers' checks, are also items commonly reported as cash. The total of these items plus undeposited coin and currency is sometimes called *cash on hand*. In addition, many companies report investments in very short-term, interest-earning securities (such as 3-month U.S. Treasury securities) as cash equivalents in the balance sheet. Deposits that are not immediately available for withdrawal or have other restrictions are sometimes referred to as time deposits. These deposits are sometimes separately classified as *temporary investments*. Examples of time deposits include certificates of deposit (CDs) and money market savings certificates. CDs, for example, generally may be withdrawn without penalty only at specified maturity dates.

Deposits in foreign banks that are subject to immediate and unrestricted withdrawal generally qualify as cash and are reported at their U.S. dollar equivalents as of the date of the balance sheet. However, cash in foreign banks that is restricted as to use or withdrawal should be designated as receivables of a current or noncurrent nature and reported subject to appropriate allowances for estimated uncollectibles.

Some items do not meet the "acceptance at face value on deposit" test and should not be reported as cash. Examples include postage stamps (which are office supplies) and postdated checks, IOUs, and not-sufficient-funds (NSF) checks (all of which are, in effect, receivables).

Cash balances specifically designated by management for special purposes should be reported separately. An example would be cash set aside specifically for the purpose of retiring a bond issue in the future; this cash is called a *sinking fund*. Restricted cash should be reported as a current item only if it is to be applied to some current purpose or obligation. Classification of the cash balance as current or noncurrent should parallel the classification applied to the liability.

A credit balance in the cash account resulting from the issuance of checks in excess of the amount on deposit is known as a cash overdraft and should be reported as a current liability.

In summary, cash is a current asset comprising coin, currency, and other items that (1) serve as a medium of exchange and (2) provide the basis for measurement in accounting. Most negotiable instruments (e.g., checks, bank drafts, and money orders) qualify as cash because they can be converted to currency on demand or are acceptable for deposit at face value by a bank. For many companies, the bulk of "cash" is held in the form of short-term, interest-earning securities. Components of cash restricted as to use or withdrawal should be disclosed or reported separately and classified as an investment, a receivable, or other asset. Exhibit 7-5 summarizes the classification of various items that have been discussed. The objective of disclosure is to provide the user of financial statements with information to assist in evaluating the entity's ability to meet obligations (i.e., its liquidity and solvency) and in assessing the effectiveness of cash management.

Compensating Balances

In connection with financing arrangements, it is common practice for a company to agree to maintain a minimum or average balance on deposit with a bank or other

EX 7-5 CLASSIFICATION OF CASH AND NONCASH ITEMS

Item	Classification
Undeposited coin and currency	Cash
Unrestricted funds on deposit at bank (demand deposits)	Cash
Petty cash and change funds	Cash
Negotiable instruments, such as checks, bank drafts, and money orders	Cash
Company checks written but not yet mailed or delivered	Cash
Restricted deposits, such as CDs and money market savings certificates (time deposits)	Investment
Deposits in foreign banks:	
Unrestricted	Cash
Restricted	Receivables
Postage stamps	Office supplies
IOUs, postdated checks, and not-sufficient-funds (NSF) checks	Receivables
Cash restricted for special purposes	Restricted cash*
Cash overdraft	Current liability

* Separately reported as current or noncurrent asset depending on the purpose for which it is restricted.

lending institution. These compensating balances are defined by the SEC as "that portion of any demand deposit (or any time deposit or certificate of deposit) maintained by a corporation . . . which constitutes support for existing borrowing arrangements of the corporation . . . with a lending institution. Such arrangements would include both outstanding borrowings and the assurance of future credit availability."[4]

Compensating balances provide a source of funds to the lender as partial compensation for credit extended. In effect, such arrangements raise the interest rate of the borrower because a portion of the amount on deposit with the lending institution cannot be used. These balances present an accounting problem from the standpoint of disclosure. Readers of financial statements are likely to assume the entire cash balance is available to meet current obligations when, in fact, part of the balance is restricted.

> **FYI**
>
> The effective interest rate on a loan can be thought of as interest ÷ "take home" amount of loan. Because a compensating balance requirement reduces the amount of the loan that can be "taken home" while still requiring that interest be paid on the entire loan, it would increase the effective interest rate.

The solution to this problem is to disclose the amount of compensating balances. The SEC recommends that any "legally restricted" deposits held as compensating balances be segregated and reported separately. If the balances are the result of short-term financing arrangements, they should be shown separately among the "cash items" in the Current Assets section; if the compensating balances are in connection with long-term agreements, they should be classified as noncurrent, either as investments or "other assets." In many instances, deposits are not legally restricted, but compensating balance agreements still exist as business commitments in connection with lines of credit. In these situations, the amounts and nature of the arrangements should be disclosed in the notes to the financial statements, as illustrated in Exhibit 7-6 for **Chiquita Brands International** (the banana company) in 2009.

[4] FASB SEC paragraph 210-10-S99-1.

EX 7-6 CHIQUITA BRANDS INTERNATIONAL—DISCLOSURE OF COMPENSATING BALANCE

Cash and equivalents include cash and highly liquid investments with a maturity of three months or less at the time of purchase. At December 31, 2009, the company had €12 million ($17 million) of cash equivalents in a compensating balance arrangement relating to an uncommitted credit line for bank guarantees used primarily for import licenses and duties in European Union countries.

Management and Control of Cash

As noted earlier, a business enterprise must maintain sufficient cash for current operations and for paying obligations as they come due. Any excess cash should be invested temporarily to earn an additional return for the shareholders. Effective cash management also requires controls to protect cash from loss by theft or fraud. Because cash is the most liquid asset, it is particularly susceptible to misappropriation unless properly safeguarded.

The system for controlling cash must be adapted to a particular business. It is not feasible to describe all features and techniques employed in businesses of various kinds and sizes. In general, however, systems of cash control deny access to the accounting records to those who handle cash. This reduces the possibility of improper entries to conceal the misuse of cash receipts and cash payments. The probability of misappropriation of cash is greatly reduced if two or more employees must conspire in an embezzlement. Furthermore, systems normally provide for separation of the receiving and paying functions. The basic characteristics of a system of cash control are as follows:

1. Specifically assigned responsibility for handling cash receipts
2. Separation of handling and recording cash receipts
3. Daily deposit of all cash received
4. Voucher system to control cash payments
5. Internal audits at irregular intervals
6. Double record of cash—bank and books, with reconciliations performed by someone outside the accounting function

These controls are more likely to be found in large companies with many employees. Small companies with few employees generally have difficulty in totally segregating accounting and cash-handling duties. Even small companies, however, should incorporate as many control features as possible.

To the extent that a company can incorporate effective internal controls, it can reduce significantly the chances of theft, loss, or inadvertent errors in accounting for and controlling cash. Even the most elaborate control system, however, cannot totally eliminate the possibilities of misappropriations or errors. The use of periodic bank reconciliations can help identify any cash shortages or errors that may have been made in accounting for cash. Another common cash control, a petty cash fund, is discussed in the Web Material associated with this chapter. The text support Web site is **www.cengage.com/international.**

Bank Reconciliations

When daily receipts are deposited and payments are made by check, the bank's statement of its transactions with the depositor can be compared with the record of cash as reported on

Employees who are responsible for handling cash in a company should not be involved in accounting activities involving the cash account.

the depositor's books. A comparison of the bank balance with the balance reported on the books is usually made monthly by means of a summary known as a bank reconciliation. A bank reconciliation is prepared to disclose any errors or irregularities in either the records of the bank or those of the business unit. It is developed in a form that points out the reasons for discrepancies in the two balances. It should be prepared by an individual who neither handles nor records cash because if a person who was embezzling from the cash account also was in charge of the reconciliation, it would be too easy to cover his or her tracks.

When the bank statement and the depositor's records are compared, certain items may appear on one but not the other, resulting in a difference in the two balances. Most of these differences result from temporary timing lags and are thus normal. Four common types of differences arise in the following situations:

1. A deposit made near the end of the month and recorded on the depositor's books is not received by the bank in time to be reflected on the bank statement. This amount, referred to as a deposit in transit, has to be added to the bank statement balance to make it agree with the balance on the depositor's books.
2. Checks written near the end of the month have reduced the depositor's cash balance but have not cleared the bank as of the bank statement date. These outstanding checks must be subtracted from the bank statement balance to make it agree with the depositor's records.
3. The bank sometimes charges a monthly fee for servicing an account. The bank automatically reduces the depositor's account balance for this bank service charge and notes the amount on the bank statement. The depositor must deduct this amount from the recorded cash balance to make it agree with the bank statement balance. The return of a customer's check for which insufficient funds are available, known as a not-sufficient-funds (NSF) check, is handled in a similar manner.
4. An amount owed to the depositor is paid directly to the bank by a third party and is added to the depositor's account. Upon receipt of the bank statement (assuming prior notification has not been received from the bank), this amount must be added to the cash balance on the depositor's books. Examples include a direct payroll deposit by an individual's employer and interest added by the bank on a savings account. Similarly, the depositor may have items deducted

> **CAUTION**
>
> In preparing a bank reconciliation, it is essential to know how the bank handled a transaction (e.g., the entry made, if any, on an NSF check) so that a proper reconciliation can be made from the company's books' perspective.

> **CAUTION**
>
> Adjustments to the book balance should reflect new information learned upon receiving the bank statement. Adjustments to the bank balance should reflect checks written and deposits made that the bank doesn't know about yet.

from the account by a third party (such as transfers to savings plans). These items must be deducted from the depositor's cash balance.

If, after considering these items, the bank statement and the book balances cannot be reconciled, a detailed analysis of both the bank's records and the depositor's books may be necessary to determine whether errors or irregularities exist on the records of either party.

Preparing a Bank Reconciliation An illustration of a common form of bank reconciliation follows. This form is prepared in two sections, the bank statement balance being adjusted to the corrected cash balance in the first section, and the book balance being adjusted to the same corrected cash balance in the second section. Any items not yet recognized by the bank (e.g., deposits in transit or outstanding checks) as well as any errors made by the bank are recorded in the first section. The second section contains any items the depositor has not yet recognized (e.g., direct deposits, NSF checks, or bank service charges) and any corrections for errors made on the depositor's books.

The reconciliation of bank and book balances to a corrected balance has two important advantages: It develops a corrected cash figure, and it shows separately all items requiring adjustment on the depositor's books.

An alternative form of reconciliation would be to reconcile the bank statement balance to the book balance. This form would not develop a corrected cash figure, however, and would make it more difficult to determine the adjustments needed on the depositor's books.

Svendsen, Inc.
Bank Reconciliation
November 30, 2013

Balance per bank statement, November 30, 2013		$2,979.72
Add: Deposits in transit	$658.50	
Charge for interest made to depositor's account by bank in error	12.50	671.00
		$3,650.72
Deduct outstanding checks:		
No. 1125	$ 58.16	
No. 1138	100.00	
No. 1152	98.60	
No. 1154	255.00	
No. 1155	192.07	703.83
Corrected bank balance		$2,946.89
Balance per books, November 30, 2013		$2,952.49
Add: Interest earned during November	$ 98.50	
Check No. 1116 to Ace Advertising for $46 recorded by depositor as $64 in error	18.00	116.50
		$3,068.99
Deduct: Bank service charges	$ 3.16	
Customer's check deposited November 25 and returned marked NSF	118.94	122.10
Corrected book balance		$2,946.89

After preparing the reconciliation, the depositor should record any items appearing on the bank statement and requiring recognition on the company's books as well as any corrections for errors discovered on its own books. The bank should be notified immediately of any bank errors. The following entries would be required on the books of Svendsen, Inc., as a result of the November 30 reconciliation:

Account	Debit	Credit
Cash	98.50	
Interest Revenue		98.50
To record interest earned during November.		
Cash	18.00	
Advertising Expense		18.00
To record correction for check in payment of advertising recorded as $64 instead of the actual amount, $46.		
Accounts Receivable	118.94	
Miscellaneous General Expense	3.16	
Cash		122.10
To record customer's uncollectible check and bank charges for November.		

STOP&THINK

Suppose that after employing the procedures outlined here, a company's bank and book balances are not the same. Further suppose that the corrected bank balance is *greater than* the corrected book balance. Which ONE of the following errors could cause this type of difference?

a) A deposit in transit made the last day of the month was omitted from the bank reconciliation. The deposit was recorded in the company's books.
b) The company mistakenly recorded a check it made out to one of its suppliers as being for $50 instead of $500. The bank cleared the check at the correct amount of $500.
c) The company mistakenly recorded a deposit made in the middle of the month as $500 instead of $50. The bank recorded the deposit at the correct amount of $50.
d) A check written three months ago, which has still not cleared the bank, was omitted from the outstanding checks list in the bank reconciliation.

After these entries are posted, the cash account will show a balance of $2,946.89. If financial statements were prepared at November 30, this is the amount that would be reported as cash on the balance sheet. It should be noted that the bank reconciliation is not presented to external users. It is used as a control procedure and as an accounting tool to determine the adjustments required to bring the cash account and related account balances up to date.

Presentation of Sales and Receivables in the Financial Statements

5 **Recognize appropriate disclosures for presenting sales and receivables in the financial statements.**

WHY **Disclosures of sales and receivables in the financial statements vary from company to company. Sales and receivables information will be in both the financial statements and in the accompanying notes.**

HOW **In the body of the financial statements, sales are generally reported net of discounts and allowances. Receivables are often reported net of their allowance account with supplemental information provided in the notes to the financial statements.**

Companies often provide a breakdown of the sources of their revenues in the body of the income statement. For example, Note 1 of **The Walt Disney Company**'s financial statements indicates four sources of revenues: media networks, parks & resorts, studio entertainment, and consumer products. As another example, **McDonald's** provides information in the notes to its financial statements partitioning revenues, operating income, and identifiable assets by geographical area (see Exhibit 7-7). This information is useful to users of the financial statements as they determine future sources of a firm's revenue. This information also allows users to determine how efficiently assets are being used to generate revenues and profits. In the case of McDonald's, we can compute the percentage of revenues generated from each geographical area and conclude that the percentage of revenues generated in Europe has increased slightly over time (from 39.2% in 2007 to 40.8% in 2009). In computing the amount of revenue dollars generated in the United States per dollar of assets, we note that the amount has decreased slightly over time (from 0.788 in 2007 to 0.762 in 2009). That amount has increased for McDonald's European operations (from 0.784 in 2007 to 0.807 in 2009). With this analysis, we can see that the European operations are generating more revenue dollars per dollar of assets than are their American counterparts.

Receivables qualifying as current items may be grouped for presentation on the balance sheet in the following classes: (1) notes receivable—trade debtors, (2) accounts receivable—trade debtors, and (3) other receivables. Alternatively, trade notes and accounts receivable can be reported as a single amount. The detail reported for other receivables depends on the relative significance of the various items included. Valuation accounts are deducted from the individual receivable balances or combined balances to which they relate. Any long-term trade and nontrade receivables would be reported as "other noncurrent assets" on the balance sheet. A company should also disclose whether restrictions have been placed on any receivables, such as when receivables have been set aside to satisfy a specific obligation or have been pledged as collateral on a loan. Finally, a company should disclose any significant concentrations of credit risk relating to its receivables. For example, if a

EX 7-7 MCDONALD'S NOTES TO CONSOLIDATED FINANCIAL STATEMENTS

Segment and geographic information

In millions	**2009**	**2008**	**2007**
U.S.	$ 7,943.8	$ 8,078.3	$ 7,905.5
Europe	9,273.8	9,922.9	8,926.2
APMEA	4,337.0	4,230.8	3,598.9
Other Countries & Corporate	1,190.1	1,290.4	2,356.0
Total revenues	$22,744.7	$23,522.4	$22,786.6
U.S.	$ 3,231.7	$ 3,059.7	$ 2,841.9
Europe	2,588.1	2,608.0	2,125.4
APMEA	989.5	818.8	616.3
Other Countries & Corporate	31.7	(43.6)	(1,704.6)
Total operating income	$ 6,841.0	$ 6,442.9	$ 3,879.0
U.S.	$10,429.3	$10,356.7	$10,031.8
Europe	11,494.4	10,532.7	11,380.4
APMEA	4,409.0	4,074.6	4,145.3
Other Countries & Corporate	3,892.2	3,497.5	3,834.2
Total assets	$30,224.9	$28,461.5	$29,391.7

significant percentage of a company's sales (and corresponding receivables) are with one debtor, that would represent a concentration of credit risk and should be disclosed.

As is explained in the Expanded Material later in the chapter, when receivables have been sold or used as collateral for loans, the details associated with the sale or borrowing transaction should be disclosed. Disclosure would include factors such as the terms of the agreement, the value of the receivables involved, and the recourse available to the lender.

Accounts and notes receivable as presented by Caterpillar, Inc., in its 2009 10-K filing are shown in Exhibit 7-8. In Exhibit 7-8, Caterpillar's note disclosure relating to its finance receivables is presented. Information relating to maturity dates of receivables, residual values of leased equipment, and credit loss estimates are presented. Notice that Caterpillar's estimate for credit losses in 2009 is substantially less than the actual write-offs during the same year.

EX 7-8 REPORTING RECEIVABLES—CATERPILLAR NOTE DISCLOSURE

TABLE III—Finance Receivables Information (Millions of dollars)
Contractual maturities of outstanding finance receivables:

	December 31, 2009			
Amounts Due In	**Retail Installment Contracts**	**Retail Finance Leases**	**Retail Notes**	**Total**
2010	$2,366	$3,189	$3,180	$ 8,735
2011	1,532	2,146	1,695	5,373
2012	917	1,124	1,084	3,125
2013	412	458	967	1,837
2014	177	193	797	1,167
Thereafter	46	154	776	976
	$5,450	$7,264	$8,499	$21,213
Residual value	—	1,181	—	1,181
Less: Unearned income	(498)	(817)	(123)	(1,438)
Total	$4,952	$7,628	$8,376	$20,956

Impaired loans and leases:

	2009	**2008**	**2007**
Average recorded investment	**$ 425**	$ 306	$ 200
At December 31:			
Recorded investment	**$ 513**	$ 479	$ 219
Impaired loans/finance leases for which there is a related allowance for credit losses	**448**	258	166
Related allowance for credit losses on impaired loans/finance leases	**117**	**59**	**35**
Impaired loans/finance leases for which there is no related allowance for credit losses	**65**	**221**	**53**

Allowance for credit loss activity:

	2009	**2008**	**2007**
Balance at beginning of year	**$ 391**	$ 351	$ 315
Provision for credit losses	**225**	192	97
Receivables written off	**(281)**	(144)	(91)
Recoveries on receivables previously written off	**28**	23	23
Other—net	**13**	(31)	7
Balance at end of year	**$ 376**	$ 391	$ 351

In estimating the allowance for credit losses, we review accounts that are past due, non-performing or in bankruptcy.

EM EXPANDED MATERIAL

In the first part of this chapter, we focused on the central activity of a business—selling a product or service and collecting the resulting receivable. We also discussed other events or activities related to this revenue/receivables/cash cycle. In this section of the chapter, we address the issue of using accounts receivable as a source of cash. Often, for a variety of reasons, a company will have an immediate need for cash. A number of methods are available to a company to convert its receivables into cash without waiting for payment from the customer. The most common of those methods are discussed here. We also discuss notes receivable and how they are valued and used as a source of cash. The Expanded Material also includes a brief discussion of the impact of uncollectible accounts on the statement of cash flows.

Receivables as a Source of Cash

6 **Explain how receivables may be used as a source of cash through secured borrowing or sale.**

WHY **A company can accelerate the cash collection process by selling its receivables or by using its receivables as collateral in obtaining a loan. The method employed and the cost to the company depend on the degree of risk to which the company wishes to expose itself.**

HOW **In the case of secured borrowing, the company is simply pledging the receivable as collateral on a loan. Receivables can also be sold to a third party, usually a bank or other financial institution. When a receivable is sold with recourse, the selling company must quantify and recognize the expected payout that will be made as a result of the recourse provision.**

As stated previously, receivables are a part of the normal revenue/receivables/cash operating cycle of a business. Frequently, this cycle takes several months to complete. Sometimes companies need immediate cash and cannot wait for completion of the normal cycle. At other times companies are not in financial stress but want to accelerate the receivables collection process, shift the risk of credit and the effort of collection to someone else, or merely use receivables from customers as a source of financing.

Receivables may be converted to cash in one of two ways: as a sale (either with or without recourse) or as a secured borrowing. The FASB specifies in Topic 860 the conditions that must be met if a transfer of receivables is to be accounted for as a sale.[5] Those conditions are as follows:

1. The transferred assets have been isolated from the transferor. That is, the transferor and its creditors cannot access the assets.
2. The transferee has the right to pledge or exchange the transferred assets.
3. The transferor does not maintain effective control over the assets through either (a) an agreement to repurchase them before their maturity or (b) the ability to cause the transferee to return specific assets.

These three conditions are designed to carefully define cases in which the transfer of a financial asset is being made with no substantial strings attached. If there are

[5] FASB ASC paragraph 860-10-40-5.

no strings attached, meaning that the transferor does not have the right to get the assets back and the transferee has the right to use the assets in any way desired, then the transfer is accounted for as a sale. If these three conditions are not met, then the transfer of receivables is accounted for as a secured borrowing. In the sections that follow, we discuss both the sale of receivables and their use as collateral in a borrowing arrangement.

Sale of Receivables without Recourse

Certain banks, dealers, and finance companies purchase receivables from companies. In many cases, these purchases are done without recourse, meaning that the purchaser assumes the risks associated with the collectibility of the receivables. If the terms of the sale are with recourse, then if the receivables are not collected, the purchaser has the right to collect from the company that originally sold the receivable. A sale of accounts receivable without recourse is commonly referred to as accounts receivable factoring, and the buyer is referred to as a *factor*.[6] Customers are usually notified that their bills are payable to the factor, and this party assumes the burden of billing and collecting accounts. The flow of activities involved in factoring is presented in Exhibit 7-9.

In many cases, factoring involves more than the purchase and collection of accounts receivable. Factoring frequently involves a continuing agreement whereby a financing institution assumes the credit function as well as the collection function. Under such an arrangement, the factor grants or denies credit, handles the accounts receivable records, bills customers, and makes collections. The business unit is relieved of all these activities, and the sale of goods provides immediate cash for business use. Because the factor absorbs the losses from bad accounts and frequently

FYI

Student loans are often factored to specialized loan servicing companies.

EX 7-9 FLOW OF ACTIVITIES INVOLVED IN FACTORING

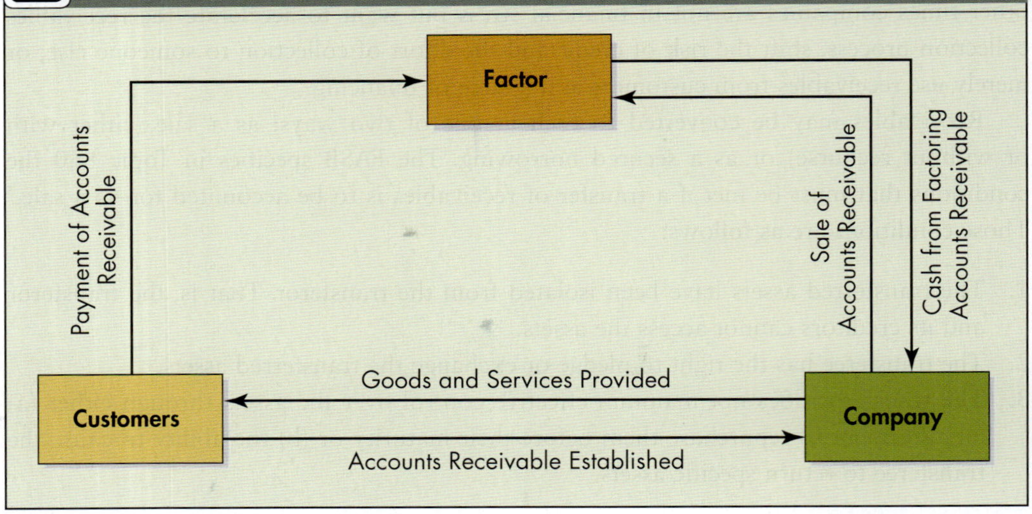

[6] Recourse is defined by the FASB as "the right of a transferee of receivables to receive payment from the transferor of those receivables for any of the following: (a) failure of the debtors to pay when due, (b) the effects of prepayments, or (c) adjustments resulting from defects in the eligibility of the transferred receivables." FASB ASC Section 860-10-20-Glossary.

assumes credit and collection responsibilities, the charges associated with factoring generally exceed the interest charges on a loan with receivables used as collateral. Often, the factor will charge a fee of 10% to 30% of the net amount of receivables purchased, except for credit card factoring where the rate is 3% to 5%. The factor may withhold a portion of the purchase price for possible future charges for customer returns and allowances or other special adjustments. Final settlement is made after receivables have been collected.

When receivables are sold outright, without recourse, Cash is debited, receivables and related allowance balances are closed, and a loss account is debited for factoring charges. When part of the purchase price is withheld by the factor, a receivable from the factor is established pending final settlement. Upon receipt of the total purchase price from the bank or finance company, the factor receivable account is eliminated. To illustrate, assume that $10,000 of receivables are factored, that is, sold without recourse, to a finance company for $8,500. An allowance for bad debts equal to $300 was previously established for these accounts. This amount will need to be written off along with the accounts receivable being sold. The finance company withheld 5% of the purchase price as protection against sales returns and allowances. The entry to record the sale of the accounts is as follows:

Cash	8,075	
Receivable from Factor	425	
Allowance for Bad Debts	300	
Loss from Factoring Receivables	1,200	
Accounts Receivable		10,000
To record the factoring of receivables. Computations: Cash = $8,500 − $425 = $8,075; Factor receivable = $8,500 × 0.05 = $425; Factoring loss = ($10,000 − $300) − $8,500 = $1,200.		

The loss from factoring is determined by comparing the book value of the receivables ($10,000 − $300) to the proceeds to be received ($8,500). Assuming there were no returns or allowances, the final settlement would be recorded as follows:

Cash	425	
Receivable from Factor		425
To record the final settlement associated with previously factored receivables.		

Sale of Receivables with Recourse

Cash can be obtained by selling receivables with recourse. This is different from factoring, which generally is on a nonrecourse basis. Selling receivables with recourse means that a purchaser (bank or finance company) advances cash in return for receivables but retains the right to collect from the seller if debtors (seller's customers) fail to make payments when due.

> **FYI**
>
> The estimation of the recourse obligation essentially involves a reexamination of the receivables being sold to determine whether the allowance for bad debts associated with those receivables is sufficient.

The FASB requires the seller to estimate the value of the recourse obligation and recognize that liability. That is, the seller must estimate the amount that will be paid to the purchaser as a result of default on the receivables that were sold. Continuing the previous example, assume that the receivables were sold with recourse and the recourse obligation has an estimated fair value of $500. In this instance, the loss to be recognized on the transaction is $1,700 and is computed as follows:

Cash received	$8,500
Estimated value of recourse obligation	(500)
Net proceeds	$8,000
Book value of the receivables	$9,700
Net proceeds to be received	(8,000)
Loss on sale of receivables	$1,700

The entry to record the sale of receivables with recourse would be as follows:

Cash	8,075	
Receivable from Factor	425	
Allowance for Bad Debts	300	
Loss on Sale of Receivables	1,700	
Accounts Receivable		10,000
Recourse Obligation		500

STOP&THINK

Why would a company ever factor receivables with recourse when it could factor those same receivables without recourse?

a) Factoring receivables without recourse is illegal in many states.
b) FASB ASC Topic 860 does not apply when receivables are factored with recourse.
c) The fee paid to the factor is lower when factoring receivables with recourse.
d) The recourse obligation is always exactly equal to the allowance for bad debts.

If in the future the estimate of the recourse obligation turns out to have been incorrect, then the company will recognize income if the actual amount paid relating to the recourse obligation is less than $500 and will recognize an additional loss if the amount turns out to be greater than $500.

As mentioned earlier, the recourse provisions of a receivable transfer may leave the transferor with such a large degree of control over or large amount of risk from the transferred receivables that the receivables should remain on the books of the transferor. Specifically, if the three conditions mentioned earlier are not met, then the transfer of receivables is accounted for as a secured borrowing, as illustrated in the next section.

Secured Borrowing

Loans are frequently obtained from banks or other lending institutions by assigning or pledging receivables as security. The loan is evidenced by a written note that provides for either a general assignment of receivables or an assignment of specific receivables. With an assignment of receivables, no special accounting problems are involved. The books simply report the loan (a debit to Cash and a credit to Notes Payable) and subsequent settlement of the obligation (a debit to Notes Payable and a credit to Cash). However, disclosure should be made on the balance sheet, by a parenthetical comment or a note, of the amount and nature of receivables pledged to secure the obligation to the lender.

The procedures involved are illustrated in the following example. It is assumed that the assignor (the borrower) collects the receivables, which is often the case.

> **FYI**
>
> Packaging and transfer of receivables is sometimes called *securitization.* In this context, when you see the term *securitization,* think of it as the process of turning receivables into cash immediately.

On July 1, 2013, Provo Mercantile Co. assigns receivables totaling $300,000 to Salem Bank as collateral on a $200,000, 12% note. Provo Mercantile does not notify its account debtors and will continue to collect the assigned receivables. Salem assesses a 1% finance charge on assigned receivables in addition to the interest on the note. Provo is to make monthly payments to Salem with cash collected on assigned receivables. The entries shown below would be made.

If in the following example Salem Bank assumes responsibility for collecting the assigned receivables, the account debtors would have to be notified to make their payments to the bank. Salem would then use a liability account (e.g., Payable to Provo Mercantile) to account for cash collections during the period. Because the receivables are still owned by Provo Mercantile, the bank would not record them as assets. Upon full payment of the note plus interest, the bank would remit to Provo Mercantile any cash collections in excess of the note, along with any uncollected accounts.

Illustrative Entries for Assignment of Specific Receivables

Provo Mercantile Co.			**Salem Bank**		
Issuance of note and assignment of specific receivables on July 1, 2013:					
Cash	197,000		Notes Receivable	200,000	
Finance Charge	3,000*		Finance Revenue		3,000*
Notes Payable		200,000	Cash		197,000
* (0.01 × $300,000)					
Collections of assigned accounts during July, $180,000 less cash discounts of $1,000; sales returns in July, $2,000:					
Cash	179,000		(No Entry)		
Sales Discounts	1,000				
Sales Returns and Allowances	2,000				
Accounts Receivable		182,000			
Paid Salem Bank amounts owed for July collections plus accrued interest on note to August 1:					
Interest Expense	2,000*		Cash	181,000	
Notes Payable	179,000		Interest Revenue		2,000
Cash		181,000	Notes Receivable		179,000
* ($200,000 × 0.12 × 1/12)					
Collections of remaining assigned accounts during August less $800 written off as uncollectible:					
Cash	117,200		(No Entry)		
Allowance for Bad Debts	800				
Accounts Receivable		118,000*			
* ($300,000 − $182,000)					
Paid Salem Bank remaining balance owed plus accrued interest on note to September 1:					
Interest Expense	210*		Cash	21,210	
Notes Payable	21,000†		Interest Revenue		210*
Cash		21,210	Notes Receivable		21,000†
* ($21,000 × 0.12 × 1/12)					
† ($200,000 − $179,000)					

In summary, receivables provide an important source of cash for many companies. The transfer of receivables to third parties in return for cash generally takes the form of secured borrowing (borrowing with the receivables pledged as collateral) or factoring (a sale without recourse). The financing arrangements are often complex and may involve a transfer of receivables on a recourse basis. Each transaction must be analyzed carefully to see if in form and substance it is a borrowing transaction or a sales transaction and treated accordingly.

Derecognition of Receivables: *IAS 39*

IASB standards address the transfer of receivables in *IAS 39*. *IAS 39* covers a lot of ground such as the accounting for investment securities, the accounting for derivatives, and the accounting for the transfer of financial assets such as receivables. As seen above in the discussion of FASB ASC Topic 860, the key accounting issue with the transfer of receivables is whether the transfer should be recorded as a sale, with the receivable then removed from the books of the transferor, or whether the transfer should be accounted for as a secured loan with the receivable remaining on the books of the transferor. Frequently the term "derecognition" is used to signify the removal of the receivable from the books of the transferor.

Recall that the purpose of the three conditions in FASB ASC Section 860-10-40 is to identify receivable transfers in which economic ownership of the receivable has been transferred. *IAS 39* contains the same concept but applied slightly differently. *IAS 39* contains a 2-step test for derecognition.

1. Determine whether the receivable transfer involves a transfer of "substantially all the risks and rewards of ownership of the [receivable]." If so, the transfer should be accounted for as a sale of the receivable, as illustrated previously. If not, go on to Step 2.
2. If the receivable transfer does not involve the transfer of substantially all the risks and rewards of ownership, determine whether control of the receivable has been transferred. If so, account for the receivable transfer as a sale. If not, the transfer is accounted for as a secured loan, as illustrated previously.[7]

The *IAS 39* 2-step test emphasizes the question of whether the risks and rewards of ownership have been transferred. With respect to receivables, the risks and rewards of ownership are the receipt, or nonreceipt, of cash depending on whether the customer who owes the receivable amount ultimately pays. For example, a transferor of a receivable who receives a nonrefundable fixed cash payment in exchange for the receivable has transferred the risks and rewards of ownership because the transferor gets to keep the nonrefundable fixed cash payment whether the customer pays the receivable amount or not. In contrast, if the transferor receives an upfront cash payment but then agrees to give back some of the cash, or to receive extra cash, depending on how much the customer ultimately pays, then the risks and rewards of ownership have not been transferred.

Compare the three criteria in *SFAS No. 140* with the 2-step test contained in *IAS 39*. As is typically the case, the U.S. standard is more detailed and the international standard is more conceptual. In the large majority of cases, the two standards will result in the same accounting treatment for a receivable transfer.

[7] *International Accounting Standard 39,* "Financial Instruments: Recognition and Measurement" (London: International Accounting Standards Board, August 18, 2005), par. 20.

Notes Receivable

7 **Describe proper accounting and valuation of notes receivable.**

WHY **Notes receivable represent a more formal obligation than does an account receivable. Notes receivable usually involve the payment of interest and a specific due date.**

HOW **Notes receivable are valued by computing the present value of the principal and interest to be received. Problems can arise in the valuation of notes receivable when the note is exchanged for goods or services and the fair value of those goods and services is difficult to determine.**

A promissory note is an unconditional written promise to pay a certain sum of money at a specified time. The note is signed by the maker and is payable to the order of a specified payee or bearer. Notes usually involve interest, stated at an annual rate and charged on the face amount of the note. Most notes are negotiable notes that are legally transferable by endorsement and delivery.

For reporting purposes, trade notes receivable should include only negotiable short-term instruments acquired from trade debtors and not yet due. Trade notes generally arise from sales involving relatively high dollar amounts when the buyer wants to extend payment beyond the usual trade credit period of 30 to 90 days. Also, sellers sometimes request notes from customers whose accounts receivable are past due. Most companies, however, have relatively few trade notes receivable.

Nontrade notes receivable should be separately designated on the balance sheet under an appropriate title. For example, notes arising from loans to customers, officers, employees, and affiliated companies should be reported separately from trade notes.

Valuation of Notes Receivable

Notes receivable are initially recorded at their present value, which may be defined as the sum of future receipts discounted to the present date at an appropriate rate of interest.[8] In a lending transaction, the present value is the amount of cash received by the borrower. When a note is exchanged for property, goods, or services, the present value equals the current cash selling price of the items exchanged. The difference between the present value and the amount to be collected at the due date or maturity date is a charge for interest.

All notes arising in arm's-length transactions between unrelated parties involve an element of interest. However, a distinction as to form is made between interest-bearing and non-interest-bearing notes. An interest-bearing note is written as a promise to pay principal (or face amount) plus interest at a specified rate. In the absence of special valuation problems discussed in the next section, the face amount of an interest-bearing note is the present value upon issuance of the note.

A non-interest-bearing note does not specify an interest rate, but the face amount includes the interest charge. Thus, the present value is the difference between the face

[8] See the text module, Time Value of Money Review, for a discussion of present value concepts and applications.

FYI

Another name for Discount on Notes Receivable is Unearned Interest Revenue.

amount and the interest included in that amount, sometimes called the implicit (or effective) interest.

In recording receipt of a note, Notes Receivable is debited for the face amount of the note. When the face amount differs from the present value, as is the case with non-interest-bearing notes, the difference is recorded as a premium or discount and amortized over the life of the note. In the example to follow, a note receivable is established with credits to sales and discount on notes receivable accounts. The amount of discount is the implicit interest on the note and will be recognized as interest revenue as the note matures.

To illustrate, assume that High Value Corporation sells goods on January 1, 2013, with a price of $1,000. The buyer gives High Value a promissory note due December 31, 2014. The maturity value of the note includes interest at 10%. Thus, High Value will receive $1,210 ($1,000 × 1.21) when the note is paid.[9] The entries below show the accounting procedures for an interest-bearing note and one written in a non-interest-bearing form.

At December 31, 2013, the unamortized discount of $110 on the non-interest-bearing note would be deducted from Notes Receivable on the balance sheet. If the non-interest-bearing note were recorded at face value with no recognition of the interest included therein, the sales price and profit to the seller would be overstated. In subsequent periods, interest revenue would be understated. Failure to record the discount would also result in an overstatement of assets.

Illustrative Entries for Notes

	Interest-Bearing Note Face Amount = Present Value = $1,000 Stated Interest Rate = 10%			**Non-Interest-Bearing Note Face Amount = Maturity = $1,210 No Stated Interest Rate**		
To record note received in exchange for goods selling for $1,000:						
2013						
Jan. 1	Notes Receivable	1,000		Notes Receivable	1,210	
	Sales		1,000	Sales		1,000
				Discount on Notes Receivable		210
To recognize interest earned for one year, $1,000 × 0.10:						
Dec. 31	Interest Receivable	100		Discount on Notes Receivable	100	
	Interest Revenue		100	Interest Revenue		100
To record settlement of note at maturity and recognize interest earned for one year, ($1,000 + $100) × 0.10:						
2014						
Dec. 31	Cash	1,210		Cash	1,210	
	Notes Receivable		1,000	Discount on Notes Receivable	110	
	Interest Receivable		100	Notes Receivable		1,210
	Interest Revenue		110	Interest Revenue		110

[9] The future value of $1 to be received two years from now, if the interest rate is 10% compounded annually, is $1.21.

Although the proper valuation of receivables calls for the amortization procedure just described, exceptions may be appropriate in some situations due to special limitations or practical considerations. Among the exceptions are the following:

> ". . . receivables and payables arising from transactions with customers or suppliers in the normal course of business which are due in customary trade terms not exceeding approximately one year."[10]

Accordingly, short-term notes and accounts receivable arising from trade sales may be properly recorded at the amounts collectible in the customary sales terms without separately recording the implicit interest embedded in those amounts.

Notes, like accounts receivable, are not always collectible. If notes receivable comprise a significant portion of regular trade receivables, a provision should be made for uncollectible amounts and an allowance account established using procedures similar to those for accounts receivable already discussed.

Special Valuation Problems

Special valuation issues arise with respect to nontrade long-term notes, such as secured and unsecured notes, debentures (bonds), equipment obligations, and mortgage notes. Examples are provided for notes exchanged for cash and for property, goods, or services.

Notes Exchanged for Cash When a note is exchanged for cash and no other rights or privileges are involved, the present value of the note is presumed to be the amount of the cash proceeds. The note should be recorded at its face amount, and any difference between the face amount and the cash proceeds should be recorded as a premium or discount on the note. The premium or discount should be amortized over the life of the note as illustrated previously for High Value Corporation. The total interest is measured by the difference in actual cash received by the borrower and the total amount to be received in the future by the lender. Any unamortized premium or discount on notes is reported on the balance sheet as a direct addition to or deduction from the face amount of the receivables, thus showing their net present value.

Notes Exchanged for Property, Goods, or Services When a note is exchanged for property, goods, or services in an arm's-length transaction, the present value of the note is usually evidenced by the terms of the note or supporting documents. There is a general presumption that the interest specified by the parties to a transaction represents fair and adequate compensation for the use of borrowed funds.[11] Valuation problems arise, however, when one of the following conditions exists:

1. No interest rate is stated.
2. The stated rate does not seem reasonable, given the nature of the transaction and surrounding circumstances.
3. The stated face amount of the note is significantly different from the current cash equivalent sales price of similar property, goods, or services, or from the current market value of similar notes at the date of the transaction.

Under any of the preceding conditions, the note should be recorded at (1) the fair value of the property, goods, or services exchanged or (2) the fair value of the note, whichever is more

[10] FASB ASC paragraph 835-30-15-3(a).
[11] FASB ASC paragraph 835-30-25-2.

clearly determinable. The difference between the face amount of the note and the recorded value is recognized as a discount or premium and is amortized over the life of the note.

> **! CAUTION**
> Make sure you are comfortable with the time value of money concepts discussed in the text module before proceeding with this example.

To illustrate, assume that on July 1, 2013, Timberline Corporation sells a tract of land purchased three years ago at a cost of $250,000. The buyer gives Timberline a 1-year note with a face amount of $310,000, bearing interest at a stated rate of 8%. An appraisal of the land prior to the sale indicated a market value of $300,000, which in this example is considered to be the appropriate basis for recording the sale as follows:

2013			
July 1	Notes Receivable	310,000	
	Discount on Notes Receivable		10,000
	Land		250,000
	Gain on Sale of Land		50,000

When the note is paid at maturity, Timberline will receive the face value ($310,000) plus stated interest of $24,800 ($310,000 × 0.08), or a total of $334,800. The interest to be recognized, however, is $34,800—the difference between the maturity value of the note and the market value of the land at the date of the exchange. Thus, the effective rate of interest on the note is 11.6% ($34,800/$300,000).

Assuming straight-line amortization of the discount and that Timberline's year-end is December 31, the following entries would be made to recognize interest revenue and to record payment of the note at maturity:

2013			
Dec. 31	Interest Receivable	12,400*	
	Discount on Notes Receivable	5,000	
	Interest Revenue		17,400
	*$310,000 × 0.08 × 6/12 = $12,400		
2013			
June 30	Cash	334,800	
	Discount on Notes Receivable	5,000	
	Notes Receivable		310,000
	Interest Receivable		12,400
	Interest Revenue		17,400

The unamortized discount balance of $5,000 would be subtracted from Notes Receivable on the December 31, 2013, balance sheet.

Imputing an Interest Rate If there is no current market price for either the property, goods, or services or the note, then the present value of the note must be determined by selecting an appropriate interest rate and using that rate to discount future receipts to the present. The imputed interest rate is determined at the date of the exchange and is not altered thereafter.

The selection of an appropriate rate is influenced by many factors, including the credit standing of the issuer of the note and prevailing interest rates for debt instruments of similar quality and length of time to maturity. The objective is as follows:

> In any event, the rate used for valuation purposes should be the rate at which the debtor can obtain financing of a similar nature from other sources at the date of the transaction.[12]

[12] FASB ASC 835-30-25-12.

SELLING A NOTE RECEIVABLE: WHAT'S IT WORTH?

As discussed earlier in the chapter, accounts and notes receivable can be used as an immediate source of cash by selling them to a factor. When a note receivable is sold, the value of the receivable depends on several factors including the interest rate on the note, the interest rate charged by the factor, and the time period involved.

Suppose for a moment that you are a bank official. What factors will affect the amount you are willing to pay to a company that wants to discount (sell) a note? First and foremost will be the creditworthiness of the maker; a second factor will be the length of time you must wait to get the money; and a third factor will be how much money you are going to receive when the note matures. Each of these factors will be reflected in your computation of the present value of that note. The steps to determine the amount to be received by the bank (the proceeds) are as follows:

1. Determine the maturity value of the note.

   Maturity value = Face amount + Interest
   Interest = Face amount × Interest rate × Interest period
   Interest period = Date of note to date of maturity

   The maturity value is the amount you will receive when the note matures.
2. Determine the amount of discount.

   Discount = Maturity value × Discount rate × Discount period
   Discount period = Date of discount to date of maturity

   Once the maturity value is determined, the second factor comes into play: how long you have to wait to get the money. This time period is termed the *discount period.* Finally, the creditworthiness of the maker enters into the equation. The riskier the maker, the higher the discount rate will be. Also affecting the discount rate are general economic variables.
3. Determine the proceeds.
   Proceeds = Maturity value − Discount

Once the proceeds are determined, the transaction can be recorded, recognizing the applicable liability and net interest revenue or expense (if a borrowing transaction) or the gain or loss (if a sales transaction).

Consider the following example. Meeker Corporation received a 3-month, $5,000, 10% note from a customer on September 1 to settle a past due accounts receivable. One month later, the note is discounted at a bank at a discount rate of 15%. The amount received from the bank would be computed as follows:

Maturity value of the note = $5,000 + ($5,000 × 0.10 × 3/12) = $5,125
Amount of discount = $5,125 × 0.15 × 2/12 = $128.13
Proceeds = $5,125 − $128.13 = $4,996.87

In this instance, Meeker would recognize a loss of $3.13 ($5,000 − $4,996.87) as a result of discounting the note.

To illustrate the process of imputing interest rates, assume that Horrocks & Associates surveyed 800,000 acres of mountain property for Mountain Meadow Ranch. On December 31, 2013, Horrocks accepted a $45,000 note as payment for services. The note is non-interest-bearing and comes due in three yearly installments of $15,000 each, beginning December 31, 2014. Assume there is no market for the note and no basis for estimating objectively the fair value of the services rendered. After considering the current prime interest rate, the credit standing of the ranch, the collateral available, the terms for repayment, and the prevailing rates of interest for the issuer's other debt, a 10% imputed interest rate is considered appropriate.

The note should be recorded at its present value and a discount recognized. The computation is based on the present value calculations as follows:

Face amount of note	$45,000
Less present value of note:	
PV_n: PMT = $15,000; N = 3; I = 10%	37,303*
Discount on note	$ 7,697

*Rounded to nearest dollar.

The entry to record the receipt of the note would be:

2013			
Dec. 31	Notes Receivable	45,000	
	Discount on Notes Receivable		7,697
	Service Revenue		37,303
	To record a non-interest-bearing note receivable at its present value based on an imputed interest rate of 10% per year.		

A schedule showing the amortization of the discount on the note follows. This type of computation is commonly referred to as the *effective interest amortization method.*

	(1) Face Amount Before Current Installment	(2) Unamortized Discount	(3) Net Amount (1) − (2)	(4) Discount Amortization 10% × (3)	(5) Payment Received
Dec. 31, 2014	$45,000	$7,697	$37,303	$3,730	$15,000
Dec. 31, 2015	30,000	3,967*	26,033	2,603	15,000
Dec. 31, 2016	15,000	1,364†	13,636	1,364	15,000
				$7,697	$45,000

*$7,697 − $3,730 = $3,967

†$3,967 − $2,603 = $1,364

At the end of each year, an entry similar to the following would be made:

2014			
Dec. 31	Cash	15,000	
	Discount on Notes Receivable	3,730	
	Interest Revenue		3,730
	Notes Receivable		15,000
	To record the first year's installment on notes receivable and recognize interest earned during the period.		

By using these procedures, at the end of the three years the discount will be completely amortized to interest revenue, the face amount of the note receivable will have been collected, and the appropriate amount of service revenue will have been recognized in the year it was earned. At the end of each year, the balance sheet will reflect the net present value of the receivable by subtracting the unamortized discount balance from the outstanding balance in Notes Receivable.

It is necessary to impute an interest rate only when the present value of the receivable cannot be determined through evaluation of existing market values of the elements of the transaction. The valuation and income measurement objectives remain the same regardless of the specific circumstances: to report notes receivable at their net present values and to record appropriate amounts of interest revenue during the collection period of the receivables.

Impact of Uncollectible Accounts on the Statement of Cash Flows

8 **Understand the impact of uncollectible accounts on the statement of cash flows.**

WHY **The accounts Allowance for Bad Debts and Bad Debt Expense must be interpreted with care when determining the amount of operating cash flows related to receivables.**

HOW **When the indirect method is used, the best way to make the appropriate cash flow adjustment for changes in the receivables balance is to incorporate the change in NET receivables (gross receivables less the allowance). When the direct method is used, recall that bad debt expense represents a reduction in net receivables that does NOT constitute a collection of cash.**

As noted in Chapter 5, the amount of reported sales or net income on an accrual basis must be adjusted for the change in the accounts receivable balances to derive the corresponding amount of cash flow from operations. The establishment of a provision for bad debts with a corresponding allowance for bad debts and the subsequent writing off of uncollectible accounts will impact the adjustments made, depending on whether the analysis considers gross or net accounts receivable balances.

To this point, we have assumed that any decrease in accounts receivable represents a payment received on account. Actually, two possibilities are associated with a decrease in receivables: Customers pay or customers never pay and the account is written off. Thus, a decrease in receivables may reflect a receipt of cash, or it may reflect the writing off of an account.

To illustrate the adjustments required for accounts receivable when preparing a statement of cash flows, consider the following information:

	Beginning Balances	Ending Balances
Accounts receivable	$20,000	$ 25,000
Allowance for bad debts	4,000	4,800
Net accounts receivable	$16,000	$ 20,200
Sales for the year		$1,000,000
Net income for the year		100,000
Bad debt expense for the year		2,000
Write-off of uncollectible amounts for the year		1,200
Cash expenses for the year		898,000

In order to focus on the impact of uncollectible accounts, the illustration assumes that all operating expenses other than bad debt expense were paid in cash. Also, it is assumed that—with the exception of accounts receivable—there were no changes in the amounts of current assets and current liabilities.

In T-account form, the receivables account and the associated allowance account appear as follows:

Accounts Receivable

Debit		Credit
Beg. bal.	20,000	
	1,000,000	
		993,800
		1,200
End. bal.	25,000	

Allowance for Bad Debts

Debit	Credit	
	Beg. bal.	4,000
1,200		2,000
	End. bal.	4,800

The accounts receivable account increased from $20,000 to $25,000. Given sales of $1,000,000, credits to Accounts Receivable must have totaled $995,000, but this $995,000 does not relate entirely to cash collections. A portion of the decline, $1,200, relates to the fact that some cash will never be collected and is no longer an asset; it must be written off. Therefore, cash collections total $993,800.

How is this information reflected in the statement of cash flows? Using the format discussed in Chapter 5, we will begin with the income statement and make adjustments as follows:

Income Statement		Adjustments		Cash Flows from Operations
Sales	$1,000,000	$(5,000)	$995,000 }	Cash collected from customers
Bad debt expense	(2,000)	800	(1,200) }	
Cash expenses	(898,000)	0	(898,000)	Cash paid for expenses
Net income	$ 100,000	$(4,200)	$ 95,800	Cash from operations

The first adjustment of ($5,000) reflects the increase in the accounts receivable account resulting from sales (the debit side of the receivables account) exceeding credits to the accounts receivable account (cash collections and actual bad debts). The second adjustment converts the accrual basis measure, the bad debt expense (the credit side of the allowance account), to its cash flow counterpart, actual bad debts (the debit side of the allowance account). These two adjustments, considered together, tell us that $993,800 ($995,000 − $1,200) was collected from customers during the period.

Using the preceding information, the net cash flow provided by operations during the period is as follows:

Direct Method	
Cash collected from customers	$993,800
Cash expenses	(898,000)
Net cash flow provided by operations	$ 95,800

Indirect Method	
Net income	$100,000
Less: Increase in accounts receivable	(5,000)
Add: Increase in allowance for bad debts	800
Net cash flows provided by operations	$ 95,800

Often, accounts receivable will be presented net of the bad debt expense. Take a look at the following T-account in which "netting" occurs.

Accounts Receivable (net)			
Beg. bal.	16,000		
Sales	1,000,000		
		Collections	993,800
		Bad debt expense	2,000
End. bal.	20,200		

What happened to the $1,200 related to the amounts written off as uncollectible? Because that amount appeared as a credit in the receivables account and a debit in the allowance account, it will net out to $0 when the two accounts are combined.

The statement of cash flows, when net accounts receivable are presented, can be prepared from the following information.

Income Statement		**Adjustments**		**Cash Flows from Operations**
Sales	$1,000,000	$(4,200)	$995,800	Cash collected from customers
Bad debt expense	(2,000)	0	(2,000)	
Cash expenses	(898,000)	0	(898,000)	Cash paid for expenses
Net income	$ 100,000	$(4,200)	$ 95,800	Cash from operations

Sales is simply adjusted for the change in the net receivables account. Why is there no adjustment to Bad Debt Expense in this case? Because when the two accounts are netted together, all adjustments are netted together as well and result in the $4,200 adjustment.

Using net receivables, the net cash flows provided by operations during the period is presented as follows:

Direct Method	
Cash collected from customers	$993,800
Cash expenses	(898,000)
Net cash flow provided by operations	$ 95,800

Indirect Method	
Net income	$100,000
Less: Increase in accounts receivable	(4,200)
Net cash flows provided by operations	$ 95,800

In the vast majority of cases, net receivables are presented and the indirect method is used. In these instances, the only adjustment required relates to the change in the net accounts receivable balance.

? SOLUTIONS TO OPENING SCENARIO QUESTIONS

1. The largest revenue amount for a bank is interest revenue on its loans. In 2009, Bank of America reported interest revenue on its loans of $48.7 billion. In addition, Bank of America reported interest revenue from investments of an additional $12.9 billion. The largest expense amount for a bank is usually its interest expense. In 2009, Bank of America reported interest expense of $30.8 billion of which $7.8 billion was interest paid to depositors. In 2009, Bank of America had the unwelcome experience of its bad debt expense for the year ($48.6 billion) exceeding its interest expense.

2. As of December 31, 2009, Bank of America had consumer loans outstanding of $739 billion and commercial loans outstanding of $323 billion. By far the largest loan category was residential mortgages/home equity loans at $391 billion. (*Note:* Because of various classifications on Bank of America's balance sheet, these numbers do NOT add up to the total reported loans receivable amount of $863 billion.)

3. The net charge-off ratio for the residential mortgage loans was just 1.74%. For home equity loans the net charge-off ratio was slightly higher at 4.56%. The net charge-off ratio for direct/indirect consumer loans was 5.46%, and the net charge-off ratio for domestic credit card loans was 12.50%.

SOLUTIONS TO STOP & THINK

1. (Page 7-5) The correct answer is A. The use of credit allows businesses to attract customers. A policy of "cash only" may cause customers to shop elsewhere, especially if all of a company's competitors are offering credit terms.

2. (Page 7-24) The correct answer is D. If an outstanding check is omitted from the outstanding check list in the reconciliation, the corrected bank balance will be greater than the corrected book balance. When a bank reconciliation does not reconcile, it is good practice to look at the reconciliation for the preceding month to see whether all outstanding checks listed in that month have subsequently cleared the bank. The other potential errors listed (a, b, and c) would all cause the corrected bank balance to be less than the corrected book balance.

3. (Page 7-30) The correct answer is C. The factor would charge a fee based on the risk he or she is assuming. Factoring without recourse involves the factor assuming all the risk associated with collections. To assume that risk, the factor will charge a higher fee. If the risk of collection remains with the company (with recourse), then the factor would be willing to charge a lower fee.

SOLUTION TO USING THE FASB'S CODIFICATION

By going to the paragraphs on regular warranties, you should run across FASB ASC paragraph 460-10-25-8 which leads to Section 605-20-25. Paragraph 4 of that Section says the following: "Costs that are directly related to the acquisition of a contract and that would have not been incurred but for the acquisition of that contract (incremental direct acquisition costs) shall be deferred and charged to expense in proportion to the revenue recognized." So, those salespersons' commissions should be deferred (recorded as a prepaid expense) and amortized to expense over the life of the associated extended warranty agreement. This matches the commission expense recognition with the timing of the recognition of the revenue from the extended warranty.

REVIEW CHAPTER 7

LEARNING OBJECTIVES

1 Explain the normal operating cycle of a business.

The operating cycle is the lifeblood of almost every business. The critical event for a business is the sale of goods or services. This sale often results in the recording of an account receivable. The account receivable is then collected, the resulting cash is reinvested in the business, and the cycle begins again.

2 Prepare journal entries to record sales revenue, including the accounting for bad debts and warranties for service or replacement.

A sale is recorded with a credit to Sales Revenue and a debit to either Accounts Receivable or Cash. The matching principle requires that expenses associated with the sale be recorded in the period of the sale. As a result, items such as bad debts and warranties must be estimated and recorded.

Bad debts are estimated using one of two methods: percentage of sales or percentage of receivables. Each of these methods involves estimating the likelihood that some receivables will not be collected. The journal entry involves a debit to Bad Debt Expense and a credit to Allowance for Bad Debts. The allowance account is a contra asset account that, when offset against the accounts receivable account, values the asset at its net realizable value.

Warranties are quantified by estimating, based on past experience, the probable amount of future warranty costs and are recorded with a debit to Warranty Expense and a credit to a liability account. When the warranty claim is presented, the liability account is reduced and a credit is made to cash, parts, labor, and so forth.

3 Analyze accounts receivable to measure how efficiently a firm is using this operating asset.

The effective management of accounts receivable is critical to the cash flows of any business. The most common tool used to monitor receivables is the average collection period, which reflects the average number of days that lapse between the time a sale is made and cash is collected. First, the accounts receivable turnover ratio is computed by dividing sales by average accounts receivable. The resulting number is divided into 365 (the number of days in a year) to compute the average collection period.

4 Discuss the composition, management, and control of cash, including the use of a bank reconciliation.

Cash management and control are critical to the success of every business. Because cash is the most liquid of assets, safeguards must be in place to ensure that cash is properly handled and accounted for. A common control involves the use of a bank reconciliation. A bank reconciliation requires the accountant to reconcile the bank's balance for cash with the company's balance. Any discrepancies are identified and appropriate corrections are made.

5 Recognize appropriate disclosures for presenting sales and receivables in the financial statements.

Disclosure of sales and receivables in the financial statements vary from company to company. In the body of the financial statements, sales are generally reported net of discounts and allowances. Receivables are often reported net of their allowance account with supplemental information provided in the notes to the financial statements.

EM EXPANDED MATERIAL

6 Explain how receivables may be used as a source of cash through secured borrowing or sale.

In most cases, a receivable is converted into cash when a customer, in the normal cycle of business, pays the company. However, companies can accelerate the cash collection process by using accounts receivable to assist in obtaining a loan. The method employed and the cost to the firm depend on the degree of risk to which the company wishes to expose itself. In the case of secured borrowing, the company is simply pledging the receivable as collateral on a loan. Receivables can also be sold to a third party, usually a bank or other financial institution. When a receivable is sold with recourse, the selling company must quantify the expected payout that will be made as a result of the recourse provision.

7 Describe proper accounting and valuation of notes receivable.

Notes receivable represent a formal borrowing arrangement between two parties. A note receivable typically specifies an interest rate and a payment date. Notes receivable are valued using techniques that compute the present value of the principal and interest to be received. Problems can arise in the valuation of notes receivable when the note is exchanged for goods or services and the fair market value of those goods and services is difficult to determine. In some instances, an effective interest rate for the note must be imputed.

8 Understand the impact of uncollectible accounts on the statement of cash flows.

The accounts Allowance for Bad Debts and Bad Debt Expense must be interpreted with care when determining the amount of cash flows related to receivables for a certain period. Different adjustments are made to the statement of cash flows, depending on whether the direct or indirect method is being used. The objective of these adjustments is to correctly identify cash collections from customers for the period.

FASB-IASB CODIFICATION SUMMARY

ifrs

Topic	FASB Accounting Standards Codification	Original FASB Standard	Corresponding IASB Standard	Differences between U.S. GAAP and IFRS
Bad debts	*Section 310-10-35 par. 7-9*	*SFAS No. 5 par. 22*	*No explicit standard*	No apparent differences
Warranties	*Section 460-10-25 par. 5-7*	*SFAS No. 5 par. 24*	*IAS 37 par. 14, 39*	No substantial differences
Compensating balances	*Section 210-10-S99 par. 1*	*SEC Regulation S-X, Rule 5-02, Caption 1*	*IAS 7 par. 48*	No substantial differences
Imputation of interest on receivables	*Section 835-30-25 par. 2, 12*	*APB No. 21 par. 9, 13*	*No explicit standard*	No apparent differences
Derecognition of receivables	*Section 860-10-40 par. 5*	*SFAS No. 140 par. 9*	*IAS 39 par. 20*	U.S. GAAP includes a list of three criteria that must be satisfied for derecognition. IFRS has a conceptual two-step test based on risks and rewards and control. In practice, the derecognition result is almost always the same.

KEY TERMS

Accounts receivable 7-4
Accounts receivable turnover 7-16
Aging receivables 7-12
Allowance method 7-9
Average collection period 7-16
Bank reconciliation 7-22
Bank service charge 7-22
Cash 7-18
Cash equivalents 7-19
Cash (sales) discount 7-7
Cash overdraft 7-19
Compensating balances 7-20
Demand deposits 7-19
Deposit in transit 7-22
Direct write-off method 7-9
Net realizable value 7-8
Nontrade receivables 7-5
Notes receivable 7-5
Not-sufficient-funds (NSF) check 7-22
Outstanding checks 7-22
Present value 7-8
Revenue 7-4
Time deposits 7-19
Trade discount 7-6
Trade receivables 7-5
Warranties 7-13

EM EXPANDED MATERIAL

Accounts receivable factoring 7-28
Assignment of receivables 7-30
Implicit (effective) interest 7-34
Imputed interest rate 7-36
Interest-bearing note 7-33
Negotiable notes 7-33
Non-interest-bearing note 7-33
Principal (face amount) 7-33
Promissory note 7-33
Selling receivables with recourse 7-29

QUESTIONS

1. Explain how each of the following factors affects the classification of a receivable: (a) the form of a receivable, (b) the source of a receivable, and (c) the expected time to maturity or collection.
2. (a) Describe the methods for establishing and maintaining an allowance for bad debts account.
   (b) How would the percentages used in estimating uncollectible accounts be determined under each of the methods?
3. In accounting for uncollectible accounts receivable, why does GAAP require the allowance method rather than the direct write-off method?
4. An analysis of the accounts receivable balance of $8,702 on the records of Jorgenson, Inc., on December 31 reveals the following:

Accounts from sales of last three months (appear to be fully collectible)	$7,460
Accounts from sales prior to October 1 (of doubtful value)	1,312
Accounts known to be worthless	320
Dishonored notes charged back to customers' accounts	800
Credit balances in customers' accounts	1,190

(a) What adjustments are required?
(b) How should the various balances be shown on the balance sheet?

5. Why should a company normally account for product warranties on an accrual basis?
6. (a) How is accounts receivable turnover computed?
   (b) How is average collection period computed?
   (c) What do these two measurements show?
7. Why is cash on hand necessary yet potentially unproductive?
8. The following items were included as cash on the balance sheet for Lawson Co. How should each of the items have been reported?
   (a) Demand deposits with bank
   (b) Restricted cash deposits in foreign banks
   (c) Bank account used for payment of salaries and wages
   (d) Cash in a special cash account to be used currently for the construction of a new building
   (e) Customers' checks returned by the bank marked "Not Sufficient Funds"
   (f) Customers' postdated checks
   (g) IOUs from employees
   (h) Postage stamps received in the mail for merchandise
   (i) Postal money orders received from customers not yet deposited
   (j) Notes receivable in the hands of the bank for collection
   (k) Special bank account in which sales tax collections are deposited
   (l) Customers' checks not yet deposited
9. Melvin Company shows in its accounts a cash balance of $66,500 with Bank A and an overdraft of $1,500 with Bank B on December 31. Bank B regards the overdraft as, in effect, a loan to Melvin Company and charges interest on the overdraft balance. How would you report the balances with Banks A and B? Would your answer be any different if the overdraft arose as a result of certain checks that had been deposited and proved to be uncollectible and if the overdraft was cleared promptly by Melvin Company at the beginning of January?
10. Mills Manufacturing is required to maintain a compensating balance of $15,000 with its bank to maintain a line of open credit. The compensating balance is legally restricted as to its use. How should the compensating balance be reported on the balance sheet and why?
11. (a) Give at least four common sources of differences between depositor and bank balances.
    (b) Which of the differences in (a) require an adjusting entry on the books of the depositor?

EM EXPANDED MATERIAL

12. How are attitudes regarding the financing of accounts receivable changing? Why do you think this is so?
13. (a) Distinguish between the practices of (1) selling receivables and (2) using receivables as collateral for borrowing.
    (b) Describe the accounting procedures to be followed in each case.
14. Under U.S. GAAP, what three conditions must be met to record the transfer of receivables with recourse as a sale?
15. Describe the 2-step test required under the provisions of *IAS 39* to determine whether a receivable should be derecognized.
16. (a) When should a note receivable be recorded at an amount different from its face amount?
    (b) Describe the procedures employed in accounting for the difference between a note's face amount and its recorded value.
17. Explain what special accounting procedures are required when receivables are assigned as collateral for a secured loan.
18. What is meant by *imputing a rate of interest?* How is such a rate determined?

PRACTICE EXERCISES

Practice 7-1
LO2

Simple Credit Sale Journal Entries
Credit sales for the year were $150,000. Collections on account were $101,000. Make the necessary summary journal entries to record this information.

Practice 7-2
LO2

Sales Discounts: Gross Method
On January 16, two credit sales were made, one for $300 and one for $400. Terms for both sales were 3/15, n/30. Cash for the $300 sale was collected on January 25; cash for the $400 sale was collected on February 14. Make all journal entries necessary to record both the sales and the cash collections. Use the gross method of accounting for sales discounts.

Practice 7-3
LO2

Sales Discounts: Net Method
Refer to Practice 7-2. Make all journal entries necessary to record both the sales and the cash collections. Use the net method of accounting for sales discounts.

Practice 7-4
LO2

Sales Returns and Allowances
On July 15, goods costing $8,400 were sold for $12,000 on account. The customer returned the goods before paying for them. Make the journal entry or entries necessary on the books of the seller to record the return of the goods. Assume that the goods are not damaged and can be resold at their normal selling price. Also assume that the selling company uses a perpetual inventory system.

Practice 7-5
LO2

Basic Bad Debt Journal Entries
Bad debt expense for the year was estimated to be $12,000. Total accounts written off as uncollectible during the year were $8,100. Make the necessary summary journal entries to record this information.

Practice 7-6
LO2

Recovery of an Account Previously Written Off
Because of the extreme deterioration in the financial condition of a customer, the customer's account in the amount of $7,500 was written off as uncollectible on July 23. By November 1, the customer's financial condition had improved such that the customer was able to pay the account in full. Make the journal entries necessary to write the account off on July 23 and then to record the collection of the account on November 1.

Practice 7-7
LO2

Bad Debts: Percentage-of-Sales Method
Bad debt expense is estimated using the percentage-of-sales method. Total sales for the year were $600,000. The ending balance in Accounts Receivable was $100,000. Historically, bad debts have been 3% of total sales. The economic circumstances of credit customers this year are about the same as they have been in past years. Total accounts written off as uncollectible during the year were $19,700. Make the necessary summary journal entries to record this bad debt-related information.

Practice 7-8
LO2

Bad Debts: Percentage-of-Accounts-Receivable Method
Bad debt expense is estimated using the percentage-of-accounts-receivable method. Total sales for the year were $600,000. The ending balance in Accounts Receivable was $200,000. An examination of the outstanding accounts at the end of the year indicates that approximately 14% of these accounts will ultimately prove to be uncollectible. Before any adjustment, the balance in Allowance for Bad Debts is $900 (credit). Total accounts written off as uncollectible during the year were $16,600. Make the necessary summary journal entries to record this bad debt-related information.

Practice 7-9
LO2

Aging Accounts Receivable
The following aging of accounts receivable is as of the end of the year:

	Overall	Less Than 30 Days	31–60 Days	61–90 Days	Over 90 Days
Ken Nelson	$ 10,000	$ 8,000		$1,000	$1,000
Elaine Anderson	40,000	31,000	$ 4,000		5,000
Bryan Crist	12,000	3,000	4,000	2,000	3,000
Renee Warner	60,000	50,000	10,000		
Nelson Hsia	16,000	10,000	6,000		
Stella Valerio	25,000	20,000		5,000	
Total	$163,000	$122,000	$24,000	$8,000	$9,000

Historical experience indicates the following:

Age of Account	Percentage Ultimately Uncollectible
Less than 30 days	2%
31 to 60 days	10
61 to 90 days	30
Over 90 days	75

Compute the appropriate amount of Allowance for Bad Debts as of the end of the year.

Practice 7-10
LO2

Estimation and Recognition of Warranty Expense
Historically, warranty expenditures have been equal to 4% of sales. Total sales for the year were $750,000. Actual warranty repairs made during the year totaled $37,400. Make the necessary summary journal entries to record this warranty-related information.

Practice 7-11
LO2

Comparison of Actual and Expected Warranty Expense
The company offers a 1-year warranty to its customers. Warranty expenditures are estimated to be 4% of sales. Sales occur evenly throughout the year. The following information relates to the company's first two years of business:

Sales—Year 1	$100,000
Actual warranty repairs—Year 1	3,000
Sales—Year 2	$150,000
Actual warranty repairs—Year 2	6,500

(1) Compute the balance in the warranty liability account at the end of Year 2. (2) Evaluate whether that balance is too high or too low given the company's experience.

Practice 7-12
LO3

Average Collection Period
Sales for the year were $400,000. The Accounts Receivable balance was $50,000 at the beginning of the year and $65,000 at the end of the year. Compute the average collection period using (1) the average accounts receivable balance and (2) the ending accounts receivable balance.

Practice 7-13
LO4

Computation of Cash Balance
Using the following information, compute the cash balance.

Restricted deposits in foreign bank accounts	$ 5,200
Cash overdraft	(1,000)
Postdated customer checks	750
Savings account balance	10,000
Coin and currency	2,300

Practice 7-14
LO4

Bank Reconciliation
The company received a bank statement at the end of the month. The statement contained the following:

Ending balance	$11,500
Bank service charge for the month	65
Interest earned and added by the bank to the account balance	45

In comparing the bank statement to its own cash records, the company found the following:

Deposits made but not yet recorded by the bank	$2,700
Checks written and mailed but not yet recorded by the bank	3,900

Before making any adjustment suggested by the bank statement, the cash balance according to the books is $10,320. What is the correct cash balance as of the end of the month? Verify this amount by reconciling the bank statement with the cash balance on the books.

EM EXPANDED MATERIAL

Practice 7-15
LO6

Sale of Receivables without Recourse
Cammo Company sold receivables (without recourse) for $53,000. Cammo received $50,000 cash immediately from the factor (the company to whom the receivables were sold). The remaining $3,000 will be received once the factor verifies that none of the receivables is in dispute. The receivables had a face amount of $60,000; Cammo had previously established an Allowance for Bad Debts of $2,500 in connection with these receivables. Make the journal entry necessary on Cammo's books to record the sale of these receivables.

Practice 7-16
LO6

Sale of Receivables with Recourse
Refer to Practice 7-15. Assume that the sale of the receivables was done *with* recourse. The estimated value of the recourse obligation is $1,300. Make the journal entry necessary on Cammo's books to record the sale of these receivables with recourse.

Practice 7-17
LO6

Accounting for a Secured Borrowing
Refer to Practice 7-15. Assume that Cammo received the entire $53,000 in cash immediately. Also assume that the transfer of receivables did *not* satisfy the three conditions contained in FASB ASC paragraph 860-10-40-5. Make the journal entry necessary on Cammo's books to record the transfer of these receivables.

Practice 7-18
LO7

Journal Entries for Interest-Bearing Note
As payment for services rendered, the company received an 18-month note on January 1. The face amount of the note is $6,000, and the stated rate of interest is 9%, compounded annually. The 9% rate is equal to the market rate. The full amount of the note, including accrued interest, will be received at the end of the 18-month period. Make *all* journal entries necessary on the books of the recipient of the note during the 18-month life of this note. Don't forget any necessary year-end adjusting entry.

Practice 7-19
LO7

Journal Entries for Non-Interest-Bearing Note
As payment for services rendered, the company received a 24-month note on January 1. The face amount of the note is $1,000; the note is non-interest-bearing. The cash price of the services rendered is $857. The market rate of interest is 8%, compounded annually. The $1,000 face amount of the note will be received at the end of the 24-month period. Make *all* journal entries necessary on the books of the recipient of the note during the 24-month life of this note. Don't forget any necessary year-end adjusting entry. The cash will be received on December 31 of the second year.

Practice 7-20
LO7

Note Exchanged for Goods or Services
In exchange for land, the company received a 12-month note on January 1. The face amount of the note is $2,000, and the stated rate of interest is 12%, compounded annually. The 12% rate is equal to the market rate. The original cost of the land was $2,450. The full amount of the note, including accrued interest, will be received at the end of the 12-month period, on December 31. Make *all* journal entries necessary on the books of the recipient of the note during the 12-month life of this note.

Practice 7-21
LO7

Effective Interest Amortization Method
As payment for services rendered, the company received a 36-month note on January 1. The face amount of the note is $1,000; the note is non-interest-bearing. There is no reasonable basis for determining the cash price of the services rendered. The market

rate of interest is 10%, compounded annually. The $1,000 face amount of the note will be received at the end of the 36-month period. Make *all* journal entries necessary on the books of the recipient of the note during the 36-month life of this note. Don't forget any necessary year-end adjusting entries.

Practice 7-22
LO8

Bad Debts and the Direct Method

	Ending Balances	Beginning Balances
Accounts receivable	$ 9,500	$13,000
Allowance for bad debts	3,100	3,000
Sales for the year	75,000	
Net income for the year	20,000	
Bad debt expense for the year	2,000	
Write-off of uncollectible amounts for the year	1,900	
Cash expenses for the year	53,000	

Prepare the Operating Activities section of the statement of cash flows using the direct method.

Practice 7-23
LO8

Bad Debts and the Indirect Method
Refer to Practice 7-22. Prepare the Operating Activities section of the statement of cash flows using the indirect method.

EXERCISES

Exercise 7-24
LO2

Sales Returns
On July 23, Louie Company sold goods costing $3,000 on account for $4,500. The terms of the sale were n/30. Payment in satisfaction of $3,000 of this amount was received on August 17. Also on August 17, the customer returned goods costing $1,000 (with a sales price of $1,500). The customer reported that the goods did not meet the required specifications.

1. Make the journal entry necessary on July 23 to record the sale. Louie uses a perpetual inventory system.
2. Make the journal entry necessary on August 17 to record the cash collection.
3. Make the journal entry necessary on August 17 to record the return of the goods.
4. What question exists with respect to the valuation of the returned inventory?

Exercise 7-25
LO2

Sales Discounts
On November 1, Rosario Company sold goods on account for $7,000. The terms of the sale were 3/10, n/40. Payment in satisfaction of $3,000 of this amount was received on November 9. Payment in satisfaction of the remaining $4,000 was received on December 9.

1. How much cash did Rosario Company collect from this $7,000 account?
2. Using the gross method, what journal entries would Rosario make on November 9 and December 9?
3. Using the net method, what journal entries would Rosario make on November 9 and December 9?

Exercise 7-26
LO4

Correct Cash Balance

Sterling Company's bank statement for the month of March included the following information:

Ending balance, March 31	$32,346
Bank service charge for March	130
Interest paid by bank to Sterling for March	107

In comparing the bank statement to its own cash records, Sterling found the following:

Deposits made but not yet recorded by the bank	$3,689
Checks written and mailed but not yet recorded by the bank	6,530

In addition, Sterling discovered that it had erroneously recorded a check for $46 that should have been recorded for $64. What is Sterling's correct Cash balance at March 31?

Exercise 7-27
LO4

Correct Cash Balance

Lewiston Corporation's bank statement for the month of April included the following information:

Bank service charge for April	$110
Check deposited by Lewiston during April was not collectible and has been marked "NSF" by the bank and returned	350

In comparing the bank statement to its own cash records, Lewiston found:

Deposits made but not yet recorded by the bank	$1,674
Checks written and mailed but not yet recorded by the bank	677

All the deposits in transit and outstanding checks have been properly recorded in Lewiston's books. Lewiston also found a check for $275, payable to Lewiston Corporation, that had not yet been deposited and had not been recorded in Lewiston's books. Lewiston's books show a bank account balance of $7,842 (before any adjustments or corrections). What is Lewiston's Corporation's correct Cash balance at April 30?

Exercise 7-28
LO4

Reporting Cash on the Balance Sheet

1. Indicate how each of the items below should be reported using the following classifications: (a) cash, (b) restricted cash, (c) temporary investment, (d) receivable, (e) liability, or (f) office supplies.

(1) Checking account at First Security	$ (20)
(2) Checking account at Second Security	350
(3) U.S. t-bills	650
(4) Payroll account	100
(5) Sales tax account	150
(6) Foreign bank account—restricted (in equivalent U.S. dollars)	750
(7) Postage stamps	22
(8) Employee's postdated check	30
(9) IOU from president's brother	75
(10) Credit memo from a vendor for a purchase return	87
(11) Traveler's check	50
(12) Not-sufficient-funds check	18
(13) Petty cash fund ($16 in currency and expense receipts for $84)	100
(14) Money order	36

2. What amount would be reported as unrestricted cash on the balance sheet?

Exercise 7-29
LO4

Composition of Cash

Ortiz Company had the following cash balances at December 31, 2013:

Undeposited coin and currency	$ 29,500
Unrestricted demand deposits	1,375,000
Company checks written (and deducted from the demand deposits amount) but not scheduled to be mailed until January 2	265,000
Time deposits restricted for use (expected use in 2014)	2,500,000

In exchange for a guaranteed line of credit, Ortiz has agreed to maintain a minimum balance of $225,000 in its unrestricted demand deposits account. How much should Ortiz report as Cash in its December 31, 2013, balance sheet?

Exercise 7-30
LO4

Restricted Cash

Baltic Group, Inc., operates Baltic Group resorts in the United States, Mexico, the Caribbean, Asia, the South Pacific, and the Indian Ocean Basin. Baltic Group routinely receives payment in advance from vacationers. In some countries, Baltic Group is required by law to deposit cash received as payment for future vacations in special accounts. Cash in these accounts is restricted as to its use.

Assume that on December 31, Baltic Group received cash totaling $7,450,000 as payment in advance for vacations at one of its resorts. The resort is in a country that requires that the cash be deposited in a special account.

1. Prepare the journal entry necessary to record receipt of the $7,450,000.
2. Explain how the $7,450,000 would be disclosed in the December 31 balance sheet.

Exercise 7-31
LO3

Analyzing Accounts Receivable

Trend Industries Company reported the following amounts on its 2012 and 2013 financial statements:

	2013	2012
Accounts receivable	$ 235,000	$ 210,000
Allowance for bad debts	12,000	8,000
Net sales	2,145,000	1,890,000
Cost of sales	1,067,000	856,000

1. Compute the accounts receivable turnover for 2013.
2. What is the average collection period during 2013? (Use 365 days.)

Exercise 7-32
LO1

Computing the Accounts Receivable Balance

The following information from Tiny Company's first year of operations is to be used in testing the accuracy of Accounts Receivable. The December 31, 2013, balance is $21,300.

(a) Collections from customers, $53,000.
(b) Merchandise purchased, $74,000.
(c) Ending merchandise inventory, $31,500.
(d) Goods sell at 60% above cost.
(e) All sales are on account.

Compute the balance that Accounts Receivable should show and determine the amount of any shortage or overage.

Exercise 7-33
LO2

Aging Accounts Receivable

Blanchard Company's accounts receivable subsidiary ledger reveals the following information:

Customer	Account Balance Dec. 31, 2013	Invoice Amounts and Dates	
Allison, Inc.	$ 8,795	$3,500	12/6/2013
		5,295	11/29/2013
Banks Bros.	5,230	3,000	9/27/2013
		2,230	8/20/2013
Barker & Co.	7,650	5,000	12/8/2013
		2,650	10/25/2013
Marrin Co.	11,285	5,785	11/17/2013
		5,500	10/9/2013
Ring, Inc.	7,900	4,800	12/12/2013
		3,100	12/2/2013
West Corp.	4,350	4,350	9/12/2013

Blanchard Company's receivable collection experience indicates that, on average, losses have occurred as follows:

Age of Accounts	Uncollectible Percentage
0–30 days	0.7%
31–60 days	1.4
61–90 days	3.5
91–120 days	10.2
Over 120 days	60.0

The Allowance for Bad Debts credit balance on December 31, 2013, was $2,245 before adjustment.

1. Prepare an accounts receivable aging schedule.
2. Using the aging schedule from (1), compute the Allowance for Bad Debts balance as of December 31, 2013.
3. Prepare the end-of-year adjusting entry.
4. (a) Where accounts receivable are few in number, such as in this exercise, what are some possible weaknesses in estimating bad debts by the aging method?
   (b) Would the other methods of estimating bad debts be subject to these same weaknesses? Explain.

Exercise 7-34

LO2

Journal Entries for Receivable Write-Offs

McGraw Medical Center has received a bankruptcy notice for Phillip Hollister. Hollister owes the medical center $1,350. The bankruptcy notice indicates that the medical center can't expect to receive payment of any of the $1,350.

1. Make the journal entry necessitated by receipt of the bankruptcy notice.
2. Six months after the medical center received the bankruptcy notice, Hollister appeared requesting medical treatment. He agreed to pay his old bill in its entirety. Make the journal entry or entries necessary to record receipt of the $1,350 payment from Hollister.

Exercise 7-35

LO1

Classifying Receivables

Classify each of the following items as: (A) Accounts Receivable, (B) Notes Receivable, (C) Trade Receivables, (D) Nontrade Receivables, or (E) Other (indicate nature of item). Because the classifications are not mutually exclusive, more than one classification may be appropriate. Also indicate whether the item would normally be reported as a current or noncurrent asset assuming a 6-month operating cycle.

1. **MasterCard** or **VISA** credit card sale of merchandise to customer
2. Overpayment to supplier for inventory purchased on account
3. Insurance claim on automobile accident
4. Charge sale to regular customer
5. Advance to sales manager
6. Interest due on 5-year note from company president, interest payable annually
7. Acceptance of 3-year note on sale of land held as investment
8. Acceptance of 6-month note for past-due account arising from the sale of inventory
9. Claim for a tax refund from last year
10. Prepaid insurance—four months remaining in the policy period
11. Overpayment by customer of an account receivable

Exercise 7-36

LO2

Analysis of Allowance for Bad Debts

The Intercontinental Publishing Company follows the procedure of debiting Bad Debt Expense for 2% of all new sales. Sales for four consecutive years and year-end allowance account balances were as follows:

Year	Sales	Allowance for Bad Debts End-of-Year Credit Balance
2010	$3,000,000	$ 44,600
2011	2,850,000	61,600
2012	3,600,000	82,800
2013	3,940,000	123,000

1. Compute the amount of accounts written off for the years 2011, 2012, and 2013.
2. The external auditors are concerned with the growing amount in the allowance account. What action do you recommend the auditors take?

Exercise 7-37

LO2

Estimating Bad Debts

Accounts Receivable of the Chalet Housing Co. on December 31, 2013, had a balance of $550,000. Allowance for Bad Debts had a $4,500 debit balance. Sales in 2013 were $3,450,000 less sales discounts of $51,000. Give the adjusting entry for estimated Bad Debt Expense under each of the following independent assumptions.

1. Of 2013 net sales, 1.5% will probably never be collected.
2. Of outstanding accounts receivable, 8% are doubtful.
3. An aging schedule shows that $41,000 of the outstanding accounts receivable are doubtful.

Exercise 7-38

LO4

REVERSE SOLVABLE

Bank Reconciliation—Analysis of Outstanding Checks

The following information was included in the bank reconciliation for Bryant, Inc., for June. What was the total of outstanding checks at the beginning of June? Assume all other reconciling items are listed.

Checks and charges recorded by bank in June, including a June service charge of $35	$16,320
Service charge made by bank in May and recorded on the books in June	30
Total of credits to Cash in all journals during June	21,705
Customer's NSF check returned as a bank charge in June (no entry made on books)	200
Customer's NSF check returned in May and redeposited in June (no entry made on books in either May or June)	275
Outstanding checks at June 30	11,470
Deposits in transit at June 30	500

Exercise 7-39
LO4

Bank Reconciliation and Adjusting Entries

The accounting department supplied the following data in reconciling the September 30 bank statement for Clegg Auto.

Ending cash balance per bank	$18,972.67
Ending cash balance per books	16,697.76
Deposits in transit	3,251.42
Bank service charge	20.00
Outstanding checks	4,163.51
Note collected by bank including $50 interest (Clegg not yet notified)	2,150.00
Error by bank—check drawn by Gregg Corp. was charged to Clegg's account	713.18

A sale and deposit of $1,628.00 were entered in the sales journal and cash receipts journal as $1,682.00.

1. Prepare the September 30 bank reconciliation.
2. Give the journal entries required on the books to adjust the cash account.

Exercise 7-40
LO2

Extended Service Contract

Hitech Appliance Company's accountant has been reviewing the firm's past television sales. For the past two years, Hitech has been offering an extended service contract on all televisions sold. With the purchase of a television, the customer has the right to purchase a 3-year service contract for an extra $75. Information concerning past television and warranty contract sales follows.

Plasma-All Model II Television	2013	2012
Television sales in units	700	590
Sales price per unit	$900	$800
Number of service contracts sold	420	380
Expenses relating to television warranties	$8,250	$4,240

Hitech's accountant has estimated from past records that the pattern of repairs has been 32% in the first year after sale, 40% in the second year, and 28% in the third year. Give the necessary journal entries related to the service contracts for 2012 and 2013. In addition, indicate how much profit on service contracts would be recognized in 2013. Assume sales of the contracts are made evenly during the year.

Exercise 7-41
LO2

Warranty Liability

In 2012, Carver Electronics Co. began selling a new computer that carried a 2-year warranty against defects. Based on the manufacturer's recommendations, Carver projects estimated warranty costs (as a percentage of dollar sales) as follows:

First year of warranty	4%
Second year of warranty	7%

Sales and actual warranty repairs for 2012 and 2013 are as follows.

	2013	2012
Sales	$850,000	$700,000
Actual warranty repairs	30,750	18,500

1. Give the necessary journal entries to record the liability at the end of 2012 and 2013.
2. Analyze the warranty liability account as of the year ended December 31, 2013, to see if the actual repairs approximate the estimate. Should Carver revise the manufacturer's warranty estimate? (Assume sales and repairs occur evenly throughout the year.)

EM EXPANDED MATERIAL

Exercise 7-42
LO8

Receivables and the Statement of Cash Flows
The following selected information is provided for Lynez Company. All sales are credit sales and all receivables are trade receivables.

Accounts receivable, January 1 net balance	$125,000
Accounts receivable, December 31 net balance	165,000
Sales for the year	800,000
Uncollectible accounts written off during the year	14,000
Bad debt expense for the year	24,000
Cash expenses for the year	681,000
Net income for the year	95,000

Using the format illustrated in the chapter and the preceding information, answer the following questions:

1. Using the *direct* method, what is the net cash flow from operations that Lynez Company would report in its statement of cash flows?
2. Assuming the use of the *indirect* method, what adjustments to net income would be required in reporting net cash flow from operations?

Exercise 7-43
LO7

Accounting for an Interest-Bearing Note
Abacus, Inc., purchased inventory costing $95,000. Terms of the purchase were 3/10, n/30. Abacus uses a perpetual inventory system. In order to take advantage of the cash discount, Abacus borrowed $75,000 from Commercial First Bank, signing a 2-month, 8% note. The bank requires monthly interest payments. Make the entries to record the following:

1. Initial purchase of inventory on account
2. Payment to the supplier within the discount period
3. Loan from the bank
4. First month's payment to the bank
5. Second and final payment to the bank

Exercise 7-44
LO7

Accounting for a Non-Interest-Bearing Note
Zobell Corporation sells equipment with a book value of $8,000, receiving a non-interest-bearing note due in three years with a face amount of $10,000. There is no established market value for the equipment. The interest rate on similar obligations is estimated at 12%. Compute the gain or loss on the sale and the discount on notes receivable, and make the necessary entry to record the sale. Also, make the entries to record the amortization of the discount at the end of the first, second, and third year using effective-interest amortization. (Round to the nearest dollar.)

Exercise 7-45
LO6

Accounting for the Sale of Accounts Receivable
On July 15, Mann Company sold $900,000 in accounts receivable for cash of $750,000. The factor withheld 10% of the cash proceeds to allow for possible customer returns or account adjustments. An Allowance for Bad Debts of $120,000 had previously been established by Mann in relation to these accounts.

1. Make the journal entry necessary on Mann's books to record the sale of the accounts.
2. Make the journal entry necessary on Mann's books to record final settlement of the factoring arrangement. No customer returns or account adjustments occurred in relation to the accounts.

PROBLEMS

Problem 7-46

LO2

SPREADSHEET

Accounting for Receivables—Journal Entries

The following transactions affecting the accounts receivable of Wonderland Corporation took place during the year ended January 31, 2013:

Sales (cash and credit)	$691,050
Cash received from credit customers, all of whom took advantage of the discount feature of the corporation's credit terms 4/10, n/30	303,800
Cash received from cash customers	310,270
Accounts receivable written off as worthless	5,250
Credit memoranda issued to credit customers for sales returns and allowances	83,800
Cash refunds given to cash customers for sales returns and allowances	13,318
Recoveries on accounts receivable written off as uncollectible in prior periods (not included in cash amount stated above)	8,290

The following two balances were taken from the January 31, 2012, balance sheet:

Accounts Receivable	$95,842
Allowance for Bad Debts	9,740 (credit)

The corporation provides for its net uncollectible account losses by crediting Allowance for Bad Debts for 1.5% of net credit sales for the fiscal period.

Instructions:

1. Prepare the journal entries to record the transactions for the year ended January 31, 2013.
2. Prepare the adjusting journal entry for estimated uncollectible accounts on January 31, 2013.

Problem 7-47

LO2

Accounting for Cash Discounts

Stockton Company sold goods on account with a sales price of $70,000 on August 17. The terms of the sale were 2/10, n/30.

Instructions:

1. Record the sale using the gross method of accounting for cash discounts.
2. Record the sale using the net method of accounting for cash discounts.
3. Assume that the payment is received on August 25. Record receipt of the payment using both the gross method and the net method.
4. Assume that payment is received on September 15. Record receipt of the payment using both the gross method and the net method. Is the account used for the net method an asset, liability, revenue, or expense?
5. Which method makes more theoretical sense—the gross method or the net method? Why? Why don't more firms use the net method?

Problem 7-48

LO2

Estimating Bad Debt Expense; Sales Method vs. Receivables Method

During 2013, Lacee Enterprises had gross sales of $247,000. At the end of 2013, Lacee had accounts receivable of $83,000 and a credit balance of $5,600 in Allowance for Bad Debts. Lacee has used the percentage-of-gross-sales method to estimate the bad debt expense. For the past several years, the amount estimated to be uncollectible has been 3%.

Instructions:

1. Using the percentage-of-gross-sales method, estimate the bad debt expense and make any necessary adjusting entries.
2. Assuming that 6% of receivables are estimated to be uncollectible and that Lacee decides to use the percentage-of-receivables method to estimate the bad debt expense, estimate the bad debt expense and make any adjusting entries.

3. Which of the two methods more accurately reflects the net realizable value of receivables? Explain.

Problem 7-49
LO2
SPREADSHEET

Estimating Uncollectible Accounts by Aging Receivables
Rainy Day Company, a wholesaler, uses the aging method to estimate bad debt losses. The following schedule of aged accounts receivable was prepared at December 31, 2013.

Age of Accounts	Amount
0–30 days	$478,600
31–60 days	172,300
61–90 days	79,200
91–120 days	21,300
Over 120 days	8,300
	$759,700

The following schedule shows the year-end receivables balances and uncollectible accounts experience for the previous five years.

Year	Year-End Receivables	0–30 Days	31–60 Days	61–90 Days	91–120 Days	Over 120 Days
2012	$780,700	0.3%	0.9%	8.7%	52.1%	84.1%
2011	750,400	0.5	0.8	9.0	49.2	80.3
2010	681,400	0.4	1.1	9.5	53.7	82.0
2009	698,200	0.4	1.0	9.9	51.3	78.5
2008	723,600	0.2	1.1	8.9	49.9	85.2

The unadjusted Allowance for Bad Debts balance on December 31, 2013, is $25,124.

Instructions: Compute the correct balance for the allowance account based on the average loss experience for the last five years and prepare the appropriate end-of-year adjusting entry.

Problem 7-50
LO2
SPREADSHEET

Warranty Liability
Sound Portal Corporation sells stereos under a 2-year warranty contract that requires Sound Portal to replace defective parts and provide free labor on all repairs. During 2012, 1,290 units were sold at $950 each. In 2013, Sound Portal sold an additional 1,100 units at $980. Based on past experience, the estimated 2-year warranty costs are $25 for parts and $30 for labor per unit. It is also estimated that 40% of the warranty expenditures will occur in the first year and 60% in the second year. Actual warranty expenditures were as follows:

	2013	2014
Stereos sold in 2012	$28,500	$37,800
Stereos sold in 2013	—	28,200

Instructions: Assuming that sales occurred on the last day of the year for both 2012 and 2013, give the necessary journal entries for the years 2012 through 2014. Analyze the warranty liability account for the year ended December 31, 2014, to see whether the actual repairs approximate the estimate. Should Sound Portal revise its warranty estimates?

Problem 7-51

LO2

SPREADSHEET

Warranty Liability

Lafayette Corporation, a client, requests that you compute the appropriate balance of its estimated liability for product warranty account for a statement as of June 30, 2013.

Lafayette Corporation manufactures television components and sells them with a 6-month warranty under which defective components will be replaced without charge. On December 31, 2012, Estimated Liability for Product Warranty had a balance of $620,000. By June 30, 2013, this balance had been reduced to $120,400 by debits for estimated net cost of components returned that had been sold in 2012.

The corporation started out in 2013 expecting 7% of the dollar volume of sales to be returned. However, due to the introduction of new models during the year, this estimated percentage of returns was increased to 10% on May 1. It is assumed that no components sold during a given month are returned in that month. Each component is stamped with a date at time of sale so that the warranty may be properly administered. The following table of percentages indicates the likely pattern of sales returns during the 6-month period of the warranty, starting with the month following the sale of components.

Month Following Sale	Percentage of Total Returns Expected
First	30%
Second	20
Third	20
Fourth through sixth—10% each month	30
	100%

Gross sales of components were as follows for the first six months of 2013:

Month	Amount	Month	Amount
January	$4,200,000	April	$3,250,000
February	4,700,000	May	2,400,000
March	3,900,000	June	1,900,000

The corporation's warranty also covers the payment of freight cost on defective components returned and on the new components sent out as replacements. This freight cost runs approximately 5% of the sales price of the components returned. The manufacturing cost of the components is roughly 70% of the sales price, and the salvage value of returned components averages 10% of their sales price. Returned components on hand at December 31, 2012, were thus valued in inventory at 10% of their original sales price.

Instructions: Using the data given, prepare a schedule for arriving at the balance of the estimated liability for product warranty account as of June 30, 2013, and give the proposed adjusting entry.

Problem 7-52

LO2, LO4, LO5, LO7

Journal Entries and Balance Sheet Presentation

The balance sheet for The Itex Corporation on December 31, 2012, includes the following cash and receivables balances.

Cash—First Security Bank		$45,000
Currency on hand		16,000
Petty cash fund		1,000
Cash in bond sinking fund		15,000
Notes receivable (including notes discounted with recourse, $15,500)		36,500
Accounts receivable	$85,600	
Less: Allowance for bad debts	4,150	81,450
Interest receivable		525

Current liabilities reported in the December 31, 2012, balance sheet included:

Obligation on discounted notes receivable	$15,500

Transactions during 2013 included the following:

(a) Sales on account were $767,000.
(b) Cash collected on accounts totaled $576,500, including accounts of $93,000 with cash discounts of 2%.
(c) Notes received in settlement of accounts totaled $82,500.
(d) Notes receivable discounted as of December 31, 2012, were paid at maturity with the exception of one $3,000 note on which the company had to pay the bank $3,090, which included interest and protest fees. It is expected that recovery will be made on this note early in 2014.
(e) Customer notes of $58,500 were discounted with recourse during the year, proceeds from their transfer being $58,500. (All discounting transactions were recorded as loans.) Of this total, $48,000 matured during the year without notice of protest.
(f) Customer accounts of $8,720 were written off during the year as worthless.
(g) Recoveries of bad debts written off in prior years were $2,020.
(h) Notes receivable collected during the year totaled $27,000 and interest collected was $2,450.
(i) On December 31, accrued interest on notes receivable was $630.
(j) Uncollectible accounts are estimated to be 5% of the December 31, 2013, Accounts Receivable balance.
(k) Cash of $35,000 was borrowed from First Security Bank with accounts receivable of $40,000 being pledged on the loan. Collections of $19,500 had been made on these receivables [included in the total given in transaction (b)], and this amount was applied on December 31, 2013, to payment of accrued interest on the loan of $600, and the balance to partial payment of the loan.
(l) The petty cash fund was reimbursed (meaning that cash was removed from the bank account and placed in the petty cash fund) based on the following analysis of expenditure vouchers:

Travel expense	$112
Entertainment expense	78
Postage expense	93
Office supplies expense	173
Cash short and over (a revenue account)	6

(m) Cash of $3,000 was added to a bond retirement fund.
(n) Currency on hand at December 31, 2013, was $12,000.
(o) Total cash payments for all expenses during the year were $665,300. Charge to General Expenses.

Instructions:

1. Prepare journal entries summarizing the preceding transactions and information.
2. Prepare a summary of current cash and receivables for balance sheet presentation.

Problem 7-53

LO4

REVERSE SOLVABLE

Compensating Balance and Effective Interest Rates

Krebsbach Company is negotiating a loan with FIS Bank. Krebsbach needs $900,000. As part of the loan agreement, FIS Bank will require Krebsbach to maintain a compensating balance of 15% of the loan amount on deposit in a checking account at the bank. Krebsbach currently maintains a balance of $50,000 in the checking account. The interest rate Krebsbach is required to pay on the loan is 12%; the interest rate FIS pays on checking accounts is 4%.

Instructions:

1. Compute the amount of the loan.
2. Determine the effective interest rate on the loan. (*Hint:* Compute the net interest paid on the loan per year and the "take-home" amount of the loan.)

Problem 7-54

LO4

SPREADSHEET

Bank Reconciliation

The cash account of Abstract, Inc., disclosed a balance of $16,348.82 on October 31. The bank statement as of October 31 showed a balance of $19,711.75. Upon comparing the statement with the cash records, the following facts were developed.

(a) Abstract's account was charged on October 26 for a customer's uncollectible check amounting to $1,927.

(b) A 2-month, 8%, $1,350 customer's note dated August 25, discounted on October 12, was dishonored October 26 and the bank charged Abstract $1,374.91, which included a protest fee of $6.91.

(c) A customer's check for $580 was entered as $530 by both the depositor and the bank but was later corrected by the bank.

(d) Check No. 661 for $1,838.00 was entered in the cash disbursements journal at $1,383.00 and Check No. 652 for $47.50 was entered as $475.00. The company uses the voucher system.

(e) Bank service charges of $54.81 for October were not yet recorded on the books.

(f) A bank memo stated that C. Castro's note for $1,800 and interest of $74.20 had been collected on October 29, and the bank charged $15.00. (No entry was made on the books when the note was sent to the bank for collection.)

(g) Receipts of October 29 for $5,450 were deposited November 1.

The following checks were outstanding on October 31:

Check	Amount	Check	Amount
No. 620	$1,075.00	No. 671	$ 567.55
No. 621	2,199.98	No. 673	337.99
No. 632	2,765.25	No. 675	375.80
No. 670	1,776.89	No. 676	1,189.49

Instructions:

1. Prepare a bank reconciliation as of October 31.
2. Give the journal entries required as a result of the preceding information.

Problem 7-55

LO4

SPREADSHEET

Reconciliation of an Individual's Bank Account

The following data were taken from Tyrone Tardieff's check register for the month of April. Tyrone's bank reconciliation for March showed one outstanding check, Check No. 78 for $57.00 (written on March 23), and one deposit in transit, Deposit No. 10499 for $96.00 (made on March 30).

Date		Item	Checks	Deposits	Balance
2013					
April	1	Beginning Balance			$175.00
	1	Deposit No. 10500		$451.61	626.61
	1	Check No. 79	$ 15.00		616.61
	4	Check No. 80	261.32		355.59
	27	Deposit No. 10501		247.28	602.87
	29	Check No. 81	214.35		389.52

The following is from Tyrone's bank statement for April:

April	1	Beginning Balance			$136.00
	3	Check No. 79	$ 15.00		121.00
	3	Deposit No. 10499		$ 96.00	217.00
	5	Check No. 80	261.32		(44.32)
	5	Automatic Loan		132.00	87.68
	5	Deposit No. 10500		457.61	545.29
	20	NSF Check	20.00		525.29
	20	Service Charge	15.00		510.29
	30	Interest		1.21	511.50

Instructions: Prepare a reconciliation of Tyrone's bank account as of April 30. Show both a corrected balance per bank and a corrected balance per books. Assume that any errors or discrepancies you find are Tyrone's fault, not the bank's.

EM EXPANDED MATERIAL

Problem 7-56

LO6

Accounting for Assignment of Accounts Receivable

On July 1, 2013, McEnroe Company used receivables totaling $150,000 as collateral on a $100,000, 15% note from Standard One Bank. The transaction is not structured such that receivables are being sold. McEnroe will continue to collect the assigned receivables. In addition to the interest on the note, Standard One also receives a 2.5% finance charge, deducted in advance on the $100,000 value of the note. Additional information for McEnroe Company is as follows:

(a) July collections amounted to $91,000, less cash discounts of $575.
(b) On August 1, paid bank the amount owed for July collections plus accrued interest on note to August 1.
(c) McEnroe collected the remaining accounts during August except for $425 written off as uncollectible.
(d) On September 1, paid bank the remaining amount owed plus accrued interest.

Instructions: Prepare the journal entries necessary to record the preceding information on the books of both McEnroe Company and Standard One Bank.

Problem 7-57

LO6

Assigning and Factoring Accounts Receivable

During its second year of operations, Shank Corporation found itself in financial difficulties. Shank decided to use its accounts receivable as a means of obtaining cash to continue operations. On July 1, 2013, Shank sold $75,000 of accounts receivable for cash proceeds of $69,500. No bad debt allowance was associated with these accounts. On December 17, 2013, Shank assigned the remainder of its accounts receivable, $250,000 as of that date, as collateral on a $125,000, 12% annual interest rate loan from Sandy Finance Company. Shank received $125,000 less a 2% finance charge. Additional information is as follows:

Allowance for Bad Debts, 12/31/2013	$3,200 (credit)
Estimated Uncollectibles, 12/31/2013	3% of Accounts Receivable
Accounts Receivable (not including factored and assigned accounts), 12/31/2013	$50,000

None of the assigned accounts has been collected by the end of the year.

Instructions:

1. Prepare the journal entries to record the receipt of cash from the (a) sale and (b) assignment of the accounts receivable.
2. Prepare the journal entry necessary to record the adjustment to Allowance for Bad Debts.

3. Prepare the Accounts Receivable section of Shank's balance sheet as it would appear after the above transactions.
4. What entry would be made on Shank's books when the sold accounts have been collected?

Problem 7-58
LO6

Selling Receivables

Freemont Factors provides financing to other companies by purchasing their accounts receivable on a nonrecourse basis. Freemont charges its clients a commission of 15% of all receivables factored. In addition, Freemont withholds 10% of receivables factored as protection against sales returns or other adjustments. Freemont credits the 10% withheld to Client Retainer and makes payments to clients at the end of each month so that the balance in the retainer is equal to 10% of unpaid receivables at the end of the month. Freemont recognizes its 15% commissions as revenue at the time the receivables are factored. Also, experience has led Freemont to establish an Allowance for Bad Debts of 4% of all receivables purchased.

On January 4, 2013, Freemont purchased receivables from Detmer Company totaling $1,500,000. Detmer had previously established an Allowance for Bad Debts for these receivables of $35,000. By January 31, Freemont had collected $1,200,000 on these receivables.

Instructions:

1. Prepare the entries necessary on Freemont's books to record the preceding information. Freemont makes adjusting entries at the end of every month.
2. Prepare the entries on Detmer's books to record the preceding information.

Problem 7-59
LO7

Accounting for a Non-Interest-Bearing Note

On January 1, 2013, Rapid River Realty sold a tract of land to three doctors as an investment. The land, purchased 10 years ago, was carried on Rapid River's books at a value of $210,000. Rapid River received a non-interest-bearing note for $275,000 from the doctors. The note is due December 31, 2014. There is no readily available market value for the land, but the current market rate of interest for comparable notes is 11%.

Instructions:

1. Give the journal entry to record the sale of land on Rapid River's books.
2. Prepare a schedule of discount amortization for the note with amounts rounded to the nearest dollar.
3. Give the adjusting entries to be made at the end of 2013 and 2014 to record the effective interest earned.

Problem 7-60
LO7

Note with Below-Market Interest Rate

On January 1, 2013, Denver Company sold land that originally cost $400,000 to Boise Company. As payment, Boise gave Denver a $600,000 note. The note bears an interest rate of 4% and is to be repaid in three annual installments of $200,000 (plus interest on the outstanding balance). The first payment is due on December 31, 2013. The market price of the land is not reliably determinable. The prevailing rate of interest for notes of this type is 14%.

Instructions: Prepare the entries required on Denver's books to record the land sale and the receipt of each of the three payments. Use the effective-interest method of amortizing any premium or discount on the note.

Problem 7-61
LO8
REVERSE SOLVABLE

Bad Debt Expense—Cash Flows

Strata Company had a $275,000 balance in Accounts Receivable on January 1. The balance in Allowance for Bad Debts on January 1 was $68,000. Sales for the year totaled $2,100,000. All sales were credit sales. Bad debt expense is estimated to be 3% of sales. Write-offs of uncollectible accounts for the year were $58,000. The debit balance in Accounts Receivable on December 31 was $335,000. All receivables are trade receivables. Strata uses the direct method in preparing its statement of cash flows.

Instructions: What is the amount of cash collected from customers?

Problem 7-62
LO2, LO4, LO6

Sample CPA Exam Questions

1. At December 31, 2013, Kale Co. had the following balances in the accounts it maintains at First State Bank:

Checking account No. 001	$175,000
Checking account No. 201	(10,000)
Money market account	25,000
90-day certificate of deposit, due February 28, 2014	50,000
180-day certificate of deposit, due March 15, 2014	80,000

   Kale classifies investments with original maturities of three months or less as cash equivalents. In its December 31, 2013, balance sheet, what amount should Kale report as cash and cash equivalents?
   (a) $190,000
   (b) $200,000
   (c) $240,000
   (d) $320,000
2. When the allowance method of recognizing uncollectible accounts is used, the entry to record the write-off of a specific account would:
   (a) decrease both accounts receivable and the allowance for uncollectible accounts.
   (b) decrease accounts receivable and increase the allowance for uncollectible accounts.
   (c) increase the allowance for uncollectible accounts and decrease net income.
   (d) decrease both accounts receivable and net income.
3. Gar Co. factored its receivables without recourse with Ross Bank. Gar received cash as a result of this transaction, which is best described as a:
   (a) loan from Ross collateralized by Gar's accounts receivable.
   (b) loan from Ross to be repaid by the proceeds from Gar's accounts receivable.
   (c) sale of Gar's accounts receivable to Ross, with the risk of uncollectible accounts retained by Gar.
   (d) sale of Gar's accounts receivable to Ross, with the risk of uncollectible accounts transferred to Ross.

CASES

Discussion Case 7-63

Should a Company Sell on Credit?
Olin Company currently makes only cash sales. Given the number of potential customers who have requested to buy on credit, Olin is considering allowing credit sales. What factors should Olin consider in making the decision whether to allow credit sales?

Discussion Case 7-64

Accounting for Potential Sales Returns
Ultimate Corporation is a computer products supplier. Ultimate sells products to dealers who then sell the products to the end users. Most of the company's competitors require dealers to pay for shipments within 45 to 60 days. Ultimate has followed a more relaxed policy; in 2013 the average length of time it took the company to collect its receivables was 158 days. (This average collection period can be computed as average accounts receivable balance/average daily sales.) It has

been suggested that in return for this lax collection policy, dealers allowed Ultimate to ship more product than the dealers needed, allowing Ultimate to recognize the excess shipments as sales. In 2014, Ultimate attempted to reduce the level of its accounts receivable by stepping up collection efforts. As a result, product returns from dealers increased significantly.

1. Assume that Ultimate's sales for the year were $1,000 with cost of sales being $600. For simplicity, also assume that all of the sales occurred on December 31 and that, on average, Ultimate expects about 15% of products sold to be returned by dissatisfied dealers or dealers who are unable to sell the products. What adjusting entry, if any, should be made at year-end to reflect the likelihood of future sales returns?
2. An allowance for sales returns is analogous to an allowance for bad debts. Most companies disclose an allowance for bad debts but very few disclose an allowance for sales returns. Why not?
3. What other more conservative accounting treatment is possible in regard to the potential sales returns?

Discussion Case 7-65

Accounting for Uncollectibles

During the audit of accounts receivable of Montana Company, the new CEO, Joe Frisco, asked why the company had debited the current-year expense for bad debts on the assumption that some accounts will become uncollectible next year. Frisco believes that the financial statements should be based on verifiable, objective evidence. In his opinion it would be more objective to wait until specific accounts become uncollectible before the expense is recorded. What accounting issues are involved? Which method of accounting for uncollectible accounts would you recommend and why?

Discussion Case 7-66

Cash Management

Jackie Wilson, manager of Expert Building Company, is a valued and trusted employee. She has been with the company from its start two years ago. Because of the demands of her job, she has not taken a vacation since she began working. She is in charge of recording collections on account, making the daily bank deposits, and reconciling the bank statement.

Early this year, clients began complaining to you, the president, about incorrect statements. As president, you check into this matter. Jackie tells you there is nothing to worry about. She asserts, "The problem is due to the slow mail; customers' payments and statements are crossing in the mail." However, because clients were not complaining last year, you doubt that the mail is the primary reason for the problem.

What might be some of the reasons for the delay? What are some other problems that might begin to occur? What can be done to remedy the problem? What should be done to make sure the problems are avoided in the future?

Discussion Case 7-67

Allocation of Cash and Near-Cash Assets

Bruno Johnson, chief financial officer of Tollerud Company, has determined that Tollerud should keep on hand $35 million in cash or near-cash assets in order to maintain proper liquidity. Bruno is now trying to determine how to allocate the $35 million among the checking account, certificates of deposit, and treasury notes. What factors should influence Bruno's decision?

Discussion Case 7-68

Did I Hide It Well Enough?

Jonathan Mitchell is the accountant for Mantua Service Company. Due to heavy investments in lottery tickets, Jonathan found himself short of cash and decided to "borrow" funds from Mantua. Jonathan received and deposited cash receipts, recorded the checks written in the cash disbursements journal, and reconciled the bank account. He made the reconciliation balance by manipulating outstanding checks in the bank reconciliation. Would this type of embezzlement be detected with a proper reconciliation of the checking account? Justify your answer.

EM EXPANDED MATERIAL

Discussion Case 7-69

Accounts Receivable as a Source of Cash

Assume you are the treasurer for Fullmer Products Inc. and one of your responsibilities is to ensure that the company always takes available cash discounts on purchases. The corporation needs $150,000 within one week in order to take advantage of current cash discounts. The lending officer at the bank insists on adequate collateral for a $150,000 loan. For various reasons, your plant assets are not available as collateral, but your accounts receivable balance is $205,000. What alternatives would you consider for obtaining the necessary cash?

Case 7-70

Deciphering Financial Statements (The Walt Disney Company)

Locate the 2009 financial statements for **The Walt Disney Company** on the Internet. Use the information contained in these statements to answer the following questions:

1. Review The Walt Disney Company's note disclosure to determine how the company recognizes revenue from its various sources.
2. Based on what you know about Disney, estimate what you think is the length of its average collection period. Once you have made that estimate, use the company's financial statements to compute the number. How does your estimate compare with the actual results?
3. Review the information relating to Disney's segment data. Which segment generates the most revenue for the company? Which segment generates the most operating income?
4. Using information from the various financial statements, compute the amount of cash collected from customers for the 2009 fiscal year.
5. How does Disney define *cash and cash equivalents*?

Case 7-71

Deciphering Financial Statements (Wal-Mart Stores, Inc.)

Use the financial information for **Wal-Mart Stores, Inc.**, given on pages 7-65 and 7-66, to answer the following questions:

1. For the most recent year given, compute Wal-Mart's average collection period. (*Hint:* Use "Net Sales" in the computation.)
2. For the most recent year given, what percentage of total current assets is accounts receivable for Wal-Mart?
3. For the most recent year given, determine the percentage of Wal-Mart's revenues that is derived from sources other than sales.

Wal-Mart Stores, Inc. and Subsidiaries
Consolidated Balance Sheets
(Amounts in millions)

January 31,	2010	2009
(Amounts in millions except per share data)		
ASSETS		
Current assets:		
Cash and cash equivalents	**$ 7,907**	$ 7,275
Receivables, net	**4,144**	3,905
Inventories	**33,160**	34,511
Prepaid expenses and other	**2,980**	3,063
Current assets of discontinued operations	**140**	195
Total current assets	**$48,331**	$48,949

Wal-Mart Stores, Inc. and Subsidiaries
Consolidated Statements of Income
(Amounts in millions)

Fiscal Years Ended January 31,	2010	2009	2008
Revenues:			
Net sales	**$405,046**	$401,087	$373,821
Membership and other income	**3,168**	3,287	3,202
	408,214	404,374	377,023
Costs and expenses:			
Cost of sales	**304,657**	304,056	284,137
Operating, selling, general and administrative expenses	**79,607**	77,520	70,934
Operating income	**$ 23,950**	$ 22,798	$ 21,952

Case 7-72

Writing Assignment (Foreign loan write-offs)

In July 1990, U.S. federal regulators ordered U.S. banks to write off 20% of their $11.1 billion in loans to Brazil and also 20% of their $2.9 billion in loans to Argentina. The action significantly affected the loan loss reserves, that is, Allowance for Bad Debts, of the banks. For example, **Citicorp** was ordered to write off loans totaling $780 million, compared to Citicorp's total loan loss reserve of $3.3 billion. However, it was reported that "the action won't automatically have any impact on bank earnings." Prepare a short report answering the following questions:

1. Why won't the ordered write-offs automatically impact bank earnings?
2. Might the ordered write-offs have an indirect impact on future bank earnings?
3. What effect would you expect to see on bank stock prices in response to this announcement?

SOURCE: Robert Guenther, "Federal Regulators Order Banks to Take Write-Offs on Loans to Brazil, Argentina," *The Wall Street Journal,* July 12, 1990, p. A3.

Case 7-73

Ethical Dilemma

You recently graduated from college with your accounting degree. Your father's best friend is the director of the accounting department of a small manufacturing firm in the area, and you accepted a position on his staff. After a month on the job, you have noticed several deficiencies in the cash controls for the company. For example, the individual making the daily deposits at the bank is also in charge of updating accounts receivable. You also notice that the petty cash fund is under general control of everyone in the office (that means that no one person has ultimate responsibility) and that vouchers are seldom completed when cash is removed from the fund. You bring your concerns to the attention of your boss, your father's friend, and he comments:

> "I appreciate your concerns. I knew when we hired you that you were sharp, but you need to understand that not everything is done by the book here. We trust our employees. If we were to enforce rigid controls on cash, it would create a nontrusting work environment. We don't want that. Sure, a little money may turn up missing now and then, but it is a small price to pay. Now, don't you worry about it anymore."

What do you do now? Would you be comfortable working in an environment where there is a lack of control on cash? If a significant sum of money were to turn up missing and the control system was unable to determine who was responsible, what would that do to the trusting work environment? And remember, big sums of money never turned up missing until you came to work at the company.

Case 7-74

Cumulative Spreadsheet Analysis

This spreadsheet assignment is a continuation of those given in earlier chapters. If you completed those assignments, you have a head start on this one. Refer to the instructions for preparing the revised financial statements for 2013 as given in part (1) of the Cumulative Spreadsheet Analysis assignment in Chapter 3.

1. Skywalker wishes to prepare a forecasted balance sheet, a forecasted income statement, and a forecasted statement of cash flows for 2014. Clearly state any additional assumptions that you make. Use the financial statement numbers for 2013 as the basis for the forecast, along with the following data:
   (a) Sales in 2014 are expected to increase by 40% over 2013 sales of $2,100.
   (b) In 2014, Skywalker expects to acquire property, plant, and equipment for $240.
   (c) The $480 in operating expenses reported in 2013 breaks down as follows: $15 depreciation expense and $465 other operating expenses.
   (d) No new long-term debt will be acquired in 2014.
   (e) No cash dividends will be paid in 2014.
   (f) New short-term loans payable will be acquired in an amount sufficient to make Skywalker's current ratio in 2014 exactly equal to 2.0.
   (g) Skywalker does not expect to repurchase additional shares of stock in 2014.
   (h) Because changes in future prices and exchange rates are impossible to predict, Skywalker's best estimate is that the balance in accumulated other comprehensive income will remain unchanged in 2014.
   (i) In the absence of more detailed information, assume that investment securities, long-term investments, other long-term assets, and intangible assets will all increase at the same rate as sales (40%) in 2014.
   (j) In the absence of more detailed information, assume that other long-term liabilities will increase at the same rate as sales (40%) in 2014.

(*Note:* The forecasted balance sheet and income statement were constructed as part of the spreadsheet assignment in Chapter 4; you can use that spreadsheet as a starting point if you have completed that assignment.) In addition, assume the following:

   (k) The investment securities are classified as available-for-sale. Thus, cash from the purchase and sale of these securities is classified as an investing activity.
   (l) Transactions impacting other long-term assets and other long-term liabilities accounts are operating activities. [*Hint:* Construction of the forecasted statement of cash flows for 2014 involves analyzing the forecasted income statement for 2014 along with the balance sheets for 2013 (actual) and 2014 (forecasted).]

   For this exercise, the current assets are expected to behave as follows:

   (m) Cash, investment securities, and inventory will increase at the same rate as sales.
   (n) The forecasted amount of accounts receivable in 2014 is determined using the forecasted value for the average collection period (computed using the end-of-period accounts receivable balance). The average collection period for 2014 is expected to be 14.08 days.

2. Repeat (1), with the following changes in assumptions:
   (a) Average collection period is expected to be 9.06 days.
   (b) Average collection period is expected to be 20 days.
3. Comment on the differences in the forecasted values of cash from operating activities in 2014 under each of the following assumptions about the average collection period: 14.08 days, 9.06 days, and 20 days.

P2 ROUTINE ACTIVITIES OF A BUSINESS

CHAPTER 8 Revenue Recognition

LEARNING OBJECTIVES

1. Identify the primary criteria for revenue recognition.
2. Discuss the revenue recognition issues, and abuses, underlying the examples used in *SAB 101*.
3. Describe the contract approach to revenue recognition that is currently being considered by the FASB and IASB.
4. Record journal entries for long-term construction-type contracts using percentage-of-completion and completed-contract methods.
5. Record journal entries for long-term service contracts using the proportional performance method.
6. Explain when revenue is recognized after delivery of goods or services through installment sales, cost recovery, and cash methods.

The rise and fall of **MicroStrategy** encapsulates the boom and bust, sprinkled with accounting scandal, associated with the high-tech economy from 1998 through 2002. At its peak, MicroStrategy was worth $31.1 billion and was trading at a price-to-sales ratio of 152 and a price-to-earnings ratio of 2,220. But in a sell-off precipitated by a revenue-related accounting restatement, the shares reached a low of $0.45 on July 26, 2002, down from their peak of $333.00 on March 10, 2000 (a 99.9% drop). In the wake of this price collapse, MicroStrategy's CEO was fined by the SEC, and the company's auditor was sued by outraged investors. An outline of MicroStrategy's rise and fall follows.

Many people have described MicroStrategy's CEO Michael Saylor as the smartest person they know.[1] He grew up outside Dayton, Ohio, the son of an Air Force sergeant, and entered MIT on an ROTC scholarship, intending to become an Air Force pilot. While at MIT, Saylor developed skills in computer simulation, and he wrote his undergraduate thesis using a computer simulation to model the reactions of different types of government systems to catastrophes such as wars or epidemics. Since a heart murmur had cut short his chances of becoming a pilot, Saylor became a computer modeler for **DuPont**.

[1] Mark Leibovich, "MicroStrategy's CEO Sped to the Brink," *The Washington Post*, January 6, 2002, p. A01. This article was the first in a 4-part series by Mr. Leibovich that ran January 6–9, 2002, in *The Washington Post*. All four articles serve as source material for this brief history of MicroStrategy.

Anton Vengo/SuperStock

In 1989, Saylor started his own computer modeling business, called MicroStrategy, in partnership with his MIT roommate, Sanju Bansal. The foundation of MicroStrategy's product line has been its corporate data mining program. The program combs through terabytes of data in an unwieldy corporate database, looking for interesting relationships. For example, MicroStrategy customers **McDonald's** and **Wal-Mart** could use the program to detect customer buying trends on, say, Monday afternoons in the summer in California compared to Texas to help in targeting local marketing efforts. This data mining program was very successful, and MicroStrategy doubled its revenues each year from 1994 through 1998, growing from 1994 revenues of $4.98 million to 1998 revenues of $106.43 million. The company went public on June 11, 1998, with the shares opening at $12 per share and ending the first day of trading at $21 per share.

In early 1999, MicroStrategy was a solid software company with an impressive record of revenue and profit growth. However, the company's price-to-sales ratio was just 12, compared to ratios routinely more than 100 for dot.com companies. This was because MicroStrategy was not benefiting from any of the "Internet halo" that seemed to surround all companies that were in any way affiliated with the Web in those days. And Michael Saylor had a vision of making his company much more than a software company. This vision is captured in the company motto: "Information like water." Saylor wanted to place the power of the data mining software that MicroStrategy provided to corporations into the hands of individuals. Accordingly, in July 1999 MicroStrategy launched Strategy.com, which promised to make personalized information available to individuals by email, through the Web, and by wireless phone. Subscribers could receive tailored messages about finance, news, weather, sports, and traffic, and that was just the beginning. By the end of 1999, Strategy.com had not yet generated a single dollar of revenue for MicroStrategy, but the initiative had brought the aura of the Internet to the valuation of MicroStrategy's stock, causing the price-to-sales ratio to increase from 12 to 150. In January 2000, while all 1,600 MicroStrategy employees were on a company cruise in the Cayman Islands, the company's stock increased in value by 19% on one day, and Michael Saylor's holdings alone increased in value by $1 billion. "We should go on cruises more often," joked Saylor.

A price-to-sales ratio of 150 means that investors expect substantial sales growth (and ultimately substantial profit and cash flow growth) in the future. It also means that any stumbling on the part of the company can result in a catastrophic drop in stock price. For example, if a company has a market value of $30 billion with a price-to-sales ratio of 150, like MicroStrategy in early 2000, then negative news about the future that causes the price-to-sales ratio to drop to a lower but still respectable level of, say, 6 (which was the price-to-sales ratio for **Coca-Cola** in early 2000) would cause the company's stock price to drop 96% to $1.2 billion. This type of precarious valuation puts huge pressure on managers to continue to report revenue growth that meets or exceeds the market's expectation. In the face of this pressure, MicroStrategy, like many firms before and many since, broke the accounting rules governing when sales can be reported.

On March, 12, 2000, MicroStrategy's chief financial officer (CFO) received a call from the partner in charge of the company's audit. The audit firm, **PricewaterhouseCoopers** (PwC), had been reviewing MicroStrategy's revenue recognition practices and believed that a restatement was necessary. This investigation had been initiated in part in response to a March 6, 2000, *Forbes* article by reporter David Raymond questioning MicroStrategy's reporting of sales.[2] MicroStrategy's board of directors was reluctant to restate revenue because preliminary revenue numbers for 1999 had already been announced, helping to drive the company's stock price to its all-time high. However, with the board finally convinced of the necessity, a press release was drafted explaining that MicroStrategy was lowering its 1999 revenues from the previously announced $205 million to between $150 and $155 million. The news announcement was issued at 8:06 a.m. on Monday, March 20, 2000. MicroStrategy's stock opened the day trading at $226.75 per share; by the end of the day, the shares had dropped 62% to $86.75 per share.

Subsequent SEC investigation confirmed that MicroStrategy had overstated its revenue, and the inquiry uncovered a number of questionable practices.[3] Two samples are given in the next page.

[2] David S. Raymond, "MicroStrategy's Curious Success," *Forbes*, March 6, 2000.

[3] Securities and Exchange Commission, *Accounting and Auditing Enforcement Release No. 1350*, Administrative Proceeding File No. 3-10388: In the Matter of MicroStrategy, Inc., December 14, 2000.

- Contract signing. *The final report on MicroStrategy from the SEC included the following: "To maintain maximum flexibility to achieve the desired quarterly financial results, MicroStrategy held, until after the close of the quarter, contracts that had been signed by customers but had not yet been signed by MicroStrategy. Only after MicroStrategy determined the desired financial results were the unsigned contracts apportioned, between the just-ended quarter and the then-current quarter, signed and given an 'effective date.' In some instances, the contracts were signed without affixing a date, allowing the company further flexibility to assign a date at a later time."*
- The NCR deal. *On October 4, 1999, MicroStrategy announced that it had sold software and services to* **NCR** *for $27.5 million under a multiyear licensing agreement. Although the deal was announced four days after the end of the third quarter and although the licensing agreement extended for several years, MicroStrategy recognized over half the amount as revenue immediately (and perhaps retroactively) and added $17.5 million to third quarter revenue. Without this $17.5 million in revenue, MicroStrategy's reported revenue for the third quarter would have been down 20% from the quarter before. The reported profit for the quarter would have instead been a loss. And perhaps worst of all, MicroStrategy would have fallen well short of analysts' expectations, sending the stock price spiraling downward. As it was, MicroStrategy's stock price soared 72% during the month of October 1999.*

The aftermath of the MicroStrategy meltdown was bad for all of the principal characters involved. Michael Saylor was judged by the SEC to have committed fraud. He paid a fine of $350,000 and was required to forfeit an additional $8.3 million in gains from stock sales. As of March 10, 2010, his stake in MicroStrategy was worth just $238 million, down from $14 billion at his company's pinnacle. In May 2001, PricewaterhouseCoopers agreed to pay $55 million to settle a class-action lawsuit brought by MicroStrategy shareholders who accused the audit firm of negligence in allowing MicroStrategy's financial reporting to go uncorrected for so long. And in August 2003, the SEC announced that it had settled a suit with the PwC partner in charge of the MicroStrategy audit, with the partner agreeing to be barred from auditing public clients. MicroStrategy itself is slowly recovering from the bursting of its revenue bubble. The company reported losses in three of the four years from 2000 through 2003, but the company has reported positive net income in each year from 2004 through 2009. And as of July 2010, the company's price-to-sales ratio was 2.36, up from its low point of just 0.25 in the wake of the revenue recognition scandal, but still a far cry from its pre-scandal peak of 152.

? QUESTIONS

1. Why do you think the price-to-sales ratio (as opposed to the price-earnings ratio) is often used in valuing the stocks of start-up technology companies, especially those related to the Internet?
2. On Monday, March 20, 2000, MicroStrategy issued a press release stating that revenues for the year 1999 were about $155 million, not $205 million as previously announced. This represented a drop of 24% in reported revenue. Why did a drop of just 24% in reported revenue result in a stock price drop of 62%? In other words, why wasn't the drop in stock price also 24%?
3. In early March 2000, MicroStrategy's board of directors received word that the company's auditor was requesting a revenue restatement. The board was reluctant to go forward with the restatement because of fears (justified, as it turns out) that the restatement would hurt the company's stock price. List and explain two or three arguments that you, as a member of the board, could have made in support of the restatement.

Answers to these questions can be found on pages 8-40–8-41.

In the MicroStrategy case, both the boom and the bust are tied to the accounting rules for revenue recognition. With high-growth companies boasting price-to-sales ratios of 150 or higher, a delay in reporting revenue from a $10 million contract can easily lead to losses in market value in excess of $1 billion. Because so much rides on how much revenue a company reports, many companies have succumbed to the temptation to either manage reported revenue or to commit outright fraud in boosting reported revenue. Because of the large number of revenue recognition abuses in the 1990s, many involving technology companies such as MicroStrategy, the SEC released *Staff Accounting Bulletin (SAB) No. 101*, "Revenue Recognition in Financial Statements," in December 1999. *SAB 101* was one of the most influential, and controversial, accounting pronouncements in the last 20 years. Following the release of *SAB 101*, the FASB, in cooperation with the IASB, has undertaken a comprehensive examination of the accounting standards related to revenue recognition. As investors struggle to guide their investment capital to its most valuable use in the uncertain, high-tech business playing field, reliable financial reporting with respect to revenue recognition is critical.

This chapter will proceed as follows. The first section includes a review of the general principles associated with revenue recognition. The next section uses selected components of *SAB 101* to provide illustrations of the difficult revenue recognition issues that can arise through a combination of complex business transactions and aggressive, or desperate, managers who are trying to meet revenue targets. The following section outlines the revised revenue recognition provisions developed in recent years by the FASB and IASB. The concluding sections cover specific revenue recognition practices and illustrate the percentage-of-completion, proportional performance, and installment sales methods of accounting.

Revenue Recognition

1 Identify the primary criteria for revenue recognition.

WHY The recognition of revenue begins the process of measuring income. Once revenue has been recognized, then expenses can be matched. In addition, without recognizing revenue, a company can't hope to report any profit. Accordingly, company accountants are typically under great pressure to recognize revenue as soon as possible.

HOW Historically, revenue has typically been recognized when two criteria have been met. The first criterion is realizability, which means that the seller has received payment or a valid promise of payment from the purchaser. The second criterion is met when the earnings process is substantially complete.

Recognition refers to the time when transactions are recorded on the books. The FASB's two criteria for recognizing revenues and gains, articulated in FASB *Concepts Statement No. 5*, were identified in Chapter 4 and are repeated here for emphasis. Revenues and gains are generally recognized when:

1. They are realized or realizable.
2. They have been earned through substantial completion of the activities involved in the earnings process.

Both of these criteria generally are met at the point of sale, which most often occurs when goods are delivered or when services are rendered to customers. Usually, assets and revenues are recognized concurrently. Thus, a sale of inventory results in an increase in Cash or Accounts Receivable and an increase in Sales Revenue. However, assets are sometimes received before these revenue recognition criteria are met. For example, if a client pays for consulting services in advance, an asset, Cash, is recorded on the books even though revenue has not been earned. In these cases, a liability, Unearned Revenue, is recorded. When the revenue recognition criteria are fully met, revenue is recognized and the liability account is reduced.

Exhibit 8-1 illustrates the time line associated with revenue recognition. At the point of sale, both revenue recognition criteria are typically satisfied. That is, the company has provided a product or service (criterion 2), and the customer has provided payment or a valid promise of payment (criterion 1). But as pointed out in the exhibit, exceptions exist, and revenue can be recognized before the point of sale, or in some conditions, the recognition of revenue must be deferred until after the point of sale.

In general, revenue is not recognized prior to the point of sale because either (1) a valid promise of payment has not been received from the customer or (2) the company has not provided the product or service. An exception occurs when the customer provides a valid promise of payment and conditions exist that contractually guarantee the sale. The most common example of this exception occurs in the case of long-term contracts where the two parties involved are legally obligated to fulfill the terms of the contract. In this case, revenue (or at least a portion of the total contract price) may be recognized prior to the point of final sale.

FYI

"Realized" or "realizable" can be interpreted as having received cash or other assets or a valid promise of cash or other assets to be received at some future time.

Another exception to the general rule occurs when either of the two revenue recognition criteria is not satisfied at the point of sale. In some cases, a product or service may be provided to the customer without receiving a valid promise of payment. In these instances, revenue is not recognized until payment or the valid promise is received. Now you are saying to yourself, "Why would anyone provide a product or service to a customer without receiving a valid promise of payment?" A common example is a family doctor

EX 8-1 REVENUE RECOGNITION TIME LINE AND CRITERIA

	Before the Point of Sale	Point of Sale	After the Point of Sale
	EXCEPTION: Revenue can be recognized prior to the point of sale *if:*	NORMAL: Revenue is generally recognized at this point in time.	EXCEPTION: The recognition of revenue must be deferred *if:*
Criterion 1: Realized	Customer provides a valid promise of payment AND	Criterion 1 is typically satisfied at this point.	Customer does not provide a valid promise at time of receipt of product or service OR
Criterion 2: Substantially complete	conditions exist that contractually guarantee subsequent sale.	Criterion 2 is typically satisfied at this point.	significant effort remains on contract.

FYI

The notes to **Walt Disney**'s financial statements provide an example of how one firm might have several different revenue recognition policies, depending on what is being sold.

who frequently provides treatment first and then tries to collect payment later.[4] Also, if a customer provides payment yet substantial services must still be provided by the company, then the recognition of revenue must be postponed until those services are provided. In any case, if both of the two revenue recognition criteria are met prior to the point of sale, revenue may be recognized. If either of the two criteria is not met at the point of sale, then the recognition of revenue must wait.

Although the point-of-sale rule has dominated the practice of revenue recognition, there have been notable variations to this rule. In fact, the cases in the far right column in Exhibit 8-1—in which revenue should be recognized after the point of sale—have proved to be very controversial. As illustrated in the MicroStrategy scenario at the beginning of the chapter, pressure to meet market and analyst revenue expectations has made companies, especially startup companies, reluctant to defer the recognition of revenue past the point of sale.

In addition, the timing of revenue recognition has become more complicated as business arrangements have become more complex. Companies frequently enter into multi-faceted transactions that specify one overall transaction price but require delivery of several different elements of value to the customer. For example, a technology services company may sign a contract, with one single overall price, with a customer to provide hardware, software, installation, service, and off-site data backup for two years. Accounting for these transactions involving "multiple deliverables" is a focus of much study and debate by both the FASB and the IASB. Multiple-deliverable arrangements will be discussed in detail later in the chapter.

Because every income statement begins with total revenue, the measurement of revenue is fundamental to the practice of accrual accounting. As you can imagine, the topic of revenue recognition has been studied very thoroughly through the years. However, from about 1995 through 2005, rapid innovations in business practices, especially involving transactions associated with technology, outstripped the FASB's ability keep up in the area of revenue recognition. In other words, the FASB's thorough and open standard-setting process was just not fast enough to address the revenue recognition abuses and deceptions that were being created seemingly on a daily basis. In order to address some of these revenue recognition abuses, the AICPA stepped in. AICPA *Statement of Position (SOP) 97-2*, "Software Revenue Recognition," was very influential in guiding revenue recognition practices adopted over the next 10 years. In *SOP 97-2* companies were given more guidance in applying the two general revenue recognition criteria through a checklist of four factors that amplify the two general criteria:[5]

(a) Persuasive evidence of an arrangement exists.
(b) Delivery has occurred.
(c) The vendor's fee is fixed or determinable.
(d) Collectibility is probable.

[4] Anyone who has visited a doctor recently can attest to the fact that most medical personnel now do all they can to secure payment or a valid promise (generally through insurance) prior to providing the service. They have learned the hard way.

[5] *American Institute of Certified Public Accountants Accounting Standards Executive Committee Statement of Position 97-2*, "Software Revenue Recognition," October 27, 1997, par. 08.

In general, the first two items relate to whether revenue has been earned, and the last two items relate to the realizability of the revenue. Although these four items were developed in the context of software revenue recognition, the principles have been extended to many other contexts. In 1999, the SEC used these four AICPA criteria as the framework for discussion of revenue recognition in *SAB 101*.

From this discussion, you should get the sense that the FASB had temporarily lost the lead in establishing the concepts and standards that define appropriate revenue recognition. This was a troubling development because other bodies such as the SEC and the AICPA tend to approach accounting standards from a practical, problem-solving viewpoint as compared to the conceptual approach preferred by the FASB. The problem-solving viewpoint is great for quick action, but it results in a set of standards that has no unifying conceptual underpinning. The FASB's approach, although sometimes excruciatingly slow, gives more predictability and logical structure to accounting standards. The FASB is currently (June 2010) engaged in a revenue recognition project in conjunction with the IASB. The FASB has tentatively decided to move away from the realizability and substantial completion criteria described above and to instead emphasize the measurement of a seller's satisfaction of performance obligations created through contracts with its customers. This new revenue recognition approach proposed by the FASB will be described later in the chapter.

SAB 101

2 Discuss the revenue recognition issues, and abuses, underlying the examples used in *SAB 101*.

WHY ***SAB 101*** **was released to curtail specific abuses in revenue recognition practices. The guiding principle behind *SAB 101* is that companies should not be granted the flexibility to decide to accelerate or delay the recognition of revenue. Instead, the economic characteristics of the transaction itself should determine when the revenue is to be recognized.**

HOW **Companies must not recognize revenue before both legal and economic ownership of goods have passed. Up-front fees should be recognized as revenue over the life of a service agreement, generally on a straight-line basis. In a multiple element transaction, the revenue associated with any specific element can be recognized separately only if that element can be sold separately.**

SAB 101 is a very interesting document. It is in a question-and-answer format. Most of the questions follow the pattern: "May a company recognize revenue in the following situation?" The answers given in *SAB 101* are invariably "No." *SAB 101* arose in response to specific abuses seen by the SEC staff. As illustrated with the MicroStrategy scenario at the beginning of the chapter, these abuses were often driven by the desire of high-flying companies to maintain their aura of invincibility by continuing to report astronomical revenue growth each quarter.

Because *SAB 101* was released to curtail specific abuses, it should not be seen as a comprehensive treatise on the entire area of revenue recognition. Remember that the vast majority of companies apply the revenue

FYI

When the SEC releases accounting guidance, it is in response to an immediate need to safeguard investors from what the SEC views as faulty, and perhaps deceptive, financial reporting practices. In these cases, the SEC sometimes grows impatient with the long deliberative process that the FASB follows before releasing a standard.

recognition criteria in a very straightforward way with no questions from their auditor, the SEC, or investors. But it is precisely in the financial reporting of high-growth, start-up companies doing innovative transactions where reliable and transparent accounting practices add greatest value. Thus, the revenue recognition issues covered in *SAB 101* may not be comprehensive, but they are extremely important.

The release by the SEC of *SAB 101* caused quite a stir in the accounting community. *SAB 101* deals with a fundamental accounting topic (revenue recognition), is blunt in its provisions, and was released without the years of discussion and lobbying typically involved in the release of an FASB statement. As a result, *SAB 101* was like a bomb going off. In the aftermath of this bomb, the FASB has undertaken a comprehensive review of the topic of revenue recognition, as mentioned above. The discussion below reflects many of the important issues addressed in *SAB 101*; as shown in a subsequent section of this chapter, these *SAB 101* issues have influenced the FASB's review of revenue recognition.

Persuasive Evidence of an Arrangement

The best evidence of a sale is that the seller and buyer have concluded a routine, arm's-length agreement that is conducted entirely according to the normal business practices of both the seller and the buyer. Two *SAB 101* questions highlight areas in which a seller might bend the revenue recognition rules to strategically time the reporting of a sale. Without a reliable internal control system, it is easier for the management of a seller to manipulate the timing of the reporting of a sale. Also, when the seller enters into side agreements with the buyer, a transaction that appears to be a sale on the surface can be transformed into a consignment arrangement.

***SAB 101*, Question 1** Company A requires each sale to be supported by a written sales agreement signed by an authorized representative of both Company A and of the customer. May Company A recognize revenue in the current quarter if the product is delivered before the end of the quarter but the sales agreement is not signed by the customer until a few days after the end of the quarter?[6]

If a company does not have a reliable, systematic, predictable procedure in place for processing customer contracts, then it becomes much easier for company executives to succumb to temptation at the end of a quarter and strategically accelerate the booking of revenue. Thus, even though *SAB 101* Question 1 seems narrowly focused, it should instead be seen as encouraging companies to implement good internal controls surrounding revenue recognition. Companies with such controls are much less likely to be called into question about their revenue recognition practices. This emphasis on internal control is a precursor to the expanded emphasis embodied in the Sarbanes-Oxley Act of 2002. Section 404 of Sarbanes-Oxley instructs the SEC to require all publicly traded companies to provide a report on the condition of the company's internal control over the financial reporting process. These financial reporting controls include company procedures to ensure that all transactions are recorded so that the public financial statements are not rendered irrelevant by secret side agreements. Proper internal controls also include procedures to ensure that no transaction takes place unless it is approved by the proper authority. In addition, a good internal control system establishes procedures to safeguard the value of the company's assets.

[6] Each of the seven *SAB 101* questions covered in this section has been simplified and adapted from its original wording. The original wording is available at **http://www.sec.gov.** Because this section does not cover all of the *SAB 101* questions, in some cases the question numbering here differs from the original numbering.

As explained in the opening scenario of the chapter, MicroStrategy executives deliberately delayed signing customer contracts near the end of a quarter until it was determined how many of the contracts were needed to meet revenue targets for the quarter.

***SAB 101*, Question 2** Company Z delivers product to a customer on a consignment basis. May Company Z recognize revenue upon delivery of the product to the customer?

Question 1 deals with internal control surrounding revenue recognition, and Question 2 addresses the issue of circumventing those controls through side agreements with customers. On its face, the answer to Question 2 is straightforward: no, revenue should not be recognized on consignment arrangements because no sale has taken place. The broader issue is that a seller can convert a "sale" into a consignment arrangement through side agreements with the customer. For example, the seller can "sell" a product to the buyer but also can guarantee a liberal return policy and not require the buyer to pay for the product until the buyer in turn sells it to a customer. Or the seller "sells" a product to the buyer but agrees to repurchase the product at the same price and provides interest-free financing to the buyer. In both of these instances, the seller may have followed the letter of its internal control policy regarding revenue recognition and contracts, but the side agreements between the seller and the buyer have transformed the deal into a consignment rather than a sale.

To illustrate the appropriate accounting for a consignment, assume that Seller Company ships goods costing $1,000 on consignment to Consignee Company. The retail price of the goods is $1,500. No sale should be recorded. However, there may be a journal entry made to reclassify the inventory, as follows:

Inventory on Consignment	1,000	
Inventory		1,000

The Coca-Cola Company was found by the SEC to have engaged in "channel stuffing" in its Japan subsidiary. On April 18, 2005, the SEC made the following statement: "The Commission found that, at or near the end of each reporting period between 1997 and 1999, Coca-Cola implemented an undisclosed 'channel stuffing' practice in Japan known as 'gallon pushing' for the purpose of pulling sales forward into a current period. To accomplish gallon pushing's purpose, Japanese bottlers were offered extended credit terms to induce them to purchase quantities of beverage concentrate the bottlers otherwise would not have purchased until a following period. . . . This practice contributed approximately $0.01 to $0.02 to Coca-Cola's quarterly earnings per share and was the difference in 8 out of the 12 quarters from 1997 through 1999 between Coca-Cola meeting and missing analysts' consensus or modified consensus earnings estimates."

Delivery Has Occurred or Service Has Been Rendered

One of the two general revenue recognition criteria is that the earnings process must be substantially completed. *SAB 101* contains four questions that relate to this issue. Questions 3 and 4 examine the notion of transfer of effective ownership of goods, and Questions 5 and 6 relate to the recognition of revenue when there are several steps in the earnings process.

***SAB 101*, Question 3** May Company A recognize revenue when it completes production of inventory for a customer if it segregates that inventory from other products in its warehouse? What if Company A ships the completed inventory to a third-party warehouse (but retains legal title to the inventory)?

SAB 101, Question 4 Company R is a retailer that offers "layaway" sales to its customers. A customer pays a portion of the sales price, and Company R sets the merchandise aside until the customer returns, pays the remainder of the sales price, and takes possession of the merchandise. When should Company R recognize revenue from a layaway sale?

Both of these questions center on so-called "bill-and-hold" arrangements. A *bill-and-hold* arrangement is exactly what the label implies: The seller bills the buyer for a purchase but holds the goods for later shipment. In general, revenue should *not* be recognized in a bill-and-hold arrangement until the seller has transferred both legal ownership, evidenced by the buyer taking title to the goods, and economic ownership, meaning that the buyer accepts responsibility for the safeguarding and preservation of the goods.

The transfer of legal title occurs in accordance with the shipping terms: Legal title passes at shipment if the terms are FOB shipping point and at customer receipt if the terms are FOB destination. Thus, in the situation described in Question 4, a layaway "sale" is not really a sale because the seller still has custody of and legal title to the goods. Accordingly, revenue from a layaway sale is not recognized until the goods are delivered to the customer.

To illustrate the appropriate accounting for a layaway sale, assume that Seller Company receives $100 cash from a customer. The $100 payment is a partial payment for goods costing $1,000 with a total retail price of $1,500. The journal entries to record the receipt of the cash and the subsequent delivery of the goods when the remaining $1,400 is collected are as follows.

	Debit	Credit
Receipt of $100 cash as initial layaway payment:		
Cash	100	
Deposits Received from Customers		100
Receipt of the final $1,400 cash payment and delivery of goods to customer:		
Cash	1,400	
Deposits Received from Customers	100	
Sales		1,500
Cost of Goods Sold	1,000	
Inventory		1,000

Whitehall Jewelers operates jewelry stores in shopping malls around the country. Before *SAB 101*, the company described its accounting practice with respect to layaway sales as follows: "Layaway receivables include those sales to customers under the Company's layaway policies that have not been collected fully as of the end of the year. Layaway receivables are net of customer payments received to date, and net of an estimate for those layaway sales which the Company anticipates will never be consummated. This estimate is based on the Company's historical calculation of layaway sales that will never be completed." In 2000, Whitehall changed its revenue recognition practice to defer recognition of layaway sales until the merchandise is delivered to the customer.

As you consider the situation in Question 3, you can see why the SEC was concerned with cases such as this. Without strict revenue recognition guidelines for bill-and-hold arrangements, a seller wishing to boost revenue near the end of a quarter could simply push some goods to the side of its warehouse and claim that the goods had been sold to a buyer and were being held for shipment. To recognize revenue in a bill-and-hold arrangement, a seller must be able to demonstrate that the goods are ready to ship, that they are segregated in fact and cannot be used to fill other orders, and most importantly, that that buyer has requested, in writing, the bill-and-hold arrangement. This is true whether the bill-and-hold goods are kept in the seller's warehouse or are shipped to an intermediate, third-party location such as a warehouse owned by a storage company.[7] In connection with the idea of the transfer of both legal and economic ownership, the seller should not recognize revenue from a sale of goods until all customer acceptance provisions have been satisfied. For example, the sales agreement for sophisticated equipment usually includes a provision that the equipment must be delivered to the buyer's location, installed, and tested to the buyer's satisfaction. In cases like this, no revenue is to be recognized until the customer acceptance provisions of the sales agreement are satisfied. The underlying idea is that the acceptance provisions must be important to the buyer or else they wouldn't have been included in the sales agreement in the first place. Accordingly, the seller has not completed the earnings process until the customer acceptance provisions have been satisfied.

To illustrate the appropriate accounting for customer acceptance provisions, assume that Seller Company receives $1,500 cash from a customer as payment in full for equipment costing $1,000. The sale is not complete until the equipment is installed at the customer's place of business. The journal entries to record the receipt of the cash and the subsequent completion of the installation follow.

Receipt of $1,500 cash as payment in full for equipment:		
Cash	1,500	
Advance Payments Received from Customers		1,500
Customer acceptance of the installed equipment is recorded:		
Advance Payments Received from Customers	1,500	
Sales		1,500
Cost of Goods Sold	1,000	
Inventory		1,000

> Before *SAB 101*, **Levitz Furniture** recognized revenue from a furniture sale when the sales order was written if the merchandise was in stock. In response to *SAB 101*, Levitz changed its revenue recognition practice so that no sale was recorded until the customer took delivery of the furniture.

***SAB 101*, Question 5** Company H requires customers to pay an up-front, nonrefundable fee in addition to monthly payments for its services. When should Company H recognize the revenue from this up-front, nonrefundable fee?

***SAB 101*, Question 6** Company A provides its customers with computer-based services over an extended period. Customers are required to prepay the entire fee for the extended service. Company A performs initial setup activities to get a customer entered into its

[7] In some legal jurisdictions, sellers must retain legal title to goods sold on credit in order to be able to enforce return of the goods if the customer doesn't pay. If retention of title is merely a tool to enforce payment on a credit sale, the seller is not necessarily blocked from recognizing revenue at the time of a credit sale.

system, and the remaining service is automated. When should Company A recognize revenue for this service?

The situations described in Questions 5 and 6 relate to the recognition of revenue when service periods cover extended periods and when there are several different activities that the seller must perform in providing the service. The concern in cases such as this is that sellers will wish to front-load the recognition of revenue; in the extreme, the seller would like to recognize all of the revenue immediately. The guidance given in *SAB 101* is that, in general, revenue should be recognized on a straight-line basis over the life of the contract and that recognition of an extra chunk of revenue for completion of a specific service act under the contract can be justified only if that service can be sold as a separate product.

In the situation described in Question 5, immediate recognition of the nonrefundable up-front fee as revenue cannot be justified because no customer would pay separately to simply be "signed up" for a service. Instead, the sign-up and payment of the up-front fee are integral parts of the entire service arrangement, and the entire package should be accounted for as a unit. An example given in *SAB 101* is the nonrefundable initiation fee paid when a customer buys a lifetime membership to a health club. The initiation fee and the subsequent monthly payments should be accounted for as a unit because no customer would pay a separate fee merely to sign up for the club without the expectation of using the club in the future. This general approach has been approved and included in the FASB Codification in FASB ASC Subtopic 605-25 (Revenue Recognition—Multiple-Element Arrangements). The terminology used in Subtopic 605-25 is that in a business arrangement with several components, revenue is recognized separately for each "unit of accounting" where a "unit of accounting" is defined as a component that has "value to the customer on a standalone basis."

ITT Educational Services offers technology-oriented degree programs to more than 30,000 students in the United States. *SAB 101* impacted the company's revenue recognition policy as follows: "Effective January 1, 2000, we implemented *SAB 101* and changed the method by which we recognize the laboratory and application fees charged to a student as revenue. We began recognizing those fees as revenue on a straight-line basis over the average student's program length of 24 months. Previously, we recognized the quarterly laboratory fee as revenue at the beginning of each academic quarter and the application fee as revenue when we received the fee."

In the situation described in Question 6, the seller might agree to spread the recognition of revenue over the life of the service contract but desire to recognize a disproportionate amount of revenue at the beginning of the contract because of the completion of the initial setup activities. Again, no customer would pay for the setup activities as a separate product, so revenue cannot be assigned specifically to the completion of that part of the agreement. Using the terminology of Subtopic 605-25, the initial setup activities are not a separate "unit of accounting." In addition, *SAB 101* also states that extra revenue cannot be recognized at the beginning of the arrangement just because proportionately more of the cost is expended during the setup activities. The recognition of revenue should be based on the amount of the expected service that has been provided, not the amount of the cost that has been incurred. Unless there is strong evidence to the contrary, revenue should be recognized on a straight-line basis, independent of the amount of cost incurred. In addition, no revenue should be recognized before the term of the agreement begins.

For example, if a licensing agreement is signed on December 10 but doesn't begin until January 1, revenue recognition should not begin until January 1.

To illustrate the appropriate accounting for a service provided over an extended period, assume that Seller Company receives $1,000 cash from a customer as the initial sign-up fee for a service. In addition to the initial sign-up fee, the customer is required to pay $50 per month for the service. The expected economic life of this service agreement is 100 months. The journal entries to record the receipt of the initial sign-up fee, the receipt of the first monthly payment, and partial revenue recognition for the initial fee after the first month are as follows:

Receipt of $1,000 cash as the initial sign-up fee:		
Cash	1,000	
Unearned Initial Sign-up Fees		1,000
Receipt of the first monthly payment of $50:		
Cash	50	
Monthly Service Revenue		50
Partial recognition of the initial sign-up fee as revenue ($1,000/100 months):		
Unearned Initial Sign-up Fees	10	
Initial Sign-up Fee Revenue		10

Genentech, Inc., is a large biotechnology company dedicated to discovering and developing pharmaceutical products. The company explains the impact of *SAB 101* as follows: "[W]e previously recognized nonrefundable, upfront product license fees as revenue when the technology was transferred and when all of our significant contractual obligations relating to the fees had been fulfilled. Effective January 1, 2000, we changed our method of accounting for non-refundable upfront product license fees and certain guaranteed payments to recognize such fees over the term of the related development collaboration when, at the execution of the agreement, the development period involves significant risk due to the incomplete stage of the product's development, or over the period of manufacturing obligation when, at the execution of the agreement, the product is approved for marketing, or nearly approvable, and development risk has been substantially eliminated. Deferred revenue related to manufacturing obligations will be recognized on a straight-line basis over the longer of the contractual term of the manufacturing obligation or the expected period over which we will supply the product."

More About Subtopic 605-25 The focus of Subtopic 605-25 is on the "unit of accounting." An element of a multiple-element arrangement is considered to be a unit of accounting if that element has standalone value. An element has standalone value if it is sold separately (by anyone, not necessarily the seller) or if the customer can resell it.

To illustrate the accounting for a multiple-element arrangement under Subtopic 605-25, assume that on April 2 Lily Kay Company sold elements A and B to a customer for a single price of $1,000; Lily Kay collected the $1,000 selling price in cash on April 2. Also assume that both element A and element B are sold separately (not necessarily by Lily Kay), so each has standalone value to the customer. Lily Kay has three different methods to use in determining the separate selling prices of the two elements. The three different methods are as follows, and are to be used in the following order.

1. Vender-specific objective evidence (VSOE). VSOE consists of the individual prices that Lily Kay itself uses in selling elements A and B. If these prices exist, then, of course, they are the best measure of the separate selling prices, for Lily Kay, of the two elements. It is possible that VSOE exists for one, or both, or neither of the two elements.
2. Third-party evidence (TPE). If Lily Kay itself does not sell one or both of the two elements separately, then the next best source of evidence for a separate selling price is the price at which the elements are sold separately by other companies.
3. Best estimate using other data. It is possible that neither Lily Kay nor a third-party competitor sells either element A or element B separately. This does not mean that the elements have no standalone value; if the customer can resell the elements separately, then they have standalone value. However, this does mean that Lily Kay must develop an estimate of what the separate selling price would be. Possible inputs into this estimation process are the cost of the element (plus a standard profit margin) and observable selling prices of similar items.

In this case, Lily Kay sometimes sells element A separately for $700 (VSOE). Also, even though neither Lily Kay nor its competitors sell element B separately, an estimate using costs and normal profit margins indicates that the separate selling price of element B would be approximately $400. Lily Kay would make the following journal entries on April 2 (to record the receipt of cash), on June 6 (to record the delivery of element A), and on July 15 (to record the delivery of element B).

April 2

Cash	1,000	
Unearned Revenue—Element A		636*
Unearned Revenue—Element B		364**

*Element A: [$700/($700 + $400)] × $1,000 = $636
**Element B: [$400/($700 + $400)] × $1,000 = $364

June 6

Unearned Revenue—Element A	636	
Revenue—Element A		636

July 15

Unearned Revenue—Element B	364	
Revenue—Element B		364

Note the impact of the accounting for the revenue associated with this multiple-element transaction. If Lily Kay's fiscal second quarter ends on June 30, then only the $636 in revenue from the delivery of element A will be included in the second quarter results, even though all of the $1,000 in cash was collected during the quarter. The amount of revenue recognized during the second quarter is determined by the relative amount of value received by the customer during that quarter.

Income Statement Presentation of Revenue: Gross or Net

Question 7 related to *SAB 101* does not deal with when revenue should be recognized but instead with how the revenue should be reported in the income statement.

***SAB 101*, Question 7** Company A operates an Internet site through which customers can order the products of traditional Company T. Company T ships the products directly to the customers, and Company A never takes title to the product. The typical sales price is $175, of which Company A receives $25. Should Company A report revenue of $175 with cost of goods sold of $150, or should Company A merely report $25 in commission revenue?

The issue dealt with in Question 7 is labeled "gross vs. net" revenue reporting. In gross reporting, Company A reports the total sales price as revenue, and the difference between the $25 proceeds to Company A and the $175 sales price is reported as cost of goods sold. Before *SAB 101*, this was the preferred accounting treatment by Internet brokers. The alternative is the net method in which Company A merely reports the $25 it receives as commission revenue. The reason that Internet companies preferred the gross presentation is illustrated by referring back to the MicroStrategy story. Recall that with MicroStrategy there was frequent reference to the company's price-to-sales ratio. Because most companies report losses in their early years, earnings-based valuation methods don't work. An alternative approach is to value the company based on its reported sales under the assumption that as the company becomes established, those sales will eventually generate positive earnings and cash flows. But a revenue-based valuation model also gives companies an incentive to maximize their reported revenue, even if there is no impact on bottom-line earnings. Thus, the gross method is preferred over the net method by companies wishing to boost reported revenue.

SAB 101 made clear that the gross method (reporting $175 in revenue and $150 in cost of goods sold in the Question 7 example) is inappropriate when a company merely serves as an agent or broker and never takes legal and economic ownership of the goods being sold. This same issue was subsequently addressed in more detail in FASB ASC Section 605-45-45 (Revenue Recognition—Principal Agent Considerations—Other Presentation Matters), where characteristics of a transaction in which a company should report revenue on a net basis are given as follows.

- The company does not maintain an inventory of the product being sold but simply forwards orders to a supplier.
- The company is not primarily responsible for satisfying customer requirements, requests, complaints, and so forth; those requirements are satisfied by the supplier of the goods.
- The company earns a fixed amount, or a fixed percentage, and doesn't bear the risk of fluctuations in the margin between the selling price and the cost of goods sold.
- The company does not bear the credit risk associated with collecting from the customer; that risk is borne by the supplier.

Enron shot to Number 5 in the *Fortune* 500 list for 2002 by virtue of its reported revenue of $139 billion. Using a gap in the accounting rules with respect to revenue reporting for energy trading companies, Enron reported its energy trades using gross reporting instead of net reporting. To illustrate, assume that Enron brokered a deal between a natural gas supplier and a local utility. Enron guaranteed a selling price of $1,000,000 to the natural gas supplier and guaranteed a purchase price of $1,050,000 to the local utility. When the natural gas supplier then provided the natural gas to the utility, Enron would keep the $50,000 excess. Because of the lack of a definite standard for revenue reporting for energy trading, Enron was able to report revenue of $1,050,000 (with cost of goods sold of $1,000,000) rather than the more appropriate reporting of simply $50,000 in commission revenue.

ifrs

This section has included a review of some of the topics addressed in *SAB 101*. Remember, *SAB 101* was never intended to be a comprehensive treatise on revenue recognition. Instead, *SAB 101* was the SEC's attempt to curtail specific accounting abuses seen in the revenue recognition practices of companies such as MicroStrategy. *SAB 101*, issued in 1999, has proved to be very influential. The big splash made by *SAB 101* prompted the FASB, followed by the IASB, to re-examine the fundamental topic of revenue recognition. The next section introduces the results of that FASB/IASB revenue recognition effort.

A Contract Approach to Revenue Recognition

3 Describe the contract approach to revenue recognition that is currently being considered by the FASB and IASB.

WHY Revenue recognition practices have arisen in a patchwork fashion over the years through the application of a general notion of "earnings process." The FASB and IASB wish to simplify revenue recognition accounting and, at the same time, put the accounting for revenue on a more sound conceptual basis.

HOW The FASB and IASB are considering a contract approach to revenue recognition. This contract approach has been reflected in all recent developments in revenue recognition, so its formal adoption will not involve any dramatic changes in current practice. The contract approach contains three basic steps: (1) identify the performance obligations accepted by a seller in its contracts with its buyers; (2) for multiple-element transactions, allocate transaction prices based on relative separate selling prices; and (3) recognize revenue when performance obligations are satisfied.

Both the FASB and IASB have conceptual frameworks that have long directed their standard setting. Key elements in these frameworks are the definitions of assets and liabilities. Both standard setters focus on correct reporting of assets and liabilities in any new standard that they contemplate. This asset-and-liability focus is at the heart of the joint FASB/IASB project on revenue recognition.[8] The insight used in the FASB/IASB project is that when a seller enters into a contract with a buyer, the seller accepts certain performance obligations (liabilities) in exchange for the promise of receiving assets from the buyer.

With this contractual performance obligation focus, the FASB and the IASB have agreed that revenue arises when a seller satisfies a performance obligation to a buyer. Although this contract approach will not change the end result of accounting for revenue in many common situations, the new approach does represent a substantial conceptual shift from the historic focus on reflecting the results of a company's earnings processes. The intent is to make the model robust enough to be used in a wide variety of settings for which there now exists a patchwork of situation-specific and industry-specific revenue recognition practices.

[8] See Proposed Accounting Standards Update—*Revenue Recognition (Topic 605): Revenue from Contracts with Customers*, June 24, 2010, FASB Web site at **http://www.fasb.org**.

For a particular contract between a buyer and a seller, the three basic steps in recognizing revenue under the contract approach are as follows:

1. Identify the performance obligations accepted by the seller. Delivery of a good or service represents a distinct performance obligation if the seller, or another company in the same line of business as the seller, sells that good or service separately. If no one sells the good or service separately, its delivery can still represent a distinct performance obligation if the good or service has a distinct function and a distinct profit margin so that it could be sold separately, if desired.
2. Allocate transaction prices based on relative separate selling prices of any distinct elements of a multiple-element arrangement. Recall that under Subtopic 605-25, data about separate selling prices are to be considered in a specific sequence: first, vender-specific objective evidence, then third-party evidence, and finally, other evidence. In their contract approach proposal, the FASB and IASB are suggesting that the same types of evidence be used. However, the emphasis in the proposal is on generating the best possible measure of the separate selling price, without specifying any particular priority among the data items used.
3. Recognize revenue as the performance obligations are satisfied. Under the contract approach proposed by the FASB and the IASB, a performance obligation is satisfied when the buyer obtains control of the good or service from the seller. This control means that the buyer can use the good or service in any way desired and can prevent others from using the good or service.

You should recognize this approach as being virtually the same as the approach explained earlier in the chapter in the discussion of multiple-element arrangements under Subtopic 605-25. This is no coincidence because the material in this Subtopic was developed and adopted at the same time the FASB and IASB were deliberating their new overall revenue recognition approach. And the general idea that no revenue should be recognized until something of value has been delivered to the customer goes back to *SAB 101* and even back to the traditional revenue recognition criteria.

The big innovation in the contract approach is the idea of performance obligations being satisfied (and revenue being recognized) as control of assets passes from the seller to the buyer. Again, the idea of "control" goes back to the Conceptual Framework definition of an asset. It will take some time for this idea to become solidified in the minds of both the accountants asked to apply these rules and the attorneys and businesspeople asked to more clearly write sales contracts to specify when "control" of the assets passes from the seller to the buyer. For example, a later section in this chapter discusses the accounting for long-term construction contracts. Currently, revenue is recognized based on the percentage of the project that has been completed by the seller, without regard to whether any ownership rights for the construction in progress have passed to the buyer. Under the proposed contract approach, this percentage-of-completion technique won't work unless long-term construction contracts are written to give access to and ownership of the asset under construction to the buyer as the project proceeds. In other words, if the FASB and IASB adopt the "passage of control" concept currently in the contract approach, sellers will need to carefully review, and perhaps revise, their existing contracts if they wish to continue recognizing revenue in the same pattern as they have in the past.

The contract approach will create other interesting differences in the accounting for sales. For example, factors related to uncertainty about cash collectibility from customers will not be reflected in a separate bad debt expense but will instead be reflected in a reduction in the initial amount recognized as revenue. The same is true for expected sales returns. For example, assume that Ashlyn Company has provided goods, on account, to customers during the month with a total billing price of $100,000. It is the end of the month, and Ashlyn is prepared to make the summary journal entry to recognize revenue from these sales of goods. [For simplicity, let's ignore the entry made to record Cost of Goods Sold.] Under the traditional approach, Ashlyn would merely have debited Accounts Receivable for $100,000 and credited Sales Revenue for $100,000. Under the contract approach, Ashlyn must incorporate expected bad debts and expected sales returns into the initial amount recognized as revenue. Assume that bad debts are expected to be 1.0% of the gross sales amount, and sales returns are expected to be 2.5% of the gross sales amount. The summary journal entry to recognize sales for the month would be as follows (ignoring the entries to record Cost of Goods Sold and the expected return of Inventory):

Accounts Receivable	96,500	
Sales Revenue [$100,000 × (100.0% – 1.0% – 2.5%)]		96,500

Another difference associated with the contract approach is the increased use of selling price estimates in accounting for multiple-element arrangements. Historically, the use of selling price estimates to account for these arrangements was almost forbidden. For example, under the provisions of pre-Codification *EITF 00-21*, if no observable price (either vendor specific or third party) were available for an undelivered element in a multiple-element arrangement, then NO revenue could be recognized, even for the delivered items with observable prices, until that undelivered item was delivered. And a price estimate could not be used in place of a verifiable, observable price. This draconian treatment has since been superseded (as discussed earlier in the treatment of Subtopic 605-25), and it will be put even further in the past as the contract approach embraces a more reasonable use of estimates in the area of revenue recognition.

To illustrate the contract approach to revenue recognition, consider the example of Wilks Company selling a plasma TV and 2-year warranty to a customer for a joint price of $2,000. For simplicity, assume that Wilks collects all of the cash up front on the contract-signing date, and also assume that the probability of product return is 0%. Wilks Company has generated the following information regarding sales of this type.

- Cost of plasma TV, $1,500
- Sales price of plasma TV if sold separately, unknown. Neither Wilks nor any of its competitors sell the plasma TV without the 2-year warranty. However, the TV has a distinct function and a distinct profit margin and could be sold separately, if desired. Wilks does sell other consumer electronic products separately. The profit margins for these products range between 16% and 22% of cost.
- Sales price of 2-year warranty if sold separately, unknown. The 2-year warranty on the plasma TV is not sold separately, but Wilks does sell warranties of various lengths for a variety of other consumer electronics products. A 2-year warranty for a refrigerator/freezer with the same wholesale cost sells for $300. Wilks estimates that the 2-year cost of repairs for the plasma TV would be about 5% higher than for a refrigerator/freezer.

When the customer signs the contract to buy the plasma TV and 2-year warranty from Wilks Company, Wilks has created two performance obligations that should be recognized as liabilities: the obligation to deliver the plasma TV and the obligation to provide two years of warranty service. The difficulty is in measuring the liabilities for the TV delivery and warranty service. Neither element has an observable price, but both elements do have standalone value to the customer. In order to allocate the total contract price of $2,000, Wilks must estimate standalone selling prices for each of the two elements. With the data given above, those estimates can be generated as follows:

TV screen delivery obligation

Low estimate: $1,500 cost + ($1,500 × 0.16) = $1,740

High estimate: $1,500 cost + ($1,500 × 0.22) = $1,830

Average: ($1,740 + $1,830) / 2 = $1,785

Warranty service obligation

$300 + ($300 × 0.5) = $315

Of course, if separate, observable selling prices were available, either from Wilks or from one of its competitors, it may be preferable to use those prices rather than these estimates.

The transaction price allocation, using the estimated separate selling prices of the TV screen and the warranty, is as follows:

TV delivery obligation $1,700 = $2,000 × [$1,785/($1,785 + $315)]

Warranty service obligation $300 = $2,000 × [$315/($1,785 + $315)]

These two quantities, $1,700 and $300, are estimates of the two performance obligations Wilks Company accepted when signing the contract. These two obligations are balanced by the asset, $2,000 in cash, that Wilks received. The journal entry to record this asset and these two liabilities created at the contract signing is as follows:

Cash	2,000	
Contract Liability—TV		1,700
Contract Liability—Warranty		300

When the plasma TV is delivered to the customer, that performance obligation has been satisfied and the associated liability has decreased to zero. Revenue is recognized when a liability created as part of a contractual arrangement with a customer has decreased. The journal entry (assuming a perpetual inventory system) is as follows:

Contract Liability—TV	1,700	
Sales Revenue		1,700
Cost of Goods Sold	1,500	
Inventory		1,500

Additional revenue will be recognized as the performance obligation associated with the warranty services is reduced. This reduction may be in a straight-line fashion, or the obligation may be reduced more, say, in the first year than in the second year; if this is true, more warranty revenue will be recognized in the first year than in the second year.

The contract approach has the benefits of being easy to understand, relatively easy to use, and generally consistent with past practice. In fact, in this simple example the contract approach may seem so much like existing practice that it doesn't seem worth the bother. However, the shift from an earnings process focus to a focus on the creation and satisfaction of performance obligation liabilities makes this revenue recognition approach both

FASB CODIFICATION

The Issue: Your sister is an economics major. She is always using sophisticated phrases such as "utility maximization," "downward-sloping demand curve," and "Pareto optimal." You wish you knew what she was talking about.

Last night she was saying something about "principal-agent models." A light went off in your head—you know that in your accounting studies you have seen something about principals and agents. You also remember that it had something to do with revenue recognition.

The Question: In the context of revenue recognition, what is a principal and what is an agent?

Searching the Codification: In the FASB Codification, all of the material about revenue recognition is in Topic 605. Good luck!

The Answer: The accounting use of the terms "principal" and "agent" is given on page 8-41.

consistent with the conceptual frameworks of the FASB and IASB and flexible enough to be applied in a wide variety of settings.

On June 24, 2010, the FASB and the IASB jointly released an Exposure Draft proposing a formal revenue recognition standard based on the contract approach. At this point, it is highly likely that some variation of the contract approach will be adopted by both the FASB and the IASB sometime in 2011 as the foundation for revenue recognition standards. As stated above, from a practical standpoint the contract approach is generally consistent with existing standards. However, some interesting differences in the accounting for bad debts and construction contracts, among other things, will result. Stay tuned.

Revenue Recognition Prior to Delivery of Goods or Performance of Services

4 **Record journal entries for long-term construction-type contracts using percentage-of-completion and completed-contract methods.**

WHY **In some instances, revenue may be recognized prior to the actual delivery of goods or services. The most common example of this is a long-term contract. The objective is to show financial statement users the economic activity of a company during the period being reported.**

HOW **Revenue may be recognized prior to delivery if four criteria are met: (1) estimates can be made of the amount of work remaining, (2) a contract exists outlining each party's responsibilities, (3) the buyer can be expected to fulfill the contract, and (4) the seller can be expected to fulfill the contract.**

At this point, it is important to remember that the contract approach to revenue recognition discussed in the previous section is still being considered and refined by the FASB and the IASB. Revenue recognition under current U.S. GAAP is still based on the historical focus on the earnings process. The next three sections explain how this general approach to revenue recognition works in three different settings.

Under some circumstances, revenue can be meaningfully reported prior to the delivery of the finished product or completion of a service contract. For example, under *IAS 41*, biological assets, such as cattle, fruit trees, and lumber forests, are recorded in the balance sheet at their fair value (less estimating selling costs) as of the balance sheet date. Increases in this fair value are recognized as gains, and decreases are recognized as losses. Accordingly, under international accounting standards, a lumber company would report the timber in its forests at fair value (less selling cost) in each balance sheet during, say, the 30-year period the timber is growing. The yearly increases or decreases in fair value would be reported in the income statement as gains or losses before the timber is ever sold or delivered to a customer. This approach is allowed in some circumstances under U.S. GAAP, but is not required.[9]

ifrs

Under U.S. GAAP, the most common occurrence of revenue recognition before final delivery is when the construction period of the asset being sold or the period of service performance is relatively long, that is, more than one year. In these cases, if a company waits until the production or service period is complete to recognize revenue, the income statement may not report meaningfully the periodic achievement of the company. Under this approach, referred to as the completed-contract method, all income from the contract is related to the year of completion, even though only a small part of the earnings may be attributable to effort in that period. Previous periods receive no credit for their efforts; in fact, they may be penalized through the absorption of selling, general and administrative, and other overhead costs relating to the contract but not considered part of the inventory cost.

Percentage-of-completion accounting, an alternative to the completed-contract method, was developed to relate recognition of revenue on long-term construction-type contracts to the activities of a firm in fulfilling these contracts. Similarly, the proportional performance method has been developed to reflect revenue earned on service contracts under which many acts of service are to be performed before the contract is completed. Examples of such service contracts include contracts covering maintenance on electronic office equipment, correspondence schools, trustee services, health clubs, professional services such as those offered by attorneys and accountants, and servicing of mortgage loans by mortgage bankers. Percentage-of-completion accounting

Keith Brofsky/Photodisc/Getty Images

Copier repair is accounted for using the proportional performance method, which allows for revenue of service contracts to be spread over the length of the contracts.

[9] See FASB ASC Section 905-330-35 (Agriculture—Inventory—Subsequent Measurement).

and proportional performance accounting are similar in their application. However, some special problems arise in accounting for service contracts. The discussion and examples in the following sections relate first to long-term construction-type contracts and then to the special problems encountered with service contracts.

General Concepts of Percentage-of-Completion Accounting

Under the percentage-of-completion method, a company recognizes revenues and costs on a contract as it progresses toward completion rather than deferring recognition of these items until the contract is completed. The amount of revenue to be recognized each period is based on some measure of progress toward completion. This requires an estimate of costs yet to be incurred. Changes in estimates of future costs arise normally, and the necessary adjustments are made in the year the estimates are revised. Thus, the revenues and costs to be recognized in a given year are affected by the revenues and costs already recognized. As work progresses on the contract, the actual costs incurred are charged to inventory. The amount of profit earned each period also is charged to this asset account. Thus, the inventory account is valued at its net realizable value: the sales (or contract) price less the cost to complete the contract and less the unearned profit on the unfinished contract. (See Chapter 9 for a review of the concepts and computations associated with net realizable value.) If a company projects a loss on the contract prior to completion, the full amount of the loss should be recognized immediately. This loss recognition results in a write-down of the asset to its estimated net realizable value. If only a percentage of the loss were recognized, the asset value would exceed the net realizable value. This would violate the lower-of-cost-or-market rule discussed more fully in Chapter 9.

STOP&THINK

Which ONE of the following is NOT a good way to measure a contract's percentage of completion?

a) The cost expended on contract work so far, relative to the estimate of the total cost to be expended on the contract.
b) The percentage of revenue that will result in the company meeting its revenue and profit goals for the period.
c) An engineer's estimate of the percentage of the work that has been completed.
d) The amount of output produced under the contract (such as the number of feet of roadway completed on a highway construction job), relative to the estimated total amount of output to be produced under the contract.

Necessary Conditions to Use Percentage-of-Completion Accounting

Most long-term construction-type contracts should be reported using the percentage-of-completion method. The guidelines presently in force, however, are not specific as to when a company must use the percentage-of-completion method and when it must use the alternative completed-contract method. The accounting standards that still govern this area were issued by the Committee on Accounting Procedure in 1955.[10] In 1981, the AICPA identified several elements that should be present if percentage-of-completion accounting is to be used.[11]

[10] Pre-Codification *Committee on Accounting Procedure, Accounting Research Bulletin No. 45*, "Long-Term Construction-Type Contracts" (New York: American Institute of Certified Public Accountants, 1955). These provisions are now contained in FASB ASC Subtopic 605-35 (Revenue Recognition—Construction-Type and Production-Type Contracts).

[11] FASB ASC paragraph 605-35-25-57. These provisions were originally found in *AICPA Statement of Position 81-1*, "Accounting for Performance of Construction-Type and Certain Production-Type Contracts" (New York: American Institute of Certified Public Accountants, 1981), par. 23.

1. Dependable estimates can be made of contract revenues, contract costs, and the extent of progress toward completion.
2. The contract clearly specifies the enforceable rights regarding goods or services to be provided and received by the parties, the consideration to be exchanged, and the manner and terms of settlement.
3. The buyer can be expected to satisfy obligations under the contract.
4. The contractor can be expected to perform the contractual obligation.

The completed-contract method should be used only when an entity has primarily short-term contracts, when the conditions for using percentage-of-completion accounting are not met, or when there are inherent uncertainties in the contract, beyond the normal business risks. By the way, under *IAS 11*, the completed-contract method is not allowed under international financial reporting standards.

For many years, income tax regulations permitted contractors wide latitude in selecting either the percentage-of-completion or completed-contract method. Beginning with the Tax Reform Act of 1986, the tax laws have limited the use of the completed-contract method and have required increased use of the percentage-of-completion method. This results in accelerated revenues from taxes without increasing the tax rates, and it also results in similar revenue recognition treatment for both taxes and financial reporting.

Measuring the Percentage of Completion

Various methods are currently used in practice to measure the earnings process. They can be conveniently grouped into two categories: input and output measures.

Input Measures Input measures are made in relation to the costs or efforts devoted to a contract. They are based on an established or assumed relationship between a unit of input and productivity. They include the widely used cost-to-cost method and several variations of efforts-expended methods.

Cost-to-cost method. Perhaps the most popular of the input measures is the cost-to-cost method. Under this method, the degree of completion is determined by comparing costs already incurred with the most recent estimates of total expected costs to complete the project. The percentage that costs incurred bear to total expected costs is applied to the contract price to determine the revenue to be recognized to date as well as to the expected net income on the project in arriving at earnings to date. Some of the costs incurred, particularly in the early stages of the contract, should be disregarded in applying this method because they do not relate directly to effort expended on the contract. These include such items as subcontract costs for work that has yet to be performed and standard fabricated materials that have not yet been installed. One of the most difficult problems in using this method is estimating the costs yet to be incurred. Engineers are often consulted to help provide estimates as to a project's percentage of completion. However difficult the estimation process may be, it is required in reporting income, regardless of how the percentage of completion is computed.

To illustrate, assume that in January 2012 Strong Construction Company was awarded a contract with a total price of $3,000,000. Strong expected to earn $400,000 profit on the contract, or in other words, total costs on the contract were estimated to be $2,600,000. The construction was completed over a 3-year period, and the cost data and cost percentages shown below were compiled during that time.

Note that the cost percentage is computed by dividing cumulative actual costs incurred by total cost, an amount that is estimated for the first two years.

Year	(1) Actual Cost Incurred	(2) Estimated Cost to Complete	(3) Total Cost (1) + (2)	(4) Cost Percentage (1)/(3)
2012	$1,040,000	$1,560,000	$2,600,000*	40
2013	910,000			
Total	$1,950,000	650,000	2,600,000*	75
2014	650,000			
Total	$2,600,000	0	2,600,000†	100

* Estimated total contract cost.

† Actual total contract cost.

Efforts-expended methods. The efforts-expended methods are based on some measure of work performed. They include labor hours, labor dollars, machine hours, or material quantities. In each case, the degree of completion is measured in a way similar to that used in the cost-to-cost approach: the ratio of the efforts expended to date to the estimated total efforts to be expended on the entire contract. For example, if the measure of work performed is labor hours, the ratio of hours worked to date to the total estimated hours would produce the percentage for use in measuring income earned.

Output Measures Output measures are made in terms of results achieved. Included in this category are methods based on units produced, contract milestones reached, and values added. For example, if the contract calls for units of output, such as miles of roadway, a measure of completion would be a ratio of the miles completed to the total miles in the contract. Architects and engineers are sometimes asked to evaluate jobs and estimate what percentage of a job is complete. These estimates are, in reality, output measures and usually are based on the physical progress made on a contract. In its current deliberations on revenue recognition (discussed in the preceding section), the FASB has indicated that "output methods often result in the most faithful depiction of the transfer of goods or services."[12]

Accounting for Long-Term Construction-Type Contracts

For both the percentage-of-completion and the completed-contract methods, all direct and allocable indirect costs of the contracts are charged to an inventory account. The difference in recording between the two methods relates to the timing of revenue and expense recognition; that is, when the estimated earned income is recognized with its related effect on the income statement and the balance sheet. During the construction period, the annual reported income under these two accounting methods will differ. However, after the contract is completed, the combined income for the total construction period will be the same under each method of accounting. The balance sheet at the end of the construction and collection periods also will be identical.

Usually, contracts require progress billings by the contractor and payments by the customer on these billings. The billings and payments are accounted for and reported in the same manner under both methods. The amount of these billings usually is specified

[12] FASB *Proposed Accounting Standards Update, Revenue Recognition (Topic 605): Revenue from Contracts with Customers*, June 24, 2010, par. 33.

by the contract terms and may be related to the costs actually incurred. Generally, these contracts require inspection before final settlement is made. The billings are debited to Accounts Receivable and credited to a deferred account, Progress Billings on Construction Contracts, that serves as an offset to the inventory account, Construction in Progress. The billing of the contract thus transfers the asset value from inventory to receivables, but because of the long-term nature of the contract, the construction costs continue to be reflected in the accounts.

To illustrate accounting for a long-term construction contract, we will continue the Strong Construction Company example mentioned earlier. Recall that construction was completed over a 3-year period and the contract price was $3,000,000. The direct and allocable indirect costs, billings, and collections[13] for 2012, 2013, and 2014 are as follows:

Year	Direct and Allocable Indirect Costs	Billings	Collections
2012	$1,040,000	$1,000,000	$ 800,000
2013	910,000	900,000	850,000
2014	650,000	1,100,000	1,350,000

The following entries for the three years would be made on the contractor's books under either the percentage-of-completion or the completed-contract method.

	2012		2013		2014	
Construction in Progress	1,040,000		910,000		650,000	
Materials, Cash, etc.		1,040,000		910,000		650,000
To record costs incurred.						
Accounts Receivable	1,000,000		900,000		1,100,000	
Progress Billings on Construction Contracts		1,000,000		900,000		1,100,000
To record billings.						
Cash	800,000		850,000		1,350,000	
Accounts Receivable		800,000		850,000		1,350,000
To record cash collections.						

No other entries would be required in 2012 and 2013 under the completed-contract method. In both years, the balance of Construction in Progress exceeds the amount in Progress Billings on Construction Contracts; thus, the latter account would be offset against the inventory account in the balance sheet.

Before proceeding further, let's examine the relationship between the accounts Construction in Progress and Progress Billings on Construction Contracts. Amounts recorded in Construction in Progress represent the costs that have been incurred to date relating to a specific contract. If the customer has not been billed, then the entire cost represents a probable future benefit to the company and should be disclosed on the balance sheet as an asset. If, however, the customer has been billed for a portion of these

[13] As a protection for the customer, long-term contracts frequently provide for an amount to be retained from the progress payments. This retention is usually a percentage of the progress billings, for example, 10% to 20%, and is paid upon final acceptance of the construction. Thus, the amount collected is often less than the amount billed in the initial years of the contract.

FYI

The reason these entries are the same under either revenue recognition method is because they are a function of the terms of the contract that specifies when payment will be made.

STOP&THINK

Progress Billings on Construction Contracts is offset against the construction in progress account. What does the resulting net figure represent?

a) The estimated fair market value of the portion of the construction that has been completed.
b) The amount of cash that has been collected under the contract.
c) The value of the completed construction for which the customer has not yet been billed.
d) The estimated amount of uncollectible accounts associated with the construction project.

costs, then the company has in effect traded one asset for another. In place of inventory, the company now has a receivable (or cash if the receivable has been collected).

Thus, if the balance in Construction in Progress exceeds the balance in Progress Billings on Construction Contracts, the excess represents the amount of the construction costs for which the customer has not been billed.[14] The amount for which the customer has been billed is included in either Accounts Receivable or Cash. If Progress Billings on Construction Contracts is greater than Construction in Progress, the difference represents a liability because the customer has been billed (and a receivable has been recorded) for more than the costs actually incurred.

Because the operating cycle of a company that emphasizes long-term contracts is usually more than one year, all of the preceding balance sheet accounts would be classified as current. The balance sheet at the end of 2013 under the completed-contract method would disclose the following balances related to the construction contract:

Current assets:		
Accounts receivable		$250,000
Construction in progress	$1,950,000	
Less: Progress billings on construction contracts	1,900,000	50,000

If the billings exceeded the construction costs, the excess would be reported in the Current Liability section of the balance sheet.

Under the completed-contract method, the following entries would be made to recognize revenue and costs and to close out the inventory and billings accounts at the completion of the contract, that is, in 2014.

Progress Billings on Construction Contracts	3,000,000	
Revenue from Long-Term Construction Contracts		3,000,000
Cost of Long-Term Construction Contracts	2,600,000	
Construction in Progress		2,600,000

The first entry represents the billings on the contract that, at the end of the contract, equal the total revenue from the contract. The second journal entry transfers the inventoried cost from the contract to the appropriate expense account on the income statement.

[14] As we will soon learn, under the percentage-of-completion method, Construction in Progress includes both costs and the portion of expected gross profit earned to date.

The income statement for 2014 would report the gross revenues and the matched costs, thus recognizing the entire $400,000 profit in one year.

Using Percentage-of-Completion Accounting: Cost-to-Cost Method

If the company used the percentage-of-completion method of accounting, the $400,000 profit would be spread over all three years of construction according to the estimated percentage of completion for each year. The information provided previously details Strong's estimated cost to complete the contract at the end of 2012 and 2013 as well as the total actual costs at the end of 2014. Recall that the percentage of completion for each year, determined on a cost-to-cost basis, is as follows:

	2012	2013	2014
Percentage of completion to date	40%	75%	100%

These percentages may be used to determine directly the gross profit that should be recognized on the income statement; that is, the income statement for 2012 would report only the gross profit from construction contracts in the amount of $160,000 (estimated gross profit—2012, $400,000 × 0.40 = $160,000). Preferably, the percentages should be used to determine both revenues and costs. The income statement will then disclose revenues, costs, and the resulting gross profit, a method more consistent with normal income statement reporting.[15] The procedures are as follows:

NASA/Space Frontiers/Getty Images

Since spacecraft like the *Endeavour* space shuttle may take many years to build, aerospace companies must account for this construction using the percentage-of-completion method.

1. Cumulative revenue to date should be computed by multiplying total estimated contract revenue by the percentage of completion. Revenue for the current period is the difference between the cumulative revenue at the end of the current period and the cumulative revenue recognized in prior periods.
2. Cumulative costs to date should be computed in a manner similar to revenue and should be equal to the total estimated contract cost multiplied by the percentage of completion on the contract. Cost for the current period is the difference between the cumulative costs at the end of the current period and the cumulative costs reported in prior periods.
3. Cumulative gross profit is the excess of cumulative revenue over cumulative costs,

[15] *Construction Contractor Guide Committee of the Accounting Standards Division, AICPA*, "AICPA Audit and Accounting Guide for Construction Contractors" (New York: American Institute of Certified Public Accountants, 1999).

and the current period gross profit is the difference between current revenue and current costs.

If the cost-to-cost method is used to estimate earned revenue, the proportional cost for each period will typically equal the actual cost incurred.

To illustrate, for 2012, 40% of the fixed contract price of $3,000,000 would be recognized as revenue ($1,200,000) and 40% of the expected total cost of $2,600,000 would be reported as cost ($1,040,000). The following revenue recognition entries would be made for each of the three years of the contract. These entries are in addition to the transaction entries illustrated previously.

	2012		2013		2014	
Cost of Long-Term Construction Contracts*	1,040,000		910,000		650,000	
Construction in Progress	160,000		140,000		100,000	
Revenue from Long-Term Construction Contracts		1,200,000		1,050,000†		750,000‡

* Actual costs.
† ($3,000,000 × 0.75) – $1,200,000 = $1,050,000.
‡ $3,000,000 – $1,200,000 – $1,050,000 = $750,000.

The gross profit recognized each year is added to the construction in progress account, thereby valuing the inventory on the books at its net realizable value. Note that the procedures used in recognizing revenue under the percentage-of-completion method do not affect the progress billings made or the amount of cash collected. These amounts are determined by contract and not by the accounting method used.

Because the construction in progress account contains costs incurred plus recognized profit (the two together equaling total revenues recognized to date), at the completion of the contract the balance in this account will exactly equal the amount in Progress Billings on Construction Contracts, because the progress billings account reflects the contract price (or total revenues). The following closing entry would complete the accounting process:

Progress Billings on Construction Contracts	3,000,000	
Construction in Progress		3,000,000

Using Percentage-of-Completion Accounting: Other Methods

If the cost-to-cost method is not used to measure progress on the contract, the proportional costs recognized under this method may not be equal to the actual costs incurred. For example, assume in 2012 that an engineering estimate measure was used, and 42% of the contract was assumed to be completed. The gross profit recognized would therefore be computed and reported as follows:

Recognized revenue (42% of $3,000,000)	$1,260,000
Cost (42% of $2,600,000)	1,092,000
Gross profit (42% of $400,000)	$ 168,000

Because some accountants believe that the amount of cost recognized should be equal to the costs actually incurred, there is an alternative to the preceding approach.[16] Under this actual cost approach, revenue is defined as the actual costs incurred on the contract plus the gross profit earned for the period on the contract. Using the data from the previous example, the revenue and costs to be reported on the 2012 income statement would be as follows:

[16] FASB ASC paragraphs 605-35-25-83 and 84.

Actual cost incurred to date	$1,040,000
Recognized gross profit (42% of $400,000)	168,000
Recognized revenue	$1,208,000

This contrasts with the $1,260,000 revenue using the proportional cost approach. Both approaches report gross profit as $168,000.

The actual cost approach and the proportional cost approach are equally acceptable. However, because the actual cost approach results in a varying gross profit percentage from period to period whenever the measurement of completion differs from that which would occur if the cost-to-cost method were used, the authors feel that the proportional cost approach is preferable. Unless a different method is explicitly stated, text examples and end-of-chapter material will assume the *proportional cost approach*.

Revision of Estimates

In the previous example, it was assumed that the estimated cost did not vary from the beginning of the contract. This rarely would be the case. As estimates change, catch-up adjustments are made in the year of the change. To illustrate the impact of changing estimates, assume that at the end of 2013, it was estimated that the remaining cost to complete the construction was $720,000 rather than $650,000. This would increase the total estimated cost to $2,670,000, reduce the expected profit to $330,000, and change the percentage of completion at the end of 2013 to 73% ($1,950,000/$2,670,000).

The following analysis shows how this change would affect the revenue and costs to be reported each year, assuming that the actual costs incurred in 2014 were $700,000.

	2012	2013	2014
Contract price	$3,000,000	$3,000,000	$3,000,000
Actual cost incurred to date	$1,040,000	$1,950,000	$2,650,000
Estimated cost to complete	1,560,000	720,000	0
Total estimated cost	$2,600,000	$2,670,000	$2,650,000
Total expected gross profit	$ 400,000	$ 330,000	$ 350,000
Percentage of completion to date	40%	73%	100%

	To Date	Recognized—Prior Years	Recognized—Current Year
2012:			
Recognized revenue ($3,000,000 × 0.40)	$1,200,000	0	$1,200,000
Cost (actual cost)	1,040,000	0	1,040,000
Gross profit	$ 160,000		$ 160,000
2013:			
Recognized revenue ($3,000,000 × 0.73)	$2,190,000	$1,200,000	$ 990,000
Cost (actual cost)	1,950,000	1,040,000	910,000
Gross profit	$ 240,000	$ 160,000	$ 80,000
2014:			
Recognized revenue	$3,000,000	$2,190,000	$ 810,000
Cost (actual cost)	2,650,000	1,950,000	700,000
Gross profit	$ 350,000	$ 240,000	$ 110,000

The entries to record revenue and cost for the three years, given the assumed estimate revision, would be as follows:

	2012		2013		2014	
Cost of Long-Term Construction Contracts	1,040,000		910,000		700,000	
Construction in Progress	160,000		80,000		110,000	
Revenue from Long-Term Construction Contracts		1,200,000		990,000		810,000

STOP&THINK

What circumstances would give rise to a loss being reported this year on a contract that is profitable overall?

a) Underestimates of the percentage completed in this period.
b) Overestimates of the percentage completed in this period.
c) Underestimates of the percentage completed in prior periods.
d) Overestimates of the percentage completed in prior periods.

In some cases, an increase in total estimated cost can result in recognition of a loss in the year of the increase. Revising the preceding example, assume that at the end of 2013 the estimated cost to complete construction was $836,000, and this was the actual cost incurred in 2014. The following analysis shows how this change in estimated cost would reduce the percentage of completion at the end of 2013 to 70%, and the cumulative profit at the end of 2013 to $150,000. Because $160,000 was already recognized as gross profit in 2012, a loss of $10,000 would be recognized in 2013.

	2012	2013	2014
Contract price	$3,000,000	$3,000,000	$3,000,000
Actual cost incurred to date	$1,040,000	$1,950,000	$2,786,000
Estimated cost to complete	1,560,000	836,000	0
Total estimated cost	$2,600,000	$2,786,000	$2,786,000
Total expected gross profit	$ 400,000	$ 214,000	$ 214,000
Percentage of completion to date	40%	70%	100%

	To Date	Recognized—Prior Years	Recognized—Current Year
2012:			
Recognized revenue ($3,000,000 × 0.40)	$1,200,000	0	$1,200,000
Cost (actual cost)	1,040,000	0	1,040,000
Gross profit	$ 160,000		$ 160,000
2013:			
Recognized revenue ($3,000,000 × 0.70)	$2,100,000	$1,200,000	$ 900,000
Cost (actual cost)	1,950,000	1,040,000	910,000
Gross profit	$ 150,000	$ 160,000	$ (10,000)
2014:			
Recognized revenue	$3,000,000	$2,100,000	$ 900,000
Cost (actual cost)	2,786,000	1,950,000	836,000
Gross profit	$ 214,000	$ 150,000	$ 64,000

The entries to record revenue and cost for the three years, given the assumed loss estimate in 2013, would be as follows:

	2012		2013		2014	
Cost of Long-Term Construction Contracts	1,040,000		910,000		836,000	
Construction in Progress	160,000			10,000	64,000	
Revenue from Long-Term Construction Contracts		1,200,000		900,000		900,000

Reporting Anticipated Contract Losses

In the example above, an increase in estimated total cost resulted in recognition of a loss in the year the estimate was revised; but overall, the contract resulted in a profit. In some cases, an increase in estimated total cost is so great that a loss on the entire contract is anticipated; that is, total estimated costs are expected to exceed the total revenue from the contract. When a loss on the total contract is anticipated, GAAP requires reporting the loss in its entirety in the period when the loss is first anticipated. This is true under either the completed-contract or the percentage-of-completion method.

For example, assume that in the earlier construction example, the estimated cost to complete the contract at the end of 2013 was \$1,300,000. Because \$1,950,000 of costs had already been incurred, the total estimated cost of the contract would be \$3,250,000 (\$1,950,000 + \$1,300,000), or \$250,000 more than the contract price. Assume also that actual costs equaled expected costs in 2014.

CAUTION

Do not confuse a loss on an entire contract with a loss for a period on a profitable contract. The accounting for these two possibilities is entirely different.

	2012	2013	2014
Contract price	\$3,000,000	\$3,000,000	\$3,000,000
Actual cost incurred to date	\$1,040,000	\$1,950,000	\$3,250,000
Estimated cost to complete	1,560,000	1,300,000	0
Total estimated cost	\$2,600,000	\$3,250,000	\$3,250,000
Total expected gross profit (loss)	\$ 400,000	\$ (250,000)	\$ (250,000)
Percentage of completion to date	40%	60%	100%

Using this example, accounting for a contract loss is illustrated first for the completed-contract method and then for the percentage-of-completion method.

Anticipated Contract Loss: Completed-Contract Method If the completed-contract method is used, the recognition of an anticipated contract loss is simple. The amount of the loss is debited to a loss account, and the inventory account, Construction in Progress, is credited by that amount to reduce the

FYI

Because the construction in progress inventory account is used to accumulate actual construction costs under the completed-contract method, this journal entry will ensure that at the end of the contract, the inventory account is not reported at an amount higher than the contract price.

inventory to its expected net realizable value. To record the anticipated loss of $250,000 on the construction contract, the following entry would be made at the end of 2013:

Anticipated Loss on Long-Term Construction Contracts	250,000	
Construction in Progress		250,000

Anticipated Contract Loss: Percentage-of-Completion Method Recognition of an anticipated contract loss under the percentage-of-completion method is more complex. To properly reflect the entire loss in the year it is first anticipated, the cumulative cost to deduct from cumulative recognized revenue cannot be the actual cost incurred but must be the cumulative recognized revenue plus the entire anticipated loss. Thus, continuing the construction contract example, the cumulative recognized revenue at the end of 2013 would be $1,800,000 (60% × $3,000,000), and the cumulative cost at the same date would be $2,050,000 ($1,800,000 + $250,000). Because the example assumes that $160,000 profit was recognized on this contract in 2012, the total loss to be recognized in 2013 is $410,000 ($160,000 + $250,000). The analysis that follows reflects the amounts to be reported for each of the three years of the contract life under the anticipated loss assumption.

	To Date	Recognized—Prior Years	Recognized—Current Year
2012:			
Recognized revenue ($3,000,000 × 0.40)	$1,200,000	0	$1,200,000
Cost (actual cost)	1,040,000	0	1,040,000
Gross profit	$ 160,000		$ 160,000
2013:			
Recognized revenue ($3,000,000 × 0.60)	$1,800,000	$1,200,000	$ 600,000
Cost (recognized revenue plus entire anticipated loss)	2,050,000	1,040,000	1,010,000
Gross profit (loss)	$ (250,000)	$ 160,000	$ (410,000)
2014:			
Recognized revenue	$3,000,000	$1,800,000	$1,200,000
Cost	3,250,000	2,050,000	1,200,000
Gross profit	$ (250,000)	$ (250,000)	$ 0

The entry to record the revenue, costs, and adjustments to Construction in Progress for the loss in 2013 would be as follows:

Cost of Long-Term Construction Contracts	1,010,000	
Revenue from Long-Term Construction Contracts		600,000
Construction in Progress		410,000

Note that the construction in progress account under both methods would have a balance of $1,700,000 at the end of 2013, computed as shown on the next page.

Completed-Contract Method
Construction in Progress

2012 cost	1,040,000	2013 loss	250,000
2013 cost	910,000		
Balance	1,700,000		

Percentage-of-Completion Method
Construction in Progress

2012 cost	1,040,000	2013 loss	410,000
2012 gross profit	160,000		
2013 cost	910,000		
Balance	1,700,000		

Accounting for Long-Term Service Contracts: The Proportional Performance Method

5 Record journal entries for long-term service contracts using the proportional performance method.

WHY **To show financial statement users the economic activity of a company during the period being reported, revenue from long-term service contracts is often recognized prior to the completion of the entire contract.**

HOW **For long-term service contracts, revenue is recognized prior to the completion of the entire contract. Estimates of completion are made based on the percentage of identical acts completed or the relative sales value of the acts completed. The amount of revenue to be recognized is computed by multiplying this ratio by the contract price.**

Thus far, the discussion in this chapter has focused on long-term construction-type contracts. As indicated earlier, another type of contract that frequently extends over a long period of time is a service contract. When the service to be performed is completed as a single act or over a relatively short period of time, no revenue recognition problems arise. The revenue recognition criteria previously defined apply, and all direct and indirect costs related to the service are charged to expense in the period the revenue is recognized. However, when several acts over a period of time are involved, the same revenue recognition problems illustrated for long-term construction-type contracts arise.

As explained in the earlier discussion of *SAB 101*, partial recognition of revenue under a multiple-element service contract is appropriate only if each element of the contract constitutes a service that can be sold separately. This approach is confirmed in FASB ASC Subtopic 605-25 (Revenue Recognition—Multiple-Element Arrangements). If a contract involves a specified number of identical or similar acts, for example, the playing of a sports contest under a season ticket arrangement, then each sports contest represents a separate product and proportional performance accounting is appropriate. In such a case, revenue should be recognized by relating the number of acts performed to the total number of acts to be performed over the contract life. If a contract involves a specified number of defined but not identical acts, revenue should be recognized using the relationship of the sales value of the individual acts to the total sales value of the service contract. If no pattern of performance can be determined, or if a service contract involves an unspecified number of similar or identical acts with a fixed period for performance, for example, a maintenance contract for electronic office equipment, the straight-line method, that is, recognizing revenue equally over the periods of performance, should be used. In Exhibit 8-2, **Microsoft**'s revenue recognition note provides an example of how a company recognizes revenue for services when a lengthy time period is involved.

Of course, proportional revenue recognition is applicable only if cash collection is reasonably assured and if losses from nonpayment can be objectively determined.

The cost recognition problems of service contracts are somewhat different from those of long-term construction-type contracts. Most service contracts involve three different types of costs: (1) initial direct costs related to obtaining and performing initial services on the contract, such as commissions, legal fees, credit investigations, and paper processing; (2) direct costs related to performing the various acts of service; and (3) indirect costs related to maintaining the organization to service the contract, for example, general and administrative expenses. Initial direct costs generally are charged, that is, matched, against revenue using the same measure used for revenue recognition. Direct costs usually are charged to expense as incurred because they relate directly to the acts for which revenue is recognized. Similarly, all indirect costs should be charged to expense as incurred. As is true for long-term construction-type contracts, any indicated loss on completion of the service contract is to be charged to the period in which the loss is first indicated. If collection of a service contract is highly uncertain, revenue recognition should not be related to performance but to the collection of the receivable using one of the methods described in the latter part of this chapter.

EX 8-2 MICROSOFT'S REVENUE RECOGNITION NOTE—PARTIAL

Revenue from multi-year licensing arrangements are accounted for as subscriptions, with billings recorded as unearned revenue and recognized as revenue ratably over the billing coverage period. Certain multi-year licensing arrangements include rights to receive future versions of software product.

To illustrate accounting for a service contract using the proportional performance method, assume a correspondence school enters into 100 contracts with students for an extended writing course. The fee for each contract is $500, payable in advance. This fee includes many different services such as providing the text material, evaluating written assignments and examinations, and awarding of a certificate. Total incremental direct costs incurred to get these 100 students to decide to sign up for the extended writing course are $5,000.[17] Direct costs for the lessons actually completed during the first period are $12,000. The separate sales value of the lessons completed during the first period is $24,000; if sold separately, the total sales value of all the lessons would be $60,000. The following entries would be made to record these transactions:

Account	Debit	Credit
Cash	50,000	
Deferred Course Revenue (liability account)		50,000
Deferred Initial Costs (asset account)	5,000	
Cash		5,000
Contract Costs (expense account)	12,000	
Cash		12,000
Deferred Course Revenue	20,000*	
Recognized Course Revenue		20,000
Contract Costs	2,000†	
Deferred Initial Costs		2,000

* Relative sales value percentage: $24,000/$60,000 = 40%; $50,000 × 0.40 = $20,000

† $5,000 × 0.40 = $2,000

[17] These "incremental direct acquisition costs" should be recorded as assets and then subsequently expensed in proportion to the amount of revenue that is recognized. See FASB ASC paragraph 605-20-25-4.

The gross profit reported on these contracts for the period would be $6,000 ($20,000 − $12,000 − $2,000). The deferred initial cost and deferred course revenues would normally be reported as current balance sheet deferrals, because the operating cycle of a correspondence school would be equal to the average time to complete a contract or one year, whichever is longer.

Revenue Recognition After Delivery of Goods or Performance of Services

6 **Explain when revenue is recognized after delivery of goods or services through installment sales, cost recovery, and cash methods.**

WHY **When a valid promise of payment has not been received, it is not appropriate to recognize revenue at the point of sale. In those instances, the recognition of revenue is deferred until cash is collected.**

HOW **Several methods exist for recognizing revenue when ultimate cash collection is in substantial doubt. The most common method, the installment sales method, results in profit being recognized based on the gross profit percentage. Under the installment sales method, a portion of every dollar collected is recorded as profit based on the gross profit percentage.**

One of the FASB's two revenue recognition criteria, listed at the beginning of this chapter, states that revenue should not be recognized until the earnings process is substantially completed. Normally, the earnings process is substantially completed by the delivery of goods or performance of services. Collection of receivables is usually routine, and any future warranty costs can be reasonably estimated. In some cases, however, the circumstances surrounding a revenue transaction are such that considerable uncertainty exists as to whether payments will indeed be received. This can occur if the sales transaction is unusual in nature or involves a customer in such a way that default carries little cost or penalty. Under these circumstances, the uncertainty of cash collection suggests that revenue recognition should await the actual receipt of cash.

There are at least three different approaches to revenue recognition that depend on the receipt of cash: installment sales, cost recovery, and cash. These methods differ as to the treatment of costs incurred and the timing of revenue recognition. They are summarized and contrasted with the full accrual method in the table below.

These methods are really not alternatives to each other; however, the guidelines for applying them are not well defined. As the uncertainty of the environment increases, GAAP would require moving from the full accrual method to installment sales, cost recovery, and, finally, a strict cash approach. The cash method is the most conservative approach, because it would not permit the deferral of any costs but would charge them to expense as those costs are paid. In the following pages, each of these revenue recognition methods will be discussed and illustrated.

Method	Timing of Revenue and/or Income Recognition	Treatment of Product Costs or Direct Costs under Service Contracts
Full accrual	At point of sale.	Charge against revenue at time of sale or rendering of service.
Installment sales	At collection of cash. Usually a portion of the cash payment is recognized as income.	Defer to be matched against a part of each cash collection. Usually done by deferring the estimated profit.
Cost recovery	At collection of cash, but only after all costs are recovered.	Defer to be matched against total cash collected.
Cash	At collection of cash.	Charge to expense as incurred.

Installment Sales Method

Traditionally, the most commonly applied method for dealing with the uncertainty of cash collections has been the installment sales method. Under this method, profit is recognized as cash is collected rather than at the time of sale.[18] The installment sales method is used most commonly in cases of real estate sales where contracts may involve little or no down payment, payments are spread over 10 to 30 or 40 years, and a high probability of default in the early years exists because of a small investment by the buyer in the contract and because the market prices of the property often are unstable. Application of the accrual method to these contracts frequently overstates income in the early years due to the failure to realistically provide for future costs related to the contract, including losses from contract defaults. The FASB considered these types of sales and concluded that accrual accounting applied in these circumstances often results in "front-end loading," that is, a recognition of all revenue at the time of the sales contract with improper matching of related costs. Thus, the Board has established criteria that must be met before real estate and retail land sales can be recorded using the full accrual method of revenue recognition. If the criteria are not fully met, then the use of the installment sales method, or in some cases the cost recovery or deposit methods, is recommended to reflect the conditions of the sale more accurately.[19] **General Growth Properties, Inc.**, a real estate development firm, provides disclosure, shown in Exhibit 8-3, relating to its revenue recognition policy. Note that General Growth Properties uses one of four revenue recognition policies (full accrual, installment, cost recovery, or percentage of completion) for its transactions, depending on whether or not the transaction meets established revenue recognition criteria.

CAUTION

Do not confuse installment sales with the installment sales method of accounting. Remember that most installment sales are accounted for using accrual accounting. Only those sales with a high degree of uncertainty as to collection are accounted for using the installment sales method.

EX 8-3 GENERAL GROWTH PROPERTIES' REVENUE RECOGNITION NOTE

Revenues from land sales are recognized using the full accrual method provided that various criteria relating to the terms of the transactions and our subsequent involvement with the land sold are met. Revenues relating to transactions that do not meet the established criteria are deferred and recognized when the criteria are met or using the installment or cost recovery methods, as appropriate in the circumstances. For land sale transactions in which we are required to perform additional services and incur significant costs after title has passed, revenues and cost of sales are recognized on a percentage of completion basis.

FYI

The installment sales method is frequently used for income tax purposes. The primary rationale for allowing its use in that setting is that when the cash is collected over an extended period, at the time the sale is made the taxpayer does not have the wherewithal to pay all of the income tax due on the total profit.

Accounting for installment sales using the deferred gross profit approach requires determining a gross profit rate for the sales of each year and establishing an accounts receivable and a deferred gross profit account identified by the year of the sale. As collections are made of a

[18] FASB ASC paragraphs 605-10-25-3 through 5 and 360-20-55-7 through 10.

[19] FASB ASC Subtopic 360-20 (Property, Plant, and Equipment—Real Estate Sales).

given year's receivables, a portion of the deferred profit equal to the gross profit rate times the collections made is recognized as income. To keep things relatively simple, the following examples of transactions and journal entries will illustrate the installment sales method assuming the sale of merchandise.

Installment Sales of Merchandise Assume that the Riding Corporation sells merchandise on the installment basis and that the uncertainties of cash collection make the use of the installment sales method necessary. The following data relate to three years of operations. To simplify the presentation, interest charges are excluded from the example.

	2012	2013	2014
Installment sales	$150,000	$200,000	$300,000
Cost of installment sales	100,000	140,000	204,000
Gross profit	$ 50,000	$ 60,000	$ 96,000
Gross profit percentage	33.333%	30%	32%
Cash collections:			
2012 sales	$ 30,000	$ 75,000	$ 30,000
2013 sales		70,000	80,000
2014 sales			100,000

The entries to record the transactions for 2012 would be as follows:

	Debit	Credit
During the year:		
Installment Accounts Receivable—2012	150,000	
Installment Sales		150,000
Cost of Installment Sales	100,000	
Inventory		100,000
Cash	30,000	
Installment Accounts Receivable—2012		30,000
End of year:		
Installment Sales	150,000	
Cost of Installment Sales		100,000
Deferred Gross Profit—2012		50,000
Deferred Gross Profit—2012	10,000*	
Realized Gross Profit on Installment Sales		10,000

* $30,000 × 33.33%

The sales and costs related to sales are recorded in a manner identical to the accounting for sales discussed in Chapter 7. At the end of the year, however, the sales and cost of sales accounts are closed to a deferred gross profit account rather than to Retained Earnings. The realized gross profit is then recognized by applying the gross profit percentage to cash collections. All other general and administrative expenses are normally written off in the period incurred.

For 2012, the income statement would begin with sales from which is subtracted deferred gross profit and to which is added realized gross profit for the year to arrive at a net figure. Cost of sales would then be subtracted along with other operating expenses (assumed to be $5,000 in this example) as illustrated:

Sales	$150,000
Less: Deferred gross profit	(50,000)
Add: Realized gross profit	10,000
	$110,000
Less: Cost of installment sales	(100,000)
Other operating expenses	(5,000)
Operating income	$ 5,000

Entries for the next two years are summarized in the schedule below.

	2013		2014	
During the year:				
Installment Accounts Receivable—2013	200,000			
Installment Accounts Receivable—2014			300,000	
Installment Sales		200,000		300,000
Cost of Installment Sales	140,000		204,000	
Inventory		140,000		204,000
Cash	145,000		210,000	
Installment Accounts Receivable—2012		75,000		30,000
Installment Accounts Receivable—2013		70,000		80,000
Installment Accounts Receivable—2014				100,000
End of year:				
Installment Sales	200,000		300,000	
Cost of Installment Sales		140,000		204,000
Deferred Gross Profit—2013		60,000		
Deferred Gross Profit—2014				96,000
Deferred Gross Profit—2012	25,000*		10,000†	
Deferred Gross Profit—2013	21,000‡		24,000§	
Deferred Gross Profit—2014			32,000#	
Realized Gross Profit on Installment Sales		46,000		66,000

* $75,000 × 0.33333 = $25,000
† $30,000 × 0.33333 = $10,000
‡ $70,000 × 0.30 = $21,000
§ $80,000 × 0.30 = $24,000
\# $100,000 × 0.32 = $32,000

If a company is heavily involved in installment sales, the operating cycle of the business is normally the period of the average installment contract. Thus, the currently accepted definition of current assets and current liabilities requires that the receivables and their related deferred gross profit accounts be reported in the Current Assets section of classified balance sheets. The deferred gross profit accounts should be reported as an offset to the related accounts receivable. Thus, at the end of 2012, the Current Assets section would include the following account balances:

CAUTION

Note that a separate deferred gross profit account is kept for each year and that accounts receivable collections must be accounted for by year. This is to ensure that the appropriate gross profit percentage is applied to the cash collected.

Installment accounts receivable	$120,000	
Less: Deferred gross profit	40,000	$80,000

Complexities of Installment Sales of Merchandise In the previous example, no provision was made for interest. In reality, installment sales contracts always include interest, either expressed or implied. The interest portion of the contract payments is recognized as income in the period in which cash is received, and the balance of the payment is treated as a collection on the installment sale. Thus, if in the example discussed previously, the

$75,000 collection of 2012 sales in 2013 included interest of $40,000, only $35,000 would be used to compute the realized gross profit from 2012 sales. The resulting journal entries made in 2013 relating to the $75,000 collection of 2012 sales would be as follows:

Cash	75,000	
Interest Revenue		40,000
Installment Accounts Receivable—2012		35,000
Deferred Gross Profit—2012	11,666*	
Realized Gross Profit on Installment Sales		11,666

* $35,000 × 0.33333 = $11,666

STOP&THINK

What does the $80,000 net amount represent?

a) The cost of the inventory associated with the $120,000 installment accounts receivable.
b) The amount of cash expected to be ultimately collected from the $120,000 installment accounts receivable.
c) The net present value of the installment accounts receivable amount of $120,000.
d) The current portion of the installment accounts receivable amount of $120,000.

Additional complexities can arise in installment sales accounting in providing for uncollectible accounts. Because of the right to repossess merchandise in the event of nonpayment, the provision for uncollectible accounts can be less than might be expected. Only the amount of the receivable in excess of the current value of the repossessed merchandise is a potential loss. Accounting for repossessions is discussed in Chapter 9. Theoretically, a proper matching of estimated losses against revenues would require allocating the expected losses over the years of collection. Practically, however, the provision is made and charged against income in the period of the sale. Thus, the accounting entries for handling estimated uncollectible accounts are the same as illustrated in Chapter 7. However, normally the impact of accounting for bad debts with respect to installment sales is not great because revenue and receivables are not recognized until the probability of cash collection is quite high.

Cost Recovery Method

Under the cost recovery method, no income is recognized on a sale until the cost of the item sold is recovered through cash receipts.[20] All cash receipts, both interest and principal portions, are applied first to the cost of those items sold. Then all subsequent receipts are reported as revenue. Because all costs have been recovered, the recognized revenue after cost recovery represents income. This method is used only when the circumstances surrounding a sale are so uncertain that earlier recognition is impossible.

Using the information from the Riding Corporation example, assume that collections are so uncertain that the use of the cost recovery method is deemed appropriate. While the entries to record the installment sale, the receipt of cash, and the deferral of the gross profit are identical for both the installment sales and cost recovery methods, the entry for recognizing gross profit differs.

In 2012 no gross profit would be recognized, because the amount of cash collected ($30,000) is less than the cost of the inventory sold ($100,000). The cash collections in 2013 relating to 2012 sales result in total cash receipts exceeding the cost of sales ($30,000

[20] FASB ASC paragraphs 360-20-55-13 through 15.

+ \$75,000 > \$100,000). Thus, in 2013 gross profit of \$5,000 would be recognized on 2012 sales. The journal entry to recognize this gross profit in 2013 follows:

Deferred Gross Profit—2012	5,000	
Realized Gross Profit on Installment Sales		5,000

Because the cash collected in 2013 for 2013 sales (\$70,000) is less than the cost of inventory sold (\$140,000), no gross profit would be recognized in 2013 on 2013 sales. In 2014 the \$30,000 collected in cash from the 2012 sales would all be recognized as gross profit. The cash collected relating to 2013 sales, \$80,000, when added to the cash received in 2013, \$70,000, exceeds the cost of the 2013 sales of \$140,000. Thus, \$10,000 of gross profit that was deferred in 2013 will be recognized in 2014. The journal entry to recognize gross profit in 2014 would be:

Deferred Gross Profit—2012	30,000	
Deferred Gross Profit—2013	10,000	
Realized Gross Profit on Installment Sales		40,000

Comparing the amount of gross profit that is recognized using the various revenue recognition methods for the period 2012–2014 indicates how the income statement can be materially impacted by the method used.

	Gross Profit Recognized		
Revenue Recognition Method	**2012**	**2013**	**2014**
Full accrual	\$50,000	\$60,000	\$96,000
Installment sales	10,000	46,000	66,000
Cost recovery	0	5,000	40,000

Cash Method

If the probability of recovering product or service costs is remote, the cash method of accounting could be used. Seldom would this method be applicable for sales of merchandise or real estate because the right of repossession would leave considerable value to the seller. However, the cash method might be appropriate for service contracts with high initial costs and considerable uncertainty as to the ultimate collection of the contract price. Under this method, all costs are charged to expense as incurred, and revenue is recognized as collections are made. This extreme method of revenue and expense recognition would be appropriate only when the potential losses on a contract cannot be estimated with any degree of certainty.

? SOLUTIONS TO OPENING SCENARIO QUESTIONS

1. First, start-up companies, particularly Internet start-ups, often have not yet reported any earnings. Thus, the price-earnings ratio is virtually worthless in estimating appropriate stock values. Second, the Internet has been, and still is, characterized by huge upside potential but great uncertainty about which Internet-related business models will ultimately succeed. In this uncertain setting, the best measure of a company's future Internet-related profitability is the size of its Internet presence now. This is measured by volume of business, or sales.
2. Here are two contributing factors.
   a. Change in expected growth trend: MicroStrategy's stock price was based on investors' forecasts of future sales and profits. Investors had extrapolated past growth trends into the future. So, the restatement of revenue not only lowered the

level of revenue, but also drastically lowered the expected future growth trend.

b. Cockroach theory: When you see one cockroach in your kitchen, what do you know? You know that there are others. The announcement of the revenue restatement called into question everything that MicroStrategy was doing. All of the company's past statements were now being reevaluated in light of this newly discovered lack of credibility.

3. Here are three possibilities.

   a. This is the ethical thing to do. All public figures should feel a fiduciary responsibility to see that those who don't have access to information are not deceived. The big guys (the banks, the institutional investors, and so forth) can take care of themselves. The small guys, who have to rely on the integrity of the big guys, are the ones who should be watched after.

   b. From a crisis management standpoint, we have seen over and over (Watergate, Enron, and any other scandal that you can think of) that the fallout from a mistake is worse if a company has tried to cover up the mistake. Just take your medicine, tell all of the bad news up front, take your lumps, and move on.

   c. Companies with more transparent reporting and with a reputation for integrity will, in the long run, have a lower cost of capital. These companies are trusted, so there is less information risk.

SOLUTIONS TO STOP & THINK

1. (Page 8-22) The correct answer is B. The other three methods are all acceptable ways to measure a contract's percentage of completion. Because this percentage can greatly influence a company's reported profits, the percentage must be arrived at objectively to avoid management pressure to bias the estimated percentage completed in order to meet profit targets.
2. (Page 8-26) The correct answer is C. When the progress billings on construction contracts account is netted against the construction in progress account, the resulting net figure represents the amount of the construction (which includes costs as well as a portion of expected profits) for which the customer has not yet been billed.
3. (Page 8-30) The correct answer is D. If estimates in prior periods were overstated by a significant amount, too much revenue (and profit) could end up being reported in the early periods. This error would require a loss to be recorded for this period so that the revenue (and profit) recognized to date would be correct.
4. (Page 8-39) The correct answer is A. The $80,000 amount represents the cost of the inventory associated with the $120,000 in sales that is reflected in the accounts receivable balance. Because collection of the receivable balance is uncertain, it is recorded at a lesser amount. This $80,000 number assumes that if worse came to worst and customers didn't pay, the seller could at least get the inventory back.

SOLUTION TO USING THE FASB'S CODIFICATION

You are in luck—Subtopic 605-45 addresses "Principal Agent Considerations." You may recall that this Subtopic came up in the text discussion of whether an Internet grocer should report revenue "gross" or "net." FASB ASC paragraph 605-45-45-1 says the following: "It is a matter of judgment whether an entity should report revenue based on either of the following: (a) The gross amount billed to a customer because it has earned revenue (as a principal) from the sale of the goods or services. (b) The net amount retained (that is, the amount billed to the customer less the amount paid to a supplier) because it has earned a commission or fee as an agent."

So, a "principal" is the primary owner of a business, the risk taker and the person ultimately responsible for the actions of the business. An "agent" merely works for a principal, doing certain tasks as directed by the principal. In some sense, the "principal" is the entrepreneur, and the "agent" is the employee.

REVIEW CHAPTER 8

LEARNING OBJECTIVES

1 Identify the primary criteria for revenue recognition.

Revenue is typically recognized and recorded when two criteria have been met. The first criterion is realizability, which means that the seller has received payment or a valid promise of payment from the purchaser. The second criterion is met when the earnings process is substantially complete. Substantial completion means that the seller has provided the product or service (or a large portion of the product or service) to the purchaser.

2 Discuss the revenue recognition issues, and abuses, underlying the examples used in *SAB 101*.

SAB 101 was released in 1999 by the SEC staff to curtail specific abuses in revenue recognition practices. *SAB 101* requires companies to implement better internal control processes so that the records about the timing of sales transactions are reliable. Companies must not recognize revenue before both legal and economic ownership of goods has passed. In addition, up-front fees should be recognized as revenue over the life of a service agreement, generally on a straight-line basis. Finally, revenue for most Internet broker arrangements should be reported net instead of gross. *SAB 101* proved to be a stimulus to the FASB and the IASB to reconsider the area of revenue recognition.

3 Describe the contract approach to revenue recognition that is currently being considered by the FASB and IASB.

With respect to revenue recognition, the FASB and IASB are considering a contract approach that is more consistent with the underlying conceptual framework of accounting standards than is the patchwork of approaches, focused on the earnings process, that have arisen over time. The contract approach uses the relative amounts of the estimated separate selling prices of the various elements in the arrangement to measure the performance obligations created when a contractual arrangement with a customer is entered into. Revenue is recognized when those performance obligations are eventually satisfied. A performance obligation is satisfied when control of the contractual good or service passes from the buyer to the seller.

4 Record journal entries for long-term construction-type contracts using percentage-of-completion and completed-contract methods.

In some instances, revenue may be recognized prior to the actual delivery of goods or services. The most common example of this is a long-term contract. In this case, revenue may be recognized prior to delivery if four criteria are met: (1) estimates can be made of the amount of work remaining, (2) a contract exists outlining each party's responsibilities, (3) the buyer can be expected to fulfill the contract, and (4) the seller can be expected to fulfill the contract. If these conditions are met, revenue may be recognized prior to the point of sale and the revenue recognition method is termed *percentage of completion*. With this method, revenue is recognized based on an estimate of the degree to which the contract is complete. Using the cost-to-cost method for estimating the degree of completion results in matching actual contract costs with estimated revenues. With long-term contracts, journal entries are required to record costs incurred, billings made to customers, and collections from customers. These entries are the same for both the percentage-of-completion method and the completed-contract method. An additional journal entry is made each period under the percentage-of-completion method to record the recognition of revenue and related expenses for the period. The amount of revenue recognized is a function of the percentage of the work completed to date.

With the completed-contract method, revenue is recognized only when the contract has been completed.

5 Record journal entries for long-term service contracts using the proportional performance method.

With long-term service contracts, revenue can be recognized prior to completion based on the degree to which the contract is completed. Estimates of completion are made based on the percentage of identical acts completed or the relative sales value of the acts completed. The amount of revenue to be recognized is computed by multiplying this ratio by the contract price.

6 Explain when revenue is recognized after delivery of goods or services through installment sales, cost recovery, and cash methods.

In some cases, it is not appropriate to recognize revenue at the point of sale when a valid promise of payment has not been received. In these instances, the recognition of revenue is deferred until cash is actually received. Several methods exist for recognizing revenue. The installment sales method recognizes profit based on a gross profit percentage. Of every dollar collected, a portion is recorded as profit based on the gross profit percentage. With the cost recovery method, cash collections are first considered to be a recovery of the costs associated with the sale. Once costs are recovered, each subsequent dollar received is recorded as profit. When the cash method is employed, profit is determined by comparing the cash received from customers with the cash expended during the period relating to inventory or services.

FASB-IASB CODIFICATION SUMMARY

ifrs

Topic	FASB Accounting Standards Codification	Original FASB Standard	Corresponding IASB Standard	Differences between U.S. GAAP and IFRS
Revenue recognition	*Topic 605*	*Contained in a large number of different standards*	*IAS 18, IAS 11*	U.S. GAAP and IFRS are generally consistent, but many detailed differences exist. The FASB and IASB are currently working on a joint revenue recognition project.
Completed-contract method	*Subtopic 605-35*	*ARB 45 and SOP 81-1*	*IAS 11*	Under IFRS, the completed contract method is not allowed.
Pre-sale revenue recognition for biological assets	*Section 905-330-35*	*SOP 85-3*	*IAS 41*	Under IFRS, changes in the fair value of biological assets are recognized as gains and losses. Under U.S. GAAP, a similar procedure is acceptable under some circumstances, but not required.
Multiple-element arrangements	*Subtopic 605-25*	*EITF 08-1*	*IAS 18*	IFRS does not contain any specific provisions related to multiple-element arrangements.

KEY TERMS

Cash method 8-40
Completed-contract method 8-21
Cost recovery method 8-39
Cost-to-cost method 8-23
Efforts-expended methods 8-24
Input measures 8-23
Installment sales method 8-36
Output measures 8-24
Percentage-of-completion accounting 8-21
Proportional performance method 8-21
Recognition 8-4

QUESTIONS

1. What are the two general revenue recognition criteria?
2. What four revenue recognition factors are identified in AICPA *Statement of Position (SOP) 97-2*, and how do these four factors relate to the two general revenue recognition criteria?
3. Why did the SEC issue *Staff Accounting Bulletin (SAB) 101*?
4. Why does Question 1 in *SAB 101* emphasize the proper signing of a sales agreement?
5. What types of side agreements can turn a sale into a consignment?
6. What is a bill-and-hold arrangement? Under what circumstances may a seller recognize revenue before shipment on a bill-and-hold arrangement?
7. What is the significance of customer acceptance provisions?
8. In general, why are up-front, nonrefundable fees not recognized as revenue immediately?
9. Under FASB ASC Subtopic 605-25, when is an element of a multiple-element arrangement considered to be a unit of accounting?
10. Under FASB ASC Subtopic 605-25, what are the three different methods for determining the separate selling price of a single element in a multiple-element transaction?
11. What are the three basic steps in applying the contract method for revenue recognition?
12. Why would a company prefer gross revenue reporting over net revenue reporting?
13. Under what conditions is percentage-of-completion accounting recommended for construction contractors?
14. Distinguish between the cost-to-cost method and efforts-expended method of measuring the percentage of completion.
15. Output measures of percentage of completion are sometimes preferred to input measures. What are some examples of commonly used output measures?
16. What is the relationship between the construction in progress account and the progress billings on construction contracts account? How should these accounts be reported on the balance sheet?
17. When a measure of percentage of completion other than cost-to-cost is used, the amount of cost charged against revenue using the percentage of completion usually will be different from the costs incurred. What accounting alternative exists to make it so that the costs charged against revenue are equal to the costs incurred?
18. The construction in progress account is used to accumulate all costs of construction. What additional item is included in this account when percentage-of-completion accounting is followed?
19. The gross profit percentage reported on long-term construction contracts often varies from year to year. What is the major reason for this variation?
20. How are anticipated contract losses treated under the completed-contract and percentage-of-completion methods?
21. What input and output measures usually are applicable to the proportional performance method for long-term service contracts?
22. The proportional performance method spreads the profit over the periods in which services are being performed. What arguments could be made against this method of revenue recognition for newly formed service-oriented companies?
23. Distinguish among the three different approaches to revenue recognition that await the receipt of cash. How does the treatment of costs incurred vary depending on the approach used?
24. Under what general conditions is the installment sales method of accounting preferred to the full accrual method?
25. The normal accounting entries for installment sales require keeping a separate record by year of receivables, collections on receivables, and the deferred gross profit percentages. Why are these separate records necessary?
26. Installment sales contracts generally include interest. Contrast the method of recognizing interest revenue from the method used to recognize the gross profit on the sale.
27. Under what conditions would the cash method of recognizing revenue be acceptable for reporting purposes?

PRACTICE EXERCISES

Practice 8-1
LO1

Basic Journal Entries for Revenue Recognition
The company collected $1,000 cash in advance from a customer for services to be rendered. Subsequently, the company rendered the services. Make the journal entries necessary to record (1) the receipt of the cash and (2) the subsequent completion of the services.

Practice 8-2
LO2

Journal Entries for a Consignment
Company S shipped goods costing $12,000 to Company T on consignment. The sales agreement states that Company T has 90 days to either sell the goods and pay Company S $18,000 for them or to return the goods to Company S. Make the journal entries necessary on the books of Company S to record (1) the original shipment of the goods to Company T and (2) the expiration of the 90-day period without the goods being returned by Company T. Company S uses a perpetual inventory system.

Practice 8-3
LO2

Journal Entries for a Layaway
On January 1, the company received layaway payments from two customers. Each customer paid $50. On December 24, the layaway period expired. On that date, the company received $300 from Customer 1 and delivered the promised merchandise (costing $200). Customer 2 did not return to make the final payment and thus forfeited the initial $50 layaway payment. Make the journal entries necessary to record (1) the receipt of the initial layaway payments, (2) the receipt of the final layaway payment and the delivery of the goods to Customer 1, and (3) the forfeit of the layaway payment by Customer 2. The company uses a perpetual inventory system.

Practice 8-4
LO2

Journal Entries for an Up-Front, Nonrefundable Fee
The company sells satellite phone service. Customers are required to pay an initial fee of $360, followed by continuing service fees of $50 per month. The initial fee is not refundable. The company's best estimate is that the average customer will continue the service for three years. On January 1, the company signed up 200 new customers. Make the journal entries necessary to record (1) the receipt of the initial fees from these 200 customers, (2) the receipt of the first monthly payment from the 200 customers, and (3) the partial recognition of the initial fees as revenue after the first month.

Practice 8-5
LO2

Revenue in a Multiple-Element Arrangement under Subtopic 605-25
On June 4, Seller Company signed a sales agreement with Buyer Company to deliver and install a piece of factory equipment. The total contract price is $300,000. Customers usually buy an equipment/installation package, but Seller Company does sell equipment without installation and also installs equipment sold by other companies. The selling price of the equipment without installation is $290,000. The separate price for installation of this piece of equipment is $20,000. How much revenue should be recognized by Seller Company when the equipment is delivered but before it is installed?

Practice 8-6
LO2

Reporting Revenue Gross and Net
Shop-at-Home Company operates a Web grocer. Customers submit their orders online to Shop-at-Home Company; Shop-at-Home then forwards the orders to a national grocery chain. The grocery chain arranges for assembly and shipment of the order. Shop-at-Home Company receives 3% of the retail value of all orders it takes. During January, Shop-at-Home Company received orders for groceries with a retail selling price of $400,000. These groceries cost the grocery store chain $280,000. The grocery store chain collected cash of $400,000 from the customers and paid the appropriate commission in cash to Shop-at-Home Company. Based on this information, make all journal entries necessary in January (1) on the books of Shop-at-Home Company and (2) on the books of the grocery store chain. Assume that the grocery store chain uses a perpetual inventory system.

Practice 8-7
LO4

Cost-to-Cost Method

The company signed an $880,000 contract to build an environmentally friendly access trail to South Willow Lake. The project was expected to take approximately three years. The following information was collected for each year of the project—Year 1, Year 2, and Year 3:

	Cost Expended During the Year	Expected Additional Cost to Completion	Support Timbers Laid during the Year	Additional Support Timbers to Be Laid	Trail Feet Constructed during the Year	Additional Trail Feet to Be Constructed
Year 1	$100,000	$450,000	150	850	3,000	15,200
Year 2	150,000	280,000	300	520	7,500	8,200
Year 3	250,000	0	500	0	8,000	0

The company uses the percentage-of-completion method of computing revenue from long-term construction contracts. Assume that the company employs the cost-to-cost method of estimating the percentage of completion. Compute the amount of revenue to be recognized in (1) Year 1, (2) Year 2, and (3) Year 3. (*Note:* Round percentage to three decimal places for percentage completed.)

Practice 8-8
LO4

Efforts-Expended Method

Refer to Practice 8-7. Assume that the company employs the efforts-expended method of estimating the percentage of completion. In particular, the company measures its progress by the number of support timbers laid in the trail. Compute the amount of revenue to be recognized in (1) Year 1, (2) Year 2, and (3) Year 3. (*Note:* Round percentage to three decimal places for percentage completed.)

Practice 8-9
LO4

Percentage of Completion Based on Output Measures

Refer to Practice 8-7. Assume that the company employs an output measure to estimate the percentage of completion. In particular, the company measures its progress by the number of trail feet that have been completed. Compute the amount of revenue to be recognized in (1) Year 1, (2) Year 2, and (3) Year 3. (*Note:* Round percentage to three decimal places for percentage completed.)

Practice 8-10
LO4

Basic Construction Journal Entries

Refer to Practice 8-7. In addition to the percentage-of-completion information, the following information is available regarding billing and cash collection for the project:

	Year 1	Year 2	Year 3
Progress billings	$200,000	$200,000	$480,000
Cash collections	180,000	170,000	530,000

Make the journal entries necessary to record the construction cost, the progress billings, and the cash collections in (1) Year 1, (2) Year 2, and (3) Year 3.

Practice 8-11
LO4

Completed-Contract Journal Entries

Refer to Practice 8-7 and Practice 8-10. Assume that the company uses the completed-contract method. Make the journal entries necessary in Year 3 to recognize revenue and costs for the completed project.

Practice 8-12
LO4

Percentage-of-Completion Journal Entries

Refer to Practice 8-7 and Practice 8-10. Assume that the company uses the percentage-of-completion method and uses a cost-to-cost approach in estimating the percentage of completion. Make the journal entries to record revenue and cost for the construction project in (1) Year 1, (2) Year 2, and (3) Year 3.

Practice 8-13

LO4

Construction Contracts: Balance Sheet Reporting

Refer to Practice 8-7, Practice 8-10, and Practice 8-12. Indicate how, and in what amount, the following accounts will be reported in the company's balance sheet for Year 1, Year 2, and Year 3: (1) Accounts Receivable, (2) Progress Billings, and (3) Construction in Progress. Assume that as of the end of Year 3, the progress billings and construction in progress accounts have not yet been closed.

Practice 8-14

LO4

Multiple Years of Revenues and Costs: Cost-to-Cost Method

The company signed a $1,800,000 contract to build an environmentally friendly access trail to Timpanogas Caves. The project was expected to take approximately three years. The following information was collected for each year of the project, Year 1, Year 2, and Year 3:

	Cost Expended during the Year	Expected Additional Cost to Completion	Trail Feet Constructed during the Year	Additional Trail Feet to Be Constructed
Year 1	$280,000	$760,000	9,800	20,300
Year 2	390,000	380,000	10,200	10,000
Year 3	370,000	0	10,000	0

The company uses the percentage-of-completion method of computing revenue from long-term construction contracts. Assume that the company employs the cost-to-cost method of estimating the percentage of completion. Make the journal entries to record revenue and cost for the construction project—(1) Year 1, (2) Year 2, and (3) Year 3. (*Note:* Round percentage to four decimal places for percentage completed.)

Practice 8-15

LO4

Multiple Years of Revenues and Costs: Output Measure

Refer to Practice 8-14. Assume that the company uses the percentage of trail feet con structed in estimating the percentage of completion. Make the journal entries to record revenue and cost for the construction project in (1) Year 1, (2) Year 2, and (3) Year 3. (*Note:* Round percentage to four decimal places for percentage completed.)

Practice 8-16

LO4

Multiple Years of Revenues and Costs: Anticipated Loss

The company signed a $1,450,000 contract to build an environmentally friendly access trail to Stansbury Peak. The project was expected to take approximately three years. The following information was collected for each year of the project—Year 1, Year 2, and Year 3:

	Cost Expended during the Year	Expected Additional Cost to Completion
Year 1	$200,000	$1,150,000
Year 2	350,000	1,020,000
Year 3	915,000	0

The company uses the percentage-of-completion method of computing revenue from long-term construction contracts, and the company employs the cost-to-cost method to estimate the percentage of completion. Make the journal entries to record revenue and cost for the construction project in (1) Year 1, (2) Year 2, and (3) Year 3. (*Note:* Round percentage to four decimal places for percentage completed.)

Practice 8-17

LO5

Journal Entries for the Proportional Performance Method

The Washington Blue Sox is a minor league baseball team. The team has 55 home games during a season and sells season tickets for $600 each. For the most recent season, the Blue Sox sold 1,900 season tickets. The total initial direct costs (in cash) related to the season tickets (including product giveaways for signing up early, costs of processing the transactions, and so forth) were $180,000. Direct costs (in cash) are $3 per customer per game. The team's fiscal year ends on June 30. As of that date, 21 of the home games have been played. Make the journal entries necessary to record (1) the receipt of the cash for the 1,900 season tickets sold, (2) the payment (in cash) for the initial direct costs, and (3) the recognition of all season ticket revenues and expenses for the fiscal year.

Practice 8-18
LO6

Installment Sales: Basic Journal Entries
The company had sales during the year of $350,000. The gross profit percentage during the year was 20%. Cash collected during the year related to these sales was 40% of the sales. Give all journal entries necessary during the year, assuming use of the installment sales method.

Practice 8-19
LO6

Installment Sales: Financial Statement Reporting
Refer to Practice 8-18. Indicate how the installment sales receivable would be reported in the balance sheet at the end of the year.

Practice 8-20
LO6

Installment Sales: Interest on Receivables
Transistor Electronics makes all of its sales on credit and accounts for them using the installment sales method. For simplicity, assume that all sales occur on the first day of the year and that all cash collections are made on the last day of the year. Transistor Electronics charges 21% interest on the unpaid installment balances. Data for Year 1 and Year 2 are as follows:

	Year 1	Year 2
Sales	$200,000	$220,000
Cost of goods sold	110,000	130,000
Cash collections (principal and interest):		
From Year 1 sales	90,000	100,000
From Year 2 sales	0	100,000

Prepare *all* necessary journal entries for (1) Year 1 and (2) Year 2.

Practice 8-21
LO6

Cost Recovery Method: Basic Journal Entries
The company had installment sales in Year 1 of $350,000, in Year 2 of $270,000, and in Year 3 of $210,000. The gross profit percentage of each year, in order, was 20%, 25%, and 30%. Past history has shown that 40% of total sales are collected in the year of the sale, 50% in the year after the sale, and no collections are made in the second year after the sale or thereafter. Because of uncertainty about cash collection, the company uses the cost recovery method. Make all necessary journal entries for (1) Year 1, (2) Year 2, and (3) Year 3.

EXERCISES

Exercise 8-22
LO5

Service Industry Accounting
The Spectrum Fitness Club charges a nonrefundable annual membership fee of $1,200 for its services. For this fee, each member receives a fitness evaluation (value $200), a monthly magazine (annual value $25), and two hours' use of the equipment each week (annual value $1,100). Each of the three elements of the annual membership can be purchased separately. The initial direct costs to obtain the membership are $180. The direct cost of the fitness evaluation is $100, and the monthly direct costs to provide the

other services are estimated to be $25 per person. Give the journal entries to record the transactions in 2013 relative to a membership sold on May 1, 2013.

Exercise 8-23
LO2

Consignment Accounting
In 2013, Rawlings Wholesalers transferred goods to a retailer on consignment. The transaction was recorded as a sale by Rawlings. The goods cost $45,000 and normally are sold at a 30% markup. In 2014, $12,000 (cost) of merchandise was sold by the retailer at the normal markup, and the balance of the merchandise was returned to Rawlings. The retailer withheld a 15% commission from payment. Prepare the journal entry in 2014 to correct the books for 2013 (assuming that the books for 2013 are already closed), and prepare the correct entries relative to the consignment sale in 2014.

Exercise 8-24
LO2
SPREADSHEET

Journal Entries for an Up-Front, Nonrefundable Fee
BodyTone Company sells lifetime health club memberships. For one up-front, nonrefundable fee, a customer becomes a lifetime member of BodyTone's network of health clubs. The fee is $2,000. The fee includes full access to all of the club facilities plus an initial comprehensive physical, mental, and spiritual wellness evaluation. The wellness evaluation is frequently sold separately for $400. Occasionally, BodyTone sells lifetime memberships without the wellness evaluation; the price is $1,750. BodyTone can reliably estimate that the average customer will use the health club facilities for five years. On January 1, 2013, BodyTone received lifetime membership payments from 300 new customers. The direct cost of providing a wellness evaluation is $70, and the direct cost of providing health club access for one person for one year is $250. All of the wellness evaluations were completed during 2013. Make all of the journal entries necessary in 2013 in connection with these 300 new memberships. Assume that all costs were incurred in cash.

Exercise 8-25
LO4

Completed-Contract Method
On January 1, 2012, the Kobe Construction Company entered into a 3-year contract to build a dam. The original contract price was $21,000,000 and the estimated cost was $19,400,000. The following cost data relate to the construction period.

Year	Cost Incurred	Estimated Cost to Complete	Billings	Cash Collected
2012	$7,200,000	$12,500,000	$7,200,000	$6,500,000
2013	6,700,000	7,800,000	6,500,000	6,400,000
2014	7,900,000	0	7,300,000	8,100,000

Prepare the required journal entries for the three years of the contract, assuming Kobe uses the completed-contract method.

Exercise 8-26
LO4

Completed-Contract Method
On June 1, 2013, bids were submitted for a construction project to build a new municipal building and fire station. The lowest bid was $5,000,000, submitted by the Shannon Construction Company. Shannon was awarded the contract. Shannon uses the completed-contract method to report gross profit. The following data are given to summarize the activities on this contract for 2013 and 2014. Give the entries to record these transactions using the completed-contract method.

Year	Cost Incurred	Estimated Cost to Complete	Billings on Contract	Collections of Billings
2013	$1,930,000	$2,420,000	$2,100,000	$1,800,000
2014	2,290,000	0	2,900,000	3,200,000

Exercise 8-27
LO4
SPREADSHEET

Percentage-of-Completion Accounting

Perfectionist Construction Company was the low bidder on an office building construction contract. The contract bid was $9,000,000, with an estimated cost to complete the project of $7,000,000. The contract period was 30 months starting May 1, 2012. The company uses the cost-to-cost method of estimating earnings. Because of changes requested by the customer, the contract price was adjusted downward to $8,600,000 on May 1, 2013.

A record of construction activities for the years 2012–2015 is as follows:

Year	Actual Cost—Current Year	Progress Billings	Cash Receipts
2012	$1,900,000	$2,500,000	$1,900,000
2013	3,600,000	3,400,000	3,100,000
2014	1,670,000	2,700,000	2,500,000
2015			1,100,000

The estimated cost to complete the contract as of the end of each accounting period is:

2012	$5,150,000
2013	1,600,000
2014	0

Calculate the gross profit for the years 2012–2014 under the percentage-of-completion method of revenue recognition. (*Note:* Round percentage to two decimal places for percentage completed.)

Exercise 8-28
LO4
REVERSE SOLVABLE

Percentage-of-Completion Analysis

Espiritu Construction Co. has used the cost-to-cost percentage-of-completion method of recognizing revenue. Tony Espiritu assumed leadership of the business after the recent death of his father, Howard. In reviewing the records, Tony finds the following information regarding a recently completed building project for which the total contract was $2,000,000.

	2012	2013	2014
Gross profit (loss)	$ 75,000	$140,000	$ (20,000)
Cost incurred	360,000	?	820,000

Espiritu wants to know how effectively the company operated during the last three years on this project and, because the information is not complete, has asked for answers to the following questions.

1. How much cost was incurred in 2013?
2. What percentage of the project was completed by the end of 2013?
3. What was the total estimated gross profit on the project by the end of 2013?
4. What was the estimated cost to complete the project at the end of 2013?

Exercise 8-29
LO4
REVERSE SOLVABLE

Percentage-of-Completion Analysis

Smokey International Inc. recently acquired the Kurtz Builders Company. Kurtz has incomplete accounting records. On one particular project, only the information below is available.

	2012	2013	2014
Costs incurred during year	$200,000	$250,000	?
Estimated cost to complete	450,000	190,000	$ 0
Recognized revenue	220,000	?	?
Gross profit on contract	?	10,000	(10,000)
Contract price	850,000		

Because the information is incomplete, you are asked the following questions assuming the percentage-of-completion method is used, an output measure is used to estimate the percentage completed, and revenue is recorded using the actual cost approach.

1. How much gross profit should be reported in 2012?
2. How much revenue should be reported in 2013?
3. How much revenue should be reported in 2014?
4. How much cost was incurred in 2014?
5. What are the total costs on the contract?
6. What would be the gross profit for 2013 if the cost-to-cost percentage-of-completion method were used rather than the output measure? (*Hint*: Ignore the revenue amount shown for 2012 and gross profit amount reported for 2013.) (*Note:* Round percentage to two decimal places.)

Exercise 8-30

LO4

Percentage-of-Completion Method with Change Orders

The Build-It Construction Company enters into a contract on January 1, 2013, to construct a 20-story office building for $42,000,000. During the construction period, many change orders are made to the original contract. The following schedule summarizes the changes made in 2013.

	Cost Incurred—2013	Estimated Cost to Complete	Contract Price
Basic contract	$8,000,000	$28,000,000	$42,000,000
Change Order 1	50,000	50,000	125,000
Change Order 2	0	50,000	0
Change Order 3	300,000	300,000	Still to be negotiated; at least cost.
Change Order 4	125,000	0	100,000

Compute the revenues, costs, and gross profit to be recognized in 2013, assuming use of the cost-to-cost method to determine the percentage completed. (*Note:* Round percentage to two decimal places.)

Exercise 8-31

LO4

Percentage of Completion Using Architect's Estimates

Southern California Builders Inc. entered into a contract to construct an office build ing and plaza at a contract price of $30,000,000. Income is to be reported using the percentage-of-completion method as determined by estimates made by the architect. The data below summarize the activities on the construction for the years 2012–2014. For the years 2012–2014, what entries are required to record this information, assuming the architect's estimate of the percentage completed is used to determine revenue (proportional cost approach)?

Year	Actual Cost Incurred	Estimated Cost to Complete	Percentage Completed—Architect's Estimate	Project Billings	Collections on Billings
2012	$7,600,000	$18,400,000	30%	$ 9,500,000	$ 9,000,000
2013	9,700,000	8,900,000	80	11,500,000	10,300,000
2014	8,800,000	0	100	9,000,000	10,700,000

Exercise 8-32

LO6

REVERSE SOLVABLE

Cost Recovery Analysis

Hatch Enterprises uses the cost recovery method for all installment sales. Complete the following table.

	2012	2013	2014
Installment sales	$92,000	$103,000	$ (1)
Cost of installment sales	(2)	62,830	74,750
Gross profit percentage	36%	(3)	35%
Cash collections:			
2012 sales	27,200	48,300	12,200
2013 sales		36,600	(4)
2014 sales			43,450
Realized gross profit on installment sales	(5)	(6)	19,250

Exercise 8-33
LO6

Cost Recovery Method

K. B. Sayer Furnishings Inc. had the following sales and gross profit percentages for the years 2012–2015.

	Sales	Gross Profit Percentage
2012	$60,000	55%
2013	65,000	51
2014	72,000	56
2015	76,000	57

Historically, 60% of sales are collected in the year of the sale, 25% in the following year, and 10% in the third year. Assuming collections are as projected, give the journal entries for the years 2012–2015, assuming the cost recovery method. (Ignore provision for bad debts.) Prepare a table comparing the gross profit recognized for 2012–2015 using the full accrual method and the cost recovery method.

Exercise 8-34
LO6

SPREADSHEET

Installment Sales Accounting

Jordan Corporation had sales in 2012 of $150,000, in 2013 of $180,000, and in 2014 of $225,000. The gross profit percentage of each year, in order, was 25%, 30%, and 35%. Past history has shown that 20% of total sales are collected in the first year, 40% in the second year, and 20% in the third year. Assuming these collections are made as projected, give the journal entries for 2012, 2013, and 2014, assuming the installment sales method. Ignore provisions for bad debts and interest.

Exercise 8-35
LO4

Reporting Construction Contracts

Kylie Builders Inc. is building a new home for Cassie Proffit at a contracted price of $200,000. The estimated cost at the time the contract is signed (January 2, 2013) is $115,000. At December 31, 2013, the total cost incurred is $60,000 with estimated costs to complete of $59,000. Kylie has billed $80,000 on the job and has received a $55,000 payment. This is the only contract in process at year-end. Prepare the sections of the balance sheet and the income statement of Kylie Builders Inc. affected by these events assuming use of (1) the percentage-of-completion method and (2) the completed-contract method. (*Note:* Round percentage to two decimal places for percentage completed.)

Exercise 8-36
LO6

REVERSE SOLVABLE

Installment Sales Analysis

Complete the following table.

	2012	2013	2014
Installment sales	$50,000	$80,000	$ (7)
Cost of installment sales	(1)	(5)	91,800
Gross profit	(2)	(6)	28,200
Gross profit percentage	(3)	25%	(8)

	2012	2013	2014
Cash collections:			
2012 sales	$ (4)	$25,000	$10,000
2013 sales		20,000	50,000
2014 sales			45,000
Realized gross profit on installment sales	1,100	10,500	(9)

Exercise 8-37

LO2

Accounting for a Bill-and-Hold Arrangement

On December 30, Shady Company segregated goods costing $530,000 for future shipment to one of its customers, Point Company. Point was billed $890,000. Make the journal entry necessary on Shady's books to record this action in each of the following situations. Treat each situation independently.

(a) Point is a regular customer, and Shady has been expecting an order for the past two weeks. To make sure that sufficient goods are available when the order from Point finally does come, Shady has segregated the goods.
(b) Normal procedure is for the purchasing agent for Point to sign a formal sales agreement as part of each purchase. That agreement is then countersigned by Shady's sales manager. The segregation of goods was arranged over the phone; Shady plans to take care of the formal paperwork next week.
(c) Point has requested, in writing, that Shady segregate the goods. Point is conducting temporary repairs to its storage warehouse, so Point has arranged to make its shipments directly from Shady's warehouse for the duration of the repairs. The goods have been carefully separated so that Shady employees don't accidentally ship them to another customer.
(d) The sales agreement between Shady and Point requires that all goods be subjected to a quality control test by Point engineers. That quality control test is not expected to occur until early January.

PROBLEMS

Problem 8-38

LO2

Consignment Accounting

Tingey Industries sells merchandise on a consignment basis to dealers. The selling price of the merchandise averages 25% above cost of merchandise. The dealer is paid a 10% commission on the sales price for all sales made. All dealer sales are made on a cash basis. The following consignment sales activities occurred during 2013.

Manufacturing cost of goods shipped on consignment	$250,000
Sales price of merchandise sold by dealers	220,000
Payments made by dealers after deducting commission	139,000

Instructions:

1. Prepare summary entries on the books of the consignor for these consignment sales transactions.
2. Prepare summary entries on the books of the dealer consignee, assuming there is only one dealer involved.
3. Prepare the parts of Tingey Industries' financial statements at December 31, 2013, that relate to these consignment sales.

Problem 8-39

LO4

Construction Accounting

Zamponi's Construction Company reports its income for tax purposes on a completed-contract basis and income for financial statement purposes on a percentage-of-completion basis. A record of construction activities for 2013 and 2014 follows:

Project	Contract Price	Cost Incurred—2013	Estimated Cost to Complete	Cost Incurred—2014	Estimated Cost to Complete
A	$1,450,000	$840,000	$560,000	$480,000	$ 0
B	1,700,000	720,000	880,000	340,000	650,000
C	850,000	160,000	480,000	431,500	58,500
D	1,200,000			280,000	520,000

General and administrative expenses for 2013 and 2014 were $60,000 for each year and are to be recorded as a period cost.

Instructions:

1. Calculate the income for 2013 and 2014 that should be reported for financial statement purposes.
2. Calculate the income for 2014 to be reported on a completed-contract basis.

Problem 8-40

LO4

SPREADSHEET

Construction Accounting

The Rushing Construction Company obtained a construction contract to build a highway and bridge over the Snake River. It was estimated at the beginning of the contract that it would take three years to complete the project at an expected cost of $50,000,000. The contract price was $60,000,000. The project actually took four years, being accepted as completed late in 2014. The following information describes the status of the job at the close of production each year.

	2011	2012	2013	2014	2015
Actual cost incurred	$12,000,000	$18,160,000	$14,840,000	$10,000,000	$ 0
Estimated cost to complete	38,000,000	27,840,000	10,555,555	0	0
Collections on contract	12,000,000	13,500,000	15,000,000	15,000,000	4,500,000
Billings on contract	13,000,000	15,500,000	17,000,000	14,500,000	0

Instructions:

1. What is the revenue, cost, and gross profit recognized for each of the years 2011–2015 under (a) the percentage-of-completion method and (b) the completed-contract method?
2. Give the journal entries for each year assuming that the percentage-of-completion method is used. (*Note:* Round percentage to nearest whole percent for percentage completed.)

Problem 8-41

LO4

Construction Accounting

Uptown Builders Company commenced doing business in January 2013. Construction activities for the year 2013 are summarized in the following table.

Project	Total Contract Price	Contract Expenditures to Dec. 31, 2013	Estimated Additional Costs to Complete Contracts	Cash Collections to Dec. 31, 2013	Billings to Dec. 31, 2013
A	$ 420,000	$340,000	$ 30,000	$270,000	$310,000
B	440,000	22,500	325,500	75,000	105,000
C	500,000	390,000	0	405,000	500,000
D	400,000	105,500	314,500	0	80,000
	$1,760,000	$858,000	$670,000	$750,000	$995,000

The company is your client. The president has asked you to compute the amounts of revenue for the year ended December 31, 2013, that would be reported under the completed-contract method and the percentage-of-completion method of accounting for long-term contracts.

The following information is available:

(a) Each contract is with a different customer.
(b) Any work remaining to be done on the contracts is expected to be completed in 2014.
(c) The company's accounts have been maintained on the completed-contract method.

Instructions:

1. Prepare a schedule computing the amount of revenue, cost, and gross profit (loss) by project for the year ended December 31, 2013, to be reported under (a) the percentage-of-completion method and (b) the completed-contract method. (*Note:* Round to two decimal places on percentages.)
2. Prepare a schedule under the completed-contract method, computing the amount that would appear on the company's balance sheet at December 31, 2013, for (a) costs in excess of billings and (b) billings in excess of costs.
3. Prepare a schedule under the percentage-of-completion method showing the computation of the amount that would appear on the company's balance sheet at December 31, 2013, for (a) costs and estimated earnings in excess of billings and (b) billings in excess of costs and estimated earnings.

Problem 8-42
LO4

Construction Accounting

The Pierson Construction Corporation contracted with the City of Plaquemine to construct a dam on the bayou at a price of $15,000,000. Pierson expects to earn $2,270,000 on the contract. The percentage-of-completion method is to be used, and the completion stage is to be determined by estimates made by the engineer. The following schedule summarizes the activities of the contract for the years 2012–2014.

Year	Cost Incurred	Engineer's Estimated Cost to Complete	Estimate of Completion	Billings on Contract	Collection on Billings
2012	$4,300,000	$8,560,000	33%	$4,000,000	$3,600,000
2013	4,100,000	4,700,000	62	5,000,000	5,100,000
2014	4,550,000	0	100	6,000,000	6,300,000

Instructions:

1. Prepare a schedule showing the revenue, cost, and the gross profit earned each year under the percentage-of-completion method, using the engineer's estimate as the measure of completion to be applied to revenues and costs.
2. Prepare all journal entries required to reflect the contract.
3. Prepare journal entries for 2014, assuming the completed-contract method is used.
4. How would the journal entries in (2) differ if the actual costs incurred were used to estimate the percentage completed for the period instead of the engineer's estimate?

Problem 8-43
LO4

Construction Accounting

Jana Crebs is a contractor for the construction of large office buildings. At the beginning of 2013, three buildings were in progress. The following data describe the status of these buildings at the beginning of the year:

	Contract Price	Costs Incurred to Jan. 1, 2013	Estimated Cost to Complete as of Jan. 1, 2013
Building 1	$ 4,000,000	$2,070,000	$1,380,000
Building 2	9,000,000	6,318,000	1,782,000
Building 3	13,150,000	3,000,000	9,000,000

During 2013, the following costs were incurred.

Building 1	$930,000 (estimated cost to complete as of December 31, 2013, $750,000)
Building 2	$1,800,000 (job completed)
Building 3	$7,400,000 (estimated cost to complete as of December 31, 2013, $2,800,000)
Building 4	$800,000 (contract price, $2,500,000; estimated cost to complete as of December 31, 2013, $1,200,000)

Instructions:

1. Compute the total revenue, costs, and gross profit in 2013. Assume that Crebs uses the cost-to-cost percentage-of-completion method. (*Note:* Round percentage to two decimal places for percentage completed.)
2. Compute the gross profit for 2013 if Crebs uses the completed-contract method.

Problem 8-44
LO4

Construction Accounting

The Kirby Construction Company was the low bidder on a specialized equipment contract. The contract bid was $5,400,000 with an estimated cost to complete the project of $4,800,000. The contract period was 34 months, beginning March 1, 2012. The company uses the cost-to-cost method to estimate profits.

A record of construction activities for the years 2012–2015 follows:

Year	Actual Cost—Current Year	Progress Billings	Cash Receipts
2012	$2,800,000	$2,600,000	$2,200,000
2013	2,200,000	2,100,000	1,900,000
2014	600,000	700,000	700,000
2015	0	0	600,000

The estimated cost to complete the contract at the end of each accounting period is:

2012	$2,200,000
2013	500,000
2014	0

Instructions:

1. What are the revenue, cost, and gross profit recognized for each of the years 2012–2014 under the percentage-of-completion method? (*Note:* Round percentage to two decimal places for percentage completed.)
2. Give the journal entries for each of the years 2012–2014 to record the information from (1).
3. Give the journal entries in 2015 to record any collections and to close out all construction accounts.

Problem 8-45
LO4

Construction Accounting

Tuscany Boatbuilders was recently awarded a $16,700,000 contract to construct a luxury liner for Queen Cruiseliners Inc. Tuscany estimates it will take 42 months to complete the contract. The company uses the cost-to-cost method to estimate profits.

The following information details the actual and estimated costs for the years 2012–2015.

Year	Actual Cost—Current Year	Estimated Cost to Complete
2012	$6,400,000	$8,700,000
2013	5,200,000	4,600,000
2014	4,100,000	1,500,000
2015	1,065,000	0

Instructions:

1. Compute the revenue, cost, and gross profit to be recognized for each of the years 2012–2015 under the percentage-of-completion method. (*Note:* Round percentage to two decimal places for percentage completed.)
2. Give the journal entries for each of the years 2012–2015 to record the information from (1).

Problem 8-46

LO6

Installment Sales Accounting

London Corporation has been using the cash method to account for income since its first year of operation in 2013. All sales are made on credit with notes receivable given by the customers. The income statements for 2013 and 2014 included the following amounts:

	2013	2014
Revenues—collection on principal	$32,000	$50,000
Revenues—interest	3,600	5,500
Cost of goods purchased*	45,200	52,020

* Includes increase in inventory of goods on hand of $2,000 in 2013 and $8,000 in 2014.

The balances due on the notes at the end of each year were as follows:

	2013	2014
Notes receivable (gross)—2013	$62,000	$36,000
Notes receivable (gross)—2014	0	60,000
Unearned interest revenue—2013	7,167	5,579
Unearned interest revenue—2014	0	8,043

Instructions: Give the journal entries for 2013 and 2014 assuming the installment sales method was used rather than the cash method. (*Note:* Round percentage to two decimal places.)

Problem 8-47

LO6

Installment Sales

Potter's Home Goods sells furniture and electronic items. The majority of its business is on credit, and the following information is available relating to sales transactions for 2012, 2013, and 2014.

	2012	2013	2014
Installment sales (net of interest)	$124,000	$138,000	$145,000
Gross profit percentage	36%	39%	38%
Cash collections on installment sales:			
Principal—2012	$ 59,300	$ 38,200	$ 18,500
Principal—2013		65,400	33,700
Principal—2014			73,450
Interest—2012	7,100	12,400	1,250
Interest—2013		6,150	15,600
Interest—2014			6,400

Instructions: Prepare the journal entries for the years 2012–2014 assuming Potter's uses the installment sales method for revenue recognition and records receivables net of interest.

Problem 8-48
LO4, LO6

Revenue Recognition Analysis

The Wasatch Construction Company entered into a $4,500,000 contract in early 2013 to construct a multipurpose recreational facility for the city of Helper. Construction time extended over a 2-year period. The table below describes the pattern of progress payments made by the city of Helper and costs incurred by Wasatch Construction by semiannual periods. Estimated costs of $3,600,000 were incurred as expected.

Period	Progress Payments for Period	Progress Cost for Period
(1) Jan. 1–June 30, 2013	$ 750,000	$ 900,000
(2) July 1–Dec. 31, 2013	1,050,000	1,200,000
(3) Jan. 1–June 30, 2014	1,950,000	1,080,000
(4) July 1–Dec. 31, 2014	750,000	420,000
Total	$4,500,000	$3,600,000

The Wasatch Construction Company prepares financial statements twice each year, June 30 and December 31.

Instructions:

1. Based on the foregoing data, compute the amount of revenue, costs, and gross profit for the four semiannual periods under each of the following methods of revenue recognition (*Note:* Round percentage to five decimal places for percentage completed.):
   (a) Percentage of completion
   (b) Completed contract
   (c) Installment sales (gross profit only)
   (d) Cost recovery (gross profit only)
2. Which method do you feel best measures the performance of Wasatch on this contract?

Problem 8-49
LO2, LO4

Sample CPA Exam Questions

1. Which of the following is used in calculating the income recognized in the fourth and final year of a contract accounted for by the percentage-of-completion method?

	Actual Total Cost	Income Previously Recognized
(a)	Yes	Yes
(b)	Yes	No
(c)	No	Yes
(d)	No	No

2. When should a lessor recognize in income a nonrefundable lease bonus paid by a lessee upon signing an operating lease?
   (a) When received
   (b) At the inception of the lease
   (c) At the expiration of the lease
   (d) Over the life of the lease

CASES

Discussion Case 8-50

Recognizing Revenue on a Percentage-of-Completion Basis

As the new controller for Enclave Construction Company, you have been advised that your predecessor classified all revenues and expenses by project, each project being considered a separate venture. All revenues from uncompleted projects were treated as unearned revenue, and all expenses applicable to each uncompleted project were treated as "work in process" inventory. Thus, the income statement for the current year includes only the revenues and expenses related to projects completed during the year.

What do you think about the use of the completed-contract method by the previous controller? What alternative approach might you suggest to company management?

Discussion Case 8-51

Let's Spread Our Losses, Too!

The Abbott Construction Company has several contracts to build sections of freeways, bridges, and dams. Because most of these contracts require more than one year to complete, the accountant, Dave Allred, has recommended use of the percentage-of-completion method to recognize revenue and income on these contracts. The president, Kathy Bahr, isn't quite sure how the accounting method works, and she indicates concern about the impact of this decision on income taxes. Bahr also inquires as to what happens when a contract results in a loss. When told by Allred that any estimated loss must be recognized when it is first identified, Bahr becomes upset. "If it is a percentage-of-completion method and we are recognizing profits in part as we go along, why shouldn't we be able to do the same for losses?"

How would you, as the accountant, answer Bahr's concerns?

Discussion Case 8-52

When Is the Membership Fee Earned?

The Superb Health Studio has been operating for five years but is presently for sale. It has opened 50 salons in various cities in the United States. The normal pattern for a new opening is to advertise heavily and sell different types of memberships: 1-year, 3-year, and 5-year. For the initial membership fee, members may use the pool, exercise rooms, sauna, and other recreational facilities without charge. If special courses or programs are taken, additional fees are charged; however, members are granted certain privileges, and the fees are less than those charged to outsiders. In addition, $10-a-month dues are charged to all members. Nonmembers may use the facilities; however, they must pay a substantial daily charge for services they receive.

Your client, Dickson Inc., is considering purchasing the chain of health studios and asks you to give your opinion on its operations. You are provided with financial statements that show a growing revenue and income pattern over the 5-year period. The balance sheet shows that the physical facilities are apparently owned rather than leased. But you are aware that health studios, like all service institutions, have some challenging revenue recognition problems.

What questions would you want answered in preparing your report for Dickson?

Discussion Case 8-53

When Is It Revenue?

Hertzel Advertising Agency handles advertising for clients under contracts that require the agency to develop advertising copy and layouts and place ads in various media, charging clients a commission of 15% of the media cost as its fee. The agency makes advance billings to its clients of estimated media cost plus its 15% commission. Adjustments to these advances usually are small. Frequently, both the billings and receipt of cash from these billings occur before the period in which the advertising actually appears in the media.

A conference meeting is held between officers of the agency and the new firm of CPAs recently engaged to perform annual audits. In this meeting, consideration is given to four possible points for measuring revenue: (1) at the time the advanced billing is made, (2) when payment is received from the client, (3) in the month when the advertising appears in the media, and (4) when the bill for advertising is received from the media, generally in the month following its appearance. The agency has been following the first method for the past several years on the basis that a definite contract exists and the revenue is earned when billed. When the billing is made, an entry is prepared to record the estimated receivable and liability to the media. Estimated expenses related to the contract are also recorded. Adjusting entries are made later for any differences between the estimated and actual amounts.

As a member of the CPA firm attending this meeting, how would you react to the agency's method of recognizing revenue? Discuss the strengths and weaknesses of each of the four methods of revenue recognition, and indicate which one you would recommend for the agency to follow.

Discussion Case 8-54

Which Method Is Appropriate?

Green Brothers Furniture sells discount furniture and offers easy credit terms. Its margins are not large, but it deals in heavy volume. Its customers are often low-income individuals who cannot obtain credit elsewhere. Green Brothers retains the title to the furniture until full payment is received, and it is not uncommon to have 20% of sales be uncollectible.

Green Brothers is considering expansion and has hired an independent auditor to review its financial statements prior to obtaining outside funding. The auditor questions the use of accrual accounting as a method for recognizing revenue and suggests that Green Brothers use the installment sales method. The auditor justifies this by stating that because of the high rate of uncollectibles, the earnings process is not substantially complete at the point of sale. Financial statements adjusted to the installment sales method result in a 17% decrease in net income for the fiscal year just ended.

The chief financial officer for Green Brothers counters that if uncollectibles can be estimated, even if that estimate is high, the use of the accrual method is appropriate. The accountant also notes that restated financial statements showing the lower net income figure will make obtaining external funding much more difficult.

Which method of revenue recognition would you argue that Green Brothers should use? Why? Remember that your decision could affect this company's ability to obtain favorable external financing.

Discussion Case 8-55

College Bound Was Bankruptcy Bound

High school students know how important it is to perform well on the educational tests required by many colleges and universities as part of the admissions process. In fact, an entire industry has developed to prepare students to take these tests. One company in this industry was **College Bound Inc.** It was a fast-growing company that claimed to be the largest educational counseling firm in the United States with 150 test centers nationally. College Bound was founded by George and Janet Ronkin because they could not find a facility that, in their opinion, could adequately prepare their own son to take the college entrance exams.

The company went public in 1988 as a penny stock, and the price of the stock soared to a high of $24 per share in August 1991. In the early months of 1992, however, the SEC began to question many of College Bound's accounting practices. As a result of its investigations, the SEC determined that much of the rapid growth in revenues reported by College Bound came as a result of "churning bank accounts." This practice involved transferring funds from the home office's bank account to various test centers and then back to the home office. College Bound was recognizing as revenue the funds being transferred back from the test centers. The money used for the "churning" was obtained via a convertible note offering in Europe.

The result of these practices was to overstate pretax profits for the fiscal year ended August 1991 by 2.5 times, or $5.2 million. The SEC alleged that the Ronkins were transferring large amounts of company money to their personal accounts. In addition to their compensation of $153,846 each, the Ronkins were said to have transferred over $500,000 to Swiss bank accounts during 1991. The court-appointed receiver, Joseph Del Raso, who was asked by the courts to monitor College Bound during bankruptcy proceedings, determined that most of the company's 150 test centers were not profitable by industry standards and closed over 100 centers in May 1992.

1. How would College Bound recognize revenue by simply transferring money from a test center to the home office? What would the journal entry be when the money was transferred from the test centers to the home office?
2. How would the accountant at the home office determine if money being received from a test center was to be recorded as revenue or as repayment of a loan?

SOURCES: Michael J. McCarthy, "College Bound Inc., Target of SEC Suit, Files for Bankruptcy Law Protection," *The Wall Street Journal*, April 30, 1992, p. A4; and Daniel Pearl, "U.S. Judge Freezes Assets of Founders of College Bound," *The Wall Street Journal*, April 24, 1992, p. C19.

Discussion Case 8-56

Keep Shipping, We Need the Revenue

Datarite, a maker of computer hardware systems, sells its products to dealers who in turn sell to the final customer. Datarite offers very liberal credit terms and allows its dealers to take up to 90 days to pay. These terms allow dealers to hold larger inventories. As the end of the fiscal year nears, Datarite needs to increase its current ratio and decrease its debt-to-equity ratio to avoid violating its debt covenants. The president of the company has asked that all dealers be shipped extra inventory. This will increase both sales and accounts receivable, thereby allowing Datarite to remain in compliance with its debt covenants. The chief financial officer remarks that shipping inventory that has not been ordered should be accounted for as consigned inventory rather than revenue.

Should the inventory shipments be accounted for as sales or as consigned inventory? Debt covenants exist to protect the interests of creditors. In this instance, are debt covenants effective in monitoring the company's activities?

Discussion Case 8-57

I Think They're Sales!

The Rain-Soft Water Company distributes its water softeners to dealers upon their request. The contract agreement with the dealers is that they may have 90 days to sell and pay for the softeners. Until the 90-day period is over, any softeners may be returned at the dealer's expense and with no further obligation on the dealer's part. If the water softeners are damaged while in the hands of a dealer, Rain-Soft agrees to accept the return of the damaged softeners with no obligation to the dealer. Past experience indicates that 75% of all softeners distributed on this basis are sold by the dealer. In June, 100 units are delivered to dealers at an average billed price of $800 each. The average cost of the softeners to Rain-Soft is $600. Based on the expected sales, Rain-Soft reports profit of $15,000.

You are asked to evaluate the income statement for its compliance with GAAP. What recommendations would you make?

Case 8-58

Deciphering Financial Statements (The Walt Disney Company)

Locate the 2009 financial statements for **The Walt Disney Company** on the Internet.

1. Locate Disney's note on revenue recognition. What is Disney's revenue recognition policy for the various business segments?
2. Relating to video and video game sales, what other points in the revenue cycle (other than when video units are made widely available for sale by retailers) could Disney have used to recognize revenue?
3. Relating to motion pictures, what other points in the revenue cycle (other than when motion pictures are exhibited) could Disney have used to recognize revenue?

Case 8-59

Deciphering Financial Statements (Siskon Gold Corporation)

Review the following note relating to revenue recognition for **Siskon Gold Corporation**, a company "engaged in the business of exploring, acquiring, developing, and exploiting precious mineral properties, principally gold."

> 2. SIGNIFICANT ACCOUNTING POLICIES
>
> *Revenue recognition*—Revenue from gold production is recognized when the finished product is poured based upon estimated weights and assays at current market prices.

1. What is the critical revenue recognition event for Siskon?
2. Is the company justified in recognizing revenue prior to the point of an actual sale? Why?
3. What potential risks exist when revenue is recognized prior to the point of sale?

Case 8-60

Deciphering Financial Statements (Ben & Jerry's Homemade, Inc.)

Ben & Jerry's Homemade, Inc., an ice cream manufacturer, was acquired by **Unilever** in 2000. Before that, Ben & Jerry's was a publicly traded company. Below is the revenue recognition note for Ben & Jerry's from its 1998 annual report:

Revenue Recognition

The Company recognizes revenue and the related costs when product is shipped. The Company recognizes franchise fees as income for individual stores when services required by the franchise agreement have been substantially performed and the store opens for business. Franchise fees relating to area franchise agreements are recognized in proportion to the number of stores for which the required services have been substantially performed. Franchise fees recognized as income and included in net sales were approximately $708,000, $553,000, and $301,000 in 1998, 1997, and 1996, respectively.

1. What is the critical event for Ben & Jerry's sale of ice cream?
2. What is the critical event for Ben & Jerry's recognition of franchise fee revenue? Note that Ben & Jerry's deals with two different types of franchise fees.

Case 8-61

Deciphering Financial Statements (Lockheed Martin Corporation)

Lockheed Martin Corporation "principally researches, designs, develops, manufactures, integrates, operates and sustains advanced technology systems and products, and provides a broad range of management, engineering, technical, scientific, logistic and information services" within its four business segments: Aeronautics, Electronic Systems, Information Systems & Global Services, and Space Systems. As a result, Lockheed has many long-term contracts. The following note is taken from Lockheed's 2009 annual report and provides a good summary of the concepts associated with revenue recognition and long-term contracts.

> *Sales and earnings*—We record sales and anticipated profits under long-term fixed-price design, development, and production (DD&P) contracts on a percentage of completion basis, generally using units-of-delivery as the basis to measure progress toward completing the contract and recognizing revenue. We include estimated contract profits in earnings in proportion to recorded sales. We record sales under certain long-term fixed-price DD&P contracts that, among other factors, provide for the delivery of minimal quantities or require a substantial level of development effort in relation to total contract value, upon achievement of performance milestones or using the cost-to-cost method of accounting where sales and profits are recorded based on the ratio of costs we incur to our estimate of total costs at completion. We record sales and an estimated profit under DD&P cost-reimbursement-type contracts as costs are incurred in the proportion that the incurred costs bear to total estimated costs. When adjustments in estimated contract revenues or estimated costs at completion are required, any changes from prior estimates are recognized by recording adjustments in the current period for the inception-to-date effect of the changes on current and prior periods. When estimates of total costs to be incurred on a contract exceed total estimates of revenue to be earned, a provision for the entire loss on the contract is recorded in the period the loss is determined. We record sales of products and services provided under essentially commercial terms and conditions upon delivery and passage of title.
>
> We consider incentives or penalties related to performance on DD&P contracts in estimating sales and profit rates, and record them when there is sufficient information to assess anticipated contract performance. We also consider estimates of award fees in estimating sales and profit rates based on actual awards and anticipated performance. We do not recognize incentive provisions that increase or decrease earnings based solely on a single significant event until the event occurs. We only include amounts representing contract change orders, claims, or other items in sales when they can be reliably estimated and realization is probable.
>
> We record revenue under contracts for services other than those associated with DD&P activities either as services are performed or when a contractually

required event has occurred, depending on the contract. The majority of our service contracts is in our Information Systems & Global Services segment. We record revenue under such services contracts on a straight-line basis over the period of contract performance, unless evidence suggests that the revenue is earned or the obligations are fulfilled in a different pattern. Costs we incur under these services contracts are expensed as incurred, except that we capitalize and recognize initial "set-up" costs over the life of the agreement. Award and incentive fees related to our performance on services contracts are recognized when they are fixed or determinable, which is typically on the date the amount is communicated to us by the customer.

1. How does Lockheed measure its percentage of completion on most of its long-term contracts?
2. For the remaining long-term contracts, how does Lockheed recognize revenue and profits?
3. If a change in the contract is made, when is that change reflected in revenues?
4. How does Lockheed normally account for revenue under its service contracts not associated with design, development, or production activities?
5. Is Lockheed's method of accounting for costs incurred under these service contracts the same as its method for recording revenue? Explain.

Case 8-62

Writing Assignment (Credit Terms and Revenue Recognition)

Many large electronics retailers offer very easy credit terms when a customer purchases their products. For example, a company might offer its customers a "$0 down, no payments for 12 months" payment option when purchasing a big-screen television. In a case such as this, when would the electronics retailer recognize revenue—at the point of sale, when payments are begun (in 12 months), or proportionally as payments are made? In no more than one page, discuss the pros and cons of each possible revenue recognition point and provide a conclusion as to when you believe an electronics retailer should recognize revenue.

Case 8-63

Ethical Dilemma (Recognizing Revenue from Gold in the Ground)

You are the president and founder of Gold Strike Inc., a mining company that acquires land and mines gold. The success of your company is largely dependent on finding large deposits of gold. To do this requires expensive geological surveys and testing. You have used an engineering firm in the past that has proven quite reliable in its estimates of gold quality and quantity.

Because of recent events around the world, the price of gold has declined approximately 15% in the past 6 months. Accounting practice allows your company to recognize revenue when the gold is mined and processed rather than waiting until it is actually sold. Because of the recent unexpected decline in gold prices, you find that your revenue has suddenly declined even though the quality and quantity of the gold being produced have been maintained.

To avoid arousing investor concerns about your business's future, you consider the following option. The engineering firm assures you that, based on its tests, large amounts of gold still exist in your mines. Because you can recognize revenue when the gold is mined and you know it is in the ground (based on your engineer's assurances), could you recognize revenue for the gold that is in the ground but has not yet been mined? Now remember, you are not talking about accounting for fictitious gold. This gold does exist (again, based on your engineer's estimates).

Case 8-64

Cumulative Spreadsheet Analysis

For the purpose of this spreadsheet assignment, assume that Skywalker is in the long-term construction business. As of the end of 2013, Skywalker has five active contracts (designated A through E). Information about each of the contracts, including forecasted information for 2014, is given below.

	A	B	C	D	E	Total
Contract price	$4,000	$1,000	$500	$1,500	$2,000	$9,000
Cumulative costs incurred, end of 2013	200	140	240	0	0	580
Estimated cost to complete, end of 2013	2,320	560	60	1,200	1,800	5,940
Estimated cost to be incurred during 2014	892	100	60	200	928	2,180
Cumulative progress billings, end of 2013	180	100	178	0	0	458
Estimated progress billings during 2014	1,300	130	120	240	966	2,756
Cumulative cash collected, end of 2013	170	80	127	0	0	377
Estimated cash to be collected during 2014	1,270	135	150	230	939	2,724

1. Using the information given, construct a spreadsheet that will compute the following. (*Note:* Skywalker uses the cost-to-cost method in estimating the percentage of completion, and 2014 total costs is based on using 2013 cumulative costs plus estimated costs to complete at the end of 2013.)
   (a) Total accounts receivable, end of 2013
   (b) Total inventory, end of 2013
   (c) Total estimated revenue to be recognized in 2014
   (d) Total estimated cost of goods sold to be recognized in 2014
   (e) Total estimated accounts receivable, end of 2014
   (f) Total estimated inventory, end of 2014
2. Repeat (1) with the following changes with respect to the estimated cost to be incurred in 2014.

	A	B	C	D	E	Total
Estimated cost to be incurred during 2014	$750	$120	$60	$200	$1,050	$2,180

3. Refer back to the original information in (1). Repeat (1) with the following changes with respect to the estimated progress billings during 2014.

	A	B	C	D	E	Total
Estimated progress billings during 2014	$1,270	$160	$140	$240	$946	$2,756

4. Refer back to (2) and (3). One of the changes results in a change in the estimated gross profit for 2014; the other change does not affect estimated gross profit for 2014. Explain this difference.

P2 ROUTINE ACTIVITIES OF A BUSINESS

CHAPTER 9 Inventory and Cost of Goods Sold

LEARNING OBJECTIVES

1. Define inventory for a merchandising business, and identify the different types of inventory for a manufacturing business.
2. Explain the advantages and disadvantages of both periodic and perpetual inventory systems.
3. Determine when ownership of goods in transit changes hands and what circumstances require shipped inventory to be kept on the books.
4. Compute total inventory acquisition cost.
5. Use the four basic inventory valuation methods: specific identification, average cost, FIFO, and LIFO.
6. Explain how LIFO inventory layers are created, and describe the significance of the LIFO reserve.
7. Choose an inventory valuation method based on the trade-offs among income tax effects, bookkeeping costs, and the impact on the financial statements.
8. Apply the lower-of-cost-or-market (LCM) rule to reflect declines in the market value of inventory.
9. Use the gross profit method to estimate ending inventory.
10. Determine the financial statement impact of inventory recording errors.
11. Analyze inventory using financial ratios, and properly compare ratios of different firms after adjusting for differences in inventory valuation methods.

EM EXPANDED MATERIAL

12. Compute estimates of FIFO, LIFO, average cost, and lower-of-cost-or-market inventory using the retail inventory method.
13. Use LIFO pools, dollar-value LIFO, and dollar-value LIFO retail to compute ending inventory.
14. Account for the impact of changing prices on purchase commitments.
15. Record inventory purchase transactions denominated in foreign currencies.

Let's go back to 1974. America was captivated by the Watergate investigation culminating in the resignation of President Nixon in August. In the spring, Hank Aaron hit his 715th career home run and broke Babe Ruth's long-standing record. Rock 'n' roll had fallen into the doldrums with best-selling songs for the year including forgettable numbers such as "Billy, Don't Be a Hero" by Bo Donaldson and the Heywoods and "Seasons in the Sun" by Terry Jacks. To add insult to injury, the first "disco" hit—"Rock the Boat" by The Hues Corporation—came out in 1974. At the movies, Americans were lining up to see disaster pictures such as *Earthquake* and *The Towering Inferno*.

From an accounting standpoint, 1974 was an interesting year because it was the first year since World War II in which consumer price inflation in the United States exceeded 10%. High inflation wreaks havoc on the reliability of historical cost financial statements. In fact, the high inflation experienced throughout the latter half of the 1970s caused the FASB to experiment with inflation-adjusted financial statements.

High inflation also magnifies the difference between the FIFO (first-in, first-out) and LIFO (last-in, first-out) inventory methods. In times of rising prices, FIFO results in low cost of goods sold because the old, lower-cost inventory is assumed to be sold. Similarly, LIFO results in high cost of goods sold because the new, higher-cost inventory is assumed to be sold. This is illustrated in Exhibit 9-1. As an example of the FIFO/LIFO difference caused by the high inflation in 1974, the 1974 cost of goods sold of **DuPont** was $600 million higher using LIFO than it would have been if DuPont had used FIFO.

By the way, 1974 happened to be the year that DuPont switched from FIFO to LIFO. DuPont was not alone—over 700 U.S. companies adopted LIFO in 1974. Why did these companies voluntarily adopt LIFO and subject themselves to higher cost of goods sold and lower reported profits? The one-word answer is taxes. The IRS requires firms using LIFO for income tax purposes to also use LIFO for financial reporting. So, if a company wants to get a reduction in taxes through higher LIFO cost of goods sold, the company must also accept a lower reported net income.[1] In DuPont's case, the adoption of LIFO in 1974 saved over $250 million in taxes but lowered its reported net income by over $300 million.

A question that has intrigued accounting researchers is whether investors viewed the 1974 LIFO adoptions as good news or bad news—good news because of the LIFO tax savings or bad news because of the reduction in reported net income. The answer to this question provides insight into whether investors are sophisticated in their knowledge of accounting. A sophisticated investor would view a LIFO adoption in a time of high inflation as good

EX 9-1 LIFO AND FIFO IN TIMES OF INFLATION

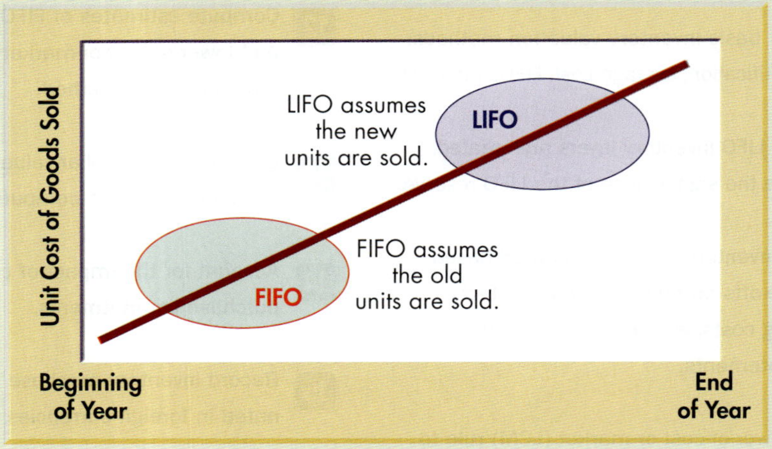

[1] This "LIFO conformity rule" is an exception—in most cases, the choice of a tax accounting method does not necessarily dictate the same choice for financial reporting.

news, realizing that the adopting firm was focusing on real cash savings (lower taxes) and not worried about just looking good in the reported financial statements. An unsophisticated investor is fixated on reported earnings and would view LIFO adoption as bad news because it lowers net income.

In 1982, Professor William E. Ricks published a study suggesting that the LIFO adoptions were viewed as bad news, implying that investors back in 1974 were unsophisticated in their understanding of LIFO and FIFO.[2] He found that the market value of firms adopting LIFO dropped an average of 2% in the week surrounding the public announcement of 1974 earnings. Many studies have reexamined this result, and the overall conclusion is that it isn't clear exactly what caused this market value drop. After a careful analysis of competing explanations, Professor John R. M. Hand concluded: "[Negative] stock returns at 1974 LIFO adoption dates appear to reflect both sophisticated and unsophisticated responses to information on LIFO adopters. It is hard to disentangle the two responses. . . ."[3]

Your job is to study this chapter and make sure that your understanding of inventory accounting puts you in the set of sophisticated users of financial statements.

? QUESTIONS

1. What causes a big difference between LIFO and FIFO?
2. What prompted so many U.S. companies to switch from FIFO to LIFO in 1974?
3. On what does an unsophisticated investor focus?

Answers to these questions can be found on page 9-63.

The time line in Exhibit 9-2 illustrates the business issues involved with inventory. The accounting questions associated with the items in the time line are as follows:

- When is inventory considered to have been purchased—when it is ordered, when it is shipped, when it is received, or when it is paid for?
- Similarly, when is the inventory considered to have been sold?
- Many costs are associated with the "value-added" process—which of these costs are considered to be part of the cost of inventory and which are simply business expenses for that period?
- How should total inventory cost be divided between the inventory that was sold (cost of goods sold) and the inventory that remains (ending inventory)?

Determining what items should be included in inventory involves more than recognizing inventory when you see it. Some inventory that should be included in a company's balance sheet cannot be found in the company's warehouses but instead is in transit in trucks, trains, or ships or is temporarily in the custody of some other company. A proper physical determination of how much inventory a company owns as of a certain date is one of the most daunting tasks of an independent external auditor.

[2] William E. Ricks, "The Market's Response to the 1974 LIFO Adoptions," *Journal of Accounting Research*, Autumn 1982, p. 367.
[3] John R. M. Hand, "1974 LIFO Excess Stock Return and Analyst Forecast Error Anomalies Revisited," *Journal of Accounting Research*, Spring 1995, p. 175.

EX 9-2 TIME LINE OF BUSINESS ISSUES INVOLVED WITH INVENTORY

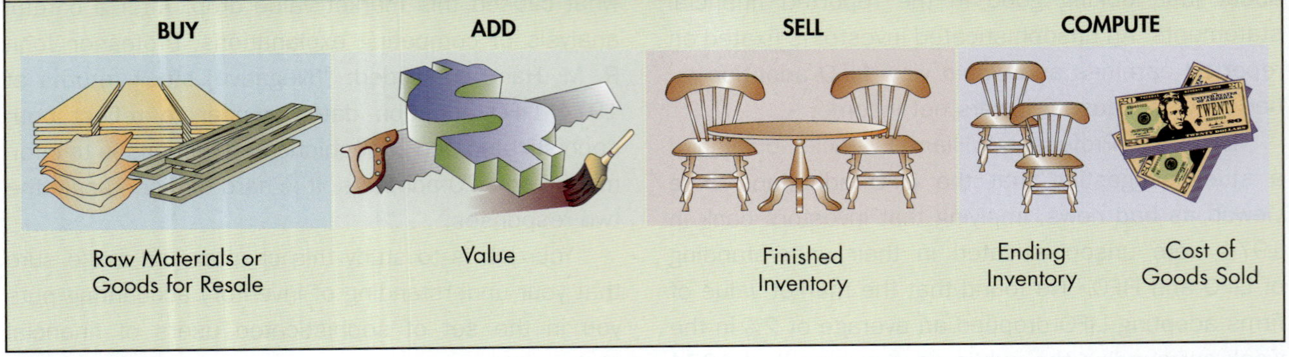

Attaching the proper costs to inventory is one of the primary functions of a cost accounting system. Advances made since 1980 in the practice of cost accounting have turned the sleepy topic of overhead allocation into a key element of product pricing and marketing focus. The important area of cost accounting is briefly covered in this chapter, but detailed treatment is left to a cost accounting course. The majority of the chapter is devoted to the topic of inventory valuation. Almost all companies in the United States use one or more of three basic inventory valuation methods: FIFO (first-in, first-out), LIFO (last-in, first-out), and average cost. The objective of inventory valuation is to divide the total cost of goods available for sale during the period into two categories: the cost associated with goods that were sold (cost of goods sold) and the cost associated with goods that still remain (ending inventory). Coverage of the LIFO inventory valuation method takes up a large proportion of the chapter because the apparently simple assumption of last-in, first-out introduces all kinds of interesting twists into inventory accounting.

The chapter continues with a discussion of the accounting treatment required when the market value of inventory declines. We then discuss a common technique used to estimate inventory—the gross profit method. In addition to providing a means of determining the amount of inventory lost in a fire or flood, the gross profit method is also used with periodic inventory systems to provide ending inventory estimates for preparing monthly or quarterly financial statements when a full physical inventory count is not feasible. Inventory estimates are also compared to perpetual inventory records to provide an early warning of unusual inventory shrinkage. Finally, external auditors and the IRS use inventory estimates to test the reasonableness of reported trends in cost of goods sold. In the Expanded Material, a more elaborate method of inventory estimation is introduced, and accounting for purchase commitments and for foreign currency inventory purchases is discussed.

What Is Inventory?

1 Define inventory for a merchandising business, and identify the different types of inventory for a manufacturing business.

WHY **Because companies hold inventory for the sole purpose of selling it, the accounting procedures for assets classified as inventory differ from those for assets that may be similar in nature but that are held to be used.**

HOW **Items held for resale in the normal course of business are classified as inventory. For a manufacturing firm, a broad array of production costs is included as part of the cost of inventory.**

The term inventory designates goods held for sale in the normal course of business and, in the case of a manufacturer, goods in production or to be placed in production. The nature of goods classified as inventory varies widely with the nature of business activities and in some cases includes assets not normally thought of as inventory. For example, land and buildings held for resale by a real estate firm, partially completed buildings to be sold in the future by a construction firm, and investment securities held for resale by a stockbroker are all properly classified as inventory by the respective firms in those industries.

For some businesses, inventory represents the most active element in business operations, being continuously acquired or produced and resold. A large part of a company's resources can be invested in goods purchased or manufactured. However, advances in information technology have made it possible for companies to more efficiently manage their inventory levels. As illustrated in Exhibit 9-3, inventory for the 50 largest companies in the United States declined from 15.8% of total assets in 1979 to 5.2% of total assets in 2006. Actually, this trend is a combination of two factors: more efficient management of inventory and a decrease in the prominence of old-style smokestack industries that carried large inventories. Companies in the growth industries of service, technology, and information often have little or no inventory.

The term *inventory* (or *merchandise inventory*) is generally applied to goods held by a merchandising firm, either wholesale or retail, when such goods have been acquired in a condition for resale. The terms *raw materials*, *work in process*, and *finished goods* refer to the inventories of a manufacturing enterprise.

Raw Materials

Raw materials are goods acquired for use in the production process. Some raw materials are obtained directly from natural sources. More often, however, raw materials are purchased from other companies and represent the finished products of the suppliers. For example, high-quality acid-free paper (like that used for this book) is the finished product of a paper mill but represents raw material to a textbook publishing company.

Although the term *raw materials* can be used broadly to cover all materials used in manufacturing, this designation is usually restricted to materials that will be physically

EX 9-3 HOW MUCH INVENTORY DO COMPANIES HAVE?

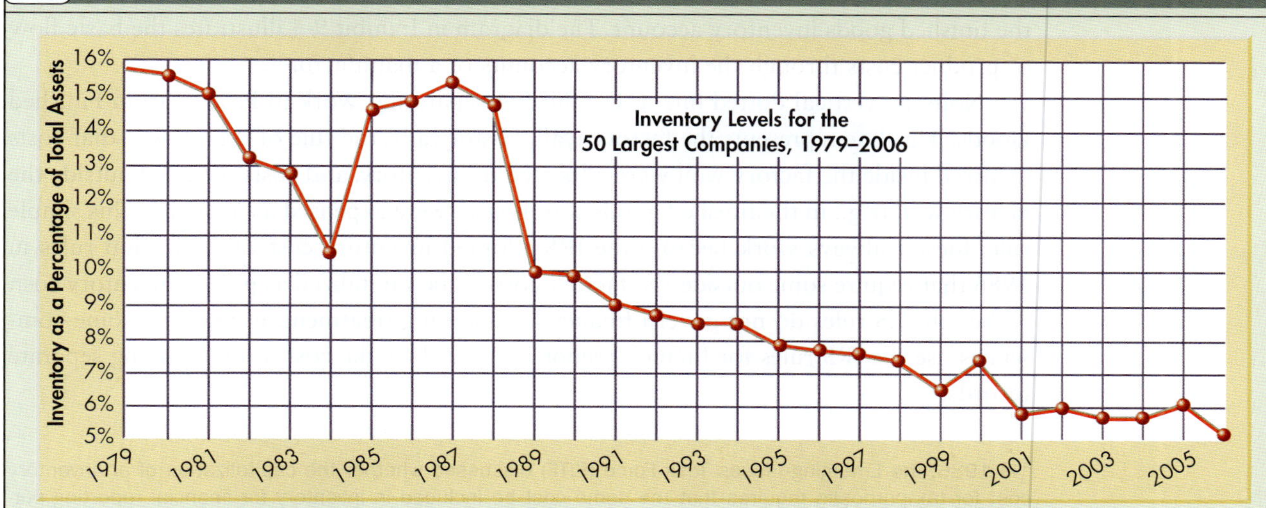

Source: Standard and Poor's *COMPUSTAT*.

incorporated in the products being manufactured. Because these materials are used directly in the production of goods, they are frequently referred to as direct materials. The term indirect materials is then used to refer to auxiliary materials, that is, materials that are necessary in the production process but are not directly incorporated in the products. Oils and fuels for factory equipment, cleaning supplies, and similar items fall into this grouping because these items are not incorporated in a product but simply facilitate production.

Although indirect materials may be summarized separately, they should be reported as a part of a company's inventories since they ultimately will be consumed in the production process. Supplies purchased for use in the delivery, sales, and general administrative functions of the enterprise should not be reported as part of the inventories, but as selling and administrative supplies. Remember, *inventory* is the label given to assets to be sold in the normal course of business or to assets to be incorporated, directly or indirectly, into goods that are manufactured and then sold.

Work in Process

Work in process, alternately referred to as *goods in process*, consists of materials partly processed and requiring further work before they can be sold. This inventory includes three cost elements.

1. *Direct materials*—the cost of materials directly identified with goods in production
2. *Direct labor*—the cost of labor directly identified with goods in production
3. *Manufacturing overhead*—the portion of factory overhead assignable to goods in production

Manufacturing overhead consists of all manufacturing costs other than direct materials and direct labor. It includes factory supplies used and labor not directly identified with the production of specific products. It also includes general manufacturing costs such as depreciation, maintenance, repairs, property taxes, insurance, and light, heat, and power, as well as a reasonable share of the managerial costs other than those relating solely to the selling and administrative functions of the business.

Finished Goods

Finished goods are the manufactured products awaiting sale. As products are completed, the costs accumulated in the production process are transferred from Work in Process to the finished goods inventory account. The diagram in Exhibit 9-4 illustrates the basic flow of product costs through the inventory accounts of a manufacturer.

Note the vertical dotted line in Exhibit 9-4 separating Work in Process from Finished Goods. This line represents the factory wall. Historically, the rule of thumb was that costs incurred inside the factory wall were allocated to inventory, and costs incurred outside the factory wall (e.g., in the finished goods warehouse) were expensed as incurred. This simple rule doesn't always work because the IRS adopted inventory cost capitalization rules in 1986 that require some outside-the-factory costs to be capitalized as part of inventory cost. Although IRS rules do not govern financial accounting treatment, in this case some companies use the IRS rules for financial reporting to reduce the cost of maintaining separate records.[4]

[4] In 1986, the Emerging Issues Task Force (EITF) discussed whether the capitalization of an inventory cost for tax purposes requires that the same cost be included in inventory for financial reporting purposes. The EITF reached a consensus that the tax treatment should be considered but should not dictate the financial accounting treatment. See FASB ASC paragraphs 330-10-55-3 and 4.

EX 9-4 INVENTORY COST FLOW

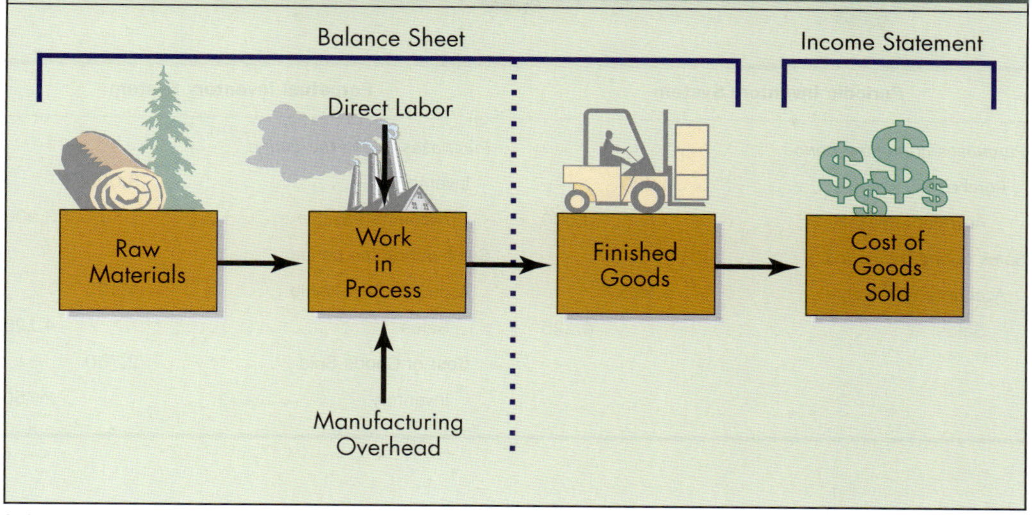

Inventory Systems

2 **Explain the advantages and disadvantages of both periodic and perpetual inventory systems.**

WHY **Understanding the costs and benefits of the periodic and perpetual inventory systems allows companies to determine which system will best fill their needs.**

HOW **A periodic inventory system is simple and inexpensive to operate but also provides relatively low-quality information. Using a perpetual inventory system can require costly technology, but the quality of the information generated by the system is high.**

Consider the last time you made a purchase. Did the business where you made the purchase keep a record of what item it sold you, or did it just record the selling price? With a traditional cash register system, the seller records only the sales price; the seller has no record of how many units of a particular inventory item have been sold. Accountants call this type of system a periodic inventory system because the only way to verify what inventory has been sold and what remains is to do a periodic physical count.

The alternative to a periodic system is a perpetual inventory system in which both the selling price and the type of item sold are recorded for each sale. A bar code scanning system is an example of a perpetual inventory system. With a perpetual system, the seller knows the number of each item sold and the number that should still be in inventory. With a perpetual system, periodic physical inventory counts are useful in revealing the amount of inventory "shrinkage"—inventory lost, stolen, or spoiled.

To illustrate the differences between periodic and perpetual inventory systems, assume the following transactions occurred during the period for CyBorg Incorporated.

Beginning inventory	50 units @ $10	$ 500
Purchases during the period	300 units @ $10	3,000
Sales during the period	275 units @ $15	4,125
Ending inventory (physical count)	70 units @ $10	700

The journal entries to record these purchases and sales for both periodic and perpetual inventory systems are as follows:

Periodic Inventory System			Perpetual Inventory System		
Purchases during the period			*Purchases during the period*		
Purchases	3,000		Inventory	3,000	
Accounts Payable		3,000	Accounts Payable		3,000
Sales during the period			*Sales during the period*		
Accounts Receivable	4,125		Accounts Receivable	4,125	
Sales		4,125	Sales		4,125
			Cost of Goods Sold	2,750	
			Inventory		2,750

There are two differences between these two sets of journal entries. First, with a perpetual system an additional entry is made upon the sale of inventory to record the cost of goods sold. With a periodic system, cost of goods sold data are not known (or at least are not recorded) at the time of the sale. The second difference is that with the periodic system the debit for the inventory purchase is to Purchases instead of to Inventory. The purchases account is a temporary holding tank for inventory costs that are allocated between Inventory and Cost of Goods Sold at the end of the period. Under a periodic system, to debit Inventory directly for the amount of purchases during the period would yield misleading information about the level of inventory because the inventory account is not reduced for the cost of goods sold during the period. With a periodic system, the inventory account remains untouched until a physical inventory count is done at the end of the period.

When a perpetual inventory system is employed, the company knows how much inventory should be on hand at any point in time. Comparing the inventory records to the result of a physical count allows the company to track discrepancies in inventory totals. Thus, even when a perpetual system is employed, physical counts of units on hand should be made at least once a year to confirm the balances on the books. The frequency of physical inventories varies depending on the nature of the goods, their rate of turnover, and the degree of internal control.[5] A plan for continuous counting of inventory items on a rotation basis is frequently employed.

Variations may be found between the recorded amounts and the amounts actually on hand as a result of recording errors, shrinkage, breakage, theft, and other causes. The inventory accounts should be adjusted to agree with the physical count when a discrepancy exists. To illustrate, cost of goods sold in the CyBorg example is computed as follows:

[5] While paying for gas and soft drinks at a mini-convenience store, one of the authors noticed the cashier marking the soft drink purchases on an inventory sheet. Aha, thought the author, this place uses a perpetual inventory system. When asked how often a physical count was done to verify the inventory records, the cashier replied, "At the end of every shift." Obviously, the store manager was using the combination of a perpetual inventory system and frequent physical counts to minimize shoplifting by customers and pilferage by employees.

	Periodic System		Perpetual System	
Beginning inventory	$ 500		$ 500	
+ Purchases	3,000		3,000	
= Cost of goods available for sale	$3,500		$3,500	
− Ending inventory	700	(count)	750	(records)
= Preliminary cost of goods sold	$2,800		$2,750	(records)
+ Cost of missing inventory	Unknown		50	($750 − $700)
= Reported cost of goods sold	$2,800		$2,800	

With the perpetual system, the accounting records contain amounts for ending inventory and cost of goods sold before the physical count is ever done. The physical count serves to verify the accounting records. And in this case, it appears that CyBorg has lost $50 in inventory: the difference between the $750 inventory recorded in the books and the $700 physically counted. The entry to adjust the perpetual system inventory account for this shrinkage would be as follows:

Cost of Goods Sold	50	
Inventory		50

As indicated, this type of inventory adjustment for shrinkage and breakage would typically be included as part of cost of goods sold on the income statement.

With the periodic system, ending inventory is known only from the physical count. In addition, cost of goods sold can be computed only after the physical count is done. No shrinkage calculation is possible with a periodic system because the accounting records contain no indication of how much inventory should be found in the physical count. In fact, with a periodic system, the label "cost of goods sold" might be better replaced by "cost of goods sold, stolen, lost, and spoiled"—all that is known is that the goods are gone. For external reporting purposes, both the periodic and perpetual systems yield the same reported cost of goods sold. However, for internal purposes, the perpetual system divides that number into cost of goods sold and cost of inventory shrinkage.

STOP&THINK

If perpetual inventory systems have so many clear advantages, why aren't they used by all companies?

a) A perpetual inventory system can increase the level of a company's bad debts.
b) Perpetual inventory systems are illegal in most countries outside the United States.
c) A perpetual inventory system is more costly to operate than a periodic system.
d) A perpetual inventory system is only appropriate for businesses with low-value identical items with a high turnover.

Practically all large trading and manufacturing enterprises and many small organizations have adopted perpetual inventory systems. With the costs of computers and point-of-sale systems so low, perpetual inventory systems are now more economical and, in today's fast-moving world, almost a necessity. These systems offer a continuous check and control over inventories. Purchasing and production planning are facilitated, adequate on-hand inventories are ensured, and losses incurred through damage and theft are fully disclosed.

Whose Inventory Is It?

3 **Determine when ownership of goods in transit changes hands and what circumstances require shipped inventory to be kept on the books.**

WHY **In general, a company reports on its balance sheet all inventory to which it holds legal title. Legal title is not necessarily determined by who has physical custody of the inventory on the balance sheet date. Accordingly, figuring out what inventory a company owns on the balance sheet date can be a challenge.**

HOW **Goods in transit belong to the seller if the shipping terms are FOB destination and to the buyer if shipping terms are FOB shipping point. Goods on consignment do NOT belong to the company with physical custody of the goods.**

As a general rule, goods should be included in the inventory of the business holding legal title. The *passing of title* is a legal term designating the point at which ownership changes. When the rule of passing title is not observed, statements should include appropriate disclosure of the special practice followed and the factors supporting such practice. Application of the legal test under a number of special circumstances is described in the following paragraphs.

Goods in Transit

When goods are in transit from the seller to the buyer, who owns them? The answer depends on the terms of the sale. When terms of sale are FOB (free on board) shipping point, title passes to the buyer with the loading of goods at the point of shipment. Because title passes at the shipping point, goods in transit at year-end should be included in the inventory of the buyer even though the buyer hasn't received them yet.

When terms of a sale are FOB destination, legal title does not pass until the goods are received by the buyer. Even though it can be difficult to determine whether goods have reached their destination by the end of the period, when the terms are FOB destination the seller should not recognize a sale, and a corresponding inventory decrease, until the goods are received by the buyer.

To summarize, when goods are shipped FOB shipping point, they belong to the buyer while they are in transit and should normally be included in the buyer's inventory while in transit. When goods are shipped FOB destination, they belong to the seller while in transit and are normally included in the seller's inventory. The impact of shipping terms on the ownership of goods in transit is summarized in Exhibit 9-5.

In some cases, title to goods may pass before shipment takes place. For example, if goods are produced on special customer order, they may be recorded as a sale as soon as they are completed and segregated from the regular inventory. If the sale is recognized upon segregation by the seller, the goods should be excluded from the seller's inventory. The buyer could recognize the goods as part of inventory as soon as they are separated.

Keep in mind that the shipping terms related to inventory are only an issue at the end of an accounting period. For most shipments, the goods will be shipped by the seller and received by the buyer in the same accounting period, thereby presenting no accounting problems.

Goods on Consignment

Goods are frequently transferred to a dealer or customer on a consignment basis. The shipper retains title and includes the goods in inventory until their sale or use by the dealer

EX 9-5 OWNERSHIP TRANSFER FOR GOODS IN TRANSIT

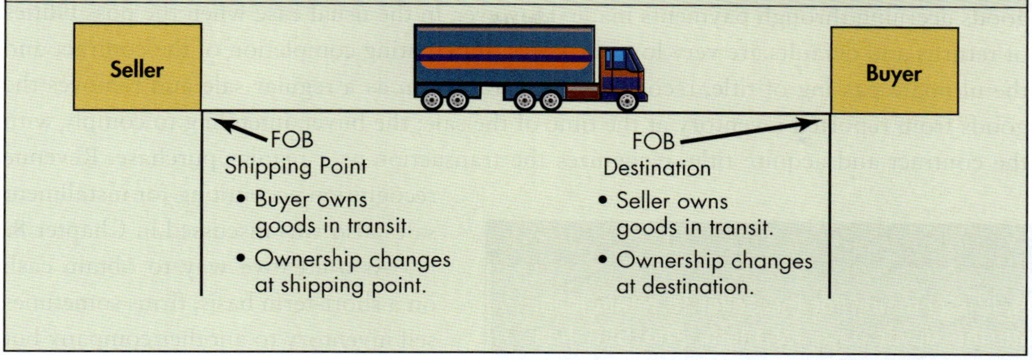

or customer. For example, **NN, Inc.**, a company that makes precision steel balls and rollers for use in manufacturing antifriction bearings, provides goods on consignment to some of its major customers. Through this arrangement, the customers are able to maintain low inventory levels. NN, Inc., benefits from this consignment arrangement because this added service improves customer satisfaction and, hopefully, increases sales. Consigned goods are properly reported by the shipper at the sum of their costs and the handling and shipping costs incurred in their transfer to the dealer or customer. The goods may be separately designated on the shipper's balance sheet as merchandise on consignment. Alternatively, the amount of inventory on consignment may be disclosed in the financial statement notes. For example, in the notes to its December 31, 2009, financial statements, NN, Inc., disclosed that $3.0 million of its $33.3 million in inventory was inventory on consignment. The dealer or customer does not own the consigned goods; hence, neither consigned goods nor obligations for such goods are reported on the dealer's or customer's financial statements. Recall that revenue recognition accounting for consignments was discussed in Chapter 8.

Other merchandise owned by a business but in the possession of others, such as goods in the hands of salespersons and agents, goods held by customers on approval, and goods held by others for storage, processing, or shipment, also should be shown as a part of the ending inventory of the business that owns the goods.

> **FYI**
>
> Twenty years ago, when auditors got together, they exchanged "war stories" about difficult inventory audits. These days you are more likely to hear auditors complaining about lawsuits and nasty computer systems.

Auditing consigned inventory presents the auditor with a special set of problems. Inventory that is on the premises may not belong to the company because the company is holding it on consignment, yet inventory that is located with a vendor on consignment, hundreds of miles away, still belongs to the company. Imagine an auditor walking out into a warehouse and seeing row upon row of inventory. "That's not ours, we are just holding it on consignment," quips the warehouse manager. Then the warehouse manager leads the auditor to the shipping platform. "See that truck just leaving the gate? That truck and hundreds more just like it contain inventory that is still ours but has been shipped on consignment. Audit that!"

Conditional Sales, Installment Sales, and Repurchase Agreements

Conditional sales and installment sales contracts may provide for a retention of title by the seller until the sales price is fully recovered. Under these circumstances, the seller, who retains title, may continue to show the goods on its records, reduced by the buyer's equity in such goods as established by collections; the buyer, in turn, can report an equity in the goods accruing through payments made. However, in the usual case when the possibilities of returns and defaults are very low, the seller, anticipating completion of the contract and the ultimate passing of title, recognizes the transaction as a regular sale and removes the goods from reported inventory at the time of the sale; the buyer, intending to comply with the contract and acquire title, recognizes the transaction as a regular purchase. Revenue recognition accounting for installment sales also was discussed in Chapter 8.

FYI

In some countries, it is common for the seller to retain legal title of goods until the buyer pays for them. The SEC has stated (in *SAB 104*) that in cases like this, it is appropriate to assume that accounting ownership changes hands at delivery if the seller's title is limited to the right to ensure recovery of the goods if payment is not made. See FASB ASC paragraph 605-10-S99-1 (Question 3).

As a creative way to obtain cash on a short-term basis, firms sometimes sell inventory to another company but at the same time agree to repurchase the inventory at some future date. The repurchase price typically includes the original selling price of the inventory plus finance and holding charges. In essence, the "selling" company has used inventory to secure a short-term loan but agrees to buy back the inventory later. For those familiar with such things, this is similar to how a pawnshop works. The FASB has decided that these arrangements should be accounted for according to their economic substance—no sale is recorded, the inventory is not removed from the selling company's balance sheet, and the seller must record a liability for the proceeds received in the "sale."[6]

What Is Inventory Cost?

4 **Compute total inventory acquisition cost.**

WHY **The cost of inventory often includes much more than just the cost of the physical materials that make up the inventory. Properly accounting for inventory costs ensures that both assets and expenses are reported correctly.**

HOW **Computing the cost of inventory, particularly inventory that is being manufactured, requires that various costs in addition to costs of the physical product be accounted for properly. In the case of manufactured inventory, material, labor, and overhead costs are assigned to inventory being produced and expensed when the inventory is sold.**

After the goods to be included as inventory have been identified, the accountant must assign a dollar value to the physical units. Both U.S. and international accounting standards agree that historical cost should normally be used in valuing inventory. Attention is directed in this section to identifying the elements that comprise inventory cost.

Items Included in Inventory Cost

Inventory cost consists of all expenditures, both direct and indirect, relating to inventory acquisition, preparation, and placement for sale. In the case of raw materials or goods

[6] FASB ASC paragraph 470-40-25-1. The FASB calls this type of transaction a "product financing arrangement."

acquired for resale, cost includes the purchase price, freight, receiving, storage, and all other costs incurred to the time goods are ready for sale. Certain expenditures can be traced to specific acquisitions or can be allocated to inventory items in some equitable manner. Other expenditures may be relatively small and difficult to allocate. Such items are normally excluded in the calculation of inventory cost and are recognized as expenses in the current period. These items are called period costs.

The charges to be included in the cost of manufactured products have already been mentioned. These costs are called product or inventoriable costs. Proper accounting for materials, labor, and manufacturing overhead items and their identification with goods in process and finished goods inventories are achieved through a cost accounting system. Certain costs relating to the acquisition or the manufacture of goods may be considered abnormal and may be excluded in arriving at inventory cost. For example, costs arising from idle capacity, excessive spoilage, and reprocessing are usually considered abnormal and are expensed in the current period.[7] Only those portions of general and administrative costs that are clearly related to procurement or production should be included in inventory cost.

Inventory costing is important for financial reporting purposes, but it is absolutely critical for making production, pricing, and strategy decisions. For example, if competitive pressures dictate that a business can sell a product for no more than $10 per unit, it is essential to that business to know whether it costs $8 or $11 to produce the unit. As mentioned earlier in the chapter, recent advances in techniques for allocating manufacturing overhead have greatly improved cost accounting systems.

Traditionally, manufacturing overhead costs have been allocated to products based on the amount of direct labor required in production. This allocation scheme often fails because direct labor can be a small part of the cost of a product that actually causes a large amount of manufacturing overhead through requiring frequent machine maintenance, lots of invoice paperwork, heavy administrative supervision, and so forth. Activity-based cost (ABC) systems strive to allocate overhead based on clearly identified cost drivers—characteristics of the production process (e.g., number of required machine reconfigurations or average frequency of production glitches requiring management intervention) that are known to create overhead costs. The real benefit of a good inventory costing system is seen in better information for internal decision making. As such, this important topic is covered fully in managerial accounting courses.

CAUTION

One last warning—don't let the short coverage of overhead allocation here deceive you. This is a vital topic that has spawned arguments, textbooks, and lots of consulting revenue for the experts.

A schedule of cost of goods manufactured is often prepared by manufacturing companies to illustrate how various costs affect inventories and, ultimately, cost of goods sold. An illustration of this schedule is presented in Exhibit 9-6.[8]

In practice, companies take different positions in classifying certain costs. For example, costs of the purchasing department, costs of accounting for manufacturing activities, and

[7] FASB ASC paragraph 330-10-30-7.

[8] To make this schedule more intuitive for the financial accounting audience using this text, the actual manufacturing overhead costs are shown. In a proper schedule of cost of goods manufactured, this total would be adjusted for the amount of over- or underapplied overhead such that the amount of applied (instead of actual) manufacturing overhead would be included in the computation of total manufacturing costs.

EX 9-6 SCHEDULE OF COST OF GOODS MANUFACTURED

Bartlett Corporation
Schedule of Cost of Goods Manufactured
For the Year Ended December 31, 2013

Direct materials:		
Raw materials inventory, January 1, 2013	$ 21,350	
Purchases	107,500	
Cost of raw materials available for use	$128,850	
Less: Raw materials inventory, December 31, 2013	22,350	
Raw materials used in production		$106,500
Direct labor		96,850
Manufacturing overhead:		
Indirect labor	$ 40,000	
Factory supervision	29,000	
Depreciation—factory buildings and equipment	20,000	
Light, heat, and power	18,000	
Factory supplies	15,000	
Miscellaneous manufacturing overhead	12,055	134,055
Total manufacturing costs		$337,405
Add: Work in process inventory, January 1, 2013		29,400
		$366,805
Less: Work in process inventory, December 31, 2013		26,500
Cost of goods manufactured		$340,305

costs of pensions for production personnel may be treated as inventoriable costs by some companies and period costs by others.

Discounts as Reductions in Cost

Discounts associated with the purchase of inventory should be treated as a reduction in the cost assigned to the inventory. Trade discounts refer to the difference between a catalog price and the price actually charged to a buyer. *Cost* is defined as the list price less the trade discount. No record needs to be made of a trade discount, and the purchases should be recorded at the net price.

Cash discounts are discounts granted for payment of invoices within a limited time period. Cash discounts are usually stated as a certain percentage to be allowed if the invoice is paid within a certain number of days, with the full amount due within another time period. For example, 2/10, n/30 (two ten, net thirty) means that 2% is allowed as a cash discount if the invoice is paid within 10 days after the invoice date but the full or "net" amount is due within 30 days.

Theoretically, inventory should be recorded at the discounted amount (i.e., the gross invoice price less the allowable discount). This net method reflects the fact that discounts not taken are in effect a finance charge incurred for failure to pay within the discount period. Discounts not taken are recorded in the discounts lost account and reported as a separate item on the income statement. Discounts lost usually represent a relatively high rate of interest. To illustrate, assume a purchase of $10,000 provides for payment on a 2/10, n/30 basis. This purchase and the payment options are illustrated in Exhibit 9-7.

If the buyer pays for the purchase by the 10th day, only $9,800 must be paid. Twenty days later the full $10,000 is due. Thus, an additional $200 must be paid in exchange for

EX 9-7 IMPACT OF CASH DISCOUNTS

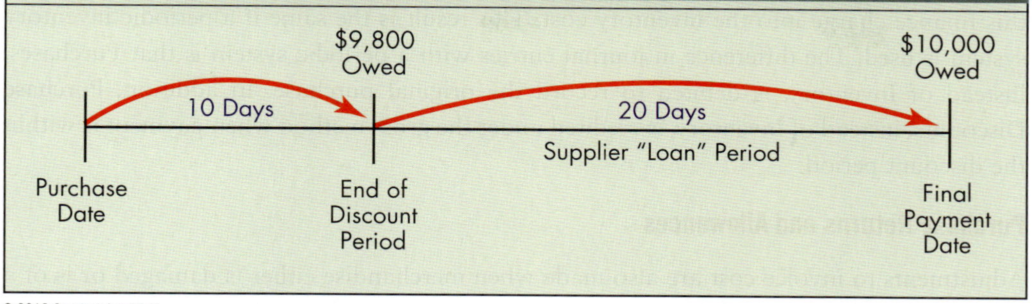

delaying payment for an extra 20 days. In essence, this is a 20-day "loan" from the supplier to the purchaser. The effective interest rate on this 20-day "loan" is 2.04% ($200/$9,800). Because there are about eighteen 20-day periods in a year, the annual interest cost on this "loan" exceeds 36%, suggesting that missing a cash discount is a very costly mistake. Failure on the part of management to take a cash discount usually represents carelessness in considering payment alternatives. If cash discounts are accounted for using the net method, the $200 cost of a missed discount is not included as part of the inventory cost but is expensed immediately as a finance charge.

Under the gross method, cash discounts are booked only when they are taken. While the net method tracks discounts not taken, the gross method provides no such information, and inventory records are maintained at the gross unit price. When a periodic system is used, cash discounts taken are reflected through a contra purchases account, Purchase Discounts. With a perpetual inventory system, discounts are credited directly to Inventory.

The net method of accounting for purchases is strongly preferred; however, many companies still follow the historical practice of recognizing cash discounts only as payments are made. The entries required for both the gross and net methods are illustrated in the following table. A perpetual inventory method is assumed.

Transaction	Purchases Reported Net			Purchases Reported Gross		
Purchase of merchandise priced at $10,000 along with a cash discount of 2%.	Inventory	9,800		Inventory	10,000	
	Accounts Payable		9,800	Accounts Payable		10,000
(a) Assuming payment of the invoice within discount period.	Accounts Payable	9,800		Accounts Payable	10,000	
	Cash		9,800	Inventory		200
				Cash		9,800
(b) Assuming payment of the invoice after discount period.	Accounts Payable	9,800		Accounts Payable	10,000	
	Discounts Lost	200		Cash		10,000
	Cash		10,000			
(c) Required adjustment at the end of the period assuming that the invoice has not been paid and the discount period has lapsed.	Discounts Lost	200		No entry required		
	Accounts Payable		200			

The difference in the two methods is that the net method shows the cost of missed discounts as a separate finance charge (Discounts Lost), whereas the gross method lumps this finance charge into the inventory cost. This result is the same if a periodic inventory system is used. The difference in journal entries with a periodic system is that Purchases, instead of Inventory, is debited to record the original purchase. In addition, Purchase Discounts, instead of Inventory, is credited under the gross method when payment is within the discount period.

Purchase Returns and Allowances

Adjustments to invoice cost are also made when merchandise either is damaged or is of a lesser quality than ordered. Sometimes the merchandise is physically returned to the supplier. In other instances, a credit is allowed to the buyer by the supplier to compensate for the damage or the inferior quality of the merchandise. A purchase allowance of $400 given for defective merchandise would be recorded as follows:

Periodic Inventory System			Perpetual Inventory System		
Accounts Payable	400		Accounts Payable	400	
Purchase Returns and Allowances. . . .		400	Inventory		400

Purchase Returns and Allowances is a contra purchases account.

The computation of total inventory acquisition cost is summarized as follows:

Invoice cost plus freight, storage, and preparation cost
– Cash discounts (only cash discounts taken if using the gross method)
– Purchase returns and allowances
= Inventory cost

Inventory Valuation Methods

5 **Use the four basic inventory valuation methods: specific identification, average cost, FIFO, and LIFO.**

WHY **In most instances, the allocation of the costs of inventory between the balance sheet and the income statement requires an assumption regarding the flow of costs. That cost flow assumption can significantly affect the numbers reported on the income statement and the balance sheet.**

HOW **The specific identification method involves matching the actual cost of inventory with the revenue generated when the product is sold. The other valuation methods—LIFO (last-in, first-out), FIFO (first-in, first-out), and average—systematically match costs with revenues based on an assumption regarding timing.**

At the end of an accounting period, total inventory cost must be allocated between inventory still remaining (to be reported on the balance sheet as an asset) and inventory sold during the period (to be reported on the income statement as the expense "cost of goods sold"). Numerous methods have evolved to make this allocation between cost of goods sold and inventory. The most common methods are as follows:

- Specific identification
- Average cost
- First-in, first-out (FIFO)
- Last-in, first-out (LIFO)

EX 9-8 FREQUENCY OF INVENTORY VALUATION METHOD USE

Frequency of Use of Inventory Valuation Methods
U.S. Companies
1979 and 2006

Inventory Method	1979 All Companies	2006 All Companies	2006 Large Companies
FIFO	75.6%	67.8%	62.2%
LIFO	25.8	13.1	26.8
Average cost	20.8	31.7	45.6
Specific identification	3.7	4.7	3.8

Source: Standard and Poor's *COMPUSTAT*.

Each of these methods has certain characteristics that make it preferable under certain conditions. All four methods have in common the fact that inventory cost is allocated between the income statement and the balance sheet. Only the specific identification method determines the cost allocation according to the physical inventory flow. Unless individual inventory items, such as automobiles, are clearly definable, inventory items are exchangeable. Thus, the emphasis in inventory valuation usually is on the accounting cost allocation, not the physical flow.

FIFO is by far the most common inventory valuation method in the United States. Exhibit 9-8 reports the frequency of use of inventory valuation methods by U.S. companies in both 1979 and 2006. The percentages sum to more than 100%, indicating that many companies use more than one inventory method, applying different methods to different classes of inventory. Recall from the opening scenario of the chapter that LIFO generates income tax savings in times of inflation. The reduction in the rate of inflation in the United States from 1979 to 2006 is probably the cause of the overall decline in usage of LIFO. Finally, notice the difference in usage of LIFO between large and small firms. This is probably the consequence of the potentially sizable bookkeeping costs of maintaining a LIFO system.

There have been few guidelines developed by the profession to assist companies in choosing among these alternative inventory valuation methods. Some argue that cost flow should mirror the physical flow of goods. Others think that inventory valuation should concentrate on matching current costs with current revenues. Still others think that the emphasis should be on the proper valuation of inventory on the balance sheet. The following discussion of the allocation methods demonstrates how each method relates to these different viewpoints.

The four methods will be illustrated using the following simple example for Dalton Company. Dalton has no beginning inventory for 2013.

	Number of Units	Unit Cost	Total Cost
Purchases:			
January 1	200	$10	$ 2,000
March 23	300	12	3,600
July 15	500	11	5,500
November 6	100	13	1,300
Total purchases	1,100		$12,400

Sales: 700 units at $15 per unit. For simplicity, assume that all sales occurred on December 31.

Specific Identification

Costs may be allocated between goods sold during the period and goods on hand at the end of the period according to the actual cost of specific units. This specific identification method requires a way to identify the historical cost of each individual unit of inventory. With specific identification, the flow of recorded costs matches the physical flow of goods.

From a theoretical standpoint, the specific identification method is very attractive, especially when each inventory item is unique and has a high cost. However, when inventory is composed of a great many items or identical items acquired at different times and at different prices, specific identification is likely to be slow, burdensome, and costly. Even a computer tracking system won't answer all these practical concerns. Consider the task of implementing a specific identification inventory system in a do-it-yourself hardware store with the requirement to specifically track all costs associated with each screwdriver, each bolt, each piece of lumber, and each can of paint.

Apart from practical concerns, when units are identical and interchangeable, the specific identification method opens the door to possible profit manipulation through the selection of particular units for delivery. Consider the Dalton Company example. If Dalton Company wants to minimize its cost of goods sold for 2013 (and thus maximize reported net income), it can strategically choose to ship the 700 units with the lowest cost. Cost of goods sold would be computed as follows:

Dalton Company
Specific Identification Method
Shipment of the Lowest Cost Units
Cost of Goods Sold Computation

	Number of Units	Unit Cost	Total Cost
Batch purchased on:			
January 1	200	$10	$2,000
July 15	500	11	5,500
Total cost of goods sold	700		$7,500

The specific identification method is the least common of the four methods discussed in this chapter. Exhibit 9-8 indicates that in 2006 it was used by only 4.7% of U.S. companies. **Amazon.com** is one company that has used the specific identification method. The company has an extremely sophisticated inventory tracking system, and this same system makes it easy to implement the specific identification method. Exhibit 9-9 provides the company's note disclosure relating to its inventory valuation method.

However, as of January 1, 2002, Amazon.com changed its inventory valuation method from specific identification to FIFO, reflecting the continuing shift away from the specific identification method for financial reporting purposes. Note that this does not mean that Amazon.com changed the way it actually tracks its goods; the switch from the specific identification method merely represents a change in assumption for financial reporting purposes.

Average Cost Method

The average cost method assigns the same average cost to each unit. This method is based on the assumption that goods sold should be charged at an average cost, with the average

EX 9-9 AMAZON.COM—INVENTORY VALUATION METHOD [BEFORE 2002]

Inventories, consisting of products available for sale, are recorded using the specific-identification method and valued at the lower of cost or market value.

being weighted by the number of units acquired at each price. Using the cost data for Dalton Company, the weighted-average cost of each unit would be computed as follows:

Total purchases: 1,100 units at a total cost of $12,400

Weighted-average cost: $12,400/1,100 units = $11.27 per unit (rounded)

Using the average cost method, cost of goods sold is simply the number of units sold multiplied by the average cost per unit: $7,890 (700 units × $11.27 per unit, rounded).

The average cost method can be supported as realistic and as paralleling the physical flow of goods, particularly where there is an intermingling of identical inventory units. Unlike the other inventory methods, the average cost approach provides the same cost for similar items of equal utility. The method does not permit profit manipulation. A limitation of the average cost method is that inventory values may lag significantly behind current prices in periods of rapidly rising or falling prices.

FYI

When Western accounting practices were first introduced into the former Soviet Union, Soviet accountants complained that LIFO and FIFO didn't make any sense. They were attracted by the logic of the average cost method.

First-In, First-Out Method

The first-in, first-out (FIFO) method is based on the assumption that the units sold are the oldest units on hand. For Dalton Company, FIFO cost of goods sold is computed as follows:

Dalton Company
FIFO Method
Cost of Goods Sold Computation

	Number of Units	Unit Cost	Total Cost
Batch purchased on:			
January 1	200	$10	$2,000
March 23	300	12	3,600
July 15	200	11	2,200
Total cost of goods sold	700		$7,800

Note that only 200 units from the July 15 batch are assumed to be sold; the remaining 300 units from that batch are assumed to be in ending inventory.

FIFO can be supported as a logical and realistic approach to the flow of costs when it is impractical or impossible to achieve specific cost identification. FIFO assumes a cost flow closely paralleling the usual physical flow of goods sold. Expense is charged with costs considered applicable to the goods actually sold. FIFO affords little opportunity for profit manipulation because the assignment of costs is determined by the order in which costs are incurred. In addition, with FIFO the units remaining in ending inventory are the most recently purchased units, so their reported cost would most closely match end-of-period replacement cost.

Last-In, First-Out Method

The last-in, first-out (LIFO) method is based on the assumption that the newest units are sold. For Dalton Company, LIFO cost of goods sold is computed as follows:

Dalton Company
LIFO Method
Cost of Goods Sold Computation

	Number of Units	Unit Cost	Total Cost
Batch purchased on:			
November 6	100	$13	$1,300
July 15	500	11	5,500
March 23	100	12	1,200
Total cost of goods sold	700		$8,000

Note that only 100 units from the March 23 batch are assumed to be sold; the remaining 200 units from that batch are assumed to be in ending inventory.

CAUTION

There is no required connection between the actual physical flow of goods and the inventory valuation method used.

LIFO is frequently criticized from a theoretical standpoint. It does not match the usual flow of goods in a business (although it does unfortunately match the flow of food in and out of a college student's refrigerator—with nasty implications for "ending inventory"). As seen in the following sections, LIFO results in old values on the balance sheet and can yield very strange cost of goods sold numbers when inventory levels decline. However, LIFO is the best method at matching current inventory costs with current revenues. The difficulties and quirks of maintaining a LIFO inventory system are detailed later in the chapter.

Comparison of Methods: Cost of Goods Sold and Ending Inventory

Recall that the purpose of an inventory valuation method is to allocate total inventory cost between cost of goods sold and inventory. For Dalton Company, total inventory cost for 2013 is $12,400. The allocation of this cost between cost of goods sold and ending inventory is shown in Exhibit 9-10 for each of the four inventory valuation methods. Note that the average cost method differs from the other three methods in that no assumption is made about the sale of specific units. Instead, all sales are assumed to be of the hypothetical "average" unit at the average cost per unit.

Use of FIFO in a period of rising prices matches oldest low-cost inventory with rising sales prices, thus expanding the gross profit margin. In a period of declining prices, oldest high-cost inventory is matched with declining sales prices, thus narrowing the gross profit margin. Using average cost, the gross profit margin tends to follow a similar pattern in response to changing prices. On the other hand, use of LIFO in a period of rising prices relates current high costs of acquiring goods with rising sales prices. Thus, LIFO tends to have a stabilizing effect on gross profit margins.

In using FIFO, inventories are reported on the balance sheet at or near current costs. With LIFO, inventories are reported at the cost of the earliest purchases. If LIFO has been

EX 9-10 COMPARISON OF INVENTORY VALUATION METHODS

Dalton Company
Comparison of Four Inventory Valuation Methods
Cost of Goods Sold and Ending Inventory

	Unit Cost	Specific Identification	Average Cost*	FIFO	LIFO
Purchased on:					
January 1	$10	200	200	200	200
March 23	12	300	300	300	200 100
July 15	11	500	500	200 300	500
November 6	13	100	100	100	100

Units sold ▭ Units remaining ▭

	Specific Identification	Average Cost*	FIFO	LIFO
Cost of goods sold (700 units):				
	200 × $10 = $ 2,000	700 × $11.27 = $ 7,890†	200 × $10 = $ 2,000	100 × $13 = $ 1,300
	500 × $11 = 5,500		300 × $12 = 3,600	500 × $11 = 5,500
			200 × $11 = 2,200	100 × $12 = 1,200
	$ 7,500	$ 7,890	$ 7,800	$ 8,000
Ending inventory (400 units):				
	300 × $12 = $ 3,600	400 × $11.27 = $ 4,510†	300 × $11 = $ 3,300	200 × $10 = $ 2,000
	100 × $13 = 1,300		100 × $13 = 1,300	200 × $12 = 2,400
	$ 4,900	$ 4,510	$ 4,600	$ 4,400
Total inventory cost:	$12,400	$12,400	$12,400	$12,400

*With the average cost method, no assumption is made about the sale of specific units. The average cost per unit is computed as follows: $12,400/1,100 units = $11.27 per unit, rounded.

†Rounded to the nearest $10.

used for a long time, the disparity between current value of inventory and reported LIFO cost can grow quite large. Use of the average method generally provides inventory values similar to FIFO values, because average costs are heavily influenced by current costs. Specific identification can produce any variety of results depending on which particular units are chosen for shipment.

When the prices paid for merchandise do not fluctuate significantly, alternative inventory methods may provide only minor differences in the financial statements. However, in periods of steadily rising or falling prices, the alternative methods may produce material differences.

Complications with a Perpetual Inventory System

In the Dalton Company example, the simplifying assumption was made that all 700 units were sold on December 31. In essence, this is the assumption made when a periodic inventory system is used. Computation of average cost and LIFO under a perpetual system is complicated because the average cost of units available for sale changes every time a purchase is made, and the identification of the "last-in" units also changes with every purchase. The complications of a perpetual system are illustrated in Exhibit 9-11,

EX 9-11 INVENTORY VALUATION METHODS AND A PERPETUAL INVENTORY SYSTEM

Dalton Company
Complications of a Perpetual Inventory System

	Unit Cost	Average Cost*	FIFO	LIFO
300 units sold on June 30:				
Purchased on:				
January 1	$10	200	200	200
March 23	12	300	100 200	300

Units sold ☐ Units remaining ☐

	Average Cost	FIFO	LIFO
Cost of goods sold (300 units):			
	300 × $11.20 = $3,360	200 × $10 = $2,000	300 × $12 = $3,600
		100 × $12 = 1,200	
	$3,360	$3,200	$3,600
Inventory on June 30 (200 units):			
	200 × $11.20 = $2,240	200 × $12 = $2,400	200 × $10 = $2,000

	Unit Cost	Average Cost†	FIFO	LIFO
400 units sold on December 31:				
Purchased on:				
Inventory on June 30	—	200 × $11.20	200 × $12 200	200 × $10 200
July 15	$11	500	300	300
November 6	13	100	100	100

Units sold ☐ Units remaining ☐

	Average Cost	FIFO	LIFO
Cost of goods sold (400 units):			
	400 × $11.30 = $4,520	200 × $12 = $2,400	100 × $13 = $1,300
		200 × $11 = 2,200	300 × $11 = 3,300
	$4,520	$4,600	$4,600
Ending inventory (400 units):			
	400 × $11.30 = $4,520	300 × $11 = $3,300	200 × $10 = $2,000
		100 × $13 = 1,300	200 × $11 = 2,200
	$4,520	$4,600	$4,200
Total inventory cost:			
Sold on June 30	$ 3,360	$ 3,200	$ 3,600
Sold on December 31.	4,520	4,600	4,600
Total cost of goods sold	$ 7,880	$ 7,800	$ 8,200
Inventory on December 31.	4,520	4,600	4,200
Total inventory cost	$12,400	$12,400	$12,400

*With the average cost method, no assumption is made about the sale of specific units. The average cost per unit is computed as follows:
[(200 x $10) + (300 x $12)]/500 units = $11.20 per unit
†[(200 x $11.20) + (500 x $11) + (100 x $13)]/800 units = $11.30 per unit

in which Dalton Company's cost of goods sold and ending inventory for 2013 are computed assuming that 300 units were sold on June 30 and 400 units were sold on December 31.

Examine Exhibit 9-11 and consider the following observations:

- Even in this more complicated example, the net result of each of the inventory valuation methods is to allocate the total inventory cost of $12,400 between cost of goods sold and ending inventory.
- For FIFO, cost of goods sold and ending inventory are the same whether a periodic system (all sales assumed to occur at year-end) or a perpetual system (sales occur throughout the year) is used. Compare Exhibits 9-10 and 9-11. This is because no matter when in the year the sales are assumed to occur, the oldest units (first in) are always the same ones.
- Because the newest units (last in) as of June 30 are not the same as the newest units on December 31, applying LIFO on a perpetual basis gives a different cost of goods sold and ending inventory than if a periodic system is used.
- Similarly, the average cost of units in inventory on June 30 ($11.20) is not the same as the average cost of all units purchased for the year ($11.27). Thus, applying average cost on a perpetual and a periodic basis yields different results.

Because of the unnecessary complications of perpetual LIFO and perpetual average cost, many businesses that use average cost or LIFO for financial reporting use a simple FIFO assumption in the maintenance of their day-to-day perpetual inventory records. These perpetual FIFO records are then converted to periodic average cost or LIFO for the financial reports.

More About LIFO

6 **Explain how LIFO inventory layers are created, and describe the significance of the LIFO reserve.**

WHY **Over the course of several years, the creation of LIFO layers can result in a substantial difference between the current market value of inventory and the reported LIFO cost of the inventory. Accordingly, it is extremely important to understand all of the financial statement implications for a company using the seemingly innocent LIFO inventory valuation assumption.**

HOW **The LIFO assumption results in "layers" of inventory being created in each year in which purchases exceed sales. In an inflationary period, the difference between the old LIFO layer costs and the current cost of inventory is called the LIFO reserve and can be thought of as an accumulated inventory holding gain. When a LIFO layer is liquidated, the associated inventory holding gain acts to artificially reduce reported cost of goods sold for the period.**

In the simple Dalton Company example of the previous section, the LIFO calculations did not seem any more difficult than the calculations using the other three methods. In a more involved example, the complexities of LIFO become apparent. In this section, a multiyear example is used to illustrate LIFO layers and LIFO liquidation. The advantages of using LIFO pools and dollar-value LIFO to reduce the recordkeeping burden associated with LIFO are illustrated later in the chapter.

LIFO Layers

The following data are for Ryanes Company for the first three years of its existence:

	2010	2011	2012
Purchases	120 units @ $ 5	150 units @ $10	160 units @ $15
Sales	100 units @ $10	120 units @ $15	120 units @ $20

! CAUTION

Pay close attention to this part of the chapter. You may think you understand LIFO, but until you work through the wrinkles and quirks presented here, you don't.

At the end of 2010, 20 units with a total cost of $100 (20 units × $5 per unit) remain in ending inventory. Are these units sold in 2011? If a FIFO assumption is made, the answer is yes. Under FIFO, the 120 units sold in 2011 are the oldest available units: the 20 units left over from 2010 plus 100 units purchased in 2011. However, if a LIFO assumption is made, the 20 units left over at the end of 2010 are not sold in 2011. Instead, the newest units are sold, and those are 120 of the units purchased in 2011. Using LIFO, cost of goods sold and ending inventory for each of the three years are as follows:

	2010		2011		2012	
LIFO cost of goods sold	100 × $5 = $500		120 × $10 = $1,200		120 × $15 = $1,800	
Ending inventory:						
Year units purchased						
2010	20 × $5 =	$100	20 × $5 =	$ 100	20 × $5 =	$ 100
2011			30 × $10 =	300	30 × $10 =	300
2012					40 × $15 =	600
Ending inventory	20 units	$100	50 units	$ 400	90 units	$1,000

Notice that each year in which the number of units purchased exceeds the number of units sold, a new LIFO layer is created in ending inventory. As long as inventory continues to grow, a new LIFO layer is created each year and the old LIFO layers remain untouched.

The creation of LIFO layers illustrates one of the drawbacks of LIFO in that after a few years, the LIFO assumption results in ending inventory containing old inventory at old prices. In the Ryanes example, 2012 ending inventory is assumed to contain inventory purchased back in 2010. And, because inventory costs have increased during the period, the $1,000 amount reported for 2012 ending inventory does not represent the current value of the 90 units of inventory. For example, if FIFO were used, the 90 units in 2012 ending inventory would be valued using the 2012 purchase price of $15 per unit, giving them a value of $1,350 (90 units × $15 per unit). The difference between the LIFO ending inventory amount and the amount obtained using another inventory valuation method (like FIFO or average cost) is called the *LIFO reserve*. In this example, the LIFO reserve is $350 ($1,350 FIFO ending inventory – $1,000 LIFO ending inventory).

EX 9-12 DUPONT'S LIFO RESERVE NOTE

9. Inventories
December 31

	2009	2008
Finished products	$2,893	$3,156
Semifinished products	2,231	2,234
Raw materials, stores and supplies	872	1,199
Total	$5,996	$6,589
Adjustment of inventories to a LIFO basis	(616)	(908)
	$5,380	$5,681

Inventory values, before LIFO adjustment, are generally determined by the average cost method, which approximates current cost. Inventories, excluding seeds and stores and supplies, are valued under the LIFO method and comprised 76 percent and 79 percent of consolidated inventories before LIFO adjustment for the periods ended December 31, 2009 and 2008, respectively.

Exhibit 9-12 contains the note disclosure of DuPont's LIFO reserve from the company's 2009 annual report. Note that DuPont uses the average cost method for maintaining its accounting records during the year and then adjusts its inventory to the LIFO method for financial reporting purposes.

Many companies that use LIFO report the amount of their LIFO reserve, either as a parenthetical note in the balance sheet or in the notes to the financial statements. The size of the LIFO reserve for several large U.S. companies is given in Exhibit 9-13. These LIFO reserve disclosures can aid financial statement users in comparing companies that use different inventory valuation methods. The disclosures can be used to recalculate LIFO ending inventory and cost of goods sold on a FIFO or average cost basis. To illustrate, the following data can be used to calculate FIFO cost of goods sold for Ryanes for 2012.

STOP&THINK

Refer to the original Ryanes Company data and compute the FIFO cost of goods sold for 2010, 2011, and 2012.

a) 2010 = $500; 2011 = $1,200; 2012 = $1,550
b) 2010 = $100; 2011 = $400; 2012 = $1,550
c) 2010 = $500; 2011 = $1,100; 2012 = $1,550
d) 2010 = $100; 2011 = $1,100; 2012 = $1,550

	2011	2012
LIFO ending inventory	$ 400	$1,000
LIFO reserve	100	350
LIFO cost of goods sold	1,200	1,800

The FIFO calculation can be done as follows:

LIFO		FIFO	
$ 400	Beginning inventory	$ 500	($400 + $100 LIFO reserve)
2,400	+ Purchases	2,400	(160 units × $15; same for LIFO and FIFO)
$2,800	= Cost of goods available	$2,900	
1,000	− Ending inventory	1,350	($1,000 + $350 LIFO reserve)
$1,800	= Cost of goods sold	$1,550	

EX 9-13 SIZE OF LIFO RESERVE FOR SELECTED U.S. COMPANIES—2009

U.S. Companies with Large LIFO Reserves for the Year 2009 (in millions of U.S. dollars)

Company Name	Reported LIFO Inventory	LIFO Reserve
Caterpillar	$6,360	$3,003
Ford Motor	5,450	798
Deere & Co.	2,397	1,367

In this simple example, purchases can be computed from the original data. Alternatively, purchases can be inferred from the beginning inventory, ending inventory, and cost of goods sold amounts. The important insight is that purchases are the same whether LIFO or FIFO is used.

LIFO Liquidation

Continuing the Ryanes Company example, assume purchases and sales for 2013 are as follows:

Purchases	60 units @ $20
Sales	150 units @ $25

Because the number of units purchased does not exceed the number sold, no new LIFO layer is added in 2013. In fact, because 2013 purchases are so low, inventory in the old LIFO layers must be sold. This is called *LIFO liquidation*. Computation of 2013 LIFO cost of goods sold is as follows:

Year Units Purchased		
2013	60 units @ $20	$1,200
2012	40 units @ $15	600
2011	30 units @ $10	300
2010	20 units @ $ 5	100
Total	150 units	$2,200

LIFO liquidation causes old LIFO layer costs to flow through cost of goods sold, sometimes with bizarre results. In this example, if Ryanes had not reduced inventory during 2013, LIFO cost of goods sold would have been $3,000 (150 units × $20 per unit). Thus, the impact of reducing inventory levels and dragging old LIFO layers into cost of goods sold is to reduce reported cost of goods sold by \$800 (\$3,000 – \$2,200). This LIFO liquidation effect would be disclosed in the notes to the financial statements.

Drastic inventory reductions can be caused by work stoppages, a slowdown in business, or financing problems. When a company has used LIFO during a period of rising prices (as illustrated in the Ryanes example), the odd result of an unfortunate inventory reduction is that LIFO liquidation causes cost of goods sold to go down and net income to go up. The potential for this LIFO liquidation effect is one reason given under IFRS for banning the use of LIFO.

John Lund/Marc Romanelli/Blend Images/Jupiter Images

Retail stores must account for interim inventory reductions due to the seasonal fluctuation of inventory levels.

Interim LIFO Liquidation Frequently, a company experiences a decline in inventory at an interim reporting date but fully expects to replenish the inventory by the end of the fiscal year. This would be common, for example, in any business with seasonal fluctuations in inventory levels. For companies using LIFO, temporary interim inventory reductions are not viewed as the liquidation of LIFO layers. To maintain the recorded historical cost of the LIFO layers, a temporary provision account is established and then reversed when the inventory is replenished.[9]

To illustrate the appropriate journal entry, assume that the LIFO liquidation for Ryanes for 2013 had actually occurred at the end of the first quarter of 2013 and that the inventory was expected to be replenished by year-end. The \$800 LIFO liquidation effect would be recorded as follows:

Cost of Goods Sold	800	
Provision for Temporary Decline in LIFO Inventory		800

The provision account represents a liability to replace the inventory at a cost exceeding its recorded LIFO amount. This provision account is recorded only for interim reports; a LIFO liquidation is recorded at the end of the fiscal year whether a year-end inventory decline is temporary or not.

LIFO and Income Taxes

The LIFO inventory method was developed in the United States during the late 1930s as a method of reducing income taxes during periods of rising prices. However, when Congress authorized the use of LIFO for income tax purposes, a unique provision was attached to the law. This provision has become known as the LIFO conformity rule and specifies that only those taxpayers who use LIFO for financial reporting purposes may use it for tax purposes. LIFO is the only accounting method that must be reported the same way for tax and book purposes. In the early years, the LIFO conformity rule was strictly applied, and companies were not permitted to report inventory values using any other method, either in the body of the financial statements or in the attached notes. In 1981, the IRS regulations were relaxed by permitting companies to provide supplemental non-LIFO disclosures

[9] FASB ASC paragraph 270-10-45-6b.

(such as the LIFO reserve disclosures discussed previously) as long as the information is not presented on the face of the income statement.[10]

> **! CAUTION**
>
> LIFO is the exception! In every other case, companies are not required to use the same accounting methods in the financial statements as they use for income tax purposes. Therefore, a financial accounting decision usually has no impact on income taxes payable—LIFO is the exception.

Prior to the relaxation of the LIFO conformity rule, the income tax regulations governed the detailed application of LIFO for financial reporting purposes as well. And in fact, the IRS rules are still very important in determining how companies apply LIFO for financial reporting. However, both the SEC and the AICPA have issued guidelines outlining how proper application of LIFO for financial reporting might differ from the IRS regulations concerning LIFO.[11] The FASB has never addressed the issue of LIFO, deciding that the AICPA and SEC guidelines on the topic are sufficient.

To illustrate how LIFO reduces taxes in times of inflation, refer back to the data for Ryanes Company. For simplicity, assume that cost of goods sold is the only expense and that the tax rate is 40%. Calculation of income taxes using both LIFO and FIFO is given in Exhibit 9-14.

From 2010 through 2012, with prices and inventory levels rising, the use of LIFO saves a total of \$140 in income taxes [(\$280 – \$240) + (\$340 – \$240)]. Because sales, collections, purchases, and payments are all the same whether LIFO or FIFO is used, the only cash flow difference between using LIFO and using FIFO is in cash paid for income taxes. Therefore, by the end of 2012, Ryanes will have additional cash of \$140 (from tax savings) if LIFO is used.

Note also that this cumulative tax savings is exactly equal to the LIFO reserve at the end of 2012 (computed to be \$350 in the previous section) multiplied by the tax rate (\$350 × 0.40 = \$140). Recall that the LIFO reserve represents the difference between the value of FIFO ending inventory and the value of LIFO ending inventory. Another way to think of the LIFO reserve is that it represents an inventory holding gain—an increase in the value of inventory because of price increases. In essence, when FIFO is used, this inventory holding gain becomes taxable income as it occurs, whereas with LIFO the inventory holding gain is not taxed until the inventory is liquidated, which happens in 2013 in this example.

The inventory liquidation in 2013 also illustrates that the use of LIFO for tax purposes results in tax deferral, not tax reduction. But because many companies have a low probability of liquidating their inventories in the foreseeable future, use of LIFO can defer payment of taxes on inventory holding gains for a long time.

LIFO Pools and Dollar-Value LIFO

As a means of simplifying the valuation process and extending its applicability to more items, the IRS developed the technique of establishing LIFO inventory pools of substantially

[10] The IRS LIFO conformity relaxation went so far as to state that, as far as the IRS is concerned, companies that use LIFO for tax purposes can prepare financial statements for external users using FIFO for inventory valuation on the balance sheet provided that LIFO cost of goods sold is reported on the income statement. However, this mismatch between the balance sheet and the income statement would be a violation of U.S. GAAP.

[11] See *Issues Paper*, "Identification and Discussion of Certain Financial Accounting and Reporting Issues Concerning LIFO Inventories" (New York: American Institute of Certified Public Accountants, 1984); and *Staff Accounting Bulletin (SAB) 58* (Topic 5.L.) (Washington, DC: Securities and Exchange Commission, March 1985). See FASB ASC paragraph 330-10-S99-1.

EX 9-14 RYANES EXAMPLE: COMPARISON OF INCOME TAXES USING LIFO AND FIFO

LIFO:

	2012		2013		2014		2015	
Sales	100 @ $10	$1,000	120 @ $15	$1,800	120 @ $20	$2,400	150 @ $25	$3,750
Cost of goods sold	100 @ $5	500	120 @ $10	1,200	120 @ $15	1,800	60 @ $20	
							40 @ $15	
							30 @ $10	
							20 @ $5	2,200
Gross profit		$ 500		$ 600		$ 600		$1,550
Income taxes (40%)		$ 200		$ 240		$ 240		$ 620

FIFO:

	2012		2013		2014		2015	
Sales	100 @ $10	$1,000	120 @ $15	$1,800	120 @ $20	$2,400	150 @ $25	$3,750
Cost of goods sold	100 @ $5	500	20 @ $5		50 @ $10		90 @ $15	
			100 @ $10	1,100	70 @ $15	1,550	60 @ $20	2,550
Gross profit		$ 500		$ 700		$ 850		$1,200
Income taxes (40%)		$ 200		$ 280		$ 340		$ 480

identical goods. The purpose of forming LIFO pools is to simplify the LIFO calculations associated with large numbers of products. The simplification results in an estimate of what cost of goods sold would be if LIFO were applied strictly and laboriously.

Even the grouping of substantially identical items into quantity pools does not produce all the benefits desired from the use of LIFO. To further simplify the recordkeeping associated with LIFO and to eliminate the issues associated with new products replacing old products, the dollar-value LIFO inventory method was developed. Under this method, LIFO layers are determined based on total dollar changes rather than quantity changes. LIFO pools and dollar-value LIFO are discussed in detail in the Expanded Material section of this chapter.

Overall Comparison of FIFO, LIFO, and Average Cost

7 Choose an inventory valuation method based on the trade-offs among income tax effects, bookkeeping costs, and the impact on the financial statements.

WHY When GAAP allows several alternative accounting treatments, the prudent manager must consider all of the effects of an accounting method choice. The choice of an inventory valuation method is especially important because there are potential cash flow effects in addition to the financial statement effects.

HOW There are a variety of advantages and disadvantages to each of the inventory valuation methods. Tax effects, bookkeeping costs, and appropriate revenue/expense matching are a few of the factors that must be considered when selecting an inventory valuation method.

EX 9-15 SUMMARY COMPARISON OF FIFO AND LIFO

	FIFO	LIFO
Income Statement	**Advantage:** • Usually corresponds with the physical flow of goods. **Disadvantages:** • Can cause older costs to be matched with current revenues. • Inventory holding gains and losses are included as part of gross profit.	**Advantages:** • Matches current costs with current revenues. • Excludes inventory holding gains and losses from gross profit. **Disadvantages:** • Usually does not correspond with the physical flow of goods. • Potential LIFO liquidation means old costs in LIFO layers can be drawn into cost of goods sold.
Balance Sheet	**Advantage:** • Ending inventory balance agrees closely with current replacement cost.	**Disadvantage:** • Ending inventory balance is composed of old costs in LIFO layers and can be substantially lower than current replacement cost. This is partially offset by supplemental disclosure.
Income Taxes	**Disadvantage:** • Yields higher taxable income in times of inflation if inventory levels are stable or increasing.	**Advantage:** • Yields lower taxable income in times of inflation if inventory levels are stable or increasing. **Disadvantage:** LIFO liquidation can result in greatly increased tax payments when inventory levels decline.

The chart in Exhibit 9-15 gives a summary comparison of the advantages and disadvantages of FIFO and LIFO. Average cost can be viewed as being somewhere between these two.

So, which inventory valuation method should a company pick? Circumstances differ from firm to firm, and the decision would be based on an analysis of the following four factors:

- Income tax effects
- Bookkeeping costs
- Impact on financial statements
- Industry comparison

Income Tax Effects

If a company has large inventory levels, is experiencing significant inventory cost increases, and does not anticipate reducing inventory levels in the future, LIFO gives substantial cash flow benefits in terms of tax deferral. This is the primary reason for LIFO adoption by most firms. For the many firms with small inventory levels or with flat or decreasing inventory costs, LIFO gives little, if any, tax benefit. Such firms are unlikely to use LIFO.

Bookkeeping Costs

As seen in this chapter, the bookkeeping associated with LIFO is a bit more complicated than with FIFO or average cost. In dollars and cents, a LIFO system costs more to operate. For this reason, LIFO is less common among small firms where any LIFO tax benefits can be swamped by increased bookkeeping costs. However, with improved information technology and with the simplifications of LIFO pools and dollar-value LIFO (discussed in the Expanded Material associated with this chapter), the incremental LIFO bookkeeping costs can be minimized.

Impact on Financial Statements

While LIFO gives tax benefits, it also gives reduced reported income and reduced reported inventory. These negative financial statement effects can harm a company by scaring off stockholders, potential investors, and banks. One way around this is to provide supplemental disclosure to allow users to see what the financial statements would look like if FIFO or average cost were used.

Industry Comparison

Although financial statement users should be sophisticated in their understanding of inventory accounting, they often are not. They ignore supplemental LIFO disclosures and just compare the unadjusted numbers. If other companies in an industry use FIFO, the reported performance of a LIFO company can look poor by comparison.

STOP&THINK

Why wouldn't it be possible to use LIFO for the income statement and FIFO for the balance sheet?

a) The amount of income taxes paid would double.
b) The ending inventory amount and the amount of cost of goods sold would always be equal.
c) Gross profit would always be negative.
d) Without a special adjustment, the balance sheet wouldn't balance.

International Accounting and Inventory Valuation

The International Accounting Standards Board (IASB) has waffled in its opinion about LIFO. In its initial standard on inventory (*IAS 2*), the IASB identified LIFO, along with FIFO, average cost, and something called the base stock method (an extreme form of LIFO), as allowable inventory valuation methods. In 1989, the IASB proposed eliminating the base stock method, and in 1991, it tentatively decided to eliminate both the base stock method and LIFO. In 1992, the IASB decided to officially endorse FIFO and average cost, to kill the base stock method, and to let LIFO live on as a second-class "allowed alternative treatment." Finally, in December 2003 the IASB adopted a revised version of *IAS 2* and did away with LIFO once and for all.

ifrs

Inventory Accounting Changes

When a company changes its method of valuing inventory, the change is accounted for as a change in accounting principle. If the change is to average cost or FIFO, both the beginning and ending inventories can usually be computed on the new basis. Thus, the effect of changing inventory methods can be determined and reported in the financial statements, as explained in Chapter 20. If the change is to LIFO from another method, however, a company's records are generally not complete enough to reconstruct the prior years' inventory layers. Therefore, the base-year layer for the new LIFO inventory is the opening inventory for the year in which LIFO is adopted (also the ending inventory for the year before LIFO is adopted). There is no adjustment to the financial statements to reflect the change to LIFO. However, the impact of the change on income for the current year must be disclosed in a note to the statements. In addition, the note should explain why there is no effect on the financial statements. Required disclosures for a change to LIFO are illustrated in Exhibit 9-16 in a description from the 2001 10-K filing of **Duane Reade**, the

EX 9-16 DUANE READE: DISCLOSURE OF CHANGE TO LIFO METHOD

Accounting Change

During the first quarter of 2002, we plan to adopt a change in accounting method to convert from our current retail dollar based first-in, first-out ("FIFO") method of inventory valuation to an item specific cost based last-in, first-out ("LIFO") method of inventory valuation. This change is expected to result in a separate one-time non-cash after tax charge of approximately $9.0 million to be recorded in the first quarter. In addition, expected 2002 inflation in inventory acquisition costs will likely result in increased charges to cost of goods to be sold during 2002. We estimate that a 1.0% inflation in the annual inventory acquisition costs in 2002 would approximate a $1.2 million reduction in fiscal 2002 net earnings. Adoption of the specific cost LIFO method will result in the recognition of the latest item costs in our reported gross margins, and will make our results more comparable to other major retailers in our industry. In an inflationary period, the LIFO method also has the added favorable impact of increasing cash flow through reduced income taxes.

largest drugstore chain in New York City. Note the company's forthright description of the income tax benefits of using LIFO when inventory costs are rising.

When inventories are a material item, a change in the inventory method by a company may impair comparability of that company's financial statements with prior years' statements and with the financial statements of other entities. Such changes require careful consideration and should be made only when management can clearly demonstrate the preferability of the alternative method.[12]

Inventory Valuation at Other than Cost

8 Apply the lower-of-cost-or-market (LCM) rule to reflect declines in the market value of inventory.

WHY **The lower-of-cost-or-market (LCM) rule reflects the conservative tradition underlying accounting. Conservatism in this context means that we quickly write down inventory when it has declined in value, but we do not recognize inventory holding gains when inventory increases in value.**

HOW **To use the lower-of-cost-or-market rule, the historical cost of the ending inventory is compared with the inventory's market value. In this context, "market value" is defined as the inventory's replacement cost, constrained by a ceiling and a floor. If market value is less than historical cost, ending inventory is written down to the market value.**

The basic procedures for allocating total cost of goods available for sale between ending inventory and cost of goods sold were explained in the previous sections. In some cases, these cost allocation procedures result in inventory cost that exceeds the current market value of the inventory. The following section discusses how to determine when inventory should be "written down" to reflect a decline in its market value. The section concludes with a discussion of inventory valuation when inventory is acquired in a nonmarket transaction (e.g., the return of defective merchandise) and a value must be assigned.

[12] FASB ASC paragraph 250-10-45-12.

Lower of Cost or Market

One of the traditional concepts of accounting is conservatism, sometimes summarized as "when in doubt, recognize all unrealized losses, but don't recognize any unrealized gains." When applied to asset valuation, conservatism results in the rule of lower of cost or market (LCM), meaning that assets are recorded at the lower of their cost or their market value.[13] LCM has the effect of recognizing unrealized decreases in the value of assets but not unrealized increases.[14]

In applying the lower-of-cost-or-market rule, the cost of the ending inventory, as determined under an appropriate cost allocation method, is compared with market value at the end of the period. If market is less than cost, an adjusting entry is made to record the loss and restate ending inventory at the lower value.[15]

What Is "Market"? The term market in "lower of cost or market" is interpreted as meaning replacement cost, with potential adjustments for a ceiling and a floor value. Replacement cost, sometimes referred to as entry cost, includes the purchase price of the product or raw materials plus all other costs incurred in the acquisition or manufacture of goods. Replacement cost is frequently a good measure of the amount of future economic benefit embodied in inventory because declines in acquisition costs (entry cost) usually indicate a decline in selling prices (exit value). However, selling prices do not always respond immediately and in proportion to changes in replacement costs. Accordingly, the following ceiling and floor constraints are placed on the use of replacement cost as the measure of the market value of inventory:[16]

- Ceiling. The market value of inventory is not greater than the net realizable value of the inventory. Net realizable value (NRV) is equal to the estimated selling price of the inventory minus any normal selling costs. The reasoning behind this ceiling is that the market value of inventory could never reasonably be considered to be more than the net amount that can be received upon sale of the inventory.
- Floor. The market value of the inventory is not less than net realizable value minus a normal profit margin. If inventory is recorded below this floor amount, then the inventory can be sold in the future netting a return that is more than the normal profit margin.

In summary, market value of inventory is never less than the floor value, is never more than the ceiling value, and is equal to replacement cost when replacement cost is between the floor and the ceiling. These relationships are summarized in Exhibit 9-17.

FYI

A good way to apply the ceiling and floor rules is to remember that the market value will always be the middle value of these three—replacement cost and ceiling and floor amounts.

[13] Historically, investment securities, inventory, and property, plant, and equipment were recorded at the lower of cost or market. With the adoption of FASB pre-Codification *Statement No. 115* in 1993, most investment securities are now recorded at their current market value whether that amount is lower or higher than cost. See FASB ASC Topic 320 (Investments—Debt and Equity Securities).

[14] For a time, the FASB required firms to make supplemental disclosure of the replacement cost of inventory. This requirement (FASB pre-Codification *Statement No. 33*) was a response to the high inflation of the late 1970s that frequently caused reported historical inventory cost to be much lower than current replacement cost. When inflation abated, interest in this supplemental disclosure waned and *Statement No. 33* was repealed.

[15] No adjustment to LIFO cost is permitted for tax purposes. Application of LCM to LIFO inventories for financial reporting purposes does not violate the "LIFO conformity" rule if IRS approval is obtained.

[16] FASB ASC Master Glossary: "Market."

EX 9-17 MARKET VALUE EQUALS REPLACEMENT COST, CONSTRAINED BY THE CEILING AND THE FLOOR

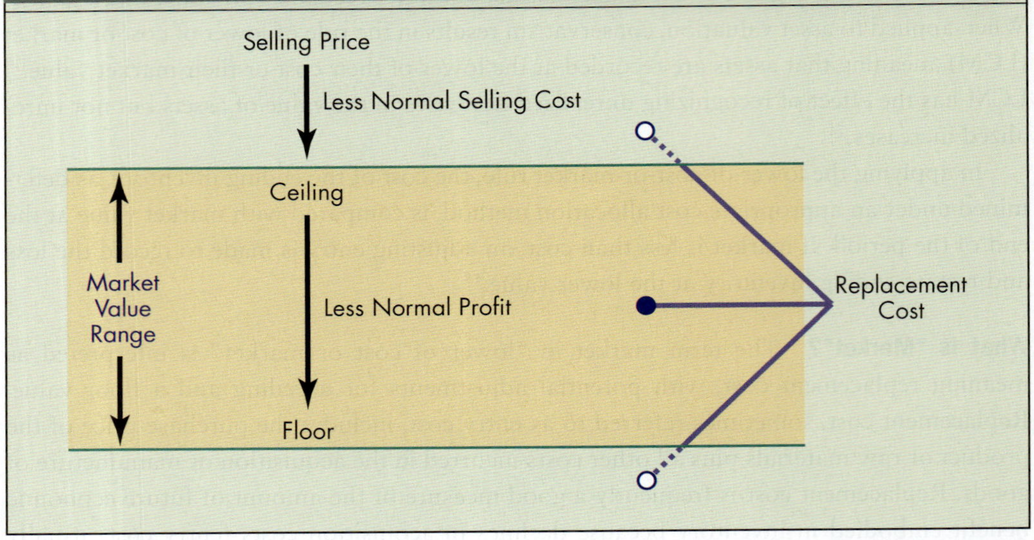

Applying the Lower-of-Cost-or-Market Method Application of the LCM rule to determine the appropriate inventory valuation may be summarized in the following steps:

1. Define pertinent values: historical cost, floor (NRV—normal profit), replacement cost, ceiling (NRV).
2. Determine "market" (replacement cost as constrained by ceiling and floor limits).
3. Compare cost with market (as defined in step 2 above), and select the lower amount.

To illustrate these steps, assume that Fezzig Company sells six products identified with the letters A through F. For each product, the selling price per unit is $1.00, selling expenses are $0.20 per unit, and the normal profit is 25% of sales, or $0.25 per unit. The historical cost and the current replacement cost are different for each product. The lower-of-cost-or-market valuation for each product is shown below with the appropriate "market" value highlighted.

Item	Historical Cost	Floor	Replacement Cost	Ceiling	Market	Lower of Cost or Market
A	$0.65	$0.55	$0.70	$0.80	$0.70	$0.65
B	0.65	0.55	0.60	0.80	0.60	0.60
C	0.65	0.55	0.50	0.80	0.55	0.55
D	0.50	0.55	0.45	0.80	0.55	0.50
E	0.75	0.55	0.85	0.80	0.80	0.75
F	0.90	0.55	1.00	0.80	0.80	0.80

A: Market is equal to replacement cost; historical cost is less than market.
B: Market is equal to replacement cost; market is less than historical cost.
C: Market is equal to the floor; market is less than historical cost.
D: Market is equal to the floor; replacement and historical costs are less than market.
E: Market is equal to the ceiling; historical cost is less than market.
F: Market is equal to the ceiling; market is less than historical and replacement costs.

For products A and B, the replacement cost is between the floor and the ceiling, so the market value is the replacement cost. For products C and D, replacement cost is below the floor, so the market value is the floor value. For products E and F, replacement cost is greater than the ceiling, so the market value is the ceiling value.

CAUTION

Don't get carried away—remember that an actual adjusting entry is made only if market value is less than historical cost. For products A, D, and E, no LCM adjustment is needed.

To see the wisdom in using the floor and ceiling values in calculating market value, consider products C and F. Without the floor, the market value for product C would be $0.50 and the inventory would be written down from the cost of $0.65 to the market value of $0.50. But this $0.50 value is too low because it would result in extra profits being recorded next period when the inventory is sold. For example, selling price of $1.00 minus selling costs of $0.20 minus recorded inventory amount of $0.50 leaves a reported profit of $0.30 per unit, whereas the normal profit is just $0.25 per unit. Without the floor, product C would be written down too much this period, resulting in unusually high profits next period.

For product F, without the ceiling value the market value would be the $1.00 replacement cost. Because this exceeds the cost of $0.90, the inventory would continue to be recorded at cost. However, the ceiling amount suggests that the maximum that can be expected to be realized upon sale of units of product F is the net realizable value of $0.80. In this case, the ceiling amount ensures that the inventory cost is written down so that reported inventory does not exceed the amount expected to be realized upon sale of the inventory.

The lower-of-cost-or-market method may be applied to each inventory item, to the major classes or categories of inventory items, or to the inventory as a whole. Application of LCM to the individual inventory items will result in the lower inventory value because increases in the market value of some inventory items are not allowed to offset decreases in the value of other items.[17]

To illustrate the difference in valuation applications, assume that Fezzig Company's inventory includes 1,000 units each of products A through F. The table on page 9-36 illustrates how the lower-of-cost-or-market valuation of Fezzig's inventory would differ, depending on whether the LCM rule is applied individually to each product or to the inventory as a whole.

If the individual product method is used, the lower-of-cost-or-market rule is applied separately to products A through F, resulting in a total LCM inventory valuation of $3,850. If the LCM rule is applied to the inventory as a whole, the aggregate market value of $4,000 is compared to the aggregate cost of $4,100, and the inventory is recorded at $4,000.

[17] The IRS requires application of the LCM rule to individual products. To reduce the burden of keeping two sets of inventory records, companies frequently use this same method for financial reporting purposes. Many disputes have arisen between taxpayers and the IRS through the years as to what constitutes a recognizable decline in inventory value. An important tax case in this area was settled by the U.S. Supreme Court in 1979. The taxpayer, **Thor Power Tool Co.**, had followed the practice of writing down the value of spare parts inventories that were being held to cover future warranty requirements. Although the sales prices did not decline, the probability of the parts being sold, and thus their net realizable value, decreased as time passed. The write-down to reflect the current decline in value is consistent with the accounting principle of recognizing declines in value as they occur. The Supreme Court, however, ruled that for tax purposes the reduction must await the actual decline in the sales price for the parts in question.

Product	Number of Units	Total Cost	Total Market	Total LCM
A	1,000	$ 650	$ 700	$ 650
B	1,000	650	600	600
C	1,000	650	550	550
D	1,000	500	550	500
E	1,000	750	800	750
F	1,000	900	800	800
	6,000	$4,100	$4,000	$3,850

The journal entry to record the write-down of the inventory on an individual item basis is usually made as follows:

Loss from Decline in Value of Inventory	250	
Inventory		250
($4,100 – $3,850)		

The loss on the decline in market value may be shown as a separate item on the income statement, or included as part of cost of goods sold. Separate reporting of the loss has the advantage of providing readers with increased information to forecast operations and cash flows. As an example, **Cisco Systems** recognized an inventory write-down of $2.77 billion in 2001 "due to a sudden and significant decrease in demand for the Company's products."[18]

Once an individual item is reduced to a lower market price, the new market price is considered to be the item's cost for future inventory valuations; cost reductions once made are not restored. Thus, inventory records must be adjusted to reflect the new values.

Rather than reducing the inventory directly, the inventory account can be maintained at cost, and an allowance for inventory decline can be used to record the decline in value. This method would generally be used when inventory is valued on a category or entire inventory basis. The entry to record the write-down on an entire inventory basis and using an allowance account would be as follows:

Loss from Decline in Value of Inventory	100	
Allowance for Decline in Value of Inventory		100
($4,100 – $4,000)		

The allowance account would be reported as an offset to the inventory account on the balance sheet. The question then arises of what to do with this allowance in subsequent years. Assume that in the subsequent year, Fezzig Company sells its entire existing inventory of products A through F. The allowance is no longer needed because the inventory to which the allowance applied has been sold. The adjusting entry necessary in the subsequent year is as follows:

Allowance for Decline in Value of Inventory	100	
Cost of Goods Sold		100

[18] According to FASB ASC paragraph 420-10-S99-3, inventory write-downs such as that made by Cisco should be classified as an increase in cost of goods sold.

The credit is entered appropriately to Cost of Goods Sold, rather than to a gain, for the following reasons:

- The recorded cost of the old inventory sold during the year, $4,100, is an overstatement of the carrying amount of the inventory. The net carrying amount is only $4,000 ($4,100 cost – $100 allowance), and Cost of Goods Sold has been overstated by the amount of the allowance.
- Recording a gain gives the misleading impression that recoveries of inventory market values are recognized as gains. On the contrary, once a particular inventory item or group of items is written down, no subsequent market value increases for those items are recognized.

The inventory at the end of the subsequent year is then evaluated to determine whether the establishment of a new Allowance for Decline in Value of Inventory is needed.[19]

CAUTION

No gains are recorded on inventory market value recoveries.

FASB CODIFICATION

The Issue: You come from the small town of Grantsville. Historically, many people in your community have been farmers. You are combining your love of accounting with your love of the farm and are doing some bookkeeping for a hometown farmer. The farmer has been asked by the local bank to prepare a balance sheet and income statement in connection with the farmer's application for a loan to finance an expansion of cultivated land for next year's planting season. The balance sheet will be dated September 30. The farmer has harvested all of her crop but has not yet sold it. The farmer is uncertain about how to report this harvested crop inventory in the balance sheet.

The Question: At what amount should harvested crop inventory be reported in the balance sheet?

Searching the Codification: If you look under the "Inventory" topic (Topic 330) in the "Assets" collection of topics in the Codification, you will see that there is an entire special topic (905) addressing agricultural accounting issues. You are interested in the "subsequent measurement" of harvested crops.

The Answer: The accounting treatment for harvested crop inventory is discussed on page 9-64.

Assigned Inventory Value: The Case of Returned Inventory

In some cases, the ceiling and floor values discussed provide guidance in assigning an appropriate inventory value when inventory cost is difficult to determine. As an illustration, consider the following data on defective inventory returned to Inigo Company by angry customers.

- Number of defective units returned: 1,000
- Selling price of normal units: $5
- Cost of normal units: $3
- Normal gross profit percentage: ($5 – $3)/$5 = 40%

[19] The two adjusting entries eliminating the allowance from the previous year and creating a new allowance can be combined into one entry that merely changes the net balance in the allowance account. However, making the two entries separately greatly clarifies the reasoning underlying the entries.

- Scrap selling price of units returned as defective: $2
- For simplicity, assume that there are no extra expenses associated with the scrap sale of units that have been returned as defective.

In this case, it is clearly wrong to record the defective inventory units at their historical cost of $3 per unit because they can be sold for only $2 per unit. No replacement cost number can be used to determine the appropriate lower-of-cost-or-market write-down because no supplier will quote a price on entire batches of defective units. Thus, the appropriate inventory valuation is somewhere between the ceiling and the floor:

Ceiling: $2 selling price – $0 selling costs = $2 net realizable value

Floor: $2 net realizable value – $0.80 normal gross profit ($2 × 40%) = $1.20

If the inventory is written down to the ceiling value of $2, the loss on the write-down is $1,000 [($3 – $2) × 1,000 units]. If the inventory is written down to the floor value, the write-down loss is $1,800 [($3 – $1.20) × 1,000 units]. The write-down loss, and profit on subsequent scrap sale of defective units, is summarized as follows:

	Write-Down to Ceiling		Write-Down to Floor	
Loss on write-down		$(1,000)		$(1,800)
Scrap sales of defective units	$2,000		$2,000	
Cost of goods sold	2,000		1,200	
Gross profit on scrap sales		0		800
Total loss on defective units		$(1,000)		$(1,000)

In the absence of a reliable replacement cost number, should the returned inventory be recorded at the ceiling value, the floor value, or somewhere in between? Or does it make any difference? You might contend that it makes no difference because the total loss on defective units is $1,000 in all cases. However, if you are the manager in charge of scrap sales and your annual bonus is based on the profit generated by your department, which inventory valuation number would you prefer? You would prefer the floor value because this lowers your cost of goods sold and allows your department to show a profit. The general point of the illustration is this: When there is some leeway in the assigning of inventory values, the assigned value can be very important in determining how profits and losses associated with the inventory are allocated among different reporting units within the business.

In summary, the absence of a reliable measure of entry values (historical cost or replacement cost) means that an inventory value must be assigned based on exit values (net realizable value and normal selling profit). The decision of what inventory value to choose within the floor-to-ceiling interval can be an interesting exercise in intracompany bargaining as managers try to set the inventory values to maximize the reported profits in their departments and push losses off to other departments. This is the same issue that arises in the context of transfer pricing (assigning inventory values to goods "sold" from one division of a company to another) and is discussed at length in courses on cost accounting.[20]

FYI

These same issues arise when assigning values to used items given in trade for new items. For example, how does a car dealer value the used car inventory accepted in trade for new cars?

Accounting for Declines in Inventory Values: *IAS 2*

The inventory write-down rule under *IAS 2* can best be labeled "lower of cost or net realizable value." This net realizable value is the same as described earlier: estimated selling price of the inventory minus any normal selling costs. Under *IAS 2,* if the selling price of inventory has declined enough (or if the normal selling costs have increased enough) that the cost of the inventory cannot be recovered, then the inventory is written down to the net realizable value. This approach is much easier to apply than the U.S. GAAP "lower-of-cost-or-market" rule—there is no ceiling, no floor, and no replacement cost. Instead, the *IAS 2* rule involves a simple comparison between cost and net realizable value. The write-down journal entry is the same as illustrated earlier.

One additional difference in the provisions of *IAS 2* is that if the depressed selling price of written-down inventory subsequently recovers, the inventory write-down loss is reversed. This reversal would probably be reported as a decrease in cost of goods sold resulting in an increase in gross profit.

Gross Profit Method

9 Use the gross profit method to estimate ending inventory.

WHY The gross profit method allows ending inventory and cost of goods sold to be approximated without performing an actual physical count.

HOW Using historical information, a gross profit percentage is estimated and applied to the current period's sales figure to obtain an estimate of cost of goods sold. This estimated cost of goods sold is subtracted from cost of goods available for sale to compute an estimate of ending inventory.

Inventory estimation techniques are used to generate inventory values when a physical inventory count is not practical and to provide an independent check of the validity of the inventory figures generated by the accounting system. The simplest inventory estimation technique is the gross profit method. The gross profit method is based on the observation that the relationship between sales and cost of goods sold is usually fairly stable. The gross profit percentage [(Sales – Cost of goods sold)/Sales] is applied to sales to estimate cost of goods sold. This cost of goods sold estimate is subtracted from the cost of goods available for sale to arrive at an estimated inventory balance.

To be useful, the gross profit percentage used must be a reliable measure of current experience. In developing a reliable rate, reference is made to past rates, and these are adjusted for changes in current circumstances. For example, the historical gross profit percentage would be adjusted if the pricing strategy has changed (e.g., because of increased competition), if the sales mix has changed, or if a different inventory valuation method has been adopted (e.g., a switch from FIFO to LIFO).

To illustrate the application of the gross profit method, consider the following information for Rugen Company.

[20] As illustrated, assigned inventory values can determine where within a company profits and losses are reported. Imagine how important this issue is in the context of tax reporting for multinational companies. Assigned inventory values determine whether a taxable profit is reported (and taxed) in a foreign subsidiary or in the U.S. parent company.

Beginning inventory, January 1	$25,000
Sales, January 1–January 31	50,000
Purchases, January 1–January 31	40,000
Historical gross profit percentages:	
Last year	40%
Two years ago	37%
Three years ago	42%

Rugen wishes to prepare financial statements as of January 31 and wants to use an estimate of ending inventory rather than performing a physical inventory count. Last year's gross profit percentage of 40% is considered to be a good estimate of the current gross profit percentage.

The inventory estimate is a 2-step process: An assumed gross profit percentage is used to determine estimated gross profit, which then allows computation of estimated cost of goods sold. That number is then used to estimate ending inventory.

Sales (actual)	$50,000	100%
Cost of goods sold (estimate)	30,000	60%
Gross profit (estimate)	$20,000	40%
Beginning inventory (actual)		$25,000
+ Purchases (actual)		40,000
= Cost of goods available for sale (actual)		$65,000
− Ending inventory (estimate)		35,000
= Cost of goods sold (estimate)		$30,000

This ending inventory estimate can now be used in the January 31 financial statements or can be compared to perpetual inventory records if they exist, or can be used as the basis of an insurance reimbursement if the inventory on January 31 is destroyed in an accident. This 2-step process is illustrated in Exhibit 9-18.

Assume that Rugen does a physical inventory count indicating that January 31 inventory is $32,000, compared to the $35,000 estimate computed above. Is this a reasonable difference, or is there reason for further investigation? One way to make this determination is to see what range of ending inventory estimates is possible given the differences observed in historical gross profit percentages. These calculations are as follows.

	Gross Profit Percentage		
	40%	**37%**	**42%**
Sales (actual)	$50,000	$50,000	$50,000
Cost of goods sold (estimate)	30,000	31,500	29,000
Gross profit (estimate)	$20,000	$18,500	$21,000
Beginning inventory (actual)	$25,000	$25,000	$25,000
+ Purchases (actual)	40,000	40,000	40,000
= Cost of goods available for sale (actual)	$65,000	$65,000	$65,000
− Ending inventory (estimate)	35,000	33,500	36,000
+ Cost of goods sold (estimate)	$30,000	$31,500	$29,000

EX 9-18 THE GROSS PROFIT METHOD

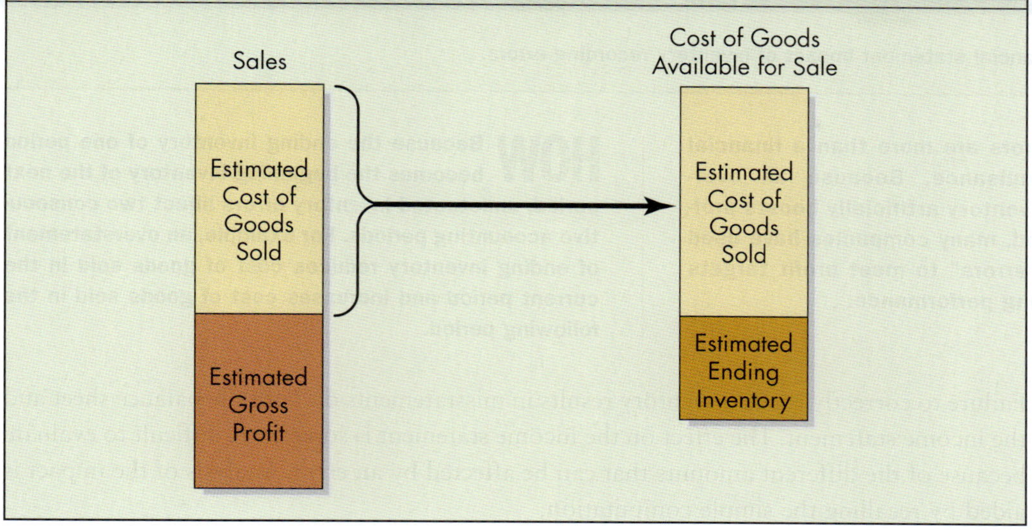

The range of estimates for January 31 inventory is from $33,500 to $36,000. The $32,000 value derived from the physical count is outside this range. Possible explanations are:

- This year's gross profit percentage is outside the historically observed range, suggesting that there has been a significant change in pricing strategy or product mix.
- Inventory shrinkage has occurred.
- Sales have been underreported. The IRS sometimes uses the gross profit method to detect underreporting of sales to avoid income taxes.

Sometimes the hardest part of applying the gross profit method is deciphering language about the relationship between sales and cost of goods sold. In the example just completed, the sales/cost of goods sold relationship was summarized by saying that the gross profit percentage is 40%. The same relationship could be described in at least two other ways:

1. Sales are made at a markup of 40% of the selling price.
2. Sales are made at a markup of 66⅔% of cost. (Gross profit/Cost = 66⅔%)

Be careful.

Like the gross profit method, the retail inventory method can be used to generate a reliable estimate of inventory position whenever desired. This method, like the gross profit method, permits the estimation of an inventory amount without the time and expense of taking a physical inventory or maintaining detailed perpetual inventory records. The retail inventory method is more flexible than the gross profit method in that it allows estimates to be based on FIFO, LIFO, or average cost assumptions, and it even permits estimation of lower-of-cost-or-market values. The retail inventory method is covered in detail in the Expanded Material associated with this chapter.

STOP&THINK

Assume that the actual amount of inventory is much lower than the estimated amount. Which ONE of the following is NOT a possible explanation?

a) The estimation process is flawed.
b) The actual amount of purchases was greater than the reported amount of purchases.
c) The missing inventory was lost or stolen.
d) The missing inventory was sold, but the sales were not reported.

Effects of Errors in Recording Inventory

10 **Determine the financial statement impact of inventory recording errors.**

WHY **Inventory errors are more than a financial statement nuisance. Because an overstatement of ending inventory artificially boosts profits in the current period, many companies have used intentional inventory "errors" to meet profit targets or to hide poor operating performance.**

HOW **Because the ending inventory of one period becomes the beginning inventory of the next period, undetected inventory errors affect two consecutive accounting periods. For example, an overstatement of ending inventory reduces cost of goods sold in the current period and increases cost of goods sold in the following period.**

Failure to correctly report inventory results in misstatements on both the balance sheet and the income statement. The effect on the income statement is sometimes difficult to evaluate because of the different amounts that can be affected by an error. Analysis of the impact is aided by recalling the simple computation:

Beginning inventory
+ Purchases
= Goods available for sale
− Ending inventory
= Cost of goods sold

For example, an overstatement of the beginning inventory will result in an overstatement of goods available for sale and cost of goods sold. Because the cost of goods sold is deducted from sales to determine the gross profit, the overstated cost of goods sold results in an understated gross profit and finally an understated net income.

FYI

Because inventory errors reverse themselves in the following year, persons using inventory fraud to overstate income must create larger and larger amounts of fictitious inventory in succeeding years to maintain the bogus income growth. This escalation is often what causes the fraud to be detected.

Sometimes an error may affect two of the amounts in such a way that they offset each other. For example, if a purchase in transit is neither recorded as a purchase nor included in the ending inventory, the understatement of purchases results in an understatement of goods available for sale; however, the understatement of ending inventory subtracted from goods available for sale offsets the error and creates a correct cost of goods sold, gross profit, and net income. Inventory and accounts payable, however, will be understated on the balance sheet.[21]

Because the ending inventory of one period becomes the beginning inventory of the next period, undetected inventory errors affect two accounting periods. If left undetected, the errors will offset each other under a FIFO or average method. Errors in LIFO layers, however, may perpetuate themselves until the layers are eliminated.

It is unwise to try to memorize the impact a particular type of inventory error has on the financial statements. It is preferable to analyze each situation. Analysis of the following three typical inventory errors provides further practice.

[21] This analysis is strictly true only if the FIFO inventory valuation method is used. With both LIFO and average cost, end-of-period purchases impact the calculation of cost of goods sold.

1. Overstatement of ending inventory through an improper physical count
2. Understatement of ending inventory through an improper physical count
3. Understatement of ending inventory through delay in recording a purchase until the following year.

The impact of the three errors on the income statement and the balance sheet in the year of the error and the following year is summarized in Exhibit 9-19.

Error 1, overstatement of ending inventory, sometimes results when a company fraudulently manipulates its inventory count. As seen in Exhibit 9-19, this ending inventory overstatement reduces cost of goods sold and increases net income in the year of the error. A counterbalancing reduction in net income occurs in the following year because beginning inventory is overstated.

STOP&THINK

Why might a manager risk his or her reputation by fraudulently overstating inventory in light of the fact that the resulting income increase is completely counterbalanced in the following year?

a) The manager is confident that operating profits next year will be strong enough to cover the impact of the counterbalancing inventory error.
b) The manager knows that not all inventory errors are counterbalancing.
c) The manager knows that inventory errors do not have any impact on reported operating profit.

Error 2, understatement of ending inventory, is the opposite of Error 1 and results in a reduction in net income in the error year. As with Error 1, a counterbalancing error occurs in the following year.

EX 9-19 ANALYSIS OF INVENTORY ERRORS

	#1 Overstatement of Ending Inventory		#2 Understatement of Ending Inventory		#3 Delay Recording Purchase	
	Error Year	**Next Year**	**Error Year**	**Next Year**	**Error Year**	**Next Year**
Beginning inventory	OK	over*	OK	under	OK	under
+ Purchases	OK	OK	OK	OK	under	over
= Goods available for sale	OK	over	OK	under	under	OK
− Ending inventory	over	OK	under	OK	under	OK
= Cost of goods sold	under	over	over	under	OK	OK
Income Statement:						
Cost of goods sold	under	over	over	under	OK	OK
Net income	over	under	under	over	OK	OK
Balance Sheet:						
Inventory	over	OK	under	OK	under	OK
Payables	OK	OK	OK	OK	under	OK
Retained earnings	over	OK	under	OK	OK	OK

*(Over) indicates overstatement, (under) indicates understatement, and (OK) indicates no effect.

Error 3, delay recording purchase or understatement of ending inventory and purchases, commonly occurs when a company fails to consider end-of-period goods in transit as part of purchases and inventory. As seen in Exhibit 9-19, this error has no impact on net income but does cause inventory and payables to be understated in the year of the error.

The correcting entry for each of these errors depends on when the error is discovered. If it is discovered in the current year, adjustments can be made to current accounts and the reported net income and balance sheet amounts will be correct. If the error is not discovered until the subsequent period, the correcting entry qualifies as a prior-period adjustment if the net income of the prior period was misstated. The error to a prior year's income is corrected through Retained Earnings. To illustrate these entries, assume that an incorrect physical count has resulted in an overstatement of ending inventory by $1,000 (Error 1). The correcting entry required, depending on when the error is discovered, would be as follows:

Error discovered in current year:		
Cost of Goods Sold	1,000	
Inventory		1,000
Error discovered in subsequent year:		
Retained Earnings	1,000	
Inventory		1,000

Using Inventory Information for Financial Analysis

11 **Analyze inventory using financial ratios, and properly compare ratios of different firms after adjusting for differences in inventory valuation methods.**

WHY **Care must be used in interpreting the results of inventory-related ratio analysis because the use of different inventory methods can make comparisons difficult.**

HOW **The inventory turnover ratio and the number of days' sales in inventory reflect the size of the inventory relative to the amount of inventory being sold. Interpretation of these ratios yields insight into the appropriateness of a company's inventory management practices.**

The inventory balances contained in the financial statements are often used to measure how efficiently the company is utilizing its inventory. The amount of inventory carried frequently relates closely to sales volume. The inventory position and the appropriateness of its size may be evaluated by computing the inventory turnover. The inventory turnover is measured by dividing cost of goods sold by average inventory [(beginning balance + ending balance) ÷ 2].

Consider the financial information relating to inventories for **Deere & Co.** provided below.

Deere & Co.
Major Classes of Inventories
(Dollars in millions)

	2009	2008
Raw materials and supplies	$ 940	$ 1,170
Work-in-process	387	519
Finished machines and parts	2,437	2,677
Total FIFO value	$ 3,764	$ 4,366
Adjustment to LIFO value	1,367	1,324
Inventories	$ 2,397	$ 3,042
Cost of sales	$16,255	$19,575

The inventory turnover rate for Deere & Co. would be computed as follows:

$$\frac{\text{Cost of goods sold}}{\text{Average inventory*}} = \frac{\$16{,}255}{\$2{,}719.5} = 5.98 \text{ times}$$

Calculation:
* 2009: ($2,397 + $3,042)/2 = $2,719.5

Inventory turnover of 5.98 times means that if Deere & Co. were to completely use up all of its inventory, and then instantaneously replace it, this process would be repeated 5.98 times during the year. The higher the inventory turnover number, the faster a company is using its inventory.

Using total inventory, this example has been simplified. If separate turnovers were computed for raw materials, work in process, and finished goods, the appropriate numerators for each computation would be raw materials used in production, cost of goods manufactured, and cost of goods sold, respectively. Note that total sales is never appropriate to use in inventory turnover calculations because sales numbers are stated in terms of selling prices, whereas inventory is stated in terms of acquisition or production cost. For example, in a retail setting, sales is a retail number and inventory is a wholesale number. Mixing them in the same calculation seriously impairs the interpretation of the inventory turnover ratio.[22]

Deere & Co. uses LIFO. From the disclosure about Deere's LIFO reserve, FIFO values for inventory and cost of goods sold can be calculated. If Deere & Co. had used FIFO instead of LIFO, inventory turnover for 2009 would have been 4.03 (instead of 5.98 under LIFO), computed as follows:

$$\frac{\text{FIFO cost of goods sold*}}{\text{FIFO average inventory}^{\dagger}} = \frac{\$16{,}212}{\$4{,}065} = 3.99 \text{ times}$$

Calculations:
*$16,255 + ($1,324 − $1,367) = $16,212
†($3,764 + $4,366)/2 = $4,065

This calculation illustrates that the ratios of two companies that are essentially the same will differ if one uses LIFO and the other uses FIFO. In any serious comparative ratio analysis, one must first make the necessary adjustments for differences in accounting methods to ensure that the accounting numbers are comparable.

Average inventories are sometimes expressed as number of days' sales in inventories. Information is thus provided concerning the average time it takes to turn over the inventory. The number of days' sales in inventory is calculated by dividing average inventory by average daily cost of goods sold. The number of days' sales in inventory also can be obtained by dividing the number of days in the year by the inventory turnover rate. The latter procedure for Deere & Co. is illustrated below, using the originally reported LIFO numbers:

CAUTION

Anyone can compute and compare a bunch of financial ratios. What sets you apart from someone without an accounting background is that you can clean up the accounting numbers, making adjustments for accounting method differences, before you compute the ratios.

Inventory turnover for the year	5.98 times
Number of days' sales in inventory (365/inventory turnover) or [average inventory/(cost of goods sold/365)]	61.0 days

[22] In spite of the incomparability of sales and inventory, in practice many inventory turnover calculations are done using sales. Obviously, not everyone in the financial community has studied this textbook . . . yet.

Number of days' sales in inventory of 61.0 days means that, on average, Deere & Co. has enough inventory to continue operations for 61.0 days using just its existing inventory.

With an increased inventory turnover, the investment necessary for a given volume of business is smaller, and consequently, the return on invested capital is higher. This assumes a company can acquire goods in smaller quantities (with more frequent orders) without paying a higher price. If merchandise must be bought in very large quantities to get favorable prices, then the savings on quantity purchases must be weighed against the savings of carrying lower inventory. Inventory investments and turnover rates vary among industries, and each business must be judged in terms of its financial structure and operations. Management must establish an inventory policy that avoids the extremes of a dangerously low stock, which may impair sales, and an overstocking of goods, which involves a heavy capital investment along with risks of spoilage, obsolescence, and price declines.

Exhibit 9-20 contains a listing of the number of days' sales in inventory of several large companies for 2009. As you can see, the numbers vary widely both across and within industries.

Required Disclosures Related to Inventories

The balance sheet typically contains a single amount for a firm's inventory. For a manufacturing firm, the breakdown of inventory into raw materials, work in process, and finished goods is detailed in the financial statement notes. Merchandising firms also sometimes provide note disclosure of the quantities of major classes of inventory. The basis of valuation (such as cost or lower of cost or market), together with the inventory valuation method (LIFO, FIFO, average, or other method), must be disclosed either in a parenthetical note in the balance sheet or in the accompanying notes. A special note is included when a firm changes its valuation method. This note describes the change, the reason for the change, and the quantitative effect of the change on the financial statements.

The amount of write-downs of inventory to lower of cost or market is also disclosed in the notes. As mentioned earlier, the amount of the write-down should be included in cost of

EX 9-20 NUMBER OF DAYS' SALES IN INVENTORY FOR SELECTED COMPANIES, 2009

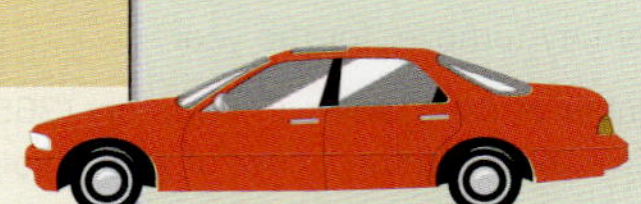

Company	Number of Days' Sales in Inventory
IBM	18.24
Dell	8.02
General Motors	37.90
Ford Motor Company	22.70
Nike, Inc.	82.78
K Swiss	144.76
Wal-Mart Stores, Inc.	40.54
Target	57.51

goods sold. If significant inventory price declines take place between the balance sheet date and the date the financial statements are issued, no adjustment of the financial statements is needed, but the declines should be disclosed as a subsequent event.

When inventories have been pledged as security on loans from banks, finance companies, or factors, the amounts pledged should be disclosed either parenthetically in the Inventory section of the balance sheet or in the notes.

EM **EXPANDED MATERIAL**

Retail Inventory Method

12 **Compute estimates of FIFO, LIFO, average cost, and lower-of-cost-or-market inventory using the retail inventory method.**

WHY **The retail inventory method is a flexible inventory estimation technique. The gross profit method is simple and intuitive, but it fails to allow for differences in inventory valuation method. The retail inventory method is a more elaborate version of the gross profit method, which can be used to estimate inventory under any of the standard valuation assumptions.**

HOW **Depending on the inventory valuation assumption, ending inventory is assumed to come from purchases made during the period, beginning inventory, or an average mixture of the two. By carefully tracking the relationship between inventory cost and retail selling price, ending inventory can be estimated under a FIFO, LIFO, or average cost assumption. In addition, by carefully handling retail price markdowns, an estimate of lower-of-cost-or-market (LCM) inventory can be generated.**

The retail inventory method is widely employed by retail firms to arrive at reliable estimates of inventory position whenever desired. This method, like the gross profit method, permits the estimation of an inventory amount without the time and expense of taking a physical inventory or maintaining detailed perpetual inventory records. The retail inventory method is more flexible than the gross profit method in that it allows estimates to be based on FIFO, LIFO, or average cost assumptions, and it even permits estimation of lower-of-cost-or-market values. The retail inventory method also offers the advantage that when a physical inventory is actually taken for financial statement purposes, the inventory can be taken at retail and then converted to cost without reference to individual costs and invoices, thus saving time and expense.[23]

When the retail inventory method is used, records of goods purchased are maintained at two amounts—cost and retail. Computers have made it feasible to maintain cost records for the thousands of items normally included in a retail inventory. A cost percentage is computed by dividing the goods available for sale at cost by the goods available for sale at retail. This cost percentage can then be applied to the ending inventory at retail, an amount that can be readily calculated by subtracting sales for the period from the total goods available for sale at retail. This process is illustrated in Exhibit 9-21.

The computation of retail inventory at the end of January is illustrated with the example for Wesley Company. The simple process illustrated in this example is based on an

[23] The retail inventory method is acceptable for income tax purposes, provided the taxpayer maintains adequate and satisfactory records supporting inventory calculations and applies the method consistently on successive tax returns.

EX 9-21 RETAIL INVENTORY METHOD

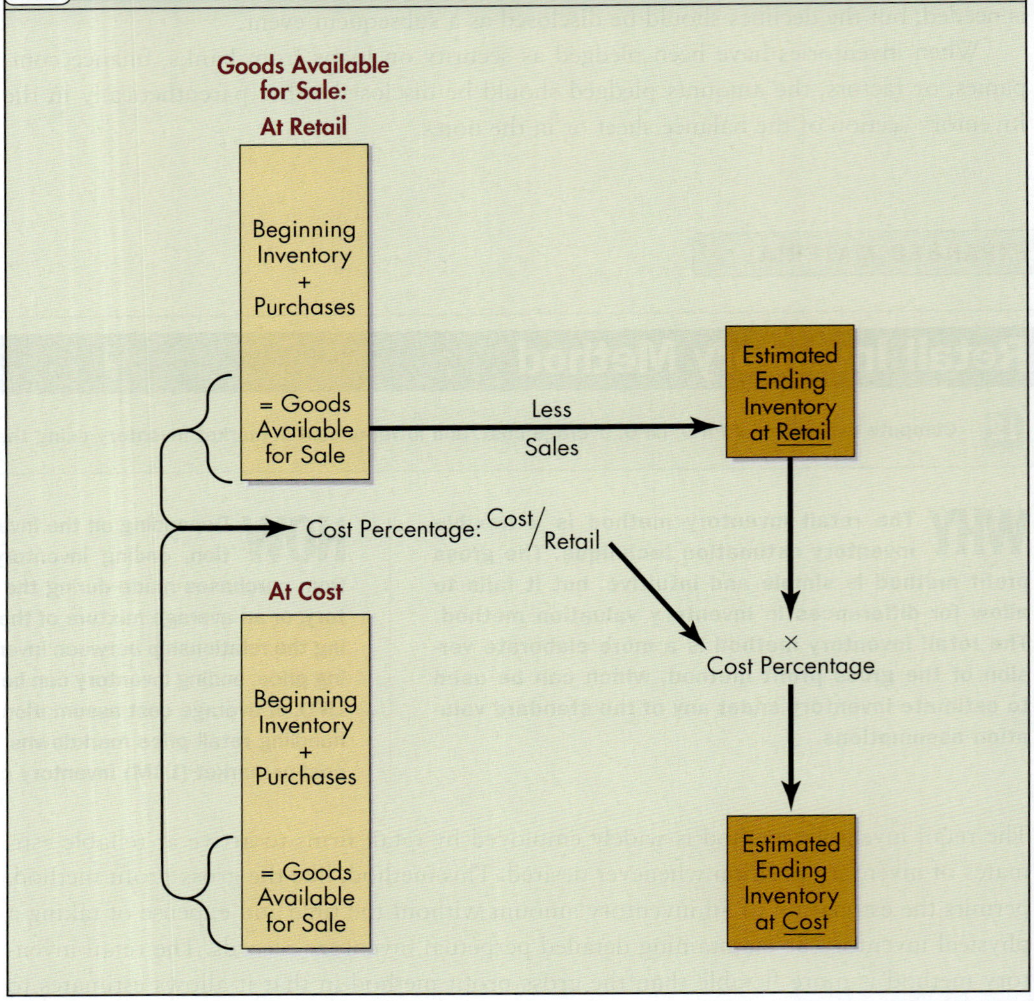

average cost assumption because beginning inventory and purchases are lumped together to compute one cost percentage.

	Cost	Retail
Inventory, January 1	$30,000	$50,000
Purchases in January	30,000	40,000
Goods available for sale	$60,000	$90,000
Cost percentage ($60,000 ÷ $90,000) = 66.7%		
Deduct sales for January		65,000
Inventory, January 31, at retail		$25,000
Inventory, January 31, at estimated cost ($25,000 × 66.7%)	$16,675	

FIFO and LIFO assumptions can be incorporated by computing different cost percentages for beginning inventory and purchases, as shown in the table on page 9-49.

	Cost	Retail
Inventory, January 1	$30,000	$50,000
Purchases in January	30,000	40,000
Goods available for sale	$60,000	$90,000
Cost percentage:		
Beginning inventory ($30,000 ÷ $50,000) = 60.0%		
Purchases ($30,000 ÷ $40,000) = 75.0%		
Deduct sales for January		65,000
Inventory, January 31, at retail		$25,000
Inventory, January 31, at estimated cost:		
FIFO ($25,000 × 75.0%)	$18,750	
LIFO ($25,000 × 60.0%)	$15,000	

With a FIFO assumption, the retail inventory is converted to cost using the cost percentage applicable to the most recently acquired goods (purchases). With a LIFO assumption, the retail-to-cost conversion for ending inventory is done using the old cost percentage (beginning inventory).

Retail Inventory Method: Lower of Cost or Market

Frequently, retail prices change after they are originally set. The following terms are used to describe these changes.

- Original retail—the initial sales price, including the original increase over cost referred to as the initial markup.
- Markups—increases that raise sales prices above original retail.
- Markdowns—decreases that reduce sales prices below original retail.

To illustrate the use of these terms, assume that merchandise costing $4 a unit is marked to sell at $6, which is the original retail price. If the retail price is subsequently increased to $7.50, this represents a retail price markup of $1.50. If the goods originally marked to sell at $6 are reduced to a sales price of $5, this represents a markdown of $1.

Retail price changes can occur because of a change in pricing strategy or because of a change in the value of the underlying inventory. These two causes of retail price changes underlie two different methods of applying the retail inventory method. To illustrate, assume that, in addition to the information given earlier, Wesley Company had retail price markups of $30,000 and markdowns totaling $20,000 during the month of January.

	Average Cost		Lower of Cost or Market	
	Cost	Retail	Cost	Retail
Inventory, January 1	$30,000	$ 50,000	$30,000	$ 50,000
Purchases in January	30,000	40,000	30,000	40,000
	$60,000	$ 90,000	$60,000	$ 90,000
Markups		30,000		30,000
Markdowns		(20,000)		
		$100,000		$120,000

	Average Cost		Lower of Cost or Market	
	Cost	Retail	Cost	Retail
Cost percentage:				
Average cost: ($60,000 ÷ $100,000) = 60.0%				
Lower of cost or market: ($60,000 ÷ $120,000) = 50.0%				
Markdowns		—		(20,000)
Goods available for sale		$100,000		$100,000
Deduct sales for January		65,000		65,000
Inventory, January 31, at retail		$ 35,000		$ 35,000
Inventory, January 31, at estimated cost:				
Average cost: ($35,000 × 60.0%)	$21,000			
Lower of cost or market: ($35,000 × 50.0%)			$17,500	

Operationally, the simple difference between the two estimates is in when the markdowns are subtracted—before computation of the cost percentage or after. And this simple computational difference reflects the two different assumptions about the cause of markups and markdowns. Subtracting the markdowns before calculation of the cost percentage is equivalent to assuming that the markdowns result from a change in pricing strategy. Under this assumption, all markups and markdowns should be reflected in the computation of the cost percentage. The resulting calculation gives an estimate of the average cost of ending inventory. Subtracting the markdowns after calculation of the cost percentage reflects the assumption that the markdowns are the result of a decline in the value of the inventory. As a result, markdowns do not affect the normal cost percentage but are instead reflected as a direct decline in the recorded value of inventory. This assumption yields an estimate of inventory at lower of cost or market.

! CAUTION

The only difference between the average cost and the lower-of-cost-or-market estimates is in the treatment of markdowns.

The illustrations in this section demonstrate the flexibility of the retail inventory method. The retail inventory method can be used to estimate ending inventory using FIFO, LIFO, average cost, and lower of cost or market.

LIFO Pools, Dollar-Value LIFO, and Dollar-Value LIFO Retail

13 Use LIFO pools, dollar-value LIFO, and dollar-value LIFO retail to compute ending inventory.

WHY **Because of the complexities associated with LIFO layers, variations of the LIFO method have been developed to allow companies to approximate the cost of their ending inventory.**

HOW **LIFO methods have been developed that compute inventory based on pools of inventory, dollar amounts of inventory, or inventory retail prices. These methods require the use of cost percentages and price indexes.**

With large and diversified inventories, application of LIFO procedures to specific goods can be extremely burdensome. In addition, if LIFO layers are defined in terms of specific products, frequent LIFO liquidations can occur as demand for individual products declines.

Two approaches have been developed to simplify the application of LIFO: LIFO pools and dollar-value LIFO. Also, the retail inventory method can be combined with the dollar-value LIFO inventory method to use retail costs to estimate LIFO ending inventory values.

LIFO Pools

As a means of simplifying the valuation process and extending its applicability to more items, the IRS developed the technique of establishing LIFO inventory pools of substantially identical goods. At the end of a period, the quantity of items in the pool is determined, and costs are assigned to those items. Units equal to the beginning quantity in the pool are assigned the beginning unit costs. If the number of units in ending inventory exceeds the number of beginning units, the additional units are regarded as an incremental layer within the pool.

To illustrate the formation of LIFO pools, the following data will be used for Elohar Company, a seller of fine neckties:

Beginning inventory:			
	Wide ties	1,000 units @ $10 =	$10,000
	Narrow ties	1,500 units @ $ 8 =	12,000
		2,500 units	$22,000
Purchases:			
January 16	Wide	800 units @ $13 =	$10,400
	Narrow	1,000 units @ $11 =	11,000
December 19	Wide	1,500 units @ $15 =	22,500
	Narrow	2,000 units @ $16 =	32,000
		5,300 units	$75,900
Sales:			
December 31	Wide	1,700 units	
	Narrow	3,200 units	
Ending inventory:			
	Wide	1,600 units	
	Narrow	1,300 units	

If the two types of neckties are accounted for separately, computations of LIFO ending inventory and cost of goods sold are as follows:

LIFO ending inventory:

Wide Ties	Narrow Ties
1,000 units @ $10 = $10,000	1,300 units @ $8 = $10,400
600 units @ $13 = 7,800	
1,600 units $17,800	

LIFO cost of goods sold:

	Wide Ties	Narrow Ties
Beginning inventory	$10,000	$12,000
+ Purchases	10,400	11,000
	22,500	32,000
= Cost of goods available	$42,900	$55,000
− Ending inventory	17,800	10,400
= Cost of goods sold	$25,100	$44,600

Total cost of goods sold: $25,100 + $44,600 = $69,700

Rather than account for the wide ties and narrow ties separately, they can be combined into one LIFO pool. This will simplify the accounting (as illustrated below) and also makes conceptual sense because the two types of ties form a natural business group. Similarly, a large appliance wholesaler might form a pool of all major kitchen appliances such as refrigerators, freezers, and ovens.

The data requirements for computing LIFO cost of goods sold with the two types of ties forming one LIFO pool are few. The three items below are all that are needed:

- Total beginning inventory: 2,500 units with a total cost of $22,000
- Number of units in the new LIFO layer: 400 units (2,900 ending – 2,500 beginning)
- Average cost per unit of ties purchased during the year: $14.32 ($75,900/5,300 units)

LIFO ending inventory using a LIFO pool is computed as follows:

Beginning inventory	2,500 units	= $22,000
New LIFO layer	400 units @ $14.32 =	5,728
		$27,728

LIFO cost of goods sold is then:

	LIFO Pool
Beginning inventory	$22,000
+ Purchases	75,900
= Cost of goods available	$97,900
– Ending inventory	27,728
= Cost of goods sold	$70,172

Remember that the purpose of forming LIFO pools is to simplify the LIFO calculations associated with large numbers of products. The simplification results in an estimate of what cost of goods sold would be if LIFO were applied strictly and laboriously. In this example, the LIFO pool cost of goods sold estimate ($70,172) differs from the total of the individual LIFO calculations ($69,700) because of the simplifying assumption of using the average cost of purchases to value the new LIFO layer.[24]

LIFO pooling was originally developed as part of the IRS regulations but was quickly adopted as acceptable for financial reporting as well. Although it is not necessary for companies to use the same pools for tax and financial reporting purposes, most companies do, even when the IRS regulations require more pools than might be necessary for accounting purposes.[25]

Because companies can choose to have many LIFO pools or, in the extreme, just one pool, what factors determine the choice of the optimal number of pools? Focusing on the income tax effect, the conventional wisdom is that the fewer pools, the better, with one pool being the best of all. This is because lumping all inventories together into one LIFO

[24] The unit cost assigned to the items in the new layer may be based on any one of the following measurements:
- The weighted-average cost of acquisitions within the period
- Actual costs of earliest acquisitions within the period (LIFO)
- Actual costs of the latest acquisitions within the period (FIFO)

[25] James M. Reeve and Keith G. Stanga, "The LIFO Pooling Decision: Some Empirical Results from Accounting Practice," *Accounting Horizons*, June 1987, p. 27.

pool allows decreases in the inventory of one product to be offset by increases in another product, making it less likely that a LIFO liquidation will result in a sudden increase in income taxes. This conventional wisdom emphasizes avoidance of LIFO liquidations but ignores the primary purpose of LIFO, which is the deferral of income taxes in normal times. Choosing the number of pools that gives maximum tax deferral in normal times (i.e., in times of steady or rising inventory levels) requires careful analysis and depends partly on whether different categories of inventory have different rates of price change.[26]

Dollar-Value LIFO

Even the grouping of substantially identical items into quantity pools does not produce all the benefits desired from the use of LIFO. For example, technological advances and marketing developments are constantly causing specific products to be phased out and replaced by something new that fills the market niche of the old product. The music store business has seen its inventory change from vinyl albums to eight-track tapes to cassettes to CDs to digital files in the past 50 years. The accounting question is whether old LIFO layers should be liquidated whenever a new product replaces an old one. To address this question, and also to further simplify the recordkeeping associated with LIFO, the dollar-value LIFO inventory method was developed. Under this method, LIFO layers are determined based on total dollar changes rather than quantity changes. The dollar-value method has become the most widely used adaptation of the LIFO concept. In a survey of LIFO users, Professors Reeve and Stanga found that 95% of the 206 companies responding to their survey used some version of the dollar-value method.[27]

With dollar-value LIFO, the unit of measurement is the dollar. All goods in the inventory pool to which dollar-value LIFO is to be applied are viewed as though they are identical items. To determine if the dollar quantity of inventory has increased during the year, it is necessary to value the ending inventory in a pool at base-year prices (i.e., those in effect when LIFO was first adopted by the company) and compare the total with that at the beginning of the year, also valued at base-year prices. If the end-of-year inventory at base-year prices exceeds the beginning-of-year inventory at base-year prices, a new LIFO layer is created. If there has been a decrease, the most recent LIFO layer (or layers) is reduced.

Dollar-value LIFO calculations are illustrated using the same Elohar Company example from the previous section.

First, the replacement cost of ending inventory is computed using prices prevailing at the end of the period. In this example, the end-of-period prices come from the December 19 purchase. For Elohar Company, the replacement cost of ending inventory is:

Ending inventory at ending prices:		
Wide ties	1,600 units @ $15 =	$24,000
Narrow ties	1,300 units @ $16 =	20,800
		$44,800

Since beginning inventory was only $22,000, it appears that there was an increase in inventory during the period, suggesting that a new LIFO layer should be added. However, the increase in inventory may be a result of price increases rather than an actual increase

[26] William R. Cron and Randall B. Hayes, "The Dollar-Value LIFO Pooling Decision: The Conventional Wisdom Is Too General," *Accounting Horizons*, December 1989, p. 57.

[27] James M. Reeve and Keith G. Stanga, "The LIFO Pooling Decision: Some Empirical Results from Accounting Practice," *Accounting Horizons*, June 1987, p. 2.

in the quantity of inventory. To make this determination, computation is made of what the value of beginning inventory would be at ending prices:

Beginning inventory at ending prices:		
Wide ties	1,000 units @ $15 =	$15,000
Narrow ties	1,500 units @ $16 =	24,000
		$39,000

After adjusting for price increases during the year, we can see that the dollar value of inventory increased by $5,800:

Ending inventory at ending prices	$44,800
− Beginning inventory at ending prices	39,000
Dollar value of new LIFO layer, at ending prices	$ 5,800

Finally, dollar-value LIFO ending inventory is computed as follows:

Beginning inventory, at base-year prices	$22,000
New LIFO layer, at ending prices	5,800
LIFO ending inventory	$27,800

This LIFO ending inventory is then used in the computation of LIFO cost of goods sold.

To summarize, the dollar-value LIFO computations are:

1. Compute ending inventory at ending prices.
2. Compute beginning inventory at ending prices.
3. Compute the difference. An increase represents a new LIFO layer.
4. LIFO ending inventory is beginning inventory at base-year prices plus the new LIFO layer.

In the example, the new LIFO layer was valued at ending prices. This is acceptable but is somewhat inconsistent with the LIFO assumption. In fact, this approach essentially results in the new layer being valued using a FIFO assumption. Alternatively, the new LIFO layer can be valued using average prices for the period, or by using the prices of the first purchases of the period. The only computational difference is that "ending prices" are replaced by "first purchase prices" or "average prices" in steps (1) and (2) above. The computations using first purchase prices to value the new LIFO layer are given below. The first purchase made during the period was on January 16.

Ending inventory at first purchase prices:		
Wide ties	1,600 units @ $13 =	$20,800
Narrow ties	1,300 units @ $11 =	14,300
		$35,100

Beginning inventory at first purchase prices:		
Wide ties	1,000 units @ $13 =	$13,000
Narrow ties	1,500 units @ $11 =	16,500
		$29,500

Ending inventory at first purchase prices	$35,100
− Beginning inventory at first purchase prices	29,500
Dollar value of new LIFO layer, at first purchase prices	$ 5,600
Beginning inventory, at base-year prices	$22,000
New LIFO layer, at first purchase prices	5,600
LIFO ending inventory	$27,600

Use of an Index

The dollar-value LIFO illustration just completed required a record of base-year prices and end-of-year prices for each individual inventory item. This technique is called the double extension method. Imagine how messy the computations would be with several thousand products. Recall that the purpose of LIFO pools and dollar-value LIFO is to reduce the bookkeeping costs associated with LIFO. Dollar-value LIFO is greatly simplified if a price index is used in place of the double extension method.

A price index is simply an overall measure of how much prices have increased during the year. A common example is the Consumer Price Index (CPI). The CPI measures how much consumer prices increase in the United States during a given period. If the CPI goes up from 100 to 103 during a year, we say that prices for the year increased by 3%, or in other words, inflation for the year was 3%.

A price index in the Elohar Company example can be computed by comparing beginning inventory at beginning prices to beginning inventory at ending prices:

Beginning inventory at ending prices:	
Wide ties	1,000 units @ $15 = $15,000
Narrow ties	1,500 units @ $16 = 24,000
	$39,000

Beginning inventory at beginning prices:	
Wide ties	1,000 units @ $10 = $10,000
Narrow ties	1,500 units @ $8 = 12,000
	$22,000

End-of-year price index: $39,000/$22,000 = 1.77, or 177

With the beginning-of-year index being 100, an end-of-year-index of 177 means that prices increased an average of 77% during the year. This index would be used in the following work sheet to compute ending inventory for Elohar Company using dollar-value LIFO:

Inventory at End-of-Year Prices		Year-End Price Index		Inventory at Base-Year Prices	Layers in Base-Year Prices		Incremental Layer Index		Dollar-Value LIFO Cost
$44,800	÷	1.77	=	$25,311	$22,000	×	1.00	=	$22,000
					3,311	×	1.77	=	5,860
					$25,311				$27,860

This ending inventory of $27,860 differs from the $27,800 computed earlier (with the new layer valued at ending prices) only because the index is rounded at 1.77 (instead of carrying it out to 1.7727272727 . . .).

Note that the index calculations in the work sheet result in the new layer being valued at ending prices. In order to value the new layer at first purchase prices, an additional index must be computed:

Beginning inventory at first purchase prices:	
Wide ties	1,000 units @ $13 = $13,000
Narrow ties	1,500 units @ $11 = 16,500
	$29,500

First purchase price index: $29,500/$22,000 = 1.34

The first purchase price index would be used to value the new LIFO layer as follows:

Inventory at End-of-Year Prices		Year-End Price Index		Inventory at Base-Year Prices	Layers in Base-Year Prices		Incremental Layer Index		Dollar-Value LIFO Cost
$44,800	÷	1.77	=	$25,311	$22,000	×	1.00	=	$22,000
					3,311	×	1.34	=	4,437
					$25,311				$26,437

To recap, the new LIFO layer can be valued using a year-end price index, a first purchase price index, or an average price index.

Dollar-Value LIFO: Multiyear Example

One more illustration of dollar-value LIFO is given below. This example illustrates how dollar-value LIFO works when LIFO layers are liquidated.

Assume the index numbers and inventories at end-of-year prices for Hsu Wholesale Co. are as follows:

Date	Year-End Price Index*	Inventory at End-of-Year Prices
December 31, 2009	1.00	$38,000
December 31, 2010	1.20	$54,000
December 31, 2011	1.32	$66,000
December 31, 2012	1.40	$56,000
December 31, 2013	1.25	$55,000

* Many published indexes appear as percentages without decimals, e.g., 100, 120, 132, 140, 125.

The work sheet in Exhibit 9-22 shows the calculation of LIFO ending inventory for Hsu for each year.

The following items should be observed in the example:

- *December 31, 2010*—With an ending inventory of $45,000 in terms of base prices, the inventory has increased in 2010 by $7,000; however, the $7,000 increase is stated in terms of base-year prices and needs to be restated in terms of 2010 year-end prices which are 120% of the base level.
- *December 31, 2011*—With an ending inventory of $50,000 in terms of base prices, the inventory has increased in 2011 by another $5,000; however, the $5,000 increase is stated in terms of base-year prices and needs to be restated in terms of 2011 year-end costs which are 132% of the base level.
- *December 31, 2012*—When the ending inventory of $40,000 (expressed in base-year dollars) is compared to the beginning inventory of $50,000 (also expressed in base-year dollars), it is apparent that the inventory has been decreased by $10,000 in base-year terms. Under LIFO procedures, the decrease is assumed to take place in the most recently added layers, reducing or eliminating them. As a result, the 2011 layer, priced at $5,000 in base-year terms, is completely eliminated, and $5,000 of the $7,000 layer from 2010 is eliminated. This leaves only $2,000 of the 2010 layer,

EX 9-22 DOLLAR-VALUE LIFO: MULTIYEAR EXAMPLE

Date	Inventory at End-of-Year Prices		Year-End Price Index		Inventory at Base-Year Prices	Layers in Base-Year Prices		Incremental Layer Index		Dollar-Value LIFO Cost
December 31, 2009	$38,000	÷	1.00	=	$38,000	$38,000	×	1.00	=	$38,000
December 31, 2010	$54,000	÷	1.20	=	$45,000	$38,000	×	1.00	=	$38,000
						7,000	×	1.20	=	8,400
						$45,000				$46,400
December 31, 2011	$66,000	÷	1.32	=	$50,000	$38,000	×	1.00	=	$38,000
						7,000	×	1.20	=	8,400
						5,000	×	1.32	=	6,600
						$50,000				$53,000
December 31, 2012	$56,000	÷	1.40	=	$40,000	$38,000	×	1.00	=	$38,000
						2,000	×	1.20	=	2,400
						$40,000				$40,400
December 31, 2013	$55,000	÷	1.25	=	$44,000	$38,000	×	1.00	=	$38,000
						2,000	×	1.20	=	2,400
						4,000	×	1.25	=	5,000
						$44,000				$45,400

plus the base-year amount. The remaining $2,000 of the 2010 layer is multiplied by 1.20 to restate it to 2010 dollars and is added to the base-year amount to arrive at the ending inventory amount of $40,400.

- *December 31, 2013*—The ending inventory of $44,000 in terms of the base prices indicates an inventory increase for 2013 of $4,000. This increase requires restatement in terms of 2013 year-end prices, which are 125% of the base level.

In some cases, the index for the first year of the LIFO layers is not 1.00. This is especially true when an externally generated index is used. When this occurs, it is simpler to convert all inventories to a base of 1.00 rather than to use the index for the initial year of the LIFO layers. The computations are done in the same manner as in the previous example except the inventory is stated in terms of the base year of the index, not the first year of the inventory layers. To illustrate, assume the same facts as stated earlier except that the base year of the external index is 2005; in 2009, the index is 1.20; and in 2010, it is 1.44. The schedule showing the LIFO inventory computations would be modified as follows for the first two years. Note that the inventory cost is the same under either situation.

Date	Inventory at End-of-Year Prices		Year-End Price Index		Inventory at Base = 1.00 (2005 Prices)	Layers in Base = 1.00 (2005 Prices)		Incremental Layer Index		Dollar-Value LIFO Cost
December 31, 2009	$38,000	÷	1.20	=	$31,667	$31,667	×	1.20	=	$38,000
December 31, 2010	$54,000	÷	1.44	=	$37,500	$31,667	×	1.20	=	$38,000
						5,833	×	1.44	=	8,400
						$37,500				$46,400

Dollar-Value LIFO Retail Method

The dollar-value LIFO procedures described in the preceding section can be combined with the retail inventory method described earlier in developing LIFO inventory values. With the dollar-value LIFO retail method, LIFO layers are stated in terms of retail values. After the LIFO retail layers have been identified and priced using a price index, a further adjustment is needed to state the inventory at cost. This is done by multiplying the retail inventory of each layer by the appropriate cost percentage.

One thing to keep in mind when computing cost percentages for the dollar-value LIFO retail method is that beginning inventory values are ignored. When LIFO is used, a new inventory layer is converted from retail to cost using the cost percentage applicable to current year purchases.

The following LIFO retail layer data for Miracle Max Department Store as of December 31, 2012, are used to illustrate the computations associated with the dollar-value LIFO retail method.

Layer Year	Year-End Price Index	Incremental Cost Percentage	Inventory at End-of-Year Retail Prices
2009	1.00	0.60	$60,000
2010	1.05	0.62	69,300
2011	1.10	0.64	77,000
2012	1.12	0.65	71,120

Assume that the 2013 year-end price index is 1.08. The incremental cost percentage and 2013 ending inventory at end-of-year retail prices are computed as follows.

	Cost	Retail
Beginning inventory, December 31, 2012	—	$ 71,120
Purchases	$59,780	$ 98,000
Incremental cost percentage: ($59,780 ÷ $98,000) = 61%		
Goods available for sale		$169,120
Deduct: Sales		90,820
Ending inventory at retail (year-end prices)		$ 78,300

From these data, a work sheet similar to that illustrated earlier for dollar-value LIFO can be constructed to determine the LIFO retail inventory layers. One additional column is necessary to record the incremental cost percentage that will convert the retail inventory to cost. It is important to note that the incremental cost percentage is used only if an incremental layer is added to the inventory in the current period. In the example, no layer was added in 2012, so the cost percentage applicable to purchases made in 2012 is not used. As seen with the dollar-value LIFO method, when an inventory layer is eliminated, it is not reintroduced in subsequent years when layers are added. This is illustrated in the example when, in 2012, the $4,000 layer formed in 2011 is eliminated. In 2013, the 2011 $4,000 layer is not resurrected. Instead, the new layer consists of 2013 percentages.

Date	End-of-Year Retail Prices		Year-End Price Index		Base-Year Retail Prices	Layers		Incremental Layer Index		Incremental Cost Percentage		Dollar-Value LIFO Retail Cost
December 31, 2009	$60,000	÷	1.00	=	$60,000	$60,000	×	1.00	×	0.60	=	$36,000
December 31, 2010	$69,300	÷	1.05	=	$66,000	$60,000	×	1.00	×	0.60	=	$36,000
						6,000	×	1.05	×	0.62	=	3,906
						$66,000						$39,906
December 31, 2011	$77,000	÷	1.10	=	$70,000	$60,000	×	1.00	×	0.60	=	$36,000
						6,000	×	1.05	×	0.62	=	3,906
						4,000	×	1.10	×	0.64	=	2,816
						$70,000						$42,722
December 31, 2012	$71,120	÷	1.12	=	$63,500	$60,000	×	1.00	×	0.60	=	$36,000
						3,500	×	1.05	×	0.62	=	2,279*
						$63,500						$38,279
December 31, 2013	$78,300	÷	1.08	=	$72,500	$60,000	×	1.00	×	0.60	=	$36,000
						3,500	×	1.05	×	0.62	=	2,279*
						9,000	×	1.08	×	0.61	=	5,929*
						$72,500						$44,208

*Rounded to nearest dollar

Purchase Commitments

14 **Account for the impact of changing prices on purchase commitments.**

WHY **When a firm commitment is made to purchase inventory in the future, the purchasing company is subject to the risk of a drop in price after a firm purchase price has already been set. Proper accounting for this risk reports any economic losses from such price drops in the period in which the price decline occurs.**

HOW **When price declines take place after a purchase commitment has been made, a loss is recorded in the period of the price decline. This loss is similar in nature to a lower-of-cost-or-market write-down.**

Extreme fluctuations in the price of inventory purchases can expose a company to excessive risk. Of the different ways to manage this risk, the simplest is a purchase commitment that locks in the inventory purchase price in advance. For example, rather than being exposed to the ups and downs of oil prices, an airline can contract in advance to purchase its next month's fuel at a set price.

The first accounting issue raised by purchase commitments is whether the company committing to the future purchase should record an asset (for the inventory to be received) and a liability (for the payment obligation) at the commitment date. This type of contract is an exchange of promises about future actions and is known as an *executory contract*. Another example of an executory contract is an employment agreement in which a firm and an employee agree to employment terms for a future

FYI

As you will see in Chapter 19, a purchase commitment is very similar to one type of derivative called a *forward contract*.

To manage their risk, airlines often contract in advance to purchase fuel at a set price.

period. Accounting rules require some executory contracts to be recognized in the financial statements.[28]

With purchase commitments, no journal entry is required to record the commitment prior to delivery of the goods. However, in an adaptation of the lower-of-cost-or-market rule, when price declines take place subsequent to such a commitment and the commitment is outstanding at the end of an accounting period, the loss is recorded just as losses on goods on hand are recognized.[29] A decline is recorded by a debit to a special loss account and a credit to either a contra asset account or an accrued liability account, such as Estimated Loss on Purchase Commitments. Acquisition of the goods in a subsequent period is recorded by a credit to Accounts Payable, a debit canceling the credit balance in the contra asset or accrued liability account, and a debit to Purchases for the difference.

To illustrate the accounting for purchase commitments, we'll use the following example. Rollins Oat Company entered into a purchase commitment on November 1, 2012, for 100,000 bushels of wheat at $3.40 per bushel to be delivered in March 2013. At the end of 2012, the market price for wheat had dropped to $3.20 per bushel. The entries to record this decline in value and the subsequent delivery of the wheat would be as follows:

2012				
Dec.	31	Loss on Purchase Commitments	20,000	
		Estimated Loss on Purchase Commitments		20,000
		(100,000 bushels × $0.20 per bushel)		
2013				
Mar.	31	Estimated Loss on Purchase Commitments	20,000	
		Purchases	320,000	
		Accounts Payable		340,000

The loss is thus assigned to the period in which the inventory price decline took place. Current loss recognition would not be appropriate when commitments can be canceled, when commitments provide for price adjustment, or when declines do not suggest reductions in sale prices. If, prior to delivery, the market price increases, the estimated loss on purchase commitments account would be reduced and a gain would be recorded. The amount of gain to be recognized is limited to the amount of loss previously recorded.

[28] A lease is a good example of an executory contract. A lease is an exchange of promises about the future—the lessor promises to provide the use of an asset (like a building) and the lessee promises to pay for the use of the asset. As discussed in Chapter 15, some leases are recognized in the financial statements (capital leases) and some are not (operating leases).

[29] FASB ASC paragraph 330-10-35-17.

Foreign Currency Inventory Transactions

15 **Record inventory purchase transactions denominated in foreign currencies.**

WHY **Foreign currency transactions expose companies to exchange rate risk during the time between the purchase and the payment of the foreign currency obligation.**

HOW **Gains or losses resulting from exchange rate changes are recognized in the period in which the exchange rate changes occur.**

The discussion of inventories thus far has centered around the purchase and valuation of inventories in a domestic environment, that is, within the United States. As noted in Chapter 1, business has become increasingly global. Exports and imports of materials and finished goods are a significant part of many companies' purchases and sales. Depending on how a purchase transaction is structured, additional gains or losses may occur in foreign inventory transactions because of fluctuations in the currency exchange rates between two countries.

Not all international transactions involve foreign currency risk. Only transactions denominated in currencies other than the U.S. dollar are foreign currency transactions for U.S. companies. For example, if a U.S. company buys inventory from a German firm, the transaction is a normal purchase (for the U.S. company) if the inventory price is set in U.S. dollars. But if the price is set in euros, the U.S. company is exposed to foreign currency exchange risk during the period the account payable is outstanding.

To illustrate the complexities associated with foreign currency transactions, assume that on November 1, 2012, Washington Company purchased inventory from Swiss Company and that the invoice was denominated in Swiss francs with a purchase price of 50,000 francs. At the time of the purchase, the exchange rate was 5 francs per U.S. dollar. This rate is called the spot rate, the rate at which the two currencies can be exchanged right now. Washington Company would make the following journal entry to record the purchase:

> **! CAUTION**
>
> If the transaction contract is written in terms of U.S. dollars, there is no foreign currency risk whether the other company is based in Azerbaijan or Zimbabwe.

2012				
Nov.	1	Inventory	10,000	
		Accounts Payable (fc)		10,000
		(50,000 francs/5 = $10,000)		

The (fc) designation is used for convenience to indicate those items that are denominated in a foreign currency. It is important to recognize, however, that the amounts in Washington's journal entry represent U.S. dollars.

The impact of a foreign currency inventory purchase is recognized when the liability is paid. If the terms call for payment of the liability on February 1, 2013, Washington Company will have to credit cash on that date, but for how much? Recall that the invoice requires payment in francs, not in dollars. Washington Company will have to purchase 50,000 francs from a foreign currency broker. How much will the company be required to pay the broker? The answer depends on the spot rate on that date. If the spot rate is 4.7 francs per U.S. dollar on February 1, 2013, then Washington Company will have to pay

$10,638 (50,000/4.7) to purchase 50,000 francs. The journal entry to record the payment to Swiss Company is as follows:

2013				
Feb.	1	Accounts Payable (fc)	10,000	
		Exchange Loss	638	
		Cash		10,638

Washington Company incurs a loss in this situation because it had a liability denominated in a currency (francs) that increased in value—the number of francs required to purchase one U.S. dollar declined. On November 1, 2012, Washington Company would have had to pay only $10,000 to purchase 50,000 francs. However, to purchase the same number of francs on February 1, 2013, requires $10,638. The exchange loss would be included as an expense in the income statement in the period incurred.

This situation could just as easily have resulted in an exchange gain for Washington Company. If the franc had weakened relative to the dollar, then fewer dollars would have been required to purchase 50,000 francs. Suppose the exchange rate for Swiss francs had been 5.1 per U.S. dollar on February 1, 2013. Washington Company would have recorded the following journal entry and recognized an exchange gain:

2013				
Feb.	1	Accounts Payable (fc)	10,000	
		Exchange Gain		196
		Cash *(50,000 francs/5.1)*		9,804

If a balance sheet date occurs while a foreign currency asset or liability is outstanding, the asset or liability is valued at the spot rate on the balance sheet date.[30] Continuing the initial example, suppose that Washington Company's fiscal year ends on December 31 and the exchange rate on December 31, 2012, is 4.8 francs per U.S. dollar. On that date, Washington Company would make the following adjusting entry to record the change in the amount of cash required to pay the liability:

2012				
Dec.	31	Exchange Loss	417	
		Accounts Payable (fc)		417
		[(50,000 francs/4.8) – $10,000 = $417]		

This journal entry adjusts the liability to its value of $10,417, given the balance sheet date spot rate, and allocates the exchange rate loss to the period in which the change in exchange rates occurred. When the liability is subsequently paid on February 1, 2013, and the spot rate is 4.7 francs per dollar, the journal entry would be as follows:

2013				
Feb.	1	Accounts Payable (fc)	10,417	
		Exchange Loss	221	
		Cash *(50,000 francs/4.7)*		10,638

Note that the exchange losses of $417 and $221 recorded on December 31 and February 1, respectively, total $638, which is the same amount that is obtained if no adjusting entry is made. The adjusting entry simply allocates the exchange loss to the appropriate accounting periods.

An obvious question at this point is, why didn't Washington Company avoid the exchange loss and pay the liability early? If Washington knew that the franc was going to

[30] FASB ASC paragraph 830-20-35-2.

become more expensive, it probably would have. However, predicting the direction and amount of change in the exchange rate for a particular currency is as difficult as predicting whether the price of a specific stock on the New York Stock Exchange is going to rise or fall, and by how much.

Foreign currency exchange risk is another form of price risk. And, just like domestic price risk, foreign currency exchange risk can be hedged. *Hedging* involves contracting with a foreign currency broker to deliver or receive a specified foreign currency at a specified future date and at a specified exchange rate. A fully hedged transaction results in no exchange gain or loss to the company. The cost of hedging is the fee charged by the broker. For that fee, the broker assumes all of the risks associated with exchange rate changes. Accounting for foreign currency hedging is discussed in Chapter 19. For coverage of how multinational companies combine the financial statements of subsidiaries located in different countries, see Chapter 22.

SOLUTIONS TO OPENING SCENARIO QUESTIONS

1. High inflation causes a big difference between the ending inventory and cost of goods sold numbers produced by LIFO and FIFO. Drastic deflation would do the same, in the opposite direction.
2. The high inflation of 1974 made it so that LIFO cost of goods sold was much greater than FIFO cost of goods sold. By adopting LIFO, companies could report higher cost of goods sold, leading to lower payment of income taxes.
3. An unsophisticated investor focuses on reported earnings without paying attention to the accounting methods and assumptions used in computing those reported earnings.

SOLUTIONS TO STOP & THINK

1. (Page 9-9) The correct answer is C. Choosing between two acceptable accounting procedures is an exercise in cost-benefit analysis. Perpetual inventory systems provide better information, but they also usually cost more to operate. For some businesses, the costs exceed the benefits, so those businesses use a periodic system. Businesses most likely to use a periodic system are those with lots of low-value identical items with a high turnover. In addition, very small businesses, because they don't make much profit, are less likely to be able to afford a computer inventory system.
2. (Page 9-25) The correct answer is C, computed as follows:

	2010	2011	2012
FIFO cost of goods sold:	100 × \$5 = \$500	20 × \$ 5 = \$ 100	50 × \$10 = \$ 500
		100 × \$10 = 1,000	70 × \$15 = 1,050
		\$1,100	\$1,550
Ending inventory:	20 × \$5 = \$100	50 × \$10 = \$ 500	90 × \$15 = \$1,350

3. (Page 9-31) The correct answer is D. Use of LIFO for the income statement and FIFO for the balance sheet would result in a cost allocation discrepancy. In essence, the FIFO inventory valuation on the balance sheet includes inventory-holding gains, but the LIFO gross profit on the income statement excludes those holding gains. Unless this discrepancy is handled appropriately, the balance sheet will not balance. A possible way to handle this discrepancy is to create a special equity item, perhaps a new type of accumulated other comprehensive income. This equity item would normally have a credit balance (unrecognized inventory holding gain), reflecting the fact that FIFO ending inventory is typically greater than LIFO ending inventory.

4. (Page 9-41) The correct answer is B. An understatement of the amount of purchases would cause the actual amount of inventory to be greater than the estimated amount. If the actual amount of inventory is much lower than the estimated amount, there are three possible explanations: (1) the estimation process is flawed, (2) inventory was lost or stolen, or (3) the missing inventory was sold but the sales were not reported. A clever fraud artist can cover his or her tracks by making sure that the reported gross profit percentage is close to industry norms and by avoiding any large swings in the level of unreported sales from one year to the next. Like anything else, successful fraud requires consistent, patient effort over the course of many years.

5. (Page 9-43) The correct answer is A. All managers are confident that any current difficulties are only temporary. They think that if they can just get past their immediate problems, business will turn around in the future. Thus, managers don't worry about the counterbalancing impact of inventory errors because they know (or think they know) that business will be better next year. In addition, when a manager is facing termination for missing this year's profit target, concerns about the counterbalancing effort of any inventory error next year are of no significance.

SOLUTION TO USING THE FASB'S CODIFICATION

In FASB ASC Subtopic 905-330 (Agriculture—Inventory), you can see Section 35 (Subsequent Measurement). Inventories of harvested crops are to be accounted for in the same way as animals held for sale. There are two acceptable treatments. First, the harvested crops (or animals) can be accounted for at lower of cost or market, just like any other inventory item. Second, the harvested crop inventory can be recorded at "sales price less estimated costs of disposal." This is a description of net realizable value.

Note that not all crops are eligible for this net realizable value reporting. The criteria listed in FASB ASC paragraph 905-330-35-3 indicate that this treatment is appropriate only for crops that are ready to ship to reliable markets.

REVIEW CHAPTER 9

LEARNING OBJECTIVES

1 Define inventory for a merchandising business, and identify the different types of inventory for a manufacturing business.

For a merchandising firm, inventory is the label given to assets sold in the normal course of business. The types of items included in the inventory of a merchandising company are determined by the nature of the business, not the nature of the items. For example, a truck is a fixed asset for an overnight mail delivery company but is inventory for a truck dealership. For a manufacturing firm, there are three types of inventory.

- *Raw materials* are goods obtained for use in the manufacturing process. Direct materials are incorporated directly into the manufactured product (e.g., steel in an automobile, wood in furniture) and indirect materials are used to facilitate production (e.g., lubricant for factory equipment, factory cleaning supplies).
- *Work in process* consists of materials only partly processed that require further work before they can be sold. The three categories of costs that go into work in process are direct materials, direct labor, and manufacturing overhead.
- *Finished goods* are the manufactured products awaiting sale. Upon sale, the cost of finished goods becomes cost of goods sold. A rough rule of thumb is that costs incurred inside the factory are assigned to the cost

of inventory, and costs incurred outside the factory are classified as selling, general, or administrative expenses.

2 **Explain the advantages and disadvantages of both periodic and perpetual inventory systems.**

The following chart summarizes the differences between periodic and perpetual inventory systems:

Periodic	Perpetual
Inventory	
Known only after an end-of-period physical count.	Known on a day-to-day basis.
Cost of Goods Sold	
Known only after an end-of-period physical count.	Known on a day-to-day basis.
Inventory Shrinkage	
Can't be calculated.	Can be calculated by comparing inventory records with physical count.
Journal Entries	
No entry made to record cost of goods sold until the end of the period.	Cost of goods sold entry made in association with each sale.
Inventory purchases debited to a temporary purchases account.	Inventory purchases debited directly to the inventory account.
Quality of Information vs. Cost to Operate	
Lower quality of information but less costly to operate.	Higher quality of information but more costly to operate.

3 **Determine when ownership of goods in transit changes hands and what circumstances require shipped inventory to be kept on the books.**

With a few exceptions, goods should be included in the reported inventory of the business that owns them, regardless of the physical location of the inventory.

- *Goods in transit.* Goods shipped FOB shipping point belong to the buyer while in transit. Goods shipped FOB destination belong to the seller while in transit.
- *Goods on consignment.* Goods on consignment should be included in the consignor's inventory. The consignee does not include the goods in inventory even though the consignee has physical possession of the goods.
- *Installment sales and conditional sales.* Even though the seller may retain legal title to the inventory until the end of the installment period, the seller should remove the goods from inventory at the time of sale if successful completion of the contract is anticipated.
- *Repurchase agreements.* When the seller promises to buy back goods at a specified price at a future date, the goods should not be removed from the seller's reported inventory. In addition, a liability is recorded for the "sales" proceeds.

4 **Compute total inventory acquisition cost.**

For purchased goods, the recorded inventory amount includes all costs related to purchase, receipt, and preparation of the goods. For manufactured inventory, cost includes direct materials, direct labor, and manufacturing overhead.

The cost of purchased inventory is summarized as follows:

Invoice cost plus freight, storage, and preparation cost
− Cash discounts
− Purchase returns and allowances
= Inventory cost

The two ways to account for cash discounts are the net method and the gross method. With the net method, the cost of missed discounts is reported as a separate financing expense. With the gross method, missed cash discounts are included as part of the cost of inventory.

The most difficult part of computing the cost of manufactured inventory is allocating manufacturing overhead. Traditionally, overhead allocation has been proportioned on the amount of direct labor associated with a product. An activity-based cost (ABC) system allocates overhead based on clearly identified cost drivers—characteristics of the production process known to create overhead costs.

5 **Use the four basic inventory valuation methods: specific identification, average cost, FIFO, and LIFO.**

Inventory valuation methods allocate total inventory cost between inventory remaining and inventory sold. The four most common methods are specific identification, average cost, first-in, first-out (FIFO), and last-in, first-out (LIFO).

- *Specific identification.* The actual physical units sold are specifically identified and their aggregate cost is reported as cost of goods sold.
- *Average cost.* The same average cost is assigned to each unit. Cost of goods sold is computed by multiplying units sold by the average cost per unit.
- *FIFO.* The units sold are assumed to be the oldest units on hand.
- *LIFO.* The units sold are assumed to be the newest units on hand.

With a perpetual inventory system, computation of average cost and LIFO is more complicated because the average cost of goods available and the identification of the newest units change with each purchase and sale. In practice, perpetual records are usually maintained on a FIFO basis and then converted to average cost or LIFO for the financial reports.

6 Explain how LIFO inventory layers are created, and describe the significance of the LIFO reserve.

A LIFO inventory layer is created in each year in which purchases exceed sales. The difference between LIFO inventory value and FIFO or average cost is called the *LIFO reserve*.

The LIFO assumption means that all sales are made from current purchases as long as purchases are greater than or equal to sales. Thus, inventory acquired in previous years remains on the books in LIFO layers.

When inventory levels decline, inventory in LIFO layers is sold, starting with the most recently created layer. In times of rising prices, these old LIFO layer costs are lower than current replacement cost. Consequently, LIFO liquidation often results in lower cost of goods sold and higher net income.

Companies using LIFO are allowed to disclose the difference between the inventory cost in old LIFO layers and the current replacement cost (approximated by FIFO or average cost inventory). These LIFO reserve disclosures can be used to compute what cost of goods sold and ending inventory would have been if the company had used FIFO (or average cost) instead of LIFO.

The primary motivation for a company to adopt LIFO is to defer payment of income taxes on inventory holding gains.

7 Choose an inventory valuation method based on the trade-offs among income tax effects, bookkeeping costs, and the impact on the financial statements.

FIFO

- *Advantages:* corresponds with physical flow of goods; ending inventory balance is close to current replacement cost
- *Disadvantages:* matches older costs with current revenues; inventory holding gains and losses are part of gross profit; no income tax deferral

LIFO

- *Advantages:* matches current costs with current revenues; excludes inventory holding gains from gross profit; income tax deferral
- *Disadvantages:* does not correspond with the physical flow of goods; potential LIFO liquidation can draw old costs into cost of goods sold; ending inventory balance can be much lower than current replacement cost

The cash flow benefits of LIFO income tax deferral must be weighed against increased bookkeeping costs and poorer reported financial statement performance. For firms with small inventory levels or low inventory cost increases, the tax deferral benefits of LIFO are probably insignificant. Currently, the LIFO method is not acceptable under IASB standards.

8 Apply the lower-of-cost-or-market (LCM) rule to reflect declines in the market value of inventory.

The lower-of-cost-or-market (LCM) rule results in recognition of decreases in the market value of inventory. Applying the LCM rule requires careful specification of the "market" value. To use the lower-of-cost-or-market rule, the cost of the ending inventory is compared with its market value. If market is less than cost, ending inventory is written down to the market value.

The market value of inventory is equal to its replacement cost, subject to floor and ceiling constraints. The ceiling constraint is that the market value of inventory is not greater than net realizable value. The floor constraint is that the market value of the inventory is not less than net realizable value minus a normal profit margin. In summary, market value of inventory is never less than the floor value, is never more than the ceiling value, and is equal to replacement cost when replacement cost is between the floor and the ceiling.

The comparable inventory write-down rule under *IAS 2* can be labeled "lower of cost or net realizable value." Under *IAS 2*, inventory write-downs can be subsequently reversed if the inventory selling price recovers.

9 Use the gross profit method to estimate ending inventory.

The gross profit method is a simple technique for estimating ending inventory. Inventory estimates are used to confirm the accounting records and to substitute for inventory counts when a physical count is not practical. The gross profit method is as follows:

- Estimate a gross profit percentage [(Sales − Cost of goods sold)/Sales] based on historical values adjusted for significant changes in pricing policy and sales mix.
- Apply the gross profit percentage to sales to estimate cost of goods sold.
- Subtract the cost of goods sold estimate from the cost of goods available for sale to arrive at an estimated ending inventory balance.

10 Determine the financial statement impact of inventory recording errors.

Undetected inventory recording errors impact financial statements in both the year of the error and the subsequent year. Depending on the nature of the error, income can be understated or overstated.

Analysis of inventory errors is aided by recalling the simple computation:

Beginning inventory
\+ Purchases
= Goods available for sale
− Ending inventory
= Cost of goods sold

Because the ending inventory of one period becomes the beginning inventory of the next period, undetected inventory errors affect two accounting periods. A common error is the overstatement of ending inventory. This error has the effect of reducing cost of goods sold and increasing net income in the year of the error. A counterbalancing reduction in net income occurs in the following year.

11 Analyze inventory using financial ratios, and properly compare ratios of different firms after adjusting for differences in inventory valuation methods.

Inventory ratios provide information on whether the level of inventory is appropriate for the volume of sales.

Inventory turnover is computed as cost of goods sold divided by average inventory, in which average inventory is usually the simple average of beginning and ending inventory. This ratio is the number of times a business completely uses and replaces its inventory during the year.

Number of days' sales in inventory is 365 divided by inventory turnover. This ratio is the number of days a firm can continue in business without buying/manufacturing additional inventory.

These ratios can differ significantly, depending on whether a company uses FIFO, LIFO, or average cost. Use the LIFO reserve disclosures to convert a company's LIFO numbers before comparing them to another company's FIFO or average cost numbers.

EM EXPANDED MATERIAL

12 Compute estimates of FIFO, LIFO, average cost, and lower-of-cost-or-market inventory using the retail inventory method.

When the retail inventory method is used, records of goods purchased are maintained at both cost and retail amounts. A cost percentage is computed by dividing the goods available for sale at cost by the goods available for sale at retail. This cost percentage is then applied to the ending inventory at retail to get an estimate of the cost of ending inventory.

Variations on the computation of the cost percentage yield inventory estimates for a variety of valuation assumptions, such as:

- *FIFO.* The cost percentage is based on current purchases.
- *LIFO.* The cost percentage is based on beginning inventory, adjusted for the addition of any new LIFO layers.
- *Average cost.* The cost percentage is computed using both beginning inventory and current purchases and includes the effects of both markups and markdowns.
- *Lower of cost or market.* The cost percentage is computed using both beginning inventory and current purchases and includes the effects of markups but not of markdowns.

13 Use LIFO pools, dollar-value LIFO, and dollar-value LIFO retail to compute ending inventory.

Use of LIFO pools simplifies LIFO by eliminating the need to keep detailed LIFO layer information on many different products. When the quantity of items in a LIFO pool increases during a year, a new LIFO layer is added. Decreases in the quantity of some items can be offset by increases in other items, reducing the frequency of LIFO liquidations. Choosing the correct number of LIFO pools to maximize the tax deferral benefits of LIFO involves analysis of the probability of LIFO liquidation and the comparative rate of price increases for different categories of inventory.

Dollar-value LIFO further simplifies LIFO bookkeeping. With dollar-value LIFO, the dollar value of inventory (instead of the physical quantity) is the basic unit of measurement.

Dollar-value LIFO is applied as follows:

- Compute the value of ending inventory using ending prices.
- Convert this value to base-year prices by dividing by the end-of-period price index.
- Compare this number to the beginning inventory (in base-year prices) to determine whether a new LIFO layer has been added.
- All LIFO layers are then converted from base-year prices using the appropriate price index from the year in which the layer was created. New layers can be valued using an end-of-period price index (a FIFO assumption), an average price index (an average cost assumption), or a first purchase price index (a LIFO assumption).

Almost all retail companies that use LIFO employ the dollar-value LIFO retail method. The dollar-value LIFO retail method is used as follows:

- A cost percentage for the current year is computed using cost and retail information for current purchases.
- A price index is used to determine whether a new LIFO layer has been created.
- The retail values of all LIFO layers are converted to cost using the appropriate cost percentages.

14 Account for the impact of changing prices on purchase commitments.

With a purchase commitment, a company locks in the cost of inventory before the inventory is actually purchased. The LCM rule is applied if prices decline between the commitment date and the purchase date. No journal entry is made to record the commitment. However, when price declines take place after a purchase commitment has been made, a loss is recorded in the period of the price decline.

15 Record inventory purchase transactions denominated in foreign currencies.

Transactions denominated in currencies other than the U.S. dollar are foreign currency transactions for U.S. companies. Foreign currency transactions expose companies to exchange rate risk during the time between the purchase and the payment of the foreign currency obligation. Gains or losses resulting from exchange rate changes are recognized in the period in which the exchange rate changes occur.

FASB-IASB CODIFICATION SUMMARY

ifrs

Topic	FASB Accounting Standards Codification	Original FASB Standard	Corresponding IASB Standard	Differences between U.S. GAAP and IFRS
LIFO	*Section 330-10-30 par. 9-11*	*ARB 43, Chapter 4*	*IAS 2 par. 23-27*	LIFO is not allowable under IFRS.
Lower of cost or market	*Section 330-10-35 par. 1-12*	*ARB 43, Chapter 4*	*IAS 2 par. 28-33*	Under IFRS, inventory is recorded at lower of cost or net realizable value, and inventory write-down losses can be reversed if the selling price subsequently recovers.
Foreign currency transactions	*Section 830-20-35 par. 2*	*SFAS No. 52 par. 16b*	*IAS 21 par. 23a, 28*	No substantial differences

KEY TERMS

Activity-based cost (ABC) system 9-13
Average cost method 9-18
Cash discount 9-14
Ceiling 9-33
Consigned goods 9-11
Cost driver 9-13
Direct materials 9-6
Dollar-value LIFO 9-29
Entry cost 9-33
Exit value 9-33
Finished goods 9-6
First-in, first-out (FIFO) method 9-19
Floor 9-33
FOB (free on board) destination 9-10
FOB (free on board) shipping point 9-10
Gross method 9-15
Gross profit method 9-39
Gross profit percentage 9-39
Indirect materials 9-6
Inventory 9-5
Inventory turnover 9-44
Last-in, first-out (LIFO) method 9-20
LIFO conformity rule 9-27
LIFO inventory pools 9-28
LIFO layer 9-24
LIFO liquidation 9-27
LIFO reserve 9-25
Lower of cost or market (LCM) 9-33
Manufacturing overhead 9-6
Market (in "lower of cost or market") 9-33
Net method 9-14
Number of days' sales in inventory 9-45
Period costs 9-13
Periodic inventory system 9-7
Perpetual inventory system 9-7
Product (inventoriable) cost 9-13
Raw materials 9-5
Replacement cost 9-33
Shrinkage 9-9
Specific identification method 9-18
Trade discount 9-14
Work in process 9-6

EM EXPANDED MATERIAL

Cost percentage 9-47
Dollar-value LIFO retail method 9-58
Double extension 9-55
Foreign currency transaction 9-61
Initial markup 9-49
Markdowns 9-49
Markups 9-49
Original retail 9-49
Price index 9-55
Purchase commitment 9-59
Retail inventory method 9-47
Spot rate 9-61

QUESTIONS

1. What four questions are associated with the accounting for inventory?
2. **General Motors**' finished goods inventory is composed primarily of automobiles. Are automobiles always classified as "inventory" on the balance sheets of all companies? Explain.
3. What is the difference between direct materials and indirect materials?
4. (a) What are the three cost elements entering into work in process and finished goods?
   (b) What items enter into manufacturing overhead?
5. What is the general rule for distinguishing between inventory-related costs that should be included in the cost of inventory and those that should be expensed as incurred?

6. A campus bookstore has a computerized inventory system. Is it more likely that the system is a periodic system or a perpetual system? Explain.
7. Would you expect to find a perpetual or a periodic inventory system used in each of the following situations?
   (a) Diamond ring department of a jewelry store
   (b) Computer department of a college bookstore
   (c) Candy department of a college bookstore
   (d) Automobile dealership—new car department
   (e) Automobile dealership—parts department
   (f) Wholesale dealer of small tools
   (g) A plumbing supply house—plastic fittings department
8. How is inventory shrinkage computed under a perpetual inventory system?
9. Under what conditions are goods in transit legally reported as inventory by the (a) seller? (b) buyer?
10. How should (a) consigned goods and (b) installment sales be treated in computing year-end inventory costs?
11. What is the appropriate way to account for inventory sold under a repurchase agreement?
12. What is an activity-based cost (ABC) system?
13. (a) What are the two methods of accounting for cash discounts? (b) Which method is generally preferred? Why?
14. What objections can be raised to the use of the specific identification method?
15. What advantages are there to using the average cost method of inventory valuation?
16. Which better matches the normal physical flow of goods—FIFO or LIFO? Which better matches current costs and current revenues?
17. Why are LIFO and average cost more complicated with a perpetual inventory system than with a periodic system?
18. (a) Under what conditions is a LIFO layer created? (b) What is meant by "LIFO reserve"?
19. (a) What is the LIFO conformity rule? (b) How has the rule changed since it was first adopted?
20. Assume there is no change in the physical quantity of inventory for the current accounting period. During a period of rising prices, which inventory valuation method (LIFO or FIFO) will result in the greater dollar value of ending inventory? The lower payment of income taxes?
21. What kinds of companies would be *least* likely to use LIFO? Explain.
22. What is the current status of LIFO under IASB standards?
23. The use of lower of cost or market is an unnecessary continuation of the tradition of conservative accounting. Comment on this view.
24. Why are ceiling and floor limitations on replacement cost considered necessary?
25. What differences result from applying lower of cost or market to individual inventory items instead of to the inventory as a whole?
26. Why would a manager care about the value assigned to inventory transferred in from another department?
27. How do the provisions of *IAS 2* differ from the lower-of-cost-or-market rule contained in U.S. GAAP?
28. What information is needed to develop a reliable gross profit percentage for use with the gross profit method?
29. State the effect of each of the following errors made by Clawson Inc. on the income statement and the balance sheet (1) of the current period and (2) of the succeeding period:
   (a) The ending inventory is overstated as a result of a miscount of goods on hand.
   (b) The company fails to record a purchase of merchandise on account, and the merchandise purchased is not recognized in recording the ending inventory.
   (c) The ending inventory is understated as a result of a miscount of goods on hand.
30. Company A has an inventory turnover ratio of 8.0 times. Company B has an inventory turnover ratio of 10.0 times. Both companies are in the same industry. Which company manages its inventory more efficiently? Explain.

EM EXPANDED MATERIAL

31. What advantages does the retail inventory method have over the gross profit method?
32. How can FIFO and LIFO assumptions be incorporated into the retail inventory method?
33. (a) How are markdowns treated when estimating average cost using the retail inventory method? (b) How are markdowns treated when estimating lower of cost or market using the retail inventory method?
34. What factors should a company consider in identifying the appropriate number of dollar-value LIFO pools?
35. What are the major advantages of dollar-value LIFO?
36. Indexes are used for two different purposes in computing the cost of LIFO layers with dollar-value LIFO. Clearly distinguish between these uses and describe how the indexes are applied.
37. Identify three different indexes that can be used in valuing a new LIFO layer with dollar-value LIFO. Which index is most consistent with the LIFO assumption?
38. When applying the dollar-value LIFO retail method: (a) How do beginning inventory values impact the computation of the cost percentage? (b) How are markdowns treated?

39. What journal entry is made when a purchase commitment is originally entered into? Explain.
40. Are all transactions with foreign companies classified as foreign currency transactions? If not, what determines if a transaction is a foreign currency transaction?
41. Why is an adjustment made on the balance sheet date to reflect exchange rate changes?

PRACTICE EXERCISES

Practice 9-1
LO2

Perpetual and Periodic Journal Entries
During the month the company purchased inventory on account for $3,000. Sales (all on account) during the period totaled $11,200. The items sold had a cost of $4,500. Cash collections on account during the period totaled $9,750. Make the journal entries necessary to record these transactions using (1) a periodic inventory system and (2) a perpetual inventory system.

Practice 9-2
LO2

Perpetual and Periodic Computations
Beginning inventory for the period was $220,000. Purchases for the period totaled $720,000 and sales were $1,250,000. A physical count of ending inventory revealed inventory of $145,000. (1) Compute cost of goods sold assuming that a periodic system is used and (2) make the journal entry to record inventory shrinkage assuming that a perpetual system is used and cost of goods sold according to the system was $710,000.

Practice 9-3
LO3

Goods in Transit and on Consignment
The company counted its ending inventory on December 31. *None of the following items were included when the total amount of the company's ending inventory was computed:*

- $15,000 in goods located in the company's warehouse that are on consignment from another company.
- $20,000 in goods that were *sold* by the company and shipped on December 30 and were in transit on December 31; the goods were received by the customer on January 2. Terms were FOB destination.
- $30,000 in goods that were *purchased* by the company and shipped on December 30 and were in transit on December 31; the goods were received by the company on January 2. Terms were FOB shipping point.
- $40,000 in goods that were *sold* by the company and shipped on December 30 and were in transit on December 31; the goods were received by the customer on January 2. Terms were FOB shipping point.

The company's reported inventory (before any corrections) was $225,000. What is the correct amount of the company's inventory on December 31?

Practice 9-4
LO4

Schedule of Cost of Goods Manufactured
The company reported the following information for the year:

Ending work-in-process inventory	$100,000
Depreciation on factory building	32,000
Salespersons' salaries	27,000
Beginning raw materials inventory	40,000
Direct labor	198,000
Factory supervisor's salary	56,000
Depreciation on company headquarters building	21,000
Beginning work-in-process inventory	76,000
Ending raw materials inventory	34,000
Indirect labor	36,000
Advertising costs	50,000
Purchases of raw materials	230,000

Prepare a schedule of cost of goods manufactured for the year.

Practice 9-5

LO4

Accounting for Purchase Discounts

On May 23, the company purchased $500,000 in inventory on account. The purchase terms are 2/10, n/30. Make the journal entries to record the purchase of and subsequent payment for these goods assuming: (1) the company uses the net method and paid for the goods on June 1, (2) the company uses the net method and paid for the goods on June 15, (3) the company uses the gross method and paid for the goods on June 1, and (4) the company uses the gross method and paid for the goods on June 15. Assume a perpetual inventory system.

Practice 9-6

LO5

Inventory Valuation: FIFO, LIFO, and Average

The company reported the following inventory data for the year:

	Units	Cost per Unit
Beginning inventory	300	$17.50
Purchases:		
March 23	900	18.00
September 16	1,200	18.25
Units remaining at year-end	400	

Compute (1) cost of goods sold and (2) ending inventory assuming (a) FIFO inventory valuation, (b) LIFO inventory valuation, and (c) average cost inventory valuation. The company uses a periodic inventory system.

Practice 9-7

LO5

Inventory Valuation: Complications with a Perpetual System

Refer to Practice 9-6. Assume that the sales occurred as follows:

	Units Sold
January 16	100
July 15	600
November 1	1,300
Total	2,000

Compute (1) cost of goods sold and (2) ending inventory assuming (a) FIFO inventory valuation, (b) LIFO inventory valuation, and (c) average cost inventory valuation. The company uses a *perpetual* inventory system.

Practice 9-8

LO6

LIFO Layers

The company started business at the beginning of Year 1. Inventory purchases and sales during the first four years of the company's business are as follows:

	Units Purchased	Cost per Unit	Units Sold
Year 1	100	$2.50	80
Year 2	160	3.00	130
Year 3	180	3.40	180
Year 4	260	4.00	200

Compute the company's ending inventory as of the end of Year 4. The company uses LIFO inventory valuation.

Practice 9-9

LO6

LIFO Reserve and LIFO Liquidation

Refer to Practice 9-8. Compute the following:

1. LIFO reserve at the end of Year 4.
2. Cost of goods sold for Year 4.
3. Cost of goods sold for Year 4 assuming that units purchased had been 150 instead of 260.

Practice 9-10

LO7

LIFO and Income Taxes

Refer to Practice 9-8. Assume that the company has no expenses except for cost of goods sold, the selling price per unit is $6 in each year, and that the income tax rate is 40%. Compute the total amount of income taxes owed for Year 1 through Year 4 assuming that (1) the company uses LIFO inventory valuation and (2) the company uses FIFO inventory valuation.

Practice 9-11

LO7

Lower of Cost or Market

The following information pertains to the company's ending inventory:

	Original Cost	Selling Price	Selling Cost	Replacement Cost	Normal Profit
Item A	$ 575	$ 700	$ 50	$ 600	$100
Item B	700	820	80	550	150
Item C	1,180	1,250	100	1,100	300

Apply lower-of-cost-or-market accounting to each inventory item individually. What *total* amount should be reported as inventory in the balance sheet?

Practice 9-12

LO8

Lower of Cost or Market: Individual vs. Aggregate

Refer to Practice 9-11. Apply lower-of-cost-or-market accounting to the inventory as a whole. What *total* amount should be reported as inventory in the balance sheet?

Practice 9-13

LO8

Lower-of-Cost-or-Market Journal Entries

The company started business at the beginning of Year 1. The company applies the lower-of-cost-or-market (LCM) rule to its inventory as a whole. Inventory cost and market values as of the end of Year 1 and Year 2 were as follows:

	Cost	Market Value
Year 1	$2,000	$1,600
Year 2	3,400	3,300

The market value numbers already include consideration of the replacement cost, the ceiling, and the floor. Make the journal entry necessary to record the LCM adjustment at the end of (1) Year 1 and (2) Year 2. The company uses an allowance account for any LCM adjustments.

Practice 9-14

LO8

Returned Inventory

The company sells large industrial equipment. A piece of equipment with an original cost of $250,000 and an original selling price of $390,000 was recently returned. It is expected that the equipment will be able to be resold for just $225,000. The company normally earns a gross profit of 35.9% of the selling price. How much loss is recorded when the inventory is returned and how much gross profit will be reported when the equipment is resold assuming that the returned inventory is recorded at (1) its original cost, (2) its net realizable value, and (3) its net realizable value minus a normal gross profit?

Practice 9-15
LO9

Gross Profit Method

On July 23, the company's inventory was destroyed in a hurricane-related flood. For insurance purposes, the company must reliably estimate the amount of inventory on hand on July 23. The company uses a periodic inventory system. The following data have been assembled:

Inventory, January 1	$1,000,000
Purchases, January 1–July 23	3,700,000
Sales, January 1–July 23	5,000,000
Historical gross profit percentages:	
Last year	60%
Two years ago	55%

Estimate the company's inventory as of July 23 using (1) last year's gross profit percentage and (2) the gross profit percentage from two years ago.

Practice 9-16
LO10

Inventory Errors

At the beginning of Year 1, the company's inventory level was stated correctly. At the end of Year 1, inventory was overstated by $2,200. At the end of Year 2, inventory was understated by $450. At the end of Year 3, inventory was correctly stated. Reported net income was $3,000 in Year 1, $3,000 in Year 2, and $3,000 in Year 3. Compute the correct amount of net income in (1) Year 1, (2) Year 2, and (3) Year 3. Ignore income taxes.

Practice 9-17
LO11

Computing Inventory Ratios

The company reported the following information for the year:

Beginning accounts receivable	$2,000
Sales	8,000
Ending inventory	3,000
Ending accounts receivable	2,400
Cost of goods sold	4,200
Beginning inventory	2,600

Compute (1) inventory turnover and (2) number of days' sales in inventory.

EM EXPANDED MATERIAL

Practice 9-18
LO12

Retail Inventory Method

The company reported the following information for the month:

	Cost	Retail
Inventory, January 1	$40,000	$60,000
Purchases in January	40,000	70,000

Sales for the month totaled $94,000. Compute the estimated cost of inventory on hand at the end of the month using the average cost assumption.

Practice 9-19
LO12

Markups and Markdowns

The company reported the following information relating to inventory for the month of April:

	Cost	Retail
Inventory, January 1	$25,000	$ 50,000
Purchases in January	40,000	70,000
Markups		30,000
Markdowns		(25,000)

Sales for the month totaled $80,000. Compute the estimated cost of inventory on hand at the end of the month using the average cost assumption.

Practice 9-20

LO13

LIFO Pools

The company has one LIFO pool. Information relating to the products in this pool is as follows:

Beginning inventory, January 1	25 units @ $20 each
Purchase, February 12	30 units @ $22 each
Purchase, February 28	45 units @ $26 each
Purchase, March 15	60 units @ $28 each
Sales for the first quarter	120 units

Compute the ending LIFO inventory value for the first quarter assuming new layers are valued based on a LIFO cost assumption.

Practice 9-21

LO13

Dollar-Value LIFO

The company manufactures a single product and has decided to adopt the dollar-value LIFO inventory method. The inventory value on that date using the newly adopted dollar-value LIFO method was $100,000. Inventory at year-end prices was $120,000, and the year-end price index was 1.05. Compute the inventory value at year-end assuming incremental layers are valued at year-end prices.

Practice 9-22

LO13

Dollar-Value LIFO Retail

The company compiled the following information concerning inventory for the current year:

Date	Year-End Price Index at Retail	Incremental Layer Index	Incremental Cost Percentage	Inventory at Retail
Jan. 1	1.00	1.00	65%	$ 80,000
Dec. 31	1.10	1.05	70%	110,000

Compute the inventory cost at year-end using the dollar-value LIFO retail method.

Practice 9-23

LO14

Purchase Commitments

On November 17 of Year 1, the company entered into a commitment to purchase 250,000 ounces of gold on February 14 of Year 2 at a price of $1,110.20 per ounce. On December 31 of Year 1, the market price of gold is $1,075.10 per ounce. On February 14, the price of gold is $1,092.00 per ounce. Make the journal entries necessary to record (1) the November 17 purchase commitment, (2) any necessary adjustment at December 31, and (3) the actual purchase (for cash) on February 14. The company uses a perpetual inventory system.

Practice 9-24

LO15

Foreign Currency Inventory Purchases

On November 6 of Year 1, the company purchased inventory (on account) from a supplier located in Indonesia. The purchase price is 100,000,000 Indonesian rupiah. On November 6, the exchange rate was 8,700 rupiah for 1 U.S. dollar. On December 31, the exchange rate was 10,000 rupiah for 1 U.S. dollar. The company paid the account on March 23 of Year 2. On that date, the exchange rate was 9,100 rupiah for 1 U.S. dollar. Make the journal entries necessary on (1) November 6, (2) December 31, and (3) March 23. The company uses a perpetual inventory system.

EXERCISES

Exercise 9-25

LO3

Passage of Title

The Anson Manufacturing Company reviewed its year-end inventory and found the following items. Indicate which items should be included in the inventory balance at December 31, 2013. Give your reasons for the treatment you suggest.

(a) A packing case containing a product costing $1,210 was standing in the shipping room when the physical inventory was taken. It was not included in the inventory because it was marked "Hold for shipping instructions." The customer's order was dated December 21, but the case was shipped and the customer billed on January 8, 2014.

(b) Merchandise costing $545 was received on December 28, 2013, and the invoice was recorded. The invoice was in the hands of the purchasing agent; it was marked "On consignment."

(c) Merchandise received on January 4, 2014, costing $905 was entered in the purchase register on January 5. The invoice showed shipment was made FOB shipping point on December 31, 2013. Because it was not on hand during the inventory count, it was not included.

(d) A special machine, fabricated to order for a particular customer, was finished and in the shipping room on December 30. The customer was billed on that date and the machine was excluded from inventory although it was shipped January 2, 2014. The customer had requested, in writing, that the special machine be held for shipment until January 2014.

(e) Merchandise costing $1,960 was received on January 3, 2014, and the related purchase invoice was recorded January 5. The invoice showed the shipment was made on December 29, 2013, FOB destination.

(f) Merchandise costing $2,400 was sold on an installment basis on December 15. The customer took possession of the goods on that date. The merchandise was included in inventory because, technically, Anson still holds legal title in order to enforce payment. Historical experience suggests that full payment on installment sales is received approximately 99% of the time.

(g) Goods costing $1,730 were sold and delivered on December 20. The goods were included in inventory because the sale was accompanied by a repurchase agreement requiring Anson to buy back the inventory in February 2014.

Exercise 9-26

LO3

Passage of Title

The management of Kauer Company has engaged you to assist in the preparation of year-end (December 31) financial statements. You are told that on November 30, the correct inventory level was 150,000 units. During the month of December, sales totaled 50,000 units including 25,000 units shipped on consignment to Towsey Company. A letter received from Towsey indicates that as of December 31, it had sold 20,000 units and was still trying to sell the remainder. A review of the December purchase orders to various suppliers shows the following:

Purchase Order Date	Invoice Date	Number of Units	Date Shipped	Date Received	Terms
Dec. 2, 2012	Jan. 3, 2013	10,000	Jan. 2, 2013	Jan. 3, 2013	FOB shipping point
Dec. 11, 2012	Jan. 3, 2013	8,000	Dec. 22, 2012	Dec. 24, 2012	FOB destination
Dec. 13, 2012	Jan. 2, 2013	13,000	Dec. 28, 2012	Jan. 2, 2013	FOB shipping point
Dec. 23, 2012	Dec. 26, 2012	12,000	Jan. 2, 2013	Jan. 3, 2013	FOB shipping point
Dec. 28, 2012	Jan. 10, 2013	10,000	Dec. 31, 2012	Jan. 5, 2013	FOB destination
Dec. 31, 2012	Jan. 10, 2013	15,000	Jan. 3, 2013	Jan. 6, 2013	FOB destination

Kauer Company uses the "passing of legal title" for inventory recognition. Compute the number of units that should be included in the year-end inventory.

Exercise 9-27

LO8

Valuation of Return

Napali Inc. sells new equipment with a $5,300 list price. A dissatisfied customer returned one piece of equipment. Napali determines that the returned equipment can be resold if it is reconditioned. The expected sales price of the reconditioned equipment is $4,500; the reconditioning expenses are estimated to be $600; and normal profit is 35% of the sales price.

1. Prepare the journal entry to record the sale of the reconditioned equipment for cash assuming that the floor value is used to record the returned equipment.
2. Prepare the journal entry to record the sale of the reconditioned equipment for cash assuming that the original list price is used to record the returned equipment.
3. Evaluate the entries.

Exercise 9-28

LO4

Recording Purchase Returns

On July 23, Stevensonville Company purchased goods on account for $6,000. Stevensonville later returned defective goods costing $450.

Record the purchase and the return of the defective goods assuming (1) a periodic inventory system and (2) a perpetual inventory system.

Exercise 9-29

LO4

Cash Discounts

Olavssen Hardware regularly buys merchandise from Dawson Suppliers. Olavssen uses the net method to record purchases and discounts. On August 15, Olavssen Hardware purchased material from Dawson Suppliers. The invoice received from Dawson showed an invoiced price of $15,536 and payment terms of 2/10, n/30. Payment was sent to Dawson Suppliers on August 28. Prepare entries to record the purchase and subsequent payment assuming a periodic inventory system. (*Note:* Round to nearest dollar.)

Exercise 9-30

LO1

Identification of Inventory Costs and Categories

The records of Burtone Company contain the following cost categories. Burtone manufactures exercise equipment and iron weights.

(a) Cost of materials used to repair factory equipment
(b) Depreciation on the fleet of salespersons' cars
(c) Cost to purchase iron
(d) Salaries of the factory supervisors
(e) Cost of heat, electricity, and insurance for the company office building
(f) Wages of the workers who shape the iron weights
(g) Property taxes on the factory building
(h) Cost of oil for the factory equipment
(i) Salary of the company president
(j) Pension benefits of workers who repair factory equipment

For each category, indicate whether the cost is an inventory cost (I) or if it should be expensed as incurred (E). For each inventory cost, indicate whether the cost is part of direct materials (DM), direct labor (DL), or manufacturing overhead (MOH).

Exercise 9-31

LO2

Perpetual and Periodic Inventory Systems

The following inventory information is for Stevenson Company.

Beginning inventory	200 units @ $8
Purchases	350 units @ $8
Ending inventory	100 units

Sales for the year totaled $5,900. All sales and purchases are on account.

1. Make the journal entries necessary to record purchases and sales during the year assuming a periodic inventory system.
2. Assume that a periodic inventory system is used. Compute cost of goods sold.
3. Assume that a perpetual inventory system is used. The perpetual records indicate that the sales of $5,900 represent 400 units with a total cost of $3,200. Make the journal entries necessary to record purchases, sales, and inventory shrinkage for the year.

Exercise 9-32
LO4
SPREADSHEET

Net and Gross Methods—Entries

On December 3, Ainge Printing purchased inventory listed at $7,400 from Craig Paper Supply. Terms of the purchase were 3/10, n/20. Ainge Printing also purchased inventory from Tippetts Ink Wholesale on December 10 for a list price of $10,300. Terms of the purchase were 3/10, n/30. On December 16, Ainge paid both suppliers for these purchases. Ainge does not use a perpetual inventory system.

1. Give the entries to record the purchases and invoice payments assuming that (a) the net method is used and (b) the gross method is used.
2. Assume that Ainge has not paid either of the invoices at December 31. Give the year-end adjusting entry if the net method is used.

Exercise 9-33
LO11

Inventory Turnover

The Rigby Supplement Company showed the following data in its financial statements.

	2013	2012
Cost of goods sold	$1,400,000	$1,125,000
Beginning inventory	275,000	175,000
Ending inventory	405,000	275,000

1. Compute the number of days' sales in average inventory for both 2012 and 2013. What can you infer from these numbers?
2. How would you interpret the answer to (1) if this company were in the business of selling fresh fruits and vegetables? What if the company sold real estate?

Exercise 9-34
LO5
SPREADSHEET

Inventory Computation Using Different Cost Flows

The Webster Store shows the following information relating to one of its products.

Inventory, January 1	250 units @ $17.00
Sales, January 8	200 units
Purchases, January 10	900 units @ $18.00
Sales, January 18	800 units
Purchases, January 20	1,200 units @ $19.50
Sales, January 25	1,000 units

What are the values of ending inventory under a periodic inventory system assuming a (1) FIFO, (2) LIFO, and (3) average cost flow? (*Note:* Round unit costs to three decimal places.)

Exercise 9-35

LO5

SPREADSHEET

Inventory Computation Using Different Cost Flows

Brooklyn Corporation had the following transactions relating to product X during September.

Date			Units	Unit Cost
September	1	Balance on hand	600 units	$1.50
	6	Purchase	200 units	2.00
	12	Sale	400 units	
	13	Sale	100 units	
	18	Purchase	250 units	3.00
	20	Purchase	150 units	3.50
	25	Sale	300 units	

Determine the ending inventory value under each of the following costing methods:

1. FIFO (perpetual)
2. FIFO (periodic)
3. LIFO (perpetual)
4. LIFO (periodic)

Exercise 9-36

LO6

REVERSE SOLVABLE

Computation of Beginning Inventory

A note to the financial statements of Highland Inc. at December 31, 2013, reads as follows:

> Because of the manufacturer's production problems for our Humdinger Limited line, our inventories were unavoidably reduced. Under the LIFO inventory accounting method currently being used for tax and financial accounting purposes, the net effect of all the inventory changes was to increase pretax income by $1,000,000 over what it would have been had the inventory of Humdinger Limited been maintained at the normal physical levels on hand at the start of the year.

The unit purchase price of the merchandise was $25 per unit during the year. Highland Inc. uses the periodic inventory system. Additional data concerning Highland's inventory were as follows:

Date	Physical Count of Inventory	LIFO Cost of Inventory
January 1, 2013	500,000 units	$?
December 31, 2013	400,000 units	$3,600,000

1. What was the unit average cost for the 100,000 units sold from the beginning inventory?
2. What was the reported value for the January 1, 2013, inventory?

Exercise 9-37

LO4, LO5

REVERSE SOLVABLE

Computation of Beginning Inventory from Ending Inventory

The Atlas Company sells product T. During a move to a new location, the inventory records for product T were misplaced. The bookkeeper has been able to gather some information from the sales records and gives you the data shown below.

July sales:

82,100 units at $9.00

July purchases:

Date		Quantity	Unit Cost
July	5	17,000	$4.50
	9	17,800	5.25
	12	18,100	5.00
	25	19,000	5.50

On July 31, 24,000 units were on hand with a total value of $129,500. Atlas has always used a periodic FIFO inventory costing system. Gross profit on sales for July was $358,100. Reconstruct the beginning inventory (quantity and dollar value) for the month of July.

Exercise 9-38
LO2

Computing Cash Expenditure for Inventory

Using the following data, compute the total cash expended for inventory in 2013.

Accounts payable:	
January 1, 2013	$ 350,000
December 31, 2013	525,000
Cost of goods sold—2013	1,125,000
Inventory balance:	
January 1, 2013	$ 600,000
December 31, 2013	540,000

Exercise 9-39
LO4, LO5
REVERSE SOLVABLE

Inventory Computation from Incomplete Records

A flood recently destroyed many of the financial records of Yak Manufacturing Company. Management has hired you to re-create as much financial information as possible for the month of July. You are able to find out that the company uses an average cost inventory valuation system. You also learn that Yak makes a physical count at the end of each month in order to determine monthly ending inventory values. By examining various documents, you are able to gather the following information:

Ending inventory at July 31	60,000 units
Total cost of units available for sale in July	$145,210
Cost of goods sold during July	$116,410
Cost of beginning inventory, July 1	$0.40 per unit
Gross profit on sales for July	$93,590

July purchases:

Date		Units	Unit Cost
July	5	55,000	$0.51
	11	53,000	0.50
	15	45,000	0.55
	16	47,000	0.53

You are asked to provide the following information.

1. Number of units on hand, July 1
2. Units sold during July

3. Unit cost of inventory at July 31
4. Value of inventory at July 31

Exercise 9-40

LO8

Lower-of-Cost-or-Market Valuation

Newcomer, Inc., values inventories using the lower-of-cost-or-market method applied to total inventory. Inventory values at the end of the company's first and second years of operation follow.

	Cost	Market
Year 1	$58,000	$53,000
Year 2	75,000	73,800

1. Prepare the journal entries necessary to reflect the proper inventory valuation at the end of each year. (Assume Newcomer uses an inventory allowance account.)
2. For Year 1, assume sales were $510,000 and purchases were $440,000. What amount would be reported as cost of goods sold on the income statement for Year 1 if: (a) the inventory decline is reported separately and (b) the inventory decline is not reported separately?

Exercise 9-41

LO8

Lower-of-Cost-or-Market Valuation

The following inventory data are available for Nordic Ski Shop at December 31.

1. Determine the value of ending inventory using the lower-of-cost-or-market method applied to (a) individual items and (b) total inventory.
2. Prepare any journal entries required to adjust the ending inventory if lower of cost or market is applied to (a) individual items and (b) total inventory.

	Cost	Market
Skis	$110,000	$124,000
Boots	85,000	76,000
Ski equipment	36,000	33,000
Ski apparel	20,000	24,000

Exercise 9-42

LO8

Lower-of-Cost-or-Market Valuation

Determine the proper carrying value of the following inventory items.

Item	Cost	Replacement Cost	Sales Price	Selling Expenses	Normal Profit
Product 431	$2.50	$2.60	$3.20	$0.45	$0.20
Product 432	1.12	1.00	1.28	0.32	0.07
Product 433	0.54	0.50	0.68	0.13	0.10
Product 434	0.75	0.85	1.07	0.23	0.04
Product 435	1.69	1.60	1.86	0.18	0.04
Product 436	2.03	1.95	2.26	0.26	0.30

Exercise 9-43
LO7

SPREADSHEET

Gross Margin Differences—FIFO vs. LIFO

Assume the Bullock Corporation had the following purchases and sales of its single product during its first three years of operation.

	Purchases		Sales	
Year	Units	Unit Cost	Units	Unit Price
1	10,000	$10	8,000	$14
2	9,000	12	9,000	17
3	8,000	15	10,000	18
	27,000		27,000	

Cost of goods sold is Bullock's only expense. The income tax rate is 40%.

1. Determine the net income (after tax) for each of the three years assuming FIFO historical cost flow.
2. Determine the net income (after tax) for each of the three years assuming LIFO historical cost flow.
3. Compare the total net income over the life of the business. How do the different cost flow assumptions affect net income and cash flows over the life of the business? From a cash flow perspective, which cost flow assumption is better? Explain.

Exercise 9-44
LO7

Income Differences—FIFO vs. LIFO

First-in, first-out has been used for inventory valuation by the Bartlett Co. since it was organized in 2010. Using the data that follow, redetermine the net incomes for each year on the assumption of inventory valuation on the last-in, first-out basis:

	2010	2011	2012	2013
Reported net income—FIFO basis	$22,300	$42,400	$ 61,350	$ 58,200
Reported ending inventories—FIFO basis	44,300	89,900	112,000	125,000
Ending inventories—LIFO basis	35,100	65,300	80,000	114,300

Exercise 9-45
LO6

LIFO Inventory Computation

White Farm Supply's records for the first three months of its existence show purchases of commodity Y2 as follows:

	Number of Units	Cost
August	5,500	$28,050
September	8,000	41,600
October	5,100	27,030

The inventory of commodity Y2 at the end of October using FIFO is valued at $36,390.

1. Assuming that none of commodity Y2 was sold during August and September, what value would be shown at the end of October if LIFO cost was assumed?
2. If White Farm uses LIFO, what disclosure could it make in its October 31 quarterly report concerning the FIFO value of inventory?

Exercise 9-46
LO6

Impact on Profit of Failure to Replace LIFO Layers

Harrison Lumber Company uses a periodic LIFO method for inventory costing. The following information relates to the plywood inventory carried by Harrison Lumber.

Plywood inventory:

Date	Quantity	LIFO Costing Layers
May 1	600 sheets	300 sheets at $ 8.00
		225 sheets at $11.00
		75 sheets at $13.00

Plywood purchases:

May 8	115 sheets at $14.00
17	95 sheets at $15.00
29	200 sheets at $14.50

All sales of plywood during May were at $20 per sheet. On May 31, there were 360 sheets of plywood in the storeroom.

1. Compute the gross profit on sales for May, as a dollar value and as a percentage of sales.
2. Assume that because of a lumber strike, Harrison Lumber is not able to purchase the May 29 order of lumber until June 10. Assuming sales remained the same, recompute the gross profit on sales for May, as a dollar value and as a percentage of sales.
3. Compare the results of (1) and (2) and explain the difference.

Exercise 9-47

LO10

Correction of LIFO Inventory

The Manwaring Products Company's inventory record appears below.

	Purchases		Sales
	Quantity	Unit Cost	Quantity
2011	8,200	$4.30	5,800
2012	8,900	4.80	9,200
2013	6,800	5.10	6,300

The company uses a LIFO cost flow assumption. It reported ending inventories as follows for its first three years of operations:

2011	$10,320
2012	9,630
2013	12,120

Determine if the Manwaring Products Company has reported its inventory correctly. Assuming that 2013 accounts are not yet closed, make any necessary correcting entries.

Exercise 9-48

LO5

Comparison of Inventory Methods

Dutch Truck Sales sells semitrailers. The current inventory includes the following five semitrailers (identical except for paint color) along with purchase dates and costs:

Semitrailer	Purchase Date	Cost
1	April 3, 2013	$73,000
2	April 10, 2013	70,000
3	April 10, 2013	71,000
4	May 4, 2013	77,000
5	May 12, 2013	78,500

On May 20, 2013, a trucking firm purchased semitrailer 3 from Dutch for $86,000.

1. Compute the gross margin on this sale assuming Dutch uses the:
   (a) FIFO inventory method
   (b) LIFO inventory method
   (c) Specific identification method
2. Which inventory method do you think Dutch should use? Why?

Exercise 9-49

LO7, LO8

Comparison of Inventory Valuation Methods

The Crevier Corporation began business on January 1, 2013. The following table shows information about inventories, as of December 31, for three consecutive years under different valuation methods. Assume that purchases are $60,000 each year. Using this information and assuming that the same method is used each year, you are to answer each of the questions that follow.

	LIFO	FIFO	Market	Lower of Cost or Market*
2013	$12,300	$15,100	$14,800	$14,500
2014	10,400	11,600	8,800	11,500
2015	11,600	13,400	13,000	12,900

* FIFO cost, item-by-item valuation.

1. Which inventory basis would result in the highest net income for 2013?
2. Which inventory basis would result in the highest net income for 2014?
3. Which inventory basis would result in the lowest net income for the three years combined?
4. For the year 2014, how much higher or lower would net income be on the FIFO cost basis than on the lower-of-cost-or-market basis?

Exercise 9-50

LO10

Effect on Net Income of Inventory Errors

The Martin Company reported income before taxes of $370,000 for 2012 and $526,000 for 2013. A later audit produced the following information:

(a) The ending inventory for 2012 included 2,000 units erroneously priced at $5.90 per unit. The correct cost was $9.50 per unit.

(b) Merchandise costing $17,500 was shipped to the Martin Company, FOB shipping point, on December 26, 2012. The purchase was recorded in 2012, but the merchandise was excluded from the ending inventory because it was not received until January 4, 2013.

(c) On December 28, 2012, merchandise costing $2,900 was sold to Deluxe Paint Shop. Deluxe had asked Martin in writing to keep the merchandise for it until January 2, when it would come and pick it up. Because the merchandise was still in the store at year-end, the merchandise was included in the inventory count. The sale was correctly recorded in December 2012.

(d) Craft Company sold merchandise costing $1,500 to Martin Company. The purchase was made on December 29, 2012, and the merchandise was shipped on December 30. Terms were FOB shipping point. Because the Martin Company bookkeeper was on vacation, neither the purchase nor the receipt of goods was recorded on the books until January 2013.

Assume that all amounts are material and a physical count of inventory was taken every December 31.

1. Compute the corrected income before taxes for each year.
2. By what amount did the total income before taxes change for the two years combined?

3. Assume all errors were found in February 2013, just after the books were closed for 2012. What journal entry would be made? Martin uses a periodic inventory system.

Exercise 9-51
LO9
REVERSE SOLVABLE

Inventory Loss—Gross Profit Method

On June 30, 2013, a flash flood damaged the warehouse and factory of Magna Corporation, completely destroying the work-in-process inventory. There was no damage to either the raw materials or finished goods inventories. A physical inventory taken after the flood revealed the following valuations:

Finished goods	$123,000
Work in process	0
Raw materials	46,100

The inventory on January 1, 2013, consisted of the following:

Finished goods	$109,000
Work in process	103,000
Raw materials	49,300
	$261,300

A review of the books and records disclosed that the gross profit margin historically approximated 42% of sales. The sales for the first six months of 2013 were $584,000. Raw materials purchases were $88,000. Direct labor costs for this period were $130,000, and manufacturing overhead has historically been applied at 70% of direct labor.

Compute the value of the work-in-process inventory lost on June 30, 2013.

Exercise 9-52
LO10

Correction of Inventory Errors

Annual income for the Stoker Co. for the period 2009–2013 appears below. However, a review of the records for the company reveals inventory misstatements as listed. Calculate corrected net income for each year.

	2009	2010	2011	2012	2013
Reported net income (loss)	$18,000	$13,000	$2,000	$ (5,800)	$16,000
Inventory overstatement, end of year		6,100			3,600
Inventory understatement, end of year	4,500			10,500	

Exercise 9-53
LO9
REVERSE SOLVABLE

Inventory Loss—Gross Profit Method

On August 15, 2013, a hurricane damaged a warehouse of Rheinhart Merchandise Company. The entire inventory and many accounting records stored in the warehouse were completely destroyed. Although the inventory was not insured, a portion could be sold for scrap. Through the use of the remaining records, the following data are assembled:

Inventory, January 1	$ 367,000
Purchases, January 1–August 15	1,385,000
Cash sales, January 1–August 15	225,000
Collection of accounts receivable, January 1–August 15	2,115,000
Accounts receivable, January 1	175,000
Accounts receivable, August 15	265,000
Salvage value of inventory	5,000
Gross profit percentage on sales	32%

Compute the inventory loss as a result of the hurricane.

Exercise 9-54
LO4

Cost of Goods Manufactured Schedule
The following quarterly cost data have been accumulated for Oakeson Mfg. Inc:

Raw materials—beginning inventory (Jan. 1, 2013)	80 units @ $6.50
Purchases	75 units @ $8.00
	120 units @ $8.50

Transferred 195 units of raw materials to work in process:

Work in process—beginning inventory (Jan. 1, 2013)	53 units @ $14.00
Direct labor	$3,100
Manufacturing overhead	$2,950
Work in process—ending inventory (Mar. 31, 2013)	47 units @ $14.25

Prepare a cost of goods manufactured schedule for Oakeson Mfg. Inc. for the quarter ended March 31, 2013. Assume the use of FIFO for raw materials inventory.

EM EXPANDED MATERIAL

Exercise 9-55
LO14

Loss on Purchase Commitments
On October 1, 2013, Sloan Oil Inc. entered into a 6-month, $650,000 purchase commitment for a supply of oil. On December 31, 2013, the market value of oil had fallen to $563,000. Make the journal entries necessary on December 31, 2013, and on March 31, 2014, assuming that the market value of the inventory on March 31 is $430,000.

Exercise 9-56
LO13

Computing Inventory Using LIFO Pools
Miller Mfg. has one LIFO pool. Information relating to the products in this pool is as follows:

Beginning inventory, January 1	60 units @ $10 each
Purchase, February 12	45 units @ $12 each
Purchase, February 28	75 units @ $18 each
Purchase, March 15	65 units @ $12.50 each
Sales for the first quarter	135 units

Compute the ending LIFO inventory value for the first quarter assuming new layers are valued based on:

1. A FIFO assumption
2. A LIFO assumption
3. An average cost assumption

Exercise 9-57
LO13

Dollar-Value LIFO Retail Method
On February 15, 2014, Rooker, Madras & Associates compiled the following information concerning inventory for five years. They used the dollar-value LIFO retail inventory method.

Date	Year-End Price Index at Retail	Incremental Layer Index	Incremental Cost Percentage	Inventory
Dec. 31, 2009	1.00	1.00	71%	$155,000
Dec. 31, 2010	1.04	1.02	72	188,600
Dec. 31, 2011	1.14	1.09	64	192,500
Dec. 31, 2012	1.12	1.11	63	194,200
Dec. 31, 2013	1.16	1.12	67	195,800

Compute the inventory cost at the end of each year under the dollar-value LIFO retail method. (*Note:* Round all dollar amounts to the nearest dollar.)

Exercise 9-58

LO13

Dollar-Value LIFO Inventory Method

The Wernli Manufacturing Company manufactures a single product. The managers, Brandon and Chris Wernli, decided on December 31, 2010, to adopt the dollar-value LIFO inventory method. The inventory value on that date using the newly adopted dollar-value LIFO method was $700,000. Additional information follows:

Date	Inventory at Year-End Prices	Year-End Price Index
Dec. 31, 2011	$803,000	1.10
Dec. 31, 2012	806,400	1.12
Dec. 31, 2013	894,000	1.20

Compute the inventory value at December 31 of each year using the dollar-value method, assuming incremental layers are valued at year-end prices.

Exercise 9-59

LO13

Dollar-Value LIFO Inventory Method

Jennifer Inc. adopted dollar-value LIFO on December 31, 2010. Data for 2010–2013 follow:

Inventory and index on the adoption date, December 31, 2010:	
Dollar-value LIFO inventory	$250,000
Price index at year-end (the base year)	1.00
Inventory information in succeeding years:	

Date	Inventory at Year-End Prices	Year-End Price Index	Average Price Index
Dec. 31, 2011	$314,720	1.12	1.04
Dec. 31, 2012	361,800	1.20	1.14
Dec. 31, 2013	353,822	1.27	1.20

1. Compute the inventory value at December 31 of each year under the dollar-value method, assuming new layers are valued using the average price index.
2. Compute the inventory value at December 31, 2013, assuming that dollar-value procedures were adopted at December 31, 2011, rather than in 2010. The beginning layer is the December 31, 2011, balance.

Exercise 9-60

LO12

Retail Inventory Method

The Help-U-Succeed Bookstore recently received a shipment of accounting textbooks from the publisher. Following the receipt of the shipment, the FASB issued a major new accounting standard that related directly to the contents of one chapter of the text. Portions of this chapter became "obsolete" immediately as a result of the FASB's action. In order to sell the books, the bookstore marked down the selling price and offered a separate supplement covering the new standard, which was provided at no cost by the publisher. Information relating to the cost and selling price of the text for the month of September is given below.

	Cost	Retail
Beginning inventory	$ 2,400	$ 3,000
Purchases	27,000	36,000
Freight-in	1,800	
Markdowns		2,600
Sales		31,200

Based on the data given, compute the estimated inventory at the end of the month using the retail inventory method and assuming:

1. Lower-of-cost-or-market valuation
2. Average cost valuation

Exercise 9-61
LO12

Retail Inventory Method

Carmel Department Store uses the retail inventory method. On December 31, 2013, the following information relating to the inventory was gathered:

	Cost	Retail
Inventory, January 1, 2013	$ 26,550	$ 45,000
Sales		430,000
Purchases	309,000	435,000
Purchase discounts	4,200	
Freight-in	5,250	
Markups		30,000
Markdowns		40,000
Sales discounts		5,000

Compute the ending inventory value at December 31, 2013, using the:

1. Average cost method
2. Lower-of-cost-or-market method

Exercise 9-62
LO12

Retail Inventory Method

The Evening Out Clothing Store values its inventory using the retail inventory method. The following data are available for the month of November 2013:

	Cost	Retail
Inventory, November 1	$107,600	$160,000
Purchases	308,608	440,000
Sales		488,000

Compute the estimated inventory at November 30, 2013, assuming:

1. FIFO
2. LIFO
3. Average cost

Exercise 9-63
LO15

Foreign Currency Purchase

Kyoto Manufacturing produces automobile mufflers, which are then sent to the United States where they are installed in domestically built cars. Truck Inc., a U.S. auto company, received a shipment of mufflers on December 15, 2012. The mufflers were subsequently paid for on January 30, 2013. The invoice was denominated in Korean won and totaled 4,500,000 won. The number of Korean won required to purchase 1 U.S. dollar fluctuated as follows:

	Exchange Rates
December 15, 2012	1,000
December 31, 2012	900
January 30, 2013	880

Provide the necessary journal entries for Truck Inc. to record the above transactions assuming Truck Inc.'s fiscal year-end is December 31.

Exercise 9-64

LO15

Foreign Currency Purchase

Wittenbecher's, a German company that supplies your firm with a necessary raw material, recently shipped 15,000 units of the material to your production facility.

1. Prepare the necessary journal entries to record the purchase of the goods and the subsequent payment 30 days later if the selling price on the invoice is $3 per unit.
2. Prepare the necessary journal entries to record the purchase of the goods and the subsequent payment 30 days later if the selling price on the invoice is 6 euros per unit. On the date of purchase, 1 euro is worth $0.50, and the rate on the date of payment is $0.60.

PROBLEMS

Problem 9-65

LO1, LO4

REVERSE SOLVABLE

Computing Cost of Goods Sold for a Manufacturing Firm

The following information is available for Granite Inc.

Products in Sample Inventory	2013	2012	2011
Raw materials:			
Beginning inventory	$ 125	$?	$ 96
Purchases	372	410	?
Materials available to use	$?	$?	$ 463
Ending inventory	136	?	?
Raw materials used	$?	$ 379	$ 369
Direct labor	318	?	307
Manufacturing overhead	398	401	?
Total manufacturing costs	$?	$1,093	$1,059
Work in process, January 1	78	?	74
	$1,155	$?	$?
Work in process, December 31	?	78	?
Cost of goods manufactured	$?	$?	$1,052
Finished goods, January 1	?	90	83
	$1,167	$?	$?
Finished goods, December 31	?	110	?
Cost of goods sold	$1,067	$1,076	$?

Instructions: Compute the missing amounts.

Problem 9-66

LO3

Whose Inventory Is It?

Streuling Inc. is preparing its 2013 year-end financial statements. Prior to any adjustments, inventory is valued at $76,050. The following information has been found relating to certain inventory transactions:

(a) Goods valued at $11,000 are on consignment with a customer. These goods are not included in the $76,050 inventory figure.
(b) Goods costing $2,700 were received from a vendor on January 5, 2014. The related invoice was received and recorded on January 12, 2014. The goods were shipped on December 31, 2013, terms FOB shipping point.
(c) Goods costing $8,500 were shipped on December 31, 2013, and were delivered to the customer on January 2, 2014. The terms of the invoice were FOB shipping point. The goods were included in ending inventory for 2013 even though the sale was recorded in 2013.
(d) A $3,500 shipment of goods to a customer on December 31, terms FOB destination, was not included in the year-end inventory. The goods cost $2,600 and were delivered to the customer on January 8, 2014. The sale was properly recorded in 2014.
(e) An invoice for goods costing $3,500 was received and recorded as a purchase on December 31, 2013. The related goods, shipped FOB destination, were received on January 2, 2014, and thus were not included in the physical inventory.
(f) Goods valued at $6,500 are on consignment from a vendor. These goods are not included in the year-end inventory figure.
(g) A $10,500 shipment of goods to a customer on December 30, 2013, terms FOB destination, was recorded as a sale in 2013. The goods, costing $8,200 and delivered to the customer on January 6, 2014, were not included in 2013 ending inventory.

Instructions:

1. Determine the appropriate accounting treatment for each of the preceding items. Justify your answers.
2. Compute the proper inventory amount to be reported on Streuling Inc.'s balance sheet for the year ended December 31, 2013.
3. By how much would net income have been misstated if no adjustments were made for the above transactions? Ignore income taxes.

Problem 9-67

LO5

Inventory Computation Using Different Cost Flows

The Gidewall Corporation uses part 210 in a manufacturing process. Information as to balances on hand, purchases, and requisitions of part 210 is given in the following table:

Date	Quantities Received	Issued	Balance	Unit Purchase Price
January 8	—	—	200	$3.10
January 29	200	—	400	3.40
February 8	—	80	320	—
March 20	—	160	160	—
July 10	150	—	310	3.50
August 18	—	110	200	—
September 6	—	75	125	—
November 14	250	—	375	4.00
December 29	—	100	275	—

Instructions: What is the closing inventory under each of the following pricing methods? (*Note:* Round unit costs to three decimal places.)

1. Perpetual FIFO
2. Periodic FIFO

3. Perpetual LIFO
4. Periodic LIFO
5. Perpetual average
6. Periodic average

Problem 9-68

LO5

Inventory Computation Using Different Cost Flows

Records of the Swain New Products Co. show the following data relative to Product M:

March	2	Inventory	450 units at $26.00
	3	Sale	400 units at $33.00
	6	Purchase	350 units at $27.50
	13	Purchase	300 units at $28.00
	20	Sale	300 units at $34.50
	25	Purchase	100 units at $27.00
	28	Sale	200 units at $35.00

Instructions: Calculate the inventory balance and the gross profit on sales for the month on each of the following bases.

1. Perpetual FIFO
2. Periodic FIFO
3. Perpetual LIFO
4. Periodic LIFO
5. Perpetual average (Carry calculations to five decimal places and round to two.)
6. Periodic average

Problem 9-69

LO5

Inventory Calculations—LIFO and FIFO

The Marci Manufacturing Co. was organized in 2011 to produce a single product. The company's production and sales records for the period 2011–2013 are summarized below.

	Units Produced		Sales	
	No. of Units	Production Costs	No. of Units	Sales Revenue
2011	330,000	$198,000	250,000	$200,000
2012	310,000	201,500	300,000	255,000
2013	290,000	179,800	270,000	210,000

All units produced in a given year are assigned the same average cost.

Instructions: Calculate the gross profit for each of the three years assuming that inventory values are calculated in terms of:

1. LIFO
2. FIFO

Problem 9-70

LO4, LO5

REVERSE SOLVABLE

Computation of Inventory from Balance Sheet and Transaction Data

A portion of the Stark Company's balance sheet appears as follows:

	December 31, 2013	December 31, 2012
Assets:		
Cash	$353,300	$100,000
Notes receivable	0	25,000
Inventory	?	199,875
Liabilities:		
Accounts payable	?	75,000

Stark Company pays for all operating expenses with cash and purchases all inventory on credit. During 2013, cash totaling $471,700 was paid on accounts payable. Operating expenses for 2013 totaled $220,000. All sales are cash sales. The inventory was restocked by purchasing 1,500 units per month and valued by using periodic FIFO. The unit cost of inventory was $32.60 during January 2013 and increased $0.10 per month during the year. Stark sells only one product. All sales are made for $50 per unit. The ending inventory for 2012 was valued at $32.50 per unit.

Instructions:

1. Compute the number of units sold during 2013.
2. Compute the December 31, 2013, accounts payable balance.
3. Compute the beginning inventory quantity.
4. Compute the ending inventory quantity and value.
5. Prepare an income statement for 2013 (including a detailed Cost of Goods Sold section and ignoring income taxes).

Problem 9-71

LO6

Impact of LIFO Inventory System

Norsk Corporation sells household appliances and uses LIFO for inventory costing. The inventory contains 10 different products, and historical LIFO layers are maintained for each of them. The LIFO layers for one of the products, Cook Right, were as follows at December 31, 2012:

2011 layer	4,600 @ $75	2002 layer	2,300 @ $58
2006 layer	4,100 @ $65	2000 layer	4.900 @ $45

Instructions:

1. What was the value of the ending inventory of Cook Right at December 31, 2012?
2. How did the December 31, 2012, quantity of Cook Right compare with the December 31, 2011, quantity?
3. What is the value of the ending inventory of Cook Right at December 31, 2013, if there are 15,600 units on hand?
4. How would net income in (3) be affected if, in addition to the quantity on hand, 950 units were in transit to Norsk Corporation at December 31, 2013? The shipment was made on December 26, 2013, terms FOB shipping point. Total invoice cost was $78,850. Ignore income taxes. Assume that all units purchased during 2013 were purchased at the same unit price as these 950 units.

Problem 9-72

LO7

Change from FIFO to LIFO Inventory

The Greenriver Manufacturing Company manufactures two products: Raft and Float. At December 31, 2012, Greenriver used the FIFO inventory method. Effective January 1, 2013, Greenriver changed to the LIFO inventory method. The retroactive effect of this change is not determinable, and as a result, the ending inventory for 2012 for which the FIFO method was used is also the beginning inventory for 2013 for the LIFO method. Any layers added during 2013 should be costed by reference to the first acquisitions of 2013.

The information below was available from Greenriver inventory records for the two most recent years:

	Raft		Float	
	Units	Unit Cost	Units	Unit Cost
2012 purchases:				
January 7	5,000	$4.00	22,000	$2.00
April 16	12,000	4.50		
November 8	17,000	5.00	18,500	2.50
December 13	10,000	6.00		

	Raft		Float	
	Units	Unit Cost	Units	Unit Cost
2013 purchases:				
February 11	3,000	7.00	23,000	3.00
May 20	8,000	7.50		
October 15	20,000	8.00		
December 23			15,500	3.50
Units on hand:				
December 31, 2012	15,000		14,500	
December 31, 2013	16,000		13,000	

Instructions: Compute the effect on net income for the year ended December 31, 2013, resulting from the change from the FIFO to the LIFO inventory method. Ignore income taxes.

Problem 9-73

LO8

Lower-of-Cost-or-Market Valuation

Witte Inc. carries four items in inventory. The following per-unit data relate to these items at the end of 2013:

	Units	Cost	Replacement Cost	Estimated Sales Price	Selling Cost	Normal Profit
Category 1:						
Commodity A	2,500	$10.50	$10.00	$13.00	$1.25	$2.00
Commodity B	1,850	7.00	6.50	9.75	0.75	1.10
Category 2:						
Commodity C	4,000	3.00	2.25	4.65	0.75	0.60
Commodity D	2,950	6.50	7.00	7.25	1.25	1.50

Instructions:

1. Calculate the value of the inventory under each of the following methods:
   (a) Cost
   (b) The lower of cost or market applied to the individual inventory items
   (c) The lower of cost or market applied to the inventory categories
   (d) The lower of cost or market applied to the inventory as a whole
2. Prepare any journal entries necessary to reflect the proper inventory valuation assuming inventory is valued at:
   (a) Cost
   (b) The lower of cost or market applied to the individual inventory items
   (c) The lower of cost or market applied to the inventory categories (*Hint:* Use a valuation allowance.)
   (d) The lower of cost or market applied to the inventory as a whole

Problem 9-74

LO5, LO8

Lower-of-Cost-or-Market Valuation

Far East Sales Co. uses the first-in, first-out method in calculating cost of goods sold for three of the products that Far East handles. Inventories and purchase information concerning these three products are given for the month of March.

On March 31, Far East's suppliers reduced their prices from the most recent purchase prices by the following percentages: product X, 15%; product Y, 12%; product Z,

9%. Accordingly, Far East decided to reduce its sales prices on all items by 10%, effective April 1. Far East's selling cost is 10% of sales price. Products X and Y have a normal profit (after selling costs) of 25% on sales prices, while the normal profit on product Z (after selling cost) is 8% of sales price.

		Product X	Product Y	Product Z
Mar. 1	Inventory	8,000 units at $7.00	4,000 units at $10.50	7,100 units at $1.60
Mar. 1–15	Purchases	10,000 units at $8.00	6,300 units at $11.00	3,400 units at $2.10
Mar. 16–31	Purchases	5,000 units at $9.00		
Mar. 1–31	Sales	17,000 units	7,000 units	5,200 units
Mar. 31	Sales price	$9.00 per unit	$12.00 per unit	$3.00 per unit

Instructions:

1. Calculate the value of the inventory at March 31, using the lower-of-cost-or-market method (applied to individual items).
2. Calculate the FIFO cost of goods sold for March and the amount of inventory write-off due to the market decline.

Problem 9-75

LO9

Trade-Ins and Repossessed Inventory

The Jamison Appliance Company began business on January 1, 2012. The company decided from the beginning to grant allowances on merchandise traded in as partial payment on new sales. During 2013, the company granted trade-in allowances of $64,035. The wholesale value of merchandise traded in was $40,875. Trade-ins recorded at $39,000 were sold for their wholesale value of $27,000 during the year. The following summary entries were made to record annual sales of new merchandise and trade-in sales for 2013.

Accounts Receivable	439,890	
Trade-In Inventory	64,035	
Sales		503,925
Cash	27,000	
Loss on Trade-In Inventory	12,000	
Trade-In Inventory		39,000

When a customer defaults on the accounts receivable contract, the merchandise is repossessed. During 2013, the following repossessions occurred:

	Original Sales Price	Unpaid Contract Balance
On 2012 contracts	$37,500	$15,600
On 2013 contracts	24,000	17,800

The wholesale value of these goods is estimated as follows:

(a) Goods repossessed during year of sale are valued at 50% of original sales price.
(b) Goods repossessed in later years are valued at 20% of original sales price.

Instructions:

1. At what values should Jamison Appliance report the trade-in and repossessed inventory at December 31, 2013?
2. Give the entry that should have been made to record the repossessions of 2013.
3. Give the entry that is required to correct the trade-in summary entries.

Problem 9-76
LO8

Inventory Transactions—Journal Entries

The Hansen Company values its inventory at the lower of FIFO cost or market. The inventory accounts at December 31, 2012, had the following balances:

Raw materials	$ 92,000
Work in process	140,510
Finished goods	195,350

The following are some of the transactions that affected the inventory of the Hansen Company during 2013.

Feb.	10	Hansen Company purchases raw materials at an invoice price of $20,000; terms 3/15, n/30. Hansen Company values inventory at the net invoice price.
Mar.	15	Hansen Company repossesses an inventory item from a customer who was overdue in making payment. The unpaid balance on the sale is $220. The repossessed merchandise is to be refinished and placed on sale. It is expected that the item can be sold for $350 after estimated refinishing costs of $90. The normal profit for this item is considered to be $65.
Apr.	1	Refinishing costs of $75 are incurred on the repossessed item.
	10	The repossessed item is resold for $350 on account, 30% down.
May	30	A sale on account is made of finished goods that have a list price of $670 and a cost of $410. A reduction of $100 off the list price is granted as a trade-in allowance. The trade-in item is to be priced to sell at $90 as is. The normal profit on this type of inventory is 25% of the sales price.
Dec.	31	The following information is available to adjust the accounts for the annual statements. (a) The raw materials inventory account has a cost balance of $105,700. Current market value is $99,700. (b) The finished goods inventory account has a cost balance of $180,250. Current market value is $195,480.

Instructions: Record this information in journal entry form, including any required adjusting entries at December 31, 2013.

Problem 9-77
LO9

REVERSE SOLVABLE

Inventory Fire Loss

Reagan Manufacturing began operations five years ago. On August 13, 2013, a fire broke out in the warehouse destroying all inventory and many accounting records relating to the inventory. The information available is presented below. All sales and purchases are on account.

	January 1, 2013	August 13, 2013
Inventory	$124,800	
Accounts receivable	152,640	$148,520
Accounts payable	91,320	105,600
Collection on accounts receivable, January 1–August 13		797,300
Payments to suppliers, January 1–August 13		463,800
Goods out on consignment at August 13, at cost		29,300

Summary of previous years' sales:

	2010	2011	2012
Sales	$842,000	$765,000	$820,000
Gross profit on sales	336,800	290,700	344,400

Instructions: Determine the inventory loss suffered as a result of the fire.

Problem 9-78

LO9

Interim Inventory Computation—Gross Profit Method

The following information was taken from the records of Prairie Company.

	Jan. 1, 2012–Dec. 31, 2012	Jan. 1, 2013–Sept. 30, 2013
Sales	$2,500,000	$1,500,000
Beginning inventory	420,000	785,000
Purchases	2,152,000	1,061,000
Freight-in	116,000	72,000
Purchase discounts	30,000	15,000
Purchase returns	40,000	13,000
Purchase allowances	8,000	5,000
Ending inventory	785,000	?
Selling and general expenses	450,000	320,000

Instructions: Using the gross profit method, compute the value to be assigned to the inventory as of September 30, 2013, and prepare an income statement for the 9-month period ending on this date.

Problem 9-79

LO9

Inventory Theft Loss

In December 2013, JB Masterpiece Merchandise Inc. had a significant portion of its inventory stolen. The company determined the cost of inventory remaining to be $32,400. The following information was taken from the records of the company:

	Jan. 1, 2013 to Date of Theft	2012
Purchases	$141,670	$156,430
Purchase returns and allowances	7,250	6,580
Sales	275,600	283,300
Sales returns and allowances	3,400	2,900
Salaries	10,100	12,900
Rent	5,340	7,120
Insurance	1,030	1,340
Utilities	1,115	1,435
Advertising	4,925	3,741
Depreciation expense	1,890	2,106
Beginning inventory	74,620	69,780

Instructions: Estimate the cost of the stolen inventory.

Problem 9-80

LO10

Inventory Error Correction

The Sonntag Corporation has adjusted and closed its books at the end of 2012. The company arrives at its inventory position by a physical count taken on December 31 of each year. In March of 2013, the following errors were discovered:

(a) Merchandise that cost $2,500 was sold for $3,400 on December 29, 2012. The order was shipped December 31, 2012, with terms of FOB shipping point. The merchandise was not included in the ending inventory. The sale was recorded on January 12, 2013, when the customer made payment on the sale.

(b) On January 3, 2013, Sonntag Corporation received merchandise that had been shipped to it on December 30, 2012. The terms of the purchase were FOB shipping point. Cost of the merchandise was $1,750. The purchase was recorded and the goods included in the inventory when payment was made in January 2013.

(c) On January 8, 2013, merchandise that had been included in the ending inventory was returned to Sonntag because the consignee had not been able to sell it. The cost of this merchandise was $1,200 with a selling price of $1,800.

(d) Merchandise costing $750, located in a separate warehouse, was overlooked and excluded from the 2012 inventory count.

(e) On December 26, 2012, Sonntag Corporation purchased merchandise costing $1,175 from a supplier. The order was shipped December 28 (terms FOB destination) and was still "in transit" on December 31. Because the invoice was received on December 31, the purchase was recorded in 2012. The merchandise was not included in the inventory count.

(f) The corporation failed to make an entry for a purchase on account of $835 at the end of 2012, although it included this merchandise in the inventory count. The purchase was recorded when payment was made to the supplier in 2013.

(g) The corporation included in its 2012 ending inventory merchandise with a cost of $1,350. This merchandise had been custom built and was being held according to the customer's written request until the customer could come and pick up the merchandise. The sale, for $1,825, was recorded in 2013.

Instructions: Give the entry in 2013 (2012 books are closed) to correct each error. Assume that the errors were made during 2012, all amounts are material, and the periodic inventory system is used.

Problem 9-81

LO11

Inventory Turnover Analysis

The following information for Whittier Technologies was taken from the company's financial statements (amounts in thousands):

	2013	2012	2011	2010
Sales	$60,000	$51,000	$39,000	$30,000
Cost of goods sold	41,200	34,900	26,500	22,200
Inventory	3,000	2,700	2,200	1,800
Accounts receivable	5,600	5,200	5,100	4,700
Accounts payable	2,500	2,100	1,900	2,400
Net income	7,260	6,540	4,950	4,100

Instructions:

1. Compute the inventory turnover and the number of days' sales in inventory for the years 2011–2013. Use average inventory in your calculations.
2. Evaluate Whittier's inventory turnover trend.

EM EXPANDED MATERIAL

Problem 9-82

LO13

Computation of LIFO Inventory with LIFO Pools

The Bergman Company sells three different products. Five years ago, management adopted the LIFO inventory method and established three specific pools of goods. Bergman values all incremental layers of inventory at the average cost of purchases within the period. Information relating to the three products for the first quarter of 2013 follows.

	Product 400	Product 401	Product 402
Purchases:			
January	1,000 @ $12.00	500 @ $25	5,000 @ $5.30
February	1,500 @ $12.50	250 @ $26	4,850 @ $5.38
March	1,200 @ $12.25	—	3,500 @ $5.45
First quarter sales (units)	2,850	775	10,750
January 1, 2013, inventory	950 @ $11.50	155 @ $24	3,760 @ $5.00

Instructions: Compute the ending inventory value for the first quarter of 2013. (*Note:* Round unit inventory values to the nearest cent and final inventory values to the nearest dollar.)

Problem 9-83

LO13

Dollar-Value LIFO Inventory Method

Bob's Repair Shop began operations on January 1, 2008. After discussing the matter with his accountant, Bob decided dollar-value LIFO should be used for inventory costing. Information concerning the inventory of Bob's Repair Shop is shown below.

Date	Inventory at Year-End Prices	Year-End Index
Dec. 31, 2008	$32,400	1.00
Dec. 31, 2009	43,100	1.16
Dec. 31, 2010	61,300	1.34
Dec. 31, 2011	52,900	1.20
Dec. 31, 2012	79,700	1.68
Dec. 31, 2013	70,800	2.10

Instructions: Compute the inventory value at December 31 of each year under the dollar-value LIFO inventory method, assuming incremental layers are valued using the year-end price index.

Problem 9-84

LO13

Dollar-Value LIFO Retail Inventory Method

In 2010, Van Hover Inc. adopted the dollar-value LIFO retail inventory method. The January 1, 2010, price index was 1.00. The following data are available for the 4-year period ending December 31, 2013.

	Cost	Retail
2010:		
Inventory, January 1	$148,050	$235,000
Purchases	393,700	635,000
Sales		590,000
Year-end price index		1.12
2011:		
Purchases	$363,000	$550,000
Sales		579,170
Year-end price index		1.08
2012:		
Purchases	$377,000	$650,000
Sales		641,955
Year-end price index		1.09

	Cost	Retail
2013:		
Purchases	$504,000	$800,000
Sales		762,500
Year-end price index		1.12

Instructions: Calculate the inventories to be reported at the end of 2010, 2011, 2012, and 2013. Incremental layers are costed at end-of-year prices.

Problem 9-85
LO14

Purchase Commitments

On November 17, 2013, Antarctic Airlines entered into a commitment to purchase 3,000 barrels of aviation fuel for $150,000 on March 23, 2014. Antarctic entered into this purchase commitment to protect itself against the volatility in the aviation fuel market. By December 31, the purchase price of aviation fuel had fallen to $40 per barrel. However, by March 23, 2014, when Antarctic took delivery of the 3,000 barrels, the price of aviation fuel had risen to $54 per barrel.

Instructions:

1. Make the journal entry necessary on November 17, 2013, to record the purchase commitment.
2. Make any adjusting entry necessary on December 31, 2013.
3. What type of account (e.g., asset, liability, revenue) is Estimated Loss on Purchase Commitments?
4. Make the journal entry to record the purchase on March 23, 2014. Antarctic uses a periodic inventory system.

Problem 9-86
LO15

Foreign Currency Transactions

Charles & Sons, a U.S. computer supplies firm, had the following transactions with foreign companies during December 2012:

(a) Goldstar Co., Ltd., a South Korea–based firm, sold 5,000 computer hard drives to Charles & Sons for 100,000 won per drive on December 12, 2012. Charles & Sons paid the bill on January 13, 2013.
(b) Charles & Sons sold 2,000 computer hard drives to a Swiss firm, Lockner Inc., on December 21, 2012. Lockner Inc. agreed to pay $135 per hard drive. Payment was received by Charles & Sons on February 4, 2013.
(c) Charles & Sons sold 2,400 computer hard drives to Geopacific, Inc., a company with headquarters in Canada, on December 28, 2012. Geopacific was billed 148 Canadian dollars per drive. Payment was received on January 10, 2013.
(d) Charles & Sons received 1,000 printers from Printco, a Japanese company, on December 28, 2012. Printco billed Charles & Sons 45,000 yen per printer. Charles & Sons paid the liability on January 14, 2013.

Exchange rates for the above transactions are as follows:

	U.S. Dollar Value of 1 Unit of Foreign Currency		
	As of Date of Sale or Purchase	As of Balance Sheet Date	As of Date of Payment or Receipt
South Korean won	$0.00103	$0.00112	$0.00115
Swiss franc	0.670	0.632	0.655
Canadian dollar	0.910	0.935	0.905
Japanese yen	0.0075	0.0069	0.0073

Instructions: Prepare the journal entries necessary for Charles & Sons to record each of the above transactions for the following: (1) date of the original transaction, (2) balance sheet date, and (3) date of payment or receipt of cash.

CASES

Discussion Case 9-87

Should We Adopt LIFO?

You are the controller of the Ford Steel Co. The economy enters a period of high inflation. Although profits are higher this year than last, you realize that the cost to replace inventory is also higher. You are aware that many companies are changing to the LIFO inventory method to save taxes in the current year, but you are concerned that what goes up will eventually come down, and when prices decline, the LIFO method will result in higher taxes. Because declining prices are usually equated with economic recession, it is likely that the higher taxes will have to be paid at a time when revenues are declining.

What factors should you consider before making a change to LIFO? Based on the above considerations, what would you recommend?

Discussion Case 9-88

Which Method Shall We Use?

The White Wove Corporation began operations in 2013. A summary of the first quarter appears below.

	Units	Total Cost
Purchases:		
January 2	250	$23,250
February 11	100	9,500
February 20	400	38,400
March 21	200	19,600
March 27	225	22,275

Other data:	Sales in Units	Sales Price per Unit	Operating Expenses
January	200	$140	$9,575
February	225	142	7,820
March	350	145	7,905

The White Wove Corporation used the LIFO perpetual inventory method and correctly computed an inventory value of $38,300 at the end of the first quarter. Management is considering changing to a FIFO costing method. It has also considered using a periodic system instead of the perpetual system presently being used. You have been hired to assist management in making the decision. What would you advise?

Discussion Case 9-89

Can I Use Both LIFO and FIFO?

Many countries around the world do not allow use of the LIFO method. The harmonization of accounting standards across countries may require a compromise on the use of LIFO concepts. Some accountants in the United States are suggesting the use of a LIFO/FIFO system that would use LIFO on the income statement and FIFO on the balance sheet. This method would not be a cost allocation method because in most cases it would not result in a clean allocation of cost of goods available for sale into ending inventory and cost of goods sold.

What theoretical arguments can be made in favor of this hybrid LIFO/FIFO system? One practical problem that would arise from using different methods for the income statement and the balance sheet is that the balance sheet wouldn't balance. How would you suggest solving this problem?

Discussion Case 9-90

How Well Am I Really Doing?

Fay Stocks sells oriental rugs. She uses the FIFO method of inventory costing. The inventory available for sale for a particular style of rug is as follows:

Inventory Date	Current Inventory	Cost
June 14	4	@ $1,200 each
June 21	3	@ $1,500 each
July 5	6	@ $1,700 each

On July 31, a wealthy customer purchases three rugs paying $2,600 for each. Fay immediately replaces those rugs with three new rugs at a cost of $2,300 apiece. In addition, Fay immediately pays income tax on the sale at a rate of 40%. (Assume that she has no other expenses.) What is Fay's net income (after taxes) from the sale of the rugs? What is Fay's net cash flow from the sale of the rugs, the payment of income taxes, and the subsequent purchase of three new rugs? Why is there a substantial difference between net income and cash flow? What other circumstances can lead to differences like those illustrated in this case?

Discussion Case 9-91

Have We Really Had a Loss?

The Destro Company is experiencing an unusual inventory situation. The replacement cost of its principal product has been declining, but because of a unique market condition, Destro has not had to reduce the selling price of the item. Eric Dona, company controller, is aware that GAAP requires the valuation of inventory at the lower of cost or market. He considers market to be replacement cost, and he is concerned that to reduce the ending inventory to replacement cost will improperly reduce net income for the current period. Has an inventory loss occurred? Discuss.

Discussion Case 9-92

But They Won't Buy Ducks Anymore!

The Bright-Lite Shirt Company buys wholesale sweatshirts, nightshirts, T-shirts, and other clothing items and, using a novel 4-color processing system, imprints hundreds of designs on the items. The printed shirts are marketed widely to sports stores, department stores, college campus outlets, variety stores, vacation shops, and so on. Gordon Smith, marketing manager, likes to have a wide variety of products on hand so orders can be promptly met. As the number of designs has grown, so has the inventory. However, the designs often exhibit "fad" characteristics, and the demand for ducks, bears, flowers, or sports heroes can change fairly rapidly.

Beverly Patton, the controller, has expressed dismay at the growing inventory and especially the issue of inventory obsolescence. Beverly is now preparing for a meeting with Bright-Lite's external auditor. The auditor is sure to ask for a write-down of inventory to the lower of cost or market. Beverly has sent a report to Gordon urging him to reduce his inventory and change his production concept. Gordon is reluctant to change because Bright-Lite has developed an excellent reputation for meeting emergency requests for inventory.

As Bright-Lite's president, which position will you support: Gordon's or Beverly's? Explain.

Discussion Case 9-93

Inventory Valuation without Records

The Ma & Pa Grocery Store has never kept many records. The proceeds from sales are used to pay suppliers for goods delivered. When the owners, Donald and Alicia Wride, need some cash, they withdraw it from the till without any record of it. The Wrides realize that eventually tax returns must be filed, but for three years, "they just haven't got around to it." Finally, the IRS catches up with the Wrides, and an audit of the company records is conducted. The auditor requests the general ledger, special journals, inventory counts, and supporting documentation—very little of which is available. Records of expenditures are extremely sketchy because most expenses are paid in cash. If you were the IRS auditor, what might you do to make a reasonable estimate of income for the company?

EM EXPANDED MATERIAL

Discussion Case 9-94

Silver's Ups and Downs

In 1979 and 1980, the Hunt brothers from Texas attempted to corner the world's silver market. Their hope was to own enough silver to be able to dictate world prices. They made purchase commitments, which locked in the price they would pay for silver. For a while, their plan worked. The price of silver rose, and the Hunt brothers used the silver they owned as collateral to purchase more silver.

Their plans were shattered when the price of silver started to decline. From a high in January 1980 of $50.35 an ounce, the price of silver fell to $10.80 in just two months. The silver they were using as collateral decreased in value, requiring the Hunt brothers to provide additional collateral. This collateral was in the form of oil, sugar, and real estate, each of which was faring poorly at the time of the silver crash. At the same time, the purchase commitments they had made required them to buy silver at prices higher than the current market value of silver. The Hunt brothers sought protection in bankruptcy court, and the scheme eventually cost them approximately $4 billion.

1. What are the risks associated with making purchase commitments?
2. Why do accounting standards require that price declines subsequent to the purchase commitment but prior to the actual purchase be recorded immediately?
3. Can firms take any action to reduce their exposure to changing prices?

Discussion Case 9-95

Can We Avoid Losses from Exchange Rate Changes?

Smith & Sons routinely purchases inventory from Matsutoshi Corp. Because of unpredictability in the foreign currency markets, transactions denominated in yen leave Smith & Sons exposed to the risks associated with exchange rate changes. Identify and discuss methods by which Smith & Sons can reduce its exposure to foreign currency losses.

Case 9-96

Deciphering Financial Statements (The Walt Disney Company)

The 2009 financial statements for The **Walt Disney Company** can be found on the Internet. Locate those financial statements and consider the following questions.

1. What inventory valuation method does Disney use?
2. How did the change in the level of inventory from September 2008 to October 2009 impact the statement of cash flows?
3. It isn't possible to compute the number of days' sales in inventory for Disney. Why not? Comment on the appropriateness of the level of detail presented in Disney's income statement.

Case 9-97

Deciphering Financial Statements (Circle K)

Circle K was once one of the largest convenience store chains in the United States. Circle K separated its products into two major categories: gasoline and merchandise (Twinkies, beef jerky, soda pop, etc.). Selected financial statement data for the year ended April 30, 1994, follow. (*Note:* More current financial statement data are no longer available because Circle K is now a subsidiary of a larger company. See the opening scenario for Chapter 5.)

	Gasoline	Merchandise
Sales	$1,562.5 million	$1,710.3 million
Cost of goods sold	1,372.1 million	1,192.6 million
End-of-year inventory	26.6 million	93.9 million

1. Compute gross profit percentage for both gasoline and merchandise. Given these numbers, what do you think the attitude of convenience stores is toward automatic pump payment systems that eliminate the need to go into the store to pay for gas?
2. Compute inventory turnover (based on end-of-year inventory) for both gasoline and merchandise.
3. Compute number of days' sales in inventory for both gasoline and merchandise. Why do you think the number of days' sales in gasoline inventory is so much lower than for merchandise?

Selected Circle K financial statement data for the years 1988 and 1993 follow. All numbers are in millions of dollars.

	1993	1988
Sales:		
Gasoline	$1,504.1	$ 964.6
Merchandise	1,541.8	1,649.2
Cost of goods sold:		
Gasoline	1,354.5	862.4
Merchandise	1,054.5	1,030.8
Ending inventory—total	131.2	191.0

For 1994, Circle K had total sales of $3,272.8. Purchases for 1994 were $2,554.0.

4. Which set of numbers—1988 or 1993—is likely to give a better estimate of the 1994 gross profit percentage? Explain.
5. Using the gross profit method, estimate Circle K's inventory as of the end of 1994.

Case 9-98

Deciphering Financial Statements (3M: Minnesota Mining and Manufacturing Company)

The **Minnesota Mining and Manufacturing Company (3M)** gives the following description of its business:

> 3M is a diversified technology company with a global presence in the following businesses: industrial and transportation; health care; display and graphics; consumer and office; safety, security and protection services; and electro and communications. 3M is among the leading manufacturers of products for many of the markets it serves. Most 3M products involve expertise in product development, manufacturing and marketing . . .

Familiar 3M products include Scotch tape and the ubiquitous Post-it notes.

Inventory data from 3M's 2009 10-K report are as follows (in millions of U.S. dollars):

	2009	2008
Cost of goods sold	$12,109	$13,379
Inventories:		
Finished goods	$ 1,255	$ 1,505
Work in process	815	851
Raw materials and supplies	569	657
Total inventories	$ 2,639	$ 3,013

1. Compute cost of goods manufactured for 2009.
2. Compute total manufacturing costs for 2009.
3. Compute number of days' sales in inventory for 2009 (use average inventory). Make the calculation using:
   (a) Total inventory
   (b) Finished goods inventory
4. Of the two numbers you computed in (3), which is more meaningful? Explain.

Case 9-99

Deciphering Financial Statements (Caterpillar and Ford Motor)

Ford Motor (automotive) and **Caterpillar** (heavy equipment) both use the LIFO inventory valuation method. Caterpillar uses it for 70% of its inventories and Ford for 28% of its inventories. Data from the 2009 10-K filings of these two companies follow (in millions of U.S. dollars):

	Ford	Caterpillar
Cost of goods sold	$100,016	$23,886
LIFO inventory, beginning	6,988	8,781
LIFO inventory, ending	5,450	6,360
LIFO reserve, beginning	850	3,183
LIFO reserve, ending	798	3,003

1. For both companies, as of the end of 2009, the existence of a LIFO reserve demonstrates that LIFO inventory is less than it would have been if FIFO had been used. For both companies, compute the ratio of LIFO inventory/FIFO inventory for 2009 ending inventory. Comment on the resulting numbers.
2. For Caterpillar, compute what 2009 cost of goods sold would have been if FIFO had been used.
3. What might have caused Caterpillar's LIFO reserve to be so much larger than Ford's?
4. If a company uses FIFO, can you use financial statement data to compute what its cost of goods sold would be using LIFO? Explain.

Case 9-100

Deciphering Financial Statements (ExxonMobil)

On December 31, 2000, the aggregate replacement cost of all of **ExxonMobil**'s crude oil and natural gas inventory was approximately $13.9 billion. By December 31, 2001, the aggregate replacement cost of ExxonMobil's inventory had fallen to $10.9 billion. This reduction in replacement cost was primarily the result of a decline in the price of crude oil. The average crude oil sales price per barrel was $21.10 in 2001, compared to $25.59 in 2000.

In spite of this $3.0 billion decline in the replacement cost of inventory, ExxonMobil was not required to make a lower-of-cost-or-market adjustment in 2001.

Instructions: Explain why you think this is so.

Case 9-101

Writing Assignment (This is not the time for "Just in Time.")

You are the assistant controller of Duo-Therm Company and are in charge of preparing the financial statements and tax returns. One of your colleagues, the assistant controller in charge of working capital management, has just returned from a 3-day seminar on just-in-time (JIT) inventory. JIT reduces inventory carrying costs by having arrangements with suppliers to deliver inventory just as it is needed for production or sale. Your colleague is excited about implementing JIT, but you are concerned that not all factors are being considered. Your company has been using LIFO for about 25 years. Prepare a memo to the controller outlining why you think just-in-time might be a bad idea.

Case 9-102

Ethical Dilemma (LIFO and the strategic timing of inventory purchases)

You have risen fast in Lam Tin Industries and are now in charge of purchasing for the entire company. Lam Tin is a privately held company, and negotiations are currently under way for Lam Tin to be acquired by Kwun Tong Company, a large publicly held firm. It is December, and the final negotiations with Kwun Tong, including the setting of the purchase price, will take place in February after the release of Lam Tin's audited financial statements for the year ended December 31.

You are puzzling over a strange request you received earlier today from Lam Tin's vice president of finance. She visited your office and asked you to delay your normal December inventory purchases until the first week in January. You explained that this would result in a reduction of year-end inventories to less than half their normal year-end level. The vice president of finance seemed pleased with this information when she left your office.

This request seemed fishy, and you pulled out your copy of Lam Tin's annual report to check a hunch. Just as you suspected, Lam Tin has been using LIFO for many years and has built up a large LIFO reserve. If you delay the December purchases until January, Lam Tin will liquidate a large portion of its old LIFO layers, resulting in a big increase in reported profit for the year. It is possible that this artificial boost in Lam Tin's profits might increase the price offered by Kwun Tong in the purchase of Lam Tin.

Should you talk over your suspicions with the vice president of finance? With Lam Tin's independent auditors? With the negotiation team from Kwun Tong? Explain.

Case 9-103

Cumulative Spreadsheet Analysis

This spreadsheet assignment is a continuation of the spreadsheet assignments given in earlier chapters. If you completed those assignments, you have a head start on this one.

Refer back to the instructions for preparing the revised financial statements for 2013 as given in (1) of the Cumulative Spreadsheet Analysis assignment in Chapter 3.

1. Skywalker wishes to prepare a *forecasted* balance sheet, a *forecasted* income statement, and a *forecasted* statement of cash flows for 2014. Use the financial statement numbers for 2013 as the basis for the forecast, along with the following additional information.

   (a) Sales in 2014 are expected to increase by 40% over 2013 sales of $2,100.
   (b) In 2014, Skywalker expects to acquire new property, plant, and equipment costing $240.
   (c) The $480 in operating expenses reported in 2013 breaks down as follows: $15 in depreciation expense and $465 in other operating expenses.
   (d) No new long-term debt will be acquired in 2014.
   (e) No cash dividends will be paid in 2014.
   (f) New short-term loans payable will be acquired in an amount sufficient to make Skywalker's current ratio in 2014 exactly equal to 2.0.
   (g) Skywalker does not anticipate repurchasing any additional shares of stock during 2014.
   (h) Because changes in future prices and exchange rates are impossible to predict, Skywalker's best estimate is that the balance in accumulated other comprehensive income will remain unchanged in 2014.
   (i) In the absence of more detailed information, assume that the balances in the investment securities, long-term investments, other long-term assets, and intangible assets accounts will all increase at the same rate as sales (40%) in 2014.
   (j) In the absence of more detailed information, assume that the balance in the other long-term liabilities account will increase at the same rate as sales (40%) in 2014.
   (k) The investment securities are classified as available-for-sale securities. Accordingly, cash from the purchase and sale of these securities is classified as an investing activity.

(l) Assume that transactions impacting other long-term assets and other long-term liabilities accounts are operating activities.

(m) Cash and investment securities accounts will increase at the same rate as sales.

(n) The forecasted amount of accounts receivable in 2014 is determined using the forecasted value for the average collection period. The average collection period for 2014 is expected to be 14.08 days. To make the calculations less complex, this value of 14.08 days is based on forecasted end-of-year accounts receivable rather than on average accounts receivable.

(*Note:* These forecasted statements were constructed as part of the spreadsheet assignment in Chapter 7; you can use that spreadsheet as a starting point if you have completed that assignment.)

For this exercise, add the following additional assumptions.

(o) The forecasted amount of inventory in 2014 is determined using the forecasted value for the number of days' sales in inventory. The number of days' sales in inventory for 2014 is expected to be 107.6 days. To make the calculations easier, this value of 107.6 days is based on forecasted end-of-year inventory rather than on average inventory.

(p) The forecasted amount of accounts payable in 2014 is determined using the forecasted value for the number of days' purchases in accounts payable. The number of days' purchases in accounts payable for 2014 is expected to be 48.34 days. To make the calculations easier, this value of 48.34 days is based on forecasted end-of-year accounts payable rather than on average accounts payable.

Clearly state any additional assumptions that you make.

2. Repeat part (1), with the following changes in assumptions:

    (a) Number of days' sales in inventory is expected to be 66.2 days.

    (b) Number of days' sales in inventory is expected to be 150.0 days.

3. Comment on the differences in the forecasted values of cash from operating activities in 2014 under each of the following assumptions about the number of days' sales in inventory: 107.6 days, 66.2 days, and 150.0 days.
4. Is there any impact on the forecasted level of accounts payable when the number of days' sales in inventory is changed? Why or why not?
5. What happens to the forecasted level of short-term loans payable when the number of days' sales in inventory is reduced to 66.2 days? Explain.

Richard Rodriguez/Fort Worth Star-Telegram/MCT via Getty Images

P2 ROUTINE ACTIVITIES OF A BUSINESS

CHAPTER 10 Investments in Noncurrent Operating Assets—Acquisition

LEARNING OBJECTIVES

1. Identify those costs to be included in the acquisition cost of different types of noncurrent operating assets.
2. Properly account for noncurrent operating asset acquisitions using various special arrangements, including deferred payment, self-construction, and acquisition of an entire company.
3. Separate costs into those that should be expensed immediately and those that should be capitalized, and understand the accounting standards for research and development and oil and gas exploration costs.
4. Recognize intangible assets acquired separately, as part of a basket purchase, and as part of a business acquisition.
5. Discuss the pros and cons of recording noncurrent operating assets at their fair values.
6. Use the fixed asset turnover ratio as a general measure of how efficiently a company is using its property, plant, and equipment.

Jerry Jones didn't win many friends in Texas when one of his first acts after buying the **Dallas Cowboys** in 1989 was to fire Tom Landry, who had been the head coach of the Cowboys ever since the team entered the NFL. Jones became even less popular when the Cowboys lost 15 of 16 games in their first year under new head coach Jimmy Johnson.[1] In those days, the Cowboys stunk as a football team but looked like a pretty shrewd business investment. When Jones, an Arkansas oil man, purchased the Cowboys for $150 million, he acquired a diverse array of assets. These assets included miscellaneous football equipment, stadium leases, radio and TV broadcast rights, cable TV rights, luxury stadium suites, player contracts, a lease on the Cowboys' luxurious Valley Ranch training facility, and the Cowboys' NFL franchise rights.

Allocating the purchase price among these assets and defining their useful lives were difficult and strategic tasks. When H. R. "Bum" Bright, Jones' predecessor, bought the Dallas Cowboys for $85 million in 1984, he was able to allocate half the purchase price to players' contracts. These

[1] William P. Barrett, "Maybe They Should Let Jerry Play," *Forbes*, February 19, 1990, p. 140.

EX 10-1 TIME LINE OF THE DALLAS COWBOYS' FRANCHISE VALUE, 1991–2009

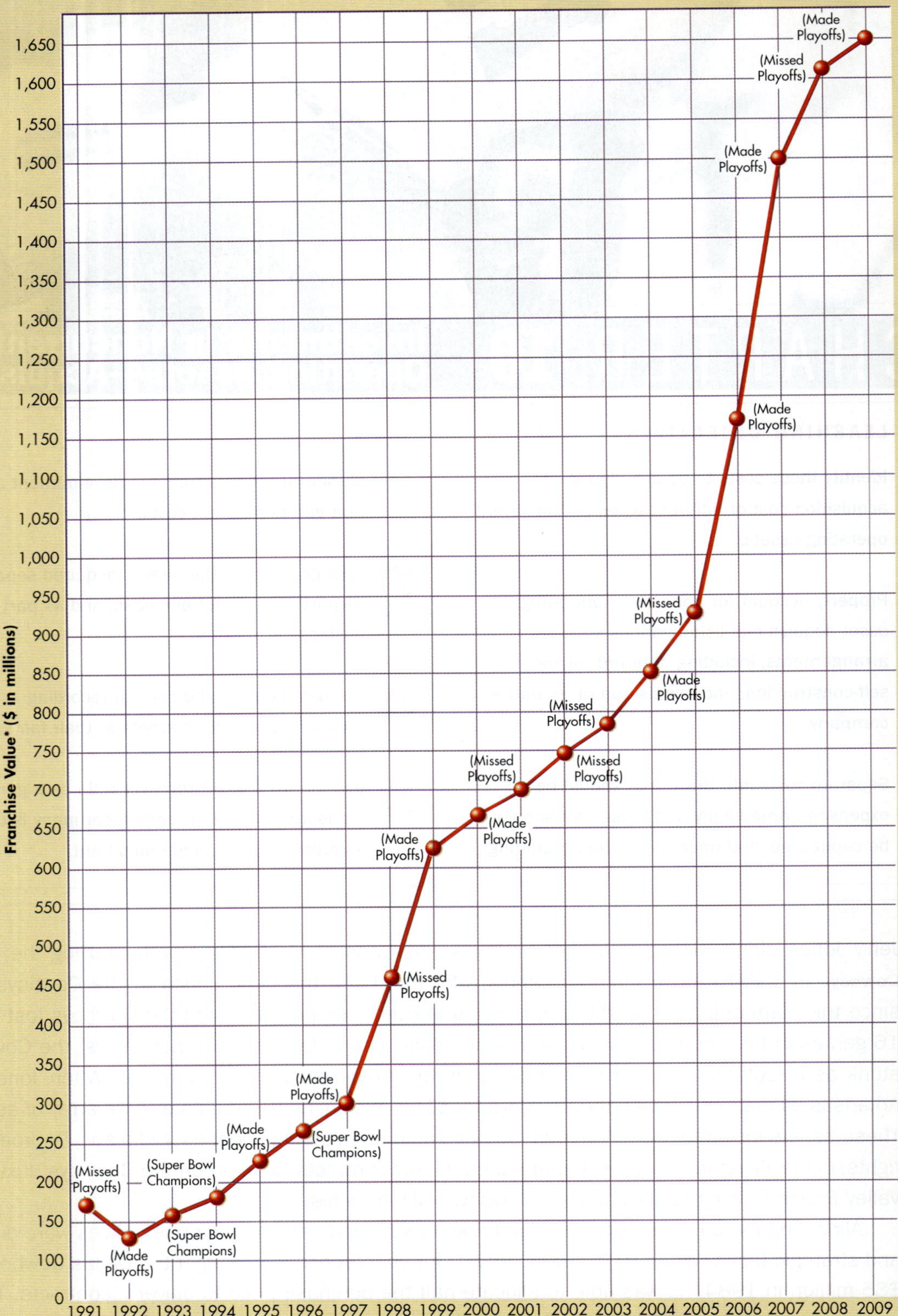

*Performance in the preceding season is shown in parentheses.

were amortizable assets that, for tax purposes, were written off over four years.[2] Jones received a similar tax break when he acquired the Cowboys.

But entrepreneurs like Jerry Jones don't get rich by relying solely on depreciation tax breaks. Jones quickly set about putting the Cowboys' finances back in the black—in 1988 the Cowboys had lost $9.5 million. Jones encouraged the team's treasurer to look for ways to cut expenses—renegotiate insurance policy premiums, seek competitive bids for printing tickets and providing training room supplies, and remove the floodlights from the parking lot of the training center. Jones also moved to increase revenues by signing leases for 99 unleased luxury boxes (generating an extra $8.5 million per year in revenue) and then building an additional 68 luxury boxes. By 1992, the Cowboys were again profitable with net income of $20.6 million.[3]

The on-field performance of the Cowboys matched their financial success. In 1990, the Cowboys improved their record to 7 and 9, and in 1991 they made the playoffs, advancing to the second round. The Cowboys' return to glory was capped in January 1993 when they returned to the Super Bowl for the first time since 1978 and routed the Buffalo Bills, 52–17. In January 1996, the Cowboys became the first NFL franchise to win three Super Bowls in a 4-year time period. The subsequent so-so on-field performance of the team (it has not been back to the Super Bowl since 1996 and made the playoffs just seven times from 1996 through 2009, winning a total of just two playoff games in that span) has not seemed to hurt its financial performance. (See Exhibit 10-1.) In a 2009 estimate by *Forbes*, the Cowboys were rated the most valuable sports franchises in North America with an estimated value of $1.65 billion.[4]

? QUESTIONS

1. From an accounting standpoint, what difficult asset valuation exercise is necessary when buying an entire business such as the Dallas Cowboys?
2. Why do buyers of a sports franchise wish to allocate as much of the purchase price as possible to the asset "players' contracts"?

Answers to these questions can be found on page 10-43.

Many billions of dollars are invested each year in new property, plant, and equipment and increasingly in intangible assets as well. A time line of the business and accounting issues associated with property, plant, and equipment is shown in Exhibit 10-2.

One of the keys to successful business is correctly choosing which long-term assets to buy. Capital budgeting and discounted cash flow analysis are essential elements in making the best choices. In addition to the difficult financial decisions surrounding long-term assets, many accounting questions are introduced when long-term items are acquired. These accounting issues include the following:

- Which costs should be capitalized as assets and which ones should be expensed?
- What costs should be included in the acquisition cost of a long-term asset?
- How should intangible assets be recorded?

[2] Hal Lancaster, "Football Team's Sale Is Strictly Business," *The Wall Street Journal*, April 18, 1989, p. B1.
[3] David Whitford, "America's Owner," *Inc.*, December 1993, p. 102.
[4] Go to **http://www.forbes.com** and look under "Lists" for the current valuation of professional sports franchises.

EX 10-2 TIME LINE OF BUSINESS AND ACCOUNTING ISSUES INVOLVED WITH LONG-TERM OPERATING ASSETS

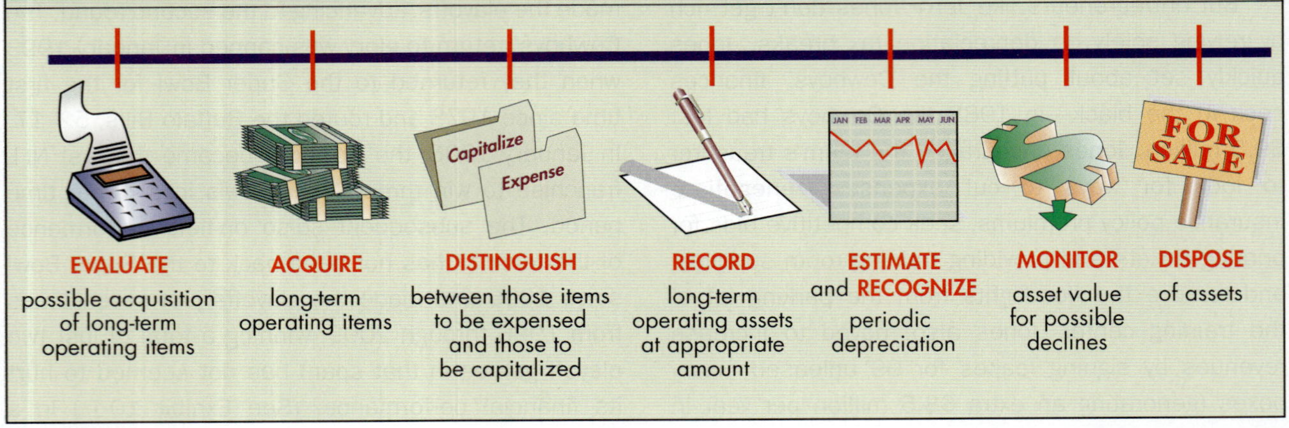

- At what amounts should long-term assets be recorded when the financing of the purchase is more complex than a simple cash payment?
- How should expenditures made subsequent to acquisition be recorded?
- What recognition should be given to changes in the market value of long-term assets?

This chapter discusses these general issues and describes many of the historic controversies that have led to changes in the accounting standards over the years. The chapter also discusses the controversial decision by the FASB to require all research and development costs to be expensed immediately (a decision that may soon be revised in order to harmonize with the international standard), the embarrassing flip-flop the FASB was forced to make on oil and gas accounting, the historical roots of the capitalization of interest, and the question of historical cost vs. current cost. Chapter 11 will address the important issues of recognizing depreciation on long-term operating assets, recording impairment losses when asset values have significantly declined, and recording the disposal of long-term operating assets.

What Costs Are Included in Acquisition Cost?

1 Identify those costs to be included in the acquisition cost of different types of noncurrent operating assets.

WHY **Costs incurred are either expensed or recorded as an asset. How these costs are classified can significantly affect both the income statement and the balance sheet.**

HOW **Noncurrent operating assets are recorded at their original purchase price plus any expenditures required to obtain and prepare the asset for its intended use. Most costs associated with internally-generated intangible assets are expensed whereas the cost of externally-purchased intangibles is generally recorded as an asset.**

Noncurrent operating assets are recorded initially at cost—the original bargained or cash sales price. In theory, the maximum price a company should be willing to pay for an operating asset is the present value of the net benefit the company expects to obtain from the use and final disposition of the asset. In a competitive economy, the market value or cost of an asset at acquisition is assumed to reflect the present value of its future benefits.

> **CAUTION**
>
> Classification of an asset as a noncurrent operating asset depends on how management intends to use the asset. For example, land held for long-term investment purposes is not an operating asset; land held for resale within a year is a current asset.

The cost of property includes not only the original purchase price or equivalent value but also any other expenditures required in obtaining and preparing the asset for its intended use. Any taxes, freight, installation, and other expenditures related to the acquisition should be included in the asset's cost. Postacquisition costs—costs incurred after the asset is placed into service—are usually expensed rather than added to the acquisition cost. Exceptions to this general rule apply to some major replacements or improvements and will be discussed later in the chapter.

Although most noncurrent operating asset categories have similar acquisition costs, over time accounting practice has identified some specific costs that are included for different asset categories. Exhibits 10-3 and 10-4 summarize the types of costs normally included as acquisition costs for each major noncurrent asset category.

Tangible Assets

Land Because land is a nondepreciable asset, costs assigned to it should be those costs that directly relate to land's unlimited life. Together with clearing and grading costs, costs of removing unwanted structures from newly acquired land are considered part of the cost to prepare the land for its intended use and are added to its purchase price. Government assessments for water lines, sewers, roads, and other such items are considered part of the land's cost because maintenance of these items is the responsibility of the government; thus, to the landowner, they have unlimited life. These types of improvements are distinguished from similar costs for landscaping, parking lots, and interior sidewalks that are installed by the owner and must be replaced over time. The improvements that owners are responsible for are generally classified as land improvements and depreciated.

Five Largest Land Accounts[5] 2006 (in millions)

Wal-Mart	$18,612
Home Depot	8,355
MGM Mirage	7,905
Peabody Energy	7,127
Lowe's	5,496

EX 10-3 ACQUISITION COSTS OF TANGIBLE NONCURRENT OPERATING ASSETS

Land	Realty used for business purposes.	**COST:** Purchase price, commissions, legal fees, escrow fees, surveying fees, clearing and grading costs, street and water line assessments.
Land improvements	Items such as landscaping, paving, and fencing that improve the usefulness of property.	**COST:** Cost of improvements, including expenditures for materials, labor, and overhead.
Buildings	Structures used to house business operations.	**COST:** Purchase price, commissions, reconditioning costs.
Equipment	Assets used in the production of goods or in providing services. Examples include automobiles, trucks, machinery, patterns and dies, and furniture and fixtures.	**COST:** Purchase price, taxes, freight, insurance, installation, and any expenditures incurred in preparing the asset for its intended use (e.g., reconditioning and testing costs).

[5] Source: Standard & Poor's *COMPUSTAT.*

EX 10-4 ACQUISITION COSTS OF GOODWILL AND OTHER INTANGIBLE ASSETS

Patent	An exclusive right granted by a national government that enables an inventor to control the manufacture, sale, or use of an invention. In the United States, legal life is 20 years from patent application date.	**COST:** Purchase price, filing and registry fees, cost of subsequent litigation to protect right. Does not include internal research and development costs.
Trademark	An exclusive right granted by a national government that permits the use of distinctive symbols, labels, and designs (e.g., McDonald's Golden Arches, Nike's Swoosh®, Apple Computer's name and logo). Legal life is virtually unlimited.	**COST:** Same as patent.
Copyright	An exclusive right granted by a national government that permits an author to sell, license, or control his or her work. In the United States, copyrights expire 70 years after the death of the author.	**COST:** Same as patent.
Franchise agreement	An exclusive right or privilege received by a business or individual to perform certain functions or sell certain products or services.	**COST:** Expenditures made to purchase the franchise. Legal fees and other costs incurred in obtaining the franchise.
Acquired customer list	A list or database containing customer information such as name, address, past purchases, and so forth. Companies that originally develop such a list often sell or lease it to other companies unless prohibited by customer confidentiality agreements.	**COST:** Purchase price when acquired from another company. Costs to internally develop a customer list are expensed as incurred.
Goodwill	Miscellaneous intangible resources, factors, and conditions that allow a company to earn above normal income with its identifiable net assets. Goodwill is recorded only when a business entity is acquired by a purchase.	**COST:** Portion of purchase price that exceeds the sum of the current market value for all identifiable net assets, both tangible and intangible.

Some of these illustrations are taken from FASB ASC Topic 805 (Business Combinations).

Five Largest Building Accounts 2006 (in millions)

Wal-Mart	$64,052
AES (electricity generation and distribution)	23,977
McDonald's	21,682
Verizon	19,207
Target	16,110

Buildings The cost of purchased buildings includes any reconditioning costs necessary before occupancy. Because self-constructed buildings have many unique costs, a separate discussion of self-constructed assets is included later in this chapter.

Equipment Equipment costs include freight and insurance charges while the equipment is in transit and any expenditures for testing and installation. Costs for reconditioning purchased used equipment are also part of the asset cost.

Intangible Assets

Intangible assets are defined as those assets (not including financial assets) that lack physical substance. Many intangible assets arise from contractual or governmental rights. A well-known example of this type of intangible asset is the right to operate a taxicab in a metropolitan area, such as New York City. Although this right is evidenced by a physical object, the taxicab medallion, it is the legal right itself that is valuable. Other intangible assets are not created by a specific contract or legal right. The existence of these intangibles is evidenced by the fact that they are bought, sold, or licensed, either separately or in conjunction with a broader assortment of assets. A good example of this type of intangible is a customer list. Magazine subscription companies, Web travel services, and real estate listing services all generate substantial revenues by selling or "leasing" their customer lists. In addition, a purchaser must pay a premium when buying an existing business location because of the value of the customer list (and customer relationships) that is tied to the business; the value of this premium should be reported as a separate intangible asset.

The most important distinction in intangible assets for accounting purposes is between those intangible assets that are internally generated and those that are externally purchased. This distinction is important because the transfer of externally purchased intangible assets in an arm's-length market transaction provides reliable evidence that the intangibles have probable future economic benefit. Such reliable evidence does not exist for most internally generated intangibles. Accordingly, most costs associated with generating and maintaining internally generated intangibles are expensed as incurred.[6] Only the actual legal and filing costs are included as part of the intangible asset cost for these internally developed items. Any costs to defend the rights in court are added to the intangible asset cost if the action is successful. If it is not successful, all asset costs related to the rights are written off as expenses.

Most externally obtained intangible assets arise in transactions involving other assets. For example, the purchase of the tangible assets of a factory building and its associated machinery also might involve the acquisition of the intangible assets of the operating permit for the factory, the water rights tied to the property, and the customer relationships developed by the prior factory owner. Accounting for this kind of "basket purchase" of assets will be discussed later in the chapter. A short description of some of the common types of intangible assets follows.

Five Largest Equipment Accounts 2006 (in millions)	
Verizon	$176,369
Qwest Communication	40,249
Dow Chemical	33,457
Intel	29,482
IBM	27,585

Five Largest Total Intangible Asset Accounts 2006 (in millions)	
AT&T	$127,397
Time Warner	92,806
Procter & Gamble	89,027
General Electric	83,928
Bank of America	78,129

Trademark A trademark is a distinctive name, symbol, or slogan that distinguishes a product or service from similar products or services. Well-known examples include Coke®, Windows®, Yahoo!®, and the Nike Swoosh®. As shown in Exhibit 10-10 later in the chapter, the value of the Coca-Cola trademark was estimated in 2009 to be in excess of $68 billion. Because the Coca-Cola trademark is an internally generated intangible asset, it is not reported in **The Coca-Cola Company**'s balance sheet. However, the company has purchased other trademarks (such as Minute Maid®), with a total cost of $6.2 billion; these are reported in The Coca-Cola Company's balance sheet, as shown in Chapter 3.

FYI

The original Coca-Cola bottling franchise sold for $1.

Franchises Franchise operations have become so common in everyday life that we often don't realize we are dealing with them. In fact, these days it is difficult to find a nonfranchise business in a typical shopping mall. When a business obtains a franchise, the recorded cost of the franchise includes any sum paid specifically for the franchise right as well as legal fees and other costs incurred in obtaining it. Although the value of a franchise at the time of its acquisition may be substantially in excess of its cost, the amount recorded should be limited to actual outlays. For example, approximately 81% of **McDonald's** locations are operated under franchise agreements. A McDonald's

[6] FASB ASC paragraph 350-20-25-3.

franchisee must contribute an initial cash amount of around $500,000, which is used to buy some of the equipment and signs and to pay the initial franchise fee. The value of a McDonald's franchise alone is much more than $500,000, but the franchisee would only record a franchise asset in his or her financial statements equal to the cost (not value) of the franchise. However, if a franchise right is included when one company purchases another company, presumably the entire value is included in the purchase price, and the fair value attributable to the franchise right is recorded as an intangible asset in the acquirer's books.

Order Backlog To some companies, especially capital equipment manufacturers, the order backlog is a key economic asset. The *order backlog* is the amount of orders the company has received for equipment that has not yet been produced or delivered. Note that these orders do not constitute sales because they do not satisfy the revenue recognition requirement that the product be completed and shipped. However, this order backlog does represent future valuable economic activity, and the contractual right to these backlogged orders constitutes an important intangible asset. In its 2009 10-K filing, **Boeing** reported the following about its order backlog:

Contractual Backlog (unaudited, in millions) Years ended December 31,	2009	2008	2007
Contractual backlog:			
Commercial Airplanes	$250,476	$278,575	$255,176
Boeing Defense, Space & Security:			
Boeing Military Aircraft	$ 26,311	$ 25,710	$ 22,974
Network & Space Systems	7,746	8,868	9,207
Global Services & Support	11,967	10,707	9,607
Total Boeing Defense, Space & Security	$ 46,024	$ 45,285	$ 41,788
Total contractual backlog	$296,500	$323,860	$296,964

As with other intangible assets, this internally generated order backlog would not be recognized as an intangible asset on Boeing's balance sheet. However, if another company were to buy Boeing, part of the purchase price would be identified with the economic value of the order backlog, and a corresponding intangible asset would be recognized in the books of the acquiring company.

Goodwill Goodwill represents the business contacts, reputation, functioning systems, staff camaraderie, and industry experience that make a business much more than just a collection of assets. As mentioned earlier, if these factors are the result of a contractual right or are associated with intangibles that can be bought and sold separately, the value of the factor should be reported as a separate intangible asset. In essence, goodwill is a residual number, the value of all of the synergies of a functioning business that cannot be specifically identified with any other intangible factor. Goodwill is recognized only when it is purchased

> **FYI**
>
> The most important recent development in accounting for intangibles is the FASB's emphasis on companies reporting separate amounts for all of the individual intangible assets that can be identified. Previously, these assets were typically tossed in with goodwill.

as part of the acquisition of another company. In other words, a company's own goodwill, its homegrown goodwill, is not recognized. Goodwill will be defined and discussed more in depth later in the chapter.

Acquisitions Other Than Simple Cash Transactions

2 **Properly account for noncurrent operating asset acquisitions using various special arrangements, including deferred payment, self-construction, and acquisition of an entire company.**

WHY **All subsequent accounting for a noncurrent operating asset depends on the amount initially recorded as the cost of that asset. Measuring that initial cost can be difficult when an acquisition involves more than a simple cash purchase.**

HOW **Conceptually, the acquisition cost of a noncurrent operating asset should reflect the cash equivalent of whatever consideration is given in exchange for the asset. Measurement of this cash equivalent sometimes involves present value calculations, estimates of fair values, and/or estimates of total self-construction cost.**

When an asset is purchased for cash, the acquisition is simply recorded at the amount of cash paid, including all outlays relating to its purchase and preparation for intended use. Assets can be acquired under a number of other arrangements, however, some of which present special problems relating to the cost to be recorded. The acquisition of assets is discussed under the following headings:

1. Basket purchase
2. Deferred payment
3. Leasing
4. Exchange of nonmonetary assets
5. Acquisition by issuing securities
6. Self-construction
7. Acquisition by donation or discovery
8. Acquisition of an asset with significant restoration costs at retirement
9. Acquisition of an entire company

Basket Purchase

In some purchases, a number of assets may be acquired in a basket purchase for one lump sum. For example, the opening scenario of this chapter described how Jerry Jones acquired football equipment, cable TV rights, player contracts, and the Cowboys' NFL franchise rights when he purchased the Dallas Cowboys. To account for the assets on an individual basis, the total purchase price must be allocated among the individual assets. When part of a purchase price can be clearly identified with specific assets, such a cost assignment should be made and the balance of the purchase price allocated among the remaining assets. When no part of the purchase price can be related to specific assets, the entire amount must be allocated among the different assets acquired. Appraisal values or similar evidence provided by a competent independent authority should be sought to support the allocation.

To illustrate the allocation of a joint asset cost, assume that land, buildings, and equipment are acquired for $160,000. Assume further that a professional appraiser valued each of the assets at the acquisition date. The cost allocation is made as follows.

Assigned to	Appraised Values	Cost Allocation According to Relative Appraised Values	Cost Assigned to Individual Assets
Land	$ 56,000	56,000/200,000 × $160,000	$ 44,800
Buildings	120,000	120,000/200,000 × $160,000	96,000
Equipment	24,000	24,000/200,000 × $160,000	19,200
	$200,000		$160,000

The entry to record this acquisition, assuming a cash purchase, is as follows.

Land	44,800	
Buildings	96,000	
Equipment	19,200	
Cash		160,000

This cost allocation of a basket purchase price is not merely a theoretical exercise. Some assets in the group may be depreciable, others nondepreciable. Depreciable assets may have different useful lives. Periodic depreciation expense can be significantly impacted by the proportion of the purchase price that is allocated to assets with relatively long useful lives.

CAUTION

In this example, each semiannual payment declines since the interest is calculated on a declining balance in Notes Payable. For example, on January 1, 2014, the total payment would be just $8,000 ($5,000 + $3,000 interest). Alternatively, a contract can provide for a constant payment, or annuity. With an annuity, the amount applied to the note principal increases (and the Interest Expense decreases) each period as the liability decreases

Deferred Payment

The acquisition of real estate or other property frequently involves deferred payment of all or part of the purchase price. The buyer signs a note or a mortgage that specifies the terms of settlement of the obligation. The debt contract may call for one payment at a given future date or a series of payments at specified intervals. Interest charged on the unpaid balance of the contract should be recognized as an expense.

To illustrate the accounting for a deferred payment purchase contract, assume that land is acquired on January 2, 2013, for $100,000; $35,000 is paid at the time of purchase, and the balance is to be paid in semiannual installments of $5,000 plus interest on the unpaid principal at an annual rate of 10%. Entries for the purchase and for the first payment on the contract follow.

Transaction	Entry		
January 2, 2013	Land	100,000	
Purchased land for $100,000, paying $35,000 down, the balance to be paid in semiannual payments of $5,000 plus interest at 10%.	Cash		35,000
	Notes Payable		65,000
June 30, 2013	Interest Expense	3,250	
Made first payment.	Notes Payable	5,000	
Amount of payment: $5,000 + $3,250 (5% of $65,000) = $8,250	Cash		8,250

In the preceding example, the contract specified both a purchase price and interest at a stated rate on the unpaid balance. Sometimes, however, a contract may simply provide for a payment or series of payments without reference to interest or may provide for a stated interest rate that is unreasonable in relation to the market. In these circumstances, the note, sales price, and cost of the property, goods, or services exchanged for the note should be recorded at the fair value of the property, goods, or services or at the current market value of the note, whichever value is more clearly determinable.[7] The following example illustrates the accounting by the purchaser in this circumstance.

Assume that certain equipment, which has a cash price of $50,000, is acquired under a deferred payment contract. The contract specifies a down payment of $15,000 plus seven annual payments of $7,189 each, or a total price, including interest, of $65,323. Although not stated, the effective interest rate implicit in this contract is 10%, the rate that discounts the annual payments of $7,189 to a present value of $35,000, the cash price less the down payment.[8] If the fair value of the asset varies from the contract price because of delayed payments, the difference should be recorded as a discount (contra liability) and amortized over the life of the contract using the implicit or effective interest rate. Using the earlier example, the entries to record the purchase, the amortization of the discount for the first two years, and the first two payments would be as follows.

Transaction	Entry		
January 2, 2013	Equipment	50,000	
Purchased equipment with a cash price of $50,000 for $15,000 down plus seven annual payments of $7,189 each, or a total contract price of $65,323.	Discount on Notes Payable	15,323	
	Notes Payable		50,323
	Cash		15,000
December 31, 2013	Notes Payable	7,189	
Made first payment of $7,189.	Cash		7,189
Amortization of debt discount: $50,323 − $15,323 = $35,000; 10% x $35,000 = $3,500	Interest Expense	3,500	
	Discount on Notes Payable		3,500
December 31, 2014	Notes Payable	7,189	
Made second payment of $7,189.	Cash		7,189
Amortization of debt discount: 10% × $31,311* = $3,131	Interest Expense	3,131	
	Discount on Notes Payable		3,131

*$50,323 − $7,189 =	$43,134	Notes payable
$15,323 − $3,500 =	11,823	Discount on notes payable
	$31,311	Present value of notes payable at end of first year

[7] FASB ASC paragraph 835-30-25-10.

[8] As illustrated in the Time Value of Money Review Module, the effective or implicit interest rate may be computed as follows:

> Business calculator keystrokes:
> First toggle to make sure that the payments are assumed to occur at the end (END) of the period.
> The difference between the cash price and the down payment is $35,000.
> PV = ($35,000); N = 7; PMT = $7,189 → I = 10.00%

Additional examples of computing an implicit rate of interest are presented in the Module.

CAUTION

The account Discount on Notes Payable is a contra liability account and is reported as an offset to Notes Payable. It represents that portion of the remaining payments on the note that will be for interest.

When there is no established cash price for the property, goods, or services and there is no stated rate of interest on the contract, or the stated rate is unreasonable under the circumstances, an imputed interest rate must be used. The imputed interest rate is an estimate of what interest rate the borrowing company would have to pay on a loan given its creditworthiness and current market interest rates.

Leasing

A lease is a contract whereby one party (the lessee) is granted a right to use property owned by another party (the lessor) for a specified period of time for a specified periodic cost. Most leases are similar in nature to rentals. These leases are called operating leases. However, other leases, referred to as capital leases, are economically equivalent to a sale of the leased asset with the lessor allowing the lessee to pay for the asset over time with a series of "lease" payments. In these circumstances, the lease payments are exactly equivalent to mortgage payments. In such cases, the leased property should be recorded as an asset on the books of the company using the asset (the lessee), not on the books of the company that legally owns the asset (the lessor). The capital lease asset is recorded at the present value of the future lease payments. Because lease accounting is a complex area, an entire chapter (Chapter 15) is devoted to accounting for leases.

FYI

In this text, the word *amortization* is used to refer to the periodic expensing of the cost of intangible assets and leasehold improvements; depreciation is used for tangible assets.

Even when a lease is not considered to be the same as a purchase and the periodic payments are recorded as rental expense, certain lease prepayments or improvements to the property by the lessee may be treated as capital expenditures. Because leasehold improvements such as partitions in a building, additions, and attached equipment revert to the owner at the expiration of the lease, they are properly capitalized on the books of the lessee and amortized over the remaining life of the lease. Some lease costs are really expenses of the period and should not be capitalized. These include improvements that are made in lieu of rent; for example, a lessee builds partitions in a leased warehouse for storage of its product, and the lessor allows the lessee to offset the cost against rental expense for the period. These costs should be expensed by the lessee.

Exchange of Nonmonetary Assets

In some cases, an enterprise acquires a new asset by exchanging or trading existing nonmonetary assets.[9] Generally, the new asset should be valued at its fair value or at the fair value of the asset given up, whichever is more clearly determinable.[10] If the nonmonetary asset is used equipment, the fair value of the new asset is generally more clearly determinable and therefore used to record the exchange. If one of the parties in the exchange could have

[9] Monetary assets are those assets whose amounts are fixed in terms of currency, by contract, or otherwise. Examples include cash and accounts receivable. Nonmonetary assets include all other assets, such as inventories, land, buildings, and equipment.
[10] FASB ASC paragraph 845-10-30-1.

chosen to receive cash instead of the nonmonetary asset, that amount of cash is a good reflection of the fair value of the assets exchanged.

It should be observed that determining the fair value of a new asset can sometimes be difficult. The quoted or list price for an asset is not always a good indicator of the market value and is often higher than the actual cash price for the asset. An inflated list price permits the seller to increase the indicated trade-in allowance for a used asset. The price for which the asset could be sold in a cash transaction is the fair value that should be used to record the acquisition.

To illustrate, assume the sticker on the window of a new car sitting in a dealer's showroom lists a total selling price of $33,500. The sticker includes a base price plus an itemized listing of all the options that have been added. If you, as a buyer, approached the dealer with your old clunker as a trade-in, you might be surprised to be offered $3,000 for a car you know is worth no more than $1,000. If you offered to pay cash for the new car with no trade-in, however, you could probably buy it for approximately $31,500 or the list price reduced by the inflated amount of allowance offered for the trade-in. The fair value of the new asset is thus not the list price of $33,500 but the true cash price of $31,500.

If the nonmonetary asset given up to acquire the new asset is also property or equipment, a sale of property occurs simultaneously with the acquisition. When an exchange of a nonmonetary asset takes place, the use of fair value results in a gain or loss on the disposal of the nonmonetary asset. Under some limited circumstances, a gain may be deferred and recognized (through lower depreciation expense) over the life of the newly acquired asset.[11] Because of the need to first discuss depreciation methods before explaining the accounting for the sale of assets, the full discussion of acquisition and disposal by exchange is covered in Chapter 11.

Acquisition by Issuing Securities

A company may acquire certain property by issuing its own bonds or stocks. When a fair value for the securities can be determined, that value is assigned to the asset; in the absence of a fair value for the securities, the fair value of the asset acquired would be used. To illustrate, assume that a company issues 1,000 shares of $1 par common stock in acquiring land; the stock has a current market price of $45 per share. An entry should be made as follows:

Land	45,000	
Common Stock		1,000
Paid-In Capital in Excess of Par		44,000

When securities do not have an established market value, appraisal of the acquired assets by an independent authority may be required to arrive at an objective determination of their fair value.

As discussed in Chapter 5, purchasing noncurrent assets in exchange for long-term debt and/or stock is an example of a significant noncash transaction. This kind of noncash transaction is not included in the body of the statement of cash flows as an investing or a financing activity. Instead, the transaction, if material, is disclosed separately.

Self-Construction

Sometimes buildings or equipment are constructed by a company for its own use. This may be done to save on construction costs, to utilize idle facilities, or to achieve a higher quality of construction.

[11] FASB ASC paragraph 845-10-30-3.

Self-Constructed Assets Like purchased assets, these are recorded at cost, including all expenditures incurred to build the asset and make it ready for its intended use. Some considerations in determining the cost of self-constructed assets are discussed in the following sections.

Overhead Chargeable to Self-Construction All costs that can be related to construction should be charged to the assets under construction. There is no question about the inclusion of charges for material and labor directly attributable to the new construction. However, there is a difference of opinion regarding the amount of overhead properly assignable to the construction activity. Some accountants take the position that assets under construction should be charged with no more than the incremental overhead, the increase in a company's total overhead resulting from the special construction activity. Others maintain that overhead should be assigned to construction just as it is assigned to normal operations. This would call for the inclusion of not only the increase in overhead resulting from construction activities but also a pro rata share of the company's fixed overhead. Common practice is to allocate both variable overhead and a pro rata share of fixed overhead to self-construction projects. An illustration of the capitalization of overhead costs is given in the December 31, 2009, 10-K filing of **Gyrodyne Company of America**. The company began in 1946 as a producer of helicopters and has since transitioned to managing real estate operations. Gyrodyne reports, "In addition to land, land development, and construction costs, real estate held for development includes legal, engineering and other related soft development costs, interest, real estate taxes, and related development and construction overhead costs which are capitalized during the development and construction period."

Savings or Loss on Self-Construction When the cost of self-construction of an asset is less than the cost to acquire it through purchase or construction by outsiders, the difference for accounting purposes is not a profit but a savings. The construction is properly reported at its actual cost. The savings will emerge as an increase in net income over the life of the asset as lower depreciation is charged against periodic revenue. Assume, on the other hand, the cost of self-construction is greater than bids originally received for the construction. There is generally no assurance that the asset under alternative arrangements might have been equal in quality to that which was self-constructed. In recording this transaction, just as in recording others, accounts should reflect those courses of action taken, not the alternatives that might have been selected. However, if there is evidence indicating cost has been materially excessive because of construction inefficiencies or failures, the asset should be evaluated for possible recording of an impairment loss. Recognition of impairment losses is discussed in Chapter 11.

Interest During Period of Construction When a construction company bids on a job, the bid includes a charge for interest that will be incurred on funds borrowed to finance the construction. The interest cost is viewed as being an integral part of the cost of construction, just like materials, labor, and equipment rental costs. In a similar way, when a company constructs an asset for its own use, long-standing accounting practice is for the company to capitalize the interest costs incurred to finance the construction.

Capitalization of interest first began with public utilities. Public utilities self-construct a large portion of their assets, so the capitalized interest amount can be very material. More importantly, public utility rates are frequently set by government bodies and are tied to the utility's rate base, which is the utility's book value of assets. The higher the rate base, the higher the utility rates. Accordingly, public utilities have a great incentive to include all possible costs, including capitalized interest, in the reported cost of their self-constructed assets.

Although capitalization of interest began with public utilities, it is now generally accepted accounting practice for all firms that construct assets for their own use. Remember that interest capitalization is not merely a ploy used by utilities to get higher rates; interest is a legitimate cost of construction, and the proper matching of revenues and expenses suggests that interest be deferred and charged over the life of the constructed asset. If buildings or equipment were acquired by purchase rather than by self-construction, a charge for interest during the construction period would be implicit in the purchase price.

Capitalization of interest is required for assets, such as buildings and equipment, that are being self-constructed for an enterprise's own use and assets that are intended to be leased or sold to others that can be identified as discrete projects. These are projects that can be clearly identified as to the assets involved. Interest should not be capitalized for inventories manufactured or produced on a repetitive basis, for assets that are currently being used, or for assets that are idle and are not undergoing activities to prepare them for use. Thus, land that is being held for future development does not qualify for interest capitalization.[12]

Once it is determined that the construction project qualifies for interest capitalization, the amount of interest to be capitalized must be determined. The following basic guidelines govern the computation of capitalized interest:

1. Interest charges begin when the first expenditures are made on the project and continue as long as work continues and until the asset is completed and actually ready for use.
2. The amount of interest to be capitalized is computed using the accumulated expenditures for the project, weighted based on when the expenditures were made during the year. *Expenditures* mean cash disbursements, not accruals.
3. The interest rates to be used in calculating the amount of interest to capitalize are, in the following order:
   (a) Interest rate incurred for any debt specifically incurred for funds used on the project.
   (b) Weighted-average interest rate from all other enterprise borrowings regardless of the use of funds.
4. If the construction period covers more than one fiscal period, accumulated expenditures include prior years' capitalized interest.

The maximum interest that can be capitalized is the total interest accrued for the year.

The following illustration demonstrates the application of these guidelines. Cutler Industries, Inc., has decided to construct a new computerized assembly plant. It is estimated that the construction period will be about 18 months and that the cost of construction will be approximately $6.4 million (excluding capitalized interest). A 12% construction loan for $2 million is obtained on January 1, 2013, at the beginning of construction.

In addition to the construction loan, Cutler has the following outstanding debt during the construction period:

5-year notes payable, 11% interest	$3,000,000
Mortgage on other plant, 9% interest	4,800,000

[12] FASB ASC paragraph 835-20-15-6.

The weighted-average interest rate on this general nonconstruction debt is computed as follows.

Nonconstruction Debt	Principal	Rate	Interest Cost
Notes payable	$3,000,000	11%	$330,000
Mortgage	4,800,000	9	432,000
	$7,800,000	9.8*	$762,000

*Weighted-average rate = $762,000 ÷ $7,800,000 = 9.8% (rounded)

The following expenditures were incurred on the project during 2013.

January 1, 2013	$1,200,000
October 1, 2013	1,800,000

Computation of the amount of interest to be capitalized for 2013 is as follows:

Expenditure Date	Amount	Interest Capitalization Rate	Fraction of the Year Outstanding	Capitalized Interest
January 1, 2013	$1,200,000	12%	12/12	$144,000
October 1, 2013	800,000	12	3/12	24,000
	1,000,000	9.8	3/12	24,500
Total capitalized interest for 2013				$192,500

Notice first that capitalized interest is computed only for the amount of time the expenditures were outstanding. The January 1 expenditures caused increased borrowing costs for the entire year, but the October 1 expenditures were outstanding for only the final three months of the year. This approach results in an approximation of the amount of interest that could have been avoided if the expenditures had been used to repay debt instead of being used for the construction project.

STOP&THINK

Which ONE of the following describes the financial statement impact of a company neglecting to capitalize interest that should be capitalized?

a) Net income overstated and total assets overstated
b) Net income understated and total assets overstated
c) Net income overstated and total assets understated
d) Net income understated and total assets understated

This approach also assumes that the most avoidable interest is the interest on the borrowing specifically for the construction project. Accordingly, the interest rate of 12% on the specific construction borrowing is used. However, the amount of that loan is only $2,000,000; expenditures above this $2,000,000 amount could have been used to repay general company debt. Therefore, the October 1 expenditure of $1,800,000 has been split into two pieces—the first $800,000 could have been used to repay the balance of the construction loan ($800,000 = $2,000,000 − $1,200,000), so the amount of avoidable interest is computed using the 12% rate. The remaining $1,000,000 could have been used to repay general company debt, so the weighted-average rate of 9.8% on general borrowing is used.

Finally, recall that the amount of interest capitalized cannot exceed total interest incurred for the year. Total interest incurred during 2013 was as follows.

Debt	Amount	Interest Rate	Annual Interest
Construction loan	$2,000,000	12%	$ 240,000
Notes payable	3,000,000	11%	330,000
Mortgage payable	4,800,000	9%	432,000
Total interest incurred			$1,002,000

Because total interest incurred exceeds the computed amount of interest to be capitalized, the entire indicated amount of $192,500 is capitalized. The journal entry to record total interest incurred by Cutler Industries during 2013 (assuming that all interest was paid in cash) is as follows.

Construction in Progress	192,500	
Interest Expense ($1,002,000 – $192,500)	809,500	
Cash		1,002,000

Assume that additional construction expenditures of $3,200,000 were made on February 1, 2014, and the project was completed on May 31, 2014.

The amount of interest to be capitalized for the year 2014 follows.

Expenditure Date	Amount	Interest Capitalization Rate	Fraction Outstanding of the Year	Capitalized Interest
Accumulated in 2013	$2,000,000	12%	5/12	$100,000
	1,192,500	9.8	5/12	48,694
February 1, 2014	3,200,000	9.8	4/12	104,533
Total capitalized interest for 2014				$253,227

Avoidable interest in 2014 includes interest on all the loans that could have been repaid with the construction expenditures made in 2013. These expenditures total $3,192,500 ($1,200,000 + $1,800,000 + $192,500) and include interest capitalized in 2013. Interest is capitalized only until May 31 (five months) when construction is completed and the building is ready for use. Because $253,227 is less than the actual annual interest of $1,002,000, the entire indicated amount of $253,227 is capitalized in 2014.

FYI

This is an unusual project indeed! It finished ahead of schedule (in only 17 months), and the actual total cost of construction (excluding capitalized interest) is only $6.2 million, $200,000 less than forecasted.

Total recorded cost of the building on May 31, 2014, when it is put into service, is $6,645,727, computed as follows.

Expenditures incurred in 2013	$3,000,000
Interest capitalized in 2013	192,500
Expenditures incurred in 2014	3,200,000
Interest capitalized in 2014	253,227
Total building cost, May 31, 2014	$6,645,727

FASB ASC Subtopic 835-20 (Interest—Capitalization of Interest) requires disclosure of the total interest expense for the year and the amount capitalized. This disclosure can be made either in the body of the income statement or in a note to the statements.

To illustrate these two methods, assume that Cutler Industries reported the 2013 interest information on the income statement and the 2014 interest information in a note.

Cutler Industries, Inc.
Income Statement
For the Year Ended December 31, 2013

Operating income		$XXX,XXX
Other expenses and losses:		
Total interest incurred	$1,002,000	
Less: Capitalized interest	192,500	809,500
Income before income taxes		$XXX,XXX
Income taxes		XXX,XXX
Net income		$XXX,XXX

Cutler Industries, Inc.
Financial Statement Notes
For the Year Ended December 31, 2014

Note X—Interest expense. Interest of $253,227 was capitalized in 2014 as part of the cost of construction for the computerized assembly plant in accordance with the requirements of FASB ASC Subtopic 835-20.

The amount of capitalized interest reported for 2009 by several large U.S. companies and its percentage of total interest reported by those companies are displayed in Exhibit 10-5. As you can see, **General Electric** capitalized only an insignificant amount of its $18,769 million in interest during 2009. On the other hand, **ExxonMobil** capitalized almost as much interest as it expensed in 2009.

EX 10-5 CAPITALIZED INTEREST FOR SEVERAL LARGE U.S. COMPANIES IN 2009 (IN MILLIONS OF U.S. DOLLARS)

Company	Capitalized Interest	Interest Expense	Capitalized as a Percentage of Total Interest
General Electric	$ 42	$18,811	0.2%
AT&T	740	3,379	18.0
ExxonMobil	429	548	43.9
McDonald's	11.7	473.2	2.4
The Walt Disney Company	57	466	10.9

Complexities arise in computing the amount of interest to capitalize when a company secures new loans in the middle of the year. These complexities and an alternate approach to computing capitalized interest are explained in the Web Material associated with this chapter (**www.cengage.com/international**).

Not everyone agrees that interest on funds used to finance the self-construction of assets should be capitalized. In fact, the original FASB vote was only four to three in favor of pre-Codification *SFAS No. 34,* which mandated the capitalization of interest in the United States back in 1979. The changing stance of the IASB and its predecessor, the IASC, perfectly illustrates the split view on interest capitalization. In the original international standard on interest capitalization *(IAS 23)*, companies were allowed to either capitalize (or *capitalise*, to use the international spelling) interest or not, but the company should be consistent in its practice. In a 1989 exposure draft, the IASC then proposed establishing a benchmark treatment requiring interest capitalization. But the revised version of *IAS 23* issued in 1993 said that all interest should be expensed, regardless of how the funds are used, with interest capitalization as an allowable alternative. Finally, in 2007 the IASB revised *IAS 23* again to require, starting on January 1, 2009, that all companies capitalize "borrowing costs" incurred in the construction of a long-term asset. An important difference between this revised version of *IAS 23* and the U.S. standard is that the international standard requires that companies capitalize the *net* amount of interest incurred rather than the *gross* amount. This means that under *IAS 23* a company capitalizes the amount of interest, computed as shown above under the explanation of the U.S. standard, *less* the amount of investment income generated by borrowed construction funds that are temporarily invested before they are needed to pay for construction expenditures. Accordingly, the amount of interest capitalized under the international standard is generally less than the amount that would be capitalized under the U.S. standard.

ifrs

Acquisition by Donation or Discovery

When property is received through donation, there is no cost that can be used as a basis for its valuation. Even though certain expenditures may have to be made incidental to the gift, these expenditures are generally considerably less than the value of the property. Here cost obviously fails to provide a satisfactory basis for asset valuation.

Property acquired through donation should be appraised and recorded at its fair value. A donation is recognized as a revenue or gain in the period in which it is received.[13] To illustrate, Netty's Ice Cream Parlor is given a donation of land and a building by an eccentric ice cream lover. The entry on Netty's books, using the appraised values of the land and the building, is as follows:

Land	400,000	
Buildings	1,500,000	
Revenue or Gain		1,900,000

Depreciation of an asset acquired by gift should be recorded in the usual manner, the value assigned to the asset providing the basis for the depreciation charge.

If a gift is contingent upon some act to be performed by the recipient, no asset should be reported until the conditions of the gift have been met. At that time, both the increase in

[13] FASB ASC paragraph 958-310-25-1.

Dave Thompson/Life File/Photodisc/Getty Images

Publicly traded oil and gas firms are required to disclose the quantity of their proved oil and gas reserves, as well as a forecast of the discounted value of future net cash flows expected to be generated by the reserves.

assets and the revenue or gain should be recognized in the accounts and in the financial statements.[14]

Occasionally, valuable resources are discovered on land already owned. The discovery greatly increases the value of the property. However, because the cost of the land is not affected by the discovery, it is common practice in the United States to ignore this increase in value. Similarly, the increase in value for assets that change over time, such as growing timber or aging wine, is ignored in common practice in the United States. Failure to recognize these discovery or accretion values ignores the economic reality of the situation and tends to materially understate the assets of the entity. Nevertheless, asset write-ups are generally not allowable under U.S. accounting standards, although they are routine in some other countries. More information on asset write-ups is given later in the chapter.

FYI

Valuation issues in transactions that are not arm's length can be very difficult. FASB ASC paragraph 845-10-S99-1 requires that when a corporation receives nonmonetary assets as an investment by a shareholder, the assets are recorded by the company at the shareholder's historical cost.

One exception to the practice of ignoring the value of assets discovered is the supplemental disclosure required regarding oil and gas reserves. Publicly traded oil and gas firms are required to disclose the amount of their proved oil and gas reserves, along with summary data on why the amount of proved reserves changed during the period. In addition, the oil and gas firms are required to disclose a forecast of the discounted value of future net cash flows expected to be generated by the reserves.[15] The oil and gas firms are skeptical about the usefulness of this disclosure as illustrated by this quote from **Chevron**'s 2009 annual report:

> The information provided does not represent management's estimate of the company's expected future cash flows or value of proved oil and gas reserves. Estimates of proved-reserve quantities are imprecise and change over time as new information becomes available. Moreover, probable and possible reserves, which may become proved in the future, are excluded from the calculations. . . . The calculations . . . should not be relied upon as an indication of the company's future cash flows or value of its oil and gas reserves.

ifrs

The international standard for recognizing increases in the value of property from growth or discovery is substantially different from U.S. practice. Under *IAS 41*, biological

[14] FASB ASC paragraph 958-605-25-11.
[15] FASB ASC paragraph 932-235-50-2.

assets, such as cattle, fruit trees, and lumber forests, are recorded in the balance sheet at their fair value (less estimating selling costs) as of the balance sheet date. Increases in this fair value are recognized as gains, and decreases are recognized as losses. Accordingly, under international accounting standards, a lumber company would report the timber in its forests at fair value (less selling cost) in each balance sheet during, say, the 30-year period the timber is growing. The yearly increases or decreases in fair value would be reported in the income statement as gains or losses. In summary, international financial reporting standards allow, and sometimes require, the recognition of changes in long-term asset values in many more cases than do U.S. standards.

FYI

In 2004, Royal Dutch/Shell Group was fined a total of $150 million by U.S. and British authorities for deceptive reporting of its proved oil and gas reserves. The company was forced to reduce its reported oil reserves by 4.47 billion barrels, a reduction of 23%. This reserve restatement knocked about 10% off the market value of the company.

Acquisition of an Asset with Significant Restoration Costs at Retirement

Sometimes, the act of acquiring a long-term operating asset legally obligates a company to incur restoration costs in the future when the asset is retired. For example, when an oil exploration firm erects an oil platform to support drilling operations, it becomes legally obligated to dismantle and remove the platform when the drilling is done.[16] Proper accounting for this obligation requires that it be recognized, at its estimated fair value, at the time that it is incurred and that the fair value of the obligation be added to the cost of acquiring the long-term operating asset.

To illustrate the initial recognition of an asset retirement obligation, assume that Bryan Beach Company purchases and erects an oil platform at a total cost of $750,000. The oil platform will be in use for 10 years, at which time Bryan Beach is legally obligated to ensure that the platform is dismantled and removed from the site. Bryan Beach can estimate the fair value of this asset retirement obligation by referring to market prices for the settlement of these obligations or by using present value techniques. If, for example, there are firms that will contract in advance to dismantle and remove an oil platform 10 years from now, Bryan Beach can use the price of those contracts to estimate the fair value of its asset retirement obligation. In this case, assume that no such market exists. However, Bryan Beach estimates that it will have to pay $100,000 to have the platform dismantled and removed from the site in 10 years. If the appropriate interest rate to use

FYI

Adding the fair value of asset retirement obligations to the cost of the associated long-term operating asset applies only to normal restoration costs that are unavoidable in the routine use of the asset. Unforeseen restoration costs, such as from a catastrophic toxic waste spill, are accounted for differently. The present value of these catastrophic cleanup costs is expensed in the period in which the unforeseen cost is incurred and the related liability is recognized.

[16] This oil platform illustration and the nuclear plant illustration used later are adapted from FASB ASC Section 410-20-55 (Asset Retirement and Environmental Obligations—Asset Retirement Obligations—Implementation Guidance and Illustration).

in computing the present value is 8%,[17] the present value of the \$100,000 obligation is computed as follows:

FV = \$100,000; I = 8%; N = 10 years → \$46,319

The journal entries to record the purchase of the oil platform and the recognition of the asset retirement obligation are as follows:

Oil Platform	750,000	
Cash		750,000
Oil Platform	46,319	
Asset Retirement Obligation		46,319

In this oil platform example, the entire asset retirement obligation was created by the initial acquisition and deployment of the long-term operating asset. In other situations, additional asset retirement obligation is created over time. For example, assume that Homer Company constructs and commences operation of a nuclear power plant. Total construction cost is \$400,000. The cost of cleaning up the routine contamination caused by the initial stockpile of nuclear material is estimated to be \$500,000; this cost will be incurred in 30 years when the plant is decommissioned. Additional contamination will occur each year that the plant is in operation. In its first year of operation, that additional contamination adds \$40,000 to the estimated cleanup cost, which will occur after 29 years (because one year has elapsed). The journal entries to record the purchase of the nuclear plant and the recognition of the initial asset retirement obligation (assuming that the appropriate interest rate is 9%) and the additional obligation created after one year are as follows:

Initial Acquisition

Nuclear Plant	400,000	
Cash		400,000
Nuclear Plant	37,686	
Asset Retirement Obligation		37,686

FV = \$500,000; I = 9%; N = 30 years → \$37,686

After One Year

Nuclear Plant	3,286	
Asset Retirement Obligation		3,286

FV = \$40,000; I = 9%; N = 29 years → \$3,286

The asset retirement cost added to the basis of the nuclear plant would be depreciated over the useful life of the plant. In addition, the amount of the asset retirement obligation would increase each year through the passage of time (because the time until the payment of the restoration costs would be shorter). Accounting for depreciation and the systematic increase in the recorded amount of the asset retirement obligation will be discussed in Chapter 11.

[17] In FASB ASC paragraphs 410-20-55-13 through 17, the FASB states that the appropriate interest rate to use is the credit-adjusted risk-free rate, meaning the rate on U.S. Treasury securities (typically 5% or less), plus premiums to reflect both the credit standing of the company doing the calculation as well as a "market-risk premium" that a third party would demand for accepting the uncertainties associated with taking on the asset retirement obligation. See the Time Value of Money Review Module of this text for more discussion on present-value calculations.

Acquisition of an Entire Company

Instead of buying selected assets from another firm, as in a basket purchase, sometimes a company will buy the entire firm. This is called a *business combination*. The procedures for accounting for a business combination are similar to those used for a basket purchase. The primary difference is that in a business combination the sum of the fair values of the identifiable assets is usually less than the total amount paid to buy the company. As discussed earlier, this excess is called *goodwill* and reflects the value of the synergy of having all of the productive assets together as a functioning unit. The accounting for business combinations and goodwill is discussed in detail later in the chapter when the acquisition of intangible assets is covered.

Capitalize or Expense?

3 **Separate costs into those that should be expensed immediately and those that should be capitalized, and understand the accounting standards for research and development and oil and gas exploration costs.**

WHY **The definition of an asset in the Conceptual Framework includes the phrase "probable future economic benefit." In practice, there has been some difficulty in using this definition to identify a cost as an asset or an expense. The FASB has created a number of more specific rules for particular types of costs.**

HOW **Postacquisition costs that increase an asset's capacity or extend its life are capitalized; routine maintenances costs are expensed. Research and development costs are always expensed except for software development costs incurred after technological feasibility has been established. Firms have the choice of either capitalizing or expensing some oil and gas exploration costs.**

The decision as to whether a given expenditure is an asset or an expense is one of the many areas in which an accountant must exercise judgment. Conceptually, the issue is straightforward: If an expenditure is expected to benefit future periods, it is an asset; otherwise, it is an expense.

In practice, the capitalize-or-expense question is much more difficult. To illustrate, look at the continuum in Exhibit 10-6.

> **FYI**
>
> This seemingly simple capitalize-or-expense issue blew up in the face of **WorldCom** in 2002 when it was revealed that the company had capitalized $3.8 billion in expenditures that it should have expensed. Uproar over this accounting abuse harmed the company's public image and hastened its bankruptcy, the largest in U.S. history to that time.

Few people would disagree with the claim that the cost of office supplies used is an expense. Once the supplies are used, they offer no more future benefit. Similarly, the cost of a building clearly should be capitalized because the building will provide economic benefit in future periods. The endpoints of the continuum are easy, but it is the vast middle ground where accountants must exercise their judgment.

The difficulty with making capitalize-or-expense decisions is that many expenditures have some probability of generating future economic benefit, but uncertainty surrounds that benefit. Research and development expenditures are a good example. Companies spend money on research and development because they expect to reap future benefits. However, there is no guarantee that the benefits will materialize. The following sections

EX 10-6 EXPENSE/ASSET CONTINUUM

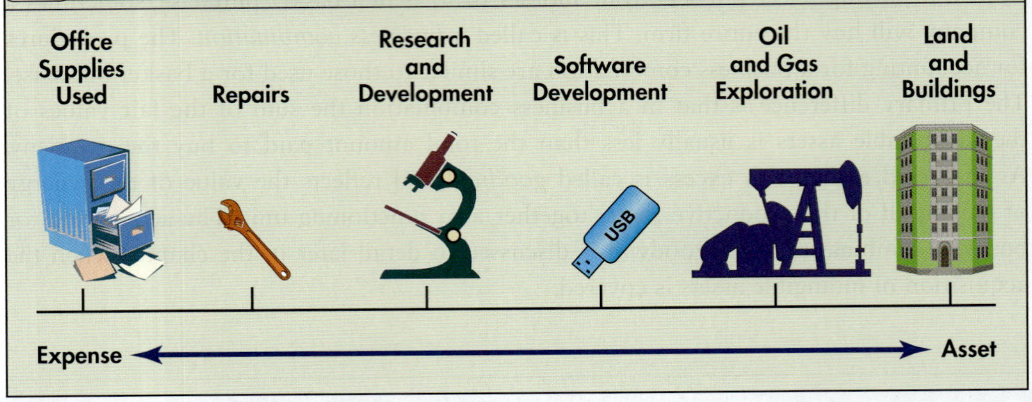

examine several categories of expenditures to give you practice in analyzing the issues relevant to a capitalize-or-expense decision.

Before examining the conceptual issues, here is one practical note. Many companies establish a lower limit on amounts that will be considered for capitalization to avoid wasting time agonizing about the proper accounting for trivial amounts. Thus, any expenditure under the established limit is always expensed currently even though future benefits are expected from that expenditure. This practice is justified on the grounds of expediency and materiality. Of course, the amount of the limit varies with the size of the company. In the published financial statements of large corporations, for example, amounts are rounded to the nearest million. Detailed accounting for amounts smaller than this will have no impact on the reported numbers. This treatment is acceptable as long as it is consistently applied and no material misstatements arise due to unusual expenditure patterns or other causes.

Postacquisition Expenditures

Over the useful lives of plant assets, regular as well as special expenditures are incurred. Certain expenditures are required to maintain and repair assets; others are incurred to increase their capacity or efficiency or to extend their useful lives. Each expenditure requires careful analysis to determine whether it should be expensed or capitalized.

The words *maintenance, repairs, renewals, replacements, additions, betterments, improvements,* and *rearrangements* are often used in describing expenditures made in the course of asset use. A more systematic way to view these postacquisition expenditures is how they relate to the components of a recorded piece of property, plant, or equipment.[18] A component is a portion of a property, plant, or equipment item that is separately identifiable and for which a separate useful life can be estimated. An example of a component is

[18] AcSEC Exposure Draft, Proposed Statement of Position, "Accounting for Certain Costs and Activities Related to Property, Plant, and Equipment" (New York: American Institute of Certified Public Accountants, June 29, 2001). On April 14, 2004, the FASB met to consider the AcSEC's final proposed Statement of Position (SOP). The Board objected to the release of the SOP, so it was withheld. Among other things, the Board members thought that intercompany differences in defining "components" would result in a lack of comparability of financial statements. The FASB may undertake a review of the accounting for property, plant, and equipment in conjunction with its general effort to increase international convergence. Ultimately, the concept of a "component" of a certain item of property, plant, or equipment may not be retained by the FASB. However, the "component" approach is part of International Financial Reporting Standards; see *IAS 16*, par. 43.

EX 10-7 SUMMARY OF EXPENDITURES SUBSEQUENT TO ACQUISITION

Type of Expenditure	Definition	Accounting Treatment
Maintenance and repairs	Normal cost of keeping property in operating condition.	Expense as incurred because the cost is intended to keep an existing component in working order.
Renewals and replacements:		
1. No extension of useful life or increase in future cash flows.	Unplanned replacement. Expenditure needed to fulfill original plans.	Expense as incurred; no new component acquired.
2. Extends useful life or increases future cash flows.	Improvement resulting from replacement with better component.	Replacement of a component. Capitalize the cost of the new component. The remaining book value of the replaced component is added to depreciation expense for the period.
Additions and betterments	Expenditures that add to asset usefulness by either extending life or increasing future cash flows.	Account for as a separate component of the asset with a separate estimated useful life.

the heating and cooling system of a building. The acquisition cost of this system can be separately identified, and typically the heating and cooling system has a different life than the building itself. In accounting for postacquisition expenditures, the important consideration is whether the expenditure results in the replacement of an existing component, the addition of a component, or is merely intended to maintain an existing component in working order. Exhibit 10-7 summarizes the accounting for these postacquisition expenditures.

Maintenance and Repairs Expenditures to maintain plant assets in good operating condition are referred to as maintenance. Among these are expenditures for painting, lubricating, and adjusting equipment. Maintenance expenditures are ordinary, recurring, and do not improve the asset or add to its life; therefore, they are recorded as expenses when they are incurred.

Expenditures to restore assets to good operating condition upon their breakdown or to restore and replace broken parts are referred to as repairs. These are ordinary and recurring expenditures that benefit only current operations; thus, they also are charged to expense immediately.

Renewals and Replacements Expenditures for overhauling plant assets are frequently referred to as renewals. These amounts should be expensed as incurred. Substitutions of parts or entire units are referred to as replacements. If a part is removed and replaced with a different part, the cost and accumulated depreciation related to the replaced part should be removed from the accounts, and the remaining book value of the replaced part is added to depreciation expense for the period. If the replacement component has a useful life different from the remaining useful life of the large plant asset of which it is a component, its cost should be accounted for as a separate depreciable asset. To illustrate replacements, assume that Mendon Fireworks Company replaces the roof of its manufacturing plant for \$40,000. Assume that the original cost of the building was \$1,600,000 and it is three-fourths depreciated. If the original roof cost \$20,000, this roof was recorded as part of the building cost, and the new roof is recorded as a separate component. The following entry could be made to remove the undepreciated book value of the old roof and record the expenditure for the new one.

Roof	40,000	
Accumulated Depreciation—Buildings (old roof)	15,000	
Depreciation Expense	5,000	
Buildings (old roof)		20,000
Cash		40,000

Additions and Betterments Enlargements and extensions of existing facilities are referred to as additions. Changes in assets designed to provide increased or improved services are referred to as betterments. If the addition or betterment does not involve a replacement of component parts of an existing asset, the expenditure should be capitalized by adding it to the cost of the asset, or, if the new component has a useful life different from the larger asset of which it is a component, establishing a separate asset account for the component. If a replacement is involved, it is accounted for as discussed in the Mendon roof example.

Research and Development Expenditures

Historically, expenditures for research and development (R&D) purposes were reported sometimes as assets and sometimes as expenses. The FASB inherited this problem from the Accounting Principles Board and made this area the subject of its first definitive standard.[19] The Board defined research activities as those undertaken to discover new knowledge that will be useful in developing new products, services, or processes or that will result in significant improvements of existing products or processes. Development activities involve the application of research findings to develop a plan or design for new or improved products and processes. Development activities include the formulation, design, and testing of products; construction of prototypes; and operation of pilot plants.

Because of the uncertainty surrounding the future economic benefit of R&D activities, the FASB concluded that research and development expenditures should be expensed in the period incurred. Among the arguments for expensing R&D costs is the frequent inability to find a definite causal relationship between the expenditures and future revenues. Sometimes very large expenditures do not generate any future revenue, but relatively small expenditures lead to significant discoveries that generate large revenues. The Board found it difficult to establish criteria that would distinguish between those research and development expenditures that would most likely benefit future periods and those that would not.[20]

Research and development costs include those costs of materials, equipment, facilities, personnel, purchased intangibles, contract services, and a reasonable allocation of indirect costs that are related specifically to research and development activities and that have no alternative future uses. Such activities include the following:

- Research aimed at discovery of new knowledge
- Search for applications of research findings
- Search for possible product or process alternatives
- Design, construction, and testing of preproduction prototypes
- Design, construction, and operation of a pilot plant

Expenditures for certain items having alternative future uses, either in additional research projects or for productive purposes, can be recorded as assets and allocated against future

[19] *Pre-Codification Statement of Financial Accounting Standards No. 2*, "Accounting for Research and Development Costs" (Stamford, CT: Financial Accounting Standards Board, 1974).
[20] FASB ASC paragraphs 730-10-05-1 through 3

projects or periods as research and development expenses. This exception permits the deferral of costs incurred for materials, equipment, facilities, and purchased intangibles, but only if an alternative use can be identified.

Computer Software Development Expenditures

The FASB's requirement that all R&D costs be expensed seemed particularly ill-suited for the many software developers that sprang up in the early 1980s. The only economic assets owned by these firms were the software they developed, and strict application of pre-Codification *Statement No. 2* dictated that all development costs be expensed. The FASB, with strong support from the SEC, reexamined the R&D issue in the context of software developers and in 1985 issued pre-Codification *Statement No. 86*, "Accounting for the Costs of Computer Software to Be Sold, Leased, or Otherwise Marketed."

The Board's conclusions concerning computer software development costs are summarized in Exhibit 10-8.

As demonstrated by Exhibit 10-8, all costs incurred up to the point where technological feasibility is established are to be expensed as research and development. These include costs incurred for planning, designing, and testing activities. In essence, the uncertainty surrounding the future benefits of these costs is so great that they should be expensed. After technological feasibility has been established, uncertainty about future benefits is decreased to the extent that costs incurred after this point can be capitalized. Capitalizable software development costs include the costs of coding and testing done after the establishment of technological feasibility and the cost to produce masters. Additional costs to actually produce software from the masters and package the software for distribution are inventoriable costs and will be expensed as part of cost of goods sold.

Considerable judgment is required to determine when technological feasibility has been established. At a minimum, technological feasibility is attained when an enterprise has produced either of the following:[21]

- A detailed program design of the software, or
- A working model of the software

International Accounting for Research and Development: *IAS 38* The IASB has established an R&D accounting rule that many think is superior to the FASB rule. *IAS 38* requires research costs to be expensed and development costs to be capitalized. *Research costs*, as defined in this standard, are those R&D costs incurred before technical and commercial feasibility has been established, and development costs are those incurred after technical and commercial

EX 10-8 DEVELOPMENT OF SUCCESSFUL SOFTWARE

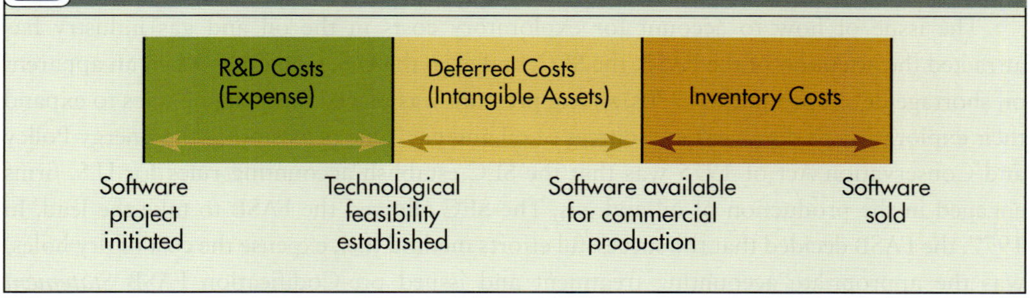

[21] FASB ASC paragraph 985-20-25-2.

feasibility. As you can see, the FASB rule for the accounting for software development costs is quite similar to the IASB standard for all research and development costs.

The Future of R&D Accounting in the United States On April 22, 2004, the FASB and the IASB held a joint meeting to discuss the convergence of their respective sets of accounting standards. One area identified as a candidate for convergence in the short term is the accounting for research and development. To date, the staffs of the FASB and the IASB are still studying this issue. Preliminary indications are that the general approach to R&D accounting in *IAS 38* will be adopted by the FASB, with the IASB borrowing some of the criteria included in pre-Codification FASB *Statement No. 86* (on computer software R&D) in order to make *IAS 38* easier to implement. However, remember that, until the FASB and the IASB come to an agreement on a joint R&D accounting standard, U.S. GAAP requires that all R&D costs be expensed except for post-feasibility computer software development costs.

Oil and Gas Exploration Costs

The nature of oil exploration is that several dry wells are drilled for each "gusher" that is discovered. The accounting question is whether the cost of the dry holes should be expensed as incurred or whether the costs should be capitalized. Two methods of accounting have been developed to account for oil and gas exploratory costs. Under the full cost method, all exploratory costs are capitalized, the reasoning being that the cost of drilling dry wells is part of the cost of locating productive wells. Under the successful efforts method, exploratory costs for dry holes are expensed, and only exploratory costs for successful wells are capitalized. Most large, successful oil companies use the successful efforts method. Exhibit 10-9 contains a description of the successful efforts method given by ExxonMobil in the notes to its 2007 financial statements.

FYI

In 1979, the SEC proposed a new method of accounting for oil and gas exploration called *reserve recognition accounting (RRA)*. RRA was a form of discovery accounting that would have recognized as an asset the value of the oil and gas discovered rather than the cost of the exploration efforts. A form of RRA lives on in the supplemental disclosures required of oil and gas firms.

For smaller companies, the full cost method has been more popular. The claim is that the full cost method encourages small companies to continue exploration by not imposing the severe penalty of recognizing all costs of unsuccessful projects as immediate expenses. Exhibit 10-9 also contains an excerpt from the 2009 financial statements of **Glen Rose Petroleum Corporation**, a small company based in Texas, which drills for oil and gas and accounts for its oil and gas operations using the full cost method.

The issue of how to account for exploratory costs in the oil and gas industry has attracted the attention of the FASB, the SEC, and even the U.S. Congress. When an apparent oil shortage developed in the 1970s, strong pressure was placed on oil companies to expand their exploration to discover new sources of oil and gas. One provision of the Energy Policy and Conservation Act of 1975 was that the SEC establish accounting rules for U.S. firms engaged in the production of oil and gas. The SEC allowed the FASB to take the lead. In 1977, the FASB decided that the successful efforts method (i.e., expense the cost of dry holes) was the appropriate accounting treatment and issued pre-Codification FASB *Statement No. 19*, "Financial Accounting and Reporting by Oil and Gas Producing Companies."

The uproar over *SFAS No. 19* was immediate and loud. Small independent oil exploration firms argued that using the successful efforts method would require them to

EX 10-9 EXXONMOBIL AND GLEN ROSE PETROLEUM—EXPLORATION COSTS

ExxonMobil

The Corporation uses the "successful efforts" method to account for its exploration and production activities. Under this method, costs are accumulated on a field-by-field basis with certain exploratory expenditures and exploratory dry holes being expensed as incurred. Costs of productive wells and development dry holes are capitalized and amortized on the unit-of-production method. The Corporation uses this accounting policy instead of the "full cost" method because it provides a more timely accounting of the success or failure of the Corporation's exploration and production activities. If the full cost method were used, all costs would be capitalized and depreciated on a country-by-country basis. The capitalized costs would be subject to an impairment test by country. The full cost method would tend to delay the expense recognition of unsuccessful projects.

Glen Rose Petroleum

We employ the full cost method of accounting for our oil and gas production assets, which are located in the southwestern United States. Under the full cost method, all costs associated with the acquisition, exploration and development of oil and gas properties are capitalized and accumulated in cost centers on a country-by-country basis. The sum of net capitalized costs and estimated future development and dismantlement costs for each cost center is depleted on the equivalent unit-of-production basis using proved oil and gas reserves as determined by independent petroleum engineers.

expense costs that they had been capitalizing, resulting in lower profits, depressed stock prices, and more difficulty in getting loans. The Department of Energy held hearings, and the Justice Department's antitrust division expressed concern. A bill was introduced in the Senate that would have made it *illegal* for the FASB to eliminate the full cost method. The SEC ran for cover and declared that in spite of the FASB standard, financial statements prepared using the full cost method would be acceptable to the SEC. In February 1979, the FASB succumbed to the pressure and issued pre-Codification *SFAS No. 25*, reinstating the full cost method.

The oil and gas controversy is a perfect illustration of the difficulties surrounding the capitalize-or-expense decision. Conceptual arguments can usually be made on both sides of the issue. Some expenditures, such as research and development and oil and gas exploration costs, are covered by specific authoritative pronouncements. Other expenditures, such as repairs or renewals, require accounting judgment. Material in the cases at the end of the chapter allows you to test your judgment on such issues as the accounting for advertising and asbestos removal.

Accounting for the Acquisition of Intangible Assets

4 **Recognize intangible assets acquired separately, as part of a basket purchase, and as part of a business acquisition.**

WHY **Intangible assets comprise an increasing portion of company assets. Because of the very nature of intangible assets, accounting for intangibles requires different rules for valuation and impairment than the rules that apply to tangible noncurrent assets.**

HOW **Internally generated intangible assets are not recognized on the balance sheet. Acquired intangible assets are valued at the amount paid to acquire them. Intangible assets are often acquired in a basket purchase, so the total purchase price is allocated on the basis of the estimated fair values of all of the assets purchased. The fair value of an intangible asset can be estimated by using market prices, by the traditional present value approach, or by the expected cash flow approach.**

One of the most striking trends in business in the past 20 years is the increasing importance of intangible assets. This trend has proved to be a difficult challenge for financial reporting. The classic financial reporting model is based on manufacturing and retail companies with a focus on inventory, accounts receivable, buildings, equipment, and so forth. In a world driven by information technology, global brand names, and human capital, this accounting model often excludes the most important economic assets of a business. For example, in 2006, it was estimated that an average of 213 gigabytes of digital information was generated for each man, woman, and child in North America.[22] In 2001, Federal Reserve economist Leonard Nakamura estimated that U.S. companies invest approximately $1 trillion per year in intangible assets and that the value of the existing stock of intangibles is $5 trillion.[23] Finally, in 2001, Professor Erik Brynjolfsson of MIT's Sloan School estimated that U.S. companies had invested $1.3 trillion over the preceding 10 years in their "organization capital," or their processes and ways of doing things effectively and efficiently; this is comparable to the amount those same companies had invested in new equipment and factories over the same period.[24]

In August 1996, the FASB began a project on the accounting for intangibles. The FASB noted, "Intangible assets make up an increasing proportion of the assets of many (if not most) entities, but despite their importance, those assets often are not recognized as such." The result of the FASB's project was a requirement that companies make greater efforts to identify and separately recognize more intangible assets. Theoretically, this requirement has existed since 1970; pre-Codification *APB Opinion No. 17* (paragraphs 24 through 26) stipulated that the cost of identifiable intangible assets should be separately recognized in the financial statements. However, in practice most companies had reported intangibles as an ill-defined conglomeration, with little detail about separate intangibles. The revised standards are contained in FASB ASC 350 (Intangibles—Goodwill and Other).

These revised standards also substantially change the practice of amortizing the cost of intangibles assets. Under these standards, many intangible assets are assumed to have indefinite useful lives and thus are not systematically amortized. The amortization (and nonamortization) of intangible assets is discussed in Chapter 11. The different types of intangible assets and the process through which they are recognized are discussed below.

Internally Generated Intangibles

One thing the new FASB standards do *not* attempt is to require companies to identify and value internally generated, or homegrown, intangibles. In most cases, these are the most valuable intangible assets that a company has. As an illustration, consider Exhibit 10-10, which lists the 10 most valuable brands in the world in 2009. Each of these brands represents a valuable economic asset that was internally generated. For example, the $68.73 billion Coca-Cola brand name has been created over the years by The Coca-Cola Company through successful business operations and relentless marketing. Because the valuation of this asset is not deemed sufficiently reliable to meet the standard for financial statement recognition, it is not included in The Coca-Cola Company's balance sheet. However, as explained later, if another company were to buy The Coca-Cola Company, an important part of recording the transaction would be allocating the total purchase price to the various economic assets acquired, including previously unrecorded intangible assets.

[22] Michelle Kessler, "Days of Officially Drowning in Data Almost upon Us," *USA Today*, March 7, 2007.
[23] Leonard I. Nakamura, "What Is the U.S. Gross Investment in Intangibles? (At Least) One Trillion Dollars a Year!" Federal Reserve Bank of Philadelphia, Working Paper No. 01-15, October 2001.
[24] Mark Kindley, "Hidden Assets," *CIO Insight*, October 1, 2001.

EX 10-10 TEN MOST VALUABLE BRANDS IN THE WORLD FOR 2009

Brand	Brand Value (in billions)
1 Coca-Cola	$68.73
2 IBM	60.21
3 Microsoft	56.65
4 General Electric	47.78
5 Nokia	34.86
6 McDonald's	32.28
7 Google	31.98
8 Toyota	31.33
9 Intel	30.64
10 Disney	28.45

Source: Interbrand at **http://www.interbrand.com**.

In the future, financial reporting will move toward providing more information about internally generated intangibles. Whether this will involve actual valuation and recognition of these intangibles in the financial statements or simply more extensive note disclosure remains to be seen.

Intangibles Acquired in a Basket Purchase

A common method of acquiring intangible assets is in conjunction with a collection of associated assets. For example, a company might pay $700,000 to purchase a patent along with a functioning factory and special equipment used in producing the patented product. Helpful information is lost if the entire $700,000 purchase price is merely recorded as a generic "asset." Accordingly, as demonstrated earlier in the chapter with a basket purchase involving only tangible assets, the total purchase price of $700,000 is allocated among all of the assets, tangible and intangible, according to the relative fair values of the assets. If the fair values of the patent, factory, and equipment are estimated to be $200,000, $450,000, and $100,000, respectively, the $700,000 cost would be allocated as follows:

	Estimated Fair Values	Cost Allocation According to Relative Estimated Values	Cost Assigned to Individual Assets
Patent	$200,000	200,000/750,000 × $700,000	$186,667
Factory	450,000	450,000/750,000 × $700,000	420,000
Equipment	100,000	100,000/750,000 × $700,000	93,333
	$750,000		$700,000

Five General Categories of Intangible Assets To aid companies in identifying different types of intangible assets that should be recognized separately, in FASB ASC Section 805-20-55, the FASB includes a description of five general categories of intangible assets. Those five general categories are:

1. *Marketing-related* intangible assets such as trademarks, brand names, and Internet domain names.
2. *Customer-related* intangible assets such as customer lists, order backlogs, and customer relationships.
3. *Artistic-related* intangible assets such as items protected by copyright.

CAUTION

Of course, an intangible can be acquired by itself. If a company buys a single intangible asset, the purchase price allocation is simple: The entire purchase price is recorded as the cost of the single intangible asset.

4. *Contract-based* intangible assets such as licenses, franchises, and broadcast rights.
5. *Technology-based* intangible assets including both patented and unpatented technologies as well as trade secrets.

These five categories do not comprise a comprehensive catalogue of all possible intangible assets. In addition, the identification of intangibles should not be viewed as merely matching up an acquired basket of assets with items from the FASB's list. As with all other assets, intangible assets must meet specific criteria to be recognized. The conceptual background for those criteria is laid out in *Concepts Statement No. 5* (paragraph 63), which indicates that to be recognized as an asset, an item must have probable future economic benefit, must be relevant to decision makers, and must be reliably measurable. In addition, intangible assets must be identifiable in order to be separately recognized in the financial statements. The criterion of identifiability is presumed to be satisfied with intangibles that are based on contracts or that are separately traded.

Contract-Based Intangibles Most of the intangible assets briefly described at the beginning of this chapter arise from contracts or other legal rights. Examples are trademarks, patents, copyrights, and franchise agreements. An intangible asset that is based on contractual or legal rights should be recognized as a separate asset, even if the right is inseparably connected with another asset. For example, the legal right to operate a specific nuclear power plant would often be sold with the nuclear power plant itself. Although these assets are not practically separable, the right to operate the factory is established by a specific legal permit and should be valued and reported separately in the books of the company that acquires the plant.

Separately Tradable Intangibles Some intangible assets arise as companies establish and maintain relationships of trust with their customers. These relationships are not imposed by legal right or contract but are voluntary and are based on past positive experiences. Companies are increasingly recognizing the value in these relationships and are even learning how to sell or rent these relationships. One example is the sale (exclusive use) or rental (nonexclusive use) of a customer database to another company. The fact that there is a market for these databases is taken as evidence that intangibles of this sort are reliably measurable assets that should be recognized as a separate asset when acquired by a company. Another example is the relationship a bank has with its depositors. Although these relationships themselves are not typically traded in separate transactions, they are inherent in the trading of portfolios of customer deposits. When a bank acquires a set of depositor liabilities from another bank, included in that transaction is the transfer of the depositor relationships to the acquiring bank. In such a transaction, a fair value should be estimated for the depositor relationships and a separate intangible asset recognized.

FYI

One of the dangers in these tradable intangibles is that the very relationship of trust that created the valuable intangible in the first place may be impaired when it is sold. For example, subscribers to a magazine may cancel their subscription when they learn that the magazine publisher has sold their subscriber database to a telemarketing firm or a political fund-raising organization.

Estimating the Fair Value of an Intangible The most difficult part of recording an amount for an intangible asset is not in identifying the asset but in estimating its fair value. The objective in estimating the fair value is to duplicate the price at which the intangible asset would change hands in an arm's-length market transaction. If there is a market for similar intangible assets, the best estimate of fair value is made with reference to these observable market prices. In the absence of such a market, present value techniques should be used to estimate the fair value. As described in *Concepts Statement No. 7*, the present value of future cash flows can be used to estimate fair value in one of two ways. In the traditional approach, which is often used in situations in which the amount and timing of the future cash flows are determined by contract, the present value is computed using a risk-adjusted interest rate that incorporates expectations about the uncertainty of receipt of the future contractual cash flows. In the expected cash flow approach, a range of possible outcomes is identified, the present value of the cash flows in each possible outcome is computed (using the risk-free interest rate), and a weighted-average present value is computed by summing the present value of the cash flows in each outcome, multiplied by the estimated probability of that outcome. To illustrate the traditional and the expected cash flow approaches, consider the following two examples.

> **FYI**
>
> In forming a corporation, certain organization costs are incurred, including legal fees, promotional costs, stock certificate costs, underwriting costs, and state incorporation fees. It can be argued that the benefits to be derived from these expenditures extend beyond the first fiscal period. However, the AICPA, with the approval of the FASB, has decided that organization costs (and the costs associated with other types of start-up activities) should be expensed as they are incurred. See FASB ASC paragraph 720-15-25-1.

Traditional approach: Intangible Asset A is the right to receive royalty payments in the future. The future royalty cash flows are $1,000 at the end of each year for the next five years. The risk-free interest rate is 5%; the receipt of these royalty cash flows is not certain, so a risk-adjusted interest rate of 12% is used in computing their present value. The fair value of Intangible Asset A is estimated as follows:

Business calculator keystrokes
N = 5 years
I = 12%
PMT = $1,000
FV = $0 (there is no additional payment at the end of five years)
PV = $3,605

If Intangible Asset A is acquired as part of a basket purchase with other assets, this $3,605 amount would be used as the estimated fair value of the intangible asset in the allocation of the total purchase price.

Expected cash flow approach: Intangible Asset B is a secret formula to produce a fast-food cheeseburger that contains 25 essential vitamins and minerals, reduces cholesterol levels, and replenishes the ozone layer. Future cash flows from the secret formula are uncertain; the following estimates have been generated, with the associated probabilities:

> **FYI**
>
> In the traditional approach to computing present values, all of the "art" goes into determining the appropriate risk-adjusted interest rate.

Outcome 1	10% probability of cash flows of $5,000 at the end of each year for 10 years
Outcome 2	30% probability of cash flows of $1,000 at the end of each year for 4 years
Outcome 3	60% probability of cash flows of $100 at the end of each year for 3 years

In the expected cash flow approach, the uncertainty of the future cash flows is not reflected in a risk-adjusted interest rate but is incorporated through the assessment of the various possible outcomes and the probabilities of each. Thus, the risk-free interest rate (5% in this case) is used in computing the present value of the cash flows in each outcome:[25]

	Present Value	Probability	Probability Weighted Present Value
Outcome 1	$38,609	0.10	$3,861
Outcome 2	3,546	0.30	1,064
Outcome 3	272	0.60	163
Total estimated fair value			$5,088

To summarize, the fair value of an intangible can be determined by referring to market prices, by computing present value using the traditional approach, or by computing present value using the expected cash flow approach. Again, these present value computation procedures are reviewed in the Time Value of Money Module of this text.

Acquired In-Process Research and Development One valuable intangible sometimes involved when one company purchases a collection of assets from another is existing research and development projects, often called *acquired in-process R&D*. For example, on October 1, 2001, **Bristol-Myers Squibb**, a large pharmaceuticals company, acquired the pharmaceuticals division of **DuPont** for $7.8 billion. Of this amount, $2.009 billion was associated with five ongoing research projects, as described in the following financial statement note:

> The [$2.009 billion] charge was associated with five research projects in the Cardiovascular, Central Nervous System, Oncology, and Anti-Infective therapeutic areas ranging from the preclinical to the phase II development stage. The amount was determined by identifying research projects for which technological feasibility has not been established and for which there is no alternative future use. The projected FDA approval dates are years 2005 through 2008, at which time the Company expects these projects to begin to generate cash flows. The cost to complete these research projects is estimated at $1.2 billion.

Acquired in-process R&D creates a somewhat embarrassing situation for financial accountants in the United States. As mentioned earlier in the chapter, under U.S. GAAP normal R&D costs are expensed as incurred. The rationale behind this treatment is that there is too much uncertainty over the future economic value of research and development. However, as demonstrated in the Bristol-Myers Squibb case, the value of ongoing R&D can be verified in a market transaction. On this issue, the FASB has provided inconsistent answers. In summary, in-process R&D is to be recognized as an intangible asset if it is acquired as part of a business combination but is to be expensed if acquired as part of a basket purchase outside of a business combination.[26]

[25] In applying the expected cash flow approach, we really should take the analysis one step further and convert the expected cash flows into "certainty equivalents." The basic idea is that there is a lower amount of cash that you would accept for sure in exchange for a higher, uncertain amount. We will leave this more complete "certainty equivalent" analysis to a more detailed course in valuation.

This patchwork approach is a perfect illustration of two general forces operating in the development of U.S. GAAP: (1) the steady influence of the desire for the FASB and the IASB to converge on a common set of high-quality international accounting standards and (2) the great caution of accountants in general and the FASB in particular when considering any change to long-standing practice. The FASB has stated that it intends to revisit this inconsistency in the future.

To summarize this section on the acquisition of intangibles as part of a basket purchase, the key point is that it is important to itemize and recognize intangible assets separately as much as possible. The total purchase price is allocated to the intangible assets according to their relative fair values. As discussed in Chapter 11, some of these intangibles will be amortized and some will not.

Intangibles Acquired in the Acquisition of a Business

In the previous section, we discussed the acquisition of intangible assets as part of a basket purchase. In this section we cover the acquisition of an entire company. When one company acquires another, the acquiring company pays for an assorted collection of tangible assets, liabilities, identifiable intangible assets, and usually an additional intangible asset, goodwill, that is essentially the synergistic value of the acquired business that can't be associated with any specific tangible or intangible asset.

One objective of the FASB standards on accounting for a business acquisition (also called a business combination) is to curtail the use of the goodwill asset account as a "kitchen sink" containing a hodgepodge of costs that would more appropriately be allocated to individual intangible assets. Goodwill is best thought of as a residual amount, the amount of the purchase price of a business that is left over after all other tangible and intangible assets have been identified. As such, goodwill is that intangible something that makes the whole company worth more than its individual parts. In general, goodwill represents all of the special advantages, not otherwise separately identifiable, enjoyed by an enterprise, such as a high credit standing, reputation for superior products and services, experience with development and distribution processes, favorable government relations, and so forth. These factors allow a business to earn above normal income with the identifiable assets, tangible and intangible, employed in the business.

The accounting for the acquisition of an entire company is very similar to the accounting for a basket purchase; the total purchase price is allocated to all of the acquired items in accordance with their estimated fair values. A key difference in the accounting for acquisition of a basket of assets and acquisition of an entire business is as follows:

- The acquisition cost is not allocated in proportion to the fair values of the identifiable assets. Instead, each identifiable asset is recorded at an amount equal to its estimated fair value; any residual is reported as goodwill.

In determining fair values of assets and liabilities for the purpose of allocating the overall acquisition price, current market values should be sought rather than the values reported in the accounts of the acquired company. Receivables should be stated at amounts expected to be realized. Inventories and securities should be restated in terms of current market values. Land, buildings, and equipment may require special appraisals in arriving at their fair values. Intangible assets, such as patents and franchises, should be included at their estimated fair values whether or not they were recorded as assets on the books of the acquired company. Care should be taken to determine that liabilities are fully recognized.

[26] See FASB ASC paragraphs 350-30-35-17A, 805-20-35-5, and 730-10-25-1 and 2.

To the extent possible, the amount paid for any existing company should be related to identifiable assets. If an excess does exist, it is recognized as an asset and called *goodwill* or "cost in excess of fair value of net assets acquired."

To illustrate the recording of the purchase of an ongoing business, assume that Airnational Corporation purchases the net assets of Speedy Freight Airlines for $1,500,000 in cash. A schedule of net assets for Speedy Freight, as recorded on Speedy Freight's books at the time of acquisition, follows.

Assets		
Cash	$ 37,500	
Receivables	246,000	
Inventory	392,000	
Land, buildings, and equipment (net)	361,200	
		$1,036,700
Liabilities		
Current liabilities	$ 86,000	
Long-term debt	183,500	269,500
Book value of net assets		$ 767,200

Analysis of the $732,800 difference between the purchase price of $1,500,000 and the net asset book value of $767,200 ($1,036,700 – $269,500) reveals the following differences between the recorded costs and market values of the assets:

	Cost	Market
Inventory	$392,000	$ 427,000
Land, buildings, and equipment	361,200	389,500
Patents	0	50,000
Purchased in-process R&D	0	400,000
Totals	$753,200	$1,266,500

The identifiable portion of the $732,800 difference amounts to $513,300 ($1,266,500 – $753,200) and is allocated to the respective items. The remaining difference of $219,500 ($732,800 – $513,300) is recorded as goodwill.

The entry to record the purchase is shown below. The estimated fair value associated with purchased in-process research and development projects is recognized as a separate intangible asset, consistent with the treatment of other research and development expenditures.

Cash	37,500	
Receivables	246,000	
Inventory	427,000	
Land, Buildings, and Equipment	389,500	
Patents	50,000	
In-Process R&D Asset	400,000	
Goodwill	219,500	
Current Liabilities		86,000
Long-Term Debt		183,500
Cash		1,500,000

After it is recognized, goodwill is left on the books at its originally recorded amount unless there is evidence that its value has been impaired. As mentioned earlier, this treatment is viewed by some as a compromise by the FASB. Whether goodwill should be amortized is an interesting theoretical discussion, but the existing standard says that goodwill is not to be amortized. Goodwill impairment is discussed in Chapter 11.

Notice that the patent asset was not recorded on the books of Speedy Freight before the acquisition. This could be because the patent cost had been fully amortized or because the patent had been developed through in-house research and development and all of those costs had been immediately expensed. However, when Speedy Freight is acquired, the patent is recognized as an identifiable economic asset.

The Speedy Freight example was simplified because Airnational purchased 100% of Speedy Freight. The accounting is changed a little if Airnational were to purchase, say, only 80% of Speedy Freight. All of the acquired assets, including goodwill, are still recognized at 100% of their fair values, but an additional item, called *noncontrolling interest*, is recognized to represent the outside ownership of the nonpurchased 20% of Speedy Freight. Noncontrolling interest is reported in the Equity section of the acquiring company's balance sheet; this topic is covered in Chapter 13.

Because goodwill is recorded on the books only when another company is acquired, one must be careful in interpreting a company's reported goodwill balance. The reported goodwill balance does not reflect the company's own goodwill but the goodwill of other companies it has acquired. So, **Microsoft**'s goodwill is not recognized on Microsoft's balance sheet, nor is **PepsiCo**'s goodwill shown on the balance sheet of PepsiCo. There is substantial goodwill on Pepsi's balance sheet, but that has arisen from the acquisitions of other companies, such as **Frito Lay**. Thus, companies with sizable economic goodwill may have no recorded goodwill at all, and the goodwill that a company does report was developed by someone else. Current accounting principles may result in misleading users of financial statements as far as goodwill is concerned. On the other hand, to allow companies to place a value on their own goodwill and record this amount on the balance sheet would introduce a significant amount of added subjectivity to the financial statements.

Bargain Purchase Occasionally, the amount paid for another company is less than the fair value of the net identifiable items of the acquired company. This condition can arise when the existing management of a company is using the assets in a suboptimal fashion. When this bargain purchase exists, the acquiring company should first review all of the fair value estimates to make sure that they are reliable. If after doing this there is still an excess of identifiable net fair value over the purchase price, any remaining excess is recognized as a gain.

To illustrate, assume that the Speedy Freight acquisition described earlier was for $1,000,000 instead of $1,500,000. The acquisition is recorded as follows:

Account	Debit	Credit
Cash	37,500	
Receivables	246,000	
Inventory	427,000	
Land, Buildings, and Equipment	389,500	
Patents	50,000	
In-Process R&D Asset	400,000	
Gain		280,500
Current Liabilities		86,000
Long-Term Debt		183,500
Cash		1,000,000

ifrs

International Accounting for Intangibles: *IAS 38* and *IFRS 3* The IASB's standard for the accounting for intangible assets is *IAS 38*. This IASB standard is very much compatible with U.S. GAAP. The international accounting standard for business combinations, *IFRS 3*, is also quite similar to the U.S. standard. This similarity in the accounting for intangibles is not accidental; the FASB and IASB worked jointly on their business combinations standards in order to eliminate almost all differences in accounting for the related intangible assets. In addition, the FASB worked with several non-U.S. standard setters in developing its standards on goodwill and intangibles. The most significant differences between U.S. GAAP and IASB standards in the accounting for intangible assets are in the testing of these assets for impairment. This topic is covered in Chapter 11.

FASB CODIFICATION

The Issue: You are the accountant for a company in the carpet cleaning business. Because of your company's innovative cleaning system (no harsh detergents, no damaging brushes, and extremely small carbon footprint), you have been very successful and have begun to drive your competitors out of business. In fact, just today your company's CEO has decided to start buying a number of your competitors. As you walked out the door at the end of the day, she said: "You had better learn how to account for a bargain purchase."

The Question: What is a bargain purchase, and why is a bargain purchase likely to arise in this situation?

Searching the Codification: Bargain purchases are covered in this chapter, but you would like to show your boss that you can find accounting standards for yourself in the authoritative literature. The best place to start is in Topic 805 (Business Combinations), which is in the "Broad Transactions" collection of topics.

The Answer: The authoritative accounting standards relative to bargain purchases are described on page 10-43.

Valuation of Assets at Fair Values

5 **Discuss the pros and cons of recording noncurrent operating assets at their fair values.**

WHY **IASB standards allow the upward revaluation of noncurrent operating assets. In a choice of reliability over relevance, U.S. accounting standards do not allow such upward revaluation.**

HOW **In those international standards allowing upward revaluation of noncurrent operating assets, the asset account is increased based on an assessment of the asset's fair value with the corresponding credit being made to a special equity account.**

Throughout this chapter, the valuation of assets has been based on historical costs. As discussed in Chapter 1, asset measurement is frequently a trade-off between relevance and reliability. Historical cost is a reliable number, but the fair value of noncurrent assets can be more relevant.

The reduction in the recorded amount of noncurrent operating assets that have declined in value has long been part of generally accepted accounting principles. Writing down assets to recognize market value declines is a reflection of the conservative bias that is a fundamental part of accounting practice. The rules governing these impairment write-downs are discussed in Chapter 11. On the other hand, asset write-ups have not been generally accepted in recent times. Before the formation of the SEC in 1934, it was common for U.S. companies to report the upward revaluation of property and equipment. However, by 1940 the SEC had effectively eliminated this practice, not by explicitly banning it but through informal administrative pressure. Much of the suspicion about asset revaluations stemmed from a Federal Trade Commission investigation, completed in 1935, that uncovered a number of cases in the public utility industry in which a utility had improperly revalued assets upward to boost its rate base. In the late 1980s, the absence of advance warning of the $500 billion collapse of the savings and loan (S&L) industry was blamed in part on the failure of S&Ls to report current market values of their loan portfolios. Reexamination of the accounting for financial institutions led to pre-Codification FASB *Statement No. 115*, which required most investment securities to be reported at their current market values; this provision continues in FASB ASC Topic 320. It is likely that the continuing call by financial statement users for current value information will result in a reconsideration of the appropriateness of historical cost accounting for noncurrent operating assets. In fact, between 1980 and 1986 the FASB required large companies to report the current value of noncurrent operating assets in a note to the statements.

ifrs

In *IAS 16*, the IASB permits the inclusion of upward revaluations of noncurrent operating assets in the financial statements as an allowable alternative to reporting the historical cost of those assets. Because fair values are often based on subjective appraisals rather than objective historical cost, accountants and auditors have traditionally been concerned that companies might use upward asset revaluations to artificially boost reported balance sheet and income statement values. This concern is reflected in the careful rules laid out in *IAS 16*, some of which are summarized here.

- If a company revalues its noncurrent operating assets to fair value, it must do so on a regular basis (not as a one-time event) and must revalue entire classes of assets rather than just picking and choosing certain assets in an effort to report the fair values of only those assets that have increased in value.
- Downward revaluations are recorded as a loss.
- Upward revaluations are recorded as a debit to the asset and a credit to a special "revaluation" equity account. This practice means that upward revaluations cannot be used to boost reported income. In addition, when an asset that has been revalued upward is subsequently sold, any associated balance in the special revaluation equity account is credited directly to retained earnings and is not reported as an income statement gain. The implication of this accounting treatment is that the choice to recognize the increase in the value of a noncurrent operating asset through an asset revaluation means that the increase will never be reported in the income statement as a gain, even when the asset is sold.

STOP&THINK

Which ONE of the following statements is true regarding the fair value of noncurrent operating assets?

a) International standards prohibit companies from recognizing the fair value of noncurrent operating assets.
b) The fair value of noncurrent operating assets can be estimated by professional appraisers, just as the pension liability is currently estimated by actuaries.
c) The fair value of noncurrent operating assets is not relevant information to most financial statement users.

One example of a company that revalues its assets on an annual basis is **Bank of China (Hong Kong) Limited** (BOC). The company indicates in the notes to its financial statements that valuations are done at least annually by external independent appraisers. As of December 31, 2009, the reported net amount of land and buildings ("premises") for BOC was HK$23.7 billion. This number is a mix of historical cost numbers and amounts obtained from professional revaluations. Without the revaluations, the net amount of land and buildings would have been HK$12.1 billion. Further explanation of the accounting for upward asset revaluations is given in Chapter 11.

IASB standards also allow investment property to be reported at fair value in the balance sheet. According to the provisions of *IAS 40*, investment property is land or a building that is held in order to earn rentals or for price appreciation, or both. This investment property can be accounted for using the traditional cost method. Alternatively, under *IAS 40*, a company can elect to use a fair value approach in which the investment property is reported in the balance sheet at its fair value, and any resulting gains or losses are reported in the income statement. This option is very important to real estate companies which are in business to make money through price appreciation; requiring these companies to report investment property at cost in the balance sheet conceals key operating information.

Measuring Property, Plant, and Equipment Efficiency

6 **Use the fixed asset turnover ratio as a general measure of how efficiently a company is using its property, plant, and equipment.**

WHY **Financial ratios allow comparisons to be made across companies and for the same company over time. Information relating to property, plant, and equipment usage allows users to determine how efficiently a company uses its noncurrent operating assets.**

HOW **A common measure of long-term asset efficiency is to determine how many sales dollars are generated by each dollar of property, plant, and equipment (also called fixed assets). When using this ratio, caution must be exercised to ensure that the resulting number is useful for comparison purposes because reported property, plant, and equipment values are sometimes substantially less than the fair values of the assets.**

The result of proper capital budgeting analysis should be a level of property, plant, and equipment that is appropriate to the amount of sales a company is doing. As with any other asset, excess funds tied up in the form of property, plant, and equipment reduce a company's efficiency, increase financing costs, and lower return on equity.

In this section, we discuss the fixed asset turnover ratio, which uses financial statement data to roughly indicate how efficiently a company is utilizing its property, plant, and equipment to generate sales. We also illustrate that careful interpretation of the fixed asset turnover ratio is necessary because the recorded book value of long-term operating assets can differ significantly from the actual value of those assets.

Evaluating the Level of Property, Plant, and Equipment

Fixed asset turnover ratio is computed as sales divided by average property, plant, and equipment (fixed assets) and is interpreted as the number of dollars in sales generated by each dollar of fixed assets. This ratio is also called *PP&E turnover*. The computation of the fixed asset turnover ratio for General Electric is given below. (All financial statement numbers are in millions.)

The fixed asset turnover ratios suggest that General Electric was more efficient at using its fixed assets to generate sales in 2008 than it was in 2009. In 2009, each dollar of fixed assets generated $2.12 in sales, down from $2.33 in 2008.

	2009	2008
Sales	$156,783	$182,515
Property, plant, and equipment:		
Beginning of year	$78,530	$77,888
End of year	$69,212	$78,530
Average fixed assets [(beginning balance + ending balance) ÷ 2]	$73,871	$78,209
Fixed asset turnover ratio	2.12	2.33

Dangers in Using the Fixed Asset Turnover Ratio

As with all ratios, the fixed asset turnover ratio must be used carefully to ensure that erroneous conclusions are not made. For example, fixed asset turnover ratio values for two companies in different industries cannot be meaningfully compared. This point can be illustrated using the fact that General Electric is composed of two primary parts: General Electric, the manufacturing company, and **GE Capital Services**, the financial services firm. The fixed asset turnover ratio computed earlier was for both parts. Because GE Capital Services does not use property, plant, and equipment for manufacturing but leases assets to other companies to earn financial revenue, one would expect GE Capital Services' fixed asset turnover ratio to be quite unlike that for a manufacturing firm. In fact, as shown next, the fixed asset turnover ratio for the manufacturing segments of General Electric was 7.89 times in 2009, more than triple the ratio value for the entire company.

Fixed Asset Turnover Ratio
General Electric—Manufacturing Segments Only

	2009	2008
Sales	$106,226	$121,753
Property, plant, and equipment:		
Beginning of year	$14,433	$14,142
End of year	$12,495	$14,433
Average fixed assets [(beginning balance + ending balance) ÷ 2]	$13,464	$14,288
Fixed asset turnover ratio	7.89	8.52

Another difficulty in comparing values for the fixed asset turnover ratio among different companies is that the reported amount for property, plant, and equipment can be a poor indicator of the actual fair value of the fixed assets being used by a company. As discussed earlier, the accounting rules in the United States require fixed assets to be written down when their value is impaired but do not allow the writing up of fixed asset amounts to reflect increases in fair value. This creates a comparability problem

STOP&THINK

Why did Safeway's accumulated depreciation decrease so dramatically from 1985 to 1986?

a) The accumulated depreciation balance fluctuates depending on the current values of property, plant, and equipment.
b) The accumulated depreciation balance represented a large cash amount that was used to finance the leveraged buyout.
c) When company ownership changes, as in a leveraged buyout, the existing assets are recorded as if they had just been purchased at their fair values (as in a business combination).
d) According to the U.S. tax code, accumulated depreciation is a deferred tax item that must be reduced when a company experiences a leveraged buyout.

when one company has relatively new fixed assets, which are recorded at close to market value, and another company has older fixed assets, which are recorded at depreciated historical cost values that may significantly understate the real value of the assets.

A graphic illustration of this comparability problem is provided by **Safeway**, the supermarket chain. Safeway was taken private in a leveraged buyout near the end of 1986. When the leveraged buyout occurred, Safeway became a new company, for accounting purposes at least, and Safeway's assets were restated to their current market values as of the leveraged buyout date. This provides a rare opportunity to see how significantly the fixed asset turnover ratio is impacted by whether a company has its fixed assets recorded at market values or at depreciated historical cost. Listed below are the cost, accumulated depreciation, and fixed asset turnover ratios for Safeway for 1985, just before the leveraged buyout, and 1986, just after the leveraged buyout.

Safeway had almost the same fixed assets in place at the end of 1986 as it had at the end of 1985; the difference in the reported numbers is due almost entirely to the revaluation that took place as part of the leveraged buyout. Notice that the book value of Safeway's fixed assets increased by more than $1 billion from 1985 to 1986. This increase reflects the impact of reporting the fixed assets at market value rather than at depreciated historical cost. Also, note the significant decline in the computed fixed asset turnover ratio: from 7.45 in 1985 to 5.44 in 1986. Actually, Safeway's use of its fixed assets was almost exactly the same in 1986 as it had been in 1985; the difference in the ratio is caused by the use of the artificially low depreciated cost numbers in 1985 to compute the ratio. In summary, the fixed asset turnover ratio can be significantly impacted by the difference between the market value of fixed assets and their reported depreciated cost. For some companies, this difference can be very large indeed.

	1986	**1985**
Cost	$3,854	$4,641
Less: Accumulated depreciation	120	2,004
Book value	$3,734	$2,637
Fixed asset turnover ratio	5.44	7.45

Another complication with analysis using the fixed asset turnover ratio is caused by leasing. As will be discussed in Chapter 15, many companies lease the bulk of their fixed assets, and, as a result, many of these assets are not included in their balance sheets. This biases the fixed asset turnover ratio for these companies upward because the sales generated by the leased assets are included in the numerator of the ratio but the leased assets generating the sales are not included in the denominator.

SOLUTIONS TO OPENING SCENARIO QUESTIONS

1. When Jerry Jones purchased the Dallas Cowboys for $150 million, his accountants were then faced with the problem of allocating this $150 million purchase price among the many and varied assets of the Cowboys such as miscellaneous football equipment, stadium leases, radio and TV broadcast rights, cable TV rights, luxury stadium suites, player contracts, a lease on the Cowboys' luxurious Valley Ranch training facility, and the Cowboys' NFL franchise rights.
2. The desire to allocate as much of the purchase price as possible to the asset "players' contracts" is motivated by tax considerations. The asset players' contracts can be written off over four years for tax purposes, thus accelerating the tax break associated with depreciation of some or all of the original purchase price.

SOLUTIONS TO STOP & THINK

1. (Page 10-16) The answer is D. Capitalized interest is not extra interest. If a company were to forget to capitalize interest that should be capitalized, interest expense would be overstated and long-term assets would be understated. Total cash flow would be unaffected, but cash from operations would be understated and cash from investing activities would be overstated.
2. (Page 10-39) The answer is B. It is unlikely that within the next 10 years U.S. companies will be required to recognize the current value of property, plant, and equipment, although such revaluation is allowable under international accounting standards. The historical cost tradition is strong in the United States, and the FASB is having enough trouble getting the business community to accept the recognition of the fair value of financial instruments and derivatives. But fair value recognition of property, plant, and equipment is only a matter of time—the information is very relevant and can be estimated by professional appraisers, just as the pension liability is currently estimated by actuaries.
3. (Page 10-42) The answer is C. One event that reduces accumulated depreciation is the disposal of old assets. This is not what happened to Safeway between 1985 and 1986. Instead, when Safeway's assets were revalued in late 1986, the accumulated depreciation account was set to zero. It was as if Safeway had disposed of all of its old assets and then repurchased them at their current market values.

SOLUTION TO USING THE FASB'S CODIFICATION

Under Topic 805 (Business Combinations), you should have seen Subtopic 805-30 (Goodwill or Gain from Bargain Purchase, Including Consideration Transferred). Section 805-30-25 includes material on "Gain from Bargain Purchase." With respect to the circumstances under which a bargain purchase might occur, the following is contained in FASB ASC paragraph 805-30-25-3: "A bargain purchase might happen, for example, in a business combination that is a forced sale in which the seller is acting under compulsion." In this particular case, your CEO expects to be able to buy her struggling competitors for a low price.

As explained in the textbook, if the purchase price is less than the fair value of the net assets of the acquired company, the difference is recognized as a "gain in earnings on the acquisition date" [FASB ASC paragraph 805-30-25-2]. In past years, this gain has sometimes been called "negative goodwill," representing the negative value associated with the acquired company created by poor management, poor reputation, and poor operating circumstances.

REVIEW CHAPTER 10

LEARNING OBJECTIVES

1 Identify those costs to be included in the acquisition cost of different types of noncurrent operating assets.

The cost of tangible noncurrent operating assets includes not only the original purchase price or equivalent value but also any other expenditures required in obtaining and preparing the asset for its intended use. For example, land cost includes surveying fees and the cost of removing old buildings. Equipment cost includes the costs of testing and installation.

Intangible noncurrent operating assets are also generally recorded at cost. The cost is the purchase price if copyrights, patents, or trademarks are purchased from another company. For internally generated intangibles, the cost often includes only the actual legal and filing costs, as well as any cost to successfully defend the rights in court.

2 Properly account for noncurrent operating asset acquisitions using various special arrangements, including deferred payment, self-construction, and acquisition of an entire company.

- *Basket purchase.* Acquisition cost is allocated to the various assets based on the relative fair values of the assets.
- *Deferred payment.* The acquisition is recorded at the discounted present value of the payments.
- *Leasing.* Property leased under a capital lease is recognized as an asset; property leased under an operating lease is not included in the balance sheet.
- *Exchange of nonmonetary assets.* The transaction is recorded at the fair value of the asset received or the asset given, whichever is more clearly determinable.
- *Acquisition by issuing securities.* The transaction is recorded at the fair value of the asset acquired or the securities issued, whichever is more clearly determinable.
- *Self-construction.* The cost of self-constructed assets includes an allocation of overhead and the cost of interest incurred to finance the construction. The amount of capitalized interest is an estimate of interest that could have been avoided if the construction expenditures had been used to repay loans instead.
- *Acquisition by donation or discovery.* Assets received as donations are recorded as revenue in an amount equal to the fair value of the assets. Discovered assets are not recognized.
- *Acquisition and an associated asset retirement obligation.* The estimated fair value of the asset retirement obligation is recognized as a liability and added to the cost of the asset acquired.
- *Acquisition of an entire company.* In a business combination accounted for as a purchase, acquired assets are recorded at their fair values, and any excess is recognized as goodwill.

3 Separate costs into those that should be expensed immediately and those that should be capitalized, and understand the accounting standards for research and development and oil and gas exploration costs.

- *Postacquisition costs.* Repair and maintenance costs are expensed. Expenditures for new components, either as replacements or as additional components, are capitalized.
- *Research and development costs.* In the United States, all general research and development expenditures are expensed as incurred. The FASB may reconsider this rule some time soon.
- *Software development costs.* In the United States, software development expenditures incurred before technological feasibility has been established are expensed; expenditures after technological feasibility has been established are capitalized.

- *Oil and gas exploration costs.* With the successful efforts method, costs of drilling dry wells are expensed immediately; with the full cost method, these costs are capitalized.

4 Recognize intangible assets acquired separately, as part of a basket purchase, and as part of a business acquisition.

In a basket purchase including intangibles, the total purchase price is allocated in proportion to the estimated fair values of all of the acquired assets, including the intangibles. Recorded intangibles can be either contract based, separately tradable, or relevant items that have probable future economic benefit and are reliably measurable. Fair values of intangibles are estimated by reference to market prices, by the traditional present value approach (using a risk-adjusted interest rate), or by the expected cash flow approach. Amounts allocated to acquired in-process research and development should be expensed immediately.

In a business acquisition, only those intangibles that are contract based or separately tradable are recognized; other intangible items are included in the recorded amount of goodwill. In the case of a bargain purchase, the fair value estimates should be carefully reviewed. If the purchase price is still less than the fair value of the net assets acquired, a gain is recognized for the difference.

5 Discuss the pros and cons of recording noncurrent operating assets at their fair values.

Recording noncurrent operating assets at their fair values represents a trade-off between relevance and reliability. In the United States, reliability concerns have resulted in the prohibition of asset write-ups. Under *IAS 16*, upward asset revaluations are an allowable alternative to reporting the historical cost of those assets.

6 Use the fixed asset turnover ratio as a general measure of how efficiently a company is using its property, plant, and equipment.

The fixed asset turnover ratio is computed as sales divided by average property, plant, and equipment (fixed assets) and is interpreted as the number of dollars in sales generated by each dollar of fixed assets. Meaningful comparison of fixed asset turnover ratios can only be done between firms in similar industries. Another difficulty in comparing values for the fixed asset turnover ratio among different companies is that the reported amount for property, plant, and equipment can be a poor indicator of the actual fair value of the fixed assets being used by a company. This is true when fixed assets have increased in value, relative to their depreciated cost, and when a significant number of assets have been leased and are not reported in the balance sheet.

FASB-IASB CODIFICATION SUMMARY

ifrs

Topic	FASB Accounting Standards Codification	Original FASB Standard	Corresponding IASB Standard	Differences between U.S. GAAP and IFRS
Interest capitalization	*Subtopic 835-20*	*SFAS No. 34*	*IAS 23*	Under IFRS, net "borrowing costs" are capitalized. The net amount is the gross interest paid less interest received on investment of idle funds.
Asset retirement obligation	*Subtopic 410-20*	*SFAS No. 143*	*IAS 16 and IAS 37*	No substantial differences

(continued)

Business combinations	*Topic 805*	*SFAS No. 141R*	*IFRS 3*	No substantial differences
Intangible assets	*Topic 350*	*SFAS No. 142*	*IAS 38*	No substantial differences
Research and development	*Topic 730*	*SFAS No.2* *SFAS No.86*	*IAS 38*	Under IFRS, development costs, which are costs incurred after technological feasibility, are capitalized. This matches U.S. GAAP for software development costs, but not for ordinary R&D.

KEY TERMS

Additions 10-26
Asset retirement obligation 10-21
Bargain purchase 10-37
Basket purchase 10-9
Betterments 10-26
Capital leases 10-12
Capitalized interest 10-15
Component 10-24
Development 10-26
Discovery 10-20
Donation 10-19
Fixed asset turnover ratio 10-40
Full cost method 10-28
Goodwill 10-35
Intangible assets 10-6
Maintenance 10-25
Noncurrent operating assets 10-4
Operating leases 10-12
Renewals 10-25
Repairs 10-25
Replacements 10-25
Research 10-26
Research and development (R&D) 10-26
Software development costs 10-27
Successful efforts method 10-28
Technological feasibility 10-27
Trademark 10-7

QUESTIONS

1. On the balance sheets of many companies, the largest classification of assets in amount is noncurrent operating assets. Name the items, other than the amount paid to the former owner or contractor, that may be properly included as part of the acquisition cost of the following property items: (a) land, (b) buildings, and (c) equipment.
2. What acquisition costs are included in (a) copyrights, (b) franchises, and (c) trademarks?
3. What procedure should be followed to allocate the cost of a basket purchase of assets among specific accounts?
4. What special accounting problems are introduced when a company purchases equipment on a deferred payment contract rather than with cash?
5. (a) Why is the "list price" of an asset often not representative of its fair market value? (b) Under these conditions, how should a fair value be determined?
6. Gaylen Corp. decides to construct a building for itself and plans to use existing plant facilities to assist with such construction. (a) What costs will enter into the cost of construction? (b) What two positions can the company take with respect to general overhead allocation during the period of construction? Evaluate each position and indicate your preference.
7. What characteristics must a construction project have before interest can be capitalized as part of the project cost?
8. What amount of interest is capitalized under *IAS 23*?
9. Parkhurst Corporation acquires land and buildings valued at $250,000 as a gift from a local philanthropist. The president of the company maintains that because there was no cost for the acquisition, neither the cost of the facilities nor depreciation needs to be recognized for financial statement purposes. Evaluate the president's position assuming (a) the donation is unconditional and (b) the donation is contingent upon the employment by the company of a certain number of employees for a 10-year period.
10. What type of asset value increases are recognized under *IAS 41*?

11. What is an asset retirement obligation? What is the proper accounting for an asset retirement obligation?
12. Why do some companies expense asset expenditures that are less than an established monetary amount?
13. Indicate the effects of the following errors on the balance sheet and the income statement in the current year and succeeding years.
    (a) The cost of a depreciable asset is incorrectly recorded as an expense.
    (b) An expense expenditure is incorrectly recorded as an addition to the cost of a depreciable asset.
14. Which of the following items would be recorded as expenses and which would be recorded as assets?
    (a) Cost of installing machinery
    (b) Cost of unsuccessful litigation to protect patent
    (c) Extensive repairs as a result of a fire
    (d) Cost of grading land
    (e) Insurance on machinery in transit
    (f) Interest incurred during construction period
    (g) Cost of replacing a major machinery component
    (h) New safety guards on machinery
    (i) Commission on purchase of real estate
    (j) Special tax assessment for street improvements
    (k) Cost of repainting offices
15. What happens to the remaining net book value of a component that is replaced?
16. (a) What type of activities are considered to be research and development activities? (b) Under what conditions, if any, are research and development costs capitalized?
17. Distinguish between the full cost and successful efforts methods of recording exploratory costs for oil and gas properties.
18. In general, how is the cost of internally generated intangibles accounted for?
19. What are the five general categories of intangible assets?
20. What two approaches are used in estimating fair values using present value computations? Briefly explain the difference between the two approaches.
21. (a) Under what conditions may goodwill be reported as an asset? (b) Roper Company engages in a widespread advertising campaign on behalf of new products, charging above normal expenditures to goodwill. Do you approve of this practice? Why or why not?
22. How is acquired in-process research and development accounted for under U.S. GAAP?
23. What argument is given for reporting noncurrent operating assets at their historical costs instead of at current values?
24. Under the provisions of *IAS 16*, what is the credit entry when noncurrent operating assets are written up to reflect an increase in market value?
25. Describe the fair value option that is available under *IAS 40* to companies that own investment property.
26. How is the fixed asset turnover ratio calculated, and what does the resulting ratio measure?
27. Briefly describe the dangers to financial statement users inherent in the use of the fixed asset turnover ratio.

PRACTICE EXERCISES

Practice 10-1

LO1

Categories of Tangible Noncurrent Operating Assets

The following costs were incurred in the most recent year:

(a) Paid $30,000 to purchase a piece of equipment. In addition, paid $1,000 to have the equipment shipped to and installed in its final location. Spent $1,750 to have the equipment tested before beginning its production use. Paid $2,000 for lubrication and normal maintenance during the first year of operation of the equipment.

(b) Paid $85,000 to buy a piece of land. Also paid $10,000 to construct a parking lot and sidewalks.

(c) Paid $50,000 to buy another piece of land. Then paid $10,000 to have an old building demolished and have the land cleared. Paid $132,000 to have a building constructed.

Compute the total cost that should be reported in each of the following categories:

1. Land
2. Buildings
3. Equipment
4. Land Improvements

Practice 10-2

LO2

Basket Purchase

The company paid $750,000 to buy a collection of assets. The assets had the following appraised values:

Equipment	$250,000
Building	425,000
Land	125,000

Compute the cost to be allocated to each asset.

Practice 10-3

LO2

Deferred Payment

The company purchased a piece of equipment. Terms of the purchase were as follows: $10,000 in cash immediately, followed by note payments of $20,000 at the end of each year for the next eight years. The market rate of interest is 9%. Make the journal entries necessary to record (1) the initial purchase and (2) the first cash payment of $20,000 at the end of the first year.

Practice 10-4

LO2

Exchange of Nonmonetary Assets

The company exchanged a piece of land for a new piece of equipment. The equipment has a list price of $100,000, and the land has a historical cost of $35,000. The land has a current market value of $97,300. Make the journal entry necessary to record the exchange.

Practice 10-5

LO2

Cost of a Self-Constructed Asset

The company constructed its own building. The cost of materials was $400,000. Labor cost incurred on the construction project was $600,000. Total overhead cost for the company for the year was $8,000,000; total labor cost (including the cost of construction) was $4,000,000. Interest incurred to finance the construction cost was $140,000. Compute the total cost of the building.

Practice 10-6

LO2

Capitalized Interest: Single-Year Computation

The company had the following loans outstanding for the entire year:

	Amount	Interest Rate
Specific construction loan	$ 100,000	10%
General loan	2,000,000	13

The company began the self-construction of a building on January 1. The following expenditures were made during the year:

January 1	$100,000
May 1	200,000
November 1	300,000
Total	$600,000

Construction was completed on December 31. Compute (1) the amount of interest capitalized during the year and (2) the recorded cost of the building at the end of the year.

Practice 10-7

LO2

Capitalized Interest: Journal Entry

Refer to Practice 10-6. Make the journal entry necessary to record *total* interest paid for the year. Assume that all of the interest was paid in cash on December 31.

Practice 10-8

LO2

Capitalized Interest: Multiple-Year Computation

Refer to Practice 10-6. Assume that construction was *not* completed on December 31 of Year 1. Also assume that the same loans were outstanding for all of Year 2. The following expenditure was made during Year 2:

July 1	$500,000

Final construction was completed on December 31 of Year 2. Compute (1) the amount of interest capitalized during Year 2 and (2) the recorded cost of the building at the end of Year 2.

Practice 10-9

LO2

Acquisition by Donation

The company has received a donation of land from a rich local philanthropist. The land originally cost the philanthropist $48,000. On the date of the donation, it had a market value of $111,000. Make the journal entry necessary on the books of the company to record the receipt of the land.

Practice 10-10

LO2

Accounting for an Asset Retirement Obligation

The company purchased a mining site that will have to be restored to certain specifications when the mining production ceases. The cost of the mining site is $800,000, and the restoration cost is expected to be $200,000. It is estimated that the mine will continue in operation for 15 years. The appropriate interest rate is 7%. Make the appropriate journal entries to record the purchase of the mining site and the recognition of the obligation to restore the mining site.

Practice 10-11

LO3

Renewals and Replacements

The company recently replaced the heating/cooling system for its building. The old system cost $160,000, and was 80% depreciated. The new system cost $210,000, which was paid in cash. The new system will extend the economic useful life of the building by five years. Make the journal entry necessary to record the removal of the old system and the installation of the new system, assuming that the separate cost of the old system is identifiable and has been accounted as part of the building cost.

Practice 10-12

LO3

Research and Development

During the year, the company made the following research and development expenditures:

Date	Amount	Comment
July 23	$120,000	Before technological feasibility established.
December 31	100,000	After technological feasibility established.

Compute the total research and development (R&D) expense for the year assuming (1) the expenditures were for normal R&D, (2) the expenditures were for software R&D, *and* (3) the expenditures were for normal R&D and the company does its accounting according to international financial reporting standards.

Practice 10-13

LO3

Oil and Gas Exploration Costs

The company started business on January 1 and during the year had oil and gas exploration costs of $500,000. Of these costs, $100,000 was associated with successful wells and $400,000 with so-called dry holes. For simplicity, assume that all of the costs were incurred on December 31. Compute the total oil and gas exploration expense to be reported for the year, assuming that (1) the company uses the successful efforts method and (2) the company uses the full cost method.

Practice 10-14

LO4

Accounting for the Acquisition of an Entire Company
Stafford Company purchased Deaver Manufacturing for $1,400,000 cash on January 1. The book value and fair value of the assets of Deaver as of the date of the acquisition follow:

	Book Value	Fair Value
Cash	$ 20,000	$ 20,000
Accounts receivable	190,000	190,000
Inventory	260,000	320,000
Patent	0	80,000
Property, plant, and equipment	600,000	750,000
Totals	$1,070,000	$1,360,000

In addition, Deaver had liabilities totaling $500,000 at the time of the acquisition. Deaver has no other separately identifiable intangible assets. Make the journal entry necessary on the books of Stafford Company to record the acquisition.

Practice 10-15

LO4

Accounting for a Bargain Purchase
Refer to Practice 10-14. Assume that the cash acquisition price is $720,000 instead of $1,400,000. Make the journal entry necessary on the books of Stafford Company to record the acquisition.

Practice 10-16

LO4

Intangibles and a Basket Purchase
The company paid $500,000 to purchase the following: a building with an appraised value of $200,000, an operating permit valued at $100,000, and ongoing research and development projects valued at $150,000. In addition, it is estimated that the fair value of the order backlog associated with the products manufactured in the building is $120,000; this order backlog is included as part of the purchase. Make the journal entry necessary to record this cash purchase.

Practice 10-17

LO4

Intangibles and a Business Acquisition
Buyer Company purchased Target Company for $800,000 cash. Target Company had total liabilities of $300,000. Buyer Company's assessment of the fair values it obtained when it purchased Target Company is as follows:

Cash	$100,000
Inventory	50,000
In-process R&D	500,000

Make the journal entry necessary to record this business acquisition.

Practice 10-18

LO6

Fixed Asset Turnover Ratio
Company A had sales for the year totaling $480,000. The net property, plant, and equipment balance at the beginning of the year was $160,000; the ending balance was $200,000. Compute the fixed asset turnover ratio.

Practice 10-19

LO6

Danger in Using Fixed Asset Turnover Ratio
Refer to Practice 10-18. Company A's competitor, Company B, had sales for the year totaling $360,000. The net property, plant, and equipment balance at the beginning of the year was $200,000; the ending balance was $220,000. Company B is a very young company; all of its fixed assets have been purchased in the past two years. In contrast, Company A's assets are 10 years old, on average. It is estimated that Company A's fixed assets had a market value of $290,000 at the beginning of the year and $310,000 at the end of the year. Which company is more efficient at using its fixed assets to generate sales, Company A or Company B? Explain.

EXERCISES

Exercise 10-20

LO2

Basket Purchase

Ratcliff Corporation purchased land, a building, a patent, and a franchise for the lump sum of $1,450,000. A real estate appraiser estimated the building to have a resale value of $600,000 (2/3 of the total worth of land and building). The franchise had no established resale value. The patent was valued by management at $337,000. Give the journal entry to record the acquisition of the assets.

Exercise 10-21

LO2

Basket Purchase

Allred Shipping Co. acquired land, buildings, and equipment at a lump-sum price of $920,000. An appraisal of the assets at the time of acquisition disclosed the following values.

Land	$250,000
Buildings	600,000
Equipment	200,000

What cost should be assigned to each asset?

Exercise 10-22

LO2

Basket Purchase in Exchange for Stock

On May 31, 2013, Julienne Corp. exchanged 20,000 shares of its $1 par common stock for the following assets:

(a) A trademark valued at $183,000.
(b) A building, including land, valued at $732,000 (20% of the value is for the land).
(c) A franchise right. No estimate of the value is available at time of exchange.

Julienne Corp. stock is selling at $53 per share on the date of the exchange. Give the entries to record the exchange on Julienne's books.

Exercise 10-23

LO4

Basket Purchase of Intangible Assets

Taraz Company paid $500,000 to purchase the following portfolio of intangibles with estimated fair values as indicated:

	Estimated Fair Value
Internet domain name	$150,000
Order backlog	100,000
In-process research and development	200,000
Operating permit	80,000

In addition, Taraz spent $300,000 to run an advertising campaign to boost its image in the local community.

Make the journal entries necessary to record the purchase of the intangibles and the payment for the advertising.

Exercise 10-24

LO4

Purchase of Intangible Assets in a Business Acquisition

Omniportal Company purchased Network Enterprises. The following fair values were associated with the items acquired in this business acquisition:

	Cost	Fair Value
Accounts receivable	$ 180,000	$ 180,000
Inventory	120,000	75,000
Government contacts	0	92,000
Equipment (net)	68,000	84,000
Short-term loan payable	(160,000)	(160,000)
Net assets	$ 208,000	$ 271,000

The fair value associated with Network Enterprises' government contacts is not based on any legal or contractual relationship. In addition, for obvious reasons, there is no open market trading for intangibles of this sort.

1. Make the journal entry necessary for Omniportal Company to record the purchase if the purchase price is $805,000 cash.
2. Assume that the purchase price is $24,300 cash. Make the journal entry necessary to record the purchase.

Exercise 10-25

LO2

Acquisition of Land and Building for Stock and Cash

Valdilla's Music Store acquired land and an old building in exchange for 50,000 shares of its common stock, par $0.50, and cash of $80,000. The auditor ascertains that the company's stock was selling for $15 per share when the purchase was made. The following additional costs were incurred to complete the transaction:

Legal cost to complete transaction	$10,000
Property tax for previous year	30,000
Cost of building demolition	21,000
Salvage value of demolished building	(6,000)

What entry should be made to record the acquisition of the property?

Exercise 10-26

LO2

Postacquisition Expenditures

GoodeHill Company replaced some parts of its factory building during 2013:

(a) The outside corrugated covering on the factory walls was removed and replaced. The job was done by an expert crew from Hollister Construction Company and will extend the life of the building by six years. The cost of the new wall was $84,000. The cost of the old wall is estimated to be $60,000. The building is 30% depreciated.

(b) Dust filters in the interior of the factory were replaced at a cost of $20,000. The new filters are expected to reduce employee health hazards and thus reduce wage and fringe benefit costs. The original filters cost $11,000. The old filters are one-fourth depreciated.

Prepare journal entries for the preceding information.

Exercise 10-27

LO2

Cost of Self-Constructed Asset

Brodhead Manufacturing Company has constructed its own special equipment to produce a newly developed product. A bid to construct the equipment by an outside company was received for $1,200,000. The actual costs incurred by Brodhead to construct the equipment were as follows:

Direct material	$320,000
Direct labor	200,000

It is estimated that incremental overhead costs for construction amount to 140% of direct labor costs. In addition, fixed costs (exclusive of interest) of $700,000 were incurred during the construction period and allocated to production on the basis of total prime costs (direct labor plus direct material). The prime costs incurred to build the new equipment amounted to 35% of the total prime costs incurred for the period. The company follows the policy of capitalizing all possible costs on self-construction projects.

To assist in financing the construction of the equipment, a $500,000, 10% loan was acquired at the beginning of the 6-month construction period. The company carries no other debt except for trade accounts payable. For simplicity, assume that all construction expenditures took place exactly midway through the project: That is, all expenditures took place with three months remaining in the construction period. Compute the cost to be assigned to the new equipment.

Exercise 10-28

LO1

Cost of Specific Plant Items

The following expenditures were incurred by Peterson Enterprises Co. in 2013:

Purchase of land	$ 282,000
Land survey	4,800
Fees for search of title for land	500
Building permit	4,000
Temporary quarters for construction crews	11,200
Payment to tenants of old building for vacating premises	4,450
Razing old building	41,000
Excavating basement	13,000
Special assessment tax for street project	2,400
Dividends	4,000
Damages awarded for injuries sustained in construction (no insurance was carried)	8,750
Costs of construction	2,395,000
Cost of paving parking lot adjoining building	55,000
Cost of shrubs, trees, and other landscaping	36,000

What is the cost of the land, land improvements, and building?

Exercise 10-29

LO2

Interest Capitalization Decision

For each of the situations described here, indicate when interest should be capitalized (C) and when it should not be capitalized (NC).

(a) Queen Company is constructing a piece of equipment for its own use. Total construction costs are expected to be $4 million, and the construction period will be one month.

(b) Ferney Company is constructing a piece of equipment for sale. Total construction costs are expected to exceed $10 million, and the construction period will be about 15 months. This is a special order. Ferney has never produced a piece of equipment like this before.

(c) Patterson Company is constructing a piece of equipment for its own use. Total construction costs are expected to be $15 million, and the construction period will be about two years. The forecasted total construction cost is only a very rough estimate because Patterson has no system in place to accumulate separately the costs associated with this project.

(d) Savis Company is constructing a piece of equipment for its own use. Total construction costs are expected to be $350, and the construction period will be nine months.

(e) Platt Company is constructing a piece of equipment for sale. Total construction costs are expected to exceed $10 million, and the construction period will be about 15 months. This particular piece of equipment is Platt's best seller.

(f) Stowell Company is in the process of renovating its corporate office building. The project will cost $7.5 million and will take about 15 months. The building will remain in use throughout the project.

(g) Jackson Company owns a piece of undeveloped land. The land originally cost $21 million. Jackson plans to hold onto the land for three to four years and then develop it into a vacation resort.

Exercise 10-30

LO2

SPREADSHEET

Capitalization of Interest

Carver Department Stores, Inc., constructs its own stores. In the past, no cost has been added to the asset value for interest on funds borrowed for construction. Management has decided to correct its policy and desires to include interest as part of the cost of a new store just being completed. Based on the following information, how much interest would be added to the cost of the store (1) in 2013 and (2) in 2014?

Total construction expenditures:	
January 2, 2013	$ 500,000
May 1, 2013	450,000
November 1, 2013	700,000
March 1, 2014	950,000
September 1, 2014	800,000
November 30, 2014	600,000
	$4,000,000

Outstanding company debt:	
Mortgage related directly to new store; interest rate, 10%; term, 5 years from beginning of construction	$1,500,000
General bond liability:	
Bonds issued just prior to construction of store; interest rate, 13% for 10 years	$ 500,000
Bonds issued prior to construction; interest rate, 12%, mature in 5 years	$ 800,000
Estimated cost of equity capital	14%

Exercise 10-31

LO3

Full Cost and Successful Efforts

Exploratory Company is an oil and gas exploration firm. During 2013, Exploratory engaged in 86 different exploratory projects, only 20 of which were successful. The total cost of this exploration effort was $24 million, $5.6 million of which was associated with the successful projects. As of the end of 2013, production had not yet begun at the successful sites.

1. Using the successful efforts method of accounting for oil and gas exploration costs, how much exploration expense would be shown in Exploratory's income statement for 2013? How much of the exploration cost will be capitalized and shown as an asset on the company's balance sheet as of December 31, 2013?
2. Repeat (1) using the full cost method.

Exercise 10-32

LO1

Determining Cost of Patent

Dean Lang Enterprises Inc. developed a new machine that reduces the time required to insert the fortunes into its fortune cookies. Because the process is considered very valuable to the fortune cookie industry, Dean Lang patented the machine. The following expenses were incurred in developing and patenting the machine:

Research and development laboratory expenses	$34,000
Metal used in the construction of the machine	6,000
Blueprints used to design the machine	2,600
Legal expenses to obtain patent	13,400
Wages paid for the employees' work on the research, development, and building of the machine (60% of the time was spent in actually building the machine)	42,000

Expense of drawing required by the patent office to be submitted with the patent application	$2,500
Fee paid to government patent office to process application	3,200

One year later, Dean Lang Enterprises Inc. paid $19,300 in legal fees to successfully defend the patent against an infringement suit by Chinese Cookie Co.

Give the entries on Dean Lang's books indicated by the preceding events. Ignore any amortization of the patent or depreciation of the machine.

Exercise 10-33

LO3

Research and Development Costs

In 2013, the Slidell Corporation incurred research and development costs as follows:

Materials and equipment	$160,000
Personnel	105,000
Indirect costs	60,000
	$325,000

These costs relate to a product that will be marketed in 2014. It is estimated that these costs will be recouped by December 31, 2017.

1. What is the amount of research and development costs that should be expensed in 2013?
2. Assume that of these costs, equipment of $80,000 can be used on other research projects. Estimated useful life of the equipment is five years with no salvage value, and it was acquired at the beginning of 2013. What is the amount of research and development costs that should be expensed in 2013 under these conditions? Assume that depreciation on all equipment is computed on a straight-line basis.

Exercise 10-34

LO3

What Are the R&D Costs?

Pringle Company has a substantial research department. Following are listed, in chronological order, some of the major activities associated with one of Pringle's research projects.

Project Started

(a) Purchased special equipment to be used solely for this project.
(b) Purchased general equipment that will be usable in Pringle's normal operations.
(c) Allocated overhead to the project.

Technological Feasibility Established

(d) Purchased more special equipment to be used solely for this project.
(e) Performed tests on an early model of the product.
(f) Allocated overhead to the project.

Product Becomes Ready for Production

(g) Incurred direct production costs.
(h) Allocated overhead to the products.

1. For each activity (a) through (h), indicate whether the cost should be capitalized (C), expensed (E), or included in cost of inventory (I).
2. Repeat (1), assuming that Pringle is a computer software development company.

Exercise 10-35

LO2

Equipment Purchase on Deferred Payment Contract

Custom Industries purchases new specialized manufacturing equipment on July 1, 2013. The equipment cash price is $96,000. Custom signs a deferred payment contract that provides for a down payment of $10,000 and a 10-year note for $112,420. The note is to be paid in 10 equal annual payments of $11,242. The payments include 5.193% interest and are made on June 30 of each year, beginning June 30, 2014. Prepare the journal entries for 2013, 2014, and 2015 related to the equipment purchase and the contract. Custom's fiscal year ends on June 30.

Exercise 10-36
LO2

Purchase on Deferred Payment Contract

HiTech Industries purchases new electronic equipment for its telecommunication system. The contractual arrangement specifies 10 payments of $8,600 each to be made over a 10-year period. If HiTech had borrowed money to buy the equipment, it would have paid interest at 9%. HiTech's accountant recorded the purchase as follows:

Equipment	86,000	
Notes Payable		86,000

Prepare the correcting acquisition entry, considering the implicit interest in the purchase.

Exercise 10-37
LO4

Purchase of a Company

Conglomerate Company purchased Individual Company for $935,000 cash. A schedule of the fair values of Individual's assets and liabilities as of the purchase date follows.

Individual Company
Schedule of Asset and Liability Fair Values

Assets		
Cash	$ 12,000	
Receivables	96,000	
Inventory	145,000	
Land, buildings, and equipment	519,000	$772,000
Liabilities		
Current liabilities	$ 75,000	
Long-term debt	116,000	191,000
Net asset fair value		$581,000

1. Make the journal entry necessary for Conglomerate Company to record the purchase.
2. Assume that the purchase price is $445,000 cash. Make the journal entry necessary to record the purchase.

Exercise 10-38
LO2

Purchase of Building with Bonds and Stock

Sayer Co. enters into a contract with Bradford Construction Co. for construction of an office building at a cost of $680,000. Upon completion of construction, Bradford agrees to accept in full payment of the contract price Sayer Co.'s 10% bonds with a face value of $350,000 and common stock with a par value of $90,000 and no established fair market value. Sayer Co.'s bonds are selling in the market at this time at 106. How would you recommend the building acquisition be recorded?

Exercise 10-39
LO4

SPREADSHEET

Purchase of a Company

Landers Inc. is considering purchasing J&B Properties, which has the following assets and liabilities.

	Cost	Fair Value
Accounts receivable	$ 210,000	$ 200,000
Inventory	250,000	260,000
Prepaid insurance	12,000	12,000

	Cost	Fair Value
Buildings and equipment (net)	$ 88,000	$ 168,000
Accounts payable	(130,000)	(130,000)
Net assets	$ 430,000	$ 510,000

1. Make the journal entry necessary for Landers Inc. to record the purchase if the purchase price is $650,000 cash.
2. Assume that the purchase price is $320,000 cash. Make the journal entry necessary to record the purchase.

Exercise 10-40

LO6

Fixed Asset Turnover

Dandy Hardware Stores reported the following asset values in 2012 and 2013:

	2013	2012
Cash	$ 40,000	$ 25,000
Accounts receivable	380,000	330,000
Inventory	590,000	410,000
Land	150,000	125,000
Buildings	500,000	450,000
Equipment	260,000	250,000

In addition, Dandy Hardware had sales of $3,500,000 in 2013. Cost of goods sold for the year was $2,200,000.

Compute Dandy Hardware's fixed asset turnover ratio for 2013.

Exercise 10-41

LO2

Asset Retirement Obligation

Simpson Company purchased a nerve gas detoxification facility. The facility cost $900,000. The cost of cleaning up the routine contamination caused by the initial location of nerve gas on the property is estimated to be $1,300,000; this cost will be incurred in 20 years when all of the existing stockpile of nerve gas is detoxified and the facility is decommissioned. Additional contamination will occur each year that the facility is in operation. In its first year of operation, that additional contamination adds $100,000 to the estimated cleanup cost, which will occur after 19 years (because one year has elapsed). Make the journal entries necessary to record the purchase of the detoxification facility and the recognition of the initial asset retirement obligation (assuming that the appropriate interest rate is 7%). Also make the journal entry to recognize the additional obligation created after one year.

Exercise 10-42

LO3

Classifying Expenditures as Assets or Expenses

One of the most difficult problems facing an accountant is the determination of which expenditures should be capitalized and which should be immediately expensed. What position would you take in each of the following instances?

(a) Painting partitions in a large room recently divided into four sections.
(b) Labor cost of tearing down a wall to permit extension of assembly line.
(c) Replacement of motor on a machine. Life used to depreciate the machine is eight years. The machine is four years old. Replacement of the motor was anticipated when the machine was purchased.
(d) Cost of grading land prior to construction.
(e) Assessment for street paving.
(f) Cost of tearing down a previously occupied old building in preparation for new construction; old building is fully depreciated.

PROBLEMS

Problem 10-43
LO1

Correcting Noncurrent Operating Asset Valuation

On December 31, 2013, Bridgeport Co. shows the following account for machinery it had assembled for its own use during 2013:

Account: MACHINERY (Job Order #1329)

Item	Debit	Credit	Balance Debit	Balance Credit
Cost of dismantling old machine	18,760		18,760	
Cash proceeds from sale of old machine		13,900	4,860	
Raw materials used in construction of new machine	83,400		88,260	
Labor in construction of new machine	55,000		143,260	
Cost of installation	13,600		156,860	
Materials spoiled in machine trial runs	3,100		159,960	
Profit on construction	22,500		182,460	
Purchase of machine tools	15,200		197,660	

An analysis of the details in the account disclosed the following:

(a) The old machine, which was removed before the installation of the new one, had been fully depreciated.
(b) Cash discounts received on the payments for materials used in construction totaled $4,500, and these were reported in the purchase discounts account.
(c) The factory overhead account shows a balance of $351,000 for the year ended December 31, 2013; this balance exceeds normal overhead on regular plant activities by approximately $22,700 and is attributable to machine construction.
(d) A profit was recognized on construction for the difference between costs incurred and the price at which the machine could have been purchased.

Instructions:

1. Determine the machinery and machine tools balances as of December 31, 2013.
2. Give individual journal entries necessary to correct the accounts as of December 31, 2013, assuming that the nominal accounts are still open.

Problem 10-44
LO1

Cost Classification for a Golf Course

The accountant for Stansbury Development Company is uncertain how to record the following costs associated with the construction of a golf course.

(a) Building artificial lakes.
(b) Moving earth around to enhance the "hilliness" of the course.
(c) Planting fairway grass.
(d) Planting trees and shrubs.
(e) Installing an automatic sprinkler system.
(f) Installing golf cart paths.
(g) Purchasing 50 wooden sand trap rakes (at $1 each).
(h) Paying attorneys' fees to prepare and file the land title.
(i) Demolishing an old house situated on the site planned for the clubhouse.

Instructions: Indicate which costs should be expensed (E), which should be capitalized and considered to be nondepreciable (CN), and which should be capitalized and depreciated (CD). Include explanations for each classification.

Problem 10-45

LO2

Acquisition of Land and Buildings

Skyline Corporation has decided to expand its operations and has purchased land in Salina for construction of a new manufacturing plant. The following costs were incurred in purchasing the property and constructing the building:

Land purchase price	$ 140,000
Payment of delinquent property taxes	22,000
Title search and insurance	7,000
City improvements for water and sewer	19,500
Building permit	6,000
Cost to destroy existing building on land ($5,000 worth of salvaged material used in new building)	24,000
Contract cost of new building	1,800,000
Land improvements—landscaping	81,600
Sidewalks and parking lot	41,000
Fire insurance on building—1 year	20,000

The depreciated value of the old building on the books of the company from which the land was purchased was $29,000. The old building was never used by Skyline.

Instructions:

1. Determine the costs of the land and land improvements. Show clearly the elements included in the totals.
2. Determine the cost of the new building. Show clearly the elements included in the total.

Problem 10-46

LO1

SPREADSHEET

Transactions Involving Property

The following transactions were completed by Millenial Toy Co. during 2013:

Mar.	1	Purchased real property for $829,700, which included a charge of $29,700 representing property tax for March 1–June 30 that had been prepaid by the vendor; 25% of the purchase price is deemed applicable to land and the balance to buildings. A mortgage of $460,000 was assumed by Millenial Toy Co. on the purchase. Cash was paid for the balance.
	30	Previous owners had failed to take care of normal maintenance and repair requirements on the building, necessitating current reconditioning at a cost of $34,200.
May	15	Demolished garages in the rear of the building, $6,600 being recovered on the lumber salvage. The company proceeded to construct a warehouse. The cost of such construction was $101,300, which was almost exactly the same as bids made on the construction by independent contractors. Upon completion of construction, city inspectors ordered extensive modifications to the building as a result of failure on the part of the company to comply with the building safety code. Such modifications, which could have been avoided, cost $12,400.
June	1	The company exchanged its own stock with a market value of $64,000 (par $4,000) for a patent and a new toy-making machine. The machine has a market value of $31,000.
July	1	The new machinery for the new building arrived. In addition to the machinery, a new franchise was acquired from the manufacturer of the machinery to produce toy robots. Payment was made by issuing bonds with a face value of $100,000 and by paying cash of $15,000. The value of the franchise is set at $50,000, while the machine's fair value is $61,000.
Nov.	20	The company contracted for parking lots and landscaping at a cost of $42,000 and $8,900, respectively. The work was completed and paid for on November 20.
Dec.	31	The business was closed to permit taking the year-end inventory. During this time, required redecorating and repairs were completed at a cost of $6,400.

Instructions: Give the journal entries to record each of the preceding transactions. (Disregard depreciation.)

Problem 10-47 **Acquisition of Land and Construction of Plant**

LO2 REVERSE SOLVABLE

Bylund Corporation was organized in June 2013. In auditing its books, you find the following land, buildings, and equipment account:

Account: LAND, BUILDINGS, AND EQUIPMENT

Date		Item	Debit	Credit	Balance Debit	Balance Credit
2013						
June	8	Organization fees paid to the state	21,000		21,000	
	16	Land site and old building	325,000		346,000	
	30	Corporate organization costs	40,000		386,000	
July	2	Title clearance fees	15,300		401,300	
Aug.	28	Cost of razing old building	15,000		416,300	
Sept.	1	Salaries of Bylund Corporation executives	100,000		516,300	
	1	Cost to acquire patent for special equipment	54,000		570,300	
Dec.	12	Stock bonus to corporate promoters, 3,000 shares of common stock, $50/share market value	150,000		720,300	
	15	County real estate tax	13,200		733,500	
	15	Cost of new building completed and occupied on this date	1,450,000		2,183,500	

An analysis of this account and of other accounts disclosed the following additional information:

(a) The building acquired on June 16, 2013, was valued at $41,000.
(b) The corporation paid $15,000 for the demolition of the old building and then sold the scrap for $7,000 and credited the proceeds to Miscellaneous Revenue.
(c) The corporation executives did not participate in the construction of the new building.
(d) The county real estate tax was for the 6-month period ended December 31, 2013, and was assessed by the county on the land.

Instructions: Prepare journal entries to correct Bylund Corporation's books.

Problem 10-48 **Acquisition of Intangible Assets**

LO2

In your audit of the books of Dyer Corporation for the year ended September 30, 2013, you found the following items in connection with the company's patents account:

(a) The company had spent $120,000 during its fiscal year ended September 30, 2012, for research and development costs and debited this amount to its patents account. Your review of the company's cost records indicated the company had spent a total of $141,500 for the research and development of its patents, of which $21,500 spent in its fiscal year ended September 30, 2012, had been debited to Research and Development Expense.
(b) The patents were issued on April 1, 2012. Legal expenses in connection with the issuance of the patents of $14,280 were debited to Legal and Professional Fees Expense.
(c) The company paid a retainer of $15,000 on October 5, 2012, for legal services in connection with a patent infringement suit brought against it. This amount was debited to Deferred Costs.
(d) A letter dated October 15, 2013, from the company's attorneys in reply to your inquiry as to liabilities of the company existing at September 30, 2013, indicated that a settlement of the patent infringement suit had been arranged. The other party had agreed to drop the suit and to release the company from all future liabilities in exchange for $23,000. Additional fees due to the attorneys amounted to $1,260.

Instructions: From the information given, prepare correcting journal entries as of September 30, 2013.

Problem 10-49
LO4

Acquisition of Intangible Assets

Transactions during 2013 of the newly organized Menlove Corporation included the following:

Jan.	2	Paid legal fees of $15,000 and stock certificate costs of $8,300 to complete organization of the corporation.
	15	Hired a clown to stand in front of the corporate office for two weeks and hand out pamphlets and candy to create goodwill for the new enterprise. Clown cost, $1,000; pamphlets and candy, $500.
Apr.	1	Patented a newly developed process with costs as follows:

Legal fees to obtain patent	$42,900
Patent application and licensing fees	6,350
Total	$49,250

		It is estimated that in six years other companies will have developed improved processes, making the Menlove Corporation process obsolete.
May	1	Acquired both a license to use a special type of container and a distinctive trademark to be printed on the container in exchange for 600 shares of Menlove Corporation no-par common stock selling for $50 per share. The license is worth twice as much as the trademark, both of which may be used for six years.
July	1	Constructed a shed for $131,000 to house prototypes of experimental models to be developed in future research projects.
Dec.	31	Incurred salaries for an engineer and chemist involved in product development totaling $175,000 in 2013.

Instructions:

1. Give journal entries to record the preceding transactions. (Ignore amortization of intangible assets.)
2. Present the Intangible Assets section of Menlove Corporation's balance sheet at December 31, 2013.

Problem 10-50
LO2
SPREADSHEET

Basket Purchase of Noncurrent Operating Assets

Bridges Wholesale Company incurred the following costs in 2013 for a warehouse acquired on July 1, 2013, the beginning of its fiscal year:

Cost of land	$132,000
Cost of building	528,000
Remodeling and repairs prior to occupancy	58,200
Escrow fee	12,000
Landscaping	31,000
Property tax for period prior to acquisition	10,000
Real estate commission	40,000

The company signed a non-interest-bearing note for $600,000 (20 × $30,000) on July 1, 2013. The implicit interest rate is 12% compounded semiannually. Payments of $30,000 are to be made semiannually beginning December 31, 2013, for 10 years.

Instructions: Give the required journal entries to record (1) the acquisition of the land and building (assume that cash is paid to equalize the cost of the assets and the present value of the note) and (2) the first two semiannual payments, including amortization of note discount.

Problem 10-51
LO3

Income Statement for Computer Software Company

Powersoft Company is engaged in developing computer software for the small business and home computer market. Most of the computer programmers are involved in developmental work designed to produce software that will perform fairly specific tasks in a user-friendly manner. Extensive testing of the working model is performed before it is released to production for preparation of masters and further testing. As a result of careful preparation, Powersoft has produced several products that have been very successful in the marketplace. The following costs were incurred during 2013:

Salaries and wages of programmers doing research	$265,000
Expenses related to projects prior to establishment of technological feasibility	82,200
Expenses related to projects after technological feasibility has been established but before software is available for production	53,800
Amortization of capitalized software development costs from current and prior years	32,150
Costs to produce and prepare software for sale	49,800
Additional data for 2013:	
Sales of products for the year	$675,000
Beginning inventory	155,000
Portion of goods available for sale sold during year	60%

Instructions: Prepare an income statement for Powersoft for the year 2013. Income tax rate is 30%.

Problem 10-52

LO3

Valuation of Property

At December 31, 2012, certain accounts included in the Noncurrent Operating Assets section of Salvino Company's balance sheet had the following balances:

Land	$150,000
Buildings	910,000
Leasehold improvements	500,000
Machinery and equipment	600,000

During 2013, the following transactions occurred.

(a) Land site 653 was acquired for $1,600,000. Additionally, to acquire the land, Salvino paid a $90,000 commission fee to a real estate agent. Costs of $25,000 were incurred to clear the land. During the course of clearing the land, timber and gravel were recovered and sold for $20,000.

(b) A second tract of land (site 654) with a building was acquired for $700,000. The closing statement indicated that the land value was $510,000 and the building value was $215,000. Shortly after acquisition, the building was demolished at a cost of $30,000. A new building was constructed for $600,000 plus the following costs.

Excavation fees	$35,000
Architectural design fees	19,000
Building permit fee	15,000
Imputed interest on funds used during construction	60,000

(Salvino had no interest-bearing debt outstanding during the construction period.)

The building was completed and occupied on September 30, 2013.

(c) A third tract of land (site 655) was acquired for $600,000 and was put on the market for resale.

(d) Extensive work was done to a building occupied by Salvino under a lease agreement that expires on December 31, 2019. The total cost of work was $150,000, which consisted of the following.

Painting ceilings	$ 10,000	(estimated useful life is 1 year)
Performing electrical work	60,000	(estimated useful life is 10 years)
Constructing extension to current working area	80,000	(estimated useful life is 30 years)
	$150,000	

The lessor paid half of the costs incurred in connection with the extension to the current working area.

(e) During December 2013, costs of $70,000 were incurred to improve leased office space. The related lease will terminate on December 31, 2015, and is not expected to be renewed.

(f) A group of new machines was purchased under a royalty agreement that provides for payment of royalties based on units of production for the machines. The invoice price of the machines was $90,000, freight costs were $2,000, unloading charges were $2,500, and royalty payments for 2013 were $13,000.

Instructions:

1. Prepare an analysis of the changes in each of the following balance sheet accounts for 2013. (Disregard the related accumulated depreciation accounts.)
   - Land
   - Buildings
   - Leasehold improvements
   - Machinery and equipment
2. List the items in the preceding information that were not used to determine the answer to (1), and indicate where, if at all, these items should be included in Salvino's financial statements.

Problem 10-53

LO2

Acquisition of Noncurrent Operating Assets

At December 31, 2012, Davis Company's noncurrent operating asset accounts had the following balances:

Category	
Land	$ 280,000
Buildings	1,150,000
Machinery and equipment	924,000
Automobiles	113,000
Leasehold improvements	277,000
Land improvements	0

Transactions for 2013 included the following:

Jan.	6	A plant facility consisting of land and a building was acquired from Matthews Corp. in exchange for 10,000 shares of Davis' common stock. On this date, Davis' stock had a market price of $73 a share. Current assessed values of land and building for property tax purposes are $195,000 and $405,000, respectively.
Mar.	25	New parking lots, streets, and sidewalks at the acquired plant facility were completed at a total cost of $141,000.
July	1	Machinery and equipment were purchased at a total invoice cost of $187,000, which included $12,000 of sales tax. Additional costs of $14,000 for delivery and $22,000 for installation were incurred.
Aug.	30	Davis purchased a new automobile for $26,400.
Nov.	4	Davis purchased for $370,000 a tract of land as a potential future building site.

Dec. 20 A machine with a cost of $22,000 and a remaining book value of $3,100 at date of disposition was scrapped without cash recovery.

Instructions: Prepare a schedule analyzing the changes in each of the noncurrent operating asset accounts during 2013. This schedule should include columns for beginning balance, increase, decrease, and ending balance for each of the noncurrent operating asset accounts.

Problem 10-54
LO2

Capitalization of Interest

Oceanwide Enterprises, Inc., is involved in building and operating cruise ships. Each ship is identified as a separate discrete job in the accounting records. At the end of 2012, Oceanwide correctly reported $5,400,000 as Construction in Progress on the following jobs.

Ship	Completion Date (end of month)	Accumulated Costs (including 2012 interest) December 31, 2012
340	October 31, 2012*	$2,300,000
341	June 30, 2013	1,150,000
342	September 30, 2013	1,200,000
343	January 31, 2014	750,000

*Ship 340 was completed and ready for use in October 2012 and will be placed in service May 1, 2013.

Construction costs for 2013, and the dates the expenditures were made, were as follows:

Ship	Date	Costs
341	April 1, 2013	$1,200,000
342	May 1, 2013	1,600,000
343	July 1, 2013	2,200,000
344	September 1, 2013	810,000
345	November 1, 2013	360,000

Oceanwide had the following general liabilities at December 31, 2013:

12%, 5-year note (maturity date—2015)	$2,000,000
10%, 10-year bonds (maturity date—2018)	8,000,000

On January 1, 2013, Oceanwide borrowed $2,000,000 specifically for the construction of ship 343. The loan was for three years with interest at 13%.

Instructions:

1. Compute the maximum interest that can be capitalized in 2013.
2. Compute the weighted-average interest rate for the general liabilities for 2013.
3. Compute the interest that Oceanwide should capitalize during 2013.

Problem 10-55
LO2

Self-Construction of Equipment

American Corporation received a $400,000 low bid from a reputable manufacturer for the construction of special production equipment needed by American in an expansion program. Because its own plant was not operating at capacity, American decided to construct the equipment itself and recorded the following production costs related to the construction:

Services of consulting engineer	$ 10,000
Work subcontracted	20,000
Materials	200,000
Plant labor normally assigned to production	65,000
Plant labor normally assigned to maintenance	100,000
Total	$395,000

Management prefers to record the cost of the equipment under the incremental cost method. Approximately 40% of the corporation's production is devoted to government supply contracts, which are all based in some way on cost. The contracts require that any self-constructed equipment be allocated its full share of all costs related to the construction.

The following information also is available.

(a) The preceding production labor was for partial fabrication of the equipment in the plant. Skilled personnel were required and were assigned from other projects. The maintenance labor amount ($100,000) represents the cost of nonproduction plant employees assigned to the construction project. Had these workers not been assigned to construction, the $100,000 cost would still have been incurred for their idle time.

(b) Payroll taxes and employee fringe benefits are approximately 30% of labor cost and are included in manufacturing overhead cost. Total manufacturing overhead for the year was $5,630,000, including the $100,000 maintenance labor used to construct the equipment.

(c) Manufacturing overhead is approximately 50% variable and is applied on the basis of production labor cost. Production labor cost for the year for the corporation's normal products totaled $6,810,000.

(d) General and administrative expenses include $22,500 of executive salary cost and $10,500 of postage, telephone, supplies, and miscellaneous expenses identifiable with this equipment construction.

Instructions:

1. Compute the amount that should be reported as the full cost of the constructed equipment to meet the requirements of the government contracts.
2. Compute the incremental cost of the constructed equipment.
3. What is the greatest amount that should be capitalized as the cost of the equipment? Why?

Problem 10-56

LO2

Asset Retirement Obligation

Madison Company has purchased land that will serve as a temporary repository for nuclear waste. The site will function for 20 years, at which time Madison will be required to completely decontaminate the land. The purchase price for the land is $700,000. Madison knows that the land will have to be decontaminated but isn't sure which of several possible approaches will be sufficient to reach the level of decontamination necessary by law. The costs of each approach, and the estimated probability that the approach will be the one used, follow:

Approach 1 15% probability of total decontamination cost of $10,000 at the end of 20 years.

Approach 2 25% probability of total decontamination cost of $250,000 at the end of 20 years.

Approach 3 60% probability of total decontamination cost of $1,200,000 at the end of 20 years.

The appropriate interest rate is 6%.

Instructions: Make the journal entries necessary to record the purchase of the land and the recognition of the asset retirement obligation.

Problem 10-57

LO4

Recording Goodwill

Aurora Corp. acquired Payette Company on December 31, 2013. The following information concerning Payette's assets and liabilities was assembled on the acquisition date:

	Per Company's Books	As Adjusted by Appraisal and Audit
Assets		
Current assets	$ 307,000	$ 340,000
Land, buildings, and equipment (net)	179,200	260,000
	$ 486,200	$ 600,000
Liabilities		
Current liabilities	(25,000)	(25,000)
Long-term liabilities	(160,000)	(160,000)
Net assets	$ 301,200	$ 415,000

Instructions:

1. Make the journal entry necessary for Aurora Corp. to record the purchase, assuming the purchase price was $1,500,000 in cash.
2. Why might Aurora be willing to pay such a high price for Payette?
3. Repeat (1), assuming the purchase price is $350,000.
4. Repeat (1), assuming the purchase price is $150,000.

Problem 10-58

LO4

Summary Entries for Interest Payments

Santa Clarita Company reported interest expense in 2013 and 2012 of $470,000 and $410,000, respectively. The balance in Accrued Interest Payable at the end of 2013, 2012, and 2011 was $51,000, $59,000, and $46,000, respectively. In addition, a note to Santa Clarita's 2013 financial statements included the following:

> Interest costs related to construction in progress are capitalized as incurred. The Company capitalized $350,000 and $260,000 of interest costs during the years 2013 and 2012, respectively.

Instructions:

1. What summary journal entries would be needed to record all information related to interest in 2013 and 2012?
2. How would interest paid be disclosed in Santa Clarita's statement of cash flows for 2013 and 2012? Santa Clarita uses the indirect method in reporting cash flow from operating activities.

Problem 10-59

LO3

REVERSE SOLVABLE

Classifying Expenditures as Assets or Expenses

As of December 31, 2013, W. W. Cole Company's total assets were $325 million and total liabilities were $180 million. Net income for 2013 was $38 million. During 2013, W. W. Cole's chief executive officer had put extreme pressure on employees to meet the profitability goal the CEO had set for them. The goal was to achieve a return on stockholders' equity in 2013 of 25% (net income/stockholders' equity). The rumor among Cole's employees is that to meet this goal, the accounting for some items may have been overly "aggressive." The following items are of concern:

(a) Research and development costs totaling $18 million were capitalized. None of these costs related to items with alternative uses. The capitalized R&D was assigned a useful life of six years; $3 million was written off during 2013.

(b) During the year, a building was acquired in exchange for 5 million shares of Cole common stock. The building was assigned a value of $27 million by the board of directors. At the time of the exchange, Cole common stock was trading on the New York Stock Exchange for $3 per share.

(c) On December 31, equipment was purchased for $1 million in cash and an agreement to pay $3 million per year for the next eight years, the first payment to be made in one year. The cost of the equipment was recorded at $25 million. The interest rate implicit in the contract was 12%.

(d) Interest of $7 million was capitalized during the year. The only items produced during the year by Cole were routine inventory items.

Instructions:

1. Ignoring any concerns raised by items (a) through (d), did W. W. Cole Company meet its profitability goal for the year?
2. After making any adjustments suggested by items (a) through (d), did W. W. Cole meet its profitability goal? (Ignore income taxes.)
3. What should prevent accounting abuses like those described above?

Problem 10-60

LO3

Classifying Expenditures as Assets or Expenses

Trevor Company completed a program of expansion and improvement of its plant during 2013. You are provided with the following information concerning its buildings account:

(a) On October 31, 2013, a 50-foot extension to the present factory building was completed at a contract cost of $462,000.

(b) During the course of construction, the following costs were incurred for the removal of the end wall of the building where the extension was to be constructed.

  (1) Payroll costs during the month of March arising from employees' time spent in removing the wall, $23,410.
  (2) Payments to a salvage company for removing unusual debris, $2,610.

(c) The cost of the original structure allocable to the end wall was estimated to be $33,900 with accumulated depreciation thereon of $17,300. Trevor Company received $6,570 from the construction company for windows and other assorted materials salvaged from the old wall.

(d) The old floor covering was replaced with a new type of long-lasting floor covering at a cost of $9,190. The cost of the old floor covering was $13,000 and accumulated depreciation was $6,250. The cost of the old floor covering had been included with the overall building cost even though the floor covering has a different useful life than the building.

(e) The interior of the plant was repainted in new bright colors for a contract price of $12,420.

(f) New and improved shelving was installed at a cost of $4,180. The cost of the old shelving was $2,200 and accumulated depreciation was $990. The cost of the old shelving had been included with the overall building cost even though the shelving has a different useful life than the building.

(g) Old electrical wiring was replaced at a cost of $13,440. Cost of the old wiring was determined to be $5,110 with accumulated depreciation to date of $1,900. Assume that the new wiring has a remaining useful life that is the same as the building.

(h) New electrical fixtures using fluorescent bulbs were installed. The new fixtures were purchased on the installment plan; the schedule of monthly payments showed total payments of $10,240, which included interest and carrying charges of $800. The old fixtures were carried at a cost of $3,300 with accumulated depreciation to date of $1,410. The old fixtures have no scrap value. Assume that the new fixtures have the same remaining useful life as the building.

Instructions: Prepare journal entries for the preceding information. Briefly justify the capitalize-or-expense decision for each item.

Problem 10-61

LO4

Acquisition and Valuation of Intangibles

Beecher's Boston Barbeque Company purchased a customer list and an ongoing research project for a total of $300,000. Beecher uses the expected cash flow approach for estimating the fair value of these two intangibles. The appropriate interest rate is 7%. The potential future cash flows from the two intangibles, and their associated probabilities, are as follows:

Customer List

Outcome 1 20% probability of cash flows of $40,000 at the end of each year for five years.

Outcome 2 30% probability of cash flows of $18,000 at the end of each year for four years.

Outcome 3 50% probability of cash flows of $9,000 at the end of each year for three years.

Ongoing Research Project

Outcome 1 10% probability of cash flows of $450,000 at the end of each year for 10 years.

Outcome 2 20% probability of cash flows of $12,000 at the end of each year for 4 years.

Outcome 3 70% probability of cash flows of $500 at the end of each year for 3 years.

Instructions: Prepare the journal entry necessary to record the purchase of the two intangibles.

Problem 10-62

LO6

Limitations of the Fixed Asset Turnover Ratio

Progressive Company reported the following asset values in 2012 and 2013:

	2013	2012
Cash	$ 50,000	$ 45,000
Accounts receivable	300,000	220,000
Inventory	650,000	510,000
Land	600,000	400,000
Buildings	900,000	800,000
Equipment	350,000	250,000

In addition, in 2013, Progressive had sales of $4,800,000; cost of goods sold for the year was $2,900,000.

As of the end of 2012, the fair value of Progressive's total assets was $3,000,000. Of the excess of fair value over book value, $100,000 resulted from the fact that Progressive uses LIFO for inventory valuation. As of the end of 2013, the fair value of Progressive's total assets was $3,800,000, and Progressive's LIFO reserve was $150,000.

Instructions:

1. Compute Progressive's fixed asset turnover ratio for 2013.
2. Using the fair value of fixed assets instead of their book values, recompute Progressive's fixed asset turnover ratio for 2013. State any assumptions that you make.
3. Progressive's primary competitor is Steady State. Steady State's fixed asset turnover ratio for 2013, based on publicly available information, is 2.5. Is Progressive more or less efficient at using its fixed assets than Steady State? Explain your answer.

Problem 10-63
LO2, LO4

Sample CPA Exam Questions

1. Cole Co. began constructing a building for its own use in January 2013. During 2013, Cole incurred interest of $50,000 on specific construction debt and $20,000 on other borrowings. The amount of interest that could have been avoided if the building construction expenditures had been used to pay off debt during 2013 was $40,000. What amount of interest cost should Cole capitalize?
   (a) $20,000
   (b) $40,000
   (c) $50,000
   (d) $70,000

2. Which of the following costs of goodwill should be capitalized?

	Maintaining Goodwill	Developing Goodwill
(a)	Yes	No
(b)	No	No
(c)	Yes	Yes
(d)	No	Yes

CASES

Discussion Case 10-64

Is There Any Goodwill?

Fugate Energy Corp. has recently purchased a small local company, Gleave Inc., for $556,950 cash. Fugate's chief accountant has been given the assignment of preparing the journal entry to record the purchase. An investigation disclosed the following information about the assets of Gleave Inc.:

(a) Gleave owned land and a small manufacturing building. The book value of the property on Gleave's records was $115,000. An appraisal for fire insurance purposes had been made during the year. The building was appraised by the insurance company at $175,000. Property tax assessment notices showed that the building's worth was five times the worth of the land.
(b) Gleave's equipment had a book value of $75,000. It is estimated by Gleave that it would take six times the amount of book value to replace the old equipment with new equipment. The old equipment is, on average, 50% depreciated.
(c) Gleave had a franchise to produce and sell solar energy units from another company in a set geographic area. The franchise was transferred to Fugate as part of the purchase. Gleave carried the asset on its books at $40,000, the unamortized balance of the original cost of $90,000. The franchise is for an unlimited time. Similar franchises are now being sold by the company for $120,000 per geographic area.
(d) Gleave had two excellent research scientists who were responsible for much of the company's innovation in product development. Each is paid $150,000 per year by Gleave. They have agreed to work for Fugate Energy at the same salary.
(e) Gleave held two patents on its products. Both had been fully amortized and were not carried as assets on Gleave's books. Gleave believes they could have been sold separately for $75,000 each.

Evaluate each of these items and prepare the journal entry that should be made to record the purchase on Fugate's books. (*Note:* Gleave has no liabilities.)

Discussion Case 10-65

But Research Is Our Only Asset!

Strategy, Inc., was organized by Elizabeth Durrant and Ramona Morales, two students working their way through college. Both Elizabeth and Ramona had used the Internet extensively while in high school and had become very proficient Web surfers. Elizabeth had a special ability for designing Web-based games that challenged the reasoning power of players. Ramona could see great potential in marketing Elizabeth's products to other Web users, and so the two began Strategy. Sales have exceeded expectations, and they have added 10 employees to their company to design additional products, debug new programs, and produce and distribute the final software products.

Because of its growing size, increased capital is needed for the company. The partners decide to apply for a $100,000 loan to support the growing cost of research. As part of the documentation to obtain the loan, the bank asks for audited financial statements for the past year. After some negotiation, Mark Dawson, CPA, is hired. Strategy had produced a preliminary income statement that reported net income of $35,000. After reviewing the statements, Dawson indicates that the company actually had a $10,000 loss for the year. The major difference relates to $45,000 of wage and material costs that Strategy had capitalized as an intangible asset but that Dawson determined should be expensed.

"It's all research and development," Dawson insisted.

"We'll easily recoup it in sales next year," countered Ramona. "I thought you accountants believed in the matching principle. Why do you permit us to capitalize the equipment we're using, but not our Web development costs? We'll never look profitable under your requirements!"

What major issues are involved in this case? Which position best reflects generally accepted accounting principles?

Discussion Case 10-66

Why Is My ROA Lower than Yours?

Terri Morton has been recently hired as a financial analyst. Her first assignment is to analyze why the reported return on assets (ROA) for Arnold Company is so much different from that of Baker Company. Arnold Company develops and markets innovative consumer products. Baker Company is a fabricator of heavy steel products. Both companies have net incomes of $1 million, but Arnold has reported total assets of only $3 million compared to $6 million for Baker. Terri suspects her new boss is using this assignment to test her understanding of financial statements. Terri's boss did give her one cryptic clue: unrecorded assets. Prepare Terri's analysis.

Discussion Case 10-67

Expensing R&D: Will It Kill Me?

In 1974, as the FASB considered requiring the expensing of all in-house research and development expenditures, the Board received many comments predicting that if firms were required to expense R&D, they would significantly cut back on research expenditures to avoid hurting reported earnings. Subsequent to the adoption of pre-Codification FASB *Statement No. 2,* such an impact proved to be difficult to document. Elliott et al. summarized and extended conflicting prior research and concluded that R&D expenditures did decrease after the adoption of FASB *Statement No. 2* but that the decrease may have been a function of the generally unfavorable economic conditions in the United States in the mid-1970s.

Would you expect that a rule requiring all firms to expense R&D outlays would cause R&D expenditures to decrease? Why or why not?

SOURCE: John Elliott, Gordon Richardson, Thomas Dyckman, and Roland Dukes, "The Impact of SFAS No. 2 on Firm Expenditures on Research and Development: Replications and Extensions," *Journal of Accounting Research*, Spring 1984, pp. 85–102.

Discussion Case 10-68

Brand Values on the Balance Sheet?

In 1996, *Financial World* magazine estimated and ranked the most valuable brand names in the world. Number 11 in the ranking was **Gillette** with an estimated value of $10.3 billion. *Financial World* explained its brand value estimation process for Gillette as follows:

- *Estimate the amount of assets used in generating the brand sales.* This estimation involves using industry sales-to-asset ratios. For Gillette, *Financial World* estimated that 1995 sales of $2.6 billion required the use of $988 million in assets.
- *Compute excess return on assets. Financial World* assumes that a generic brand name will generate a return on assets of 5%. Gillette's 1995 operating profit of

$961 million exceeds this 5% return by $912 million [$961 million − ($988 million assets × 0.05)].

- *Estimate after-tax return. Financial World* puts Gillette's tax rate at 37%, yielding an after-tax excess return of $575 million [$912 million × (1 − 0.37)].
- *Multiply the after-tax excess return by the brand's strength multiple.* The *strength multiple* takes into account the brand's leadership, stability, market size, internationality, trend, and legal protection. *Financial World* placed Gillette's strength multiple at 17.9 (quite high). This yields the final estimate of the brand value: $10.3 billion ($575 million excess after-tax return × 17.9).

Comment on the relevance and reliability of the $10.3 billion Gillette brand value calculated by *Financial World.* Under what circumstances would you be willing to recognize this value in the financial statements?

SOURCE: See "Behind the Numbers," *Financial World*, July 8, 1996, p. 54.

Discussion Case 10-69

Asset Write-Ups

Rouse Company, a real estate developer, is well known as one of the few U.S. companies to have reported the current value of property and equipment in its financial statements. As mentioned in the text of the chapter, *IAS 16* permits the inclusion of upward asset revaluations, based on appraisals, in the financial statements. And *IAS 40* allows real estate companies to both record investment property in the balance sheet at its fair value and include the associated unrealized gains in the income statement.

In Germany, as in the United States, upward revaluations are not allowed. In fact, before being replaced by IASB standards, German rules were seen as encouraging write-downs, resulting in the creation of so-called hidden reserves, which constitute a systematic understatement of assets. In March 1993, **Daimler-Benz** disclosed that it had hidden reserves of $2.45 billion.

1. Why might real estate companies be among the leaders in encouraging the disclosure of the current value of property and equipment?
2. If German companies have "hidden reserves," why do you think Daimler-Benz chose to reveal the magnitude of its hidden reserves in March 1993? What is the advantage of having hidden reserves?
3. As an auditor, how would you feel about auditing the financial statements of a company that uses appraisal values instead of historical costs?

Case 10-70

Deciphering Financial Statements (The Walt Disney Company)

Locate the 2009 financial statements for **The Walt Disney Company** on the Internet.

Use those financial statements and consider the following questions.

1. As illustrated in Exhibit 10-10, **Interbrand** estimates the value of the Disney brand name in 2009 at $28.45 billion. Search Disney's financial statements and notes—what is Disney's estimate of the value of the Disney name?
2. What summary journal entry did Disney make to record interest incurred during fiscal 2009? (*Hint:* Don't forget to distinguish between interest incurred and cash paid for interest.)
3. Find Disney's note about intangible assets. What is Disney's amortization policy for intangible assets? How often does Disney review its intangible assets to determine if their carrying values are recorded accurately?
4. According to the statement of cash flows, in 2009 Disney spent $1,753 million on investments in parks, resorts, and other property. Use the notes to the financial statements to determine how much of this total related to each of Disney's operating segments.

Case 10-71

Writing Assignment (Is It an Asset or Not?)

Hunter Company has developed a computerized machine to assist in the production of appliances. It is anticipated that the machine will do well in the marketplace; however, the company lacks the necessary capital to produce the machine. Rosalyn Finch, secretary-treasurer of Hunter Company, has offered to transfer land to the company to be used as collateral for a bank loan. In exchange for the land transfer, Rosalyn will receive a 5-year employment contract and a percentage of any profits earned from sales of the new machine. The title to the land is to be transferred unconditionally. If Hunter defaults on the employment contract, a lump-sum cash settlement for lost wages will be paid to Rosalyn.

The land transfer may be a good business move, but it raises a number of sticky accounting issues. Hunter's controller has given you the task of writing a memo that summarizes the options available in accounting for the land transfer. Your memo should outline the arguments both for and against recording the land as an asset on Hunter's books. Also discuss how the land should be valued if it is recorded as an asset.

Case 10-72

Ethical Dilemma (Dumping Costs into a Landfill)

On St. Patrick's Day 1992, **Chambers Development Company**, one of the largest landfill and waste management firms in the United States, announced that it had been improperly capitalizing costs associated with landfill development. Chambers announced that it was immediately expensing over $40 million in executive salaries, travel expenses, and public relations costs that had been capitalized as part of the cost of landfills. Wall Street fear over what this move meant for Chambers' track record of steady earnings growth sent Chambers' stock price plunging 62% in one day—total market value declined by $1.4 billion.

Imagine that it is early 1992 and you have just been assigned to work on the Chambers Development audit. In the course of your audit, you find a number of irregular transactions, including the questionable capitalization of costs as described above. Chambers' accounting staff tells you that the company has always capitalized these costs. You do a little historical investigation and find that if all the questionable costs had been expensed as you think they should have been, the $362 million expense would completely wipe out all the profit reported by Chambers since it first went public in 1985. You are reluctant to approach your superior, the audit partner on the job, because you know that a large number of the financial staff working for Chambers are former partners in the audit firm you work for. However, you know that ignoring something like this can lead to a catastrophic audit failure.

Draft a memo to the audit partner summarizing your findings.

Case 10-73

Cumulative Spreadsheet Analysis

This spreadsheet assignment is a continuation of the spreadsheet assignments given in earlier chapters. If you completed those assignments, you have a head start on this one.

Refer back to the instructions for preparing the revised financial statements for 2013 as given in (1) of the Cumulative Spreadsheet Analysis assignment in Chapter 3.

1. Skywalker wishes to prepare a *forecasted* balance sheet, a *forecasted* income statement, and a *forecasted* statement of cash flows for 2014. Use the financial statement numbers for 2013 as the basis for the forecast, along with the following additional information.
   (a) Sales in 2014 are expected to increase by 40% over 2013 sales of $2,100.
   (b) In 2014, new property, plant, and equipment acquisitions will be in accordance with the information in (q).
   (c) The $480 in operating expenses reported in 2013 breaks down as follows: $15 in depreciation expense and $465 in other operating expenses.
   (d) No new long-term debt will be acquired in 2014.
   (e) No cash dividends will be paid in 2014.
   (f) New short-term loans payable will be acquired in an amount sufficient to make Skywalker's current ratio in 2014 exactly equal to 2.0.
   (g) Skywalker does not anticipate repurchasing any additional shares of stock during 2014.
   (h) Because changes in future prices and exchange rates are impossible to predict, Skywalker's best estimate is that the balance in accumulated other comprehensive income will remain unchanged in 2014.

(i) In the absence of more detailed information, assume that the balances in Investment Securities, Long-Term Investments, and Other Long-Term Assets will all increase at the same rate as sales (40%) in 2014. The balance in Intangible Assets will change in accordance with item (r).

(j) In the absence of more detailed information, assume that the balance in the other long-term liabilities account will increase at the same rate as sales (40%) in 2014.

(k) The investment securities are classified as available-for-sale securities. Accordingly, cash from the purchase and sale of these securities is classified as an investing activity.

(l) Assume that transactions impacting other long-term assets and other long-term liabilities accounts are operating activities.

(m) Cash and investment securities accounts will increase at the same rate as sales.

(n) The forecasted amount of accounts receivable in 2014 is determined using the forecasted value for the average collection period. The average collection period for 2014 is expected to be 14.08 days. To make the calculations less complex, this value of 14.08 days is based on forecasted end-of-year accounts receivable rather than on average accounts receivable.

(o) The forecasted amount of inventory in 2014 is determined using the forecasted value for the number of days' sales in inventory. The number of days' sales in inventory for 2014 is expected to be 107.6 days. To make the calculations simpler, this value of 107.6 days is based on forecasted end-of-year inventory rather than on average inventory.

(p) The forecasted amount of accounts payable in 2014 is determined using the forecasted value for the number of days' purchases in accounts payable. The number of days' purchases in accounts payable for 2014 is expected to be 48.34 days. To make the calculations simpler, this value of 48.34 days is based on forecasted end-of-year accounts payable rather than on average accounts payable.

(*Note*: These forecasted statements were constructed as part of the spreadsheet assignment in Chapter 9; you can use that spreadsheet as a starting point if you have completed that assignment.)

For this exercise, make the following additional assumptions:

(q) The forecasted amount of property, plant, and equipment (PP&E) in 2014 is determined using the forecasted value for the fixed asset turnover ratio. The fixed asset turnover ratio for 2014 is expected to be 3.518 times. To make the calculations simpler, this ratio of 3.518 is based on forecasted end-of-year gross property, plant, and equipment balance rather than on the average balance. (*Note:* For simplicity, ignore accumulated depreciation in making this calculation.)

(r) Skywalker has determined that no new intangible assets will be acquired in 2014. For this assignment, ignore amortization of the existing intangible asset account balance.

Clearly state any additional assumptions that you make.

2. Assume the same scenario as (1), and show the impact on the financial statements with the following changes in assumptions:

   (a) Fixed asset turnover ratio is expected to be 4.500.

   (b) Fixed asset turnover ratio is expected to be 2.500.

3. Comment on the differences in the forecasted values of cash provided by operating activities in 2014 under each of the following assumptions about the fixed asset turnover ratio: 3.518 times, 4.500 times, and 2.500 times. Explain how a change in the fixed asset turnover ratio impacts cash provided by operations.

AP Photo/Ron Heflin

P2 ROUTINE ACTIVITIES OF A BUSINESS

CHAPTER 11 Investments in Noncurrent Operating Assets—Utilization and Retirement

LEARNING OBJECTIVES

1. Use straight-line, accelerated, use-factor, and group depreciation methods to compute annual depreciation expense.
2. Apply the productive-output method to the depletion of natural resources.
3. Incorporate changes in estimates and methods into the computation of depreciation for current and future periods.
4. Identify whether an asset is impaired, and measure the amount of the impairment loss using both U.S. GAAP and IASB standards.
5. Discuss the issues impacting proper recognition of amortization or impairment for intangible assets.
6. Account for the sale of depreciable assets in exchange for cash and in exchange for other depreciable assets.

EM EXPANDED MATERIAL

7. Compute depreciation for partial periods, using both straight-line and accelerated methods.
8. Understand the depreciation methods underlying the MACRS income tax depreciation system.

Garbage—that's how H. Wayne Huizenga made his first splash on the national scene. In the early 1960s, he started with one garbage truck in southern Florida. Huizenga went on to buy up hundreds of local garbage companies across the country, combining them into **Waste Management Inc.** (which later merged with USA Waste Services but kept the Waste Management name), the largest trash hauler in the world.

After his retirement from the trash business in 1984, Huizenga's eye fell on a small, 20-store, video chain in Dallas called **Blockbuster Video**.[1] By the end of 1987, Huizenga had acquired control of Blockbuster and had increased the number of stores to 130. Through a combination of aggressive expansion and the acquisition of existing video chains, Blockbuster soon became the nation's largest video chain. By the end of 2007, there were 7,830 Blockbuster Video stores, primarily located in the United States, Great Britain, and Canada.

[1] Eric Calonius, "Meet the King of Video," *Fortune*, June 4, 1990, p. 208.

On May 8, 1989, a **Bear Stearns** investment report was released that was critical of some of Blockbuster's accounting practices, particularly its depreciation policies. The report suggested that the 40-year life Blockbuster used for amortizing goodwill was much too long; to quote from the report: "Have you ever seen a 40-year-old videotape store?" Five years was suggested as a more reasonable amortization period. The report also criticized Blockbuster for increasing the depreciation period for videotapes from 9 months to 36 months.[2] Revising both these items to use the shorter amortization periods would have cut Blockbuster's 1988 net income almost in half—from $0.57 per share to $0.32 per share.

Release of the Bear Stearns report caused Blockbuster's stock price to drop from $33.50 to $26.25 in two days, a 22% drop. (See Exhibit 11-1.) This represented a total decline in market value of approximately $200 million. Wayne Huizenga was livid. In a meeting with stock analysts, he showed a letter from the SEC ordering Blockbuster to use the longer videotape amortization period. He criticized the Bear Stearns researchers for not understanding his business and said that their report wasn't "worth the powder to blow it to hell."[3] Huizenga was vindicated when within two weeks of the release of the report, Blockbuster's stock had regained most of the 22% loss.

In 1994, Wayne Huizenga left Blockbuster after presiding over its acquisition by **Viacom** in a deal valued at over $8 billion. This completed an incredible run by Huizenga: He had entered, dominated, and successfully exited two very different industries, garbage and video rentals. So, what was next? Selected as America's number 1 entrepreneur by *Success* magazine in 1995, it was certain that Wayne Huizenga would not just sit around and count his money (about $1.4 billion). At one time he owned three professional sports teams in southern Florida: the Miami Dolphins (football), the Florida Marlins (baseball), and the Florida Panthers (hockey). His new company, **AutoNation**, is busy doing for auto dealerships what Huizenga already did for garbage hauling and video stores: taking fragmented businesses across the country and consolidating them into a nationwide network. Currently, AutoNation is the largest automotive retailer in the United States with 246 new vehicle franchises as of December 31, 2009. At age 66, after creating three Fortune 1000 companies from scratch, Mr. Huizenga announced that he was stepping down from the board of AutoNation in April 2004.

EX 11-1 BLOCKBUSTER VIDEO DAILY STOCK PRICES IN MAY 1989

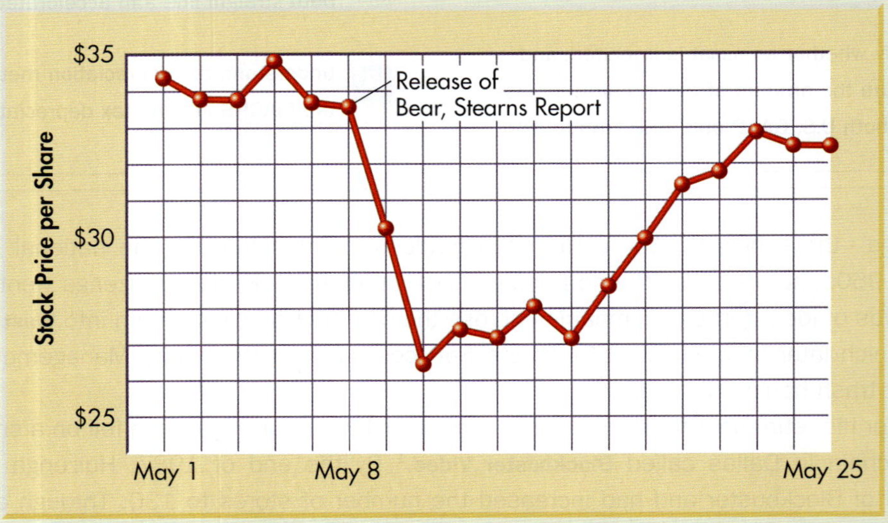

[2] Dana Weschsler, "Earnings Helper," *Forbes*, June 12, 1989, p. 15. As explained later in the chapter, GAAP has been changed, and goodwill is no longer amortized but is instead tested for impairment on a regular basis.
[3] Duncan Maxwell Anderson and Michael Warshaw, "The #1 Entrepreneur in America," *Success*, March 1995, p. 32.

QUESTIONS

1. Why would the Bear Stearns report cause Blockbuster's stock price to decline by 22%?
2. Look carefully at Exhibit 11-1 to see the behavior of Blockbuster's stock price around the release of the Bear Stearns report. When did "the market" better understand Blockbuster's accounting for depreciation—on May 7, just before the release of the Bear Stearns report, or on May 10, two days after the release of the report? Explain your answer.

Answers to these questions can be found on page 11-41.

A fundamental task of accrual accounting is appropriately allocating the cost of long-lived assets to expense. If you are a Venetian shipmaster setting the price that you will charge for the use of your ship on a spice-trading voyage to the Orient, you must somehow allocate the cost of the ship over the expected number of voyages the ship can complete. If you are a Silicon Valley research firm, proper measurement of annual income requires you to allocate the cost of your research patents over their expected economic life. Computing asset depreciation is an exercise in accounting judgment, and, as illustrated in the Blockbuster/Bear Stearns example, reasonable people can disagree, with huge implications for reported profits.

Three different terms are used to describe the process of allocating the cost of long-lived assets to periodic expense. The allocation of tangible property costs is referred to as depreciation. For minerals and other natural resources, the cost allocation process is called depletion. For intangible assets, such as patents and copyrights, the process is referred to as amortization. Sometimes amortization is used generically to encompass all three terms.

This chapter discusses what happens to a long-lived asset after acquisition. The first decision facing management relates to estimating and recognizing the expense associated with a long-lived asset's use. We will cover the common depreciation methods and the depletion of natural resources. We will also address the issues associated with the proper treatment of changes in depreciation estimates. The chapter also describes when an impairment loss should be recognized and the proper accounting for the retirement of depreciable assets. The chapter includes discussion of three types of intangibles: those that are amortized, those that are not amortized but are tested for impairment, and goodwill, which is not amortized and is tested for impairment using a special test. The time line in Exhibit 11-2 illustrates the issues to be discussed. The Expanded Material at the end of the chapter offers more detail on depreciating assets acquired and retired in midyear and on the modified accelerated cost recovery system (MACRS), a depreciation system used for income tax purposes.

EX 11-2 TIME LINE OF BUSINESS ISSUES INVOLVED WITH LONG-TERM OPERATING ASSETS

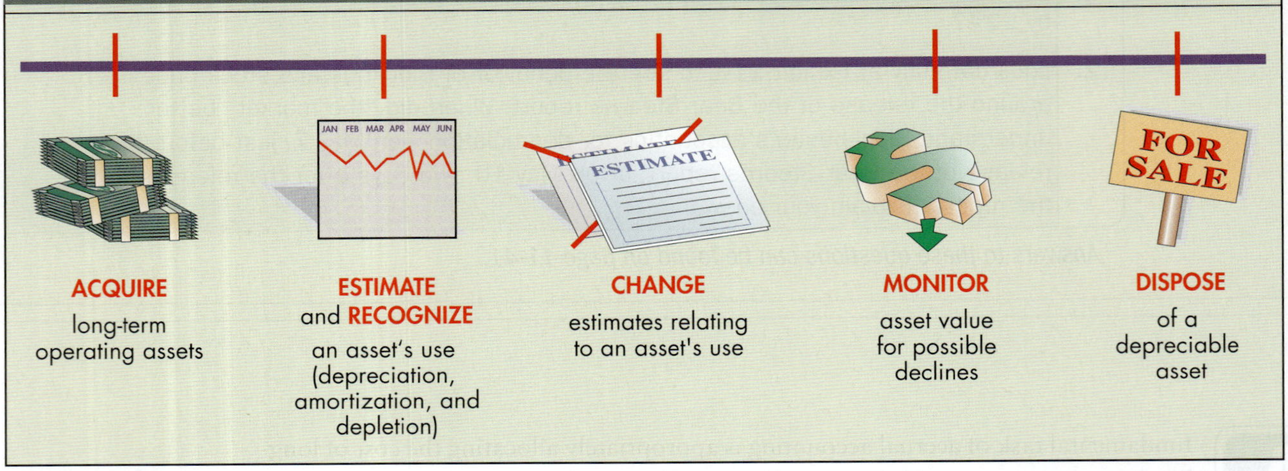

Depreciation

1 Use straight-line, accelerated, use-factor, and group depreciation methods to compute annual depreciation expense.

WHY **The conduct of business operations involves the use, and eventual wearing out, of plant and equipment, as well as some intangible assets. Conceptually, the amount of these assets consumed in doing business during a period should be reported as an expense of that period. In practice, accountants estimate this cost by using a systematic method to allocate the recorded cost of these assets to expense over the life of the asset.**

HOW **Four factors are used to compute depreciation expense: asset cost, salvage value, useful life, and pattern of use. The amount of depreciation expense recognized for a particular period depends on the depreciation method used.**

FYI

Depreciation expense was not widely reported in income statements until the early 1900s. The passage of the Sixteenth Amendment in 1913, allowing the taxation of income, spurred companies to demand some depreciation deduction for the use of long-term assets.

Depreciation is *not* a process through which a company accumulates a cash fund to replace its long-lived assets. Depreciation is also *not* a way to compute the current value of long-lived assets. Instead, depreciation is the systematic allocation of the cost of an asset over the different periods benefited by the use of the asset. Accumulated depreciation is not an asset replacement fund but is the sum of all the asset cost that has been expensed in prior periods. Similarly, the book value of an asset (historical cost less accumulated depreciation) is the asset cost remaining to be allocated to future periods but is not an estimate of the asset's current value.

Depreciation expense is the recognition of the using up of the service potential of an asset. The nature of depreciation expense is conceptually no different from the expenses that recognize the expiration of insurance premiums or prepaid rent; the practical difference is that noncurrent assets are depreciated over several years, whereas prepaid rent is usually expensed over a period of months.

Factors Affecting the Periodic Depreciation Charge

Four factors are taken into consideration in determining the appropriate amount of annual depreciation expense.

- Asset cost
- Residual or salvage value
- Useful life
- Pattern of use

Asset Cost The cost of an asset includes all the expenditures relating to its acquisition and preparation for use as described in Chapter 10. The cost of property less the expected residual value, if any, is the depreciable cost or depreciation base, that is, the portion of asset cost to be expensed in future periods.

Residual or Salvage Value The residual (salvage) value of property is an estimate of the amount for which the asset can be sold when it is retired. The residual value depends on the retirement policy of the company as well as market conditions and other factors. If, for example, the company normally uses equipment until it is physically exhausted and no longer serviceable, the residual value, represented by the scrap or junk value that can be salvaged, may be quite small. If, however, the company normally replaces its equipment after a short period of use, the residual value, represented by the selling price or trade-in value, may be relatively high.

From a theoretical point of view, any estimated residual value should be subtracted from cost in arriving at the portion of asset cost to be charged to depreciation. In practice, however, residual values are frequently ignored in determining periodic depreciation charges. This practice is acceptable when residual values are relatively small or are not subject to reasonable estimation.

> **! CAUTION**
>
> Ignoring small residual values bothers some students who want to compute depreciation correctly to the penny. Remember that depreciation is an *estimate*—forget the pennies.

Useful Life Noncurrent operating assets other than land have a limited useful life as a result of certain physical and functional factors. The physical factors that limit the service life of an asset are (1) wear and tear, (2) deterioration and decay, and (3) damage or destruction. Everyone is familiar with the processes of wear and tear that render an automobile, a building, or furniture no longer usable. A tangible asset, whether used or not, also is subject to deterioration and decay through aging. Finally, fire, flood, earthquake, or accident may reduce or terminate the useful life of an asset.

The primary functional factor limiting the useful lives of assets is obsolescence. An asset may lose its usefulness when as a result of altered business requirements or technological progress, it no longer can produce sufficient revenue to justify its continued use. Although the asset is still physically usable, its inability to produce sufficient revenue has cut short its economic life. Look around: How many old personal computers are stored in corners, still perfectly operational, but unable to run the software that is currently being used?

Amos Morgan/Digital Vision/Getty Images

Computers have short useful lives due to the quick progress of technology.

Both physical and functional factors must be considered in estimating the useful life of a depreciable asset. This recognition requires estimating what events will take place in the future and requires careful judgment on the part of the accountant. Physical factors are more readily apparent than functional factors in predicting asset life. When functional factors are expected to hasten the retirement of an asset, these also must be considered.

In practice, many companies as a matter of policy dispose of certain classes of assets after a predetermined period without regard to the serviceability of individual assets within a class. Company automobiles, for example, may be replaced routinely every two or three years.

The useful life of a depreciable plant asset may be expressed in terms of either an estimated time factor or an estimated use factor. The time factor may be a period of months or years; the use factor may be a number of hours of service or a number of units of output. The cost of the asset is allocated in accordance with the lapse of time or extent of use. The rate of cost allocation may be modified by other factors, but basically depreciation must be recognized on a time or use basis.

Pattern of Use To match asset cost against revenues, periodic depreciation charges should reflect as closely as possible the pattern of use. If the asset produces a varying revenue pattern, the depreciation charges should vary in a corresponding manner. When depreciation is measured in terms of a time factor, the pattern of use must be estimated. Because of the difficulty in identifying a pattern of use, several somewhat arbitrary methods have come into common practice. Each method represents a different pattern and is designed to make the time basis approximate the use basis. The time factor is employed in two general classes of methods: straight-line depreciation and accelerated depreciation. When depreciation is measured in terms of a use factor, the units of use must be estimated. The depreciation charge varies periodically in accordance with the services provided by the asset. As illustrated later, the use factor is employed in service-hours depreciation and in productive-output depreciation.

Recording Periodic Depreciation

The general form of the journal entry used to recognize depreciation is as follows:

Depreciation Expense	xx	
Accumulated Depreciation		xx

In manufacturing operations, depreciation is sometimes charged to a production overhead account and then allocated to the cost of inventory. This merely extends the period of deferral; instead of going straight to an expense account, depreciation goes to inventory and then to expense (Cost of Sales).

The allowance account that is credited in recording periodic depreciation is commonly titled *Accumulated Depreciation*. The accumulation of expired cost in a separate account rather than crediting the asset account directly permits identification of the original cost of the asset and the accumulated depreciation. Companies are required to disclose both cost and accumulated depreciation for plant assets on the balance sheet or in the notes to the financial statements. This enables the user to estimate the relative age of plant assets and provides some basis for predicting future cash outflows for the replacement of plant assets.

Methods of Depreciation

There are a number of different methods for computing depreciation expense. The depreciation method used in any specific instance is a matter of judgment and, conceptually, should be selected to most closely approximate the actual pattern of use expected from the asset. In practice, most firms select one depreciation method, such as straight-line, and use it for substantially all their depreciable assets. The following methods are described in this section.

Time-Factor Methods

- Straight-line depreciation
- Accelerated methods
  - Sum-of-the-years'-digits depreciation
  - Declining-balance depreciation

Use-Factor Methods

- Service-hours depreciation
- Productive-output depreciation

Group and Composite Methods

The examples that follow assume the acquisition of a polyurethane plastic-molding machine at the beginning of 2013 by Schuss Boom Ski Manufacturing, Inc., at a cost of $100,000 with an estimated residual value of $5,000. The following symbols are used in the formulas for the development of depreciation rates and charges:

C = Asset cost
R = Estimated residual value
n = Estimated life in years, hours of service, or units of output
r = Depreciation rate per period, per hour of service, or per unit of output
D = Periodic depreciation charge

Time-Factor Methods The most common methods of cost allocation are related to the passage of time. A productive asset is used up over time, and possible obsolescence due to technological changes is also a function of time. Of the time-factor depreciation methods, straight-line depreciation is by far the most popular.

The use of accelerated depreciation methods is based largely on the assumption that there will be rapid reductions in a depreciable asset's efficiency, output, or other benefits in the early years of that asset's life. As assets age, they often require increased charges for maintenance and repairs. Charges for depreciation decline, then, as the economic advantages afforded through ownership of the asset decline. The most commonly used accelerated method is the declining-balance method; the sum-of-the-years'-digits method is also sometimes used.

Straight-line depreciation. Straight-line depreciation relates depreciation to the passage of time and recognizes equal depreciation in each year of the life of the asset. The simple assumption behind the straight-line method is that the asset is equally useful during each time period, and depreciation is not affected by asset productivity or efficiency variations.

In applying the straight-line method, an estimate is made of the useful life of the asset, and the depreciable asset cost (the difference between the asset cost and residual value) is divided by the useful life of the asset in arriving at the periodic depreciation amount.

Using data for the machine acquired by Schuss Boom Ski Manufacturing and assuming a 5-year life, annual depreciation is computed as follows:

$$D = \frac{C - R}{N}, \text{ or } \frac{\$100{,}000 - \$5{,}000}{5 \text{ years}} = \$19{,}000 \text{ per year}$$

A table summarizing annual depreciation for the entire life of the asset, using the straight-line method, follows.

End of Year	Computation		Depreciation Amount	Accumulated Depreciation	Asset Book Value
					$100,000
2013	$95,000/5	=	$19,000	$19,000	81,000
2014	95,000/5	=	19,000	38,000	62,000
2015	95,000/5	=	19,000	57,000	43,000
2016	95,000/5	=	19,000	76,000	24,000
2017	95,000/5	=	19,000	95,000	5,000
			$95,000		

It was indicated earlier that residual value is frequently ignored when it is a relatively minor amount. If this were done in the preceding example, depreciation would be $20,000 per year instead of $19,000.

When assets are acquired or disposed of in the middle of a year, depreciation for the partial year should be recognized. The examples in this chapter assume that partial-year depreciation is recognized for the number of months an asset was held during the year. A variety of other approaches to computing partial-year depreciation are covered in the Expanded Material at the end of the chapter.

Sum-of-the-years'-digits depreciation. The sum-of-the-years'-digits depreciation method yields decreasing depreciation in each successive year. The computations are done by applying a series of fractions, each of a smaller value, to depreciable asset cost. The numerator of the fraction is the number of years remaining in the asset life as of the beginning of the year. The denominator of the fraction is the sum of all the digits from one to the original useful life. There is no great conceptual insight behind this method; it is merely a clever arithmetic scheme that gives decreasing depreciation each year and results in the entire depreciable cost being allocated over the asset's useful life.

In the Schuss Boom example, the useful life is five years, so the denominator of the fraction is 15(1 + 2 + 3 + 4 + 5). Annual depreciation is computed as follows:

End of Year	Computation		Depreciation Amount	Accumulated Depreciation	Asset Book Value
					$100,000
2013	$95,000 × 5/15	=	$31,667	$31,667	68,333
2014	95,000 × 4/15	=	25,333	57,000	43,000
2015	95,000 × 3/15	=	19,000	76,000	24,000
2016	95,000 × 2/15	=	12,667	88,667	11,333
2017	95,000 × 1/15	=	6,333	95,000	5,000
			$95,000		

Note that under this method, annual depreciation expense declines by 1/15 of the depreciation asset base each year, or by $6,333 (by $6,334 in 2014 and 2017 due to effects of rounding).

> **FYI**
>
> The famous mathematician Carl Friedrich Gauss deduced this formula in 1878 during a test in school when he was 10 years old.

When an asset has a long useful life, such as 20 years, computing the sum of the years' digits can be cumbersome. The following formula is a shortcut to computing the sum of the years' digits:

$$\frac{[n(n+1)]}{2} = (1 + 2 + 3 + \cdots + n)$$

With a useful life of 20 years, the sum-of-the-years'-digits denominator determined by the formula is [20 (20 + 1)]/2 = 210. The fraction applied to depreciable cost in the first year would be 20/210, in the second year, 19/210, and so forth.

Declining-balance depreciation. The declining-balance depreciation methods provide decreasing charges by applying a constant percentage rate to a declining asset book value. The most popular rate is two times the straight-line rate, and this method is often called double-declining-balance depreciation. The percentage to be used is double the straight-line rate, calculated for various useful lives as follows:

Estimated Useful Life in Years	Straight-Line Rate	2 Times Straight-Line Rate
3	33 1/3%	66 2/3%
5	20	40
7	14 2/7	28 4/7
8	12 1/2	25
10	10	20
20	5	10

Residual value is not used in the computations under this method; however, it is generally recognized that depreciation should not continue once the book value is equal to the residual value. Depreciation using the double-declining-balance method for the Schuss Boom asset described earlier is summarized in the following table:

End of Year	Computation		Depreciation Amount	Accumulated Depreciation	Asset Book Value
					$100,000
2013	$100,000 × 40%	=	$40,000	$40,000	60,000
2014	60,000 × 40%	=	24,000	64,000	36,000
2015	36,000 × 40%	=	14,400	78,400	21,600
2016	21,600 × 40%	=	8,640	87,040	12,960
2017	12,960 × 40%	=	5,184	92,224	7,776
			$92,224		

It should be noted that the rate of 40% is applied to the decreasing book value of the asset each year. This results in a declining amount of depreciation expense. In applying this rate, the book value after five years exceeds the residual value by $2,776 ($7,776 – $5,000). This condition arises whenever residual values are relatively low in amount. Companies

> **CAUTION**
>
> With both the straight-line and sum-of-the-years'-digits methods, the residual value is subtracted from the asset cost before calculating depreciation. Residual value is not subtracted when using the double-declining-balance method.

> **STOP&THINK**
>
> Imagine that at the beginning of 2013, Schuss Boom had five different machines: one brand new, and the others one year, two years, three years, and four years old. Which depreciation method—straight-line, sum-of-the-years'-digits, or double-declining-balance—would give the highest total depreciation expense in 2013?
>
> a) Straight-line gives the highest total depreciation expense in 2013.
> b) Sum-of-the-years'-digits gives the highest total depreciation expense in 2013.
> c) Double-declining-balance gives the highest total depreciation expense in 2013.
> d) All three depreciation methods give the same total depreciation expense in 2013.

usually switch to the straight-line method when the remaining annual depreciation computed using straight line exceeds the depreciation computed by continuing to apply the declining-balance rate. In the Schuss Boom example, the depreciation expense for the year 2017 would be $7,960 if a switch was made from the double-declining-balance to the straight-line method. This would reduce the book value of the asset to its $5,000 residual value. In this example, the switch would be made in the last year of the asset's life, and the final year's depreciation expense is simply the amount necessary to reduce the asset's book value to its residual value. However, if the asset in the example had a lower residual value, the switch could have been made in the fourth year. For example, assume the asset is expected to have no residual value. The book value under the double-declining-balance method at the end of the third year as shown previously is $21,600; thus, the straight-line depreciation for the fourth and fifth years would be $10,800 ($21,600/2); because the straight-line depreciation of $10,800 exceeds the double-declining depreciation of $8,640, the straight-line amount would be used.

Evaluation of time-factor methods. Exhibit 11-3 illustrates the pattern of depreciation expense for the time-factor methods discussed in the preceding sections. Note that when the straight-line method is used, depreciation is a constant or fixed charge each period. When the life of an asset is affected primarily by the lapse of time rather than by the degree of use, recognition of depreciation as a constant charge is generally appropriate. However, when the straight-line method is used, net income measurements become particularly sensitive to changes in the volume of business activity. With above normal activity, there is no increase in the depreciation charge; with below normal activity, there is no decrease in the depreciation charge.

As mentioned, straight-line depreciation is the most widely used procedure for financial reporting purposes. It is readily understood and frequently parallels asset use. It has the advantage of simplicity and under normal conditions offers a satisfactory means of cost allocation. Normal asset conditions exist when (1) assets have been accumulated over a period of years so that the total of depreciation plus maintenance is comparatively even from period to period and (2) service potentials of assets are being steadily reduced by functional as well as physical factors. The absence of either of these conditions may suggest the use of some depreciation method other than straight line.

EX 11-3 TIME-FACTOR METHODS: DEPRECIATION PATTERNS COMPARED

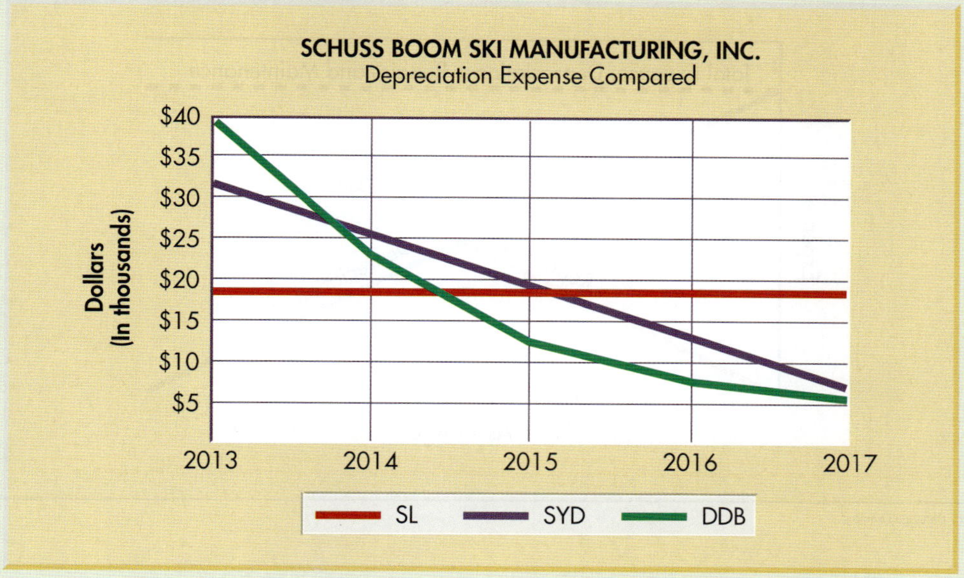

Accelerated methods can be supported as reasonable approaches to cost allocation when the annual benefits provided by an asset decline as it grows older. These methods, too, are suggested when an asset requires increasing maintenance and repairs over its useful life.[4] When straight-line depreciation is employed, the combined charges for depreciation, maintenance, and repairs will increase over the life of the asset; when an accelerated method is used, the combined charges will tend to be equalized. Exhibit 11-4 illustrates this relationship.

Other factors suggesting the use of an accelerated method include (1) the anticipation of a significant contribution in early periods with the extent of the contribution to be realized in later periods being less definite and (2) the possibility that inadequacy or obsolescence may result in premature retirement of the asset.

Use-Factor Methods Use-factor depreciation methods view asset exhaustion as related primarily to asset use or output and provide periodic charges varying with the degree of such service. Service life for certain assets can best be expressed in terms of hours of service but for others in terms of units of production.

Service-hours depreciation. Service-hours depreciation is based on the theory that the purchase of an asset represents the purchase of a number of hours of direct service. This method requires an estimate of the life of the asset in terms of service hours. Depreciable

[4] The following is found in FASB ASC paragraph 360-10-35-7: "The declining-balance method is an example of one of the methods that meet the requirements of being systematic and rational. If the expected productivity or revenue-earning power of the asset is relatively greater during the earlier years of its life, or maintenance charges tend to increase during later years, the declining-balance method may provide the most satisfactory allocation of cost. That conclusion also applies to other methods, including the sum-of-the-years'-digits method, that produce substantially similar results."

EX 11-4 ACCELERATED DEPRECIATION AND REPAIRS AND MAINTENANCE EXPENSE

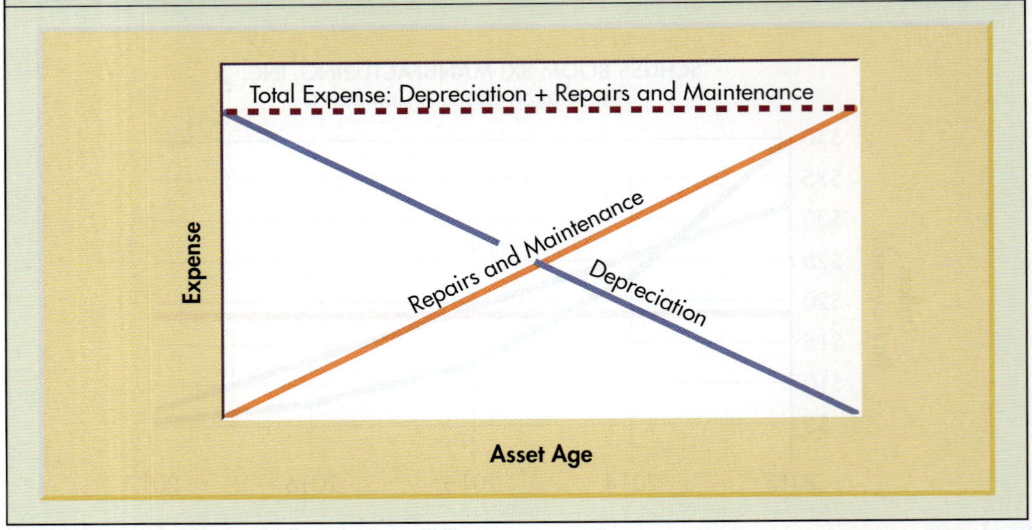

cost is divided by total service hours in arriving at the depreciation rate to be assigned for each hour of asset use. The use of the asset during the period is measured, and the number of service hours is multiplied by the depreciation rate in arriving at the periodic depreciation charge. Depreciation charges against revenue fluctuate periodically according to how much the asset is used.

Using the Schuss Boom asset data previously given and an estimated service life of 20,000 hours, the rate to be applied for each service hour is determined as follows:

$$r \text{ (per hour)} = \frac{C - R}{n}, \text{ or } \frac{\$100{,}000 - \$5{,}000}{20{,}000 \text{ hours}} = \$4.75 \text{ per hour}$$

Computation of annual depreciation is summarized in the following table.

End of Year	Service Hours	Computation		Depreciation Amount	Accumulated Depreciation	Asset Book Value
						$100,000
2013	3,000	3,000 × $4.75	=	$14,250	$14,250	85,750
2014	5,000	5,000 × 4.75	=	23,750	38,000	62,000
2015	5,000	5,000 × 4.75	=	23,750	61,750	38,250
2016	4,000	4,000 × 4.75	=	19,000	80,750	19,250
2017	3,000	3,000 × 4.75	=	14,250	95,000	5,000
	20,000			$95,000		

In this illustration, the original estimate of service hours is correct, and the asset is retired after 20,000 hours are reached in the fifth year. Such precise estimation would seldom be found in practice. Procedures for handling changes in estimates are discussed later in the chapter.

Recall that straight-line depreciation resulted in annual depreciation of $19,000 regardless of fluctuations in how much the asset was used. When asset life is affected directly by the degree of use and when there are significant fluctuations in such use, the service-hours method, which recognizes hours used instead of hours available for use, normally provides the more appropriate charge to operations.

FYI

The productive-output method approximates the technique used to depreciate the cost of producing a motion picture. This technique is discussed in Discussion Case 11-74.

Productive-output depreciation. Productive-output depreciation is based on the theory that an asset is acquired for the service it can provide in the form of production output. This method requires an estimate of the total unit output of the asset. Depreciable cost divided by the total estimated output gives the equal charge to be assigned for each unit of output. The measured production for a period multiplied by the charge per unit gives the charge to be made against revenue. Depreciation charges fluctuate periodically according to the contribution the asset makes in unit output.

Using the Schuss Boom asset data and an estimated productive life of 25,000 units, the rate to be applied for each unit produced is determined as follows:

$$r \text{ (per hour)} = \frac{C - R}{n}, \text{ or } \frac{\$100{,}000 - \$5{,}000}{25{,}000 \text{ units}} = \$3.80 \text{ per unit}$$

A table for the productive-output method would be similar to that prepared for the service-hours method.

Evaluation of use-factor methods. When quantitative measures of asset use can be reasonably estimated, the use-factor methods provide highly satisfactory approaches to asset cost allocation. Depreciation as a fluctuating charge tends to follow the revenue curve: High depreciation charges are assigned to periods of high activity; low charges are assigned to periods of low activity. When the useful life of an asset is affected primarily by the degree of its use, recognition of depreciation as a variable charge is particularly appropriate.

However, certain limitations in applying the use-factor methods need to be noted. Asset performance in terms of service hours or productive output is often difficult to estimate. Measurement solely in terms of these factors could fail to recognize special conditions, such as increasing maintenance and repair costs, as well as possible inadequacy and obsolescence. Furthermore, when service life expires even in the absence of use, a use-factor method may conceal actual fluctuations in earnings; by relating periodic depreciation charges to the volume of operations, periodic operating results may be smoothed out, thus creating a false appearance of stability.

Group and Composite Methods It was assumed in preceding discussions that depreciation expense is associated with individual assets and is applied to each separate unit. This practice is called unit depreciation. From a practical standpoint, it often makes sense to compute depreciation for an entire group of assets as if the group were one asset. Group cost allocation procedures are referred to as group depreciation when the assets in the group are similar (e.g., all of a company's delivery vans) and composite depreciation when the assets in the group are related but dissimilar (e.g., all of a company's desks, chairs, and computers). In the following discussion, the term *group depreciation* will be used generically to refer to both methods.

The group depreciation procedure treats a collection of assets as a single group. Depreciation is accumulated in a single account, and the depreciation rate is based on the average life of assets in the group. Group depreciation is generally computed as an adaptation of the straight-line method, and the illustrations in this chapter assume this approach. A group rate is established by initially analyzing the various assets or classes of assets in use and computing the depreciation as an average of the straight-line annual depreciation as follows:

Asset	Cost	Residual Value	Depreciable Cost	Estimated Life in Years	Annual Depreciation Expense (Straight-Line)
A	$ 2,000	$ 120	$ 1,880	4	$ 470
B	6,000	300	5,700	6	950
C	12,000	1,200	10,800	10	1,080
	$20,000	$1,620	$18,380		$2,500

Group depreciation rate to be applied to cost: $2,500/$20,000 = 12.5%

Average life of assets: $18,380/$2,500 = 7.352 years

The rate of 12.5% applied to the cost of the existing assets, $20,000, results in annual depreciation of $2,500. Annual depreciation of $2,500 will accumulate to a total of $18,380 in 7.352 years; hence, 7.352 years is the average life of the assets.

After the group rate of 12.5% has been set, it is used to compute annual depreciation for all assets subsequently included in the group. For example, if Asset D is acquired for $5,000, the total cost of the assets in the group becomes $25,000 ($2,000 + $6,000 + $12,000 + $5,000), and annual depreciation expense is $3,125 ($25,000 × 0.125). The group rate is ordinarily left the same in subsequent years in the absence of significant changes in the lives of assets included in the group. It is assumed that the assets are replaced with similar assets when retired. The group rate should be reviewed periodically to confirm that it is still appropriate for the assets in the group.

Because the accumulated depreciation account under the group procedure applies to the entire group of assets, it is not related to any specific asset. Thus, no book value can be calculated for any specific asset, and there are no fully depreciated assets. No gains or losses are recognized at the time individual assets are retired. For example, if asset B is sold for $3,500 after two years of use, the entry to record the sale using the group depreciation method would be as follows:

Cash	3,500	
Accumulated Depreciation	2,500	
Equipment		6,000

Because no gain or loss is recognized, the debit to Accumulated Depreciation is the difference between the cost of the asset and the cash received. Gains and losses due solely to normal variations in asset lives are not recognized.

In instances when assets in a group are continued in use after their cost has been assigned to operations, no further depreciation charges are recognized. On the other hand, when all the assets in a group are retired before their costs have been assigned to

FASB CODIFICATION

The Issue: You are interviewing for a job with a mid-size accounting firm. Just before lunch you had a fairly unpleasant interview with a person who has been with the firm for six years. He decided to test your knowledge of depreciation methods, so he asked you to list all of the depreciation methods you know. When you mentioned "group depreciation," he stopped you and challenged you to name one industry that uses group depreciation. He said that in his long experience in the "real world," he has never seen a company using group depreciation. You can hear this person down the hall boasting to his colleagues about how he "stumped" the job applicant with a simple question about depreciation.

You feel that your credibility is at stake. You have just 30 minutes until your afternoon set of interviews begins.

The Question: According to the authoritative accounting literature, what industry uses group depreciation?

Searching the Codification: You have found that with respect to questions about accounting standards and practices, your best online friend is the FASB's Codification. You know that depreciation expense relates to property, plant, and equipment, which is discussed in Topic 360 of the Codification. You also know that depreciation expense is an issue of "subsequent measurement," which is found in Section 35 of whatever subtopic it is under. So, start with Topic 360 and start looking for some descriptions of depreciation standards in specific industries.

The Answer: The use of group depreciation in a specific industry is described on page 11–42.

operations, a special charge related to such retirement would be recognized, either as a loss or as an addition to depreciation expense.

Depreciation and *IAS 16*

Some items of property, plant, and equipment are composed of identifiable subitems. A perfect example is a building which has a roof, a heating/cooling system, windows, a general supporting structure, and so forth. Those subitems almost certainly do not depreciate over the same life. However, standard U.S. practice has been to treat the building as one composite asset depreciated as a group. An alternate approach is to depreciate each subitem, or component, separately. This component approach was mentioned briefly in Chapter 10. Mandatory use of the component approach was proposed by the AICPA in 2001 but rejected by the FASB in 2004; under current U.S. GAAP companies are allowed, but not required, to use the component approach.

In contrast, the component approach is required under IASB standards. The following requirement is contained in *IAS 16:*

> Each part of an item of property, plant and equipment with a cost that is significant in relation to the total cost of the item shall be depreciated separately.[5]

[5] *International Accounting Standard 16*, "Property, Plant and Equipment" (London: International Accounting Standards Board, December 9, 2004), par. 43.

Conceptually, the component approach presents no great difficulty because it merely requires that the standard depreciation calculations be applied separately to each significant component of a larger asset, such as a building. In practice, there is a slight increase in bookkeeping effort to keep track of the separate components.

Depreciation and Accretion of an Asset Retirement Obligation

As discussed in Chapter 10, the act of acquiring a long-term operating asset sometimes legally obligates a company to incur restoration costs in the future when the asset is retired. The fair value of this obligation is estimated when the asset is acquired; the fair value of the obligation is recognized as a liability and is added to the cost of the acquired asset. To continue the example introduced in Chapter 10, assume that Bryan Beach Company purchases and erects an oil platform at a total cost of $750,000. The oil platform will be in use for 10 years, at which time Bryan Beach is legally obligated to ensure that the platform is dismantled and removed from the site. Bryan Beach estimates that it will have to pay $100,000 to have the platform dismantled and removed from the site in 10 years. If the appropriate interest rate to use in computing the present value of the restoration obligation is 8%, the present value of the $100,000 obligation is computed as follows:

$$FV = \$100{,}000;\ I = 8\%;\ N = 10 \text{ years} \rightarrow \$46{,}319$$

The journal entries to record the purchase of the oil platform and the recognition of the asset retirement obligation are as follows:

Oil Platform	750,000	
Cash		750,000
Oil Platform	46,319	
Asset Retirement Obligation		46,319

The cost of the oil platform asset, including the estimated retirement obligation, is depreciated just like any other long-term asset. If straight-line depreciation is used and a zero residual value is assumed, the depreciation entry each year is as follows:

Depreciation Expense [($750,000 + $46,319)/10]	79,632	
Accumulated Depreciation—Oil Platform		79,632

In addition to this entry, each year an entry must be made to recognize the increase in the present value of the asset retirement obligation as the time until the obligation must be satisfied grows closer. This increase is similar to interest expense, but the FASB ruled that it should not be classified as interest expense.[6] Instead, the expense is called *accretion expense* and is recognized through the following journal entry:

Accretion Expense ($46,319 × 0.08)	3,706	
Asset Retirement Obligation		3,706

[6] FASB ASC paragraph 410-20-35-5.

Depletion of Natural Resources

2 Apply the productive-output method to the depletion of natural resources.

WHY **The cost associated with the use of a natural resource should be reported as an expense in the period in which the resource is used. As with depreciation, accountants estimate this cost by using a systematic method to allocate the recorded cost of these assets to expense over the life of the asset.**

HOW **Depletion expense (the term used to represent the using up of a natural resource) is computed by estimating the amount of natural resource consumed during the period in relation to the amount of natural resource that existed as of the beginning of the period. This proportion of the cost of the resource (as of the beginning of the period) is expensed.**

Natural resources, also called *wasting assets*, are consumed as the physical units representing these resources are removed and sold. The withdrawal of oil or gas, the cutting of timber, and the mining of coal, sulfur, iron, copper, or silver ore are examples of processes leading to the exhaustion of natural resources. Depletion expense is a charge for the "using up" of the resources.

The computation of depletion expense is an adaptation of the productive-output method of depreciation. Perhaps the most difficult problem in computing depletion expense is estimating the amount of resources available for economical removal from the land. Generally, a geologist, mining engineer, or other expert is called upon to make the estimate, and it is subject to continual revision as the resource is extracted or removed.

Developmental costs, such as costs of drilling, sinking mine shafts, and constructing roads, should be capitalized and added to the original cost of the property in arriving at the total cost subject to depletion. These costs are often incurred before normal activities begin.

To illustrate the computation of depletion expense, assume the following facts: Land containing mineral deposits is purchased at a cost of $5,500,000. After all of the mineral deposits have been extracted, it is expected that the land will have a residual value of $250,000. The natural resource supply is estimated at 1,000,000 tons. The unit-depletion charge and the total depletion charge for the first year, assuming the withdrawal of 80,000 tons, are calculated as follows:

Depletion charge per ton: ($5,500,000 − $250,000) ÷ 1,000,000 = $5.25

Depletion charge for the first year: 80,000 tons × $5.25 = $420,000

The following entries should be made to record these events:

Mineral Deposits	5,500,000	
Cash		5,500,000
Depletion Expense	420,000	
Accumulated Depletion (or Mineral Deposits)		420,000

If the 80,000 tons are sold in the current year, the entire $420,000 would be included as part of the cost of goods sold. If only 60,000 tons are sold, $105,000 is reported as part of ending inventory on the balance sheet.

When buildings and improvements are constructed in connection with the removal of natural resources and their usefulness is limited to the duration of the project, it is reasonable to recognize depreciation on such properties on an output basis consistent with the charges to be recognized for the natural resources themselves. For example, assume that buildings are constructed at a cost of $250,000; the useful lives of the buildings are expected to terminate upon exhaustion of the natural resource consisting of 1,000,000 units. Under these circumstances, a depreciation charge of $0.25 ($250,000/1,000,000) should accompany the depletion charge recognized for each unit. When improvements provide benefits expected to terminate prior to the exhaustion of the natural resource, the cost of such improvements should be allocated on the basis of the units to be removed during the life of the improvements or on a time basis, whichever is considered more appropriate.

Changes in Estimates of Cost Allocation Variables

3 Incorporate changes in estimates and methods into the computation of depreciation for current and future periods.

WHY Depreciation expense involves making estimates relating to pattern of use, estimated useful life, and salvage value. Almost inevitably, actual experience will indicate that one or more of these estimates is incorrect. This does NOT suggest a past error that must be fixed, but it does suggest the need for a revised depreciation estimate for the current and future periods to reflect the updated information.

HOW Changes in estimated salvage value or useful life and changes in depreciation method are reflected in the computation of depreciation expense for the current and future periods. The undepreciated book value is allocated over the remaining life based on the revised estimates or method.

The allocation of asset costs benefiting more than one period cannot be precisely determined at acquisition because so many of the variables must be estimated. Only one factor in determining the periodic charge for depreciation, amortization, or depletion is based on historical information: asset cost. Other factors—residual value, useful life or output, and the pattern of use or benefit—must be estimated. The question frequently facing accountants is how adjustments to these estimates, which arise as time passes, should be reflected in the accounts. A change in estimate is reported in the current and future periods rather than as an adjustment of prior periods. This type of adjustment is made for residual value and useful-life changes. A change in depreciation method (e.g., from double-declining-balance to straight-line) based on a revised expected pattern of use is also reported in the current and future periods rather than as an adjustment of prior periods.[7]

Change in Estimated Life

To illustrate the procedure for a change in estimated life affecting allocation of asset cost, assume that a company purchased $50,000 of equipment and estimated a 10-year life. Using the straight-line method with no residual value, the annual depreciation would be $5,000. After four years, accumulated depreciation would amount to $20,000, and the remaining undepreciated book value would be $30,000. Early in the fifth year, a reevaluation of the life indicates only four more years of service can be expected from the asset. An adjustment must therefore be made for the fifth and subsequent years to reflect the change. A new annual depreciation charge is calculated by dividing the remaining book

[7] FASB ASC paragraph 250-10-45-19.

value by the remaining life of four years. This would result in an annual charge of $7,500 for the fifth through eighth years ($30,000/4 = $7,500).

Year	Computation		Depreciation Amount	Accumulated Depreciation
1	$50,000/10	=	$ 5,000	$ 5,000
2	$50,000/10	=	5,000	10,000
3	$50,000/10	=	5,000	15,000
4	$50,000/10	=	5,000	20,000
5	($50,000 – $20,000)/4	=	7,500	27,500
6	($50,000 – $20,000)/4	=	7,500	35,000
7	($50,000 – $20,000)/4	=	7,500	42,500
8	($50,000 – $20,000)/4	=	7,500	50,000
			$50,000	

Note that no attempt is made to go back and "fix" the first four years. The $5,000 depreciation charge recognized in those years was computed using the best information available. When revised information becomes available in the fifth year, the impact is reflected in the current and future periods.

Change in Estimated Units of Production

Another change in estimate occurs in accounting for natural resources when the estimate of the recoverable units changes as a result of further discoveries, improved extraction processes, or changes in sales prices that indicate changes in the number of units that can be extracted profitably. A revised depletion rate is established by dividing the remaining resource cost balance by the estimated remaining recoverable units.

To illustrate, assume the facts used in the earlier depletion example. Land is purchased at a cost of $5,500,000 with estimated net residual value of $250,000. The original estimated supply of natural resources in the land is 1,000,000 tons. As indicated previously, the depletion rate under these conditions would be $5.25 per ton, and the depletion charge for the first year when 80,000 tons were mined would be $420,000. Assume that in the second year of operation, 100,000 tons of ore are withdrawn, but before the books are closed at the end of the second year, appraisal of the expected recoverable tons indicates a remaining tonnage of 950,000. The new depletion rate and the depletion charge for the second year would be computed as follows:

Cost assignable to recoverable tons as of the beginning of the second year:	
Original costs applicable to depletable resources	$5,250,000
Deduct: Depletion charge for the first year	420,000
Balance of cost subject to depletion	$4,830,000
Estimated recoverable tons as of the beginning of the second year:	
Number of tons withdrawn in the second year	100,000
Estimated recoverable tons as of the end of the second year	950,000
Total recoverable tons as of the beginning of the second year	1,050,000

Depletion charge per ton for the second year: $4,830,000/1,050,000 = $4.60

Depletion charge for the second year: 100,000 × $4.60 = $460,000

Sometimes an increase in estimated recoverable units arises from additional expenditures for capital developments. When this occurs, the additional costs should be added to the remaining recoverable cost and divided by the number of tons remaining to be extracted. To illustrate this situation, assume in the preceding example that $525,000 of additional costs had been incurred at the beginning of the second year. The preceding computation of depletion rate and depletion expense would be changed as follows:

Cost assignable to recoverable tons as of the beginning of the second year:	
Original costs applicable to depletable resources	$5,250,000
Add: Additional costs incurred in the second year	525,000
	$5,775,000
Deduct: Depletion charge for the first year	420,000
Balance of cost subject to depletion	$5,355,000
Estimated recoverable tons as of the beginning of the second year (as stated previously)	1,050,000
Depletion charge per ton for the second year: $5,355,000/1,050,000 = $5.10	
Depletion charge for the second year: 100,000 × $5.10 = $510,000	

Accounting is made up of many estimates. The procedures outlined in this section are designed to prevent the continual restating of reported income from prior years. Adjustments to prior-period income figures are made only if actual errors have occurred, not when reasonable estimates have been made that later prove inaccurate.

Change in Depreciation Method

Another change in estimate occurs when the actual pattern of consumption of an asset doesn't match the pattern of consumption implicit in the depreciation method used. For example, an asset for which straight-line depreciation has been used might be observed to be wearing out in an accelerated fashion. Accordingly, a change in depreciation method is indicated.

To illustrate, assume that an asset is purchased for $120,000 with a 12-year expected useful life and zero expected salvage value. Straight-line depreciation is used with the asset resulting in annual depreciation expense of $10,000 [($120,000 − $0)/12 years]. After two years of use, the asset has a remaining book value of $100,000 ($120,000 − $10,000 depreciation for Year 1 − $10,000 depreciation for Year 2) and a remaining useful life of 10 years. Observation of the pattern of consumption of this asset for these two years indicates that the double-declining-balance method of depreciation would yield a better estimate of periodic depreciation. This change in estimate related to the pattern of asset consumption is reflected in the year in which the change is implemented (Year 3 in this example) and the subsequent years. Depreciation expense for Year 3 is computed as follows:

- Straight-line rate = 100%/Remaining life = 100%/10 years = 10%
- Double the straight-line rate = 10% × 2 = 20%
- Remaining book value = $100,000 (computation shown above)
- Year 3 depreciation expense = $100,000 × 0.20 = $20,000

When a change in estimate impacting the computation of depreciation expense is made, the current-year impact of the change on net income must be disclosed in the notes to the financial statements. When the change is implemented through a change in depreciation method, the note disclosure must also include an explanation of the change. Further discussion of accounting changes is contained in Chapter 20.

Impairment of Tangible Assets

4 **Identify whether an asset is impaired, and measure the amount of the impairment loss using both U.S. GAAP and IASB standards.**

WHY **To avoid misleading financial statement users with overly optimistic data, noncurrent operating assets should not be reported in the balance sheet at an amount substantially in excess of their current value. Under U.S. GAAP, noncurrent operating assets are reviewed for possible substantial declines in value (called impairment) whenever there is a significant change in operations or in the way an asset is used.**

HOW **An asset is impaired when the undiscounted sum of future cash flows from the asset is less than the reported book value. An impaired asset is written down to its fair value.**

Events sometimes occur after the purchase of an asset and before the end of its estimated life that impair its value and require an immediate write-down of the asset rather than making a normal allocation of cost over a period of time. Until 1995, the authoritative accounting literature did not include a clear statement of accounting standards governing the recognition of asset impairment.

As an example, in 1994, **Eli Lilly**, a large pharmaceutical company, paid $4.1 billion to acquire **PCS Health Systems**, a company that helps insurance companies and HMOs manage their prescription drug benefit plans. By the second quarter of 1997, it had become apparent that the PCS acquisition was not turning out as planned. The movement toward managed health care had not been as fast as Lilly had expected, and the ominous possibility of increased government regulation of prescription drug benefit plans had tempered enthusiasm about PCS's prospects. In reviewing the acquisition, Eli Lilly decided that it should recognize a loss and reduce the recorded value of PCS's assets by $2.4 billion.

As illustrated by the Eli Lilly/PCS Health Systems case, whether to recognize the impairment of operating assets is not a simple decision. In addition, once the decision to recognize the impairment has been made, one is still faced with the question of the amount of the write-down. This section discusses the concepts and procedures associated with the recognition of an asset impairment.

FYI

In a final act of surrender, Eli Lilly sold its PCS division to Rite Aid on January 22, 1999, for just $1.6 billion.

Accounting for Asset Impairment

Guidance on the accounting for asset impairment addresses the following four questions:[8]

1. When should an asset be reviewed for possible impairment?
2. When is an asset impaired?
3. How should an impairment loss be measured?
4. What information should be disclosed about an impairment?

[8] FASB ASC Subtopic 360-10 (Property, Plant, and Equipment—Overall), various subsections on "Impairment."

1. When Should an Asset Be Reviewed for Possible Impairment? Conducting an impairment review of every asset at the end of every year would be unlikely to provide sufficiently improved financial information to justify the cost of the reviews. Instead, companies are required to conduct impairment tests whenever there has been a material change in the way an asset is used or in the business environment. In addition, if management obtains information suggesting that the market value of an asset has declined, an impairment review should be conducted.

2. When Is an Asset Impaired? According to the FASB, an entity should recognize an impairment loss only when the undiscounted sum of estimated future cash flows from an asset is less than the book value of the asset. As illustrated in the following example, this is rather a strange impairment threshold; a more intuitive test would be to compare the book value to the fair value of the asset. Because the undiscounted cash flows do not incorporate the time value of money, the sum of undiscounted future cash flows will always be greater than the fair value of the asset.

3. How Should an Impairment Loss Be Measured? The impairment loss is the difference between the book value of the asset and the fair value. The fair value can be approximated using the present value of estimated future cash flows from the asset.

4. What Information Should Be Disclosed about an Impairment? Disclosure should include a description of the impaired asset, reasons for the impairment, a description of the measurement assumptions, and the business segment or segments affected. An impairment loss should be included as part of income from continuing operations, and note disclosure of the amount should be made if the impairment loss is not shown as a separate income statement item.

> **! CAUTION**
>
> The existence of an impairment loss is determined using undiscounted future cash flows. The amount of the impairment loss is measured using fair value, or *discounted,* future cash flows.

Application of the impairment rules is illustrated with the following example. Guangzhou Company purchased a building five years ago for $600,000. The building has been depreciated using the straight-line method with a 20-year useful life and no residual value. Several other buildings in the immediate area have recently been abandoned, and Guangzhou has decided that the building should be evaluated for possible impairment. Guangzhou estimates that the building has a remaining useful life of 15 years, that net cash inflow from the building will be $25,000 per year, and that the fair value of the building is $230,000.

Annual depreciation for the building has been $30,000 ($600,000/20 years). The current book value of the building is computed as follows:

Original cost	$600,000
Accumulated depreciation ($30,000 × 5 years)	150,000
Book value	$450,000

The book value of $450,000 is compared to the $375,000 ($25,000 × 15 years) undiscounted sum of future cash flows to determine whether the building is impaired. The sum of future cash flows is less, so an impairment loss should be recognized. The loss is equal to the $220,000 ($450,000 − $230,000) difference between the book value of the building and its fair value. The impairment loss would be recorded as on page 11-23.

Accumulated Depreciation—Building	150,000	
Loss on Impairment of Building	220,000	
Building ($600,000 − $230,000)		370,000

The new recorded value of $230,000 ($600,000 − $370,000) is considered to be the cost of the asset. After an impairment loss is recognized, no restoration of the loss is allowed even if the fair value of the asset recovers.

The odd nature of the undiscounted cash flow threshold can be seen if the facts in the Guangzhou example are changed slightly. Assume that net cash inflow from the building will be $35,000 per year and that the fair value of the building is $330,000. With these numbers, no impairment loss is recognized, even though the fair value of $330,000 is less than the book value of $450,000 because the undiscounted sum of future cash flows of $525,000 ($35,000 × 15 years) exceeds the book value.

In many cases, it is more appropriate to estimate a range of possible future cash flows rather than to make a specific point estimate. In the preceding example, assume that instead of estimating future cash flows of $25,000 per year, it is estimated that the following two cash flow scenarios are possible, with the indicated probabilities:

STOP&THINK

Which ONE of the following statements best describes the effect of the undiscounted cash flow threshold used in the impairment test?

a) Use of the undiscounted cash flow threshold means that an asset must suffer a significant drop in fair value before an impairment loss is recognized.
b) Use of the undiscounted cash flow threshold means that any drop in fair value, no matter how small, will result in the recognition of an impairment loss.
c) Use of the undiscounted cash flow threshold means that impairment losses will occasionally be recognized even when assets have increased in value.
d) Use of the undiscounted cash flow threshold means that it is unlikely that any company will ever recognize an impairment loss.

	Future Cash Inflows	Probability
Scenario 1	$20,000 per year for 15 years	85%
Scenario 2	50,000 per year for 15 years	15%

In applying the impairment test, the weighted-average undiscounted cash flows are computed as follows:

	Undiscounted Future Cash Inflows	Probability	Probability-Weighted Future Cash Flows
Scenario 1	$20,000 × 15 years = $300,000	85%	$255,000
Scenario 2	50,000 × 15 years = 750,000	15%	112,500
Total			$367,500

The $367,500 probability-weighted sum of undiscounted future cash flows is compared to the $450,000 book value of the building, indicating that the asset is impaired ($367,500 < $450,000). Assume that in this case there is no observable market value of the building and that the market value must be estimated using present value techniques. If the risk-free interest rate is 6.0%, the expected present value is computed as shown on page 11-24.

	Future Cash Inflows	Present Value (6.0% discount rate)	Probability	Probability-Weighted Present Value
Scenario 1	$20,000 × 15 years	$194,245	85%	$165,108
Scenario 2	50,000 × 15 years	485,612	15%	72,842
Estimated fair value				$237,950

The impairment loss would be recorded as follows:

Accumulated Depreciation—Building	150,000	
Loss on Impairment of Building ($450,000 − $237,950)	212,050	
Building ($600,000 − $237,950)		362,050

International Accounting for Asset Impairment: *IAS 36*

The IASB's standard for impairment is *IAS 36*, "Impairment of Assets." This international standard is, from a conceptual standpoint, superior to the impairment standard embodied in U.S. GAAP. The IASB standard requires that a company recognize an impairment loss whenever the "recoverable amount" of an asset is less than its book value. *Recoverable amount* is defined as the higher of the selling price of the asset or the discounted future cash flows associated with the asset's use. Both of these measures are based on the discounted value of the future cash flows from the asset, which means that the IASB has completely rejected the conceptually unappealing undiscounted cash flow threshold adopted by the FASB.

IAS 36 also differs from U.S. GAAP in that the international standard allows for the reversal of an impairment loss if events in subsequent years suggest the asset is no longer impaired. Therefore, if an asset has increased in value and is no longer deemed to be impaired, the portion of the impairment loss that has been recovered should be reversed and recognized as a gain. Under the FASB standard, no subsequent recovery of an impairment loss is allowed.

Accounting for Upward Asset Revaluations: *IAS 16*

As mentioned in Chapter 10, an allowable alternative under *IAS 16* is to recognize increases in the value of long-term operating assets. Because the accounting procedures associated with asset revaluation are similar to those used to recognize an asset impairment, they are illustrated in this section.

Recognizing an Upward Asset Revaluation Earlier, we used an example of a building purchased by Guangzhou Company to illustrate the accounting for an asset impairment. Recall that after five years, the book value of that building was as follows:

Original cost	$600,000
Accumulated depreciation ($30,000 × 5 years)	150,000
Book value	$450,000

Now assume that Guangzhou Company uses international accounting standards, the building's fair value is $540,000, and Guangzhou employs the allowable alternative under international standards, electing to recognize this increase in asset value. The journal entry to recognize the asset revaluation is as follows:

Accumulated Depreciation—Building	150,000	
Revaluation Equity Reserve		90,000
Building ($600,000 − $540,000)		60,000

After the entry is posted, the balance in the accumulated depreciation account is $0, and the balance in the building account is $540,000 ($600,000 − $60,000), resulting in a net recorded amount of $540,000. As discussed in Chapter 13, the revaluation equity reserve is a separate category of equity and reflects the increase in the reported value of the total assets of the company stemming from increases in the market value of long-term operating assets. After the revaluation, annual depreciation expense is computed based on the revalued amount; the revalued amount is depreciated over the remaining estimated life of the asset.

! CAUTION

Remember that the upward revaluation of long-term operating assets is an allowable alternative under international accounting standards but is *not* allowable under U.S. GAAP.

Recording the Disposal of a Revalued Asset An interesting twist in the provisions of *IAS 16* makes it somewhat costly for a company to revalue its assets upward. To illustrate, assume that, immediately after revaluing its building to $540,000, Guangzhou Company sells the building for $540,000 in cash. This disposal would be recorded as follows:

Cash	540,000	
Building		540,000
Revaluation Equity Reserve	90,000	
Retained Earnings		90,000

Note that because Guangzhou chose to revalue the asset, the $90,000 "gain" from the increase in the value of the asset is never reported as a gain in Guangzhou's income statement. The "gain" is initially reflected as an increase in the equity reserve; on disposal, the "gain" is transferred directly to Retained Earnings, bypassing the income statement completely. Thus, although *IAS 16* gives companies the benefit of recognizing increases in the value of long-term operating assets, the provisions of *IAS 16* also impose a cost in the sense that these increases are then never reflected as increases in earnings in the income statement.

Amortization and Impairment of Intangibles

5 **Discuss the issues impacting proper recognition of amortization or impairment for intangible assets.**

WHY **Because intangible assets do not necessarily wear out as do physical assets, their periodic amortization and tests for impairment must be handled more delicately than the corresponding tests for tangible assets. In particular, careful consideration must be given to whether an intangible asset has a finite or an infinite life.**

HOW **An intangible asset with a finite life is amortized over its estimated useful life, usually with zero residual value and using the straight-line method. These intangibles are tested for impairment using the standard 2-step impairment test. An intangible asset with an indefinite life is not amortized. These intangibles are tested for impairment simply by comparing their carrying value to their estimated fair value. Goodwill is tested for impairment using a special fair value test tied to the reporting unit to which the goodwill is assigned.**

For accounting purposes, recorded intangible assets come in three varieties:

- *Intangible assets that are amortized.* The impairment test for these intangibles is the same as the 2-step test described earlier in the chapter for tangible long-term operating assets.
- *Intangible assets that are not amortized.* The impairment test for these intangibles involves a simple 1-step comparison of the book value to the fair value.
- *Goodwill, which according to FASB ASC Topic 350 (Intangibles—Goodwill and Other) is not amortized.* The goodwill impairment test is a process that first involves estimating the fair value of the entire reporting unit to which the goodwill is allocated.

In accounting for an intangible asset after its acquisition, a determination first must be made as to whether the intangible asset has a finite life. If no economic, legal, or contractual factors cause the intangible to have a finite life, then its life is said to be indefinite, and the asset is not to be amortized until its life is determined to be finite. An indefinite life is one that extends beyond the foreseeable horizon.[9] An example of an intangible asset that has an indefinite life is a broadcast license that includes an extension option that can be renewed indefinitely. If an intangible asset is determined to have a finite life, the asset is to be amortized over its estimated life; the useful life estimate should be reviewed periodically.[10]

Amortization and Impairment of Intangible Assets Subject to Amortization

The very nature of intangible assets makes estimating their useful lives a difficult problem. The useful life of an intangible asset may be affected by a variety of economic, legal, regulatory, and contractual factors. These factors, including options for renewal or extension, should be evaluated in determining the appropriate period over which the cost of the intangible asset should be allocated. A patent, for example, has a legal life of 20 years from the date of application in the United States; but if the competitive advantages afforded by the patent are expected to terminate after five years, the patent cost should be amortized over the shorter period.

Intangible assets are to be amortized by the straight-line method unless there is strong justification for using another method. Amortization, like depreciation, may be charged as an operating expense of the period or allocated to production overhead if the asset is related directly to the manufacture of goods. Because companies must disclose both the original cost and the accumulated amortization for amortizable intangibles, the credit entry should be made to a separate accumulated amortization account.

To illustrate the accounting for amortizable intangibles, consider the following example. Ethereal Company markets products to real-estate agents and to new homeowners. Ethereal purchased a customer list for $30,000 on January 1, 2013. Because of turnover among real-estate agents and because new homeowners gradually become established homeowners, the list is expected to have economic value for only four years. As with all amortizable intangibles, the presumption is that the residual value of the customer list is zero; in this case there is no evidence to rebut this presumption. Similarly,

[9] FASB ASC paragraph 350-30-35-4.

[10] Before the adoption of pre-Codification *SFAS No. 142* in 2001 (which is the basis for FASB ASC Topic 350), intangible assets were amortizable over a maximum period of 40 years. The FASB considered imposing a maximum amortization period of 20 years on intangibles. However, the final standard does not include any arbitrary cap on the useful life of amortizable intangible assets.

there is no evidence to justify the use of any amortization method other than straight line. On December 31, 2013, the following journal entry is made to recognize amortization expense:

Amortization Expense ($30,000/4 years)	7,500	
Accumulated Amortization—Customer List		7,500

During 2014, before amortization expense for the year is recognized, the customer list intangible asset is tested for impairment. The impairment test is the same as that explained previously for tangible long-term operating assets. The impairment test for the real-estate customer list was prompted by a substantial downturn in the real-estate market in the area. At the time of the impairment test, the book value of the intangible asset is $22,500 ($30,000 − $7,500). It is estimated that the customer list will generate future cash flows of $5,000 per year for the next three years and that the fair value of the customer list on December 31, 2014, is $12,000. The customer list intangible asset is impaired because the $15,000 ($5,000 × 3 years) sum of the future undiscounted cash flows is less than the book value of $22,500. The amount of the impairment loss is the $10,500 ($22,500 − $12,000) difference between the book value and the fair value and is recorded as follows:

Impairment Loss ($22,500 − $12,000)	10,500	
Accumulated Amortization—Customer List	7,500	
Customer List ($30,000 − $12,000)		18,000

The $12,000 fair value is the new basis for the intangible asset; no entry is made to recognize any subsequent recovery in the value of the intangible. Amortization in subsequent years will be based on the new book value of $12,000 and the estimated remaining useful life of three years. In the notes to the financial statements for 2014, Ethereal Company would be required to disclose the amount of amortization expense it expects to recognize for all of its intangibles in each year for the next five years.

Impairment of Intangible Assets Not Subject to Amortization

Some intangibles are identified as having indefinite lives and are not amortized. The FASB described the following examples of intangibles with indefinite lives:

- *Broadcast license.* Broadcast licenses often have a renewal period of 10 years. Renewal is virtually automatic if the license holder maintains an acceptable level of service to the public. Accordingly, there is no foreseeable end to the useful life of the broadcast license; it has an indefinite life.
- *Trademark.* A trademark right is granted for a limited time, but trademarks can be renewed almost routinely. If economic factors suggest that the trademark will continue to have value in the foreseeable future, then its useful life is indefinite.[11]

Intangibles with indefinite lives are not amortized. However, an intangible with an indefinite life is evaluated at least annually to determine (1) whether the end of the useful life is now foreseeable and amortization should begin and/or (2) whether the intangible is impaired. The impairment test is a very simple one: The fair value of the intangible is compared to its book value, and if the fair value is less than the book value, an impairment loss is recognized for the difference.

[11] FASB ASC paragraphs 350-30-55-11 through 13 and 20 through 22.

STOP&THINK

Why wouldn't the regular 2-step impairment test (using the undiscounted sum of future cash flows) work for intangible assets that are not amortized?

a) The undiscounted sum of future cash flows is zero.
b) The undiscounted sum of future cash flows is always equal to the book value of the intangible asset, by definition.
c) The undiscounted sum of future cash flows is infinite.
d) The undiscounted sum of future cash flows is always less than the fair value of the asset.

To illustrate, assume that Impalpable Company has a broadcast license that has no foreseeable end to its useful life. The broadcast license is recorded at its original acquisition cost of $60,000. In the past, it was estimated that the broadcast license would generate cash flows of $7,000 per year. Recent changes in the broadcast environment have reduced the cash flows expected to be generated by the license. The data gathered by Impalpable Company suggest that, although the useful life of the license is still indefinite, the possible future cash flows will be reduced to either $2,000 per year (with 70% probability) or to $4,000 per year (with 30% probability). The risk-free interest rate to be used in the probability-weighted present value calculation is 5%. The estimate of the fair value of the intangible is computed as follows:

	Future Cash Inflows	Present Value* of Indefinite Annual Cash Flows	Probability	Probability-Weighted Present Value
Scenario 1	$2,000 per year	$40,000	70%	$28,000
Scenario 2	$4,000 per year	80,000	30%	24,000
Total estimated fair value				$52,000

*The present value of a stream of indefinite, or infinite, annual cash flows is simply (Annual cash flow/Discount rate).

Because the estimated fair value of the broadcast license is less than its book value ($52,000 < $60,000), the intangible asset is impaired. The impairment loss is recognized with the following journal entry:

Impairment Loss ($60,000 − $52,000)	8,000	
Broadcast License		8,000

As with the recognition of other impairment losses, the $52,000 fair value is the new basis for the intangible asset; no entry is made to recognize any subsequent recovery in the value of the intangible.

Impairment of Goodwill

When goodwill is recognized in conjunction with the acquisition of a business, that goodwill is assigned to an existing "reporting unit" of that business. For example, if **Disney** were to acquire another TV network in addition to its existing ABC network, any goodwill associated with the acquisition would be assigned to Disney's Media Networks segment. If necessary, goodwill created in an acquisition can be split up and assigned to several different existing operating segments.

As discussed in Chapter 10, for accounting purposes goodwill is computed as the residual amount left over after the purchase price of a business has been allocated to all of the identifiable tangible and intangible assets. This residual nature of goodwill is the key to testing whether goodwill is impaired after its acquisition. Clearly, by definition goodwill cannot be valued by itself but is instead the remaining value not explained by the fair values of all of the identifiable assets. The procedures in testing goodwill for impairment stem from this idea and are outlined as follows:

Procedures in Testing Goodwill for Impairment

1. Compute the fair value of each reporting unit to which goodwill has been assigned. This can be done by using the present value of expected future cash flows or earnings or revenue multiples.
2. If the fair value of the reporting unit exceeds the net book value of the assets (including goodwill) and liabilities of the reporting unit, the goodwill is assumed to *not* be impaired and no impairment loss is recognized.
3. If the fair value of the reporting unit is less than the net book value of the assets and liabilities of the reporting unit, then a new fair value of goodwill is computed. The value of goodwill cannot be measured directly. Instead, goodwill value is always a residual amount; it is the amount of fair value of a reporting unit that is left over after the values of all identifiable assets and liabilities of the reporting unit have been considered. Accordingly, the fair values of all assets and liabilities of the reporting unit are estimated, these amounts are compared to the overall fair value of the reporting unit, and the implied amount of goodwill is computed.
4. If the implied amount of goodwill computed in (3) is less than the amount initially recorded, a goodwill impairment loss is recognized for the difference.

To illustrate the goodwill impairment test, assume that Buyer Company acquired Target Company on January 1, 2013. As part of the acquisition, $1,000 in goodwill was recognized; this goodwill was assigned to Buyer's Manufacturing reporting unit. For 2013, earnings from the Manufacturing reporting unit were $350. Separately traded companies with operations similar to the Manufacturing reporting unit have market values approximately equal to six times earnings (i.e., their price-earnings ratios are 6.0). As of December 31, 2013, book and fair values of assets and liabilities of the Manufacturing reporting unit are as follows:

	Book Values	Fair Values
Identifiable assets	$3,500	$4,000
Goodwill	1,000	?
Liabilities	2,000	2,000

Procedure 1 Using the earnings multiple, the fair value of the Manufacturing reporting unit is estimated to be $2,100 ($350 × 6). This fair value estimation could also be done using cash flow estimates and present value techniques.

Procedure 2 The net book value of the assets and liabilities of the Manufacturing reporting unit is computed as follows:

Assets ($3,500 + $1,000) − Liabilities ($2,000) = $2,500

Because the estimated fair value of the reporting unit ($2,100) is less than the net book value of the reporting unit ($2,500), further computations are needed to determine the amount of a goodwill impairment loss, if any.

STOP&THINK

It has been suggested that the goodwill impairment test is a costly one to apply in practice. Which one of the four procedures of the goodwill impairment test do you think is the most costly to perform?

a) Compute the fair value of each reporting unit to which goodwill has been assigned.
b) Compare the fair value of the reporting unit to the net book value of the assets (including goodwill) and liabilities of the reporting unit.
c) Estimate the fair value of all assets and liabilities of the reporting unit and use these amounts to compute the implied amount of goodwill.
d) Compare the newly computed estimate of goodwill to the recorded amount of goodwill.

FYI

During 2002, **Time Warner** (formerly known as AOL Time Warner) recognized goodwill impairment losses totaling $98.884 billion. The goodwill initially arose as part of the ill-fated acquisition of Time Warner by AOL.

Procedure 3 Using the $2,100 estimated fair value of the Manufacturing reporting unit, along with the estimated fair values of the identifiable assets and liabilities, the implied fair value of goodwill is computed as follows:

Estimated fair value of Manufacturing reporting unit	$2,100
Fair value of identifiable assets – fair value of liabilities ($4,000 – $2,000) . .	2,000
Implied fair value of goodwill	$ 100

Procedure 4 The implied fair value of goodwill is less than the recorded amount of goodwill ($100 < $1,000). Accordingly, the goodwill is impaired. The journal entry necessary to recognize the goodwill impairment loss is as follows:

Goodwill Impairment Loss	900	
Goodwill ($1,000 – $100)		900

The total amount of goodwill impairment losses should be reported as a separate line item in the income statement.

ifrs

International Accounting for Intangible Impairment: *IAS 36*

As explained in the preceding section, U.S. GAAP contains three different impairment tests for intangible assets—one for intangibles with finite lives, a different one for intangible assets with indefinite lives, and a third test for goodwill. Well, the good news with respect to international financial reporting standards is that there is basically just one impairment test for intangibles, explained in *IAS 36*, and this is the same impairment test used with tangible assets: the recorded amount of the intangible asset is compared to its "recoverable amount." As explained earlier, the recoverable amount is the higher of the fair value of the intangible (less the cost to sell the intangible) and the value of the intangible in use.[12] If the recoverable amount is less than the recorded amount, the intangible is impaired, and an impairment loss is recognized. When testing goodwill for impairment, the test is applied to the business unit to which the goodwill has been assigned. Goodwill is impaired if the recoverable amount of the entire business unit is less than the recorded amount of the net assets of the unit (including goodwill); this test is similar to the goodwill impairment test under U.S. GAAP.

[12] The difference between "fair value" and "value in use" is that "fair value" is a market-based quantity reflecting what market participants outside a company would pay to buy the intangible. In contrast, "value in use" is a company-specific quantity based on the present value of the discounted cash flows expected to be generated by the intangible given how the company plans to use that intangible internally. "Value in use" is usually greater than "fair value" because if the internal value of an asset is less than its value in the external market, the company would likely have already sold the asset.

Asset Retirements

6 **Account for the sale of depreciable assets in exchange for cash and in exchange for other depreciable assets.**

WHY **Depreciation expense is not expected to perfectly reflect declines in an asset's market value. A gain or loss on disposal (or exchange) reflects the difference between an asset's book value and its fair value on the date it is sold or exchanged.**

HOW **When a noncurrent operating asset is disposed or exchanged, it is removed from the books and replaced with the assets received in exchange, which are recorded at their fair values. If the fair value of the assets received exceeds the book value of the assets given, then a gain is recognized; if the reverse is true, a loss is recognized. In some special cases, assets received are recorded at the BOOK value of the assets given in exchange.**

Assets may be retired by sale, exchange, or abandonment. Generally, when an asset is disposed of, any unrecorded depreciation or amortization for the period is recorded at the date of disposition. A book value as of the date of disposition can then be computed as the difference between the cost of the asset and its accumulated depreciation. If the disposition price exceeds the book value, a gain is recognized. If the disposition price is less than the book value, a loss is recorded. As part of the disposition entry, the balances in the asset and accumulated depreciation accounts for the asset are canceled. The following sections illustrate the asset retirement process under varying conditions.

Asset Retirement by Sale

If the proceeds from the sale of an asset are in the form of cash or a receivable, the recording of the transaction follows the order outlined in the previous paragraph. For example, assume that on July 1, 2013, Landon Supply Co. sells for $43,600 machinery that is recorded on the books at cost of $83,600 with accumulated depreciation as of January 1, 2013, of $50,600. The company depreciates its machinery using a straight-line, 10% rate. Before recording the asset sale, a half-year of depreciation is recognized representing use of the asset for the first six months of the year.

The following entries would be made to record this transaction:

Depreciation Expense—Machinery	4,180	
Accumulated Depreciation—Machinery		4,180
To record depreciation for six months in 2013 ($83,600 × 0.10 × 6/12).		
Cash	43,600	
Accumulated Depreciation—Machinery	54,780	
Machinery		83,600
Gain on Sale of Machinery		14,780*
To record sale of machinery at a gain.		

*Sales price	$43,600
Book value ($83,600 − $54,780)	28,820
Gain on sale	$14,780

Asset Classification as Held for Sale

Often a plan is made to dispose of an asset before the actual sale takes place. Special accounting is required if the following conditions are satisfied:

- Management commits to a plan to sell a long-term operating asset.
- The asset is available for immediate sale.
- An active effort to locate a buyer is underway.
- It is probable that the sale will be completed within one year.

If these criteria are satisfied, two uncommon accounting actions are required. During the interval between being classified as held for sale and actually being sold

1. No depreciation is to be recognized, and
2. The asset is to be reported at the lower of its book value or its fair value (less the estimated cost to sell).[13]

To illustrate the accounting for a long-term asset that is classified as held for sale, assume that as of July 1, 2013, Haan Company has a building with a cost of $100,000 and accumulated depreciation of $35,000. Haan commits to a plan to sell the building by March 1, 2014. On July 1, 2013, the building has an estimated fair value of $40,000, and it is estimated that selling costs associated with the disposal of the building will be $3,000. On July 1, 2013, Haan must make the following journal entry:

Building—Held for Sale	37,000	
Loss on Held-for-Sale Classification	28,000	
Accumulated Depreciation—Building	35,000	
Building		100,000

After this journal entry is made, the building is recorded at its net realizable value of $37,000 ($40,000 selling price − $3,000 selling costs). If the net realizable value had been greater than the book value of $65,000 ($100,000 − $35,000), no journal entry would have been made. This measurement approach is exactly the same as that used to record inventory at the lower of cost or market, as illustrated in Chapter 9.

CAUTION

Recognition of this loss did *not* involve use of the 2-step impairment test explained earlier. Instead, the net selling price of the asset held for sale is compared directly to the book value; no comparison is made to the sum of future undiscounted cash flows.

On December 31, 2013, no adjusting entry is made for depreciation of the building. As mentioned, no depreciation expense is recognized on a long-term asset classified as held for sale. The rationale behind this approach is that because the asset is now designated for disposal, the key accounting point is no longer long-term cost allocation using depreciation but is instead proper current valuation of the asset. Accordingly, in the Haan Company example, the $37,000 carrying value of the building on December 31, 2013, would be compared to a revised estimate of the selling price (less selling cost) on that date. If this revised estimate is even lower than $37,000, an additional loss would be recognized. If the estimated net selling price had increased since the initial loss was recognized, a gain would be recognized to the extent of the $28,000 loss initially recognized.

[13] FASB ASC paragraph 360-10-35-43.

For example, if the estimated selling price as of December 31, 2013, was $58,000 (with $3,000 estimated selling costs), the following journal entry would be necessary:

Building Held for Sale	18,000	
Gain on Recovery of Value—Held for Sale		18,000

Computation of gain: ($58,000 − $3,000) − $37,000 = $18,000

A gain is recognized only to the extent that it offsets a previously recognized loss. For example, if the net selling price of the building on December 31, 2013, was estimated to be $80,000, a gain of only $28,000 would be recognized instead of the entire indicated gain of $43,000 ($80,000 – $37,000).

! CAUTION

This partial recovery of the loss recognized on the held-for-sale classification is not the usual practice with impairment losses. For regular long-term assets (not being held for sale), no recovery of impairment losses is allowed.

Asset Retirement by Exchange for Other Nonmonetary Assets

As indicated in Chapter 10, when operating assets are acquired in exchange for other nonmonetary assets, the new asset acquired is generally recorded at its fair value or the fair value of the nonmonetary asset given in exchange, whichever is more clearly determinable. However, if the exchange has no real commercial substance, the asset received is sometimes recorded at the BOOK value (not fair value) of the asset given.

The entries required to record the exchange of most nonmonetary assets are identical to those illustrated in the previous section except that a nonmonetary asset is received in exchange rather than cash or receivables. Gains and losses arising from these exchanges are recognized when the exchange takes place.

To illustrate, assume in the earlier example that the retirement of the described asset was done by exchanging it for delivery equipment that had a market value of $43,600. The entries would be the same as illustrated except that instead of a debit to Cash, Delivery Equipment would be debited for $43,600. The gain would still be computed by comparing the book value of the machine and the market value of the asset acquired in the exchange. (*Note:* In the examples in this section, the entry to record depreciation expense for the first six months of the year will not be shown.)

Delivery Equipment	43,600	
Accumulated Depreciation—Machinery	54,780	
Machinery		83,600
Gain on Exchange of Machinery		14,780

If the machinery's market value were more clearly determinable than the value of the delivery equipment, the value of the machinery would be used to compute the gain or loss and to determine the value for the delivery equipment. Assume that the delivery equipment is used and has no readily available market price, but the machinery had a market value of $25,000. Under these circumstances, a loss of $3,820 ($28,820 – $25,000) would be indicated, and the entry to record the exchange would be as follows:

Delivery Equipment	25,000	
Accumulated Depreciation—Machinery	54,780	
Loss on Exchange of Machinery	3,820	
Machinery		83,600

Often the exchange of nonmonetary assets includes a transfer of cash because the nonmonetary assets in most exchange transactions do not have identical market values. The cash part of the transaction adjusts the market values of the assets received to those of the assets given up. Thus, if in the previous example the machinery (with a market value of $25,000) were given in exchange for the delivery equipment and $3,000 cash, the entry would be as follows:

Cash	3,000	
Delivery Equipment ($25,000 − $3,000 cash received)	22,000	
Accumulated Depreciation—Machinery	54,780	
Loss on Exchange of Machinery	3,820	
Machinery		83,600

Remember that for most exchanges of nonmonetary assets, the asset received is recorded on the books at its fair value on the date of exchange. An exception to this general rule is explained in the next section.

Nonmonetary Exchange without Commercial Substance

Not all exchanges of nonmonetary assets involve substantive business transactions. For example, the Tri-City Cadillac dealership has a blue DeVille in its inventory but really wishes that it had a red one in stock. Another dealership in a nearby town has a red DeVille and is willing to exchange its car for Tri-City's blue one. This exchange of nonmonetary assets is not intended to be an earnings transaction for either party. Using the FASB's terminology, this exchange has no "commercial substance" because it does nothing to affect the risk, timing, or amount of Tri-City's cash flows.[14] Another example of such an exchange without commercial substance would occur if two manufacturing companies exchanged similar equipment that both companies used in similar ways in their production processes.

To illustrate the application of the notion of "commercial substance" to the accounting for nonmonetary exchanges, three examples follow. In the first example, no cash is involved in the exchange. In the second example, the exchange includes a "small" transfer of cash. In the third example, cash makes up a "large" part of the value of the transaction.

Example 1—No Cash Involved Republic Manufacturing Company owns a molding machine which it has decided to exchange for a similar machine owned by Logan Square Company. The following cost and market data relate to the two machines:

	Republic	Logan
Costs of machines to be exchanged	$46,000	$54,000
Accumulated depreciation on machines to be exchanged	32,000	37,700
Book values of machines to be exchanged	14,000	16,300
Fair values of machines to be exchanged	16,000	16,000

This exchange does not have commercial substance because the machines are essentially the same, will be used in the same way, and have the same fair values. In short, this exchange will not affect the risk, timing, or amount of either company's cash flows. In such a case, both companies will record the asset received at the book value of the asset or assets given up. The entry on Republic's books to record the exchange is on page 11-35.

[14] FASB ASC Section 845-10-30 (Nonmonetary Transactions—Overall—Initial Measurement).

Machinery (new)	14,000	
Accumulated Depreciation—Machinery (old)	32,000	
Machinery (old)		46,000

The entry on Logan's books to record the exchange is as follows:

Machinery	16,000	
Accumulated Depreciation—Machinery (old)	37,700	
Loss on Exchange of Machinery	300	
Machinery (old)		54,000

CAUTION

Indicated losses are *always* recognized. Indicated gains are sometimes recognized and sometimes not.

Note that in Republic's entry, no gain is recognized even though there is an indicated gain because the fair value of the asset received is $2,000 more than the book value of the asset given. The exchange does not have commercial substance, so no gain is recognized and the new asset is slotted into Republic's accounting records at the same book value as the old asset.

For Logan's entry, the fair value of the asset exchanged is less than its book value, so there is an indicated loss. The loss is recognized, and the newly acquired molding machine is recorded on Logan's books at its fair value. This is a good example of conservatism in accounting: Losses are recognized as soon as they are objectively determinable; gains are not recognized until realized. Another way to view the recognition of this loss is that the exchange prompted a reevaluation of the recorded amount of the machine, suggesting that Logan should recognize a loss similar to an impairment loss.

Example 2—Transfer of a "Small" Amount of Cash in the Exchange Assume the same facts as in Example 1, except that it is agreed that Republic's machine has a fair value of $16,000 and Logan's machine is worth $17,000. To make the exchange equal, Republic agrees to pay Logan $1,000 cash. The entry on Republic's books for Example 2 is as follows:

Machinery (new)	15,000	
Accumulated Depreciation—Machinery (old)	32,000	
Machinery (old)		46,000
Cash		1,000

As was true for Example 1, Republic does not recognize any of the indicated gain. The fair value of the assets surrendered ($16,000 + $1,000) exceeds their book values ($14,000 + $1,000), indicating a $2,000 gain. The exchange does not have commercial substance because the machines are essentially the same except for a minor difference ($1,000) in fair value. Technically, the immediate payment of the $1,000 in cash impacts the risk, timing, and amount of both companies' cash flows, but the impact is not significant. The indicated gain, therefore, is not recognized. The new machine is recorded at $15,000, equal to the book value of the assets given in the exchange.

In example 2, the book value of Logan's machine is less than the fair value, indicating a $700 gain ($17,000 − $16,300). Because Logan received cash as part of the transaction, a portion of the $700 indicated gain should be recognized as having been earned.[15]

[15] FASB ASC paragraph 845-10-30-6.

The amount to be recognized is computed using the following formula:

$$\text{Recognized gain} = \frac{\text{Cash received}}{\text{Cash received} + \text{Fair value of acquired asset}} \times \text{Total indicated gain}$$

Using the figures from example 2, Logan would recognize $41 of the indicated gain, computed as follows:

$$\frac{\$1{,}000}{\$1{,}000 + \$16{,}000} \times \$700 = \$41$$

The recorded value of the molding machine on Logan's books is $15,341, the book value of the packaging machine exchanged less the cash received plus the gain recognized ($16,300 − $1,000 + $41). Another way of computing the recorded value is by deducting the deferred gain from the fair value of the asset received ($16,000 − $659, or $15,341).

The entry on Logan's books to record the exchange is as follows:

Cash	1,000	
Machinery (new)	15,341	
Accumulated Depreciation—Machinery (old)	37,700	
Machinery (old)		54,000
Gain on Exchange of Machinery		41

The effect of this treatment is to defer a portion of the indicated gain and reduce the recorded book value of the new machinery. In essence, the deferred gain will be recognized over time through lower depreciation charges.

Example 3—Transfer of a "Large" Amount of Cash in the Exchange Assume the same facts as in Example 2 except that it is agreed that Republic's machine has a fair value of $12,750 and that Republic must pay $4,250 cash to make the exchange equal; remember that in Example 2 the fair value of Logan's machine was $17,000. In this case, the cash comprises a "large" part of the fair value of the exchange. When cash comprises a large part of the transaction, the exchange has commercial substance, all gains and losses are recognized, and assets received are recorded at their fair values. The entry on Republic's books for Example 3 is as follows:

ifrs

Machinery (new)	17,000	
Accumulated Depreciation—Machinery (old)	32,000	
Loss on Exchange of Machinery	1,250	
Machinery (old)		46,000
Cash		4,250

The entry on Logan's books for the exchange is as follows:

Cash	4,250	
Machinery (new)	12,750	
Accumulated Depreciation—Machinery (old)	37,700	
Machinery (old)		54,000
Gain on Exchange of Machinery		700

The question that remains is how much cash constitutes an amount large enough to have a significant impact on the risk, amount, or timing of the cash flows of the companies involved in the exchange. In Example 3, the $4,250 in cash comprises 25% ($4,250/$17,000) of the transaction. A 25% threshold is used by the FASB to distinguish a small amount of cash from a large amount of cash. So, if the amount of cash is 25% or more of the fair value of the transaction, then the transaction is accounted for as a monetary transaction.[16]

[16] FASB ASC paragraph 845-10-25-6.

EM **EXPANDED MATERIAL**

The kind of depreciation that businesspeople are most interested in is income tax depreciation. By lowering taxable income, tax depreciation reduces the payments for income taxes. The Expanded Material for this chapter shows how the MACRS income tax depreciation system is derived from the financial reporting depreciation methods illustrated earlier. An important part of MACRS is the depreciation computation for assets acquired or disposed of in the middle of the year. Accordingly, computation of depreciation for partial periods is also explained in more detail.

Depreciation for Partial Periods

7 **Compute depreciation for partial periods, using both straight-line and accelerated methods.**

WHY **To simplify depreciation computations, reasonable assumptions may be made regarding how much depreciation to recognize in the year an asset is purchased or sold rather than tracking exact purchase and sales dates.**

HOW **A common simplifying assumption is the half-year convention: One-half of a year's depreciation is recognized on all assets purchased or sold during the year. Alternatively, fractional calculations can be made using any one of the time-factor depreciation methods covered in the chapter.**

Most of the illustrations in this chapter have assumed that assets were purchased on the first day of a company's fiscal period. In reality, of course, asset transactions occur throughout the year. When a time-factor method is used, depreciation on assets acquired or disposed of during the year may be based on the number of days the asset was held during the period. When the level of acquisitions and retirements is significant, however, companies often adopt a less burdensome policy for recognizing depreciation for partial periods. Some alternatives found in practice include the following:

1. Depreciation is recognized to the nearest whole month. Assets acquired on or before the 15th of the month are considered owned for the entire month; assets acquired after the 15th are not considered owned for any part of the month; assets sold after the 15th are considered owned for the entire month.
2. Depreciation is recognized to the nearest whole year. Assets acquired during the first six months are considered held for the entire year; assets acquired during the last six months are not considered in the depreciation computation. Conversely, no depreciation is recorded on assets sold during the first six months, and a full year's depreciation is recorded on assets sold during the last six months.
3. One-half year's depreciation is recognized on all assets purchased or sold during the year. A full year's depreciation is taken on all other assets. This approach is required for income tax purposes and is illustrated in the next section.
4. No depreciation is recognized on acquisitions during the year, but depreciation for a full year is recognized on retirements.
5. Depreciation is recognized for a full year on acquisitions during the year, but no depreciation is recognized on retirements.

> **! CAUTION**
>
> Remember that depreciation is an estimate, and computing depreciation for the exact number of days or months gives only an illusion of precision.

Alternatives 2 through 5 are attractive because of their simplicity. Alternative 1 makes the most intuitive sense, and its use is assumed in the examples and problems in the text unless otherwise noted.

If a company uses the sum-of-the-years'-digits method of depreciation and recognizes a partial year's depreciation on assets in the year purchased, the depreciation expense for the second year must be determined by the following allocation procedure. To illustrate, the example used earlier in the chapter of the asset acquired by Schuss Boom Ski Manufacturing will be used. To repeat, the asset cost $100,000 and has an estimated residual value of $5,000 and an estimated useful life of five years. Assume that the asset was purchased three-fourths of the way through the fiscal year. The computation of depreciation expense for the first two years, using sum-of-the-years'-digits depreciation, is as follows:

First year:		
Depreciation for full year ($95,000 × 5/15)	$31,667	
One-fourth year's depreciation ($31,667/4)		$ 7,917
Second year:		
Depreciation for balance of first year ($31,667 − $7,917)		$23,750
Depreciation for second full year ($95,000 × 4/15)	$25,333	
One-fourth year's depreciation ($25,333/4)		6,333
Total depreciation—second year		$30,083

From this point, each year's depreciation will be $6,333 less than the previous year's depreciation. This difference equals 1/15 of the original depreciable asset base of $95,000. A summary of the depreciation charges for the 5-year period is as follows:

	Depreciation	Asset Book Value (Cost Less Accumulated Depreciation)
Year 1	$ 7,917	$92,083
Year 2	30,083	62,000
Year 3	23,750	38,250
Year 4	17,417	20,833
Year 5	11,083	9,750
Year 6	4,750	5,000
Total	$95,000	

Year 5 depreciation is $6,334 less than the previous year due to effects of rounding.

Alternatively, depreciation for Years 2 through 6 can be computed using the standard sum-of-the-years'-digits computation with the numerator being the number of years remaining in the asset's useful life as of the beginning of the year. For Year 2, the number of years remaining in the asset's useful life at the beginning of the year is 4.75. The depreciation for Year 2 is $95,000 × 4.75/15 = $30,083.

If a company uses a declining-balance method of depreciation, the computation of depreciation when partial years are involved is relatively straightforward. After Year 1's depreciation is computed, the remaining years are calculated in the same manner as illustrated earlier in the chapter; a constant percentage is multiplied by a declining book value. Again assuming a purchase three-fourths of the way through the fiscal year and the use of alternative 1, the double-declining-balance depreciation expense for the Schuss Boom asset would be as shown on page 11-39, assuming a switch to straight-line depreciation in Year 5.

Year	Computation		Depreciation Amount	Asset Book Value
1	$100,000 × 0.40 × 1/4	=	$10,000	$90,000
2	$90,000 × 0.40	=	36,000	54,000
3	$54,000 × 0.40	=	21,600	32,400
4	$32,400 × 0.40	=	12,960	19,440
5	($19,440 – $5,000)/1.75	=	8,251*	11,189
6	$11,189 – $5,000	=	6,189	5,000
			$95,000	

*Rounded.

Income Tax Depreciation

8 **Understand the depreciation methods underlying the MACRS income tax depreciation system.**

WHY **The depreciation tax rules are designed to simplify the depreciation calculations and to accelerate depreciation enabling companies to get their depreciation tax deductions sooner.**

HOW **Depreciation for tax purposes is based on the 200% declining-balance depreciation method with no residual value and a half-year convention. The Internal Revenue Service has established different classes of assets with varying depreciation lives.**

The Economic Recovery Tax Act (ERTA) of 1981 introduced an adaptation of the declining-balance depreciation method to be used for income tax purposes. It is referred to as the accelerated cost recovery system (ACRS). Subsequent revisions to the income tax laws have altered the original provisions. Because the Tax Reform Act of 1986 made several significant changes to ACRS, the new system is now referred to as the modified accelerated cost recovery system (MACRS).

The term *cost recovery* was used in the tax regulations to emphasize that ACRS is not a standard depreciation method because the system is not based strictly on asset life or pattern of use. ACRS has largely replaced traditional depreciation accounting for income tax purposes. Its original purpose was to both simplify the computation of tax depreciation and provide for a more rapid write-off of asset cost to reduce income taxes and thus stimulate investment in noncurrent operating assets. Simplification was to be achieved by using one of three cost recovery periods for all assets rather than a specific useful life for each class of asset as previously prescribed by the income tax regulations. In addition, salvage values were to be ignored. A more rapid write-off was achieved by allowing companies to write off most machinery and equipment over three to five years, and all real estate over 15 years, even though previously prescribed income tax class lives were for much longer periods.

FYI

Firms can choose MACRS for tax purposes and another method for financial reporting. Unlike LIFO elections, there is no necessary connection between income tax depreciation and depreciation for financial reporting.

The subsequent modifications to ACRS by Congress have tended to dampen both of its original objectives, primarily because tightening tax depreciation rules is a way to increase tax revenues without increasing income tax rates.[17] The original three recovery periods have been replaced with six recovery periods for personal property, such as equipment, automobiles, and furniture, and two periods for real property or land and buildings.[18] At the same time, the recovery periods for most assets have been extended so that less rapid write-off of asset cost is permitted.

Exhibit 11-5 illustrates the cost recovery periods and depreciation methods under MACRS. For personal property, the appropriate cost recovery period is determined by reference to the IRS class lives defined in the tax regulations. The real property recovery periods relate to the type of real property involved rather than class lives. ACRS initially provided for 150% declining-balance depreciation. The 1986 Reform Act increased the number of asset recovery periods and extended the recovery periods for most assets. The effects of these changes were partially offset by changing the method of depreciation for most personal property to the 200% (or double-) declining-balance method.

The MACRS method for personal property also incorporates a half-year convention, meaning that one-half of a year's depreciation is recognized on all assets purchased or sold during the year. To illustrate, assume that office equipment is purchased for $100,000 on October 1, 2013. The office equipment has a $5,000 estimated residual value. The equipment is 5-year property according to the IRS classification. Using the half-year convention, the double-declining-balance method, and ignoring the residual value, the MACRS depreciation for the equipment would be computed as follows:

Year	Computation		MACRS Depreciation Amount	Asset Book Value
1	$100,000 × 0.40 × 1/2	=	$ 20,000	$80,000
2	80,000 × 0.40	=	32,000	48,000
3	48,000 × 0.40	=	19,200	28,800
4	28,800 × 0.40	=	11,520	17,280
5	17,280/1.5	=	11,520	5,760
6	Remaining book value	=	5,760	0
			$100,000	

FYI

Of course, regular taxpayers aren't prepared to do these calculations. The IRS has summarized the MACRS method in a series of tables listing the percentage of the original asset cost that should be depreciated each year.

Even though the asset was purchased three-fourths of the way through the year, for tax purposes $20,000 is reported as the cost recovery in the first year rather than $10,000 determined by computing depreciation to the nearest month. Note that a switch to the straight-line method was made in Year 5. If the double-declining-balance method had been applied to this year, only $6,912 ($17,280 × 0.40) would have been reported rather than $11,520 using straight-line for the remaining one and one-half years.

[17] For example, the Revenue Reconciliation Act of 1993 increased the recovery period for nonresidential real property from 31.5 years to 39 years. *RIA United States Tax Reporter, Tax Bulletin*, No. 33, August 12, 1993.

[18] *Personal property* is a general term that encompasses all property other than real property (land and buildings).

EX 11-5 MACRS COST RECOVERY PERIODS AND DEPRECIATION METHODS

IRS–Defined Class Lives	MACRS Cost Recovery Period	Depreciation Method	Examples of Assets
Personal Property:			
4 years or less	3.0 years	200% declining balance	Race horses
4 to < 10 years	5.0	200 declining balance	Cars, trucks, office machinery
10 to < 16 years	7.0	200 declining balance	Office furniture, most factory machinery
16 to < 20 years	10.0	200 declining balance	Ships
20 to < 25 years	15.0	150 declining balance	Service station
More than 25 years	25.0	150 declining balance	Water treatment facilities
Real Property—Buildings:			
Residential rental	27.5	Straight line	
Nonresidential	39.0	Straight line	

SOLUTIONS TO OPENING SCENARIO QUESTIONS

1. The stock price decline was likely caused by a number of factors. First, if investors were convinced that they had previously been valuing Blockbuster's stock based on artificially inflated earnings, the stock price would drop upon realization of that fact. In addition, if this announcement caused investors to doubt the integrity of Blockbuster's management, the stock price would drop in anticipation of the uncovering of even more bad news.
2. Interpretation of daily stock price movements is a very uncertain business in spite of the impression you might get from Wall Street analysts every evening on the news. With that said, here is one explanation for the pattern in Blockbuster's stock price movement around the release of the Bear Stearns report. First, investors understood the valuation implications of Blockbuster's depreciation practices before the release of the report on May 8. In response to the report, investors panicked and drove the price down. Over the course of the next two weeks, investors re-evaluated their valuation of Blockbuster and decided that they had been correct in the first place. The fact that the stock price ended up a little below where it had stood before the report indicates, perhaps, a little lingering uncertainty about Blockbuster.

SOLUTIONS TO STOP & THINK

1. (Page 11-10) The correct answer is D. Total depreciation expense for the five assets is computed below. (*Note*: With double-declining-balance, the depreciation for the 4-year-old asset is the amount that reduces the book value to the residual value of $5,000.) For each depreciation method, total annual depreciation expense for the five assets is the same—$95,000. For a company with a stable base of assets, all depreciation methods yield the same

Age of Asset	Straight-Line	Sum-of-the-Years'-Digits	Double-Declining-Balance
Brand new	$19,000	$31,667	$40,000
One year old	19,000	25,333	24,000
Two years old	19,000	19,000	14,400
Three years old	19,000	12,667	8,640
Four years old	19,000	6,333	7,960
Total depreciation	$95,000	$95,000	$95,000

total depreciation expense. If a company is growing, and thus has more new assets than old assets, the accelerated methods yield higher total depreciation expense than does straight-line.

2. (Page 11-23) The correct answer is A. The undiscounted sum of future cash flows is always greater than an asset's fair value because the undiscounted amount does not reflect the time value of money. Accordingly, in order for the undiscounted sum of future cash flows to be less than an asset's book value, the fair value of the asset must be substantially less than the book value.

3. (Page 11-28) The correct answer is C. For an intangible asset with an indefinite life, there is no foreseeable end to the future cash flows to be generated by the asset. Accordingly, the undiscounted sum of future cash flows will always be infinite, and, using the 2-step impairment test, no impairment loss would ever be recognized. This is an unreasonable outcome, so a separate impairment test, using the discounted present value of the future cash flows, is used.

4. (Page 11-30) The correct answer is C. Procedure 3 is the most costly to perform. In many cases, Procedure 1 can be done using simple earnings or revenue multiples to estimate the fair value of the reporting unit. Procedure 2 is a simple calculation using the estimated fair value and the reported amounts of assets and liabilities for the reporting unit. Once Procedure 3 is completed, Procedure 4 simply involves the comparison of two numbers. However, Procedure 3 requires the estimation of the fair value of ALL the assets and liabilities of the reporting unit. Because of the difficulty of performing Procedure 3, Topic 350 allows a company to use the same detailed asset and liability valuations from one year to the next if the economic situation of the reporting unit has not changed much, if the composition of the assets and liabilities has not changed much, and if the previous impairment test threshold was exceeded by a substantial margin.

SOLUTION TO USING THE FASB'S CODIFICATION

Under Topic 360 (Property, Plant, and Equipment), you see a number of industries listed—agriculture, airlines, contractors, and so forth. Let's start with agriculture. In Section 35 (Subsequent Measurement) under Subtopic 905-360, you see subsections on topics such as breeding animals, production animals, and trees and vines. This doesn't look like the right place.

The next industry listed is airlines covered in Subtopic 908-360. In Section 35 on subsequent measurement, you see a subsection on "Depreciation Methods." There you find the following: "A depreciation method may be applied to a single asset (unit depreciation) or to a group or pool of assets that are similar in nature (group depreciation). An air carrier can use unit or group depreciation methods on different groups of assets . . . Under the group method, the airline depreciates the aggregate cost of a group of equipment that is fairly homogeneous, despite differences in the service lives of individual items. Group depreciation usually is applied to groups of assets that are significant in number but have relatively small unit values, such as rotable parts and assemblies."

So, here is one example, the airline industry, where group depreciation is so routine that it is mentioned in the authoritative accounting standards.

REVIEW CHAPTER 11

LEARNING OBJECTIVES

1 **Use straight-line, accelerated, use-factor, and group depreciation methods to compute annual depreciation expense.**

The four factors that are considered in computing annual depreciation are asset cost, residual (or salvage) value, useful life, and pattern of use. The most common methods for computing annual depreciation are as follows:

Time-Factor Methods

- *Straight-line depreciation.* The difference between asset cost and residual value is divided by the useful life of the asset.
- *Accelerated methods*
  - *Sum-of-the-years'-digits depreciation.* The depreciable asset cost is multiplied by a fraction; the numerator is the number of years remaining in the asset life as of the beginning of the year, and the denominator is the sum of all the digits from 1 to the original useful life.
  - *Declining-balance depreciation.* The asset book value is multiplied by a constant percentage rate derived from the useful life. The most commonly used percentage is double the straight-line rate.

Use-Factor Methods

- *Service-hours depreciation.* Depreciable cost is divided by total expected lifetime service hours to compute a per-hour depreciation rate. The number of service hours in a period multiplied by the rate yields the periodic depreciation charge.
- *Productive-output depreciation.* This is similar to service-hours depreciation except the rate is based on expected number of output units during the life of the asset.

Group and Composite Methods

A collection of assets is depreciated as one group. A group rate, derived from an initial analysis of the type of assets in the group, is multiplied by the total cost of group assets to compute periodic depreciation expense. Gains and losses resulting from normal variations in asset lives are not recognized.

2 **Apply the productive-output method to the depletion of natural resources.**

The depletion rate is based on total development cost of the natural resource divided by the estimated amount of resource units to be removed. Periodic depletion expense is the depletion rate multiplied by the number of units removed during the period. Structures and improvements related specifically to removal of the natural resource should be depreciated based on the fraction of natural resources extracted during the period.

3 **Incorporate changes in estimates and methods into the computation of depreciation for current and future periods.**

A change in estimate impacts the current and future periods and is not used to adjust amounts reported in prior periods. The undepreciated book value is allocated over the remaining life based on the revised estimates. Changes in depreciation method are accounted for as changes in estimates and are reflected in the current and future periods.

4 **Identify whether an asset is impaired, and measure the amount of the impairment loss using both U.S. GAAP and IASB standards.**

Under U.S. GAAP, assets are reviewed for possible impairment whenever there is a significant change in operations or in the way an asset is used. An asset is impaired when the undiscounted sum of future cash flows from the asset is less than the reported book value. An impaired asset is written down to its fair value. IASB standards differ from U.S. GAAP in that the discounted sum of future cash flows—rather than the undiscounted sum—is used to determine whether an impairment loss exists. International standards also allow for the upward revaluation of long-term operating assets that have increased in value.

5 Discuss the issues impacting proper recognition of amortization or impairment for intangible assets.

An intangible asset with a finite life is amortized over its estimated useful life, usually with zero residual value and using the straight-line method. These intangibles are tested for impairment using the standard 2-step impairment test. An intangible asset with an indefinite life is not amortized. Instead, these intangibles are tested for impairment simply by comparing their carrying value to their estimated fair value. Goodwill is not amortized. Goodwill is tested for impairment each year using a process that starts with an estimate of the fair value of the entire reporting unit to which the goodwill was assigned when it was acquired.

6 Account for the sale of depreciable assets in exchange for cash and in exchange for other depreciable assets.

Indicated losses are always recognized. In cash transactions and in other exchanges involving commercial substance, indicated gains are recognized and all assets exchanged are recorded on the books of the company receiving them at their fair values. Some nonmonetary exchanges do not have commercial substance, meaning that they do not impact the risk, timing, or amount of the cash flows of the parties in the exchange. In this case, the assets received are recorded at the book value of the assets given up in the exchange.

EM EXPANDED MATERIAL

7 Compute depreciation for partial periods, using both straight-line and accelerated methods.

Depreciation is not always computed for the exact number of days or months an asset is owned. One common simplifying assumption is the half-year convention: One-half of a year's depreciation is recognized on all assets purchased or sold during the year.

8 Understand the depreciation methods underlying the MACRS income tax depreciation system.

MACRS is based on the 200% declining-balance depreciation method with no residual value and a half-year convention. To streamline the system, the IRS has established eight classes of assets with set depreciation lives.

FASB-IASB CODIFICATION SUMMARY

ifrs

Topic	FASB Accounting Standards Codification	Original FASB Standard	Corresponding IASB Standard	Differences between U.S. GAAP and IFRS
Impairment of tangible assets	*Subtopic 360-10 various subsections on "Impairment"*	*SFAS No. 144*	*IAS 36*	Under U.S. GAAP, the impairment test is a 2-step test. Under IFRS, the impairment test involves just one step, a comparison of the book value to the "recoverable amount" of the asset.
Impairment of intangible assets	*Topic 350*	*SFAS No. 142*	*IAS 36*	U.S. GAAP includes three different impairment tests for intangibles. Under IFRS, there is just one test, which is the same as is used for tangible assets.
Upward revaluation	*Not part of U.S. GAAP*	*Not part of U.S. GAAP*	*IAS 16*	Upward revaluations of property, plant, and equipment are generally not allowable under U.S. GAAP.
Asset retirement obligations	*Subtopic 410-20*	*SFAS No. 143*	*IAS 16 and IAS 37*	No substantial differences
Assets classified as held for sale	*Section 360-10-45*	*SFAS No. 144*	*IFRS 5*	No substantial differences

KEY TERMS

Accelerated depreciation 11-7
Amortization 11-3
Book value 11-4
Composite depreciation 11-13
Declining-balance depreciation 11-9
Depletion 11-3
Depreciation 11-3
Double-declining-balance depreciation 11-9
Gain 11-31
Group depreciation 11-13
Impairment 11-21
Indicated gain 11-35
Indicated loss 11-35
Loss 11-31
Natural resources 11-17
Productive-output depreciation 11-13
Residual (salvage) value 11-5
Service-hours depreciation 11-11
Straight-line depreciation 11-7
Sum-of-the-years'-digits depreciation 11-8
Time-factor depreciation 11-7
Unit depreciation 11-13
Use-factor depreciation 11-11
Useful life 11-5

EM EXPANDED MATERIAL

Accelerated cost recovery system (ACRS) 11-39
Half-year convention 11-40
Modified accelerated cost recovery system (MACRS) 11-39

QUESTIONS

1. Distinguish among depreciation, depletion, and amortization expenses.
2. What factors must be considered in determining the periodic depreciation charges that should be made for a company's depreciable assets?
3. What role does residual, or salvage, value play in the various methods of time-factor depreciation?
4. Distinguish between the functional and physical factors affecting the useful life of a tangible noncurrent operating asset.
5. Distinguish between time-factor and use-factor methods of depreciation.
6. Briefly describe group depreciation, and describe how asset retirements are recorded under this method.
7. Describe the component approach to computing depreciation.
8. How does the recognition of an asset retirement obligation impact periodic depreciation expense? Interest expense?
9. Describe the proper accounting treatment for a change in estimated useful life.
10. What procedures must be followed when the estimate of recoverable natural resources is changed due to subsequent development work?
11. Under U.S. GAAP, what test is used to determine whether a long-term tangible asset is impaired? How is an impairment loss measured?
12. How does the international accounting standard for asset impairment differ from the standard used in the United States?
13. If a non-U.S. company chooses to revalue a long-term operating asset upward in accordance with *IAS 16*, how is the unrealized "gain" on the revaluation recognized in the financial statements?
14. Briefly describe the three types of intangible assets in terms of amortization and impairment.
15. Briefly describe the four procedures followed in testing goodwill for impairment.
16. Under *IAS 36*, there is basically one impairment test for intangible assets. Briefly describe the structure of that test.
17. What two unusual accounting actions are taken when a long-term operating asset is classified as held for sale?
18. Under what circumstances is a gain recognized when a productive asset is exchanged for a similar productive asset? A loss?

EM EXPANDED MATERIAL

19. Why isn't depreciation expense always computed for the exact number of days an asset is owned?
20. What were the original reasons for the development of the ACRS income tax depreciation method?

PRACTICE EXERCISES

Practice 11-1
LO8

Recording Depreciation Expense

Depreciation expense for the year was $1,000. Make the necessary journal entry.

Practice 11-2
LO1

Computing Straight-Line Depreciation

The company acquired a machine on January 1 at an original cost of $108,000. The machine's estimated residual value is $20,000, and its estimated life is five years.

(1) Compute the annual straight-line depreciation amount, (2) make the journal entry necessary to record depreciation expense for the first year, and (3) compute the machine's book value at the end of the first year.

Practice 11-3

LO1

Computing Sum-of-the-Years'-Digits Depreciation

The company acquired a machine on January 1 at an original cost of $115,000. The machine's estimated residual value is $20,000, and its estimated life is five years. Assume that the company uses sum-of-the-years'-digits depreciation. Compute (1) depreciation expense for each year of the machine's 5-year life and (2) book value at the end of each year of the machine's 5-year life.

Practice 11-4

LO1

Computing Double-Declining-Balance Depreciation

The company acquired a machine on January 1 at an original cost of $100,000. The machine's estimated residual value is $10,000, and its estimated life is four years. The company uses double-declining-balance depreciation and switches to straight-line in the final year of the machine's life. Compute (1) depreciation expense for each year of the machine's 4-year life and (2) book value at the end of each year of the machine's 4-year life.

Practice 11-5

LO1

Computing Service-Hours Depreciation

The company acquired a machine on January 1 at an original cost of $81,000. The machine's estimated residual value is $15,000, and its estimated life is 20,000 service hours. The actual usage of the machine was as follows: Year 1, 9,000 hours; Year 2, 5,000 hours; Year 3, 4,000 hours; Year 4, 2,000 hours. Compute (1) depreciation expense for each year of the machine's life and (2) book value at the end of each year of the machine's life.

Practice 11-6

LO1

Computing Productive-Output Depreciation

The company acquired a machine on January 1 at an original cost of $70,000. The machine's estimated residual value is $5,000, and its estimated lifetime output is 13,000 units. The actual output of the machine was as follows: Year 1, 3,000 units; Year 2, 5,000 units; Year 3, 2,000 units; Year 4, 3,000 units. Compute (1) depreciation expense for each year of the machine's life and (2) book value at the end of each year of the machine's life.

Practice 11-7

LO1

Computing Group Depreciation

The company has decided to use group depreciation based on the straight-line depreciation method. The initial pool of assets on which the group depreciation rate is based is as follows:

	Acquisition Cost	Salvage Value	Useful Life
Asset 1	$64,000	$ 4,000	6 years
Asset 2	90,000	10,000	10
Asset 3	42,000	6,000	9
Asset 4	30,000	0	5

Compute the group depreciation rate.

Practice 11-8

LO1, LO6

Group Depreciation: Recording Asset Sales

Refer to Practice 11-7. (1) Make the journal entry to record the sale of Asset 3 after two years for $22,000 cash. (2) Compute depreciation expense in the third year if Asset 5 is purchased at the beginning of the year for $50,000. This purchase is made at the same time that Asset 3 is sold.

Practice 11-9

LO1

Asset Retirement Obligation

On January 1, Lewis Company purchased land it will use as a landfill for the next 12 years. The cost of the land was $525,000. At the end of 12 years, Lewis Company will be required to spend $250,000 to landscape and reforest the landfill site. The appropriate discount rate is 6%. Because the useful life of the land is limited in this case, the cost of the land is depreciated. Lewis uses the straight-line method. Compute the amount of depreciation expense and accretion expense in Year 1.

Practice 11-10
LO2

Computing Depletion Expense

On January 1, the company purchased a mine for $100,000. At that time, it was estimated that the mine contained 5,000 tons of ore. It is also estimated that the mine will have a residual value of $20,000 when all of the ore is extracted. During the year, the company extracted 900 tons of ore from the mine. (1) Compute depletion expense for the year and (2) make the journal entry necessary to record the depletion expense.

Practice 11-11
LO3

Change in Estimated Life

The company purchased a machine for $40,000. The machine had an estimated residual value of $4,000 and an estimated useful life of nine years. After three full years of experience with the machine, it was determined that its total useful life would be only seven years instead of nine. In addition, a revised estimate of $8,000 was made for the residual value, instead of the original $4,000. Compute depreciation expense for the fourth year. The company uses straight-line depreciation.

Practice 11-12
LO3

Change in Estimated Units of Production

On January 1 of Year 1, the company purchased a mine for $300,000. At that time, it was estimated that the mine contained 2,000 tons of ore. During Year 1, the company extracted 900 tons of ore from the mine. On January 1 of Year 2, the company spent $120,000 on mine improvements. During Year 2, the company extracted 600 tons of ore. On December 31 of Year 2, it was estimated that the mine contained 700 tons of ore. Compute depletion expense for (1) Year 1 and (2) Year 2.

Practice 11-13
LO3

Change in Depreciation Method

On January 1, the company purchased a machine for $80,000. The machine had an estimated useful life of eight years and an estimated salvage value of $8,000. After three full years of using the machine, the company changed its depreciation method from straight-line to double-declining-balance. Compute depreciation expense for the fourth year.

Practice 11-14
LO4

Determining Whether a Tangible Asset Is Impaired

The cost and the accumulated depreciation for a piece of equipment are $1,500,000 and $600,000, respectively. Management is concerned that the equipment has become impaired. Management hired several independent appraisers who agreed that the current value of the equipment is $500,000. Management also estimates that the equipment will generate cash inflows of $65,000 per year for the next 14 years. Is the equipment impaired? Explain.

Practice 11-15
LO4

Recording a Tangible Asset Impairment

A building has a cost of $1,500,000 and accumulated depreciation of $250,000. The fair value of the building is estimated to be $600,000. The building is expected to generate net cash inflows of $40,000 per year for the next 30 years. (1) Determine whether the building is impaired and (2) if it is impaired, make the journal entry necessary to record the impairment loss.

Practice 11-16
LO4

Recording Upward Asset Revaluations

A building has a cost of $500,000 and accumulated depreciation of $40,000. The current value of the building is estimated to be $730,000. The company that owns the building is based in Genovia and uses international financial reporting standards. The company has chosen to recognize increases in the value of long-term operating assets. Make the necessary journal entry.

Practice 11-17
LO5

Recording Amortization Expense

On January 1, the company purchased the rights to a valuable Internet domain name for $250,000. Given current market conditions, the company estimates that these rights have an economic life of four years at which time they will have no residual value. Make the journal entry necessary to recognize amortization expense for the year.

Practice 11-18
LO5

Goodwill Impairment

Buyer Company acquired Target Company on January 1. As part of the acquisition, $2,000 in goodwill was recognized; this goodwill was assigned to Buyer's Manufacturing reporting unit. On December 31, it was estimated that the future cash flows expected to be generated by the Manufacturing reporting unit are $700 at the end of each year for the next 10 years. The appropriate interest rate is 10%. The fair values and book values of the assets and liabilities of the Manufacturing reporting unit are as follows:

	Book Values	Fair Values
Identifiable assets	$7,000	$8,000
Goodwill	2,000	?
Liabilities	4,000	4,000

Make the journal entry necessary to recognize any goodwill impairment loss.

Practice 11-19
LO6

Exchange of Assets

A building has a cost of $700,000 and accumulated depreciation of $340,000. The building is exchanged for land. Make the necessary journal entry if (1) the land has a market value of $400,000 and (2) the land has a market value of $200,000.

Practice 11-20
LO6

Classifying an Asset as Held for Sale

On October 1, 2013, the company has a building with a cost of $375,000 and accumulated depreciation of $225,000. The company commits to a plan to sell the building by February 1, 2014. On October 1, 2013, the building has an estimated selling price of $145,000, and it is estimated that selling costs associated with the disposal of the building will be $9,000. On December 31, 2013, the estimated selling price of the building has increased to $170,000, with estimated selling costs remaining at $9,000. Make the journal entries necessary to record (1) the initial classification of the building as held for sale on October 1, 2013, and (2) any adjustment necessary on December 31, 2013. Remember that no depreciation expense is recognized once an asset is classified as held for sale.

Practice 11-21
LO6

Exchange of Assets

The company exchanged an asset for a similar asset. The exchange was with another company in the same line of business. The old asset had a cost of $1,000 and accumulated depreciation of $850. The old asset had a market value of $400 on the date of the exchange. Make the journal entry necessary to record the exchange assuming that (1) the company received the new machine and no cash, (2) the company received the new machine and a "large" amount of cash of $300, and (3) the company received the new machine and a "small" amount of cash of $80. [*Hint:* In all three cases, the total market value of assets received (cash plus new asset) is the same as the market value of the asset given up ($400).]

EM EXPANDED MATERIAL

Practice 11-22
LO7

Depreciation for Partial Periods

The company purchased a machine on April 1 for $100,000. The machine has an estimated useful life of five years and an estimated salvage value of $15,000. The company computes partial-year depreciation to the nearest whole month. Compute the amount of depreciation expense for this year *and* next year using (1) sum-of-the-years'-digits depreciation and (2) double-declining-balance depreciation.

Practice 11-23
LO8

Income Tax Depreciation

The company purchased a ship for $850,000. The ship has an estimated residual value of $100,000. Compute the amount of MACRS depreciation deduction for the first two years of the life of the ship.

EXERCISES

Exercise 11-24

LO5

Impairment of Goodwill

Largest Company acquired Large Company on January 1. As part of the acquisition, $10,000 in goodwill was recognized; this goodwill was assigned to Largest's Production reporting unit. During the year, the Production reporting unit reported revenues of $13,000. Publicly traded companies with operations similar to those of the Production unit had price-to-revenue ratios averaging 1.60. The fair values and book values of the assets and liabilities of the Production reporting unit are as follows:

	Book Values	Fair Values
Identifiable assets	$21,300	$20,500
Goodwill	10,000	?
Liabilities	7,600	7,600

Make the journal entry necessary to recognize any goodwill impairment loss.

Exercise 11-25

LO5

Impairment of Intangibles

An intangible asset cost $300,000 on January 1, 2013. On January 1, 2014, the asset was evaluated to determine whether it was impaired. As of January 1, 2014, the asset was expected to generate future cash flows of $25,000 per year (at the end of the year). The appropriate discount rate is 5%.

1. Give the entries to record amortization in 2013 and any impairment loss in 2014 assuming that as of January 1, 2013, the asset was assumed to have a total useful life of 10 years and that as of January 1, 2014, there were nine years remaining.
2. Give the entries to record amortization in 2013 and any impairment loss in 2014 assuming that as of January 1, 2013, the asset was assumed to have an indefinite useful life and that as of January 1, 2014, the remaining life was still indefinite.

Exercise 11-26

LO4

Recording an Impairment Loss

Della Bee Company purchased a manufacturing plant building 10 years ago for $2,600,000. The building has been depreciated using the straight-line method with a 30-year useful life and 10% residual value. Della Bee's manufacturing operations have experienced significant losses for the past two years, so Della Bee has decided that the manufacturing building should be evaluated for possible impairment. Della Bee estimates that the building has a remaining useful life of 15 years, that net cash inflow from the building will be $100,000 per year, and that the fair value of the building is $760,000.

1. Determine whether an impairment loss should be recognized.
2. If an impairment loss should be recognized, make the appropriate journal entry.
3. How would your answer to (1) change if the fair value of the building was $1,120,000?

Exercise 11-27

LO4

Impairment and Revaluation Under International Accounting Standards

Use the information given in Exercise 11-26 and assume that Della Bee Company is located in Hong Kong and uses International Financial Reporting Standards. Della Bee also has chosen to recognize increases in the value of long-term operating assets in accordance with the allowable alternative under *IAS 16*.

1. Determine whether an impairment loss should be recognized.

2. If an impairment loss should be recognized, make the appropriate journal entry.
3. What journal entry would Della Bee make if the fair value of the building was $2,500,000?

Exercise 11-28

LO5

Accounting for Patents

The Rockington Co. applied for and received numerous patents at a total cost of $31,195 at the beginning of 2008. It is assumed the patents will have economic value for their remaining legal life of 16 years. At the beginning of 2010, the company paid $9,350 in successfully prosecuting an attempted infringement of these patent rights. At the beginning of 2013, $32,400 was paid to acquire patents that could make its own patents worthless; the patents acquired have a remaining life of 15 years but will not be used.

1. Give the entries to record the expenditures relative to patents.
2. Give the entries to record patent amortization for the years 2008, 2010, and 2013.

Exercise 11-29

LO6

Exchange of Machinery

Assume that Coaltown Corporation has a machine that cost $52,000, has a book value of $35,000, and has a fair value of $40,000. The machine is used in Coaltown's manufacturing process. For each of the following situations, indicate the value at which the company should record the new asset and why it should be recorded at that value.

(a) Coaltown exchanged the machine for a truck with a list price of $43,000.
(b) Coaltown exchanged the machine with another manufacturing company for a similar machine with a list price of $41,000.
(c) Coaltown exchanged the machine for a newer model machine from another manufacturing company. The new machine had a list price of $62,000, and Coaltown paid a "large" amount of cash of $15,000.
(d) Coaltown exchanged the machine plus a "small" amount of cash of $3,000 for a similar machine from Newton Inc., a manufacturing company. The newly acquired machine is carried on Newton's books at its cost of $55,000 with accumulated depreciation of $42,000; its fair value is $43,000. In addition to determining the value, give the journal entries for both companies to record the exchange.

Exercise 11-30

LO6

Exchange of Truck

On January 2, 2013, Joshon Hardware Company traded with a dealer an old delivery truck for a newer model. Data relative to the old and new trucks follow:

Old truck:	
Original cost	$22,750
Accumulated depreciation as of January 2, 2013	19,000
New truck:	
List price	$24,000
Cash price without trade-in	23,100
Cash paid with trade-in	20,900

1. Give the journal entries on Joshon's books to record the purchase of the new truck.
2. Give the journal entries on Joshon's books if the cash paid was $18,000 and that amount is considered "large."

Exercise 11-31

LO6

Long-Term Operating Asset Held for Sale

On April 1, 2013, Brandoni Company has a piece of machinery with a cost of $100,000 and accumulated depreciation of $75,000. On April 1, Brandoni decided to sell the machine within one year. As of April 1, 2013, the machine had an estimated selling price of $10,000 and a remaining useful life of two years. It is estimated that selling costs associated with the disposal of the machine will be $1,000. On December 31, 2013, the estimated selling price of the machine had increased to $15,000, with estimated selling costs increasing to $1,600.

1. Make the entry to record the initial classification of the machine as held for sale on April 1, 2013.
2. Make the entry to record depreciation expense on the machine for the period April 1 through December 31, 2013.
3. Make the entry, if any, needed on December 31, 2013, to reflect the change in the expected selling price.

Exercise 11-32
LO6

Recording the Sale of Equipment with Note

On December 31, 2013, Debenham Corporation sold an old machine for $15,000, having an original cost of $84,000 and a book value of $9,000. The terms of the sale were as follows: $3,000 down payment, $6,000 payable on December 31 of the next two years. The sales agreement made no mention of interest; however, 8% would be a fair rate for this type of transaction. Give the journal entries on Debenham's books to record the sale of the machine and receipt of the two subsequent payments. (*Note:* Round to the nearest dollar.)

Exercise 11-33
LO2

SPREADSHEET

Depletion Expense

On January 2, 2012, Adelaide Rose purchased land with valuable natural ore deposits for $13 million. The estimated residual value of the land was $4 million. At the time of purchase, a geological survey estimated 3 million tons of removable ore were under the ground. Early in 2012, roads were constructed on the land to aid in the extraction and transportation of the mined ore at a cost of $975,000. In 2012, 75,000 tons were mined. In 2013, Adelaide fired her mining engineer and hired a new expert. A new survey made at the end of 2013 estimated 4.5 million tons of ore were available for mining. In 2013, 265,000 tons were mined. Assuming that all the ore mined was sold, how much was the depletion expense for 2012 and 2013?

Exercise 11-34
LO3

Change in Estimated Useful Life

Finn Corporation purchased a machine on July 1, 2010, for $225,000. The machine was estimated to have a useful life of 12 years with an estimated salvage value of $15,000. During 2013, it became apparent that the machine would become uneconomical after December 31, 2017, and that the machine would have no scrap value. Finn uses the straight-line method of depreciation for all machinery. What should be the charge for depreciation in 2013 using the new estimates for useful life and salvage value?

Exercise 11-35
LO3

Change in Estimated Useful Life

Goff Corporation purchased a machine on January 1, 2008, for $250,000. At the date of acquisition, the machine had an estimated useful life of 20 years with no salvage value. The machine is being depreciated on a straight-line basis. On January 1, 2013, as a result of Goff's experience with the machine, it was decided that the machine had an estimated useful life of 15 years from the date of acquisition. What is the amount of depreciation expense on this machine in 2013 using a new annual depreciation charge for the remaining 10 years?

Exercise 11-36
LO1

REVERSE SOLVABLE

Inferring Useful Lives

The information that follows is from the balance sheet of Hampton Company for December 31, 2013, and December 31, 2012.

	Dec. 31, 2013	Dec. 31, 2012
Equipment—cost	$ 680,000	$ 680,000
Accumulated depreciation—equipment	(250,000)	(160,000)
Buildings—cost	2,450,000	2,450,000
Accumulated depreciation—buildings	(340,000)	(230,000)

Hampton did not acquire or dispose of any buildings or equipment during 2013. Hampton uses the straight-line method of depreciation. If residual values are assumed to be 10% of asset cost, what is the average useful life of Hampton's (1) equipment and (2) buildings?

Exercise 11-37

LO1, LO2

Asset Retirement Obligation

On January 1, 2013, Major Company purchased a uranium mine for $800,000. On that date, Major estimated that the mine contained 1,000 tons of ore. At the end of the productive years of the mine, Major Company will be required to spend $4,200,000 to clean up the mine site. The appropriate discount rate is 8%, and it is estimated that it will take approximately 14 years to mine all of the ore. Major uses the productive-output method of depreciation. During 2013, Major extracted 100 tons of ore from the mine.

1. Compute the amount of depreciation (or depletion) expense for 2013.
2. Compute the amount of accretion expense for 2013.

Exercise 11-38

LO1

Productive-Output Depreciation and Asset Retirement

Equipment was purchased at the beginning of 2011 for $100,000 with an estimated product life of 300,000 units. The estimated salvage value was $4,000. During 2011, 2012, and 2013, the equipment produced 80,000 units, 120,000 units, and 40,000 units, respectively. The machine was damaged at the beginning of 2014, and the equipment was scrapped with no salvage value.

1. Determine depreciation using the productive-output method for 2011, 2012, and 2013.
2. Give the entry to write off the equipment at the beginning of 2014.

Exercise 11-39

LO1

Service-Hours Depreciation

Jen and Barry's Ice Milk Company used cash to purchase a new ice milk mixer on January 1, 2013. The new mixer is estimated to have a 20,000-hour service life. Jen and Barry's depreciates equipment on the service-hours method. The total price paid for the machine was $57,000. This price included $2,000 freight in, $1,800 installation costs, and $3,000 for a 2-year maintenance contract.

During 2013, Jen and Barry's used the machine for 2,500 hours; in 2014, 3,000 hours. Prepare all related journal entries for the purchase of equipment, annual depreciation, and maintenance expense for 2013 and 2014.

Exercise 11-40

LO1

Group Depreciation

Allwood, Inc., a small furniture manufacturer, purchased the following assets at the end of 2012.

Description	Cost	Salvage	Life
Delivery truck	$37,000	$8,000	7 years
Circular saws	725	180	5 years
Workbench	460	—	10 years
Forklift	11,000	950	6 years

Compute the following amounts for 2013 using group depreciation on a straight-line basis:

1. Depreciation expense
2. Group depreciation rate
3. Average life of the assets

Exercise 11-41

LO1

Group Depreciation Entries

Lundquist, Inc., uses the group depreciation method for its furniture account. The depreciation rate used for furniture is 21%. The balance in the furniture account on December 31, 2012, was $125,000, and the balance in Accumulated Depreciation—Furniture was $61,000.

The following purchases and dispositions of furniture occurred in the years 2013–2015 (assume that all purchases and disposals occurred at the beginning of each year).

Year	Assets Purchased—Cost (Cash)	Assets Sold	
		Cost	Selling Price (Cash)
2013	$35,000	$27,000	$8,000
2014	27,600	15,000	6,000
2015	24,500	32,000	8,000

1. Prepare the summary journal entries Lundquist should make each year (2013–2015) for the purchase, disposition, and depreciation of the furniture.
2. Prepare a summary of the furniture and accumulated depreciation accounts for the years 2013–2015.

Exercise 11-42

LO3

Change in Depreciation Method

Franklin Company purchased a machine on January 1, 2010, paying $150,000. The machine was estimated to have a useful life of eight years and an estimated salvage value of $30,000. In early 2012, the company elected to change its depreciation method from straight-line to sum-of-the-years'-digits for future periods. What should be the charge for depreciation for 2012?

Exercise 11-43

LO1

Depreciation of Special Components

Jackson Manufacturing acquired a new milling machine on April 1, 2008. The machine has a special component that requires replacement before the end of the useful life. The asset was originally recorded in two accounts, one representing the main unit and the other for the special component. Depreciation is recorded by the straight-line method to the nearest month, residual values being disregarded. On April 1, 2014, the special component is scrapped and is replaced with a similar component. This component is expected to have a residual value of approximately 25% of cost at the end of the useful life of the main unit, and because of its materiality, the residual value will be considered in calculating depreciation. Specific asset information is as follows:

Main milling machine:	
Purchase price in 2008	$71,200
Residual value	$6,200
Estimated useful life	10 years
First special component:	
Purchase price	$12,000
Residual value	$500
Estimated useful life	6 years
Second special component:	
Purchase price	$16,500

What are the depreciation charges to be recognized for the years (1) 2008, (2) 2014, and (3) 2015?

Exercise 11-44

LO1

Computation of Asset Cost and Depreciation Expense

A machine is purchased at the beginning of 2013 for $38,400. Its estimated life is eight years. Freight costs on the machine are $3,000. Installation costs are $1,600. The machine is estimated to have a residual value of $600 and a useful life of 32,000 hours. It was used 3,000 hours in 2013.

1. What is the cost of the machine for accounting purposes?

2. Compute the depreciation charge for 2013 using (a) the straight-line method and (b) the service-hours method.

Exercise 11-45
LO1

Computation of Depreciation Expense

Limestone Construction purchased a concrete mixer on July 15, 2013. Company officials revealed the following information regarding this asset and its acquisition:

Purchase price	$196,000
Residual value	$20,000
Estimated useful life	9 years
Estimated service hours	50,000
Estimated production in units	375,000 yards

The concrete mixer was operated by construction crews in 2013 for a total of 6,500 hours, and it produced 49,500 yards of concrete.

It is company policy to take a half-year's depreciation on all assets for which it used the straight-line or double-declining-balance depreciation method in the year of purchase.

Calculate the resulting depreciation expense for 2013 under each of the following methods, and specify which method allows the greatest depreciation expense.

1. Double-declining-balance
2. Productive-output
3. Service-hours
4. Straight-line

EM EXPANDED MATERIAL

Exercise 11-46
LO8

MACRS Computation

Olympus Equipment Company purchased a new piece of factory equipment on May 1, 2013, for $29,200. For income tax purposes, the equipment is classified as a 7-year asset. Because this is similar to the economic life expected for the asset, Olympus decides to use the tax depreciation for financial reporting purposes. The equipment is not expected to have any residual value at the end of the seven years. Prepare a depreciation schedule for the life of the asset using the MACRS method of cost recovery.

Exercise 11-47
LO7

Computation of Depreciation Expense

Feng Company purchased a machine for $180,000 on September 1, 2013. It is estimated that the machine will have a 10-year life and a salvage value of $18,000. Its working hours and production in units are estimated at 36,000 and 750,000, respectively. It is the company's policy to depreciate assets for the number of months they are held during a year. During 2013, the machine was operated 1,500 hours and produced 21,000 units. Which of the following methods will give the greatest depreciation expense for 2013: (1) double-declining-balance (2) sum-of-the-years'-digits, (3) productive-output, or (4) service-hours? (Show computations for all four methods.)

Exercise 11-48
LO8

Computation of Book and Tax Depreciation

Rocky Point Foundry purchased factory equipment on March 15, 2012. The equipment will be depreciated for financial purposes over its estimated useful life, counting the year of acquisition as a half-year. The company accountant revealed the following information regarding this machine:

Purchase price	$110,000
Residual value	$17,000
Estimated useful life	12 years

1. What amount should Rocky Point Foundry record for depreciation expense for 2013 using the (a) double-declining-balance method and (b) sum-of-the-years'-digits method?
2. Assuming the equipment is classified as 8-year property under the modified accelerated cost recovery system (MACRS), what amount should Rocky Point Foundry deduct for depreciation on its tax return in 2013?

PROBLEMS

Problem 11-49

LO1

SPREADSHEET

Time-Factor Methods of Depreciation

A delivery truck was acquired by Navarro Inc. for $80,000 on January 1, 2013. The truck was estimated to have a 3-year life and a trade-in value at the end of that time of $20,000. The following depreciation methods are being considered:

(a) Depreciation is to be calculated by the straight-line method.
(b) Depreciation is to be calculated by the sum-of-the-years'-digits method.
(c) Depreciation is to be calculated by the double-declining-balance method.

Instructions: Prepare tables reporting periodic depreciation and asset book value over a 3-year period for each method listed.

Problem 11-50

LO1

Depreciation Under Different Methods

On January 1, 2010, Ron Shelley purchased a new tractor to use on his farm. The tractor cost $100,000. Ron also had the dealer install a front-end loader on the tractor. The cost of the front-end loader was $7,000. The shipping charges were $600, and the cost to install the loader was $800. The estimated life of the tractor was eight years, and the estimated service-hour life of the tractor was 12,500 hours. Ron estimated that he could sell the tractor for $15,000 at the end of eight years or 12,500 hours. The tractor was used for 1,725 hours in 2013. A full year's depreciation was taken in 2010, the year of acquisition.

Instructions: Compute depreciation expense for 2013 under each of the following methods:

1. Straight-line
2. Double-declining-balance
3. Sum-of-the-years'-digits
4. Service-hours

Problem 11-51

LO1

Maintenance Charges and Depreciation of Components

A company buys a machine for $61,700 on January 1, 2010. The maintenance costs for the years 2010–2013 are as follows: 2010, $4,900; 2011, $4,700; 2012, $12,400 (includes $7,800 for cost of a new motor installed in December 2012); 2013, $4,800.

Instructions:

1. Assume the machine is recorded in a single account at a cost of $61,700. Although it was not accounted for separately, the old motor (replaced at the end of 2012) had a cost of $7,100. Straight-line depreciation is used, and the asset is estimated to have a useful life of 11 years. It is assumed there will be no residual value at the end of the useful life. What are the total expenses related to the machine for each of the first four years?
2. Assume the cost of the frame of the machine was recorded in one account at a cost of $54,600 and the motor was recorded in a second account at a cost of $7,100. Straight-line depreciation is used with a useful life of 13 years for the frame and four years for the motor. Neither item is assumed to have any residual

value at the end of its useful life. What are the total expenses related to the machine?

3. Evaluate the two methods.

Problem 11-52
LO1

Depreciation and the Steady State

Lyell Company started a newspaper delivery business on January 1, 2010. On that date, the company purchased a small pickup truck for $14,000. Lyell planned to depreciate the truck over three years and assumed an $800 residual value. During 2010 and 2011, Lyell's business expanded. On January 1, 2011, Lyell purchased a second truck, identical to the first. On January 1, 2012, Lyell purchased a third truck, again identical to the first two. During 2012, Lyell's growth leveled off. However, on January 1, 2013, Lyell bought another truck to replace the one (purchased in 2010) that had just worn out. All trucks purchased cost the same amount as the first truck.

Instructions:

1. Compute depreciation expense for 2010, 2011, 2012, and 2013 using the following:
   (a) Straight-line method
   (b) Sum-of-the-years'-digits method
2. What general conclusions can be drawn from your calculations in (1)?

Problem 11-53
LO1
SPREADSHEET

Group Depreciation and Asset Retirement

Wright Manufacturing Co. acquired 20 similar machines at the beginning of 2008 for a total cost of $150,000. The machines have an average life of five years and no residual value. The group depreciation method is employed in writing off the cost of the machines. They were retired as follows:

2 machines at the end of 2010
4 machines at the end of 2011
8 machines at the end of 2012
6 machines at the end of 2013

Assume the machines were not replaced.

Instructions: Give the entries to record the retirement of the machines and the periodic depreciation for the years 2008–2013 inclusive.

Problem 11-54
LO1

Group Depreciation

Machines are acquired by Milestone Corporation on April 1, 2013, as follows:

Machine	Cost	Estimated Residual Value	Estimated Life in Years
511	$27,000	$ 5,000	11
512	31,000	7,000	6
513	52,000	10,000	7
514	38,000	None	8
515	23,000	4,000	5

Instructions:

1. Calculate the group depreciation rate for this group.
2. Calculate the average life in years for the group.
3. Give the entry to record the group depreciation for the year ended December 31, 2013.

Problem 11-55

LO3

Changes in Estimates

The following independent cases describe facts concerning the ownership of racing bicycles.

(a) Piero Niccolo, winner of the 2011 Milan–San Remo cycling classic, purchased a new Fierro bicycle for $6,500 at the beginning of 2011. The bicycle was being depreciated using the straight-line method over an estimated useful life of four years, with a $1,500 salvage value. At the beginning of 2013, the Italian superstar paid $900 to upgrade the bicycle. As a result, the useful life of the bicycle was extended by one year. The salvage value remained $1,500.

(b) Bart Gysel, winner of his country's own Tour of Flanders cycling classic in 2011, purchased a new Lampacht bicycle for $7,400 at the beginning of 2010. The bicycle was being depreciated using the double-declining-balance method over an estimated useful life of seven years, with a $2,000 salvage value. At the beginning of 2011, when the Belgian superstar won at Flanders, the salvage value of his Lampacht (eventual selling price) jumped to $3,000.

(c) Jacques Arouet, winner of the 2010 and 2011 Paris–Roubaix cycling classics, purchased a new Tonnerre bicycle for $8,000 in 2009. The French superstar did not use his new bicycle during the 2009 season. However, in 2010 and 2011, Arouet used his bicycle to win Paris–Roubaix and logged 7,500 and 9,000 kilometers, respectively, each year. Arouet estimated that the bicycle had a productive life of 25,000 kilometers. He did not use the bike in 2012, but in 2013 he decided to upgrade the bike with $1,750 of new components, giving the bicycle an additional 11,000 kilometers of productive use. During the 2013 season, he logged 11,500 kilometers on the bike. The estimated salvage value of the bicycle is $1,500.

Instructions: In each case, compute the depreciation for 2013.

Problem 11-56

LO1, LO2

Financial Statements for Mining Company

Roscoe Corp. was organized on January 2, 2013. It was authorized to issue 74,000 shares of common stock. On the date of organization, it sold 20,000 shares at $50 per share and gave the remaining shares in exchange for certain land-bearing recoverable ore deposits estimated by geologists at 900,000 tons. The property is deemed to have a value of $2,700,000 with no residual value.

During 2013, purchases of mine buildings and equipment totaled $350,000. During the year, 75,000 tons were mined; 8,000 tons of this amount were unsold on December 31, the balance of the tonnage being sold for cash at $17 per ton. Expenses incurred and paid for during the year, exclusive of depletion and depreciation, were as follows:

Mining	$173,500
Delivery	20,000
General and administrative	19,500

Cash dividends of $2 per share were declared on December 31, payable January 15, 2014.

It is believed that buildings and sheds will be useful only over the life of the mine; hence, depreciation is to be recognized in terms of mine output.

Instructions: Prepare an income statement and a balance sheet for 2013. Ignore income taxes.

Problem 11-57

LO1, LO2

Depletion Expense

In 2009, Heslop Mining Company purchased property with natural resources for $5,400,000. The property was relatively close to a large city and had an expected residual value of $700,000.

The following information relates to the use of the property:

(a) In 2009, Heslop spent $300,000 in development costs and $500,000 in buildings on the property. Heslop does not anticipate that the buildings will have any utility after the natural resources are depleted.
(b) In 2010 and 2012, $200,000 and $700,000, respectively, were spent for additional developments on the mine.
(c) The tonnage mined and estimated remaining tons for years 2009–2013 are as follows:

Year	Tons Extracted	Estimated Tons Remaining
2009	0	4,000,000
2010	1,200,000	2,800,000
2011	1,100,000	1,800,000
2012	800,000	900,000
2013	900,000	0

Instructions: Compute the depletion and depreciation expense for the years 2009–2013.

Problem 11-58
LO1, LO2

Depletion and Depreciation

In 2008, Sunbeam Corporation acquired a silver mine in eastern Alaska. Because the mine is located deep in the Alaskan frontier, Sunbeam was able to acquire the mine for the low price of $50,000. In 2009, Sunbeam constructed a road to the silver mine costing $5,000,000. Improvements to the mine made in 2009 cost $750,000. Because of the improvements to the mine and to the surrounding land, it is estimated that the mine can be sold for $600,000 when mining activities are complete.

During 2010, five buildings were constructed near the mine site to house the mine workers and their families. The total cost of the five buildings was $1,500,000. Estimated residual value is $250,000. In 2008, geologists estimated 4 million tons of silver ore could be removed from the mine for refining. During 2011, the first year of operations, only 5,000 tons of silver ore were removed from the mine. However, in 2012, workers mined 1 million tons of silver. During that same year, geologists discovered that the mine contained 3 million tons of silver ore in addition to the original 4 million tons. Improvements of $275,000 were made to the mine early in 2012 to facilitate the removal of the additional silver. Early in 2012, an additional building was constructed at a cost of $225,000 to house the additional workers needed to excavate the added silver. This building is not expected to have any residual value.

In 2013, 2.5 million tons of silver were mined and costs of $1,100,000 were incurred at the beginning of the year for improvements to the mine.

Instructions:

1. Compute the depreciation and depletion charges for 2011, 2012, and 2013.
2. Give the journal entries to record the depreciation and depletion charges for 2013.

Problem 11-59
LO1, LO2

Computation of Depreciation and Depletion

The following independent situations describe facts concerning the ownership of various assets.

(a) Dickenton Company purchased a tooling machine in 1998 for $85,000. The machine was being depreciated on the straight-line method over an estimated useful life of 30 years with no salvage value. At the beginning of 2013, when the machine had been in use for 15 years, Dickenton paid $17,000 to overhaul the machine. As a result of this improvement, Dickenton estimated that the useful life of the machine would be extended an additional five years.

(b) Andresen Manufacturing Co., a calendar-year company, purchased a machine for $50,000 on January 1, 2011. At the date of purchase, Andresen incurred the following additional costs:

Loss on sale of old machinery	$3,000
Freight cost	900
Installation cost	1,900
Testing costs prior to regular operation	800

The estimated salvage value of the machine was $8,000, and Andresen estimated that the machine would have a useful life of 15 years, with depreciation being computed using the straight-line method. In January 2013, accessories costing $2,925 were added to the machine to reduce its operating costs. These accessories neither prolonged the machine's life nor did they provide any additional salvage value.

(c) On July 1, 2013, Schiff Corporation purchased equipment at a cost of $48,000. The equipment has an estimated salvage value of $6,000 and is being depreciated over an estimated life of five years under the double-declining-balance method of depreciation. For the six months ended December 31, 2013, Schiff recorded a half-year's depreciation.

(d) Quinn Company acquired a tract of land containing an extractable natural resource. Geological surveys estimate that the recoverable reserves will be 4,000,000 tons and that the land will have a value of $800,000 after restoration. Relevant cost information follows:

Land	$14,000,000
Tons mined and sold in 2013	950,000

(e) In January 2013, Bradley Corporation entered into a contract to acquire a new machine for its factory. The machine, which had a cash price of $150,000, was paid for as follows:

Down payment	$ 40,000
400 shares of Bradley common stock with an agreed-upon value of $325 per share	130,000
	$170,000

Prior to the machine's use, installation costs of $10,000 were incurred. The machine has an estimated useful life of 16 years and an estimated salvage value of $20,000. The straight-line method of depreciation is used.

Instructions: In each case, compute the amount of depreciation or depletion for 2013.

Problem 11-60

LO1

Depreciation and the Cash Flow Statement

Oakeson Company is a manufacturing firm. Work-in-process and finished goods inventories for December 31, 2013, and December 31, 2012, follow:

	Dec. 31, 2013	Dec. 31, 2012
Work-in-process inventory (including depreciation)	$ 70,000	$ 75,000
Finished goods inventory (including depreciation)	123,000	110,000

Depreciation is a major portion of Oakeson's overhead, and the inventories listed above include depreciation in the amounts shown on page 11-60.

	Dec. 31, 2013	Dec. 31, 2012
Depreciation included in work-in-process inventory	$15,000	$12,500
Depreciation included in finished goods inventory	26,000	29,000

Oakeson's net income for 2013 was $90,000. Cost of goods sold for the year included $22,000 in depreciation.

Instructions: Compute net cash flow from operating activities for Oakeson Company for 2013. Assume that the levels of all current assets (except for inventories) and all current liabilities were unchanged from beginning of year to end of year.

Problem 11-61

LO4

Impairment

Deedle Company purchased four convenience store buildings on January 1, 2007, for a total of $13,000,000. The buildings have been depreciated using the straight-line method with a 20-year useful life and 5% residual value. As of January 1, 2013, Deedle has converted the buildings into Internet Learning Centers where classes on Internet usage will be conducted six days a week. Because of the change in the use of the buildings, Deedle is evaluating the buildings for possible impairment. Deedle estimates that the buildings have a remaining useful life of 10 years, that their residual value will be zero, that net cash inflow from the buildings will total $800,000 per year, and that the current fair value of the four buildings totals $5,000,000.

Instructions:

1. Make the appropriate journal entry, if any, to record an impairment loss as of January 1, 2013.
2. Compute total depreciation expense for 2013.
3. Repeat (1) and (2) assuming that the net cash inflow from the buildings totals $1,100,000 per year. The fair value of the four buildings totals $6,000,000.

Problem 11-62

LO4

Impairment: U.S. GAAP and IASB Standards

JJS Corporation purchased a building on January 1, 2009, for a total of $12,000,000. The building has been depreciated using the straight-line method with a 20-year useful life and no residual value. As of January 1, 2013, JJS is evaluating the building for possible impairment. The building has a remaining useful life of 12 years and is expected to generate cash inflows of $850,000 per year. The estimated fair value of the building on January 1, 2013, is $6,800,000.

Instructions:

1. Determine whether the building is impaired as of January 1, 2013. Make your determination using the provisions of both U.S. GAAP and *IAS 36*. Compare your answers.
2. Assume that JJS uses U.S. GAAP. Compute depreciation expense for 2013. (*Note*: Don't forget the new information on the expected useful life of the building.)
3. Assume that JJS is a non-U.S. company and uses international accounting standards. Compute depreciation expense for 2013.
4. Assume that JJS is a non-U.S. company and uses international accounting standards. Further assume that the building has a fair value of $14,000,000 on January 1, 2013, and that JJS chooses to upwardly revalue its long-term operating assets when they increase in value. Compute depreciation expense for 2013.

Problem 11-63

LO5

Accounting for Patents

On January 3, 2005, Merris Company spent $89,000 to apply for and obtain a patent on a newly developed product. The patent had an estimated useful life of 10 years.

At the beginning of 2009, the company spent $16,000 in successfully prosecuting an attempted infringement of the patent. At the beginning of 2010, the company purchased for $37,000 a patent that was expected to prolong the life of its original patent by five years. On July 1, 2013, a competitor obtained rights to a patent that made the company's patent obsolete.

Instructions: Give all the entries that would be made relative to the patent for the period 2005–2013, including entries to record the purchase of the patent, annual patent amortization, and ultimate patent obsolescence. (Assume the company's accounting period is the calendar year.)

Problem 11-64

LO5

Intangible Impairment

On December 31, 2012, Magily Company acquired the following three intangible assets:

(a) *A trademark for $30,000*. The trademark has seven years remaining in its legal life. It is anticipated that the trademark will be renewed in the future, indefinitely, without problem.
(b) *Goodwill for $150,000*. The goodwill is associated with Magily's Abacus Manufacturing reporting unit.
(c) *A customer list for $22,000*. By contract, Magily has exclusive use of the list for five years. Because of market conditions, it is expected that the list will have economic value for just three years.

On December 31, 2013, before any adjusting entries for the year were made, the following information was assembled about each of the intangible assets:

(a) Because of a decline in the economy, the trademark is now expected to generate cash flows of just $1,000 per year. The useful life of the trademark still extends beyond the foreseeable horizon.
(b) The cash flow expected to be generated by the Abacus Manufacturing reporting unit is $25,000 per year for the next 22 years. Book values and fair values of the assets and liabilities of the Abacus Manufacturing reporting unit are as follows:

	Book Values	Fair Values
Identifiable assets	$270,000	$300,000
Goodwill	150,000	?
Liabilities	180,000	180,000

(c) The cash flows expected to be generated by the customer list are $12,000 in 2014 and $8,000 in 2015.

Instructions: The appropriate discount rate for all items is 6%. Make all journal entries necessary on December 31, 2013, in connection with these three intangible assets.

Problem 11-65

LO6

REVERSE SOLVABLE

Exchange of Assets

A review of the books of Lakeshore Electric Co. disclosed that there were five transactions involving gains and losses on the exchange of fixed assets. The transactions were recorded as indicated in the following ledger accounts:

Cash

(b)	5,000	(e)	1,000
(c)	6,000		

Buildings and Equipment

(a)	10,000	(c)	118,000
(b)	25,000	(d)	850,000
(d)	550,000		

Acum. Depr.—Buildings and Equipment

Debit		Credit	
(c)	110,000		
(d)	390,000		

Intangible Assets

Debit		Credit	
(e)	1,000		

Gain on Exchange of Buildings and Equipment

Debit		Credit	
		(a)	10,000
		(b)	30,000
		(d)	90,000

Loss on Exchange of Buildings and Equipment

Debit		Credit	
(c)	2,000		

Investigation disclosed the following facts concerning these dealer-to-dealer transactions:

(a) Exchanged a piece of equipment with a $50,000 original cost, $20,000 book value, and $30,000 fair value for a piece of similar equipment owned by Highlite Electric, which had a $60,000 original cost, $10,000 book value, and a $30,000 fair value.

(b) Exchanged a machine—cost, $70,000; book value, $10,000; fair value, $40,000—for a similar machine—fair value, $35,000—and a "small" amount in cash, $5,000.

(c) Exchanged a building—cost, $150,000; book value, $40,000; fair value, $30,000—for a building with fair value of $24,000 plus cash of $6,000.

(d) Exchanged a factory building—cost, $850,000; book value, $460,000; fair value, $550,000—for equipment owned by Romeo Inc. That had an original cost of $900,000, accumulated depreciation of $325,000, and fair value of $550,000. The transaction is deemed to have commercial substance.

(e) Exchanged a patent—cost, $12,000; book value, $6,000; fair value, $3,000—and cash of $1,000 for another patent with fair value of $4,000.

Instructions: Analyze each recorded transaction as to its compliance with generally accepted accounting principles. Prepare adjusting journal entries where required.

Problem 11-66
LO6

SPREADSHEET

Exchange of Assets

Wild Expansion Co. acquired the following assets in exchange for various nonmonetary assets.

2013

Mar. 15 Acquired from another company a large lathe in exchange for three small lathes. The small lathes had a total cost of $28,000 and a remaining book value of $15,000. The new lathe had a market value of $23,000, approximately the same value as the three small lathes. This transaction is deemed NOT to have commercial substance.

June 1 Acquired 175 acres of land by issuing 3,200 shares of common stock with par value of $1 and market value of $75. Market analysis reveals that the market value of the stock was a reasonable value for the land.

July 15 Acquired a used piece of heavy, earth-moving equipment, market value, $120,000, by exchanging a used molding machine with a market value of $20,000 (book value, $12,000; cost, $50,000) and land with a market value of $135,000 (cost, $110,000). Cash of $35,000 was received by Wild Expansion Co. as part of the transaction.

Aug. 15 Acquired a patent, franchise, and copyright for two used milling machines. The book value of each milling machine was $4,000, and each originally cost $8,500. The market value of each machine is $9,000. It is estimated that the patent and franchise have about the same market values, and the market value of the copyright is 50% of the market value of the patent.

Nov. 1 Acquired a new packaging machine for four old packaging machines. The old machines had a total cost of $72,000 and a total remaining book value of $20,000. The new packaging machine has an indicated market value of $60,000, approximately the same value as the four machines. This transaction is deemed to have commercial substance.

Instructions: Prepare the journal entries required on Wild Expansion Co.'s books to record the exchanges.

Problem 11-67

LO1, LO6

Computation of Depreciation and Amortization

Information pertaining to Hedlund Corporation's property, plant, and equipment for 2013 follows.

Account balances at January 1, 2013:	**Debit**	**Credit**
Land	$ 150,000	
Buildings	1,200,000	
Accumulated Depreciation—Buildings		$263,100
Machinery and Equipment	900,000	
Accumulated Depreciation—Machinery and Equipment		250,000
Automotive Equipment	115,000	
Accumulated Depreciation—Automotive Equipment		84,600

Depreciation data:	**Depreciation Method**	**Useful Life**
Buildings	150% declining-balance	25 years
Machinery and Equipment	Straight-line	10 years
Automotive Equipment	Sum-of-the-years'-digits	4 years
Leasehold Improvements	Straight-line	—

The salvage values of the depreciable assets are immaterial. Depreciation is computed to the nearest month.

Transactions during 2013 and other information are as follows:

(a) On January 2, 2013, Hedlund purchased a new car for $20,000 cash and trade-in of a 2-year-old car with a cost of $18,000 and a book value of $5,400. The new car has a cash price of $24,000; the market value of the trade-in is not known.

(b) On April 1, 2013, a machine purchased for $23,000 on April 1, 2008, was destroyed by fire. Hedlund recovered $15,500 from its insurance company.

(c) On May 1, 2013, costs of $168,000 were incurred to improve leased office premises. The leasehold improvements have a useful life of eight years. The related lease terminates on December 31, 2019.

(d) On July 1, 2013, machinery and equipment were purchased at a total invoice cost of $280,000; additional costs of $5,000 for freight and $25,000 for installation were incurred.

(e) Hedlund determined that the automotive equipment comprising the $115,000 balance at January 1, 2013, would have been depreciated at a total amount of $18,000 for the year ended December 31, 2013.

Instructions:

1. Compute the total depreciation and amortization expense that would appear on Hedlund's income statement for the year ended December 31, 2013. Also compute the accumulated depreciation and amortization that would appear on the balance sheet at December 31, 2013.
2. Compute the total gain or loss from disposal of assets that would appear in Hedlund's income statement for the year ended December 31, 2013.
3. Prepare the Noncurrent Operating Assets section of Hedlund's December 31, 2013, balance sheet.

Problem 11-68

LO1, LO6

Comprehensive Depreciation and Amortization

At December 31, 2012, Oteron Company's noncurrent operating asset and accumulated depreciation and amortization accounts had balances as follows:

Category	Cost of Asset	Accumulated Depreciation and Amortization
Land	$ 430,000	
Buildings	1,500,000	$320,500
Machinery and equipment	825,000	174,300
Automobiles and trucks	146,000	94,600
Leasehold improvements	205,000	102,500

Category	Depreciation Method	Useful Life
Land improvements	Straight-line	15 years
Buildings	150% declining-balance	30 years
Machinery and equipment	Straight-line	12 years
Automobiles and trucks	150% declining-balance	6 years
Leasehold improvements	Straight-line	8 years

Depreciation is computed to the nearest month. The salvage values of the depreciable assets are immaterial.

Transactions during 2013 and other information are as follows:

(a) On January 6, 2013, a plant facility consisting of land and a building was acquired from Windop Corp. for $800,000. Of this amount, 25% was allocated to land.

(b) On April 6, 2013, new parking lots, streets, and sidewalks at the acquired plant facility were completed at a total cost of $210,000. These expenditures had an estimated useful life of 15 years.

(c) The leasehold improvements were completed on December 31, 2009, and had an estimated useful life of eight years. The related lease, which would have terminated on December 31, 2015, was renewable for an additional 4-year term. On April 29, 2013, Oteron exercised the renewal option.

(d) On July 1, 2013, machinery and equipment were purchased at a total invoice cost of $275,000. Additional costs of $15,000 for delivery and $25,000 for installation were incurred.

(e) On August 30, 2013, Oteron purchased a new automobile for $18,000.

(f) On September 30, 2013, a truck with a cost of $21,000 and a carrying amount of $10,841 on the date of sale was sold for $12,500. Depreciation for the nine months ended September 30, 2013, was $2,502.

(g) On December 20, 2013, a machine with a cost of $19,000 and a carrying amount of $3,275 at date of disposition was scrapped without cash recovery.

Instructions: Compute total depreciation and amortization expense for the year ended December 31, 2013.

Problem 11-69

LO2, LO3

Sample CPA Exam Questions

1. In January 2013, Vorst Co. purchased a mineral mine for $2,820,000 with removable ore estimated at 1,200,000 tons. After it has extracted all the ore, Vorst believes it will be able to sell the property for $300,000. During 2013, Vorst incurred $360,000 of development costs preparing the mine for production and removed and sold 60,000 tons of ore. In its 2013 income statement, what amount should Vorst report as depletion?
   (a) $135,000
   (b) $144,000

(c) $150,000
(d) $159,000

2. Turtle Co. purchased equipment on January 2, 2011, for $50,000. The equipment had an estimated 5-year service life with an expected salvage value of $0. Turtle's policy for 5-year assets is to use the double-declining-balance depreciation method for the first two years of the asset's life and then switch to the straight-line depreciation method. In its December 31, 2013, balance sheet, what amount should Turtle report as accumulated depreciation for equipment?
(a) $30,000
(b) $38,000
(c) $39,200
(d) $42,000

EM EXPANDED MATERIAL

Problem 11-70
LO8

Tax Depreciation Methods and the Time Value of Money

The following two depreciation methods are acceptable for tax purposes:

(a) *Straight line with a half-year convention*. The half-year convention is the assumption that all assets are acquired in the middle of the year. Therefore, a half-year's depreciation is allowed in the first year.
(b) *200% declining balance with a half-year convention*. There is a switch to straight-line depreciation on the remaining cost when straight line yields a larger amount than does 200% declining balance.

On January 1, 2013, Stratford Company purchased a piece of equipment for $425,000. The equipment has an estimated useful life of five years and no estimated residual value.

Instructions:

1. For tax purposes, depreciation reduces taxes payable by reducing taxable income. If the tax rate is 40%, for example, a $100 depreciation deduction will reduce taxes by $40. Ignoring the time value of money, calculate the total reduction in taxes Stratford will realize through the recovery of the asset cost over the life of the equipment. Assume that the tax rate is 40%. Is the answer the same for each of the two acceptable depreciation methods?
2. For each of the acceptable methods, compute the present value (as of January 1, 2013) of the depreciation tax savings. Assume that the appropriate interest rate is 10% and that the tax savings occur at the end of the year.
3. Should a company be required to use the same depreciation method in its financial statements as it uses for tax purposes?

CASES

Discussion Case 11-71

We Don't Need No Depreciation!

The managements of two different companies argue that because of specific conditions in their companies, recording depreciation expense should be suspended for 2013. Evaluate carefully their arguments.

(a) The president of Guzman Co. recommends that no depreciation be recorded for 2013 because the depreciation rate is 5% per year, and price indexes show that prices during the year have risen by more than this figure.
(b) The policy of Liebnitz Co. is to recondition its building and equipment each year so that they are maintained in perfect repair. In view of the extensive periodic costs incurred in 2013, officials of the company believe that the need for recognizing depreciation is eliminated.

Discussion Case 11-72

Is It Really Worth that Much?

Ferris Bueller, Inc., owns a building in Des Moines, Iowa, that was built at a cost of $5,000,000 in 2000. The building was used as a manufacturing facility from 2003 to 2012. However, economic conditions have made it necessary to consolidate Ferris Bueller's operations, and the building has been leased as of January 1, 2013, as a warehouse for 10 years at an annual rental of $240,000. Taxes, insurance, and normal maintenance costs are to be paid by the lessee. At the end of the 10-year period, Ferris Bueller may offer the lessee a renewal of the lease or again use the building in its operations. The building is being depreciated on a straight-line basis over a 40-year life.

In early 2013, Julie Ramos, a new staff accountant for Ferris Bueller, was assigned to review the building accounts and raised a question to Alison Crowther, her supervisor, concerning the carrying value of the Des Moines building. As of January 1, 2013, Julie feels the Des Moines building was impaired and should be written down in value. Alison is unsure about the current position of the FASB on this issue and invites Julie to prepare a memorandum recommending a specific write-down amount, with supporting justification. Prepare the memorandum, assuming current interest rates are 10%.

Discussion Case 11-73

Which Depreciation Method Should We Use?

Atwater Manufacturing Company purchased a new machine especially built to perform one particular function on the assembly line. A difference of opinion has arisen as to the method of depreciation to be used in connection with this machine. Three methods are now being considered:

(a) The straight-line method
(b) The productive-output method
(c) The sum-of-the-years'-digits method

List separately the arguments for and against each of the proposed methods from both the theoretical and practical viewpoints.

Discussion Case 11-74

How Do We Charge that Motion Picture Cost to Revenue?

In today's high-tech, high-cost entertainment industry, motion pictures often have costs in the tens of millions of dollars. Of course, it is hoped that these movies will be box office winners and that the revenues will exceed the cost outlay. With first runs, reruns, DVD sales and rentals, and so forth, it has become increasingly difficult to determine how the initial cost should be amortized against the revenue. Considering this industry and its characteristics, what amortization method would you suggest for these movie production costs?

Discussion Case 11-75

Let's Take a Bath!

Professor Linda DeAngelo found evidence suggesting that when the management of a company is ousted under fire, the new management tends to take an earnings "bath" after gaining control. A "bath" is a large reduction in earnings due to asset write-downs, reorganization charges, discontinuance of segments, and other extraordinary charges.

As an example, **Circle K Corporation** declared Chapter 11 bankruptcy and changed management during fiscal 1990. For the year, Circle K reported a reorganization and restructuring charge of $639 million, consisting primarily of write-downs of long-term assets. This contributed to a net loss for the year of $773 million, compared to average net income for the previous four years of about $40 million per year. Why might the new management of a company want to "take a bath" in its first year?

SOURCES: Linda DeAngelo, "Managerial Compensation, Information Costs, and Corporate Governance," *Journal of Accounting and Economics 10*, January 1988, pp. 3–36.

The Circle K Corporation, 1990 Annual Report.

Discussion Case 11-76

But What Is a Reasonable Life for My Airplane?

Different airlines depreciate the same airplanes but using different useful-life and residual value assumptions. For example, airlines have depreciated the same **Boeing** aircraft over lives ranging from 14 years to 28 years. What might cause a firm to decide to increase the estimated useful life of a depreciable asset?

Case 11-77

Deciphering Financial Statements (The Walt Disney Company)

Locate the 2009 financial statements for **The Walt Disney Company** on the Internet and consider the following questions:

1. What depreciation method does Disney use for its parks, resorts, and other property? For its film and television costs?
2. Where do you have to look to find out that Disney's 2009 total depreciation and amortization expense was $1,631 million?
3. As of October 3, 2009, what percentage of film and television production costs was expected to be amortized within the next three years?
4. In 2006, Disney acquired **Pixar**. The following information concerning the acquisition is summarized from Disney's 2006 annual report:

On May 5, 2006, the Company completed an all stock acquisition of Pixar, a digital animation studio. The acquisition price was $7.5 billion, and the Company allocated the purchase price to the tangible and identifiable assets acquired and liabilities assumed based on their fair values, which were determined primarily through third-party appraisals. The following table summarizes the allocation of the purchase price (in millions):

Cash and cash equivalents	$ 11
Investments	1,073
Prepaid and other assets	45
Film costs	538
Buildings and equipment	225
Intangibles	233
Goodwill	5,557
Total assets acquired	$7,682
Liabilities	$ 64
Deferred income taxes	123
Total liabilities assumed	$ 187
Net assets acquired	$7,495

The goodwill on Disney's 2005 consolidated balance sheet was $16.974 billion, and, as seen in the table above, $5.557 billion of goodwill was associated with the Pixar purchase in 2006. In the consolidated balance sheet of Disney's 2009 financial statements, the original cost associated with total goodwill was $21.683 billion. If $5.557 billion of goodwill from the Pixar purchase was added to Disney's 2005 total goodwill (giving a total of $22.531 billion), why you think Disney's 2009 total goodwill was only $21.683 billion?

Case 11-78

Deciphering Financial Statements (Delta Air Lines)

The following information is from the June 30, 1998, balance sheet for **Delta Air Lines** (all dollar amounts are in millions):

	1998	1997
Flight equipment	$11,180	$9,619
Less: Accumulated depreciation	3,895	3,510

Delta also included this note to its financial statements:

Depreciation and Amortization—Effective July 1, 1998, the Company increased the depreciable life of certain new generation aircraft types from 20 to 25 years. Owned flight equipment is depreciated on a straight-line basis to a residual value equal to 5% of cost.

1. Assume that all flight equipment will be affected by this policy change. The new policy will not be reflected in the 1998 financial statements, as the policy was changed on July 1, 1998. Estimate the total depreciation expense recognized by Delta on flight equipment for the year ended June 30, 1998, using the old 20-year life and the new 25-year life. Assume there were no flight equipment retirements during the year and new acquisitions are depreciated for half the year.
2. How reasonable is the assumption that there were no flight equipment retirements in 1998?

Case 11-79

Writing Assignment (One depreciation method, please!)

The FASB frequently receives recommendations about areas it should consider for study. Depreciation accounting has not been addressed as a separate topic by the FASB, and several alternative methods are used for recording this expense on the books. Assume that a group of financial analysts recommends to the FASB that a study be made of depreciation accounting with the objective of selecting one method as the only acceptable one. The analysts reason that only then will comparability in financial statements be achieved. You have recently been hired as a member of the FASB's research staff. Write a summary memo presenting the arguments for and against the FASB following the recommendation by the analysts.

Case 11-80

Ethical Dilemma (Profit manipulation during labor negotiations)

You and your partner own a small data-entry company. You contract with businesses to manually enter data, such as library card catalogs and medical records, into a computer database. Your most significant physical assets are a large office building you own, along with the computer hardware and software necessary for operations. Your business has been running for five years, and you now have 100 employees. Operating cash flow has always been healthy, and you and your partner have been able to withdraw significant amounts of cash from the business. Recently, you have seen growing discontent among your employees because of their low wages and lack of fringe benefits. You and your partner are preparing for the first meeting with an employee grievance committee.

Your partner has taken responsibility for preparing the company's financial statements. You are embarrassed to admit that this is the first set of financial statements you have ever examined—you have never sought bank financing and all equity funding has come from you and your partner. You are surprised when you first review the statements because they reveal that the company has experienced significant losses in each of its five years of operation.

A closer look at the statements reveals that your partner has used the double-declining-balance method of depreciation for your office building and computer equipment. He has also assumed very short useful lives and zero residual values. Your calculations indicate that using the straight-line method with more realistic useful life and residual value assumptions would increase profits dramatically, even to the extent that substantial profits would be reported in each of the first five years of operation.

The meeting with the employee grievance committee is tomorrow. Your partner has been your friend since first grade. What, if anything, should you do?

Case 11-81

Cumulative Spreadsheet Analysis

This spreadsheet assignment is a continuation of the spreadsheet assignments given in earlier chapters. If you completed those assignments, you have a head start on this one.

Refer back to the instructions for preparing the revised financial statements for 2013 as given in (1) the Cumulative Spreadsheet Analysis assignment in Chapter 3.

1. Skywalker wishes to prepare a *forecasted* balance sheet, a *forecasted* income statement, and a *forecasted* statement of cash flows for 2014. Use the financial statement numbers for 2013 as the basis for the forecast, along with the following additional information.

   (a) Sales in 2014 are expected to increase by 40% over 2013 sales of $2,100.
   (b) In 2014, new property, plant, and equipment acquisitions will be in accordance with the information in (q).
   (c) The $480 in operating expenses reported in 2013 breaks down as follows: $15 in depreciation expense and $465 in other operating expenses.
   (d) No new long-term debt will be acquired in 2014.
   (e) No cash dividends will be paid in 2014.
   (f) New short-term loans payable will be acquired in an amount sufficient to make Skywalker's current ratio in 2014 exactly equal to 2.0.
   (g) Skywalker does not expect to repurchase additional shares of stock in 2014.
   (h) Because changes in future prices and exchange rates are impossible to predict, Skywalker's best estimate is that the balance in accumulated other comprehensive income will remain unchanged in 2014.
   (i) Assume that the balances in Investment Securities, Long-Term Investments, and Other Long-Term Assets will increase at the same rate as sales (40%) in 2014. The balance in Intangible Assets will change in accordance with item (r).
   (j) Assume that the balance in the other long-term liabilities account will increase at the same rate as sales (40%) in 2014.
   (k) The investment securities are classified as available-for-sale securities. Accordingly, cash from the purchase and sale of these securities is classified as an investing activity.
   (l) Assume that transactions impacting other long-term assets and other long-term liabilities accounts are operating activities.
   (m) Cash and investment securities accounts will increase at the same rate as sales.
   (n) The forecasted amount of accounts receivable in 2014 is determined using the forecasted value for the average collection period. The average collection period for 2014 is expected to be 14.08 days. To make the calculations less complex, this value of 14.08 days is based on forecasted end-of-year accounts receivable rather than on average accounts receivable.
   (o) The forecasted amount of inventory in 2014 is determined using the forecasted value for the number of days' sales in inventory. The number of days' sales in inventory for 2014 is expected to be 107.6 days. To make the calculations simpler, this value of 107.6 days is based on forecasted end-of-year inventory rather than on average inventory.
   (p) The forecasted amount of accounts payable in 2014 is determined using the forecasted value for the number of days' purchases in accounts payable, which is expected to be 48.34 days. To make the calculations simpler, this value of 48.34 days is based on forecasted end-of-year accounts payable rather than on average accounts payable.
   (q) The forecasted amount of property, plant, and equipment (PP&E) in 2014 is determined using the forecasted value for the fixed asset turnover ratio, which is expected to be 3.518 times. To make the calculations simpler, this ratio of 3.518 is based on forecasted end-of-year gross property, plant, and equipment rather than on the average balance. (*Note*: For simplicity, ignore accumulated depreciation in making this calculation.)
   (r) Skywalker has determined that no new intangible assets will be acquired in 2014. Intangible assets are amortized according to the information in (t).

(*Note*: These forecasted statements were constructed as part of the spreadsheet assignment in Chapter 10; you can use that spreadsheet as a starting point.)

For this exercise, make the following additional assumptions:

(s) In computing depreciation expense for 2014, use straight-line depreciation and assume a 30-year useful life with no residual value. Gross PP&E acquired during the year is only depreciated for half the year. In other words, depreciation expense for 2014 is the sum of two parts: (1) a full year of depreciation on the beginning balance in PP&E, assuming a 30-year life and no residual value, and (2) a half-year of depreciation on any new PP&E acquired during the year, based on the change in the gross PP&E balance.

(t) Skywalker assumes a 20-year useful life for its intangible assets. Assume that the $100 in intangible assets reported in 2013 is the original cost of the intangibles. Include the amortization expense with the depreciation expense in the income statement.

Clearly state any additional assumptions that you make.

2. Assume the same scenario as (1), and show the impact on the financial statements with the following changes in assumptions:
   (a) Estimated useful life of property, plant, and equipment is 15 years.
   (b) Estimated useful life of property, plant, and equipment is 60 years.
3. Comment on the differences in the forecasted values of cash from operating activities in 2014 under each of the following assumptions about the estimated useful life of PP&E: 15 years, 30 years, and 60 years. Explain exactly why a change in depreciation life has an impact on cash from operating activities.

P3 ADDITIONAL ACTIVITIES OF A BUSINESS

Jin Lee/Bloomberg via Getty Images

CHAPTER 12 Debt Financing

LEARNING OBJECTIVES

1. Understand the various classification and measurement issues associated with debt.
2. Account for short-term debt obligations, including those expected to be refinanced, and describe the purpose of lines of credit.
3. Apply present value concepts to the accounting for long-term debts such as mortgages.
4. Understand the various types of bonds; compute the price of a bond issue; and account for the issuance, interest, and redemption of bonds.
5. Discuss the use of the fair value option for financial assets and liabilities.
6. Explain various types of off-balance-sheet financing, and understand the reasons for this type of financing.
7. Analyze a firm's debt position using ratios.
8. Review the notes to financial statements, and understand the disclosure associated with debt financing.

EM EXPANDED MATERIAL

9. Understand the conditions under which troubled debt restructuring occurs, and be able to account for troubled debt restructuring.

Analysis of the data gathered in the U.S. census of 1880 took almost 10 years. For the census of 1890, the U.S. government commissioned Herman Hollerith to provide data tabulation machines to speed up the process. This system of mechanized data handling saved the Census Bureau $5 million and slashed the data analysis time by two years. In 1924, Hollerith's company adopted the name **International Business Machines Corporation (IBM)**. IBM became the largest office machine producer in the United States with sales of more than $180 million in 1949.

In 1950, there was great resistance to the idea of electronic computers at IBM. IBM's engineers were specialists in electromechanical devices and were uncomfortable working with vacuum tubes, diodes, and magnetic recording tapes. In addition, there were many questions about the customer demand for electronic computers. One IBM executive forecast that the size of the total worldwide market for computers was no more than five. However, following significant internal debate, IBM pressed forward with the production of its first electronic computer, the 701. Through the 1960s and 70s, with its aggressive leasing program, emphasis on sales and service, and continued investment in research and development, IBM established a dominant (some claimed a monopolistic) position in the mainframe computer market.

When the IBM personal computer was released in 1981, it quickly became the industry standard for PCs. By 1986, IBM held 40% of the PC market. Amid this success, IBM made what, in retrospect, was a crucial error—it chose to focus on producing and selling hardware and to leave software development, by and large, to others. In fact, IBM did not develop the operating system for its first PC, instead electing to use a system called DOS, licensed from a 32-person company named **Microsoft**. In the early 1990s, as profits of software developers such as Microsoft exploded, the profits of IBM slumped badly. In 1990, IBM reported an operating profit of $11 billion. Operating profit in 1991 fell to $942 million, and operations showed a loss of $45 million in 1992, which was IBM's first operating loss ever. As of December 31, 1992, the total market value of IBM stock was $29 billion, down from $106 billion in 1987 when IBM was the most valuable company in the world.

Interestingly, in the midst of these problems—decreasing market share, lower profit margins, and record losses—IBM found high demand for its record-setting bond issue. In 1993, IBM issued $1.25 billion of 7-year notes and $550 million of 20-year debentures. At the time, this was the largest U.S. bond issue in history. The stated interest rates were 6.375% for the notes and 7.50% for the bonds. On their issue date, these two bond issues provided investors with a yield just 0.7% above that provided by U.S. Treasury instruments with comparable maturity periods. Because of IBM's financial woes and increased risk at the time, many thought that the difference would be much higher. Nonetheless, investors' concerns about IBM's future did increase the perceived risk associated with loaning money to the company. In January 1993, **Standard & Poor**'s downgraded IBM's credit rating from the highest rating, AAA, to AA–. In March 1993, **Moody's Investor's Service** also lowered IBM's rating from A–1 to AA–2.[1] Prior to these downgrades, IBM was able to finance debt in the market at approximately 0.5% above the U.S. Treasury yield.[2]

In a bid to turn IBM around, the board of directors looked outside the company for a new CEO in 1993. They picked Louis V. Gerstner, Jr., who had been the CEO at **RJR Nabisco** for four years. In his 1997 address to IBM's shareholders, Mr. Gerstner looked back on the task that had faced him when he took the reins in 1993. When he came aboard, he reported, IBM's board was considering dismantling the company, thinking that a collection of smaller, more nimble businesses would hopefully be worth more to IBM's shareholders than the lumbering, inefficient parent company. Mr. Gerstner changed the direction of the company, deciding to keep the company together and to rely on IBM's unique market position in terms of product breadth and strong customer ties.

Under Mr. Gerstner's leadership, IBM recovered. Mr. Gerstner led the company, as the chairman of the board of directors, through 2002. Exhibit 12-1 shows the relationship between IBM's total short- and long-term debt, its total assets, and its market value from 1992 through 2007. Note that IBM's total short- and long-term debt and total market value were almost equal in 1992. Although the company's assets and debt have remained relatively constant over the 16-year period, the firm's market value increased significantly peaking at $208 billion on December 31, 2001, before easing in the wake of the burst of the dot.com bubble.

An examination of IBM's 2009 liabilities reveals the following (in millions):

Current liabilities:	
Taxes	$ 3,826
Short-term debt	4,168
Accounts payable	7,436
Compensation and benefits	4,505
Deferred income	10,845
Other accrued expenses and liabilities	5,223

[1] These bond rating scales have since been modified.

[2] Thomas T. Vogel, Jr., and Leslie Scism, "Investors Snap Up $1.8 Billion of IBM Securities as Corporations Scramble to Best Higher Interest Rates," *The Wall Street Journal*, June 9, 1993, p. C16.

EX 12-1 IBM'S TOTAL DEBT, TOTAL ASSETS, AND TOTAL MARKET VALUE OF EQUITY

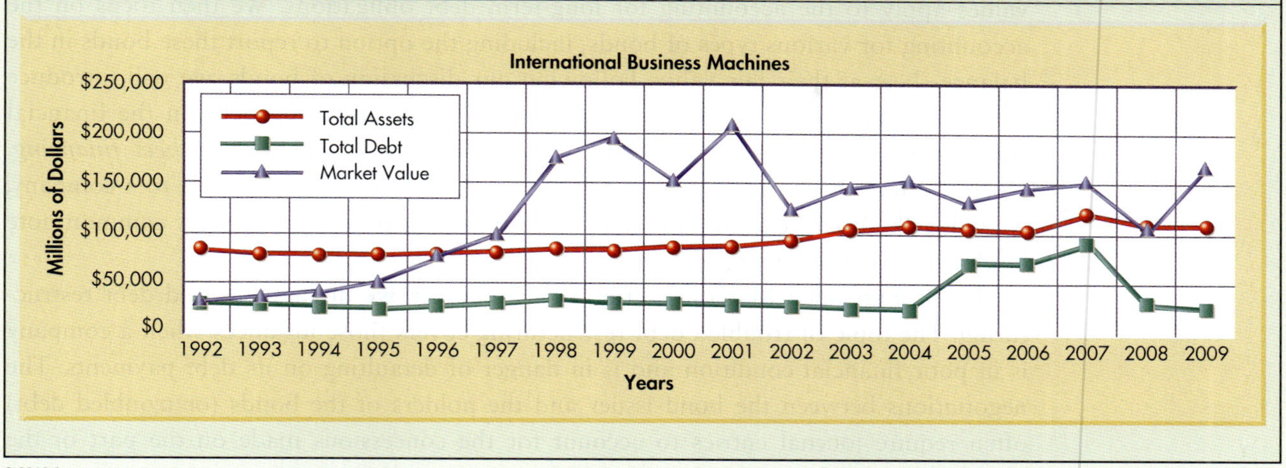

Long-term:	
Long-term debt	21,932
Retirement and nonpension postretirement benefit obligations	15,953
Deferred income	3,562
Other liabilities	8,819

IBM's largest liability is its long-term debt. A review of this debt reveals debentures, some of which will mature as far out as 2096. In addition, the long-term debt includes notes and foreign currency debt denominated in euros, Japanese yen, and Swiss francs.

In this chapter, we will discuss many of these liabilities. A discussion of the liabilities relating to compensation (compensation and benefits and retirement and nonpension postretirement benefits) will be saved for Chapter 17.

QUESTIONS

1. What was the interest rate impact of the downgrading of IBM's debt by the bond rating agencies?
2. Why is the market interest rate on corporate bonds ALWAYS higher than the market interest rate associated with comparable U.S. Treasury bonds?
3. In 2009, IBM's long-term debt and its long-term retirement obligation were the two largest liabilities on the balance sheet. However, the financial characteristics of these two obligations are dramatically different. On what important dimension do these two long-term obligations differ?

Answers to these questions can be found on page 12-54.

In addition to the routine notes and debentures issued by IBM, a long list of more creative types of debt-financing instruments has been created by the U.S. financial industry. For years, we've had convertible bonds, junk bonds, zero-interest bonds, and commodity-backed bonds, to name a few. The objective of each of these debt instruments is to assist a company in raising needed funds for its business. In this chapter, we will discuss various methods available to companies for borrowing money. We begin with a quick review of liabilities: what they are and how they are measured. Then we will discuss short-term obligations and lines of credit. We then review the concept of present value and examine a mortgage to illustrate how present values apply to the accounting for long-term debt obligations. We then focus on the accounting for various types of bonds, including the option to report these bonds in the balance sheet at their fair value. Following our discussion of bonds, we will introduce some common methods that companies use to avoid disclosing debt on the financial statements. These methods are collectively referred to as *off-balance-sheet financing*. Once you have been exposed to various types of debt financing available to a company, we will talk about how one can analyze a firm's debt position as well as common note disclosures associated with debt.

In the Expanded Material section of the chapter, we discuss troubled debt restructuring. The topic of troubled debt restructuring covers those instances when a company is in poor financial condition and is in danger of defaulting on its debt payments. The negotiations between the bond issuer and the holders of the bonds (or troubled debt) often require journal entries to account for the concessions made on the part of the bondholders.

A time line illustrating the business issues associated with long-term financing is given in Exhibit 12-2. The first action is to choose the appropriate form of financing. For example, a company must decide whether to negotiate a private loan with a bank or to seek public financing through the issuance of bonds. After the debt is issued, it is usually serviced through periodic interest payments, although some forms of long-term debt defer payment of all interest until the end of the loan period. An important part of issuing and monitoring long-term debt is the accounting for the specific features of the debt. As discussed in this chapter, bonds require specialized accounting procedures to ensure that the proper amount of interest expense is reported in the income statement and that the long-term debt obligation is reported at the appropriate amount in the balance sheet. Finally, the long-term debt is repaid, either as originally scheduled or, sometimes, in advance.

EX 12-2 TIME LINE OF BUSINESS ISSUES ASSOCIATED WITH LONG-TERM DEBT

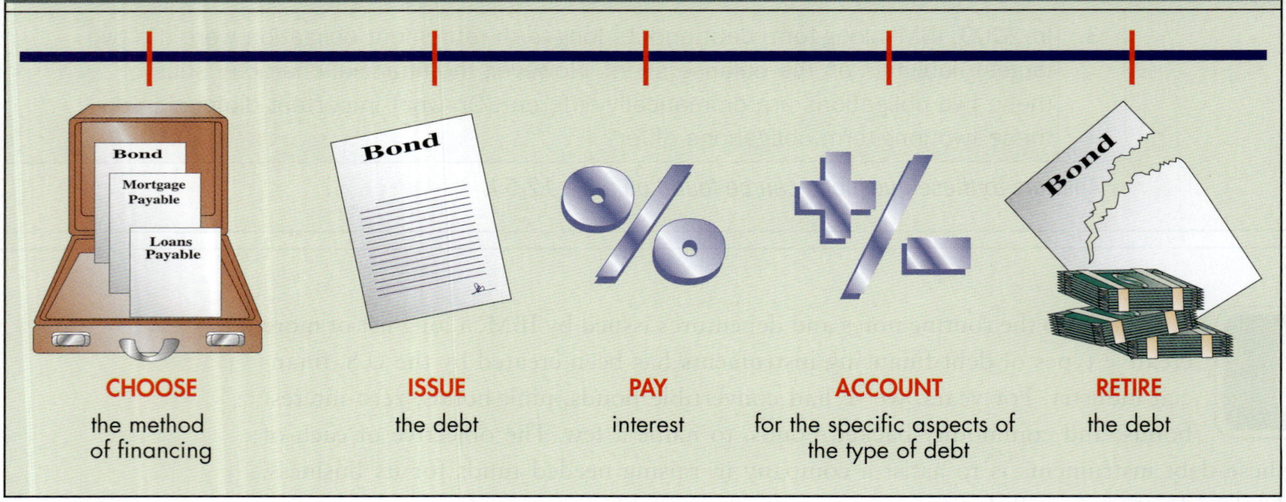

Classification and Measurement Issues Associated with Debt

1 **Understand the various classification and measurement issues associated with debt.**

WHY **To effectively evaluate a firm's liquidity and solvency positions, all current and future obligations must be identified and quantified. Obligations due in the future must be measured in present value terms.**

HOW **Theoretically, all debt should be recorded at its present value. However, most current obligations arising in the normal course of business are not discounted. Obligations that cannot be measured with certainty are estimated and recorded at an approximate amount.**

Before we get into the specifics of debt, let's first take a moment and review just what liabilities are and how they are classified and measured.

Definition of Liabilities

The FASB has defined liabilities as "probable future sacrifices of economic benefits arising from present obligations of a particular entity to transfer assets or provide services to other entities in the future as a result of past transactions or events."[3] This definition contains significant components that need to be explained before individual liability accounts are discussed.

A liability is a result of *past transactions or events*. Thus, a liability is not recognized until incurred. This part of the definition excludes contractual obligations from an exchange of promises if performance by both parties is still in the future. Such contracts are referred to as *executory contracts*. Determining when an executory contract qualifies as a liability is not always easy. For example, the signing of a labor contract that obligates both the employer and the employee does not give rise to a liability in current accounting practice, nor does the placing of an order for the purchase of merchandise. However, under some conditions, the signing of a lease is recognized as an event that requires the current recognition of a liability even though a lease is essentially an executory contract.

A liability must involve a *probable future transfer of assets or services*. Although liabilities result from past transactions or events, an obligation may be contingent upon the occurrence of another event sometime in the future. When occurrence of the future event seems probable, the obligation is defined as a *liability*. Although the majority of liabilities are satisfied by payment of cash, some obligations are satisfied by transferring other types of assets or by providing services. For example, revenue received in advance requires recognition of an obligation to provide goods or services in the future. Usually, the time of payment is specified by a debt instrument, for example, a note requiring payment of interest and principal on a given date or series of dates. Some obligations, however, require the transfer

> **FYI**
>
> The FASB is considering a change in the conceptual framework definition of a liability. The change intends to extend the definition of a liability beyond obligations to transfer assets or services to also include obligations to deliver a certain dollar value of equity shares.

[3] *Statement of Financial Accounting Concepts No. 6*, "Elements of Financial Statements" (Stamford, CT: Financial Accounting Standards Board, December 1985), par. 35. As discussed in this chapter and in Chapter 13 on equity financing, the FASB is currently considering a revision of this liability definition.

Keith Brofsky/Photodisc/Getty Images

A liability, such as a bank loan, has the following characteristics: (1) is a result of past transactions or events, (2) involves a probable future transfer of assets or services, and (3) is the obligation of a particular entity.

of assets or services over a period of time, but the exact dates cannot be determined when the liability is incurred, for example, obligations to provide parts or service under a warranty agreement.

A liability is the *obligation of a particular entity*, that is, the entity that has the responsibility to transfer assets or provide services. As long as the payment or transfer is probable, it is not necessary that the entity to whom the obligation is owed be identified. Thus, a warranty to make any repairs necessary to an item sold by an entity is an obligation of that entity even though it is not certain which customers will receive benefits. Generally, the obligation rests on a foundation of legal rights and duties. However, obligations created, inferred, or construed from the facts of a particular situation may also be recognized as liabilities. For example, if a company regularly pays vacation pay or year-end bonuses, accrual of these items as a liability is warranted even though no legal agreement exists to make these payments.

Although the FASB's definition is helpful, the question of when a liability exists is not always easy to answer. Examples of areas in which there are continuing controversies include the problems associated with off-balance-sheet financing, deferred income taxes, leases, pensions, and even some equity securities, such as redeemable preferred stock. Once an item is accepted as having met the definition of a liability, there is still the need to appropriately classify, measure, and report the liability.

Classification of Liabilities

For reporting purposes, liabilities are usually classified as current or noncurrent. The distinction between current and noncurrent liabilities was introduced and explained in Chapter 3, where it was pointed out that the computation of working capital is considered by many to be a useful measure of the liquidity of an enterprise.

As noted in Chapter 3, the same rules generally apply for the classification of liabilities as for assets. If a liability arises in the course of an entity's normal operating cycle, it is considered current if current assets will be used to satisfy the obligation within one year or one operating cycle, whichever period is longer. On the other hand, bank borrowings, notes, mortgages, and similar obligations are related to the general financial condition of the entity, rather than directly to the operating cycle, and are classified as current only if they are to be paid with current assets within one year.

When debt that has been classified as noncurrent will mature within the next year, the liability should be reported as a current liability in order

FYI

The classification of a liability as current or noncurrent can impact significantly a company's ability to raise additional funds. Most lending institutions and investors look carefully at the current ratio—current assets divided by current liabilities—as a measure of liquidity.

to reflect the expected drain on current assets. However, if the liability is to be paid by transfer of noncurrent assets that have been accumulated for the purpose of liquidating the liability, the obligation continues to be classified as noncurrent.

The distinction between current and noncurrent liabilities is important because of the impact on a company's current ratio. This fundamental measurement of a company's liquidity is computed by dividing total current assets by total current liabilities.

> **STOP&THINK**
>
> Look at Exhibit 12-3. The 2009 current ratio of **Wal-Mart** is only 0.87. How will Wal-Mart most likely meet its current obligations as they come due?
>
> a) By the issuance of new shares of common stock
> b) By liquidating long-term assets such as land or buildings
> c) Wal-Mart will probably not be able to meet its current obligations as they come due.
> d) Through the generation of operating cash flow in the normal course of business

The current ratio is a measure of an entity's ability to meet current obligations. Care must be taken to determine that proper items have been included in the current asset and current liability categories. Historically, the rule of thumb has been that a current ratio below 2.0 suggests the possibility of liquidity problems. However, advances in information technology have enabled companies to be much more effective in minimizing the need to hold cash, inventories, and other current assets. As a result, current ratios for successful companies these days are frequently less than 1.0. Current ratios for selected U.S. companies are given in Exhibit 12-3. Note that ALL of the companies have current ratios substantially below the 2.0 historical benchmark, and the current ratio of **Delta Air Lines** is only 0.79.

A reasonable margin of current assets over current liabilities suggests that a company will be able to meet maturing obligations even in the event of unfavorable business conditions or losses on such assets as securities, receivables, and inventories. A current ratio of 1.4 means, for example, that a company could liquidate its total current liabilities 1.4 times using only its current assets.

EX 12-3 CURRENT RATIOS FOR SELECTED U.S. COMPANIES FOR FISCAL 2009

	Current Ratio
Coca-Cola	1.28
Delta Air Lines	0.79
Dow Chemical	1.49
IBM	1.36
McDonald's	1.14
Microsoft	1.82
Wal-Mart	0.87

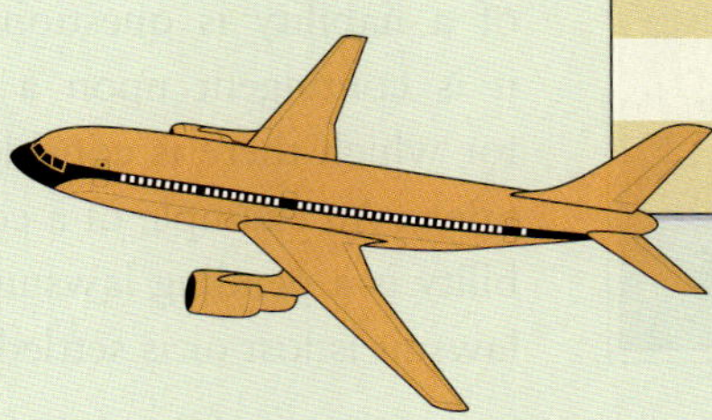

Measurement of Liabilities

The distinction between current and noncurrent liabilities is also an important consideration in the measurement of liabilities. Obviously, before liabilities can be reported on the financial statements, they must be stated in monetary terms. The fair value measurement used for liabilities is typically the present value of the future cash outflows to settle the obligation. Generally, this is the amount of cash required to pay someone else to accept responsibility for the obligation today.

If a claim isn't to be paid until sometime in the future, as is the case with noncurrent liabilities, either the claim should provide for interest to be paid on the debt or the obligation should be reported at the discounted value of its maturity amount. Current obligations that arise in the course of normal business operations are generally due within a short period, for example, 30 to 60 days, and normally are not discounted.[4] Thus, trade accounts payable are not reported at their present value even though they carry no interest provision. However, this is an exception to the general rule; most nonoperating business transactions, such as the borrowing of money, purchasing of assets over time, and long-term leases, do involve the computation of present values. The obligation in these instances is the present value of the future resource outflows. The use of present value concepts with long-term debt obligations is illustrated in detail later in the chapter.

For measurement purposes, liabilities can be divided into three categories:

1. Liabilities that are definite in amount
2. Estimated liabilities
3. Contingent liabilities

The measurement of liabilities always involves some uncertainty because a liability, by definition, involves a future outflow of resources. However, for the first category, both the existence of the liability and the amount to be paid are determinable because of a contract, trade agreement, or general business practice. An example of a liability that is definite in amount is the principal payment on a note.

The second category includes items that are definitely liabilities; that is, they involve a definite future resource outflow, but the actual amount of the obligation cannot be established currently. In this situation, the amount of the liability is estimated so that the obligation is reflected in the current period, even though at an approximated value. A warranty obligation that is recorded on an accrual basis is an example of an estimated liability.

Generally, liabilities from both of the first two categories are reported on the balance sheet, either as current or noncurrent liabilities, whichever is appropriate. However, items that resemble liabilities but are contingent upon the occurrence of some future event are not recorded until it is probable that the event will occur. Even though the amount of the potential obligation may be known, the actual existence of a liability is questionable because it is contingent upon a future event for which there is considerable uncertainty. An example of a contingent liability is a pending lawsuit. Only if the lawsuit is lost or is settled out of court

! CAUTION

A contingent liability results only when there is a significant degree of uncertainty as to the outcome of the event associated with the potential liability. Recall from its definition that a liability involves a "probable future sacrifice. . . ." If the contingent event is probable, it meets the definition of a liability and should be recorded as such.

[4] FASB ASC paragraph 835-30-15-3a.

will a sacrifice of economic benefits be necessary. Although not recorded in the accounts, some contingent liabilities should be disclosed in the notes to the financial statements as discussed and illustrated in Chapter 19.

Accounting for Short-Term Debt Obligations

2 **Account for short-term debt obligations, including those expected to be refinanced, and describe the purpose of lines of credit.**

WHY **Obligations due within one year or within the company's operating cycle are classified as current. This classification allows financial statement users to assess the company's liquidity position.**

HOW **The most common current liabilities include accounts payable, wages payable, interest payable, taxes payable, and other short-term operating accruals. Short-term obligations expected to be refinanced on a long-term basis should be classified as noncurrent if certain criteria are met.**

As noted in the previous section, liabilities that have been classified as current are typically not discounted, that is, they are not reported at their present value. Instead, they are reported on the balance sheet at their face value. Representative of this type of debt are accounts payable, notes payable, and miscellaneous operating payables including salaries, payroll taxes, property and sales taxes, and income taxes. Short-term obligations that are expected to be refinanced require special consideration. Problems that can arise in determining the balances to be reported for these various types of debt are described in the following sections.

Short-Term Operating Liabilities

Businesses with good internal processes purchase most goods and services on credit. The term account payable usually refers to the amount due for the purchase of materials by a manufacturing company or merchandise by a wholesaler or retailer. Other obligations, such as salaries and wages, rent, interest, and utilities, are reported as separate liabilities in accounts descriptive of the nature of the obligation. Accounts payable are not recorded when purchase orders are placed but instead when legal title to the goods passes to the buyer. The rules for the customary recognition of legal passage of title were presented in Chapter 9. If goods are in transit at year-end, the purchase should be recorded if the shipment terms indicate that title has passed. This means that care must be exercised to review the purchase of goods and services near the end of an accounting period to ensure a proper cutoff and reporting of liabilities and inventory. It is customary to report accounts payable at the expected amount of the payment. Because the payment period is normally short, no recognition of interest is required.

Short-Term Debt

Companies often borrow money on a short-term basis for operating purposes other than for the purchase of materials or merchandise involving accounts payable. Collectively, these obligations may be referred to as *short-term debt*. In most cases, such debt is evidenced by a promissory note, a formal written promise to pay a sum of money in the future, and is usually reflected on the debtor's books as Notes payable.

Notes issued to trade creditors for the purchase of goods or services are called trade notes payable. Nontrade notes payable are notes issued to banks or to officers and stockholders for loans to the company and those issued to others for the purchase of noncurrent operating assets. It is normally desirable to classify current notes payable on the balance sheet as trade or nontrade because such information would reveal to statement users the sources of indebtedness and the extent to which the company has relied on each source in financing its activities.

The problems encountered in the valuation of notes payable are the same as those discussed in Chapter 7 with respect to notes receivable. Thus, a short-term note payable is recorded and reported at its present value, which is normally the face value of the note. This presumes that the note bears a reasonable stated rate of interest. However, if a note has no stated rate of interest, or if the stated rate is unreasonable, then the face value of the note would need to be discounted to its present value to reflect the effective rate of interest implicit in the note. This is accomplished by debiting Discount on Notes Payable when the note is issued and by writing off the discount to Interest Expense over the life of the note in the same manner as was illustrated for the discount on notes receivable in Chapter 7.

Discount on Notes Payable is a contra account to Notes Payable and would be reported on the balance sheet as follows; the $90,000 net amount represents the present value of the note.

Current liabilities:		
Notes payable	$100,000	
Less: Discount on notes payable	10,000	$90,000

Short-Term Obligations Expected to Be Refinanced

Misclassification of debt can create serious problems for users of financial statements. Because the "current" classification is reserved for those obligations that will be satisfied with current assets within a year, a short-term obligation that is expected to be refinanced on a long-term basis should not be reported as a current liability. This applies to the currently maturing portion of a long-term debt and to all other short-term obligations except those arising in the normal course of operations that are due in customary terms. Similarly, it should not be assumed that a short-term obligation will be refinanced and therefore classified as a noncurrent liability unless the refinancing arrangements are secure. Thus, to avoid potential manipulation, the refinancing expectation must be realistic, not just a mere possibility.

An example will illustrate this last point and show the importance of proper classification. Assume that a company borrows a substantial amount of money that it expects to pay back at the end of five years. The president of the company signs a 6-month note, which the loan officer at the bank verbally agrees will be renewed "automatically" until the actual maturity date in five years. The only current obligation expected is payment of the accrued interest each renewal period. Under these circumstances, the company reports the obligation as noncurrent, except for the accrued interest obligation. Assume further that the loan officer leaves the bank and that the new bank official will not allow the short-term note to be refinanced. The financial picture of the company is now dramatically changed. What was considered a long-term obligation because of refinancing expectations is suddenly a current liability requiring settlement with liquid assets in the near future.

The authoritative guideline for classifying short-term obligations expected to be refinanced is contained in FASB ASC Topic 470 (Debt). According to the FASB, both of the following conditions must be met before a short-term obligation may be properly excluded from the current liability classification.[5]

[5] FASB ASC paragraph 470-10-45-14.

1. Management must *intend to refinance* the obligation on a long-term basis.
2. Management *must demonstrate an ability to refinance* the obligation.

Concerning the second point, an ability to refinance may be demonstrated by either of the following:

(a) Actually refinancing the obligation during the period between the balance sheet date and the date the statements are issued.
(b) Reaching a firm agreement that clearly provides for refinancing on a long-term basis.

The terms of the refinancing agreement should be noncancelable as to all parties and extend beyond the current year. In addition, the company should not be in violation of the agreement at the balance sheet date or the date of issuance, and the lender or investor should be financially capable of meeting the refinancing requirements.

If an actual refinancing does occur before the balance sheet is issued, the portion of the short-term obligation that is to be excluded from current liabilities cannot exceed the proceeds from the new debt or equity securities issued to retire the old debt. For example, if a $400,000 long-term note is issued to partially refinance $750,000 of short-term obligations, only $400,000 of the short-term debt can be excluded from current liabilities.

An additional question relates to the timing of the refinancing. If the obligation is paid prior to the actual refinancing but before the issuance of the financial statements, the obligation should be included in current liabilities on the balance sheet.[6] To illustrate, assume that the liabilities of CareFree Inc. at December 31, 2012, include a note payable for $200,000, due January 15, 2013. The management of CareFree intends to refinance the note by issuing 10-year bonds. The bonds are actually issued before the issuance of the December 31, 2012, balance sheet on February 15, 2013. If the bonds are issued prior to payment of the note, the note should be classified as noncurrent on the December 31, 2012, balance sheet. If payment of the note precedes the issuance of the bonds, however, the note should be included in current liabilities as of December 31, 2012.

The international standard for classification of short-term obligations to be refinanced is slightly different. According to *IAS 1*, for the obligation to be classified as long term the refinancing must take place by the balance sheet date, not the later date when the financial statements are finalized. In other words, under the international standard post-balance-sheet-date events are NOT considered when determining whether a refinanceable obligation is reported as current or noncurrent. The FASB is considering adopting this more stringent condition.

ifrs

Normally, classified balance sheets are presented showing a total for Current Liabilities. If a short-term obligation is excluded from that category due to refinancing expectations, disclosure should be made in the notes to the financial statements. The note should include a general description of the refinancing agreement.

Lines of Credit

Some companies have temporary borrowing needs necessitated by the seasonal nature of their business. **Toys "R" Us** is an example of this type of business. Even nonseasonal companies have predictable short-term funding needs that they prefer to arrange for in advance. A way to handle these temporary funding needs is to arrange lines of credit with banks. The lines of credit can be used for automatic borrowing as cash is needed, and then the loans can be repaid when cash is plentiful. For example, in 2009, Toys "R" Us had a

[6] FASB ASC paragraph 470-10-45-15.

$2 billion line of credit to finance seasonal inventory buildup and store construction costs. IBM also has lines of credit established with numerous banks that allow it to quickly borrow money. A line of credit is a negotiated arrangement with a lender in which the terms are agreed to prior to the need for borrowing. When a company finds itself in need of money, an established line of credit allows the company access to funds immediately without having to go through the credit approval process. IBM disclosed the following in the notes to its 2009 financial statements:

LINES OF CREDIT

The company maintains a five-year, $10 billion Credit Agreement (the "Credit Agreement"), which expires on June 28, 2012. The total expense recorded by the company related to this facility was $6.3 million in 2009, $6.2 million in 2008 and $6.2 million in 2007. The amended Credit Agreement permits the company and its Subsidiary Borrowers to borrow up to $10 billion on a revolving basis. Borrowings of the Subsidiary Borrowers will be unconditionally backed by the company. The company may also, upon the agreement of either existing lenders, or of the additional banks not currently party to the Credit Agreement, increase the commitments under the Credit Agreement up to an additional $2.0 billion. Subject to certain terms of the Credit Agreement, the company and Subsidiary Borrowers may borrow, prepay and reborrow amounts under the Credit Agreement at any time during the Credit Agreement. Interest rates on borrowings under the Credit Agreement will be based on prevailing market interest rates, as further described in the Credit Agreement. The Credit Agreement contains customary representations and warranties, covenants, events of default, and indemnification provisions. The company believes that circumstances that might give rise to breach of these covenants or an event of default, as specified in the Credit Agreement are remote. The company's other lines of credit, most of which are uncommitted, totaled approximately $9,790 million and $11,031 million at December 31, 2009 and 2008, respectively. Interest rates and other terms of borrowing under these lines of credit vary from country to country, depending on local market conditions.

($ in millions) **At December 31:**	**2009**	**2008**
Unused lines:		
From the committed global credit facility	$ 9,910	$ 9,888
From other committed and uncommitted lines	7,405	8,376
Total unused lines of credit	$17,314	$18,264

The line of credit itself is *not* a liability. However, once the line of credit is used to borrow money, the company has a formal liability that will be reported as either a current or long-term liability, depending on the repayment terms of the agreement. A sample of U.S. companies with large unused lines of credit is given in Exhibit 12-4. Note especially that the lines of credit are quite large relative to the amount of outstanding debt; in the case of **Sears**, use of the full amount of credit would increase its amount of outstanding debt by 75%. Details regarding the terms of the line of credit, for example, the used and unused portions and the applicable interest rates, are disclosed in the financial statement notes.

EX 12-4 UNUSED LINES OF CREDIT—2009

(numbers in billions of dollars)

Company	Unused Line of Credit	Outstanding Short-Term and Long-Term Debt
IBM	$17.3	$ 26.1
ExxonMobil	4.8	9.6
General Electric	9.0	12.2
General Electric Capital Services	51.7	461.4
Sears	2.5	3.3

Maintaining a line of credit is not costless. Banks typically charge a small amount, a fraction of 1% per year, in exchange for the commitment to provide a company with guaranteed credit. For example, on December 31, 2009, **McDonald's** had a $1.3 billion line of credit (expiring in 2012) that had a fee of 0.05% per year. Of course, if McDonald's uses the line of credit, interest on the borrowed amount would have to be paid in addition to this fee. The fee is the cost that McDonald's pays in order to have guaranteed access to credit. The cost of maintaining this $1.3 billion credit line for one year is $650,000 ($1.3 billion × 0.0005).

PhotoLink/Photodisc/Getty Images

Seasonal businesses often use lines of credit to handle temporary borrowing needs.

Present Value of Long-Term Debt

3 Apply present value concepts to the accounting for long-term debts such as mortgages.

WHY **Conceptually, a liability should be reported at the amount that would satisfy the obligation on the balance sheet date. For a long-term obligation, this amount is the present value of the future payments to be made.**

HOW **When a payment is made on a long-term debt, present value calculations are used to determine the portion of the payment that is applied to reduce the liability and the amount that is included as interest expense on the income statement.**

The reporting of long-term debt obligations is more complex than for short-term obligations because the sum of the future cash payments to be made on a long-term debt is not a good measure of the actual economic obligation. For example, repaying a 30-year, $200,000 mortgage with a 7% interest rate will require monthly payments totaling $479,018 over the 30-year life of the mortgage. However, the entire obligation could be settled with one payment of $200,000 today. In reporting long-term debt obligations, the emphasis is on reporting what the real economic value of the obligation is today, not what the total debt payments will be in the future.

To illustrate the application of present value concepts to the accounting for long-term debt, a simple mortgage example will be used. A mortgage is a loan backed by an asset that serves as collateral for the loan. If the borrower cannot repay the loan, the lender has the legal right to claim the mortgaged asset and sell it in order to recover the loan amount. Mortgages are generally payable in equal installments; a portion of each payment represents interest on the unpaid mortgage balance, and the remainder of the payment is designated as repayment of part of the principal of the loan. As an example, assume that on January 1, 2013, Crystal Michae purchases a house for $250,000 and makes a down payment of $50,000. The remaining $200,000 of the purchase price is financed through a mortgage on the house. The mortgage is payable over 30 years at a rate of $2,057 monthly. The interest rate is 12% compounded monthly, and the first payment is due on February 1, 2013. An interest rate of 12% compounded monthly is the same as 1% per month (12%/12 months). (See the Time Value of Money Review module for a review of present value concepts.)

As the mortgage payments are made, each monthly payment of $2,057 must be divided between principal and interest. The interest is based on 1% of the mortgage balance at the beginning of the month. On February 1, the interest is $2,000 ($200,000 × 0.01), and the principal portion of the payment is $57 (or $2,057 − $2,000). In March, the interest is $1,999, 1% of $199,943 ($200,000 − $57), and this pattern continues monthly. The division of these payments into interest and principal components for the first five monthly payments is shown in Exhibit 12-5. This process is called loan (or mortgage) amortization.

If Crystal were to maintain a set of personal financial records, she would make the following journal entry on February 1:

Interest Expense	2,000	
Mortgage Payable	57	
Cash		2,057

As with other forms of long-term financing, a mortgage obligation is reported in a company's balance sheet at its present value, which approximates the cash amount that would fully satisfy the obligation today. So, for example, if Crystal were to prepare a quarterly balance sheet as of April 1, 2013 (after the third payment was made), she would show a mortgage liability of $199,827 (see Exhibit 12-5). Because most mortgages are payable in monthly installments, the principal payments for the next 12 months following the balance sheet date must be shown in the Current Liability section as the current portion of a long-term debt. The remaining portion is classified as a long-term liability.

A secured loan is similar to a mortgage in that it is a loan backed by certain assets as collateral. If the borrower cannot repay the loan, the lender can claim the securing assets. Secured loans are more common among firms experiencing financial difficulties. The fact

EX 12-5 LOAN (MORTGAGE) AMORTIZATION SCHEDULE

Date	(1) Payment Amount	(2) Interest Expense (4) × 0.01	(3) Amount Applied to Reduce Principal (1) − (2)	(4) Balance
January 1, 2013	—	—	—	$200,000
February 1, 2013	$2,057	$2,000	$57	199,943
March 1, 2013	2,057	1,999	58	199,885
April 1, 2013	2,057	1,999	58	199,827
May 1, 2013	2,057	1,998	59	199,768
June 1, 2013	2,057	1,998	59	199,709

that the loan is secured reduces the risk to the lender and therefore reduces the interest cost for the borrower. For example, in its 2009 annual report, Delta Air Lines disclosed the following regarding its secured loans:

> In December 2009, we entered into a $100 million first-lien revolving credit facility, which is guaranteed by the Guarantors and is secured by a first lien on certain aircraft, engines and related assets owned by Mesaba and us . . . In December 2009, we also entered into a $150 million first-lien revolving credit facility, which is guaranteed by the Guarantors and is secured by a first lien on certain aircraft, engines and related assets owned by Delta and Comair.

Financing with Bonds

4 **Understand the various types of bonds; compute the price of a bond issue; and account for the issuance, interest, and redemption of bonds.**

WHY **Bonds come in a variety of shapes and sizes, but all bonds share one feature—the borrowing of money now with some form of repayment in the future. Because bonds represent long-term obligations, bond accounting involves extensive use of present value calculations.**

HOW **Bonds typically involve interest-only payments during the bond life with a lump-sum payment at maturity for the face amount of the bond. Present value techniques are used to determine the present value of the bond issue as well as the amount to be recorded as periodic interest expense.**

The long-term financing of a corporation is accomplished either through the issuance of long-term debt instruments, usually bonds or notes, or through the sale of additional stock. The issuance of bonds or notes instead of stock may be preferred by management and stockholders for the following reasons:

1. Present owners remain in control of the corporation.
2. Interest is a deductible expense in arriving at taxable income; dividends are not.
3. Current market rates of interest may be favorable relative to stock market prices.
4. The charge against earnings for interest may be less than the amount of dividends that might be expected by shareholders.

There are, however, certain limitations and disadvantages of financing with long-term debt securities. Debt financing is possible only when a company is in satisfactory financial condition and can offer adequate security to creditors. Furthermore, interest obligations must be paid regardless of the company's earnings and financial position. If a company has operating losses and is unable to raise sufficient cash to meet periodic interest payments, secured debt holders may take legal action to assume control of company assets.

A complicating factor is that the distinction between debt and equity securities may become fuzzy. Usually, a debt instrument has a fixed interest rate and a definite maturity date when the principal must be repaid. Also, holders of debt instruments generally have no voting privileges. A traditional equity security, on the other hand, has no fixed repayment obligation or maturity date, and dividends on stock become obligations only after being formally declared by the board of directors of a corporation. In addition, common stockholders generally have voting and other ownership privileges. The problem is that certain convertible debt securities have many equity characteristics, and some preferred stocks have many of the characteristics of debt. This makes it important to recognize the distinction between debt and equity and to provide the accounting treatment that is most appropriate under the specific circumstances.

> **FYI**
>
> Often, companies in poor financial condition can still obtain financing. However, the terms of the debt are typically very restrictive and the interest rate is very high. Bonds issued by high-risk companies are often classified as ***junk bonds***. Junk bonds are discussed later in this chapter.

Accounting for Bonds

Conceptually, bonds and long-term notes are similar types of debt instruments. There are some technical differences, however. For example, the trust indenture, (i.e., the bond contract) associated with bonds generally provides more extensive detail than the contract terms of a note, often including restrictions on the payment of dividends or incurrence of additional debt. The length of time to maturity is also generally longer for bonds than for notes. Some bonds do not mature for 20 years or longer, while most notes mature in one to five years. Other characteristics of bonds and notes are similar. Therefore, although the discussion that follows deals specifically with bonds, the accounting principles and reporting practices related to bonds can also be applied to long-term notes.

There are three main considerations in accounting for bonds:

1. Recording the issuance or purchase
2. Recognizing the applicable interest during the life of the bonds
3. Accounting for the retirement of bonds either at maturity or prior to the maturity date

Before these considerations are discussed, the nature of bonds and the determination of bond market prices will be reviewed.

Nature of Bonds

The power of a corporation to create bond indebtedness is found in the corporation laws of a state and may be specifically granted by charter. In some cases, formal authorization by a majority of stockholders is required before a board of directors can approve a bond issue.

Borrowing by means of bonds involves the issuance of certificates of indebtedness. Bond certificates, commonly referred to simply as *bonds*, are frequently issued in denominations of $1,000, referred to as the face value, par value, or maturity value of the bond, although in some cases bonds are issued in varying denominations.

The group contract between the corporation and the bondholders is known as the bond indenture. The indenture details the rights and obligations of the contracting parties, indicates the property pledged as well as the protection offered on the loan, and names the bank or trust company that is to represent the bondholders.

Bonds may be sold by the company directly to investors, or they may be underwritten by investment bankers or a syndicate. The underwriters may agree to purchase the entire bond issue or that part of the issue not sold by the company, or they may agree simply to manage the sale of the security on a commission basis, often referred to as a "*best efforts*" *basis*.

Most companies attempt to sell their bonds to underwriters to avoid incurring a loss after the bonds are placed on the market. An interesting example of this occurred when IBM went to the bond market for the first time and issued a record $1 billion worth of bonds and long-term notes. After the issue was released by IBM to the underwriters, interest rates soared as the Federal Reserve Bank sharply increased its discount rate. The market price of the IBM securities fell, and the brokerage houses and investment bankers participating in the underwriting incurred a loss in excess of $50 million on the sale of the securities to investors.

Issuers of Bonds Bonds and similar debt instruments are issued by private corporations; the U.S. government; state, county, and local governments; school districts; and government-sponsored organizations, such as the Federal Home Loan Bank and the Federal National Mortgage Association. As of December 2009, the Securities Industry and Financial Markets Association estimated that the amount of outstanding bonds for corporations was $6.9 trillion.

The U.S. government's debt includes not only U.S. Treasury bonds but also U.S. Treasury bills, which are notes with less than one year to maturity date, and U.S. Treasury notes, which mature in one to seven years. Outstanding U.S. government debt securities as of December 2009 totaled $9.2 trillion.

Debt securities issued by state, county, and local governments and their agencies are collectively referred to as municipal debt. A unique feature of municipal debt is that the interest received by investors from such securities is exempt from federal income tax. Because of this tax advantage, "municipals" generally carry lower interest rates than debt securities of other issuers, enabling these governmental units to borrow at favorable interest rates. The tax exemption is in reality a subsidy granted by the federal government to encourage capital investment in state and local governments. Municipal bonds outstanding as of December 2009 were $2.8 trillion.

Types of Bonds Bonds may be categorized in many different ways, depending on the characteristics of a particular bond issue. The major distinguishing features of bonds are identified and discussed in the following sections.

Term versus serial bonds. Bonds that mature on a single date are called term bonds. When bonds mature in installments, they are referred to as serial bonds. Serial bonds are much less common than term bonds.

Secured versus unsecured bonds. Bonds issued by private corporations may be either secured or unsecured. Secured bonds offer protection to investors by providing some form of security, such as a mortgage on real estate or a pledge of other collateral. A first-mortgage bond represents a first claim against the property of a corporation in the event of the company's inability to meet bond interest and principal payments. A second-mortgage bond is a secondary claim ranking only after the claim of the first-mortgage bond or senior issue has been completely satisfied. A collateral trust bond is usually secured by stocks and bonds of other corporations owned by the issuing company. Such securities are generally transferred to a trustee, who holds them as collateral on behalf of the bondholders and, if necessary, will sell them to satisfy the bondholders' claim.

Unsecured bonds are not protected by the pledge of any specific assets and are frequently termed debenture bonds, or debentures. Holders of debenture bonds simply rank as general creditors along with other unsecured parties. The risk involved in these securities varies with the financial strength of the debtor. Debentures issued by a strong company may involve little risk; debentures issued by a weak company whose properties are already heavily mortgaged may involve considerable risk. Quality ratings for bonds are published by both Moody's and Standard & Poor's investor service companies. For example, Moody's bond ratings range from (Aaa), for prime or high-quality bonds to (C), for very high-risk bonds. Standard & Poor's range is from AAA, AA, A, BBB, and so forth, to D.

Registered versus bearer (coupon) bonds. Registered bonds call for the registry of the owner's name on the corporation books. Transfer of bond ownership is similar to that for stock. When a bond is sold, the corporate transfer agent cancels the bond certificate surrendered by the seller and issues a new certificate to the buyer. Interest checks are mailed periodically to the bondholders of record. Bearer bonds, or coupon bonds, are not recorded in the name of the owner; title to these bonds passes with delivery. Each bond is accompanied by coupons for individual interest payments covering the life of the issue. Coupons are clipped by the owner of the bond and presented to a bank for deposit or collection. The issue of bearer bonds eliminates the need for recording bond ownership changes and preparing and mailing periodic interest checks. Coupon bonds fail to offer the bondholder the protection found in registered bonds in the event the bonds are lost or stolen. In some cases, bonds provide interest coupons but require registry as to principal. Here, ownership safeguards are provided while the time-consuming routines involved in making interest payments are avoided. Bonds of recent issue are registered rather than coupon bonds.

Zero-interest bonds and bonds with variable interest rates. In recent years, some companies have issued long-term debt securities that do not bear interest. Instead, these securities sell at a significant discount that provides an investor with a total interest payoff at maturity. These bonds are known as zero-interest bonds or deep-discount bonds. Another type of zero-interest bond delays interest payments for a period of time.

Because of potentially wide fluctuations in interest rates, some bonds and long-term notes are issued with variable (or floating) interest rates. Over the life of these obligations, the interest rate changes as prevailing market interest rates increase or decrease. A variable interest rate security benefits the investor when interest rates are rising and the issuer when interest rates are falling.

Junk bonds. High-risk, high-yield bonds issued by companies that are heavily in debt or otherwise in weak financial condition are often referred to as junk bonds. These bonds are rated Ba2 or lower by Moody's and BB or lower by Standard & Poor's. Junk bonds typically yield higher interest rates, some yielding in excess of 20%.

Junk bonds are issued in at least three types of circumstances. First, they are issued by companies that once had high credit ratings but have fallen on hard times. As an example,

Standard & Poor's issued a rating of B for debt issued by **Little Traverse Bay Band of Odawa Indians**, owners of a hotel and casino resort in Michigan, and provided the following information:

> Standard & Poor's Ratings Services assigned its 'B' rating to Harbor Springs, Mich.-based Little Traverse Bay Band of Odawa Indians' $195 million senior notes due 2013. At the same time, Standard & Poor's assigned its 'B' issuer credit rating to the Tribe. The outlook is negative.
>
> The ratings on the Tribe reflect very high leverage during the construction period of the Tribe's expansion project, a narrow gaming operation, a competitive marketplace that is facing additional intermediate-term gaming supply, and challenges managing a larger gaming facility. These are only partially tempered by the escrowing of the first four interest payments on the notes, totaling $33 million, and stable cash flow from the existing gaming facility.

Second, junk bonds are issued by emerging growth companies, such as **Amazon.com**'s issue of junk bonds priced at $275 million in 1998, that lack adequate cash flow, credit history, or diversification to permit them to issue higher grade (i.e., lower risk) bonds (Amazon's fortunes have since changed with the company reporting its first positive cash flow from operations in 2002 and its first positive net income in 2003). The third circumstance is that junk bonds are issued by companies undergoing restructuring, often in conjunction with a leveraged buyout (LBO).

Convertible and commodity-backed bonds. Bonds may provide for their conversion into some other security at the option of the bondholder. Such bonds are known as convertible bonds. The conversion feature generally permits the owner of bonds to exchange them for common stock. The bondholder is thus able to convert the claim into an ownership interest if corporate operations prove successful and conversion becomes attractive; in the meantime, the special rights of a creditor are maintained. Bonds may also be redeemable in terms of commodities, such as oil or precious metals. These types of bonds are referred to as commodity-backed bonds.

Callable bonds. Bond indentures frequently give the issuing company the right to call and retire the bonds prior to their maturity. Such bonds are termed callable bonds. When a corporation wishes to reduce its outstanding indebtedness, bondholders are notified of the portion of the issue to be surrendered, and they are paid in accordance with call provisions. Interest does not accrue after the call date.

Mortgage-backed securities. One of the culprits of the 2008 worldwide financial crises was mortgage-backed securities. In many cases, these securities are just a special form of secured bonds. The underlying collateral for these bonds is the collection of mortgages owned by the issuing entity (either a private company or, more often, a U.S. government sponsored entity such as the Federal National Mortgage Association, or Fannie Mae). Problems with this type of secured bond arise when the people who own the mortgaged homes can no longer make their payments. These defaults cause the portfolio of mortgage loans to have decreased value as collateral for the mortgage-backed bonds.

FASB CODIFICATION

The Issue: You are in charge of preparing the financial statements for the start-up company for which you work. The CEO has just come to your office to criticize your liability classification of the subordinated debentures that the company has issued. These debentures are "subordinated" to the company's other loans, meaning that those other loans must be repaid first before the subordinated debentures are repaid. As a result, from an economic standpoint, the holders of the subordinated debentures are close to being common stockholders. Your CEO thinks that these debentures should be reported in the equity section of your company's balance sheet. She points out, correctly, that banks often classify subordinated debentures as "equity" in the definition of debt covenant calculations for borrowers. Your accounting instinct tells you that subordinated debentures must be classified as liabilities, but you don't have any authoritative support for your position.

The Question: Where can one find the authoritative statement requiring subordinated debt to be classified as a liability in the balance sheet?

Searching the Codification: Of course, we are going to start by looking in FASB ASC Topic 470 (Debt). Here is a hint—the classification of subordinated debt was addressed by the SEC in a Staff Accounting Bulletin.

The Answer: The authoritative guidance for the balance sheet classification of subordinated debt is given on page 12-55.

Market Price of Bonds

The market price of bonds varies with the safety of the investment and the current market interest rate for similar instruments. When the financial condition and earnings of a corporation are such that payment of interest and principal on bond indebtedness is virtually ensured, the interest rate a company must offer to sell a bond issue is relatively low. As the risk factor increases, a higher interest return is necessary to attract investors. The amount of interest paid on bonds is a specified percentage of the face value. This percentage is termed the stated rate, or contract rate. This rate, however, may not be the same as the prevailing or market rate for bonds of similar quality and length of time to maturity at the time the issue is sold. Furthermore, the market rate fluctuates constantly. These factors often result in a difference between bond face values and the prices at which the bonds actually sell in the market.

The purchase of bonds at face value implies agreement between the bond's stated rate of interest and the prevailing market rate of interest. If the stated rate exceeds the market rate, the bonds will sell at a premium; if the stated rate is less than the market rate, the bonds will sell at a discount. The bond premium or the bond discount is the amount needed to adjust the stated rate of interest to the actual market rate of interest or yield for that particular bond. Thus, the stated rate adjusted for the premium or the discount gives the actual rate of return on the bonds, known as the

> **CAUTION**
>
> When the stated interest rate on a company's bonds is less than the market rate for similar bonds, investors will pay less than the face value of the bond because they are going to receive a lower interest payment. The amount paid below the face value is termed a *discount*. The reverse is true for a premium.

market, yield, or effective interest rate. A declining market rate of interest subsequent to issuance of the bonds results in an increase in the market value of the bonds; a rising market rate of interest results in a decrease in their market value.

Bond prices are quoted in the market as a percentage of face value. For example, a bond quotation of 96.5 means the market price is 96.5% of face value; thus, the bond is trading at a discount. A bond quotation of 104 means the market price is 104% of face value; thus, the bond is trading at a premium. U.S. government note and bond quotations are made in 32s rather than 100s. This means that a government bond selling at 98.16 (sometimes written 98:16) is selling at 98 16/32, or in terms of decimal equivalents, 98.5%.

The market price of a bond at any date can be determined by discounting the maturity value of the bond and each remaining interest payment at the market rate of interest for similar debt on that date. The present value calculations explained in the Time Value of Money Review module can be used for computing bond market prices.

To illustrate the computation of a bond market price, assume 10-year, 8% bonds of $100,000 are to be sold on the bond issue date. Further assume that the effective interest rate for bonds of similar quality and maturity is 10%, compounded semiannually.

The computation of the market price of the bonds may be divided into two parts:

Part 1 Present value of principal (maturity value):		
Maturity value of bonds after 10 years, or 20 semiannual periods	$100,000	
Effective interest rate = 10% per year, or 5% per semiannual period; *FV* = $100,000; *N* = 20; *I* = 5%		$37,689
Part 2 Present value of 20 interest payments:		
Semiannual payment, 4% of $100,000	$ 4,000	
Effective interest rate, 10% per year, or 5% per semiannual period; *PMT* = $4,000; *N* = 20; *I* = 5%		49,849
Total present value (market price) of bond		$87,538

The market price for the bonds would be $87,538, the sum of the present values of the two parts. Because the effective interest rate is higher than the stated interest rate, the bonds would sell at a $12,462 discount at the issuance date. It should be noted that if the effective rate on these bonds were 8% instead of 10%, the sum of the present values of the two parts would be $100,000, meaning that the bonds would sell at their face value, or at par. If the effective interest rate were less than 8%, the market price of the bonds would be more than $100,000, and the bonds would sell at a premium.

The bonds of public corporations are traded on various bond exchanges, which are similar to stock exchanges. Exhibit 12-6 presents a selection of bond listings as of July 12, 2010.

EX 12-6 BOND LISTING

	Price	Coupon %	Maturity Date	Yield to Maturity %	Current Yield%	Rating
Hewlett-Packard	116.26	5.400	1-Mar-2017	2.703	4.645	A
Hewlett-Packard	116.71	5.500	1-Mar-2018	3.029	4.712	A
Delta Airlines	103.50	6.417	2-Jul-2012	4.533	6.200	BB
Atlantic Richfield	118.55	8.750	1-Mar-2032	7.063	7.381	A

Source: finance.yahoo.com/bonds, July 12, 2010. Data provided by ValuBond.

STOP&THINK

In computing the market price for bonds, what is the only thing for which the stated rate of interest is used?

a) Computing the amount of the periodic interest payments
b) Computing the amount of the maturity value
c) Computing the present value of the periodic interest payments
d) Computing the present value of the maturity value

Notice that **Hewlett-Packard** has more than one bond issue listed; the first listing is for bonds that mature in 2017, and the second listing is for bonds that mature in 2018. The current yield for the first Hewlett-Packard bond listing is 4.645, which means that if the bonds were purchased at their closing price of 116.26, the interest payments would give the investor a 4.645% annual return. These Hewlett-Packard bonds were trading at a premium, which means that the coupon rate on these bonds of 5.400% is higher than was the market rate required on bonds of similar riskiness. The yield to maturity percentage is the overall rate of return that would be earned by an investor (through receipt of periodic interest payments as well as the maturity amount) who purchases the bonds today and holds them until their maturity. The yield to maturity percentage can be thought of as the rate of return necessary to induce an investor to buy the bonds, given the riskiness of the bond issuer.

Issuance of Bonds

Bonds may be sold directly to investors by the issuer or they may be sold in the open market through securities exchanges or through investment bankers. Regardless of how they are placed, when bonds are issued (sold), the issuer must record the receipt of cash and recognize the long-term liability. The purchaser must record the payment of cash and the bond investment.

FYI

Where capital markets are less well developed, banks are the major source of debt financing of companies. As economies develop, such as in China, the relative amount of bond financing increases.

An issuer normally records the bond obligation at its face value—the amount that the company must pay at maturity. Hence, when bonds are issued at an amount other than face value, a bond discount or premium account is established for the difference between the cash received and the bond face value. The premium is added to or the discount is subtracted from the bond face value to report the bonds at their present value. Although an investor could also record the investment in bonds at their face value by using a premium or discount account, traditionally investors record their bond investments at cost, that is, the face value net of any premium or discount.

Bonds issued or acquired in exchange for noncash assets or services are recorded at the fair value of the bonds unless the value of the exchanged assets or services is more clearly determinable. A difference between the face value of the bonds and the cash value of the bonds or the value of the property acquired is recognized as bond discount or bond premium. When bonds and other securities are acquired for a lump sum, an apportionment of such cost among the securities is required.

As indicated earlier, bonds may be issued at par, at a discount, or at a premium. They may be issued on an interest payment date or between interest dates, which calls for the recognition of accrued interest. Each of these situations will be illustrated using the following data: \$100,000, 8%, 10-year bonds are issued; semiannual interest of \$4,000 (\$100,000 × 0.08 × 6/12) is payable on January 1 and July 1.

Bonds Issued at Par on Interest Date When bonds are issued at par, or face value, on an interest date, there is no premium or discount to be recognized nor any accrued interest at the date of issuance. The appropriate entries for the first year on the issuer's books and on the investor's books, assuming the data in the preceding paragraph and issuance on January 1 at par value, are as follows.

	Issuer's Books			Investor's Books		
Jan. 1	Cash	100,000		Bond Investment	100,000	
	Bonds Payable		100,000	Cash		100,000
July 1	Interest Expense	4,000		Cash	4,000	
	Cash		4,000	Interest Revenue		4,000
Dec. 31	Interest Expense	4,000		Interest Receivable	4,000	
	Interest Payable		4,000	Interest Revenue		4,000

Bonds Issued at Discount on Interest Date Now assume that the bonds were issued on January 1 but that the effective rate of interest was 10%, requiring recognition of a discount of $12,462 ($100,000 − $87,538; see computations on page 12-21). The appropriate entries on January 1 follow. The interest entries on July 1 and December 31 are illustrated in a later section of this chapter that discusses the amortization of discounts and premiums.

	Issuer's Books			Investor's Books		
Jan. 1	Cash	87,538		Bond Investment	87,538	
	Discount on Bonds Payable	12,462		Cash		87,538
	Bonds Payable		100,000			

Bonds Issued at Premium on Interest Date Again using the preceding data, assume that the bonds were sold at an effective interest rate of 7%. Using present value techniques, it can be computed that the bond will sell for a premium of $7,106. In this case, the entries on January 1 are as follows:

	Issuer's Books			Investor's Books		
Jan. 1	Cash	107,106		Bond Investment	107,106	
	Premium on Bonds Payable		7,106	Cash		107,106
	Bonds Payable		100,000			

Bonds Issued at Par between Interest Dates When bonds are issued between interest dates, an adjustment is made for the interest accrued between the last interest payment date and the date of the transaction. A buyer of the bonds pays the amount of accrued interest along with the purchase price and then receives the accrued interest plus interest earned subsequent to the purchase date when the next interest payment is made. This practice avoids the problem an issuer of bonds would have in trying to split interest payments for a given period between two or more owners of the securities. To illustrate, if the bonds in the previous example were issued at par on March 1, the appropriate entries are as follows.[7]

	Issuer's Books			Investor's Books		
Mar. 1	Cash	101,333		Bond Investment	100,000	
	Bonds Payable		100,000	Interest Receivable	1,333	
	Interest Payable		1,333*	Cash		101,333
*($100,000 × 0.08 × 2/12)						
July 1	Interest Expense	2,667†		Cash	4,000	
	Interest Payable	1,333		Interest Receivable		1,333
	Cash		4,000	Interest Revenue		2,667
†($100,000 × 0.08 × 4/12)						

Bond Issuance Costs The issuance of bonds normally involves costs to the issuer for legal services, printing and engraving, taxes, and underwriting. Traditionally, these costs have been offset against any premium or added to any discount arising on the issuance and thus netted against the face value of the bonds. In *Statement of Financial Accounting Concepts No. 3* (paragraph 161), the FASB stated that "deferred charges" such as bond issuance costs fail to meet the definition of assets. In its recent consideration of the accounting for the issuance of debt and equity financing, the FASB has made a preliminary determination that all issuance costs, for both debt and equity financing, should be expensed as incurred. However, this decision has not yet been formalized into an official standard. Accordingly, until such time as the FASB releases a formal standard, these bond issuance costs will still be reported as assets by some companies.[8]

Accounting for Bond Interest

With coupon bonds, cash is paid by the issuing company in exchange for interest coupons on the interest dates. Payments on coupons may be made by the company directly to bondholders, or payments may be cleared through a bank or other disbursing agent. Subsidiary records with bondholders are not maintained because coupons are redeemable by bearers. In the case of registered bonds, interest checks are mailed either by the company or its agent. When bonds are registered, the bonds account requires subsidiary ledger support. The subsidiary ledger shows holdings by individuals and changes in such holdings. Checks are sent to bondholders of record as of the interest payment dates.

When bonds are issued at a premium or discount, the market acts to adjust the stated interest rate to a market or effective interest rate. Because of the initial premium or discount, the periodic interest payments made over the bond's life by the issuer do not represent the total interest expense for the periods involved. An adjustment to the interest

[7] As an alternative, the accrued interest could be initially credited to Interest Expense by the issuer and debited to Interest Revenue by the investor. When the first interest payment is made, the debit to Interest Expense for the issuer, when combined with the initial entry, would result in the proper amount of interest expense being recognized. A similar procedure can be applied by the investor in determining interest revenue.

[8] FASB ASC paragraph 835-30-45-3. In some cases, these bond issuance costs, or "deferred charges," can be thought of as "points," or interest paid in advance, that are then capitalized and expensed over the life of the bond. The FASB also states that debt issuance costs for financial liabilities that are reported at fair value should be expensed as incurred. This "fair value option" is discussed in more detail later in the chapter.

expense associated with the cash payment is necessary to reflect the effective interest being incurred on the bonds. This adjustment is referred to as bond premium or discount amortization. This periodic adjustment results in a gradual adjustment of the bond's carrying value toward the bond's face value.

A premium on issued bonds recognizes that the stated interest rate is higher than the market interest rate. Amortization of the premium reduces the interest expense below the amount of cash paid. A discount on issued bonds recognizes that the stated interest rate is lower than the market interest rate. Amortization of the discount increases the amount of interest expense above the amount of cash paid. In summary, the amortization of a discount or premium on bonds accomplishes two things: The bond's carrying value is gradually adjusted to be equal to the maturity value, and the periodic interest expense is adjusted to reflect the fact that the effective interest rate on the bonds is either higher (with a discount) or lower (with a premium) than the actual amount of cash paid each period.

Two main methods are used to amortize the premium or discount: (1) the straight-line method and (2) the effective-interest method. The straight-line method is explained first because the computations are simpler. This method is acceptable, however, only when its application results in periodic interest expense that does not differ materially from the amounts that would be reported using the effective-interest method.[9]

Straight-Line Method The straight-line method provides for the recognition of an equal amount of premium or discount amortization each period. The amount of monthly amortization is determined by dividing the premium or discount at purchase or issuance date by the number of months remaining to the bond maturity date. For example, if a 10-year, 10% bond issue with a maturity value of $200,000 was sold on the issuance date at 103, the $6,000 premium would be amortized evenly over the 120 months until maturity, or at a rate of $50 per month ($6,000/120). If the bonds were sold three months after the issuance date, the $6,000 premium would be amortized evenly over 117 months, or at a rate of $51.28 per month ($6,000/117). The amortization period is always the time from original sale to maturity. The premium amortization would reduce both interest expense on the issuer's books and interest revenue on the investor's books. A discount amortization would have the opposite results: Both accounts would be increased.

To illustrate the accounting for bond interest using straight-line amortization, consider again the earlier example of the $100,000, 8%, 10-year bonds issued on January 1. When sold at a $12,462 discount, the appropriate entries to record interest on July 1 and December 31 would be as follows:

	Issuer's Books			Investor's Books		
July 1	Interest Expense	4,623		Cash	4,000	
	Discount on Bonds Payable		623*	Bond Investment	623	
	Cash		4,000†	Interest Revenue		4,623

*$12,462/120 × 6 months = $623 (rounded) discount amortization for 6-month period
†$100,000 × 0.08 × 6/12 = $4,000 cash

	Issuer's Books			Investor's Books		
Dec. 31	Interest Expense	4,623		Interest Receivable	4,000	
	Discount on Bonds Payable		623	Bond Investment	623	
	Interest Payable		4,000	Interest Revenue		4,623

[9] FASB ASC paragraphs 835-30-35-2 through 4.

FYI

As explained in Chapter 14, this amortization of bond premiums and discounts on the books of the investor is most important when the bond investment is classified as held to maturity. For trading and available-for-sale securities, the bond investment is revalued at the end of each period and reported at its fair value.

Note that the discount amortization has the effect of increasing the effective interest rate over the life of the bond from the 8% stated rate to the 10% market rate of interest that the bonds were sold to yield. Over the life of the bond, the $12,462 discount will be charged to interest expense for the issuer and recognized as interest revenue by the investor.

To illustrate the entries that would be required to amortize a bond premium, consider again the situation in which the 8% bonds were sold to yield 7%, or $107,106. The $7,106 premium would be amortized on a straight-line basis as follows:

	Issuer's Books			Investor's Books		
July 1	Interest Expense	3,645		Cash	4,000	
	Premium on Bonds Payable	355*		Bond Investment		355
	Cash		4,000	Interest Revenue		3,645
Dec. 31	Interest Expense	3,645		Interest Receivable	4,000	
	Premium on Bonds Payable	355		Bond Investment		355
	Interest Payable		4,000	Interest Revenue		3,645

*$7,106/120 × 6 months = $355 (rounded) premium amortization for 6-month period

The amortization of the premium has the effect of reducing the amount of interest expense or interest revenue over the life of the bond to the actual yield or market rate of the bonds, 7%.

Effective-Interest Method The effective-interest method of amortization uses a uniform interest rate based on a changing loan balance and provides for an increasing premium or discount amortization each period. The mortgage (or loan) amortization schedule in Exhibit 12-5 on page 12-15 employs the effective-interest method. In order to use this method, the effective-interest rate for the bonds must be known. This is the rate of interest at bond issuance that discounts the maturity value of the bonds and the periodic interest payments to the market price of the bonds. This rate is used to determine the amount of revenue or expense to be recorded on the books.

To illustrate the amortization of a bond discount using the effective-interest method, consider once again the $100,000, 8%, 10-year bonds sold for $87,538, based on an effective interest rate of 10%. The discount amortization for the first six months using the effective-interest method is computed as follows:

Bond balance (carrying value) at beginning of first period	$87,538
Effective rate per semiannual period	5%
Stated rate per semiannual period	4%
Interest amount based on carrying value and effective rate ($87,538 × 0.05)	$ 4,377
Interest payment based on face value and stated rate ($100,000 × 0.04)	4,000
Discount amortization—difference in interest based on effective rate and stated rate	$ 377

This difference between the amount paid (received) and the compound interest expense (revenue) is the discount amortization for the first period using the effective-interest method. For the second semiannual period, the bond carrying value increases by the amount of discount amortized. The amortization for the second semiannual period would be computed as follows:

CAUTION

Students often interchange the stated and market interest rates when computing interest expense for the period. Remember that the stated rate is used only once—to determine the amount of cash paid or received as interest. The market, or effective, rate is used to calculate the amount of interest expense or interest revenue.

Bond balance (carrying value) at beginning of second period ($87,538 + $377)	$87,915
Interest amount based on carrying value and effective rate ($87,915 × 0.05)	$ 4,396
Interest payment based on face value and stated rate ($100,000 × 0.04)	4,000
Discount amortization—difference in interest based on effective rate and stated rate	$ 396

The amount of interest to be recognized each period is computed at a uniform rate on an increasing balance. This results in an increasing discount amortization over the life of the bonds, which is graphically demonstrated and compared with straight-line amortization in Exhibit 12-7.

STOP&THINK

When preparing a bond amortization schedule like the one that follows, there are certain numbers within that schedule that you know without having to do any elaborate computations. Which ONE of the following numbers can be determined using a very simple computation?

a) The periodic interest expense
b) The periodic interest payment
c) The periodic premium (or discount) amortization
d) The carrying value of the bond

The entries for amortizing the discount would be the same as those shown for straight-line amortization; only the amounts would be different.

Premium amortization would be computed in a similar way except that the interest payment based on the stated interest rate would be higher than the interest amount based on the effective rate. For example, assume that the $100,000, 8%, 10-year bonds were sold on the issuance date for $107,106, thus providing an effective interest rate of 7%. The premium amortization for the first and second 6-month periods would be computed as follows (amounts are rounded to the nearest dollar):

Bond balance (carrying value) at beginning of first period	$107,106
Effective rate per semiannual period	3.5%
Stated rate per semiannual period	4.0%
Interest payment based on face value and stated rate ($100,000 × 0.04)	$ 4,000
Interest amount based on carrying value and effective rate ($107,106 × 0.035)	3,749
Premium amortization—difference in interest based on stated rate and effective rate	$ 251
Bond balance (carrying value) at beginning of second period ($107,106 – $251)	$106,855
Interest payment based on face value and stated rate ($100,000 × 0.04)	$ 4,000
Interest amount based on carrying value and effective rate ($106,855 x 0.035)	3,740
Premium amortization—difference in interest based on stated rate and effective rate	$ 260

As illustrated, as the investment or liability balance is reduced by the premium amortization, the interest, based on the effective rate, also decreases. The difference between the interest payment and the effective interest amount increases in a manner similar to

EX 12-7 COMPARISON OF STRAIGHT-LINE AND EFFECTIVE-INTEREST AMORTIZATION METHODS

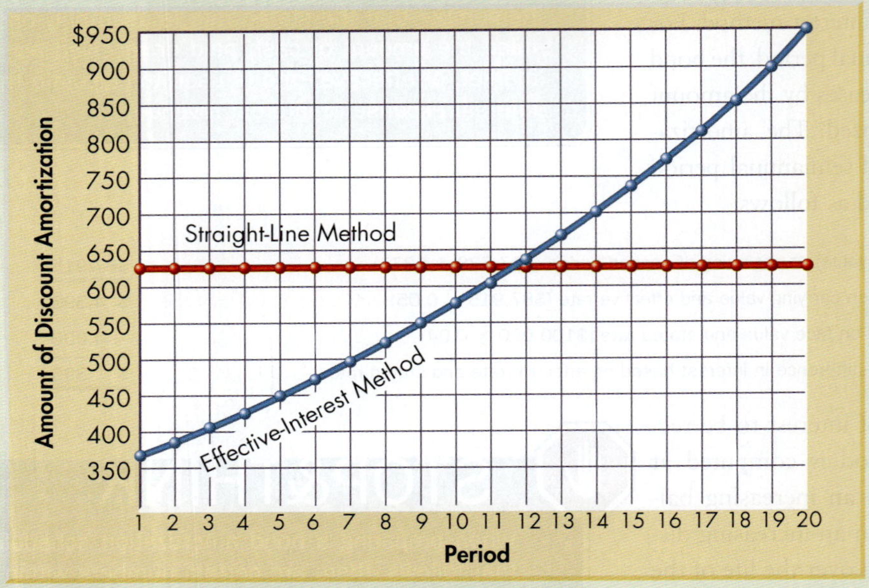

discount amortization. Bond amortization tables may be prepared to determine the periodic adjustments to the bond carrying value, that is, the present value of the bond. A partial bond amortization table follows.

Because the effective-interest method adjusts the stated interest rate to an effective interest rate, it is theoretically more accurate as an amortization method than is the straight-line method. Note that the total amortization over the life of the bond is the same under either method; only the interim amounts differ. The effective-interest method is the recommended amortization method. However, as stated previously, the straight-line method may be used by a company if the interim results of using it do not differ materially from the amortization using the effective-interest method.

Amortization of Bond Premium—Effective-Interest Method $100,000, 10-Year Bonds, Interest at 8% Payable Semiannually, Sold at $107, 106 to Yield 7%

Interest Payment	A Interest Paid (0.04 × $100,000)	B Interest Expense (0.035 × Bond Carrying Value)	C Premium Amortization (A − B)	D Unamortized Premium (D − C)	E Bond Carrying Value ($100,000 + D)
				$7,106	$107,106
1	$4,000	$3,749 (0.035 × $107,106)	$251	6,855	106,855
2	4,000	3,740 (0.035 × $106,855)	260	6,595	106,595
3	4,000	3,731 (0.035 × $106,595)	269	6,326	106,326
4	4,000	3,721 (0.035 × $106,326)	279	6,047	106,047
5	4,000	3,712 (0.035 × $106,047)	288	5,759	105,759

Cash Flow Effects of Amortizing Bond Premiums and Discounts

The amortization of a bond discount or premium does not involve the receipt or payment of cash and, like other noncash items, must be considered in preparing a statement of cash flows. Recall that when the indirect method is used to report cash flows from operating activities, net income is adjusted for noncash items. When a bond discount is amortized, interest expense reported on the income statement is higher than interest paid, and net income, on a cash basis, is understated. The appropriate adjustment is to add the amount of discount amortization back to net income. The reverse is true in the case of a bond premium. That is, the amount of bond premium amortization is subtracted from net income to arrive at cash flow from operations.

Using the direct method requires conversion of individual accrual-basis revenue and expense items to a cash basis. Thus, to convert interest expense to cash paid for interest, the expense reported on the income statement is decreased by the amount of discount amortization for the period or increased by the amount of premium amortization.

The following example illustrates the adjustments necessary when preparing a statement of cash flows. Consider the information used in the previous examples related to a bond discount: The company issues $100,000, 8%, 10-year bonds when the effective rate of interest is 10%. The bonds are issued at a price of $87,538. The calculations for the discount amortization during the first year are on page 12-26. The amount of discount amortized during the first year is $773 ($377 + $396). The amount of interest expense disclosed on the income statement for the year is $8,773 ($4,377 + $4,396), and the amount of cash paid to bondholders is $8,000 (if, for simplicity, we assume that the second payment of $4,000 is made on December 31). To keep the example simple, assume that the company reported net income of $90,000 for the year and that sales for the year (all cash) were $98,773, meaning that the $8,773 in interest expense was the only expense. An analysis of the cash flow impact of the discount amortization is included in the following matrix:

Income Statement		**Adjustments**	**Cash Flows from Operations**	
Sales	$98,773	None	$98,773	Cash collected from customers
Interest expense	*(8,773)*	*+ $773 (bond discount amortization; not a cash item)*	*(8,000)*	*Cash paid for interest*
Net income	$90,000	+ $773 net adjustment	$90,773	Cash flow from operations

Reporting using the indirect method, the amount of discount amortized ($773) is added back to net income. Reporting using the direct method, the amount of the discount is subtracted from reported interest expense to convert that amount to a cash basis as follows: $8,773 interest expense − $773 discount amortization = $8,000 cash paid for interest. In this case, in which only one bond issue is involved, cash paid for interest could instead be computed by multiplying the stated interest rate by the face value of the bonds ($100,000 × 0.08).

Retirement of Bonds at Maturity

In most cases, bonds include a specified termination or maturity date. At that time, the issuer must pay the current investors the maturity, or face, value of the bonds. When bond discount or premium and issuance costs have been properly amortized over the life of the bonds, bond retirement at maturity simply calls for elimination of the liability or the investment by a cash transaction, illustrated as follows assuming a $100,000 bond:

Issuer's Books			Investor's Books		
Bonds Payable	100,000		Cash	100,000	
Cash		100,000	Bond Investment		100,000

FYI

In 1975, high interest rates had caused a decline in the market value of bonds issued during the 1960s. Many companies were retiring these bonds early in order to be able to report accounting gains on the retirement. In order to stop companies from including these gains as part of ordinary income from continuing operations, the FASB decreed that they be classified as extraordinary. In 2002, the FASB rescinded this special accounting for gains and losses on early extinguishment of debt.

There is no recognition of any gain or loss on retirement because the carrying value is equal to the maturity value, which is also equal to the market value of the bonds at that point in time.

Any bonds not presented for payment at their maturity date should be removed from the Bonds Payable balance on the issuer's books and reported separately as Matured Bonds Payable; these are reported as a current liability except when they are to be paid out of a bond retirement fund. Interest does not accrue on matured bonds not presented for payment. If a bond retirement fund is used to pay off a bond issue, any cash remaining in the fund may be returned to the cash account.

CAUTION

Note that a gain or loss is determined by comparing the carrying value of the bond to its fair value. If a company can retire a bond for less than its carrying value, a gain results. If the company must pay more than the carrying value, the result is a loss.

Extinguishment of Debt Prior to Maturity

When debt is retired, or "extinguished," prior to the maturity date, a gain or loss must be recognized for the difference between the carrying value of the debt security and the amount paid to satisfy the obligation.

The problems that arise in retiring bonds or other forms of long-term debt prior to maturity are described in the following sections. Bonds may be retired prior to maturity in one of the following ways.

1. Bonds may be *redeemed* by the issuer by purchasing the bonds on the open market or by exercising the call provision that is frequently included in bond indentures.
2. Bonds may be *converted*, that is, exchanged for other securities.
3. Bonds may be *refinanced* (sometimes called *refunded*) by using the proceeds from the sale of a new bond issue to retire outstanding bonds.

Redemption by Purchase of Bonds in the Market Corporations frequently purchase their own bonds in the market when prices or other factors make such actions desirable. When bonds are purchased, amortization of bond premium or discount and issue costs should be brought up to date. Purchase by the issuer calls for the cancellation of the bond's face value together with any related premium, discount, or issue costs as of the purchase date.

To illustrate a bond redemption prior to maturity, assume that $100,000, 8% bonds of Triad Inc. are not held until maturity but are redeemed by the issuer on February 1, 2013, at 97. The carrying value of the bonds on both the issuer's and investor's books is $97,700 as of February 1. Interest payment dates on the bonds are January 31 and July 31. Entries on both the issuer's and investor's books at the time of redemption are as follows:

	Issuer's Books			**Investor's Books**		
Feb. 1	Bonds Payable	100,000		Cash	97,000	
	Discount on Bonds Payable		2,300	Loss on Sale of Bonds	700	
	Cash		97,000	Bond Investment—Triad Inc.		97,700
	Gain on Bond Redemption		700*			

Computation:

*Carrying value of bonds, February 1, 2013	$97,700
Purchase (redemption) price	97,000
Gain on bond redemption	$ 700

If the redemption had occurred between interest payment dates, adjusting entries would have to be made to recognize the accrued interest and to amortize the bond discount or premium.

Redemption by Exercise of Call Provision A call provision gives the issuer the option of retiring bonds prior to maturity. Frequently, the call must be made on an interest payment date, and no further interest accrues on the bonds not presented at this time. When only a part of an issue is to be redeemed, the bonds called may be determined by lot.

The inclusion of call provisions in a bond agreement is a feature favoring the issuer. The company is in a position to terminate the bond agreement and eliminate future interest charges whenever its financial position makes such action feasible. Furthermore, the company is protected in the event of a fall in the market interest rate by being able to retire the old issue from proceeds of a new issue paying a lower rate of interest. A bond contract normally requires payment of a premium if bonds are called. A bondholder is thus offered special compensation if the investment is terminated early.

FYI

Until the issuance of pre-Codification FASB *Statement No. 125* in 1996, early extinguishment of debt could also be accomplished through *in-substance defeasance*. This process involved transferring assets into an irrevocable trust, using those assets to satisfy the cash flow requirements of a certain debt obligation, and removing both the assets and the associated debt from the balance sheet. The requirement now is that the assets and debt in an in-substance defeasance arrangement still be reported in the balance sheet.

When bonds are called, the difference between the amount paid and the bond carrying value is reported as a gain or a loss on both the issuer's and investor's books. Any interest paid at the time of the call is recorded as a debit to Interest Expense on the issuer's books and a credit to Interest Revenue on the investor's books. The entries to be made are the same as illustrated previously for the purchase (redemption) of bonds by the issuer.

Convertible Bonds Convertible debt securities raise specific questions as to the nature of the securities, that is, whether they should be considered debt or equity securities, the valuation of the conversion feature, and the treatment of any gain or loss on conversion.

Convertible debt securities usually have the following features:[10]

1. An interest rate lower than the issuer could establish for nonconvertible debt
2. An initial conversion price higher than the market value of the common stock at time of issuance
3. A call option retained by the issuer

The popularity of these securities may be attributed to the advantages to both an issuer and a holder. An issuer is able to obtain financing at a lower interest rate because of the value of the conversion feature to the holder. Because of the call provision, an issuer is in a position to exert influence on the holders to exchange the debt for equity securities if stock values increase; the issuer has had the use of relatively low interest rate financing if stock values do not increase. On the other hand, the holder has a debt instrument that, barring default, ensures the return of investment plus a fixed return and, at the same time, offers an option to transfer his or her interest to equity capital should such transfer become attractive.

Accounting for convertible debt issuance when the conversion feature is nondetachable. Differences of opinion exist as to whether convertible debt securities should be treated by an issuer solely as debt or whether part of the proceeds received from the issuance of debt should be recognized as equity capital. One view holds that the debt and the conversion privilege are inseparably connected, and, therefore, the debt and equity portions of a security should not be separately valued. A holder cannot sell part of the instrument and retain the other. An alternate view holds that there are two distinct elements in these securities and that each should be recognized in the accounts: The portion of the issuance price attributable to the conversion privilege should be recorded as a credit to Paid-In Capital; the balance of the issuance price should be assigned to the debt. This would decrease the premium otherwise recognized in the debt or perhaps result in a discount.

These views are compared in the example that follows. Assume that 500 ten-year bonds, face value $1,000, are sold at 105, or a total issue price of $525,000 (500 × $1,000 × 1.05). The bonds contain a conversion privilege that provides for exchange of a $1,000 bond for 20 shares of stock, par value $1. The interest rate on the bonds is 8%. It is estimated that without the conversion privilege, the bonds would sell at 96. Assume that a separate value of the conversion feature cannot be determined. The journal entries to record the issuance on the issuer's books under the two approaches are as follows:

Debt and Equity Not Separated			**Debt and Equity Separated**		
Cash	525,000		Cash	525,000	
Bonds Payable		500,000	Discount on Bonds Payable	20,000*	
Premium on Bonds Payable		25,000	Bonds Payable		500,000
			Paid-In Capital Arising from Bond Conversion Feature		45,000†

Computations:

*Par value of bonds (500 × $1,000)	$500,000	†Total cash received on sale of bonds	$525,000
Selling price of bonds without conversion feature ($500,000 × 0.96)	480,000	Selling price without conversion feature	480,000
Discount on bonds without conversion feature	$ 20,000	Amount applicable to conversion feature (equity portion)	$ 45,000

[10] FASB ASC paragraph 470-20-25-11.

The periodic charge for interest will differ, depending on which method is employed. To illustrate the computation of interest charges, assume that the straight-line method is used to amortize bond premium or discount. Under the first approach, the annual interest charge would be $37,500 ($40,000 paid less $2,500 premium amortization). Under the second approach, the annual interest charge would be $42,000 ($40,000 paid plus $2,000 discount amortization).

The provisions of FASB ASC Section 470-20-25 (Debt—Debt with Conversion and Other Options—Recognition) state that when convertible debt is sold at a price or with a value at issuance not significantly in excess of the face value, "no portion of the proceeds from the issuance . . . should be accounted for as attributable to the conversion feature."[11] On the other hand, there would seem to be strong theoretical support for separating the debt and equity portions of the proceeds from the issuance of convertible debt on the issuer's books. Despite these theoretical arguments, current practice follows the provisions in Topic 470, and no separation is usually made between debt and equity when the conversion feature of the debt is not detachable, or separately tradable, from the debt instrument itself. This is true even when separate values are determinable.[12]

Accounting for convertible debt issuance when the conversion feature is detachable. Sometimes, bonds are issued in conjunction with stock warrants. The warrants allow the holder to buy shares of stock at a set price. The bonds and the warrants are issued as elements of a single security; in essence, the combination of the bonds and the stock warrants is economically equivalent to a convertible debt security. The practical difference is that investors can trade the stock warrants separately from the bonds themselves. In this case, the issuer of the bonds and the stock warrants is required to allocate the joint issuance price between the two instruments; the bonds are accounted for as debt, and the stock warrants are accounted for as part of paid-in capital as illustrated in the "Debt and Equity Separated" journal entry shown previously. The FASB has expressed a preliminary preference for ultimately requiring the proceeds of ***all*** convertible debt issues to be separated into their debt and equity components. If the value of the convertibility feature cannot be separately determined, as in the preceding example, the "with-and-without" method of allocating the bond proceeds between the debt and the equity components can be used. This is the method illustrated earlier in the "Debt and Equity Separated" example. An alternative method of separating the proceeds, the "relative-fair-value" method, is recommended by the FASB when reliable fair values of both the bond and the conversion feature can be determined.[13] This relative-fair-value method is illustrated in the section on accounting for stock warrants in Chapter 13. The Board has not yet produced a formal standard on this issue.

Accounting for convertible debt issuance according to *IAS 32*. *IAS 32*, "Financial Instruments: Disclosure and Presentation," does not differentiate between convertible debt with nondetachable and detachable conversion features. Instead, *IAS 32* states that for all convertible debt issues, the issuance proceeds should be allocated between the debt and equity. Accordingly, the international standard mandates that in all cases, the "Debt and Equity Separated" journal entry illustrated previously should be used.

ifrs

[11] FASB ASC paragraphs 470-20-25-10 and 12.

[12] Separation is required when the initial conversion price is *lower* than the market value of the common stock at the time of issuance. These convertible bonds are said to be "in the money" at the date of issuance, and the accounting standards refer to this as a "beneficial conversion feature." According to FASB ASC paragraph 470-20-25-5, the magnitude of the excess of the market value over the conversion price at issuance is to be recognized as additional paid-in capital.

[13] FASB ASC paragraph 470-20-30-1.

Accounting for conversion. When conversion takes place, a special valuation question must be answered: Should the issuer of the convertible bonds use the fair value of the securities to compute a gain or loss on the date of the conversion? This question has two answers, and the correct answer depends on the nature of the conversion feature as of the issuance date of the convertible bonds. If, as of the issuance date, the probability of eventual conversion of the convertible bonds was deemed to be "at least reasonably possible," then the conversion is really just a routine transition in the life of the convertible bonds, and no gain or loss is recognized upon conversion.[14] For example, consider a convertible bond for which, as of the issuance date, the fair value of the common stock into which the bond can be converted is close to the fair value of the convertible bond itself. In such a case, it is "at least reasonably possible" that at some time during the life of the convertible bond, the fair value of the common stock will increase and create conditions favorable to the conversion of the bonds by the bondholder. Upon conversion of these bonds, no gain or loss would be recognized on the books of the bond issuer. Instead, the carrying value of the bonds is simply transferred from the bond-related accounts to the common stock accounts.

To illustrate bond issuer accounting for a conversion when no gain or loss is recognized, assume HiTec Co. offers bondholders 40 shares of HiTec Co. common stock, $1 par, in exchange for each $1,000, 8% bond held. An investor exchanges bonds with a face value of $10,000 (carrying value as of the conversion date, $9,850) for 400 shares of common stock having a market price at the time of the exchange of $26 per share. To keep things simple, assume that the exchange is completed at an interest payment date AFTER interest has been paid and properly recorded, including bond discount amortization. Also assume that, as of the issuance date, the fair value of 40 shares of HiTec Co. common stock was close to the issuance price of the convertible bonds. In this case, no gain or loss is recognized on the conversion date. The bond's carrying value is transferred to the common stock accounts on the theory that the company, upon issuing the bonds, is aware of the fact that bond proceeds are at least reasonably likely to ultimately represent the consideration identified with stock. Thus, when bondholders exercise their conversion privileges, the value identified with the obligation is transferred to the common stock that replaces it. The conversion is recorded as follows:

Bonds Payable	10,000	
Common Stock, $1 par		400
Paid-In Capital in Excess of Par		9,450
Discount on Bonds Payable		150

The accounting for the conversion is different if, as of the issuance date, there is not a reasonable possibility that the convertible bonds will eventually be converted. This occurs if, for example, the fair value of the common stock into which the bond can be converted is substantially lower than the fair value of the convertible bond itself on the issuance date. In this case, the most likely future for the convertible bonds is that they will never be converted into common stock. Thus, it is a significant event if and when they are converted. Refer again to the HiTec example, but now assume that, as of the issuance date, the fair value of 40 shares of HiTec Co. common stock was substantially below the issuance price of the convertible bonds. The subsequent "unexpected" conversion is recorded as shown on page 12-35.

[14] FASB ASC paragraphs 470-20-40-4 and 5.

Bonds Payable	10,000	
Loss on Conversion of Bonds	550*	
Common Stock, $1 par		400
Paid-In Capital in Excess of Par		10,000
Discount on Bonds Payable		150
Computation:		
*Market value of stock issued (400 shares at $26)		$10,400
Face value of bonds payable	$10,000	
Less unamortized discount	150	9,850
Loss to company on conversion of bonds		$ 550

In summary, if subsequent conversion is at least reasonably possible as of the issuance date, then no gain or loss is recognized upon that subsequent conversion. If subsequent conversion was unexpected as of the issuance date, the fair value of the shares issued on conversion is used to compute a gain or loss on the conversion date.

From the standpoint of the bondholder, or investor, the exchange of the bonds for common stock of HiTec Co. represents a nonmonetary exchange of one asset for another. Nonmonetary exchanges were discussed in Chapter 10. The general rule is that an asset received in a nonmonetary exchange is to be recorded on the books at its fair value on the exchange date, and any gain or loss arising from a difference between this fair value and the carrying value of the exchanged asset is to be recognized. An exception to this rule occurs when the exchange lacks "commercial substance" meaning that the cash flows expected to come from the newly received asset have the same risk, timing, and amount as the cash flows that had been expected from the exchanged asset.[15] In the case of a bond conversion into common stock, cash flows from a bond investment have substantially different risk, timing, and amount compared to cash flows from a common stock investment, so the exchange does have commercial substance.

Refer again to the HiTec example. Assume that the bond investment carrying value is the same on the books of the investor as it is on the books of the issuer. The exchange is recorded on the books of the investor as follows:

Investment in HiTec Co. Common Stock	10,400	
Bond Investment—HiTec Co.		9,850
Gain on Conversion of HiTec Co. Bonds		550

Bond Refinancing Cash for the retirement of a bond issue is frequently raised through the sale of a new issue and is referred to as bond refinancing, or refunding. Bond refinancing may take place when an issue matures, or bonds may be refinanced prior to their maturity when the interest rate has dropped and the interest savings on a new issue will more than offset the cost of retiring the old issue. To illustrate, assume that a corporation has outstanding $1,000,000 of 12% bonds callable at 102 and with a remaining 10-year term, and similar 10-year bonds can be marketed currently at an interest rate of only 10%. Under these circumstances it would be advantageous to retire the old issue with the proceeds from a new 10% issue because the future savings in interest will exceed by a considerable amount the premium to be paid on the call of the old issue.

The desirability of refinancing may not be so obvious as in the preceding example. In determining whether refinancing is warranted in marginal cases, careful consideration must be given to factors such as the different maturity dates of the two issues, possible

[15] FASB ASC paragraphs 845-10-301 through 4.

future changes in interest rates, changed loan requirements, different indenture provisions, income tax effects of refinancing, and legal fees, printing costs, and marketing costs involved in refinancing.

When refinancing takes place before the maturity date of the old issue, the call premium and unamortized discount and issue costs of the original bonds are considered in computing the gain or loss on bond retirement.[16]

Reporting Some Equity-Related Items as Liabilities

As discussed more fully in Chapter 13, the FASB has decided that certain equity-related items should actually be reported in the balance sheet as liabilities.[17] These items are as follows:

- Mandatorily redeemable preferred shares
- Financial instruments (such as written put options) that obligate a company to repurchase its own shares
- Financial instruments that obligate a company to issue a certain dollar value of its own shares

These items share the characteristic that, although related to equity shares, they each obligate the company to deliver items of a set value (either cash or equity shares) some time in the future. Again, each of these items will be illustrated in detail in Chapter 13.

Fair Value Option

5 **Discuss the use of the fair value option for financial assets and liabilities.**

WHY **To allow companies to reflect in the financial statements the offsetting economic effects of hedging activities, the FASB permits companies to report financial assets and financial liabilities in the balance sheet at their fair value rather than their historical cost.**

HOW **Fluctuations in fair values create unrealized economic gains and losses. When financial assets and liabilities are reported in the balance sheet at their fair value, the associated unrealized economic gains and losses are reported in the income statement.**

For many assets and liabilities, the FASB and IASB have determined that fair value is the most relevant measurement attribute. Recall that fair value is defined as "the price that would be received to sell an asset or paid to transfer a liability in an orderly transaction between market participants at the measurement date."[18] Because accounting has long been founded on a backbone of historical cost, the FASB and IASB are transitioning cautiously, item by item, to fair value.

In 2007, with pre-Codification *SFAS No. 159*, the FASB took a bold step toward increased use of fair value by allowing companies a fair value option for the reporting of financial assets and liabilities.[19] Under the fair value option, a company has the option to report, at each balance sheet date, any or all of its financial assets and liabilities at their

[16] FASB ASC paragraph 470-50-40-2.

[17] FASB ASC Topic 480 (Distinguishing Liabilities from Equity).

[18] FASB ASC Master Glossary, "Fair Value."

[19] Pre-Codification *Statement of Financial Accounting Standards No. 159*, "The Fair Value Option for Financial Assets and Financial Liabilities—Including an amendment of FASB Statement No. 115" (Norwalk, CT: Financial Accounting Standards Board, February 2007). This guidance is now found in the "Fair Value Option" subsections of FASB ASC Topic 825 (Financial Instruments).

fair values on the balance sheet date. This is a very interesting accounting rule because a company can choose to report some financial assets and liabilities of a certain type at fair value while at the same time continuing to use another basis, such as historical cost, for other financial assets and liabilities of exactly the same type.

You should be asking yourself: Why did the FASB give companies this financial reporting flexibility? The FASB stated its reason as follows: "The objective is to improve financial reporting by providing entities with the opportunity to mitigate volatility in reported earnings caused by measuring related assets and liabilities differently without having to apply complex hedge accounting provisions." The best way to understand this rationale is through a simple example as given below.

Lily Kay Company has a very simple structure—the company has one asset, a Lusvardi Company bond that it purchased (on the day it was issued) as an investment, and one liability, one of its own bonds that Lily Kay issued to finance the purchase of the Lusvardi bond investment. Both bonds have the same terms: $1,000 face value, 20-year life, 10% coupon rate, and single interest payments made at the end of each year. Given the general level of interest rates in the economy and the riskiness of both Lily Kay Company and Lusvardi Company, both bonds were associated with a market interest rate of 10% when they were issued. Accordingly, both bonds were issued at par of $1,000. Lily Kay Company's balance sheet on the day it purchased the Lusvardi bond with the $1,000 cash raised by issuing its own bond is as follows:

Assets		Liabilities and Equity	
Lusvardi bond	$1,000	Bonds payable	$1,000
		Equity	0

As seen earlier, a risk associated with bonds is that their value fluctuates when market interest rates fluctuate. If, for example, the market interest rate associated with the Lusvardi bond asset were to increase to 12%, the value of the bond would decrease by $149 to $851.[20] This would represent an economic loss to Lily Kay Company. However, in the same way that the fair value of the bond asset is impacted by market interest rates, the fair value of the bond liability is also impacted by market interest rates. If the market interest rate associated with the Lily Kay Company bond were to also increase to 12%, the fair value of the bond would decrease to $851. This $149 decrease represents an economic gain because Lily Kay Company could pay a third party just $851 to take over its bond obligation, which is currently reported in its balance sheet at $1,000. The $149 loss on the bond asset is exactly offset by the $149 gain on the bond liability. Lily Kay Company's balance sheet would then appear as follows:

Assets		Liabilities and Equity	
Lusvardi bond	$851	Bonds payable	$851
		Equity	0

Under the FASB's fair value option, both the $149 loss and the $149 gain from the fair value fluctuations would be reported in Lily Kay Company's income statement. The net impact on income is $0, so retained earnings (and total equity in this case because there was no initial shareholder investment) stays at its initial balance of $0.

[20] $N = 20, I = 12\%, PMT = \$100, FV = \$1{,}000 \rightarrow PV = \$851.$

In this case, the bond liability serves as a hedge for fluctuations in the value of the bond asset. A hedge is an action taken to reduce the risk associated with a related investment or action. For example, if an airline company is worried about future fluctuations in the price of aviation fuel, the airline can enter into hedging arrangements whereby it enters into contracts to buy its fuel in the future at a price that is set now. Hedging is discussed in more detail in Chapter 19.

Now, assume that Lily Kay Company were required to report the Lusvardi bond asset at its fair value of $851 but were also required to report the bond liability at its historical issuance amount of $1,000. The resulting balance sheet would appear as follows:

Assets		Liabilities and Equity	
Lusvardi bond	$851	Bonds payable	$1,000
		Equity	(149)

The negative equity of $149 represents the recognized loss associated with the decline in fair value of the bond asset. And because the accounting requirement is that the bond liability be reported at its historical issuance amount of $1,000, the corresponding, and offsetting, economic gain is not recognized. Requiring one side of the balance sheet to include fair values but the other side to report historical amounts results in misleading reporting because the hedging effect of the related asset and liability is not reflected in the financial statements.

As explained more fully in Chapter 19, accounting rules and procedures exist which allow for the impact of hedging activities to be reflected in the financial statements. These accounting rules are found in FASB ASC Topic 815 (Derivatives and Hedging). However, the bookkeeping requirements underlying the accounting for hedges often prove to be extremely onerous. As shown in the simple Lily Kay example, for some cases the economic effect of hedging can be reflected quite nicely and simply in the financial statements by allowing companies the option of fair value reporting for both financial assets and financial liabilities. Thus, the intent of the fair value option is to simplify the accounting for economic hedges.

Please note that hedging reduces risk, it doesn't guarantee profits. In the example given above when the market interest rate increased to 12% for both the Lusvardi bond asset and the Lily Kay bond liability, the economic loss on the asset was offset by an economic gain on the liability. However, it could just as easily have been the case that the market interest rate decreased for both the bond asset and the bond liability. For example, assume that the market interest rate on both the Lusvardi bond asset and the Lily Kay bond liability decreased to 8%. The fair value of both the asset and the liability would then be $1,196.[21] In this case, an economic gain of $196 on the bond asset would be offset by an economic loss of $196 because of an increase in the fair value of the bond liability. The resulting balance sheet would appear as follows:

Assets		Liabilities and Equity	
Lusvardi bond	$1,196	Bonds payable	$1,196
		Equity	0

In retrospect, from a reporting standpoint, Lily Kay might wish it had not elected the fair value option for the bonds payable. Then the economic gain of $196 from the increase

[21] $N = 20$, $I = 8\%$, $PMT = \$100$, $FV = \$1{,}000 \rightarrow PV = \$1{,}196$.

in the value of the asset would have been reported but the offsetting loss would not have been reported. To prevent companies from using hindsight to selectively enhance reported results using the fair value option, a company must designate whether it is using the fair value option with respect to a financial asset or financial liability when the initial transaction to create the item occurs.[22] A company can't wait to see which way interest rates go and then cherry pick the economic gains while ignoring the economic losses.

In the examples given in this section, the gains and losses on the Lusvardi and Lily Kay bonds were exactly offsetting, meaning that the market interest rates for the two bonds moved together. This might be the case if the change in interest rates were caused by general economic factors that affected both companies equally. However, if the change in market interest rates is caused by firm-specific factors, there is no reason to think that they would move together. For example, assume that the financial condition of Lusvardi Company weakened, resulting in an increase in the market interest rate associated with the company's bonds from 10% to 12%. At the same time, assume that the financial condition of Lily Kay Company strengthened, resulting in a decrease in the market interest rate from 10% to 8%. The resulting balance sheet would appear as follows:

Assets		Liabilities and Equity	
Lusvardi bond	$851	Bonds payable	$1,196
		Equity	(345)

The $345 economic loss is a combination of the $149 loss from the weakening of Lusvardi Company and a $196 economic loss from the strengthening of Lily Kay Company as evidenced by the drop in the market interest rate from 10% to 8%. The $149 loss is easy to understand, but the $196 loss requires further explanation. How can an improvement in a company's economic circumstances result in a loss? Remember that losses and gains are reported from the standpoint of the shareholders. In this example, the shareholders of Lily Kay are now obligated to make 10% interest payments on the Lily Kay bonds for the next 20 years when in fact the circumstances of the company suggest that it need pay only 8%. In other words, Lily Kay Company is obligated to make above-market interest payments for the next 20 years. This represents a transfer of wealth from the shareholders, who are paying too much interest, to the bondholders, who are collecting too much interest. From an accounting standpoint, the important thing to note here is that use of the fair value option results in all of these interesting and relevant economic facts being reflected immediately in the financial statements.

Off-Balance-Sheet Financing

6 **Explain various types of off-balance-sheet financing, and understand the reasons for this type of financing.**

WHY **Off-balance-sheet financing is a set of accounting techniques companies employ to avoid recognizing economic obligations as liabilities in the balance sheet.**

HOW **By carefully structuring transactions, companies can comply with accounting rules while at the same time avoiding the balance sheet recognition of economic obligations. However, a careful review of note disclosure will often allow financial statement users to assess the potential financial statement impact of these off-balance-sheet transactions.**

[22] FASB ASC paragraph 825-10-25-4.

A major issue facing the accounting profession today is how to deal with companies that do not disclose all their debt in order to make their financial position look stronger. This is often referred to as off-balance-sheet financing. Traditionally, leasing has been one of the most common forms of off-balance-sheet financing. The primary techniques that have been used to borrow money while keeping the debt off the balance sheet are

1. Leases
2. Unconsolidated subsidiaries
3. Variable interest entities (VIEs)
4. Joint ventures
5. Research and development arrangements
6. Project financing arrangements

Leases

A lease is merely a seller-sponsored technique through which a buyer can finance the use of an asset. For accounting purposes, leases are considered to be either rentals (called *operating leases*) or asset purchases with borrowed money (called *capital leases*). A company using a leased asset tries to have the lease classified as an operating lease in order to keep the lease obligation off the balance sheet. The proper accounting treatment depends on whether the lease contract transfers effective ownership of the leased asset. Capital leases are accounted for as if the lease agreement transfers ownership of the leased asset from the lessor (the owner of a leased asset) to the lessee (the user of the leased asset). Operating leases are accounted for as rental agreements.

The four lease classification criteria are as follows:

1. Lease transfers ownership
2. Lease includes a bargain purchase option
3. Lease covers 75% or more of the economic life of the asset
4. Present value of lease payments is 90% or more of the asset value

If any one of these criteria is met, the lease is classified as a capital lease by the lessee; if none of the criteria are met, the lease is accounted for as an operating lease. An operating lease is accounted for as a rental, with neither the leased asset nor (more importantly to the lessee) the lease liability appearing on the lessee's balance sheet. The vast majority of leases, probably in excess of 90%, are accounted for as operating leases, with the obligation to make the future lease payments excluded from balance sheet recognition. Accounting for leases is discussed in great detail in Chapter 15.

Unconsolidated Subsidiaries

In 1987, the FASB issued pre-Codification *Statement No. 94* requiring all majority-owned subsidiaries to be consolidated.[23] Prior to the issuance of FASB *Statement No. 94*, subsidiaries involved in operations unrelated to the parent company's primary focus were not required to be consolidated. For example, **IBM Credit LLC** and **GE Capital Services** are each financing subsidiaries of their respective parent companies. The tremendous debt associated with these financing subsidiaries was not recognized on the balance sheets of their parent companies prior to 1987 because the subsidiaries were involved in nonhomogeneous operations. However, with the issuance of *Statement No. 94*, even these subsidiaries

[23] Pre-Codification *Statement of Financial Accounting Standards No. 94*, "Consolidation of All Majority-Owned Subsidiaries" (Stamford, CT: Financial Accounting Standards Board, 1987).

are now consolidated. Thus, the FASB eliminated one opportunity that companies have used for off-balance-sheet financing.

The objective of consolidated financial statements is to show the net assets that are owned *or* controlled by a company and its subsidiaries. For accounting purposes, a controlling interest in a subsidiary's net assets is presumed to exist when ownership by the parent company exceeds 50%. Of course, there are some instances when control can be achieved with less than 50% ownership, such as when a parent owns a large portion of a subsidiary, say 40%, and also controls access to important inputs to and outputs from the subsidiary's production process. This difficult issue of defining "control" is something that the FASB, now in conjunction with the IASB, continues to re-evaluate from time to time.

Under current accounting rules, companies are able to avoid recognizing debt associated with subsidiaries that are less than 50% owned by the company. As described in Chapter 14, unconsolidated subsidiaries using the equity method are those subsidiaries for which the parent company owns between 20% and 50% of the outstanding shares. With this level of ownership, the presumption is that the parent influences but does not control the subsidiary. The equity method of accounting dictated for these subsidiaries provides that the parent reports, as an asset, its share of the net assets (assets minus liabilities) of the subsidiary; none of the individual liabilities of the subsidiary are reported in the parent company's balance sheet. Even with less than 50% ownership, a parent can often effectively control a subsidiary. For example, **Coca-Cola** owns just 34% of its major U.S. bottler but still effectively controls the operations of this bottler. Because Coca-Cola owns less than 50%, however, the parent company is not required to report the liabilities of the bottler in its balance sheet. To illustrate the potential impact of unconsolidated subsidiaries on the reported amount of a company's debt, consider that Coca-Cola's reported liabilities as of December 31, 2009, were $23.325 billion, whereas the actual liabilities of Coca-Cola and its unconsolidated bottlers totaled $58.382 billion.[24] The topic of consolidation is briefly introduced in Chapter 14 and is covered extensively in advanced accounting courses.

Variable Interest Entities (VIEs)

An important category of unconsolidated subsidiaries is variable interest entities (VIEs). Much of the dissatisfaction about Enron's accounting leading up to its 2001 accounting scandal and bankruptcy centered around its use of so-called "special-purpose entities" (SPEs). A post-Enron revision of the accounting rules has changed the practice and terminology associated with these entities; they are now called *variable interest entities*. However, the fundamental concept of a variable interest entity is the same as a special-purpose entity. To illustrate how a VIE can serve as a form of off-balance-sheet financing, consider the following example. Sponsor Company requires the use of a building costing $100,000. Rather than buy the building (with borrowed money), Sponsor facilitates the establishment of VIE Company. VIE Company is started with a $10,000 investment from a private investor (who is not associated with Sponsor Company), along with a $90,000 bank loan. VIE now has $100,000 in cash with which it purchases the $100,000 building needed by Sponsor. VIE then leases the building to Sponsor, with the lease terms carefully crafted to allow for the lease to be accounted for as an operating lease. After this series of

[24] In February 2010, Coca-Cola announced that it intended to purchase the North American operations of its largest bottler. Apart from the operational reasons for making this acquisition, this transaction will bring over $10 billion of liabilities onto Coca-Cola's balance sheet that had previously been hidden in its unconsolidated subsidiary.

transactions, the building-related and lease-related items on the balance sheets of Sponsor and VIE are as follows:

Sponsor		VIE	
Assets:		Assets:	
....	$0	Building	$100,000
Liabilities:		Liabilities:	
....	0	Bank loan	90,000
		Equity:	
		Paid-in capital	10,000

As you can see, with the help of VIE, Sponsor now has use of the building but without any debt on its balance sheet. If VIE were classified as being "controlled" by Sponsor, then VIE's books would be consolidated with those of Sponsor, and both the building and the bank loan would appear on Sponsor's consolidated balance sheet. Thus, the creation of an "independent" VIE is another way to engage in off-balance-sheet financing.

From this simple example, you can see that the following issues are crucial in the accounting for a VIE:

- How much outside equity financing of the VIE is necessary for the VIE to be considered an independent entity? The 10% financing in this case ($10,000/$100,000) coincides with the general guideline contained in FASB ASC Topic 810 (Consolidation).[25]
- If the sponsor is contingently liable for the VIE's debt, is the VIE an independent entity? When the sponsor guarantees, or cosigns, the debt of the VIE, the VIE certainly is less like an entity independent of the sponsor. According to FASB rules, loan cosigning by the sponsor can be evidence that the risks of ownership are actually borne by the sponsor and not the VIE equity investor. If the risks of ownership are borne by the sponsor, then the sponsor would be required to report in its balance sheet both the assets and liabilities of the VIE.

FYI

Enron also used its SPEs to engage in strategically timed purchases of assets so that Enron could avoid reporting losses on declines in the values of the assets. Also, Enron used SPEs to take the other side of a number of hedging transactions, as discussed in Chapter 19. The provisions of FASB ASC Subtopic 810-10 are now designed to prevent, or at least reduce, all of these abuses.

The accounting rules that existed for special-purposes entities allowed sponsor companies to carefully design their SPEs so that they could be accounted for as separate companies. In the wake of the Enron scandal and the unwelcome focus on SPEs as a tool for financial statement manipulation, the FASB has not only changed the terminology (from SPE to VIE) but has also substantially tightened the accounting rules to prevent variable interest entities from serving as forms of off-balance-sheet financing. The focus of the current FASB rules is on the expected profits and losses of the special entity; the entity expected to bear the majority of the expected losses or reap the majority of the expected gains should include the assets and liabilities of the VIE in its balance sheet, independent of technical voting control.

SIC 12 Consolidation—Special Purpose Entities was issued internationally in December 1998. *SIC 12* is a good example of a principles-based standard. The gist of *SIC 12* is contained in its paragraph 8, reproduced here in its entirety: "An SPE [special-purpose

[25] FASB ASC paragraph 810-10-25-45.

entity] shall be consolidated when the substance of the relationship between an entity and the SPE indicates that the SPE is controlled by that entity." If, in the judgment of the accountant, an entity "controls" an SPE, then the entity is required to consolidate the SPE, meaning that all of its assets and liabilities are included in the balance sheet of the controlling entity. In this context, "control" is not limited to voting control. For example, if a special-purpose entity has been set up with all of its operating decisions determined in advance by rigid policies, then the company that established the special-purpose entity and the "autopilot" operating policies effectively controls the SPE no matter what its ownership percentage is. This concept of "control" is an essential one, but further discussion is outside the scope of this text.

ifrs

Joint Ventures

Companies will, on occasion, join forces with other companies to share the costs and benefits associated with specifically defined projects. These joint ventures are often developed to share the risks associated with high-risk projects. For example, following the identification of the human genome's complete structure, pharmaceutical companies have been forming joint ventures. These joint ventures are intended to perform research to identify the exact structure of proteins manufactured by specific genes associated with specific diseases. The ultimate objective is to use this detailed understanding of the biochemistry underlying specific diseases to be able to design chemical treatments, or, even better, cures. Start-up costs for this type of joint venture can easily exceed $100 million. By involving several pharmaceutical companies, the costs, risks, and results can be shared.

Because the benefits of these joint ventures are uncertain, companies could incur substantial liabilities with few, if any, assets resulting from their efforts. As a result (as is sometimes the case with unconsolidated subsidiaries), a joint venture is sometimes carefully structured to ensure that its liabilities are not disclosed in the balance sheets of the companies that are partners.

A common form of a joint venture is a 50/50 partnership between two companies. For example, before its merger with **Chevron** in 2001, **Texaco** had two 50/50 joint venture partnerships: one with Chevron and one with **Saudi Refining, Inc.** The Chevron joint venture was called **Caltex** and engaged in oil exploration, refining, and marketing in Africa, Asia, the Middle East, Australia, and New Zealand. The joint venture with Saudi Refining was called **Star** and marketed gasoline in the eastern United States. The advantage of a 50/50 joint venture is that both companies can account for their investment using the equity method. Thus, joint ventures are often just a special type of unconsolidated subsidiary. For example, the Caltex and Star joint ventures had total long-term liabilities in excess of $3 billion, none of which were reported in Texaco's balance sheet. The accounting for joint ventures is discussed in more detail in Chapter 14.

> **FYI**
>
> Many U.S. automobile companies have formed joint ventures with foreign car companies to develop and manufacture cars. For example, **Ford Motor Co.** has teamed up with **Mazda** in joint ventures in both North America and Asia.

Research and Development Arrangements

Another way a company may obtain off-balance-sheet financing is with research and development arrangements. These involve situations in which an enterprise obtains the results of research and development activities funded partially or entirely by others. The main accounting issue is whether the arrangement is, in essence, a means of borrowing to fund research and development or if it is simply a contract to do research for others.[26] In deciding on the appropriate accounting treatment, a major consideration is whether the enterprise is obligated to repay the funds provided by the other parties regardless of the outcome of the research and development activities. If there is an obligation to repay, the enterprise should estimate and recognize that liability and record the research and development expenses in the current year in accordance with FASB ASC Topic 730 (Research and Development). If the financial risk associated with the research and development is transferred from the enterprise to other parties and there is no obligation to them, then a liability need not be reported by the enterprise.

Research and development arrangements may take a variety of forms, including a limited partnership. For example, assume that Kincher Company formed a limited partnership for the purpose of conducting research and development. Kincher is the general partner and manages the activities of the partnership. The limited partners are strictly investors. The question is this: Should Kincher record the research and development expenses and the obligation to the investors on its books? The answer depends on an assessment of who is at risk and whether Kincher is obligated to repay the limited partners regardless of the results of the research and development. If the limited partners are at risk and have no guarantee or claim against Kincher Company for any of the funds contributed, the debt and related expenses need not be reported on Kincher's books.

Project Financing Arrangements

At times, companies become involved in long-term commitments that are related to project financing arrangements. As an example, assume that Striker Corporation, a large construction company, has decided to establish a separate company, Paveway, in order to undertake a highway construction project. Paveway is to be organized as a separate legal entity, and all loans acquired by Paveway will specifically state that they are to be repaid from the cash flows of Paveway itself, with the assets of Paveway serving as collateral for the loans. It is likely that Striker would have a contingent obligation to satisfy the debt of Paveway even though the debt itself is intended to be repaid from Paveway cash flows. In this case, Striker would disclose this commitment in a note to the financial statements. This type of arrangement is another form of off-balance-sheet financing.[27]

Reasons for Off-Balance-Sheet Financing

Companies might use one of the preceding or other techniques to avoid including debt on the balance sheet for several reasons. It may allow a company to borrow more than it otherwise could due to debt-limit restrictions. Also, if a company's financial position looks stronger, it will usually be able to borrow at a lower cost.

Whatever the reasons, the problems of off-balance-sheet financing are serious. Many investors and lenders aren't sophisticated enough to see through the off-balance-sheet borrowing tactics and therefore make ill-informed decisions. For example, in periods of economic downturn, a company with hidden debt may find it is not able to meet its obligations and, as a result, may suffer severe financial distress or, in extreme cases, business failure. In turn, unsuspecting creditors and investors may sustain substantial losses that could have been avoided had they known the true extent of the company's debt.

[26] FASB ASC Subtopic 730-20 (Research and Development—Research and Development Arrangements).
[27] FASB ASC Topic 440 (Commitments).

Analyzing a Firm's Debt Position

7 **Analyze a firm's debt position using ratios.**

WHY **Assessing a firm's liquidity and solvency allows investors and creditors to evaluate the potential return on their investment.**

HOW **The results of debt-related ratio analysis allow users to compare a firm's debt position over time or at the same time across companies.**

Those parties considering investing in, or lending money to, a firm are particularly interested in that firm's obligations and capital structure. The term *leverage* refers to the relationship between a firm's debt and assets or its debt and stockholders' equity. A firm that is highly leveraged has a large amount of debt relative to its assets or equity. A common measure of a firm's leverage is the debt-to-equity ratio, calculated by dividing total liabilities by total stockholders' equity. As an example, consider the following information from the 2009 annual report of IBM.

(In millions)	2009	2008
Long-term debt	$21,932	$22,689
Total liabilities	86,267	95,939
Total stockholders' equity	22,755	13,584
Income before income taxes	18,138	16,715
Interest expense	402	673

IBM's debt-to-equity ratios for 2009 and 2008 are as follows:

2009: $82,267/$22,755 = 3.62
2008: $95,939/$13,584 = 7.06

A debt-to-equity ratio exceeding 1.0 indicates that the firm has more liabilities than stockholders' equity. For IBM, the debt-to-equity ratio has decreased substantially from 2008 to 2009. Investors generally prefer a higher debt-to-equity ratio to obtain the advantages of financial leverage, while creditors favor a lower ratio to increase the safety of their debt. Debt-to-equity ratios for a number of U.S. companies are presented in Exhibit 12-8.

As these data illustrate, what constitutes an acceptable debt-to-equity ratio depends to a great extent on the industry in which a company operates. For example, financial institutions, such as **Bank of America**, typically have very high debt-to-equity ratios because the financial assets held by such institutions provide very good collateral for loans. Note that **General Electric**, which has a large amount of financial assets and liabilities in its GE Capital Services subsidiary, has a debt-to-equity ratio indicative of a financial institution. At the other end of the spectrum, companies with few tangible assets to offer as loan collateral typically have lower debt-to-equity ratios. The extreme example of this is **Yahoo!** with a debt-to-equity ratio of just 0.19.

Because there is no hard and fast rule for what is included in the word *debt*, alternative definitions and interpretations of the debt-to-equity ratio have developed. For example, the ratio is often varied to include only long-term debt. If this definition were used for IBM, the debt-to-equity ratio for the 2-year period would be:

2009: $21,932/$22,755 = 0.96
2008: $22,689/$13,584 = 1.67

EX 12-8 DEBT-TO-EQUITY RATIOS FOR SELECTED U.S. COMPANIES FOR FISCAL 2009 ($ IN MILLIONS)

Company (Industry)	Total Liabilities	Total Equity	Debt-to-Equity Ratio
Bank of America (banking)	$1,991,855	$231,444	8.61
Disney (entertainment)	29,383	33,734	0.87
General Electric (diversified industrial and financing)	656,682	125,136	5.25
McDonald's (fast food)	16,191	14,034	1.15
Merck (pharmaceuticals)	23,468	18,282	1.28
Microsoft (software)	38,330	39,558	0.97
Yahoo! (Internet portal)	2,417	12,519	0.19

Note that the debt-to-equity ratios differ dramatically depending on how "debt" is defined: The debt-to-equity ratio is 3.62 if debt is defined to include all liabilities but is only 0.96 if debt is defined to include just long-term debt. Because there is no requirement for companies or analysts to compute ratios in particular ways, you are certain to encounter various different measures of the debt-to-equity ratio. The point to be remembered is this: Make sure you understand the inputs to a ratio before you try to interpret the output. Debt to one person may not mean the same thing to another. Another common variation of the leverage measure is to compare total liabilities to total assets. This measure, frequently called the *debt ratio*, was introduced in Chapter 3.

FYI

The sum of a company's income before income taxes and interest expense is often called *EBIT* (*earnings before interest and taxes*).

Another measure of a company's performance relating to debt is the number of times interest is earned. This measure compares a company's interest obligations with its earnings ability. Times interest earned is calculated by adding a company's income before income taxes and interest expense and then dividing by the interest expense for the period. In the case of IBM, times interest earned for 2009 and 2008 is computed as follows:

2009: ($18,138 + $402)/$402 = 46.1
2008: ($16,715 + $673)/$673 = 25.8

The number of times interest is earned reflects the company's ability to meet interest payments and the degree of safety afforded the creditors. Note that in 2009, IBM offered creditors a much larger margin of safety than in 2008. In 2009, IBM's operations generated 46.1 times the amount needed to be able to pay the company's interest obligation for the year, while in 2008, IBM generated "only" 25.8 times the needed amount (still a healthy cushion).

Disclosing Debt in the Financial Statements

8 **Review the notes to financial statements, and understand the disclosure associated with debt financing.**

WHY **Disclosures in the notes to the financial statements relating to debt financing provide additional details that may not be captured in the recognized numbers in the financial statements.**

HOW **Common disclosure associated with long-term debt includes information relating to maturities, interest rates, conversion privileges, and debt covenants.**

In disclosing details about long-term debt in the notes to the financial statements, the nature of the liabilities, maturity dates, interest rates, methods of liquidation, conversion privileges, sinking fund requirements, borrowing restrictions, assets pledged, dividend limitations, and other significant matters should be indicated. The portion of long-term debt coming due in the current period should also be disclosed.

Bond liabilities are often combined with other long-term debt for balance sheet presentation, with supporting details disclosed in a note. An example of such a note

EX 12-9 IBM—DISCLOSURE OF LONG-TERM DEBT

IBM—Disclosure of Long-Term Debt

At December 31:	Maturities	2009	2008
U.S. Dollar Notes and Debentures (average interest rate at December 31, 2009):			
3.33%	2010–2012	$ 5,456*	$10,496
4.99%	2013–2014	3,332	5,053
6.63%	2015–2019	5,396	5,511
7.00%	2025	600	600
6.22%	2027	469	469
6.50%	2028	313	313
5.875%	2032	600	600
8.00%	2038	187	1,000
5.60%	2039	1,518	—
7.00%	2045	27	150
7.125%	2096	350	850
		18,247	25,041
Other currencies (average interest rate at December 31, 2009, in parentheses):			
Euros (4.4%)	2010–2014	3,427	3,330
Japanese yen (1.5%)	2010–2014	1,565	1,457
Swiss francs (3.4%)	2011–2015	484	470
Other (5.5%)	2010–2013	285	203
		24,008	30,502
Less: Net unamortized discount		527	81
Add: Fair value adjustment**		673	1,210
		24,154	31,631
Less: Current maturities		2,222	8,942
Total		$21,932	$22,689

* $1.6 billion in debt securities issued by IBM International Group Capital LLC, which is an indirect, 100 percent owned finance subsidiary of the company, is included in 2010–2012. Debt securities issued by IBM International Group Capital LLC are fully and unconditionally guaranteed by the company.

** The portion of the fixed-rate debt obligations that is hedged is reflected in the Consolidated Statement of Financial Position as an amount equal to the sum of the debt's carrying value plus a fair value adjustment representing changes in the fair value of the hedged debt obligations attributable to movements in benchmark interest rates.

taken from the 2009 annual report of IBM is presented in Exhibit 12-9. Note that IBM enters into long-term borrowing arrangements using a variety of different instruments and in a variety of different currencies. In U.S. dollars, IBM has both long-term debentures (unsecured bonds) and notes. The 7.125% debenture issue is interesting because it doesn't mature until 2096. IBM obtains loans denominated in foreign currencies for a variety of reasons. First, some countries are reluctant to allow large multinational corporations such as IBM to do business in their countries without using local financing. It helps IBM establish good local relations if it uses local financial institutions as much as possible. Also, some of IBM's foreign subsidiaries are relatively self-contained, meaning that almost all operating, investing, and financing activities are handled locally. Sometimes IBM gets foreign currency financing because the interest rate is low. (Look at the 1.5% average rate on the Japanese yen loans.) Finally, foreign currency financing is a way for IBM to hedge, or protect itself, against fluctuations in the value of foreign currencies. For example, if IBM has assets denominated in Thai baht and the baht decreases in value, IBM will have lost money. However, if IBM has an equal amount of loans denominated in Thai baht, the loss from the decrease in the value of the Thai baht assets will be offset by the gain from the decrease in value of the Thai baht liabilities. This is called a *hedge* and results in IBM being immune from the effects of exchange rate changes, up or down.

EM **EXPANDED MATERIAL**

To this point in the chapter, we have covered the most common issues associated with debt: issuance, the payment of interest, and its retirement. In this Expanded Material, we will introduce and discuss an issue that does not occur frequently but, when it does occur, has a significant impact. The issue to be discussed is troubled debt restructuring: how to account for concessions made on the debt of firms in poor financial condition.

Accounting for Troubled Debt Restructuring

9 **Understand the conditions under which troubled debt restructuring occurs, and be able to account for troubled debt restructuring.**

WHY **When a firm finds itself in financial trouble, actions taken to alleviate some of the distress are to retire some of the firm's debt at a reduced amount or to restructure the terms of the debt.**

HOW **When debt is restructured, the terms of the debt are modified. These modifications might include forgoing interest payments, reducing the interest rate on the debt, reducing the amount of the principal, or a combination of these options. This restructuring provides an economic benefit to the firm, and that benefit must be carefully reflected in either an immediate or a gradual future increase in reported income.**

A significant accounting problem is created when economic conditions make it difficult for an issuer of long-term debt to make the cash payments required under the terms of the debt instrument. These payments include interest payments, principal payments on installment obligations, periodic payments to bond retirement funds, or even payments to retire debt at maturity. To avoid bankruptcy proceedings or foreclosure on the debt, investors may agree to make concessions and revise the original terms of the debt to permit the issuer to recover from financial problems. The revision of debt terms in such situations, referred to as troubled debt restructuring, can take many different forms. For example, there may be a suspension of interest payments for a period of time, a reduction in the interest rate, an extension of the maturity date of the debt, or even an exchange of assets or equity securities for the debt. The primary accounting question in these cases, on both the books of the issuer and the investor, is whether a gain or loss should be recognized upon the restructuring of the debt.

In FASB ASC Subtopic 470-60 (Debt—Troubled Debt Restructurings by Debtors), the FASB defined *troubled debt restructuring* as a situation in which "the creditor for economic or legal reasons related to the debtor's financial difficulties grants a concession to the debtor that it would not otherwise consider . . . That concession either stems from an agreement between the creditor and the debtor or is imposed by law or a court."[28] The key word in this definition is *concession*. If a concession is not made by creditors, accounting for the restructuring follows the procedures discussed for extinguishment of debt prior to maturity.

The major issue addressed by the FASB in Subtopic 470-60 is whether a troubled debt restructuring agreement should be viewed as a significant economic transaction. It was decided that if it is considered to be a significant economic transaction, entries should be made on the issuer's books to reflect any gain or loss. If the restructuring is not considered to be a significant economic transaction, no entries are required. The accounting treatment thus depends on the nature of the restructuring. The FASB conclusions are summarized in the table below.

For the issuer, each type of restructuring is discussed and illustrated in the following sections. For the investor, the procedures associated with an asset swap and an equity swap are discussed in this chapter. The complexities associated with a modification of terms from the point of view of the investor (or creditor) are discussed in Chapter 14 where we discuss the accounting for the impairment of a loan, which is addressed in FASB ASC Subtopic 310-40 (Receivables—Troubled Debt Restructurings by Creditors).

Type	Restructuring Considered Significant Economic Transaction: Gain or Loss Recognized	Restructuring Not Considered Significant Economic Transaction: No Gain or Loss Recognized
Transfer of assets in full settlement (asset swap)	XXX	
Grant of equity interest in full settlement (equity swap)	XXX	
Modification of terms: Total payment under new structure exceeds debt carrying value		XXX
Modification of terms: Total payment under new structure is less than debt carrying value.	XXX	

[28] FASB ASC paragraphs 470-60-15-5 and 6.

Transfer of Assets in Full Settlement (Asset Swap)

A debtor that transfers assets, such as real estate, inventories, receivables, or investments, to a creditor to fully settle a payable usually will recognize two types of gains or losses: (1) a gain or loss on disposal of the asset and (2) a gain arising from the concession granted in the restructuring of the debt. The computation of these gains and/or losses is made as follows:

Carrying value of assets being transferred	
	Difference represents gain or loss on disposal
Market value of asset being transferred	
	Difference represents gain on restructuring
Carrying value of debt being liquidated	

The gain or loss on disposal of an asset is usually reported as an ordinary income item unless it meets criteria for reporting it as an unusual or irregular item. Similarly, the gain on restructuring is typically considered to be part of ordinary income.

An investor always recognizes a loss on the restructuring due to the concession granted unless the investment has already been written down in anticipation of the loss. The computation of the loss is made as follows:

Carrying value of investment liquidated	
	Difference represents loss on restructuring
Market value of asset being transferred	

The classification of this loss depends on the criteria being used to recognize irregular or extraordinary items. However, usually the loss is anticipated as market values of the investment decline, and it is recognized as an ordinary loss, either prior to the restructuring or as part of the restructuring.

> **STOP&THINK**
>
> From the standpoint of the debtor, which ONE of the following is NOT possible on an asset swap done as part of a debt restructuring?
>
> a) Loss on disposal of the asset and loss on the debt restructuring
>
> b) Gain on disposal of the asset and gain on the debt restructuring
>
> c) Loss on disposal of the asset and gain on the debt restructuring

To illustrate these points, assume that Stanton Industries is behind in its interest payments on outstanding bonds of $500,000 and is threatened with bankruptcy proceedings. The carrying value of the bonds on Stanton's books is $545,000 after deducting the unamortized discount of $5,000 and adding unpaid interest of $50,000. To settle the debt, Stanton transfers long-term investments it holds in Worth common stock with a carrying value of $350,000 and a fair value of $400,000 to all investors on a pro rata basis.

Assume that Realty Inc. holds $40,000 face value of Stanton's bonds. Because of the troubled financial condition of Stanton Industries, Realty Inc. has previously recognized as a loss a $5,000 decline in the value of the debt and is carrying the investment at $35,000 on its books plus interest receivable of $4,000. The entry on Stanton's books to record the asset transfer would be as follows:

Stanton Industries (Issuer)			**Realty Inc. (Investor)**		
Interest Payable	50,000		Long-Term Investments—		
Bonds Payable	500,000		Worth Common Stock	32,000[†]	
Discount on Bonds Payable		5,000	Loss on Restructuring of Debt	7,000	
Long-Term Investments—			Bond Investment—Stanton Industries		35,000
Worth Common Stock		350,000	Interest Receivable		4,000
Gain on Disposal of Worth Common Stock		50,000*			
Gain on Restructuring of Debt		145,000*			

*Carrying value of Worth common	$350,000	$50,000 gain on disposal
Market value of Worth common	$400,000	$145,000 gain from restructuring
Carrying value of debt liquidated	$545,000	

[†]Percentage of debt held by Realty Inc.: $40,000/$500,000 = 8%
Market value of long-term investment received in settlement of debt: 0.08 × $400,000 = $32,000

Grant of Equity Interest (Equity Swap)

A debtor that grants an equity interest to the investor as a substitute for a liability must recognize a gain equal to the difference between the fair value of the equity interest and the carrying value of the liquidated liability. A creditor (investor) must recognize a loss equal to the difference between the same fair value of the equity interest and the carrying value of the debt as an investment. For example, assume that Stanton Industries transferred 20,000 shares of common stock to satisfy the $500,000 face value of bonds. The par value of the common stock per share is $1, and the market value at the date of the restructuring is $20 per share. Assume that the other facts described in the preceding illustration of an asset swap are unchanged. The entry on Stanton's books to record the grant of the equity interest is as follows:

Stanton Industries (Issuer)			**Realty Inc. (Investor)**		
Interest Payable	50,000		Long-Term Investments—Stanton		
Bonds Payable	500,000		Common Stock	32,000	
Discount on Bonds Payable		5,000	Loss on Restructuring of Debt	7,000	
Common Stock		20,000	Bond Investment—Stanton Industries		35,000
Paid-In Capital in Excess of Par		380,000	Interest Receivable		4,000
Gain on Restructuring of Debt		145,000*			

*Market value of common stock	$400,000	$145,000 gain from restructuring
Carrying value of debt liquidated	$545,000	

The entry on Stanton's books for an equity swap differs from that made for the asset swap because there can be no gain or loss on exchange of a company's own stock.

Modification of Debt Terms

There are many ways debt terms may be modified to aid a troubled debtor. Modification may involve either the interest or the maturity value or both. Interest concessions may involve a reduction of the interest rate, forgiveness of unpaid interest, or a moratorium on interest payments for a period of time. Maturity value concessions may involve an extension of the maturity date or a reduction in the amount to be repaid at maturity. Basically, the FASB decided that most modifications of debt did not result in a significant economic transaction for the issuer of the debt and thus did not give rise to a gain or loss at the date of restructuring. It argued that the new terms were merely an extension of an existing debt and that the modifications should be reflected in future periods through modified interest charges based on computed implicit interest rates. The only exception to this general rule occurs if the total payments to be made under the new structure, including all future interest payments, are less than the carrying value of the debt at the time of restructuring. Under this exception, the difference between the total future cash payments required and the carrying value of the debt is recognized immediately as a gain on the debtor's books. These provisions are summarized here:

Description of the Restructuring	Accounting Treatment
Substantially modify the loan terms.	Make a journal entry.
The sum of the future payments (undiscounted) does ***not*** exceed the carrying value of the loan.	New carrying value of the loan equals the undiscounted future payments.
	No interest expense in subsequent periods.
Slightly modify the loan terms.	***No*** journal entry.
The sum of the future payments (undiscounted) still exceeds the carrying value of the loan.	However, a new "implicit" interest rate is computed and used to compute interest expense in subsequent periods.

To illustrate the accounting for a "substantial" restructuring, assume the interest rate on the Stanton Industries bonds (see page 12-51) is reduced from 10% to 7%, the maturity date is extended from three to five years from the restructuring date, and the past interest due of $50,000 is forgiven. The total future payments to be made after this restructuring are as follows:

Maturity value of bonds	$500,000
Interest—0.07 × $500,000 × 5 years	175,000
Total payments to be made after restructuring	$675,000

Because the $675,000 exceeds the carrying value of $545,000 [($500,000 − $5,000) + $50,000], no gain is recognized on the books of Stanton Industries at the time of restructuring.

However, if, in addition to the preceding changes, $200,000 of maturity value is forgiven, the future payments would be reduced as follows:

Maturity value of bonds ($500,000 − $200,000)	$300,000
Interest—0.07 × $300,000 × 5 years	105,000
Total payments to be made after restructuring	$405,000

Now the carrying value exceeds the future payments by $140,000, and this gain would be recognized by Stanton as follows:

Interest Payable	50,000	
Bonds Payable	500,000	
Discount on Bonds Payable		5,000
Restructured Debt		405,000
Gain on Restructuring of Debt		140,000

In this case, the total future cash flows to be repaid are less than the amount that is owed, meaning that the implicit interest rate is negative. In order to raise the rate to zero, the carrying value must be reduced to the cash to be realized and a gain recognized for the difference. All interest payments in the future are offset directly to the debt account. No interest expense will be recognized in the future because of the extreme concessions made in the restructuring. By charging all interest payments to the debt account, the balance remaining at the maturity date will be the maturity value of the debt.

When terms are modified just "slightly," the total carrying value of the restructured debt is not changed, and no gain is recognized. The amount recognized as interest expense in the remaining periods of the debt instrument's life is based on a computed implicit interest rate. The implicit interest rate is the rate that equates the present value of all future debt payments to the present carrying value of the debt. The interest expense for each period is equal to the carrying value of the debt for the period involved times the implicit interest rate. The computation of the implicit interest rate can be complex and usually requires the use of a business calculator. Computing implicit interest rates (internal rates of return) is explained in the Time Value of Money Review module.

To illustrate the computation of an implicit interest rate, the initial restructuring of Stanton Industries described above will be used. The question to be answered is what rate of interest will equate the total future payments of $675,000 to the present carrying value of $545,000. Interest is paid and compounded semiannually.

Business Calculator Keystrokes

PV = – $545,000 (this is the carrying value of the loan; enter as a negative number)
PMT = $17,500 ($500,000 × 0.07 × 6/12)
FV = $500,000 (amount to be paid in a lump sum at the loan maturity date)
N = 10 (the total loan term is 5 years; interest payments are semiannual)
I = ???

The solution returned by the calculator is 2.47% for each 6-month period.

Using the Excel RATE Function

Excel Label	Your Input
Nper	10
Pmt	17,500
Pv	–545,000
Fv	500,000
Type	0

Press "Enter" to see the answer of 2.47%.

Using this rate, the recorded interest expense for the first six months would be $13,462, or 2.47% of $545,000. Because the actual cash payment for interest is $17,500, the carrying value of the debt will decline by $4,038 ($17,500 – $13,462). The interest expense for the second semiannual period will be less than for the first period because of the decrease in the carrying value of the debt [(\$545,000 − \$4,038) × 0.0247 = \$13,362 interest expense]. These computations are the same as those required in applying the effective-interest method of amortization described earlier. Continuation of the procedure for the 10 periods would leave a balance of \$500,000, the maturity value, in the liability account of Stanton Industries. The entries to record the restructuring on Stanton's books and the first two interest payments would be as follows:

Account	Debit	Credit
Bonds Payable	500,000	
Interest Payable	50,000	
Discount on Bonds Payable		5,000
Restructured Debt		545,000
Interest Expense	13,462	
Restructured Debt	4,038	
Cash		17,500
Interest Expense	13,362	
Restructured Debt	4,138	
Cash		17,500

Any combination of these methods of bond restructuring may be employed. Accounting for these multiple restructurings can become very complex and must be carefully evaluated. As stated previously, the accounting for a modification of terms by the creditor is discussed in Chapter 14.

SOLUTIONS TO OPENING SCENARIO QUESTIONS

1. A bond rating downgrade indicates that a company's riskiness has increased. Accordingly, the downgrades increased the market interest rate on IBM's debt. Prior to the downgrades, the market interest rate on IBM's debt was approximately 0.5% above the interest rate on comparable U.S. Treasury bonds. After the downgrades, this spread grew to 0.7%.
2. The interest rate that investors must be paid to get them to purchase a bond is related to the riskiness of the bond issuer. Historically, investors have viewed U.S. Treasury bonds as being essentially riskless. As a result, the market interest rate on U.S. Treasury bonds is sometimes called the "risk-free rate." Because there is some risk associated with the bonds of all issuing corporations, the market interest rate associated with corporate bonds is higher than the rate on comparable U.S. Treasury bonds.
3. The long-term debt obligation is fixed, in monetary terms, by a variety of contracts. IBM has virtually no uncertainty about the amounts it owes under these contracts. In contrast, the retirement obligation is an estimate based on expected employee life spans, future health care cost trends, and so forth. IBM has great uncertainty about the amounts it will ultimately pay for these retirement obligations.

SOLUTIONS TO STOP & THINK

1. (Page 12-7) The correct answer is D. The current ratio is just one indicator of a company's ability to meet its current obligations. Another indicator is the ability of the company to generate operating cash flow. In fact, from a practical standpoint, current obligations are satisfied with normal ongoing operating cash flow rather than through the liquidation of a company's existing current assets. Because Wal-Mart has the ability to generate a stable stream of operating cash flow, the company is still able to meet its current obligations even though its current ratio is just 0.87.

2. (Page 12-22) The correct answer is A. Do not confuse the market and the stated rates. The stated rate is only used for computing the amount of the interest payments. The market rate is used for computing the present value amounts of the principal and interest payments.
3. (Page 12-27) The correct answer is B. The periodic interest payment is the same each period and is equal to the bond maturity value multiplied by the coupon rate.
4. (Page 12-50) The correct answer is A. The gain or loss on disposal of an asset is computed by comparing the carrying value with its market value. The market value could be greater than or less than book value. Regarding the restructuring, there can only be a gain for the debtor. Remember what we are doing here—getting the creditor to forgive the debt. That means the debtor will be able to retire debt at less than its carrying value. The debtor is getting a good deal—and this good deal is classified as a gain.

SOLUTION TO USING THE FASB'S CODIFICATION

The "Debt—Overall" subtopic (470-10) includes a section (S99) on SEC material. Under the heading "SEC Staff Guidance" you can see a reference to "Staff Accounting Bulletins." One of the topics under that heading is "SAB Topic 4.A, Subordinated Debt." The authoritative GAAP reference is FASB ASC paragraph 470-10-S99-2, and the guidance is as follows: "Subordinated debt may not be included in the stockholders' equity section of the balance sheet. Any presentation describing such debt as a component of stockholders' equity must be eliminated. Furthermore, any caption representing the combination of stockholders' equity and only subordinated debts must be deleted."

Note that this classification restriction is imposed on those who prepare financial statements. In contrast, users of financial statements, such as banks and financial analysts, are free to reclassify balance sheet items in any way they choose. Thus, for purposes of debt covenant calculations, banks often exclude goodwill from the balance sheet assets and reclassify subordinated debt from a liability to equity.

REVIEW CHAPTER 12

LEARNING OBJECTIVES

1 Understand the various classification and measurement issues associated with debt.

Debt can be classified as either current or noncurrent. Debt is considered current if it will be paid within one year or the current operating cycle, whichever period is longer. Theoretically, all debt should be recorded at its present value. However, most current obligations arising in the normal course of business are not discounted. Some obligations cannot be measured with certainty. These obligations are estimated and recorded at an approximate amount.

2 Account for short-term debt obligations, including those expected to be refinanced, and describe the purpose of lines of credit.

Short-term debt obligations can result from operations or from nonoperating activities. The most common example of a short-term obligation resulting from operations is accounts payable. Other short-term operating liabilities include wages payable, interest payable, and taxes payable. Notes payable involve a more formal credit arrangement. These notes typically specify an interest rate and a payment date. Notes payable can be classified as trade or nontrade. Short-term obligations expected to be refinanced on a long-term basis should be classified as noncurrent if certain criteria are met.

Negotiating a line of credit allows a company to arrange the source of its financing in advance of the time that the funds are actually needed.

3 Apply present value concepts to the accounting for long-term debts such as mortgages.

The present value of a long-term obligation is the amount of cash it would take today to completely satisfy the obligation. Mortgages and secured loans are loans that are backed by specific assets as collateral. These types of loans reduce the risk to the lender because the securing assets can be seized if the loan payments are not made. In accounting for the repayment of a mortgage obligation, each payment amount must be divided between the amount paid for interest and the amount paid for principal.

4 Understand the various types of bonds; compute the price of a bond issue; and account for the issuance, interest, and redemption of bonds.

Bonds come in various shapes and sizes. They are issued by governments and corporations; they can be secured or unsecured, term or serial, registered or coupon—to name a few of the variations. All bonds share one feature: the borrowing of money now with some form of repayment in the future.

Most bonds also involve periodic interest payments. The market price of a bond is determined using present value techniques that incorporate the market rate of interest and the stated rate of the bond. The difference between the market and stated rates will result in a premium or discount. This premium or discount is amortized over time.

When bonds are retired, the debt is removed from the books of the debtor when cash is paid. Bonds can be refinanced at or prior to maturity. Any gain on the early retirement of debt is reported as an ordinary item on the income statement.

5 Discuss the use of the fair value option for financial assets and liabilities.

Under the fair value option, a company has the option to report, at each balance sheet date, any or all of its financial assets and liabilities at their fair values on the balance sheet date. The resulting unrealized gains and losses are reported in the income statement. This simple procedure allows companies to include the economic effects of hedging activities in the financial statements.

6 Explain various types of off-balance-sheet financing, and understand the reasons for this type of financing.

Off-balance-sheet financing is a method companies employ to avoid disclosing obligations in the financial statements. Common examples of off-balance-sheet financing include leasing, unconsolidated subsidiaries, variable interest entities, joint ventures, research and development arrangements, and project financing arrangements. Most areas involving off-balance-sheet financing have been addressed by the FASB, and disclosure associated with the financing arrangement is often required in the notes to the financial statements.

7 Analyze a firm's debt position using ratios.

Ratios can be used to compare a firm's debt position over time or at the same time across companies. The most common measure of a firm's debt position is the debt-to-equity ratio. This ratio compares a firm's liabilities and its stockholders' equity. A common variation on this ratio is to include only long-term debt in the numerator. Times interest earned is another ratio often used to evaluate a company's debt position. This ratio is computed by dividing a firm's income before interest expense and taxes by interest expense for the period.

8 Review the notes to financial statements, and understand the disclosure associated with debt financing.

Common disclosure associated with long-term debt includes information relating to maturities, interest rates, conversion privileges, and debt covenants. The portion of long-term debt coming due in the current period is also disclosed.

EM EXPANDED MATERIAL

9 Understand the conditions under which troubled debt restructuring occurs, and be able to account for troubled debt restructuring.

When a firm finds itself in financial trouble, options used to alleviate some of the distress are to retire the debt at a reduced amount or to restructure the terms of its debt. Debt can be retired immediately at a reduced value with assets or by trading the debt for stock ownership. Another option for restructuring debt is to modify the terms of the debt. These modifications might include forgoing interest payments, reducing the interest rate on the debt, reducing the amount of the principal, or a combination of these options. If these modifications result in the total payments under the new structure being greater than the carrying value of the debt, no gain is recognized. A gain is recognized, however, if the total payments are less than the debt's current carrying value.

FASB-IASB CODIFICATION SUMMARY

ifrs

Topic	FASB Accounting Standards Codification	Original FASB Standard	Corresponding IASB Standard	Differences between U.S. GAAP and IFRS
Short-term obligations expected to be refinanced	*Section 470-10-45 par. 14*	*SFAS No. 6 par. 10-11*	*IAS 1 par. 72*	Under IFRS, for a short-term obligation to be classified as long term, the refinancing must take place by the balance sheet date.
Splitting convertible debt proceeds into debt and equity	*Subtopic 470-20*	*APB Opinion No. 14*	*IAS 32 par. 28-32*	Under IFRS, ALL convertible debt issues are divided into their debt and equity components. This separation is only done under certain circumstances under U.S. GAAP.
Consolidation of variable interest entities (VIE)	*Section 810-10-25 par. 20 through 59*	*FIN 46R*	*SIC 12*	Under IFRS, a VIE is consolidated when the economic substance of the relationship indicates that the VIE is controlled. Compared to U.S. GAAP, this is very much a principles-based approach.
Fair value option	*Topic 825, "Fair Value Option" subsections*	*SFAS No. 159*	*IFRS 9*	There is a fair value option for financial assets under IFRS, but as of 2010 there was not yet a fair value option for financial liabilities.
Troubled debt restructuring	*Subtopic 470-60*	*SFAS No. 15*	*IAS 39 par. 39 through 41*	No substantial differences

KEY TERMS

Account payable 12-9
Amortization 12-25
Bearer (coupon) bonds 12-18
Bond certificates 12-16
Bond discount 12-20
Bond indenture 12-17
Bond issuance costs 12-24
Bond premium 12-20
Bond refinancing 12-35
Callable bonds 12-19
Collateral trust bond 12-18
Commodity-backed bonds 12-19
Convertible bonds 12-19
Convertible debt securities 12-31
Debenture bonds, or debentures 12-18
Debt-to-equity ratio 12-45
Effective-interest method 12-26
Face value, par value, or maturity value 12-17
Hedge 12-38
Joint venture 12-43
Junk bonds 12-18
Liabilities 12-5
Line of credit 12-12
Loan (mortgage) amortization 12-14
Long-term debt 12-15
Market, yield, or effective interest rate 12-21
Mortgage 12-14
Municipal debt 12-17
Nontrade notes payable 12-9
Notes payable 12-9
Off-balance-sheet financing 12-40
Promissory note 12-9
Registered bonds 12-18
Secured bonds 12-17
Secured loan 12-14
Serial bonds 12-17
Stated (contract) rate 12-20
Straight-line method 12-25
Term bonds 12-17
Times interest earned 12-46
Trade notes payable 12-9
Trust indenture 12-16
Unsecured bonds 12-18
Variable interest entity (VIE) 12-41
Zero-interest (deep-discount) bonds 12-18

EM EXPANDED MATERIAL

Troubled debt restructuring 12-49

QUESTIONS

1. Identify the major components included in the definition of *liabilities* established by the FASB.
2. (a) What is meant by *executory contract*?
   (b) Do these contracts fit the definition of liabilities included in this chapter?
3. Distinguish between current and noncurrent liabilities.
4. At what amount should liabilities generally be reported?
5. Under what circumstances is a short-term loan classified among the long-term liabilities on the balance sheet?
6. How does the international standard for classification of short-term obligations to be refinanced differ from U.S. GAAP?
7. What is a line of credit?
8. Why is it important to use present value concepts in properly valuing long-term liabilities?
9. When money is borrowed and monthly payments are made, how does one determine the portion of the payment that is interest and the portion that is principal?
10. Distinguish between (a) secured and unsecured bonds, (b) collateral trust and debenture bonds, (c) convertible and callable bonds, (d) coupon and registered bonds, (e) municipal and corporate bonds, and (f) term and serial bonds.
11. What is meant by *market rate of interest*, *stated or contract rate*, and *effective rate*? Which of these rates changes during the lifetime of the bond issue?
12. What amortization method for premiums and discounts on bonds is recommended in FASB ASC Section 835-30-35 (Interest—Imputation of Interest—Subsequent Measurement)? Why? When can the alternative method be used?
13. List three ways that bonds are commonly retired prior to maturity. How should the early extinguishment of debt be presented on the income statement?
14. What purpose is served by issuing callable bonds?
15. What are the distinguishing features of convertible debt securities? What questions relate to the nature of this type of security?
16. How does the accounting for convertible debt under *IAS 32* differ from the accounting prescribed by U.S. GAAP?
17. The conversion of convertible bonds to common stock may be viewed as an exchange involving no gain or loss or as a transaction for which market values should be recognized and a gain or loss reported. What arguments support each of these views for the issuer?
18. What is meant by *refinancing* or *refunding* a bond issue? When may refinancing be advisable?
19. Briefly explain the “fair value option.”
20. Why did the FASB decide to allow the fair value option?

21. What provision of the fair value option prevents companies from using hindsight to selectively enhance reported results using the fair value option?
22. Why is off-balance-sheet financing popular with many companies? What problems are associated with the use of this method of financing?
23. How can a variable interest entity (VIE) be used as a vehicle for off-balance-sheet financing?
24. What is a joint venture, and how can a joint venture be a form of off-balance-sheet financing?

EM EXPANDED MATERIAL

25. What distinguishes a troubled debt restructuring from other debt restructurings?
26. What is the recommended accounting treatment for bond restructurings effected as
    (a) An asset swap?
    (b) An equity swap?
    (c) A modification of terms?

PRACTICE EXERCISES

Practice 12-1

LO1

Working Capital and Current Ratio

Using the following information, compute (1) working capital and (2) current ratio.

Deferred sales revenue	$ 900
Accounts payable	1,100
Accounts receivable	1,750
Cash	400
Sales	10,000
Accrued wages payable	375
Sales returns and allowances	700
Bonds payable (to be repaid in 6 months)	1,000
Bonds payable (to be repaid in 5 years)	4,000

Practice 12-2

LO2

Short-Term Obligations Expected to Be Refinanced

The company has the following three loans payable scheduled to be repaid in February of next year. As of December 31 of this year, compute (1) total current liabilities and (2) total noncurrent liabilities.

(a) The company intends to repay Loan A, for $10,000, when it comes due in February. In the following September, the company intends to get a new loan for $8,000 from the same bank.
(b) The company intends to refinance Loan B for $15,000 when it comes due in February. The refinancing contract, for $18,000, will be signed in May, *after* the financial statements for this year have been released.
(c) The company intends to refinance Loan C for $20,000 before it comes due in February. The actual refinancing, for $17,500, took place in January, *before* the financial statements for this year have been released.

Practice 12-3

LO2

Total Cost of Line of Credit

The company arranged a line of credit for $500,000 on January 1. The commitment fee is 0.05% (five one-hundredths of 1%) of the total credit line. In addition, the company must pay interest of 5.9% (compounded annually) on any actual loans acquired under the credit line arrangement. This year, the company borrowed $260,000 under the agreement on May 1; this loan was still outstanding at the end of the year. Compute the total cost of the credit line (including interest) for the year.

Practice 12-4

LO3

Computation of Monthly Payments

Florence Clark purchased a house for $300,000. She paid cash of 10% of the purchase price and signed a mortgage for the remainder. She will repay the mortgage in monthly payments for 30 years, with the first payment to occur in one month. The interest rate is 5.4% compounded monthly. What is the amount of her monthly payment?

Practice 12-5
LO3
Present Value of Future Payments
Refer to Practice 12-4. What is the present value of Florence's monthly mortgage payments after 12 payments have been made?

Practice 12-6
LO4
Market Price of a Bond
The company intends to issue 20-year bonds with a face value of $1,000. The bonds carry a coupon rate of 9%, and interest is paid semiannually. On the issue date, the market interest rate for bonds issued by companies with similar risk is 12% compounded semiannually. Compute the market price of one bond on the date of issue.

Practice 12-7
LO4
Market Price of a Bond
The company intends to issue 10-year bonds with a face value of $1,000. The bonds carry a coupon rate of 13%, and interest is paid semiannually. On the issue date, the market interest rate for bonds issued by companies with similar risk is 8% compounded semiannually. Compute the market price of one bond on the date of issue.

Practice 12-8
LO4
Accounting for Issuance of Bonds
Bonds with a face value of $1,000 were issued for $1,083. Make the necessary journal entry on the books of the issuer.

Practice 12-9
LO4
Accounting for Issuance of Bonds
Bonds with a face value of $1,000 were issued for $920. Make the necessary journal entry on the books of the issuer.

Practice 12-10
LO4
Bond Issuance between Interest Dates
The company had planned to issue bonds with a face value of $100,000 on January 1. Because of regulatory delays, the bonds were not issued until February 1. The bonds have a coupon rate of 9%, which is equal to the market rate of interest (for companies of similar risk) on the issue date of February 1. Interest is to be paid semiannually; the first interest payment of $4,500 [$100,000 × 0.09 × 6/12] will be made on July 1, as originally scheduled. Make the journal entry necessary on the books of the issuer on February 1 to record the issuance of these bonds.

Practice 12-11
LO4
Straight-Line Amortization
On January 1, the company issued 10-year bonds with a face value of $400,000. The bonds carry a coupon rate of 10%, and interest is paid semiannually. On the issue date, the market interest rate for bonds issued by companies with similar risk was 12% compounded semiannually. The issuance price of the bonds was $354,120. Make the journal entries needed on the books of the issuer to record the first two interest payments on June 30 and December 31. Use straight-line amortization of the bond discount.

Practice 12-12
LO4
Effective-Interest Amortization
On January 1, the company issued 10-year bonds with a face value of $400,000. The bonds carry a coupon rate of 10%, and interest is paid semiannually. On the issue date, the market interest rate for bonds issued by companies with similar risk was 12% compounded semiannually. The issuance price of the bonds was $354,120. Make the journal entries needed on the books of the issuer to record the first two interest payments on June 30 and December 31. Use effective-interest amortization of the bond discount.

Practice 12-13
LO4
Bond Premiums and Discounts on the Cash Flow Statement
The company has bonds outstanding with a face value of $50,000 and an unamortized premium of $2,350 at the beginning of the year and $2,000 as of the end of the year.

Sales (all for cash) were $42,000 for the year. Total interest expense of $4,650 was reported for the year. Because interest expense is the only expense for this company, net income for the year was $37,350 ($42,000 – $4,650). Prepare the Operating Activities section of the cash flow statement using both (1) the direct method and (2) the indirect method.

Practice 12-14

LO4

Market Redemption of Bonds

The company has outstanding bonds payable with a total face value of $100,000. On July 1, the company redeemed the bonds by purchasing them on the open market for a total of $102,700. Make the necessary journal entry on the issuer's books to record the redemption of the bonds assuming that (1) the bonds have an unamortized discount of $1,800 and (2) the bonds have an unamortized premium of $1,800.

Practice 12-15

LO4

Accounting for Issuance of Convertible Bonds

The company issued convertible bonds with a total face value of $100,000 for $111,000. If the bonds had been issued without the conversion feature, their issuance price would have been $101,000. Make the journal entry necessary to record the issuance of the bonds.

Practice 12-16

LO4

Accounting for Conversion of Convertible Bonds

The company has convertible bonds with a total face amount of $100,000 and a carrying value of $98,500. The bonds are converted into 2,000 shares of $1 par common stock. Each share of stock had a market value of $55 on the date of conversion. Make the journal entry to record the conversion. (*Note:* On the bond issuance date, it had been less than reasonably possible that the bonds would eventually be converted. In other words, ultimate conversion had been viewed as an unlikely event.)

Practice 12-17

LO5

Fair Value Option

The company has one asset, a bond (called Bond B) that it purchased (on the day it was issued) as an investment, and one liability, one of its own bonds (called Bond X) that the company issued to finance the purchase of the Bond B investment. The company had no initial shareholder investment. Both bonds have the same terms: $1,000 face value, 30-year life, 8% coupon rate, and single interest payments made at the end of each year. On their issuance dates, both bonds were associated with a market interest rate of 8%. The company has determined to account for both the bond asset and the bond liability using the fair value option. (1) Prepare a balance sheet for the company as of the issuance date of investment Bond B and the company's own Bond Payable X. (2) On the very next day, the market interest rate with respect to Bond B had risen to 13% and the market interest rate with respect to Bond Payable X had risen to 11%. Prepare the company's balance sheet.

Practice 12-18

LO7

Debt-to-Equity Ratio

Consider the following information:

Short-term debt	$ 17,300
Interest expense	8,200
Total current liabilities	27,000
Long-term debt	93,000
Cash	6,200
Total liabilities	130,000
Total stockholders' equity	85,000
Income before income taxes	17,500

Compute the debt-to-equity ratio assuming that (1) *debt* is defined to include all liabilities, (2) *debt* is defined to include just interest-bearing debt, and (3) *debt* is defined to include just long-term, interest-bearing debt.

Practice 12-19
LO7

Times Interest Earned Ratio

Refer to Practice 12-18. Compute the times interest earned ratio.

EM EXPANDED MATERIAL

Practice 12-20
LO9

Debt Restructuring: Asset Swap

The company has bonds payable with a total face value of $100,000 and a carrying value of $103,000. In addition, unpaid interest on the bonds has been accrued in the amount of $6,000. The lender has agreed to the settlement of the bonds in exchange for land worth $90,000. The land has a historical cost of $64,000. Make the journal entry necessary on the books of the borrower to record this settlement of the bonds payable.

Practice 12-21
LO9

Debt Restructuring: Equity Swap

The company has bonds payable with a total face value of $150,000 and a carrying value of $142,000. In addition, unpaid interest on the bonds has been accrued in the amount of $8,000. The lender has agreed to the settlement of the bonds in exchange for 20,000 shares of $1 par common stock. The shares have a current market value of $140,000. Make the journal entry necessary on the books of the borrower to record this settlement of the bonds payable.

Practice 12-22
LO9

Debt Restructuring: Substantial Modification

On January 1, the company obtained a $10,000, 8% loan. The $800 interest is payable at the end of each year, with the principal amount to be repaid in five years. As of the end of the year, the first year's interest of $800 is not yet paid because the company is experiencing financial difficulties. The company negotiated a restructuring of the loan. The payment of all of the interest ($4,000 = $800 × 5 years) will be delayed until the end of the loan term. In addition, the amount of principal repayment will be dropped from $10,000 to $5,000. (1) Make the journal entry necessary on the company's books to record this debt restructuring. (2) Compute the amount of interest expense that will be recognized *next* year.

Practice 12-23
LO9

Debt Restructuring: Slight Modification

Refer to Practice 12-22. Assume all of the same facts except that the principal repayment amount will be dropped to $8,000 (from $10,000) instead of to $5,000. (1) Make the journal entry necessary on the company's books to record this debt restructuring. (2) Compute the amount of interest expense that will be recognized *next* year.

EXERCISES

Exercise 12-24
LO4

Convertible Bonds

Clarkston Inc. issued $1,000,000 of convertible 10-year, 11% bonds on July 1, 2012. The interest is payable semiannually on January 1 and July 1. The discount in connection with the issue was $9,500, which is amortized monthly using the straight-line basis. The debentures are convertible after one year into five shares of the company's $1 par common stock for each $1,000 of bonds.

On August 1, 2013, $100,000 of the bonds were converted. Interest has been accrued monthly and paid as due. Any interest accrued at the time of conversion of the bonds is paid in cash.

Prepare the journal entries on Clarkston's books to record the conversion, amortization, and interest on the bonds as of August 1 and August 31, 2013. (*Note:* Round to the nearest dollar.) (*Note:* On the bond issuance date, it had been at least reasonably possible that the bonds would eventually be converted.)

Exercise 12-25

LO4

Issuance of Convertible Bonds

Joy Insurance decides to finance expansion of its physical facilities by issuing convertible debenture bonds. The terms of the bonds follow: maturity date 10 years after May 1, 2012, the date of issuance; conversion at option of holder after two years; 20 shares of $1 par value stock for each $1,000 bond held; interest rate of 12% and call provision on the bonds of 102. The bonds were sold at 101.

1. Give the entry on Joy's books to record the sale of $1,800,000 of bonds on July 1, 2012; interest payment dates are May 1 and November 1.
2. Assume the same condition as in (1) except that the sale of the bonds is to be recorded in a manner that will recognize a value related to the conversion feature. The estimated sales price of the bonds without the conversion feature is 98.

Exercise 12-26

LO4

Issuance and Reacquisition of Bonds

On January 1, 2012, Housen Company issued 10-year bonds of $500,000 at 102. Interest is payable on January 1 and July 1 at 10%. On April 1, 2013, Housen Company reacquires and retires 50 of its own $1,000 bonds at 98 plus accrued interest. The fiscal period for Housen Company is the calendar year.

Prepare entries to record (1) the issuance of the bonds, (2) the interest payments and adjustments relating to the debt in 2012, (3) the reacquisition and retirement of bonds in 2013, and (4) the interest payments and adjustments relating to the debt in 2013. Assume the premium or discount is amortized on a straight-line basis. (*Note:* Round to the nearest dollar.)

Exercise 12-27

LO4

Sale of Bond Investment

Jennifer Stack acquired $50,000 of Oldtown Corp. 9% bonds on July 1, 2010. The bonds were acquired at 92; interest is paid semiannually on March 1 and September 1. The bonds mature September 1, 2017. Stack's books are kept on a calendar-year basis. On February 1, 2013, Stack sold the bonds for 97 plus accrued interest. Assuming straight-line amortization and no reversing entry at January 1, 2013, give the entry to record the sale of the bonds on February 1. (*Note:* Round to the nearest dollar.)

Exercise 12-28

LO4

Selling Bonds at Par, Premium, or Discount

In each of the following independent cases, state whether the bonds were issued at par, a premium, or a discount. Explain your answers.

(a) Pop-up Manufacturing sold 1,500 of its $1,000, 8% stated-rate bonds when the market rate was 7%.
(b) Splendor, Inc., sold 500 of its $2,000, 8 3/4% bonds to yield 9%.
(c) Cards Corporation issued 1,000 of its 9%, $100 face value bonds at an effective rate of 9 1/2%.
(d) Floppy, Inc., sold 3,000 of its 10% bonds with a face value of $2,500 at a time when the market rate was 9%.
(e) Cintron Co. sold 5,000 of its 12% contract-rate bonds with a stated value of $1,000 at an effective rate of 12%.

Exercise 12-29

LO4

Computation of Market Values of Bond Issues

What is the market value of each of the following bond issues? (*Note:* Round to the nearest dollar.)

(a) 10% bonds of $1,000,000 sold on bond issue date; 10-year life; interest payable semiannually; effective rate, 12%.
(b) 9% bonds of $200,000 sold on bond issue date; 5-year life; interest payable semiannually; effective rate, 8%.
(c) 8% bonds of $150,000 sold 30 months after bond issue date; 15-year life; interest payable semiannually; effective rate, 10%.

Exercise 12-30
LO4

Discount and Premium Amortization

Tanzanite Corporation issued $500,000 of 7% debentures to yield 11%, receiving $424,624. Interest is payable semiannually, and the bonds mature in five years.

1. What entries would be made by Tanzanite for the first two interest payments, assuming premium or discount amortization on interest dates by (a) the straight-line method and (b) the effective-interest method? (*Note:* Round to the nearest dollar.)
2. What entries would be made on the books of the investor for the first two interest receipts, assuming premium or discount amortization on interest dates and that one party obtained all the bonds and used the straight-line method of amortization? (*Note:* Round to the nearest dollar.)
3. If the sale is made to yield 5%, $543,760 being received, what entries would be made by Tanzanite for the first two interest payments, assuming premium or discount amortization on interest dates by (a) the straight-line method and (b) the effective-interest method? (*Note:* Round to the nearest dollar.)

Exercise 12-31
LO4

SPREADSHEET

Bond Interest and Premium or Discount Amortization

Assume that $280,000 of Denham Springs School District 8% bonds are sold on the bond issue date for $257,196. Interest is payable semiannually, and the bonds mature in 15 years. The purchase price provides a return of 9% on the investment.

1. What entries would be made on the investor's books for the receipt of the first two interest payments, assuming premium or discount amortization on each interest date by (a) the straight-line method and (b) the effective-interest method? (*Note:* Round to the nearest dollar.)
2. What entries would be made on Denham Springs School District's books to record the first two interest payments, assuming premium or discount amortization on each interest date by (a) the straight-line method and (b) the effective-interest method? (*Note:* Round to the nearest dollar.)

Exercise 12-32
LO4

Amortization of Bond Premium or Discount

On January 1, 2012, Terrel Company sold $100,000 of 10-year, 8% bonds at 93.5, an effective rate of 9%. Interest is to be paid on July 1 and December 31. Compute the amount of premium or discount amortization in 2012 and 2013 using (1) the straight-line method and (2) the effective-interest method. Make the journal entries to record the amortization when the effective-interest method is used.

Exercise 12-33
LO3

Mortgage Amortization Schedule

On July 1, 2013, Ketchikan Inc. borrowed $90,000 to finance the purchase of machinery. The terms of the mortgage require payments to be made at the end of every month with the first payment of $1,589 being due on July 31, 2013. The length of the mortgage is seven years, and the mortgage carries an interest rate of 12% compounded monthly.

1. Prepare a mortgage amortization schedule for the last six months of 2013.
2. How much interest expense will be reported in 2013 in connection with this mortgage?
3. What amount will be reported in Ketchikan's balance sheet as mortgage liability at the end of 2013?

Exercise 12-34
LO3

Accounting for Mortgages

On January 1, 2013, Lily Company purchased a building for $2,000,000. The company made a 25% down payment and took out a mortgage payable over 30 years with monthly payments of $11,006.47. The first payment is due February 1, 2013. The mortgage interest rate is 8%.

1. Determine how much of the first two mortgage payments would be applied to interest expense and how much would be applied to reducing the principal. (*Note:* The 8% interest rate is compounded monthly.)
2. Make the journal entry necessary to record the first mortgage payment on February 1, 2013.

Exercise 12-35
LO5

Fair Value Option

Ryan Marie Company has one asset, a bond issued by Miles Company that Ryan Marie purchased (on the day it was issued) as an investment. Ryan Marie also has only one liability, one of its own bonds that was to finance the purchase of the Miles bond investment. The company had no initial shareholder investment. Both bonds have the same terms: $1,000 face value, 10-year life, 11% coupon rate, and single interest payments made at the end of each year. On their issuance dates, both bonds were associated with a market interest rate of 8%. The company has determined to account for both the bond asset and the bond liability using the fair value option.

1. Prepare a balance sheet for Ryan Marie Company as of the date it both purchased the Miles bond investment and issued its own bonds payable.
2. On the very next day, the market interest rate with respect to the Miles bond investment had risen to 13%, and the market interest rate with respectto Ryan Marie's bond had risen to 11%. Prepare the company's balance sheet.
3. Repeat (2) but this time assume that the market interest rate for the Miles bond had gone down to 6%, and the market interest rate of the Ryan Marie bond had increased to 14%.
4. Repeat (2) but this time assume that the market interest rate for the Miles bond had increased to 14%, and the market interest rate of the Ryan Marie bond had gone down to 6%.

Exercise 12-36
LO4

Retirement of Bonds

The December 31, 2012, balance sheet of Spring Company includes the following items:

8% bonds payable due December 31, 2019	$200,000
Premium on bonds payable	8,750

The bonds were issued on December 31, 2011, at 105, with interest payable on June 30 and December 31 of each year. The straight-line method is used for premium amortization.

On April 1, 2013, Spring retired $100,000 of these bonds at 99 plus accrued interest. Prepare the journal entries to record retirement of the bonds, including accrual of interest since the last payment and amortization of the premium.

Exercise 12-37
LO4

Retirement and Refinancing of Bonds

Chiam Corporation has $300,000 of 12% bonds, callable at 102, with a remaining 10-year term, and interest payable semiannually. The bonds are currently valued on the books at $290,000, and the company has just made the interest payment and adjustments for amortization of any premium or discount. Similar bonds can be marketed currently at 10% and would sell at par.

1. Give the journal entries to retire the old debt and issue $300,000 of new 10% bonds at par.
2. In what year will the reduction in interest offset the cost of refinancing the bond issue?

Exercise 12-38
LO4

Retirement of Debt before Maturity

The Long-Term Debt section of Rodman Company's balance sheet as of December 31, 2012, included 8% bonds payable of $600,000 less unamortized discount of $44,000. Further examination revealed that these bonds were issued to yield 11%. The amortization of the bond discount was recorded using the effective-interest method. Interest was paid on January 1 and July 1 of each year. On July 1, 2013, Rodman retired the bonds at 104 before maturity.

Prepare the journal entries to record the July 1, 2013, payment of interest, including the amortization of the discount since December 31, 2012, and the early retirement on the books of Rodman Company.

Exercise 12-39
LO4

Zero-Coupon Bonds
George's Inc. is considering issuing bonds to finance the acquisition of a nationwide chain of distributors of George's products. George's is contemplating two different types of bonds to raise the required $180 million purchase price. The first is a traditional 10-year, 14% bond with semiannual interest payments. The second is a 10-year, zero-coupon bond.

Assuming the market rate of interest is 14%, compute the face value of the bond issuance and make the journal entries necessary to record the issuance if (a) a traditional bond is issued and (b) a zero-coupon bond is issued.

EM EXPANDED MATERIAL

Exercise 12-40
LO9

Modification of Debt Terms
Moriarty Co. is experiencing financial difficulties. Income has exhibited a downward trend, and the company reported its first loss in company history this past year. The firm has been unable to service its debt and, as a result, has missed two semiannual interest payments. In an attempt to turn the company around, management has negotiated a modification of its debt terms with bondholders. These modified terms are effective January 1, 2013. The bonds are $10,000,000, 10-year, 10% bonds that were issued on January 2, 2008, and currently have an unamortized premium of $210,000. Prepare the necessary journal entries on Moriarty's books for each of the following independent situations.

(a) Bondholders agree to forgive past-due interest and reduce the interest rate on the debt from 10% to 5%.
(b) Bondholders agree to forgive past-due interest and forgive $3,000,000 of the face amount of the debt.
(c) Bondholders agree to forgive past-due interest, reduce the interest rate on the debt from 10% to 6%, and forgive $2,000,000 of the face value of the debt.

Exercise 12-41
LO9

Troubled Debt Restructuring—Asset Swap
McKeon Machine Company has outstanding a $210,000 note payable to Tejon Investment Corporation. Because of financial difficulties, McKeon negotiates with Tejon to exchange inventory of machine parts to satisfy the debt. The cost of the inventory transferred is carried on McKeon's books at $160,000. The estimated retail value of the inventory is $195,000. McKeon uses a perpetual inventory system. Prepare journal entries for the exchange on the books of McKeon Machine Company according to the requirements of FASB *Statement No. 15*.

Exercise 12-42
LO9

Troubled Debt Restructuring—Equity Swap
MedQuest Enterprises is threatened with bankruptcy due to its inability to meet interest payments and fund requirements to retire $5,000,000 of long-term notes. The notes are all held by Dynasty Insurance Company. In order to prevent bankruptcy, MedQuest has entered into an agreement with Dynasty to exchange equity securities for the debt. The terms of the exchange are as follows: 300,000 shares of $1 par common stock, current market value $10 per share, and 24,000 shares of $10 par preferred stock, current market value $65 per share. Prepare journal entries for the exchange on the books of MedQuest Enterprises according to the requirements of ASC Subtopic 470-60.

PROBLEMS

Problem 12-43
LO2, LO7

Short-Term Loans Expected to Be Refinanced
The following information comes from the financial statements of Randall Stewart Company.

Current assets	$ 80,000
Accounts payable	55,000
Short-term loan payable*	65,000
Long-term debt	110,000
Other long-term liabilities	10,000
Total stockholders' equity	180,000

*Randall Stewart has arranged with its bank to refinance its short-term loan when it becomes due in three months. The new loan will have a term of five years.

Instructions:

1. Compute the following ratio values.
   (a) Current ratio
   (b) Debt-to-equity ratio
   (c) Debt ratio
2. If you were the auditor of Randall Stewart's financial statements, how would you convince yourself of the validity of the refinancing agreement?

Problem 12-44
LO3

Amortizing a Mortgage and the Effect on the Financial Statements

On January 1, 2013, Picard Inc. purchased a new piece of equipment from LaForge Engineering to expand its production facilities. The equipment was purchased at a cost of $800,000. Picard financed the purchase with an $800,000 mortgage to be repaid in annual payments over five years at a rate of 10%. The mortgage was arranged through Pulaski Bank. The annual payments of $211,038 are to be made on December 31 of each year.

Instructions:

1. Prepare a mortgage amortization schedule for the 5-year life of the mortgage.
2. Assuming the equipment is expected to last for five years (with zero salvage value), determine the net amount at which the equipment will be reported on the balance sheet at the end of each year for its 5-year life using straight-line depreciation.
3. Compare the liability amount to be disclosed on the balance sheet at the end of each year for the 5-year mortgage term with the asset amount to be disclosed at the end of the same years. Identify the primary reasons for the differences each year.

Problem 12-45
LO4

Bond Issuance and Adjusting Entries

On January 1, 2013, Encino Company issued bonds with a face value of $1,000,000 and a maturity date of December 31, 2022. The bonds have a stated interest rate of 8%, payable on January 1 and July 1. They were sold to SeaRay Company for $820,744, a yield of 11%. It cost Encino $40,000 to issue the bonds. This amount was deferred and amortized over the life of the issue using the straight-line method. Assume that both companies have December 31 year-ends and that Encino uses the effective-interest method to amortize any premium or discount and SeaRay uses the straight-line method.

Instructions:

1. Make all entries necessary to record the sale and purchase of the bonds on each company's books.
2. Prepare the adjusting entries as of December 31, 2013, for both companies. Assume SeaRay is carrying the bonds as a long-term held-to-maturity security.

Problem 12-46
LO4

Computation of Bond Market Price and Amortization of Premium or Discount

Lighthouse Enterprises decided to issue $1,400,000 of 10-year bonds. The interest rate on the bonds is stated at 10%, payable semiannually. At the time the bonds were sold, the market rate had increased to 12%.

Instructions:

1. Determine the maximum amount an investor should pay for these bonds. (*Note:* Round to the nearest dollar.)
2. Assuming that the amount in (1) is paid, compute the amount at which the bonds would be reported by the investor after being held for one year. Use two recognized methods of handling amortization of the difference in cost and maturity value of the bonds and give support to the method you prefer. (*Note:* Round to the nearest dollar.)

Problem 12-47

LO4

SPREADSHEET

Premium or Discount Amortization Table

Bray Co. acquired $30,000 of Honey Sales Co.'s 7% bonds, interest payable semiannually, bonds maturing in five years. The bonds were acquired at $32,626, a price to return approximately 5%.

Instructions:

1. Prepare tables to show the periodic adjustments to the investment account and the annual bond earnings, assuming adjustment by each of the following methods: (a) the straight-line method and (b) the effective-interest method. (*Note:* Round to the nearest dollar.)
2. Assuming the use of the effective-interest method, prepare journal entries for each company for the first year.

Problem 12-48

LO4

Amortizing Deferred Interest Bonds

R. J. Winter Co. recently issued $100,000, 10-year deferred interest bonds. The bonds have a stated rate of 10%, and interest is to be paid in 10 semiannual payments beginning in Year 6. The market rate of interest on the date of issuance was 8%.

Instructions:

1. Compute the maximum amount an investor should pay for these bonds. (*Note:* Round to the nearest dollar.)
2. Prepare a bond amortization schedule for R. J. Winter, assuming the effective-interest method is used. (*Note:* Round to the nearest dollar.)

Problem 12-49

LO4

SPREADSHEET

Cash Flow Effects of a Bond Premium

On January 1, 2013, Datalink Inc. issued $100,000, 10%, 10-year bonds when the market rate of interest was 8%. Interest is payable on June 30 and December 31. The following financial information is available:

Sales	$300,000
Cost of sales	180,000
Gross profit	120,000
Interest expense	?
Depreciation expense	(14,500)
Other expenses	(82,000)
Net income	?

	Dec. 31, 2013	Jan. 1, 2013
Accounts receivable	$55,000	$48,000
Inventory	87,000	93,000
Accounts payable	60,000	58,000

All purchases of inventory are on account. Other expenses are paid for in cash.

Instructions:

1. Prepare the journal entry to record the issuance of the bonds on January 1, 2013.
2. Compute (a) the amount of cash paid to bondholders for interest during 2013, (b) the amount of premium amortized during 2013, assuming Datalink uses the straight-line method for amortizing bond premiums and discounts, and (c) the amount of interest expense for 2013.
3. Prepare the Cash Flows from Operating Activities section of Datalink's statement of cash flows using (a) the direct method and (b) the indirect method.

Problem 12-50

LO4

Bond Entries—Issuer

On April 1, 2003, Rowe Tool Company authorized the sale of $5,000,000 of 6% convertible bonds with interest payment dates of April 1 and October 1. The bonds were sold on July 1, 2003, and mature on April 1, 2023. The bond discount totaled $398,200. The bond contract entitles the bondholders to receive 20 shares of $1 par value common stock in exchange for each $1,000 bond. On April 1, 2013, the holders of bonds with total face value of $700,000 exercised their conversion feature. On July 1, 2013, Rowe Tool Company reacquired bonds, face value $600,000, on the open market. The balances in the equity accounts as of December 31, 2012, were

Common stock, $1 par, authorized 3 million shares, issued and outstanding, 300,000 shares	$ 300,000
Paid-in capital in excess of par	6,400,000

Market values of the common stock and bonds were as follows:

Date	Bonds (per $1,000)	Common Stock (per share)
April 1, 2013	$1,120	$52
July 1, 2013	1,200	61

Instructions: Prepare journal entries on the issuer's books for each of the following transactions. (Use the straight-line amortization method for the bond discount.)

1. Sale of the bonds on July 1, 2003.
2. Interest payment on October 1, 2003.
3. Interest accrual on December 31, 2003, including bond discount amortization for the six months since the bond issuance.
4. Conversion of bonds on April 1, 2013. (Assume that interest and discount amortization are correctly shown as of April 1, 2013. No gain or loss on conversion is recognized.)
5. Reacquisition and retirement of bonds on July 1, 2013. (Assume that interest and discount amortization are correctly reported as of July 1, 2013.)

Problem 12-51

LO4

Bond Entries—Issuer

Greenwood Company sold $4,000,000 of 7% first-mortgage bonds on October 1, 2005, at $3,479,683 plus accrued interest. The bonds were dated July 1, 2005; interest payable semiannually on January 1 and July 1; redeemable after June 30, 2010, to June 30, 2013, at 101, and thereafter until maturity at 100; and convertible into $1 par value common stock as follows:

- Until June 30, 2010, at the rate of five shares for each $1,000 bond.
- From July 1, 2010, to June 30, 2013, at the rate of four shares for each $1,000 bond.
- After June 30, 2013, at the rate of three shares for each $1,000 bond.

The bonds mature 10 years from their issue date. The company adjusts its books monthly and closes its books as of December 31 each year.

The following transactions occur in connection with the bonds.

2011
July 1 Converted $1,500,000 of bonds into stock with no gain or loss recognized.

2012
Dec. 31 Reacquired $1,000,000 face value of bonds at 99.75 plus accrued interest. These were immediately retired.

2013
July 1 Called the remaining bonds for redemptions and paid accrued interest. For purposes of obtaining funds for redemption and business expansion, a $3,000,000 issue of 9% bonds was sold at 97. These bonds are dated July 1, 2013, and are due in 20 years.

Instructions: Prepare journal entries necessary for Greenwood Company in connection with the preceding transactions, including monthly adjustments, where appropriate, as of the following dates. Assume bond discount amortization is made using the straight-line method. (*Note:* Round to the nearest dollar.)

1. October 1, 2005
2. December 31, 2005
3. July 1, 2011
4. December 31, 2012
5. July 1, 2013

Problem 12-52
LO4

Bond Entries—Investor

On June 1, 2012, Chloe Inc. purchased as a long-term investment 800 of the $1,000 face value, 9% bonds of Logan Corporation for $731,052. The bonds were purchased to yield 11% interest. Interest is payable semiannually on December 1 and June 1. The bonds mature on June 1, 2018. Chloe uses the effective-interest method of amortization. On November 1, 2013, Chloe sold the bonds for $756,400. This amount includes the appropriate accrued interest. Chloe intended to hold these bonds until they matured, so year-to-year market value fluctuations were ignored in accounting for the bonds.

Instructions: Prepare a schedule showing the income or loss before income taxes from the bond investment that Chloe should record for the years ended December 31, 2012, and 2013.

Problem 12-53
LO4

Bond Entries—Investor

On May 1, 2010, Glacier Bay Co. acquired $30,000 of Horizon Corp. 8% bonds at 97 plus accrued interest. Interest on bonds is payable semiannually on March 1 and September 1, and bonds mature on September 1, 2013.

On May 1, 2011, Glacier Bay Co. sold bonds of $10,000 for 103 plus accrued interest. On July 1, 2012, bonds of $15,000 were exchanged for 2,000 shares of Horizon Corp. common, no par value, quoted on the market on this date at $9. Interest was received on bonds to date of exchange.

On September 1, 2013, remaining bonds were redeemed and accrued interest was received.

Instructions: Give journal entries for 2010–2013 to record the preceding transactions on the books for Glacier Bay Co., including any adjustments that are required at the end of each fiscal year ending on December 31. Assume bond premium or discount amortization is by the straight-line method. Ignore any potential impact of year-to-year market value changes on the accounting for the bonds.

Problem 12-54
LO4

Note Payable Entries—Investor and Issuer

Fitzgerald Inc. issued $750,000 of 8-year, 11% notes payable dated April 1, 2009. Interest on the notes is payable semiannually on April 1 and October 1. The notes were sold on April 1, 2009, to an underwriter for $720,000 net of issuance costs. The notes were then offered for sale by the underwriter, and on July 1, 2009, L. Baum purchased the entire issue as a long-term investment. Baum paid 101 plus accrued interest for the notes. On June 1, 2012, Baum sold the investment in Fitzgerald notes to J. Gott as a short-term investment. Gott paid 96 plus accrued interest for the notes as well as $1,500 for brokerage fees. Baum paid $1,000 brokerage fees to sell the notes. Gott held the investment until April 1, 2013, when the notes were called at 104 by Fitzgerald.

Instructions: Prepare all journal entries required on the books of Fitzgerald Inc. for 2009 and 2013, on the books of Baum for 2009 and 2012, and on the books of Gott for 2012 and 2013. Assume that each entity uses the calendar year for reporting purposes and that issue costs are netted against the note proceeds by Fitzgerald. Any required amortization is made using the straight-line method. Ignore any potential impact of year-to-year market value changes on the accounting for the notes by the investors.

Problem 12-55

LO4

REVERSE SOLVABLE

Adjustment of Bond Investment Account

In auditing the books for Stiller Corporation as of December 31, 2013, before the accounts are closed, you find the following long-term investment account balance:

Account: INVESTMENT IN WILSON CHEMICAL 9% BONDS (MATURITY DATE, JUNE 1, 2017)

Date		Item	Debit	Credit	Balance	
					Debit	Credit
2013						
Jan.	21	Bonds, $300,000 par, acquired at 103 plus accrued interest	312,773		312,773	
Mar.	1	Proceeds from sale of bonds, $150,000 par and accrued interest		159,000	153,773	
June	1	Interest received		6,750	147,023	
Nov.	1	Amount received on call of bonds, $80,000 par, at 102 plus accrued interest		84,600	62,423	
Dec.	1	Interest received		3,150	59,273	

Instructions:

1. Give the entries that should have been made relative to the investment in bonds, including any adjusting entries that would be made on December 31, the end of the fiscal year. (Assume that bond premium or discount amortization is by the straight-line method and ignore any potential impact of year-to-year market value changes on the accounting for the bonds.)
2. Give the journal entries required at the end of 2013 to correct and bring the accounts up to date in view of the entries actually made.

Problem 12-56

LO4

Reacquisition of Bonds

Gerona Company authorized the sale of $300,000 of 10%, 10-year debentures on January 1, 2008. Interest is payable on January 1 and July 1. The entire issue was sold on April 1, 2008, at 103 plus accrued interest. On April 1, 2013, $100,000 of the bond issue was reacquired and retired at 99 plus accrued interest. On June 30, 2013, the remaining bonds were reacquired at 98 plus accrued interest and refunded with an issue of $200,000 of 9% bonds which were sold at 100.

Instructions: Give the journal entries for 2008 and 2013 (through June 30) on Gerona Company's books. The company's books are kept on a calendar-year basis. (*Note:* Round to the nearest dollar. Assume straight-line amortization of the premium or discount. Ignore any potential impact of year-to-year market value changes on the accounting for the bonds.)

Problem 12-57

LO4

Deferred Interest Bonds and the Selling of Assets

At the beginning of 2011, Wheel R. Dealer purchased the net assets of Consolidated Corp. by issuing 10-year, 10% bonds with a face value of $100,000,000, with semiannual interest payments made on June 30 and December 31 and no interest payments made until 2016. Dealer hopes to sell off assets of Consolidated and realize enough cash to buy back the bonds on the open market prior to interest payments becoming due in 2016. At the end of 2013, Dealer sold net assets with a carrying value of $85,000,000 for $70,000,000 and used the proceeds to retire the bond issue.

Instructions:

1. Prepare the journal entry to record the issuance of the bonds on January 2, 2011, assuming a market rate of 8%.
2. Prepare the journal entry to record the sale of the net assets.
3. Compute the market value of the bonds on January 3, 2014, the day of retirement, assuming a market rate of 14%.
4. Prepare the journal entry to record the retirement of the bond issue on January 3, 2014, assuming a carrying value of $96,000,000 and the market value as computed in (3).
5. Explain how Mr. Dealer can buy his bonds back three years after their initial sale for less than he originally sold them for and without ever having made an interest payment.
6. Should Mr. Dealer be able to reduce the liability to market value even if he does not retire the bonds?

Problem 12-58

LO4

Convertible Bonds

Von Surf Co. issued $1,200,000 of convertible 10-year debentures on July 1, 2012. The debentures provide for 8% interest payable semiannually on January 1 and July 1. The discount in connection with the issue was $18,000, which is being amortized monthly on a straight-line basis.

The debentures are convertible after one year into nine shares of the Von Surf Co.'s $1 par value common stock for each $1,000 of debentures.

On August 1, 2013, $200,000 of debentures were turned in for conversion into common stock. Interest has been accrued monthly and paid as due. Accrued interest on debentures is paid in cash upon conversion.

Instructions: Prepare the journal entries to record the conversion, amortization, and interest in connection with the debentures as of August 1, 2013, August 31, 2013, and December 31, 2013, including closing entries for year-end. Note: On the bond issuance date, it had been at least reasonably possible that the bonds would eventually be converted. (*Note:* Round to the nearest dollar.)

Problem 12-59

LO4

Early Extinguishment and Conversion of Bonds

On January 1, 2012, Brewster Company issued 2,000 of its 5-year, $1,000 face value, 11% bonds dated January 1 at an effective annual interest rate (yield) of 9%. Interest is payable each December 31. Brewster uses the effective-interest method of amortization. On December 31, 2013, the 2,000 bonds were extinguished early through acquisition in the open market by Brewster for $1,980,000 plus accrued interest.

On July 1, 2012, Brewster issued 5,000 of its 6-year, $1,000 face value, 10% convertible bonds dated July 1 at an effective annual interest rate (yield) of 12%. Interest is payable every June 30 and December 31. The bonds are convertible at the investor's option into Brewster's common stock at a ratio of 10 shares of common stock for each bond. On July 1, 2013, an investor in Brewster's convertible bonds tendered 1,500 bonds for conversion into 15,000 shares of Brewster's common stock, which had a fair market value of $105 and a par value of $1 at the date of conversion.

Instructions:

1. Make all necessary journal entries for the issuer and the investor to record the issuance of both the 11% and the 10% bonds. Ignore any potential impact of year-to-year market value changes on the investor accounting for the bonds.

2. Make all necessary journal entries on the issuer's books to record the early extinguishment of both debt instruments assuming:
   (a) On the bond issuance date, it had been less than reasonably possible that the bonds would eventually be converted. In other words, ultimate conversion had been viewed as an unlikely event.
   (b) On the bond issuance date, it had been at least reasonably possible that the bonds would eventually be converted.

Problem 12-60

LO4

Sample CPA Exam Questions

1. On December 31, 2014, Moss Co. issued $1,000,000 of 11% bonds at 109. Each $1,000 bond was issued with 50 detachable stock warrants, each of which entitled the bondholder to purchase one share of $5 par common stock for $25. Immediately after issuance, the market value of each warrant was $4. On December 31, 2014, what amount should Moss record as discount or premium on issuance of bonds?
   (a) $40,000 premium
   (b) $90,000 premium
   (c) $110,000 discount
   (d) $200,000 discount

2. On July 31, 2014, Dome Co. issued $1,000,000 of 10%, 15-year bonds at par and used a portion of the proceeds to call its 600 outstanding 11%, $1,000 face value bonds, due on July 31, 2022, at 102. On that date, unamortized bond premium relating to the 11% bonds was $65,000. In its 2014 income statement, what amount should Dome report as gain or loss, before income taxes, from retirement of bonds?
   (a) $53,000 gain
   (b) $0
   (c) ($65,000) loss
   (d) ($75,000) loss

EM EXPANDED MATERIAL

Problem 12-61

LO9

Troubled Debt Restructuring—Modification of Terms

Volatile Company, after having experienced financial difficulties in 2011, negotiated with two major creditors and arrived at an agreement to restructure its debts on December 31, 2011. The two creditors were M. Voisin and G. Stock. Voisin was owed principal of $325,000 and interest of $40,000 but agreed to accept equipment worth $70,000 and notes receivable from Volatile Company's customers worth $275,000. The equipment had an original cost of $95,000 and accumulated depreciation of $35,000. Stock was owed $650,000 and agreed to extend the terms and to accept immediate payment of $200,000 and the remaining agreed-upon balance of $477,403 to be paid on December 31, 2013. All payments were made according to schedule.

Instructions: Prepare Volatile's journal entries to record the restructuring on December 31, 2011, and the entries necessary to make the adjustments and record payments on December 31, 2012, and 2013.

Problem 12-62

LO9

Troubled Debt Restructuring—Modification of Terms

In the latter part of 2012, New Iberia Company experienced severe financial pressure and was in default of meeting interest payments on long-term notes of $4,500,000 due on December 31, 2017. The interest rate on the debt was 10%, payable semiannually on June 30 and December 31. In an agreement with Loans-R-Us Corporation, New Iberia obtained acceptance of a change in principal and interest terms for the remaining 5-year life of the notes. The changes in terms are as follows:

(a) A reduction of principal of $500,000.
(b) A reduction in the interest rate to 7%.
(c) New Iberia agreed to pay on December 31, 2012, both the $450,000 of interest in arrears and the normal interest payment under the old terms.

Instructions:

1. Compute the total dollar difference in cash payments by New Iberia over the 5-year period as a result of the restatement of terms.
2. Prepare the journal entries for the restructuring of the debt, payment of interest under the old terms, and the first two interest payments under the new terms that New Iberia would make. (*Note:* The implicit interest rate is 4.2% compounded semiannually.)

CASES

Discussion Case 12-63

What Is a Liability?

Professional athletes regularly sign long-term multimillion-dollar contracts in which they promise to play for a particular team for a specified time period. Owners of these teams often sign long-term leases for the use of playing facilities for a specified time period. GAAP often requires the leases to be booked as liabilities but does not require the obligations associated with pro athletes' contracts to be recorded.

Discuss the reasons for the differing treatment of these two seemingly similar events. Do you think the accounting treatment currently required by GAAP in these instances satisfies the needs of investors and creditors?

Discussion Case 12-64

Leave My Current Ratio Alone!

Soto Inc., a closely held corporation, has never been audited and is seeking a large bank loan for plant expansion. The bank has requested audited financial statements. In conference with the president and majority stockholder of Soto, the auditor is informed that the bank looks very closely at the current ratio. The auditor's proposed reclassifications and adjustments include the following:

(a) A note payable issued 4 1/2 years ago matures in six months from the balance sheet date. The auditor wants to reclassify it as a current liability. The controller says no because "we are probably going to refinance this note with other long-term debt."
(b) An accrual for compensated absences. Again the controller objects because the amount of the pay for these absences cannot be estimated. "Some employees quit in the first year and don't get vacation, and it is impossible to predict which employees will be absent for illness or other causes. Without being able to identify the employees, we can't determine the rate of compensation."

If you were the auditor, how would you respond to the controller?

Discussion Case 12-65

What Is Meant by Valuing Liabilities at Fair Value?

John Jex, CPA, had just delivered a keynote address to a banker's organization on the merits of valuing loan portfolio assets at fair values that reflected changing interest rates. During the question-and-answer period, he was asked why bank liabilities should not be valued using current interest rates if assets are to be revalued for interest rate changes. His answer did not seem to satisfy the banker, and the meeting soon adjourned. After the meeting, John was asked by a listener to explain the impact that changing interest rates would have on liabilities if a revaluation were to occur. How would you respond to such a request?

EM EXPANDED MATERIAL

Discussion Case 12-66

Do We Really Have Income?

Jefferson Corporation has $20,000,000 of 10% bonds outstanding. Because of cash flow problems, the company is behind in interest payments and in contributions to its bonds retirement fund. The market value of the bonds has declined until it is currently only 50% of the face value of the bonds. After lengthy negotiations, the principal bondholders have agreed to exchange their bonds for preferred stock that has a current market value of $10,000,000. The accountant for Jefferson Corporation recorded the transaction by charging Bond Liability for the entire $20,000,000 and crediting Preferred Stock for the same amount. This entry thus transfers the amount received by the company from debt to equity.

The CPA firm performing the annual audit, however, does not agree with this treatment. The auditors argue that this transfer represents a troubled debt restructuring due to the significant concessions made by the bondholders, and under these conditions, the FASB requires Jefferson to use the market value of the preferred stock as its recorded value. The difference between the $20,000,000 face value of the bonds and the $10,000,000 market value of the preferred stock is a reportable gain.

The controller of Jefferson, L. Rogers, is flabbergasted. "Here we are, almost bankrupt, and you tell us we must report the $10,000,000 as a gain. I don't care what the FASB says; that's a ridiculous situation. You can't be serious."

The auditor in charge of the engagement is adamant. "We really have no choice. You have had a forgiveness of debt for $10,000,000. You had use of the money, and based on current conditions, you won't have to pay it back. That situation looks like a gain to me."

What position do you think should be taken? Consider the external users of the financial statements and their needs in your discussion.

Case 12-67

Deciphering Financial Statements (The Walt Disney Company)

Locate **The Walt Disney Company**'s 2009 annual report on the Internet and answer the following questions.

1. What is the largest liability listed in Disney's 2009 balance sheet?
2. By what percentage did Disney change its total borrowings (current and long-term) in 2009?
3. In the notes to the financial statements, Disney outlines how the company has borrowed money. What form of borrowing constitutes the greatest portion of Disney's total borrowing?

Case 12-68

Deciphering Financial Statements (Boston Celtics)

In December of 2002, the Boston Celtics were purchased by a private investment group. Now that the Celtics are owned by a private group, their financial statements are not publicly available. However, prior to their going private, their financial statements were publicly available. A portion of those financial statements (the Liabilities and Equity section of the balance sheet) is shown below. **Celtics Basketball Holdings Limited Partnership** was the name of the entity under which the results of the Boston Celtics were reported prior to their going private.

Review the Liabilities and Equity section of the balance sheet and answer the following questions.

1. What is Deferred Game Revenues? How would that liability have arisen?
2. What does the account Deferred Compensation represent? Note that this account has both a current and noncurrent portion.
3. As of June 30, 2001, what did the Celtics report as total assets?
4. Consider your answer to part (3) in light of the $50,000,000 amount of outstanding notes payable. If you were a creditor of the Celtics, would you be concerned? How is it possible for the organization to continue to function with such a large partners' deficit?

Celtics Basketball Holdings, LP Liabilities and Partners' Capital (Deficit)

	June 30, 2001	June 30, 2000
CURRENT LIABILITIES		
Accounts payable and accrued expenses	$ 23,506,664	$ 24,478,303
Deferred game revenues	6,498,726	9,204,607
Deferred compensation—current portion	1,226,316	1,278,410
TOTAL CURRENT LIABILITIES	$ 31,231,706	$ 34,961,320
NOTES PAYABLE TO BANK	50,000,000	50,000,000
DEFERRED COMPENSATION—noncurrent portion	5,182,821	6,369,646
OTHER NON-CURRENT LIABILITIES		708,000
PARTNERS' CAPITAL (DEFICIT)		
Celtics Basketball Holdings, L.P.:		
General Partner	1,015	1,008
Celtics Pride GP—Limited Partner	(29,111,174)	(29,437,209)
Castle Creek Partners, L.P.—Limited Partner	(31,144,430)	(31,493,235)
	(60,254,589)	(60,929,436)
Celtics Basketball, L.P.—General Partner	1,081	1,074
TOTAL PARTNERS' CAPITAL (DEFICIT)	$(60,253,508)	$(60,928,362)

Case 12-69

Deciphering Financial Statements (Hewlett-Packard & Dell)

Review the 2009 balance sheet data for **Hewlett-Packard (HP)** and **Dell** shown below.

(in millions)	Hewlett-Packard	Dell
Current assets	$52,539	$24,245
Current liabilities	43,003	18,960
Total liabilities	74,282	28,011
Total stockholders' equity	40,517	5,641
Retained earnings	29,936	22,110

1. Compute each company's current ratio for 2009. Based on the result, which company appears to be more liquid?
2. Compute each company's debt-to-equity ratio for 2009. Which company appears to have the most debt in relation to stockholders' equity?
3. Which company has a larger amount of long-term debt in its financing mix?
4. Why would HP have a larger amount in retained earnings at the end of 2009 relative to Dell?
5. How can Dell have $22,110 million in retained earnings and only $5,641 million of total stockholders' equity?

Case 12-70

Deciphering Financial Statements (Altria Group)

Examine the partial balance sheet of **Altria Group** shown below and answer the following questions.

1. Current assets for Altria Group (parent company of **Philip Morris**) totaled $5,773 (in millions) at the end of 2009. Compute the company's current ratio.
2. Why would Altria classify its liabilities into two different categories?
3. Compute Altria's debt-to-equity ratio for 2009 using (a) only long-term debt and (b) all liabilities in your computations. Why the huge difference in your answers?

When interpreting a debt-to-equity ratio computed by someone else, what should be your first question?

at December 31,	2009	2008
Liabilities		
Consumer products		
Current portion of long-term debt	$ 775	$ 135
Accounts payable	494	510
Accrued liabilities:		
Marketing	467	374
Taxes, except income taxes	318	98
Employment costs	239	248
Settlement charges	3,635	3,984
Other	1,354	1,128
Dividends payable	710	665
Total current liabilities	$ 7,992	$ 7,142
Long-term debt	11,185	6,839
Deferred income taxes	4,383	351
Accrued pension costs	1,157	1,393
Accrued postretirement health care costs	2,326	2,208
Other liabilities	1,248	1,208
Total consumer products liabilities	28,291	19,141
Financial services		
Debt		500
Deferred income taxes	4,180	4,644
Other liabilities	102	102
Total financial services liabilities	4,282	5,246
Total liabilities	32,573	24,387
Contingencies (Note 22)		
Redeemable noncontrolling interest	32	
Stockholders' Equity		
Common stock, par value $0.33 1/3 per share (2,805,961,317 shares issued)	$ 935	$ 935
Additional paid-in capital	5,997	6,350
Earnings reinvested in the business	22,599	22,131
Accumulated other comprehensive losses	(1,561)	(2,181)
Cost of repurchased stock (729,932,673 shares in 2009 and 744,589,733 shares in 2008)	(23,901)	(24,407)
Total stockholders' equity attributable to Altria Group, Inc.	4,069	2,828
Noncontrolling interests	3	
Total stockholders' equity	$ 4,072	$ 2,828
Total Liabilities and Stockholders' Equity	$36,677	$27,215

Case 12-71

Writing Assignment (I like these "no interest" bonds)

J. R. Chump, president of ProKeeper Industries, is contemplating the issuance of long-term debt to finance plant expansion and renovation. In the past, his company has issued traditional debt instruments that require regular interest payments and a retirement of the principal on the maturity date. However, he has noticed that several competitors have recently issued bonds that either do not require interest payments or defer interest payments for several years. He has asked you, his chief financial officer, to prepare a short memo addressing the following questions.

1. Why would a company issue bonds that require interest payments if bonds that do not require interest payments are being sold in the open market?
2. If the company were to issue 10-year bonds with a face value of $100,000 and the market rate of interest is 10%, what would be the proceeds from the sale if the bonds were zero-interest bonds? What would be the proceeds if the annual interest payments did not begin for five years and the stated rate of interest were 10%? What would be the proceeds if the bonds paid interest annually for 10 years at 10%?
3. What factors must a business consider when determining the interest terms associated with long-term debt?

Case 12-72

Ethical Dilemma (Keeping our debt covenants)

You are the chief financial officer of a local manufacturing company, Larsen Enterprises. This company is run by two brothers, Steve and John Larsen. The Larsen brothers have built this company up from a small 5-man shop to a company now employing over 200 people. The national economy has recently taken a turn for the worse, which has affected the Larsens' business. In fact, the company's performance of late has been such that it is in jeopardy of violating several of its debt covenants (promises made to the lending institution). If the company violates these covenants, the bank has the option of calling the debt due immediately. If the debt is called, Larsen is not sure what will happen, but it will certainly not be good.

The covenant that is in jeopardy relates to the current ratio. If the current ratio drops below 2, Larsen Enterprises is considered in technical default on its debt. Steve and John have come to you and asked you to suggest ways in which the current ratio, which currently stands at 1.9, could be increased.

Take a moment and think of ways in which the current ratio might be manipulated. Identify specific actions that the Larsen brothers might take to increase the current ratio. Is it in the best interests of shareholders and lending institutions for Steve and John to make business decisions that have cosmetic effects on the financial statements?

Case 12-73

Cumulative Spreadsheet Analysis

This spreadsheet assignment is a continuation of the spreadsheet assignments given in earlier chapters. If you completed those assignments, you have a head start on this one.

Refer back to the instructions for preparing the revised financial statements for 2013 as given in (1) of the Cumulative Spreadsheet Analysis assignment in Chapter 3.

1. Skywalker wishes to prepare a *forecasted* balance sheet, a *forecasted* income statement, and a *forecasted* statement of cash flows for 2014. Use the financial statement numbers for 2013 as the basis for the forecast, along with the following additional information.

   (a) Sales in 2014 are expected to increase by 40% over 2013 sales of $2,100.
   (b) In 2014, new property, plant, and equipment acquisitions will be in accordance with the information in (q).
   (c) The $480 in operating expenses reported in 2013 breaks down as follows: $15 in depreciation expense and $465 in other operating expenses.
   (d) New long-term debt will be acquired in 2014 in accordance with (u).
   (e) No cash dividends will be paid in 2014.
   (f) New short-term loans payable will be acquired in an amount sufficient to make Skywalker's current ratio in 2014 exactly equal to 2.0.
   (g) Skywalker does not anticipate repurchasing any additional shares of stock during 2014.
   (h) Because changes in future prices and exchange rates are impossible to predict, Skywalker's best estimate is that the balance in accumulated other comprehensive income will remain unchanged in 2014.

(i) In the absence of more detailed information, assume that the balances in Investment Securities, Long-Term Investments, and Other Long-Term Assets will all increase at the same rate as sales (40%) in 2014. The balance in Intangible Assets will change in accordance with item (r).

(j) In the absence of more detailed information, assume that the balance in the other long-term liabilities account will increase at the same rate as sales (40%) in 2014.

(k) The investment securities are classified as available-for-sale securities. Accordingly, cash from the purchase and sale of these securities is classified as an investing activity.

(l) Assume that transactions impacting other long-term assets and other long-term liabilities accounts are operating activities.

(m) Cash and investment securities accounts will increase at the same rate as sales.

(n) The forecasted amount of accounts receivable in 2014 is determined using the forecasted value for the average collection period. The average collection period for 2014 is expected to be 14.08 days. To make the calculations less complex, this value of 14.08 days is based on forecasted end-of-year accounts receivable rather than on average accounts receivable.

(o) The forecasted amount of inventory in 2014 is determined using the forecasted value for the number of days' sales in inventory. The number of days' sales in inventory for 2014 is expected to be 107.6 days. To make the calculations simpler, this value of 107.6 days is based on forecasted end-of-year inventory rather than on average inventory.

(p) The forecasted amount of accounts payable in 2014 is determined using the forecasted value for the number of days' purchases in accounts payable. The number of days' purchases in accounts payable for 2014 is expected to be 48.34 days. To make the calculations simpler, this value of 48.34 days is based on forecasted end-of-year accounts payable rather than on average accounts payable.

(q) The forecasted amount of property, plant, and equipment (PP&E) in 2014 is determined using the forecasted value for the fixed asset turnover ratio. The fixed asset turnover ratio for 2014 is expected to be 3.518 times. To make the calculations simpler, this ratio of 3.518 is based on forecasted end-of-year gross property, plant, and equipment balance rather than on the average balance. (*Note*: For simplicity, ignore accumulated depreciation in making this calculation.)

(r) Skywalker has determined that no new intangible assets will be acquired in 2014. Intangible assets are amortized according to the information in (t).

(s) In computing depreciation expense for 2014, use straight-line depreciation and assume a 30-year useful life with no residual value. Gross PP&E acquired during the year is only depreciated for half the year. In other words, depreciation expense for 2014 is the sum of two parts: (1) a full year of depreciation on the beginning balance in PP&E, assuming a 30-year life and no residual value, and (2) a half-year of depreciation on any new PP&E acquired during the year, based on the change in the gross PP&E balance.

(t) Skywalker assumes a 20-year useful life for its intangible assets. Assume that the $100 in intangible assets reported in 2013 is the original cost of the intangibles. Include the amortization expense with the depreciation expense in the income statement.

(*Note*: These forecasted statements were constructed as part of the spreadsheet assignment in Chapter 11; you can use that spreadsheet as a starting point if you have completed that assignment.)

For this exercise, make the following additional assumptions:

(u) New long-term debt will be acquired (or repaid) in an amount sufficient to make Skywalker's debt ratio (total liabilities divided by total assets) in 2014 exactly equal to 0.80.

(v) Assume an interest rate on short-term loans payable of 6.0% and on long-term debt of 8.0%. Only a half-year's interest is charged on loans taken out during the year. For example, if short-term loans payable at the end of 2014 is $15 and given that short-term loans payable at the end of 2013 were $10, total short-term interest expense for 2014 would be $0.75 [($10 × 0.06) + ($5 × 0.06 × 1/2)].

Clearly state any additional assumptions that you make.

2. Repeat (1) with the following changes in assumptions.
   (a) The debt ratio in 2014 is exactly equal to 0.70.
   (b) The debt ratio in 2014 is exactly equal to 0.90.
3. Comment on the differences in the forecasted values of cash from operating activities in 2014 under each of the following assumptions about the debt ratio: 0.70, 0.80, and 0.90. Explain exactly why a change in debt ratio has an impact on cash from operating activities.

P3 ADDITIONAL ACTIVITIES OF A BUSINESS

CHAPTER 13 Equity Financing

LEARNING OBJECTIVES

1. Identify the rights associated with ownership of common and preferred stock.
2. Record the issuance of stock for cash, on a subscription basis, and in exchange for noncash assets or for services.
3. Use both the cost and par value methods to account for stock repurchases.
4. Account for the issuance of stock rights and stock warrants.
5. Compute the compensation expense associated with the granting of employee stock options.
6. Determine which equity-related items should be reported in the balance sheet as liabilities.
7. Distinguish between stock conversions that require a reduction in retained earnings and those that do not.
8. List the factors that impact the Retained Earnings balance.
9. Properly record cash dividends, property dividends, small and large stock dividends, and stock splits.
10. Explain the background of unrealized gains and losses recorded as part of accumulated other comprehensive income, and list the major types of equity reserves found in foreign balance sheets.
11. Prepare a statement of changes in stockholders' equity.

Bill Gates is one of the two richest people in the United States. (The other one is mentioned further down—keep reading.) **Microsoft**, the company Bill Gates founded with partner Paul Allen in 1975, was originally best known for developing the first-generation DOS operating system used with **IBM** personal computers and their clones. Microsoft subsequently came to dominate (some would say monopolize) the software market with popular software packages such as Word®, Excel®, and PowerPoint®, based on its Windows® operating system.

In 1985, Microsoft decided to issue its stock publicly for the first time. Before this time, Microsoft had stock outstanding, but the stock was held by company officials and employees and was not publicly traded. A key consideration, of course, was what price to charge when issuing the shares.

Lou Dematteis/Reuters/Landov

EX 13-1 MICROSOFT'S PRICE PER SHARE OF STOCK

An initial price range of $16 to $19 per share was set, based on Microsoft's earnings per share and the price-earnings (P/E) ratios for similar firms that already had publicly traded stock. The large amount of interest in the Microsoft stock issue resulted in the final offering price being raised to $21 per share. On March 13, 1986, Microsoft shares were first publicly traded, and by the end of the first day of trading, the shares were at $27.75.[1] If you had purchased one of those initial shares for $21 in 1986, by December 1999 it would have been worth almost $15,000. (See Exhibit 13-1.) By December 2000, that same share of stock would have declined in value to $5,489 as a result of both the bursting of the dot.com bubble and the continued uncertainty about Microsoft's future caused by the antitrust lawsuits against the company. In May 2010, Microsoft had recovered some of its lost value, with one of the initial shares being worth $8,320.

A share of Microsoft stock does not trade for $8,320 because, since 1986, Microsoft has split its stock several times. A split is like cutting a pie into more pieces—the number of shares is increased and the price of each share is reduced proportionately. Most firms use stock splits to maintain their per-share price in the range that is considered normal, usually between $20 and $80 per share in the United States.

A glaring exception to this price-per-share range is stock of **Berkshire Hathaway**, which is headed by Warren Buffett, who annually vies with Bill Gates for the title of richest person in the United States. Buffett's company is involved in a number of diverse lines of business. Its largest operations are in property and casualty insurance; **Geico** is owned by Berkshire Hathaway. However, it also produces and sells **Kirby** vacuums, **See's Candies**, and **World Book** encyclopedias. In addition, Berkshire Hathaway has a substantial investment portfolio: It owns 12.7% of **American Express**, 9.9% of **BYD Company**, 8.6% of **Coca-Cola**, 8.8% of **Kraft Foods**, 6.5% of **Wells Fargo**, and 19% of the **Washington Post**.[2] In fact, a whole industry has built up around financial analysts who interpret the investment choices made by Warren Buffett.

Because Berkshire Hathaway has been very profitable and has never split its stock, its price per share has risen higher than any other stock on the New York Stock Exchange. On May 14, 2010, Berkshire Hathaway shares closed at $114,150 each.[3]

By the way, in the 2009 annual *Forbes* survey of America's richest people, Bill Gates ($50.0 billion) beat out Warren Buffett ($40.0 billion) as the richest person in the United States for the 16th straight year.[4]

? QUESTIONS

1. If you had purchased Microsoft stock in December 1999 and sold it in May 2010, what percentage return on your investment would you have earned during that time interval?
2. What is Berkshire Hathaway's relationship with the *Washington Post*?
3. In the year 2010, Microsoft's price per share was around $29, whereas the price per share for Berkshire Hathaway was about $114,150. What additional information would you need to determine which company had a higher total market value?

Answers to these questions can be found on page 13-54.

[1] Bro Uttal, "Inside the Deal That Made Bill Gates $350,000,000," *Fortune*, July 21, 1986, p. 23.

[2] From the 2009 Annual Report of Berkshire Hathaway.

[3] In May 1996, the shareholders of Berkshire Hathaway approved the creation of a new class of shares, called *Class B shares*. Originally, each of these shares had 1/30 the value of the original Class A shares. A 50-for-1 stock split of these shares in January 2010 now makes each B share worth 1/1,500 the value of the A shares. These actions were taken to head off some investment companies that had started buying Berkshire Hathaway shares, carving them up, and selling shares of the shares.

[4] In the 2009 *Forbes survey*, Warren Buffett was ahead of Paul Allen ($11.5 billion), who was Bill Gates' partner in the founding of Microsoft. Also, the six heirs to Sam Walton's Wal-Mart fortune had a combined net worth of $90 billion, making them the wealthiest family in America.

Owner investments are reported in the Equity section of the balance sheet. For example, when a corporation issues new shares of stock to the public, the proceeds are recorded in the Equity section. These invested funds are called *contributed*, or *paid-in, capital*. Owners also contribute funds to a company by allowing profits to be reinvested. In a corporation, these reinvested profits are called *retained earnings*. In sole proprietorships and partnerships, paid-in capital and retained earnings are lumped together into a single capital account. This chapter emphasizes the accounting for equity of corporations.

In a simple world, the Equity section of a corporation's balance sheet would include only the two sections just mentioned, paid-in capital and retained earnings. However, the increasing complexity of worldwide business necessitates a number of other equity items. For example, some equity-related items must be reported as liabilities in the balance sheet. In addition, unrealized gains or losses on some investment securities are shown in a separate equity category, as is the impact of foreign currency fluctuations on the equity of foreign subsidiaries. The items that can appear in the Equity section are summarized in Exhibit 13-2 and are discussed in the remainder of the chapter.

Although many items affect owners' equity, the major decisions associated with owner investment are illustrated in the time line in Exhibit 13-3. Note that many of the issues associated with transactions involving owners may or may not occur during any given period. Dividends may or may not be paid, and options may or may not be granted. This chapter discusses many of the possible actions that may be taken by management that will affect owners' equity.

EX 13-2 EQUITY ITEMS

Stockholders' Equity

Contributed capital:
  Preferred stock
  Common stock
  Additional paid-in capital
Retained earnings
Less: Treasury stock
Accumulated other comprehensive income:
  Foreign currency translation adjustment
  Unrealized gains and losses on available-for-sale securities
  Unrealized gains and losses on some derivatives
Noncontrolling interest
Total stockholders' equity

EX 13-3 TIME LINE OF ISSUES ASSOCIATED WITH OWNERS' EQUITY

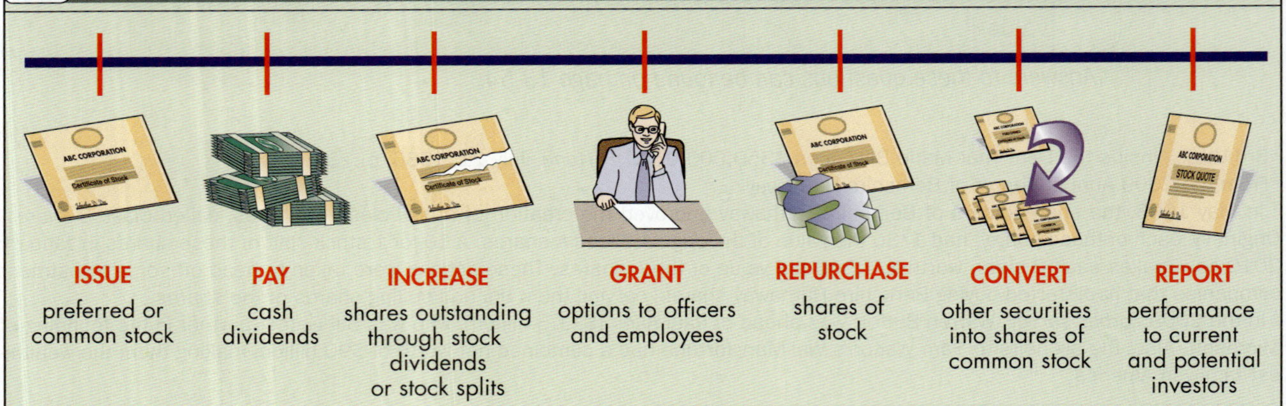

Nature and Classifications of Paid-In Capital

1 **Identify the rights associated with ownership of common and preferred stock.**

WHY The providers of a company's financing (both debt and equity) need to know who else has provided financing to the company and in what amount. This information, coupled with knowledge of the rights held by each class of capital provider, allows any given capital provider to assess the risks and potential returns associated with the investment.

HOW Holders of common stock are the true owners of the business and have voting rights in corporate matters. Preferred shareholders do not typically possess voting rights but do have preference when it comes to the receipt of dividends.

A corporation is a legal, artificial entity that has an existence separate from its owners and may engage in business within prescribed limits just as if it were a real person. The modern corporation makes it possible for large amounts of resources to be assembled under one management. These resources are transferred to the corporation by individual owners, and in exchange for these resources, the corporation issues stock certificates evidencing ownership interests.[5] Stockholders elect a board of directors whose members oversee the strategic and long-run planning for the corporation. The directors select managers who supervise the day-to-day operations of the corporation.

Corporations are typically created under the incorporating laws of one of the 50 states. Because the states do not follow a uniform incorporating act, the conditions under which corporations may be created and under which they may operate are somewhat varied. Many businesses are incorporated in Delaware because constraints on cash dividends are loose, and Delaware laws governing corporations are generally seen as being "pro business." In fact, of the 1,471 publicly traded companies in the United States with market values greater than $1 billion as of the end of the first quarter of 2004, more than 50% (752 of 1,471) were incorporated in Delaware.

In theory, regulation of corporations is strictly a state matter falling outside the jurisdiction of federal authorities. However, in practice almost all issues of stock to the public fall under the jurisdiction of the federal Securities and Exchange Commission (SEC). Exceptions are made when an issue is small (less than $1 million in any 12-month period), is made only to "accredited" investors (informed investors such as banks, investment companies, issuing company officers, and individuals with net worth exceeding $1 million), or is made only to residents of a single state.

FYI

Boards of directors are composed of top managers of the company, top executives from other companies, prominent civic officials, and major shareholders. For example, the 2010 board of The Coca-Cola Company included Peter Ueberroth, former head of the Los Angeles Olympics Committee (1984) and former commissioner of Major League Baseball, and Alexis Herman, former U.S. Secretary of Labor and former director of Public Liaison for the White House.

When a corporation is formed, a single class of stock, known as *common stock*, is usually issued. Corporations may later find that there are advantages to issuing one or more

[5] Briefly, the advantages of organizing a business as a corporation instead of as a sole proprietorship or partnership are that the investors in a corporation have limited liability (they can lose only what they put in; their other personal assets are safe), and ownership interest is easily transferable (there is no need to get approval from the other shareholders before selling your shares). The primary disadvantage is that corporate income is taxed twice: once at the corporate level and again at the individual level when shareholders receive cash dividends.

additional classes of stock with varying rights and priorities. Stock with certain preferences (rights) over common stock is called *preferred stock*.

Common Stock

The owners of the common stock of a corporation can be thought of as the true owners of the business. If the corporation does poorly, the common stockholders are likely to lose some or all of their investment because they can receive cash from the corporation only after the claims of all other parties (i.e., lenders, employees, government, preferred stockholders) are satisfied. On the other hand, if the corporation does well, the common stockholders reap the benefit because they own all assets in excess of those needed to satisfy the fixed claims of others. In summary, the common stockholders bear the greatest risk, but they also stand to receive the highest return on their investment.

Unless restricted by terms of the articles of incorporation, certain basic rights are held by each common stockholder. These rights are as follows:

1. To vote in the election of directors and in the determination of certain corporate policies such as the management compensation plan or major corporate acquisitions.
2. To maintain one's proportional interest in the corporation through purchase of additional common stock if and when it is issued. This right is known as the *preemptive right* and ensures that a common stockholder's ownership percentage cannot be diluted against his or her will. In recent years, some states have eliminated the preemptive right.

FYI

Outside the United States, corporations sometimes have different classes of shares for local investors and for foreign investors. For example, Chinese corporations can have two classes of shares that trade on the Shanghai and Shenzhen stock exchanges: A shares, which only Chinese citizens (and selected foreign institutional investors) can own, and B shares, which can be purchased by foreigners. In February 2001, regulations were loosened, allowing Chinese citizens with approved foreign currency accounts to trade in B shares. Chinese B shares traded on The Stock Exchange of Hong Kong are called *H shares*. Shares of Chinese companies that trade on a U.S. exchange are called *N shares* (for "New York").

Usually, each corporation has only one class of common stock. However, a recent phenomenon is the creation of multiple classes of common stock, each with slightly different ownership privileges. For example, **Google** has two classes of common stock. Google Class B common is held almost exclusively by insiders and is not publicly traded. Each share of Class B common has 10 votes in board elections, compared to one vote for each share of the publicly traded Class A common. With this share structure, Google is able to raise equity funding through issuance of Class A shares without seriously diluting voting control. Berkshire Hathaway, discussed in the opening scenario of this chapter, has created some Class B common shares that have 1/1,500 the value of the Class A shares—for those investors (such as you and the authors) who might not have the $114,150 necessary to buy one share of Berkshire's Class A shares. However, to repeat, most corporations have only one class of common stock.

Par or Stated Value of Stock

The journal entry to record the issuance of common stock in exchange for cash frequently looks something like this:

Cash	XXX	
Common Stock (at par value)		XXX
Additional Paid-In Capital		XXX

Historically, par value was equal to the market value of the shares at issuance. Par value was also sometimes viewed by the courts as the minimum contribution by investors.[6] Accordingly, when corporate assets were insufficient to cover corporate liabilities, investors who had contributed less than par value were required to cover the shortfall. As a consequence, corporations began to issue shares with lower par values in order to protect investors. In addition, state incorporation laws were written to prevent payment of cash dividends whenever operating losses reduced corporate equity below total par value of shares issued. Lower par values allowed corporations more flexibility in their cash dividend policy.

Today, most stocks have either a nominal par value or no par value at all. No-par stock sometimes has a stated value that, for financial reporting purposes, functions exactly like a par value. As can be seen from Exhibit 13-4, 84.6% of publicly traded stocks in the United States have par values of $1 or less.

FYI

Legal capital constraints are not usually a limiting factor for payment of cash dividends. More frequently, payment of dividends is restricted by debt covenants imposed by lenders. A typical debt covenant might require maintenance of a debt-to-equity ratio below a certain amount.

Preferred Stock

The term *preferred stock* is somewhat misleading because it gives the impression that preferred stock is better than common stock. Preferred stock isn't better—it's different. In fact, a useful way to think of preferred stock is that preferred stockholders give up many of the rights of ownership in exchange for some of the protection enjoyed by creditors.

The rights of ownership given up by preferred stockholders are:

- *Voting.* In most cases, preferred stockholders are not allowed to vote for the board of directors. Voting rights can exist under circumstances specific to each preferred stock issue. For example, some preferred stockholders are granted corporate voting rights if the company fails to pay them cash dividends for, say, two consecutive quarters. When a company fails to pay preferred dividends, those dividends are said to have been "passed."
- *Sharing in success.* The cash dividends received by preferred stockholders are usually fixed in amount. Therefore, if the company does exceptionally well, preferred stockholders do not get to share in the success. As a result of this cap on dividends, the market value of preferred stock does not typically vary with the success of the company as does the price of common stock. Instead, the market value of preferred stock varies with changes in interest rates, in much the same way as bond prices change.

The protections enjoyed by preferred stockholders, relative to common stockholders, are:

- *Cash dividend preference.* Preferred stockholders are entitled to receive their full cash dividend before any cash dividends are paid to common stockholders.
- *Liquidation preference.* If the company goes bankrupt, preferred stockholders are entitled to have their investment repaid, in full, before common stockholders receive anything.

[6] For a more complete discussion of the legal significance of par value, see Philip McGough, "The Legal Significance of the Par Value of Common Stock: What Accounting Educators Should Know," *Issues in Accounting Education,* Fall 1988, pp. 330–350.

EX 13-4 PAR VALUES OF PUBLICLY TRADED STOCKS

Par or Stated Values
Publicly Traded Stocks in the United States
For the Year 2003

	All Firms	Only Firms with Market Value Greater Than $1 Billion
Less than $0.01	24.4%	9.9%
Exactly $0.01	36.7	38.0
Between $0.01 and $1.00	15.3	18.8
Exactly $1.00	8.2	13.2
Greater than $1.00	15.4	20.1

Source: Standard & Poor's *COMPUSTAT.*

A later section in the chapter discusses in more detail the securities, such as preferred stock, that share the characteristics of both debt and equity. As financial markets become more sophisticated, the line between debt and equity continues to blur and disclosure issues associated with these hybrid securities become even more important.

Preferred stock is generally issued with a par value. When preferred stock has a par value, the dividend is stated in terms of a percentage of par value. When preferred stock is no par, the dividend must be stated in terms of dollars and cents. Thus, holders of 5% preferred stock with a $50 par value are entitled to an annual dividend of $2.50 per share before any distribution is made to common stockholders; holders of $5 no-par preferred stock are entitled to an annual dividend of $5 per share before dividends are paid to common stockholders.

A corporation may issue more than one class of preferred stock. For example, **Citigroup** described 14 classes of preferred stock in the notes to its 2008 financial statements; only four classes remained outstanding at the end of 2009. The classes vary in terms of dividend rates, redemption requirements, convertibility, and other features.

Cumulative and Noncumulative Preferred Stock When a corporation fails to declare dividends on cumulative preferred stock, such dividends accumulate and require payment in the future before any dividends may be paid to common stockholders.

For example, assume that Good Time Corporation has outstanding 100,000 shares of 9% cumulative preferred stock, $10 par. Dividends were last paid in 2010. Total dividends of $300,000 are declared in 2013 by the board of directors. The majority of this amount will be paid to the preferred shareholders as follows:

	Dividends to Preferred Shareholders	Dividends to Common Shareholders	Total Dividends
Cumulative dividend for 2011	$ 90,000	—	$ 90,000
Cumulative dividend for 2012	90,000	—	90,000
Dividends for 2013	90,000	$30,000	120,000
Total	$270,000	$30,000	$300,000

Dividends on cumulative preferred stock that are passed are referred to as dividends in arrears. Although these dividends are not a liability until declared by the board of directors, this information is important to stockholders and other users of the financial statements. The amount of dividends in arrears is disclosed in the notes to the financial statements. For example, **Harrah's Entertainment, Inc.**, a large U.S. corporation that owns several casinos, hotels, and golf courses, disclosed in the notes to its 2009 financial statements that it had $652.6 million of dividends in arrears..

With noncumulative preferred stock, it is not necessary to provide for passed dividends. A dividend omission on preferred stock in any one year means it is irretrievably lost. Dividends may be declared on common stock as long as the preferred stock receives the preferred rate for the current period. Thus, in the previous example, if the preferred stock were noncumulative, the 2013 dividends would be distributed as follows:

	Dividends to Preferred Shareholders	Dividends to Common Shareholders	Total Dividends
Dividend passed in 2011	—	—	—
Dividend passed in 2012	—	—	—
Dividends for 2013	$90,000	$210,000	$300,000
Total	$90,000	$210,000	$300,000

Preferred stock contracts normally provide for cumulative dividends. Also, courts have generally held that dividend rights on preferred stock are cumulative in the absence of specific provisions to the contrary.

Participating Preferred Stock Dividends on preferred stock are generally of a fixed amount. However, participating preferred stock issues provide for additional dividends to be paid to preferred stockholders after dividends of a specified amount are paid to the common stockholders. A participative provision makes preferred stock more like common stock. Although once quite common, participating preferred stocks are now relatively rare.

Convertible Preferred Stock Preferred stock is convertible when it can be exchanged by its owner for some other security of the issuing corporation. Conversion rights generally provide for the exchange of preferred stock into common stock. Conversion of preferred stock into common stock would be attractive when the company has done well, allowing the preferred shareholders to escape from the preferred dividend limits. In some instances, preferred stock may be convertible into bonds, thus allowing investors the option of changing their positions from stockholders to creditors. The journal entries required for stock conversions are illustrated later in the chapter. Consideration of convertible preferred stock is important in the calculation of diluted earnings per share; this is discussed in Chapter 18.

Callable Preferred Stock Many preferred issues are callable, meaning they may be called and canceled at the option of the corporation. The call price is usually specified in the original agreement and provides for payment of dividends in arrears as part of the repurchase price.

Redeemable Preferred Stock Redeemable preferred stock is preferred stock that is redeemable at the option of the stockholder or upon other conditions not within the control of the issuer (e.g., redemption on a specific date or upon reaching a certain level of earnings). This feature makes redeemable preferred stock somewhat like a loan in that the issuing corporation may be forced to repay the stock proceeds. The FASB currently requires disclosure of the extent of redemption requirements for all issues of preferred stock that are callable or redeemable.[7] As described in a later section in this chapter, preferred stock that *must* be redeemed, called mandatorily redeemable preferred stock, is reported as a liability in the balance sheet instead of as equity.

Current Developments in the Accounting for Preferred Stock Since 1990 the FASB has been wrestling with the sticky issue of separating debt financing from equity financing. Their most current attempt is a *Preliminary Views* document, "Financial Instruments with Characteristics of Equity," released on November 30, 2007. This document explains that many provisions of existing U.S. GAAP conflict with the Conceptual Framework definition of a liability, so a substantial reworking of the liability/equity distinction, with perhaps an accompanying change in the Conceptual Framework, is necessary.

In the *Preliminary Views* document, the FASB recommended the "basic ownership approach" to identifying equity. This approach hinges on the idea that equity claims are those that remain when all other claims have been satisfied. Thus, the only elements of financing that should be identified as "equity" are the most basic elements which are left when all claims with a higher priority have been satisfied.[8]

Application of this basic ownership approach would result in a very restrictive definition of equity. In fact, *all* preferred stock, whether redeemable or not, would be reported as a liability under this approach. User comments to both the FASB and the IASB have been overwhelmingly against this "basic ownership approach." Instead, users prefer a "perpetual approach," which describes an equity instrument as one for which there is no requirement to repay the invested funds, and the holder of the instrument is entitled to some assets if the company is liquidated. Preferred shares would be classified as equity under this "perpetual approach." Both the FASB and the IASB are leaning toward the "perpetual approach." However, remember that no final decision has been made, so stay tuned. For the time being, most preferred stock is classified as equity.

Issuance of Capital Stock

2 **Record the issuance of stock for cash, on a subscription basis, and in exchange for noncash assets or for services.**

WHY **To avoid misstating the amount of financing provided by the shareholders in a corporation, issued shares must be carefully valued whenever anything other than cash is received in exchange for the shares. In addition, to avoid inflating the apparent amount of equity funds received by a corporation, stock subscriptions receivable (but not yet received) do not result in a net increase in equity.**

HOW **Issued stock is recorded using the fair value of the assets or services received in exchange for the shares or the fair market value of the shares issued, whichever is more objectively determinable. Stock subscriptions receivable are *not* reported as an asset.**

Stock can be issued in exchange for cash, on a subscription basis, in exchange for noncash consideration, or as part of a business combination. The accounting for each of these possibilities is described on the following pages.

[7] FASB ASC paragraphs 505-10-50-4 and 5.

[8] *Preliminary Views*, "Financial Instruments with Characteristics of Equity" (Norwalk, CT: Financial Accounting Standards Board, November 2007), par. D11.

Capital Stock Issued for Cash

The issuance of stock for cash is recorded by a debit to Cash and a credit to Capital Stock for the par or stated value.[9] When the amount of cash received from the sale of stock is more than the par or stated value, the excess is recorded separately as a credit to an additional paid-in capital account. This account is carried on the books as long as the stock to which it relates is outstanding. When stock is retired, the Capital Stock balance as well as any related Additional Paid-In Capital balance is generally canceled.

To illustrate, assume that Goode Corporation issued 4,000 shares of $1 par common stock on April 1, 2011, for $45,000 cash. The entry to record the transaction is as follows:

2011			
Apr. 1	Cash	45,000	
	Common Stock		4,000
	Paid-In Capital in Excess of Par		41,000

If, in the example, the common stock were no-par stock but with a $1 stated value, the entry would be the same except that the $41,000 would be designated Paid-In Capital in Excess of Stated Value. Generally, stock is assigned a par or a stated value. However, if there is no such value assigned, the entire amount of cash received on the sale of stock is credited to the capital stock account, and no additional paid-in capital account is associated with the stock. Assuming Goode Corporation's stock was no-par common without a stated value, the entry to record the sale of 4,000 shares for $45,000 would be as follows:

2011			
Apr. 1	Cash	45,000	
	Common Stock		45,000

Capital Stock Sold on Subscription

Capital stock may be issued on a subscription basis. A subscription is a legally binding contract between the subscriber (purchaser of stock) and the corporation (issuer of stock). The contract states the number of shares subscribed, the subscription price, the terms of payment, and other conditions of the transaction. A subscription gives the corporation a legal claim for the contract price and gives the subscriber the legal status of a stockholder unless certain rights as a stockholder are specifically withheld by law or by terms of the contract. Ordinarily, stock certificates evidencing share ownership are not issued until the full subscription price has been received by the corporation.

The following entries illustrate the recording and issuance of capital stock sold on subscription.

November 1–30: Received subscriptions for 5,000 shares of $1 par common at $12.50 per share with 50% down, balance due in 60 days.

Common Stock Subscriptions Receivable	62,500	
Common Stock Subscribed		5,000
Paid-In Capital in Excess of Par		57,500
Cash	31,250	
Common Stock Subscriptions Receivable		31,250

[9] *Capital stock* is a general term; when it is used in account titles in the text, it represents either preferred stock or common stock. When an illustration is meant to apply specifically to preferred or common stock, the appropriate term is used in the account title.

December 1–31: Received balance due on one-half of subscriptions and issued stock to the fully paid subscribers, 2,500 shares.

Cash	15,625	
Common Stock Subscriptions Receivable		15,625
Common Stock Subscribed	2,500	
Common Stock		2,500

Contributed capital would be reported in the Stockholders' Equity section of the December 31 balance sheet as follows:

Stockholders' Equity

Contributed capital:	
Common stock, $1 par, 2,500 shares issued and outstanding	$ 2,500
Common stock subscribed, 2,500 shares	2,500
Paid-in capital in excess of par	57,500
	$62,500
Less: Common stock subscriptions receivable	15,625
Total contributed capital	$46,875

Capital Stock Subscriptions Receivable should normally not be shown as an asset but as an offset to equity.[10] This treatment is deemed appropriate because the legal penalty against subscribers who don't fully pay the contract price is often minimal, increasing the probability that the issuer of the stock may not fully collect on the subscriptions receivable. SEC rules allow subscription amounts receivable as of the balance sheet date to be shown as a current asset if the full contract price is collected prior to the date the financial statements are actually issued. For example, **Nebo Products**, a Draper, Utah-based importer of hand tools and camping gear (manufactured in Taiwan, China, and India), reported stock subscriptions receivable totaling $1,302,586 in its December 31, 2001, balance sheet. Of this amount, $201,664 was reported as a current asset, and $1,100,922 was reported as a subtraction from stockholders' equity. By way of explanation, Nebo reported the following in its 2001 annual report: "From January 2002 to March 25, 2002 [the date on the audit opinion], the company collected a total of $201,664 of stock subscriptions receivable."

Subscription Defaults If a subscriber defaults on a subscription by failing to make a payment when it is due, a corporation may (1) return to the subscriber the amount paid, (2) return to the subscriber the amount paid less any reduction in price or expense incurred on the resale of the stock, (3) declare the amount paid by the subscriber as forfeited, or (4) issue to the subscriber shares equal to the number paid for in full. The practice followed will depend on the policy adopted by the corporation within the legal limitations set by the state in which it is incorporated.

Capital Stock Issued for Consideration Other Than Cash

When capital stock is issued for consideration in the form of property other than cash or for services received, the fair market value of the stock or the fair market value of the property or services, whichever is more objectively determinable, is used to record

[10] FASB ASC paragraph 505-10-45-2.

the transaction. If a quoted market price for the stock is available, that amount should be used as a basis for recording the exchange. Otherwise, it may be possible to determine the fair market value of the property or services received, for example, through appraisal by a competent outside party.

To illustrate, assume that AC Company issues 200 shares of $0.50 par value common stock in return for land. The company's stock is currently selling for $50 per share. The entry on AC Company's books would be as follows:

Land	10,000	
Common Stock		100
Paid-In Capital in Excess of Par		9,900

If, on the other hand, the land has a readily determinable market price of $12,000 but AC Company's common stock has no established fair market value, the transaction would be recorded as follows:

Land	12,000	
Common Stock		100
Paid-In Capital in Excess of Par		11,900

If no readily determinable value is available for either the stock or the property or services received, the accepted procedure is to have the value of the property or services independently appraised. If the transaction is material, the source of the appraisal should be disclosed in the financial statements.

When stock is issued in exchange for services, the journal entry is similar to that just illustrated. Assume that AC Company decides not to pay a key employee in cash but instead grants the employee 100 shares of $0.50 par common stock, with a market value of $50 per share, as payment of salary. The transaction would be recorded as follows:

Salary Expense	5,000	
Common Stock		50
Paid-In Capital in Excess of Par		4,950

This entry is interesting because it is so noncontroversial. However, if AC Company were to pay the employee with stock options instead of with actual shares of stock, the accounting would be highly controversial. Accounting for stock options given as employee compensation is discussed later in the chapter.

Issuance of Capital Stock in a Business Combination

Corporations often merge; the combination of **Mars** and **Wrigley** in a $22 billion deal in 2008 is one recent example. The union of two corporations is called a business combination. The combination can be accomplished by one corporation paying cash to buy out the shareholders of the other, by an exchange of stock whereby all the shareholders of the two separate corporations become joint shareholders of the new combined company, or by a mixture of a cash buyout and a stock swap.

The accounting for a business combination assumes that one of the companies is dominant and is acquiring the other company. The assets of the company being acquired are revalued to their fair value. In addition, the acquiring company records goodwill if the value of the cash and stock given in the acquisition exceeds the fair value of the net assets acquired. Accounting for business combinations is discussed in detail in advanced accounting texts. Accounting for the acquisition of a business and any resulting goodwill was covered in Chapters 10 and 11.

Stock Repurchases

3 Use both the cost and par value methods to account for stock repurchases.

WHY There is really no good reason to have two different methods for accounting for stock repurchases. However, given that the two exist, it is important to understand the differences between them. For example, use of the par value method can have a significant impact on the reported amount of a company's retained earnings.

HOW The cost method is quite simple with the amount paid to repurchase the shares recorded in a contra-equity account. The par value method treats a stock repurchase similar to the retirement of stock, and Paid-In Capital in Excess of Par and (sometimes) Retained Earnings are debited.

For a variety of reasons, a company may find it desirable to reacquire shares of its own stock. **ExxonMobil**, for example, has been the most aggressive company in buying back its own stock. As of December 31, 2009, Exxon Mobil had spent a cumulative net amount of $166.4 billion in buying back its own shares. Coca-Cola, another company well known for stock repurchasing, had spent more than $25.4 billion as of December 31, 2009, in buying back its own stock. In general, companies acquire their own stock to:

1. Provide shares for incentive compensation and employee savings plans.
2. Obtain shares needed to satisfy requests by holders of convertible securities (bonds and preferred stock).
3. Reduce the amount of equity relative to the amount of debt.
4. Invest excess cash temporarily.
5. Remove some shares from the open market in order to protect against a hostile takeover.
6. Improve per-share earnings by reducing the number of shares outstanding and returning inefficiently used assets to shareholders.
7. Display confidence that the stock is currently undervalued by the market.

Whatever the reason, a company's stock may be reacquired by exercise of call or redemption provisions or by repurchase of the stock in the open market. State laws normally prohibit the repurchase of stock if the repurchase would impair the ability of creditors to be repaid. In many states, the total amount spent to repurchase shares cannot exceed the sum of additional paid-in capital and retained earnings. In addition, share repurchases at exorbitant prices are banned because they dilute the stock value for the remaining shareholders.

In accounting for the reacquisition of stock, remember that reacquisitions do not give rise to income or loss. A company issues stock to raise capital. In reacquiring shares of its stock, the company is merely reducing its invested capital. Gains or losses arise from the operating and investing activities of the business, not from transactions with shareholders.

A company's stock may be reacquired for immediate retirement or be reacquired and held as treasury stock for subsequent disposition, either eventual retirement or reissuance. There are two methods of accounting for treasury stock transactions: the cost method and the par value method. After a short discussion of treasury stock, these methods will be discussed in detail.

Treasury Stock

When a company's own stock is reacquired and held in the name of the company, it is referred to as treasury stock. Treasury shares may subsequently be reissued or formally retired. Before discussing how to account for treasury stock, three important features should be noted:

- Treasury stock should not be viewed as an asset; instead, it should be reported as a reduction in total owners' equity.
- There is no income or loss on the reacquisition, reissuance, or retirement of treasury stock.
- Retained earnings can be decreased by treasury stock transactions but is never increased by such transactions.

CAUTION

Reacquisition of shares may reduce retained earnings, but it can *never* increase retained earnings.

Two methods for recording treasury stock transactions are generally accepted: (1) the cost method, which records the treasury stock in a special equity account until the shares are reissued or retired; and (2) the par (or stated) value method, which accounts for the purchase of treasury stock as if the shares were being retired.

Cost Method of Accounting for Treasury Stock Under the cost method, the purchase of treasury stock is recorded by debiting a treasury stock account for the total amount paid to repurchase the shares. The treasury stock account is reported as a deduction from total stockholders' equity on the balance sheet.

The cost method of accounting for treasury stock transactions is illustrated in the following example:

2012—*Newly organized corporation issued 10,000 shares of common stock, $1 par, at $15:*

Cash	150,000	
Common Stock		10,000
Paid-In Capital in Excess of Par		140,000

Net income for the first year of business was $30,000.

2013—*Reacquired 1,000 shares of common stock at $40 per share:*

Treasury Stock	40,000	
Cash		40,000

2013—Sold 200 shares of treasury stock at $50 per share:

Cash	10,000	
Treasury Stock (200 × $40)		8,000
Paid-In Capital from Treasury Stock		2,000

Because the treasury stock is reissued at a price greater than the $40 repurchase price, the excess is recorded in an additional paid-in capital account. (*Note:* No gain is recorded.)

2013—*Sold 500 shares of treasury stock at $34 per share:*

Cash	17,000	
Paid-In Capital from Treasury Stock	2,000	
Retained Earnings	1,000	
Treasury Stock (500 × $40)		20,000

Because the treasury stock is reissued at a price less than the $40 repurchase price, Retained Earnings is debited for the difference, or as in this example, any paid-in capital from prior treasury stock reissuances may first be debited.

2013—*Retired remaining 300 shares of treasury stock (3% of original issue of 10,000 shares):*

Common Stock	300	
Paid-In Capital in Excess of Par	4,200	
Retained Earnings [300 × ($40 − $15)]	7,500	
Treasury Stock (300 × $40)		12,000

FYI

In the 1980s, a large number of "greenmail" treasury stock transactions occurred. A firm repurchased its shares from a troublesome shareholder at a price significantly greater than the market value. In many cases, the "greenmail" in excess of the market value of the repurchased shares had to be expensed.

Alternatively, the entire $11,700 difference between Common Stock and the cost to acquire the treasury stock may be debited to Retained Earnings.

It should be noted that in the example, all treasury stock was acquired at $40 per share. If several acquisitions of treasury stock are made at different prices, the resale or retirement of treasury shares must be recorded using the actual cost to reacquire the shares being sold or retired (specific identification) or using the basis of a cost flow assumption, such as FIFO or average cost.

Par (or Stated) Value Method of Accounting for Treasury Stock If the par (or stated) value method is used, the purchase of treasury stock is regarded as a withdrawal of a group of stockholders. Similarly, the sale or reissuance of treasury stock, under this approach, is viewed as the admission of a new group of stockholders, requiring entries giving effect to the investment by this group. Thus, the purchase and sale are viewed as two separate and unrelated transactions.

Using the data given for the cost method illustration, the following entries would be made for 2013 under the par value method:

2013—*Reacquired 1,000 shares of common stock at $40 per share:*

Treasury Stock	1,000	
Paid-In Capital in Excess of Par	14,000	
Retained Earnings [1,000 × ($40 − $15)]	25,000	
Cash		40,000

Sold 200 shares of treasury stock at $50 per share:

Cash	10,000	
Treasury Stock		200
Paid-In Capital in Excess of Par		9,800

Sold 500 shares of treasury stock at $34 per share:

Cash	17,000	
Treasury Stock		500
Paid-In Capital in Excess of Par		16,500

Retired remaining 300 shares of treasury stock:

Common Stock	300	
Treasury Stock		300

Evaluating the Cost and Par Value Methods Less than 10% of large U.S. companies use the par value method. Using the numbers from the example just given, the following comparison shows the impact on stockholders' equity of the two approaches after the original stock repurchases have occurred but prior to the reissuance or retirement of the treasury shares.

Comparison of Stockholders' Equity

	Cost Method	Par Value Method
Contributed capital:		
Common stock	$ 10,000	$ 10,000
Paid-in capital in excess of par	140,000	126,000
Total contributed capital	$150,000	$136,000
Retained earnings	30,000	5,000
Total contributed capital and retained earnings	$180,000	$141,000
Less: Treasury stock	40,000	1,000
Total stockholders' equity	$140,000	$140,000

Note that total stockholders' equity is the same regardless of which method is used. As the example shows, however, there may be differences in the relative amounts of contributed capital and retained earnings reported. Note again that retained earnings may be decreased by treasury stock transactions but can never be increased by buying or selling treasury stock. Exhibit 13-5 lists the 10 largest companies in the United States (in terms of their April 2010 market value) and their stock repurchases, according to reported information. It is interesting to note that three of these 10 companies—Microsoft, **Wal-Mart**, and **Bank of America**—use the par value method of accounting for their treasury stock purchases. Note also that Berkshire Hathaway, **Apple**, and Google do not repurchase shares of their own stock. Because of poor operating performance associated with the 2008 worldwide financial meltdown, Bank of America did not buy back shares in 2008 or 2009, but did engage in stock buybacks in the years before 2008.

STOP&THINK

After looking at this comparison, why do you think so few companies use the par value method?

a) Use of the cost method usually increases reported earnings.
b) Use of the par value method usually involves reducing retained earnings.
c) Use of the par value method requires the company to pay more for the repurchased shares.
d) Use of the par value method increases long-term debt.

EX 13-5 TREASURY STOCK PURCHASES FOR THE 10 LARGEST U.S. COMPANIES

Rank	Market Value (in $billions)	Repurchases During the Year	Balance Sheet Amount	Accounting Method
1. ExxonMobil	$308.77	$19,703	$166,410	Cost
2. Microsoft	254.52	2,611	0	Par Value
3. Wal-Mart	205.37	7,397	0	Par Value
4. Berkshire Hathaway	190.86	0	0	?
5. Apple	189.51	0	0	?
6. Procter & Gamble	184.47	6,370	55,961	Cost
7. Johnson & Johnson	174.90	2,130	19,780	Cost
8. General Electric	169.65	214	32,238	Cost
9. Google	169.38	0	0	?
10. Bank of America	167.63	0	0	Par Value

Retirement of Repurchased Shares If shares of stock are reacquired at par (or stated) value and then retired, the capital stock account is debited and the cash account is credited. However, if the purchase price of the stock exceeds the par value, the excess amount may be (1) charged to any paid-in capital balances applicable to that class of stock, (2) allocated between Paid-In Capital and Retained Earnings, or (3) charged entirely to Retained Earnings.[11] The alternative used depends on the existence of previously established paid-in capital amounts and on management's preference.

Stock Rights, Warrants, and Options

4 Account for the issuance of stock rights and stock warrants.

WHY **Stock rights, warrants, and options are separate equity instruments with unique characteristics. Accordingly, for a financial statement user to understand the potential impact of these items on the issuing company's financial structure, these items must be recognized or disclosed separately.**

HOW **When stock warrants are issued in connection with debt or preferred stock, a portion of the total issuance proceeds should be allocated to the stock warrants based on the relative fair value of the warrants.**

A corporation may issue rights, warrants, or options that permit the purchase of the company's stock for a specified period (the exercise period) at a certain price (the exercise price). Although the terms *rights, warrants*, and *options* are sometimes used interchangeably, a distinction may be made as follows:

- Stock rights—issued to existing shareholders to permit them to maintain their proportionate ownership interests when new shares are to be issued. (Some state laws require this preemptive right.)
- Stock warrants—sold by the corporation for cash, generally in conjunction with the issuance of another security.
- Stock options—granted to officers or employees, usually as part of a compensation plan.

A company may offer rights, warrants, or options to raise additional capital, to encourage the sale of a particular class of securities, or as compensation for services received. The exercise period is generally longer for warrants and options than for rights. Warrants and rights may be traded independently among investors, whereas options generally are restricted to a particular person or specified group to whom the options are granted. The accounting considerations relating to stock rights, warrants, and options are described in the following sections.

Stock Rights

When announcing rights to purchase additional shares of stock, the directors of a corporation specify a date on which the rights will be issued. All stockholders of record on the issue date are entitled to receive the rights. Thus, between the announcement date and the issue date, the stock is said to sell *rights-on*. After the rights are issued, the stock sells *ex-rights*, and the rights may be sold separately by those receiving them from the corporation. An expiration date is also designated when the rights are announced, and rights not exercised by this date are worthless.

[11] FASB ASC paragraph 505-30-30-8.

When rights are issued to stockholders, only a memorandum entry is made on the issuing company's books stating the number of shares that may be claimed under the outstanding rights. This information is required so the corporation may retain sufficient unissued or reacquired stock to meet the exercise of the rights. Upon surrender of the rights and the receipt of payments as specified by the rights, the stock is issued. At this time, a memorandum entry is made to record the decrease in the number of rights outstanding accompanied by an entry to record the stock sale. The entry for the sale is recorded the same as any other issue of stock, with appropriate recognition of the cash received, the par, or stated, value of the stock issued, and any additional paid-in capital. Information concerning outstanding rights should be reported with the corporation's balance sheet so that the effects of the future exercise of remaining rights may be determined.

FYI

A company would include warrants to encourage investors to purchase the company's bonds. Of course, another way to encourage investors to purchase the bonds is to increase the interest rate paid on the bonds. Therefore, warrants can be viewed as decreasing the interest rate that must be paid.

Stock Warrants

Warrants may be sold in conjunction with other securities as a "sweetener" to make the purchase of the securities more attractive. For example, warrants to purchase shares of a corporation's common stock may be issued with bonds to encourage investors to purchase the bonds. A warrant has value when the exercise price is less than the market value, either present or potential, of the security that can be purchased with the warrants. Warrants issued with other securities may be detachable or nondetachable. Detachable warrants are similar to stock rights because they can be traded separately from the security with which they were originally issued. Nondetachable warrants cannot be separated from the security with which they were issued.

Part of the issuance price of debt securities is assigned to any detachable stock warrants and classified as part of owners' equity.[12] The value assigned to the warrants is determined by the relative fair value method which is illustrated in the following equation:

$$\text{Value assigned to warrants} = \text{Total issue price} \times \frac{\text{Market value of warrants}}{\text{Market value of security without warrants} + \text{Market value of warrants}}$$

Although the FASB's standards are directed only to warrants attached to debt, it appears logical to extend the conclusions of that opinion to warrants attached to preferred stock. Thus, if a market value exists for the warrants at the issuance date, a separate equity account is credited with that portion of the issuance price assigned to the warrants. If the warrants are exercised, the value assigned to the common stock is the value allocated to the warrants plus the cash proceeds from the issuance of the common stock. If the warrants are allowed to expire, the value assigned to the warrants may be transferred to a permanent paid-in capital account.

FYI

From an investor standpoint, both the preferred shares and the detachable warrants are recorded at their fair values.

[12] FASB ASC paragraph 470-20-25-2.

Accounting for detachable warrants attached to a preferred stock issue is illustrated as follows. Assume that Stewart Co. sells 1,000 shares of $50 par preferred stock for $58 per share. As an incentive to purchase the stock, Stewart Co. gives the purchaser detachable warrants enabling holders to subscribe to 1,000 shares of $2 par common stock for $25 per share. The warrants expire after one year. Immediately following the issuance of the preferred stock, the warrants are selling at $3, and the fair market value of the preferred stock without the warrant attached is $57. The proceeds of $58,000 should be allocated by Stewart Co. as follows:

$$\text{Value assigned to the warrants} = \$58{,}000 \times \frac{\$3}{\$57 + \$3} = \$2{,}900$$

The entry on Stewart's books to record the sale of the preferred stock with detachable warrants is as follows:

Cash	58,000	
Preferred Stock, $50 par		50,000
Paid-In Capital in Excess of Par—Preferred Stock		5,100
Common Stock Warrants		2,900

If the warrants are exercised, the entry to record the issuance of common stock would be as follows:

Common Stock Warrants	2,900	
Cash	25,000	
Common Stock, $2 par		2,000
Paid-In Capital in Excess of Par—Commo n Stock		25,900

This entry would be the same regardless of the market price of the common stock at the issuance date.

If the warrants in the example were allowed to expire, the following entry would be made:

Common Stock Warrants	2,900	
Paid-In Capital from Expired Warrants		2,900

ifrs

Under current U.S. GAAP, if warrants are nondetachable, the securities are considered inseparable, and no allocation is made to recognize the value of the warrant. The entire proceeds are assigned to the security to which the warrant is attached. Thus, for nondetachable warrants, the accounting treatment is similar to that for convertible securities, such as convertible bonds. Clearly, from a conceptual standpoint this inconsistency is not justified because the economic value of a warrant exists, even if the warrant cannot be traded separately or "detached." This is essentially the same argument made for recognizing the conversion feature of a convertible security. Notwithstanding this argument, a separate instrument does not exist for a nondetachable warrant, and current practice in the United States does not require a separate value to be assigned to these warrants. In its October 2000 *Exposure Draft*, "Accounting for Financial Instruments with Characteristics of Liabilities, Equity, or Both," the FASB recommended the relative fair value method for allocating the proceeds for all securities that combine different elements of debt, preferred stock, and common stock. But so far no such comprehensive standard has been adopted in the United States. In contrast, *IAS 32* requires all compound financial instruments to be recorded as separate debt and equity components.

Accounting for Share-Based Compensation

5 Compute the compensation expense associated with the granting of employee stock options.

WHY **Share-based compensation comprises an important component of the compensation packages of many employees in the United States, especially for upper-level management of large corporations and for employees at all levels in technology-based startup companies. Fair and accurate reporting of the total compensation expense for these companies requires that share-based compensation be reported as an expense in the income statement.**

HOW **The fair value of share-based compensation is estimated as of the date the compensation is granted. This fair value is then expensed over the service period required of the employee to earn the compensation.**

During 1994, debate over the proper accounting for employee stock options escalated into a full-scale war, with the FASB pitted against the business community and, ultimately, the Congress of the United States. The subject of all the controversy was this: Should the fair value of stock options granted to employees be estimated and recognized as part of compensation expense? In his letter to the shareholders in Berkshire Hathaway's 1993 annual report, Warren Buffett approvingly summarized the position of the FASB:

> If options aren't a form of compensation, what are they? If compensation isn't an expense, what is it? And if expenses shouldn't go into the calculation of earnings, where in the world should they go?[13]

In spite of this logic, the FASB surrendered to the pressure and did not require the recognition of a stock option expense because "the debate threatened the future of accounting standard-setting in the private sector,"[14] meaning that Congress had suggested the possibility of abolishing the FASB if it didn't toe the line on stock option accounting. The FASB's compromise was to encourage companies to recognize a stock option expense or, if they didn't, then to disclose an estimate of this expense in the notes to the financial statements. Almost all companies chose the disclosure route.

> **FYI**
>
> Employee stock options are *not* the same as the call and put stock options traded on major exchanges. Traded option contracts can exist between any two parties. Call options entitle the owner to buy shares of a certain stock at a set "exercise" price. Put options entitle the owner to sell shares at a set price.

In 2002, stock option accounting again became a hot issue in the wake of the financial accounting scandals that began to bubble to the surface in 2001. Many financial statement users pointed to stock option accounting as another example of poor accounting rules that allowed companies to hide their activities from investors and creditors. In this case, the activity being hidden was the granting of stock options to top corporate executives.

So, in 2003 the FASB again added stock option accounting to its agenda but quickly found that the strong feelings against expensing the cost of stock options had not died down. When the FASB issued an Exposure Draft in March 2004 that basically repeated its position

[13] Berkshire Hathaway Annual Report—1993.

[14] Pre-Codification *Statement of Financial Accounting Standards No. 123*, "Accounting for Stock-Based Compensation" (Norwalk, CT: Financial Accounting Standards Board, 1995), par. 60.

from back in 1994, yet another firestorm of protest arose. The FASB received 14,239 comment letters in response to this Exposure Draft; by comparison, issuance of a typical Exposure Draft rarely elicits more than 100 comment letters, and usually the FASB receives just 20 or 30 comment letters. Business lobbying of Congress against the FASB's Exposure Draft prompted passage of a House Resolution mandating alternative accounting that would have greatly reduced companies' reported stock option compensation expense; mercifully, this bill died in the Senate.

In opposing the FASB's proposal to require expensing the fair value of stock options granted to employees, businesses concocted a marvelous array of pseudo-theoretical arguments that we, the authors, would rather not repeat here. Theoretical arguments aside, the vast majority of corporations in the United States opposed the FASB's attempt to require recognition of a stock option compensation expense for a simple reason: Recognition of a stock option compensation expense would reduce reported earnings. The area of stock option accounting is a perfect illustration of why we need an independent financial accounting standard setter such as the FASB—financial statement users need informative and unbiased information about companies, which those companies would sometimes prefer not to include in the financial statements. In December 2004, the FASB adopted pre-Codification *Statement No. 123* (revised 2004), "Share-Based Payment," which requires the expensing of the fair value of stock options granted as compensation. This standard is now found in FASB ASC Topic 718 (Compensation—Stock Compensation).

The recognition and disclosure requirements for stock option compensation plans are illustrated in the following example. A simple plan is illustrated first, followed by some exposure to the accounting for more complex plans.

Basic Stock Option Compensation Plan

On January 1, 2011, the board of directors of Neff Company authorized the grant of 10,000 stock options to supplement the salaries of certain employees. Each stock option permits the purchase of one share of Neff common stock at a price of $50 per share; the market price of the stock on January 1, 2011, is also $50 per share. (This is typical of many actual stock option plans for real companies. For example, in its 2009 annual report, **Toys "R" Us** states that options granted under its Management Equity Plan have an exercise price equal to the stock's fair market value on the grant date.) The options vest, or become exercisable, beginning on January 1, 2014, and only if the employees stay with the company for the entire 3-year vesting period. The options expire on December 31, 2014.

Neff is required to estimate the fair value of the options as of the grant date. Clearly, each option has value because the stock price could increase above $50 during the 3-year period and the options give the employees the right to buy the stock at the fixed exercise price of $50. Computation of the fair value of the options involves consideration of factors such as the expected volatility of the stock price and the length of time the options are valid. For example, the higher the volatility of the stock price, the higher the value of the option, because there is a better chance that the stock price will increase significantly. Of course, increased volatility also means that there is an increased probability that the stock price will decrease. However, this doesn't negatively impact the option value, because the employees can choose not to exercise the option if the share price drops below the option price of $50. Also, an option with a longer term has increased value because there is a better chance of a significant stock price increase over a long time period than there is over a short one. Exact computation of option values involves formulas derived using stochastic calculus (the famous Black-Scholes model) or discrete probability lattice models (such as the binomial model). Unfortunately, we don't have time to cover stochastic calculus in this text. However, commercially available software packages make option valuation no more difficult than using a spreadsheet.

> **FYI**
>
> In general, an employee has taxable income in the amount of the difference between the option exercise price and the stock price on the date the options are exercised. The worst-case scenario occurs when an employee exercises options, holds the stock, and the stock subsequently declines drastically in value. If the stock price has declined enough, selling the stock might not generate enough cash even to pay the tax.

For the Neff Company example, assume that an option-pricing formula is used to estimate a grant date value of $10 for each of the employee stock options. Thus, the total fair value of the options granted is $100,000 (10,000 × $10) as of the grant date. Once the options granted have been valued, the remaining accounting problem is determining when the compensation expense should be recognized. The compensation should be charged to the periods in which the employees perform the services for which the options are granted. In the Neff example, no specific service period is mentioned, so compensation cost is allocated over the 3-year period between the January 1, 2011, grant date and the January 1, 2014, vesting date. The journal entry to record the recognition of compensation expense for 2011 is as follows:

2011				
Dec.	31	Compensation Expense ($100,000/3 years)	33,333	
		Paid-In Capital from Stock Options		33,333

Note that this paid-in capital is *not* from the investment of cash in the business but instead represents an investment of work by the employees covered under the stock option plan.

Similar entries would be made in 2012 and 2013. At the end of the 3-year service period, the balance in the additional paid-in capital from stock options account is $100,000, which is equal to the grant date value of the options.

The journal entry to record the exercise of all 10,000 of the options on December 31, 2014, to purchase shares of Neff's no-par common stock would be as follows:

2014				
Dec.	31	Cash (10,000 × $50)	500,000	
		Paid-In Capital from Stock Options	100,000	
		Common Stock (no par)		600,000

If the options had been allowed to expire unexercised, the following journal entry could be made on December 31, 2014, the end of the exercise period, to reclassify the paid-in capital from the stock options:

2014				
Dec.	31	Paid-In Capital from Stock Options	100,000	
		Paid-In Capital from Expired Options		100,000

Required Disclosure The following note disclosure (illustrated for 2011) is required each year:

Employee Stock Options

	Shares	Exercise Price
Outstanding at January 1, 2011	0	—
Granted during 2011	10,000	$50
Exercised during 2011	0	—
Forfeited during 2011	0	—
Outstanding at December 31, 2011	10,000	$50
Options exercisable at December 31, 2011	0	
Weighted-average fair value of options granted during 2011	$10	
Compensation expense associated with the stock option plan in 2011	$33,333	

The note should also include a general description of the employee stock option plan as well as a description of the techniques used in estimating the fair value of the options.

IASB Standard The release of pre-Codification FASB *Statement No. 123* (revised 2004) is an excellent example of how the convergence between FASB and IASB standards is improving the quality of both sets of standards. In February 2004, the IASB adopted *International Financial Reporting Standard (IFRS) 2*, "Share-Based Payment." This standard requires essentially the same expensing of stock options as initially proposed by the FASB back in 1994. Because the granting of employee stock options is much less common outside the United States, the IASB did not experience nearly as much opposition to its stock option expensing proposal as did the FASB. And once the IASB had adopted its standard, the FASB could wave the flag of "international harmonization" to aid in promulgating the U.S. stock option expensing standard over the protests of the U.S. business community and Congress.

Accounting for Performance-Based Plans

The simple example above is based on a simple stock option plan. In such a plan, the plan terms (i.e., the option exercise price and the number of options granted) are fixed as of the date the options are granted. In a performance-based stock option plan, the plan terms are dependent on how well the individual or company performs after the date the options are granted. In the simple stock option plan of Neff Company that is illustrated above, Neff's employees needed only to stay with the company for the entire 3-year vesting period in order to receive the full value of the options. With a performance-based plan, the terms of the option depend on how well an employee performs or how well the company performs during the vesting period. To illustrate, assume that the terms of the Neff Company stock-based compensation plan are as follows:

- On January 1, 2011, the board of directors of Neff Company authorized the grant of stock options to supplement the salaries of certain employees.
- Each stock option permits the purchase of one share of Neff common stock at a price of $50 per share; the market price of the stock on January 1, 2011, is also $50 per share.
- The options vest, or become exercisable, beginning on January 1, 2014, and only if the employees stay with the company for the entire 3-year vesting period. The options expire on December 31, 2014.

- The number of options granted, instead of being fixed at 10,000 as in the earlier example, is contingent on Neff's level of sales for 2013. If Neff's sales for 2013 are less than $50 million, only the 10,000 options will vest. If Neff's 2013 sales are between $50 million and $80 million, an additional 2,000 options will vest, making a total of 12,000. Finally, if Neff's 2013 sales exceed $80 million, a total of 15,000 options will vest.

> **CAUTION**
>
> Stock price and option fair value changes after the grant date do not impact compensation expense.

For the Neff performance-based stock option plan, the computation of compensation expense is done by combining the value of the options on the grant date with the number of options that are probable to vest. As in the earlier example, application of an option valuation method results in a computed value for each option of $10 as of the grant date. The number of options probable to vest depends, of course, on the probable level of 2013 sales. As of December 31, 2011, when compensation expense for the first year must be recorded, Neff forecasts that 2013 sales will be around $60 million, indicating that 12,000 options will vest. Recognition of compensation expense for 2011 involves recognizing one-third of the $120,000 (12,000 × $10) total estimated expense for the 3-year service period. Note that the change in Neff's stock price during the year (from $50 to $56) does not affect the calculation. The options are valued once, at the grant date, and that value is used for the life of the options. The journal entry to recognize compensation expense is as follows:

2011			
Dec. 31	Compensation Expense ($120,000/3 years)	40,000	
	Paid-In Capital from Stock Options		40,000

Events in 2012 lead Neff to lower its forecast of 2013 sales. As of December 31, 2012, Neff expects 2013 sales to be only $40 million. Accordingly, it is probable that only 10,000 options will vest on January 1, 2014. The new estimate for total compensation expense for the 3-year service period is $100,000 (10,000 × $10). Because two-thirds of the service period has elapsed, aggregate compensation expense recognized should be $66,667 ($100,000 × 2/3). Because compensation expense of $40,000 was recognized in 2011, the necessary journal entry in 2012 is as follows:

2012			
Dec. 31	Compensation Expense ($66,667 − $40,000)	26,667	
	Paid-In Capital from Stock Options		26,667

Upon close examination, it can be seen that this computation of compensation expense differs from that typically encountered in situations with changing accounting estimates. Usually, the effects of changes in estimates are spread over current and future periods. In this case, such a procedure would result in 2012 compensation expense of $30,000, an allocation of the remaining compensation expense of $60,000 ($100,000 – $40,000) evenly over the remaining two years of the service period, 2012 and 2013. However, a so-called "catch-up adjustment" is required when recognizing compensation expense related to performance-based option plans. The catch-up adjustment makes the cumulative expense recognized equal to the amount it would have been had the updated estimate for 2013 sales been used all along.

Actual sales for 2013 are $85 million (Neff had a pretty good year). As a result, according to the terms of the performance-based plan, 15,000 options will vest as of

January 1, 2014. Because the entire service period has elapsed, aggregate compensation expense recognized should be \$150,000 (15,000 × \$10). Because compensation expense of \$66,667 (\$40,000 + \$26,667) has already been recognized in 2011 and 2012, the necessary journal entry in 2013 is as follows:

2013			
Dec. 31	Compensation Expense (\$150,000 − \$66,667)	83,333	
	Paid-In Capital from Stock Options		83,333

The journal entry to record the exercise of all 15,000 of the options on December 31, 2014, to purchase shares of Neff's no-par common stock would be as follows:

2014			
Dec. 31	Cash (15,000 × \$50)	750,000	
	Paid-In Capital from Stock Options	150,000	
	Common Stock (no par)		900,000

Accounting for Awards That Call for Cash Settlement

Neff Company's stock-based compensation plans discussed above stipulated that the compensation would be paid in the form of stock options. Because settlement of these stock options requires Neff to issue its own stock and does not require any transfer of assets, the stock options are considered to be equity instruments. When a stock-based compensation plan calls for a cash settlement or gives the employee the option of choosing a cash settlement instead of receiving stock options, work by employees during the service period creates a liability for the firm because the firm is obligated to transfer assets (cash) in the future.

To illustrate the accounting for share-based compensation plans that call for settlement in cash, assume that Neff Company, the company used in the earlier example on stock option plans, has decided that instead of granting its employees 10,000 stock options, it will grant an equal number of cash stock appreciation rights (SARs). A cash SAR awards an employee a cash amount equal to the market value of the issuing firm's shares above a specified threshold price. Neff Company promises that after January 1, 2014, it will pay the exerciser of each cash SAR an amount equal to the excess of the share price on the exercise date over the \$50 threshold price. The cash SARs vest beginning on January 1, 2014, only for the employees who stay with the company for the entire 3-year vesting period. The cash SARs expire on December 31, 2014. From an employee's standpoint, this cash SAR plan is economically equivalent to the basic stock option plan illustrated earlier in the chapter.

STOP&THINK

Assume that Neff's managers are greedy, unscrupulous scoundrels. Which ONE of the following might Neff's performance-based stock option plan cause Neff's management (the ones who are receiving the stock options) to do?

a) Delay the recognition of 2012 sales into 2013, and accelerate the recognition of 2014 sales into 2013.
b) Accelerate the recognition of 2013 sales into 2012, and delay the recognition of 2013 sales into 2014.
c) Accelerate the recognition of 2013 sales into 2012, and delay the recognition of 2011 sales into 2012.
d) Accelerate the recognition of 2012 sales into 2011, and delay the recognition of 2010 sales into 2011.

From the standpoint of Neff's accounting treatment, the cash SAR plan is different from the stock option plan discussed previously because the cash SAR plan creates a liability to transfer cash. All journal entries to record compensation expense for 2011, 2012, and 2013 and for the redemption of the cash SARs on December 31, 2014, are given on the next page.

Assume the following information:

Fair value of one SAR:	
January 1, 2011	$10
December 31, 2011	6
December 31, 2012	7
December 31, 2013	9

The forecast of the cash settlement amount is updated at the end of each period using current data to estimate the fair value of each SAR. This fair value is impacted by the existing stock price, the amount of time remaining until the award settlement date, and the volatility of the underlying stock price. As of December 31, 2011, because the estimated fair value of each SAR is \$6, the best estimate of the amount of cash that will be transferred when the cash SARs are exercised is \$60,000 (10,000 × \$6). The journal entry to recognize 2011 compensation expense is as follows:

2011				
Dec.	31	Compensation Expense (\$60,000/3 years)	20,000	
		Share-Based Compensation Liability		20,000

As of December 31, 2012, the estimated fair value of each SAR is \$7. The new estimate for total compensation expense for the 3-year service period is \$70,000 (10,000 × \$7). Because two-thirds of the service period has elapsed, aggregate compensation expense recognized should be \$46,667 (\$70,000 × 2/3). Because compensation expense of \$20,000 was recognized in 2011, the necessary journal entry in 2012 is as follows:

2012				
Dec.	31	Compensation Expense (\$46,667 − \$20,000)	26,667	
		Share-Based Compensation Liability		26,667

Except for the account titles, this catch-up adjustment is exactly like those illustrated previously.

The estimated fair value of each SAR is \$9 on December 31, 2013. Aggregate compensation expense for the 3-year service period is \$90,000 (10,000 × \$9). Because compensation expense of \$46,667 (\$20,000 + \$26,667) has already been recognized in 2011 and 2012, the necessary journal entry in 2013 is as follows:

2013				
Dec.	31	Compensation Expense (\$90,000 − \$46,667)	43,333	
		Share-Based Compensation Liability		43,333

Between the time the cash SARs vest and the time they are exercised, the company's stock price can still move, affecting the ultimate amount of cash paid out for the cash SARs. The impact of these post-vesting price movements on the cash SAR payable account are recognized as compensation expense in the year the price movements occur. The share price on December 31, 2014 is \$61, meaning that Neff will pay \$11 (\$61 − \$50) for each SAR. The required entry in 2014, to reflect this information is:

2014				
Dec.	31	Compensation Expense {[10,000 × (\$61 − \$50)] − \$90,000}	20,000	
		Share-Based Compensation Liability		20,000

The entry to record the cash payments made to holders of the 10,000 cash SARs that vested on January 1, 2014, and were exercised on December 31, 2014, is shown on p. 13-28.

2014			
Dec. 31	Share-Based Compensation Liability	110,000	
	Cash [10,000 × ($61 − $50)]		110,000

If the exercise period extended beyond 2014 and if cash SARs remained outstanding, an entry would be made at the end of each year to revise the estimated amount of the cash SAR liability. These revisions are recognized as part of compensation expense for the period.

Broad-Based Plans

Some employers grant employee stock options and employee stock purchase rights to substantially all employees. Under FASB ASC Topic 718 (Compensation—Stock Compensation), compensation expense is recognized if employees are allowed to purchase shares for more than a 5% discount from the market price.[15] The rationale is that allowing employees to purchase stock for an excessive discount is just an alternative way to grant compensation.

Reporting Some Equity-Related Items as Liabilities

6 Determine which equity-related items should be reported in the balance sheet as liabilities.

WHY **In the increasingly complex world of corporate finance, companies are using their own equity shares in many different ways. Accordingly, accountants must carefully examine the economic nature of financing arrangements, rather than just the labels placed on the arrangements, in order to decide whether an item should be reported as a liability or as equity in the balance sheet.**

HOW **Obligations that require a company to deliver financial instruments or cash of a fixed monetary value in the future should be reported in the balance sheet as liabilities. In addition, a company obligation to repurchase its own shares should be reported as a liability.**

In the field of finance, a *debt claim* is one that entitles the debt holders to a fixed payment when company assets are sufficient to meet that payment; if company assets are below that amount, the debt holders get all of the assets. An *equity claim* is one that entitles the equity holders to all company assets in excess of the debt holders' portion. The definitions of liabilities and equities given by the FASB in its *Statement of Accounting Concepts No. 6* embody similar notions: Equity is defined as the residual amount of assets left after deducting the liability claims.

Although examples of pure equity (common stock) and pure debt (a bank loan) are easy to distinguish, many securities are in a middle ground and have characteristics of both debt and equity. For example, preferred stock is like debt in that the payments (both dividend and liquidation amounts) are capped, but it is also like equity because the payments aren't guaranteed and have lower priority than debt claims. As another example, convertible debt may be exchanged for equity if the issuing firm performs well; as the performance of the issuing firm improves, the convertible debt gradually changes in nature from debt to equity.

These examples illustrate that the line between a liability and an equity can be very unclear. As mentioned several times earlier in the chapter, for several years the FASB has

[15] FASB ASC paragraph 718-50-25-1a(2).

been performing a fundamental review of the accounting distinction between debt and equity. As a result of this review, the FASB has decided that certain equity-related items should actually be reported in the balance sheet as liabilities.[16] These items are as follows.

- Mandatorily redeemable preferred shares
- Financial instruments (such as written put options) that obligate a company to repurchase its own shares
- Financial instruments that obligate a company to issue a certain dollar value of its own shares

These items share the characteristic that, although related to equity shares, they each obligate the company to deliver items of a set value (either cash or equity shares) some time in the future. Each of these items is illustrated below.

In addition, this section includes a brief description of noncontrolling interest which has historically been called *minority interest*. Noncontrolling interest is an item that has often in the past been classified as a liability but that should now be classified as equity.

Mandatorily Redeemable Preferred Shares

As mentioned above, preferred stock embodies some of the characteristics of a debt instrument because preferred shareholders are typically not entitled to additional payments based on the success of the issuing company. In some cases, the ownership contract associated with preferred shares stipulates that those shares must be redeemed by the issuing company at a specified future date. For example, consider preferred shares that are issued now in exchange for $1,000 cash but the issuing company agrees that in 10 years it will redeem those shares for, say, $1,100 cash. In this case, you can call these financial instruments "shares" if you like, but the more you consider them, the more they resemble a liability. In fact, mandatorily redeemable preferred shares are a textbook example of a financial instrument that fits the Conceptual Framework definition of a liability: ". . . present obligation to transfer assets . . . in the future as a result of past transactions or events."

Historically, the SEC required that firms not include mandatorily redeemable preferred stock under the Stockholders' Equity heading. Instead, mandatorily redeemable preferred stock was listed above the Equity section in a gray area between the liabilities and equities; this reporting of mandatorily redeemable preferred stock as neither debt nor equity was referred to as "mezzanine" treatment. The FASB now requires mandatorily redeemable preferred shares to be reported as liabilities in the balance sheet. For example, in 2004, **Critical Path**, a seller of messaging technology, reported the following in its balance sheet (in thousands of U.S. dollars):

Total liabilities	$ 59,011
Mandatorily redeemable preferred stock	122,377
Total shareholders' deficit	(112,189)
Total liabilities, mandatorily redeemable preferred stock and shareholders' deficit	$ 69,199

Under FASB ASC Topic 480, Critical Path, and all other U.S. companies, are now required to include mandatorily redeemable preferred stock in the computation of total liabilities.

An example of the new presentation required under FASB ASC Topic 480 (pre-Codification *Statement No. 150)* can be found in the financial statements of **American**

[16] FASB ASC Topic 480 (Distinguishing Liabilities from Equity).

Physicians Service Group, an insurance and financial services company. The Liabilities section of the company's 2009 balance sheet is as follows (in thousands of U.S. dollars):

Reserve for loss and loss adjustment expense	$ 88,668
Unearned premiums	36,341
Reinsurance premiums payable	30
Funds held under reinsurance treaties	2,379
Accrued expenses and other liabilities	6,465
Mandatorily redeemable preferred stock	6,679
Total liabilities	$140,562

To understand the journal entries associated with mandatorily redeemable preferred shares, consider the following simple example. On January 1, 2011, Tarazi Company issued mandatorily redeemable preferred shares in exchange for $100 cash. No dividends are to be paid on these shares, and they must be redeemed in exactly one year, on January 1, 2012, for $110. You can see that the interest rate implicit in this agreement is 10%; Tarazi is agreeing to pay $10 in interest in order to use the $100 issuance proceeds for one year. The journal entries to record the issuance, accrual of interest, and redemption of these preferred shares are as follows:

2011			
Jan. 1	Cash	100	
	Mandatorily Redeemable Preferred Shares (liability)		100
Dec. 31	Interest Expense ($100 × 0.10)	10	
	Mandatorily Redeemable Preferred Shares (liability)		10
2012			
Jan. 1	Mandatorily Redeemable Preferred Shares (liability)	110	
	Cash		110

A related class of shares is called "temporary equity." Shares classified as "temporary equity" are shares, either common or preferred, that can be redeemed at the option of the shareholders. According to SEC *Accounting Series Release (ASR) No. 268*, "Presentation in Financial Statements of 'Redeemable Preferred Stocks,'" such securities are to be reported in the balance sheet outside of the Stockholders' Equity section, similar to the "mezzanine" treatment described above.[17]

Written Put Options

As discussed in a previous section, most successful companies have approved extensive programs of share repurchases. One such company is **Dell Computer**. In the past, as part of this effort Dell wrote put options allowing other parties to sell Dell's shares back to Dell at set prices on specific dates. For example, on February 2, 2001, Dell had obligated itself to repurchase 122 million shares of its own stock at an average repurchase price of $44 per share. Because this obligation was in the form of a put option, Dell was not certain that it would have to repurchase the shares. In fact, Dell was hoping that its share price would stay above $44 per share so that the options would never be exercised. In the extreme, if Dell's share price were to drop to $0, the company would have had to buy back 122 million worthless shares for a total of $5.4 billion ($44 per share × 122 million shares). Of course, it was unlikely that Dell's share price would drop all the way to $0, and if that

[17] This standard can be found in FASB ASC paragraph 480-10-S99-1.

were to actually happen, the company would have more pressing things to worry about than honoring its obligation under these put contracts. Accordingly, the fair value of Dell's obligation was somewhere between $0 (if the share price stayed above $44) and $5.4 billion (if the share price dropped all the way to $0). Precise estimation of the fair value of the put options involves the use of option-pricing formulas, as discussed earlier.

Why would Dell write these put options in the first place? The reason is that when Dell writes the put options, the party buying the options (usually a large financial institution) pays Dell some cash up front (equal to the fair value of the options on that date) for the right to be able to sell Dell shares to Dell at a set price in the future. Dell takes the cash and hopes that its share price stays high. The financial institution pays the cash and hopes that Dell's share price will go down.

Historically, companies have often recorded these put options as part of equity. However, the FASB now instructs companies to record the fair value of the obligation under written put options on a company's own shares as a liability.[18]

To understand the journal entries associated with written put options, consider the following simple example. On January 1, 2011, Kamili Company wrote a put option agreeing to purchase one share of its own stock for $100 on December 31, 2012, at the option of the purchaser of the put option. The market price of Kamili's shares on January 1, 2011, was $100. Given the past volatility in Kamili's share price and the 2-year period until the option expiration date, there is some chance that Kamili's shares will actually be trading for less than $100 on December 31, 2012. If this is the case, the put option holder will exercise the option to sell a share of Kamili stock to Kamili for $100 at a time when the shares are worth less than $100. Assume that the use of an option-pricing formula indicates that, as of January 1, 2011, this put option has a fair value of $20. The journal entry that Kamili would make to record the writing of the put option is as follows:

2011				
Jan.	1	Cash	20	
		Put Option (liability)		20

By December 31, 2011, Kamili's share price has declined to $88 per share. Accordingly, the odds that the share price will be less than $100 on December 31, 2012, have increased, making it more likely that the put option holder will find it attractive to exercise the option and require Kamili to repurchase one of its own shares at an amount greater than its market value. Assume that an option-pricing formula suggests that the fair value of the put option on December 31, 2011, is $30, up from $20 at the beginning of the year. The necessary adjusting entry is as follows:

2011				
Dec.	31	Loss on Put Option	10	
		Put Option (liability) ($30 − $20 already recognized)		10

On December 31, 2012, the put option expiration date, the market price of Kamili stock is $82 per share. At this price, the put option holder of course decides to exercise the option and sell one share of Kamili stock to Kamili for $100. One way to think of this transaction is that the put option holder can go out into the market, buy a share of Kamili stock for $82, and then exercise the put option to require Kamili to buy that same share of stock for $100. Accordingly, the option holder will net a gain of $18 on the option exercise

[18] FASB ASC paragraph 480-10-25-8.

date. In this case, this is less than the option holder expected to gain, as evidenced by the fact that the option holder paid $20 to purchase this option back on January 1, 2011.

The journal entry that Kamili would make to record the purchase of one share of its stock in conjunction with the exercise of the put option is as follows:

2012			
Dec. 31	Treasury Stock (the fair value of the share repurchased)	82	
	Put Option (liability)	30	
	Gain on Put Option		12
	Cash		100

The $12 gain on the put option reflects the fact that Kamili's estimated obligation under the put option decreased from $30 at the beginning of the year to just $18 ($100 – $82) at the option exercise date.

Obligation to Issue Shares of a Certain Dollar Value

Companies occasionally agree to satisfy their obligations by delivering shares of their own stock rather than by paying cash. This is especially true for startup companies that are trying to conserve their limited cash supply. Depending on how the contract is written, this promise to deliver shares of one's stock to satisfy an obligation can be recorded as equity or as a liability. The two following examples illustrate this distinction.

Example 1: On October 1, 2011, Lily Company, a software startup firm, experienced trouble with its office air conditioning system. The repair bill is $5,000. Rather than pay this amount in cash, Lily has agreed to deliver 200 shares of its no-par common stock to the repairperson on February 1, 2012. On October 1, 2011, Lily's shares have a market value of $25 per share. The journal entries that Lily would make to record the repairs and the delivery of the shares are as follows:

2011			
Oct. 1	Maintenance Expense (200 shares × $25)	5,000	
	Common Stock Issuance Obligation (equity)		5,000
2012			
Feb. 1	Common Stock Issuance Obligation (equity)	5,000	
	Common Stock		5,000

The account "Common Stock Issuance Obligation (equity)" is similar to the common stock subscribed account introduced earlier in the chapter; both are included in the Equity section of the balance sheet. An obligation that requires a company to deliver a fixed number of its shares should be classified as equity because the party to whom the shares must be delivered is at risk to the same extent as are the existing shareholders. If Lily's shares go down in value between October 1, 2011, and February 1, 2012, the repairperson suffers in that the value of the shares received will be less than $5,000. Similarly, if Lily's shares go up in value, the repairperson benefits. In short, once Lily has made the promise to deliver a fixed number of shares to the repairperson, he or she experiences the same ups and downs in economic circumstances as do the existing shareholders of Lily Company. Accordingly, on the December 31, 2011, balance sheet, Lily Company will report this obligation to deliver a fixed number of its shares as part of equity.

Example 2: As in Example 1, on October 1, 2011, Lily Company received air conditioning repair services costing $5,000. Again, the company, wishing to conserve cash, promises to pay the repair bill with shares of its own stock on February 1, 2012. However, in this example, Lily doesn't fix the number of shares to be handed over on February 1 but instead promises to deliver shares with a market value of $5,000 on February 1. On October 1, 2011, Lily's shares have a market value of $25 per share, and on February 1, 2012, the shares have a market value of $20 per share. The journal entries that Lily would make to record the repairs and the delivery of the shares are as follows:

2011				
Oct.	1	Maintenance Expense	5,000	
		Common Stock Issuance Obligation (liability)		5,000
2012				
Feb.	1	Common Stock Issuance Obligation (liability)	5,000	
		Common Stock (250 shares × $20)		5,000

The account "Common Stock Issuance Obligation (liability)" would be reported as a liability on Lily's December 31, 2011, balance sheet. Because Lily has an obligation to deliver shares with a fixed monetary amount, the repairperson really doesn't care whether Lily's shares increase or decrease in value between October 1, 2011, and February 1, 2012. No matter what happens to the value of Lily's shares, the repairperson gets $5,000 worth of shares. Between October 1, 2011, and February 1, 2012, the repairperson does not share in the risks and rewards of ownership in Lily Company, so the obligation to deliver the shares is reported as a liability rather than as equity.

By the way, this provision will ultimately require a change in the Conceptual Framework. Currently, the Conceptual Framework definition of a liability includes only obligations to "transfer assets or provide services." The FASB may revise this definition to include obligations to transfer shares without transferring the risks and rewards of ownership. However, as mentioned several times earlier in the chapter, the FASB is currently undertaking a comprehensive review of the definitions of liability and equity items which probably will require more extensive changes in the conceptual definitions of those items.

Noncontrolling Interest

A consolidated balance sheet is the combined balance sheet for both a parent company and all of the subsidiaries that it controls. A consolidated balance sheet includes *all* assets and liabilities of the parent and the subsidiaries it controls. Thus, even though the parent owns only, say, 80% of a subsidiary, *all* of that subsidiary's assets and liabilities are included in the consolidated total. The intuition here is that the parent, with its 80% ownership, completely controls the assets of the subsidiary even though it doesn't own them completely.

The fact that all of the assets and liabilities of a subsidiary owned less than 100% by the parent are in the consolidated total means that the consolidated balance sheet includes assets for which the acquisition was financed by funds coming not from consolidated liabilities and not from parent equity but instead from the shareholders who, in the example given above, own the other 20% of the subsidiary. These are called minority shareholders, and the financing provided by them is called minority interest. Minority interest is the amount of equity investment made by outside shareholders to consolidated subsidiaries that are not 100% owned by the parent.

The FASB uses the term noncontrolling interest to replace "minority interest" and directs that this item be classified in the consolidated balance sheet as part of equity.[19] This treatment brings U.S. GAAP in line with International Financial Reporting Standards contained in *IAS 27*.

[19] FASB ASC paragraph 810-10-45-16.

Other than bringing consistent treatment within the set of U.S. companies and consistency with international standards, no one is really pleased with the classification of noncontrolling interest as part of equity. Everyone realizes that the claims of the noncontrolling, or minority, shareholders are fundamentally different from the claims of the shareholders who directly control the parent and indirectly control the subsidiaries in the consolidated group. However, the claim of the noncontrolling shareholders also isn't a liability. If it isn't equity and it isn't a liability, what is it? Historically, noncontrolling, or minority, interest has been reported as a liability, an equity, and as an in-between item in the "mezzanine" that was mentioned earlier. Given the existing Conceptual Framework, classifying noncontrolling interest as equity is the best the FASB can do. As part of the FASB's general reexamination of the difference between liability and equity items, the Conceptual Framework definitions may be revised to clarify the status of noncontrolling interest.

Stock Conversions

7 Distinguish between stock conversions that require a reduction in retained earnings and those that do not.

WHY **When stock is converted from one class or type to another, contributed capital accounts will be affected as par values are transferred.**

HOW **In most instances, contributed capital amounts are simply reclassified. When total paid-in capital associated with stock that is to be converted is less than the total par value of the post-conversion shares, the retained earnings account is debited for the difference.**

As noted earlier, stockholders may be permitted by the terms of their stock agreement or by special action of the corporation to exchange their holdings for stock of other classes. No gain or loss is recognized by the issuer on these conversions, because it is an exchange of one form of equity for another. In certain instances, the exchanges may affect only corporate contributed capital accounts; in other instances, the exchanges may affect both capital and retained earnings accounts.

To illustrate the different conditions, assume that the capital of Sorensen Corporation on December 31, 2013, is as follows:

Preferred stock, $50 par, 10,000 shares	$ 500,000
Paid-in capital in excess of par—preferred	100,000
Common stock, $1 par, 100,000 shares	100,000
Paid-in capital in excess of par—common	2,900,000
Retained earnings	1,000,000

Each preferred share is convertible into four common shares at any time at the option of the shareholder.

Case 1: One Preferred Share for Four Common Shares ($1 par)

On December 31, 2013, 1,000 shares of preferred stock are exchanged for 4,000 shares of common. The amount originally paid for the 1,000 preferred shares, $60,000, is now the consideration identified with 4,000 shares of common stock with a total par value of $4,000. The conversion is recorded as shown on page 13-35.

Preferred Stock, $50 par	50,000	
Paid-In Capital in Excess of Par—Preferred	10,000	
Common Stock, $1 par		4,000
Paid-In Capital in Excess of Par—Common		56,000

Case 1 is the usual case because par values for preferred stocks are typically high relative to par values of common stocks. This is so because preferred stock par values are still approximately equal to the market value of the preferred stock at the issue date, whereas the par value of common stocks is usually set at some very low value (as discussed earlier in the chapter).

Case 2: One Preferred Share for Four Common Shares ($20 par)

In Case 2, assume that the par value of the common shares is $20. In converting 1,000 shares of preferred for 4,000 shares of common, an increase in common stock at par of $80,000 (4,000 × $20) must be recognized, although it is accompanied by a decrease in the preferred equity of only $60,000. This type of conversion is generally recorded as follows:

Preferred Stock, $50 par	50,000	
Paid-In Capital in Excess of Par—Preferred	10,000	
Retained Earnings	20,000	
Common Stock, $20 par		80,000

The problems relating to the conversion of bonds for capital stock were described in Chapter 12.

For an investor, conversion of preferred stock for common stock often requires only retitling the investment account because both types of investment are carried at fair market value in the books of the investor. A special journal entry may be required if the conversion is also associated with a change in the investor's classification of the investment (e.g., from trading security to available-for-sale security). Investment reclassification is discussed in Chapter 14.

Factors Affecting Retained Earnings

8 List the factors that impact the Retained Earnings balance.

WHY In a simple case, the retained earnings account is exactly what the name implies: the cumulative amount of a company's earnings that have been retained in the business instead of being paid out as cash dividends. However, because many other transactions can impact retained earnings, and sometimes in very significant ways, it is important to understand all factors affecting retained earnings.

HOW All income-related effects on a company's equity are reflected in retained earnings. In addition, certain other equity impacts, such as treasury stock transactions and stock conversions, can reduce, but *never* increase, retained earnings.

The retained earnings account is essentially the meeting place of balance sheet and income statement accounts. In successive periods, retained earnings are increased by income and decreased by losses and dividends. As a result, the Retained Earnings balance represents the net accumulated earnings of a corporation.

A number of other factors can affect retained earnings in addition to net income, losses, and dividends. These factors include prior-period adjustments for corrections of errors, quasi-reorganizations, stock dividends, and treasury stock transactions. The transactions and events that increase or decrease retained earnings may be summarized as follows:

Retained Earnings

Decreases	*Increases*
Error corrections	Error corrections
Some changes in accounting principle	Some changes in accounting principle
Net loss	Net income
Cash dividends	Quasi-reorganizations
Stock dividends	
Treasury stock transactions	
Stock conversions	

Net Income and Dividends

The primary source of retained earnings is the net income generated by a business. The retained earnings account is increased by net income and is reduced by net losses from business activities. When operating losses or other debits to Retained Earnings produce a debit balance in this account, the debit balance is referred to as a *deficit*.

Dividends are distributions to the stockholders of a corporation in proportion to the number of shares held by the respective owners. Distributions may take the form of cash, other assets, notes (in essence, these are deferred cash dividends), and stock dividends. Most dividends involve reductions in retained earnings. Exceptions include some large stock dividends, which involve a reduction in additional paid-in capital, and liquidating dividends, which represent a return of invested capital to stockholders and call for reductions in contributed capital.

Use of the term *dividend* without qualification normally implies the distribution of cash. Dividends in a form other than cash, such as property or stock dividends, should be designated by their special form. Distributions from a capital source other than retained earnings should carry a description of their special origin, for example, liquidating dividend or dividend distribution of paid-in capital.

Prior-Period Adjustments

In some situations, errors made in past years are discovered and corrected in the current year by an adjustment to the retained earnings account, referred to as a *prior-period adjustment*. Several types of errors can occur in measuring the results of operations and the financial status of an enterprise. Accounting errors can result from mathematical mistakes, a failure to apply appropriate accounting procedures, or a misstatement or omission of certain information. In addition, a change from an accounting principle that is not generally accepted to one that is accepted is considered a correction of an error.[20]

Fortunately, most errors are discovered during the accounting period, prior to closing the books. When this is the case, corrections can be made by making correcting entries directly to the accounts. This is much better than error correction by prior-period adjustment, because the error is fixed immediately and it isn't advertised to the world through disclosure of a retained earnings adjustment.

Sometimes errors go undetected during the current period, but they are offset by an equal misstatement in the subsequent period. When this happens, the under- or overstatement of income in one period is counterbalanced by an equal over- or understatement of

[20] FASB ASC Topic 250 (Accounting Changes and Error Corrections).

income in the next period. After the closing process is completed for the second year, the retained earnings account is correctly stated. If a counterbalancing error is discovered during the second year, however, it should be corrected at that time.

When errors of past periods are not counterbalancing, retained earnings will be misstated until a correction is made in the accounting records. If the error is material, a prior-period adjustment should be made directly to the retained earnings account. If an error resulted in an understatement of income in previous periods, a correcting entry would be needed to increase Retained Earnings; if an error overstated income in prior periods, then Retained Earnings would have to be decreased. These adjustments for corrections in net income of prior periods typically would be shown as a part of the total change in retained earnings as follows:

Retained earnings, unadjusted beginning balance	$XXX
Add or deduct prior-period adjustments	XX
Retained earnings, adjusted beginning balance	$XXX
Add current year's net income or deduct current year's net loss	XX
	$XXX
Deduct dividends	XX
Retained earnings, ending balance	$XXX

An example of a prior-period adjustment made to correct an error is in the August 2006 financial statements of **Apollo Group**, an education provider and parent company of the University of Phoenix. In 2006, Apollo made prior-period adjustments to reflect errors in the accounting for share-based compensation and the allowance for doubtful accounts. The adjustment also reflected corrections needed to change the accounting for cash, revenue, property and equipment, leases, and other investments to be in accordance with GAAP. The company corrected these errors by reducing its beginning Retained Earnings balance by $72.7 million.

ifrs

FYI

The provisions of *IAS 8* regarding prior-period adjustments are the same as those under U.S. GAAP.

Another type of prior-period adjustment occurs when a company changes an accounting method or principle. When there is a change in accounting principle or method, a company is required to determine how the income statement would have been different in past years if the new accounting method had been used all along. To improve comparability, income statements for all years presented (for example, for all three years if three years of comparative data are provided) must be restated using the new accounting method. The beginning balance of Retained Earnings for the oldest year presented reflects an adjustment for the cumulative income effect of the accounting change on the net incomes of all preceding years for which a detailed income statement is not presented.

Techniques for analyzing and correcting errors are covered in detail in Chapter 20. Chapter 20 also covers prior-period adjustments associated with changes in accounting principle.

Other Changes in Retained Earnings

The most common changes in retained earnings result from earnings (or losses) and dividends. Other changes may result from treasury stock transactions (explained earlier in the chapter) or from a quasi-reorganization, which is performed only under special circumstances in which a business seeks a "fresh start." Quasi-reorganizations are covered in the Web Material (see **www.cengage.com/international**) associated with this chapter.

Retained Earnings Restrictions

A company's Retained Earnings balance has historically served as a constraint on the payment of cash dividends and on the repurchase of treasury shares. For example, the General Corporation Law of the state of California states that

> Neither a corporation nor any of its subsidiaries shall make any distribution to the corporation's shareholders [unless] . . . the amount of the retained earnings of the corporation immediately prior thereto equals or exceeds the amount of the proposed distribution. (Division 1, Chapter 5, Section 500)

However, in most states this constraint is no longer absolute. California law allows the payment of cash dividends even if the preceding retained earnings provision is not satisfied, as long as the total equity and working capital of the corporation are at specified levels. Other states, with Delaware often being viewed as the leader, have even less restrictive laws.

This flexibility in state laws doesn't mean that the level of retained earnings is not important. Banks and other lenders often place retained earnings restrictions in their loan contracts. For example, **Coinmach Service Corp.**, a Plainview, New York-based company that provides outsourced laundry equipment services for multi-family housing properties, disclosed the following in its 2007 financial statements:

> The covenant described above in the indenture governing the 11% Senior Secured Notes relating to restrictions on our ability to pay dividends permits quarterly dividend payments for the life of the notes in an amount equal to the difference between our distributable cash flow and our consolidated interest expense, so long as we satisfy an interest coverage test for the preceding fiscal quarter and no default is continuing.

In addition, industry regulations, such as banking codes, can also restrict the amount of retained earnings that can be used to support dividend payments. This is illustrated in a note from the 2009 financial statements of **Dimeco Inc.**, a bank that has been based in Pennsylvania since 1905.

> The Pennsylvania Banking Code restricts the availability of capital funds for payment of dividends by all state-chartered banks to the surplus of the Bank. Accordingly, at December 31, 2009, the balance in the capital surplus account totaling approximately $1,756,000 is unavailable for dividends.

Retained earnings may also be restricted at the discretion of the board of directors. For example, the board may designate a portion of retained earnings as restricted for a particular purpose, such as expansion of plant facilities.

If restrictions on retained earnings are material, they are generally disclosed in a note to the financial statements. Occasionally, the restricted portion of retained earnings is reported on the balance sheet separately from the unrestricted amount that is available for dividends. The restricted portion may be designated as appropriated retained earnings and the unrestricted portion as unappropriated (or free) retained earnings. Whatever the form of disclosure, the main idea behind restrictions on retained earnings is to notify stockholders that some of the assets that might otherwise be available for dividend distribution are being retained within the business for specific purposes.

FASB CODIFICATION

The Issue: You have been working as a part-time accountant for a small electronics company. Your company makes remote control devices for home entertainment systems. The company has suffered five very tough years and has a large negative retained earnings balance to show for it. However, recent successes suggest that profits will be substantially improved in the future.

Unfortunately, the large negative retained earnings balance makes your company's reported financial statements look terrible. The company's CEO has come to you to see if you have any ideas about removing this accumulated deficit from the company's books. The CEO knows that the company's financial statements can be "refreshed" by going through a formal legal reorganization, but she is hoping that you can come up with a less costly process that will directly address the accumulated deficit on the balance sheet.

The Question: Is there a way to eliminate a negative retained earnings balance without going through a formal legal reorganization of the company?

Searching the Codification: Here are two hints. First, you are looking for "reorganizations," which are transactions that have a broad impact on the financial statements. Hence, you should look under the collection of topics labeled "Broad Transactions." Second, you don't want a "real" reorganization. You are looking for an imitation or informal reorganization. Another way to say this is "quasi-reorganization."

The Answer: The accounting technique for eliminating a large negative retained earnings balance is described on pages 13-54–13-55.

Accounting for Dividends

9 **Properly record cash dividends, property dividends, small and large stock dividends, and stock splits.**

WHY **Dividends are a return on investment to the owners of shares of stock. This return on investment is accounted for differently depending on the type of dividend being given.**

HOW **The declaration of a dividend results in a reduction in the retained earnings account balance. The amount of the reduction depends on the type of dividend. In most instances, retained earnings is reduced for the fair value of the dividend.**

Among the powers delegated by the stockholders to the board of directors is the power to control the dividend policy. Whether dividends will or will not be paid, as well as the nature and the amount of dividends, are matters that the board determines. In setting dividend policy, the board of directors must answer two questions:

1. Do we have the legal right to declare a dividend?
2. Is a dividend distribution financially advisable?

In answering the first question, the board of directors must observe the state incorporation laws governing the payment of dividends. The availability of capital as a basis for dividends is a determination to be made by the legal counsel, not by the accountant. The accountant must report accurately the sources of each capital increase or decrease; the legal counsel investigates the availability of such sources as bases for dividend distributions.

> **FYI**
>
> It has been recommended that the format of the Stockholders' Equity section in the balance sheet be changed to give emphasis to the specific legal restrictions on cash distributions to shareholders. See Michael L. Roberts, William D. Samson, and Michael T. Dugan, "The Stockholders' Equity Section: Form without Substance?" *Accounting Horizons*, December 1990, p. 35.

The board of directors must also consider the second question (i.e., does the payment of a dividend make financial sense?). Literally thousands of research papers by finance professors have examined the issue of the "best" corporate dividend policy. Full discussion of this issue is a topic for a corporate finance class. Three general observations are made here:

- Old stable companies pay out a large portion of their income as cash dividends.
- Young growing companies pay out a small portion of their income as cash dividends. They keep the funds inside the company for expansion.
- Once a company has established a certain level of cash dividends, any subsequent reduction is seen as very bad news by investors. Accordingly, companies are quite cautious about raising their dividends, waiting until they are sure they can maintain the increased level permanently.

When a dividend is legally declared and announced, it cannot be revoked. The amount of the dividend is thereafter reported as a dividends payable liability until it is paid to the shareholders.

Recognition and Payment of Dividends

Three dates are essential in the recognition and payment of dividends: (1) date of declaration, (2) date of record, and (3) date of payment. Dividends are made payable to stockholders of record as of a date following the date of declaration and preceding the date of payment.

> **FYI**
>
> After the record date, stock no longer carries a right to dividends and it sells at a lower price. Stock on the New York Stock Exchange is normally quoted ex-dividend several trading days prior to the record date because of the time required to deliver the stock and to record the stock transfers.

The liability for dividends payable is recorded on the declaration date and is canceled on the payment date. No entry is required on the record date, but a list of the stockholders is made as of the close of business on this date. These are the persons who receive dividends on the payment date. For example, on May 10, 2010, American Express paid a quarterly cash dividend of $0.18, or 18 cents, per share to shareholders of record as of April 1, 2010. These dividends were declared on March 22, 2010.

Cash Dividends

The most common type of dividend is a cash dividend. For the corporation, these dividends involve a reduction in Retained Earnings and in Cash. For the investor, a cash dividend generates cash and is recognized as dividend revenue. Entries to record the declaration and payment of a $100,000 cash dividend by a corporation follow:

Declaration of Dividend:		
Dividends (or Retained Earnings)	100,000	
Dividends Payable		100,000
Payment of Dividend:		
Dividends Payable	100,000	
Cash		100,000

In most circumstances, the declaration of a dividend is viewed as a noncancelable, legal obligation to pay the dividend to the shareholders. However, this is not always true, as demonstrated by this December 11, 2001, press release from **Enron**:

> HOUSTON—Enron Corp. (NYSE: ENE) announced today that previously declared dividends will not be paid on the corporation's common stock, the Cumulative Second Preferred Convertible Stock, the Enron Capital LLC 8% Cumulative Guaranteed Monthly Income Preferred Shares, and the Enron Capital Resources, L.P. 9% Cumulative Preferred Securities, Series A.

This press release was made about a week after Enron filed for Chapter 11 bankruptcy, probably to head off an additional landslide of lawsuits. Obviously, if the dividends had been paid to the shareholders, the creditors, who were resigned to recovering just pennies on the dollar for the amounts owed to them, would have sued to reclaim the assets paid out as dividends.

Property Dividends

A distribution to stockholders that is payable in some asset other than cash is generally referred to as a property dividend. Frequently, the assets to be distributed are securities of other companies owned by the corporation. The corporation thus transfers to its stockholders the ownership interest in such securities. Property dividends occur most frequently in closely held corporations.

This type of transfer is sometimes referred to as a nonreciprocal transfer to owners inasmuch as nothing is received by the company in return for its distribution to the stockholders. These transfers should be recorded using the fair value (as of the day of declaration) of the assets distributed and a gain or loss recognized for the difference between the carrying value on the books of the issuing company and the fair value of the assets.[21] Property dividends are valued at carrying value if the fair value is not determinable.

To illustrate the entries for a property dividend, assume that Bigler Corporation owns 100,000 shares in Tri-State Oil Co., carrying value $2,700,000, current fair market value $3,000,000, or $30 per share, which it wishes to distribute to its stockholders. There are 1,000,000 shares of Bigler Corporation stock outstanding. Accordingly, a dividend of 1/10 of a share of Tri-State Oil Co. stock is declared on each share of Bigler Corporation stock outstanding. The entries for Bigler for the dividend declaration and payment are as follows:

Declaration of Dividend:		
Dividends (or Retained Earnings)	3,000,000	
Property Dividends Payable		2,700,000
Gain on Distribution of Property Dividends		300,000
Payment of Dividend:		
Property Dividends Payable	2,700,000	
Investment in Tri-State Oil Co. Stock		2,700,000

[21] FASB ASC paragraph 845-10-30-1.

Stock Dividends

A corporation may distribute to stockholders additional shares of the company's own stock as a stock dividend. A stock dividend involves no transfer of cash or any other asset to shareholders. In essence, a stock dividend results in the same pie (the company) being cut up into more pieces (shares outstanding), with each shareholder owning the same proportion of the pieces as before the stock dividend. From a shareholder's standpoint, receipt of a stock dividend is an economic nonevent.

Fear that investors were being deceived into thinking that receipt of a stock dividend actually represented income led to development of the rules governing how the issuing company must account for stock dividends. As described by Professor James Tucker, stock dividends acquired a shady reputation in the late 1800s because they were viewed as being similar to "stock watering."[22] *Stock watering* is the practice of issuing stock without receiving adequate compensation in return, thus diluting the value of the shares. In addition, in the 1920s and 1930s, accountants and regulatory authorities became concerned that companies issuing stock dividends were wrongly leading investors to believe that receiving a stock dividend was equivalent to receiving a cash dividend. This impression was particularly easy to convey when a company had a practice of issuing small, regular stock dividends (e.g., a 2.5% annual stock dividend). Also, from the issuing company's standpoint, a stock dividend involved no cash outlay, and the standard accounting treatment required only a small reduction in Retained Earnings equal to the par value of the newly issued shares.

The Committee on Accounting Procedure (CAP) issued *Accounting Research Bulletin (ARB) No. 11* in September 1941, which made it considerably more difficult for firms to issue small stock dividends by requiring a reduction in Retained Earnings equal to the market value of the newly issued shares. To see what a difference this makes, recall that par values are typically around $1 per share, whereas market values usually range between $20 and $80 per share. Professor Stephen Zeff cites *ARB No. 11* as one of the earliest examples of the economic consequences of accounting standards, in this case, the use of an accounting standard to reduce the incidence of small, regular stock dividends.[23]

Small versus Large Stock Dividends In accounting for stock dividends, a distinction is made between a small and a large stock dividend.[24] Recall that the specific objective of the Committee on Accounting Procedures was to discourage regularly recurring small stock dividends. As a general guideline, a stock dividend of less than 20%–25% of the number of shares previously outstanding is considered a small stock dividend. Stock dividends involving the issuance of more than 20%–25% are considered large stock dividends.[25]

With a small stock dividend, companies must transfer from Retained Earnings to Capital Stock and Additional Paid-In Capital an amount equal to the fair market value of the additional shares issued. Such a transfer is consistent with the general public's view of a stock dividend as a distribution of corporate earnings at an amount equivalent to the fair

[22] James J. Tucker III, "The Role of Stock Dividends in Defining Income, Developing Capital Market Research and Exploring the Economic Consequences of Accounting Policy Decisions," *The Accounting Historians Journal*, Fall 1985, pp. 73–94.

[23] Stephen A. Zeff, "Towards a Fundamental Rethinking of the Role of the 'Intermediate' Course in the Accounting Curriculum," in *The Impact of Rule-Making on Intermediate Financial Accounting Textbooks*, Daniel J. Jensen, ed. (Columbus, OH: 1982), pp. 33–51.

[24] FASB ASC paragraph 505-20-25-3.

[25] In *Accounting Series Release No. 124*, the SEC specified that for publicly traded companies, stock dividends of 25% or more should be accounted for as large stock dividends and those of less than 25% as small stock dividends.

market value of the shares received. The following example illustrates the entries for the declaration and issuance of a small stock dividend.

Assume that stockholders' equity for the Fuji Company on July 1 is as follows:

Common stock, $1 par, 100,000 shares outstanding	$ 100,000
Paid-in capital in excess of par	1,100,000
Retained earnings	750,000

The company declares a 10% stock dividend, or a dividend of 1 share of common for every 10 shares held. Before the stock dividend, the stock is selling for $22 per share. After the 10% stock dividend, each original share worth $22 will become 1.1 shares, each with a value of $20 ($22/1.1). The stock dividend is to be recorded at the market value of the new shares issued, or $200,000 (10,000 new shares at the postdividend price of $20). The entries to record the declaration of the dividend and the issuance of stock by Fuji Company are as follows:

Declaration of Dividend:		
Retained Earnings	200,000	
Stock Dividends Distributable		10,000
Paid-In Capital in Excess of Par		190,000
Issuance of Dividend:		
Stock Dividends Distributable	10,000	
Common Stock, $1 par		10,000

If a balance sheet is prepared after the declaration of a stock dividend but before issue of the shares, Stock Dividends Distributable is reported in the Stockholders' Equity section as an addition to capital stock outstanding.

Because the focus of the CAP was on reducing the number of small stock dividends, the accounting requirements governing large stock dividends are less specific than those for small stock dividends. Accordingly, the existing standard is quite general, as follows:

> . . . there is no need to capitalize retained earnings, other than to the extent occasioned by legal requirements. (FASB ASC 505-20-30-6)

In practice, this standard results in the par or stated value of the newly issued shares being transferred to the capital stock account from either the retained earnings or paid-in capital in excess of par accounts.[26] To illustrate, assume that Fuji Company declares a large stock dividend of 50%, or a dividend of one share for every two held. Legal requirements call for the transfer to Capital Stock of an amount equal to the par value of the shares issued. Entries for the declaration of the dividend and the issuance of the 50,000 new shares (100,000 × 0.50) are as follows:

Declaration of Dividend:		
Retained Earnings	50,000	
Stock Dividends Distributable		50,000
OR		
Paid-In Capital in Excess of Par	50,000	
Stock Dividends Distributable		50,000
Issuance of Dividend:		
Stock Dividends Distributable	50,000	
Common Stock, $1 par		50,000

[26] Some large stock dividends are effected by reducing both paid-in capital in excess of par and retained earnings by a total of the par value of the newly issued shares.

Stock Dividends versus Stock Splits A corporation may effect a stock split by reducing the par or stated value of each share of capital stock and proportionately increasing the number of shares outstanding. For example, a corporation with 1,000,000 shares of $3 par stock outstanding may split the stock on a 3-for-1 basis. After the split, the corporation will have 3,000,000 shares of $1 par stock outstanding, and each stockholder will have three shares for every one previously held. However, each share now represents only one-third of the capital interest it previously represented; furthermore, each share of stock can be expected to sell for approximately one-third of its previous market price. From an investor's perspective, therefore, a stock split can be viewed the same as a stock dividend.

STOP&THINK

You are hired as an accounting consultant by a company that is considering issuing either a 20% stock dividend or a 25% stock dividend. From an accounting standpoint, which would you recommend?

a) If the company wishes to minimize the impact of the stock dividend on reported profits for the current year, declare a 20% stock dividend.
b) If the company wishes to minimize the impact of the stock dividend on reported profits for the current year, declare a 25% stock dividend.
c) If the company is confident about its future ability to generate profits and pay cash dividends, declare a 20% stock dividend as a way to proclaim this confidence in a public way.
d) If the company is confident about its future ability to generate profits and pay cash dividends, declare a 25% stock dividend as a way to proclaim this confidence in a public way.

Although a stock dividend can be compared to a stock split from the investor's point of view, its effects on corporate capital differ from those of a stock split. A stock dividend results in an increase in the number of shares outstanding, and because the par or stated value of each share is unchanged, the Capital Stock balance also increases. In contrast, a stock split merely divides the existing Capital Stock balance into more parts, with a reduction in the par or stated value of each share. Because a stock split does not involve any transfers among the capital accounts, no journal entry is necessary. Instead, the change in the number of shares outstanding, as well as the change in the par or stated value, may be recorded by means of a memorandum entry.

Exhibit 13-6 provides a comparative example of the effects of a 100% stock dividend and a 2-for-1 stock split.

FYI

A *reverse stock split* is the consolidation of shares outstanding into a smaller number of shares. Conventional wisdom is that shares trading for less than $10 are viewed with some skepticism, and a reverse split can make the stock look more respectable. Whatever the conventional wisdom, a reverse stock split is almost always viewed as bad news by investors.

The simple example in Exhibit 13-6 illustrates that, from an accounting perspective, the effects of a large stock dividend can be very different from the effects of a stock split even though both result in the creation of the same number of new shares. The required transfer from Retained Earnings (or Paid-In Capital in Excess of Par) can significantly impact the Stockholders' Equity section of the balance sheet. For example, in the illustration in Exhibit 13-6, the 100% stock dividend may hinder the issuing firm's ability to pay future cash dividends because the Retained Earnings balance is so drastically reduced; no such constraint arises when the issuance of the new shares is accounted for as a 2-for-1 stock split.

Although stock splits and stock dividends are distinctly different in an accounting sense, the terms "stock split" and "stock dividend" are used interchangeably in the

EX 13-6 COMPARATIVE EXAMPLE—STOCK DIVIDEND VERSUS STOCK SPLIT

Stockholders' Equity*	
Common stock, $5 par, 50,000 shares outstanding	$250,000
Paid-in capital in excess of par	400,000
Retained earnings	300,000
Total stockholders' equity	$950,000

*Prior to stock dividend or stock split.

Stockholders' Equity After 100% Stock Dividend		Stockholders' Equity After 2-for-1 Stock Split	
Common stock, $5 par, 100,000 shares outstanding	$500,000	Common stock, $2.50 par, 100,000 shares outstanding	$250,000
Paid-in capital in excess of par*	400,000	Paid-in capital in excess of par	400,000
Retained earnings	50,000	Retained earnings	300,000
Total stockholders' equity	$950,000	Total stockholders' equity	$950,000

*Some or all of the $250,000 transfer to common stock at par could have been made from paid-in capital in excess of par.

financial press and sometimes even in the issuing company's annual report. For example, *The Wall Street Journal*'s description of a distribution as a split or dividend agrees with the actual accounting for the distribution only about 25% of the time.[27]

Liquidating Dividends

A liquidating dividend is a distribution representing a return to stockholders of a portion of contributed capital. Whereas a normal cash dividend provides a return on investment and is accounted for by reducing Retained Earnings, a liquidating dividend provides a return of investment. A liquidating dividend is accounted for by reducing Paid-In Capital.

To illustrate, assume that Stubbs Corporation declared and paid a cash dividend and a partial liquidating dividend amounting to $150,000. Of this amount, $100,000 represents a regular $10 cash dividend on 10,000 shares of common stock. The remaining $50,000 represents a $5-per-share liquidating dividend, which is recorded as a reduction to Paid-In Capital in Excess of Par. The entries would be as follows:

Declaration of Dividend:		
Dividends (or Retained Earnings)	100,000	
Paid-In Capital in Excess of Par	50,000	
Dividends Payable		150,000
Payment of Dividend:		
Dividends Payable	150,000	
Cash		150,000

[27] See Graeme Rankine and Earl K. Stice, "The Market Reaction to the Choice of Accounting Method for Stock Splits and Large Stock Dividends," *Journal of Financial and Quantitative Analysis*, 1997.

USING STOCK DIVIDENDS AS SIGNALS

The accounting treatment of stock dividends makes their declaration an interesting way to send a good news signal to the market. The reasoning goes like this: Because cash dividend payments are often restricted to the amount of retained earnings, the reduction in Retained Earnings required in accounting for a stock dividend might make it more difficult to declare cash dividends in the future. Accordingly, only firms with favorable future prospects would be likely to declare stock dividends. These firms would be confident that future earnings would bolster the Retained Earnings balance, making up for the reduction required by the stock dividend declaration.

So, according to this reasoning, if you see a firm declaring a stock dividend, you can conclude that the management of that firm must be confident that future earnings will be adequate to cover future cash dividends. This signaling view of stock dividends is supported by the fact that stock prices of companies instantly go up when they announce plans to issue a stock dividend. The accompanying graph shows the size of the positive market reaction to a stock dividend announcement, based on the size of the stock dividend.

Questions:

1. Assume that there is validity to this signaling theory of stock dividends. Which would be a stronger signal, a 20% stock dividend or a 25% stock dividend?
2. Again, assuming validity to the signaling theory, which would be a stronger signal, a 100% stock dividend or a 2-for-1 stock split?

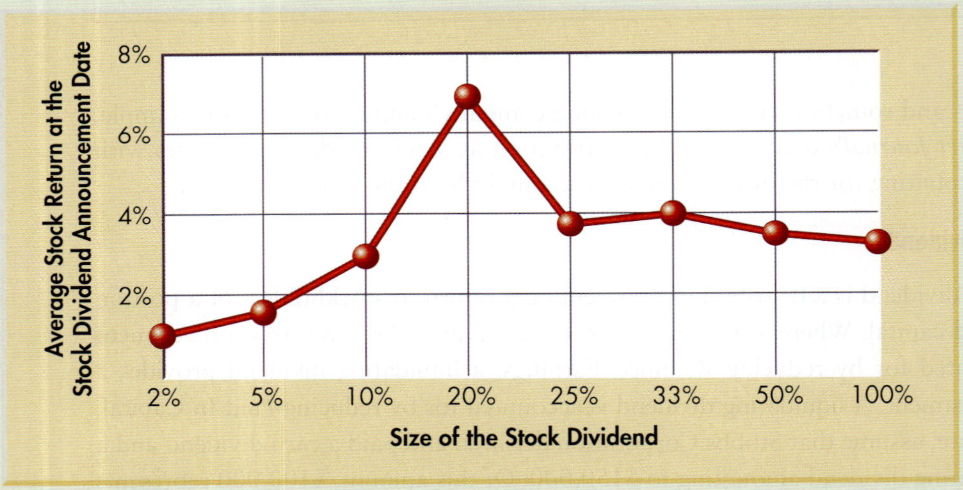

Sources: Graeme Rankine and Earl K. Stice, "Accounting Rules and the Signaling Properties of 20% Stock Dividends," *The Accounting Review*, January 1997; Graeme Rankine and Earl K. Stice, "The Market Reaction to the Choice of Accounting Method for Stock Splits and Large Stock Dividends," *Journal of Financial and Quantitative Analysis*, 1997.

Stockholders should be notified as to the allocation of the total dividend payment, so they can determine the amount that represents revenue and the amount that represents a return of investment.

In addition to the two major categories of contributed capital and retained earnings, the Equity section of a U.S. balance sheet often includes a number of miscellaneous items. These items are gains or losses that bypass the income statement when they are recognized

Other Equity Items

10 **Explain the background of unrealized gains and losses recorded as part of accumulated other comprehensive income, and list the major types of equity reserves found in foreign balance sheets.**

WHY **Some economic gains and losses that are reflected in the balance sheet (with changes in recorded asset values) are not included in the computation of net income and thus are not recorded in the Retained Earnings section of stockholders' equity. Instead, the equity impact of those economic gains and losses is shown in the equity account, Accumulated Other Comprehensive Income.**

HOW **Unrealized economic gains and losses stemming from the impact of foreign currency exchange rate changes on the value of foreign subsidiaries, from changes in the market value of an available-for-sale investment portfolio, and from fluctuations in the value of some derivatives, are not recorded in the income statement but do impact the accumulated other comprehensive income equity account directly.**

and are reported as part of accumulated other comprehensive income. A further discussion of these items follows. In addition, the following section includes a discussion of equity reserves, which are common in the balance sheets of foreign companies that do not use U.S. accounting principles.

FASB ASC Topic 220 requires that all companies provide a statement of comprehensive income. An example of Microsoft's 2009 statement of comprehensive income is included in Exhibit 13-7. A discussion of the most common elements affecting comprehensive income follows.

Equity Items That Bypass the Income Statement and Are Reported as Part of Accumulated Other Comprehensive Income

Since 1980, the Equity sections of U.S. balance sheets have begun to fill up with a strange collection of items, each the result of an accounting controversy. These items are summarized in the following sections.

Foreign Currency Translation Adjustment The foreign currency translation adjustment arises from the change in the equity of foreign subsidiaries (as measured in terms of U.S.

EX 13-7 MICROSOFT'S STATEMENT OF COMPREHENSIVE INCOME

Microsoft
Statement of Comprehensive Income
For the Year Ended June 30, 2009

(In millions)	2009	2008	2007
Net income	14,569	17,681	14,065
Other comprehensive income:			
Net unrealized gains on derivatives	302	18	14
Net unrealized gains/(losses) on investments	(233)	(653)	326
Translation adjustments and other	(240)	121	85
Comprehensive income	14,398	17,167	14,490

dollars) that occurs as a result of changes in foreign currency exchange rates. For example, if the Japanese yen weakens relative to the U.S. dollar, the equity of Japanese subsidiaries of U.S. firms will decrease, in dollar terms. Before 1981, these changes were recognized as losses or gains in the income statement. Multinational firms disliked this treatment because it added volatility to reported earnings. The FASB changed the accounting rule, and now these changes are reported as direct adjustments to equity, insulating the income statement from this aspect of foreign currency fluctuations.[28] Computation of this foreign currency translation adjustment is explained in Chapter 22.

Unrealized Gains and Losses on Available-for-Sale Securities Available-for-sale securities are those that were not purchased with the immediate intention to resell but that a company also doesn't necessarily plan to hold forever. These securities, along with trading securities (those purchased as part of an active buying and selling program), are reported on the balance sheet at their current market values. The unrealized gains and losses from market value fluctuations in trading securities are included in the income statement, but the unrealized gains and losses from market value fluctuations in available-for-sale securities are shown as a direct adjustment to equity. When the FASB was considering requiring securities to be reported at their market values, companies complained about the income volatility that would be caused by recognition of changes in the market value of securities. The FASB made the standard more acceptable to businesses by allowing unrealized gains and losses on available-for-sale securities to bypass the income statement and go straight to the Equity section.[29] Accounting for securities is covered in Chapter 14.

Unrealized Gains and Losses on Derivatives A derivative is a financial instrument, such as an option or a future, that derives its value from the movement of a price, an exchange rate, or an interest rate associated with some other item. For example, as discussed earlier in the chapter, an option to purchase a stock becomes more valuable as the price of the stock increases. Similarly, the right to purchase foreign currency at a fixed exchange rate becomes more valuable as that foreign currency becomes more expensive. As will be discussed in Chapter 19, companies often use derivatives to manage their exposure to risk stemming from changes in prices and rates. Frequently, derivatives are used to manage risk associated with sales or purchases that will not occur until a future period. In these cases, in order to ensure proper matching of gains and losses, derivative gains and losses are sometimes deferred and reported as part of accumulated other comprehensive income.

To illustrate the computation and reporting of comprehensive income, consider the following example. The last few lines of Kendall Company's income statement were as follows:

Income before income taxes		$2,000
Income tax expense		(800)
Income from continuing operations		$1,200
Income from discontinued operations:		
Income from operations (including loss on disposal of $200)	$ 250	
Income tax expense	(100)	
Income from discontinued operations		150
Net income		$1,350

[28] FASB ASC Subtopic 830-30 (Foreign Currency Matters-Translation of Financial Statements).
[29] FASB ASC paragraph 320-10-35-1b.

In addition, Kendall had the following items impacting comprehensive income:

	Amount This Year (Before Taxes)
Unrealized gain (loss) on available-for-sale securities	$100
Unrealized gain (loss) on derivative instruments	(20)
Foreign currency translation adjustment, increase (decrease) in stockholders' equity	300

Assume that the income tax rate for all items is 40%. Kendall Company would report its comprehensive income for the year as follows.

Net income	$1,350
Other comprehensive income:	
Unrealized gain on available-for-sale securities [$100 × (1 − 0.40)]	60
Unrealized loss on derivative instruments [$20 × (1 − 0.40)]	(12)
Foreign currency translation adjustment [$300 × (1 − 0.40)]	180
Comprehensive income	$1,578

In this illustration, each of the other comprehensive income items is shown net of income taxes. An alternative approach is to report all of the items before tax and then show the total income tax effect of the other comprehensive income items as a single separate line in the computation of comprehensive income.

In this case, comprehensive income is composed of three primary components:

- Income from continuing operations
- Income from discontinued operations
- Other comprehensive income

The most important source of income is income from continuing operations because this income not only arises from the core business of the company but also represents the potential for a continuing stream of income in the future. Other comprehensive income arises from events (such as changes in security values, changes in foreign exchange rates, and so forth) that are not part of a company's core operations and that also fluctuate, almost randomly, from positive to negative from year to year. The reporting of comprehensive income allows the financial statement user to see all of the wealth changes that impacted the company during the year but to also distinguish between those wealth changes that are expected to persist in the future and those that are transitory, 1-year items.

FYI

The income tax effects of other comprehensive income items are usually deferred and don't impact the amount of current income taxes payable. Deferred income taxes are discussed in Chapter 16.

Balance Sheet Reporting The accumulated amount of comprehensive income is reflected in the Equity section of the balance sheet in two ways:

- Net income (less dividends) is cumulated in retained earnings.
- Other comprehensive income is cumulated in accumulated other comprehensive income.

In essence, you can think of the accumulated other comprehensive income account as the "retained earnings" of other comprehensive income items. To illustrate, refer back to the Kendall Company example. Assume that the beginning balance in Retained Earnings was $5,000, the beginning balance in Accumulated Other Comprehensive Income was an equity reduction of $500, and the dividends paid for the year were $400. The Equity section of Kendall's balance sheet at the end of the year would include the following two items:

Retained earnings ($5,000 + $1,350 − $400)	$5,950
Accumulated other comprehensive income [−$500 + $60 − $12 + $180]	(272)

International Accounting: Equity Reserves

As discussed earlier in this chapter, state incorporation laws link the ability of a firm to pay cash dividends to the Retained Earnings balance. In other words, total equity is divided into two parts: the equity that is available to be distributed to shareholders and the equity that is not available for distribution. Restriction of the distribution of equity ensures that an equity "cushion" exists for the absorption of operating losses, thus increasing the chances of creditors to be fully repaid.

Laws in foreign countries are often more explicit than U.S. state incorporation laws in linking the payment of cash dividends to the amount of distributable equity. Equity is divided among various equity reserve accounts, each with legal restrictions dictating whether it can be distributed to shareholders. In that type of legal environment, the accounting for equity accounts directly influences a firm's ability to pay dividends and thus becomes an important part of corporate financing policy.

A brief summary of accounting for equity reserves is given in the following sections. The discussion is based on equity accounting practice in the United Kingdom. Because of the worldwide British influence left from the days of the British Empire, the U.K. model is widely used.

The major types of equity reserve accounts are illustrated in Exhibit 13-8. Remember that the most important distinction is whether the reserve is part of distributable or nondistributable equity.

Par Value and Share Premium These accounts correspond closely with U.S. practice, with the share premium account being the same as the paid-in capital in excess of par account. Usually, a country's laws restrict the ability of a firm to "refund" any of this paid-in capital, so these two accounts are part of nondistributable equity.

EX 13-8 EQUITY RESERVES

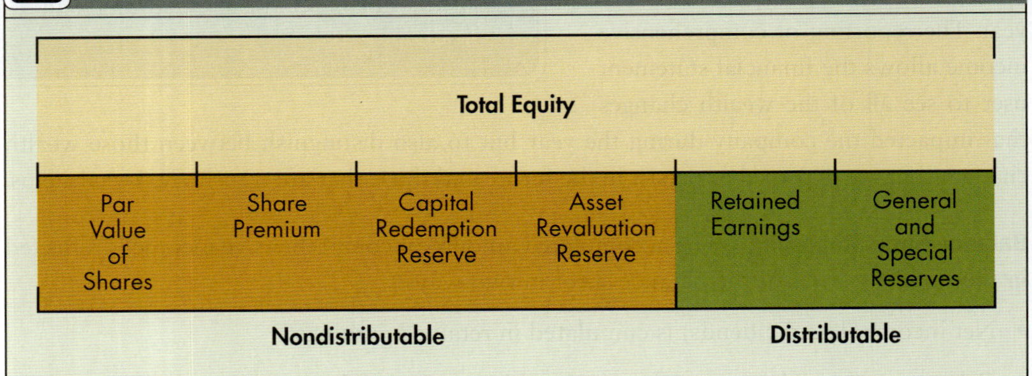

Capital Redemption Reserve When shares are reacquired, total equity is reduced. To protect the ability of creditors to be fully repaid, these reductions are usually considered to be reductions in distributable equity. To reflect this fact in the accounts, an amount equal to the par value of the shares reacquired is transferred from Retained Earnings (part of distributable equity) to Capital Redemption Reserve (part of nondistributable equity).

Asset Revaluation Reserve In many countries, property, plant, and equipment can be written up to its current market value. The recognition of this unrealized gain increases equity. The question is whether the additional equity can be used to support additional cash dividend payments. The answer is no. A revaluation reserve is established as part of nondistributable equity, and unrealized gains from increases in fixed asset market values are credited to the revaluation reserve.

General and Special Reserves As discussed earlier, the board of directors can voluntarily restrict the use of retained earnings for the payment of cash dividends. These restrictions can later be rescinded. In the United States, these restrictions can be disclosed in a financial statement note or recognized as a formal appropriation of a portion of retained earnings. In many foreign countries, these restrictions are acknowledged by transferring part of retained earnings to a general or a special reserve account. Note that these reserves are still part of distributable equity; the board of directors can remove the restrictions at any time.

Some of the reserves mentioned are illustrated with the accounts of **Swire Pacific Limited** shown in Exhibit 13-9. Swire Pacific Limited is based in Hong Kong and is one of the largest companies in the world. The primary operations of the company are in the regions of Hong Kong, China, and Taiwan, where it has operated for more than 125 years. Swire operates **Cathay Pacific Airways** and has extensive real estate holdings in Hong Kong.

As you can see from the amounts included in its calculation, the "revenue reserve" is generally equivalent to what we call "retained earnings." The "investment revaluation reserve" is equivalent to the accumulated unrealized gain or loss on available-for-sale securities. Thus, the legal limit on dividend payments by Swire Pacific is HK$14.151 billion.

EX 13-9 EQUITY SECTION FOR SWIRE PACIFIC LIMITED

(In millions of HK dollars)	Revenue Reserve	Share Premium Account	Capital Redemption Reserve	Investment Revaluation Reserve
At 1st January 2009	13,292	342	49	(41)
Profit for the year	3,989	—	—	—
Other comprehensive income				
Net fair value gains on available-for-sale assets				
– recognised during the year	—	—	—	55
– transferred to operating profit	—	—	—	(16)
Total comprehensive income for the year	3,989	—	—	39
2008 final dividend	(2,227)	—	—	—
2009 interim dividend	(903)	—	—	—
At 31st December 2009	14,151	342	49	(2)

Disclosures Related to the Equity Section

11 **Prepare a statement of changes in stockholders' equity.**

WHY **The statement of stockholders' equity provides users with a summary of changes in the equity accounts of a company.**

HOW **This statement allows users to determine whether or not changes in equity were as a result of contributed capital transactions, transactions affecting retained earnings, or events affecting accumulated other comprehensive income.**

In accounting for capital stock, it should be recognized that stock may be

- Authorized but unissued
- Subscribed for and held for issuance pending receipt of cash for the full amount of the subscription price
- Outstanding in the hands of stockholders
- Reacquired and held by the corporation for subsequent reissuance
- Canceled by appropriate corporation action

Thus, a corporation must maintain an accurate record of all transactions involving capital stock. Separate general ledger accounts are required for each source of capital including each class of stock. In addition, subsidiary records are needed to keep track of individual stockholders and stock certificates.

Contributed capital and its components should be disclosed separately from retained earnings on the balance sheet. Within the Contributed Capital section, it is important to identify the major classes of stock and the additional paid-in capital. Although it is common practice to report a single amount for additional paid-in capital, separate accounts should be provided in the ledger to identify the individual sources of additional paid-in capital, for example, Paid-In Capital in Excess of Par or Stated Value, Paid-In Capital from Treasury Stock, or Paid-In Capital from Stock Options.

For each class of stock, a description of the major features should be disclosed, such as par or stated value, dividend preference, or conversion terms. The number of shares authorized, issued, and outstanding should also be disclosed.

As an illustration, the Stockholders' Equity section from the balance sheet of IBM as of December 31, 2009, is presented in Exhibit 13-10. Many companies do not provide as much detail on the balance sheet as is illustrated for IBM.

EX 13-10 IBM'S STOCKHOLDERS' EQUITY SECTION

(Dollars in millions)	**2009**	**2008**
Stockholders' equity		
Common stock, par value $0.20 per share and additional paid-in capital	41,810	39,129
Shares authorized: 4,687,500,000		
Shares issued (2009—2,127,016,668; 2008—2,096,981,860)		
Retained earnings	80,900	70,353
Treasury stock, at cost (shares: 2009—821,679,245; 2008—757,885,937)	(81,243)	(74,171)
Accumulated other comprehensive income/(loss)	(18,830)	(21,845)
Total IBM Stockholders' equity	22,637	13,465
Noncontrolling interests (Note N)	118	119
Total equity	22,755	13,584

Readers of financial statements should be provided with an explanation of the changes in individual equity balances during the period. When stockholders' equity is composed of numerous accounts, as in the following example, a statement of changes in stockholders' equity is usually presented. The statement of changes in stockholders' equity for IBM for 2009 is illustrated in Exhibit 13-11.

EX 13-11 STATEMENT OF STOCKHOLDER'S EQUITY FOR IBM

(Dollars in millions)	Common Stock and Additional Paid-In Capital	Retained Earnings	Treasury Stock	Accumulated other (Losses) Comprehensive Income/(Loss)	Total IBM Stockholders' Equity	Non-controlling Interests	Total Equity
2009							
Equity, January 1, 2009.	$39,129	$70,353	($74,171)	($21,845)	$13,465	$119	$13,584
Net income plus other comprehensive income/(loss):							
Net income		13,425			13,425		$13,425
Other comprehensive income/(loss), net of tax:							
Net unrealized gains/(losses) on cash flow hedge derivatives (net of tax benefit of $256)				(556)	(556)		$ (556)
Foreign currency translation adjustments (net of tax benefit of $57)				1,732	1,732		1,732
Retirement-related benefit plans:							
Prior service costs/(credits) (net of tax expense of $146)				229	229		229
Net (losses)/gains (net of tax expense of $439)				994	994		994
Curtailments and settlements (net of tax benefit of $33)				(93)	(93)		(93)
Amortization of prior service (credits)/costs (net of tax benefit of $55)				(107)	(107)		(107)
Amortization of net gains/(losses) (net of tax expense of $402)				704	704		704
Net unrealized gains/(losses) on marketable securities (net of tax expense of $71)				111	111		111
Total other comprehensive income/(loss)					3,015		$ 3,015
Subtotal: Net income plus other comprehensive income/(loss). . . .					$ 16,440		$16,440
Cash dividends declared—common stock.		(2,860)			(2,860)		(2,860)
Common stock issued under employee plans (30,034,808 shares).	3,011				3,011		3,011
Purchases (1,550,846 shares) and sales (6,408,265 shares) of treasury stock under employee plans—net		(19)	462		443		443
Other treasury shares purchased, not retired (68,650,727 shares).			(7,534)		(7,534)		(7,534)
Changes in other equity.	(330)				(330)		(330)
Changes in noncontrolling interests . .						(1)	(1)
Equity, December 31, 2009.	$41,810	$80,900	($81,243)	($18,830)	$22,637	$118	$22,755

SOLUTIONS TO OPENING SCENARIO QUESTIONS

1. Your return would have been a negative 44.5% = ($8,320 − $15,000)/$15,000.
2. In 2009, Berkshire Hathaway owned 19% of the shares of the company that publishes the *Washington Post.*
3. You would also need to know how many shares of stock of each company were outstanding. In May 2010, Microsoft had about 8.76 billion shares outstanding and the total market value of the company was $254 billion. Also in May 2010, Berkshire Hathaway had just 1.6 million shares outstanding, and the total market value of the company was $189 billion.

SOLUTIONS TO STOP & THINK QUESTIONS

1. (Page 13-17) The answer is B. When a company's stock price has increased since the time the stock was originally issued (as is true for most companies), the par value method reduces retained earnings when shares are repurchased. Reduced retained earnings can hinder a firm's ability to pay cash dividends. The cost method does not involve a reduction in retained earnings until the repurchased shares are actually retired.
2. (Page 13-26) The answer is A. Because the number of options granted depends on reported sales in 2013, the greedy, unscrupulous managers of Neff will do their best to boost the reported sales for 2013. They can do this by delaying the recognition of some 2012 sales and reporting them in 2013, and by accelerating the recognition of some 2014 sales and reporting them in 2013.
3. (Page 13-44) The answer is C. The surprising answer to this question is discussed in the boxed item "Using Stock Dividends as Signals" in this chapter. A 20% stock dividend, because it requires the transfer of the market value of the new shares from retained earnings, causes a much larger decrease in retained earnings than does a 25% stock dividend that only requires the transfer of the par value. If a firm is nervous about the size of its dividend pool, it should not declare a 20% stock dividend, as this could drastically reduce retained earnings. However, if a company is confident about its future ability to generate profits and pay cash dividends and it wants to proclaim this confidence in a public way, then it should declare a 20% stock dividend. This blatant reduction in the retained earnings safety net shows management's optimism about the future.

SOLUTION TO USING THE FASB'S CODIFICATION

Under Topic 852 (Reorganizations), you should have seen Subtopic 852-20 (Quasi-Reorganizations). Section 852-20-05 contains the following: "This Subtopic addresses the accounting applicable to a corporate readjustment procedure in which, without the creation of a new corporate entity and without the intervention of formal court proceedings, an entity restates its balance sheet to fair value. This corporate readjustment procedure may eliminate an accumulated deficit." Well, this sounds like what we are looking for.

The quasi-reorganization process is described in Section 852-20-25 as follows: "If a corporation elects to restate its assets, capital stock, additional paid-in capital, and retained earnings or accumulated deficit through a readjustment and therefore avail itself of permission to relieve its future income account or retained earnings account of charges that would otherwise be made against it, it shall make a clear report to its shareholders of the restatements proposed to be made, and obtain their formal consent. It shall present a fair balance sheet as at the date of the readjustment, in which the adjustment of carrying amounts is reasonably complete, in order that there may be no continuation of the circumstances that justify charges to additional paid-in capital. When the amounts to be written off in a readjustment have been determined, they shall be charged first against retained earnings to the full extent of such retained earnings; any balance may then be charged against additional paid-in capital." In other words, in a quasi-reorganization, assets are revalued to reflect their fair values. This may require significant write-downs of assets against retained earnings, thus initially increasing the accumulated deficit. The total deficit is then written off (retained earnings is adjusted to a zero balance) against paid-in capital balances, giving the company's balance sheet a substantially restructured equity section with, as of the quasi-reorganization date, a fresh start with respect to retained earnings.

REVIEW CHAPTER 13

LEARNING OBJECTIVES

1 Identify the rights associated with ownership of common and preferred stock.

Common stockholders are the true owners of the business. They are the first to lose their investment when a business does poorly, and they are the ones who get rich when a business does well. Common stockholders vote in the election of members of the board of directors.

Preferred stockholders usually cannot vote in director elections. Preferred stock dividends must be paid in full before any common stock dividends can be paid. Preferred stock can be cumulative, participating, convertible, callable, redeemable, or some combination of these.

Par values of common stocks are usually very low (less than $1). Par values of preferred stocks often approximate the issuance price.

2 Record the issuance of stock for cash, on a subscription basis, and in exchange for noncash assets or for services.

When stock is sold for cash, the amount of the proceeds is usually divided between par value (or stated value) and additional paid-in capital.

When stock is sold on a subscription basis, any unpaid subscription amount (Stock Subscriptions Receivable) is reported as a subtraction from stockholders' equity.

When stock is issued in exchange for non-cash assets or for services, the transaction is recorded using the fair market value of the assets or services or the fair market value of the stock, whichever is more objectively determinable.

3 Use both the cost and par value methods to account for stock repurchases.

When capital stock is acquired and retired, the capital stock account is reduced, and Retained Earnings can be reduced for all or part of the excess over par value paid to reacquire the stock. Additional paid-in capital created at the issuance of the stock can also be reduced or eliminated when the stock is reacquired.

Treasury stock is stock reacquired but not immediately retired. When the par value method is used, the treasury shares are accounted for in a manner similar to a stock retirement. When the cost method is used, the entire cost to reacquire the treasury shares is shown in a contra equity account until the shares are reissued or retired.

4 Account for the issuance of stock rights and stock warrants.

Stock rights are issued to existing shareholders to allow them to purchase sufficient shares to maintain their proportionate interest when new shares are issued. Only memorandum entries are needed to record the issuance of stock rights.

Stock warrants are issued in conjunction with other securities to make those other securities more attractive to investors. The proceeds of the security issuance are allocated between the security and a detachable stock warrant.

No allocation is done for nondetachable warrants.

5 Compute the compensation expense associated with the granting of employee stock options.

With a simple stock-based compensation plan, total compensation expense is the number of options granted multiplied by the fair value of each option as of the grant date. This expense is allocated over the service period.

With a performance-based stock option plan, total compensation expense is equal to the fair value of each option as of the grant date multiplied by the number of options that are probable to be awarded. This amount is reevaluated at the end of each year, and a catch-up adjustment is made to compensation expense.

Some stock-based compensation plans call for payment in cash such as with cash stock appreciation rights (SARs). These obligations are remeasured at the end of each year, and a catch-up adjustment is made to compensation expense.

6 Determine which equity-related items should be reported in the balance sheet as liabilities.

Certain equity-related items are reported in the balance sheet as liabilities. These items are as follows.

- Mandatorily redeemable preferred shares
- Financial instruments (such as written put options) that obligate a company to repurchase its own shares
- Financial instruments that obligate a company to issue a certain dollar value of its own shares

In addition, the FASB has clarified that noncontrolling interest should be classified as equity in the consolidated balance sheet.

7 Distinguish between stock conversions that require a reduction in retained earnings and those that do not.

When total paid-in capital (par value plus additional paid-in capital) associated with stock that is to be converted is less than the total par value of the postconversion shares, the retained earnings account is debited for the difference.

8 List the factors that impact the Retained Earnings balance.

Retained earnings is reduced by the following:

- Some error corrections
- Some changes in accounting principle
- Net losses
- Cash dividends
- Stock dividends
- Treasury stock transactions
- Preferred stock conversions

Retained earnings is increased by the following:

- Some error corrections
- Some changes in accounting principle
- Net income
- Quasi-reorganizations

The Retained Earnings balance is often a constraint on the amount of cash dividends a firm can pay because of state incorporation law restrictions. In addition, a firm may voluntarily restrict the use of retained earnings.

9 Properly record cash dividends, property dividends, small and large stock dividends, and stock splits.

A dividend payable is recorded on the dividend declaration date and is removed from the books when the dividend is distributed. When a property dividend is paid, a gain or loss is recorded on the declaration date to recognize the difference between the book value and fair value of the asset to be distributed as the property dividend.

A stock dividend is a distribution of additional shares to stockholders without receiving any cash in return. In essence, a stock dividend results in company ownership being divided into more pieces, with each stockholder owning a proportionately increased number of shares.

Stock dividends and stock splits are accounted for as follows:

- *Small stock dividend (less than 20%–25%):* Retained Earnings is reduced by the market value of the new shares created.
- *Large stock dividend (more than 20%–25%):* Retained Earnings and/or Additional Paid-In Capital is reduced by the par value of the new shares created.
- *Stock split:* No journal entry is made. A memorandum entry records the facts that the par value of each share is reduced and the number of outstanding shares is increased.

10 Explain the background of unrealized gains and losses recorded as part of accumulated other comprehensive income, and list the major types of equity reserves found in foreign balance sheets.

Unrealized gains and losses that bypass the income statement and are recognized as direct equity adjustments as part of accumulated other comprehensive income are as follows:

- *Foreign currency translation adjustment.* Changes in the equity of foreign subsidiaries resulting from foreign currency exchange rate fluctuations.
- *Unrealized gains and losses on available-for-sale securities.* Unrealized gains and losses from market value fluctuations of available-for-sale securities.
- *Unrealized gains and losses on derivatives.* Unrealized gains and losses from market value fluctuations of derivative instruments that are intended to manage risks associated with future sales or purchases.

The Equity sections of foreign balance sheets often include a number of equity reserves. These reserves are designed to carefully divide equity into the portion that is available for distribution to shareholders and the portion that is nondistributable. Some of these equity reserves are the capital redemption reserve, the asset revaluation reserve, and general and special reserves.

11 Prepare a statement of changes in stockholders' equity.

A statement of changes in stockholders' equity outlines the changes during a given period in the different equity categories.

FASB-IASB CODIFICATION SUMMARY

ifrs

Topic	FASB Accounting Standards Codification	Original FASB Standard	Corresponding IASB Standard	Differences between U.S. GAAP and IFRS
Stock warrants	*Section 470-20-25 par. 2*	*APB Opinion No. 14 par. 16*	*IAS 32 par. 28*	Under IFRS, all compound financial instruments, such as stock warrants, are to be separated into separate debt and equity components. Under U.S. GAAP, this is required only if the stock warrants are "detachable."
Stock-based compensation	*Topic 718*	*SFAS No. 123R*	IFRS 2	No substantial differences
Reporting equity-related items as liabilities	*Topic 480*	*SFAS No. 150*	*IAS 32*	No substantial differences
Noncontrolling interest	*Section 810-10-45 par. 16*	*SFAS No. 160 par. 5*	*IAS 27 par. 27*	No substantial differences

KEY TERMS

QUESTIONS

1. What basic rights are held by each common stockholder?
2. What is the historical significance of par value?
3. What rights of ownership are given up by preferred shareholders? What additional protections are enjoyed by preferred shareholders?
4. What was the user response to the FASB proposal, in its November 2007 *Preliminary Views* document, that preferred stock be classified in the balance sheet as a liability?
5. How is stock valued when it is issued in exchange for noncash assets or for services?
6. Why might a company repurchase its own stock?
7. (a) What is the basic difference between the cost method and the par value method of accounting for treasury stock? (b) How will total stockholders' equity differ, if at all, under the two methods?
8. There is frequently a difference between the purchase price and the selling price of treasury stock. Why isn't this difference shown as a gain or a loss on the income statement?
9. Explain the difference in the accounting for detachable and nondetachable warrants.
10. What option value is used in the computation of compensation expense associated with a basic stock-based compensation plan?
11. With a performance-based stock option plan, a catch-up adjustment is necessary when the probable number of options that will vest changes from one year to the next. Describe this catch-up adjustment.
12. When a stock-based award calls for settlement in cash, how is the obligation accounted for?
13. How should mandatorily redeemable preferred shares be reported in the balance sheet?
14. When a corporation writes a put option on its own shares, what does the corporation receive? What does the corporation agree to do?
15. What distinguishes a situation in which an obligation to issue shares is recorded as equity from a situation in which an obligation to issue shares is recorded as a liability?
16. What is noncontrolling interest?
17. How are errors corrected when they are discovered in the current year? in a subsequent year?
18. How can retained earnings be restricted by law? In what other ways can retained earnings be restricted?
19. The following announcement appeared on the financial page of a newspaper: The board of directors of Benton Co., at its meeting on June 15, 2013, declared the regular quarterly dividend on outstanding common stock of $1.40 per share, payable on July 10, 2013, to the stockholders of record at the close of business June 30, 2013.
    (a) What is the purpose of each of the three dates given in the announcement?
    (b) When would the common stock of Benton Co. normally trade "ex-dividend"?
20. The directors of The Dress Shoppe are considering declaring either a stock dividend or a stock split. They have asked you to explain the difference between a stock dividend and a stock split and the accounting for a small stock dividend versus a large stock dividend.

21. (a) What is a liquidating dividend? (b) Under what circumstances are such distributions made?
22. What three types of unrealized gains and losses are shown as direct equity adjustments (part of accumulated other comprehensive income), bypassing the income statement? Briefly explain each.
23. In accounting for the equity of foreign companies, what is the primary purpose of equity reserves?

PRACTICE EXERCISES

Practice 13-1

LO1

Computation of Dividends, Common and Preferred

The company has 10,000 shares of 6%, $100 par preferred stock outstanding. In addition, the company has 100,000 shares of common stock outstanding. The company started business on January 1, 2012. Total cash dividends paid during 2012 and 2013 were $55,000 and $107,000, respectively. Compute the total dividends paid to preferred shareholders and to common shareholders in both years, assuming that (1) the preferred stock is noncumulative and (2) the preferred stock is cumulative.

Practice 13-2

LO2

Issuance of Common Stock

The company issued 10,000 shares of $1 par common stock for cash of $40 per share. Make the necessary journal entry.

Practice 13-3

LO2

Accounting for Stock Subscriptions

The company received subscriptions for 20,000 shares of $1 par common stock for $25 per share. The company received 40% of the subscription amount immediately and the remainder two months later. Make the journal entries necessary to record the initial subscriptions (and cash receipt) and the subsequent receipt of the remaining cash.

Practice 13-4

LO2

Issuing Stock in Exchange for Services

The company is experiencing a cash flow shortfall and has asked certain key employees to accept shares of common stock (instead of cash) in payment of salaries. The employees accepted 35,000 shares of $0.50 par common stock in place of salaries of $623,000. Make the necessary journal entry.

Practice 13-5

LO3

Accounting for Treasury Stock: Cost Method

The company repurchased 10,000 shares of $1 par common stock for a total of $300,000. None of the shares were retired. A month later, the company sold 4,000 of these shares for $144,000. The shares were initially issued for $20 per share. Make the necessary journal entries to record the repurchase of the 10,000 shares and the subsequent sale of the 4,000 shares.

Practice 13-6

LO3

Accounting for Treasury Stock: Par Value Method

Refer to Practice 13-5. Make the necessary journal entries using the par value method.

Practice 13-7

LO4

Accounting for Stock Warrants

The company issued 40,000 shares of 7%, $50 par preferred stock. Associated with each share of stock was a detachable common stock warrant. Each warrant entitles the holder to purchase one share of the company's $1 par common stock for $20 per share. Each unit (one share of preferred stock and one warrant) was issued for $55. It is estimated that each warrant could have been issued for $3 if issued alone, and the preferred stock could have been issued for $52 if issued alone. Some time after the issuance, all of the warrants were exercised. Make the journal entries necessary to record both the issuance of the preferred stock-warrant units and the subsequent exercise of the warrants.

Practice 13-8
LO5

Accounting for a Basic Stock-Based Compensation Plan

On January 1, the company granted 150,000 stock options to key employees. Each option allows an employee to buy one share of $1 par common stock for $25, which was the market price of the shares on the grant date of January 1. In order to be able to exercise the options, the employees must remain with the company for three entire years. It is estimated that the fair value of each option on the date of grant was $4. At the end of three years, all of the options were exercised when the market price of the shares was $38 per share. Make all of the journal entries necessary with respect to these options in the first year. Also make the journal entry that would be made at the end of three years to record the exercise of the options.

Practice 13-9
LO5

Accounting for a Performance-Based Stock Option Plan

Refer to Practice 13-8. Assume that the stock-based compensation plan is performance based. As of the end of the first year, the number of options that are probable to vest is 150,000. At the end of the second year, the number of options that are probable to vest is 120,000. As in Practice 13-8, the options have a 3-year service period. Make the journal entries necessary at the end of the first year and the second year to recognize the compensation expense associated with this performance-based plan.

Practice 13-10
LO5

Accounting for Cash Stock Appreciation Rights

Refer to Practice 13-8. Assume that the stock-based compensation plan involves stock appreciation rights (SARs). At the end of three years, the employees are given a cash award equal to the excess of the fair value at that time of 150,000 shares of stock above the threshold price of $25. The estimated fair value of each SAR is $8 at the end of the first year and $5 at the end of the second year. The service period is three years. Make the journal entries necessary at the end of the first year and the second year to recognize the compensation expense associated with these stock appreciation rights.

Practice 13-11
LO6

Accounting for Mandatorily Redeemable Preferred Shares

On January 1, Year 1, the company issued mandatorily redeemable preferred shares in exchange for $2,000 cash. No dividends are to be paid on these shares, and they must be redeemed in exactly two years, on January 1, Year 3, for $2,332.80. The interest rate implicit in this agreement is 8%. Make the journal entries to record the issuance, accrual of interest in Year 1 and Year 2, and redemption of these preferred shares on January 1, Year 3.

Practice 13-12
LO6

Accounting for a Written Put Option

On January 1, Year 1, the company wrote a put option agreeing to purchase 100 shares of its own stock for $50 per share on December 31, Year 2, at the option of the purchaser of the put option. The market price of the company's shares on January 1, Year 1, was $50 per share. As of January 1, Year 1, this put option has a fair value of $1,200. Because the company's shares increased in value during Year 1, the put option has a fair value of just $350 on December 31, Year 1. On December 31, Year 2, the company's shares have a market price of $46 per share, so the purchaser of the put option exercised the option on that date. Make the journal entries necessary on January 1, Year 1, on December 31, Year 1, and on December 31, Year 2 on the books of the company that wrote the put option.

Practice 13-13
LO7

Accounting for Stock Conversion

Stockholders of the company converted 12,000 shares of $40 par preferred stock into 60,000 shares of $1 par common stock. The preferred shares were originally issued for $44 per share. Make the journal entry necessary to record the conversion.

Practice 13-14
LO8

Prior-Period Adjustments

The Retained Earnings balance at the end of last year was $42,000. In June of this year, well after last year's books were closed, it was found that a mistake had been made in computing depreciation expense last year. The mistake resulted in reported depreciation expense that was $4,000 too high last year. Net income for this year was $12,000; cash dividends declared and paid this year totaled $4,500. Show the computation of the correct ending balance in Retained Earnings for this year. Ignore income taxes.

Practice 13-15
LO9

Accounting for Declaration and Payment of Dividends
On August 17, the company declared cash dividends of $35,000. The dividends were paid on September 16. Make the journal entries necessary to record both events.

Practice 13-16
LO9

Accounting for Property Dividends
On January 1, the company purchased 10,000 shares of Wilsonville Company stock for $20 per share as an available-for-sale investment. In March, the company decided to distribute the Wilsonville shares as a property dividend to its stockholders. The Wilsonville shares had a market price of $27 per share on the date the property dividend was declared on March 23. The Wilsonville property dividend was distributed on April 15. Make the journal entries necessary to record the declaration and distribution of this property dividend.

Practice 13-17
LO9

Accounting for Small Stock Dividends
The company had 40,000 shares of $1 par common stock outstanding. When each share of stock had a market value of $44, the company declared and distributed a 10% stock dividend. After the distribution of the dividend shares, each share of stock had a market value of $40. Make the journal entries necessary to record the declaration and distribution of this stock dividend.

Practice 13-18
LO9

Large Stock Dividends and Stock Splits
The company had 10,000 shares of $1 par common stock outstanding. When each share of stock had a market value of $130, the company decided to reduce the price per share of stock to $65 by doubling the number of shares outstanding. Make the journal entries necessary to record the declaration of the decision to double the number of shares and to distribute the shares assuming that (1) the distribution is accounted for as a large stock dividend and (2) the distribution is accounted for as a stock split.

Practice 13-19
LO9

Accounting for Liquidating Dividends
The board of directors of the company has decided that the interests of the shareholders will be best served if the company is liquidated in an orderly fashion, with the proceeds to be distributed to the shareholders. As the first installment in this liquidation, a total dividend of $500,000 was distributed to the shareholders. Of this amount, $30,000 is a regular dividend, and $470,000 is a liquidating dividend. Make the journal entries necessary to record the declaration and payment of this combined dividend.

Practice 13-20
LO10

Comprehensive Income
The company started business on January 1, 2011. Net income and dividends for the first three years of the company's existence are as follows:

	Net Income (Loss)	Dividends
2011	$(1,500)	$ 0
2012	600	150
2013	2,100	550

The company has some foreign subsidiaries and also maintains a portfolio of available-for-sale securities. During 2011, 2012, and 2013, the U.S. dollar value of the equity of the foreign subsidiaries and the market value of the securities in the available-for-sale portfolio fluctuated as shown on p. 13-62.

	Change in U.S. Dollar Value	Change in Value of Portfolio
2011	Increase of $320	Decrease of $900
2012	Decrease of $680	Decrease of $400
2013	Decrease of $170	Increase of $560

Compute comprehensive income for each of the three years: 2011, 2012, and 2013.

Practice 13-21
LO10

Accumulated Other Comprehensive Income
Refer to Practice 13-20. Compute the balance in (1) Retained Earnings and (2) Accumulated Other Comprehensive Income as of the end of each year: 2011, 2012, 2013.

Practice 13-22
LO10

International Equity Reserves
The company, based in the United Kingdom, has the following equity accounts:

Retained earnings	$1,000
Asset revaluation reserve	3,200
Par value of shares	100
Special reserve	400
Share premium	1,700
Total equity	$6,400

Compute the amount of (1) nondistributable and (2) distributable equity.

Practice 13-23
LO11

Statement of Changes in Stockholders' Equity
Beginning balances in the equity accounts were as follows:

Common stock, at par	$ 2,000
Paid-in capital in excess of par	14,000
Accumulated other comprehensive income	(3,500)
Retained earnings	18,000
Treasury stock	(6,000)
Total stockholders' equity	$24,500

The following is true for the year:

(a) Net income was $6,300.
(b) Equity increased $200 from an increase in value of available-for-sale securities.
(c) Dividends were $2,000.
(d) Treasury stock of $1,600 was purchased. Assume the cost method.
(e) Shares of stock for $800 were issued. Par value was $50.

Prepare a statement of changes in stockholders' equity for the year.

EXERCISES

Exercise 13-24
LO4

Stock Rights
In 2013, Calton Inc. had 100,000 shares of $1.50 par value common stock outstanding. Calton issued 100,000 stock rights. Five rights, plus $50 in cash, are required to purchase one new share of Calton common stock. On the date the rights were issued, Calton common stock was selling for $55 per share.

What entries must Calton make to record the issuance of the stock rights?

Exercise 13-25

LO5

Stock Appreciation Rights

San Juan Corporation established a stock option plan that provides for cash payments to employees based on the appreciation of stock prices from an established threshold price. The plan was instituted on January 1, 2013, and provides benefits to employees who work for the succeeding three years. Cash payments to employees will be made on January 1, 2016, and will equal the excess of the stock price over the threshold price on that date. In total, 15,000 of these cash stock appreciation rights (SARs) were granted to employees.

The threshold price established for the SARs is $10 per share. The estimated fair value of each SAR on selected dates in 2013–2015 was as follows:

December 31, 2013	$ 6
December 31, 2014	10
December 31, 2015	8

Prepare the journal entries on San Juan's books for the years 2013, 2014, 2015, and 2016 related to this plan.

Exercise 13-26

LO2

Issuance of Common Stock

Verdero Company is authorized to issue 100,000 shares of $2 par value common stock. Verdero has the following transactions:

(a) Issued 20,000 shares at $30 per share; received cash.
(b) Issued 250 shares to attorneys for services in securing the corporate charter and for preliminary legal costs of organizing the corporation. The value of the services was $9,000.
(c) Issued 300 shares, valued objectively at $10,000, to the employees instead of paying them cash wages.
(d) Issued 12,500 shares of stock in exchange for a building valued at $295,000 and land valued at $80,000. (The building was originally acquired by the investor for $250,000 and has $100,000 of accumulated depreciation; the land was originally acquired for $30,000.)
(e) Received cash for 6,500 shares of stock sold at $38 per share.
(f) Issued 4,000 shares at $45 per share; received cash.

Make the journal entries necessary for Verdero Company to record each transaction.

Exercise 13-27

LO7

Convertible Preferred Stock

Stockholders' equity for Channa Co. on December 31 was as follows:

Preferred stock, $14 par, 25,000 shares issued and outstanding	$ 350,000
Paid-in capital in excess of par—preferred stock	100,000
Common stock, $9 par, 125,000 shares issued and outstanding	1,125,000
Paid-in capital in excess of par—common stock	875,000
Retained earnings	1,600,000

Preferred stock is convertible into common stock.

Provide the entry made on Channa Co.'s books assuming that 6,000 shares of preferred are converted under each assumption listed:

1. Preferred shares are convertible into common on a share-for-share basis.
2. Each share of preferred stock is convertible into 4.0 shares of common.
3. Each share of preferred stock is convertible into 1.5 shares of common.

Exercise 13-28

LO1

Preferred Stock—Cumulative and Noncumulative

Anderson Company paid dividends at the end of each year as follows: 2011, $150,000; 2012, $240,000; and 2013, $560,000. Determine the amount of dividends per share paid on common and preferred stock for each year, assuming independent capital structures as follows:

(a) 300,000 shares of no-par common; 10,000 shares of $100 par, 9% noncumulative preferred.
(b) 250,000 shares of no-par common; 20,000 shares of $100 par, 9% noncumulative preferred.
(c) 250,000 shares of no-par common; 20,000 shares of $100 par, 9% cumulative preferred.
(d) 250,000 shares of $1 par common; 30,000 shares of $100 par, 9% cumulative preferred.

Exercise 13-29

LO3

Acquisition and Retirement of Stock

Holanna Company reported the following balances related to common stock as of December 31, 2012:

Common stock, $1 par, 200,000 shares issued and outstanding	$ 200,000
Paid-in capital in excess of par	2,400,000

The company purchased and immediately retired 21,000 shares at $19 on August 1, 2013, and 34,000 shares at $9 on December 31, 2013. Make the entries to record the acquisition and retirement of the common stock. (Assume all shares were originally sold at the same price.)

Exercise 13-30

LO3

Treasury Stock: Par Value and Cost Methods

The stockholders' equity of Thomas Company as of December 31, 2012, was as follows:

Common stock, $1 par, authorized 275,000 shares; 240,000 shares issued and outstanding	$ 240,000
Paid-in capital in excess of par	3,840,000
Retained earnings	900,000

On June 1, 2013, Thomas reacquired 15,000 shares of its common stock at $16. The following transactions occurred in 2013 with regard to these shares.

July	1	Sold 5,000 shares at $20.
Aug.	1	Sold 7,000 shares at $14.
Sept.	1	Retired 1,000 shares.

1. Using the cost method to account for treasury stock:
   (a) Prepare the journal entries to record all treasury stock transactions in 2013.
   (b) Prepare the Stockholders' Equity section of the balance sheet at December 31, 2013, assuming Retained Earnings of $1,005,000 (before the effects of treasury stock transactions).
2. Using the par value method to account for treasury stock:
   (a) Prepare the journal entries to record all treasury stock transactions in 2013.
   (b) Prepare the Stockholders' Equity section of the balance sheet at December 31, 2013, assuming Retained Earnings of $1,005,000 (before the effects of treasury stock transactions).

Exercise 13-31

LO2

Issuance of Capital Stock with Subscriptions

Palo Verde Company was incorporated on January 1, 2013, with the following authorized capitalization:

- 25,000 shares of common stock, stated value $6 per share
- 8,000 shares of 8% cumulative preferred stock, par value $20 per share

Make the entries required for each of the following transactions:

(a) Issued 14,000 shares of common stock for a total of $518,000 and 5,000 shares of preferred stock at $25 per share.

(b) Subscriptions were received for 3,000 shares of common stock at a price of $41. A 25% down payment is received.
(c) Collected the remaining amount owed on the stock subscriptions and issued the stock.
(d) Sold the remaining authorized shares of common stock at $53 per share.

Exercise 13-32
LO5

Accounting for a Performance-Based Stock Option Plan
Rhiener Corporation initiated a performance-based employee stock option plan on January 1, 2012. The performance base for the plan is net sales in the year 2014. The plan provides for stock options to be awarded to the employees as a group on the following basis:

Level	Net Sales Range	Options Granted
1	<$250,000	10,000
2	$250,000–$499,999	20,000
3	$500,000–$1,000,000	30,000
4	>$1,000,000	40,000

The options become exercisable on January 1, 2015. The option exercise price is $20 per share. On January 1, 2012, each option had a fair value of $9. The market prices of Rhiener stock on selected dates in 2012–2014 were as follows:

January 1, 2012	$25
December 31, 2012	30
December 31, 2013	35
December 31, 2014	32

Year 2014 sales estimates as of selected dates were as follows:

January 1, 2012	$400,000
December 31, 2012	450,000
December 31, 2013	550,000

Actual sales for 2014 were $700,000. Calculate the compensation expense Rhiener should report for the years 2012, 2013, and 2014 related to this performance-based stock option plan.

Exercise 13-33
LO5

Accounting for a Basic Stock-Based Compensation Plan
On January 1, 2012, Obregon Supply Company established a stock-based compensation plan for its senior employees. A total of 45,000 options was granted that permit employees to purchase 45,000 shares of $2 par common stock at $29 per share. Each option had a fair value of $7 on the grant date. Options are exercisable beginning on January 1, 2015, and can be exercised anytime during 2015. The market price for Obregon common stock on January 1, 2012, was $32.

Assume that all options were exercised on December 31, 2015. Prepare all entries required for the years 2012–2015.

Exercise 13-34
LO4

Accounting for Stock Warrants
Western Company wants to raise additional equity capital. After analysis of the available options, the company decides to issue 1,500 shares of $20 par preferred stock with detachable warrants. The package of the stock and warrants sells for $90. The warrants enable the holder to purchase 1,500 shares of $2 par common stock at $30 per share. Immediately following the issuance of the stock, the stock warrants are selling at $9 per share. The market value of the preferred stock without the warrants is $85.

1. Prepare a journal entry for Western Company to record the issuance of the preferred stock and the attached warrants.
2. Assuming that all the warrants are exercised, prepare a journal entry for Western to record the exercise of the warrants.
3. Assuming that only 70% of the warrants are exercised (and the remaining 30% lapse), prepare the journal entries for Western to record the exercise and expiration of the warrants.

Exercise 13-35
LO11

Analysis of Owners' Equity

From the following information, reconstruct the journal entries that were made by Rivers Corporation during 2013.

	Dec. 31, 2013		Dec. 31, 2012	
	Amount	**Shares**	**Amount**	**Shares**
Common stock	$175,000	7,000	$150,000	6,000
Paid-in capital in excess of par	54,250	—	36,000	—
Paid-in capital from treasury stock	1,000	200	—	—
Retained earnings	76,500*	—	49,000	—
Treasury stock	15,000	300	—	—

*Includes net income of $40,000 for 2013. There were no dividends. Assume that revenues and expenses were closed to a temporary account, Income Summary. Use this account to complete the closing process. At the beginning of 2013, 2,500 shares of common stock (issued when the company was formed) were purchased for $90,000; these were retired later in the year. The cost method is used to record treasury stock transactions. Treasury stock purchased during the year was purchased at a cost of $50 per share.

Exercise 13-36
LO10, LO11

Equity Adjustments

The following data are for Radial Company:

Contributed capital and retained earnings	$417,000
Foreign currency translation adjustment	72,000
Unrealized gain on available-for-sale securities	95,000

(*Note*: The currencies in the countries where Radial has foreign subsidiaries have strengthened relative to the U.S. dollar.)

Compute total stockholders' equity for Radial Company.

Exercise 13-37
LO11

Reporting Stockholders' Equity

Kenny Co. began operations on January 1, 2012, by issuing at $15 per share one-half of the 950,000 shares of $1 par value common stock that had been authorized for sale. In addition, Kenny has 500,000 shares of $5 par value, 6% preferred shares authorized. During 2012, Kenny had $1,025,000 of net income and declared $237,500 of dividends.

During 2013, Kenny had the following transactions:

Jan.	10	Issued an additional 100,000 shares of common stock for $17 per share.
Apr.	1	Issued 150,000 shares of the preferred stock for $8 per share.
July	19	Authorized the purchase of a custom-made machine to be delivered in January 2014. Kenny restricted $295,000 of retained earnings for the purchase of the machine.
Oct.	23	Sold an additional 50,000 shares of the preferred stock for $9 per share.
Dec.	31	Reported $1,215,000 of net income and declared a dividend of $635,000 to stockholders of record on January 15, 2014, to be paid on February 1, 2014.

1. Prepare the Stockholders' Equity section of Kenny's balance sheet for December 31, 2012.

2. Prepare a statement of changes in stockholders' equity for 2013.
3. Prepare the Stockholders' Equity section of Kenny's balance sheet for December 31, 2013.

Exercise 13-38
LO8
REVERSE SOLVABLE

Correcting the Retained Earnings Account

The retained earnings account for Carlitos Inc. shows the following debits and credits. Indicate all entries required to correct the account. What is the corrected amount of retained earnings?

Account: Retained Earnings

Date	Item	Debit	Credit	Balance	
				Debit	Credit
Jan. 1	Balance				291,700
(a)	Loss from fire	3,175			288,525
(b)	Goodwill impairment	32,200			256,325
(c)	Stock dividend	50,000			206,325
(d)	Loss on sale of equipment	17,550			188,775
(e)	Officers' compensation related to income of prior periods—accrual overlooked	210,400		21,625	
(f)	Loss on retirement of preferred shares at more than issuance price	28,000		49,625	
(g)	Paid-in capital in excess of par		79,500		29,875
(h)	Stock subscription defaults		3,725		33,600
(i)	Gain on retirement of preferred stock at less than issuance price		14,700		48,300
(j)	Gain on early retirement of bonds at less than book value		8,100		56,400
(k)	Gain on life insurance policy settlement		7,800		64,200
(l)	Correction of prior-period error		31,050		95,250

Exercise 13-39
LO8

Reporting Errors from Previous Periods

Endicott Company's December 31, 2012, balance sheet reported retained earnings of $86,500, and net income of $124,000 was reported in the 2012 income statement. While preparing financial statements for the year ended December 31, 2013, Tom Dryden, accountant for Endicott Company, discovered that net income for 2012 had been overstated by $36,000 due to an error in recording depreciation expense for 2012. Net income for 2013 was $106,000, and dividends of $30,000 were declared and paid in 2013.

1. What effect, if any, would the $36,000 error made in 2012 have on the company's 2013 financial statements?
2. Compute the amount of retained earnings to be reported in Endicott Company's December 31, 2013, balance sheet.

Exercise 13-40
LO9
SPREADSHEET

Stock Dividends and Stock Splits

The capital accounts for Alston Market on June 30, 2013, are as follows:

Common stock, $6 par, 50,000 shares issued and outstanding	$ 300,000
Paid-in capital in excess of par	600,000
Retained earnings	1,840,000

Shares of the company's stock are selling at this time at $66. What entries would you make in each of the following cases?

(a) A 10% stock dividend is declared and issued.
(b) A 50% stock dividend is declared and issued.
(c) A 2-for-1 stock split is declared and issued.

Exercise 13-41
LO9

Stock Dividends
The balance sheet of Carmen Corporation shows the following:

Common stock, $1 stated value, 80,000 shares issued and outstanding	$ 80,000
Paid-in capital in excess of stated value	1,120,000
Retained earnings	350,000

A 25% stock dividend is declared, with the board of directors authorizing a transfer from Retained Earnings to Common Stock at the stated value of the shares.

1. Provide entries to record the declaration and issuance of the stock dividend.
2. What was the effect of the issuance of the stock dividend on the ownership equity of each stockholder in the corporation?
3. Provide entries to record the declaration and issuance of the dividend if the board of directors had elected to declare a 15% stock dividend instead of 25%. The market value of the stock is $10 per share after the 15% stock dividend is issued.

Exercise 13-42
LO9

Small Stock Dividend
Zenon Company has 450,000 shares of $1 par value common stock outstanding. In declaring and distributing a 10% stock dividend, Zenon initially issued only 40,000 new shares; the other stock dividend shares have not yet been issued as of the end of the year. Prepare all journal entries necessary to record the declaration and distribution of the stock dividend. The market price of the shares is $21 per share after the 10% stock dividend is issued.

Exercise 13-43
LO1

Dividends—Different Classes of Stock
Solar Storm Inc. began operations on June 30, 2011, and issued 60,000 shares of $1 par common stock on that date. On December 31, 2011, Solar Storm declared and paid $24,200 in dividends. After a vote of the board of directors, Solar Storm issued 25,000 shares of 7% cumulative, $10 par, preferred stock on January 1, 2013. On December 31, 2013, Solar Storm declared and paid $16,500 in dividends, and on December 31, 2014, Solar Storm declared and paid $41,300 in dividends. Determine the amount of dividends to be distributed to each class of stock for each of Solar Storm's dividend payments.

Exercise 13-44
LO9

Liquidating Dividend
Van Etten Company declared and paid a cash dividend of $3.25 per share on its $1 par common stock. Van Etten has 100,000 shares of common stock outstanding and total paid-in capital from common stock of $800,000. As part of the dividend announcement, Van Etten stated that retained earnings served as the basis for only $0.50 per share of the dividend; investors should consider the remainder to be a return of investment. Prepare the journal entries necessary on Van Etten's books to record the declaration and distribution of this dividend.

Exercise 13-45
LO9

Property Dividends
Phelps Company distributed the following dividends to its stockholders:

(a) 450,000 shares of Bedrock Corporation stock, carrying value of investment, $975,000; fair market value, $1,350,000.
(b) 220,000 shares of Great Basin Company stock, a closely held corporation. The shares were purchased by Phelps three years ago at $6.25 per share, but no current market price is available.

Indicate the journal entries to account for the declaration and the payment of the dividends.

Exercise 13-46
LO9

Cash Dividend Computations
Consistent Company has been paying regular quarterly dividends of $2.00 and wants to pay the same amount in the third quarter of 2013. Given the following information,

(1) what is the total amount that Consistent will have to pay in dividends in the third quarter in order to pay $2.00 per share, and (2) what is the total amount of dividends to be distributed during the year assuming no equity transactions occur after June 30?

2013

Jan. 1 Shares outstanding, 800,000; $2 par (1,500,000 shares authorized).

Feb. 15 Issued 50,000 new shares at $10.50.

Mar. 31 Paid quarterly dividends of $2.00 per share.

May 12 Converted $1,000,000 of $1,000 bonds to common stock at the rate of 100 shares of stock per $1,000 bond.

June 15 Issued an 11% stock dividend.

30 Paid quarterly dividends of $2.00 per share.

PROBLEMS

Problem 13-47

LO2, LO9, LO11

SPREADSHEET

Journalizing Stock Transactions

Lighthouse Company began operations on January 1. Authorized were 25,000 shares of $1 par value common stock and 5,000 shares of 10%, $100 par value convertible preferred stock. The following transactions involving stockholders' equity occurred during the first year of operations:

Jan. 1 Issued 1,000 shares of common stock to the corporation promoters in exchange for property valued at $23,000 and services valued at $5,000. The property had cost the promoters $18,000 three years before and was carried on the promoters' books at $15,000.

Feb. 23 Issued 1,500 shares of convertible preferred stock with a par value of $100 per share. Each share can be converted to five shares of common stock. The stock was issued at a price of $120 per share, and the company paid $6,000 to an agent for selling the shares.

Mar. 10 Sold 2,500 shares of the common stock for $26 per share. Issue costs were $2,000.

Apr. 10 Sold 5,000 shares of common stock under stock subscriptions at $37 per share. No shares are issued until a subscription contract is paid in full. No cash was received.

July 14 Exchanged 1,200 shares of common stock and 190 shares of preferred stock for a building with a fair market value of $72,000. The building was originally purchased for $65,000 by the investors and has a book value of $48,000. In addition, 900 shares of common stock were sold for $27,000 in cash.

Aug. 3 Received payments in full for half of the stock subscriptions and payments on account on the rest of the subscriptions. Total cash received was $138,000. Shares of stock were issued for the subscriptions paid in full.

Dec. 1 Declared a cash dividend of $10 per share on preferred stock, payable on December 31 to stockholders of record on December 15, and a $1.20-per-share cash dividend on common stock, payable on January 5 of the following year to stockholders of record on December 15. (No dividends are paid on unissued subscribed stock.)

31 Paid the preferred stock dividend.

31 Received notice from holders of stock subscriptions for 1,000 shares that they would not pay further on the subscriptions because the price of the stock had fallen to $19 per share. The amount still due on those contracts was $35,000. Amounts previously paid on the contracts are forfeited according to the agreements.

Net income for the first year of operations was $80,000. Assume that revenues and expenses were closed to a temporary account, Income Summary. Use this account to complete the closing process.

Instructions:

1. Prepare journal entries to record the preceding transactions on Lighthouse's books.
2. Prepare the Stockholders' Equity section of the balance sheet at December 31 for Lighthouse.

Problem 13-48
LO2, LO11

Stockholders' Equity Transactions and Balance Sheet Presentation

Atlantic Pacific Corporation was organized on September 1, 2013, with authorized capital stock of 150,000 shares of 7% cumulative preferred stock with a $40 par value and 1,000,000 shares of no-par common stock with a $2 stated value. During the balance of the year, the following transactions relating to capital stock were completed:

Oct.	1	Received subscriptions for 200,000 shares of common stock at $39, payable $20 down and the balance in two equal installments due November 1 and December 1. On the same date, 17,800 shares of common stock were issued to Alan Williams in exchange for his business. Assets transferred to the corporation were valued as follows: land, $195,000; buildings, $216,000; equipment, $62,000; merchandise, $105,000. Liabilities of the business assumed by the corporation were mortgage payable, $46,000; accounts payable, $14,000; accrued interest on mortgage, $900. The fair value of the net assets is considered to be a reliable reflection of the value of the business; no goodwill is recognized.
	3	Received subscriptions for 110,000 shares of preferred stock at $51, payable $21 down and the balance in two equal installments due November 1 and December 1.
Nov.	1	Collected amounts due on this date from all common and preferred stock subscribers.
	12	Received subscriptions for 390,000 shares of common stock at $42, payable $20 down and the balance in two equal installments due December 1 and January 1.
Dec.	1	Collected amounts due on this date from all common stock and preferred stock subscribers and issued stock fully paid for.

Instructions:

1. Prepare journal entries to record these transactions.
2. Prepare the Contributed Capital section of stockholders' equity for the corporation as of December 31, including any equity offsets.

Problem 13-49
LO2, LO8, LO9, LO11

REVERSE SOLVABLE

Reconstruction of Equity Transactions

Manti Company had the following account balances on its balance sheet at December 31, 2013, the end of its first year of operations. All stock was issued on a subscription basis.

Common stock subscriptions receivable	$150,000
Common stock, $1 par	3,000
Common stock subscribed	9,000
Paid-in capital in excess of par—common	348,000
8% preferred stock, $100 par	120,000
Paid-in capital in excess of par—8% preferred	60,000
10% preferred stock, $50 par	25,000
Retained earnings	10,000

The reported net income for 2013 was $55,000. Assume that revenues and expenses were closed to a temporary account, Income Summary. Use this account to complete the closing process.

Instructions: From the data given, reconstruct in summary form the journal entries to record all transactions involving the company's stockholders. Indicate the amount of dividends distributed on each class of stock.

Problem 13-50
LO2, LO3, LO9, LO11

Comprehensive Analysis and Reporting of Stockholders' Equity

Keystone Company has two classes of capital stock outstanding: 10%, $40 par preferred and $1 par common. During the fiscal year ended November 30, 2013, the company was active in transactions affecting the stockholders' equity. Page 13-71 summarizes these transactions.

Type of Transaction	Number of Shares	Price per Share
(a) Issue of preferred stock	6,000	$47
(b) Issue of common stock	40,000	76
(c) Reacquisition and retirement of preferred stock	3,000	50
(d) Purchase of treasury stock—common (reported at cost)	15,000	80
(e) Stock split—common (par value reduced to $0.50)	2 for 1	
(f) Reissuance of treasury stock—common (after stock split)	15,000	56

Balances of the accounts in the Stockholders' Equity section of the November 30, 2012, balance sheet were

Preferred stock, 40,000 shares	$ 1,600,000
Common stock, 250,000 shares	250,000
Paid-in capital in excess of par—preferred	200,000
Paid-in capital in excess of par—common	18,250,000
Retained earnings	960,000

Dividends were paid at the end of the fiscal year on the common stock at $1.20 per share and on the preferred stock at the preferred rate. Net income for the year was $800,000.

Instructions: Based on the preceding data, prepare the Stockholders' Equity section of the balance sheet as of November 30, 2013. For shares retired, assume that the most recently issued shares are retired first. (*Note*: A work sheet beginning with November 30, 2012, balances showing transactions for the current year will facilitate the preparation of this section of the balance sheet.)

Problem 13-51

LO4, LO5, LO11

Accounting for Various Capital Stock Transactions

The Stockholders' Equity section of Webster Inc. showed the following data on December 31, 2012: common stock, $3 par, 300,000 shares authorized, 250,000 shares issued and outstanding, $750,000; paid-in capital in excess of par, $7,050,000; additional paid-in capital from stock options, $150,000; retained earnings, $480,000. The stock options were granted to key executives and provided them the right to acquire 30,000 shares of common stock at $35 per share. The options had a value of $5 each on the grant date.

The following transactions occurred during 2013.

Mar.	31	Key executives exercised 4,500 options outstanding at December 31, 2012. The market price per share was $44 at this time.
Apr.	1	The company issued bonds of $2,000,000 at par, giving each $1,000 bond a detachable warrant enabling the holder to purchase two shares of stock at $40 each for a 1-year period. Market values immediately following issuance of the bonds were $4 per warrant and $998 per $1,000 bond without the warrant.
June	30	The company issued rights to stockholders (one right on each share, exercisable within a 30-day period) permitting holders to acquire one share at $40 with every 10 rights submitted. Shares were selling for $43 at this time. All but 6,000 rights were exercised on July 31, and the additional stock was issued.
Sept.	30	All warrants issued with the bonds on April 1 were exercised.
Nov.	30	The market price per share dropped to $33, and options came due. Because the market price was below the option price, no remaining options were exercised.

Instructions:

1. Provide entries to record these transactions.
2. Prepare the Stockholders' Equity section of the balance sheet as of December 31, 2013 (assume net income of $210,000 and no dividend declarations for 2013).

Problem 13-52
LO2, LO3, LO7, LO8, LO9, LO11

Accounting for Various Capital Stock Transactions

Pineview Co., organized on June 1, 2012, was authorized to issue stock as follows:

- 80,000 shares of preferred 9% stock, convertible, $100 par
- 500,000 shares of common stock, $2.50 stated value

During the remainder of Pineview Co.'s fiscal year ended May 31, 2013, the following transactions were completed in the order given:

(a) 30,000 shares of preferred stock were subscribed for at $105, and 90,000 shares of common stock were subscribed for at $26. Both subscriptions were payable 30% upon subscription, the balance in one payment.
(b) The second subscription payment was received, except one subscriber for 6,000 shares of common stock defaulted on payment. The full amount paid by this subscriber was returned, and all of the fully paid stock was issued.
(c) 15,000 shares of common stock were reacquired by purchase at $28. (Treasury stock is recorded at cost.)
(d) Each share of preferred stock was converted into four shares of common stock.
(e) The treasury stock was exchanged for machinery with a fair market value of $430,000.
(f) There was a 2-for-1 stock split, and the stated value of the new common stock is $1.25.
(g) Net income was $83,000. Assume that revenues and expenses have been closed to a temporary account, Income Summary.

Instructions:

1. Give the journal entries to record these transactions. (For net income, give the entry to close the income summary account to Retained Earnings.)
2. Prepare the Stockholders' Equity section as of May 31, 2013.

Problem 13-53
LO2, LO3

Issuance, Repurchase, and Resale of Capital Stock

Lupito Company had the following transactions occur during 2013:

(a) Issued 8,000 shares of common stock to the founders for land valued at $275,000. Par value of the common stock is $1 per share.
(b) Issued 4,000 shares of $100 par preferred stock for cash at $120.
(c) Sold 2,500 shares of common stock to the company president for $45 per share.
(d) Purchased 750 shares of outstanding preferred stock issued in (b) for cash at par.
(e) Purchased 2,000 shares of the outstanding common stock issued in (a) for $39 per share.
(f) Reissued 400 shares of repurchased preferred stock at $112.
(g) Reissued 500 shares of reacquired common stock for $45 per share.
(h) Repurchased 200 shares of the common stock sold in (g) for $43 per share. These same 200 shares were later reissued for $35 per share.

Instructions:

1. Prepare the necessary entries to record the preceding transactions involving Lupito's preferred stock. Assume that the par value method is used for recording treasury stock.
2. Prepare the necessary entries for the common stock transactions assuming that the cost method is used for recording treasury stock.

Problem 13-54
LO2, LO3, LO11

Treasury Stock Transactions

Transactions that affected Barter Company's stockholders' equity during 2013, the first year of operations, follow.

(a) Issued 30,000 shares of 9% preferred stock, $20 par, at $26.
(b) Issued 50,000 shares of $3 par common stock at $33.

(c) Purchased and immediately retired 4,000 shares of preferred stock at $28.
(d) Purchased 6,000 shares of its own common stock at $35.
(e) Reissued 1,000 shares of treasury stock at $37.

No dividends were declared in 2013, and net income for 2013 was $185,000.

Instructions:

1. Record each of the transactions. Assume that treasury stock acquisitions are recorded at cost.
2. Prepare the Stockholders' Equity section of the balance sheet at December 31, 2013.

Problem 13-55

LO5

Accounting for Stock Options

The board of directors of Muir Company adopted a fixed stock option plan to supplement the salaries of certain executives of the company. Options to buy common stock were granted as follows:

Date	Employee	Number of Shares	Exercise Price	Price of Shares at Date of Grant	Option Value at Date of Grant
Jan. 1, 2010	D. R. Call	80,000	$30	$32	$ 9
Jan. 1, 2011	J. K. Neilson	45,000	38	41	10
Jan. 1, 2012	B. D. Gwynn	25,000	43	47	11

Options are nontransferable and can be exercised beginning three years after date of grant, provided the executive is still employed by the company. Stock options were exercised as follows:

Date	Employee	Number of Shares	Price of Shares at Date of Exercise
Dec. 31, 2013	D. R. Call	80,000	$48
Dec. 31, 2014	J. K. Neilson	45,000	43
Dec. 31, 2015	B. D. Gwynn	25,000	49

Stock of the company has a $1 par value. The accounting period for the company is the calendar year.

Instructions:

1. Provide all entries that would be made on the books of Muir relative to the stock option plan for the period 2010 to 2015 inclusive.
2. Prepare the required note disclosure relative to the stock option plan for the year 2012 and for the year 2014.

Problem 13-56

LO5

Performance-Based Stock Options

Globe Corporation, a new environmental control company, initiated a performance-based stock option plan for its management on January 1, 2012. The plan provided for the granting of a variable number of stock options to management personnel who worked for the entire 4-year period ending December 31, 2015, depending on the net income earned by the company in 2015. No options were granted for the first $50,000 of net income. Thereafter, the following options were available based on the level of net income in 2015.

$50,000–$99,999	12,000 stock options
$100,000–$124,999	24,000 stock options
$125,000–$149,999	36,000 stock options
$150,000 or more	60,000 stock options

The exercise price for the $5 par common stock was $20 per share. The fair value of the options on the grant date was $9.

Assume the market price for the Globe stock and Globe's forecasted 2015 net income were as follows at each of the following dates:

	Stock Price	Forecasted 2015 Income
January 1, 2012	$24	$120,000
December 31, 2012	31	140,000
December 31, 2013	26	170,000
December 31, 2014	32	135,000
December 31, 2015	33	145,000 (actual)

Instructions: Prepare journal entries related to the stock options of Globe for the period 2012–2015 assuming that all available options are exercised on December 31, 2015.

Problem 13-57

LO2, LO9

SPREADSHEET

Analysis of Stock Transactions

You have been asked to audit Greystone Company. During the course of your audit, you are asked to prepare comparative data from the company's inception to the present. You have determined the following:

(a) Greystone Company's charter became effective on January 2, 2009, when 2,000 shares of no-par common and 1,000 shares of 7% cumulative, nonparticipating, preferred stock were issued. The no-par common stock had no stated value and was sold at $120 per share, and the preferred stock was sold at its par value of $100 per share.

(b) Greystone was unable to pay preferred dividends at the end of its first year. The owners of the preferred stock agreed to accept two shares of common stock for every 50 shares of preferred stock owned in discharge of the preferred dividends due on December 31, 2009. The shares were issued on January 2, 2010. The fair market value was $100 per share for common on the date of issue.

(c) Greystone Company acquired all of the outstanding stock of Booth Corporation on May 1, 2011, in exchange for 1,000 shares of Greystone common stock.

(d) Greystone split its common stock 3 for 2 on January 1, 2012, and 2 for 1 on January 1, 2013.

(e) Greystone offered to convert 20% of the preferred stock to common stock on the basis of two shares of common for one share of preferred. The offer was accepted, and the conversion was made on July 1, 2013.

(f) No cash dividends were declared on common stock until December 31, 2011. Cash dividends per share of common stock were declared as follows:

	June 30	Dec. 31
2011	—	$3.19
2012	$1.75	2.75
2013	1.25	1.25

Instructions: Compute the following:

1. The number of shares of each class of stock outstanding on the last day of each year from 2009 through 2013.
2. Total cash dividends applicable to common stock for each year from 2011 through 2013.

Problem 13-58

LO2, LO3, LO9, LO11

SPREADSHEET

Accounting for Stock Transactions

Morris Corporation is publicly owned, and its shares are traded on a national stock exchange. Morris has 16,000 shares of $2 stated value common stock authorized. Only 75% of these shares have been issued, and of the shares issued, only 11,000 are outstanding. On December 31, 2012, the Stockholders' Equity section revealed that the balance in Paid-In Capital in Excess of Stated Value was $416,000, and the Retained Earnings balance was $110,000. Treasury stock was purchased at an average cost of $37.50 per share.

During 2013, Morris had the following transactions:

Jan. 15 Morris issued, at $55 per share, 800 shares of $50 par, 5% cumulative preferred stock; 2,000 shares are authorized.

Feb. 1 Morris sold 1,500 shares of newly issued $2 stated value common stock at $42 per share.

Mar. 15 Morris declared a cash dividend on common stock of $0.15 per share, payable on April 30 to all stockholders of record on April 1.

Apr. 15 Morris reacquired 200 shares of its common stock for $43 per share. Morris uses the cost method to account for treasury stock.

30 Morris paid dividends.

30 Employees exercised 1,000 options granted in 2008 under a fixed stock option plan. When the options were granted, each option entitled the employee to purchase one share of common stock for $50 per share. The share price on the grant date was $51 per share. On April 30, when the market price was $55 per share, Morris issued new shares to the employees. The fair value of the options at the grant date was $6.

May 1 Morris declared a 10% stock dividend to be distributed on June 1 to stockholders of record on May 7. The market price of the common stock was $55 per share on May 1 (before the stock dividend). (Assume that treasury shares do not participate in stock dividends.)

31 Morris sold 150 treasury shares reacquired on April 15 and an additional 200 shares costing $7,500 that had been on hand since the beginning of the year. The selling price was $57 per share.

June 1 Morris distributed the stock dividend.

Sept. 15 The semiannual cash dividend on common stock was declared, amounting to $0.15 per share. Morris also declared the yearly dividend on preferred stock. Both are payable on October 15 to stockholders of record on October 1.

Oct. 15 Morris paid dividends.

Net income for 2013 was $50,000. Assume that revenues and expenses were closed to a temporary account, Income Summary. Use this account to complete the closing process.

Instructions:

1. Compute the number of shares and dollar amount of treasury stock at the beginning of 2013.
2. Make the necessary journal entries to record the transactions in 2013 relating to stockholders' equity.
3. Prepare the Stockholders' Equity section of Morris Corporation's December 31, 2013, balance sheet.

Problem 13-59

LO2, LO3, LO9

Accounting for Stock Transactions

Valentine Corporation was organized on June 30, 2010. After 2 1/2 years of profitable operations, the Equity section of Valentine's balance sheet was as follows:

Contributed capital:	
Common stock, $5 par, 500,000 shares authorized, 300,000 shares issued and outstanding	$ 1,500,000
Paid-in capital in excess of par	11,000,000
Retained earnings	3,600,000
Total stockholders' equity	$16,100,000

During 2013, the following transactions affected stockholders' equity:

Jan.	31	Reacquired 20,000 shares of common stock at $41; treasury stock is recorded at cost.
Apr.	1	Declared a 30% stock dividend. (Applies to all issued stock.)
	30	Declared an $0.80 cash dividend. (Applies only to outstanding stock.)
June	1	Issued the stock dividend and paid the cash dividend.
Aug.	31	Sold all treasury stock at $49.

Instructions: Provide the journal entries to record the stock transactions.

Problem 13-60

LO9

Stock Dividend and Cash Dividend

On January 1, 2013, Cozumel Company had 100,000 shares of $0.50 par value common stock outstanding. The market value of Cozumel's common stock was $18 per share. Cozumel's Retained Earnings balance on January 1 was $460,000. During 2012, Cozumel had declared and paid cash dividends of $0.75 per share. Net income for 2013 is expected to be $130,000. Cozumel has a large loan from McGraw Bank; part of the loan agreement stipulates that Cozumel must maintain a minimum Retained Earnings balance of $350,000.

Cozumel's board of directors is debating whether to declare a stock dividend in addition to its $0.75 per share annual cash dividend. Three proposals have been presented: (1) no stock dividend, (2) a 10% stock dividend, and (3) a 25% stock dividend.

Instructions: As a shareholder in Cozumel Company, which of the three proposals do you favor? Support your answer.

Problem 13-61

LO2, LO3, LO8, LO9, LO11

Stockholders' Equity Transactions

Squires Inc. was organized on January 2, 2012, with authorized capital stock consisting of 40,000 shares of 10%, $200 par value preferred, and 300,000 shares of no-par, no stated value common. During the first two years of the company's existence, the following selected transactions took place:

2012		
Jan.	2	Sold 15,000 shares of common stock at $14.
	2	Sold 4,000 shares of preferred stock at $211.
Mar.	2	Sold common stock as follows: 11,300 shares at $19; 3,900 shares at $24.
July	10	Acquired a nearby piece of land, appraised at $500,000, for 800 shares of preferred stock and 34,000 shares of common. (Preferred stock was recorded at $211, the balance being assigned to common.)
Dec.	16	Declared the regular preferred dividend and a $1.75 common dividend.
	28	Paid dividends declared on December 16.
	31	Assume that revenues and expenses were closed to a temporary account, Income Summary. The income summary account showed a credit balance of $600,000, which was transferred to Retained Earnings.
2013		
Feb.	27	Reacquired 11,000 shares of common stock at $18. The treasury stock is carried at cost. (State law requires that an appropriation of Retained Earnings be made for the purchase price of treasury stock. Appropriations are to be returned to Retained Earnings upon resale of the stock.)
June	17	Resold 8,000 shares of the treasury stock at $21.
July	31	Resold all of the remaining treasury stock at $16.
Sept.	30	Sold 17,000 additional shares of common stock at $22.
Dec.	16	Declared the regular preferred dividend and a $0.70 common dividend.
	28	Dividends declared on December 16 were paid.
	31	The income summary account showed a credit balance of $550,000, which was transferred to Retained Earnings.

Instructions:

1. Give the journal entries to record these transactions.
2. Prepare the Stockholders' Equity section of the balance sheet as of December 31, 2013.

Problem 13-62

LO3, LO7, LO8, LO9, LO11

Accounting for Stockholders' Equity

A condensed balance sheet for Sharp Tax Inc. as of December 31, 2010, follows. Capital stock authorized consists of 750 shares of 8%, $100 par, cumulative preferred stock and 15,000 shares of $50 par common stock.

Information relating to operations of the succeeding three years follows the condensed balance sheet.

Sharp Tax Inc.
Condensed Balance Sheet
December 31, 2010

Assets		Liabilities and Stockholders' Equity	
Assets	$525,000	Liabilities	$120,000
		8% preferred stock, $100 par	75,000
		Common stock, $50 par	150,000
		Paid-in capital in excess of par—common	30,000
		Retained earnings	150,000
Total assets	$525,000	Total liabilities and stockholders' equity	$525,000

	2011	2012	2013
Dividends declared on December 20, payable on January 10 of the following year:			
Preferred stock	8% cash	8% cash	8% cash
Common stock	$1.00 cash 50% stock	$1.25 cash	$1.00 cash
Net income for year	$67,500	$39,000	$51,000

2012

Feb. 12 Accumulated depreciation was reduced by $72,000 following an income tax investigation. (Assume that this was an error that qualified as a prior-period adjustment.) Additional income tax of $22,500 for prior years was paid.

Mar. 3 Purchased 300 shares of common stock at $54 per share; treasury stock is recorded at cost, and retained earnings are appropriated equal to such costs.

2013

Aug. 10 All the treasury stock was resold at $59 per share, and the retained earnings appropriation was canceled.

Sept. 12 By vote of the stockholders, each share of the common stock was exchanged by the corporation for four shares of no-par common stock with a stated value of $15.

Instructions:

1. Make the journal entries to record these transactions for the 3-year period ended December 31, 2013. (Assume that revenues and expenses were closed to a temporary account, Income Summary, at the end of each year. Use this account to complete the closing process.)
2. Prepare the Stockholders' Equity section of the balance sheet as it would appear at the end of 2011, 2012, and 2013.

Problem 13-63

LO8, LO9

Retained Earnings and the Statement of Cash Flows

The following items relate to the activities of Schmidt Company for 2013:

(a) Cash dividends declared and paid on common stock during the year totaled $90,000. In addition, on January 15, 2013, dividends of $25,000 that were declared in 2012 were paid.

(b) Retained earnings of $145,000 were appropriated during the year in anticipation of a major capital expansion in future years.
(c) Depreciation expense was $59,000.
(d) Equipment was purchased for $215,000 in cash.
(e) Early in the year, a 10% stock dividend was declared and distributed. This stock dividend resulted in the distribution of 40,000 new shares of $1 par common stock. The market value per share immediately after the stock dividend was $55.
(f) Cash revenues for the year totaled $582,000.
(g) Cash expenses for the year totaled $305,000.
(h) Old machinery was sold for its book value of $20,000.
(i) Near the end of the year, a 2-for-1 stock split was declared. The 440,000 shares of $1 par common stock outstanding at the time were exchanged for 880,000 shares with a par value of $0.50.
(j) Cash dividends totaling $27,000 were declared and paid on preferred stock.
(k) Land was acquired in exchange for 5,000 shares of $0.50 par value common stock. The land had a fair market value of $170,000.
(l) Assume no changes in current operating receivable and payable balances during the year.

Instructions: Prepare a statement of cash flows for Schmidt Company for the year ended December 31, 2013. Use the indirect method for reporting cash flows from operating activities.

Problem 13-64

LO2, LO8, LO9, LO11

Reporting Stockholders' Equity

The Stockholders' Equity section of Nilsson Corporation's balance sheet as of December 31, 2012, is as follows:

Common stock ($5 par, 500,000 shares authorized, 275,000 issued and outstanding)	$1,375,000	
Paid-in capital in excess of par	550,000	
Total paid-in capital		$1,925,000
Unappropriated retained earnings	$1,335,000	
Appropriated retained earnings	500,000	
Total retained earnings		1,835,000
Total stockholders' equity		$3,760,000

Nilsson Corporation had the following stockholders' equity transactions during 2013:

Jan.	15	Completed the building renovation, for which $500,000 of retained earnings had been restricted. Paid the contractor $485,000, all of which is capitalized.
Mar.	3	Issued 100,000 additional shares of the common stock for $8 per share.
May	18	Declared a dividend of $1.50 per share to be paid on July 31, 2013, to stockholders of record on June 30, 2013.
June	19	Approved additional building renovation to be funded internally. The estimated cost of the project is $400,000, and retained earnings are to be restricted for that amount.
July	31	Paid the dividend.
Nov.	12	Declared a property dividend to be paid on December 31, 2013, to stockholders of record on November 30, 2013. The dividend is to consist of 35,000 shares of Hampton Inc. stock that are currently recorded in Nilsson's books at $9 per share. The fair market value of the stock on November 12 is $13 per share.
Dec.	31	Reported $885,000 of net income on the December 31, 2013, income statement. (Assume that revenues and expenses were closed to a temporary account, Income Summary. Use this account to complete the closing process.) In addition, the stock was distributed in satisfaction of the property dividend. The Hampton stock closed at $14 per share at the end of the day's trading.

Instructions:

1. Make all necessary journal entries for Nilsson to account for the transactions affecting stockholders' equity.
2. Prepare the December 31, 2013, Stockholders' Equity section of the balance sheet for Nilsson.

Problem 13-65

LO2, LO3, LO4

Auditing Stockholders' Equity

You have been assigned to the audit of Packer Inc., a manufacturing company. You have been asked to summarize the transactions for the year ended December 31, 2013, affecting stockholders' equity and other related accounts. The Stockholders' Equity section of Packer's December 31, 2012, balance sheet follows:

Stockholders' Equity	
Contributed capital:	
Common stock, $2 par value, 300,000 shares authorized, 75,000 shares issued, 73,850 shares outstanding	$ 150,000
Paid-in capital in excess of par	1,800,000
Paid-in capital from treasury stock	25,000
Total contributed capital	$1,975,000
Retained earnings	295,741
Total contributed capital and retained earnings	$2,270,741
Less: Cost of 1,150 shares of treasury stock	74,750
Total stockholders' equity	$2,195,991

You have extracted the following information from the accounting records and audit working papers.

2013		
Jan.	15	Packer reissued 850 shares of treasury stock for $50 per share. The 1,150 shares of treasury stock on hand at December 31, 2012, were purchased in one block in 2012. Packer used the cost method for recording the treasury shares purchased.
Feb.	2	Sold 80, $1,500, 9% bonds due February 1, 2016, at 103 with one detachable stock warrant attached to each bond. Interest is payable annually on February 1. The fair market value of the bonds without the stock warrants is 97. The detachable warrants have a fair value of $90 each and expire on February 1, 2014. Each warrant entitles the holder to purchase 15 shares of common stock at $50 per share.
Mar.	6	Subscriptions for 1,800 shares of common stock were issued at $53 per share, payable 45% down and the balance by March 20.
	20	The balance due on 1,500 shares was received and those shares were issued. The subscriber who defaulted on the 300 remaining shares forfeited the down payment in accordance with the subscription agreement.
Nov.	1	There were 65 stock warrants detached from the bonds and exercised.

Instructions: Provide journal entries required to summarize the preceding transactions.

Problem 13-66

LO3, LO4, LO5, LO10

Sample CPA Exam Questions

1. On January 2, 2014, Kine Co. granted Morgan, its president, compensatory stock options to buy 1,000 shares of Kine's $10 par common stock. The options call for a price of $20 per share and are exercisable beginning on December 31, 2014. The options can be exercised any time during the three years beginning with this date. Morgan exercised the options on December 31, 2014. The market price of the stock was $40 on January 2, 2014, and $70 on December 31, 2014. The fair value of the options was $25. By what net amount should stockholders' equity increase as a result of the grant and exercise of the options?

   (a) $20,000
   (b) $25,000
   (c) $30,000
   (d) $50,000

2. A company issued rights to its existing shareholders without consideration. The rights allowed the recipients to purchase unissued common stock for an amount

in excess of par value. When the rights are issued, which of the following accounts will be increased?

	Common Stock	Additional Paid-In Capital
(a)	Yes	Yes
(b)	Yes	No
(c)	No	No
(d)	No	Yes

3. If a corporation sells some of its treasury stock at a price that exceeds its cost, this excess should be
   (a) reported as a gain in the income statement.
   (b) treated as a reduction in the carrying amount of remaining treasury stock.
   (c) credited to Additional Paid-In Capital.
   (d) credited to Retained Earnings
4. Which of the following should be reported as a stockholders' equity contra account?
   (a) Discount on convertible bonds
   (b) Premium on convertible bonds
   (c) Cumulative foreign exchange translation loss
   (d) Organization costs

CASES

Discussion Case 13-67

Should I Throw the Stock Warrants Away?

A stock warrant entitles the owner to buy a specified number of shares of stock at a specified price. Landon Davis owns 1,000 stock warrants. Each warrant entitles him to buy one share of Plum Street Company common stock for $50. The current market price of a share of Plum Street common is $40. Because the warrant price is higher than the current market price, Landon has decided that his warrants are worthless and is going to throw them away. Do the warrants have any value? How would you explain to Landon the factors that influence the value of a stock warrant?

Discussion Case 13-68

Treasury Stock Transactions—You Can't Lose!

The following is adapted from an article appearing in *Forbes:*

> The board of **Hospital Corporation of America (HCA)** authorized the buyback of 12 million of the firm's own shares at a total cost of $564 million. However, after the stock market crash of 1987, HCA's shares were trading at only 31 1/8. So, HCA was now out $190.5 million on its investment—right? Common sense would answer yes, but beyond common sense lurks the logic of accounting. According to generally accepted accounting principles, HCA didn't lose a penny on the buyback. Call it a no-risk investment. In this era of stock market volatility, stock buybacks offer firms the opportunity to tell shareholders that they have a terrific investment—without ever having to own up to the bad news if it turns sour.

Consider the criticism in the preceding paragraph and evaluate the reasonableness of the accounting for treasury stock transactions.

SOURCE: Penelope Wang, "Losses? What Losses?" *Forbes,* February 8, 1988, p. 118.

Discussion Case 13-69

Who Gets the Cash Dividend?

On March 23, 2013, the board of directors of Mycroft Company declared a quarterly cash dividend on its $1 par common stock of $0.50 per share, payable on May 10, 2013, to the shareholders of record on April 14, 2013. Before April 9, Mycroft's shares traded in the stock market "with dividend," meaning that the quoted stock price included the right to receive the dividend. After April 9, the shares traded "ex-dividend," meaning that the quoted price did not include the right to receive the dividend. Before April 9, Mycroft's shares were selling for $30 per share. What should happen to Mycroft's stock price on April 9, the ex-dividend date? What should happen to Mycroft's stock price on March 23, the dividend declaration date?

Discussion Case 13-70

Stock Split or Stock Dividend?

In early 2013, the $20 par common stock of Driftwood Construction Company was selling in the range of $100 to $130 per share, with 146,000 shares outstanding. On May 1, 2013, Driftwood's board of directors decided that, effective May 10, 2013, Driftwood stock would be split 2 for 1. Before making the public announcement, the board had to decide whether to do the split as a "true" stock split and reduce the par value per share to $10 or to accomplish the split through a 100% stock dividend.

Why does Driftwood's board of directors want to double the number of shares outstanding? What factors should Driftwood's board consider in deciding between a true 2-for-1 split and a 100% stock dividend?

Discussion Case 13-71

Out of Sight, Out of Mind

Historically, in some countries payments of bonuses to directors were deducted directly from Retained Earnings rather than being charged to income of the year. Does this treatment make it more or less likely that bonuses will be paid to directors? Can accounting standards be neutral in their impact on economic decision making by companies? Should they be neutral?

Case 13-72

Deciphering Financial Statements (The Walt Disney Company)

The 2009 financial statements for **The Walt Disney Company** can be found on the Internet. Locate those financial statements and consider the following questions.

1. What is the par value of Disney's common stock? What was the average issuance price of Disney's common stock?
2. Does Disney use the cost method or the par value method of accounting for treasury stock? As of October 3, 2009, what was the average cost of the repurchased shares held in treasury?
3. Combining information from questions (1) and (2), estimate the decrease in Disney's retained earnings if all of the treasury shares were retired.
4. From Disney's foreign currency translation adjustment, deduce whether the foreign currencies got stronger or weaker in 2009 (relative to the U.S. dollar) in the countries where Disney has subsidiaries. (*Hint*: Find the detail about accumulated other comprehensive income that is included at the bottom of the statement of stockholders' equity.)

Case 13-73

Deciphering Financial Statements (Swire Pacific Limited)

The equity categories for **Swire Pacific Limited** are illustrated in Exhibit 13-9, on page 13-51. Using the information in the exhibit, answer the following questions:

1. Recall that the primary purpose of defining different reserve categories is to distinguish between distributable and nondistributable equity. As of December 31, 2009, how much of Swire Pacific's equity is distributable?
2. What is the U.S. equivalent of Swire Pacific's revenue reserve?
3. What do you think is the purpose of the capital redemption reserve?

Case 13-74

Writing Assignment (Strategic accounting: par value or cost method?)

J. D. Michael Company has been very successful in recent years. Cash flow from operations is more than sufficient to cover the cost of all capital expenditures as well as regular cash dividends. J. D. Michael has decided to use some of its extra cash to begin a program of repurchasing its own shares in the open market. The shares will not be retired but will be held for potential reissue. Because J. D. Michael has never repurchased its own shares before, it has not had to make a choice between the par value and cost methods of accounting for treasury stock.

As the resident expert on accounting in the company, you have been asked to draft a 1-page memo to the board of directors recommending either the cost method or the par value method of accounting for treasury stock. Your memo should address issues like the prevailing practice, the likely effect on the financial statements (particularly the Equity section), and the potential impact of the treasury stock accounting treatment on the ability to maintain steady cash dividend payments in the future.

Case 13-75

Ethical Dilemma (Stock dividend instead of cash: The investors will never know!)

Best Ski Manufacturer usually pays a cash dividend sufficient to give investors a dividend yield (annual dividend divided by stock price) of around 6%. Last quarter, Best Ski Manufacturer paid a quarterly cash dividend of $1 per share. Its stock price is currently at $65 per share.

In the current quarter, Best Ski has suddenly experienced a big slowdown in ski equipment orders. The vice president of finance unequivocally stated that Best Ski just didn't have the cash to pay another cash dividend of $1 per share. She suggested that Best Ski make a public announcement explaining the situation to shareholders. This suggestion infuriated the chief executive officer, who subsequently insisted that nothing be done to make the shareholders nervous or pessimistic about Best Ski's future prospects.

The controller (your boss) came to the rescue with an accounting solution to the problem. He proposed that Best Ski declare a 10% stock dividend in place of the regular quarterly cash dividend. He said that a stock dividend is merely a cosmetic increase in the number of shares, with no associated cash flow, either into or out of the company. However, he claimed that investors would never know the difference between a cash dividend and a stock dividend. The controller's suggestion was met with enthusiasm by the board of directors.

The shareholder relations department is drafting a press release to announce the 10% stock dividend. Because of your accounting expertise, you have been asked to help with the wording of the memo. What wording would you suggest?

Case 13-76

Cumulative Spreadsheet Analysis

This spreadsheet assignment is a continuation of the spreadsheet assignments given in earlier chapters. If you completed those assignments, you have a head start on this one.

Refer back to the instructions for preparing the revised financial statements for 2013 as given in (1) of the Cumulative Spreadsheet Analysis assignment in Chapter 3.

1. Skywalker wishes to prepare a *forecasted* balance sheet, a *forecasted* income statement, and a *forecasted* statement of cash flows for 2014. Use the financial statement numbers for 2013 as the basis for the forecast, along with the following additional information.
   (a) Sales in 2014 are expected to increase by 40% over 2013 sales of $2,100.
   (b) In 2014, new property, plant, and equipment acquisitions will be in accordance with the information in (q).
   (c) The $480 in operating expenses reported in 2013 breaks down as follows: $15 in depreciation expense and $465 in other operating expenses.
   (d) New long-term debt will be acquired in 2014 in accordance with (u).
   (e) Cash dividends will be paid in 2014 in accordance with (w).
   (f) New short-term loans payable will be acquired in an amount sufficient to make Skywalker's current ratio in 2014 exactly equal to 2.0.
   (g) Skywalker anticipates repurchasing additional shares of stock during 2014 in accordance with (x).

(h) Because changes in future prices and exchange rates are impossible to predict, Skywalker's best estimate is that the balance in accumulated other comprehensive income will remain unchanged in 2014.
(i) In the absence of more detailed information, assume that the balances in Investment Securities, Long-Term Investments, and Other Long-Term Assets will all increase at the same rate as sales (40%) in 2014. The balance in Intangible Assets will change in accordance with item (r).
(j) In the absence of more detailed information, assume that the balance in the other long-term liabilities account will increase at the same rate as sales (40%) in 2014.
(k) The investment securities are classified as available-for-sale securities. Accordingly, cash from the purchase and sale of these securities is classified as an investing activity.
(l) Assume that transactions impacting other long-term assets and other long-term liabilities accounts are operating activities.
(m) Cash and investment securities will increase at the same rate as sales.
(n) The forecasted amount of accounts receivable in 2014 is determined using the forecasted value for the average collection period. The average collection period for 2014 is expected to be 14.08 days. To make the calculations less complex, this value of 14.08 days is based on forecasted end-of-year accounts receivable rather than on average accounts receivable.
(o) The forecasted amount of inventory in 2014 is determined using the forecasted value for the number of days' sales in inventory. The number of days' sales in inventory for 2014 is expected to be 107.6 days. To make the calculations simpler, this value of 107.6 days is based on forecasted end-of-year inventory rather than on average inventory.
(p) The forecasted amount of accounts payable in 2014 is determined using the forecasted value for the number of days' purchases in accounts payable. The number of days' purchases in accounts payable for 2014 is expected to be 48.34 days. To make the calculations simpler, this value of 48.34 days is based on forecasted end-of-year accounts payable rather than on average accounts payable.
(q) The forecasted amount of property, plant, and equipment (PP&E) in 2014 is determined using the forecasted value for the fixed asset turnover ratio. The fixed asset turnover ratio for 2014 is expected to be 3.518 times. To make the calculations simpler, this ratio of 3.518 is based on forecasted end-of-year gross property, plant, and equipment balance rather than on the average balance. (*Note*: For simplicity, ignore accumulated depreciation in making this calculation.)
(r) Skywalker has determined that no new intangible assets will be acquired in 2014. Intangible assets are amortized according to the information in (t).
(s) In computing depreciation expense for 2014, use straight-line depreciation and assume a 30-year useful life with no residual value. Gross PP&E acquired during the year is only depreciated for half the year. In other words, depreciation expense for 2014 is the sum of two parts: (1) a full year of depreciation on the beginning balance in PP&E, assuming a 30-year life and no residual value, and (2) a half-year of depreciation on any new PP&E acquired during the year, based on the change in the gross PP&E balance.
(t) Skywalker assumes a 20-year useful life for its intangible assets. Assume that the $100 in intangible assets reported in 2013 is the original cost of the intangibles. Include the amortization expense with the depreciation expense in the income statement.
(u) New long-term debt will be acquired (or repaid) in an amount sufficient to make Skywalker's debt ratio (total liabilities divided by total assets) in 2014 exactly equal to 0.80.

(v) Assume an interest rate on short-term loans payable of 6.0% and on long-term debt of 8.0%. Only a half-year's interest is charged on loans taken out during the year. For example, if short-term loans payable at the end of 2014 is \$15 and given that short-term loans payable at the end of 2013 were \$10, total short-term interest expense for 2014 would be \$0.75 [(\$10 × 0.06) + (\$5 × 0.06 × 1/2)].

(*Note*: These forecasted statements were constructed as part of the spreadsheet assignment in Chapter 12; you can use that spreadsheet as a starting point if you have completed that assignment.)

For this exercise, make the following additional assumptions:

(w) Skywalker has decided to begin paying cash dividends in 2014. Skywalker intends to maintain a dividend payout ratio (cash dividends divided by net income) of 40%. (*Note:* Make sure you adjust your spreadsheet formula so that if net income happens to be negative, cash dividends are no lower than \$0.)

(x) Skywalker has decided to continue its stock repurchase program in 2014. Skywalker intends to spend \$50 repurchasing shares during the year. Skywalker accounts for treasury stock purchases using the cost method.

Clearly state any additional assumptions that you make.

2. According to the forecast for 2014, state whether Skywalker is expected to issue new shares of stock. Would your answer change if Skywalker were not to repurchase the shares as described in (x)?
3. Repeat (2), with the following changes in assumptions:

   (a) The debt ratio in 2014 is exactly equal to 0.70.
   (b) The debt ratio in 2014 is exactly equal to 0.95.

4. Comment on how it is possible for a company to have negative net paid-in capital when net paid-in capital is equal to paid-in capital minus treasury stock.

P3 ADDITIONAL ACTIVITIES OF A BUSINESS

CHAPTER 14 Investments in Debt and Equity Securities

LEARNING OBJECTIVES

1. Determine why companies invest in other companies.
2. Understand the varying classifications associated with investment securities.
3. Account for the purchase of debt and equity securities.
4. Account for the recognition of revenue from investment securities.
5. Account for the change in fair value of investment securities.
6. Account for the sale of investment securities.
7. Record the transfer of investment securities between categories.
8. Properly report purchases, sales, and changes in fair value of investment securities in the statement of cash flows.
9. Explain the proper classification and disclosure of investments in securities.

EM EXPANDED MATERIAL

10. Account for the impairment of a loan receivable.

Many companies invest in other companies. In some cases, the investor may own another company in its entirety; for example, **The Walt Disney Company** owns 100% of the **American Broadcasting Company (ABC)**. In other cases, the investor may own just a portion of another company as is the case with **Berkshire Hathaway**, which owns more than 8% of **The Coca-Cola Company**, 13% of **American Express**, and more than 6% of **Wells Fargo**. In other instances, investors may purchase debt rather than equity interests. Exhibit 14-1 lists selected U.S. companies with investment account balances.

> **FYI**
>
> **Citigroup** is the first company in history to exceed $1 trillion in total assets. As of December 31, 2009, the company reported total assets of $1.857 trillion and total liabilities of $1.702 trillion.

EX 14-1 INVESTMENT IN DEBT AND EQUITY SECURITIES—2009

Company	Total Investments (in billions)	Percentage of Total Assets
Berkshire Hathaway	$126.3	42.5%
Coca-Cola	8.9	18.4%
Microsoft	30.3	38.9%
Citigroup	870.9	46.9%
Verizon	4.0	1.8%

As the exhibit illustrates, company investment in other companies can be quite substantial. Berkshire Hathaway, a company whose major stockholder, Warren Buffett, is the second richest person in America, is a holding company that basically buys ownership in other companies. **Microsoft**, whose major stockholder, Bill Gates, is the richest person in America, makes more money than it can reinvest in its own company. As a result, it invests in other companies, sometimes in order to exercise strategic influence on companies that are developing new technologies. **College Retirement Equities Fund (CREF)** is a company established to assist in the retirement plans for employees of nonprofit educational and research organizations. College professors and others have money withheld from their salaries and forwarded to CREF, which invests that money. As of December 31, 2009, CREF had more than $100 billion, or 99.7% of the company's total assets, invested in the debt and equity securities of other companies. Exhibit 14-2 displays the asset portion of CREF's balance sheet as of December 31, 2009. How do companies like CREF, Berkshire Hathaway, and Microsoft account for their huge investments in securities? That topic is the focus of this chapter.

EX 14-2 COLLEGE RETIREMENT EQUITIES FUND PARTIAL BALANCE SHEET

(In millions)—2009	
Investments	
Portfolio investments	$101,439
Cash	36
Dividends and interest receivable	119
Receivable from securities sold	98
Other	17
TOTAL ASSETS	$101,709

QUESTIONS

1. What is the important difference between Disney's investment in ABC and Berkshire Hathaway's investment in Coca-Cola?
2. What is the important difference between the investing operations of Berkshire Hathaway and the investing operations of Microsoft?
3. Whose money does CREF invest?

Answers to these questions can be found on pages 14-48–14-49.

Accounting for investments in debt and equity securities has generated a great deal of interest for many years. The primary area of concern is the recognition and disclosure of changes in fair value. Because the value of investment securities can change dramatically in a short period of time, accounting information that reflects this change in value is useful to businesses and financial statement users. To address the issue of valuation, the FASB issued pre-Codification *Statement of Financial Accounting Standards No. 115*, "Accounting for Certain Investments in Debt and Equity Securities." The major effect of this standard, issued in 1993, was to require businesses to record many of their investment securities at fair value. This position differs from previous standards in that increases, as well as decreases, in the value of certain securities are reported in the financial statements. The fair value requirements of pre-Codification *SFAS No. 115* were augmented in 2006 by the refined definition of fair value and the increased disclosure requirements included in pre-Codification *Statement of Financial Accounting Standards No. 157*, "Fair Value Measurements." The provisions of both of these standards are now contained in FASB ASC Topic 320 (Investments—Debt and Equity Securities).

In this chapter, we discuss why and how companies invest in other companies. We will also address the accounting issues associated with investments in both debt and equity securities. Accounting for these investments involves several activities. These activities are summarized in Exhibit 14-3. Each of the issues presented in Exhibit 14-3 will be addressed in turn. Following the discussion of these issues, the Expanded Material section of the chapter discusses the accounting for the impairment of a loan receivable.

EX 14-3 TIME LINE OF BUSINESS ISSUES INVOLVED WITH INVESTMENT SECURITIES

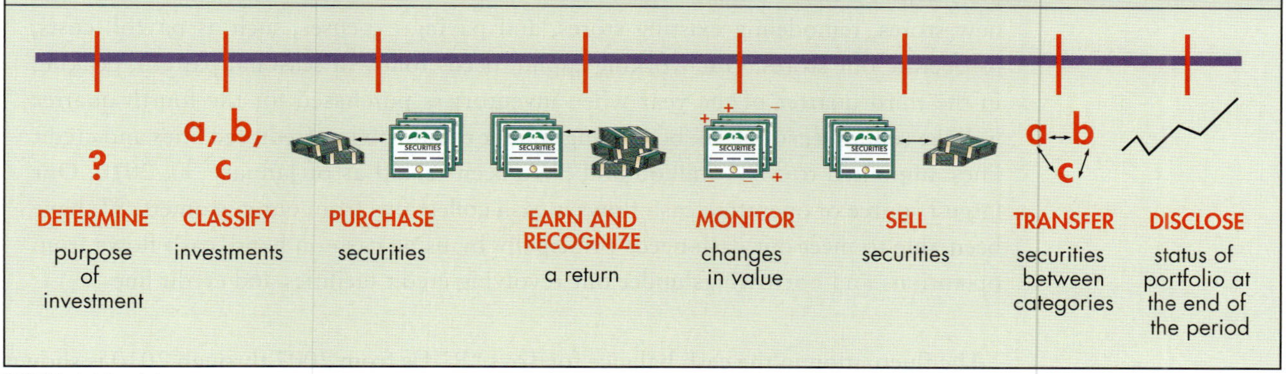

Why Companies Invest in Other Companies

1 **Determine why companies invest in other companies.**

WHY **Proper accounting treatment must incorporate the idea of management intent. In the area of accounting for investments in other companies, management's objective in making an investment impacts how the investment itself and the economic gains and losses from the investment are reported in the financial statements.**

HOW **Sometimes management intent with respect to an investment can be determined through explicit statements by management. In other cases, the nature and size of the investment give an indication of management intent.**

Companies invest in the debt and equity securities of other companies for a host of reasons. Five of the more common reasons are discussed in this section.

Safety Cushion

Microsoft holds more cash and short-term investments than just about any company. As of June 30, 2009, Microsoft reported holding $31.4 billion in cash and short-term investments. Of this amount, only $2.064 billion was actually composed of cash; the remainder was a mixture of certificates of deposit, U.S. Treasury securities, corporate notes and bonds, and other short-term interest-earning securities. In essence, Microsoft has stored a substantial amount of cash in the form of interest-earning loans to banks, governments, and other corporations. In *Time* magazine (January 13, 1997), it was reported that Bill Gates has a rule that Microsoft must always have a large enough liquid investment balance to operate for a year without any revenue. Thus, this large investment balance is a safety cushion to ensure that Microsoft can continue to operate even in the face of extreme adversity. Other companies have much smaller safety cushions, but the general principle is that investments are sometimes made to give a company a ready source of funds on which it can draw when needed.

Cyclical Cash Needs

Some companies operate in seasonal business environments that need cyclical inventory buildups requiring large amounts of cash, followed by lots of sales and cash collections. For example, the following is an excerpt from the January 30, 2010, 10-K filing of **Toys "R" Us**, the large retail toy chain:

> In general, our primary uses of cash are providing for working capital, which principally represents the purchase of inventory, servicing debt, financing construction of new stores, remodeling existing stores, and paying expenses, such as payroll costs, to operate our stores. Our working capital needs follow a seasonal pattern, peaking in the third quarter of the year when inventory is purchased for the fourth quarter holiday selling season. Peak borrowings under our revolving credit facilities and credit lines amounted to $784 million and have been repaid as of January 30, 2010. Our largest source of operating cash flows is cash collections from our customers. We have been able to meet our cash needs principally by using cash on hand, cash flows from operations and borrowings under our revolving credit facilities and credit lines.

The fluctuation in the cash balance for Toys "R" Us from 2007 through 2010 is shown in Exhibit 14-4. During those periods of time when excess cash exists for a company such

EX 14-4 CYCLICAL CASH BALANCE: TOYS "R" US

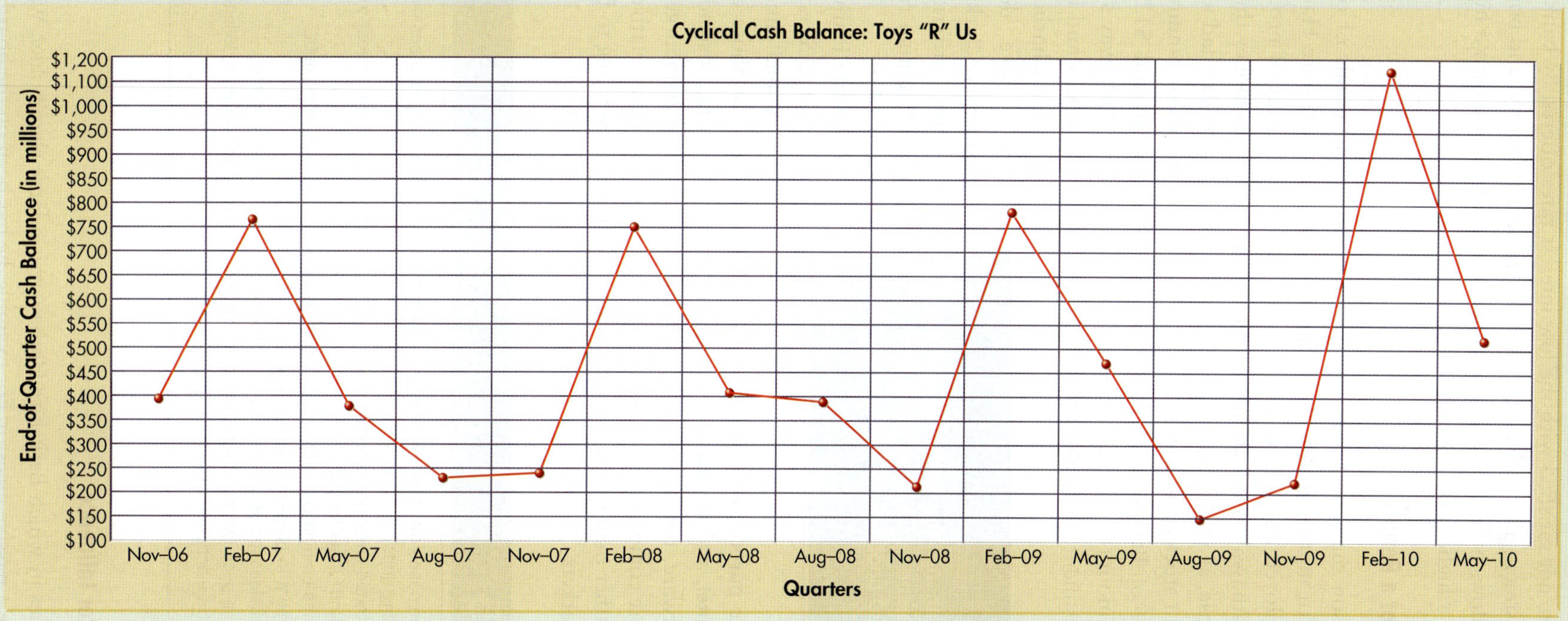

as Toys "R" Us, the company can invest that money and earn a return. Of course, most companies are not satisfied with the low interest rates offered by bank deposits and turn to other investment alternatives. Investing in the stocks (equity) and bonds (debt) of other companies allows a firm to store its cyclical cash surplus and earn a higher rate of return by accepting a higher degree of risk.

Investment for a Return

Another reason that companies invest in the stocks and bonds of other companies is simply to earn money. Although companies owned by Berkshire Hathaway at the end of 2009 employed 257,000 employees who provide a variety of products and services, Berkshire Hathaway is still commonly viewed as making its money through investments. This is because, as of December 31, 2009, Berkshire Hathaway had invested an average of $63,641 in stocks and bonds for each ownership share outstanding. In other words, with a share of Berkshire Hathaway stock selling for around $120,000, more than half of the amount required to buy a share of Berkshire Hathaway stock represents an indirect investment, through Berkshire Hathaway, in the stocks and bonds that Warren Buffett and Charlie Munger (Buffett's partner) have decided are good investments. Berkshire Hathaway's investment criteria, reprinted from the 2009 annual report, are listed in Exhibit 14-5.

> **FYI**
>
> Warren Buffett is proud that although the Berkshire Hathaway headquarters staff must oversee an empire that employs 257,000 people, only about 20 people work in the corporate offices.

Berkshire Hathaway is the exception; most U.S. corporations engage in only a small amount of investment solely for the purpose of earning a return. This is so because those companies, such as Microsoft, **Intel**, and **McDonald's**, are not experts in investing. Instead, they are good at creating software, developing computer chips, and selling hamburgers. Thus, it makes sense for those companies to concentrate on operating decisions relative to their respective businesses rather than to spend management's valuable time trying to figure out the stock and bond markets.

EX 14-5 BERKSHIRE HATHAWAY INC. ACQUISITION CRITERIA

1. Large purchases (at least $75 million of pre-tax earnings unless the business will fit into one of our existing units),
2. Demonstrated consistent earning power (future projections are of *no* interest to us, nor are "turnaround" situations),
3. Businesses earning good returns on equity while employing little or no debt,
4. Management in place (we can't supply it),
5. Simple businesses (if there's lots of technology, we won't understand it),
6. An offering price (we don't want to waste our time or that of the seller by talking, even preliminarily, about a transaction when price is unknown).

Investment for Influence

For companies in which Berkshire Hathaway is a large shareholder, Warren Buffett is not content to be a passive investor. For example, he has been on the board of directors of The Coca-Cola Company, **The Gillette Company**, and **The Washington Post Company**. In general,

EX 14-6 THE COCA-COLA COMPANY'S OWNERSHIP PERCENTAGE OF MAJOR BOTTLERS OF ITS PRODUCTS

Bottler	Location	Coca-Cola's Ownership Percentage
Coca-Cola Enterprises	United States, Canada, and Great Britain (largest bottler of Coca-Cola products in the world)	34%
Coca-Cola Amatil	Australia, New Zealand, and Pacific Islands	30
Coca-Cola FEMSA	Mexico, Central and South America	32
Coca-Cola Hellenic Bottling Company	Europe (primarily eastern)	23

companies can invest in other companies for many reasons other than to earn a return. Some reasons are to ensure a supply of raw materials, to influence the board of directors, or to diversify product offerings. For example, Coca-Cola historically has not bottled its own soft drinks; those bottling franchises are owned by independent bottlers all over the world. However, to ensure that the bottling segment of the soft drink supply chain remains predictably open to Coca-Cola, Coca-Cola owns sizable portions of a number of the major bottlers of its soft drinks. Some of these bottlers, their location, and Coca-Cola's ownership percentage are listed in Exhibit 14-6.[1]

To summarize, large investments in other companies are often made for business reasons such as to be able to exercise influence over the conduct of that company's operations.

Purchase for Control

Warren Buffett first invested in **GEICO** insurance in 1951, soon after graduating from Columbia. He describes the company as his "first business love," partly stemming from his admiration of its basic strategy of being the low-cost provider of a necessary product. In 1976, Buffett decided that Berkshire Hathaway should buy a large number of GEICO shares. At the beginning of 1995, Berkshire Hathaway owned almost 50% of GEICO and obviously exercised significant influence over the operation of the company. In 1995, Buffett decided to buy the remaining shares of GEICO, making GEICO a wholly owned subsidiary of Berkshire Hathaway.

STOP&THINK

As of December 31, 2009, **Ford Motor** owned 11% of **Mazda**. Which ONE of the following possible motivations do you think is the primary motivation for this investment by Ford?

a) Safety cushion
b) Cyclical cash needs
c) Investment for a return
d) Investment for influence

When a company purchases enough of another company to be able to control operating, investing, and financing decisions, different accounting treatment is required for that acquisition. For accounting purposes, a parent company is required to report the results

[1] In February 2010, Coca-Cola announced that it intended to purchase the North American operations of its largest bottler, Coca-Cola Enterprises. Coca-Cola's announced intention for the acquisition is to create operational efficiencies and to increase its control of its product's bottling in the key North American market.

of all of its subsidiaries of which it owns more than 50% as if the parent and subsidiaries were one company. For example, Berkshire Hathaway has a controlling interest in a host of different subsidiaries incorporated in many different states and countries scattered from Omaha, Nebraska, to Cologne, Germany. The financial performances of these subsidiaries are included in the financial statements of Berkshire Hathaway. This is the reason the financial statements of most large corporations are called *consolidated financial statements*: They include aggregated, or consolidated, results for both the parent and all of its majority-owned subsidiaries.

Classification of Investment Securities

2 Understand the varying classifications associated with investment securities.

WHY **Investment securities are classified based on management's intent in holding the securities. How the securities are classified will influence how the securities are accounted for, the resulting financial statement numbers, and the financial ratios computed using those numbers.**

HOW **Based on management intent, investment securities are classified as either equity method, trading, available-for-sale, or held-to-maturity securities.**

As mentioned previously, FASB ASC Topic 320 addresses the valuation of securities. The statement applies to all debt securities and to equity securities for which a readily determinable fair value is available.[2] If, however, the investment in equity securities of a company is large enough, a different method of accounting (called the "equity method") for equity securities is applied.

Before we discuss the various classifications of securities under the provisions of Topic 320, let's first review what debt and equity securities are.

Debt Securities

From Chapter 12 you will recall that debt securities are financial instruments issued by a company that typically have the following characteristics: (1) a maturity value representing the amount to be repaid to the debt holder at maturity, (2) an interest rate (either fixed or variable) that specifies the periodic interest payments, and (3) a maturity date indicating when the debt obligation will be redeemed.

Equity Securities

Equity securities represent ownership in a company. These shares of stock typically carry with them the right to collect dividends and to vote on corporate matters. In addition, equity securities are an attractive investment because of the potential for significant increases in the price of the security. Features of equity securities were covered in detail in Chapter 13.

Sophisticated trading markets for both debt and equity securities have developed over time, with the New York Stock Exchange, the New York Bond Exchange, and NASDAQ being the premier trading exchanges for stocks and bonds.

[2] FASB ASC paragraph 320-10-15-5.

EX 14-7 CLASSIFICATIONS OF DEBT AND EQUITY SECURITIES

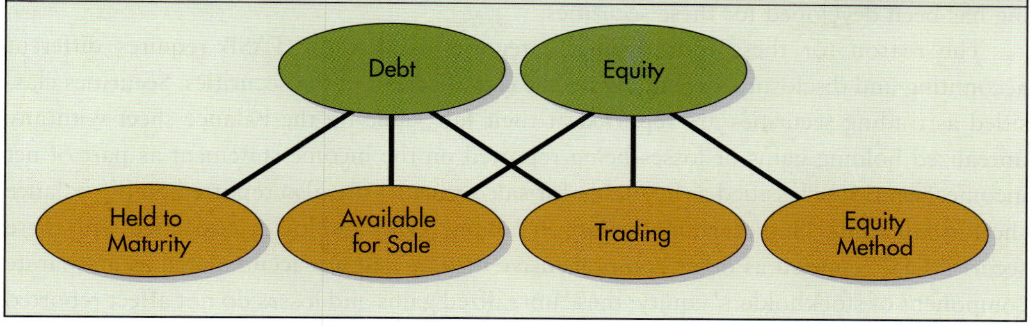

For accounting purposes, debt and equity securities falling under the scope of FASB ASC Topic 320 can be classified into one of four categories: held to maturity, available for sale, trading, and equity method. Exhibit 14-7 illustrates the major classifications of debt and equity securities.

Held-to-Maturity Securities

Held-to-maturity securities are debt securities purchased by a company with the intent and ability to hold those securities until they mature.[3] Note that this category includes only debt securities because equity securities typically do not mature. Note also that the company must have the intention of holding the security until it matures. Simply intending to hold a security for a long period of time does not qualify for inclusion in this category.

Available-for-Sale Securities

Debt securities that are not being held until maturity and are not classified as trading securities are considered, by default, to be "available-for-sale" securities.[4] Available-for-sale securities are also equity securities that are not considered trading securities and are not accounted for using the equity method. Most of the typical company's investment securities are classified as available for sale. This is because the typical company uses its investment securities as a store of excess cash and is not actively managing the investment portfolio to make profits on stock trading.

Trading Securities

Trading securities are debt and equity securities purchased with the intent of selling them in the near future. Trading involves frequent buying and selling of securities, generally for the purpose of "generating profits on short-term differences in price."[5]

Equity Method Securities

Equity method securities are equity securities purchased with the intent of being able to control or significantly influence the operations of the investee. As a result, a large block of stock (presumed to be at least 20% of the outstanding stock unless there exists evidence to the contrary) must be owned to be classified as an equity method security.[6] Because the

[3] FASB ASC paragraph 320-10-25-1c.
[4] FASB ASC paragraph 320-10-25-1b.
[5] FASB ASC paragraph 320-10-25-1a.
[6] FASB ASC paragraph 323-10-15-8.

intent associated with these securities is not simply to earn a return on an investment but includes being able to affect the operations of the investee, a different method of accounting has been developed for these securities.

The reason for these four distinct categories is that the FASB requires different accounting and disclosure, depending on the classification of the securities. Securities classified as trading securities are reported at their fair value on the balance sheet with any unrealized holding gains or losses being reported on the income statement as part of net income. Securities classified as available-for-sale securities are also reported on the balance sheet at fair value. However, any unrealized holding gains and losses associated with these securities are reported as other comprehensive income and are accumulated as a separate component of stockholders' equity; these unrealized gains and losses do not affect reported net income for the period. Held-to-maturity securities are reported on the balance sheet at their amortized cost and are not reported at fair value. The accounting for held-to-maturity securities is generally the mirror image of the accounting by an issuer of long-term debt as discussed in Chapter 12. Equity method securities are not reported at their fair value on the balance sheet. Instead, the investment account is increased or decreased as the net assets of the investee increase and decrease. Exhibit 14-8 summarizes the accounting treatment for debt and equity securities.

Why the Different Categories?

Why does the FASB have these different categories for classifying securities? Why didn't they just make the rule that all increases and decreases in fair value go on the income statement? If you think about the classification scheme, it makes a lot of sense. Take, for example, held-to-maturity securities. Companies plan on holding these securities until they mature (hence the name). The company has no intention of realizing any changes in fair value on these securities between the purchase date and the maturity date, so there is no reason to recognize any changes in fair value prior to the maturity date. Similarly, companies hold equity method securities not to realize changes in the fair value of those securities but to maintain some level of influence over the investee. Thus, the fair value of the investment is not of primary importance to the investor. In summary, because appreciation in price is not a major reason for holding held-to-maturity and equity method securities, adjustments for temporary changes in fair value are not required.

Trading securities are purchased with the intent of realizing profits in the short term. Thus, changes in fair value are recorded in the period in which they occur, whether that change has been realized through an arm's-length transaction or not. Because an unrealized gain (or loss) can be turned into a realized gain (or loss) with a simple phone call to a

EX 14-8 THE DIFFERENT ACCOUNTING TREATMENTS FOR DEBT AND EQUITY SECURITIES

Classification of Securities	Types of Securities	Disclosure on the Balance Sheet	Treatment of Temporary Changes in Fair Value
Held to maturity	Debt	Amortized cost	Not recognized
Available for sale	Debt and equity	Fair value	Reported in stockholders' equity
Trading	Debt and equity	Fair value	Reported on the income statement
Equity method	Equity	Historical cost adjusted for changes in the net assets of the investee	Not recognized

portfolio manager, it makes sense to include the change in fair value on the income statement of the period in which the change occurs.

> **FYI**
>
> Who decides how a security is to be classified? Management does. Management's intent is the key factor in determining the reasons for holding certain securities. As you can guess, judgment plays a significant role in this classification.

What about available-for-sale securities? Why not treat increases and decreases in fair value on this type of security similar to the treatment for trading securities? The answer lies in the probability of realizing those changes in fair value. With trading securities, it is likely that those changes in fair value will be realized sooner rather than later; that is the reason they are called *trading securities*. The same likelihood of realization is not as certain with available-for-sale securities. Because it is less certain that the changes in fair value of available-for-sale securities will actually be realized in the current period, the FASB elected to bypass the income statement and require these increases in value to be reported directly in the Stockholders' Equity section of the balance sheet as part of Accumulated Other Comprehensive Income. In addition, although these unrealized gains and losses are excluded from net income, they are included in the computation of comprehensive income. Because available-for-sale securities are not purchased with the primary intent of making money on short-term price fluctuations, it seems reasonable to exclude unrealized gains and losses on these securities from the computation of the periodic net income.

The Fair Value Option

As explained in Chapter 12, in 2007 the FASB took a bold step toward increased use of fair value by allowing companies a fair value option for the reporting of financial assets and liabilities.[7] Under the fair value option, a company has the option to report, at each balance sheet date, any or all of its financial assets and liabilities at their fair values on the balance sheet date. The unrealized gains and losses from changes in the fair values of financial assets and liabilities accounted for using the fair value option are reported in the income statement. As illustrated in Chapter 12, this fair value option allows companies to reflect in the income statement, without complicated hedge accounting procedures, the offsetting economic effects of the hedging of corresponding financial assets and liabilities.

The election of this fair value option for an investment security trumps the classification of the security as described above (trading, available for sale, held to maturity, and equity method). Accordingly, even though a security is classified as available for sale, if the company elects the fair value option for that security then the unrealized gains and losses are included in earnings in the income statement rather than in other comprehensive income as is typically required for available-for-sale securities. Similarly, equity method or held-to-maturity securities, which typically are NOT reported in the balance sheet at fair value, are reported at fair value if the company has elected the fair value option with respect to those particular securities. In essence, all investment securities for which the fair value option is elected are accounted for in the same way as the trading security accounting illustrated later in the chapter.

[7] *Pre-Codification Statement of Financial Accounting Standards No. 159*, "The Fair Value Option for Financial Assets and Financial Liabilities—Including an Amendment of FASB Statement No. 115" (Norwalk, CT: Financial Accounting Standards Board, February 2007). This guidance is now found in the "Fair Value Option" subsections of FASB ASC Topic 825 (Financial Instruments).

Classification of Investment Securities According to IFRS

ifrs

The classification of investment securities under International Financial Reporting Standards, specifically *IFRS 9*, is very similar to the classification categories under U.S. GAAP. In fact, it is apparent that *IFRS* has been heavily influenced by pre-Codification *SFAS No. 115* (adopted in 1993 and now included in Topic 320). The same categories of trading, available-for-sale, and held-to-maturity investments exist. Under IFRS, the available-for-sale category exists but is typically referred to by a description rather than a label.

The fair value option for financial assets, as described above, also exists in IFRS under the provisions of IFRS 9.[8] In fact, Sir David Tweedie, the chairman of the IASB, has stated several times that he thinks that the perfect accounting standard for the accounting for all investment securities would consist of just two paragraphs. The first paragraph would say that *all* investment securities should be reported on the balance sheet at fair value, with unrealized gains and losses from changes in fair value to be reported through "profit and loss" (the income statement); this is the fair value option comprehensively applied to all investment securities. The second paragraph of this perfect accounting standard would say: "Reread Paragraph 1."

Purchase of Securities

3 **Account for the purchase of debt and equity securities.**

WHY **As with any other asset, the original cost of investment securities must be recognized when the securities are acquired.**

HOW **Debt and equity securities are accounted for at acquisition cost. For debt securities, this cost must be adjusted for accrued interest imbedded in the purchase price.**

The purchase of debt and equity securities is recorded at cost just like the purchase of any other asset. But because debt securities are bought and sold between interest payment dates, accounting for the amount of accrued interest since the last payment date adds a minor complexity.

Purchase of Debt Securities

The purchase of debt securities is recorded at cost, which includes brokerage fees, taxes, and other charges incurred in their acquisition. When debt securities are acquired between interest payment dates, the amount paid for the securities is increased by a charge for accrued interest to the date of purchase. This charge should not be reported as part of the investment cost. Two assets have been acquired—the security and the accrued interest receivable—and should be reported in two separate asset accounts. Upon receipt of the interest, Interest Receivable is closed and Interest Revenue is credited for the amount of interest earned since the purchase date. Instead of recording the interest as a receivable (asset approach), Interest Revenue may be debited for the accrued interest paid at the time of purchase. The subsequent collection of interest would then be credited in full to Interest Revenue. The latter procedure (revenue approach) is usually more convenient.

[8] Initially, the fair value option under IFRS has applied only to financial assets. In May 2010, the IASB released an exposure draft proposing extension of the fair value option to financial liabilities.

To illustrate the entries for the acquisition of debt securities, assume that $100,000 in U.S. Treasury notes are purchased at 104¼ (debt securities are normally quoted at a price per $100 face value) on May 1. Interest is 9% payable semiannually on January 1 and July 1. Accrued interest of $3,000 would thus be added to the purchase price. The debt securities are classified by the purchaser as trading securities because management will sell the securities if a change in the price will result in a profit. The entries to record the purchase of the notes and the subsequent collection of interest under the alternate procedures would be as follows:

Asset Approach

May 1	Investment in Trading Securities	104,250	
	Interest Receivable	3,000	
	Cash		107,250
July 1	Cash	4,500	
	Interest Receivable		3,000
	Interest Revenue		1,500

Revenue Approach

May 1	Investment in Trading Securities	104,250	
	Interest Revenue	3,000	
	Cash		107,250
July 1	Cash	4,500	
	Interest Revenue		4,500

The important point is that under either approach, the interest revenue recognized for the period is equal to the interest earned, not the amount received. In this case, the company earned $1,500, representing interest for the period May 1 to June 30.

Purchase of Equity Securities

Shares of stock are usually purchased for cash through stock exchanges (e.g., New York, NASDAQ, or regional exchanges) and from individuals and institutional investors rather than from the corporations themselves. The investment is recorded at the amount paid, including brokers' commissions, taxes, and other fees incidental to the purchase price. Even when part of the purchase price is deferred, the full cost should be recorded as the investment in stock, with a liability account established for the amount yet to be paid. If stock is acquired in exchange for properties or services instead of cash, the fair value of the consideration given or the value at which the stock is currently selling, whichever is more clearly determinable, should be used as the basis for recording the investment. If two or more securities are acquired for a lump-sum price, the cost should be allocated to each security in an equitable manner, as illustrated in Chapter 10 with the basket purchase of long-term operating assets.

Ryan McVay/Photodisc/Getty Images

Stock purchased for cash through stock exchanges is recorded at the amount paid, including brokers' commissions, taxes, and other fees at the amount paid.

To illustrate the accounting for the purchase of equity securities, assume that Gondor Enterprises purchased 300 shares of Boromir Co. stock at $75 per share and 500 shares of Faramir Inc. stock at $50 per share. Gondor classifies the Boromir stock as a trading security because management has no intention of holding these securities for a long period of time and will sell them as soon as it is economically advantageous for the company. The Faramir stock is classified as available for sale.[9] The journal entry to record the purchases would be as follows:

Investment in Trading Securities—Boromir Co.	22,500*	
Investment in Available-for-Sale Securities—Faramir Inc.	25,000†	
Cash		47,500

Computations:

*300 × $75 = $22,500

†500 × $50 = $25,000

Recognition of Revenue from Investment Securities

4 Account for the recognition of revenue from investment securities.

WHY **In order to properly characterize the performance of different types of investment securities, revenue from investment securities must be carefully computed and labeled.**

HOW **For trading and available-for-sale debt securities, the amount of interest revenue is a function of the stated rate of interest on those debt securities. In the case of held-to-maturity securities, any premium or discount associated with the initial purchase must be amortized and included in the computation of interest revenue. For equity securities classified as trading or available for sale, dividends declared by the investee are recorded as revenue. If an investment is accounted for using the equity method, the amount of revenue recognized by the investor is a function of the income earned by the investee and the percentage of ownership of the investor.**

A primary reason that companies invest in the debt or equity securities of other companies is to earn a return in the form of either interest or dividends. In the case of debt securities, the computation of that return is complicated because a difference often exists between the purchase price and the maturity value of the debt instrument. The resulting premium or discount can affect the amount of interest revenue recognized in each future period—depending on how the securities are classified when purchased. For equity securities, the recognition of revenue from an investment depends on the level of ownership in the investee. Each of these issues is discussed in the following sections.

Recognition of Revenue from Debt Securities

Recall from Chapter 12 that debt securities carry with them a stated rate of interest that when multiplied by the maturity value of the securities indicates the amount of cash to be received in interest each year. Often, interest is received on a semiannual basis. When interest is received, Cash is debited and Interest Revenue is credited. However, when debt securities are acquired at a higher or lower price than their maturity value and the debt securities are classified as held to maturity, periodic amortization of the premium or accumulation

[9] Historically, brokerage fees and other costs involved with purchasing investment securities have been included in the initial recorded cost of the securities. However, for securities accounted for using the fair value option, brokerage fees and other upfront costs are to be expensed when incurred; see FASB ASC paragraph 825-10-25-3. This immediate expensing of upfront fees also applies to trading securities. The historical approach of including upfront fees as part of the initial recorded amount for the securities still applies to available-for-sale and held-to-maturity securities; see FASB ASC paragraphs 310-20-15-2 through 4.

of the discount with corresponding adjustments to interest revenue is required. One could amortize a premium or discount associated with trading or available-for-sale securities. But recall that one of the primary reasons for this amortization process is to ensure that the carrying value of held-to-maturity securities is equal to its maturity value on the maturity date. If securities are not classified as being held to maturity, the amortization process becomes less relevant.[10]

As explained in Chapter 12, a premium or discount results when the stated rate of interest and the market rate of interest on the date of acquisition of the debt security are different. If the stated rate of interest is higher than the prevailing market rate, investors will pay a higher price for the debt security (a premium) to receive the higher interest payments. When the market rate of interest is higher than the stated rate, investors will pay less than the face amount of the debt security, resulting in a discount.

FYI

You will need to be comfortable with present value computations if you are to understand the calculations that follow. The Time Value of Money Review module contains an overview of the time value of money.

The present value computations associated with computing the value of a debt security were illustrated in Chapter 12 and an example is included here. Assume that on January 1, 2012, Silmaril Technologies purchased 5-year, 10% bonds with a face value of $100,000 and interest payable semiannually on January 1 and July 1. The market rate on bonds of similar quality and maturity is 8%. Silmaril computes the market price of the bonds as follows:

Present value of principal:		
Maturity value of bonds after 5 years	$100,000	
Present value of $100,000: *FV* = $100,000; *N* = 10; *I* = 4%		$ 67,556
Present value of interest payments:		
Semiannual payment, 5% of $100,000	$ 5,000	
Present value of 10 payments of $5,000: *PMT* = $5,000; *N* = 10; *I* = 4%		40,554
Total present value (market price) of the bonds (rounded)		$108,110

We will use two examples to illustrate the accounting for interest revenue. First, we will assume that Silmaril intends to take advantage of short-term price fluctuations (thereby making them trading securities), and second, we will assume that Silmaril intends, and has the ability, to hold the bonds until they mature (making them held-to-maturity securities).

Interest Revenue for Debt Securities Classified as Trading Recall from Chapter 12 that the investor typically does not use a premium or discount account but instead records the investment at cost and nets the face value and any premium or discount. Silmaril would make the following journal entry to record the initial purchase of the bonds:[11]

Investment in Trading Securities	108,110	
Cash		108,110

When interest payments are received, the journal entry to record their receipt would be

Cash	5,000	
Interest Revenue		5,000

[10] In all examples that follow as well as in the end-of-chapter material, we will assume that premiums and discounts associated only with held-to-maturity securities are amortized.

[11] The journal entries would be similar had the security been classified as available for sale. The only difference would be in the account title.

Interest Revenue for Debt Securities Classified as Held to Maturity The entry to record the initial purchase of the bonds had they been originally classified as held to maturity would be

Investment in Held-to-Maturity Securities	108,110	
Cash		108,110

To determine the amount of premium to amortize each period, Silmaril would prepare an amortization table, as illustrated. This table is based on the effective-interest method of amortization.[12]

Amortization of Bond Premium—Effective-Interest Method
$100,000, 5-Year Bonds, Interest at 10% Payable Semiannually,
Sold at $108,110 to Yield 8% Compounded Semiannually

Interest Payment	A Interest Received (0.05 × $100,000)	B Interest Revenue (0.04 × Bond Carrying Value)	C Premium Amortization (A − B)	D Unamortized Premium (D − C)	Bond Carrying Value ($100,000 + D)
				$8,110	$108,110
1	$5,000	$4,324	$676	7,434	107,434
2	5,000	4,297	703	6,731	106,731
3	5,000	4,269	731	6,000	106,000
4	5,000	4,240	760	5,240	105,240
5	5,000	4,210	790	4,450	104,450
6	5,000	4,178	822	3,628	103,628
7	5,000	4,145	855	2,773	102,773
8	5,000	4,111	889	1,884	101,884
9	5,000	4,075	925	959	100,959
10	5,000	4,041*	959	0	100,000

*Rounding differences are adjusted with last entry.

STOP&THINK

Theoretically, we should amortize the discount or premium associated with trading and available-for-sale debt securities just as we do with held-to-maturity securities. In this simple example, why don't we?

a) Both trading and available-for-sale debt securities are adjusted to fair value at the end of each reporting period.
b) Most U.S. companies don't hold any trading or available-for-sale debt securities.
c) Neither trading nor available-for-sale debt securities are ever sold at premiums or discounts to face value.
d) Companies avoid amortizing discounts and premiums on trading and available-for-sale debt securities for income tax reasons.

When the first interest payment of $5,000 is received from the bond issuer, Silmaril would make the following journal entry:

Cash	5,000	
Interest Revenue		4,324
Investment in Held-to-Maturity Securities		676

Subsequent receipts of interest would be recorded with a similar journal entry, the only difference being that the amount amortized would differ, depending on which interest payment was received.

[12] As explained in Chapter 12, the straight-line method of interest amortization can be used when the results do not differ materially from effective-interest amortization. However, in all the examples that follow as well as in the end-of-chapter material, we will use the effective-interest method.

Recognition of Revenue from Equity Securities

Once an equity security is purchased, one of two basic methods must be used to account for the revenue earned on that investment depending on the control or degree of influence exercised by the acquiring company (investor) over the acquired company (investee). In those instances where the level of ownership in the investee is such that the investor is able to control or significantly influence decisions made by the investee, the use of the equity method is appropriate. The accounting procedures associated with the equity method are outlined in FASB ASC Topic 323 (Investments—Equity Method and Joint Ventures). When the acquiring company does not exercise significant influence over the investee, the equity securities are classified as trading or available-for-sale securities.

The ability of the investor to exercise significant influence over such decisions as dividend distribution and operational and financial administration may be indicated in several ways: representation on the investee's board of directors, participation in policy-making processes, material intercompany transactions, interchange of managerial personnel, or technological dependency of investee on investor. Another important consideration is the extent of ownership by an investor in relation to the concentration of other stockholdings. While it is clear that ownership of more than 50% of common stock virtually assures control by the acquiring company, ownership of 50% or less may give effective control if the remaining shares of the stock are widely held and no significant blocks of stockholders are consistently united in their ownership. The FASB recognizes that the degree of influence and control will not always be clear and that judgment will be required in assessing the status of each investment. To achieve a reasonable degree of uniformity in the application of its position, the FASB has set 20% as an ownership standard; the ownership of 20% or more of the voting stock of the company carries the presumption, in the absence of evidence to the contrary, that an investor has the ability to exercise significant influence over that company. Conversely, ownership of less than 20% leads to the presumption that the investor does not have the ability to exercise significant influence unless such ability can be demonstrated.[13] Again, the 20% criterion is only a guideline, and judgment is required in determining the appropriate accounting method in cases where ownership is 50% or less.[14]

Both the FASB and the IASB are currently deliberating the issue of control in the context of whether a sizeable equity investment should be accounted for using the equity method (which is illustrated in this chapter) or consolidation (which is outside the scope of this book). In their discussions of control, the FASB and IASB have described control as the power to direct the affairs of another company to the extent that profits or returns of that company are significantly affected. The current thinking of the FASB and the IASB is that one company has control over another when it has more than half of the voting rights, when it possesses substantive contractual control of key activities, or when it has a large minority voting interest in the election of the Board of Directors and no other party or organized group of parties has a significant voting interest. Thus, one company could be classified as "controlling" another with less than 50% ownership. For example, Coca-Cola might be classified as controlling the bottling subsidiaries listed in Exhibit 14-6. As of 2010, the FASB and IASB were still considering this area. The existing standard is that control exists when one company owns more than 50% of another.

[13] FASB ASC paragraphs 322-10-15-6 through 8.
[14] FASB ASC paragraph 323-10-15-10.

Until the FASB provides a definitive standard addressing the issue of control, the percentage-of-ownership criterion is widely accepted as the basis for determining the appropriate method of accounting for long-term investments in equity securities when the investor does not possess absolute voting control. If it is determined that control exists, the combined financial results are reported in consolidated financial statements. If significant influence exists, the equity method of accounting is applied to the investment. If not, then the securities are classified as either trading or available for sale. Note that because preferred stock is generally nonvoting stock and does not provide for significant influence, it is always classified as either trading or available for sale.

In the case of consolidation, the investor and investee are referred to respectively as the parent company and the subsidiary company. Where control exists, preparation of consolidated financial statements is required. This means that the financial statement balances of the parent and subsidiary companies are combined, or consolidated, for financial reporting purposes even though the companies continue to operate as separate entities. In the consolidation process, any intercompany transactions are eliminated, for example, any sales and purchases between the parent and subsidiary companies. By eliminating all intercompany transactions, the combined balances or consolidated totals appropriately reflect the financial position and results of operation of the total economic unit. This treatment reflects the fact that majority ownership of common stock assures control by the parent over the decision-making processes of the subsidiary. The important point is this: The process of consolidation builds on the journal entries made when the equity method is applied. In fact, the equity method of accounting is often referred to as a "one-line consolidation." Coca-Cola provides an example of an instance where the company owned a greater than 50% interest in a subsidiary and yet did not prepare consolidated financial statements for the subsidiary. Recall from our previous discussion of acquiring companies for influence that Coca-Cola owned 30% of Coca-Cola Amatil, an Australian-based bottler. In past years, Coca-Cola's ownership interest in Coca-Cola Amatil exceeded 50%, yet the company did not consolidate. The reason Coca-Cola did not consolidate was that, as the company indicated in the notes to its financial statements, its control was considered temporary.

> **FYI**
>
> Remember, consolidation is not an alternative to the equity method. It constitutes procedures employed in addition to those used with the equity method.

Previous accounting standards allowed separate reporting for certain majority-owned subsidiaries if those subsidiaries had "nonhomogeneous" operations, a large minority interest, or a foreign location. Separate reporting by subsidiaries occurred most often when the operations of the subsidiary and parent were significantly different (i.e., nonhomogeneous). Typically, the subsidiary was engaged in finance, insurance, leasing, or real estate, while the parent company was a manufacturer or merchandiser. Examples include **General Electric Capital Services (GECS)** and **IBM Credit Corporation**, which are finance companies that are wholly owned by **General Electric** and **IBM**, respectively. Traditionally, the financial statements of these subsidiaries were not consolidated with those of their respective parent companies.

Since the issuance of pre-Codification *Statement of Financial Accounting Standards No. 94*, the FASB has required the consolidation of all majority-owned subsidiaries unless control is temporary or does not rest with the majority owner (as, for instance, when the subsidiary is in legal reorganization or in bankruptcy) and is considering expanding the concept of control to encourage the consolidation of subsidiaries for which a parent

EX 14-9 EFFECT OF OWNERSHIP INTEREST AND CONTROL OR INFLUENCE ON ACCOUNTING FOR LONG-TERM INVESTMENTS IN COMMON STOCKS

Ownership Interest	Control or Degree of Influence	Accounting Method	Applicable Standard
More than 50%	Control	Equity method and consolidation procedures	FASB ASC *Topic 810*
20 to 50%	Significant influence	Equity method	FASB ASC *Topic 323*
Less than 20%	No significant influence	Account for as trading or available for sale	FASB ASC *Topic 320*

company has control even with a less-than-majority ownership interest.[15] Thus, even though a subsidiary has nonhomogeneous operations, a large minority interest, or a foreign location, it should be consolidated. The reporting entity is to be the total economic unit consisting of the parent and all of its subsidiaries.

To summarize, in the absence of persuasive evidence to the contrary, equity securities are classified as trading or available for sale when ownership is less than 20%; the equity method is used when ownership is such that the investor has the ability to significantly influence or control the investee's operations; in those instances where control is deemed to exist, the equity method, along with additional consolidation procedures, is used. These relationships dealing with the effect of ownership interest and control or influence and the proper accounting method to be used are summarized in Exhibit 14-9. Note that the percentages are given only as guidelines. Subjective assessment of the ability of an investor to influence or control an investee should also be considered when determining the appropriate accounting for the investment.

We will first discuss and illustrate the accounting and reporting issues associated with the recognition of revenue on trading and available-for-sale equity securities. The more complex equity method will then be discussed.

Revenue for Equity Securities Classified as Trading and Available for Sale When an investment in another company's stock does not involve either a controlling interest or significant influence, it is classified as either trading or available for sale. Recall that equity securities cannot be classified as held to maturity. Revenue is recognized when dividends are declared (if the investor knows about the declaration) or when the dividends are received from the investee. Continuing a previous example, assume that Gondor Enterprises receives the following dividends from its investees:

Company	Classification	Number of Shares Held	Dividends Received per Share
Boromir Co.	Trading securities	300	$2.00
Faramir Inc.	Available-for-sale securities	500	3.75

The journal entry to record receipt of the dividends would be:

Cash	2,475*	
Dividend Revenue		2,475

*[(300 × $2.00) + (500 × $3.75) = $2,475]

[15] Pre-Codification *Statement of Financial Accounting Standards No. 94,* "Consolidation of All Majority-Owned Subsidiaries" (Stamford, CT: Financial Accounting Standards Board, 1987).

Revenue for Securities Classified as Equity Method Securities The equity method of accounting for long-term investments in common stock reflects the economic substance of the relationship between the investor and investee rather than the legal distinction of the separate entities. The objective of this method is to reflect the underlying claim by the investor on the net assets of the investee company.

Under the equity method, the investment is initially recorded at cost, just as any other investment. However, with the equity method, the investment account is periodically adjusted to reflect changes in the underlying net assets of the investee. The investment balance is increased to reflect a proportionate share of the earnings of the investee company or decreased to reflect a share of any losses reported. If preferred stock dividends have been declared by the investee, they must be deducted from income reported by the investee before computing the investor's share of investee earnings or losses. When dividends are received by the investor, the investment account is reduced. Thus, the equity method results in an increase in the investment account when the investee's net assets increase; similarly, the investment account decreases when the investee records a loss or pays out dividends.

We will illustrate the equity method with a simple example. Assume that BioTech Inc. purchased 40% of the outstanding stock of Medco Enterprises on January 1 of the current year by paying $200,000. During the year, Medco reported net income of $50,000 and paid dividends of $10,000. BioTech would make the following journal entries during the year:

Investment in Medco Enterprises Stock	200,000	
Cash		200,000
To record the purchase of 40% of Medco stock.		
Investment in Medco Enterprises Stock	20,000	
Income from Investment in Medco Enterprises Stock ($50,000 × 0.40)		20,000
To record the recognition of revenue from investment in Medco.		
Cash ($10,000 × 0.40)	4,000	
Investment in Medco Enterprises Stock		4,000
To record the receipt of a dividend on Medco stock.		

Notice that Medco Enterprises' book value increased by $40,000 during the year ($50,000 in income less $10,000 dividend). BioTech's investment in Medco increased by 40% of this amount ($16,000 = $20,000 − $4,000). The equity method of accounting maintains a relationship between the book value of the investee and the investment account on the books of the investor. As the subsidiary's book value changes, so does the investment account on the books of the parent company.

Comparing the Provisions of FASB ASC Topics 320 and 323 To contrast and illustrate the accounting entries under various methods, assume that Powell Corporation purchases 5,000 shares of San Juan Company common stock on January 2 at $20 per share, including commissions and other costs. San Juan has a total of 25,000 shares outstanding; thus, the 5,000 shares represent a 20% ownership interest. We will illustrate the accounting differences in revenue recognition for equity securities by assuming that (1) the securities are classified as available for sale and (2) the securities are classified as equity method securities and accounted for using the equity method. The appropriate entries under both assumptions are shown in Exhibit 14-10. The actual method used would depend on the degree of influence exercised by the investor as indicated by a consideration of all relevant factors, as well as the percentage owned. Exhibit 14-10 highlights the basic differences in accounting for investments using FASB ASC Topics 320 (on standard investments in debt and equity securities) and 323 (on the equity method used when an investment is made in order to create significant influence). Under both methods, the investment is originally

EX 14-10 JOURNAL ENTRIES TO RECORD REVENUE RECOGNITION USING FASB ASC TOPICS 320 AND 323

Available for Sale (Topic 320)			**Equity Method (Topic 323)**		
Jan. 2 Purchased 5,000 shares of San Juan Company common stock at $20 per share:					
Investment in Available-for-Sale Securities	100,000		Investment in San Juan Company Stock	100,000	
Cash		100,000	Cash		100,000
Oct. 31 Received dividend of $0.80 per share from San Juan Company ($0.80 × 5,000 shares):					
Cash	4,000		Cash	4,000	
Dividend Revenue		4,000	Investment in San Juan Company Stock		4,000
Dec. 31 San Juan Company announced earnings for the year of $60,000:					
No entry			Investment in San Juan Company Stock	12,000	
			Income from Investment in San Juan Company Stock (0.20 × $60,000)		12,000

recorded at cost. Dividends received are recognized as dividend revenue for the available-for-sale securities and as a reduction in the investment account under the equity method.

The investor's percentage of the earnings of the investee company are recorded as income and as an increase to the investment account under the equity method, whereas no entry is required for this event when the securities are classified as available for sale. If the securities had been classified as trading, the journal entries to recognize revenue would have been identical to those made for the available-for-sale securities.

Equity Method: Purchase for More than Book Value When a company is purchased by another company, the purchase price usually differs from the recorded book value of the underlying net assets of the acquired company. For example, assume that Snowbird Company purchased 100% of the common stock of Ski Resorts International for $8 million, although the book value of Ski Resorts' net assets is only $6.5 million. In effect, Snowbird is purchasing some undervalued assets, above-normal earnings potential, or both.

As explained in Chapter 10, if the purchase price of an ongoing business exceeds the recorded value, the acquiring company must allocate this purchase price among the assets acquired using their current market values as opposed to the amounts carried on the books of the acquired company. If part of the purchase price cannot be allocated to specific assets, either tangible or intangible, that amount is recorded as goodwill. If the fair values of the acquired assets have decreased, the assets acquired might be recorded at an amount less than their carrying value on the books of the acquired company. Whether assets are increased or decreased as a result of the purchase, future income determination will use the new (adjusted) values to determine the depreciation and amortization charges.

When only a portion of a company's stock is purchased and the equity method is used to reflect the income of the partially owned company, an adjustment to the investee's reported income, similar to that just described, may be required. To determine whether such an adjustment is necessary, the acquiring company must compare the purchase price of the common stock with the recorded net asset value of the acquired company at the date of purchase. If the purchase price exceeds the investor's share of book value, the computed excess must be analyzed in the same way as described above for a 100% purchase. Although no entries to adjust asset values are made on the books of either company, an adjustment to the investee's reported income is required under the equity method for the investor to reflect the economic reality of paying more for the investment than the underlying net book value. If depreciable assets had been adjusted to higher market values on the books of the investee to reflect the price paid by the investor, additional depreciation would have been taken by the investee company. Similarly, if the purchase price reflected amortizable intangibles, additional amortization would have been required. These adjustments would have reduced the reported income of the investee. To reflect this condition, an adjustment is made by the investor to the income reported by the investee in applying the equity method. This adjustment serves to meet the objective of computing the income reported using the equity method in the same manner as would be done if the company were 100% purchased and consolidated financial statements were prepared.

To illustrate, assume that the book value of common stockholders' equity (net assets) of Stewart Inc. was $500,000 at the time Phillips Manufacturing Co. purchased 40% of its common shares for $250,000. Based on a 40% ownership interest, the market value of the net assets of Stewart Inc. would be $625,000 ($250,000/0.40), or $125,000 more than the book value. Assume that a review of the asset values discloses that the market value of depreciable properties exceeds the carrying value of these assets by $50,000. The remaining $75,000 difference ($125,000 – $50,000) is attributed to a special operating license. Assume further that the average remaining life of the depreciable assets is 10 years and that the license is to be amortized over 20 years. Phillips Manufacturing Co. would adjust its share of the annual income reported by Stewart Inc. to reflect the additional depreciation and the amortization of the license as follows:

Additional depreciation ($50,000 × 0.40)/10 years	$2,000
License amortization ($75,000 × 0.40)/20 years	1,500
	$3,500

Each year for the first 10 years, Phillips would make the following entry in addition to entries made to recognize its share of Stewart Inc.'s income and dividends:

Income from Investment in Stewart Inc. Stock	3,500	
Investment in Stewart Inc. Stock		3,500
To adjust share of income on Stewart Inc. common stock for proportionate depreciation on excess market value of depreciable property, $2,000, and for amortization of the unrecorded license, $1,500.		

After the 10th year, the adjustment would be for $1,500 until the license amount is fully amortized.

To complete the illustration, assume that the purchase was made on January 2, 2013; Stewart Inc. declared and paid dividends of $70,000 to common stockholders during 2013, and it reported net income of $150,000 for the year ended December 31, 2013. At the end of 2013, the investment in Stewart Inc. common stock would be reported on the balance sheet of Phillips Manufacturing Co. at $278,500, computed as follows:

Investment in Stewart Inc. Common Stock

Acquisition cost	$250,000	
Add: Share of 2013 earnings of investee company ($150,000 × 0.40)	60,000	$310,000
Less: Dividends received from investee ($70,000 × 0.40)	$ 28,000	
Additional depreciation of undervalued assets	2,000	
Amortization of unrecorded license	1,500	31,500
Year-end carrying value of investment (equity in investee company)		$278,500

This illustration assumes that the fiscal years of the two companies coincide and that the purchase of the stock is made at the beginning of the year. If a purchase is made at a time other than the beginning of the year, the income earned up to the date of the purchase is assumed to be included in the cost of purchase. Only income earned by the investee subsequent to acquisition should be recognized by the investor.

The adjustments for additional depreciation and intangible asset amortization are needed only when the purchase price is greater than the underlying book value at the date of acquisition. If the purchase price is less than the underlying book value at the time of acquisition, it is assumed that specific assets of the investee are overvalued. An adjustment is necessary to reduce the depreciation included in the reported income of the investee. The journal entry to reflect this adjustment is the reverse of the one illustrated previously. The computations would also be similar except that the adjustments for overvalued assets would be added to (instead of subtracted from) the carrying value of the investment.

FYI

Goodwill associated with an equity method investment is not tested for impairment using the techniques described in Chapter 11. Instead, as described later in the chapter, the entire equity method investment is considered to see whether any declines in value are permanent.

If the excess of the investment cost over the share of the book value of the net assets of the investee is attributable to goodwill, the computation of investment income is simplified. This is so because this goodwill, just like goodwill recorded in connection with the acquisition of an entire business, is not amortized. Accordingly, in the Phillips Manufacturing example if the $75,000 excess had been attributed to goodwill instead of to the operating license, income for the investment in the first year would have been $58,000 ($60,000 − $2,000) rather than $56,500 ($60,000 − $2,000 − $1,500).

Equity Method: Joint Ventures As explained in Chapter 12, a *joint venture* is a form of off-balance-sheet financing. What was not mentioned in Chapter 12 is that joint ventures are accounted for using the equity method. The manner in which joint ventures serve as a form of off-balance-sheet financing is illustrated in the following example. Owner A Company and Owner B Company each own 50% of Ryan Julius Company, which does research and marketing for the products of both Owner A and Owner B. Ryan Julius has assets of $10,000 and liabilities of $9,000. Because neither Owner A nor Owner B owns more than 50% of Ryan Julius, both companies would account for their investment using the equity method. The balance sheets of both companies would include the following with respect to their investment in Ryan Julius:

Owner A Balance Sheet

Investment in Ryan Julius [($10,000 − $9,000) × 0.50]	$500

Owner B Balance Sheet

Investment in Ryan Julius [($10,000 − $9,000) × 0.50]	$500

The off-balance-sheet financing aspect of joint ventures can be seen in that the $9,000 in liabilities of Ryan Julius are not reported in the balance sheet of either of the companies that own Ryan Julius. In this way, Owner A and Owner B have used the Ryan Julius joint venture to jointly borrow $9,000 without either one of them being required to report the liability in its balance sheet. As mentioned in Chapter 12, before their merger, **Chevron** and **Texaco** had a 50-50 joint venture partnership, **Caltex**. The Caltex joint venture had total liabilities in excess of $6 billion, none of which were reported in either Chevron's or Texaco's balance sheet.

Not all joint ventures have the 50-50 ownership structure illustrated here. If the owner of a joint venture is, say, 70-30, the minority owner will still account for the joint venture using the equity method, but the majority owner will be required to consolidate the joint venture and list all of the assets and liabilities of the joint venture in its (the majority owner's) balance sheet.

Equity Method Accounting According to IFRS

ifrs

Equity method accounting under IFRS is the same, in all important respects, as under U.S. GAAP. The relevant standard is *IAS 28*. Under IFRS, the term "associate" is used for what is called an "equity method investee" under U.S. GAAP. If this were an advanced accounting text, we would probably discuss the proportionate consolidation for joint ventures that is allowed under *IAS 31*; proportionate consolidation is allowed only in specialized industries under U.S. GAAP. However, because this is not an advanced accounting text, we will leave the very interesting proportionate consolidation discussion to another day.

Accounting for the Change in Value of Securities

5 **Account for the change in fair value of investment securities.**

WHY **For most investment securities, the most relevant measure of value is fair value. In addition, for those investment securities tradeable in public markets, fair value is also a reliable measure of value. Accordingly, most investment securities are reported in the balance sheet at fair value, with unrealized economic gains and losses being reported either in the income statement or as other comprehensive income.**

HOW **Temporary changes in the value of debt and equity securities classified as trading or available for sale are accounted for through the use of a market adjustment account. The use of this account results in these securities being reported at fair value on the balance sheet. For trading securities, the increase or decrease in fair value is reported as a gain or loss on the income statement. In the case of available-for-sale securities, the change in fair value is recognized as other comprehensive income, which is then accumulated as part of stockholders' equity. Temporary changes in fair value for held-to-maturity securities and equity method securities are not recognized.**

The fair value of debt and equity securities can rise and fall on a daily basis. Some of these changes in fair value can be considered temporary while others might be of a more permanent nature. Prior to 1993, when pre-Codification FASB *Statement No. 115* was issued, if temporary price changes occurred, only declines (and their subsequent recovery) in value of securities were recognized in the financial statements. The existing standard requires, for many types of debt and equity securities, both increases and decreases in fair value to be reflected in the financial statements. This section of the chapter deals with accounting for temporary changes in a security's fair value. We also briefly discuss the accounting for permanent declines in fair value.

Accounting for Temporary Changes in the Fair Value of Securities

Recall from our previous discussion that all publicly traded debt securities and those publicly traded equity securities not being held with the intent to influence the investee are to be classified into one of three categories. Those categories and their required disclosures were summarized in Exhibit 14-8.

The following example will be used throughout this section to illustrate accounting for changes in fair value. Eastwood Incorporated purchased five different securities on March 23, 2013. A schedule showing the type and cost of each security, along with its fair value on December 31, 2013, is as follows:

Security	Classification	Cost	Fair Value, Dec. 31, 2013
1	Trading	$ 8,000	$ 7,000
2	Trading	3,000	3,500
3	Available for sale	5,000	6,100
4	Available for sale	12,000	11,500
5	Held to maturity	20,000*	19,000

*Security 5 was purchased at face value. If the security were purchased at a price other than face value, the amortization procedures described previously would be employed.

The entry to record the initial purchase would be as follows:

Investment in Trading Securities	11,000	
Investment in Available-for-Sale Securities	17,000	
Investment in Held-to-Maturity Securities	20,000	
Cash		48,000

Securities 1 and 2 are classified by management as trading securities because management has no intention of holding these securities for a long period of time and will sell them as soon as it is economically advantageous for the company. Securities 3 and 4 are deemed by management to be available-for-sale securities. Management purchased security 5 at face value and intends to hold it until it matures.

During an accounting period, the fair value of securities will rise and fall. Only at the end of the period, when financial statements are prepared, is a company required to account for any change in fair value. At the end of the accounting period, the fair value of the portfolio of securities for certain categories is compared with the historical cost and an adjustment is made for the difference.

Trading Securities At the end of 2013, the fair value of the trading securities portfolio has decreased by $500 ($11,000 cost less $10,500 fair value). As a result, the following journal entry would be made:

Unrealized Loss on Trading Securities	500	
Market Adjustment—Trading Securities		500

The loss of $500 reflects the fact that the fair value of the trading securities portfolio has declined during the period. The loss is classified as unrealized because these securities have not been sold. This entry introduces a valuation account, *Market Adjustment—Trading Securities*. This account is

FYI

Once the adjusting entry is made, the trading securities account and the market adjustment account should always sum to the fair value of the trading securities. The same is true for available-for-sale securities.

combined with Investment in Trading Securities and is reported on the balance sheet. The use of a valuation account allows the company to maintain a record of historical cost. To determine realized and unrealized holding gains and losses, a record of historical cost is necessary. The unrealized loss on the trading securities account would be reported on the income statement under Other Expenses and Losses or would be combined with dividend and interest revenue in one item called Net Investment Income.

Available-for-Sale Securities For available-for-sale securities, adjustments similar to those illustrated for trading securities would be made; the only difference would be that instead of any unrealized gain or loss being disclosed on the income statement, it would be reported as part of other comprehensive income and then accumulated directly in stockholders' equity as part of Accumulated Other Comprehensive Income. Continuing the Eastwood example, at the end of 2013, its available-for-sale portfolio had increased from $17,000 to $17,600. This $600 increase in fair value of the securities above their cost would be recorded with the following journal entry:

Market Adjustment—Available-for-Sale Securities	600	
Unrealized Increase/Decrease in Value of Available-for-Sale Securities		600

Note that the unrealized increase/decrease in value of the available-for-sale securities account would serve to increase the amount of stockholders' equity, which is consistent with the fact that an asset has increased in value. The $600 increase would *not* be included in the computation of net income, but it would be in Other Comprehensive Income and added to net income when computing comprehensive income for the year.

Held-to-Maturity Securities Security 5 has decreased in value from $20,000 to $19,000. However, because this security is classified as held to maturity, no adjustment is made for the difference between carrying value and fair value. Exhibit 14-11 summarizes how the securities and the resulting increases and decreases in fair value would be reported in the financial statements of Eastwood Inc. for 2013.

At the end of 2014, similar adjustments must be made to reflect changes in fair value. Assume the following fair values at the end of 2014:

Security	Classification	Cost	Fair Value, Dec. 31, 2014
1	Trading	$ 8,000	$ 7,700
2	Trading	3,000	3,600
3	Available for sale	5,000	6,500
4	Available for sale	12,000	10,700
5	Held to maturity	20,000	20,700

By the end of 2014, the trading securities portfolio had increased to a fair value of $11,300 ($7,700 + $3,600). Comparing this amount to the historical cost of $11,000 indicates that Market Adjustment—Trading Securities should have a debit balance of $300. Because its current balance is a $500 credit (carried over from 2013), an adjusting entry must be made. The adjusting entry is as follows:

Market Adjustment—Trading Securities	800	
Unrealized Gain on Trading Securities		800

EX 14-11 FINANCIAL STATEMENT DISCLOSURE OF SECURITIES

Eastwood Inc.
Balance Sheet (Partial)
December 31, 2013

Assets:			
Investment in trading securities, at cost	$11,000		
Less: Market adjustment—trading securities	(500)	$10,500	
Investment in available-for-sale securities, at cost	$17,000		
Add: Market adjustment—available-for-sale securities	600	17,600	
Investment in held-to-maturity securities, at amortized cost		20,000	$48,100
Stockholders' Equity:			
Add: Unrealized increase in fair value of available-for-sale securities		$ 600	

Eastwood Inc.
Income Statement (Partial)
For the Year Ended December 31, 2013

Other expenses and losses:	
Unrealized loss on trading securities	$ 500

The balance in Market Adjustment—Trading Securities, which appears here in T-account form, would be added to Investment in Trading Securities and reported on the balance sheet. The $800 unrealized gain would be included in the computation of net income for 2014.

Market Adjustment—Trading Securities

		12/31/2013 Balance	500
12/31/2014 Adjustment	800		
12/31/2014 Balance	300		

At the end of 2014, the fair value of the available-for-sale securities has decreased from $17,600 to $17,200. Because fair value now exceeds historical cost by $200, the market adjustment account should have a $200 debit balance. Its current balance, carried over from 2013, is $600 (debit). The journal entry made at the end of 2014 to adjust the account is as follows:

Unrealized Increase/Decrease in Value of Available-for-Sale Securities	400	
Market Adjustment—Available-for-Sale Securities		400

The effect on the market adjustment—available-for-sale securities account is reflected in the following T-account. Again, no adjustment is made for changes in the fair value of held-to-maturity securities. The $400 unrealized decrease would be subtracted from net income in computing comprehensive income for 2014.

Market Adjustment—Available-for-Sale Securities

12/31/2013 Balance	600		
		12/31/2014 Adjustment	400
12/31/2014 Balance	200		

The financial statements for Eastwood Inc. at the end of 2014 would include the effects of each of the above adjusting entries as shown in Exhibit 14-12.

EX 14-12 FINANCIAL STATEMENT DISCLOSURE OF SECURITIES

Eastwood Inc.
Balance Sheet (Partial)
December 31, 2014

Assets:			
Investment in trading securities, at cost	$11,000		
Add: Market adjustment—trading securities	300	$11,300	
Investment in available-for-sale securities, at cost	$17,000		
Add: Market adjustment—available-for-sale securities	200	17,200	
Investment in held-to-maturity securities, at amortized cost		20,000	$48,500
Stockholders' Equity:			
Add: Unrealized increase in fair value of available-for-sale securities		$ 200	

Eastwood Inc.
Income Statement (Partial)
For the Year Ended December 31, 2014

Other expenses and losses:	
Unrealized gain on trading securities	$ 800

Equity Method Securities Assume that security 5 is an equity method security rather than a held-to-maturity security. As with held-to-maturity securities, no journal entries are made to reflect changes in fair value of equity method securities. Thus, the $20,700 fair value of the securities on December 31, 2014, would not be used to adjust the reported balance sheet amount of the equity method securities. However, the $20,700 fair value would be disclosed in the notes to the financial statements. For example, in the notes to its 2009 financial statements, Coca-Cola disclosed that its investment in its bottler **Coca-Cola Enterprises** was recorded in the Coca-Cola balance sheet at just $25 million but that the current market value of the investment was $3.4 billion.

Accounting for "Other-Than-Temporary" Declines in the Fair Value of Securities

Sometimes the fair value of investments declines due to economic circumstances that are unlikely to improve. For example, in 2001 the value of numerous Internet stocks decreased significantly without much expectation that they would ever recover. If a decline in the fair value of an individual security is judged to be other than temporary, regardless of whether the security is debt or equity and regardless of whether it is being accounted for as a trading, available-for-sale, held-to-maturity, or equity method security, the cost basis of that security should be reduced by crediting the investment account rather than a market adjustment account. In addition, the write-down should be recognized as a loss and charged against current income. The new cost basis for the security may not be adjusted upward to its original cost for any subsequent increases in fair value. If, however, the security is classified as a trading security or an available-for-sale security, a market adjustment account may be used to record future increases and decreases in fair value.

Determining whether a decline in fair value is other than temporary may sound like an impossible task because no one can predict which way market prices will move in the future. Also, investors are always confident that their carefully chosen investments that have declined in value will recover soon. In *Staff Accounting Bulletin (SAB) No. 59*,[16] the SEC staff suggests that one consider the following in determining whether a decline in fair value is other than temporary:

- How long has the fair value of the security been below its original cost? A rule of thumb (not in the official GAAP provisions) is that securities that have had fair values less than their costs for over six months have probably experienced an "other-than-temporary" decline in fair value.
- What is the current financial condition of the investee and its industry? If the investee has experienced losses for several years, and if the investee's entire industry has performed poorly, the decline in fair value is probably other than temporary.
- Will the investor's plans involve holding the security long enough for it to recover its value? For example, if a security has declined in fair value by 40% and the investor plans to sell the security in five months, it is unlikely that the security will recover its fair value in that time.

FYI

Because of the permanent change in the operations of some industries (e.g., travel and tourism-related industries) in the wake of the September 11, 2001, attack on the World Trade Center, accountants and auditors were particularly careful in determining whether investments in companies in these industries had suffered "other-than-temporary" declines in value.

FASB CODIFICATION

The Issue: You are the accounting expert in a mid-sized technology company that has a substantial investment portfolio. The company maintains this portfolio in order to have sufficient liquidity to take advantage of any favorable acquisition opportunities in your volatile industry. In recent years, the balance sheet value of your portfolio has fluctuated substantially because of the ups and downs in the market. Your CEO hates this "mark-to-market" accounting. She has heard that if you were to classify your debt securities as held to maturity, you wouldn't be required to report these balance sheet fluctuations.

You have been trying to convince the CEO that the held-to-maturity classification is extremely restrictive, but she has not been persuaded by your arguments. What you need is some authoritative support showing that very few debt security investments can be classified as held to maturity.

The Question: Under what circumstances can debt securities NOT be classified as held to maturity?

Searching the Codification: The location of the authoritative guidance on the accounting for investment securities is Topic 320 (Investments—Debt and Equity Securities). The relevant section is 320-10-25 on "Recognition."

The Answer: The authoritative guidance for classifying debt securities as held to maturity is given on page 14-49.

[16] This SEC guidance is contained in the formal U.S. GAAP provisions in FASB ASC paragraph 320-10-299-1.

Sale of Securities

6 **Account for the sale of investment securities.**

WHY **Careful accounting for the sale of investment securities, coupled with careful accounting for changes in fair value of investment securities, allow the financial statement user to compute the total economic return on an investment security portfolio for the reporting period.**

HOW **When an investment security is sold, its carrying value is removed from the books, and the difference between carrying value and the cash received is recorded as a realized gain or loss.**

When securities are sold, an entry must be made to remove the carrying value of the security from the investor's books and to record the receipt of cash. The difference between the carrying value and the cash received is a realized gain or loss. For trading and available-for-sale securities, the carrying value will be equal to the security's original cost. The carrying value of held-to-maturity and equity method securities will change as any premium or discount is amortized (in the case of held-to-maturity securities) or when the book value of the investee changes (in the case of equity method securities).

How does the market adjustment account come into play when a security is sold? Simply put, it does not. The market adjustment account is adjusted only at the end of each accounting period prior to the issuance of financial statements. The market adjustment account is used to reflect the fair value of the securities portfolio as of the end of the period; it is not to be associated with transactions that are measuring the amount of realized gains or losses. This approach makes practical sense if you think of a large company with an investment portfolio containing several hundred different securities. The significant effort required to associate a specific portion of the market adjustment account with each individual security (and to maintain this identification as hundreds or even thousands of securities are traded during the year) would not result in any improvement in the reported financial result.

At this point, it is important to distinguish between a realized and an unrealized gain or loss. A realized gain or loss occurs when an arm's-length transaction has occurred and a security has actually been sold. When the sale occurs, any difference between the carrying value of the security and the selling price is recognized on the income statement. An unrealized gain or loss arises when the fair value of a security changes, yet the security is still being held by the investor. As discussed previously, these unrealized gains and losses may or may not be recognized, depending upon the security's classification or whether the company has elected the fair value option with respect to that security.

In the case of a debt security, an entry must be made prior to recording the sale to record any interest earned to the date of the sale and to amortize any premium or discount. For example, continuing the Silmaril

STOP&THINK

What is the difference between *realized* and *recognized*?

a) *Realized* relates to the past, whereas *recognized* relates to the future.
b) *Realized* relates to trading securities, whereas *recognized* relates to available-for-sale securities.
c) *Realized* relates to the collection of cash, whereas *recognized* relates to the recording of an accounting journal entry.
d) *Realized* relates to financial statements, whereas *recognized* relates to income taxes.

Technologies example from page 14-15, assume that the debt securities are sold on April 1, 2014, for $103,000, which includes accrued interest of $2,500. The carrying value of the debt securities on January 1, 2014, is $105,240. Interest revenue of $2,105 ($105,240 × 0.08 × 3/12) would be recorded, and a receivable relating to interest of $2,500 would be established. The investment account would be reduced by $395 to reflect the amortization of the premium for the 3-month period between January 1 and April 1.

Interest Receivable	2,500	
Investment in Held-to-Maturity Securities		395
Interest Revenue		2,105

A second entry would remove the book value of the investment from Silmaril's books, record the receipt of cash of $103,000, eliminate the Interest Receivable balance, and record a loss equal to the difference between the investment's carrying value and the amount of cash received (net of interest).

Cash	103,000	
Realized Loss on Sale of Securities	4,345	
Interest Receivable		2,500
Investment in Held-to-Maturity Securities		104,845

These two entries could easily be combined into a single journal entry:

Cash	103,000	
Realized Loss on Sale of Securities	4,345	
Investment in Held-to-Maturity Securities		105,240
Interest Revenue		2,105

Impact of Sale of Securities on Unrealized Gains and Losses

The sale of a portion of an investment securities portfolio during the year complicates the computation and interpretation of the unrealized increases and decreases in the fair value of trading and available-for-sale securities. To illustrate, consider the following simple example. At the beginning of Year 1, Levi Company purchased a portfolio of trading securities for $10. At the end of Year 1, the portfolio had a value of $12. At the end of Year 2, the entire portfolio is sold for $9. The surprisingly difficult question is this: What is the amount of the unrealized gain or loss on the portfolio for Year 2? If you quickly answered "$3 unrealized loss," you need to read the following discussion carefully.

At the end of Year 1, the market adjustment account has a $2 debit balance to reflect the $2 increase ($10 ↑ to $12) in the fair value of the trading portfolio during Year 1. In addition, at the end of Year 2, the market adjustment account must have a $0 balance because the cost of the remaining trading securities ($0) is exactly equal to the fair value of those securities ($0). The necessary adjustment to the market adjustment account during Year 2 can be identified using the following T-account:

Market Adjustment—Trading

End of Year 1	2		
		2	Necessary Adjustment in Year 2
End of Year 2	0		

The required journal entry is as follows:

Unrealized Loss—Trading	2	
Market Adjustment—Trading		2

The reason that the unrealized loss for Year 2 is not equal to the $3 decline ($12 − $9) in the portfolio for the year is that a portion of that decline is included in the *realized* loss recorded when the trading securities are sold. The realized loss is the $1 difference between the original cost of the securities ($10) and their selling price ($9). The realized loss is recorded with the following entry:

Cash	9	
Realized Loss—Trading	1	
Investment Securities—Trading		10

The realized and unrealized losses in Year 2 in this case can be thought of as follows:

- *Realized loss* is the difference between the selling price and the original cost of the securities.
- *Unrealized loss* is the amount needed to adjust the end-of-year market adjustment account to its appropriate balance. More intuitively, in this simple example, it represents the reversal of the cumulative unrealized gains and losses recognized in past years on securities that were sold during this year. This reversal is needed to avoid double counting because those cumulative unrealized gains and losses from past years will impact the computation of the gain or loss realized this year.

As you can see, the interpretation of the unrealized loss is quite difficult. In a more complicated example, in which only a portion of the securities portfolio is sold, the unrealized gain or loss becomes a mixture of unrealized gains and losses for the year for securities still held at the end of this year and a reversal of unrealized gains and losses from past years for securities sold this year. What you should remember is that with an active securities portfolio, for which many purchases and sales of securities occur throughout the year, the computed amount of unrealized gain or loss for the year has no easy interpretation.

Lest you be discouraged by the unwelcome news contained in the previous paragraph, rest assured that the accounting system for investment securities actually does yield meaningful information. This can be seen by computing the total of the realized and unrealized gains and losses for the year. In this case, the sum of the $1 realized loss and the $2 unrealized loss is a total loss of $3 for the year. This total is exactly equal to the economic performance of the portfolio during the year; the portfolio decreased from a fair value of $12 at the beginning of the year to $9 at the end of the year. So, even though the interpretation of the unrealized gain or loss by itself is somewhat difficult, the sum of the realized and unrealized gains and losses is always easy to interpret in that the sum is equal to the total economic return on the portfolio for the year.

The preceding discussion dealt with trading securities. The concept is exactly the same for available-for-sale securities. The only difference is that the unrealized "gains" and "losses" are not included in the income statement. However, it is still true that the sum of the realized gains and losses and the unrealized increases and decreases for an available-for-sale portfolio is equal to the economic return on the portfolio during the year. For example, in 2007 Berkshire Hathaway reported a net realized gain of $5,598 million and a net unrealized loss of $2,981 million on its available-for-sale portfolio. The combination of these two numbers reveals that the total economic return for the portfolio during 2007 was a gain of $2,617 million ($5,598 million gain − $2,981 million loss).

Derecognition

On July 17, 2008, two large financial industry trade groups implored the FASB to rethink an accounting rule change that would hurt the financial ratios of financial institutions, cause some of them to violate loan covenants, "force some banks to tighten their lending requirements," and "make it more cumbersome for [the financial institutions] to raise capital."[17] These consequences would arise, it was claimed, from an FASB rule that would require financial institutions to change the accounting for $10.5 trillion in asset-backed securities. The financial institutions had accounted for the transfer of these securities as sales, removing them from their books as illustrated in the previous section. The new FASB rule would require that these transfers instead be accounted for as loans (with the securities serving as collateral), with the security assets returned to the balance sheets of the financial institutions, balanced by a $10.5 trillion liability for the loans. There is a HUGE difference between accounting for a security transfer as a sale and accounting for it as a collateralized loan. This is another example of the practice of off-balance-sheet financing that was introduced in Chapter 12. By the way, on July 30, 2008, the FASB decided to delay the rule change until 2010, giving the financial institutions some time to figure out how to explain to the users of their financial statements what had been going on with the missing $10.5 trillion.

As explained in Chapter 7 and according to FASB ASC Topic 860 (Transfers and Servicing), a transfer of a financial asset is accounted for as a sale (resulting in derecognition) when the transfer satisfies each of the following three conditions.[18]

- Legal control—The transferor has given up legal claim to the assets, meaning that even if it declares bankruptcy its creditors cannot go after the transferred assets.
- Actual control—The transferor cannot prevent the transferee from using the transferred assets however desired, such as selling them or pledging them as collateral for a loan.
- Effective control—The transferor does not have the right to force the transferee to return the assets, such as with a repurchase agreement.

The international standard governing derecognition is in *IAS 39*. Whereas Topic 860 focuses on the transfer of control, *IAS 39* focuses on the transfer of risks and rewards. Under the provisions of *IAS 39*, the transfer of a financial asset is recorded as a sale "if the entity transfers substantially all the risks and rewards of ownership of the financial asset."[19]

ifrs

[17] Marine Cole, "Securities Groups to FASB: Push Back Deadline for FAS 140," *Financial Week*, July 17, 2008.
[18] FASB ASC paragraph 860-10-40-5.
[19] *International Accounting Standard 39*, "Financial Instruments: Recognition and Measurement" (London: International Accounting Standards Board, August 18, 2005), par. 20.

Transferring Securities between Categories

7 **Record the transfer of investment securities between categories.**

WHY When securities are reclassified, recognition of previously unrecognized changes in fair value must be made to ensure that securities are recorded at fair value on the date of the reclassification. This procedure also ensures that category changes cannot be used to hide unrealized losses.

HOW If the reclassification involves a movement to or from the trading classification, any change in fair value not previously recognized in income is recognized in the current period. If the reclassification is from held to maturity to available for sale, changes in fair value since the investment's acquisition are recorded as a separate component of stockholders' equity. If an available-for-sale security is reclassified as a held-to-maturity security, all previously recorded changes in fair value are amortized over the remaining life of the investment.

On occasion, management will change its intentions with respect to holding certain securities. For example, a company may originally purchase securities for the purpose of making effective use of excess cash; subsequently, the company may decide to pursue a long-term business relationship with the investee. As a result, the company may reclassify the security from a trading security to an available-for-sale security. In addition, a company may initially purchase an equity security as a short-term investment and subsequently elect to increase its ownership interest to the point where the equity method is appropriate. This section of the chapter discusses the procedures employed when a security is transferred between investment security categories. Transitions to and from the equity method are covered in the Web Material (see **www.cengage.com/international**) associated with this chapter. By the way, investment securities for which the fair value option has been elected must always be accounted for according to that choice; the fair value election is irrevocable.

Transferring Debt and Equity Securities between Categories

If a company reclassifies a security, the security is accounted for at the fair value at the time of the transfer.[20] Because these securities are maintained on the books at their historical cost, the historical cost of the securities must be removed from the "old" category, and the securities are recorded in the "new" category at their current fair value. The change in value that has occurred is accounted for differently, depending on the category being transferred to and the category being transferred from. Exhibit 14-13 summarizes how these unrealized gains and losses are accounted for in each category.

To illustrate each type of transfer, we will use the data from the Eastwood Inc. example as of December 31, 2014 (page 14-28). Recall that on that date Eastwood Inc. had the following securities:

Security	Classification	Cost	Fair Value, Dec. 31, 2014
1	Trading	$ 8,000	$ 7,700
2	Trading	3,000	3,600
3	Available for sale	5,000	6,500
4	Available for sale	12,000	10,700
5	Held to maturity	20,000	20,700

[20] FASB ASC paragraph 320-10-35-10.

EX 14-13 ACCOUNTING FOR TRANSFERS OF SECURITIES BETWEEN CATEGORIES

Transferred	Treatment of the Change in Value
From trading	Any unrealized change in value not previously recognized will be recognized in net income in the current period. Previously recognized changes in value are not to be reversed.
To trading	Any unrealized change in value not previously recognized will be recognized in net income in the current period.
From held to maturity to available for sale	Recognize any unrealized change in value in a stockholders' equity account.
From available for sale to held to maturity	Any unrealized change in value recorded in a stockholders' equity account is to be amortized over the security's remaining life using the effective-interest method.*

* FASB ASC paragraph 320-10-35-10d.

During 2015, Eastwood Inc. elects to reclassify certain of its securities. The category being transferred from and to along with the fair value for each security on the date of the transfer is as follows:

Security	Transferring from	Transferring to	Fair Value, Date of Transfer
2	Trading	Available for sale	$ 3,800
3	Available for sale	Held to maturity	5,900
4	Available for sale	Trading	10,300
5	Held to maturity	Available for sale	20,400

The different types of reclassifications are illustrated in the following sections.

From the Trading Security Category Assume that Eastwood elects to reclassify security 2 from a trading security to an available-for-sale security. The security's historical cost is removed from the trading security classification, along with the associated $600 market adjustment (as of December 31, 2014), and the security is recorded at its current fair value as an available-for-sale security. The $200 difference between the fair value as of December 31, 2014, and the fair value at the date of transfer is recorded as an unrealized gain. The following journal entry illustrates this procedure:

Investment in Available-for-Sale Securities	3,800	
Market Adjustment—Trading Securities		600
Unrealized Gain on Transfer of Securities		200
Investment in Trading Securities		3,000

Alternatively, Eastwood could have recognized the $800 difference between fair value and historical cost as an unrealized gain at the time of the transfer and made an adjustment to the market adjustment—trading securities account at the end of the period. The net result of either approach would be the same. In the remainder of the examples that follow, we will adjust the market adjustment account on the date of the transfer.

Into the Trading Security Category Suppose Eastwood Inc. elects to reclassify security 4 from an available-for-sale security to a trading security. Recall that unrealized holding gains and losses associated with available-for-sale securities are recorded in the stockholders' equity account, Unrealized Increase/Decrease in Value of Available-for-Sale Securities. The amount in this account associated with security 4 is removed, and the security is recorded as a trading security at its current fair value.

Investment in Trading Securities	10,300	
Market Adjustment—Available-for-Sale Securities	1,300	
Unrealized Loss on Transfer of Securities	1,700	
Unrealized Increase/Decrease in Value of Available-for-Sale Securities		1,300
Investment in Available-for-Sale Securities		12,000

With this journal entry, security 4 is recorded as a trading security at its current fair value of $10,300. The carrying value of security 4 (historical cost less market adjustment) as an available-for-sale security is eliminated from the company's books. Because the security is now classified as a trading security, all changes in fair value should be reflected in the income statement. Thus, this journal entry transfers the unrealized changes in value from the stockholders' equity account to the income statement and recognizes the additional $400 decline in value since the last balance sheet date. The amount of the unrealized increase/decrease is determined by comparing the security's historical cost, obtained from subsidiary records, with its carrying value as of December 31, 2014. In this example, the unrealized decrease is $1,300 ($12,000 less $10,700). The final result of this journal entry is to reclassify the security and to record on the income statement the decline in fair value since the purchase of the security.

From the Held-to-Maturity to the Available-for-Sale Category Although transfers of debt securities from the held-to-maturity category should not occur often, they will happen on occasion. FASB ASC Topic 320 lists a number of circumstances that might lead a firm to reclassify a held-to-maturity security.[21] In this instance, Eastwood Inc. has elected to reclassify security 5 from a security being held until maturity to one that is available to be sold. Recall that security 5's fair value on the date of the transfer is $20,400. The security is recorded as an available-for-sale security at its current fair value with any difference between its carrying cost and its fair value being recorded as an unrealized increase/decrease in value of available-for-sale securities. The following journal entry will accomplish these objectives:

Investment in Available-for-Sale Securities	20,400	
Unrealized Increase/Decrease in Value of Available-for-Sale Securities		400
Investment in Held-to-Maturity Securities		20,000

Because security 5 was originally classified as held to maturity, no adjustment has been made in prior periods to record any changes in value. Thus, there is no market adjustment account related to this transfer.

From the Available-for-Sale to the Held-to-Maturity Category Eastwood Inc. elects to reclassify security 3 from one that is available to be sold to a security that will be held until maturity. Recall that security 3 was originally purchased for $5,000, had a fair value on December 31, 2014, of $6,500, and has a fair value on the date of the transfer of $5,900. The following entry should be made:

Investment in Held-to-Maturity Securities	5,900	
Unrealized Increase/Decrease in Value of Available-for-Sale Securities	600	
Investment in Available-for-Sale Securities		5,000
Market Adjustment—Available-for-Sale Securities		1,500

The debit to Unrealized Increase/Decrease in Value of Available-for-Sale Securities reflects the fact that the security has declined in value by $600 since the last balance sheet date. The $1,500 credit to the market adjustment account removes the previously

[21] FASB ASC paragraph 320-10-25-6.

recorded increase in value for this security ($6,500 − $5,000) while it was classified as available for sale. The combination of these amounts illustrates that security 3 has increased in value by $900 ($5,900 − $5,000) since its acquisition.

> **STOP&THINK**
>
> Which ONE of the following statements is correct with respect to ALL transfers of investment securities from one category to another?
>
> a) All unrealized losses as of the date of transfer are recognized immediately as part of income.
>
> b) All unrealized gains as of the date of transfer are recognized immediately as part of income.
>
> c) All unrealized losses as of the date of transfer are recognized immediately as part of other comprehensive income.
>
> d) All transferred securities are recorded at their fair value on the date of transfer.

Once the security is classified as held to maturity, increases and decreases in its value will not be reflected in the financial statements. The treatment of the $900 unrealized increase in value (gain) existing at the transfer date is a bit of a problem because, on the one hand, the gain can't be ignored because it occurred while the security was classified as available for sale, but, on the other hand, the gain would never have been recognized if the security had always been classified as held to maturity. Any unrealized increases and decreases in value that have been recorded to date (while the security has been available to be sold) must be amortized over the remaining life of the security using the effective-interest method and offset against (or added to) any interest revenue received on the debt security. The unamortized balance of an unrealized gain or loss continues to be reported as part of Accumulated Other Comprehensive Income in the Equity section of the balance sheet.[22] In addition, because the security is now classified as held to maturity, the company must also begin amortizing it down to its eventual maturity value. For example, if security 3 has a maturity value of $4,500, Eastwood Inc. must amortize, as a premium, the $1,400 difference between the security's carrying value and its maturity value ($5,900 less $4,500), as discussed previously. Thus, the interest revenue from security 3 will be adjusted for two types of amortization: the unrealized gain (increasing interest revenue) that existed at the transfer date and the carrying value to the maturity value (reducing interest revenue).

Investment Securities and the Statement of Cash Flows

8 **Properly report purchases, sales, and changes in fair value of investment securities in the statement of cash flows.**

WHY **The classification of a security indicates how management is using the investment in that security as part of the company's business strategy and therefore determines where the cash flows associated with that security are reported in the statement of cash flows.**

HOW **The purchase and sale of available-for-sale, held-to-maturity, and equity method securities are reported in the Investing Activities section of the statement of cash flows. The cash flows associated with the purchase and sale of trading securities and securities for which the fair value option has been elected are shown in the Operating or Investing Activities section depending on the reason the securities were acquired. If the cash flows are classified as operating activities, adjustments must be made for unrealized gains and losses when the indirect method is used to compute operating cash flow.**

The purchase and sale of available-for-sale, held-to-maturity, and equity method securities are reported in the Investing Activities section of the statement of cash flows. In contrast, the cash flows associated with the purchase and sale of trading securities (and fair value

[22] FASB ASC paragraph 320-10-35-10d.

option securities) are shown in the Operating or Investing Activities depending on the reason the securities were acquired.[23] This difference stems from the fact that a company that maintains a trading securities portfolio or that chooses to account for certain investment securities using the fair value option often considers as part of its business operations the attempt to make money through the correct timing of purchases and sales of these securities.

The difficulties in reporting the cash flows associated with investment securities are associated with the proper treatment of both realized and unrealized gains and losses. In addition, a special adjustment must be made to operating cash flow associated with equity method securities because the cash received in the form of dividends is not equal to the income reported from the investment. These issues are discussed in the following sections.

Cash Flows from Gains and Losses on Available-for-Sale Securities

Caesh Company came into existence with a $1,000 cash investment by owners on January 1, 2013, and entered into the following transactions during 2013:

Cash sales	$ 1,700
Cash expenses	(1,400)
Purchase of investment securities	(600)
Sale of investment securities (costing $200)	170

The investment securities are classified as available for sale. In addition, the market value of the remaining securities was $500 on December 31, 2013. Given these transactions, Caesh Company's net income for 2013 can be computed as follows:

Sales	$ 1,700
Expenses	(1,400)
Operating income	$ 300
Realized loss on sale of securities ($200 − $170)	(30)
Net income	$ 270

In addition, Caesh Company will report a $100 unrealized increase in the fair value of its available-for-sale portfolio. This $100 increase is the difference between the $500 ending fair value of the portfolio and the $400 cost ($600 − $200 sold) of the portfolio. This $100 unrealized increase is not included in the computation of net income but is reported as an increase in the Accumulated Other Comprehensive Income portion of equity.

Recall from Chapter 5 that the general treatment of gains and losses in the Operating Activities section of the statement of cash flows is that gains are subtracted and losses are added when the indirect method is used. This approach stems from the fact that the cash flow effects of the transactions creating the gains and losses will be reported in the Investing Activities section, so the impact of those gains and losses must be removed from the Operating Activities section. With this in mind, the statement of cash flows for Caesh Company for 2013 can be prepared as follows:

Operating activities:		
Net income	$ 270	
Plus: Realized loss on sale of securities	30	$ 300
Investing activities:		
Purchase of investment securities	$(600)	
Sale of investment securities	170	(430)
Financing activities:		
Initial investment by owners		1,000
Net increase in cash		$ 870

[23] FASB ASC paragraph 320-10-45-11.

As you can see, the realized gains and losses from the sale of available-for-sale securities are treated in exactly the same way, and for exactly the same reasons, as the gains and losses from the sale of property, plant, and equipment that were discussed in Chapter 5.

Cash Flows from Gains and Losses on Trading Securities

If the investment securities purchased by Caesh Company are classified as trading securities and are deemed to have been acquired for operating purposes, the cash flows associated with the purchase and sale of the securities are reported in the Operating Activities section of the statement of cash flows. In addition, net income is $370 instead of $270 because the $100 unrealized increase in the fair value of the portfolio is reported as an unrealized gain in the income statement. The statement of cash flows appears as follows:

Operating activities:		
Net income	$ 370	
Purchase of investment securities	(600)	
Sale of investment securities	170	
Plus: Realized loss on sale of securities	30	
Less: Unrealized gain on trading securities	(100)	$ (130)
Investing activities		0
Financing activities:		
Initial investment by owners		1,000
Net increase in cash		$ 870

The realized loss on the sale of the securities is added back because all of the cash flow effects of the sale are reflected in the $170 cash proceeds, which are reported separately; to fail to adjust for the realized loss, which is included in net income, would double count this $30. The unrealized gain is subtracted in the computation of operating cash flow, but the subtraction occurs for a different reason than to avoid double counting. Instead, the $100 unrealized gain is subtracted in the computation of operating cash flow because the gain increases income but does not result in any cash flow this period. The increased cash flow will come in the future when the securities are sold for a higher price, at which time the cash proceeds will be reported as a separate item. Similarly, the amount of an unrealized loss on trading securities would be added back in the computation of cash from operating activities.

FYI

Alternatively, the $600 cash outflow for the purchase of investment securities, the $170 cash inflow from the sale of trading securities, and the $30 realized loss can all be netted together and reported as a net cash outflow from the $400 increase in the cost of the trading securities portfolio. If this is done, the fact that securities are sold for more or less than their cost is reflected in the amount of the realized gain or loss, which is already imbedded in net income.

Equity Method Securities and Operating Cash Flow

When a company owns equity method securities, an adjustment to operating cash flow must be made to reflect the fact that the cash received from the securities in the form of dividends is not equal to the income from the securities included in the computation of net income. To illustrate, assume that Daltone Company owns 30% of the outstanding shares of Chase Company. Chase Company's net income for the year was $100,000, and cash dividends paid were $40,000. Daltone would include $30,000 ($100,000 × 0.30) in its income statement as income from the investment. However, Daltone received only $12,000 ($40,000 × 0.30) in cash dividends from its investment in Chase. Accordingly, Daltone would report a subtraction in the Operating Activities section of its statement of cash flows for the $18,000 ($30,000 − $12,000) difference between the income reported and the cash dividends received.

Classification and Disclosure

9 Explain the proper classification and disclosure of investments in securities.

WHY **Companies that have investment securities typically have not just one or two investments but instead have complicated portfolios of investments. Note disclosure is necessary to give financial statement users a sufficient understanding of the performance and status of these portfolios. In addition, because the fair values of investment securities are determined in a variety of ways, financial statement users need disclosure to help them determine the reliability of the reported numbers.**

HOW **Realized gains and losses on the sale of investment securities are reported in the income statement in the period of the sale. Unrealized gains and losses on trading securities are also reported in the income statement. Unrealized increases and decreases on securities classified as available for sale are reported as other comprehensive income and are accumulated in the Stockholders' Equity section of the balance sheet. Companies are also required to give additional note disclosure regarding their investment portfolios, including details on Level 1, Level 2, and Level 3 fair values.**

We have discussed the treatment of the gains and losses (both realized and unrealized) associated with selling, valuing, and/or reclassifying securities. Gains and losses from the sale of securities and unrealized gains and losses from changes in fair value while holding trading securities are reported in the income statement as Other Revenues and Expenses, or are combined with dividend and interest revenue and reported as Net Investment Income. Unrealized gains and losses on available-for-sale securities are reported in the Accumulated Other Comprehensive Income section of stockholders' equity and are included as Other Comprehensive Income in the computation of comprehensive income. As with any asset, significant permanent declines in the value of investments are recognized as a loss in the year they occur. Berkshire Hathaway, for example, includes a one-line summary of all of its realized gains and losses for the year in its income statement and discloses further details in the notes. The relevant note disclosure for Berkshire Hathaway for 2009 is included in Exhibit 14-14. Note that Berkshire Hathaway has cumulative unrealized gains on its debt and equity investments totaling almost $36 billion. How is it possible that none of this unrealized amount shows up on Berkshire Hathaway's income statement? The company classifies its securities as either held to maturity (for some debt securities), available for sale (for most debt and equity securities), or equity method (for some large investments).

Although the unrealized increases associated with the available-for-sale securities are not reported on the income statement, they are included in the computation of comprehensive income. Berkshire Hathaway's statement of comprehensive income is included in Exhibit 14-15.

The total unrealized increase reported for the available-for-sale portfolio is $20,375 million ($17,607 million + $2,768 million). The "reclassification" item reported in the

EX 14-14 BERKSHIRE HATHAWAY—NOTE DISCLOSURE RELATING TO INVESTMENTS (PARTIAL)

4) Investments in fixed maturity securities

Investments in securities with fixed maturities as of December 31, 2009 are summarized below (in millions).

	Amortized Cost	Unrealized Gains	Unrealized Losses*	Fair Value
December 31, 2009				
U.S. Treasury, U.S. government corporations and agencies	$ 2,362	$ 46	$ (1)	$ 2,407
States, municipalities and political subdivisions	3,689	275	(1)	3,963
Foreign governments	11,518	368	(42)	11,844
Corporate bonds	13,094	2,080	(502)	14,672
Mortgage-backed securities	3,961	310	(26)	4,245
	$34,624	$ 3,079	$ (572)	$37,131

**Includes $471 million at December 31, 2009 related to securities that have been in an unrealized loss position for 12 months or more.*

5) Investments in equity securities

Investments in equity securities as of December 31, 2009 are summarized below (in millions).

	Cost Basis	Unrealized Gains	Unrealized Losses	Fair Value
December 31, 2009				
American Express Company	$ 1,287	$ 4,856	$ —	$ 6,143
The Coca-Cola Company	1,299	10,101	—	11,400
Kraft Foods Inc.	4,330	—	(789)	3,541
The Procter & Gamble Company	4,962	78	—	5,040
Wells Fargo & Company	7,394	2,721	(1,094)	9,021
Other	17,935	7,118	(1,164)	23,889
	$37,207	$24,874	$(3,047)	$59,034

**Included in Other assets.*

Unrealized losses at December 31, 2009 included $1,864 million related to securities that have been in an unrealized loss position for 12 months or more. Approximately 90% of the gross unrealized losses at December 31, 2009 were concentrated in four issuers. We use no bright-line test in determining whether impairments are temporary or other than temporary. We consider several factors in determining other-than-temporary impairment losses including the current and expected long-term business prospects of the issuer, the length of time and relative magnitude of the price decline and our ability and intent to hold the investment until the price recovers. In our judgment, the future earnings potential and underlying business economics of these companies are favorable and we possess the ability and intent to hold these securities until their prices recover. Changing market conditions and other facts and circumstances may change the business prospects of these issuers as well as our ability and intent to hold these securities until the prices recover. Accordingly, other-than-temporary impairment charges may be recorded in future periods with respect to one or more of these securities.

(6) Other Investments

A summary of other investments follows (in millions).

	Cost	Unrealized Gains/Losses	Fair Value	Carrying Value
December 31, 2009				
Fixed maturity and equity	$21,089	$ 5,879	$26,968	$26,014
Equity method	5,851	1,721	7,572	6,586
	$26,940	$ 7,600	$34,540	$32,600

Fixed maturity and equity investments in the preceding table include our investments in The Goldman Sachs Group, Inc. ("GS") and The General Electric Company ("GE"), which were acquired in 2008 and investments in Swiss Reinsurance Company Ltd. ("Swiss Re") and The Dow Chemical Company ("Dow") that were made in 2009. In addition, fixed maturity and equity investments include investments in Wm. Wrigley Jr. Company ("Wrigley") that we acquired in both 2008 and 2009.

EX 14-14 CONTINUED

(7) Investment gains/losses

Investment gains/losses are summarized below (in millions).

	2009	2008	2007
Fixed maturity securities —			
Gross gains from sales and other disposals	$ 357	$ 212	$ 657
Gross losses from sales and other disposals	(54)	(20)	(35)
Equity securities —			
Gross gains from sales and other disposals	701	1,256	4,880
Gross losses from sales	(617)	(530)	(7)
Other	(69)	255	103
	$ 318	$1,173	$5,598

Net investment gains/losses are reflected in the Consolidated Statements of Earnings as follows.

	2009	2008	2007
Insurance and other	$251	$1,166	$5,405
Finance and financial products	67	7	193
	$318	$1,173	$5,598

statement of comprehensive income includes the reversal of prior-year unrealized losses on securities that were sold during the year.

Appropriate presentation of individual securities on the balance sheet depends on the intent of management. If management intends or is willing to sell the securities within one year or the current operating cycle, whichever is longer, the security is classified as a current asset. Because trading securities are short term by definition, they are always classified as current. Held-to-maturity securities are always classified as noncurrent unless they mature within a year. Available-for-sale securities are classified as current or noncurrent, depending on the intentions of management.

EX 14-15 BERKSHIRE HATHAWAY—STATEMENT OF COMPREHENSIVE INCOME FOR 2009

	2009	2008	2007
Comprehensive income attributable to Berkshire:			
Net earnings	$ 8,055	$ 4,994	$13,213
Other comprehensive income:			
Net change in unrealized appreciation of investments	17,607	(23,342)	2,523
Applicable income taxes	(6,263)	8,257	(872)
Reclassification of investment appreciation in net earnings	2,768	895	(5,494)
Applicable income taxes	(969)	(313)	1,923
Foreign currency translation	851	(2,140)	456
Applicable income taxes	(17)	118	(26)
Prior service cost and actuarial gains/ losses of defined benefit plans	(41)	(1,071)	257
Applicable income taxes	(1)	389	(102)
Other	(206)	(60)	(22)
Other comprehensive income, net	13,729	(17,267)	(1,357)
Comprehensive income attributable to Berkshire	$21,784	$(12,273)	$11,856

In addition to the reporting required in the income statement, balance sheet, and statement of cash flows, the following additional disclosures are required in the financial statement notes:

1. Trading securities:
   - The change in net unrealized holding gain or loss that is included in the income statement.
2. Available-for-sale securities:
   - Aggregate fair value, gross unrealized holding gains and gross unrealized holding losses, and amortized cost basis by major security type. For debt securities, the company should disclose information about contractual maturities.
   - The proceeds from sales of available-for-sale securities and the gross realized gains and losses on those sales and the basis on which cost was determined in computing realized gains and losses.
   - The change in net unrealized holding gain or loss on available-for-sale securities that has been included in stockholders' equity during the period.
3. Held-to-maturity securities:
   - Aggregate fair value, gross unrealized holding gains and gross unrealized holding losses, and amortized cost basis by major security type. In addition, the company should disclose information about contractual maturities.
4. Transfers of securities between categories:
   - Gross gains and losses included in earnings from transfers of securities from available-for-sale into the trading category.
   - For securities transferred from held-to-maturity, the company should disclose the amortized cost amount transferred, the related realized or unrealized gain or loss, and the reason for transferring the security.

In Exhibit 14-16, an excerpt from the note on the fair value of investment securities is taken from the 2009 annual report of Wells Fargo & Company, a major company in the banking industry. In particular, note the extended disclosure regarding the Level 3 items, as described more fully in the Fair Value Module in this textbook.

The IASB does not currently have a fair value measurement and disclosure standard comparable to U.S. GAAP. International Financial Reporting Standards do, of course, include many fair value measurements, including those associated with investment securities as explained earlier in this chapter. However, the IASB has not yet adopted a single, comprehensive fair value measurement and disclosure standard. In particular, the IASB does not currently have any disclosure requirement comparable to the Level 1, Level 2, and Level 3 disclosures illustrated in Exhibit 14-16. As of July 2010, the IASB was considering this issue. Of course, the provisions outlying the disclosures required under U.S. GAAP are an important springboard in those considerations.

ifrs

EX 14-16 WELLS FARGO—NOTE DISCLOSURE FOR INVESTMENT SECURITIES (PARTIAL)

Assets and Liabilities Recorded at Fair Value on a Recurring Basis

The table below presents the balances of assets and liabilities measured at fair value on a recurring basis.

(in millions)	Level 1	Level 2	Level 3	Netting[1]	Total
Balance at December 31, 2009					
Trading assets (excluding derivatives)[2]	$ 2,386	20,497	2,311	—	25,194
Derivatives (trading assets)	340	70,938	5,682	(59,115)	17,845
Securities of U.S. Treasury and federal agencies	1,094	1,186	—	—	2,280
Securities of U.S. states and political subdivisions	4	12,708	818	—	13,530
Mortgage-backed securities:					
Federal agencies	—	82,818	—	—	82,818
Residential	—	27,506	1,084	—	28,590
Commercial	—	9,162	1,799	—	10,961
Total mortgage-backed securities	—	119,486	2,883	—	122,369
Corporate debt securities	—	8,968	367	—	9,335
Collateralized debt obligations	—	—	3,725	—	3,725
Other	—	3,292	12,587	—	15,879
Total debt securities	1,098	145,640	20,380	—	167,118
Marketable equity securities:					
Perpetual preferred securities	736	834	2,305	—	3,875
Other marketable equity securities	1,279	350	88	—	1,717
Total marketable equity securities	2,015	1,184	2,393	—	5,592
Total securities available for sale	3,113	146,824	22,773	—	172,710
Mortgages held for sale	—	33,439	3,523	—	36,962
Loans held for sale	—	149	—	—	149
Mortgage servicing rights (residential)	—	—	16,004	—	16,004
Other assets[3]	1,932	11,720	1,690	(6,812)	8,530
Total	$ 7,771	283,567	51,983	(65,927	277,394
Other liabilities[4]	$(6,527)	(81,613)	(7,942)	73,299	(22,783)

(1) Derivatives are reported net of cash collateral received and paid and, to the extent that the criteria of the accounting guidance covering the offsetting of amounts related to certain contracts are met, positions with the same counterparty are netted as part of a legally enforceable master netting agreement.
(2) Includes trading securities of $24.0 billion and $19.5 billion at December 31, 2009 and 2008, respectively.
(3) Derivative assets other than trading and principal investments are included in this category.
(4) Derivative liabilities are included in this category.

Table of Contents

Note 16: Fair Values of Assets and Liabilities (*continued*)

The changes in Level 3 assets and liabilities measured at fair value on a recurring basis are summarized as follows:

(in millions)	Balance beginning of year	Total net gains (losses) included in: Net income	Total net gains (losses) included in: Other comprehensive income	Purchases, sales, issuances and settlements net	Net transfers into and/ or out of Level 3[1]	Balance end of year	Net unrealized gains (losses) included in net income related to assets and liabilities held at period end[2]
Year ended December 31, 2009							
Trading assets (excluding derivatives)	$ 3,495	202	2	(1,749)	361	2,311	276[3]
Securities available for sale:							
Securities of U.S. states and political subdivisions	903	23	—	25	(133)	818	(8)

EX 14-16 CONTINUED

(in millions)	Balance beginning of year	Total net gains (losses) included in: Net income	Total net gains (losses) included in: Other comprehensive income	Purchases, sales, issuances and settlements net	Net transfers into and/ or out of Level 3[(1)]	Balance end of year	Net unrealized gains (losses) included in net income related to assets and liabilities held at period end[(2)]
Mortgage-backed securities:							
Federal agencies	4	—	—	—	(4)	—	—
Residential	3,510	(74)	1,092	(759)	(2,685)	1,084	(227)
Commercial	286	(220)	894	41	798	1,799	(112)
Total mortgage-backed securities	3,800	(294)	1,986	(718)	(1,891)	2,883	(339)
Corporate debt securities	282	3	61	(7)	28	367	—
Collateralized debt obligations	2,083	125	577	623	317	3,725	(84)
Other	12,799	136	1,368	584	(2,300)	12,587	(94)
Total debt securities	19,867	(7)	3,992	507	(3,979)	20,380	(525)
Marketable equity securities:							
Perpetual preferred securities	2,775	104	144	(723)	5	2,305	(1)
Other marketable equity securities	50	—	(2)	63	(23)	88	—
Total marketable equity securities	2,825	104	142	(660)	(18)	2,393	(1)
Total securities available for sale	$ 22,692	97	4,134	(153)	(3,997)	22,773	(526)
Mortgages held for sale	$ 4,718	(96)	—	(921)	(178)	3,523	(109)[(4)]
Mortgage servicing rights (residential)	14,714	(4,970)	—	6,260	—	16,004	(1,534)[(4)]
Net derivative assets and liabilities	37	1,439	—	(2,291)	(17)	(832)	(799)[(5)]
Other assets (excluding derivatives)	1,231	10	—	132	—	1,373	12
Other liabilities (excluding derivatives)	(638)	(630)	—	168	(10)	(1,110)	(606)

(1) The amounts presented as transfers into and out of Level 3 represent fair value as of the beginning of the quarter in which each transfer occurred.

(2) Represents only net gains (losses) that are due to changes in economic conditions and management's estimates of fair value and excludes changes due to the collection/ realization of cash flows over time.

(3) Included in other noninterest income in the income statement.

(4) Included in mortgage banking in the income statement.

(5) Represents total unrealized losses of $3.3 billion and $571 million, net of losses of $8 million and gains of $23 million related to sales, in 2008 and 2007, respectively.

EM EXPANDED MATERIAL

To this point in the chapter, we have talked about securities for which there is a tradeable market. In some instances, a company may invest in another firm in the form of a nonmarketable security. The most common example of this type of security would be a loan. In this Expanded Material, we deal with the most complex issue associated with these nonmarketable securities: impairment.

Accounting for the Impairment of a Loan

10 **Account for the impairment of a loan receivable.**

WHY On some occasions, particularly in the case of loans made to other companies, a market value may not exist for the investment. In these instances, the investor must assess the collectibility of the investment, and if it is determined that an "impairment" exists, an adjustment to the value of the receivable must be made.

HOW Impairment is measured by comparing the present value of expected future cash flows with the carrying value of the investment.

A common example of an investment for which there might be no market value would be a loan receivable. Accounting for loans receivable is straightforward except for impairment.[24] Loans may arise by a company lending money to a borrower or by selling inventory and assets in return for a receivable. An entry to Loans Receivable is thus offset by a credit to Sales, Cash, or a surrendered asset. Financial institutions engage in such loans on a regular basis. A critical issue with these loans is when cost should be abandoned as the valuation basis. In other words, when should the loan be written down, or written off?

Because it is assumed that no ready market exists for these loans, the market valuations prescribed by FASB ASC Topic 320 cannot apply.

Loans receivable are thus carried at a cost valuation unless evidence exists of a probable impairment. FASB ASC Topic 310 (Receivables) defines impairment as follows:

> A loan is impaired when, based on current information and events, it is probable that a creditor will be unable to collect all amounts due according to the contractual terms of the loan agreement.[25]

All amounts due according to contractual terms include both interest and principal payments. Troubled debt restructuring is direct evidence of impairment; however, impairment may occur even though a formal restructuring has not occurred. If sufficient write-down has not previously been made, the restructuring will give rise to an additional decrease in the value of the loan receivable.

Measurement of Impairment

A creditor shall measure impairment for loans with no market value at the present value of expected future cash flows discounted at the loan's effective interest rate, that is, the rate implicit in the original loan contract. The impairment is recorded by creating a valuation allowance account and charging the estimated loss to Bad Debt Expense. Thus, accounting for loans receivable is similar to accounting for accounts receivable except that the measurement method is more specifically defined by the FASB.

If a loan agreement is restructured in a troubled debt restructuring, the interest rate to be used to discount the new modified contract terms is based on the original contract rate, not the rate specified in the restructuring agreement. The selection of the discount rate to use was one of the difficult issues addressed by the FASB. The continued use of the original loan rate is consistent with the historic cost principle. The estimate of future cash

[24] See Chapter 7 for discussion of notes receivable.
[25] FASB ASC paragraph 310-10-35-16.

flows is based on the creditor's best estimate based on reasonable and supportable assumptions and projections. Any future changes in the estimates or timing of future cash flows result in a recalculation of the impairment and an adjustment of the receivable and valuation allowance accounts with a charge or credit to Bad Debt Expense. Income arising from the passage of time will be recognized as part of interest revenue in each respective reporting period.

> **FYI**
>
> Again, you will need to be comfortable with present values if you are to understand the computations in this section. See the Time Value of Money Review module if you need a review.

Example of Accounting for Loan Impairment

Assume that Malone Enterprises reports a loan receivable from Stockton Co. in the amount of $500,000. The initial loan's repayment terms include a 10% interest rate plus annual principal payments of $100,000 on January 1 each year. The loan was made on January 1, 2011. Stockton made the $50,000 interest payment in 2011 but did not make the $100,000 principal payment nor the $50,000 interest payment for 2012. Malone is preparing its annual financial statements on December 31, 2012. The loan receivable has a carrying value of $550,000 including the $50,000 interest receivable for 2012. Stockton is having financial difficulty, and Malone has concluded that the loan is impaired. Analysis of Stockton's financial conditions indicates the principal and interest currently due can probably be collected, but it is probable that no further interest can be collected. The probable amount and timing of the collections is determined to be as follows:

December 31, 2013	$175,000
December 31, 2014	200,000
December 31, 2015	175,000
	$550,000

The present value at December 31, 2012, of the expected future cash flows discounted at 10% is $455,860, calculated as follows:

Date	Payment	Time of Discount	Present Value @ 10%
Dec. 31, 2013	$175,000	1 year	$159,091
Dec. 31, 2014	200,000	2 years	165,289
Dec. 31, 2015	175,000	3 years	131,480
Present value at December 31, 2012			$455,860

The impairment loss to be reported for 2012 is $94,140, or the $550,000 carrying value less the present value of $455,860. The journal entry to record the impairment is as follows:

2012			
Dec. 31	Bad Debt Expense	94,140	
	Allowance for Loan Impairment		94,140

The allowance would be reported as an offset to the loan receivable account.

> **FYI**
>
> If you look closely, you will realize that the computations being made in this table are conceptually identical to those done in the bond amortization table on page 14-16.

If Stockton makes the payments as projected, the accounting for the cash received and the recognition of interest revenue is computed by constructing an amortization schedule similar to that illustrated here.

Interest Revenue from Loan Impairment

Date	(1) Loan Receivable before Current Payment	(2) Allowance for Loan Impairment	(3) Net Receivable (1) − (2)	(4) Interest Revenue 10% × (3)	(5) Payment Received
Dec. 31, 2013	$550,000	$94,140	$455,860	$45,586	$175,000
Dec. 31, 2014	375,000	48,554*	326,446	32,645	200,000
Dec. 31, 2015	175,000	15,909†	159,091	15,909	175,000
				$94,140	$550,000

*$94,140 − $45,586 = $48,554

†$48,554 − $32,645 = $15,909

The entries on December 31, 2013, to record the receipt of the 2013 loan payment and to recognize interest revenue for the year are as follows:

2013			
Dec. 31	Cash	175,000	
	Loan Receivable		175,000
	Allowance for Loan Impairment	45,586	
	Interest Revenue*		45,586

*Alternatively, a company may show all changes in present value as an adjustment to Bad Debt Expense in the same manner in which impairment initially was recognized.[26]

The T-accounts for the loan receivable and allowance accounts for 2012 and 2013 are as follows:

Loan Receivable

Debit		Credit	
Beg. Bal.	550,000		
		12/31/2013	175,000
Bal.	375,000		

Allowance for Loan Impairment

Debit		Credit	
		12/31/2012	94,140
12/31/2013	45,586		
		Bal.	48,554

Similar entries would be made at the end of 2014 and 2015 using the amounts included in the preceding schedule. Note that computation of the amortization of the allowance for loan impairment account is identical to the computation for the amortization of Discount on Notes Receivable used in Chapter 7. If all payments are made as scheduled, the loan receivable and allowance accounts will both be closed out as of December 31, 2015.

[26] FASB ASC paragraph 310-10-35-40.

? SOLUTIONS TO OPENING SCENARIO QUESTIONS

1. Disney owns 100% of ABC. As a result, the shareholders of Disney, through their board of directors, control the strategic decisions of ABC. In contrast, Berkshire Hathaway owns just over 8% of Coca-Cola. Berkshire Hathaway may be able to influence the actions of Coca-Cola but certainly not control them.

2. The primary business activity of Berkshire Hathaway is to invest in other companies and earn a return from those investments.

In contrast, Microsoft's primary business activity is the development and sale of software. Microsoft's investments serve as both a temporary storage place for excess cash as well as strategic investments in order to exercise influence on the operations of other companies.

3. CREF invests the retirement funds of educators. Many college professors have their retirement funds invested through CREF.

SOLUTIONS TO STOP & THINK

1. (Page 14-7) The correct answer is D. The investment by Ford in Mazda is part of a broader strategic alliance. Ford and Mazda are partners in a joint venture in Thailand, have joint plans for production and sales in China, and are partners in production facilities in the United States. In addition, this investment by Ford gives the company a presence in Japan, the homeland of the company's primary foreign competitors, Toyota and Honda. Before the fourth quarter of 2008, Ford's ownership of Mazda was 33%. As discussed in this chapter, for accounting purposes the ownership threshold for "significant influence" is assumed to be 20%. However, it is clear that Ford's 11% ownership of Mazda exists to give Ford significant influence.

2. (Page 14-16) The correct answer is A. Recall that both trading and available-for-sale debt securities are reported in the balance sheet at fair value. Accordingly, after carefully amortizing a discount or premium on these debt securities, the securities would then just be adjusted to current fair value anyway. However, in a more comprehensive example, achieving a proper split between interest revenue and unrealized holding gains and losses would require that the discount or premium first be amortized before adjusting the security to fair value.

3. (Page 14-30) The correct answer is C. Recognized is an accounting term, which indicates that a transaction has been recorded using a journal entry. In the context of investment securities, realized means that a gain or loss amount has actually been confirmed through the sale of the securities.

4. (Page 14-37) The correct answer is D. As seen in the examples, all transferred securities are recorded at their fair value on the date of transfer. Depending on the type of transfer, unrealized gains and losses will be treated in a variety of ways.

SOLUTION TO USING THE FASB'S CODIFICATION

Under FASB ASC Section 320-10-25 you can see material labeled "Restrictions on Classification of a Debt Security as Held-to-Maturity." Paragraph 320-10-25-3 confirms what you have been telling your CEO: "Use of the held-to-maturity category is restrictive because the use of amortized cost must be justified for each investment in a debt security."

This section also lists circumstances when the held-to-maturity classification is definitely NOT appropriate. For example, paragraph 320-10-25-4b identifies potential "needs for liquidity" as a circumstance in which a debt security must NOT be classified as held to maturity. Because the securities in your company's investment portfolio are held to provide liquidity for potential business acquisitions, the held-to-maturity classification is NOT appropriate.

REVIEW CHAPTER 14

LEARNING OBJECTIVES

1 Determine why companies invest in other companies.

Companies invest in the debt and equity securities of other businesses for a variety of reasons. The most common reason is to earn a return on idle cash. Other reasons for investing in other companies include establishing a business relationship through ownership, diversifying seasonal or industry risk, and gaining access to a company's research or technology. The intended outcome of investing in other companies is to enhance the overall return to shareholders.

2 Understand the varying classifications associated with investment securities.

Securities are classified based on management's intent in holding the securities. If a firm invests in the equity securities of another company with the intent of influencing or controlling the decisions and activities of that company, the investment is accounted for using the equity method. Investments in debt and equity securities where the intent is to sell those securities should the need for cash arise or to take advantage of increases in value are classified as trading securities. Debt securities that are intended to be held until they mature are classified as held-to-maturity securities. All remaining investment securities are classified as available for sale.

3 Account for the purchase of debt and equity securities.

Debt and equity securities are accounted for at cost, which includes brokerage fees, taxes, and other charges incurred at acquisition. In the case of debt securities, accrued interest presents an additional complexity. The amount of interest accrued prior to the purchase date must be accounted for separately from the cost of the investment.

4 Account for the recognition of revenue from investment securities.

The method for recognizing revenue from investments depends on how the investment was originally classified. For debt securities, the revenue recognized is termed *interest revenue*. For trading and available-for-sale debt securities, the amount of interest revenue is a function of the stated rate of interest associated with the debt interest. In the case of held-to-maturity securities, any premium or discount associated with the initial purchase must be amortized and offset against interest revenue. For equity securities classified as trading or available for sale, dividends declared by the investee are recorded as revenue. If an investment is accounted for using the equity method, then the amount of revenue recognized is a function of the percentage of ownership. The net income of the investee is multiplied by the ownership interest and recorded as revenue.

5 Account for the change in fair value of investment securities.

Temporary changes in the fair value of debt and equity securities classified as trading or available for sale are accounted for through the use of a market adjustment account. The use of this account results in securities being valued at fair value on the balance sheet. For trading securities, the increase or decrease in fair value is reported on the income statement. In the case of available-for-sale securities, the change in fair value is disclosed as a separate component of stockholders' equity. Temporary changes in fair value for held-to-maturity securities and equity method securities are not recognized. If a decline in the fair value of an investment is judged to be permanent, the amount of the decline is recorded in the current period's income, and the investment's cost basis is adjusted.

6 **Account for the sale of investment securities.**

When an investment is sold, its carrying value is removed from the books, and the difference between carrying value and the cash received is recorded as a realized gain or loss. In the case of debt securities, an adjustment may be required to record interest revenue earned but not received prior to the sale and to amortize any premium or discount.

7 **Record the transfer of investment securities between categories.**

On occasion, management may elect to reclassify certain of its investment securities. If the reclassification involves a movement to or from the trading classification, any change in fair value not previously recognized in income is recorded in the current period. If the reclassification is from held to maturity to available for sale, changes in fair value since the investment's acquisition are recorded as a separate component of stockholders' equity. If an available-for-sale security is reclassified as a held-to-maturity security, all previously recorded changes in fair value are amortized over the remaining life of the investment.

8 **Properly report purchases, sales, and changes in fair value of investment securities in the statement of cash flows.**

The purchase and sale of available-for-sale, held-to-maturity, and equity method securities are reported in the Investing Activities section of the statement of cash flows. The cash flows associated with the purchase and sale of trading securities and securities accounted for using the fair value options are shown in the Operating or Investing Activities section depending on the reason the securities were acquired. For available-for-sale securities, realized losses are added and realized gains are subtracted when computing cash from operating activities. With trading securities, unrealized gains are also subtracted, and unrealized losses are also added if those trading securities are considered to be part of operating activities. With equity method securities, an adjustment to operating cash flow must be made to reflect the fact that the cash received from the securities in the form of dividends is not equal to the income from the securities included in the computation of net income.

9 **Explain the proper classification and disclosure of investments in securities.**

Realized gains and losses on the sale of investment securities are disclosed on the income statement in the period of the sale. Unrealized gains and losses on trading securities are also disclosed on the income statement. Unrealized increases and decreases on securities being classified as available for sale are disclosed in the Stockholders' Equity section of the balance sheet. Additional note disclosure relating to investment securities is required, and the appropriate disclosure varies, depending on the classification of the security. For investment securities reported at fair value, the magnitude of the fair values determined using Level 1, Level 2, and Level 3 inputs is disclosed.

EM EXPANDED MATERIAL

10 **Account for the impairment of a loan receivable.**

On some occasions, particularly in the case of loans made to other companies, a market value may not exist for the investment. In these instances, the investor must regularly assess the collectibility of the investment, and if it is determined that an "impairment" exists, an adjustment to the value of the receivable must be made. Impairment is measured by comparing the present value of expected future cash flows with the carrying value of the investment.

FASB-IASB CODIFICATION SUMMARY

Topic	FASB Accounting Standards Codification	Original FASB Standard	Corresponding IASB Standard	Differences between U.S. GAAP and IFRS
Classification as trading, available for sale, or held to maturity	*Section 320-10-25 par. 1*	*SFAS No. 115 par. 6-12*	*IFRS 9 par 4.1, 5.4.4*	No substantial differences
Equity method	*Topic 323*	*APB Opinion No. 18*	*IAS 28*	No substantial differences
Fair value option	*Topic 825, "Fair Value Option" subsections*	*SFAS No. 159*	*IFRS 9*	There is a fair value option for financial assets under IFRS, but as of 2010 there was not yet a fair value option for financial liabilities.
Derecognition of investment securities	*Topic 860*	*SFAS No. 140*	*IAS 39 par. 20*	Under U.S. GAAP, the transfer of a financial asset is recorded as a sale if control of the asset passes from the transferor to the transferee. Under IFRS, the transfer is recorded as a sale if the risks and rewards associated with the cash flows from the financial assets pass from the transferor to the transferee.
Classification of cash flows from the purchase and sale of investment securities	*Section 320-10-45 par. 11*	*SFAS No. 115 par. 18*	*IAS 7 par. 15-16*	Under IFRS, cash flows from the purchase and sale of trading securities are classified under operating activities; for other security categories, the cash flows are investing activities. Under U.S. GAAP, trading security cash flows may be operating or investing, depending on management intent.
Loan impairment	*Section 310-10-35*	*SFAS No. 114*	*IAS 39 par. 58 through 65*	No substantial differences

KEY TERMS

Available-for-sale securities 14-9
Control 14-17
Debt securities 14-8
Derecognition 14-33
Equity method 14-17
Equity method securities 14-9
Equity securities 14-8
Held-to-maturity securities 14-9
Parent company 14-18
Significant influence 14-17
Subsidiary company 14-18

QUESTIONS

1. Why might a company invest in the securities of another company?
2. What securities fall under the scope of FASB ASC Topic 320?
3. What criteria must be met for a security to be classified as held to maturity?
4. What criteria must be met for a security to be classified as a trading security?
5. What is "the fair value option"?
6. How does the classification of investment securities under International Financial Reporting Standards (trading, available for

sale, and held to maturity) differ from the classification under U.S. GAAP?

7. (a) When computing the price to be paid for a debt security, the stated rate of interest is used to determine what value? (b) How does the market or effective rate affect a debt security's value?
8. How does one compute the interest revenue to be recognized on a debt security if the effective-interest method is being used?
9. What other factors are considered when determining whether effective control exists when the investor does not possess absolute voting control?
10. (a) What factors may indicate the ability of an investor owning less than a majority voting interest to exercise significant influence on the investee's operating and financial policies? (b) What factors may indicate the investor's inability to exercise significant influence?
11. How is a joint venture a form of off-balance-sheet financing?
12. In the United States, we use the term "equity method investee" to describe a company in which another company has purchased between 20 and 50% of the shares and is thus able to exert significant influence. What term is used for an "equity method investee" in International Financial Reporting Standards?
13. How are changes in value reported in the financial statements for trading securities? Available-for-sale securities? Held-to-maturity securities?
14. What type of account is Market Adjustment? How is it disclosed on the financial statements?
15. How is an "other-than-temporary" decline in the value of investments recorded?
16. What impact does the sale of investment securities during the year have on the computation of unrealized gains and losses on trading securities? On unrealized increases and decreases on available-for-sale securities?
17. When transferring securities between categories, how is the transfer accounted for? At what value are the securities recorded?
18. How are realized gains and losses on trading securities handled in the statement of cash flows? How are unrealized gains and losses on trading securities handled?
19. Are trading, available-for-sale, and held-to-maturity securities disclosed on the balance sheet as current or long-term assets?
20. Where are the cash flow effects of purchases and sales of equity securities reported?
21. What additional disclosures are recommended under FASB *Statement No. 115* for trading, available-for-sale, and held-to-maturity securities?

EM EXPANDED MATERIAL

22. Why is the impairment of a loan accounted for differently from the decline in value of a debt security?

PRACTICE EXERCISES

Practice 14-1
LO3

Purchasing Debt Securities

On January 1, Issuing Company issued $100,000 in debt securities. The stated interest rate on the debt securities is 8%, with interest payable semiannually, on June 30 and December 31. On February 1, Purchasing Company purchased the bonds from the private investor who acquired them when they were originally issued. Purchasing Company paid the private investor an amount equal to the face value of the securities plus accrued interest. The securities were purchased as trading securities. Make the journal entries necessary on Purchasing Company's books to record the security purchase and the receipt of interest on June 30 using (1) the asset approach and (2) the revenue approach.

Practice 14-2
LO3

Purchasing Equity Securities

The company purchased 2,000 shares of equity securities for $27 per share. The shares were purchased as an available-for-sale investment. Make the journal entry necessary to record the purchase.

Practice 14-3
LO3

Computing the Value of Debt Securities

On January 1, the company purchased debt securities with a face value of $100,000. The securities mature in seven years. The securities have a stated interest rate of 8%, and interest is paid semiannually. The prevailing market interest rate on these debt securities is 12% compounded semiannually. Compute the fair value of the securities.

Practice 14-4
LO4

Interest Revenue for Held-to-Maturity Securities
On January 1, the company purchased debt securities for cash of $25,518. The securities have a face value of $20,000, and they mature in 15 years. The securities have a stated interest rate of 10%, and interest is paid semiannually, on June 30 and December 31. The prevailing market interest rate on these debt securities is 7% compounded semiannually. The securities were purchased as a held-to-maturity investment. Make the journal entries to record (1) the purchase of the securities, (2) the June 30 receipt of interest, and (3) the December 31 receipt of interest.

Practice 14-5
LO2, LO4

Cost Method, Equity Method, and Consolidation
Identify how each of the following investments in equity securities should be classified by the investor company:

	Number of Shares Owned by Investor Company	Total Shares of Investee Company Outstanding
1	1,200	10,000
2	6,000	8,000
3	20,000	55,000

Practice 14-6
LO4

Revenue for Trading and Available-for-Sale Securities
The company owns 2,000 shares of Stock A and 6,000 shares of Stock B. The company received dividends of $1.75 per share from Stock A and $0.97 per share from Stock B. The company classifies Stock A as a trading security and Stock B as an available-for-sale security. Make the journal entry or entries necessary to record the receipt of the cash dividends.

Practice 14-7
LO4

Revenue for Equity Method Securities
On January 1 of Year 1, Burton Company purchased 2,000 shares of the 8,000 outstanding shares of Company A for a total of $54,000. The purchase price was equal to 25% of the book value of Company A's equity. Company A's net income in Year 1 was $40,000; net income in Year 2 was $50,000. Dividends per share paid by Company A were $1.60 in Year 1 and $2.00 in Year 2. Make all journal entries necessary on Burton's book to record its investment in Company A in Year 1 and Year 2.

Practice 14-8
LO4

Equity Method: Excess Depreciation
On January 1 of Year 1, Stratton Company purchased 5,000 shares of the 15,000 outstanding shares of Company B for a total of $82,000. At the time of the purchase, the book value of Company B's equity was $202,000. Any excess of investment purchase price over the book value of Company B's equity is attributable to a building owned by Company B. The building has a remaining useful life of 11 years. Company B's net income in Year 1 was $72,000. Dividends per share paid by Company B were $1.65 in Year 1. (1) Make all journal entries necessary on Stratton's books to record its investment in Company B in Year 1. (2) Compute the Year 1 ending balance in Stratton Company's investment in Company B account.

Practice 14-9
LO4

Equity Method: Cost Greater than Book Value
On January 1 of Year 1, Dridge Company purchased 2,500 shares of the 10,000 outstanding shares of Company C for a total of $100,000. At the time of the purchase, the

book value of Company C's equity was $300,000. Company C assets having a fair value greater than book value at the time of the acquisition were as follows:

Asset	Book Value	Fair Value	Remaining Life
Inventory	$ 40,000	$ 50,000	less than 1 year
Building	200,000	250,000	10 years
Goodwill	0	40,000	indefinite

Company C's net income in Year 1 was $70,000. Dividends per share paid by Company C were $2.00 in Year 1. (1) Make all journal entries necessary on Dridge's books to record its investment in Company C in Year 1. Assume that the goodwill is not impaired. (2) Compute the Year 1 ending balance in Dridge Company's investment in Company C account.

Practice 14-10
LO5

Changes in Value: Trading Securities
On December 1, the company purchased securities for $3,850. On December 31, the company still held the securities. Make the necessary adjusting journal entry to record a change in value of the securities assuming that their December 31 fair value was (a) $5,200 and (b) $2,600. In addition, before considering the impact of the change in value of the securities, the net income for the company was $3,000. Compute net income assuming that the December 31 fair value of the securities was (c) $5,200 and (d) $2,600. Ignore income taxes. Assume that the securities are classified as trading.

Practice 14-11
LO5

Changes in Value: Available-for-Sale Securities
Refer to Practice 14-10. Make the adjusting journal entries for (a) and (b) and the computations for (c) and (d), assuming that the securities are classified as available for sale.

Practice 14-12
LO5

Changes in Value: Held-to-Maturity Securities
Refer to Practice 14-10. Make the adjusting journal entries for (a) and (b) and the computations for (c) and (d), assuming that the securities are classified as held to maturity. The changes in value are not deemed to be "other than temporary."

Practice 14-13
LO5

Changes in Value: Equity Method
Refer to Practice 14-10. Make the adjusting journal entries for (a) and (b) and the computations for (c) and (d), assuming that the securities are accounted for using the equity method. Ignore the impact of the investee company income and dividends. The changes in value are not deemed to be "other than temporary."

Practice 14-14
LO6

Sale of Securities
During Year 1, the company purchased 1,000 shares of stock for $24 per share. Near the end of Year 1, the company sold 400 shares. Make the journal entry to record the sale, assuming that the shares were sold for (1) $27 per share and (2) $20 per share. The shares were classified as trading securities.

Practice 14-15
LO6

Sale of Securities and the Market Adjustment Account
The company purchased the following securities during Year 1:

Security	Classification	Cost	Fair Value (Dec. 31, Year 1)
A	Trading	$ 9,000	$10,000
B	Trading	10,000	16,000

On July 23, Year 2, the company sold all of the shares of security B for a total of $9,500. As of December 31, Year 2, the shares of security A had a fair value of $5,800. No other activity occurred during Year 2 in relation to the trading security portfolio. (1) What amount should the company report as *realized gain or loss* in the Year 2 income statement? Clearly indicate whether the amount is a gain or a loss. (2) What amount should the company report as *unrealized gain or loss* in the Year 2 income statement? Clearly indicate whether the amount is a gain or a loss.

Practice 14-16
LO7

Transfer between Categories: To and from Trading
The company purchased the following securities during Year 1:

Security	Classification	Cost	Fair Value (Dec. 31, Year 1)
A	Trading	$5,000	$4,000
B	Available for sale	6,000	8,000

In Year 2, the company reclassified both of these securities. Security A was reclassified as available for sale; the fair value of security A at the time of the reclassification was $5,500. Security B was reclassified as trading; the fair value of security B at the time of the reclassification was $4,100. Make the journal entries necessary to record both of these reclassifications.

Practice 14-17
LO7

Transfer between Categories: Available for Sale
The company purchased the following securities during Year 1:

Security	Classification	Cost	Fair Value (Dec. 31, Year 1)
A	Available for sale	$ 8,200	$ 7,100
B	Held to maturity	10,000	13,500

In Year 2, the company reclassified both of these securities. Security A was reclassified as held to maturity; the fair value of security A at the time of the reclassification was $8,850. Security B was reclassified as available for sale; the fair value of security B at the time of the reclassification was $9,450. Make the journal entries necessary to record both of these reclassifications. (*Note*: The held-to-maturity securities were acquired at their face value, so there has been no amortization.)

Practice 14-18
LO8

Cash Flow and Available-for-Sale Securities
The company entered into the following transactions during the year:

Purchase of investment securities	$400
Sale of investment securities	470

The company had no investment securities at the beginning of the year. The cost of the investment securities sold was $350. The fair value of the remaining securities was $65 on December 31. The net income for the year was $880. Assume that net income does not include any noncash items and does not reflect gains or losses related to investment securities.

Assume that the securities are classified as available for sale. Compute (1) cash flow from operating activities and (2) cash flow from investing activities.

Practice 14-19
LO8

Cash Flow and Trading Securities
Refer to Practice 14-18. Assume that the securities are classified as trading and that they were purchased for operating purposes. Compute (1) cash flow from operating activities and (2) cash flow from investing activities.

Practice 14-20
LO9

Disclosure: Computation of Total Economic Gain
During Year 1, Walters Company purchased 6,000 shares of Company A common stock for $25 per share and 10,000 shares of Company B common stock for $32 per share.

These investments are classified as available-for-sale securities. At December 31, Year 1, Walters Company appropriately recorded a $95,000 debit to Market Adjustment—Available-for-Sale Securities. On March 23, Year 2, the 6,000 shares of Company A common stock were sold for $41 per share. The fair value of the Company B shares on December 31, Year 2, was $38 per share. (1) Prepare *all* journal entries *needed in Year 2* related to these securities. (2) Compute the total increase in economic value generated by Walters' stock portfolio during Year 2.

EM EXPANDED MATERIAL

Practice 14-21
LO10

Loan Impairment: Initial Measurement

On January 1 of Year 1, the lending company made a $10,000, 8% loan. The $800 interest is receivable at the end of each year, with the principal amount to be received at the end of five years. As of the end of Year 1, the first year's interest of $800 has not yet been received because the borrower is experiencing financial difficulties. The lending company negotiated a restructuring of the loan. The payment of all of the interest ($4,000 = $800 × 5 years) will be delayed until the end of the 5-year loan term. In addition, the amount of principal repayment will be dropped from $10,000 to $5,000. Make the journal entry necessary on the lending company's books to record this loan impairment on December 31 of Year 1. (*Note*: *No* interest revenue has been recognized in Year 1 in connection with the loan.)

Practice 14-22
LO10

Loan Impairment: Subsequent Interest Revenue

Refer to Practice 14-21. Make all journal entries necessary on the lending company's books in connection with the loan during Year 2, Year 3, Year 4, and Year 5. Assume that all cash payments are received according to the renegotiated schedule.

EXERCISES

Exercise 14-23
LO4

Investment in Equity Securities

On January 10, 2013, Delta Corporation acquired 12,000 shares of the outstanding common stock of Kennedy Company for $600,000. At the time of purchase, Kennedy Company had outstanding 48,000 shares with a book value of $2.4 million. On December 31, 2013, the following events took place:

(a) Kennedy reported net income of $180,000 for the calendar year 2013.
(b) Delta received from Kennedy a dividend of $0.55 per share of common stock.
(c) The fair value of Kennedy Company stock had temporarily declined to $41 per share.

Give the entries that would be required to reflect the purchase and subsequent events on the books of Delta Corporation, assuming that (1) the security is classified as available for sale and (2) the equity method is appropriate.

Exercise 14-24
LO4

Investment in Equity Securities—Fair Value Different from Book Value

On January 3, 2013, McDonald Inc. purchased 40% of the outstanding common stock of Old Farms Co., paying $128,000 when the book value of the net assets of Old Farms equaled $250,000. The difference was attributed to equipment, which had a book value of $60,000 and a fair value of $100,000, and to buildings, with a book value of $50,000 and a fair value of $80,000. The remaining useful life of the equipment and buildings was 4 years and 12 years, respectively. During 2013, Old Farms reported net income of $80,000 and paid dividends of $50,000.

Prepare the journal entries made by McDonald Inc. during 2013 related to its investment in Old Farms.

Exercise 14-25
LO4

Investment in Equity Securities—Unrecorded Intangible

Alpha Co. acquired 20,000 shares of Beta Co. on January 1, 2012, at $12 per share. Beta Co. had 80,000 shares outstanding with a book value of $800,000. The difference between the book value and fair value of Beta Co. on January 1, 2012, is attributable to a broadcast license intangible asset. Beta Co. recorded earnings of $360,000 and $390,000 for 2012 and 2013, respectively, and paid per-share dividends of $1.60 in 2012 and $2.00 in 2013. Assuming a 20-year straight-line amortization policy for the broadcast license, give the entries to record the purchase in 2012 and to reflect Alpha's share of Beta's earnings and the receipt of the dividends for 2012 and 2013.

Exercise 14-26
LO4

Accounting Methods for Equity Securities

For each of the following independent situations, determine the appropriate accounting method to be used: cost or equity. For cost method situations, determine whether the security should be classified as trading or available for sale. For equity method situations, determine whether consolidated financial statements would be required. Explain the rationale for your decision.

(a) ATV Company manufactures and sells 4-wheel recreational vehicles. It also provides insurance on its products through its wholly owned subsidiary, RV Insurance Company.
(b) Buy Right Inc. purchased 20,000 shares of Big Supply Company common stock to be held as a long-term investment. Big Supply has 200,000 shares of common stock outstanding.
(c) Super Tire Manufacturing Co. holds 5,000 shares of the 10,000 outstanding shares of nonvoting preferred stock of Valley Corporation. Super Tire considers the investment as being long-term in nature.
(d) Takeover Company owns 15,000 of the 50,000 shares of common stock of Western Supply Company. Takeover has tried and failed to obtain representation on Western's board of directors. Takeover intends to sell the securities if it cannot obtain board representation at the next stockholders' meeting, scheduled in three weeks.
(e) Espino Inc. purchased 50,000 shares of Independent Mining Company common stock. Independent has a total of 125,000 common shares outstanding. Espino has no intention to sell the securities in the foreseeable future.

Exercise 14-27
LO5, LO6

Accounting for Securities

During 2012, the first year of its operations, Profit Industries purchased the following securities:

Security	Classification	Cost	Fair Value, Dec. 31, 2012	Fair Value, Dec. 31, 2013
A	Trading	$18,000	$13,000	$ 9,000
B	Trading	8,000	9,000	10,000
C	Available for sale	17,000	15,000	17,000
D	Available for sale	24,000	28,000	13,000

During 2013, Profit sold one-half of security A for $8,000 and one-half of security D for $15,000.

Provide the journal entries required to do the following:

1. Adjust the portfolio of securities to its fair value at the end of 2012.
2. Record the sale of security A and security D.
3. Adjust the portfolio of securities to its fair value at the end of 2013.

Exercise 14-28
LO8

Investment Securities and the Statement of Cash Flows

Indicate how each of the following transactions or events would be reflected in a statement of cash flows prepared using the indirect method. Each transaction or event is independent of the others. For items (a) and (d), assume that the balance in the market adjustment account was zero at the beginning of the year. In all cases, assume that trading securities were acquired for operating purposes.

(a) At year-end, the trading securities portfolio has an aggregate cost of $185,000 and an aggregate fair value of $150,000.
(b) During the year, trading securities and available-for-sale securities were purchased for $50,000 and $70,000, respectively. The securities were paid for in cash.
(c) Trading securities on hand at the beginning of the period (cost $40,000) were sold for $62,000 cash.
(d) At year-end, the trading securities portfolio has an aggregate cost of $170,000 and an aggregate fair value of $190,000.

Exercise 14-29
LO3, LO4, LO6

Recording Securities Transactions

The following transactions of Kelsey, Inc., occurred within the same accounting period:

(a) Purchased $55,000 U.S. Treasury 6% bonds, paying 102 plus accrued interest of $1,400. Kelsey uses the revenue approach to record accrued interest on purchased bonds. Kelsey classified this security as a trading security.
(b) Purchased 2,100 shares of Dulce Co. common stock at $67 per share. Kelsey classifies this stock as an available-for-sale security.
(c) Received semiannual interest on the U.S. Treasury bonds.
(d) Sold 400 shares of Dulce at $81 per share.
(e) Sold $20,000 of U.S. Treasury 6% bonds at 101 plus accrued interest of $180.
(f) Purchased an $18,000, 6-month certificate of deposit. The certificate is classified as a trading security.

Prepare the entries necessary to record these transactions.

Exercise 14-30
LO4

SPREADSHEET

Amortization of a Discount on a Debt Security

On January 1, 2013, Cougar Creations Inc. purchased $100,000 of 5-year, 8% bonds when the effective rate of interest was 10%, paying $92,277. Interest is to be paid on July 1 and December 31.

1. Prepare an interest amortization schedule for the bonds.
2. Prepare the journal entries made by Cougar Creations on July 1 and December 31 of 2013 to recognize the receipt of interest and to amortize the discount.

Exercise 14-31
LO5

Valuation of a Debt Security

Using the information from Exercise 14-30, provide the journal entry that would be necessary to properly value the debt security if, on December 31, 2013, the bond's fair value was $96,500. Assume the security was initially classified as follows:

1. A trading security
2. An available-for-sale security
3. A held-to-maturity security

Exercise 14-32
LO3, LO5

SPREADSHEET

Trading Securities

During 2013, Litten Company purchased trading securities as a short-term investment. The costs of the securities and their fair values on December 31, 2013, follow:

Security	Cost	Fair Value, Dec. 31, 2013
A	$ 65,000	$ 75,000
B	100,000	54,000
C	220,000	226,000

At the beginning of 2013, Litten had a zero balance in the market adjustment—trading securities account. Before any adjustments related to these trading securities, Litten had net income of $287,000.

1. What is net income after making any necessary trading security adjustments? (Ignore income taxes.)
2. What would net income be if the fair value of security B were $95,000?

Exercise 14-33
LO5

Valuation of Securities

Truss Builders Co. reported the following selected balances on its financial statements for each of the four years 2011–2014:

	2011	2012	2013	2014
Market adjustment—Available-for-sale securities	$0	$ 6,200	$4,600	$ (800)
Market adjustment—Trading securities	0	(1,800)	300	1,550

Based on these balances, reconstruct the valuation entries that must have been made each year.

Exercise 14-34
LO3, LO5, LO6

Accounting for Trading Securities

During 2012, Spelling Inc. purchased the following trading securities:

Security	Cost	Fair Value, Dec. 31, 2012
Bizarre Corp. common	$31,000	$33,000
8% U.S. Treasury notes	16,000	9,000
PhalCo bonds	22,000	25,000

At the beginning of 2012, Spelling had a zero balance in Market Adjustment—Trading Securities.

1. What entry would be made at year-end, assuming the preceding values?
2. What entry would be made during 2013, assuming one-half of the Bizarre Corp. common stock is sold for $17,000?
3. Give the entry that would be made at the end of 2013, assuming the following situations:
   (a) The fair value of remaining securities is $50,000.
   (b) The fair value of remaining securities is $52,500.
   (c) The fair value of remaining securities is $56,000.

Exercise 14-35
LO5

Debt and Equity Securities

American Steel Corp. acquired the following securities in 2013:

Security	Classification	Cost	Fair Value, Dec. 31, 2013
A	Trading	$10,000	$12,000
B	Trading	16,000	10,000
C	Available for sale	12,000	15,000
D	Available for sale	20,000	15,000
E	Held to maturity	20,000	22,000

At the beginning of 2013, American Steel had a zero balance in each of its market adjustment accounts.

1. What entry or entries would be made at the end of 2013, assuming the preceding fair values?
2. If net income before any adjustments related to investment securities was $100,000, what would reported income be after adjustments? (Ignore income taxes.)

Exercise 14-36
LO4

Amortization of a Premium on a Debt Security

On January 1, 2013, Randy Incorporated purchased $600,000 of 20-year, 10% bonds when the market rate of interest was 8%. Interest is to be paid on June 30 and December 31 of each year.

1. Prepare the journal entry to record the purchase of the debt security classified as held to maturity.
2. Prepare the journal entry to record the receipt of the first two interest payments, assuming that Randy accounts for the debt security as held to maturity and uses the effective-interest method.

Exercise 14-37
LO3, LO4, LO6

Accounting for the Purchase and Sale of Securities

During January 2013, Aragorn Inc. purchased the following securities:

Security	Classification	No. of Shares	Total Cost
Gimli Corporation stock	Trading	500	$ 9,000
Legolas International Inc. stock	Available for sale	1,000	22,000
Glorfindel Enterprises stock	Available for sale	2,500	42,500
Mirkwood Co. bonds	Held to maturity	—	24,000
U.S. Treasury bonds	Trading	—	11,000

During 2013, Aragorn received interest from Mirkwood and the U.S. Treasury totaling $3,630. Dividends received on the stock held amounted to $1,760. During November 2013, Aragorn sold 200 shares of the Gimli stock at $17 per share and 250 shares of the Glorfindel stock at $19 per share.

Give the journal entries required by Aragorn to record the (1) purchase of the debt and equity securities; (2) receipt of interest and dividends during 2013; and (3) sale of the equity securities during November.

Exercise 14-38
LO5

Temporary and "Other-Than-Temporary" Changes in Value

The securities portfolio for Malibu Industries contained the following trading securities:

Securities (common stock)	Initial Cost	Fair Value, Dec. 31, 2012	Fair Value, Dec. 31, 2013
Brooks Co.	$15,000	$18,000	$22,300
Sonoma Co.	12,000	8,000	5,300
Taylor Co.	24,000	20,000	25,700

1. Assuming that all changes in fair value are considered temporary, what is the effect of the changes in value on the 2012 and 2013 financial statements? Give the valuation entries for these years, assuming that the market adjustment account has a $0 balance at the beginning of 2012.
2. Assume that at December 31, 2013, management believed that the fair value of the Sonoma Co. common stock reflected an "other-than-temporary" decline in the value of that stock. Give the entries to be made on December 31, 2013, under this assumption.

Exercise 14-39

LO8

Gain and Losses and the Statement of Cash Flows

Miss Maggie Company entered into the following transactions during the year:

Purchase of trading securities	$500
Sale of trading securities	220
Purchase of available-for-sale securities	900
Sale of available-for-sale securities	470

Miss Maggie had no investment securities at the beginning of the year. The cost of the trading securities sold was $300; the cost of the available-for-sale securities sold was $150. The fair value of the remaining securities on December 31 was as follows: trading securities, $310; available-for-sale securities, $460. The net income for the year was $985. Assume that net income does not include any noncash items except for those related to investment securities. In all cases, assume that trading securities were acquired for operating purposes.

Compute (1) cash flow from operating activities and (2) cash flow from investing activities.

Exercise 14-40

LO5, LO6

Reclassification of Securities

Bicknel Technologies Inc. purchased the following securities during 2012:

Security	Classification	Cost	Fair Value, Dec. 31, 2012
A	Trading	$ 2,000	$ 4,000
B	Trading	7,000	6,000
C	Available for sale	18,000	16,000
D	Available for sale	5,000	4,000
E	Held to maturity	14,000	15,000

At the beginning of 2012, Bicknel Technologies had a zero balance in each of its market adjustment accounts. During 2013, after the 2012 financial statements had been issued, Bicknel determined that security B should be reclassified as an available-for-sale security and security C should be reclassified as a trading security. The fair values on the date of the transfer are $5,500 for security B and $17,000 for security C.

Prepare the journal entries to do the following:

1. Adjust the portfolio of securities to its fair value at December 31, 2012.
2. Reclassify security B as an available-for-sale security in 2013.
3. Reclassify security C as a trading security in 2013.

Exercise 14-41

LO5, LO7

Reclassification of Securities

Kyoto Inc. had the following portfolio of securities at the end of its first year of operations:

Security	Classification	Cost	Year-End Fair Value
A	Trading	$ 8,000	$13,000
B	Trading	15,000	18,000

1. Provide the entry necessary to adjust the portfolio of securities to its fair value.
2. In the following year, Kyoto elects to reclassify security B as an available-for-sale security. On the date of the transfer, security B's fair value is $16,500. Provide the journal entry to reclassify security B.

EM EXPANDED MATERIAL

Exercise 14-42
LO10

SPREADSHEET

Accounting for the Impairment of a Loan

Tortuga Enterprises loaned $350,000 to Turner Inc. on January 1, 2012. The terms of the loan require principal payments of $70,000 each year for five years plus interest at the market rate of interest of 6%. The first principal and interest payment is due on January 1, 2013. Turner made the required payments during 2013 and 2014. However, during 2014 Turner began to experience financial difficulties, requiring Tortuga to reassess the collectibility of the loan. On December 31, 2014, Tortuga determines that the remaining principal payments will be collected, but the collection of interest is unlikely.

1. Compute the present value of the expected future cash flows as of December 31, 2014.
2. Provide the journal entry to record the loan impairment as of December 31, 2014.
3. Provide the journal entries for 2015 to record the receipt of the principal payment on January 1 and the recognition of interest revenue as of December 31, assuming that Tortuga's assessment of the collectibility of the loan has not changed.

PROBLEMS

Problem 14-43
LO3, LO5, LO6

Accounting for Trading Securities

Fox Company made the following transactions in the common stock of NOP Company:

July 10, 2011	Purchased 10,000 shares at $45 per share.
Sept. 29, 2012	Sold 2,000 shares for $51 per share.
Aug. 17, 2013	Sold 2,500 shares for $33 per share.

The end-of-year market prices for the shares were as follows:

December 31, 2011	$47 per share
December 31, 2012	39 per share
December 31, 2013	31 per share

Instructions: Prepare the necessary entries for 2011, 2012, and 2013, assuming the NOP stock is classified as a trading security.

Problem 14-44
LO3, LO4, LO5, LO6

SPREADSHEET

Recording and Valuing Trading Securities

Myers & Associates reports the following information on its December 31, 2011, balance sheet:

Trading securities (at cost)	$225,850	
Less: Market adjustment—trading securities	2,260	$223,590

Supporting records of Myers' trading securities portfolio show the following debt and equity securities:

Security	Cost	Fair Value
200 shares Conway Co. common	$ 25,450	$ 24,300
$80,000 U.S. Treasury 7% bonds	79,650	77,400
$120,000 U.S. Treasury 7 1/2% bonds	120,750	121,890
Total	$225,850	$223,590

Interest dates on the treasury bonds are January 1 and July 1. Myers & Associates uses the revenue approach to record the purchase of bonds with accrued interest.

During 2012 and 2013, Myers & Associates completed the following transactions related to trading securities:

2012

Jan.	1	Received semiannual interest on U.S. Treasury bonds. Assume that the appropriate adjusting entry was made on December 31, 2011.
Apr.	1	Sold $60,000 of the 7 1/2% U.S. Treasury bonds at 102 plus accrued interest. Brokerage fees paid were $200.
May	21	Received dividend of $0.25 per share on the Conway Co. common stock. The dividend had not been recorded on the declaration date.
July	1	Received semiannual interest on U.S. Treasury bonds and then sold the 7% bonds at 97 1/2. Brokerage fees paid were $250.
Aug.	15	Purchased 100 shares of Nieman Inc. common stock at $116 per share.
Nov.	1	Purchased $50,000 of 8% U.S. Treasury bonds at 101 plus accrued interest. Interest dates are January 1 and July 1.
Dec.	31	Market prices of securities were Conway Co. common, $110; 7 1/2% U.S. Treasury bonds, 101 3/4; 8% U.S. Treasury bonds, 101; Nieman Inc. common, $116.75.

2013

Jan.	2	Recorded the receipt of semiannual interest on the U.S. Treasury bonds.
Feb.	1	Sold the remaining 7 1/2% U.S. Treasury bonds at 101 plus accrued interest. Brokerage fees paid were $300.

Instructions:

1. Prepare journal entries for the preceding transactions and to accrue interest on December 31, 2012. Ignore any amortization of premium or discount on U.S. Treasury bonds. Give computations in support of your entries.
2. Show how trading securities would be presented on the December 31, 2012, balance sheet.

Problem 14-45

LO3, LO4, LO5, LO6

Accounting for Debt and Equity Securities

During 2013, Rooster Company purchased 5,000 shares of Hen Company common stock for $18 per share and 3,200 shares of Egg Company common stock for $21 per share. These investments are intended to be held as ready sources of cash and are classified as trading securities.

Also in 2013, Rooster purchased 6,400 shares of Chicken Company common stock for $27 per share and $80,000 of treasury notes at 103. These securities are classified as available for sale.

During 2013, Rooster received the following interest and dividend payments on its investments:

Hen Company	$2.50 per share dividend
Egg Company	$1.25 per share dividend
Chicken Company	$1.00 per share dividend
Treasury notes	8% annual interest earned for 6 months

Fair values of the securities at December 31, 2013, were as follows:

Hen Company	$21 per share
Egg Company	$16 per share
Chicken Company	$24 per share
Treasury notes	104

On March 23, 2014, the 3,200 shares of Egg common stock were sold for $16 per share. On June 30, 2014, the treasury notes were sold at 102 plus accrued interest.

Fair values of remaining securities at December 31, 2014, were as follows:

Hen Company	$20 per share
Chicken Company	$30 per share

Instructions:

1. Prepare all 2013 and 2014 journal entries related to these securities.
2. Describe how the following items would be treated on Rooster Company's statement of cash flows for the year ended December 31, 2014. Rooster uses the indirect method of reporting cash flows from operating activities. In all cases, assume that trading securities were acquired for operating purposes.
   (a) Proceeds from the sale of Egg shares and any realized gain or loss from the sale.
   (b) Proceeds from the sale of the treasury securities and any realized gain or loss from the sale.
   (c) Any unrealized gain or loss on the remaining securities.

Problem 14-46

LO3, LO4, LO5, LO6, LO9

Journal Entries and Balance Sheet Presentation for Investments in Securities

On December 31, 2011, Durst Company's balance sheet showed the following balances related to its securities accounts:

Trading securities . . .	$155,000	
Less: Market adjustment—trading securities . . .	(7,250)	$147,750
Available-for-sale securities . . .	$108,000	
Add: Market adjustment—available-for-sale securities . . .	10,000	118,000
Interest receivable—NYC water bonds . . .		1,250

Durst's securities portfolio on December 31, 2011, was made up of the following securities:

Security	Classification	Cost	Market
1,000 shares Herzog Corp. stock . . .	Trading	$75,000	$76,250
800 shares Taylor Inc. stock. . .	Trading	55,000	52,825
10% New York City water bonds (interest payable semiannually on January 1 and July 1). . .	Trading	25,000	18,675
1,000 shares Martin Inc. stock. . .	Available for sale	59,000	65,000
2,000 shares Outdoors Unlimited Inc. stock . . .	Available for sale	49,000	53,000

During 2012, the following transactions took place:

Jan.	3	Received interest on the New York City water bonds.
Mar.	1	Purchased 300 additional shares of Herzog Corp. stock for $22,950, classified as a trading security.
Apr.	15	Sold 400 shares of the Taylor Inc. stock for $69 per share.
May	4	Sold 400 shares of the Martin Inc. stock for $62 per share.
July	1	Received interest on the New York City water bonds.
Oct.	30	Purchased 1,500 shares of Cook Co. stock for $83,250, classified as a trading security.

The fair values of the stocks and bonds on December 31, 2012, are as follows:

Herzog Corp. stock	$76.60 per share
Taylor Inc. stock	$68.50 per share
Cook Co. stock	$55.25 per share
New York City water bonds	$20,555
Martin Inc. stock	$61.00 per share
Outdoors Unlimited Inc. stock	$27.00 per share

Instructions:

1. Make all necessary journal entries for 2012, including any year-end accrual or adjusting entries.
2. Show how the investment securities would be presented on the balance sheet at December 31, 2012. Assume that the available-for-sale securities are classified as current assets.

Problem 14-47

LO3, LO4, LO5, LO7

REVERSE SOLVABLE

Journal Entries for Trading Securities

During 2013 and 2014, Foley Co. made the following journal entries to account for transactions involving trading securities:

2013

			Debit	Credit
(a)	Nov. 1	Investment in Trading Securities—7% U.S. Treasury Bonds	52,417	
		Cash		52,417
		To record the purchase of $50,000 of U.S. Treasury bonds at 102.50. Interest is payable semiannually on January 1 and July 1.		
(b)	Dec. 31	Unrealized Increase/Decrease in Value of Available-for-Sale Securities	2,227	
		Market Adjustment—Trading Securities		2,227
		To record the decrease in fair value of the current investment securities based on the following data.		

	Cost	Market	Market Adjustment
Lawlor Co. stock	$ 26,420	$ 25,260	$1,160 Cr.
Hurst Co. stock	34,850	36,200	1,350 Dr.
7% U.S. Treasury bonds	52,417	50,000	2,417 Cr.
Total	$113,687	$111,460	$2,227 Cr.

The beginning balance in Market Adjustment—Trading Securities was a $900 credit. There were no other entries in 2013.

2014

			Debit	Credit
(c)	Jan. 1	Cash	1,750	
		Interest Revenue		1,750
		To record interest revenue for 6 months.		
(d)	July 1	Cash	1,750	
		Interest Revenue		1,750
		To record interest revenue for 6 months.		
(e)	Dec. 6	Investment in Available-for-Sale Securities—Lawlor Co.	26,420	
		Investment in Trading Securities—Lawlor Co.		26,420
		To reclassify Lawlor Co. stock from trading securities to available-for-sale securities. Market price was $26,100 at the date of reclassification.		
(f)	Dec. 31	Unrealized Increase/Decrease in Value of Available-for-Sale Securities	937	
		Market Adjustment—Available-for-Sale Securities		220
		Market Adjustment—Trading Securities		717
		To record the decrease in fair value of available-for-sale securities based on the following data.		

	Cost	Market	Market Adjustment
Hurst Co. stock	$ 34,850	$ 35,350	$ 500 Dr.
7% U.S. Treasury bonds	52,417	51,200	1,217 Cr.
Lawlor Co. stock	26,420	26,200	220 Cr.
Total	$113,687	$112,750	$ 937 Cr.

There were no other entries in 2014.

Instructions: For each incorrect entry, give the entry that should have been made. Assume the revenue approach is used. Ignore any premium or discount amortization on U.S. Treasury bonds.

Problem 14-48
LO5

Valuation of Equity Securities

The investment portfolio of Morris Inc. on December 31, 2012, contains the following securities:

- Opus Co. common, 3% ownership, 5,000 shares; cost, $100,000; fair value, $95,000; classified as a trading security.
- Garrod Inc. preferred, 2,000 shares; cost, $40,000; fair value, $43,000; classified as a trading security.
- Sherrill Inc. common, 30% ownership, 20,000 shares; cost, $1,140,000; fair value, $1,130,000; classified as an influencing investment.
- Jennings Co. common, 15% ownership, 25,000 shares; cost, $67,500; fair value, $50,000; classified as an available-for-sale security.

Instructions:

1. Give the valuation adjustment required at December 31, 2012, assuming that all investments were purchased in 2012 and none of the indicated declines in fair value are considered other than temporary.
2. Assume that the Jennings Co.'s common stock market decline is considered other than temporary. Give the valuation entry required at December 31, 2012, under this change in assumption.
3. Assume that the fair values for the long-term investment portfolio at December 31, 2013, were as follows:

Opus Co. common	$ 102,000
Garrod Inc. preferred	43,000
Sherrill Inc. common	1,115,000
Jennings Co. common	45,000

Give the valuation entries at December 31, 2013, assuming that the investment categories remain the same and that all declines in 2012 and 2013 are temporary except for the 2012 decline in Jennings Co. stock.

Problem 14-49
LO4, LO5

Investments in Common Stock

Both Seco Inc. and Hillsborough Corp. have 100,000 shares of no-par common stock outstanding. World Inc. acquired 10,000 shares of Seco stock for $6 per share and 30,000 shares of Hillsborough stock for $12 per share in 2012. Both securities are being held as long-term investments. Changes in retained earnings for Seco and Hillsborough for 2012 and 2013 are as follows:

	Seco Inc.	Hillsborough Corp.
Retained earnings (deficit), January 1, 2012	$175,000	$ (45,000)
Net income, 2012	40,000	70,000
Cash dividends, 2012	(37,500)	—
Retained earnings, December 31, 2012	$177,500	$ 25,000
Net income, 2013	70,000	40,000
Cash dividends, 2013	(45,000)	(20,000)
Retained earnings, December 31, 2013	$202,500	$ 45,000
Fair value of stock: December 31, 2012	$ 7.50	$ 13.00
December 31, 2013	6.50	15.00

Instructions: Give the entries required on the books of World Inc. for 2012 and 2013 to account for its investments.

Problem 14-50

LO3, LO4, LO5

Long-Term Investments in Stock—Equity Method

On January 1, 2013, Standard Co. bought 40% of the outstanding common stock of Exchange Corp. for $380,000 cash. Standard Co. accounts for this investment by the equity method. At the date of acquisition of the stock, Exchange Corp.'s net assets had a carrying value of $630,000. Assets with an average remaining life of five years have a current fair value that is $160,000 in excess of their carrying values. The remaining difference between the purchase price and the value of the underlying stockholders' equity cannot be attributed to any identifiable tangible or intangible asset. Accordingly, the remaining difference is allocated to goodwill. At the end of 2013, Exchange Corp. reports net income of $210,000. During 2013, Exchange Corp. declared and paid cash dividends of $30,000.

Instructions: Give the entries necessary to reflect Standard Co.'s investment in Exchange Corp. for 2013.

Problem 14-51

LO4, LO5

Investment in Common Stock

On July 1 of the current year, Melissa Co. acquired 25% of the outstanding shares of common stock of International Co. at a total cost of $700,000. At the time, the equity (net assets) of Melissa totaled $2,400,000, meaning that the $700,000 purchase price was greater than 25% of Melissa's net assets. Melissa was willing to pay more than book value for the International Co. stock for the following reasons:

(a) International owned depreciable plant assets (10-year remaining economic life) with a current fair value of $60,000 more than their carrying amount.
(b) International owned land with a current fair value of $300,000 more than its carrying amount.
(c) There are no other identifiable tangible or intangible assets with fair value in excess of book value. Accordingly, the remaining excess, if any, is to be allocated to goodwill.

International Co. earned net income of $527,000 evenly over the current year ended December 31. On December 31, International declared and paid a cash dividend of $105,000 to common stockholders. Fair value of Melissa's share of the stock at December 31 is $761,000. Both companies close their accounting records on December 31.

Instructions:

1. Compute the total amount of goodwill of International Co. based on the price paid by Melissa Co.
2. Prepare all journal entries in Melissa's accounting records relating to the investment for the year ended December 31 under the cost method of accounting, classifying the securities as available for sale.
3. Prepare all journal entries in Melissa's accounting records relating to the investment for the year ended December 31 under the equity method of accounting.

Problem 14-52

LO3, LO4

Investment in Common Stock—Fair Value Less than Book Value

JJJ Inc. purchased 35% of ABC Co. on January 4, 2013, for $280,000 when ABC's book value was $810,000. On that day, the fair value of the net assets of ABC equaled their book values with the following exceptions:

	Book	Fair Value
Equipment	$175,000	$140,000
Buildings	40,000	65,000

The equipment has a remaining useful life of 10 years, and the building has a remaining useful life of 20 years. ABC reported the following related to operations for 2013 and 2014:

	Net Income (Loss)	Dividends
2013	$ 80,000	$15,000
2014	(10,000)	8,000

Instructions: Provide the entries made by JJJ Inc. relating to its investment in ABC for the years 2013 and 2014.

Problem 14-53

LO5, LO7

Reclassification of Securities

Willow Creek Incorporated had the following portfolio of securities on December 31, 2012:

Security	Classification	Cost	Fair Value, Dec. 31, 2012
A	Trading	$18,000	$23,000
B	Trading	31,000	37,000
C	Available for sale	3,000	6,000
D	Available for sale	12,000	14,000
E	Available for sale	34,000	28,000
F	Held to maturity	65,000	67,000

The balances in the market adjustment accounts as of January 1, 2012, were as follows:

Market Adjustment—Trading Securities	$9,000 Dr.
Market Adjustment—Available-for-Sale Securities	3,600 Cr.

During 2013, Willow Creek determined that certain securities should be reclassified. Those reclassifications are as follows:

Security	Old Classification	New Classification	Fair Value at Date of Reclassification
A	Trading	Available for sale	$24,400
C	Available for sale	Trading	5,200
D	Available for sale	Held to maturity	15,000
F	Held to maturity	Trading	63,500

Instructions:

1. Make the necessary journal entries to adjust Willow Creek's portfolio of securities to fair value as of December 31, 2012.
2. Make the necessary journal entries to reclassify the securities in 2013.

Problem 14-54

LO5, LO6, LO7

Accounting for Marketable Equity Securities

Trans America Trust Co. owns both trading and available-for-sale securities. The securities shown on page 14-70 were owned on December 31, 2012.

Trading Securities:

Security	Shares	Total Cost	Fair Value, Dec. 31, 2012	Market Adjustment
Albert Groceries, Inc.	600	$ 9,000	$11,500	$2,500 Dr.
West Data, Inc.	1,000	27,000	18,000	9,000 Cr.
Steel Co.	450	9,900	10,215	315 Dr.
Total		$45,900	$39,715	$6,185 Cr.

Available-for-Sale Securities:

Security	Shares	Total Cost	Fair Value, Dec. 31, 2012	Market Adjustment
Dairy Products	2,000	$ 86,000	$ 90,000	$ 4,000 Dr.
Vern Movies, Inc.	15,000	390,000	365,000	25,000 Cr.
Disks, Inc.	5,000	60,000	80,000	20,000 Dr.
Total		$536,000	$535,000	$ 1,000 Cr.

The following transactions occurred during 2013:

(a) Sold 500 shares of West Data, Inc., for $9,500.
(b) Sold 200 shares of Disks, Inc., for $3,000.
(c) Transferred all shares of Albert Groceries, Inc., to the available-for-sale portfolio when the total fair value was $12,900.
(d) Transferred the remaining shares of Disks, Inc., to the trading securities portfolio when the market price was $20 per share. These shares were subsequently sold for $18 per share.

At December 31, 2013, market prices for the remaining securities were as follows:

Security	Market Price per Share
Albert Groceries, Inc.	$22
West Data, Inc.	15
Steel Co.	21
Dairy Products	46
Vern Movies, Inc.	31

Instructions: Prepare all journal entries necessary to record Trans America Trust Co.'s marketable equity securities transactions and year-end adjustments for 2013. Assume that all declines in fair value are temporary.

Problem 14-55
LO4, LO5

Accounting for Long-Term Investments

On January 2, 2011, Weston Company acquired 20% of the 200,000 shares of outstanding common stock of Startile Corp. for $18 per share. The purchase price was equal to Startile's underlying book value. Weston plans to hold this stock to influence the activities of Startile.

The following data are applicable for 2011 and 2012:

	2011	2012
Startile dividends (paid Oct. 31)	$28,000	$ 29,000
Startile earnings	93,000	105,000
Startile stock market price at year-end	21	20

On January 2, 2013, Weston Company sold 12,000 shares of Startile stock for $23 per share. During 2013, Startile reported net income of $80,000, and on October 31, 2013, Startile paid dividends of $22,000. At December 31, 2013, after a significant stock market decline, which is expected to be temporary, Startile's stock was selling for $14 per share. After selling the 12,000 shares, Weston does not expect to exercise significant influence over Startile, and the shares are classified as available for sale.

Instructions:

1. Make all journal entries for Weston Company for 2011, 2012, and 2013, assuming the 20% original ownership interest allowed significant influence over Startile.
2. Make the year-end valuation adjusting entries for Weston Company for 2011, 2012, and 2013, assuming the 20% original ownership interest did not allow significant influence over Startile.

Problem 14-56
LO8, LO9

Investment Securities and the Statement of Cash Flows

Julie Company came into existence with a $2,000 cash investment by owners on January 1, 2013, and entered into the following transactions during 2013:

Sales	$ 3,200
Cash expenses	(2,700)
Purchase of building on January 1	550
Purchase of trading securities	500
Sale of trading securities (cost, $200)	340
Purchase of available-for-sale securities	300
Sale of available-for-sale securities (cost, $100)	60

The following additional information is available:

Balance in accounts receivable on December 31	$190
Depreciation expense recognized for the year	50
Fair value of remaining trading securities on December 31	210
Fair value of remaining available-for-sale securities on December 31	270

Instructions:

1. Prepare an income statement for 2013.
2. Prepare a complete statement of cash flows for 2013. Use the indirect method of reporting cash from operating activities. In all cases, assume that trading securities were acquired for operating purposes.
3. Prepare a balance sheet as of December 31, 2013.

Problem 14-57
LO2

Sample CPA Exam Questions

1. A company should report the marketable equity securities that it has classified as trading at:
   (a) Lower of cost or market, with holding gains and losses included in earnings.
   (b) Lower of cost or market, with holding gains included in earnings only to the extent of previously recognized holding losses.
   (c) Fair value, with holding gains included in earnings only to the extent of previously recognized holding losses.
   (d) Fair value, with holding gains and losses included in earnings.
2. Nola Co. has a portfolio of marketable equity securities which it does not intend to sell in the near term. How should Nola classify these securities, and how should it report unrealized gains and losses from these securities?

	Classify as	Report as
(a)	Trading securities	Component of income from continuing operations
(b)	Available-for-sale securities	Separate component of stockholders' equity
(c)	Trading securities	Separate component of stockholders' equity
(d)	Available-for-sale securities	Component of income from continuing operations

3. Kale Co. purchased bonds at a discount on the open market as an investment and intends to hold these bonds to maturity. Kale should account for these bonds at:
   (a) Cost.
   (b) Amortized cost.
   (c) Fair value.
   (d) Lower of cost or market.

EM EXPANDED MATERIAL

Problem 14-58
LO10

Accounting for the Impairment of a Loan

Halstead Associates loaned Stevens Company $600,000 on January 1, 2011. The terms of the loan were payment in full on January 1, 2016, plus annual interest payments at 10%. The interest payment was made as scheduled on January 1, 2012; however, due to financial setbacks, Stevens was unable to make its 2013 interest payment. Halstead considers the loan impaired and projects the following cash flows from the loan as of December 31, 2013, and 2014. Assume that Halstead accrued the interest at December 31, 2012, but did not continue to accrue interest due to the impairment of the loan.

Projected Cash Flows:

Date of Flow	Amount Projected as of Dec. 31, 2013	Amount Projected as of Dec. 31, 2014
Dec. 31, 2014	$ 40,000	$ 40,000
Dec. 31, 2015	120,000	140,000
Dec. 31, 2016	150,000	220,000
Dec. 31, 2017	200,000	200,000
Dec. 31, 2018	90,000	

Instructions:

1. Prepare the valuation adjusting entry at December 31, 2013.
2. Prepare the journal entry to record the $40,000 receipt on December 31, 2014.
3. Prepare the valuation adjusting entry at December 31, 2014.
4. Prepare the 2015 journal entries, assuming the receipt of $140,000 as scheduled; also assume that estimates for future cash flows remain the same as they were at the end of 2014.

CASES

Discussion Case 14-59

But Do We Really Have "Mark to Market" Accounting Now?

The movement toward the use of fair value for investments has been given the label "mark to market." Previously, marketable equity securities were valued at the lower of cost or market. The shift to fair value, whether higher or lower than cost, is a significant departure from the past. Even though all investments classified as trading or available for sale are now valued at fair values, only market changes for trading securities affect the income statement. To many accounting theorists, this is indeed a cop-out on the part of the FASB. These accountants reason that if market changes are going to be recognized on the balance sheet, they should be recognized on the income statement as well. This position was held by the two FASB members who voted against the issuance of pre-Codification *Statement No. 115*. This is also the approach taken in the "fair value option" and, as noted in the chapter, is the common-sense approach advocated by Sir David Tweedie, chairman of the IASB.

Evaluate the rationale for this compromise position. What arguments for the two different approaches (income and equity) do you think are most persuasive and why? What future events could cause standard setters to revise this approach?

Discussion Case 14-60

Why Is 49% Ownership Enough?

In 1986, **The Coca-Cola Company** borrowed $2.4 billion to purchase several large soft drink bottling operations. Then a separate company, **Coca-Cola Enterprises**, was formed to bottle and distribute Coke throughout the country. The Coca-Cola Company sold 51% of Coca-Cola Enterprises to the public and retained a 49% ownership. The $2.4 billion debt incurred to finance the purchase was transferred to the balance sheet of Coca-Cola Enterprises.

While 49% ownership did not guarantee control, it did give The Coca-Cola Company significant influence over the bottling company. For example, The Coca-Cola Company determines the price at which it will sell concentrate to Coca-Cola Enterprises and reviews Coca-Cola Enterprises' marketing plan. In addition, The Coca-Cola Company's chief operating officer initially was chairman of Coca-Cola Enterprises, and many current or former Coca-Cola Company officials have served on Coca-Cola Enterprises' board of directors.

SOURCE: *The Wall Street Journal*, October 15, 1986, pp. A1 and A12.

1. From an accounting standpoint, what is the significance of owning more than 50% of a company's stock?
2. Why would The Coca-Cola Company elect to own less than 50% of its distribution network?
3. In the consolidation process, the parent's and the subsidiary's individual asset and liability account balances are added together and reported on the consolidated financial statements, whereas with the equity method, the net investment is reported as an asset on the investor company's balance sheet. Why would The Coca-Cola Company want to avoid consolidation?

Discussion Case 14-61

Which Method of Accounting for Investments Is Appropriate?

International Inc. owns companies or the stock of companies in countries all over the world. International is reviewing its methods of accounting for those companies and has asked you to provide input as to whether the cost method, the equity method, or consolidation is appropriate for each of the following subsidiaries. Provide justification for your suggestions.

1. Subsidiary 1: This subsidiary, MEOil, is an oil company located in the Middle East. A growing anti-American sentiment in the country in which the company is located has led International to remove all non-native employees. There is a growing fear that the government may nationalize MEOil. International Inc. owns 75% of the oil company.
2. Subsidiary 2: Ecological Inc., a company that produces environmentally safe products, has production facilities in more than 10 states. The ownership of the company is widely held, with International Inc. holding the largest block of stock. International has succeeded in placing its president and vice president in two of the five board of directors' seats of Ecological Inc. International owns 15% of Ecological Inc.'s outstanding stock.

3. Subsidiary 3: International Inc. recently purchased 100% of the outstanding stock of Harmon National Bank. This subsidiary represents International's first purchase of a nonmanufacturing facility, and management has expressed concern about the comparability of the different accounting methods used by financial institutions.
4. Subsidiary 4: International has been involved in a takeover battle with Beatrix Inc. involving Campton Soups. Beatrix recently purchased 50% of the stock of Campton. International has owned 30% of Campton's stock for five years.

Discussion Case 14-62

What Is the Difference in Accounting between the Cost and Equity Methods?
Logical Corporation, a producer of medical products, disclosed the following investments in affiliates in the notes to its July 31, 2013, financial statements:

	2013	2012
Investments (if classified as available for sale)	$ 822,188	$ 50,000
Investments (if using the equity method)	1,677,181	2,009,647

Discuss the factors that determine whether Logical uses the cost or the equity method in accounting for its investment in affiliates. What events are recorded when the security is accounted for as an available-for-sale security? What events are recorded when the equity method is used? What does the investment account represent when the security is classified as available for sale? What does it represent using the equity method?

Discussion Case 14-63

How Different Are International Standards?
You have been approached about doing a consulting job for Choi Hung Company, which is based in southern China. Choi Hung reports its financial results using International Financial Reporting Standards. The consulting job involves sorting through Choi Hung's purchases and sales of investment securities for the past three years to make sure that the reported results are in conformity with international standards. An acquaintance has advised you not to take this consulting job because "you are trained in U.S. GAAP and don't know anything about international standards." How might you respond?

Case 14-64

Deciphering Financial Statements (The Walt Disney Company)
Locate **Disney**'s 2009 financial statements and related notes on the Internet and answer the following questions:

1. Locate Disney's note that discusses investments. What amount of the investment portfolio is classified as available for sale? Now look at Disney's balance sheet. What percentage of the total investment account is classified as available-for-sale securities? What types of securities constitute the balance in that account?
2. Locate Disney's note that discusses what types of securities are included in "Investments" on the balance sheet. Also examine the note that defines cash and cash equivalents. Are all of Disney's investment securities listed under Investments in the balance sheet?
3. Review the note on "Fair Value Measurement" to determine the fair value of investments on October 3, 2009. Why is this number so much less than that reported as Investments on the balance sheet?

Case 14-65

Deciphering Financial Statements (Intel)
The note shown on page 14-75 is taken from **Intel**'s 2009 annual report.

Note 7: Available-for-Sale Investments

Available-for-sale investments as of December 26, 2009 and December 27, 2008 were as follows:

	2009				2008			
(In Millions)	Adjusted Cost	Gross Unrealized Gains	Gross Unrealized Losses[1]	Fair Value	Adjusted Cost	Gross Unrealized Gains	Gross Unrealized Losses	Fair Value
Commercial paper	$ 5,444	$ —	$ —	$ 5,444	$ 3,244	$ 4	$ —	$ 3,248
Corporate bonds	3,688	38	(14)	3,712	6,323	5	(139)	6,189
Government bonds[2]	2,205	11	(1)	2,215	546	2	—	548
Bank time deposits[3]	1,317	1	—	1,318	606	2	—	608
Marketable equity securities	387	386	—	773	393	2	(43)	352
Asset-backed securities	154	—	(18)	136	374	—	(43)	331
Money market fund deposits	65	—	—	65	419	—	—	419
Total available-for-sale investments	$13,260	$436	$(33)	$13,663	$11,905	$15	$(225)	$11,695

[1] As of December 26, 2009, unrealized non-credit components of other-than-temporary impairments recognized on available-for-sale investments were insignificant.

[2] Includes bonds issued or deemed to be guaranteed by non-U.S. governments, FDIC-insured corporate bonds, U.S. agency securities, and U.S. Treasury securities.

[3] Bank time deposits were primarily issued by institutions outside the U.S. as of December 26, 2009 and December 27, 2008.

As of December 26, 2009, we had $33 million of gross unrealized losses on available-for-sale investments, which included $26 million of gross unrealized losses related to individual securities that had been in a continuous loss position for 12 months or more.

As of December 26, 2009, a majority of our available-for-sale investments in an unrealized loss position were rated AA-/Aa3 or better. With the exception of a limited number of investments for which we have recognized other-than-temporary impairments, we have not seen significant liquidation delays, and for those that have matured we have received the full par value of our original debt investments.

We sold available-for-sale investments, primarily marketable equity securities, for proceeds of $192 million in 2009 ($1.2 billion in 2008 and $1.7 billion in 2007, primarily marketable debt instruments). The gross realized gains on sales of available-for-sale investments totaled $43 million in 2009 ($38 million in 2008 and $138 million in 2007) and were primarily related to our sales of marketable equity securities.

1. What amount of gains and losses on available-for-sale securities is reported in Intel's 2009 income statement? How much is realized? How much is unrealized?
2. Judging from the comparison of book values to fair values, what portion of Intel's available-for-sale portfolio performed the best in 2009?

Case 14-66

Writing Assignment (Going around the income statement)

The accounting provisions in FASB ASC Topic 320 outline two different treatments for unrealized gains and losses depending on whether the security is classified as trading or available for sale. Unrealized gains and losses for trading securities are reported on the income statement, while unrealized gains and losses for available-for-sale securities are reported as other comprehensive income and then become part of accumulated other comprehensive income in stockholders' equity.

Your assignment is to develop an argument, in writing, for including unrealized gains and losses for available-for-sale securities on the income statement. Include in your 1-page paper reasons as to why the FASB might have chosen the reporting rules that it did and be able to refute the Board's reasoning.

Case 14-67

Ethical Dilemma (Reclassifying securities for gain)

You are the chief financial officer of a large manufacturing company. As CFO, you are responsible for investing excess cash in marketable securities and then handling the accounting for those securities. Your firm has a policy of classifying all securities as being available for sale. At the end of the year, preliminary financial results indicate that your company will be slightly below targeted net income. The board of directors has given you the task of determining how income might be increased without (and the board emphasized this point) going outside of the rules.

You determine that one method of increasing net income would be to reclassify all available-for-sale securities that have experienced an increase in fair value as if they were purchased as trading securities.

1. Would this reclassification achieve the desired results?
2. Is this reclassification within the rules?
3. Is this reclassification consistent with the intent of FASB *Statement No. 115*?
4. If you were the company's external auditor, what questions might you have regarding this reclassification?

Case 14-68

Cumulative Spreadsheet Analysis

This assignment is based on the spreadsheet prepared in (1) of the cumulative spreadsheet assignment for Chapter 13. Review that assignment for a summary of the assumptions made in preparing a forecasted balance sheet, income statement, and statement of cash flows for 2014 for Skywalker Company. This assignment involves changing assumption (h) in the Chapter 13 assignment.

	Original Cost	Fair Value, 12/31/2013
Security A	$10	$22
Security B	25	18
Security C	5	8
Security D	40	15
Total	1	7
	$81	$70

[*Note*: These numbers imply that the accumulated other comprehensive income balance of $132 (credit) as of December 31, 2013, includes a debit amount of $11($81 − $70) from available-for-sale securities.]

As mentioned in the Chapter 13 assignment, Skywalker intends to invest another $28 in available-for-sale securities (security F) in 2014 in order to increase the total value of the portfolio by 40% to $98 ($70 + $28).

Because Skywalker cannot predict future stock prices, the best forecast is that the fair values of Securities A through E will remain the same during 2014 and that the fair value of security F, to be acquired in 2014 for $28, will remain at $28.

Revise the spreadsheet made in (1) of the Chapter 13 assignment in accordance with the above and following assumptions. In each case, any gains or losses expected to be realized in 2014 should be reported in a separate income statement line, "Investment income, net."

1. Skywalker intends to sell security A in 2014 at an anticipated price of $22. That $22 will be used to buy security G. Skywalker's best forecast is that the fair value of security G will remain at $22 through the end of 2014.
2. How does the sale of security A in (1) impact expected cash from operating activities in 2014? Explain.
3. Repeat (1) and (2) assuming that, instead of selling security A, Skywalker intends to sell security D in 2014 at an anticipated price of $15, which will be used to buy security G. Skywalker's best forecast is that the fair value of security G will remain at $15 through the end of 2014.

P3 ADDITIONAL ACTIVITIES OF A BUSINESS

CHAPTER 15 Leases

LEARNING OBJECTIVES

1. Describe the circumstances in which leasing makes more business sense than does an outright sale and purchase.
2. Understand the accounting issues faced by the asset owner (lessor) and the asset user (lessee) in recording a lease transaction.
3. Outline the types of contractual provisions typically included in lease agreements.
4. Apply the lease classification criteria in order to distinguish between capital and operating leases.
5. Properly account for both capital and operating leases from the standpoint of the lessee (asset user).
6. Properly account for both capital and operating leases from the standpoint of the lessor (asset owner).
7. Prepare and interpret the lease disclosures required of both lessors and lessees.
8. Compare the treatment of accounting for leases in the United States with the requirements of international accounting standards.

EM EXPANDED MATERIAL

9. Record a sale-leaseback transaction for both a seller-lessee and a purchaser-lessor.

Which company owns the largest number of commercial jets in the world? Did you guess **Delta**, **United**, or **American**? Those are good guesses. As of December 31, 2009, those three airlines, which are the three largest in the United States, owned the following number of aircraft:

	Number of Aircraft Owned on December 31, 2009
Delta	677
American	590
United	209

The company that owns the most commercial jets, however, is **General Electric**. Through its GE Capital Aviation Services subsidiary, General Electric owns over 1,800 aircraft that it leases to more than 225 customer airlines in over 70 countries. Aircraft leasing companies own about 40% of the passenger jets flying today. The leasing companies buy the jets from **Boeing** or **Airbus** and in turn lease them to an airline. Not one to let a good business opportunity slip away, Boeing is also in the leasing business. In a move that was seen by many as putting itself in close competition with companies that already buy its planes and lease them to airlines, Boeing restructured Boeing Capital Corporation in 1999 in an effort to become a major player in the airplane financing business.[1]

Airlines use these leasing arrangements as an alternative to obtaining loans to buy the planes themselves. Large stable airlines typically sign long-term leases of 15 to 20 years. Smaller airlines trying to establish a market toehold are likely to sign more expensive short-term leases of four to eight years.[2] The flexibility that lease financing gives to airlines was illustrated in the wake of the September 11, 2001, World Trade Center attack when the business of most airlines suffered substantially. Airlines were able to cancel or renegotiate their leases to adapt to this lower passenger traffic. Of course, the leasing companies were also impacted; they began to scrutinize the financial condition of their potential customer airlines more carefully. In fact, in October 2001, **International Lease Finance Corporation (ILFC)** (which leases 985 aircraft worldwide, mostly outside the United States) shipped 30 pilots to Zurich to snatch 19 of ILFC's planes that had been leased to **Swissair**. Like auto repossession specialists, the pilots boarded the planes and flew them to France. The reason for the repossession was that ILFC's planes appeared to be in danger of being dragged into the bankruptcy proceedings of Swissair.[3]

As an accountant, a question you might ask yourself while flying at 35,000 feet is whether your airline reports its leased planes as assets on its balance sheet. The answer is sometimes yes but often no. In the case of Delta, a company that leased 306 airplanes (or 31% of its fleet) as of December 31, 2009, only 93 of those leased aircraft were reported on the company's balance sheet. The remaining 213 planes, for which Delta had made contractual promises to pay billions of dollars in the future, were not reported on the balance sheet as assets, nor were the future lease payments reported as a liability. The only financial statement indication that these planes even exist is buried in the lease note to Delta's financial statements.

So, when is a leased airplane an asset? Keep reading; that question is what this chapter is all about.

? QUESTIONS

1. How is it that General Electric owns so many more airplanes than does American Airlines?
2. Why do airlines find it attractive to lease rather than buy their airplanes?
3. Do leased airplanes appear as assets in the balance sheets of the airlines that are using the planes? Explain.

Answers to these questions can be found on page 15-42.

[1] Jeff Cole, "Boeing Overhauls Financing Operation, Heightening Rivalry with Its Lessors," *The Wall Street Journal*, October 4, 1999, p. A3.

[2] John H. Taylor, "Fasten Seat Belts, Please," *Forbes*, April 2, 1990, p. 84.

[3] J. Lynn Lunsford, "With Airlines in a Dive, Secretive Leasing Firm Plays a Crucial Role," *The Wall Street Journal*, February 12, 2002, p. A1.

A lease is a contract specifying the terms under which the owner of property, the lessor, transfers the right to use the property to a lessee. In this chapter, we will focus on how leases are accounted for from both the lessor's and the lessee's perspectives. We will discuss the issues associated with classifying a lease as a debt-financed purchase of property (capital lease) or as a rental (operating lease) and the disclosure issues associated with that classification. In addition, we will illustrate how businesses can have definite obligations to pay significant amounts of money in the future relating to operating lease obligations yet not recognize those obligations as liabilities on the balance sheet.

Historically, a major challenge for the accounting profession has been to establish accounting standards that prevent companies from using the legal form of a lease to avoid recognizing future payment obligations as a liability. "Off-balance-sheet financing" continues to be a perplexing problem for the accounting profession, and leasing is probably the oldest and most widely used means of keeping debt off the balance sheet. This chapter will discuss in detail and analyze the criteria established by the FASB in an attempt to bring more long-term leases onto the balance sheet as well as specific accounting procedures used for leased assets. In addition, we will discuss how international financial reporting standards differ from those in the United States.

FYI

The Committee on Accounting Procedure (CAP) addressed the issue of leasing in 1949 with *ARB No. 38*. The APB, formed in 1959, issued four opinions on the subject. The FASB issued pre-codification *Statement No. 13* on leases in 1976 and has subsequently issued over a dozen amendments and interpretations of the lease accounting rules.

Economic Advantages of Leasing

1 **Describe the circumstances in which leasing makes more business sense than does an outright sale and purchase.**

WHY **Accountants get very excited about the interesting accounting issues surrounding leases. But we should remember that leases actually serve very important business purposes that have nothing to do with accounting.**

HOW **The lessee (the party using the leased asset) enjoys flexibility and reduced risk through leasing rather than buying. The lessor (the party that owns the leased asset) uses the attractiveness of leasing to increase sales and establish long-term relationships with customers.**

Before discussing the accounting treatment of leases, it is important first to consider the valid business reasons for entering into a lease agreement. It would be unfair and incorrect to imply that the only reason companies lease property is to avoid reporting the lease obligation in the financial statements. Although the accounting ramifications are an important consideration in structuring a deal as a lease, other financial and tax considerations also play an important role in the leasing decision.

Every situation is different, but there are three primary advantages to the lessee of leasing over purchasing.

1. *No down payment.* Most debt-financed purchases of property require a portion of the purchase price to be paid immediately by the borrower. This provides

Skip Nall/Photodisc/Getty Images

Car leasing provides increased sales for automakers while making payments more affordable for car owners.

added protection to the lender in the event of default and repossession. Lease agreements, in contrast, frequently are structured so that 100% of the value of the property is financed through the lease. This aspect of leasing makes it an attractive alternative to a company that does not have sufficient cash for a down payment or wishes to use available capital for other operating or investing purposes. Of course, many leases also require a down payment; as an example, look carefully at the fine print the next time you see a car lease advertisement on television.

2. *Avoid risks of ownership*. There are many risks accompanying the ownership of property. These risks include casualty loss, obsolescence, changing economic conditions, and physical deterioration. If the market value of a leased asset decreases dramatically, the lessee may terminate the lease, although usually with some penalty. On the other hand, if you own the asset, you are stuck with it when the market value declines.
3. *Flexibility*. Business conditions and requirements change over time. If assets are leased, a company can more easily replace assets in response to these changes. This flexibility is especially important in businesses where innovation and technological change make the future usefulness of particular equipment or facilities highly uncertain. A prime example of this condition in recent years has been in high-tech industries with rapid change in areas such as computer technology, robotics, and telecommunications. Flexibility is a primary reason for the popularity of automobile leasing. Car buyers like the flexibility of choosing a brand-new car every two or three years as their leases run out.

The lessor also may find benefits to leasing its property rather than selling it. Advantages of the lease to the lessor include the following:

1. *Increased sales*. For the reasons suggested in the preceding paragraphs, customers may be unwilling or unable to purchase property. By offering potential customers the option of leasing its products, a manufacturer or dealer may significantly increase its sales volume.
2. *Ongoing business relationship with lessee*. When property is sold, the purchaser frequently has no more dealings with the seller of the property. In leasing situations, however, the lessor and lessee maintain contact over a period of time, and long-term business relationships often can be established through leasing.
3. *Residual value retained*. In many lease arrangements, title to the leased property never passes to the lessee. The lessor benefits from economic conditions that may result in a significant residual value at the end of the lease term. The lessor may lease the asset to another lessee or sell the property and realize an immediate gain. For example,

new car leasing provides auto dealers with a supply of 2- to 3-year-old used cars, which can then be sold or leased again.

> **! CAUTION**
>
> The sooner you get comfortable with the terms *lessee* and *lessor*, the better. The *lessor* is the legal owner of the leased asset; the *lessee* is the party that will use the leased asset.

In summary, a leasing arrangement is often a sound business practice for both the lessee and the lessor. The remainder of the chapter discusses the intricate and interesting accounting implications of leases.

Simple Example

2 **Understand the accounting issues faced by the asset owner (lessor) and the asset user (lessee) in recording a lease transaction.**

WHY **For the lessor, the key accounting issue is whether or not a sale should be recognized on the date the lease is signed. For the lessee, the key accounting issue is whether the leased asset and the lease payment obligation should be recognized on the balance sheet.**

HOW **Capital leases are accounted for as if the lease agreement transfers ownership of the leased asset from the lessor to the lessee. Operating leases are accounted for as rental agreements.**

A simple example will be used to introduce the accounting issues associated with leases. Owner Company owns a piece of equipment with a market value of $10,000 and an estimated useful life of five years. User Company wishes to acquire the equipment for use in its operations. One option for User Company is to purchase the equipment from Owner by borrowing $10,000 from a bank at an interest rate of 10%. User can use the $10,000 to buy the equipment from Owner and can repay the principal and interest on the bank loan in five equal annual installments of $2,638.

Alternatively, User Company can lease the asset from Owner for five years, making five annual "rental" payments of $2,638. From User's standpoint, the lease is equivalent to purchasing the asset, the only difference being the legal form of the transaction. User will still use the equipment for five years and will still make payments of $2,638 per year. From Owner's standpoint, the primary difference in the transaction is that now Owner is not just selling the equipment but is also substituting for the bank in providing financing.

With this lease arrangement, the key accounting issue for Owner Company is as follows:

- On the date the lease is signed, should Owner Company recognize an equipment sale?

The correct answer to this question hinges on factors that have been discussed in previous chapters in connection with inventory sales and revenue recognition.

- Has effective ownership of the equipment been passed from Owner to User?
- Is the transaction complete, meaning does Owner have any significant responsibilities remaining in regard to the equipment?
- Is Owner reasonably certain that the five annual payments of $2,638 can be collected from User?

The key accounting issue for User Company is as follows:

- On the date the lease is signed, should User recognize the leased equipment as an asset and the obligation to make the lease payments as a liability?

The correct answer to this question also hinges on whether effective ownership, as opposed to legal ownership, of the equipment changes hands when Owner and User sign the lease agreement.

Accounting for leases is a classic illustration of the accounting aphorism "substance over form." The legal form of the lease is that Owner Company maintains ownership of the equipment, but whether the lease transfers economic ownership of the asset from Owner to User depends on the specifics of the lease agreement. Consider the following four independent scenarios:

- The lease agreement stipulates that Owner is to maintain legal title to the equipment for the 5-year lease period, but title is to pass to User at the end of the lease.
- The lease agreement stipulates that Owner is to maintain legal title to the equipment for the 5-year lease period, but at the end of the lease period User has the option to buy the equipment for $1.
- The useful life of the equipment is just five years. Accordingly, when the lease term is over, the equipment can no longer be used by anyone else.
- Present value calculations suggest that payment of the five annual $2,638 lease payments is equivalent to paying $10,000 for the equipment on the lease-signing date.

In each of these four scenarios, the economic substance of the lease is that the lease signing is equivalent to the transfer of effective ownership, and the fact that Owner retains legal title of the equipment during the lease period is a mere technicality. On the other hand, if the lease agreement does not provide for the transfer of the legal title at the end of the lease, if the lease covers only a fraction of the useful life of the equipment, and if the lease payments are not large enough to "pay" for the equipment, then economically the lease is just a rental, not a transfer of ownership.

For accounting purposes, leases are separated into two groups, capital leases and operating leases. Capital leases are accounted for as if the lease agreement transfers ownership of the asset from the lessor to the lessee. In the preceding example, if the lease is accounted for as a capital lease, Owner Company would recognize the sale of the equipment on the lease-signing date and would recognize earned interest revenue as the five annual lease payments are collected. On the lease-signing date, User Company would recognize the leased asset, as well as the liability for the future lease payments, on its balance sheet.

Operating leases are accounted for as rental agreements, with no transfer of effective ownership associated with the lease. In the foregoing example, if the lease is accounted for as an operating lease, Owner Company recognizes no sale on the lease-signing date. Instead, lease rental revenue is recognized each year when the lease payment is collected. User Company recognizes no leased asset and no lease liability but reports only a periodic lease rental expense equal to the annual lease payments.

From this simple introduction, you may receive the misleading impression that accounting for leases is straightforward and noncontroversial. In fact, most companies using assets under lease agreements go to great lengths to ensure that they can account for the bulk of their leases as operating leases because it allows them to keep both the asset and the associated liability off the balance sheet. Keeping the asset off the balance sheet improves financial ratio measures of efficiency, and keeping the liability off the balance sheet improves measures of leverage. For companies that lease a large portion of the assets that they use, the accounting standards associated with leasing are the most critical accounting standards that they apply.

The following sections contain a more detailed description of the kinds of provisions found in lease agreements. In addition, the specific accounting rules used to distinguish between operating leases and capital leases will be explained.

Nature of Leases

3 **Outline the types of contractual provisions typically included in lease agreements.**

WHY **The specific contractual provisions in a lease determine whether or not the lease involves a transfer of economic ownership.**

HOW **The key contractual provisions of a lease are cancellation provisions, bargain purchase option (if any), lease term, residual value (and whether it is guaranteed or unguaranteed), and the minimum lease payments.**

Leases vary widely in their contractual provisions. Reasons for this variability include cancellation provisions and penalties, bargain renewal and purchase options, lease term, economic life of assets, residual asset values, minimum lease payments, interest rates implicit in the lease agreement, and the degree of risk assumed by the lessee, including payments of certain costs such as maintenance, insurance, and taxes. These and other relevant facts must be considered in determining the appropriate accounting treatment of a lease.

The many variables affecting lease capitalization have been given precise definitions that must be understood in order to account for the various types of leases found in practice. Each of these variables is defined and briefly discussed in the following sections.

Cancellation Provisions

Some leases are noncancelable, meaning that these lease contracts are cancelable only on the outcome of some remote contingency or that the cancellation provisions and penalties of these leases are so costly to the lessee that, in all likelihood, cancellation will not occur. All cancelable leases are accounted for as operating leases; some, but not all, noncancelable leases are accounted for as capital leases.

> **CAUTION**
>
> To determine whether a bargain purchase option exists, the parties to the lease must be able to make a reasonable estimate as to what the fair value of the leased asset will be at the end of the lease.

Bargain Purchase Option

Leases often include a provision giving the lessee the right to purchase leased property at some future date. If the specified purchase option price is expected to be considerably less than the fair value at the date the purchase option may be exercised, the option is called a bargain purchase option. By definition, a bargain purchase option is one that is expected to be exercised. Accordingly, a lease agreement including a bargain

FYI

The lease term is an important concept in capital lease accounting for lessees because it can determine the period over which the leased asset is depreciated.

purchase option is likely to result in the transfer of asset ownership from the lessor to the lessee. Noncancelable leases with bargain purchase options are accounted for as capital leases.

Lease Term

An important variable in lease agreements is the lease term, that is, the time period from the beginning to the end of the lease. The beginning of the lease term occurs when the leased property is transferred to the lessee. The end of the lease term is more flexible because many leases include provisions allowing the lessee to extend the lease period. For accounting purposes, the end of the lease term is defined as the end of the fixed noncancelable lease period plus all renewal option periods that are likely to be exercised. A bargain renewal option is one with such an attractive lease rate, or other favorable provision, that at the inception of the lease, it is likely that the lease will be renewed beyond the fixed lease period. If a bargain purchase option is included in the lease contract, the lease term includes any renewal periods preceding the date of the bargain purchase option but does not extend beyond the date of the bargain purchase option.

Residual Value

The market value of the leased property at the end of the lease term is referred to as its *residual value*. In some leases, the lease term extends over the entire economic life of the asset or the period in which the asset continues to be productive, and there is little, if any, residual value. In other leases, the lease term is shorter, and a significant residual value does exist. If the lessee can purchase the asset at the end of the lease term at a materially reduced price from its residual value, a bargain purchase option is present, and it can be assumed that the lessee would exercise the option and purchase the asset.

CAUTION

The residual value risk for unguaranteed residual values is borne by the lessor; the residual value risk for guaranteed residual values is borne by the lessee.

Some lease contracts require the lessee to guarantee a minimum residual value. If the market value at the end of the lease term falls below the guaranteed residual value, the lessee must pay the difference. This provision protects the lessor from loss due to unexpected declines in the market value of the asset. For example, assume that the car you lease is expected to have a \$15,000 residual value at the end of the lease term and that you guarantee that amount to the car dealership. However, at the end of the lease term, the residual value of the car is only \$10,000. You are then obligated to pay the dealership the \$5,000 difference because the dealership is, in effect, guaranteed the full amount of the residual value that was estimated at the beginning of the lease. You may buy the car for the \$15,000 guaranteed amount, but the lease terms do not require the purchase.

If there is no bargain purchase option or guarantee of the residual value, the lessor reacquires the property at the end of the lease term and may offer to renew the lease, lease the asset to another lessee, or sell the property. The actual amount of the residual value is unknown until the end of the lease term; however, it must be estimated at the inception of the lease. The residual value under these circumstances is referred to as the unguaranteed residual value.

Minimum Lease Payments

The rental payments required over the lease term plus any amount to be paid for the residual value either through a bargain purchase option or a guarantee of the residual value are referred to as the minimum lease payments. Lease payments sometimes include charges for items such as insurance, maintenance, and taxes incurred for the leased property. These are referred to as executory costs, and they are not included as part of the minimum lease payments. In addition, building lease payments are often composed of a fixed minimum amount with additional payments made based on sales by the lessee. The additional payments are not considered part of the minimum lease payment.

To illustrate the computation of minimum lease payments, assume that Dorney Leasing Co. owns and leases road equipment for three years at $3,000 per month. Included in the lease payment is $500 per month for executory costs to insure and maintain the equipment. At the end of the 3-year period, Dorney is guaranteed a residual value of $10,000 by the lessee.

Minimum lease payments:	
Rental payments exclusive of executory costs ($2,500 × 36)	$ 90,000
Guaranteed residual value	10,000
Total minimum lease payments	$100,000

How did Dorney decide that a $2,500 monthly lease payment would be sufficient? Calculation of the appropriate lease payment involves consideration of the fair value of the leased equipment, the guaranteed residual value, the lease term, and the appropriate interest rate. Dorney computed the $2,500 monthly lease payment by using an interest rate of 12% compounded monthly (1% per month) and a fair value of the road equipment of $82,258. The computation is as follows:

Present value of 36 monthly payments of $2,500 ($3,000 less executory costs of $500) at 1% interest (12% compounded monthly) paid at the end of each month:	
PMT = $2,500, *N* = 36, *I* = 1%, *PV*	$75,269
Present value of $10,000 guaranteed residual value at the end of three years at 12% compounded monthly:	
FV = $10,000, *N* = 36, *I* = 1%, *PV*	6,989
Present value of minimum lease payments	$82,258

Of course, this computation is backwards; in actuality, Dorney would use the $82,258 fair value and the interest rate of 12% compounded monthly to compute the desired monthly lease payment of $2,500. The interest rate used is called the implicit interest rate: the rate used by the lessor in calculating the desired lease payment.

FYI

If the lessee cannot ascertain the lessor's implicit rate, the incremental borrowing rate is used in the lessee's present value calculations. Two reasons the lessee would not be able to compute the implicit rate are if the asset being leased does not have a readily determinable fair value or if a reliable estimate of residual value cannot be obtained.

As discussed later in the chapter, the present value of the minimum lease payments is also an important quantity for the lessee. A complication arises because the implicit interest rate used by the lessor in calculating the lease payments may not be the appropriate discount rate for the lessee. For purposes of computing the present value of the minimum lease payments, the lessee uses the *lower* of the implicit interest rate used by the lessor and the lessee's own incremental borrowing rate. The lessee's incremental borrowing rate is the rate at which the lessee could borrow the amount of money necessary to purchase the leased asset, taking into consideration the lessee's financial situation and the current conditions in the marketplace.

The use of present value formulas and tables in discounting minimum lease payments is illustrated later in the chapter.

Lease Classification Criteria

4 Apply the lease classification criteria in order to distinguish between capital and operating leases.

WHY The lease classification criteria were designed by the FASB to capture the idea of the transfer of economic ownership. In practice, these criteria are often used by companies in designing leases to make sure that they get the accounting treatment (either capital or operating) that they desire.

HOW If a lease involves a transfer of ownership, a bargain purchase option, a lease term greater than or equal to 75% of the economic life of the leased asset, or minimum payments with a present value of at least 90% of the fair value of the leased asset, then the lease is accounted for as a capital lease. Otherwise, the lease is accounted for as an operating lease.

Leasing was one of the topics on the original agenda of the FASB, and in 1976 the Board issued pre-codification *Statement No. 13*, "Accounting for Leases." The objective of the FASB in issuing *Statement No. 13* was to reflect the economic reality of leasing by requiring that some long-term leases be accounted for as capital acquisitions by the lessee and sales by the lessor. To accomplish this objective, the FASB identified criteria to determine whether a lease is merely a rental contract (an operating lease) or is, in substance, a purchase of property (a capital lease). The lease classification criteria and their applicability to lessees and lessors are summarized in Exhibit 15-1. These criteria are now found in FASB ASC Topic 840.

EX 15-1 LEASE CLASSIFICATION CRITERIA

Capital Lease		Operating Lease
Yes ←	Title Transfer?	→ No
Yes ←	Bargain Purchase Option?	→ No
Yes ←	Lease Term ≥ 75% of Life?	→ No
Yes ←	Present Value of Payments ≥ 90% of Fair Value?	→ No

Additional *revenue recognition* criteria applicable to lessors:

1. Collectibility of the minimum lease payments is reasonably predictable.
2. No important uncertainties surround the amount of unreimbursable costs yet to be incurred by the lessor.

- **Lessee:** Capital lease if any one of general criteria is met.
- **Lessor:** Capital lease if any one of general criteria is met and both revenue recognition criteria are met.

General Classification Criteria—Lessee and Lessor

The four general criteria that apply to all leases for both the lessee and lessor relate to transfer of ownership, bargain purchase options, economic life, and fair value. The transfer of ownership criterion is met if the lease agreement includes a clause that transfers full ownership of the property to the lessee by the end of the lease term. Of all the classification criteria, transfer of ownership is the most objective and therefore the easiest to apply.

The second general criterion is met if the lease contains a bargain purchase option that makes it reasonably assured that the property will be purchased by the lessee at some future date. This criterion is more difficult to apply than the first criterion because the future fair value of the leased property must be estimated at the inception of the lease and compared with the purchase option price to determine whether a bargain purchase is indeed indicated.

The third criterion relates to the economic life of the asset. This criterion is met if the lease term is equal to 75% or more of the estimated economic life of the leased property. As defined earlier, the lease term includes renewal periods if renewal seems assured. The economic life criterion is somewhat subjective because of the uncertainty of an asset's economic life. This criterion does not apply to land leases because land has an unlimited life.

FYI

The FASB's intent was that these general criteria would require most long-term leases to be accounted for as capital leases. However, companies have been clever in how they construct lease agreements, so most leases are accounted for as operating leases.

The fourth general criterion focuses on the fair value of the property in relation to the provisions of the lease. This criterion is met if, at the beginning of the lease term, the present value of the minimum lease payments equals or exceeds 90% of the fair value of the leased asset. If the lessee is obligated to pay, in present value terms, almost all the fair value of the leased property, the lease is in substance a purchase of the property. The key variable in this criterion is the discounted minimum lease payments.

The rate used to discount the future minimum lease payments is critical in determining whether the fair value criterion is met. The lower the discount rate used, the higher the present value of the minimum lease payments and the greater the likelihood that the fair value criterion of 90% will be met. As explained earlier, the FASB specified that the lessor should use the implicit interest rate of the lease agreement. The lessee also uses the lessor's implicit interest rate if it is known and if it is lower than the lessee's incremental borrowing rate. If the lessee cannot determine the lessor's implicit interest rate, the lessee must use its incremental borrowing rate.

STOP&THINK

How exactly does using a higher incremental borrowing rate reduce the likelihood that a lessee will be required to account for a lease as a capital lease?

a) A higher incremental borrowing rate increases the incidence of bargain purchase options.
b) A higher incremental borrowing rate increases the expected useful life of the leased asset.
c) The use of a higher discount rate increases the likelihood that the lease will be canceled.
d) The use of a higher discount rate lowers the computed present value of the minimum payments.

Because incremental borrowing rates are often higher than the implicit interest rates and because lessees generally do not want to capitalize leases, many lessees use the borrowing rate and do not attempt to estimate the implicit rate. In the 1980s, the FASB

> **FYI**
>
> During World War II, the United Kingdom was in dire need of warships. The problem was that the United Kingdom had no money, and U.S. law prohibited the United States from loaning money to another country for purchasing ships. The solution: An 1892 statute that allowed the secretary of war to lease U.S. military property. Thus was born the famous Lend-Lease Bill, which allowed the United States to provide warships to the United Kingdom.

proposed tightening the capital lease criteria by requiring lessees to estimate the implicit interest rate in all cases. The FASB dropped the proposal when criticism of this proposed provision became widespread.

The four criteria outlined represent the FASB's attempt to precisely delineate the difference between operating and capital leases. In practice, companies have become very skilled at structuring lease agreements according to whether they want to account for the lease as an operating or a capital lease. In essence, the precise nature of the FASB's four criteria provides a legalistic framework that firms easily circumvent through clever structuring of the lease. As a result, the goal of lease accounting that represents substance over form is not entirely met.

ifrs

An alternative to the FASB's precise framework is the IASB approach, which relies more on accounting judgment. The international accounting standard on leases (*IAS 17*, "Accounting for Leases") states simply: "A lease is classified as a finance (i.e., capital) lease if it transfers substantially all the risks and rewards incident to ownership."[4] This type of standard places the responsibility of distinguishing between operating and capital/finance leases on the accountant. Paragraph 10 in *IAS 17* does provide some guidance on distinguishing between operating and finance leases. The paragraph gives the following examples of situations that "would normally lead to a lease being classified as a finance lease."

(a) the lease transfers ownership of the asset to the lessee by the end of the lease term;

(b) the lessee has the option to purchase the asset at a price that is expected to be sufficiently lower than the fair value at the date the option becomes exercisable for it to be reasonably certain, at the inception of the lease, that the option will be exercised;

(c) the lease term is for the major part of the economic life of the asset even if title is not transferred;

(d) at the inception of the lease the present value of the minimum lease payments amounts to at least substantially all of the fair value of the leased asset

As you can recognize as you read the *IAS 17* list, the IASB guidance is exactly the same, in spirit, to the FASB guidance. However, the "75% of economic life" criterion of the FASB becomes a "major part of the economic life" in IFRS. Similarly, the "90% of fair value" criterion of the FASB becomes "substantially all of the fair value" under IFRS. The international standard on lease accounting is a classic example of the principles-based approach in IFRS compared to the rules-based approach in U.S. GAAP.

Revenue Recognition Criteria—Lessor

In addition to meeting one of the four general criteria, a lease must meet two additional revenue recognition criteria to be classified by the lessor as a capital lease.[5] As indicated in Exhibit 15-1, the first of the two revenue recognition criteria relates to collectibility. Collection of the minimum lease payments must be reasonably predictable.

[4] *International Accounting Standard No. 17*, "Accounting for Leases" (London: International Accounting Standards Board, revised December 2003).

[5] FASB ASC paragraph 840-10-25-42. If the lease involves real estate, these revenue recognition criteria are more complex and depend on whether the lease involves just land, land and buildings, or just part of a building. See FASB ASC paragraphs 840-10-25-54 through 69.

The second additional criterion requires substantial completion of performance by the lessor. This means that any unreimbursable costs yet to be incurred by the lessor under the terms of the lease are known or can be reasonably estimated at the lease inception date. If the leased asset is constructed by the lessor, this criterion is applied at the later of the lease inception date or the date construction is completed.

Application of General Lease Classification Criteria

To illustrate the application of the lease classification criteria, four different leasing situations are presented in Exhibit 15-2. A summary analysis of each lease also is presented in the exhibit. Following is a brief explanation of the analysis for each of the four leases.

Lease 1 will be treated as an operating lease by the lessee but as a capital lease by the lessor. The lease does not meet any of the first three general criteria. Because the lessee does not know the implicit interest rate of the lessor, the incremental borrowing rate is used to test for the present value criterion. The present value of the minimum lease payments using the incremental borrowing rate is less than 90% of the fair value of the property; thus, the present value criterion is not met for the lessee. Because the lessor uses the implicit interest rate, the present value criterion is met. The two additional criteria applicable to the lessor are also met.

Lease 2 will be treated as a capital lease by both the lessee and the lessor because title passes to the lessee at the end of the lease term and the additional lessor criteria are both met. Because of the difference in the present value calculations, if the title had not passed, Lease 2 would be treated as an operating lease by the lessee but as a capital lease by the lessor.

Lease 3 will be treated as a capital lease by the lessee but as an operating lease by the lessor. The bargain purchase option criterion is met as is the present value criterion.

EX 15-2 APPLICATION OF LEASE CLASSIFICATION CRITERIA TO LEASE SITUATIONS

Lease Provisions	Lease 1	Lease 2	Lease 3	Lease 4
Cancelable	No	No	No	Yes
Title passes to lessee	No	Yes	No	Yes
Bargain purchase option	No	No	Yes	No
Lease term	10 years	10 years	8 years	10 years
Economic life of asset	14 years	15 years	13 years	12 years
Present value of minimum lease payments as a percentage of fair value—incremental borrowing rate	80%	79%	95%	76%
Present value of minimum lease payments as a percentage of fair value—implicit interest rate	92%	91%	92%	82%
Lessee knows implicit interest rate	No	No	Yes	Yes
Rental payments collectible and lessor costs certain	Yes	Yes	No	Yes
Analysis of Leases:				
Lessee				
Treat as capital lease	No	Yes	Yes	No
Criteria met	None	Title	Bargain purchase, present value	Must be noncancelable
Lessor				
Treat as capital lease	Yes	Yes	No	No
First four criteria met	Present value	Title, present value	Bargain purchase, present value	Must be noncancelable
Lessor criteria met	Yes	Yes	No	n/a

However, because there is some uncertainty as to the collectibility of the rental payments and the amount of lessor costs to be incurred, the lease fails to meet the revenue recognition criteria applicable to the lessor.

Lease 4 will be treated as an operating lease by both the lessee and the lessor. The lease is a cancelable lease, and even though title passes to the lessee at the end of the lease, it would be classified as a rental agreement.

Accounting for Leases—Lessee

5 Properly account for both capital and operating leases from the standpoint of the lessee (asset user).

WHY **Operating lease accounting is by far the biggest form of off-balance-sheet financing. It is important to understand both why lessees desire operating lease accounting and how leases can be carefully constructed to allow for operating lease accounting.**

HOW **For a lessee, an operating lease is accounted for as a rental, with the lease payment amount being recognized as rent expense. With a capital lease, an asset and a liability are recognized on the lease-signing date.**

All leases as viewed by the lessee may be divided into two types: operating leases and capital leases. If a lease meets any one of the four general classification criteria discussed previously, it is treated as a capital lease. Otherwise, it is accounted for as an operating lease.

Accounting for operating leases involves the recognition of rent expense over the term of the lease. The leased property is not reported as an asset on the lessee's balancesheet, nor is a liability recognized for the obligation to make future payments for use of the property. Information concerning the lease is limited to disclosure in notes to the financial statements. Accounting for a capital lease essentially requires the lessee to report on the balance sheet the present value of the future lease payments, both as an asset and a liability. The asset is amortized as though it had been purchased by the lessee. The liability is accounted for in the same manner as would be a mortgage on the property. The difference in the impact of these two treatments on the financial statements of the lessee often can be significant, as illustrated here.

Accounting for Operating Leases—Lessee

Operating leases are considered to be simple rental agreements with debits being made to an expense account as the payments are made. For example, assume the lease terms for manufacturing equipment are $40,000 a year on a year-to-year basis. The entry to record the lease payment for a year would be as follows:

Rent Expense	40,000	
Cash		40,000

Lease payments frequently are made in advance. If the lease period does not coincide with the lessee's fiscal year or if the lessee prepares interim reports, a prepaid rent account would be required to record the unexpired portion of the lease payment at the end of the accounting period involved. The prepaid rent account would be adjusted at the end of each period.

Operating Leases with Varying Lease Payments Some operating leases specify lease terms that provide for varying lease payments over the lease term. Most commonly, these types of agreements call for lower initial payments and scheduled increases later in the life of the lease. They may even provide an inducement to prospective lessees in the form of a "rent holiday" (free rent). In some cases, however, the lease may provide for higher initial payments. In cases with varying lease payments, periodic expense should be recognized on a straight-line basis.[6]

When recording lease payments under these agreements, differences between the actual payments and the debit to expense would be reported as Rent Payable or Prepaid Rent, depending on whether the payments were accelerating or declining. For example, assume the terms of the lease for an aircraft by International Airlines provide for payments of $150,000 a year for the first two years of the lease and $250,000 for each of the next three years. The total lease payments for the five years would be $1,050,000, or $210,000 a year on a straight-line basis. The required entries in the first two years would be as follows:

Rent Expense	210,000	
Cash		150,000
Rent Payable		60,000

The entries for each of the last three years are as follows:

Rent Expense	210,000	
Rent Payable	40,000	
Cash		250,000

The portion of Rent Payable due in the subsequent year would be classified as a current liability.

This process of making appropriate accrual adjustments to report rent expense of an equal amount each period seems simple. However, in February 2005 the chief accountant of the SEC wrote a letter to the AICPA explaining that many U.S. companies had been improperly reporting lease-related rent expense because of a failure to make these simple accrual adjustments.[7]

As explained later in the chapter, a large amount of detail concerning operating leases is disclosed in the notes to the financial statements. This disclosure includes summary information about lease provisions and a schedule of future minimum lease payments associated with operating leases.

Accounting for Capital Leases—Lessee

Capital leases are considered to be more like a purchase of property than a rental. Consequently, accounting for capital leases by lessees requires entries similar to those required for the purchase of an asset with long-term credit terms. The amounts to be recorded as an asset and as a liability are the present values of the future minimum lease payments as previously defined. The discount rates used by lessees to record capital leases are the same as those used to apply the classification criteria previously discussed, that is, the lower of the implicit interest rate (if known) and the incremental borrowing rate. The

[6] Periodic lease expense is recognized on a straight-line basis "unless another systematic and rational basis is more representative of the time pattern in which use benefit is derived from the leased property, in which case that basis shall be used." FASB ASC paragraph 840-20-25-1.

[7] Letter from Donald T. Nicolaisen, chief accountant of the SEC, to Robert J. Kueppers, chairman of the Center for Public Company Audit Firms at the American Institute of Certified Public Accountants, February 7, 2005, available at **http://www.sec.gov/info/accountants/staffletters/cpcaf020705.htm**.

FASB CODIFICATION

The Issue: You are part of the management team of a start-up company. Your company has outgrown its existing facility and has decided to move to a larger building. You have agreed with a real estate management company to lease a building that the real estate management company will build to your specifications. This is called a "build-to-suit" lease. You personally have carefully negotiated the lease terms so that your company will account for the lease as an operating lease.

During the 3-month construction period, and before you have moved in and started using the building, the lease contract requires you to make monthly lease payments. Note that these payments are made BEFORE you start using the building.

The Question: What is the proper accounting treatment for these lease payments made BEFORE you start using the building under the operating lease agreement?

Searching the Codification: This is a question we would love to address using the "Search" box in the top right corner of the FASB ASC home page. However, the search facility doesn't work when you are using the "Basic View" version; this is one of the things you get when you pay your $800+ to upgrade to the "Professional View." But we can still answer this question using the menus and our knowledge of the transaction. Let's proceed step by step.

- Of course, we'll start by going to Topic 840, Leases.
- Because the lease we are talking about is an operating lease, let's choose Subtopic 840-20, Operating Leases.
- Now things get tough. However, we can narrow our search by realizing that we are talking about how to account for something that happens at the beginning of the lease agreement. So, we want to look in either Recognition or Initial Measurement.
- Under both of the options, we have to remember that we are talking about the accounting rules from the standpoint of the lessee.
- You are close—go ahead and find out how the lessee in an operating lease arrangement is to account for early lease payments made under a build-to-suit lease.

The Answer: The correct treatment is described on page 15-42.

minimum lease payments consist of the total rental payments, bargain purchase options, and lessee-guaranteed residual values.[8]

Illustrative Entries for Capital Leases Assume that Marshall Corporation leases equipment from Universal Leasing Company with the following terms:

- Lease period: 5 years, beginning January 1, 2013. Noncancelable.
- Rental amount: $65,000 per year payable annually in advance; includes $5,000 to cover executory costs.
- Estimated economic life of equipment: 5 years.
- Expected residual value of equipment at end of lease period: None.

[8] An important exception to the use of the present value of future minimum lease payments as a basis for recording a capital lease is included in FASB ASC paragraph 840-30-30-3, as follows: "If the present value of the minimum lease payments exceeds the fair value of the leased property at lease inception, the amount measured initially as the asset and obligation shall be the fair value." In this case, an implicit interest rate would have to be computed using the fair value of the asset.

Because the lease payments are payable in advance, one way to compute the present value of the lease is to add the amount of the first payment (made on the lease-signing date) to the present value of the annuity of the four remaining payments.[9] Assuming that Marshall Corporation's incremental borrowing rate and the implicit interest rate on the lease are both 10%, the present value for the lease would be \$250,192 computed as follows using a business calculator:

Toggle so that the payments are assumed to occur at the beginning (BEG) of the period.

$$PMT = \$60{,}000;\ N = 5;\ I = 10\% \rightarrow PV = \$250{,}192$$

The journal entries to record the lease at the beginning of the lease term would be

2013				
Jan.	1	Leased Equipment	250,192	
		Obligations under Capital Leases		250,192
		To record the lease.		
	1	Lease Expense	5,000	
		Obligations under Capital Leases	60,000	
		Cash		65,000
		To record the first lease payment (including executory costs of \$5,000).		

FYI

When a lease is capitalized, the asset is included on the balance sheet and written off over time. The word *amortization*, instead of *depreciation*, is typically used when describing the systematic expensing of the cost of a leased asset.

The term *lease expense* is used to record the executory costs related to the leased equipment, such as insurance and taxes. It is possible to record the lease liability at the gross amount of the payments (\$300,000 = 5 × \$60,000) and offset it with a discount account—Discount on Lease Contract. The net method is more common in accounting for leases by the lessee and will be used in this chapter.

Once the leased asset and the lease liability are recorded, periodic entries must be made to recognize the gradual depreciation of the leased asset and the payment (with interest) of the lease liability. The asset value is amortized in accordance with the lessee's normal method of depreciation for owned assets. The amortization period to be used depends on which of the criteria is used to qualify the lease as a capital lease. If the lease qualifies under the ownership transfer or bargain purchase option criteria, the economic life of the asset should be used because it is assumed that the lessee will take ownership of the asset for the remainder of its useful life at the end of the lease term. If the lease fails to satisfy the ownership transfer or bargain purchase option criteria but does qualify under either the lease term or present value of minimum lease payments criteria, the length of the lease term should be used for amortization purposes. In the Marshall Corporation example, the equipment lease qualifies for capitalization under the lease term criterion because the lease period is equal to the economic life of the equipment. Accordingly, the equipment is amortized over the economic life of five years.

[9] The annuity present value tables assume that the payments occur at the end of the period. To compute the present value of an annuity when the payments occur at the beginning of the period, split the annuity into a payment now plus the remaining payments. For example:

$PVn = \$60{,}000 + [\$60{,}000\ PVAF_{\overline{4}|10\%}]$

$PVn = \$60{,}000 + [\$60{,}000(3.1699)]$

$PVn = \$250{,}194$ (differs from \$250,192 because of rounding in the tables)

EX 15-3 SCHEDULE OF LEASE PAYMENTS [5-YEAR LEASE, $60,000 ANNUAL PAYMENTS (NET OF EXECUTORY COSTS), 10% INTEREST]

Date	Description	Amount	Interest Expense*	Principal	Lease Obligation
1/1/2013	Initial balance				$250,192
1/1/2013	Payment	$ 60,000		$ 60,000	190,192
12/31/2013	Payment	60,000	$19,019	40,981	149,211
12/31/2014	Payment	60,000	14,921	45,079	104,132
12/31/2015	Payment	60,000	10,413	49,587	54,545
12/31/2016	Payment	60,000	5,455	54,545	0
		$300,000	$49,808	$250,192	

*Preceding lease obligation × 10%.

The recorded amount of the lease liability should be reduced each period as the lease payments are made. Interest expense on the unpaid balance is computed and recognized. The lessee's incremental borrowing rate, or the lessor's implicit interest rate if lower, is the interest rate that should be used in computing interest expense. Exhibit 15-3 shows how the $60,000 payments (excluding executory costs) would be allocated between payment on the obligation and interest expense. To simplify the schedule, it is assumed that all lease payments after the first payment are made on December 31 of each year. If the payments were made in January, an accrual of interest at December 31 would be required.

If the normal company depreciation policy for this type of equipment is straight line, the required entry at December 31, 2013, for amortization of the leased asset would be as shown below.

2013			
Dec. 31	Amortization Expense on Leased Equipment	50,038*	
	Accumulated Amortization on Leased Equipment		50,038

*Computation: $250,192/5 = $50,038

Similar entries would be made for each of the remaining four years. Although the credit could be made directly to the asset account, the use of a contra asset account provides the necessary disclosure information about the original lease value and accumulated amortization to date.

In addition to the entry recording amortization, another entry is required at December 31, 2013, to record the second lease payment, including a prepayment of 2014's executory costs. As indicated in Exhibit 15-3, the interest expense for 2013 would be computed by multiplying the incremental borrowing rate of 10% by the initial present value of the obligation less the immediate $60,000 first payment, or ($250,192 − $60,000) × 0.10 = $19,019.

2013			
Dec. 31	Prepaid Executory Costs	5,000	
	Obligations under Capital Leases	40,981	
	Interest Expense	19,019	
	Cash		65,000

Because of the assumption that all lease payments after the first payment are made on December 31, the portion of each payment that represents executory costs must be recorded as a prepayment and charged to lease expense in the following year.

Based on the preceding journal entries and using information contained in Exhibit 15-3, the December 31, 2013, balance sheet of Marshall Corporation would include information concerning the leased equipment and related obligation as illustrated here:

Marshall Corporation
Balance Sheet (Partial)
December 31, 2013

Assets		**Liabilities**	
Current assets:		Current liabilities:	
Prepaid executory costs—		Obligations under capital	
leased equipment.	$ 5,000	leases, current portion	$ 45,079
Land, buildings, and equipment:		Noncurrent liabilities:	
Leased equipment.	$250,192	Obligations under capital	
Less: Accumulated amortization	50,038	leases, exclusive of $45,079	
Net value	$200,154	Included in current liabilities	$104,132

Note that the principal portion of the payment due December 31, 2014, is reported as a current liability on the December 31, 2013, balance sheet.[10]

The income statement would include the amortization on leased property of $50,038, interest expense of $19,019, and executory costs of $5,000 as expenses for the period. The total expense of $74,057 exceeds the $65,000 rental payment made in the first year. As the amount of interest expense declines each period, the total expense will be reduced and, for the last two years, will be less than the $65,000 payments (Exhibit 15-4). The total amount debited to expense over the life of the lease will be the same regardless of whether the lease is accounted for as an operating lease or as a capital lease. If an accelerated depreciation method of amortization is used, the difference in the early years between the expense and the payment would be even larger.

In addition to the amounts recognized in the capital lease journal entries previously given, a note to the financial statements would be necessary to explain the terms of the lease and future minimum lease payments in more detail.

Accounting for Leases with a Bargain Purchase Option Frequently, the lessee is given the option of purchasing the property at some future date at a bargain price. As discussed previously, the present value of the bargain purchase option is part of the minimum lease payments and should be included in the capitalized value of the lease. Assume in the preceding example that there is a bargain purchase option of $75,000 exercisable after

[10] There have been some theoretical arguments advanced against this method of allocating lease obligations between current and noncurrent liabilities. See Robert J. Swieringa, "When Current Is Noncurrent and Vice Versa," *The Accounting Review*, January 1984, pp. 123–130. Professor Swieringa identifies two methods of making the allocation: the "change in present value" (CPV) approach that is used in the example and the "present value of the next year's payment" (PVNYP) approach that allocates a larger portion of the liability to the current category. A later study shows that the CPV method is followed almost universally in practice. See A. W. Richardson, "The Measurement of the Current Portion of Long-Term Lease Obligations—Some Evidence from Practice," *The Accounting Review*, October 1985, pp. 744–752. While there is theoretical support for both positions, this text uses the CPV method in chapter examples and problem materials.

EX 15-4 SCHEDULE OF EXPENSES RECOGNIZED—CAPITAL AND OPERATING LEASES COMPARED

	Expenses Recognized—Capital Lease				Expenses Recognized—Operating Lease	
Year	Interest	Executory Costs	Amortization	Total		Difference
2013	$19,019	$ 5,000	$ 50,038	$ 74,057	$ 65,000	$ 9,057
2014	14,921	5,000	50,038	69,959	65,000	4,959
2015	10,413	5,000	50,038	65,451	65,000	451
2016	5,455	5,000	50,038	60,493	65,000	(4,507)
2017	0	5,000	50,040*	55,040	65,000	(9,960)
	$49,808	$25,000	$250,192	$325,000	$325,000	$ 0

*Rounded.

5 years, and the economic life of the equipment is expected to be 10 years. The other lease terms remain the same. The present value of the minimum lease payments would be increased by the present value of the bargain purchase amount of $75,000, or $46,569, computed as follows:

Toggle back so that the payments are assumed to occur at the end (END) of the period.

FV = $75,000; *N* = 5; *I* = 10% → *PV* = $46,569

> **FYI**
>
> In FASB ASC paragraph 840-30-35-14, the FASB states that no gain or loss should be recognized when a leased asset is purchased. As with the exchange of similar assets, the fair value of the equipment on the purchase date is ignored unless evidence of significant impairment exists. See Chapter 11.

The total present value of the future minimum lease payments is $296,761 ($250,192 + $46,569). This amount will be used to record the initial asset and liability. The asset balance of $296,761 will be amortized over the asset life of 10 years because of the existence of the bargain purchase option; this makes the transaction, in reality, a sale. The liability balance will be reduced as shown in Exhibit 15-5.

At the date of exercising the option, the net balance in the leased equipment asset account and its related accumulated amortization account would be transferred to the regular equipment account. The entries at the exercise of the option would be as follows:

2017			
Dec. 31	Obligations under Capital Leases	68,182	
	Interest Expense	6,818	
	Cash		75,000
	To record exercise of bargain purchase option.		
	Equipment	148,381	
	Accumulated Amortization on Leased Equipment	148,380*	
	Leased Equipment		296,761
	To transfer remaining balance in leased asset account to equipment account.		

*Computation:
Accumulated amortization: $296,761/10 years = $29,676 per year;
5 years × $29,676 per year = $148,380.

EX 15-5 SCHEDULE OF LEASE PAYMENTS [5-YEAR LEASE WITH BARGAIN PURCHASE OPTION OF $75,000 AFTER FIVE YEARS, $60,000 ANNUAL PAYMENTS (NET OF EXECUTORY COSTS), 10% INTEREST]

Date	Description	Amount	Interest Expense	Principal	Lease Obligation
1/1/2013	Initial balance				$296,761
1/1/2013	Payment	$ 60,000		$ 60,000	236,761
12/31/2013	Payment	60,000	$23,676	36,324	200,437
12/31/2014	Payment	60,000	20,044	39,956	160,481
12/31/2015	Payment	60,000	16,048	43,952	116,529
12/31/2016	Payment	60,000	11,653	48,347	68,182
12/31/2017	Payment	75,000	6,818	68,182	0
		$375,000	$78,239	$296,761	

If the equipment is not purchased and the lease is permitted to lapse, a loss equal to the $73,381 difference ($148,381 − $75,000) between the equipment's remaining book value and the remaining balance in the lease liability account (including accrued interest) would have to be recognized by the following entry:

2017			
Dec. 31	Loss from Failure to Exercise Bargain Purchase Option	73,381	
	Obligations under Capital Leases	68,182	
	Interest Expense	6,818	
	Accumulated Amortization on Leased Equipment	148,380	
	Leased Equipment		296,761

Accounting for Leases with a Lessee-Guaranteed Residual Value If the lease agreement requires the lessee to guarantee a residual value, the lessee treats the guarantee similar to a bargain purchase option and includes the present value of the guarantee as part of the capitalized value of the lease. At the expiration of the lease term, the amount of the guarantee will be reported as a liability under the lease. In addition, the remaining book value of the leased asset will be equal to the guaranteed residual value. If the fair value of the leased asset is less than the guaranteed residual value, a loss is reported for the difference, and the lessee must make up the difference with a cash payment.

Accounting for Purchase of Asset During Lease Term When a lease does not provide for a transfer of ownership or a purchase option, it is still possible that the lessee may purchase leased property during the term of the lease. Usually the purchase price will differ from the recorded lease obligation at the purchase date. No gain or loss should be recorded on the purchase, but the difference between the purchase price and the obligation still on the books should be charged or credited to the acquired asset's carrying value.[11]

To illustrate, assume that on December 31, 2015, rather than making the lease payment due, the lessee purchased the leased property in the Marshall Corporation example described on page 15-16 for $120,000. At that date, the remaining liability recorded on the

[11] FASB ASC paragraph 840-30-35-15.

lessee's books is $114,545 (lease obligation of $104,132 + interest payable of $10,413; see Exhibit 15-3) and the net book value of the recorded leased asset is $100,078, the original capitalized value of $250,192 less $150,114 amortization ($50,038 × 3). The entry to record the purchase on the lessee's books would be as follows:

2015			
Dec. 31	Interest Expense	10,413	
	Obligations under Capital Leases	104,132	
	Equipment	105,533	
	Accumulated Amortization on Leased Equipment	150,114	
	Leased Equipment		250,192
	Cash		120,000

The purchased equipment is capitalized at $105,533, which is the book value of the leased asset, $100,078, plus $5,455, the excess of the purchase price over the carrying value of the lease obligation ($120,000 − $114,545).

Treatment of Leases on Lessee's Statement of Cash Flows

Operating leases present no special problems to the lessee in preparing a statement of cash flows. The lease payments reduce, and thus require no adjustment to, net income under the indirect method except for accrued or prepaid rent expense. The cash payments would be reported as operating expense outlays under the direct method.

Adjustments for capital leases by the lessee, however, are more complex. The amortization of leased assets would be treated the same as depreciation, that is, added to net income under the indirect method and ignored under the direct method. The portion of the cash payment allocated to interest expense would require no adjustment under the indirect method and would be reported as part of the cash payment for interest expense under the direct method. The portion of the cash payment allocated to the lease liability would be reported as a financing outflow under either method. The signing of a capital lease would not be reported as either an investing or financing activity because it is a noncash transaction. The impact of a capital lease on the lessee's statement of cash flows is summarized in Exhibit 15-6.

EX 15-6 IMPACT OF A CAPITAL LEASE ON THE LESSEE'S STATEMENT OF CASH FLOWS

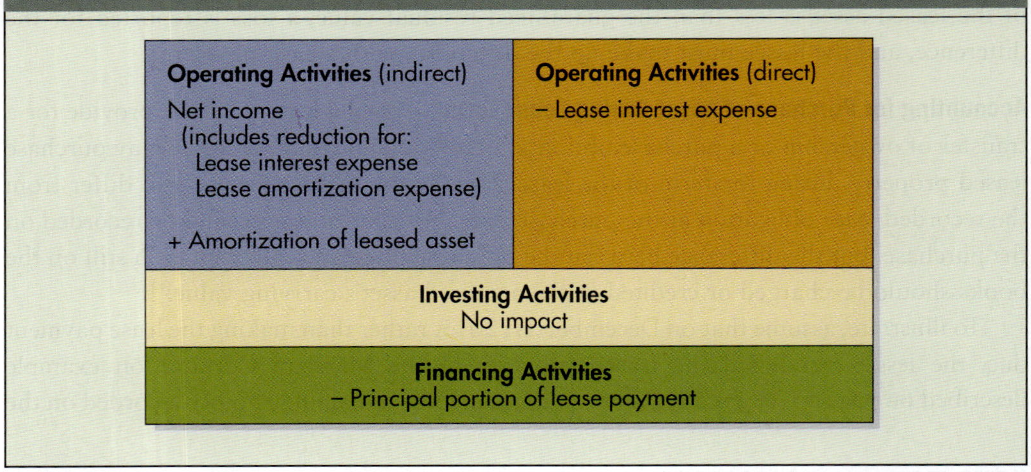

To illustrate the impact of a capital lease on the lessee's statement of cash flows, refer back to the Marshall Corporation example starting on page 15-16. Assume that in 2013, Marshall Corporation's income before any lease-related expenses is $200,000. For simplicity, ignore income taxes and executory costs. Net income for the year can be computed as follows:

Income before lease-related expenses	$200,000
Lease-related interest expense	(19,019)
Lease-related amortization expense	(50,038)
Net income	$130,943

The statement of cash flows for Marshall Corporation for 2013, displaying only the lease-related items and using the indirect method to report cash flow from operating activities, would appear as follows:

Operating activities:	
Net income	$ 130,943
Add: Amortization of asset leased under capital lease	50,038
Net cash flow from operating activities	$ 180,981
Investing activities:	
No lease-related items	
Financing activities:	
Repayment of lease liability ($60,000 + $40,981)	$(100,981)

In addition, the supplemental disclosure to the statement of cash flows would include the following two lease-related items:

- Significant noncash transaction: During 2013 the company leased equipment under a capital lease arrangement. The present value of the minimum future payments under the lease was $250,192 on the lease-signing date.
- Cash paid for interest was $19,019.

Accounting for Leases—Lessor

6 **Properly account for both capital and operating leases from the standpoint of the lessor (asset owner).**

WHY **Just as lessees often desire operating lease treatment as a form of off-balance-sheet financing, lessors often desire capital lease treatment in order to be able to recognize a sale immediately. An interesting twist in the accounting rules allows a lessor to treat a lease as a capital lease while at the same time the lessee treats the same lease as an operating lease.**

HOW **For a lessor, an operating lease is accounted for as a rental, with the lease payment amount being recognized as rent revenue. The lessor continues to depreciate the leased asset. For a lessor, there are two types of capital leases: direct financing leases and sales-type leases. With a direct financing lease, a lease receivable is recognized on the lease-signing date. Interest revenue on the receivable balance is recognized during the lease term. With a sales-type lease, in addition to interest revenue over the life of the lease, a profit is recognized on the lease-signing date equal to the difference between the fair value of the leased asset and its cost.**

The lessor in a lease transaction gives up the physical possession of the property to the lessee. If the transfer of the property is considered temporary in nature, the lessor will continue to carry the leased asset as an owned asset on the balance sheet; the revenue from the lease will be reported as it is earned; and depreciation of the leased asset will be matched against the revenue. This type of lease is described as an *operating lease*, and cash receipts from the lessee are treated similar to the operating lease procedures described for the lessee. However, if a lease has terms that make the transaction similar in substance to a sale or a permanent transfer of the asset to the lessee, the lessor should no longer report the asset as though it were owned but should reflect the transfer to the lessee.

As indicated earlier, if a lease meets one of the four general lease classification criteria that apply to both lessees and lessors plus both of the revenue recognition criteria that apply to the lessor only (i.e., collectibility and substantial completion), it is classified by the lessor as a capital lease and recorded as either a direct financing lease or a sales-type lease.

Direct financing leases involve a lessor who is primarily engaged in financing activities, such as a bank or finance company. The lessor views the lease as an investment. The revenue generated by this type of lease is interest revenue. Sales-type leases, on the other hand, involve manufacturers or dealers who use leases as a means of facilitating the marketing of their products. Thus, there are two different types of revenue generated by this type of lease: (1) an immediate profit or loss, which is the difference between the cost of the property being leased and its sales price, or fair value, at the inception of the lease and (2) interest revenue earned over time as the lessee makes the lease payments that pay off the lease obligation plus interest.

> **FYI**
>
> The sale of new cars provides a good example of a sales-type lease. **Ford Motor** has a financing subsidiary to handle leasing. When a car is leased from a dealership, the auto company earns a profit on the lease as well as interest from the lease contract.

For either an operating, direct financing, or sales-type lease, a lessor may incur certain costs, referred to as initial direct costs, in connection with obtaining the lease. These costs include the costs to negotiate the lease, perform the credit check on the lessee, and prepare the lease documents.[12]

Initial direct costs are accounted for differently, depending on which of the three types of leases is involved. Exhibit 15-7 summarizes the accounting treatment for initial direct costs. These costs will be discussed further as each type of lease is presented.

Accounting for Operating Leases—Lessor

Accounting for operating leases for the lessor is very similar to that described for the lessee. The lessor recognizes revenue as the payments are received. If there are significant variations in the payment terms, entries will be necessary to reflect a straight-line pattern of revenue recognition. Initial direct costs incurred in connection with an operating lease are deferred and amortized on a straight-line basis over the term of the lease, thus matching them against rent revenue.

To illustrate accounting for an operating lease on the lessor's books, assume that the equipment leased for five years by Universal Leasing Company to Marshall Corporation (page 15-16) on January 1, 2013, for $65,000 a year, including executory costs of $5,000 per year, had a cost of $400,000 to the lessor, Universal Leasing. Initial direct costs of $15,000 were incurred to obtain and finalize the lease. The equipment has an estimated life of 10 years, with no residual value. Assuming no purchase or renewal options or guarantees

[12] FASB ASC paragraph 840-20-25-17.

EX 15-7 ACCOUNTING FOR INITIAL DIRECT COSTS

Type of Lease	Accounting Treatment of Initial Direct Costs
Operating (840-20-35-2)	Recorded as an asset and amortized over lease term.
Direct financing (840-30-35-23)	Recorded as an asset and amortized over lease term, reducing interest revenue.
Sales-type (840-30-25-6)	Immediately recognized as a reduction in manufacturer's or dealer's profit.

by the lessee, the lease does not meet any of the four general classification criteria and would be treated as an operating lease. The entries to record the payment of the initial direct costs and the receipt of the lease payments by Universal Leasing would be as follows:

2013			
Jan. 1	Deferred Initial Direct Costs	15,000	
	Cash		15,000
1	Cash	65,000	
	Rent Revenue		60,000
	Executory Costs		5,000

The $5,000 payment received from the lessee to reimburse the executory costs may be reflected as a credit (reduction) to the executory costs account, as shown here, or as a credit to a separate revenue account against which the executory costs can be matched.

Assuming the lessor depreciates the equipment on a straight-line basis over its expected life of 10 years and amortizes the initial direct costs on a straight-line basis over the 5-year lease term, the depreciation and amortization entries at the end of the first year would be as follows:

2013			
Dec. 31	Amortization of Initial Direct Costs	3,000	
	Deferred Initial Direct Costs		3,000
31	Depreciation Expense on Leased Equipment	40,000	
	Accumulated Depreciation on Leased Equipment		40,000

If the rental period and the lessor's fiscal year do not coincide or if the lessor prepares interim reports, an adjustment would be required to record the unearned rent revenue at the end of the accounting period. Amortization of the initial direct costs would be adjusted to reflect a partial year.

Accounting for Direct Financing Leases

Accounting for direct financing leases for lessors is very similar to that used for capital leases by lessees but with the entries reversed to provide for interest revenue rather than interest expense and reduction of a lease payment receivable rather than a lease liability. The lease payment receivable is reported at its present value; this is the standard practice followed with all long-term receivables, as explained in Chapter 7. The lease payment receivable is sometimes recorded by the lessor at the gross amount of the lease payments with an offsetting valuation account for the unearned interest, or aggregate amount of interest that will be earned by the lessor over the course of the lease. Unearned interest revenue is computed as the difference between the total expected lease payments and the fair value, or cost, of the leased asset. This approach is illustrated for the first year in the following example. Although the remainder of the journal entries in the chapter report the lease payment receivable at its net present value, note that in each case the receivable could be shown at its gross amount less an adjustment for unearned interest revenue.

Illustrative Entries for Direct Financing Leases Referring to the lessee example on page 15-16, assume that the cost of the equipment to the Universal Leasing Company was the same as its fair value, $250,192, and that the purchase by the lessor had been entered into Equipment Purchased for Lease. The entry to record the initial lease would be this:

2013			
Jan. 1	Lease Payments Receivable	250,192	
	Equipment Purchased for Lease		250,192

or, if the lease payment receivable is recorded at its gross amount:

Jan. 1	Lease Payments Receivable	300,000	
	Equipment Purchased for Lease		250,192
	Unearned Interest Revenue		49,808

The first payment would be recorded as follows:

Jan. 1	Cash	65,000	
	Lease Payments Receivable		60,000
	Executory Costs		5,000

The lessor is paying the executory costs but charging them to the lessee. The lessor can record the receipt of the executory costs by debiting Cash and crediting the Executory Costs Expense account. As the lessor pays the costs, the expense account is debited. The lessor is serving as a conduit for these costs to the lessee and will have an expense only if the lessee fails to make the payments. Interest revenue will be recognized over the lease term as shown in Exhibit 15-8.

At the end of the first year, the following entries would be made to record the receipt of the second lease payment, to recognize the interest revenue for 2013, and to recognize the advance payment for next year's executory costs as a deferred credit.

2013			
Dec. 31	Cash	65,000	
	Lease Payments Receivable		40,981
	Interest Revenue		19,019
	Deferred Executory Costs (a liability)		5,000

EX 15-8 SCHEDULE OF LEASE RECEIPTS AND INTEREST REVENUE [5-YEAR LEASE, $60,000 ANNUAL PAYMENTS (EXCLUSIVE OF EXECUTORY COSTS), 10% INTEREST]

Date	Description	Interest Revenue*	Payment Receipt	Reduction in Receivable	Lease Payments Receivable
1/1/2013	Initial balance				$250,192
1/1/2013	Receipt		$ 60,000	$ 60,000	190,192
12/31/2013	Receipt	$19,019	60,000	40,981	149,211
12/31/2014	Receipt	14,921	60,000	45,079	104,132
12/31/2015	Receipt	10,413	60,000	49,587	54,545
12/31/2016	Receipt	5,455	60,000	54,545	0
		$49,808	$300,000	$250,192	

*Preceding lease payment receivable × 10%.

or, if the lease payment receivable is recorded at its gross amount:

Dec. 31	Cash	65,000	
	Lease Payments Receivable		60,000
	Deferred Executory Costs (a liability)		5,000
31	Unearned Interest Revenue	19,019	
	Interest Revenue		19,019

Notice that unlike the operating lease example, no annual depreciation expense is recorded by the lessor in association with an asset leased under a capital lease agreement. This is because the asset has been "sold" to the lessee and removed from the lessor's books.

Based on the journal entries, the asset portion of the balance sheet of the lessor at December 31, 2013, will report the lease receivable as follows:

Universal Leasing Company
Balance Sheet (Partial)
December 31, 2013

Assets

Current assets:	
Lease payments receivable	$ 45,079
Noncurrent assets:	
Lease payments receivable (exclusive of $45,079 included in current assets)	$104,132

If a direct financing lease contains a bargain purchase option, the present value of the option is added to the receivable. The periodic entries and computations are made as though the bargain purchase amount was an additional rental payment.

Lessor Accounting for Direct Financing Leases with Residual Value If leased property is expected to have residual value, the present value of the expected residual value is added to the receivable account. It does not matter whether the residual value is guaranteed or unguaranteed. If guaranteed, it is treated in the accounts exactly like a bargain purchase option. If unguaranteed, the lessor is expected to have an asset equal in value to the residual amount at the end of the lease term.

CAUTION

The fair value in this example ($296,761) is different from the fair value in the previous example ($250,192) because, in the previous example, the asset was assumed to be worthless at the end of the lease term. In this example, the asset is estimated to have a residual value of $75,000. The present value of that $75,000 (i.e., $46,569) accounts for the difference.

To illustrate the recording of residual values, assume the same facts for the Universal Leasing Company as the example on pages 15-20–15-21 except that the asset has a residual value at the end of the 5-year lease term of $75,000 (either guaranteed or unguaranteed) rather than a bargain purchase option. Assume the cost of the equipment to the Universal Leasing Company was again the same as its fair value, $296,761.

The entries to record this lease and the first payment follow:

2013			
Jan. 1	Lease Payments Receivable	296,761	
	Equipment Purchased for Lease		296,761
1	Cash	65,000	
	Lease Payments Receivable		60,000
	Executory Costs		5,000

The computation of interest revenue would be identical to the interest expense computation illustrated in Exhibit 15-5 for the lessee.

At the end of the first year, the lessor would make the following entries:

2013			
Dec. 31	Cash	65,000	
	Lease Payments Receivable		36,324
	Deferred Executory Cost		5,000
	Interest Revenue		23,676

At the end of the lease term, the lessor would make the following entry to record the recovery of the leased asset, assuming the residual value was the same as originally estimated:

2017			
Dec. 31	Equipment	75,000	
	Lease Payments Receivable		68,182
	Interest Revenue		6,818

Initial Direct Costs Related to Direct Financing Leases If the lessor incurs any initial direct costs in conjunction with a direct financing lease, those costs are recorded as a separate asset, increasing the net lease investment. Because the initial net lease investment is increased but the lease payments remain the same, the existence of initial direct costs results in a lower implicit interest rate earned by the lessor. Including initial direct costs as part of the initial net lease investment effectively spreads the initial costs over the lease term and reduces the amount of interest revenue that would otherwise be recognized.

Accounting for Sales-Type Leases—Lessor

Accounting for sales-type leases adds one more dimension to the lessor's revenue, an immediate profit or loss arising from the difference between the sales price of the leased property and the lessor's cost to manufacture or purchase the asset. If there is no difference between the sales price and the lessor's cost, the lease is not a sales-type lease. The lessor also will recognize interest revenue over the lease term for the difference between the sales price and the gross amount of the minimum lease payments. The three values that must be identified to determine these income elements, therefore, can be summarized as follows:

1. The minimum lease payments as defined previously for the lessee, that is, rental payments over the lease term net of any executory costs plus the amount to be paid under a bargain purchase option or guarantee of the residual value.
2. The fair value of the asset.
3. The cost or carrying value of the asset to the lessor increased by any initial direct costs to lease the asset.

The manufacturer's or dealer's profit is the difference between the fair value of the asset and the cost or carrying value of the asset to the lessor. If cost exceeds the fair value, a loss will be reported. The difference between the gross rentals and the fair value of the asset is interest revenue and arises because of the time delay in paying for the asset as described by the lease terms. The relationship between these three values can be demonstrated as follows:

(1) Minimum lease payments	
	Financial Revenue (Interest)
(2) Fair value of leased asset	
	Manufacturer's or Dealer's Profit (Loss)
(3) Cost or carrying value of leased asset to lessor	

To illustrate this type of lease, assume that the lessor for the equipment described on page 15-16 is American Manufacturing Company rather than Universal Leasing. The fair value of the equipment is equal to its present value (the future lease payments discounted at 10%), or $250,192. This computation is reversed from what would happen in practice; normally, the fair value is known, and the minimum lease payments are set at an amount that will yield the desired rate of return to the lessor.

Assume that the equipment cost American Manufacturing $160,000 and initial direct costs of $15,000 were incurred. The three values and the related revenue amounts would be as follows:

(1) Minimum lease payments: ($65,000 − $5,000) × 5	$300,000	
		$49,808 (Interest Revenue)
(2) Fair value of equipment	$250,192	
		$75,192 (Manufacturer's Profit)
(3) Cost of leased equipment to lessor, plus initial direct costs	$175,000	

Illustrative Entries for Sales-Type Leases The interest revenue ($49,808) is the same as that illustrated for a direct financing lease on page 15-25, and it is recognized over the lease term by the same entries and according to Exhibit 15-8. The manufacturer's profit is recognized as revenue immediately in the current period by including the fair value of the asset as a sale and debiting the cost of the equipment carried in Finished Goods Inventory to Cost of Goods Sold. The initial direct costs previously deferred are recognized as an expense immediately by increasing Cost of Goods Sold by the amount expended for these costs. This reduces the amount of immediate profit to be recognized. The reimbursement of executory costs is treated in the same way as illustrated for direct financing leases.

The entries to record this information on American Manufacturing Company's books at the beginning of the lease term would be as follows:

2013			
Jan. 1	Lease Payments Receivable	250,192	
	Sales		250,192
1	Cost of Goods Sold	175,000	
	Finished Goods Inventory		160,000
	Deferred Initial Direct Costs		15,000
1	Cash	65,000	
	Lease Payments Receivable		60,000
	Executory Costs		5,000

The first journal entry records the sale and recognizes a receivable, reported at its present value. The second journal entry simply removes the inventory and deferred direct costs from the books of the lessor and recognizes the cost of goods sold. The final entry records the first payment. The example does not show the payment for the initial direct costs. The deferred initial direct costs account would have been charged at the time these costs were paid.

The 2013 income statement would include the sales and cost of goods sold amounts yielding the manufacturer's profit of $75,192 and interest revenue of $19,019. A note to the statements would describe in more detail the nature of the lease and its terms.

! CAUTION

The sales account is always credited for the present value of the minimum lease payments.

i FYI

These journal entries to record a sales-type lease may seem complex, but look more carefully—these are exactly the entries one makes when reporting a credit sale and a subsequent partial payment.

Accounting for Sales-Type Leases with a Bargain Purchase Option or Guarantee of Residual Value If the lease agreement provides for the lessor to receive a lump-sum payment at the end of the lease term in the form of a bargain purchase option or a guarantee of residual value, the minimum lease payments include these amounts. The receivable is thus increased by the present value of the future payment, and sales are increased by the present value of the additional amount.

To illustrate a sales-type lease with a bargain purchase option, assume that American Manufacturing was the lessor on the lease described on page 15-16 and in Exhibit 15-5.

The initial entries when either a bargain purchase option or a guarantee of residual value of $75,000 is payable at the end of the 5-year lease term would be as follows:

2013			
Jan. 1	Lease Payments Receivable	296,761	
	Sales		296,761
1	Cost of Goods Sold	175,000	
	Finished Goods Inventory		160,000
	Deferred Initial Direct Costs		15,000
1	Cash	65,000	
	Lease Payments Receivable		60,000
	Executory Costs		5,000

Because the lease now includes a bargain purchase option, Sales increases by $46,569 (present value of the bargain purchase amount) over the amount recognized in the previous example. The manufacturer's profit is also increased by this amount.

Accounting for Sales-Type Leases with Unguaranteed Residual Value When a sales-type lease does not contain a bargain purchase option or a guaranteed residual value but the economic life of the leased asset exceeds the lease term, the residual value of the property will remain with the lessor. As indicated earlier, this is called an *unguaranteed residual value*. Because the sales amount reflects the present value of the minimum lease payments, an unguaranteed residual value would not be included in the sales amount. However, the cost of goods sold would be reduced by the present value of the unguaranteed residual value to recognize the fact that the lessor will be receiving back the $75,000 leased asset (worth a present value of $46,569) at the end of the lease term. In essence, this $46,569 residual value is not "sold" but is merely loaned to the lessee for the period of the lease, after which it will be returned to the lessor. The entry to record the initial lease described earlier with an unguaranteed residual value follows:

2013			
Jan. 1	Lease Payments Receivable	250,192	
	Sales		250,192
1	Cost of Goods Sold ($175,000 − $46,569)	128,431	
	Finished Goods Inventory ($160,000 − $46,569)		113,431
	Deferred Initial Direct Costs		15,000
1	Lease Payment Receivable	46,569	
	Finished Goods Inventory		46,569

The only difference between accounting for an unguaranteed residual value and a guaranteed residual value or bargain purchase option is that rather than increasing Sales by the present value of the residual value, the present value of the unguaranteed residual value is deducted from the cost of the leased equipment sold. This reduction occurs because the portion of the leased asset represented by the unguaranteed residual value will be returned at the end of the lease term and therefore is not "sold" on the lease-signing date. The $46,569 in inventory represented by the present value of the unguaranteed residual value has not been sold but has been exchanged for a receivable of equal amount.

Note that the gross profit on the transaction is the same regardless of whether the residual value is guaranteed or unguaranteed, as follows:

	Guaranteed Residual Value	Unguaranteed Residual Value
Sales	$296,761	$250,192
Cost of goods sold	175,000	128,431
Gross profit	$121,761	$121,761

Third-Party Guarantees of Residual Value When a lease is used by the seller as a means to provide financing to the buyer and to increase sales, the seller wants to account for the lease as a sales-type lease, not as an operating lease, so that the revenue from the sale can be recognized immediately. On the other hand, the buyer would prefer to account for the lease as an operating lease to keep the lease obligation off the balance sheet. A third-party guarantee of residual value is a clever trick that companies have devised to get around the accounting rules and allow the desires of both the seller-lessor and the buyer-lessee to be satisfied.

Consider the example just given in which the guaranteed residual value is $75,000. In this case, the fair value of the equipment on the lease-signing date is $296,761. From the lessor's standpoint, the present value of the minimum lease payments, including the guaranteed residual value, is also $296,761. Accordingly, the lease meets the 90% of fair value criterion, and the lease is accounted for as a sales-type lease.

Here is where the fun begins. The lessee, instead of guaranteeing the residual value itself, can pay an insurance company or investment firm to guarantee the residual value. For a fee, the insurance company bears the risk that the residual value of the leased asset might fall below the guaranteed residual value. If this happens, the insurance company, not the lessee, will make up the difference. By the purchase of this "insurance policy," the lessee removes the guaranteed residual value from its calculation of the present value of the minimum lease payments. Without the guaranteed residual value, the present value of the minimum lease payments is only $250,192, just 84% ($250,192/$296,761) of the fair value of the leased asset. As a result, the lessee accounts for the lease as an operating lease.

In summary, a third-party guarantee of residual value allows the seller-lessor to recognize the entire profit from the lease transaction immediately but also permits the buyer-lessee to treat the lease as an operating lease and keep the lease liability off the balance sheet.

Obviously these "insurance policies" are designed to take advantage of the precision of the FASB 90% criterion. As U.S. companies transition to IFRS, it is likely that the number of these third-party guarantee arrangements will decrease because the principles-based nature of the IASB's lease classification standard will require accountants to be very skeptical of transactions designed to mask the economic substance of a lease.

Sale of Asset During Lease Term

If the lessor sells an asset to the lessee during the lease term, a gain or loss is recognized on the difference between the receivable balance and the selling price of the asset. Thus, if the leased asset described in Exhibit 15-8 is sold on December 31, 2015, for $140,000 before the $60,000 rental payment is made, a gain of $25,455 would be reported. The following journal entry would be made to record the sale:

2015			
Dec. 31	Cash	140,000	
	Interest Revenue		10,413
	Lease Payments Receivable		104,132
	Gain on Sale of Leased Asset		25,455

Although the lessor does recognize a gain or loss on the sale, as mentioned earlier, the lessee accounts for the transaction as an exchange of similar assets and defers any gain or loss through an adjustment in the value placed on the purchased asset.

Treatment of Leases on Lessor's Statement of Cash Flows

Operating leases present no special problems to the lessor in preparing a statement of cash flows except for initial direct costs. Because initial direct costs are recognized as an asset when the lease is an operating lease, the payment of these costs would be reported as an investing cash outflow. Under the indirect method, the amortization of initial direct costs would be added to net income in the same way income is adjusted for depreciation. Under the direct method, the amortization would be ignored. The lease payment receipts would be reported as part of net income and would require no adjustment under the indirect method and would be reported as part of the revenue receipts under the direct method.

Capital leases must be analyzed carefully to determine their impact on the statement of cash flows. Direct financing leases would require adjustments similar to those made by the lessee for capital leases except that for the lender (lessor), the transaction is viewed as an investing activity rather than a financing activity as was the case for the borrower (lessee). The portion of the receipt that represents interest will be included in net income and requires no adjustment under the indirect method. It would be part of cash inflows from interest under the direct method. The portion of the lease payment representing the principal would be reported as a cash inflow from investing activities.

Under sales-type leases, the manufacturer's profit, net of initial direct costs, is reported in net income, but the cash inflow comes as the lease payments are received. Under the indirect method, this requires a deduction from net income for the manufacturer's profit at the inception of the lease. This would automatically occur as the changes in inventory, deferred initial costs, and net lease payments receivable are reflected in the Operating section of the statement of cash flows. Because the transaction is being accounted for as a sale, all further receipts under the indirect method are reported as operating inflows either as interest revenue or as reductions in the net lease payments receivable. Under the direct method, the entire lease receipt would be included in cash flows from operating activities. A summary of the treatment of lease impact on the statement of cash flows is included in Exhibit 15-9.

To illustrate the impact of a lease on the lessor's statement of cash flows, refer back to the American Manufacturing Company sales-type lease example starting on page 15-20. Assume that in 2013, American Manufacturing's income before any lease-related items is $200,000. For simplicity, ignore income taxes and executory costs and assume that all of the nonlease items included in income are cash items. Net income for the year can be computed as follows:

Income before lease-related items	$ 200,000
Lease-related sales	250,192
Lease-related cost of goods sold	(175,000)
Lease-related interest revenue	19,019
Net income	$ 294,211

The computation of cash from operating activities for American Manufacturing Company for 2013, using the indirect method to report cash flow from operating activities, would appear as follows:

Operating activities:	
Net income	$ 294,211
Less: Increase in lease payments receivable ($250,192 − $60,000 − $40,981)	(149,211)
Plus: Decrease in finished goods inventory	175,000
Net cash flow from operating activities	$ 320,000

Note that the total operating cash flow of $320,000 is equal to the $200,000 income before lease-related items (which were assumed to be all cash items) plus the two $60,000 lease payments received during the year. This illustrates again that a sales-type lease impacts the lessor's financial statements in the same way as any other long-term credit sale.

EX 15-9 SUMMARY OF LEASE IMPACT ON STATEMENT OF CASH FLOWS

	Operating Activities			
	Indirect Method	Direct Method	Investing Activities	Financing Activities
Lessee:				
Operating lease payments	NI	− Cash		
Capital lease:				
Lease payments—interest	NI	− Cash		
Lease payments—principal				− Cash
Amortization of asset	+ NI	No impact		
Lessor:				
Operating lease:				
Initial direct costs (IDC)			− Cash	
Amortization of IDC	+ NI	No impact		
Lease receipts	NI	+ Cash		
Direct financing lease:				
Initial direct costs			− Cash	
Amortization of IDC	+ NI	No impact		
Lease receipts—interest	NI	+ Cash		
Lease receipts—principal			+ Cash	
Sales-type lease:				
Initial direct costs			− Cash	
Manufacturer's or dealer's profit (net of IDC)	− NI	No impact		
Lease receipts—interest	NI	+ Cash		
Lease receipts—principal	+ NI	+ Cash		

Key:
NI = Included in net income
+ NI = Added as an adjustment to net income
− NI = Deducted as an adjustment to net income
+ Cash = Reported as a receipt of cash
− Cash = Reported as a payment of cash

Disclosure Requirements for Leases

7 Prepare and interpret the lease disclosures required of both lessors and lessees.

WHY **Because a key characteristic of an operating lease, from the standpoint of the lessee, is that the lease-related asset and liability are off the balance sheet, it is important for the financial statement user to be able to interpret the associated note disclosure to detect the existence of these off-balance-sheet items.**

HOW **The lessee is required to provide enough note disclosure to allow the financial statement users to quantify the magnitude of the off-balance-sheet operating leases. The lessor is also required to provide enough disclosure to allow the financial statement user to figure out the extent to which lease-related sales and rentals have impacted the lessor's financial statements.**

The FASB has established specific disclosure requirements for all leases, regardless of whether they are classified as operating or capital leases. The required information supplements the amounts recognized in the financial statements and usually is included in a single note to the financial statements.

The following information is required for all leases that have initial or remaining noncancelable lease terms in excess of one year:

Lessee

1. Gross amount of assets recorded as capital leases, along with related accumulated amortization.
2. Future minimum rental payments required as of the date of the latest balance sheet presented in the aggregate and for each of the five succeeding fiscal years. These payments should be separated between operating and capital leases. For capital leases, executory costs should be excluded.
3. Rental expense for each period for which an income statement is presented. Additional information concerning minimum rentals, contingent rentals, and sublease rentals is required for the same periods.
4. A general description of the lease contracts, including information about restrictions on such items as dividends, additional debt, and further leasing.
5. For capital leases, the amount of imputed interest necessary to reduce the lease payments to present value.

Exhibit 15-10 presents a note accompanying the 2009 financial statements of Delta Air Lines, illustrating the required lessee disclosures for both operating and capital leases.

Several points should be highlighted relating to Delta's lease disclosure. First, compare the minimum lease payments for Delta's capital leases to the payments to be made for its operating leases. The expected payments for operating leases exceed those for capital leases by a factor of more than 13. Note also that Delta discloses the portion of the minimum lease payments on its capital leases that represents interest. With the information in this note, we can approximate the impact that the obligations related to Delta's operating leases would have on its balance sheet if those leases were capitalized.

To approximate the present value of these future operating lease payments, we can make some simplifying assumptions:

- The appropriate interest rate for discounting future cash flows is 10%.
- The uneven stream of future operating lease payments by Delta is roughly equivalent to \$1,310 million per year for nine years. This rough approximation stems from the fact that the payments in the first five years average \$1,310 million per year and the total of the payments is \$11,790 million, which is roughly equal to \$1,310 million a year for nine years.

Given these simplifying assumptions, it is easy to compute that the present value of an annuity of \$1,310 million per year for nine years is \$7.5 billion if the interest rate is 10%. This \$7.5 billion approximates the economic value of Delta's obligations under its operating leases.

If Delta were required to report these future obligations as liabilities, there would be a noticeable impact on the company's reported liabilities—long-term debt would increase from \$17.2 billion to \$24.7 billion. For this reason, companies go to great lengths to structure leases so that the leases can be classified as operating leases and the lease obligation can be excluded from the balance sheet.

Lessor

1. The following components of the net investment in sales-type and direct financing leases as of the date of each balance sheet presented:
   (a) Future minimum lease payments receivable with separate deductions for amounts representing executory costs and the accumulated allowance for uncollectible minimum lease payments receivable

EX 15-10 DELTA AIR LINES—LESSEE DISCLOSURE

NOTE 7. LEASE OBLIGATIONS

We lease aircraft, airport terminals and maintenance facilities, ticket offices and other property and equipment from third parties. Rental expense for operating leases, which is recorded on a straight-line basis over the life of the lease term, totaled $1.3 billion and $798 million for the years ended December 31, 2009 and 2008, respectively, $470 million for the eight months ended December 31, 2007 and $261 million for the four months ended April 30, 2007. Amounts due under capital leases are recorded as liabilities on our Consolidated Balance Sheets. Assets acquired under capital leases are recorded as property and equipment on our Consolidated Balance Sheets. Amortization of assets recorded under capital leases is included in depreciation and amortization expense on our Consolidated Statements of Operations. Many of our facility, aircraft and equipment leases include rental escalation clauses and/or renewal options. Our leases do not include residual value guarantees.

The following tables summarize, as of December 31, 2009, our minimum rental commitments under capital leases and noncancelable operating leases (including certain aircraft under Contract Carrier agreements) with initial or remaining terms in excess of one year:

Capital Leases

Years Ending December 31, (in millions)	Capital Leases
2010	$148
2011	146
2012	119
2013	87
2014	67
Thereafter	337
Total minimum lease payments	904
Less: amount of lease payments representing interest	(396)
Present value of future minimum capital lease payments	508
Plus: unamortized premium, net	25
Less: current obligations under capital leases	(88)
Long-term capital lease obligations	$445

Operating Leases

Years Ending December 31, (in millions)	Delta Lease Payments	Contract Carrier Aircraft Lease Payments[1]	Total
2010	$1,082	$ 507	$ 1,589
2011	910	497	1,407
2012	806	490	1,296
2013	711	460	1,171
2014	634	451	1,085
Thereafter	3,700	1,542	5,242
Total minimum lease payments	$7,843	$3,947	$11,790

[1] These amounts represent the minimum lease obligations under our Contract Carrier agreements with Atlantic Southeast Airlines, Inc. ("ASA"), Chautauqua Airlines, Inc. ("Chautauqua"), Freedom Airlines, Inc. ("Freedom"), Pinnacle Airlines, Inc. ("Pinnacle"), Shuttle America Corporation ("Shuttle America") and SkyWest Airlines, Inc. ("SkyWest Airlines").

At December 31, 2009, we operated 213 aircraft under operating leases and 93 aircraft under capital leases. Our Contract Carriers under capacity purchase agreements operated 450 aircraft under operating leases. Leases for aircraft operated by us and our Contract Carriers have expiration dates ranging from 2010 to 2025. During the four months ended April 30, 2007, we recorded estimated claims relating to the restructuring of the financing arrangements for many of our aircraft and the rejection of certain of our leases in connection with our bankruptcy proceedings.

(b) Unguaranteed residual values accruing to the benefit of the lessor
(c) Unearned revenue (the difference between the gross lease payments and the present value of the lease payments)
(d) For direct financing leases only, initial direct costs

2. Future minimum lease payments to be received for each of the five succeeding fiscal years as of the date of the latest balance sheet presented, including information on contingent rentals
3. The amount of unearned revenue included in income to offset initial direct costs for each year for which an income statement is prepared
4. For operating leases, the cost of assets leased to others and the accumulated depreciation related to these assets
5. A general description of the lessor's leasing arrangements

An example of lessor disclosure of sales-type and direct financing leases for International Lease Finance Corporation, one of the major lessors of airplanes mentioned at the beginning of this chapter, is shown in Exhibit 15-11.

EX 15-11 INTERNATIONAL LEASE FINANCE CORPORATION—LESSOR DISCLOSURE

Note E — Net Investment in Finance and Sales-type Leases

The following lists the components of the net investment in finance and sales-type leases:

	December 31, 2009	December 31, 2008
Total lease payments to be received	$171,549	$165,503
Estimated residual values of leased flight equipment (unguaranteed)	138,665	195,737
Less: Unearned income	(49,133)	(59,481)
Net investment in finance and sales-type leases	$261,081	$301,759

At December 31, 2009, minimum future lease payments on finance and sales-type leases are as follows:

2010	$ 39,323
2011	32,333
2012	32,040
2013	24,526
2014	21,596
Thereafter	21,731
Total minimum lease payments to be received	$ 171,549

International Accounting of Leases

8 **Compare the treatment of accounting for leases in the United States with the requirements of international accounting standards.**

WHY **The IASB's lease accounting standard is very similar, in concept, to the U.S. standard. However, a big practical difference is that the U.S. standard provides precise guidelines and thresholds in the four lease criteria described earlier. In contrast, the international standard is an example of a "principles-based" standard.**

HOW **In practice, international lease accounting is the same as lease accounting in the United States with the one noticeable difference being that, internationally, capital leases are called *finance leases.***

As mentioned earlier in the chapter, the international accounting standard on leases (*IAS 17*) relies on the exercise of accounting judgment to distinguish between operating and capital leases. *IAS 17* states that a finance lease, which is the same as our capital lease, is "a lease that transfers substantially all the risks and rewards incident to ownership of an asset." This standard has been criticized because it leaves the classification of a lease as either operating or capital almost exclusively up to the accountant (subject to the approval of an external auditor). However, before finding fault with *IAS 17*, remember that the four lease classification criteria adopted as part of pre-codification *Statement No. 13* have not been successful in preventing U.S. companies from cleverly constructing most leases to be classified as operating.

In October 2002, the FASB circulated a proposal regarding principles-based accounting standards. As envisioned by their proponents, principles-based standards would involve fewer rigid thresholds and rules (such as the four lease classification criteria) and would rely more on accountants exercising professional judgment in the interpretation and execution of the standards.[13] *IAS 17* is just such a principles-based standard. The entire idea of principles-based standards is still being debated, but the area of lease accounting provides a good illustration of the limitation of principles-based standards. Although *IAS 17* is indeed a principles-based standard, when the rule is actually applied in practice around the world, accountants often sneak a peek at the four lease classification criteria included in FASB ASC paragraph 840-10-25-1 in order to be able to use the *IAS 17* "principle" in the context of an actual lease contract. As U.S. companies switch to IFRS, it is likely that accountants and auditors will continue to reference the FASB's four lease classification criteria for help in applying the principles of *IAS 17*.

A very interesting lease accounting proposal has been circulating for a number of years among accounting standard setters around the world. The standard setters of the United States, the United Kingdom, Canada, Australia, and New Zealand sponsored a research project that resulted in a new lease accounting proposal in 1996. This proposal, titled "Accounting for Leases: A New Approach," notes that current lease accounting standards fail in their objective of requiring companies to recognize significant rights and obligations as assets and liabilities in the balance sheet. The proposal also suggests that the lease accounting rules be simplified as follows: All lease contracts are to be accounted for as capital leases.

To illustrate the dramatic impact that this "new approach" would have on the reporting of leases for lessees, consider the following table:

Fair value of leased asset = $10,000	Present value of minimum lease payments = $8,999	Present value of minimum lease payments = $9,001
Lease obligation reported under current U.S. GAAP	$ 0	$9,001
Lease obligation that would be reported under the New Approach for lease accounting	$8,999	$9,001

In each of the two cases, the fair value of the leased asset is $10,000. In the first case, the present value of the minimum lease payments is $8,999, which is 89.9% of the fair value of the leased asset. The present value of the minimum payments is less than 90% of the fair value of the leased asset, and, assuming that none of the other capital lease criteria are

[13] Proposal—"Principles-Based Approach to U.S. Standard Setting" (Norwalk, CT: Financial Accounting Standards Board, October 21, 2002).

satisfied, the lease would be accounted for as an operating lease under U.S. GAAP. With the lease classified as an operating lease, the lessee would not report any obligation for the future lease payments. Under the new approach, an $8,999 obligation would be reported for the present value of the future minimum lease payments. In the second case, the present value of the lease payments is $9,001, which is more than 90% of the fair value of the leased asset. This lease would be classified as a capital lease under existing U.S. GAAP, and the $9,001 obligation would be reported under both U.S. GAAP and the new approach. Note that under the new approach, the small $2 change in the present value of the lease payments, from $8,999 to $9,001, is reflected in the correspondingly small increase in the recorded amount of the lease obligation. However, under U.S. GAAP, this small change in the present value of the payments results in a huge change in the reported liability. Whenever there is a knife-edge accounting rule such as this, one can be sure that companies will be very careful, and inventive, in making certain that the present value of their lease payments is just below the 90% threshold.

More recently, the FASB and IASB have both endorsed the idea that all leases should be capitalized. The terminology currently being used by the FASB is that the signing of a lease creates a "right-of-use asset" and a "lease obligation." The FASB and IASB expect to circulate an exposure draft along these lines in 2010 and hope to adopt final standards in 2011.

This proposal to capitalize all leases is still in the discussion stage. Given the great efforts that U.S. companies now expend to keep leases off the balance sheet, a proposal to capitalize all leases is sure to touch off one of the largest accounting debates in the past 30 years.

EM EXPANDED MATERIAL

Lease agreements can be very complicated. Some of these complications have been specifically designed to circumvent the accounting rules and allow for favorable classification of leases. One example is the third-party guarantee of residual values mentioned earlier in the chapter. Another example is the sale-leaseback transaction described in this section. It is a transaction that usually has the effect of sweeping assets and liabilities right off a company's balance sheet even as those assets continue to be used exactly as they were before.

Sale-Leaseback Transactions

9 Record a sale-leaseback transaction for both a seller-lessee and a purchaser-lessor.

WHY Sale-leaseback transactions are common because they can serve both a valid business purpose and an attractive accounting purpose.

HOW A sale-leaseback is a transaction in which one party sells an asset to another, and then the first party immediately leases the asset back and continues to use it. Any gain realized on a sale-leaseback by the seller-lessee is deferred and amortized over the life of the lease. A loss on the sale is recognized immediately. If the lease is structured appropriately, the seller-lessee can account for the lease as an operating lease; in this case, the sale-leaseback serves to remove the asset and any associated liability from the balance sheet without impacting the continued use of the asset.

A common type of lease arrangement is referred to as a sale-leaseback transaction. Typical of this type of lease is an arrangement whereby one party sells the property to a second party, and then the first party leases the property back. Thus, the seller becomes a seller-lessee and the purchaser a purchaser-lessor.

The accounting problem raised by this transaction is whether the seller-lessee should recognize the profit from the original sale immediately or defer it over the lease term. The FASB rule is that if the initial sale produces a profit, it should be deferred and amortized in proportion to the amortization of the leased asset if it is a capital lease or in proportion to the rental payments if it is an operating lease. If the transaction produces a loss because the fair value of the asset is less than its carrying value, an immediate loss should be recognized.[14]

There are two exceptions to the profit deferral rule. First, if the seller-lessee's remaining ownership rights are "minor" after the sale-leaseback transaction, then the sale and leaseback are separate transactions, and any profit on the sale is recognized immediately. Second, if the profit on the sale is "large," defined as larger than the present value of the minimum payments on the leaseback, then the "excess" profit (the amount greater than the present value of the minimum leaseback payments) is recognized at the time of the sale with the remainder of the profit deferred and recognized according to the normal process.

STOP&THINK

Why would a company sell an asset and then turn right around and lease that same asset back?

a) To increase the reported amount of total liabilities.
b) To decrease the reported amount of total liabilities.
c) To increase the reported amount of total assets.
d) To increase the reported amount of current liabilities.

To illustrate the accounting treatment for a sale at a gain, assume that on January 1, 2013, Hopkins Inc. sells equipment having a carrying value of $750,000 on its books to Ashcroft Co. for $950,000 and immediately leases back the equipment. The following conditions are established to govern the transaction:

1. The term of the lease is 10 years, noncancelable. A down payment of $200,000 is required plus equal lease payments of $107,107 at the beginning of each year. The implicit interest rate is 10%.
2. The equipment has a fair value of $950,000 on January 1, 2013, and an estimated economic life of 20 years. Straight-line depreciation is used on all owned assets.
3. Hopkins has an option to renew the lease for $10,000 per year for 10 years, the rest of its economic life. Title passes at the end of the lease term.

Analysis of this lease shows that it qualifies as a capital lease under both the lease term and present value of payments criteria. It meets the 75% of economic life criterion because of the bargain renewal option, which makes both the lease term and the economic life of the equipment 20 years. It meets the 90% of fair value criterion because the present value of the lease payments is equal to the fair value of the equipment ($950,000).[15] The

[14] FASB ASC paragraph 840-40-25-3 and paragraph 840-40-35-1.

[15] Computation of present value of lease:

(a) Present value of 10 years' rentals:
Payments at the beginning of the period (BEG): PMT = $107,107, N = 10, I = 10% → $723,939.

(b) Present value of second 10 years' rentals:
Payments at the beginning of the period (BEG): PMT = $10,000, N = 10, I = 10% → $67,590, present value at beginning of second 10 years' lease period. Present value at beginning of lease, 10 years earlier: FV = $67,590, N = 10, I = 10% → $26,059.

(c) Total present value, $723,939 + $26,059 + $200,000 down payment = $950,000 (rounded).

journal entries for the first year of the lease for Hopkins, the seller-lessee, and Ashcroft, the purchaser-lessor, follow:

Hopkins Inc. (Seller-Lessee)

2013			
Jan. 1	Cash	950,000	
	Equipment		750,000
	Unearned Profit on Sale-Leaseback		200,000
	To record original sale of equipment.		
1	Leased Equipment	950,000	
	Obligations under Capital Lease		642,893
	Cash ($200,000 + $107,107)		307,107
	To record lease of equipment, including down payment and first payment.		
Dec. 31	Amortization Expense on Leased Equipment	47,500	
	Accumulated Amortization on Leased Equipment		47,500
	To record amortization of equipment over 20-year period ($950,000/20).		
31	Interest Expense	64,289	
	Obligations under Capital Lease	42,818	
	Cash		107,107
	To record second lease payment (interest expense: $642,893 × 0.10 = $64,289).		
31	Unearned Profit on Sale-Leaseback	10,000	
	Revenue Earned on Sale-Leaseback		10,000
	To record recognition of revenue over 20-year life in proportion to the amortization of the leased asset.		

Ashcroft Co. (Purchaser-Lessor)

Jan. 1	Equipment	950,000	
	Cash		950,000
	To record purchase of equipment.		
1	Cash	307,107	
	Lease Payments Receivable	642,893	
	Equipment		950,000
	To record direct financing sale-leaseback to Hopkins Inc. Gross receivable = (10 × $107,107) + (10 × $10,000) = $1,171,070		
Dec. 31	Cash	107,107	
	Lease Payments Receivable		42,818
	Interest Revenue		64,289
	To record receipt of second lease payment (see computations for Hopkins Inc.).		

The amortization entries and recognition of the deferred gain on the sale for Hopkins Inc. would be the same each year for the 20-year lease term. The interest expense and interest revenue amounts would decline each year using the effective interest method of computation.

If the lease had not met the criteria, it would have been recorded as an operating lease. The gain on the sale would have been deferred and recognized in proportion to the lease payments. The yearly gain recognition amounts would closely parallel that just illustrated because both the amortization of a leased asset and the pattern of lease payments typically follow a straight-line process.

If the initial sale had been at a loss, an immediate recognition of the loss would have been recorded.

ifrs

The provisions of *IAS 17* regarding the deferral of sale profits on a sale-leaseback are essentially the same as under U.S. GAAP. The wording in *IAS 17* is somewhat different (and, frankly, a bit more clear) than in FASB ASC Subtopic 840-40, but the international accounting is basically the same as that required under U.S. GAAP.

SOLUTIONS TO OPENING SCENARIO QUESTIONS

1. American Airlines leases many of the airplanes that it uses. It leases these planes from financing companies, such as GE Capital Aviation Services, that buy the airplanes from the manufacturer and then make money by leasing the planes to airlines.
2. By leasing many of their airplanes, the airlines give themselves financing flexibility. If they experience a decline in the need for aircraft, it is much easier to get out of a lease than it is to sell an unneeded plane in order to pay off the loan used to buy the plane in the first place.
3. As illustrated with data from Delta Air Lines, some leased airplanes are reported as an asset in the leasing airline's balance sheet and some are not. This chapter explains the accounting rules that determine when a leased asset is reported on the leasing company's balance sheet as an asset.

SOLUTIONS TO STOP & THINK

1. (Page 15-11) The correct answer is D. The use of a higher discount rate results in a lower computed present value. A lower present value reduces the probability that a lease will satisfy the 90% of market value criterion and thus reduces the likelihood that the lease will be classified as a capital lease.
2. (Page 15-40) The correct answer is B. One reason for a firm to do a sale-leaseback is to remove an asset (and the associated payment obligation) from the balance sheet. A carefully constructed sale-leaseback deal results in the lease being classified as an operating lease—with the leased asset and the lease liability disclosed only in the financial statement notes.

   Another reason to do a sale-leaseback is to put the property in the hands of a professional property management firm, allowing the company to concentrate on its core business. For example, imagine a large engineering consulting firm with an office building located on a prime piece of land in a large city. What does an engineering consulting firm know about maximizing the use of the property? Nothing. But it needs the office building. So, the firm sells the building and property to a property management firm and then leases them back. The engineering consulting firm is now concentrating on what it does best—engineering—and the property is being managed by a firm of professionals.

SOLUTION TO USING THE FASB'S CODIFICATION

You should have found the following in FASB ASC paragraph 840-20-25-8: "If a build-to-suit lease is classified as an operating lease, the lessee shall consider construction period lease payments made before the beginning of the lease term to be prepaid rent."

So, if these payments are prepaid rent, they should then be added in with all of the other lease/rent payments so that the total amount is recognized as expense in a straight-line fashion over the lease term.

REVIEW CHAPTER 15

LEARNING OBJECTIVES

1 **Describe the circumstances in which leasing makes more business sense than does an outright sale and purchase.**

The three primary advantages to a lessee of leasing over purchasing are that a lease often involves no down payment, leasing avoids the risks of ownership, and leasing gives the lessee flexibility to change assets when technology or preferences change.

The economic advantages to a lessor include an increase in sales by providing financing to customers who might not otherwise be able to buy, establishment of an ongoing relationship with customers, and retention of the residual value of the leased asset after the lease term is over.

2 **Understand the accounting issues faced by the asset owner (lessor) and the asset user (lessee) in recording a lease transaction.**

For the lessor, the key accounting issue is whether or not a sale should be recognized on the date the lease is signed. The proper accounting hinges on whether the lease signing transfers effective ownership of the leased asset, whether the lessor has any significant additional responsibilities remaining after the lease is signed, and whether payment collectibility is reasonably assured.

For the lessee, the key accounting issue is whether the leased asset and the lease payment obligation should be recognized on the balance sheet. Again, the proper accounting treatment depends on whether the lease signing transfers effective ownership of the leased asset.

Capital leases are accounted for as if the lease agreement transfers ownership of the leased asset from the lessor to the lessee. Operating leases are accounted for as rental agreements.

3 **Outline the types of contractual provisions typically included in lease agreements.**

- *Cancellation provisions*. A noncancelable lease agreement is one that can be canceled by the lessee only under very unusual circumstances. Only noncancelable leases can be classified as capital leases.
- *Bargain purchase option*. If the lessee has the option to purchase the leased asset in the future at an amount low enough such that exercise of the option is likely, a bargain purchase option exists.
- *Lease* term. The lease term includes the noncancelable lease period plus any periods covered by bargain renewal options that include favorable lease terms (e.g., low lease payments) that make it likely that the lessee will renew the lease.
- *Residual* value. The residual value is the value of the leased asset at the end of the lease term. Sometimes, the lease agreement requires that the lessee guarantee the residual value; if the residual value falls below the guaranteed amount, the lessee must pay the lessor the difference.
- *Minimum lease payments*. The minimum lease payments include the periodic lease payments plus any bargain purchase option amount or the amount of any guaranteed residual value. The lessor computes the present value of the minimum lease payments using the implicit interest rate. The lessee computes the present value using the lower of the implicit interest rate and the lessee's own incremental borrowing rate.

4 **Apply the lease classification criteria in order to distinguish between capital and operating leases.**

The four general lease classification criteria, applicable to both lessors and lessees, are as follows:

- *Transfer of ownership*. The lease includes a provision that title to the leased asset passes to the lessee by the end of the lease term.
- *Bargain purchase option*. A bargain purchase option exists that makes it reasonably assured that the lessee will acquire the asset.

- *75% of economic life*. The lease term is equal to 75% or more of the economic life of the leased asset.
- *90% of asset value*. The present value of the minimum lease payments is greater than or equal to 90% of the fair value of the leased asset on the lease-signing date.

If any one of these criteria is met, the lease is classified as a capital lease by the lessee. For the lessor, the lease is a capital lease if, in addition to one of the general criteria, both of the revenue recognition criteria are met:

- *Collection* of the minimum lease payments is reasonably assured.
- The *lessor* has substantially completed its obligations to the lessee as of the date of the lease signing; no significant work remains to be done.

5 Properly account for both capital and operating leases from the standpoint of the lessee (asset user).

An operating lease is accounted for as a rental, with the lease payment amount being recognized as rent expense. With a capital lease, an asset and a liability are recognized on the lease-signing date. The asset is subsequently amortized over the lease term or, if the ownership transfer or bargain purchase option criteria are met, over the economic life of the asset. The lease payments are recorded as reductions in the balance of the lease liability, with a part of the payment being classified as interest expense.

6 Properly account for both capital and operating leases from the standpoint of the lessor (asset owner).

An operating lease is accounted for as a rental, with the lease payment amount being recognized as rent revenue. The lessor continues to depreciate the leased asset.

For a lessor, there are two types of capital leases: direct financing leases and sales-type leases. With a direct financing lease, a lease receivable is recognized on the lease-signing date. Interest revenue on the receivable balance is recognized during the lease term. With a sales-type lease, in addition to interest revenue over the life of the lease, a profit is recognized on the lease-signing date equal to the difference between the fair value of the leased asset and its cost.

With operating leases and direct financing leases, initial direct costs are capitalized and amortized over the lease term. With a sales-type lease, initial direct costs are immediately recognized as a reduction in the sale profit.

7 Prepare and interpret the lease disclosures required of both lessors and lessees.

Required disclosures for lessees include the following:

- Gross amount and accumulated amortization associated with assets leased under capital leases
- Rental expense associated with operating leases
- Schedule of future minimum lease payments for both capital and operating leases

Required disclosures for lessors include the following:

- Schedule of future minimum lease payments to be received for both capital and operating leases
- Cost and accumulated depreciation of assets leased to others under operating leases

8 Compare the treatment of accounting for leases in the United States with the requirements of international accounting standards.

IAS 17 does not include specific lease classification criteria; instead, it states that a capital lease is "a lease that transfers substantially all the risks and rewards incident to ownership of an asset." A proposal is now circulating internationally that suggests that all leases longer than one year should be capitalized.

EM **EXPANDED MATERIAL**

9 **Record a sale-leaseback transaction for both a seller-lessee and a purchaser-lessor.**

A sale-leaseback is a transaction in which one party sells an asset to another, and then the first party immediately leases the asset back and continues to use it. Apart from a couple of exceptions, any gain realized on a sale-leaseback by the seller-lessee is deferred and amortized over the life of the lease. A loss on the sale is recognized immediately.

FASB-IASB CODIFICATION SUMMARY

ifrs

Topic	FASB Accounting Standards Codification	Original FASB Standard	Corresponding IASB Standard	Differences between U.S. GAAP and IFRS
Lease classification criteria	*Section 840-10-25 par. 1*	*SFAS No. 13 par. 7*	*IAS 17 par. 8-10*	In substance, the standards are the same. IFRS provides less detail.
Lease discount rate (for lessees)	*Section 840-10-25 par. 31*	*SFAS No. 13 par. 7*	*IAS 17 par. 20*	In IFRS, no explicit mention is made of using the lower of the implicit rate or the incremental borrowing rate. Instead, the implicit rate is to be used if known.
Revenue recognition criteria (for lessor)	*Section 840-10-25 par. 42*	*SFAS No. 13 par. 8*	*IAS 17 par. 42*	Substantially the same. Rather than the two explicit criteria, IFRS merely says that a sale in a sales-type lease is recognized "in accordance with the policy followed by the entity for outright sales."
Initial direct costs (for lessors)	*Section 840-20-35 par. 2* *Section 840-30-35 par. 23* *Section 840-30-25 par. 6*	*SFAS No. 13 par. 19* *SFAS No. 13 par. 18* *SFAS No. 13 par. 17*	*IAS 17 par. 38, 42*	No substantial differences
Sale-leaseback accounting	*Section 840-40-25 par. 3* *Section 840-40-35 par. 1*	*SFAS No. 13 par. 7*	*IAS 17 par. 58-63*	No substantial differences

KEY TERMS

Bargain purchase option 15-7
Bargain renewal option 15-8
Direct financing leases 15-24
Executory costs 15-9
Guaranteed residual value 15-8
Implicit interest rate 15-9
Incremental borrowing rate 15-10
Initial direct costs 15-24
Lease 15-3
Lease term 15-8
Lessee 15-3
Lessor 15-3
Minimum lease payments 15-9
Noncancelable 15-7
Sales-type leases 15-24
Unguaranteed residual value 15-8

EM EXPANDED MATERIAL

Sale-leaseback 15-40

QUESTIONS

1. What are the principal advantages to a lessee in leasing rather than purchasing property?
2. What are the principal advantages to a lessor in leasing rather than selling property?
3. Conceptually, what is the difference between a capital lease and an operating lease?
4. What is a bargain purchase option?
5. How is the lease term measured?
6. (a) What discount rate is used to determine the present value of a lease by the lessee?
   (b) by the lessor?
7. What criteria must be met before a lease can be properly accounted for as a capital lease on the books of the lessee?
8. In determining the classification of a lease, a lessor uses the criteria of the lessee plus two additional criteria. What are these additional criteria, and why are they included in the classification of leases by lessors?
9. What is the basic difference between an operating lease and a capital lease from the viewpoint of the lessee?
10. If an operating lease requires the payment of uneven rental amounts over its life, how should the lessee recognize rental expense?
11. What amount should be recorded as an asset and a liability for capital leases on the books of the lessee?
12. Why do asset and liability balances for capital leases usually differ after the first year?
13. A capitalized lease should be amortized in accordance with the lessee's normal depreciation policy. What time period should be used for lease amortization?
14. The use of the capital lease method for a given lease will always result in a lower net income than the operating lease method. Do you agree? Explain fully.
15. (a) How does a capital lease for equipment affect the lessee's statement of cash flows?
    (b) How would the treatment on the statement of cash flows differ if the contract was identified as a purchase of equipment with a down payment and a long-term note payable for the balance?
16. Distinguish a sales-type lease from a direct financing lease.
17. Unguaranteed residual values accrue to the lessor at the expiration of the lease. How are these values treated in a sales-type lease?
18. Under what circumstances are the minimum lease payments for the lessee different from those of the lessor?
19. Why is the principal portion of a lease receipt of a financing lease treated as an investment inflow on the lessor's books while the principal portion of a lease payment is treated as a financial cash outflow on the lessee's books?
20. Describe the specific lease disclosure requirements for lessees.
21. What disclosures are required by the FASB for lessors under sales-type and direct financing leases?
22. How does the lease classification standard in *IAS 17* differ from that in FASB ASC Topic 840?
23. What lease accounting proposal has been circulating among the members of the international accounting community?

EM EXPANDED MATERIAL

24. When should the profit or loss be recognized by the seller-lessee in a sale-leaseback arrangement?

PRACTICE EXERCISES

Practice 15-1
LO3

Present Value of Minimum Payments
A lease involves payments of $2,000 per month for two years. The payments are made at the end of each month. The lease also involves a guaranteed residual value of $20,000 to be paid at the end of the 2-year period. The appropriate interest rate is 12% compounded monthly. Compute the present value of the minimum payments.

Practice 15-2
LO3

Computation of Payments
The lessor is computing the appropriate monthly lease payment. The fair value of the leased asset is $75,000. The guaranteed residual value at the end of the lease term is $12,000. The appropriate interest rate is 12% compounded monthly. The lease term is 36 months, and the lease payments occur at the end of each month. What is the appropriate amount of the monthly payment?

Practice 15-3

LO3

Computation of Implicit Interest Rate
A lease involves payments of $1,000 per month for five years. The payments are made at the end of each month. The lease also involves a guaranteed residual value of $10,000 to be paid at the end of the 5-year period. The fair value of the leased asset is $35,000. Compute the interest rate implicit in the lease.

Practice 15-4

LO3

Incremental Borrowing Rate and Implicit Interest Rate
A lease involves payments of $16,000 per month for four years. The payments are made at the end of each month. The lease also involves a guaranteed residual value of $50,000 to be paid at the end of the 4-year period. Compute the present value of the minimum payments (1) using the rate implicit in the lease of 9% compounded monthly and (2) the lessee's incremental borrowing rate of 12% compounded monthly.

Practice 15-5

LO4

Lease Criteria
The lessor leased equipment to the lessee. The fair value of the equipment is $246,000. Lease payments are $35,000 per year, payable at the *end* of the year, for 10 years. The interest rate implicit in the lease is 9%. At the end of 10 years, the lessor will repossess the equipment. The lease does *not* include a bargain purchase option, and the equipment has a total estimated useful life of 15 years. Is the lease an operating lease or a capital lease? Explain.

Practice 15-6

LO5

Journal Entries for an Operating Lease—Lessee
On January 1, the lessee company signed an operating lease contract. The lease contract calls for $3,000 payments at the end of each year for 10 years. The rate implicit in the lease is 10%. Make the journal entries necessary on the books of the lessee company (1) on the lease-signing date and (2) to record the first lease payment.

Practice 15-7

LO5

Operating Lease with Varying Payments—Lessee
The company is a lessee and signed a 3-year operating lease that calls for a payment of $20,000 at the end of the first year and payments of $80,000 at the end of each year for the second and third years. Make the journal entries necessary to record the lease payments at the end of each of the three years.

Practice 15-8

LO5

Journal Entries for a Capital Lease—Lessee
Refer to Practice 15-6. Assume that the lease is to be accounted for as a capital lease. Also assume that the leased asset is to be amortized over the 12-year asset life rather than the 10-year lease term. Make the journal entries necessary on the books of the lessee company (1) on the lease-signing date and (2) at the end of the first year, including the recording of the first lease payment.

Practice 15-9

LO5

Accounting for a Bargain Purchase Option—Lessee
A lease involves payments of $10,000 per year for six years. The payments are made at the end of each year. The lease involves a bargain purchase option of $6,000 to be exercised at the end of the 6-year period. The total economic life of the leased asset is nine years. The interest rate implicit in the lease is 12% compounded annually. Make the journal entries necessary on the books of the lessee company (1) on the lease-signing date and (2) at the end of the first year, including the recording of the first lease payment.

Practice 15-10

LO5

Purchasing a Leased Asset During the Lease Term—Lessee
On December 31, the company, a lessee, purchased some machinery that it had been leasing under a capital lease arrangement. The leased asset and lease liability were originally recorded at $1,000,000. At the time of the purchase, the accumulated amortization on the leased asset was $400,000, and the remaining balance of the lease liability was $650,000. The leased asset was purchased for $720,000 cash. Make the necessary journal entry on the books of the lessee.

Practice 15-11

LO5

Leases on a Statement of Cash Flows—Lessee

Refer to Practice 15-6. Net income for the year was $10,000. Except for lease-related items, there were no changes in current operating assets or liabilities during the year, no purchases or sales of property, plant, or equipment, and no dividends paid, stock issued, or loans obtained or repaid. Prepare a complete statement of cash flows using the indirect method of reporting operating cash flow assuming that the lease is accounted for as (1) an operating lease (net income was $10,000) and (2) a capital lease (net income was $9,621). (*Note*: The capital lease entries for the year are made in Practice 15-8.)

Practice 15-12

LO6

Journal Entries for an Operating Lease—Lessor

On January 1, the lessor company purchased a piece of equipment for $24,000. The equipment has an expected life of four years with zero salvage value. The lessor company immediately leased the equipment under an operating lease agreement. The lease calls for the lessor company to receive lease payments of $6,800 per year to be received at the beginning of the year. Make the journal entries necessary on the books of the lessor company to record (1) the purchase of the equipment for cash, (2) the lease signing (including receipt of the first lease payment), and (3) depreciation of the leased equipment.

Practice 15-13

LO6

Journal Entries for a Direct Financing Lease—Lessor

Refer to Practice 15-12. Assume that the lease is accounted for as a direct financing lease instead of as an operating lease. The interest rate implicit in the lease is 9%. Make the journal entries necessary on the lessor's books to record (1) the signing of the lease, (2) the receipt of the initial $6,800 lease payment on the lease-signing date, and (3) the recognition of interest revenue at the end of the first year.

Practice 15-14

LO6

Direct Financing Lease with a Residual Value

On January 1, the lessor company purchased a piece of equipment for $100,000. The equipment has an expected salvage value of $3,974; this amount is *not* guaranteed. The lessor company immediately leased the equipment under a direct financing lease agreement. The lease calls for the lessor company to receive annual lease payments of $15,600 per year for 10 years, to be received at the beginning of the year; at the end of 10 years, the equipment is returned to the lessor company. The interest rate implicit in the lease is 12%. Make the journal entries necessary on the lessor's books to record (1) the signing of the lease, (2) the receipt of the initial $15,600 lease payment on the lease-signing date, (3) the recognition of interest revenue at the end of the first year, and (4) the journal entry at the end of 10 years to record the final interest revenue accrual and the recovery of the equipment, assuming that the salvage value was equal to its estimated amount. (*Hint*: Interest revenue in the 10th year is $426.)

Practice 15-15

LO6

Journal Entries for a Sales-Type Lease—Lessor

On January 1, the lessor company purchased a piece of equipment for $7,000 as inventory. The lessor company immediately leased the equipment under a sales-type lease agreement; the cash selling price of the equipment is $10,000. The lease calls for the lessor company to receive five annual lease payments of $2,600 per year, to be received at the beginning of the year. The interest rate implicit in the lease is 15%. Make the journal entries necessary on the books of the lessor company to record (1) the lease signing (including receipt of the first lease payment) and (2) the recognition of interest revenue at the end of the first year.

Practice 15-16

LO6

Sales-Type Lease with a Bargain Purchase Option

On January 1, the lessor company purchased a piece of equipment for $6,000 as inventory. The lessor company immediately leased the equipment under a sales-type lease agreement. The lease calls for the lessor company to receive five annual lease payments of $2,500 per year, to be received at the beginning of the year. In addition to the five annual payments of $2,500 at the beginning of each year, the lessor is to receive a bargain purchase option amount of $500 at the end of five years. The interest rate implicit in the lease is 12%. Make the journal entries necessary on the books of the lessor company to record (1) the lease signing (including receipt of the first lease payment) and (2) the recognition of interest revenue at the end of the first year.

Practice 15-17

LO6

Sales-Type Lease with an Unguaranteed Residual Value
Refer to Practice 15-16. Assume the same facts except that the $500 bargain purchase option is instead a $500 *unguaranteed* residual value. Make the journal entries necessary on the books of the lessor company to record (1) the lease signing (including receipt of the first lease payment) and (2) the recognition of interest revenue at the end of the first year.

Practice 15-18

LO5, LO6

Third-Party Guarantees of Residual Value
On January 1, the lessor company purchased a piece of equipment for $9,000 as inventory. The lessor company immediately leased the equipment under a sales-type lease agreement. The lease calls for the lessor company to receive six annual lease payments of $3,000 per year, to be received at the beginning of the year. In addition to the six annual payments of $3,000 at the beginning of each year, the lessor is to receive a *guaranteed* residual value of $4,000 at the end of six years. The fair value on the date of the lease signing is equal to the present value of the lessor's minimum payments; the interest rate implicit in the lease is 11%. The equipment has a useful life of 10 years, there is no bargain purchase option, and the title does not transfer at the end of the lease term. Also, the residual value is guaranteed by a third-party insurance company, not by the lessee company. Make the journal entries necessary to record the lease signing, including the first lease payment, (1) on the books of the *lessor* company and (2) on the books of the *lessee* company.

Practice 15-19

LO6

Selling a Leased Asset During the Lease Term—Lessor
On December 31 of Year 1, the company, a lessor, sold some machinery that it had been leasing under a direct financing lease arrangement. On January 1 of Year 1 (after receipt of the lease payment for the year), the following account balances were associated with the lease:

Gross Lease Payments Receivable	$234,000
Unearned Interest Revenue	40,000
Present Value of Lease Payments Receivable	$194,000

The interest rate implicit in the lease is 10%. The leased machinery is sold for $130,000 cash. Make the journal entry or entries necessary on the books of the lessor to record this sale. (*Note*: Don't forget any necessary year-end adjustment.)

Practice 15-20

LO6

Leases on a Statement of Cash Flows—Lessor
On January 1, the lessor company purchased some equipment (for cash) that the company then immediately leased. The lease contract calls for the receipt of $5,000 payments at the end of each year for eight years. The residual value of the equipment at the end of the 8-year lease term is expected to be $6,500. The rate implicit in the lease is 13%. Except for lease-related items, there were no changes in current operating assets or liabilities during the year; no purchases or sales of property, plant, or equipment; and no dividends paid, stock issued, or loans obtained or repaid. The equipment has a total useful life of 12 years with no salvage value. Prepare a complete statement of cash flows for the lessor using the indirect method of reporting operating cash flow assuming that the lease is accounted for as (1) an operating lease (net income was $30,000) and (2) a direct financing lease (net income was $30,640).

Practice 15-21
LO5, LO7

Debt-to-Equity Ratio Adjusted for Operating Leases
As of December 31, the company has total assets of $10,000 and total liabilities of $4,000. Future minimum payments on operating leases for which the company is the lessee are $600 per year for the next 15 years. Assume that the lease payments occur at the end of the year. The appropriate discount rate is 8%. Calculate (1) the company's debt-to-equity ratio using its reported numbers and (2) the company's debt-to-equity ratio assuming that the operating leases were accounted for as capital leases.

EM EXPANDED MATERIAL

Practice 15-22
LO9

Sale-Leaseback Transactions—Lessor and Lessee
On January 1, Seller-Lessee sold a building to Buyer-Lessor for $200,000. The building had originally cost Seller-Lessee $230,000 and had accumulated depreciation of $70,000 on the date of the sale. On the day of the sale, Seller-Lessee leased the building back from Buyer-Lessor. The lease calls for annual lease payments of $23,750 at the end of each year for the next 25 years. The interest rate implicit in the lease is 11%. On January 1, the building had a fair value of $200,000 and a remaining useful life of 25 years (with zero expected salvage value). Make all lease-related journal entries necessary for the year on the books of (1) Seller-Lessee and (2) Buyer-Lessor.

EXERCISES

Exercise 15-23
LO5

Entries for Lease—Lessee
On January 2, 2013, Jacques Company entered into a noncancelable lease for new equipment. The equipment was built to Jacques Company's specifications and is in an area in which rental to another lessee would be difficult. Rental payments are $600,000 a year for 10 years, payable in advance. The equipment has an estimated economic life of 20 years. The taxes, maintenance, and insurance are to be paid directly by Jacques Company, and the title to the equipment is to be transferred to Jacques at the end of the lease term. Assume the cost of borrowing funds for this type of an asset by Jacques Company is 12%.

1. Give the entry on Jacques' books that should be made at the inception of the lease.
2. Give the entries for 2013 and 2014, assuming the second payment and subsequent payments are made on December 31 and assuming double-declining-balance amortization.

Exercise 15-24
LO5

Entries for Lease—Lessee
Bingham Smelting Company entered into a 15-year noncancelable lease beginning January 1, 2013, for equipment to use in its smelting operations. The term of the lease is the same as the expected economic life of the equipment. Bingham uses straight-line depreciation for all plant assets. The provisions of the lease call for annual payments of $290,000 in advance plus $20,000 per year to cover executory costs, such as taxes and insurance, for the 15-year period of the lease. At the end of the 15 years, the equipment is expected to be scrapped. The incremental borrowing rate of Bingham is 10%. The lessor's computed implicit interest rate is unknown to Bingham.

Record the lease on the books of Bingham and give all the entries necessary to record the lease for its first year plus the entry to record the second lease payment on December 31, 2013. (*Note:* Round to the nearest dollar.)

Exercise 15-25
LO5

Entries for Operating Lease—Lessee
Mighty Inc. leases some of the equipment it uses. The lease term is five years, and the lease payments are to be made in advance as shown in the following schedule.

SPREADSHEET

January 1, 2013	$ 60,000
January 1, 2014	60,000
January 1, 2015	90,000
January 1, 2016	110,000
January 1, 2017	140,000
Total	$460,000

The equipment is to be used evenly over the 5-year period. For each of the five years, give the entry that should be made at the time the lease payment is made to allocate the proper share of rent expense to each period. The lease is classified as an operating lease by Mighty Inc.

Exercise 15-26

LO5, LO7

Impact of Capitalizing the Value of Operating Leases

The following information comes from the 2013 financial statements of Jessica Hatch Company:

Total liabilities	$250,000
Total stockholders' equity	110,000

In addition, Jessica Hatch has a large number of operating leases. The future payments on these operating leases are disclosed in the notes to the financial statements as follows:

Year	Payment
2014	$ 30,000
2015	30,000
2016	30,000
2017	30,000
2018	30,000
Thereafter	330,000

All of these lease payments occur at the end of the year. The incremental borrowing rate of Jessica Hatch Company is 10%. This is also the implicit rate in all of the leases that Jessica Hatch signs.

1. Compute the debt-to-equity ratio (total liabilities/total equity).
2. Compute the debt ratio (total liabilities/total assets).
3. Assuming that Jessica Hatch's operating leases are accounted for as capital leases, compute the debt-to-equity ratio.
4. Assuming that Jessica Hatch's operating leases are accounted for as capital leases, compute the debt ratio.

Exercise 15-27

LO5, LO6

Entries for Lease—Lessor and Lessee

Doxey Company purchased a machine on January 1, 2013, for $2,500,000 for the express purpose of leasing it. The machine was expected to have a 9-year life from January 1, 2013, no salvage value, and to be depreciated on a straight-line basis. On March 1, 2013, Doxey leased the machine to Mondale Company for $600,000 a year for a 4-year period ending February 28, 2017. The appropriate interest rate is 12% compounded annually. Doxey paid a total of $30,000 for maintenance, insurance, and property taxes on the machine for the year ended December 31, 2013. Mondale paid $600,000 to Doxey on March 1, 2013. Doxey retains title to the property and plans to lease it to someone else after the 4-year lease period. Give all the 2013 entries relating to the lease on (1) Doxey Company's books and (2) Mondale Company's books. Assume both sets of books are maintained on the calendar-year basis.

Exercise 15-28
LO5, LO7

SPREADSHEET

Schedule of Lease Payments

Stagg Construction Co. is leasing equipment from Cloud Inc. The lease calls for payments of $50,000 a year plus $3,000 a year executory costs for five years. The first payment is due on January 1, 2013, when the lease is signed, with the other four payments coming due on December 31 of each year. Stagg has also been given the option of purchasing the equipment at the end of the lease at a bargain price of $95,000. Stagg has an incremental borrowing rate of 9%, the same as the implicit interest rate of Cloud. Stagg has hired you as an accountant and asks you to prepare a schedule showing how the lease payments will be split between principal and interest and the outstanding lease liability balance over the life of the lease.

Exercise 15-29
LO4

Criteria for Capitalizing Leases

Atwater Manufacturing Co. leases its equipment from Westside Leasing Company. In each of the following cases, assuming none of the other criteria for capitalizing leases are met, determine whether the lease would be a capital lease or an operating lease under FASB ASC Topic 840. Your decision is to be based only on the terms presented, considering each case independently of the others.

(a) At the end of the lease term, the market value of the equipment is expected to be $20,000. Atwater has the option of purchasing it for $5,000.
(b) The fair value of the equipment is $75,000. The present value of the lease payments is $67,000 (excluding any executory costs).
(c) Ownership of the property automatically passes to Atwater at the end of the lease term.
(d) The economic life of the equipment is 12 years. The lease term is 8 years.
(e) The lease requires payments of $9,000 per year in advance plus executory costs of $500 per year. The lease period is three years, and Atwater's incremental borrowing rate is 12%. The fair value of the equipment is $28,000.
(f) The lease requires payments of $6,000 per year in advance, which includes executory costs of $500 per year. The lease period is three years, and Atwater's incremental borrowing rate is 10%. The fair value of the equipment is $16,650.

Exercise 15-30
LO5

Capital Lease with Guaranteed Residual Value—Lessee

Mario Automobile Company leases automobiles under the following terms. A 3-year lease agreement is signed in which the lessor receives annual rental of $4,000 (in advance). At the end of the three years, the lessee agrees to make up any deficiency in residual value below $3,500. The cash price of the automobile is $13,251. The implicit interest rate is 12%, which is known to the lessee, and the lessee's incremental borrowing rate is 14%. The lessee estimates the residual value at the end of three years to be $4,200 and depreciates its automobiles on a straight-line basis.

1. Give the entries on the lessee's books required in the first year of the lease, including the second payment on April 30, 2014. Assume the lease begins May 1, 2013, the beginning of the lessee's fiscal year.
2. What balances relative to the lease would appear on the lessee's balance sheet at the end of Year 3?
3. Assume that at the end of the three years, the automobile is sold by the lessee (with the permission of the lessor) for $3,800. Prepare the entries to record the sale and settlement with the lessor.

Exercise 15-31
LO5, LO7

Cash Flow Treatment of Capital Leases—Lessee

The following information relates to a capital lease between Glass Electric Co. (lessee) and Williams Manufacturing Inc. (lessor). The lease term began on January 1, 2013. Glass capitalized the 10-year lease and recorded $150,000 as an asset. The annual lease payment, made at the beginning of each year, is $22,193 at 10% interest. Glass uses the straight-line method to depreciate its owned assets. How will this lease be reported on Glass' statement of cash flows for 2013 if the second lease payment is made on December 31, 2013, and Glass uses the indirect method?

Exercise 15-32

LO6

Cash Flow Treatment of Capital Leases—Lessor

On January 1, 2013, Warr Delivery Company purchased some equipment for $64,768 in cash. Warr Delivery immediately leased the equipment; Warr Delivery is the lessor. The lease contract calls for the receipt of $14,000 payments at the end of each year for five years. The residual value of the equipment at the end of the 5-year lease term is expected to be $15,868. The rate implicit in the lease is 9%. Except for lease-related items, there were no changes in current operating assets or liabilities during the year; no purchases or sales of property, plant, or equipment; and no dividends paid, stock issued, or loans obtained or repaid. The equipment has a total useful life of eight years with no salvage value. Prepare a complete statement of cash flows for Warr Delivery for 2013 using the indirect method of reporting operating cash flow assuming that the lease is accounted for as (1) an operating lease (net income was $70,000), (2) a direct financing lease (net income was $69,925), and (3) a sales-type lease (net income was $69,925; for comparability, make the unreasonable assumption that sales and cost of good sold are the same amount).

Exercise 15-33

LO6

SPREADSHEET

Direct Financing Lease with Residual Value

Massachusetts Casualty Insurance Company decides to enter the leasing business. It acquires a specialized packaging machine for $600,000 cash and leases it for a period of six years, after which the machine is to be returned to the insurance company for disposition. The expected unguaranteed residual value of the machine is $40,000. The lease terms are arranged so that a return of 12% is earned by the insurance company.

1. Calculate the annual lease payment, payable in advance, required to yield the desired return.
2. Prepare entries for the lessor for the first year of the lease, assuming the machine is acquired and the lease is recorded on January 1, 2013. The first lease payment is made on January 1, 2013, and subsequent payments are made each December 31.
3. Assuming that the packaging machine is sold by Massachusetts to the lessee at the end of the six years for $58,000, give the required entry to record the sale.

Exercise 15-34

LO6

Direct Financing Lease—Lessor

Deseret Finance Company purchased a printing press to lease to Quality Printing Company. The lease was structured so that at the end of the lease period of 15 years, Quality would own the printing press. Lease payments required in this lease were $190,000 (excluding executory costs) per year, payable in advance. The cost of the press to Deseret was $1,589,673, which is also its fair value at the time of the lease.

1. Why is this a direct financing lease?
2. Give the entry to record the lease transaction on the books of Deseret Finance Company.
3. Give the entry at the end of the first year on Deseret Finance Company's books to recognize interest revenue.

Exercise 15-35

LO6

Table for Direct Financing Lease—Lessor

Wenville Savings and Loan Company acquires a piece of specialized manufacturing equipment for $2,000,000 that it leases on January 1, 2013, to a local factory for $466,646 per year, payable in advance. Because of rapid technological developments, the equipment is expected to be replaced after four years. It is expected that the machine will have a residual value of $450,000 to Wenville Savings at the end of the lease term. The implicit rate of interest in the lease is 8%.

1. Prepare a 4-year table for Wenville Savings and Loan similar to Exhibit 15-8.
2. How would the table differ if the local factory guaranteed the residual value to Wenville?

Exercise 15-36
LO5, LO6

Effect of Lease on Reported Income—Lessee and Lessor

On February 20, 2013, Hudson Inc. purchased a machine for $2,100,000 for the purpose of leasing it. The machine is expected to have a 12-year life, has no residual value, and is depreciated on the straight-line basis to the nearest month. The machine was leased to Donah Company on March 1, 2013, for a 5-year period at a monthly rental of $34,000. Assume that the lease payments are made at the end of the month and that the appropriate interest rate is 11% compounded monthly. There is no provision for the renewal of the lease or purchase of the machine by the lessee at the expiration of the lease term. Hudson paid $72,000 of commissions associated with negotiating the lease in February 2013.

1. What expense should Donah record as a result of the lease transaction for the year ended December 31, 2013?
2. What income or loss before income taxes should Hudson record as a result of the lease transaction for the year ended December 31, 2013?

Exercise 15-37
LO6

Entry for Sale by Lessor

Smithston Corporation leased equipment to Dayplanner Co. on January 1, 2013. The terms of the lease called for annual lease payments to be made at the first of each year. Smithston's implicit interest rate for the transaction is 12%. On July 1, 2015, Dayplanner purchased the equipment and paid $116,000 to complete the transaction. After the 2015 payment was made, the following balance relating to the leased equipment was on the books of Smithston as of January 1, 2015:

Lease Payments Receivable (net)	$151,500

Prepare the journal entry that should be made by Smithston to record the sale, including the accrual of interest through July 1.

Exercise 15-38
LO6

Sales-Type Lease—Lessor

Salcedo Co. leased equipment to Erickson Inc. on April 1, 2013. The lease, appropriately recorded as a sale by Salcedo, is for an 8-year period ending March 31, 2019. The first of eight equal annual payments of $350,000 (excluding executory costs) was made on April 1, 2013. The cost of the equipment to Salcedo is $1,880,000. The equipment has an estimated useful life of eight years with no residual value expected. Salcedo uses straight-line depreciation and takes a full year's depreciation in the year of purchase. The cash selling price of the equipment is $2,053,800.

1. Give the entry required to record the lease on Salcedo's books.
2. How much interest revenue will Salcedo recognize in 2013?

Exercise 15-39
LO6

Sales-Type Lease—Lessor

Loco Leasing and Manufacturing Company uses leases as a means of financing sales of its equipment. Loco leased a machine to Potomac Construction for $15,000 per year, payable in advance, for a 10-year period. The cost of the machine to Loco was $86,000. The fair value at the date of the lease was $100,000. Assume a residual value of $0 at the end of the lease.

1. Give the entry required to record the lease on Loco's books.
2. How much profit will Loco recognize initially on the lease, excluding any interest revenue?
3. How much interest revenue would be recognized in the first year?

Exercise 15-40
LO5

Entry for Purchase by Lessee

Cordon Enterprise Company leases many of its assets and capitalizes most of the leased assets. At December 31, the company had the following balances on its books in relation to a piece of specialized equipment:

Leased Equipment	$80,000
Accumulated Amortization—Leased Equipment	49,300
Obligations under Capital Leases	26,000

Amortization has been recorded up to the end of the year, and no accrued interest is involved. At December 31, Cordon decided to purchase the equipment for $32,000 and paid cash to complete the purchase. Give the entry required on Cordon's books to record the purchase.

Exercise 15-41
LO3, LO6
REVERSE SOLVABLE

Computation of Implicit Interest Rate
Moor Leasing leases equipment to Wong Manufacturing. The fair value of the equipment is $527,169. Lease payments, excluding executory costs, are $60,000 per year, payable in advance, for 15 years. What is the implicit rate of interest Moor Leasing should use to record this capital lease on its books?

Exercise 15-42
LO5, LO7
SPREADSHEET

Lease Disclosure on the Financial Statements
Acme Enterprises leased equipment from Monument Equipment Co. on January 1, 2013. The terms of the lease agreement require five annual payments of $20,000 with the first payment being made on January 1, 2013, and each subsequent payment being made on December 31 of each year. Because the equipment has an expected useful life of five years, the lease qualifies as a capital lease for Acme. Acme does not know Monument's implicit interest rate and therefore uses its own incremental borrowing rate of 12% to calculate the present value of the lease payments. Acme uses the sum-of-the-years'-digits method for amortizing leased assets. The expected salvage value of the leased asset is $0.

1. Prepare a schedule that shows the lease obligation balance in each year of the lease.
2. Prepare an asset amortization schedule for the leased asset.
3. Compare the amount shown on the year-end balance sheet for the leased asset with that of the lease obligation for the years 2013 through 2017 and explain why the amounts differ.

Exercise 15-43
LO5, LO7

Lease Disclosures—Lessee
The following lease information was obtained by a staff auditor for a client, Kroller Inc., at December 31, 2013. Indicate how this information should be presented in Kroller's 2-year comparative financial statements. Include any notes to the statements required to meet generally accepted accounting principles. Lease payments are made on December 31 of each year.

Leased building; minimum lease payments per year; 10 years remaining life on December 31, 2012	$ 45,000
Executory costs per year	2,000
Capitalized lease value, 12% interest	343,269
Accumulated amortization of leased building at December 31, 2013	114,423
Amortization expense for 2013	22,885
Obligations under capital leases; balance at December 31, 2013	239,770
Obligations under capital leases; balance at December 31, 2012	254,259

EM EXPANDED MATERIAL

Exercise 15-44
LO9

Sale-Leaseback Transaction
Smalltown Grocers sold its plant facilities to United Grocers, Inc., for $813,487. United immediately leased the building back to Smalltown for 20 annual payments of $96,000 with the first payment due immediately. The terms of the lease agreement provide a bargain purchase option wherein Smalltown has the option of purchasing the building at

the end of the lease term for $100,000. If United's implicit interest rate is 12% (lower than Smalltown's incremental borrowing rate), prepare the entries that should be made by United to record the purchase of the building and the receipt of the first two payments from Smalltown Grocers, assuming this leasing arrangement qualifies as a capital lease for United.

Exercise 15-45
LO9

Sale-Leaseback Accounting
On July 1, 2013, Flashlight Corporation sold equipment it had recently purchased to an unaffiliated company for $480,000. The equipment had a book value on Flashlight's books of $390,000 and a remaining life of six years. On that same day, Flashlight leased back the equipment at $95,000 per year, payable in advance, for a 6-year period. Flashlight's incremental borrowing rate is 11%, and it does not know the lessor's implicit interest rate. What entries are required for Flashlight to record the transactions involving the equipment during the first full year, assuming the second lease payment is made on June 30, 2014? Ignore consideration of the lessee's fiscal year. The lessee uses the double-declining-balance method of depreciation for similar assets it owns outright.

PROBLEMS

Problem 15-46
LO4, LO5

Entries for Capital Lease—Lessee; Lease Criteria
Extractor Company leased a machine on July 1, 2013, under a 10-year lease. The economic life of the machine is estimated to be 15 years. Title to the machine passes to Extractor Company at the expiration of the lease, and thus, the lease is a capital lease. The lease payments total $194,000 per year (which includes executory costs of $6,000 per year), all payable in advance annually. The incremental borrowing rate of the company is 9%, and the lessor's implicit interest rate is unknown. Extractor Company uses the straight-line method of amortization and the calendar year for reporting purposes.

Instructions:

1. Give all entries on the books of the lessee relating to the lease for 2013.
2. Assume that the lessor retains title to the machine at the expiration of the lease, that there is no bargain renewal or purchase option, and that the fair value of the equipment is $1,420,000 as of the lease date. Using the criteria for distinguishing between operating and capital leases according to FASB ASC Topic 840, what would be the amortization expense for 2013?

Problem 15-47
LO5, LO6

Operating Lease—Lessee and Lessor
York Industries leases a large specialized machine to Echo Company at a total rental of $1,400,000, payable in five annual installments in the following declining pattern: 24% in the first two years, 20% in the third and fourth years, and 12% in the last year. The lease begins January 1, 2013. In addition to the rent, Echo is required to pay annual executory costs of $18,000 to cover unusual repairs and insurance. The lease does not qualify as a capital lease for reporting purposes. York incurred initial direct costs of $18,000 in obtaining the lease. The machine cost York $1,900,000 to construct and has an estimated life of eight years with an estimated residual value of $120,000. York uses the straight-line depreciation method on its equipment. Both companies report on a calendar-year basis.

Instructions:

1. Prepare the journal entries on York's books for 2013 and 2017 related to the lease.
2. Prepare the journal entries on Echo's books for 2013 and 2017 related to the lease.

Problem 15-48

LO5

Entries for Capital Lease—Lessee

Aldridge Enterprises has a long-standing policy of acquiring company equipment by leasing. Early in 2013, the company entered into a lease for a new milling machine. The lease stipulates that annual payments will be made for five years. The payments are to be made in advance on December 31 of each year. At the end of the 5-year period, Aldridge may purchase the machine. Company financial records show the incremental borrowing rate to be less than the implicit interest rate. The estimated economic life of the equipment is 12 years. Aldridge uses the calendar year for reporting purposes and straight-line depreciation for other equipment. In addition, the following information about the lease is also available:

Annual lease payments	$55,000
Purchase option price	$25,000
Estimated fair value of machine after five years	$75,000
Incremental borrowing rate	10%
Date of first lease payment	Jan. 1, 2013

Instructions:

1. Compute the amount to be capitalized as an asset for the lease of the milling machine.
2. Prepare a schedule that shows the computation of the interest expense for each period.
3. Give the journal entries that would be made on Aldridge's books for the first two years of the lease.
4. Assume that the purchase option is exercised at the end of the lease. Give the Aldridge journal entry necessary to record the exercise of the option. The actual fair value of the milling machine at the end of the lease is $95,000. On the date the purchase option is exercised, the undiscounted sum of future cash flows expected from the machine is $125,000.

Problem 15-49

LO5

Entries for Capital Lease—Lessee; Guaranteed Residual Value

For some time, Ulrich Inc. has maintained a policy of acquiring company equipment by leasing. On January 1, 2013, Ulrich entered into a lease with Riverbottoms Fabricators for a new concrete truck that had a selling price of $315,000. The lease stipulates that annual payments of $61,800 will be made for six years. The first lease payment is made on January 1, 2013, and subsequent payments are made on December 31 of each year. Ulrich guarantees a residual value of $33,535 at the end of the 6-year period. Ulrich has an incremental borrowing rate of 11%, and the implicit interest rate to Riverbottoms is 10% after considering the guaranteed residual value. The economic life of the truck is eight years. Ulrich uses the calendar year for reporting purposes and straight-line depreciation to depreciate other equipment.

Instructions:

1. Compute the amount to be capitalized as an asset on the lessee's books for the concrete truck. Ulrich knows that Riverbottoms' implicit interest rate is 10%.
2. Prepare a schedule showing the reduction of the liability by the annual payments after considering the interest charges.
3. Give the journal entries that would be made on Ulrich's books for the first two years of the lease.
4. Assume that the lessor sells the truck for $24,000 at the end of the 6-year period
to a third party. Give the Ulrich journal entries necessary to record the payment to satisfy the residual guarantee and to write off the leased equipment accounts.

Problem 15-50

LO5, LO6

Accounting for Direct Financing Lease—Lessee and Lessor

Trost Leasing Company buys equipment for leasing to various manufacturing companies. On October 1, 2012, Trost leases a press to Shumway Shoe Company. The cost of the machine to Trost was $392,220, which approximated its fair value on the lease date. The lease payments stipulated in the lease are $66,000 per year in advance for the 10-year period of the lease. The payments include executory costs of $6,000 per year. The expected economic life of the equipment is also 10 years. The title to the equipment remains in the hands of Trost Leasing Company at the end of the lease term, although only nominal residual value is expected at that time. Shumway's incremental borrowing rate is 10%, and it uses the straight-line method of depreciation on all owned equipment. Both Shumway and Trost have fiscal years ending September 30, and lease payments are made on this date.

Instructions:

1. Prepare the entries to record the lease and the first lease payment on the books of the lessor and lessee, assuming the lease meets the criteria of a direct financing lease for the lessor and a capital lease for the lessee.
2. Compute the implicit rate of interest of the lessor.
3. Give all entries required to account for the lease on both the lessee's and lessor's books for the fiscal years 2013, 2014, and 2015.

Problem 15-51

LO5, LO6

Lease Computations—Lessee and Lessor

Enco Tech Corporation is in the business of leasing new sophisticated satellite systems. As a lessor of satellites, Enco Tech purchased a new system on December 31, 2013. The system was delivered the same day (by prior arrangement) to Ocular Investment Company, a lessee. The corporation accountant revealed the following information relating to the lease transaction:

Cost of system to Enco Tech	$840,000
Estimated useful life and lease term	6 years
Expected residual value (unguaranteed)	$60,000
Enco Tech's implicit rate of interest	12%
Ocular's incremental borrowing rate	14%
Date of first lease payment	Dec. 31, 2013

Additional information is as follows:

(a) At the end of the lease, the system will revert to Enco Tech.
(b) Ocular is aware of Enco Tech's rate of implicit interest.
(c) The lease rental consists of equal annual payments.
(d) Enco Tech accounts for leases using the direct financing method. Ocular intends to record the lease as a capital lease. Both the lessee and the lessor report on a calendar-year basis and elect to depreciate all assets on the straight-line basis.

Instructions:

1. Compute the annual lease payment under the lease. (*Note:* Round to the nearest dollar.)
2. Compute the amounts of the lease payments receivable that Enco Tech should recognize at the inception of the lease.
3. What are the total expenses related to the lease that Ocular should record for the year ended December 31, 2014?

Problem 15-52

LO6

Sales-Type Lease—Lessor

Aquatran Incorporated uses leases as a method of selling its products. In early 2013, Aquatran completed construction of a passenger ferry for use between Manhattan and Staten Island. On April 1, 2013, the ferry was leased to the Manhattan Ferry Line on a contract specifying that ownership of the ferry will transfer to the lessee at the end of the lease period. Annual lease payments do not include executory costs. Other terms of the agreement are as follows:

Original cost of the ferry	$1,500,000
Fair value of ferry at lease date	$2,107,102
Lease payments (paid in advance)	$225,000
Estimated residual value	$78,000
Incremental borrowing rate—lessee	10%
Date of first lease payment	April 1, 2013
Lease period	20 years

Instructions:

1. Compute the amount of financial revenue that will be earned over the lease term and the manufacturer's profit that will be earned immediately by Aquatran.
2. Give the entry to record the signing of the lease on Aquatran's books. Compute the implicit rate of interest on the lease.
3. Give the journal entries necessary on Aquatran's books to record the lease for the first three years, exclusive of the initial entry. Aquatran's accounting period is the calendar year.
4. Indicate the balance of Lease Payments Receivable at December 31, 2015.

Problem 15-53

LO6

Sales-Type Lease—Lessor

New World Enterprises adopted the policy of leasing as the primary method of selling its products. The company's main product is a small jet airplane that is very popular among corporate executives. New World constructed such a jet for Corporate Air Company (CAC) at a cost of $6,456,239. Financing of the construction was at a 12% rate. The terms of the lease provided for annual advance payments of $985,630 to be paid over 15 years with the ownership of the airplane transferring to CAC at the end of the lease period. It is estimated that the plane will have a residual value of $950,000 at that date. The lease payments began on October 1, 2013. New World incurred initial direct costs of $100,000 in finalizing the lease agreement with CAC. The sales price of similar airplanes is $7,867,200.

Instructions:

1. Compute the amount of manufacturer's profit that will be earned immediately by New World.
2. Prepare the journal entry to record the lease on New World's books at October 1, 2013.
3. Prepare the journal entries to record the lease on New World's books for the years 2013–2015 exclusive of the initial entry. New World's accounting period is the calendar year.
4. How much revenue did New World earn from this lease for each of the first three years of the lease?

Problem 15-54

LO5, LO6

Entries for Capital Lease—Lessee and Lessor

Alta Corporation entered into an agreement with Snowfire Company to lease equipment for use in its ski manufacturing facility. The lease is appropriately recorded as a purchase by Alta and as a sale by Snowfire. The agreement specifies that lease payments will be made on an annual basis. The cost of the machine is reported as inventory on Snowfire's accounting records. Because of extensive changes in ski manufacturing technology, the machine is not expected to have any residual value. Alta uses straight-line depreciation and computes depreciation to the nearest month. After three years, Alta purchases the machine from Snowfire.

Annual lease payments do not include executory costs. Other terms of the agreement are as follows:

Machine cost recorded in inventory	$3,700,000
Price at purchase option date	$3,250,000
Lease payments (paid in advance)	$710,000
Contract interest rate	10%
Contract date/first lease payment	Oct. 1, 2013
Date of Alta purchase	Oct. 1, 2016
Lease period	8 years

Instructions: Prepare journal entries on the books of both the lessee and the lessor as follows:

1. Make entries in 2013 to record the first lease payment, and make adjustments necessary at December 31, the end of each company's fiscal year.
2. Record all entries required in 2014.
3. Prepare the entries in 2016 to record the sale (on Snowfire's books) and purchase (on Alta's books), assuming that no previous entries have been made during the year in connection with the lease.

Problem 15-55
LO5, LO6

Accounting for Capital Lease—Lessee and Lessor

Mullen Equipment Company both leases and sells its equipment to its customers. The most popular line of equipment includes a machine that costs $280,000 to manufacture. The standard lease terms provide for five annual payments of $110,000 each (excluding executory costs), with the first payment due when the lease is signed and subsequent payments due on December 31 of each year. The implicit rate of interest in the contract is 10% per year. Walton Tool Co. leases one of these machines on January 2, 2013. Initial direct costs of $20,000 are incurred by Mullen on January 2, 2013, to obtain the lease. Walton's incremental borrowing rate is determined to be 12%. The equipment is very specialized, and it is assumed it will have no salvage value after five years. Assume that the lease qualifies as a capital lease and a sales-type lease for lessee and lessor, respectively. Also assume that both the lessee and the lessor are on a calendar-year basis and that the lessee is aware of the lessor's implicit interest rate.

Instructions:

1. Give all entries required on Walton's books to record the lease of equipment from Mullen for the year 2013. The depreciation on owned equipment is computed once a year on the straight-line basis.
2. Give entries required on Mullen's books to record the lease of equipment to Walton for the year 2013.
3. Prepare the balance sheet section involving lease balances for both the lessee's and lessor's financial statements at December 31, 2013.
4. Determine the amount of expense Walton will report relative to the lease for 2013 and the amount of revenue Mullen will report for the same period.

Problem 15-56
LO5, LO6, LO7

Accounting for Leases—Lessee and Lessor with Third-Party Guarantee

Atwater Equipment Co. manufactures, sells, and leases heavy construction equipment. England Construction Company, a regular customer, leased equipment on July 1, 2013, that had cost Atwater $252,000 to manufacture. The lease payments are $63,161, beginning on July 1, 2013, and continuing annually with the last payment being made on July 1, 2017. If England were to purchase the equipment outright, the fair value would be $291,881. Because of the heavy wear expected on construction equipment, the lease contains a guaranteed residual value clause wherein the lessee guarantees a residual value on June 30, 2018, of $65,000. England contracted with Weathertop Financial Services to serve as a third-party guarantor of the residual value. Atwater's implicit interest rate is 12%, which is lower than England's incremental borrowing rate of 14%.

Instructions:

1. Assuming that the equipment reverts to Atwater upon completion of the lease term and that the equipment has an expected useful life of 10 years, prepare the entries that should be made on the books of both Atwater and England in recording the lease on July 1, 2013. (*Note*: England knows the implicit interest rate for the lease.)
2. Prepare the journal entries that should be made by Atwater and England on July 1, 2014. Ignore fiscal year considerations.
3. What financial statement disclosure should be made by Weathertop in its role as a third-party guarantor?

Problem 15-57

LO5, LO6

Accounting for Lease—Lessee and Lessor

Gryphon Manufacturing Company manufactures and leases a variety of items. On January 2, 2013, Gryphon leased a piece of equipment to Scissor Industries Co. The lease is for seven years for an annual amount of $43,500, payable in advance. The lease payment includes executory costs of $2,500 per year. The equipment has an estimated useful life of 12 years, and it was manufactured by Gryphon at a cost of $180,000. It is estimated that the equipment will have a residual value of $90,000 at the end of the 7-year lease term. There is no provision for purchase or renewal by Scissor at the end of the lease term. However, a third party has guaranteed the residual value of $90,000. The equipment has a fair value at the lease inception of $250,274. The implicit rate of interest in the contract is 12%, the same rate at which Scissor can borrow money at its bank. All lease payments after the first one are made on December 31 of each year. Both companies use the straight-line method of depreciation.

Instructions:

1. Give all the entries relating to the lease on the books of the lessor and lessee for 2013.
2. Show how the lease would appear on the balance sheet of Gryphon Manufacturing Company and Scissor Industries Co. (if applicable) as of December 31, 2013.
3. Assume that Gryphon sold the equipment at the end of the 7-year lease for $110,000. Give the entry to record the sale, assuming that all lease entries have been properly made.

Problem 15-58

LO6

Cash Flow Treatment of Capital Lease—Lessor

The following information relates to a capital lease between Bradford Electric Co. (lessee) and Widstoe Manufacturing Inc. (lessor). The lease term began on January 1, 2013. Widstoe recorded the lease as a sale and made the following entries related to the lease during 2013. Assume this was the only lease Widstoe had during the year.

Date		Account	Debit	Credit
Jan.	1	Deferred Initial Direct Costs	6,000	
		Cash		6,000
	1	Lease Payments Receivable	88,000	
		Sales		88,000
	1	Cost of Goods Sold	70,000	
		Inventory		64,000
		Deferred Initial Direct Costs		6,000
	1	Cash	11,132	
		Lease Payments Receivable		11,132
Dec.	31	Cash	11,132	
		Lease Payments Receivable		11,132
	31	Lease Payments Receivable	6,242	
		Interest Revenue		6,242

Instructions:

1. Prepare the partial Operating Activities section of the statement of cash flows for 2013 for Widstoe Manufacturing Inc. under the indirect method. Widstoe reported net income of $148,504 inclusive of the lease revenue in the preceding entries.
2. Prepare the partial Operating Activities section of the statement of cash flows for 2013 for Widstoe Manufacturing Inc. under the direct method. Assume that cash provided by operating activities exclusive of the lease transactions is $124,262.

Problem 15-59

LO7

Disclosure Requirements—Operating Leases

Jaquar Mining and Manufacturing Company leases from Emory Leasing Company three machines under the following terms.

- Machine 1: Lease period—10 years, beginning April 1, 2007; lease payment—$18,000 per year, payable in advance.
- Machine 2: Lease period—10 years, beginning July 1, 2011; lease payment—$30,000 per year, payable in advance.
- Machine 3: Lease period—15 years, beginning January 1, 2012; lease payment—$12,500 per year, payable in advance.

All of the leases are classified as operating leases.

Instructions: Prepare the note to the 2013 financial statements that would be required to disclose the lease commitments of Jaquar Mining and Manufacturing Company. Jaquar uses the calendar year as its accounting period.

Problem 15-60

LO5, LO7

Capitalizing the Value of Operating Leases

The following information comes from the financial statements of Marci Sinclair Company.

Total liabilities	$ 300,000
Total stockholders' equity	220,000
Property, plant, and equipment	290,000
Sales	1,400,000

In addition, Marci Sinclair has a large number of operating leases. The payments on these operating leases total $55,000 per year for the next 10 years. All of these lease payments occur at the end of the year. The incremental borrowing rate of Marci Sinclair Company is 11%. This is also the rate implicit in all of the leases that Marci Sinclair signs.

Instructions:

1. Compute the following ratio values:
   (a) Debt ratio (total liabilities/total assets).
   (b) Debt ratio, assuming that Marci Sinclair's operating leases are accounted for as capital leases.
   (c) Asset turnover (sales/total assets).
   (d) Asset turnover, assuming that Marci Sinclair's operating leases are accounted for as capital leases.
2. Briefly describe how the accounting for assets used under operating leases distorts the values of financial ratios.

EM EXPANDED MATERIAL

Problem 15-61

LO9

Sale-Leaseback of a Building

On January 3, 2013, Wayside Inc. sold a building with a book value of $1,800,000 to Birchman Industries for $1,735,500. Wayside immediately entered into a leasing agreement wherein Wayside would lease the building back for an annual payment of $320,049. The term of the lease is eight years, the expected remaining useful life of the building. The first annual lease payment is to be made immediately, and future payments will be made on January 1 of each succeeding year. Birchman's implicit interest rate is 13%.

Instructions:

1. Prepare the journal entries that both Wayside and Birchman should make on January 3, 2013, relating to this sale-leaseback transaction.
2. Prepare the journal entries that both parties should make at the end of 2013 to accrue interest and to amortize the leased building. (Assume a salvage value of $0 and use of the straight-line method.)

Problem 15-62
LO3, LO9

Sample CPA Exam Questions

1. In a sale-leaseback transaction, a gain resulting from the sale should be deferred at the time of the sale-leaseback and subsequently amortized when:
   I. The seller-lessee has transferred substantially all the risks of ownership.
   II. The seller-lessee retains the right to substantially all of the remaining use of the property.
   (a) I only.
   (b) II only.
   (c) Both I and II.
   (d) Neither I nor II.

2. At the inception of a capital lease, the guaranteed residual value should be:
   (a) Included as part of minimum lease payments at present value.
   (b) Included as part of minimum lease payments at future value.
   (c) Included as part of minimum lease payments only to the extent that guaranteed residual value is expected to exceed estimated residual value.
   (d) Excluded from minimum lease payments.

CASES

Discussion Case 15-63

How Should the Lease Be Recorded?

Louise Corporation entered into a leasing arrangement with Wilder Leasing Corporation for a certain machine. Wilder's primary business is leasing; it is not a manufacturer or dealer. Louise will lease the machine for a period of three years, which is 50% of the machine's economic life. Wilder will take possession of the machine at the end of the initial 3-year lease. Louise does not guarantee any residual value for the machine.

Louise's incremental borrowing rate is 10%, and the implicit rate in the lease is 8½%. Louise has no way of knowing the implicit rate used by Wilder. Using either rate, the present value of the minimum lease payments is between 90% and 100% of the fair value of the machine at the date of the lease agreement.

Louise has agreed to pay all executory costs directly, and no allowance for these costs is included in the lease payments.

Wilder is reasonably certain that Louise will pay all lease payments, and because Louise has agreed to pay all executory costs, there are no important uncertainties regarding costs to be incurred by Wilder.

1. With respect to Louise (the lessee), answer the following:
   (a) What type of lease has been entered into? Explain the reason for your answer. How should Louise compute the appropriate amount to be recorded for the lease or asset acquired?
   (c) What accounts will be created or affected by this transaction, and how will the lease or asset and other costs related to the transaction be matched with earnings?
   (d) What disclosures must Louise make regarding this lease or asset?

2. With respect to Wilder (the lessor), answer the following:
   (a) What type of leasing arrangement has been entered into? Explain the reason for your answer.
   (b) How should this lease be recorded by Wilder, and how are the appropriate amounts determined?
   (c) How should Wilder determine the appropriate amount of earnings to be recognized from each lease payment?
   (d) What disclosures must Wilder make regarding this lease?

Discussion Case 15-64

Should We Buy or Lease?

Meeker Machine and Die Company has learned that a sophisticated piece of computer-operated machinery is available to either buy or rent. The machinery will result in three employees being replaced, and quality of the output has been tested to be superior in every demonstration. There is no doubt that this machinery represents the latest in technology; however, new inventions and research make it difficult to estimate when the machinery will be made obsolete by new technology. The physical life expectancy of the machine is 10 years; however, the estimated economic life is between two and five years.

Meeker has a debt-to-equity ratio of 0.75. If the machine is purchased and the minimum down payment is made, the outstanding loan balance on the machine will cause the debt-to-equity ratio to increase to 1.1. The monthly payments if the machine is purchased are 20% lower than the lease payments if it is leased. The incremental borrowing rate for Meeker is 11%. The rate implicit in the lease is 12%. What factors should Meeker consider in deciding how to finance the acquisition of the machine?

Discussion Case 15-65

More Leases Mean Lower Profits

Digital X-Ray, Inc., has introduced a new line of equipment that may revolutionize the medical profession. Because of the new technology involved, potential users of the equipment are reluctant to purchase the equipment, but they are willing to enter into a lease arrangement as long as they can classify the lease as an operating lease. The new equipment will replace equipment that Digital X-Ray, Inc., has been selling in the past. It is estimated that a 25% loss of actual equipment sales will occur as a result of the leasing policy for the new equipment.

Management must decide how to structure the leases so that they can treat them as operating leases. Some members of management want to structure the leases so that Digital X-Ray, Inc., as lessor, can classify the lease as a sales-type lease and thus avoid a further reduction of income. Others believe that they should treat the leases as operating leases and minimize the income tax liability in the short term. They are uncertain, however, as to how the financial statements would be affected under these two different approaches. They also are uncertain as to how leases could be structured to permit the lessee to treat the lease as an operating lease and the lessor to treat it as a sales-type lease. You are asked to respond to their questions.

Discussion Case 15-66

Structuring a Lease to Avoid Liability Recognition

Johnson Pharmaceuticals needs cash. One option being considered by the board of directors is to sell the plant facilities to a group of venture capitalists and then lease the facilities back for a long-term period with the option of repurchasing the plant facilities at the end of the lease.

The chairman has commented that this option will provide Johnson Pharmaceuticals the needed cash but will result in a large lease liability on the balance sheet. As the chief financial officer, you comment that if the company carefully structures the terms of the lease agreement, it may be able to avoid recognizing the lease liability.

The chairman has asked you to prepare a memo discussing the specific ways in which a lease agreement can be structured to avoid recognizing the liability on the balance sheet.

Discussion Case 15-67

REVERSE SOLVABLE

The Risks of Leasing: The Case of SUVs

On January 1, 2013, Skull Valley Motors leased a Lincoln Navigator to T. K. "Pusan Boots" Denny. The lease is a 3-year lease requiring a payment of $695 at the end of each month for 36 months. The cash price of the Navigator was $46,000. Skull Valley Motors expects to be able to sell the Navigator for $30,652 when it is returned at the end of the 3-year lease term.

1. What interest rate (compounded monthly) was used in the computation of the $695 monthly payment amount?
2. On December 31, 2015, Skull Valley Motors learned that the Navigator could be sold for only $25,000 at auction instead of the anticipated $30,652. With this actual residual value, what rate of return (compounded monthly) did Skull Valley earn on this 3-year Navigator lease?
3. Assume that Skull Valley did not know about the decline in residual value until the Navigator was sold at auction for $25,000 in 2015. How much net profit, in total, was recognized during the 3-year life of the lease, excluding the final sale of the Navigator at auction? How much gain or loss was recognized when the Navigator was sold for $25,000 at auction?
4. Refer to (2). If the rate of return on the lease is so low, why would Skull Valley Motors continue in the leasing business at all?

SOURCE: Emily Thornton, Joann Muller, Jeff Green, and Heather Timmons, "Losing at the Leasing Game," *Business Week*, October 16, 2000, p. 48.

EM EXPANDED MATERIAL

Discussion Case 15-68

Recognizing Profits on a Sale-Leaseback Transaction

John Carson, president of Carson Enterprises, recently arranged a financing deal with a group of foreign investors whereby he sold his movie company for $13,000,000 and immediately leased the company back, recognizing a $4,000,000 profit on the sale. Mr. Carson has just entered your office to tell you, his accountant, the good news.

After hearing the details of the transaction, you tell Mr. Carson that he must defer recognizing the gain immediately and instead recognize it piecemeal over the term of the lease agreement. Mr. Carson counters that if he had simply sold the company to the investors, he would be able to book the profits. He asks you: "What difference does it make if I lease the company back or not? Shouldn't the sale and the lease be treated as two separate transactions?" How do you respond?

Case 15-69

Deciphering Financial Statements (The Walt Disney Company)

Look in the historical archives of the SEC's EDGAR online database of financial statements and locate the 2004 financial statements for **The Walt Disney Company**. In Note 4 to the financial statements, Disney briefly outlines a rather complicated lease it arranged in regard to the Disneyland Paris theme park assets of **Euro Disney**. To summarize:

- The theme park assets are owned by an unnamed financing company.
- A wholly owned subsidiary of Disney, called Disney SCA, has leased the theme park assets from the owner under a 12-year, noncancelable lease.
- Euro Disney has subleased the theme park assets from Disney SCA.

1. With this leasing and subleasing, who will actually use the theme park assets?
2. Regarding the lease agreement between the owner of the assets and Disney SCA, does it appear that the lease includes a bargain purchase option?
3. Why do you think Euro Disney just didn't lease the theme park assets directly from the owner?

Case 15-70

Deciphering Financial Statements (International Lease Finance Corporation)
As mentioned in the chapter, **International Lease Finance Corporation** leases airplanes to airlines. Disclosure regarding International's leases is reproduced in Exhibit 15-11 in the text.

1. By examining the stream of expected future lease payments as of the end of 2008 and 2009, estimate how much business in new capital leases the company generated during 2009.
2. Comment on the relationship between the amount of total lease payments to be received and the estimated residual values as of the end of 2008 and 2009.

Case 15-71

Deciphering Financial Statements (FedEx)
The following summary data are from the May 31, 2009, balance sheet of **FedEx**. All numbers are in millions.

Total current assets	$ 7,116
Property, plant, and equipment (net)	13,417
Other long-term assets	3,711
Total assets	$24,244
Current liabilities	$ 4,524
Long-term debt	1,930
Other long-term liabilities	4,164
Total liabilities	$10,618
Stockholders' equity	$13,626
Total sales	$35,497

A summary of future minimum lease payments under capital leases and noncancelable operating leases with an initial or remaining term in excess of one year at May 31, 2009 is as follows (in millions):

		Operating Leases		
	Capital Leases	Aircraft and Related Equipment	Facilities and Other	Total Operating Leases
2010	$164	$ 512	$1,247	$ 1,759
2011	20	526	1,086	1,612
2012	8	504	947	1,451
2013	119	499	817	1,316
2014	2	472	694	1,166
Thereafter	15	2,458	4,894	7,352
Total	328	$4,971	$9,685	$14,656
Less amount representing interest	34			
Present value of net minimum lease payments	$294			

Instructions: Compute the following ratio values.

1. Debt ratio (total liabilities/total assets).
2. Debt ratio assuming that FedEx's operating leases are accounted for as capital leases.
3. Asset turnover (sales/total assets).
4. Asset turnover assuming that FedEx's operating leases are accounted for as capital leases.

Case 15-72

Deciphering Financial Statements (McDonald's Corporation)
The franchise arrangement between **McDonald's** and its franchisees is summarized in the following note from McDonald's 2009 annual report.

Conventional franchise arrangements generally include a lease and a license and provide for payment of initial fees, as well as continuing rent and royalties to the Company based upon a percent of sales with minimum rent payments that parallel the Company's underlying leases and escalations (on properties that are leased). Under this arrangement, franchisees are granted the right to operate a restaurant using the McDonald's System and, in most cases, the use of a restaurant facility, generally for a period of 20 years. These franchisees pay related occupancy costs including property taxes, insurance and maintenance. Affiliates and developmental licensees operating under license agreements pay a royalty to the Company based upon a percent of sales, and may pay initial fees.

The results of operations of restaurant businesses purchased and sold in transactions with franchisees were not material to the consolidated financial statements for periods prior to purchase and sale. Revenues from franchised restaurants consisted of:

In millions	2009	2008	2007
Rents	$4,841.0	$4,612.8	$4,177.2
Royalties	2,379.8	2,275.7	1,941.1
Initial fees	65.4	73.0	57.3
Revenues from franchised restaurants	$7,286.2	$6,961.5	$6,175.6

Future minimum rent payments due to the Company under existing franchise arrangements are:

In millions	Owned sites	Leased sites	Total
2010	$ 1,218.1	$ 1,076.0	$ 2,294.1
2011	1,177.3	1,042.9	2,220.2
2012	1,144.5	1,011.5	2,156.0
2013	1,105.1	972.4	2,077.5
2014	1,062.1	924.8	1,986.9
Thereafter	8,495.8	6,782.5	15,278.3
Total minimum payments	$14,202.9	$11,810.1	$26,013.0

At December 31, 2009, net property and equipment under franchise arrangements totaled $13.1 billion (including land of $3.8 billion) after deducting accumulated depreciation and amortization of $6.5 billion.

Instructions: From this information, answer the following questions.

1. McDonald's arrangement with its franchisees is that the franchisees agree to pay a minimum rent plus additional amounts if sales are above a certain level. Compare the minimum amount to be received from rent payments in 2010 with the total amount received from franchised and affiliated restaurants in 2009. How significant are these additional amounts?
2. As indicated in the franchise note, McDonald's owns some of its sites and leases others. An important comparison is the relationship between future minimum lease payments McDonald's must make and future minimum payments to be received from franchisees. The future payments (in millions of dollars) McDonald's must make on its leased restaurant sites are summarized as follows.

In millions	Restaurant
2010	$ 1,064.7
2011	1,002.4
2012	928.1
2013	859.8
2014	783.9
Thereafter	5,794.5
Total minimum payments	$10,433.4

Comparing the payments to be made for leased sites and the minimum payments (plus the additional percentage from royalties) to be collected from franchisees for leased sites, it looks as if McDonald's is guaranteed to make money every year on its leased sites. What would have to happen for McDonald's to *lose* money on these leased sites?

Case 15-73 **Writing Assignment (All leases are sales-type leases!)**

You are the accountant for Clear Water Bay Company, an equipment manufacturer. In order to help customers finance their purchases, Clear Water Bay often leases, rather than sells, the equipment. Clear Water Bay structures the lease agreements so that most of its equipment leases are classified as operating leases. This is because customers strongly prefer this treatment in order to keep the lease obligations off their balance sheets. This treatment does result in a delay in Clear Water Bay's ability to report profits from the sales, but this delay has been viewed as part of the cost of keeping customers happy.

The president of Clear Water Bay just returned from a weeklong accounting and finance seminar at a prominent university. She is excited about the session she attended on the accounting for leases. She was told, or thinks she was told, that there is no need for Clear Water Bay to report its leasing arrangements as operating leases—according to U.S. GAAP, lessors can always classify a lease as a sales-type lease even when the lessee classifies the same lease as an operating lease. The president tells you to get to work restating Clear Water Bay's most recent financial statements to reflect reclassification of all Clear Water Bay's leases from operating leases to sales-type leases.

Write a memo to the president clarifying the accounting rules governing sales-type and operating leases. Carefully explain the circumstances in which the same lease can be classified as a sales-type lease by the lessor and an operating lease by the lessee.

Case 15-74 **Ethical Dilemma (Using operating leases to fool the bank)**

You are the chief financial officer for RAM Solutions, a small but rapidly growing retail computer hardware chain. You are trying to figure out how to finance the new buildings that are scheduled to be purchased this year. The difficulty is that RAM has an existing loan with Commercial Security Bank (CSB) that requires RAM to maintain an interest coverage ratio (Operating income/Interest expense) of 2.0 or greater. Forecasts for next year are as follows:

Forecasted operating income	$15,000,000
Forecasted interest expense (assuming no new borrowing)	7,000,000
Cost of purchasing new buildings	50,000,000

If you borrow the $50 million needed to finance the new buildings, the increased interest expense will cause you to be in violation of the interest coverage constraint.

The controller has suggested an accounting solution to this dilemma: lease the new buildings, carefully constructing the lease agreements so that the leases will be accounted for as operating leases. The leasing arrangements will be economically similar to purchase of the buildings with borrowed money, but the annual payments will be reported as rent expense instead of interest expense. Accordingly, the interest coverage loan covenant will be completely sidestepped.

You personally negotiated the loan with Commercial Security Bank, and you know that the intent of the loan covenant was to prevent RAM from incurring large fixed obligations that might endanger the repayment of the CSB loan. Operating lease payments are fixed obligations, just like interest payments, and you are uneasy about using this accounting trick to get around the loan covenant. However, there does not seem to be any other solution. What should you do?

Case 15-75

Cumulative Spreadsheet Analysis

This assignment is based on the spreadsheet prepared in (1) of the cumulative spreadsheet assignment for Chapter 13. Review that assignment for a summary of the assumptions made in preparing a forecasted balance sheet, income statement, and statement of cash flows for 2014 for Skywalker Company. This assignment involves revisiting assumptions (q) and (u) in the Chapter 13 assignment.

Skywalker would like to know how its forecasted financial statements would look if it decided to lease all new property, plant, and equipment under operating leases. Before 2014, all of Skywalker's property, plant, and equipment purchases had been 100% financed using long-term debt. This same assumption underlies the forecast prepared in (1) of the Chapter 13 assignment.

1. Using the same instructions given in (1) of the Chapter 13 spreadsheet assignment, forecast the following values for 2014:

   Forecasted balance sheet for 2014:

   (a) Property, plant, and equipment
   (b) Accumulated depreciation
   (c) Long-term debt

   Forecasted income statement for 2014:

   (d) Depreciation and amortization expense
   (e) Other operating expenses
   (f) Interest expense
   (g) Income tax expense
   (h) Net income

   Forecasted statement of cash flows for 2014:

   (i) Cash from operating activities
   (j) Cash from investing activities
   (k) Cash from financing activities

   Financial ratios for 2014:

   (l) Debt ratio (Total liabilities/Total assets)
   (m) Asset turnover (Sales/Total assets)

2. Repeat (1), but now assume that all new property, plant, and equipment expected to be acquired during 2014 will be acquired under an operating lease arrangement. Assume that the annual operating lease payment for property, plant, and equipment is 15% of the purchase price of the asset and that the new property, plant, and equipment that Skywalker will lease in 2014 will not all be leased at the start of the year but will be added evenly throughout the year. Mathematically, this is the same as assuming that new assets leased during the year are leased, on average, for half the year. (*Note*: Operating lease payments are classified in the income statement as "Other operating expenses.") Under this leasing arrangement, the forecasted balance in long-term debt at the end of 2014 should be the amount forecasted previously (assuming an 80% debt ratio), less the amount of recognized long-term debt that can be avoided through the leasing arrangement.
3. Comment on the differences between the numbers in (1) and (2).

P3 ADDITIONAL ACTIVITIES OF A BUSINESS

Ken Cedeno Bloomberg News/Bloomberg/Getty Images

CHAPTER 16 Income Taxes

LEARNING OBJECTIVES

1. Understand the concept of deferred taxes and the distinction between permanent and temporary differences.
2. Compute the amount of deferred tax liabilities and assets including the use of a valuation allowance and the uncertainty of tax positions.
3. Explain the provisions of tax loss carrybacks and carryforwards, and be able to account for these provisions.
4. Schedule future tax rates, and determine the effect on deferred tax assets and liabilities.
5. Determine appropriate financial statement presentation and disclosure associated with deferred tax assets and liabilities.
6. Comply with income tax disclosure requirements associated with the statement of cash flows.
7. Describe how, with respect to deferred income taxes, international accounting standards have converged toward the U.S. treatment.

Accounting for deferred taxes is both complicated and controversial. You will learn about a few of the complications in this chapter. The controversy has stemmed from the FASB's attempts to use accounting theory to define exactly what the phrase "income tax expense" means. Because of the idiosyncrasies of the income tax code, there are many cases in which income is earned this year but is not taxed until a future year; this gives rise to a deferred income tax liability equal to the amount of additional tax expected to be paid in the future based on business activities completed this year. Similarly, there are many cases in which a company can create a business expense this year but the tax code does not allow for the deduction of that expense until a future year; this gives rise to a deferred income tax asset equal to the expected future tax savings from business activities completed this year. "Income tax expense" for this year must reflect ALL of the tax consequences, both current and deferred, of business activities undertaken this year.

In February 1992, the FASB issued pre-Codification *Statement No. 109*, "Accounting for Income Taxes," in response to five years of complaints and controversy surrounding the standard it superseded, pre-Codification FASB *Statement No. 96. Statement No. 96* was so unpopular that some observers predicted it would result in an unraveling of public confidence in the FASB, with the possibility that the FASB would be replaced just as its two predecessor bodies, the Committee on Accounting Procedure (CAP) and the Accounting Principles Board (APB), had been. The two primary complaints against *Statement No. 96* were that it was overly complicated and that it severely restricted the recognition of deferred tax assets.

Issued in 1987, *Statement No. 96* mandated that the deferred tax amounts reported on the balance sheet should be valued using expected future tax rates. Previously, deferred tax items had been valued using tax rates in effect when the deferred taxes arose in past years. This accounting change, coupled with the fact that the Tax Reform Act of 1986 had lowered the maximum corporate tax rate from 46% to 34%, caused significant downward revisions in the reported amounts of deferred taxes. For a firm with a deferred tax liability, the combined result was a decrease in the reported liability (a debit) and the recognition of a corresponding one-time gain (a credit). The business press of the period was full of articles warning investors of the large cosmetic accounting gains that companies were expected to report.[1] **General Electric** adopted *Statement No. 96* in 1987; as a result, General Electric's finance subsidiary showed a gain of $518 million, increasing the subsidiary's net income by 106%. **IBM** adopted *Statement No. 96* in 1988 and showed a gain of $315 million. **Exxon** made the adoption in 1989 and increased net income by 18% with a $535 million gain.

In response to one of the major criticisms of *Statement No. 96, Statement No. 109*, as explained more fully in this chapter, allows the recognition of most deferred tax assets. Once again, the business press warned investors to beware of firms reporting one-time accounting gains because of the change in accounting for deferred taxes.[2] These gains come about because previously unrecorded deferred tax assets are recognized (a debit), along with a corresponding gain (a credit). For example, on September 30, 1992, IBM announced that it would report a $1.9 billion gain as a result of adopting *Statement No. 109*. Interestingly, this gain was used to partially offset a $2.1 billion write-off of buildings and equipment.[3]

? QUESTIONS

1. Why was the release of pre-Codification FASB *Statement No. 96* in 1987 a dangerous event for the FASB?
2. Adoption of FASB *Statement No. 96* resulted in big one-time gains for many firms. What external event resulted in these gains?
3. How did adoption of pre-Codification *FASB Statement No. 109* result in big one-time gains for many firms?

Answers to these questions can be found on page 16-35.

[1] For an example, see Lee Berton, "FASB Is Expected to Issue Rule Allowing Many Firms to Post Big, One-Time Gains," *The Wall Street Journal,* November 4, 1987, p. 4.

[2] See Mary Beth Grover, "Cosmetics," *Forbes,* March 30, 1992, p. 78.

[3] See Michael W. Miller and Laurence Hooper, "IBM Announces Write-Off for Total of $2.1 Billion," *The Wall Street Journal,* September 30, 1992, p. A3.

This chapter begins with a discussion of the reasons for differences between financial reporting income and taxable income. This discussion leads into the topic of deferred taxes and how differences in the timing of the recognition of revenues and expenses for tax and financial reporting purposes cause differences between income tax payable and income tax expense for a period. Accounting for these deferred tax assets and liabilities comprises the bulk of this chapter. Additional topics covered include net operating loss carrybacks and carryforwards and their relationship to deferred taxes, the effect of deferred taxes on the statement of cash flows, common deferred tax items for large corporations, the accounting for uncertain tax positions, and the disclosure requirements associated with deferred taxes. We will also discuss how the international standards for deferred tax accounting have become more similar to U.S. GAAP over the past few years.

Deferred Income Taxes: An Overview

1 **Understand the concept of deferred taxes and the distinction between permanent and temporary differences.**

WHY **In order to properly inform financial statement users about all of the income tax consequences associated with operations during the current period, the delayed, or deferred, income tax consequences must be reflected in the balance sheet and the income statement.**

HOW **Permanent differences between financial income and tax income provide no difficult accounting issues; income tax expense is based strictly on taxable income. Temporary differences can create the need to recognize additional income tax expense, with an associated deferred tax liability, or to recognize a reduction in income tax expense, with an associated deferred tax asset.**

When taking introductory financial accounting courses, many students are surprised to learn that corporations in the United States compute two different income numbers: financial income for reporting to stockholders and taxable income for reporting to the Internal Revenue Service (IRS). The existence of these two "sets of books" seems unethical to some, illegal to others. However, the difference between the information needs of the stockholders and the efficient revenue collection needs of the government makes the computation of the two different income numbers essential. The different purposes of these reporting systems were summarized by the U.S. Supreme Court in the **Thor Power Tool** case (1979):

> The primary goal of financial accounting is to provide useful information to management, shareholders, creditors, and others properly interested; the major responsibility of the accountant is to protect these parties from being misled. The primary goal of the income tax system, in contrast, is the equitable collection of revenue.

CAUTION

Although the emphasis in this chapter is on accounting for federal income taxes, most states also assess a tax on income. The conceptual issues are applicable to both federal and state taxes. Often, state income tax laws are patterned after the federal law. Multinational companies are also often subject to foreign income taxation. Having multiple taxing jurisdictions complicates the establishment of income tax accounting standards and increases the materiality of income tax payments.

In summary, U.S. corporations compute income in two different ways, and rightly so. The existence of these two different numbers that can each be called "income before taxes" makes it surprisingly difficult to define what is meant by "income tax

STOP&THINK

This discussion mentions two sets of books, the financial accounting and the income tax records. Which ONE of the following is the most important third set of accounting records in a well-run business?

a) Managerial accounting records
b) State sales tax records
c) CEO astrological chart records
d) Corporate property tax records

expense" and to compute an appropriate balance sheet value for income tax liabilities and prepaid income tax assets. This accounting difficulty stems from two basic considerations:

1. How to account for revenues and expenses that have already been recognized and reported to shareholders in a company's financial statements but will not affect taxable income until subsequent years.
2. How to account for revenues and expenses that have already been reported to the IRS but will not be recognized in the financial statements until subsequent years.

Accounting for deferred income taxes focuses on temporary differences between financial accounting income and taxable income. For example, the income tax rules allow companies to deduct depreciation faster than is typically done for the financial accounting books. Over the life of the asset, the amount of depreciation is the same for both sets of books, but *temporarily*, there is a difference between the cumulative depreciation deduction reported in the tax books and the amount of cumulative depreciation expense recognized in the financial accounting books. It is this temporary difference that results in deferred income taxes. The accounting for deferred taxes is summarized in Exhibit 16-1.

Two simple examples will be used to illustrate the accounting issues resulting from this difference between financial accounting income and taxable income.

Example 1. Simple Deferred Income Tax Liability

In 2013, Ibanez Company earned revenues of $30,000. Ibanez has no expenses other than income taxes. Assume that in this case, the income tax law specifies that income is taxed when received in cash and that Ibanez received $10,000 cash in 2013 and expects to receive $20,000 in 2014. The income tax rate is 40%, and we will assume for the moment that the tax rate is expected to remain the same into the foreseeable future.

EX 16-1 A SUMMARY OF TEMPORARY DIFFERENCES AND DEFERRED INCOME TAXES

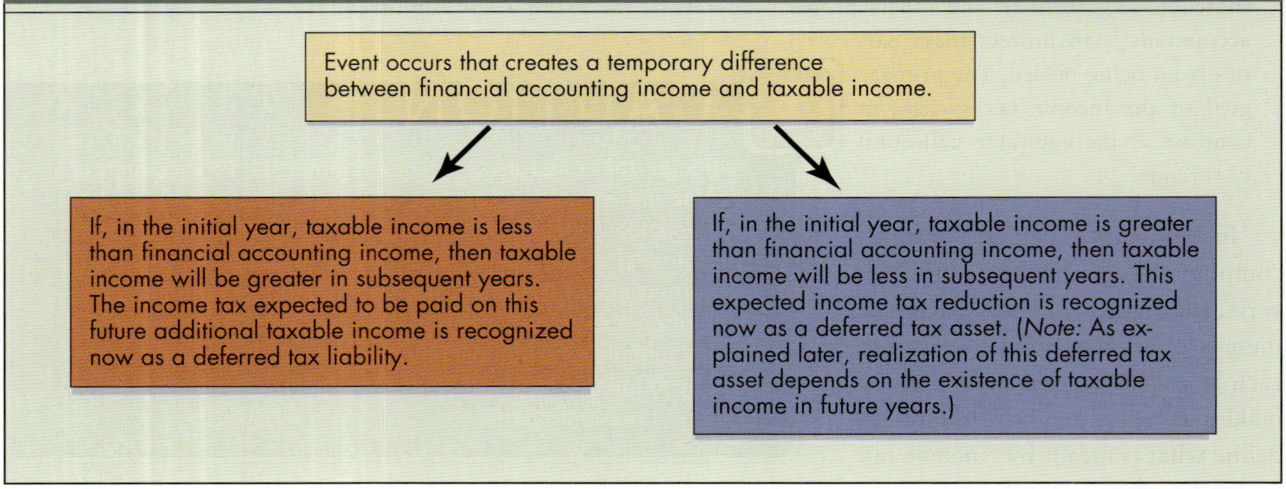

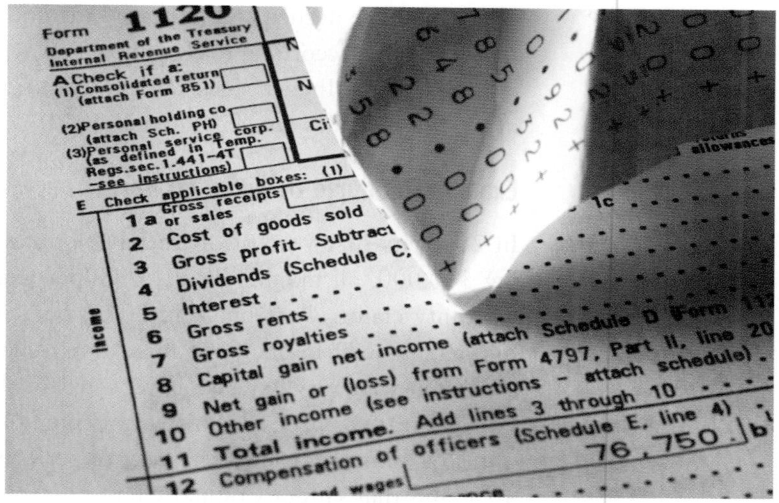

C. Sherburne/PhotoLink/Photodisc/Getty Images

Corporations keep two "sets of books" to compute income—one for reporting financial income and the other for reporting taxable income to the IRS.

The two amounts to be determined are total income tax liability at the end of the year and total income tax expense for the year. Obviously, the income tax liability is at least $4,000 because that is how much the IRS is expecting based on Ibanez's reported taxable income of $10,000. In addition, it would be misleading to the shareholders not to tell them of the expected tax to be paid on the additional $20,000 to be received in cash in 2014. Remember, this $20,000 in income has been reported to the shareholders because it was earned in 2013, but it has not yet been reported to the IRS. The expected tax on the $20,000 is $8,000 ($20,000 × 0.40) and is called a *deferred tax liability*. It is a liability because it requires a payment in the future (hence the word *deferred*) as a result of a past transaction (the past transaction is the earning of the income). This liability can be thought of as the expected income tax on income earned but not yet taxed. The journal entry to record all the tax-related information for Ibanez for 2013 is as follows:

Income Tax Expense ($4,000 current year + $8,000 deferred)	12,000	
Income Taxes Payable		4,000
Deferred Tax Liability		8,000

It is important to recognize the difference between the two recorded liabilities. Income taxes payable is an existing legal liability that the IRS fully expects to collect by March 15, 2014 (corporations pay taxes at different times than do individuals). Deferred tax liability is not an existing legal liability; as far as the IRS is concerned, it doesn't exist. However, because Ibanez knows that $20,000 of the revenues earned in 2013 will be taxed in 2014, recognition of the deferred tax liability is necessary to ensure that all expenses associated with 2013 revenues are reported in the 2013 income statement and that all obligations are reported on the December 31, 2013, balance sheet.

FYI

Although accounting standard-setting bodies have not expressed interest in abandoning deferred income tax accounting, many writers through the years have suggested that basing income tax expense on the actual tax payments is the most practical way of reporting income taxes. If this solution were to become the standard, there would be no need for a chapter on income taxes in an intermediate financial accounting text. This would undoubtedly please authors, faculty, and students alike.

As can be seen from the income tax journal entries for 2013, total income tax expense of $12,000 is the sum of the current and deferred tax expenses. The 2013 income statement for Ibanez Company is as follows:

Revenues		$30,000
Income tax expense:		
Current	$4,000	
Deferred	8,000	12,000
Net income		$18,000

Some have argued that reported income tax expense should just be the amount currently payable according to IRS rules. This type of disclosure would lead to a rude surprise in 2014 for the Ibanez shareholders: Ibanez will owe $8,000 in income tax in 2014 even if no new revenues are generated in 2014.

Example 2. Simple Deferred Tax Asset

In 2013, its first year of operations, Gupta Company generated service revenues totaling $60,000, all taxable in 2013. Gupta Company offers a warranty on its service. No warranty claims were made in 2013, but Gupta estimates that in 2014 warranty costs of $10,000 will be incurred for claims relating to 2013 service revenues. The $10,000 estimated warranty expense is reported in the 2013 financial statements as required by GAAP. For tax purposes, however, assume that the IRS does not allow any tax deduction until the actual warranty services are performed. Also assume that the income tax rate is 40% and that Gupta Company had no expenses in 2013 other than warranty costs and income taxes.

Income taxes payable as of the end of 2013 is $24,000 ($60,000 × 0.40) because Gupta is required to report $60,000 in revenues to the IRS but is not allowed to take any warranty deduction until 2014. What about the $10,000 warranty deduction Gupta expects to take in 2014? Gupta can expect this deduction to lower the 2014 tax bill by $4,000 ($10,000 × 0.40). This $4,000 is called a *deferred tax asset* and represents the expected benefit of a tax deduction for an expense item that has already been incurred and reported to the shareholders but is not yet deductible according to IRS rules. In effect, Gupta is paying taxes this year in anticipation of lower taxes next year—a prepayment of taxes. The journal entry to record all the tax-related information for Gupta for 2013 is as follows:

Income Tax Expense ($24,000 current – $4,000 deferred benefit)	20,000	
Deferred Tax Asset	4,000	
Income Taxes Payable		24,000

Total income tax expense of $20,000 is the difference between the current tax expense and the deferred tax benefit. The 2013 income statement for Gupta Company is as follows:

Revenues		$60,000
Warranty expense		10,000
Income before taxes		$50,000
Income tax expense:		
Current	$24,000	
Deferred benefit	(4,000)	20,000
Net income		$30,000

As explained in detail later in the chapter, deferred tax assets can be much more complicated than this simple example indicates. The two most common complications revolve around (1) the likelihood that a company will be able to realize the deferred tax asset in the future (a company that experiences repeated operating losses, for example, may not be able to take full advantage of the deferred tax asset) and (2) changing tax rates (a change in future tax rates affects the amount of deferred tax assets and liabilities). As mentioned at the start of this chapter, dissatisfaction over the FASB's handling of these issues related to the accounting for deferred income tax assets contributed to the acrimonious demise of pre-Codification *Statement No.* 96 in 1992.

Permanent and Temporary Differences

Before more detailed deferred tax examples are presented, some of the specific differences between financial accounting standards and tax rules will be described.

Some differences between financial and taxable income are permanent differences. These differences are caused by specific provisions of the tax law that exempt certain types of revenues from taxation and prohibit the deduction of certain types of expenses. Nontaxable revenues and nondeductible expenses are never included in determining taxable income, but they are included in determining financial income under GAAP. Permanent differences are created by political and social pressures to favor certain segments of society or to promote certain industries or economic activities. Examples of nontaxable revenues include proceeds from life insurance policies, interest received on municipal bonds, and a portion of the dividend revenue received by one corporation from its investments in other corporations. Examples of nondeductible expenses include fines for violation of laws and payment of life insurance premiums. Permanent differences also arise because income tax rates are different in different jurisdictions. For example, the state of Texas has no state income tax while the corporate income tax rate for income generated in New York is 7.1%. Permanent differences do not create accounting problems. Because they are never included in the computation of taxable income, they have no impact on either current or future (deferred) tax obligations.

> **FYI**
>
> Although permanent differences do not create financial accounting problems, that doesn't mean that they aren't important. The dream of a tax accountant is to be able to structure a company's transactions so that all of the revenue differences are permanent ones, meaning that the revenue is never taxed.

More commonly, differences between pretax financial income and taxable income arise from business events that are recognized for both financial reporting and tax purposes but in different time periods. In some cases, income tax payments are deferred to a period later than when the effect of the event on financial income is recognized. In other cases, income tax payments are required before the effect of the event on financial income is recognized. These differences are referred to as temporary differences because, over time, their impact on financial income and taxable income will be the same.

A common example of a temporary difference, and one that historically has been the most significant for U.S. companies, is the computation of depreciation. As indicated in Chapter 11, depreciation for federal income tax purposes is referred to as *cost recovery* and has varied over time as to the degree of acceleration in the recovery of asset costs. On the other hand, the most common depreciation method used to determine financial income is the straight-line method, which recognizes an even amount of depreciation expense each year the asset is in service. In the early years of an asset's life, straight-line depreciation reported on the income statement usually is less than the cost recovery deduction on the income tax return. In the latter portion of an asset's life, however, this pattern reverses; that is, the depreciation expense on the income statement exceeds the cost recovery deduction on the tax return.

There are many other temporary differences in addition to depreciation, and new income tax laws continue to create new ones as income taxes are used to meet changing economic and policy objectives. Some examples of temporary differences are given in Exhibit 16-2. This list is just a sample of the differences between financial accounting standards and income tax laws that can create temporary differences between financial and taxable income.

EX 16-2 EXAMPLES OF TEMPORARY DIFFERENCES

1. Differences That Create Deferred Tax Liabilities for Future Taxable Amounts
   (a) Revenues or gains are taxable *after* they are recognized for financial reporting purposes.
   - Installment sales method or cash basis used for tax purposes but accrual method of recognizing sales revenue used for financial reporting purposes.
   - Unrealized gain on trading securities recognized as a gain in the period in which the value increases for financial reporting purposes but becomes a taxable gain only when the securities are sold.

   (b) Expenses or losses are deductible for tax purposes *before* they are recognized for financial reporting purposes.
   - MACRS used for tax purposes but straight-line method of depreciation used for financial reporting purposes.
   - Intangible drilling costs for extractive industry written off as incurred for tax purposes but capitalized for financial reporting purposes.
2. Differences That Create Deferred Tax Assets for Future Deductible Amounts
   (a) Revenues or gains are taxable *before* they are recognized for financial reporting purposes.
   - Rent revenue received in advance of period earned recognized as revenue for tax purposes but deferred to be recognized in future periods for financial reporting purposes.
   - Subscription revenue received in advance of period earned recognized as revenue for tax purposes but deferred to be recognized in future periods for financial reporting purposes.

   (b) Expenses or losses are deductible for tax purposes *after* they are recognized for financial reporting purposes.
   - Warranty expense or bad debt expense deductible for tax purposes only when actually incurred but accrued in the year of sale for financial reporting purposes.
   - Restructuring charge deductible for tax purposes only when expenses actually incurred or losses actually realized but accrued in the year of the restructuring for financial reporting purposes.
   - Unrealized loss on trading securities recognized as a loss in the period in which the value decreases for financial reporting purposes but becomes a tax deductible loss only when the securities are sold.

STOP&THINK

How can a company have both deferred tax assets and deferred tax liabilities at the same time?

a) A company can have both deferred tax assets and deferred tax liabilities at the same time only if it has negative retained earnings.
b) A company can have both deferred tax assets and deferred tax liabilities at the same time only if the effective income tax rate is greater than 50%.
c) Deferred tax assets and deferred tax liabilities result from different transactions, so a company can have both at the same time.
d) Actually, a company *cannot* have both deferred tax assets and deferred tax liabilities at the same time.

The examples in Exhibit 16-2 are presented in two major categories. The first category includes differences, called taxable temporary differences, that will result in taxable amounts in future years. Income taxes expected to be paid on future taxable amounts are reported on the balance sheet as a deferred tax liability. The second category includes differences, called deductible temporary differences, that will result in deductible amounts in future years. Income tax benefits (savings) expected to be realized from future deductible amounts are reported on the balance sheet as a deferred tax asset. Exhibit 16-3 provides examples of deferred tax assets and deferred tax liabilities taken from the 2009 financial statements of several large U.S. companies. The large deferred tax liabilities of the capital-intensive companies listed in Exhibit 16-3 highlight the importance of deferred tax liabilities arising from depreciation. The $25,636 million deferred tax liability recognized by **Berkshire Hathaway** stems from its large investment portfolio. Increases in the value of investments are recognized for financial reporting purposes as they occur but are not taxed until the investments are sold; this gives rise to deferred tax liabilities.

EX 16-3 SELECTED DEFERRED TAX ASSETS AND DEFERRED TAX LIABILITIES FOR 2009

(Numbers in millions)

Company	Deferred Tax Assets*	Deferred Tax Liabilities
Berkshire Hathaway	$ 6,941	$25,636
ExxonMobil	16,318	34,033
Ford Motor	9,636	8,571
General Electric	26,052	28,225
Union Pacific	339	11,130

*Where applicable, deferred tax assets are reported net of any associated valuation allowance. Valuation allowances are discussed later in the chapter.

Illustration of Permanent and Temporary Differences

To illustrate the effect of permanent and temporary differences on the computation of income taxes, assume that for the year ended December 31, 2013, Monroe Corporation reported income before taxes of $420,000. Assume that this amount includes $20,000 of nontaxable revenues and $5,000 of nondeductible expenses, both permanent differences. In addition, assume that Monroe has one temporary difference: The depreciation (cost recovery) deduction on the 2013 income tax return exceeds depreciation expense on the income statement by $30,000. Assuming a corporate income tax rate of 35% for 2013, income taxes payable for the year would be computed as follows:

Pretax financial income (from income statement)		$420,000
Add (deduct) permanent differences:		
Nontaxable revenues	$(20,000)	
Nondeductible expenses	5,000	(15,000)
Financial income subject to tax		$405,000
Add (deduct) temporary differences:		
Excess of tax depreciation over book depreciation		(30,000)
Taxable income		$375,000
Tax on taxable income (income taxes payable): $375,000 × 0.35		$131,250

CAUTION

It is important that you be able to distinguish among the terms *pretax financial income, pretax financial income subject to tax,* and *taxable income*. This simple illustration highlights these terms and will make the later discussion clearer. Where there are no permanent differences, pretax financial income and pretax financial income subject to tax are the same. Unless otherwise noted, the shorter term is used in the remainder of the chapter.

As illustrated, the permanent differences are not included in either the financial income subject to tax or the taxable income. In addition, because these permanent differences never reverse, they have no impact on income taxes payable in subsequent periods and are thus not associated with any deferred tax consequences. Temporary differences are the cause of the complexity and controversy in accounting for income taxes because they impact financial income and taxable income in different periods. In general, the accounting for temporary differences is referred to as interperiod tax allocation.

Annual Computation of Deferred Tax Liabilities and Assets

2 **Compute the amount of deferred tax liabilities and assets including the use of a valuation allowance and the uncertainty of tax positions.**

WHY **Although they are not perfectly measured, deferred tax assets and liabilities fit the conceptual framework definitions of assets and liabilities and should therefore be included in the balance sheet.**

HOW **Computing the amount of deferred tax assets and liabilities involves identifying the temporary differences, computing the amounts of any deferred tax liability and deferred tax asset, and reducing the amount of the deferred tax asset using a valuation allowance account, if necessary.**

As illustrated with the earlier examples, the basic concepts underlying deferred tax accounting are fairly simple. The examples that follow introduce some of the complexities associated with the specific provisions of FASB ASC Topic 740 (Income Taxes). Before launching into these examples, take a moment to reflect on how lucky you are not to have taken this class a few years ago. At that time, this chapter was based on pre-Codification *Statement No. 96*, which was much more difficult to understand and to implement and was hated by practitioners, financial statement users, students, and professors alike.

Topic 740 reflects the Board's preference for the asset and liability method of interperiod tax allocation, which emphasizes the measurement and reporting of balance sheet amounts. The major advantages of the asset and liability method of accounting for deferred taxes are as follows:

1. Because the assets and liabilities recorded under this method are in agreement with the FASB definitions of financial statement elements, the method is conceptually consistent with other standards.
2. The asset and liability method is a flexible method that recognizes changes in circumstances and adjusts the reported amounts accordingly. This flexibility may improve the predictive value of the financial statements.

One drawback of the asset and liability method is that in some ways, it is still too complicated (even after the significant simplification implemented in the wake of pre-Codification *Statement No. 96*). Many financial statement users claim that they ignore deferred tax assets and liabilities anyway, and thus, efforts devoted to deferred tax accounting are just a waste of time. For example, one financial statement analysis textbook reports that "because of the uncertainty over whether (and when) a deferred tax liability will be paid, some individuals elect to exclude deferred tax liabilities from liabilities when performing analysis."[4] On the other hand, research using stock market data suggests that investors compute values of companies as if the reported deferred tax liabilities are bona fide liabilities.[5]

[4] Charles H. Gibson, *Financial Statement Analysis: Using Financial Accounting Information*, 6th ed. (Cincinnati, OH: South-Western Publishing Co., 1995), p. 321.

[5] Dan Givoly and Carla Hayn, "The Valuation of the Deferred Tax Liability: Evidence from the Stock Market," *The Accounting Review*, April 1992, pp. 394–410.

The following list summarizes the procedure to be followed each year to compute the amount of deferred tax liabilities and assets to be included in the financial statements.[6]

1. Identify the types and amounts of existing temporary differences.
2. Measure the deferred tax liability for taxable temporary differences using applicable current and future tax rates.
3. Measure the deferred tax asset for deductible temporary differences using applicable current and future tax rates.
4. Reduce deferred tax assets by a valuation allowance if it is more likely than not (a likelihood of more than 50%) that some portion or all of the deferred tax assets will not be realized. The valuation allowance should reduce the deferred tax asset to the amount that is more likely than not to be realized.

Several examples will illustrate the computation of deferred tax assets and liabilities.

Example 3. Deferred Tax Liability

If a company has only deferred tax liabilities to consider, the accounting for deferred taxes is relatively straightforward. To illustrate, assume that Roland Inc. begins operations in 2013. For 2013, Roland computes pretax financial income of $75,000. The only difference between financial accounting income and taxable income is depreciation. Roland uses the straight-line method of depreciation for financial reporting purposes and an accelerated cost recovery method on its tax return. The depreciation amounts for existing plant assets for the years 2013 through 2016 are as follows:

Year	Financial Reporting	Income Tax Reporting
2013	$ 25,000	$ 40,000
2014	25,000	30,000
2015	25,000	25,000
2016	25,000	5,000
	$100,000	$100,000

The enacted tax rate for 2013 and future years is 40%. Roland's taxable income for 2013 is $60,000, computed as follows:

Financial income subject to tax	$ 75,000
Deduct temporary difference:	
Excess of tax depreciation over book depreciation	(15,000)
Taxable income	$ 60,000
Tax ($60,000 × 0.40)	$ 24,000

Thus, Roland records a current liability of $24,000. At the end of 2013, aggregate tax depreciation exceeds aggregate book depreciation by $15,000 ($40,000 – $25,000). This taxable temporary difference will result in a taxable amount of $15,000 in future years as the difference reverses. With the currently enacted 40% tax rate, income tax on this future taxable amount will total $6,000 ($15,000 × 0.40). Accordingly, a deferred tax liability of $6,000 will be reported on the December 31, 2013, balance sheet. Because the depreciable

[6] FASB ASC paragraph 740-10-30-5.

asset is a noncurrent operating asset, the associated deferred tax liability is also classified as noncurrent.

The journal entry to record Roland's income taxes for 2013 would be as follows:

Income Tax Expense ($24,000 current + $6,000 deferred)	30,000	
Income Taxes Payable		24,000
Deferred Tax Liability—Noncurrent		6,000

Income taxes would be shown on Roland's 2013 income statement as follows:

Income before income taxes		$75,000
Current	$24,000	
Deferred	6,000	30,000
Net income		$45,000

The December 31, 2013, balance sheet would report a current liability of $24,000 for income taxes payable and, as noted above, a noncurrent deferred tax liability of $6,000.

So as to not unnecessarily complicate this example, we will assume that Roland earns financial income subject to tax of $75,000 in each of the years 2014 through 2016. In 2014, Roland reports taxable income of $70,000, computed as follows:

STOP&THINK

How might the current and deferred income tax numbers for 2013 change if the 2013 income tax rate were 40% but Roland expected tax rates in future periods to be 30% instead of 40%?

a) The numbers would be the same.
b) Both the current and deferred amounts would be multiplied by 30% instead of 40%.
c) The current amount would be multiplied by 30% instead of 40%.
d) The deferred amount would be multiplied by 30% instead of 40%.

Financial income subject to tax	$75,000
Deduct temporary difference:	
Excess of tax depreciation over book depreciation	(5,000)
Taxable income	$70,000
Tax ($70,000 × 0.40)	$28,000

Roland's current taxes payable are $28,000. In each subsequent year following the initial deferral, the ending deferred tax liability is determined and compared with the beginning balance. The difference between the beginning and ending balances is recorded as an adjustment to the deferred tax liability account. At the end of 2014, aggregate tax depreciation exceeds aggregate book depreciation by $20,000 ($70,000 – $50,000). The deferred tax liability account, therefore, must be adjusted to a balance of $8,000 ($20,000 × 0.40). The amount of the adjustment is $2,000 ($8,000 less the beginning balance of $6,000). The following journal entry records the current payable and the adjustment to the deferred tax liability account:

Income Tax Expense ($28,000 current + $2,000 deferred)	30,000	
Income Taxes Payable		28,000
Deferred Tax Liability—Noncurrent		2,000

Because the depreciation expense for tax and financial reporting purposes is the same for 2015, no adjustment to the deferred tax liability account would be necessary for that year. Income for tax purposes would be equal to financial accounting income, and tax expense and taxes payable would be recorded with the journal entry shown on page 16-13.

Income Tax Expense	30,000	
Income Taxes Payable ($75,000 × 0.40)		30,000

For 2016, income for tax purposes would be equal to $95,000, computed as follows:

Financial income subject to tax	$75,000
Add reversal of temporary difference:	
Excess of book depreciation over tax depreciation	20,000
Taxable income	$95,000
Tax ($95,000 × 0.40)	$38,000

Therefore, current taxes payable would be $38,000. The accumulated difference of $20,000 in the deferred tax account reverses, and aggregate tax depreciation and aggregate book depreciation are the same ($100,000). Thus, the journal entry to record the current year's payable as well as to reduce the deferred tax liability to zero would be as shown:

Income Tax Expense ($38,000 current – $8,000 deferred benefit)	30,000	
Deferred Tax Liability—Noncurrent	8,000	
Income Taxes Payable		38,000

The income tax benefit reduces the current income tax expense for 2016. The T-account summarizing the changes in the deferred tax liability account from 2013 to 2016 is as follows:

Deferred Tax Liability

		6,000	for 2013
		6,000	balance, end of 2013
		2,000	for 2014
		8,000	balance, end of 2014
		0	for 2015
		8,000	balance, end of 2015
for 2016	8,000		
		0	balance, end of 2016

Effect of Currently Enacted Changes in Future Tax Rates The example assumed a constant future tax rate of 40%. If changes in future tax rates have been enacted, the deferred tax liability (or asset) is measured using the enacted tax rate for the future years when the temporary difference is expected to reverse. To illustrate, assume that in 2013, Congress enacts legislation that reduces corporate tax rates for 2014 and subsequent years. In the Roland Inc. example, all of the temporary difference reverses in 2016, and the deferred tax liability should be measured using the tax rate enacted for that year. If the enacted tax rate for 2016 is 35%, the deferred tax liability at the end of 2013 would be $5,250 ($15,000 × 0.35), rather than $6,000 as computed earlier. At the end of 2014, the deferred tax liability would be $7,000 ($20,000 × 0.35), and the required adjustment would be $1,750 ($7,000 – $5,250).

IAS 12 is very similar to, but not exactly the same as, U.S. GAAP regarding the use of future tax rates. Under U.S. GAAP, as described in the previous paragraph, measurement of deferred tax liabilities and assets is done using the income tax rates that had been enacted as of the measurement date. This provision has the objective of measuring the deferred tax items at the tax rates that are expected to be in effect when the temporary items reverse, which will not be the same as the income tax rate for the current year if future tax rate changes have already been enacted into law. IFRS carries this concept one step further. Under *IAS 12*, deferred tax items are to be measured at income tax rates "that

ifrs

> **! CAUTION**
>
> The entire effect of a change in rates is reflected in tax expense on income from continuing operations even if some of the deferred tax balances relate to "below-the-line" or accumulated other comprehensive income items. See FASB ASC paragraph 740-10-45-17.

have been enacted or substantively enacted by the end of the reporting period." The "substantively enacted" part of this IFRS provision refers to cases in which governments in some jurisdictions announce an income tax rate change but the formal legal enactment of the change does not occur for several months. This is an example of the international standard taking a step back from legal literalism in order to capture the economic essence of a transaction or an event.

Subsequent Changes in Enacted Tax Rates When rate changes are enacted after a deferred tax liability or asset has been recorded, Topic 740 requires that the beginning deferred account balance be adjusted to reflect the new tax rate. Again using the Roland Inc. example, assume that the enacted tax rate for 2016 changed from 40% to 35% during 2014. The balance in the deferred tax liability at the beginning of 2014 is $6,000 ($15,000 × 0.40). The following adjusting entry would be made to reflect the newly enacted 35% tax rate for 2016:

Deferred Tax Liability—Noncurrent	750	
Income Tax Benefit—Rate Change (reduction in income tax expense)		750
($15,000 × 0.05)		

The income effect of the change is reflected in income tax expense. In this case, the effect is a tax benefit resulting from a lower tax rate and would be shown as a reduction in income tax expense on the 2014 income statement.

Example 4. Deferred Tax Asset

Assume that Sandusky Inc. begins operations in 2013. For 2013, Sandusky computes pretax financial income of $22,000. The only difference between financial and taxable income is the recognition of warranty expense. Sandusky accrues estimated warranty expense in the year of sale for financial reporting purposes but deducts only actual warranty expenditures for tax purposes. Accrued warranty expense for 2013 was $18,000; no actual warranty expenditures were made in 2013. Therefore, taxable income in 2013 is $40,000, computed as follows:

Financial income subject to tax	$22,000
Add temporary difference:	
Excess of warranty expense over warranty deductions	18,000
Taxable income	$40,000
Tax ($40,000 × 0.40)	$16,000

The difference in 2013 between warranty expense for financial reporting and tax purposes is a deductible temporary difference because it will result in future tax deductions of $18,000. The deferred tax asset implied by this difference is $7,200 ($18,000 × 0.40). Warranty expenditures for 2013 sales are expected to be $6,000 in each of the years 2014 through 2016. Because the underlying warranty obligation is assumed to be one-third current and two-thirds noncurrent, the associated deferred tax asset would be classified in the same ratio.

The future tax deduction of $18,000 will provide a tax benefit only if Sandusky has taxable income in future periods against which the deduction can be offset. Accordingly, to record a deferred tax asset, one must assume that sufficient taxable income will exist in future years. Conditions under which this assumption may or may not be reasonable are described later in the chapter in the section entitled "Valuation Allowance for Deferred Tax Assets."

Assuming that future taxable income will be sufficient to allow for full realization of the tax benefits of the $18,000 future tax deduction (and let's assume, just to keep things simple, that financial income subject to tax is $22,000 in each of the next three years), the journal entry to record Sandusky's income taxes for 2013 would be as follows:

Income Tax Expense ($16,000 current − $7,200 deferred benefit)	8,800	
Deferred Tax Asset—Current	2,400*	
Deferred Tax Asset—Noncurrent	4,800†	
Income Taxes Payable		16,000

*One-third of underlying warranty obligation is current (1/3 × $7,200).

†Two-thirds of underlying warranty obligation is noncurrent (2/3 × $7,200).

Sandusky's 2013 income statement would present income tax expense as follows:

Income before income taxes		$22,000
Income tax expense:		
Current	$16,000	
Deferred (benefit)	(7,200)	8,800
Net income		$13,200

Sandusky's December 31, 2013, balance sheet would report deferred tax assets of $2,400 under current assets and $4,800 under noncurrent assets. Income taxes payable for 2013 would be shown with current liabilities.

In subsequent periods, Sandusky's taxable income would be less than reported pretax financial income because the deductible temporary differences would begin to reverse. In the years 2014 through 2016, taxable income would be equal to $16,000, computed as follows:

Income subject to tax	$22,000
Reversal of temporary difference:	
Excess of warranty deductions over warranty expense	(6,000)
Taxable income	$16,000
Tax ($16,000 × 0.40)	$ 6,400

The amount of the deductible temporary difference would decline each year, affecting first the amount classified as noncurrent and finally eliminating the current portion of the deferred tax asset account. The following table illustrates the journal entries that would be made each year:

	2014		2015		2016	
Income Tax Expense	6,400		6,400		6,400	
Income Taxes Payable		6,400		6,400		6,400
Income Tax Expense	2,400		2,400		2,400	
Deferred Tax Asset—Current		2,400		2,400		2,400
Deferred Tax Asset—Current	2,400		2,400			
Deferred Tax Asset—Noncurrent		2,400		2,400		

The first journal entry records the current period's tax liability. The second journal entry recognizes that the current portion of the deferred tax asset has expired. The final journal entry simply reclassifies the deferred tax asset from noncurrent to current, indicating that a portion of the deductible temporary difference will reverse in the upcoming period.

Example 5. Deferred Tax Liabilities and Assets

Hsieh Company began operation on January 1, 2013. For 2013, Hsieh reported pretax financial income of $38,000. As of December 31, 2013, the actual differences between Hsieh Company's financial accounting and income tax records for 2013 and the estimated differences for 2014 through 2016 are summarized as follows:

	Financial Reporting		Income Tax Reporting	
	Depreciation Expense	Warranty Expense	Depreciation Deduction	Warranty Deduction
2013 (actual)	$25,000	$18,000	$40,000	$ 0
2014 (estimated)	25,000	0	30,000	6,000
2015 (estimated)	25,000	0	25,000	6,000
2016 (estimated)	25,000	0	5,000	6,000

The enacted income tax rate for all years is 40% (note that Example 5 simply combines Examples 3 and 4). For 2013, taxable income would be computed as follows:

Financial income subject to tax	$ 38,000
Add (deduct) temporary differences:	
Excess of warranty expense over warranty deductions	18,000
Excess of tax depreciation over book depreciation	(15,000)
Taxable income	$ 41,000
Tax ($41,000 × 0.40)	$ 16,400

As of December 31, 2013, aggregate tax depreciation exceeds aggregate book depreciation by $15,000 ($40,000 – $25,000). As explained previously, this represents a future taxable amount. The income tax expected to be paid on this amount is $6,000 ($15,000 × 0.40). This $6,000 is a deferred tax liability as of December 31, 2013. Because the difference relates to a noncurrent item, the deferred tax liability is a noncurrent liability.

As of December 31, 2013, Hsieh has recognized an $18,000 warranty expense for financial accounting purposes, which it plans to deduct for tax purposes over the next three years. Assuming that future taxable income will be sufficient to allow the tax benefit of this deduction to be fully realized, this future deductible amount creates a deferred tax asset of $7,200 ($18,000 × 0.40). Because the underlying warranty liability is part current ($6,000) and part noncurrent ($12,000), the deferred tax asset would also be classified as part current ($2,400 = $6,000 × 0.40) and part noncurrent ($4,800 = $12,000 × 0.40). The journal entries to record Hsieh's current taxes payable as well as the deferred portion of its 2013 income tax expense are as follows:

	Debit	Credit
Income Tax Expense	16,400	
Income Taxes Payable		16,400
Deferred Tax Asset—Current	2,400	
Deferred Tax Asset—Noncurrent	4,800	
Income Tax Benefit (a subtraction from income tax expense)		1,200
Deferred Tax Liability—Noncurrent		6,000

Note that this journal entry is a combination of the journal entries associated with the deferred taxes from Examples 3 and 4. For reporting purposes, current deferred tax assets and current deferred tax liabilities are netted against one another and reported as a single amount. Similarly, noncurrent deferred tax assets and liabilities are netted and reported as a single amount.[7] In this example, the amounts to be reported on Hsieh's December 31, 2013, balance sheet are a $2,400 current deferred tax asset and a $1,200 noncurrent deferred tax liability ($6,000 liability − $4,800 asset). The income tax benefit would be shown as a $1,200 reduction of current income tax expense in the 2013 income statement.

Deferred Tax Classification under IFRS Under IFRS, deferred tax assets and liabilities are to be classified as noncurrent assets and liabilities. As seen in the examples explained earlier, under U.S. GAAP, the deferred tax items are classified as current or noncurrent based on the classification of the underlying item that gives rise to the deferred income tax asset or liability. The IFRS classification provision is contained in *IAS 1*, which outlines, among other things, the basic structure of the financial statements.

ifrs

Valuation Allowance for Deferred Tax Assets

A deferred tax asset represents future income tax benefits. But the tax benefits will be realized only if there is sufficient taxable income from which the deductible amount can be deducted. Topic 740 requires that the deferred tax asset be reduced by a valuation allowance if, based on all available evidence, it is "more likely than not" that some portion or all the deferred tax asset will not be realized. As applied to deferred tax assets, "more likely than not" means a likelihood of more than 50%.[8] The valuation allowance is a contra asset account that reduces the asset to its expected realizable value. Before we get into the details of the valuation allowance, it is important for you to realize that for most companies, and for profitable companies in particular, the valuation allowance is not an issue. The valuation allowance becomes an issue when future profitability is in doubt.

In the Hsieh Company example (Example 5 on page 16-16), it was assumed that there would be sufficient taxable income to allow for the full realization of the benefits from the $18,000 warranty deduction, and thus, no valuation allowance was established. Some possible sources of taxable income to be considered in evaluating the realizable value of a deferred tax asset are as follows:[9]

1. Future reversals of existing taxable temporary differences
2. Future taxable income exclusive of reversing temporary differences
3. Taxable income in prior (carryback) years

The first source of future taxable income, reversals of taxable temporary differences, can be identified without making assumptions about the profitability of future operations. In 2013, Hsieh Company has a $15,000 excess of aggregate tax depreciation over aggregate book depreciation, which will result in a future taxable amount. The reversal of this temporary difference will provide taxable income in the future against which the $18,000 warranty deduction can be offset. If it appears more likely than not that no other income will be available, then only $15,000 of the $18,000 warranty deduction is expected to be realized. Accordingly, the total deferred tax asset is $7,200 ($18,000 × 0.40), but the realizable amount is only $6,000 ($15,000 × 0.40). The $1,200 difference would be recorded as a valuation allowance, an offset to the reported deferred tax asset. Two journal entries

[7] FASB ASC paragraph 740-10-45-6.
[8] FASB ASC paragraph 740-10-30-5e.
[9] FASB ASC paragraph 740-10-30-18.

can be used to record this deferred tax information. First, the deferred tax asset and liability are recognized, as follows.

Deferred Tax Asset—Current	2,400	
Deferred Tax Asset—Noncurrent	4,800	
Income Tax Benefit (a subtraction from income tax expense)		1,200
Deferred Tax Liability—Noncurrent		6,000

Note that this is the same as the deferred tax journal entry shown earlier. The second journal entry represents the fact that it is more likely than not that $1,200 of the deferred tax asset will not be realized.

Income Tax Expense	1,200	
Allowance to Reduce Deferred Tax Asset to Realizable Value—Current		400
Allowance to Reduce Deferred Tax Asset to Realizable Value—Noncurrent		800

For classification purposes, the valuation allowance is allocated proportionately between the current and noncurrent portions of the deferred tax asset.[10] In this example, because one-third of the deferred tax asset is current ($6,000/$18,000), one-third, or $400 ($1,200 × 1/3), of the valuation allowance is classified as current. Of course, these two journal entries can be combined into one. The net effect of the two entries is that there is no deferred tax component of income tax expense—the $6,000 income tax expense associated with the deferred tax liability is exactly offset by the $6,000 ($7,200 − $1,200) income tax benefit (net) associated with the realizable portion of the deferred tax asset.

STOP&THINK

In what way do the data regarding deferred tax assets and liabilities provide valuable information to current and potential investors and creditors?

a) Data regarding deferred tax assets and liabilities allow investors and creditors to better compute cost of goods sold.
b) Data regarding deferred tax assets and liabilities allow investors and creditors to better estimate bad debt expense.
c) Data regarding deferred tax assets and liabilities allow investors and creditors to better estimate future tax-related cash flows.
d) Data regarding deferred tax assets and liabilities allow investors and creditors to better compute earnings before interest and taxes.

In 2014 and subsequent years, the company should reconsider available evidence to determine whether the valuation account should be adjusted.

The other two sources through which the benefit of a deferred tax asset can be realized include taxable income expected from profitable operations in future years and taxable income in prior carryback years. This latter source relates to specific carryback provisions of the tax law, which are explained later in the chapter.

Topic 740 stipulates that both positive and negative evidence be considered when determining whether deferred tax assets will be fully realized.[11] Examples of negative evidence include cumulative losses in recent years, a history of the expiration of unused tax loss carryforwards, and unsettled circumstances that might cause a currently profitable company to report losses in future years. Positive evidence includes the existence of an order backlog sufficient to yield enough taxable income for the deferred tax asset to be realized, the existence of appreciated assets, and a strong earnings history.

[10] FASB ASC paragraph 740-10-45-5.
[11] FASB ASC paragraph 740-10-30-17.

The FASB was very reluctant to allow firms to consider possible future taxable income when evaluating the realizability of deferred tax assets because, as stated in pre-Codification FASB *Statement No. 96*:

> Incurring losses or generating profits in future years are future events that are not recognized in financial statements for the current year. Those future events shall not be anticipated, regardless of probability, for purposes of recognizing and measuring a deferred tax liability or asset in the current year. The tax consequences of those future events shall be recognized and reported in the financial statements in future years when the events occur.[12]

However, because many firms complained that it was unfair to require them to report deferred tax liabilities but not allow them to report deferred tax assets, the FASB reconsidered and revised its position. Topic 740 explicitly allows a firm to consider potential future income in evaluating the realizability of deferred tax assets.

Valuation Allowance under *IAS 12* Simply stated, under the provisions of *IAS 12,* there is no valuation allowance. Instead, deferred tax assets are recognized only "to the extent that it is probable that taxable profit will be available against which the deductible temporary difference can be utilised." Thus, under U.S. GAAP, all deferred tax assets are initially recognized and then are reduced by a valuation allowance if it is more likely than not that there will not be sufficient future taxable income to allow for the realization of the deferred tax asset. Under IFRS, deferred tax assets are only recognized in the first place if their realization is probable; there is no need for a valuation allowance. However, much more important than the procedural difference between U.S. GAAP and IFRS is the difference in probability thresholds for ultimate deferred tax asset recognition. Under U.S. GAAP, the realizability of the deferred tax asset must be more likely than not, interpreted as a probability of 50%. Under IFRS, the realizability must be "probable." Although no one has put a definitive probability percentage on "probable," everyone agrees that probable is more than 50%, usually substantially more. Thus, the international standard is stricter than is U.S. GAAP with respect to the recognition of deferred tax assets.

Accounting for Uncertain Tax Positions In spite of the voluminous nature of the tax code, there are still many areas in which the deductibility of certain expenses or losses and the claiming of some tax credits are in question. Professional tax preparers are constantly giving advice to clients regarding aggressive tax positions that may, upon close scrutiny, be rejected by the Internal Revenue Service. Tax preparers are not required to be absolutely certain that a position will be sustained by the IRS in order to be justified in recommending that tax position to a client. According to U.S. Treasury Department regulations, a tax preparer or a taxpayer can justifiably advocate an aggressive tax position, without fear of legal or professional censure, if there is "substantial authority" to support a position.[13] "Substantial authority" is generally defined in practice as being a greater than 40% probability of having the tax position sustained.

The existence of aggressive tax positions that are not certain to be sustained upon IRS scrutiny raises the financial accounting question of whether the tax benefit associated with

[12] Pre-Codification FASB *Statement No. 96*, "Accounting for Income Taxes" (Stamford, CT: Financial Accounting Standards Board, 1987), par. 15.
[13] *IRC Section 6662(d).*

these tax positions should be recognized as a reduction in income tax expense. Topic 740 states that the tax benefit associated with an uncertain tax benefit can be recognized only if it is *more likely than not* that the position will be sustained upon audit by the IRS. You can see that, under this interpretation, there will be some uncertain tax positions that might be taken by taxpayers but the tax benefits are not immediately recognized for financial accounting purposes because those benefits are not yet more likely than not.

Some examples of areas where tax benefits might be considered uncertain include the following:

- Classifying a revenue transaction as tax exempt (when it may not be)
- Electing not to file a tax return in a certain jurisdiction (when filing might be appropriate)
- Establishing a capitalization threshold for routine property and equipment purchases (when the tax law does not prescribe a threshold)

Topic 740 requires the use of a 2-step process to determine the recognition of any tax benefit associated with an uncertain tax position. The two steps relating to recognition and measurement are as follows:

1. Step 1—Determine if it is more likely than not that a tax position would be sustained if it were examined, and it must be assumed that the tax position will be examined. Remember, more likely than not means a likelihood of greater than 50%. If a tax position meets this criterion, then the analysis moves to Step 2.
2. Step 2—The measurement of the tax benefit is based on a probability assessment of the likelihood of specific outcomes and the amounts associated with those outcomes. The amount of the benefit is measured by taking the largest amount of tax benefit that is greater than 50% likely of being realized upon settlement.

An example is used to illustrate this 2-step process. Company A has taken a tax position on an issue for which the tax law is subject to interpretation. For tax purposes, Company A has claimed a deduction in the current period that results in a $100 reduction in taxes to be paid this period. If this expenditure is reviewed, it is possible that the IRS may disallow all or part of the deduction. Company A must now determine how much should be reported as Income Tax Expense on the income statement and as Income Taxes Payable on the balance sheet.

Case 1: Highly certain tax position. In this example, if the probability that the tax benefit of $100 would be achieved were greater than 50%, this would be deemed a "highly certain" tax position. A "highly certain" tax position is one in which the position is based on clear and unambiguous tax law and where it is more likely than not that (that is, a greater than 50% probability) the position taken and the amount in question would be upheld if reviewed. In this instance, there would be no additional tax liability recognized because the amount of tax benefit claimed on the tax return and the amount of benefit expected to be received based on the tax position analysis are the same.

Case 2: Uncertain tax position—more likely than not. Suppose instead that there is a range of possible outcomes associated with this tax position. The company is required to provide an assessment of both the probability of an outcome as well as the amount of allowable reduction in taxes associated with that probability. Assume the assessment of probabilities as shown on page 16-21.

There is a xx% probability that	The allowable reduction in taxes payable will be	The cumulative probability of occurrence is
10%	$100	10%
20	80	30
25	60	55
20	40	75
15	20	90
10	0	100

If Company A determines that the technical merits of its position exceed the more-likely-than-not threshold (Step 1), the amount of tax benefit to be recognized for financial statement purposes in this example is $60, the amount at which the cumulative probability exceeds 50% (Step 2). What this means is that Company A would now need to record an additional tax liability, called an *unrecognized tax benefit*, for the $40 difference—the difference between the actual reduction in taxes (or tax benefit) on the income tax return filed this period and the expected amount of benefit based on this tax position analysis.[14]

The required journal entry is as follows:

Income Tax Expense	40	
Unrecognized Tax Benefit		40

The account, Unrecognized Tax Benefit, is a liability and would be classified as current if payment is anticipated within one year. It is important to note that liabilities relating to uncertain tax positions are not to be combined with deferred tax assets or liabilities for disclosure purposes.

Case 3: Uncertain tax position—NOT more likely than not. If the company completes Step 1 of the analysis and determines that it is NOT more likely than not that the tax position will be sustained (that is, there is a less than 50% chance the position will be supported upon review), then the entire amount of the position must be recognized as a liability with the following journal entry:

Income Tax Expense	100	
Unrecognized Tax Benefit		100

Topic 740 also requires note disclosure relating to the beginning balance of unrecognized tax benefits, additions based on tax positions related to the current year, additions related to tax positions for prior years, reductions for tax positions of prior years, and adjustments related to any settlements made during the year.

Exhibit 16-4 includes a portion of the financial statement note disclosure about uncertain tax positions made by **General Mills** in its May 30, 2010, financial statements. Note that a $30.7 million tax benefit, and then a $52.6 million tax expense, were recorded in consecutive years with respect to the same uncertain tax position. Clearly, a substantial amount of complex judgment must be used in assessing the probabilities and amounts associated with these uncertain tax positions.

[14] FASB ASC paragraph 740-10-25-16.

EX 16-4 GENERAL MILLS DISCLOSURE ABOUT UNCERTAIN TAX POSITIONS—2010

NOTE 14. INCOME TAXES (in part)

The IRS has concluded its field examination of our 2006 and prior federal tax years, which resulted in payments of $17.6 million in fiscal 2009 and $56.5 million in fiscal 2008 to cover the additional U.S. income tax liability plus interest related to adjustments during these audit cycles. The IRS also proposed additional adjustments for the fiscal 2002 to 2006 audit cycles related to the amount of capital loss and depreciation and amortization we reported as a result of our sale of noncontrolling interest in our GMC subsidiary. The IRS has proposed adjustments that effectively eliminate most of the tax benefits associated with this transaction. We believe our positions are supported by substantial technical authority and are vigorously defending our positions. We are currently in negotiations with the IRS Appeals Division for fiscal 2002 to 2006. We have determined that a portion of this matter should be included as a tax liability and have accordingly included it in our total liabilities for uncertain tax positions. The IRS initiated its audit of our fiscal 2007 and 2008 tax years during fiscal 2009.

In the third quarter of fiscal 2008, we recorded an income tax benefit of $30.7 million as a result of a favorable U.S. district court decision on an uncertain tax matter. In the third quarter of fiscal 2009, the U.S. Court of Appeals for the Eighth Circuit issued an opinion reversing the district court decision. As a result, we recorded $52.6 million (including interest) of income tax expense related to the reversal of cumulative income tax benefits from this uncertain tax matter recognized in fiscal years 1992 through 2008. We expect to make cash tax and interest payments of approximately $31.7 million in connection with this matter . . .

In Millions	Fiscal Year 2010	Fiscal Year 2009
Balance, beginning of year	$ 570.1	$ 534.6
Tax position related to current year:		
Additions	19.7	66.8
Tax positions related to prior years:		
Additions	7.1	48.9
Reductions	(37.6)	(63.7)
Settlements	(1.9)	(13.0)
Lapses in statutes of limitations	(4.5)	(3.5)
Balance, end of year	$ 552.9	$ 570.1

FASB CODIFICATION

The Issue: Your brother-in-law is a bit of a know-it-all. He has heard that you are taking an accounting class. He thinks he is an accounting expert because he took, and passed (barely), an intermediate financial accounting class several years ago. He is now trying to embarrass you at a family gathering by showing how much more he knows about accounting than you do.

He has just thrown the following question at you: "What is INTRAperiod tax allocation?" Fortunately, he has been called away to a phone call. You have five minutes to go online and use the FASB's Codification to avoid the humiliation of being bested by your obnoxious brother-in-law.

The Question: What is INTRAperiod tax allocation?

Searching the Codification: Your initial thought is that your brother-in-law has made a mistake. The accounting for temporary differences and deferred income taxes is called INTERperiod tax allocation. But because of the wicked smile he gave you when he asked the question, you know there is a trick here. The best place to start your search is FASB ASC Topic 740. Good luck!

The Answer: A discussion of INTRAperiod tax allocation is given on page 16-36.

Carryback and Carryforward of Operating Losses

3 **Explain the provisions of tax loss carrybacks and carryforwards, and be able to account for these provisions.**

WHY For some startup businesses, and even for some established businesses experiencing difficult economic conditions, the cash flow savings associated with the deduction of tax losses comprise an extremely important portion of the business's total economic value.

HOW If a business reports a tax loss, the U.S. tax code allows the business to carry back this loss up to two years to obtain a refund of taxes previously paid or to carry forward the loss up to 20 years in order to reduce the tax payments to be made in future periods. A tax carryforward results in a reduction in the current period's income tax expense and the recognition of a deferred tax asset.

Because income tax is based on the amount of taxable income reported, no tax is payable if a company experiences an operating loss. As an incentive to those businesses that experience alternate periods of income and losses, U.S. tax laws provide a way to ease the risk of loss years. This is done through a carryback and carryforward provision that permits a company to apply a net operating loss occurring in one year against income of other years. Specifically, the Internal Revenue Code provides for a 2-year carryback and a 20-year carryforward.[15]

Net Operating Loss (NOL) Carryback

If you were profitable in prior periods and, as a result, paid taxes, you can get a refund of some or all those tax payments in the period in which you incur an operating loss. A net operating loss (NOL) carryback is applied to the income of the two preceding years in reverse order, beginning with the second year and moving to the first year. If unused net operating losses are still available, they may be carried forward up to 20 years to offset any future income. Amended income tax returns must be filed for each year to which the carryback is applied to receive refunds of previously paid income taxes. Net operating loss carrybacks result in a journal entry establishing a current receivable for the tax refund claim. The benefit that arises from such refunds is used to reduce the loss in the current period. This treatment is supported in theory because it is the current year's operating loss that results in the tax refund.

To illustrate, assume that Prairie Company had the following pattern of income and losses for the years 2012 through 2014:

Year	Income (Loss)	Income Tax Rate	Income Tax
2012	$ 10,000	35%	$3,500
2013	14,000	30	4,200
2014	(19,000)	30	0

[15] Before 1997, the carryback period was 3 years and the carryforward period was 15 years. Also, as an alternative, a taxpayer can elect to forgo the carryback and carry the entire loss forward for up to 20 years. This election is seldom made because carrybacks result in current refunds of taxes. In recognition of the economic damage caused by the September 11, 2001, World Trade Center attack, the Job Creation and Worker Assistance Act of 2002 extended the carryback period for NOLs created in 2001 or 2002 from two years to five years.

The $19,000 net operating loss in 2014 would be carried back to 2012 first and then to 2013. An income tax refund claim of $6,200 would be filed for the two years [$3,500 + 0.30($9,000)]. The entry to record the income tax receivable in 2014 would be as follows:

Income Tax Refund Receivable	6,200	
Income Tax Benefit from NOL Carryback		6,200

The refund will be reflected on the income statement as a reduction of the operating loss as follows:

Net operating loss before income tax benefit	$(19,000)
Income tax benefit from NOL carryback	6,200
Net loss	$(12,800)

The 2014 net operating loss reduces the 2012 taxable income to zero and the 2013 taxable income to $5,000 ($14,000 – $9,000). If another net operating loss occurs next year (in 2015), it may be carried back to the remaining $5,000 from 2013.

Net Operating Loss (NOL) Carryforward

If an operating loss exceeds income for the two preceding years, the remaining unused loss may be applied against income earned over the next 20 years as a net operating loss (NOL) carryforward. Under the provisions of Topic 740, a deferred tax asset is recognized for the potential future tax benefit from a loss carryforward. Full realization of the benefit, however, depends on the company having income equal to the carryforward in the next 20 years. As is true for other deferred tax assets, a valuation allowance is used to reduce the asset if it is more likely than not that some or all of the future benefit will not be realized.

STOP&THINK

These net operating loss carrybacks sound like a great feature of the tax law. However, what did the company have to do to take advantage of this aspect of the law?

a) Experience a tax loss
b) Experience substantial taxable income
c) Experience a financial accounting loss
d) Experience substantial financial accounting income

To illustrate the carryforward provisions, let's continue the previous example and assume that in 2015 Prairie Company incurred an operating loss of $35,000. This loss would be carried back to the years 2013 and 2014 in that order. However, the only income remaining against which operating losses can be applied is $5,000 from 2013. After applying $5,000 to the 2013 income, $30,000 is left to carry forward against future income. The tax benefit from the carryback is $1,500 ($5,000 × 0.30). Assuming the enacted tax rate for future years is 30%, the potential tax benefit from the carryforward is $9,000 ($30,000 × 0.30). The entry in 2015 to record the tax benefits would be as follows:

Income Tax Refund Receivable	1,500	
Deferred Tax Asset—NOL Carryforward	9,000	
Income Tax Benefit from NOL Carryback		1,500
Income Tax Benefit from NOL Carryforward		9,000

The deferred tax asset of $9,000 would be reported on the balance sheet as a current asset if it is expected to be realized in 2016. Any portion that is expected to be realized after 2016 would be classified as noncurrent. The $10,500 in tax benefits would be shown on the 2015 income statement as a reduction of the operating loss.

Assuming that Prairie becomes profitable in future periods, the deferred tax asset associated with the NOL carryforward would be used to offset any taxes payable resulting from profitable operations. As an example, assume that Prairie reports taxable income of $50,000 in 2016. Rather than pay $15,000 ($50,000 × 0.30) in taxes, Prairie would be allowed to offset the deferred tax asset against the liability. The journal entry made by Prairie associated with its tax liability would then be as follows:

The IRS provides a 2-year carryback and a 20-year carryforward provision that allows a company to apply a net operating loss occurring in one year against income of other years.

Income Tax Expense	15,000	
Income Taxes Payable		6,000
Deferred Tax Asset—NOL Carryforward		9,000

The journal entry recorded at the end of 2015 indicates that it is more likely than not that the carryforward benefit will be realized in full. If, however, it is more likely than not that some portion or all of the deferred tax asset will not be realized, a valuation allowance account is needed to reduce the asset to its estimated realizable value. For example, assume that Prairie Company's recent losses resulted from a declining market for its products and that the weight of available evidence indicates continuing losses in subsequent years. As a result, management believes it is more likely than not that none of the asset will be realized. In this case, the journal entry to record the carryback and carryforward would be as follows:

Income Tax Refund Receivable	1,500	
Deferred Tax Asset—NOL Carryforward	9,000	
Income Tax Benefit from NOL Carryback		1,500
Allowance to Reduce Deferred Tax Asset to Realizable Value—NOL Carryforward		9,000

As a result of this entry, the net deferred tax asset is zero—the expected realizable value. If market conditions improve and the company does have taxable income in subsequent years, the valuation allowance account would be decreased (debited) and an income tax benefit account would be credited.

FYI

Under certain conditions, a company may acquire another company's NOL carryforwards as part of an acquisition or a merger. In some situations, these unused carryforwards are a company's most valuable "asset" to another company.

Under pre-Codification *APB Opinion No. 11*, future tax benefits from an NOL carryforward could be reported as an asset only if future income were "assured beyond reasonable doubt." Although such a criterion is not easily met, there were cases in which NOL carryforward benefits were reported as an asset. In pre-Codification *Statement No. 96*, the FASB was even more restrictive and prohibited reporting income tax benefits from carryforwards as an asset under any circumstances. The adoption of the more-likely-than-not approach for deferred tax assets in pre-Codification *Statement No. 109* in 1992 led the Board to conclude that a similar approach should be used for net operating loss carryforwards. That is, NOL carryforwards are reported as assets if it is more likely than not that future income will be sufficient to allow for the realization of the tax benefit. This is a significant change in accounting for NOL carryforwards. Under *Statement No. 109*, millions of dollars of previously unreported income tax carryforwards are now included in the assets of companies. For example, IBM indicated in the notes to its 1990 financial statements that in addition to $110 million of unrecognized deferred tax assets under FASB *Statement No. 96*, it had $700 million of unrecognized tax credit carryforwards. As reported at the beginning of the chapter, IBM announced in September 1992 that it would recognize a gain of $1.9 billion as a result of the deferred tax assets it would be able to recognize because of its adoption of *Statement No. 109*.

Deferred tax asset valuation allowances were discussed in the preceding section. Four U.S. companies with deferred tax asset valuation allowances are given in Exhibit 16-5. As the exhibit indicates, a very common reason for a company to have a deferred tax asset valuation allowance is that it has state, federal, or foreign NOL carryforwards that it doesn't think it will be able to use before they expire.

EX 16-5 EXAMPLE OF DEFERRED TAX ASSET VALUATION ALLOWANCES 2009

For the Year 2009 (in millions)	Deferred Tax Assets	Valuation Allowance	Reason Given for Need for Valuation Allowance
AT&T Inc.	$18,085	$1,182	Certain state NOL carryforwards may expire unused.
Verizon	17,562	2,942	Certain state and foreign NOL carryforwards may expire unused.
ExxonMobil	17,813	1,495	No reason given
IBM	11,788	812	Certain state and foreign NOL carryforwards may expire unused.

Scheduling for Enacted Future Tax Rates

4 Schedule future tax rates, and determine the effect on deferred tax assets and liabilities.

WHY When future tax rates are expected to be different from current tax rates, proper recognition of deferred tax assets and liabilities requires careful determination of when the temporary differences will reverse and what the tax rates will be in those periods.

HOW Deferred tax assets and liabilities are recorded at the tax rates expected to be in effect in the future when the temporary differences reverse. With varying future tax rates, the scheduled timing of the reversal of temporary differences must be determined in order to match the appropriate tax rate with the deferred tax assets and liabilities.

Recall that the two major complaints about FASB *Statement No. 96* were that it did not allow for the recognition of most deferred tax assets and that it was too complicated. The complaints about nonrecognition of deferred tax assets came primarily from companies and users of financial statements who thought the inconsistent treatment of deferred tax assets and liabilities was misleading and unfair. Complaints about the complexities of pre-Codification *Statement No. 96* came primarily from preparers of financial statements. Those complaints focused on one topic: scheduling of the periods in which temporary differences are expected to reverse. Under the provisions of *Statement No. 96*, scheduling was required each year to determine which deferred tax assets could be realized because no future income could be assumed, and these assets were realizable only through the carryback and carryforward provisions of the tax law. In addition, under the provisions of *Statement No. 96*, scheduling was necessary to determine how deferred tax assets and liabilities should be classified based on the expected period of their reversal.

In 1992, the FASB eliminated much of the need for scheduling through the "more-likely-than-not" criterion for future income and because deferred tax assets and liabilities are classified according to the classification of the underlying items instead of according to the expected reversal period. However, scheduling is still required in a limited number of cases. One such case arises when differences in enacted future tax rates make it necessary to schedule the timing of a reversal in order to match that reversal with the tax rate expected to be in effect when it occurs.

Consider again the Hsieh Company example introduced on page 16-17. When that example was covered before, it was assumed that the enacted income tax rate was 40% for all periods. Assume now that the enacted tax rates are as follows: 2013, 40%; 2014, 35%; 2015, 30%; and 2016, 25%. As of December 31, 2013, using the 40% rate to value the deferred tax asset stemming from the future deductible amount of $18,000 and the deferred tax liability resulting from the future taxable amount of $15,000 would be misleading because it is known that the tax rate will not be 40% when those temporary differences reverse. A more accurate valuation can be obtained by applying tax rates expected to be in effect when the differences reverse, as follows:

	Enacted Tax Rate	Deductible Amount	Asset Valuation	Taxable Amount	Liability Valuation
2014	35%	$ 6,000	$2,100	$ 0	$ 0
2015	30	6,000	1,800	0	0
2016	25	6,000	1,500	15,000	3,750
Total		$18,000	$5,400	$15,000	$3,750

The noncurrent deferred tax liability is $3,750 ($15,000 × 0.25), which is the expected tax to be paid on the taxable amount when it is taxed in 2016. The current deferred tax asset is $2,100 ($6,000 × 0.35), and the noncurrent deferred tax asset is $3,300 [($6,000 × 0.30) + ($6,000 × 0.25)]. The journal entry to record the deferred portion of income tax expense for 2013 would be as follows:

Deferred Tax Asset—Current	2,100	
Deferred Tax Asset—Noncurrent	3,300	
Income Tax Benefit (a subtraction from income tax expense)		1,650
Deferred Tax Liability—Noncurrent		3,750

In this example, it was assumed that future income is more likely than not to be sufficient to allow for full deductibility of the $6,000 deductible amount each year. Accordingly, the tax benefit is computed as the deductible amount times the tax rate for that year. However, if the future income was not deemed sufficient to allow for offset of the deductible amounts and if the deferred tax asset could be realized only through the carryback provision of the tax law, the deferred tax asset would be valued using the tax rate in the carryback year. For example, if future income is unlikely but 2013 taxable income exceeds $18,000, then the deductible amounts will be realized only through carryback and offset against 2013 taxable income. If this is the case, the deferred tax asset would be valued using the tax rate in effect for 2013, the carryback year.

Financial Statement Presentation and Disclosure

5 **Determine appropriate financial statement presentation and disclosure associated with deferred tax assets and liabilities.**

WHY **Accounting for income taxes is a complex area with current and deferred tax effects as well as state, federal, and international income tax obligations. Significant supplemental disclosure is necessary to allow a financial statement user to understand the impact of income taxes on a company's financial position and performance.**

HOW **Deferred tax assets and liabilities are reported on the balance sheet as either current or noncurrent, based on the classification of the underlying asset or obligation. Additional disclosure is required relating to the tax expense for the period, deferred tax expense, benefits associated with tax loss carryforwards, the effect of changes in tax rates, and adjustments associated with the valuation allowance account.**

On classified balance sheets, deferred tax assets and liabilities must be reported as either current or noncurrent. As discussed previously, FASB ASC Topic 740 provides for some offsetting of deferred assets and liabilities. For offsetting to be acceptable, the asset and liability must both be current or both be noncurrent. A current asset cannot be offset against a noncurrent liability. Most companies are subject to state and municipal income taxes as well as federal income taxes. If a business enterprise pays income taxes in more than one tax jurisdiction, no offsetting is permitted across jurisdictions.

The income statement must show, either in the body of the statement or in a note, the following selected components of income taxes related to continuing operations:[16]

1. Current tax expense or benefit
2. Deferred tax expense or benefit
3. Investment tax credits
4. Government grants recognized as tax reductions
5. Benefits of operating loss carryforwards
6. Adjustments of a deferred tax liability or asset for enacted changes in tax laws or rates or a change in the tax status of an enterprise
7. Adjustments in the beginning-of-the-year valuation allowance because of a change in circumstances

The kind of disclosure typically made for income taxes is illustrated by an excerpt from the notes to the 2009 financial statements of ExxonMobil, presented in Exhibit 16-6.

The current portion of income tax expense (with an $838 million tax benefit for U.S. federal and $15.830 billion tax expense for non-U.S. income taxes in the ExxonMobil example) can be viewed as the one place in the financial statements where the financial accounting records and the tax records coincide. Roughly speaking, the $838 million tax benefit that ExxonMobil reports as the consolidated current portion of U.S. federal income

[16] FASB ASC paragraph 740-10-50-9.

EX 16-6 EXXONMOBIL—DISCLOSURE FOR PROVISION FOR INCOME TAXES

18. Income, Sales-Based and Other Taxes

	2009			2008			2007		
(Millions of dollars)	**U.S.**	**Non-U.S.**	**Total**	**U.S.**	**Non-U.S.**	**Total**	**U.S.**	**Non-U.S.**	**Total**
Income taxes									
Federal and non-U.S.									
Current	$ (838)	$15,830	$14,992	$ 3,005	$ 31,377	$ 34,382	$ 4,666	$24,329	$ 28,995
Deferred—net	650	(665)	(15)	168	1,289	1,457	(439)	415	(24)
U.S. tax on non-U.S. operations	32	—	32	230	—	230	263	—	263
Total federal and non-U.S.	(156)	15,165	15,009	3,403	32,666	36,069	4,490	24,744	29,234
State	110	—	110	461	—	461	630	—	630
Total income taxes	(46)	15,165	15,119	3,864	32,666	36,530	5,120	24,744	29,864
Sales-based taxes	6,271	19,665	25,936	6,646	27,862	34,508	7,154	24,574	31,728
All other taxes and duties									
Other taxes and duties	581	34,238	34,819	1,663	40,056	41,719	1,008	39,945	40,953
Included in production and manufacturing expenses	699	1,318	2,017	915	1,720	2,635	825	1,445	2,270
Included in SG&A expenses	197	538	735	209	660	869	215	653	868
Total other taxes and duties	1,477	36,094	37,571	2,787	42,436	45,223	2,048	42,043	44,091
Total	$7,702	$70,924	$78,626	$13,297	$102,964	$116,261	$14,322	$91,361	$105,683

tax for 2009 is the same number that would appear on a hypothetical ExxonMobil 2009 consolidated tax return for the U.S. federal jurisdiction under the heading of "Total Tax Refund" for the year. A careful look at Exhibit 16-6 reveals that this isn't all of the tax ExxonMobil paid during the year. First, additional income taxes of $32 million (extra income tax that must be paid to the U.S. government for income earned in a foreign country) and $110 million (state income taxes) were also payable for 2009. Also, note that because of the existence of deferred taxes, the amount of reported income tax expense (related to U.S. federal income taxes) is $650 million more than the amount of income tax actually owed for the year. In addition, to highlight the large taxes associated with its industry, ExxonMobil reports that in 2009 it owed a total of $63.507 billion ($25.936 + $37.571) worldwide for sales-based taxes, other taxes, and duties.

As another example of disclosure, see Exhibit 16-7, which is a portion of IBM's 2009 financial statement note related to income taxes. IBM reported in the notes to its 2009 financial statements that it had a valuation allowance for its deferred tax assets of $812 million on December 31, 2009. The note also indicates that the valuation allowance is principally associated with foreign and state loss carryforwards and state credit carryforwards that IBM believes it is more likely than not that it won't be able to use.

Firms also disclose the specific accounting differences between the financial statements and the tax return that give rise to deferred tax assets and deferred tax liabilities. The most common source of deferred tax items is depreciation. As an illustration, IBM provides significant disclosure as to the specific makeup of its deferred tax assets and liabilities. This disclosure is reproduced in Exhibit 16-7. Overall, as of December 31, 2009, IBM had $10.976 billion in deferred tax assets (net of a $812 million valuation allowance) and $5.578 billion in deferred tax liabilities. In contrast, for ExxonMobil, the total deferred tax

EX 16-7 IBM—DISCLOSURE FOR DEFERRED TAX ASSETS AND LIABILITIES

The significant components of deferred tax assets and liabilities that are recorded in the Consolidated Statement of Financial Position were as follows:

Deferred Tax Assets

($ in millions) **At December 31:**	**2009**	**2008**
Retirement benefits	$ 3,921	$ 5,215
Share-based and other compensation	1,853	2,579
Domestic tax loss/credit carryforwards	859	862
Deferred income	847	739
Foreign tax loss/credit carryforwards	680	642
Bad debt, inventory and warranty reserves	605	561
Capitalized research and development	539	795
Depreciation	485	388
Other	1,999	1,863
Gross deferred tax assets	11,788	13,644
Less: valuation allowance	812	720
Net deferred tax assets	$10,976	$12,924

Deferred Tax Liabilities

($ in millions) **At December 31:**	**2009**	**2008**
Leases	$2,129	$1,913
Depreciation	1,138	941
Goodwill and intangible assets	639	552
Software development costs	409	449
Retirement benefits	389	104
Other	874	697
Gross deferred tax liabilities	$5,578	$4,656

The valuation allowance at December 31, 2009, principally applies to certain foreign, state and local loss carryforwards that, in the opinion of management, are more likely than not to expire unutilized. However, to the extent that tax benefits related to these carryforwards are realized in the future, the reduction in the valuation allowance will reduce income tax expense. The year-to-year change in the allowance balance was an increase of $92 million.

liability as of December 31, 2009 (not shown in Exhibit 16-6), was $34.033 billion; of this amount, 59.4%, or $20.210 billion, arose from accelerated tax depreciation.

In addition to the disclosures already described, the reported amount of income tax expense related to continuing operations must be reconciled with the amount of income tax expense that would result from applying federal tax rates to pretax financial income from continuing operations. This reconciliation provides information to readers of the financial statements regarding how the entity has been affected by special provisions of the tax code such as permanent differences, tax credits, and so forth. To illustrate, Exhibit 16-8 is the income tax rate reconciliation for Berkshire Hathaway for 2009. The company begins by reporting that its 2009 income tax expense would have been $4,043 million ($11,552 million × 0.35) if the federal tax rate of 35.0% had been applied to all of its earnings before income taxes. Berkshire Hathaway's effective tax rate for the year of 30.6% is computed by dividing reported income tax expense by earnings before income taxes ($3,538 million/$11,552 million). By looking at Exhibit 16-8, you can see that this difference between the 35.0% statutory rate and the 30.6% effective rate is *not* caused by temporary differences (except for the tax rate changes affecting these temporary differences as noted in the footnote to the exhibit). As illustrated in this chapter, temporary differences affect whether income tax is payable this year but do not affect whether the income tax expense is accrued this year. The items included in Exhibit 16-8 reflect permanent differences between the tax that Berkshire Hathaway must pay and the tax the company would pay if all income were taxed at the 35.0% rate. For example, Berkshire Hathaway owed an extra $81 million in income taxes for the year because state income taxes must be paid on top of the 35.0% federal income tax. In addition, lower income tax rates in foreign countries resulted in Berkshire Hathaway's saving $92 million in income tax for the year. Offsetting these extra taxes is the fact that some of Berkshire Hathaway's 2009 income will never be taxed. Berkshire Hathaway saved $33 million in income taxes because some of its interest income (on municipal securities) is not taxable. Also, dividends paid by one corporation to another are partially excluded from tax; this tax provision yielded a permanent $479 million tax savings to Berkshire Hathaway in 2009.

STOP&THINK

What is the rationale behind excluding from a corporation's taxable income dividends received from another corporation?

a) The dividend exclusion increases the progressive nature of income tax rates.
b) The dividend exclusion is necessary to avoid the recognition of unrealizable deferred tax assets.
c) Without the exclusion, corporate income would be subject to triple taxation.
d) It is futile to search for any underlying rationale in income tax rules.

EX 16-8 BERKSHIRE HATHAWAY—RECONCILIATION OF EFFECTIVE TAX RATE TO FEDERAL STATUTORY RATE

Charges for income taxes are reconciled to hypothetical amounts computed at the U.S. federal statutory rate in the table shown below (in millions).

	2009	2008	2007
Earnings before income taxes	$11,552	$7,574	$20,161
Hypothetical amounts applicable to above computed at the federal statutory rate	$ 4,043	$2,651	$ 7,056
Tax-exempt interest income	(33)	(88)	(33)
Dividends received deduction	(479)	(415)	(306)
State income taxes, less federal income tax benefit	81	162	152
Foreign tax rate differences	(92)	(59)	(36)
Effect of income tax rate changes on deferred income taxes*	—	—	(90)
Non-taxable exchange of investment	—	(154)	—
Other differences, net	18	(119)	(149)
Total income taxes	$ 3,538	$1,978	$ 6,594

** Relates to adjustments made to deferred income tax assets and liabilities in 2007 upon the enactment of reductions to corporate income tax rates in the United Kingdom and Germany.*

Deferred Taxes and the Statement of Cash Flows

6 Comply with income tax disclosure requirements associated with the statement of cash flows.

WHY **The FASB decided that all cash flows associated with income statement expenses were to be reported in the statement of cash flows as operating activities. Because many financial statement users view income taxes as a nonoperating item, it is useful to these users to have separate disclosure of the amount of cash paid for income taxes.**

HOW **The amount of cash paid for income taxes must be disclosed in the financial statements. With the direct method, the amount of cash paid for income taxes is disclosed in the body of the statement of cash flows. With the indirect method, disclosure of cash paid for income taxes is typically made in the notes to the financial statements.**

FASB ASC Topic 230 (Statement of Cash Flows) requires separate disclosure of the amount of cash paid for income taxes during a period. This separate disclosure is required for just two items: cash paid for income taxes and cash paid for interest. Financial statements are used to assess the amount and timing of future cash flows, and in the case of interest and income taxes, the FASB argued that this specific cash flow information should be readily available and easily disclosed by most firms.[17] As an example, **Disney** discloses in its financial statements that for the year ended October 3, 2009, it reported income tax expense of \$2,049 million (on the income statement) and cash paid during the year for income taxes of \$1,609 million (on the statement of cash flows).

Income taxes affect the Operating Activities section of the statement of cash flows.[18] When the direct method is used, cash paid for income taxes is shown as a separate line item. When the indirect method is used, the treatment of income taxes is a bit more complicated. Adjustments to convert net income into cash from operations are needed for changes in income taxes payable and receivable accounts and for changes in deferred tax asset and liability accounts. In addition, supplemental disclosure of the amount of cash paid for income taxes is required.

As an illustration of how income taxes are handled in the statement of cash flows, consider the following information for Collazo Company for 2013:

Revenue (all cash)		\$30,000
Income tax expense:		
Current	\$10,300	
Deferred	1,700	12,000
Net income		\$18,000

In addition, Collazo had the balance sheet amounts shown on page 16-33 at the beginning and end of the year.

[17] FASB ASC paragraph 230-10-50-2.

[18] The FASB considered allocating income taxes paid among the Operating, Investing, and Financing Activities sections of the statement of cash flows. For example, any income tax effects from the disposal of equipment could be disclosed in the Investing Activities section. However, it was concluded that this allocation would be unnecessarily complex, with the cost of doing it outweighing the benefit. See pre-Codification FASB *Statement No. 95*, par. 92.

	December 31, 2013	December 31, 2012
Income tax refund receivable	$2,000	$ 0
Income taxes payable	0	1,000
Deferred tax liability	9,700	8,000

Using the format developed in Chapter 5, we will analyze the income statement and convert the accrual basis number to the cash basis, as demonstrated in the following table:

Income Statement		Adjustments	Statement of Cash Flows	
Revenue (all cash)	$ 30,000	—	$ 30,000	Cash collected from customers
Income tax expense—current	(10,300)	− $2,000—Increase in tax receivable	(13,300)	Cash paid for taxes
Income tax expense—deferred	(1,700)	− 1,000—Decrease in taxes payable + 1,700—Increase in deferred tax liability	0	
Net income	$ 18,000	− $1,300—Total adjustments	$ 16,700	Cash flow from operations

Using the resulting information, the Operating Activities section of Collazo's statement of cash flows is as follows if the direct method is used:

Cash collected from customers	$ 30,000
Income taxes paid	(13,300)
Cash provided by operating activities	$ 16,700

If the indirect method is used, the Operating Activities section is as follows:

Net income	$18,000
(Increase) decrease in income tax refund receivable	(2,000)
Increase (decrease) in income taxes payable	(1,000)
Increase (decrease) in deferred tax liability	1,700
Cash provided by operating activities	$16,700

In addition, if the indirect method is used, the amount of cash paid for income taxes, $13,300, must be separately disclosed either in the statement of cash flows or in the notes to the financial statements.

International Accounting for Deferred Taxes

7 **Describe how, with respect to deferred income taxes, international accounting standards have converged toward the U.S. treatment.**

WHY **Accounting for income taxes is an area where there have historically been large differences in standards around the world. In this particular area, the U.S. approach has gradually become the worldwide standard.**

HOW **Historically, companies around the world have used the no-deferral, the partial recognition, and the comprehensive recognition approaches to deferred tax accounting. Since the substantial revision of *IAS 12* in 1996, deferred tax accounting around the world has converged toward the comprehensive recognition approach employed in the United States.**

In the past, accounting standards around the world have differed substantially in the area of deferred taxes. However, over the past 15 years, the U.S. approach to deferred tax accounting has become used almost everywhere. This section discusses the different approaches that have been used around the world and recent developments in the international harmonization of deferred tax accounting.

ifrs

The approach to deferred tax accounting used in the United States (and discussed in this chapter) is sometimes called the *comprehensive recognition approach* because it requires recognition of all temporary differences between financial accounting income and taxable income. At the other extreme, the *no-deferral approach* recognizes none of the differences. These two approaches are described in this section.

No-Deferral Approach

The simplest approach to accounting for differences between financial accounting and taxable income is just to ignore the differences and report income tax expense equal to the amount of tax payable for the year. Historically, this no-deferral approach was quite common around the world. In countries where there is a close correspondence between financial accounting standards and tax rules, the no-deferral approach yields financial statement numbers that are not that much different from what would be generated using the full-blown deferred tax accounting practices used in the United States. The no-deferral approach has become almost extinct now (except in smaller, privately held companies) as companies seek to converge to the prevailing international practice; the no-deferral approach has been formally frowned upon since the original issuance of *IAS 12* in 1979.

Comprehensive Recognition Approach

The IASB has embraced the comprehensive recognition approach to deferred tax accounting that underlies FASB ASC Topic 740 in the United States. The original version of *IAS 12* required that deferred taxes be included in the computation of income tax expense and that deferred taxes be reported on the balance sheet, but it left open the method used to compute the deferred taxes. In 1996, the IASC (predecessor to the IASB) revised *IAS 12*; the accounting required in the revised version is very similar to the deferred tax accounting practices that have been described throughout this chapter. The good news for U.S. accountants and accounting students is that the world appears to have come around to the U.S. way of accounting for deferred taxes, so we don't have to learn very much in order to understand international accounting for deferred taxes.

Partial Recognition Approach

Historically, the United Kingdom employed an innovative technique for accounting for deferred taxes that results in a deferred tax liability being recorded only to the extent that the deferred taxes are actually expected to be paid in the future. To use the U.K. terminology, deferred income taxes are recognized only if they are expected to "crystallise." An equivalent concept in the United States might be "realized." For example, if a company is growing and continually purchasing new assets, as deferred taxes on the older assets reverse, they will be offset by taxes being deferred on the new assets. In such cases, if the firm is assumed to be a going concern, the tax deferral may continue indefinitely as new assets replace old ones. In the United Kingdom, it is said that this type of deferred tax liability will not crystallise, and so historically it was not recognized. Only if it is expected that deferrals on new assets will not offset older assets will crystallisation occur—and then a deferred tax liability would be recognized. The reasoning behind the U.K. approach to deferred tax liabilities is actually quite interesting: If a liability is deferred indefinitely, the present value of that liability is zero. This concept highlights a common criticism of U.S. deferred tax accounting—no accounting recognition is given to the fact that by deferring income tax payments, firms are decreasing the present value of their tax obligation. Despite its conceptual attractiveness, the U.K. partial recognition approach was dropped in the interest of international harmonization. In its description of its new standard (*FRS 19*), the Accounting Standards Board (ASB) of the United Kingdom gives this lukewarm evaluation of the comprehensive recognition approach:

> In recent years, the partial provision method of accounting for deferred tax . . . has lost favour internationally, primarily because it is subjective (relying heavily on management expectations about future events) and inconsistent with other areas of accounting. Other major standard-setters and *IAS 12* (revised 1996) now require deferred tax to be provided for in full. Whilst the ASB could see the merits of the partial provision method, it accepted some of the arguments against it and concluded that deferred tax was not an area where a good case could be made for taking a stand against the direction of international opinion.[19]

In summary, both the no-deferral and partial recognition approaches have been used around the world in the past, but *IAS 12* now requires the comprehensive recognition approach that is employed in the United States. It appears that the international differences in accounting for deferred income taxes will be relatively small in future years.

SOLUTIONS TO OPENING SCENARIO QUESTIONS

1. Financial statement users and preparers complained about pre-Codification *Statement No. 96* on both practical and conceptual grounds. These complaints were so heated that the FASB's credibility was damaged. For a time, there were suggestions that, because of its "mishandling" of the accounting for deferred taxes, the FASB should be replaced with a different standard setter.
2. Pre-Codification *Statement No. 96* required that deferred tax liabilities be valued using current income tax rates instead of the tax rates that existed when the deferred tax liability was first recognized. Because the Tax Reform Act of 1986 had lowered corporate income tax rates, *Statement No. 96* resulted in recognition of a reduction in the recorded amount of deferred tax liabilities and a corresponding gain.
3. Under FASB Pre-Codification *Statement No. 96*, deferred tax assets were generally not recognized; in fact, this was one of the complaints about *Statement No. 96*. With the adoption of pre-Codification FASB *Statement No. 109*, these deferred tax assets were recognized on the balance sheet along with the recognition of a corresponding gain.

SOLUTIONS TO STOP & THINK

1. (Page 16-4) The correct answer is A. An obvious third set of books for a well-run company, arguably the most important, is the managerial accounting system. Of course, the managerial records would be tailored to the needs of each company. Different aspects of the managerial records would emphasize CONTROL, EVALUATION, and PLANNING. A small business would combine the functions of all three sets of books—financial, tax, and managerial—into one set of reports. As a company's information needs become more sophisticated, there is increased divergence among these three sets of books.
2. (Page 16-8) The correct answer is C. Deferred tax assets and deferred tax liabilities result from different types of transactions. For example, a deferred tax asset can result from warranties, while a deferred tax liability can result from

[19] **http://www.asb.org.uk.** *FRS 19*, "Deferred Tax," background to FRS requirements.

accelerated depreciation of a depreciable asset. The differences between GAAP and tax law provide numerous instances that can result in either deferred tax assets or deferred tax liabilities.

3. (Page 16-12) The correct answer is D. As will be pointed out in an upcoming section of the text, deferred tax assets and deferred tax liabilities are to be measured using tax rates expected to be applicable in the period of the reversal. Thus, if rates in the future are expected to be 30%, then the deferred amount would be multiplied by 30% instead of 40%.

4. (Page 16-18) The correct answer is C. One of the key purposes of financial statements, according to the Conceptual Framework, is to aid investors and creditors in assessing the amounts, timing, and uncertainty of future cash flows. By reporting to financial statement users the existence of additional future cash flows (deferred tax liabilities) and additional future cash savings (deferred tax assets), deferred tax accounting helps users assess future cash flows.

5. (Page 16-24) The correct answer is A. Although carrybacks and carryforwards work to the benefit of the company in that it is able to either receive a refund of taxes previously paid or to reduce the amount of taxes to be paid in the future, one must remember that the company had to report a net operating loss in order to take advantage of this feature of the tax law. The carryback and carryforward provisions ease the pain of an operating loss.

6. (Page 16-31) The correct answer is C. Dividends paid to shareholders are already double taxed. The corporation must pay tax on the income, leaving less income to pay to shareholders as dividends. Then the shareholders must pay income tax when they receive the dividends. When a corporation is a shareholder and receives dividends, then that dividend income would be taxed for a third time without the special tax provision excluding the dividends from income taxation for the receiving corporation.

SOLUTION TO USING THE FASB'S CODIFICATION

You should have found Topic 740 in the "Expenses" collection of topics. And right there in the topic table of contents is Subtopic 740-20 (Income Taxes—Intraperiod Tax Allocation). A quick look at the "Overview and Background" section reveals the following in FASB ASC paragraph 740-20-05-2: "This Subtopic addresses the process of intraperiod tax allocation that allocates total income tax expense or benefit of an entity for a period to different components of comprehensive income and shareholders' equity. This includes allocating income tax expense or benefit for the year to: (a) continuing operations, (b) discontinued operations, (c) extraordinary items, (d) other comprehensive income, and (e) items charged or credited directly to shareholders' equity." Ahh, this makes sense. The IRS doesn't care whether you classify a certain income-generating event as an extraordinary item or a discontinued operation—you still have to pay tax on any income generated. Intraperiod tax allocation is the process of assigning your total tax bill to the different categories of income. So, when your brother-in-law comes back in the room, try to be gracious in victory.

REVIEW CHAPTER 16

LEARNING OBJECTIVES

1 Understand the concept of deferred taxes and the distinction between permanent and temporary differences.

Deferred taxes result from the different objectives being used and applied for computing taxable income and income for financial reporting purposes. Because of differences between the tax code and GAAP, the accounting treatment for certain issues will differ. These differences can result in temporary timing differences that will eventually reverse or permanent differences that will not reverse. Temporary timing differences that result in taxable income in the future are termed *taxable temporary differences* and result in deferred tax liabilities. Those differences that result in expected deductible amounts in the future are termed *deductible temporary differences* and result in deferred tax assets.

2 Compute the amount of deferred tax liabilities and assets including the use of a valuation allowance and the uncertainty of tax positions.

Computing the amount of deferred tax assets and liabilities involves four steps: (1) identify the types and amounts of temporary timing differences, (2) compute the deferred tax liability associated with taxable temporary differences using current and future tax rates, (3) compute the amount of deferred tax asset associated with deductible temporary differences using current and future tax rates, and (4) reduce the amount of deferred tax asset if it is more likely than not that some or all of the asset may not be realized, using a valuation allowance account. The claiming of uncertain tax deductions may require the recognition of an unrecognized tax benefit liability to the extent that the claimed deduction is in excess of the deduction that is more likely than not to be sustained upon taxing authority review.

3 Explain the provisions of tax loss carrybacks and carryforwards, and be able to account for these provisions.

Tax law requires corporations to pay taxes if they report taxable income. If a business reports a loss, the tax code allows that business to offset the loss against income in other years. The business is allowed to carry back its net operating losses up to 2 years to obtain a refund of taxes previously paid or to carry forward an operating loss up to 20 years in order to reduce the tax liability associated with future periods. A carryforward results in a deferred tax asset and may require the use of a valuation allowance account if it is more likely than not that the deferred asset may not be realized.

4 Schedule future tax rates, and determine the effect on deferred tax assets and liabilities.

Deferred tax assets and liabilities are recorded at the tax rates expected to be in effect in the periods of reversal. Thus, if Congress enacts rate changes or the corporation's taxable income level results in different expected future tax rates, these differing rates must be reflected in the valuation of deferred tax assets and liabilities.

5 Determine appropriate financial statement presentation and disclosure associated with deferred tax assets and liabilities.

Deferred tax assets and liabilities are disclosed on the balance sheet as either current or noncurrent, based on the classification of the underlying asset or obligation. Additional disclosure is required relating to the tax expense (or benefit) for the period, deferred tax expense (or benefit), benefits associated with tax loss carryforwards, the effect of changes in tax rates, and adjustments associated with the valuation allowance account.

6 Comply with income tax disclosure requirements associated with the statement of cash flows.

The amount of cash paid for income taxes must be disclosed using either the direct or indirect methods. With the direct method, the amount of cash paid for income taxes would be disclosed directly on the statement of cash flows. Under the indirect method, adjustments are made to net income for changes in receivable and payable balances associated with current and deferred tax assets and liabilities. Thus, with this method, the actual amount paid for taxes may not be disclosed in the body of the statement of cash flows. If this is the case, disclosure of cash paid for taxes is required in the notes to the financial statements or at the bottom of the statement of cash flows.

7 Describe how, with respect to deferred income taxes, international accounting standards have converged toward the U.S. treatment.

Historically, companies around the world have used the no-deferral, the partial recognition, and the comprehensive recognition approaches to deferred tax accounting. With the revision of *IAS 12* in 1996, it now appears that deferred tax accounting around the world is converging toward the comprehensive recognition approach employed in the United States.

FASB-IASB CODIFICATION SUMMARY

ifrs

Topic	FASB Accounting Standards Codification	Original FASB Standard	Corresponding IASB Standard	Differences between U.S. GAAP and IFRS
Use of currently enacted tax rates	*Section 740-10-10 par. 3*	*SFAS No. 109 par. 18*	*IAS 12 par. 46*	Under U.S. GAAP, currently enacted tax rates for future years are used in valuing deferred tax assets and liabilities. Under IFRS, tax rates that have been "substantively enacted" are also used. Substantively enacted tax rates are future tax rates that have been announced by the government but that have not yet been formally enacted into law.
Current/noncurrent classification of deferred tax assets and liabilities	*Section 740-10-45 par. 4*	*SFAS No. 109 par. 41*	*IAS 1 par. 56*	Under U.S. GAAP, deferred tax assets and liabilities are classified current or noncurrent based on the classification of the associated asset or liability. Under IFRS, all deferred tax items are classified as noncurrent.
Recognition of deferred tax assets	*Section 740-10-30 par. 5e*	*SFAS No. 109 par. 17e*	*IAS 12 par. 24*	Under U.S. GAAP, deferred tax assets are recognized if it is "more likely than not" (50%+ probability) that the future tax benefits will be realized. Under IFRS, the probability threshold is "probable," which is generally seen to be higher than "more likely than not."
Uncertain tax positions	*Topic 740*	*FASB FIN No. 48*	*No specific accounting standard in IAS*	Under IFRS, there is no standard regarding the recognition of a tax liability related to an uncertain tax position.
Cash paid for income taxes	*Section 230-10-50 par. 2*	*SFAS No. 95 par. 121*	*IFRS 7 par. 35*	Both U.S. GAAP and IFRS require separate disclosure of the amount of cash paid for income taxes. Under IFRS, this amount may be allocated among operating, investing, and financing activities.

KEY TERMS

Asset and liability method of interperiod tax allocation 16-10
Deductible temporary differences 16-8
Effective tax rate 16-31
Financial income 16-3
Interperiod tax allocation 16-10
Net operating loss (NOL) carryback 16-23
Net operating loss (NOL) carryforward 16-24
Permanent differences 16-7
Taxable income 16-3
Taxable temporary differences 16-8
Temporary differences 16-7
Uncertain tax position 16-20
Valuation allowance 16-17

QUESTIONS

1. Accounting methods used by a company to determine income for financial reporting purposes frequently differ from those used to determine taxable income. What is the justification for these differences?
2. Distinguish between a nondeductible expense and a temporary difference that results in a taxable income greater than pretax financial income reported in the income statement.
3. Distinguish between taxable temporary differences and deductible temporary differences, and give at least two examples of each type.
4. One possibility for reporting income tax expense in the income statement for a given year is to merely report the amount of income tax payable in that year. What is wrong with this approach?
5. What are the major advantages of the asset and liability method?
6. What is a drawback of the asset and liability method?
7. Describe how a change in enacted future tax rates is accounted for under the asset and liability method.
8. When is a valuation allowance necessary?
9. How does the FASB define the probability term "more likely than not" in Topic 740?
10. What are the sources of income through which the tax benefit of a deferred tax asset can be realized?
11. In applying the net operating loss carryback and carryforward provisions, what order of application is followed for federal tax purposes?
12. How is the classification of assets (current or noncurrent) arising from NOL carryforwards determined under FASB ASC Topic 740?
13. Under what conditions would scheduling the temporary difference reversals be required under Topic 740?
14. How would you define "uncertain" tax position?
15. What are the two steps that are required in determining the amount of tax benefit to be recognized in association with an uncertain tax position?
16. "In practice, the provisions for accounting for uncertain tax positions are relatively easy to apply." Do you agree or disagree? Explain.
17. What was the most significant change in accounting for income tax carryforwards between pre-Codification *Statement No. 96* and pre-Codification *Statement No. 109*? (*Note:* Pre-Codification *Statement No. 109* is the source for most of the existing provisions in FASB ASC Topic 740.)
18. How do changes in the balances of deferred income taxes affect the amount of cash paid for income taxes?
19. If a company experiences a current operating loss, it may carry the loss backward and forward. What impact do these carrybacks and carryforwards have on the reported operating loss? on the statement of cash flows?
20. What rules govern the netting of deferred tax assets and deferred tax liabilities?
21. In the past, why was accounting for income taxes not as significant an issue in some foreign countries as it is in the United States?
22. In 1996, the IASB revised *IAS 12*. Did that revision make the international standard for deferred tax accounting more or less similar to the U.S. standard?
23. Briefly describe the partial recognition approach to accounting for deferred income taxes.

PRACTICE EXERCISES

Practice 16-1
LO1

Simple Deferred Tax Liability

The company had sales for the year of $100,000. Of these sales, only $70,000 was collected in cash. The other $30,000 is expected to be collected in cash next year. For this business, the tax rules stipulate that income is not taxed until it is collected in cash. The only expense is income tax expense, and the tax rate is 35% this year and in all future years. Make all journal entries necessary to record income tax expense for the year.

Practice 16-2
LO1

Simple Deferred Tax Asset
The company had sales for the year of $200,000. Expenses (except for income taxes) for the year totaled $170,000. Of this $170,000 in expenses, $12,000 is bad debt expense. The tax rules applicable to this company stipulate that bad debts are not tax deductible until the accounts are actually written off. None of the accounts were written off this year but are expected to be written off next year or the following year. The tax rate is 30% this year and in all future years. Make all journal entries necessary to record income tax expense for the year. Assume that the company has been profitable and is expected to be profitable in the future.

Practice 16-3
LO1

Permanent and Temporary Differences
The company reported pretax financial income in its income statement of $50,000. Among the items included in the computation of pretax financial income were the following:

Interest revenue from municipal bonds	$10,000
Nondeductible expenses	17,000
Warranty expenses (not deductible until actually provided; none provided this year)	8,000

The income tax rate is 30%. Compute the following: (1) financial income subject to tax, (2) taxable income, (3) income tax expense, and (4) net income.

Practice 16-4
LO2

Deferred Tax Liability
On January 1, the company purchased investment securities for $1,000. The securities are classified as trading. By December 31, the securities had a fair value of $1,800 but had not yet been sold. Excluding the trading securities, income before taxes for the year was $10,000. Assume that there are no other book-tax differences. The income tax rate is 40% for the current year and all future years. Prepare the journal entry or entries necessary to record income tax expense for the year.

Practice 16-5
LO2

Deferred Tax Liability
On January 1, 2013, the company purchased a piece of equipment for $75,000. The equipment has a 5-year useful life and $0 residual value. The company uses straight-line depreciation for financial accounting purposes. Assume that the depreciation deduction for income tax purposes is as follows: 2013 = $25,000; 2014 = $20,000; 2015 = $15,000; 2016 = $10,000; and 2017 = $5,000. Assume that revenue in each year 2013–2017 is $50,000, that the revenue is the same for both tax and financial reporting purposes, and that the only expenses are depreciation and income taxes. The income tax rate is 40% in all years. Prepare the journal entry or entries to record income tax expense in each year 2013–2017.

Practice 16-6
LO2

Variable Future Tax Rates
Refer to Practice 16-4. Assume that the income tax rate is 40% for the current year but that the enacted tax rate for all future years is 46%. Prepare the journal entry or entries necessary to record income tax expense for the year.

Practice 16-7
LO2

Change in Enacted Tax Rates
Refer to Practice 16-5. Assume that on January 1, 2015, Congress changes the enacted tax rate. Make the journal entry necessary to record this tax rate change on January 1, 2015, assuming that (1) the new tax rate is 30% and (2) the new tax rate is 43%.

Practice 16-8
LO2

Deferred Tax Asset
On January 1, the company purchased investment securities for $1,000. The securities are classified as trading. By December 31, the securities had a fair value of $100 but

had not yet been sold. Excluding the trading securities, income before taxes for the year was $5,000. Assume that there are no other book-tax differences. The income tax rate is 45% for the current year and all future years. Assume that the company has been profitable in past years and is more likely than not to be profitable in future years. Prepare the journal entry or entries necessary to record income tax expense for the year.

Practice 16-9

LO2

Deferred Tax Asset

The company started business on January 1 and had revenues of $60,000 for the year. In addition to income tax expense, the company's only other expenses are as follows:

- *Bad debt expense of $10,000.* Tax rules do not allow any deduction until the bad debts are actually written off. During the year, bad debts totaling $2,000 were written off.
- *Postretirement health care benefit expense of $15,000.* Tax rules do not allow any deduction until the actual retiree health care expenditures are made. No expenditures were made during the year.

The income tax rate is 41% for the current year and all future years. Assume that the company is more likely than not to be profitable in future years. Prepare the journal entry or entries necessary to record income tax expense for the year.

Practice 16-10

LO2

Deferred Tax Liabilities and Assets

On January 1, the company purchased investment securities for $2,000. The securities are classified as trading. By December 31, the securities had a fair value of $4,200 but had not yet been sold. The company also recognized a $7,000 restructuring charge during the year. The restructuring charge is composed of an impairment write-down on a manufacturing facility. Tax rules do not allow a deduction for the write-down unless the facility is actually sold; the facility was not sold by the end of the year. Excluding the trading securities and the restructuring charge, income before taxes for the year was $25,000. Assume that there are no other book-tax differences. The income tax rate is 40% for the current year and all future years. Prepare the journal entry or entries necessary to record income tax expense for the year. State any assumptions you must make.

Practice 16-11

LO2

Deferred Tax Liabilities and Assets

On January 1, the company purchased investment securities for $1,000. The securities are classified as trading. By December 31, the securities had a fair value of $700 but had not yet been sold. On January 1, the company also purchased a piece of equipment for $10,000. The equipment has a 4-year useful life and $0 residual value. The company uses straight-line depreciation for financial accounting purposes. Assume that the depreciation deduction for income tax purposes is $3,300 in the first year of the life of the equipment. Excluding the trading securities and the depreciation, income before taxes for the year was $4,000. Assume that there are no other book-tax differences. The income tax rate is 40% for the current year and all future years. Prepare the journal entry or entries necessary to record income tax expense for the year. State any assumptions you must make.

Practice 16-12

LO2

Valuation Allowance

Refer to Practice 16-8. The company had no taxable income in past years. Analysis of prospects for the future indicates that it is more likely than not that total taxable income in the foreseeable future will be no more than $400. Assume that the income tax expense journal entry required in Practice 16-8 has already been made. Make any necessary adjusting entry.

Practice 16-13

LO2

Valuation Allowance

Refer to Practice 16-9. The company had no taxable income in past years. Analysis of prospects for the future indicates that it is more likely than not that total taxable income in the foreseeable future will be no more than $20,000. Assume that the income tax expense journal entry required in Practice 16-9 has already been made. Make any necessary adjusting entry.

Practice 16-14 **LO2**

Uncertain Tax Positions

The company has taken a tax position that is subject to review by the Internal Revenue Service. The company determines that there is a 40% probability that the position will not be sustained upon review. Is this a "highly certain" tax position? Why or why not?

Practice 16-15 **LO2**

Uncertain Tax Position

The company has determined that there is an 80% likelihood that its position on a tax issue will be upheld upon review by taxing authorities and that the entire amount of the position, $100,000, will be allowed. Is this a "highly certain" tax position? Why or why not?

Practice 16-16 **LO2**

Uncertain Tax Position

The company is evaluating its tax position on a certain issue and has determined that although it is more likely than not that its position will be sustained, it is less certain about the amount that will be sustained. It has provided the following probability estimates and amounts:

There is a xx% probability that	The allowable reduction in taxes payable will be	The cumulative probability of occurrence is
15%	$100	15%
20	80	35
10	60	45
15	40	60
20	20	80
20	0	100

Determine the amount of the unrecognized tax benefit liability and provide the journal entry required to recognize the liability associated with the unrecognized tax benefit.

Practice 16-17 **LO3**

Net Operating Loss Carryback

Taxable income and income tax rates for 2011–2013 for the company have been as follows:

Year	Taxable Income	Income Tax Rate	Total Tax Paid
2011	$ 75,000	25%	$18,750
2012	50,000	30	15,000
2013	(93,000)	35	0

Make the journal entry necessary to record any net operating loss (NOL) carryback in 2013.

Practice 16-18 **LO3**

Net Operating Loss Carryforward

Refer to Practice 16-17. Assume that the net operating loss in 2013 was $150,000 instead of $93,000. Make the journal entry necessary to record (1) any net operating loss (NOL) carryback in 2013 and (2) any net operating loss (NOL) carryforward created in 2013. The enacted tax rate for future years is 35%. State any assumptions you must make.

Practice 16-19 **LO3**

Net Operating Loss Carryforward

Taxable income and income tax rates for 2011–2016 for the company have been as seen on page 16-43.

Year	Taxable Income	Income Tax Rate	Total Tax Paid
2011	$ 30,000	30%	$9,000
2012	15,000	35	5,250
2013	20,000	35	7,000
2014	(100,000)	40	?
2015	50,000	35	?
2016	(200,000)	30	?

Make the journal entry necessary to record any net operating loss (NOL) carryforward created in 2016. The enacted tax rate for future years is 40%.

Practice 16-20

LO4

Scheduling for Enacted Future Tax Rates

Refer to Practice 16-5. Assume that the enacted tax rates are as follows:

2013	40%
2014	37
2015	37
2016	37
2017	31

For simplicity, assume that temporary differences reverse in a FIFO pattern; that is, assume that the first temporary difference created is the first to reverse. Prepare the journal entry or entries to record income tax expense in 2013.

Practice 16-21

LO5

Reporting Deferred Tax Assets and Liabilities

Refer to Practice 16-11. (1) What deferred tax amount or amounts would appear on the balance sheet? (2) Prepare the financial statement note disclosure needed to identify the sources of the deferred tax amounts. Refer to Exhibit 16-7.

Practice 16-22

LO5

Computation of Effective Tax Rate

Refer to Practice 16-3. Compute the effective tax rate.

Practice 16-23

LO5

Reconciliation of Statutory Rate and Effective Rate

The company reported sales of $60,000. Other income statement items for the year were as follows:

Interest revenue from municipal bonds	$ 7,000
Depreciation expense (tax depreciation was $36,000)	25,000
Expenses not deductible for tax purposes	18,000
Warranty expenses (not deductible until actually provided; $2,000 provided this year)	10,000

The income tax rate is 35%. (1) Compute the effective tax rate and (2) provide a reconciliation of the statutory tax rate of 35% to the effective tax rate.

Practice 16-24

LO6

Deferred Taxes and Operating Cash Flow

The company assembled the following information with respect to operating cash flow for the year:

Net income	$10,000
Depreciation	2,000
Increase in accounts receivable	1,200
Decrease in inventory	850

Decrease in accounts payable	$ 300
Increase in income taxes payable	40
Increase in deferred tax liability	1,430

Compute cash flow from operating activities.

Practice 16-25
LO6

Cash Paid for Income Taxes
The company reported the following balance sheet information:

	2013	2012
Income taxes payable	$ 17,000	$22,000
Deferred income tax liability	130,000	90,000

Total income tax expense for 2013 was $60,000. Compute the amount of cash paid for income taxes in 2013.

EXERCISES

Exercise 16-26
LO6

Cash Flow and Income Taxes
Victoria Clothing reported the following amounts related to income taxes on its 2013 income statement.

Income tax benefit from NOL carryback	$12,000
Income tax benefit from NOL carryforward	28,000

Victoria also reported the following on its December 31, 2012 and 2013, balance sheets.

	2013	2012
Deferred tax asset—NOL carryforward	$28,000	$ 0
Income tax refund receivable	12,000	4,000

1. If Victoria uses the indirect method of reporting cash flows, what information concerning income taxes would Victoria include in its statement of cash flows and related disclosure?
2. If Victoria uses the direct method of reporting cash flows, what information concerning income taxes would Victoria include in its statement of cash flows and related disclosure?

Exercise 16-27
LO6

Cash Flow and Income Taxes
Joyce Smithers Inc. reported the following amounts related to income taxes on its 2013 income statement.

Income tax expense—current	$32,000
Income tax expense—deferred	(8,000)

Smithers also reported the following amounts on its December 31, 2012 and 2013, balance sheets:

	2013	2012
Deferred tax liability	$26,000	$34,000
Income taxes payable	10,000	4,000

If Smithers uses the indirect method of reporting cash flows, what information concerning income taxes would it include in its statement of cash flows and related disclosure?

Exercise 16-28

LO2

Changing Tax Rates

Goshute Company computed pretax financial income of $50,000 for the year ended December 31, 2013. Taxable income for the year was $15,000. Accumulated temporary differences as of December 31, 2012, were $120,000. A deferred tax liability of $48,000 was included on the December 31, 2012, balance sheet. Accumulated temporary differences as of December 31, 2013, are $155,000. The differences are related to noncurrent items.

1. Prepare the journal entries necessary to record income tax for 2013. The enacted income tax rate is assumed to be 40% for 2013 and future years.
2. On January 1, 2014, the income tax rate is changed to 32% for 2014 and all future years. Prepare the necessary journal entry, if any.

Exercise 16-29

LO1

Identification of Temporary Differences

Indicate which of the following items are temporary differences and which are nontaxable or nondeductible. For each temporary difference, indicate whether the item considered alone would create a deferred tax asset or a deferred tax liability.

(a) Tax depreciation in excess of book depreciation, $150,000.
(b) Excess of income on installment sales over income reportable for tax purposes, $130,000.
(c) Premium payment for life insurance policy on president, $95,000.
(d) Rent collected in advance of period earned, $75,000.
(e) Warranty provision accrued in advance of period paid, $40,000.
(f) Interest revenue received on municipal bonds, $30,000.

Exercise 16-30

LO1

Calculation of Taxable Income

Using the information given in Exercise 16-29 and assuming pretax financial income of $2,900,000, calculate taxable income.

Exercise 16-31

LO2

SPREADSHEET

Deferred Tax Asset Valuation Allowance

Relevan Company computed a pretax financial loss of $15,000 for the first year of its operations ended December 31, 2013. Included in the loss was $42,000 in uncollectible accounts expense that was accrued on the books in 2013 using an allowance system based on a percentage of sales. For income tax purposes, deductions for uncollectible accounts are allowed when specific accounts receivable are determined to be uncollectible and written off. No accounts receivable have been written off as uncollectible in 2013.

1. Prepare the journal entries necessary to record income taxes for the year. The enacted income tax rate is 35% for 2013 and all future years. Assume that it is more likely than not that future taxable income will be sufficient to allow for the full realization of any deferred tax assets. Accounts Receivable and the related allowance account are reported under current assets on the balance sheet.
2. Repeat (1), assuming that it is more likely than not that future taxable income will be zero before considering the actual bad debt losses in future years.

Exercise 16-32

LO3, LO4

Net Operating Loss (NOL) Carryback and Carryforward

The following historical financial data are available for Lexis Company.

Year	Income	Tax Rate	Tax Paid
2010	$500,000	35%	$175,000
2011	150,000	30	45,000
2012	30,000	30	9,000

In 2013, Lexis Company suffered a $1 million net operating loss. The company will use the carryback provision of the tax law.

1. Using the information given, calculate the refund due for the loss carryback and the amount of the loss available to carry forward to future periods. Assume that the enacted tax rate for 2013 and all future years is 40%.
2. Prepare journal entries to record the loss carryback and carryforward. Assume that it is more likely than not that future taxable income will be sufficient to allow for the full realization of any deferred tax assets.
3. Evaluate the reasonableness of the assumption in (2).

Exercise 16-33
LO3, LO4

Net Operating Loss (NOL) Carryback and Carryforward

The following historical financial data are available for the Bradshaw Manufacturing Company.

Year	Income	Tax Rate	Tax Paid
2010	$175,000	40%	$70,000
2011	230,000	42	96,600
2012	310,000	30	93,000

In 2013, Bradshaw suffered an $820,000 net operating loss due to an economic recession. The company elects to use the carryback provision in the tax law.

1. Using the information given, calculate the refund due arising from the loss carryback and the amount of the loss available to carry forward to future periods. Assume that the enacted tax rate is 34% for 2013 and all future years.
2. Prepare the entry necessary to record the loss carryback and carryforward. Assume that there will be sufficient taxable income in the carryforward period to realize all benefits from NOL carryforwards.
3. Using the answers from (1) and (2), prepare the bottom portion of the 2013 income statement reflecting the effect of the loss carryback and carryforward.

Exercise 16-34
LO2

Deferred Tax Asset

Lofthouse Machinery Co. includes a 2-year warranty on its machinery sales. At the end of 2013, an analysis of the warranty records reveals an accumulated temporary difference of $120,000 for warranty expenses; book expenses related to warranties have exceeded tax deductions allowed. The enacted income tax rate for 2013 and future years is 40%. Management concludes that it is more likely than not that Lofthouse will have future income to realize the future tax benefit from this temporary difference. They also conclude that 20% of the warranty liability is current and 80% is noncurrent.

1. How would the deferred tax information be reported on the Lofthouse balance sheet at December 31, 2013?
2. If management assumed that only 70% of the tax benefit from the temporary difference could be realized, how would the deferred tax information be reported on the balance sheet at December 31, 2013? (Recall that the valuation allowance is allocated proportionately between the current and noncurrent portions of the deferred tax asset.)

Exercise 16-35
LO2

Deferred Tax Asset

Pro-Tech-Tronics Company computed pretax financial income of $35,000 for the first year of its operations ended December 31, 2013. Unearned rent revenue of $55,000 had been recognized as taxable income in 2013 when the cash was received but had not yet been recognized in the financial accounting records.

The unearned rent is expected to be recognized on the books in the following pattern.

2014	$15,000
2015	20,000
2016	12,000
2017	8,000
Total	$55,000

The enacted tax rates for this year and the next four years are as follows:

2013	34%
2014	34
2015	30
2016	30
2017	37

Prepare the journal entries necessary to record income taxes for 2013. Assume that there will be sufficient income in each future year to realize any deductible amounts.

Exercise 16-36

LO2

Deferred Tax Liability

Hinton Exploration Company reported pretax financial income of $637,000 for the calendar year 2013. Included in the Other Income section of the income statement was $98,000 of interest revenue from municipal bonds held by the company. The income statement also included depreciation expense of $580,000 for a machine that cost $3,250,000. The income tax return reported $650,000 as MACRS depreciation on the machine.

The enacted tax rate is 40% for 2013 and future years. Prepare the journal entry or entries necessary to record income taxes for 2013.

Exercise 16-37

LO2

Deferred Tax Liability

Faro Inc. began operating on January 1, 2013. At the end of the first year of operations, Faro reported $400,000 income before income taxes on its income statement but only $320,000 taxable income on its tax return. Analysis of the $80,000 difference revealed that $45,000 was a permanent difference and $35,000 was a temporary tax liability difference related to a current asset. The enacted tax rate for 2013 and future years is 35%.

1. Prepare the journal entries to record income taxes for 2013.
2. Assume that at the end of 2014, the accumulated temporary tax liability difference related to future years is $70,000. Prepare the journal entry to record any adjustment to deferred tax liabilities at the end of 2014.

Exercise 16-38

LO2

Deferred Tax Assets and Liabilities

Flatworld Shipping Company reports taxable income of $912,000 on its income tax return for the year ended December 31, 2013, its first year of operations. Temporary differences between financial income and taxable income for the year are as follows:

Tax depreciation in excess of book depreciation	$ 95,000
Accrual for product liability claims in excess of actual claims (estimated product claims payable is a current liability)	180,000
Reported installment sales income in excess of taxable installment sales income (installments receivable is a current asset)	315,000

The enacted income tax rate is 35% for 2013 and all future years. Prepare the journal entries necessary to record income taxes for 2013.

Exercise 16-39

LO2

Deferred Tax Assets and Liabilities

Fibertek, Inc., computed a pretax financial income of $40,000 for the first year of its operations ended December 31, 2013. Included in financial income was $25,000 of nondeductible expenses, $22,000 gross profit on installment sales that was deferred for tax purposes until the installments were collected, and $18,000 in bad debt expense that had been accrued on the books in 2013.

The temporary differences are expected to reverse in the following patterns:

Year	Gross Profit on Collections	Bad Debt Write-Offs
2014	$ 5,000	$ 6,000
2015	7,000	12,000
2016	4,000	
2017	6,000	
Totals	$22,000	$18,000

The enacted tax rates for this year and the next four years are as follows:

2013	40%
2014	35
2015	32
2016	30
2017	32

Prepare the journal entries necessary to record income taxes for 2013. Assume that there will be sufficient income in each future year to realize any deductible amounts. For classification purposes, the bad debt write-offs are considered to be associated with a current asset, and the receivable for installment sales is classified as both current and noncurrent, depending on the expected timing of the receipt.

Exercise 16-40
LO2

Determinants of "More Likely than Not"

Fulton Company computed a pretax financial loss of $18,000 for the first year of its operations ended December 31, 2013. This loss did not include $25,000 in unearned rent revenue that was recognized as taxable income in 2013 when the cash was received.

1. Prepare the journal entries necessary to record income tax for the year. The income tax rate is 40%. Assume it is more likely than not that future taxable income will be sufficient to allow for the full realization of any deferred tax assets and that unearned rent revenue is a current liability.
2. If future taxable income from operations was not expected to be sufficient to allow for the full realization of any deferred tax assets, what other sources of income may be considered to determine the need for a valuation allowance?

Exercise 16-41
LO2, LO4

Computation of Deferred Asset and Liability Balances

Dixon Type and Supply Company reported taxable income of $75,000 for 2013, its first fiscal year. The enacted tax rate for 2013 is 40%. Enacted tax rates and deductible amounts for 2014–2017 are as follows:

	Enacted Tax Rate	Deductible Amount
2014	35%	$14,000
2015	32	24,000
2016	30	16,000
2017	32	40,000

1. Prepare the journal entries necessary to record income taxes for 2013. Assume that there will be sufficient income in each future year to realize any deductible amounts. For classification purposes, assume that all deductible amounts relate to noncurrent items.

2. Repeat (1), assuming it is more likely than not that taxable income for all future periods will be zero or less.

Exercise 16-42

LO2, LO4

Computation of Deferred Asset and Liability Balances

Friedman Construction reported taxable income of $50,000 for 2013, its first fiscal year. The enacted tax rate for 2013 is 40%. Enacted tax rates and deductible amounts for 2014–2016 are as follows:

	Enacted Tax Rate	Deductible Amount
2014	38%	$12,000
2015	35	15,000
2016	36	18,000

1. Prepare the journal entries necessary to record income taxes for 2013. Assume that there will be sufficient income in each future year to realize any deductible amounts. For classification purposes, assume that all deductible amounts relate to noncurrent items.
2. Repeat (1), assuming that it is more likely than not that taxable income for all future periods will be zero or less.

PROBLEMS

Problem 16-43

LO1, LO2

SPREADSHEET

Life Cycle of a Temporary Difference

A. J. Johnson & Co. recorded certain revenues on its books in 2013 and 2014 of $15,400 and $16,600, respectively. However, such revenues were not subject to income taxation until 2015. The company records reveal pretax financial income and taxable income for the 3-year period as follows:

	Financial Income	Taxable Income
2013	$44,200	$28,800
2014	38,200	21,600
2015	21,100	53,100

Assume that Johnson's tax rate is 35% for all periods.

Instructions: Prepare the journal entries necessary at the end of each year to record income taxes.

Problem 16-44

LO2

Deferred Tax Liability

Polytechnic Corporation reported taxable income of $2,340,000 for the year ended December 31, 2013. The controller is unfamiliar with the required treatment of temporary and permanent differences in reconciling taxable income to pretax financial income and has contacted your firm for advice. You are given company records that list the following differences.

Tax depreciation in excess of book depreciation	$310,000
Proceeds from life insurance policy upon death of officer	145,000
Interest revenue on municipal bonds	107,000

Instructions:

1. Compute pretax financial income.

2. Given an income tax rate of 35%, prepare the journal entry or entries to record income taxes for the year.
3. Prepare a partial income statement beginning with Income from continuing operations before income taxes.

Problem 16-45

LO2, LO4

Deferred Tax Liability

Olympus Motors, Inc., computed a pretax financial income of $90,000 for its first year of operations ended December 31, 2013. In preparing the income tax return for the year, the tax accountant determined the following differences between 2013 financial income and taxable income.

Nondeductible expenses	$25,000
Nontaxable revenues	15,500
Temporary difference—installment sales reported in financial income but not in taxable income	32,000

The temporary difference is expected to reverse in the following pattern as the cash is collected:

2014	$ 7,000
2015	16,500
2016	8,500
Total	$32,000

The enacted tax rates for this year and the next three years are as follows:

2013	40%
2014	35
2015	33
2016	30

Instructions:

1. Prepare journal entries to record income taxes payable and deferred income taxes.
2. Prepare a partial income statement for Olympus Motors beginning with Income from continuing operations before income taxes for the year ended December 31, 2013.

Problem 16-46

LO2, LO4

Deferred Tax Asset

Davidson Gasket Inc. computed a pretax financial loss of $25,000 for the first year of its operations, ended December 31, 2013. Analysis of the tax and book bases of its liabilities disclosed $55,000 in unearned rent revenue on the books that had been recognized as taxable income in 2013 when the cash was received. Also disclosed was $20,000 in warranties payable that had been recognized as expense on the books in 2013 when product sales were made but that are not deductible on the tax return until paid.

These temporary differences are expected to reverse in the following pattern.

Year	Rent Earned on Books	Warranty Payments
2014	$13,000	$ 5,000
2015	25,000	8,000
2016	12,000	7,000
2017	5,000	
Totals	$55,000	$20,000

The enacted tax rates for this year and the next four years are as follows:

2013	38%
2014	36
2015	32
2016	30
2017	30

Instructions:

1. Prepare journal entries to record income taxes payable and deferred income taxes. Assume there will be sufficient income in each future year to realize any deductible amount.
2. Prepare the income statement for Davidson Gasket Inc. beginning with Loss from continuing operations before income taxes for the year ended December 31, 2013.
3. If future taxable income from operations was not expected to be sufficient to allow for the full realization of any deferred tax assets, what other sources of income may be used to avoid establishing a valuation allowance?

Problem 16-47

LO2

Deferred Tax Assets and Liabilities

As of December 31, 2013, its first year in business, Kukui Company had taxable temporary differences totaling $110,000. Of this total, $45,000 relates to current items. Kukui also had deductible temporary differences totaling $42,000, $14,000 of which relates to current items. Pretax financial income for the year was $200,000. The enacted tax rate for 2013 and all future years is 35%.

Instructions:

1. Prepare the journal entries to record income taxes for 2013.
2. Repeat (1), but assume that all the taxable temporary differences are noncurrent and that all the deductible temporary differences are current.

Problem 16-48

LO2, LO4

SPREADSHEET

Netting of Deferred Tax Assets and Liabilities

Stratco Corporation computed a pretax financial income of $40,000 for the first year of its operations ended December 31, 2013. Included in financial income was $50,000 of nontaxable revenue, $20,000 gross profit on installment sales that was deferred for tax purposes until the installments were collected, and $50,000 in warranties payable that had been recognized as expense on the books in 2013 when product sales were made.

The temporary differences are expected to reverse in the following pattern:

Year	Gross Profit on Collections	Warranty Payments
2014	$ 5,000	$ 9,000
2015	7,000	16,500
2016	2,000	20,500
2017	6,000	4,000
Totals	$20,000	$50,000

The enacted tax rates for this year and the next four years are as follows:

2013	40%
2014	35
2015	32
2016	30
2017	30

Instructions:

1. Prepare journal entries to record income taxes payable and deferred income taxes. Assume that there will be sufficient income in each future year to realize any deductible amount.
2. Prepare the income statement for Stratco beginning with Income from continuing operations before income taxes for the year ended December 31, 2013.

Problem 16-49

LO2

Valuation Allowance

Cheng Company computed taxable income of $8,000 for the first year of its operations ended December 31, 2013. Tax depreciation exceeded depreciation for financial reporting purposes by $24,000. Receipt of $13,000 cash was reported as revenue for tax purposes but is reported as a current liability, Unearned Revenue, for financial reporting. The enacted tax rate for 2013 and all future years is 35%.

Instructions:

1. Prepare the journal entries to record income taxes for 2013. Assume that it is more likely than not that future taxable income will be sufficient to allow for the full realization of any deferred tax assets.
2. Repeat (1), assuming that it is more likely than not that future taxable income will be zero, exclusive of the expected reversal of the depreciation temporary difference.

Problem 16-50

LO4

SPREADSHEET

Adjustment for Changing Tax Rates

Hermann Company analyzed its temporary differences as of December 31, 2013. The enacted tax rate was 35% for 2013 and all future tax years.

The total amount of taxable temporary differences as of the end of 2013 was $540,000. All the temporary differences relate to noncurrent items.

Instructions:

1. Assume that in early 2014 the taxing authority changed the rates for 2014 and beyond to 30%. Prepare the 2014 journal entry to record the tax rate decrease.
2. Assume that instead of being decreased, the tax rate was increased to 40% in early 2014. Prepare the 2014 journal entry to record the tax rate increase.

Problem 16-51

LO3, LO4

Operating Loss Carryback and Carryforward

The following information is taken from the financial statements of Aruban Enterprises.

Year	Taxable and Pretax Financial Income	Income Tax Rate	Income Tax Paid
2009	$ 32,000	40%	$12,800
2010	29,300	35	10,255
2011	33,100	40	13,240
2012	22,500	34	7,650
2013	(94,300)	35	0

The company elects to use the carryback provisions of the tax law.

Instructions:

1. Given the information from the financial statements, compute the amount of income tax refund due as a result of the operating loss in 2013.
2. What is the amount, if any, of the operating loss carryforward? How would the operating loss carryforward be reflected in the financial statements?

3. Assume the foregoing information except as follows:
   (a) The loss in 2013 was $39,000. Calculate the refund due and prepare the journal entry to record the claim for income tax refund.
   (b) In addition to (a), there was a loss of $28,000 in 2014. How much could be carried back, and how much could be carried forward?

Problem 16-52

LO3, LO4

NOL Carryback and Carryforward

The financial history below shows the income and losses for Irontree Company for the 10-year period 2004–2013.

Assume that no adjustments to taxable income are necessary for purposes of the NOL carryback and that the company elects to use the carryback provisions of the tax code.

Year	Taxable and Pretax Financial Income (before NOL)	Income Tax Rate	Income Tax Paid
2004	$ 14,200	48%	$ 6,816
2005	17,600	48	8,448
2006	20,500	42	8,610
2007	(29,300)	42	0
2008	13,900	42	5,838
2009	(25,100)	44	0
2010	23,500	44	?
2011	40,650	38	15,447
2012	(64,400)	38	0
2013	72,000	38	?

Instructions:

1. Given the foregoing information, compute the amount of income tax refund for each year as a result of each NOL carryback and the amount of the carryforward (if any).
2. How would the NOL carryforward as of December 31, 2012, be reflected in the 2012 financial statements?
3. Calculate the amount of income tax paid, showing the benefit of the NOL carryforward, for the years 2010 and 2013.
4. For 2013, give the entry (or entries) to record income taxes, assuming that the deferred tax asset stemming from the 2012 NOL carryforward was fully recognized in 2012.

Problem 16-53

LO1, LO5

Sample CPA Exam Questions

1. At December 31, 2013, Bren Co. had the following deferred income tax items:
   - A deferred income tax liability of $15,000 related to a noncurrent asset
   - A deferred income tax asset of $3,000 related to a noncurrent liability
   - A deferred income tax asset of $8,000 related to a current liability

   Which of the following should Bren report in the noncurrent section of its December 31, 2013, balance sheet?
   (a) A noncurrent asset of $3,000 and a noncurrent liability of $15,000.
   (b) A noncurrent liability of $12,000.
   (c) A noncurrent asset of $11,000 and a noncurrent liability of $15,000.
   (d) A noncurrent liability of $4,000.

2. For the year ended December 31, 2013, Grim Co.'s pretax financial statement income was $200,000 and its taxable income was $150,000. The difference is due to the following:

Interest on municipal bonds	$ 70,000
Premium expense on keyman life insurance	(20,000)
Total	$ 50,000

Grim's enacted income tax is 30%. In its 2013 income statement, what amount should Grim report as current provision for income tax expense?
(a) $45,000
(b) $51,000
(c) $60,000
(d) $66,000

CASES

Discussion Case 16-54

What Are Deferred Income Taxes?

Hurst Inc. is a new corporation that has just completed a highly successful first year of operations. Hurst is a privately held corporation, but its president, Byron Hurst, has indicated that if the company continues to do as well for the next four or five years, it will go public. By all indications, the company should continue to be highly profitable on both a short-term and a long-term basis.

The controller of the new company, Lori James, plans on using the MACRS method of depreciating Hurst's assets and using the installment sales method of recognizing income for tax purposes. For financial statement presentation, straight-line depreciation will be used, and all sales will be fully recognized in the year of sale. There are no other differences between book and taxable income.

Hurst has hired your firm to prepare its financial statements. You are now preparing the income statement. The controller wants to show, as income tax expense, the amount of the tax liability actually due. "After all," James reasons, "that's the amount we'll actually pay, and in light of our plans for continued expansion, it's highly unlikely that the temporary differences will ever reverse."

Draft a memo to the controller outlining your reaction to the plan. Give reasons in support of your decision.

Discussion Case 16-55

Why Aren't Deferred Taxes Discounted?

Tyler Dee is the controller for Martinez Company, a major employer in the area. Tyler has just come from a meeting of a local civic group. The meeting was an opportunity for Tyler to present and explain Martinez's financial statements for the fiscal year recently ended. A significant amount of time was spent discussing the large deferred tax liability reported by Martinez. Several members of the civic group questioned Tyler about the nature of this liability. In particular, Tyler was asked why the liability wasn't discounted to reflect the time value of money. Tyler had no real answer, except to mumble something like, "That's just the way the standard is written."

How might Tyler have better explained the lack of discounting of deferred taxes?

Discussion Case 16-56

Raising Tax Rates: Does It Help Me or Hurt Me?

When the corporate tax rate was lowered from 46% to 34% in 1986, most firms that had adopted the asset and liability method of deferred tax accounting reported one-time gains as a result of the revaluation of their deferred tax items. In fact, one writer claimed that this lowering of income tax rates "freed a large chunk of money that had been accumulated to pay deferred taxes at the former higher rate."

In early 1993, Congress was considering raising the corporate income tax rate. One proposal was to raise the top corporate rate from 34% to 36%. Accounting experts pointed out that the increase in the tax rate would cause some firms to report one-time losses and other firms to report one-time gains.

1. Why did the lowering of tax rates in 1986 result in most firms reporting gains, whereas an increase in tax rates in 1993 would cause some firms to report gains and some firms to report losses?
2. Comment on the writer's statement that the lowering of income tax rates "freed a large chunk of money."

SOURCES: Rick Wartzman, "Rise in Corporate Taxes Would Force Many Big Companies to Take Charges," *The Wall Street Journal*, February 11, 1993, p. A2; Lee Berton, "FASB Is Expected to Issue Rule Allowing Firms to Post Big, One-Time Gains," *The Wall Street Journal*, November 4, 1987, p. 4.

Discussion Case 16-57

Is a Valuation Allowance Needed?

Assume that you go to work for one of the large accounting firms upon your graduation from college and that for your first assignment, you are asked to review the deferred income tax asset account to determine whether a valuation allowance seems to be warranted. You remember talking about deferred income taxes in your intermediate financial accounting class, but the problems always told you whether an allowance was required or not. Now you must examine the facts to help determine the need for an allowance. What factors would you consider in making your recommendation?

Case 16-58

Deciphering Financial Statements (The Walt Disney Company)

The 2009 financial statements for **The Walt Disney Company** can be found on the Internet.

1. Using the financial statements and information contained in the notes, determine how much income tax expense Disney reported for the fiscal year ended October 3, 2009.
2. Referring to the note on income taxes, how much of the tax expense relates to current items, and how much relates to deferred items?
3. Disney notes that its effective income tax rate for 2009 was 36.2%. Using information from the income statement, determine how that number was computed.
4. Note that Disney has a valuation allowance of $388 million. In the journal entry establishing this allowance account, what would have been the debit and the credit?
5. Why was Disney's effective income tax rate higher than the U.S. federal income tax rate of 35.0% in 2009? [*Hint*: Look at Note 10 (Income Taxes).]
6. Explain why the effective income tax rate differs from company to company.
7. Do differences in effective tax rates reflect the impact of *temporary* book-tax differences or *permanent* book-tax differences? Explain.
8. How much cash did Disney pay for income taxes during 2009?

Case 16-59

Deciphering Financial Statements (Sara Lee Corporation)

Sara Lee Corporation owns the following brands: Ball Park franks, Sara Lee bakery goods, Hillshire Farm, Jimmy Dean, Kiwi shoe care products, and many other products. The following information relates to the company's deferred taxes.

Sara Lee Corporation and Subsidiaries
Income Taxes

Current and deferred tax provisions (benefits) were (in millions):

	2009		2008		2007	
	Current	**Deferred**	**Current**	**Deferred**	**Current**	**Deferred**
U.S.	$ 89	$(61)	$310	$(247)	$ 18	$(144)
Foreign	214	(22)	168	(32)	123	4
State	4	0	(10)	12	(4)	(8)
	$307	$(83)	$468	$(267)	$137	$(148)

Cash payments for income taxes from continuing operations were $273 in 2009, $459 in 2008, and $378 in 2007.

Based on this information, answer the feollowing questions:

1. Provide the journal entry(ies) made by Sara Lee to record the 2009 income tax expense (net) of $224 million. Remember to allocate the expense and benefit between current and deferred.
2. Provide the journal entry made by Sara Lee to record the payment of income taxes during the year 2009.

Case 16-60

Writing Assignment (Uncertain Tax Positions)

FASB ASC Topic 740 discusses uncertain tax positions and highly certain tax positions. In one page or less, discuss the difference between an uncertain tax position and a highly certain tax position.

Case 16-61

Writing Assignment (Crystallisation)

As discussed in the chapter, deferred taxes in the United Kingdom have historically been computed in a slightly different manner than in the United States. The concept underlying this "crystallisation" approach is that if a liability is deferred indefinitely, then the present value of that liability is zero. No deferred tax liability is recognized if the accumulated deferred tax amount is expected to increase each year, thus delaying indefinitely the ultimate liquidation of this obligation.

In one page or less, address the following questions regarding how crystallisation relates to accounts payable.

1. How might this same concept be applied to the recognition of a liability for accounts payable? That is, if accounts payable are expected to increase each year, should the crystallisation concept apply to this liability?
2. How reasonable does this approach seem?

Case 16-62

Ethical Dilemma (The valuation allowance)

You have just completed a preliminary draft of the year-end financial statements and notes and have distributed it to members of the board of directors for the upcoming board meeting. At the meeting, board members will have an opportunity to analyze, ask questions, and offer suggestions regarding the content of the statements and the accompanying notes.

According to your computations, the company will be reporting yet another loss—the third in as many years. The company has taken full advantage of the carryback provisions of the tax law. With this year's loss, the company will carry forward some of the loss. As a result, you have correctly recorded a deferred tax asset. However, because of continued losses, you have used a valuation allowance account to reduce the amount of the deferred tax asset.

At the board meeting, initial questions focus on the company's profitability or lack thereof. Following this discussion, an astute member of the board questions the use of a valuation allowance account. You explain that if losses continue, the entire amount of the deferred asset may not be realized and that it is your professional opinion that sufficient evidence exists to justify the use of a valuation allowance account.

Immediately, the board begins to question your assumption of future losses. "Of course we will be profitable next year," says one board member. "We have a plan to turn this company around," says another. You overhear another whisper to his colleague, "If the accountants don't think we are going to make money in the future, why are they staying?"

You have heard this talk about a turnaround in prior years, yet management seems unsuccessful in implementing desired changes. In past years, you have always had prior years' profits against which you could offset losses. But now the accounting department, of which you are the head, has openly questioned management's intentions to report profits in the future. Now the board is questioning your loyalty to the company as well as your judgment.

1. What other factors might be considered when valuing the deferred tax asset account?
2. As the accountant, is it your place to question management's ability to turn a company around?
3. What effect did the journal entry involving the valuation allowance account have on this year's income statement? Did net income go up or down? With this journal entry, are you contributing to the company's loss?

Case 16-63

Cumulative Spreadsheet Analysis

This assignment is based on the cumulative spreadsheet assignment for Chapter 13. Review that assignment for a summary of the assumptions made in preparing a forecasted balance sheet, income statement, and statement of cash flows for 2014 for Skywalker Company. This assignment involves computations related to deferred income taxes and the amount of cash paid for income taxes.

Skywalker would like to estimate the amount of cash it will pay for income taxes in 2014. The only difference between financial accounting income and taxable income for Skywalker is in the area of depreciation. Skywalker uses straight-line depreciation for financial reporting purposes and an accelerated method for tax reporting. This difference has created a deferred tax liability, which is included in the balance sheet's "Other long-term liabilities." The following information is for December 31, 2013:

Accumulated depreciation, financial accounting records	$27.00
Accumulated depreciation, tax records	$50.00
Expected future income tax rate	33.0%

Construct a spreadsheet that will allow you to answer the following questions.

1. Given this information, what is Skywalker's deferred tax liability as of December 31, 2013? (Carry calculations to two decimal places.)
2. In 2014, depreciation expense for income tax purposes is expected to be 1.5 times as much as depreciation expense computed for financial reporting purposes. Estimate the amount of cash that Skywalker will pay for income taxes in 2014. Report your answer with two decimal places, and assume the following:
   (a) Amortization expense is the same for book and for tax purposes.
   (b) All current income taxes are paid in cash during the year.
   (c) These calculations do not impact the overall total forecast for "Other long-term liabilities" for 2014; the balance is still expected to increase at the same rate as sales.
3. Repeat (2), assuming the following:
   (a) Depreciation expense for income tax purposes will be the same as depreciation expense computed for financial reporting purposes.
   (b) Depreciation expense for income tax purposes will be 2.0 times as much as depreciation expense computed for financial reporting purposes.
4. Comment on what implicit assumption underlies your answer to (3b).

P3 ADDITIONAL ACTIVITIES OF A BUSINESS

CHAPTER 17 Employee Compensation—Payroll, Pensions, and Other Compensation Issues

LEARNING OBJECTIVES

1. Account for payroll and payroll taxes, and understand the criteria for recognizing a liability associated with compensated absences.
2. Compute performance bonuses, and recognize the issues associated with postemployment benefits.
3. Understand the nature and characteristics of employer pension plans, including the details of defined benefit plans.
4. Use the components of the pension-related asset/liability and changes in the components to compute the periodic expense associated with pensions and to compute the impact on other comprehensive income.
5. Prepare required disclosures associated with pensions, and understand the accounting treatment for pension settlements and curtailments.
6. Explain the differences in accounting for pensions and postretirement benefits other than pensions.

Press reports in the United States often talk about the rising "national debt." As of September 30, 2009, borrowing from the public by the U.S. Treasury totaled $7.583 trillion. This obligation is the most publicized liability of the U.S. government, but it is not the only large one. As of the same date, the present value of the government liability under military and civilian pension plans and for veterans' benefits was $5.284 trillion.[1] These liabilities are certainly large (a trillion dollar bills laid end to end would stretch from the earth to the moon and back 197 times), but all other U.S. government liabilities are surpassed by the Social Security and Medicare obligations. Of course, in one sense it is not correct to view Social Security as a pension plan or Medicare as a company retiree health care plan; those plans are a social insurance arrangement in which current workers pay for the benefits of past workers in the hopes that they (the current workers) will be

[1] *Financial Report of the United States Government—2009* (Washington, DC: Department of the Treasury).

supported by the contributions of future workers. With that qualification, it is still interesting to evaluate the funding status of Social Security and Medicare as if they were private company plans. As of September 30, 2009, the U.S. Treasury estimated that the present value of future Social Security benefits to current and future participants in the plan (over an infinite horizon) exceeded the present value of expected future contributions from those workers and their employers by $17.5 trillion. And the present value of the Medicare obligation to those same people (in excess of their expected contributions) is $89.5 trillion!

A widely recognized phenomenon of the past 100 years has been the increasing life expectancy of people in almost all countries of the world. For example, in 1900 the average life expectancy of people in the United States was 47.3 years; by 2005 it had increased to 77.8 years.[2] As people live longer, they must deal with the problem of financing their extended retirement years. The magnitude of the problem in the United States will increase in the next 10 to 15 years as the "baby boomer" population of the 1940s and 1950s moves into retirement. It is estimated that the proportion of the U.S. population that is over 65 will increase from the current 12% to 20% by the year 2030.

As a country's population ages, an increasingly large share of the country's resources must be used to honor obligations to retired people. This is also true of a business enterprise. For example, it has been reported that approximately $1,100 of the sales price of each **General Motors** vehicle must be used to satisfy the pension and health care claims of retired workers who no longer work at General Motors.

Complex accounting issues associated with employee compensation do not begin, however, when an employee retires. As introduced in Chapter 13, stock compensation has become an increasingly complex and controversial issue. In addition, companies must address issues associated with the computation of performance bonuses and liabilities associated with sick and vacation pay. Finally, the compensation issues associated with payroll, such as the differing employee and employer payroll taxes, introduce added complexity to the topic of employee compensation.

The event line displayed in Exhibit 17-1 outlines the various issues associated with employee compensation. Naturally, immediate compensation for services provided is the issue with which we all are most familiar. The next issue on the event line relates to accruing an obligation for sick days, vacation days, and other types of compensated absences. These obligations are accrued in the current period and are often related to the amount of time an employee has been employed. Stock options and other types of performance bonuses, which often are accounted for at the end of an accounting period, constitute the next event. In some instances, employees may leave an employer prior to retirement yet still be entitled to certain benefits. These benefits are known as *postemployment benefits* and are different from the final event listed—pensions and other postretirement benefits.

EX 17-1 EMPLOYEE COMPENSATION EVENT LINE

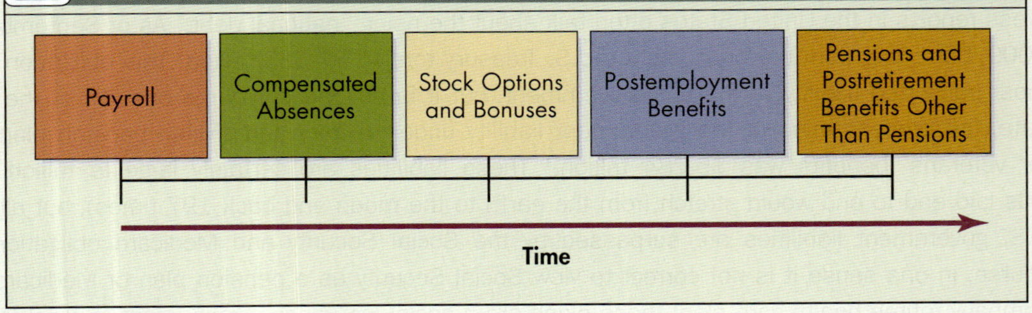

[2] *Health, United States, 2008*, National Center for Health Statistics, Centers for Disease Control and Prevention, U.S. Department of Health and Human Services, (Table 26. Life expectancy at birth, at 65 years of age, and at 75 years of age, by race and sex: United States, selected years 1900–2005).

? QUESTIONS

1. The U.S. federal government has two obligations that each total over $5 trillion. One of these obligations is the "national debt." What is the other?
2. How will the changing age mix of the U.S. population over the next 30 years make the satisfaction of retired workers' Social Security claims more difficult?
3. In addition to the pension costs associated with retired workers, what other substantial cost must General Motors bear with respect to retired workers?

Answers to these questions can be found on page 17-46.

This chapter will proceed in the order of the employee compensation event line. We first focus on payroll, followed by issues related to compensated absences. Stock options and bonuses are then briefly discussed. Issues related to postemployment benefits are then reviewed, followed by a detailed discussion of pensions, including a discussion of the international standards for pension accounting. Postretirement benefits other than pensions are discussed in the final section of this chapter.

Routine Employee Compensation Issues

1 **Account for payroll and payroll taxes, and understand the criteria for recognizing a liability associated with compensated absences.**

WHY **Even routine employee compensation issues involve much more than merely recognizing an expense for an employee's total salary or wage. Proper reporting of compensation requires an understanding of these issues.**

HOW **In addition to salary or wage expense, a company must recognize payroll tax expense for Social Security and unemployment taxes. A company must also carefully record amounts withheld from an employee's salary or wage for income taxes and other items. Finally, an adjusting entry for vacation and sick days earned during a year must be made.**

In the area of employee compensation, the complexities associated with pensions have received a great deal of attention in recent years. Before we turn our attention to pensions, we will first discuss employee compensation issues associated with the current pay period. Along with accounting for current payroll issues, we will discuss issues associated with compensated absences: sick pay, vacation pay, and so on.

Payroll and Payroll Taxes

In an ongoing entity, salaries and wages of officers and other employees accrue daily. Normally, no entry is made for these expenses until payment is made. A liability for unpaid salaries and wages is recorded, however, at the end of an accounting period when a more precise matching of revenues and expenses is desired. An estimate of the amount of unpaid wages and salaries is made, and an adjusting entry is prepared to recognize the amount due. Usually, the entire accrued amount is identified as salaries payable with no attempt to identify the withholdings associated with the accrual. When payment is made in the subsequent period, the amount is allocated between the employee and other entities such as government taxing units, unions, and insurance companies.

For example, assume that a company has 15 employees who are paid every two weeks. At December 31, four days of unpaid wages have accrued. Analysis reveals that the 15 employees earn a total of $1,000 a day. Thus, the adjusting entry at December 31 would be as follows:

Salaries and Wages Expense	4,000	
Salaries and Wages Payable		4,000

When payment is made, Salaries and Wages Payable will be debited for $4,000.

Social Security and income tax legislation impose five taxes based on payrolls:

1. Federal old-age, survivors', and disability (tax to both employer and employee)
2. Federal hospital insurance (tax to both employer and employee)
3. Federal unemployment insurance (tax to employer only)
4. State unemployment insurance (tax to employer only)
5. Individual income tax (tax to employee only but withheld and paid by employer)

Federal Old-Age, Survivors', and Disability Tax The Federal Insurance Contributions Act (FICA), generally referred to as Social Security legislation, provides for FICA taxes from both employers and employees to provide funds for federal old-age, survivors', and disability benefits for certain individuals and members of their families. At one time, only employees were covered by this legislation; however, coverage now includes most individuals who are self-employed.

Provisions of the legislation require an employer of one or more employees, with certain exceptions, to withhold FICA taxes from each employee's wages. The amount of the tax is based on a tax rate and wage base as currently specified in the law. The tax rate and wage base both have increased dramatically since the inception of the Social Security program in the 1930s. The initial rate of FICA tax was 1% in 1937; the rate in effect for 2010 was 6.20%. During that same period, the annual wages subject to FICA tax increased from $3,000 to $106,800. The taxable wage base is subject to yearly increases based on cost-of-living adjustments in Social Security benefits.

The employer remits the amount of FICA tax withheld for all employees, along with a matching amount, to the federal government. The employer is required to maintain complete records and submit detailed support for the tax remittance. The employer is responsible for the full amount of the tax even if employee contributions are not withheld.

Federal Hospital Insurance The Federal Insurance Contributions Act (FICA) also includes a provision for Medicare tax. This tax differs from the tax previously discussed in that the tax is applied to all wages earned; there is no upper limit. The tax rate for 2010 was 1.45% for both the employer and the employee.[3]

Federal Unemployment Insurance The Federal Social Security Act and the Federal Unemployment Tax Act (FUTA) provide for the establishment of unemployment insurance plans. Employers with insured workers employed in each of 20 weeks during a calendar year or who pay $1,500 or more in wages during any calendar quarter are affected.

[3] For illustrative purposes and end-of-chapter exercises and problems, a combined FICA rate of 7.65% will be used.

Under present provisions of the law, the federal government taxes eligible employers on the first $7,000 paid to every employee during the calendar year. The rate of tax in effect since 1985 has been 6.2%, but the employer is allowed a tax credit limited to 5.4% for taxes paid under state unemployment compensation laws. No tax is levied on the employee. When an employer is subject to a tax of 5.4% or more as a result of state unemployment legislation, the federal unemployment tax is 0.8% of the qualifying wages.

Payment to the federal government is required quarterly. Unemployment benefits are paid by the individual states. Revenues collected by the federal government under the acts are used to meet the cost of administering state and federal unemployment plans as well as to provide supplemental unemployment benefits.

State Unemployment Insurance State unemployment compensation laws are not the same in all states. In most states, laws call for tax only on employers, but in a few states, taxes are applicable to both employers and employees. Each state law specifies the classes of exempt employees, the number of employees required or the amount of wages paid before the tax is applicable, and the contributions that are to be made by employers and employees. Exemptions are frequently similar to those under the federal act. Tax payment is generally required on or before the last day of the month following each calendar quarter.

Although the normal tax on employers may be 5.4%, states have merit rating or experience plans providing for lower rates based on employers' individual employment experiences. Employers with stable employment records are taxed at a rate in keeping with the limited amount of benefits required for their former employees; employers with less satisfactory employment records contribute at a rate more nearly approaching 5.4% in view of the higher amount of benefits paid to their former employees. Savings under state merit systems are allowed as credits in the calculation of the federal contribution, so the federal tax does not exceed 0.8% even though an employer entitled to a lower rate under the merit rating system makes payment of less than 5.4%.

Income Tax Federal income taxes on the wages of individuals are collected in the period in which the wages are paid. The "pay-as-you-go" plan requires employers to withhold income tax from wages paid to their employees. Most states and many local governments also impose income taxes on the earnings of employees that the employer must withhold and remit. Withholding is required not only of employers engaged in a trade or business but also of religious and charitable organizations, educational institutions, social organizations, and governments of the United States, the states, the territories, and their agencies, instrumentalities, and political subdivisions. Certain classes of wage payments are exempt from withholding although they are still subject to income tax.

An employer must meet withholding requirements under the law even if wages of only one employee are subject to such withholdings. The amounts to be withheld by the employer are developed from formulas provided by the law or from tax withholding tables made available by the government. Withholding is based on the length of the payroll period, the amount earned, and the number of withholding exemptions claimed by the employee. Taxes required under FICA (both employee and employer portions) and income tax that has

FYI

Not all countries require employers to withhold income tax from employees. For example, in Hong Kong an employee is entirely responsible to accumulate sufficient funds to pay the 15% flat income tax due at the end of the year. Financial institutions are happy to arrange "tax loans" for those who forget to set aside the money to pay their taxes.

been withheld by the employer are paid to the federal government at the same time. These combined taxes are deposited in an authorized bank quarterly, monthly, or several times each month, depending on the amount of the liability. Quarterly and annual statements providing a summary of all wages paid by the employer must also be filed.

Accounting for Payroll Taxes To illustrate the accounting procedures for payroll taxes, assume that salaries for the month of January for a retail store with 15 employees are $16,000. The state unemployment compensation law provides for a tax on employers of 5.4%. Income tax withholdings for the month are $1,600. Assume that FICA rates are 7.65% for employer and employee. Entries for the payroll and the employer's payroll taxes follow:

Salaries Expense	16,000	
FICA Taxes Payable		1,224
Employees Income Taxes Payable		1,600
Cash		13,176
To record payment of payroll and related employee withholdings.		
Payroll Tax Expense	2,216*	
FICA Taxes Payable		1,224
State Unemployment Taxes Payable		864
Federal Unemployment Taxes Payable		128
To record the payroll tax liability of the employer.		

*Computation:

Tax under FICA (0.0765 × $16,000)	$1,224
Tax under state unemployment insurance legislation (0.054 × $16,000)	864
Tax under FUTA [0.008 (0.062 – credit of 0.054) × $16,000]	128
Total payroll tax expense	$2,216

When tax payments are made to the proper agencies, the tax liability accounts are debited and Cash is credited.

The employer's payroll taxes, as well as the taxes withheld from employees, are based on amounts paid to employees during the period regardless of the basis employed for reporting income. When financial reports are prepared on the accrual basis, the employer will have to recognize both accrued payroll and the employer's payroll taxes relating thereto by adjustments at the end of the accounting period.

CAUTION

Don't forget that to ensure that the financial statements are properly stated, an adjusting entry is required at the end of an accounting period if salaries and wages are owed.

For example, assume that the salaries and wages accrued at December 31 were $9,500. Of this amount, $2,000 was subject to unemployment tax and $6,000 to FICA tax. Although the salaries and wages will not be paid until January of the following year, the concept of matching requires these costs to be allocated in the period in which they were incurred. This allocation is accomplished with an adjusting entry. The adjusting entry for the employer's payroll taxes would be as follows:

Payroll Tax Expense	583*	
FICA Taxes Payable		459
State Unemployment Taxes Payable		108
Federal Unemployment Taxes Payable		16
To accrue the payroll tax liability of the employer.		

*Computation:

Tax under FICA (0.0765 × $6,000)	$459
Tax under state unemployment insurance legislation (0.054 × $2,000)	108
Tax under FUTA (0.008 × $2,000)	16
Total payroll tax expense	$583

Agreements with employees may provide for payroll deductions and employer contributions for other items, such as group insurance plans, pension plans, savings bond purchases, or union dues. Such agreements call for accounting procedures similar to those described for payroll taxes.

Compensated Absences

Compensated absences include payments by employers for vacation, holiday, illness, or other personal activities. Employees often earn paid absences based on the time employed. Generally, the longer an employee works for a company, the longer the vacation allowed or the more liberal the time allowed for illnesses. At the end of any given accounting period, a company has a liability for earned but unused compensated absences. The matching principle requires that the estimated amounts earned be charged against current revenue and a liability established for that amount.[4] The difficult part of this accounting treatment is estimating how much should be accrued. The FASB requires a liability to be recognized for compensated absences that (1) have been earned through services already rendered, (2) vest or can be carried forward to subsequent years, and (3) are estimable and probable.

For example, assume that a company has a vacation pay policy for all employees. If all employees had the same anniversary date for computing time in service, the computations would not be too difficult. However, most plans provide for a flexible employee starting date. To compute the liability, a careful inventory of all employees must be made to include the number of years of service, rate of pay, carryover of unused vacation from prior periods, turnover, and the probability of taking the vacation.

To illustrate the accounting for compensated absences, assume that S&N Corporation has 20 employees who are paid an average of $700 per week. During 2012, employees earned a total of 40 vacation weeks but took only 30 weeks of vacation that year. They took the remaining 10 weeks of vacation in 2013 when the average rate of pay was $800 per week. The entry to record the accrued vacation pay on December 31, 2012, follows:

Wages Expense	7,000	
Vacation Wages Payable		7,000
To record accrued vacation wages ($700 × 10 weeks).		

This entry assumes that wages expense has already been recorded for the 30 weeks of vacation taken during 2012. Therefore, the income statement would reflect the total wages expense for the entire 40 weeks of vacation earned during the period. On its December 31, 2012, balance sheet, S&N would report a current liability of $7,000 to reflect the obligation for the 10 weeks of vacation pay that are owed. In 2013, when the additional vacation weeks are taken and the payroll is paid, S&N would make the following entry:

Wages Expense	1,000	
Vacation Wages Payable	7,000	
Cash		8,000
To record payment at current rates of previously earned vacation time ($800 × 10 weeks).		

[4] FASB ASC paragraphs 710-10-25-1 through 3, Compensated Absences.

Because the vacation weeks have now been used, this entry eliminates the liability. An adjustment to Wages Expense is required because the liability was recorded at the rates of pay in effect during the time the compensation (vacation pay) was earned. However, the cash is being paid at the current rate, which requires an adjustment to Wages Expense. If the rate of pay for the 10 weeks of vacation taken in 2013 had remained the same as the rate used to record the accrual on December 31, 2012, there would not have been an adjustment to Wages Expense. The entry to record payment in 2013 would simply be a debit to the payable and a credit to Cash for $7,000.

An exception to the requirement for accrual of compensated absences, such as vacation pay, is made for sick pay. The FASB decided that sick pay should be accrued only if it vests with the employee, that is, the employee is entitled to compensation for a certain number of "sick days" regardless of whether the employee is actually absent for that period. Upon

FASB CODIFICATION

The Issue: You are an accounting student and are generally acknowledged to be the best accounting student on campus. Your organic chemistry professor (you are taking a broad set of elective courses to enhance your accounting training), Harold Pearl, has come to you with an accounting question. Professor Pearl reports that he had a very unpleasant conversation with the university accountant the day before. The accountant says that because Professor Pearl receives a university "sabbatical" once every seven years, the cost of that "sabbatical" must be partially accrued (whatever that means; Professor Pearl is not sure) in each of the six years leading up to the "sabbatical" year. The result is that the university compensation cost related to Professor Pearl in each year is one-sixth higher than Professor Pearl's actual annual cash compensation. As a result, Professor Pearl's cash compensation must be reduced by 17% ... immediately.

Professor Pearl is dismayed. To him, this seems unfair. He reports to you that this "sabbatical" year is not a year in which he relaxes on the beach. Sure, he has no classes that year. However, during that year he is required to appear at the organic chemistry lab each day and mentor chemistry graduate students. He enjoys the work, but it is not as if he were really taking the year off. He wants you to help him convince the university accountant that it is not right to "accrue," in advance, the cost of his "sabbatical" year salary.

The Question: Should a university accrue an expense, in advance, for faculty who receive a periodic sabbatical year?

Searching the Codification: There are two ways to find the answer to Professor Pearl's question. First, the brute force approach is to just type "sabbatical" into the search bar at the top right of the FASB ASC home page. Unfortunately, this doesn't work when using the Basic View (free) version of the Codification. So, the second approach is to look through the menu of the 71X (Compensation) family of topics. Here are some hints. This looks like a general compensation issue not related to pensions, stock compensation, or severance benefits (euphemistically called "nonretirement postemployment benefits"). Next, this is an overall issue, not one related to airlines or regulated industries. Final hint: This is an issue of when the sabbatical year cost should be recognized (accrued now or recognized in the sabbatical year itself).

The Answer: The correct treatment is described on page 17-47.

leaving the firm, the employee would be compensated for any unused sick time. If the sick pay does not vest, it is recorded as an expense only when actually paid.[5]

Although compensated absences are not deductible for income tax purposes until the vacation, holiday, or illness occurs and the payment is made, GAAP requires them to be recognized as liabilities on the financial statements.

Nonroutine Employee Compensation Issues

2 Compute performance bonuses, and recognize the issues associated with postemployment benefits.

WHY **The full cost of employee services includes payments, or promises of payments, associated with bonuses and stock options, as well as termination benefits.**

HOW **The compensation expense associated with a bonus is recognized in the period in which it is earned. Computation of compensation expense associated with stock options requires that the fair value of the options be estimated; details on the accounting for stock-based compensation are included in Chapter 13. The total termination benefits payable to employees are recognized when the termination news is communicated to the employees.**

In addition to routine compensation issues that are addressed on a regular basis, several other compensation issues arise, often at the end of the period. These issues, performance-based incentive plans either in the form of stock or bonus, are discussed in this section. We conclude this section with a discussion of the compensation issues that may arise following employment but prior to retirement.

Stock-Based Compensation and Bonuses

As discussed in Chapter 13, stock options are often a part of an employee's compensation package. While stock option compensation (particularly performance based) is more common for upper management and directors, many companies have stock option plans available for all employees. The amount of compensation expense reported related to stock-based compensation is a function of the fair value of the options on the date they are granted and the type of stock-based compensation plan. With a simple stock-based compensation plan, total compensation expense is the number of options granted multiplied by the fair value of each option as of the grant date. This expense is allocated over the period of time that the employees have to stay with the company in order to earn the options. With a performance-based stock option plan, total compensation expense is equal to the fair value of each option as of the grant date multiplied by the number of options that are probable to be awarded. This amount is re-evaluated at the end of each year. Some stock-based compensation plans call for payment in cash such as with cash stock appreciation rights (SARs). These liability amounts are remeasured

FYI

The existence of an earnings-based bonus plan is intended to encourage managers to work harder and smarter to improve the company's performance. However, such a plan also increases managers' incentive to manipulate reported earnings. In fact, one of the factors looked at by auditors in evaluating the risk of financial statement fraud in a company is whether the company has an earnings-based management bonus plan.

[5] FASB ASC paragraphs 710-10-25-6 through 8, Sick Pay Benefits.

at the end of each year, and a catch-up adjustment is made to compensation expense. Refer back to Chapter 13 for a discussion of the details associated with stock-based compensation.

In addition to stock options, employees often earn bonuses based on a company's performance over a given period of time. This additional compensation should be recognized in the period in which it is earned. Bonuses are often based on some measure of the employer's income. For example, assume that Photo Graphics, Inc., gives its store managers a 10% bonus based on individual store earnings. The bonus is to be based on income after deduction for the bonus but before deduction for income taxes. Assume furthermore that income for a particular store is \$100,000 before charging any bonus or income taxes. The bonus would be calculated as follows:

$$\begin{aligned} B &= 0.10(\$100{,}000 - B) \\ B &= \$10{,}000 - 0.10B \\ B + 0.10B &= \$10{,}000 \\ 1.10B &= \$10{,}000 \\ B &= \$9{,}091 \text{ (rounded)} \end{aligned}$$

The bonus would be reported on the income statement as an operating expense, and the bonus payable would be shown as a current liability on the balance sheet unless the bonus was paid immediately in cash. As an example of a bonus plan, **ExxonMobil** disclosed in its 2010 proxy statement filed with the SEC that it has a management bonus plan targeted at its top managers. The plan grants a certain number of "earnings bonus units" to the managers; a manager is entitled to receive cash equal to ExxonMobil's cumulative reported net earnings per share for the next three years up to a cap amount of \$5.75 for each award unit granted in 2009. ExxonMobil's CEO, Rex W. Tillerson, received \$2,400,000 in earnings-based bonus in 2009; his salary for the year was \$2,057,000.

Postemployment Benefits

In a business world where downsizing has become commonplace, an employee cannot count on remaining with one employer for his or her entire career. In addition, employees are making job changes for reasons such as to facilitate career advancement and to enhance their family's quality of life. For these reasons and others, compensation issues following employment but preceding retirement have increased in magnitude. The most common situation in which this issue arises is when an employee is terminated. Examples of the types of benefits typically granted to terminated employees include supplemental unemployment benefits, severance benefits, disability-related benefits, job training and counseling, and continuation

EX 17-2 NOTE DISCLOSURE FOR POSTEMPLOYMENT BENEFITS—NCR

Employee Severance Costs

In the first quarter of 2007, the Company initiated the manufacturing realignment related to its ATM products, which included outsourcing of certain manufacturing activities in the Americas region and shifting other manufacturing activities from high cost to low cost geographies primarily in the EMEA [Europe, Middle East, and Africa] and APJ [Asia Pacific Japan] regions. As a result of this realignment, the Company recorded \$46 million for employee severance and other termination benefits in cost of products in the Condensed Consolidated Statements of Operations in the first quarter of 2007.

of benefits such as health care benefits and life insurance coverage.[6] These are exactly the type of benefits that are often granted to employees as part of a restructuring. Thus, a postemployment benefit obligation would often comprise part of a restructuring charge. In a restructuring, the postemployment benefit obligation is recognized only when the termination is approved by management, the details of the termination are set, and the employees have been notified.[7]

STOP&THINK

Which ONE of the following is NOT a criterion used in identifying a postemployment benefit obligation?

a) The employer's obligation is proportional to the amount of the employee's salary or wage.
b) The employer's obligation relates to rights that vest.
c) The payment of the liability is probable, and the amount can be reasonably estimated.
d) The employer's obligation in the future relates to services already provided by the employee.

The same criteria used in accounting for compensated absences are applied to postemployment benefits. Those criteria are (1) the employer's obligation in the future relates to services already provided by the employee, (2) the employer's obligation relates to rights that vest, and (3) the payment of the liability is probable and the amount can be reasonably estimated.[8] If these criteria are met, then entries made are similar to those illustrated previously for compensated absences. To illustrate the magnitude of postemployment benefits, consider the disclosure provided by **NCR** in the notes to its 2007 first quarter report, shown in Exhibit 17-2.

Accounting for Pensions

3 **Understand the nature and characteristics of employer pension plans, including the details of defined benefit plans.**

WHY **The promises made to employees in a company's pension plan can constitute a huge economic liability. The size of this liability is determined by the details of the plan. Stockholders and creditors need to know how much of the company's future cash flows will be required to be used to satisfy pension promises.**

HOW **With a defined contribution pension plan, pension expense is equal to the amount of the required contribution each year. With a defined benefit plan, annual pension expense is composed of a number of factors, the most important being the implicit interest charge on the actuarial present value of the pension obligation, the present value of new pension benefits earned during the year, offset by a measure of the return on the pension fund for the year.**

Financing retirement years is accomplished by establishing some type of pension plan that sets aside funds during an employee's working years so that at retirement the funds and earnings from investment of the funds may be returned to the employee in lieu of earned wages. In the United States, three major categories of pension plans have emerged:

1. Government plans, primarily Social Security
2. Individual plans, such as individual retirement accounts (IRAs)
3. Employer plans

The third category, employer pension plans, involves several difficult and controversial accounting and reporting issues.

[6] FASB ASC paragraphs 712-10-25-1 through 5, Other Postemployment Benefits.
[7] FASB ASC paragraphs 420-10-25-4 through 10, One-time Employee Termination Benefits.
[8] FASB ASC paragraph 712-10-25-4.

A related accounting issue is the employer's accounting for postretirement benefits other than pensions. These benefits extend beyond the active years of employment and include such items as health care, life insurance, legal services, special discounts on items produced or sold by the employer, and tuition assistance. For both pensions and for other postretirement benefits, the accounting objective is to properly measure both the balance sheet obligation and the current year earnings impact of the value of these promises.

Nature and Characteristics of Employer Pension Plans

The subject of employers' accounting for pensions is very complex, partly because of the many variations in plans that have been developed. Most pension plans are specifically designed for one employer and are known as single-employer pension plans. If several companies contribute to the same plan, it is called a *multiemployer pension plan*. This chapter, like the accounting standards, focuses on accounting for single-employer pension plans.

Funding of Employer Pension Plans The basic purpose of all employer pension plans is the same: to provide retirement benefits to employees. A principal issue concerning pension plans is how to provide sufficient funds to meet the needs of retirees. The Social Security system of the federal government has frequently been criticized because it is not a "funded" plan. FICA taxes (contributions) paid by employers and employees in the current year are used to pay benefits to individuals who are currently retired. This means that the current employees must have faith that a future generation will do the same for them. Such a system creates much doubt and uncertainty.

Private plans are not permitted to operate in this way. Federal law, such as the Employee Retirement Income Security Act (ERISA) of 1974, requires companies to fund their pension plans in an orderly manner so that the employee is protected at retirement. Some pension plans are funded entirely by the employer and are referred to as noncontributory pension plans. In other cases, the employee also contributes to the cost of the pension plan, referred to as a contributory pension plan.[9] The amounts and timing of contributions depend on the particular circumstances and plan provisions. While the provisions of pension plans vary widely and in many cases are very complex, there are two basic classifications of pension plans: (1) defined contribution plans and (2) defined benefit plans.

Defined Contribution Pension Plans Defined contribution pension plans are relatively simple in their construction and raise very few accounting issues for employers. Under these plans, the employer pays a periodic contribution amount into a separate trust fund, which is administered by an independent third-party trustee. The contribution may be defined as a fixed amount each period, a percentage of the employer's income, a percentage of employee earnings, or a combination of these or other factors. As contributions to the fund are made, they are invested by the fund administrator. When an employee retires, the accumulated value in the fund is used to determine the pension payout to the employee. The employee's retirement income therefore depends on how the fund has been managed. If investments have been made wisely, the employee will fare better than if the investments have been managed poorly. In effect, the investment risk is borne by the employee. The employer's obligation extends only to making the specified periodic contribution. This amount is charged to pension expense, and no further accounting is required for the plan. As an example of this type of plan, many college professors belong to

[9] Employee contributions are not considered in subsequent discussions and examples because the chapter is concerned with employers' accounting for pensions.

a defined contribution plan called **TIAA/CREF**. The college or university makes contributions on behalf of the professor, who then must rely on the good judgment of the TIAA/CREF fund managers to ensure his or her retirement security. As of September 2009, TIAA/CREF was the largest private pension plan in the world with assets in excess of $402 billion held on behalf of 3.8 million active and retired employees.

Keith Brofsky/Photodisc/Getty Images

Pensions represent a substantial liability for many companies.

Defined Benefit Pension Plans Defined benefit pension plans are much more complex than defined contribution plans. Under defined benefit plans, the employee is guaranteed a specified retirement income often related to his or her number of years of employment and average salary over a certain number of years. The periodic amount of the employer's contribution is based on the expected future benefits to be paid to employees and is affected by a number of variables. Because the benefits are defined, the contributions (funding) must vary as conditions change. Exhibit 17-3 illustrates the basic nature of a defined benefit plan. A defined contribution plan could be illustrated in the same manner except that the contributions (rather than the benefits) would be defined. This difference, however, is significant and accounts for the complexity of defined benefit plans.

> **FYI**
>
> In a sense, all pension plans are funded completely by the employee. When considering an acceptable level of compensation, both the firm and the employee should consider total compensation: current salary, fringe benefits, and deferred compensation. A higher employer pension contribution presumably means lower current compensation.

Under defined benefit plans, the investment risk is, in substance, borne by the employer. While a separate trust fund usually is maintained for contributions and investment earnings, the employer ultimately is responsible to ensure that employees receive the defined benefits provided by the plan. A pension fund may be viewed essentially as funds set aside to meet the employer's future pension obligation just as funds may be set aside for other purposes, for example, to retire bonds at maturity. One major difference, however, is that a future obligation to retire bonds is a definite amount, while the employer's future obligation for retirement benefits is based on many estimates and assumptions. In addition, U.S. federal law requires minimum pension plan funding, whereas sinking fund requirements are privately negotiated between the borrower and the bondholders.

Defined benefits. Defined benefit pension plans provide for an increase in future retirement benefits as additional services are rendered by an employee. In effect, the employee's total compensation for a period consists of current wages or salaries plus deferred compensation represented by the right to receive a defined amount of future benefits. The amount of future benefits earned by employees for a particular period is determined by actuaries, not accountants. However, an understanding of the basic concepts

EX 17-3 DEFINED BENEFIT PENSION PLANS

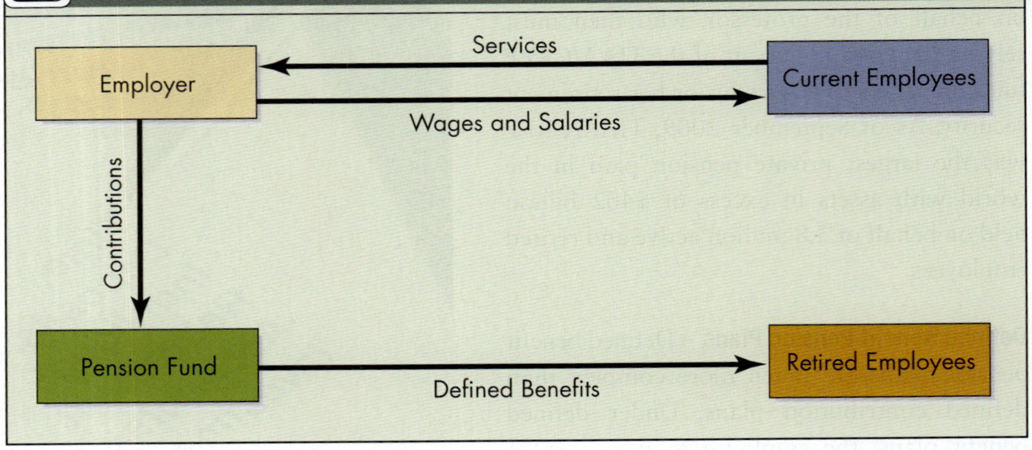

used in measuring future retirement benefits is necessary for understanding the accounting issues relating to pensions.

The amount of future benefits earned for a period is based on the plan's benefit formula, which specifies how benefits are attributed (assigned) to years of employee service. Some plans attribute equal benefits to each year of service rendered, for example, a pension benefit of $100 per month for each year of employee service rendered. Thus, an employee who retires after 30 years of service would be entitled to a monthly benefit of $3,000 ($100 per month × 30 years of service). The benefit attributed to each year of service would be $100 multiplied by the number of months of life expectancy after retirement. Some plans attribute different benefits to different years of service, for example, a pension benefit of $100 per month for each year of service up to 20 years and $120 per month for each additional year of service. Many plans include a benefit formula based on current or future employee earnings. For example, a plan might provide monthly benefits of 2% of an employee's average annual earnings for the five years preceding retirement.

The measurement of future benefits is highly subjective. The amount of benefits earned by employees for a period is based on many variables, including the average age of employees, length of service, expected turnover, vesting provisions, and life expectancy. Thus, one must estimate how many of the current employees will retire and

FYI

The issue of risk and who bears it is very important. With a defined benefit plan, the employee is not completely free of risk; receipt of the benefit payments might be in jeopardy if the employing firm goes bankrupt. To mitigate this risk, Congress created the **Pension Benefit Guaranty Corporation (PBGC)**, a federally supported pension plan insurer. The PBGC collects insurance premiums from participating companies and is given a high-priority claim against company assets in case of bankruptcy.

STOP&THINK

Many companies are changing their plans from defined benefit to defined contribution. Why would employers do this?

a) The total cost of a defined contribution plan is always lower.
b) The U.S. government has mandated a gradual switch from defined benefit to defined contribution plans.
c) A defined contribution pension plan is an attractive form of off-balance-sheet financing.
d) A shift from a defined benefit to a defined contribution plan shifts the investment risk from the company to the employee.

when they will retire, the number of employees who will leave the company prior to retirement, the life expectancy of employees after retirement, and other relevant factors.

Vesting of pension benefits. A key element in all pension plans is the vested benefits provision. *Vesting* occurs when an employee has met certain specified requirements and is eligible to receive pension benefits at retirement regardless of whether the employee continues working for the employer. In early pension plans, vesting did not occur for many years. In extreme cases, vesting occurred only when an employee reached retirement. A major outcome of federal regulation is the much earlier vesting privileges for employees. Most pension plans provide for full vesting after 10 years of employment. Colleges and universities typically require professors to remain at the school for three to five years in order for pension contributions to vest. It is not uncommon for a professor to forfeit nonvested pension contributions when moving from one school to another.

Funding of defined benefit plans. The periodic amounts to be contributed to a defined benefit plan by the employer are directly related to the future benefits expected to be paid to current employees. The methods of funding pension plans vary widely. Most defined benefit plans require periodic contributions that accumulate to the balance needed to pay the promised retirement benefits to employees. Some plans specify an even amount for each year of employee service. Others require a lower amount in the early years of employee service, with an accelerating schedule over the years. Still other plans provide for a higher amount at first and then a declining pattern of funding. The contribution amounts are determined by actuarial formulas and must be adjusted as estimates and assumptions are revised to reflect changing conditions.

All funding methods are based on present values. The additional future benefits earned by employees each year must be discounted to their present value, referred to as the actuarial present value, using an assumed rate of return on pension fund investments. In many cases, employers contribute an amount equal to the present value of future benefits attributed to current services. As noted, however, funding patterns vary, and the amount contributed for a particular period may be less than or greater than the present value of the additional benefits earned for the period. Assume, for example, that the present value of future benefits earned in the current period is determined to be $30,000, using a discount rate of 10%. If the funding method requires a contribution of only $25,000 for the period, the employer has an unfunded obligation of $5,000. At the end of the following year, this obligation will have increased to $5,500 to reflect the interest cost of 10%. When contributions exceed the present value of the future benefits, lower contributions will be required in subsequent periods as a result of earnings on the "overfunded" amount.

The Pension Benefit Guaranty Corporation is charged with monitoring the funding status of defined benefit pension plans in the United States. As of December 31, 2009, the PBGC protects the retirement incomes of about 44 million working Americans in 29,000 defined benefit pension plans. The PBGC provides federal insurance for participants in U.S. pension plans much as the FDIC provides insurance for bank depositors. The PBGC is not funded by general tax revenues; instead, it collects insurance premiums from employers, receives income on investments, and receives funds from pension plans that it takes over. In 2009, the PBGC was directly responsible for the future benefits of 1.3 million active and retired workers whose pension plans had failed. The PBGC Web site lists an interesting rogue's gallery of companies that have declared bankruptcy and passed responsibility for their employees' pensions to the PBGC. The list includes Circuit City, Polaroid, Lehman Brothers ... and many more.

Issues in Accounting for Defined Benefit Plans

Although the provisions of defined benefit pension plans can be extremely complex and the application of accounting standards to a specific plan can be highly technical, the accounting issues themselves are identified easily. Following is a list of these issues, all of which relate to accounting and reporting by employers.

1. The amount of net periodic pension expense to be recognized on the income statement
2. The amount of pension liability or asset to be reported on the balance sheet
3. Accounting for pension settlements, curtailments, and terminations
4. Disclosures needed to supplement the amounts reported in the financial statements

The issue of funding pension plans is purposely omitted from the list. Funding decisions are affected by tax laws, governmental regulations, actuarial computations, and contractual terms, not by accounting standards. They should not directly affect the amount that is reported as net periodic pension expense under the accrual concept.

The next section of the chapter illustrates the basic computational and accounting issues related to pensions in the context of a simple illustration. The simple example is then followed by a more complex illustration that introduces the intricacies for which pension accounting is famous.

Simple Illustration of Pension Accounting

Thakkar Company has established a defined benefit pension plan. As of January 1, 2013, only one employee, Lorien Bach, is enrolled in the plan. Some characteristics of the plan and of Bach as of January 1, 2013, are outlined as follows:

- Bach is 35 years old and has worked for Thakkar for 10 years.
- Bach's salary for 2012 was $40,000.
- Thakkar's pension plan pays a benefit based on an employee's highest salary. Pension payments begin after an employee turns 65, and payments are made at the end of the year. The annual payment is equal to 2% of the highest salary times number of years with the company.
- Bach is an unusually predictable person; it is known with certainty that she will not quit, be fired, or die before age 65. Also, it is known with certainty that she will live exactly 75 years and will therefore collect 10 annual pension payments after she retires. Bach's benefits are already fully vested.
- In valuing pension fund liabilities, Thakkar uses a discount rate of 10%.
- As of January 1, 2013, Thakkar Company has a pension fund containing $10,000. During 2013, Thakkar made additional contributions to the fund totaling $1,500. Also, the fund earned a return of $1,200 during the year. Over the long run, Thakkar expects to earn an average return of 12% on pension fund assets.

Estimation of Pension Obligation The first step in estimating Thakkar Company's pension obligation is to compute the amount of the annual pension payment to be made to Bach when she retires. The amount of the payment depends on Bach's years of service and highest salary. As of January 1, 2013, Bach has put in 10 years of service and, assuming that her most recent salary of $40,000 is her highest salary to date, the forecasted amount of her annual pension payment can be computed as follows:

$$(2\% \times 10 \text{ years}) \times \$40,000 = \$8,000$$

It is known that Bach will live long enough after retirement at age 65 to collect 10 annual pension payments; thus, the total amount of pension benefits that Thakkar expects to pay to Bach is $80,000 (10 years × $8,000). However, $80,000 is an overstatement of the value of Thakkar's pension obligation because the payments won't begin for another 30 years. To properly compute the present value of the payments to Bach, allowance must be made for the fact that the first payment won't be made until Bach is 66 years old (recall that pension payments are made at the end of the year), the payments are spread over 10 years, and Thakkar Company's discount rate is 10%. This discount rate can be thought of as the rate of interest Thakkar could earn on a portfolio of high-quality fixed-income investments (such as highly rated corporate bonds).[10] In *IAS 19*, the IASB recognizes that not all countries have an active market in high-quality corporate bonds. In such markets, the IASB requires the use of the rate on government bonds. In the Web Material (**www.cengage.com/international**) associated with this chapter, it is shown that, using the 10% discount rate, the present value of the expected pension payments to Bach is equal to $2,817.

ifrs

The $2,817 amount can be thought of as follows: If Thakkar Company deposited $2,817 on January 1, 2013, in a bank account yielding 10%, by the end of 30 years when Bach retires, that $2,817 will have accumulated to an amount large enough to support payments of $8,000 per year to Bach for the succeeding 10 years. The $2,817 is the actuarial present value of Thakkar's pension obligation. An actuarial present value takes into account both time value of money considerations and actuarial assumptions (i.e., how long until Bach retires, how long Bach will live after retirement). In practice, such calculations are performed by professionals called *actuaries*. Financial accountants do not need to know how to perform the detailed actuarial present value calculations, but they should understand the general concepts underlying the calculations.

The $2,817 pension obligation just computed is called the accumulated benefit obligation (ABO). The ABO is the actuarial present value of the expected future pension payments, using the current salary as the basis for forecasting the amount of the pension benefit payments. The ABO approach ignores the impact of expected future salary increases on the amount of the benefit payments. An alternative measure of the pension obligation that does consider the impact of future salary increases is called the projected benefit obligation (PBO).

FYI

Over the past 10 years, *Job Rated Almanac* has rated being an actuary as one of the top jobs in America based on income, outlook, physical demands, stress, and security. How much do actuaries make? Starting salaries are around $54,000, with top salaries exceeding $130,000. Training in math, computers, communication, and business are needed to become a successful actuary.

To illustrate the difference between the PBO and the ABO, assume that Thakkar Company expects Bach's 2012 salary of $40,000 to increase 5% every year until retirement. As a result, Bach's salary is expected to increase to $172,877 by the year 2042, Bach's last year of employment.[11] The pension benefit payment based on this salary is as follows:

$$(2\% \times 10 \text{ years}) \times \$172{,}877 = \$34{,}575 \text{ (rounded)}$$

The PBO at January 1, 2013, is $12,176 (see the Web Material associated with this chapter for details of the computation). This is the present value of the 10 future annual

[10] FASB ASC paragraph 715-30-35-43

[11] PV = $40,000, N = 30, I = 5% → FV = $172,877

EX 17-4 THAKKAR COMPANY—PROJECTED BENEFIT OBLIGATION, JANUARY 1, 2013

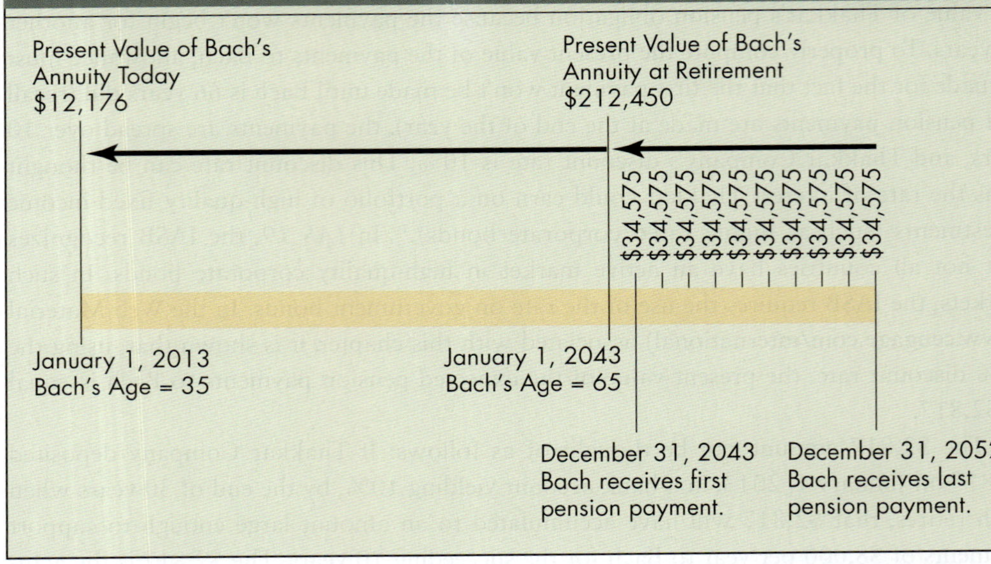

payments of $34,575 that Bach is expected to receive. The diagram in Exhibit 17-4 illustrates the relationship between the future payments and the PBO.

Both the PBO and the ABO computations are based on the amount of pension benefits that have already been earned—in this case, on the 10 years of service Bach has provided to Thakkar. The difference between the PBO and the ABO comes in the estimate of Bach's highest salary. The ABO computations ignore likely future salary increases; the PBO computations include estimates of those increases. The quantitative difference between these two approaches can be substantial. For Thakkar, the $2,817 ABO is substantially lower than the $12,176 value computed for the PBO.

The numerical relationship between the ABO and the PBO can be presented as follows:

Accumulated benefit obligation, January 1, 2013	$ 2,817
Additional amounts related to projected pay increases	9,359
Projected benefit obligation, January 1, 2013	$12,176

So which is a better measure of a firm's pension obligation, the PBO or the ABO? FASB ASC Topic 715 identifies the PBO as the measure appropriate for use in the financial statements. The ABO is not involved in any of the pension-related recognition provisions, but it is disclosed in the notes to the financial statements. This choice of the PBO as the primary measure of a firm's pension obligation was not without some controversy.[12] It was argued that use of the PBO is not appropriate because it embodies future salary increases and that the historical cost accounting model does not include recognition of future events. This argument was countered with the observation that the use of a discount rate also results in recognition of future events because the discount rate includes a premium for expected future inflation. It was argued that to allow recognition of the impact of expected future inflation but not to allow consideration of expected salary increases would result in a gross

[12] Adoption of FASB *Statement No. 87* (the source of the standards in FASB ASC Topic 715) was opposed by three of the seven members of the Board. A description of the dissenting views is included at the end of the primary text of this pre-codification *Statement* (following paragraph 77).

understatement of the pension obligation in some cases. Hence, the PBO is the primary measure of a firm's pension obligation.

As of January 1, 2013, the pension obligation for Thakkar, as measured by the PBO, is $12,176, and from the information given at the beginning of the illustration, the total fair value of the pension fund is $10,000. One possible way to present this information on a balance sheet is to list the pension fund among the noncurrent assets and the pension obligation as a noncurrent liability. However, FASB standards stipulate that these two items be offset against one another and requires that a single net amount be shown as either a net pension asset or a net pension liability.[13] Thakkar would calculate the appropriate balance sheet amount in the following way:

PBO, January 1, 2013	$12,176
Pension fund at fair value, January 1, 2013	10,000
Pension-related liability, January 1, 2013	$ 2,176

If the fair value of the pension fund had exceeded the projected benefit obligation, the resulting net asset would have been labeled Pension-Related Asset.

Why does Topic 715 require offsetting pension obligations and pension funds instead of separate recognition of each? The answer is, in one word, tradition. Accepted practice before *Statement No. 87* was adopted in 1985 was to offset pension obligations and pension funds; to avoid too great a change, the FASB decided to maintain that method. *Statement No. 87* was viewed as an improvement over prior standards but not too different from those standards to preserve the "gradual, evolutionary" nature of accounting standard setting.[14] The existing standard in Topic 715 preserves that traditional method of reporting. The separate components of the pension-related liability or asset are disclosed in the notes to the financial statements in a manner similar to the table shown previously.

Computation of Pension Expense for 2013 In the simple Thakkar Company example, measurement of pension expense[15] for the year involves consideration of three factors:

1. Implied interest on the beginning-of-the-period pension obligation (which increases the PBO)
2. New pension benefits earned by employees through service during the year (which increase the PBO)
3. Investment return on the pension fund (which increases the fair value of the pension fund)

These three factors will be considered in turn.

Interest cost. The projected benefit obligation on January 1, 2013, is $12,176. This represents an amount owed by Thakkar to its employee, Bach. The 10% discount rate used in the computation of the PBO is called the obligation discount rate and can be viewed as the implied interest rate on this debt. In a sense, employees have agreed to loan the company money (by deferring the receipt of some of their compensation) to be repaid

[13] FASB ASC paragraph 715-30-25-1. In a more complicated example, additional pension-related items would also be included in the balance sheet; these items are reported in the accumulated other comprehensive income portion of equity. These items are discussed later in the chapter.
[14] Pre-codification *Statement of Financial Accounting Standards No. 87*, par. 107.
[15] To avoid confusion, the text discussion refers to *pension expense* instead of *pension cost*. Periodic pension cost may be expensed immediately or it may be capitalized as part of an asset such as inventory. In all of our examples, we will assume that pension costs are expensed immediately.

when they retire. As is the case with all loans, there is a charge for interest for the time period for which the money is loaned. Accordingly, one aspect of annual pension expense is the increase in the PBO resulting from implicit interest on this pension obligation, computed as follows:

PBO, Beginning of Period	×	Discount Rate	=	Interest Cost
$12,176	×	0.10	=	$1,218 (rounded)

Service cost. Bach's work for Thakkar Company during the year results in an increase in the forecasted annual pension benefit payments from Thakkar to Bach because those payments are now computed based on 11 years of service instead of 10 years. The impact of this extra year of service is to increase the December 31, 2013, projected benefit obligation by $1,339 over what it would have been if Bach had just vacationed for the entire year. (See the Web Material associated with this chapter for the detailed present value computations.) Therefore, the service cost element of pension expense for the year is $1,339. In practice, of course, service cost computations are very complex and are done by actuaries.

Return on the pension fund. Pension expense is reduced by the return on the pension fund for the year. Just as liabilities and assets are offset to arrive at a net measure of accrued pension liability or prepaid pension cost, the return on the pension fund is offset against interest and service costs to compute a single net pension expense number. FASB ASC paragraphs 715-30-35-22 and 23 indicate that instead of using the actual return, the expected long-term return should be used; more about why this number is used will be discussed shortly. This return is typically computed by multiplying the fair value of the pension fund as of the beginning of the year by some estimate of the average rate of return the pension fund is expected to earn over the long run. For Thakkar Company, this long-term expected rate of return has been estimated to be 12%, and for this introductory example, we will assume that expected return and actual return are equal. Accordingly, for 2013, Thakkar's net pension expense is reduced by $1,200 ($10,000 × 0.12).

In addition to these changes in the PBO and the pension fund, two additional events are common when dealing with pension plans: contributions to the plan and benefits paid from the plan. Contributions increase the amount in the pension fund; in this example, contributions of $1,500 were made during the year. Benefits paid from the plan have two effects: They reduce the amount in the pension fund, and they reduce the PBO. The reason the PBO is reduced is that if the benefits have been paid, they are no longer projected to be paid. In this simplified example, no benefits were paid during the year.

To review, the PBO is a present value measure of the future benefits expected to be paid to employees based on their employment to date but taking into consideration, if applicable, expected increases in wages that would affect their retirement benefits. The measurement is based on actuarial estimation of such factors as life expectancy, employee turnover, and interest rates. The projected benefit obligation increases each year as additional benefits are earned by employees through another year of service (service cost) and by the passage of time that brings employees one year closer to receiving their benefits (interest cost). The PBO decreases each year by the pension payments to retired employees. In addition, the obligation may increase or decrease by changes in any of the actuarial assumptions enumerated previously. These changes can be summarized as shown on page 17-21.

Project benefit obligation, beginning of year	+	Service cost and interest cost	−	Retirement benefits paid	±	Change in actuarial assumptions	=	Projected benefit obligation, end of year

The fair value of the pension fund is based on its market value at a given measurement date. The fair value of the pension fund increases each year by employer contributions to the fund and decreases by the retirement benefits paid. The fair value also changes by the amount of earnings on the pension fund, including changes in the market value of the fund. These changes can be summarized as follows:

Fair value of pension fund, beginning of year	+	Employer contributions	−	Retirement benefits paid	±	Actual return on pension fund	=	Fair value of pension fund, end of year

Exhibit 17-5 illustrates how service costs, interest costs, and return on the pension fund change the PBO and the fair value of the pension fund (FVPF) and how those changes are combined to be reflected on the income statement.

Net pension expense for 2013 for Thakkar is computed as follows:

Interest cost	$ 1,218
Service cost	1,339
Less: Expected return on the pension fund	(1,200)
Net pension expense	$ 1,357

Note that benefits paid have no effect on the net pension liability as they reduce the FVPF and the PBO by the same amount. Also note that the amount of contributions to the pension fund is not reflected on the income statement. That amount would be disclosed as a cash outflow on the statement of cash flows.

EX 17-5 ANALYSIS OF PENSION COMPONENTS

Components Pension	Fair Value of Pension Fund		Projected Benefit Obligation		Balance Sheet: Pension-Related Liability	Income Statement: Pension Expense
January 1 balance	$10,000	+	$(12,176)	=	$(2,176)	
Service costs			(1,339)			$1,357
Interest costs			(1,218)			
Expected* return	1,200					
Contributions	1,500					
Benefits paid	0		0			
December 31 balance	$12,700	+	$(14,733)	=	$(2,033)	

*In this example, expected return and actual return are equal.

The Thakkar Company illustration contains only the most basic elements of accounting for pensions. In more complex cases, pension expense is affected by amortization of deferred gains and losses from prior periods, amortization of the impact of a change in the terms of the pension plan, and amortization of the impact of changes in the actuarial assumptions. The accounting for these components of pension expense is illustrated in a subsequent example.

Computation of Pension-Related Liability As of December 31, 2013, the PBO for Thakkar is $14,733 (see the Web Material associated with this chapter for the detailed calculations), and the total FVPF is $12,700 ($10,000 + $1,200 return + $1,500 new contributions). As illustrated previously, the PBO and the FVPF are offset to arrive at a single balance sheet amount. As of December 31, 2013, Thakkar Company would perform the following calculation:

PBO, December 31, 2013	$ 14,733
Pension fund at fair value, December 31, 2013	(12,700)
Pension-related liability, December 31, 2013	$ 2,033

The net accrued pension liability of $2,033 would typically be shown in the Noncurrent Liability section of Thakkar's balance sheet.[16] The preceding table would be included in the notes to the financial statements.

Basic Pension Journal Entries The basic accounting entries for pensions are straightforward. An entry is made to accrue the pension expense, and another entry is made to record the contribution to the pension fund. For convenience, a single account, the pension-related asset/liability account, is used to reflect changes in the net pension asset or liability. Because Thakkar started the year with a credit balance of $2,176 in this account, it is a liability account in this example. Thakkar Company would make the following journal entries for 2013:

Pension Expense	1,357	
Pension-Related Asset/Liability		1,357
To record 2013 pension expense.		
Pension-Related Asset/Liability	1,500	
Cash		1,500
To record 2013 contribution to pension plan.		

As a result of these entries, pension expense of $1,357 would be reported as an expense on the income statement. The combined effect of the two entries is to decrease the Pension-Related Liability account by $143 ($1,500 − $1,357); the balance in Pension-Related Liability is $2,033 ($2,176 beginning balance − $143 decrease). In a more complicated example, the summary journal entry to recognize pension expense can also involve either a debit or credit to other comprehensive income and/or accumulated other comprehensive income. This is illustrated in the following examples.

Key Points from the Thakkar Company Example Before considering a more complicated example, take a moment now to review some important points illustrated with the Thakkar Company example.

[16] FASB ASC paragraph 715-20-45-3. A portion of the pension-related liability is reported as current to the extent that the present value of benefits to be paid in the next 12 months exceeds the fair value of the plan assets.

- The actuarial computations are complicated, even in the simplest possible example. For proof, see the Web Material associated with this chapter. The good news is that in real life these computations are done by actuaries.
- The balance sheet and income statement amounts related to pensions are sensitive to the actuarial assumptions made.
- The balance sheet amount is a combination of two items: the projected benefit obligation and the fair value of the pension fund. The details of the computation are disclosed in the notes to the financial statements.
- Net pension expense is also a conglomeration of several items. The three main items are interest cost, service cost, and expected return on the pension fund.

In the next section, the discussion of pension accounting continues with a more complex example. That example provides detailed coverage of the treatment of deferred items and illustrates the impact of pension accounting on the Accumulated Other Comprehensive Income section of stockholders' equity. A work sheet approach that greatly simplifies the handling of complex pension situations is introduced.

Comprehensive Pension Illustration

4 **Use the components of the pension-related asset/liability and changes in the components to compute the periodic expense associated with pensions and to compute the impact on other comprehensive income.**

WHY **A company's pension obligation and pension fund are long-term items. As a result, pension accounting seeks to minimize the temporary impact of fluctuations in short-term interest rates and investment returns. However, this admirable objective substantially complicates the accounting for pensions. The deferred impact of these temporary items is reported in equity as part of accumulated other comprehensive income.**

HOW **The pension-related asset/liability account reflects the difference between the present value of the amount expected to be paid in the future (PBO) and the fair value of the pension fund. Pension expense is the sum of service cost and interest cost, with a subtraction for the expected return on the pension fund. The computation of pension expense is also impacted by the amortization of prior service cost and of any deferred gain or loss in excess of the corridor amount. Deferred gains and losses are reported in the current period as other comprehensive income. The unamortized balance in prior service cost and deferred gains/losses is reported as part of accumulated other comprehensive income.**

The Thakkar Company example included only three factors in the computation of pension expense. In a more general case, a company could recognize as many as five different components of net periodic pension expense. The five components are as follows:

1. Service cost
2. Interest cost
3. Actual return on the pension fund (if any)
4. Amortization of prior service cost (if any)
5. Deferral of current period gain or loss and amortization of deferred net gain or loss

The PBO and the FVPF are used extensively in computing pension cost. Because the FASB (in Topic 715) requires the pension fund (FVPF) and the obligation (PBO) to be offset against each other, they are not reported separately on the employer's balance sheet.

However, detailed records of these and other pension-related balances must be maintained to compute pension cost. These detailed records include accounts for the following three items:

1. Projected Benefit Obligation
2. Fair Value of Pension Fund
3. Accumulated Other Comprehensive Income (AOCI)
   (a) Deferred pension gains and losses
   (b) Prior service cost

Exhibit 17-6 contains a summary of the important elements that impact the reported amounts of these pension-related balance sheet items. These different elements will be discussed in the following example. Throughout the discussion of the components of pension expense, an illustration for a hypothetical company, Thornton Electronics, Inc., will be used.

EX 17-6 OVERVIEW OF WORK SHEET FORMAT

	Pension-Related Asset/Liability		Accumulated Other Comprehensive Income	
Dec. 1 Balance Sheet	**Projected Benefit Obligation (−)**	**Fair Value of Pension Fund (+)**	**Deferred Gain/Loss (+/−)**	**Prior Service Cost (+)**
Income Statement	− Service Cost	+ Actual Return on Pension Fund	+/− Difference Between Actuarial Estimates with Actual Experience	− Amortization of Prior Service Cost
	− Interest Cost		+/− Amortization of Gain/Loss	
	+ Benefits Paid	− Benefits Paid		
Statement of Cash Flows		+ Contributions		
Dec. 31 Balance Sheet	**Projected Benefit Obligation (−)**	**Fair Value of Pension Fund (+)**	**Deferred Gain/Loss (+/−)**	**Prior Service Cost (+)**

Note: All signs are relative to the balance sheet. Positive amounts are debits; negative amounts are credits.

Thornton Electronics—2013

Thornton's pension-related balances as of January 1, 2013, are as follows:

Item	Where Reported	Amount
Projected benefit obligation	Notes	$1,500,000
Fair value of pension fund	Notes	1,385,000
Pension-related liability	Balance Sheet	115,000
Prior service cost (Accumulated other comprehensive income; subtraction from equity)	Balance Sheet	75,000

The PBO, the FVPF, and the net pension liability have been explained previously. Prior service cost is described below.

Prior Service Cost When a pension plan is initially adopted or amended to provide increased benefits, employees are granted additional benefits for services performed in years prior to the plan's adoption or amendment. The cost of these additional benefits to the employer is called *prior service cost*. The amount of prior service cost is determined by actuaries and represents the increase in the PBO arising from the adoption or amendment of the plan. Although prior service cost initially arises from a plan adoption or amendment made in the current period, the accounting profession has been in general agreement that the cost should not be recognized as part of expense at the plan's adoption or amendment date but should be amortized over future periods. This treatment assumes that an adoption or amendment is not part of the normal, ongoing cost of the pension plan and so should not be included in its entirety in the computation of net pension expense for the current period. Instead, the cost represented by a plan adoption or amendment is recognized in the current period as a reduction in other comprehensive income. The prior service cost amount is then amortized in subsequent years, increasing net pension expense in those years. Assuming that the plan adoption occurred on December 31, 2012, the journal entry to record the plan adoption is as follows:

> **STOP&THINK**
>
> What is the relationship between prior service cost and the measurement of the projected benefit obligation (PBO)?
>
> a) There is no relationship between prior service cost and the PBO.
> b) The projected benefit obligation includes some amount related to prior service cost.
> c) Prior service cost includes some amount related to the projected benefit obligation.
> d) The projected benefit obligation and prior service cost are always equal to each other.

Other Comprehensive Income	75,000	
Projected Benefit Obligation		75,000
To record December 31, 2012, prior service cost arising from plan amendment.		

As shown in Exhibit 17-6, prior service cost is an element of the Accumulated Other Comprehensive Income section of equity; the other comprehensive income amount of $75,000 recognized in the journal entry above was closed, at 2012 year-end, to the prior service cost portion of accumulated other comprehensive income. The projection benefit obligation amount is used in computing the net pension-related asset or liability that is reported in the balance sheet.

Under *IAS 19*, "Employee Benefits," prior service cost is often accounted for differently from that explained above. According to paragraph 96 of *IAS 19*, past service cost (equivalent to prior service cost) is recognized as an expense over the period when the retroactive benefits vest. If the retroactive benefits vest over some future time period, then the accounting will be very much like that illustrated above. However, if the retroactive benefits vest immediately, then under *IAS 19* the entire amount of past service cost is expensed immediately.

ifrs

The January 1, 2013, pension information for Thornton Electronics would appear in a pension work sheet as shown in Exhibit 17-7.

The work sheet is divided into two sections: the Financial Statement Accounts section, which shows the net effect of pension-related items on the balance sheet and income

EX 17-7 THORNTON ELECTRONICS, INC.—PENSION WORK SHEET, JANUARY 1, 2013

	Financial Statement Accounts				Detailed Accounts		
					Pension Asset/Liability		AOCI
	Net Pension Expense	Cash	Pension-Related Asset/ (Liability)	Accumulated Other Comprehensive Income	Projected Benefit Obligation	Fair Value of Pension Fund	Prior Service Cost
Balance, January 1, 2013			(115,000)	75,000	(1,500,000)	1,385,000	75,000

Note: Positive amounts are debits; negative amounts are credits.

statement, and the Detailed Accounts section, which lists detailed pension information, to be disclosed in the notes to the financial statements. The formal balance sheet account, Pension-Related Asset/(Liability), summarizes in one number the projected benefit obligation and the fair value of pension fund information contained in the detailed records. The equity account Accumulated Other Comprehensive Income includes deferred gains and losses associated with pension-related items such as the pension plan adoption mentioned earlier. In the work sheet, a credit amount is indicated by parentheses, and the numbers without parentheses are debits.

Information summarizing the 2013 pension activity of Thornton Electronics follows:

Service cost as reported by actuaries	$75,000
Contributions to pension plan	$115,000
Benefits paid to retirees	$125,000
Fair value of pension fund at December 31, 2013	$1,513,500
Obligation discount rate	11.0%
Long-term expected rate of return on the pension fund	10.0%

FYI

Many different interest rates are used throughout the accounting standards. The obligation discount rate can vary over time; thus, the computation of the benefit obligation may vary from one year to another as a result of the change in interest rates. An increase in the rate lowers the present value of the liability; a decrease in the rate increases it. In formulating *Concepts Statement No. 7*, the FASB studied the different ways in which accountants use interest rates.

The 2013 pension information has been entered in the pension work sheet shown in Exhibit 17-8. Each entry is explained below.

Service Cost Recall that service cost is the present value of additional benefits earned by employees during the period. As explained earlier, service cost for the period is determined by actuaries based on the pension plan's benefit formula. Thornton Electronics' actuaries reported 2013 service cost of $75,000. This $75,000 is recorded in work sheet entry (a) as an increase in net periodic pension expense (a debit which ultimately reduces the retained earnings portion of equity when the expense is closed to Retained Earnings) and an increase to the PBO (a credit).

a. Pension Expense	75,000	
Projected Benefit Obligation		75,000
To record 2013 service cost.		

EX 17-8 THORNTON ELECTRONICS, INC.—PENSION WORK SHEET FOR 2013

	Financial Statement Accounts				Detailed Accounts		
					Pension Asset/Liability		AOCI
	Net Pension Expense	Cash	Pension-Related Asset/(Liability)	Accumulated Other Comprehensive Income	Projected Benefit Obligation	Fair Value of Pension Fund	Prior Service Cost
Balance, January 1, 2013			(115,000)	75,000	(1,500,000)	1,385,000	75,000
(a) Service cost	75,000				(75,000)		
(b) Interest cost	165,000				(165,000)		
(c) Actual return	(138,500)					138,500	
(d) Benefits paid					125,000	(125,000)	
(e) PSC amortization	13,636						(13,636)
(f) Pension contribution		(115,000)				115,000	
Balance, December 31, 2013	115,136	(115,000)	(101,500)	61,364	(1,615,000)	1,513,500	61,364

Notes: Positive amounts are debits; negative amounts are credits.
The gray area indicates that no changes are made directly to these accounts. These accounts simply reflect changes that are made to the detailed accounts.

Interest Cost The interest cost represents the fact that the present value of Thornton's pension obligation is increased by the interest on the beginning PBO. The obligation discount rate is used to discount the PBO and to compute the interest cost. The interest cost for 2013 is $1,500,000 × 0.11, or $165,000. The interest cost is shown in entry (b) as a debit to the net periodic pension expense and a credit to the PBO.

b. Pension Expense	165,000	
Projected Benefit Obligation		165,000
To record 2013 interest cost.		

Actual Return on the Pension Fund The assets created by employer contributions to a pension plan usually earn a return that reduces the reported amount of annual pension expense. The return is composed of elements such as interest revenue, dividends, rentals, and changes in the market value of the assets. If a decline in the market value of the pension fund exceeds the earnings on the assets, the actual return will be a negative figure that would increase the pension expense rather than decrease it. The actual return can be computed by comparing the fair value of the pension fund at the beginning and end of the year. After adjusting for current-year contributions and benefits paid to retirees, any change is the actual return on the pension fund. The actual return on the pension fund for Thornton Electronics in 2013 is $138,500, computed as follows:

Fair value of pension fund, December 31, 2013	$1,513,500
Fair value of pension fund, January 1, 2013	1,385,000
Increase in fair value	$ 128,500
Add benefits paid	125,000
Deduct contributions made	(115,000)
Actual return on the pension fund	$ 138,500

The actual return on the pension fund assets is always computed in determining net periodic pension expense. However, as illustrated later, the actual return may be adjusted to the expected return when there is a difference between the two amounts. In this case, the actual return of $138,500 is equal to the expected return ($1,385,000 × 0.10).

The actual return of $138,500 is shown in entry (c) as a credit to the net periodic pension expense (representing a decrease in the expense and, ultimately, an increase in retained earnings) and a debit to the fair value of pension assets (representing an increase in the asset).

c. Pension Fund	138,500	
Pension Expense		138,500
To record 2013 actual return on pension fund.		

Note that benefits paid from fund assets do not reduce the account Cash; benefit payments are shown in entry (d) as a decrease in both the pension fund and the remaining PBO. The benefit payments are made by the pension plan trustee to the retired employees using the assets in the pension fund, so the company itself does not make those direct cash payments. Instead, the entry to reduce cash because of company contributions to the pension fund is shown later.

d. Projected Benefit Obligation	125,000	
Pension Fund		125,000
To record 2013 benefits paid.		

Amortization of Prior Service Cost Prior service cost (PSC) is the cost of benefits granted to employees for past service when a pension plan is adopted or amended. As illustrated in Exhibit 17-7, the prior service cost amount is initially recorded as a credit (increase) to the PBO and a debit (reduction) to Other Comprehensive Income. This other comprehensive income reduction is eventually closed to Accumulated Other Comprehensive Income, reducing this equity account. This deferred loss is then spread out, or amortized to pension expense, over future periods.

The FASB states that prior service cost should be amortized by "assigning an equal amount to each future period of service of each employee active at the date of the amendment who is expected to receive benefits under the plan."[17] The future period of service is referred to as the expected service period. Because employees will have varying years of remaining service, this amortization method will result in a declining amortization charge.

When a company has many employees retiring or terminating in a systematic pattern, a method similar to the sum-of-the-years'-digits depreciation method can be used. The FASB has provided an illustration of how this computation can be made.[18] Assume that Thornton Electronics, Inc., has 150 employees who are expected to receive benefits for prior services under an amendment adopted at the end of 2012. Ten percent of the employees (15 employees) are expected to leave (either retire or quit with vesting privileges) in each of the next 10 years. Employees hired after the plan's amendment date do not affect the amortization. The formula for the sum-of-the-years'-digits depreciation method illustrated in Chapter 11 can be used with a slight modification to reflect the decreased number of employees each period. Thus, the total service years for Thornton Electronics, Inc., could be computed with the following formula:

$$\frac{N(N+1)}{2} \times D = \text{Total future years of service}$$

[17] FASB ASC paragraph 715-30-35-11.

[18] Ibid., Appendix B, illustration 3. FASB ASC paragraphs 715-30-55-93 through 100.

where

N = number of remaining years of service
D = decrease in number of employees working each year

Therefore

$$\frac{10(11)}{2} \times 15 = 825$$

The numerator would begin with the total employees at the time of the plan's amendment and decline by D each period. Under these assumptions, 825 service years will be rendered by the affected employees. The fraction used to determine the amortization has a numerator that declines by 15 employees each year and a denominator that is the sum of the service years, or 825. If the increase in the projected benefit obligation, or prior service cost, arising from the plan's amendment at the end of 2012 was $75,000, the amortization for 2013 would be 150/825 × $75,000, or $13,636. In the following two years, the amount amortized would be 135/825 × $75,000, or $12,273, and 120/825 × $75,000, or $10,909, respectively.

Although the FASB has indicated a preference for this sum-of-the-years'-digits–type method of amortization, the consistent use of an alternative amortization approach that more rapidly reduces the prior service cost is acceptable. An example of such an alternative is the straight-line amortization of prior service cost over the average remaining service period of the employees. To illustrate the straight-line approach using the Thornton Electronics example, the average remaining service life would be 5.5 years (825/150 employees), and $13,636 ($75,000/5.5) would be amortized for each full year.

A separate amortization schedule is necessary for each amendment of the plan. There is no need to alter the schedule for new employees because they would not receive benefits from prior services. If the planned termination or retirement pattern does not occur, adjustments may be necessary later to completely amortize the prior service cost.

For the Thornton Electronics example, the amortization amount based on the number of service years remaining is used. For 2013, this amount is $13,636. In entry (e) of Exhibit 17-8, the $13,636 is shown as an increase in net periodic pension expense (with a debit) and an increase in accumulated other comprehensive income (with a credit).

e. Pension Expense	13,636	
Accumulated Other Comprehensive Income		13,636
To record 2013 amortization of prior service cost.		

Recall that prior service cost is a subcategory of Accumulated Other Comprehensive Income, an equity account. Thus, a credit to Accumulated Other Comprehensive Income reduces the amount of unamortized prior service cost, but this then means that the subtraction from equity is smaller; equity is increased. The prior service cost amount is systematically amortized until the entire equity subtraction has been transferred from accumulated other comprehensive, through pension expense and net income, and into retained earnings. The amortization process increases pension expense each year, but there is no net annual effect on equity (or on annual comprehensive income); instead, the net annual equity effect is that a portion of the equity reduction is transferred from accumulated other comprehensive income to retained earnings each year. The entire reduction in equity, and in comprehensive income, caused by the granting of retroactive benefits upon the plan adoption was recognized immediately when the plan adoption journal entry was initially made, as illustrated earlier.

Plan Contributions Federal government pension funding rules in the United States make U.S. companies with defined benefit pension plans contribute minimum amounts to their pension funds each year. Under the Pension Protection Act of 2006, companies are required to contribute an amount equal to their service cost and interest cost each year plus an additional contribution designed to eliminate any remaining shortfall within seven years. These shortfalls could arise, for example, if the investment performance of the pension plan is worse than expected. Of course, if past superior pension fund performance has created a surplus in the pension fund, subsequent contributions can be cut back or even eliminated for a time.

In the Thornton example, the cash contribution to the pension fund is $115,000. The necessary journal entry is shown as entry (f) in the work sheet in Exhibit 17-8 and is as follows:

f. Pension Fund	115,000	
Cash		115,000
To record 2013 contribution to the pension plan.		

Note the large shaded area on the left side, the Financial Statement Accounts side, of the work sheet. This shaded area represents the fact that the detailed factors that impact the pension-related asset/liability and the pension-related portion of accumulated other comprehensive income during the year are not recorded directly in those accounts but are instead recorded in the detailed accounts contained on the right side of the work sheet. The year-end balance sheet balances in the work sheet ($101,500 for the pension-related liability and $61,364 for accumulated other comprehensive income) reflect the totals from the detailed accounts. The pension-related liability balance is the combination of the end-of-year projected benefit obligation and the fair value of the pension fund ($1,615,000 liability and $1,513,500 asset). In this simple example, the accumulated other comprehensive income balance includes only the unamortized prior service cost.

Summary Journal Entries The six detailed journal entries described above and illustrated in the pension work sheet in Exhibit 17-8 can be summarized in two summary journal entries, as follows:

Pension Expense	115,136	
Pension-Related Asset/Liability		101,500
Accumulated Other Comprehensive Income		13,636
Summary journal entry to recognize pension expense for 2013.		
Pension-Related Asset/Liability	115,000	
Cash		115,000
Summary journal to record pension fund contribution for 2013.		

In the first journal entry, the amount credited to Pension-Related Asset/Liability is calculated strictly by reference to the three primary components of pension expense: service cost, interest cost, and the actual return on the pension fund. In this case, that total is $101,500 ($75,000 + $165,000 − $138,500). The remaining amount of pension expense in this example, prior service cost amortization of $13,636, represents a reclassification from accumulated other comprehensive income to pension expense (which is then closed to Retained Earnings). Additional components of pension expense and their impact on this summary journal entry are illustrated in later examples.

Financial Statement Reporting The four numbers on the Financial Statement Accounts side of the work sheet are reported in Thornton's financial statements, as follows:

- *Net pension expense.* The $115,136 expense is reported as part of compensation expense in Thornton's income statement.
- *Cash.* The $115,000 negative cash amount associated with Thornton's defined benefit pension plan is reported as a cash outflow from operating activities in Thornton's statement of cash flows.
- *Pension-related liability.* The $101,500 pension-related liability is reported in Thornton's balance sheet.
- *Accumulated other comprehensive income.* The $61,364 debit balance in Accumulated Other Comprehensive Income is reported as a subtraction from equity in Thornton's balance sheet.

Note again that the left side of the work sheet includes the items to be reported in Thornton's financial statements and the right side of the work sheet represents the underlying detail that is used to construct the necessary financial statement note disclosure.

Thornton Electronics–2014

The Thornton Electronics example continues with the following information for 2014:

Service cost as reported by actuaries	$87,000
Contributions to pension plan	$75,000
Benefits paid to retirees	$132,000
Actual return on pension fund	$26,350
Actuarial change increasing projected benefit obligation	$80,000
Obligation discount rate	11.0%
Long-term expected rate of return on pension fund	10.0%

The pension work sheet to record the 2014 pension information is shown in Exhibit 17-9. Entries (a) through (e) are similar to those shown previously for 2013. Note that the amount of prior service cost (PSC) amortization has decreased because the remaining service years of the employees in place at the time of the plan amendment have declined; referring back to the earlier discussion, the amount is computed as follows: 135/825 × $75,000 = $12,273. Entries (f) and (g) relate to deferred gains and losses and are explained below.

Deferral of Gains and Losses Because pension costs include many assumptions and estimates, frequent adjustments must be made for variations between the actual results and the estimates or projections that were used in determining net periodic pension expense for previous periods. For example, the market value of the pension fund may increase at a much higher or lower rate than anticipated, the employee turnover rate may differ from that projected in earlier periods, or the interest rate may differ significantly from expectations. Such differences between expected results and actual experience give rise to a deferred pension gain or loss.

Treatment of these pension gains and losses has been a subject of controversy throughout the FASB's long study of pension accounting. Immediate recognition as part of annual pension expense is opposed by many accountants who are concerned about the volatility of pension expense. However, these pension gains and losses do represent economic events that should be reflected in the financial statements. The FASB decided to minimize the volatility of net periodic pension expense by allowing deferral of some gains and losses and amortization over future periods rather than requiring recognition of gains and losses in

EX 17-9 THORNTON ELECTRONICS, INC.—PENSION WORK SHEET FOR 2014

	Financial Statement Accounts				Detailed Accounts			
					Pension Asset/Liability		AOCI	
	Net Pension Expense	Cash	Pension-Related Asset/(Liability)	Accumulated Other Comprehensive Income	Projected Benefit Obligation	Fair Value of Pension Fund	Prior Service Cost	Deferred Pension (Gain)/Loss
Balance, January 1, 2013			(101,500)	61,364	(1,615,000)	1,513,500	61,364	
(a) Service cost	87,000				(87,000)			
(b) Interest cost	177,650				(177,650)			
(c) Actual return	(26,350)					26,350		
(d) Benefits paid					132,000	(132,000)		
(e) PSC amortization	12,273						(12,273)	
(f) Deferred loss	(125,000)							125,000
(g) PBO change					(80,000)			80,000
(h) Pension contribution		(75,000)				75,000		
Balance, December 31, 2014	125,573	(75,000)	(344,800)	254,091	(1,827,650)	1,482,850	49,091	205,000

Notes: Positive amounts are debits; negative amounts are credits.
The gray area indicates that no changes are made directly to these accounts. These accounts simply reflected changes that are made to the detailed accounts.

the period they arise.[19] These pension gains and losses are recognized in other comprehensive income instead of in the computation of net pension expense. The cumulative amount of these deferred gains and losses is included in the accumulated other comprehensive income portion of equity in the balance sheet.

Although actuarial estimates may change for several reasons, only two will be considered in this illustration: (1) the current-year difference between the actual and expected return on the pension fund and (2) actuarial changes in determining the PBO.

Deferral of Current-Year Difference between Actual and Expected Return on the Pension Fund As mentioned earlier, in estimating the return on the pension fund, the expected long-term rate of return on assets should be used rather than a more volatile short-term rate. Thus, in the short run, the actual return on the pension fund usually will differ from the expected return. By deferring the difference between the expected return and the actual return, pension expense will tend to be reduced by the expected long-term rate of return rather than by the more volatile short-term return rates. If the actual return on the pension fund exceeds the expected return, the difference is a deferred gain; if the expected return exceeds the actual return, the difference is a deferred loss. The deferred gain or loss is recognized as part of other comprehensive income in the current period; the cumulative amount is reported as accumulated other comprehensive income in the Equity section of the balance sheet. The financial statement impact of deferred pension gains and losses can be summarized as shown on page 17-33.

[19] Alternatively, a company may elect to recognize all gains or losses immediately. If this election is made, the company must (1) apply the immediate recognition method consistently, (2) recognize all gains or losses immediately, and (3) disclose the fact that immediate recognition is being followed. FASB ASC paragraph 715-30-35-20. For purposes of this chapter, all illustrations and end-of-chapter material will assume that the deferred recognition method is used.

	Income Statement	Balance Sheet
Deferred gain	**Increases** pension expense	**Increases** AOCI
Debit net pension expense		
Credit other comprehensive income (OCI)		
Deferred loss	**Decreases** pension expense	**Decreases** AOCI
Credit net pension expense		
Debit other comprehensive income (OCI)		

Now, look at this chart in terms of computing comprehensive income, which is the sum of two things: net income and other comprehensive income. When a gain is deferred, pension expense is increased (reducing net income), but the "other comprehensive income" portion of comprehensive income is increased. The net effect is that there is no overall impact on the amount of comprehensive income, but merely in the mix between net income and other comprehensive income. The same is true, in the opposite direction, with a deferred loss. So, the deferred gain and the deferred loss amount are actually included in the computation of comprehensive income but are excluded in the computation of the "net income" portion of comprehensive income.

The expected return on the pension fund is computed by multiplying the market-related value of the pension fund by the expected long-term rate of return. The FASB defines *market-related value of the pension fund* as either (1) the fair market value of the pension fund at the beginning of the current year or (2) a weighted-average value based on market values of the pension fund over a period not to exceed five years.[20] If asset values have been increasing, the weighted-average value will be lower than the beginning fair market value, resulting in a lower expected return.

When the actual return on the pension fund exceeds the expected return, the excess is called a *deferred gain*. This amount is added in the computation of pension expense. The reason the deferred gain increases pension expense is because the "gain" (actually it is better-than-expected pension fund performance) is not allowed to reduce pension expense this period. The result is to increase pension expense and to report the deferred gain as an increase in other comprehensive income. When the actual return is less than the expected return, the difference is called a *deferred loss*. This amount is subtracted in the computation of pension expense because the "loss" (worse-than-expected pension fund performance) is not allowed to increase pension expense this period. The deferred loss is reported as a reduction in other comprehensive income. Because the actual return on the pension fund is deducted in computing pension expense, the net effect of the deferred pension gain or loss adjustment is that the expected return, rather than the actual return, is used to reduce pension expense, thus achieving a smoothing of pension expense over time.

FYI

The net result of using the expected return on the pension fund instead of the actual return is that reported pension expense equals what it would be if the pension fund were to perform exactly as expected, with any large differences amortized to expense in future years, as illustrated later in the chapter.

To illustrate the computation of the deferred pension gain or loss

[20] Different methods of calculating market-related value may be used for different classes of assets. However, a company must apply the methods consistently from year to year.

arising from differences between the actual and expected return, assume that Thornton Electronics computes the expected return on the pension fund using the fair market value of the pension fund at the beginning of the year. The expected return on the pension fund for 2014 is $151,350 ($1,513,500 × 0.10). Because the actual return for the year of only $26,350 is much less than the expected return, the $125,000 difference is treated as a deferred pension loss and results in a reduction in pension expense.

As mentioned, combining the effects of the actual return and the deferred loss results in a net reduction in pension expense equal to the expected return of $151,350 (actual return of $26,350 + deferred loss of $125,000). The deferred loss is recorded in entry (f) in the 2014 pension work sheet as a credit (decrease) to annual Pension Expense and a debit to Other Comprehensive Income. Once this debit to Other Comprehensive Income is closed at year end to Accumulated Other Comprehensive Income, the cumulative amount is called Deferred Net Pension Gain/Loss and is part of accumulated other comprehensive income in the Equity section of the balance sheet.

f. Other Comprehensive Income	125,000	
Pension Expense		125,000
To record 2014 deferred loss stemming from the actual return on the pension fund being less than expected.		

Differences in Actuarial Estimates of PBO As indicated earlier, the actuarial computation of the projected benefit obligation involves many estimates, including future interest rates, life expectancy rates, and future salary rates. The effects of changing these estimates are deferred and accumulated for possible amortization to pension expense over future periods. During 2014, Thornton's actuaries reevaluated their actuarial assumptions in light of experience with Thornton's employees and calculated that the projected benefit obligation should be increased by $80,000. This increase is identified as a loss and is deferred to future periods. The deferred loss arising from the adjustment to the PBO becomes part of the deferred net pension gain or loss for possible future amortization. This adjustment is shown as entry (g) in the 2014 work sheet, as follows.

g. Other Comprehensive Income	80,000	
Projected Benefit Obligation		80,000
To record 2014 impact of a revision in actuarial estimates associated with the projected benefit obligation.		

This change in actuarial estimate is recorded in work sheet entry (g) as a credit (increase) to the PBO and a debit to Other Comprehensive Income. Note that the change has no impact on pension expense for 2014; the reduction in equity bypasses expense and net income and retained earnings and is instead eventually reflected in accumulated other comprehensive income. However, the change will impact future years in two ways. First, because the PBO is higher, interest cost in future years will be higher. Second, depending on future developments, the deferred loss may be amortized to pension expense in future years. Circumstances under which deferred losses and gains are amortized are described later in the chapter.

From the work sheet in Exhibit 17-9, it can be seen that a $75,000 contribution to the pension fund is recorded in entry (h) as illustrated previously.

Summary Journal Entries The eight detailed journal entries described above and illustrated in the pension work sheet in Exhibit 17-9 can be summarized in three summary journal entries, as shown on page 17-35.

Pension Expense	125,573	
Other Comprehensive Income	125,000	
Pension-Related Asset/Liability		238,300
Accumulated Other Comprehensive Income		12,273
Summary journal entry to recognize pension expense for 2014.		
Pension-Related Asset/Liability	115,000	
Cash		115,000
Summary journal to record pension fund contribution for 2014.		
Other Comprehensive Income	80,000	
Pension-Related Asset/Liability		80,000
To record 2014 impact of a revision in actuarial estimates associated with the projected benefit obligation.		

In the first journal entry, the amount credited to Pension-Related Asset/Liability is calculated strictly by reference to the three primary components of pension expense: service cost, interest cost, and the actual return on the pension fund. In this case, that total is $238,300 ($87,000 + $177,650 − $26,350). In addition, as illustrated previously, prior service cost amortization of $12,273 represents a reclassification from accumulated other comprehensive income to pension expense. Finally, the deferred loss resulting from the underperformance of the pension fund reduces pension expense in the current period and instead is recognized as negative other comprehensive income for the year which is then closed to Accumulated Other Comprehensive Income as part of the regular closing of the accounts.

The pension fund contribution journal entry is recorded as illustrated previously. Also, in this year, one additional summary entry is needed to reflect the $80,000 increase in the projected benefit obligation from the change in actuarial assumptions. This change does not impact pension expense in the current year but does reduce comprehensive income by $80,000.

Financial Statement Reporting The four numbers on the Financial Statement Accounts side of the work sheet are reported in Thornton's financial statements, as follows:

- *Net pension expense.* The $125,573 expense is reported as part of compensation expense in Thornton's income statement. Note that the combination of $26,350 actual return plus the $125,000 deferred loss means that the total amount subtracted in the computation of pension expense is $151,350 ($26,350 + $125,000), which is the expected return on the pension fund for the year.
- *Cash.* The $75,000 negative cash amount associated with Thornton's defined benefit pension plan is reported as a cash outflow from operating activities in Thornton's statement of cash flows.
- *Pension-related liability.* The $344,800 pension-related liability is reported in Thornton's balance sheet.
- *Accumulated other comprehensive income.* The $254,091 debit balance in Accumulated Other Comprehensive Income is reported as a subtraction from equity in Thornton's balance sheet.

Note again that the left side of the work sheet includes the items to be reported in Thornton's financial statements, and the right side of the work sheet represents the underlying detail that is used to construct the necessary financial statement note disclosure.

Under old U.S. GAAP rules that were superseded in 2006, the cumulative portion of the deferred gains and losses was combined with the net pension-related asset or liability in the balance sheet. As a result, the reported balance sheet pension item was an unsavory conglomeration of asset, liability, and equity items, all rolled into one number. The resulting mysterious, and often misleading, nature of this number was a primary motivation behind the change in the rules in 2006. In addition, the old rules were viewed as deficient because the most basic facts about a defined benefit pension plan—is the plan overfunded or underfunded, and by how much—were not reflected in the balance sheet. This old, confusing method of accounting is still the accounting mandated under *IAS 19*. Under this approach, the number recognized in Thornton's balance sheet as of the end of 2014 would be a net liability of $90,709 ($344,800 − $254,091). Under this approach, the negative equity, or debit, items shown as accumulated other comprehensive income separately in the balance sheet would essentially be considered assets (also debits) and used to offset the pension-related liability. This approach was long viewed with disdain by accountants and accounting students in the United States, and there was joy when the FASB eliminated this approach in 2006. The IASB is close to completely revamping its accounting for defined benefit pension plans. The proposed changes are really quite exciting. But you will have to work through the next section (Thornton Electronics for 2015) before we'll tell you about them.

Thornton Electronics—2015

The Thornton Electronics pension information for 2015 follows:

Service cost as reported by actuaries	$115,000
Contributions to pension plan	$80,000
Benefits paid to retirees	$140,000
Actual return on pension fund	$175,500
Obligation discount rate	11.0%
Long-term expected rate of return on the pension fund	10.0%
Accumulated benefit obligation, December 31, 2015	$1,795,150

EX 17-10 THORNTON ELECTRONICS, INC.—PENSION WORK SHEET FOR 2015

	Financial Statement Accounts				Detailed Accounts			
					Pension Asset/Liability		AOCI	
	Net Pension Expense	Cash	Pension-Related Asset/(Liability)	Accumulated Other Comprehensive Income	Projected Benefit Obligation	Fair Value of Pension Fund	Prior Service Cost	Deferred Pension (Gain)/Loss
Balance, January 1, 2015			(344,800)	254,091	(1,827,650)	1,482,850	49,091	205,000
(a) Service cost	115,000				(115,000)			
(b) Interest cost	201,042				(201,042)			
(c) Actual return	(175,500)					175,500		
(d) Benefits paid					140,000	(140,000)		
(e) PSC amortization	10,909						(10,909)	
(f) Deferred gain	27,215							(27,215)
(g) Amortization of deferred loss	4,447							(4,447)
(h) Pension contribution		(80,000)				80,000		
Balance, December 31, 2015	183,113	(80,000)	(405,342)	211,520	(2,003,692)	1,598,350	38,182	173,338

Notes: Positive amounts are debits; negative amounts are credits.
The blue area indicates that no changes are made directly to these accounts. These accounts simply reflected changes that are made to the detailed accounts.

This information is recorded in the 2015 pension work sheet shown in Exhibit 17-10. Entries (a) through (f) are similar to those made in 2014. Again, note that the prior service cost amortization amount is lower than in prior years, reflecting the continuing decline in the expected remaining service lives of those employees who were in place when the plan's amendment was initiated; the amount, as computed earlier, is 120/825 × $75,000 = $10,909. Entry (f) reflects the fact that the actual return on the pension fund of $175,500 for the year exceeded the expected return of $148,285 ($1,482,850 × 0.10). The excess of $27,215 is considered an unexpected gain and is credited to Other Comprehensive Income. The same amount is debited to the net periodic pension expense.

Entry (g) relates to amortization of deferred pension gains and losses and will now be explained.

Amortization of Deferred Net Pension Gain or Loss from Prior Years Under certain conditions, an employer's net periodic pension expense will include the amortization of deferred net pension gain or loss. The deferred pension gain or loss from prior years (recognized in accumulated other comprehensive income) is amortized over future years if it accumulates to more than an amount defined by the FASB as a corridor amount. Amortization is only required for a deferred net gain or loss that exceeds 10% of the greater of the PBO or the market-related value of the pension fund as of the beginning of the year. The rationale behind this approach is that the deferred gains and losses are not a concern as long as they are small, indicating that the estimates are close to being correct. The 10% rule used in defining the corridor amount is just an arbitrary attempt to define "small." Over time, if the estimates are not systematically bad, one would expect the total deferred net gain or loss to fluctuate randomly around zero.

If the deferred net gain or loss does exceed the corridor amount, that is an indication that the estimates have been systematically incorrect and the cumulative deferred amounts should begin to be recognized. The FASB indicated that any systematic method of amortizing the deferred net gain or loss that equaled or exceeded the straight-line amortization over the remaining expected service years of the employees would be acceptable as long as the procedure is applied consistently to both gains and losses. The amortization of a deferred gain reduces the net periodic pension expense, and the amortization of a deferred loss increases the net periodic pension expense. It is important to remember that only deferred gains and losses from prior years are subject to amortization. Accordingly, the corridor comparison applies only to the beginning balances in Projected Benefit Obligation, Fair Value of Pension Fund, and the deferred net pension gain/loss accounts.

This corridor amortization is a compromise between immediate recognition of gains and losses (which is viewed as causing too much volatility in earnings) and permanent deferral. Permanent deferral makes sense as long as the gains and losses tend to cancel out, but it becomes less reasonable when a "large" deferred gain or loss accumulates. The corridor amount is simply an arbitrary definition of what amount of deferred gain or loss is considered "large."

STOP&THINK

When would a company find itself exceeding the corridor amount?

a) Only when the company has pension fund assets in excess of total stockholders'equity
b) Only when the company is off in its pension estimates by a significant amount or by smaller regular amounts over a long period of time
c) Only when the company has pension fund assets in excess of 10% of total assets
d) Only when the company has a projected benefit obligation in excess of 10% of total liabilities

To illustrate the computation of the corridor amount, Thornton would apply the 10% corridor threshold to the projected benefit obligation at the beginning of the year because the PBO exceeds the market value of the pension fund at the beginning of the year.[21] Thus, the corridor amount is $182,765 ($1,827,650 × 0.10). Because the deferred loss at January 1, 2015, is $205,000, only the excess of $22,235 ($205,000 – $182,765) is subject to amortization. The average remaining employee service life on January 1, 2015, is assumed to be five years, so the 2015 amortization is $4,447 ($22,235/5). This amount represents amortization of a deferred loss and is an addition to the other components in computing pension expense. The loss amortization is recorded in entry (g) in the 2015 pension work sheet as a debit to the net periodic pension expense and a credit to Accumulated Other Comprehensive Income, resulting in a reclassification out of Accumulated Other Comprehensive Income and into pension expense. Note the size of the loss amortization amount ($4,447) in relation to the size of the deferred loss itself ($205,000). Clearly, this deferral of gains and losses and subsequent corridor amortization accomplishes the goal of reducing volatility in annual pension expense.

Pension Expense	4,447	
Accumulated Other Comprehensive Income		4,447
To record 2015 amortization of deferred net pension loss in excess of the corridor amount.		

Summary Journal Entries The eight detailed journal entries described above and illustrated in the pension work sheet in Exhibit 17-10 can be summarized in two summary journal entries, as follows:

Pension Expense	183,113	
Other Comprehensive Income		27,215
Pension-Related Asset/Liability		140,542
Accumulated Other Comprehensive Income		15,356
Summary journal entry to recognize pension expense for 2015.		
Pension-Related Asset/Liability	80,000	
Cash		80,000
Summary journal to record pension fund contribution for 2015.		

In the first journal entry, the amount credited to Pension-Related Asset/Liability is calculated strictly by reference to the three primary components of pension expense: service cost, interest cost, and the actual return on the pension fund. In this case, that total is $140,542 ($115,000 + $201,042 – $175,500). In addition, in this year, there are two types of amortization—prior service cost amortization of $10,909 and deferred loss amortization of $4,447. Both of these amortization amounts, totaling $15,356, represent a reclassification from accumulated other comprehensive income to pension expense. Finally, the deferred gain of $27,215 resulting from the overperformance of the pension fund increases pension expense (and reduces net income) in the current period but is also recognized as an increase in other comprehensive income for the year. From this final aspect of the summary journal entry, it can be seen that ultimately NET income is impacted by the expected return on the pension fund but COMPREHENSIVE income is impacted by the actual return.

Financial Statement Reporting The four numbers on the Financial Statement Accounts side of the work sheet are reported in Thornton's financial statements, as shown on page 17-39.

[21] For simplicity, the fair market value of pension assets is used as the market-related value. Recall that an alternative measure is the weighted average of the fair market value of pension assets from prior years.

- *Net pension expense.* The $183,113 expense is reported as part of compensation expense in Thornton's income statement. Note that the combination of $175,500 actual return less the $27,215 deferred gain means that the net amount subtracted in the computation of pension expense is $148,285 ($175,500 – $27,215), which is the expected return on the pension fund for the year.
- *Cash.* The $80,000 negative cash amount associated with Thornton's defined benefit pension plan is reported as a cash outflow from operating activities in Thornton's statement of cash flows.
- *Pension-related liability.* The $405,342 pension-related liability is reported in Thornton's balance sheet. This liability represents substantial underfunding of Thornton's pension plan. It is likely that if this were a real company the federal pension regulations would require substantial increases in the pension contribution amount to alleviate this underfunding.
- *Accumulated other comprehensive income.* The $211,520 debit balance in Accumulated Other Comprehensive Income is reported as a subtraction from equity in Thornton's balance sheet.

Revolutionary IASB April 2010 Exposure Draft Perhaps this "corridor amortization" was the last straw in what many view as an arbitrary, ad hoc, and opaque load of accounting compromises. In any event, the IASB decided to do a complete review of pension accounting, and the FASB has agreed to let the IASB take the lead on this. In April 2010, the IASB released a bold exposure draft; the stated IASB goal is to approve a final accounting standard revision in mid 2011. Key elements of this exposure draft are as follows.

- Balance sheet reporting of the net pension liability/asset with adjustments, for example, if the company is constrained in how soon it can recover any pension plan overfunding.
- Use of actual return on the pension fund rather than expected return.
- No accumulated other comprehensive income. The amount of any PBO changes because of, say, changes in actuarial assumptions would be shown as part of other comprehensive income and then would be closed straight to retained earnings rather than to accumulated other comprehensive income.
- Decomposition of the pension expense components. Service cost is shown in the income statement as part of compensation expense. Net interest cost (roughly speaking, the difference between interest cost and return on the pension fund) is shown as part of the net financing cost of the business, along with general company interest expense.

Remember, this is an exposure draft and not a final standard. Also, because international convergence pressure will be on the FASB to adopt any revised IASB standard, the U.S. business community will be active in lobbying the IASB for or against the standard. So, there could be changes, even substantial changes, before the final standard is released in 2011. Stay tuned.

FYI

Sir David Tweedie, Chairman of the IASB, is known for his witty, concise, and controversial statements about accounting standards. In a televised interview, he said the following about the usefulness of the numbers generated under the corridor approach: "You may as well take the [cumulative deferred gain or loss], divide it by the cube root of the number of miles to the moon, and multiply it by your shoe size. I mean, it doesn't mean a thing."

Disclosure of Pension Plans

5 **Prepare required disclosures associated with pensions, and understand the accounting treatment for pension settlements and curtailments.**

WHY **For some companies, the company pension plan can have a substantial impact on the company's future cash flows and its exposure to investment risk. In addition, pension accounting summarizes a huge amount of information into one number on the balance sheet (net pension asset or liability) and one number on the income statement (net pension expense). Detailed disclosure is necessary to understand a company's pension plan.**

HOW **A company with a defined benefit pension plan must disclose how the balances in the projected benefit obligation and the pension fund changed during the year. In addition, the company must disclose details about the computation of pension expense. This disclosure must also be shown for postretirement benefit plans other than pensions. The company must also disclose data about its estimates so that financial statement users can perform some sensitivity analysis. Finally, the company must disclose information about its investment strategy and about the cash flow impact of its postretirement plans.**

The disclosure requirements relating to pensions are discussed in FASB ASC Topic 715. The FASB requires information similar to that presented in the work sheet that was used throughout the chapter for calculating pension costs. Specifically, the major disclosure requirements for most publicly traded companies are as follows:

1. A reconciliation between the beginning and ending balances for the projected benefit obligation
2. A reconciliation between the beginning and ending balances in the fair value of the pension fund
3. A disclosure of the accumulated benefit obligation
4. The funded status of the plans and the amounts recognized in the balance sheet
5. The components of pension expense for the period
6. Any effects on other comprehensive income for the period and the details of the existing balances in accumulated other comprehensive income
7. The assumptions used relating to the following items:
   (a) Discount rate
   (b) Rate of compensation increase
   (c) Expected long-term rate of return on the pension fund
8. Disclosure of the percentage of the different types of investments held in the pension fund along with a narrative description of investment strategy
9. For each of the next five years, disclose an estimate of the amount of cash to be paid in benefits (from the pension fund assets) and the amount of cash to be contributed by the company to the pension fund
10. For postretirement benefits (discussed later in this chapter): assumed health care cost trend rates and their effect on service and interest costs and the ABO if the assumed health care cost trend rates were one percentage point higher

As you can see, the work sheet used in this chapter provides much of the information required for disclosure. In addition to the disclosure requirement for defined benefit pension plans, there are also disclosure requirements for defined contribution plans. Specifically, an employer must disclose the amount of pension expense recognized for defined contribution plans separately from the amount of expense recognized for defined benefit plans. In addition, the nature and effect of any significant changes during the period should be disclosed.

For Thornton Electronics, most of the information needed for the disclosure of the details of the computation of annual pension expense and reconciliation of the funded status of the pension plan can be obtained from the 2015 pension work sheet in Exhibit 17-10. In addition, the accumulated benefit obligation (ABO) of $1,795,150 is disclosed.

Companies with more than one pension plan may combine the amounts of all pension plans. However, in those cases when the ABO exceeds the FVPF, that information must be disclosed separately in the notes. In addition, companies may combine the disclosure relating to their U.S. and non-U.S. plans unless the obligation associated with the non-U.S. plans is significant or the terms of the non-U.S. plans differ substantially from those of the U.S. plans. *In addition,* companies must separate the disclosures relating to pensions and postretirement benefits other than pensions (these benefits are discussed in the next section). This type of disclosure is illustrated in Exhibit 17-11 using an excerpt from the notes to the 2009 financial statements of General Motors.

Note that General Motors reports information for its U.S. and non-U.S. pension plans separately. Also note that the period covered is only six months (from July 10, 2009 through December 31, 2009). Usually, a note such as this includes two full years of data. However, because of the bankruptcy and reorganization of General Motors in 2009, the note here includes just the post-reorganization details.

Pension Settlements and Curtailments

If a pension plan is settled or the benefits are curtailed, a question arises as to how the employer should treat a resulting gain or loss. Settlement of a pension plan occurs when an employer takes an irrevocable action that relieves the employer of primary responsibility for all or part of the obligation. Examples of a settlement transaction include the employer's purchase of an annuity from an insurance company that would cover employees' vested benefits or a lump-sum cash payment to the employees in exchange for their rights to receive specified pension benefits. A curtailment of a pension plan arises from an event that significantly reduces the benefits that will be provided for present employees' future services. Curtailments include (1) the termination of employees' services earlier than expected, for example, as a result of closing a plant or discontinuing a segment of the business and (2) the termination or suspension of a pension plan so that employees do not earn additional benefits for future services.[22]

As discussed throughout this chapter, in Topic 715 the FASB provides for delayed recognition of pension gains and losses arising from the ordinary operations of the pension plan. In addition, the statement provides for delayed recognition of prior service cost. Thus, at any given time, deferred gains, losses, and prior service cost usually exist.

The FASB felt it was clear that if a pension plan is completely terminated and all pension obligations are settled and pension funds are disbursed, previously deferred pension amounts should be recognized. What wasn't clear, however, is what happens when partial settlements or curtailments take place. The rules are discussed below.

Settlements Pension plans occasionally become overfunded because a rising stock market causes the value of the pension fund to exceed the pension obligation. To take advantage of this situation, companies sometimes settle their pension plans by purchasing annuity contracts from insurance companies for less than the amount in the pension

[22] FASB ASC paragraph 715-30-15-6.

EX 17-11 NOTE DISCLOSURE FOR U.S. AND NON-U.S. PENSION PLANS—GENERAL MOTORS

	Successor			
	U.S. Plans Pension Benefits	Non-U.S. Plans Pension Benefits(a)	U.S. Plans Other Benefits	Non-U.S. Plans Other Benefits
	July 10, 2009 Through December 31, 2009			
Change in benefit obligations				
Beginning benefit obligation	$ 98,012	$ 21,392	$ 27,639	$ 3,420
Service cost	216	157	62	17
Interest cost	2,578	602	886	94
Plan participants' contributions	—	4	172	—
Amendments	(13)	(9)	1	(89)
Actuarial (gains) losses	3,102	1,592	1,732	64
Benefits paid	(3,938)	(714)	(1,700)	(70)
Medicare Part D receipts	—	—	84	—
IUE-CWA & USW related liability transfer	—	—	514	—
Foreign currency translation adjustments	—	1,469	—	376
Delphi benefit guarantee and other	1,365	—	—	—
UAW retiree medical plan settlement	—	—	(25,822)	—
Curtailments, settlements, and other (b)	249	(119)	2,220	(15)
Ending benefit obligation	101,571	24,374	5,788	3,797
Change in plan assets				
Beginning fair value of plan assets	78,493	8,616	10,702	—
Actual return on plan assets	9,914	1,201	1,909	—
Employer contributions	31	4,287	1,528	70
Plan participants' contributions	—	4	172	—
Benefits paid	(3,938)	(714)	(1,700)	(70)
UAW hourly retiree medical plan asset settlement	—	—	(12,586)	—
Foreign currency translation adjustments	—	765	—	—
Other	—	(132)	6	—
Ending fair value of plan assets	84,500	14,027	31	—
Ending funded status	$(17,071)	$(10,347)	$ (5,757)	$(3,797)
Amounts recorded in the consolidated balance sheet are comprised of:				
Noncurrent asset	$ —	$ 98	$ —	—
Current liability	(93)	(337)	(685)	(161)
Noncurrent liability	(16,978)	(10,108)	(5,072)	(3,636)
Net amount recorded	$(17,071)	$(10,347)	$ (5,757)	$(3,797)
Amounts recorded in Accumulated other comprehensive Income (loss) are comprised of:				
Net actuarial loss (gain)	$ (3,803)	$ 833	$ 212	$ 65
Net prior service cost (credit)	(13)	(9)	(1)	(89)
Total recorded in Accumulated other comprehensive income (loss)	$ (3,816)	$ 824	$ 211	$ (24)

fund. Subject to regulations such as ERISA, the excess funds can then be used for other corporate purposes.

The accounting issue surrounding settlements centers on whether the gain should be recognized immediately or deferred and recognized in future periods. The FASB decided that if the settlement (1) was an irrevocable action, (2) relieved the employer of primary responsibility for the pension benefit obligation, and (3) eliminated significant risks related to the obligation and the assets used to effect the settlement, the previously deferred net gain or loss should be recognized in the current period. If only part of the projected benefit obligation (PBO) is settled, a pro rata portion of the gain should be recognized currently.[23]

Curtailments As indicated previously, a pension plan curtailment is an event that significantly reduces the expected years of future service of present employees or eliminates for a significant number of employees the accrual of defined benefits for their future services. Examples include termination of employees' services earlier than expected, such as occurs when a segment of the business is discontinued, or termination or suspension of a plan so that it earns no further benefits for future services.

Any prior service cost associated with years of service no longer expected to be rendered as a result of the curtailment is recognized as a loss. In addition, the projected benefit obligation of the pension plan may be changed as a result of the curtailment, giving rise to an additional gain or loss. The FASB provided for offsetting previously deferred pension gains and losses against the gain or loss from changes in the projected benefit obligation and called the difference *curtailment gains or losses*. If the sum of all gains and losses attributed to the curtailment, including the write-off of prior service cost, is a loss, it is recognized in the period when it is probable that the curtailment will occur and the effects are estimable. If the sum of all gains and losses attributed to the curtailment is a gain, it is recognized when the related employees are terminated or when the plan's suspension or amendment is adopted.[24]

Postretirement Benefits Other than Pensions

6 **Explain the differences in accounting for pensions and postretirement benefits other than pensions.**

WHY **For many companies, other postretirement benefits, such as health care benefits for retirees, now represent a bigger economic obligation than the pension obligation.**

HOW **Accounting for other postretirement benefits is quite similar to the accounting for a defined benefit pension plan. One practical difference is that other postretirement benefits are often not a function of salary level. Also, other postretirement benefit plans are often not funded.**

FASB ASC Section 715-60-05 includes an overview of the accounting standards for postretirement benefits other than pensions. Although the primary focus is on health care benefits, the rules also apply to other postretirement benefits, such as the cost of life insurance contracts, legal assistance benefits, and tuition assistance. The rules relate only to single-employer–defined benefit postretirement plans. The benefits are defined either in monetary amounts, such as a designated amount of life insurance, or as benefit coverage, such as specified coverage for hospital or doctor care. In general, the costs of these benefits are accounted for by employers in the same way as pension costs, that is, on an accrual basis. However, as noted later, there are some important differences between pensions and other postretirement benefits.

Nature of Postretirement Health Care Plans

There are a number of unique features of postretirement health care benefits as compared with pension benefits. Because the details of the accounting rules are reflected in these

[23] FASB ASC paragraph 715-30-35-79.
[24] FASB ASC paragraphs 7-15-30-35-92 through 94.

features, they will be considered first before the differences between accounting for pensions and other postretirement benefits are discussed.

Informal Rather than Formal Plans Many company postretirement benefit plans are not written into formal contracts. Companies often begin paying for postretirement health care benefits as a continuation of health care coverage for active employees. In some cases, the practice becomes part of union contract bargaining, and informal plans are changed to formal, union-negotiated contractual plans. Even though a plan may be informal, and thus not legally binding, the courts have sometimes interpreted the informal plan as a contract and have required companies to honor the plan. Historically, General Motors has had the largest postretirement benefit plan in the United States, with that nonpension postretirement obligation peaking at $81.5 billion on December 31, 2005. Interestingly, in the past, General Motors has clearly indicated in its financial statement notes that although it is reporting a liability for these postretirement benefits, it does not recognize these benefits as a legal obligation. In the notes to the 1998 financial statements, the management of General Motors stated the following:

> GM has disclosed in the consolidated financial statements certain amounts associated with estimated future postretirement benefits other than pensions and characterized such amounts as "accumulated postretirement benefit obligations," "liabilities," or "obligations." Notwithstanding the recording of such amounts and the use of these terms, GM does not admit or otherwise acknowledge that such amounts or existing postretirement benefit plans of GM (other than pensions) represent legally enforceable liabilities of GM.

This note is especially interesting in light of what occurred between General Motors (GM) and the United Auto Workers (UAW) since 2005. Because of continued large operating losses, GM sought concessions from the UAW to reduce benefits costs. Under an agreement worked out in 2005 and approved in court in 2006, GM retirees were required to begin to pay deductibles, premiums, and copayments for the first time. It was estimated that the changes would save GM about $1 billion per year and reduce GM's recognized liability for retiree medical care by $17.4 billion. Subsequently, in the final negotiations over the General Motors bankruptcy, these retiree health care benefits were sacrificed by GM employees in an effort to help save the restructured company. As seen in Exhibit 17-11, employee concessions had reduced the obligation to $5.8 billion by the end of 2009. (*Note:* GM's retiree health care obligation is also discussed at the beginning of Chapter 20.)

Nonfunded Rather than Funded Plans Most company plans for postretirement benefits are not funded. Thus, companies rely on current revenues to meet current costs of the plan. Unlike pension contributions, postretirement benefit plan contributions usually are not deductible for income tax purposes. As discussed earlier, ERISA, a federal law, requires companies to fund their pension liability during an employee's working years. There has been no similar federal legislation to encourage funding of postretirement benefit costs. In some instances, a separate insurance carrier is used to cover the risk. In many cases, especially for larger companies, a form of self-insurance has developed.

Pay-as-You-Go Accounting Rather than Accrual Accounting Because postretirement benefit plans usually are not funded, almost all companies previously charged these costs against revenue in the period the benefit costs were incurred rather than in the period when the employee service was rendered. This policy results in uneven charges against revenue and does not recognize a liability for unfunded postretirement benefits. Before the adoption of pre-codification *SFAS No. 106* in 1990, the total of unfunded postretirement benefits for all companies was estimated to amount to more than $1 trillion.[25]

Uncertainty of Future Benefits Rather than Clearly Defined Benefits Defined benefit pension plans establish terms that make the amount of their future pension obligation measurable with reasonably high reliability. Salary trends, mortality tables, and discount rates are reasonably objective and have been used in accounting for defined benefit pension plans. Health care costs, however, involve many variables that make accrual accounting difficult to implement. Over the years, factors such as longer life expectancy, improved medical treatment facilities, and early retirements have combined to cause health care costs for retired employees to increase dramatically. The amount of these costs absorbed by government Medicare programs has varied over time and will continue to vary as Congress works to bring government finances under control. As the Medicare plans cover fewer of these costs, employers and individuals are required to absorb higher costs.

Other variables that must be considered before an accrual entry can be made for postretirement benefits include age of retirees, geographic location of retirement, geographic differences in health costs, dependent coverage, gender of retiree, costs of new medical technology, emergence of new diseases, retirement dates, and so forth. Estimating future benefit costs based on these variables can be costly and time consuming for companies. However, the alternative is to throw up your hands in despair and record nothing at all. This unacceptable alternative was what existed before 1990.

Nonpay-Related Rather than Pay-Related Benefits Most postretirement benefits are granted to employees after a certain number of service years or when an employee reaches a specified preretirement age. The amount of benefits to be received is usually unrelated to the level of compensation. The date when an employee becomes eligible for these benefits is known as the full eligibility date. No postretirement benefits are granted unless the employee meets this service or age requirement. After that date is reached, the employee is eligible to receive 100% of the postretirement benefits regardless of any future service or regardless of pay level reached. Thus, the period over which an employee earns postretirement benefits extends from the hire date to the full eligibility date.

In contrast, because most pension plans increase an employee's benefits for each additional year of service rendered and for salary increases, the employee continues to earn pension benefits until retirement. Accordingly, the period over which postretirement benefits are earned differs from that over which pension benefits are earned. There are, of course, many exceptions to this description of pensions and postretirement benefits. Some pension plans are nonpay related, and some health care postretirement benefit plans are pay related.

Overview of the Accounting for Postretirement Benefits Other than Pensions

Most companies adopted accrual accounting for postretirement benefits beginning with their 1993 financial statements. The same five components for net periodic pension expense listed on page 17-23 are required for net periodic postretirement benefit expense. Service cost and prior service cost are charged (attributed) to the years from the hire date to the full eligibility date rather than from the hire date to the retirement date as is true

[25] Lee Berton, "FASB Plan Would Make Firms Deduct Billions for Potential Retiree Benefits," *The Wall Street Journal*, August 17, 1988, p. 3.

for pension expenses.[26] Any retirement benefit fund assets may be offset against retirement benefit obligations if the assets are clearly restricted for the payment of postretirement benefits.

The disclosure required for postretirement benefit plans includes all requirements for pension plans plus information about health cost trend assumptions and sensitivity analysis of how postretirement expenses and the postretirement obligation would vary if the health care costs trend rate were increased by 1%.The details of accounting for postretirement benefits other than pensions are included in the Web Material associated with this chapter.

SOLUTIONS TO OPENING SCENARIO QUESTIONS

1. The "national debt," which represents the total amount borrowed by the U.S. federal government in the form of U.S. Treasury notes, bills, bonds, and so forth, totaled $7.6 trillion on September 30, 2009. At that same time, the federal government's pension obligation to its employees totaled $5.3 trillion. Note that this $5.3 trillion is NOT the Social Security obligation; instead, this is the amount of pension benefits owed to U.S. federal employees.
2. By the year 2030, it is estimated that 20% of the U.S. population will be over 65 years old. With this high proportion of older people in the population, the Social Security payroll taxes of each working person will be required to cover the Social Security benefits of more retired people. In 1950, each retired person was supported by 16 workers. In 2004, the ratio was 3.3 workers per retiree. In 2025, the ratio will reach two workers per retiree and remain at that level for the foreseeable future. Social Security reform is a political football that neither major political party has mustered the will to attack.
3. General Motors must cover both the pension and the health care costs of its retired workers. In fact, in recent years at General Motors the cost of covering the health care costs of retired workers has exceeded the pension costs. Exhibit 20-1 in Chapter 20 illustrates how the bankruptcy and reorganization of General Motors in 2009 drastically reduced the company's obligation for retiree health care.

SOLUTIONS TO STOP & THINK

1. (Page 17-11) The correct answer is A. Notice that the definition of a liability closely parallels the criteria used in accounting for postemployment benefits. The benefits are probable future sacrifices of economic benefit resulting from past transactions. The definitions provided in the Conceptual Framework have been used extensively by the FASB in addressing complex accounting issues.
2. (Page 17-14) The correct answer is D. With a defined benefit plan, the employer bears the majority of the investment risk. With a defined contribution plan, the risk shifts to the employee. Companies would prefer that, where possible, employees bear the investment risk.
3. (Page 17-25) The correct answer is B. Prior service cost is the present value of pension benefits granted to existing employees on the date a plan is initiated. As a result, this amount is included in the computation of the projected benefit obligation (PBO).

[26] If the period of service needed to earn the postretirement benefits does not include previous years, the attribution period will be from a later date, referred to as the *beginning of the credited service period*. FASB ASC paragraph 715-60-35-66.

4. (Page 17-37) The correct answer is B. A company would exceed the corridor amount only when it was off in its estimates by a significant amount over a long period of time. Because the corridor amount is 10% of a very large number (either plan assets or PBO), a company would have to have made a series of bad estimates. Typically, a company will monitor the amount of its unrealized gains and losses and adjust its estimates to compensate.

SOLUTION TO USING THE FASB'S CODIFICATION

The accounting for sabbatical leaves is discussed in FASB ASC paragraph 710-10-25-4: "The appropriate accounting for a sabbatical leave depends on the purpose of the leave. If a sabbatical leave is granted only to perform research or public service to enhance the reputation of or otherwise benefit the employer, the compensation is not attributable to services already rendered (see paragraph 710-10-25-1(a)); a liability shall not be accrued in advance of the employee's services during such leave. If the leave is granted to provide compensated unrestricted time off for past service and the other conditions for accrual are met, a liability for sabbatical leave shall be accrued."

So, because Professor Pearl will be required to stay on campus and conduct research, at the direction of the university, during the "sabbatical" leave, the anticipated compensation cost for Professor Pearl is NOT judged to be incurred during the six years leading up to the "sabbatical" year, but instead is a cost to be recognized during the "sabbatical" year itself. The university accountant who is using Professor Pearl's future "sabbatical" as a reason to cut his compensation this year is twisting the accounting rules. In fact, it is more accurate to state that the university accountant doesn't understand the accounting rules. He or she needs to get more familiar with the use of the FASB's Codification.

REVIEW CHAPTER 17

LEARNING OBJECTIVES

1 Account for payroll and payroll taxes, and understand the criteria for recognizing a liability associated with compensated absences.

Accounting for payroll and payroll taxes is a routine event that occurs at the end of every pay period. In addition to accounting for the taxes withheld from employees, care must be taken to ensure that employer payroll taxes are considered. Employers are responsible for FICA as well as state and federal unemployment taxes. As employees work, they often earn the right to receive, in the future, time off for sickness or vacation. These days are referred to as *compensated absences* and must be accounted for as expenses in the period in which the employee earns those rights.

2 Compute performance bonuses, and recognize the issues associated with postemployment benefits.

In addition to regular payroll, employees may have the opportunity to receive additional compensation based on the achievement of performance goals. This additional compensation often takes the form of bonuses or stock options. The accounting for stock options requires estimates as to future value and can become quite complex. In some cases, employees will leave a firm, either voluntarily or involuntarily. Benefits promised to these employees following employment but prior to retirement must be accounted for in a fashion similar to the accounting for compensated absences.

3 **Understand the nature and characteristics of employer pension plans, including the details of defined benefit plans.**

Pension plans can be structured as either defined benefit plans or defined contribution plans. With *defined contribution plans*, the employee receives, upon retirement, the funds that have accumulated over time. Accounting for defined contribution plans is straightforward. *Defined benefit plans* are more challenging in that the value of the benefits are often difficult to measure. These benefits are often a function of years of service, future salary levels, and life expectancy. Actuaries are employed to provide estimates as to projected future benefits.

4 **Use the components of the pension-related asset/liability and changes in the components to compute the periodic expense associated with pensions and to compute the impact on other comprehensive income.**

The prepaid/accrued pension account reflects the difference between the present value of the amount expected to be paid in the future (PBO) and the fair value of the pension fund (FVPF) set aside to meet that obligation. Additional pension-related factors are reported as part of accumulated other comprehensive income. These additional factors include prior service costs and deferred gains/losses related to differences between expected and actual returns on the pension fund.

Each year, an assessment is made as to the additional benefits owed as a result of another year of service, the effects of being a year closer to paying out benefits, and the return received as a result of setting aside funds to meet these future obligations. The additional factors mentioned in the previous paragraph also affect the amount reported on the income statement in that they each may require adjustment over time.

5 **Prepare required disclosures associated with pensions, and understand the accounting treatment for pension settlements and curtailments.**

Detailed disclosure relating to pensions is required. The assumptions made by actuaries relating to expected return on assets, discount rates, and projected increases in salaries are required to be disclosed. In addition, firms are required to disclose the components of the pension-related asset or liability from the balance sheet as well as the periodic pension expense amount disclosed on the income statement. Most of the required disclosures can be provided through presentation of a work sheet such as those illustrated in the chapter.

In the event that the benefits associated with a pension plan are curtailed, any prior service cost associated with the curtailment is recognized as a loss and offset against adjustments required to the PBO. Pension settlements often give rise to gains or losses. The FASB determined that those gains and losses resulting from irrevocable actions by the company that relieve the company of future obligations are to be recognized immediately.

6 **Explain the differences in accounting for pensions and postretirement benefits other than pensions.**

Although many of the concepts used in accounting for pensions are similar to those used in accounting for postretirement benefits other than pensions, there are some important differences. A common difference, unrelated to the accounting for these benefits, relates to other postretirement benefits being largely unfunded by companies. Other differences relate to other postretirement benefits often not being a function of salary levels and to the difficulty of measuring these other benefits.

FASB-IASB CODIFICATION SUMMARY

Topic	FASB Accounting Standards Codification	Original FASB Standard	Corresponding IASB Standard	Differences between U.S. GAAP and IFRS
Compensated absences	*Section 710-10-25 par. 1-8*	*SFAS No. 43 par. 6-16*	*IAS 19 par. 11-16*	No substantial differences
Postemployment benefits	*Section 712-10-05 par. 2-6* *Section 712-10-15 par. 3-5* *Section 712-10-25 par. 1-5*	*SFAS No. 112 par. 1-6* *SFAS No. 88 par. 15*	*IAS 19 par. 132-140*	No substantial differences
Discount rate for projected benefit obligation	*Section 715-30-35 par. 43*	*SFAS No. 87 par. 44*	*IAS 19 par.78*	IFRS allows use of the interest rate on government bonds in countries lacking a developed corporate bond market.
Prior service cost	*Section 715-30-35 par. 10-11*	*SFAS No. 87 par. 24-25*	*IAS 19 par.96*	Under IFRS, the "past" service cost amount is recognized as an expense immediately IF the benefits are immediately vested.
Balance sheet numbers: one net number for the difference between PBO and the pension fund, with AOCI shown separately	*Section 715-30-25 par. 1, 4*	*SFAS No. 87 par. 35, 38*	*IAS 19 par.54*	Under current IFRS, the reported balance sheet number is the sum of the PBO, the pension fund, and AOCI associated with the pension plan.
Settlements and curtailments	*Various sections in Subtopics 715-30 and 715-60; illustrations in Section 715-30-55*	*SFAS No. 88*	*IAS 19 par.109-115*	No substantial differences
Disclosure	*Sections 715-29-50 715-30-50 715-60-50*	*SFAS No. 132(R)*	*IAS 19 par.120-125*	No substantial differences
Postretirement benefits other than pensions	*Subtopic 715-60*	*SFAS No. 106*	*In general, no distinction between pensions and other postretirement benefits. Guidance on medical benefits found in IAS 19 par.88-91*	Differences similar to the differences in accounting for pensions.

KEY TERMS

Accumulated benefit obligation (ABO) 17-17
Actual return on the pension fund 17-27
Actuarial present value 17-15
Compensated absences 17-7
Contributory pension plan 17-12
Corridor amount 17-37
Curtailment of a pension plan 17-41
Deferred net pension gain or loss 17-34
Deferred pension gain or loss 17-31
Defined benefit pension plans 17-13
Defined contribution pension plans 17-12
Expected return on the pension fund 17-33
Expected service period 17-28
Fair value of the pension fund 17-21
Full eligibility date 17-45
Market-related value of the pension fund 17-33
Net periodic pension expense 17-16
Noncontributory pension plans 17-12
Obligation discount rate 17-19
Pension fund 17-13
Pension plan 17-11
Pension-related asset/liability 17-22
Postretirement benefits other than pensions 17-12
Prior service cost 17-25
Projected benefit obligation (PBO) 17-17
Service cost 17-20
Settlement of a pension plan 17-41
Single-employer pension plans 17-12
Vested benefits 17-15

QUESTIONS

1. Gross payroll is taxed by both federal and state governments. Identify these taxes and indicate who bears the cost of the tax, the employer or the employee.
2. How should compensated absences be accounted for?
3. The sales manager for Off-Road Enterprises is entitled to a bonus equal to 12% of profits. What difficulties may arise in the interpretation of this profit-sharing agreement?
4. Distinguish between (a) a defined benefit pension plan and a defined contribution pension plan, (b) a contributory pension plan and a noncontributory pension plan, and (c) a multi-employer pension plan and a single-employer pension plan.
5. What is meant by the word *vesting*?
6. What factors must actuaries consider in determining the amount of future benefits under a defined benefit pension plan?
7. What four accounting issues were addressed by the FASB in relation to defined benefit pension plans?
8. Distinguish between the accumulated benefit approach and the projected benefit approach in determining the amount of future benefits earned by employees under a defined benefit pension plan.
9. List and briefly describe the five basic components of net periodic pension expense.
10. Explain how prior service costs arise (a) at the inception of a pension plan and (b) at the time of a plan's amendment.
11. How is the service cost portion of net periodic pension expense to be measured?
12. Does pension expense include the actual return on plan assets or the expected return? Explain.
13. Is prior service cost recognized as an expense in the period in which it initially arises?
14. The FASB permits the use of an average market value of plan assets for some pension computations. In other cases, the fair market value at a specific measurement date must be used. Under what circumstances is the average market value permissible?
15. Which pension-related items impact the reported amount of accumulated other comprehensive income?
16. Why is a corridor amount identified in recognizing gain or loss from pension plans?
17. What is the function of the pension disclosure requirement included in the pension standards?
18. Distinguish between a pension settlement and a pension curtailment.
19. What is meant by *postretirement benefits*, and what is the primary issue in accounting for their costs?
20. Describe the differences between pension plans and other postretirement benefit plans.
21. What is the *full eligibility date*, and why is it an important date in accounting for postretirement benefits?
22. Describe the major differences between the accounting for pensions and other postretirement benefits.

PRACTICE EXERCISES

Practice 17-1
LO1

Wages and Wages Payable
The company pays its employees each Monday for the work performed during the preceding 5-day work week. Total payroll for one week is $25,000. December 31 fell on a Wednesday. (1) Make the journal entry necessary to record wages payable as of December 31. (2) Make the journal entry necessary on the following January 5 to record payment of wages for the preceding week. Assume that this is a very strict company and that there were no holidays during the week.

Practice 17-2
LO1

Accounting for Payroll Taxes
Total wages and salaries for the month of January were $50,000. Because it is January, no employee has yet reached the FICA tax cap amount, so the full FICA tax percentage is applicable to the entire amount of wages and salaries. The same is true of the federal unemployment tax amount. The state requires a 5.4% employer tax on all wages and salaries. Income taxes withheld from employees' pay during the month totaled $7,000. Make the summary journal entries to record payment of wages and salaries and recognition of total salary and wage expense (including payroll tax expense) for the month.

Practice 17-3
LO1

Compensated Absences
During Year 1 (the first year of the company's existence), employees of the company earned vacation days as follows:

Employee	Average Wage per Day	Vacation Days Earned This Year	Vacation Days Taken This Year
1	$160	10	10
2	200	15	10
3	250	20	5

(1) Make the journal entry necessary at the end of Year 1 to record the unused vacation days earned during the year and (2) make the journal entry necessary in Year 2 to record the use of all of these vacation days. Assume that all employees received a 10% pay raise in Year 2.

Practice 17-4
LO2

Earnings-Based Bonus
The manager is entitled to a bonus equal to 5% of her store's earnings. The difficult part is that calculation of the store's earnings includes a subtraction for the amount of the bonus. The store's earnings before the bonus total $200,000. Calculate the store manager's bonus.

Practice 17-5
LO2

Postemployment Benefits
The company has decided to restructure operations at one of its stores. As part of this restructuring, the company has determined that the store facility is impaired. The store originally cost $3,000,000 and has accumulated depreciation of $1,300,000. The fair value of the store is determined to be $800,000. In addition, 32 employees at the store are being terminated. As part of the severance package, each employee is entitled to job training benefits (costing $500 per employee), supplemental health care and life insurance benefits for six months (costing $3,300 per employee), and two months' salary (averaging $5,000 per employee). Make the journal entry or entries necessary to record this restructuring.

Practice 17-6
LO3

Computing the Accumulated Benefit Obligation (ABO)
Wu Company has established a defined benefit pension plan for its lone employee, Ronald Dalton. Annual payments under the pension plan are equal to Ronald's highest

lifetime salary multiplied by (2% × number of years with the company). As of the beginning of 2013, Ronald had worked for Wu Company for 10 years. His salary in 2012 was $50,000. Ronald is expected to retire in 25 years, and his salary increases are expected to average 3% per year during that period. Ronald is expected to live for 15 years after retiring and will receive the first annual pension payment one year after he retires. Compute Wu Company's accumulated benefit obligation (ABO) as of January 1, 2013, assuming (1) an 8% discount rate and (2) a 12% discount rate.

Practice 17-7

LO3

Computing the Projected Benefit Obligation (PBO)

Refer to Practice 17-6. Compute Wu Company's projected benefit obligation (PBO) as of January 1, 2013, assuming (1) an 8% discount rate and (2) a 12% discount rate.

Practice 17-8

LO3

Simple Computation of the Net Pension Asset or Liability

On January 1 of Year 1, the company had a projected benefit obligation (PBO) of $10,000 and a pension fund with a fair value of $9,200. There was no prior service cost, nor were there deferred pension gains or losses. The following information relates to the pension plan during the year:

Service cost	$1,200
Actual return on the pension fund	$250
Benefits paid to retirees	$100
Contribution to the pension fund	$1,050
Discount rate for PBO	9%
Expected return on pension fund	10%

Compute (1) the pension-related amount that should be reported on the company's balance sheet on January 1 of Year 1, (2) the PBO as of December 31, and (3) the fair value of the pension fund as of December 31.

Practice 17-9

LO3

Simple Computation of Pension Expense

Refer to Practice 17-8. Compute pension expense for the year.

Practice 17-10

LO3

Basic Pension Journal Entries

Refer to Practice 17-8. Make two *summary* journal entries necessary with respect to the pension plan for the year.

Practice 17-11

LO3

Simple Pension Work Sheet

Refer to Practice 17-8. Enter all of the pension information, including the beginning balances, in a pension work sheet. Use the pension work sheet to display the computation of pension expense for the year as well as the ending balances for all pension-related items.

Practice 17-12

LO4

Amortization of Prior Service Cost

On January 1, the company adopted a new defined benefit pension plan. Existing employees were given credit in the new plan for their past service to the company. This created an immediate projected benefit obligation of $1,000,000. The company has 30 employees; three of these employees are expected to leave the company each year for the next 10 years. Using the amortization method that is similar to sum-of-the-years'-digits depreciation, compute the amount of prior service cost that should be amortized for the year.

Practice 17-13

LO4

Difference Between Actual and Expected Return on Pension Fund

As of January 1, the company had the following pension-related balances:

Projected benefit obligation (PBO)	$(15,000)
Fair value of pension fund	$17,000
Deferred net pension (gain)/loss	$(1,100)
Discount rate for the PBO	8%

During the year, service cost was $1,500. The actual return on the pension fund was $700. Compute pension expense for the year and the ending balance in deferred net pension (gain)/loss assuming that (1) the expected return on the pension fund is 10% and (2) the expected return on the pension fund is 12%.

Practice 17-14
LO4

Impact of Changes in Actuarial Estimates

Refer to Practice 17-6 and Practice 17-7. Assume that as of January 1, 2013, Wu Company changed the discount rate it uses to compute the PBO from 8% to 12%. Assume that before this change, Wu Company had the following pension-related balances:

Projected benefit obligation (PBO)	$(26,169)
Fair value of pension fund	23,000
Deferred net pension (gain)/loss	1,100
Prior service cost	2,000

Compute (1) the pension-related asset/liability balance and accumulated other comprehensive income balance that would be reported in the balance sheet *before* the change to 12%, (2) the PBO balance after the change to 12%, (3) interest cost for 2013, and (4) the pension-related asset/liability balance and accumulated other comprehensive income balance that would be reported in the balance sheet immediately *after* the change to 12% (before the impact of any other 2013 transactions).

Practice 17-15
LO4

Pension Work Sheet

On January 1 of Year 1, the company had a projected benefit obligation (PBO) of $10,000 and a pension fund with a fair value of $9,200. Prior service cost was $2,000; it was being amortized on a straight-line basis over the 5-year average remaining life of the affected employees. The balance in the deferred pension gain was $700. The following information relates to the pension plan during the year:

Service cost	$1,200
Actual return on the pension fund	$1,550
Benefits paid to retirees	$300
Contribution to the pension fund	$1,050
Discount rate for PBO	8%
Expected return on pension fund	11%

Enter all of the pension information, including the beginning balances, in a pension work sheet. Use the work sheet to display the computation of pension expense for the year as well as the ending balances for all pension-related items.

Practice 17-16
LO4

The Corridor Amount

The company had the following pension-related balances as of January 1:

Projected benefit obligation (PBO)	$(20,000)
Fair value of pension fund	23,000
Deferred net pension loss	3,100
Prior service cost	1,000

The average remaining service life of employees working on January 1 is six years. Compute the amount of the deferred net pension loss that should be amortized during the year.

Practice 17-17
LO4

Reconciliation of Beginning and Ending PBO Balances

On January 1 of Year 1, the company had a projected benefit obligation (PBO) of $10,000 and a pension fund with a fair value of $9,200. Prior service cost was $2,000; it was being amortized on a straight-line basis over the 5-year average remaining life of the affected employees. The balance in the deferred pension gain was $700. The following information relates to the pension plan during the year:

Service cost	$1,200
Actual return on the pension fund	$1,550
Benefits paid to retirees	$300
Contribution to the pension fund	$1,050
Discount rate for PBO	8%
Expected return on pension fund	11%

Prepare the note disclosure necessary to reconcile the beginning balance in the PBO and the ending balance in the PBO.

Practice 17-18

LO4

Reconciliation of Beginning and Ending Pension Fund Balances
Refer to Practice 17-17. Prepare the note disclosure necessary to reconcile the beginning balance in the pension fund and the ending balance in the pension fund.

EXERCISES

Exercise 17-19

LO2

Calculation of Bonus
Illinois Wholesale Company has an agreement with its sales manager entitling that individual to 7% of company earnings as a bonus. Company income for the calendar year before bonus and income tax is $350,000. Income tax is 30% of income after bonus.

1. Compute the amount of bonus if the bonus is calculated on income before deductions for bonus and income tax.
2. Compute the amount of bonus if the bonus is calculated on income after deduction for bonus but before deduction for income tax.

Exercise 17-20

LO1

SPREADSHEET

Monthly Payroll Entries
Aggie Co. sells agricultural products. Aggie pays its salespeople a salary plus a commission. The salary is the same for each salesperson, $1,000 per month. The commission varies by length of employment and is a percentage of the company's total gross sales. Each salesperson starts with a commission of 1.0%, which is increased an additional 0.5% for each full year of employment with Aggie, to a maximum of 5.0%. The total gross sales for the month of January were $120,000.

Aggie has six salespeople as follows:

	Number of Years Employment
Frank	10
Sally	9
Tina	8
Barry	6
Mark	3
Lisa	0.75

Assume that the FICA rate is 7.65%, the FUTA rate is 6.2%, and the state unemployment rate is 5.4%. (Assume that the federal government allows the maximum credit for state unemployment tax paid.) The federal income tax withholding rate is 30%. Compute the January salaries and commissions expense, and make any necessary entries to record the payroll transactions including cash payment of all the taxes payable.

Exercise 17-21
LO1

SPREADSHEET

Compensated Absence—Vacation Pay

General Aviation Company employs six people. Each employee is entitled to three weeks' paid vacation every year the employee works for the company. The conditions of the paid vacation are (a) for each full year of work, an employee will receive three weeks of paid vacation (no vacation accrues for a portion of a year), (b) each employee will receive the same pay for vacation time as the regular pay in the year taken, and (c) unused vacation pay can be carried forward. Based on the following data, compute the liability for vacation pay as of December 31, 2013.

Employee	Starting Date	Cumulative Vacation Taken as of December 31, 2013	Weekly Salary
Marci Clark	December 21, 2006	14 weeks	$850
Bradford Sayer	July 17, 2010	5 weeks	725
Sorena Williams	April 8, 2012	None	650
Jonathan Beecher	December 17, 2005	18 weeks	800
Brian Giles	July 17, 2011	1 week	450
Dale Murphy	May 31, 2013	None	500

Exercise 17-22
LO3

Computation of Pension Service Cost

Pension plan information for Naperville Window Company is as follows:

January 1, 2013	PBO	$4,780,000
	ABO	$3,950,000
During 2013	Pension benefits paid to retired employees	$315,000
December 31, 2013	PBO	$5,425,000
	ABO	$4,245,000
Obligation discount rate		10%

Assuming no change in actuarial assumptions, what is the pension service cost for 2013?

Exercise 17-23
LO4

Computation of Actual Return on the Pension Fund

Longlee Electrical Company maintains a fund to cover its pension plan. The following data relate to the fund for 2013:

January 1	FVPF	$875,000
	Market-related value of the pension fund (5-year weighted average)	715,000
During year	Pension benefits paid	62,000
	Contributions made to the fund	70,000
December 31	FVPF	980,000
	Market-related value of the pension fund (5-year weighted average)	730,000

Compute the 2013 actual return on the pension fund for Longlee Electrical.

Exercise 17-24
LO3

Computing Defined Benefit Pension Payments

Francisco Company has established a defined benefit pension plan for its lone employee, Derrald Ryan. Annual payments under the pension plan are equal to 3% of Derrald's highest lifetime salary multiplied by the number of years with the company. Derrald's salary in 2012 was $75,000. Derrald is expected to retire in 20 years, and his salary increases are expected to average 4% per year during that period. As of the beginning of 2013, Derrald had worked for Francisco Company for 12 years.

1. What is the amount of the annual pension payment that should be used in computing Francisco's accumulated benefit obligation (ABO) as of January 1, 2013?

2. What is the amount of the annual pension payment that should be used in computing Francisco's projected benefit obligation (PBO) as of January 1, 2013?

Exercise 17-25
LO4

Computation of Pension Expense and Summary Journal Entries

The accountants for Eden Financial Services provide you with the following detailed information at December 31, 2013. Based on these data, prepare the summary journal entries related to the recognition of pension expense and the pension contribution for 2013.

Service cost	$ 52,000
Actual return on pension plan assets	81,000
Interest cost	59,000
Excess of expected return over actual return on pension plan assets	15,000
Amortization of deferred pension loss from prior years	24,000
Amortization of prior service cost	36,000
Contribution to pension fund	100,000

Exercise 17-26
LO4

Computing the Amount of Pension-Related Asset/Liability

Using the information given for the following three independent cases, compute the amount of pension-related asset/liability that would be reported on the balance sheet. Clearly indicate whether the amount would be shown as an asset or as a liability. Also compute the amount of pension-related accumulated other comprehensive income that would be reported on the balance sheet.

	Case 1	Case 2	Case 3
Prior service cost	$ 310	$ 190	$ 50
PBO	1,000	900	1,000
Deferred net pension gain	70	120	200
ABO	750	800	850
FVPF	700	1,300	900

Exercise 17-27
LO5

Pension-Related Balance Sheet Items

From the following information for each of three independent cases, prepare the pension note disclosure that outlines the items that go into the computation of the pension-related asset or liability reported in the balance sheet as well as the pension-related accumulated other comprehensive income reported in the balance sheet.

	(in thousands)		
	Case 1	Case 2	Case 3
Projected benefit obligation	$12,500	$6,290	$890
Accumulated benefit obligation	9,700	4,100	750
Fair value of the pension fund	15,300	4,200	650
Market-related value of the pension fund	12,800	5,000	560
Deferred net (gain) or loss from prior years	(200)	(850)	100
Prior service cost	800	2,300	125

Exercise 17-28
LO4

Pension Expense Computation

Fredco's defined benefit pension plan had a PBO of $10,000,000 at the beginning of the year. This was based on a 10% discount rate (obligation discount rate). The fair value of pension plan assets at the beginning of the year was $10,400,000. These assets were expected to earn a long-term rate of return on the fair value of 8%. During the year, service cost was $750,000. At the beginning of the year, prior service cost was $25,000; this entire remaining amount will be amortized this period. There was no deferred net pension gain (loss) at the beginning of the year. The actual return on pension plan assets for the year was $900,000. The ABO was $9,500,000 at the beginning of the year. Compute Fredco's net periodic pension expense for the year.

Exercise 17-29

LO4

Computations Associated with Deferred Gains and Losses

The computation of pension expense includes (1) a deferral of the difference between actual and expected return on the pension fund and (2) amortization of deferred pension gains and losses. Determine the proper addition (deduction) to pension expense related to deferred gains and losses and their amortization under each of the following independent conditions.

	A	B	C	D
(1) Actual return on the pension fund	$200,000	$200,000	$500,000	$500,000
(2) Expected return on the pension fund	$180,000	$230,000	$400,000	$550,000
(3) Deferred (gain) loss at beginning of year	$200,000	$275,000	$(100,000)	$(175,000)
(4) Average service life of employees used for amortization	10 years	5 years	8 years	12 years
(5) Corridor amount	$100,000	$150,000	$50,000	$175,000

Exercise 17-30

LO4

Amortization of Deferred Gain on the Pension Fund

Melba Enterprises has a deferred gain of $425,000 relating to its pension plan as of January 1, 2013. Management has chosen to amortize this deferral on a straight-line basis over the 10-year average remaining service life of its employees, subject to the limitation of the corridor amount. Additional facts about the pension plan as of January 1, 2013, are as follows:

PBO	$2,050,000
ABO	1,900,000
Fair value of the pension fund	1,500,000
Market-related value of the pension fund (5-year weighted average)	1,350,000

Compute the minimum amortization of deferred gain to be recognized by Melba in 2013.

Exercise 17-31

LO4

Return on the Pension Fund—Expected and Actual

Rasband Photography has a pension plan covering its 100 employees. Rasband anticipates an 11% return on its pension fund. The fund trustee furnishes Rasband with the following information relating to the pension fund for 2013:

January 1	FVPF	$1,500,000
	Market-related value of the pension fund (5-year weighted average)	1,350,000
During year	Actual return on the pension fund	110,000
December 31	FVPF	1,620,000
	Market-related value of the pension fund (5-year weighted average)	1,480,000

Compute the difference between the actual and expected return on the pension fund. How should the difference be treated in determining pension expense for 2013? Rasband bases expected return on the market-related value of the pension fund.

Exercise 17-32

LO4

Amount of Funding and Amortization of Prior Service Cost

Da Vinci Inc. has a workforce of 400 employees. A new pension plan is negotiated on January 1, 2013, with the labor union. Based on the provisions of the pension agreement, prior service cost related to the new plan amounts to $4,823,000. The cost is to be funded evenly with annual contributions over a 10-year period, with the first payment due at the end of 2013. The cost is to be amortized over the average remaining service life of the covered employees. The interest rate for funding purposes is 12%. It is anticipated that, on the average, 10 employees will retire each year over the next 40 years.

1. Compute the annual amount Da Vinci will pay to fund its prior service cost.
2. Compute the amount of amortization of prior service cost for 2013, 2015, and 2020.

Exercise 17-33
LO4

Amortization of Prior Service Cost—Plan Amendment

Queensland Company has five employees belonging to its pension plan. One employee is expected to retire each year over the next five years.

On January 1, 2013, Queensland initiated an amendment to its pension plan that increased the PBO for the plan by $620,000. If Queensland amortizes the prior service cost of the pension plan using the sum-of-the-years'-digits method, determine the amortization for the each of the next five years.

Exercise 17-34
LO4

Amortization of Prior Service Cost—Straight-Line Method

Osvaldo Awning Co. has prior service cost of $1,262,000 arising from a pension plan amendment. The board of directors decided to amortize this cost over the average remaining service period for its 45 employees on a straight-line basis. It is assumed that employees will retire at the rate of three employees each year over a 15-year period.

1. Compute the average remaining service life and the annual amortization of prior service cost for Osvaldo.
2. Assume that pension expense other than amortization of prior service cost was $460,000 for the year and also assume that all of this amount is associated with service cost, interest cost, and actual return on plan assets (meaning that actual return equaled expected return this year). Also assume that $520,000 was contributed by the employer to the pension fund. Prepare the summary journal entries to record pension expense and the pension contribution for the current year.

Exercise 17-35
LO4

SPREADSHEET

Preparing a Pension Work Sheet

The following information relates to the defined benefit pension plan of Mascare Company.

January 1, 2013:	
PBO	$9,000
FVPF	$11,000
Expected return on plan assets	8%
Obligation discount rate	10%
For the year ended December 31, 2013:	
Service cost	$1,200
Benefit payments to retirees	500
Contributions to pension fund	100
Actual return on plan assets	1,500

Prepare a pension work sheet for Mascare Company for 2013.

Exercise 17-36
LO1

Recording Payroll and Payroll Taxes

Express Company paid one week's wages of $21,200 in cash (net pay after all withholdings and deductions) to its employees. Income tax withholdings were equal to 17% of the gross payroll, and the only other deductions were 7.65% for FICA tax and $160 for union dues. Give the entries that should be made on the company's books to record the payroll and the tax accruals to be recognized by the employer, assuming that the company is subject to unemployment taxes of 5.4% (state) and 0.8% (federal). Assume that all wages for the week are subject to FICA and unemployment taxes.

PROBLEMS

Problem 17-37

LO1

Accrued Payroll and Payroll Taxes

Joey Department Store's employees are paid on the 6th and 22nd of each month for the period ending the last day of the previous month and the 15th of the current month, respectively. An analysis of the payroll on Monday, October 6, 2013, revealed the following data.

	Gross Pay	FICA	Federal Income Tax	State Income Tax	Net Insurance	Pay
Office staff salaries	$15,450	$ 810	$ 2,400	$ 450	$ 410	$11,380
Officer salaries	31,000	286	6,300	1,000	500	22,914
Sales salaries	20,000	834	4,200	690	480	13,796
Totals	$66,450	$1,930	$12,900	$2,140	$1,390	$48,090

It is determined that for the September 30 pay period, no additional employees exceeded the wage base for FICA purposes than had done so in prior pay periods. All of the officer salaries, 75% of the office staff salaries, and 40% of the sales salaries for the payroll period ending September 30 were paid to employees who had exceeded the wage base for unemployment taxes. Assume the unemployment tax rates in force are as follows: federal unemployment tax, 0.8%, and state unemployment tax, 5.4%.

Instructions: Prepare the adjusting entries that would be required at September 30, the end of Joey's fiscal year, to reflect the accrual of the payroll and any related payroll taxes. Separate salaries and payroll tax expense accounts are used for each of the three employee categories: office staff, officer, and sales.

Problem 17-38

LO1

Accounting for Payroll

Bags, Inc., a manufacturer of suitcases, has 10 employees; five are paid on a salary basis, and five are hourly employees. The employees and their compensation are as follows:

	Annual Salary
Ken Scott (president)	$91,500
Tatia Furgins	57,000
Jennifer Poulns	48,750
Robyn Meek	23,800
Kyle Roberts	13,900
	Rate per Hour
Richard Dean (50 hours per week)	$14.00
Denise Ray (40 hours per week)	11.50
Dale Frank (40 hours per week)	9.75
Bryan Leslie (30 hours per week)	4.50
Albert Lamb (20 hours per week)	3.65

The salaried employees are covered by a comprehensive medical and dental plan. The cost of the plan is $45 per employee and is deducted from each paycheck. The hourly employees are covered only by a medical plan. The cost is calculated at 3.5% of gross pay and is deducted from each check. The FICA rate is 7.65%, and FUTA is 6.2%, with the maximum credit for state unemployment allowed. The state unemployment tax is 5.4%. No employee has reached the FICA, FUTA, or SUTA salary limits. In addition, each of the hourly employees, except Albert, belongs to the Suitcase Workers of America Union. Union dues are $5.65 per month and are deducted and paid on behalf of the hourly employees. The income tax withholding rate is 28% for employees with annual incomes above $29,500 and 15% for employees with annual incomes of $29,500 or less.

Hourly employees are paid weekly on Friday, January 6, 13, 20, and 27. Salaried employees are paid twice a month, on January 13 and 27. Assume that payroll taxes and all employee withholdings and deductions are paid on the 15th and the last day of each month, for the current month.

Instructions: Make all entries related to Bags, Inc.'s, payroll for January 6, January 13, and January 15.

Problem 17-39

LO1

Compensated Absences

Ludwig Electronics Inc. has a plan to compensate its employees for certain absences. Each employee can receive five days' sick leave each year plus 10 days' vacation. The benefits carry over for two additional years, after which the provision lapses on a FIFO flow basis. Thus, the maximum accumulation is 45 days. In some cases, the company permits vacations to be taken before they are earned. Payments are made based on current compensation levels, not on the level in effect when the absence time was earned.

Employee	Days Accrued Jan. 1, 2013	Daily Rate Jan. 1, 2013	Days Earned 2013	Days Taken 2013	Days Accrued Dec. 31, 2013	Daily Rate Dec. 31, 2013
A	20	$68	15	13	22	$70
B	15	74	15	15	15	76
C	25	62	7	32	0	Terminated, June 15— Rate = $64
D	–5	56	15	20	–10	58
E	40	78	15	5	50	82
F	Hired July 1	60	8	2	6	60

Instructions:

1. How much is the liability for compensated absences at December 31, 2013?
2. Prepare a summary journal entry to record compensation absence payments during the year and the accrual at the end of the year. Assume that the payroll liability account is charged for all payments made during the year for both sick and vacation leaves. The average rate of compensation for the year may be used to value the hours taken except for Employee C, who took leaves at the date of termination. The end-of-year rate should be used to establish the ending liability.

Problem 17-40

LO3

SPREADSHEET

Summary Entries to Record Pension Expense and Funding of Pension Costs

United Rental Company reported the following information related to its pension plan for the years 2013–2016. The fund is administered by a separate outside trustee.

Year	Pension Expense	Contribution	Benefit Payments to Retirees	Actual Return on the Pension Fund
2013	$720,400	$675,000	$350,000	$320,000
2014	810,100	700,000	350,000	350,000
2015	695,700	725,000	300,000	410,000
2016	790,000	680,000	375,000	505,000

Instructions:

1. Prepare the required summary journal entries for each year to record pension expense and the pension contribution. Throughout this example, assume that the actual return on the pension fund is equal to the expected return in each year, that there is no existing balance in deferred gain or loss related to the pension, and that there is no prior service cost.
2. Assuming that United had pension-related liability of $41,000 at January 1, 2013, compute the pension-related asset/liability balance at December 31, 2016.
3. Assuming that the fair value of the pension fund at January 1, 2013, was $3,200,000, compute the fair value of the pension fund at December 31, 2016.

Problem 17-41
LO4

Computation of Prior Service Cost Funding and Amortization

Staybrite Electronics Co. amended its pension plan effective January 1, 2013. The increase in the PBO occurring as a result of the plan amendment is $6,290,000. Staybrite arranged to fund the prior service cost by equal annual contributions over the next 15 years at 10% interest. The first payment will be made December 31, 2013. The company decides to amortize the prior service cost on a straight-line basis over the average remaining service life of its employees. The company has 225 employees at January 1, 2013, who are entitled to the benefits of the amendment. It is estimated that, on the average, 15 employees will retire each year.

Instructions:

1. Compute the amount Staybrite will pay each year to fund the prior service cost arising from the plan's amendment.
2. Compute Staybrite's annual prior service cost amortization based on average remaining years of employee service.

Problem 17-42
LO4

Deferred Gains and Losses

McGrath Financial Corp. has a defined benefit pension plan. As of January 1, 2013, the following balances were computed for the pension plan:

Deferred pension gain	$ 420,000
Fair value of the pension fund	3,300,000
Market-related value of the pension fund (5-year weighted average)	2,850,000
PBO	3,900,000
ABO	3,500,000

It was anticipated that the pension plan would earn 12% of the market-related value of the pension fund in 2013. The actual return on the pension fund was $315,000. The company has elected to amortize the deferred pension gains and losses over 10 years.

Instructions:

1. Compute the amount of deferred gain or loss for 2013.
2. Compute the amount of amortization of deferred pension gain or loss for 2013.
3. Computed pension expense is $534,000. However, this computation ignores any deferred gains or losses for the year (meaning that actual, rather than expected, return on the pension fund was included in the computations) as well as any amortization of deferred gains or losses from prior years. What is pension expense after considering the impact of deferred gains and losses and their amortization?
4. What is the deferred pension gain or loss that McGrath will carry forward to 2014?

Problem 17-43
LO4

Computation, Recording, and Funding of Pension Expense

Averon Industrial, Inc., computed the following components of pension expense for the years 2013–2015:

Components of Pension Expense	2013	2014	2015
	(in thousands)		
Service cost	$330	$415	$580
Interest cost	150	170	220
Actual return on the pension fund	35	50	40
Expected return on the pension fund	30	45	50
Amortization of deferred pension (gain) or loss—above corridor amount	(20)	(10)	18
Amortization of prior service cost	70	90	90
Amount contributed to fund	520	580	750

Instructions:

1. Compute the net periodic pension expense for the years 2013–2015.
2. Prepare the summary journal entries to record the computed pension expense in (1) and the funding of the pension plan.
3. If the pension-related asset balance at January 1, 2013, was $75,000, compute the balance of the pension-related asset/liability account at December 31, 2015. Also compute the balance in pension-related accumulated other comprehensive income at December 31, 2015; the balance on January 1, 2013 was a debit of $600,000.

Problem 17-44

LO4

REVERSE SOLVABLE

Computation of Prior Service Cost Amortization

The information below was provided relative to the pension plan for Atlas Wholesale Company for the years 2013–2015.

	January 1, 2013	December 31, 2013	December 31, 2014	December 31, 2015
PBO	$27,525	$28,900	$30,200	$31,500
Fair value of the pension fund	23,600	27,730	29,830	29,730
Service cost plus interest cost less actual return on plan assets		215	1,710	3,810
Contributions made to pension fund		2,970	2,510	2,410
Deferred net pension loss (gain)	2,520	1,145	1,445	3,795
Prior service cost	420	0	0	0

Instructions:

1. Compute the amount of net periodic pension expense for each of the three years. Assume that the deferred net pension loss relates only to the difference between the actual and expected return on the pension fund. Also note that this deferred loss is never amortized in 2013, 2014, or 2015 because it is always less than the 10% corridor amount (although it will be amortized in 2016).
2. Prepare the journal entries for recording the net pension expense and the pension funding for the three years.
3. Identify the pension balance sheet accounts and their amounts as of December 31, 2015.

Problem 17-45

LO5

Disclosure of Pension Plan Information

The following information relates to the pension plan of Circle Manufacturing Company at December 31, 2013:

	(in thousands)
Balances at December 31, 2013:	
PBO	$12,950
Fair value of the pension fund	11,600
Prior service cost	0
Deferred net pension loss (arose in 2013)	220
2013 activity:	
Service cost	$ 950
Interest cost	1,300
Actual return on the pension fund	1,020
Expected return on the pension fund	1,110
Amortization of prior service cost	80

Instructions: Prepare the pension note at December 31, 2013, that discloses the component parts of pension expense as well as the items that combine to yield the net amounts reported in the balance sheet.

Problem 17-46
LO4

Preparing a Pension Work Sheet

The following data relate to the defined benefit pension plan of Haan Company:

Balances at January 1, 2013:	
PBO	$3,500
Prior service cost	$150
Fair value of pension assets	$3,000
ABO	$2,800
Expected return on plan assets	7%
Obligation discount rate	10%
Activity for 2013:	
Service cost	$400
Benefit payments to retirees	170
Contributions to pension fund	230
Actual return on plan assets	130
Prior service cost amortization	40

Instructions: Prepare a pension work sheet for Haan Company for 2013.

Problem 17-47
LO4

Comprehensive Computation of Pension Cost Components

The actuaries for Interconnect Cable Company provided its accountants with the following information (in thousands of $) related to the company's pension plan:

December 31, 2012:	
Increase in PBO arising from plan's amendment	$684
January 1, 2013:	
PBO	$2,700
Fair value of the pension fund	$1,860
Market-related value of the pension fund (5-year weighted average)	$1,600
Obligation discount rate	10%
Average service life for amortization of deferred gain and prior service costs	14 years
Deferred pension gain—prior year	$70
Expected rate of return	9%

For year 2013:	
Benefit payments to retirees	$173
Contributions to pension plan	290
December 31, 2013:	
PBO	$2,917
Fair value of pension plan assets	2,137

Instructions: Based on the data provided, prepare a pension work sheet for Interconnect Cable Company for 2013. The 5-year weighted-average value of plan assets is used in computing the expected return.

Problem 17-48
LO4

Pension Cost Components and Reconciliation of Funded Status

As of January 1, 2013, information related to the defined benefit pension plan of Leffingwell Company was as follows:

PBO	$1,615,000
Fair value of pension assets	1,513,500
Prior service cost	105,000
Deferred net pension gain or loss	0

Pension data for the years 2013 and 2014 are listed as follows:

2013 Pension plan information:	
Service cost as reported by actuaries	$87,000
Contributions to pension plan	$120,000
Benefits paid to retirees	$132,000
Actual return on pension plan assets	$26,350
Amortization of prior service cost	$21,000
Actuarial change increasing PBO	$80,000
Obligation discount rate	11%
Long-term expected rate of return on pension plan assets	10%
2014 Pension plan information:	
Service cost as reported by actuaries	$115,000
Contributions to pension plan	$125,000
Benefits paid to retirees	$140,000
Actual return on pension plan assets	$180,000
Amortization of prior service cost	$18,667
Obligation discount rate	11%
Long-term expected rate of return on pension plan assets	10%

As of January 1, 2014, the remaining expected service life of employees was 5.0 years. Also, Leffingwell uses the fair market value of pension plan assets at the beginning of the year as the market-related value of pension plan assets.

Instructions:

1. For both 2013 and 2014, prepare the pension note that discloses the component parts of pension expense as well as the items that combine to yield the net amounts reported in the balance sheet.
2. Prepare the summary journal entries for recording net pension expense and pension funding for 2013 and 2014.

CASES

Discussion Case 17-49

Recognition or Disclosure?

Before 2006, U.S. accounting standards did not require companies to report the funding status of a defined benefit pension plan (overfunded if the plan assets exceed the projected benefit obligation and underfunded if the plan assets are less than the PBO) in the balance sheet. Some preparers and users of financial statements believe that it isn't absolutely necessary to reflect the pension plan funding status on the face of the balance sheet. Instead, they believe that mere note disclosure of the funding status is enough. Other preparers and users view it as essential to explicitly require a net pension-related asset or liability to be recognized in an amount equal to the funding status of the defined benefit plan. Is note disclosure sufficient for financial statement users, or is it important that information be actually recognized in the financial statements themselves?

Discussion Case 17-50

What Theoretical Support Is There for the Pension Standards?

The topic of pensions and other postretirement benefits was considered at length in an accounting theory class. The discussion centered on the following terms:

(a) Representational faithfulness
(b) Substance over form
(c) Verifiability
(d) Usefulness
(e) Present value
(f) Conservatism
(g) Adequate disclosure

How are these terms helpful in justifying the accounting for pension and other postretirement benefit plans on the employer's books? Based on your understanding of these terms, assess the U.S. accounting treatment of pension and other postretirement benefit plans.

Discussion Case 17-51

How Much Do You Need to Save for Retirement?

You plan to retire at age 65. You anticipate needing $5,000 per month ($60,000 per year) after you retire. You expect to live for 20 years after you retire. You will work for 40 years, from age 25 to 65. Your average salary per working year will be $100,000. You estimate that you can earn an average of 8% per year on your investments. This considers inflation by using a "real" interest rate (nominal rate of 11% less an expected inflation rate of 3%). Assume that all cash flows occur at the end of the year and ignore income taxes. Before doing any calculations, estimate what fraction of your annual income you will need to save to have $60,000 per year for each year of your retirement life. After you make your estimate, compute what percentage of your annual salary during your 40 working years you must invest to be able to withdraw $60,000 per year for the 20 years after you retire. What if you wait until you are 30 to start saving? 35? 40? Was your initial guess too high or too low?

Discussion Case 17-52

Does Accounting Have Political Consequences?

Let's go back in time to 1990. C. B. Seabright, a U.S. congresswoman, has just received from her staff an analysis of pre-codification FASB *Statement No. 106*, "Employers' Accounting for Postretirement Benefits Other Than Pensions." This is the standard that switched accounting for retiree health care benefit plans from a pay-as-you-go basis to an accrual basis (like that used for defined benefit pension plans). Seabright is very influential in the formation of tax legislation and in federal regulation of employer-provided health care plans. How might pre-codification FASB *Statement No. 106* impact Seabright's legislative agenda?

Case 17-53

Deciphering Financial Statements (The Walt Disney Company)

Locate the information relating to pensions and other postretirement benefits found in **The Walt Disney Company**'s annual report (which can be found on the Internet at **http://www.disney.com**) and answer the following questions.

1. What is Disney's PBO at the end of fiscal 2009 (October 3, 2009)?
2. Determine whether Disney's actual return on its pension fund was greater than or less than its expected return in 2009.
3. Because of the high costs associated with medical benefits, Disney has elected to follow a strategy adopted by a number of firms. That strategy has been to not offer those benefits to new employees. In its 1994 annual report, Disney stated that "employees hired after January 1, 1994, are not eligible for postretirement medical benefits." How might the financial accounting rules have caused Disney to make this change in policy in 1994?
4. At the end of 2009, Disney's pension plans appear to be slightly underfunded. What can you say about the status of its postretirement medical benefits plans?

Case 17-54

Deciphering Financial Statements (Northrop Grumman)

Northrop Grumman is a leading aerospace/defense company. The company has developed the F-16 fighter, the Apache helicopter, the AWACS early warning airborne radar, and the B-2 Stealth bomber. Grumman, one of the predecessor companies of Northrop Grumman, was the primary contractor for the Lunar Excursion Module (LEM) that landed Neil Armstrong and Buzz Aldrin on the moon in 1969. Information relating to Northrop Grumman's pension and other postretirement benefit plans follows.

	Pension Benefits			Medical and Life Benefits		
$ in millions	**2009**	**2008**	**2007**	**2009**	**2008**	**2007**
Components of Net Periodic Benefit Cost						
Service cost	$ 661	$ 721	$ 786	$ 48	$ 55	$ 52
Interest cost	1,350	1,335	1,250	164	166	164
Expected return on plan assets	(1,559)	(1,895)	(1,774)	(48)	(64)	(58)
Amortization of						
Prior service cost (credit)	50	40	40	(59)	(65)	(65)
Net loss from previous years	337	24	48	28	22	25
Other	17		2			
Net periodic benefit cost	$ 856	$ 225	$ 352	$133	$114	$118

	Pension Benefits		Medical and Life Benefits	
$ in millions	**2009**	**2008**	**2009**	**2008**
Change in Projected Benefit Obligation				
Projected benefit obligation at beginning of year	$22,147	$22,069	$2,716	$2,812
Service cost	661	721	48	55
Interest cost	1,350	1,335	164	166
Plan participants' contributions	16	14	106	78
Plan amendments	5	73		30
Actuarial loss (gain)	869	(818)	15	(170)
Benefits paid	(1,359)	(1,179)	(289)	(269)
Acquisitions, curtailments, divestitures and other	34	(68)	20	14
Projected benefit obligation at end of year	23,723	22,147	2,780	2,716
Change in Plan Assets				
Fair value of plan assets at beginning of year	18,501	22,891	718	951
Gain/(loss) on plan assets	2,945	(3,500)	126	(238)

$ in millions	Pension Benefits 2009	Pension Benefits 2008	Medical and Life Benefits 2009	Medical and Life Benefits 2008
Employer contributions	858	320	162	181
Plan participants' contributions	16	14	106	78
Benefits paid	(1,359)	(1,179)	(289)	(269)
Acquisitions, curtailments, divestitures and other	12	(45)	20	15
Fair value of plan assets at end of year	20,973	18,501	843	718
Funded status	$(2,750)	$(3,646)	$(1,937)	$(1,998)
Amounts Recognized in the Consolidated Statements of Financial Position				
Non-current assets	$ 264	$ 266	$ 36	$ 24
Current liability	(47)	(45)	(66)	(66)
Non-current liability	(2,967)	(3,867)	(1,907)	(1,956)

The following table shows those amounts expected to be recognized in net periodic benefit cost in 2010:

$ in millions	Pension Benefits	Medical and Life Benefits
Amounts Expected to be Recognized in 2010 Net Periodic Benefit Cost		
Net loss	$244	$26
Prior service cost (credit)	47	(60)

The accumulated benefit obligation for all defined benefit pension plans was $22.1 billion and $20.4 billion at December 31, 2009 and 2008, respectively.

$ in millions	Pension Benefits 2009	Pension Benefits 2008	Medical and Life Benefits 2009	Medical and Life Benefits 2008
Amounts Recorded in Accumulated Other Comprehensive Loss				
Net actuarial loss	$(4,648)	$(5,509)	$(451)	$(539)
Prior service cost and net transition obligation	(242)	(287)	298	357
Income tax benefits related to above items	1,923	2,286	61	72
Unamortized benefit plan costs	$(2,967)	$(3,510)	$ (92)	$(110)

Based on this information, answer the following questions:

1. Is Northrop Grumman's pension plan overfunded or underfunded? How can you tell?
2. Are Northrop Grumman's medical and life benefits programs overfunded or underfunded? Explain.
3. As of the end of 2009, does Northrop Grumman's pension-related accumulated other comprehensive income increase or decrease its stockholders' equity?
4. During 2009, was the actual return on Northrop Grumman's pension fund more or less than the expected return? What about in 2008? Explain.

Case 17-55

Deciphering Financial Statements (General Motors)

Direct your attention to the company with perhaps the largest private pension plan in the world—**General Motors**. GM's note relating to its pension plan is included in Exhibit 17-11 on page 17-42. Use that information to answer the following questions.

1. Compute GM's total PBO as of December 31, 2009. How much has GM set aside in its pension fund to offset the PBO?
2. Now consider GM's postretirement benefits other than pensions. What is GM's TOTAL estimated obligation related to pensions and other postretirement benefits?
3. Why do you think there is a separation into U.S. and non-U.S. plans?
4. For the interval July 10, 2009 to December 31, 2009, compare GM's service cost to the amount of benefits paid to retirees. What can you draw from this comparison?
5. Evaluate the funded status of GM's "other benefits" plans. Treat the U.S. and non-U.S. plans as one large plan.

Case 17-56

Writing Assignment (Pensions in foreign countries)

In the United States, accounting for pensions has received a great deal of attention. In other countries, pension accounting is given much less attention. In one page, examine the reasons that would explain why pension accounting is given much less emphasis in most foreign countries as compared to the emphasis it receives in the United States.

Case 17-57

Cumulative Spreadsheet Analysis

This assignment is a detailed examination of Skywalker's pension-related items. As of December 31, 2013, the $253 in "Other long-term liabilities" reported by Skywalker (see Chapter 13) included an amount for a net pension liability. In addition, Skywalker's $456 in "Other operating expenses" for 2013 included an amount for net pension expense.

The following information relates to Skywalker's pension plan as of December 31, 2013.

Fair value of pension fund assets	$200
Discount rate used in valuing the PBO	7%
Long-term expected rate of return on pension fund assets	9%
Total annual pension payment earned by Skywalker's employees so far	$50
Number of years that employees are expected to receive pension payments after retirement	30 years
Number of years until first pension payment is to be received	11 years

Construct a spreadsheet to calculate the following:

1. Given the information above, compute the net pension liability that Skywalker will report as of December 31, 2013. (*Note:* Be careful in computing the PBO; remember that the standard annuity formula yields the present value of the annuity one year *before* the first payment is received.)
2. Compute a forecast of Skywalker's net pension liability as of December 31, 2014, and net pension expense for 2014 using the following information:
   - By working an extra year in 2014, the total annual pension payment earned by Skywalker's employees is expected to increase from $50 to $55.
   - Skywalker's employees will be one year closer to receiving the first pension payment.
   - No pension benefits are expected to be paid to employees in 2014.
   - Skywalker expects to contribute $50 to the pension plan during 2014.
   - Skywalker's best estimate is that the pension fund assets will earn in 2014 an amount equal to the long-term expected rate of return.
3. Repeat (1) and (2) using the following information:
   (a) The discount rate is 8%, and the long-term expected rate of return on the pension fund assets is 12%.
   (b) The discount rate is 5%, and the long-term expected rate of return on the pension fund assets is 11%.

P4 OTHER DIMENSIONS OF FINANCIAL REPORTING

Myrleen Ferguson Cate/PhotoEdit

CHAPTER 18 Earnings Per Share

LEARNING OBJECTIVES

1. Know the difference between a simple and a complex capital structure, and understand how dilutive securities affect earnings per share computations.
2. Compute basic earnings per share, taking into account the sale and repurchase of stock during the period as well as the effects of stock splits and stock dividends.
3. Use the treasury stock method to compute diluted earnings per share when a firm has outstanding stock options, warrants, and rights.
4. Use the if-converted method to compute diluted earnings per share when a company has convertible preferred stock or convertible bonds outstanding.
5. Factor into the diluted earnings per share computations the effect of actual conversion of convertible securities or the exercise of options, warrants, or rights during the period, and understand the antidilutive effect of potential common shares when a firm reports a loss from continuing operations.
6. Determine the order in which multiple potentially dilutive securities should be considered in computing diluted earnings per share.
7. Understand the disclosure requirements associated with basic and diluted earnings per share computations.

EM EXPANDED MATERIAL

8. Make complex earnings per share computations involving multiple potentially dilutive securities.

With 1.3 billion people and an economy that is growing at almost 10% per year, China's energy needs are exploding. And in today's world, that means that China has an increasing appetite for imported oil. In fact, China is the second largest consumer of oil in the world, after the United States. This thirst for imported oil is having a noticeable impact on China's geopolitics. China is taking an increased interest in what happens in the oil-producing areas of the world ... in the Persian Gulf, in Nigeria, and in Venezuela.[1]

Of course, the Chinese government would like to maximize its domestic production of oil in order to lessen the country's dependence on foreign oil. **Sinopec**, **PetroChina**, and **CNOOC** are the Big Three in the Chinese oil industry. All three of these companies arose out of the Chinese government's Ministry of Petroleum. For many years, these oil companies were a cross between a business entity and a government agency. Today, even though these companies are still majority owned by the Chinese government, they are each publicly listed and are each operated as business enterprises.

China Petroleum & Chemical Corporation (Sinopec)

Sinopec Group is a holding company created by the Chinese government. The primary subsidiary of Sinopec Group is the China Petroleum & Chemical Corporation, usually called "Sinopec Corp." or just "Sinopec." Sinopec was incorporated as a separate company on February 28, 2000, and executed an initial public offering (IPO) of "H shares" (shares of a Chinese company that are publicly traded on the Stock Exchange of Hong Kong) in October 2000. After the IPO, Sinopec shares were listed in Hong Kong, New York, and London. In July 2001, Sinopec issued "A shares" (shares of a Chinese company that are publicly traded inside China) in Shanghai. In its early years, Sinopec was primarily a "downstream" oil company, meaning that it used petroleum as an input into its refining and petrochemical operations. In 1998, the Chinese government required Sinopec to exchange some of its refining assets for "upstream," or oil-producing, assets. Today, Sinopec is an integrated petroleum and petrochemical company, meaning that it explores for oil, refines oil, transports oil, and produces and distributes petrochemical products. Sinopec operates over 29,000 retail gasoline stations in China. Sinopec is particularly strong in the southeast part of China.

PetroChina Company Limited (PetroChina)

China National Petroleum Corporation (CNPC) is a large state-owned enterprise authorized by the Chinese central government. CNPC created PetroChina as a separate corporation in November 1999. PetroChina was listed on the New York and Hong Kong stock exchanges in April 2000 and on the Shanghai Stock Exchange in November 2007. In contrast to Sinopec, PetroChina was primarily an upstream oil company in its early years. In 1998 PetroChina exchanged some of its oilfield assets for some of Sinopec's refining assets, creating an integrated petroleum and petrochemical company. This interesting move essentially created two large competitors, both majority owned by the Chinese central government. PetroChina is particularly strong in the north and northeast part of China. PetroChina operates China's largest oilfield, the Daqing field in northeastern China, which is the fourth-largest producing oil field in the world.

China National Offshore Oil Corporation (CNOOC)

China National Offshore Oil Corporation (CNOOC) is the state-owned parent of CNOOC Limited, which is publicly listed in Hong Kong and New York. CNOOC is the smallest of the Big Three and has historically focused on developing China's offshore oil and gas resources. Since its IPO in 2001, CNOOC has made efforts to expand its operations overseas. Its most public attempt, ultimately an unsuccessful one, was its bid to buy Unocal, the U.S. oil company. CNOOC's US$18.5 billion bid topped the bid of ChevronTexaco, but U.S. political forces, opposed to the purchase of a U.S. oil firm by a company controlled by the Chinese government, ultimately caused CNOOC to withdraw its bid.

With the increasing demand for oil by the Chinese economy, how fast are the profits of these Chinese state-owned oil companies expected to grow? A good way to assess the market consensus on this topic is to look at the relation between the earnings per share and stock prices of these companies. Those numbers, with the corresponding numbers for **ExxonMobil**, are shown in Exhibit 18-1.

Several interesting insights come from the data in Exhibit 18-1. First, note that the earnings per share of the Chinese oil companies are quite small; with the yuan/dollar exchange rate of 7.2941 at that time, the

[1] Gal Luft, "Fueling the dragon: China's race into the oil market," Institute for the Analysis of Global Security, 2003/2004, http://www.iags.org/china.htm.

EX 18-1 EARNINGS PER SHARE AND P/E RATIOS FOR CHINESE OIL COMPANIES (FOR 2007)

	Sinopec	PetroChina	CNOOC	ExxonMobil
Earnings pre share	¥0.63	¥0.75	¥0.72	$7.36
Market price pre share	¥12.51	¥14.79	¥14.13	$93.69
Price/earnings (P/E) ratio	19.9	19.7	19.6	12.7
Total market value of shares (in billion)	¥1,084.62	¥2,706.18	¥625.85	$504.24

As of December 31, 2007, one U.S. dollar was the equivalent of ¥7.2941 (Chinese yuan).

earnings per share of each of the Chinese oil companies is about 10 U.S. cents compared to $7.36 for ExxonMobil. This same relative relation holds for the market prices of the companies' shares; the price of the shares of the Chinese oil companies, after conversion to U.S. dollars, is less than $2 per share, compared to $93.69 per share for ExxonMobil. However, a look at the final row in Exhibit 18-1 demonstrates that this large difference merely reflects the fact that Chinese oil companies have many, many shares outstanding. In fact, if you add up the total market values of each of the three Chinese oil companies, and then convert that total into U.S. dollars, you will see that these three companies, as a group, are worth more ($605.5 billion) than ExxonMobil ($504.2 billion).

Now, what about the expected profitability growth of the Chinese oil companies? The expected growth is reflected in the price/earnings (P/E) ratio, which is equal to the company's market price per share divided by its earnings per share. One of the primary factors influencing P/E ratios is expected future earnings growth. In general, companies or industries in which expected future earnings growth is expected to be high are characterized by high P/E ratios. An example is any kind of high technology industry such as software development or pharmaceuticals. Conversely, in industries where expected future earnings growth is low, P/E ratios are low. Examples of these industries are traditional manufacturing businesses such as automobiles or heavy equipment. The P/E ratio of the Big Three Chinese oil companies are all approximately 20, substantially higher than the P/E ratio of about 13 for ExxonMobil. At least as far as the international investment community is concerned, the earnings per share of the Chinese oil companies are expected to grow rapidly in the future.

? QUESTIONS

1. In general, what does a firm's P/E ratio reflect?
2. Why is the earnings per share of ExxonMobil so much higher than the earnings per share of the three Chinese oil companies?

Answers to these questions can be found on page 18-27.

Simple and Complex Capital Structures

1 **Know the difference between a simple and a complex capital structure, and understand how dilutive securities affect earnings per share computations.**

WHY From the standpoint of a common stockholder, a fundamental and understandable measure of a company's operating performance is the earnings generated for each share of common stock outstanding. The existence of potential shareholders, such as option holders or holders of convertible securities, makes this important computation of earnings per share of common stock more complicated.

HOW A complex capital structure is one in which stock options or convertible securities (bonds or preferred stock) exist. With a complex capital structure, the computation of earnings per share must include consideration of the potential impact of options and convertible securities on both earnings available to common stockholders and on the number of common shares outstanding.

Earnings per share figures were historically computed and used primarily by financial analysts. Sometimes the computation was disclosed in the unaudited section of the annual report along with a message from the company's president. However, because this measurement was not reviewed by an independent third party, figures used to develop EPS were often different from those attested to by the auditor. The situation became more complex when some companies and analysts began computing EPS not only on the basis of common shares actually outstanding but also on the basis of what shares would be outstanding if certain convertible securities were converted and if certain stock options were exercised. Usually, the conversion or exercise terms were very favorable to the holders of these securities, and EPS would decline if common stock were issued on conversion or exercise. This result, a reduced EPS, is referred to as a dilution of earnings. In some cases, however, the exercise of options or conversion of securities might result in an increased EPS. This result is referred to as an antidilution of earnings. Securities that would lead to dilution are referred to as dilutive securities, and those that would lead to antidilution are referred to as antidilutive securities. Rational investors would not convert or exercise antidilutive securities because they could do better by purchasing common stock in the marketplace.

FYI

Although EPS is a common measure used to assess a firm's profitability, the FASB specifically stated that under no circumstances was cash flow per share to be reported. The FASB did not want financial statement users to consider cash flow per share as an alternative to earnings per share.

These forward-looking computations of EPS attempt to provide information as to what future EPS might be, assuming conversions and exercises took place. Because these "as if" conditions are based on assumptions, they can be computed in several ways. This is where the accounting standards come in. The standard in the United States is found in FASB ASC Topic 260, Earnings per Share. The corresponding international standard is *IAS 33*. In the area of earnings per share, U.S. GAAP and IFRS are very similar. In fact, the corresponding standards, both issued in 1997, were among the very first projects in which the FASB and IASB worked closely together. The differences between the two standards lie in technical areas that are outside the scope of this chapter.

A company's capital structure may be classified as simple or complex. If a company has only common stock, or common and nonconvertible preferred stock outstanding and there are no convertible securities, stock options, warrants, or other rights outstanding, it is classified as a company with a simple capital structure. Earnings per share is computed

Duncan Smith/Photodisc/Getty Images

The earnings per share figure can significantly influence a firm's perceived value in the stock market.

by dividing income available to common shareholders by the weighted-average number of common shares outstanding for the period. No future-oriented "as if" conditions need to be considered. If net income includes extraordinary gains or losses or other below-the-line items, as discussed in Chapter 4, a separate EPS figure is required for each major component of income, as well as for net income. These historical EPS amounts are referred to as basic earnings per share.

Even if convertible securities, stock options, warrants, or other rights do exist, the capital structure may be classified as simple if there is no potential dilution to EPS from the conversion or exercise of these items. Potential EPS dilution exists if the EPS would decrease or the loss per share would increase as a result of the conversion of securities or exercise of stock options, warrants, or other rights based on the conditions existing at the financial statement date. A company with potential earnings per share dilution is considered to have a complex capital structure.

For those companies with a complex capital structure, the computation of both basic EPS and diluted EPS provides financial statement users with endpoints as to EPS. The basic EPS computation uses the results of actual transactions to determine both the numerator and the denominator in the EPS calculation. Diluted EPS is computed by making assumptions regarding transactions that did not occur. Why worry about transactions that did not occur? We can answer this question with an example. Suppose an individual is given stock options to purchase shares of stock in a company at $10 per share. The current market price for the company's stock is $15 per share. Why wouldn't the individual exercise the options and purchase the stock? The most likely reason is that the individual is contractually constrained from exercising the options until a certain time (this is a common feature of employee stock options). Or perhaps the individual is uncertain about the future of the stock and wants to wait to see whether it will go down in value or perhaps go even higher. Thus, even though the transaction (exercising the options) didn't occur, it could have occurred and, given the current level of the stock price, it is likely that it will occur in the future. The FASB requires events such as this to be included in the diluted EPS computation to disclose to financial statement users the effects of transactions that, although they did not occur, will likely occur in the future.

To summarize, the basic EPS computation uses the results of actual transactions and events to compute an EPS figure. Diluted EPS involves making assumptions about transactions relating to a company's stock that, based on information available now, will likely occur in the future. In other words, diluted EPS provides financial statement users a "worst-case" estimate as to EPS with the computations made by assuming that all events relating to the exercising of existing options or the conversion of existing securities that will likely occur in the future have in fact already occurred.

FASB CODIFICATION

The Issue: You are the controller for Della Bee Enterprises, a private company. The company is a corporation, so there are ownership shares outstanding. However, all of these shares are held by a few family members and a handful of trusted employees (like yourself). Your summer accounting intern has just told you that the income statements that you have been preparing for the past five years are incomplete because those statements do not include earnings per share data. You told the intern that private companies are not required to include EPS in their income statements. However, you don't know this for sure. You would like to be able to prove to the know-it-all intern that you are right.

The Question: In order to comply with U.S. GAAP, are private companies required to provide EPS data on their income statements?

Searching the Codification: What you are looking for is some description of the "scope" of the FASB ASC Earnings per Share topic. The "scope" of a standard is a description of the transactions and entities that are subject to the accounting rules included in that standard. In the FASB's ASC, scope descriptions are always sections denoted by the number 15. So, go into Topic 260, Earnings per Share, and look around for any scope descriptions.

The Answer: The correct treatment is described on page 18-28.

Basic Earnings per Share

2 **Compute basic earnings per share, taking into account the sale and repurchase of stock during the period as well as the effects of stock splits and stock dividends.**

WHY **Although the computation of diluted earnings per share is complicated and exciting (as illustrated in the next section), the simple computation of earnings per weighted-average common share outstanding during the year is extremely informative.**

HOW **Basic EPS is computed by dividing income available to common shareholders by the weighted-average number of common shares outstanding. If a company splits its stock or declares a stock dividend, a retroactive recognition of this change must be made in determining the weighted-average number of shares outstanding.**

The basic EPS computation presents no problem when only common stock has been issued and the number of shares outstanding has remained the same for the entire period. The numerator is the net income (loss) for the period, and the denominator is the number of shares outstanding for the entire period. Frequently, however, either the numerator, the denominator, or both must be adjusted because of the circumstances described in the following sections.

Issuance or Reacquisition of Common Stock

When common shares have been issued or have been reacquired by a company during a period, the resources available to the company have changed, and this change should affect earnings. To illustrate, suppose a company doubles the number of shares it has outstanding through the sale of additional stock. With the proceeds from the sale, one would expect the company to be able to invest in additional productive assets and thereby increase net income. Thus, income is not higher because the company suddenly became more profitable. Instead, income is higher because the company had more resources available for its use. This sale of stock must be factored into the EPS computation to provide a measure of per-share profitability given the resources available. Under these circumstances, a weighted average for shares outstanding should be computed.

The weighted-average number of shares can be computed by determining "month-shares" of outstanding stock and dividing by 12 to obtain the weighted average for the year. For example, if a company has 10,000 shares outstanding at the beginning of the year, issues 5,000 more shares on May 1, and reacquires 2,000 shares on November 1, the weighted-average number of shares would be computed as follows. Note that a separate period computation is required each time stock is sold or reacquired.

			Month-Shares
Jan. 1 to May 1		10,000 × 4 months	40,000
May 1 to Nov. 1	(10,000 + 5,000)	15,000 × 6 months	90,000
Nov. 1 to Dec. 31	(15,000 − 2,000)	13,000 × 2 months	26,000
Total month-shares			156,000
Weighted-average number of shares: 156,000/12			13,000

The same answer can be obtained by applying a weight to each period equivalent to the portion of the year since the last change in shares outstanding, as follows:

Jan. 1 to May 1	10,000 × 4/12 year	3,333
May 1 to Nov. 1	15,000 × 6/12 year	7,500
Nov. 1 to Dec. 31	13,000 × 2/12 year	2,167
Weighted-average number of shares		13,000

If stock transactions occurred during a month, the weighted-average computation could be made either on a daily basis or to the nearest month. In examples and end-of-chapter material in this text, assume computations to the nearest month unless otherwise specified.

Stock Dividends and Stock Splits

When the number of common shares outstanding has changed during a period as a result of a stock dividend, a stock split, or a reverse split, a retroactive recognition of this change must be made in determining the weighted-average number of shares outstanding. Without this retroactive recognition, comparing a share of stock at the beginning of the period to a share of stock at the end of the period (after a stock split or stock dividend) would be like comparing apples and oranges, or perhaps more accurately, like comparing a whole pie to a piece of pie. To illustrate, assume that a company had 2,600 shares outstanding as of January 1 and the following events affecting common stock occurred during the year:

Date	Economic Event	Change in Shares Outstanding
Feb. 1	Exercise of stock option	+ 400
May. 1	10% stock dividend (3,000 × 10%)	+ 300
Sept. 1	Sale of stock for cash	+ 1,200
Nov. 1	Purchase of treasury stock	− 400
Dec. 1	3-for-1 stock split	+ 8,200

The computation of the weighted-average number of shares for the year would be as follows:

Dates	Shares Outstanding		Stock Dividend		Stock Split		Portion of Year		Average
Jan. 1 to Feb. 1	2,600	×	1.10	×	3.0	×	1/12	=	715
Feb. 1—option	400								
Feb. 1 to May 1	3,000	×	1.10	×	3.0	×	3/12	=	2,475
May 1—stock dividend	300								
May 1 to Sept. 1	3,300			×	3.0	×	4/12	=	3,300
Sept. 1—sale	1,200								
Sept. 1 to Nov. 1	4,500			×	3.0	×	2/12	=	2,250
Nov. 1—treasury stock	(400)								
Nov. 1 to Dec. 1	4,100			×	3.0	×	1/12	=	1,025
Dec. 1—split	8,200								
Dec. 1 to Dec. 31	12,300					×	1/12	=	1,025
Weighted-average number of shares									10,790

In the preceding illustration, the shares outstanding for January 1 to May 1 were multiplied by 1.10 to reflect the 10% stock dividend, and the shares outstanding for January 1 to December 1 were multiplied by 3 to reflect the 3-for-1 stock split. When comparative financial statements are presented, the common shares outstanding for all periods shown must be adjusted to reflect any stock dividend or stock split in the current period.

Only with the retroactive recognition of changes in the number of shares can EPS presentations for prior periods be stated on a basis comparable with the EPS presentation for the current period. Similar retroactive adjustments must be made even if a stock dividend or stock split occurs after the end of the period but before the financial statements are prepared; disclosure of this situation should be made in a note to the financial statements. As an example, consider the disclosure provided by **Nike** relating to its EPS: For the fiscal year ended May 31, 2006, the company reported basic EPS of $5.37. In its 2007 annual report, the company reported basic EPS of just $2.69 for the fiscal year ended May 31, 2006. In the notes accompanying its 2007 financial statements (shown in Exhibit 18-2), Nike explains the reason for the restatement of EPS for 2006: it split its shares 2-for-1 during fiscal 2007.

! CAUTION

As the example illustrates, stock splits and stock dividends must be incorporated to calculate weighted-average shares outstanding. This procedure must be applied for all periods included in the financial statements. Thus, the EPS figures computed in the current period may have to be changed in subsequent years if stock splits or stock dividends occur.

Preferred Stock Included in Capital Structure

Basic EPS reflects only income available to common stockholders; it does not include preferred stock. It would be inappropriate to report EPS on preferred stock in view of the limited dividend rights of such stock. When a capital structure includes preferred stock, dividends on preferred stock should be deducted from income before extraordinary or other special items and from net income in arriving at the earnings related to common shares. If preferred dividends are not cumulative, only the dividends declared on preferred

EX 18-2 NIKE NOTE DISCLOSURE RELATING TO STOCK SPLITS

Note 1. STOCK SPLIT On February 15, 2007 the Board of Directors declared a two-for-one stock split of the Company's Class A and Class B common shares, which was effected in the form of a 100% common stock dividend distributed on April 2, 2007. All references to share and per share amounts in the consolidated financial statements and accompanying notes to the consolidated financial statements have been retroactively restated to reflect the two-for-one stock split.

stock during the period are deducted. If preferred dividends are cumulative, the full amount of dividends on preferred stock for the period, whether declared or not, should be deducted from income in arriving at the earnings or loss balance related to the common stock. If there is a loss for the period, preferred dividends for the period, including any undeclared dividends on cumulative preferred stock, are added to the loss in arriving at the full loss related to the common stock.

STOP&THINK

Why must basic EPS associated with prior periods be adjusted for stock splits or stock dividends that occurred in the current period?

a) Without adjustment, the cash flow impact of stock splits and stock dividends would not be reflected in the EPS numbers.
b) Without adjustment, net income for the current period would be overstated.
c) Without adjustment, the stock splits and stock dividends would not be properly reflected in the Equity section of the balance sheet.
d) Without adjustment, the comparison with prior-year EPS numbers would be misleading.

To illustrate the computation of EPS at December 31, 2013, for a company with a simple capital structure for a comparative 2-year period, assume the following data.

Summary of Changes in Capital Balances

	8% Cumulative Preferred Stock $100 Par		Common Stock $0.10 Par		
	Shares	**Amount**	**Shares**	**Amount**	**Retained Earnings**
Dec. 31, 2011, balances	10,000	$1,000,000	200,000	$1,000,000	$4,000,000
June 30, 2012, issuance of 100,000 shares of common stock			100,000	600,000	
June 30, 2012, dividend on preferred stock, 8%					(80,000)
June 30, 2012, dividend on common stock, $0.30					(90,000)
Dec. 31, 2012, net income for year, including extraordinary gain of $75,000					380,000
Dec. 31, 2012, balances	10,000	$1,000,000	300,000	$1,600,000	$4,210,000
May 1, 2013, 50% stock dividend on common stock			150,000	15,000	(15,000)
Dec. 31, 2013, net loss for year					(55,000)
Dec. 31, 2013, balances	10,000	$1,000,000	450,000	$1,615,000	$4,140,000

Because comparative statements are presented, the denominator of weighted-average shares outstanding for 2012 must be adjusted for the 50% stock dividend issued in 2013 as follows:

2012		
Jan. 1–June 30	200,000 × 1.5 (50% stock dividend in 2013) × 6/12 year	150,000
July 1–Dec. 31	[200,000 + 100,000 (issuance of stock on June 30, 2012)] × 1.5 (50% stock dividend in 2013) × 6/12 year	225,000
		375,000
2013		
Jan. 1–May 1	300,000 × 1.5 (50% stock dividend in 2013) × 4/12 year	150,000
May 1–Dec. 31	450,000 (300,000 + 150,000) × 8/12 year	300,000
		450,000

Continuing the example, EPS for 2012 is shown separately for income from continuing operations, the extraordinary gain, and net income. The preferred dividends must be deducted from both income from continuing operations and net income in computing EPS for these income components. For 2013, the reported net loss must be increased by the full amount of the preferred dividend even though the dividend was not declared. If the preferred stock were noncumulative, no adjustment for the undeclared preferred dividend would be necessary in 2013. The adjusted income (loss) figures for computing basic EPS are determined as follows:

2012	
Income from continuing operations ($380,000 net income – $75,000 extraordinary gain)	$ 305,000
Less: Preferred dividend	80,000
Income from continuing operations identified with common stock	$ 225,000
Net income	$ 380,000
Less: Preferred dividend	80,000
Net income identified with common stock	$ 300,000
2013	
Net loss	$ (55,000)
Less: Preferred dividend	(80,000)
Net loss identified with common stock	$(135,000)

The basic EPS amounts can now be computed as follows:

2012	
Basic earnings per common share:	
Continuing operations ($225,000/375,000)	$ 0.60
Extraordinary gain ($75,000/375,000)	0.20
Net income per share ($300,000/375,000)	$ 0.80
2013	
Basic loss per share ($135,000/450,000)	$(0.30)

Participating Securities and the Two-Class Method

Sometimes a company issues more than one class of stock with ownership privileges. For example, as discussed in Chapter 13, **Google** has both Class A and Class B common stock. In Google's case, both classes of common stock have the same dividend rights, so the earnings that can be claimed by the two classes of shareholders are the same. As a result, the computed and reported amounts of earnings per share for both classes of Google common stock are the same. However, different classes of stock don't always have the same claim upon dividends. In such a case, earnings attributable to each share of the different classes of stock are different and EPS is computed using the two-class method.

In addition to different classes of common stock, a company can also have preferred stock that includes characteristics similar to that of common stock. In particular, as described in Chapter 13, a company can issue participating preferred stock. With participating preferred stock, the preferred stockholders receive additional dividends, beyond their base amount, once the common stockholders receive a certain level of dividends. In essence, participating preferred stockholders share in the success of the company in the same way that common stockholders do. This sharing in the profits of the company should be reflected in the computation of earnings per share.

To illustrate earnings per share computations when two classes of stock share in the profits, consider the data below for Lily Kay Company.

- Common shares outstanding: 100,000 for the entire year
- Participating preferred shares outstanding: 50,000 shares for the entire year
- Net income: $500,000
- Dividends on participating preferred shares: $2.00 per share plus a per-share increase 50% as large as the per-share increase of common dividends above $1.00 per share. Thus, if the common dividend is $1.20 per share, the participating preferred dividend is $2.10 per share [$2.00 + 0.50($1.20 − $1.00)].
- Common dividends paid for the year: $1.80 per share making a total of $180,000 ($1.80 per share × 100,000 shares)
- Participating preferred dividends paid for the year: $2.40 per share making a total of $120,000 ($2.40 per share × 50,000 shares)

To compute basic earnings per share, it is necessary to allocate the undistributed earnings to the two classes of stock. In this case, undistributed earnings total $200,000 ($500,000 net income − $180,000 common dividends − $120,000 participating preferred dividends). The allocation of this $200,000 in undistributed earnings is done assuming that the $200,000 "belongs" to the common and preferred shareholders in the proportion that would exist if those undistributed earnings were paid out as dividends. The excess dividends paid so far have been $80,000 for common shares [$180,000 total common dividends less $100,000 ($1.00 per share × 100,000 shares) baseline common dividends] and $20,000 for participating preferred shares [$120,000 total preferred dividends less $100,000 ($2.00 per share × 50,000 shares) baseline preferred dividends]. Thus, 80% of the excess dividends [$80,000 ÷ ($80,000 + $20,000)] have gone to common shareholders and 20% have gone to participating preferred shareholders. The undistributed earnings of $200,000 are allocated as follows:

	Preferred Stock	Common Stock
Total undistributed earnings	$200,000	$200,000
Allocation percentage	×0.20	×0.80
Allocation of undistributed earnings	$ 40,000	$160,000
Number of shares	÷50,000	÷100,000
Undistributed earnings per share	$ 0.80	$ 1.60

The basic earnings per share amounts are computed and reported as follows:

	Participating Preferred Stock	Common Stock
Distributed earnings	$2.40	$1.80
Undistributed earnings	0.80	1.60
Basic earnings per share	$3.20	$3.40

Similar computations are performed if there are two classes of common stock with different dividend rights.

Diluted Earnings per Share—Options, Warrants, and Rights

3 **Use the treasury stock method to compute diluted earnings per share when a firm has outstanding stock options, warrants, and rights.**

WHY **Stock options (and warrants and rights) represent potential new shares of common stock that can become actual common shares whether the existing common shareholders approve or not. Because the exercise of these options can potentially impact the portion of the earnings that will flow to the existing common shareholders, those shareholders should be made aware of the magnitude of that potential dilution.**

HOW **If the option exercise price is less than the end-of-period market price for the period, the option, warrant, or right is considered dilutive and is included in computing diluted EPS. This also coincides with the economic circumstance in which the options are most likely to be exercised. The treasury stock method involves determining the number of incremental shares that would be issued assuming that the options, warrants, or rights were exercised and the proceeds used to repurchase treasury shares in the market at the market price prevailing at the end of the period.**

When a company has a complex capital structure, additional information may be provided to users of the financial statements to reflect all potential dilution arising from the assumption that additional common stock is issued from exercise of options or conversion of convertible securities. Dilution occurs if inclusion of a potentially dilutive security reduces the basic EPS or increases the basic loss per share. If the opposite results occur, the security is classified as an antidilutive security. If a company reports a below-the-line item (i.e., discontinued operations or an extraordinary item), the "control number" used in determining whether a security is dilutive or not is "Income from continuing operations."[2] In general, securities classified as antidilutive are not included in computing diluted EPS.

! CAUTION

You must continually remind yourself when dealing with diluted EPS that the events you are analyzing *did not* occur; bonds were not converted; options were not exercised; and so on. Diluted EPS is providing information *as if* these events occurred.

The adjustment of the numerator and/or denominator of basic EPS to compute diluted EPS depends on the nature of the security and its terms. The adjustment process consists of a "what-if" scenario. What would happen to the numerator and denominator if options had been exercised and

[2] FASB ASC paragraph 260-10-45-18.

convertible securities had been converted at the beginning of the year being evaluated? The two major types of potentially dilutive securities are (1) common stock options, warrants, and rights and (2) convertible bonds and convertible preferred stock. Because the purpose of a diluted EPS figure is to disclose how an exercise or conversion would affect future EPS, all computations of diluted EPS are made as if the exercise or conversion took place at the beginning of the company's fiscal year or at the issue date of the stock option or convertible security, whichever comes later. Thus, if a convertible bond has been outstanding the entire year, the diluted EPS computation will be made as if the conversion of the bonds took place at the beginning of the year. However, if the convertible bond is issued on May 1 and the fiscal year is the calendar year, all conversion computations will be made for eight months, or two-thirds of a year.

Stock Options, Warrants, and Rights

As explained in Chapter 13, stock options, warrants, and rights provide no cash yield to investors, but they have value because they permit the acquisition of common stock at specified prices for a certain period of time. As noted previously, options, warrants, and rights are included in the computation of diluted EPS for a particular period only if they are dilutive. If the price for which stock can be acquired (exercise price) is lower than the average market price for the period, the options, warrants, or rights probably would be exercised and their effect would be dilutive. If the exercise price is higher than the average market price, no exercise would take place; thus, there is no potential dilution from these securities.

It is assumed that exercise of options, warrants, or rights takes place as of the beginning of the year or at the date they are issued, whichever comes later. Additional cash resources would thus have been available for the company's use. To compute diluted EPS when these types of securities exist, either net income must be increased to take into consideration the increase in revenue such additional resources would produce or the cash must be assumed to be used for some non-revenue-producing purpose. The FASB selected the latter approach and recommended it be assumed that the cash proceeds from the exercise of options, warrants, or rights be used to purchase common stock on the market (treasury stock) at the average market price. It is further assumed that the shares of treasury stock are issued to those exercising their options, warrants, or rights, and the remaining shares required to be issued will be added as incremental shares to the actual number of shares outstanding to compute diluted EPS. This method of including warrants, options, and rights in the EPS computation is known as the treasury stock method.

To illustrate, assume that at the beginning of the current year, employees were granted options to acquire 5,000 shares of common stock at $40 per share. The average market price of the stock for the year is $50, so exercise is assumed and the effect will be dilutive.[3] The proceeds received by the corporation from the issuance of stock to the employees would be $200,000 (5,000 shares × $40 exercise price). Because the average market price of the stock was $50, these proceeds would purchase 4,000 shares of treasury stock ($200,000/$50). If it is assumed that these 4,000 shares are repurchased in the market, the net increase in shares outstanding would be just 1,000: the 5,000 shares issued to the employees who exercised the options less the 4,000 shares that were repurchased

[3] FASB ASC subparagraph 260-10-45-23(b). Over the years, the FASB has waffled back and forth between using the average market price for the year and the ending market price for the year in implementing the treasury stock method. The FASB has recommended the use of the ending market price (in an Exposure Draft released for comment on August 7, 2008), but that proposal has been pushed to the back burner while other more pressing issues are discussed. The examples and exercises in this chapter use average market price for the period, which is what is currently required under both U.S. GAAP and IFRS.

using the proceeds from the exercise of the options. Accordingly, the number of shares of stock for computing diluted EPS would be increased by 1,000 shares.[4]

Illustration of Diluted Earnings per Share with Stock Options

The use of the treasury stock method in computing diluted EPS is illustrated with the following data for Rasband Corporation.

Summary of relevant information:		
Net income for the year		$ 92,800
Common shares outstanding (no change during year)		100,000
Options outstanding to purchase common shares		20,000
Exercise price per share on options		$6
Average market price for the period for common shares		$10
Basic earnings per share:		
Net income for the year		$ 92,800
Actual number of shares outstanding		÷100,000
Basic EPS ($92,800/100,000)		$ 0.93
Application of proceeds from assumed exercise of options outstanding to purchase treasury stock:		
Proceeds from assumed exercise of options outstanding (20,000 × $6)		$120,000
Number of outstanding shares assumed to be repurchased with proceeds from options ($120,000/$10)		12,000
Number of shares to be used in computing diluted earnings per share:		
Actual number of shares outstanding		100,000
Incremental shares:		
Issued on assumed exercise of options	20,000	
Less: Assumed repurchase of shares from proceeds of options	12,000	8,000
Total		108,000
Diluted EPS ($92,800/108,000)		$ 0.86

If the stock options had been issued to the company's employees on April 1 of the current year, the incremental shares would be three-fourths of 8,000, or 6,000 shares, and the diluted EPS would be $0.88 ($92,800/106,000).

If the market price of the company's stock is less than the option exercise price, the treasury stock computation would cause the EPS to increase when compared to basic EPS because the incremental shares would be negative rather than positive. To illustrate, assume that the average market price for Rasband Corporation is $5 rather than $10. In this case, 24,000 shares could be purchased with the $120,000 proceeds from the stock options. Because only 20,000 shares would be issued on exercise of the options, the number of shares for computing diluted EPS would be 96,000 and the diluted EPS would be $0.97. When compared with basic EPS of $0.93, the result is antidilution.

[4] In this example, the amount of the proceeds from the hypothetical exercise of the options by the employees is set at the exercise price of $40 per share. According to the FASC ASC paragraph 260-10-45-29, for employee stock options the hypothetical proceeds should be increased by the future compensation expense expected to be recognized in connection with the options before their exercise. Also, the hypothetical proceeds are to be increased by the value of any excess tax benefits expected to be generated by the future exercise of the options. In other words, the hypothetical exercise amount is the total amount of value expected to accrue to the company through the eventual exercise of the options by the employees—exercise price plus the value of future employee services plus the value of excess tax benefits. For simplicity, the examples in this chapter ignore the unrecognized compensation expense and the expected excess tax benefits.

Don't make the mistake of viewing this as just one more example of accounting conservatism in that options that would decrease earnings per share are included in the calculation but that options that would increase earnings per share are excluded. Actually, this is an example of when the accounting rules do a good job at reflecting underlying economic reality. Options that are "in the money" (the stock price is currently greater than the exercise price) are likely to be exercised in the future. Thus, it makes sense to include these options in the calculation of diluted earnings per share. On the other hand, options that are currently "out of the money" (the stock price is currently less than the exercise price) are less likely to be exercised in the future. So, the notion of how likely it is that the options will be exercised corresponds exactly with whether the options are dilutive or antidilutive.

Thus, the test for antidilution of stock options, warrants, and rights is simply to compare the average market price with the exercise price. If the market price exceeds the exercise price, the options are dilutive and would be included "as if" they are exercised in computing diluted EPS. If the average market price is less than the exercise price, the options are antidilutive and would not be used in computing diluted EPS.

> **FYI**
>
> If stock options, warrants, or rights are determined to be dilutive, then only the *denominator* is affected in the diluted EPS computation.

Diluted Earnings per Share—Convertible Securities

4 **Use the if-converted method to compute diluted earnings per share when a company has convertible preferred stock or convertible bonds outstanding.**

WHY **Convertible securities represent potential new shares of common stock that can become actual common shares whether the existing common shareholders approve or not. Because the conversion of these securities can potentially impact the portion of the earnings that will flow to the existing common shareholders, those shareholders should be made aware of the magnitude of that potential dilution.**

HOW **For convertible bonds, interest expense (net of tax) must be added back to the numerator, and the number of shares that would be issued upon conversion is included in the denominator. For convertible preferred stock, preferred dividends must be added back to income available to common shareholders, and the denominator is increased by the number of shares that would be issued upon conversion.**

To compute diluted EPS when convertible securities exist, adjustments must be made both to net income and to the number of shares of common stock outstanding. These adjustments must reflect what these amounts would have been if the conversion had taken place at the beginning of the current year or at the date of issuance of the convertible securities, whichever comes later. This method of including convertible securities in the EPS computation is referred to as the if-converted method. If the securities are bonds, net income is adjusted by adding back the interest expense, net of tax, to net income; the number of shares of common stock outstanding is increased by the number of shares that would have been issued on conversion.[5] Any amortization of initial premium or discount

[5] In addition to adjustments for interest, adjustments to net income for nondiscretionary or indirect items would have to be made in many situations. These items would include profit-sharing bonuses and other payments whose amount is determined by the net income reported. For simplicity, no indirect effects are illustrated in this chapter.

is included in the interest expense added back. If the convertible securities are shares of preferred stock, no reduction is made from net income for preferred dividends, as is done with the computation of basic EPS; the number of shares of common stock outstanding is increased by the number of shares that would have been issued on conversion. Because preferred stock dividends are not deductible as an expense for tax purposes, no adjustment for tax effects is required. If the convertible securities were issued during the year, adjustments would be made for only the portion of the year since the issuance date.

To test for dilution, each potentially dilutive convertible security must be evaluated individually. If there is only one such security, comparison is made of EPS before considering the convertible security with the EPS after including it. As indicated earlier, if the EPS decreases or loss per share increases, the convertible security is defined as dilutive. Antidilutive securities are excluded from the computation of diluted EPS. We will now look at an example of the two most common types of dilutive securities: convertible bonds and convertible preferred stock.

FYI

If convertible securities are determined to be dilutive, both the *numerator* and the *denominator* are affected in the diluted EPS computation.

Illustration of Diluted Earnings per Share with Convertible Securities

The following examples for Reid Corporation illustrate the computation of diluted EPS when convertible securities exist.

Summary of relevant information:		
8% convertible bonds issued at par		$ 500,000
Net income for the year		$ 83,000
Common shares outstanding (no change during year)		100,000
Conversion terms of convertible bonds—80 shares for each $1,000 bond		
Assumed tax rate		30%
Basic earnings per share:		
Net income		$ 83,000
Actual number of shares outstanding		÷ 100,000
Basic EPS ($83,000/100,000)		$ 0.83
Diluted earnings per share:		
Net income		$ 83,000
Add interest on convertible bonds, net of income tax:		
Interest ($500,000 × 8%)	$40,000	
Less: Income tax savings ($40,000 × 30%)	12,000	28,000
Adjusted net income		$ 111,000
Actual number of shares outstanding		100,000
Additional shares issued on assumed conversion of bonds (500 × 80)		40,000
Adjusted number of shares		140,000
Diluted EPS ($111,000/140,000)		$ 0.79

Computation of Diluted Earnings per Share for Securities Issued during the Year

If the convertible bonds had been issued by Reid Corporation on June 30 of the current year, the adjustment would be made to reflect only the period subsequent to the issuance date, or one-half of a year.

Diluted earnings per share:		
Net income		$ 83,000
Add interest on convertible bonds, net of income tax:		
Interest ($500,000 × 8% × 1/2 year)	$20,000	
Less: Income tax ($20,000 × 30%)	6,000	14,000
Adjusted net income		$ 97,000
Actual number of shares outstanding		100,000
Additional shares issued on assumed conversion of bonds (500 × 80 × 1/2)		20,000
Adjusted number of shares		120,000
Diluted EPS ($97,000/120,000)		$ 0.81

Convertible preferred stock is treated in a manner similar to that for convertible debt securities (bonds). To illustrate application of the if-converted method to preferred stock, assume the same facts as given previously for Reid Corporation except that instead of 8% convertible bonds, the company has 8% preferred stock outstanding, par value $500,000, convertible into 40,000 shares of common stock. Note that because Reid would have no bond interest under the change in assumptions, the reported net income would be $111,000 ($83,000 + $28,000 bond interest net of tax savings). Assume the preferred stock was outstanding for the entire year.

CAUTION

Remember that with convertible preferred stock, preferred dividends were initially subtracted from income to arrive at income available to common shareholders. If we assume conversion, those dividends must be added back. Also remember that no tax effect is associated with preferred dividends.

Basic earnings per share:	
Net income, without the deduction for interest on bonds	$ 111,000
Less: Preferred dividends	40,000
Net income identified with common stock	$ 71,000
Actual number of shares outstanding	÷ 100,000
Basic EPS ($71,000/100,000)	$ 0.71
Diluted earnings per share:	
Net income assuming no payment of preferred dividends due to conversion	$ 111,000
Actual number of shares outstanding	100,000
Additional shares issued on assumed conversion of preferred stock	40,000
Adjusted number of shares	140,000
Diluted EPS ($111,000/140,000)	$ 0.79

In this example, diluted EPS ($0.79) is more than basic EPS ($0.71). Thus, the convertible preferred stock is antidilutive and would not be considered in the computation of EPS. Assuming that the corporation had no other potentially dilutive securities outstanding, only basic EPS would be presented on the income statement.

Shortcut Test for Antidilution

It is possible to determine whether a convertible security is antidilutive without actually computing diluted EPS assuming conversion. If a company has net income rather than loss, the antidilutive test is performed by computing what the conversion contributes to per-share earnings. For example, if the 8% bonds are converted, net income to the common shareholders increases by $28,000, and the number of common shares outstanding increases by 40,000 shares. The contribution of this conversion to earnings is $0.70 ($28,000/40,000) per share. Because this amount is less than the preconversion basic EPS of $0.83, the bonds are dilutive. On the other hand, if the preferred stock is converted, the preferred dividends of $40,000 would no longer be deducted from net income in computing EPS, and the number of common shares outstanding would increase by 40,000 shares. The contribution of this conversion to earnings is $1.00 ($40,000/40,000) per share. Because the preferred stock conversion contributes more per share than preconversion basic earnings of $0.71, the preferred stock is antidilutive.

Effect of Actual Exercise or Conversion

5 **Factor into the diluted earnings per share computations the effect of actual conversion of convertible securities or the exercise of options, warrants, or rights during the period, and understand the antidilutive effect of potential common shares when a firm reports a loss from continuing operations.**

WHY **The diluted EPS computation is intended to present the worst-case scenario for the common shareholders. Of course, the worst-case scenario doesn't always actually occur. However, for comparability across companies, the diluted EPS should always reflect the worst that could have happened, whether that actually happened during the period or not.**

HOW **If conversion or exercise actually takes place during a period, an adjustment to the computation of diluted EPS must be made to reflect what the EPS would have been if conversion or exercise had taken place at the beginning of the period or the issuance date if issued during the period. When a company reports a net loss, no presentation of diluted EPS is required because inclusion of stock options or convertible securities would decrease the loss per share and thus always would be antidilutive.**

Recall that if additional shares are issued as a result of securities being converted, those newly issued shares would be included in the computation of the weighted-average number of shares outstanding for the period. In addition, however, an adjustment must be made to reflect what the EPS would have been if conversion or exercise had taken place at the beginning of the period or issuance date, whichever comes later. This adjustment is required for all securities actually converted or exercised during the period for computing diluted EPS whether dilutive or not.

When options or warrants are exercised, the adjustment for the period before exercise for diluted EPS uses the market price at exercise date. To illustrate the computation of diluted EPS when stock options are exercised during the year, assume the following data for Weatherby, Inc.

Summary of relevant information:	
Net income for the year	$2,300,000
Common shares outstanding at beginning of year	400,000
Options outstanding at beginning of year to purchase common shares	100,000
Exercise price per share on options	$ 9.00
Proceeds from actual exercise of options on October 1 of current year	$ 900,000
Market price of common stock at exercise date, October 1	$ 15.00
Number of shares to be used in computing basic earnings per share:	
Actual number of shares outstanding for full year	400,000
Weighted-average shares issued on October 1 (100,000 × 3/12)	25,000
Weighted-average number of shares for basic EPS	425,000
Basic EPS ($2,300,000/425,000)	$ 5.41

Number of shares to be used in computing diluted earnings per share:

Weighted-average number of shares for basic EPS		425,000
Incremental shares if options had been exercised on January 1 (included whether dilutive or not):		
Issued on assumed exercise of options	100,000	
Less: Assumed repurchase of shares with proceeds ($900,000/$15)	60,000	
Incremental shares assumed to be issued	40,000	
Weighted average of incremental shares assumed to be issued (40,000 × 9/12)		30,000
Weighted-average number of shares for diluted EPS		455,000
Diluted EPS ($2,300,000/455,000)		$ 5.05

Mandatorily Convertible Securities Typically, convertible preferred stock and convertible bonds are converted at the option of the security holders. However, in some cases convertible instruments must be converted upon the occurrence of some event or upon the passing of a specified amount of time. In a 2008 Exposure Draft, the FASB proposed new EPS treatment for mandatorily convertible bonds and preferred stock. The proposal is that for computation of diluted EPS these instruments be treated as if they had been converted at the beginning of the period in which the conditions were satisfied to make them mandatorily convertible. This means that from that period forward, the completed conversion of these instruments would be assumed in the computation of diluted EPS. This is also consistent with SEC guidance (FASB ASC paragraph 260-10-S99-2). As of this writing, the final adoption of this provision by the FASB is not certain, but it is likely.

STOP&THINK

In the case of securities actually converted during the year, why must we assume conversion occurred at the beginning of the period in the computation of diluted EPS when we know it did not?

a) Without this assumption, the number of shares in the denominator will not be comparable with prior years.
b) Without this assumption, the ending retained earnings balance will not be calculated correctly.
c) The diluted EPS computation is intended to present the worst-case scenario for the common shareholders.
d) The diluted EPS computation is intended to reflect the most likely scenario for the common shareholders.

Effect of a Loss from Continuing Operations on Earnings per Share

If a company reports a loss from continuing operations—referred to as the *control number*—no dual computation of EPS is necessary because inclusion of convertible securities would decrease the loss per share and thus always would be antidilutive. This is the case even if, as a result of below-the-line items such as discontinued operations, the firm reports net income. To illustrate this situation, assume the following data for Boggs Co.

Summary of relevant information:

Loss from continuing operation	$(50,000)
Extraordinary gain	75,000
Net income	$ 25,000
Number of shares of stock outstanding—full year	100,000
Number of shares of convertible preferred stock	10,000
Conversion terms—2 shares of common for 1 share of preferred	
Dividends on preferred stock	$ 8,000

The computation of basic and diluted EPS would be as follows:

Basic loss per share:	
Loss from continuing operations	$ (50,000)
Dividends on preferred stock	(8,000)
Total loss to common shareholders	$ (58,000)
Actual number of shares outstanding	100,000
Basic loss per share—from continuing operations ($58,000/100,000)	$ (0.58)
Basic EPS—extraordinary gain ($75,000/100,000)	0.75
Basic EPS—net income available to common shareholders ($17,000/100,000)	$ 0.17
Diluted loss per share:	
Loss from continuing operations	$ (50,000)
Actual number of shares outstanding	100,000
Incremental shares on assumed conversion of preferred stock	20,000
Adjusted number of shares	120,000
Diluted loss per share ($50,000/120,000)	$ (0.42)

Because the diluted loss per share from continuing operations is less than the basic loss per share from continuing operations, only information relating to basic EPS computations would be reported on the income statement. This is the case even though net income is positive. The comparison for determining dilution is made using the control number, income (or loss) from continuing operations, not net income.

FYI

Options are also ignored when a company reports a loss from continuing operations. This is done because the options most likely to be exercised, those in the money, would spread the loss among a greater number of shares and reduce the loss per share. Because of this counterintuitive impact, all potentially dilutive securities are ignored when a company reports a loss from continuing operations.

Multiple Potentially Dilutive Securities

6 **Determine the order in which multiple potentially dilutive securities should be considered in computing diluted earnings per share.**

WHY **For a company with several different potentially dilutive securities, it can be difficult to identify the lowest diluted EPS number among all of the possible combinations. A systematic ordering of the potentially dilutive securities greatly simplifies this process.**

HOW **In those instances when a firm has multiple potentially dilutive securities, the individual effect of each security is computed, and the securities are considered in turn beginning with the security with the least favorable effect on basic EPS. The procedure is repeated until the diluted EPS figure is lower than the next security's incremental EPS impact.**

The illustrations in the chapter thus far have dealt primarily with one type of potentially dilutive security at a time. For a company having several different issues of convertible securities and/or stock options and warrants, the FASB requires selection of the combination of securities producing the *lowest possible EPS figure.* To avoid having to test a large number of different combinations to find the lowest one, companies can compute the incremental EPS for each potentially dilutive security. Because the smaller the incremental computation, the greater the impact on basic EPS, the securities are then ranked in order from the smallest incremental EPS to the largest.[6] Then each security—beginning with the one having the smallest incremental EPS—is introduced into the computation until the EPS is lower than the next security's incremental computation. At that point, all remaining securities in the list would be antidilutive. Any dilutive stock options and warrants are considered first before introducing convertible securities into the computations.

To illustrate, assume that a company had no stock options but did have four convertible securities that would have the following effects on diluted EPS if each were considered separately.

	Effects of Assumed Conversion		
	Increase in Net Income	Increase in No. of Shares	Incremental EPS
Convertible Security A	$ 75,000	50,000	$1.50
Convertible Security B	150,000	60,000	2.50
Convertible Security C	110,000	20,000	5.50
Convertible Security D	600,000	100,000	6.00

Assume further that basic EPS was $6.50 ($2,275,000 income divided by 350,000 outstanding shares). Each of the four securities considered separately results in an incremental EPS figure lower than basic EPS and thus would be potentially dilutive. However, when considering all four securities together, only the first two (A and B) would be dilutive and therefore included in diluted EPS. This is determined by adding one security at a time to the basic EPS figure as follows:

	Net Income (Adjusted)	No. of Shares (Adjusted)	Diluted EPS
Simple capital structure	$2,275,000	350,000	$6.50
Convertible Security A	75,000	50,000	
	$2,350,000	400,000	5.88
Convertible Security B	150,000	60,000	
	$2,500,000	460,000	5.43
Convertible Security C	110,000	20,000	
	$2,610,000	480,000	5.44
Convertible Security D	600,000	100,000	
	$3,210,000	580,000	5.53

It would not be necessary to continue the computation beyond Security B because the EPS at that point ($5.43) is lower than the incremental EPS impact of Security C ($5.50). Inclusion of Securities C and D would be antidilutive as the computations show.

When a company has multiple potentially dilutive convertible securities, an orderly approach to computing EPS is necessary. Exhibit 18-3 should prove helpful in understanding the above illustration and in solving complex EPS problems. The exhibit summarizes the steps in computing basic and diluted EPS.

[6] FASB ASC paragraph 260-10-45-18.

EX 18-3 STEPS IN COMPUTING EARNINGS PER SHARE

1. Compute basic EPS using a weighted-average number of shares for common stock outstanding during the year.
2. For companies with complex capital structures, determine whether stock options, warrants, rights, and convertible securities are potentially dilutive.
   (a) Stock options, warrants, and rights: Dilutive if the exercise price is less than the average market price of the common stock.
   (b) Convertible securities: Compute incremental EPS for each security individually. Those with an incremental value greater than basic EPS after considering any stock options, warrants, or rights are antidilutive and are excluded.
3. Compute diluted EPS:
   (a) Include all dilutive stock options, warrants, and rights first. Apply proceeds using the treasury stock method at the average common stock market price for the period to compute incremental shares.
   (b) Include potentially dilutive convertible securities one at a time, beginning with the security that has the smallest incremental EPS. Compute a new EPS figure. Continue selecting and applying convertible securities until the next security in the list has an incremental EPS value greater than the last computed EPS. Discontinue the process at that point. All other securities in the list are antidilutive for purposes of computing the lowest possible diluted EPS figure.
4. Report basic and diluted EPS on the face of the income statement.

To illustrate the steps in Exhibit 18-3 for computing basic and diluted EPS, assume the following facts related to Wildwood, Inc.

Summary of relevant information:

Net income for the year	$136,000
Common shares outstanding (no change during the year)	125,000
Options outstanding to purchase common shares	30,000
Exercise price per share on options	$10
Average market price for the period for common shares	$15
9% convertible bonds, issued at par	$600,000
Conversion terms for bonds, 100 shares for each $1,000 bond	
Tax rate	30%

Step 1—Compute basic earnings per share:

Net income for the year	$ 136,000
Actual number of shares outstanding	÷ 125,000
Basic EPS ($136,000/125,000)	$ 1.09

Step 2—Determine whether stock options and convertible bonds are dilutive:

(a) Stock options: The options are dilutive because the exercise price is less than the average market price.

(b) Convertible bonds: The bonds are potentially dilutive because the EPS impact of $0.63, as computed in the following table, is less than basic EPS of $1.09. As shown in step 3 below, not only are the convertible bonds potentially dilutive, but they are also actually dilutive since the incremental EPS impact of $0.63 is less than the adjusted EPS of $1.01.

Net Income Impact	Number of Shares	EPS Impact
$600,000 × 0.09 × (1 − 0.30) = $37,800	60,000	$0.63

Step 3—Compute diluted earnings per share:

Description		Net Income	Number of Shares	EPS
Basic EPS		$136,000	125,000	$1.09
Options as if exercised at beginning of year:				
Number of shares assumed issued	30,000			
Less: Number of treasury shares assumed Repurchased [(30,000 × $10)/$15]	(20,000)			
Incremental shares	10,000		10,000	
		$136,000	135,000	$1.01
9% Convertible bonds		37,800	60,000	
Diluted EPS		$173,800	195,000	$0.89

Financial Statement Presentation

7 Understand the disclosure requirements associated with basic and diluted earnings per share computations.

WHY Because of the great interest of financial statement users in earnings per share data, both basic and diluted EPS are highlighted by being included directly in the income statement.

HOW Both basic and diluted EPS are reported on the face of the income statement for those companies with a complex capital structure. For companies with a simple capital structure, only basic EPS is reported. Companies reporting below-the-line items on their income statement may report the per-share effects of these items either on the face of the income statement or in the notes.

Companies with a simple capital structure are required to present basic EPS on the face of the income statement. For those companies with a complex capital structure, both basic and diluted EPS for both income from continuing operations and net income are to be disclosed on the face of the income statement. When earnings of a period include income or loss from discontinued operations or extraordinary items, EPS amounts for these line items may be presented either on the face of the income statement or in the notes to the financial statements.

Firms are also required to provide the following disclosure items in the notes to the financial statements:[7]

1. A reconciliation of both the numerators and the denominators of the basic and diluted EPS computations for income from continuing operations. The example from step 3 in the Wildwood, Inc., example illustrates the type of reconciliation required.
2. The effect that preferred dividends have on the EPS computations.
3. Securities that could potentially dilute basic EPS in the future that were not included in computing diluted EPS this period because those securities were antidilutive for the current period.
4. Disclosure of transactions that occurred after the period ended but prior to the issuance of financial statements that would have materially affected the number of common shares outstanding or potentially outstanding such as the issuance of stock options.

Earnings per share data should be presented for all periods covered by the income statement. If potential dilution exists in any of the periods presented, the dual presentation

[7] FASB ASC paragraph 260-10-50-1.

of basic and diluted EPS should be made for all periods presented.[8] If basic EPS and diluted EPS are the same amount, one amount can be presented on the income statement. Whenever net income of prior periods has been restated as a result of a prior-period adjustment, the EPS for these prior periods should be restated and the effect of the restatements disclosed in the current year.[9] Exhibit 18-4 illustrates the disclosure required when presenting earnings per share, using information from H. J. Heinz's 2009 annual report.

Note that Heinz subtracts preferred dividends in computing basic EPS, includes the incremental number of shares associated with dilutive securities, and does not include some options in the calculations because their effect would have been anitdilutive.

It is important that great care be exercised in interpreting EPS data regardless of the degree of refinement applied in the development of the data. These EPS figures are the products of the principles and practices employed in the accounting process and are subject to the same limitations found in the net income measurement reported on the income statement.

EX 18-4 H. J. HEINZ NOTE DISCLOSURE RELATING TO EARNINGS PER SHARE

14. INCOME PER COMMON SHARE

The following are reconciliations of income to income applicable to common stock and the number of common shares outstanding used to calculate basic EPS to those shares used to calculate diluted EPS.

Fiscal Year Ended	**April 29, 2009**	**April 30, 2008**	**May 2, 2007**
(Amounts in thousands)	**(52 Weeks)**	**(52 Weeks)**	**(52 Weeks)**
Income from continuing operations	$923,072	$844,925	$791,602
Preferred dividends	12	12	13
Income from continuing operations applicable to common stock	$923,060	$844,913	$791,589
Average common shares outstanding—basic	313,747	317,019	328,625
Effect of dilutive securities:			
Convertible preferred stock	106	109	123
Stock options, restricted stock and the global stock purchase plan	4,210	4,589	3,720
Average common shares outstanding—diluted	318,063	321,717	332,468
Income/(Loss) Per Common Share:			
Diluted			
Continuing operations	$ 2.90	$ 2.63	$ 2.38
Discontinued operations	—	—	(0.02)
Net Income	$2.90	$ 2.63	$ 2.36
Average common shares outstanding—Diluted	318,063	321,717	332,468
Basic			
Continuing operations	$2.94	$2.67	$2.41
Discontinued operations	—	—	(0.02)
Net Income	$2.94	$2.67	$ 2.39
Average common shares outstanding—Basic	313,747	317,019	328,625
Cash dividends per share	$ 1.66	$ 1.52	$ 1.40

Diluted earnings per share is based upon the average shares of common stock and dilutive common stock equivalents outstanding during the periods presented. Common stock equivalents arising from dilutive stock options, restricted common stock units, and the global stock purchase plan are computed using the treasury stock method.

Options to purchase an aggregate of 3.7 million, 6.1 million and 9.1 million shares of common stock as of April 29, 2009, April 30, 2008 and May 2, 2007, respectively, were not included in the computation of diluted earnings per share because inclusion of these options would be anti-dilutive. These options expire at various points in time through 2016.

[8] FASB ASC paragraph 260-10-45-7.
[9] FASB ASC paragraph 260-10-45-25.

EM EXPANDED MATERIAL

In this Expanded Material, we take the opportunity to combine most of the complexities associated with EPS computations into one example. This example reviews basic and diluted EPS computations and considers stock options, convertible preferred stock, and convertible debt. As you will see, care must be exercised in determining whether a security is dilutive.

Comprehensive Illustration Using Multiple Potentially Dilutive Securities

8 **Make complex earnings per share computations involving multiple potentially dilutive securities.**

WHY **The correct computation of diluted EPS is almost hopelessly complex for a company with several potentially dilutive securities UNLESS those computations are done in the correct order.**

HOW **The diluted EPS computations are greatly simplified if they are done in the correct sequence with the securities with the lowest incremental EPS being considered first, then the next lowest, and so forth.**

The steps outlined in Exhibit 18-3 (page 18-22) for computing EPS for multiple securities are used in the comprehensive problem that follows. Circle West Transportation Company has the following outstanding stocks and bonds at January 1, 2013. All securities had been sold at par or face value.

Date of Issue	Type of Security	Par or Face Value	No. of Shares or Total Face Value	Conversion Terms
2002–2012	Common stock	$ 0.25	200,000	None
May 1, 2007	12% debentures	1,000	$750,000	None
Jan. 1, 2011	6% cumulative preferred stock	100	40,000	4 shares of common for each preferred share
Jan. 1, 2012	6% debentures	1,000	$1,000,000	15 shares of common for each $1,000 debenture
June 30, 2012	10% debentures	1,000	$600,000	30 shares of common for each $1,000 debenture
Dec. 31, 2012	8% cumulative preferred stock	50	12,500	None

Circle West also had stock options outstanding at January 1, 2013, for the purchase of 20,000 shares of common stock. During 2013, options were granted for an additional 40,000 shares. The terms of these stock options are as follows:

Date of Issue	Exercisable Date	Exercise Price	Number of Options
Jan. 1, 2010	Oct. 1, 2013	$30	20,000
Oct. 1, 2013.	June 30, 2015	60	40,000

Common stock market prices for 2013 were as follows:

Average for year	$61
Average for first 9 months of year	62
Oct. 1 price	62
Dec. 31 price	61

During 2013, Circle West issued the following common stock:

Apr. 1	30,000 shares sold at $56.
Oct. 1	20,000 shares issued from exercise of Jan. 1, 2010, options.

On December 1, 2013, Circle West paid a full year's dividend on the 6% preferred stock and on the 8% preferred stock. Assume that the company had net income of $1,026,000 in 2013, all from income from continuing operations. The income tax rate is 30%.

The steps for computing EPS will be applied to the data for Circle West Transportation Company to compute the various EPS amounts.

Step 1—Compute basic earnings per share:

Net income				$1,026,000
Less: Preferred dividends:				
6% stock (40,000 × $100 × 0.06)			$240,000	
8% stock (12,500 × $50 × 0.08)			50,000	290,000
Net income identified with common stock				$ 736,000
Weighted-average number of shares:				
Jan. 1 to Apr. 1		200,000 × 3/12	50,000	
Apr. 1 to Oct. 1	(200,000 + 30,000)	230,000 × 6/12	115,000	
Oct. 1 to Dec. 31	(230,000 + 20,000)	250,000 × 3/12	62,500	
Total weighted-average number of shares			227,500	
Basic earnings per share ($736,000/227,500)				$ 3.24

Step 2—Determine whether options and convertible securities are dilutive:

(a) Stock options: Both stock options are dilutive because the exercise prices ($30 and $60) are less than the applicable market prices ($62 on October 1 for the exercised options and $61 average market price for the year for the unexercised options).

(b) Convertible securities:

	Net Income Impact	Number of Shares	Incremental EPS
6% preferred stock	$240,000	160,000	$1.50
10% debentures	42,000*	18,000	2.33
6% debentures	42,000†	15,000	2.80

*$600,000 × 0.10 × (1 − 0.30)
†$1,000,000 × 0.06 × (1 − 0.30)

All three convertible securities are potentially dilutive because their impact on EPS is less than the $3.24 basic EPS. Whether the securities are actually dilutive depends on the comparison with the recomputed EPS, as shown in step 3.

Step 3—Compute diluted earnings per share:

Description	Net Income	Number of Shares	Part of Year	Weighted Average Shares	EPS
Basic earnings per share	$ 736,000			227,500	$3.24
Jan. 1, 2010, options—exercised Oct. 1, as if exercised Jan. 1, 2013:					
Number of shares assumed issued		20,000			
Less: Number of treasury shares assumed repurchased (20,000 × $30)/$62		(9,677)			
Incremental shares		10,323	9/12	7,742	
Oct. 1, 2013, options:					
Number of shares assumed issued		40,000			
Number of treasury shares assumed repurchased (40,000 × $60)/$61		(39,344)			
Incremental shares		656	3/12	164	
	$ 736,000			235,406	$3.13
6% preferred stock	240,000	160,000	12/12	160,000	
	$ 976,000			395,406	$2.47
10% debentures	42,000		12/12	18,000	
Diluted EPS	$1,018,000			413,406	$2.46

6% debentures: Because incremental EPS value of $2.80 exceeds latest EPS of $2.46, the debentures are antidilutive and not included in diluted EPS.

Circle West would report basic EPS of $3.24 and diluted EPS of $2.46. In addition, Circle West would provide note information similar to that developed in step 3.

SOLUTIONS TO OPENING SCENARIO QUESTIONS

1. A P/E ratio reflects the relationship between a company's current earnings and its current stock price. In general, a higher P/E ratio is indicative of a company for which the market has higher growth expectations. Lower P/E ratios are associated with companies with lower growth prospects.
2. The Chinese oil companies have many, many more shares outstanding than does ExxonMobil. Thus, when the amount of earnings is divided by the number of shares, the resulting earnings per share is a low number. Think of it like this: Who has more money—a person with $1,000,000 in $100 dollar bills or a person with $1,000,000 in $1 bills? Of course, both people have the same amount of money, a million dollars. The difference is that the second person has his or her wealth divided up into many, many more little pieces.

SOLUTIONS TO STOP & THINK

1. (Page 18-9) The correct answer is D. If prior-period income statements were not adjusted for stock splits and stock dividends occurring in the current period, the comparisons of per-share information across periods would be meaningless in determining trend information. The per-share computations provide financial statement users with a measure of profitability scaled by the number of ownership shares in the company. If the number of shares should change over time (without any new investment, such as with stock splits and stock dividends),

that new information should be reflected in the current period's financial statements.

2. (Page 18-19) The correct answer is C. The diluted EPS computation is intended to present the worst-case scenario for the common shareholders. Of course, the worst-case scenario doesn't always actually occur. However, for comparability across companies, the diluted EPS should always reflect the worst that could have happened, whether that actually happened during the period or not. Recall that diluted EPS assumes conversion occurs at the beginning of the period or the date of issuance, whichever comes later. The computations associated with basic EPS already include the time period relating to the actual conversion. For diluted EPS, we must make an additional adjustment to include the time period for which the convertible securities (or options) were outstanding during the period.

SOLUTION TO USING THE FASB'S CODIFICATION

The only Subtopic under Topic 260, Earnings per Share, is Subtopic 10—General. Under that subtopic, there is a section on scope. The required statement on scope is FASB ASC paragraph 260-10-15-2: "The guidance in the Earnings per Share Topic requires presentation of earnings per share (EPS) by all entities that have issued common stock or potential common stock (that is, securities such as options, warrants, convertible securities, or contingent stock agreements) if those securities trade in a public market either on a stock exchange (domestic or foreign) or in the over-the-counter market, including securities quoted only locally or regionally. This Topic also requires presentation of EPS by an entity that has made a filing or is in the process of filing with a regulatory agency in preparation for the sale of those securities in a public market."

So, because Della Bee Enterprises does not have shares that trade on any exchange, and is not in the process of preparing to go public, the company does NOT need to present EPS data. You are right, and the intern is wrong.

REVIEW CHAPTER 18

LEARNING OBJECTIVES

1 Know the difference between a simple and a complex capital structure, and understand how dilutive securities affect earnings per share computations.

FASB ASC Topic 260, Earnings per Share, requires two EPS computations: basic and diluted. *Dilution* relates to those convertible securities and stock options that, if exercised, would result in a decrease in EPS. A simple capital structure exists when a company has no convertible securities, stock options, warrants, or other rights outstanding. A company with convertible securities or stock options that would, if exercised, result in a dilution in EPS is considered to have a complex capital structure.

2 Compute basic earnings per share, taking into account the sale and repurchase of stock during the period as well as the effects of stock splits and stock dividends.

Basic EPS is computed by dividing income available to common shareholders by the weighted-average number of common shares outstanding. If a company splits its stock or declares a stock dividend, a retroactive recognition of this change must be made in determining the weighted-average number of shares outstanding. When comparative financial statements are presented, the common shares outstanding for all periods shown must be adjusted to reflect any stock dividend or stock split in the current period.

3 **Use the treasury stock method to compute diluted earnings per share when a firm has outstanding stock options, warrants, and rights.**

If a firm has stock options, warrants, or rights outstanding, a determination must be made as to their potential effects on EPS. If the exercise price is less than the average market price for the period, the option, warrant, or right is considered dilutive and would be included in computing diluted EPS. The treasury stock method involves determining the number of incremental shares that would be issued assuming that the options, warrants, or rights were exercised and the proceeds used to buy treasury shares on the market.

4 **Use the if-converted method to compute diluted earnings per share when a company has convertible preferred stock or convertible bonds outstanding.**

A company with convertible securities may be required to adjust both the numerator and the denominator in computing diluted EPS if those convertible securities are determined to be potentially dilutive. In the case of convertible bonds, interest expense (net of tax) must be added back to the numerator, and the number of shares that would be issued upon conversion would be included in the denominator. For convertible preferred stock, preferred dividends must be added back to income available to common shareholders, and the denominator would be increased by the number of shares that would be issued upon conversion.

5 **Factor into the diluted earnings per share computations the effect of actual conversion of convertible securities or the exercise of options, warrants, or rights during the period, and understand the antidilutive effect of potential common shares when a firm reports a loss from continuing operations.**

If conversion or exercise actually takes place during a period, an adjustment must be made to reflect what the EPS would have been if conversion or exercise had taken place at the beginning of the period or issuance date, whichever comes later.

In the case of a firm reporting a loss from continuing operations, no dual presentation of EPS is required because inclusion of stock options or convertible securities would decrease the loss per share and thus always would be antidilutive.

6 **Determine the order in which multiple potentially dilutive securities should be considered in computing diluted earnings per share.**

In those instances when a firm has multiple potentially dilutive securities, the FASB requires a systematic procedure for determining the order in which the various securities are considered. The individual effect of each security is computed, and the securities are considered in turn beginning with the security with the least favorable effect on basic EPS. The procedure is repeated until the diluted EPS figure is lower than the next security's incremental impact.

7 **Understand the disclosure requirements associated with basic and diluted earnings per share computations.**

Basic and diluted EPS are required to be disclosed on the face of the income statement for those companies with a complex capital structure. Firms reporting below-the-line items on their income statement may report the per-share effects of these items either on the face of the income statement or in the notes. In addition, a schedule reconciling both the numerator and the denominator for the basic and diluted per-share computations must be provided in the notes to the financial statements.

EM EXPANDED MATERIAL

8 **Make complex earnings per share computations involving multiple potentially dilutive securities.**

For firms with stock options, warrants, rights, convertible preferred stock, and/or convertible bonds, the computations associated with diluted EPS can become quite complex. For those items that are dilutive or potentially dilutive, considering them in the proper sequence will ensure that diluted EPS is properly calculated.

FASB-IASB CODIFICATION SUMMARY

Topic	FASB Accounting Standards Codification	Original FASB Standard	Corresponding IASB Standard	Differences between U.S. GAAP and IFRS
Computing basic earnings per share	*Section 260-10-45 par. 10-11*	*SFAS No. 128 par. 8-9*	*IAS 33 par. 9-29*	No substantial differences
Computing diluted earnings per share	*Section 260-10-45 par. 16-17*	*SFAS No. 128 par. 11, 13*	*IAS 33 par. 30-44*	No substantial differences
Participating securities and the two-class method	*Section 260-10-45 par. 59A-66*	*SFAS No. 128 par. 60-61 EITF 03-06*	*IAS 33 par. A13-A14*	No substantial differences
Treasury stock method for options	*Section 260-10-45 par.23, 25*	*SFAS No. 128 par. 17-18*	*IAS 33 par. 45-48*	No substantial differences
If-converted method for convertible securities	*Section 260-10-45 par. 40-42*	*SFAS No. 128 par. 26-28*	*IAS 33 par. 49-51*	No substantial differences
Impact of actual conversion or exercise	*Section 260-10-45 par. 17*	*SFAS No. 128 par. 13*	*IAS 33 par. 38*	No substantial differences
Proper order of consideration for multiple potentially dilutive securities	*Section 260-10-45 par. 18*	*SFAS No. 128 par. 14-15*	*IAS 33 par. 44*	No substantial differences
Disclosures associated with basic and diluted EPS	*Section 260-10-50 par. 1-2*	*SFAS No. 128 par. 40-41*	*IAS 33 par. 70-73A*	No substantial differences

KEY TERMS

Antidilution of earnings 18-4
Antidilutive securities 18-4
Basic earnings per share 18-5
Complex capital structure 18-5
Dilution of earnings 18-4
Dilutive securities 18-4
If-converted method 18-15
Simple capital structure 18-4
Treasury stock method 18-13
Two-class method 18-11

QUESTIONS

1. Earnings per share computations have received increased prominence on the income statement. How would an investor use such information in making investment decisions?
2. What limitations should be recognized in using EPS data?
3. Why are EPS figures computed on the basis of common stock transactions that have not yet happened rather than on the basis of strictly historical common stock data?
4. What distinguishes a simple capital structure from a complex capital structure?

5. An enterprise split its common stock 3 for 1 on July 1. Its accounting year ends December 31. Prior to the split, there were 10,000 shares of common stock outstanding. What is the weighted-average number of shares that should be used to compute EPS in the current and preceding years?
6. Why are EPS figures adjusted retroactively for stock dividends, stock splits, and reverse stock splits?
7. What is the two-class method?
8. What is meant by *dilution of EPS*?
9. What is an *antidilutive security*? Why are such securities generally excluded from the computation of EPS?
10. What is the *treasury stock method* of accounting for outstanding stock options, warrants, and rights in computing diluted EPS?
11. Convertible debt that is dilutive requires an adjustment to income. What is the nature of the adjustment?
12. What is the meaning of the if-converted method of computing EPS?
13. If stock options are actually exercised during the year, how is diluted EPS affected?
14. Why are all convertible securities and options antidilutive when a company is operating at a loss?

EM EXPANDED MATERIAL

15. If a company has multiple potentially dilutive securities, how are the computations made to ensure obtaining the lowest EPS figure?

PRACTICE EXERCISES

Practice 18-1
LO2

Shares Outstanding: Issuance and Reacquisition
On January 1, the company had 200,000 common shares outstanding. On April 1, the company issued 60,000 additional shares. On August 1, the company reacquired 100,000 shares. What was the weighted-average number of shares outstanding for the year?

Practice 18-2
LO2

Shares Outstanding: Stock Dividends and Stock Splits
On January 1, the company had 150,000 common shares outstanding. During the year, the following events occurred:

March 1: 2-for-1 stock split
June 1: Issued 45,000 additional shares
September 1: 20% stock dividend

What was the weighted-average number of shares outstanding for the year?

Practice 18-3
LO2

Impact of Preferred Stock on Basic EPS
On January 1, the company had 100,000 common shares outstanding. This same number of common shares was outstanding throughout the year. The company also had 30,000 shares of 5%, $100 par preferred stock outstanding throughout the year. The company did *not* declare any common or preferred dividends during the year. Net income for the year was $220,000. Compute basic earnings per share, assuming that (1) the preferred stock is not cumulative and (2) the preferred stock is cumulative.

Practice 18-4
LO2

Computation of Basic EPS
On January 1, the company had 200,000 common shares outstanding. On April 1, the company issued 60,000 additional shares. On August 1, the company performed a 2-for-1 stock split. The company also had 20,000 shares of 8%, $50 par preferred stock outstanding throughout the year. The company declared the required preferred dividend during the year. Net income for the year was $300,000. Compute basic earnings per share.

Practice 18-5
LO2

Two-Class Method
The company had the following shares of stock outstanding during the year. Data regarding dividend privileges and net income are also given.

- Common shares outstanding: 320,000 for the entire year
- Participating preferred shares outstanding: 100,000 shares for the entire year

- Net income: $1,000,000
- Dividends on participating preferred shares: $1.00 per share plus a per-share increase 80% as large as the per-share increase of common dividends above $0.50 per share
- Common dividends paid for the year: $1.00 per share

Compute basic earnings per share for both the common shares and the participating preferred shares.

Practice 18-6
LO3

Diluted EPS and Stock Options

The company had 200,000 shares of common stock outstanding throughout the year. In addition, as of January 1, the company had issued stock options that allowed employees to purchase 50,000 shares of common stock. The option exercise price is $10 per share. The company has no other potentially dilutive securities. Net income for the year was $400,000. Compute diluted earnings per share, assuming that (1) the average stock price for the year was $16 and (2) the average stock price for the year was $8.

Practice 18-7
LO3

Stock Options Issued During the Year

Refer to Practice 18-6. Assume that the options were issued on September 1 instead of being outstanding throughout the year. Compute diluted earnings per share, assuming that (1) the average stock price for the year and for the September 1–December 31 period was $5 and (2) the average stock price for the year and for the September 1–December 31 period was $14.

Practice 18-8
LO4

Diluted EPS and Convertible Preferred Stock

The company had 100,000 shares of common stock outstanding throughout the year. In addition, as of January 1, the company had issued 10,000 convertible preferred shares (cumulative, 5%, $100 par). The company has no other potentially dilutive securities. Net income for the year was $400,000. Compute diluted earnings per share, assuming that (1) each preferred share was convertible into four shares of common stock and (2) each preferred share was convertible into one share of common stock.

Practice 18-9
LO4

Convertible Preferred Stock Issued During the Year

Refer to Practice 18-8. Assume that the convertible preferred stock was issued on February 1. Also assume that the issuance agreement stipulates that the preferred stockholders are entitled to their entire preferred dividend for the year even though the shares are issued on February 1. Compute diluted earnings per share, assuming that (1) each preferred share was convertible into five shares of common stock and (2) each preferred share was convertible into one share of common stock.

Practice 18-10
LO4

Diluted EPS and Convertible Bonds

The company had 50,000 shares of common stock outstanding throughout the year. In addition, as of January 1, the company had issued 100 convertible bonds ($1,000 face value, 10%). The company has no other potentially dilutive securities. Net income for the year was $100,000. The income tax rate is 30%. Compute diluted earnings per share, assuming that (1) each bond was convertible into 50 shares of common stock and (2) each bond was convertible into 20 shares of common stock.

Practice 18-11
LO4

Convertible Bonds Issued During the Year

Refer to Practice 18-10. Assume that the convertible bonds were issued on October 1. Compute diluted earnings per share, assuming that (1) each bond was convertible into 100 shares of common stock and (2) each bond was convertible into 15 shares of common stock.

Practice 18-12
LO4

Shortcut Antidilution Tests

Net income for the company for the year was $300,000, and 100,000 shares of common stock were outstanding during the year. The income tax rate is 30%. For each of the following potentially dilutive securities, perform the shortcut antidilution test to determine whether the security is dilutive. Assume that each of the securities was issued on or before January 1. Treat each security independently; in other words, when testing one security, assume that the others do not exist.

1. 10,000 convertible preferred shares (cumulative, 5%, $100 par). Each preferred share is convertible into one share of common stock.
2. 500 convertible bonds ($1,000 face value, 10%). Each bond is convertible into 25 shares of common stock.
3. 20,000 convertible preferred shares (cumulative, 10%, $50 par). Each preferred share is convertible into four shares of common stock.
4. 2,000 convertible bonds ($1,000 face value, 8%). Each bond is convertible into 15 shares of common stock.

Practice 18-13

LO5

Basic and Diluted EPS and Actual Conversion of Stock Options

The company had 100,000 shares of common stock outstanding on January 1. In addition, as of January 1, the company had issued stock options that allowed employees to purchase 40,000 shares of common stock. The option exercise price is $10 per share. The options were exercised on April 1. The average stock price for the year was $16; the stock price on the option exercise date (April 1) was $15. The company has no other potentially dilutive securities. Net income for the year was $200,000. Compute (1) basic earnings per share and (2) diluted earnings per share.

Practice 18-14

LO5

Basic and Diluted EPS and Actual Conversion of Convertible Preferred

The company had 200,000 shares of common stock outstanding on January 1. In addition, as of January 1, the company had issued 5,000 convertible preferred shares (cumulative, 5%, $100 par). These preferred shares were converted on September 1. Each preferred share was converted into five shares of common stock. The preferred dividends for the entire year were paid in full *before* the conversion. The company has no other potentially dilutive securities. Net income for the year was $300,000. Compute (1) basic earnings per share and (2) diluted earnings per share.

Practice 18-15

LO5

Basic and Diluted EPS and Actual Conversion of Convertible Bonds

The company had 100,000 shares of common stock outstanding on January 1. In addition, as of January 1, the company had issued 500 convertible bonds ($1,000 face value, 10%). The company has no other potentially dilutive securities. The bonds were converted on August 1; 40 shares of common stock were issued in exchange for each bond. Accrued interest on the bonds was recognized and paid on that date. Net income for the year was $400,000. The income tax rate is 40%. Compute (1) basic earnings per share and (2) diluted earnings per share.

Practice 18-16

LO5

Diluted EPS and a Loss

The company reported a net loss of $300,000 for the year and 100,000 shares of common stock were outstanding during the year. The income tax rate is 30%. For each of the following potentially dilutive securities, compute (1) basic EPS and (2) diluted EPS. Assume that each of the securities was issued on or before January 1. Treat each security independently; in other words, when doing the EPS computations for one security, assume that the others do not exist.

(a) 10,000 convertible preferred shares (cumulative, 5%, $100 par). Each preferred share is convertible into three shares of common stock.
(b) 500 convertible bonds ($1,000 face value, 10%). Each bond is convertible into 25 shares of common stock.
(c) Stock options that allow employees to purchase 40,000 shares of common stock. The option exercise price is $10 per share. The average stock price for the year was $16.

Practice 18-17
LO6

Multiple Potentially Dilutive Securities

The company reported net income of $300,000 for the year and 100,000 shares of common stock were outstanding during the year. The income tax rate is 40%. The company has the following potentially dilutive securities. Assume that each of the securities was issued on or before January 1. Compute (1) basic EPS and (2) diluted EPS.

(a) Stock options that allow employees to purchase 30,000 shares of common stock. The option exercise price is $10 per share. The average stock price for the year was $18.
(b) 10,000 convertible preferred shares (cumulative, 5%, $100 par). Each preferred share is convertible into four shares of common stock.
(c) 500 convertible bonds ($1,000 face value, 10%). Each bond is convertible into 40 shares of common stock.

Practice 18-18
LO6

Multiple Potentially Dilutive Securities

The company reported net income of $430,000 for the year and 120,000 shares of common stock were outstanding during the year. The income tax rate is 30%. The company has the following potentially dilutive securities. Assume that each of the securities was issued on or before January 1. Compute (1) basic EPS and (2) diluted EPS.

(a) Stock options that allow employees to purchase 20,000 shares of common stock. The option exercise price is $10 per share. The average stock price for the year was $8.
(b) 5,000 convertible preferred shares (cumulative, 5%, $100 par). Each preferred share is convertible into five shares of common stock.
(c) 1,000 convertible bonds ($1,000 face value, 10%). Each bond is convertible into 22 shares of common stock.

Practice 18-19
LO7

EPS and Financial Statement Presentation

The income statement for the company is as follows:

Sales	$1,000,000
Operating expenses	600,000
Operating income	$ 400,000
Interest expense	80,000
Income before income taxes	$ 320,000
Income tax expense (40%)	128,000
Income from continuing operations	$ 192,000
Extraordinary loss (net of taxes)	(50,000)
Discontinued operations (net of taxes)	(35,000)
Net income	$ 107,000

The company had 100,000 common shares outstanding for the entire year. In addition, for the entire year, the company had stock options outstanding that allow employees to purchase 50,000 shares of common stock. The option exercise price is $10 per share, and the average stock price for the year was $14. Compute and list all earnings per share numbers that the company is required to report.

EM EXPANDED MATERIAL

Practice 18-20
LO8

Comprehensive Calculation of Diluted EPS

Refer to Practice 18-17. Assume that the company issued 25,000 new shares of common stock on June 1 and that the company issued a 2-for-1 stock split on December 1. Compute (1) basic EPS and (2) diluted EPS. (*Note*: The shares in the option, convertible preferred, and convertible bond descriptions are in terms of January 1 shares. The number of shares in each case—and the exercise price in the case of the options—would be adjusted to reflect the December 1 2-for-1 split. The average stock price of $18 for the year does *not* reflect the 2-for-1 stock split.)

EXERCISES

Exercise 18-21

LO3

Number of Shares—Stock Options

Barone Company has employee stock options outstanding to purchase 40,000 common shares at $14 per share. All options were outstanding during the entire year. The average price of the company's common stock for the year was $20. Compute the incremental shares that would be used in arriving at diluted EPS. Barone has 80,000 shares outstanding at the date the options are granted.

Exercise 18-22

LO3

Number of Shares—Stock Options

On January 1, 2013, Primavera Corporation had 55,000 shares of common stock outstanding that did not change during 2013. In 2012, Primavera granted options to certain executives to purchase 12,000 shares of its common stock at $6 each. The average market price of common was $8.00 per share for 2013. Compute the number of shares to be used in computing diluted EPS for 2013.

Exercise 18-23

LO2

Weighted-Average Number of Shares

Transactions involving the common stock account of Higrade Gas Company during the 2-year period 2013 to 2014 were as follows:

2013

Jan. 1	Had a balance of 200,000 shares of $10 par common stock.
Apr. 1	Converted $2,500,000 of convertible bonds with 50 shares issued for each $1,000 bond.
July. 1	Declared a 10% stock dividend.
Oct. 1	Employees exercised options to purchase 7,000 shares for $20 a share.

2014

Apr. 1	Declared a 2-for-1 stock split.
Oct. 1	Sold 170,000 shares for $30 a share.

From the information given, compute the comparative number of weighted-average shares outstanding for 2013 and 2014 to be used for basic EPS computations at the end of 2014.

Exercise 18-24

LO2

Weighted-Average Number of Shares

Compute the weighted-average number of shares outstanding for Steadman Company, which has a simple capital structure, assuming that the following transactions in common stock occurred during the calendar year.

Date	Transactions in Common Stock	Number of Shares $10 Par Value
Jan. 1	Shares outstanding	76,000
Feb. 1	Issued for cash	48,000
May 1	Acquired treasury stock	(20,000)
Aug. 1	20% stock dividend	20% of shares outstanding
Sept. 1	Resold part of treasury stock shares	15,000
Nov. 1	Issued 3-for-1 stock split	

Exercise 18-25
LO2

REVERSE SOLVABLE

Weighted-Average Number of Shares

Assume that the following transactions affected owners' equity for De Soto Inc. during 2013.

Feb. 1	Sold 40,000 shares of common stock in the market.
Apr. 1	Purchased 3,000 shares of common stock to be held as treasury stock. Paid cash dividends of $0.50 per share.
May 1	Split common stock 2 for 1.
July 1	Sold 15,000 shares of common stock.
Oct. 1	Issued a 10% stock dividend.
Dec. 31	Paid a cash dividend of $0.70 per share. The total amount paid for dividends on December 31 was $407,330.

Compute the weighted-average number of shares to be used in computing basic EPS for 2013. Because no beginning share figures are available, you must work backward from December 31, 2013, to compute shares outstanding.

Exercise 18-26
LO2

Basic Earnings per Share—Simple Capital Structure

The income statement for Fignon Co. for the year ended December 31, 2013, reported the following.

Income from continuing operations before income taxes	$35,000
Income taxes	14,000
Income from continuing operations	$21,000
Loss from disposal of segment (net of income taxes)	(4,200)
Net income	$16,800

Compute basic EPS amounts for 2013 under each of the following assumptions (consider each assumption separately):

(a) The company has only one class of common stock with 20,000 shares outstanding.

(b) The company has shares outstanding as follows: preferred 8% stock, $15 par, cumulative, 5,000 shares; common, $12 par, 20,000 shares. Only the current year's preferred dividends are unpaid.

(c) Same as (b) except that Fignon Co. also has preferred 7% stock, $10 par, noncumulative, 6,000 shares, and only $3,000 in dividends on the noncumulative preferred has been declared.

Exercise 18-27
LO2

Basic Earnings per Share—Simple Capital Structure

At December 31, 2013, Marquis Corporation had 100,000 shares of common stock issued and outstanding, 60,000 of which had been issued and outstanding throughout the year and 40,000 of which had been issued on October 1, 2013. Income before income taxes for the year ended December 31, 2013, was $636,400. In 2013 and 2014, a dividend of $70,000 was paid on 70,000 shares of 10% cumulative preferred stock, $10 par.

On May 1, 2014, there were 20,000 additional shares issued. Total income before income taxes for 2014 was $461,000, which included an extraordinary gain before income taxes of $42,000. Assuming a 30% tax rate, what is Marquis's basic earnings per common share for 2013 and for 2014, rounded to the nearest cent? Show computations in good form.

Exercise 18-28
LO2, LO4, LO5

Earnings per Share with Actual Conversion

Atlas, Inc., has the following capital structure at January 1, 2013.

	Outstanding
Common stock, $10 par	800,000 shares
11% stated interest rate convertible bonds issued at par; each $1,000 bond is convertible into 80 shares of common stock	$5,000,000

During 2013, Atlas had the following stock transactions:

May 1	Issued 50,000 shares of common stock for $30 per share.
Aug. 1	Purchased 100,000 shares of treasury stock at $35 per share.
Oct. 1	Converted $2,000,000 of bonds.

Net income for 2013 was $950,000. The income tax rate was 30%. Compute basic and diluted EPS for Atlas for 2013.

Exercise 18-29

LO4, LO5

Earnings and Loss per Share—Convertible Preferred Stock, Operating Loss

During all of 2013, Cougar Inc. had outstanding 180,000 shares of common stock and 16,000 shares of $5 preferred stock. Each share of the preferred stock is convertible into five shares of common stock. For 2013, Cougar had a $200,000 loss from operations; no dividends were paid or declared.

Compute the basic and diluted earnings (loss) per share for Cougar, assuming that (1) the preferred stock is noncumulative and (2) the preferred stock is cumulative.

Exercise 18-30

LO4

SPREADSHEET

Diluted Earnings per Share—Convertible Bonds

Delgado Manufacturing Company reports long-term liabilities and stockholders' equity balances at December 31, 2013, as follows:

Convertible 5% bonds (par)	$ 800,000
Common stock, $25 par, 100,000 shares issued and outstanding	2,500,000

Additional information is determined as follows:

Conversion term of bonds—50 shares for each $1,000 bond	
Income before extraordinary items—2013	$ 199,800
Extraordinary gain (net of tax)	43,520
Net income—2013	$ 243,320

Compute the basic and diluted EPS for the company for 2013, assuming that the income tax rate is 30%. No changes occurred in the debt and equity balances during 2013.

Exercise 18-31

LO4

Diluted Earnings per Share—Convertible Bonds

On January 2, 2013, McGregor Co. issued at par $45,000 of 9% bonds convertible in total into 4,000 shares of McGregor's common stock. No bonds were converted during 2013. Throughout 2013, McGregor had 10,000 shares of common stock outstanding. McGregor's 2013 net income was $75,000. McGregor's tax rate is 30%.

No other potentially dilutive securities other than the convertible bonds were outstanding during 2013. For 2013, compute McGregor's basic and diluted EPS.

Exercise 18-32

LO3, LO4

Dilutive Securities

Kingston Corporation has basic earnings per common share of $1.54 for the year ended December 31, 2013. For each of the following independent examples, decide whether the convertible security would be dilutive or antidilutive in computing diluted EPS. Consider each example individually. The tax rate is 35%.

(a) 7 1/2% debentures, $500,000 face value are convertible into common stock at the rate of 25 shares for each $1,000 bond.
(b) $6 preferred stock (no par) is convertible into common stock at the rate of three shares of common stock for one share of preferred stock. There are 30,000 shares of preferred stock outstanding.
(c) Options to purchase 150,000 shares of common stock are outstanding. The exercise price is $22 per share; average market price is $27 per share.
(d) $800,000 of 11% debentures are convertible at the rate of 25 shares of common stock for each $1,000 bond.
(e) Preferred 7% stock, $100 par, 10,000 shares outstanding is convertible into 5 shares of common stock for each share of preferred stock.

Exercise 18-33

LO1, LO2, LO4, LO7

SPREADSHEET

Earnings per Share

At December 31, 2013, the books of Yorke Corporation include the following balances:

Long-term liabilities:	
Bonds payable, 8%, each $1,000 bond is convertible into 50 shares of common stock; bonds sold at par and were issued November 3, 2012	$ 500,000
Stockholders' equity:	
Preferred stock, 7%, $50 par, cumulative, nonconvertible, 10,000 shares outstanding	500,000
Paid-in capital in excess of par, preferred stock	300,000
Common stock, $10 par, authorized 300,000 shares; 199,500 shares outstanding	1,995,000
Paid-in capital in excess of par, common stock	450,000
Retained earnings	519,000

The records of Yorke reveal the following additional information.

(a) Had 150,000 shares of common stock outstanding January 1, 2013.
(b) Sold 40,000 shares of common stock for cash on April 30, 2013.
(c) Issued 5% stock dividend on July 1, 2013.
(d) Had income before extraordinary items (after tax) of $715,000.
(e) Had extraordinary loss (net of tax), $16,000.
(f) Had income tax rate, 30%.
(g) Bond indenture does not provide for increase in shares at conversion due to stock dividends declared subsequent to the bond issue date.

1. Is this a simple or complex capital structure?
2. Compute all EPS amounts as required by FASB *ASC Topic 260.* How should the EPS data be presented?

EM EXPANDED MATERIAL

Exercise 18-34

LO2, LO3, LO4, LO6, LO8

Earnings per Share—Convertible Securities

Information relating to the capital structure of Harry Porter Corporation at December 31, 2012 and 2013, is as follows:

	Outstanding
Common stock	270,000 shares
Convertible preferred stock noncumulative (issued in 2011)	24,000 shares
7.5% convertible bonds (issued in 2012)	$900,000
Stock options to purchase 32,000 shares at $12. The average market price of Harry Porter stock during 2013 was $18.	

Harry Porter Corporation paid dividends of $4 per share on its preferred stock. The preferred stock is convertible into 48,000 shares of common stock. The 7.5% convertible bonds are convertible into a total of 26,000 shares of common stock. The net income for the year ended December 31, 2013, is $760,000. Assume that the income tax rate is 30%. Compute basic and diluted EPS for the year ended December 31, 2013.

PROBLEMS

Problem 18-35
LO2

SPREADSHEET

Weighted-Average Number of Shares

Outdoor Recreation Products Inc. had 50,000 shares of common stock outstanding at the end of 2012. During 2013 and 2014, the following transactions took place.

2013

Mar. 31	Sold 10,000 shares at $24.
Apr. 26	Paid cash dividend of $0.45 per share.
July. 31	Paid cash dividend of $0.20 per share and issued a 5% stock dividend.
Nov. 1	Sold 12,000 shares at $25.

2014

Feb. 28	Purchased 8,000 shares of common stock to be held in treasury.
Mar. 1	Paid cash dividend of $0.50 per share.
Apr. 30	Issued 4-for-1 stock split.
Nov. 1	Sold 5,000 shares of treasury stock.
Dec. 20	Declared cash dividend of $0.15 per share.

Outdoor Recreation Products Inc. has a simple capital structure.

Instructions: Compute the weighted-average number of shares for 2013 and 2014 to be used in the EPS computation at the end of 2014.

Problem 18-36
LO2

Basic Earnings per Share—Simple Capital Structure

The following condensed financial statements for Hudson Corporation were prepared by the accounting department.

Hudson Corporation
Income Statement
For the Year Ended December 31, 2013

Sales		$11,000,000
Cost of goods sold		8,500,000
Gross profit on sales		$ 2,500,000
Expenses:		
Selling expense	$730,000	
Administrative expense	370,000	
Interest expense	50,000	1,150,000
Income from continuing operations before income taxes		$ 1,350,000
Income taxes		420,000
Income from continuing operations		$ 930,000
Extraordinary loss, net of tax savings		(80,000)
Net income		$ 850,000

Hudson Corporation
Balance Sheet
December 31, 2013

Assets	$6,850,000
Liabilities:	
Current liabilities	$1,200,000
6% bonds, due December 31, 2017	600,000
Stockholders' equity:	
Common stock, $10 par, 250,000 shares authorized, issued and outstanding	2,500,000
Additional paid-in capital	750,000
Retained earnings	1,800,000
Total liabilities and stockholders' equity	$6,850,000

Instructions: Compute the basic EPS under each of the following independent assumptions (the company has a simple capital structure).

1. No change in the capital structure occurred in 2013.
2. On December 31, 2012, there were 160,000 shares outstanding. On May 1, 2013, 60,000 shares were sold at par, and on October 1, 2013, 30,000 shares were sold at par.
3. On December 31, 2012, there were 200,000 shares outstanding. On July 1, 2013, the company issued a 25% stock dividend.

Problem 18-37
LO2

Basic Earnings per Share—Simple Capital Structure

Great Northern Inc. reported the following comparative information in the Stockholders' Equity section of its 2014 balance sheet.

	December 31,		
	2014	2013	2012
12% preferred stock, $50 par	$ 82,500	$ 67,500	$ 50,000
Paid-in capital in excess of par—preferred	13,400	9,200	5,000
Common stock, $5 par*	410,600	399,600	325,000
Paid-in capital in excess of par—common	64,300	58,800	35,000
Paid-in capital from treasury stock	1,800	800	800
Retained earnings	471,200	396,460	180,200
Total stockholders' equity	$1,043,800	$932,360	$596,000

*Par value after June 1, 2014, stock split.

In addition, company records show that the following transactions involving stockholders' equity were recorded in 2013 and 2014.

2013

May 1	Sold 4,500 shares of common stock for $12, par value $10.
June 30	Sold 350 shares of preferred stock for $62, par value $50.
Aug. 1	Issued an 8% stock dividend on common stock. The market price of the stock was $15.
Sept. 1	Declared cash dividends of 12% on preferred stock and $1.50 on common stock.
Dec. 31	Income before extraordinary items for the year totaled $316,200. In addition, Great Northern had an extraordinary gain of $12,500, net of tax.

2014

Jan. 31	Sold 1,100 shares of common stock for $15.
May 1	Sold 300 shares of preferred stock for $64.

June	1	Issued a 2-for-1 split of common stock, reduced par value to $5.
Sept.	1	Purchased 500 shares of common stock for $9 to be held as treasury stock.
Oct.	1	Declared cash dividends of 12% on preferred stock and $2 per share on outstanding common stock.
Nov.	1	Sold 500 shares of treasury stock for $11.
Dec.	31	Net income for the year included an extraordinary loss, net of income tax, of $19,000.

Instructions: Compute the basic EPS amounts for 2013 and 2014 to be presented in the income statement for 2014.

Problem 18-38
LO3

Diluted Earnings per Share—Stock Options

The records of Eureka Gold Company reveal the following capital structure as of December 31, 2012.

$9 preferred stock, $100 par, 5,000 shares issued and outstanding	$ 500,000
Additional paid-in capital on preferred stock	110,000
Common stock, $10 par, 175,000 shares issued and outstanding	1,750,000
Additional paid-in capital on common stock	550,000
Retained earnings	778,000

To stimulate work incentive and to bolster trade relations, Eureka Gold on May 1, 2013, issued stock options to selected executives, creditors, and others allowing the purchase of 32,000 shares of common stock for $26 a share. Market prices for the stock at various times during 2013 were:

Option issuance date	$24
Average for the year	62

A dividend on preferred stock was paid during the year, and there are no dividends in arrears at year-end. There are no other capital transactions during the year. Net income for 2013 was $500,000.

Instructions: Compute basic and diluted EPS for 2013.

Problem 18-39
LO3

Diluted Earnings per Share—Stock Options

Kulkulcan Technology Co. provides the following data at December 31, 2013.

Operating revenue	$1,460,000
Operating expenses	$790,000
Income tax rate	35%
Common stock outstanding during the entire year	34,000 shares

On January 1, 2013, there were options outstanding to purchase 9,000 shares of common stock at $20 per share. The average market price for the year was $26 per share. The balance sheet reports $510,000 of 7% nonconvertible bonds at December 31, 2013. (Interest expense is included in operating expenses.)

Instructions:

1. Compute basic EPS for 2013.
2. Compute diluted EPS for 2013.

Problem 18-40
LO3, LO5
SPREADSHEET

Diluted Earnings per Share with Exercise of Stock Options

As of January 1, 2013, Anvil Corporation had 25,000 shares of $10 par common stock outstanding. The company had issued stock options in 2011 to its management personnel, permitting them to acquire 4,000 shares of common stock at $12 per share. At the time of the issuance, common stock was selling for $12 per share. The market price of common stock was $25 on September 1, 2013, and the average price for 2013 was $27. Income before extraordinary items for 2013 was $142,400. The company also had an extraordinary gain of $21,000, net of taxes. Terms of the options make them currently exercisable. On September 1, 2013, options to acquire 1,500 shares were exercised. The other 2,500 options are still outstanding at December 31, 2013.

Instructions: Compute basic and diluted EPS for the year ended December 31, 2013.

Problem 18-41

LO5

Diluted Earnings per Share—Conversion of Debentures

The following information relates to the December 31, 2012, balance sheet for Chiapucci Incorporated.

6% convertible 10-year debentures issued at par	$1,000,000
Common stock, $12 par, 110,000 shares issued and outstanding	$1,320,000
Retained earnings	842,000
Total stockholders' equity	$2,162,000

The convertible debentures include terms stating that each $1,000 bond can be converted into 30 shares of common stock.

The following events occurred during 2013.

(a) On August 31, 2013, the complete issue of convertible debentures was converted into common stock.

(b) Chiapucci reported net income of $540,000 in 2013. The company's income tax rate was 30%.

(c) No other common stock transactions took place during the year other than the debenture conversion.

Instructions:

1. Compute basic and diluted EPS for the year ended December 31, 2013.
2. Assume that Chiapucci had a net loss of $220,000. Show why the convertible debentures are antidilutive under loss conditions.

Problem 18-42

LO2, LO3, LO4, LO6

Diluted Earnings per Share—Complex Capital Structure

Hillcrest Corporation's capital structure is as follows:

	December 31,	
	2014	2013
Outstanding shares of:		
Common stock	310,000	220,000
Nonconvertible, noncumulative preferred stock	12,000	12,000
10% convertible bonds	$800,000	$800,000

The following additional information is available.

(a) On September 1, 2014, Hillcrest sold 90,000 additional shares of common stock.

(b) Net income for the year ended December 31, 2014, was $920,000.

(c) During 2014, Hillcrest declared and paid dividends of $6 per share on its preferred stock.

(d) The 10% bonds are convertible into 50 shares of common stock for each $1,000 bond.

(e) Unexercised options to purchase 25,000 shares of common stock at $24.00 per share were outstanding at the beginning and end of 2014. The average market price of Hillcrest's common stock for 2014 was $34 per share.

(f) Warrants to purchase 36,000 shares of common stock at $36 per share were attached to the preferred stock at the time of issuance. The warrants, which expire on December 31, 2019, were outstanding at December 31, 2014.

(g) Hillcrest's effective income tax rate was 30% for 2013 and 2014.

Instructions:

1. For the year ended December 31, 2014, compute basic EPS.
2. Compute diluted EPS for 2014.

Problem 18-43

LO2, LO3, LO4, LO5, LO6

Earnings per Share—Complex Capital Structure

The Stockholders' Equity section of Alta Company's balance sheet as of December 31, 2013, contains the following:

$2 cumulative preferred stock, $25 par, convertible, 1,600,000 shares authorized, 1,400,000 shares issued, 750,000 converted to common, 650,000 shares outstanding	$16,250,000
Common stock, $0.25 par, 15,000,000 shares authorized, 8,800,000 shares issued and outstanding	2,200,000
Additional paid-in capital	32,750,000
Retained earnings	40,595,000
Total stockholders' equity	$91,795,000

Included in Alta Company's liabilities are 9% convertible subordinated debentures, face value $20,000,000, issued at par in 2012. The debentures are due in 2019 and, until then, are convertible into the common stock of Alta Company at the rate of 60 shares of common stock for each $1,000 debenture. To date, none has been converted.

On April 2, 2013, Alta Company issued 1,400,000 shares of convertible preferred stock at $40 per share. Quarterly dividends to December 31, 2013, have been paid on these shares. The preferred stock is convertible into common stock at the rate of two shares of common for each share of preferred. On October 1, 2013, 150,000 shares and on November 1, 2013, 600,000 shares of the preferred stock were converted into common stock.

During July 2012, Alta Company granted options to its officers and key employees to purchase 500,000 shares of the company's common stock at a price of $20 per share. No options were exercised in 2013.

During 2013, dividend payments for the Alta common stock were as follows.

	Dividend per Share
First quarter	$0.10
Second quarter	0.15
Third quarter	0.10
Fourth quarter	0.15

The average market price for the company's common stock for the year was $25. Alta Company's net income for the year ended December 31, 2013, was $12,750,000. The provision for income tax was computed at a rate of 30%.

Instructions: Compute basic and diluted EPS for the year ended December 31, 2013.

EM EXPANDED MATERIAL

Problem 18-44

LO2, LO3, LO4, LO6, LO8

Earnings per Share—Complex Capital Structure

At December 31, 2013, Hemington Company had 320,000 shares of common stock outstanding. Hemington sold 80,000 shares on October 1, 2014. Net income for 2014 was $1,985,000; the income tax rate was 35%. In addition, Hemington had the following debt and equity securities on its books at December 31, 2013.

(a) 30,000 shares of $100 par, 8% cumulative preferred stock.
(b) 25,000 shares of 10% convertible cumulative preferred stock, par $100, sold at 110. Each share of preferred stock is convertible into three shares of common stock.
(c) $1,500,000 face value of 9% bonds sold at par.

(d) \$2,500,000 face value of 7% convertible bonds sold to yield 8%. Unamortized bond discount is \$150,000 at December 31, 2013. Each \$1,000 bond is convertible into 22 shares of common stock.

Also, options to purchase 20,000 shares of common stock were issued May 1, 2014. Exercise price is \$20 per share; market value at date of option was \$19; average market value for the year (and for the period May 1 through December 31), \$25.

Instructions: For the year ended December 31, 2014, compute basic and diluted EPS.

Problem 18-45
LO4, LO6, LO8

Earnings per Share—Multiple Convertible Securities

Data for Schrute Powder Company at the end of 2014 follow. All bonds are convertible as indicated and were issued at their face amounts.

Description of Bonds	Amount	Date Issued	Conversion Terms
10-year, $6\frac{1}{2}$% convertible bonds	\$ 600,000	Jan. 1, 2008	110 shares of common for each \$1,000 bond
20-year, 7% convertible bonds	1,200,000	Jan. 1, 2009	45 shares of common for each \$1,000 bond
25-year, $10\frac{1}{2}$% convertible bonds	900,000	June 30, 2013	36 shares of common for each \$1,000 bond

Additional information:

Common shares outstanding at December 31, 2013	880,000
Net income for 2014	\$1,315,000
Income tax rate	40%

Instructions:

1. Compute basic and diluted EPS for 2014, assuming that no additional shares of common stock were issued during the year.
2. Compute basic and diluted EPS, assuming that the 10-year bonds were converted on July 1, 2014, and that net income for the year was \$1,326,700 (reflects reduction in interest due to bond conversion).

Problem 18-46
LO2, LO3, LO4, LO5, LO6, LO8

Earnings per Share—Multiple Convertible Securities

Kishkumen Company had the following capital structure at December 31, 2013 and 2014:

	2014	2013
Shares of stock outstanding:		
Common stock	776,490	550,000
\$7 convertible preferred stock	11,000	24,000
Bonds outstanding:		
$7\frac{1}{4}$%, 10-year convertible bonds	\$1,650,000	\$2,200,000

The following additional information is available.

(a) The conversion terms of the preferred stock and bonds at January 1, 2014, were as follows: Preferred stock, five shares of common for each share of preferred; convertible bonds, 38 shares of common for each \$1,000 bond. These terms are to be adjusted for any issued stock dividends or stock splits.

(b) On May 1, 2014, Kishkumen sold an additional 70,000 shares of common stock, and on August 1, 2014, a 10% stock dividend on common shares was declared.

(c) On October 1, 2014, 13,000 shares of preferred stock were converted to 71,500 shares of common stock (5.5 shares common for each share of preferred). The preferred stock was issued at $100 par in 2010.
(d) On December 1, 2014, 25% of the convertible bonds were converted (41.8 shares of common for each bond converted). The bonds were issued at par in 2013.
(e) On December 31, 2014, Kishkumen declared and paid a $7-per-share dividend on outstanding preferred stock. Income for the year was $2,300,000.
(f) Stock options (issued and unexercised) to purchase 70,000 shares of common stock at $30 per share were outstanding at the beginning of 2014. Average market price for 2014 was $46.36. The number of shares was adjusted to 77,000 and the exercise price was adjusted to $27.27 in response to the 10% stock dividend.
(g) Stock warrants to purchase 50,000 shares of common stock at $45 per share were initially attached to the preferred stock. This was adjusted to 55,000 shares at $40.91 per share in response to the 10% stock dividend. The warrants expire on December 31, 2018, and were outstanding at December 31, 2014.
(h) The effective tax rate was 30% for both years.
(i) On February 1, 2015, before the 2014 financial statements were issued, Kishkumen split its common stock 2 for 1.

Instructions: For the year ended December 31, 2014, compute basic and diluted EPS.

CASES

Discussion Case 18-47

But Why Is EPS Different if Income Is the Same?

Fredrica Brown has $200,000 that she plans to invest in growth stocks. She has narrowed her choices to two companies in the same industry, White Inc. and Adam Inc. Each company has a documented history of growth and an established, strong position within the industry. Last year, each company reported net income of $10 million and a return on owners' investment of 17%; however, White reported EPS of $1.32, and Adam reported EPS of $2.75.

Fredrica requests that you explain why the EPS differs when other measures of activity and profitability are similar. What factors contribute to and limit the comparability of these data?

Discussion Case 18-48

But Let's Maintain Earnings per Share

On January 1, 2011, Farnsworth Company had 1,000,000 shares of common stock and 100,000 shares of $8 cumulative preferred stock issued and outstanding. A principal goal of Farnsworth's management is to maintain or increase EPS.

On January 1, 2012, Farnsworth Company retired 50,000 shares of the preferred stock with excess cash and additional funds provided from the sale of a subsidiary.

At the beginning of 2013, the company borrowed $5,000,000 at 10% and used the proceeds to retire 200,000 shares of common stock. Operating income, before interest and income taxes (income tax rate is 30%), is as follows:

	2013	2012	2011
Operating income	$6,500,000	$7,000,000	$7,500,000

Did Farnsworth Company maintain its EPS even though income declined? What was the impact of the preferred and common stock transactions on EPS?

Discussion Case 18-49

How Does a Complex Capital Structure Affect EPS?

Big Horn Construction Company has gradually grown in size since its inception in 1919. The third generation of Jensens who now manage the enterprise are considering selling a large block of stock to raise capital for new equipment purchases and to help finance several big projects. The Jensens are concerned about how the EPS information should be presented on the income statement and have many questions concerning the nature of EPS.

1. Discuss the EPS presentation that would be required if Big Horn Construction has (a) a simple capital structure or (b) a complex capital structure. What factors determine whether a capital structure is simple or complex?
2. Assume that Big Horn Construction Company has a complex capital structure. Discuss the effect, if any, of each of the following transactions on the computation of EPS.
   (a) The firm acquires some of its outstanding common stock to hold as treasury stock.
   (b) The firm pays a dividend of $0.50 per common stock share.
   (c) The firm declares a dividend of $0.75 per share on cumulative preferred stock.
   (d) A 3-for-1 common stock split occurs during the year.
   (e) Retained earnings are appropriated for a disputed construction contract that may be litigated.

Discussion Case 18-50

What Is Dilution?

You have just finished presenting a summary of this year's financial results to the board of directors. Included in your presentation was an income statement including both basic and diluted EPS figures. One of the board members comments that he understands basic EPS but has no clue as to what diluted EPS is referring to. He actually wondered aloud whether this diluted EPS computation was part of some "full-employment for accountants" project. He asks you to explain the concept of dilution and what diluted EPS is trying to measure.

Case 18-51

Deciphering Financial Statements (The Walt Disney Company)

Review the information relating to EPS found in **The Walt Disney Company**'s 2009 income statement and notes to the financial statements on the Internet.

Answer the following questions.

1. Using the information provided on the face of the income statement relating to net income and average number of shares outstanding, verify Disney's reported basic EPS figure.
2. From the statement of cash flows, we see that Disney paid dividends of $648 million in 2009. Using the average number of Disney common shares outstanding from the EPS computation in (1), compute the approximate dividends paid per share. Using this number, compute the dividend payout ratio for Disney. (*Note*: Dividend payout ratio is dividends per share divided by earnings per share.) Comment on your results.
3. Can you determine from the notes Disney has effected any stock splits recently. How do stock splits affect the presentation of the prior year's information?

Case 18-52

Writing Assignment (U.S. GAAP and IFRS)

The project for developing the current standards for earnings per share reporting was the first major project in which the FASB and the IASB collaborated in a formal way. Of course, now the FASB and the IASB have a very formal joint program to increase the international harmonization of accounting standards.

In two pages or less, address the following question: Why is it important for the FASB to work with the IASB to harmonize international accounting standards?

Case 18-53

Ethical Dilemma (Are there other options?)

After computing the current period's basic and diluted EPS figures, you notice that while basic EPS continues its upward trend, diluted EPS has dropped slightly. In discussions with your manager regarding reasons for the decline, you identify numerous potentially dilutive securities that were considered in computing diluted EPS. Because the company has multiple dilutive securities, those securities were considered in turn, beginning with the convertible security that had the least favorable impact on EPS. As a result of considering the potentially dilutive securities in this order, convertible bonds that were potentially dilutive were not included in the computations because they became antidilutive after considering the effect of other convertible securities.

Your manager takes the position that if a security is dilutive when compared to basic EPS, then it should be included in the diluted EPS computations. He maintains that each dilutive security should be considered independently of the others. Including these convertible bonds in the diluted EPS computations would result in maintaining an upward trend for diluted EPS.

1. Is there merit to your manager's position? That is, does the approach he is advocating make some sense?
2. Do the accounting standards allow for this flexibility in interpretation?
3. Prepare your defense for when your manager insists that diluted EPS be computed using his approach. What will you say to convince him that his approach is not acceptable?

Case 18-54

Cumulative Spreadsheet Analysis

This assignment is an exercise in computing diluted EPS. In prior years, Skywalker has had a simple capital structure. That may change in 2014; Skywalker is considering the following actions at the beginning of 2014.

- Issue options granting top-level managers the opportunity to purchase a total of 2,000,000 shares of Skywalker common stock for $25 per share.
- Exchange $600 million in existing long-term debt (with an interest rate of 8%) for $600 million in 8% convertible bonds (600,000 bonds, each with a $1,000 face value).

Without these changes, Skywalker expects to have net income of $15,890,000 in 2014; the net income forecast reflects the expectation that Skywalker will be subject to a 33% tax rate in 2014. (*Note*: This $15,890,000 forecasted net income for 2014 comes from the assumptions outlined in Chapter 13; all numbers in Chapter 13 are in millions of dollars.) As of the end of 2013, Skywalker had 10,000,000 common shares outstanding.

Using these data, construct a spreadsheet to answer the following questions.

1. What is Skywalker's basic EPS expected to be in 2014?
2. What is Skywalker's diluted EPS expected to be in 2014 if the options and convertible bonds are issued on January 1, 2014, the average stock price is expected to be $20 per share for 2014, and each bond is convertible into 40 shares of common stock?
3. What is Skywalker's diluted EPS expected to be in 2014 if the options and convertible bonds are issued on January 1, 2014, the average stock price is expected to be $40 per share during 2014, and each bond is convertible into 35 shares of common stock?
4. Assuming that Skywalker issues the options and convertible bonds on January 1, 2014, complete the following table.

Diluted Earnings per Share in 2014

		Forecasted Average Market Price		
		$20	**$30**	**$40**
Common	20			
Shares	35			
Per bond	40			

P4 OTHER DIMENSIONS OF FINANCIAL REPORTING

CHAPTER 19 Derivatives, Contingencies, Business Segments, and Interim Reports

LEARNING OBJECTIVES

DERIVATIVES

1. Understand the business and accounting concepts connected with derivatives and hedging activities.
2. Identify the different types of risk faced by a business.
3. Describe the characteristics of the following types of derivatives: swaps, forwards, futures, and options.
4. Define *hedging*, and outline the difference between a fair value hedge and a cash flow hedge.
5. Account for a variety of different derivatives and for hedging relationships.

CONTINGENCIES

6. Apply the accounting rules for contingent items to the areas of lawsuits and environmental liabilities.

SEGMENT REPORTING

7. Prepare the necessary supplemental disclosures of financial information by product line and by geographic area.

INTERIM REPORTING

8. Recognize the importance of interim reports, and outline the difficulties encountered when preparing those reports.

This chapter is a little different from the other chapters in the text. The chapter is composed of four modules: derivatives, contingencies, segment reporting, and interim reporting. Each of the modules is self-contained and can be studied independently. So do as much or as little of this chapter as your instructor thinks best. Of course, you are free to sneak a look at any of the modules that your instructor does not assign.

AP Photo/Al Behrman

DERIVATIVES

Procter & Gamble (P&G) is a sophisticated marketer of consumer products such as Tide®, Pampers®, Folgers®, and Crest®. Apparently this sophistication hasn't always extended to P&G's understanding of derivative financial instruments. In November 1993, P&G agreed to buy a complex derivative that would give the company lower current interest payments in exchange for an agreement to make higher payments in the future depending on the future level of interest rates.[1] When interest rates increased after the derivative was purchased, P&G learned a rough lesson relative to the risk associated with speculative derivatives. After the smoke had cleared, the increased interest payments from the derivative arrangement had cost P&G $195.5 million. A note written by former P&G chairman Edwin Artzt after this fiasco said that the officials who bought the derivative were like "farm boys at a country carnival."[2]

FYI

The largest part of Enron's business before its bankruptcy in 2001 was the trading of derivative contracts. When the scandals swirling around Enron caused the company to lose credibility with its customers, its derivative trading activity plummeted literally overnight.

Procter & Gamble is just one in a long list of organizations that lost large amounts of money by trading in derivatives: **Dell Computer**, **Orange County**, **Fannie Mae**, and on and on. The combination of the complexity of derivatives, which are frequently misunderstood even by corporate treasurers and portfolio managers, and the lack of disclosure about derivatives created a dangerous environment in which users of financial statements could be completely unaware of huge company risks. This is exactly the type of situation the SEC was created to address. Accordingly, in recent years the FASB, with the blessing and prodding of the SEC, has significantly improved the accounting for and disclosure of derivative financial instruments. However, don't get the impression that improved accounting disclosure has led to complete understanding of derivatives. Even with this improved accounting, overly aggressive use of derivatives contributed to the worldwide financial institution meltdown in the second half of 2008.

The first module in this chapter explains the general nature of derivatives, the types of risk companies face and how different types of derivatives can be used to hedge those risks, and the standards governing the accounting for derivatives.

[1] Kelley Holland, Linda Himelstein, and Zachary Schiller, "The Bankers Trust Tapes," *Business Week*, October 16, 1995, p. 106.

[2] Carol J. Loomis, "Like Farm Boys at a Country Carnival," *Fortune*, November 27, 1995, p. 34.

Simple Example of a Derivative

1 **Understand the business and accounting concepts connected with derivatives and hedging activities.**

WHY **Let's be honest—most of us don't even know what a derivative is. Before we can account for derivatives, we need to know what they are and what business purpose they serve.**

HOW **A derivative is a financial instrument or other contract that derives its value from the movement of prices, interest rates, or exchange rates associated with an underlying item. For example, an option to buy a piece of land is a derivative. The option itself increases in value as the piece of land increases in value. Uncertainty about the future fair value of assets and liabilities or about future cash flows exposes firms to risk. One way to manage the risk associated with fair value and cash flow fluctuations is through the use of derivatives.**

Assume that you are an employee of Nauvoo Software Solutions. On October 1, 2013, you purchase 100 shares of stock in the company at the market price of $50 per share, making the total purchase price $5,000. If you were to prepare a personal balance sheet, how would you report these shares? Obviously, the 100 shares of Nauvoo stock would be reported as a $5,000 asset.

Now assume that you are nervous about possible price fluctuations in the stock. On January 1, 2014, you need to make a college tuition payment of $5,000 on behalf of your daughter, and you must make certain that you have $5,000 on that date. You can't sell the Nauvoo shares now (and put the $5,000 cash under your mattress) because your employment contract states that any shares you purchase from the company must be held for at least three months before you can sell them. Your risk management dilemma is as follows: You must hold the Nauvoo shares as an asset for the next three months, but a downward movement in the stock price between now and January 1 would be disastrous for you.

The answer to your problem is the following agreement: If the price of Nauvoo stock is above $50 per share on January 1, you agree to pay a cash amount equal to that excess (multiplied by 100 shares) to John Bennett, a local stock speculator. If the price of Nauvoo stock goes below $50, John Bennett agrees to pay you a cash amount equal to the deficit (multiplied by 100 shares). As detailed later in the chapter, the broad name given to agreements such as this is a *derivative*. A derivative is a financial instrument or other contract that derives its value from the movement of the price, foreign exchange rate, or interest rate on some other underlying asset or financial instrument.

How does this derivative agreement solve your risk management dilemma? Look at the following chart:

	Stock Price on January 1		
	$45	**$50**	**$55**
Value of shares	$4,500	$5,000	$5,500
Receipt from (payment to) Bennett	500	0	(500)
Net amount	$5,000	$5,000	$5,000

Because of the structure of the agreement, you wind up with $5,000 on January 1 no matter what happens to the price of Nauvoo stock between now and then. After the fact, a derivative contract is sometimes a good deal and sometimes a bad one. If the price actually increases to $55, it would have been better had you not entered into the agreement. Because of the absolute necessity of having $5,000 on January 1, however, you are willing to trade off any stock profits you might make for the right to receive payments that will reimburse your stock losses.[3]

> **FYI**
>
> In the past, a derivative instrument such as this was said to have "off-balance-sheet risk" because it could fluctuate in value after the initial agreement date, but these fluctuations would not be reflected in the balance sheet. As explained later, the accounting standards have been changed to bring these fluctuations onto the balance sheet.

How much money will change hands between you and John Bennett on October 1, the day you enter into the derivative contract? In other words, do you have to pay John Bennett anything up front to get him to sign the agreement, or does he have to pay you? The valuation of derivatives is way beyond the scope of this book, but two of the factors that would be considered are the expected return on Nauvoo stock over the 3-month period (on average, stock prices move up 3% or 4% per quarter) and the difference in the way you and John Bennett view risk. If you are very nervous about risk and John Bennett is not, he has the advantage in the bargaining and may be able to extract an up-front payment from you. For simplicity, the valuation assumptions made in this chapter will be very basic; for more advanced treatment you will need to talk to your finance professor. The simplest assumptions are that you and John Bennett have the same risk preferences and that the $50 price of the stock on October 1 is equal to the expected price on January 1. If these two assumptions hold, the money exchanged at the signing of the agreement on October 1 is $0 because the probability of your being required to make a payment to Bennett on January 1 is equal to the probability that he will have to make a payment to you.

Another way to describe the arrangement between you and John Bennett is as follows: You have agreed, three months in advance, to sell 100 shares of Nauvoo stock to John Bennett at a price of $50 per share. A forward sale such as this is similar to what the finance people call a *short sale.* To demonstrate that a forward sale is equivalent to the original exchange of cash payments you and John Bennett agreed to, consider the following:

> If the shares are worth, say, $5,500 on January 1, John Bennett will pay you $5,000 for the shares and then be able to immediately sell them for $5,500, netting a cash increase of $500. At the same time, you will have received $5,000, which is $500 less than you would have received if you had simply sold the shares in the market. In place of executing the forward sale, the same cash flow effects are achieved if you simply give John Bennett $500 in cash.

The same analysis could be done to show that requiring John Bennett to buy the shares for $5,000 when they are worth just $4,500 is equivalent to a simple cash transfer of $500 from John Bennett to you. A general characteristic of derivative arrangements is that although they are phrased in terms of the exchange of some underlying item (shares of stock, interest payments, pounds of orange juice concentrate, Japanese yen), they are often settled by a simple exchange of cash.

[3] Another question is why John Bennett, the speculator, would be willing to enter into this agreement. An arrangement such as this is one way for a speculator to make money if a price or rate moves in the direction he or she thinks it will. In this case, John Bennett's valuation analysis has led him to believe that the price of Nauvoo stock will move up in the next three months, and the derivative is a way for Bennett to make money if his analysis is correct.

Now, let's talk about some accounting. What journal entry would you be required to make to recognize the signing of the agreement on October 1? The answer is that you make no journal entry. No cash changes hands; you and John Bennett have merely exchanged promises about some future action. This type of contract is called an executory contract and is very common in business. Another example of an executory contract is an operating lease, a promise to make payments in the future in exchange for the promise to receive the use of an asset in the future. Like an operating lease, the derivative contract is "off balance sheet" on the day it is signed.

On December 31, 2013, the price of Nauvoo stock is $47 per share, making your investment in Nauvoo shares worth $4,700 ($47 × 100). The payment exchange with John Bennett is to be made on the following day. With the price per share at $47, it appears that you will receive a payment from Bennett of $300 [($50 − $47) × 100]. How should this information be reflected in the Assets section of your December 31, 2013, balance sheet? Four possibilities are outlined below.

	Option 1	Option 2	Option 3	Option 4
Nauvoo stock	$5,000	$4,700	$5,000	$4,700
Derivative payment receivable	$0	$0	$300	$300
Valuation of stock	Cost	Fair value	Cost	Fair value
Recognition of derivative receivable?	No	No	Yes	Yes

Option 4 provides the best information because it reports the fair value of both the stock investment and the derivative payment receivable. Historically, the generally accepted treatment in the United States was Option 2, with some added disclosure about the derivative agreement.[4] The FASB has now adopted a standard that results in Option 4, the recognition of the fair value of derivatives in the financial statements.[5]

The remainder of this module details how derivatives are used to hedge risk and how information about derivatives should be reported in the financial statements.

Types of Risk

2 Identify the different types of risk faced by a business.

WHY **Because the use of derivatives helps companies to manage their risks, an important element in understanding derivatives is understanding the risks they help to manage.**

HOW **Four important risks faced by businesses are price risk (uncertainty about the future price of an asset), credit risk (uncertainty over whether other people or companies will do what they have agreed to do), interest rate risk (uncertainty about future interest rates), and exchange risk (uncertainty about future foreign exchange rates).**

Most firms use derivatives as a tool for managing risk. Accordingly, before discussing the different types of derivatives, we will briefly outline the various types of risk.

[4] Pre-Codification *Statement of Financial Accounting Standards No. 119*, "Disclosure about Derivative Financial Instruments and Fair Value of Financial Instruments" (Norwalk, CT: Financial Accounting Standards Board, 1994).
[5] FASB ASC Topic 815 (Derivatives and Hedging).

Price Risk

Price risk is the uncertainty about the future price of an asset. It was uncertainty about the future price of Nauvoo Software Solutions stock that prompted the derivative contract in the preceding example. Firms can be exposed to price risk with existing assets, such as financial securities or inventory, or with assets to be acquired in the future, such as equipment to be purchased next month.

Credit Risk

Credit risk is the uncertainty that the party on the other side of an agreement will abide by the terms of the agreement. The most common example of credit risk is the uncertainty over whether a credit customer will ultimately pay his or her account. Banks are in the business of properly evaluating credit risk, and the success or failure of a bank depends largely on how good the bank's credit analysts are at identifying who will repay a loan and who won't. Credit risk analysis is a specialized skill, and many retail companies, through the acceptance of credit card purchases, have contracted their credit risk analysis to **Visa**, **MasterCard**, **Discover**, or **American Express**. In the Nauvoo stock and derivative contract example, the credit risk is the possibility that John Bennett, the party on the other side of the agreement, will not make the payments required under the agreement.

Interest Rate Risk

Interest rate risk is the uncertainty about future interest rates and their impact on future cash flows as well as on the fair value of existing assets and liabilities. A variable-rate mortgage is a good illustration of one type of interest rate risk. The periodic interest payments on the variable-rate mortgage will fluctuate in the future, depending on the level of future interest rates. A fixed-rate mortgage is a good example of another type of interest rate risk. If interest rates decrease, the present value of future fixed payments to be made under a fixed-rate mortgage will increase. Thus, the fair value of the mortgage liability increases; this is the downside of obligating yourself to a fixed stream of interest payments when there is a possibility that interest rates may go down in the future. In summary, interest rate risk exposes a firm to uncertainty about future cash flows as well as uncertainty about the fair value of assets and liabilities that have values tied to the level of interest rates.

Exchange Rate Risk

Exchange rate risk is the uncertainty about future U.S. dollar cash flows arising when assets and liabilities are denominated in a foreign currency. For example, many compensation packages for U.S. citizens working in foreign countries include an end-of-contract bonus payment if the employee sticks it out and stays on the foreign assignment for the entire length of the contract. If this bonus is denominated in the currency of the foreign country, the employee knows with certainty the future amount of his or her foreign currency bonus, but the U.S. dollar value bonus depends on the exchange rate prevailing when the bonus is received. U.S. multinational firms face the same risk when sales, purchases, loans, and investments are denominated in foreign currencies.

FYI

Other types of risk include liquidity risk, theft risk, competitive risk, and business cycle risk. See Johnson and Swieringa, "Derivatives, Hedging and Comprehensive Income," *Accounting Horizons*, December 1996, p. 109.

Some degree of risk is an unwanted but common side effect of doing business. For example, the variation in the cost of jet fuel is a nuisance and a worry to the major airlines. Similarly, fluctuations in the U.S. dollar/Japanese yen exchange rate wreak havoc on the competitive plans of both U.S. and Japanese car manufacturers. On the other hand, managing risk is the very reason for the existence of some businesses. Much of the revenue generated by a bank arises because the bank has expertise in evaluating and managing credit, interest rate, and exchange rate risk. The following sections discuss derivatives and hedging from the standpoint of a manufacturing, retailing, or service firm that is trying to use these techniques to reduce the risks that arise as part of doing business. Coverage of the more complicated risk management strategies of banks and financial institutions is outside the scope of this text.

Types of Derivatives

3 Describe the characteristics of the following types of derivatives: swaps, forwards, futures, and options.

WHY **Understanding the use of and accounting for derivatives requires an understanding of the common types of derivatives: swaps, forwards, futures, and options.**

HOW **A swap is an agreement to exchange payments in the future, usually a fixed payment for a variable payment, or vice versa. A forward is an agreement to exchange an item at a set date in the future at a price that is set now. A future is quite similar to a forward except that the terms of futures contracts are standardized and these contracts are traded in markets. An option is the right, but not the obligation, to buy or sell an asset at a specified price in the future.**

Recall that a derivative is a financial instrument or other contract that derives its value from the movement of the price, exchange rate, or interest rate on some other underlying asset or financial instrument. In addition, a derivative does not require a firm to take delivery or make delivery of the underlying asset or financial instrument; in situations in which actual delivery is required, the underlying item can easily be converted into cash.[6] For example, you may have heard about the buying and selling of pork belly futures. These contracts (futures contracts are explained later) can qualify as derivatives because, fortunately, they do not require the holder to either deliver or take delivery of a truckload of pork bellies. Instead, these contracts are settled by cash payments, much as the Nauvoo stock derivative contract was settled, not with the delivery of any shares of stock, but by a cash payment.

The most common types of derivatives are swaps, forwards, futures, and options. Each type is explained.

Swap

A swap is a contract in which two parties agree to exchange payments in the future based on the movement of some agreed-upon price or rate. A common type of swap is an interest rate swap. In an interest rate swap, two parties agree to exchange future interest payments on a given loan amount; usually, one set of interest payments is based on a fixed interest rate and the other is based on a variable interest rate. To illustrate,

[6] FASB ASC paragraph 815-10-15-83.

assume that Pratt Company has a good working relationship with a bank that issues only variable-rate loans. Pratt takes advantage of its relationship at the bank and on January 1, 2013, receives a 2-year, $100,000 loan, with interest payments occurring at the end of each year. The interest rate for the first year is the prevailing market rate of 10%, and the rate in the second year will be equal to the market interest rate on January 1 of that year. Pratt is reluctant to bear the risk associated with the uncertainty about what the interest payment in the second year will be. So Pratt enters into an interest rate swap agreement with another party (not the bank) whereby Pratt agrees to pay a fixed interest rate of 10% on the $100,000 loan amount to that party in exchange for receiving from that party a variable amount based on the prevailing market rate multiplied by $100,000. This is called a *pay-fixed, receive-variable swap*.

Instead of exchanging the entire amount of the interest payments called for under the swap contract, Pratt would probably settle the agreement by exchanging a small cash payment, depending on what has happened to interest rates. Accordingly, Pratt will receive an amount equal to [$100,000 × (Jan. 1, 2014, interest rate − 10%)] if the January 1, 2014, interest rate is more than 10% and will pay the same amount if the rate is less than 10%. The interest swap payment will be made in 2014. To see the impact of this interest rate swap, consider the following table:

	Interest Rate on January 1, 2014		
	7%	10%	13%
Variable-rate interest payment in 2014	$ (7,000)	$(10,000)	$(13,000)
Receipt (payment) for interest rate swap	(3,000)	0	3,000
Net interest payment in 2014	$(10,000)	$(10,000)	$(10,000)

The interest rate swap agreement has changed Pratt's uncertain future interest payment into a payment of $10,000 no matter what the prevailing interest rates are in 2014. Why didn't Pratt just go out and get a fixed-rate loan in the first place? Sometimes, in this case because of Pratt's special relationship with the bank, it is easier to get one type of loan or investment security than another. A derivative instrument can effectively change the loan that you got into the loan that you want.

Forwards

A forward contract is an agreement between two parties to exchange a specified amount of a commodity, security, or foreign currency at a specified date in the future with the price or exchange rate being set now. To illustrate, assume that on November 1, 2013, Clayton Company sold machine parts to Maruta Company for ¥30,000,000 to be received on January 1, 2014. The current exchange rate is ¥120 = $1. To ensure the dollar amount that will be received, Clayton enters into a forward contract with a large bank, agreeing that on January 1 Clayton will deliver ¥30,000,000 to the bank and the bank will give U.S. dollars in exchange at the rate of ¥120 = $1, or $250,000 (¥30,000,000/¥120 per $1). This forward contract guarantees

CAUTION

Don't forget that one of the characteristics of a derivative, whether it relates to yen, wheat, pork bellies, or stock index levels, is that it can be, and usually is, settled in the end with a cash payment instead of with actual delivery of the underlying item.

the U.S. dollar amount that Clayton will receive from the receivable denominated in Japanese yen.

Operationally, this forward contract would usually be settled as follows. Given the exchange rate on January 1, 2014, if ¥30,000,000 is worth less than $250,000, the bank will pay Clayton the difference in cash (U.S. dollars). If ¥30,000,000 is worth more than $250,000, Clayton pays the difference to the bank in cash. Therefore, no yen need be delivered as part of the contract; the contract is settled with a U.S. dollar cash payment.

The impact of the forward exchange contract is shown in the following table:

	Exchange Rate on January 1		
	¥118 = $1	**¥120 = $1**	**¥122 = $1**
Value of ¥30,000,000	$254,237	$250,000	$245,902
Clayton receipt (payment) to settle forward contract	(4,237)	0	4,098
Net U.S. dollar receipt by Clayton	$250,000	$250,000	$250,000

If Clayton is nervous about exchange rate changes, why agree to denominating the transaction in Japanese yen in the first place? The answer is that some types of transactions and some products are routinely negotiated in terms of a certain currency. For example, almost all crude oil sales are denominated in U.S. dollars, regardless of the countries of the companies conducting the transaction. In addition, if denominating a sale in a certain currency will make the customer feel more comfortable, companies are likely to follow the policy that "the customer is always right."

In this simple example, the forward exchange rate of ¥120 = $1 is equal to the prevailing exchange rate, called the spot rate, on the date the forward contract is signed. Usually, the forward rate would differ from the spot rate in order to compensate the bank for providing this risk-reduction service to Clayton. For example, a forward rate of ¥121 = $1 means that the bank would receive cash payments from Clayton when the

STOP&THINK

What type of credit risk is associated with a forward contract?

a) The risk that the party required to make the settlement payment will refuse to pay
b) The risk that the price, interest rate, or exchange rate will increase
c) The risk that the price, interest rate, or exchange rate will decrease
d) The risk that overall company net income will decrease between now and the contract settlement date

F. Schussler/PhotoLink/Photodisc/Getty Images

A wheat futures contract can protect the farmer from wide fluctuations in wheat prices.

dollar value of ¥30,000,000 was higher than $247,934 (¥30,000,000/¥121 per $1). With this lower threshold (instead of $250,000), it would be more likely that the bank would receive cash from Clayton to settle the forward contract. In this chapter, we will make the simplifying assumption that spot rates and forward rates are equal to one another.

Futures

A futures contract is a contract, traded on an exchange, that allows a company to buy or sell a specified quantity of a commodity or a financial security at a specified price on a specified future date. A futures contract is very similar to a forward contract with the difference being that a forward contract is a private contract negotiated between two parties, whereas a futures contract is a standardized contract that is sponsored by a trading exchange and can be traded among different parties many times in a single day. So, with a forward contract, you know the party with whom you will be exchanging cash to settle the contract; with a futures contract, all these cash settlements are handled through the exchange and you never know, or care, who is on the other side of the contract.

As an example of the use of a futures contract, assume that Hyrum Bakery uses 1,000 bushels of wheat every month. On December 1, 2013, Hyrum decides to protect itself against price movements for its January 1, 2014, wheat purchase because long-term spring weather forecasts often come out in December, causing wide fluctuations in wheat prices. To protect against these fluctuations, Hyrum buys a futures contract on December 1 that obligates it to purchase 1,000 bushels of wheat on January 1, 2014, at a price of $4 per bushel (which is also the prevailing price of wheat on December 1). This is a standardized exchange-traded futures contract, so Hyrum has no idea who is on the other side of the agreement; that is, Hyrum doesn't know who is promising to deliver the wheat.

FYI

The difference between a *forward contract* and a *futures contract* is similar to the difference between investing as a partner in a company and buying stock in a company. When you invest, you personally negotiate the amount you will invest and your percentage ownership, and you know who sold you the investment. When you buy stock, you buy a standardized chunk of a company and because the shares are purchased through an exchange, you have no idea who owned the shares before you bought them.

FYI

Hedging future purchases is where derivative use sometimes is abused. The people in the corporate finance office start to think that they can forecast changes in wheat prices, so they buy forward contracts far in excess of that needed to hedge future wheat purchases. These extra contracts are speculations on the movement of wheat prices, and they expose the company to substantial speculative risk.

As with other derivatives, a wheat futures contract is usually settled by a cash payment at the end of the contract instead of by actual delivery of the wheat. Settlement of Hyrum's futures contract would be as follows. If the price of wheat is less than $4 per bushel on January 1, Hyrum will make a cash payment of that difference, multiplied by 1,000 bushels. If the price of wheat is more than $4 per bushel on January 1, Hyrum will receive a cash payment equal to that difference multiplied by 1,000 bushels.[7] The effect of the futures contract is illustrated in the table shown on page 19-11.

[7] For exchange-traded futures contracts, cash settlements usually are not deferred until the end of the contract but occur at the end of every day based on price movements during that day.

	Wheat Price on January 1		
	$3.80	$4.00	$4.20
Cost to purchase 1,000 bushels	$(3,800)	$(4,000)	$(4,200)
Hyrum receipt (payment) to settle futures contract	(200)	0	200
Net cost of January wheat	$(4,000)	$(4,000)	$(4,000)

Option

An option is a contract giving the owner the right, but not the obligation, to buy or sell an asset at a specified price any time during a specified period in the future. Options come in two general types: call options and put options. A call option gives the owner the right to buy an asset at a specified price, and a put option gives the owner the right to sell an asset at a specified price. In exchange for the rights inherent in the option, the owner of the option pays an amount in advance to the party on the other side of the transaction, who is called the *writer of the option*. Like a futures contract, many options are standardized contracts that are traded on organized exchanges.

An option differs from the derivative instruments discussed previously because it protects the owner against unfavorable movements in prices or rates while allowing the owner to benefit from favorable movements. With the swaps, forwards, and futures discussed earlier, the protection from unfavorable movements was "paid for" by sacrificing the benefits from favorable movements. With an option, the protection is "paid for" with an up-front cash payment when the option is purchased.

Because of the asymmetrical nature of options, the owner of an option and the writer of an option are in very different positions. With a call option, for example, the owner of the option can buy the designated asset at a fixed price no matter how high the market price of the asset goes. If the market price of the asset decreases, the option owner can just throw the option away because it is cheaper to buy the asset at the low market price. So, the maximum amount that the owner of an option can lose is the price paid to buy the option. On the other side of the transaction, the writer of the option has no such downside protection. No matter how high market prices increase, the writer of a call option must sell the asset at the fixed option price. So, there is no limit to the amount that a call option writer can lose.[8] Because this discussion of derivative instruments focuses on the use of derivatives for risk management and risk reduction, only buyers of options will be considered.

To illustrate the use of options in managing risk, assume that, on October 1, 2013, Woodruff Company decides that it will need to purchase 1,000 ounces of gold for use in its computer chip manufacturing process in January 2014. Gold is selling for $1,100 per ounce on October 1, 2013. For cash flow reasons, Woodruff plans to delay the purchase of the gold until January 1, 2014, and is concerned about potential increases in the market price of gold between October 1, 2013, and January 1, 2014.

To reduce the price risk associated with the gold, Woodruff enters into a call option contract on October 1. The contract gives Woodruff the right, but not the obligation, to purchase 1,000 ounces of gold at a price of $1,100 per ounce. The option period extends

[8] The losses of the writer of a put option are limited to the full amount of the option price. Even if the asset becomes completely worthless, the put option writer must buy it at the option price.

to January 1, 2014, and Woodruff has to pay $20,000 to buy this option.[9] In exchange for this $20,000 payment, the option arrangement protects Woodruff from unfavorable movements in the price of gold but also allows Woodruff to benefit from favorable movements. This can be seen from the following table:

	Gold Price (per ounce) on January 1		
	$1,000	**$1,100**	**$1,200**
Cost of 1,000 ounces of gold if			
• Buy gold at January 1 price	$1,000,000	$1,100,000	$1,200,000
• Exercise option	$1,100,000	$1,100,000	$1,100,000
Will option be exercised?	No	Same either way	Yes
Cost of gold	$1,000,000	$1,100,000	$1,100,000

! CAUTION

Remember that an option is a right, not an obligation. The owner of the option can always throw it away and forget the whole deal.

The existence of the option contract means that Woodruff will pay no more than $1,100,000 for the gold. Because the option is a right and not an obligation, Woodruff can ignore it, as in the preceding case in which the January 1 price of gold is $1,000 per ounce, and just buy gold at the market price prevailing on January 1. Remember that this ability to enjoy protection from unfavorable price changes but to benefit from favorable price changes was not free; it cost Woodruff $20,000 at the beginning of the option period. As with the other derivative instruments, this option can be settled on January 1 by a direct cash payment from the option writer to Woodruff in place of the actual delivery of the gold. If the cost of 1,000 ounces of gold is more than $1,100,000 on January 1, the option writer pays Woodruff the difference.

Types of Hedging Activities

4 Define *hedging*, and outline the difference between a fair value hedge and a cash flow hedge.

WHY **Hedging is the structuring of transactions to reduce risk. Because derivatives are often used as hedges, an understanding of derivative accounting requires an understanding of hedging.**

HOW **A business can carefully structure its transactions to hedge, or partially offset, many of its risks. Derivatives can be used as fair value hedges (where the change in the fair value of the derivative offsets changes in fair values of assets or liabilities) and cash flow hedges (where cash flows from the derivative offset variability in the cash flows from forecasted transactions).**

[9] Computation of option values was outlined in Chapter 13, but a detailed treatment is beyond the scope of this text. Briefly, the price that must be paid to purchase a call option is higher when the option exercise price is lower, when the length of the option is longer, and when the movement of the price of the underlying asset (gold in this example) is more volatile.

The preceding illustrations of the different types of derivatives—swaps, forwards, futures, and options—also illustrated how these derivatives are used in hedging activities. Broadly defined, hedging is the structuring of transactions to reduce risk. Hedging occurs naturally as part of many business activities, examples of which follow.

- In the retail sale of gasoline, one risk to the gasoline retailer is that movement in worldwide oil prices will cause variation in the cost to purchase gasoline. This "cost of goods sold" risk is partially offset by the fact that the retail selling price of gasoline also goes up when oil prices rise. So, the increase in the cost is offset by the increase in the selling price.
- Banks are vulnerable to interest rate increases because this increases the amount they must pay to get the use of depositors' money. However, this risk is hedged because an interest rate increase also allows a bank to raise the rates it charges on its loans.
- Multinational companies can be impacted by changes in exchange rates. If a U.S. multinational has a subsidiary in France, a decline in the value of the euro will cause the dollar value of the subsidiary's euro-denominated assets to decline. This loss is partially offset, however, because the dollar value of the subsidiary's euro-denominated liabilities will also decline.

Derivatives can be used in hedging activities through the acquisition of a derivative with the characteristic that changes in the value of the derivative are expected to offset changes in the value of the item being hedged. Let's review how derivatives were used as hedges in each of the derivative illustrations given in the preceding section.

- *Pratt swap.* The interest rate swap was structured to offset changes in the variable-rate interest payments.
- *Clayton forward.* The forward currency contract was entered into to offset changes in the dollar value of the receivable denominated in Japanese yen.
- *Hyrum future.* The wheat futures contract was acquired to offset movements in the expected purchase price of the following month's supply of wheat.
- *Woodruff option.* The gold call option was purchased to offset the negative impact on the cost of gold for production purposes of changes in the market price of gold.

The FASB has defined two of the broad categories of hedging activities as follows:[10]

- *Fair value hedges.* A fair value hedge is a derivative that offsets, at least partially, the change in the fair value of an asset or a liability. A derivative can also serve as a hedge of the fair value of firm commitments even though the assets and liabilities associated with a firm commitment are not recognized until the actual transaction date.
- *Cash flow hedges.* A cash flow hedge is a derivative that offsets, at least partially, the variability in cash flows from forecasted transactions that are probable.

FYI

Historically, cash flow hedges have been very controversial. Firms have claimed to be using derivatives to hedge forecasted transactions when in fact the dollar value of supposed hedging activity has been far greater than any possible future transactions. Using a derivative in this way transforms the derivative from a hedging tool into a speculative investment.

[10] FASB ASC paragraph 815-20-35-1.

The FASB has identified a third category of hedges related to foreign currency risk. Some of these hedges are fair value hedges, and some are cash flow hedges. In addition, some of these hedges relate to the foreign currency risk associated with the net investment in foreign subsidiaries. This category of hedges is covered in more detail in advanced accounting courses.

The next section illustrates the proper accounting for derivatives, particularly those designated as hedges.

Accounting for Derivatives and for Hedging Activities

5 **Account for a variety of different derivatives and for hedging relationships.**

WHY **In practice, the accounting for derivatives is extremely complex. However, as you will see in this section, it is not too hard to gain a solid understanding of the basics of derivative accounting.**

HOW **If a derivative is not a hedge, changes in the fair value of the derivative are reported as gains or losses in the income statement. If a derivative is a fair value hedge, changes in the fair value of the derivative are reported as gains or losses in the income statement and are offset by gains or losses on changes in the fair value of the asset or liability being hedged. If a derivative is a cash flow hedge, changes in the fair value of the derivative are deferred and reported as part of other comprehensive income. These deferred gains and losses are recognized in income on the forecasted date of the cash flows being hedged.**

Several factors combined in 1993 and 1994 to move the accounting for derivatives to the top of the FASB's agenda. First was the tremendous proliferation in the use of derivatives by U.S. businesses. Second was the derivative-related catastrophes experienced by companies such as Procter & Gamble. And third was the SEC's urging for improvement in the accounting for derivatives. In October 1994, the FASB released pre-Codification *Statement No. 119* with the main focus being on improved disclosure (not recognition) for the 1994 fiscal year. *Statement No. 119* was viewed as a temporary stopgap standard.

A more comprehensive recognition standard for derivatives, FASB pre-Codification *Statement No. 133*, was adopted in June 1998; its effective date was subsequently delayed to fiscal years beginning after June 15, 2000. The delay was motivated by two reasons: Companies wanted more time to figure out how to implement the standard and they did not want to implement the standard before January 1, 2000, because of "Y2K" concerns with their computer systems. The adoption of FASB *Statement No. 133* was not the end of the quest for better derivative accounting. A special Derivatives Implementation Group (DIG) was established by the FASB with the sole purpose of handling derivative accounting issues. Until it stopped meeting in June 2009, the DIG had commented on 190 different issues relative to accounting for derivatives. So keep in mind that the brief treatment of derivative accounting in this chapter is just an overview. However, this overview does cover the key elements of accounting for derivatives.

Overview of Accounting for Derivatives and Hedging Activities

The accounting difficulty caused by derivatives is illustrated in this simple matrix:

	Historical Cost	Subsequent Changes in Value
Traditional assets and liabilities	Focus	Frequently ignored
Derivatives	Small or zero	Everything

As the matrix shows, the historical cost focus of traditional accounting is misplaced with derivatives because derivatives often have little or no up-front historical cost. With derivatives, the subsequent changes in prices or rates are critical to determining the value of the derivative, yet these changes are frequently ignored in traditional accounting.

Because derivatives do not mesh well with the traditional accounting model, the FASB has endorsed a different approach, based on two simple notions:

1. *Balance sheet.* Derivatives should be reported in the balance sheet at their fair value as of the balance sheet date. No other measure of value is relevant for derivatives.
2. *Income statement.* When a derivative is used to hedge risk, the gains and losses on the derivative should be reported in the same income statement in which the income effects on the hedged item are reported. This sometimes requires unrealized gains and losses being temporarily deferred in an accumulated other comprehensive income account that is reported as part of equity.

A consequence of this approach is that the appropriate treatment of changes in the fair value of a derivative depends on whether the derivative serves as a hedge and, if so, the type of hedge, as follows:

- *No hedge.* All changes in the fair value of derivatives that are not designated as hedges are recognized as gains or losses in the income statement in the period in which the value changes. In a sense, a derivative that does not serve as a hedge can be thought of as a speculation about the direction of movement of some price or rate.

- *Fair value hedge.* Changes in the fair value of derivatives designated as fair value hedges are recognized as gains or losses in the period of the value change. These derivative gains or losses are offset (either in whole or in part) by the recognition of gains or losses on the change in fair value of the item being hedged. The net effect is that when gains or losses on derivatives designated as fair value hedges exceed the gains or losses on the item being hedged, the excess affects reported net income.

- *Cash flow hedge.* Changes in the fair value of derivatives designated as cash flow hedges are recognized as part of the accumulated other comprehensive income account. In effect, this treatment defers recognition of the gain or loss and classifies the deferred item as an equity adjustment. These deferred derivative gains and losses are recognized in net income in the period in which the hedged cash flow transaction was forecasted to occur.

FYI

Assessing hedge effectiveness when the critical elements of the hedged item and the hedging derivative are not the same involves statistical procedures and can be quite difficult. For a discussion, see John D. Finnerty and Dwight Grant, "Alternative Approaches to Testing Hedge Effectiveness under SFAS No. 133," *Accounting Horizons,* June 2002, p. 95.

An important aspect of this approach is that derivatives must be identified as hedges of specific items at the beginning of the hedging relationship. Firms cannot wait until after they see the results for the period to decide whether they want to designate certain derivatives as hedges. The designation of a derivative as a hedge should be supported with formal documentation.

To account for a derivative as a hedge, a company must define, in advance, how it will determine whether the derivative is functioning as an effective hedge. For the simple examples given in this chapter, hedge effectiveness is easy to assess because the terms of the derivatives have been constructed to exactly match the amount and timing of the underlying hedged item. Partial hedge ineffectiveness would occur if, for example, the derivative maturity date did not exactly match the date of a forecasted purchase. Similarly, hedge ineffectiveness occurs when the amount in the derivative agreement (such as the number of units of foreign currency or of pounds of a commodity) is either more or less than the amount of the underlying hedged item. Derivative gains or losses associated with hedge ineffectiveness are recognized in income immediately in the period in which they occur.

Disclosure Companies are required to provide a description of their risk management strategy and how derivatives fit into that strategy. For both fair value and cash flow hedges, companies also must disclose the amount of derivative gains or losses that are included in income because of hedge ineffectiveness. Finally, for cash flow hedges, a company must describe the transactions that will cause deferred derivative gains and losses to be recognized in net income and disclose the amount of deferred gains or losses that are expected to be recognized in net income in the next 12 months.[11]

Another item that is often referred to in the business press is the *notional amount* of the derivative instrument. The notional amount is the total face amount of the asset or liability that underlies the derivative contract. For example, with a forward contract, the notional amount is the U.S. dollar value of the commodity or currency to be exchanged. The notional amount of derivative instruments is often reported and is frequently misleading. For example, the Clayton forward contract described earlier in the chapter has a notional amount of $250,000 (¥30,000,000/¥120 per $1) but has a fair value of $0 on the day the forward agreement is signed, and in the example, the total cash payment stemming from the derivative does not exceed $4,237. In summary, notional amounts grossly overstate both the fair value and the potential cash flows of derivatives.

> **FYI**
>
> A favorite ploy of financial reporters is to report the notional amount of derivatives in order to exaggerate their importance.

The accounting for derivatives will be illustrated using the information from the previous four derivative examples.

Illustrations of Accounting for Derivatives and Hedging Activities

Pratt Swap On January 1, 2013, Pratt Company received a 2-year, $100,000, variable-rate loan and entered into an interest rate swap agreement. The journal entry to record this information follows:

2013			
Jan. 1	Cash	100,000	
	Loan Payable		100,000

[11] FASB ASC paragraph 815-30-50-1.

No entry is made to record the swap agreement because as of January 1, 2013, the swap has a fair value of $0. The value is zero because the interest rate on January 1, 2013, is 10%, and if it is assumed that the best forecast of the future interest rate is the current rate of 10%, it is expected that, on average, no payments will be exchanged under the swap agreement.[12]

Assume now that the actual market interest rate on December 31, 2013, is 11%. With this rate, Pratt will receive a $1,000 payment [$100,000 × (0.11 − 0.10)] at the end of 2014 under the swap agreement. Accordingly, on December 31, 2013, Pratt has a $1,000 receivable under the swap agreement, and the receivable has a present value of $901 (FV = $1,000, N = 1, I = 11%, PV = $901). The impact of the change in interest rates on the interest rate swap and on reported interest expense is accounted for as follows:

	2013 Balance Sheet	2013 Income Statement
Underlying item	No change in the reported loan balance	No impact on 2013 interest expense; the impact will show up in 2014 interest expense
Derivative	Creation of a $901 receivable under the interest rate swap	Deferred gain of $901 on the interest rate swap; gain recognized in 2014 to offset increased interest expense

The interest rate swap asset is reported at its present value of $901 in the December 31, 2013, balance sheet. However, the $901 gain from the increase in the value of the swap is not included in the 2013 income statement. The swap is intended to offset changes in interest expense in 2014. Accordingly, the gain on the swap is deferred so that it can be offset against the increased interest expense to be reported in 2014. The deferral of the gain merely means that it is temporarily reported as an increase in equity under Accumulated Other Comprehensive Income. The deferred gain would also be included as an addition in the statement of comprehensive income (but not in the normal income statement) for 2013.

The journal entry to record Pratt's 2013 interest payment, along with the adjusting entry to recognize the change in the fair value of the swap, is as follows:

2013			
Dec. 31	Interest Expense	10,000	
	Cash ($100,000 × 0.10)		10,000
	Interest Rate Swap (asset)	901	
	Other Comprehensive Income		901

The journal entries necessary in Pratt's books at the end of 2014 are as follows:

2014			
Dec. 31	Interest Expense	11,000	
	Cash ($100,000 × 0.11)		11,000
	Cash (from swap agreement)	1,000	
	Interest Rate Swap (asset)		901
	Other Comprehensive Income ($901 × 0.11; rounded)		99
	Accumulated Other Comprehensive Income	1,000	
	Interest Expense		1,000
	Loan Payable	100,000	
	Cash		100,000

[12] As mentioned earlier, detailed treatment of the valuation of derivatives is outside the scope of this text. Remember that the valuation assumptions used here represent a simplification.

The $99 credit to Other Comprehensive Income represents the increase in the value of the swap payment receivable stemming from the passage of time. Also, recall that Other Comprehensive Income is closed to the equity account Accumulated Other Comprehensive Income at the end of each year. The debit to Accumulated Other Comprehensive Income of $1,000 removes this amount from the Accumulated Other Comprehensive Income portion of equity and transfers it, after the accounts are closed, to Retained Earnings.

An important thing to notice in these journal entries is that net interest expense is $10,000 because of the hedging effect of the swap. Also notice that the value changes in a derivative designated as a cash flow hedge are deferred in comprehensive income and then reflected in earnings in the period when the hedged cash flow occurs.

Clayton Forward On November 1, 2013, Clayton Company sold machine parts to Maruta Company for ¥30,000,000 to be received on January 1, 2014. On the same date, Clayton also entered a yen forward contract. The journal entry to record this information is as follows:

2013			
Nov. 1	Yen Receivable (¥30,000,000/¥120 per $1)	250,000	
	Sales		250,000

No entry is made to record the forward contract because as of November 1, 2013, the forward has a fair value of $0. The value is zero because settlement payments are made under the contract only if the exchange rate on January 1, 2014, differs from ¥120 = $1. If the current exchange rate of ¥120 = $1 is assumed to be the best forecast of the future rate, it is expected that, on average, no payments will be exchanged under the forward contract.

Assume now that the actual exchange rate on December 31, 2013, is ¥119 = $1. At this exchange rate, Clayton will have a loss on the forward contract and be required to make a $2,101 payment [(¥30,000,000/¥119 per $1) – $250,000] on January 1, 2014, to settle the forward contract. Accordingly, on December 31, 2013, Clayton has a $2,101 loss and payable under the forward contract. However, there is also an increase in the yen receivable and a corresponding gain on foreign exchange due to the change in yen value relative to the U.S. dollar. The impact of the change in the yen exchange rate on both the yen receivable and the value of the forward contract is accounted for as follows:

	2013 Balance Sheet	2013 Income Statement
Underlying item	Increase of $2,101 in the value of the yen receivable	Exchange gain of $2,101
Derivative	Creation of a $2,101 liability	Loss on forward contract of $2,101 under the forward contract

FYI

These journal entries illustrate that, after the fact, hedging is not always a good idea. In the Clayton example, the forward contract hedge wipes out the gain on the increase in the value of the yen receivable. The advantage of a hedge is that it reduces volatility, but that sometimes means canceling out gains.

The forward contract liability is reported at its fair value of $2,101 in the December 31, 2013, balance sheet. In addition, the $2,101 loss on the forward contract is included in the 2013 income statement, thus offsetting the gain reported from the increase in dollar value of the yen receivable. This accounting treatment accurately reflects the intent of the forward contract hedge; that is, unrealized gains and losses from changes in value of the forward contract are meant to offset similar changes in value in the item of concern, the yen receivable.

The adjusting entries to recognize the change in the fair value of the forward contract and in the U.S. dollar value of the yen receivable are as follows:

2013			
Dec. 31	Loss on Forward Contract	2,101	
	Forward Contract (liability)		2,101
	Yen Receivable	2,101	
	Gain on Foreign Currency		2,101

The increase in the yen receivable reflects the $2,101 increased dollar value of the receivable after the change in the exchange rate to ¥119 = $1. This gain is offset by the loss from the change in value of the forward contract. The forward contract is a fair value hedge of the value of the receivable, so both changes in value are recognized in earnings.

The journal entries necessary in Clayton's books on January 1, 2014, to record receipt of the yen payment and settlement of the yen forward contract are as follows:

2014			
Jan. 1	Cash (¥30,000,000/¥119 per $1)	252,101	
	Yen Receivable		252,101
	Forward Contract (liability)	2,101	
	Cash (forward contract settlement)		2,101

It should be noted that the Clayton forward contract does not qualify for hedge accounting under FASB ASC Topic 815. The FASB explicitly excluded foreign currency–denominated assets and liabilities from the set of items that can be considered as items underlying a hedge.[13] Thus, derivatives that serve as economic hedges of foreign currency assets and liabilities are accounted for as speculations, with all gains and losses recognized as part of income immediately. However, because the accounting standards [in Topic 830 (Foreign Currency Matters)] already require that foreign currency assets and liabilities be revalued at current exchange rates at the end of each period, with the resulting exchange gains and losses recognized in income, the net effect is the same as if the foreign currency derivatives were accounted for as fair value hedges after all. This fact can be seen by reviewing the Clayton forward example: The gains and losses from both the foreign currency receivable and the yen forward contract are recognized in income immediately, effectively offsetting one another.[14]

By excluding derivatives associated with foreign currency assets and liabilities from the hedge accounting rules of Topic 815, the FASB has reduced the disclosure burden of companies that use such derivatives as hedges. The fair value option of Section 825-10-25, which was discussed in detail in Chapter 12, is another effort by the FASB to allow companies to report the economic effects of hedging activity without the elaborate documentation that is required under Topic 815.

[13] FASB ASC paragraph 815-20-25-43.

[14] As mentioned earlier, in this chapter we make the simplifying assumption that spot rates and forward rates are equal to one another. When this is not true, the foreign currency and derivative gains and losses will not exactly offset because foreign currency assets and liabilities are valued using the spot rate and derivative instruments are valued using the forward rate.

Hyrum Future On December 1, 2013, Hyrum Company decided to hedge against potential fluctuations in the price of wheat for its forecasted January 2014 purchases and bought a futures contract entitling and obligating Hyrum to purchase 1,000 bushels of wheat on January 1, 2014, for $4.00 per bushel. No entry is made to record the futures contract because, as of December 1, 2013, the future has a fair value of $0. The value is zero because settlement payments are made under the contract only if the price of wheat on January 1, 2014, differs from $4.00 per bushel. If the current price of $4.00 per bushel is assumed to be the best forecast of the future price, it is expected that, on average, no payments will be exchanged under the futures contract.

Assume that the actual price of wheat on December 31, 2013, is $4.40 per bushel. At this price, Hyrum will receive a $400 payment [1,000 bushels × ($4.40 – $4.00)] on January 1, 2014, to settle the futures contract. Accordingly, on December 31, 2013, Hyrum has a $400 receivable under the futures contract. The impact of the change in wheat prices on the wheat futures contract and on the anticipated cost of wheat purchases in January 2014 is accounted for as follows:

	2013 Balance Sheet	2013 Income Statement
Underlying item	No impact; the higher-priced wheat won't be purchased until January 2014	No impact on 2013 cost of goods sold; the impact will show up in 2014 cost of goods sold
Derivative	Creation of a $400 receivable under the wheat futures contract	Deferred gain of $400 on the wheat futures contract; gain recognized in 2014 to offset increased cost of goods sold

The wheat futures asset is reported at its fair value of $400 in the December 31, 2013, balance sheet. However, the $400 gain from the increase in the value of the futures contract is not included in the 2013 income statement. The futures contract is intended to offset changes in the purchase price of wheat in January 2014. Accordingly, the gain on the futures contract is deferred so that it can be offset against the increased cost of goods sold to be reported in 2014. As with the interest rate swap discussed earlier, the deferral of the gain means that it is temporarily reported as an increase in equity under Accumulated Other Comprehensive Income.

! CAUTION

It is *not* the case that derivative losses are reported immediately and derivative gains are deferred. If wheat prices had declined, Hyrum would have experienced a loss on the wheat futures contract, which would have been deferred until 2014.

The adjusting entry to recognize the change in the fair value of the futures contract is as follows:

2013			
Dec. 31	Wheat Futures Contract (asset)	400	
	Other Comprehensive Income		400

The gain from the increase in the value of Hyrum's futures contract is deferred as part of other comprehensive income. The wheat futures contract is a cash flow hedge, with the futures contract payment intended to offset the increased amount that Hyrum will have to pay to make its forecasted purchase of 1,000 bushels of wheat on January 1, 2014.

The journal entries necessary in Hyrum's books on January 1, 2014, to record the purchase of 1,000 bushels of wheat in the open market and cash settlement of the wheat futures contract are as follows:

2014			
Jan. 1	Wheat Inventory	4,400	
	Cash (1,000 bushels × $4.40)		4,400
	Cash (futures contract settlement)	400	
	Wheat Futures Contract (asset)		400
	Accumulated Other Comprehensive Income	400	
	Gain on Futures Contract		400

The gain on the futures contract is recognized in earnings on January 1, 2014, the forecasted date of the transaction that was hedged. To the extent that the wheat inventory is used to make bread and that bread is sold in 2014, the gain on the futures contract will offset the increased cost of goods sold arising from the increase in the price of wheat to $4.40 per bushel.

Woodruff Option On October 1, 2013, Woodruff Company paid $20,000 to purchase a call option to buy 1,000 ounces of gold at a price of $1,100 per ounce some time before January 1, 2014. This option is intended to protect Woodruff against increases in the price of the gold that it needs for 2014. Because Woodruff paid cash for the gold call option, the following journal entry is made on October 1:

2013			
Oct. 1	Gold Call Option (asset)	20,000	
	Cash		20,000

Assume that the actual price of gold on December 31, 2013, is $1,128 per ounce. At this gold price, Woodruff will receive a $28,000 payment [($1,128 × 1,000 ounces) − ($1,100 × 1,000 ounces)] on January 1, 2014, to settle the call option. Accordingly, on December 31, 2013, the call option is worth $28,000. The impact of the change in the price of gold on the gold call option and on the anticipated cost of gold purchases in January 2014 is accounted for as follows:

	2013 Balance Sheet	2013 Income Statement
Underlying item	No impact; the higher-priced gold won't be purchased until January 2014	No impact on 2013 cost of goods sold; the impact will show up in 2014 cost of goods sold
Derivative	Increase from $20,000 to $28,000 of the recorded value of the gold call option	Deferred gain of $8,000 on the gold call option; gain recognized in 2014 to offset increased cost of goods sold

The gold call option is reported at its fair value of $28,000 in the December 31, 2013, balance sheet. This represents an $8,000 increase ($28,000 − $20,000) over the amount originally paid for the option. However, the $8,000 gain from the increase in the value of the call option is not included in the 2013 income statement. The call option is intended to offset changes in the purchase price of gold in January 2014. Accordingly, the gain on the call option is deferred so that it can be offset against the increased production costs to be reported in 2014.

The adjusting entry to recognize the change in the fair value of the option is as follows:

2013			
Dec. 31	Gold Call Option ($28,000 − $20,000)	8,000	
	Other Comprehensive Income		8,000

The journal entries necessary in Woodruff's books on January 1, 2014, to record the purchase of 1,000 ounces of gold and the cash settlement of the option contract are as follows:

2014			
Jan. 1	Gold Inventory	1,128,000	
	Cash (1,000 ounces × $1,128)		1,128,000
	Cash (gold call option settlement)	28,000	
	Gold Call Option (asset)		28,000
	Accumulated Other Comprehensive Income	8,000	
	Gain on Gold Call Option		8,000

As mentioned previously, the gain from the increase in the value of the gold call option would be offset against the increased production costs in January 2014 resulting from the increase in the price of gold. The $8,000 gain does not completely offset the $28,000 increase in production costs because Woodruff had to pay $20,000 to purchase the gold call option in the first place.

FASB CODIFICATION

The Issue: You have been doing some part-time bookkeeping for a local ski resort. Because of your accounting background, the general manager of the resort has come to rely on your understanding of business transactions. A salesperson for a local brokerage firm has just visited the general manager. The salesperson was trying to sell the general manager on the idea of a "weather derivative" to help manage the risk the ski resort faces from low or late snowfall. The general manager had never heard of such a thing. The general manager has asked you to find out if there is such a thing as a "weather derivative."

The Question: Is there such a thing as a "weather derivative"?

Searching the Codification: Of course, the quickest way to find out the answer to this question is to just do a general search online. However, that wouldn't be nearly as sophisticated, or fun, as searching the FASB Codification. In addition, if you can find some coverage of "weather derivatives" in the Codification, you will know that this is a mainstream transaction, common enough to be addressed by the FASB. This is a good opportunity to just relax and scan through Topic 815 (Derivatives and Hedging—Broad Transactions).

The Answer: The existence of weather derivatives is discussed on page 19–38.

Summary

The centerpiece of accounting for derivatives and hedging activities is that derivatives are recognized as assets and liabilities and reported on the balance sheet at their fair values. For a derivative designated as a fair value hedge, changes in fair value are included in earnings and offset against changes in fair value of the hedged item. For a cash flow hedge, gains and losses are deferred in accumulated other comprehensive income and recognized in earnings on the forecasted date of the hedged transaction. In formulating an International Financial Reporting Standard for derivatives, the International Accounting Standards Board (IASB) drew heavily on the work done by the FASB. The general provisions of *IAS 39* are very similar to the provisions of FASB ASC Topic 815.

ifrs

CONTINGENCIES

During 1983, **Pennzoil** initiated negotiations for the acquisition of **Getty Oil**. Before the Pennzoil-Getty deal could be closed, **Texaco** swooped in and bought Getty right out from underneath Pennzoil's nose for $10.2 billion. Pennzoil immediately sued Texaco for $14 billion in damages caused by Texaco's interference in Pennzoil's attempted acquisition of Getty. In December 1985, a Houston jury awarded $10.5 billion to Pennzoil. The case was appealed in both 1986 and 1987, with judgment in each instance against Texaco. With the uncertainty of a multibillion-dollar judgment hanging over its head, Texaco found it increasingly difficult to calm the fears of its suppliers and creditors. Texaco played its trump card in April 1987 and declared Chapter 11 bankruptcy. This action forced Pennzoil to the bargaining table, and in December 1987 the two companies negotiated a $3 billion payment to settle the case. Texaco made the payment on April 7, 1988.[15]

In addition to illustrating the strategic use of Chapter 11 bankruptcy, the Texaco-Pennzoil case serves as a classic example of the difficulties surrounding the accounting for contingencies. Among the interesting accounting questions here are the following:

- During the 4.5-year life of this lawsuit, when should Texaco have recognized a liability, and for what amount?
- At the same time, when should Pennzoil have recognized an asset for the receivable from Texaco?

As the Texaco-Pennzoil case suggests, uncertainty about the future sometimes makes it difficult to identify a company's assets and liabilities. The definitions of assets and liabilities given in the conceptual framework discussed in Chapter 1 use the word "probable"; an asset is a probable future economic benefit, and a liability is a probable future economic sacrifice. In this module, the specific accounting rules governing the accounting for contingent items will be discussed. These rules will be illustrated with coverage of the accounting for lawsuits and for environmental liabilities.

[15] Edward B. Deakin, "Accounting for Contingencies: The Pennzoil-Texaco Case," *Accounting Horizons*, March 1989, p. 21.

Accounting for Contingencies: Probable, Possible, and Remote

6 **Apply the accounting rules for contingent items to the areas of lawsuits and environmental liabilities.**

WHY **Understanding the accounting for contingent items is extremely important in a broader sense because many issues in accounting revolve around probabilities and uncertainty.**

HOW **If a contingent liability is probable and can be reasonably estimated, it should be recognized in the financial statements. If a contingent liability is only possible, it should be disclosed in the financial statement notes. Contingent liabilities that are remote should not, in general, be disclosed. Contingent assets are generally not recognized until any remaining uncertainty is very small.**

A contingency is defined in FASB ASC Topic 450 (Contingencies) as follows:

> . . . an existing condition, situation, or set of circumstances involving uncertainty as to possible gain . . . or loss . . . to an entity that will ultimately be resolved when one or more future events occur or fail to occur.[16]

As defined, contingencies may relate to either assets or liabilities and to either a gain or loss. The primary focus of this module is on contingent losses that might give rise to a liability, but the accounting for contingent gains is also discussed briefly.

Historically, when the existence of an obligation depended on the occurrence of a future event, recognition of the liability was deferred until the event occurred. This approach can fail to reflect the existence of significant obligations that are highly likely to materialize and that exist because of past transactions or events. For example, Texaco's contingent obligation to Pennzoil arose because of Texaco's interference in Pennzoil's attempted acquisition of Getty Oil, a past event. The future events determining whether Texaco would have to make payments to Pennzoil were the court verdicts. For Texaco to fail to record its liability until the day the $3 billion was actually paid to Pennzoil would be grossly misleading to users of the financial statements.

FASB ASC Topic 450 specifies different accounting for contingent items based on the probability of the occurrence of the resolving future event. The likelihood of the event and the accounting actions recommended are shown in Exhibit 19-1.

If the occurrence of an event that would create a liability is probable and if the amount of the obligation can be reasonably estimated, the contingency should be recognized as a liability. Many estimated liabilities are in reality probable contingent liabilities because the existence of the obligation depends on some future event occurring. For example, the estimated amount of warranty liability is a probable contingent liability because warranties depend on the need to provide future repairs or service. In addition, a pension obligation depends on employees staying with the company long enough to earn full pension benefits, and frequent-flier trips are contingent on whether customers accumulate enough miles for free trips and whether they actually claim their free trips.

The rules governing accounting for contingent assets are somewhat confused. The wording in FASB ASC Topic 450 about contingent gains goes back to *ARB No. 50*, which was originally adopted in 1958. *ARB No. 50* says that contingent gains (and, by extension,

[16] FASB ASC Section 450-10-20—Glossary.

EX 19-1 ACCOUNTING FOR CONTINGENCIES

Contingent Losses:

Likelihood	**Accounting Action**
Probable	Recognize a probable liability if the amount can be reasonably estimated. If not estimable, disclose facts in a note. FASB ASC paragraph 450-20-25-2.
Reasonably possible	Disclose a possible liability in a note. FASB ASC paragraph 450-20-50-3.
Remote	Make no recognition or disclosure unless contingency represents a guarantee. Then note disclosure is required. FASB ASC paragraph 460-10-50-2.

Contingent Gains:

Likelihood	**Accounting Action**
Probable plus	Recognize a contingent asset if the probability of its occurrence is very high (more than probable) and if the amount can be reasonably estimated. Otherwise, disclose the facts in a note. FASB ASC paragraph 450-30-25-1.
Reasonably possible	Disclose a possible asset in a note, but be careful to avoid misleading implications. In practice, possible contingent gains are often not disclosed. FASB ASC paragraph 450-30-50-1.
Remote	Make no recognition or disclosure.

contingent assets) are not to be recognized before they are "realized." This appears to be in conflict with the asset definition in *Concepts Statement No. 6*, which says that an asset is a "probable future economic benefit." The international rules add another view. In *IAS 37*, paragraph 33, we read that a contingent asset should be recognized when it "is virtually certain." The only thing we can conclude with certainty from all of this is that the probability threshold for the recognition of a contingent asset is higher than that for a contingent liability. This reflects the conservatism that has been at the roots of accounting for years.

If a contingent liability is *reasonably possible*, defined as more than remote but less than likely, it should be disclosed in a note to the financial statements. Possible gains are often not disclosed to avoid any misleading implications about the likelihood that the gain will eventually be realized. If a contingent item is *remote*, that is, the chance of occurrence is slight, there is no requirement that it be disclosed unless it is a contingent liability under a guarantee arrangement such as guaranteeing, or co-signing, the loan of another party. The requirement to disclose certain contingencies that have a remote probability of occurrence does NOT exist in *IAS 37*.

ifrs

The timing of the disclosures made in the Texaco-Pennzoil case illustrates the different treatment of contingent losses and contingent gains. As seen in Exhibit 19-2, the initial lawsuit was filed in early 1984, and Texaco was careful to mention the possibility of a loss in its 1984 and 1985 financial statements. Pennzoil made no mention of the contingent gain in its 1984 or its 1985 financial statements. In the body of the 1986 annual report, Texaco management took two pages to discuss the Pennzoil litigation. In addition, the financial statements included another page in the notes discussing the case. Texaco's management concluded the discussion by stating that the Pennzoil litigation could materially affect Texaco. At the same time, the uncertainty surrounding Texaco's future, given the large judgment hanging over its head, caused Texaco's auditor to render a qualified audit opinion. While Texaco's financial statements were being drastically

EX 19-2 ACCOUNTING TREATMENT IN THE TEXACO-PENNZOIL CASE

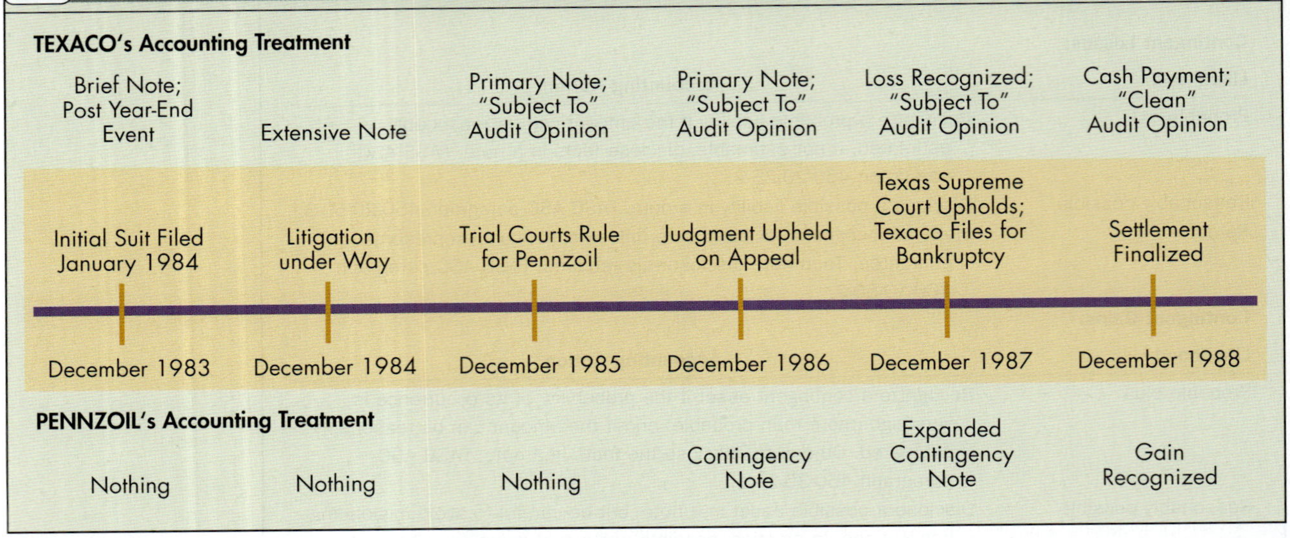

impacted by this contingent loss, Pennzoil's financial statements included just a brief note about the contingent gain. In 1987, Texaco formally recognized the $3 billion liability and filed for Chapter 11 bankruptcy. Pennzoil did not recognize the gain until 1988 when the payment was actually received. This case nicely illustrates the asymmetry between the treatment of contingent losses and the treatment of contingent gains.

As described here, the accounting for contingent liabilities and contingent assets is inconsistent with fair value measurement.[17] Even a contingent liability with remote probability of realization has a fair value which would be reflected if, for example, another company were to accept responsibility for that contingency. As FASB standards move increasingly to a fair value measurement standard, it is likely that the area of accounting for contingencies will be revisited.

FASB ASC Topic 450 does not provide specific guidelines as to how the words *probable*, *possible*, and *remote* should be interpreted in terms of probability percentages. For example, is a 60% likelihood "probable" or just "possible"? Surveys of statement preparers and users reveal a great diversity in the numerical interpretations of these probability terms as used in the accounting standards. Thus, the contingency standard that seems fairly easy to apply given the straightforward guidelines outlined in Exhibit 19-1 is actually very difficult to apply consistently in practice. This is illustrated below with a discussion of the accounting for lawsuits and environmental liabilities.

> **FYI**
>
> In the area of deferred taxes, the FASB has introduced a fourth probability term, "more likely than not," defined as a probability level of 50%. Use of the more-likely-than-not criterion is discussed in Chapter 16.

Accounting for Lawsuits

The United States is the land of the lawsuit. Companies are sued by customers who claim they were injured by defective products, auditors are sued by stockholders who claim

[17] See FASB ASC paragraphs 450-20-05-4 through 7

they were injured by defective financial statements, and parents are sued by children who claim they were injured by defective upbringing. Typically, a lawsuit takes a long time to wind its way through the courts. Even after a decision has been handed down by a lower court, many appeal opportunities are available. Thus, both the amount and timing of a loss arising from litigation are generally highly uncertain. Some companies carry insurance to protect themselves against these losses, so the impact of the losses on the financial statements is minimized. For uninsured risks, however, a decision must be made as to when the liability for litigation becomes probable, and thus, a recorded loss. In ASC Topic 450, the FASB identifies several key factors to consider in making the decision. These include the following:[18]

1. The nature of the lawsuit
2. Progress of the case in court, including progress between date of the financial statements and their issuance date
3. Views of legal counsel as to the probability of loss
4. Prior experience with similar cases
5. Management's intended response to the lawsuit

If analysis of these and similar factors results in the judgment that a loss is probable and the amount of the loss can be reasonably estimated, the liability should be recorded. A settlement after the balance sheet date but before the statements are issued would be evidence that the loss was probable at year-end, and it would result in reporting the loss in the current financial statements.

Another area of potential liability involves unasserted claims; that is, a cause of action has occurred but no claim has yet been asserted. For example, a person may be injured on a company's property, but as of the date the financial statements are issued, no legal action has been taken. As another example, a violation of a government regulation may have occurred, but no federal action has yet been taken. If it is probable that a substantiated claim will be filed and upheld and the amount of the claim can be reasonably estimated, accrual of the liability should be made. If the amount cannot be reasonably estimated, note disclosure is required. If assertion of the claim is judged not to be at least reasonably possible, no accrual or disclosure is necessary.

As a practical matter, it should be noted that a company would be very unlikely to record a loss from unasserted claims or from pending litigation unless negotiations for a settlement had been substantially completed. When that is the case, the loss is no longer a contingency but an estimated loss.

Once a company has determined that the facts and circumstances require that it recognize a liability, the company must then generate a reasonable estimate of the amount of the liability. Even though the company doesn't know the exact amount of the future payout, it can usually specify a range of possible payouts. Under U.S. GAAP, the company should choose the amount within the range that is the best estimate. If no amount in the range is any better than any other amount, the company should recognize the lowest amount in the range and then disclose the potential additional loss exposure.[19]

ifrs

Under IFRS, the estimation process for recognizing an amount associated with a probable future payout differs substantially from U.S. GAAP. The focus in *IAS 37* is on recognizing the fair value of the obligation. Accordingly, the company is expected to

[18] Ibid., par. 36.FASB ASC paragraph 450-20-55-12.
[19] FASB ASC paragraph 450-20-30-1.

estimate the amount that would have to be paid right now in order to settle the obligation or to transfer the obligation to a third party.[20] This estimate involves consideration of the possible payouts, the probabilities of each, and the time value of money if the payout is expected to stretch over a long time period. As you can see, this process results in a recognized liability with much more economic meaning than does the U.S. GAAP process of picking either the single most likely outcome or the lowest in a range of equally probable outcomes.

Disclosure Some companies do not disclose any information regarding potential liabilities from lawsuits. Others provide a brief, general description of pending lawsuits. Sometimes companies provide fairly specific information about pending actions and claims. However, companies must be careful not to increase their chances of losing pending lawsuits, and they generally do not disclose dollar amounts of potential losses, which might be interpreted as an admission of guilt and a willingness to pay a certain amount. As an illustration, **ExxonMobil** disclosed the information in Exhibit 19-3 in its 1991, 1997, 2007, and 2009 annual reports in connection with lawsuits filed as a result of the *Valdez* oil spill. Note that, in 1991, Exxon sounds quite optimistic that it has settled the bulk of the claims related to the oil spill and that any further claims "will not have a materially adverse effect" upon the company. This optimistic disclosure is particularly interesting in light of the $5 billion adverse judgment discussed in the 1997 disclosure (although the amount of this judgment was later reduced by order of the U.S. Supreme Court).

Another example of disclosure relating to contingent liabilities can be found in the financial statements of **Altria**, maker of Marlboro cigarettes. The company's 2009 financial statements contain more than 20 pages of disclosure relating to thousands of lawsuits (in various stages of litigation) against the company involving billions of dollars in damage awards. In Item 3. *Legal Proceedings*, the company gives the following statement:

> Altria Group, Inc. and its subsidiaries record provisions in the consolidated financial statements for pending litigation when they determine that an unfavorable outcome is probable and the amount of the loss can be reasonably estimated. At the present time, while it is reasonably possible that an unfavorable outcome in a case may occur, except as discussed elsewhere in this Item 3. *Legal Proceedings*: (i) management has concluded that it is not probable that a loss has been incurred in any of the pending tobacco-related cases; (ii) management is unable to estimate the possible loss or range of loss that could result from an unfavorable outcome in any of the pending tobacco-related cases; and (iii) accordingly, management has not provided any amounts in the consolidated financial statements for unfavorable outcomes, if any. Legal defense costs are expensed as incurred.
>
> Altria Group, Inc. and its subsidiaries have achieved substantial success in managing litigation. Nevertheless, litigation is subject to uncertainty and significant challenges remain. It is possible that the consolidated results of operations, cash flows or financial position of Altria Group, Inc., or one or more of its subsidiaries, could be materially affected in a particular fiscal quarter or fiscal year by an unfavorable outcome or settlement of certain pending litigation.

[20] IAS 37 paragraphs 36 through 47.

EX 19-3 EXXON—1991, 1997, 2007, AND 2009 DISCLOSURE CONCERNING *EXXON VALDEZ* OIL SPILL

Disclosure in 1991 (in part)

On March 24, 1989, the Exxon Valdez, a tanker owned by Exxon Shipping Company, a subsidiary of Exxon Corporation, ran aground on Bligh Reef in Prince William Sound off the port of Valdez, Alaska, and released approximately 260,000 barrels of crude oil. More than 315 lawsuits, including class actions, have been brought in various courts against Exxon Corporation and certain of its subsidiaries.

On October 8, 1991, the United States District Court for the District of Alaska approved a civil agreement and consent decree. . . . These agreements provided for guilty pleas to certain misdemeanors, the dismissal of all felony charges and the remaining misdemeanor charges by the United States, and the release of all civil claims against Exxon . . . by the United States and the state of Alaska. The agreements also released all claims related to or arising from the oil spill by Exxon. . . .

Payments under the plea agreement totaled $125 million—$25 million in fines and $100 million in payments to the United States and Alaska for restoration projects in Alaska. Payments under the civil agreement and consent decree will total $900 million over a ten-year period. The civil agreement also provides for the possible payment, between September 1, 2002, and September 1, 2006, of up to $100 million for substantial loss or decline in populations, habitats, or species in areas affected by the oil spill which could not have been reasonably anticipated on September 25, 1991.

The remaining cost to the corporation from the Valdez accident is difficult to predict and cannot be determined at this time. It is believed the final outcome, net of reserves already provided, will not have a materially adverse effect upon the corporation's operations or financial condition.

Disclosure in 1997 (in part)

On September 24, 1996, the United States District Court for the District of Alaska entered a judgment in the amount of $5.058 billion in the Exxon Valdez civil trial that began in May 1994. The District Court awarded approximately $19.6 million in compensatory damages to fisher plaintiffs, $38 million in prejudgment interest on the compensatory damages and $5 billion in punitive damages to a class composed of all persons and entities who asserted claims for punitive damages from the corporation as a result of the Exxon Valdez grounding. The District Court also ordered that these awards shall bear interest from and after entry of the judgment. The District Court stayed execution on the judgment pending appeal based on a $6.75 billion letter of credit posted by the corporation. Exxon has appealed the judgment. The corporation continues to believe that the punitive damages in this case are unwarranted and that the judgment should be set aside or substantially reduced by the appellate courts. Since it is impossible to estimate what the ultimate earnings impact will be, no charge was taken in 1996 or 1997 related to these verdicts.

Disclosure in 2007 (in part)

A number of lawsuits, including class actions, were brought in various courts against Exxon Mobil Corporation and certain of its subsidiaries relating to the accidental release of crude oil from the tanker Exxon Valdez in 1989. All the compensatory claims have been resolved and paid. All of the punitive damage claims were consolidated in the civil trial that began in 1994. The first judgment from the United States District Court for the District of Alaska in the amount of $5 billion was vacated by the United States Court of Appeals for the Ninth Circuit as being excessive under the Constitution. The second judgment in the amount of $4 billion was vacated by the Ninth Circuit panel without argument and sent back for the District Court to reconsider in light of the recent U.S. Supreme Court decision in Campbell v. State Farm. The most recent District Court judgment for punitive damages was for $4.5 billion plus interest and was entered in January 2004. The Corporation posted a $5.4 billion letter of credit. ExxonMobil and the plaintiffs appealed this decision to the Ninth Circuit, which ruled on December 22, 2006, that the award be reduced to $2.5 billion. On January 12, 2007, ExxonMobil petitioned the Ninth Circuit Court of Appeals for a rehearing en banc of its appeal. On May 23, 2007, with two dissenting opinions, the Ninth Circuit determined not to re-hear ExxonMobil's appeal before the full court. ExxonMobil filed a petition for writ of certiorari to the U.S. Supreme Court on August 20, 2007. On October 29, 2007, the U.S. Supreme Court granted ExxonMobil's petition for a writ of certiorari. Oral argument was held on February 27, 2008. While it is reasonably possible that a liability for punitive damages may have been incurred from the Exxon Valdez grounding, it is not possible to predict the ultimate outcome or to reasonably estimate any such potential liability.

Disclosure in 2009 (in part)

A number of lawsuits, including class actions, were brought in various courts against ExxonMobil Corporation and certain of its subsidiaries relating to the accidental release of crude oil from the tanker Exxon Valdez in 1989. All the compensatory claims and the punitive damage award have been paid.

In June 2008, the FASB released an Exposure Draft that seeks to improve the disclosures associated with loss contingencies. Among other things, the FASB proposal would require companies to provide more detailed, systematic loss contingency disclosure, including a table summarizing the reasons for any increases or decreases in a company's recognized losses relative to contingencies. The FASB expects to issue a final standard on improved loss contingency disclosure in 2010.

Accounting for Environmental Liabilities

An area that is receiving increasing attention in our society, both politically and from an accounting perspective, is the environment. Most citizens recognize the need to protect our environment and, in many instances, to recover from past environmental abuses. What is not so obvious are the staggering costs associated with environmental liabilities. As but one example, current legislation in the United States mandates the cleanup of existing toxic waste sites. The Environmental Protection Agency (EPA) is empowered to clean up waste sites and then can charge the cleanup costs to those parties the EPA deems responsible. This can cost companies $25 to $100 million or more for each polluted site. The total environmental cleanup obligation in the United States has been estimated to be at least $750 billion and may perhaps exceed $1 trillion.[21]

Even though environmental costs represent one of the critical issues facing businesses today, many, if not most, companies do not fully reflect those costs in their financial statements. The primary reason is that these loss contingencies often cannot be reasonably estimated. As discussed earlier in this chapter, if a liability cannot be reasonably estimated, no amount can be recognized.

In recent years, accounting standard setters have issued several statements and Exposure Drafts designed to improve the environmental liability information reported in the financial statements and notes. The SEC staff has issued *Staff Accounting Bulletin (SAB) No. 92*, which sets forth the SEC's interpretation of GAAP regarding contingent liabilities, with particular applicability to companies having environmental liabilities. In 1996, the AICPA issued *Statement of Position (SOP) 96-1*, "Environmental Remediation Liabilities (Including Auditing Guidance)." *SOP 96-1* outlines key events that can be used to determine whether an environmental liability is probable. For example, if a company acknowledges that it has some responsibility for environmental damage and if an initial cleanup feasibility study has been completed, it is reasonable to assume that the contingent liability is probable and the firm should recognize its share of the total cost. In addition, because a big part of dealing with the cleanup of an environmental site involves legal recovery of cleanup costs from other firms that initially refused to pay for their share of the cleanup, firms are allowed to recognize these potential recoveries as assets if they are probable.

The FASB has codified the accounting standards related to environmental remediation costs in FASB ASC Subtopic 410-30 (Environmental Obligations). Accounting standards related to asset retirement obligations (costs associated with cleaning up after retiring a long-term asset) are included in FASB ASC Subtopic 410-20 (Asset Retirement Obligations) and are discussed in Chapters 10 and 11.

[21] American Society of Civil Engineers, **http://www.asce.org/pressroom/publicpolicy/vgwaste.cfm**, July 8, 2002.

SEGMENT REPORTING

Who sells more soft drinks, **Coca-Cola** or **PepsiCo**? Coke sells more soft drinks in the United States, with a 2009 market share of 41.9%, compared to 29.9% for Pepsi.[22] So how is it that PepsiCo employs 203,000 people, whereas Coke employs just 92,800? The answer is that PepsiCo does much more than sell soft drinks. PepsiCo's revenue is split 50–50 between its food (**Frito-Lay** and **Quaker Oats**) and soft drink (Pepsi-Cola) segments. Which business strategy is more successful, the concentrated strategy of Coke or the diversified strategy of Pepsi? In recent years, the focused approach of Coke has been the winner; the May 2009 market value of The Coca-Cola Company was $122 billion, which is greater than the $107 billion of PepsiCo. An attempt at increased focus was behind the October 1997 strategic change of direction at PepsiCo involving the spinoff of its restaurant businesses (**Pizza Hut**, **Taco Bell**, and **KFC**) to focus more attention on soft drinks and snack foods.[23]

Like PepsiCo, many businesses today are large, complex organizations engaged in a variety of activities that bear little relationship to each other. For example, a company might manufacture airplane engines, operate a real estate business, and manage a professional hockey team. Such companies, referred to as diversified companies, or conglomerates, operate in multiple industries and do not fit into any one specific industry category. The different segments of a diversified company often operate in distinct and separate markets, involve different management teams, and experience different growth patterns, profit potentials, and degrees of risk. In effect, the segments of the company behave almost like, and in some cases are, separate companies within an overall corporate structure. Yet, if only total company information is presented for a highly diversified company, the different degrees of risk, profitability, and growth potential for major segments of the company cannot be analyzed and compared.

Business Segments

7 **Prepare the necessary supplemental disclosures of financial information by product line and by geographic area.**

WHY **For companies with several different lines of business, the overall financial statements have limited usefulness. In order to generate their forecasts and their industry comparative analyses, financial statement users need detailed information by business segment and by geographic area.**

HOW **Companies are required to disclose the following information for each business segment: revenues, operating profit, assets, capital expenditures, and certain income statement items such as depreciation and interest revenue and expense. Companies are to define their reportable business segments using the same practice that is used internally.**

Historically, the United States has led the world in the quality and quantity of financial information required to be disclosed about business segments. In 1939, U.S. companies were encouraged to make separate disclosures concerning operations of foreign business segments because of the "disturbed conditions abroad"—polite language for World

[22] "Top-10 CSD [Carbonated Soft-Drinks] for 2009," *Beverage Digest*, March 24, 2010.

[23] Lori Bongiorno, "Fiddling with the Formula at Pepsi?" *Business Week*, October 14, 1996, p. 42; and Nikhil Deogun, "Pepsi Has Had Its Fill of Pizza, Tacos, Chicken," *The Wall Street Journal*, January 24, 1997, p. B1.

War II.[24] Increased creation of firms with many diverse lines of business in the 1960s caused the APB to issue a nonbinding statement encouraging diversified companies to provide summary business segment information to financial statement users. The segment disclosure rules were refined and made mandatory in 1976 with the issuance of pre-Codification *Statement No. 14* by the FASB.

Information to be disclosed in the financial statement notes under the provisions of FASB *Statement No. 14* included revenues, operating profit, and identifiable assets for each significant industry segment of a company. Other provisions of *Statement No. 14* required disclosure of revenues from major customers and information about foreign operations and export sales.

Although the disclosure required of U.S. companies under pre-Codification *Statement No. 14* was more extensive than the segment disclosure required by the accounting standards of any other country in the world, financial statement users have consistently requested that firms be required to disclose more. In 1994, the AICPA Special Committee on Financial Reporting (often called the *Jenkins Committee*) made the improvement of segment reporting its first recommendation. In response to this push for even better segment reporting, the FASB issued pre-Codification *Statement No. 131* in June 1997. In an early example of international cooperation in creating accounting standards, the FASB worked closely with the Accounting Standards Board in Canada and with the International Accounting Standards Board in developing the segment reporting standard. The provisions of pre-Codification *Statement No. 131* are now contained in FASB ASC Topic 280 (Segment Reporting).

ifrs

According to the provisions of FASB ASC Topic 280, companies are required to disclose the following information concerning business segments:

1. Total segment operating profit or loss
2. Amounts of certain income statement items such as operating revenues, depreciation, interest revenue, interest expense, tax expense, and significant noncash expenses
3. Total segment assets
4. Total capital expenditures
5. Reconciliation of the sum of segment totals to the company total for each of the following items:
   - Revenues
   - Operating profit
   - Assets

In addition to these five items, companies must also disclose how operating segments are identified. Segments are to be identified using the same criteria, whatever they might be, used by management to distinguish business segments for internal reporting purposes. The objective of this requirement is to provide external users with the same type of information about business segments that is used internally. Some companies were concerned about this definition of reportable business segments because they have dozens or even hundreds of internally reportable segments. The FASB responded to this concern by specifying how large a segment must be for separate disclosure to be required. Specifically, a segment is reportable if it meets any one of the following three criteria:

[24] The information in this historical review is adapted from the following source: *Research Report* (prepared by Paul Pacter), "Reporting Disaggregated Information" (Norwalk, CT: Financial Accounting Standards Board, February 1993).

- *Revenue test.* A segment should be reported if its total revenue (both to external customers and to other internal segments) is 10% or more of the company's total revenue (external and internal).
- *Profit test.* A segment should be reported if the absolute value of its operating profit (or loss) is more than 10% of the total of the operating profit for all segments that reported profits (or the total of the losses for all segments that reported losses).
- *Asset test.* A segment should be reported if it contains 10% or more of the combined assets of all operating segments.

The FASB also decided that segments can be combined for reporting purposes, even if they are treated as separate segments internally, if the segments have similar products or services, similar processes, similar customers, similar distribution methods, and are subject to similar regulations.

Companies typically define their business segments in terms of product lines or geographic areas. For those firms defining their segments along product lines, the FASB requires additional disclosure of revenues and long-lived assets for the company's home country and for all foreign operations combined. If one foreign country comprises a material portion of operations, separate revenue and long-lived asset disclosure should be made for that country. A company may consider also showing revenue and long-lived asset subtotals for "groups" of countries, such as for Europe or Asia.

FYI

The FASB received more than 200 comment letters in response to its June 1996 Exposure Draft for pre-Codification *Statement No. 131.* A key concern of businesses was that the Exposure Draft required them to disclose information that might be used by competitors. In response to these concerns, the FASB dropped the original proposal that firms be required to report research and development expenditures and liabilities by segment.

For companies defining their business segments geographically, additional revenue information must be disclosed by product line. This product line information is provided on a companywide basis, however, not by geographic segment.

Companies are also required to disclose supplemental information about major customers. If revenues from any one customer are more than 10% of total revenue, this fact must be disclosed (although the name of the customer isn't disclosed) along with the amount of the revenue and the names of the operating segments in which the revenue is reported.

To illustrate the type of business segment disclosure provided under FASB ASC Topic 280, the segment information given in the 2009 annual report of PepsiCo will be used. PepsiCo discloses that it has six reportable segments, as follows:

- Frito-Lay North America (PepsiCo defines North America to be the United States and Canada.)
- Quaker Foods North America
- Latin America Foods
- PepsiCo Americas Beverages
- Europe
- Asia, Middle East & Africa

EX 19-4 NET SALES, OPERATING PROFIT, AND TOTAL ASSETS BY REPORTABLE SEGMENT, FOR PEPSICO

BUSINESS SEGMENTS

Net Revenue: (In millions of dollars)	**2009**	**2008**	**2007**
Frito-Lay North America	$13,224	$12,507	$11,586
Quaker Foods North America	1,884	1,902	1,860
Latin America Foods	5,703	5,895	4,872
PepsiCo Americas Beverages	10,116	10,937	11,090
Europe	6,727	6,891	5,896
Asia, Middle East & Africa	5,578	5,119	4,170
Total division	$43,232	$43,251	$39,474

Operating Profit: (In millions of dollars)	**2009**	**2008**	**2007**
Frito-Lay North America	$ 3,258	$ 2,959	$ 2,845
Quaker Foods North America	628	582	568
Latin America Foods	904	897	714
PepsiCo Americas Beverages	2,172	2,026	2,487
Europe	932	910	855
Asia, Middle East & Africa	716	592	466
Total division	$ 8,610	$ 7,966	$ 7,935

Total Assets: (In millions of dollars)	**2009**	**2008**	**2007**
Frito-Lay North America	$ 6,337	$ 6,284	$ 6,270
Quaker Foods North America	997	1,035	1,002
Latin America Foods	3,575	3,023	3,084
PepsiCo Americas Beverages	7,670	7,673	7,780
Europe	9,321	8,840	7,330
Asia, Middle East & Africa	4,937	3,756	3,683
Total division	$32,837	$30,611	$29,149

Exhibit 19-4 contains information on PepsiCo's sales and operating profit by segment. Notice that the bulk of PepsiCo's sales and operating profit occur in North America. In addition to this sales, operating profit, and total asset disclosure, PepsiCo gives information, by segment, on amortization of intangibles, depreciation, and capital spending.

Application of accounting principles to individual segments of a business presents some unique problems. For example, if a firm uses LIFO and all of the inventory is part of one LIFO pool for financial reporting purposes, how is LIFO to be applied in calculating cost of goods sold for individual segments? Another example is the allocation of income tax expense to different segments when the income tax return is prepared for the entire company as a whole. Because of difficulties such as these, the FASB states in Topic 280 that, for segment reporting purposes, firms are to report to external users using the same accounting practices that are used for internal purposes. What this means is that the financial data reported in the segment disclosures won't always conform with GAAP. The FASB views this as part of the price to be paid to reduce the incremental bookkeeping cost required for firms to provide segment information. With the release of *IFRS 8* in November 2006, the IASB adopted this same method of identifying reportable segments.

ifrs

In summary, consider the question of how much segment information is enough. Of course, when asked whether they want more information or less, financial statement users will always reply that they want more. Ultimately, every user would like unlimited access to the accounting records of all companies. Understandably, companies are reluctant to disclose everything to everyone. The FASB must set segment reporting standards to balance users' desire for relevant data against firms' legitimate concern about disclosing proprietary information.

STOP&THINK

How could The Coca-Cola Company use PepsiCo's reported segment information to aid it in formulating its competitive strategy?

a) To compute total company sales
b) To compute total company return on equity
c) To compute segment profit margins
d) To determine segment advertising strategies

INTERIM REPORTING

The Business Roundtable is an organization of approximately 160 CEOs of top U.S. corporations. On August 20, 1990, The Business Roundtable sent a letter to one of the commissioners of the SEC.[25] The letter was critical of the work of the FASB and suggested that FASB rules were burdening U.S. business "with a costly reporting infrastructure that overloads the user with data but provides very little insight into the economic condition or results of the enterprise." The Roundtable also complained that FASB rules were putting U.S. firms at a competitive disadvantage overseas where foreign accounting standard setters are more sympathetic to business concerns.

One of the specific problem areas identified by The Business Roundtable was quarterly reporting. The Roundtable described quarterly reports as being very costly in terms of preparation and counterproductive because they cause management to focus on short-term earnings rather than long-term growth. The Roundtable pointed out that many foreign companies (such as those in the United Kingdom) are required to report only semiannually.

This concern about the counterproductivity of quarterly reporting was echoed by Peter A. Magowan, then-CEO of **Safeway**, the large supermarket chain based in Oakland, California. In November 1986, Safeway was taken private in a $5.3 billion leveraged buyout (LBO). In looking back on the success of the restructuring that followed the LBO, Magowan reported that one of the key advantages enjoyed by Safeway was that as a private company, it was no longer locked into the cycle of fixation on reported quarterly earnings. According to Magowan, this freedom from pressure to report ever-increasing quarterly profits made it possible for Safeway to institute aggressive pricing, store expansion, and increased spending for training and technology—all actions that would hurt reported profits in the short run but were for the long-term good of the company.[26]

In spite of concerns that quarterly reports lead to a myopic focus on short-term profits by management, they are still required disclosure in the United States. Publicly traded firms must file quarterly financial statements with the SEC in a 10-Q filing within 40 days of the end of the quarter for large firms and 45 days for smaller firms. An outline of the special problems associated with the preparation of interim reports is given in this module.

[25] John S. Reed, Chairman, Accounting Principles Task Force of The Business Roundtable; letter dated August 20, 1990, addressed to Philip R. Lochner, Jr., Commissioner, Securities and Exchange Commission.

[26] Peter A. Magowan, "The Case for LBOs: The Safeway Experience," *California Management Review*, Fall 1989, p. 9. In April 1990, Safeway again issued shares to the public.

Interim Reports

8 **Recognize the importance of interim reports, and outline the difficulties encountered when preparing those reports.**

WHY **In this age of instant information, it just isn't reasonable to expect financial statement users to wait an entire year between receipt of financial statements for a company. SEC regulations require publicly traded companies to release financial statements each quarter. The preparation of these interim financial statements involves difficult issues of estimation and allocation.**

HOW **Interim financial statements are prepared using the "integral part of annual period" concept. Using this concept, each quarter is not viewed as a separate period but as an integral part of the year, and estimates are used to appropriately allocate a share of the annual results to each quarter. Quarterly reports are typically not audited, but they still are to be prepared in accordance with GAAP.**

Statements showing financial position and operating results for intervals of less than a year are referred to as interim financial statements. Interim reports are considered essential in providing investors and others with timely information as to the position and progress of an enterprise. Notwithstanding the need for interim reports, significant difficulties are associated with them. One problem is caused by the seasonal factors of certain businesses. For example, in some companies, revenues fluctuate widely among interim periods; in other businesses, significant fixed costs are incurred during a single period but are to benefit several periods. Not only must costs be allocated to appropriate periods of benefit but also they must be matched against the realized revenues for the interim period to determine a reasonable income measurement.

In preparing interim reports, adjustments for accrued items, generally required only at year-end, must be considered at the end of each interim period. Because of the additional time and extra costs involved to develop complete information, many estimates of expenses are made for interim reports. The increased number of estimates adds an element of subjectivity to these reports. Another problem is that extraordinary items or the disposal of a business segment will have a greater impact on an interim period's earnings than on the results of operations for an entire year. In analyzing interim financial statements, special attention should be given to these and similar considerations.

ifrs

Two prominent viewpoints exist in relation to the reporting of interim results. One viewpoint is that each reporting interval is to be recognized as a separate accounting period. Thus, the results of operations for each interim period are determined in essentially the same manner as for the annual accounting period. Under this approach, the same judgments, estimations, accruals, and deferrals are recognized at the end of each interim period as for the annual period. This is the approach followed in *IAS 34*.

The other viewpoint, and the one accepted by the FASB, is that the interim period is an integral part of the annual period.[27] Essentially, the revenues and expenses for the total period are allocated among interim periods on some reasonable basis, for example, time, sales volume, or productive activity. Under the integral part of annual period concept, the same general accounting principles and reporting practices employed for annual reports are to be utilized for interim statements, but modifications may be required so the interim

[27] FASB ASC paragraphs 270-10-45-1 and 2.

results will better relate to the total results of operations for the annual period. As an example of the type of modification that may be required, assume that a company uses the LIFO method of inventory valuation and encounters a situation where liquidation of the base period inventory occurs at an interim date but the inventory is expected to be replaced by the end of the annual period. Under these circumstances, the inventory reported at the interim date should not reflect the LIFO liquidation, and the cost of goods sold for the interim period should include the expected cost of replacing the liquidated LIFO base.

Another example of a required modification deals with a change in accounting principle during an interim period. As explained in Chapter 20, these changes should follow the provisions of FASB ASC Topic 250 (Accounting Changes and Error Corrections). Those provisions state that the change should be applied retroactively to all of the results reported.[28]

To illustrate the added insight that quarterly information can provide, quarterly data for **Toys "R" Us** from its 2009 annual report are provided in Exhibit 19-5. The retail toy business is very seasonal, and this fact is reflected in the quarterly numbers for Toys "R" Us. Reported revenue is at its maximum in the quarter that concludes at the end of January (the fourth quarter), which encompasses the Christmas selling season. Anyone reading only the annual net income numbers of Toys "R" Us misses the potentially valuable information contained in the wide variation in net income from quarter to quarter.

> **STOP&THINK**
>
> What is the biggest barrier to the release of *daily* financial statements by publicly traded companies?
>
> a) Generation of daily stock price data
> b) Generation of daily accounting estimates
> c) Generation of daily sales data
> d) Generation of daily cost of goods sold data

Notice that Toys "R" Us' quarterly results are labeled "unaudited." Obviously, the small amount of information provided about each quarter does not "present fairly" the results of Toys "R" Us' operations for that quarter. Accordingly, quarterly reports

EX 19-5 SUMMARY QUARTERLY DATA FOR TOYS "R" US

Quarterly Financial Data
(In millions)

The following table sets forth certain unaudited quarterly financial information:

	First Quarter	Second Quarter	Third Quarter	Fourth Quarter
2009 Net Sales	$2,477	$2,567	$2,667	$5,857
2009 Gross Margin	890	951	950	1,987
2009 Net Earnings/(Loss)	(35)	27	(67)	387
2008 Net Sales	2,719	2,771	2,773	5,461
2008 Gross Margin	977	1,014	960	1,797
2008 Net Earnings/(Loss)	(36)	13	(104)	345

[28] FASB ASC paragraphs 250-10-45-14 through 16.

are almost always labeled "unaudited" because they do not fairly present a firm's operations, cash flows, and financial position in the same way as do the annual financial statements that are audited. Quarterly reports submitted to the SEC in the 10-Q filing are not required to be audited although they are to be prepared in accordance with GAAP.

SOLUTIONS TO STOP & THINK

1. (Page 19-9) The correct answer is A. Credit risk is the uncertainty over whether the party on the other side of an agreement will abide by the terms of the agreement. A forward contract is a private agreement negotiated between two parties. There is always the possibility that the party required to make the settlement payment at the end of the forward contract will refuse to pay. Accordingly, there is credit risk associated with a forward contract.
2. (Page 19-35) The correct answer is C. PepsiCo's segment information can tell Coke where Pepsi is enjoying the most soft drink success, where PepsiCo is weak, and what PepsiCo's profit margins are. The profit margin information is probably the most useful to Coca-Cola. Without any disclosure by Pepsi, market research can probably tell Coca-Cola where Pepsi's strengths and weaknesses are with regard to sales. However, the information about Pepsi's costs and profits is hard to find out unless Pepsi discloses it.
3. (Page 19-37) The correct answer is B. Technically, it is possible right now for most large firms to prepare daily financial statements. And many firms actually do compile daily sales and gross profit reports. However, it isn't clear whether making the estimates necessary to prepare full financial statements would provide useful information. As discussed in the chapter, even the preparation of quarterly reports requires more estimates and approximations than does the preparation of the annual report. The cost of the timeliness of daily reports very likely exceeds any associated benefit.

SOLUTION TO USING THE FASB'S CODIFICATION

In FASB ASC Topic 815 (Derivatives and Hedging), you can see listed Subtopic 815-45 (Weather Derivatives). This is a good indication that "weather derivatives" actually exist. Clicking on the Glossary yields the following definition of a "weather derivative": "A forward-based or option-based contract for which settlement is based on a climatic or geological variable. One example of such a variable is the occurrence or nonoccurrence of a specified amount of snow at a specified location within a specified period of time."

Section 815-45-55 provides some illustrations of accounting for a weather derivative. The weather derivative used in the illustration is based on daily temperature. The firms involved in the weather derivative arrangement are described as follows: "Entity A is a construction materials entity that has its sales decrease during cold winters or a chemical manufacturer that has its natural gas consumption costs increase during cold winters. Entity B is a natural gas distribution entity that experiences lower revenues during warm winters." Whether the company receives cash or pays cash under the weather derivative contract depends on the average temperature for a specified period.

REVIEW CHAPTER 19

DERIVATIVES

1 Understand the business and accounting concepts connected with derivatives and hedging activities.

Uncertainty about the future fair value of assets and liabilities or about future cash flows exposes firms to risk. One way to manage this risk is through the use of derivatives. A *derivative* is a financial instrument or other contract that derives its value from the movement of prices, interest rates, or exchange rates associated with an underlying item. Many derivatives are executory contracts, meaning that they are not a transaction but are an exchange of promises about future actions.

2 Identify the different types of risk faced by a business.

Of the many types of risk faced by a firm, four important types are as follows:

- *Price risk.* Uncertainty about the future price of an asset
- *Credit risk.* Uncertainty over whether the party on the other side of a transaction will abide by the terms of the agreement
- *Interest rate risk.* Uncertainty about future interest rates and their impact on cash flows and the fair value of financial instruments
- *Exchange rate risk.* Uncertainty about the future U.S. dollar cash flows stemming from assets and liabilities denominated in foreign currencies

3 Describe the characteristics of the following types of derivatives: swaps, forwards, futures, and options.

- *Swap.* Contract in which two parties agree to exchange payments in the future based upon some price or rate. A good example is the exchange of a stream of variable-rate interest payments for a stream of fixed-rate payments. A swap can transform the stream of future cash flows that you have into the cash flow stream that you want.
- *Forwards.* Agreement between two parties to exchange a specified amount of a commodity, security, or foreign currency at a specified date with the price or rate being set now. Forward contracts are usually settled with cash payments instead of by actual delivery of the underlying asset.
- *Futures.* Very similar to a forward contract, with the difference being that a futures contract is a standardized instrument that is sponsored by and traded on an organized exchange.
- *Option.* Contract giving the owner the right, but not the obligation, to buy or sell an asset at a specified exercise price. A *call option* gives the owner the right to buy an asset; a *put option* gives the owner the right to sell an asset. The buyer of an option must pay cash in advance for the option; in exchange, the buyer is protected against unfavorable price or rate movements but can still benefit from favorable movements.

4 Define *hedging*, and outline the difference between a fair value hedge and a cash flow hedge.

Hedging is the structuring of transactions to reduce risk. Much hedging occurs naturally in business as increases in costs or in the value of liabilities are offset by related increases in revenues or in the value of assets. Derivatives are also used for hedging. The FASB has identified two general types of hedges for which derivatives can be used:

- *Fair value hedge.* The change in the fair value of the derivative offsets changes in fair values of assets or liabilities
- *Cash flow hedge.* Cash flows from the derivative offset variability in the cash flows from forecasted transactions

5 **Account for a variety of different derivatives and for hedging relationships.**

The fair value of all derivatives is to be recognized and reported in the balance sheet. Changes in fair value are reported as follows:

- *Derivative is not a hedge.* Changes in fair value are reported as gains or losses in the income statement.
- *Derivative is a fair value hedge.* Changes in fair value are reported as gains or losses in the income statement and are offset by gains or losses on changes in the fair value of the asset or liability being hedged.
- *Derivative is a cash flow hedge.* Changes in fair value are deferred and reported in comprehensive income (an equity adjustment). These deferred gains and losses are recognized in income on the forecasted date of the cash flows being hedged.

CONTINGENCIES

6 **Apply the accounting rules for contingent items to the areas of lawsuits and environmental liabilities.**

If a contingent liability is probable and can be reasonably estimated, it should be recognized in the financial statements. If a contingent liability is only possible, it should be disclosed in the financial statement notes. Contingent liabilities that are remote should not, in general, be disclosed. Contingent assets are generally not recognized until any remaining uncertainty is very small.

In accounting for lawsuits, firms are usually reluctant to disclose specific amounts or to overestimate the likelihood of losing the suit because they don't want to increase their chances of losing the lawsuit or of paying a large judgment amount.

Accounting for environmental remediation liabilities is complicated by the fact that the future cost of the cleanup is very difficult to estimate. In addition, each cleanup project is surrounded by suits and countersuits between government agencies and the responsible firms and among the responsible firms themselves. The SEC requires substantial disclosure of the details of a firm's environmental cleanup projects.

SEGMENT REPORTING

7 **Prepare the necessary supplemental disclosures of financial information by product line and by geographic area.**

Historically, segment reporting in the United States has been more extensive than in any other country. The FASB worked with the AcSB in Canada and with the IASB to improve segment reporting worldwide.

Under the provisions of FASB ASC Topic 280, companies are required to disclose the following information for each business segment: revenues, operating profit, assets, capital expenditures, and certain income statement items such as depreciation and interest revenue and expense.

Companies are to define their reportable business segments using the same practice that is used internally. The objective of this requirement is to provide external users the same type of segment information used inside the company.

INTERIM REPORTING

8 **Recognize the importance of interim reports, and outline the difficulties encountered when preparing those reports.**

In the United States, publicly traded firms are required to file quarterly summary financial statements with the SEC in a filing called a *10-Q*. These interim financial statements are prepared using the "integral part of annual period" concept. Using this concept, each quarter is not viewed as a separate period but as an integral part of the year, and estimates are used to appropriately allocate a share of the annual results to each quarter. Quarterly reports are typically not audited, but they still are to be prepared in accordance with GAAP.

FASB-IASB CODIFICATION SUMMARY

ifrs

Topic	FASB Accounting Standards Codification	Original FASB Standard	Corresponding IASB Standard	Differences between U.S. GAAP and IFRS
Accounting for derivatives	*Topic 815*	*SFAS No. 133*	*IAS 39*	No substantial differences at the conceptual level, but numerous technical differences that are beyond the scope of this book.
Recognition of contingent liabilities and contingent assets	*Contingent liabilities: Section 450-20-25* *Contingent assets: Section 450-30-25*	*SFAS No. 5 par. 3 and 17*	*IAS 37 par. 10,27-28,31,34*	Generally the same. Under IFRS, there is no requirement to disclose contingent guarantee obligations when their likelihood is remote.
Measurement of contingent liabilities	*Section 450-20-30 par. 1*	*FIN No. 14 par. 3*	*IAS 37 par. 36-47*	Under U.S. GAAP, the estimated liability is the low end of the estimated range if each estimate in the range is equally likely. Under IFRS, the estimated liability is the amount required to settle the obligation.
Segment reporting	*Topic 280*	*SFAS No. 131*	*IFRS 8*	No substantial differences
Relation between interim reporting and annual reporting	*Section 270-10-45 par. 1-2*	*APB Opinion No. 28 par. 9*	*IAS 34 par. 28*	Under U.S. GAAP, an interim period is viewed as a subcomponent of the annual period. Under IFRS, accounting principles are applied to an interim period in the same way they are applied to an annual period.

KEY TERMS

Call option 19-11
Cash flow hedge 19-13
Conglomerates 19-31
Contingent gains 19-24
Contingent losses 19-24
Credit risk 19-6
Derivative 19-3
Exchange rate risk 19-6
Executory contract 19-5
Fair value hedge 19-13
Forward contract 19-8
Futures contract 19-10
Hedging 19-13
Integral part of annual period concept 19-36
Interest rate risk 19-6
Interest rate swap 19-7
Interim financial statements 19-36
Notional amount 19-16
Option 19-11
Price risk 19-6
Put option 19-11
Swap 19-7

QUESTIONS

DERIVATIVES

1. How does a derivative differ from other financial instruments and contracts?
2. Why is a derivative often an executory contract? Give another example of an executory contract.
3. Briefly describe the four types of risk discussed in the chapter.
4. Why would a company enter into an interest rate swap?
5. What is the difference between a forward contract and a futures contract?

6. How does an option differ from the other types of derivatives discussed in the chapter?
7. Describe the purpose of a cash flow hedge, and give an example of a cash flow hedge.
8. Why is traditional historical cost accounting inappropriate when accounting for derivative contracts?
9. When does partial hedge ineffectiveness occur?
10. Derivatives are to be reported in the balance sheet at their fair value on the balance sheet date. How are unrealized gains and losses on derivatives recognized in the financial statements?
11. What is the notional amount of a derivative? How can the notional amount be misleading?
12. A derivative used as an economic hedge of foreign currency risk associated with a foreign currency–denominated asset or liability is not accounted for as a hedge under the provisions of FASB ASC Topic 815 (Derivatives and Hedging). How are these derivatives accounted for?
13. How does the accounting for a speculative derivative investment differ from that for a derivative that serves as a hedge?
14. What international standard governs the accounting for derivatives? How does this standard differ from U.S. GAAP?

CONTINGENCIES

15. How should contingent liabilities that are reasonably possible of becoming liabilities be reported in the financial statements?
16. Describe the appropriate treatment of contingent gains.
17. What factors are important in deciding whether a pending lawsuit should be reported as a liability on the balance sheet?
18. What factors must a company consider in estimating the amount to recognize for a probable contingent liability?
19. Under what circumstances should the existence of an environmental liability be considered "probable"?

SEGMENT REPORTING

20. In what ways can segment information assist in the analysis of a company's financial statements?
21. How is a business segment to be identified under the provisions of FASB ASC Topic 280 (Segment Reporting)?
22. How large must an internally defined segment be for separate financial statement disclosure to be required?
23. Is segment information prepared according to GAAP? Explain.

INTERIM REPORTING

24. Distinguish between the two primary viewpoints concerning the preparation of interim financial statements.
25. Why should investors be careful in interpreting interim reports?

PRACTICE EXERCISES

Practice 19-1
LO3

Understanding the Terms of an Interest Rate Swap

On January 1 of Year 1, the company entered into a 2-year $100,000 variable interest rate loan. In the first year of the loan, the interest rate is 10%. In its second year, the interest rate is equal to the prime lending rate on January 1 of Year 2. The company does not want to bear the risk associated with the uncertain interest rate in the second year. Accordingly, on January 1 of Year 1, the company enters into a pay-fixed, receive-variable interest rate swap with a speculator. This swap obligates the company to pay the speculator a fixed amount of $10,000 ($100,000 × 0.10) on December 31 of Year 2. In return, the company will receive from the speculator on December 31 of Year 2 a variable amount equal to $100,000 multiplied by the prime lending rate on January 1 of Year 2. This amount received from the speculator is exactly enough to pay the interest due on the variable-rate loan in Year 2. Typically, interest rate swaps such as this are settled with a single net cash payment rather than the actual payment of $10,000 and receipt of the variable amount. What net amount will the company pay or receive on December 31 of Year 2 if the prime lending rate on January 1 of Year 2 is (1) 8%, (2) 12%, and (3) 10%?

Practice 19-2
LO3

Understanding the Impact of an Interest Rate Swap
Refer to Practice 19-1 and complete the following:

1. Compute the total amount (including all swap-related cash flows) that the company will pay in interest in Year 2, assuming that the prime lending rate on January 1 of Year 2 is (a) 8%, (b) 12%, and (c) 10%. Comment on your computations.
2. When the speculator entered into the interest rate swap agreement on January 1 of Year 1, which direction did the speculator think that interest rates were going to go—up or down? Explain.

Practice 19-3
LO3

Understanding the Terms of a Forward Contract
The company is a golf course developer that constructs approximately 15 courses per year. Next year, the company will buy 5,000 trees to install in the courses it builds. In recent years, the price of trees has fluctuated wildly. To eliminate this uncertainty, the company has found a reputable financial institution that will enter into a forward contract for 5,000 trees. On January 1 of Year 1, the company agrees to buy 5,000 trees on January 1 of Year 2 from the financial institution. The price is set at $400 per tree. Of course, the financial institution doesn't own any trees. As with most derivative contracts, this agreement will be settled by an exchange of cash on January 1 of Year 2 based on the price of trees on that date. What net amount will the golf course developer pay or receive on January 1 of Year 2 under the forward contract if the price of each tree on that date is (1) $250, (2) $600, and (3) $400? Remember that the forward contract was for 5,000 trees.

Practice 19-4
LO3

Understanding the Impact of a Forward Contract
Refer to Practice 19-3 and complete the following:

1. Compute the total amount (including all forward-related cash flows) that the golf course developer will pay to buy 5,000 trees in Year 2, assuming that the price of a tree on January 1 of Year 2 is (a) $250, (b) $600, and (c) $400. Comment on your computations.
2. When the financial institution entered into the tree forward contract on January 1 of Year 1, which direction did the financial institution think that tree prices were going to go—up or down? Explain.

Practice 19-5
LO3

Understanding the Terms of a Futures Contract
The mining company produces 25,000 pounds of copper each month in its mining operations. To eliminate the price risk associated with copper sales, on December 1 of Year 1, the mining company entered into a futures contract to sell 25,000 pounds of copper on January 1 of Year 2. The futures price is $0.77 per pound. The futures contract is managed through an exchange, so the mining company does not know the party on the other side of the contract. As with most derivative contracts, this futures contract will be settled by an exchange of cash on January 1 of Year 2 based on the price of copper on that date. What net amount will the mining company pay or receive on January 1 of Year 2 under the futures contract if the price of copper per pound on that date is (1) $0.62, (2) $0.88, and (3) $0.77? Remember that the futures contract is for 25,000 pounds and that the mining company is selling the copper.

Practice 19-6
LO3

Understanding the Impact of a Futures Contract
Refer to Practice 19-5 and complete the following:

1. Compute the total amount (including all futures-related cash flows) that the mining company will receive to sell 25,000 pounds of copper in January of Year 2, assuming that the price of copper per pound on January 1 of Year 2 is (a) $0.62, (b) $0.88, and (c) $0.77. Comment on your computations.
2. Assume that the party on the other side of the futures contract was a speculator. When that speculator entered into the copper futures contract on December 1 of

Year 1, which direction did the speculator think that copper prices were going to go—up or down? Explain.

Practice 19-7

LO3

Understanding the Terms of an Option Contract

The company makes colorful 100% cotton shirts that are very popular among sophisticated business executives. The company uses 100,000 pounds of cotton each month in its production process. On December 1 of Year 1, the company purchased a call option to buy 100,000 pounds of cotton on January 1 of Year 2. The option exercise price is $0.39 per pound. It cost the company $2,500 to buy this option. As with most derivative contracts, this option contract will be settled by an exchange of cash on January 1 of Year 2 based on the price of cotton on that date. What net amount will the shirt company pay or receive on January 1 of Year 2 under the option contract if the price of cotton per pound on that date is (1) $0.52, (2) $0.30, and (3) $0.39? Remember that the option contract is for 100,000 pounds and that the shirt company has the option to buy the cotton.

Practice 19-8

LO3

Understanding the Impact of an Option Contract

Refer to Practice 19-7 and complete the following:

1. Compute the total amount (including all option-related cash flows) that the shirt company will pay to buy 100,000 pounds of cotton in January of Year 2, assuming that the price of cotton per pound on January 1 of Year 2 is (a) $0.52, (b) $0.30, and (c) $0.39. Comment on your computations.
2. Assume that the party who wrote the cotton call option contract was a speculator. When that speculator wrote the cotton call option on December 1 of Year 1, which direction did the speculator think that cotton prices were going to go—up or down? Explain.

Practice 19-9

LO4

Understanding the Impact of Overhedging: Interest Rate Swap

Refer to Practice 19-1 and Practice 19-2. What would be the impact on the company's total cash payment in Year 2 if the pay-fixed, receive-variable interest rate swap had been based on a loan amount of $300,000 instead of $100,000? In other words, what would be the company's total cash payment in Year 2 if the variable-rate loan is $100,000 but the interest rate swap is for a $300,000 loan and the January 1 of Year 2 prime lending rate is (1) 8%, (2) 12%, and (3) 10%? Comment on your computations.

Practice 19-10

LO4

Understanding the Impact of Partial Hedging: Forward Contract

Refer to Practice 19-3 and Practice 19-4. What would be the impact on the golf course developer's total cash payment to purchase trees in Year 2 if the forward contract had been for just 1,500 trees rather than the full 5,000 trees expected to be purchased in Year 2? In other words, what would be the golf course developer's total cash payment in Year 2 if it purchases 5,000 trees but the forward contract is for 1,500 trees and the January 1 of Year 2 tree price is (1) $250, (2) $600, and (3) $400? Comment on your computations.

Practice 19-11

LO5

Overview of Accounting for Derivatives: Fair Value Hedge

On December 1 of Year 1, the company made a $100,000 investment in a highly risky Internet stock. The investment is classified as a trading security. Part of the investment agreement prevents the company from selling the investment before January 1 of Year 2. To remove uncertainty about fluctuations in the value of the investment, the company entered into a forward contract with a speculator. Under the forward contract, the company will sell the investment to the speculator on January 1 of Year 2 for $100,000. (*Note*: For simplicity, ignore the inconsistency in the fact that the securities are classified as trading yet the forward contract guarantees that the company will not earn any return when the securities are sold.) Make all journal entries necessary on December 31 of Year 1 in connection with both the investment securities and the forward contract, assuming that the market value of the securities on December 31 is (1) $130,000, (2) $75,000, and (3) $100,000.

Practice 19-12
LO5

Overview of Accounting for Derivatives: Cash Flow Hedge
A farmer expects to sell 5,000 bushels of corn on January 1 of Year 2. On December 1 of Year 1, the farmer enters into a futures contract to sell the corn on January 1 of Year 2 at $2.30 per bushel. The market price of corn on December 1 was also $2.30 per bushel. Make all journal entries necessary on December 31 of Year 1 in connection with the futures contract, assuming that the market price of corn per bushel on December 31 is (1) $2.55, (2) $2.10, and (3) $2.30.

Practice 19-13
LO5

Computing the Notional Amount
Compute the notional amount of the derivative contract for each of the following:

1. The interest rate swap contract. See Practice 19-1.
2. The tree forward contract. See Practice 19-3.
3. The copper futures contract. See Practice 19-5.
4. The corn futures contract. See Practice 19-12.

Practice 19-14
LO5

Accounting for an Interest Rate Swap
Refer to Practice 19-1. Make any necessary journal entry on the borrowing company's books on December 31 of Year 1 in connection with the interest rate swap, assuming that the prime lending rate on December 31 is (1) 8%, (2) 12%, and (3) 10%. Even though the swap payment is not made until December 31 of Year 2, for simplicity ignore the time value of money.

Practice 19-15
LO5

Accounting for a Forward Contract
Refer to Practice 19-3. Make any necessary journal entry on the golf course developer's books on December 31 of Year 1 in connection with the tree forward contract, assuming that the price per tree on that date is (1) $250, (2) $600, and (3) $400.

Practice 19-16
LO5

Accounting for a Futures Contract
Refer to Practice 19-5. Make any necessary journal entry on the mining company's books on December 31 of Year 1 in connection with the copper futures contract, assuming that the price of copper per pound on that date is (1) $0.62, (2) $0.88, and (3) $0.77.

Practice 19-17
LO5

Accounting for an Option Contract
Refer to Practice 19-7. Make any necessary journal entry on the shirt company's books on December 31 of Year 1 in connection with the cotton option contract, assuming that the price of cotton per pound on that date is (1) $0.52, (2) $0.30, and (3) $0.39. Remember that the cotton option was purchased for $2,500.

Practice 19-18
LO5

Accounting for a Foreign Currency Futures Contract
On December 1 of Year 1, Lorien Company made a credit sale to a Thai company. The amount of the sale was 100,000 Thai baht. Lorien will collect the account on January 1 of Year 2. On December 1, the exchange rate was 40 Thai baht for 1 U.S. dollar. On December 1, Lorien entered into a futures contract to sell 100,000 Thai baht on January 1 of Year 2 at an exchange rate of 40 Thai baht for 1 U.S. dollar. Make all journal entries necessary on December 31 of Year 1 in connection with both the account receivable and the futures contract, assuming that the exchange rate for 1 U.S. dollar on December 31 is (1) 50 Thai baht, (2) 37 Thai baht, and (3) 40 Thai baht.

Practice 19-19
LO5

Accounting for a Derivative Speculation
The company specializes in speculating on the direction of movements in the price of gold. On December 1 of Year 1, the company entered into a futures contract to sell 100 ounces of gold at $1,119 per ounce on January 1 of Year 2. The company expected the price of gold to decline between December 1 and January 1. The market price of gold on December 1 of Year 1 was $1,119 per ounce. Make all journal entries necessary on December 31 of Year 1 in connection with the futures contract, assuming that the price per ounce of gold on December 31 is (1) $1,050, (2) $1,213, and (3) $1,119.

Practice 19-20
LO6

Contingent Liabilities
The company has the following three potential obligations. Describe how each will be reported in the financial statements.

1. The company has guaranteed a loan for one of its suppliers. If the supplier fails to repay the loan, the company will be required to repay it. Currently, the probability of the supplier defaulting on the loan is considered remote.
2. The company has been sued by a group of shareholders who claim that they were deceived by the company's financial reporting practices. It is possible that the company will lose this lawsuit.
3. The company is involved in litigation over who must clean up a toxic waste site near one of the company's factories. It is probable, but not certain, that the company will be required to pay for the cleanup.

Practice 19-21
LO6

Accounting for Contingent Losses and Contingent Gains
In each of the following cases, make the necessary journal entry, if any. If no journal entry is necessary, describe how the item would be reported in the financial statements.

1. The company has sued another company for patent infringement and won a preliminary judgment of $800,000 in the case. This judgment is under appeal. The company's attorneys agree that it is possible (not probable) that the sued company will win this appeal.
2. The company has long owned a manufacturing site that has now been discovered to be contaminated with toxic waste. The company has acknowledged its responsibility for the contamination. An initial cleanup feasibility study has shown that it will cost at least $450,000 to clean up the toxic waste.
3. The company has been sued for patent infringement and lost the case. A preliminary judgment of $290,000 was issued and is under appeal. The company's attorneys agree that it is possible (not probable) that the company will lose this appeal.

Practice 19-22
LO7

Segment Reporting
Rainbow Company has internally organized itself into the following seven segments:

	Total Revenues	Operating Profit	Total Assets
Segment 1	$1,000	$150	$ 600
Segment 2	600	30	100
Segment 3	500	80	200
Segment 4	700	100	300
Segment 5	200	20	800
Segment 6	100	10	110
Segment 7	80	15	100
Total	$3,180	$405	$2,210

Segments 3 and 4 have similar products, use similar processes, and distribute their products through similar channels.

Rainbow Company is concerned about reporting segment information for each segment. According to FASB ASC Topic 280 (Segment Reporting), which of the segments should be separately reported?

Practice 19-23
LO8

Interim Reporting
The company has historically reported bad debt expense of 1% of sales in each quarter. For the current year, the company followed the same procedure in the first three quarters of the year. However, in the fourth quarter, the company, in consultation with its auditor,

determined that bad debt expense for the year should be $280. Sales in each quarter of the year were as follows: first quarter, $2,000; second quarter, $1,600; third quarter, $2,200; fourth quarter, $3,000. Make the adjusting journal entry necessary to record bad debt expense in the fourth quarter.

EXERCISES

Exercise 19-24
LO5

Derivatives: Accounting for a Speculation

Warsaw Signal Company specializes in predicting price movements in the soybean market. On November 1, 2013, it was convinced that soybean prices were too low. Accordingly, Warsaw entered into futures contracts to purchase 50,000 bushels of soybeans at $5.00 per bushel on January 1, 2014. The market price of soybeans on November 1, 2013 was $5.00 per bushel.

1. Make the adjusting journal entry necessary on December 31, 2013, if the market price of soybeans is $4.75 per bushel on that date.
2. Make the adjusting journal entry necessary on December 31, 2013, if the market price of soybeans is $5.20 per bushel on that date.

Exercise 19-25
LO5
SPREADSHEET

Derivatives: Accounting for Swaps

On January 1, 2013, Slidell Company received a 2-year, $500,000 loan, with interest payments occurring at the end of each year and the principal to be repaid on December 31, 2014. The interest rate for the first year is the prevailing market rate of 8%, and the rate in 2014 will be equal to the market interest rate on January 1, 2014. In conjunction with this loan, Slidell enters into an interest rate swap agreement to receive a swap payment (based on $500,000) if the January 1, 2014, interest rate is greater than 8% and will make a swap payment if the rate is less than 8%. The interest swap payment will be made on December 31, 2014.

Make all journal entries necessary on Slidell's books in 2013 and 2014 to record this loan and the interest rate swap. On January 1, 2014, the interest rate is 6%.

Exercise 19-26
LO5

Derivatives: Accounting for Options

Far West Clothing Mills uses approximately 300,000 pounds of cotton each month to make the cotton fabric used in its patented no-wrinkle, long-sleeved white shirts. On December 1, 2013, Far West purchased an option to buy 300,000 pounds of cotton on January 1, 2014, at a price of $0.50 per pound. The market price on December 1 is $0.50 per pound. Far West had to pay $2,000 to purchase the cotton option. Far West designated the option as a hedge against price fluctuations for its January purchases of cotton.

Make all journal entries necessary on Far West's books on December 1, 2013, December 31, 2013, and January 1, 2014, to record this option and to record the purchase of 300,000 pounds of cotton on January 1. On December 31, 2013, and on January 1, 2014, the market price of cotton is $0.42 per pound.

Exercise 19-27
LO5

Derivatives: Accounting for Forward Contracts

On September 1, 2013, Ramus Company purchased machine parts from Ho Man Tin Company for 6,000,000 Hong Kong dollars to be paid on January 1, 2014. The exchange rate on September 1 is HK$7.7 = $1. On the same date, Ramus enters into a forward contract and agrees to purchase HK$6,000,000 on January 1, 2014, at the rate of HK$7.7 = $1.

Make all journal entries necessary on Ramus' books on three dates—September 1, 2013, December 31, 2013, and January 1, 2014—to record this purchase and the forward contract. On December 31, 2013, and on January 1, 2014, the exchange rate is HK$8.0 = $1. Ramus uses a perpetual inventory system.

Exercise 19-28
LO5

Derivatives: Accounting for Futures Contracts

Shelby Organics produces bottled orange juice. Orange juice concentrate is typically bought and sold by the pound, and Shelby uses 50,000 pounds of orange juice concentrate each month. On December 1, 2013, Shelby entered into an orange juice concentrate futures contract to buy 50,000 pounds of concentrate on January 1 at a price of $0.95 per pound, which is also the market price of concentrate on December 1. Shelby designates the futures contract as a hedge of the forecasted purchase of orange juice concentrate in January.

Make all journal entries necessary on Shelby's books on December 1, 2013, December 31, 2013, and January 1, 2014, to record this futures contract and to record the purchase of 50,000 pounds of orange juice concentrate on January 1. On December 31, 2013, and on January 1, 2014, the market price of concentrate is $0.85 per pound.

Exercise 19-29
LO4

Derivatives: Identifying a Hedge

Shank Company manufactures candy. On September 1, Shank purchased a futures contract that obligates it to sell 150,000 pounds of sugar on September 30 at $0.41 per pound. Shank typically purchases 150,000 pounds of sugar per month to use as a raw material in the candy production process. It purchased the futures contract to hedge against movements in the price of sugar during the month of September.

In Shank's case, the sugar futures contract does not hedge against movements in the price of sugar. Demonstrate this by computing the net cost of the 150,000 pounds of sugar purchased in September under three sets of circumstances, at the price per pound of $0.38, $0.41, and $0.44.

Exercise 19-30
LO5

Derivatives: Notional Amounts

Refer back to Exercises 19-27 and 19-28.

1. What is the notional value of the Hong Kong dollar forward contract described in Exercise 19-27? What is the fair value of the forward contract on December 31, 2013?
2. What is the notional value of the orange juice concentrate futures contract described in Exercise 19-28? What is the fair value of the futures contract on December 31, 2013?

Exercise 19-31
LO8

Interim Reporting: Interim LIFO Liquidation

On December 31, 2012, Courtney Company had LIFO ending inventory consisting of 800 units with a LIFO cost of $15 per unit. During the first quarter of 2013, Courtney sold 1,400 units. As of March 31, 2013, the inventory of Courtney is 650 units, and the current purchase price of inventory is $38 per unit. The reduction in the level of inventory is temporary, and Courtney fully expects inventory levels to be at or above 800 units by December 31, 2013. The recorded cost of goods sold for Courtney for the first quarter of 2013 is $49,750 [(1,250 × $38) + (150 × $15)]. What adjusting entry, if any, should Courtney make on March 31, 2013, to correctly apply LIFO to the reporting of quarterly results?

Exercise 19-32
LO8

Interim Reporting: Interim Income Statements

The income statement of Heifer Technology Inc. for the year ended December 31, 2013, is given below. Using the yearly income statement and the supplemental information, reconstruct the third-quarter interim statement for Heifer.

Supplemental information:

(a) Assume a 35% tax rate.
(b) Third-quarter sales were 30% of total sales.
(c) For interim reporting purposes, a gross profit rate of 41% can be justified.
(d) Variable operating expenses are allocated in the same proportion as sales. Fixed operating expenses are allocated based on the expiration of time. Of the total operating expenses, $70,000 relate to variable expenses.
(e) The equipment was sold June 1, 2013.
(f) The extraordinary loss occurred September 1, 2013.

Heifer Technology Inc.
Income Statement
For the Year Ended December 31, 2013

Sales	$1,200,000
Cost of goods sold	710,000
Gross profit on sales	$ 490,000
Operating expenses	104,000
Operating income	$ 386,000
Gain on sale of equipment	22,000
Income from continuing operations before income taxes	$ 408,000
Income taxes	142,800
Income from continuing operations	$ 265,200
Extraordinary loss (net of income tax savings of $45,000)	(80,000)
Net income	$ 185,200

Exercise 19-33

LO7

Segment Reporting: Types of Information Disclosed by Business Segment

Companies are required to disclose selected results in the financial statements for significant business segments. This information often takes the form of industry segment reporting by diversified companies, but it also can be by geographic areas.

Locate the annual report of **The Walt Disney Company** on the Internet at **http://www.disney.com** and identify the kind of segment disclosure Disney provides. Is this information useful to prospective investors? Why or why not?

Exercise 19-34

LO7

Segment Reporting: Reporting Segment Information

Multitasking Industries sells five different types of products. Internally, Multitasking is divided into five different divisions based on these five different product lines. Multitasking has prepared the following information to disclose to external users in the notes to its 2013 financial statements:

Multitasking Industries
Business Segment Information
For the Year Ended December 31, 2013
(in millions of dollars)

	Division 1	Division 2	Division 3	Division 4	Division 5	Total
Revenues	$320	$ 750	$ 94	$290	$105	$1,559
Operating profit	51	104	14	20	7	196
Total assets	530	2,110	372	415	280	3,707

According to the provisions of FASB ASC Topic 280 (Segment Reporting), what additional information must Multitasking provide?

Exercise 19-35

LO6

Contingencies: Types of Liabilities

For each of the following scenarios, identify whether the event described is an actual liability, a contingent liability, or not a liability.

(a) Apple Inc. has used the toxic substance, iocaine powder, in its production process. Recently adopted federal regulations require companies to clean up any factory sites contaminated with iocaine. Apple has begun a preliminary investigation into the iocaine contamination at its factory sites.

(b) Banana Corp. financed its warehouse facilities with a long-term mortgage that calls for semiannual payments of $7,000. The mortgage's current outstanding balance is $98,000.

(c) Orange Company sells computer systems and supplies. It offers its customers a 1-year, money-back guarantee. In the past, approximately 10% of customers have exercised this return privilege.
(d) Kiwi Industries manufactures and distributes outdoor recreational equipment. An individual recently filed a lawsuit as a result of injuries sustained while using Kiwi equipment. Attorneys for Kiwi believe the chance of losing the case is minimal.
(e) Berry Incorporated, a newly formed company, has an unfunded pension plan that calls for retirement benefits to be paid to employees who retire after a minimum of 10 years of employment with the company.
(f) John Townson, a successful entrepreneur, has expressed a desire to establish university scholarships for disadvantaged youth in his community. He has been contacted by numerous universities, but as of yet, nothing firm has been established.

Exercise 19-36
LO6

Contingencies: Contingent Liabilities

Bell Industries is a multinational company. In preparing the annual financial statements, the auditors met with Bell's attorneys to discuss various legal matters facing the firm. For each of the following independent items, determine the appropriate disclosure:

(a) Bell is being sued by a distributor for breach of contract. The attorneys believe there is a 30% chance Bell will lose the suit.
(b) One of Bell's subsidiaries has been accused by a federal agency of violating numerous environmental laws. The company faces significant fines if found guilty. The attorneys believe that the subsidiary has complied with all applicable laws, and they therefore place the probability of incurring the fines at less than 10%.
(c) A subsidiary operating in a foreign country whose government is unstable was recently taken over by the government and nationalized. Bell is negotiating with representatives of that government, but company attorneys believe the probability of the company losing possession of its assets is approximately 90%.

Exercise 19-37
LO6

Contingencies: Disclosure of Contingencies

A lawsuit has been filed against See-Me-Here, Inc., a manufacturer of video postcards, by See-Me-Wherever, another manufacturer of video postcards. The suit alleges patent right infringements by See-Me-Here and asks for compensatory damages. For the following possible situations, determine whether See-Me-Here should report the information concerning the lawsuit as a liability on the balance sheet, and if so, how much; disclose it in a note; or do nothing. Give reasons for your answers.

(a) The suit hasn't been filed, but See-Me-Here's legal counsel has informed management that an unintentional patent infringement has occurred.
(b) See-Me-Here's legal counsel believes an out-of-court settlement is probable and will cost See-Me-Here approximately $700,000.
(c) See-Me-Here's legal counsel believes it is probable that the case will result in an undeterminable loss to See-Me-Here.
(d) See-Me-Here's legal counsel is convinced that the suit will result in a loss to See-Me-Here but isn't sure of the dollar damages.
(e) See-Me-Here's legal counsel believes there is a remote chance for a loss to occur.
(f) See-Me-Here's legal counsel believes it is reasonably possible that the case will result in a $2,800,000 loss to See-Me-Here.

Exercise 19-38
LO6

Contingencies: Contingent Losses

Conrad Corporation sells motorcycle helmets. In 2013, Conrad sold 4 million helmets before discovering a significant defect in their construction. By December 31, 2013, two lawsuits had been filed against Conrad. The first lawsuit, which Conrad has little chance of winning, is expected to settle out of court for $750,000 in January 2014. Conrad's attorneys think the company has a 50–50 chance of winning the second lawsuit, which is for $400,000. What accounting treatment should Conrad give the pending lawsuits in the 2013 year-end financial statements? (Include any necessary journal entries.)

PROBLEMS

Problem 19-39
LO4

Derivatives: Identifying a Hedge

Kanesville Company is still new at using derivatives to hedge business risk. Kanesville has entered into five derivative agreements in an attempt to hedge five specific items. The derivatives, and associated items, are briefly described here:

(a) *Euro futures contract*. If the U.S. dollar value of €500,000 is higher than $300,000 on July 31, Kanesville must pay the difference; if the U.S. dollar value is less than $300,000, Kanesville receives the difference. This futures contract is intended to hedge a €500,000 account payable due to be paid on July 31.

(b) *Copper forward contract*. If the price of copper is more than $1.10 per pound on August 31, Kanesville must pay the difference (multiplied by 100,000 pounds); if the price is less than $1.10, Kanesville receives the difference. This forward contract is intended to hedge Kanesville's expected purchases of copper (as a raw material) for the month of August.

(c) *Japanese yen futures contract*. If the U.S. dollar value of ¥10 million is higher than $90,000 on July 15, Kanesville receives the difference; if the U.S. dollar value is less than $90,000, Kanesville must pay the difference. This futures contract is intended to hedge Kanesville's expected purchase of some equipment from a Japanese company on July 15 for ¥5 million.

(d) *Interest rate swap*. If the interest rate on March 31 of next year is more than 12%, Kanesville receives the difference (on a principal amount of $2,000,000); if the interest rate is less than 12%, Kanesville must pay the difference. This interest rate swap is intended to hedge a $2,000,000 variable-rate loan. The loan is expected to be fully repaid this year on May 10.

(e) *Call option on Williams Company stock*. If the price of a share of Williams Company stock is more than $60 on September 24, Kanesville receives the difference (multiplied by 25,000 shares); if the price of the stock is less than $60, the option is worthless and will be allowed to expire. This call option is intended to hedge an investment in 25,000 shares of Williams Company stock.

Instructions: For each of these five pairs (derivative and associated item), state whether the derivative serves as an effective hedge. Explain your answer.

Problem 19-40
LO5

SPREADSHEET

Derivatives: Accounting for Swaps

On January 1, 2013, Nathan Company received a 5-year, $7,000,000 loan, with interest payments occurring at the end of each year and the principal to be repaid on December 31, 2017. The interest rate for the first year is the prevailing market rate of 8%, and the rate in each succeeding year will be equal to the market interest rate on January 1 of that year. In conjunction with this loan, Nathan enters into an interest rate swap agreement whereby, in each year of the loan starting with 2014, Nathan will receive a swap payment (based on $7,000,000) if the January 1 interest rate is more than 8% and will make a swap payment if the rate is less than 8%. The swap payments are made at the end of the year.

On January 1, 2014, the interest rate is 11%, and on December 31, 2014, the interest rate is 7%.

Instructions: Make all journal entries necessary on Nathan's books in 2013 and 2014 to record this loan and the interest rate swap. For purposes of estimating future swap payments, assume that the current interest rate is the best forecast of the future interest rate.

Problem 19-41
LO5

Derivatives: Accounting for Forward Contracts

Candra Christensen Cuisine operates a chain of fine seafood restaurants. The company makes very detailed long-term plans. On October 1, 2013, Candra Christensen determined that it would need to purchase 800,000 pounds of New England lobster on January 1, 2015. Because of the fluctuations in the price of New England lobster, on October 1 the company negotiated a special forward contract with Lisa Investment Bank for Candra Christensen to purchase 800,000 pounds of New England lobster on January 1, 2015, at a price of $9,600,000. The price of New England lobster was $12 per pound on October 1. Lisa Investment Bank has a staff of financial analysts who specialize in forecasting lobster prices. These analysts are predicting a drop in worldwide lobster prices between October 1, 2013, and January 1, 2015.

On December 31, 2013, the price of a pound of New England lobster is $15. On December 31, 2014, the price of a pound of New England lobster is $9. The appropriate discount rate throughout this period is 10%.

Instructions: Make all journal entries necessary on Candra Christensen's books in 2013, 2014, and 2015 to record the forward contract and the purchase of the lobster. For purposes of estimating future settlement payments under the forward contract, assume that the current price of lobster is the best forecast of the future price.

Problem 19-42
LO5

Derivatives: Accounting for Futures Contracts

On January 1, 2013, Jessica Marie Company sold equipment to Gwang Ju Company for 30,000,000 Korean won, with payment to be received in two years on January 1, 2015. The exchange rate on January 1, 2013, is 800 won = $1. On the same date, Jessica Marie enters into a futures contract and agrees to sell 30,000,000 won on January 1, 2015, at the rate of 800 won = $1.

On December 31, 2013, the exchange rate is 790 won = $1. On December 31, 2014, the exchange rate is 830 won = $1. The appropriate discount rate throughout this period is 10%.

Instructions: Make all journal entries necessary on Jessica Marie's books in 2013, 2014, and 2015 to record this sale, the futures contract, and the collection of the receivable. For purposes of estimating future settlement payments under the futures contract, assume that the current exchange rate is the best forecast of the future exchange rate. (*Note:* Don't forget to record the receivable at its present value.)

Problem 19-43
LO5
SPREADSHEET

Derivatives: Accounting for Options

Pratt Agriculture sells approximately 600,000 bushels of grain each month. On January 1, 2013, Pratt purchased an option to sell 600,000 bushels of grain on January 1, 2015, at a price of $1.25 per bushel. The market price on January 1, 2013, is $1.25 per bushel. Pratt had to pay $90,000 to purchase this grain put option, which it designated as a hedge against price decreases for its January 2015 sales of grain.

On December 31, 2013, the price of grain is $1.75 per bushel. Because there is still time for the price of grain to potentially fall below $1.25 per bushel before the option expires (thus making it advantageous to exercise the put option), the option has a value on December 31, 2013, of $23,000. (*Note*: This December 31, 2013, option value already takes into account an appropriate adjustment for the time value of money.) On December 31, 2014, the price of grain is $1.35 per bushel.

Instructions: Make all journal entries necessary on Pratt's books in 2013, 2014, and 2015 to record this option and the sale of 600,000 bushels of grain in January 2015.

Problem 19-44
LO5

Derivatives: Notional Amounts

Refer to Problems 19-41 and 19-42.

Instructions:

1. What is the notional value of the lobster forward contract described in Problem 19-41? What is the fair value of the forward contract during its life?
2. What is the notional value of the Korean won futures contract described in Problem 19-42? What is the fair value of the futures contract during its life?

Problem 19-45
LO5

Derivatives: Accounting for a Speculation
Martins Cove Company employs 25 analysts who closely track news about supply and demand for livestock and agricultural commodities. Martins Cove uses that information to enter into futures contracts based on its prediction of which way agriculture prices are heading. On December 1, 2013, Martins Cove entered into the following three contracts:

Type of Contract	Quantity	Futures Price per Pound	Market Price per Pound on Dec. 1, 2013
Purchase feeder cattle	250,000 pounds	$1.65	$1.65
Sell pork bellies	800,000	0.45	0.45
Purchase milk.	500,000	0.70	0.70

All three of the contracts are to be settled on January 1, 2014.

Instructions:

1. Make the adjusting journal entries necessary on December 31, 2013, assuming the following market prices per pound on that date: feeder cattle, $1.53; pork bellies, $0.55; and milk, $0.67.
2. Martins Cove has much information about agricultural products. What advantages are there to using this information to trade derivative contracts rather than buying and selling cattle, hogs, and milk directly? What are the disadvantages?

Problem 19-46
LO6

Contingencies: Contingent Liabilities
Southern Outpost Co. has several contingent liabilities at December 31, 2013. The auditor obtained the following brief description of each liability:

(a) In May 2012, Southern Outpost became involved in litigation. In December 2013, the court assessed a judgment for $600,000 against Southern. Southern is appealing the amount of the judgment. Its attorneys believe it is probable that they can reduce the assessment on appeal by 50%. Southern has made no entries pending completion of the appeal process, which is expected to take at least a year.

(b) In July 2013, Duval County brought action against Southern for polluting the St. Johns River with its waste products. It is reasonably possible that Duval County will be successful, but the amount of damages Southern might have to pay should not exceed $280,000. Southern has made no entry to reflect the possible loss.

(c) Southern Outpost has signed as guarantor for a $70,000 loan by Guaranty Bank to Northern Supply Inc., a principal supplier to Southern. At this time, there is a only a remote likelihood that Southern Outpost will have to make payments on behalf of Northern Supply.

Instructions:

1. What amount should be reported as a liability on the December 31, 2013, balance sheet for each of these items?
2. What note disclosure should be included as part of the balance sheet for each of these items?
3. Prepare the journal entries necessary to adjust Southern's books to reflect your answers in (1) and (2).

Problem 19-47
LO6

Contingencies: Entries and Disclosure
This chapter briefly outlined the legal history of the case between **Pennzoil** and **Texaco**. Texaco was ordered to pay $10.5 billion to Pennzoil in 1985. Subsequent appeals in 1986 and 1987 affirmed the judgment against Texaco. The two companies agreed in late 1987 to a settlement of $3 billion, and in 1988 Texaco paid Pennzoil.

Instructions:

1. In 1984, when the lawsuit was initially filed, how should Texaco have disclosed the event? If a journal entry is required, prepare it.
2. In 1986, following the initial jury award and Texaco's failure to have the judgment reversed on appeal, how should Texaco have disclosed the event? If a journal entry is required, prepare it.
3. In 1987, following the $3 billion agreement between Texaco and Pennzoil, how should Texaco have disclosed the event? If a journal entry is required, prepare it.
4. Prepare the journal entry to record Texaco's settlement in 1988.
5. How should Pennzoil have disclosed this event during the years 1984 through 1987?

Problem 19-48

LO6

Contingencies: Accounting for Environmental Liabilities and Other Events

Mercury Rising Inc. manufactures thermometers for use in labs. Management has prepared financial statements for the year ended 2013 for review by the auditors. The audit team has questioned several items in the financial statements and has asked for your advice concerning the proper treatment of these items. Each of the items being questioned follows.

(a) In November 2013, attorneys for current and former employees of Mercury Rising Inc. filed a class action lawsuit, alleging that exposure to mercury has caused significant medical problems. Attorneys for Mercury Rising Inc. are uncertain as to the outcome of the case. However, similar lawsuits against other firms in the mercury industry have resulted in significant payments by the employer.

(b) On January 12, 2014, a fire at a production facility damaged a number of adjacent buildings (owned by other businesses). Mercury's insurance policy does not cover damage to the property of others. Insurance companies for those other businesses have billed Mercury for the estimated cost of $5.3 million required to restore the damaged buildings.

(c) One of Mercury's production plants is located on the shores of Lake Hogwarts. The lake has been rising for a number of years, and the company has installed dikes to prevent flooding. The dikes are currently operating at or near capacity. Weather forecasters have predicted that the lake will rise another eight inches this coming summer. If this occurs, significant damage will likely result from stressing the dikes beyond capacity.

(d) A national magazine printed an article regarding the dangers of mercury and specifically named Mercury Rising Inc. as a "killer of innocent victims." Attorneys for Mercury filed suit for libel and were awarded $2.1 million in damages on December 16, 2013. The magazine has indicated it would appeal the verdict.

Instructions: Determine how each of these events should be disclosed in the financial statements of Mercury Rising Inc. for the year ended December 31, 2013. Provide support for your position.

Problem 19-49

LO7

Segment Reporting: Reporting Segment Data

ProCom Industries operates in several different industries. Total sales for ProCom are $14,000,000, and total common costs are $6,500,000 for 2013. For internal reporting purposes, ProCom allocates common costs based on the ratio of a segment's sales to total sales. Additional information regarding the different segments follows:

	Segment 1	Segment 2	Segment 3	Segment 4	Other Segments
Contribution to total sales	25%	12%	31%	23%	9%
Costs specific to the segment	$1,100,000	$1,000,000	$1,300,000	$880,000	$400,000

Instructions:

1. Compute the operating profit that would be reported internally for each of the four segments.
2. Comment on whether it is appropriate for ProCom to report segment information in the external financial statements using the same common cost allocation method that is used for internal reports.

Problem 19-50

LO7

Segment Reporting: Product Line and Country Disclosure

Chatterton Company has two different product lines and makes significant sales in both the United States and Brazil. Chatterton has compiled the following information:

	Revenue	Operating Profit	Depreciation	Plant and Equipment	Total Assets	Total Liabilities	Capital Expenditure
Product X/U.S.	$500	$110	$10	$ 90	$150	$ 60	$30
Product X/Brazil	210	60	12	70	135	70	20
Product Y/U.S.	300	80	40	200	640	325	80
Product Y/Brazil	120	40	35	130	410	250	60

Instructions:

SPREADSHEET

1. Assume that Chatterton has structured its company internally into divisions based on the two products, X and Y. Prepare the segment disclosure necessary under the provisions of FASB ASC Topic 280.
2. Assume that Chatterton has structured its company internally into two divisions, one for operations in the United States and one for operations in Brazil. Prepare the segment disclosure necessary under the provisions of FASB ASC Topic 280.

Problem 19-51

LO8

Interim Reporting: Forecasting Fourth-Quarter Sales

Harper Company sells toys, so its sales are heavily concentrated in the last quarter of the year because of holiday buying. Harper reported total sales for the past three years as follows (all numbers are in thousands):

	Quarter Ending				
	March 31	June 30	September 30	December 31	Total
2011	$ 6,000	$ 6,000	$ 6,000	$12,000	$30,000
2012	8,000	8,000	8,000	16,000	40,000
2013	10,000	10,000	10,000	20,000	50,000

To make advance arrangements with suppliers, you have been asked to forecast Harper's fourth-quarter sales for the year 2014.

Instructions:

1. Ignore the quarterly sales data given by Harper. Forecast fourth-quarter 2014 sales using just the annual sales data. Describe your assumptions.
2. Repeat (1), but this time use the quarterly sales data.
3. Repeat (2), but also incorporate the fact that first-quarter sales in 2014 were $14,000.
4. Comment on the usefulness of quarterly data.

Problem 19-52

LO6, LO8

Sample CPA Exam Questions

1. Eagle Co. has cosigned the mortgage note on the home of its president, guaranteeing the indebtedness in the event that the president should default. Eagle considers the likelihood of default to be remote. How should the guarantee be treated in Eagle's financial statements?
   (a) Disclosed only.
   (b) Accrued only.
   (c) Accrued and disclosed.
   (d) Neither accrued nor disclosed.
2. In FASB ASC Topic 270 (Interim Reporting), the FASB concludes that interim financial reporting should be viewed primarily in which of the following ways?
   (a) As useful only if activity is spread evenly throughout the year.
   (b) As if the interim period were an annual accounting period.
   (c) As reporting for an integral part of an annual period.
   (d) As reporting under a comprehensive basis of accounting other than GAAP.

CASES

Discussion Case 19-53

Derivatives: What Risks Do We Face?

Palmer Equipment Company is a multinational firm that sells exercise equipment to fitness clubs and to individuals. When customers buy Palmer's equipment, they typically pay 20% down and pay the balance within one year. Palmer's primary market is the United States, where it makes 60% of its sales. Palmer makes 10% of its sales in Japan and 30% in Europe. All foreign sales are denominated in the local currencies.

All of the equipment that Palmer sells is manufactured in southern China. Palmer doesn't own the factories but contracts with various factory owners for the manufacture and delivery of equipment. Palmer's equipment purchase contracts are denominated in Hong Kong dollars.

Palmer has obtained its long-term debt financing from a mixture of U.S., Japanese, and German banks. About half of the loans from U.S. banks are variable-rate loans; the remainder of Palmer's bank loans have fixed rates.

Recently, Palmer has seen its earnings fluctuate wildly from one year to the next. As the recently appointed head of the corporate risk management committee, you have been asked by Jefferson Todd Palmer, CEO of Palmer Equipment, to briefly summarize the different types of risk that Palmer faces.

Discussion Case 19-54

Derivatives: Are Derivatives Just Another Way to Gamble?

Laurie Seals and Julie Winn are roommates at Upland State College. Laurie majors in political science, and Julie is an accounting major. Recently, one of Laurie's political science classes has been discussing the impact of derivative trading losses on the finances of several public institutions in the United States, including city governments and public colleges. The political science class has decided that derivatives are nothing more than a sophisticated form of gambling and that their trading in the United States should be banned.

How should Julie explain to Laurie that derivatives serve a vital business purpose?

Discussion Case 19-55

Contingencies: When Is a Loss a Loss?

How should Newport Company report each of the following contingencies?

(a) A reasonably possible threat of expropriation exists for one of Newport's manufacturing plants located in a foreign country. Any compensation from the foreign government would be less than the plant's carrying amount (book value).

(b) Potential costs exist due to the discovery of a safety hazard related to one of Newport's products. These costs are probable and can be reasonably estimated.
(c) One of Newport's warehouses located at the base of a mountain can no longer be insured against rockslide losses. As of yet, no rockslide losses have occurred.

Discussion Case 19-56

Contingencies: Accounting Standards in Court

Judge Daniel H. Wells is currently deliberating over a suit filed by three stockholders against Transcontinental Corporation. The stockholders allege that Transcontinental's year-end balance sheet was misleading because it did not accurately reflect the company's financial position. The stockholders claim that they relied on the published financial statements and subsequently lost money on their investments in Transcontinental. The primary point at issue is that Transcontinental did not disclose anything about a contingent liability relating to a significant pending lawsuit with a supplier, which Transcontinental subsequently lost. The three stockholders contend that this information was material and relevant and should have been disclosed.

Tomorrow, Transcontinental's accountant will take the stand. Before the lawyers for the opposing parties begin their questioning of the accountant, Judge Wells intends to ask a few questions to determine whether Transcontinental was negligent in its accounting practices. What questions should Judge Wells ask?

Discussion Case 19-57

Contingencies: Do We Need Specific Standards for Environmental and Other Contingent Liabilities?

Many state and federal laws place possible future liabilities on companies as a result of environmental pollution, gender discrimination, safety requirements, and other social responsibilities. In general, these items are part of those potential losses and liabilities covered by FASB ASC Topic 450 (Contingencies). Some companies are reporting these items as liabilities; others are waiting for more specific guidelines by the FASB before reporting them. Should the FASB adopt specific guidelines for reporting these liabilities, or should the decision be left to companies based on the general conceptual guidelines of Topic 450?

Discussion Case 19-58

Segment Reporting: By Product Line or by Country?

Eliza Snow is the controller for Lorenzo Manufacturing. Lorenzo has five different product lines and conducts significant operations in six different countries. Lorenzo's internal organization is set up so that a division manager is in each of the six different countries, with responsibility for sale of all five products in that country. Internal accounting reports are prepared based on this same organizational structure.

Snow has heard rumors that the FASB rules will require Lorenzo to externally report summary segment information by product line. Snow is very upset because this is completely at odds with what Lorenzo does internally. She estimates that compiling segment information by product line will require at least a week's worth of work by her and her entire staff.

Does Snow have a correct understanding of the provisions of FASB ASC Topic 280 (Segment Reporting)? Explain.

Discussion Case 19-59

Interim Reporting: The Quarterly Report Must Be Exactly Like the Annual Report!

J. M. Grant has recently been elected to the board of directors of Montrose Company. The other directors of Montrose are beginning to regret this action. Grant has proved to be very opinionated, very stubborn, and quite old fashioned. Every decision by the board members since Grant joined the board has taken two to three times as long as it should have because Grant seems to disagree with everything that everyone else says.

The most recent crisis is over the preparation of the quarterly report. Grant was shocked to learn that quarterly reports do not include the same detail as is contained in the annual report and that estimates and assumptions are used extensively in preparing the summary information that goes into the quarterly report. The last straw for Grant was when he learned that the quarterly report is not audited. Grant has absolutely refused to accept this slipshod method of quarterly reporting and has vowed that he will bottle up board action on all other decisions until the board agrees to the preparation of a quarterly report that contains the same detail, the same accounting practices, and the same type of audit opinion as the annual report.

You have been appointed by the board to reason with Grant. What will you tell him?

Case 19-60

Deciphering Financial Statements (The Walt Disney Company)

Locate the 2009 financial statements for **The Walt Disney Company** on the Internet.

Once you have located those financial statements, consider the following questions.

1. In Note 17 on derivative instruments, Disney explains how the company manages interest rate risk and foreign exchange risk. What types of instruments does Disney use to manage foreign exchange risk? What specific currency risk is Disney trying to hedge against? Does Disney speculate with its foreign currency transactions?
2. What types of instruments does Disney use to manage interest rate risk?
3. What interesting details about pending lawsuits does Disney include in the notes to the financial statements?
4. Disney has five primary business segments: Media Networks, Parks and Resorts, Studio Entertainment, Consumer Products, and Interactive Media. Which of these five yields the highest return on assets (Operating income/Identifiable assets)? (*Note*: Use information from the financial statement notes.)
5. Find Disney's Quarterly Financial Summary. Do you detect any seasonal pattern in Disney's revenues? Explain.

Case 19-61

Deciphering Financial Statements (Interim Reporting: Toys "R" Us)

Toys "R" Us is the biggest toy store chain in the United States, with significant operations outside the United States as well. The following quarterly financial data were taken from the 2009 annual report of Toys "R" Us.

	First Quarter	Second Quarter	Third Quarter	Fourth Quarter
2009 Net Sales	$2,477	$2,567	$2,667	$5,857
2009 Gross Margin	890	951	950	1,987
2009 Net Earnings/(Loss)	(35)	27	(67)	387
2008 Net Sales	2,719	2,771	2,773	5,461
2008 Gross Margin	977	1,014	960	1,797
2008 Net Earnings/(Loss)	(36)	13	(104)	345

1. Does Toys "R" Us have any seasonal pattern in its sales?
2. Compute gross profit (or margin) percentage (Gross margin/Sales) for each quarter for fiscal years 2008 and 2009. Is the gross profit percentage in the fourth quarter substantially different from other quarters?
3. Assume that first-quarter sales for fiscal 2010 are $2,700 million. What is your prediction of fourth-quarter sales?

Case 19-62

Deciphering Financial Statements (Derivatives: IBM)

In Note L to its 2009 financial statements, **IBM** includes disclosure about its derivatives as follows:

Fair Values of Derivative Instruments on the Consolidated Statement of Financial Position
($ in millions)

	Fair Value of Derivative Assets			Fair Value of Derivative Liabilities		
At December 31, 2009:	**Designated as Hedging Instruments**	**Not Designated as Hedging Instruments**	**Total**	**Designated as Hedging Instruments**	**Not Designated as Hedging Instruments**	**Total**
Interest rate contracts:						
Prepaid expenses and other current assets	$ 43	$ —	$ 43	$ —	$ —	$ —
Investments and sundry assets	383	—	383	—	—	—
Other liabilities	—	—	—	2	—	2
Foreign exchange contracts:						
Prepaid expenses and other current assets	74	151	225	—	—	—
Investments and sundry assets	156	26	182	—	—	—
Other accrued expenses and liabilities	—	—	—	602	304	906
Other liabilities	—	—	—	423	224	647
Equity contracts:						
Prepaid expenses and other current assets	—	5	5	—	—	—
Other accrued expenses and liabilities	—	—	—	—	0	0
Fair value of derivative assets and liabilities	$656	$182	$838	$1,027	$528	$1,555
Total debt designated as hedging instruments:						
Short-term debt	NA	NA	NA	$1,440	—	$1,440
Long-term debt	NA	NA	NA	2,618	—	2,618
Total			**$838**			**$5,613**

The Effect of Derivative Instruments on the Consolidated Statement of Earnings
($ in millions)

For the year ended December 31, 2009:

	Gain (Loss) Recognized in Earnings		
Derivative Instruments in Fair Value Hedges	**Consolidated Statement of Earnings Line Item**	**Recognized on Derivatives(2)**	**Attributable to Risk Being Hedged(3)**
Interest rate contracts	Cost of financing	$(172)	$344
	Interest expense	(97)	193
Total		**$(269)**	**$537**

	Gain (Loss) Recognized in Earnings and Other Comprehensive Income			
Derivative Instruments in Cash Flow Hedges	**Effective Portion Recognized in AOCI**	**Consolidated Statement Of Earnings Line Item**	**Effective Portion Reclassified from AOCI to Earnings**	**Ineffectiveness and Amounts Excluded from Effectiveness Testing(4)**
Interest rate contracts	$ (0)	Interest income	$ (13)	$—
Foreign exchange contracts	(718)	Other (income) and expense	143	(3)
		Cost of sales	(49)	
		SG&A expense	14	
Total	**$(718)**		**$ 94**	**$(3)**

	Gain (Loss) Recognized in Earnings and Other Comprehensive Income			
Derivative Instruments in Net Investment Hedges	**Effective Portion Recognized in AOCI**	**Consolidated Statement of Earnings Line Item**	**Effective Portion Reclassified from AOCI to Earnings**	**Ineffectiveness and Amounts Excluded from Effectiveness Testing(5)**
Foreign exchange contracts	$234	Interest income	$—	$1
		Other (income) and expense	$—	$—

Derivative Instruments Not Designated as Hedging Instruments(1)	**Consolidated Statement of Earnings Line Item**	**Gain (Loss) Recognized in Earnings**
Foreign exchange contracts	Other (income) and expense	$(128)
Equity contracts	SG&A expense	177
Total		**$ 50**

Note: AOCI represents Accumulated other comprehensive income/(loss) in Consolidated Statement of Changes in Equity.

(1) See pages 76 and 77 for additional information on the purpose for entering into derivatives not designated as hedging instruments.
(2) Includes changes in clean fair values of the derivative instruments in fair value hedging relationships and the periodic accrual for coupon payments required under these derivative contracts.
(3) Includes basis adjustments to the carrying value of the hedged item recorded during the period and amortization of basis adjustments recorded on de-designated hedging relationships during the period.
(4) Amount of gain (loss) recognized in income represents ineffectiveness on hedge relationships.
(5) Amount of gain (loss) recognized in income represents amounts excluded from effectiveness assessment.

At December 31, 2009, in connection with cash flow hedges of anticipated royalties and cost transactions, the company recorded net losses of $718 million (before taxes) in accumulated other comprehensive income/(loss); $427 million of losses are expected to be reclassified to net income within the next 12 months, providing an offsetting economic impact against the underlying anticipated transactions. At December 31, 2009, net losses of approximately $18 million (before taxes) were recorded in accumulated other comprehensive income/(loss) in connection with cash flow hedges of the company's borrowings; $10 million of losses are expected to be reclassified to net income within the next 12 months, providing an offsetting economic impact against the underlying transactions.

For the 12 months ending December 31, 2009, there were no significant gains or losses recognized in earnings representing hedge ineffectiveness or excluded from the assessment of hedge effectiveness (for fair value hedges), or associated with an underlying exposure that did not or was not expected to occur (for cash flow hedges); nor are there any anticipated in the normal course of business.

1. IBM reports that it uses both fair value and cash flow hedges in its debt risk management program. Most of these hedges are accomplished through interest rate swaps. Some of the interest rate swaps are pay-fixed, receive-variable swaps, and some are pay-variable, receive-fixed swaps. Which of these two types of swaps are fair value hedges, and which are cash flow hedges? Explain.
2. IBM lists $2,618 million in long-term debt as a hedge. What does this debt hedge, and how does the debt serve as an effective hedge?
3. As of December 31, 2009, IBM has recognized $736 million in net unrealized losses associated with cash flow hedges. Of these net losses, how much is related to cash flow transactions expected to occur within one year?
4. What type of disclosure would give the best indication of IBM's exposure to foreign exchange and interest rate risk?

Case 19-63 **Deciphering Financial Statements (Segment Reporting: PepsiCo)**

Refer to the 2009 segment information for **PepsiCo** given in Exhibit 19-4.

1. Compute operating profit margin (Operating profit/Net revenue) for 2009 for each of the following: (a) Frito-Lay North America, (b) Quaker Foods North America, (c) Latin America Foods, (d) PepsiCo Americas Beverages, (e) Europe, and (f) Asia, Middle East & Africa
2. For each of the segments listed in (1), compute asset turnover (Net revenue/Total assets).

3. Given your calculations in (1) and (2), what is your analysis of the different segments of PepsiCo?

Case 19-64

Writing Assignment (The FASB is an eco-villain!)

You are one of the seven members of the FASB. The FASB was recently criticized in a cover story in a major newsmagazine. The topic was "accounting for environmental liabilities." The main point of the article was that the accounting for potential environmental liabilities is governed by the obscure terms "probable, possible, and remote." In addition, the article claimed that firms could avoid recognizing a liability for future environmental cleanup costs by simply arguing that the costs cannot be "reasonably estimated."

Of course, the charges in the newsmagazine cover story were repeated in the network TV news programs. Various accounting academics appeared on the morning news shows to pontificate about the slowness of the FASB to address the vital area of environmental accounting. Environmental groups have started picketing outside FASB headquarters, shouting that the FASB is conspiring with "Big Business" to hide the corporate responsibility for cleaning up the environment.

You have been chosen to write the FASB's response to this criticism. Address your memo to the editor of the weekly newsmagazine and restrict it to 1 page or less.

(*Note*: This scenario is hypothetical—you are not a member of the FASB, the FASB's environmental accounting practices have not been the subject of a *Time* or *Newsweek* cover story, and environmental groups have not picketed the FASB. Yet.)

Case 19-65

Ethical Dilemma (Once a hedge, always a hedge)

You are the controller/treasurer for a small import-export company. You make all the finance and accounting decisions. Your company makes sales in Germany, Poland, and the Czech Republic. Historically, your Polish sales have been denominated in zlotys. Early this year, you decided to enter into some zloty futures contracts to protect against the effect of changes in the dollar/zloty exchange rate on the cash flows from next year's sales in Poland. In accordance with proper accounting procedure, you formally designated the futures contracts as a cash flow hedge.

In December of this year, your customers in Poland notified you that they are nervous about the impact of European currency consolidation on the strength of the zloty, and they wish all future sales prices to be denominated in U.S. dollars. The good news is that this action removes the need to worry about the effect of exchange rate changes on Polish sales. The bad news is that you have already entered into the futures contracts and, at the end of the year, the futures have a fair value of $5 million (liability).

Your dilemma is this: The futures no longer serve as a hedge because future Polish sales will be denominated in U.S. dollars. However, if you account for the futures as speculative investments, you will be forced to recognize a loss in earnings this year of $5 million. This entire hedging operation was your idea, and you convinced the president of the company that you knew what you were doing and there was no chance of a major loss. If this loss is recognized, reported profits for the year will be wiped out, and the company will show a net loss for the first time in its history.

What should you do?

Case 19-66

Cumulative Spreadsheet Analysis

This assignment is an exercise in simple derivative valuation. Skywalker is considering using derivative contracts in 2014 to hedge interest rate risk. However, before entering into any derivative contract agreements, the management of Skywalker wishes to better understand how the values of derivative financial instruments fluctuate.

For 2014, Skywalker is considering converting $600 of its long-term debt into 3-month renewable debt; by so doing, Skywalker will be able to receive various preferential privileges from its lender. However, Skywalker doesn't want to bear the associated interest rate risk that would arise from the interest rate on the debt being reset at the prevailing market interest rate every three months as the loan is renewed. As a result, Skywalker has inquired about entering into an interest rate swap with another financial institution. The terms of the swap would be as follows: loan amount, $600; swap interest rate, 8%.

Skywalker would pay a fixed amount of $12 ($600 × 0.08 × 3/12) to the financial institution each quarter; in exchange, Skywalker would receive a variable amount equal to $600 multiplied by the current market interest rate (for a 3-month period). This is called a pay-fixed, receive-variable swap. Skywalker could then use the variable amount received to pay the variable interest amount on its 3-month renewable loan.

In practice, the swap will be settled by Skywalker's paying an amount equal to [$600 × (0.08 − Market interest rate) × 3/12] when interest rates are below 8% and receiving the same amount when interest rates are above 8%.

The financial staff at Skywalker have done some research on the historical behavior of interest rates and have prepared the table at the left. The data in this table mean that if, for example, the current market interest rate is 8.0%, the probability that the market interest rate will still be 8.0% in three months is 30%. In addition, there is a 5% probability that the market rate will increase to 8.3% in three months, and a 3% probability that the market rate will decrease to 7.6% in three months.

Interest Rate Expected to Prevail in 3 Months	Probability
Current rate + 0.5%	2%
Current rate + 0.4%	3
Current rate + 0.3%	5
Current rate + 0.2%	10
Current rate + 0.1%	15
Current rate	30
Current rate − 0.1%	15
Current rate − 0.2%	10
Current rate − 0.3%	5
Current rate − 0.4%	3
Current rate − 0.5%	2

Using these data, construct a spreadsheet to answer the following questions:

1. What is the value of the pay-fixed, receive-variable swap contract to Skywalker if there are three months remaining in the contract term and the current market interest rate is 8.0%? Be sure to indicate whether the swap contract is an asset or a liability for Skywalker.
2. Repeat (1) using the following assumptions about the current market interest rate: (a) 7.2%, (b) 8.1%, and (c) 9.0%
3. Comment on the relative sizes of the fair values of the derivative contract and the notional value of the contract.

P4 OTHER DIMENSIONS OF FINANCIAL REPORTING

CHAPTER 20 Accounting Changes and Error Corrections

LEARNING OBJECTIVES

1. Understand the two different types of accounting changes that have been identified by accounting standard setters.
2. Recognize the difference between a change in accounting estimate and a change in accounting principle, and know how a change in accounting estimate is reflected in the financial statements.
3. Prepare the retrospective adjustment of prior periods' financial statements, and any necessary cumulative adjustment, associated with a change in accounting principle.
4. Report pro forma results for prior years following a business combination.
5. Recognize the various types of errors that can occur in the accounting process, understand when errors counterbalance, and be able to correct errors when necessary.

Statement of Financial Accounting Standards No. 106, "Employers' Accounting for Postretirement Benefits Other Than Pensions," was issued in 1992 (and is now included in the FASB Codification as Section 715-60). These "postretirement benefits other than pensions" are primarily retiree health care costs. The overall impact of this standard on corporate profits established a record for a new accounting rule and was estimated to result in a decrease in the reported profits of major U.S. companies by as much as $1 trillion.[1] As an example of the effect, the standard required **General Motors** to recognize a liability relating to retiree health care benefits of $33 billion.

The amazing thing about the accounting change mandated by the FASB back in 1992 is that before the rule change, the liability amount recorded by all U.S. companies for their retiree health care obligations totaled exactly zero. Nil. Nada. Zilch. Let's be honest: This wasn't very informative accounting for these obligations. The economic obligations certainly existed before 1992, but the accounting rules did not require companies to report the obligations in their balance sheets.

For General Motors, the after-tax income effect of the adoption of *Statement No. 106* was to decrease earnings by $21 billion and decrease earnings per share (EPS) by $33.38. Because this

[1] Lee Berton and Robert J. Brennan, "New Medical-Benefits Accounting Rule Seen Wounding Profits, Hurting Shares," *The Wall Street Journal,* April 22, 1992, p. C1.

Andrew Sacks/Stone/Getty Images

retiree health care obligation had been built up over many years preceding the mandated accounting change in 1992, it makes sense to ask whether the entire estimated after-tax cost of $21 billion should have been reported by General Motors as an expense in the year of adoption, or whether there was a more informative way to recognize this cost. This issue, the proper reporting of accounting changes, is discussed in this chapter.

The retiree health care obligation created by General Motors through the company's promises to its employees over the years, and finally recognized in the financial statements starting in 1992, has had an extremely interesting and controversial history. The controversy swirls around the claim that these health care promises contributed to the eventual bankruptcy of General Motors. And part of the blame is placed at the feet of the accounting profession. The fact that, before 1992, the true cost of these health care promises was not included in the financial statements may have led pre-1992 GM decision makers to have the mistaken impression that the promises were "free." The cost of these "free" benefits eventually helped kill the company.

In the negotiations over the General Motors bankruptcy, these retiree health care benefits were sacrificed by GM employees in an effort to help save the restructured company. Exhibit 20-1 shows that the recorded obligation went from $0 in 1991 (because of the flaw in the accounting rules described above), to a high of over $80 billion in 2005, and then back to almost $0 in 2009 (because GM's employees agreed to release the financially ruined company from its previous promises).

EX 20-1 HISTORY OF GENERAL MOTORS' REPORTED RETIREE HEALTH CARE OBLIGATION (IN MILLIONS)

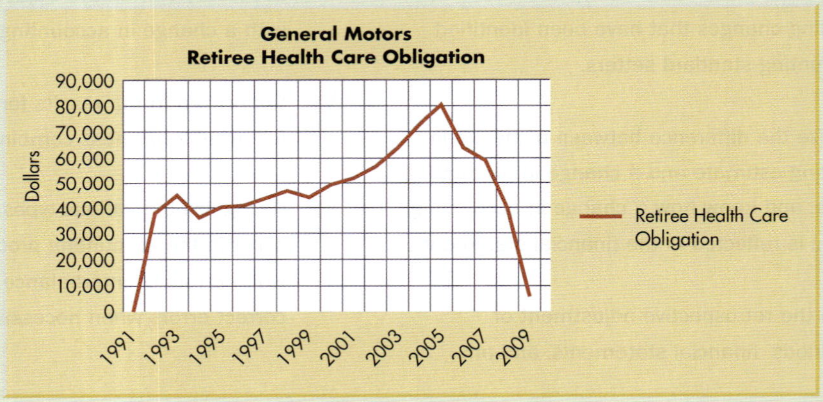

? QUESTIONS

1. Before FASB *Statement No. 106,* companies typically recognized no cost and no liability for their retiree health care benefit plans. List several reasons for a firm to reduce its retiree health benefits in response to the FASB's requirement that companies recognize the cost and obligation associated with such plans.
2. FASB *Statement No. 106* resulted in firms reporting lower earnings and higher liabilities. Would you expect stock prices to decline for companies with large retiree health care plans? Would you expect it to be harder for these firms to obtain loans?
3. General Motors was required to recognize a one-time $21 billion expense upon its adoption of FASB *Statement No. 106.* This $21 billion represented the cumulative after-tax cost of GM's retiree health care plan for all years preceding 1992. How else might GM have recorded this $21 billion?

Answers to these questions can be found on page 20-27.

A company's financial statements sometimes report significantly different results from year to year. This may be due to changes in economic circumstances, but it also may be due to changes in accounting methods or corrections of errors in recording past transactions.

Changing the accounting methods used can have a dramatic impact on a company's financial statements. Because of this impact, one can argue that accounting changes detract from the informational characteristics of comparability and consistency discussed in Chapter 1. So why are these accounting changes made? The main reasons for such changes can be summarized as follows:

1. A company, as a result of experience or new information, may change its estimates of revenues or expenses—for example, the estimate of uncollectible accounts receivable or the estimated service lives of depreciable assets.
2. Due to changes in economic conditions, companies may need to change methods of accounting to more clearly reflect the current economic situation.
3. Accounting standard-setting bodies may require the use of a new accounting method or principle, such as new reporting requirements for postretirement benefits.
4. Management may be pressured to report profitable performance. Clever accounting changes can result in higher net income, thereby reflecting favorably on management.

Whatever the reason, accountants must keep the primary qualitative characteristic of usefulness in mind. They must determine whether the reasons for accounting changes are appropriate and then how best to report the changes to facilitate understanding of the financial statements.

The detection of errors in accounting for past transactions presents a similar problem. The errors must be corrected and appropriate disclosures made so that readers of the financial statements will clearly understand what has happened. The purpose of this chapter is to discuss the different types of accounting changes and error corrections and the related accounting procedures that should be used.

Accounting Changes

1 Understand the two different types of accounting changes that have been identified by accounting standard setters.

WHY **Changes in accounting estimates are made routinely and are a natural result of the improved information that comes through experience. Changes in accounting principle occur relatively infrequently and are the result of either the adoption of a new accounting standard by the FASB or a shift from one acceptable principle to another.**

HOW **These two types of accounting "changes"—change in estimate and change in principle—are substantially different from one another. Accordingly, the accounting treatment of these two types of changes is substantially different, as explained in subsequent sections.**

The accounting profession has identified two main categories of accounting changes:[2]

1. Change in accounting estimate
2. Change in accounting principle

[2] *FASB ASC Section 250-10-20,* Presentation—Accounting Changes and Error Corrections—Overall—Glossary. [*SFAS No. 154,* "Accounting Changes and Error Corrections: A Replacement of APB Opinion No. 20 and FASB Statement No. 3," May 2005, par. 2.] A third category of accounting changes, changes in reporting entity, is much less common and is not covered in any detail in this chapter.

As pointed out in Chapter 1, a major objective of published financial statements is to provide users information to help them predict, compare, and evaluate future earning power and cash flows of the reporting entity. When a reporting entity adjusts its past estimates of revenues earned or costs incurred or changes its accounting principles from one method to another, it becomes more difficult for a user to predict the future from past historical statements. The basic accounting issue is whether accounting changes should be reported as adjustments of the prior periods' statements (thus increasing their comparability with current and future statements) or whether the changes should affect only the current and future years.

Several alternatives have been suggested for reporting accounting changes.

1. Restate the financial statements presented for prior periods to reflect the effect of the change. Adjust the beginning retained earnings balance of the earliest period reported for the cumulative effect of the change in all preceding years.
2. Make no adjustment to statements presented for prior periods. Report the cumulative effect of the change in the current year as a direct entry to Retained Earnings.
3. Same as (2), except report the cumulative effect of the change as a special item in the income statement instead of directly to Retained Earnings.
4. Report the cumulative effect in the current year as in (3) but also present limited pro forma information for all prior periods included in the financial statements reporting "what might have been" if the change had been made in the prior years.
5. Make the change effective only for current and future periods with no catch-up adjustment.

Each of these methods for reporting an accounting change has been used by companies in the past, and arguments can be made for each of the approaches. For example, some accountants argue that accounting principles should be applied consistently for all reported periods. Therefore, if a new accounting principle is used in the current period, the financial statements presented for prior periods should be restated so that the results shown for all reported periods are based on the same accounting principles. Other accountants contend that restating financial statements may dilute public confidence in those statements. Principles applied in earlier periods were presumably appropriate at that time and should be considered final. In addition, restating financial statements is costly, requires considerable effort, and is sometimes impossible due to lack of data.

Consider the General Motors (GM) example at the beginning of this chapter. How should the liability and the effect on earnings have been reported? Specifically, what would have been the appropriate journal entry? Obviously, GM would recognize a liability of $33 billion. Because GM will not receive a tax deduction for the other postretirement benefits until those expenses are actually paid, GM would also recognize a deferred tax asset of $12 billion. This deferred tax asset would be recognized because GM expensed the cost of the benefits now for financial accounting purposes but does not expect to receive the tax deduction for those expenses until they are paid in the future: Recall from Chapter 16 that this would result in taxable income being higher than financial income in the current period, resulting in a deferred tax asset. As a result, the journal entry would appear as follows:

Deferred Tax Asset	12 billion	
????	21 billion	
Other Postretirement Benefits Liability		33 billion

What account should replace the question marks? Should it be an income statement account, a balance sheet account, or some other type of account? In accordance with the accounting rules in existence at the time, General Motors debited an expense called "Cumulative Effect of an Accounting Change" and reported the $21 billion reduction in earnings as a below-the-line item on the income statement. International practice is different with respect to the handling of this type of accounting change. Under the provisions of *International Accounting Standard (IAS) 8*, companies would debit the beginning balance in the retained earnings account, reasoning that the adjustment was related to prior periods and the income from those prior periods had been previously closed to the retained earnings account. In addition, all income statements presented for prior years would be retrospectively restated as if the new standard had always been in effect; this is alternative (1) described above.

ifrs

FYI

Cumulative effects of changes in accounting principles used to be shown as below-the-line items on the income statement.

As part of its continuing effort to harmonize U.S. GAAP with International Accounting Standards, the FASB adopted *Statement No. 154* in May 2005. This statement changed the U.S. approach to accounting for accounting changes and error corrections to be in conformity with *IAS 8*. The coverage in this chapter reflects this new standard which now forms the basis of FASB Codification Topic 250, "Accounting Changes and Error Corrections."

Change in Accounting Estimate

2 **Recognize the difference between a change in accounting estimate and a change in accounting principle, and know how a change in accounting estimate is reflected in the financial statements.**

WHY **Preparation of accrual-based financial statements requires that estimates be made. When those good faith estimates are found in later periods to have been inaccurate, no attempt is made to go back and "fix" previously issued financial statements because those statements reflect the best information that was available at the time.**

HOW **A change in accounting estimate does not involve a restatement of prior periods' financial statements. Instead, the effects of these types of changes are reflected in the current and future periods.**

Contrary to what many people believe, accounting information cannot always be measured and reported precisely. Also, to be reported on a timely basis for decision making, accounting data often must be based on estimates of future events. The financial statements incorporate these estimates, which are based on the best professional judgment given the information available at that time. At a later date, however, additional experience or new facts sometimes make it clear that the estimates need to be revised to more accurately reflect the existing business circumstances. When this happens, a change in accounting estimate occurs.

Examples of areas for which changes in accounting estimates often are needed include the following:

1. Uncollectible receivables
2. Useful lives of depreciable or intangible assets

3. Residual values for depreciable assets
4. Warranty obligations
5. Quantities of mineral reserves to be depleted
6. Actuarial assumptions for pensions or other postemployment benefits
7. Number of periods benefited by deferred costs

Exhibit 20-2 provides examples of disclosure relating to estimates contained in the 2009 annual reports of two companies: **H. J. Heinz Company** and **McDonald's**. Even though the companies had different auditors (**PricewaterhouseCoopers** and **Ernst & Young**, respectively), it is surprising how similar the note disclosures are.

STOP&THINK

Why aren't changes in estimates accounted for by restating prior years' financial statements?

a) The data necessary to perform restatements typically are not available.
b) Restating prior years' financial statements would force most companies to make a large penalty payment to the Internal Revenue Service.
c) With most restatements, the deferred tax consequences would cause an unusually large reduction in retained earnings.
d) With restatements, prior-period financial statements would be constantly revised, reducing the reliance placed on them by investors and creditors.

Accounting for a change in estimate has already been discussed in Chapter 4 and throughout the text in areas for which changes in estimates are common. By way of review, all changes in estimates should be reflected either in the current period or in current and future periods. No retroactive adjustments or pro forma (as-if) statements are to be prepared for a change in accounting estimate. Changes in estimates are considered to be part of the normal accounting process, not corrections or changes of past periods. However, disclosures such as the ones in Exhibit 20-3, reported by **United Airlines**, are useful in helping readers of financial statements understand the impact of changes in estimates.

Some changes in accounting principle are actually just another form of a change in estimate. For example, if a company changes its depreciation method, it is really making a statement about a change in the expected usage pattern with respect to that asset. As required by the Accounting Changes and Error Corrections Topic (250) of the FASB ASC,

EX 20-2 H. J. HEINZ COMPANY AND MCDONALD'S—DISCLOSURE RELATING TO ESTIMATES

NOTES TO CONSOLIDATED FINANCIAL STATEMENTS
H. J. Heinz Company and Subsidiaries
I. Significant Accounting Policies

Use of Estimates: The preparation of financial statements, in conformity with accounting principles generally accepted in the United States of America, requires management to make estimates and assumptions that affect the reported amounts of assets and liabilities, the disclosure of contingent assets and liabilities at the date of the financial statements, and the reported amounts of revenues and expenses during the reporting period. Actual results could differ from these estimates.

McDonald's Corporation
Summary of Significant Accounting Policies

Estimates in financial statements
The preparation of financial statements in conformity with accounting principles generally accepted in the U.S. requires management to make estimates and assumptions that affect the amounts reported in the financial statements and accompanying notes. Actual results could differ from those estimates.

EX 20-3 UNITED AIRLINES—DISCLOSURE OF CHANGE IN ESTIMATE

UAL Corporation (the "Company") follows a deferred revenue accounting policy to record the fair value of its Mileage Plus frequent flyer obligation. The Company defers the portion of the sales proceeds of ticketed revenue on United and our alliance partners, as well as revenue associated with mileage sales to third parties, that represents the estimated air transportation fair value of the miles awarded. This deferred revenue is then recognized when the miles are redeemed.

Some of these miles will never be redeemed by Mileage Plus members, and the Company recognizes an estimate of revenue from the expected expired miles, which is referred to as breakage, over an estimated redemption period. The Company reviews its breakage estimates annually based upon the latest available information regarding mileage redemption and expiration patterns.

During the first quarter of 2010 the Company obtained additional historical data, previously unavailable, which has enabled the Company to refine its breakage estimates. This new data indicates that a larger number of miles than previously estimated are expected to expire. As a result, the Company has changed its estimate of Mileage Plus breakage on a prospective basis, effective beginning in the first quarter of 2010. In addition to this change in estimate, the Company is making an improvement to the accounting model for Mileage Plus breakage that is inseparable from the change in estimate.

These changes will result in the recognition of approximately $64 million of incremental passenger revenue in the first quarter of 2010, reducing the net amount of revenue that we otherwise would have deferred to future periods.

a change in depreciation method is accounted for as a change in estimate and is called "a change in accounting estimate effected by a change in accounting principle."

To illustrate a change in accounting estimate effected by a change in accounting principle, assume that Telstar Company, a high-power telescope sales and manufacturing firm, elected in 2013 to change from the double-declining-balance method of depreciation to the straight-line method to make its financial reporting more consistent with the majority of its competitors. Telstar's depreciable assets have a cost of $500,000 and, to keep things simple, assume that they were all acquired on January 1, 2010, have an expected useful life of 10 years, and have an expected salvage value of zero. For tax purposes, assume that Telstar had elected to use the straight-line method and will continue to do so. Assume further that Telstar presents comparative income statements for three years and that the past difference in book and tax depreciation is the only difference in accounting treatment impacting Telstar's financial and taxable income.

These and other assumptions are necessary because, in most instances, a change in accounting principle involves temporary differences between book and tax income, creating the need for interperiod tax allocation. The exact amounts of any deferred income tax liabilities or potential deferred income tax assets are dependent on several factors, such as current tax laws and current and future tax rates. Therefore, in this chapter, including the end-of-chapter material, the impact of income tax either is ignored or the assumed amounts are provided to simplify the illustrations and focus on the effects of accounting changes and error corrections.

For Telstar, the greater accelerated depreciation charged on the books in prior years, as compared to the straight-line tax depreciation taken, resulted in a previously recorded deferred tax asset. The income tax rate is assumed to be 30%. This and other relevant information for Telstar is presented below.

Year	Double-Declining-Balance Depreciation (used for books)	Straight-Line Depreciation (used for taxes)	Depreciation Difference	Deferred Tax Effects	Effects on Income (net of taxes)
2010	$100,000	$ 50,000	$50,000	$15,000	$35,000
2011	80,000	50,000	30,000	9,000	21,000
2012	64,000	50,000	14,000	4,200	9,800
Cumulative before 2013	$244,000	$150,000	$94,000	$28,200	$65,800

The data indicate that cumulative depreciation expense for the years prior to 2013 would have been $94,000 ($244,000 – $150,000) less if the straight-line method had been used. Thus, income would have been $94,000 higher, less the applicable income taxes of $28,200, leaving a net income difference of $65,800. The total impact on Telstar's balance sheet as of January 1, 2013, is as follows:

ASSETS	
Gross Property, Plant, and Equipment	No impact
Accumulated Depreciation	*$94,000 higher with double declining balance*
Net Property, Plant, and Equipment	$94,000 lower with double declining balance
Deferred Tax Asset	*$28,200 higher with double declining balance*
Total Assets	$65,800 lower with double declining balance
LIABILITIES	
No impact	
EQUITIES	
Retained Earnings	$65,800 lower with double declining balance

Because a change in depreciation method is to be accounted for as "a change in accounting estimate effected by a change in accounting principle," no attempt is made to go back and change the depreciation and deferred tax information reported in 2010, 2011, and 2012. Instead, the change is accounted for in the current and future periods as illustrated in Chapter 11 in the discussion of changes in depreciation lives. The remaining depreciable book value as of January 1, 2013, is depreciated over the remaining life of seven years using the new straight-line method. Depreciation expense for 2013 is computed as follows:

[($500,000 – $244,000) – $0 salvage value]/7 years = $36,571

The table below shows the depreciation amount that would be reported in the books and for income tax purposes after the accounting change. You can see that the lower depreciation expense reported under the straight-line method applied on the books results in the gradual reversal of the deferred tax asset that had been recognized previously. By the end of seven years (in 2019), the deferred tax effects will have completely reversed.

Year	First Double-Declining-Balance and then Straight-Line Depreciation (used for books)	Straight-Line Depreciation (used for taxes)	Depreciation Difference	Deferred Tax Effects	Effects on Income (net of taxes)
Cumulative before 2013	$244,000	$150,000	$ 94,000	$28,200	$65,800
2013	36,571	50,000	(13,429)	(4,029)	(9,400)
2014	36,571	50,000	(13,429)	(4,029)	(9,400)
.					
.					
.					
2019 (adjusted for rounding)	36,574	50,000	(13,426)	(4,026)	(9,400)
Cumulative through 2019	$500,000	$500,000	$ 0	$ 0	$ 0

Change in Accounting Principle

3 **Prepare the retrospective adjustment of prior periods' financial statements, and any necessary cumulative adjustment, associated with a change in accounting principle.**

WHY **An extremely important characteristic of good financial reports is that they are based on consistent application of accounting principles so that the results and financial position in the current year can be meaningfully compared to the preceding years.**

HOW **A change in accounting principle is implemented by recomputing all financial statement amounts for the preceding years (at least those that will be included in the current year's comparative financial statements). These recomputed amounts are included in the comparative financial statements reported this year. Any income effect in even earlier years is shown as an adjustment to the beginning balance in retained earnings for the earliest year reported.**

A change in accounting principle involves a change from one generally accepted principle or method to another.[3] A change in principle does not include the initial adoption of an accounting principle as a result of transactions or events that had not occurred (or were immaterial) in previous periods. A change from a principle that is not generally accepted to one that is generally accepted is considered to be an error correction rather than a change in accounting principle.

As indicated in previous chapters, companies may select among alternative accounting principles to account for business transactions. For example, for financial reporting purposes, inventory may be accounted for using FIFO, LIFO, or other acceptable methods. These alternative methods are often equally available to a given company, but in most instances, criteria for selection among the methods are inadequate. As a result, companies have found it rather easy to justify changing from one accounting principle or method to another.

The effect of a change from one accepted accounting principle to another is reflected by retrospectively adjusting the financial statements for all years reported, and reporting the cumulative effect of the change in the income for all preceding years as an adjustment to the beginning balance in retained earnings for the earliest year reported. For example, in a standard set of financial statements presenting balance sheets for two years and income statements and statements of cash flows for three years, all of the statements would be redone using the new accounting principle. In addition, the statement of stockholders' equity that is typically included with the financial statements would reflect the cumulative effect on income in prior years with an adjustment to beginning retained earnings in the first of the three years reported.

To illustrate the general treatment of a change in accounting principle, assume that as of January 1, 2013, Forester Company changed from the LIFO inventory costing method to the FIFO method for both financial reporting and income tax purposes. There are no deferred tax consequences because both the old and new methods apply to both financial and tax reporting. However, additional taxes will be payable for prior years as a result of the change in inventory method used for tax purposes. The income tax rate is 30%. The following balance sheet and income statement data are based on LIFO as shown on page 20-10.

[3] The classification "change in accounting principle" includes changes in methods used to account for transactions. No attempt is made in FASB ASC Topic 250 to distinguish between a principle and a method.

	If Continued Using LIFO	As Originally Reported Using LIFO	
Balance Sheet	**2013**	**2012**	**2011**
Cash	$ 150	$ 120	$ 100
Inventory	3,800	3,000	2,500
Total assets	$3,950	$3,120	$2,600
Income taxes payable	$ 165	$ 105	$ 90
Paid-in capital	1,645	1,260	1,000
Retained earnings	2,140	1,755	1,510
Total liabilities and equities	$3,950	$3,120	$2,600
Income Statement	**2013**	**2012**	**2011**
Sales	$1,500	$1,200	$1,000
Cost of goods sold	950	850	700
Gross profit	$ 550	$ 350	$ 300
Income tax expense	165	105	90
Net income	$ 385	$ 245	$ 210

The data for 2011 and 2012 are the actual financial statements that were released for those years. The LIFO data for 2013 are the financial statements that would have been released had Forester decided to continue using LIFO.

The following LIFO and FIFO inventory valuation data have been assembled:

	LIFO	FIFO	Difference
January 1, 2011, inventory	$2,100	$2,350	$250
December 31, 2011, inventory	2,500	2,900	400
December 31, 2012, inventory	3,000	3,600	600
December 31, 2013, inventory	3,800	4,500	700

As discussed in Chapter 9, the excess of FIFO inventory valuation over LIFO inventory valuation is called the LIFO reserve and can be thought of as inventory holding gains (during times of inflation) that are recognized when FIFO is used (reducing reported cost of goods sold) but that are not recognized when LIFO is used. The LIFO financial statement data and the inventory valuation differences can be used to construct the FIFO financial statements for 2011–2013, as follows:

	After Changing to FIFO	If Originally Used FIFO	
Balance Sheet	**2013**	**2012**	**2011**
Cash	$ 150	$ 120	$ 100
Inventory	4,500	3,600	2,900
Total assets	$4,650	$3,720	$3,000
Income taxes payable	$ 195	$ 105	$ 90
FIFO taxes payable	180	180	120
Paid-in capital	1,645	1,260	1,000
Retained earnings	2,630	2,175	1,790
Total liabilities and equities	$4,650	$3,720	$3,000

(Continued)

Income Statement	2013	2012	2011
Sales	$1,500	$1,200	$1,000
Cost of goods sold	850	650	550
Gross profit	$ 650	$ 550	$ 450
Income tax expense	195	165	135
Net income	$ 455	$ 385	$ 315

Details of the computations of retained earnings and the FIFO taxes payable amounts are given below.

Retained Earnings As of January 1, 2011, a retrospective switch to FIFO means that cumulative before-tax profits from the years before 2011 are increased by $250, corresponding to the amount of the LIFO reserve on that date. The increase in cumulative after-tax profits is $175 ($250 × [1 − 0.30]). Accordingly, retained earnings as of January 1, 2011, is increased by $175. The computation of the ending balance in retained earnings for 2011 would be shown as follows in the 2013 3-year comparative statement of stockholders' equity for Forester.

Retained earnings, January 1, 2011, as originally reported	$1,300
Add adjustment for cumulative effect on prior years of retrospectively applying the FIFO method of inventory valuation	175
Adjusted retained earnings, January 1, 2011	$1,475
Add net income for 2011 (under FIFO)	315
Retained earnings, December 31, 2011	$1,790

FIFO Taxes Payable Because the switch is being made for both book and tax purposes, the increase in taxable profits of $250 creates a "FIFO taxes payable" of $75 ($250 × 0.30) corresponding to the tax that is now owed on excess FIFO profits from the years before 2011. In addition, the $45 increased tax expense for 2011 ($135 FIFO − $90 LIFO) represents additional FIFO taxes payable as of the end of 2011. The total of $120 ($75 + $45) is reported in the revised December 31, 2011, balance sheet. This amount increases by $60 ($165 FIFO taxes in 2012 − $105 LIFO taxes in 2012), to $180, by the end of 2012 to reflect the additional FIFO taxes payable created in 2012.

The primary financial statements reported in 2013 are the three years of retrospectively prepared FIFO-based financial statements. The disadvantage of this retrospective approach is that the comparative balance sheet and income statement for 2012 that are included in the 2013 financial statements are different from the balance sheet and income statement for 2012 that were originally released the year before. Some financial statement users may be confused by the fact that, for example, Forester's 2012 net income of $245 as originally reported has been retrospectively changed to $385 in the financial statements released in 2013. This disadvantage is outweighed by the fact that the comparative financial statements released in 2013 all reflect the FIFO method of inventory valuation, and so those financial statements can be meaningfully compared from one year to the next.

In addition to the preparation of retrospectively adjusted primary financial statements, the change in accounting principle from LIFO to FIFO also necessitates note disclosure that shows the impact of the change on each financial statement item in each year reported. The information on page 20-12 would be reported in the financial statements notes in 2013, the year of the change. Note that because balance sheet data are typically reported only for two years, disclosure of the balance sheet comparisons for 2011 is not needed.

For 2013	Computed Using LIFO	As Reported Using FIFO	Effect of Change
Balance Sheet			
Cash	$ 150	$ 150	$ 0
Inventory	3,800	4,500	700
Total assets	$3,950	$4,650	$ 700
Income taxes payable	$ 165	$ 195	$ 30
FIFO taxes payable	0	180	180
Paid-in capital	1,645	1,645	0
Retained earnings	2,140	2,630	490
Total liabilities and equities	$3,950	$4,650	$ 700
Income Statement			
Sales	$1,500	$1,500	$ 0
Cost of goods sold	950	850	(100)
Gross profit	$ 550	$ 650	$ 100
Income tax expense	165	195	30
Net income	$ 385	$ 455	$ 70

For 2012	As Originally Reported	Using FIFO	Effect of Change
Balance Sheet			
Cash	$ 120	$ 120	$ 0
Inventory	3,000	3,600	600
Total assets	$3,120	$3,720	$ 600
Income taxes payable	$ 105	$ 105	$ 0
FIFO taxes payable	0	180	180
Paid-in capital	1,260	1,260	0
Retained earnings	1,755	2,175	420
Total liabilities and equities	$3,120	$3,720	$ 600
Income Statement			
Sales	$1,200	$1,200	$ 0
Cost of goods sold	850	650	(200)
Gross profit	$ 350	$ 550	$ 200
Income tax expense	105	165	60
Net income	$ 245	$ 385	$ 140

For 2011	As Originally Reported	Using FIFO	Effect of Change
Income Statement			
Sales	$1,000	$1,000	$ 0
Cost of goods sold	700	550	(150)
Gross profit	$ 300	$ 450	$ 150
Income tax expense	90	135	45
Net income	$ 210	$ 315	$ 105

Impractical to Determine Period-Specific Effects Sometimes the cumulative effect of a change in accounting principle can be determined, but it is impractical to determine the precise periods when past differences arose. For example, it is possible that in a case such as the Forester example just given, the company may be able to determine the LIFO and FIFO inventory valuations on January 1, 2013, when the accounting change is made, but not be able to determine differences in prior years. In such a case, the beginning balance sheet accounts, including beginning retained earnings, are adjusted for the earliest year in which the necessary data are available. If Forester were only able to determine the January 1, 2013, inventory balances under LIFO ($3,000) and FIFO ($3,600), the following retained earnings computation would be presented for 2013:

Retained earnings, January 1, 2013, as originally reported	$1,755
Add adjustment for cumulative effect on prior years of retrospectively applying the FIFO method of inventory valuation	420
Adjusted retained earnings, January 1, 2013	$2,175
Add net income for 2013 (under FIFO)	455
Retained earnings, December 31, 2013	$2,630

FASB CODIFICATION

The Issue: You are the newly hired accountant for Deedle Development, a real estate company that develops time share units in beautiful but out-of-the-way places. One of your company's current projects is a multi-stage development on the hillside overlooking picturesque South Willow Lake located in the Stansbury Mountains southwest of Grantsville, Utah. In past years, for financial reporting purposes Deedle has accounted for this development as a three-phase project, even though one of the phases involves the construction of two separate buildings. Legal fees and development costs have been appropriately allocated among the three phases. Starting this year, Deedle has decided to account for the South Willow development as a four-phase project. This change was not prompted by any changes in the project design or timeline; instead, Deedle's management has merely decided that separation of the costs (and revenues) of the development into four phases will more accurately reflect the economics of the project.

The Question: Is this change from three phases to four phases to be accounted for as a change in estimate (prospectively), or a change in principle (retrospectively)?

Searching the Codification: There are three ways to search for the answer to this question.

- Scan the table of contents for Topic 250, Accounting Changes and Error Corrections. Because this question appears to be specific to a particular industry (real estate), Topic 250 might list guidance on industry-specific issues.
- Scan the table of contents for the collection of Industry topics in the Codification; these have topic numbers in the 900s. You will find a number of industry topics specific to real estate.
- Use the "Search" box in the top right corner of the Codification home page. Try the search term "time share."

The Answer: The correct treatment is described on page 20-28.

Prospective Application In other cases, it is simply impossible to determine the past impact of an accounting change. For example, a change to the LIFO method of inventory valuation is usually made effective with the beginning inventory in the year of change rather than with some prior year because of the difficulty in identifying prior-year LIFO layers or dollar-value pools. Thus, the beginning inventory in the year of change becomes the same as the previous inventory valued using another costing method, such as FIFO, and this becomes the base LIFO layer. The LIFO assumption is then applied prospectively, meaning that it is used from that time forward.

Accounting Change Mandated by a Change in Accounting Standards Most changes in accounting principle are recognized in connection with a company's adoption of a mandated new accounting principle. For example, the opening scenario of this chapter describes the large impact on companies when they adopted *SFAS No. 106* and were required to recognize a large liability for their previously unrecognized obligation for retirees' health care. Almost all standards include specific instructions about how to account for the necessary change in accounting principle. In the unlikely event that a new standard does not include specific instructions on how to report the impact of the change, FASB ASC 250-10-45 (paragraphs 3 and 5) states that the presumption is that the change is to be accounted for retrospectively, as illustrated earlier.

Pro Forma Disclosures after a Business Combination

4 **Report pro forma results for prior years following a business combination.**

WHY **A business combination can drastically change the size and economic character of an accounting entity. To give financial statement users some basis on which to perform a time-series analysis of this new entity, supplemental accounting disclosure is needed.**

HOW **After a business combination, supplemental disclosure of revenues and net income must be made as if the combination had occurred at the beginning of both the combination year and the preceding year.**

A business combination can substantially alter the size and mix of the operations reported in a single set of financial statements. For example, on January 11, 2001, **America Online** merged with **Time Warner** to form **AOL Time Warner**. This merger was accounted for as the acquisition of Time Warner by America Online. A comparison of the financial statements for AOL before and after this acquisition is quite startling. For example, AOL revenues in 2000 were \$6.886 billion. Revenues in 2001, the year after the merger, were \$38.234 billion. Assets in 2000 were \$10.673 billion; assets in 2001 were \$208.559 billion. Clearly, investors are not able to decipher this drastic change in the make-up of an economic entity without substantial supplemental disclosure. (*Note*: Setting the accounting aside, this merger was a disaster from a business standpoint. In 2003, after recognizing a record-breaking loss of \$99 billion in 2002, the merger company dropped the "AOL" from the name and reverted to the name "Time Warner.")

The supplemental disclosure required following a business combination is explained in FASB ASC Section 805-10-50.[4] The combined company is required to disclose pro forma results for the year of the combination as if the combination had occurred at the beginning

[4] FASB ASC paragraphs 805-10-50-1,2.

of the year. In addition, the same pro forma disclosure is required for the preceding year, as if the business combination had occurred at the beginning of that year. At a minimum, a company must include revenue and net income for the respective periods in this pro forma disclosure.[5] Preparing these pro forma disclosures involves more than simply adding together the sales and net income amounts from the financial statement prepared by the separate companies before they combined. For example, depreciation expense must be recomputed using the fair value amounts recorded for the depreciable assets of the acquired company when the purchase was recorded.

To illustrate the adjustments that must be made in preparing these pro forma disclosures, assume that on December 31, 2013, Sump Pump Company acquired Rock Wall Company for $500,000. This amount exceeded the recorded value of Rock Wall Company's net assets by $100,000 on the acquisition date. The entire excess was attributable to a piece of Rock Wall's equipment that had a remaining useful life of five years as of the acquisition date. Information reported for the two companies for 2012 and 2013 was as follows:

	2013	2012
Sump Pump Company:		
Revenue	$3,500,000	$3,000,000
Net income	250,000	200,000
Rock Wall Company:		
Revenue	$ 250,000	$ 400,000
Net income	40,000	75,000

The necessary pro forma information that would be included in the notes to Sump Pump Company's 2013 financial statements is as follows:

	2013 Reported Results	2013 Results for Combined Companies	2012 Reported Results	2012 Results for Combined Companies
Revenue	$3,500,000	$3,750,000	$3,000,000	$3,400,000
Net income	250,000	270,000	200,000	255,000

2013 combined income computation:

$250,000 + $40,000 − extra depreciation ($100,000/5 years) = $270,000

2012 combined income computation:

$200,000 + $75,000 − extra depreciation ($100,000/5 years) = $255,000

[5] Companies sometimes change their structures or report their operations in such a way that the financial statements are, in effect, those of a different reporting entity. Specifically, a change in reporting entity includes (1) presenting consolidated or combined statements in place of statements of individual companies, (2) changing specific subsidiaries composing the group of companies for which consolidated statements are presented, and (3) changing the companies included in combined financial statements. In these cases, the financial statements must be adjusted retroactively to disclose what the statements would have looked like if the current entity had been in existence in the prior years. Thus, previous years' financial statements presented for comparison with the current year (the year of change) must be restated to reflect results of operations, financial condition, and cash flows as if the current reporting entity had been in existence in those years.

Error Corrections

5 **Recognize the various types of errors that can occur in the accounting process, understand when errors counterbalance, and be able to correct errors when necessary.**

WHY **A financial statement error can impact the interpretation of the financial statements in the year of the error and in all subsequent years when the error year is used for comparison.**

HOW **For financial reporting purposes, when an error is detected, all financial statements presented for comparative purposes are corrected and restated. For bookkeeping purposes, most errors that go undetected counterbalance over a 2-year period; those errors that impact income and that have not counterbalanced are corrected by making a direct adjustment to retained earnings.**

Error corrections are not considered accounting changes, but their treatment is specified in FASB ASC Topic 250. Accounting errors made in prior years are corrected from a reporting standpoint by restating the financial statements for all years presented and, if needed, by reporting an adjustment to the beginning retained earnings for the earliest year reported. Basically, errors in the financial statements are fixed in subsequent years by releasing corrected financial statements and providing note disclosure of the line-by-line impact of the errors. This reporting is essentially the same as the reporting required for a change in accounting principle, as discussed in the preceding section.

From a bookkeeping standpoint, errors that have not already been "counterbalanced" or reversed are reported as prior-period adjustments and debited or credited directly to Retained Earnings for the current year. Examples of errors include mathematical mistakes, improper application of accounting principles, omissions of material facts, or fraudulent financial reporting. These bookkeeping corrections will be illustrated in this section. As you will soon see, the bookkeeping correction of accounting errors is a good test of how well you understand your debits and credits.

Types of Errors

There are a number of different kinds of errors. Some errors are discovered in the period in which they are made and are easily corrected. Others may not be discovered currently and are reflected on the financial statements until discovered. Some errors are never discovered; however, the effects of these errors may be counterbalanced in subsequent periods, and after this takes place, account balances are again accurately stated. Errors may be classified as follows:

1. *Errors discovered currently in the course of normal accounting procedures.* Examples of this type of error are clerical errors, such as an addition error, posting to the wrong account, misstating an account, or omitting an account from the trial balance. These types of errors usually are detected during the regular summarizing process of the accounting cycle and are readily corrected.
2. *Errors limited to balance sheet accounts.* Examples include debiting Accounts Receivable instead of Notes Receivable, crediting Interest Payable instead of Notes Payable, or crediting Interest Payable instead of Salaries Payable. Another example is not recording the exchange of convertible bonds for stock. Such errors are frequently discovered and corrected in the period in which they are made. When such errors

are not found until a subsequent period, corrections must be made at that time and balance sheet data subsequently restated for comparative reporting purposes.

3. *Errors limited to income statement accounts.* The examples and correcting procedures for this type of error are similar to those in (2). For example, Office Salaries may be debited instead of Sales Salaries. This type of error should be corrected as soon as it is discovered. Even though the error would not affect net income, the misstated accounts should be restated for analysis purposes and comparative reporting.
4. *Errors affecting both income statement accounts and balance sheet accounts.* Certain errors, when not discovered currently, result in the misstatement of net income and thus affect both the income statement accounts and the balance sheet accounts. The balance sheet accounts are carried into the succeeding period; hence, an error made currently and not detected will affect future earnings. Such errors may be classified into two groups:
   (a) *Errors in net income that, when not detected, are automatically counterbalanced in the following fiscal period.* Net income amounts on the income statements for two successive periods are inaccurately stated; certain account balances on the balance sheet at the end of the first period are inaccurately stated, but the account balances in the balance sheet at the end of the succeeding period will be accurately stated. In this class are errors such as the misstatement of inventories and the omission of adjustments for prepaid and accrued items at the end of the period.
   (b) *Errors in net income that, when not detected, are not automatically counterbalanced in the following fiscal period.* Account balances on successive balance sheets will be inaccurately stated until such time as entries are made compensating for or correcting the errors. In this class are errors such as the recognition of capital expenditures as expenses and the omission of charges for depreciation and amortization.

When errors affecting income are discovered, careful analysis is necessary to determine the required action to correct the account balances. As indicated, most errors will be caught and corrected prior to closing the books. The few material errors not detected until subsequent periods and those that have not already been counterbalanced must be treated as prior-period adjustments.

The following sections describe and illustrate the procedures to be applied when error corrections require prior-period adjustments. It is assumed that each of the errors is material. Errors that are discovered usually affect the income tax liability for a prior period. Amended tax returns are usually prepared either to claim a refund or to pay any additional tax assessment. For simplicity, the examples on the following pages and in the exercises and problems at the end of the chapter ignore the income tax effects of errors.

Illustrative Example of Error Correction

Assume that Supply Master, Inc., began operations at the beginning of 2011. An auditing firm is engaged for the first time in 2013. Before the accounts are adjusted and closed for 2013, the auditor reviews the books and accounts and discovers the errors summarized on pages 20-18 and 20-19. Effects of these errors on the financial statements, before any correcting entries, are indicated as follows: A plus sign (+) indicates an overstatement and a minus sign (−) indicates an understatement. Each error correction is discussed in the following paragraphs.

(1) Understatement of Merchandise Inventory It is discovered that the merchandise inventory as of December 31, 2011, was understated by $1,000. The effects of the misstatement were as shown on page 20-18.

	Income Statement	Balance Sheet
2011	Cost of goods sold overstated (ending inventory too low) Net income understated	Assets understated (inventory too low) Retained earnings understated
2012	Cost of goods sold understated (beginning inventory too low) Net income overstated	Balance sheet items not affected, retained earnings understatement for 2011 being corrected by net income overstatement for 2012

Because this type of error counterbalances after two years, no correcting entry is required in 2013.

Analysis Sheet to Show Effects

	At End of 2011					
	Income Statement			Balance Sheet		
	Section		Net Income	Section		Retained Earnings
(1) Understatement of merchandise inventory of $1,000 on December 31, 2011.	Cost of Goods Sold	+	–	Current Assets	–	–
(2) Failure to record merchandise purchases on account of $850 in 2011; purchases were recorded in 2012.	Cost of Goods Sold	–	+	Current Liabilities	–	+
(3) Failure to record merchandise sales on account of $1,800 in 2012. (It is assumed that the sales for 2012 were recognized as revenue in 2013.)						
(4) Failure to record accrued sales salaries of $450 on December 31, 2011; expense was recognized when payment was made.	Selling Expense	–	+	Current Liabilities	–	+
(5) Failure to record prepaid taxes of $275 on December 31, 2011; amount was included in Miscellaneous General Expense.	General Expense	+	–	Current Assets	–	–
(6) Failure to record accrued interest on notes receivable of $150 on December 31, 2011; revenue was recognized when collected in 2012.	Other Revenue	–	–	Current Assets	–	–
(7) Failure to record unearned service fees of $225 on December 31, 2012; amount received was included in Miscellaneous Revenue.						
(8) Failure to record depreciation of delivery equipment. On December 31, 2011, $1,200.	Selling Expense	–	+	Noncurrent Assets	+	+
On December 31, 2012, $1,200.						
(9) Incorrectly capitalizing an expenditure for operating expenses on January 1, 2011; depreciation expense of $400 was incorrectly recognized in 2011 and 2012.	Operating Expense	–	+	Noncurrent Assets	+	+

! CAUTION

Errors (1) through (6) provide examples of errors that will counterbalance over two periods. However, errors that will "fix themselves" still result in misstated financial statements for each year of the 2-year period. Investors and creditors may make ill-advised decisions based on those misstated financial statements.

If the error had been discovered in 2012 instead of 2013, an entry would have been made to correct the account balances so that operations for 2012 would be reported accurately. The beginning inventory for 2012 would have been increased by $1,000, the amount of the asset understatement, and Retained Earnings would have been credited for this amount, representing the income understatement in 2011. The correcting entry in 2012 would have been as follows:

> **! CAUTION**
>
> This entry is made only if the error is identified at the end of 2012.

Merchandise Inventory.	1,000	
Retained Earnings		1,000

This correcting entry is the same whether the company uses a periodic or a perpetual inventory system. As seen with error (2), the correcting entry is sometimes different, depending on what type of inventory system the company uses.

of Errors on Financial Statements

At End of 2012				At End of 2013			
Income Statement		**Balance Sheet**		**Income Statement**		**Balance Sheet**	
Section	**Net Income**	**Section**	**Retained Earnings**	**Section**	**Net Income**	**Section**	**Retained Earnings**
Cost of Goods Sold −	+						
Cost of Goods Sold +	−						
Sales −	−	Accounts Receivable −	−	Sales +	+		
Selling Expense +	−						
General Expense −	+						
Other Revenue +	+						
Other Revenue +	+	Current Liabilities −	+	Other Revenue −	−		
		Noncurrent Assets +	+			Noncurrent Assets +	+
Selling Expense −	+	Noncurrent Assets +	+			Noncurrent Assets +	+
Operating Expense +	−	Noncurrent Assets +	+			Noncurrent Assets +	+

(2) Failure to Record Merchandise Purchases It is discovered that purchase invoices as of December 28, 2011, for $850 had not been recorded until 2012. The goods had been included in the inventory at the end of 2011. The effects of failure to record the purchases were as shown on page 20-20.

	Income Statement	Balance Sheet
2011	Cost of goods sold understated (purchases too low)	Liabilities understated (accounts payable too low)
	Net income overstated	Retained earnings overstated
2012	Cost of goods sold overstated (purchases too high)	Balance sheet items not affected, retained earnings overstatement for 2011 being corrected by net income understatement for 2012
	Net income understated	

Because this is a counterbalancing error, no correcting entry is required in 2013.

If the error had been discovered in 2012 instead of 2013, a correcting entry would have been necessary. In 2012, Purchases was debited and Accounts Payable was credited for $850 for merchandise acquired in 2011 and included in the ending inventory of 2011. Retained Earnings would have to be debited for $850, representing the net income overstatement for 2011, and Purchases would have to be credited for the same amount to reduce the balance in 2012. The correcting entry in 2012, assuming the company uses a periodic inventory system, would have been as follows:

Retained Earnings	850	
Purchases		850

If the company had used a perpetual system, the incorrect purchase would have been debited directly to Inventory. Accordingly, the correcting entry would have been made in 2012:

Retained Earnings	850	
Inventory		850

(3) Failure to Record Merchandise Sales It is discovered that sales on account of $1,800 for the last week of December 2012 had not been recorded until 2013. The goods sold were not included in the inventory at the end of 2012. The effects of the failure to report the revenue in 2012 follow:

	Income Statement	Balance Sheet
2012	Revenue understated (sales too low)	Assets understated (accounts receivable too low)
	Net income understated	Retained earnings understated

When the error is discovered in 2013, Sales is debited for $1,800 and Retained Earnings is credited for this amount, representing the net income understatement for 2012. The following entry is made:

Sales	1,800	
Retained Earnings		1,800

(4) Failure to Record Accrued Expense Accrued sales salaries of $450 as of December 31, 2011, were overlooked in adjusting the accounts. Sales Salaries is debited for salary payments. The effects of the failure to record the accrued expense of $450 as of December 31, 2011, were as shown on page 20-21.

	Income Statement	Balance Sheet
2011	Expenses understated (sales salaries too low)	Liabilities understated (accrued salaries not reported)
	Net income overstated	Retained earnings overstated
2012	Expenses overstated (sales salaries too high) Net income understated	Balance sheet items not affected, retained earnings overstatement for 2011 being corrected by net income understatement for 2012

No entry is required in 2013 to correct the accounts for the failure to record the accrued expense at the end of 2011, the misstatement in 2011 having been counterbalanced by the misstatement in 2012. However, if comparative income statements were presented in 2013, then the amounts reported for sales salaries in 2011 and 2012 would be corrected. If the error had been discovered in 2012, an entry would have been required to correct the accounts for the failure to record the accrued expense at the end of 2011 if the net income for 2012 is not to be misstated. If accrued expenses are to be properly recorded at the end of 2012, Retained Earnings would be debited for $450, representing the net income overstatement for 2011, and Sales Salaries would be credited for the same amount, representing the amount to be subtracted from salary expenses in 2012. The correcting entry made in 2012 follows:

Retained Earnings	450	
Sales Salaries		450

(5) Failure to Record Prepaid Expense It is discovered that Miscellaneous General Expense for 2011 included taxes of $275 that should have been deferred in adjusting the accounts on December 31, 2011. The effects of the failure to record the prepaid expense were as follows:

	Income Statement	Balance Sheet
2011	Expenses overstated (miscellaneous general expense too high)	Assets understated (prepaid taxes not reported)
	Net income understated	Retained earnings understated
2012	Expenses understated (miscellaneous general expense too low) Net income overstated	Balance sheet items not affected, retained earnings understatement for 2011 being corrected by net income overstatement for 2012

Because this is a counterbalancing error, no entry to correct the accounts is required in 2013.

If the error had been discovered in 2012 instead of 2013, a correcting entry would have been necessary. If prepaid taxes had been properly recorded at the end of 2012, Miscellaneous General Expense would have to be debited for $275, the expense relating to operations of 2012, and Retained Earnings would have to be credited for the same amount, representing the net income understatement for 2011. The following correcting entry would have been made in 2012:

Miscellaneous General Expense	275	
Retained Earnings		275

(6) Failure to Record Accrued Revenue Accrued interest on notes receivable of $150 was overlooked in adjusting the accounts on December 31, 2011. The revenue was recognized when the interest was collected in 2012. The effects of the failure to record the accrued revenue follow:

	Income Statement	Balance Sheet
2011	Revenue understated (interest revenue too low)	Assets understated (interest receivable not reported)
	Net income understated	Retained earnings understated
2012	Revenue overstated (interest revenue too high) Net income overstated	Balance sheet items not affected, retained earnings understatement for 2011 being corrected by net income overstatement for 2012

Because the balance sheet items at the end of 2012 were correctly stated, no entry to correct the accounts is required in 2013.

If the error had been discovered in 2012 instead of 2013, an entry would have been necessary to correct the account balances. If accrued interest on notes receivable had been properly recorded at the end of 2012, Interest Revenue would have to be debited for $150, the amount to be subtracted from receipts of 2012, and Retained Earnings would have to be credited for the same amount, representing the net income understatement for 2011. The correcting entry in 2012 would have been as follows:

Interest Revenue	150	
Retained Earnings		150

(7) Failure to Record Unearned Revenue Fees of $225 received in advance for miscellaneous services as of December 31, 2012, were overlooked in adjusting the accounts. Miscellaneous Revenue had been credited when fees were received. The effects of the failure to recognize the unearned revenue of $225 at the end of 2012 were as follows:

	Income Statement	Balance Sheet
2012	Revenue overstated (miscellaneous revenue too high)	Liabilities understated (unearned service fees not reported)
	Net income overstated	Retained earnings overstated

An entry is required to correct the accounts for the failure to record the unearned revenue at the end of 2012 if the net income for 2013 is not to be misstated. If the unearned revenue was properly recorded at the end of 2013, Retained Earnings would be debited for $225, representing the net income overstatement for 2012, and Miscellaneous Revenue would be credited for the same amount, representing the revenue that is to be identified with 2013. The correcting entry follows:

Retained Earnings	225	
Miscellaneous Revenue		225

CAUTION

Error (8) does not counterbalance in the following year. Thus, financial statements have the potential to be misstated for several years. In this example, the error could continue until the delivery equipment is removed from the books.

(8) Failure to Record Depreciation Delivery equipment was acquired at the beginning of 2011 at a cost of $6,000. The equipment has an estimated 5-year life. Its depreciation of $1,200 was overlooked at the end of 2011 and 2012. The effects of the failure to record depreciation for 2011 were as follows:

	Income Statement	Balance Sheet
2011	Expenses understated (depreciation of delivery equipment too low)	Assets overstated (accumulated depreciation of delivery equipment too low)
	Net income overstated	Retained earnings overstated
2012	Expenses not affected	Assets overstated (accumulated depreciation of delivery equipment too low)
	Net income not affected	Retained earnings overstated

It should be observed that the misstatements arising from the failure to record depreciation are not counterbalanced in the succeeding year.

Failure to record depreciation for 2012 affected the statements as follows:

	Income Statement	Balance Sheet
2012	Expenses understated (depreciation of delivery equipment too low)	Assets overstated (accumulated depreciation of delivery equipment too low)
	Net income overstated	Retained earnings overstated

When the omission is recognized, Retained Earnings must be decreased by the net income overstatements of prior years and Accumulated Depreciation must be increased by the depreciation that should have been recorded. The correcting entry in 2013 for depreciation that should have been recognized for 2011 and 2012 is as follows:

Retained Earnings	2,400	
Accumulated Depreciation—Delivery Equipment		2,400

(9) Incorrectly Capitalizing an Expenditure Operating expenses of $2,000 were paid in cash at the beginning of 2011. However, the payment was incorrectly recorded as the purchase of equipment. The "equipment" was assumed to have an estimated 5-year life with $0 residual value, and depreciation of $400 was recognized at the end of 2011 and 2012. The effects of this incorrect capitalization of an expenditure were as follows:

	Income Statement	Balance Sheet
2011	Expenses understated (operating expenses too low, partially offset by depreciation expense)	Assets overstated (asset, net of accumulated depreciation, is recorded when there should not be any asset)
	Net income overstated	Retained earnings overstated
2012	Expenses overstated (depreciation too high)	Assets overstated (asset is still incorrectly recorded, though the net amount is less)
	Net income understated	Retained earnings overstated

When the error is discovered, Retained Earnings must be decreased by the net income overstatement of 2011 (partially offset by the net income understatement in 2012) and the accounts related to the "equipment" (Equipment and Accumulated Depreciation) must be eliminated. The correcting entry in 2013 is as follows:

Retained Earnings	1,200	
Accumulated Depreciation—Equipment	800	
Equipment		2,000

Required Disclosure for Error Restatements

If an error (either accidental or intentional in nature) is subsequently discovered that affected a prior period, the nature of the error, its effect on previously issued financial statements, and the effect of its correction on current period's net income and EPS should be disclosed in the period in which the error is corrected.[6] In addition, any comparative financial statements provided must be corrected.

An example of the disclosure provided when an error correction is made through a prior-period adjustment is given in Exhibit 20-4; the error correction (intentional errors in this instance) was made in 2000 by **Xerox Corporation**. Xerox provides extensive disclosure as to the effect of the errors on the income statement and the balance sheet for each year affected. Recall that Xerox's accounting difficulties were discussed in Chapter 6. As you read over the businesslike description of the accounting errors uncovered at Xerox, keep in mind that underlying this dry verbiage lie the destroyed careers of many accountants and managers at Xerox who stepped over the earnings management line into the area of earnings misstatement (see Chapter 6). Between the lines of this note one can also sense the lost trust of Xerox shareholders, customers, suppliers, and regulators.

Summary of Accounting Changes and Error Corrections

The summary listed below presents the appropriate accounting procedures applicable to each of the four main categories covered in FASB ASC Topic 250, Accounting Changes and Error Corrections. Naturally, accountants must apply these guidelines with judgment and should seek to provide the most relevant and reliable information possible.

Summary of Procedures for Reporting Accounting Changes and Error Corrections

Category	Accounting Procedures
I. Change in estimate	1. Adjust either current-period results or current- and future-period results. 2. No separate cumulative adjustment or restated financial statements.
II. Change in accounting principle	1. Direct cumulative adjustment to beginning retained earnings balance of earliest year presented in the financial statements. 2. Restate financial statements to reflect new principle for comparative purposes.
III. Pro forma disclosures after a business combination	1. Supplemental disclosure for the year of the combination and the preceding year of revenues and net income as if the combination had occurred at the beginning of both the combination year and the preceding year.
IV. Error corrections	1. If detected in period error occurred, correct accounts through normal accounting cycle adjustments. 2. If detected in a subsequent period, adjust for effect of material errors by making prior-period adjustments directly to Retained Earnings balance for the years affected by those errors. If the error relates to a year that is not presented in the financial statements, the Retained Earnings balance for the earliest year presented is adjusted. Also correct each item presented in comparative financial statements. 3. Once an error is discovered in previously issued financial statements, the nature of the error, its effect on the financial statements, and its effect on the current period's income and EPS should be disclosed.

[6] FASB ASC paragraph 250-10-50-7.

EX 20-4 XEROX CORPORATION—DISCLOSURE OF ERROR CORRECTION

2. Restatement

We have restated our Consolidated Financial Statements for the fiscal years ended December 31, 1999 and 1998 as a result of two separate investigations conducted by the Audit Committee of the Board of Directors. These investigations involved previously disclosed issues in our Mexico operations and a review of our accounting policies and procedures and application thereof. As a result of these investigations, it was determined that certain accounting practices and the application thereof misapplied GAAP and certain accounting errors and irregularities were identified. The Company has corrected the accounting errors and irregularities in its Consolidated Financial Statements. The Consolidated Financial Statements have been adjusted as follows:

In fiscal 2000 the Company had initially recorded charges totaling $170 ($120 after taxes) which arose from imprudent and improper business practices in Mexico that resulted in certain accounting errors and irregularities. Over a period of years, several senior managers in Mexico had collaborated to circumvent certain of Xerox's accounting policies and administrative procedures. The charges related to provisions for uncollectible long-term receivables, the recording of liabilities for amounts due to concessionaires and, to a lesser extent, for contracts that did not fully meet the requirements to be recorded as sales-type leases. The investigation of the accounting issues discovered in Mexico has been completed. The Company has restated its prior year Consolidated Financial Statements to reflect reductions to pre-tax income of $53 and $13 in 1999 and 1998, respectively. It is not practical to determine what portion, if any, of the approximate remaining $101 of the Mexican charge reflected in adjusted 2000 results of operations relates to prior years.

In connection with our acquisition of the remaining 20 percent of Xerox Limited from Rank Group, Plc in 1997, we recorded a liability of $100 for contingencies identified at the date of acquisition. During 1998, we determined that the liability was no longer required. During 1998 and 1999, we charged to the liability certain expenses incurred as part of the consolidation of our European back-office operations. This reversal should have been recorded as a reduction of Goodwill and Deferred tax assets. Therefore, we have restated our previously reported Consolidated Financial Statements to reflect decreases of $67 to Goodwill and $33 of Deferred tax assets and increases in Selling, administrative and general expenses of $76 in 1999 and $24 in 1998.

In addition to the above items, we have made adjustments in connection with certain misapplications of GAAP under SFAS No. 13, "Accounting for Leases." These adjustments primarily relate to the accounting for lease modifications and residual values as well as certain other items. The following table presents the effects of all of the aforementioned adjustments on pre-tax income (loss).

	Year Ended December 31,		
	2000	**1999**	**1998**
Increase (decrease) to pre-tax income (loss):			
Mexico	$ 69	$ (53)	$ (13)
Rank Group acquisition	6	(76)	(24)
Lease issues, net	87	83	(165)
Other, net	10	(82)	18
Total	$172	$(128)	$(184)

These adjustments resulted in the cumulative net reduction of Common shareholders' equity and Consolidated Tangible Net Worth (as defined in our $7 Billion Revolving Credit Agreement) of $137 and $76, respectively, as of December 31, 2000.

Retained earnings at December 31, 1997 was restated from $3,960 to $3,852 as a result of the effect of these aforementioned adjustments on years prior to 1998.

The following tables present the impact of the adjustments and restatements on a condensed basis.

(Continued)

EX 20-4 XEROX CORPORATION—DISCLOSURE OF ERROR CORRECTION (CONTINUED)

	Amount Previously Reported	As Adjusted
(in millions, except per share amounts)		
Year ended December 31, 2000:*		
Statement of operations:		
Revenues	$18,632	$18,701
Costs and expenses	19,188	19,085
Income (loss) from continuing operations	(384)	(257)
Basic loss per share	$ (0.63)	$ (0.44)
Diluted loss per share	$ (0.63)	$ (0.44)
Balance Sheet:		
Current finance receivables, net	$ 5,141	$ 5,097
Inventories, net	1,930	1,932
Equipment and operating leases, net	717	724
Deferred taxes and other current assets	1,284	1,247
Finance receivables due after one year, net	8,035	7,957
Intangible and other assets, net	3,062	3,061
Goodwill, net	1,639	1,578
Other current liabilities	1,648	1,630
Deferred taxes and other liabilities	1,933	1,876
Common shareholders' equity	3,630	3,493

	Amount Previously Reported	As Adjusted
(in millions, except per share amounts)		
Year ended December 31, 1999:**		
Statement of operations:		
Revenues	$19,548	$19,567
Costs and expenses	17,512	17,659
Income (loss) from continuing operations	1,424	1,339
Basic earnings per share	$ 2.09	$ 1.96
Diluted earnings per share	$ 1.96	$ 1.85
Balance Sheet:		
Accounts receivable, net	$ 2,622	$ 2,633
Current finance receivables, net	5,115	4,961
Inventories, net	2,285	2,290
Equipment and operating leases, net	676	695
Finance receivables due after one year, net	8,203	8,058
Intangible and other assets, net	2,831	2,810
Goodwill, net	1,724	1,657
Other current liabilities	2,163	2,176
Deferred taxes and other liabilities	2,623	2,521
Common shareholders' equity	4,911	4,648
Year ended December 31, 1998:**		
Statement of operations:		
Revenues	$19,747	$19,593
Costs and expenses	18,984	19,014
Income (loss) from continuing operations	585	463
Basic earnings per share	$ 0.82	$ 0.63
Diluted earnings per share	$ 0.80	$ 0.62

*As reported in the Company's unaudited financial statements included in its report on Form 8-K dated April 19, 2001.

**Revenues and costs and expenses have been reclassified to reflect the Change in classification of shipping and handling costs as discussed in Note 1.

SOLUTIONS TO OPENING SCENARIO QUESTIONS

1. Reducing retiree health benefits would reduce the earning impact and the size of the liability to be reported under FASB *Statement No. 106.* Without the changes, firms might fear that the adverse financial statement effects would lower their stock price, reduce their ability to maintain management bonuses, or make it more difficult to obtain loans. In one sense, the existence of such consequences is counterintuitive, because FASB *Statement No. 106* mandated only a change in accounting for retiree benefit plans—plans that have been in existence for years. However, the fact that firms seemed to be willing to change their retiree plans in response to a change in accounting again supports the belief that the way something is accounted for has real economic consequences.

   Another reason that a company might have reduced its retiree health benefits in response to the adoption of FASB *Statement No. 106* is that, in the absence of the accounting requirement, the company had never before quantified the cost of the promises it was making to its workers. FASB *Statement No. 106* forced some companies to face economic reality and acknowledge that they could no longer make these costly promises to employees.

2. In a perfect world, one would expect no impact on stock prices or on the ability to get loans. This is because the impact of retiree health care plans on the financial condition of a company would have already been taken into account by sophisticated investors and bankers who are known to use all sorts of data not found in financial statements when doing their financial analyses. However, the world is not perfect, and it is possible that the financial effects of retiree health care plans either were not fully factored into investment decisions, or the estimates of those effects were systematically in error. There is some evidence that firms found that they had been underestimating the cost of their retiree health care plans. If this is true, FASB *Statement No. 106* could have impacted stock prices and creditworthiness of firms with large retiree health care plans.

3. General Motors could have recognized this $21 billion after-tax cost as correction of a past error with a restatement of past income statements to reflect the cost in the years in which it occurred. As explained in this chapter, this approach, the restatement approach, is the approach now required by the FASB.

SOLUTIONS TO STOP & THINK

1. (Page 20-6) The correct answer is D. Changes in estimates are made on an ongoing basis and are a routine part of the accounting process. Each year, estimates as to the percentage of accounts receivable that will be uncollected, the amount of warranty claims that will be serviced, and percentage of costs incurred on long-term contracts, to name a few, must be reassessed. If previously issued financial statements were required to be restated in every case where an estimate was changed, then prior-period statements would continually be reissued. Investors and creditors would be unable to rely on the information provided by companies because they would know that the information would be changing. It is a good thing that accounting standards do not require financial statements to be restated for every change in estimate.

SOLUTION TO USING THE FASB'S CODIFICATION

Your search of the Codification will lead you to Topic 978, Real Estate—Time-Sharing Activities. The table of contents for this topic reveals that there is material specific to Topic 250, Accounting Changes and Error Corrections. Paragraph 978-250-35-2 says the following (in part): "A change in the delineation of a project or its phases without a significant change in facts and circumstances related to the project's development shall be accounted for as a change in the method of applying an accounting principle under Subtopic 250-10. An example of this latter change would be a decision to divide the same development of a project into more or fewer phases, which would be a change only in how the project is accounted for rather than a change in the nature (that is, the facts and circumstances) of the project itself."

So, Deedle Development's change in accounting for the South Willow project from three phases to four phases would be accounted for as a change in accounting principle and thus would be applied retrospectively.

REVIEW CHAPTER 20

LEARNING OBJECTIVES

1 Understand the two different types of accounting changes that have been identified by accounting standard setters.

The accounting profession has identified two different types of accounting changes: change in accounting estimate and change in accounting principle. The distinction between the two is important because different accounting treatment and disclosure are required for each type of accounting change.

2 Recognize the difference between a change in accounting estimate and a change in accounting principle, and know how a change in accounting estimate is reflected in the financial statements.

A change in accounting estimate does not involve a restatement of prior periods' financial statements. Instead, the effects of these types of changes are reflected in the current and future periods. Previous chapters discussed the accounting for common areas involving changing estimates. Examples include bad debt expense (Chapter 7), depreciation (Chapter 10), and actuarial assumptions (Chapter 17). A change in depreciation method is accounted for as a change in estimate and is called "a change in accounting estimate effected by a change in accounting principle."

3 Prepare the retrospective adjustment of prior periods' financial statements, and any necessary cumulative adjustment, associated with a change in accounting principle.

A change in accounting principle is implemented by recomputing all financial statement amounts for the preceding years (at least those that will be included in the current year's comparative financial statements). These recomputed amounts are included in the comparative financial statements reported this year. Any income effect in even earlier years is shown as an adjustment to the beginning balance in Retained Earnings for the earliest year reported. Note disclosure gives a line-by-line comparison between these retrospectively adjusted financial statements and the financial statements (using the former accounting principles) that were originally reported.

4 Report pro forma results for prior years following a business combination.

After a business combination, supplemental disclosure for the year of the combination and the preceding year is required. Pro forma disclosure of revenues and net income must be made as if the combination had occurred at the beginning of both the combination year and the preceding year.

5 Recognize the various types of errors that can occur in the accounting process, understand when errors counterbalance, and be able to correct errors when necessary.

Numerous errors can occur during the accounting process. Many of those errors will be discovered and corrected in the normal course of business. Some errors will be detected after the books have been closed for an accounting period, thereby requiring an adjustment to the Retained Earnings balance. Most errors that go undetected counterbalance over a 2-year period, but those that do not often require a cumulative adjustment once they have been detected. When an error is detected, all financial statements presented for comparative purposes are corrected and restated.

FASB-IASB CODIFICATION SUMMARY

ifrs

Topic	FASB Accounting Standards Codification	Original FASB Standard	Corresponding IASB Standard	Differences between U.S. GAAP and IFRS
Disclosure after a business combination	*Section 805-10-50 par. 1-2*	*SFAS No. 141(R) par. 68*	*IFRS 3 par. 59-63 and B64-B67*	No substantial Differences
Change in accounting principle	*Section 250-10-45 par. 1-16* *Section 250-10-50 par. 1- 3*	*SFAS No. 154 par. 4-18* *APB No. 28 par. 28*	*IAS 8 par. 14-31*	No substantial Differences
Change in accounting estimate	*Section 250-10-45 par. 17-20* *Section 250-10-50 par. 4- 5*	*SFAS No. 154 par. 19-22* *SFAS No. 157 par. 20*	*IAS 8 par. 32-40*	No substantial Differences
Correction of an error	*Section 250-10-45 par. 22-28* *Section 250-10-50 par. 7-11*	*SFAS No. 154 par. 25-26* *SFAS No. 16 par. 10-15* *APB No. 9 par. 17-18* *APB No. 9 par. 26-27* *APB No. 28 par. 29*	*IAS 8 par. 41-49*	No substantial Differences

KEY TERMS

Accounting changes 20-3

Accounting errors 20-16

Change in accounting estimate 20-5

Change in accounting principle 20-9

QUESTIONS

1. How do accounting changes detract from the informational characteristics of comparability and consistency as described in FASB *Concepts Statement No. 2*?
2. What are the two categories of accounting changes? Explain briefly why such changes are made.
3. What alternative procedures have been suggested as solutions for reporting accounting changes?

4. (a) List several examples of areas for which changes in accounting estimates are often made. (b) Explain briefly the proper accounting treatment for a change in estimate. (c) Why is this procedure considered proper for recording changes in accounting estimates?
5. What is the proper way to account for a change in depreciation method?
6. (a) List several examples of changes in accounting principle that a company may make. (b) Explain briefly the proper accounting treatment for recognizing currently a change in accounting principle.
7. Why does a change in accounting principle require justification?
8. (a) When should the effects of a change in accounting principle be reported only as a direct adjustment to the current year's beginning Retained Earnings balance? (b) When should the effects of a change in accounting principle be reported only prospectively?
9. Dallas Company purchased a delivery van in 2010. At the time of purchase, the van's service life was estimated to be seven years with a salvage value of $500. The company has been using the straight-line method of depreciation. During 2013, the company determined that because of extensive use, the van's service life would be only five years with no salvage value. Also, the company has decided to change the depreciation method used from straight-line to the sum-of-the-years'-digits method. How would these changes be treated?
10. Describe the required disclosures following a business combination.
11. Describe the effect of each of the following:
    a. Depreciation is changed from the straight-line method to an accelerated method.
    b. Depreciation is changed from an accelerated method to the straight-line method.
    c. Income on construction contracts that had been reported on a completed-contract basis is now reported on the percentage-of-completion basis.
    d. The valuation of inventories is changed from a FIFO to a LIFO basis.
    e. It is determined that warranty expenses in prior years should have been 5% of sales instead of 4%.
    f. The valuation of inventories is changed from a LIFO to a FIFO basis.
    g. Your accounts receivable clerk has learned that a major customer has declared bankruptcy.
    h. Your patent lawyer informs you that your rival has perfected and patented a new invention making your product obsolete.
12. (a) How are accounting errors to be treated?
    (b) What are counterbalancing errors?
13. Mendez Manufacturing Company failed to record accrued interest for 2010, $800; 2011, $700; and 2012, $950. What is the amount of overstatement or understatement of the retained earnings account at December 31, 2013?
14. Goods purchased FOB shipping point were shipped to Merkley & Co. on December 31, 2013. The purchase was recorded in 2013, but the goods were not included in ending inventory. (a) What effect would this error have had on reported income for 2013 had it not been discovered? (b) What entry should be made on the books to correct this error, assuming that the books have not yet been closed for 2013?

PRACTICE EXERCISES

Practice 20-1
LO2

Change in Depreciation Life

On January 1, 2009, the company purchased equipment for $200,000. Originally, the equipment had a 12-year expected useful life and $8,000 residual value. The company uses straight-line depreciation. On January 1, 2013, the company realized that the equipment would have a total useful life of 15 years instead of 12 years and that the residual value would be $30,000 instead of $8,000. Compute depreciation expense for 2013. (*Note*: If you need some hints on how to do this exercise, look back at Chapter 11.)

Practice 20-2
LO2

Change from Double-Declining-Balance to Straight-Line Depreciation

On January 1, 2010, the company purchased equipment for $600,000. The equipment has a 20-year expected useful life and $0 residual value. Initially, the company used double-declining-balance depreciation. On January 1, 2013, the company changed to straight-line depreciation. The expected useful life and residual value are unchanged. Compute depreciation expense for 2013. Ignore income taxes.

Practice 20-3

LO2

Deferred Tax Impact of a Change in Depreciation Method
Refer to Practice 20-2. Assume that before 2013 the company used straight-line depreciation for tax purposes while using double-declining-balance depreciation for book purposes. The change to straight-line depreciation in 2013 is made for book purposes; the company continues to use straight-line depreciation for tax purposes. The income tax rate is 40%. (1) Compute the amount of the deferred tax asset or liability that would be included in the December 31, 2012, balance sheet and (2) compute the amount of the deferred tax asset or liability that would be included in the December 31, 2013, balance sheet.

Practice 20-4

LO2

Change from Straight-Line to Double-Declining-Balance Depreciation
On January 1, 2010, the company purchased equipment for $600,000. The equipment has an 8-year expected useful life and $0 residual value. Initially, the company used straight-line depreciation. On January 1, 2013, the company changed to double-declining-balance depreciation. Compute depreciation expense for 2013. Ignore income taxes.

Practice 20-5

LO3

Change from LIFO to FIFO: First Year Retained Earnings
As of January 1, 2013, the company decided to change from the LIFO method of inventory valuation to the FIFO method. The change is being made for both book and tax purposes. Data for the past four years (including 2013) are as follows:

	2013	2012	2011	2010
Sales	$2,000	$1,500	$1,200	$1,000
Cost of goods sold—LIFO	1,200	900	720	600
Ending inventory—LIFO	200	150	120	100
Ending income taxes payable—LIFO	n/a	240	192	160
Ending retained earnings—LIFO	1,668	1,188	828	540
Cost of goods sold—FIFO	1,170	880	710	595
Ending inventory—FIFO	300	220	170	140

The ending income taxes payable—LIFO amount is not given because, in 2013, income taxes payable will be computed using the newly adopted FIFO numbers. As you can see from the prior years, it is the practice of the company to pay all income taxes in the subsequent year.

The company's income tax rate is 40%, and the company has no expenses except for cost of goods sold and income tax expense. Compute the retrospectively recalculated Retained Earnings balance as of January 1, 2011, after the change to FIFO is made.

Practice 20-6

LO3

Change from LIFO to FIFO: Year-by-Year Retained Earnings Calculations
Refer to Practice 20-5. Compute (1) the retrospectively recalculated Retained Earnings balances as of December 31, 2011, and December 31, 2012, and (2) the Retained Earnings balance as of December 31, 2013, after the change to FIFO is made. Note that the company does not pay dividends.

Practice 20-7

LO3

Change from LIFO to FIFO: Year-by-Year Income Taxes Payable Calculations
Refer to Practice 20-5. Compute TOTAL income taxes payable, after the change to FIFO is made, as of December 31, 2011, December 31, 2012, and December 31, 2013. Recall that the change to FIFO will necessitate the payment of any tax savings that had been created by the use of LIFO.

Practice 20-8

LO3

Change from LIFO to FIFO: Income Statement Comparative Disclosure
Refer to Practice 20-5. Prepare the comparative note disclosure that would be provided in the notes to the 2013 financial statements with respect to the income statements for 2011, 2012, and 2013.

Practice 20-9
LO3

Change from LIFO to FIFO: Impractical to Identify Yearly Differences

Refer to Practice 20-5. Assume that the detailed information listed in Practice 20-5 is not available. Instead, the company only knows that the beginning inventory for 2013 is $150 using LIFO and $220 using FIFO. Show the retained earnings computation for 2013 that would be included in the statement of stockholders' equity for the year.

Practice 20-10
LO4

Disclosures Following a Business Combination

On December 31, 2013, Big Company acquired Tiny Company for $150,000. This amount exceeded the recorded value of Tiny Company's net assets by $30,000 on the acquisition date. The entire excess was attributable to a Tiny Company building that had a remaining useful life of 20 years as of the acquisition date. Information reported for the two companies for 2012 and 2013 was as follows:

	2013	2012
Big Company:		
Revenue	$500,000	$400,000
Net income	60,000	50,000
Tiny Company:		
Revenue	$ 75,000	$ 90,000
Net income	12,000	20,000

Prepare the necessary pro forma information that would be included in the notes to Big Company's 2013 financial statements. For simplicity, ignore income taxes.

Practice 20-11
LO5

Misstatement of Inventory

The company miscounted its inventory at the end of the year. The correct amount of inventory was $100,000. The error was not discovered until the following May when the books for the preceding year were already closed. Make the correcting entry necessary the following May, assuming that the incorrectly reported amount of inventory at the end of the preceding year was (1) $75,000 and (2) $110,000. Ignore income taxes.

Practice 20-12
LO5

Failure to Record Inventory Purchases

The company purchased inventory for $10,000 on December 28. The inventory purchase was not recorded until the following January 5. However, the inventory was appropriately included in the inventory count on December 31. The error was not discovered until the following May when the books for the preceding year had already been closed. Make the correcting entry necessary the following May, assuming that the company uses (1) the periodic inventory method and (2) the perpetual inventory method. Ignore income taxes.

Practice 20-13
LO5

Failure to Record Inventory Purchases and Inventory

Refer to Practice 20-12. Assume that in addition to failing to record the purchase, the company also failed to include the inventory in the ending inventory count. Make the correcting entry necessary the following May, assuming that the company uses (1) the periodic inventory method and (2) the perpetual inventory method. Ignore income taxes.

Practice 20-14
LO5

Misstatement of Sales

The company miscounted its total credit sales in the last two weeks of the year. The correct amount of credit sales for this period was $310,000. The error was not discovered until the following year when the books for the preceding year were already closed. Make the correcting entry necessary the following year, assuming the facts that follow. Ignore income taxes and assume (perhaps unreasonably) that no errors occurred in recording expenses associated with the sales.

(a) The incorrectly reported amount of credit sales was $260,000, and the error was found when the accounts were collected in cash.

(b) The incorrectly reported amount of credit sales was $260,000, and *none* of these credit sales had been collected in cash by the time the error was discovered.
(c) The incorrectly reported amount of credit sales was $325,000, and the error was found when the accounts were collected in cash.
(d) The incorrectly reported amount of credit sales was $325,000, and *none* of these credit sales had been collected in cash by the time the error was discovered.

Practice 20-15
LO5

Failure to Record Accrued Expense
In December 2012, the company neglected to accrue a $1,000 expense for rent. The expense was recognized in January 2013 when the rent was paid in cash. Make the necessary correcting entry, assuming that (1) the error was found in May 2013 after the 2012 books had been closed and (2) the error was found in May 2014 after the 2013 books had been closed. Ignore income taxes.

Practice 20-16
LO5

Failure to Record Prepaid Expense
In December 2012, the company paid $1,800 for insurance for the first six months of 2013. This payment was mistakenly recorded as insurance expense in 2012. Make the necessary correcting entry, assuming that (1) the error was found in August 2013 after the 2012 books had been closed and (2) the error was found in August 2014 after the 2013 books had been closed. Ignore income taxes.

Practice 20-17
LO5

Failure to Record Accrued Revenue
In December 2012, the company failed to recognize $5,700 in consulting revenue earned during 2012. This revenue was recognized when the cash was received in January 2013. Make the necessary correcting entry, assuming that (1) the error was found in May 2013 after the 2012 books had been closed and (2) the error was found in May 2014 after the 2013 books had been closed. Ignore income taxes.

Practice 20-18
LO5

Failure to Record Unearned Revenue
In December 2012, the company received $6,000 for services to be provided in early 2013. This payment was mistakenly recorded as service revenue in 2012. Make the necessary correcting entry, assuming that (1) the error was found in May 2013 after the 2012 books had been closed and (2) the error was found in May 2014 after the 2013 books had been closed. Ignore income taxes.

Practice 20-19
LO5

Failure to Record Depreciation
In January 2011, the company purchased equipment for $10,000. The equipment has a useful life of 10 years with $0 expected salvage value. The company uses straight-line depreciation. The company mistakenly failed to record depreciation expense on this equipment. Make the necessary correcting entry, assuming that (1) the error was found in May 2013 after the 2012 books had been closed and (2) the error was found in May 2014 after the 2013 books had been closed. Ignore income taxes.

Practice 20-20
LO5

Immediately Expensing Equipment that Is Subsequently Sold
On January 1, 2010, equipment was purchased for $20,000. The entire purchase price was expensed immediately. The equipment has a useful life of 10 years with $0 expected salvage value. The company uses straight-line depreciation. On January 1, 2013, the equipment was sold for $11,000 cash. The incorrect expensing of the purchase price, along with the subsequent failure to recognize depreciation, was discovered in May 2013 after the books for 2012 had been closed. (1) Make the necessary correcting entry in 2013 and (2) describe any necessary corrections to the 2013 comparative income statement (which includes 2011 and 2012).

Practice 20-21
LO5

Incorrect Capitalization
In January 2011, the company made $24,000 in expenditures. These expenditures should have been expensed immediately. Instead, the company recorded this $24,000 payment as a purchase of equipment with a useful life of 12 years and $0 expected

salvage value. The company uses straight-line depreciation. The company proceeded to depreciate this "equipment." Make the necessary correcting entry, assuming that (1) the error was found in May 2013 after the 2012 books had been closed and (2) the error was found in May 2014 after the 2013 books had been closed. Ignore income taxes.

Practice 20-22
LO5

Disclosure of a Prior-Period Adjustment
Refer to Practice 20-21. Assume that the error was found in May 2013. Net income for 2013 (correctly stated) was $50,000. Dividends for 2013 were $15,000. The Retained Earnings balance as originally reported at the end of 2012 was $130,000. Prepare a statement of retained earnings for 2013.

EXERCISES

Exercise 20-23
LO2

Change in Accounting Estimate
On January 1, 2013, management of Micro Storage Inc. determined that a revision in the estimates associated with the depreciation of storage facilities was appropriate. These facilities, purchased on January 5, 2011, for $300,000, had been depreciated using the straight-line method with an estimated salvage value of $30,000 and an estimated useful life of 20 years. Management has determined that the storage facilities' expected remaining useful life is 10 years and that they have an estimated salvage value of $40,000.

1. How much depreciation was recognized by Micro Storage in 2011 and 2012?
2. How much depreciation will be recognized by Micro Storage in 2013 as a result of the changes in estimates?
3. What journal entry is required to account for the changes in estimates at the beginning of 2013?

Exercise 20-24
LO2

Change in Accounting Estimate
Albrecht Inc. began business in 2010. An examination of the company's allowance for bad debts account reveals the following.

	Estimated Bad Debts	Actual Bad Debts
2010	$11,000	$4,500
2011	13,000	6,800
2012	16,500	8,950
2013	No adjustment yet	9,500

In the past, the company has estimated that 3% of credit sales would be uncollectible. The accountant for Albrecht has determined that the percentage used in estimating bad debts has been inappropriate. She would like to revise the estimate downward to 1.5%. The company president has stated that if the previous estimates of bad debt expense were incorrect, the financial statements should be restated using the more accurate estimate.

1. Assuming that credit sales for 2013 are $650,000, provide the adjusting entry to record bad debt expense for the year.
2. What catch-up entry, if any, would be made to correct the inaccurate estimates for previous years?
3. How would you respond to the president's request to restate the prior years' financial statements?

Exercise 20-25

LO2

Change in Accounting Estimate

Danje Corporation purchased a machine on January 1, 2010, for $3,600,000. At the date of acquisition, the machine had an estimated useful life of 10 years with no residual value. The machine is being depreciated on a straight-line basis. On January 1, 2013, Danje determined, as a result of additional information, that the machine had an estimated useful life of 15 years from the date of acquisition with no residual value.

What is the amount of depreciation expense on the machine that should be charged to Danje Corporation's income statement for the year ended December 31, 2013?

Exercise 20-26

LO2

Change in Estimate of Natural Resources

Hollow Mining Company purchased a tract of land with estimated copper ore deposits totaling 1,500,000 tons. The purchase price for the land was $4.8 million. During the first year of operation, Hollow mined and sold 160,000 tons of ore. During the second year, Hollow mined and sold 210,000 tons of ore. At the beginning of the third year, new geological engineering estimates determined that a total of 790,000 tons of copper ore remained. During Year 3, 245,000 tons of ore were mined and sold.

1. What was the original depletion rate used by Hollow in Years 1 and 2?
2. Make the accounting entries for depletion expense for Hollow Mining Company at the end of Years 1 and 2.
3. What is the depletion rate, carried to four decimals, for Year 3, and what accounting entry should be made to reflect the change in accounting estimate in Year 3? (*Note:* Round to four decimal places.)

Exercise 20-27

LO2

Change in Accounting Estimate and in Depreciation Method

Manchester Manufacturing purchased a machine on January 1, 2009, for $100,000. At the time, it was determined that the machine had an estimated useful life of 10 years and an estimated residual value of $4,000. The company used the double-declining-balance method of depreciation. On January 1, 2013, the company decided to change its depreciation method from double-declining balance to straight line. The machine's remaining useful life was estimated to be five years with a residual value of $1,000.

Give the entry required to record the company's depreciation expense for 2013.

Exercise 20-28

LO2

SPREADSHEET

Change in Depreciation Method

Modern Lighting Inc. has in the past depreciated its computer hardware using the straight-line method, assuming a 10% salvage value and an expected useful life of five years. As a result of the rapid obsolescence associated with the computer industry, Modern Lighting has determined that it receives most of the benefit from its computer systems in the first few years of ownership. Therefore, as of January 1, 2013, Modern Lighting proposes changing to the sum-of-the-years'-digits method for depreciating its computer hardware. The following information is available regarding all of Modern Lighting's computer purchases:

	Cost
2010	$45,000
2011	25,000
2012	30,000

1. Compute the depreciation taken by Modern Lighting during 2010, 2011, and 2012. Assume that all purchases were made at the beginning of the year.
2. Compute the amount of depreciation expense for 2010–2012, assuming the sum-of-the-years'-digits had been used.
3. Compute the amount of depreciation expense for 2013.

Exercise 20-29
LO3

Change in Accounting Principle without Detailed Prior-Year Information

Refer to Exercise 20-30. Assume that the detailed information for 2011 and 2012 is not available. During 2013, dividends of $20,000 were paid (compared to dividends of $16,500 in both 2011 and 2012). Based on this information, prepare the retained earnings statement for 2013. (*Note*: Do NOT prepare the comparative retained earnings statements for 2011 and 2012.) The December 31, 2012, Retained Earnings balance as reported using LIFO was $290,000.

Exercise 20-30
LO3

Change in Accounting Principle

Keairnes Supplies decided to change from LIFO to FIFO as of January 1, 2013. The change is being made for both book and tax purposes.

Year	Net Income Computed Using LIFO	Excess of LIFO Cost of Goods Sold over FIFO Cost of Goods Sold	Income Effect (Net of Tax)
Prior to 2011		$14,000	$ 9,000
2011	$68,000	7,200	4,800
2012	61,500	8,750	5,250
2013	86,000	10,500	7,500
		$40,450	$26,550

1. Using LIFO, the beginning retained earnings as of January 1, 2011, was $182,000. Compute adjusted beginning retained earnings, using FIFO, as of January 1, 2011.
2. The 3-year comparative income statement for 2013 includes net income for 2011, 2012, and 2013. In that comparative income statement, prepared after the change for FIFO has been adopted, what amount of net income will be reported for each year?

Exercise 20-31
LO2, LO3

SPREADSHEET

Changes in Accounting Estimates and Accounting Principles

Due to changing economic conditions and to making its financial statements more comparable to those of other companies in its industry, the management of Kelsea Inc. decided on January 1, 2013, to review its accounting practices.

Kelsea decided to change its allowance for bad debts from 2% to 4.5% of its outstanding receivables balance.

Kelsea decided to begin using the straight-line method of depreciation on its building instead of the sum-of-the-years'-digits method. The change will be effective as of January 1, 2013. Based on further information, it also was decided that the building has 10 more years of useful life as of January 2, 2013. Kelsea bought the building on January 1, 2003, at a cost of $550,000. At that time, Kelsea estimated it would have a 15-year useful life. The building has no expected salvage value. Prior years' depreciation is as follows:

Year	Depreciation	Year	Depreciation
2003	$68,750	2008	$45,833
2004	64,167	2009	41,250
2005	59,583	2010	36,667
2006	55,000	2011	32,083
2007	50,417	2012	27,500

Kelsea determined that starting with the current year, it would depreciate the company's printing press using hours of use as the depreciation base. The press, which had been purchased on January 1, 1998, at a cost of $930,000, was being depreciated for 25 years using the straight-line method. No salvage value was anticipated. It is estimated that this type of press provides 200,000 total hours of use and, as of

January 1, 2013, it had been used 76,000 hours. At the end of 2013, the plant manager determined that the press had been run 6,250 hours during the year. Ignore income taxes relating to this change.

1. Evaluate each of the foregoing changes and determine whether it is a change in estimate or a change in accounting principle.
2. Give the journal entries required at December 31, 2013, to account for bad debt expense and depreciation expense given the preceding changes. Kelsea's receivable balance at December 31, 2013, was $345,000. Allowance for Bad Debts carried a $1,000 debit balance before adjustment.

Exercise 20-32

LO5

REVERSE SOLVABLE

Analysis of Errors

State the effect of each of the following errors made in 2012 on the balance sheets and the income statements prepared in 2012 and 2013.

(a) The ending inventory is understated as a result of an error in the count of goods on hand.
(b) The ending inventory is overstated as a result of the inclusion of goods acquired and held on a consignment basis. No purchase was recorded on the books.
(c) A purchase of merchandise at the end of 2012 is not recorded until payment is made for the goods in 2013; the goods purchased were included in the inventory at the end of 2012.
(d) A sale of merchandise at the end of 2012 is not recorded until cash is received for the goods in 2013; the goods sold were excluded from the inventory at the end of 2012.
(e) Goods shipped to consignees in 2012 were reported as sales; goods in the hands of consignees at the end of 2012 were not recognized for inventory purposes; sale of such goods in 2013 and collections on such sales were recorded as credits to the receivables established with consignees in 2012.
(f) The total of one week's sales during 2012 was credited to Gain on Sale—Machinery.
(g) No depreciation is taken in 2012 for equipment sold in April 2012. The company reports on a calendar-year basis and computes depreciation to the nearest month.
(h) No depreciation is taken in 2012 for equipment purchased in October 2012. The company reports on a calendar-year basis and computes depreciation to the nearest month.
(i) Customer notes receivable are debited to the accounts receivable account.

Exercise 20-33

LO5

REVERSE SOLVABLE

Error Analysis

In early 2012, while reviewing Huffman Inc.'s 2011 financial records, the accountant discovered several errors. For each of the following errors, indicate the effect on net income (i.e., understatement, overstatement, or no effect) for both 2011 and 2012, assuming that no correction had been made and the company uses a periodic system for inventory.

(a) Certain items of ending inventory were accidentally not counted at the end of 2011.
(b) Machinery was sold in May 2011, but the company continued to deduct depreciation for the remainder of 2011, although the asset was removed from the books in May.
(c) The 2011 year-end purchases of inventory were not recorded until the beginning of 2012, although the inventory was correctly counted at the end of 2011.
(d) Goods sold on account in 2011 were not recorded as sales until 2012.
(e) Insurance costs incurred but unpaid in 2011 were not recorded until paid in 2012.
(f) Interest revenue in 2011 was not recorded until 2012.
(g) The 2011 year-end purchases were not recorded until the beginning of 2012. The inventory associated with these purchases was omitted from the ending inventory count in 2011.

(h) A check for January 2012 rent was received and recorded as revenue at the end of 2011.

(i) Interest accrued in 2011 on a note payable was not recorded until it was paid in 2012.

Exercise 20-34
LO5

SPREADSHEET

Error Disclosure

Comparative statements for Bodie Corporation are as follows:

Bodie Corporation
Income Statements and Statement of Retained Earnings
For the Years Ended December 31

	2012	2011
Sales	$4,600,000	$4,350,000
Cost of goods sold	2,346,000	2,305,500
Gross profit	$2,254,000	$2,044,500
Expenses	1,598,000	1,533,000
Net income	$ 656,000	$ 511,500
Beginning retained earnings	$1,441,000	$1,077,500
Net income	656,000	511,500
Dividends	(157,000)	(148,000)
Ending retained earnings	$1,940,000	$1,441,000

In 2012, Bodie Corporation discovers that ending inventory for 2011 was understated by $77,000.

Prepare comparative income and retained earnings statements for 2011 and 2012. Ignore income tax effects, and assume that the 2012 books have not been closed.

Exercise 20-35
LO5

REVERSE SOLVABLE

Accounting Errors

The following errors in the accounting records of the Chipp & Simon Partnership were discovered on January 10, 2013.

Year of Error	Ending Inventories Overstated	Accrued Rent Depreciation Understated	Accrued Interest Revenue Not Recorded	Expense Not Recorded
2010	$42,000		$11,000	
2011		$18,000	31,000	
2012	34,000			$7,000

The partners share net income and losses as follows: 65%, Chipp; 35%, Simon.

1. Prepare a correcting journal entry on January 10, 2013, assuming that the books were closed for 2012.
2. Prepare a correcting journal entry on January 10, 2013, assuming that the books are still open for 2012 and that the partnership uses the perpetual inventory system.

Exercise 20-36
LO5

REVERSE SOLVABLE

Journal Entries to Correct Accounts

The first audit of the books for Ringer Company was made for the year ended December 31, 2013. In reviewing the books, the auditor discovered that certain adjustments had been overlooked at the end of 2012 and 2013 and that other items had been improperly recorded. Omissions and other failures for each year are summarized as follows:

	2012	2013
Sales Salaries Payable	$1,800	$1,400
Interest Receivable	700	550
Prepaid Insurance	450	250
Advances from Customers	1,900	2,200
(Collections from customers had been included in sales but should have been recognized as advances from customers because goods were not shipped until the following year.)		
Equipment	1,600	1,300
(Expenditures had been recognized as repairs but should have been recognized as cost of equipment; the depreciation rate on such equipment is 10% per year, but depreciation in the year of the expenditure is to be recognized at 5%.)		

Prepare journal entries to correct revenue and expense accounts for 2013, and record assets and liabilities that require recognition on the balance sheet as of December 31, 2013. Assume that the nominal accounts for 2013 have not yet been closed into the income summary account.

PROBLEMS

Problem 20-37

LO2

Change in Depreciation Estimates and Depreciation Method

Yuki, Inc., acquired the following assets on January 1, 2010.

Equipment, estimated useful life 5 years; residual value $13,000	$513,000
Building, estimated useful life 40 years; no residual value	900,000

The equipment has been depreciated using the sum-of-the-years'-digits method for the first three years. In 2013, the company decided to change the method of depreciation to straight line. No change was made in the estimated service life or residual value. The company also decided to change the total estimated useful life of the building from 40 to 45 years with no change in the estimated residual value. The building is depreciated on the straight-line method. The company has 200,000 shares of capital stock outstanding. Partial results of operations for 2013 and 2012 are as follows:

	2013	2012
Income before depreciation	$956,000	$890,000

Instructions:

1. Compute depreciation expense for 2012 and 2013.
2. Compute earnings per share for 2012 and 2013. (Ignore income tax effects.)

Problem 20-38

LO2, LO3

Accounting Changes

Barney Corporation began business on January 1, 2011. The company has released the following financial statements for 2011 and 2012 and has prepared the following proposed statements for 2013.

Barney Corporation
Comparative Balance Sheets
December 31

	2013	2012	2011
Assets			
Cash	$249,000	$219,000	$165,000
Capitalized exploration costs	60,000	45,000	30,000
Equipment	150,000	150,000	150,000
Accumulated depreciation—equipment	(45,000)	(30,000)	(15,000)
Total assets	$414,000	$384,000	$330,000
Liabilities and Stockholders' Equity			
Current liabilities	$177,000	$177,000	$147,000
Common stock	165,000	165,000	165,000
Retained earnings	72,000	42,000	18,000
Total liabilities and stockholders' equity	$414,000	$384,000	$330,000

Barney Corporation
Comparative Income Statements
For the Years Ended December 31

	2013	2012	2011
Sales	$315,000	$300,000	$255,000
Cost of goods sold	$240,000	$225,000	$189,000
Administrative expenses	12,500	23,500	28,000
Amortization of capitalized exploration costs	17,500	12,500	5,000
Depreciation expense—equipment	15,000	15,000	15,000
Total costs	$285,000	$276,000	$237,000
Net income	$ 30,000	$ 24,000	$ 18,000

Barney Corporation acquired the equipment for $150,000 on January 1, 2011, and began depreciating the equipment over a 10-year estimated useful life with no salvage value, using the straight-line method of depreciation. The capitalized exploration costs reflect oil and gas drilling costs that Barney has capitalized under the full cost method.

As of January 1, 2013, Barney has decided to make the following accounting changes.

(a) For justifiable reasons, Barney Corporation changed to the double-declining-balance method of depreciation for the equipment as of January 1, 2013.

(b) For justifiable reasons, Barney Corporation changed from the full cost to the successful efforts method of accounting for oil and gas drilling costs as of January 1, 2013. Because none of Barney's drilling so far can be classified as "successful," all drilling costs would be expensed as incurred under the successful efforts method.

Instructions: In 3-year comparative format, prepare the balance sheets, statements of income, and statements of retained earnings that would be reported in 2013 for the years 2011, 2012, and 2013. Barney has not yet paid any dividends. Make sure to correctly treat the accounting changes mentioned above. (Ignore any income tax effects.)

Problem 20-39

LO2

SPREADSHEET

Change in Depreciation Estimates and Depreciation Method
The following information relates to depreciable assets of Strata Technologies.

(a) Machine A was purchased for $80,000 on January 1, 2008. The entire cost was erroneously expensed in the year of purchase. The machine had a 16-year useful life and no residual value.
(b) Machine B cost $220,000 and was purchased January 1, 2009. The straight-line method of depreciation was used. At the time of purchase, the expected useful life was 10 years with no residual value. In 2013, it was estimated that the total useful life of the asset would be only seven years and that there would be a $12,000 residual value.
(c) Building C was purchased January 1, 2010, for $750,000. The straight-line method of depreciation was originally chosen. The building was expected to be useful for 25 years and to have zero residual value. On January 1, 2013, a change was made from the straight-line depreciation method to the sum-of-the-years'-digits method. Estimates relating to the useful life and residual value remained the same.

Income before depreciation expense was $620,000 for 2013. Depreciation on assets other than those described totaled $65,000. (*Note*: Ignore all income tax effects.)

Instructions:

1. Compute total depreciation expense for 2013.
2. Prepare the statement of retained earnings for 2013. The beginning Retained Earnings balance, before considering items (a) through (c) above, was $890,000. For this problem, assume that only the statements for 2013 are presented, so any prior-period adjustment to retained earnings is done as of January 1, 2013. Strata declared and paid dividends totaling $210,000 in 2013.
3. Make the January 1, 2013, correcting journal entry necessary with respect to item (a), the erroneous expensing of the machine cost.

Problem 20-40

LO2

Change in Accounting Estimates and Depreciation Method
Johnston Doors began operations on January 1, 2010. On that day, Johnston purchased the following assets, both of which were depreciated using the straight-line method.

Equipment:	Cost, $48,000; estimated salvage value, $5,000; estimated useful life, 10 years.
Building:	Cost, $85,000; estimated salvage value, $15,000; estimated useful life, 15 years.

As of January 1, 2014, Johnston reviewed its accounting records and determined that the building should have a total useful life of 20 years. In addition, because of significant wear on the equipment, Johnston has decided to use the sum-of-the-years'-digits method for depreciating equipment.

Johnston also has found that its estimated bad debt expense has been consistently higher than actual bad debts. Management proposes lowering the percentage from 3% of credit sales to 2%. If 2% had been used since 2010, the balance in Allowance for Bad Debts at the beginning of 2014 would have been $3,200 rather than $6,900. Credit sales for 2014 totaled $250,000, and accounts written off as uncollectible during 2014 totaled $5,500.

Instructions: (Ignore income tax effects.)

1. What is the proper accounting treatment for each of the proposed changes?
2. Prepare the journal entries necessary to record the depreciation expense for 2014 for both the equipment and the building.
3. Prepare the journal entry to record the write-off of accounts deemed uncollectible during 2014 and the adjusting entry at year-end to record the bad debt expense for the period.
4. What adjustment is made to the allowance account at the beginning of 2014 as a result of changing the bad debt estimate percentage?

Problem 20-41
LO2

Reporting Accounting Changes
The following are two independent, unrelated sets of facts concerning accounting changes.

(a) Case 1: Runyon Development Company determined that the amortization rate on its patents is unacceptably low due to current advances in technology. The company decided at the beginning of 2013 to decrease the estimated useful life on all existing patents from 10 years to seven years. Patents were purchased on January 1, 2008, for $3,000,000. The estimated residual value is $0.

(b) Case 2: Cartwright Corporation decided on January 1, 2013, to change its depreciation method for manufacturing equipment from an accelerated method to the straight-line method. The straight-line method is to be used for new acquisitions as well as for previously acquired equipment. As of January 1, 2013, the total historical cost of depreciable assets is $800,000; accumulated depreciation on those assets is $343,000. The expected remaining useful life of Cartwright's depreciable assets as of January 1, 2013, is 10 years; the expected salvage value is $25,000.

Instructions: For each of the cases:

1. Identify the type of accounting change.
2. Explain how the accounting change should be reported in 2013.
3. Explain the effect of the change on the December 31, 2013, balance sheet and the 2013 income statement.

Problem 20-42
LO3

Change in Accounting Principle
During 2013, Magma Company changed its inventory valuation method from LIFO to FIFO. The following information shows the effect of this change.

Year	Net Income Computed Using LIFO	Excess of LIFO Cost of Goods Sold over LIFO Cost of Goods Sold	Income Effect (Net of Tax)
Prior to 2011		$130,000	$95,700
2011	$310,000	52,000	38,500
2012	240,000	66,000	45,000
2013	500,000	96,000	80,000

Instructions:

1. Before the change from LIFO to FIFO, the Retained Earnings balance on January 1, 2011, was $700,000. Magma Company does not pay any dividends. Prepare the comparative statement of retained earnings, reflecting the change to FIFO, for 2011, 2012, and 2013.
2. What additional information would you need to prepare all the necessary disclosures to include in the notes to the 2013 financial statements?

Problem 20-43
LO2

Change in Accounting Estimate
On January 3, 2012, Airflow Corporation, a company selling stunt kites, purchased a large number of personal computers. The cost of these computers was $170,000. On the date of purchase, Sandy's management estimated that the computers would last approximately four years and would have a salvage value at that time of $20,000. The company used the double-declining-balance method to depreciate the computers.

During January 2013, Airflow's management realized that technological advancements had made the computers virtually obsolete. The new salvage value is estimated to be $1,000. Management proposed changing the estimated useful life of the computers to two years.

Instructions: Prepare the journal entry necessary at the end of 2013 to record depreciation on the computers.

Problem 20-44

LO3

Change in Accounting Principle—LIFO to FIFO

On January 1, 2013, Down Under, Inc. decided to change from the LIFO method of inventory valuation to the FIFO method. The net income (using LIFO) for the four years Down Under has been in business is as follows:

2010	$120,000	2012	$156,000
2011	138,000	2013	180,000

Analysis of the inventory records revealed that the following inventories were on hand at the end of each year as valued under both the LIFO and FIFO methods.

	LIFO Method	FIFO Method
January 1, 2010	$ 0	$ 0
December 31, 2010	178,000	208,000
December 31, 2011	220,000	216,000
December 31, 2012	252,000	290,000
December 31, 2013	295,000	349,000

For simplicity, assume that Down Under's sales for each year are $500,000. The income tax rate is 40%. Down Under has only two expenses—cost of goods sold and income tax expense.

Instructions:

1. Prepare the 3-year comparative income statement for 2013 which will include FIFO numbers for 2013 and retrospectively adjusted FIFO numbers for 2011 and 2012. [*Hint*: You will have to work backwards to figure out income tax expense (using net income) and then calculate cost of goods sold using pretax income and sales.]
2. Prepare the 3-year comparative retained earnings statement for Down Under for 2013. Note that the company started business on January 1, 2010. Dividends declared and paid have been as follows: 2010—$10,000; 2011—$15,000; 2012—$15,000; 2013—$25,000.
3. Prepare the year-by-year income statement note disclosure that Down Under must provide in the notes to its 2013 financial statements.

Problem 20-45

LO5

Correction of Errors

Hiatt Textile Corporation is planning to expand its current plant facilities and is in the process of obtaining a loan at City Bank. The bank has requested audited financial statements. Hiatt has never been audited before. It has prepared the following comparative financial statements for the years ended December 31, 2013 and 2012.

Hiatt Textile Corporation
Comparative Balance Sheets
December 31, 2013 and 2012

	2013	2012
Assets		
Current assets:		
Cash	$ 602,500	$ 400,000
Accounts receivable	980,000	740,000
Allowance for bad debts	(92,500)	(45,000)
Inventory	517,500	505,000
Total current assets	$2,007,500	$1,600,000

	2013	2012
Plant assets:		
Property, plant, and equipment	$ 417,500	$ 423,750
Accumulated depreciation	(304,000)	(266,000)
Total plant assets	$ 113,500	$ 157,750
Total assets	$2,121,000	$1,757,750
Liabilities and Stockholders' Equity		
Liabilities:		
Accounts payable	$ 303,500	$ 490,250
Stockholders' equity:		
Common stock, par value $25; authorized, 30,000 shares; issued and outstanding, 26,000 shares	$ 650,000	$ 650,000
Retained earnings	1,167,500	617,500
Total stockholders' equity	$1,817,500	$1,267,500
Total liabilities and stockholders' equity	$2,121,000	$1,757,750

Hiatt Textile Corporation
Comparative Income Statements
For the Years Ended December 31, 2013 and 2012

	2013	2012
Sales	$2,500,000	$2,250,000
Cost of goods sold	1,075,000	987,500
Gross margin	$1,425,000	$1,262,500
Operating expenses	$ 575,000	$ 512,500
General and administrative expenses	300,000	262,500
	$ 875,000	$ 775,000
Net income	$ 550,000	$ 487,500

The following facts were uncovered during the audit.

(a) On January 20, 2012, Hiatt had charged a 5-year fire insurance premium to expense. The total premium amounted to $15,500.

(b) Over the last two years, the amount of loss due to bad debts has steadily decreased. Hiatt has decided to reduce the amount of bad debt expense from 2% to 1.5% of sales, beginning with 2013. (A charge of 2% has already been made for 2013.)

(c) The inventory account (maintained on a periodic basis) has been in error the last two years. The errors were as follows:

2012:	Ending inventory overstated by $37,750
2013:	Ending inventory overstated by $49,500

(d) A machine costing $75,000, purchased on January 4, 2012, was incorrectly charged to operating expense. The machine has a useful life of 10 years and a residual value of $12,500. The straight-line depreciation method is used by Hiatt.

Instructions:

1. Prepare the journal entries to correct the books at December 31, 2013. The books for 2013 have not been closed. (Ignore income taxes.)
2. Prepare a schedule showing the computation of corrected net income for the years ended December 31, 2012 and 2013, assuming that any adjustments are to be reported on the comparative statements for the two years. Begin your schedule with the net income for each year. (Ignore income taxes.)

Problem 20-46

LO5

REVERSE SOLVABLE

Analysis and Correction of Errors

A CPA was engaged by Blackbird Company in 2013 to examine its books and records and to make whatever corrections are necessary. An examination of the accounts discloses the following.

(a) Dividends had been declared on December 15 in 2010 and 2011 but had not been entered in the books until paid.

(b) Improvements in buildings and equipment of $10,800 had been debited to expense at the end of April 2009. Improvements are estimated to have 12-year life. The company uses the straight-line method in recording depreciation and computes depreciation to the nearest month.

(c) The physical inventory of merchandise had been understated by $3,200 at the end of 2010 and by $4,750 at the end of 2011.

(d) The merchandise inventories at the end of 2011 and 2012 did not include merchandise that was then in transit and to which the company had title. These shipments of $2,100 and $2,900 were recorded as purchases in January of 2012 and 2013, respectively.

(e) The company had failed to record sales commissions payable of $3,600 and $1,100 at the end of 2011 and 2012, respectively.

(f) The company had failed to recognize supplies on hand of $850 and $1,720 at the end of 2011 and 2012, respectively.

The retained earnings account appeared as shown below on the date the CPA began the examination.

Account: RETAINED EARNINGS

Date		Item	Debit	Credit	Balance	
					Debit	Credit
2010						
Jan.	1	Balance				65,000
Dec.	31	Net income for year		28,000		93,000
2011						
Jan.	10	Dividends paid	15,500			77,500
Mar.	6	Stock sold—excess over par		21,000		98,500
Dec.	31	Net loss for year	17,800			80,700
2012						
Jan.	10	Dividends paid	15,500			65,200
Dec.	31	Net loss for year	19,300			45,900

Instructions:

1. Journalize the necessary corrections.
2. Prepare a statement of retained earnings covering the 3-year period beginning January 1, 2010. The statement should report the corrected Retained Earnings balance on January 1, 2010, the annual changes in the account, and the corrected Retained Earnings balances as of December 31, 2010, 2011, and 2012.
3. Set up an account for retained earnings before correction, and post correcting data to this account for (1). Balance the account, showing the corrected retained earnings as of January 1, 2013.

Problem 20-47
LO5

REVERSE SOLVABLE

Correction of Errors

Hinckley Company is in the process of adjusting its books at the end of 2013. Hinckley's records reveal the following information:

(a) Hinckley failed to accrue sales commissions at the end of 2011 and 2012 as follows:

2011	$44,000
2012	30,000

In each case, the sales commissions were paid (and expensed) in January of the following year.

(b) Errors in ending inventories for the last three years were discovered to be as follows:

2011	$41,300 understated
2012	54,200 overstated
2013	15,000 understated

The incorrect amount has already been recorded for 2013.

Instructions:

1. Prepare the necessary journal entries at December 31, 2013, to record the preceding information. Assume that the books are still open for 2013. Ignore all income tax effects.
2. Assume that the unadjusted retained earnings balance at the beginning of 2013 was $1,265,000 and that the unadjusted net income for 2013 was $300,000. Also assume that dividends of $175,000 were declared during 2013. Prepare a statement of retained earnings for Hinckley Company for 2013, reflecting appropriate adjustments from (1). Assume that there are no income taxes.

Problem 20-48
LO2, LO3, LO5

Sample CPA Exam Questions

1. On January 1, 2011, Frank Company purchased equipment for $200,000. The equipment has an 8-year expected useful life and a $10,000 expected residual value. Initially, Frank Company used double-declining-balance depreciation. On January 1, 2013, Frank Company changed to straight-line depreciation. The expected useful life and residual value are unchanged. Compute depreciation expense for 2013.
   (a) $28,125
   (b) $17,083
   (c) $12,813
   (d) $23,750
2. Jean Company decided to change from LIFO to FIFO as of January 1, 2013. The change is being made for both book and tax purposes. LIFO and FIFO data for 2013 and preceding years are given below.

Year	Net Income Computed Using LIFO	Excess of LIFO Cost of Goods Sold over FIFO Cost of Goods Sold	Income Effect (Net of Tax)
Prior to 2011		$12,500	$ 7,500
2011	$62,500	6,250	3,750
2012	54,500	7,500	4,500
2013	78,000	11,250	6,750
		$37,500	$22,500

Using the provisions of FASB ASC Topic 250 *Statement No. 154*, compute Jean Company's net income for 2013. Remember that Jean Company switched to FIFO on January 1, 2013.
(a) $84,750
(b) $100,500
(c) $85,500
(d) $93,750

3. Goods sold FOB destination were shipped by Brook Company (the seller) on December 31, 2013. The sale was recorded in 2013, and the goods were not included in 2013 ending inventory. The shipment arrived on January 4, 2014. The goods cost $3,000, and the sales price was $4,400. As a result of this transaction, was net income overstated or understated, and by how much? Ignore income taxes.
(a) Reported net income was correct.
(b) Net income in 2013 was overstated by $4,400.
(c) Net income in 2013 was understated by $3,000.
(d) Net income in 2013 was overstated by $1,400.

CASES

Discussion Case 20-49

Accounting Changes

Situation A: Tucker Corporation has determined that the depreciable lives of several operating machines are too long and thus do not fairly match the cost of the assets with the revenues produced. Tucker therefore decides to reduce the depreciable lives of these machines by three years.

Situation B: Trent Company decides that at the beginning of the year, it will adopt the FIFO method of inventory valuation. Trent had previously used LIFO.

What types of accounting changes are involved in the two situations? Describe the method of reporting the changes under current GAAP.

Discussion Case 20-50

Change in Accounting Principle or Change in Accounting Estimate?

Jill Stanton, president of Central Company, is confused about why your accounting firm has recommended that she report certain events as changes in principle instead of changes in estimate, which is what Jill thought they should be. She has asked you for an explanation. Describe a change in an accounting principle and a change in accounting estimate. Explain how each is reported in the income statement of the period of change.

Discussion Case 20-51

Why Do They Make the Change?

An interesting phenomenon can sometimes occur when companies are in danger of not meeting their projected earnings goals. Management suddenly realizes that they have been far too conservative in their previous estimates associated with bad debts, estimated useful lives of equipment, and residual values, to name a few. With this newfound realization, management proceeds to revise these estimates to, as is often stated, "more closely reflect economic reality."

What is the primary difference in financial statement disclosure between a change in estimate and a change in principle? Why do you think managers who are in danger of not meeting their goals would prefer to revise an accounting estimate rather than change an accounting principle?

Discussion Case 20-52

How Long Can Airplanes Fly?

Airline A depreciates its airplanes over a 15-year period and estimates a salvage value of 10% of the cost of the plane. At the same time, Airline B depreciates identical airplanes over a 25-year period and provides for a 15% salvage value. These different assumptions resulted in markedly different operating results. For example, if one airplane costs $10 million, Airline A would depreciate $260,000 more per year for 15 years than would Airline B.

Which company's estimate of useful life more closely reflects reality? Would you feel comfortable as a passenger in an airplane that is 25 years old? Does the fact that Airline B subsequently went out of business provide any information as to why its estimates were so substantially different from those of financially sound Airline A?

Case 20-53

Deciphering Financial Statements (Bausch & Lomb Inc.)

Bausch & Lomb, maker of eye-care products, found itself in the news because of certain procedures that were outside accepted accounting and business practices. The note below from its 1995 annual report provides information about the company's problems.

Prior Period Adjustment

BAUSCH & LOMB INCORPORATED (DEC)
NOTES TO FINANCIAL STATEMENTS

Note 2. Restatement of Financial Information

The Company has restated its financial statements for the years ended December 31, 1994 and December 25, 1993. This action was taken as a result of an ongoing investigation which identified uncertainties surrounding the execution of a fourth quarter 1993 contact lens sales program and the improper recording of 1993 sunglass sales in Southeast Asia. In the fourth quarter of 1993 a marketing program was initiated to implement a business strategy to shift responsibility for the sale and distribution of a portion of the U.S. Traditional contact lens business to optical distributors. Subsequently, this strategy proved unsuccessful and, in the 1994 third quarter, led to the implementation of a new pricing policy for traditional contact lenses and a decision to accept on a one-time basis returns from these distributors. The investigation of this marketing program disclosed instances where unauthorized terms may have been or were offered which were inconsistent with the stated terms and conditions of the program. The resulting uncertainties relating to the execution of this marketing program led to a decision to restate the 1993 financial statements to account for shipments under the program as consigned inventory and to record revenues when the products were sold by the distributors to their customers and to reverse the effect of subsequent product returns and pricing adjustments related to this program which had been previously recognized in 1994. The investigation of Southeast Asia sunglass sales disclosed that in certain instances distributor transactions recorded as revenues in 1993 had not actually resulted from a sale to those customers, and thus were improperly recorded. The 1993 financial statements have been restated to reverse the improperly recorded sales with a corresponding restatement of the 1994 financial statements to reverse the effect of sales returns previously recognized in that period. In the opinion of management, all material adjustments necessary to correct the financial statements have been recorded. The impact of these adjustments on the Company's financial results as originally reported is summarized below:

Dollar Amounts in Thousands (Except Per Share Data)	1994		1993	
	As Reported	**As Restated**	**As Reported**	**As Restated**
Net Sales:				
Healthcare	$1,227,648	$1,249,923	$1,191,467	$1,169,192
Optics	622,904	642,763	680,717	660,858
Total	$1,850,552	$1,892,686	$1,872,184	$1,830,050
Business Segment Earnings:				
Healthcare	$ 73,466	$ 91,541	$ 210,393	$ 192,318
Optics	64,148	72,075	87,456	79,529
Total	$ 137,614	$ 163,616	$ 297,849	$ 271,847
Net Earnings	$ 13,478	$ 31,123	$ 156,547	$ 138,902
Net Earnings Per Share	$ 0.23	$ 0.52	$ 2.60	$ 2.31
Retained Earnings At End of Year	$ 846,245	$ 846,245	$ 889,325	$ 871,680

Review this information to answer the questions that follow.

1. What exactly was the company doing that was wrong?
2. Compare the "As Reported" and "As Restated" columns to determine what income was included in both categories over the combined 2-year period. What did the company gain?

3. If this error had been uncovered in 1994 after the 1993 reporting year had been closed, what journal entry would have been made to correct the error?
4. When this error was uncovered in 1995 after the 1994 reporting year had been closed, what journal entry was made to correct the error?

Case 20-54

Deciphering Financial Statements (The Walt Disney Company)
Locate the 2009 financial statements for **The Walt Disney Company** on the Internet. Once you have located these financial statements, consider the following questions.

1. Review the notes to the financial statements and determine whether the company had any accounting changes for any of the years reported. (*Note*: Most, if not all, of these changes will be as a result of accounting rule changes by the FASB.) To what did those changes relate?
2. Briefly describe the nature of any changes identified in (1).

Case 20-55

Writing Assignment (Counterbalancing errors)
As stated in the chapter, most accounting-related errors are detected and corrected in the current period. Of those that go undetected, some will fix themselves over two periods, while other errors may remain undetected for years.

The objective of this writing assignment is to have you think about what it is that is different between those errors that will counterbalance and those that carry over from period to period. In a short memo, identify these differences considering such issues as whether the accounts involved are balance sheet and/or income statement accounts, whether they are current and/or noncurrent accounts, and whether they involve revenue or expense accounts. Finally, provide a systematic method for analyzing an error to determine if it counterbalances or if a journal entry is necessary to correct the books.

Case 20-56

The Debate (Restating prior years' financial statements)
This chapter began with an illustration of the impact that *Statement No. 106* had on the earnings of several companies. Recall that **General Motors** reported a $33 billion decline in income in 1992. One-time "hits" such as this can make comparison of financial statements and ratios over time difficult.

This debate relates to the different methods for dealing with changes in accounting principle by either making a cumulative adjustment or restating the financial statements.

Divide your group into two teams.

- One team will argue that when a new standard is issued, all prior years' financial statements being disclosed with the current year's information should be restated to comply with the new standard. This is the approach now required under FASBASC Topic 250.
- The other team will argue that a cumulative adjustment that summarizes the new standard's effect on prior periods is sufficient. This is the approach that was required at the time GM adopted *Statement No. 106.*

Case 20-57

Ethical Dilemma (Changing a change in principle)
Your company has recently decided to change its method of depreciating long-term assets to be consistent with major competitors. While your company has used the straight-line method in the past, most other companies in the industry use a declining-balance method. Preliminary computations indicate that changing this accounting principle will reduce EPS by about 10% in the current year. Naturally, those to whom you report would like to know if there is any way to lessen the impact of this change.

You know that other factors in computing depreciation expense are the estimates of useful life and salvage value. You reason that if the estimated useful life of all long-term assets is reassessed with minor modifications being made to these estimated lives, then switching the depreciation method will not decrease net income this period.

1. Can the plan of reassessing the estimated lives of long-term assets achieve the desired result of allowing the firm to change depreciation accounting methods to a declining-balance method without reducing net income this period?
2. Will the firm have a higher cash inflow as a result of either the change in principle or the change in estimate?
3. Should the level of a company's income determine the accounting methods that it uses and the accounting estimates that it makes? Why or why not?

Case 20-58

Cumulative Spreadsheet Analysis

This spreadsheet assignment is an extension of the spreadsheet assignment given in Chapter 13, part (1). Refer back to the instructions given in Chapter 13. That spreadsheet can form the foundation for this assignment.

1. In addition to preparing forecasted financial statements for 2014, Skywalker also wishes to prepare forecasted financial statements for 2015. All assumptions applicable to 2014 are assumed to be applicable to 2015. Sales in 2015 are expected to be 40% higher than sales in 2014. (Clearly state any additional assumptions that you make.)
2. Assume that Skywalker expects the number of days' sales in inventory in both 2014 and 2015 to be 60 days instead of 107.6 days. This change should make the forecasted level of the short-term loans payable in your spreadsheet negative for both 2014 and 2015.
   (a) Explain why this change causes negative short-term loans payable.
   (b) Because a negative amount of short-term loans payable is not possible, adjust your spreadsheet so that the value of short-term loans payable cannot be less than zero. What is the forecasted current ratio for 2014 and 2015 after you make this adjustment?

P4 OTHER DIMENSIONS OF FINANCIAL REPORTING

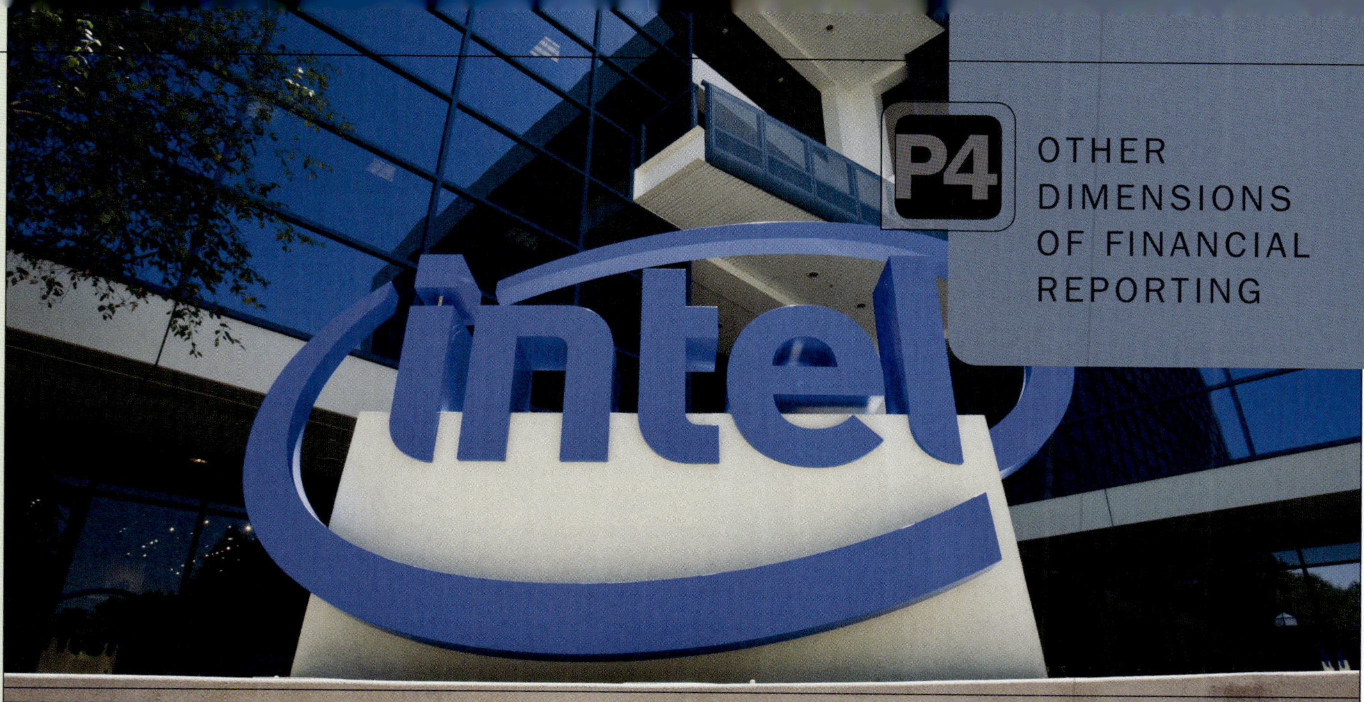

CHAPTER 21 Statement of Cash Flows Revisited

LEARNING OBJECTIVES

1. Prepare a complete statement of cash flows and provide the required supplemental disclosures.
2. Understand the differences among cash flow statements prepared according to U.S. GAAP and IASB standards.
3. Incorporate material from the entire text into the preparation of a statement of cash flows.
4. Perform a detailed case analysis of a company's operations and performance using cash flow data.

In 1968, Robert Noyce and Gordon Moore left their jobs as engineers at **Fairchild Semiconductor** to start their own firm. They saw a business opportunity in using semiconductor technology to build a better, cheaper alternative to the magnetic core memory that was, at the time, the dominant computer memory technology. Their problem was that the cost of semiconductor memory was 100 times the cost of magnetic core memory.

With $2.5 million in financing from a venture capitalist, Noyce and Moore founded **Intel**, short for integrated electronics. Andy Grove soon joined Intel, and together these three solved the computer memory problem. The 1103, introduced in 1970, quickly became the world's largest selling semiconductor device.

> **FYI**
> The name "Intel" had to be purchased from a hotel chain.

But cheaper computer memory was not to be the innovation that put Intel on the map. In 1971, a Japanese calculator company asked Intel to design a set of custom computer chips. In response, Intel created the first microprocessor, the 4004. However, the design contract stipulated that the rights for the completed microprocessor were owned by **Busicom**, the calculator company. Intel bought back the rights to the microprocessor for $60,000.

SiliconValleyStock/Alamy

The 4004 chip was smaller than a thumbnail and cost $200, yet it provided as much computing power as the first electronic computer. The first electronic computer, made in 1946, required 18,000 vacuum tubes and occupied 3,000 cubic feet of space.

Intel continued to develop its microprocessor technology. In the mid-1970s, the idea of combining a processor, a keyboard, and a monitor for sale as a personal computer for home use was presented to Intel Chairman Gordon Moore. He asked: "What's it good for? And the only answer was that a housewife could keep her recipes on it. I personally didn't see anything useful in it, so we never gave it another thought."

In 1981, Intel combined with **IBM** to develop the first personal computer using the 8088 processor. After that, microprocessor technology accelerated dramatically. The rate of change, both in terms of time and in terms of capacity, for microprocessors gave rise to Moore's Law (a phrase coined by Gordon Moore)—every two years computing power will double.

While the capacity of chips has increased, their costs have decreased. In 1991, the 486 cost $225 per MIPS (million instructions per second). The Pentium II costs about $2 per MIPS. Moore made the following comparison, "If the auto industry advanced as rapidly as the semiconductor industry, a Rolls Royce would get a half a million miles per gallon, and it would be cheaper to throw it away than to park it."

By April 2010, Intel's total market value had grown to almost $126 billion, and the market value of the computer giant IBM that Intel had partnered with to produce the first IBM PC had grown to nearly $165 billion.

The fact that Intel is a very successful company can be seen quite easily by looking at the company's cash flow statement. Exhibit 21-1 contains Intel's statement of cash flows for the three years ending December 26, 2009. When looking at a statement of cash flows, the first thing to find is the company's cash from operating activities. For Intel, operating cash flow in 2009 was $11.2 billion, up 2% from the $10.9 billion in 2008.

FYI

Intel defines a microprocessor as follows: "A microprocessor is an integrated circuit built on a tiny piece of silicon. It contains thousands, or even millions, of transistors, which are interconnected via superfine traces of aluminum. The transistors work together to store and manipulate data so that the microprocessor can perform a wide variety of useful functions. The particular functions a microprocessor performs are dictated by software."

The next thing you should look at is the operations-related investing cash needs of the company. For Intel in 2009, investing cash flow related to the operations of the company totaled $5.4 billion and was the sum of the cash paid to buy new property, plant, and equipment and the cash used to make business acquisitions. These items are sometimes called the capital expenditures (or capex) of a business. A comparison of operating cash flow to the capital expenditures yields the company's free cash flow. For 2009, Intel's free cash flow was $5.8 billion ($11.2 billion operating cash inflow minus $5.4 billion capital expenditures cash outflow). Intel's large amount of free cash flow means that the company is a cash cow. The company's operations are generating so much cash that the capital expenditures required for the company's expansion plans can be completely paid for with cash left over.

FYI

The sum of the market values of Intel and IBM is only $23 billion greater than the $268 billion April 2010 market value of software giant Microsoft, which was a small 30-person software company when it was chosen by IBM to provide the operating system for the first IBM PC.

Finally, in our simple analysis, let's see what Intel is doing with its surplus cash flow. In the Financing Activities section, we see that in 2009 Intel spent $1.8 billion buying back shares of its own stock and $3.1 billion paying cash dividends to the remaining

EX 21-1 INTEL'S STATEMENT OF CASH FLOWS FOR 2009 (IN MILLIONS)

Intel Corporation Consolidated Statements of Cash Flows

Consolidated Statements of Cash Flows (USD $) In Millions	12 Months Ended		
	Dec. 26, 2009	Dec. 27, 2008	Dec. 29, 2007
Statements of Cash Flows [Abstract]			
Cash and cash equivalents, beginning of year	$ 3,350	$ 7,307	$ 6,598
Cash flows provided by (used for) operating activities:			
Net income	4,369	5,292	6,976
Adjustments to reconcile net income to net cash provided by operating activities:			
Depreciation	4,744	4,360	4,546
Share-based compensation	889	851	952
Restructuring, asset impairment, and net loss on retirement of assets	368	795	564
Excess tax benefit from share-based payment arrangements	(9)	(30)	(118)
Amortization of intangibles and other acquisition-related costs	308	256	252
(Gains) losses on equity method investments, net	147	1,380	(3)
(Gains) losses on other equity investments, net	23	376	(154)
(Gains) losses on divestitures	0	(59)	(21)
Deferred taxes	271	(790)	(443)
Changes in assets and liabilities:			
Trading assets	299	193	(1,429)
Accounts receivable	(535)	260	316
Inventories	796	(395)	700
Accounts payable	(506)	29	102
Accrued compensation and benefits	247	(569)	354
Income taxes payable and receivable	110	(834)	(248)
Other assets and liabilities	(351)	(189)	279
Total adjustments	6,801	5,634	5,649
Net cash provided by operating activities	11,170	10,926	12,625
Cash flows provided by (used for) investing activities:			
Additions to property, plant and equipment	(4,515)	(5,197)	(5,000)
Acquisitions, net of cash acquired	(853)	(16)	(76)
Purchases of available-for-sale investments	(8,655)	(6,479)	(11,728)
Maturities and sales of available-for-sale investments	7,756	7,993	8,011
Purchases of trading assets	(4,186)	(2,676)	0
Maturities and sales of trading assets	2,543	1,766	0
Loans receivable	(343)	0	0
Investments in non-marketable equity investments	(250)	(1,691)	(1,459)
Return of equity method investment	449	316	0
Proceeds from divestitures	0	85	32
Other investing activities	89	34	294
Net cash used for investing activities	(7,965)	(5,865)	(9,926)
Cash flows provided by (used for) financing activities:			
Increase (decrease) in short-term debt, net	(87)	(40)	(39)
Proceeds from government grants	0	182	160
Excess tax benefit from share-based payment arrangements	9	30	118
Issuance of long-term debt	1,980	0	125
Proceeds from sales of shares through employee equity incentive plans	400	1,105	3,052
Repurchase and retirement of common stock	(1,762)	(7,195)	(2,788)
Payment of dividends to stockholders	(3,108)	(3,100)	(2,618)
Net cash used for financing activities	(2,568)	(9,018)	(1,990)
Net increase (decrease) in cash and cash equivalents	637	(3,957)	709
Cash and cash equivalents, end of year	$ 3,987	$ 3,350	$ 7,307
Cash paid during the year for:			
Interest, net of amounts capitalized of $86 in 2009 ($86 in 2008 and $57 in 2007)	$ 4	$ 6	$ 15
Income taxes, net of refunds	$ 943	$ 4,007	$ 2,762

shareholders. What else could Intel do with this $5.8 billion in free cash flow? Anything it wants. The amount of free cash flow is an indication of the flexibility a company has. If Intel wants to expand more quickly, it has the cash flow to do so. If the company wants to increase cash dividends, it can do so. If the company wants to repay its loans more quickly, it can do that. In short, because of its substantial free cash flow, Intel can do anything.

? QUESTIONS

1. What is Moore's Law?
2. What is the meaning of the term "capex"?
3. What is free cash flow?
4. How much did Intel pay for income taxes in 2009? (*Hint:* Look at the supplemental disclosure at the bottom of the company's statement of cash flows.)

Answers to these questions can be found on page 21-45.

The title of this chapter is "Statement of Cash Flows Revisited." Hopefully, you recall that we introduced the statement of cash flows back in Chapter 5. Since that basic coverage, we have learned a lot of accounting. We now know about leases, goodwill impairment, accounting for bad debts, and a host of other accounting items. The purpose of this chapter is to revisit the statement of cash flows and add some of the accounting complexities that we skipped over in our earlier discussion. If you need a quick refresher course on the basics of the statement of cash flows, look back at Chapter 5.

Preparing a Complete Statement of Cash Flows

1 Prepare a complete statement of cash flows and provide the required supplemental disclosures.

WHY **A complete statement of cash flows provides an excellent summary of all of the activities—operating, investing, and financing—undertaken by a company during a period.**

HOW **Most of the information to prepare the three sections of the cash flow statement comes from the following portions of the balance sheet and the income statement:**

- **Operating—income statement and current assets and liabilities**
- **Investing—long-term assets**
- **Financing—long-term liabilities and owners' equity**

Preparation of a complete cash flow statement is not finished until each income statement item has been considered, all changes in balance sheet items have been explained, and the net change in cash has been exactly reconciled.

In this section, we will work through a comprehensive problem to illustrate the preparation of a complete statement of cash flows. This same process was illustrated in Chapter 5 using a basic example. For this more complex example, we will use financial statement and transaction information for Western Resources, a hypothetical company, for fiscal year 2013. During fiscal 2013, Western Resources completed the following transactions (in summary form).

(1) Sales on account, $688,800.
(2) Collections on account, $692,300.
(3) Received payments from customers in advance for services to be delivered in the future (i.e., unearned sales revenue, $72,000).
(4) Performed services related to sales revenue unearned in prior years, $65,000.
(5) Cost of goods sold, $524,100.
(6) Purchased inventory on account, $522,600.
(7) Paid accounts payable (all related to inventory), $529,300.
(8) Purchased buildings and equipment for cash, $117,000.
(9) Purchased land for $108,500, the seller accepting in payment $40,000 of common stock and $68,500 in cash.
(10) On December 31, purchased available-for-sale securities for cash, $2,000. The existing available-for-sale securities (recorded at $10,000) did not change in value during the year.
(11) Sold a building for cash of $10,000 (original cost, $40,000; accumulated depreciation, $26,000).
(12) On January 1, sold long-term investments recorded at $96,000 for $102,500.
(13) Borrowed short-term debt, $7,500.
(14) Borrowed long-term debt, $20,000.
(15) Issued common stock, $10,000.
(16) Repurchased common stock, $3,200.
(17) Recorded depreciation expense on property, plant, and equipment and amortization expense on patent, $20,900 and $5,000, respectively.
(18) Paid interest on debt, $3,600.
(19) Paid operating and administrative expenses, $150,900. For simplicity, assume that all of these amounts were payments in advance.
(20) Recorded a restructuring charge of $11,700. The entire amount related to a liability for employee severance benefits, none of which have been paid as of the end of the year.
(21) Incurred operating and administrative expenses, $146,400.
(22) Computed the amount of income tax that must be paid as a result of taxable transactions occurring this year, $21,300.
(23) Computed total income tax expense for the year, $24,000. [*Note*: This is higher than the amount in (22) because the income tax code allows taxation of some income earned this year to be deferred to the future.]
(24) Paid income taxes, $23,500.
(25) Declared a dividend of $25,100. During the year, paid $20,700 of this dividend.

A work sheet summarizing the beginning balances in Western Resources' balance sheet accounts for fiscal 2013, the journal entries to record the 25 summary transactions for the year, and the ending preclosing account balances is given in Exhibit 21-2.

From the work sheet in Exhibit 21-2, the information regarding the transactions impacting the cash account can be isolated. This is the information needed to construct the statement of cash flows for Western Resources. A summary and categorization of all the transactions impacting cash is given in Exhibit 21-3.

As you can see, if one has access to the detailed transaction data from the cash account, preparing a statement of cash flows is easy. In fact, if transactions are properly coded as operating, investing, or financing when they are first input into an accounting system, the preparation of a statement of cash flows is no more complicated than a simple 3-way sort of the transactions.

EX 21-2 WORK SHEET ANALYZING WESTERN RESOURCES' FISCAL 2013 TRANSACTIONS

Western Resources
Work Sheet
December 31, 2013
(Amounts in millions)

Account Title	Beginning Balance Debits	Beginning Balance Credits	Transactions During the Year Debits	Transactions During the Year Credits	Ending Balance Debits	Ending Balance Credits
Cash	55,000		(2) 692,300	(7) 529,300	50,600	
			(3) 72,000	(8) 117,000		
			(11) 10,000	(9) 68,500		
			(12) 102,500	(10) 2,000		
			(13) 7,500	(16) 3,200		
			(14) 20,000	(18) 3,600		
			(15) 10,000	(19) 150,900		
				(24) 23,500		
				(25) 20,700		
Available-for-Sale Securities	10,000		(10) 2,000		12,000	
Accounts Receivable	70,500		(1) 688,800	(2) 692,300	67,000	
Inventories	76,500		(6) 522,600	(5) 524,100	75,000	
Prepaid Operating Expenses	12,000		(19) 150,900	(21) 146,400	16,500	
Long-Term Investments	106,000			(12) 96,000	10,000	
Land	75,000		(9) 108,500		183,500	
Buildings and Equipment	345,000		(8) 117,000	(11) 40,000	422,000	
Accumulated Depreciation		198,500	(11) 26,000	(17) 20,900		193,400
Patents	40,000			(17) 5,000	35,000	
Accounts Payable		97,700	(7) 529,300	(6) 522,600		91,000
Short-Term Debt		17,000		(13) 7,500		24,500
Income Taxes Payable		9,500	(24) 23,500	(22) 21,300		7,300
Unearned Sales Revenue		25,000	(4) 65,000	(3) 72,000		32,000
Obligation for Employee Severance		0		(20) 11,700		11,700
Dividends Payable		0		(25) 4,400		4,400
Long-Term Debt		0		(14) 20,000		20,000
Deferred Income Tax Liability		14,500		(23) 2,700		17,200
Common Stock		250,000		(9) 40,000		300,000
				(15) 10,000		
Retained Earnings		234,300				229,800
Treasury Stock	56,500		(16) 3,200		59,700	
Sales				(1) 688,800		
				(4) 65,000		
Cost of Goods Sold			(5) 524,100			
Operating and Administrative Expenses			(21) 146,400			
Depreciation Expense			(17) 20,900			
Amortization Expense			(17) 5,000			
Interest Expense			(18) 3,600			
Loss on Sale of Building			(11) 4,000			
Restructuring Charge			(20) 11,700			
Gain on Sale of Long-Term Investment				(12) 6,500		
Income Tax Expense			(22) 21,300			
			(23) 2,700			
Dividends			(25) 25,100			
Totals	846,500	846,500	3,915,900	3,915,900	931,300	931,300

EX 21-3 SUMMARY OF CASH TRANSACTIONS FOR WESTERN RESOURCES FOR FISCAL 2013

Transaction Number	Cash Flows Relating To	Type of Activity	Amount of Cash Inflow	Amount of Cash Outflow
(2)	Collections on account	Operating	$692,300	
(3)	Collections in advance	Operating	72,000	
(7)	Paid for inventory	Operating		$529,300
(8)	Paid for buildings and equipment	Investing		117,000
(9)	Paid for land (partial payment in cash)	Investing		68,500
(10)	Purchased available-for-sale securities	Investing		2,000
(11)	Sold building	Investing	10,000	
(12)	Sold long-term investment	Investing	102,500	
(13)	Borrowed short-term debt	Financing	7,500	
(14)	Borrowed long-term debt	Financing	20,000	
(15)	Issued common stock	Financing	10,000	
(16)	Repurchased common stock (treasury stock)	Financing		3,200
(18)	Paid interest on debt	Operating		3,600
(19)	Paid operating and administrative expenses	Operating		150,900
(24)	Paid income taxes	Operating		23,500
(25)	Paid a dividend to shareholders	Financing		20,700

Preparing a Statement of Cash Flows in the Absence of Detailed Transaction Data

In this section, we discuss how a statement of cash flows is prepared if we do not have ready access to detailed cash inflow and outflow information or if cash transactions are not coded as being operating, investing, or financing. A solid understanding of the process needed to construct a cash flow statement is important for several reasons. First, the majority of cash flow statements are prepared using the indirect method. Without a detailed understanding of how this type of statement is prepared, your ability to understand and interpret the numbers is severely limited. Second, an understanding of the intricacies of the statement of cash flows allows you to see how individual transactions can affect all of the financial statements. Thus, when we analyze the statement of cash flows, we are also looking at the income statement and the balance sheet. Finally, small companies that are not publicly traded frequently prepare only balance sheets and income statements, so external users of financial statements, such as banks and potential investors, are required to construct cash flow statements using partial information.

If we do not have access to detailed cash flow information, the preparation of a statement of cash flows involves analyzing the income statement and comparative balance sheets to determine how a business generated and used cash. A company's cash inflow and outflow can be determined through a careful analysis of each account contained in these statements. Our knowledge of the activities associated with each balance sheet and income statement account, coupled with our knowledge of the relationship between these two financial statements, allows us to infer the cash flow effects of the various transactions of a business during a period.

For example, consider the accounts receivable account. We know that an increase in Accounts Receivable is associated with a credit sale. Similarly, we know that a decrease in Accounts Receivable usually means that cash was collected. Accordingly, if you know the beginning and ending balances for the accounts receivable account (from comparative balance sheets) and you know sales for the period (from the income statement), you can then infer the cash collected from customers during the period.

To illustrate, consider the following information taken from Western Resources' beginning and ending balance sheets and income statement for fiscal 2013. Remember that we are assuming that the detailed transaction information is not available to us; we have only the summary information available in the resulting financial statements.

Beginning accounts receivable (initial amount owed to Western Resources)	$ 70,500
+ Sales during the year ($688,800 + $65,000)	753,800
= Total amount owed to Western Resources by customers	$824,300
− Ending accounts receivable (amount not yet collected)	67,000
= Cash collections for goods and services already provided	$757,300

In addition to cash collected from customers who have already received services, Western Resources also received an additional $7,000 from customers in advance; this is the increase in the unearned sales revenue account ($32,000 − $25,000). This $7,000 must be added to the previous figure to arrive at total cash collections for the period.

Cash collections for goods and services already provided	$757,300
+ Increase in unearned sales revenue for the period	7,000
Total cash collections for the period	$764,300

Because we know what was owed to Western Resources at the start of the period, what was owed to it at the end of the period, what happened to the unearned sales revenue account during the period, and sales that were made during the period, we can infer the amount of cash that must have been collected during the period. As you can see from this analysis, we don't necessarily need the detailed cash account information to prepare a statement of cash flows. We can use our knowledge of business and accounting to infer those details.

CAUTION

Some students are skeptical of this analysis because it appears to exclude cash sales since they are never recorded as part of Accounts Receivable. Think of a cash sale as a credit sale with an extremely short collection period.

A similar analysis is conducted for every balance sheet account. We use our knowledge of the relationship between the income statement and balance sheet accounts and couple it with our knowledge of what accounts are associated with operating, investing, and financing activities. Consider another example, common stock. First, we know that changes in the common stock account are considered to be financing activities. Second, we know that increases are associated with the issuance of shares of stock. Finally, we know that decreases to the common stock account are associated with the retirement of previously issued shares of stock. Using comparative balance sheet information for the common stock account of Western Resources in fiscal 2013, we can infer the stock-related activities that occurred during the period.

	Beginning Balance	Ending Balance	Change
Common Stock	$250,000	$300,000	$50,000 Increase

From this information, it is reasonable to infer that Western Resources issued stock in exchange for $50,000 during the year. Of course, it is possible that some of these shares were not issued in exchange for cash. For example, we know from transaction (9) that $40,000 of this increase in common stock arose as part of a noncash exchange for land. As will be illustrated later, information about significant noncash transactions such as this must be disclosed somewhere in the financial statement notes and would be used to modify the analysis. By the way, note that we don't use information from the income statement in analyzing transactions impacting the common stock account because transactions in a company's own stock are not reflected in the income statement.

As one other illustration, consider Western Resources' buildings and equipment account. This account is associated with investing activities: Increases in buildings and equipment correspond to purchases of new buildings and equipment and decreases relate to the sale of old buildings and equipment. Western Resources' financial statement notes reveal that a building with an original cost of $40,000 and accumulated depreciation of $26,000 was sold during 2013 for $10,000. Based on this information, and using information from the comparative balance sheets, we can infer that the following buildings and equipment purchases were made during the period.

	Beginning buildings and equipment balance	$345,000
+	Purchases during the period	?
−	Disposals during the period	(40,000)
=	Ending buildings and equipment balance	$422,000

Calculation reveals that the unknown amount is $117,000, which is the amount of buildings and equipment purchased during fiscal 2013. Again, we see that we don't need the detail of the cash account to be able to infer the cash inflow and outflow for the company. Our knowledge of accounting allows us to do a little detective work and infer what transactions impacted Western Resources' cash account.

A 6-Step Process for Preparing a Statement of Cash Flows

The following 6-step process outlines a systematic method that can be used in analyzing the income statement and comparative balance sheets in preparing a statement of cash flows.

1. Compute how much the cash balance changed during the year. The statement of cash flows is not complete until the sum of cash from operating, investing, and financing activities exactly matches the total change in the cash balance during the year.
2. Convert the income statement from an accrual-basis to a cash-basis summary of operations. This is done in three steps.
   (a) Eliminate expenses that do not involve the outflow of cash, such as depreciation expense.
   (b) Eliminate gains and losses associated with investing or financing activities to avoid counting these items twice.
   (c) Adjust for changes in the balances of current operating assets and operating liabilities (usually, but not always, current) because these changes indicate cases in which the operating cash flow associated with an item does not match the revenue or expense reported for that item.

   The final result of these adjustments is that net income is converted into cash flow from operating activities.
3. Analyze the long-term assets to identify the cash flow effects of investing activities. Changes in property, plant, and equipment as well as in long-term investments could indicate that cash has either been spent or been received. Also, examine certain investment securities accounts because purchases and sales of some investment securities are classified as investing activities.
4. Analyze the long-term debt and stockholders' equity accounts to determine the cash flow effects of any financing transactions. These transactions include borrowing or

repaying debt, issuing or buying back stock, and paying dividends. Also examine changes in short-term loan accounts; borrowing and repaying under short-term arrangements are also classified as financing activities.

5. Make sure that the total net cash flow from operating, investing, and financing activities is equal to the net increase or decrease in cash as computed in step 1. Then prepare a formal statement of cash flows by classifying all cash inflows and outflows according to operating, investing, and financing activities. The net cash flows from each of the three main activities should be highlighted.
6. Prepare supplemental disclosure, including the disclosure of any significant investing or financing transactions that did not involve cash. This disclosure is made outside the cash flow statement itself. The types of transactions disclosed in this way include the purchase of land by issuing stock and the retirement of bonds by issuing stock. In addition, supplemental disclosure of cash paid for interest expense and taxes is required.

An Illustration of the 6-Step Process

We will illustrate this 6-step process using the information from the Western Resources example presented earlier. Remember that we will prepare the statement of cash flows without reference to the detailed cash flow information. Thus, we are going to have to make inferences about cash flows by examining the balance sheet and income statement accounts.

Step 1. Compute How Much the Cash Balance Changed During the Year Recall that Western Resources began the year with a cash balance of $55,000 and ended with a cash balance of $50,600. Thus, our target in preparing the statement of cash flows is to explain why the cash account decreased by $4,400 during the year.

Step 2. Convert the Income Statement from an Accrual-Basis to a Cash-Basis Summary of Operations Recall that converting accrual net income into cash from operations involves eliminating noncash expenses, removing the effects of gains and losses, and adjusting for the impact of changes in current operating asset and liability balances. These adjustments are shown in the work sheet, Exhibit 21-4, and are explained below.

Depreciation and amortization (adjustments A1 and A2). The first two adjustments involve adding the amounts of depreciation and amortization expense. Because these expenses do not involve an outflow of cash and because depreciation and amortization were initially subtracted to arrive at net income, these adjustments effectively eliminate depreciation and amortization from the computation of cash from operations. In the far right column of the work sheet in Exhibit 21-4, adjustment A1 results in a $0 (−$20,900 + $20,900 = $0) cash flow effect from depreciation; the same is true of the $5,000 amortization expense. These adjustments are often the largest adjustments that are made. For example, in 2009, **Time Warner** reported net income of $2.5 billion and cash flow from operations of $3.4 billion; its adjustment for depreciation and amortization involved adding $7.6 billion.

Gains and losses (adjustments B1 and B2). Adjustment must also be made for any gains or losses included in the computation of net income. To illustrate the need for this type of adjustment, consider the case of a company that sells some equipment and records a gain on the sale. The cash flow effect of the equipment sale is shown in the Investing Activities section of the cash flow statement. To avoid counting this twice, the gain should be excluded

EX 21-4 ADJUSTMENTS TO CONVERT WESTERN RESOURCES' ACCRUAL NET INCOME INTO CASH FROM OPERATIONS—WORK SHEET

	Income Statement			Adjustments	Cash Flow from Operations
Sales	$ 753,800	C1	3,500	Decrease in accounts receivable	$ 764,300
		C2	7,000	Increase in unearned sales revenue	
Cost of Goods Sold	(524,100)	C3	1,500	Decrease in inventory	(529,300)
		C4	(6,700)	Decrease in accounts payable	
Operating and Administrative Expenses	(146,400)	C5	(4,500)	Increase in prepaid expenses	(150,900)
Depreciation Expense	(20,900)	A1	20,900	Not a cash flow item	0
Amortization Expense	(5,000)	A2	5,000	Not a cash flow item	0
Interest Expense	(3,600)		0	No adjustment	(3,600)
Loss on Sale of Building	(4,000)	B1	4,000	Avoid double counting	0
Restructuring Charge	(11,700)	C6	11,700	Increase in obligation	0
Gain on Sale of Long-Term Investment	6,500	B2	(6,500)	Avoid double counting	0
Income Tax Expense	(24,000)	C7	(2,200)	Decrease in income taxes payable	(23,500)
		C8	2,700	Increase in deferred tax liability	
Net Income	$ 20,600		36,400		$ 57,000

from the Operating Activities section. However, the gain has already been added in the computation of net income. To exclude the gain from the Operating Activities section, it must be subtracted from net income. If there had been a loss on the equipment sale, that loss would be added back to net income in the Operating Activities section so that it would not impact cash flows from operations.

FYI

Treatment of gains and losses on investments in the cash flow statement can actually be a bit more complicated than illustrated here. The correct treatment depends on what type of security the investment is (trading, available for sale, etc.) and whether the gain or loss is realized or unrealized. This topic is covered in Chapter 14.

In 2013, Western Resources reported a $4,000 loss on the sale of a building. The entire $10,000 cash proceeds from this sale are reported as a cash inflow in the Investing Activities section. To remove this loss from impacting the computation of operating cash flow, it is added (adjustment B1) in Exhibit 21-4. In 2013 Western Resources reported a gain of $6,500 from selling a long-term investment; this gain is subtracted (adjustment B2) in the Operating Activities section. The full $102,500 cash flow impact of the sale of this investment is reported in the Investing Activities section.

Changes in current assets and liabilities. The remaining adjustments (C1–C8 in Exhibit 21-4) are needed because the computation of accrual net income involves reporting revenues and expenses when economic events occur, not necessarily when cash is received or paid. The timing differences between the receipt or payment of cash and the earning of revenue or the incurring of an expense are reflected in the shifting balances in the current operating assets and liabilities. This is illustrated through a discussion of each of Western Resources' current operating asset and liability accounts.

Accounts receivable (adjustment C1). Recall from our analysis earlier in the chapter that the amount of cash Western Resources collected from customers in 2013 differed from sales for the period. In fact, collections exceeded sales by $3,500, which explains why the accounts receivable account decreased by $3,500. In computing cash from operations, an adjustment must be made to increase the accrual-basis sales figure to its cash-basis counterpart. The $3,500 decrease in accounts receivable is added, as shown in Exhibit 21-4.

Unearned sales revenue (adjustment C2). In converting the accrual-based sales into cash collected from customers, we must also make an adjustment for cash received from customers in advance of the revenue being earned. The unearned sales revenue account increased by $7,000 (from $25,000 to $32,000), representing cash received from customers in 2013 that won't be reflected in sales and included in the computation of net income until a subsequent year. The $7,000 increase reflects an additional amount of cash not yet included in the computation of 2013 net income and is added in the computation of cash from operations, as shown in Exhibit 21-4. This adjustment for unearned revenue is typically a significant item in the cash flow statement of Microsoft because a portion of the selling price of software is considered to be advance payment for technical and support services. In 2009, **Apple**'s operating cash flow increased by $6.9 billion because of an increase in unearned revenue.

Inventory (adjustment C3). The statement of cash flows should reflect the amount of cash paid for inventory during the year, which is not necessarily the same as the cost of inventory sold. Western Resources' inventory decreased by $1,500 (from $76,500 to $75,000) during 2013, indicating that the amount of inventory purchased during 2013 was less than the amount of inventory sold. Accordingly, in the computation of cash from operations, we must reduce the cost of goods sold number to reflect the fact that part of the inventory sold this period was actually purchased last period. To reduce cost of goods sold (which is subtracted in the computation of net income), the adjustment involves adding $1,500, as shown in Exhibit 21-4. As mentioned earlier in the chapter, the inventory increases experienced by rapidly growing companies result in a decrease in cash from operations because the cash is tied up in the form of inventory. In its February 2008 cash flow statement, **Home Depot** reported a reduction of $491 million in cash from operations stemming from increased inventories.

Accounts payable (adjustment C4). The balance in Western Resources' accounts payable account decreased by $6,700 during 2013. This decrease occurred because Western Resources paid for more than it bought from its suppliers during the year. The adjustment necessary to reflect this additional cash outflow is to subtract $6,700 in computing cash from operations, shown as adjustment C4 in Exhibit 21-4. On the other hand, an increase in the accounts payable account results in more operating cash flow because cash that otherwise would have been used to pay bills is kept within the business. **Enron**, in its 2000 annual report, provides an example of just how significant this source of cash can be. In computing cash provided by operations, Enron added $7.167 billion to reflect the effect of an increase in its accounts payable account balance. Perhaps hinting at the troubles that lay ahead in 2001 for Enron, operating cash flow for 2000 would have been negative (by about $3 billion!) without this addition for an increase in accounts payable.

Prepaid operating expenses (adjustment C5). Prepaid operating expenses increased by $4,500 (from $12,000 to $16,500) during 2013. Prepaid expenses are increased when a company pays cash in advance for a service that it will use later. Thus, an increase in prepaid expenses indicates that Western Resources paid $4,500 over and above its obligation for operating expense services used during the year. Accordingly, the increase in prepaid expenses is subtracted in computing cash from operations, as shown in adjustment C5.

Restructuring charge (adjustment C6). Recall from Chapter 4 that a restructuring charge is an accounting estimate of the decrease in value of some assets and the creation of future obligations as a result of the decision to restructure parts of a business. The important point to note is that this charge is an accounting estimate, not necessarily an immediate cash payment. From Western Resources' balance sheet, we can see that the $11,700 obligation for employee severance benefits recognized in connection with the restructuring charge is still unpaid as of the end of the year. In computing cash from operating activities, the unpaid portion of an obligation associated with a restructuring charge should be added back to net income. In Exhibit 21-4, this adjustment (C6) is shown as an addition of $11,700, resulting in a net cash flow effect from the restructuring charge of $0 this year. Restructuring charges also involve asset write-downs, and these also do not require an immediate cash outlay.

Interest expense. Because an interest payable account does not exist, we can safely assume that all interest expense was paid for in cash. Therefore, there is no need for an adjustment. If there were an interest payable account, the reasoning used when analyzing the accounts payable account would apply.

Income tax expense (adjustments C7 and C8). Computation of cash paid for income taxes requires two adjustments. First, as explained in Chapter 16, the amount of income tax expense reported in the financial statements is not the same as the amount of income tax that is owed to the taxing authorities for the year. Accrual accounting requires the immediate recognition of *all* of the tax effects stemming from a transaction, whether those effects will occur this year or in a subsequent year. Thus, it is quite common for companies to recognize a liability for income taxes that relates to income that was earned in the current year but, according to the tax rules, won't become taxable until a subsequent year. This type of liability is called a *deferred income tax liability.* In 2013 the deferred income tax liability for Western Resources increased by $2,700, indicating that some of the $24,000 income tax expense reported won't actually become payable to the taxing authorities until some future year. This means that income taxes owed for 2013 operations are just $21,300:

Reported income tax expense	$24,000
Less: Increase in deferred income tax liability	2,700
Taxes owed for current year operations	$21,300

The effect of the increase in the deferred income tax liability is to reduce the amount of cash paid for income taxes this year; this is shown in adjustment C8. In addition, the Western Resources balance sheet indicates that income taxes payable, which is the liability that relates to the income taxes that are payable to the taxing authorities right now, decreased by $2,200 during the year. An operating accrual such as income taxes payable is reduced by paying additional cash; this is reflected in adjustment C7.

> **FYI**
>
> The matrix used to illustrate the analysis associated with the Operating Activities section is just one way to do this analysis. A T-account approach is illustrated later in this chapter.

The direct and indirect methods. The final task in reporting cash flow from operations relates to preparing the Operating Activities section of the statement of cash flows. Two alternative reporting methods are available: the indirect method and the direct method.

The indirect method begins with net income as reported in the income statement and then details the adjustments needed to arrive at cash flow from operations. Continuing the Western Resources illustration, the indirect method involves reporting the information

EX 21-5 OPERATING CASH FLOW ITEMS REPORTED UNDER THE INDIRECT METHOD—WORK SHEET

	Income Statement	Adjustments			Cash Flow from Operations
Sales	$ 753,800	C1	3,500	Decrease in accounts receivable	$ 764,300
		C2	7,000	Increase in unearned sales revenue	
Cost of Goods Sold	(524,100)	C3	1,500	Decrease in inventory	(529,300)
		C4	(6,700)	Decrease in accounts payable	
Operating and Administrative Expenses	(146,400)	C5	(4,500)	Increase in prepaid expenses	(150,900)
Depreciation Expense	(20,900)	A1	20,900	Not a cash flow item	0
Amortization Expense	(5,000)	A2	5,000	Not a cash flow item	0
Interest Expense	(3,600)		0	No adjustment	(3,600)
Loss on Sale of Building	(4,000)	B1	4,000	Avoid double counting	0
Restructuring Charge	(11,700)	C6	11,700	Increase in obligation	0
Gain on Sale of Long-Term Investment	6,500	B2	(6,500)	Avoid double counting	0
Income Tax Expense	(24,000)	C7	(2,200)	Decrease in income taxes payable	(23,500)
		C8	2,700	Increase in deferred tax liability	
Net Income	$ 20,600		36,400		$ 57,000

shown in the shaded segment of the work sheet in Exhibit 21-5. The actual format of the Operating Activities section of the cash flow statement, using the indirect method, is shown in Exhibit 21-6.

Because understanding the adjustments made under the indirect method requires some practice, it is useful at this point to review the rationale behind each addition and subtraction reported in Exhibit 21-6:

- *Add the amount of depreciation and amortization expense.* These amounts are added back to net income because no cash flow was associated with these expenses in the current period.
- *Subtract the amount of gains and add the amount of losses* because the full cash effect of these items is reported in the Investing Activities section. Because gains and losses

EX 21-6 CASH FROM OPERATING ACTIVITIES: INDIRECT METHOD

Cash flows from operating activities:		
Net income.		$20,600
Adjustments:		
Add Depreciation expense	$20,900	
Add Amortization expense	5,000	
Add Loss on sale of building	4,000	
Subtract Gain on sale of long-term investment	(6,500)	
Add Decrease in accounts receivable	3,500	
Add Increase in unearned sales revenue	7,000	
Add Decrease in inventory	1,500	
Subtract Decrease in accounts payable	(6,700)	
Subtract Increase in prepaid expenses	(4,500)	
Add Increase in restructuring charge obligation	11,700	
Subtract Decrease in income taxes payable	(2,200)	
Add Increase in deferred income tax liability	2,700	36,400
Net cash provided by operating activities		$57,000

are included in the computation of net income, failing to adjust for them here would result in their being double counted.

- *Add the decrease in Accounts Receivable.* The accounts receivable account decreases when customers pay for more than they purchased this year. Thus, Western Resources has more cash than it would have had if customers had not paid down their accounts.
- *Add the increase in Unearned Sales Revenue.* Unearned Sales Revenue goes up when customers pay for goods or services in advance. Thus, an increase in Unearned Sales Revenue represents cash collected over and above the sales amount.
- *Add the decrease in Inventory.* By allowing the Inventory amount to decrease, Western Resources has conserved cash that otherwise would have been used to purchase inventory.
- *Subtract the decrease in Accounts Payable.* Western Resources paid extra cash to reduce the balance in Accounts Payable.
- *Subtract the increase in Prepaid Operating Expenses.* Western Resources paid extra cash by prepaying for services that it won't use until a future period.
- *Add the increase in Obligation for Employee Severance.* A restructuring charge does not involve an immediate outlay of cash. The increase in this liability indicates that Western Resources has not yet paid any cash associated with the restructuring, so the amount of the increase is added in computing operating cash flow.
- *Subtract the decrease in Income Taxes Payable.* Western Resources paid extra cash to reduce the balance in Income Taxes Payable.
- *Add the increase in Deferred Income Tax Liability.* A portion of income tax expense relates to income taxes that will not become payable until a future year. Accordingly, this portion of income tax expense does not involve a current cash outlay and is added back in computing operating cash flow.

The direct method involves simply reporting the information contained in the last column of the adjustment work sheet, shown as the shaded portion in Exhibit 21-7. The resulting Operating Activities section is given in Exhibit 21-8.

EX 21-7 OPERATING CASH FLOW ITEMS REPORTED UNDER THE DIRECT METHOD

	Income Statement	Adjustments			Cash Flow from Operations
Sales	$ 753,800	C1	3,500	Decrease in accounts receivable	$ 764,300
		C2	7,000	Increase in unearned sales revenue	
Cost of Goods Sold	(524,100)	C3	1,500	Decrease in inventory	(529,300)
		C4	(6,700)	Decrease in accounts payable	
Operating and Administrative Expenses	(146,400)	C5	(4,500)	Increase in prepaid expenses	(150,900)
Depreciation Expense	(20,900)	A1	20,900	Not a cash flow item	0
Amortization Expense	(5,000)	A2	5,000	Not a cash flow item	0
Interest Expense	(3,600)		0	No adjustment	(3,600)
Loss on Sale of Building	(4,000)	B1	4,000	Avoid double counting	0
Restructuring Charge	(11,700)	C6	11,700	Increase in obligation	0
Gain on Sale of Long-Term Investment	6,500	B2	(6,500)	Avoid double counting	0
Income Tax Expense	(24,000)	C7	(2,200)	Decrease in income taxes payable	(23,500)
		C8	2,700	Increase in deferred tax liability	
Net Income	$ 20,600		36,400		$ 57,000

EX 21-8 CASH FROM OPERATING ACTIVITIES: DIRECT METHOD

Cash flows from operating activities:	
Collections from customers	$ 764,300
Payments for inventory	(529,300)
Payments for operating and administrative expenses	(150,900)
Payments for interest	(3,600)
Payments for income taxes	(23,500)
Net cash provided by operating activities	$ 57,000

Some rules of thumb for the indirect method. Because the indirect method is the more commonly used of the two methods and because the adjustments required under the indirect method are sometimes difficult to understand, we outline some simple rules to aid in your understanding.

Item	Direction of Change	Necessary Adjustment
Current operating asset	Increase	Subtract the increase
Current operating asset	Decrease	Add the decrease
Current or noncurrent operating liability	Increase	Add the increase
Current or noncurrent operating liability	Decrease	Subtract the decrease

Examples of noncurrent operating liabilities that necessitate adjustments in the computation of operating cash flow are deferred income tax liability and obligation for employee severance, as illustrated in the Western Resources example.

More important than memorizing whether an increase is added or subtracted is understanding the business rationale for doing so. When a current operating asset increases, cash that otherwise would have been available for buying equipment or paying dividends is tied up in the form of that current operating asset. Thus, the current operating asset increase means a decrease in the cash generated by operations. As an example, an Accounts Receivable increase during the year means that cash that could be used for other purposes has not yet been collected from customers. On the other hand, an Accounts Receivable decrease means that, in addition to collecting all cash from sales during the period, the business has also collected enough extra cash to reduce the outstanding balance in Accounts Receivable. In short, current operating assets represent cash tied up in noncash form; an increase in current operating assets means more cash tied up, and a decrease means cash has been freed for other purposes.

In the case of operating liabilities (current and noncurrent), an increase means that more cash is available to the business because the cash was not used to pay the liability. For example, an increase in Accounts Payable means that the amount of cash used to pay suppliers was less than the amount of purchases made during the period. This results in an increase in cash from operations because more cash is available to be used for other purposes within the business. A decrease in Accounts Payable means that extra cash was paid to reduce the balance in the liability account; this extra cash is therefore not available for other uses in the business and represents a decrease in the cash generated by operating activities.

Some old-fashioned people will tell you that it is a waste of time to learn about the direct method because all companies use the indirect method. Well, those old-fashioned people are wrong on two counts. First, there are a few companies that use the direct method, although so few well-known companies use the direct method that it is difficult to find an example. As a matter of fact, the first hit in an April 2010 search of the SEC archives for companies using the direct method was **PT Telekomunikasi Indonesia**, the largest telecommunications company in Indonesia. Not exactly a household name in the United States. Second, both the FASB and the IASB are formally on record as preferring the direct method over the indirect method. And, as described in more detail later in the chapter, the FASB and the IASB currently are circulating a proposal that would make the direct method *mandatory*. So, the best thing for you to do is to use the matrix format illustrated in this textbook and become comfortable with both the direct and indirect methods.

Step 3. Analyze the Long-Term Assets to Identify the Cash Flow Effects of Investing Activities Western Resources reports four long-term asset accounts.

- Long-Term Investments
- Land
- Buildings and Equipment
- Patents

We will analyze each of these in turn to determine how much cash flow was associated with each during 2013.

Long-term investments. The long-term investments account was reduced by $96,000 ($106,000 − $10,000) during the year. This could be a combination of the purchase of new investments and the sale of old investments. We must rely on supplemental information outside the financial statements to determine whether any new long-term investments were purchased during the year. In this case, none were, indicating that the entire $96,000 reduction in the account balance represents the book value of long-term investments sold during the year. To calculate the amount of cash collected from this sale, we must use income statement information to determine whether there was a gain or loss on the sale. Computation of the cash proceeds is as follows:

Book value of long-term investments sold	$ 96,000
Plus: Gain on sale	6,500
Cash proceeds	$102,500

Land. The land account increased by $108,500 ($183,500 – $75,000) during the year. Again, this could be a combination of purchases and sales of land. Because there is no indication of land sales during the year, we conclude that the $108,500 represents the price of new land purchased during the year. One additional element arises in this case; the entire purchase price was not paid in cash. Supplemental information tells us that payment for the land was a combination of $68,500 of cash and common stock valued at $40,000. Only the $68,500 cash outlay for the land will be shown in the cash flow statement; the $40,000 in common stock exchanged for the land will be disclosed separately in the notes to the financial statements, as illustrated later.

Buildings and equipment. The balance in Western Resources' buildings and equipment account increased by $77,000 ($422,000 – $345,000) during 2013. In the absence of any other information, this increase would suggest that Western Resources purchased buildings and equipment with a cost of $77,000. In this case, however, additional information is available, indicating that buildings and equipment with an original cost of $40,000 were sold for $10,000 during the year. This $10,000 cash proceeds from the sale is a cash inflow from investing activities. When this information is combined with the fact that the beginning balance in PP&E was $345,000, we can make the following computation:

Beginning buildings and equipment balance	$345,000
− Original cost of buildings and equipment sold during the year	(40,000)
= Ending buildings and equipment balance without additional purchases	$305,000

The actual ending balance sheet for Western Resources reports a buildings and equipment balance of $422,000. We can therefore infer that Western Resources purchased buildings and equipment for $117,000 ($422,000 − $305,000) to account for the difference. This $117,000 purchase of buildings and equipment represents cash used for investing activities.

A useful way to summarize all purchase and sale information for buildings and equipment is to reconstruct the T-accounts for both the buildings and equipment account and the associated accumulated depreciation account. Those T-accounts appear as follows:

Buildings and Equipment

	Debit	Credit	
Beginning	345,000		Historical cost of items sold
Purchases	[117,000]	40,000	
Ending	422,000		

Accumulated Depreciation

	Debit	Credit	
		198,500	Beginning
Accum. depr. on items sold	[26,000]	20,900	Depr. exp.
		193,400	Ending

The amounts in boxes (amount of purchases and amount of accumulated depreciation associated with the items sold) are those amounts that can be inferred given the other information. With this information, we can compute whether the sale of buildings and equipment resulted in a gain or in a loss as follows:

Cash proceeds (given earlier)	$10,000
Book value of items sold ($40,000 − $26,000)	14,000
Loss on sale of buildings and equipment	$ (4,000)

The existence of a $4,000 loss is confirmed by examination of the Western Resources income statement information. Note that with the income statement information and the amounts inferred using these T-accounts, we could have traced backward and computed the cash proceeds from the sale of the buildings and equipment. The T-accounts are very useful devices for structuring the information that we have so that we can infer the missing values needed to complete the statement of cash flows.

Patents. Finally, the patents account began the year with a $40,000 balance and ended with a $35,000 balance. This decrease arose as follows:

Beginning Patents	$40,000
− Patent amortization recognized during the year	(5,000)
+ New patents purchased during the year	???
= Ending Patents	$35,000

The numbers indicate that no new patents were purchased during the year. Thus, there were no investing cash flow implications for the change in the patent balance because the entire change in the patent balance is explained by the patent amortization expense for the year.

One additional item must be considered before we can complete the Investing Activities section of the statement of cash flows. Although investment securities are not always long-term assets, their purchase and sale are sometimes reported as investing activities. Specifically, purchases and sales of available-for-sale and held-to-maturity securities are reported as part of investing activities whereas purchases and sales of trading securities are usually part of operating activities.[1] For Western Resources, the balance in the available-for-sale securities account increased by $2,000 ($12,000 − $10,000). As explained in Chapter 14, this increase could have arisen because of an increase in the market value of existing available-for-sale securities. If this were the case, no cash flow impact would be reported. In this case, we have to rely on other information to confirm that the increase came from the purchase of new securities for cash. This $2,000 cash outflow for the purchase of available-for-sale securities is reported as part of investing activities.

The Investing Activities section of the statement of cash flows for Western Resources is as follows:

Cash flows from investing activities:	
Sold building	$ 10,000
Sold long-term investment	102,500
Purchased available-for-sale securities	(2,000)
Purchased land	(68,500)
Purchased buildings and equipment	(117,000)
Net cash used by investing activities	$ (75,000)

This Investing Activities section, which we just constructed using balance sheet, income statement, and financial statement note information, would be identical to one prepared using detailed cash transaction data. With a solid understanding of accounting, we can infer the cash flow effects of transactions without having access to all the details.

Step 4. Analyze the Long-Term Debt and Stockholders' Equity Accounts to Determine the Cash Flow Effects of any Financing Transactions Long-term debt accounts increase when a company borrows more money—an inflow of cash—and decrease when the company pays back the debt—an outflow of cash. In the case of Western Resources, we observe that the company's balance in Long-Term Debt increased by $20,000 ($20,000 − $0) during the year. Accordingly, we can infer that Western Resources borrowed an additional $20,000 during 2013. This $20,000 in new borrowing represents cash provided by financing activities. The same analysis applies to short-term debt; the increase of $7,500 ($24,500 − $17,000) during the year represents a cash inflow from financing activities arising from new short-term loans.

The $50,000 ($300,000 − $250,000) increase in Western Resources' common stock account during the year potentially represents a cash inflow from the issuance of new shares of stock. However, as mentioned earlier, additional information indicates that $40,000 of this increase arose from the exchange of common stock for land. Accordingly, the actual cash generated by the issuance of new shares during the year is just $10,000 ($50,000 − $40,000). This cash inflow is reported as part of cash from financing activities.

When companies repurchase some of their own common stock during the year, the price paid to repurchase the stock is shown as a reduction in stockholders' equity and is usually labeled *treasury stock*. Thus, an increase in the treasury stock account reflects a cash repurchase of the company's own shares. The balance in Western Resources' treasury stock account increased by $3,200 ($59,700 − $56,500) during the year. Thus, Western

[1] FASB ASC paragraph 320-10-45-11.

Resources should report a cash outflow of $3,200 from treasury stock purchases in the Financing Activities section.

The retained earnings account increases from the recognition of net income (an operating activity), decreases as a result of net losses (also an operating activity), and decreases through the payment of dividends (a financing activity). In the absence of detailed information, it is possible to infer the amount of dividends declared by identifying the unexplained change in the retained earnings account balance. An efficient way to do this is to recreate the retained earnings T-account as follows:

Retained Earnings

		234,300	Beginning
Dividends declared	25,100	20,600	Net income
		229,800	Ending

The increase in the Western Resources' dividends payable account during the year indicates that not all of the $25,100 in dividends declared were paid in cash during the year. Computation of the amount of cash paid for dividends during the year is as follows:

Dividends declared	$25,100
Less: Increase in dividends payable	4,400
Cash paid for dividends	$20,700

Of course, it is usually the case that the amount of dividends paid is disclosed somewhere in the financial statements. However, you never know the level of detailed information to which you will have access. After all, it is a relatively simple (and fun!) analytical exercise.

The following information summarizes the cash flow effects of Western Resources' financing activities during 2013:

Cash flows from financing activities:	
Issued common stock	$ 10,000
Borrowed short-term debt	7,500
Borrowed long-term debt	20,000
Paid dividends	(20,700)
Treasury stock purchases	(3,200)
Net cash provided by financing activities	$ 13,600

Again, and not surprisingly, this section of Western Resources' statement of cash flows would be identical to the one prepared using the detailed cash information. We hope that you are convinced that if you know enough about accounting, you can conduct some powerful analyses using very limited information.

Step 5. Prepare a Formal Statement of Cash Flows Based on our analyses of the income statement and balance sheet accounts, we have identified all inflows and outflows of cash for Western Resources for 2013, and we have categorized those cash flows based on the type of activity. The resulting statement of cash flows (prepared using the indirect method, which is by far the more common method of presentation) is shown in Exhibit 21-9.

The FASB's decision to classify interest paid as part of operating activities was a controversial one. In fact, many users do not consider cash paid for either interest or

EX 21-9 STATEMENT OF CASH FLOWS FOR WESTERN RESOURCES FOR FISCAL 2013

Western Resources
Statement of Cash Flows
For the Year Ended December 31, 2013

Cash flows from operating activities:		
Net income		$ 20,600
Adjustments:		
Add Depreciation expense	$ 20,900	
Add Amortization expense	5,000	
Add Loss on sale of building	4,000	
Subtract Gain on sale of long-term investment	(6,500)	
Add Decrease in accounts receivable	3,500	
Add Increase in unearned sales revenue	7,000	
Add Decrease in inventory	1,500	
Subtract Decrease in accounts payable	(6,700)	
Subtract Increase in prepaid expenses	(4,500)	
Add Increase in restructuring charge obligation	11,700	
Subtract Decrease in income taxes payable	(2,200)	
Add Increase in deferred income tax liability	2,700	36,400
Net cash provided by operating activities		$ 57,000
Cash flows from investing activities:		
Sold building	$ 10,000	
Sold long-term investment	102,500	
Purchased available-for-sale securities	(2,000)	
Purchased land	(68,500)	
Purchased buildings and equipment	(117,000)	
Net cash used by investing activities		(75,000)
Cash flows from financing activities:		
Issued common stock	$ 10,000	
Borrowed short-term debt	7,500	
Borrowed long-term debt	20,000	
Paid dividends	(20,700)	
Treasury stock purchases	(3,200)	
Net cash provided by financing activities		13,600
Net decrease in cash		$ (4,400)
Beginning cash balance		55,000
Ending cash balance		$ 50,600

income taxes to be part of operating cash flow. As a compromise, the FASB requires companies to separately disclose the amount of cash paid for interest and for income taxes during the year. This allows users to recast and reclassify the reported cash flow numbers into the format they think is more useful. When the direct method is used, the amounts of cash paid for interest and for income taxes are part of the Operating Activities section, so no additional disclosure is needed. When the indirect method is used, as in Exhibit 21-9, these amounts must be shown separately, either at the bottom of the cash flow statement or in an accompanying note. For example, as you saw in Exhibit 21-1, Intel uses the indirect method and discloses separately at the bottom of its statement of cash flows that \$4 million and \$943 million were paid in 2009 for interest and income taxes, respectively.

Remember, if you have access to the details of the cash account, a statement of cash flows can be easily prepared. Also, if operating cash flow is reported using the direct method, the cash flow statement can be easily understood. However, it is likely that at some point you will need to construct a cash flow statement using summary balance sheet and income statement data. In addition, most cash flow statements that you encounter will use the indirect method. The adjustments required to compute cash flow numbers can be confusing if you have no understanding of the "why" behind the adjustments. This section has covered the "gory" details of preparing a statement of cash flows to help you gain an understanding of why the adjustments are made.

Step 6. Prepare Supplemental Disclosure Three categories of supplemental disclosure are associated with the statement of cash flows. These are as follows:

- Cash paid for interest and income taxes
- Reconciliation schedule
- Noncash investing and financing activities

Cash paid for interest and income taxes. As mentioned previously, the FASB requires separate disclosure of the cash paid for interest and for income taxes during the year. When the direct method is used, the amounts of cash paid for interest and for income taxes are part of the Operating Activities section, so no additional disclosure is needed. When the indirect method is used, these amounts must be shown separately, either at the bottom of the cash flow statement or in an accompanying note. In the case of Western Resources, the supplemental information might be presented as follows:

Supplemental Disclosure:	
Cash paid for interest	$ 3,600
Cash paid for income taxes	23,500

Reconciliation schedule. An important aspect of the indirect method is that it highlights the differences between net income and cash from operations. This comparison is absent when the direct method is used. The FASB concluded that this comparison is of such value to financial statement users that when the direct method is used, a schedule should be included that reconciles net income to cash from operations. Fortunately, you don't have to learn anything new because the schedule is the same as the Operating Activities section prepared using the indirect method (the middle column in our work sheets). So, when a company uses the direct method, in essence it provides both operating cash flow computations: the direct method in the body of the cash flow statement and the indirect method as a supplemental schedule. When the indirect method is used, no additional reconciliation schedule is necessary.

Noncash investing and financing activities. When a company has significant noncash transactions, such as purchasing property, plant, and equipment by issuing debt or in exchange for shares of stock, these transactions must be disclosed in the notes to the financial statements. In 2013, Western Resources had one such transaction: the exchange of common stock for land valued at $40,000. The existence of this transaction would be reported in the financial statements either as a note at the bottom of the statement of cash flows or in a separate financial statement note. As another example of this type of noncash transaction, **Wal-Mart** discloses at the bottom of its January 2010 statement of cash flows that during the year it used capital lease arrangements to acquire property, plant, and equipment worth $61 million. A capital lease is a long-term, noncancelable lease that effectively serves as mortgage financing for the acquisition of assets. Acquiring assets using capital leases does not require the immediate outlay of cash in the full amount of the lease, so a capital lease constitutes a significant noncash transaction. Capital leases were explained in detail in Chapter 15.

FASB CODIFICATION

The Issue: As a part-time job while you are attending school, you are the accountant for a local equipment rental company. The company needs financing for a major expansion and so is preparing to seek a sizeable bank loan. You have been asked to prepare the financial statements in advance of this loan application. Most of this preparation is routine, but you have come across one vexing issue. The company has two types of equipment. One type is maintained strictly for rental purposes; these items are rarely sold. Items in this set include large construction cranes and concrete pumper extensions. The other type of equipment is usually rented for a few months and then sold. Items in this set include pressure washers and concrete saws.

You are wondering how the cash spent to buy these two different types of equipment should be classified in the statement of cash flows. Are these operating cash outflows or investing cash outflows? You could call the local CPA who sometimes does consulting work for your company, but you would prefer to add to your personal credibility by finding out the answer yourself.

The Question: When equipment is purchased to then be rented, and sometimes sold, should the cash paid to purchase the equipment be classified as an operating cash outflow or as an investing cash outflow?

Searching the Codification: OK, let's just dig in and find the answer. Start by locating Topic 230 under the "Presentation" tab in the FASB ASC home page. None of those industry-specific sets of standards seem applicable here, so click to open up the menu under "Overall." This is a presentation matter and relates to how cash flows should be classified. Finally, the issue here is how the cash flows associated with a certain activity (purchase of equipment to be rented and then, perhaps, sold) should be classified when there appear to be two classes of cash flows (operating and investing) involved.

The Answer: The correct treatment is described on page 21-45.

International Cash Flow Statements

2 **Understand the differences among cash flow statements prepared according to U.S. GAAP and IASB standards.**

WHY **The primary differences in cash flow reporting around the world relate to alternative classifications of selected cash transactions such as payment of interest and income taxes.**

HOW **Relative to U.S. GAAP, *IAS 7* allows greater flexibility in classifying cash transactions such as interest and dividends paid and received and income taxes paid. In the United Kingdom, *FRS 1* specifies eight different categories for classifying cash flow transactions.**

With the adoption of pre-codification *FASB Statement No. 95* in 1987, the FASB set the benchmark for cash flow reporting around the world. Before that time, cash flow reporting was either ignored or done using an antiquated "funds flow" approach. It wasn't until 1992 that the International Accounting Standards Board (IASB) adopted a comparable cash flow standard, *IAS 7*. In this section, the provisions of *IAS 7* are compared to those of U.S. GAAP (now contained in FASB ASC Topic 230). In addition, the U.K. standard for cash flow reporting is also examined. As will be seen, the primary differences in cash flow reporting around the world relate to alternative classifications of selected cash transactions.

International Accounting Standard 7

IAS 7 closely matches the provisions of the U.S. cash flow reporting standard, with the primary difference being greater flexibility in classifying cash transactions as either operating, investing, or financing. The IASB opted to allow more company discretion in deciding how to classify items such as interest and dividends paid and received. Within the FASB, there was great debate about how these items should be classified, but the final version of the U.S. standard mandates that these items be classified as operating activities. The more flexible standard of the IASB is discussed next.

Interest and Dividends Received When the FASB adopted pre-codification *SFAS No. 95* in 1987, three of the seven Board members objected to the classification of interest and dividends received as operating activities. Those three Board members argued that interest and dividends received were investing activities since they represent returns on investments in debt and equity securities. Ultimately, the majority of the FASB decided that, because interest and dividends received are included in the computation of net income, they should be classified as operating activities. In *IAS 7*, the IASB acknowledges the merits of both sides of the philosophical debate over classifying interest and dividends received, as discussed earlier, and allows companies to classify them as either operating or investing activities.

Interest Paid The same three FASB members also objected to the classification of interest paid as an operating activity. They contended that interest paid is the cost of obtaining financing and should be classified as a financing activity. Again, the majority of the FASB voted to classify interest paid as an operating activity because it is included in the computation of net income. The provisions of *IAS 7* allow interest paid to be classified as either an operating activity or a financing activity; whichever classification is chosen, it should be applied on a consistent basis.

Dividends Paid *IAS 7* allows dividends paid to be classified as either a financing activity (as in the United States) or as an operating activity. The rationale for allowing dividend payments to be classified as operating activities is that this classification helps investors determine whether the operations of the business have the ability to generate enough cash to support the continued payment of dividends. This reasoning seems a little dubious and has led some to criticize *IAS 7* of not being an effective accounting standard because it allows too much classification flexibility.

Income Taxes According to *IAS 7*, the amount of income taxes paid should be reported as an operating activity unless the income taxes can be specifically identified with a financing or an investing activity. For example, if the disposal of equipment results in a gain on which income taxes are paid, those income taxes could be classified as a cash outflow from an investing activity. The FASB considered this approach and rejected it as being too complex and arbitrary and not worth the benefit that it might provide to financial statement users. No matter how income taxes are classified, *IAS 7* requires separate disclosure of the total amount of income taxes paid for the period.

United Kingdom Cash Flow Standard, *FRS 1*

The accounting standard setters in the United Kingdom first adopted a cash flow standard in 1991. In recognition of the fact that the cash flow statement has become an increasingly important addition to the set of primary financial statements, the U.K. Accounting Standards Board (ASB) revised its standard in 1996. The revised version of *Financial Reporting Standard (FRS) 1* specifies eight different categories for classifying cash flow transactions and represents the most innovative and, probably, the most useful standard for cash flow reporting currently in existence in the world. Because of the flexibility in the current version of *IAS 7*, both the U.S. approach in FASB ASC Topic 230 and the U.K. approach in *FRS 1* are in conformity with the international standard.

The Eight Cash Flow Categories The eight cash flow categories specified in *FRS 1* are as follows:

1. Operating activities
2. Returns on investments and servicing of finance
3. Taxation
4. Capital expenditure and financial investment
5. Acquisitions and disposals
6. Equity dividends paid
7. Management of liquid resources
8. Financing

The U.K. amount reported as cash from operating activities excludes items such as interest and income taxes that are included in the U.S. measure of operating cash flow but that are widely viewed as being nonoperating activities. As a result, the U.K. measure of "operating" cash flow is more precise than is the U.S. measure. For example, as discussed earlier, reasonable people can disagree about the classification of interest and dividends received and interest paid. In recognition of this fact, *FRS 1* dictates that these items be reported in a separate category. Income taxes paid and dividends paid are also reported in their own separate categories. Finally, *FRS 1* requires U.K. companies to report an amount called *management of liquid resources*, which summarizes the net amount of cash used to purchase and sell short-term investment securities; in the United States no separate category is reported because these items are typically considered to be cash equivalents.

Example: Tesco **Tesco** is one of the largest supermarket chains in the United Kingdom, and the company is also expanding its international operations, nonfood business, and service businesses. Tesco's 2009 cash flow statement is reproduced in Exhibit 21-10. In the notes to its financial statements, Tesco reports the following about the standards it used in preparing its 2009 financial statements:

> The consolidated financial statements have been prepared in accordance with International Financial Reporting Standards (IFRS) and International Financial Reporting Interpretation Committee (IFRIC) interpretations as endorsed by the European Union.

EX 21-10 STATEMENT OF CASH FLOWS FOR TESCO FOR FISCAL 2009

Tesco
Group Cash Flow Statement
53 weeks ended 28 February 2009

	2009 £ million	2008 £ million
Cash flows from operating activities		
Cash generated from operations	4,978	4,099
Interest paid	(562)	(410)
Corporation tax paid	(456)	(346)
Net cash from operating activities	**3,960**	**3,343**
Cash flows from investing activities		
Acquisition of subsidiaries, net of cash acquired	(1,275)	(169)
Purchase of property, plant and equipment and investment property	(4,487)	(3,442)
Proceeds from sale of property, plant and equipment	994	1,056
Purchase of intangible assets	(220)	(158)
Increase in loans to joint ventures	(242)	(36)
Investments in joint ventures and associates	(30)	(61)
Investments in short-term investments	(1,233)	(360)
Proceeds from sale of short-term investments	360	—
Dividends received	69	88
Interest received	90	128
Net cash used in investing activities	**(5,974)**	**(2,954)**
Cash flows from financing activities		
Proceeds from the issue of ordinary share capital	130	138
Proceeds from sale of ordinary share capital to minority interests	—	16
Increase in borrowings	7,387	9,333
Repayment of borrowings	(2,733)	(7,593)
New finance leases	—	119
Repayment of obligations under finance leases	(18)	(32)
Dividends paid	(883)	(792)
Dividends paid to minority interests	(3)	(2)
Own shares purchased	(265)	(775)
Net cash from financing activities	**3,615**	**412**
Net increase in cash and cash equivalents	**1,601**	801
Cash and cash equivalents at beginning of year	1,788	1,042
Effect of foreign exchange rate changes	120	(55)
Cash and cash equivalents at end of year	**3,509**	**1,788**

However, as mentioned above, the international standard contained in *IAS 7* is quite flexible. It appears that Tesco's cash flow statement is an artful combination of adherence to IFRS while at the same time providing almost all the information required under the U.K. standard in *FRS 1*. For example, note the following:

- Tesco reports two operating cash flow numbers—"cash generated from operations" and "net cash from operating activities." The primary number is "net cash from operating activities," and this number satisfies the general requirements of *IAS 7*, but the "cash generated from operations" number is in conformity with the required categorizations under *FRS 1*.

- To allow financial statement users to recreate the other categories required under *FRS 1*, Tesco separately lists cash paid for interest, cash paid for taxes, cash received for dividends, and cash received for interest. This separate disclosure allows for the computation of the *FRS 1* numbers "returns on investments and servicing of finance" and "taxation."
- The line items reported in the "Cash Flows from Investing Activities" section allow the financial statement user to compute the cash flows associated with acquisitions and disposals as well as with net capital expenditures. Again, this satisfies the requirements of both *IAS 7* and *FRS 1*.

Summary of FRS 1 As seen in Tesco's cash flow statement, the provisions of *FRS 1* result in companies in the United Kingdom providing a more detailed breakdown of the types of activities that create cash inflows and outflows than is required under either U.S. GAAP or IFRS. In terms of benefits to financial statement users, it appears that the focus on cash flow reporting required by *FRS 1* makes the U.K. standard the premier cash flow standard in the world.

FASB-IASB Project on Financial Statement Presentation As mentioned in Chapter 3, the FASB and IASB are in the middle of major project aimed at restructuring the way information is displayed in the three primary financial statements. The focus of this effort is to give financial statement users a coherent picture, across all three financial statements, of a company's operating, investing, and financing activities. The FASB and IASB plan to have a final standard issued in 2011.

So, will you have to learn a completely new set of statement of cash flows principles? No. And even better, you already have a good idea of what the future statement of cash flows is going to look like because the joint FASB–IASB proposal is staying close to what you have just read about with respect to the U.K. standard, *FRS 1*. This should not be too surprising because we (the authors) having been saying for several editions of this textbook that *FRS 1* is (to quote ourselves) "the premier cash flow standard in the world." Some of the changes that will be seen in U.S. GAAP are as follows.

- This with be a true cash flow statement, not a "cash and cash equivalents" flow statement. Accordingly, the statement will focus on cash only, and any changes in short-term liquid investments will be shown separately, as in the "management of liquid resources" section required under *FRS 1*.
- The FASB and IASB have tentatively agreed to require the direct method of reporting operating cash flow. However, there will also be an additional requirement to show a reconciliation between operating cash flow and operating income. This reconciliation will look very much like the indirect method.
- Cash flows related to income taxes are to be reported separately, as under *FRS 1*.
- Cash flows associated with non-operating income, such as dividends and interest received on investments, are to be reported outside of operating activities.
- The cash flows associated with financing activities, such as interest paid, are to be reported outside of operating activities.

In summary, there will be significant changes to the details of the statement of cash flows, but your study of this chapter prepares you completely for understanding those changes.

Expanded Illustration of Statement of Cash Flows

3 **Incorporate material from the entire text into the preparation of a statement of cash flows.**

WHY Preparing a complete statement of cash flows for a company with many accounts and a variety of complex transactions requires a systematic approach to ensure that you don't miss anything.

HOW Preparation of a complex statement of cash flows is greatly aided by T-account analysis of each balance sheet account.

The basic techniques for preparing a statement of cash flows were first explained in Chapter 5 and then reviewed in the first part of this chapter. More complex circumstances have been addressed as the topics have come up in subsequent chapters. Here we present an expanded problem that illustrates many of the cash flow issues that have been treated in the text. The example also demonstrates a T-account approach to preparing the statement of cash flows.

The following comparative balance sheets for December 31, 2013, and December 31, 2012, are for Willard Company.

Willard Company
Comparative Balance Sheet
December 31, 2013 and 2012

	2013	2012
Assets		
Cash and cash equivalents	$ 42,400	$ 180,000
Investment securities (net)	47,000	0
Accounts receivable	400,000	345,000
Allowance for bad debts	(20,000)	(31,000)
Inventories	680,000	643,000
Property, plant, and equipment	810,500	743,400
Accumulated depreciation	(229,000)	(228,000)
Total assets	$1,730,900	$1,652,400
Liabilities and Stockholders' Equity		
Accounts payable	$ 46,000	$ 103,000
Short-term notes payable	100,000	120,000
Accrued liabilities	76,500	48,000
Bonds payable	250,000	278,000
Discount on bonds payable	(19,600)	(20,800)
Deferred income tax liability	108,000	97,000
Total liabilities	$ 560,900	$ 625,200
Common stock, $10 par	$ 840,000	$ 790,000
Paid-in capital in excess of par	52,000	20,000
Retained earnings	301,000	217,200
Other equity	(23,000)	0
Total stockholders' equity	$1,170,000	$1,027,200
Total liabilities and stockholders' equity	$1,730,900	$1,652,400

Additional information includes:

1. Net income for the year ended December 31, 2013, was $175,300. There were no extraordinary items.
2. During 2013, uncollectible accounts receivable of $43,000 were written off. Bad debt expense for the year was $32,000.
3. During 2013, machinery and land were purchased at a total cost of $115,100.
4. Machinery with a cost of $48,000 and a book value of $4,200 was sold for $3,600.
5. The bonds payable mature at the rate of $28,000 every year.
6. In January 2013, the company issued an additional 1,000 shares of its common stock at $14 per share.
7. In May 2013, the company declared and issued a 5% stock dividend on its outstanding stock; there were 80,000 shares of stock outstanding at the time, and the market value per share after the stock dividend was issued was $17.
8. During the year, cash dividends of $20,000 were paid on the common stock.
9. In November 2013, 1,000 shares of treasury stock were purchased for $20 per share. Willard uses the cost method.
10. The notes payable relate to operating activities.
11. During 2013, a prior-period adjustment was made to correct an understatement of depreciation on equipment. The amount of the adjustment was $3,500 after taxes.
12. During the year, investment securities were purchased for $50,000. As of December 31, 2013, the securities have a market value of $47,000. The securities are classified as available-for-sale securities.
13. Depreciation expense for the year totaled $41,300.

The preparation of the statement of cash flows will be illustrated using the indirect method of determining cash flows from operations. The analysis uses T-accounts, which are shown below and on the following page. Explanations for the individual adjustments and the related entries that are recorded in the T-accounts follow the T-accounts. These entries and T-accounts are only presented to aid in the preparation of the statement of cash flows; the entries are not actually posted to the accounts and the T-accounts do not represent actual ledger accounts. The letter preceding each explanation corresponds with that used in the T-accounts.

Cash Flows—Operating

	Debit		Credit
(a)	175,300	(o)	66,000
(g)	600	(p)	37,000
(h)	41,300	(q)	57,000
(l)	1,200	(r)	20,000
(m)	11,000		
(s)	28,500		
	77,900		

Cash Flows—Investing

	Debit		Credit
(g)	3,600	(f)	115,100
		(i)	50,000
			161,500

Cash Flows—Financing

	Debit		Credit
(n)	14,000	(b)	20,000
		(e)	20,000
		(k)	28,000
			54,000

Cash Flows—Summary

	Debit	Credit	
	77,900		Operating
		161,500	Investing
		54,000	Financing
(t)	137,600		Net Decrease in Cash
	215,500	215,500	

Cash and Cash Equivalents

Beg. bal.	180,000	(t)	137,600
End. bal.	42,400		

Investment Securities (net)

Beg. bal.	0	(j)	3,000
(i)	50,000		
End. bal.	47,000		

Accounts Receivable (net)

Beg. bal.	314,000		
(o)	66,000		
End. bal.	380,000		

Inventories

Beg. bal.	643,000		
(p)	37,000		
End. bal.	680,000		

Property, Plant, and Equipment

Beg. bal.	743,400	(g)	48,000
(f)	115,100		
End. bal.	810,500		

Accumulated Depreciation

(g)	43,800	Beg. bal.	228,000
		(d)	3,500
		(h)	41,300
		End. bal.	229,000

Accounts Payable

(q)	57,000	Beg. bal.	103,000
		End. bal.	46,000

Short-Term Notes Payable

(r)	20,000	Beg. bal.	120,000
		End. bal.	100,000

Accrued Liabilities

		Beg. bal.	48,000
		(s)	28,500
		End. bal.	76,500

Bonds Payable

(k)	28,000	Beg. bal.	278,000
		End. bal.	250,000

Discount on Bonds Payable

Beg. bal.	20,800	(l)	1,200
End. bal.	19,600		

Deferred Income Tax Liability

		Beg. bal.	97,000
		(m)	11,000
		End. bal.	108,000

Common Stock, $10 par

		Beg. bal.	790,000
		(c)	40,000
		(n)	10,000
		End. bal.	840,000

Paid-In Capital in Excess of Par

		Beg. bal.	20,000
		(c)	28,000
		(n)	4,000
		End. bal.	52,000

Retained Earnings

(b)	20,000	Beg. bal.	217,200
(c)	68,000	(a)	175,300
(d)	3,500		
		End. bal.	301,000

Other Equity

Beg. bal.	0		
(e)	20,000		
(j)	3,000		
End. bal.	23,000		

(a) Net income is recorded as follows:

Cash Flows—Operating	175,300	
Retained Earnings		175,300

(b) Cash dividends paid are recorded as follows:

Retained Earnings	20,000	
Cash Flows—Financing		20,000

(c) The 5% stock dividend results in a transfer of Retained Earnings to Common Stock at Par and to Paid-In Capital in Excess of Par. However, the stock dividend has no effect on cash. The amount of the transfer is the number of new shares (80,000 × 0.05 = 4,000) multiplied by the market value of the new shares ($17):

Retained Earnings	68,000	
Common Stock, $10 par		40,000
Paid-In Capital in Excess of Par		28,000

(d) The recognition that depreciation had been understated in prior periods is recorded by a debit to Retained Earnings and a credit to Accumulated Depreciation. This correction of earnings of prior periods has no effect on cash:

Retained Earnings	3,500	
Accumulated Depreciation		3,500

(e) The purchase of the treasury shares is a financing activity and, because the cost method is used, is recorded as follows:

Other Equity	20,000	
Cash Flows—Financing		20,000

(f) The purchase of the machinery and land is recorded as follows:

Property, Plant, and Equipment	115,100	
Cash Flows—Investing		115,100

(g) The amount of cash received in the sale of machinery was $3,600, and this is shown as cash provided by investing activities. The sale involved a loss of $600. Because this loss reduced net income but involved no cash effects beyond the $3,600 received, the $600 must be added to cash flows from operating activities to avoid understating the cash effect of the transaction:

Cash Flows—Investing	3,600	
Accumulated Depreciation	43,800	
Cash Flows—Operating	600	
Property, Plant, and Equipment		48,000

(h) Depreciation reduces net income but does not involve cash, so the following adjustment to cash flows is necessary:

Cash Flows—Operating	41,300	
Accumulated Depreciation		41,300

(i) The purchase of investment securities that are available-for-sale or held-to-maturity is an investing activity; purchase of trading securities is usually an operating activity. The necessary entry is:

Investment Securities—Available-for-Sale	50,000	
Cash Flows—Investing		50,000

(j) A decline in the market value of the investment securities caused them to be written down. Because the securities are classified as available-for-sale, the $3,000 write-down reduced equity but did not impact net income; no cash is involved:

Other Equity	3,000	
Investment Securities—Available-for-Sale		3,000

(k) Bonds retired for $28,000 during the year resulted in an outflow of cash for financing activities:

Bonds Payable	28,000	
Cash Flows—Financing		28,000

(l) The amortization of bond discount represents another item that reduced net income but did not involve cash. The necessary adjustment to cash flows is as follows:

Cash Flows—Operating	1,200	
Discount on Bonds Payable		1,200

(m) The $11,000 increase in Deferred Income Tax Liability is added back to cash flows provided by operating activities because it represents income taxes recognized as an expense of the current period for which no cash was paid:

Cash Flows—Operating	11,000	
Deferred Income Tax Liability		11,000

(n) The issuance of new common stock is shown as an increase in cash from financing activities:

Cash Flows—Financing	14,000	
Common Stock, $10 par		10,000
Paid-In Capital in Excess of Par		4,000

Cash flows from operating activities must be adjusted for changes in the levels of current assets and current liabilities. These adjustments follow. The simplest way to handle bad debt expense and account write-offs is to make the adjustment using the net receivable balance. If this is done and the indirect method is used, no special adjustments are required.

(o)	Accounts Receivable (net)	66,000	
	Cash Flows—Operating		66,000
(p)	Inventories	37,000	
	Cash Flows—Operating		37,000
(q)	Accounts Payable	57,000	
	Cash Flows—Operating		57,000
(r)	Short-Term Notes Payable	20,000	
	Cash Flows—Operating		20,000
(s)	Cash Flows—Operating	28,500	
	Accrued Liabilities		28,500

After all changes in account balances for the year have been reconciled, the balances in the three cash flows T-accounts are transferred to a summary account. The $137,600 excess credit amount in this summary account represents a net decrease in cash for the year. The final entry records this decrease in the cash account and completes the analysis:

(t)	Net Decrease in Cash	137,600	
	Cash and Cash Equivalents		137,600

The formal statement of cash flows is prepared using the data in the three cash flows T-accounts.

Willard Company
Statement of Cash Flows
For the Year Ended December 31, 2013

Cash flows from operating activities:	
Net income	$ 175,300
Adjustments:	
Loss on sale of machinery	600
Depreciation expense	41,300
Amortization of bond discount	1,200
Increase in deferred income tax liability	11,000
Increase in net accounts receivable	(66,000)
Increase in inventories	(37,000)

(Continued)

Decrease in accounts payable	(57,000)	
Decrease in short-term notes payable	(20,000)	
Increase in accrued liabilities	28,500	
Net cash provided by operating activities		$ 77,900
Cash flows from investing activities:		
Purchase of machinery and land	$(115,100)	
Sale of machinery	3,600	
Purchase of investment securities	(50,000)	
Net cash used in investing activities		(161,500)
Cash flows from financing activities:		
Payment of cash dividends	$ (20,000)	
Purchase of treasury stock	(20,000)	
Retirement of bonds payable	(28,000)	
Issuance of common stock	14,000	
Net cash used in financing activities		(54,000)
Net decrease in cash		$(137,600)
Cash and cash equivalents, beginning of year		180,000
Cash and cash equivalents, end of year		$ 42,400

An essential element in the preparation of a statement of cash flows is the systematic consideration of every single item listed in the balance sheet and the income statement. An advantage of the T-account approach illustrated in this Willard Company example is that the approach forces you to explain the changes in balance during the year of every single balance sheet account. Use of a systematic approach such as this ensures that you don't overlook any potential inflows or outflows of cash as you prepare the statement of cash flows.

Cash Flow Analysis

4 **Perform a detailed case analysis of a company's operations and performance using cash flow data.**

WHY **Analysis of cash flow data can add additional insight into the performance of a company, over and above what can be learned by analyzing the balance sheet and the income statement.**

HOW **For many nonpublic companies in the United States, only a balance sheet and an income statement are prepared internally. Using the techniques illustrated in this chapter and throughout the text, these balance sheet and income statement data can be used to generate cash flow data.**

In this section, we will use the tools that we have developed for preparing a statement of cash flows to perform a detailed case analysis of a company's operations and performance. This analysis will be done using case data for a fictitious company, Kamila Software.

This section is structured as follows. First, background data, financial statements, and more detailed specifics about Kamila Software are given. Then a decision context will be explained in which we will take on the role of consultants. In our consulting role, we will be asked to consider several specific aspects of Kamila Software's performance and finally to make a recommendation about Kamila's financial viability and attractiveness as a business partner. This case material is then followed by a detailed solution and an explanation.

Ryan McVay/Photodisc/Getty Images

Cash flow data are extremely useful in analyzing a company's operations and gauging its performance.

Kamila Software: Background, Financial Statements, and Extra Details

Kamila Software develops, produces, and sells software. The company headquarters is located in Panaca, Nevada. In addition to developing, producing, and selling software, Kamila also maintains a team of consultants who are engaged in a variety of systems consulting projects, some lasting for several years. Five years ago, Kamila established an office in Kazakhstan; this office employs programmers who are integrated online with programming teams working at company headquarters in Panaca.

Kamila's headquarters campus consists of two buildings. The company office building houses the company executives, the administrative staff, and all of the programmers and consultants. The company factory, situated next door, contains the machinery for actually burning the software CDs in large quantities and for packaging the software. The factory building also contains the storage and shipping warehouse.

Kamila Software's balance sheets (for 2010 through 2013) and income statements (for 2011 through 2013) are contained in Exhibits 21-11 and 21-12, respectively.

EX 21-11 KAMILA SOFTWARE BALANCE SHEETS: 2010–2013

Balance Sheet	2013	2012	2011	2010
Cash	$ 23	$ 10	$ 15	$ 10
Accounts receivable	600	60	100	80
Inventory	5	50	30	20
Capitalized software development costs, net	192	255	165	67
Gross PPE	360	500	500	440
Accumulated depreciation	(116)	(129)	(82)	(35)
Total assets	$1,064	$ 746	$728	$582
Accounts, salaries, and miscellaneous operating payables	$ 100	$ 75	$ 30	$ 20
Rent payable	100	0	0	0
Unearned consulting revenue	20	80	100	150
Warranty obligation	38	118	113	50
Dividends payable	50	0	0	0
Long-term debt	264	270	275	280
Environmental obligation	58	153	52	17
Paid-in capital	397	171	127	100
Retained earnings	37	(121)	31	(35)
Total liabilities and equities	$1,064	$ 746	$728	$582

EX 21-12 KAMILA SOFTWARE INCOME STATEMENTS: 2011–2013

Income Statement	2013	2012	2011
Software sales revenue	$1,050	$ 700	$1,000
Consulting revenue	350	200	300
Total revenue	$1,400	$ 900	$1,300
Cost of software sales	$ (220)	$ (150)	$ (210)
Salary and administrative expense	(600)	(150)	(450)
Rental expense	(100)	(100)	(100)
Software research expense	(20)	(200)	(150)
Warranty expense	(40)	(70)	(100)
Environmental expense	(25)	(150)	(50)
Foreign exchange gain (loss)	15	0	0
Gain (loss) on PPE disposal	10	0	0
Amortization of software development costs	(143)	(110)	(52)
Depreciation expense	(45)	(47)	(47)
Interest expense	(24)	(25)	(25)
Total expenses	(1,192)	(1,002)	(1,184)
Net income	$ 208	$ (102)	$ 116

Additional details about Kamila Software's operations in 2011 through 2013 are as follows:

1. In 2013, Kamila's accounts receivable balance includes amounts related to both regular software sales and consulting projects. In prior years, the accounts receivable balance included only receivables from regular software sales. The year-by-year detail is as follows:

	2013	2012	2011	2010
Regular software sales	$400	$60	$100	$80
Consulting projects	200	0	0	0
Total accounts receivable	$600	$60	$100	$80

2. Over the past three years (2011 through 2013), Kamila's systems consultants have worked on a total of nine different projects (designated A through I). The total contract price, and the amount of revenue recognized in each year with respect to these projects, are given in the following table.

	Total Contract Price	Revenue Recognized Each Year		
		2013	2012	2011
A	$200	$ 0.0	$ 0.0	$200.0
B	150	7.5	45.0	45.0
C	100	5.0	55.0	5.0
D	500	100.0	100.0	50.0
E	300	75.0	0.0	0.0
F	250	62.5	0.0	0.0
G	100	25.0	0.0	0.0
H	200	50.0	0.0	0.0
I	100	25.0	0.0	0.0
Total		$350.0	$200.0	$300.0

3. Both of Kamila's buildings are leased. Both leases were signed on January 1, 2010. The factory is leased under a capital lease arrangement; the office building is leased under an operating lease arrangement. The office building lease payments are $100 per year. Under the office building lease contract, Kamila can elect to defer an annual payment for one year in exchange for a 20% payment surcharge. The factory lease payment is $30 per year. The required lease payment disclosure is given below.

A summary of future minimum lease payments under capital leases and noncancellable operating leases with a remaining term in excess of one year at December 31, 2013, is as follows:

	Capital Leases	Operating Leases
2014	$ 30	$ 220
2015	30	100
2016	30	100
2017	30	100
2018	30	100
Thereafter	330	1,100
	$480	$1,720

At December 31, 2013, the present value of future minimum lease payments for capital lease obligations was $264.

4. In December 2013, Kamila sold some land that it had held since the company's inception. The land was in the neighboring town of Pioche, Nevada, and had been sometimes spoken of as a spot for future expansion. The land had a historical cost of $50 and was appraised at $80 just before the sale. In the same transaction, Kamila also sold some of its manufacturing equipment. No property, plant, or equipment was purchased in 2013.
5. An important part of Kamila's business is developing new software. As required under FASB ASC Section 985-20-25, Kamila expenses all software research costs incurred up until technological feasibility has been established. Software development costs incurred after technological feasibility are capitalized and amortized over three years.
6. In order to increase customer satisfaction in its software, Kamila offers a broad warranty with each piece of software it sells. This warranty has become Kamila's trademark. Under the warranty, Kamila not only agrees to replace defective software, but also agrees to reimburse customers for the reasonable costs they incur as a result of a failure by a piece of Kamila software still under warranty. For example, Kamila has paid a customer for the direct and indirect costs associated with an inventory outage when Kamila's inventory software failed. Kamila has also paid for extra accounting help at a company that used a failed piece of Kamila payroll software.
7. One of the unfortunate facts about Kamila's software production process is that a variety of toxic materials are generated as by-products. These toxic materials include benzene, dioxin, and iocaine powder. Some of these toxic materials have leaked into the ground under Kamila's factory. The management of Kamila is aware that Kamila's factory site will eventually have to be completely cleaned up. In fact, Kamila pays an outside cleanup firm to do some environmental remediation work each year. An estimate of the total cleanup cost is used at the end of each year to calculate an annual environmental cleanup expense.

8. Of the "Accounts, Salaries, and Miscellaneous Operating Payables" balance of $100 at December 31, 2013, a total of $25 relates to Kamila's Kazakhstan office. Kamila had some contract disputes in 2012 with its Kazakh employees and so has withheld $25 in salaries (for about 18 months now) pending a resolution of the disputes. Actually, the original amount withheld was the equivalent of $40 (which is included in the December 31, 2012, Salaries Payable amount); however, because the salaries are payable in Kazakh tenge and the tenge has declined in value drastically over the past 18 months, the recorded amount of the obligation is now just $25.

The Decision Context: Is Kamila a Financially Viable Software Partner?

It is May 15, 2014, and you have been hired by a large manufacturer, ManuFab, Inc., which is considering entering into a long-term strategic alliance with Kamila Software. Specifically, ManuFab is planning to adopt robotic technology in its manufacturing facilities and will need continuing technical software design, programming, and support for the foreseeable future. It is extremely important to ManuFab to have a financially viable software partner. Kamila Software is the lead candidate for this partnership.

The in-house analysis team at ManuFab is very positive about Kamila Software based on a traditional financial statement analysis. You sense that you have been hired primarily to provide an "independent" outside stamp of approval to bolster ManuFab's management team's proposal to the board of directors. Keep in mind that ManuFab's in-house analysis suggests that this alliance with Kamila is a winner. Your evidence to the contrary, if you find any, must be clear and persuasive.

Consider the following issues as you prepare your recommendation to ManuFab's board regarding the advisability of entering into a long-term strategic alliance with Kamila Software.

1. What traditional financial ratios indicate that Kamila Software is in strong financial health?
2. Using the financial statement data and additional information that you have, prepare a complete statement of cash flows (operating, investing, and financing) for Kamila Software for 2011, 2012, and 2013.
3. Compare actual cash flows to the income statement amounts for the following items. In particular, look at the trends over the 3-year period from 2011 through 2013.
   (a) Software sales
   (b) Consulting project revenue
   (c) Software development costs
   (d) Warranties
   (e) Environmental cleanup
4. Kamila Software is a private company and has never been audited by external auditors. Is there any specific evidence in Kamila's reported financial statements that the company's accounting practices are aggressive or deceptive?
5. What is your overall recommendation—should ManuFab enter into a long-term strategic alliance with Kamila Software? Explain your recommendation.

Kamila Software: Solution

The discussion and analysis of the Kamila Software case follows the sequence given in the questions above.

Traditional Financial Ratios A quick indication of Kamila's performance measured using traditional financial ratios comes from computing the company's return on equity for the three years 2011, 2012, and 2013. In these calculations, average total equity is used in the denominator.

	2013	2012	2011
Return on equity	86.0%	(98.1%)	104.0%

This is quite an erratic series, but the very strong numbers in 2011 and 2013 may indicate that 2012 was just a one-time blip. The average annual return on equity for these three years is 30.6%, which is very strong.

Another factor to consider in deciding whether to enter into a partnership with Kamila Software is the company's financial structure. Kamila's debt ratio for the past four years is as follows:

	2013	2012	2011	2010
Debt ratio	59.2%	93.3%	78.3%	88.8%

These numbers definitely show a more comfortable position in 2013 relative to the preceding years. One can interpret these numbers as suggesting that Kamila is in a strong financial position to move forward in the years following 2013.

In terms of profitability measures, of course the net loss in 2012 is of some concern. However, the strong profits in 2013 suggest that Kamila has put the 2012 problems into the past. The gross profit percentage for software sales is very stable, as shown below.

	2013	2012	2011
Software gross profit percentage	79.0%	78.6%	79.0%

In summary, Kamila has an extremely high return on equity, has reduced its leverage to a normal level, and has demonstrated very stable profitability in its software sales. The bad year in 2012 may have just been an aberration.

Statement of Cash Flows The balance sheet and income statement data, coupled with the additional data given and with the cash flow statement preparation skills covered earlier in the chapter, lead to the statements of cash flows for Kamila Software for 2011, 2012, and 2013 contained in Exhibit 21-13. In terms of preparing these statements of cash flows, most of the items are straightforward, and you should be able to figure everything out by looking at the balance sheets and income statements. Additional explanation of a few items is given below.

Foreign currency gain in 2013. Note that the foreign currency gain is NOT subtracted in the computation of operating cash flow. The foreign currency gain does not involve any cash flow (just a reduction in the reported value of salaries payable), so there is a temptation to eliminate it as a noncash item. However, eliminating the gain but retaining the $15 reduction in salaries payable (a subset of the total operating payables amount) gives the impression of a cash outflow; in the indirect method calculations, a salaries payable reduction leads to a decrease in operating cash flow. So, we can subtract the gain and also adjust the change in salaries payable to reflect this noncash reduction, or we can simply include the total change in salaries payable and leave the gain in net income in

EX 21-13 KAMILA SOFTWARE STATEMENTS OF CASH FLOWS: 2011–2013

	2013	2012	2011
Operating Activities			
Net income	208	(102)	116
Plus depreciation	45	47	47
Plus amortization of software development costs	143	110	52
Less gain/plus loss on PPE disposal	(10)	0	0
(Increase) decrease in accounts receivable	(540)	40	(20)
(Increase) decrease in inventory	45	(20)	(10)
Increase (decrease) in accounts payable, etc.	25	45	10
Increase (decrease) in rent payable	100	0	0
Increase (decrease) in unearned revenue	(60)	(20)	(50)
Increase (decrease) in warranty obligation	(80)	5	63
Increase (decrease) in environmental obligation	(95)	101	35
Net cash flow from operating activities	(219)	206	243
Investing Activities			
Cash received from sale of PPE	92	0	0
Cash paid to purchase PPE	0	0	(60)
Cash paid for capitalized software development costs	(80)	(200)	(150)
Net cash flow from investing activities	12	(200)	(210)
Financing Activities			
Issuance (repayment) of long-term debt	(6)	(5)	(5)
Cash from issuance of shares of stock	226	44	27
Cash paid for dividends	0	(50)	(50)
Net cash flow from financing activities	220	(11)	(28)
Net change in cash	13	(5)	5
Beginning cash balance	10	15	10
Ending cash balance	23	10	15

the computation of operating cash flow. Basically, the reduction in salaries payable looks like an outflow of cash, but it isn't, and the gain looks like an inflow of cash, but it isn't. Leaving both of these items in the calculation of operating cash flow allows them to offset one another. This treatment is similar to what is sometimes done with the realized and unrealized gains and losses on trading securities in the computation of operating cash flow, as explained in Chapter 14.

Cash from the sale of property, plant, and equipment in 2013. From Note 4 given on page 21-36, it appears that land costing $50 was sold for $80. The gain on this portion of the sale was $30. This sale occurred in conjunction with the sale of some manufacturing equipment. The book value of the equipment sold can be computed using the following T-accounts.

Property, Plant, and Equipment

Beginning	500		
		50	Cost of land
		??	Cost of equipment
Ending	360		

Accumulated Depreciation

		129	Beginning
Accum. depr. on equip. sold	??	45	Depr. exp.
		116	Ending

From these T-accounts, we can compute that the cost of the equipment sold was $90 and the accumulated depreciation was $58, making a book value of $32 ($90 – $58). From the income statement, we see that there was an overall gain of $10 on the sale of the land and equipment. Because there was a gain of $30 ($80 appraised value – $50 cost) on the land alone, the equipment portion of the sale must have resulted in a loss of $20. The total cash proceeds from the sale can be computed as follows:

	Land	Equipment
Book value	$50	$ 32
Plus gain/minus loss	30	(20)
Cash proceeds	$80	$ 12

The total cash proceeds is $92 ($80 land + $12 equipment), which is reported in the Investing Activities section of Kamila's 2013 statement of cash flows.

Cash paid for capitalized software development costs. The amount of cash paid for capitalized software development costs is computed using the beginning and ending balances in the capitalized software development cost asset account and the annual amount of costs amortized, as follows:

Capitalized Software Development Costs, net	2013	2012	2011
Beginning balance	$255	$165	$ 67
Less amortization for the year	143	110	52
Balance without any additions for the year	$112	$ 55	$ 15
Cash paid for software development costs capitalized during the year	**80**	**200**	**150**
Ending balance	$192	$255	$165

In these calculations, all of the information comes from the balance sheet and the income statement with the exception of cash paid for capitalized software development costs, which is the plug figure in each annual computation.

Cash paid for dividends. As illustrated in earlier examples, the amount of dividends can be computed using the change in retained earnings during the year. The computation for 2013 is shown below.

Retained Earnings

	Debit	Credit	
Beginning—2013	121		
Dividends—2013	50	208	Net income—2013
		37	Ending—2013

The plug figure in the T-account is the $50 in dividends declared during 2013. However, note in the balance sheet that the dividends payable account increases from $0 to $50 during the year. Accordingly, for the year 2013, the amount of cash paid for dividends was $0 because the entire $50 in dividends declared for the year was still unpaid as of year-end.

Overall, Kamila's statement of cash flows presents very bad news. Operating cash flow drops from a positive amount of $243 and $206 in 2011 and 2012, respectively, to a negative amount of $219 in 2013. In light of these numbers, the net loss reported in 2012 no longer looks like a one-time stumble from which Kamila has recovered. Instead, the loss in 2012 was just a precursor to the substantial negative operating cash flow in 2013. In fact, we now look with some skepticism upon the positive net income of $208 reported by Kamila in 2013. The negative operating cash flow for 2013 makes us wonder whether Kamila achieved the positive reported income through aggressive accrual accounting assumptions rather than through improved operating performance. We need to do some further analysis on individual items in order to see whether our suspicions are justified.

Comparison of Cash Flow and Accrual Amounts When a company has a strong incentive to favorably bias its accrual assumptions in order to make it look good on paper for an initial public offering (IPO) or a big loan application, cash flow data can provide a reality check on the underlying performance of the company. A comparison of cash flow and accrual amounts for several important items for Kamila Software is given below.

Software sales. The Operating Activities sections of the statements of cash flows shown in Exhibit 21-13 are prepared using the indirect method. In this case, we can gain additional insight into Kamila Software's operations by doing some direct method calculations. The annual calculations of cash collected for software sales are as follows:

Software Sales	2013	2012	2011
Reported software sales	$1,050	$700	$1,000
Plus beginning accounts receivable for software sales	60	100	80
Less ending accounts receivable for software sales	(400)	(60)	(100)
Cash collected for software sales	$ 710	$740	$ 980

The news is not good. Software sales revenue, as reported in the income statement, made a recovery in 2013. However, the cash flow data suggest that Kamila's fortunes have been steadily declining since 2011. These numbers give us some cause for concern and make us wonder whether the accrual numbers in the income statement have been boosted through favorable revenue recognition assumptions.

Consulting revenue. The annual calculations of cash collected from consulting customers are as follows:

Consulting Revenue	2013	2012	2011
Reported consulting revenue	$ 350	$ 200	$ 300
Plus beginning accounts receivable for consulting	0	0	0
Less ending accounts receivable for consulting	(200)	0	0
Less beginning unearned consulting revenue	(80)	(100)	(150)
Plus ending unearned consulting revenue	20	80	100
Cash collected from consulting customers	$ 90	$ 180	$ 250

As with the cash collected from software customers, the cash flow numbers for consulting have been steadily deteriorating since 2011. The income statement gives the impression that 2013 was a recovery year. In contrast, the cash flow numbers suggest that 2013 represents the continuation of a negative trend.

Software development costs. The calculation of the amount of cash paid for capitalized software development was illustrated previously. The software research costs are expensed as incurred. Accordingly, the computation of total cash paid for software research and development for each year is as follows:

Total Software Development Costs	2013	2012	2011
Cash paid for capitalized software development costs	$ 80	$200	$150
Cash paid for software research costs expensed immediately	20	200	150
Total cash paid for software research and development	$100	$400	$300

A generous and optimistic way to interpret this trend is that Kamila is becoming more efficient at doing software research and development and was therefore able to cut down on expenditures in 2013. However, a more likely interpretation is that the continued downturn in business, indicated by the cash inflow calculations illustrated above, led Kamila to cut back drastically on software research and development in 2013. This is an ominous sign in terms of Kamila's ability to stay competitive and innovative in future years.

Warranties. The warranty expense estimates reported in Kamila Software's income statement indicate that the expense has declined steadily in each year since 2011. The cash outflow numbers, computed below, show exactly the opposite.

Warranties	2013	2012	2011
Beginning warranty obligation	$118	$ 113	$ 50
Plus warranty expense	40	70	100
Less ending warranty obligation	(38)	(118)	(113)
Cash paid for warranties	$120	$ 65	$ 37

One could make the argument that the increase in cash paid for warranties is just a natural result of the delayed nature of the warranties—the sales are first made and then the warranty-related expenditures occur in subsequent years. To explore this possibility, a subsequent section contains a brief analysis of the accrual assumptions underlying the reported warranty expense.

Environmental cleanup. The annual cash flow calculations for environmental remediation costs are as follows:

Environmental Cleanup	2013	2012	2011
Beginning environmental obligation	$153	$ 52	$ 17
Plus environmental expense	25	150	50
Less ending environmental obligation	(58)	(153)	(52)
Cash paid for environmental remediation	$120	$ 49	$ 15

As with the warranty expenditures, the cash paid for environmental remediation has increased each year, with a very large increase in 2013. This is just one more piece of cash flow evidence that suggests that 2013 was a catastrophic year for Kamila Software.

Evaluation of Accounting Practices As mentioned earlier, the cash flow numbers can provide a reality check when there is a chance that the accrual assumptions have been strategically biased by management. In the case of Kamila Software, the cash flow data certainly do indicate that 2013 was a terrible year rather than an awesome recovery year as suggested in the income statement. Because the cash flow data have raised our suspicions, this section contains a closer look at some of Kamila's accrual assumptions.

Consulting revenue. The total contract price and annual revenue numbers for Kamila's nine consulting contracts (A through I) can be used to compute the annual completion percentage for each contract as follows:

Percentage Completed	2013	2012	2011
A	0%	0%	100%
B	5	30	30
C	5	55	5
D	20	20	10
E	25	0	0
F	25	0	0
G	25	0	0
H	25	0	0
I	25	0	0

Because our suspicions about Kamila's accrual assumptions have been aroused, given the poor operating cash flow performance in 2013, let's look at these completion percentages with a skeptical eye. First, we note that Kamila did not complete any contracts in 2013. The small amounts estimated for Contracts B and C make us wonder whether these contracts are really even active any more. But the most troubling evidence is the 25% assumed completion percentage for each one of the five contracts begun in 2013 (Contracts E through I). It is highly unlikely that each one of these contracts would be exactly one quarter completed. It is more likely that Kamila has hurriedly signed these contracts and then made arbitrary estimates of completion in order to bolster reported revenue. This scenario is supported by the cash flow evidence, which indicates that cash collected from consulting customers in 2013 was at an all-time low of $90.

Operating lease payment. In the income statement, we see that Kamila reported rental expense of $100 associated with its operating lease in 2013. Because the rent payable amount at the end of 2013 is $100, we can deduce that Kamila didn't actually make any operating lease payment in 2013. This deduction is supported by the lease note disclosure, which shows that Kamila must pay $220 in 2013. This $220 includes the $100 late payment for 2013, the $100 regular payment for 2014, and a $20 late payment fee as mentioned in the description of the lease contract. The fact that no payment was made in 2013 is consistent with the other evidence suggesting that Kamila was desperately trying to cut back on cash expenditures during the year. From an accrual accounting standpoint, the expense for the year should probably be $120 (with a corresponding $120 rent payable) to reflect both the regular payment amount and the $20 late fee.

Proportion of software R&D expenditures capitalized and expensed. In the previous section, we computed the total cash paid for software research and development for each year, and we were disturbed to see a substantial drop in R&D spending in 2013. Using those same numbers, the percentage of software R&D expenditures that were capitalized in each year can be computed as follows:

	2013	2012	2011
Percentage of software R&D capitalized	80%	50%	50%

By assuming that 80% of the R&D in 2013 was completed after technological feasibility was established, Kamila was able to capitalize \$80 (\$100 × 0.80) in R&D costs, rather than the \$50 (\$100 × 0.50) that would have been capitalized if the same percentage had been used in 2013 that had been used in 2011 and 2012. Kamila may have used this generous 80% assumption in order to reduce reported software research expense and thus boost reported profit in 2013.

Warranty expense as a percentage of software sales. Kamila's reported warranty expense, as a percentage of sales, is as follows:

	2013	2012	2011
Warranty expense as a percentage of software sales	3.8%	10.0%	10.0%

The cash flow numbers indicate that Kamila spent \$120 on warranty-related costs in 2013, up from \$65 in 2012. At the same time warranty costs were going up, Kamila's estimate of warranty expense, as a percentage of software sales, was reduced dramatically, from 10.0% to 3.8%. Again, this looks like a favorable accrual assumption made to boost reported income in 2013.

Environmental expense. Kamila's reported environmental expense, as a percentage of sales, is as follows:

	2013	2012	2011
Environmental expense as a percentage of software sales	2.4%	21.4%	5.0%

As with warranties, the cash paid for environmental remediation costs was actually up in 2013 compared to 2012, from \$49 to \$120. At the same time, environmental expense as a percentage of software sales was reduced to 2.4%. These calculations make it appear that 2012 was a "big-bath" year, with a large expense recognized in 2012 in order to be able to recognize lower expenses in subsequent years.

Overall Recommendation The evidence is overwhelming—ManuFab should NOT enter into a strategic partnership with Kamila Software. The operating cash flow evidence indicates that 2013 was a very bad year for Kamila. These cash flow data caused us to look closely at Kamila's accrual assumptions in 2013, and we found that those assumptions were favorably biased to make 2013 look like a year of record-breaking profits. Our recommendation to ManuFab? Stay away from Kamila Software.

The point of the Kamila Software case analysis is to show you how useful your cash flow analysis skills can be. Many people are skilled in computing and interpreting traditional financial ratios based on the balance sheet and the income statement. You can set yourself apart as a true master of the financial statements if you have the added skill of performing cash flow analysis.

SOLUTIONS TO OPENING SCENARIO QUESTIONS

1. Moore's Law is a prediction by Intel cofounder Gordon Moore that computing power would double every two years. Moore's Law is cited in a host of variations—density of transistors, memory capacity, and so forth. And sometimes the doubling time period is given as 18 months rather than two years.
2. "Capex," short for "capital expenditures," is the amount of cash paid by a company to buy new property, plant, and equipment and to make business acquisitions.
3. "Free cash flow" is the difference between the cash flow generated by operations and the cash flow used for capital expenditures. Free cash flow represents the discretionary cash flow generated by the company, above the cash needed for regular business operations and long-term asset acquisition.
4. As seen at the bottom of Intel's statement of cash flows shown in Exhibit 21-1, cash paid for income taxes in 2009 was $943 million.

SOLUTION TO USING THE FASB'S CODIFICATION

FASB ASC paragraph 230-10-45-22 says the following: "Certain cash receipts and payments may have aspects of more than one class of cash flows. For example, a cash payment may pertain to an item that could be considered either inventory or a productive asset. If so, the appropriate classification shall depend on the activity that is likely to be the predominant source of cash flows for the item. For example, the acquisition and sale of equipment to be used by the entity or rented to others generally are investing activities. However, equipment sometimes is acquired or produced to be used by the entity or rented to others for a short period and then sold. In those circumstances, the acquisition or production and subsequent sale of those assets shall be considered operating activities."

So, the key issue here is the "predominant source of cash flows for the item." For the large equipment purchased strictly for rental, the equipment itself is a long-term asset of the company, and its purchase is an investing cash outflow. For the small equipment that is purchased to be rented for a short time and then sold, the equipment is more like inventory. Accordingly, the cash used to purchase these equipment items is a cash outflow from operating activities.

REVIEW CHAPTER 21

LEARNING OBJECTIVES

1 Prepare a complete statement of cash flows and provide the required supplemental disclosures.

Basic information to prepare the three sections of the cash flow statement comes from the following portions of the balance sheet and the income statement:

- Operating—income statement and current assets and liabilities
- Investing—long-term assets
- Financing—long-term liabilities and owners' equity

Preparation of a complete cash flow statement is not done until each income statement item has been considered, all changes in balance sheet items have been explained, and the net change in cash has been exactly reconciled.

Six steps to preparing a cash flow statement are as follows:

1. Determine the change in cash (including cash equivalents). This is the target number.
2. Operating activities—analyze each income statement item and the changes in all current operating assets and operating liabilities (current and noncurrent).
3. Investing activities—analyze the changes in all noncurrent assets as well as changes in all nonoperating current assets.
4. Financing activities—analyze the changes in all noncurrent liabilities, all owners' equity accounts, and all nonoperating current liabilities.
5. Prepare a formal statement of cash flows, reconciling the beginning and ending cash balances. If the sum of operating, investing, and financing activities does not equal the total balance sheet change in cash, something in the cash flow statement is wrong. Fix it.
6. Prepare supplemental disclosure, including the disclosure of any significant investing or financing transactions that did not involve cash.

2 **Understand the differences among cash flow statements prepared according to U.S. GAAP and IASB standards.**

The primary differences in cash flow reporting around the world relate to alternative classifications of selected cash transactions. *IAS 7* closely matches the provisions of the U.S. cash flow reporting standard, with the difference being greater flexibility in classifying cash transactions such as interest and dividends paid and received and income taxes paid. In the United Kingdom, *Financial Reporting Standard (FRS) 1* specifies eight different categories for classifying cash flow transactions and represents the most innovative and, probably, the most useful standard for cash flow reporting currently in existence in the world.

3 **Incorporate material from the entire text into the preparation of a statement of cash flows.**

Preparation of a complex statement of cash flows is greatly aided by T-account analysis of each balance sheet account. Once the cash flow implications of each balance sheet account change have been categorized, the formal statement of cash flows can be prepared from the summary T-accounts for operating, investing, and financing activities.

4 **Perform a detailed case analysis of a company's operations and performance using cash flow data.**

Analysis of cash flow data can add additional insight into the performance of a company, over and above what can be learned by analyzing the balance sheet and the income statement. Cash flow analysis is particularly important when a company has a special incentive (such as an upcoming IPO or loan application) to favorably bias the accrual assumptions.

FASB-IASB CODIFICATION SUMMARY

ifrs

Topic	FASB Accounting Standards Codification	Original FASB Standard	Corresponding IASB Standard	Differences between U.S. GAAP and IFRS
Definition of cash equivalents	*Section 230-10-20 (Glossary) – Cash equivalents*	*SFAS No. 95 par. 8*	*IAS 7 par. 7*	No substantial differences
Noncash investing and financing activities	*Section 230-10-50 par. 3*	*SFAS No. 95 par. 32*	*IAS 7 par. 43*	No substantial differences
Direct and indirect methods	*Section 230-10-45 par. 25,28*	*SFAS No. 95 par. 27-28*	*IAS 7 par. 18-19*	No substantial differences
Classification of interest paid	*Section 230-10-45 par. 17(d)*	*SFAS No. 95 par. 23(d)*	*IAS 7 par. 33*	U.S. GAAP – operating IFRS – operating or financing
Classification of income taxes paid	*Section 230-10-45 par. 17(c)*	*SFAS No. 95 par. 23(c)*	*IAS 7 par. 35*	U.S. GAAP – operating IFRS – operating, investing, or financing
Classification of interest received	*Section 230-10-45 par. 16(b)*	*SFAS No. 95 par. 22(b)*	*IAS 7 par. 33*	U.S. GAAP – operating IFRS – operating or investing
Classification of dividends received	*Section 230-10-45 par. 16(b)*	*SFAS No. 95 par. 22(b)*	*IAS 7 par. 33*	U.S. GAAP – operating IFRS – operating or investing
Classification of dividends paid	*Section 230-10-45 par. 15(a)*	*SFAS No. 95 par. 20(a)*	*IAS 7 par. 34*	U.S. GAAP – financing IFRS – operating or financing

QUESTIONS

1. When preparing a statement of cash flows, the sum of cash flow from operations, cash flow from investing, and cash flow from financing should equal what number?
2. What is the most common event that causes the accounts receivable account to increase? decrease?
3. What is the most common event that causes the inventory account to increase? decrease?
4. What is the most common event that causes the accounts payable account to increase? decrease?
5. What is the most common event that causes the equipment account to increase? decrease?
6. What is the most common event that causes the accumulated depreciation account to increase? decrease?
7. What is the most common event that causes the long-term debt account to increase? decrease?
8. What is the most common event that causes the capital stock account to increase? decrease?
9. What is the most common event that causes the retained earnings account to increase? decrease?
10. When using the indirect method, why is depreciation added back to the net income figure when computing cash flow from operations?
11. When using the indirect method, why is a gain subtracted from net income and a loss added to net income when computing cash flow from operations?

12. Why is an increase in accounts receivable shown as a decrease in cash when computing cash flow from operations?
13. Why is a decrease in inventory shown as an increase in cash when computing cash flow from operations?
14. Why is a decrease in accounts payable shown as a decrease in cash when computing cash flow from operations?
15. When the indirect method is used to report cash flow from operations, what two operating cash flow items must be disclosed either on the cash flow statement or in the notes?
16. With respect to the statement of cash flows, what is a reconciliation schedule, and when is it required?
17. The international cash flow standard (*IAS 7*) treats several items differently than does the U.S. cash flow standard. Identify those items, and discuss how they are treated differently.
18. What are the eight categories in a statement of cash flows prepared according to the U.K. standard (*FRS 1*)?

PRACTICE EXERCISES

Use the following information for Practices 21-1 through 21-3.

The company provides the following information:

	December 31	January 1
Accounts Payable	$68,600	$72,300
Inventory	47,800	43,100
Accounts Receivable	95,000	99,700

(a) All purchases of inventory were on account.
(b) Sales for the year were $995,000.
(c) Cost of goods sold for the year was $451,000.

Practice 21-1
LO1

Cash Collected from Customers
Compute how much cash was collected from customers during the year.

Practice 21-2
LO1

Amount of Inventory Purchases
Compute how much inventory was purchased during the year. (*Hint:* Remember that all purchases of inventory were on account.)

Practice 21-3
LO1

Cash Paid for Inventory
Using your answer to Practice 21-2, compute how much cash was paid for inventory during the year.

Practice 21-4
LO1

Cash Paid for Expenses
During the year, the company expensed $140,600 in other operating expenses. The beginning and ending balances in the prepaid expenses account were $14,100 and $12,500, respectively. Compute the amount of cash paid for other operating expenses for the year.

Practice 21-5
LO1

Depreciation Expense
If depreciation expense is $20,000 and the beginning and ending accumulated depreciation balances are $100,000 and $110,000, respectively, how much cash was paid for depreciation?

Practice 21-6

LO1

REVERSE SOLVABLE

Cash Paid for Equipment

The company began the year with a balance in its equipment account of $928,500. During the year, equipment with an original cost of $106,000 was sold. The ending balance in the equipment account was $880,000. How much equipment was purchased during the year?

Practice 21-7

LO1

REVERSE SOLVABLE

Proceeds from Sale of Equipment

During the year, the company sold equipment that originally cost $61,000. Accumulated depreciation associated with the equipment was $17,500. A gain of $8,500 on the sale of the equipment was recognized. How much cash was received from the sale?

Practice 21-8

LO1

REVERSE SOLVABLE

Loan Repayment

The company began the year with a balance in its long-term debt account of $235,400. During the year, additional debt of $172,000 was incurred. The ending balance in the long-term debt account was $365,000. How much long-term debt was repaid during the year?

Practice 21-9

LO1

REVERSE SOLVABLE

Cash Paid for Dividends

The company began the year with a balance in its retained earnings account of $955,500. At the end of the year, net income of $176,000 was closed into the retained earnings account. The ending balance in the retained earnings account was $1,070,500. Dividends of how much were paid during the year? (*Note*: All dividends that were declared were paid.)

Practice 21-10

LO2

Statement of Cash flows in the United Kingdom

Using the following information, compute cash flow from operating activities under (1) the U.S. approach and (2) the U.K. approach.

(a) Cash paid to purchase inventory	$ 7,800
(b) Cash received from sale of a building	5,600
(c) Cash paid for interest	450
(d) Cash paid to repay a loan	1,000
(e) Cash collected from customers	10,000
(f) Cash received from issuance of new shares of common stock	1,200
(g) Cash paid for dividends	780
(h) Cash paid for income taxes	1,320
(i) Cash paid to purchase machinery	1,950

EXERCISES

Exercise 21-11

LO1

REVERSE SOLVABLE

SPREADSHEET

Analysis of the Accounts Receivable Account

Yosef Company reports the following information:

Credit sales for the year	$457,200
Accounts receivable, end of year	77,500
Cash collections during the year	415,000

Compute the balance in Accounts Receivable as of the beginning of the year.

Exercise 21-12
LO1

Preparing a Complete Statement of Cash Flows

The following are financial statements for Germaine Company:

Germaine Company
Comparative Balance Sheet
December 31, 2013 and 2012
(Dollars in thousands)

	2013	2012
Assets		
Cash	$ 22	$ 16
Accounts receivable	225	245
Inventory	105	125
Prepaid general expenses	21	12
Plant assets	1,025	1,000
Accumulated depreciation—plant assets	(530)	(585)
Total assets	$ 868	$ 813
Liabilities and Stockholders' Equity		
Accounts payable	$ 70	$ 45
Interest payable	15	12
Income taxes payable	80	77
Bonds payable	105	97
Common stock	362	354
Retained earnings	236	228
Total liabilities and stockholders' equity	$ 868	$ 813

Germaine Company
Condensed Income Statement
For the Year Ended December 31, 2013
(Dollars in thousands)

Sales		$1,450
Cost of goods sold		990
Gross profit		$ 460
Operating expenses:		
Depreciation expense	$ 55	
General expenses	340	
Interest expense	12	
Income tax expense	15	422
Net income		$ 38

The following information is also available for 2013:

(a) Plant assets were sold for their book value of $180 during the year. The assets had an original cost of $290.
(b) Cash dividends totaling $30 were paid during the year.
(c) All accounts payable relate to inventory purchases.
(d) All purchases of plant assets were cash transactions.

Prepare a statement of cash flows for 2013 using the indirect method.

Exercise 21-13
LO1

Statement of Cash Flows—Direct Method

Using the information given in Exercise 21-12, prepare a statement of cash flows for 2013 for Germaine Company using the direct method.

Exercise 21-14
LO1
SPREADSHEET

Computing Cash from Operations

Executive Inc. had the following operating balances for 2013:

	December 31, 2013	January 1, 2013
Accounts Payable	$54,400	$62,800
Inventory	21,800	29,900
Accounts Receivable	73,600	77,200

All purchases of inventory were on account.

Executive provides the following income statement information for 2013:

Revenues	$ 740,000
Cost of goods sold	(360,000)
Other expenses	(104,000)
Depreciation expense	(87,000)
Loss on sale of equipment	(9,000)
Net income	$ 180,000

Compute cash from operations.

Exercise 21-15
LO1
SPREADSHEET

Preparing a Complete Statement of Cash Flows

Sunnyvale Corporation prepared the following balance sheet data for 2013 and 2012:

	Dec. 31, 2013	Dec. 31, 2012
Cash and cash equivalents	$ 518,500	$ 675,000
Accounts receivable	360,000	345,000
Merchandise inventory	750,000	654,000
Prepaid insurance	4,500	6,000
Buildings and equipment	5,515,500	4,350,000
Accumulated depreciation—buildings and equipment	(2,235,000)	(1,995,000)
Total assets	$ 4,913,500	$ 4,035,000
Accounts payable	$ 613,500	$ 945,000
Salaries payable	75,000	105,000
Notes payable—bank (current)	150,000	600,000
Notes payable—bank (long-term)	1,500,000	—
Common stock	2,400,000	2,400,000
Retained earnings (deficit)	175,000	(15,000)
Total liabilities and stockholders' equity	$ 4,913,500	$ 4,035,000

Cash needed to purchase new equipment and to improve the company's working capital position was raised by borrowing from the bank with a long-term note. Equipment costing $75,000 with a book value of $15,000 was sold for $18,000; the gain on the sale was included in net income. The company paid cash dividends of $90,000 and reported earnings of $280,000 for 2013. There were no entries in the retained earnings account other than to record the dividends and net income for the year.

Prepare a statement of cash flows for 2013 using the indirect method.

Exercise 21-16
LO1
REVERSE SOLVABLE

Working Backwards from Operating Cash Flow to an Income Statement
Thornton Inc. had the following operating balances for 2013:

	December 31, 2013	January 1, 2013
Accounts Payable	$58,200	$61,500
Inventory	39,400	37,300
Accounts Receivable	87,000	89,100
Prepaid Expenses	12,500	14,100

Additional information for Thornton is as follows:

(a) All purchases of inventory were on account.
(b) Depreciation Expense of $96,000 was recognized during 2013.
(c) Equipment was sold during 2013, and a gain of $3,000 was recognized.

Thornton provides the following cash flow information for 2013:

Cash collected from customers	$ 950,000
Cash paid for inventory	(410,000)
Cash paid for other expenses	(139,000)
Cash from operations	$ 401,000

Prepare an income statement for Thornton for 2013.

Exercise 21-17
LO1
REVERSE SOLVABLE

Working Backwards from Cash from Operations to Net Income
Patriot Corporation's statement of cash flows shows cash flow from operations of $322,000. The following items also appear on Patriot's balance sheet and income statement:

Depreciation expense	$78,000
Accounts receivable increase	23,000
Inventory decrease	41,000
Accounts payable decrease	11,000

What is Patriot's net income?

PROBLEMS

Problem 21-18
LO1

Cash Flow from Operations—Direct Method
The following combined income and retained earnings statement, along with selected balance sheet data, is provided for Gemini Corporation:

Gemini Corporation
Combined Income and Retained Earnings Statement
For the Year Ended December 31, 2013

Revenues:		
Net sales revenue		$340,000
Other revenues		6,000*
Total revenues		$346,000
Expenses:		
Cost of goods sold	$188,000	
Selling and administrative expenses	52,600	
Depreciation expense	13,500	
Interest expense	3,200	
Total expenses		257,300

(Continued)

Income before income taxes	$ 88,700
Income taxes	21,850
Net income	$ 66,850
Retained earnings, January 1, 2013	56,000
	$122,850
Dividends declared and paid	16,000
Retained earnings, December 31, 2013	$106,850

*Gain on sale of equipment (cost, $20,000; book value, $12,000; sales price, $18,000).

Balance Sheet Amounts

	Beginning of Year	End of Year
Accounts receivable	$47,000	$53,000
Inventory	73,400	75,400
Prepaid expenses	4,500	3,600
Accounts payable	31,800	38,300
Interest payable	5,500	4,300
Income taxes payable	2,900	7,200

Instructions:

1. Using the direct method, compute the amount of net cash provided by (used in) operating activities for Gemini Corporation for 2013.
2. What is the impact of dividends paid on net cash flow from operations? Explain.

Problem 21-19
LO1

Cash Flow from Operations—Comparison of Indirect and Direct Methods

The statement of cash flows for Riker Company (prepared using the indirect method) follows. Consider the following additional information:

(a) Sales for the year totaled $812,350. Cost of goods sold was $500,000. Operating expenses were $100,000. Interest expense was $23,000. Income tax expense was $40,430.

(b) Of the decrease in accounts payable, 80% is related to inventory purchases; the remaining 20% related to operating expenses.

(c) Depreciation and amortization are period costs; they do not enter into the computation of cost of goods sold.

Riker Company
Statement of Cash Flows (Indirect Method)
For the Year Ended December 31, 2013

Cash flows from operating activities:		
Net income		$ 68,850
Adjustments:		
Depreciation expense	$ 65,000	
Amortization expense	10,000	
Loss on sale of machine	7,400	
Gain on retirement of long-term debt	(2,330)	
Increase in accounts receivable	(8,600)	
Decrease in inventory	12,430	
Decrease in prepaid operating expenses	1,680	
Decrease in accounts payable	(2,400)	

(Continued)

Increase in interest payable	$ 500	
Increase in income taxes payable	2,500	$ 86,180
Net cash provided by operating activities		$155,030
Cash flows from investing activities:		
Sale of machine	$ 12,000	
Purchase of fixed assets	(78,000)	
Net cash used in investing activities		(66,000)
Cash flows from financing activities:		
Retirement of long-term debt	$(65,000)	
Payment of dividends	(27,000)	
Net cash used in financing activities		(92,000)
Net decrease in cash		$ (2,970)
Cash at beginning of year		5,320
Cash at end of year		$ 2,350

Instructions: Prepare the Operating Activities section of the statement of cash flows for Riker Company using the direct method.

Problem 21-20
LO1
REVERSE SOLVABLE

Preparation of Income Statement Using Balance Sheet and Cash Flow Data
The following financial statements are for Troi Company. Consider the following additional information:

(a) All accounts payable relate to inventory purchases.
(b) Property, plant, and equipment sold had an original cost of $75,000 and a book value of $22,000.

Troi Company
Comparative Balance Sheet
December 31, 2013 and 2012

	2013	2012
Assets		
Cash	$ 4,000	$ 3,400
Accounts receivable	25,000	18,000
Inventory	30,000	34,000
Prepaid general expenses	5,700	5,000
Property, plant, and equipment	305,000	320,000
Accumulated depreciation	(103,500)	(128,900)
Patent	36,000	40,000
Total assets	$ 302,200	$ 291,500
Liabilities and Stockholders' Equity		
Accounts payable	$ 25,000	$ 22,000
Wages payable	12,000	10,300
Interest payable	2,800	4,000
Dividends payable	14,000	—
Income taxes payable	1,600	1,200
Bonds payable	100,000	120,000
Common stock	50,000	50,000
Retained earnings	96,800	84,000
Total liabilities and stockholders' equity	$ 302,200	$ 291,500

Troi Company
Statement of Cash Flows
For the Year Ended December 31, 2013

Cash flows from operating activities:		
Cash collected from customers		$685,300
Cash payments for:		
Inventory purchases	$300,000	
General expenses	102,000	
Wages expense	150,000	
Interest expense	11,000	
Income tax expense	23,900	586,900
Net cash provided by operating activities		$ 98,400
Cash flows from investing activities:		
Sale of property, plant, and equipment	$ 27,200	
Purchase of property, plant, and equipment	(60,000)	
Net cash used in investing activities		(32,800)
Cash flows from financing activities:		
Retirement of bonds payable	$ (23,000)	
Payment of dividends	(42,000)	
Net cash used in financing activities		(65,000)
Net increase in cash		$ 600
Cash at beginning of year		3,400
Cash at end of year		$ 4,000

Instructions: Prepare the income statement for Troi Company for the year ended December 31, 2013.

Problem 21-21

LO1

REVERSE SOLVABLE

Preparation of Balance Sheet Using Cash Flow and Income Statement Data

Terra Company just completed its first year of operations. The company's income statement and statement of cash flows are provided.

Income Statement

Sales	$140,000
Gain on sale of equipment	2,000
Cost of goods sold	(86,000)
Depreciation expense	(16,000)
Interest expense	(8,400)
Other expenses	(34,000)
Net income (loss)	$ (2,400)

Statement of Cash Flows

Operating Activities		
Collected from customers	$ 132,000	
Paid for inventory	(87,000)	
Paid for interest	(7,000)	
Paid for other expenses	(30,000)	$ 8,000
Investing Activities		
Purchase of buildings and equipment	$(175,000)	
Sale of equipment	19,000	(156,000)

(Continued)

Financing Activities		
Sale of stock	$ 100,000	
Issuance of bonds	88,000	
Payment of dividends	(4,000)	184,000
Net increase in cash for the period		$ 36,000

The following information is also available:

(a) Equipment with an original cost of $21,000 and a book value of $17,000 was sold during the year.
(b) All sales of inventory are on account.
(c) Purchases of inventory on account totaled $93,300.

Instructions: Prepare a balance sheet for Terra Company as of December 31.

Problem 21-22
LO1, LO3

Comprehensive Statement of Cash Flows
The following schedule shows the account balances of Beneficio Corporation at the beginning and end of the fiscal year ended October 31, 2013.

Debits	October 31, 2013	October 31, 2012
Cash and Cash Equivalents	$ 222,000	$ 50,000
Investment Securities—Trading	10,000	40,000
Accounts Receivable	148,000	100,000
Inventories	291,000	300,000
Prepaid Insurance	2,500	2,000
Land and Building	195,000	195,000
Equipment	305,000	170,000
Discount on Bonds Payable	8,500	9,000
Treasury Stock (at cost)	5,000	10,000
Cost of Goods Sold	539,000	
Selling and General Expenses	287,000	
Income Taxes	35,000	
Unrealized Loss on Trading Securities	4,000	
Loss on Sale of Equipment	1,000	
Total debits	$2,053,000	$876,000
Allowance for Bad Debts	$ 8,000	$ 5,000
Accumulated Depreciation—Building	26,250	22,500
Accumulated Depreciation—Equipment	39,750	27,500
Accounts Payable	55,000	60,000
Notes Payable—Current	70,000	20,000
Miscellaneous Expenses Payable	18,000	8,700
Taxes Payable	35,000	10,000
Unearned Revenue	1,000	9,000
Notes Payable—Long-Term	40,000	60,000
Bonds Payable—Long-Term	250,000	250,000
Deferred Income Tax Liability	47,000	53,300
Common Stock, $2 par	359,400	200,000
Retained Earnings Appropriated for Possible Building Expansion	43,000	33,000
Unappropriated Retained Earnings	34,600	112,000

(Continued)

Debits	October 31, 2013	October 31, 2012
Paid-In Capital in Excess of Par Value	$ 116,000	$ 5,000
Sales	898,000	
Gain on Sale of Investment Securities	12,000	
Total credits	$2,053,000	$876,000

The following information was also available:

(a) All purchases and sales were on account.
(b) Equipment with an original cost of $15,000 was sold for $7,000.
(c) Selling and general expenses include the following:

Building depreciation	$ 3,750
Equipment depreciation	25,250
Bad debt expense	4,000
Interest expense	18,000

(d) A 6-month note payable for $50,000 was issued toward the purchase of new equipment.
(e) The long-term note payable requires the payment of $20,000 per year plus interest until paid.
(f) Treasury stock was sold for $1,000 more than its cost.
(g) During the year, a 30% stock dividend was declared and issued. At the time, there were 100,000 shares of $2 par common stock outstanding. However, 1,000 of these shares were held as treasury stock at the time and were prohibited from participating in the stock dividend. Market price was $10 per share after the stock dividend was issued.
(h) Equipment was overhauled, extending its useful life at a cost of $6,000. The cost was debited to Accumulated Depreciation—Equipment.
(i) Beneficio has determined that its purchases and sales of trading securities are operating activities.

Instructions: Prepare a *complete* statement of cash flows for the year ended October 31, 2013, using the *indirect* method of reporting cash flows from operations.

Problem 21-23

LO1, LO3

Complete Statement of Cash Flows

Below are balance sheet and income statement data for Blue Panel Corporation. (*Note*: For the balance sheet data, the end-of-year information is in the left column.)

Balance Sheet

	2013	2012
Cash	$ 8,261	$ 1,506
Investment securities (available-for-sale)	300	250
Accounts receivable	2,200	1,365
Paid-in capital	7,200	6,000
Inventory	4,874	5,168
Prepaid selling and administrative expenses	208	224
Retained earnings (deficit)	8,768	(2,042)
Accumulated depreciation	3,200	2,780
Accounts payable	370	450
Unearned revenue	110	170
Income taxes payable	78	54

(Continued)

	2013	2012
Other long-term liabilities	$ 490	$ 185
Property, plant, and equipment	12,000	8,400
Long-term debt	7,952	9,816
Accumulated other comprehensive income (credit balance)	50	0
Intangible assets	375	500

Income Statement (for 2013)

Sales		$57,860
Cost of goods sold	$32,600	
Loss on sale of property, plant, and equipment	80	
Selling and administrative expenses	6,550	
Amortization expense	125	
Depreciation expense	2,355	
Income tax expense	2,400	
Total expenses and losses		44,110
Net income		$13,750

Additional information for Blue Panel Corporation is as follows:

(a) Property, plant, and equipment with an original historical cost of $2,100 was sold during 2013.
(b) All accounts payable relate to inventory purchases.
(c) The "Other long-term liabilities" item is Blue Panel's pension liability. Pension expense is reported as part of selling and administrative expenses.
(d) During 2013, Blue Panel issued shares of common stock to an investor in exchange for property, plant, and equipment valued at $800.
(e) The accumulated other comprehensive income relates solely to the available-for-sale investment securities.

Instructions: Prepare a *complete* statement of cash flows for 2013 for Blue Panel Corporation. Use the *direct* method for reporting cash flows from operating activities.

Problem 21-24
LO1, LO3

Complete Statement of Cash Flows

The balance sheet and income statement data for Howard Bannister Company follow. (*Note*: For the balance sheet data, the end-of-year information is in the left column.)

Balance Sheet

	2013	2012
Cash	$ 228	$ 120
Investment securities (available-for-sale)	170	250
Accounts receivable	400	568
Paid-in capital	4,900	3,000
Inventory	2,795	2,259
Retained earnings (deficit)	(132)	117
Accumulated depreciation	900	1,090
Accounts payable	300	270
Unearned revenue	92	106
Property, plant, and equipment	7,000	5,900

(Continued)

	2013	2012
Long-term debt	$5,247	$5,164
Accumulated other comprehensive income (all related to available-for-sale securities)	70	100
Investments (accounted for using the equity method)	784	750

Income Statement (for 2013)		
Sales		$22,535
Income from investments (accounted for using the equity method)		100
Realized gain on sale of available-for-sale securities		45
Cost of goods sold	$14,800	
Impairment loss	170	
Selling and administrative expenses	3,380	
Depreciation expense	1,068	
Income tax expense	1,200	
Total expenses and losses		20,618
Net income		$ 2,062

Additional information for Howard Bannister Company is as follows:

(a) All accounts payable relate to inventory purchases.
(b) Equipment with an original historical cost of $1,200 was judged to be impaired during 2013. The fair value of the equipment on the date the impairment was recognized was $210.
(c) Howard Bannister made *only* two purchases of property, plant, and equipment during the year. One purchase was for $2,300 cash. The other purchase, for $650, was completely financed with a mortgage. The mortgage is shown as part of "Long-term debt" on the balance sheet.
(d) No available-for-sale securities were purchased *before* January 1, 2012. Available-for-sale investment securities sold during 2013 had an original cost of $65.
(e) The accumulated other comprehensive income balance represents an increase, or credit, to equity.

Instructions: Prepare a *complete* statement of cash flows for 2013 for Howard Bannister Company. Use the *direct* method for reporting cash flows from operating activities.

Problem 21-25
LO1, LO3

Complete Statement of Cash Flows
Below are balance sheet and income statement data for Supersonic Corporation. (*Note*: For the balance sheet data, the end-of-year information is in the left column.)

Balance Sheet	2013	2012
Cash	$4,443	$3,130
Accounts receivable	804	728
Allowance for bad debts	110	92
Investment securities (trading)	80	105
Inventory	1,587	2,134
Prepaid selling and administrative expenses	26	43

(Continued)

	2013	2012
Investment securities (available-for-sale)	$ 245	$ 200
Property, plant, and equipment	9,400	8,250
Accumulated depreciation	3,300	2,780
Investment in Micro Inc.	280	0
Capitalized software development costs	106	0
Deferred income tax asset	116	90
Intangible assets	682	740
Accounts payable	360	490
Interest payable	75	110
Income taxes payable	54	36
Sales revenue received in advance	1,820	1,480
Dividends payable	270	125
Long-term debt	2,085	3,227
Net pension liability	910	830
Convertible preferred stock	0	600
Common stock (no par)	5,335	3,450
Retained earnings	3,450	2,200

Income Statement (for 2013)

Sales		$38,730
Income from Micro Inc.		60
Gain on sale of property, plant, and equipment		250
Cost of goods sold	$23,200	
Selling and administrative expenses	7,840	
Pension expense	210	
Interest expense	370	
Depreciation expense	940	
Amortization expense	112	
Unrealized holding loss on investment securities	35	
Income tax expense	2,800	
Total expenses and losses		35,507
Net income		$ 3,533

Additional information for Supersonic Corporation is as follows:

(a) Bad debt expense of $185 is included in selling and administrative expenses.
(b) Property, plant, and equipment was sold during 2013 for $900 cash.
(c) All accounts payable relate to inventory purchases.
(d) During 2013, Supersonic capitalized $75 of interest associated with the construction of a building. None of the interest payable relates to this capitalized interest.
(e) On July 15, 2013, Supersonic repurchased shares of its own stock for $130. On December 19, 2013, Supersonic resold the shares for $90. Supersonic uses the cost method for accounting for treasury stock.
(f) On November 17, 2013, Supersonic declared and issued a 10% stock dividend. The number of shares of common stock outstanding increased from 200 to 220. After the stock dividend, the market price per share of common stock was $60.

(g) During the year, Supersonic capitalized $160 in expenditures for software. The capitalized costs are being amortized over the estimated useful life of the development costs.

(h) On January 1, 2013, Supersonic signed an agreement to lease a piece of equipment. The lease is being accounted for as a capital lease. The annual lease payment is $50. The present value of the minimum lease payments is $257. The leased asset has been included in property, plant, and equipment, and the lease liability is included in long-term debt. The lease term is nine years, and the implicit interest rate is 13%.

(i) Supersonic uses the LIFO method of inventory valuation. During the year, Supersonic dipped into its LIFO layers. As a result, cost of goods sold was $128 lower than it otherwise would have been.

(j) On January 1, 2013, Supersonic purchased 30% of Micro Inc. for $240 cash. At the time, the book value of Micro's net assets was $800. Net income for 2013 for Micro Inc. was $200.

(k) During the year, all of the convertible preferred stock was converted into shares of Supersonic common stock.

Instructions: Prepare a *complete* statement of cash flows for 2013 for Supersonic Corporation. Use the *direct* method for reporting cash flows from operating activities.

P4 OTHER DIMENSIONS OF FINANCIAL REPORTING

Alexey Zarubin/Alamy

CHAPTER 22 Accounting in a Global Market

LEARNING OBJECTIVES

1. Understand the importance and potential impact of a common worldwide set of accounting standards.
2. Outline the history of the IASB.
3. Identify key differences between U.S. GAAP and IFRS.
4. Convert foreign currency financial statements into U.S. dollars using the translation method.

Henry Ford's Model T is sometimes mistakenly viewed as the first automobile built. Although the Model T, first sold in 1908 with a base sticker price of $260, may rightly be considered the first car produced for the masses, the first automobile was actually produced 22 years earlier in Germany. In 1886, Carl Benz patented the world's first 3-wheel motor carriage. This motorized tricycle is considered by many as the first automobile. Later in that same year and also in Germany, Gottlieb Daimler equipped a horse-drawn coach with a fast-running engine to produce his first 4-wheeled automobile. Daimler had patented the world's first motorcycle the previous year.

In 1894, Carl Benz manufactured the first production car, the Velo-Motorwagon. In 1896, Daimler produced the world's first truck. Daimler and Benz competed with one another for years, both for customers and on race tracks. Auto racing was seen by both as the best way to advertise their products. It was through auto racing that Gottlieb Daimler met Emil Jellinek. Jellinek raced Daimler cars in France and in 1900 had established an auto dealership in Monaco for selling Daimler automobiles. He obtained the exclusive rights to sell Daimler cars in Austria-Hungary, France, Belgium, and the United States. Because Daimler had already sold the rights to sell Daimler cars in France, the Daimler car line was renamed Mercedes after Jellinek's 10-year-old daughter.

Benz and Daimler continued to compete against one another until the First World War, at which point most German factories were converted to war production. During the hyperinflation in Germany that followed the First World War, Daimler issued its own currency because confidence in the German mark was so low. In 1926, Daimler and Benz merged to form **Daimler-Benz AG** with corporate headquarters located in Berlin.

And while all this was happening in Europe, what was going on in the United States? Piano maker William Steinway acquired the Daimler patent licenses for the United States in 1888 and founded the **Daimler Motor Company** in New York that same year. But it wasn't until 1906 that the first Mercedes was produced in America—appropriately called the American Mercedes. And in 1912, a young man named Walter Chrysler became the production manager at **Buick Motor Company**, a subsidiary of **General Motors Company**. Within five years, Chrysler had become president and general manager of Buick. In 1920, because of differences with General Motors President William Durant, Chrysler left General Motors to take charge of a floundering car company that would in 1925 become **Chrysler Motor Company**.

> **FYI**
>
> The AG stands for Aktiengesellschaft, which is the German word for *stock company*, or *corporation*.

During the next 65 years, Daimler-Benz and Chrysler competed for market share in the global automotive market, and both companies had their fair share of financial difficulties. Daimler-Benz suffered through another world war, and Chrysler avoided bankruptcy in 1980 only because the U.S. federal government guaranteed Chrysler's debt.

In the fall of 1993, Daimler-Benz became the first German company to list its shares on the New York Stock Exchange (NYSE). In those days, non-U.S. companies listed on the NYSE were required to provide financial information prepared according to U.S. GAAP. For 1993, Daimler-Benz reported a profit of DM 615 million using German accounting principles.[1] For the same year, the net *loss* for Daimler-Benz was DM 1,839 million according to U.S. GAAP. As you can see, in those days there were very significant differences between reported results using U.S. GAAP and, in this case, German GAAP. As a result, the Securities and Exchange Commission (SEC) required foreign companies with shares traded in the United States to report and reconcile the differences in their reported net income to what their net income would have been using U.S. GAAP. A sample of this reconciliation for Daimler-Benz for 1993, included in SEC Form 20-F, appears in Exhibit 22-1.

A close look at Exhibit 22-1 reveals why Daimler-Benz might have been reluctant to report income using U.S. GAAP. The DM 2.454 billion reduction in

EX 22-1 DAIMLER-BENZ'S FORM 20-F RECONCILIATION FOR 1993

(In millions of DM)	
Consolidated net income in accordance with German HGB (Commercial Code)	**615**
—Minority interest	(13)
Adjusted net income under German GAAP	602
—Changes in appropriated retained earnings: provisions, reserves and valuation differences	(4,262)
	(3,660)
Additional adjustments:	
Long-term contracts	78
Goodwill and business acquisitions	(287)
Pensions and other postretirement benefits	(624)
Foreign currency translation	(40)
Financial instruments	(225)
Other valuation differences	292
Deferred taxes	2,627
Consolidated loss in accordance with U.S. GAAP	(1,839)

[1] DM stands for Deutsche mark, which was the currency in Germany until 1999 when Germany adopted the euro as its legal tender.

net income in converting from German GAAP to U.S. GAAP is caused primarily by a removal from income of DM 4.262 billion in "appropriated retained earnings." This innocent-sounding adjustment actually represents the removal of some serious income manipulation that was allowable under German GAAP. In good years, German companies often overstated their expenses by creating provisions (liability accounts such as "provision for future environmental cleanup costs"), by creating reserves (separate categories of equity, as described in Chapter 13), or by writing down the value of assets. Created in good years, these so-called "hidden reserves" could be reversed in bad years, thus increasing income. In 1993, Daimler-Benz took advantage of German GAAP and reversed DM 4.262 billion in hidden reserves, thus increasing reported net income and covering up an operating loss. Under the more restrictive standards of U.S. GAAP at the time, this huge reversal of hidden reserves was not allowable, necessitating the large adjustment shown in Exhibit 22-1.

In 1998, companies founded by Gottlieb Daimler, Carl Benz, and Walter Chrysler combined forces to become, in terms of 1998 revenues, the fourth largest company in the world—**DaimlerChrysler**. The merger came under fire right from the start. Chrysler supporters cried that Daimler had paid too small a price for Chrysler, while Daimler supporters worried that the price was too high. In addition, in the aftermath of the merger, the expected synergies between the two companies' product lines did not emerge as powerfully as hoped. After a rocky 9-year "marriage," the two companies split up with Daimler selling Chrysler to **Cerberus Capital Management**, a large U.S. private equity firm, in 2007. On April 30, 2009, in the wake of the implosion of the worldwide economy and the associated collapse of the market for new cars in the United States, Chrysler declared bankruptcy. After a restructured Chrysler emerged from bankruptcy proceedings, it was owned by an interesting collection of stakeholders of the former company: 2.5% by the Canadian government, 10% by the U.S. government, 20% by the Italian automaker **Fiat**, and 67.5% by the employee and retiree health care plan of Chrysler's auto workers.

As illustrated in Daimler-Benz's 1993 reconciliation of German GAAP net income to U.S. GAAP net income, the divergent national accounting practices that existed around the world before the widespread acceptance of IASB standards had an extremely significant impact on reported financial statements. Cross-border mergers such as that between Daimler-Benz and Chrysler illustrate the increasing integration of the worldwide economy. Other examples of cross-border mergers are the purchase of the quintessential American company **Anheuser-Busch** (brewer of Budweiser) by **InBev**, a Belgian company, and the purchase of U.S. wireless company **Voicestream** by German company **Deutsche Telekom**. With this global business integration, accounting differences have become impossible to ignore. This chapter reviews the efforts of the Financial Accounting Standards Board (FASB) and the International Accounting Standards Board (IASB) to accelerate the harmonization of accounting standards around the world.

This chapter also includes a discussion of an important issue faced by U.S. multinational companies operating through foreign subsidiaries around the world. In order to consolidate these foreign results into the financial reports of their overall operations, U.S. multinational companies with foreign subsidiaries must convert the subsidiary financial reports into U.S. dollars. This process is called *translation* and is explained in this chapter.

? QUESTIONS

1. What is the purpose of the SEC's Form 20-F?
2. Can U.S. companies create "hidden reserves"? Explain.

Answers to these questions can be found on page 22-22.

The Need for One Worldwide Financial Accounting Standard

1 Understand the importance and potential impact of a common worldwide set of accounting standards.

WHY **Fundamentally, the purpose of financial statements is to communicate. Globalization of business operations and of capital markets has created the need for companies to communicate with one common financial accounting language to investors and other stakeholders around the world.**

HOW **An educated preparer or user of financial statements must understand the impact that differing accounting standards can have on the reported numbers.**

Companies of all sizes and types are operating in the international environment. Well-conceived global financing strategies are an important part of successful international operations. For a U.S. firm, these strategies might include a stock listing on a foreign exchange, such as the Tokyo Stock Market or the London Stock Exchange; selling bonds and other debt securities in countries other than or in addition to the United States; and borrowing from non-U.S. financial institutions. For example, **Disney** has significant currency hedging operations with respect to the euro, the British pound, the Japanese yen, and the Canadian dollar.

Similarly, to raise debt or equity capital, many non-U.S. firms, such as **Sony**, **Cadbury**, and **Toyota**, list their securities on U.S. exchanges and borrow from U.S. financial institutions. For example, Daimler lists its shares on three different stock exchanges around the world—New York, Frankfurt, and Stuttgart. The number of non-U.S. companies listed on the New York Stock Exchange is substantial. As detailed in Exhibit 22-2, 414 foreign share issues were trading on the NYSE as of April 30, 2008, including 77 from Canadian companies and 41 from Chinese companies.

International financing strategies impose a variety of financial reporting standards on these multinational corporations. Firms such as Daimler and Disney must produce financial statements for users not only in their own countries but also in other countries. The significant differences in accounting standards that have existed throughout the world have complicated both the preparation of financial statements and the understanding of those financial statements by users.

Dangers of Differing National Accounting Standards

Chapter 23 follows this chapter and pulls together the techniques of analyzing financial statement data that have been included throughout the text. Learning Objective #2 of Chapter 23 contains an extended example showing the impact that the use of differing accounting methods can have on a financial statement analysis comparison. The two fictitious companies in that example are Sai Kung Company and Tuen Mun Limited. As you will see when you study Chapter 23, a careful comparison of the financial statements for Sai Kung and Tuen Mun reveals that the companies are economically identical. However, as you can see from the sampling of financial ratios in Exhibit 22-3, on paper the companies appear to be anything but identical.

The differences between the two sets of financial statements are caused by differences in accounting treatment. In fact, as shown in Chapter 23, the differences in these ratios are caused by just four accounting differences: classification of investment securities, inventory valuation method, depreciation life assumption, and lease classification. In this example, these four accounting differences cause significant differences between the financial

EX 22-2 NUMBER OF FOREIGN COMPANIES LISTED ON THE NEW YORK STOCK EXCHANGE BY COUNTRY OF ORIGIN

Country of Origin	Number of Listed Companies
Argentina	11
Australia	5
Bahamas	4
Bermuda	30
Brazil	32
Canada	77
Chile	14
China	41
France	8
Germany	9
Greece	10
Hong Kong	5
India	12
Ireland	6
Italy	4
Japan	19
Korea	8
Mexico	17
Netherlands	9
Puerto Rico	6
Russia	5
South Africa	6
Spain	5
Switzerland	8
Taiwan	5
United Kingdom	29
Others (representing 21 countries)	29
Total	414

Source: http://www.nyse.com. List is current as of April 30, 2008.

statements of two otherwise essentially identical companies. The differences in accounting method have made Tuen Mun appear to be a superior company on almost every dimension. Tuen Mun has better return on equity, better profitability, and better overall efficiency. In addition, Tuen Mun appears to be a less risky company because its leverage is lower and its liquidity, as indicated by the current ratio, is higher.

The point of this example (and don't forget to work through the details when you get to Chapter 23) is that ratio comparisons can yield misleading implications if the ratios come from companies with differing accounting practices. And historically, this is exactly the situation that existed between different countries around the world. For example, Japanese financial reporting standards were known for being extremely conservative, so net income numbers for companies from Japan always looked lower than their U.S. or UK counterparts even though the companies might have been economically identical. The Daimler-Benz example that opened this chapter demonstrates the huge difference in reported net income that could result from the strategic use of hidden reserves which were created under the financial accounting rules then in existence under German GAAP.

A key function of accounting standards is to create a common set of rules to be used by all companies so that outsiders, who do not have control over or access to the detailed

EX 22-3 COMPARISON OF THE FINANCIAL RATIOS OF SAI KUNG COMPANY AND TUEN MUN LIMITED

	Sai Kung	Tuen Mun
Return on equity	9.1%	35.2%
Return on sales	2.5%	12.9%
Asset turnover	1.18	1.28
Assets-to-equity ratio	3.09	2.14
Number of days' sales in inventory	63.9	98.6
Fixed asset turnover	1.67	2.07
Debt ratio	67.6%	53.2%
Debt-to-equity ratio	2.09	1.14
Times interest earned	1.90	6.17
Return on assets	2.9%	16.5%
Current ratio	1.5	1.8

Ratio values are computed using the detailed financial statement data given in Chapter 23, Learning Objective #2.

financial records, can receive financial reports that are comparable among all of the different companies that they might want to analyze. Without this comparability, financial reports are virtually worthless. As the globalization of business has forced investors, creditors, and other stakeholders to perform an increasing number of cross-border financial statement comparisons, the need for a common set of global standards has become apparent. For a number of years, both the FASB and the IASB vied for the honor of being the provider of that worldwide set of standards. The IASB won. The next section gives a brief history of the IASB.

Brief History of the IASB and Its Standards (IFRS)

2 Outline the history of the IASB.

WHY **It is likely that within the next five years all publicly traded companies in the United States will be required to prepare their financial statements using IFRS as issued by the IASB.**

HOW **Over the past 20 years, the IASB has made great strides in improving the quality of its financial reporting standards and in improving the transparency of its standard-setting process. The IASB's standards, collectively called IFRS, are now generally accepted around the world.**

Both the FASB and the IASC (predecessor of the IASB) were established in 1973. For many years, there was a real question about which set of accounting standards would become the worldwide standard—U.S. GAAP set by the FASB or IFRS (International Financial Reporting Standards) set by the IASB based in London.[2] Until the mid-1990s, the FASB was clearly the dominant accounting standard setter in the world. The FASB had the advantage of being an independent board with broad representation from the U.S. business

[2] The original standards of the IASC were, and are, called International Accounting Standards (IAS). These standards maintain this title even though most of them have been subsequently amended, sometimes substantially, by the IASB. The body of standards issued by the IASC/IASB is now referred to as "IFRS" whether the label of the actual standard is IAS or IFRS.

community. In contrast, the IASC was a consortium of national CPA organizations, and committee members served part time while maintaining their connections with their firms and their clients. In addition, the FASB standards, by and large, were viewed as being conceptually consistent with an underpinning of the Conceptual Framework. The early IASC standards were really just a compilation of the diverse accounting practices from around the world with some expression of a preferred alternative but no coherent conceptual foundation. Finally, the IASC's set of standards was viewed as being incomplete with the most conspicuous deficiency being the lack of a standard on financial instruments.[3]

In spite of its head start, the FASB began to give ground to the IASC in terms of international acceptance. Part of this was due to international reluctance to allow the "Americans" to become the worldwide standard setter. As one French accounting standard setter put it, the French will never accept U.S. GAAP as the worldwide standard precisely because they will not bow to U.S. dominance no matter how reasonable are the standards themselves.[4] But more important than this international aversion to U.S. dominance was the improvement in the IASC standards themselves. All during the 1990s, the IASC worked to eliminate the large number of alternative accounting treatments allowable under IAS and also to improve the overall quality of the standards. The immediate goal of the IASC was to have its set of standards endorsed by the International Organization of Securities Commissions (IOSCO), which includes as one of its members the U.S. Securities and Exchange Commission. Although the IASC never received the unqualified endorsement of its set of standards that it hoped to receive from the IOSCO, its efforts to satisfy IOSCO greatly enhanced the perceived quality of both the IASC's standards and of the organization itself.

In 2001, the IASC made a strong bid to become THE international accounting standard setter through a substantial organizational restructuring. To symbolize this change, the group's name was changed to the International Accounting Standards Board. The similarity with the name of the FASB is no coincidence. With this restructuring, the IASB became an operational clone of the FASB. The Board members were to be full time, just as the FASB Board members have always been. The Board members are not to represent specific national constituencies, unlike the IASC and also unlike what was envisioned under several IASC restructuring proposals. Like the FASB, the IASB Board members come from a much broader background than the CPA community (this continued a trend that had already been started in the IASC). The 15 Board members of the IASB come from many countries and represent a variety of professional backgrounds. As of May 2010, the 15 Board members included individuals from the United States, the United Kingdom, France, Sweden, China, Australia, South Africa, Brazil, and Japan.[5] Many of the Board members are CPAs with audit experience, but in May 2010 the IASB also included a financial analyst and several people with national regulatory experience. And the IASB deliberative process was to be much more along the lines of the FASB's operating procedure—public meetings, open debate, lots of public input into the process, transparent decisions, and so forth.

In 2002, the IASB and the FASB entered into a joint agreement, called the Norwalk Agreement, in which they pledged to work together to develop a set of "fully compatible" accounting standards as soon as possible, and to continue to work together to make sure that those standards stay compatible. This joint effort is proceeding along two fronts. First,

[3] Kees Camfferman and Stephen A. Zeff, *Financial Reporting and Global Capital Markets: A History of the International Accounting Standards Committee, 1973–2000* (Oxford University Press, 2007), p. 10. This book is the definitive and authoritative history of the IASC.

[4] Summer Research Symposium, Hong Kong University of Science and Technology, Hong Kong, 1998.

[5] The IASB will be expanded to 16 members by 2012.

the IASB and the FASB identified several accounting standard issues on which they could achieve full compatibility without too much difficulty. These issues included the accounting for some inventory costs, accounting for the exchange of nonmonetary assets, and the reporting of accounting changes, all of which have been completed, and the computation of earnings per share, which is still in progress. Second, the IASB and the FASB are working together on larger projects involving fundamental issues such as revenue recognition, the accounting for business combinations, and a joint conceptual framework.

In spite of this surface appearance of amiable cooperation between the IASB and the FASB, the IASB has been very aggressive at promoting its standards as THE worldwide standard. For a time, the IASB Web site was almost like a scoreboard proudly proclaiming the number of countries that had accepted IASB standards as their national standard. But as it has become apparent that the IASB would eventually become the source for worldwide accounting standards and that the FASB would fade in influence, the FASB appears to have gracefully accepted this and has worked closely with the IASB on their many joint projects.

This shift from the FASB to the IASB as the acknowledged source of high-quality global accounting standards is illustrated by an historic announcement by the SEC in 2007 that approved the use of IASB standards for the financial reports of non-U.S. companies with shares traded on U.S. stock exchanges. This change took effect in 2008. Specifically, on March 4, 2008, Chapter II of Title 17 of the CFR (Code of Federal Regulations) was amended by the SEC to allow non-U.S. companies to use International Financial Reporting Standards, instead of U.S. GAAP, in their financial statement filings with the SEC. Before this, non-U.S. companies wishing to have their shares traded in the United States had to provide U.S. shareholders with a summary showing what key reported financial statement numbers would have been had the company used U.S. GAAP. An example of this disclosure, called Form 20-F, was shown for Daimler-Benz in Exhibit 22-1.

An even more earth-shaking development occurred on August 27, 2008. Here is the first paragraph of an article that appeared in *The Wall Street Journal* the next day:

> "The Securities and Exchange Commission signaled the demise of U.S. accounting standards, kicking off a process Wednesday that could ultimately require all publicly listed American companies to follow an international model instead."[6]

Additional details from this landmark SEC announcement revealed a "time line" for the rapid shift from U.S. GAAP to IFRS, with all U.S. publicly traded companies being required to use IASB standards by 2014. As explained in detail in the opening scenario of Chapter 1 of this textbook, this rosy "time line" exploded in a blaze of controversy in October 2008. In brief, external pressure caused the IASB to short-circuit its due process deliberations and cave in to European bank urgings for a favorable accounting standard change. This blatant politicization of the accounting standard-setting process caused many in the U.S. business community to rethink the transfer of sovereignty over U.S. accounting standards from the FASB, which can be closely monitored by the SEC, to the IASB, which is completely outside any U.S. regulatory jurisdiction. The revised "work plan" of the SEC promises that no switch from U.S. GAAP to IFRS will occur until 2015, at the earliest.

FYI

Look again at the opening scenario for Chapter 1 to see the details of the October 2008 IASB debacle.

[6] Kara Scannell and Joanna Slater, "SEC Moves to Pull Plug on U.S. Accounting Standards," *The Wall Street Journal*, August 28, 2008, p. A1.

Although the details of the U.S. transition to some form of IFRS are uncertain, it is now very likely that all publicly traded U.S. companies will be using IFRS very early in your career. Of course, some skeptics are claiming that U.S. investors and accountants will find the new international financial statements hard to understand. But you won't be one of those without understanding. As you will see in the U.S. GAAP/IFRS comparison summary in the next learning objective in this chapter, this textbook has already given you very thorough exposure to IFRS.

Summary of U.S. GAAP/IFRS Differences

3 Identify key differences between U.S. GAAP and IFRS.

WHY **Students of accounting in the United States must know U.S. GAAP as well as IFRS.**

HOW **Throughout this textbook, you have learned U.S. accounting rules as well as key areas of difference between U.S. GAAP and IFRS. Once a person understands U.S. GAAP in a certain area, it doesn't take much additional study to understand any significant differences under IFRS.**

In almost every chapter in this textbook, you have been presented with comparisons of the important differences between U.S. GAAP and IFRS. A summary of those differences is included on the next few pages. Before you become overwhelmed by this list of differences, you should stop for a moment and consider the much longer list that could be made of the similarities between U.S. GAAP and IFRS. The large majority of accounting standards and treatments discussed in this long, long textbook are the same under both sets of standards. And as you will be reminded as you look through the list below, once you understand U.S. GAAP, the IFRS differences are reasonable alternatives that fit comfortably under the conceptual umbrella of generally accepted accounting principles.

The following comparisons also include side-by-side references to both the current FASB Codification and the historical standards from which the Codification was generated. Most practicing accountants still think in terms of the old standard numbers. For example, if you say "Statement 133," a seasoned accountant will immediately think, "Derivatives!" In contrast, those of us friendly with the FASB's Codification associate "Topic 815" with "derivatives." The following summary tables can help as you attempt to communicate with accountants who received their education before the Codification.

Topic	U.S. GAAP	IASB
Chapter 1: Financial Reporting		
Accounting standard setter	Financial Accounting Standards Board (FASB)	International Accounting Standards Board (IASB)
Financial accounting standards	FASB Accounting Standards Codification (ASC)	• International Financial Reporting Standards (IFRS) • International Accounting Standards (IAS)
Group to address issues of interpretation or for which no formal standard currently exists	Emerging Issues Task Force (EITF)	• International Financial Reporting Interpretations Committee (IFRIC) • Standing Interpretations Committee (SIC) before 2002

ifrs

Topic	FASB Accounting Standards Codification	Original FASB Standard	Corresponding IASB Standard	Differences between U.S. GAAP and IFRS
Chapter 3: The Balance Sheet and Notes to the Financial Statements				
Classified balance sheet	*Section 210-10-05 par. 4* *Section 210-10-45 par. 1 through 12*	*ARB 43 Ch, 3A par. 4-8*	*IAS 1 par. 60-61*	No substantial differences in the descriptions and definitions of current assets and current liabilities
Classification of short-term obligations to be refinanced	*Section 470-10-45 par. 14*	*SFAS No. 6 par. 10-11*	*IAS 1 par. 72*	Under IFRS, for a short-term obligation to be classified as long term, the refinancing must take place by the balance sheet date.
Upward revaluation	*Topic 855*	*SFAS No. 165*	*IAS 10*	No substantial differences
Chapter 4: The Income Statement				
Discontinued operations	*Subtopic 205-20*	*SFAS No. 144*	*IFRS 5*	Under IFRS, a discontinued operation must be a major line of business or geographic segment. Also, under IFRS, separate disclosure must be made of the cash flows of the discontinued operations.
Extraordinary items	*Subtopic 225-20*	*APB Opinion No. 30*	*IAS 1 par. 87*	Under IFRS, no income or expense items are allowed to be classified as "extraordinary."
Change in accounting principle	*Section 250-10-45 par. 1-16* *Section 250-10-50 par. 1- 3*	*SFAS No. 154 par. 4-18* *APB No. 28 par. 28*	*IAS 8 par. 14-31*	No substantial differences
Chapter 5: Statement of Cash Flows and Articulation				
Definition of cash equivalents	*Section 230-10-20 (Glossary) – Cash equivalents*	*SFAS No. 95 par. 8*	*IAS 7 par. 7*	No substantial differences
Noncash investing and financing activities	*Section 230-10-50 par. 3*	*SFAS No. 95 par. 32*	*IAS 7 par. 43*	No substantial differences
Direct and indirect methods	*Section 230-10-45 par. 25,28*	*SFAS No. 95 par. 27-28*	*IAS 7 par. 18-19*	No substantial differences
Classification of interest paid	*Section 230-10-45 par. 17(d)*	*SFAS No. 95 par. 23(d)*	*IAS 7 par. 33*	U.S. GAAP – operating IFRS – operating or financing
Classification of income taxes paid	*Section 230-10-45 par. 17(c)*	*SFAS No. 95 par. 23(c)*	*IAS 7 par. 35*	U.S. GAAP – operating IFRS – operating, investing, or financing
Classification of interest received	*Section 230-10-45 par. 16(b)*	*SFAS No. 95 par. 22(b)*	*IAS 7 par. 33*	U.S. GAAP – operating IFRS – operating or investing
Classification of dividends received	*Section 230-10-45 par. 16(b)*	*SFAS No. 95 par. 22(b)*	*IAS 7 par. 33*	U.S. GAAP – operating IFRS – operating or investing
Classification of dividends paid	*Section 230-10-45 par. 15(a)*	*SFAS No. 95 par. 20(a)*	*IAS 7 par. 34*	U.S. GAAP – financing IFRS – operating or financing

Topic	U.S. GAAP	IASB Standard
Chapter 6: Earnings Management		
General characterization of the standards	Rules oriented. U.S. GAAP contains about 25,000 pages with lots of detailed guidance.	Principles oriented. IFRS contains just 2,500 pages with many detailed accounting decisions left up to the professional judgment of the accountant.

Topic	FASB Accounting Standards Codification	Original FASB Standard	Corresponding IASB Standard	Differences between U.S. GAAP and IFRS
Fair Value Module				
Fair values in financial reporting	*Topic 820*	*SFAS No. 157*	*Exposure Draft: Fair Value Measurement, May 2009*	No substantial differences. Both the FASB and the IASB plan to have revised fair value standards finalized by the end of 2010; the revised standards will be mutually consistent.
Chapter 7: The Revenue/Receivables/Cash Cycle				
Bad debts	*Section 310-10-35 par. 7-9*	*SFAS No. 5 par. 22*	*No explicit standard*	No apparent differences
Warranties	*Section 460-10-25 par. 5-7*	*SFAS No. 5 par. 24*	*IAS 37 par. 14, 39*	No substantial differences
Compensating balances	*Section 210-10-S99 par. 1*	*SEC Regulation S-X, Rule 5-02, Caption 1*	*IAS 7 par. 48*	No substantial differences
Imputation of interest on receivables	*Section 835-30-25 par. 2, 12*	*APB No. 21 par. 9, 13*	*No explicit standard*	No apparent differences
Derecognition of receivables	*Section 860-10-40 par. 5*	*SFAS No. 140 par. 9*	*IAS 39 par. 20*	U.S. GAAP includes a list of three criteria that must be satisfied for derecognition. IFRS has a conceptual 2-step test based on risks and rewards and control. In practice, the derecognition result is almost always the same.
Chapter 8: Revenue Recognition				
Revenue recognition	*Topic 605*	*Contained in a large number of different standards*	*IAS 18, IAS 11*	U.S. GAAP and IFRS are generally consistent, but many detailed differences exist. The FASB and IASB are currently working on a joint revenue recognition project.
Completed-contract method	*Subtopic 605-35*	*ARB 45 and SOP 81-1*	*IAS 11*	Under IFRS, the completed contract method is not allowed.
Pre-sale revenue recognition for biological assets	*Section 905-330-35*	*SOP 85-3*	*IAS 41*	Under IFRS, changes in the fair value of biological assets are recognized as gains and losses. Under U.S. GAAP, a similar procedure is acceptable under some circumstances, but not required.

Topic	FASB Accounting Standards Codification	Original FASB Standard	Corresponding IASB Standard	Differences between U.S. GAAP and IFRS
Multiple-element arrangements	*Subtopic 605-25*	*EITF 08-1*	*IAS 18*	IFRS does not contain any specific provisions related to multiple-element arrangements.
Chapter 9: Inventory and Cost of Goods Sold				
LIFO	*Section 330-10-30 par. 9-11*	*ARB 43, Chapter 4*	*IAS 2 par. 23-27*	LIFO is not allowable under IFRS.
Lower of cost or market	*Section 330-10-35 par. 1-12*	*ARB 43, Chapter 4*	*IAS 2 par. 28-33*	Under IFRS, inventory is recorded at lower of cost or net realizable value, and inventory write-down losses can be reversed if the selling price subsequently recovers.
Foreign currency transactions	*Section 830-20-35 par. 2*	*SFAS No. 52 par. 16b*	*IAS 21 par. 23a, 28*	No substantial differences
Chapter 10: Investments in Noncurrent Operating Assets—Acquisition				
Interest capitalization	*Subtopic 835-20*	*SFAS No. 34*	*IAS 23*	Under IFRS, net "borrowing costs" are capitalized. The net amount is the gross interest paid less interest received on investment of idle funds.
Asset retirement obligation	*Subtopic 410-20*	*SFAS No. 143*	*IAS 16 and IAS 37*	No substantial differences
Business combinations	*Topic 805*	*SFAS No. 141R*	*IFRS 3*	No substantial differences
Intangible assets	*Topic 350*	*SFAS No. 142*	*IAS 38*	No substantial differences
Research and development	*Topic 730*	*SFAS No.2 SFAS No.86*	*IAS 38*	Under IFRS, development costs, which are costs incurred after technological feasibility, are capitalized. This matches U.S. GAAP for software development costs, but not for ordinary R&D.
Chapter 11: Investments in Noncurrent Operating Assets—Utilization and Retirement				
Impairment of tangible assets	*Subtopic 360-10 various subsections on "Impairment"*	*SFAS No. 144*	*IAS 36*	Under U.S. GAAP, the impairment test is a 2-step test. Under IFRS, the impairment test involves just one step, a comparison of the book value to the "recoverable amount" of the asset.
Impairment of intangible assets	*Topic 350*	*SFAS No. 142*	*IAS 36*	U.S. GAAP includes three different impairment tests for intangibles. Under IFRS, there is just one test, which is the same as is used for tangible assets.
Upward revaluation	*Not part of U.S. GAAP*	*Not part of U.S. GAAP*	*IAS 16*	Upward revaluations of property, plant, and equipment are generally not allowable under U.S. GAAP.

Topic	FASB Accounting Standards Codification	Original FASB Standard	Corresponding IASB Standard	Differences between U.S. GAAP and IFRS
Asset retirement obligations	*Subtopic 410-20*	*SFAS No. 143*	*IAS 16 and IAS 37*	No substantial differences
Assets classified as held for sale	*Section 360-10-45*	*SFAS No. 144*	*IFRS 5*	No substantial differences
Chapter 12: Debt Financing				
Short-term obligations expected to be refinanced	*Section 470-10-45 par. 14*	*SFAS No. 6 par. 10-11*	*IAS 1 par. 72*	Under IFRS, for a short-term obligation to be classified as long term, the refinancing must take place by the balance sheet date.
Splitting convertible debt proceeds into debt and equity	*Subtopic 470-20*	*APB Opinion No. 14*	*IAS 32 par. 28-32*	Under IFRS, ALL convertible debt issues are divided into their debt and equity components. This separation is only done under certain circumstances under U.S. GAAP.
Consolidation of variable interest entities (VIE)	*Section 810-10-25 par. 20 through 59*	*FIN 46R*	*SIC 12*	Under IFRS, a VIE is consolidated when the economic substance of the relationship indicates that the VIE is controlled. Compared to U.S. GAAP, this is very much a principles-based approach.
Fair value option	*Topic 825, "Fair Value Option" subsections*	*SFAS No. 159*	*IFRS 9*	There is a fair value option for financial assets under IFRS, but as of 2010 there was not yet a fair value option for financial liabilities.
Troubled debt restructuring	*Subtopic 470-60*	*SFAS No. 15*	*IAS 39 par. 39 through 41*	No substantial differences
Chapter 13: Equity Financing				
Stock warrants	*Section 470-20-25 par. 2*	*APB Opinion No. 14 par. 16*	*IAS 32 par. 28*	Under IFRS, all compound financial instruments, such as stock warrants, are to be separated into separate debt and equity components. Under U.S. GAAP, this is required only if the stock warrants are "detachable."
Stock-based compensation	*Topic 718*	*SFAS No. 123R*	IFRS 2	No substantial differences
Reporting equity-related items as liabilities	*Topic 480*	*SFAS No. 150*	*IAS 32*	No substantial differences
Noncontrolling interest	*Section 810-10-45 par. 16*	*SFAS No. 160 par. 5*	*IAS 27 par. 27*	No substantial differences

Topic	FASB Accounting Standards Codification	Original FASB Standard	Corresponding IASB Standard	Differences between U.S. GAAP and IFRS
Chapter 14: Investments in Debt and Equity Securities				
Classification as trading, available for sale, or held to maturity	*Section 320-10-25 par. 1*	*SFAS No. 115 par. 6-12*	*IFRS 9 par 4.1, 5.4.4*	No substantial differences
Equity method	*Topic 323*	*APB Opinion No. 18*	*IAS 28*	No substantial differences
Fair value option	*Topic 825, "Fair Value Option" subsections*	*SFAS No. 159*	*IFRS 9*	There is a fair value option for financial assets under IFRS, but as of 2010 there was not yet a fair value option for financial liabilities.
Derecognition of investment securities	*Topic 860*	*SFAS No. 140*	*IAS 39 par. 20*	Under U.S. GAAP, the transfer of a financial asset is recorded as a sale if control of the asset passes from the transferor to the transferee. Under IFRS, the transfer is recorded as a sale if the risks and rewards associated with the cash flows from the financial assets pass from the transferor to the transferee.
Classification of cash flows from the purchase and sale of investment securities	*Section 320-10-45 par. 11*	*SFAS No. 115 par. 18*	*IAS 7 par. 15-16*	Under IFRS, cash flows from the purchase and sale of trading securities are classified under operating activities; for other security categories, the cash flows are investing activities. Under U.S. GAAP, trading security cash flows may be operating or investing, depending on management intent.
Loan impairment	*Section 310-10-35*	*SFAS No. 114*	*IAS 39 par. 58 through 65*	No substantial differences
Chapter 15: Leases				
Lease classification criteria	*Section 840-10-25 par. 1*	*SFAS No. 13 par. 7*	*IAS 17 par. 8-10*	In substance, the standards are the same. IFRS provides less detail.
Lease discount rate (for lessees)	*Section 840-10-25 par. 31*	*SFAS No. 13 par. 7*	*IAS 17 par. 20*	In IFRS, no explicit mention is made of using the lower of the implicit rate or the incremental borrowing rate. Instead, the implicit rate is to be used if known.
Revenue recognition criteria (for lessor)	*Section 840-10-25 par. 42*	*SFAS No. 13 par. 8*	*IAS 17 par. 42*	Substantially the same. Rather than the two explicit criteria, IFRS merely says that a sale in a sales-type lease is recognized "in accordance with the policy followed by the entity for outright sales."

Topic	FASB Accounting Standards Codification	Original FASB Standard	Corresponding IASB Standard	Differences between U.S. GAAP and IFRS
Initial direct costs (for lessors)	*Section 840-20-35 par. 2* *Section 840-30-35 par. 23* *Section 840-30-25 par. 6*	*SFAS No. 13 par. 19* *SFAS No. 13 par. 18* *SFAS No. 13 par. 17*	*IAS 17 par. 38, 42*	No substantial differences
Sale-leaseback accounting	*Section 840-40-25 par. 3* *Section 840-40-35 par. 1*	*SFAS No. 13 par. 7*	*IAS 17 par. 58-63*	No substantial differences
Chapter 16: Income Taxes				
Use of currently enacted tax rates	*Section 740-10-10 par. 3*	*SFAS No. 109 par. 18*	*IAS 12 par. 46*	Under U.S. GAAP, currently enacted tax rates for future years are used in valuing deferred tax assets and liabilities. Under IFRS, tax rates that have been "substantively enacted" are also used. Substantively enacted tax rates are future tax rates that have been announced by the government but that have not yet been formally enacted into law.
Current/ noncurrent classification of deferred tax assets and liabilities	*Section 740-10-45 par. 4*	*SFAS No. 109 par. 41*	*IAS 1 par. 56*	Under U.S. GAAP, deferred tax assets and liabilities are classified current or noncurrent based on the classification of the associated asset or liability. Under IFRS, all deferred tax items are classified as noncurrent.
Recognition of deferred tax assets	*Section 740-10-30 par. 5e*	*SFAS No. 109 par. 17e*	*IAS 12 par. 24*	Under U.S. GAAP, deferred tax assets are recognized if it is "more likely than not" (50%+ probability) that the future tax benefits will be realized. Under IFRS, the probability threshold is "probable," which is generally seen to be higher than "more likely than not."
Uncertain tax positions	*Topic 740*	*FASB FIN No. 48*	*No specific accounting standard in IAS*	Under IFRS, there is no standard regarding the recognition of a tax liability related to an uncertain tax position.
Cash paid for income taxes	*Section 230-10-50 par. 2*	*SFAS No. 95 par. 121*	*IFRS 7 par. 35*	Both U.S. GAAP and IFRS require separate disclosure of the amount of cash paid for income taxes. Under IFRS, this amount may be allocated among operating, investing, and financing activities.
Chapter 17: Employee Compensation—Payroll, Pensions, and Other Compensation Issues				
Compensated absences	*Section 710-10-25 par. 1-8*	*SFAS No. 43 par. 6-16*	*IAS 19 par. 11-16*	No substantial differences

Topic	FASB Accounting Standards Codification	Original FASB Standard	Corresponding IASB Standard	Differences between U.S. GAAP and IFRS
Postemployment benefits	*Section 712-10-05 par. 2-6 Section 712-10-15 par. 3-5 Section 712-10-25 par. 1-5*	*SFAS No. 112 par. 1-6 SFAS No. 88 par. 15*	*IAS 19 par. 132-140*	No substantial differences
Discount rate for projected benefit obligation	*Section 715-30-35 par. 43*	*SFAS No. 87 par. 44*	*IAS 19 par.78*	IFRS allows use of the interest rate on government bonds in countries lacking a developed corporate bond market.
Prior service cost	*Section 715-30-35 par. 10-11*	*SFAS No. 87 par. 24-25*	*IAS 19 par.96*	Under IFRS, the "past" service cost amount is recognized as an expense immediately IF the benefits are immediately vested.
Balance sheet numbers: one net number for the difference between PBO and the pension fund, with AOCI shown separately	*Section 715-30-25 par. 1, 4*	*SFAS No. 87 par. 35, 38*	*IAS 19 par.54*	Under current IFRS, the reported balance sheet number is the sum of the PBO, the pension fund, and AOCI associated with the pension plan.
Settlements and curtailments	*Various sections in Subtopics 715-30 and 715-60; illustrations in Section 715-30-55*	*SFAS No. 88*	*IAS 19 par.109-115*	No substantial differences
Disclosure	*Sections 715-29-50 715-30-50 715-60-50*	*SFAS No. 132(R)*	*IAS 19 par.120-125*	No substantial differences
Differences similar to the differences in accounting for pensions.	*Subtopic 715-60*	*SFAS No. 106*	In general, no distinction between pensions and other postretirement benefits. Guidance on medical benefits found in IAS 19 par. 88-91	Differences similar to the differences in accounting for pensions.
Chapter 18: Earnings per Share				
Computing basic earnings per share	*Section 260-10-45 par. 10-11*	*SFAS No. 128 par. 8-9*	*IAS 33 par. 9-29*	No substantial differences
Computing diluted earnings per share	*Section 260-10-45 par. 16-17*	*SFAS No. 128 par. 11, 13*	*IAS 33 par. 30-44*	No substantial differences

Topic	FASB Accounting Standards Codification	Original FASB Standard	Corresponding IASB Standard	Differences between U.S. GAAP and IFRS
Participating securities and the two-class method	*Section 260-10-45 par. 59A-66*	*SFAS No. 128 par. 60-61 EITF 03-06*	*IAS 33 par. A13-A14*	No substantial differences
Treasury stock method for options	*Section 260-10-45 par.23, 25*	*SFAS No. 128 par. 17-18*	*IAS 33 par. 45-48*	No substantial differences
If-converted method for convertible securities	*Section 260-10-45 par. 40-42*	*SFAS No. 128 par. 26-28*	*IAS 33 par. 49-51*	No substantial differences
Impact of actual conversion or exercise	*Section 260-10-45 par. 17*	*SFAS No. 128 par. 13*	*IAS 33 par. 38*	No substantial differences
Proper order of consideration for multiple potentially dilutive securities	*Section 260-10-45 par. 18*	*SFAS No. 128 par. 14-15*	*IAS 33 par. 44*	No substantial differences
Disclosures associated with basic and diluted EPS	*Section 260-10-50 par. 1-2*	*SFAS No. 128 par. 40-41*	*IAS 33 par. 70-73A*	No substantial differences
Chapter 19: Derivatives, Contingencies, Business Segments, and Interim Reports				
Accounting for derivatives	*Topic 815*	*SFAS No. 133*	*IAS 39*	No substantial differences at the conceptual level, but numerous technical differences that are beyond the scope of this book.
Recognition of contingent liabilities and contingent assets	*Contingent liabilities: Section 450-20-25 Contingent assets: Section 450-30-25*	*SFAS No. 5 par. 3 and 17*	*IAS 37 par. 10,27-28,31,34*	Generally the same. Under IFRS, there is no requirement to disclose contingent guarantee obligations when their likelihood is remote.
Measurement of contingent liabilities	*Section 450-20-30 par. 1*	*FIN No. 14 par. 3*	*IAS 37 par. 36-47*	Under U.S. GAAP, the estimated liability is the low end of the estimated range if each estimate in the range is equally likely. Under IFRS, the estimated liability is the amount required to settle the obligation.
Segment reporting	*Topic 280*	*SFAS No. 131*	*IFRS 8*	No substantial differences
Relation between interim reporting and annual reporting	*Section 270-10-45 par. 1-2*	*APB Opinion No. 28 par. 9*	*IAS 34 par. 28*	Under U.S. GAAP, an interim period is viewed as a subcomponent of the annual period. Under IFRS, accounting principles are applied to an interim period in the same way they are applied to an annual period.

Topic	FASB Accounting Standards Codification	Original FASB Standard	Corresponding IASB Standard	Differences between U.S. GAAP and IFRS
Chapter 20: Accounting Changes and Error Corrections				
Disclosure after a business combination	*Section 805-10-50 par. 1-2*	*SFAS No. 141(R) par. 68*	*IFRS 3 par. 59-63 and B64-B67*	No substantial differences
Change in accounting principle	*Section 250-10-45 par. 1-16* *Section 250-10-50 par. 1- 3*	*SFAS No. 154 par. 4-18* *APB No. 28 par. 28*	*IAS 8 par. 14-31*	No substantial differences
Change in accounting estimate	*Section 250-10-45 par. 17-20* *Section 250-10-50 par. 4- 5*	*SFAS No. 154 par. 19-22* *SFAS No. 157 par. 20*	*IAS 8 par. 32-40*	No substantial differences
Correction of an error	*Section 250-10-45 par. 22-28* *Section 250-10-50 par. 7-11*	*SFAS No. 154 par. 25-26* *SFAS No. 16 par. 10-15* *APB No. 9 par. 17-18* *APB No. 9 par. 26-27* *APB No. 28 par. 29*	*IAS 8 par. 41-49*	No substantial differences
Chapter 21: Statement of Cash Flows Revisited				
Definition of cash equivalents	*Section 230-10-20 (Glossary) – Cash equivalents*	*SFAS No. 95 par. 8*	*IAS 7 par. 7*	No substantial differences
Noncash investing and financing activities	*Section 230-10-50 par. 3*	*SFAS No. 95 par. 32*	*IAS 7 par. 43*	No substantial differences
Direct and indirect methods	*Section 230-10-45 par. 25,28*	*SFAS No. 95 par. 27-28*	*IAS 7 par. 18-19*	No substantial differences
Classification of interest paid	*Section 230-10-45 par. 17(d)*	*SFAS No. 95 par. 23(d)*	*IAS 7 par. 33*	U.S. GAAP – operating IFRS – operating or financing
Classification of income taxes paid	*Section 230-10-45 par. 17(c)*	*SFAS No. 95 par. 23(c)*	*IAS 7 par. 35*	U.S. GAAP – operating IFRS – operating, investing, or financing
Classification of interest received	*Section 230-10-45 par. 16(b)*	*SFAS No. 95 par. 22(b)*	*IAS 7 par. 33*	U.S. GAAP – operating IFRS – operating or investing
Classification of dividends received	*Section 230-10-45 par. 16(b)*	*SFAS No. 95 par. 22(b)*	*IAS 7 par. 33*	U.S. GAAP – operating IFRS – operating or investing
Classification of dividends paid	*Section 230-10-45 par. 15(a)*	*SFAS No. 95 par. 20(a)*	*IAS 7 par. 34*	U.S. GAAP – financing IFRS – operating or financing
Chapter 22: Accounting in a Global Market				
Foreign currency translation	*Subtopic 830-30*	*SFAS No. 52*	*IAS 21*	No substantial differences

Foreign Currency Financial Statements

4 **Convert foreign currency financial statements into U.S. dollars using the translation method.**

WHY **Almost every large U.S. corporation has foreign subsidiaries. Anyone associated with the financial statements of a large multinational should understand how the financial statements of the foreign subsidiaries are folded into those of the parent.**

HOW **Assets and liabilities are translated using the current exchange rate prevailing as of the balance sheet date. Income statement items are translated at the average exchange rate for the year. Dividends are translated using the exchange rate prevailing on the date the dividends were declared. Capital stock is translated at the historical rate, that is, the rate prevailing on the date the subsidiary was acquired or the stock was issued. Retained earnings is translated in the first year using historical rates, but in subsequent years, it is computed by taking the balance in Retained Earnings from the prior period's translated financial statements, adding translated net income, and subtracting translated dividends. The translation adjustment is recognized as a separate component of the U.S. parent company's stockholders' equity and included as part of accumulated other comprehensive income.**

In Chapter 9 (inventory purchases) and Chapter 19 (derivatives), the issues associated with foreign exchange rates and their impact on accounting for transactions were introduced. In this section, the concepts associated with foreign currency are extended to include entire foreign currency financial statements. Foreign currency financial statements are financial statements prepared in a currency other than the U.S. dollar. For example, **IBM** has many European subsidiaries whose internal financial statements are prepared in euros. Those financial statements, when submitted to IBM headquarters in Armonk, New York, must be converted into U.S. dollars. There are two methods for converting foreign currency financial statements: translation and remeasurement. Translation is used when the foreign subsidiary is a relatively self-contained unit that is independent from the parent company's operations. Remeasurement is appropriate when the subsidiary does not operate independently of the parent company. The translation process simply converts the foreign currency financial statements into U.S. dollars for consolidation with the parent company's statements; remeasurement involves remeasuring the financial statements as though the transactions had been originally recorded in U.S. dollars.

To determine the correct method of conversion, the functional currency of the foreign subsidiary must first be determined. In most instances, the functional currency is the currency in which most of the subsidiary's transactions are denominated.[7] If the functional currency is the local currency, the subsidiary is considered to be self-contained, and its financial statements are translated into U.S. dollars. If the functional currency is the U.S. dollar, the subsidiary is considered to be just a branch office of the parent, and the financial statements are remeasured into U.S. dollars. Most foreign entities are self-contained and use their local currency as the functional currency; thus, their financial statements are converted into U.S. dollars by translation. Therefore, this chapter

[7] FASB ASC Subtopic 830-30 (Foreign Currency Matters—Translation of Financial Statements).

discusses the translation process. Coverage of remeasurement is left to an advanced accounting course.

Translation

Translation involves converting financial statement information from a subsidiary's functional currency to the parent company's reporting currency using the current exchange rate. The specifics follow:

- Assets and liabilities are translated using the current exchange rate prevailing as of the balance sheet date.
- Income statement items are translated at the average exchange rate for the year.
- Dividends are translated using the exchange rate prevailing on the date the dividends were declared.
- Capital stock is translated at the historical rate, that is, the rate prevailing on the date the subsidiary was acquired or the stock was issued.
- Retained earnings is translated in the first year using historical rates, but in subsequent years, it is computed by taking the U.S. dollar balance in Retained Earnings from the prior period's translated financial statements, adding translated net income and subtracting translated dividends.

Double-entry accounting works the same for foreign subsidiaries as it does for U.S. companies: When a local currency trial balance is prepared, debits equal credits. However, as a result of the translation process, debits in the translated U.S. dollar trial balance typically will not equal credits. The balancing figure is called a translation adjustment and is recognized as part of the U.S. parent company's stockholders' equity.

To illustrate the translation process, consider the following example. USA Company purchased Swiss Inc. on January 1, 2013, for 50,000 francs. On that date, the exchange rate for 1 Swiss franc was $0.25, so the acquisition price was equivalent to $12,500. On December 31, 2013, the following trial balance for Swiss Inc. is available. The current exchange rate is $0.28, and the average exchange rate for the year was $0.27. Dividends were declared and paid when the exchange rate was $0.275.

Cash	10,000	francs	Accounts Payable	50,000	francs
Accounts Receivable	35,000		Long-Term Debt	80,000	
Inventory	65,000		Capital Stock	30,000	
Equipment	90,000		Retained Earnings	20,000	
Cost of Goods Sold	60,000		Sales	120,000	
Expenses	30,000				
Dividends	10,000				
Total debits	300,000	francs	Total credits	300,000	francs

If Swiss Inc. determines its functional currency to be the Swiss franc, translation is required to convert the financial statements into U.S. dollars for consolidation with USA Company's financial statements. As stated previously, the current rate is used to translate assets and liabilities, and the average rate is used to translate income statement items. The translation process is as shown on page 22-21.

December 31, 2013	Trial Balance (In Swiss francs)	Exchange Rate	Trial Balance (In U.S. dollars)
Cash	10,000	$0.28	$ 2,800
Accounts Receivable	35,000	0.28	9,800
Inventory	65,000	0.28	18,200
Equipment	90,000	0.28	25,200
Cost of Goods Sold	60,000	0.27	16,200
Expenses	30,000	0.27	8,100
Dividends	10,000	0.275	2,750
	300,000		$83,050
Accounts Payable	50,000	$0.28	$14,000
Long-Term Debt	80,000	0.28	22,400
Capital Stock	30,000	0.25	7,500
Retained Earnings	20,000	0.25	5,000
Sales	120,000	0.27	32,400
Translation Adjustment			1,750
	300,000		$83,050

Note that the retained earnings amount in the trial balance is the BEGINNING retained earnings for the year. We know this because we see both retained earnings and the detailed revenue, expense, and dividend accounts listed in the same trial balance. Once the books are closed so that the ending Retained Earnings balance is recorded in the accounts, the revenue, expense, and dividend accounts are zero.

In this example, Swiss Inc. requires an additional credit of $1,750 to balance the U.S. dollar trial balance. This translation adjustment can be thought of as a deferred gain. USA Company invested 50,000 francs in Swiss Inc. when 1 franc was worth $0.25. By year-end, each franc was worth $0.28, suggesting that USA Company had experienced a gain of approximately $1,500 [50,000 francs × ($0.28 – $0.25)]. The reason the deferred gain is not exactly equal to $1,500 is that the investment just didn't sit there during the year, but transactions occurred (sales, expenses, and dividends) that impacted the amount of USA Company's net franc investment.

The U.S. dollar amounts for the Swiss Inc. financial statement items are added to USA Company's amounts as part of the consolidation process. In addition, the translation adjustment is shown as a separate item in USA Company's Equity section as part of accumulated other comprehensive income. The annual change in the translation adjustment is recognized as part of other comprehensive income (essentially, a deferred gain or loss) rather than as an income statement gain or loss because the only way the foreign currency gain can be realized is through liquidation

FYI

For comparison, remeasurement uses historical rates in converting assets such as equipment and land. The historical rate is also used for converting the associated depreciation expense.

FYI

With remeasurement, the adjustment needed to balance the foreign subsidiary's U.S. dollar trial balance is recognized as a foreign currency gain or loss and is included in the income statement of the U.S. parent company.

of all the assets and liabilities of the foreign subsidiary. If the foreign subsidiary is a self-contained going concern, as it is assumed to be when the functional currency is the local currency and translation is used, it makes sense to defer the translation gain (or loss) because actual liquidation and conversion of the foreign subsidiary's net assets into U.S. dollars is not expected any time soon.

FASB CODIFICATION

The Issue: You and some old friends from high school have been sitting around talking about old times. Inevitably, the conversation has turned to accounting. You mentioned that you have learned how to translate foreign currency balance sheets and income statements into U.S. dollars. This pronouncement brought some "oohs" and "aahs" from your friends. But one friend cut short the respectful exclamations when he said: "Listen, don't talk to me about the balance sheet and the income statement. I care about the statement of cash flows. Tell me how to translate a statement of cash flows into U.S. dollars."

Well, the gauntlet has been thrown down. You have asked for a laptop so that you can go online, look at the FASB's Codification, and answer your friend's challenge.

The Question: How is a foreign currency statement of cash flows translated into U.S. dollars?

Searching the Codification: The Codification's foreign currency material is contained in Topic 830 (Foreign Currency Matters). Let's hope there is something there about the statement of cash flows.

The Answer: The procedure necessary to translate a foreign currency statement of cash flows into U.S. dollars is described below.

SOLUTIONS TO OPENING SCENARIO QUESTIONS

1. The SEC's Form 20-F provides a reconciliation between the reported net income of a non-U.S. company and what that net income would have been had the company used U.S. GAAP. The company is also required to provide a reconciliation of stockholders' equity. Since 2008, non-U.S. companies using IFRS have been able to have their shares traded on U.S. exchanges without providing a supplemental 20-F reconciliation.
2. Yes, U.S. companies can create "hidden reserves." Recall that hidden reserves are simply overstatements of expenses that can be reversed in future years to bolster income. A prime example of a "hidden reserve" used by U.S. companies is an overly large restructuring charge. Similarly, an excessive bad debt allowance can serve as a "hidden reserve."

SOLUTION TO USING THE FASB'S CODIFICATION

Under Topic 830, you can see Subtopic 230 (Statement of Cash Flows). A quick look through that subtopic reveals FASB ASC paragraph 830-230-45-1: "A statement of cash flows of an entity with foreign currency transactions or foreign operations shall report the reporting currency equivalent of foreign currency cash flows using the exchange rates in effect at the time of the cash flows. An appropriately weighted average exchange rate for the period may be used for translation if the result is substantially the same as if the rates at the dates of the cash flows were used. (That is, paragraph 830-30-45-3 applies to cash receipts and cash payments.) The statement of cash flows shall report the effect of exchange rate changes on cash balances held in foreign currencies as a separate part of the reconciliation of the change in cash and cash equivalents during the period."

So, the translated statement of cash flows is generated using much the same process as with the income statement. For cash flows occurring evenly throughout the year (such as cash collected from customers and cash paid to suppliers), an average rate for the year can be used. For discrete cash flows on a specific date (such as loan proceeds or dividend payments), the exchange rate on that date should be used. Finally, the impact of exchange rates changes on the U.S. dollar value of cash balances is to be shown as a separate line item in the statement of cash flows.

REVIEW CHAPTER 22

LEARNING OBJECTIVES

1 Understand the importance and potential impact of a common worldwide set of accounting standards.

Financial ratio comparisons can yield misleading implications if the ratios come from companies with differing accounting practices. Historically, this is exactly the situation that existed between different countries around the world. A key function of accounting standards is to create a common set of rules to be used by all companies so that outsiders can receive financial reports that are comparable among all of the different companies that they might want to analyze. Globalization of business has forced investors, creditors, and other stakeholders to perform an increasing number of cross-border financial statement comparisons, and the need for a common set of global standards has become apparent.

2 Outline the history of the IASB.

The IASC (predecessor of the IASB) was created by national CPA organizations from around the world, and the committee members did their work on a part-time basis. The early standards of the IASC were compilations of accounting practices around the world with, perhaps, a preferred treatment identified. In order to get the stamp of approval on its standards from IOSCO (an international association of securities regulators such as the SEC in the United States), the IASC improved its standards and created a comprehensive set of standards. In 2001, the IASC was restructured into the IASB with full-time Board members representing a broad business constituency. In 2002, the IASB and the FASB signed the Norwalk Agreement pledging to work together to develop a single set of high-quality accounting standards to be used around the world. The SEC is currently considering whether and when to require the adoption of IASB standards by all publicly traded U.S. companies.

3 Identify key differences between U.S. GAAP and IFRS.

Almost every chapter in this textbook contains a comparison of the important differences between U.S. GAAP and IFRS. A summary of those differences is included in Learning Objective #3.

4 Convert foreign currency financial statements into U.S. dollars using the translation method.

A foreign subsidiary's functional currency is the currency in which most of the subsidiary's transactions are denominated. If the functional currency is the local currency, the subsidiary is considered to be self-contained and its financial statements are converted into U.S. dollars through a process called *translation*. The financial statements of most foreign subsidiaries of U.S. companies are translated as follows:

- Assets and liabilities are translated using the current exchange rate prevailing as of the balance sheet date.
- Income statement items are translated at the average exchange rate for the year.
- Dividends are translated using the exchange rate prevailing on the date the dividends were declared.

- Capital stock is translated at the historical rate, that is, the rate prevailing on the date the subsidiary was acquired or the stock was issued.
- Retained earnings is translated in the first year using historical rates, but in subsequent years, it is computed by taking the balance in Retained Earnings from the prior period's translated financial statements, adding translated net income, and subtracting translated dividends.

The translation adjustment is a balancing figure and can be thought of as a deferred gain or loss stemming from the impact of exchange rate changes on the value of the U.S. parent's investment in the foreign subsidiary. The translation adjustment is recognized as a separate component of the U.S. parent company's stockholders' equity and included as part of accumulated other comprehensive income.

FASB-IASB CODIFICATION SUMMARY

ifrs

Topic	FASB Accounting Standards Codification	Original FASB Standard	Corresponding IASB Standard	Differences between U.S. GAAP and IFRS
Foreign currency translation	*Subtopic 830-30*	*SFAS No. 52*	*IAS 21*	No substantial differences

KEY TERMS

Functional currency 22-19

International Organization of Securities Commissions (IOSCO) 22-7

Remeasurement 22-19

Translation 22-19

Translation adjustment 22-20

QUESTIONS

1. Why is there a need for one set of worldwide financial accounting standards?
2. What kind of people served on the IASC when it was initially established?
3. Briefly describe the nature of the early IASC standards.
4. In the 1990s, what organization provided a push to the IASC to improve the quality of its standards?
5. Briefly describe the structural changes that accompanied the renaming of the IASC to the IASB.
6. What is the Norwalk Agreement?
7. What historic announcement did the SEC make in 2007 regarding IFRS?
8. What announcement did the SEC make on August 27, 2008?
9. What happened in October 2008 to derail the SEC's time line for transition to IFRS?
10. How do accounting differences impact the usefulness of financial ratio comparisons?
11. A foreign subsidiary's functional currency determines whether its financial statements should be translated or remeasured. Identify the primary factor in determining a subsidiary's functional currency. What other factors can influence management's determination as to the subsidiary's functional currency?
12. When financial statements are translated, which exchange rate is used for translating assets and liabilities? Which exchange rate is used for translating common stock? Which exchange rate is used for translating income statement items?
13. When financial statements are translated, what is the difference between the resulting debits and credits called? Where is this difference reported on the balance sheet?

PRACTICE EXERCISES

Practice 22-1

LO4

Foreign Currency Translation

U.S. Multi Company established a foreign subsidiary, called ForSub Company, on January 1, 2013. The local currency is the crown; on the date the subsidiary was established, the exchange rate was 2 crowns to 1 U.S. dollar. U.S. Multi invested U.S.$6,000 to get things started. In addition, a local loan in the amount of 8,000 crowns, equivalent to U.S.$4,000, was obtained. ForSub used the 20,000 crowns in initial financing to acquire the following assets:

	(in crowns)
Cash	2,000
Accounts receivable	4,000
Inventory	6,000
Land	8,000
Total assets	20,000

During 2013, ForSub conducted *no business operations* beyond the purchase of the assets listed above. Prepare a translated balance sheet, in U.S. dollars, for ForSub as of December 31, 2013, assuming that on that date the exchange rate is (1) 4 crowns to each U.S. dollar and (2) 1 crown to each U.S. dollar. (*Note*: Don't forget the Liability and Equity sections of the balance sheet.)

Practice 22-2

LO4

Foreign Currency Translation

Refer to Practice 22-1. Now, instead of assuming that ForSub conducted no business operations during 2013, assume that ForSub conducted the following business operations during 2013:

(a) Sales were 100,000 crowns.
(b) Expenses totaled 90,000 crowns.
(c) Dividends paid were 2,000 crowns.

The December 31, 2013, balance sheet differs from the January 1 balance sheet and is as follows:

	(in crowns)
Cash	3,000
Accounts receivable	6,000
Inventory	11,000
Land	8,000
Total assets	28,000

Prepare a translated balance sheet, in U.S. dollars, for ForSub as of December 31, 2013. Also prepare a translated income statement for 2013. Assume the following exchange rates:

End of year	4.0
Average for the year	3.0
Rate when dividends were paid	3.5

EXERCISES

Exercise 22-3
LO4

Translating Foreign Currency Financial Statements

The following trial balance in Japanese yen for World Mind Company, a Japanese subsidiary of American Mind Company, is available.

	(In Japanese yen)
Cash	¥ 7,000,000
Accounts Receivable	17,200,000
Inventory	23,500,000
Equipment	32,300,000
Cost of Goods Sold	28,550,000
Expenses	18,900,000
Dividends	6,000,000
Total debits	¥133,450,000
Accounts Payable	¥ 32,000,000
Long-Term Debt	15,000,000
Capital Stock	16,500,000
Retained Earnings	13,750,000
Sales	56,200,000
Total credits	¥133,450,000

The exchange rate when the subsidiary was purchased was $0.0059. The current exchange rate is $0.008, the average exchange rate for the year is $0.0072, and the exchange rate on the date dividends were declared and paid was $0.0074. The computed Retained Earnings balance from the previous year's translated financial statements was $130,000.

1. Prepare a translated trial balance for World Mind Company using the information provided.
2. Prepare a combined income and retained earnings statement and a balance sheet for World Mind Company using the information contained in the translated trial balance.

Exercise 22-4
LO4

Translating Foreign Currency Financial Statements

On January 3, 2013, Pecos Yo Company purchased International Metals, a Canadian company. On the day of the purchase, the exchange rate for 1 Canadian dollar was U.S.$0.79. International Metals' balance sheet on the date of the purchase follows.

	(In Canadian dollars)
Assets	
Cash	$ 58,000
Accounts receivable	112,500
Inventory	91,800
Plant assets	145,400
Total assets	$407,700
Liabilities and Equity	
Accounts payable	$165,600
Long-term debt	98,000

(continued)

	(In Canadian dollars)
Capital stock	65,100
Retained earnings	79,000
Total liabilities and equity	$407,700

Prepare a translated balance sheet as of January 3, 2013.

PROBLEMS

Problem 22-5
LO4

Translating Foreign Currency Financial Statements

Crab Beach Systems, a U.S. multinational producer of computer hardware, has subsidiaries located throughout the world. The company recently received year-end financial statements from its Swiss subsidiary, Doghead Technology. Doghead was purchased by Crab Beach on January 1, 2012. Doghead's financial statements are prepared and submitted to Crab Beach headquarters in Swiss francs. The accountant in charge of translating the financial statements has been unable to locate last year's translated financial statements. Instead, the only data available from last year are the financial statements prepared in francs. Doghead's adjusted trial balances as of December 31, 2012 and 2013, in Swiss francs, are as follows:

	Trial Balance Dec. 31, 2013	Trial Balance Dec. 31, 2012
Cash	925,000	750,000
Accounts Receivable	1,875,000	1,215,000
Inventory	2,115,000	1,850,000
Equipment	1,025,000	975,000
Cost of Goods Sold	7,985,000	6,505,000
Expenses	4,234,000	3,156,000
Dividends	900,000	500,000
Total debits	19,059,000	14,951,000
Accounts Payable	2,100,000	1,825,000
Long-Term Debt	1,000,000	1,125,000
Capital Stock	1,200,000	1,200,000
Retained Earnings (balance at beginning of year)	640,000	301,000
Sales	14,119,000	10,500,000
Total credits	19,059,000	14,951,000

Relevant exchange rates for 2013 and 2012 are as follows. The numbers shown are the U.S. dollar equivalent of one franc.

	2013	2012
January 1	$0.196	$0.175
Date of dividend payment	0.205	0.188
Average rate for the year	0.210	0.178
December 31	0.228	0.196

Instructions: Using the information given, prepare a translated income and retained earnings statement and balance sheet, in U.S. dollars, for Doghead Technology for 2013.

Problem 22-6
LO4
REVERSE SOLVABLE

Translating Foreign Currency Financial Statements

Kingscraft Inc., a company with headquarters in London, England, is a fully owned subsidiary of Dover Company. The accountant for Dover just received Kingscraft's financial statements and must translate them from British pounds into U.S. dollars to prepare consolidated financial statements. Income statement and balance sheet data for the year just ended, along with relevant exchange rates, are as follows:

	(in pounds)
Revenues	£445,000
Cost of goods sold	260,000
Gross margin	£185,000
Other expenses	80,000
Net income	£105,000
Cash	£ 46,000
Accounts receivable	102,000
Inventory	84,000
Plant and equipment	172,000
Total assets	£404,000
Current liabilities	£ 62,000
Long-term debt	54,000
Common stock	90,000
Retained earnings	198,000
Total liabilities and equity	£404,000

Exchange rates follow. The numbers shown are the U.S. dollar equivalent of one pound.

On date of purchase	$2.03
Average rate for the year	1.87
On the balance sheet date	1.84
On date of dividend payment	1.89

In addition, dividends of 60,000 pounds were paid during the year. Kingscraft's translated financial statements at year-end result in a translation adjustment with a debit balance of $73,000.

Instructions: Determine Kingscraft's Retained Earnings balance, in U.S. dollars, at the beginning of the year.

CASES

Discussion Case 22-7

Are International Ratios Comparable?

As the world economy becomes more integrated, one question facing financial analysts is whether financial ratios can be compared across national boundaries. For example, at one time the average P/E ratio for Japanese companies was around 60, and the average for U.S. companies was between 15 and 20. (A P/E ratio in excess of 30 is considered quite high in the United States.) This dramatic variation was a result of differences in the two national economies and in their accounting methods. One of the accounting differences is that Japanese companies generally depreciate their fixed assets over shorter lives than do U.S. companies.

In addition to differences in accounting methods, what other challenges are faced by financial analysts in comparing the financial ratios of a U.S. company to those of a Japanese, German, or British company?

Discussion Case 22-8

Fear of Reporting Under U.S. GAAP

You are on the board of directors of a large German corporation. You are in the years before 2008 when the SEC required all U.S.-listed companies to prepare reports using U.S. GAAP. For several years, the board has been discussing the possibility of listing the company's shares on the New York Stock Exchange. The CEO has approached the SEC several times asking for permission to list in the United States without also being required to reconcile its reported income to U.S. GAAP. So far, the SEC has refused to compromise. As a result, the CEO has decreed that the company will not list its shares in the United States.

You know that the reason the CEO is so vehemently opposed to reporting net income under U.S. GAAP is that doing so would reveal the income manipulation that your company has engaged in during the past few years. Historically, your company has overstated expenses, thereby creating a large amount of "hidden reserves." During the past two years, those hidden reserves have been reversed, increasing reported income and covering up mounting operating losses.

You are fearful of the company's survivability in the long run as long as operating losses are being covered up instead of addressed head on. The board of directors meets tomorrow, and one of the items on the agenda is yet another proposal to list shares on the New York Stock Exchange. What points should you bring up during that discussion?

Discussion Case 22-9

Translation or Remeasurement?

As the chief financial officer for Harvestors Inc., you are responsible for preparing its consolidated financial statements. Your first problem is how to consolidate the French subsidiary it purchased during the past year. You recently received the subsidiary's year-end financial statements and find that they are stated in euros. Before you can consolidate the financial statements, you must first convert them from euros to U.S. dollars. You know that foreign financial statements can be either translated or remeasured, and you must now determine which method is appropriate.

What factors should you consider in determining whether the financial statements should be translated or remeasured? Who has the final say in determining which method is used? What are the major differences between translation and remeasurement?

Case 22-10

Deciphering Financial Statements (The Walt Disney Company)

Locate the 2009 financial statements for **The Walt Disney Company** on the Internet.

Once you have located those financial statements, consider the following question. From Disney's foreign currency translation adjustment, deduce whether the foreign currencies got stronger or weaker in 2009 (relative to the U.S. dollar) in the countries where Disney has subsidiaries.

Case 22-11

Writing Assignment (Choosing the Functional Currency)

You are on the accounting staff at Jeff Pong Company. Jeff Pong is based in California and has recently acquired a subsidiary, Mak Hung Enterprises, located in Guangzhou, China. The board of directors of Jeff Pong is curious about how the Chinese currency (yuan) financial statements of Mak Hung will be consolidated with Jeff Pong's U.S. dollar financial statements. Yesterday, your boss, the controller, made a presentation to the board explaining the adjustments that will be made to Mak Hung's financial statements to restate them from IFRS to U.S. GAAP.

The controller has asked you to write a memo to the board explaining how the yuan financial statements, once restated to be in conformity with U.S. GAAP, will be converted into U.S. dollars. The controller has decided that Mak Hung's functional currency is the yuan. Make sure you explain to the board what a functional currency is, how it is determined, and what implications it has for the way financial statements are converted into U.S. dollars.

P4 OTHER DIMENSIONS OF FINANCIAL REPORTING

Kristoffer Tripplaar/Alamy

CHAPTER 23 Analysis of Financial Statements

LEARNING OBJECTIVES

1. Organize a systematic financial ratio analysis using common-size financial statements and the DuPont framework.
2. Recognize the potential impact that differing accounting methods can have on the financial ratios of otherwise essentially identical companies.
3. Perform a simple valuation of a company using financial statement data.

Home Depot is the leading retailer in the do-it-yourself home improvement market. As of January 31, 2010, Home Depot had 2,244 stores throughout the United States, Canada, China, and Mexico. With each store averaging 105,000 square feet (and an additional 24,000 square feet in the outside garden center), that is a lot of shelf space filled with paint, lumber, hardware, and plumbing fixtures. If plumbing fixtures don't seem very exciting to you, consider this: Home Depot is the 118th largest company in the United States (in terms of market value), with a 2010 market value of $61 billion.[1] In fiscal 2010, Home Depot's sales reached $66.2 billion.[2]

Home Depot's prospects weren't always so rosy. Back in 1985, when sales were only $700 million, Home Depot experienced severe profitability problems that threatened to terminate the company's expansion in its infancy. For example, Home Depot's gross profit percentage (gross profit/sales) had decreased from 27.3% to 25.9%. This decrease of 1.4 percentage points doesn't seem like much until you calculate that this decrease, with sales of $700 million, caused a gross profit reduction of $9.8 million ($700 million × 0.014) and reduced total operating profit by 34%. Overall, Home Depot's net income in 1985 was only $8.2 million, down 42% from the year before.

[1] 2010 Forbes Global 2000 listing. This list can be viewed by accessing Forbes' Web site at **http://www.forbes.com**.
[2] 2010 10-K filing of The Home Depot, Inc.

Home Depot also experienced cash flow problems, in large part due to rapid increases in the level of inventory. Part of this inventory increase was the natural result of Home Depot's expansion. But Home Depot stores were also starting to fill up with excess inventory because of lax inventory management. In 1983, the average Home Depot store contained enough inventory to support average sales for 75 days. By 1985, the number of days' sales in inventory had increased to 83 days. Combined with Home Depot's rapid growth, this inventory inefficiency caused total inventory to increase by $69 million in 1985, and this increase in inventory was instrumental in Home Depot's negative cash from operations of $43 million. Driven by this declining profitability and negative cash flow, Home Depot's stock value took a dive in 1985, and the beginning of 1986 found Home Depot wondering where it would find the investors and creditors to finance its aggressive expansion plans.

In 1986, however, Home Depot pulled off an incredible turnaround. Gross profit percentage went back up to 27.5%, operating income almost tripled compared to 1985, and net income increased from $8.2 million to $23.9 million. A computerized inventory management program was instituted, and the number of days' sales in inventory dropped to 80 days. Improved profitability and more efficient management of inventory combined to transform the negative $43 million operating cash flow in 1985 into positive cash from operations of $66 million in 1986. Home Depot even used a clever sale-leaseback arrangement to get $32 million of debt off its balance sheet.[3]

? QUESTIONS

1. Company A had sales of $1,000 and a gross profit percentage of 20%. By how many dollars would total gross profit increase if the gross profit percentage were to increase from 20% to 23%?
2. What was the primary cause of Home Depot's negative operating cash flow of $43 million in 1985?
3. By how much did Home Depot's operating cash flow increase from 1985 to 1986?

Answers to these questions can be found on page 23-27.

The Home Depot example illustrates how financial statement information can be used to evaluate the health of a business and identify specific areas that need improvement. This final chapter in the textbook covers financial statement analysis and reinforces the principle that the entire purpose of preparing financial statements is so that the statements can be used. This chapter summarizes the discussions of financial ratios that have appeared throughout the text and presents a coherent framework in which ratios can be systematically analyzed. The chapter also illustrates how differing accounting assumptions impact the values of financial ratios. The chapter concludes with a brief introduction to the use of financial statement data in valuing a company.

[3] The troubles of Home Depot in 1985 are the subject of a popular Harvard Business School case: Professor Krishna Palepu, "The Home Depot, Inc.," Harvard Business School, 9-188-148.

Framework for Financial Statement Analysis

1 **Organize a systematic financial ratio analysis using common-size financial statements and the DuPont framework.**

WHY **Financial statements are made to be used. Information can be extracted from the financial statements much more efficiently through a structured approach rather than just computing a hodgepodge of ratios.**

HOW **Common-size financial statements are computed by dividing all financial statement amounts for a given year by sales for that year. The DuPont framework decomposes return on equity (ROE) into three areas: profitability, efficiency, and leverage. The informativeness of financial ratios is greatly enhanced when they are compared with past values and with values for other firms in the same industry.**

Financial statement analysis is the examination of both the relationships among financial statement numbers and the trends in those numbers over time. One purpose of financial statement analysis is to use the past performance of a company to predict its future profitability and cash flows. Another purpose of financial statement analysis is to evaluate the performance of a company with an eye toward identifying problem areas. For example, the Home Depot numbers from 1985 indicated that the company had an inventory management problem that was severely reducing cash from operations. Home Depot's management used this information to spur inventory management improvements, and Home Depot's investors and creditors used the information in forecasting cash from operations for subsequent years. In summary, financial statement analysis is both diagnostic, identifying where a firm has problems, and prognostic, predicting how a firm will perform in the future.

Most pieces of information are meaningful only when they can be compared to some benchmark. For example, if you ask your friend how she feels and she says, "38," you will have some difficulty interpreting the information. If you know, however, that she felt 32 yesterday and that the happiest people you know are between 39 and 41, you can reasonably infer that your friend was unhappy yesterday but is feeling much better today. Similarly, the informativeness of financial ratios is greatly enhanced when they are compared with past values and with values for other firms in the same industry.

To enhance users' ability to do time-series comparisons, the SEC requires comparative financial reporting. Annual statements, for example, must include income and cash flow statements for three years and balance sheets for two years. These are minimum standards. Many companies include comparative statistics for 10 years in their annual reports.

Industry comparisons can be made by comparing financial statements for specific companies in an industry and by comparing a company's ratios with overall industry averages. The *COMPUSTAT* database from which the information in many of the exhibits in this text has been extracted is one source of industry data. Other well-known commercial sources for industry benchmark ratios include **Value Line** and **Dun & Bradstreet**.

FYI

Financial information is almost always compared to what was reported the previous year. For example, when Home Depot publicly announced on November 17, 2009, that its third-quarter sales were $16.4 billion, the press release also stated that this amount represented an 8.0% decrease from the prior year.

The Accounting Principles Board stated that comparisons between financial statements are most informative and useful under the following conditions:[4]

1. The presentations are in good form; that is, the arrangement within the statements is identical.
2. The content of the statements is identical; that is, the same items from the underlying accounting records are classified under the same captions.
3. Accounting principles are not changed, or, if they are changed, the financial effects of the changes are disclosed.
4. Changes in circumstances or in the nature of the underlying transactions are disclosed.

To the extent that the foregoing criteria are not met, comparisons may be misleading. Consistent practices and procedures are also important, especially when comparisons are made for a single enterprise. The potential impact of accounting differences on financial ratio comparisons is illustrated in a later section in this chapter.

Financial statement analysis is sometimes wrongly viewed as just the computation of a bunch of financial ratios: Take every financial statement number and divide it by every other number. This is a very inefficient and ineffective approach to analyzing a set of financial statements. This shotgun approach usually fails to lead to any concrete conclusions. This section of the chapter introduces the DuPont framework, which is one useful way to structure the analysis of financial ratios. In addition, this section explains the use of common-size financial statements, which are easy to prepare, easy to use, and should be the first step in any comprehensive financial statement analysis.

CAUTION

This chapter presents only an introduction to financial statement analysis. A good source for further information is Palepu and Healy, *Business Analysis and Valuation: Using Financial Statements, Text and Cases*, South-Western: Mason, Ohio, 2008 Fourth Edition.

Common-Size Financial Statements

The first problem encountered when using comparative data to analyze financial statements is that the scale, or size, of the numbers is usually different. If a firm has more sales this year than last year, it is now a larger company, and the levels of expenses and assets this year can't be meaningfully compared to the levels last year. In addition, if a company is of medium size in its industry, how can its financial statements be compared to those of the larger firms? The quickest and easiest solution to this comparability problem is to divide all financial statement numbers for a given year by sales for the year. The resulting financial statements are called common-size financial statements, with all amounts for a given year being shown as a percentage of sales for that year.

Exhibit 23-1 is a common-size income statement for Colesville Corporation, a hypothetical example. To illustrate the usefulness of a common-size income statement, consider the question of whether Colesville's gross profit in 2013 is too low. In comparison to the gross profit of $1,280,000 in 2011, the $1,700,000 gross profit for 2013 looks pretty good. Sales in 2013 are higher than sales in 2011, however, so the absolute levels of gross profit in the two years cannot be compared. But looking at the common-size information it is seen that gross profit is 33.7% of sales in 2011, compared to 29.8% in 2013. The

[4] *Statement of the Accounting Principles Board No. 4*, "Basic Concepts and Accounting Principles Underlying Financial Statements of Business Enterprises" (New York: American Institute of Certified Public Accountants, 1970), pars. 95–99.

common-size information reveals something that was not apparent in the raw numbers: In 2011, an item selling for $1 yielded an average gross profit of 33.7 cents; in 2013, an item selling for $1 yielded an average gross profit of 29.8 cents. Is this good or bad? Well, in 2013, Colesville made less gross profit from each dollar of sales than in 2011, so this is bad news. The good news is that gross profit as a percentage of sales is improved in 2013 relative to 2012 (27.3%).

Each item in the income statement can be analyzed in the same way. In 2013, bottom-line net income was 3.2% of sales, compared to just 1.6% in 2011. How can the gross profit percentage be better in 2011 while the net income percentage is worse? The answer lies in an examination of the remaining income statement items. Total operating expenses were 35.8% of sales in 2011, compared to just 26.6% in 2013. With a common-size income statement, each of the income statement items can be examined in this way, yielding much more information value than just looking at the raw income statement numbers.

A full analysis of Colesville's common-size income statement requires a comparison to industry averages. Assume that for companies in Colesville's industry, gross profit averages 31.5% of sales. Combined with the information previously discussed, this suggests that Colesville was outperforming its industry in 2011, suffered serious gross profit problems in 2012, and has started a slow comeback in 2013.

At this point, you should be saying to yourself: Yes, but what is the exact explanation for Colesville's drop in gross profit percentage from 2011? And how was Colesville able to reduce operating expenses? These questions illustrate the usefulness and the limitation of financial statement analysis. Our analysis of Colesville's income statement has pointed out two areas in which Colesville has experienced significant income statement change in the past two years, but the only way to find out why these financial statement numbers changed is to gather information from outside the financial statements: Ask management, read press releases, talk to financial analysts who follow the firm, and/or read industry newsletters. In short, financial statement analysis may not give you all the final answers, but it can guide you toward the questions you should be asking.

EX 23-1 COMMON-SIZE INCOME STATEMENT

Colesville Corporation
Comparative Income Statements
For the Years Ended December 31

	2013	%	2012	%	2011	%
Net sales	$5,700,000	100.0	$6,600,000	100.0	$3,800,000	100.0
Cost of goods sold	4,000,000	70.2	4,800,000	72.7	2,520,000	66.3
Gross profit on sales	$1,700,000	29.8	$1,800,000	27.3	$1,280,000	33.7
Selling expenses	$1,120,000	19.6	$1,200,000	18.2	$ 960,000	25.3
General expense	400,000	7.0	440,000	6.7	400,000	10.5
Total operating expenses	$1,520,000	26.6	$1,640,000	24.9	$1,360,000	35.8
Operating income (loss)	$ 180,000	3.2	$ 160,000	2.4	$ (80,000)	(2.1)
Other revenue (expense)	80,000	1.4	130,000	2.0	160,000	4.2
Income before taxes	$ 260,000	4.6	$ 290,000	4.4	$ 80,000	2.1
Income taxes	80,000	1.4	85,000	1.3	20,000	0.5
Net income	$ 180,000	3.2	$ 205,000	3.1	$ 60,000	1.6

Minor adjustments to percentage computations have been made to counteract the cumulative effect of rounding.

FYI

A common-size balance sheet can also be prepared using total assets to standardize each amount instead of using total sales. If this is done, the asset percentages are good indications of the company's asset mix.

A common-size balance sheet also expresses each amount as a percentage of sales for the year. As an illustration, a comparative balance sheet for Colesville Corporation with each item expressed in both dollar amounts and percentages is shown in Exhibit 23-2.

The most informative section of the common-size balance sheet is the Assets section, which can be used to determine how efficiently a company is using its assets. For example, compare total assets for Colesville in 2012 and 2013. Colesville has total assets of $2,278,000 in 2013. Is Colesville managing its assets more efficiently than in 2012 when total assets were $2,191,000? Comparing the raw numbers cannot give a clear answer because Colesville's level of sales is different in the two years. The common-size balance sheet indicates that each dollar of sales in 2012 required assets of 33.2 cents, whereas each dollar of sales in 2013 required assets of 40.0 cents. So, in which of the two years is Colesville more efficient at using its assets to generate sales? In 2012, when each dollar of sales required a lower level of assets. Examination of the individual asset accounts suggests that the primary reason for less efficient total asset usage in 2013 is land, building, and equipment: A dollar of sales in 2012 required only 16.3 cents of land, building, and equipment, compared to 22.4 cents in 2013.

DuPont Framework

As discussed in Chapter 3, return on equity (net income/equity) is the single measure that summarizes the financial health of a company. Return on equity can be interpreted as the number of cents of net income an investor earns in one year by investing one dollar in the company. As a very rough rule of thumb, return on equity (ROE) consistently above 15% is a sign of a company in good health; ROE consistently below 15% is a sign of trouble.

EX 23-2 COMMON-SIZE BALANCE SHEET

Colesville Corporation
Comparative Balance Sheets
December 31

	2013	%	2012	%	2011	%
Assets						
Current assets	$ 855,000	15.0	$ 955,500	14.5	$ 673,500	17.7
Land, building, and equipment (net)	1,275,000	22.4	1,075,000	16.3	925,000	24.4
Intangible assets	100,000	1.8	100,000	1.5	100,000	2.6
Other assets	48,000	0.8	60,500	0.9	61,500	1.6
Total assets	$2,278,000	40.0	$2,191,000	33.2	$1,760,000	46.3
Liabilities and Stockholders' Equity						
Current liabilities	$ 410,000	7.2	$ 501,000	7.6	$ 130,000	3.4
Noncurrent liabilities	400,000	7.0	600,000	9.1	400,000	10.5
Total liabilities	$ 810,000	14.2	$1,101,000	16.7	$ 530,000	13.9
Paid-in capital	$1,100,000	19.3	$ 800,000	12.1	$1,000,000	26.3
Retained earnings	368,000	6.5	290,000	4.4	230,000	6.1
Total stockholders' equity	$1,468,000	25.8	$1,090,000	16.5	$1,230,000	32.4
Total liabilities and stockholders' equity	$2,278,000	40.0	$2,191,000	33.2	$1,760,000	46.3

Minor adjustments to the percentage computations have been made to counteract the cumulative effect of rounding.

Return on equity for Colesville Corporation for the years 2013 and 2012 is computed as follows.

	2013	2012
Net income	$ 180,000	$ 205,000
Stockholders' equity	$1,468,000	$1,090,000
Return on equity	12.3%	18.8%

So, what can we say about Colesville's overall performance in 2013? It was bad relative to the rough ROE benchmark of 15%, and it was bad relative to ROE in 2012 of 18.8%. How do we pin down the exact reason(s) for the poor performance in 2013? That's what this section is about.

The DuPont framework (named after a system of ratio analysis developed internally at **DuPont** around 1920) provides a systematic approach to identifying general factors causing ROE to deviate from normal. The DuPont system also provides a framework for computing financial ratios to yield more in-depth analysis of a company's areas of strength and weakness. The insight behind the DuPont framework is that ROE can be decomposed into three components as shown in Exhibit 23-3.

EX 23-3 ANALYSIS OF ROE USING THE DUPONT FRAMEWORK

Return on Equity	=	Profitability	×	Efficiency	×	Leverage
	=	Return on Sales	×	Asset Turnover	×	Assets-to-Equity Ratio
	=	$\frac{\text{Net Income}}{\text{Sales}}$	×	$\frac{\text{Sales}}{\text{Assets}}$	×	$\frac{\text{Assets}}{\text{Equity}}$

For each of the three ROE components—profitability, efficiency, and leverage—one ratio summarizes a company's performance in that area. These ratios are as follows:

- *Return on sales* is computed as net income divided by sales and is interpreted as the number of pennies in profit generated from each dollar of sales.
- *Asset turnover* is computed as sales divided by assets and is interpreted as the number of dollars in sales generated by each dollar of assets.
- *Assets-to-equity ratio* is computed as assets divided by stockholders' equity and is interpreted as the number of dollars of assets a company is able to acquire using each dollar invested by stockholders.

The DuPont analysis of Colesville's ROE for 2013 and 2012 is as follows:

Return on Equity		=	$\frac{\text{Net Income}}{\text{Sales}}$	×	$\frac{\text{Sales}}{\text{Assets}}$	×	$\frac{\text{Assets}}{\text{Equity}}$
2013	12.3%	=	$\frac{\$180{,}000}{\$5{,}700{,}000}$	×	$\frac{\$5{,}700{,}000}{\$2{,}278{,}000}$	×	$\frac{\$2{,}278{,}000}{\$1{,}468{,}000}$
		=	3.16%	×	2.50	×	1.55
2012	18.8%	=	$\frac{\$205{,}000}{\$6{,}600{,}000}$	×	$\frac{\$6{,}600{,}000}{\$2{,}191{,}000}$	×	$\frac{\$2{,}191{,}000}{\$1{,}090{,}000}$
		=	3.11%	×	3.01	×	2.01

The results of the DuPont analysis suggest that Colesville's ROE is lower in 2013, not because of a decrease in profitability of sales but because of the following.

1. In 2013, assets are used less efficiently to generate sales. Each $1 of assets generated $3.01 in sales in 2012 but only $2.50 in sales in 2013.
2. In 2013, Colesville is less effective at leveraging stockholders' investment. By use of borrowing, Colesville was able to turn each $1 of invested funds in 2012 into $2.01 of assets, which is more than the $1.55 in assets in 2013.

This preliminary DuPont analysis is only the beginning of a proper ratio analysis. If a DuPont analysis suggests problems in any of the three ROE components, there are further ratios in each area that can shed more light on the exact nature of the problem. A sampling of those ratios is discussed next. Many of these ratios were introduced in prior chapters.

Profitability Ratios If the DuPont calculations had shown that Colesville had a profitability problem in 2013, a common-size income statement could have been used to identify which expenses were causing the problem. Referring back to the common-size income statement in Exhibit 23-1, cost of goods sold as a percentage of sales is lower in 2013 than in 2012 (70.2% vs. 72.7%). This positive development is partially offset by higher 2013 selling expenses (19.6% vs. 18.2%) and higher general expenses (7.0% vs. 6.7%). To summarize, the return on sales gives an overall indication of whether a firm has a problem with the profitability of each dollar of sales; the common-size income statement can be used to pinpoint exactly which expenses are causing the problem.

Efficiency Ratios The asset turnover ratio suggests that Colesville is less efficient at using its assets to generate sales in 2013 than it was in 2012. Which assets are causing this problem? One way to get a quick indication is to review the common-size balance sheet in Exhibit 23-2. The common-size balance sheet numbers indicate that in 2013, Colesville has a much larger amount of land, buildings, and equipment as a percentage of sales (22.4%) than in 2012 (16.3%), suggesting that Colesville is using its land, buildings, and equipment less efficiently in 2013. If the individual current assets were listed on the balance sheets (only total current assets are reported on the balance sheets in Exhibit 23-2), a similar analysis could be done with each individual current asset account.

In addition to the common-size balance sheet, specific financial ratios have been developed to indicate whether a firm is holding too much or too little of a particular asset. A selection of the most common of these ratios is discussed next. Many of the detailed asset balances used in the following calculations are not listed in Colesville's summary balance sheets contained in Exhibit 23-2.

Accounts receivable turnover. The amount of receivables usually bears a close relationship to the volume of credit sales. The appropriateness of the level of receivables may be evaluated by computing the accounts receivable turnover. This ratio is computed by dividing sales by the average accounts receivable for the year. The sales amount is used because companies typically don't separately disclose the amount of credit sales. The computations for Colesville Corporation for 2012 and 2013 follow.

	2013	2012
Sales	$5,700,000	$6,600,000
Net receivables:		
Beginning of year	$ 375,000	$ 333,500
End of year	$ 420,000	$ 375,000
Average receivables		
[(beginning balance + ending balance)/2]	$ 397,500	$ 354,250
Accounts receivable turnover	14.3 times	18.6 times

Receivables turnover represents the average number of sales/collection cycles completed by the firm during the year. The higher the turnover, the more rapid is a firm's average collection period for receivables. The numbers indicate that Colesville collected its receivables more rapidly in 2012 (18.6 times) than in 2013 (14.3 times).

> **! CAUTION**
>
> If sales occur seasonally, the ending balance in receivables may be unusually large (if many sales occur near the end of the year) or small (if the year-end occurs during a natural business lull). Averaging the beginning and ending balance will not correct for seasonality because the same thing happens each year. If quarterly data are available, the average of the quarterly balances can be used to correct for seasonality

The average accounts receivable balance is used in the calculation because of the desire to compare sales, which were made throughout the year, with the average level of receivables outstanding throughout the year. The ending balance in receivables may not be a good reflection of the normal receivable balance prevailing during the year. For example, if a business grows significantly during the year, the ending balance in the receivables account is greater than the average prevailing balance during the year. The opposite is true if the business shrinks during the year. Using the average receivables balance is a way to adjust for changes in the size of a business during the year. Similar adjustments are made with other ratios that compare end-of-year balance sheet amounts to sales made or expenses incurred throughout the year.

Average collection period. Average receivables are sometimes expressed in terms of the average collection period, which shows the average time required to collect receivables. Average receivables outstanding divided by average daily sales gives the average collection period. This measure is computed for Colesville as illustrated here.

	2013	2012
Average receivables	$ 397,500	$ 354,250
Sales	$5,700,000	$6,600,000
Average daily sales (sales/365)	$ 15,616	$ 18,082
Average collection period		
(average receivables/average daily sales)	25.5 days	19.6 days

This same measurement can be obtained by dividing the number of days in a year by the receivables turnover.

What constitutes a reasonable average collection period varies with individual businesses. For example, if the credit sale contract gives customers 60 days to pay, a 40-day average collection period would be reasonable. If customers are supposed to pay in 30 days, however, a 40-day average collection period would indicate slow collections.

Inventory turnover. The amount of inventory carried relates closely to sales volume. The inventory position and the appropriateness of its size may be evaluated by computing the inventory turnover. The inventory turnover is computed by dividing cost of goods sold by average inventory. Inventory turnover for Colesville is computed as follows:

	2013	2012
Cost of goods sold	$4,000,000	$4,800,000
Inventory:		
Beginning of year	$ 330,000	$ 125,000
End of year	$ 225,000	$ 330,000
Average receivables		
[(beginning balance + ending balance)/2]	$ 277,500	$ 227,500
Inventory turnover	14.4 times	21.1 times

CAUTION

Be careful when using ratios computed by someone else or extracted from a published source. Make sure you know exactly what formula was used to compute the ratio.

Inventory turnover sometimes is computed using sales instead of cost of goods sold. This is not entirely correct because sales is a retail number and both cost of goods sold and inventory are wholesale numbers. However, when it comes to ratios, people are free to perform the calculations any way they wish. The most important thing is that the computation is made the same way and is compared with other values computed in the same way.

Number of days' sales in inventory. Average inventories are sometimes expressed as the number of days' sales in inventory. Information is thus afforded concerning the average time it takes to turn over the inventory. The number of days' sales in inventory is calculated by dividing average inventory by average daily cost of goods sold. The number of days' sales also can be obtained by dividing the number of days in the year by the inventory turnover rate. The latter procedure for Colesville is illustrated here.

	2013	2012
Inventory turnover for year	14.4 times	21.1 times
Number of days' sales in inventory		
(365/inventory turnover)	25.3 days	17.3 days

Colesville is holding a 25-day supply of inventory in 2013 compared to a 17-day supply in 2012. Is the 2013 level too high? The important thing with inventory, receivables, cash, and all other assets is for a company to hold just enough but not too much. For example, the 17-day supply of inventory in 2012 might be too low, exposing Colesville to the risk of running out of inventory. As mentioned earlier, drawing meaningful conclusions requires that the ratio values be compared to an industry benchmark to find out what level of inventory is normal for Colesville's industry.

Fixed asset turnover. In addition to analyzing the level of the individual current assets, ratios can be used to determine whether the level of long-term assets is appropriate. As mentioned previously, the common-size balance sheet indicates that in 2013 Colesville has a much larger amount of land, buildings, and equipment, as a percentage of sales (22.4%), than in 2012 (16.3%). An alternate way to represent this same information is to compute the fixed asset turnover. Fixed asset turnover is computed as sales divided by average long-term assets and is interpreted as the number of dollars in sales generated by each dollar invested in fixed assets. The computation for Colesville follows.

STOP&THINK

You have probably heard of just-in-time inventory systems. What would a just-in-time system do to a company's number of days' sales in inventory?

a) Increase it
b) Reduce it
c) Leave it unchanged

	2013	2012
Sales	$5,700,000	$6,600,000
Land, building, and equipment:		
Beginning of year	$1,075,000	$ 925,000
End of year	$1,275,000	$1,075,000
Average fixed assets		
[(beginning balance + ending balance)/2]	$1,175,000	$1,000,000
Fixed asset turnover	4.85 times	6.60 times

As suggested by the common-size balance sheet, Colesville is less efficient at using its fixed assets to generate sales in 2013 than it was in 2012.

Other measures of activity. The efficiency ratios just outlined are not the only ratios that can be used to evaluate how efficiently a company is using its resources. For example, in its 2010 annual report, Home Depot reports that its average weekly sales per store is $563,000 and its annual sales per square foot of store space is $279. The key thing to remember with ratios is that there are no rules limiting the ratios that can be computed; users and managers are free to calculate and use any ratios they think will aid their understanding of the company.

Margin vs. turnover. Profitability and efficiency combine to determine a company's return on assets. Return on assets is computed as net income divided by total assets and is the cents amount of net income generated by each dollar of assets. The return on assets is impacted by both the profitability of each dollar of sales and the efficiency of using assets to generate sales. Return on assets for Colesville is computed as follows:

	2013	2012
Net income	$ 180,000	$ 205,000
Total assets:		
Beginning of year	$2,191,000	$1,760,000
End of year	$2,278,000	$2,191,000
Average total assets		
[(beginning balance + ending balance)/2]	$2,234,500	$1,975,500
Return on assets	8.1%	10.4%

Even though profitability, as measured by return on sales, is approximately the same in 2013 and 2012, the return on assets is higher in 2012 because in that year Colesville was more efficient at using assets to generate sales.

> **FYI**
>
> Thomas Selling and Clyde Stickney have documented the trade-off between margin and turnover described above. They report that industries with high levels of fixed costs and other barriers to entry are characterized by a low asset turnover and high profit margins. Industries with low fixed costs and commodity like products have a high asset turnover and low profit margins. See *Financial Analysts Journal* (January–February 1989), p. 43.

The profitability of each dollar in sales is sometimes called a company's margin. The degree to which assets are used to generate sales is called turnover. The nature of business is that some industries, such as the supermarket industry, are characterized by low margin but high turnover. Other industries, such as the jewelry store business, are characterized by high margin but low turnover. The important point to remember is that companies with a low margin can still earn an acceptable level of return on assets if they have a high turnover. This is illustrated with the information for selected U.S. companies given in Exhibit 23-4. Notice the wide variation in return on sales, ranging from negative 2.7% for **Safeway** to 24.9% for **Microsoft**. Notice also that the variation in return on assets is less (if you leave out the bad year for Safeway). The companies with a high return on sales (Microsoft and **McDonald's**) have a low asset turnover, whereas those with a low return on sales (Home Depot and **Wal-Mart**) have a high turnover. Margin isn't everything, nor is turnover everything—the important thing is how they combine to generate return on assets.

Leverage Ratios Leverage ratios are an indication of the extent to which a company is using other people's money to purchase assets. Leverage is borrowing so that a company can purchase more assets than the stockholders are able to pay for through their own investment. The assets-to-equity ratios for Colesville for 2012 and 2013 indicate that leverage was higher in 2012. Higher leverage increases return on equity through the following chain of events.

EX 23-4 RETURN ON SALES AND ASSET TURNOVER FOR SELECTED U.S. COMPANIES IN 2009

Company	Return on Sales	Asset Turnover	Return on Assets
Microsoft	24.9%	0.75	18.7%
Home Depot	4.0%	1.62	6.5%
McDonald's	20.0%	0.75	15.1%
Safeway	(2.7%)	2.73	(7.3%)
Wal-Mart	3.5%	2.37	8.4%

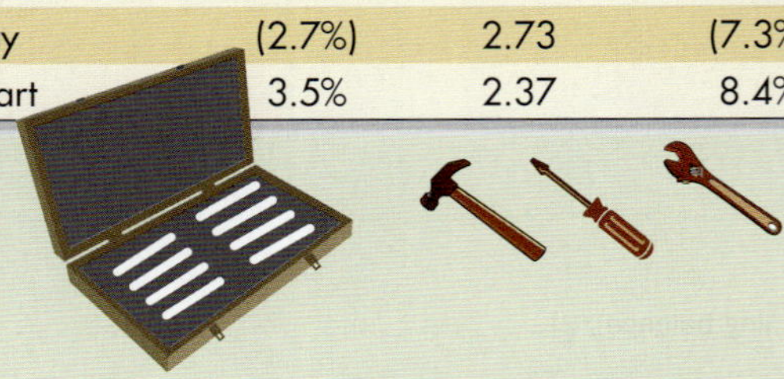

- More borrowing means that more assets can be purchased without any additional equity investment by stockholders.
- More assets means that more sales can be generated.
- More sales means that net income should increase.

Investors generally prefer high leverage to increase the size of their company without increasing their investment, but lenders prefer low leverage to increase the safety of their loans. The field of corporate finance deals with how to optimally balance these opposing tendencies and choose the perfect capital structure for a firm. As a general rule of thumb, most large U.S. companies borrow about half the funds they use to purchase assets.

Two common leverage ratios, debt ratio and debt-to-equity ratio, are explained here.

Debt ratio. Debt ratio is computed as total liabilities divided by total assets and can be interpreted as the percentage of total funds, both borrowed and invested, that a company acquires through borrowing. Debt ratios for Colesville for 2012 and 2013 are computed here.

	2013	2012
Total liabilities	$ 810,000	$1,101,000
Total assets	$2,278,000	$2,191,000
Debt ratio	35.6%	50.3%

Debt-to-equity ratio. Another common way to measure the level of leverage is the debt-to-equity ratio, computed as total liabilities divided by total equity. This ratio is computed for Colesville as follows:

	2013	2012
Total liabilities	$810,000	$1,101,000
Stockholders' equity	$1,468,000	$1,090,000
Debt-to-equity ratio	0.55	1.01

STOP&THINK

Company Z has an assets-to-equity ratio of 2.5. What are its debt and debt-to-equity ratios?

a) Debt ratio = 0.60; debt-to-equity ratio = 1.50
b) Debt ratio = 0.40; debt-to-equity ratio = 0.60
c) Debt ratio = 0.60; debt-to-equity ratio = 1.00
d) Debt ratio = 1.50; debt-to-equity ratio = 0.60

The assets-to-equity ratio used in the DuPont framework, the debt ratio, and the debt-to-equity ratio measure the same thing: the level of borrowing relative to funds (borrowing and investment) used to finance the company. The most important thing to remember, as stated before, is that you use comparable ratios when analyzing a company. It doesn't matter whether you use the debt ratio or the debt-to-equity ratio, but make sure you don't compare one company's debt ratio to another company's debt-to-equity ratio.

To illustrate the impact of financial leverage on stockholders, assume that Company A has stockholders' equity of $500,000 and has no liabilities. The company estimates that its income before income taxes will be $80,000 without any borrowed capital.

Income taxes are estimated to be 30% of income; therefore, net income is estimated to be \$56,000 [\$80,000 − (0.30 × \$80,000)]. This would result in a return on equity of 11.2% (\$56,000/\$500,000).

Exhibit 23-5 illustrates the effects of borrowing an extra \$1 million at 12% interest under the assumptions (1) that the \$1,000,000 in additional assets earns a before-tax return on assets of 15%, more than the cost of the borrowed funds and (2) that the additional assets earn a before-tax return of 5%, less than the cost of the borrowed funds. In the first case, because the company can earn a higher return from the new \$1,000,000 in assets than it must pay to use the borrowed money, return on equity increases from 11.2% to 15.4%. In essence, the stockholders get to keep the difference between what they can earn from the assets and what they must pay the lender to borrow the money. On the other hand, the risk of financial leverage can be seen under the second assumption as the return on equity decreases from 11.2% to 1.4%.

Times interest earned. A measure of the debt position of a company in relation to its earnings ability is the number of times interest is earned. The times interest earned calculation is made by dividing income before any charges for interest or income taxes by the interest requirements for the period. The resulting figure reflects the company's ability to meet interest payments and the degree of safety afforded the creditors. The times interest earned ratio for Colesville is computed as follows:

	2013	2012
Income before income taxes	\$260,000	\$290,000
Add interest: 10% of long-term debt		
\$400,000 × 0.10	40,000	
\$600,000 × 0.10		60,000
Earnings before interest and taxes	\$300,000	\$350,000
Times interest earned	7.5 times	5.8 times

Pretax income was used in the computation because income tax applies only after interest is deducted, and it is pretax income that protects creditors. The times interest

EX 23-5 THE POSITIVE AND NEGATIVE ASPECTS OF FINANCIAL LEVERAGE

	Assumption 1: Borrowed Capital Earns 15%	Assumption 2: Borrowed Capital Earns 5%
Income before interest and taxes:		
Without borrowed funds	\$ 80,000	\$ 80,000
On \$1,000,000 borrowed	150,000	50,000
	\$230,000	\$130,000
Interest (12% × \$1,000,000)	120,000	120,000
Income before taxes	\$110,000	\$ 10,000
Income taxes (30%)	33,000	3,000
Net income	\$ 77,000	\$ 7,000
Stockholders' equity	\$500,000	\$500,000
Return on equity	15.4%	1.4%

earned ratio indicates that Colesville's creditors are happier in 2013 because their interest requirements are covered 7.5 times, offering a larger margin of safety than in 2012. However, this high times interest earned value might also indicate that Colesville has not properly leveraged its investment capital in 2013. Again, the appropriate level of times interest earned represents a balancing of the desire of investors to leverage their investment with the desire of creditors for safety concerning the collection of their loans.

A computation similar to times interest earned, but more inclusive, is the fixed charge coverage. Fixed charges include such obligations as interest on bonds and notes, lease obligations, and any other recurring financial commitments. The number of times that fixed charges are covered is calculated by adding the fixed charges to pretax income and then dividing the total by the fixed charges.

Other Common Ratios

Not all commonly used ratios fit into the DuPont framework. Ratios for measuring liquidity, cash flow, dividend payments, and stock price performance are outlined in this section.

Current ratio. An important concern about any company is its liquidity, or the ability to meet its current obligations. If a firm cannot meet its obligations in the short run, it may not be around to enjoy the long run. The most commonly used measure of liquidity is the current ratio. Current ratio is computed by dividing total current assets by total current liabilities. For Colesville, current ratios for December 31, 2012, and December 31, 2013, are computed as follows:

	2013	2012
Current assets	$855,000	$955,500
Current liabilities	$410,000	$501,000
Debt ratio	2.09	1.91

Historically, the rule of thumb has been that a current ratio below 2.0 suggests the possibility of liquidity problems. However, advances in information technology have enabled companies to be much more effective in minimizing the need to hold cash, inventories, and other current assets. As a result, current ratios for successful companies these days are frequently less than 1.0. As mentioned previously in relation to other ratios, the best way to interpret a current ratio is to compare the value to the current ratio for the same firm in previous years and to different companies in the same industry. Current ratios for selected U.S. companies are given in Exhibit 23-6.

Cash flow adequacy ratio. The current ratio is an indirect measure of a company's ability to meet its upcoming obligations. Ratios based on cash flow from operations give a more direct indication of a company's ability to generate sufficient cash to satisfy predictable cash requirements. One overall indicator of cash flow sufficiency is the cash flow adequacy ratio.[5] This ratio is computed by dividing cash flow from operating activities by the total primary cash requirements, defined as the sum of dividend payments, long-term asset purchases, and long-term debt repayments. The following information for Colesville Corporation is needed to compute this ratio.

[5] See Chapter 5 for a summary of other cash flow ratios.

EX 23-6 CURRENT RATIOS FOR SELECTED U.S. COMPANIES IN 2009

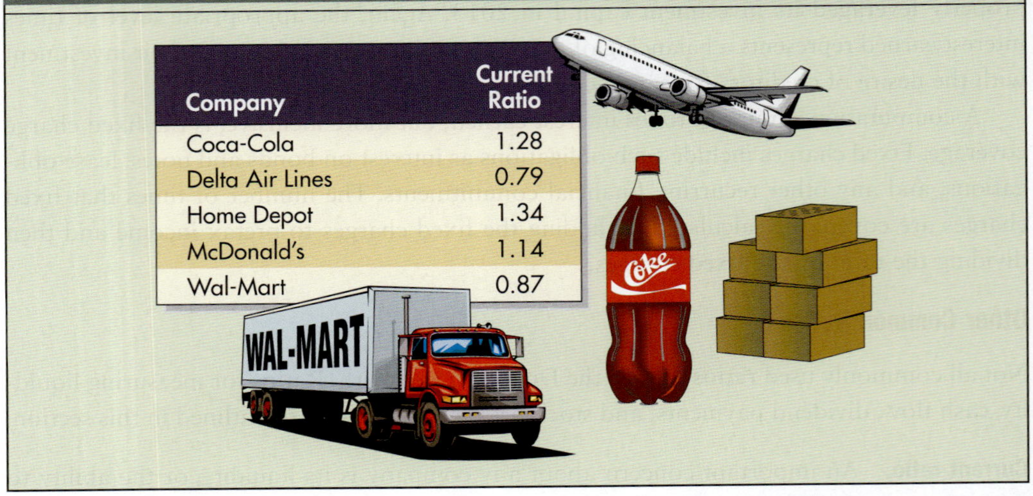

Company	Current Ratio
Coca-Cola	1.28
Delta Air Lines	0.79
Home Depot	1.34
McDonald's	1.14
Wal-Mart	0.87

	2013	2012
Net income	$180,000	$ 205,000
Depreciation expense	100,000	80,000
(Increase) Decrease in noncash current assets	60,000	(231,500)
Increase (Decrease) in current liabilities	(91,000)	371,000
Cash from operating activities	$249,000	$ 424,500
Long-term asset purchases	$300,000	$ 230,000
Long-term debt repayments	200,000	0
Dividends paid	102,000	145,000
Total primary cash requirements	$602,000	$ 375,000

Note that long-term asset purchases in 2013 and 2012 were enough to offset the depreciation of assets for the year and increase the level of net land, buildings, and equipment.

The computation of the cash flow adequacy ratio is as follows:

	2013	2012
Cash from operating activities	$249,000	$424,500
Total primary cash requirements	$602,000	$375,000
Cash flow adequacy ratio	0.41	1.13

Because the cash flow adequacy ratio in 2013 is less than 1.0, Colesville was not able to satisfy its primary cash requirements with cash generated by operations. A look at Colesville's balance sheets in Exhibit 23-2 indicates that the shortfall has been partially compensated for by the issuance of additional stock in 2013. One study has shown that for a sample of Fortune 500 companies, the cash flow adequacy ratio averaged 0.88.[6]

[6] Don E. Giacomino and David E. Mielke, "Cash Flows: Another Approach to Ratio Analysis," *Journal of Accountancy*, March 1993, pp. 55–58.

Earnings per share. Earnings per share (EPS) is such a fundamental number that we usually forget that it is a financial ratio. The necessary adjustments for dilutive securities and so forth were covered fully in Chapter 18 and are not repeated here. For Colesville, EPS for 2013 and 2012 is computed as follows:

	2013	2012
Net income	$180,000	$205,000
Weighted shares outstanding	90,000	75,000
Earnings per share	$ 2.00	$ 2.73

Dividend payout ratio. All net income belongs to the stockholders. Cash dividends are the portion of net income paid to the stockholders in the form of cash. An important ratio in analyzing a firm's dividend policy is the dividend payout ratio, computed as dividends divided by net income. Colesville's dividend payout ratios for 2013 and 2012 are computed as follows:

	2013	2012
Dividends	$102,000	$145,000
Net income	$180,000	$205,000
Dividend payout ratio	56.7%	70.7%

In general, high-growth firms have low dividend payout ratios (Microsoft didn't begin paying cash dividends to its common stockholders until 2003), and low-growth stable firms have higher dividend payout ratios.

Price-earnings ratio. The market price of a share of stock is often expressed as a multiple of earnings to indicate how attractive the market views the stock as an investment. This ratio is called the *price-earnings ratio*, or *P/E ratio*, and is computed by dividing the market price per share of stock by the EPS. In the United States, P/E ratios typically range between 10.0 and 30.0. Assuming market values per share of Colesville stock at the end of 2013 of $29 and at the end of 2012 of $60, P/E ratios would be computed as follows:

> **FYI**
>
> Finance and accounting professors often prefer to compute the inverse of the P/E ratio, called the *earnings-price (EP) ratio*. There are some interesting econometric reasons that EP is better than P/E, but so far the business press and most businesspeople have stuck with the P/E ratio.

	2013	2012
Market value per share	$29.00	$60.00
Earnings per share	$ 2.00	$ 2.73
Price-earnings ratio	14.5	22.0

High P/E ratios are generally associated with firms for which strong future growth is predicted.

Book-to-market ratio. The ratio of book value to market value, called the *book-to-market ratio*, is frequently used in investment analysis. The book-to-market ratio reflects the difference between a company's balance sheet value and the company's actual market value. A company's book-to-market ratio is almost always less than 1.0. This is so because many assets are reported at historical cost, which is usually less than market value, and other assets are not included in the balance sheet at all. Research has shown that firms with high book-to-market ratios tend to have high stock returns in future years.[7] One possible reason for this is that the accounting book value reflects fundamental underlying value and a high book-to-market ratio indicates that the market is currently undervaluing a company. For Colesville Corporation, the book-to-market ratio is computed as follows:

	2013	2012
Book value of stockholders' equity	$1,468,000	$1,090,000
Year-end shares outstanding	100,000	70,000
Market value per share	× $29	× $60
Total market value of equity	$2,900,000	$4,200,000
Book-to-market ratio	0.51	0.26

FASB CODIFICATION

The Issue: To you, it seems to create a lot of extra work to have to provide financial statements for several past years instead of just one year. You wonder who made up this requirement, and do companies really have to provide several years of data.

The Question: Where is the authoritative guidance saying that comparative financial statements are to be presented?

Searching the Codification: Well, we aren't going to use the Codification for this one. If we did, we would find this generic statement in FASB ASC paragraph 205-10-45-1: "The presentation of comparative financial statements in annual and other reports enhances the usefulness of such reports and brings out more clearly the nature and trends of current changes affecting the entity. Such presentation emphasizes the fact that statements for a series of periods are far more significant than those for a single period and that the accounts for one period are but an installment of what is essentially a continuous history."

Somewhere we read (actually, it was in Chapter 3 of this book) that the detailed comparative financial statement requirements come from the SEC. U.S. Federal regulations are contained in the Code of Federal Regulations (CFR). The regulations related to the public trading of securities are contained in Title 17, Commodity and Securities Exchanges. So, get your favorite search engine and type in the following search string:

"CFR Title 17 consolidated balance sheet"

Have fun!

The Answer: The correct treatment is described on page 23-28.

[7] See Eugene F. Fama and Kenneth R. French, "The Cross-Section of Expected Stock Returns," *The Journal of Finance*, June 1992, p. 427.

A summary of the financial ratios discussed in this section is presented in Exhibit 23-7. This overview of financial ratios is intended to emphasize the point that the preparation of the financial statements by the accountant is not the end of the process but just the beginning. Those financial statements are then analyzed by investors, creditors, and management to detect signs of existing deficiencies in performance and to predict how the firm will perform in the future. As repeated throughout this section, proper interpretation of a ratio depends on comparing the ratio value to the value for the same firm in previous years and to values for other firms in the same industry. In addition, diversity or inconsistency in accounting practice can harm the comparability of ratio values. This point is illustrated in the next section.

Impact of Alternative Accounting Methods

2 **Recognize the potential impact that differing accounting methods can have on the financial ratios of otherwise essentially identical companies.**

WHY **Naïve financial statement users can be excused for not knowing that reported financial statement numbers, and the financial ratios computed using those numbers, can be significantly impacted by accounting assumptions. But as someone who has reached this chapter in this textbook, you have no excuse.**

HOW **Before computing all of the financial ratios described in the preceding section, a careful financial statement user should make adjustments for accounting differences among the companies being analyzed.**

This section illustrates the impact of accounting method differences on reported financial statement numbers and the resulting financial ratios. The balance sheets and income statements for 2013 for two hypothetical companies, Sai Kung Company and Tuen Mun Limited, both of which started business on January 1, 2013, are shown on page 23-21. To keep things simple, there are no income taxes in the example.

The following additional information relates to Sai Kung and Tuen Mun.

1. Sai Kung and Tuen Mun both purchased investment securities for $275. In both cases, the fair value of the securities dropped to $200. Sai Kung classifies the securities as trading; Tuen Mun classifies them as available for sale.
2. Sai Kung uses LIFO, and Tuen Mun uses FIFO. If Sai Kung had used FIFO, ending inventory would have been $1,000.
3. Both companies purchased similar buildings and equipment for $3,000 at the start of the year. Sai Kung assumes a 10-year useful life; Tuen Mun uses a 30-year life.
4. Both companies leased additional buildings and equipment at the beginning of the year. The annual lease payment is $150. The present value of the lease obligation on the lease signing date was $1,000. The terms of the leases are very similar. Sai Kung classifies its lease as a capital lease; Tuen Mun classifies its lease as an operating lease.

EX 23-7 SUMMARY OF SELECTED FINANCIAL RATIOS

Ratio	Formula	Description
(1) Return on equity	Net income / Stockholders' equity	Number of pennies earned during the year on each dollar invested.
	DuPont Framework	
(2) Return on sales	Net income / Sales	Number of pennies earned during the year on each dollar of sales.
(3) Asset turnover	Sales / Total assets	Number of dollars of sales during the year generated by each dollar of assets.
(4) Assets-to-equity ratio	Total assets / Stockholders' equity	Number of dollars of assets acquired for each dollar of funds invested by stockholders.
Efficiency:		
(5) Accounts receivable turnover	Sales / Average accounts receivable	Number of sales/collection cycles completed during the year.
(6) Average collection period	Average accounts receivable / Average daily sales	Average number of days that elapse between sale and cash collection.
(7) Inventory turnover	Cost of goods sold / Average inventory	Number of purchase/sale cycles completed during the year.
(8) Number of days' sales in inventory	Average inventory / Average daily cost of goods sold	Average number of days of sales that can be made using only the supply of inventory on hand.
(9) Fixed asset turnover	Sales / Average fixed assets	Number of dollars of sales during the year generated by each dollar of fixed assets.
Leverage:		
(10) Debt ratio	Total liabilities / Total assets	Percentage of funds needed to purchase assets that were obtained through borrowing.
(11) Debt-to-equity ratio	Total liabilities / Stockholders' equity	Number of dollars of borrowing for each dollar of equity investment.
(12) Times interest earned	Earnings before interest and taxes / Interest expense	Number of times that interest payments could be covered by operating earnings.
	Other Financial Ratios	
(13) Return on assets	Net income / Total assets	Number of pennies of income generated by each dollar of assets.
(14) Current ratio	Current assets / Current liabilities	Measure of liquidity; number of times current assets could cover current liabilities.
(15) Cash flow adequacy ratio	Cash flow from operations / (Purchases of long-term assets + Repayments of long-term debt + Cash dividend payments)	Number of times that cash from operations can cover predictable cash requirements.
(16) Earnings per share	Net income / Weighted number of shares outstanding	Dollars of net income attributable to each share of common stock.
(17) Dividend payout ratio	Cash dividends / Net income	Percentage of net income paid out to the stockholders as dividends.
(18) Price-earnings ratio	Market price per share / Earnings per share	Amount investors are willing to pay for each dollar of earnings; indication of growth potential.
(19) Book-to-market ratio	Stockholders' equity / Market value of shares outstanding	Number of dollars of book equity for each dollar of market value.

	Sai Kung	Tuen Mun
Cash	$ 100	$ 100
Investment securities	200	200
Accounts receivable	500	500
Inventory	700	1,000
Total current assets	$ 1,500	$ 1,800
Buildings and equipment (net)	2,700	2,900
Capital lease assets	900	0
Total assets	$ 5,100	$ 4,700
Current liabilities	$ 1,000	$ 1,000
Long-term debt	1,500	1,500
Capital lease obligations	950	0
Total liabilities	$ 3,450	$ 2,500
Paid-in capital	$ 1,500	$ 1,500
Retained earnings	150	775
Other equity	0	(75)
Total equities	$ 1,650	$ 2,200
Total liabilities and equities	$ 5,100	$ 4,700
Sales	$ 6,000	$ 6,000
Cost of goods sold	4,000	3,700
Gross profit	$ 2,000	$ 2,300
Depreciation expense	(400)	(100)
Lease expense	0	(150)
Other operating expenses	(1,125)	(1,125)
Operating income	$ 475	$ 925
Interest expense:		
Long-term debt ($1,500 × 0.10)	(150)	(150)
Capital lease ($1,000 ×0.10)	(100)	0
Loss on investment securities	(75)	0
Net income	$ 150	$ 775

A careful comparison of the financial statements for Sai Kung and Tuen Mun reveals that the companies are economically identical. The differences between the two sets of financial statements are caused by differences in accounting treatment. Consider the following:

1. Both companies have a $75 economic loss on investment securities. Sai Kung recognizes this loss in its income statement; Tuen Mun recognizes the loss as an equity adjustment.
2. If both companies had used FIFO, ending inventory, cost of goods sold, and gross profit would have been the same for both.
3. The purchased buildings and equipment are similar; the difference is that Sai Kung recognized $300 ($3,000/10) of depreciation in 2013, whereas Tuen Mun assumed a longer life and recognized depreciation of $100 ($3,000/30).
4. The leased buildings and equipment are also similar, as are the terms of the lease contracts. Because Sai Kung accounts for the lease as a capital lease, it recognizes depreciation expense of $100 ($1,000/10 years) and interest expense of $100 ($1,000 × 0.10). Tuen Mun accounts for the lease as an operating lease and reports lease expense equal to the annual lease payment of $150.

In this example, these four accounting differences cause significant differences between the financial statements of two otherwise essentially identical companies. To illustrate the impact of these accounting differences on the financial ratios of the two companies, ratios (1) through (14) in Exhibit 23-7 are computed and compared for Sai Kung and Tuen Mun. When required, end-of-year amounts are used in place of average balances.

		Sai Kung	Tuen Mun
(1)	Return on equity	9.1%	35.2%
(2)	Return on sales	2.5%	12.9%
(3)	Asset turnover	1.18	1.28
(4)	Assets-to-equity ratio	3.09	2.14
(5)	Accounts receivable turnover	12.0	12.0
(6)	Average collection period	30.4	30.4
(7)	Inventory turnover	5.71	3.7
(8)	Number of days' sales in inventory	63.9	98.6
(9)	Fixed asset turnover	1.67	2.07
(10)	Debt ratio	67.6%	53.2%
(11)	Debt-to-equity ratio	2.09	1.14
(12)	Times interest earned	1.90	6.17
(13)	Return on assets	2.9%	16.5%
(14)	Current ratio	1.5	1.8

The differences in accounting method have made Tuen Mun appear to be a superior company on almost every dimension. Tuen Mun has better return on equity, better profitability, and better overall efficiency. In addition, Tuen Mun appears to be a less risky company because its leverage is lower and its liquidity, as indicated by the current ratio, is higher.

The point of this example is that ratio comparisons can yield misleading implications if the ratios come from companies with differing accounting practices. Frequently, financial ratios from companies are compared without adjusting for underlying accounting differences. Be careful.

Introduction to Equity Valuation

3 Perform a simple valuation of a company using financial statement data.

WHY Various models exist for estimating values of equity securities. Proper equity valuation is a challenging art, and comparison of estimated values to actual market values can yield insights into what market participants are currently expecting about the future performance of a company.

HOW By using numbers from the financial statements such as net income, operating cash flow, and dividends, you can generate an estimate of the market value of a company. Four models used in estimating values of equity securities are constant future dividends, constant dividend growth, price-earnings multiple, and discounted free cash flow.

In Chapter 12, we discussed the valuation of bonds. You saw that once you are given the appropriate market interest rate to use in valuing bonds, the calculation of the current value of the bond is quite straightforward. The ease of this process stems from the fact that the future cash flows associated with the bonds are certain because they are set as part of the original bond contract. Thus, the art of bond trading really boils down to being able to determine what the correct market interest rate is, given the riskiness of the bond being valued; after that is done, the actual calculation of the bond value is simple arithmetic.

Valuing stocks is much more difficult than valuing bonds. When valuing stocks, not only does one need to determine the appropriate interest rate to use, but also one must estimate uncertain future cash flows. Because accounting numbers are frequently used in equity valuation models, we introduce the topic of equity valuation here. Realize that this is a basic introduction. The experts in equity valuation are the finance professors, and this topic is covered at length in finance courses.

To illustrate several simple equity valuation models, we use the following information for McDonald's as of the end of 2009.

	2009	2008	2007	2006
Diluted earnings per share	$4.11	$ 3.76	$1.98	$2.83
Dividends per share	2.05	1.625	1.50	1.00

For simplicity, we will assume that the required rate of return on equity capital for McDonald's is 15%. Don't be deceived by the seemingly casual manner in which we are assuming a 15% rate of return—in any valuation exercise, determining the correct required rate of return, given the riskiness of the company being valued, is crucial to arriving at a reasonable valuation. Entire courses in finance are devoted to learning how to properly compute required rates of return on equity investments.

Constant Future Dividends In this simple model, the equity shares are valued as if the current cash dividend amount is a guaranteed fixed payment to be received each year forever. Valuation in this case is easy; the future dividend stream is a perpetuity (an annuity of infinite length). The appropriate valuation formula is as follows:

$$\text{Price} = \frac{\text{Dividends}}{r}$$

where r is the required rate of return on equity capital.

Using this simple model, the implied price per share for McDonald's is computed as follows:

$$\text{Price} = \$2.05 \div 0.15 = \$13.67$$

Constant Dividend Growth In this simple model (sometimes called the Gordon growth model), dividends are assumed to grow at a constant rate forever. The valuation formula is as follows:

$$\text{Price} = \frac{\text{Forecasted Dividend Next Year}}{r - g}$$

where g is the expected future dividend growth rate.

FYI

Including the 50% increase in dividends during 2007 in the computation of the average dividend growth for McDonald's would have been a bad idea because it is safe to assume that McDonald's (or any company for that matter) will not be able to increase its dividends by 50% every year. In addition, in our simple model, a long-term dividend growth rate in excess of the required return yields a counterintuitive negative value. And if you look at the mathematics underlying this simple model, a long-term growth rate in excess of the required rate of return actually implies an infinite stock value, suggesting that such a high sustainable growth rate is impossible.

For McDonald's, the dividend growth rate from 2006 to 2009 averaged 27% per year with the dividend growth rate in 2007 reaching 50%. This 27% average annual growth rate is extremely high, so high that it is clearly not sustainable. For example, if McDonald's were to continue increasing its dividends at this rate, in 50 years the dividend per share would be more than $300,000. Even the long-run dividend growth rate for McDonald's (over the past 12 years) has exceeded 20%. For this example, we will assume a slower future McDonald's dividend growth rate of 12% per year. Using this value, the implied price per share is computed as follows:

$$\text{Price} = (\$2.05 \times [1 + 0.120]) \div (0.150 - 0.120) = \$76.53$$

Price-Earnings Multiple Market prices incorporate all kinds of information. For example, the market prices for firms in a given industry include average investor expectations about future earnings growth in that industry and required rates of return for firms in that industry. This information is summarized in the price-earnings (P/E) ratio, computed as (price per share ÷ earnings per share). Rather than directly estimating growth rates and required rates of return, an investor can value a company's shares by using the information in the P/E ratio as follows:

$$\text{Price} = \text{Earnings} \times \text{P/E Ratio}$$

P/E ratios for a selection of restaurant chains as of the end of 2009 are as follows.

Brinker International	23.6
Darden Restaurants	16.6
Starbucks	49.5
Yum! Brands	18.2

These companies are considered to be competitors of McDonald's. **Brinker International** operates restaurants all over world under the names Chili's, Macaroni Grill, and others. **Darden Restaurants** operates under the names Red Lobster and Olive Garden, among others. **Starbucks** sells coffee in more than 11,000 locations worldwide. **Yum! Brands** operates over 37,000 fast-food locations worldwide under the names KFC, Pizza Hut, Taco Bell, A&W, and more.

Using the average of these ratios (27.0), the implied price per share for McDonald's is computed as follows:

$$\text{Price} = \$4.11 \times 27.0 = \$110.97$$

Discounted Free Cash Flow In theory, a company should be worth the discounted value of the future cash flows to be generated by the company. A way to look at this directly is to compute the discounted present value of free cash flow. In this context, free cash flow is defined as:

Cash from operating activities
− Cash paid for capital expenditures
= Free cash flow

Free cash flow for McDonald's for 2007, 2008, and 2009 is computed as follows.

(millions of dollars)	2009	2008	2007
Cash from operating activities	$5,751.0	$5,917.2	$4,876.3
— Capital expenditures	1,952.1	2,135.7	1,946.6
Free cash flow	$3,798.9	$3,781.5	$2,929.7

In order to use this discounted free cash flow model, we need to make forecasts about the following:

- Future growth rates in free cash flow
- Forecasting horizon
- What happens in the "terminal year"

Future Growth Rates Free cash flow increased by 29.1% from 2007 to 2008 but increased only 0.5% from 2008 to 2009. Growth rates in the preceding five years suggest that McDonald's free cash flow has been growing over 20% per year. For our analysis, we will assume a slowdown in future growth and will use the 14.8% average increase from 2007 to 2009.

Forecasting Horizon We should extend our free cash flow growth rate forecasts for as many years in the future for which we have reliable data. Also, as shown in the next section, our forecasts only need to extend for as long as we think the firm can generate above-normal cash flows from new investments. We will choose a 3-year forecasting horizon to keep the illustration simple; in this case, the choice is arbitrary.

Terminal Year Bill Gates of Microsoft may be the smartest person in the United States—he is certainly the richest. If you were to go into partnership with Bill and give him $1 billion, he probably would have enough great business ideas in his head that he could take that $1 billion and start an innovative business that would generate cash flows with a present value far in excess of $1 billion. Now, what if you were to give him another $10 billion? Does he have enough good ideas to be able to use that additional $10 billion to generate excess profits? What if you next gave him another $100 billion? The point is this: Eventually, even Bill Gates is going to run out of innovative ideas. At that time, any additional investment funds you give him will be used in just an average way, earn an average return, and the present value of the cash flows from the investment will exactly equal the amount of the investment. To use a phrase often used in finance, all that will be left will be "zero net present value" projects—projects that return exactly the average required rate of return.

The key thing to remember: You don't increase the value of your business by engaging in average, "zero net present value" projects. With such projects, the discounted value of future cash flows is completely offset by the initial cost of the project. Instead, you increase the value of your business by using investment funds in innovative ways that earn above-normal returns. Once a business has run out of innovative ideas, growth via new projects will not increase its value because the discounted present value of new projects is exactly offset by the initial cost of the projects. So, once the terminal year is reached, when it is expected that the company will have no new above-average ideas, the valuation impact of any additional growth can be ignored. For illustration purposes, we will assume that McDonald's will run out of innovative ideas after three years (from 2009), at the end of 2012. After that, free cash flow will be assumed to be constant forever.

FYI

Remember that this is merely an introduction to equity valuation using discounted cash flow analysis. In this example, we have used a short forecasting horizon and an unsophisticated cost of capital number, and we have assumed (without stating it) that McDonald's has no debt. In your finance and financial statement analysis courses, you will learn how to enhance this simple model.

The forecasted free cash flow for McDonald's, given our assumptions, is given in Exhibit 23-8. Remember, in this example we are picturing ourselves as standing at the end of 2009 looking into McDonald's future. The exhibit also illustrates the calculation of the present value of these forecasted free cash flows.

At the end of 2009, McDonald's had 1,077 million shares outstanding. Thus, the estimated price per share is computed as follows.

Price = \$36,551 million ÷ 1,077 million shares = \$33.94

Comparison of the Valuation Models The computed prices for McDonald's shares at the end of 2009, using each of the four models, are as follows.

	Estimated Price
Model 1 (constant future dividends)	$ 13.67
Model 2 (constant dividend growth)	76.53
Model 3 (price-earnings multiple)	110.97
Model 4 (discounted free cash flow)	33.94

EX 23-8 FORECASTED FREE CASH FLOW FOR MCDONALD'S

Present Value of Forecasted Free Cash Flow for McDonald's
2009 Free Cash Flow Value — \$3,798.9 million
3 Years of 14.8% Growth; Constant Free Cash Flow Thereafter
15% Required Rate of Return

(millions of dollars)	2010	2011	2012	2013	2014
Free cash flow	$ 4,361	$5,007	$5,748	$ 5,748	$5,748
Present value as of the end of 2009; using 15% rate of return	$ 3,792	$3,786	$3,779	$25,194*	
Total present value	$36,551				

Note: All numbers shown are rounded.

*This is the present value of the cash flows to occur after it is assumed that McDonald's runs out of new ideas (at the end of 2012). The present value of this perpetuity (an annuity of infinite length) extending from 2013 into the future is computed in two steps:

1. As of the end of 2012, the perpetuity of \$5,748 per year forever has a present value of \$38,320, computed as \$5,748/0.15.
2. In order to add the \$38,320 value of the perpetuity to the present value of the other free cash flows, it must be discounted back as a lump sum three more years to the end of 2009, resulting in the \$25,194 shown above.

The actual market price of a share of McDonald's stock at the end of 2009 was $61.91.

This valuation exercise should leave you feeling dissatisfied for two reasons. First, our estimates are all over the map, ranging from $13.67 per share to $110.97 per share. Second, except for the constant dividend growth model, our estimated values are not even close to the actual $61.91 value of McDonald's shares at the end of 2009. You should come away from this simple valuation exercise with the following three lessons.

Equity valuation is difficult. Proper use of the price-earnings multiple model would involve considering which of the four benchmark companies we used in computing an average P/E ratio might be the best match with McDonald's. Also, we would probably look at the accounting practices of each of the benchmark companies to determine if their net incomes were reflecting their underlying business performance in the same way as McDonald's. To fully implement the discounted free cash flow model, we would be required to gather information on McDonald's expansion plans in order to give more sophisticated estimates of future growth rates. In addition, we would have to make a more informed decision rather than just assuming that McDonald's will run out of innovative ideas in three years. And we would put a lot more work into calculating the cost of capital.

Price-earnings valuation is simple and often relatively accurate, but it begs the question of identifying the underlying determinants of value. The price-earnings multiple model frequently yields a price that is not far off the actual market price because, with this model, we are allowing the market to do most of the work for us in terms of forecasting industry growth rates, setting an appropriate rate of return, and so forth. This model is often used in getting a ballpark estimate for the appropriate price of a company's shares, especially when a company is issuing shares for the first time. However, this model is a black box that avoids consideration of the fundamental operating performance forecasts for a company.

The most useful part of equity valuation is often what it reveals about what investors must believe about a stock in order to give it its current market price. One thing we learn from the McDonald's discounted free cash flow valuation is that investors must believe that McDonald's free cash flow is going to grow faster than 14.8%, or McDonald's is not going to run out of innovative ideas in three years, or both. In fact, it would require assumptions more like 12.7% growth for the next 20 years to yield an estimated price close to McDonald's actual market price. Thus, this valuation analysis can yield interesting insights into how a company is currently viewed by market participants.

? SOLUTIONS TO OPENING SCENARIO QUESTIONS

1. Total gross profit would increase by $30, from $200 ($1,000 × 0.20) to $230 ($1,000 × 0.23).
2. The primary cause of Home Depot's negative operating cash flow of $43 million in 1985 was an increase in inventory during the year of $69 million.
3. Home Depot's operating cash flow increased by $109 million, from a negative $43 million in 1985 to a positive $66 million in 1986.

SOLUTIONS TO STOP & THINK

1. (Page 23-11) The correct answer is B. The objective of a just-in-time inventory system is to reduce the level of inventory as far as possible. Reduced inventory means a lower number of days' sales in inventory.

2. (Page 23-13) The correct answer is A. With an assets-to-equity ratio of 2.5, hypothetical Company Z has the following simplified balance sheet:

Assets	2.5
Liabilities	1.5
Equities	1.0

Assets-to-equity ratio: 2.5 ÷ 1.0 = 2.5
Debt ratio: 1.5 ÷ 2.5 = 0.60
Debt-to-equity ratio: 1.5 ÷ 1.0 = 1.5

It is always true (prove it to yourself using algebra) that the debt-to-equity ratio is equal to the assets-to-equity ratio minus 1.

SOLUTION TO USING THE FASB'S CODIFICATION

Hopefully you found the following.

Title 17 CFR Section 210.3-01: "There shall be filed, for the registrant and its subsidiaries consolidated, audited balance sheets as of the end of each of the two most recent fiscal years."

With the clue that the balance sheet requirement is in Section 210.3-01, you may then have been able to find the requirements for the income statement and statement of cash flows as well.

Title 17 CFR Section 210.3-02: "There shall be filed, for the registrant and its subsidiaries consolidated and for its predecessors, audited statements of income and cash flows for each of the three fiscal years preceding the date of the most recent audited balance sheet being filed."

REVIEW **CHAPTER 23**

LEARNING OBJECTIVES

1 Organize a systematic financial ratio analysis using common-size financial statements and the DuPont framework.

Financial statement analysis is used to predict a company's future profitability and cash flows from its past performance and to evaluate the performance of a company with an eye toward identifying problem areas. The informativeness of financial ratios is greatly enhanced when they are compared with past values and with values for other firms in the same industry.

Common-size financial statements are computed by dividing all financial statement amounts for a given year by sales for that year. A common-size income statement reveals the number of pennies of each expense for each dollar of sales. The Assets section of a common-size balance sheet tells how many pennies of each asset are needed to generate each dollar of sales.

The DuPont framework decomposes return on equity (ROE) into three areas:

- *Profitability.* Return on sales is computed as net income divided by sales and is interpreted as the number of pennies in profit generated from each dollar of sales.
- *Efficiency.* Asset turnover is computed as sales divided by assets and is interpreted as the number of dollars in sales generated by each dollar of assets.

- *Leverage.* Assets-to-equity ratio is computed as assets divided by equity and is interpreted as the number of dollars of assets a company is able to acquire using each dollar invested by stockholders.

If a company has a profitability problem, the common-size income statement is the best tool for detecting which expenses are responsible. Financial ratios for detailed analysis of a company's efficiency and leverage have been developed; a number of them are summarized in Exhibit 23-7.

Margin is the profitability of each dollar in sales, and turnover is the degree to which assets are used to generate sales. Companies with a low margin can still earn an acceptable level of return on assets if they have a high turnover.

2 Recognize the potential impact that differing accounting methods can have on the financial ratios of otherwise essentially identical companies.

Ratio comparisons can yield misleading implications if the ratios come from companies with differing accounting practices. Adjustments for accounting differences should be made before financial ratios are compared.

3 Perform a simple valuation of a company using financial statement data.

Four models used in estimating values of equity securities are as follows.

- Constant future dividends
- Constant dividend growth
- Price-earnings multiple
- Discounted free cash flow

Three lessons to be learned from simple equity valuation are as follows.

- Equity valuation is difficult.
- Price-earnings valuation is simple and often relatively accurate, but it begs the question of identifying the underlying determinants of value.
- The most useful part of equity valuation is often what it reveals about what investors must believe about a stock in order to give it its current market price.

KEY TERMS

Common-size financial statements 23-4
DuPont framework 23-7
Financial statement analysis 23-3
Margin 23-12
Perpetuity 23-23
Turnover 23-12

QUESTIONS

1. Financial statement analysis can be used to identify a company's weak areas so that management can work for improvement. Can financial statement analysis be used for any other purpose? Explain.
2. Why are comparative financial statements considered more meaningful than statements prepared for a single period? What conditions increase the usefulness of comparative statements?
3. An analysis of a company's financial ratios reveals the underlying reasons for profitability and efficiency problems. Do you agree or disagree? Explain.
4. What is a *common-size financial statement*? What are its advantages?
5. What is the purpose of the DuPont framework?
6. (a) How is the inventory turnover computed? (b) What precautions are necessary in arriving at the inventory number to be used in the turnover calculation? (c) How would you interpret a rising inventory turnover rate?
7. Indicate how each of the following measurements is calculated, and appraise its significance.
   (a) Times interest earned
   (b) Return on equity
   (c) Earnings per share
   (d) Price-earnings ratio

(e) Dividend payout ratio
(f) Book-to-market ratio

8. Explain how the turnover of assets can affect return on assets.
9. Under what conditions is the return on assets equal to the ROE?
10. How do accounting differences impact the usefulness of financial ratio comparisons?
11. What variables are used to determine a share price when using the constant dividend growth model?
12. In using the discounted free cash flow valuation model, what is the significance of the terminal year?
13. What are three lessons one can learn by studying basic equity valuation models?

PRACTICE EXERCISES

Practice 23-1
LO1

Preparing a Common-Size Income Statement

Company A reported the following income statement data for the most recent three years:

	Year 3	Year 2	Year 1
Sales	$ 350,000	$ 260,000	$ 300,000
Cost of goods sold	(163,000)	(144,000)	(156,000)
Operating expenses:			
Marketing expense	(21,000)	(21,000)	(22,000)
R&D expense	(27,000)	(6,000)	(14,000)
Administrative expense	(45,000)	(50,000)	(48,000)
Operating income	$ 94,000	$ 39,000	$ 60,000
Interest expense	(6,000)	(11,000)	(7,000)
Income before income taxes	$ 88,000	$ 28,000	$ 53,000
Income tax expense	(25,000)	(8,000)	(20,000)
Net income	$ 63,000	$ 20,000	$ 33,000

Prepare a common-size income statement for each year.

Practice 23-2
LO1

Interpreting a Common-Size Income Statement

Refer to Practice 23-1. Briefly explain why overall profitability declined in Year 2 and then went back up in Year 3.

Practice 23-3
LO1

Preparing a Common-Size Balance Sheet

Company A reported the following balance sheet data for the most recent three years:

	Year 3	Year 2	Year 1
Cash	$ 8,000	$ 8,000	$ 6,000
Accounts receivable	18,000	37,000	18,000
Inventory	36,000	47,000	36,000
Current assets	$ 62,000	$ 92,000	$ 60,000
Property, plant, and equipment (net)	138,000	126,000	123,000
Total assets	$200,000	$218,000	$183,000
Accounts payable	$ 28,000	$ 39,000	$ 21,000
Short-term debt	15,000	20,000	15,000
Current liabilities	$ 43,000	$ 59,000	$ 36,000
Long-term debt	52,000	65,000	58,000
Total liabilities	$ 95,000	$124,000	$ 94,000
Paid-in capital	19,000	19,000	19,000
Retained earnings	86,000	75,000	70,000
Total liabilities and equities	$200,000	$218,000	$183,000

Prepare the Assets section of a common-size balance sheet for each year. (*Note*: Refer to Practice 23-1 for sales data.)

Practice 23-4

LO1

Interpreting a Common-Size Balance Sheet

Refer to Practice 23-3. Briefly explain why overall efficiency declined in Year 2 and then went back up in Year 3.

Practice 23-5

LO1

Computing the DuPont Framework Ratios

Refer to Practices 23-1 and 23-3. Compute the following ratios for Year 1, Year 2, and Year 3 for Company A:

1. Return on equity
2. Return on sales
3. Asset turnover
4. Assets-to-equity ratio

Practice 23-6

LO1

Interpreting the DuPont Framework Ratios

Refer to Practice 23-5. Interpret the changes in the DuPont framework ratios from Year 1 to Year 2 and from Year 2 to Year 3.

Practice 23-7

LO1

Accounts Receivable Ratios

Refer to Practices 23-1 and 23-3. Compute the following ratios for Year 2 and Year 3 for Company A:

1. Accounts receivable turnover
2. Average collection period

Practice 23-8

LO1

Inventory Ratios

Refer to Practices 23-1 and 23-3. Compute the following ratios for Year 2 and Year 3 for Company A:

1. Inventory turnover
2. Number of days' sales in inventory

Practice 23-9

LO1

Fixed Asset Turnover

Refer to Practices 23-1 and 23-3. Compute fixed asset turnover for Year 2 and Year 3 for Company A.

Practice 23-10

LO1

Margin and Turnover

Refer to Practice 23-5. Company B and Company C had the following DuPont framework ratio values for Year 3:

	Company B	Company C
Return on sales	7.8%	24.7%
Asset turnover	2.75	0.87
Assets-to-equity ratio	1.90	1.90

Which company—A, B, or C—had the highest ROE in Year 3? Comment on your results.

Practice 23-11

LO1

Debt Ratio and Debt-to-Equity Ratio

Refer to Practices 23-1 and 23-3. Compute the following ratios for Year 1, Year 2, and Year 3 for Company A:

1. Debt ratio
2. Debt-to-equity ratio

Practice 23-12
LO1

Times Interest Earned

Refer to Practices 23-1 and 23-3. Compute times interest earned for Year 1, Year 2, and Year 3 for Company A.

Practice 23-13
LO1

Current Ratio

Refer to Practices 23-1 and 23-3. Compute the current ratio for Year 1, Year 2, and Year 3 for Company A.

Practice 23-14
LO1

Cash Flow Adequacy Ratio

The company reported the following information with respect to its statement of cash flows:

Cash from issuance of additional shares of stock	$1,000
Decrease in inventory	75
Cash used to purchase property, plant, and equipment	400
Net income	780
Cash used to repay long-term loans	600
Increase in accounts payable	100
Depreciation	300
Cash dividends paid	200
Increase in accounts receivable	150

Compute the company's cash flow adequacy ratio.

Practice 23-15
LO1

Earnings per Share and Dividend Payout Ratio

	Company S	Company T
Net income	$1,000	$15,000
Dividends	50	6,000
Weighted shares outstanding	200	10,000

Compute (1) earnings per share and (2) dividend payout ratio for Companies S and T. Indicate which of the two companies is more likely to be an older company in a low-growth industry.

Practice 23-16
LO1

Price-Earnings Ratio and Book-to-Market Ratio

	Company M	Company N
Net income	$5,000	$65,000
Stock price per share	$64.00	$35.00
Weighted shares outstanding	625	125,000
Total stockholders' equity	$56,000	$600,000

Compute (1) the price-earnings ratio and (2) the book-to-market ratio for Companies M and N. Indicate which of the two companies is more likely to be in a high-growth industry.

Practice 23-17

LO3

Equity Valuation Using Dividends and P/E Ratio

The following information has been collected regarding John Scott Company:

Most recent annual cash dividend per share	$0.65
Dividend growth rate over the past five years	7%
Most recent earnings per share	$1.53
Average P/E ratio of similar firms	18
Required rate of return on equity capital	12%

Estimate a price per share for John Scott's stock using the following equity valuation models.

1. Constant future dividends
2. Constant dividend growth
3. Price-earnings multiple

Practice 23-18

LO3

Equity Valuation Using Discounted Free Cash Flow

The following information has been collected regarding Burton Dee Company:

Free cash flow	$3,500
Annual growth rate in free cash flow over the past five years	25%
Number of shares outstanding	3,000
Required rate of return on equity capital	12%
Length of time until terminal year	4 years

Estimate a price per share for Burton Dee's stock using the discounted free cash flow model.

EXERCISES

Exercise 23-19

LO1

REVERSE SOLVABLE

DuPont Framework

Using the following data, estimate the return on equity (ROE) for the following industries.

	Assets-to-Equity Ratio	Asset Turnover	Return on Sales
Retail jewelry stores	1.6	1.5	0.040
Retail grocery stores	1.8	5.6	0.014
Electric service companies	2.6	0.5	0.069
Legal services firms	1.7	3.5	0.073

Exercise 23-20

LO1

Effect of Leverage

Trunks Company estimates that pretax earnings for the year ended December 31, 2013, will be $230,000 if it operates without borrowed capital. Income tax is 40% of earnings. Average stockholders' equity for 2013 is $740,000. Assuming that the company is able to borrow $800,000 at 12% interest, indicate the effects on net income and return on equity if borrowed capital earns (1) 15% and (2) 8%. Explain the cause of the variations.

Exercise 23-21

LO3

Equity Valuation

The following information has been collected about DeeAnn Company:

Most recent annual cash dividend per share	$0.35
Dividend growth rate over the past five years	5%
Most recent earnings per share	$2.80

(Continued)

Average P/E ratio of similar firms	19
Required rate of return on equity capital	14%
Free cash flow for most recent year	$12,800
Annual growth rate in free cash flow over past five years	25%
Number of shares outstanding	4,000
Length of time until terminal year	4 years

Estimate a price per share for DeeAnn's stock using the following equity valuation models.

1. Constant future dividends
2. Constant dividend growth
3. Price-earnings multiple
4. Discounted free cash flow
5. Which of the four estimates do you think is most reliable? Why?

Exercise 23-22
LO1
SPREADSHEET

Ratios for Receivables and Fixed Assets

The following financial statement data are for Moonbeam Inc.

	2013	2012	2011
Sales	$275,000	$220,000	$180,000
Accounts receivable (net)	75,000	65,000	30,000
Property, plant, and equipment (net)	190,000	155,000	160,000

For 2012 and 2013, compute:

(a) Accounts receivable turnover
(b) Average collection period
(c) Fixed asset turnover

Use the average of the beginning and ending asset balances in computing the ratios.

Exercise 23-23
LO1
SPREADSHEET

Analysis of Inventory

Income statements for Eldermon Sales Company follow. Analyze the inventory position at the end of each year as well as the profitability of inventory sales in each year. What conclusions would you make concerning the inventory trend?

	2013	2012	2011
Sales	$125,000	$100,000	$75,000
Cost of goods sold:			
Beginning inventory	$ 30,000	$ 25,000	$ 5,000
Purchases	105,000	80,000	85,000
	$135,000	$105,000	$90,000
Ending inventory	45,000	30,000	25,000
	$ 90,000	$ 75,000	$65,000
Gross profit	$ 35,000	$ 25,000	$10,000

Exercise 23-24
LO1

Common-Size Balance Sheets

The following data are taken from the comparative balance sheets prepared for Gubler Wholesale Company.

	2013	2012
Cash	$ 43,000	$ 22,000
Accounts receivable (net)	31,000	42,000
Inventories	71,000	33,000
Property, plant, and equipment (net)	106,000	59,000
Total assets	$251,000	$156,000

Sales for 2013 were $1,200,000. Sales for 2012 were $1,000,000.

1. Prepare the Assets section of common-size balance sheets for Gubler Wholesale Company for 2013 and 2012.
2. Overall, Gubler Wholesale is less efficient at using its assets to generate sales in 2013 than in 2012. What asset or assets are responsible for this decreased efficiency?

Exercise 23-25

LO1

SPREADSHEET

REVERSE SOLVABLE

Margin and Turnover

The following information is obtained from the primary financial statements of two retail companies. One company markets its gift merchandise in a resort area; the other company is a discount household goods store. Neither company has any debt. By analyzing these data, indicate which company is more likely to be the gift shop and which is the discount household goods store. Support your answer.

	Company A	Company B
Revenue	$6,000,000	$6,000,000
Average total assets	1,200,000	6,000,000
Net income	125,000	600,000

Exercise 23-26

LO1

SPREADSHEET

Equity Ratios

Montpelier Lumber Corp. reported the following information.

	2013	2012	2011
8% bonds payable	$ 800,000	$ 800,000	$ 800,000
Common stock, $1 par	250,000	220,000	220,000
Additional paid-in capital	2,000,000	1,430,000	1,430,000
Retained earnings	250,000	150,000	100,000
Net income	190,000	110,000	90,000
Dividends	90,000	60,000	40,000
Year-end stock price per share	22	25	12

Compute the following for each year, 2011–2013.

1. Return on equity
2. Times interest earned (ignore income taxes)
3. Earnings per share
4. Dividend payout ratio
5. Price-earnings ratio
6. Book-to-market ratio

Exercise 23-27
LO1

SPREADSHEET

REVERSE SOLVABLE

Debt Covenants and Financing Alternatives

Cubicle Company is in need of another factory building. The building will cost $500,000. Cubicle is considering the following possible financing alternatives to acquire the building.

(a) Lease the building under an operating lease.
(b) Issue common stock in the amount of $500,000.
(c) Negotiate a long-term bank loan for $500,000.
(d) Negotiate a long-term bank loan for $350,000 and increase short-term borrowing by $150,000.

Currently, Cubicle has current assets of $600,000, noncurrent assets of $975,000, current liabilities of $280,000, and noncurrent liabilities of $410,000. Under existing loan covenants, Cubicle must maintain a current ratio of 2.0 or more and a debt-to-equity ratio of less than 0.80. Which, if any, of the financing alternatives will allow Cubicle to avoid violating the loan covenants?

Exercise 23-28
LO1

SPREADSHEET

REVERSE SOLVABLE

Analysis of Financial Data

The December 31, 2013, balance sheet of Copepper's Inc. and additional information follow. These are the only accounts on Copepper's balance sheet.

Amounts indicated by a question mark (?) can be calculated from the additional information given.

Assets		Liabilities and Stockholders' Equity	
Cash	$ 25,000	Accounts payable	$?
Accounts receivable (net)	?	Income taxes payable (current)	25,000
Inventory	?	Long-term debt	?
		Common stock	300,000
Property, plant, and equipment (net)	294,000	Retained earnings	?
	$432,000		$?

Additional information follows:

Current ratio (at year-end)	1.5 to 1
Total liabilities divided by total stockholders' equity	0.8
Inventory turnover based on sales and ending inventory	15 times
Inventory turnover based on cost of goods sold and ending inventory	10.5 times
Gross margin for 2013	$315,000

1. What was Copepper's December 31, 2013, balance in Accounts Payable?
2. What was Copepper's December 31, 2013, balance in Retained Earnings?
3. What was Copepper's December 31, 2013, balance in Inventory?

Exercise 23-29
LO1

Common-Size Income Statements

Comparative income statements for Xenon Corporation for 2013 and 2012 follow.

	2013	2012
Sales	$950,000	$600,000
Cost of goods sold	595,000	325,000
Gross profit	$355,000	$275,000
Selling and general expenses	115,000	94,000
Operating income	$240,000	$181,000
Interest expense	45,000	35,000

(Continued)

	2013	2012
Income before income taxes	$195,000	$146,000
Income taxes	72,000	57,000
Net income	$123,000	$ 89,000

1. Prepare common-size income statements for Xenon Corporation for 2013 and 2012.
2. Return on sales for Xenon is lower in 2013 than in 2012. What expense or expenses are causing this lower profitability?

PROBLEMS

Problem 23-30
LO1

Common-Size Income Statements

Operations for Probe Corporation for 2012 and 2013 are summarized here.

	2013	2012
Net sales	$280,000	$230,000
Cost of goods sold	198,000	110,000
Gross profit	$ 82,000	$120,000
Selling and general expenses	50,000	53,000
Operating income	$ 32,000	$ 67,000
Other expenses	40,000	28,000
Income (loss) before income taxes	$ (8,000)	$ 39,000
Income taxes (refund)	(3,000)	16,000
Net income (loss)	$ (5,000)	$ 23,000

Instructions:

1. Prepare common-size income statements for 2013 and 2012.
2. Comment on Probe's profitability in 2013 relative to 2012.

Problem 23-31
LO1

Common-Size Balance Sheets

As of December 31, 2013, balance sheet data for Stay-Trim Company and Tone-Up Company are as follows:

	Stay-Trim Company	Tone-Up Company
Assets		
Current assets	$ 51,000	$ 240,000
Long-term investments	5,000	280,000
Land, buildings, and equipment (net)	48,000	520,000
Intangible assets	1,000	100,000
Other assets	5,000	60,000
Total assets	$110,000	$1,200,000
Liabilities and Stockholders' Equity		
Current liabilities	$ 15,000	$ 180,000
Long-term liabilities	25,000	300,000
Deferred revenues	5,000	70,000
Total liabilities	$ 45,000	$ 550,000

(Continued)

	Stay-Trim Company	Tone-Up Company
Preferred stock	$ 5,000	$ 100,000
Common stock	30,000	200,000
Additional paid-in capital	20,000	185,000
Retained earnings	10,000	165,000
Total stockholders' equity	$ 65,000	$ 650,000
Total liabilities and stockholders' equity	$110,000	$1,200,000

Instructions:

1. Prepare comparative common-size balance sheets for these two companies using total assets.
2. What conclusions can be drawn from these comparative common-size balance sheets?

Problem 23-32

LO1

DuPont Analysis of Three Companies

Financial information (in thousands of dollars) relating to three different companies follows.

	Company A	Company B	Company C
Net sales	$ 60,000	$28,000	$21,000
Net income	9,600	1,850	360
Total assets	155,400	21,500	3,200
Total equity	61,000	11,300	1,690

Instructions:

1. Compute the following ratios:
   (a) Return on sales
   (b) Asset turnover
   (c) Assets-to-equity ratio
   (d) Return on assets
   (e) Return on equity
2. Assume that the three companies are (a) a large department store, (b) a large grocery store, and (c) a large utility. Based on the above information, identify each company. Explain your answer.

REVERSE SOLVABLE

Problem 23-33

LO1

Analysis of Inventory and Receivables

Inventory and receivable balances and gross profit data for Mountain Electric follow.

	2013	2012	2011
Balance sheet data:			
Inventory, December 31	$230,000	$180,000	$140,000
Accounts receivable, December 31	120,000	95,000	60,000
Income statement data:			
Net sales	$630,000	$560,000	$510,000
Cost of goods sold	325,000	290,000	265,000
Gross profit	$305,000	$270,000	$245,000

Instructions: Compute the following ratios for 2013 and 2012.

1. Accounts receivable turnover
2. Average collection period (Use the receivables balance at the end of the year.)
3. Inventory turnover
4. Number of days' sales in inventory (Use the inventory balance at end of year.)

Problem 23-34

LO1

Inventory Turnover

The following data are taken from Clayburgh Corporation's records for the years ended December 31, 2013, 2012, and 2011.

	2013	2012	2011
Finished goods inventory	$ 60,000	$ 40,000	$ 30,000
Goods in process inventory	60,000	65,000	60,000
Raw materials inventory	60,000	40,000	35,000
Sales	400,000	340,000	300,000
Cost of goods sold	225,000	230,000	210,000
Cost of goods manufactured	260,000	250,000	200,000
Raw materials used in production	150,000	130,000	120,000

Instructions:

1. Compute turnover rates for 2013 and 2012 for the following:
   (a) Finished goods
   (b) Goods in process
   (c) Raw materials
2. Analyze the turnover results as to reasonableness and the message they send to a statement reader.

Problem 23-35

LO1

Comparative Ratio Analysis

The following are comparative data for Sunshine State Equipment, Inc., for the 3-year period 2011–2013.

Income Statement Data

	2013	2012	2011
Net sales	$1,400,000	$1,100,000	$1,220,000
Cost of goods sold	760,000	600,000	610,000
Gross profit on sales	$ 640,000	$ 500,000	$ 610,000
Selling, general, and other expenses	340,000	280,000	250,000
Income before taxes	$ 300,000	$ 220,000	$ 360,000
Income taxes	120,000	89,000	152,000
Net income	$ 180,000	$ 131,000	$ 208,000
Dividends paid	155,000	150,000	208,000
Net increase (decrease) in retained earnings	$ 25,000	$ (19,000)	$ 0

Balance Sheet Data

	2013	2012	2011
Assets			
Cash	$ 50,000	$ 40,000	$ 75,000
Accounts receivable (net)	300,000	320,000	250,000
Inventory	380,000	420,000	350,000
Prepaid expenses	30,000	10,000	40,000
Land, buildings, and equipment (net)	760,000	600,000	690,000
Intangible assets	110,000	100,000	125,000
Other assets	70,000	10,000	20,000
	$1,700,000	$1,500,000	$1,550,000
Liabilities and Stockholders' Equity			
Accounts payable	$ 120,000	$ 185,000	$ 220,000
Wages, interest, and dividends payable	25,000	25,000	25,000
Income tax payable	29,000	5,000	30,000
Miscellaneous current liabilities	10,000	4,000	10,000
8% bonds payable	300,000	300,000	250,000
Deferred revenues (long term)	10,000	10,000	25,000
No-par common stock, $10 stated value	500,000	400,000	400,000
Additional paid-in capital	510,000	400,000	400,000
Retained earnings	196,000	171,000	190,000
	$1,700,000	$1,500,000	$1,550,000

Instructions:

1. From the foregoing data, calculate financial ratios for the three years 2011–2013 as follows (for all ratios using balance sheet amounts, use the end-of-year balance):
   (a) Return on equity
   (b) Return on sales
   (c) Asset turnover
   (d) Assets-to-equity ratio
   (e) Return on assets
   (f) Current ratio
   (g) Dividend payout ratio
2. Based on the ratios calculated in (1), evaluate Sunshine State Equipment, Inc., in 2013 as compared with 2012.

Problem 23-36
LO1

Comparative Ratio Analysis

Use the comparative data for Sunshine State Equipment, Inc., as given in Problem 23-35. In addition, the year-end price per share of Sunshine's stock was $50 for 2011, $25 for 2012, and $35 for 2013.

Instructions:

1. Compute financial ratios for the three years 2011–2013 as follows (for ratios normally using average balances, assume that 2010 figures are the same as 2011):
   (a) Accounts receivable turnover
   (b) Average collection period
   (c) Inventory turnover
   (d) Number of days' sales in inventory

(e) Fixed asset turnover
(f) Debt ratio
(g) Debt-to-equity ratio
(h) Times interest earned (Assume that Bonds Payable is the only interest-bearing liability.)
(i) Earnings per share
(j) Price-earnings ratio
(k) Book-to-market ratio

2. Based on the ratios calculated in (1), evaluate Sunshine State Equipment, Inc., in 2013 as compared with 2012.

Problem 23-37

LO1, LO2

REVERSE SOLVABLE

Accounting Differences and Ratio Analysis

The following three ratios have been computed using the financial statements for the year ended December 31, 2013, for Fun Science Company:

Current ratio = (Current assets/Current liabilities)
= $62,000/$41,000
= 1.51

Debt-to-equity ratio = (Total liabilities/Stockholders' equity)
= $103,000/$115,000
= 0.90

Return on sales = (Net income/Sales)
= $53,000/$550,000
= 9.6%

The following additional information has been assembled:

(a) Fun Science uses the LIFO method of inventory valuation. Beginning inventory was $23,000, and ending inventory was $32,000. If Fun Science had used FIFO, beginning inventory would have been $41,000 and ending inventory would have been $57,200.

(b) Fun Science's sole depreciable asset was purchased on January 1, 2010. The asset cost $140,000 and is being depreciated over seven years with no estimated salvage value. Although the 7-year life is within the acceptable range, most firms in Fun Science's industry depreciate similar assets over five years.

(c) For 2013, Fun Science decided to recognize a $24,000 liability for future environmental cleanup costs. Most other firms in Fun Science's industry have similar environmental cleanup obligations but have decided that the amounts of the obligations are not reasonably estimable at this time; on average, these firms recognized only 10% of their total environmental cleanup obligation.

Instructions:

1. How would the values for the three ratios just computed differ if Fun Science had used FIFO, depreciated the asset over five years, and recognized only 10% of its environmental cleanup obligation? Do not think of these as accounting changes; compute how the financial statements would differ if the alternate accounting methods had been used to begin with. Ignore any income tax effects.
2. What dangers are there in comparing a company's financial ratios with summary industry ratios?

Problem 23-38

LO1

Sample CPA Exam Questions

1. A company pays $75,000 in cash to pay a current account payable. Would this transaction increase, decrease, or have no effect on the current ratio that now stands at 2:1?
   (a) Increase
   (b) Decrease
   (c) No effect

2. A company purchases equipment by making a down payment and financing the remainder through a 4-year bank loan, due in monthly installments. What effect would this transaction have on the company's current ratio, which currently stands at 1.5:1?
(a) Increase
(b) Decrease
(c) No effect
3. A firm borrows $200,000 from a bank. The principal and interest on the loan are due in 18 months. Would this transaction increase, decrease, or have no effect on the debt ratio (Total liabilities/Total assets) that now stands at 36%?
(a) Increase
(b) Decrease
(c) No effect

CASES

Discussion Case 23-39

Are International Ratios Comparable?

As the world economy becomes more integrated, one question facing financial analysts is whether financial ratios can be compared across national boundaries. For example, at one time the average P/E ratio for Japanese companies was around 60, and the average for U.S. companies was between 15 and 20. (A P/E ratio in excess of 30 is considered quite high in the United States.) This dramatic variation was a result of differences in the two national economies and in their accounting methods. One of the accounting differences is that Japanese companies generally depreciate their fixed assets over shorter lives than do U.S. companies.

In addition to differences in accounting methods, what other challenges are faced by financial analysts in comparing the financial ratios of a U.S. company to those of a Japanese, German, or British company?

Discussion Case 23-40

Analyzing Earnings

Royer Donahoe owns two businesses, a drug store and a retail department store.

	Drug Store	Department Store
Net sales	$1,050,000	$670,000
Cost of goods sold	1,000,000	600,000
Average total assets	50,000	200,000
Other expenses	39,500	36,500

Which business is more profitable? Which business is more efficient? Overall, which business would you consider to be a more attractive investment?

Discussion Case 23-41

Can a Ratio Be Too Good?

Tony Christopher is analyzing the financial statements of Shaycole Company and has computed the following ratios.

	Shaycole	Industry Comparison
Current ratio	4.7	1.9
Inventory turnover	14.8 times	6.1 times
Accounts receivable turnover	27.4 times	8.7 times
Debt-to-equity ratio	0.117	0.864

Andy Martinez, Tony's colleague, tells Tony that Shaycole looks great. Andy points out that although Shaycole's ratios deviate significantly from the industry norms, all deviations suggest that Shaycole is doing better than other firms in its industry. Is Andy right?

Discussion Case 23-42

Evaluating Alternative Investments

Judy Snow is considering investing $10,000 and wishes to know which of two following companies offers the better alternative.

Hoffman Company earned net income of $63,000 last year on average total assets of $280,000 and average stockholders' equity of $210,000. The company's shares are selling for $100 per share; 6,300 shares of common stock are outstanding.

McMahon Company earned $24,375 last year on average total assets of $125,000 and average stockholders' equity of $100,000. The company's common shares are selling for $78 per share; 2,500 shares are outstanding.

Which stock should Snow buy?

Case 23-43

Deciphering Financial Statements (The Walt Disney Company)

Locate the 2009 financial statements for **The Walt Disney Company** on the Internet.

Once you have located those financial statements, consider the following questions.

1. Disney has five primary business segments: Media Networks, Parks and Resorts, Studio Entertainment, Consumer Products, and Interactive Media. Which of these five has the best 2009 profitability as measured by return on sales?
2. Which of Disney's five segments has the best overall asset efficiency in 2009 as measured by asset turnover?
3. Which of Disney's five segments best combines margin and turnover in 2009 to yield the highest return on assets?
4. Discuss why ROE cannot be computed for each segment. What is Disney's overall ROE in 2009?

Case 23-44

Deciphering Financial Statements (McDonald's)

Shown on the next page are comparative income statements for **McDonald's** for 2007, 2008, and 2009.

1. There are two kinds of McDonald's restaurants—restaurants that McDonald's itself owns and restaurants owned by McDonald's franchisees. For each of the three years, prepare a mini income statement for McDonald's containing the following items:

	Sales by company-operated restaurants
Less:	Food & paper
Less:	Payroll & employee benefits
Less:	Occupancy & other operating expenses
=	Operating income from company-operated restaurants

2. From the mini income statements prepared in (1), prepare common-size income statements for McDonald's company-operated restaurants for the three years 2007–2009.
3. Comment on the common-size income statements prepared in (2).
4. Where does McDonald's get more of its total operating income—from company-owned restaurants or from franchise operations?

McDonald's
Consolidated Statement of Income

Statement of Income Alternative (USD $) In Millions, except Per Share data	12 Months Ended Dec. 31, 2009	Dec. 31, 2008	Dec. 31, 2007
Revenues			
Sales by Company-operated restaurants	$15,458.5	$16,560.9	$16,611.0
Revenues from franchised restaurants	7,286.2	6,961.5	6,175.6
Total revenues	22,744.7	23,522.4	22,786.6
Company-operated restaurant expenses			
Food & paper	5,178	5,586.1	5,487.4
Payroll & employee benefits	3,965.6	4,300.1	4,331.6
Occupancy & other operating expenses	3,507.6	3,766.7	3,922.7
Franchised restaurants-occupancy expenses	1,301.7	1,230.3	1,139.7
Selling, general & administrative expenses	2,234.2	2,355.5	2,367.0
Impairment and other charges (credits), net	(61.1)	6.0	1,670.3
Other operating (income) expense, net	(222.3)	(165.2)	(11.1)
Total operating costs and expenses	15,903.7	17,079.5	18,907.6
Operating income	6,841.0	6,442.9	3,879.0
Interest expense-net of capitalized interest of $11.7, $12.3 and $6.9	473.2	522.6	410.1
Nonoperating (income) expense, net	(24.3)	(77.6)	(103.2)
Gain on sale of investment	(94.9)	(160.1)	0
Income from continuing operations before provision for income taxes	6,487.0	6,158.0	3,572.1
Provision for income taxes	1,936.0	1,844.8	1,237.1
Income from continuing operations	4,551.0	4,313.2	2,335.0
Income from discontinued operations (net of taxes of $34.5)	0	0	60.1
Net income	$ 4,551.0	$ 4,313.2	$ 2,395.1

Case 23-45

Deciphering Financial Statements (Coke vs. Pepsi)

The following information is from the 2009 annual reports of **The Coca-Cola Company** and of **PepsiCo** (all amounts are in millions of U.S. dollars). The information for PepsiCo is separated into overall results and results for just the beverage segments. Coca-Cola reports that substantially all of its operations are beverage-related.

1. Using the overall data, compute return on equity, return on sales, asset turnover, and assets-to-equity ratio for both PepsiCo and Coca-Cola.

	PepsiCo		Coca-Cola
	Overall	Beverages	Overall
Sales	$43,232	$22,421	$30,990
Operating income	8,044	3,820	8,231
Net income	5,946	—	6,824
Identifiable operating assets	32,837	21,928	41,916
Total assets	39,848	—	48,671
Total equity	16,908	—	24,799

2. Using the Beverages segment data for PepsiCo, compute return on beverage sales, beverage asset turnover, and return on beverage assets for both PepsiCo

and Coca-Cola. Because Coca-Cola has only one operating segment, the overall results are the same as the beverage segment results. Use operating income and identifiable operating assets in your calculations (in place of net income and total assets, respectively).

3. Some writers have claimed that Coca-Cola has outperformed PepsiCo historically because Coke has concentrated on the profitable soft drink business, whereas PepsiCo has diversified into snack foods. Evaluate this claim in light of your calculations in (1) and (2).

Case 23-46

Deciphering Financial Statements (Safeway)
Below are sales data, in nominal dollars, for **Safeway**, the supermarket chain, from 1981 through 2009 (in millions of U.S. dollars). In addition, the consumer price index (CPI) for each year is given (1982–1984 = 100).

Year	Sales	CPI	Year	Sales	CPI
1981	$16,580	90.9	1996	$17,269	156.9
1982	17,633	96.5	1997	22,484	160.5
1983	18,585	99.6	1998	24,484	163.0
1984	19,642	103.9	1999	28,860	166.6
1985	19,651	107.6	2000	31,977	172.2
1986	20,312	109.6	2001	34,301	177.1
1987	18,301	113.6	2002	34,917	179.9
1988	13,612	118.3	2003	35,727	184.0
1989	14,325	124.0	2004	35,823	188.9
1990	14,874	130.7	2005	38,416	195.3
1991	15,119	136.2	2006	40,185	201.6
1992	15,152	140.3	2007	42,286	207.3
1993	15,215	144.5	2008	44,104	215.3
1994	15,627	148.2	2009	40,851	214.5
1995	16,398	152.4			

Nominal dollar sales are just the regular sales as reported. Constant dollar sales are sales adjusted to the price level of a common comparison year in order to remove the distortions caused by inflation. Nominal dollar sales are converted into constant dollar sales by dividing by the price index for the year in which the sales were made and multiplying by the price index in the comparison year.

1. Use the CPI to restate all the Safeway sales numbers in terms of 2009 dollars.
2. In terms of nominal dollar sales, Safeway's sales have been growing steadily since 1988 (until the recession year of 2009). Do the constant dollar sales data give the same picture? Explain.
3. In the latter part of 1986, Safeway underwent a leveraged buyout and began to get rid of a number of its stores. Is there any evidence of this in the nominal dollar sales data? In the constant dollar sales data?

Case 23-47

Ethical Dilemma (Does the Bonus Plan Reward the Right Thing?)
Roaring Springs Booksellers is a mail-order book company. Customers choose their purchases from a catalog and send in their order by mail, fax, phone, or e-mail. Roaring Springs then assembles the books from its warehouse inventory, packs the order, and ships it to the customer within three working days. This rapid turnaround time on orders requires Roaring Springs to have a large warehouse staff; wage expense averages almost 20% of sales.

Each member of the top management of Roaring Springs receives an annual bonus equal to 1% of his or her salary for every 0.1% that Roaring Springs' return on sales exceeds 5.0%. For example, if return on sales is 5.3%, each top manager would receive a bonus of 3% of salary. Historically, return on sales for Roaring Springs has ranged from 4.5% to 5.5%.

The management of Roaring Springs has come up with a plan to dramatically increase return on sales, perhaps to as high as 6.5% to 7.0%. The plan is to acquire a sophisticated, computerized packing machine that can receive customer order information, mechanically assemble the books for each individual order, box the order, print an address label, and route the box to the correct loading dock for pickup by the delivery service. Acquisition of this machine will allow Roaring Springs to lay off 100 warehouse employees, resulting in a significant savings in wage expense. Top management intends to acquire the machine using new investment capital from stockholders. In this way, there will be no increase in interest expense. Because the depreciation expense on the new machine will be much less than the savings in reduced wage expense, return on sales will increase.

All top managers of Roaring Springs are excited about this plan: It could increase their bonuses to as much as 20% of salary. As assistant to the chief financial officer of Roaring Springs, you have been asked to prepare a briefing for the board of directors explaining exactly how this new packing machine will increase return on sales. As part of your preparation, you decide to examine the impact of the machine acquisition on the other two components of the DuPont framework—efficiency and leverage. You find that even with the projected increase in return on sales, the decrease in asset turnover and in the assets-to-equity ratio will cause total ROE to decline from its current level of 18.0% to around 14.0%.

Your presentation is scheduled for the next board of directors meeting in two weeks. What should you do?

Case 23-48

Cumulative Spreadsheet Analysis

This spreadsheet assignment is an extension of the spreadsheet assignment given in Chapter 20, part (1). Refer back to the instructions given in Chapter 20. If you completed the spreadsheet assignment for Chapter 20, that spreadsheet can form the foundation for this assignment.

1. In addition to preparing forecasted financial statements for 2014 and 2015, Skywalker also wishes to prepare forecasted financial statements for 2016, 2017, and 2018. All assumptions applicable to 2014 and 2015 are assumed to be applicable to the subsequent years. Refer back to Chapter 13, part (1), for an explanation of each of the assumptions. Sales in each year are expected to be 40% higher than sales in the year before. [*Note*: For this part of the assignment, use the original 107.6-day value for the number of days' sales in inventory; ignore the change assumed in (2) of the Chapter 20 assignment.] Clearly state any additional assumptions that you make.
2. As a company matures, it expects to generate enough cash from its operating activities to pay for a significant portion of its investing activities. Comment on whether it appears that Skywalker will reach that condition between 2013 and 2018.
3. Repeat (1), with the following changes in assumptions:

Average collection period	9.06 days
Number of days' sales in inventory	66.23 days
Fixed asset turnover	3.989 times
Gross profit percentage	27.55%
Other operating expenses/sales	19.86%
Number of days' purchases in accounts payable	50.37 days

(*Note*: After making these changes in ratio values, your spreadsheet may have negative amounts for Short-Term Loans Payable. This is impossible. Adjust your spreadsheet so that Short-Term Loans Payable is never less than zero. This will require a relaxation of the requirement that the current ratio be at least 2.0.)

4. Discuss why Skywalker has a projected current ratio of less than 2.0 in some years when using the ratios in (3).
5. Which company would you rather loan money to: a company with the projected financial statements prepared in (1) or a company with the projected financial statements prepared in (3)? Explain your answer.

APPENDIX AP

Summary of U.S. GAAP/IFRS Differences

Topic	U.S. GAAP	IASB
Chapter 1: Financial Reporting		
Accounting standard setter	Financial Accounting Standards Board (FASB)	International Accounting Standards Board (IASB)
Financial accounting standards	FASB Accounting Standards Codification (ASC)	• International Financial Reporting Standards (IFRS) • International Accounting Standards (IAS)
Group to address issues of interpretation or for which no formal standard currently exists	Emerging Issues Task Force (EITF)	• International Financial Reporting Interpretations Committee (IFRIC) • Standing Interpretations Committee (SIC) before 2002

Topic	FASB Accounting Standards Codification	Original FASB Standard	Corresponding IASB Standard	Differences between U.S. GAAP and IFRS
Chapter 3: The Balance Sheet and Notes to the Financial Statements				
Classified balance sheet	*Section 210-10-05 par. 4* *Section 210-10-45 par. 1 through 12*	*ARB 43 Ch, 3A par. 4-8*	*IAS 1 par. 60-61*	No substantial differences in the descriptions and definitions of current assets and current liabilities
Classification of short-term obligations to be refinanced	*Section 470-10-45 par. 14*	*SFAS No. 6 par. 10-11*	*IAS 1 par. 72*	Under IFRS, for a short-term obligation to be classified as long term, the refinancing must take place by the balance sheet date.
Upward revaluation	*Topic 855*	*SFAS No. 165*	*IAS 10*	No substantial differences
Chapter 4: The Income Statement				
Discontinued operations	*Subtopic 205-20*	*SFAS No. 144*	*IFRS 5*	Under IFRS, a discontinued operation must be a major line of business or geographic segment. Also, under IFRS, separate disclosure must be made of the cash flows of the discontinued operations.
Extraordinary items	*Subtopic 225-20*	*APB Opinion No. 30*	*IAS 1 par. 87*	Under IFRS, no income or expense items are allowed to be classified as "extraordinary."
Change in accounting principle	*Section 250-10-45 par. 1-16* *Section 250-10-50 par. 1- 3*	*SFAS No. 154 par. 4-18* *APB No. 28 par. 28*	*IAS 8 par. 14-31*	No substantial differences

Topic	FASB Accounting Standards Codification	Original FASB Standard	Corresponding IASB Standard	Differences between U.S. GAAP and IFRS
Chapter 5: Statement of Cash Flows and Articulation				
Definition of cash equivalents	*Section 230-10-20 (Glossary) – Cash equivalents*	*SFAS No. 95 par. 8*	*IAS 7 par. 7*	No substantial differences
Noncash investing and financing activities	*Section 230-10-50 par. 3*	*SFAS No. 95 par. 32*	*IAS 7 par. 43*	No substantial differences
Direct and indirect methods	*Section 230-10-45 par. 25,28*	*SFAS No. 95 par. 27-28*	*IAS 7 par. 18-19*	No substantial differences
Classification of interest paid	*Section 230-10-45 par. 17(d)*	*SFAS No. 95 par. 23(d)*	*IAS 7 par. 33*	U.S. GAAP – operating IFRS – operating or financing
Classification of income taxes paid	*Section 230-10-45 par. 17(c)*	*SFAS No. 95 par. 23(c)*	*IAS 7 par. 35*	U.S. GAAP – operating IFRS – operating, investing, or financing
Classification of interest received	*Section 230-10-45 par. 16(b)*	*SFAS No. 95 par. 22(b)*	*IAS 7 par. 33*	U.S. GAAP – operating IFRS – operating or investing
Classification of dividends received	*Section 230-10-45 par. 16(b)*	*SFAS No. 95 par. 22(b)*	*IAS 7 par. 33*	U.S. GAAP – operating IFRS – operating or investing
Classification of dividends paid	*Section 230-10-45 par. 15(a)*	*SFAS No. 95 par. 20(a)*	*IAS 7 par. 34*	U.S. GAAP – financing IFRS – operating or financing

Topic	U.S. GAAP	IASB Standard
Chapter 6: Earnings Management		
General characterization of the standards	Rules oriented. U.S. GAAP contains about 25,000 pages with lots of detailed guidance.	Principles oriented. IFRS contains just 2,500 pages with many detailed accounting decisions left up to the professional judgment of the accountant.

Topic	FASB Accounting Standards Codification	Original FASB Standard	Corresponding IASB Standard	Differences between U.S. GAAP and IFRS
Fair Value Module				
Fair values in financial reporting	*Topic 820*	*SFAS No. 157*	*Exposure Draft: Fair Value Measurement, May 2009*	No substantial differences. Both the FASB and the IASB plan to have revised fair value standards finalized by the end of 2010; the revised standards will be mutually consistent.
Chapter 7: The Revenue/Receivables/Cash Cycle				
Bad debts	*Section 310-10-35 par. 7-9*	*SFAS No. 5 par. 22*	*No explicit standard*	No apparent differences
Warranties	*Section 460-10-25 par. 5-7*	*SFAS No. 5 par. 24*	*IAS 37 par. 14, 39*	No substantial differences

Topic	FASB Accounting Standards Codification	Original FASB Standard	Corresponding IASB Standard	Differences between U.S. GAAP and IFRS
Compensating balances	*Section 210-10-S99 par. 1*	*SEC Regulation S-X, Rule 5-02, Caption 1*	*IAS 7 par. 48*	No substantial differences
Imputation of interest on receivables	*Section 835-30-25 par. 2, 12*	*APB No. 21 par. 9, 13*	*No explicit standard*	No apparent differences
Derecognition of receivables	*Section 860-10-40 par. 5*	*SFAS No. 140 par. 9*	*IAS 39 par. 20*	U.S. GAAP includes a list of three criteria that must be satisfied for derecognition. IFRS has a conceptual 2-step test based on risks and rewards and control. In practice, the derecognition result is almost always the same.
Chapter 8: Revenue Recognition				
Revenue recognition	*Topic 605*	*Contained in a large number of different standards*	*IAS 18, IAS 11*	U.S. GAAP and IFRS are generally consistent, but many detailed differences exist. The FASB and IASB are currently working on a joint revenue recognition project.
Completed-contract method	*Subtopic 605-35*	*ARB 45 and SOP 81-1*	*IAS 11*	Under IFRS, the completed contract method is not allowed.
Pre-sale revenue recognition for biological assets	*Section 905-330-35*	*SOP 85-3*	*IAS 41*	Under IFRS, changes in the fair value of biological assets are recognized as gains and losses. Under U.S. GAAP, a similar procedure is acceptable under some circumstances, but not required.
Multiple-element arrangements	*Subtopic 605-25*	*EITF 08-1*	*IAS 18*	IFRS does not contain any specific provisions related to multiple-element arrangements.
Chapter 9: Inventory and Cost of Goods Sold				
LIFO	*Section 330-10-30 par. 9-11*	*ARB 43, Chapter 4*	*IAS 2 par. 23-27*	LIFO is not allowable under IFRS.
Lower of cost or market	*Section 330-10-35 par. 1-12*	*ARB 43, Chapter 4*	*IAS 2 par. 28-33*	Under IFRS, inventory is recorded at lower of cost or net realizable value, and inventory write-down losses can be reversed if the selling price subsequently recovers.
Foreign currency transactions	*Section 830-20-35 par. 2*	*SFAS No. 52 par. 16b*	*IAS 21 par. 23a, 28*	No substantial differences
Chapter 10: Investments in Noncurrent Operating Assets—Acquisition				
Interest capitalization	*Subtopic 835-20*	*SFAS No. 34*	*IAS 23*	Under IFRS, net "borrowing costs" are capitalized. The net amount is the gross interest paid less interest received on investment of idle funds.
Asset retirement obligation	*Subtopic 410-20*	*SFAS No. 143*	*IAS 16 and IAS 37*	No substantial differences

Topic	FASB Accounting Standards Codification	Original FASB Standard	Corresponding IASB Standard	Differences between U.S. GAAP and IFRS
Business combinations	*Topic 805*	*SFAS No. 141R*	*IFRS 3*	No substantial differences
Intangible assets	*Topic 350*	*SFAS No. 142*	*IAS 38*	No substantial differences
Research and development	*Topic 730*	*SFAS No.2* *SFAS No.86*	*IAS 38*	Under IFRS, development costs, which are costs incurred after technological feasibility, are capitalized. This matches U.S. GAAP for software development costs, but not for ordinary R&D.
Chapter 11: Investments in Noncurrent Operating Assets—Utilization and Retirement				
Impairment of tangible assets	*Subtopic 360-10 various subsections on "Impairment"*	*SFAS No. 144*	*IAS 36*	Under U.S. GAAP, the impairment test is a 2-step test. Under IFRS, the impairment test involves just one step, a comparison of the book value to the "recoverable amount" of the asset.
Impairment of intangible assets	*Topic 350*	*SFAS No. 142*	*IAS 36*	U.S. GAAP includes three different impairment tests for intangibles. Under IFRS, there is just one test, which is the same as is used for tangible assets.
Upward revaluation	*Not part of U.S. GAAP*	*Not part of U.S. GAAP*	*IAS 16*	Upward revaluations of property, plant, and equipment are generally not allowable under U.S. GAAP.
Asset retirement obligations	*Subtopic 410-20*	*SFAS No. 143*	*IAS 16 and IAS 37*	No substantial differences
Assets classified as held for sale	*Section 360-10-45*	*SFAS No. 144*	*IFRS 5*	No substantial differences
Chapter 12: Debt Financing				
Short-term obligations expected to be refinanced	*Section 470-10-45 par. 14*	*SFAS No. 6 par. 10-11*	*IAS 1 par. 72*	Under IFRS, for a short-term obligation to be classified as long term, the refinancing must take place by the balance sheet date.
Splitting convertible debt proceeds into debt and equity	*Subtopic 470-20*	*APB Opinion No. 14*	*IAS 32 par. 28-32*	Under IFRS, ALL convertible debt issues are divided into their debt and equity components. This separation is only done under certain circumstances under U.S. GAAP.
Consolidation of variable interest entities (VIE)	*Section 810-10-25 par. 20 through 59*	*FIN 46R*	*SIC 12*	Under IFRS, a VIE is consolidated when the economic substance of the relationship indicates that the VIE is controlled. Compared to U.S. GAAP, this is very much a principles-based approach.

Topic	FASB Accounting Standards Codification	Original FASB Standard	Corresponding IASB Standard	Differences between U.S. GAAP and IFRS
Fair value option	*Topic 825, "Fair Value Option" subsections*	*SFAS No. 159*	*IFRS 9*	There is a fair value option for financial assets under IFRS, but as of 2010 there was not yet a fair value option for financial liabilities.
Troubled debt restructuring	*Subtopic 470-60*	*SFAS No. 15*	*IAS 39 par. 39 through 41*	No substantial differences
Chapter 13: Equity Financing				
Stock warrants	*Section 470-20-25 par. 2*	*APB Opinion No. 14 par. 16*	*IAS 32 par. 28*	Under IFRS, all compound financial instruments, such as stock warrants, are to be separated into separate debt and equity components. Under U.S. GAAP, this is required only if the stock warrants are "detachable."
Stock-based compensation	*Topic 718*	*SFAS No. 123R*	IFRS 2	No substantial differences
Reporting equity-related items as liabilities	*Topic 480*	*SFAS No. 150*	*IAS 32*	No substantial differences
Noncontrolling interest	*Section 810-10-45 par. 16*	*SFAS No. 160 par. 5*	*IAS 27 par. 27*	No substantial differences
Chapter 14: Investments in Debt and Equity Securities				
Classification as trading, available for sale, or held to maturity	*Section 320-10-25 par. 1*	*SFAS No. 115 par. 6-12*	*IFRS 9 par 4.1, 5.4.4*	No substantial differences
Equity method	*Topic 323*	*APB Opinion No. 18*	*IAS 28*	No substantial differences
Fair value option	*Topic 825, "Fair Value Option" subsections*	*SFAS No. 159*	*IFRS 9*	There is a fair value option for financial assets under IFRS, but as of 2010 there was not yet a fair value option for financial liabilities.
Derecognition of investment securities	*Topic 860*	*SFAS No. 140*	*IAS 39 par. 20*	Under U.S. GAAP, the transfer of a financial asset is recorded as a sale if control of the asset passes from the transferor to the transferee. Under IFRS, the transfer is recorded as a sale if the risks and rewards associated with the cash flows from the financial assets pass from the transferor to the transferee.

Topic	FASB Accounting Standards Codification	Original FASB Standard	Corresponding IASB Standard	Differences between U.S. GAAP and IFRS
Classification of cash flows from the purchase and sale of investment securities	*Section 320-10-45 par. 11*	*SFAS No. 115 par. 18*	*IAS 7 par. 15-16*	Under IFRS, cash flows from the purchase and sale of trading securities are classified under operating activities; for other security categories, the cash flows are investing activities. Under U.S. GAAP, trading security cash flows may be operating or investing, depending on management intent.
Loan impairment	*Section 310-10-35*	*SFAS No. 114*	*IAS 39 par. 58 through 65*	No substantial differences
Chapter 15: Leases				
Lease classification criteria	*Section 840-10-25 par. 1*	*SFAS No. 13 par. 7*	*IAS 17 par. 8-10*	In substance, the standards are the same. IFRS provides less detail.
Lease discount rate (for lessees)	*Section 840-10-25 par. 31*	*SFAS No. 13 par. 7*	*IAS 17 par. 20*	In IFRS, no explicit mention is made of using the lower of the implicit rate or the incremental borrowing rate. Instead, the implicit rate is to be used if known.
Revenue recognition criteria (for lessor)	*Section 840-10-25 par. 42*	*SFAS No. 13 par. 8*	*IAS 17 par. 42*	Substantially the same. Rather than the two explicit criteria, IFRS merely says that a sale in a sales-type lease is recognized "in accordance with the policy followed by the entity for outright sales."
Initial direct costs (for lessors)	*Section 840-20-35 par. 2* *Section 840-30-35 par. 23* *Section 840-30-25 par. 6*	*SFAS No. 13 par. 19* *SFAS No. 13 par. 18* *SFAS No. 13 par. 17*	*IAS 17 par. 38, 42*	No substantial differences
Sale-leaseback accounting	*Section 840-40-25 par. 3* *Section 840-40-35 par. 1*	*SFAS No. 13 par. 7*	*IAS 17 par. 58-63*	No substantial differences
Chapter 16: Income Taxes				
Use of currently enacted tax rates	*Section 740-10-10 par. 3*	*SFAS No. 109 par. 18*	*IAS 12 par. 46*	Under U.S. GAAP, currently enacted tax rates for future years are used in valuing deferred tax assets and liabilities. Under IFRS, tax rates that have been "substantively enacted" are also used. Substantively enacted tax rates are future tax rates that have been announced by the government but that have not yet been formally enacted into law.

Topic	FASB Accounting Standards Codification	Original FASB Standard	Corresponding IASB Standard	Differences between U.S. GAAP and IFRS
Current/noncurrent classification of deferred tax assets and liabilities	*Section 740-10-45 par. 4*	*SFAS No. 109 par. 41*	*IAS 1 par. 56*	Under U.S. GAAP, deferred tax assets and liabilities are classified current or noncurrent based on the classification of the associated asset or liability. Under IFRS, all deferred tax items are classified as noncurrent.
Recognition of deferred tax assets	*Section 740-10-30 par. 5e*	*SFAS No. 109 par. 17e*	*IAS 12 par. 24*	Under U.S. GAAP, deferred tax assets are recognized if it is "more likely than not" (50%+ probability) that the future tax benefits will be realized. Under IFRS, the probability threshold is "probable," which is generally seen to be higher than "more likely than not."
Uncertain tax positions	*Topic 740*	*FASB FIN No. 48*	*No specific accounting standard in IAS*	Under IFRS, there is no standard regarding the recognition of a tax liability related to an uncertain tax position.
Cash paid for income taxes	*Section 230-10-50 par. 2*	*SFAS No. 95 par. 121*	*IFRS 7 par. 35*	Both U.S. GAAP and IFRS require separate disclosure of the amount of cash paid for income taxes. Under IFRS, this amount may be allocated among operating, investing, and financing activities.
Chapter 17: Employee Compensation—Payroll, Pensions, and Other Compensation Issues				
Compensated absences	*Section 710-10-25 par. 1-8*	*SFAS No. 43 par. 6-16*	*IAS 19 par. 11-16*	No substantial differences
Postemployment benefits	*Section 712-10-05 par. 2-6* *Section 712-10-15 par. 3-5* *Section 712-10-25 par. 1-5*	*SFAS No. 112 par. 1-6* *SFAS No. 88 par. 15*	*IAS 19 par. 132-140*	No substantial differences
Discount rate for projected benefit obligation	*Section 715-30-35 par. 43*	*SFAS No. 87 par. 44*	*IAS 19 par.78*	IFRS allows use of the interest rate on government bonds in countries lacking a developed corporate bond market.
Prior service cost	*Section 715-30-35 par. 10-11*	*SFAS No. 87 par. 24-25*	*IAS 19 par.96*	Under IFRS, the "past" service cost amount is recognized as an expense immediately IF the benefits are immediately vested.
Balance sheet numbers: one net number for the difference between PBO and the pension fund, with AOCI shown separately	*Section 715-30-25 par. 1, 4*	*SFAS No. 87 par. 35, 38*	*IAS 19 par.54*	Under current IFRS, the reported balance sheet number is the sum of the PBO, the pension fund, and AOCI associated with the pension plan.

Topic	FASB Accounting Standards Codification	Original FASB Standard	Corresponding IASB Standard	Differences between U.S. GAAP and IFRS
Settlements and curtailments	*Various sections in Subtopics 715-30 and 715-60; illustrations in Section 715-30-55*	*SFAS No. 88*	*IAS 19 par.109-115*	No substantial differences
Disclosure	*Sections 715-29-50 715-30-50 715-60-50*	*SFAS No. 132(R)*	*IAS 19 par.120-125*	No substantial differences
Differences similar to the differences in accounting for pensions.	*Subtopic 715-60*	*SFAS No. 106*	In general, no distinction between pensions and other postretirement benefits. Guidance on medical benefits found in IAS 19 par. 88-91	Differences similar to the differences in accounting for pensions.
Chapter 18: Earnings per Share				
Computing basic earnings per share	*Section 260-10-45 par. 10-11*	*SFAS No. 128 par. 8-9*	*IAS 33 par. 9-29*	No substantial differences
Computing diluted earnings per share	*Section 260-10-45 par. 16-17*	*SFAS No. 128 par. 11, 13*	*IAS 33 par. 30-44*	No substantial differences
Participating securities and the two-class method	*Section 260-10-45 par. 59A-66*	*SFAS No. 128 par. 60-61 EITF 03-06*	*IAS 33 par. A13-A14*	No substantial differences
Treasury stock method for options	*Section 260-10-45 par.23, 25*	*SFAS No. 128 par. 17-18*	*IAS 33 par. 45-48*	No substantial differences
If-converted method for convertible securities	*Section 260-10-45 par. 40-42*	*SFAS No. 128 par. 26-28*	*IAS 33 par. 49-51*	No substantial differences
Impact of actual conversion or exercise	*Section 260-10-45 par. 17*	*SFAS No. 128 par. 13*	*IAS 33 par. 38*	No substantial differences
Proper order of consideration for multiple potentially dilutive securities	*Section 260-10-45 par. 18*	*SFAS No. 128 par. 14-15*	*IAS 33 par. 44*	No substantial differences
Disclosures associated with basic and diluted EPS	*Section 260-10-50 par. 1-2*	*SFAS No. 128 par. 40-41*	*IAS 33 par. 70-73A*	No substantial differences

Topic	FASB Accounting Standards Codification	Original FASB Standard	Corresponding IASB Standard	Differences between U.S. GAAP and IFRS
Chapter 19: Derivatives, Contingencies, Business Segments, and Interim Reports				
Accounting for derivatives	*Topic 815*	*SFAS No. 133*	*IAS 39*	No substantial differences at the conceptual level, but numerous technical differences that are beyond the scope of this book.
Recognition of contingent liabilities and contingent assets	*Contingent liabilities: Section 450-20-25* *Contingent assets: Section 450-30-25*	*SFAS No. 5 par. 3 and 17*	*IAS 37 par. 10,27-28,31,34*	Generally the same. Under IFRS, there is no requirement to disclose contingent guarantee obligations when their likelihood is remote.
Measurement of contingent liabilities	*Section 450-20-30 par. 1*	*FIN No. 14 par. 3*	*IAS 37 par. 36-47*	Under U.S. GAAP, the estimated liability is the low end of the estimated range if each estimate in the range is equally likely. Under IFRS, the estimated liability is the amount required to settle the obligation.
Segment reporting	*Topic 280*	*SFAS No. 131*	*IFRS 8*	No substantial differences
Relation between interim reporting and annual reporting	*Section 270-10-45 par. 1-2*	*APB Opinion No. 28 par. 9*	*IAS 34 par. 28*	Under U.S. GAAP, an interim period is viewed as a subcomponent of the annual period. Under IFRS, accounting principles are applied to an interim period in the same way they are applied to an annual period.
Chapter 20: Accounting Changes and Error Corrections				
Disclosure after a business combination	*Section 805-10-50 par. 1-2*	*SFAS No. 141(R) par. 68*	*IFRS 3 par. 59-63 and B64-B67*	No substantial differences
Change in accounting principle	*Section 250-10-45 par. 1-16* *Section 250-10-50 par. 1- 3*	*SFAS No. 154 par. 4-18* *APB No. 28 par. 28*	*IAS 8 par. 14-31*	No substantial differences
Change in accounting estimate	*Section 250-10-45 par. 17-20* *Section 250-10-50 par. 4- 5*	*SFAS No. 154 par. 19-22* *SFAS No. 157 par. 20*	*IAS 8 par. 32-40*	No substantial differences
Correction of an error	*Section 250-10-45 par. 22-28* *Section 250-10-50 par. 7-11*	*SFAS No. 154 par. 25-26* *SFAS No. 16 par. 10-15* *APB No. 9 par. 17-18* *APB No. 9 par. 26-27* *APB No. 28 par. 29*	*IAS 8 par. 41-49*	No substantial differences
Chapter 21: Statement of Cash Flows Revisited				
Definition of cash equivalents	*Section 230-10-20 (Glossary) – Cash equivalents*	*SFAS No. 95 par. 8*	*IAS 7 par. 7*	No substantial differences

Topic	FASB Accounting Standards Codification	Original FASB Standard	Corresponding IASB Standard	Differences between U.S. GAAP and IFRS
Noncash investing and financing activities	*Section 230-10-50 par. 3*	*SFAS No. 95 par. 32*	*IAS 7 par. 43*	No substantial differences
Direct and indirect methods	*Section 230-10-45 par. 25,28*	*SFAS No. 95 par. 27-28*	*IAS 7 par. 18-19*	No substantial differences
Classification of interest paid	*Section 230-10-45 par. 17(d)*	*SFAS No. 95 par. 23(d)*	*IAS 7 par. 33*	U.S. GAAP – operating IFRS – operating or financing
Classification of income taxes paid	*Section 230-10-45 par. 17(c)*	*SFAS No. 95 par. 23(c)*	*IAS 7 par. 35*	U.S. GAAP – operating IFRS – operating, investing, or financing
Classification of interest received	*Section 230-10-45 par. 16(b)*	*SFAS No. 95 par. 22(b)*	*IAS 7 par. 33*	U.S. GAAP – operating IFRS – operating or investing
Classification of dividends received	*Section 230-10-45 par. 16(b)*	*SFAS No. 95 par. 22(b)*	*IAS 7 par. 33*	U.S. GAAP – operating IFRS – operating or investing
Classification of dividends paid	*Section 230-10-45 par. 15(a)*	*SFAS No. 95 par. 20(a)*	*IAS 7 par. 34*	U.S. GAAP – financing IFRS – operating or financing
Chapter 22: Accounting in a Global Market				
Foreign currency translation	*Subtopic 830-30*	*SFAS No. 52*	*IAS 21*	No substantial differences

CHECK FIGURES

CF

Chapter 1

E1–4 2. e, k, n
E1–5 5. False
E1–7 4. a, d, g, l

Chapter 2

E2–19 Total Debit = $113,300
E2–20 3. Dividends = $20,250 (Debit)
E2–22 Net Income Increase for 2012 = $6,400
E2–23 (c) Receivable from Insurance Company = $7,000 (Debit)
E2–24 2. Interest Revenue = $3,200 – $800 + $2,100 = $4,500
E2–25 (b) Prepaid Selling Expense = $1,500 (Debit)
E2–26 1. (d) Prepaid Rent = $2,800 (Debit)
E2–27 (b) Adjustment = $3,900
E2–28 1. Insurance Expense = $500 (Debit)
E2–29 (f) Other Assets = $13,000 (Debit)
E2–30 1. Sales Commissions Payable = $5,900 (Credit)
E2–31 Dividends = $29,200 (Credit)
E2–32 1. (q) Retained Earnings—Balance Carried Forward
P2–33 1. May 18 Accounts Receivable = $21,000 (Debit)
P2–35 1. (e) Sales Revenue = $12,160 (Debit)
P2–36 (c) Mar. 1 Cash = $5,400 (Debit)
P2–37 (c) Discount on Notes Payable = $900 (Debit)
P2–38 1. (d) Utilities Expense = $2,700 (Debit)
P2–39 2. (c) Selling Expenses = $3,840 (Debit)
P2–40 1. (a) No adjustment needed
P2–42 2. (c) Bad Debt Expense = $1,850 (Debit)

Chapter 3

E3–26 Total Current Assets = $84,300
E3–28 7. (f) or (h)
E3–29 (i) $43,911
E3–30 1. (a) Inventory = $59,300
E3–32 (b) Note Disclosure
E3–33 Inventory Asset = 25.9%
E3–34 ROA = 12%
E3–35 Working Capital = $160,000
P3–37 1. Total Current Liabilities = $88,000
P3–38 Total Liabilities = $268,370
P3–39 Total Assets = $956,000
P3–40 Bonds Payable = $200,000
P3–41 Total Liabilities and Owners' Equity = $1,254,300
P3–42 Total Liabilities = $344,500
P3–43 Total Assets = $857,000
P3–44 Retained Earnings = $179,650
P3–45 Total Liabilities = $49,830
P3–46 Total Current Liabilities = $138,000

Chapter 4

E4–25 Forecasted Net Income 2014 = $151
E4–26 Forecasted Total Liabilities and Stockholders' Equities 2014 = $1,190
E4–27 2. Comprehensive Income = $12,313
E4–28 Selling Expenses = $208,000
E4–31 Income Taxes = $47,560
E4–32 1. Corrected Net Income = $2,980
E4–35 Revised Net Income 2012 = $124,600
E4–36 Income from Continuing Operations = $169,000
E4–37 Net Income = $87,000
P4–40 Net Income = $805,100
P4–41 1. Income Statement—Time of Sale: 2013 Gross Profit = $72,000
P4–42 2. Net Income = $21,350
P4–43 Retained Earnings, July 31, 2013 = $3,167,500
P4–44 Net Income = $145,800
P4–46 1. (a) Gross Profit Percentage on Sales for 2011 = 55.0%
P4–47 Net Income = $823,075
P4–48 Net Income = $24,780
P4–49 Net Income = $14,340
P4–50 Net Income = $87,874
P4–51 Net Income = $118,400
P4–52 Forecasted Net Income 2014 = $120

Chapter 5

E5–23 (j) Investing activity
E5–24 3. 2012 = 8.66
E5–27 Net Cash Provided by Operating Activities = $146,300
E5–28 Net Cash Provided by Operating Activities = $19,760
E5–29 2. Cash from Operating Activities = $814,000
E5–30 3. Cost of Goods Sold = $290,000
E5–31 1. Total Liabilities and Stockholders' Equity for 2014 = $1,190
E5–32 2. Net Cash Provided by Operating Activities 2012 = $239
E5–33 1. Cash collected in 2013 = $3,909,000
E5–34 Net Increase in Cash and Cash Equivalents = $61,700
E5–35 Cash Balance at End of Year = $139,500
E5–36 Net Cash Provided by Operating Activities = $150,700
E5–37 Net Cash Provided by Operating Activities = $36,400

E5–38 Net Cash Provided by Operating Activities = $150,700
E5–39 Cash from Operating Activities = $1,547,000
P5–40 2. Net Cash Provided by Operating Activities = $137,350
P5–41 Cash and Cash Equivalents at End of Year = $42,000
P5–42 Cash Balance at End of Year = $36,800
P5–43 Net Increase in Cash = $45,000
P5–44 Cash Balance at End of Year = $490,300
P5–45 Cash & Cash Equivalents at End of Year = $15,000
P5–46 Net Decrease in Cash & Cash Equivalents = $(5,050)
P5–47 1. Net Increase in Cash & Cash Equivalents = $118,400
P5–48 2. Cash & Cash Equivalents at End of Year = $176,400
P5–49 3. Cost of Goods Sold = $217,000
P5–50 1. Net Cash from Operating Activities for 2012 = $51,000
P5–51 Net Cash from Operating Activities for 2013 = $135
P5–52 1. (e) 2013 = 0.77
P5–53 1. Net Cash Provided by Operating Activities = $270

Chapter 6

No check figures necessary.

Chapter 7

E7–24 3. Sales Returns and Allowances = $1,500 (Debit)
E7–25 1. Total Cash Collected = $6,910
E7–27 Correct Balance = $7,657
E7–28 1. (11) (a)
E7–30 1. Restricted Cash = $7,450,000 (Debit)
E7–31 1. Average Net Receivables = $212,500
E7–33 2. Total = $2,642.87
E7–34 2. Cash = $1,350 (Debit)
E7–35 7. B, D, Noncurrent asset
E7–36 1. Accounts Written Off for 2011: $40,000
E7–37 1. Bad Debt Expense = $50,985 (Debit)
E7–38 Outstanding Checks at the Beginning of June = $5,880
E7–39 Corrected Book Balance = $18,773.76
E7–40 Profit from Service Contracts in 2013 = $7,050
E7–41 2. Balance in Liability Account at End of 2013: $121,250
E7–42 1. Cash Flow from Operating Activities = $55,000
E7–43 3. Notes Payable = $75,000 (Credit)
E7–44 End of Third Year, Interest Revenue = $1,071 (Credit)
E7–45 1. Cash = $675,000 (Debit)
P7–46 2. Bad Debt Expense = $4,265 (Debit)
P7–47 1. Gross Method: Sales = $70,000 (Credit)
P7–48 1. Bad Debt Expense = $7,410 (Debit)
P7–49 Balance for Estimated Uncollectible = $28,420
P7–50 Balance in Liability Account at End of 2014 = $36,950
P7–51 Required Adjustment to Liability Account = $301,353
P7–52 (i) Interest Revenue = $630 (Credit)
P7–54 1. Corrected Book Balance = $14,873.80
P7–55 Corrected Book Balance = $487.43
P7–56 Standard One Bank: (b) Cash = $91,675 (Debit)
P7–57 1. (b) Cash = $122,500 (Debit)
P7–58 2. Jan. 31, Receivable from Factor = $120,000 (Credit)
P7–59 1. Gain on Sale of Land = $13,196 (Credit)
P7–60 Total Discounted Value = $503,090
P7–61 Cash Collected from Customers = $1,982,000

Chapter 8

E8–22 Dec. 31 Equipment Use Costs = $100 (Debit)
E8–25 2013 loss recognition, Construction in Progress = $700,000 (Credit)
E8–27 2014 (100% Completed) Gross Profit Recognized in Current Year = $268,440
E8–28 4. Estimated Cost to Complete Contract as of End of 2013 = $656,667
E8–29 3. $370,000
E8–30 Gross Profit to Be Recognized in 2013 = $1,366,185
E8–31 2013 Cost of Long-Term Construction Contracts = $13,160,000 (Debit)
E8–32 Realized Gross Profit 2013 = $16,620
E8–33 Realized Gross Profit 2013 = $22,150 (Credit)
E8–34 Deferred Gross Profit—2014 = $15,750 (Debit)
E8–35 1. Balance Sheet: Construction in Progress = $100,840
E8–36 7. $120,000 ($91,800 + $28,200)
P8–39 1. Net Income 2014 = $254,500
P8–40 1. a. Total Estimated Cost 2014 = $55,000,000
P8–41 1. a. Gross Profit for Project A = $45,938
P8–42 4. Revenue from Long-Term Construction Contracts 2013 = $4,602,769 (Credit)
P8–43 2. Adjusted Gross Profit = $832,000
P8–44 1. Percentage of Completion for 2012 = 56.00%
P8–45 1. Percentage of Completion for 2012 = 42.38%
P8–47 Deferred Gross Profit—2012 = $21,348 (Debit)
P8–48 1. (b) Gross Profit = $900,000

Chapter 9

E9–25 d. Excluded
E9–26 Ending Inventory Quantity as of Dec. 31 = 126,000 units
E9–27 2. Cash = $4,500 (Debit)
E9–28 2. Inventory = $6,000 (Debit)
E9–29 Aug. 15 Purchases = $15,225 (Debit)
E9–30 (f) I, DL
E9–31 1. Purchases = $2,800 (Debit)
E9–32 1. a. Dec. 10 Purchases = $9,991 (Debit)

E9–33 1. 2013: 89 days
E9–34 2. LIFO Ending Inventory = $6,050
E9–35 1. Ending Inventory Value = $1,275
E9–36 2. Jan. 1, 2013, Inventory = $5,100,000
E9–37 Quantity Available for Sale = 106,100 units
E9–38 Cash Expended for Inventory—2013 = $890,000
E9–39 Purchases: Total Cost = $104,210
E9–40 2. (b) Cost of Goods Sold = $387,000
E9–41 1. (a) $239,000
E9–42 Product 435, LCM = 1.64
E9–43 1. Net Income Total = $70,200
E9–44 Net Income—LIFO Basis, 2013 = $79,500
E9–45 1. FIFO Inventory, Oct. 31 = $36,390
E9–46 1. Gross Profit as a Percent of Sales = 32.88% of Sales
E9–47 Overstated Inventory for 2013 = $540
E9–48 1. (a) $13,000
E9–49 2. Cost of Goods Sold, LCM = $63,000
E9–50 3. Inventory for Feb. 28 = $23,300 (Debit)
E9–51 Work-in-Process Inventory Lost = $62,480
E9–52 Corrected Net Income for 2013 = $1,900
E9–53 Total Sales = $2,430,000
E9–54 Cost of Goods Manufactured = $7,582
E9–55 Dec. 31, 2013, Loss on Purchase Commitments = $87,000 (Debit)
E9–56 3. $1,331
E9–57 Dec. 31, 2011, Dollar-Value LIFO Retail Cost = $120,229
E9–58 Dec. 31, 2013, Dollar-Value LIFO Cost = $752,000
E9–59 1. Dec. 31, 2012, Dollar-Value LIFO Cost = $305,610
E9–60 2. Ending Inventory at Average Cost = $4,456
E9–61 2. $26,400
E9–62 1. $78,557
E9–63 Jan. 30, 2013, Exchange Loss = $114 (Debit)
E9–64 2. Cash = $54,000 (Credit)
P9–65 Cost of Goods Sold 2011 = $1,045
P9–66 2. Total = $92,050
P9–67 3. Dec. 29 Balance = $987.50
P9–68 1. Mar. 28 Balance = $8,300.00
P9–69 2. FIFO Gross Profit on Sales—2013 = $39,900
P9–70 4. Ending Inventory Value = $192,950
P9–71 1. 2002 Layer = $133,400
P9–72 Ending Inventory If Using LIFO Inventory Method = $124,500
P9–73 1. (d) $70,375
P9–74 2. Total Cost of Goods Sold = $211,320
P9–75 3. Trade-In Inventory = $11,160 (Credit)
P9–76 Dec. 31 (b) No Adjustment Required
P9–77 2011 = 38% gross profit percentage
P9–78 Net Income = $85,000
P9–79 Cost of Stolen Inventory = $35,096
P9–80 (g) Retained Earnings = $475 (Credit)
P9–81 2011 Inventory Turnover = 13.25
P9–82 Product 402 Ending Inventory = $32,762
P9–83 Dec. 31, 2013, Dollar-Value LIFO Cost = $33,924
P9–84 Dec. 31, 2012, Dollar-Value LIFO Retail Cost = $149,637
P9–85 4. Mar. 23, 2014, Purchases = $150,000 (Debit)
P9–86 2. Printco: Exchange Gain = $27,000 (Credit)

Chapter 10

E10–20 Land = $300,000 (Debit)
E10–21 Cost Assigned to Land = $219,048
E10–22 Value Assigned to Franchise = $145,000
E10–24 2. Gain = $154,000 (Credit)
E10–27 Interest Charges Capitalized = $25,000
E10–28 Total Land = $335,150
E10–30 (1) Total Capitalized Interest for 2013 = $92,267
E10–31 2. Exploration Expense = $0
E10–32 R&D Expense = $50,800 (Debit)
E10–33 2. Total = $261,000
E10–35 2015 Interest Expense = $4,114 (Debit)
E10–36 Discount on Notes Payable = $30,808 (Debit)
E10–37 1. Goodwill = $354,000 (Debit)
E10–38 Premium on Bonds Payable = $21,000 (Credit)
P10–43 1. Raw Materials = $78,900
P10–45 1. Total Cost of Land = $207,500
P10–46 Mar. 30 Buildings = $34,200 (Debit)
P10–47 Organization Expenses = $211,000 (Debit)
P10–48 (b) Patents = $14,280 (Debit)
P10–49 1. Jan. 2 Organization Expenses = $23,300 (Debit)
P10–50 Building Cost = $528,000
P10–51 Net Income = $129,941
P10–53 Land Increase = $237,250
P10–54 1. Total Interest Accrued = $1,300,000
P10–57 1. Goodwill = $1,085,000 (Debit)
P10–59 1. ROE = 26.2%
P10–60 (b) Loss on Removal of Wall = $26,020 (Debit)

Chapter 11

E11–26 1. Book Value = $1,820,000
E11–27 3. Building = $100,000 (Credit)
E11–28 2. 2013 Amortization Expense = $5,563 (Debit)
E11–30 2. Gain on Trade-In of Truck = $1,350 (Credit)
E11–32 Gain on Sale of Equipment = $4,700 (Credit)
E11–34 Charge for 2013 = $36,250
E11–36 1. 6.8 Years
E11–38 1. Depreciation Rate = $320
E11–39 Dec. 31, 2013, Depreciation Expense = $6,750 (Debit)
E11–40 1. $5,973
E11–41 1. 2013 Depreciation Expense = $27,930 (Debit)
E11–42 Depreciation for 2012 = $25,714
E11–43 2014 Depreciation Expense = $9,940
E11–44 Machine Cost = $43,000
E11–45 1. $21,778
E11–46 2015 Cost Recovery Amount = $5,108
E11–47 4. $6,750
E11–48 1. (a) $16,836 for 2013
P11–50 1. $11,675
P11–53 2009: Accumulated Depreciation—Machinery = $30,000 (Credit)
P11–54 2. 7.06 years
P11–55 (b) 2011 = $3,773
P11–56 Net Income = $717,449

P11–57 2012 Depletion = $1,392,000
P11–58 2. Depreciation Expense = $525,000 (Debit)
P11–59 (b) Depreciation Expense for Year 2013 = $3,265
P11–60 Net Cash Flow Provided by Operating Activities = $103,500
P11–61 2. Depreciation Expense = $500,000
P11–62 3. Depreciation Expense = $566,667
P11–63 Dec. 31, 2009, Amortization Expense = $11,567 (Debit)
P11–64 (c) Amortization Expense = $7,333 (Debit)
P11–65 (b) Cash = $5,000 (Credit) (To reverse entry made incorrectly on Lakeshore's books.)
P11–66 June 1 Land = $240,000 (Debit)
P11–67 Total Depreciation and Amortization Expense for 2013 = $200,789
P11–68 Depreciation on Machinery and Equipment for 2013 = $81,875

Chapter 12

E12–24 8/1/13 Discount on Bonds Payable = $847 (Credit)
E12–25 1. Interest Payable = $36,000 (Credit)
E12–26 (3) Gain on Bond Redemption = $1,875 (Credit)
E12–29 (a) Market Price = $885,295
E12–30 1. a. Discount on Bonds Payable = $7,538 (Credit)
E12–32 (1) $650
E12–33 2. Interest Expense 2013 = $5,295
E12–34 2. Mortgage Payable = $1,006.47 (Debit)
E12–36 Gain on Early Retirement of Bonds = $5,219 (Credit)
E12–37 1. Loss on Early Retirement of Debt = $16,000 (Debit)
E12–40 (a) Total Payments = $12,500,000
E12–42 Gain on Restructuring of Debt = $440,000 (Credit)
P12–43 (c) Debt Ratio = 0.57
P12–44 2. Book Value 2014 = $480,000
P12–46 1. Maximum Amount Investor Should Pay = $1,239,413
P12–48 1. $73,037
P12–49 2. c. $8,641
P12–51 1. Accrued Interest = $70,000
P12–52 2013 Income before Taxes = $50,400
P12–57 1. Market Value = $73,037,000
P12–59 2. a. Gain on Bond Retirement, Brewster = $121,190

Chapter 13

E13–25 2015 Compensation Expense = $20,000 (Debit)
E13–27 2. Retained Earnings = $108,000 (Debit)
E13–28 b. 2012 Preferred Dividends per Share = $9.00
E13–29 Dec. 31 Cash = $306,000 (Credit)
E13–30 1. (b) Total Stockholders' Equity = $5,043,000
E13–31 (c) Common Stock Subscribed = $18,000 (Debit)
E13–32 2013 Compensation Expense = $120,000
E13–33 Compensation Expense = $105,000 (Debit)
E13–34 1. Paid-In Capital in Excess of Par—Preferred = $92,074 (Credit)
E13–35 Common Stock = $62,500 (Debit)
E13–36 Total Stockholders' Equity = $584,000
E13–37 1. Total Stockholders' Equity = $7,912,500
E13–38 Corrected Retained Earnings = $34,350
E13–39 2. Dec. 31, 2013, Retained Earnings = $126,500
E13–40 (a) Paid-In Capital in Excess of Par = $270,000 (Credit)
E13–41 3. Retained Earnings = $120,000 (Debit)
E13–42 Retained Earnings = $945,000 (Debit)
E13–44 Paid-In Capital in Excess of Par = $275,000 (Debit)
E13–46 (1) Dividends Paid in Third Quarter = $2,109,000
P13–47 2. Total Stockholders' Equity = $555,380
P13–48 2. Total Contributed Capital = $26,022,000
P13–49 Dividends Paid to Common Stockholders = $32,900
P13–50 Total Stockholders' Equity = $24,022,000
P13–51 Apr. 1, 2013, Discount on Bonds Payable = $7,984
P13–52 2. Total Contributed Capital = $5,344,000
P13–53 (f) Treasury Stock—Preferred = $40,000 (Credit)
P13–54 2. Retained Earnings = $177,000
P13–55 1. 2013 Compensation Expense = $241,667 (Debit)
P13–56 2015 Compensation Expense = $81,000
P13–57 2. 2013 Dividends Applicable to Common Stock = $23,300
P13–58 3. Treasury Stock = $32,150
P13–59 6/1/13 Dividends Payable = $224,000 (Debit)
P13–61 2. Total Stockholders' Equity = $3,043,110
P13–62 2. 2012 Total Stockholders' Equity = $524,550
P13–63 Net Cash Provided by Operating Activities = $277,000
P13–64 2. Total Retained Earnings = $1,702,500
P13–65 3/6/13 Common Stock Subscribed = $3,600 (Credit)

Chapter 14

E14–25 Annual Amortization = $2,000
E14–27 3. Unrealized Gain on Trading Securities = $6,000 (Credit)
E14–29 (c) Interest Revenue = $1,650 (Credit)
E14–31 1. Unrealized Gain on Trading Securities = $2,964 (Credit)
E14–32 2. Total Cost = $385,000
E14–34 2. Realized Gain on Sale of Securities = $1,500 (Credit)
E14–35 2. Adjusted net income = $96,000
E14–36 1. Investment in Held-to-Maturity Securities = $718,764 (Debit)
E14–37 3. Realized Loss on Sale of Securities = $200 (Debit)
E14–40 2. Unrealized Loss on Transfer of Securities = $500 (Debit)
E14–41 1. Unrealized Gain on Trading Securities = $8,000 (Credit)
E14–42 2. Bad Debt Expense = $11,662 (Debit)

P14–43 Dec. 31, 2013, Unrealized Loss on Trading Securities = $29,000 (Debit)
P14–44 1. Jan. 1, 2012, Cash = $7,300 (Debit)
P14–47 (b) Market Adjustment—Trading Securities = $160 (Credit)
P14–49 2012 Dividend Revenue = $3,750 (Credit)
P14–50 Net Annual Adj. to Income = $12,800
P14–51 1. Goodwill = $40,000
P14–52 Diff. Between FV & BV = $(3,500)
P14–54 (c) Unrealized Gain on Transfer of Securities = $1,400 (Credit)
P14–55 2. 2013 Adjustment Required = $192,000

Chapter 15

E15–23 PV = $3,796,920
E15–24 PV = $2,426,343
E15–25 Debit Rent Exp. each year = $92,000
E15–28 12/31/14 Interest Exp. = $17,447
E15–30 2. Net Balance = $4,200
E15–33 1. $125,898
E15–34 3. Interest Rate = 10%
E15–35 1. 12/31/15 Interest Revenue = $65,430
E15–36 2. Income from Operating Lease = $182,167
E15–37 Interest Revenue = $9,090 (Credit)
E15–38 2. Interest Revenue Recognized = $127,785
E15–39 3. Implicit Interest Rate = 10.5%
E15–40 Cost of Owned Equip. = $36,700
E15–41 Interest Rate = 9%
E15–42 3. Dec. 31, 2015, Book Value of Asset = $16,150
E15–43 2013 Noncurrent Liabilities = $223,542
E15–44 Interest Revenue = $86,098
P15–46 2. Amortization for Period = $65,755
P15–47 2. 2017 Cash = $186,000 (Credit)
P15–48 2. 12/31/15 Int. Exp. = $11,424
P15–49 1. PV of Lease = $315,001
P15–50 2. Interest Rate = 11%
P15–51 1. PV of Residual Value = $30,396
P15–52 1. Manufacturer's Profit = $607,102
P15–53 1. Manufacturer's Profit = $1,310,961
P15–54 3. Interest Exp. = $201,858
P15–55 1. Dec. 31 Amortization Expense on Leased Equipment = $91,738 (Debit)
P15–56 1. PV of Guaranteed Residual Value = $36,881
P15–58 1. Cash Provided by Operating Activities = $140,526
P15–59 Future Minimum Rental Payments = $426,500

Chapter 16

E16–26 2. $4,000
E16–27 Increase in Income Tax Pay. = $6,000
E16–28 1. Inc. Tax Exp. = $20,000 (Debit)
E16–30 Taxable Income = $2,800,000
E16–31 1. Inc. Tax Benefit = $5,250 (Credit)
E16–32 1. Refund Due = $54,000
E16–33 1. 2012 Refund Due = $93,000
E16–34 1. Current Deferred Tax Asset = $9,600
E16–35 Inc. Tax Benefit = $17,660 (Credit)
E16–36 Inc. Taxes Payable = $187,600 (Credit)
E16–37 1. Income Tax Exp. = $124,250 (Debit)
E16–38 Net Current Deferred Tax Liability = $47,250
E16–39 Inc. Taxes Pay. = $24,400 (Credit)
E16–40 1. Inc. Tax Benefit = $7,200 (Credit)
E16–41 1. Inc. Taxes Pay. = $30,000 (Credit)
E16–42 2. Inc. Tax Benefit = $5,490 (Debit)
P16–43 2015 Inc. Tax Benefit = $11,200 (Credit)
P16–44 1. Pretax Financial Income = $2,902,000
P16–45 1. Taxable Income = $67,500
P16–46 2. Net Loss = $(19,760)
P16–48 2. Net Income = $41,390
P16–49 1. Def. Tax Asset—Current = $4,550 (Debit)
P16–50 1. Inc. Tax Benefit—Rate Change = $27,000 (Credit)
P16–51 1. Tax Refund Due Aruban = $20,890
P16–52 1. Inc. Tax Refund Due in 2007 = $13,362

Chapter 17

E17–19 1. $24,500
E17–20 Salaries & Comm. Expense = $33,000 (Debit)
E17–21 Total Liability for Vacation Pay = $17,850
E17–22 Pension Service Cost = $482,000
E17–23 Actual Return on Pension Fund = $97,000
E17–24 1. $27,000
E17–25 Pension Expense = $75,000
E17–27 Case 1, Pension-related asset = $2,800
E17–28 Pension Expense = $943,000
E17–30 Amortization = $22,000
E17–31 Difference = $38,500
E17–32 1. $853,595
E17–33 2013 Amortization Amount = $206,667
E17–34 1. $157,750
E17–36 FICA Taxes Payable = $2,169 (Credit)
P17–37 Salaries Payable = $66,450 (Credit)
P17–38 Jan. 6 Payroll Tax Exp. = $243.48 (Debit)
P17–39 1. Total Accrued = $6,150
P17–40 1. 2013 Cash = $675,000 (Credit)
P17–41 2. 8 years
P17–42 1. Difference = $(27,000)
P17–43 1. 2013 Interest Cost = $150
P17–44 1. 2013 Net periodic pension expense = $2,010
P17–45 2013 Net Pension Expense = $1,220
P17–48 2013 Net Pension Expense = $134,300

Chapter 18

E18–21 Incremental Shares = 12,000
E18–22 Number of shares to be used in computing diluted EPS = 58,000
E18–23 Weighted Avg. No. of Common Shares, 2014 = 771,500
E18–24 Weighted Avg. Shares Outstanding = 399,000
E18–25 Weighted Avg. Shares, 2013 = 567,966
E18–26 (c) Income from Continuing Operations = $0.60
E18–27 2013 EPS = $5.36
E18–28 Basic EPS = $1.14
E18–29 1. Basic Loss per Share = $(1.11)
E18–30 Basic EPS = $2.43
E18–31 Basic EPS = $7.50

E18–32 e. $1.40
E18–33 Basic EPS = $3.58
E18–34 Basic EPS = $2.46
P18–35 2013 Weighted Avg. No. of Shares = 249,500
P18–36 1. Net Income = $850,000
P18–37 Basic EPS 2013 = $4.18
P18–38 Basic EPS = $2.60
P18–39 1. Basic EPS = $12.81
P18–40 Basic EPS = $6.41
P18–41 2. Basic Loss per Share = $(1.83)
P18–42 1. Basic EPS = $3.39
P18–43 Basic EPS = $1.46
P18–44 Basic EPS = $4.40
P18–45 1. Basic EPS = $1.49
P18–46 Basic EPS = $1.64

Chapter 19

E19–25 Dec. 31, 2013, Int. Exp. = $40,000 (Debit)
E19–26 Dec. 31, 2013, Cotton Call Option (asset) = $2,000 (Credit)
E19–27 Dec. 31, 2013, Gain on Foreign Currency = $29,221 (Credit)
E19–28 Dec. 31, 2013, Futures Contract (liability) = $5,000 (Credit)
E19–29 Net Cost at $0.38 = $(52,500)
E19–31 COGS = $3,450 (Debit)
E19–32 Gross Profit = $147,600
P19–39 (b) Net Cost on Aug. 31 at $1.00 = $(90,000)
P19–40 Dec. 31, 2013, Interest Rate Swap (asset) = $651,514 (Debit)
P19–42 Dec. 31, 2013, Int. Revenue = $3,099 (Credit)
P19–43 Jan. 1, 2013, Grain Put Option = $90,000 (Debit)
P19–46 1. (c) $0
P19–49 1. Segment 2 Operating Profit = $(100,000)

Chapter 20

E20–23 1. $13,500 per Year
E20–24 1. Bad Debt Exp. = $9,750 (Debit)
E20–25 Depreciation to Date = $1,080,000
E20–26 1. $3.20 per Ton
E20–27 Book Value, Jan. 1, 2013 = $40,960
E20–28 1. 2012 Depreciation = $18,000
E20–29 2013 Retained Earnings = $382,550
E20–30 1. Adjusted Retained Earnings Beg. Bal. = $191,000
E20–31 2. Bad Debt Expense = $16,525 (Debit)
E20–34 2011 COGS = $2,228,500
E20–35 1. Simon, Capital = $20,650 (Debit)
E20–36 2012 Depreciation = $80
P20–37 2013 Sum-of-Years' Digits Dep. = $50,000
P20–38 2013 Retained Earnings (Deficit) = ($3,000)
P20–39 Machine B Dep. Exp. = $40,000
P20–40 3. Allowance for Bad Debts = $5,500 (Debit)
P20–41 Case 1, 2. Patents = $750,000 (Credit)
P20–42 2013 FIFO Net Income = $580,000
P20–43 2013 Dep. Exp. = $65,000
P20–44 2012 FIFO Net Income = $181,200
P20–45 1. c. Retained Earnings = $37,750 (Debit)
P20–46 2. Retained Earnings Dec. 31, 2013 = $33,020
P20–47 1. a. Retained Earnings = $30,000 (Debit)

Chapter 21

E21–11 Accounts Receivable, Beg. Bal. = $35,300
E21–12 Net Increase in Cash and Cash Equivalents = $6
E21–13 Cash Receipts from Customers = $1,470
E21–14 Cash Paid for Inventory = $360,300
E21–15 Net Cash Provided by Operating Activities = $106,000
E21–16 Cost of Goods Sold = $404,600
E21–17 Net Income = $237,000
P21–18 Cash Payments for Inventory = $183,500
P21–19 Cash Payments for Income Taxes = $37,930
P21–20 Gross Profit = $385,300
P21–21 Inventory = $7,300
P21–22 Net Cash Provided by Operations = $83,000
P21–23 Cash Paid for Inventory = $32,386
P21–24 Cash Flow from Investing Activities = ($1,783)
P21–25 Cash Flow from Financing Activities = ($2,252)

Chapter 22

E22–3 2. Ending retained earnings = $148,600
E22–4 Total assets (U.S. $) = $322,083
P22–5 Total assets = $1,354,320
P22–6 Total debits (U.S. $) = $1,565,560

Chapter 23

E23–19 Electric Service Companies ROE = 9.0%
E23–20 W/O Borrowed Capital, Net Income = $138,000
E23–22 2013 A/R Turnover = 3.93 times
E23–23 2011 Inventory Turnover—Average = 2.4
E23–24 2013 Total Assets = 20.9% of Sales
E23–25 Company A, Return on Sales = 2.08%
E23–26 2013 ROE = 7.6%
E23–27 Operating Lease, Debt-to-Equity Ratio = 0.78
E23–28 1. Current Liabilities = $92,000
E23–29 2013 Net Income = 12.9% of Sales
P23–31 Stay-Trim Total Liabilities = 41%
P23–32 Company A, Asset Turnover = 0.39
P23–33 1. 2013 Avg. Receivables = $107,500
P23–34 2013 Raw Materials Turnover = 3.0 times
P23–35 1. (a) 2013 ROE = 14.9%
P23–36 b. 2012 Avg. Collection Period = 94.6 days
P23–37 1. (a) Beg. Retained Earnings Increases by $18,000

GLOSSARY

G

accelerated cost recovery system (ACRS) Adaptation of the declining-balance depreciation method introduced for tax purposes in 1981 and subsequently modified.

accelerated depreciation Method of computing depreciation that yields higher annual depreciation in the early years of an asset's life than in later years.

account A record used to classify and summarize the effects of transactions.

accounting A service activity whose "function is to provide quantitative information, primarily financial in nature, about economic entities that is intended to be useful in making economic decisions—in making reasoned choices among alternative courses of action" (*Statement of the Accounting Principles Board No. 4*, par. 40).

accounting changes A general term used to describe the use of different estimates or accounting principles or reporting entities from those used in a prior year.

accounting errors Incorrect accounting treatment resulting from mathematical mistakes, improper application of accounting principles, or omissions of material facts.

accounting periods The time intervals used for financial reporting; due to the need for timely information, the life of a business or other entity is divided into specific accounting periods for external reporting purposes. One year is the normal reporting period, although most large U.S. companies also provide quarterly statements.

Accounting Principles Board (APB) A board of the AICPA that issued Opinions establishing accounting standards during the period 1959–1973.

accounting (cycle) process The procedures used for analyzing, recording, classifying, and summarizing the information to be presented in accounting reports; also referred to as the *accounting cycle*.

Accounting Standards Updates Accounting standards researched and established by the Financial Accounting Standards Board.

accounting system The procedures and methods used, including data processing equipment, to collect and report accounting data.

accounts payable Amounts due for the purchase of materials by a manufacturing company or merchandise by a wholesaler or retailer.

accounts receivable Trade receivables that are not evidenced by a formal agreement or "note"; accounts receivable are usually unsecured "open accounts" and represent an extension of short-term credit to customers.

accounts receivable factoring The sale of receivables without recourse for cash to a third party, usually a bank or other financial institution.

accounts receivable turnover An analytical measurement of how rapidly customers' accounts are being collected. The net accounts receivable turnover formula is net sales divided by average trade accounts receivable for a period.

accrual accounting A basic assumption that revenues are recognized when earned and expenses are recognized when incurred without regard to when cash is received or paid.

accumulated benefit obligation (ABO) The actuarial present value of pension benefits based on the plan formula for employee service earned to date using the existing salary structure; used to compute the minimum liability.

acid-test ratio A financial ratio used as a measure of short-term liquidity; also called *quick ratio*.

activity-based cost (ABC) system Cost system that allocates overhead based on clearly identified characteristics of the production process that are known to create overhead costs.

actual return on the pension fund A component of net periodic pension expense measured by the difference between the fair value of pension plan assets at the end of the period and the fair value at the beginning of the period, adjusted for contributions and payments of benefits during the period.

actuarial present value The present value of pension obligations determined by using stated actuarial assumptions and estimates.

additional paid-in capital The investment by stockholders in excess of the amounts assignable to capital stock as par or stated value, as well as invested capital from other sources, such as sale of treasury stock.

additions Enlargements and extensions of existing facilities.

adjusting entries Entries required at the end of each accounting period to update the accounts as necessary and to fully recognize, on an accrual basis, revenues and expenses for the period.

aging receivables The most commonly used method for establishing an allowance for bad debts account based on outstanding receivables. This method involves analyzing individual accounts to determine those not yet due and those past due. Past-due accounts are classified in terms of length of the period past due.

allowance method A method of recognizing the estimated losses from uncollectible accounts as expenses during the period in which the sales occur; this method is required by GAAP.

American Accounting Association (AAA) An organization primarily for accounting professors. The AAA's role in establishing accounting standards includes research projects to help the FASB and a forum for representing different points of view on various issues.

American Institute of Certified Public Accountants (AICPA) A professional organization for CPAs in which membership is voluntary. It publishes a monthly journal, the *Journal of Accountancy*.

amortization (1) The process of allocating the cost of intangible assets to periodic expense. (2) An adjustment to interest expense (for either a premium or a discount) to reflect the effective interest being incurred on bonds. This periodic adjustment results in the convergence of the carrying value of a bond to its face value over time.

annuity A series of equal payments over a specified number of equal time periods.

annuity due A type of annuity in which periodic receipts or payments are made at the beginning of the period and one period of the annuity term remains after the last payment.

antidilution of earnings Assumed conversion of convertible securities or exercise of stock options that results in an increase in earnings per share (or decrease in loss per share).

antidilutive securities Securities whose assumed conversion or exercise results in an antidilution of earnings per share.

appropriated retained earnings Amount of retained earnings restricted (i.e., made unavailable for dividend payments) at the discretion of the board of directors.

arm's-length transactions Exchanges between parties who are independent of each other. A traditional assumption in accounting is that recorded transactions and events are executed between independent parties, each of which is acting in its own best interest.

articulation The idea that the three primary financial statements are not isolated lists of numbers but are an integrated set of reports on a company's financial health.

asset A resource of an entity.

asset and liability method of interperiod tax allocation A method of income tax allocation that determines deferred tax assets or tax liabilities based on the expected future benefit or obligation associated with temporary difference reversals. If tax rates change, the asset or liability balances are adjusted to reflect the tax rates legislated to be in effect in the year when reversal is expected to occur.

asset mix The proportion of total assets in each asset category.

asset retirement obligation Obligation incurred in the act of acquiring a long-term operating asset to restore costs in the future when the asset is retired. Required to be recognized at its estimated fair value when it is incurred and be added to the cost of acquiring the long-term operating asset.

asset turnover Financial ratio measuring how efficiently a company uses its assets to generate sales. The ratio formula is total sales divided by total assets.

assignment of receivables The borrowing of money with receivables pledged as security on the loan.

available-for-sale securities Investment securities not intended for immediate trading but, in the case of debt securities, not intended to be held until maturity.

average collection period Average number of days that lapse between the time that a sale is made and the time that cash is collected. Computed by dividing average receivables outstanding by average daily sales.

average cost method An inventory valuation method that assigns the same average cost to each unit sold and to each item in the inventory.

balance sheet A statement that reports, as of a given point in time, the assets, liabilities, and owners' equity of a business.

bank reconciliation A process that identifies differences between the cash balance on the depositor's books and the balance reported on the bank statement. The reconciliation provides information needed to adjust the book balance to a corrected cash amount.

bank service charge Monthly fee sometimes charged by a bank to service the depositor's account.

bargain purchase option A lease provision that allows for the purchase of a leased asset in the future by the lessee at a price so low that the lessee is almost certain to exercise the option.

bargain renewal option A lease provision that allows for renewal of the lease by the lessee at significantly reduced lease payments from the original lease. The bargain terms strongly imply that the lease will be renewed.

basic earnings per share An earnings per share computation that considers only common stock issued and outstanding. It is computed as the net income less preferred dividends divided by the weighted-average common shares outstanding for the period.

basket purchase The purchase of a number of assets for one lump-sum purchase price.

bearer (coupon) bonds Bonds whose ownership is determined by possession and for which interest is paid to the holder (bearer) of an interest coupon.

betterments Changes in assets designed to provide increased or improved services.

big bath The concept that a company expecting to have a series of hits to earnings in future years is better off to try to recognize all of the bad news in one year, leaving future years unencumbered by continuing losses.

board of directors Group elected by the shareholders to oversee the strategic and long-run planning for the corporation.

bond certificates Certificates of indebtedness issued by a company or government agency guaranteeing payment of a principal amount at a specified future date plus periodic interest; usually issued in denominations of $1,000.

bond discount The difference between the face value and the sales price when bonds are sold below their face value.

bond indenture The contract between the issuing entity and the bondholders specifying the terms, rights, and obligations of the contracting parties.

bond issuance costs Costs incurred by the issuer for legal services, printing and engraving, taxes, and underwriting in connection with the sale of a bond.

bond premium The difference between the face value and the sales price when bonds are sold above their face value.

bond refinancing Issuing new bonds to replace outstanding bonds either at maturity or prior to maturity.

book value The long-term asset cost remaining to be allocated to future periods; computed as historical cost less accumulated depreciation.

book-to-market ratio A financial ratio measuring the deviation between accounting book value of equity and market value of equity. The ratio formula is book equity divided by market equity.

business combination The combining of two businesses accomplished through the exchange of cash or an exchange of stock.

business (source) document Business record used as the basis for analyzing and recording transactions; examples include invoices, check stubs, receipts, and similar business papers.

call option Contract giving the owner the right, but not the obligation, to buy an asset at a specified price.

callable A security, such as a bond or a preferred stock, that can be redeemed and canceled at the option of the issuing company.

callable bonds Bonds for which the issuer reserves the right to pay the obligation prior to the maturity date.

callable obligation A debt instrument that is (1) payable on demand or (2) has a specified due date but is payable on demand if the debtor defaults on the provisions of the loan agreement.

capital lease A lease that is economically equivalent to the purchase of the leased asset.

capital stock The portion of the amount invested by stockholders that is designated as par or stated value.

capitalized interest Interest incurred during the self-construction of an asset that is considered to be part of the asset cost.

cash Coin, currency, and other items that are acceptable for deposit at face value; serves as a medium of exchange and provides a basis of measurement for accounting.

cash (sales) discount A reduction in sales price allowed if payment is received within a specified period, usually offered to customers to encourage prompt payment.

cash dividend The payment of cash to shareholders in proportion to the number of shares owned.

cash equivalents Short-term, highly liquid investments that can be converted easily to cash. Generally, only investments that on the day of acquisition have less than three months remaining to maturity qualify as cash equivalents.

cash flow adequacy ratio Computed as cash from operations divided by expenditures for fixed asset additions and acquisitions of new businesses; indicates whether a business is a "cash cow."

cash flow hedge Derivative that offsets the variability in cash flows from forecasted transactions that are probable.

cash flow-to-net income ratio Financial ratio used to analyze the cash flow relationship between cash from operations and reported net income; computed as cash from operations divided by net income.

cash method The method of accounting under which all costs are charged to expense as incurred and revenue is recognized as collections are made.

cash overdraft A credit balance in the cash account; results from checks being written for more than the cash amount on deposit; should be reported as a current liability.

cash times interest earned ratio A measure used to indicate a company's interest-paying ability; computed as pretax cash flow divided by cash paid for interest.

cash-basis accounting A system of accounting in which revenues and expenses are recorded as they are received and paid.

ceiling The net realizable value; used as an upper limit in defining market when valuing inventory at the lower of cost or market.

certified public accountant (CPA) An accountant who has met specified professional requirements established by the AICPA and local and state societies. A CPA often does not work for a single business enterprise but provides a variety of professional services for many different individual and business clients. A key service provided by CPAs is the performance of independent audits of financial statements.

change in accounting estimate A specific type of accounting change that modifies predictions of future events, for example, the useful life of a depreciable asset; changes in estimates are to be reflected in current and future periods.

change in accounting principle A specific type of accounting change that uses an accounting principle or method different from that used previously, for example, using straight-line depreciation instead of the declining-balance method. Generally, changes in principle require the reporting of a cumulative effect of the change in the current year's income statement as well as pro forma information.

closing entries Entries that reduce all temporary accounts to a zero balance at the end of each accounting period, transferring the preclosed balances to a permanent account.

collateral trust bond Bonds that are secured by the stocks and bonds of other corporations owned by the issuer but held in trust for the benefit of the bondholders.

commodity-backed (asset-linked) bonds Bonds that may be redeemed in terms of commodities, such as oil or precious metals.

common stock The class of stock issued by corporations that represents the basic ownership of the company; allows shareholders the right to vote and to receive dividends if declared, although the right to dividends is generally secondary to that of preferred stockholders.

common-size financial statements Financial statements standardized by a measure of size, either sales or total assets. All amounts are stated in terms of a percentage of the size measure.

comparability A quality of useful accounting information based on the premise that information is more useful when it can be related to a benchmark or standard, such as data for other firms within the same industry.

comparative financial statements Statements that enable users to analyze performance over multiple periods and identify significant trends that might affect future performance.

compensated absences Payments by employers for vacation, holiday, illness, or other personal activities.

compensating balances The portion of a demand deposit that must be maintained as support for existing borrowing arrangements.

completed-contract method An accounting method that recognizes revenues and expenses on long-term construction contracts only when completed.

complex capital structure A corporate structure that includes convertible securities and/or stock options, warrants, or rights that could result in the issuance of additional common stock through exercise or conversion.

component A portion of a property, plant, or equipment item that is separately identifiable and for which a separate useful life can be estimated.

composite depreciation Computation of depreciation on an entire group of related but dissimilar assets as if the group were one asset.

compound interest Interest that is calculated by adding the amount of interest earned for a certain period to the principal. Interest for the subsequent period is then computed on this sum, which includes both principal and accumulated interest.

comprehensive income A concept of income measurement and reporting that includes all changes in owners' equity except investments by and distributions to owners.

conceptual framework A theoretical foundation underlying accounting standards and practice. The framework established by the FASB encompasses the objectives, fundamental concepts, and implementation guidelines described in FASB *Concepts Statement Nos. 1–7.*

conglomerates Complex companies that operate in multiple industries.

conservatism The notion that when doubt exists concerning two or more reporting alternatives, users should select the alternative with the least favorable impact on reported income, assets, and liabilities.

consigned goods Inventory that is physically located at a dealer but whose ownership is retained by the shipper until the dealer sells the inventory.

consistency A quality of useful accounting information requiring that accounting methods be followed consistently from one period to the next.

consolidated financial statements Financial statements that combine the financial results of a parent company and its subsidiaries.

contingent gains Circumstances involving potential gains that will not be resolved until some future event occurs.

contingent liability A potential obligation whose existence is uncertain because it depends on the outcome of a future event, such as a pending lawsuit. The amount of the potential obligation may or may not be determinable.

contingent losses Circumstances involving potential losses that will not be resolved until some future event occurs.

contra account An account used to record subtractions from a related account. Also called an *offset account.*

contributed capital The portion of corporate capital that represents investments by the stockholders. Also referred to as *paid-in capital.*

contributory pension plan A pension plan in which employees make contributions to the plan and thus bear part of the cost.

control The ability of an investor to decisively influence the operating, investing, and financing decisions made by an investee.

control account A general ledger account that summarizes the detailed information in a subsidiary ledger.

convertible Securities, such as bonds and preferred stock, whose terms permit the holder to convert the investment into common stock of the issuing company.

convertible bonds Bonds that provide for conversion into common stock at the option of the bondholder.

convertible debt securities Securities that have an interest rate lower than the issuer could establish for nonconvertible debt, an initial conversion price higher than the market value of the common stock at time of issuance, and a call option retained by the issuer.

corporation A business entity that is a separate legal entity owned by its shareholders.

corridor amount An amount established as a minimum before amortization of pension gains and losses is required. Only amortization of unrecognized pension gains and losses that exceed 10% of the greater of the projected benefit obligation or the market-related asset value as of the beginning of the period is included in the net periodic pension expense. Any systematic method of amortization that exceeds the minimum may be used as long as it is consistently applied to both gains and losses and it is disclosed in the statements.

cost driver Characteristic of the production process that is known to create overhead costs.

cost method Method of accounting for treasury stock purchases in which the entire cost of the treasury stock is shown as a subtraction from equity.

cost of capital The cost a company bears to obtain external financing.

cost of debt financing The after-tax interest cost associated with obtaining external financing through borrowing.

cost of equity financing The expected return (both as dividends and as an increase in the market value of the investment) necessary to induce investors to provide equity capital.

cost percentage A percentage computed by dividing the goods available for sale at cost by the goods available for sale at retail.

cost recovery method A revenue recognition method that requires recovery of the total cost (investment) prior to the recognition of revenue.

cost-to-cost method A method for determining the percentage of completion for long-term construction contracts using a ratio of the actual cost incurred to date to the estimated total costs.

credit An entry on the right side of an account.

credit risk Uncertainty that the party on the other side of an agreement will abide by the terms of the agreement.

creditors Outside parties who are owed money by a company.

cumulative preferred stock Preferred stock that has a right to receive current dividends as well as any dividends in arrears before common stockholders receive any dividends.

current asset Cash or assets that are reasonably expected to be converted into cash during the normal operating cycle of a business or within one year, whichever period is longer.

current liability Obligations that are reasonably expected to be paid within one year.

current ratio Current assets divided by current liabilities.

current replacement cost The cash equivalent price that would be paid currently to purchase or replace goods or services.

curtailment of a pension plan An event that significantly reduces the expected number of years of future services of present employees or eliminates for a significant number of employees the accrual of defined benefits for their future services.

debenture bonds, or debentures Another name for unsecured bonds which are not protected by the pledge of any specific assets.

debit An entry on the left side of an account.

debt ratio A financial ratio used to measure the degree of leverage of a company. The debt ratio formula is total liabilities divided by total assets.

debt securities Financial instruments issued by a company that typically have the following characteristics: (1) a maturity value, (2) an interest rate (either fixed or variable) that specifies the periodic interest payments, and (3) a maturity date.

debt-to-equity ratio A ratio that measures the relationship between the debt and equity of an entity. The debt-to-equity formula is total debt divided by total stockholders' equity.

declining-balance depreciation Computation of periodic depreciation expense with a decreasing amount of depreciation recognized in each successive period, based on depreciation of a fixed percentage of a declining book value.

deductible temporary differences Differences between financial and taxable income that will result in deductible amounts in future years; expected benefits (tax savings) are reported on the balance sheet as deferred tax assets.

deferred income tax asset Expected future benefits from tax deductions that have been recognized as expenses in the income statement but not yet deducted for income tax purposes.

deferred income tax liability Expected future income taxes to be paid on income that has been recognized in the income statement but not yet taxed. Deferred income tax liabilities often arise from the temporary tax shielding provided by accelerated depreciation.

deferred net pension gain or loss Cumulative amount after Other Comprehensive Income is closed at year end to Accumulated Other Comprehensive Income.

deferred pension gain or loss Differences between expected results and actual experience in pension market value.

deficit A negative retained earnings balance caused by an excess of dividend payments and losses over net income.

defined benefit pension plans Pension plans that define the benefits that employees will receive at retirement. In these plans, it is necessary to determine what the contribution should be to meet the future benefit requirements. FASB *Statement No. 87* deals primarily with this type of pension plan.

defined contribution pension plans Pension plans that specify the employer's contributions based on a formula that includes such factors as age, length of service, employer's profits, and compensation levels. FASB *Statement No. 87* does not deal with these types of plans. The pension expense is the amount funded each year.

demand deposits Funds deposited in a bank that can be withdrawn upon demand.

depletion Process of allocating the cost of mineral and other natural resource assets to periodic expense.

deposit in transit A deposit made near the end of the month and recorded on the depositor's books but is not received by the bank in time to be reflected on the bank statement.

depreciation Process of allocating the cost of tangible long-term assets to periodic expense.

derecognition The process of designing QSPEs to use as financing vehicles to get cash through borrowing without showing the borrowing on the balance sheet.

derivative A financial instrument, such as an option or a future, that derives its value from the movement of a price, an exchange rate, or an interest rate associated with some other item.

detachable warrants Stock warrants that can be traded separately from the security with which they were originally issued.

development Activities that involve applying research findings to develop a plan or design for new or improved products and processes; includes the formulation, design, and testing of products; construction of prototypes; and operation of pilot plants.

dilution of earnings A reduction in earnings per share (or increase in loss per share) resulting from the assumption that convertible securities have been converted or that options and warrants have been exercised or other shares have been issued upon the fulfillment of certain conditions.

dilutive securities Securities whose assumed exercise or conversion results in a reduction in earnings per share (or increase in loss per share).

direct financing leases A lease in which the lessor is primarily engaged in financial activities and views the lease as an investment.

direct materials Materials used directly in the production of goods; the primary physical materials making up the final product.

direct method An approach to calculating and reporting cash flow from operating activities that itemizes the major operating cash receipt and cash payment categories.

direct write-off method A method of recognizing the actual losses from uncollectible accounts as expenses during the period in which the receivables are determined to be uncollectible; this method is not in accordance with GAAP.

disclosure Reporting the details of a transaction in the notes to the financial statements. Disclosure is sometimes used in place of recognition; that is, instead of including the results of a transaction in the financial statements themselves, it is disclosed in the notes.

discontinued operations The disposal of a separately identifiable component of a business either through sale or abandonment. The operations and cash flows of the component must be clearly distinguishable, both physically and operationally, from other activities of the company.

discovery The finding of valuable resources located on property that is already owned.

dividends in arrears Dividends on cumulative preferred stock that are passed or not paid. Dividends in arrears must be paid before any dividends can be paid to common stockholders.

dollar-value LIFO An adaptation of LIFO that measures inventory by total dollar amount rather than by individual units. LIFO incremental layers are determined based on total dollar changes.

dollar-value LIFO retail method A method in which LIFO layers are stated in terms of retail values.

donation The receipt of assets without being required to give goods or services in return.

double extension A technique that requires a record of base-year prices and end-of-year prices for each individual inventory item.

double-declining-balance depreciation Computation of periodic depreciation expense with depreciation equal to double the straight-line rate multiplied by a declining book value.

double-entry accounting A system of recording transactions in a way that maintains the equality of the accounting equation:
Assets = Liabilities + Owners' Equity.

DuPont framework Systematic approach to identifying general factors impacting return on equity; decomposes return on equity into profitability, efficiency, and leverage components.

earnings management continuum A continuum that describes earnings management ranging from savvy timing of transactions to outright fraud; in most companies, if practiced at all, does not extend beyond savvy transaction timing.

earnings per share (EPS) Income for the period reported on a per-share-of-common-stock basis. The presentation of earnings per share on the income statement is required by generally accepted accounting principles. Separate

EPS amounts are required for income from continuing operations and for each irregular or extraordinary component of reported income.

economic entity A specific reporting unit, separate and distinct from its owners or other entities.

effective rate of interest The interest rate used in compound interest problems.

effective tax rate Rate computed by dividing reported income tax expense by earnings before income taxes.

effective-interest method An amortization method that provides for recognition of an equal rate of amortization of bond premium or discount each period; uses a constant interest rate times a changing investment balance.

efforts-expended methods Methods for determining the percentage of completion for long-term construction contracts using an estimate of work or service performed. The estimates may be based on labor hours, labor dollars, or estimates of experts.

Emerging Issues Task Force (EITF) A task force of representatives from the accounting profession and industry created by the FASB to take timely action on emerging issues of financial reporting. The EITF identifies significant emerging issues and develops consensus positions when possible.

entry cost The acquisition cost of an asset.

equity The residual interest in the assets of an entity that remains after deducting its liabilities; sometimes referred to as *net assets*.

equity method The method of accounting for long-term investments in the stock of another company where significant influence exists (generally, 20%–50% ownership); the initial investment is recorded at cost but is increased by a proportionate share of investor's income and decreased by dividends and a proportionate share of losses to reflect the underlying claim by the investor on the net assets of the investee company.

equity method securities Equity securities purchased with the intent of being able to control or significantly influence the operations of the investee.

equity reserve A partition of total equity common in the financial statements of foreign companies. Each equity reserve has specific legal restrictions dictating whether it can be distributed to shareholders.

equity securities Securities that represent ownership in a company. These shares of stock typically carry with them the right to collect dividends and to vote on corporate matters.

estimated liability A liability for an indefinite amount that must be estimated.

exchange rate risk Uncertainty about future U.S. dollar cash flows arising when assets and liabilities are denominated in a foreign currency.

executory contract An exchange of promises to engage in a transaction in the future.

executory costs Costs to maintain leased property such as repairs, insurance, and taxes.

exit value The value received for an asset when sold.

expected return on the pension fund An amount calculated as a basis for determining the extent of delayed recognition of the effects of changes in the fair value of pension plan assets. The expected return on pension plan assets is determined based on the pension plan's expected long-term rate of return and market-related value.

expected service period Estimated number of years an employee will work before receiving pension benefits. Can be estimated as the average computed life based on the total expected future years of service divided by the number of employees. The expected future years of service may be computed by the formula $[N(N + 1)/2] \times D$, where N equals the number of years over which service is to be performed and D is the decrease in number of employees through retirement or termination of services per year.

expense recognition The process of determining the period in which expenses are to be recorded. Expense recognition is divided into three categories: (1) direct matching, (2) systematic and rational allocation, and (3) immediate recognition.

expenses Outflows or other "using up" of assets of an entity or incurrences of liabilities (or a combination of both) from delivering or producing goods, rendering services, or carrying out other activities that constitute the entity's ongoing major or central operations.

Exposure Draft A preliminary statement of a standard that includes specific recommendations made by the FASB. Reaction to the Exposure Draft is requested from the accounting and business communities, and the comments received are carefully considered before a final Statement of Financial Accounting Standards is issued.

extraordinary items Gains or losses resulting from events and transactions that are both unusual in nature and infrequent in occurrence or otherwise defined as an extraordinary item per accounting standards.

fair value The cash equivalent price that could be obtained by selling an asset in an orderly transaction.

face value, par value, or maturity value The amount that will be paid on a bond at the maturity date.

fair value hedge Derivative that offsets the change in the fair value of an asset or a liability.

fair value of the pension fund Value based on the pension fund's market value at a given measurement date that increases each year by employer contributions to the fund and decreases by the retirement benefits paid; also changes by the amount of earnings on the pension fund, including changes in its market value.

feedback value A key ingredient of relevant accounting information; helps to confirm or change a decision maker's beliefs based on whether the information matches what was expected.

financial accounting The activity associated with the development and communication of financial information for external users.

Financial Accounting Foundation (FAF) An organization responsible for selecting members of the FASB, GASB, and their advisory councils.

Financial Accounting Standards Board (FASB) The organization responsible for studying accounting issues and establishing accounting standards to govern financial reporting in the United States.

financial capital maintenance A concept under which income is defined as the excess of net assets at the end of an accounting period over the net assets at the beginning of the period, excluding effects of transactions with owners.

financial income Income reported on the financial statements as opposed to taxable income that is reported to taxing authorities in accordance with tax regulations.

financial ratios Mathematical relationships between financial statement amounts, used to quantify various characteristics of a company's performance such as efficiency and profitability.

financial statement analysis Examination of the relationships among financial statement numbers and the trends in those numbers over time.

financing activities One of three major categories included in a statement of cash flows; includes transactions and events whereby cash is obtained from or repaid to owners and creditors.

finished goods Manufactured products for which the manufacturing process is complete.

first-in, first-out (FIFO) method An inventory valuation method that assumes that the units sold are the first ones purchased or manufactured.

fixed asset turnover ratio A ratio that uses financial statement data to roughly indicate how efficiently a company is utilizing its property, plant, and equipment to generate sales; computed as sales divided by net property, plant, and equipment.

floor The net realizable value less a normal profit; used as a lower limit in defining market when valuing inventory at the lower of cost or market.

FOB (free on board) destination Terms of sale under which title of goods passes to the purchaser at the point of destination.

FOB (free on board) shipping point Terms of sale under which title of goods passes to the purchaser at the point of shipment.

foreign currency transaction For a U.S. company, a transaction denominated in a currency other than the U.S. dollar.

foreign currency translation adjustment Equity item arising from the change in the equity of foreign subsidiaries resulting from changes in foreign currency exchange rates.

forward contract Agreement between two parties to exchange a specified amount of a commodity, security, or foreign currency at a specified date with the price being set now.

full cost method A method of accounting developed to account for oil and gas exploratory costs by capitalizing all exploratory costs; the reasoning is that the cost of drilling dry wells is part of the cost of locating productive wells.

full disclosure principle A basic accounting concept that requires that all relevant information be presented in an unbiased, understandable, and timely manner.

full eligibility date The date at which an employee attains full eligibility for the benefits that employee is expected to earn under the terms of a postretirement benefit plan.

functional currency Currency in which most of a foreign subsidiary's transactions are denominated.

future value of an annuity due A value that is calculated by selecting the appropriate table value for an ordinary annuity for one additional period (n + 1) and subtracting the extra payment.

future values The value of money in the future.

futures contract Contract, traded on an exchange, that allows a company to buy a specified quantity of a commodity or a financial security at a specified price on a specified future date.

GAAP oval Represents the flexibility a manager has, within GAAP, to report one earnings number from among many possibilities based on different methods and assumptions.

gain Amount by which the proceeds from disposing of an asset exceed the book value of the asset.

general journal An accounting record used to record all business activities for which a special journal is not maintained.

general ledger A collection of all the accounts used by a business that could appear on the financial statements.

Generally Accepted Accounting Principles (GAAP) Accounting standards recognized by the accounting profession as required in the preparation of financial statements for external users. Currently, the FASB is the principal issuer of generally accepted accounting principles.

general-purpose financial statements A balance sheet, income statement, and statement of cash flows.

going concern An entity that is expected to continue in existence for the foreseeable future.

goodwill A residual number, the value of all of the synergies of a functioning business that cannot be specifically identified with any other intangible factor, that is recognized only when it is purchased as part of the acquisition of another company.

Governmental Accounting Standards Board (GASB) An independent private organization responsible for establishing standards in state and local governmental areas.

gross method A method of inventory accounting that records inventory cost before considering cash discounts.

gross profit Revenue from net sales minus cost of goods sold.

gross profit method An inventory estimation technique based on the relationship between gross profit and sales. The gross profit percentage is used to estimate cost of goods sold, which in turn, is used to estimate the value of the inventory not yet sold.

gross profit percentage Gross profit divided by sales; a measure of the profitability of sales in relation to the cost of the goods sold.

group depreciation Computation of depreciation on an entire group of similar assets as if the group were one asset.

guaranteed residual value A guarantee by lessee of a minimum value for the residual value of a leased asset. If the residual value is less than the guarantee, the lessee must pay the difference to the lessor.

half-year convention Assumption sometimes used in computing depreciation; one-half of a year's depreciation is recognized for assets acquired or disposed of during a year.

hedge To hide.

hedging Structuring transactions to reduce risk.

held-to-maturity securities Debt securities purchased by a company with both the intent and ability to hold the securities to maturity.

historical cost The cash equivalent price of goods or services at the date of acquisition.

if-converted method A method used to adjust the earnings per share computation to consider the impact of the possible conversion of convertible securities. Under this method, the earnings per share computation is made as if the convertible securities were converted at the beginning of the year or the date the convertible security was issued, whichever is later.

impairment Reduction in the expected cash flow to be generated by a long-term asset sufficient to warrant reducing the recorded value of the asset.

implicit (effective) interest The actual interest rate earned or paid on a note, bond, or similar instrument.

implicit interest rate The interest rate that would discount the minimum lease payments to the fair market value of the leased asset at the lease signing date.

imputed interest rate A rate of interest assigned to a note when there is no current market price for either the property, goods or services, or the note. The assigned rate of interest is used to discount future receipts or payments to the present in computing the present value of the note.

income A measure of a company's "well-offness." It is often defined as the amount that an entity could return to its investors and still be as well-off at the end of the period as it was at the beginning.

income from continuing operations A measure of the profitability of a firm's operations. The number is obtained by subtracting expenses and losses from revenues and gains. Income from continuing operations is always disclosed after taxes have been subtracted.

income smoothing The practice of carefully timing the recognition of revenues and expenses to even out the amount of reported earnings from one year to the next.

incremental borrowing rate The interest rate at which the lessee could borrow the amount of money necessary to purchase the leased asset, taking into consideration the lessee's financial situation and the current conditions in the marketplace.

indicated gain The excess of the market value over the book value of the asset given up in an exchange of assets.

indicated loss The excess of the book value over the market value of the asset given up in an exchange of assets.

indirect materials Materials that are necessary to facilitate the production process but are not directly incorporated in the final product.

indirect method An approach to calculating and reporting cash flow from operating activities that reconciles net income with operating cash flow; net income is adjusted for noncash revenues and expenses, for any gains or losses associated with investing and financing activities, and for changes in current operating assets and liabilities that indicate noncash sources of revenues and expenses.

initial direct costs Costs such as commissions, legal fees, and preparation of documents that are incurred by the lessor in negotiating and completing a lease transaction.

initial markup The original increase over cost.

input measures Measures of the earnings process in percentage-of-completion accounting based on cost or efforts devoted to a contract.

installment sales method A revenue recognition method that recognizes revenue and related expenses as cash is received.

intangible assets Legal or economic rights controlled by a company that are expected to generate future economic benefits.

integral part of annual period concept Concept guiding the preparation of interim statements; accounting practices may be slightly modified to make sure the interim results relate properly to the annual results.

interest Payment for the use of money.

interest rate risk Uncertainty about future interest rates and their impact on future cash flows as well as on the fair value of existing assets and liabilities.

interest rate swap Contract in which two parties agree to exchange future interest payments on a given loan amount; usually, one set of interest payments is fixed and the other is variable.

interest-bearing note A note written in a form in which the maker promises to pay the face amount plus interest at a specified rate; in this form, the face amount is usually equal to the present value upon issuance of the note.

interim financial statements Statements showing financial position and operating results for an interval of less than a year.

internal earnings target An important tool in motivating managers to increase sales efforts, control costs, and use resources more efficiently.

Internal Revenue Service (IRS) U.S. government agency responsible for administering U.S. income tax rules.

International Accounting Standards Board (IASB) International group, based in London, representing accounting bodies in over 100 countries formed to develop accounting standards that can serve as the basis for harmonizing conflicting national standards.

International Organization of Securities Commissions (IOSCO) International securities regulation firm, including member groups such as the U.S. Securities and Exchange Commission, that approves and endorses the overall quality of accounting standards.

interperiod tax allocation An accounting method that recognizes the tax effect of temporary differences between financial and taxable income in the financial statements rather than reporting as tax expense the actual tax liability in each year. The allocation may be made either by (1) the deferred method or (2) the asset and liability method. The latter method is currently required by GAAP.

intraperiod income tax allocation A method of income statement presentation of irregular or extraordinary items in which the tax effect of each of these special items is reported with the individual item rather than in the income tax expense related to current operations.

inventory Assets held for sale in the normal course of business; also, assets held to be used as materials in a production process.

inventory turnover Measured by dividing cost of goods sold by average inventory; used to evaluate whether the level of inventory is appropriate, given the volume of business.

investing activities One of three major categories included in a statement of cash flows; primarily includes purchases and sales of noncurrent assets such as land, buildings, and nontrading financial instruments.

investors Owners and potential owners of a company.

joint venture A separate economic entity created when companies join forces with other companies to share the costs and benefits associated with a specifically defined project.

journal entry A recording of a transaction in which debits equal credits; it usually includes a date and an explanation of the transaction.

journals Accounting records in which transactions are first entered, providing a chronological record of business activity.

junk bonds High-risk, high-yield bonds issued by companies in a weak financial condition.

large stock dividend A stock dividend of 25% or more of the shares outstanding.

last-in, first-out (LIFO) method An inventory valuation method that assumes that the units sold are the most recent ones purchased or manufactured.

lease A contract specifying the terms under which the owner of the property, the lessor, transfers the right to use the property to a lessee.

lease term The noncancelable period of a lease designated in the lease contract plus the period of any bargain renewal periods over which the lease is likely to be renewed.

ledger A collection of accounts maintained by a business.

lessee The party using property that is owned by another party (lessor).

lessor The owner of leased property who transfers the right to use the property to a second party (lessee).

leverage The degree to which a company uses borrowed funds instead of invested funds. By adding borrowed funds to their own capital, owners are said to "leverage" their investment.

liabilities The claims of creditors against an entity's resources: technically defined by the FASB as "probable future sacrifices of economic benefits arising from present obligations of a particular entity to transfer assets or provide services to other entities in the future as a result of past transactions or events."

LIFO conformity rule A federal tax regulation that requires the use of LIFO for financial reporting purposes if LIFO is used for income tax purposes.

LIFO inventory pool A group of inventory items having common characteristics and assumed to be the same when applying LIFO.

LIFO layer An incremental group of LIFO inventory items created in any year in which the number of units purchased or produced exceeds the number sold.

LIFO liquidation Reduction or elimination of old LIFO layers because total purchases or production in the current period is less than sales.

LIFO reserve The difference between LIFO ending inventory and the amount obtained using another method such as FIFO or average cost.

line of credit A negotiated arrangement with a lender in which the terms are agreed to prior to the need for actual borrowing.

liquidating dividend A distribution to stockholders representing a return of a portion of their contributed capital.

liquidity The ability of a company to pay its short-term obligations.

loan (mortgage) amortization The process by which payments on a loan are allocated between principal and interest components.

loan covenant Provision of a loan contract restricting the actions of the borrower or allowing for some monitoring of the borrower's actions.

long-term debt Obligations that are not expected to be paid in cash or other current assets within one year or the normal operating cycle.

loss Amount by which the proceeds from disposing of an asset are less than the book value of the asset.

lower of cost or market (LCM) Generally accepted method for valuation of inventories in which assets are recorded at the lower of their cost or market value; this method can be applied to inventories on an aggregate or individual item basis.

maintenance Expenditures made to maintain plant assets in good operating condition.

management accounting The activity associated with financial reporting for internal users.

manufacturing overhead All manufacturing costs other than direct materials and direct labor.

margin Profitability of each dollar in sales; another term for *return on sales*.

markdowns Decreases that reduce sales prices below original retail.

market (in "lower of cost or market") The replacement cost adjusted for an upper and lower limit that reflects the estimated net realizable value.

market, yield, or effective interest rate The actual rate of interest earned or paid on a bond.

market-related value of the pension fund Value of pension plan assets used in computing the expected return. Either of the following can be used as the market-related value: (1) the fair market value of pension plan assets as of the beginning of the year or (2) a weighted-average value based on the market value of plan assets over a preceding period not exceeding five years.

markups Increases that raise sales prices above original retail.

matching A basic accounting concept that is applied to determine when expenses are recognized (recorded). Under this principle, expenses for a period are determined by associating or "matching" them with specific revenues over a particular time period.

materiality An important constraint underlying the reporting of accounting information; it relates to how large an item is in terms of a dollar amount. Accounting standards do not need to be applied to items that are considered to be immaterial.

minimum lease payments The lease payments required over the lease term plus any amount to be paid for the residual value either through a bargain purchase option or a guarantee of residual value.

minority interest The amount of equity investment made by outside shareholders to consolidated subsidiaries that are not 100% owned by the parent.

modified accelerated cost recovery system (MACRS) Modification of the ACRS tax depreciation method that is based on declining-balance depreciation, fixed cost recovery periods, and no residual values.

mortgage A loan backed by an asset with the asset title pledged to the lender.

multiple-step form A format of the income statement that lists operating revenues and expenses first, resulting in operating income. From this figure, gains and losses are then added or subtracted to arrive at income from continuing operations. Irregular and extraordinary items are then added or subtracted to arrive at net income.

municipal debt Debt securities issued by state, county, and local governments and their agencies.

natural resources Products of the earth, such as oil, gold, and timber. Also called *wasting assets*.

negotiable notes Notes that are legally transferable by endorsement and delivery.

net method A method of inventory accounting that records inventory net of any cash discounts.

net operating loss (NOL) carryback The amount of operating loss that can be carried back and offset against the income of earlier profitable years to obtain a refund of previously paid income taxes.

net operating loss (NOL) carryforward The amount of operating loss that can be carried forward and offset against income of future profitable years to reduce the tax liability for those years.

net periodic pension expense The amount recognized in an employer's financial statements as an expense of a pension plan for a period. Components of net periodic pension expense are service cost, interest cost, actual return on plan assets, pension gain or loss, amortization of unrecognized prior service cost, and amortization of deferred gain or loss in excess of the corridor amount.

net realizable value The amount of cash expected to be received from the conversion of assets in the normal course of business; net realizable value equals selling price less normal selling costs for inventory and equals gross receivables less the allowance for bad debts for accounts receivable.

neutrality A key ingredient of reliable accounting information requiring that information be presented in an unbiased manner; neutrality relates to the concept of fairness to users.

nominal (temporary) accounts Accounts that are closed to a zero balance at the end of an accounting period.

noncancelable A lease contract that can be canceled only under very unlikely circumstances or with extremely expensive penalties to the lessee.

noncash investing and financing activities Investing and financing transactions that affect a company's financial position but not the cash flows during the period; an example is the purchase of land by issuing stock.

noncontributory pension plans Plans in which the employer bears the total cost of the plan.

noncontrolling interest The term used by the FASB to replace "minority interest" and directs that this item be classified in the consolidated balance sheet as part of equity.

noncumulative preferred stock Preferred stock that has no claim on any prior year dividends that may have been "passed."

noncurrent operating assets Assets used in the normal course of business that are expected to have a useful life exceeding one year, or one operating cycle, whichever is longer.

nondetachable warrants Stock warrants that cannot be traded separately from the security with which they were originally issued.

non-interest-bearing note A note written in a form in which the face amount includes an interest charge; in this form, the difference between the face amount and the present value of the note is the implicit or effective interest.

nonreciprocal transfer to owners Transfer of cash or property to shareholders in which nothing is received by the company in return.

nontrade notes payable Notes issued to nontrade creditors for purposes other than to purchase goods or services.

nontrade receivables Any receivables arising from transactions that are not directly associated with the normal operating activities of a business.

notes payable Formal written promises to pay a sum of money in the future. Notes payable are generally evidenced by a promissory note.

notes receivable Receivables that are evidenced by a formal written promise to pay a certain sum of money at a specified date.

notional amount Total face amount of the asset or liability that underlies a derivative contract.

not-sufficient-funds (NSF) check A check that is not honored by a bank because of insufficient cash in the maker's account.

number of days' sales in inventory Measured by dividing average inventory by average daily cost of goods sold; used to evaluate whether the level of inventory is appropriate, given the volume of business.

objective acceleration clause A clause in a debt agreement that identifies specific conditions that will cause the debt to be callable immediately.

obligation discount rate The 10% discount rate used in the computation of the projected benefit obligation and viewed as the implied interest rate on this debt.

off-balance-sheet financing Procedures used by companies to avoid disclosing all of their debt on the balance sheet to make their financial position look stronger.

operating activities One of three major categories included in a statement of cash flows; includes transactions and events that normally enter into the determination of net income, including interest and taxes.

operating income A measure of the performance of a company's business operations. The formula is revenues minus cost of goods sold and operating expenses. Also called *earnings before interest and taxes*.

operating lease A lease that is economically equivalent to the rental of the leased asset.

option Contract giving the owner the right, but not the obligation, to buy or sell an asset at a specified price any time during a specified period.

ordinary annuity A type of annuity in which periodic receipts or payments are made at the end of each period and the last payment coincides with the end of the annuity term.

original retail The initial sales price, including the original increase over cost referred to as the *initial markup*.

other comprehensive income The summary typically provided by companies as part of their statement of stockholders' equity showing changes in owners' equity exclusive of net income and contributions by and distributions to owners; required by the FASB beginning in 1998.

output measures Measures of the earnings process in percentage-of-completion accounting based on units produced, contract milestones reached, or values added.

outstanding checks Checks written near the end of the month that have reduced the depositor's cash balance but have not yet cleared the bank as of the bank statement date.

paid-in capital The portion of corporate capital that represents investments by the stockholders. Also referred to as *contributed capital*.

par value A nominal value that is assigned to stock by the terms of a corporation's charter.

par (or stated) value method Method of accounting for treasury stock purchases in which the repurchased shares are accounted for as if they were being retired.

parent company A company that exercises control over another company, known as a subsidiary, through majority ownership (more than 50%) of the subsidiary's voting stock.

participating preferred stock Preferred stock that provides for additional dividends to be paid to preferred stockholders after dividends of a specified amount are paid to common stockholders.

partnership A business entity owned by two or more people.

pension fund Fund set aside to meet the employer's future pension obligation.

pension plan An agreement, usually written, that provides for benefits to employees upon retirement from active employment. The plan usually includes provisions as to how the benefits are to be funded, who receives benefits, the amount of benefits to be paid, and restrictions on investments of pension plan assets.

pension-related asset/liability An account used to reflect changes in the net pension asset or liability.

percentage-of-completion accounting An accounting method for long-term construction contracts that recognizes revenue and related expenses prior to delivery of the goods. Recognition is based on either an input or output measure of the earning process.

performance-based stock option plan A plan in which the terms are dependent on how well the individual or company performs after the date the options are granted.

period cost Cost that is recognized as an expense during the period in which it is incurred; not included as part of inventory cost.

periodic inventory system A method of accounting for inventory in which cost of goods sold is determined and inventory is adjusted to the proper balance at the end of the accounting period. Purchases are recorded in the purchases account, and ending inventory is determined by a physical count.

permanent differences Nondeductible expenses or nontaxable revenues that are recognized for financial reporting purposes but that are never part of taxable income.

perpetual inventory system A method of accounting for inventory in which detailed records of each inventory purchase and sale are maintained. This system provides a current record of inventory on hand and cost of goods sold to date.

perpetuity Annuity of infinite length.

physical capital maintenance A concept under which income is defined as the excess of physical productive capacity at the end of an accounting period over the physical productive capacity at the beginning of the period, excluding the effects of transactions with owners.

post-balance sheet event Event occurring between the balance sheet date and the date financial statements are issued and made available to external users. Also called a *subsequent event*.

post-closing trial balance A list of all real accounts and their balances after the closing process has been completed.

posting The process of summarizing transactions by transferring amounts from the journals to the ledger accounts.

postretirement benefits other than pensions Benefits other than pensions provided by an employer to former employees. Includes health insurance, life insurance, and disability payments. Current standards require these benefits to be accrued in a manner similar to pension costs.

predictive value Helps a decision maker predict future consequences based on information about past transactions and events.

preferred stock A class of stock that usually confers dividend and liquidation rights that take precedence over those of common stock; preferred stockholders usually aren't allowed to vote in the selection of the board of directors.

prepaid expenses Payments that a company makes in advance for items normally charged to expenses.

present value The amount of net future cash inflows or outflows discounted to their present value at an appropriate rate of interest.

present value of an annuity due A value that is calculated by selecting the appropriate table value for an ordinary annuity for one less period ($n - 1$) and adding the extra payment.

price index An overall measure of how much prices have increased during the year.

price risk Uncertainty about the future price of an asset.

price-earnings (P/E) ratio A measure of the relationship between the market price of a company's stock and its profitability. The formula is the market price per share of common stock divided by the earnings per share of common stock.

principal (face amount) The amount, excluding interest, that the maker of a note or the issuer of a bond agrees to pay at the maturity date; this amount is printed on the note or bond contract.

prior service cost The present value of the increased benefits granted by a pension plan's amendment (or initial adoption of a plan). Recognized as a component of net periodic pension expense through amortization over the future service life of the covered employees.

prior-period adjustment An adjustment made directly to the retained earnings account to correct errors made in prior accounting periods.

pro forma cash flow statement A forecast or projection of the amounts that will be in the cash flow statement in a future period.

pro forma earnings number The regular GAAP earnings number with some revenues, expenses, gains, or losses excluded because companies claim that the GAAP results do not fairly reflect the company's performance.

product (inventoriable) cost Costs included in the total cost of manufactured inventory.

productive-output depreciation Computation of periodic depreciation expense based on how many units of output were produced during the period relative to estimated total lifetime output units.

projected benefit obligation (PBO) The actuarial present value of pension benefits using the benefits/years of service approach that requires assumptions about future compensation levels, such as increases over time by interest, amendments to the plan, additional service years, and changes in actuarial assumptions.

promissory note A formal written promise to pay a certain amount of money at a specified future date.

property dividend A dividend paid in the form of some asset other than cash.

proportional performance method An accounting method for recording service revenue and related expenses prior to completion of a service contract.

proprietorship A business entity owned by one person.

purchase commitment An advance commitment to purchase inventory in the future at a set price.

put option Contract giving the owner the right, but not the obligation, to sell an asset at a specified price.

quick ratio A financial ratio used as a measure of short-term liquidity. Also called *acid-test ratio.*

raw materials Inventory acquired by a manufacturer for use in the production process.

real (permanent) accounts Accounts that are not closed to a zero balance at the end of each accounting period.

recognition The process of formally recording an item in the accounting records and eventually reporting it in the financial statements; includes both the initial recording of an item and any subsequent changes related to that item.

redeemable preferred stock Preferred stock that may be redeemed at the option of the holder, at a fixed price on a specific date, or upon other conditions not solely within the control of the issuer.

registered bonds Bonds for which the bondholders' names and addresses are kept on file by the issuing company.

relevance One of two primary qualities inherent in useful accounting information; essentially, information is relevant if it will affect a decision. The key ingredients of relevance are feedback value, predictive value, and timeliness.

reliability One of two primary qualities inherent in useful accounting information; to be reliable, information must contain the key ingredients of verifiability, neutrality, and representational faithfulness.

remeasurement Method of converting a foreign subsidiary's financial statements into U.S. dollars; used when most of the subsidiary's transactions are denominated in U.S. dollars.

renewals Expenditures made for overhauling plant assets.

repairs Expenditures made to restore assets to good operating condition upon their breakdown or to restore and replace broken parts.

replacement cost The cost that would be required to replace an existing asset.

replacements Expenditures to purchase substitutions of parts or entire units of plant assets.

representational faithfulness A key ingredient of reliable accounting information requiring that the amounts and descriptions reported in the financial statements reflect the actual results of economic transactions and events.

research Investigation to discover new knowledge that will be useful in developing new products, services, or processes or that will result in significant improvements of existing products or processes.

research and development (R&D) Activities undertaken to discover new knowledge or apply research findings in developing new products, services, processes, or significant improvements of existing ones and to formulate, design, and test products; construct prototypes; and operate pilot plants.

residual (salvage) value Estimate of the amount for which an asset can be sold when it is retired.

restructuring charge An estimate of the costs expected to be incurred as a result of a plan to significantly modify a company's operations.

retail inventory method An inventory method that permits the estimation of an inventory amount without the time and expense of taking a physical inventory or maintaining detailed perpetual inventory records.

retained earnings The portion of owners' equity that represents the net accumulated earnings of a corporation.

return on assets A financial ratio used to measure the degree to which assets have been used to generate profits. The return on assets formula is net income divided by total assets.

return on equity A financial ratio used to measure the degree to which funds invested by owners have been used to generate profits. The return on equity formula is net income divided by total equity.

return on sales A measure of the profitability of a company that relates net income to the sales of the company. The formula is net income divided by net sales.

revenue recognition A basic accounting concept that is applied to determine when revenue should be recognized (recorded). Generally, under this principle, revenues are recognized when two criteria are met: The earnings process is substantially complete, and the revenues are realized, or realizable.

revenues Inflows or other enhancements of assets of an entity or settlements of its liabilities (or a combination of both) from delivering or producing goods, rendering services, or other activities that constitute the entity's ongoing major or central operations.

sale-leaseback An arrangement in which one party sells an asset and then immediately leases back and uses the same asset. The seller becomes the seller-lessee and the purchaser is the purchaser-lessor.

sales-type leases A lease in which the lessor is a manufacturer or dealer utilizing the lease to facilitate the sale of goods.

secured bonds Bonds for which assets are pledged to guarantee repayment.

secured loan A loan backed by certain assets as collateral.

Securities and Exchange Commission (SEC) A U.S. government agency created to regulate the issuance and trading of securities in the United States. As part of this function, the SEC is vitally interested in financial accounting and reporting standards. The SEC has the legal authority to establish accounting standards, but it has historically relied heavily on the private sector to perform this function.

selling receivables with recourse A purchaser advances cash in return for receivables but retains the right to collect from the seller if debtors fail to make payments when due.

serial bonds Bonds that mature in a series of installments at future dates.

service cost A component of net periodic pension expense representing the actuarial present value of benefits accruing to employees for services rendered during that period.

service-hours depreciation Computation of periodic depreciation expense based on how many hours of service were used during the period relative to estimated total lifetime service hours.

settlement of a pension plan An irrevocable action taken by an employer that relieves the employer of primary responsibility for all or part of the pension obligation. Examples include purchasing from an insurance company an annuity that would cover employees' vested benefits or a lump-sum payment to employees in exchange for their rights to receive specified pension benefits.

shrinkage The amount of inventory that is lost, stolen, or spoiled.

significant influence The ability of an investor to impact the operating, investing, and financing decisions of an investee but not absolutely determine those decisions.

simple capital structure A corporate structure that includes only common and nonconvertible preferred stock and has no convertible securities, stock options, warrants, or other rights outstanding.

simple interest A type of interest that is computed using the formula: $i = p \times r \times t$.

single-employer pension plans Pension plans established for a single employer. FASB *Statement No. 87* primarily refers to this type of plan.

sinking fund Assets that have been accumulated in order to repay a loan.

small stock dividend A stock dividend of less than 25% of the shares outstanding.

software development costs Costs that are examined in FASB *Statement No. 86*.

source document Also known as a "business document," it is the first record of each transaction.

special journal An accounting record used to list a particular type of frequently recurring transaction.

specific identification method Inventory valuation method that assigns the actual cost of inventory items sold to cost of goods sold.

spot rate The exchange rate at which currencies can be traded immediately.

stable monetary units An accounting assumption that the measuring unit maintains constant purchasing power; based on this assumption, U.S. financial statements have traditionally reported items in nominal dollars without adjustment for changes in purchasing power.

stakeholders All parties interested in the performance of a company.

stated (contract) rate The rate of interest printed on the bond.

stated value A nominal value that may be assigned to no-par stock by the board of directors of a corporation; similar in concept to par value.

statement of cash flows One of the three primary financial statements. The cash flow statement provides information about the cash receipts (inflows) and cash payments (outflows) of a company during a period of time. The statement is separated into cash flows from operating, investing, and financing activities.

statement of changes in owners' equity A report that shows the total changes in all owners' equity accounts during a period of time; provides a reconciliation of the beginning and ending owners' equity amounts.

statement of changes in stockholders' equity A report that summarizes the reasons for the changes in all equity accounts during a period of time.

Statements of Financial Accounting Concepts A set of guidelines established by the FASB to provide a conceptual framework for establishing and administering accounting standards.

stock appreciation rights (SARs) Awards an employee a cash amount equal to the market value of the issuing firm's shares above a specified threshold price.

stock options Rights granted to officers or employees as part of a compensation plan; the options allow for the purchase of shares at a specified exercise price.

stock rights Rights issued to existing shareholders to buy shares of stock in order to maintain their proportionate ownership interests.

stock split A reduction in the par or stated value of stock accompanied by a proportionate increase in the number of shares outstanding.

stock warrants Rights to purchase shares of stock; warrants are generally issued in conjunction with the issuance of another security.

stockholders' (shareholders') equity Total owners' equity of a corporation.

straight-line depreciation Computation of periodic depreciation expense with an equal amount of depreciation recognized in each year.

straight-line method An amortization method that provides for recognition of an equal amount of bond premium or discount amortization each period.

subjective acceleration clause A clause in a debt agreement that identifies general conditions that can cause the debt to be callable immediately, but violation of the conditions cannot be determined objectively.

subscription A contract between the purchaser of stock and the issuer in which the purchaser promises to buy shares of the issuing company's stock.

subsequent event Event occurring between the balance sheet date and the date financial statements are issued and made available to external users. Also called a *post-balance sheet event.*

subsidiary company A company that is owned or controlled by another company, known as the parent company.

subsidiary ledgers A grouping of supporting accounts that in total equal the balance of a control account in the general ledger.

successful efforts method An accounting method developed to account for oil and gas exploratory costs that expenses costs related to dry holes and capitalizes only exploratory costs for successful wells; used by most large, successful oil companies.

sum-of-the-years'-digits depreciation Computation of periodic depreciation expense with a decreasing amount of depreciation recognized in each successive period, based on a fraction derived from the sum of the digits from 1 to the asset's original useful life.

swap Contract in which two parties agree to exchange payments in the future based on the movement of some agreed-upon price or rate.

taxable income Income as defined by income tax regulations as the basis for determining the income tax liability for a given entity.

taxable temporary differences Differences between financial and taxable income that result in future taxable amounts; income taxes expected to be paid on future taxable amounts are reported in the balance sheet as a deferred tax liability.

technological feasibility Stage attained in software development when an enterprise has produced either a detailed program design or a working model.

temporary differences Differences between pretax financial income and taxable income arising from business events that are recognized for both financial and tax purposes, but in different time periods. For example, it is common for a temporary difference to result from depreciation expense on equipment.

term bonds Bonds that mature in one lump sum at a specified future date.

time deposits Funds deposited in a bank that legally require prior notification before they can be with-drawn.

time-factor depreciation Computation of periodic depreciation expense based on the passage of time.

timeliness Quality of information that is provided on a timely basis.

times interest earned An indicator of a company's ability to meet interest payments; calculated as income before income taxes plus interest expense divided by interest expense for the period.

trade discount A reduction in the "list" sales price of an item to the "net" sales price actually charged the customer; trade discounts are generally dependent on the volume of business or size of order from the customer.

trade notes payable A note issued to trade creditors for the purchase of goods or services.

trade receivables Receivables associated with the normal operating activities of a business (e.g., credit sales of goods or services to customers).

trademark A distinctive name, symbol, or slogan that distinguishes a product or service from similar products or services.

trading securities Debt and equity securities that are purchased with the intent of selling them in the near future to generate profits from short-term changes in market prices.

transaction approach A method of determining income by defining the financial statement effects of certain events classified as revenues, gains, expenses, and losses. Also known as the *matching method*, this is the traditional accounting approach to measuring and defining income.

transactions Exchanges of goods or services between/among two or more entities or some other event having an economic impact on a business enterprise.

translation Method of converting a foreign subsidiary's financial statements into U.S. dollars; used when most of the subsidiary's transactions are denominated in the local (foreign) currency.

translation adjustment Balancing figure to equate a foreign subsidiary's U.S. dollar debits and credits; can be thought of as an unrealized gain or loss from the impact of exchange rate changes on the U.S. dollar value of a foreign subsidiary's equity.

treasury stock Stock issued but subsequently bought back by the same company and held for possible future reissuance or retirement.

treasury stock method A method of recognizing the use of proceeds that would be obtained upon exercise of options and warrants in computing earnings per share. It assumes that any proceeds would be used to purchase common stock at current market prices.

trial balance A list of all accounts and their balances.

troubled debt restructuring A situation involving a concession by creditors to allow debtors to eliminate or significantly modify debt obligations due to the debtor's financial difficulties.

trust indenture A legal agreement specifying how a bond fund should be administered by its trustees.

turnover The degree to which assets are used to generate sales.

two-class method When different classes of stock don't always have the same claim upon dividends. In such a case, earnings attributable to each share of the different classes of stock are different and EPS is computed using this method.

uncertain tax positions Might be taken by taxpayers but the tax benefits are not immediately recognized for financial accounting purposes because those benefits are not yet more likely than not.

unearned revenues Amounts received before the actual earning of revenues.

unguaranteed residual value A residual value of leased property that reverts to the lessor at the end of the lease term. Because there is no guarantee of the residual value, market factors and asset condition determine the value of the leased asset at the end of the lease.

unit depreciation Computation of depreciation on an individual asset as a separate unit.

unrecorded liabilities Liabilities created by expenses being incurred prior to being paid or recorded.

unrecorded receivables Revenues that have been earned but have not yet been collected or recorded.

unsecured (debenture) bonds Bonds for which no specific collateral has been pledged.

use-factor depreciation Computation of periodic depreciation expense based on how much the asset is used during the period.

useful life Length of time over which a long-term asset is forecasted to provide economic benefits.

valuation allowance A contra-asset account that reduces an asset to its expected realizable value. This type of account is used, for example, in valuing accounts receivable and deferred tax assets.

variable interest entity (VIE) A category of unconsolidated subsidiaries, formerly called *special-purpose entities*.

verifiability A key ingredient of reliable accounting information; reported information should be based on objectively determined facts that can be verified by other accountants using the same measurement methods.

vested benefits The amount of pension benefits an employee will retain if employment with the employer is terminated.

warranties Obligations of a company to provide free service on units failing to perform satisfactorily or to replace defective goods.

weighted-average cost of capital The average of the cost of debt and equity financing, weighted by the proportion of each type of financing.

window dressing Practice of companies to boost their reported earnings when the companies enter phases in which it is critical that reported earnings look good.

work in process Inventory of a manufacturer that is partly processed and requires further work before it can be sold.

working capital Current assets less current liabilities; a measure of liquidity.

zero-interest (deep-discount) bonds Bonds that do not bear interest but instead are sold at significant discounts, providing the investor with a total interest payoff at maturity.

SUBJECT INDEX

SI

A

E

G

H

I

M

N

O

P

S

T

U

V

W

COMPANY INDEX

CI

A

B

C

D